The Zondervan Pictorial Encyclopedia of the Bible

Volume Two
D-G

The Zondervan Pictorial Encyclopedia of the Bible

IN FIVE VOLUMES

General Editor
MERRILL C. TENNEY

Associate Editor
STEVEN BARABAS

Volume Two • D-G

ZONDERVAN PUBLISHING HOUSE
OF THE ZONDERVAN CORPORATION
GRAND RAPIDS, MICHIGAN 49506

The Zondervan Pictorial Encyclopedia of the Bible

Grand Rapids, Michigan

Third printing 1978

Library of Congress Cataloging in Publication Data

The Zondervan Pictorial Encyclopedia of the Bible.

1. Bible—Dictionaries. I. Tenney, Merrill Chapin, 1904- ed.
BS440.Z63 220.3 74-6313

ISBN 0-310-33188-9

Printed in the United States of America

Abbreviations

I. General

A — Codex Alexandrinus
AA — *Alttestamentliche Abhandlungen*
AAA — *Annals of Archaeology and Anthropology*
AASOR — *Annual of the American Schools of Oriental Research*
ABR — *Australian Biblical Review*
ABW — Austin: *Birds of the World*
ad loc. — at the place
AFO — *Archiv für Orientforschung*
AG — Arndt and Gingrich: *A Greek-English Lexicon of the NT and Other Early Christian Literature*
AIs — de vaux: *Ancient Israel*
AJA — *American Journal of Archaeology*
AJP — *American Journal of Philology*
AJS — *American Journal of Anthropology*
AJSL — *American Journal of Semitic Languages and Literature*
AJT — *American Journal of Theology*
Akkad. — Akkadian
al. — *alii*, others
Aleph — Codex Sinaiticus
Alf — Alford: *Greek Testament Commentary*
Am. Trans. — Smith and Goodspeed, *The Complete Bible, An American Translation*
ANEA — *Ancient Near Eastern Archaeology*
ANEP — Pritchard: *The Ancient Near East in Pictures*
ANET — Pritchard: *Ancient Near Eastern Texts*
ANF — Roberts and Donaldson: *The Ante-Nicene Fathers*
ANT — James: *The Apocryphal New Testament*
AOTS — Thomas: *Archaeology and Old Testament Study*
APEF — *Annual of the Palestine Exploration Fund*
APOT — Charles: *Apocrypha and Pseudepigrapha of the Old Testament*
Ap. Lit. — Apocalyptic Literature
Apoc. — Apocrypha
Aq. — Aquila's *Greek Translation of the Old Testament*
ARAB — Luckenbill: *Ancient Records of Assyria and Babylonia*
Arab. — Arabic
Aram. — Aramaic
ARC — *Archaeology*
ARE — Breasted: *Ancient Records of Egypt*
ARM — *Archives royales de Mari*
Arndt — Arndt-Gingrich: *Greek-English Lexicon*
A-S — Abbott-Smith: *Manual Greek Lexicon of the New Testament*
ASV — American Standard Version
AThR — *Anglican Theological Review*
B — Codex Vaticanus
(b.) — born
BA — *Biblical Archaeologist*
BAAE — Badawy: *Architecture in Ancient Egypt and the Near East*
BAB — Barton: *Archaeology and the Bible*
BASOR — *Bulletin of the American Schools of Oriental Research*
BC — Foakes-Jackson and Lake: *The Beginnings of Christianity*
BDB — Brown, Driver and Briggs: *Hebrew-English Lexicon of the Old Testament*
BDT — Harrison: *Baker's Dictionary of Theology*
Beng. — Bengel's *Gnomon*
BETS — *Bulletin of the Evangelical Theological Society*
Bibl. Stud. — *Biblische Studien*
BJRL — *Bulletin of the John Rylands Library*
Blunt — Blunt: *Dictionary of Doctrinal and Historical Theology*
BrAP — *Brooklyn Museum Aramaic Papyri*
BS — *Bibliotheca Sacra*
BT — *Babylonian Talmud*
BTh — *Biblical Theology*
BV — Berkeley Version
BW — *Biblical World*
BWANT — *Beitrage zur Wissenschaft vom Alten und Neuen Testament*
BWL — *Babylonian Wisdom Literature*
BZ — *Biblische Zeitschrift*
BZF — *Biblische Zeitfragen*
C — Codex Ephraemi Syri
c. — *circa*, about
CA — *Current Anthropology*
CAH — *Cambridge Ancient History*
CanJTh — *Canadian Journal of Theology*
CBQ — *Catholic Biblical Quarterly*
CBSC — *Cambridge Bible for Schools and Colleges*

CD	Barth: *Church Dogmatics*
CDC	Cairo Genizah Document of the Damascus Covenanters
CE	*Catholic Encyclopedia*
cent.	century
cf.	*confer*, compare
CGT	*Cambridge Greek Testament*
ch., chs.	chapter, chapters
ChT	*Christianity Today*
CIG	*Corpus Inscriptionum Graecarum*
CIL	*Corpus Inscriptionum Latinorum*
CNFI	*Christian News from Israel*
col.	column
ConTM	*Concordia Theological Monthly*
Corp Herm	*Corpus Hermeticum*
Crem	Cremer: *Biblico-Theological Lexicon of the New Testament Greek*
CSEG	*Corpus Scriptorum Ecclesiasticorum Graecorum*
CSEL	*Corpus Scriptorum Ecclesiasticorum Latinorum*
D	Codex Bezae
(d.)	died, or date of death
DDB	*Davis' Dictionary of the Bible*
De Leg Agr	Cicero: *De Lege Agraria*
Deiss BS	Deissmann: *Bible Studies*
Deiss LAE	Deissmann: *Light From the Ancient East*
DMM	Drumm: *Mammoths and Mastodons*
DOTT	*Documents from Old Testament Times*
DSS	Dead Sea Scrolls
DWGH	Dunbar and Waage: *Historical Geology*
E	east
EB	*Etudes Bibliques*
EBi	*Encyclopedia Biblica*
EBr	*Encyclopedia Britannica*
ed., edd.	edited, edition, editor, editions
EDB	*Encyclopedic Dictionary of the Bible*
e.g.	*exampli gratia*, for example
EGT	Nicoll: *Expositor's Greek Testament*
Egyp.	Egyptian (adj. only)
Eng.	English
Eng. VSS	English versions of the Bible
ENC	*Encounter*
EQ	*Evangelical Quarterly*
ERV	English Revised Version
ESAR	*Economic Survey of Ancient Rome*
esp.	especially
et al.	*et alibi, et alii*, and others
ETh	*Evangelische Theologie*
Ethio.	Ethiopian
ETSB	*Evangelical Theological Society Bulletin*
Euseb. Hist.	Eusebius: *History of the Christian Church*
ExB	*The Expositor's Bible*
EXP	*The Expositor*
ExpT	*The Expository Times*
f., ff.	following (verse or verses, pages, etc.)
fem.	feminine

FFR	Filby: *The Flood Reconsidered*
fig.	figuratively, figurative
FLAP	Finegan: *Light From the Ancient Past*
FR	*Fortnightly Review*
ft.	foot, feet
Ger.	German (sing. only—adj.)
Gordon	Gordon: *Ugaritic Manual*
Gr.	Greek (sing. only—adj.)
GR	*Gordon Review*
GTT	Simons: *Geographical and Topigraphical Texts of the Old Testament*
HAT	*Handbuch zum Alten Testament*
HBD	*Harper's Bible Dictionary*
HBH	*Halley's Bible Handbook*
HDAC	Hastings: *Dictionary of the Apostolic Church*
HDB	Hastings: *Dictionary of the Bible*
HDBrev.	Hastings: *Dictionary of the Bible,* rev. by Grant Rawley
HDCG	Hastings: *Dictionary of Christ and the Gospels*
Heb.	Hebrew (sing. only—adj.)
Hel.	Hellenistic
HERE	Hastings: *Encyclopedia of Religion and Ethics*
HEV	Euselius: *Historia Ecclesiastica*
HGEOTP	Heidel: *The Gilgamesh Epic and Old Testament Parallels*
HGHL	Smith: *Historical Geography of the Holy Land*
Hitt.	Hittite
HJ	*Hibbert Journal*
HJP	Schürer: *A History of the Jewish People in the Time of Christ*
HKAT	*Handkommentar zum Alten Testament*
HNT	Leitzmann: *Handbuch zum Neuen Testament*
HPN	Gray: *Studies in Hebrew Proper Names*
HR	Hatch and Redpath: *Concordance to the Septuagint*
HTR	*Harvard Theological Review*
HUCA	*Hebrew Union College Annual*
IAE	*Iscrizioni Antico-Ebraici Palestinesi*
IBA	*Interpreter's Bible*
IB	Wiseman: *Illustrations from Biblical Archaeology*
ibid.	*ibidem*, in the same place
ICC	*International Critical Commentary*
id.	*idem*, the same
IDB	*Interpreter's Dictionary of the Bible*
i.e.	*id est*, that is
IEJ	*Israel Exploration Journal*
illus.	illustration
ILOT	Driver: *Introduction to the Literature of the Old Testament*
impf.	imperfect
infra	below
in loc.	*in loco*, in the place cited
inscr.	inscription
INT	*Interpretation*
Intro.	Introduction

IPN — *Die israelitischen Persoanennamen im Rahmen der germein semitischen Namengehbung*
Iren. Her. — Irenaeus: *Against Heresies*
ISBE — *International Standard Bible Encyclopedia*
IVF — Inter-Varsity Fellowship
JA — *Journal Asiatique*
JAF — *Journal of American Folklore*
JAOS — *Journal of American Oriental Society*
JASA — *Journal of the American Scientific Affiliation*
JB — *Jerusalem Bible*
JBL — *Journal of Biblical Literature*
JBR — *Journal of Bible and Religion*
JCS — *Journal of Cunieform Studies*
JEA — *Journal of Egyptian Archaeology*
Jew Enc. — *Jewish Encyclopedia*
JFB — Jamieson, Fausset and Brown: *Commentary on the Old and New Testaments*
JNES — *Journal of Near Eastern Studies*
Jos. Antiq. — Josephus: *The Antiquities of the Jews*
Jos. Apion — Josephus: *Against Apion*
Jos. Life — Josephus: *Life*
Jos. War — Josephus: *The Jewish War*
JPOS — *Journal of the Palestine Oriental Society*
JPS — Jewish Publication Society Version of the Old Testament
JQR — *Jewish Quarterly Review*
JR — *Journal of Religion*
JRAI — *Journal of the Royal Anthropological Institute*
JRS — *Journal of Roman Studies*
JSOR — *Journal of the Society of Oriental Research*
JSS — *Journal of Semitic Studies*
JT — *Jerusalem Talmud*
JTS — *Journal of Theological Studies*
JTVI — *Journal of the Transactions of the Victoria Institute*
KAHL — Kenyon: *Archaeology in the Holy Land*
KAT — *Kommentar zum Alten Testament*
KB — Koehler-Baumgartner: *Lexicon in Veteris Testament Libros*
KD — Keil and Delitzsch: *Commentary on the Old Testament*
KHC — *Kurzer Hand-Kommentar zum Alten Testament*
KJV — King James Version
KWNT — Keitel: *Wortenbuch zum Neuen Testament*
lang. — language
Lat. — Latin
lex. — lexicon
lit. — literature
LSJ — Liddell, Scott, Jones: *Greek-English Lexicon*
LT — Edersheim: *The Life and Times of Jesus the Messiah*
LXX — Septuagint
M — Mishna
m. — mile(s)
masc. — masculine
MCh — *Modern Churchman*
Met. — Ovid: *Metamorphoses*
Meyer — Meyer: *Critical and Exegetical Commentary on the New Testament*
mg. — margin
MM — Moulton and Milligan: *The Vocabulary of the Greek Testament*
MNT — Moffatt: *New Testament Commentary*
MPL — *Migne Patrologia Latina*
MS(S) — manuscript(s)
MST — McClintock and Strong: *Cyclopedia of Biblical, Theological, and Ecclesiastical Literature*
MT — Masoretic text
MWPE — Martin and Wright: *Pleistocene Extinction*
N — north
NASB — *New American Standard Bible*
NBC — Davidson: *New Bible Commentary*
NBD — Douglas: *New Bible Dictionary*
NCE — *The New Catholic Encyclopedia*
n.d. — no date
NE — northeast
NEB — *New English Bible*
Nestle — Nestle (ed.) *Novum Testamentum Graece*
NIC — *New International Commentary*
NKZ — *Neue kirchliche Zeitschrift*
no. — number
NovTest — *Novum Testamentum*
NSI — Cooke: *Handbook of North Semitic Inscriptions*
NT — New Testament
NTS — *New Testament Studies*
NTSp — Hennecke: *New Testament Apocrypha*
NW — northwest
ODCC — *Oxford Dictionary of the Christian Church*
OED — *Oxford English Dictionary*
OIC — Oriental Institute Communications (or Institute-University of Chicago)
op. cit. — *opere citato*, in the work cited above
OT — Old Testament
Oxyr. Pap. — *Oxyrhynchus Papyri*
p., pp. — page, pages
Pal. — Palestine
PBFIE — Patten: *The Biblical Flood and the Ice Epoc*
PCDZ — Pennak: *Collegiate Dictionary of Zoology*
Peake — Black and Rowley: *Peake's Commentary on the Bible*
PEFQSt — Palestine Exploration Fund Memoirs, *Palestine Quarterly Statement*
PEQ — *Palestine Exploration Quarterly*
PJB — *Palastina-Jahrbuch*
prob. — probably
PSBA — *Proceedings of the Society of Biblical Archaeology*
Pseudep. — Pseudepigrapha
PTR — *Princeton Theological Review*

Q	Quelle ("Saying" source in the Gospels)
QDAP	*Quarterly of the Department of Antiquities of Palestine*
1QH	Thanksgiving Hymns
1QIs[a]	Isaiah Scroll (published American Schools of Oriental Research)
1QIs[b]	Isaiah Scroll (published by E. L. Sukenik)
1QM	War Scroll
4Q Num[b]	Numbers
1Qp Hab	Habakkuk Commentary
1QS	Manual of Discipline
1QSa	Rule of the Congregation
4Q Sam[a]	Samuel A text from Qumran Cave 4
4Q Sam[b]	Samuel B text from Qumran Cave 4
RAHR	*American Historical Review*
RB	*Revue Biblique*
RCUSS	Ramm: *The Christian View of Science and Scripture*
RE	Hauck-Herzog: *Realencyclopädie für protestantiche Theologie und Kirche*
REJ	*Revue des etudes Juives*
rev.	revised, reviser, revision
RGG	*Die Religion in Geschichte und Gegenwart*
RHA	*Révue Hittite et Asianique*
RHD	*Random House Dictionary*
RHPR	*Révue d'Historie et de Philosophie religieuse*
Rom.	Roman (sing. only—adj.)
RS	*Révue Semitique*
RSV	Revised Standard Version
RTP	*Révue de Theologie et de Philosophie*
RTWB	Richardson: *A Theological Wordbook of the Bible*
RV	Revised Version
RVmg.	Revised Version margin
S	south
SBK	Strack and Billerbeck: *Kommentar zum Neuen Testament aus Talmud und Midrash*
SE	southeast
sec.	section
Sem.	Semitic (sing. only—adj.)
SHERK	*The New Schaff-Herzog Encyclopedia of Religious Knowledge*
sing.	singular
SJT	*Scottish Journal of Theology*
SOTI	Archer: *A Survey of Old Testament Introduction*
SPEAK	Stanek: *The Pictorial Encyclopedia of the Animal Kingdom*
ST	*Studia Theologica*
Sumer.	Sumerian (sing. only—adj.)
SUT	Supplements to *Vetus Testamentum*
s.v.	*sub verbo*, under the word
SW	southwest
SWP	*Survey of Western Palestine*
Syr.	Syriac (sing only—adj.)
Symm.	Symmachus
Tac. Ann.	Tacitus, *Annals*
Targ.	Targum
TCERK	Loetscher: *The Twentieth Century Encyclopedia of Religious Knowledge*
TDNT	Kittel: *Theological Dictionary of the New Testament* (English Edition)
Theod	Theodotion
Theol.	*Theology*
ThLZ	*Theologische Literaturzeitung*
ThR	*Theologische Rundschaw*
ThT	*Theology Today*
TR	Textus Receptus
tr.	translation, translator, translated
Trench	Trench: *Synonyms of the New Testament*
TSBA	*Transactions of the Society of Biblical Archaeology*
TWNT	Kittel: *Theologisches Worterbuch zum Neuen Testament*
VB	Allmen: *Vocabulary of the Bible*
UBD	Unger: *Unger's Bible Dictionary*
UC	*Vigiliae Christianae*
UIGOT	Unger: *Introductory Guide to the Old Testament*
u.s.	*ut supra*, as above
UT	*Ugaritic Textbook*
v., vv.	verse, verses
VetTest	*Vetus Testamentum*
viz.	*videlicet*, namely
vol.	volume
VS(S)	Version(s)
vs.	versus
Vul.	Vulgate
W	west
WBC	Pfeiffer and Harrison: *Wycliffe Bible Commentary*
WC	*Westminster Commentaries*
WesBC	*Wesleyan Bible Commentary*
WH	Westcott and Hort, *The New Testament in Greek*
WTJ	*Westminster Theological Journal*
ZAS	*Zeitschrift für Aegyptische Sprache und Altertumskunde*
ZAW	*Zeitschrift für die Alttestamentliche Wissenschaft*
ZDMG	*Zeitschrift der Deutschen Morgenlandischen Gesellschaft*
ZDPV	*Zeitschrift der Deutschen Palestina-Vereins*
ZNW	*Zeitschrift für die neutestamentliche Wissinschaft*
ZST	*Zeitschrift für systematische Theologie*
ZTSf Aeg. Spr.	*Zeitschrift fur Aegyptische Sprache*

II. Books of the Bible

Old Testament

Gen	1 Kings	Eccl	Obad
Exod	2 Kings	S of Sol	Jonah
Lev	1 Chron	Isa	Mic
Num	2 Chron	Jer	Nah
Deut	Ezra	Lam	Hab
Josh	Neh	Ezek	Zeph
Judg	Esth	Dan	Hag
Ruth	Job	Hos	Zech
1 Sam	Ps (Pss)	Joel	Mal
2 Sam	Prov	Amos	

New Testament

Matt	2 Cor	1 Tim	2 Pet
Mark	Gal	2 Tim	1 John
Luke	Eph	Titus	2 John
John	Phil	Philem	3 John
Acts	Col	Heb	Jude
Rom	1 Thess	James	Rev
1 Cor	2 Thess	1 Pet	

III. The Apocrypha

1 Esd	1 Esdras
2 Esd	2 Esdras
Tobit	Tobit
Jud	Judith
Add Esth	Additions to Esther
Wisd Sol	Wisdom of Solomon
Ecclus	Ecclesiasticus (Wisdom of Jesus the Son of Sirach)
Baruch	Baruch
Ep Jer	Epistle of Jeremy
Pr Azar	Prayer of Azariah
S Th Ch	Song of the Three Children (or Young Men)
Sus	Susanna
Bel	Bel and the Dragon
Pr Man	Prayer of Manasseh
1 Macc	1 Maccabees
2 Macc	2 Maccabees

IV. The Pseudepigrapha

As Moses	Assumption of Moses
2 Baruch	2 Baruch
3 Baruch	3 Baruch
1 Enoch	1 Enoch
2 Enoch	2 Enoch
4 Ezra	4 Ezra
Jub	Book of Jubilees
L Aristeas	Letter of Aristeas
Life AE	Life of Adam and Eve
3 Macc	3 Maccabees
4 Macc	4 Maccabees
Mart Isa	Martyrdom of Isaiah
Pirke Aboth	Pirke Aboth
Pss Sol	Psalms of Solomon
Sib Oracles	Sibylline Oracles
Story Ah	Story of Ahikar
Test Benj	Testament of Benjamin
Test XII Pat	Testaments of the Twelve Patriarchs
Zad Frag	Zadokite Fragments

A small house shrine used in worshiping Dagon, found at Beth-shan. ©*U.M.P.*

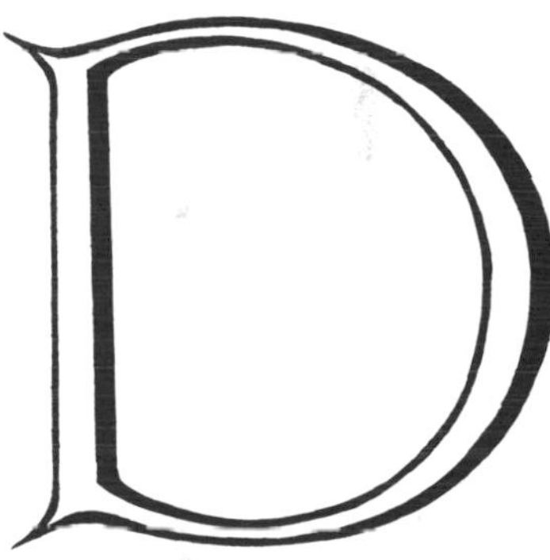

D (DEUTERONOMIST). The supposed source, author, editor, material, or outlook peculiar to Deuteronomy. Characteristic are the centralization of worship (Deut 12:5-7), the Holy War demanding the massacre of the inhabitants of the land (Deut 7, 20), and the concept of earthly reward for doing right (Deut 11:13-17).

DABAREH. KJV form of DABERATH in Joshua 21:28.

DABBESHETH dăb' ə shĕth (דבשת). KJV DABBASHETH. A town in the territory of Zebulun (Josh 19:11) between Sarid and Jokneam, perhaps a little E of the brook Kishon. Exact location unknown.

DABERATH dā' bə răth (דברת, prob. *pasture land*).

A town W of Mt. Tabor, in Issachar's territory (1 Chron 6:72) allotted to the Bershonite Levites (Josh 21:27, 28 KJV DABAREH, and apparently on Zebulun's border (Josh 19:10, 12). This place has been suggested as the site of Sisera's defeat by Barak, Jael's exploit being connected with it (Josh 4). Its site is supposed to have been that of the village of Deburiyeh.

R. F. GRIBBLE

DABRIA **dăb′ rĭ ə.** One of five men trained to "write rapidly," commissioned to write down the apocalyptic vision of Esdras on "many writing tablets" (2 Esd 14:24).

DACOBI. KJV form of AKKUB.

DAGGER. *See* ARMS, ARMOR.

DAGON **dā′ gŏn** (דגין from דגן "grain"). The god Dagon is associated in the OT with the Philistines (1 Chron 10:10), particularly in the centers Gaza (Judg 16:23) and Ashdod (1 Sam 5:2-7). For a brief period the Ark of God was captured by the Philistines and deposited in Dagon's temple in Ashdod (1 Sam 5). The presence of the Ark in the same sanctuary with the idol of Dagon gave rise to a series of judgments on the idol including the severing of its hands and head. In a remarkably similar manner the Philistine capture of Samson, the man of God, brought disaster to the temple of Dagon in Gaza (Judg 16:23ff). Because of his association in the OT with Philistines who live by the sea and because of the popular etymology of Dagon (deriving it from *dag* "fish") it has been argued that the god Dagon was a sea god. Extra-Biblical evidence does not favor this view, nor does the correct etymology (deriving Dagon from *dagan* "grain"). Dagon under his Amorite form *Dagan* was venerated from before 2000 B.C. His temple in Ugarit has been dated to c. 2000 B.C., and he was widely worshiped among Amorites in Mesopotamia in the age of Hammurabi of Babylon and the kingdom of Mari (c. 1850-1750 B.C.). During the Amarna Age (c. 1500-1200 B.C.) Dagon was venerated as a grain god at Ugarit and was considered to be the father of the chief god Baal-Hadd. C. H. Gordon has claimed that the divine name Daguna (= Dagon) appears in Minoan Linear A tablets on Crete c. 1500 B.C. The popularity of Dagon in Pal. during the Late Bronze Age is attested both by personal names of Palestinian princes (Dagan-takala in El Amarna tablets) and the spread of place names such as Beth-Dagon, of which there were at least three: (1) in Judah (Josh 15:41), (2) near Joppa (Annals of Sennacherib), and (3) in Asher (19:27). In Mesopotamia Dagon's consort was the goddess Shala, who was possibly of Hurrian extraction. In the Old Babylonian period in the region of Mari, Dagon was considered the father of the storm god, just as at Ugarit Baal the storm god is "son of Dagon." In this same Middle Euphrates region Dagon bore the epithet "King of the Land," under which epithet the *ziqqurat* of Mari was dedicated to him. In the Babylonian god list An:*Anum* Dagon is equated with Enlil, the god of the wind. In Pal. he appears to have yielded place as a vegetation fertility god in some locales to Baal, but have held his own against Baal in others. *See* PHILISTINES.

BIBLIOGRAPHY. H. Schmökel, *Der Gott Degan* (diss. Heidelberg, 1928); *Reallexikon der Assyriologie* II, 99-101; E. Dhorme, "Les avatars du dieu Dagan," RHR 138 (1950), 129-144; H. W. Haussig (ed.), *Wörterbuch der Mythologie* I/1, 49ff. (D. O. Edzard), 276ff. (M. H. Pope).

H. A. HOFFNER, JR.

DAGON, TEMPLES OF **dā′ gŏn** (דגון). Dagon was the chief god of the Philistines (Judg 16:23). Two locations use the name of Dagon: Beth-dagon (בת-דגין) in Judah near Gederoth (Josh 15:41), now Beit Dajan; and a town in the area of the tribe of Asher (Josh 19:27) near the sea coast, prob. the modern Beit Dajan SE of Joppa. The name ארע דגין was applied to the area of Joppa and Dor c. 300 B.C. These uses indicate the widespread worship of Dagon by the inhabitants. Dagon was most prominent in the time of Saul (2 Sam 5:1-7), because by this time Philistine power was reaching down into the Jordan Valley and moving southward toward the Dead Sea. The following shows the development in the cultus of Dagon and the principal centers of worship in the Syro-Palestinian area.

I. The problem of the origin of the name
II. The meaning of the name
III. Philistine Dagon
IV. Temples
  1. Ugarit
  2. Ashdod
  3. Gaza
  4. Bethshan
V. Conclusions

I. The problem of the origin of the name. The problem is twofold: the apparent confusion of the basis of the meaning of the name and, second, its origin. Etymologically the name has been thought to have come from דג plus ין, meaning, according to Jerome, "fish of sorrow," i.e., to the devotees because of the burdens of idolatry (*see* Macalister, *The Philistines, Their History and Civilization*, 100, n. 1), and by others from *dagan*, grain (Philo Byblius). In the Middle Ages, the name was thought by the rabbis to have been derived from דג *fish*, but as early as Jerome and Josephus "Dagon" was not known as a fish god. The popular derivation prob. resulted from the similarity to *dag*. The meaning must be sought in the area of association with earlier eras and in other areas, coming in by migrations of peoples. Some have considered *on* as indicative of a diminutive, whereas others see *dāgôn* as derived from a root represented in Arab. by *dagga* with the aspect of "cloudy." This suggests the proper basis for the derivation of the name in the light of historical usage of the name.

II. The meaning of the name. Sargon I (c. 2360 B.C.) in his account of the campaign to the upper Euphrates country and Cilicia (Gadd-Legrain, *Ur Excavation Texts*, 119, 350) relates his stop at Tutuli (modern Hit) to worship

Dagon. His son Naram-Sin conquered the same territory and claimed it was a gift to him by Dagon, which implies that the worship of Dagon had spread westward beyond the western Syrian mountains. As to the usage of the name, indicative of the early existence and long persistence of the cult, besides the late 3rd millennium usages, the name occurs in the Ur III period, the Isin-Larsa period, and well beyond the Hammurabi epoch (from 1530 B.C.; Montalbano, "Canaanite Dagon," CBQ, 13: 384-393). It is possible on the basis of certain specific uses of the name to derive its meaning. Naram-Sin's texts of the conquest of Syria (Gelb, *Inscriptions from Alishar*, 6) cannot be used to describe Dagon as the war god, for this function was served by Ninurta. Dagon could not have achieved widespread popularity in a role secondary to the chief Ninurta. It is first in the Ur III period that a suggestion as to meaning is given. His "wife's" name is written as *Ša-la-aš*, prob. equivalent to *Ša-la*, the wife of Adad the weather God (Montalbano, ibid., 386). Final confirmation is found in the Hammurabi period where, in a letter to Zimrilim (c. 1730 B.C.) of Mari, Dagon is equated with Enlil the Babylonian storm god (CBQ, 13:388). The victory cited in the letter was promised from Dagon for suggested reverence on achievement of victory, which reverence was made in offerings in the temple of Dagon, most likely at Tirqa, c. 60 m. N of Mari, which could be called the locus of the cult of Dagon. The letter strongly suggests a palace revolt of some kind. By this equation is shown the nature of Dagon as the weather god of the Upper Euphrates River country between the Ḥabur River and Tutuli.

Dagon is mentioned in the Amarna Tablets by the name *Dagan-takala* (*Tell El Amarna Tablets of the British Museum*, 74:3; 129:2) c. 1375 B.C., and c. 1400 B.C. at Ugarit on commemorative sacrificial stelae (*Syria*, 16: 179, 180). In other Ras Shamra texts, Dagon is presented as the father of Baal, the Canaanite storm god, who had a temple erected to him in Ugarit, prob. from the Middle Bronze period. Thus down to the 2nd millennium B.C. and later, as Assyro-Babylonian records show, Dagon was widely popular for a time span of some 1500 years. It is in the Amarna era that his worship appears to have reached widespread permanence in Syro-Palestinian areas. It is necessary to find the causes of his adoption by Palestinians and the significance of his name. The temples dedicated to his name show distinctly the influence of the occupying power.

In Syria, as in the upper Euphrates, Dagon was associated with the weather gods (Gordon, *Ugaritic Literature* lists Dagon with his son twelve times). Adad, another Babylonian-Assyrian weather god, was associated with Dagon, and Adad was assimilated into Syria as Hadad and then became the son of Dagon (CBQ, 13:396). Hadad became the Baal of Ugarit. Thus the transference of a fixed association tending toward Dagon's identity as a weather god is established. In Pal. and Syria weather is important from the standpoint of rain for the crops. It is not too difficult to transfer the power of Dagon from a weather god to the status of a grain god, particularly since good harvests generally coincided with the appeals to him for rain so the grainfields would flourish. In Ugarit was found a word for grain that is synonymous with the name of Dagon (Gordon, *Ugaritic Handbook* III, 223, n. 519). Baal, his "son," by virtue of the process of amalgamation begun with Dagon, was known both as the god of weather and productivity (CBQ, 13:397).

Therefore Dagon as a storm god of upper Euphrates country was brought into Syro-Pal. by conquerors from Mesopotamia, was adopted there, and by a process of accretion became also the storm god. Along with the usage of the upper Euphrates area, one must look for a word that would provide a root for the name, perhaps best supplied in the root *dg*, cognate to Arab. *dagga*, *dagā*, ("cloudy," "rainy"). The final long syllable *ôn* derives from the Akkad. *an*, but not the Aram. long *â* (*ân*), as is shown by the frequency of the short *a* in the Assyrian inscrs. The *a* of the second syllable became accented (á) in Heb. and then became long (ā/ô). The *Dagan* form from Akkad. is confirmed by the Arab. and the *an* ending most likely came from a 2nd millennium form ending in *an* or *annum*, expanding the original word. The name *Dāgôn* is thus a first millennium form that underwent first tone shift and then quality shift of an original short vowel.

III. Philistine Dagon. The references to Dagon in the Bible are Judges 16:23; ten in 1 Samuel 5:2-7 and 1 Chronicles 10:10 (cf. also the coupling of his name with בית in Josh 15:41; 19:27). The first was in Judah and the second in Simeon, both tribes that bordered Philistine territory; and the references in Judges and 1 Samuel fit better the later date of the Exodus and conquest. In the days of Abraham, the Philistines were not the warriors as later in the days of Samson and Samuel when they were distinctly aggressive to acquire territory—first in Egypt where they were repulsed by Rameses III. The Philistines later settled in Pal. but some were subsequently hired by the Pharaoh as mercenaries (Wright, "Philistine Coffins and Mercenaries," BA, XXII, 65) and, as such were quartered at Bethshan. This town was controlled by the Pharaoh of Egypt as indicated by a door lintel inscr. left there by one of his officers. This was also the era of Egyp. hegemony over the land, particularly along the trade routes (*see* Albright, AJA, LIV [1950], 162-176). But the evidence of Philistine pottery, which shows Aegean affinities, does not appear in Pal. from before the 13th cent. B.C., which requires that the period of the judges be moved down in time since the first and earliest reference to the warrior Philistines as established in Philistia (Josh 13:2, 13) occurs in the era of the conquest (cf. BA, XXII, 61, 62), esp. n. 11). Since also Rameses II (1290-1224) and Merneptah (1224-1216) beat off the "sea peoples," among whom were the *Peleste* (or the Philistines), it appears that the 13th cent. B.C. is established for the advent of these people in Pal.

How did the Philistines take up the worship of Dagon? The answer is found first in a tablet found at Ugarit dated to the 18th dynasty (c. 1580-1350 B.C.), which includes the name of Ashdod with those of Askelon and Akko as Palestinian cities (BA, XXVI, 135-136), indicating commercial relations with the area, naming linen as an article of that commerce, and also naming the governor of Ashdod. It would seem that since Dagon appeared earlier in Syria and later in Pal., and since there is provable commercial traffic, Dagon migrated with those traders and their families from Ugarit. It is probable that trade was established much earlier and continued for a considerable time. Since the Philistine plain had been a grain growing area for some time, this was a most likely area for a weather god to come to active acknowledgment. Since a temple to Dagon was erected at Ugarit as early as the 12th dynasty (1991-1786 B.C., *Syria,* 13:20 and 16:177ff.), Ugarit was known to the Palestinians from the Amarna age (Dussaud, *Decouverts du Ras Shamra,* 28), indicative of a commerce wider than just with Ashdod. The presence of an invoice or receipt tablet in 12th cent. B.C. Taanach (BA, XXX, 21, 22) in Ugaritic confirms the commerce of the area of Pal. with Ugarit and widens the understanding of the scope of Ugarit's cultural influence. Thus it may be assumed that the worship of Dagon traveled southward earlier than the Amarna period, perhaps as early as the 16th cent. B.C. when, still within the era of Egyp. hegemony, commercial relations were established and continued thereafter. Indications of Egyp. influence in Ugarit in the area and era in question is seen in the Mani Stele (Dussaud, op cit., 28) in its dedication to "Seth Zapouna," an Egyp. god that is equivalent to Baal Zaphon, thus using a form of localized paraphrase, which pinpoints the locale.

It would seem evident that the Dagon of the Philistines was the same as the Syrian type and perhaps the aspect emphasized would be that of fertility since Philistia was a grain-producing area.

IV. The temples of Dagon. Temples to this god existed in Ugarit (Dussaud, op. cit.), in Bethshan (1 Chron 10:10; cf. 1 Sam 31:7-10), in Gaza (Judg 16:23) and in Ashdod (1 Sam 5:1-7).

1. *Ugarit.* The peculiarity about the temple of Dagon is that it is of the same size and arrangements and orientation as the temple of Baal (*Syria,* 16:177; *Ugaritica,* III, fig. 9). It is situated c. 170 ft. E-SE of the temple of Baal and was discovered after that of Baal. Dussaud remarked that the honors the father had received were accorded likewise to the son (op. cit., 29). The temple was situated within an open court where the religious ceremonies were performed and in which was situated the altar. That of the Baal temple had two steps; prob. that of Dagon had steps also. Beyond the altar was the holy place and back of that the holy of holies itself.

One is at once impressed with the similarity of these temples to the later Ishtar temple of Assur (13th cent. B.C.; *Syria* 16:406, 407 and Andrae, *Das Wiedererstandene Assur,* 109, for plan and 110 for perspective). The striking and common element is the arrangement of the altar; one entered the holy of holies and then turned to the right to view the altar and the idol, which was on a platform served by a series of steps.

Since the Baal temple was built after that to Dagon, and since inscriptional evidence points to the founding of the latter c. 1910 B.C. (*Syria* 13:20), the temple of Dagon began its history late in the 20th cent. B.C.

That the identification of the temple with Dagon is certain is seen by the finding of two dedicatory stelae on the site. One stele (A), complete, is that of a woman, reading:

> *The stele that Tryl erected to Dagan. A monument (commemorating)* [*a head of small*] *and a head of large cattle as food* (Gordon, *Ugaritic Literature,* 108).

The other (B), incomplete, reads in part:

> *The monument that* -zn *erected to Dagan, his master, (commemorating)* [*a head of small and a head of large*] *cattle in the* mhrt *(temple refectory?) (Ibid.)*

The stelae had the usual rounded heads and a tennon at the bottom to fit into a stone socket (*Syria* 16, plate XXXI).

2. *Ashdod.* Excavations were conducted at Ashdod May-June, 1962 (IEJ 12:147-150) and June-July, 1963 (IEJ 13:340-342). In the first campaign, the only Philistine pottery finds occurred in a large pit. In the second season two levels of Philistine occupation dating to the 12th and 11th centuries B.C. were exposed, the principal structure being a fortress. So far no temple has appeared (cf. Judg 16:23), but such may be unearthed in the future (*see* BA, XXVI, 134ff.). The fortress testifies to the prowess of the Philistines.

3. *Gaza.* Excavations of this city by Phythian-Adams, "Reports on Soundings at Gaza" (PEQ, 1923, 11-36), give no data since the soundings were limited by present occupation. As this was a Philistine city, one would expect a temple to occur in this city, and perhaps future excavations will disclose it.

4. *Bethshan.* Of the four temples found by the Museum of the University of Pennsylvania excavations in 1925-1926, the two temples of Rameses III (1175-1144) are from the era of Philistine occupation (Rowe, *The Four*

Canaanite Temples of Beth-shan, 22). The southern temple is of minor hypo-style construction on an irregular plan. The outer walls are of mud brick on basalt stone bases; the central hall is divided into side aisles and a central one by three columns in each of two rows that support the clerestory above the center aisle. Between the columns in each row are dwarf walls separating the clerestory aisle from the side aisles (*see* Rowe, op. cit., 24, fig. 5 and plate X). This central hall measures 71 ft E to W and 25 ft. N to S. It is flanked by two small and one long storeroom on the N and by two small ones on the S, plus a third room to their E, which opens off the E end of the central hall. At this end of the hall is a transept, longer toward the S than to the N. At its E wall is a type of pedestal on a raised floor level at the E end of the hall and extends around both to the north and south sides of the transept. From the center aisle, steps ascend to this level with a small, low pedestal immediately in front of them. In a general way this is similar to the pedestal feature at Ugarit and at Assur. The low pedestal on the upper level may have carried an idol but there is no evidence of any curtain at the near columns.

The clerestory wall was of brick construction supported by wood beams bearing on the wood columns below. The clay roof was supported on a framework of beams and branches.

Since the southern temple is the larger of the two, and since Dagon was the chief god of the Philistines, it may be assumed that this was the temple of Dagon. It was here that the head of Saul was fastened (1 Chron 10:10).

The reconstruction of the northern temple may be seen in Rowe, op. cit., 33, figure; plate XII. This is similar to the southern temple but having one less column in each row, a slightly higher platform for the idol, and no store rooms. The identity as the house of Ashtaroth (1 Sam 31:10) seems assured by the finding of the figures of Antit, the warrior goddess, dressed as an ashteroth. Here was placed the armor of Saul by the Philistines (1 Chron 10:10).

V. Conclusions. The similarities among the separate temples vary somewhat, but one may note that those of Ugarit and Assyria are closest, whereas those of Ashdod and Bethshan are most alike. This conclusion is based on the fact that, although no temple of Dagon at Gaza has been found yet, Judges 16:25-30 indicates that there were pillars in it, perhaps somewhat in arrangement as those at Bethshan. There was most likely a large forecourt framed by a colonnade, indicated by the large number of observers (3000) on the roofs, with the court side being supported by a series of columns according to the Egyp. style. The temple itself under this arrangement would have been fitted into one side. It was there that Samson was placed and, pushing down the columns, initiated a domino-like action of destruction that brought down the temple and court colonnade.

An Astarte plaque, associated with Dagon worship.

A comparison of the Ugaritic and Assyrian temples show preference for the Mesopotamian model, whereas those of the Philistines reveal a preference for the Egypt. type. This latter conclusion is based on the usage in Egypt of the clerestory and a more open sanctuary. Therefore, the temple plans followed the typical arrangement of the political area exerting greatest influence over the respective areas. Ugarit derived her religion and temple from Mesopotamia; the Philistines owed their allegiance to Egypt and took inspiration from her architecture.

The use in Solomon's Temple of a plan akin to the temple of Dagon in Ugarit is dictated by the requirements of the worship of Yahweh, and this arrangement was not available in the examples from Egypt. A "wall of separation" between the worshiper and Yahweh was required, but even in this arrangement, it is not the heavy masonry dividing wall characteristic of the examples from the north.

BIBLIOGRAPHY. R. A. S. Macalister, *The Philistines, Their History and Civilization* (1913); Phythian-Adams, "Report on Soundings at Gaza," PEQ (1923), 11-36; "Beth-dagon vs. Beth-gallim," BASOR 18 (1925), 10; "Dagan," H. Schmökel, *Realexikon für Assyriologie*, II (1934), 99-101; R. Dussaud, "Two Stelae to Dagan," *Syria,* XVI (1935), 179, 180; A. Rowe, *The Four Canaanite Temples of Bethshan*, I (1940); R. Dussaud, *Les*

Decouverts de Ras Shamra et l'OT (1941); F. J. Montalbano, "Canaanite Dagon: Origin, Nature," CBQ (1951), 13:381-397; Y. Yadin, "Excavations at Hazor," BA (1956), XIX:2-12; "Excavations at Ashdod," IEJ (1962), 12:147-150; (1963), 13: 340-342; BA (1963) XXVI:134ff.; M. Dothan, "2000 ans de l'ancienne cité," BETS (1965), 71.

H. G. STIGERS

DAILY BREAD. *See* LORD'S PRAYER, THE.

DAINTIES, DAINTY (MEATS). Three Heb. words referring to tasty, delightful food are so tr. Each occurs only in the pl. מַטְעַמּוֹת "tasty, savory food" is built on the root טעם "to taste." Six times in Genesis 27 *mat'amôt* refers to the "savory food" which Rebekah and Jacob used to deceive Isaac. Rebekah made this favorite dish out of two kids of the goats (KJV v. 9). In Proverbs 23:3 "dainties" (RSV "delicacies") of the ruler are described as "deceptive food." Verse 6 warns about the dainties and bread of one with an evil eye.

מַנְעַמִּים "delicacies, dainties," from נעם "be pleasant, delightful" occurs only in Psalm 141:4. The psalmist prays that Jehovah will preserve his heart from evil deeds and from partaking of their "dainties." The food is clearly portrayed as a lure to unrighteous fellowship.

מַעֲדַנִּים, "dainty (food), delight," can have a good connotation. Proverbs 29:17 speaks of the delight which a disciplined son brings his father. Food does not seem to be involved. When Jacob blesses Asher, he predicts that he will "yield royal dainties" (Gen 49:20). This same identification of royalty and *ma'ădannîm* occurs in Lamentations 4:5, where "wearers of scarlet" are mentioned.

H. M. WOLFE

DAISAN. KJV Apoc. form of REZIN.

DAKUBI. ASV form of AKKUB.

DALAIAH. KJV form of DELAIAH in 1 Chronicles 3:24.

DALE, THE KING'S (עֵמֶק הַמֶּלֶךְ). Where Abraham met the king of Sodom and Melchizedek (Gen 14:17, KJV KING'S DALE; ASV KING'S VALE; RSV KING'S VALLEY), and where Absalom erected a pillar to himself (2 Sam 18:18, RSV KING'S VALLEY). Josephus (Antiq. VII, x, 3) says it was two furlongs from Jerusalem.

DALETH. The fourth letter in the Heb. alphabet (ד), originally shaped like a triangle with no projecting leg at the right-hand corner (such as characterized the letter *rēsh*) until the 7th century B.C. and thereafter (when it became more easily confused with (ר), *rēsh*, even though the latter normally had a longer tail projecting from its lower right angle). Later on, when "square Heb." characters developed (apparently in Aram. circles during the 6th cent.), *daleth* assumed the shape of an upside-down "L" (with the short horizontal arm projecting leftward); oddly enough, *rēsh* also assumed a similar shape (ר), except that the angle corner was somewhat rounded, and never developed a tittle (or projection to the right of the vertical stroke) as *daleth* did. This letter was pronounced *d* as in Eng., although in later times it spirantized to the *th* sound in the Eng. "this" when it was preceded by a vowel sound. As a numerical sign, *daleth* represented the number four.

G. L. ARCHER

DALILA. Douay VS form of DELILAH.

DALMANUTHA dăl' mə nōō' thə (Δαλμανουθά). Only in Mark 8:10 in the NT, the name of a village near the W shore of the Sea of Galilee.

Jesus and His disciples came to this place (εἰς μέρη Δαλμανουθά) following the feeding of the 4,000, an area seemingly contingent or identical with Magadan in the Matthew 15:39 parallel passage (Μαγαδάν; variant, Μαγδαλά) in both of which passages the τὰ μέρη and τὰ ὅρια used respectively indicating "regions" suggest the same area, although the names vary.

The ruins on the W shore of the lake N of Tiberias near modern Mejdel (Magdala) may be the location.

The textual variants for Dalmanutha in Mark 8:10 are several, including Magedan, Melegada and Magdala. Rendell Harris has argued that Dalmanutha is in the text because of an inadvertently repeated לחניתא, the real name having disappeared. However, Dalman notes that τὰ μέρη as "districts" is a Graecism, not capable of being reproduced literally in Aram. The variant Magdala may have been the original reading (Mark 8:10mg.).

BIBLIOGRAPHY. G. Dalman, *Die Worte Jesu* (1930), 52f.; B. Hjerl-Hansen, "Dalmanutha," RBL III (1946), 372-384; D. Baly, *Geographical Companion to the Bible* (1963), 120; C. E. B. Canfield, *Saint Mark,* CGT Commentary (1963), 257.

W. H. MARE

DALMATIA dăl mā' shə (Δαλματία). Dalmatia (2 Tim 4:10) was a district in the southern part of Illyricum, a somewhat vaguely defined area of coast and mountain hinterland that lay E of the Adriatic Sea confronting Italy. Rome first compelled the warlike tribes of this area to acknowledge her sovereignty in the middle years of the 2nd cent. B.C. Subjugation was precarious and far from complete, and the Dalmatians remained a military problem until Octavian, the future emperor Augustus, brought the area more firmly under Rom. control. The Pax Romana was finally established by his successor, Tiberius. It was a vital area in the prosecution of Rome's project of a Rhine-Danube frontier.

Paul's brief and unexplained reference to Illyricum in writing to Rome (Rom 15:19) may mean that the apostle himself had founded Christian churches in the southern and more Hellenized parts of the region. He possibly visited the area from Macedonia after his Ephesian ministry (Acts 20:1).

E. M. BLAIKLOCK

DALPHON **dăl′ fŏn** (דַּלְפוֹן, perhaps from a root meaning *dripping, weeping*). The second of ten sons of Haman killed by the Jews in Susa (Esth 9:7).

DAMARIS **dám ə rĭs** (Δάμαρις; meaning uncertain; prob. *wife* from the poetic Gr. δάμαρ).

One of Paul's converts at Mars Hill in Athens (Acts 17:34). Beyond this we know nothing of her. Since Luke singled her out as one of several converts and since she was named with Dionysius, one of the judges of the Athenian court, she may have been a woman of high social rank. There is no evidence that she was the wife of Dionysius as some have contended. Since a respectable woman of Athens generally would not have attended such a public gathering, some have suggested that she was one of the ἑταίραι, an educated courtesan, a woman of low moral character. This is possible but the evidence is not conclusive.

H. J. MILES

DAMASCUS **də măs′ kəs** (Gr. Δαμασκός; Heb. דַּמֶּשֶׂק, and perhaps מֶשֶׁק; Gen 15:2) (1) the well-known city NE of Mt. Hermon, (2) the general geographic region, and (3) at times, the state of which the city was the capital.

A. Locale. Damascus is located in a plain of about 2200 ft. elevation surrounded on three sides by mountains: Mt. Hermon and the Anti-Lebanon range on the W, a ridge jutting from the range on the N, and Jebel Aswad (Mt. Aswad) which separates it from the fertile Hauran (Biblical Bashan) on the S. Toward the E marshy lakes and low hills separate the region from the desert. Rainfall is a sparse ten inches per year so that agriculture must depend upon irrigation waters from the streams flowing off the Anti-Lebanon (El-Barada, *The Cool*, Biblical Abana) and from Mt. Hermon (El-Awaj, *The Crooked*, Biblical Pharpar). By careful usage these transform the plain into a green garden, surrounded by barren, brown hills and desert sands. Agricultural products include olives, various fruits, almonds, walnuts, pistachios, grains, tobacco, cotton, flax, and hemp.

B. History. 1. *Prior to 1200 B.C.* Earliest history of Damascus is known only from occasional references in documents of surrounding peoples and by inferences from the general state of affairs. The general region (called Abina, Apina, Aba, Abu, Api, Upe, etc.) is referred to in the Egyp. Execration texts (18th and 19th centuries B.C.) and in the Mari Letters (c. 18th cent. B.C.). Biblical "Mesheq" may be a name for Damascus from the time of Abraham (Gen 15:2: Heb. text). The name "Damascus" first appears among the conquests of Thutmoses III (1484-1450 B.C.). It remained a part of the Egyp. empire until Akhenaton (c. 1372-1354 B.C.). With the collapse of Egyp. power under Akhenaton, the Hittites penetrated as far S as Damascus, but Damascus does not seem to have been incorporated into the Hitt. empire as were regions further N. Seti I (1312-1298 B.C.) returned Damascus to the Egyp. sphere of influence, but in the latter part of the reign of Ramses II (1301-1225 B.C.) Egyp. power in Asia again faltered.

2. *From 1200 B.C. to the Assyrian Conquest (732 B.C.).* The extensive migrations of people of the late 13th cent. B.C. jolted Egypt and destroyed the Hitt. empire. They left the Hebrews, the Aramaeans, the Philistines, and numerous other peoples settled in new homelands. They set the stage for the Biblical conflicts between the Hebrews and the Aramaeans, esp. those of Damascus. The Heb. tribes lay directly across the trade routes extending SW from Damascus, thus assuring enmity between the two. Likewise Damascus was a threat to Assyrian trade routes to the Mediterranean.

Saul fought against Aramaean kingdoms such as Zobah (1 Sam 14:47). David incorporated a number of Aramaean kingdoms, including Damascus, into his empire (2 Sam 8:5, 6). But,

Ruins of Roman gate on or at the entrance to the "Street called Straight" in Damascus (Photo 1966). ©Lev

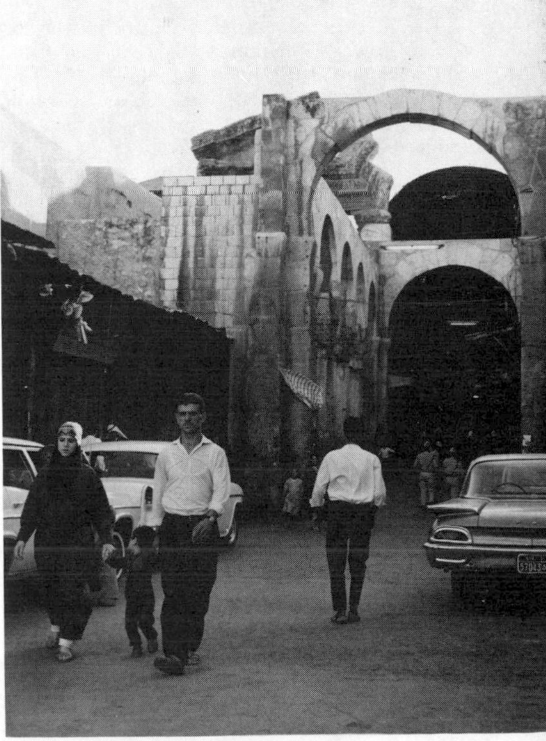

shortly afterward, Damascus regained her independence under Rezon and took the lead in Syrian resistance to Heb. domination (1 Kings 11:23-25; c. 940 B.C.). The death of Solomon and the subsequent division of the Heb. kingdom ended all Heb. pretensions of an empire in Syria. Under Rezon, Hezion and Tabrimmon (the latter two known from 1 Kings 15:18 and the Ben-hadad Stele; some identify Rezon and Hezion), Damascus became the leader of the Aramaean states of Syria.

History of Damascus now turns on three kings, Ben-hadad I (i.e. Hadad-ezer or Adad-idri; 883-843 B.C.), Hazael (843-c. 801 B.C.), and Ben-hadad II. Their policies were (1) suppression of the Hebrews in order to keep the southeastern trade routes open, and (2) maintenance of an anti-Assyrian coalition of Syrian states—including the Hebrews whenever possible.

Under Ben-hadad I, Damascus dominated Syria and was easily able to intervene in Heb. affairs (cf. 1 Kings 15:16-22; c. 879). The dynasty of Omri offered more effective resistance; Ahab defeated Ben-hadad I twice in battle (c. 855 and 854; 1 Kings 20:1-21, 23-34). However, the following year, Ahab and Ben-hadad were allies against Assyria at the Battle of Qarqar (853 B.C.). Ben-hadad remained the soul of resistance to Assyria through three more hard-fought campaigns (849, 848, 845) and seems to have been generally successful in checking Assyrian expansion. He also saw his great enemy, Ahab, die in the battle of Ramoth-gilead (c. 851; 22:34-36). Ben-hadad was killed by the usurper, Hazael.

The role of the prophet Elisha in Hazael's rise to power (2 Kings 8:10-15) is significant. This incident also gives a graphic view of Heb. fear of Hazael (v. 12). Hazael decisively defeated the Hebrews; he suppressed Jehu and reduced Jehoahaz to vassalage (13:1-9). Against the Assyrians, he was less successful. Shalmaneser III boasted of slaying some 16,000 of Hazael's men, besieging Damascus, despoiling gardens outside the wall, and plundering the region as far S as the Hauran.

Ben-hadad II was defeated both by the Hebrews and the Assyrians. Adad-Nirari III of Assyria boasts of besieging Damascus and receiving tribute. Then a revitalized Israel, under Joash and Jeroboam II, not only gained independence but even succeeded in making Damascus the vassal state (14:28).

The end for Damascus came when Ahaz of Judah called for Assyrian help against Israel under Pekah and Damascus under Rezon (Biblical Rezin; 16:5-9). Tiglath-pileser III (i.e. Pul; 745-727 B.C.), in response, defeated Israel annexing part of her territory and then sacked Damascus putting an end to her history as an independent Aramaean state.

3. *Under Foreign Rule (732 B.C.-A.D. 636).* Damascus' economic importance endured through Assyrian, Babylonian, and Persian rule until Antioch became the commercial leader of Syria in the Hel. Age. Warfare between the Ptolemies of Egypt and the Seleucids left Damascus under Seleucid control. However, after Rom. intervention Damascus was at various times controlled by the Nabateans (c. 85 B.C. and the time of Paul), by Herod, and even by Cleopatra. Other times Damascus was a "free" member of the Decapolis, but finally became a part of the Rom. empire under Nero after being temporarily controlled by Augustus and Tiberius. With the division of the Rom. empire, Damascus became one of the major frontier cities of the Byzantine empire.

4. *Arab rule (A.D. 636-present).* Arab rule began with the Battle of Yarmuk in 636. Since then Damascus has generally retained her economic importance and at times has added an important political and cultural role. Her period as capital of the Umayyad Empire (639-744) and the 14th cent. under the control of the Egyp. Mamelukes was brilliant. Her most serious disaster was the sacking at the hands of Timur's Mongols in 1401. In modern times, Damascus has regained her role as leading city and capital of Syria though her former economic importance is shared with Aleppo.

C. Description and remains. Modern Damascus combines clean, wide thoroughfares with the narrow, crowded lanes of the older quarters of the city. Traditional handicraft industries can be seen within walking distance of the site of the annual Damascus trade fair.

Historic remains and sacred sites abound in the region. Moslem pilgrims can visit Adam's Cave at Jebel Qasiyun, the Cave of Blood where Abel was murdered, the Cavern of Gabriel, and Moses' Tomb. The Umayyad Mosque built on the site of the basilica of St. John the Baptist—which in turn occupied the site of a classical temple of Jupiter—still shows some elements of the old pagan temple. Moslem tradition asserts that the Prophet Jesus (i.e. Jesus of Nazareth) will return to the Minaret of Jesus of this mosque to fight the Anti-Christ.

For the Christian there is the street called Straight, the place in the wall—including the very window—from which Paul was lowered in a basket, the site of Paul's vision, and the house of Ananias. All of these are of dubious authenticity.

For the historian there are the Citadel chiefly from the 13th cent. but built on the site of a Rom. fortress, portions of the city wall, and the National Museum. For the student of Biblical backgrounds, the Museum features the Mari Room with an outstanding collection of statues and objects, and the Ras Shamra Room containing the major finds from Ugarit. Also of interest is the reconstruction of the Dura Europa synagogue and the objects from Palmyra (Tadmor). *See* ARAM, ARAMEANS.

BIBLIOGRAPHY. "Damascus," HDB (1900);

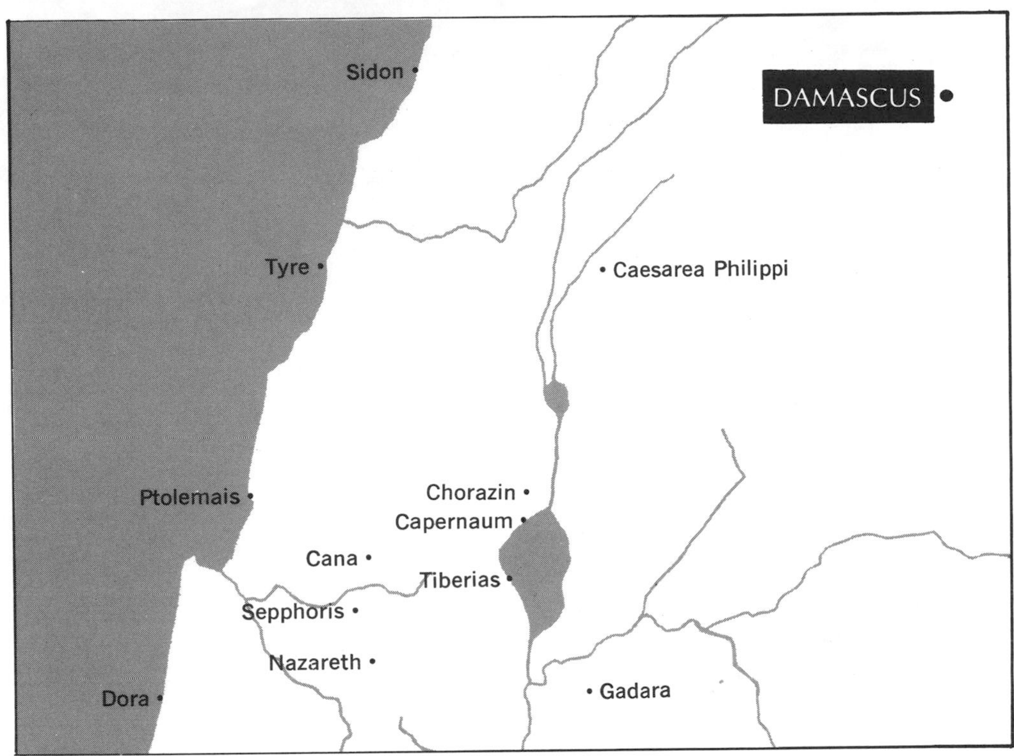

BASOR, 87 (1947), 23-29; M. F. Unger, *Israel and the Aramaeans of Damascus* (1957); "Damascus," *Encyclopedia of Islam* (1965); M. F. Unger, "Damascus," *The Biblical World* (1966); C. Thubron, *Mirror to Damascus* (1967).

A. BOWLING

DAMASCUS, COVENANT OF. The name of a Jewish community which cherished the priestly traditions of the sons of Zadok. Its existence became known through the discovery of two fragmentary MSS written between the 10th and 12th centuries A.D., found in 1896-1897 in the genizah of the Ibn-Ezra Synagogue in Cairo. These documents are usually called the Zadokite Fragments, but sometimes referred to as the Damascus Document or the Zadokite Work. They refer to the community as the "New Covenant in the Land of Damascus." The community has also been called the community of the Zadokites, or the New Covenanters. Affinities between this group and the Qumran community are striking and indisputable. Many characteristic expressions of the Zadokite Fragments are found in the DSS.

F. B. HUEY, JR.

DAMN, DAMNABLE, DAMNATION (ἀπώλεια, *destruction, ruin, loss*; κρίμα, *judgment, verdict, condemnation*; κρίσις, *judgment*; κρίνω, *to judge*; κατακρίνω, *to condemn*).

These words appear in the KJV, but not in the RSV. "Damnable" is found only in 2 Peter 2:1, where the apostle warns of false teachers who will secretly bring in "damnable heresics" (RSV "destructive heresies"). The word "damnable" does not really express the force of the Gr. word used, *apōleia,* which implies that the leading characteristic of the heresies of which the apostle speaks is that they lead men to destruction or perdition. The same Gr. word is tr. "damnation" in 2 Peter 2:3, where the apostle says of the false teachers that "their damnation slumbereth not" (RSV "their destruction has not been asleep")—that is, destruction will certainly overtake them.

In the KJV the word "damnation" is used ten times and "damned" three times as trs. of the Gr. word *krínō* and its cognates, which the KJV renders "judge" eighty-seven times, "judgment" forty-one times, "condemn" twenty-two times, and "condemnation" eight times. There is no good reason why on thirteen occasions the stronger words "damnation" and "damned" should be used. They have a connotation today that they did not have in 1611. The Lat. word *damnare,* from which "damnation" is derived, means "to judge," "condemn." Under the influence of theology, however, the Eng. words derived from it acquired the sense of "condemnation to eternal punishment in hell," which they have today, but which the KJV trs. did not have in mind.

In Matthew 23:14 Jesus warned the Pharisees that because of their hypocrisy they would receive "the greater condemnation," not "the greater damnation" (KJV); and in Matthew 23:33 He asked them how they were "to escape being sentenced to hell," not how they were to

Excavation at Dan. This was the platform on which Jeroboam's golden calves were located. ©*Lev*

"escape the damnation of hell" (KJV).

The Lord did not warn that those guilty of blasphemy against the Holy Ghost are in danger of "eternal damnation" (KJV), but rather that they are "guilty of an eternal sin" (RSV) (Mark 3:29); that is, this sin belongs to the sphere of the world to come.

The KJV of Mark 16:16 says that "he that believeth not shall be damned"; the RSV has, correctly, "will be condemned."

Jesus foretold that some day all men shall rise from their graves, the good to a resurrection of life, the evil to a "resurrection of judgment" (KJV "resurrection of damnation") (John 5:29).

Paul says of some Jews who have slandered him that their condemnation (KJV "damnation") is just (Rom 3:8); that is, the judgment of God which will fall upon them is just.

In Romans 13:2 Christians are urged to obey the state, for those who resist it will incur "judgment" (KJV "damnation").

The Christian who has doubts about what he eats is "condemned" (KJV "damned") (Rom 14:23)—that is, he is condemned both by his own conscience and the Word of God.

The Christian who observes the Lord's Supper carelessly brings "judgment" (KJV "damnation") upon himself (1 Cor 11:29)—exposing himself to severe temporal judgments from God.

God will send upon unbelievers and evildoers in the tribulation period a strong delusion "so that all may be condemned" (KJV "damned") (2 Thess 2:12).

Young widows who have violated their first pledge incur "condemnation," not "damnation" (KJV) (1 Tim 5:12). *See* Condemn.

BIBLIOGRAPHY. R. Bridges and L. A. Weigle, *The Bible Word Book* (1960), 92, 93; TNDT, III (1965), 921-942.

S. Barabas

DAN. *See* Vedan.

DAN (CITY) (Heb. דָּן), a city of the northern extremity of ancient Israel, situated on the S base of Mount Hermon close to one of the tributaries of the Jordan River, the Nahr Leddan. It was commonly used as a symbol of the extent of Israelite territory in the phrase, "from Dan to Beer-sheba" (Judg 20:1, et al.). The mound where the ancient city stood is presently known as Tell el-Qādi and rises about seventy-five ft. above the grass land roundabout. In ancient Canaanite times it was known as Laish (variant, Leshem Heb. לישה, variant, Heb. לשם, as in Judg 18:7; variant, Josh 19:47). The name was prob. derived from an old Sem. word for "lion" (Heb. ליש, Isa 30:6, et al.). It is known that the site was occupied as early as the Bronze Age and prob. was inhabited by 3500 B.C. The town was on the trade route to the Syrian coast; specifically, it was about midway between ancient Aram, Tyre and Sidon. It is above the great valley of Beth-Rehob which stretches from N to S between Mt. Lebanon and Mt. Hermon. It was in this region that Abraham and his retinue pursued the Elamite king, Chedorlaomer (Gen 14:14). The Danite conquest of the city is reviewed in Judges 18 which also states, "they dwelt in security, after the manner of the Sidonians, quiet and unsuspecting, lacking nothing that is in the earth, and possessing wealth" (v. 7). After the revolt of Jeroboam, Dan along with Bethel became the locations of the two shrines which he set up with golden calves prob. as symbols of Baal worship (1 Kings 12:29). So ingrained did this worship at the shrines become that even the massacre of Baal worshipers by Jehu did not stamp out the worship at Dan (2 Kings 10:28-31). Subsequently it was one of the towns taken by the Syrian king, Ben-hadad, in fulfillment of the warning in 2 Kings 10:32, "the LORD began to cut off parts of Israel." Dan was recaptured by Israel under Jeroboam II (14:25), but was again captured by the Assyrian Tiglath-pileser III (745-727 B.C.). In accord with his usual policy often depicted on Assyrian reliefs of the period, he deported the inhabitants of captured towns, thus the Israelites were carried off to resettle the cities of the Medes (2 Kings 17:6). Dan is mentioned in the extrabiblical sources as early as the conquest annals of Thutmose III (1490-1436 B.C.), in which it appears as *R w ś* (L/Ra-wish). It is also mentioned by Josephus, as the area in which Titus, at his father Vespasian's orders, stamped out a revolt in the Fall of A.D. 67. (Jos. War IV, I, 1ff.)

W. WHITE, JR.

DANCING. Several Heb. words describe the joyous, rhythmic movements of the dance, which evidently played a significant part in Israelite life and religion. רקד, *to skip about*, means *to dance, leap* in the Piel. It is used of children's merriment (Job 21:11) and is the opposite of mourning (Eccl 3:4). Ugaritic *mrqdm* are dancers, appearing with drums, cymbals and lyre. חול (חיל), basically means *to whirl, dance, writhe*. Cf. Akkad. *hâlu, to tremble, writhe*. Dancing described by חיל and its cognates can be performed in praise of Yahweh (Ps 149:3; 150:4) or in idol worship. When David and Saul returned victoriously from battle with the Philistines, women joyously met them dancing to the accompaniment of singing and musical instruments (1 Sam 18:6).

The root כרר, denotes a whirling type of dance. (Cf. Aram. *karkara* "to turn," and Ugar. *krkr* "to twist, twiddle fingers.") This word describes David's lengthy dance before the Ark (2 Sam 6:14, 16). Verse 16 also includes the Piel of פזז, "to show agility, leap (in dancing)." The dancing of the whirling dervishes of Islam seems to afford some parallel to this type. Another word, שחק, basically "to laugh, play," can describe singing and dancing (1 Sam 18:7; 2 Sam 6:5, 21).

The religious involvements of dancing are clear from several passages already cited. Added to these could be the dance led by Miriam's timbrel playing celebrating Israel's preservation at the Sea of Reeds (Exod 15:20). Judges 21:16-24 records the dancing of girls connected with the annual feast at Shiloh. There is likewise evidence based on post-OT practice that dancing may have taken place during other religious celebrations, such as the Feast of Tabernacles.

Some feel that the root of the basic word for festival or pilgrim feast, חג, may be related to dancing. David surprised the Amalekites as they were eating, drinking, and חגגים, "reeling, dancing" (1 Sam 30:16). Cf. Psalm 107:27 where "reeling" on the sea as drunkards is the meaning for חגג. "Circling in the sacred dance" has been suggested as the meaning of חגג (BDB p. 290), but this is doubtful based on its usage.

The Psalms scarcely mention dancing, but do frequently describe religious processions. It is possible that dancing was included on these occasions, inasmuch as singers and instrumentalists are mentioned (Ps. 68:25). If Psalm 132 commemorates 2 Samuel 6, the procession in vv. 8 to 10 could include a repetition of the dance of David in 2 Samuel 6:14-16.

Pagan societies utilized the dance for various purposes, including religious ritual. The prophets of Baal employed a kind of limping dance while imploring their god on Mt. Carmel (1 Kings 18:26). In Babylon, dancing was so closely tied to the religious cult that it could not be properly called an independent activity. Egyptian paintings and reliefs portray the dancing of girls to the beating of drums and other instruments.

Gordon has related the dancing of David (2 Sam 6:16) to the war dances used by the Spartans of Tyrtaeus. These dances were performed in time to the elegiac poems composed by the Spartan leader. Just as David used poetry to inspire and teach his troops (1:18ff.), so he may have utilized the dance. He could have learned this technique from his tenure among the Philistines, whose Aegean connections are well-known.

In the NT ὀρχέομαι can be used of the playful dancing of children (Luke 7:32) or of the performance of the daughter of Herodias (Matt 14:6; Mark 6:22). The latter dance was undoubtedly a sensuous display before the immoral king. Luke 15:25 refers to the joyous dancing celebrating the return of the prodigal son.

While the mode of dancing is not known in detail, it is clear that men and women did not generally dance together, and there is no real evidence that they ever did. Social amusement was hardly a major purpose of dancing, and the modern method of dancing by couples is unknown. *See* FEASTS.

BIBLIOGRAPHY. W. O. E. Oesterley, *The Sacred Dance* (1923); J. Pedersen, *Israel* III-IV (1940), 759; W. Sorell, "Israel and the Dance"; D. D. Runes, ed., *The Hebrew Impact on Western Civilization* (1951), 505-511; C. Gordon, "David the Dancer," M. Haran, ed., *Yehezkel Kaufmann Jubilee* (1960), 46-49; H. W. F. Saggs, *The Greatness That Was Babylon* (1962), 190.

H. M. WOLF

DANDLE. To dandle is affectionately to move a child up and down on one's knees or in one's arms. The word is used to tr. two Heb. words: (1) שׁעשׁע, *to sport, take delight in* (Isa 66:12; used in KJV, ASV, RSV), LXX παρακαλέω, *to comfort*, and (2) טפח, *to hold in spread hands, spread* (Lam 2:22 ASV and RSV); KJV *swaddled.* Both contexts illustrate God's care for His children by the loving care of a parent.

DANIEL, BOOK OF Dăn'yĕl (דניאל), LXX Δανιήλ. This book was placed in the *Ketubim* or third section of the Heb. Canon, but in Eng. VSS it occurs as the fourth major composition in the prophetic writings, following the order of the Alexandrian canon.

1. Historical background
2. Unity
3. Authorship and special problems
4. Date
5. Place of origin
6. Destination
7. Occasion
8. Purpose
9. Canonicity
10. Text
11. Content
12. Theology and Interpretation

1. Historical background. The period of time covered by the historical and visionary sections of the book is slightly in excess of the full period of Heb. exile in Babylonia. Daniel was apparently taken by Nebuchadnezzar to Babylon along with other Judean hostages in 605 B.C., following a Babylonian attempt to subjugate Judah. This would indicate that he was descended from a noble family, since normally only prominent persons were taken captive in this manner. According to the book, the attributive author was trained for service in the royal court, and it was not long before he gained an outstanding reputation as a seer and wise man. With divine help he was able to recall and interpret visions which other men had had, and subsequently he experienced several visions himself by which he was able to predict the future triumph of the Messianic kingdom. The book covers the activities of Daniel under successive rulers including Belshazzar and Darius the Mede. His last recorded vision occurred on the banks of the river Tigris in the third year of Cyrus, i.e., 536 B.C. Thus the historical period involved corresponds to slightly more than the full extent of the Heb. exile, after the decree of Cyrus had been promulgated in 538 B.C. The background of both the historical and visionary sections is clearly Babylonian, and there is no question as to whether the author was ever in any other place than Babylonia during his mature years. Babylonian traditions and imagery are clearly in evidence, and the book reflects precisely the same historical background as that found in Ezekiel. Quite possibly the Book of Daniel covers a greater length of time than that of his contemporary Ezekiel, since the latter has no specific references to the Pers. regime as master of the contemporary political scene.

2. Unity. The book falls quite readily into two distinct sections comprising chs. 1 to 6, which consist of narratives set against an historical background, and chs. 7 to 12, which contain the visions experienced by Daniel. There seems little doubt that similarity of subject matter was the primary reason for such an arrangement. Although a general chronological order was followed in the first six chs., it was modified in the remainder of the book in favor of relating the various visions to one another in terms of theme and content rather than the actual time when they occurred. This division indicates that the Book of Daniel was compiled as a literary bifid, furnishing in effect a two-volume work whose parts could circulate independently if necessary and still provide an adequate understanding of the prophet's activities and outlook. The compilation of works in bifid form was by no means uncommon in antiquity, and in the case of large books like Isaiah it served to reduce the composition to more manageable proportions without at the same time losing any of the essential teachings of the author concerned. Elementary though this bifid division is, a great many scholars have failed to recognize it as a genuine literary structure. Consequently a number of contributing authors have been suggested for the book in some circles, ranging up to nine different hands. Yet, concurrent with theories of multiple authorship have been staunch avowals of the unity of Daniel from both liberal and conservative sources. The wide diversity of opinion regarding the unity of the book is unfortunately self-defeating, and reflects unfavorably upon the critical methods employed. It is now no longer possible to maintain the diversity of authorship of the work on the ground that it contains two languages, an Aram. section (Dan 2:4b-7:28) enclosed by a Heb. prologue and epilogue (1:1-2:4a; 8:1-12:13). As the result of archeological discoveries it is now known that the ancient Mesopotamian writers not infrequently enclosed the main body of a unified literary work within a linguistic form of a contrasting nature in order to heighten the general effect. This is true of such notable compositions as the Code of Hammurabi, where the principal prose section was prefaced and concluded by means of poetic material. Exactly the same compositional technique can be seen in the Book of Job, where a prose prologue and epilogue enclose a large poetic section. The Book of Daniel is yet another example of a unified and consciously constructed literary integer involving different linguistic components, and once the underlying compositional traditions are recognized, the need for postulating a diversity of authorship on this ground disappears.

3. Authorship and special problems. The question of the authorship of Daniel is closely linked with considerations of date, particularly since modern critical scholarship has been virtually unanimous in its rejection of the book as a 6th cent. B.C. document written by Daniel. If the book was composed by an unknown author during the Maccabean period with the aim of encouraging faithful Jews in their resistance to the Hellenizing policies of Antiochus IV Epiphanes (cf. 1 Macc 2:59, 60), as critics have long maintained, it must have been written about 165 B.C., and therefore could not possibly have been the work of Daniel. So diametrically opposed are these views of authorship that the problems which they raise must be given some consideration. The traditional opinion of authorship maintained that the book was in its final form during or shortly after the lifetime of Daniel, and that both the historical experiences through which he passed and the visions received were of a genuine nature. In ascribing authorship to Daniel within this general period the traditional view does not overlook the possibility that Daniel may have had scribal assistance in the compilation of his work, esp. if the finished product can be regarded in any sense as his memoirs. In any event, however, the traditional view could not place the extant form of the book later than half a cent. after the time of Daniel's death.

The critical view of authorship and date can be said to have begun with Porphyry, a 3rd cent. A.D. neo-Platonic philosopher, who took special issue with the leading tenets of Christianity. His comments on Daniel have only survived in quotation form, but show that his objections to the traditional view were based on the *a priori* supposition that there could be no predictive element as such in prophecy. Hence the predictions in Daniel relating to post-Babylonian kings and wars were not really prophecies so much as historical accounts, and therefore of a late date. In assigning the work to the time of Antiochus IV Epiphanes, Porphyry held that the author of Daniel had lied so as to revive the hopes of contemporary Jews in the midst of their hardships. As a result the Book of Daniel contained a number of historical errors because of its distance in time from the original events.

This view has been reflected in one way or another ever since in rationalistic attacks upon Daniel. The shallowness of its basic philosophical pre-supposition is readily apparent from even a casual perusal of OT prophetic lit., where the speakers not only dealt with contemporary events but also pronounced upon happenings in the future, some of which had no particular relationship to the circumstances of their own time. The reason for this, stated simply, is that the Heb. prophets would have had little sympathy for the modern antithesis between forthtelling and foretelling, if only because of the fact that, for them, the future was inherent in the present in a special revelational manner. Rather more serious attention should be paid to the suggestion of Porphyry that the author of Daniel committed specific historical errors. This allegation is curious, since modern critics have regarded him as an extremely talented Jew, and who therefore could be expected to write authoritatively. Furthermore, no intelligent 2nd cent. B.C. Jew could possibly have committed the kind of mistakes alleged if he had ever read the Book of Ezra, which covered the history of the early Pers. period. Nor would the Jews of the Maccabean age have recognized the book as canonical had it actually contained the kind of errors proposed, since they had access to the writings of such ancient historians as Herodotus, Ctesias, Berossus and Menander, who preserved correct chronological and historical traditions. By contrast however, 2nd cent. B.C. Palestinians rejected such works as 1 Maccabees as being unworthy of inclusion in the Heb. canon, which by this time had become closed by common consent.

Characteristic of the sort of historical error popularly supposed to be present in Daniel is the assertion that the reference in Daniel 1:1 can be regarded only as anachronistic, since it implies that Jerusalem had been captured in the third year of Jehoiakim (605 B.C.), and this conflicts with Jeremiah 25:1, 9; 46:2, which spoke in the following year as though Jerusalem had yet to fall to the Chaldean armies. This apparent discrepancy of one year rests on a misunderstanding of chronological reckoning in antiquity. The Babylonian scribes used an accession-year system of computation, reckoning the year in which the king ascended the throne as the "year of the accession to the kingdom," and this was followed by the first, second and subsequent years of rule. The Palestinian scribes, by contrast, tended to follow the non-accession patterns of reckoning found in Egypt, in which the year when royal rule began was regarded as the first of the reign. Quite obviously therefore, Jeremiah reckoned according to the current Palestinian pattern, while Daniel followed the one used in Babylonia. As a result, the fourth year of Jeremiah 25:1 is actually identical with the third year of Daniel 1:1. Both writers were clearly using systems of reckoning with which they were familiar, and which fully accorded with their different cultural backgrounds. It should also be noted that the reference in Daniel does not affirm that Jerusalem was destroyed in 605 B.C., but states only that Nebuchadnezzar took with him certain hostages to Babylonia as a token of good faith on the part of Jehoiakim.

Another supposed historical error on the part of the author has been seen in his use of the term "Chaldean" in an ethnic sense and in a restricted context to indicate a group of "wise men," a usage which does not occur elsewhere in the OT and which pointed allegedly to a late date of composition. This difficulty can be dismissed immediately when it is realized that the 5th cent. B.C. historian Herodotus spoke consistently of the Chaldeans in his *Persian Wars*, acknowledged their priestly office, and stated that some of their cultic procedures went back at least to the time of Cyrus. Furthermore, Assyrian annals employed the term "Chaldean" (*kaldu*) in an ethnic sense and under Nabopolassar of Babylon (626-605 B.C.), a native Chaldean, the designation became extremely reputable, reflecting OT usage.

Further critical objections to the historicity of Daniel have been raised in connection with the relationship between Belshazzar and Nabonidus. In the Book of Daniel the former was king of Babylon, whereas in contemporary cuneiform writings it was Nabonidus who occupied the Babylonian throne (c. 555-539 B.C.). Obviously a contemporary writer would not have made so elementary a mistake, it was argued, and thus the book must be a late product. Babylonian historical sources show that Nabonidus came to power at a time of considerable unrest in the Chaldean period. Amel-Marduk (562-560 B.C.), the successor of Nebuchadnezzar, was assassinated by Neriglissar (560-556 B.C.), who then set out with an army to Cilicia in an attempt to stem the rising power of the Lydians. His son, Labashi-Marduk, reigned for less than a year before being overthrown by Nabonidus, who in turn marched to Cilicia and appears to have achieved some sort of political settlement between Lydia and the Medes. The latter then began to threaten Babylonia, and when its inhabitants refused to accept certain reforms proposed by Nabonidus he promptly made his son Belshazzar co-regent and left for Syria. He campaigned there and in N Arabia for a decade while the feud between himself and the Babylonian priesthood gradually simmered down. About 544 B.C. political conditions in Babylonia made his return possible, but by then the country was weak and hopelessly divided politically. Against this historical background it was perfectly correct for the author of Daniel to speak of Belshazzar as "king," since he was in fact co-regent, and to observe that Daniel ruled "as one of three" (Dan 5:29), the absent partner being Nabonidus. The reference in Daniel 5:18 to Belshazzar as a son of Nebuchadnezzar is also correct according to Sem. usage, since "son" often was used as the equivalent of "descendant." Nitocris, the mother of Belshazzar, was apparently the daughter of Nebuchadnezzar, which again supports the tradition contained in Daniel. As far as incidental historical accuracy is concerned, the author was sufficiently well informed about 6th cent. B.C. life in Babylonia to represent Nebuchadnezzar as being able to formulate and change Babylonian law with absolute sovereignty (2:12, 13, 46), while showing that Darius the Mede was powerless to alter the rigid laws of the Medes and Persians (6:8, 9). Again he was quite correct in recording the change from punishment by fire in the time of the Babylonians (ch. 3) to punishment by being thrown into a lion's den under the Persians (ch. 6), since fire was sacred to the Zoroastrians. Similarly, the author of the work knew precisely why the image of Nebuchadnezzar had been set up in the plain of Dura. Archeological excavations have shown that this enterprising king undertook considerable restoration of ancient buildings during his reign, one of the more notable instances being at Ur. Nebuchadnezzar also instigated a thoroughgoing reformation of religious calendars and cultic practices, and from the evidence presented by the excavation of the temple at Ur it appears that the general tendency of his cultic reforms was in the direction of greater public participation in what hitherto had been rather esoteric sacrificial and other rites. The erecting of a large image in the plain of Dura served to establish general congregational worship by the public, with the king rather than the priesthood as the representative of the god. Substituting this form of congregational worship, Nebuchadnezzar displaced the secret rituals performed by the priests and brought religion within the reach of the lowliest citizen in the empire. All of the foregoing is of immediate significance for the 6th cent. B.C., but is of no relevance whatever for the Maccabean period. Critics of the traditional date and composition of Daniel have long employed the circumstances surrounding the insanity of Nebuchadnezzar as an indication of the unhistorical nature of the book, since such a mental affliction was sup-

A general view of the ruins of Babylon, locale of the Book of Daniel. ©M.P.S.

posedly not recorded in non-Biblical sources. The latter is by no means true, however, for three centuries after the time of Nebuchadnezzar a Babylonian priest named Berossus preserved a tradition that Nebuchadnezzar became ill suddenly toward the end of his reign, which was mentioned by Josephus as well as by the 2nd cent. B.C. writer Abydenus. The garbled nature of Berossus' report lends strength to the view that the illness was a form of madness. In Mesopotamia this kind of affliction was dreaded above all others because it was thought to be the direct result of demon possession. Consequently, madmen were immediately deprived of normal social contacts lest they should cause others to be possessed, and the affliction in its various forms was treated with superstitious dread. For such an ailment to overtake a Babylonian king was unthinkable, but even if it occurred it could never have been recorded as such in the annals. More than three centuries later only the most discreet of references to this calamity was deemed advisable and this attitude contrasts markedly with the concise, objective Heb. report in ch. 4. That this latter described accurately a genuine though rare psychotic condition is evident from the way in which the latter is still seen occasionally today, and can be recognized clearly even from the Daniel narrative alone. The condition is a rare form of monomania known as *boanthropy*, in which the sufferer imagines himself to be an ox and behaves accordingly. The present writer has actually encountered one such case in a British mental institution, and despite the fact that the patient was receiving professional care he manifested all the physical attitudes described in Daniel, including the eating of grass and the drinking of rain water, these latter two items forming his entire diet. Some light may perhaps be thrown on the historical situation by a damaged tablet which Sir Henry Rawlinson recovered from the period of Nebuchadnezzar II. When tr. it read in part: "For four years . . . in all my dominions I did not build a high place of honor, the precious treasures of my kingdom I did not lay out. In the worship of Merodach . . . I did not sing his praises . . . nor did I clear out the canals." If this is a genuine contemporary record it could well be a direct allusion to this embarrassing interlude in the reign of Nebuchadnezzar.

From the fourth Qumran cave came a papyrus scrap containing the "prayer of Nabonidus," and this discovery has prompted the suggestion that the disease described in Daniel 4 was wrongly attributed to Nebuchadnezzar evidently by another author writing long after the events described. The papyrus fragment in question preserved a prayer supposedly uttered by Nabonidus "the great king, (who) prayed when he was smitten with a serious inflammation by command of the most high God in the city of Teima." This affliction evidently occurred during the years when Nabonidus was in voluntary exile from Babylonia, and was living in Arabia. The fragment recorded that Nabonidus confessed his sin when a Jewish priest from the exiles in Babylonia had been sent to him, and the priest then furnished a partial interpretation of the significance of the illness.

Those scholars who have studied this material have supposed that the author of the papyrus had preserved an "older" tradition, regarding Nabonidus rather than Nebuchadnezzar II as the victim of illness. The substitution of the latter in the Daniel account was thought to have occurred long after the original story had been brought to Pal. where recollections of Nabonidus soon faded. There are obvious difficulties in such a position, however. Precisely why the author of Daniel should have used the "prayer of Nabonidus" as the basis for the fourth ch. of his book, and then altered the names, the locale, and even the nature of the disease itself, is extremely difficult to explain. Furthermore, there was already a strong historical tradition associating Nabonidus with Teima and because of the brutality with which Nabonidus established himself at the site it is highly unlikely that either he or the events themselves would be forgotten, particularly among the Arab tribes of the area. Again, while Nabonidus was undoubtedly strong-willed and self-assertive as well as being a man of culture and antiquarian tastes, there is no tradition extant which at any time described him as a madman, cruel though he may have been occasionally. Furthermore, the "prayer of Nabonidus" contains pathological elements which are certainly unknown to modern medicine, whereas the account in Daniel describes a well-attested and readily-recognizable psychotic condition.

It seems clear that two very different traditions are involved. The Qumran scrap seems to preserve an account of some ailment, whether of a staphylococcal nature or not, which afflicted Nabonidus during his years at Teima, and because of certain unrealistic elements it can only be assigned to the realm of legend and folklore. By contrast, the account in Daniel is of an attestable clinical nature, and forms part of a larger tradition which associated madness with Nebuchadnezzar II. Compositions such as *Susanna* and *Bel and The Dragon* show that the Book of Daniel attracted a good deal of legendary material and it may well be that the Qumran fragment is another hitherto undiscovered element of this apocryphal corpus. However, in the view of the present writer, the "prayer of Nabonidus" more prob. constitutes a near contemporary of the apocryphal composition entitled *The Prayer of Manasses*, written in the cent. between 250 and 150 B.C. and closely related to it in both form and content. There is clearly no connection between the "prayer of Nabonidus" and the fourth ch. of Daniel, and it is therefore extremely difficult to see how the Qumran fragment can underlie the Daniel tradition in any sense. The fact that the "prayer of Nabonidus" was first discovered at Qumran might well indicate that it originated during the Maccabean period, and it may possibly have been composed by the Qumran secretaries themselves. There is no single element in it which requires a date of composition significantly earlier than the Maccabean period, and it could possibly have been written as late as 100 B.C.

One of the most tenacious arguments against the historicity and traditional authorship of Daniel has involved the identity of Darius the Mede. Since this man is not mentioned as such by name other than in the Book of Daniel, and the contemporary cuneiform inscrs. leave no room for a king of Babylon between Nabonidus-Belshazzar and the accession of Cyrus of Persia, his historicity has been denied on the ground that the events dealing with him in Daniel represent a mixture of confused traditions. However, because the narratives relating to Darius the Mede have all the appearances of a genuine historical record, it may be instructive to examine the evidence a little more closely. According to Daniel 5:30, 31, Darius the Mede received the government on the death of Belshazzar, being made ruler of the Chaldeans (Dan 9:1) at the age of sixty-two

(5:31). He was accorded the title of "king" (6:6, 9, 25) and the years were reckoned in Babylonian fashion according to his reign (11:1). He appointed 120 subordinate governors of provincial districts under three presidents of whom Daniel was one (6:2). Darius was a contemporary of Cyrus the Persian, and during his rule Daniel came into even greater prominence than before.

Those who have taken the Daniel narrative as historical have made numerous attempts to identify Darius the Mede with persons mentioned in Babylonian cuneiform texts. Since he was a contemporary of Cyrus he clearly cannot be identified with Darius I, son of Hystaspes, who ruled over Babylonia and Persia from 521 to 486 B.C. Darius the Mede has also been identified with Cyrus the Great, who on his defeat of Astyages, king of Media, in 549 B.C. was accorded the title "king of the Medes" by Nabonidus of Babylon. Cyrus is known to have been in his early sixties when he conquered Babylon, and according to contemporary inscrs. he appointed many of his subordinates to positions of high office in the provincial government. Such a view would require that the phrase "and the reign of Cyrus" (6:28) be tr. "in the reign of Cyrus," using two names for one person. This device is quite permissible linguistically, and would accord with the suggestion by D. J. Wiseman that Darius the Mede and Cyrus the Great should be regarded as alternative titles for the same individual, in exactly the same way as James VI of Scotland was known as James I of England. This theory is unfortunately weak in that nowhere was Cyrus named as "son of Ahasuerus" (cf. Dan 1:1), though it may be, of course, that this title was a term used of the royal succession. However, even though Cyrus was considered the king of Media, he was again never described in contemporary inscrs. as "of the seed of a Mede."

Probably the best approach to the problem is to follow J. C. Whitcomb and identify Darius the Mede with Gubaru the governor of Babylon and the "Regions beyond the River" under Cyrus. The Nabonidus Chronicle mentioned two persons connected with the fall of Babylon, namely Ugbaru and Gubaru, and faulty tr. of the Chronicle since 1882 has tended to confuse their identities. It was on the basis of this misunderstanding that scholars such as H. H. Rowley assumed that they were actually one person, the Gobryas of Xenophon's *Cyropaedia*, who died after the fall of Babylon in 539 B.C. The tr. of the Chronicle by Sidney Smith in 1924, however, distinguished between Ugbaru and Gubaru, and it is now apparent that the former, who was governor of Gutium and an ally of Cyrus, took a prominent part in the capture of Babylon and then died shortly afterward, presumably of wounds sustained in the battle. Whereupon the other victorious leader Gubaru, who with Ugbaru was apparently responsible for diverting the river Euphrates so that his soldiers could capture the city by infiltrating along the dried-up river bed, was appointed by Cyrus as the governor of Babylon. He appears to have held this position for fourteen years, and was mentioned in a number of cuneiform texts. One of the Nabonidus tablets discovered at Haran referred to the "king of the Medes" in the tenth year of the reign of Nabonidus (546 B.C.), and while this text does not throw any light on the identity of Darius the Mede it does at least show that the title was in existence after Cyrus had conquered Media, perhaps as the designation of a provincial governor. Certainly the evidence presented by the Nabonidus Chronicle would not permit Darius the Mede to be regarded as a "conflation of confused traditions" as Rowley maintained, but instead offers definite possibilities of the identification of Darius with an historical personage, namely Gubaru. Subsequent cuneiform discoveries may well clarify the situation completely.

At the end of the 19th cent. liberal scholars were fond of adducing as proof of a Maccabean date certain of the linguistic features found in Daniel. Thus, in 1891 S. R. Driver could pronounce quite confidently that the Gr. words demanded, the Heb. supported and the Aram. permitted a date of composition after the conquest of Pal. by Alexander the Great in 332 B.C. This opinion was widely quoted, and H. H. Rowley in particular tried to substantiate these conclusions in some of his publications. However, with more information concerning the history of the Aram. language now on hand, the opinions of Driver and others have undergone sobering modifications. Certain Aram. forms which originally were regarded as late in date have been discovered in the Ras Shamra texts of the Amarna Age, and include specific ones found in the Book of Daniel. As a spoken language Aram. was already current in the 3rd millennium B.C., and was the dialect favored by Laban (Gen 31:47) in the following millennium. Of the four groups of Aram. as established by linguistic research, Old Aram., the language of the N Syrian inscrs. from the 10th to the 8th centuries B.C., formed the basis for official Aram. This latter was already in use by government personnel during the Assyrian period (c. 1100-605 B.C.), and when the Persians gained control of the Near E it became the approved language of diplomatic and other communications. Even before the end of the Assyrian empire, Aram. "dockets" were already being attached to cuneiform tablets to indicate names and dates connected with the texts as well as a summary of their contents. During the Hel. period official Aram. continued in use on dockets as well as on coins, papyri, and a variety of inscrs. Recent studies have shown that the Aram. of Daniel was the kind which developed in government circles from the 7th cent. B.C. and subsequently became widespread in the Near E. The linguistic forms are also closely related to the language of the 5th cent. B.C. Elephantine papyri from Egypt, as well as to the appropriate sections of Ezra. The Heb. portions of Daniel have affinity with the linguistic forms of Ezekiel, Haggai, Ezra, and Chronicles, and not with the later linguistic characteristics of Ecclesiasticus as preserved in rabbinic quotations. Furthermore, it is now seen inadvisable to distinguish at all sharply between the eastern and western branches of the Aram. language, as older scholars were accustomed to do, and this weakens even further the argument for a later rather than an earlier date of composition. Scholars now realize that Pers. loan words in Daniel are consistent with an earlier date for the book instead of one in the Maccabean age. Thus the term "satrap," once thought to be Gr., is now known to have been derived from the old Pers. *Kshathrapan*, which also occurred in the cuneiform texts as *satarpanu*, from which the Gr. form emerged. The Pers. terms in Daniel are actually old Pers. in nature, that is to say, words which occurred specifically within the history of the language up to 300 B.C. To this extent at the very least the Aram. of Daniel is decidedly pre-Hel. in nature, and reflects clearly the classical period when the language was the *lingua franca* of the Pers. empire. From the foregoing evidence it will be obvious that the kind of Aram. used in Daniel is a forceful argument for an earlier rather than a later date of composition, and strongly supports the traditional view of authorship by Daniel in 6th cent. B.C. Babylonia.

The fact that Gr. names were used for certain musical instruments in Daniel, tr. as "harp," "sakbut," and "psaltery," was formerly much in vogue as an argument for a Maccabean date for the writing of the book. However, this view no longer constitutes a serious problem, since archeological discoveries have revealed something of the extent to which Gr. culture had infiltrated the Near E long before the Pers. period. It is now known that, despite their ostensible Gr. nature, the instruments in question are of undoubted Mesopotamian origin. Thus the "harp" was one of the numerous Asiatic forerunners of the Gr. *kithara*; the "sakbut" was most prob. similar to, or derived from, the *sabitu* or Akkad. seven-stringed lyre, while the "psaltery" was the old Pers. *santir* or dulcimer which was frequently portrayed on 1st millennium B.C. reliefs in Assyria.

In the light of the foregoing evidence it would appear that it is both unnecessary and undesirable for the authorship of the Book of Daniel to be assigned to any other place and time than the Babylonia of the 6th cent. B.C. This being the case, there can be little objection to the view that the book was written by Daniel, whether with or without scribal assistance, during or immediately after the period of time which the work purports to cover.

4. Date. Because questions of authorship and historicity are closely connected with the dating of the book the historical, archeological and linguistic evidence adduced in the previous section strongly confirms the traditional date assigned to Daniel. While the problems associated with Darius the Mede are not yet completely resolved, the situation is by no means as fictitious historically as Rowley and others have maintained. All the evidence to date indicates that Darius the Mede must once again be regarded as an historical personage and it is not too much to hope that future cuneiform discoveries will vindicate his historicity and reveal his identity.

As far as the languages of the Book of Daniel are concerned, the most recent studies place the Aram. firmly within the tradition of chancellery usage from the 7th cent. B.C. onward, and indicate a positive *terminus ad quem* in the pre-Hel. period at the absolute latest. The Heb. linguistic forms also accord with the traditions of the exilic and postexilic period as found in Ezekiel, Haggai and Ezra, and not with a considerably later stage in the language. From this it would appear that the book emerged from a period in the 6th to 5th centuries B.C. rather than from the Maccabean

Cylinder seal and impression showing Darius I, King of Babylon, hunting. The winged-disk emblem of Ahuramazda, a national god of ancient Persia, is above him. The trilingual inscription gives his name and title ("the great king") in Old Persian, Elamite and Babylonian Cuneiform. From Thebes 521-486 B.C. ©*B.M.*

age. Some liberal scholars have adduced as evidence for a Maccabean dating the fact that the name of Daniel was omitted from the list of noteworthy Israelites (Ecclus 44:1ff.). Since the latter was in extant form by 180 B.C., it has been argued the omission implies that Ben Sira knew nothing either of Daniel or his book. Aside from any other considerations it is simply inconceivable that a person such as Daniel, whose prophecy had already attracted significant legendary accretions, would be entirely unknown to an erudite 2nd cent. B.C. Jew, particularly if, as liberal critics claimed, the sagas of Daniel were on the point of being written and accepted with great enthusiasm by oppressed Jews. When the list of notables as preserved by Ben Sira is examined even superficially, it will be observed that not merely was the name of Daniel omitted but also those of Job, all the Judges except Samuel, King Asa, Jehoshaphat, Mordecai and even Ezra himself. Quite clearly an appeal to ignorance has to be abandoned in favor of some other principle of selectivity whose nature is unknown. There are, however, references to Daniel and his book in 1 Maccabees 2:59ff., Baruch 1:15-3:3 and Sibylline Oracles III, 397ff., all of which are at least 2nd cent. B.C. compositions and attest to the familiarity of the Daniel tradition at that time.

Much of the most damaging evidence to the liberal assessment of the date of Daniel has been provided by the Qumran discoveries. It is now clear that the sect originated in the 2nd cent. B.C. and that all its Biblical MSS were copies, not originals. The nature of Jewish compositions aspiring to canonicity was that they were allowed to circulate for a period of time so that their general consonance with the law and the other canonical writings could become established. Once this had taken place the works were accorded a degree of popular canonicity as distinct from a conciliar pronouncement. Under normal circumstances a moderate interval of time was required for this process, though some prophecies were doubtless recognized early for what they were by those who heard them. Nevertheless, the written form generally only gained acceptance as the Word after some time had elapsed, but once this had happened it was transmitted with scrupulous care. Daniel was represented at Qumran by several MSS in good condition as well as by numerous fragments, thus showing the popularity of the work. Since all of these are copies, the autograph must clearly be earlier than the Maccabean period. Two fragments of Daniel recovered from 1Q proved to be related palaeographically to the large Isaiah scroll, and another was akin to the script of the Habakkuk *pesher* (*see* DEAD SEA SCROLLS). If this relationship is as genuine as palaeographers think, the liberal dating of Daniel will need radical upward adjustment, since the Book of Isaiah was certainly written several centuries before the earliest date to which the large Isaiah scroll (1QIsa) can be assigned on any grounds. A Maccabean dating for Daniel has now to be abandoned, if only because there could not possibly be a sufficient interval of time between the composition of Daniel and its appearance in the form of copies in the library of a Maccabean religious sect.

While at the time of writing the Daniel MSS from Qumran have yet to be published and evaluated it is clearly fatuous even in the light of current knowledge for scholars to abandon the Maccabean dating of certain Psalms which have long been regarded as demonstrably late, and yet adhere to it rigidly with regard to the Book of Daniel. For the sake of consistency alone, if the "late" Psalms are to be assigned now to the Pers. period, precisely the same should be done for the Book of Daniel. That scholarly prejudice is largely involved is seen in the fact that critics can argue from the reference to Jaddua (Jos. Antiq. XI, 7, 2) to an earlier rather than a later date for the list of high priests (Neh 12:10, 22), and yet completely ignore or dismiss the tradition preserved in the next section (Jos. Antiq. XI, 8, 5) which relates that after Jaddua had met Alexander the Great outside Jerusalem and had instructed him in the cultic procedures of Jewish sacrifice, the Book of Daniel was shown to the conqueror. If one tradition concerning Jaddua is acceptable, logical consistency would again demand that another concerning the same individual be given at least some consideration.

From the foregoing evidence it can be stated that a Maccabean date for Daniel is now absolutely precluded by the discoveries at Qumran. Whatever the critical objections to the traditional date, they will have to be modified radically in the light of this situation. Since the choice of date is between a Maccabean and a 6th cent. B.C. one, the demonstrated inadequacy of the former leaves the latter as the only acceptable alternative.

5. Place of origin. On the basis of a 6th cent. B.C. date of composition, the place of origin is clearly Babylonia. Indeed on any dating sequence there can be no real question as to the Babylonian background of the work. There is no single element which is consistent with a Palestinian compositional milieu, and the book consistently breathes the air of the Neo-Babylonian and Pers. periods. The city of Babylon itself seems the most probable place of compilation.

6. Destination. Liberal scholars who have suggested a Maccabean origin for the book have thought that it was intended as a "tract for the times" to encourage oppressed Palestinian Jews as they resisted the program of Hellenizing which Antiochus IV Epiphanes was imposing upon his realm. Since the work has been shown to belong properly to the 6th cent. B.C., the book can have been meant only for the exiles in Babylonia, evidently with the avowed purpose of showing that foreign captivity and a living faith in God were by no means as incompatible as some exiles imagined.

7. Occasion. The contents of Daniel arose out of the experiences of the seer in the Babylonian court, and comprise memoirs and visions. The various chs. represent the outstanding occurrences in the life of Daniel, which covers fully the period of the Exile in Babylonia. It is difficult to say whether the book was prompted by any specific occurrence, since it appears to be a straightforward record of notable events in the life of an outstanding servant of God. In the historical section the specific occasion was invariably one of pagan culture or superstition being confronted by the power of the Israelite God. In the visions the events of future times were the dominant concern, and whether these were occasioned by specific happenings in the life of Daniel or not is unknown.

8. Purpose. The overall aim of the book is to show the superiority of the Israelite God over the heathen idols of Mesopotamia. Daniel also makes it clear that, although the Babylonians had been the means of punishment for Israel, they also would pass from the historical scene. The visions go even further in predicting the time when the Messiah's work would begin, showing that in the latter days God would establish a permanent kingdom. Despite the fact that the chosen people would not remain unscathed throughout their existence, their destiny was bound up with that of the Messiah. A living faith in the power of God would be more than a match for whatever difficulties might arise, as exemplified in the life of Daniel himself.

9. Canonicity. From its inception the work was apparently assigned to the third division of the Heb. canon, the Writings, presumably on the basis that Daniel could not be regarded as a prophet in the sense of Isaiah or Ezekiel, since he was not the mediator of revelation from God to a theocratic community. This conviction evidently underlay the pronouncement of the Talmud (Bab. Bath. 15a) which nevertheless testifies to the esteem in which Daniel was held. In the LXX version the book was placed among the prophetic writings following Ezekiel but preceding the Twelve, a position which was adopted by the English VSS.

10. Text. The MT is in good condition, and the LXX and other VSS do not suggest the presence of significant textual corruptions. The LXX has survived in one MS only, and indicates that the VS was characterized by expansions. It was displaced in the Early Church by the more literal VS of Theodotion, from which Patristic writers usually quoted. Legendary accretions such as the *Song of the Three Young Men* and *Bel and The Dragon* formed part of some VSS, including the LXX.

11. Content. The book can be analyzed as follows:

A. Daniel and his friends come to prominence in Babylon (1:1-21).

B. The vision of the image recalled and interpreted (2:1-49).

C. Image-worship in the plain of Dura and its consequences for Daniel and his friends (3:1-30).

D. A vision of the impending illness of Nebuchadnezzar (4:1-37).

E. The explanation of the cryptic text and the fall of Babylon (5:1-31).

F. Daniel in the den of lions (6:1-28).

G. A vision of four great beasts and their significance (7:1-28).

H. A vision of future kingdoms (8:1-27).

I. Confession, followed by a vision relating to the coming of the Messiah (9:1-27).

J. A divine message is given to Daniel which serves to introduce the prophecies of chs. 11 and 12 (10:1-21).

K. The wars of Syria and Egypt and the sealing of the prophecy (11:1-12:13).

12. Theology and interpretation. The theological standpoint of Daniel has much in common with that of Ezekiel. God is viewed as a transcendent Being who by nature is superior to all the gods of the heathen. Because God is all-powerful, events work out according to a predetermined divine purpose, and this is consistent with 8th cent. prophetic thought, which maintained that God was in firm control of the trend of events. In the same way Daniel thought of the Messianic kingdom as the conclusion of the age, and as a matter for divine rather than human decision. Although the coming kingdom was contemplated in largely material terms, the concepts of resurrection in ch. 12 are an advance on the eschatology of the preexilic prophets. The angelology of Daniel is similar to that of Ezekiel, and although somewhat vague on occasions it recognizes that angels possessed personalities and even names. However, the angelology is by no means as elaborate as that of later Jewish apocalyptic works such as 1 Enoch. The apocalyptic character of the visions should be distinguished carefully from oriental apocalypticism generally, since Daniel contains no dualism of the kind found in Zoroastrian religion and does not reflect an ethical passivity which would preclude Daniel from announcing divine judgment upon individuals or nations.

The apocalyptic sections of the book have been widely discussed, partly because of the interpretation to be assigned to the four kingdoms of ch. 2, where critics have divided Medo-Persia into two separate empires, making the kingdoms Babylonia, Media, Persia and Greece respectively. However, the history of the Median kingdom precludes such a division, so that the order of the empires would be Babylonia, Medo-Persia, Greece and Rome.

The identity of the fourth kingdom is important for the later visions of Daniel. It is quite different in nature from the "he-goat" (Dan 8:5), and thus cannot represent Greece, as liberal scholars have maintained. Again, the "little horn" (8:9), representing Antiochus IV Epiphanes, is not the same as the "little one" (7:8), and is also different from the successor to the ten kings (7:24). The "little horn" emerging from the fourth beast was represented in conflict with the saints of God before the establishing of the divine kingdom (7:21).

Attempting to interpret the prophecies, some conservative scholars have seen the predictions concerning the image (2:31-49), the four beasts (7:2-27), and the seventy weeks (9:24-27) culminating in the incarnation of Christ and the birth of the Christian Church. On this view the stone (2:34, 35) points to the coming of Christ, while the ten horns of the fourth beast (7:24), the little horn (7:8), and the concept of "time, two times, and half a time" (7:25) are interpreted symbolically. The Messianic work is accomplished during a period of seventy sevens (9:24), presumably dating from the decree of Cyrus in 538 B.C., including the work of Ezra, and culminating in the advent and ascension of Christ. The death of the Messiah causes Jewish sacrifices to cease, and the "one who makes desolate" (9:27) is Titus, who destroyed Jerusalem in A.D. 70. Other conservatives have related the apocalyptic passages to the Second Advent of Christ rather than the incarnation, and have seen in the image of Daniel two successive forms of the Satan-dominated kingdom of men represented by the empires of Babylon, Medo-Persia, Greece and Rome, the latter being protracted in some form until the Second Coming of Christ. This ends with the rise of the ten kings (2:41-44; cf. Rev 17:12) who are destroyed by Christ at His Second Coming. The divine kingdom is then established (cf. Matt 6:10; Rev 20:1-6) which becomes a "great mountain," filling the whole earth (Dan 2:35). Daniel 7:25 shows an advance in thought over Daniel 2, however, with the antichrist being introduced as the eleventh horn who persecutes the saints for "a time, and times and half a time" i.e. three and a half years (cf. Dan 7:6; 8:5 and Rev 12:14). One like a son of man (Dan 7:13) achieves the ultimate destruction of the antichrist, the four kingdoms, and the ten kings. The seventy sevens of years is reckoned on this view from the decree of Artaxerxes I in 444 B.C. to rebuild Jerusalem (Neh 2:1-8) and concludes with the founding of the millennial kingdom (Dan 9:24). A gap is held to separate the end of the sixty-ninth week from the beginning of the seventieth (9:62), since Christ set the abomination of desolation at the end of the present age (cf. 9:27, Matt 24:15). The millennial interpreters see in the seventieth week a seven-year period just prior to the Second Coming of Christ during which interval the antichrist arises and persecutes the saints of God. The transition from the purely historical situation represented by the Persian, Greek, Ptolemaic and Seleucid regimes, culminating in the persecutions of Antiochus IV Epiphanes (Dan 11:2-35a) is marked by the phrase "for it is yet for the time appointed" (11:35b), which introduces the specifically eschatological situation relating to the Second Coming of Christ. Some premillennial interpreters have seen the "king of the north" subduing the antichrist along with the "king of the south" before being destroyed himself (cf. 11:40-45; Ezek 39:4, 17), but ultimately the antichrist recovers and begins his era of world domination (Dan 11:44; cf. Rev 13:3; 17:8). The great tribulation of three and a half years (Dan 7:25) or 1260 days (Rev 12:6) ends with the bodily resurrection of those saints who have died in the tribulation (Dan 12:2, 3; cf. Rev 7:9-14). After a short interval in which the Temple is cleansed (Dan 12:11) the fullness of the millennial kingdom is ushered in (12:12).

BIBLIOGRAPHY. R. D. Wilson, *Studies in the Book of Daniel*, I (1917); II (1938); J. A. Montgomery, *The Book of Daniel*, ICC (1927); R. P. Dougherty, *Nabonidus and Belshazzar* (1929); H. H. Rowley, *Darius the Mede and the Four World Empires in the Book of Daniel* (1935); F. Rosenthal, *Die Aramaistische Forschung* (1939); E. J. Young, *The Prophecy of Daniel* (1949); H. C. Leupold, *Exposition of Daniel* (1949); R. D. Culver, *Daniel and the Latter Days* (1954); J. C. Whitcomb, *Darius the Mede* (1959); S. B. Frost, IDB, I, 761-768; D. J. Wiseman, et al., *Notes on Some Problems in the Book of Daniel* (1965); R. K. Harrison, *Introduction to the Old Testament* (1969), 1105-1138.

R. K. HARRISON

DANIEL (MAN) (דניאל, *God is my judge*, LXX Δανιήλ, *Daniēl*). 1. The second son of David (1 Chron 3:1, the Chileab of 2 Sam 3:3).

2. A priest of the postexilic period (Ezra 8:2; Neh 10:6).

3. The exilic seer traditionally credited with authorship of the Book of Daniel. This man is commonly accorded the status of a prophet, but this is technically incorrect. His life experiences show that he was more of a statesman in a foreign court than a mediator of divine revelation to a theocratic community. Yet it is also true that his outlook contains elements which are in full accord with the highest spiritual traditions of Heb. prophecy generally.

Daniel seems to have been born into an unidentified family of Judean nobility somewhat prior to Josiah's reformation in 621 B.C. While nothing is known about the life and career of Daniel aside from what is narrated in the canonical book of that name, the fact that he was among the first selection of Jewish captives taken to Babylon in 605 B.C. by Nebuchadnezzar indicates that he claimed considerable social standing. The advance of the Babylonians against the Egyptians, who had marched to Haran to assist the beleaguered remnants of the Assyrian armies, has been well documented by cuneiform texts. The discovery in 1956 by D. J. Wiseman of four additional tablets of the Babylonian Chronicle in the British Museum archives furnished an account of the shattering defeat which the Babylonians inflicted upon the Egyptians at Carchemish in 605 B.C. One result of this victory was that the Babylonians seem to have demanded hostages of Judah as evidence of good faith toward Babylonia, and it was this group which went into captivity in the third year of Jehoiakim (Dan 1:1, 3), including the young man Daniel. For a three-year period he was instructed in all the lore of the Chaldeans (Dan 1:4, 5) in preparation for the royal service. He was also given the Babylonian name of Belteshazzar, the Heb. form most prob. being a transliteration of *balatṣu-uṣur* or "protect his life," the name of the protective deity having been omitted in the Heb. However, despite his superficial conformity to the court customs of Babylonia, Daniel remained true to his Jewish heritage. Thus, when he and his three friends Shadrach, Meshach and Abednego were invited to accept the royal food and drink, they declined courteously rather than violate the ancient dietary laws of Leviticus since the food in question (1:8) had been tainted through contact with idols. God honored the witness of this group by giving them outstanding learning abilities (1:20), enabling them to qualify as official "wise men" after three years (1:20; cf. 2:13). In addition, Daniel received the ability to experience visions and interpret dreams.

In 602 B.C. Nebuchadnezzar was troubled by a dream which he had promptly forgotten on waking (2:5, 8). The priestly diviners were ordered to disclose the nature of the dream and interpret its meaning, and when they proved unequal to this challenge they were promptly sentenced to death. This unfortunate fate included Daniel also, but after prayer God revealed the dream and its meaning to him (2:11, 18, 19). It depicted a fourfold image representing the four world empires of Babylon, Persia, Greece, and Rome which would precede the introduction of the Messianic kingdom. Nebuchadnezzar was so impressed with this performance that he made Daniel chief over the wise men (2:48) and offered him the governorship of the province of Babylon, a position which Daniel assigned to his three friends (2:49). Toward the end of Nebuchadnezzar's reign (604-562 B.C.) Daniel was called upon to interpret the dream of the fallen tree (4:8-27). It required both courage and tact for Daniel to tell the king that for a specified period he would be afflicted with a mental condition, a prediction which was fulfilled within a year (4:28-33). When Nabonidus, the last ruler of imperial Babylon, retired to Teima in Arabia c. 556 B.C., his son Belshazzar acted as coregent. About 555 B.C. Daniel saw a vision of four great beasts (7:1-14) which paralleled Nebuchadnezzar's earlier dream of the composite image. In the meantime Babylonian political power was diminishing and being overshadowed by the rising influence of Cyrus (559-530 B.C.). About 552 B.C. Daniel had a vision of a ram and a he-goat which related to the fortunes of Persia and Greece (8:20, 21) down to the Maccabean period (Dan 8:25). Late in 539 B.C. Gubaru and Ugbaru led the armies of Cyrus to victory over the Chaldeans, and during the drunken revelries which immediately preceded the fall of Babylon, Daniel was summoned to the court and asked to explain the "handwriting on the wall." He predicted a Medo-Persian victory, condemned the dissolute Belshazzar, and witnessed the collapse of the regime that very night (5:23-31). On assuming his office as king of Babylon, Darius the Mede (prob. Gubaru) invited Daniel to become one of his three "presidents" (6:2). Jealous colleagues tried to cause the downfall of Daniel through charges of corruption (6:4), and when this failed they instituted a royal edict prohibiting all prayers or petitions except those addressed to King Darius himself. The intractable laws of the Medes and Persians left Darius no course but to throw Daniel into a den of lions for breaking them. God intervened to save His servant but allowed the fate intended for Daniel to overtake his accusers. As the Israelite exile in Babylon drew to a close in 538 B.C., the angel Gabriel answered Daniel's prayers by revealing the time span "seventy weeks" or 490 years (9:24-27) intervening between the decree enabling Jerusalem to be rebuilt and the time when the Messiah's work would begin. Daniel continued to function as a wise man during the early years of Cyrus (6:28), and having seniority in this position he would doubtless have been accorded great veneration by the superstitious Persians. What appears to be the last recorded event in the life of the seer occurred in the third year of Cyrus (536 B.C.), when Daniel saw a vision of the conflict between the archangel Michael and the demonic powers of society. This unfolded in terms of the history of Near Eastern nations, dealing at some length with the persecutions of Antiochus Epiphanes (175 B.C.) and the rise of the eschatological antichrist. It culminated in a revelation concerning resurrection and the final judgment of God (10:10-12:4), during which Daniel was assured that, although he would die before all this was fulfilled, he would nevertheless receive his reward at the consummation (12:13). It seems probable that Daniel was well over eighty when he died. He left behind an impressive reputation for inspiring faith through the exercise of courage when confronted by mortal danger. He also manifested complete

Damascus Gate. ©K.T.

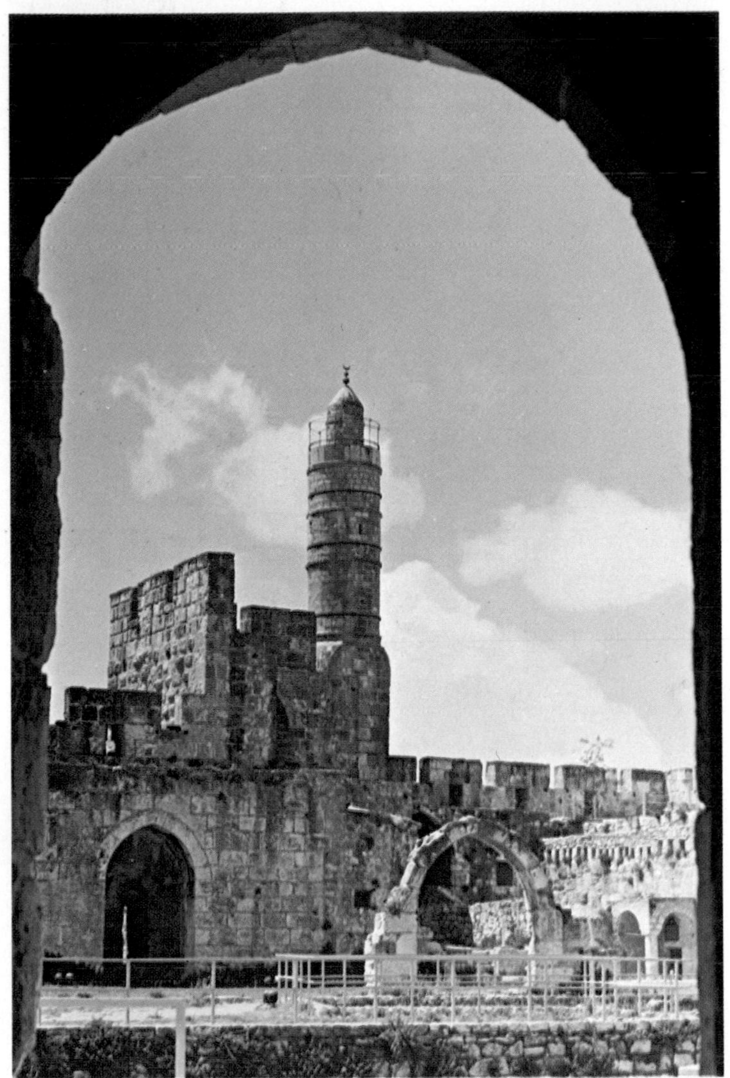

David's Tower, Jerusalem. ©*Frank Raymond*

Qumran Caves near Jericho. ©*Frank Raymond*

Dead Sea. © *Frank Raymond*

Dome of the Rock, Jerusalem. ©*Frank Raymond*

This woman, returning from a visit to the market in Jerusalem, is typically dressed. © *K.T.*

The garb of this modern-day Arab on a Jerusalem street is reminiscent of Bible days. © *K.T.*

An Egyptian idol. ©*O.I.U.C.*

A fishing boat on the Gulf of Aquabah. © *Frank Raymond*

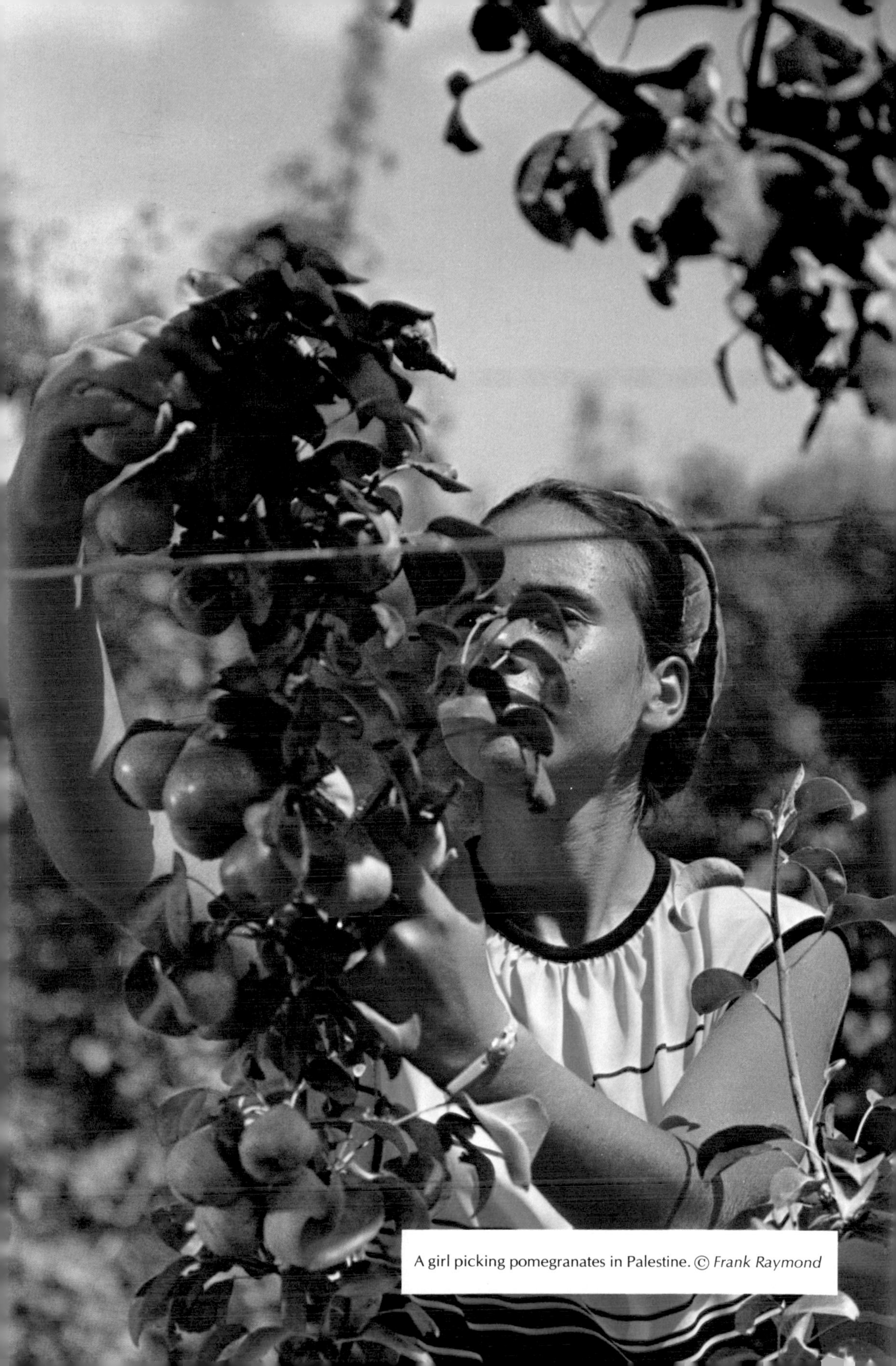

A girl picking pomegranates in Palestine. © *Frank Raymond*

The Golden Gate entrance into the Old City of Jerusalem. © *Frank Raymond*

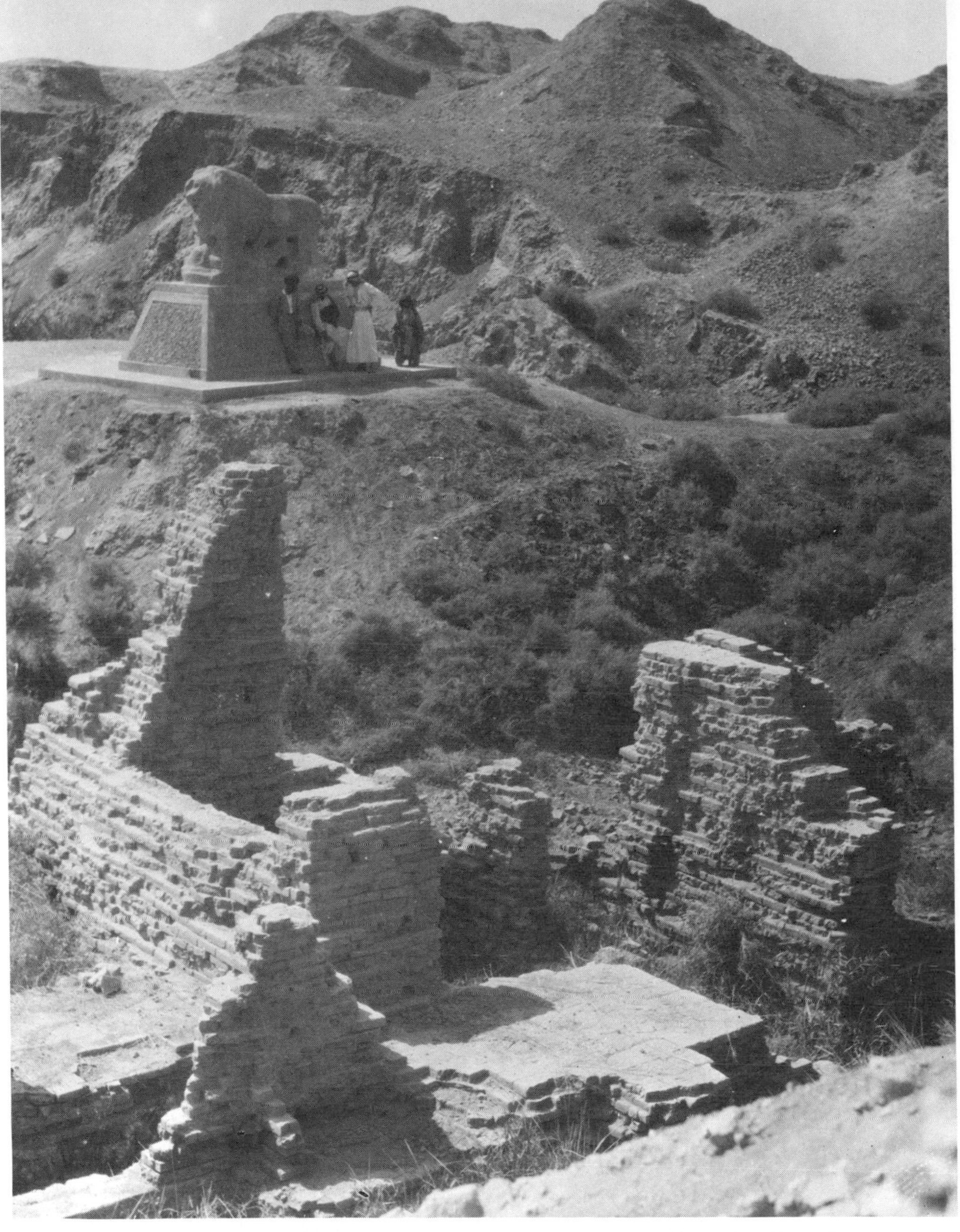

The Lion Monument in the ruins of Babylon, supposedly marking the site of Daniel's den of lions. ©*M.P.S.*

dedication to the ideals of God in a pagan society, and set an example of persistence in prayer. His popularity in later times among the Jews is indicated by the numerous legendary accretions, as well as MSS and fragments of the book discovered at Qumran.

The Ugaritic *Legend of Aqht* referred to an ancient Phoenician king named *Dnil* (vocalized as *Dan'el* or *Dani'el*) who was reputedly wise and upright. The reference to "Daniel" in Ezekiel 14:14 may point to some such antediluvian person, and not a contemporary of Ezekiel. So also in Ezekiel 28:3 where the prophet also mocked Tyre sarcastically because she was "wiser than Daniel."

BIBLIOGRAPHY. E. J. Young, *The Prophecy of Daniel* (1949); E. W. Heaton, *The Book of Daniel* (1956).

R. K. Harrison

DANITES, the tribe descended from the older son of Bilhah, Jacob's concubine (Gen 30:1-6).

1. The name means "judging" or a "judge." Rachel saw in the birth of this child God's acceptance of her claim to motherhood and the evidence that He had heard her prayer.

2. In Jacob's blessing (49:16f.), Dan was placed after the last two sons of Leah, although he was born before them. The blessing again played on the meaning of the name: "Dan shall judge his people," apparently meaning that the tribe would govern itself without the help of others. To this brief prediction, based on the name, Jacob added the cryptic statement: "Dan shall be a serpent in the way, an adder by the path, that bites the horse's heels, so that his rider falls backward." This is regarded as a description of the cerastes, a small and venomous snake which hides itself in hollow places from which it makes its sudden attack on the passer-by. The prophecy clearly suggests that Dan would show the subtilty and venom of a snake in dealing with his enemies. Why Dan's blessing is followed by the words, "I wait for thy salvation, O LORD," might be regarded as applicable to all the tribes, but is uncertain. It may be connected with Rachel's impatient and desperate plan for motherhood which was followed by the birth of Dan, but this would seem far-fetched.

3. Although the second largest of the tribes (62,700) at the time of the Exodus (Num 1:39), and one of the tribes which increased slightly during the years of wandering (26:43) being second only to Judah in the census, Dan's position in both listings is after the Leah and Rachel tribes but first of the four handmaid tribes. Its prince in the time of Moses was Ahiezer (Num 1:12). In the encampments Dan's standard, which included Asher and Naphtali, was on the N side of the Tabernacle. In the line of march Dan headed the last of the four standards (Num 10:25f.). Likewise when the offerings for the dedication of the altar were presented, Dan offered on the tenth day (Num 7:66ff.), being followed by Asher and Naphtali. At the great ceremony at Ebal, Dan was among the tribes which were to pronounce the curses (Deut 27:13).

4. Dan was mentioned briefly in Moses' blessing of the tribes (Deut 33:22). The comparison with "a lion's whelp" suggests vigor and ferocity; and the words, "that leaps forth from Bashan" suggest events which took place after the conquest of Laish (Judg 18).

5. At the distribution of the land by Joshua, Dan's lot was the last (Josh 19:40-48). Their portion was between Judah on the S and Ephraim on the N, with Benjamin to the E and the sea to the W. Seventeen cities assigned to Dan are listed. These were cramped quarters, because of the resistance of the Amorites (Judg 1:34), and because the Philistines were in possession of much of their seacoast (3:3). Only a brief reference is made to the way in which they remedied the situation (Josh 19:47).

6. The most spectacular event (or series of events) in their history was their trek to the N. Instead of endeavoring to gain possession of all their allotted portion in the land of Canaan, they secured for themselves by violent means lands in the far N which had not been occupied by an Israelite tribe. They sent out five spies to search out for them an inheritance in which to dwell (Judg 18:1ff.). The spies came first to the house of Micah in Mount Ephraim. Instead of being shocked that Micah had installed a Levite as his priest and had "a house of gods, an ephod, and teraphim," they sought counsel concerning their journey and its possible results. Having received the rather oracular answer, "Go in peace. The journey on which you go is under the eye of the LORD" (v. 6), they went to Laish, which apparently was under the nominal protection of Zidon; and discovering that it was likely to fall an easy prey to an invader, they brought back a most favorable report and declared that God would bless them. Thereupon 600 armed men of Zorah and Eshtaol, apparently with families and livestock (18:21), departed for Laish. En route they came to the house of Micah, guided there by the spies, and possessing themselves of Micah's priest and objects of idol worship, they went to Laish, surprised and destroyed it, and then named it Dan. The story of this successful foray ends with the statement that they "set up the graven image" as the evidence and guarantee of their conquest; and finally the name of the priest whom they had taken away from Micah is given, Jonathan, the son of Gershom, the son of Moses (if this is the correct reading rather than the Masoretic emendation, "Manasseh") and it is stated that he and his sons were priests to the tribe of Dan "until the day of the captivity of the land" (Judg 18:30, 31). The parallel statement, "as long as the house of God was at Shiloh," may be defined as ending with the disastrous battle in the days of Eli (1 Sam 4:10), when the Ark was taken by the Philistines and Shiloh apparently destroyed. Many scholars find here a reference to the invasion of Tiglath-pileser in 734 B.C., which would indicate a late date of composition for this narrative.

7. The conquest of Laish in the time of the Judges apparently was followed by the gradual removal from there of many or most of the tribe, although there is nothing concerning this in the Bible. Samson was a Danite and in his day there were many Danites still living in the portion assigned to them by Joshua. Zorah, Eshtaol, Timnah, Eltekeh, and Ekron were "Danite" cities (Josh 19:41-46; cf. 21:23), although the last was in the days of Samson one of the five cities of the lords of the Philistines (Judg 13:2, 25) and others were more or less under their control. If the "camp of Dan" (Heb. Mahaneh-dan) (v. 25) is the same as the Mahaneh-dan mentioned in Judges 18:12, the inference is justified that the conquest of Laish took place before the time of Samson. The meaning of Judges 5:17 is too uncertain to be referred to in this connection.

8. Dan is not listed in the genealogies of 1 Chronicles (1-8), but 28,600 Danites came to

David in Hebron to make him king over all Israel (1 Chron 12:35). The listing of the Danites after Issachar, Zebulun and Naphtali and before Asher indicates that by the time of David, the Danites were regarded as a northern tribe, which meant that by the time of David or long before, the Danites had completed the trek, the beginning of which is described in the Book of Judges. A hint of this is the statement in the letter of Hiram king of Tyre to Solomon, that he was sending Solomon a skillful workman whose father was a Tyrian but his mother a Danite (2 Chron 2:14), such a mixed marriage being more likely to take place after the trek to the N.

9. The well-known idolatry of the Danites was prob. mainly responsible for Jeroboam placing one of his golden calves at Dan (2 Kings 10:29), although the location prob. figured to some extent, Dan and Bethel being on the northern and southern boundaries of the northern kingdom.

10. In Ezekiel's vision of the Holy Land and the Holy City, Dan is named as occupying the northernmost portion (Ezek 48:1). Dan was one of the so-called "lost tribes" which were carried away by the Assyrians and disappeared. But it is to be remembered that, when Ezra came to Jerusalem, the Israelites offered in sacrifice "twelve bullocks for all Israel" (Ezra 8:35), and that the aged Anna, who was present when the infant Jesus was presented to the Lord, was of the tribe of Asher (Luke 2:36). Paul also, speaking before Agrippa referred to the promise to which "our twelve tribes, instantly serving God day and night, hope to come" (Acts 26:7 KJV). This would seem to indicate that there was a remnant of grace in the northern kingdom, including Danites, after the carrying away, even as there had been 7,000 in the days of Elijah who had not bowed the knee to Baal (1 Kings 19:18). Yet it is remarkable that in Revelation 7 the name of Dan does not appear, a fact which is prob. responsible for the ancient tradition that the antichrist was to come from the tribe of Dan.

11. The phrase "from Dan to Beersheba," which occurs a number of times, refers to Israel in its utmost bounds and therefore presupposes the trek to the N, and appears first in Judges 20:1. (This may indicate that the near-extermination of the tribe of Benjamin took place after the events recounted in chs. 17, 18.) Compare the words "from Geba to Beersheba" (2 Kings 23:8) which describe the limits of the southern kingdom in the days of Josiah.

12. The mention of Dan in Genesis 14:14 as the limit of Abraham's pursuit of the four kings who had invaded Pal., has caused much discussion; it is one of the stock arguments against the Mosaic authorship of the Pentateuch. Some scholars believe that this is a different Dan, although there is no clear documentary evidence of the existence of such a city. One may well say with W. H. Green: "If the Dan of later times is here meant, the strong probability is that the older name [Laish?] was in the original text, and in the course of transcription one more familiar was substituted for it. The proofs of Mosaic authorship are too numerous and strong to be outweighed by a triviality like this."

13. In Deuteronomy 34:1 the mention of Dan, which seems clearly to be to the northern city, need occasion no difficulty, since here again the more modern name for Laish may have been substituted by a later copyist. It is not unlikely that this concluding chapter of the Pentateuch may have been written substantially later than the time of Moses, as the closing verses may perhaps imply (vv. 9-12); the statement reads more like history than prediction. This short chapter is then to be regarded as a biographical addendum supplied by a writer later than Moses, as is natural for any obituary tribute of this type.

BIBLIOGRAPHY. C. F. Keil, *The Book of Judges* (1875), 429-442; W. H. Green, *The Unity of Genesis* (1895), 202; F. W. Farrar, *Judges* in *A Bible Commentary for Bible Students*, ed. by C. J. Ellicott, vol. II, 253-260. For the critical view, compare: G. F. Moore, *Judges*, ICC (1900), 365-408; C. F. Burney, *Judges* (1920), 408-436; J. Garstang, *Joshua-Judges* (1931), 229f., 245-257; H. H. Rowley, *From Joseph to Joshua* (1952), 79-86.

O. T. Allis

DAN-JAAN **dăn jā′ ən** (דן יען). The KJV tr. of a locality somewhere between Gilead and Sidon, as based on the fact that David's census takers, setting out from Aroer near the river Arnon went to Gilead, coming to this place and to Sidon's vicinity (2 Sam 24:6). It could be the well-known Dan of Scripture (also connected with Sidon, Judg 18:28f.), but perhaps a town in Dan's environs. Because one LXX reading of 1 Kings 15:29 and 2 Chronicles 16:4 mentions coming to Dan, and going round to Sidon, some suggest: "To Dan and Ijon (Jaan)," as the true sense. Jaan as a proper name is a possibility. RSV has "Dan."

R. F. Gribble

DANNAH **dăn′ ə** (דנה). A town of the hill country of Judah; perhaps less than five m. E of Kirjath-sepher (Debir, Josh 15:15). Location uncertain.

DAPHNE **dăf′ nĭ** (Δάφνη). A park or pleasure resort in a suburb of Syrian Antioch, consecrated by Seleucus I to the royal gods and esp. to Apollo (Apoc., 2 Macc 4:33). It was a beautiful precinct of temples and gardens with associated theaters and stadia, similar to Delphi and all other religious centers of the Greeks in which worship of the Olympian gods, ritual, drama, and sport were inevitably linked. Daphne became a haunt of pleasure seekers and merry-making Antiochenes and tourists, winning a worldwide reputation for vice and carnality. Gibbon gave a description of the place in his *Decline and Fall of the Roman Empire* (II, ch. 23, pp. 395, 396, J. B. Bury, ed., Everyman's Ed).

BIBLIOGRAPHY. R. Stillwell, *Antioch on the Orontes* (1934).

E. M. BLAIKLOCK

DAPPLED dap′ ld (ברד, *spotted, marked,* from the root ברד, *hail;* LXX ποικίλοι, *many-colored, spotted*). A term used to describe some horses in a vision of Zechariah (6:3, 6 KJV *grisled,* ASV *grizzled*). The RSV trs. the same Heb. word "mottled" in Genesis 31:10, 12 (KJV *grisled,* ASV *grizzled*).

J. B. SCOTT

DARDA där də (דרדע ; LXX, Δαρδα, Gr. has several spellings), perhaps, *full of wisdom;* or, by change of last letter, it could be *thistle*).

A son of Mahol (1 Kings 4:31), a Judahite of the family of Zerah (1 Chron 2:6). The name is given as Dara in the above Chronicles reference (which could be a copyist's error), where a fifth man, Zimri, is added and all five listed as sons of Zerah. Of the five in Chronicles, four are also named in the above Kings passage. That the Kings reference makes them sons of Mahol, and the Chronicles reference, sons of Zerah, can be explained by understanding that Mahol was their proximate father, and Zerah the Ezrahite, a remote ancestor.

R. F. GRIBBLE

DARIC. *See* COINS.

DARIUS də rī′ əs. In addition to DARIUS THE MEDE (q.v.), it is the name of two Pers. kings mentioned in Haggai, Zechariah, Ezra, and Nehemiah.

1. Darius I Hystaspes (521-486 B.C.), fourth ruler of the Pers. empire (after Cyrus, Cambyses, and Gaumata; cf. Dan 11:2, which lists three kings *after* Cyrus and *before* the "richer" king, who is obviously Xerxes). He often is referred to as "Darius the Great" because of his brilliant achievements as restorer of the empire after Gaumata, the Pseudo-Smerdis, usurped the throne from CAMBYSES (q.v.). The Achaemenid dynasty would prob. have ended with Cambyses had not Darius, one of his officers, son of Hystaspes (a satrap) and great-grandson of Ariyaramnes (brother of Cyrus I), retained the loyalty of the Pers. army. Within two months he had killed Gaumata (522 B.C.) and during the next two years defeated nine kings in nineteen battles to secure his throne. His own account of these victories is recorded in a large trilingual (Old Persian, Akkadian, and Elamite) cuneiform inscr. on the face of the Behistun Rock.

In one of these campaigns a Babylonian

The Apadana, or audience hall, of Darius and Xerxes at Persepolis. Excavated by the Oriental Institute. ©O.I.U.C.

Darius sits on his throne holding a long scepter. © *OIUC*

usurper claiming the title Nebuchadnezzar IV was trapped with his followers within Babylon. After a long siege the city was taken and three thousand of its leading citizens were crucified as a warning to other potential rebels (Herodotus, III, 159). This helps to explain the amazing zeal of Tattenai to obey a decree of Darius I about a year later to which the following warning was appended "whosoever shall alter this word, let timber be pulled down from his house, and being set up, let him be hanged thereon; and let his house be made a dunghill for this" (Ezra 6:11-13 KJV).

The beginning of the inscription of DARIUS, *King of Persia* (521-486 B.C.), *on the rock of Behistun.*

/ a da m / d a ra ya wa u š / h̬ š a ya th i ya
I (AM) DARIUS THE KING
/ wa za r ka / h̬ š a ya th i ya / h̬ š a ya th i y a n a m /
THE GREAT (ONE). THE KING (OF) KINGS,
h̬ š a ya th i ya / p a r sa i y / h̬ š a ya th i ya /
THE KING (OF) PERSIA, THE KING (OF)
da h y u n a m / wi š t a s pa h y a / p u thra /
COUNTRIES, HYSTASPES' SON,
a r š a ma h y a / na p a / ha h̬ a m n i š i ya
ARSAMES' GRANDSON, THE ACHAMENIDIAN.

Translation of part of an inscription of Darius in ancient Persian (after Pfeiffer).

The remaining years of his reign were devoted to the reorganization of the empire into twenty satrapies and many provinces; the establishment of a highly efficient postal system similar to the 19th cent. American pony express (Herodotus VIII, 98; cf. Esth 8:10); the building of a fabulous new capital at Persepolis; the conquest of NW India (c. 514 B.C.); the redigging of an ancient canal from the Nile to the Red Sea (c. 513 B.C.); the conquest of Libya, Thrace, and Macedonia (c. 512 B.C.); the crushing of revolts among Ionian Greeks (500-493 B.C.); and the ill-fated expeditions against Greece (493 and 490 B.C.). Returning to Persia in defeat he died in 486 B.C. while preparing for yet another attack upon Greece.

Darius was buried in a rock-hewn tomb at Naqsh-i-Rustam, a few m. NE of Persepolis. The trilingual inscr. includes these words: "Says Darius the king: By the favor of Ahuramazda I am of such a sort that I am a friend to right, I am not a friend to wrong; it is not my desire that the weak man should have wrong done to him by the mighty; nor is that my desire, that the mighty man should have wrong done to him by the weak."

Early in his reign, just after securing his throne, Darius I became God's instrument for encouraging the Jews to complete their second Temple. In 520 B.C., Tattenai, the recently-appointed Pers. governor of W Euphrates

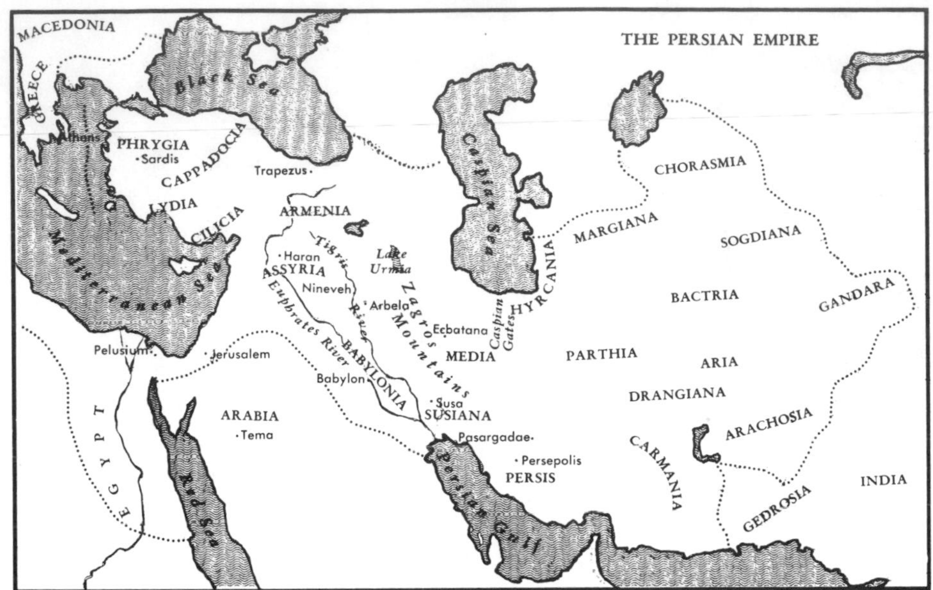

Under Darius the Great the empire reached its height of expansion. In contrast with Cyrus' policy of clemency, Darius sought to exercise more direct control.

provinces (formerly included in the realm of Darius the Mede), challenged the Jews who had started to build their Temple through the encouragement of Haggai and Zechariah (Ezra 5:1-3). Their explanation that Cyrus had given Sheshbazzar (Zerubbabel) official permission to build the Temple was forwarded to Darius I with a request to investigate. Providentially the work was not halted during the long process of searching for Cyrus' decree (Ezra 5:5).

The transition of royal power from Cambyses to Darius I was so traumatic that it is a testimony to Pers. efficiency that the document was ever discovered. An expanded form of the decree of Cyrus on a parchment scroll had been filed away in a branch library in the distant city of Ecbatana (Ezra 6:2). Darius I then proceeded to issue his own decree, commanding Tattenai to assist the Jews in their work on the Temple and to provide expenses from the tribute that came from the western provinces (Ezra 6:6-12). Doubtless, the king was sufficiently polytheistic (in spite of his devotion to Zoroastrianism) to suspect that Jehovah could either help or injure his dynasty (6:10).

With this substantial material assistance (and with additional words from the Lord during Darius' fourth year [518 B.C., cf. Zech 7:1-8:23]), the Jews completed the Temple in his sixth year (Feb/March, 516 B.C.). Nothing further is known of the experiences of the Jews during the subsequent thirty years of the reign of Darius I.

2. Darius II Ochus (423-404 B.C.), seventh ruler of the Pers. empire, and son of Artaxerxes I by a Babylonian concubine. His cruel and scheming queen, Parysatis, was frequently the real ruler. The empire disintegrated at an accelerated pace under his administration, with revolts in Sardis, Media, Cyprus, Cadusia and Egypt. In the latter case, the Jewish colony at Elephantine lost their temple (on an island in the Nile of Upper Egypt) and wrote desperate letters to Jerusalem and Samaria for help, all in vain.

It was prob. during the reign of Darius II that Nehemiah went to Jerusalem the second time and found that many abuses had arisen (Neh 13:6ff.). Also, it was during his reign that the names of some Jewish priests were recorded (Neh 12:22). Some have insisted that this must have been Darius III Codomannus (335-331 B.C.), because the same v. mentions a high priest Jaddua, and Josephus states that Jaddua was high priest in 332 B.C. (Antiq. XI. viii. 4). If we assume that Josephus was historically accurate at this point (and this assumption carries with it very embarrassing implications for destructive critics, since Josephus states in the following paragraph that this Jaddua presented a copy of the Book of Dan to Alexander the Great!), he could have been referring to another high priest of the same name or to the same Jaddua at a very advanced age. The Elephantine papyri mention Jaddua's father Johanan, as being high priest in 408 B.C. (cf. ANET, p. 492). Therefore, Jaddua could easily have been high priest in 404, esp. since he was only five generations removed from Joshua (Neh 12:10, 11), who was high priest until at least 519 (Zech 1:7; 6:11). Consequently, there is no valid reason for denying that this king was Darius II and that Nehemiah could have written this v. as well as all the other vv. of his book.

BIBLIOGRAPHY. A. T. Olmstead, *History of the Persian Empire* (1948); J. B. Pritchard (ed.), *Ancient Near Eastern Texts* (1950); G. C. Cameron, "Darius Carved History on Ageless Rock" *National Geographic Magazine* (Dec., 1950); R. Ghirshman, *Iran* (1954); J. Finegan, *Light From the Ancient Past* (1959); Pfeiffer and Vos, *The Wycliffe Historical Geography of Bible Lands* (1967).

J. C. WHITCOMB

DARIUS THE MEDE də rī′ əs (דריוש). Medo-Pers. governor ("king") of Babylonia under Cyrus the Great mentioned esp. in the sixth ch. of Daniel. Immediately following the death of "Belshazzar the Chaldean king" in Oct. 539 B.C., Darius the Mede is said to have "received the kingdom" (Dan 5:31), prob. having been made "king over the realm of the Chaldeans" (9:1) by Cyrus the Great (1:21; 6:28). He is best remembered for the unalterable decree which his officers tricked him into signing, which resulted in Daniel being cast into a den of lions (6:7-18). In contrast to Nebuchadnezzar, this ruler was helpless to reverse his own decree, vividly illustrating the inferiority of the silver kingdom of Medo-Persia to the golden kingdom of Babylon in the matter of royal sovereignty. Compare Daniel 3:29; Esther 1:19; 8:8, and the testimony of Diodorus Siculus (xvii, 30), that Darius III (335-331) wanted to free a man he had condemned, but realized that "it was not possible to undo what was done by royal authority."

Darius the Mede is not to be confused with the later Pers. monarch, Darius I Hystaspes (521-486 B.C.), for he was of Median extraction ("of the seed of the Medes," Dan 9:1 KJV), and his father's name was Ahasuerus (the Heb. equivalent of "Xerxes," the name of the son of Darius I. See Esth 1:1). Darius the Mede was born in the year 601/600 B.C., for at the fall of Babylon in 539 B.C. he was sixty-two (Dan 5:31).

A major assumption of negative higher criticism has been that the Book of Daniel was authored by an unknown writer of the Maccabean age (c. 164 B.C.) who mistakenly thought that an independent Median kingdom ruled by Darius the Mede followed the fall of Babylon and preceded the rise of Persia under Cyrus. Darius the Mede, however, is not depicted in the book as a universal monarch. His subordinate position (under Cyrus) is clearly implied in the statement that he "*was made king* (Heb. passive, *homlak*) over the realm of the Chaldeans" (9:1 KJV). Also, the fact that Belshazzar's kingdom was "given to the Medes and *Persians*" (5:28) and that Darius found himself incapable of altering the "law of the Medes and *Persians*" (6:15) renders the critical view untenable.

The early 20th cent. publication of additional cuneiform texts from this period has enabled one to understand much better the circumstances surrounding the fall of Babylon in 539 B.C. It seems quite probable that Darius the Mede was another name for GUBARU, the governor under Cyrus who appointed sub-governors in Babylonia immediately after its conquest ("Nabonidus Chronicle," ANET, 306; cf. Dan 6:1). This same Gubaru (not to be confused with UGBARU, governor of Gutium, the general under Cyrus who conquered Babylon and died three weeks later, according to the Nabonidus Chronicle) is frequently mentioned in cuneiform documents during the following fourteen years as "Governor of Babylon and the Region Beyond the River" (i.e., the entire Fertile Crescent). Gubaru thus ruled over the vast and populous territories of Babylonia, Syria, Phoenicia, and Pal., and his name was a final warning to criminals throughout this area (cf. J. C. Whitcomb, *Darius the Mede* [1963], pp. 10-24). The fact that he is called "king" in the sixth ch. of Daniel is not an inaccuracy, even though he was a subordinate of Cyrus. Similarly, Belshazzar was called "king," even though he was second ruler of the kingdom under Nabonidus (5:29).

The Book of Daniel gives more information concerning the personal background of Darius the Mede than of Belshazzar or even of Nebuchadnezzar; for he is the only monarch in the book whose age, parentage, and nationality are recorded. Although he was a subordinate ruler like Belshazzar, it is evident that he ruled Babylonia with far greater zeal and efficiency than did his profligate predecessor; and even more important, he honored the God of Daniel (6:25-27). *See* DANIEL, BOOK OF.

BIBLIOGRAPHY. R. D. Wilson, *Studies in the Book of Daniel: A Discussion of the Historical Questions* (1917); H. H. Rowley, *Darius the Mede and the Four World Empires of the Book of Daniel* (1935); E. J. Young, *The Prophecy of Daniel* (1949); J. C. Whitcomb, Jr., *Darius the Mede: A Study in Historical Identification* (1963); D. J. Wiseman, et al., *Notes on Some Problems in the Book of Daniel* (1965), 9-16.

J. C. WHITCOMB

DARK, DARKNESS (חשך, *darkness, obscurity*; ערפל, *cloud, heavy cloud*; σκότος, σκοτία). Darkness first appears in Scripture as a description of the chaotic condition of the world before God created light (Gen 1:2, 3). The subsequent division between light and darkness resulted in "day" and "night." Darkness has a certain reality, being more than the absence of light (Isa 45:7). The regular succession of darkness and light is under God's control, who can modify it as He wills. A day is lengthened to afford victorious Israel more time (Josh 10:12, 13), whereas darkness shrouds the scene of Christ's death (Matt 27:45). Thick darkness plagued the Egyptians for three days (Exod 10:22). Mines are characterized by darkness (Job 28:3) as is Sheol (10:21, 22; Ps 88:11-13). Even darkness can not hide from God, to whom all is light (Ps 139:11, 12). The blind are said to be in darkness (Isa 42:7; 49:9).

Metaphorically darkness symbolizes distress (Isa 5:30; 9:1), mourning (47:5), perplexity

(Job 5:14), ignorance (Job 12:24, 25; Matt 4:16), and captivity (Ezek 34:12). Statements made in secret are called "in the dark" (Matt 10:27). The judgment and terror of the day of the Lord are likened to darkness (Amos 5:18). In the spiritual sphere, darkness denotes sin and godlessness, everything that is opposed to God, including demonic forces (Isa 9:1; 42:7). Darkness represents the condition of the spiritually unenlightened (John 1:4, 5), who are blinded by the power of Satan (Acts 26:18). The eye which is evil fills the body with spiritual darkness (Matt 6:33). In general, the world loves darkness rather than the reproof of the light (John 3:19, 20). The unregenerate can even be directly called "darkness" (Eph 5:8).

Evil spirits are the "powers of darkness," against which believers must be armed (Eph 6:11, 12). The wicked will be cast into this "darkness outside" (Matt 8:12; 22:13). Believers must beware lest they walk in darkness and mar their fellowship with God (1 John 1:6).

The term ערפל, "cloud, heavy cloud," can describe the place where God dwells (Exod 20:18; 1 Kings 8:12). It is parallel to חשך (Isa 60:2), where the darkness of the nations will be dispelled by the glory of Jehovah (cf. Rev 21:23-25).

Some scholars would include צלמות among words meaning "darkness." Thomas claims that it is the strongest word for darkness and does not really mean "shadow of death" (Ps 23:4). Relating the word to Akkad. *ṣalāmu* "to be dark," he feels that it should be tr. "very deep shadow, thick darkness." צלמות is parallel to חשך in Psalm 107:10 and several times in Job.

BIBLIOGRAPHY. D. Winton Thomas "צלמות in the Old Testament," JSS 7 (1962), 191-200; C. H. Dodd, *The Interpretation of the Fourth Gospel* (1953), 201-212.

H. M. WOLF

DARKON där' kŏn (דרקון). The sons of Darkon were a body of descendants of Solomon's servants who returned from Babylonian exile with Zerubbabel and his associates (Ezra 2:56; Neh 7:58).

E. RUSSELL

DARK SAYINGS. *See* RIDDLE.

DART. Several words are so rendered although none is unambiguously a dart. שבטים, is used in 2 Samuel 18:14 as Joab kills Absalom. Usually, שבט means "rod, scepter, staff." שלח, in 2 Chronicles 32:5 is some sort of "missile, weapon," based on the root "to send." מסע, in Job 41:26, a hapax legomenon, is one of the weapons which cannot affect Leviathan. "Missile" or "dart" may be correct. תותח, is prob. a "club, mace," but its parallelism to "javelin" in Job 41:29, lends some weight to the rendering "dart." כידון, ordinarily tr. "javelin," could also be a dart (1 Sam 17:45).

The Gr. βέλος, is used in Ephesians 6:16 of the "flaming darts" which Satan unleashes in his attacks on believers. Here again, "arrows" may be intended.

See ARMOR, ARMS.

H. WOLF

DATES (תמר). Dates as such, are not mentioned, though they are by inference—for the palm trees described are obviously date palms (*Phoenix dactylifera.*)

The harmful "strong drink" referred to (Prov 20:1) is prob. date brandy. On the other hand, the date honey of 2 Chronicles 31:5 would do nothing but good. Long-lasting dried dates were handy to carry on long camel journeys across the deserts.

Dates are borne in huge clusters—these hang down among the leaves. The fruits are the main food of some Arabian tribes. *See also* PALM TREE; FOOD.

W. E. SHEWELL-COOPER

DATHAN dā' thən (דתן, meaning unknown). Dathan with two other Reubenites joined the Levite Korah in leading a rebellion of 250 chosen men against the leadership of Moses and Aaron. Numbers (16:1, 12, 24, 25, 27) says Moses prayed and the next morning said, "You have gone too far" (16:7). Dathan and Abiram were sent for, but would not come. They said Moses brought them into the wilderness to kill them, while he was a prince over them. Korah assembled all the congregation against Moses and Aaron, but the glory of the Lord appeared to them all, and Moses and Aaron prayed God would not be angry with all for one. The 250 leaders brought censers with incense. Then fire from the Lord consumed these would-be priests. Dathan and Abiram and their families were swallowed by the earth into Sheol, with Korah and his men.

The people resented this punishment. God threatened them, but Aaron made atonement for them, while 14,700 more died. Later Moses reminded Israel of this discipline of the Lord (Deut 11:2, 6).

The causes of the rebellion were wilderness weariness, envy of Aaron (Ecclus 45:6, 20), jealousy against divinely appointed leadership (Ps 106:16, 17; Jude 11). The penalty was as for treason, sin at the cost of their lives.

W. G. BROWN

DATHEMA dăth' ə mə (Δάθεμα). A fortress (1 Macc 5:29) in Gilead where the Jews found refuge from the Syrians. They were besieged there by the Syrians until Judas Maccabeus and his brother Jonathan rescued them. The town lay a night's march from Bosora. Attempts to locate it have failed. Some think it is the modern Remtheh (Syr. of 1 Macc has "Rametha") or Dameh, if the Syr. is a mistake for "Damtha." Another possibility is Athaman, E of el-Muzerib.

H. WOLF

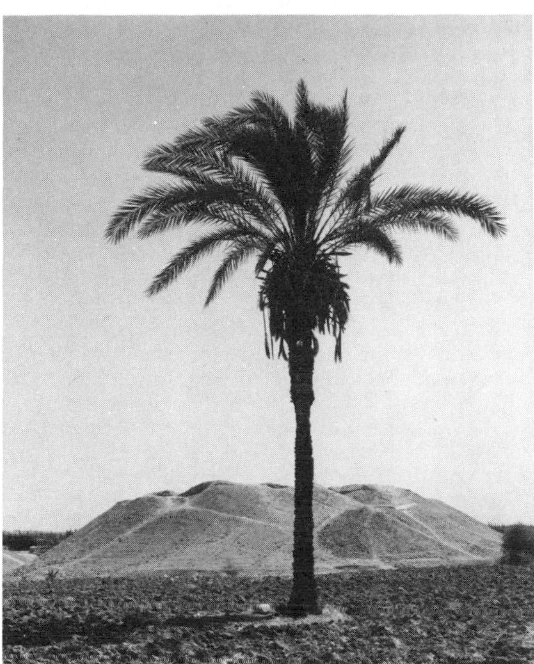

A date palm. ©Lev

DAUGHTER (Heb. בַּת, the regular fem. form of the common Sem. בֵּן, "son"). It is used irrespective of age for a proximate circle of female relatives, even for members of a group as "daughters of Zion" (Isa 3:16, et al.). Any female relative thus defined was prohibited from marriage or sexual activity with any male to whom she held the relationship. The Levitical code is very clear on this point (Lev 18:9-18). Although applied to classes of females, "daughters of X," the term is considerably less common than such constructions as "son/sons." The word is compounded in some names as, Bath-rab-bim=daughter of a multitude; Bath-shua=daughter of Shua; Bath-sheba=daughter of abundance. In some rare occasions the KJV mistakes "bath" for *beth* and thus transliterations such as Bath-Zachariah (1 Macc 6:32, 33) occur. In the NT the common Gr. θυγάτηρ, "daughter" is used throughout (Matt 9:18, et al.) and as in the LXX to tr. Heb. *bāt*. (Matt 21:5, et al.). *See* FAMILY.

W. WHITE, JR.

DAUGHTER-IN-LAW (Heb. כַּלָּה, "bride," before marriage, "reserved one," after marriage, "newly married woman"). The same prohibitions against incest stipulated in the Levitical code for daughters are applied to daughters-in-law (Lev 18:15; 20:12). The daughter-in-law, unlike the concubine, was removed from her father's house as soon as the bride-price, the payment to reimburse the father-in-law for her economic services was paid (Gen 29:21-30). The NT term Gr. νύμφη, means primarily "bride" (Rev 21:9, et al.) and secondarily, "daughter-in-law" (Matt 10:35).

W. WHITE, JR.

DAVID dā′ vĭd (דָּוִד, *beloved one*?). The son of Jesse of Bethlehem.

- I. The life of David
  - A. His family
  - B. The days before his kingship
    - 1. The anointing of David
      - a. God's choice made known
      - b. God's favor shown
    - 2. David's rapid rise and Saul's jealousy
      - a. The Goliath victory
      - b. David before Saul
        - (1) Friendship with Jonathan
        - (2) Popularity brings a negative reaction
        - (3) Saul's plot to destroy David
      - c. David's flight from Saul
    - 3. David's life as a fugitive
      - a. The mustering of a force
      - b. Saul's hot pursuit
      - c. David and Abigail
      - d. The end of the pursuit
      - e. David as an ally to Philistines
    - 4. The death of Saul and Jonathan
      - a. The word from Samuel
      - b. The battle with the Philistines
  - C. The reign of David
    - 1. The years in Hebron
      - a. News of Saul's death
      - b. David anointed by the people
      - c. The war between the two houses
      - d. David firmly established
    - 2. David in Jerusalem
      - a. The capture of the city
      - b. David's wars
      - c. David's sin
      - d. David's peace
        - (1) The moving of the Ark
        - (2) The plans for a sanctuary
        - (3) David keeps his promise to Jonathan
      - e. David's family troubles
        - (1) Amnon and Tamar
        - (2) Absalom's revenge
        - (3) Absalom's treachery
        - (4) David's flight from Absalom
        - (5) The fall of Absalom
      - f. Sheba's rebellion
      - g. Unsettled accounts
      - h. David's folly in taking census
      - i. Preparations for the Temple
      - j. David's last days
- II. David's influence on the history of Israel
  - A. The estimate of David in Israel
    - 1. His high regard among the people
    - 2. His high regard in God's eyes
  - B. The concept of the throne of David and its perpetuity
  - C. David and the worship in Israel
  - D. The effect of David's walk before God on Israel

Sculpture of The Young Shepherd in the Louvre, Paris, reminiscent of David's younger life © *R.B.*

III. David in the prophets
  A. Isaiah
    1. The house of David
    2. The throne of David
    3. The tabernacle of David
    4. The city of David
    5. The sure mercies of David
    6. The God of David
  B. Jeremiah
    1. The throne of David
    2. The house of David
    3. The righteous branch of David
    4. David as king
    5. The covenant with David
    6. Seed of David
  C. The other prophets on David
    1. Ezekiel
    2. Hosea
    3. Amos
    4. Zechariah
IV. David in the New Testament
  A. The gospels
    1. Jesus the Christ, as heir of David
    2. The city of David
    3. The superiority of Christ over David
    4. Other references to David
  B. The Acts
    1. The superiority of Christ over David
    2. David, an inspired writer of Scripture
    3. The tabernacle of David
  C. The epistles
  D. The Revelation
    1. Christ called heir of David
    2. Christ called the Root and Offspring of David.

I. THE LIFE OF DAVID

A. His family. The genealogy of David is given several times in Scripture, the first being in Ruth 4:18-22. He is a direct descendant of Judah, Perez, Hezron, Ram, Amminadab, Nahshon, Salmon, Boaz (the husband of Ruth), Obed (the son of Boaz and Ruth), and Jesse, his father (cf. 1 Chron 2:5-16; Matt 1:3-6; Luke 3:31-33).

B. The days before his kingship. 1. *The anointing of David.* a. GOD'S CHOICE MADE KNOWN. When God determined to reject Saul as the king of Israel, He sent Samuel with oil to anoint another: one of the sons of Jesse of Bethlehem. When Samuel arrived at Jesse's home, he had the sons of Jesse brought forward one by one. Samuel favored Eliab, the eldest, but God showed him that he should not look on the outside but in the heart for truly kingly qualities. God passed by seven of the sons of Jesse until only the youngest, David, remained.

David was then keeping the sheep of his father, and Jesse did not consider it important to bring him before Samuel. He was described as ruddy and beautiful of countenance. When Samuel insisted and David was brought before him, God indicated that this was His choice. David was anointed that day, and the Spirit of the Lord came upon him mightily. It is not certain that his family understood at that time why he was anointed (1 Sam 16:1-13).

b. GOD'S FAVOR SHOWN. In the meantime God's spirit departed from Saul and an evil spirit from God came and troubled him. On the advice of some to call a harpist to soothe him, one young man in the court recommended David as a cunning player and a mighty man of valor, a man of war and prudent in speech. Saul sent for David, thus giving him an early opportunity to see and know court life.

Jesse sent David with an ass loaded with bread, wine, and a kid. When he arrived before Saul, Saul loved him at first sight and made David his armorbearer. Saul sought and received Jesse's permission for David to stand before him.

Whenever the evil spirit fell on Saul, David was at hand with his harp to soothe him. He undoubtedly composed many Psalms in this period (16:14-23).

2. David's rapid rise and Saul's jealousy. a. THE GOLIATH VICTORY. When the Philistines gathered to do battle with Israel in the valley of Elah, Goliath, a giant of the Philistines, came out and threatened Israel.

Jesse was by now quite old and his three older sons were fighting with Saul. He sent David to the front to see how his sons were doing. He sent with him corn and bread for the brothers and cheeses for their captain. David went, leaving the sheep with a keeper and found his brothers in the camp.

As he was talking with them, Goliath came out and threatened as before. When David heard Goliath's boasting, he was indignant.

Eliab was disgusted with David for his interest in these matters and accused David of vain curiosity, but David gave his brother no heed. The men in the camp told David that Saul had promised to give his daughter and great riches to the slayer of Goliath.

David's words of indignation against Goliath reached Saul and Saul sent for him. When David assured Saul he would fight Goliath, Saul listened. David related to Saul how he had cared for the sheep and protected them against a lion and a bear. He gave all the glory to God for his victories over the wild beasts. He confessed that he believed the same God would now deliver him from Goliath. Saul was convinced and sent him out to face the giant.

David rejected the use of Saul's armor and took those weapons with which he was familiar, his staff, some stones and a sling—the weapons of a shepherd.

When Goliath saw this boy, he ridiculed and threatened him. David, not being afraid, affirmed his faith in God. He knew that God would give him the victory so that all might know that there is a God in Israel and that God's people might know that God does not save by sword and spear, but by his own strength.

David ran to meet Goliath and killed him with the first stone. He then cut off Goliath's head with his own sword. Israel won the day in battle (17:1-51).

b. DAVID BEFORE SAUL. (1) *Friendship with Jonathan.* David remained in Saul's court and a great friendship blossomed between him and Saul's son Jonathan. The two made a covenant and Jonathan sealed it by giving to David his robe, apparel, sword, bow and girdle (18:1-4).

(2) *Popularity brings a negative reaction.* David behaved wisely before Saul and the people and was set over all of Saul's men. This pleased the people, but trouble developed because the women began to praise David more than Saul. Saul became jealous, seeing his throne threatened. He no longer trusted David.

Soon Saul tried to kill David and David fled. Now Saul's fear of David increased since it was evident that God was with David but no longer with Saul. He demoted David to captain over a thousand men, but still he conducted himself wisely and God was with him. This troubled Saul even more, for now all Israel and Judah loved David (18:5-16).

(3) *Saul's plot to destroy David.* Though Saul offered Merab, his eldest daughter, to David, he did not keep the bargain. She married another. Then Michal, a second daughter, was offered as bait to get David to fight the Philistines. David bargained for her for a dowry of one hundred foreskins of the Philistines. Saul hoped by this that David would be killed in the attempt to get the foreskins.

David not only got the one hundred foreskins, but one hundred more, and Michal was given to him. Saul understandably feared

A "modern David," a shepherd boy with sling. ©*M.P.S.*

David even more now and was his enemy. Yet David, acting wisely, grew ever more popular (18:17-30).

Saul also tried to turn Jonathan against David. However, Jonathan warned David to avoid Saul and at the same time tried to persuade his father that David was good to the king. Saul assented for a short time and David was temporarily restored to the court.

As soon as war began again, David's popularity rose and Saul was again aroused to jealousy. He tried to kill David in his bed while he slept, but Michal helped him escape (19:1-17).

c. DAVID'S FLIGHT FROM SAUL. David first went to Samuel at Ramah, and together they fled to Naioth. When Saul heard he was hiding there, he sent a force to capture him. These men sent by Saul were made helpless when the Spirit of prophecy fell on them by Samuel's command. Saul, when he came personally to capture David, fell under the same power (19:18-23).

David now fled from Naioth back to Jonathan. Jonathan found it hard to believe that his father really hated David and promised to find out the truth. The truth was that Saul did hate David. Jonathan himself was nearly killed by his father who was now in a rage.

David and Jonathan then made a pact in which Jonathan expressed assurance that David would one day be king, and David promised to protect Jonathan's seed forever. Then David fled (20:1-42). He was now an outlaw and went first to Nob to get help from Ahimelech, the priest. He lied to Ahimelech, not telling the priest that he fled from Saul. He deceived Ahimelech to get aid for himself and those with him. His lie later was fatal to Ahimelech. The priest gave him some of the holy bread and Goliath's sword, but Doeg, a servant of Saul, saw it all.

David next fled to the king of Gath but when he saw he was not welcome there, he feigned madness and escaped (21:1-15).

3. *David's life as a fugitive.* a. THE MUSTERING OF A FORCE. David went to the cave of Adullam and his family joined him there.

Others in distress also came to David. Soon he had a fighting force of four hundred men. All who came seemed to be of one mind with David in his cause (22:1, 2; 1 Chron 12:16).

From there David and his men went to Mizpeh of Moab where he left his parents. Gad, the prophet, warned David to leave there and go to Judah, and thus he came to the forest of Hereth (1 Sam 22:3-5).

b. SAUL'S HOT PURSUIT. Meanwhile Saul learned of David's maneuvers. He complained that his own men did not help him and that they failed to inform him that his own son was working against him. Doeg then volunteered information about the events at Nob. As a result, in his frustration, Saul had all the priests of Nob killed. One son of Ahimelech, Abiathar, escaped with the ephod and joined David (22:6-23).

During this time, David took the city of Keilah from the Philistines, and Saul, hearing of this, came to Keilah to capture David. David learned from God that the people of Keilah would betray him, so he fled with some six hundred men.

He fled to the hill country of the wilderness of Ziph where he hid in the woods. It was here that he saw Jonathan for the last time.

When the Ziphites offered to help Saul capture David, David moved to Maon in the Arabah south of the desert. Saul pursued and nearly caught David there on a mountain. Just as Saul was about to succeed in capturing David this time, he received word to return and fight off an attack of the Philistines. Understandably David called the place, Sela-hammahlekoth (the rock of escape) (23:1-29).

Next, David fled to En-gedi. Saul took three thousand men to capture him there. While Saul rested in a cave in which David hid, he was put into David's hands by God. Though David's men urged him to kill the king, he refused, respecting God's anointed. He did cut off Saul's robe but later even that bothered David's conscience.

When Saul had left the cave, David showed from a distance how he had spared the king's life. Saul, under great stress and emotion, seemed to see his own wrong, and even confessed that he believed David would be king. The change, however, was not long-lasting (24:1-22).

c. DAVID AND ABIGAIL. At this time Samuel died and was buried at Ramah, and David went to the wilderness of Paran. There was a citizen of Maon named Nabal who had great possessions. Nabal was rich but also miserly and evil. David asked Nabal for some help for his men in return for the years his men had protected Nabal's sheep and shepherds. Nabal, instead, ridiculed David which infuriated him. David armed his men and started out to get revenge on Nabal.

Meantime, Abigail, Nabal's wife, who was both lovely and wise, heard of Nabal's folly and went to meet David to make peace. She met him and pleaded for mercy urging David not to blot his own good name by shedding innocent blood. She expressed confidence that God would bless David. David reacted favorably to her pleas and spared Nabal and his sons, accepting her gifts. All this time Nabal was drunk and unaware of what had transpired. The next day, when he learned the truth, he was stricken and died. David later married Abigail. About the same time, Saul gave Michal, David's wife to another man (25:1-44).

d. THE END OF THE PURSUIT. The Ziphites continued to aid Saul by reporting David's whereabouts. Again Saul took some three thousand men and went after David. This time David carefully followed Saul's progress by means of his own spies.

One evening as Saul slept, David and Abishai went into the camp where he lay. God had caused deep sleep to fall on all the camp. David took Saul's spear and water jug, though Abishai urged him to kill his enemy. When David had left the camp he called to Saul and chided Abner for not guarding his master. Saul realizing that a second time David had spared his life, seemed convinced that David meant him no ill. He returned home and never pursued David again. However, David, distrusting Saul thoroughly now, fled to the Philistines and dwelt at Gath with the king Achish (26:1-27:2).

e. DAVID AS ALLY TO PHILISTINES. Achish was impressed with David and gave him Ziklag as a home. David, while pretending to be his friend, raided Philistine towns in the neighborhood. He left no survivors to tell tales. He reported dutifully to Achish that he was raiding cities of Judah. In this period many men of Judah and Israel joined David, even some of Saul's own people, men of Benjamin (1 Chron 12:1-17).

When the Philistines later prepared to war on Israel, Achish wanted to take David to battle with him but the war lords of the Philistines wisely refused him. David was forced to stay away from this battle providentially, for in it Saul and Jonathan would die (1 Sam 28:1, 2; 1 Chron 12:19-22).

When David returned to Ziklag he and his men discovered that the city had been raided and their families carried away. Bitterly they followed in pursuit and finally found the Amalekite raiders and destroyed them recapturing their own families. He sent gifts from the spoils to the elders of Judah to gain their favor. In this battle a principle was established by David whereby those who fought and those who guarded the supplies would share alike in the booty. From Ziklag David had learned the value of leaving some men behind to guard (1 Sam 30:1-31).

4. *The death of Saul and Jonathan.* a. A WORD FROM SAMUEL. Saul became afraid of the Philistines and perhaps had premonitions of his own death. He no longer had Samuel to consult and so he went to a witch at Endor for some word from Samuel of his own fate. He tricked her into attempting to call forth Samuel's spirit and surprisingly, to her and Saul, God obliged. Samuel foretold Saul's death (28:3-25).

b. THE BATTLE WITH THE PHILISTINES. In battle the next day Saul and his sons were killed. Israel fled in confusion, leaving Saul's body behind. The Philistines, in mockery, hung his body and those of his sons on the wall at Beth-shan. In an act of great devotion, the people of Jabesh-gilead bravely took the bodies from the wall and gave them proper burial. David later showed his appreciation to them for their devotion.

Jonathan's nurse, on hearing of the defeat, picked up Jonathan's son Mephibosheth and fled, but the boy fell in flight and was permanently lamed (31:1-13; 2 Sam 4:4).

C. The reign of David. 1. *The years in Hebron.* a. NEWS OF SAUL'S DEATH. While David was at Ziklag, news came from Saul's camp that Saul was defeated and killed. The newsbearer thought he was bringing good news. He even claimed to have killed Saul whom he had found in pain. He hoped for reward, but his reward was execution. David wanted no friend who despised the Lord's anointed. The fact that the newsbearer was an Amalekite did not help, of course.

At this time David composed a beautiful lamentation over the memory of Saul and Jonathan. This first example of David's psalm writing in Scripture is representative of his great inspiration as is seen in the Psalms credited to him (2 Sam 1:1-27).

b. DAVID ANOINTED BY THE PEOPLE. At God's instruction, David went up to Hebron and there was anointed the king of Judah. He showed his character by honoring the men of Jabesh-gilead for their bravery and asked for their support. About the same time Abner took

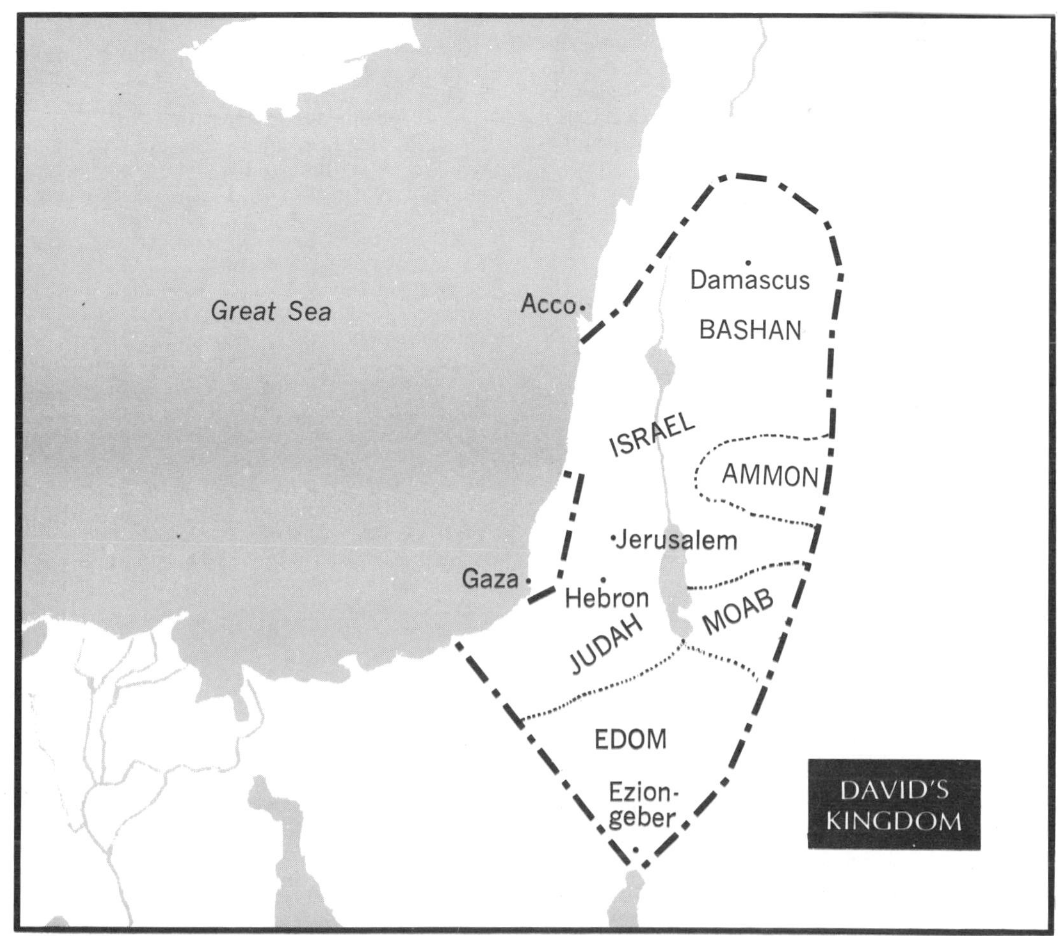

Saul's son Ish-bosheth and made him king over the rest of Israel. David remained at Hebron and Ish-bosheth at Mahanaim (2:8-10).

c. THE WAR BETWEEN THE TWO HOUSES. Soon a showdown between David and Ish-bosheth was inevitable and the two armies met at Gibeon by the pool. David's men led by Joab defeated Abner. In this battle Joab's brother was killed by Abner as he pursued Abner. Joab never forgot this deed (2:12-32).

From that time Saul's house weakened and David's increased in strength. David remained at Hebron seven and one-half years. In all, six sons were born to him there. Three of them, Amnon, Absalom and Adonijah would later play significant roles in his life (3:1-5; 1 Chron 3:1-4a).

As Abner came to dominate Saul's house, Ish-bosheth resented his power and accused him of taking Saul's concubines, an act tantamount to treason. Abner angrily sold out to David. He sent word to David of his plans to have all Israel subject to David. David agreed to a meeting, providing he could have back Michal, Saul's daughter, as a wife.

In the meeting, Abner agreed to a covenant that made David king of all Israel. Joab, who had been away at the time, pursued Abner on his return to Mahanaim and treacherously killed him. He had never forgiven Abner for killing his brother in battle. David, innocent of any guilt in this, openly condemned Joab. He lamented publicly for Abner that all Israel might know his own innocence (2 Sam 3:6-39).

After this, Ish-bosheth was also killed. His head was brought to David for a reward, but those seeking the reward were rewarded as the Amalekite had been—David had them killed (4:5-12).

d. DAVID FIRMLY ESTABLISHED. Now the elders of Israel came and made covenant with David. He was anointed king of all Israel (5:1-3).

2. *David in Jerusalem.* a. THE CAPTURE OF THE CITY. To inaugurate his kingship, David desired to capture the city of Jerusalem, a Jebusite city which David had known from the days of shepherding his father's sheep. He took the stronghold by entering through the tunnels that led out to the spring of Gihon. Those tunnels and the spring are visible today. David increased the size of the city by building up a fill on the steep sides of the hill, called the Millo (from the Heb. מלוא meaning "a fill") (2 Sam 5:6-10; 1 Chron 11:4-9).

b. DAVID'S WARS. In quick succession David conquered Israel's enemies. First he fought and defeated the Philistines. While the Philistines held Bethlehem, David unconsciously expressed a desire for water from the well there. Three brave men went in to get the water. When David saw their devotion, he poured out the water as an offering to God. Now David was victorious at Baal-perazim, Geba (Gibeon) and Gezer. Finally he took their chief city, Gath.

During this time, Hiram, king of Tyre, undoubtedly saw the wisdom of befriending David and sent him cedars to build his house in Jerusalem (2 Sam 5:11, 12, 17-25; 8:1; 21:15-22; 1 Chron 11:15-19; 12:8-15; 14:1, 2, 8-17; 20:4-8).

David next turned to fight the Ammonites when the latter treated his ambassadors disgracefully. The king of Ammon, Hanun, hired the Syrians to fight against David. At Medeba, David beat them soundly (10:1-19; 1 Chron 19:1-19).

c. DAVID'S SIN. The next spring, when David should have been in battle against Ammon, he sent Joab and remained at home. While Joab had Rabbah of Ammon under siege David lusted after and finally seduced Bathsheba, the wife of a Hitt. soldier in his ranks named Uriah. She became pregnant.

To cover his sin he sought to have Uriah have intercourse with his own wife, hoping he would think she was pregnant by him, but Uriah proved a loyal soldier and would not sleep with his wife while his brothers fought in battle.

Now David added sin to sin and plotted Uriah's death. He commanded Joab to put Uriah in the heat of battle and order a retreat, leaving him to the mercy of the Ammonites. When news of Uriah's death came to David, he took Bathsheba as his wife.

But God did not overlook David's actions. He sent Nathan the prophet who put the finger of guilt on David. David's immediate response was confession of his sin (cf. Ps 51). Unlike Saul he could see his own faults. Though forgiven, David was told that his own house would display the sins he had sought to cover. Blood and sex would blight his house.

David went out to battle later and won over Rabbah but it was for him a bitter victory (2 Sam 12:1-31; 1 Chron 20:1).

Among the nations captured by David were Syria, Moab, Ammon, Philistia, Amalek and Zobah. To crown his great victories, David composed a Psalm of Thanksgiving which is closely related to Psalm 18 (2 Sam 8:13-18; 11:15-18; 1 Chron 18:3-17; 2 Sam 22:1-51).

d. DAVID'S PEACE. (1) *The moving of the Ark.* Peace settled over the land and David began to give attention to other matters. He desired to move the Ark to Jerusalem, for it had remained in Kiriath-jearim since Samuel's day.

David did not heed the Mosaic law of instruction for moving the Ark, and as a result one of the men moving it was killed by God. After the Ark rested for three months at the home of Obed-edom, David brought it into the city by the proper means. On that day there was a great celebration in Jerusalem and David composed a Psalm of Praise for the occasion.

Rules and appointments were made for the

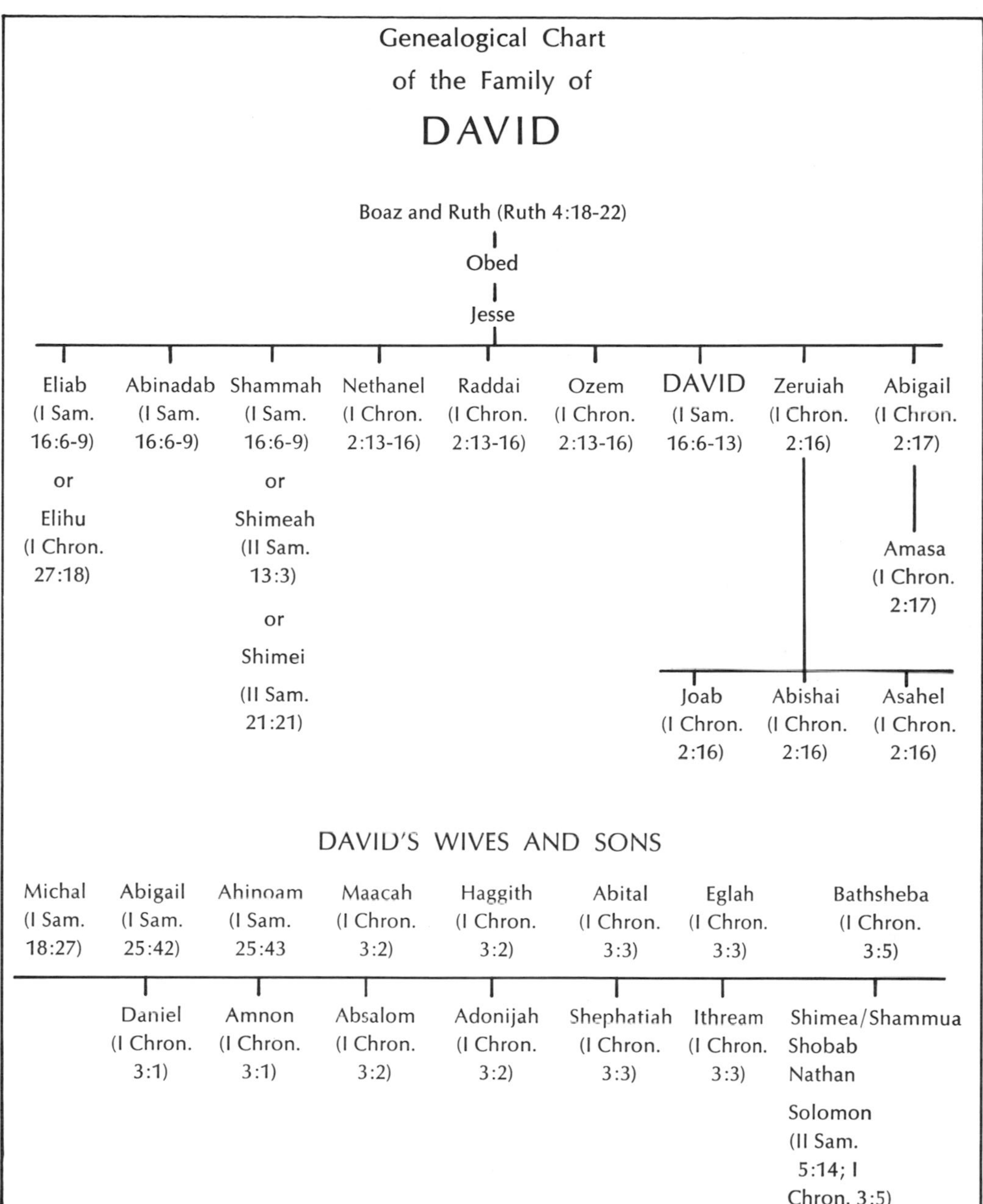

care of the Ark and for the first time proper worship of God in Jerusalem was conducted (2 Sam 6:1-7:29; 2 Chron 13:1-17:27).

(2) *Plans for a sanctuary.* David was not content for the Ark to remain in a tent. He desired to build a permanent structure. However, the Lord would not permit David to do this, and through Nathan told David that not he but his son would build God's house (2 Sam 7:1-29).

(3) *David keeps his promise to Jonathan.* At this time he showed his faithfulness to the memory of his friend Jonathan by allowing the crippled Mephibosheth, Jonathan's son, to sit at David's own table, much as David once had sat at Saul's table with Jonathan (9:1-13).

e. DAVID'S FAMILY TROUBLES. (1) *Amnon and Tamar.* From this time David's sins of the past began to be seen in his own family. One of his sons born at Hebron, Amnon, fell in love with his half-sister, Tamar. He seduced her and afterward cast her off. David knew of this evil but failed to discipline Amnon (12:24, 25; 13:1-22).

(2) *Absalom's revenge.* Absalom, the full brother of Tamar, seeing Amnon go unpunished, plotted revenge. After two years he had Amnon killed. David again displayed weakness, letting Absalom flee, and did not seek to gain his respect. Only after Joab insisted did David call Absalom back to Jerusalem. Even then David refused to see him.

Absalom, a fiery individual, again took matters into his own hand and burned Joab's fields to get his attention. At Joab's insistence David finally received Absalom in the court (13:23-29; 14:1-33).

(3) *Absalom's treachery.* Absalom in these years had grown to distrust his father and now plotted his overthrow. He told the people how much better he would run the kingdom if he were ruler. It worked to a degree and he was able to sow seeds of rebellion (15:1-6).

After about four years Absalom was able to get enough of a following to try to take the kingdom for himself. He went to his home town, Hebron, and there was acclaimed king by his followers. Ahithophel, David's counselor, sided with him (15:27-37).

(4) *David's flight.* When David heard the news he fled Jerusalem with a small following. Ittai and others went with him to show their support, but David would not permit the priest Zadok to bring the Ark. Among David's supporters was Hushai, a man whom David asked to remain in Jerusalem to attempt to foil the good counsel of Ahithophel.

As they left the city, Shimei, a descendant of Saul, cursed David. David received this as a rebuke from God and did not punish Shimei. Absalom entered the city with Ahithophel at his side.

Ahithophel counseled Absalom wisely to pursue with a few men and attack David while he was weary and discouraged. But Hushai, David's friend, pretending loyalty to Absalom, counter-advised him to wait until he had mustered a large force. This would, of course, give David time to reorganize and also give the people time to come to David's aid. Absalom followed Hushai's advice and sealed his own doom. Hushai sent word to David of all that had transpired (15:37-17:29).

(5) *The fall of Absalom.* When the battle was fought, David was not permitted to go. He pled for the troops to spare Absalom's life, but Absalom was killed by Joab who ignored David's pleas. When David received news of the victory he was grieved by word of Absalom's death. Joab, in his brusque manner, rebuked David for his mourning on the day of victory and David smiled before the people through a veil of tears. He was once again restored as king in Jerusalem (18:1-19:43).

f. SHEBA'S REBELLION. A short-lived attempt to rebel soon followed. Sheba, a Benjaminite, sought to lead the ten tribes away from David, but it failed. In the battle, Joab killed Amasa whom David had appointed as commander. Joab took command and put down the revolt himself (20:1-22).

g. UNSETTLED ACCOUNTS. In a series of acts David now sought revenge on Saul's house for the slaying of the Gibeonites during Saul's life. He killed seven descendants of Saul but spared Mephibosheth. David also had Saul and Jonathan buried in the family sepulcher of Kish, the father of Saul (21:1-14).

h. THE CENSUS. For some reason, David took a census of the people at this time. The Bible does not give the reason why it displeased God. God had not ordered it, and apparently the pride of David was involved.

As a consequence of David's action in this matter, God punished Israel. David was given three choices: either seven years of famine, or three months of war, or three days of pestilence. He chose the latter and still seventy thousand were killed. When it seemed as though the whole city of Jerusalem would be destroyed God stopped the angel of destruction as he stood on the threshing floor of Araunah which overlooked the hill on which the city of Jerusalem was built (24:1-25; 1 Chron 21:1-30).

i. PREPARATION FOR THE TEMPLE. God sent Gad the prophet to instruct David to acquire the property belonging to Araunah (or Ornan, according to Chronicles). He did so and built an altar there. This would be the future site of Solomon's Temple.

Before his death David made preparations for the Temple. He gave to Solomon specific instructions, insisting that Solomon strictly abide by the law of Moses (1 Chron 22:1-19). The various duties in the Temple were preassigned to the Levites. David established the order for the Temple services and appointed chiefs of the tribes to oversee the treasury. He publicly announced to the people that Solomon should be his successor, giving Solomon and the officers specific instructions on how to build the Temple. On a closing day of ceremony, David made prayers of thanksgiving and offered many sacrifices (23:1-29:22a).

j. DAVID'S LAST DAYS. In David's last days he was not to be spared trouble. Being very old he was given a young virgin to warm his body.

In these days, Adonijah, a son of David, sought to take over the kingdom. At the foot of the hill in Jerusalem at a well called En-rogel, he tried to have himself made king. He succeeded in getting both Joab and Abiathar the priest to follow him, but Zadok and Nathan would not desert David's son Solomon.

Nathan and Bathsheba moved quickly and told David of the plot. David immediately ordered Solomon brought to the spring of Gihon, within earshot of En-rogel, and there had him publicly acclaimed king. The plan worked and all those following Adonijah fled, fearing David's wrath.

Interior view of the Citadel or so-called "Tower of David" in Jerusalem.
©Three Lions

David then charged Solomon before his death to be strong and keep the law of God.

After forty years as king: seven in Hebron and thirty-three in Jerusalem, David died and was buried in Jerusalem, the city of David. Solomon reigned after him (1 Kings 1:1-2:11; 1 Chron 29:22b-30).

II. David's influence on the history of Israel

A. The estimate of David in Israel. 1. *His high regard among the people.* Respect for the good name of David was great after his death. Solomon was careful that he cleared his father from all guilt in the ignominious death of Abner (1 Kings 2:32, 33). Solomon further showed his respect for his father in sparing the life of Abiathar though he had taken part in Adonijah's attempt to usurp the kingdom from Solomon. He spared Abiathar's life because he had always been faithful to David and had suffered with him (2:26). Solomon, by the same token, executed Shimei for having ill-treated his father when Absalom was in rebellion (2:44-46).

The respect for David, however, extended far beyond the person and time of Solomon. Hiram was later kind to Solomon for David's sake (5:1). Furthermore, in the days of Josiah, long after, Josiah sought after the God of David (2 Chron 34:3).

Even David's enemies respected him. It took the news of his death to embolden Hadad to leave his retreat in Egypt where he had fled from David (1 Kings 11:21). Later, Jeroboam, after leading a rebellion against David's grandson, feared greatly that the people would return to David's house and risked the wrath of God to form a new worship to prevent the people from going to David's city (12:27).

2. *His high regard in God's eyes.* Similarly, God often expressed his own high regard for his servant David. David, we are told, was hand-picked by the Lord to be over God's people (8:16). Thereafter, God was known as the God of David by the people (2 Kings 20:5; 2 Chron 21:12).

The favor God showed to David can be seen in His promise of peace to David's seed forever (1 Kings 2:33). This favor of God toward David is expressed in terms both of loving kindness and goodness (3:6; 8:66).

B. The concept of the throne of David and its perpetuity. Solomon was established as the rightful successor to David before David's death. Soon after his death, the concept of the throne of David was developed and became a permanent part of the covenant involving God's goodness to His people.

Solomon sat on David's throne, a gift to Israel from God (3:6; 5:7). He was known for his great discretion and understanding which was indicated early in his reign. He humbly acknowledged that God had raised him up to fulfill His promise to David.

There was, however, much more to the concept of the throne of David than his successor-son. God had established David's throne forever (2:45). Solomon, recognizing this, as soon as he was made king, sought for God's assurance. He desired that God would perform his whole promise to David, that there fail not an heir on the throne (8:25, 26).

God clearly honored this promise through all the history of Judah. When it appeared, in the days of Athaliah, that the seed of David might be completely destroyed, David's spears and shields were used to put his seed (Jehoash) on the throne in spite of Athaliah's power (2 Kings 11:10). Jehoash (or Joash) was made king on the basis of God's promise to David (2 Chron 23:3).

In the days of Hezekiah the king and Isaiah the prophet (2 Kings 19:34), God determined to defend Jerusalem for David's sake.

Nevertheless, the promise of God to bless the throne of David was not unconditionally given. For David's throne to be blessed, the successors had to walk uprightly as David had done (1 Kings 9:5). When Solomon failed to walk purely before God as David had walked, God determined to rend the kingdom and leave for David's seed only Judah (11:13). Yet, for David's sake, even this he would not do in Solomon's day (11:12, 24).

Though rent asunder, the throne of David remained a reality and God was determined that David should always have a lamp before God in Jerusalem (11:36). This promise became a constant reminder of hope to God's people thereafter (15:4, 5; 2 Kings 8:19; 2 Chron 21:7). Beyond the days of trial gleamed the constant hope that David's seed would not be afflicted forever (1 Kings 11:39).

The split-off tribes were, in essence, put under the same conditions for blessings as Judah. The perpetuity of Jeroboam's throne depended on his doing right as David had done (11:38). But Jeroboam led the northern tribes away from the worship ordained by Moses and later is pictured as having led a revolt against God's will (2 Chron 13:6-8). God clearly disapproved of Jeroboam's innovations in worship and forewarned, through an unnamed prophet, that a descendant of David would one day destroy the altar Jeroboam had built at Bethel. That seed was to be Josiah (1 Kings 13:2). This underlines the temporal nature of the throne of Jeroboam in contrast with the eternal nature of David's throne.

To this day, the concept of the throne of David is alive in the hearts of the Jewish people who still await the birth of David's son, the Messiah. For Christians, of course, this promise is already fulfilled in Jesus Christ who is David's Seed forever. (See IV below.)

C. David and the worship in Israel. Nowhere can the influence of David be seen more clearly and felt more strongly than in the worship of God's people in the Temple that David had planned (2 Chron 1:4).

1. *David and the Temple of Solomon.* In a sense, this Temple rightly could be called the Temple that David built. It was his desire to build it and his influence was heavily felt in its construction, as to form and usage.

Although David had desired to build the Temple (1 Kings 8:18) and God approved that desire, yet He would not permit David to do so (5:3; 8:18). Instead, God told David that Solomon was to build it (1 Kings 5:5; 2 Chron 6:10), and promised to put His name in the house that Solomon was to build (1 Kings 8:15, 24). Solomon was conscious of this promise at the dedication of the Temple (2 Chron 1:9). In the later history of Judah this promise, that God's name would be in the Temple, was highly regarded by the faithful (2 Kings 21:7; 2 Chron 33:7).

The skills and devotion of David are seen throughout the construction of the Temple. David had dedicated gold, silver, and vessels for the House of God (1 Kings 7:51) which things Solomon brought in when the Temple was completed (2 Chron 5:1). For the construction itself, David had already provided skilled workmen (2:7).

2. *David and the worship in the Temple.* David is said to have made the musical instruments which were used to praise God and give God thanks (7:6). He also had written the words of praise for the Temple worship (29:30), and to him are credited many of the Psalms in the Bible which were used in worship by God's people. He also ordered the courses for the priests (8:14).

David's influence was felt in later years as equally as it had been in the days of Solomon, his son. Jehoiada the priest in the days of Joash, when a brief revival of true worship was observed, appointed officers of the house of the Lord under the hand of the priests even as David had ordered (23:18). Later, in the greater revival of Hezekiah's time, the musical instruments for God's house, which David had ordered, were again ordered by Hezekiah (29:25-27). Also the words of praise David had prepared for the Temple worship were used by Hezekiah (29:30). It could be said in Hezekiah's day that not since the days of Solomon had there been such a worship in Jerusalem (30:26).

Still later in the last revival of the kingdom of Judah, in Josiah's day, once again the courses for the house of God and the singers were according to or followed the instructions of David (35:4, 15).

Finally, in the Restoration in the time of Ezra and Nehemiah this same respect for David's influence in worship can be seen. Temple worship was according to the order of David. The musical instruments used were still those specified by David, and the singing followed David's own teaching (Ezra 3:10; Neh 12:24, 36, 45, 46).

D. The effect on Israel of David's walk before God. David's walk before God is seen as an example of the integrity God demanded of all the kings of Israel. God, on numerous occasions, declared that David walked before him in integrity of heart. He was upright in all that God commanded, keeping God's ordinances (1 Kings 9:4).

God showed great lovingkindness to David for this walk, and made clear that the condition of God's continued blessing on His covenant with David depended on such conduct in his seed after him (2 Chron 7:18).

At first, Solomon walked in the statutes of David. But in the long run he failed to live up to David's standards (1 Kings 11:1). As a result Solomon caused all Israel to depart from David's righteous walk (11:33).

In Israel, after the divided kingdom, Jeroboam was the first of a long list of kings who were described as not being like David, who had kept God's commandments and followed after God with the whole heart (14:8). Thus it became the standard of all the kings of Judah and Israel to be judged in the light of the works and heart of David before God (15:3, 11; 2 Kings 14:3; 16:2; 18:3; 22:2; 1 Chron 17:1, 2; 2 Chron 7:17, 18; 28:1; 29:2; 34:2).

III. DAVID IN THE PROPHETS

In the following prophets, various expressions are used in connection with David.

A. Isaiah. 1. *The house of David.* There are ten references to David in Isaiah. The first two are in ch. seven. Here the context is the threat of allied Syria and Israel against Jerusalem. At that time, the seed of David on the throne was the unworthy Ahaz. God's Word in this time of danger to Jerusalem was addressed to the house of David (7:2). When Ahaz refused to ask a sign of God as the Lord had commanded, then Isaiah, God's prophet, ignoring Ahaz, spoke words of hope to the house of David (7:13). These words were the words foretelling the birth of the Christ by the virgin (7:14). The only other reference to the house of David occurs in 22:22, where Eliakim is spoken of as receiving the keys of the house of David on his shoulders. This term is used several times in the historical books of the OT to designate David's kingdom (1 Kings 12:19, 20, 26; 13:2; 14:8; 2 Chron 10:16; 21:7; Neh 12:37).

2. *The throne of David* (Isa 9:7). This passage, clearly Messianic, predicts the coming of a child who shall be mighty God and rule in peace on the throne of David. He will establish and uphold David's throne with justice and righteousness forever.

3. *The tabernacle of David* (16:5). Similarly, this passage is Messianic and points to the same kingdom and throne. The future King is described as sitting in the tent of David in truth, seeking justice and doing righteousness.

In all three of the above categories one sees that the use of David's name so far in Isaiah is in regard to the future blessing on God's people. David's characteristics, noted in Kings and Chronicles after his death are here shown to be a type of the more perfect King to come.

4. *City of David* (22:9). When the city of Jerusalem was under siege it was described as the city of David, thus recalling the covenant of God with David. The term "city of David" applied to Jerusalem is of frequent occurrence in Kings and Chronicles (1 Kings 3:1; 8:1; 2 Kings 8:24; 9:28; 2 Chron 5:2; 8:11; etc.).

5. *The sure mercies of David* (Isa 37:35; 55:3). God indicates His mercy on Jerusalem for David's sake. This provokes the promise from God to defend the city in Hezekiah's day. Later (55:3), God spoke of the sure mercies of David as pertaining to His covenant with David and his seed.

6. *The God of David* (Isa 38:5). It follows then that long after the time of David, it was comforting to such a descendant of David as good King Hezekiah to have God describe Himself as "the God of David your father."

B. Jeremiah. 1. *The throne of David* (Jer 13:13; 17:25; 22:2, 4, 30; 29:16; 33:17; 36:30). This is Jeremiah's favorite term for the successors to David in Jerusalem. It is, in most contexts, simply used to describe the kings who followed David and perpetuated the kingdom. One passage (33:17) is in the context of a Messianic prophecy which related the throne of David to the promise of God that a seed shall not fail David.

2. The house of David (21:12). Jeremiah used the term to address the king on the throne.

3. *The righteous Branch of David* (23:5; 33:15). This term as used in Jeremiah clearly refers to the promised seed of David and heir to his throne. It is a Messianic term. The term undoubtedly refers to the ultimate fulfillment of the eternal seed of David, the Christ.

4. *David as king* (30:9). In accord with the above, David is described here as the future king of Israel. Jeremiah thus applies the term "David" to the Messiah Himself.

5. *Covenant with David* (33:21). In the same context mentioned twice above, assurance was given that God would not break His covenant with David, that he would have a seed forever on his throne.

6. *Seed of David* (33:22, 26). In a way reminiscent of God's promise to Abraham, God spoke of the seed of David as immeasurable and sure of perpetuity as kings over the seed of Abraham, Isaac and Jacob.

For the most part then, Jeremiah's use of the name David is for Messianic prophecy, relating the promise of God to David. The ultimate promise of God is to send His Messiah to save all of His people.

C. The other prophets. 1. *Ezekiel* (34:23; 37:24, 25). Ezekiel always uses the name "David" with the idea of the servant of God in a Messianic and eschatological sense.

2. *Hosea* (3:5). This prophet in referring to King David looks to the future when David will reign as king over God's people. This also is an eschatological view.

3. *Amos* (6:5; 9:11). In the first passage Amos refers to David's reputation as a musician. In the other, he speaks of the Tabernacle of David to be restored to its former glory. This latter passage came at the end of the prophecy of Amos, in the concluding section of hope for the future. Here a great contrast is seen between the Messianic hope and the contemporary evil of Israel in Amos' day.

4. *Zechariah* (12:7, 8, 10, 12; 13:1). Zechariah uses the term "house of David" five times in one passage which speaks of the restoration of glory to David's house in the latter days.

In all these prophets there is a continuation of the concept first seen in the life of David and immediately thereafter, that David's seed would be the channel of God's blessings on His people.

IV. David in the New Testament

A. The gospels. 1. *Jesus the Christ, as heir of David.* It is notable that all the gospel writers seek to make clear the relation between the Lord Jesus and David. With great frequency Matthew and the other writers note this relationship by the term "the son of David" which is applied to Jesus. Thereby they show that Jesus is the fulfillment of the OT prophecies concerning the eternal kingdom of David. The great thesis of the gospels is that Jesus fulfills exactly all of the conditions and promises of God's covenant with David, that a seed should never fail on his throne. Jesus is the seed of David and the eternal King whom God had promised (Matt 1:1; 9:27; 12:23; Mark 10:48; 12:35; Luke 18:38, 39; 20:41). Both Mark and John indicate that the Jewish leaders of Jesus' day fully expected the Christ to be the seed of David (John 7:42; Mark 11:10).

When Matthew began his gospel, he felt it important to establish this fact. In great detail he listed the generations of Jesus, showing that he was indeed the direct descendant of David (Matt 1). Joseph was specifically called the son of David (1:20) and the husband of Mary, Jesus' mother.

Luke in a similar approach gathers together evidence for the fulfillment of God's promise to David in the coming of Jesus (Luke 1:27, 32, 69; 2:4).

2. *The city of David.* One noticeable difference between the gospels and the OT is the reference to the city of David in the NT. While in the OT this constantly refers to Jerusalem, in the NT it consistently refers to Bethlehem (Luke 2:4, 11; John 7:42).

3. *The superiority of Christ over David.* Most important however, in the whole matter of the NT concept of Jesus as the fulfillment of God's covenant with David, is the lesson taught by the Lord to the Pharisees. Jesus taught them that the Christ while properly the son of David and heir of David is, even in the OT, most certainly shown to be above and superior to David. He is indeed the Son of God. All three of the synoptic gospels record this most important lesson (Matt 22:45; Mark 12:35, 37; Luke 20:41, 44).

4. *Other references to David.* Jesus refers to David in two more contexts. Once he uses an event in David's life to show the propriety of His disciples plucking and eating grain on the Sabbath (Matt 12:3; etc.). Once he speaks of David as the psalm writer who wrote in the Spirit (Matt 22:43; etc.).

We conclude then that the dominant Davidic theme in the gospels is the complete fulfillment of all God had promised in reference to David and his kingdom in the coming of Jesus Christ.

B. The Acts. 1. *The superiority of Christ over David.* This theme from the gospels (see above) becomes a major theme in the Early Church. Both Peter and Paul demonstrated that the prophecies about David were by no means fulfilled in David himself but *only* in Jesus Christ. They particularly stressed this in reference to the resurrection (Acts 2:29, 34; 13:36). Paul, furthermore, at Antioch of Pisidia when addressing the Israelites, spoke of David as the king and a man after God's own heart. However, he taught that only in Jesus Christ and His Resurrection could we know the sure mercies of David which God had promised (Acts 13:16-34).

2. David, an inspired writer of Scripture by the Holy Spirit. In two places Luke makes mention of David as a writer inspired by the Holy Spirit in the writing of the Psalms (Acts 1:16; 4:25).

3. The Tabernacle of David. James, quoting Amos 9:11, 12, which spoke of the Tabernacle of David to be built again relates the rebuilding of the Tabernacle of David to the election of the Gentiles. The Gentiles were to have full part in David's kingdom as Amos had foretold (Acts 15:16-18).

C. The epistles. In the epistles also, Christ is demonstrated as being of the seed of David according to the flesh (Rom 1:3; 2 Tim 2:8). In several other passages mention is made of David: one in connection with forgiveness of sins as demonstrated in David's life and Psalms (Rom 4:6) and another listing David as among the faithful of the OT period (Heb 11:32). Psalms 69 and 95 are specifically ascribed to David (Rom 11:9; Heb 4:7).

D. The Revelation. 1. *Christ called heir of David* (Rev 3:7). The inheritance of David is spoken of as the key of David which is described as being in Christ's hands.

2. Christ called the Root and Offspring of David (Rev 5:5; 22:16). In keeping with the gospels and epistles, the Book of Revelation also clearly teaches that Jesus is the true fulfillment and ultimate application of all God's promises to David. He is the eternal seed in whom all the promises and hopes pertaining to David's throne are to be found.

BIBLIOGRAPHY. F. Josephus, *Antiquities of the Jews* and *A History of the Jews,* V. ix; VII. viii-xv; W. De Burgh, *The Messianic Prophecies of Isaiah* (1863), 81-107; A. Edersheim, *Bible History* IV (1890), 81; V (1890), 58; A. Edersheim, *History of the Jewish Nation* (1896), 306-308, 390-392; T. Meek, *Hebrew Origins* (1936), 146ff; J. Finegan, *Light from the Ancient Past* (1946), 141, 149, 150, 151; H. Rowley, *The Rediscovery of the Old Testament* (1946), 37ff., 217ff.; W. Albright, *The Archaeology of Palestine* (1949), 122; A. Pieters, *Notes on Old Testament History* (1950), 141-175; G. Wright, *The Old Testament Against Its Environment* (1950), 65ff., 88ff.; H. Rowley, *The Old Testament and Modern Study* (1951), 13ff., 97ff., 183; S. Driver, *An Introduction to the Literature of the Old Testament* (1956), 377-385, 533, 534; W. Albright, *From the Stone Age to Christianity* (1957), 253f., 293f.; D. Baly, *The Geography of the Bible* (1957), 141, 142; Wright and Fuller, *The Book of the Acts of God* (1957), 112, 113, 117-119; Margolis and Marx, *History of the Jewish People* (1958), 40-60; D. Thomas, *Documents From Old Testament Times* (1958), 195-201; E. Young, *An Introduction to the Old Testament* (1958), 194-199, 201-203, 313-320, 357-360; J. Bright, *A History of Israel* (1960), 163-190, 272, 352-355, 440ff.; K. Kenyon, *Archaeology in the Holy Land* (1960), 240-245; W. Eichrodt, *Theology of the Old Testament,* I (1961), 446ff.; C. Pfeiffer, *Patriarchal Age* (1961), 101; J. Gray, *Archaeology in the Old Testament* (1962), 128ff.; C. Pfeiffer, *Exile and Return* (1962), 20; C. Pfeiffer, *Ras Shamra and the Bible* (1962), 41, 43, 44, 48; J. Thompson, *The Bible and Archaeology* (1962), 96-100; F. F. Bruce, *Israel and the Nations* (1963), 26-35; R. Carlson, *David, the Chosen King* (1964); A. Sachar, *A History of the Jews* (1965), 33-37; J. Bosch, *David—the Biography of a King* (1966); J. Bowker, "Psalm LX", *Vet Test,* XVII (1967), 34-41; H. Rowley, "Notes," *Vet Test* (1967), 30 (See Jan. 1963); R. Clements, *Absalom and David* (1967), 47-88; National Geographic Society, *Everyday Life in Bible Times* (1967), 207-218; C. Pfeiffer, *Jerusalem Through the Ages* (1967), 15-18.

J. B. SCOTT

DAVID, CITY OF (עִיר דּוִד, *town* [*-quarter*] *of David* [q.v.], i.e., *beloved* or *uncle,* K. Kitchen, *Ancient Orient and OT,* p. 85). The oldest, or SE, portion of Jerusalem, on the original Mt. Zion.

The City of David is equated with the מְצוּדָה, "place difficult of approach" (KB), "fortress," of Zion (q.v.) (2 Sam 5:7). Such a mountain fortress at Jerusalem dated back to patriarchal and Canaanite days (Gen 14:18, Salem; cf. Ps 76:2). It occupied the approximately one-quarter m. of sharply sloped ridge between the Kidron Valley on the E and the Tyropoeon Valley on the W, to the N of their junction with the Hinnom Valley. The location was determined by the presence at its NE end, in the Kidron Valley, of the Gihon spring, which was the area's only perennial source for water. Earlier excavators had limited the City of David to the crest, barely 100 yards wide from a gate on the W (Crowfoot, 1927) to a wall and towers on the E (Macalister, (1923-1926); but, while a Canaanite shaft had been cut out through the rock to the water of the spring, this would have left the top of the shaft outside the wall, some eighty ft. to its E, and undefendable. More recent archeologists have demonstrated that the main walls, from c. 1800 B.C. to the fall of Jerusalem to Nebuchadnezzar in 586 B.C., were fifty yards more nearly toward the bottom of the slope, with houses crowding the ascents (K. Kenyon [1961]).

This city David captured from the Jebusites in 1003 B.C. (2 Sam 5:7), renamed it after himself, and settled in it, making it his capital (v. 9). His subsequent building projects included a palace (1 Chron 15:1) and Millo [q.v.], lit., "a filling," which may refer to massive 10th cent. retaining walls with which the previous system of Canaanite terraces on the slopes was strengthened (Kenyon, BA, 27

Above: Site of the City of David at Jerusalem, showing SE corner of city wall and Temple area.
Below: The Mosque marking the Tomb of David on Mount Zion. ©*M.P.S.*

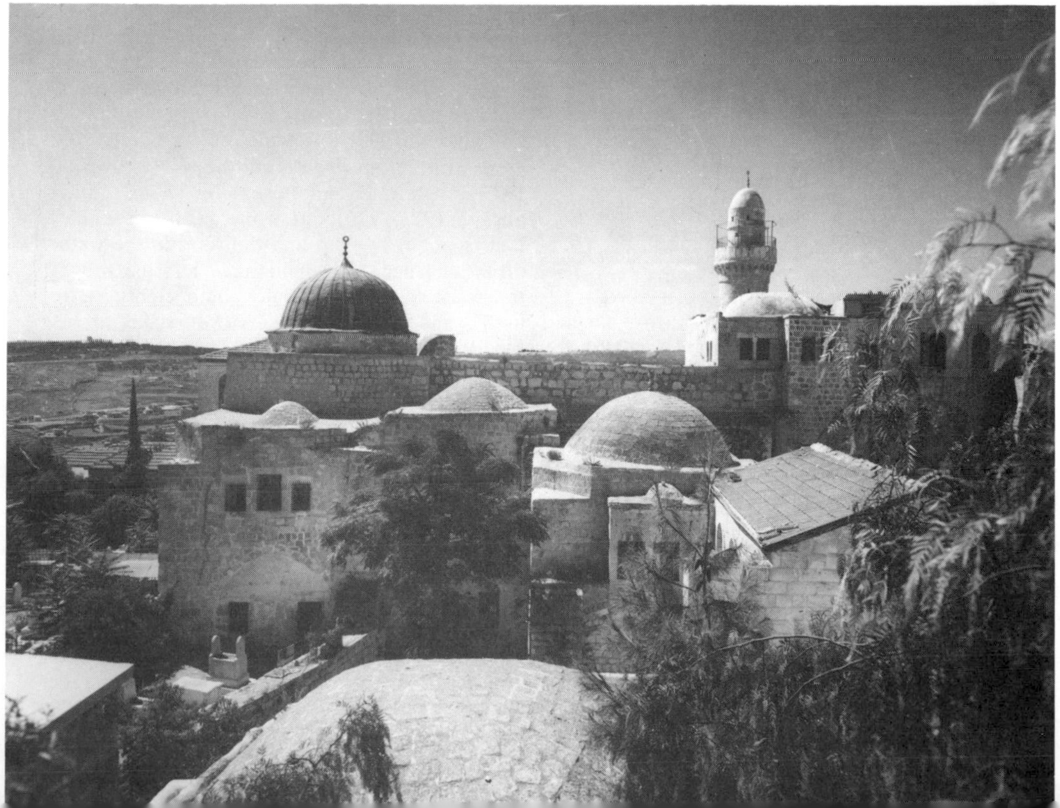

[1964], 43). David brought God's Ark into his City of David (1 Chron 15:1, 29), where it remained until 959 B.C. and its removal by Solomon to the new Temple he had built for it on Mt. Moriah to the N (1 Kings 8:1; 2 Chron 5:2). Solomon seems also to have constructed an acropolis or palace area, with casemate walls, on the crest of the City of David (Kenyon, p. 41), though his palace for the daughter of Pharaoh was not there (1 Kings 9:24), but between Moriah and Zion (?), because of the holiness of these places as caused by the presence of the Ark (2 Chron 8:11).

Scripture notes the burial within the City of David of David himself (1 Kings (2:10), of Solomon (11:43), of most of the kings of Judah down to Jothan, d. 736 B.C. (2 Chron 12:16; 14:1; 16:14; 21:1, 20; 24:25; 27:9), and of other important figures such as Jehoiada the priest (24:16). Certain "barrel vaults," now partly cut away, near the S end of the city may be their remains. King Hezekiah strengthened it before the Assyrian crisis of 701 B.C. (32:5) and brought water down its W side via his tunnel from Gihon (32:30) and thus included the Pool of Siloam and the King's Garden at the southern tip within the walls (Neh 3:15; Isa 22:9-11). Babylon destroyed the city in 586 B.C.

Nehemiah's refortification in 444 embraced only the crest of the City of David, the walls of Crowfoot and Macalister (Neh 3:15; 12:37). Later expansion was to the hill W of the Tyropoeon Valley, on which Josephus located (falsely) the "Tomb of David" (War, V, 4, 1) and to which, with the abandonment of the original City of David after A.D. 70, the name Zion was attached.

The NT speaks of Bethlehem as the πόλις Δαυίδ, "city of David" (Luke 2:11).

BIBLIOGRAPHY. J. Simons, *Jerusalem in the OT* (1952), 60-64; M. Avi-Yonah, *Jerusalem* (1960); K. Kenyon, "Excavation in Jerusalem," BA, 27 (1964), 34-52.

J. B. PAYNE

DAVID, ROOT OF. The term occurs in Revelation 5:5 and 22:16 in reference to Jesus Christ. For further information, *see* DAVID, IV, D, 2.

DAVID, TOWER OF (מִגְדַּל דָּוִד, *wall-* or *watchtower* of David q.v.). A famous Davidic fortress, built in תַּלְפִּיּוֹת, *courses of stones* (KB) and hung with shields, but now unknown except as a symbol of strength (S of Sol 4:4). "David's Tower" by Jerusalem's Jaffa Gate is only medieval, built on a Herodian substructure.

DAWN, DAWNING. DAWN, THE (שַׁחַר, *dawn, morning* ἀνατολή Luke 1:78) שחר is ordinarily tr. "morning" in the KJV or "dayspring" (Job 38:12). The RSV alternates between "dawn" and "morning." That it should be rendered "dawn" is evident from passages such as Judges 19:25, "As the dawn began to break," and Job 3:9, "the eyelids of the morning." The light of dawn can be a symbol for truthfulness and discernment (Isa 8:19, 20).

נֶשֶׁף, tr. "dawn" in Job 7:4 and Psalm 119:147, is more precisely "twilight" denoting the faint light at either dawn or sunrise. In Luke 1:78 "the dawn from heaven" (AG p. 62) is a fig. reference to the coming of Messiah.

H. M. WOLF

DAY (יוֹם ; ἡμέρα). The Bible includes a number of different uses of the word. 1. It often refers to the hours of daylight between dawn and dusk (Gen 1:5; 8:22; Acts 20:31; etc.). In OT times this was divided into morning, noon, and evening (Ps 55:17), or the time of the day might be indicated by the use of such expressions as sunrise, heat of the day, cool of the day, sunset, and the like. The Babylonians reckoned their days from sunrise to sunrise; the Romans, from midnight to midnight; the Greeks and the Jews, from sunset to sunset. The first mention in the Bible of a twelve-hour day is found in John 11:9. The division of the day into twelve-hour periods came from the Babylonians.

2. The concept of a legal or civil day, the period between two successive sun risings, goes back to the creation story (Gen 1:14, 19) and is found throughout the Bible (Luke 9:37; Acts 21:26). The only day of the week to which the Jews gave a name was the Sabbath; they used ordinal numbers for the days, although the day before the Sabbath was often called the day of Preparation (Matt 27:62; Mark 15:42; Luke 23:54; John 19:31, 42). The night was subdivided into watches—first, middle, and morning. The Romans had four watches. Acts 23:23 shows that the night also was divided into twelve hours.

3. The word often is used in the sense of an indefinite period of time: the whole creative period (Gen 2:4), day of God's wrath (Job 20:28), day of trouble (Ps 20:1), day of the Lord of hosts (Isa 2:12), day of salvation (2 Cor 6:2) day of Jesus Christ (Phil 1:6).

The pl. is sometimes used in the sense of "time of," as in the "days of Abraham" (Gen 26:18), the "days of Noah" (Matt 24:37), or of the span of human life, as in "the days of Adam . . . were eight hundred years" (Gen 5:4), "I will lengthen your days" (1 Kings 3:14).

The eternal God is called "the Ancient of Days" (Dan 7:9, 13).

4. Many times the word is used fig When Jesus said, "We must work the works of him who sent me, while it is day; night comes, when no one can work" (John 9:4), "day" means the time of opportunity for service. Jesus said that because His disciples saw "the light of this world" as they walked "in the

day" (John 11:9), and He Himself claimed to be "the light of the world" (John 8:12). Paul called Christians "sons of light and sons of the day," contrasting them with those who were "of the night or of darkness" (1 Thess 5:5). When Paul wrote, "the night is far gone, the day is at hand" (Rom 13:12), he meant by "day" the time of eschatological salvation. There will be perpetual day in the final state of perfection (Rev 21:25).

5. There are special days set aside for and belonging in a peculiar sense to Jehovah, such as the Sabbath day (Gen 2:3; Exod 20:8-11), the Passover (Exod 12:14), and the Day of Atonement (Lev 16:29-31). On these days no labor was to be done and special rituals were observed.

6. In both Testaments is frequent mention of "the day of the Lord" and similar terms used to designate it. This is not a particular day, but a period of time at the end of history when God will bring judgment upon godless peoples and vindicate His name (Isa 2:12; 13:9; Ezek 7:7, 8; Matt 24; 25; 2 Thess 2:1-12). After this supernatural intervention of God in history, He will set up His eternal kingdom (Rev 20-22), and all things will be consummated in Christ (Eph 1:10).

7. The phrase, "the last days," seems to include in its broadest meaning the whole period from the cross to the Second Advent (Acts 2:17; 2 Tim 3:1; Heb 1:2; 2 Peter 3:3, 4).

BIBLIOGRAPHY. Crem (1892), 275-277; BDB (1952), 398-401; O. Cullmann, *Christ and Time* (1950); Arndt (1957), 346-348; W. G. Kummel, *Promise and Fulfilment* (1961); TWNT, II (1964), 243-253.

S. BARABAS

DAY, JOSHUA'S LONG, an event mentioned in a poetic passage in Joshua 10:12, 13. When Joshua and the Israelites began to conquer the hill country of Judah from the Canaanite tribes the town of Gibeon made peace with the invaders. A coalition of petty kings, Adonizedek of Jerusalem, Hoham of Hebron, Piram of Jarmuth, Japhia of Lachish, and Debir of Eglon together with five chieftains of the Amorites met Joshua in battle at Gibeon (10:1-10). There the Lord rained down hailstones and killed many of the enemy. Then Joshua, before Israel, prays to God with a short poem. "Sun, stand thou still at Gibeon, and thou Moon in the valley of Aijalon." So the sun stood still and the moon remained (10:12, 13). It seems as though the parallelism and the sense of Scripture connects the movement of sun and moon. The next statement, v. 14, states that "There has been no day like it before or since." There is no doubt that the Scripture narrative means to be understood in the sense of a supernatural, miraculous event. However, the long day is not mentioned anywhere else in Scripture. Needless to add, this passage has been of great interest throughout the ages of Biblical study. It is so simple and straightforward that it admits to little emendation. On the other hand, it is clear that the victory thus won by Israel was the direct result of the sovereign work of God. The short poem is a hymn of praise for God's providential provision. The mechanics of that action are not told, but only its result in a victory for the children of Israel.

W. WHITE, JR.

DAY, LAST. *See* ESCHATOLOGY.

DAY OF ATONEMENT. *See* ATONEMENT, DAY OF.

DAY OF CHRIST. *See* DAY OF THE LORD.

DAY OF JEHOVAH. *See* DAY OF THE LORD.

DAY OF JUDGMENT. *See* ESCHATOLOGY.

DAY OF THE LORD (YAHWEH) (יום יהוה; LXX ἡ ἡμέρα [τοῦ] Κυρίου). Together with associated expressions like "the day of the wrath of Yahweh" and "that day," it designates God's decisive intervention in history for judgment. (Elsewhere decisive events are called "days," cf. "the day of Midian" in Isa 9:4; "the day of Jezreel" in Hos 1:11. Heb. has no special word for "hour.")

The expression was evidently current in the time of Amos in the 8th cent. B.C., indicating the time when Yahweh would avenge His people on their enemies. Amos turns it back upon those who use it, for the day will bring judgment upon sinful Israel as well (Amos 5:18-20; 6:3; 8:9; chs. 1 and 2). Already Amos's vision of the day oscillates between battles, natural disasters and supernatural calamities, but he ends on a note of hope. The day will usher in a new age (9:11f., which is interpreted christologically in Acts 15:16f.).

The expression figures a great deal in subsequent prophecy. The theme of judgment is developed by Isaiah (cf. chs. 2 and 22), but like other prophetic books Isaiah telescopes numerous themes together. Most prophets look forward to the day of the Lord, but there is a sense in which it was fulfilled in the fall of Jerusalem in 587 B.C. (Lam 1:21; Ezek 34:12). Sometimes the prophet foretells the impending judgment of a particular nation: Babylon (Isa 13:1, 6, 9, 13); Edom (Isa 34:8f.; 63:4); Egypt (Jer 46:10; Ezek 30:3ff.); the Philistines (Jer 47:4). After describing the horrors of the day in great detail, Zephaniah (Zeph 1) mentions by name the surrounding nations (cf. 2; cf. 3:8) before announcing the judgment and restoration of Jerusalem (ch. 3). Obadiah 15 announces that "the day of the LORD is near upon all the nations." Zechariah 12-14 paints a vivid and detailed picture of the desolation of Jerusalem on that day.

The day of the Lord is also associated with universal restoration, and in places is connected with the Messiah. "In that day the root of Jesse shall stand as an ensign to the peoples; him shall the nations seek, and his dwellings shall be glorious. In that day the Lord will extend his hand yet a second time to recover the remnant which is left of his people" (Isa 11:10, 11; cf. 61:2; Luke 4:18f.). Isaiah 2:2-4 (cf. Mic 4:1-3) looks forward to "the latter days" of universal peace and prosperity, when the Lord shall judge between the nations.

Malachi stresses the unbearable judgment and purging as well as the healing and joy that the day will bring (3:2; 4:1f.). He also speaks of the messenger, "Elijah," who will herald the day (Mal 3:1; 4:5). The latter is identified with John the Baptist in Matthew 11:10; 17:10-13; Mark 1:2; 9:11-13; Luke 1:17, 76; 7:27.

Joel's description of the day of the Lord might at first seem to refer to a plague of locusts (Joel 1:15; 2:1f., 11), but the vision merges into one of cosmic, supernatural events and final judgment (3:14ff.). Against the background of heavenly portents the promise is given that "all who call upon the name of the LORD shall be delivered" (2:32), and God will pour out His spirit "on all flesh" (2:28). Acts 2:17-21 sees the prophecy being fulfilled at Pentecost.

Jeremiah speaks of "that time" and "those days" rather than of the day of the Lord (cf. Jer 3:16ff.; 4:11; 50:4). The thought seems to be the same. He announces that "the days are coming" when God will make a new covenant, by which He will write His law on men's hearts and fulfill the covenant promise: "I will be their God, and they shall be my people" (31:31-34).

The expression is not found in Daniel who speaks rather of "that time" when "shall arise Michael . . . who has charge of your people. And there shall be a time of trouble, such as never has been since there was a nation till that time; but at that time your people shall be delivered, every one whose name shall be found written in the book. And many of those who sleep in the dust of the earth shall awake, some to everlasting life, and some to shame and everlasting contempt" (12:1f; cf. 9:26; 10:14; 11:27, 35, 40; 12:4, 9, 13 where mention is also made of the "end").

The expression virtually disappears in late Jewish lit. which ceases to use the name of Yahweh. The terminology survives in (e.g.) 2 Baruch 48:47; 49:2; 55:6. It is revived in the NT (2 Pet 3:10, 12; Rev 6:17; 16:14) where it is also connected with the return of Christ both in language and imagery (Matt 24; 25; Mark 13; Luke 17:22-31; 21; 1 Cor 1:8; 5:5; 2 Cor 1:14; Phil 1:6, 10; 2:16; 1 Thess 5:2; 2 Thess 2:2).

OT prophecy stresses the imminence of the day of the Lord. Men need to prepare for it without delay. God's justice and judgment are certain, as is His mercy. Sometimes prophetic utterances found partial fulfillment in particular events. But these are, in fact, foretastes or trailers of the decisive acts of God in the coming of Christ, the outpouring of the Spirit and Christ's return in final judgment and glory.

BIBLIOGRAPHY. L. Cerný, *The Day of Yahweh and Some Relevant Problems* (1948); G. Delling, ἡμέρα in TDNT, II, 943-953; E. Jenni, "Day of the Lord" IDB, I, 784f.; H. H. Rowley, *The Faith of Israel* (1956), 177-201; S. Mowinckel, *He that Cometh* (1956), passim; G. von Rad, "The Origin of the Concept of the Day of Yahweh," JSS, IV (1959), 97-108; *Old Testament Theology*, II (1965), 119-125; D. S. Russell, *The Method and Message of Jewish Apocalyptic* (1964) passim.

C. BROWN

DAY'S JOURNEY (דרך יום, ἡμέρας ὁδός). The distance that a person can normally travel in one day. This would necessarily vary with the terrain and the method of travel—whether on foot, with an animal, with a caravan; also whether the journey was made in leisure or in haste. Herodotus in one place (IV 101) says that he reckons a day's journey at twenty-five m.; in another place (V 53), at eighteen m. Mention is made of a day's journey (Num 11:31; 1 Kings 19:4; Jon 3:4; Luke 2:44); of a three days' journey (Gen 30:36; Exod 3:18; 5:3; 8:27; Num 10:33; Jon 3:3); and of a seven days' journey (Gen 31:23; 2 Kings 3:9). It is said that Laban pursued Jacob from Haran to Gilead, a distance of 350 m., in seven days —or an average of fifty m. a day (Gen 31:23).

J. C. CONNELL

DAYS, LAST. *See* ESCHATOLOGY.

DAYSMAN. KJV word for UMPIRE.

DAYSPRING (שחר, *dawn, dayspring*; Job 38:12, KJV. Ἀνατολή Luke 1:78, RSVmg.). For initial discussion, *see* DAWN. Some feel that the primary use of שחר is as the name of the Amorite god Shahar, the Venus star at dawn. Ugaritic mythology describes the birth of Shahar and Shalem, his twin, to the Canaanite god El. Reflection of this myth may appear in Job 3:9 and 41:18, where "the eyelids of שחר" are mentioned, and in the phrase "the wings of שחר" (Ps 139:9). Job 41:18 compares the eyes of Leviathan with the eyelids of שחר. Frequently, the passage has been tr. "eyelids of the morning," a reference to the rays of the sun at dawn. עפעפים can mean "eyelashes" as well as "eyelids," which would perhaps fit the imagery better. The simile regarding Leviathan does indeed suggest the sun rather than a star, since flashing brightness is demanded by the context. On the other hand, reference to Canaanite deities is not unknown in the OT. It is difficult, however, to regard שחר as primarily denoting a god, since the word means "dawn" also in Ugaritic.

BIBLIOGRAPHY. C. H. Gordon, *Ugaritic Literature* (1949), 60-62; J. Gray, "The Desert

God Attr in the Literature and Religion of Canaan," JNES VIII (1949), 72-83.

H. M. WOLF

DAY STAR, DAY-STAR, Gr. φωσφόρος, literally "bearer of light," name applied to Venus in classical Gr. astronomy. It is hapax legomenon in 2 Peter 1:19. The name is utilized by the Ger. alchemist Hennig Brandt (17th cent.) for the element phosphorus (P) in A.D. 1669. There is some evidence that it was applied to the sun by certain Hel. astrological writers, but its primary reference from early Hel. times onward was to Venus, the morning star (planet). Such usages in the NT are prob. snatches of liturgical or doxological phrases used by the Apostolic Church and obliquely referring to OT passages such as Numbers 24:17. The tr. of the RSV, "morning star" is to be preferred.

W. WHITE, JR.

DAY, THAT (THE). *See* DAY OF THE LORD.

DEACON, DEACONESS (Gr. διάκονος, *servant, table-waiter*, Luke 10:40; 17:8f.; 22:25ff.; John 2:5, 9); of royal servants (Matt 22:13); of service or ministry in general (Mark 10:43-45 [Jesus]; Acts 1:17, 25 [apostles]; Rom 11:13 [Paul]); of local Christian leaders, possibly an official title (Phil 1:1, 1 Tim 3:8, 12, 13 [*See also* MINISTRY]). In Romans 13:4 the word is applied to secular rulers.

1. Origin. In Gr. thought, service (*diakonía*) was considered unworthy of the dignity of free men (Plato, *Gorg*. 492b, "How can a man be happy when he has to serve someone?"), except when rendered to the state (Demosth. 50, 2; Plato, Leg. 955). In Hel. times the term *diákonos* is applied to certain cult officials (MM p. 149); more generally, Epictetus described the wise man as a servant of God (Diss. III, 22, 69 et al., see Kittel, II, p. 82). Judaism viewed service much more positively, but the LXX used other terms to describe it (*diákonos* only in Esth 1:10; 2:2; 6:1, 3, 5; Prov 10:4; *diakonía* in Esth 6:3, 5). The Suffering Servant of Isaiah 40ff. (*Yebed Yavé*) is described in the LXX as slave (*doûlos toû Theoû*, 42:19) or "child" (*paîs*, 52:13) rather than as *diákonos*. Some aspects of the OT concern for the poor perhaps anticipate the charitable functions of the Christian deacon. The relationship of the "ruler of the synagogue" (*hyperétēs*, Luke 4:20) and his attendant (*ḥazzān*) shows certain similarities to the later correlation between the Christian bishop and his deacons, but the functions involved were very different and there is no evidence of any causal link between the two sets of offices.

2. Christ as deacon. The unique source of all Christian *diakonía*, and its perfect prototype, is found in Him who, being Lord, made himself servant (*diákonos*, Rom 15:8) and slave (*doûlos*, Phil 2:6). By His incarnation as the messianic servant of the Father and by His messianic suffering, Christ completely inverted the servant-master relationship and transvaluated the dignity and honor of serving and suffering. Contrasting his own servant-role with both the power structures of Gentile authority and the ambitious strife of the disciples, He affirmed that "whoever would be great among you, must be your servant (*diákonos*), and whoever would be first among you must be slave (*doûlos*) of all. For the Son of man also came not to be served but to serve (*diakonêsai*) and to give his life a ransom for many" (Mark 10:35-45, cf. 9:35; Matt 20:20-28). Luke, who places the episode in the table context of the Last Supper, concludes the account with the declaration of Christ, "But I am among you as one who serves" (Luke 22:27, *ho diakonôn*). In the fourth gospel the same servant-nature of the Son is dramatically illustrated by His washing the disciples' feet prior to the Supper (John 13:1-11).

All three synoptic gospels refer to the women who followed Jesus and ministered to Him (Luke 8:3; Matt 27:55; Mark 15:41); Peter's mother-in-law, healed of her fever, arose and ministered to the disciples (Matt 8:15; Mark 1:31; Luke 4:39). Whereas the master customarily dines before his servant and expects the required attentions as a matter of course (Luke 17:8), at the final marriage feast the Master Himself will seat His faithful servants at His table, don the apron of table service and wait upon them (Luke 12:37, cf. John 12:25f.).[1] In the judgment described in Matthew 25:31-46, the Son of man will separate the sheep from the goats on the basis of *diakonía*: the Son acknowledges those who ministered to Him (25:44) in feeding, clothing, sheltering and visiting "one of the least of these my brethren."

From these teachings it becomes clear that all Christian *diakonía*, and indeed the whole Christian life, is a participation by grace in the Servanthood of the Son of man. This diaconate-in-Christ marks the entire Church; we are partakers in the communal life and in the corporate servanthood and suffering of the Suffering Servant (cf. Phil 2:5-11; Col 1:24-28). According to Romans 12:7 and 1 Peter 4:7, this *diakonía* is a distinctive gift of the Spirit within the Body of Christ, along with (or manifested in) such gifts as helps, liberality, mercy, and hospitality.

3. Christian ministry. Throughout the NT the Gr. terms "deacon" (*diákonos*) and "deaconate" (*diakonía*, ministry) are consistently

[1] A curious rabbinic parallel occurs in the Mishnah: when Rabban Gamaliel II astonished his fellow rabbis by rising and serving them at table, Rabbi Jehoshua commented that "Abraham was greater than he, and he served at table," while another confrere added, "God himself spreads the table before all men, and should not Rabban Gamaliel therefore arise and serve us?" (SBK II, p. 257).

used in the broad sense implied in the above data; of the more than 100 occurrences of the terms, few even hint at the ecclesiastical office which later developed. The noun *diakonía* is used of financial aid (2 Cor 8:4; 11:8; Rom 15:25; the offering is both *diakonía* and *koinōnía*, Rom 15:26; 2 Cor 8:4), of beneficence (Acts 6:1), and of personal assistance with regard to temporal needs or in evangelistic and missionary efforts (Acts 19:22; 1 Cor 6:15; 2 Tim 4:11; Rev 2:19). The title *diákonos* is applied to Christ (see above), the Twelve (Acts 1:17, 25), Paul (1 Cor 3:5) minister of God (2 Cor 6:4); of Jesus Christ (11:23); of new covenant (3:6); of Gospel (Eph 3:7, Col 1:23); of the Church (Col 1:25), Timothy (1 Thess 3:2; 1 Tim 4:6; Acts 19:22, with Erastus), Tychicus (Col 4:7; Eph 6:21) and Epaphras (Col 1:7). Thus the term is applied to an area of ministry which includes the apostle, missionary, evangelist and prophet—in effect, all the varied forms of Christian ministry (1 Cor 12:5; Eph 4:12).

Some have seen in Acts 6 the initiation of the diaconate as a church office, since the passage employs the noun *diakonía* (6:1, 4) and the verb *diakoneîn* (6:2), and introduces the significant distinction between the "ministry of the Word" (6:4) and the "ministry of tables" (6:1, 2). But the seven are nowhere called "deacons"; Philip is in fact called an evangelist" (21:8) and subsequent accounts emphasize the role of the seven in disputing, teaching, preaching and baptizing.

The salutation of Philippians 1:1 seems to refer to the diaconate as a specific and relatively defined function within the congregation, closely associated with the bishop (or overseer), perhaps esp. in administration of the contribution for which Paul thanks the Philippians. The same quasi-official use reappears in 1 Timothy 3:8-13, again closely linked to the bishop. The requisites for the choice of deacons fit those required for the administration of congregational funds and for house-to-house visitation, two functions typically ascribed to the deacon in patristic lit. (Hipp. Ap. Tr. 9, 21, 23-25, 30). These two passages stand alone as instances of a more technical official sense of the term. Patristic lit. illustrates the progressive definition of its official character, along with the gradual distinction of the bishop and presbyter to constitute a threefold ministry in which the deacon assists the bishop.

4. Deaconess. The synoptic gospels give curious emphasis to the *diakonía* of certain women (see above). In Romans 16:1 Phoebe is described as a *diákonos* (RSV, "deaconess"), but since the form is masculine, without article, and since the first indications of an office of "deaconess" appear only in the 3rd cent., it is highly doubtful that the v. refers to a specific and definite church office. The "women" of 1 Timothy 3:11 prob. refer to the wives of deacons rather than to deaconesses. These passages, however, plus the role of widows indicated in 1 Timothy 5:3-16 and 1 Corinthians 7:8 may point to the earliest origins of the development of the later office of deaconess.

BIBLIOGRAPHY. B. Reicke, *Diakonie, Festfreude und Zelos* (1951); G. Kittel, TWNT II, (1964), 81-93; J. McCord and T. H. L. Parker, *Service in Christ* (1966); H. von Campenhausen, *Ecclesiastical Authority and Spiritual Power in the Church of the First Three Centuries* (1969).

J. STAM

DEAD (מת, מתים ; רפאים; *shades, ghosts,* νεκρός, *dead, lifeless*). מת is the general OT word for "dead," applied to men or animal alike (Exod 21:35). Occasionally, it can refer to someone in a prospective sense, such as God's warning to Abimelech that he was a dead man because of Sarah (Gen 20:3). A leper is also called "one dead" (Num 12:12). The phrase "dead dog" refers to a particularly worthless and lowly individual, sometimes an opponent of the king (1 Sam 24:14; 2 Sam 9:8; 16:9). Physical deformity or vile character can be involved in that expression.

Hebrew law had strict requirements relating to defilement through contact with dead bodies. The high priest could not go near the dead (Lev 21:11); neither could a Nazirite during the days of his separation to Jehovah (Num 6:6). Individuals who touched the dead were unclean seven days (19:11) and had to perform a purification ritual or face death (19:13). Hyssop dipped in water was sprinkled upon the defiled person and the place where the man died (19:18).

Mourning for the dead was common. This involved donning of special apparel and anointing with oil (2 Sam 14:2), weeping in a house of mourning, and eating and drinking for the dead (Jer 16:5-8; 22:10). Ezekiel was forbidden to remove his shoes or cover his lips when his wife died (Ezek 24:17). Burial of the dead was the usual custom (but note 1 Sam 31:12).

The dead are forgotten (Ps 31:12) and, in a sense, without knowledge (Eccl 9:5). They do not praise the Lord (Ps 115:17). Their abode is "the dark places" of Sheol (143:3). Glimpses of the resurrection of the dead appear in the OT (Isa 26:19; Dan 12:2).

In several instances רפאים appeal parallel to the dead as the inhabitants of Sheol (Ps 88:11; Isa 26:14). The exact meaning of the word is not known, though perhaps is related to רפה "to sink, relax." In Ugaritic they appear as the "deities, shades of the dead."

The return of spirits from the dead (1 Sam 28:8f.) was accomplished through the "lady of the *'ôḇ*." This enigmatic term is prob. related to Hitt. *api,* referring to the sacrificial pit where necromancy took place.

NT usage of the dead includes the idea of being spiritually dead in sin (Matt 8:22; Eph 2:1). Believers, however, are to be dead to sin (Rom 6:11). This sense of "lifeless, inactive" is applied to dead faith (James 2:26), dead works of the law (Heb 9:14) and to the church of Sardis (Rev 3:1). The Resurrection of Christ and of the dead is a vital NT doctrine (1 Cor 15:20, 52).

BIBLIOGRAPHY. J. Gray, "The Rephaim," PEQ 84 (1949), 127-139; J. B. Payne, *The Theology of the Older Testament* (1962), 443-463.

H. M. WOLF

DEAD SEA, an intensely saline lake occupying the southern end of the Jordan Valley, called in Scripture the Salt Sea (ים המלח, Gen 14:3; Num 34:3, 12; Deut 3:17; Josh 3:16; 15:2, 5; 18:19); the Sea of Arabah or (KJV) Plain (ים הערבה, Deut 3:17; 4:49; Josh 3:16; 2 Kings 14:25); and the East(ern) Sea (הים הקד מוני, Ezek 47:18; Joel 2:20). Other names include the Arab. Bahr Lût, "the Sea of Lot," Lake Asphaltites (Josephus Antiq I. 9. 1) and the "Sea of Sodom" (Talmud).

The Dead Sea is a remarkable geographical feature and a pivot point of history. Filling a segment of the great Afro-Asian Rift Zone and the deepest of continental depressions, with a shoreline 1300 ft. below the Mediterranean surface and a floor plunging 1300 ft. deeper, it forms a sheet of greenish water extending almost fifty m. from the muddy salt flats of the Jordan delta in the N to the scrubby marshland of the Sebkha in the S. Constricted by the mountain walls of Judaea and Jordan, it is scarcely eleven m. across at its broadest and narrows to two where the Lisan or "Tongue" Peninsula divides the 294 square m. of the deep northern basin from the 99 square m. of the shallow southern basin. Yet this harsh lifeless sea is notable for its geological structure, its hydrology, its natural resources, and its role in Biblical history.

1. Origin and structure. If the geological signs have been read right, the Dead Sea was initially formed when a Miocene "earth storm" trapped the fringe of the ancient Mediterranean (or "Tethys") between the walls of the subsiding Rift, and when the inland sea that once extended from the slopes of Hermon to the central Arabah subsequently shrank into the residual water bodies of Huleh, Galilee and the Salt Sea. The earth storm left its legacy of abrupt walls, plunging strata and crustal weakness. Tethys left its deposits as the thick strata of hard limestone and soft chalk that form the Judean hills and cap the continental crystallines and "Nubian sandstones" of Trans-Jordan, while the trace of fluctuating shorelines is left in elevated terrace and crumbling deposit. A gross oversimplification, for the pattern was complicated and modified by cross currents of crustal movement and climatic change—particularly the alternation of pluvial and arid phases that correlated with the advance and retreat of the European ice sheets.

During the three major pluvial periods the Dead Sea expanded to form terraces high in the walls of the Rift, while a simultaneous acceleration of erosion creased the valley slopes with wadis and spread thick deposits across the valley floor—masses of gravel that choked the wadi exits, beds of rock salt and gypsum, shale and clay, sand and soft chalk, along with the ash gray or yellowish marls that form the Lisan peninsula and bleach the terrace lands of the Jordan. Subsequently exposed and eroded during arid phases, such marls crumbled into the intricate chaos of corrugated "badlands" that flank the Ghor, and the Jordan carved the jungled trench of the Zor. Crustal deformations depressed and tilted the northern basin of the Dead Sea, perhaps simultaneously upthrusting the mass of rock salt and gypsum that forms Mt. Sodom (Jebel Usdum). The subsequent breaching of the Sodom-Lisan ridge and the flooding of the southern basin may well be events of historic times, hypothetically burying the Vale of Siddim with its ruined cities (cf. Gen 14:3).

Sodom and Gomorrah apart, instability is a recurrent feature of this structural "shatter belt." Intermittent earthquakes, submerged trees, a Rom. road traced to the vanished Lisan crossing, the fording of this now deeper sill as late as 1846—all manifest the continuance of ancient crustal weakness. The faulting was complicated. Apart from the primary faults that shaped the Ghor, the downward pull of subsidence tilted the flanking strata into plunging monoclines, while diagonal "hinge faults" splintered the adjacent scarps to form the Plain of Moab and create zones of weakness subsequently deepened into the sawcut river gorges of the Moab scarp.

2. Springs and seepages. Crustal weakness also released a variety of subsurface materials. The rock salt of Mt. Sodom, pressured and plastic, apparently exuded through broken cap rock, while springs—hot and cold, fresh and mineral—issued forth. Patches of greenery mark the sites of fresh-water springs such as those of Zo'ar and En-gedi, while hot and sulphurous waters like those of Zerka Ma'in long have been accounted therapeutic. Submarine sources send salt water as well as fresh welling into the sea floor, contributing, moreover, such minerals as bromide and sulphur that exclude all but a modicum of bacterial life, and impart the distinctively bitter taste and nauseous smell of Dead Sea water. Exhalations of gas and seepages of petroleum and esp. bitumen occur, the latter impregnating chalk and limestone to furnish trader and artisan with coal-like "Dead Sea stone" and welling to the sea's surface particularly after earthquakes; the "slime pits" (Gen 14:10) may well have been bitumen seeps. In all likelihood—since volcanic eruption is geologically improbable—it was an earthquake accompanied by the explosive ejection of gas, bitumen and rock salt that wrought destruction to Sodom and Gomorrah.

The Dead Sea, looking southeast, with the mountains of Moab in the background.
©*Lev*

3. The salty sea. While the sea derives something of its saltiness from surface or subterranean springs along with sporadic runnels from Sodom rock salt, some salinity is added from the soils of the arid watershed. The four permanent streams that drain the rainier uplands of Moab—the 'Udhemi, Zerqa, Arnon and Zered—along with countless intermittent wadis, all carry their quota of salts, while the Jordan, which supplies about 6,500,000 of the 7,000,000 tons of daily inflow, has a high content of sodium and magnesium chloride.

Nevertheless the salt sea would be fresh or only mildly saline had it an outlet: but the landlocked basin in a hot and arid climate forms a superb evaporating pan. The desert climate, accentuated by the rain shadow of the Judean uplands and the hot, gusty winds that pour downslope to the Ghor, is here intense. Scarcely four erratic inches of unreliable precipitation fall annually at the northern end, while the S has less than two. Dry heat accelerates evaporation. Relative humidity is only fifty-seven per cent, average annual temperatures (though reduced by the inclusion of moderate winters and the marked nocturnal cooling of the desert) reach 77°F in places, with individual days soaring to 124°F in the almost non-existent shade—to say nothing of fiercer heat in the glaring sunlight. True enough, occasional winds from the moderate N and regular onshore breezes generated particularly by the northern basin may temper the heat, but they also increase the evaporation. Though this is reduced by high barometric pressure and its own concomitants of light surface mists and high salinity, evaporation remains intense enough to balance the daily inflow of 7,000,000 tons and maintain a fairly constant level. There are seasonal and long term oscillations, of course, which render the 1963 mean of "1308 ft. below" somewhat theoretical: winter levels seasonally rise some ten to fifteen ft. above those of summer, while cycles of relative wetness or drought in the Jordan catchment area—along with more hypothetical crustal deformations—may produce cumulative changes. The rising trend of recent centuries gave way to sinking shorelines after 1929, and measurements since 1900 record a rise of thirty-seven, and fall of sixteen ft. Walled in to E and W, the shoreline perforce expands or contracts at its shelving ends, sometimes inundating the Sebkha for several miles.

4. Mineral extraction is concentrated at these shallow ends. The western shore has long yielded "Dead Sea stone," and salt has been collected for distant markets and temple sacrifice from Sodom and the southwestern Lisan. Arabs and Romans inherited an ancient trade and the Madeba mosaic depicts the passage of a salt-laden Byzantine vessel. Massive extraction awaited the rising demand for chemicals—esp. fertilizers—and in the Mandate period the Dead Sea became a treasure trove. Apart from such crystallized minerals as gypsum (calcium sulphate) and common salt (sodium chloride), which veneer the lake floor, the water—surpassed only by Turkey's Lake Van—sustains a twenty-five per cent concentration of mineral salts, a percentage rising to thirty in the shallow southern basin and thirty-three at depth. As individual elements it is chlorine, potassium, and sodium which are dominant, with sixty-seven, sixteen and ten per cent respectively, while bromine, potassium, calcium and sulphur are present in the small but essential amounts critical for combination into the immense tonnages of salts that saturate the sea—22,000,000,000 tons of magnesium chloride, 11,000,000,000 tons of common salt, 6,000,000,000 tons of calcium chloride, 2,000,000,000 tons of potassium chloride, 980,000,000 tons of magnesium bromide, and 200,000,000 tons of gypsum. Furthermore, the mass of Jebel Usdum preserves a vast residue of rock salt from a larger sea.

Initiated by the Palestine Potash Company at Kallia in 1929, extraction was expanded in 1934 to the subsidiary but ampler site of Sodom, now the focus of production. With the wreckage of Kallia behind the Jordanian lines, and with the Beersheba road completed in 1952, the present pattern took shape. A bromide factory built in 1955 has been merged with a revived and expanded "Dead Sea Works," rock salt quarried from Sodom, and a complex of evaporating pans extended around and into the water. The brine, conducted into pans, deposits common salt before evaporating to leave the carnallite which yields first potash and then bromine. With potash production multiplied fourfold between 1960 and 1965 and doubling again to 1,000,000 tons by 1971, with the addition of table salt refining, with natural gas delivered from the newly-discovered Arad field and with bromine-bottling established at Beersheba, a distinctive industrial complex has emerged.

5. Agricultural resources, by contrast, are uninviting. Even the Bedouin flocks find little sustenance in scanty grass and thorny scrub which occasionally thickens into a scatter of acacia, and in ancient times, when irrigation agriculture was patchily intensive at wadi mouths, most of the region was apparently used only intermittently from peripheral upland settlements. Even the tangle of reed and tamarisk typical of wetter patches may cover soils of repellent saltiness, and "Dead Sea fruit" (*Calotropis procera*) is an appropriate metaphor—a ball of threads and air. Nevertheless, islands of greenery, often dominated by *spina Christi,* occur around fresh water springs, which (skillfully utilized) can sustain a varied range of crops and livestock.

A series of actual or potential settlement sites are aligned along the Dead Sea shores. Little significant development has characterized the eastern side, for (despite the ampler streams of Moab) cliffs crowd the shoreline to eliminate route ways, and the gorges that cleave the sandstone cliffs offer little in the way of level and cultivable land. Settlement, however, could lodge at the northern end where the well-watered Plain of Moab gave Israel a base (Num 22:1), at Callirhoe (prob. Zara S of the Zerqa Ma'in) and particularly in the fertile depression extending from the backslope of the Lisan Peninsula to the delta of the Wadi el-Heso or Zered. Though this oasis belt has a considerable potential for intensive and varied production, it lacks the essential stimuli of access to markets and cultural or historical conditioning: despite some cropping and grazing it remains only patchily developed. However, the descent of five streams from the adjacent escarpment has suggested one hypothetical location for the five cities of the plain.

The western shore, by contrast, is better developed: water supplies may be meager but the mountains shelve less brusquely to the lake, and ancient route ways could not only thread the beach but penetrate the Judean uplands from the three oases of 'Ain Feshkah, En-gedi, and Jericho. Jericho lay eight m. to the N, but springs such as 'Ain Feshka near Qumran, 'Ain el-Ghuweir, 'Ain el-Turaba and esp. the splendid oasis of En-gedi enabled settlement to lodge along the shoreline. Three elevated springs sent water cascading from the cliffs to the sea, sustaining the irrigation settlement of Hazazon-tamar (En-gedi) in Abraham's day (Gen 14:7; 2 Chron 20:2): gracious with vineyards and gardens in Solomon's time (S of Sol 1:14), it now nourishes a kibbutz, rich with tropical oasis crops.

6. Historical role. Typically enough, En-gedi's backdrop is a barren chaos of crags and wadis that gave refuge before ever the fugitive David sought its fastnesses (1 Sam 23:29), a barrenness reinforcing the general impression of lifeless shores around a lifeless sea. In Scripture the region is characteristically a scene of judgment or of battle. Chedorlaomer overwhelmed the Palestinian kings and swept Lot into brief captivity (Gen 14:12) and somewhere hereabouts—perhaps beneath the southern embayment—lay the cities whose destruction reverberated through history and prophecy. The eastern escarpment, seamed by the canyons of the Arnon and the Zered, recalls the thrust and counterthrust of Edom, Moab and Israel, as do the heights behind En-gedi (2 Chron 20:2).

The Qumran caves, where the Dead Sea Scrolls were discovered. In foreground is Cave #4, where the main library of the Essenes was found. ©*M.P.S.*

The Moab rim gave Moses a glimpse of the Promised Land across the Rift, while the plains of Moab and Jericho witnessed the passage of the invader. The hot springs of Callirhoe gave momentary relief to the dying Herod, while among the opposing cliffs of Judea, the Qumran community meditated and wrote. The fortress of Machaerus, traditional site of John's beheading, crested the eastern scarp, while the westerr shores were dominated by the outthrust mesa of Masada, grimly reminiscent of the Zealots' last stand as the Temple lay in ruins. But, in a vision of Messianic healing, the role of the Dead Sea changes. The harsh wadi of the Kidron fills with the fresh waters of healing that flow from the Temple to the Sea, and though the marshes still yield their salt, the once lifeless waters now swarm with shoals of fish (Ezek 47:9, 10).

BIBLIOGRAPHY. W. F. Lynch, *Official Report of the United States Expedition to the Dead Sea* (1849); G. A. Smith, *Historical Géographv of the Holy Land* (1931); F. M. Abel, *Geographie de la Palestine* (1933-1938); (British) Naval Intelligence Division, B. R. 514, Geographical Handbook Series, *Palestine and Transjordan* (1943); D. Baly, *Geography of the Bible* (1957); *Geographical Companion to the Bible* (1963); E. Orni and E. Efrat, *Geography of Israel* (1966).

G. R. LEWTHWAITE

DEAD SEA SCROLLS. The popular name given to a collection of MS material belonging originally to an ancient religious community living near the Dead Sea.

1. Early discoveries
2. Further excavations
3. Dating the scrolls
4. Contents of manuscripts
5. Manuscript scraps
6. The Qumran settlement
7. The Qumran brotherhood
   a. Origins
   b. Community life
   c. Relation to Essenes
   d. Qumran and Christianity
8. The scrolls and the Bible

1. Early discoveries. The exact date when the material was found is uncertain, but is thought to have been early in 1947. A Bedouin goatherd searching for lost animals entered one of the caves high in the marly cliffs of the Wadi Qumran, a m. or so W of the NW corner of the Dead Sea and a little over eight m. S of Jericho. There he stumbled upon several jars somewhat over two ft. in height and almost ten inches wide, containing leather scrolls wrapped in linen cloth. They were removed from the cave and subsequently smuggled to an antique dealer in Bethlehem, who bought

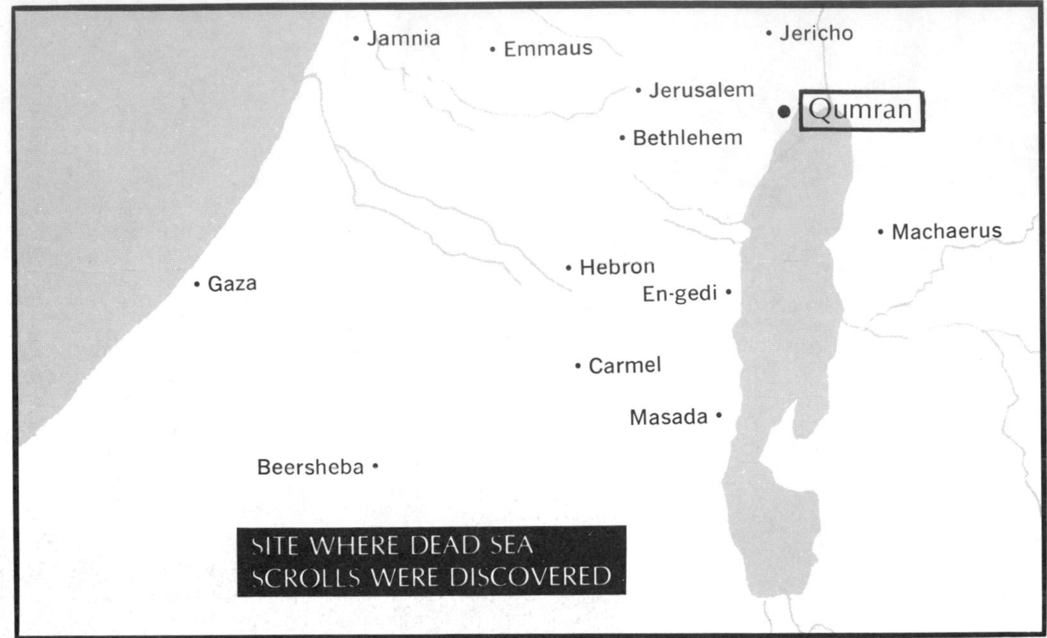

some of them, while the rest came into the possession of the archbishop of the Syrian Orthodox monastery in Jerusalem.

Several scholars examined the scrolls during 1947, some of whom discredited the MSS as forgeries. But the late E. L. Sukenik of the Hebrew University of Jerusalem recognized the antiquity of the scrolls and was able to purchase three of them. Other MSS were taken to the American Schools of Oriental Research, where the acting Director, J. C. Trever, realized their value and promptly photographed them, sending some prints to W. F. Albright, the eminent Biblical archeologist. The opinion of the latter that the scrolls represented the most important discovery ever made in OT MSS has been amply confirmed by subsequent researches.

By the time the value of the scrolls had become apparent, the Arab-Israeli war of 1948 made it impossible for the original cave (1Q) to be located and explored scientifically. However, this was accomplished in 1949 by G. L. Harding of the Jordanian Department of Antiquities and R. de Vaux of the *École Biblique* in Jerusalem who recovered several hundred fragments of Biblical, non-Biblical and apocryphal writings, some of which were unknown previously. The cave had formed the repository of a library comprising about 200 scrolls, and may have been discovered on an earlier occasion if a report of Eusebius is correct that Origen (A.D. 185-254) had employed a Gr. tr. of the Psalms, recovered from a cave near Jericho. This may also have been the same library as the "little house of books" which a shepherd found near Jericho about A.D. 800, and which was subsequently reported to the Nestorian Patriarch Timothy I.

The Palestinian conflict made it desirable for the scrolls in possession of the Syrian archbishop to be brought to the U.S. in 1948, where they were published by M. Burrows, J. C. Trever and W. H. Brownlee. They included a complete scroll of the prophecy of Isaiah (1QIs[a]), a commentary on the Book of Habakkuk (1QpHab), and a document which Burrows styled the "Manual of Discipline" (1QS), because it contained the rules for community life at Qumran. One scroll, at first believed to be an apocalypse of Lamech, could not be opened at the time, and it was only in 1956 that the MS was unrolled and found to comprise an Aram. paraphrase of early chs. of the Book of Genesis. It was published in 1956 under the title, *A Genesis Apocryphon.*

The scrolls acquired by E. L. Sukenik included a fragmentary scroll of Isaiah (1QIs[b]), a War Scroll (1QM) and four portions of a collection of Thanksgiving Hymns or *Hodayoth* (1QH). The entire group was published in 1954 after Sukenik's death by his son, Y. Yadin, under the title *Osar Hammegilloth Haggenuzoth* or "treasury of the hidden scrolls." The fragments recovered from the first Qumran cave were published in 1955 by D. Barthélemy and J. T. Milik under the designation, *Qumran Cave I.*

2. Further explorations. Toward the end of 1951 some new MS fragments were found by Bedouins in two caves of the Wadi Murabba'at, about eleven m. S of 1Q and two m. W of the Dead Sea. Clandestine investigators anticipated

The interior of Cave 4, where archeologists found scrolls lying on the ground.

the official excavation of the caves in 1952, but despite this, several Biblical MSS of the Masoretic textual variety were found, including a scroll of the minor prophets, potsherds inscribed in Gr. and Heb., two Gr. literary papyri in fragmentary condition, coins from the Second Jewish Revolt (A.D. 132-135) which dated the occupational level accurately in the Rom. period, and other less significant artifacts. Important sources for a study of the Second Jewish Revolt against Rome were some papyrus letters in Heb., two of which were signed by Simon Bar-Kokhba and addressed to a certain Joshua ben Galgola, apparently the commander of the military outpost at the Wadi Murabba'at.

Another MS discovery was made in 1952 in the ruins of a monastery about eight m. NE of Bethlehem at a site known as Khirbet Mird. These documents were much later in date than those recovered from other sites, being assigned to a period between the 5th and 9th centuries A.D. The Biblical MSS were of Christian origin, written in both Greek and Palestinian Syriac. The literary material from the Wadi Murabba'at and Khirbet Mird, though interesting and important archeologically, is not directly related to the scrolls and fragments from Qumran.

From 1952, serious attempts were made to locate and explore other caves in the rugged terrain near the Wadi Qumran, the result of which has been that eleven caves have been discovered in the vicinity and have yielded a varied assortment of MSS, fragments, pottery and the like. The second Qumran cave (2Q), discovered in 1952, had already been looted by Ta'amireh Bedouin tribesmen before the official party arrived, and only a few tiny fragments of MSS were found at the site. The third cave (3Q), located about one m. N of 1Q, contained 274 Heb. and Aram. fragments as well as two copper scrolls. The latter had become oxidized, and great technical difficulties confronted those attempting to unroll them. Early in 1956 the rolls were specially treated and cut into strips at the Manchester College of Technology. A textual loss of under five percent occurred in the process, and when tr. the rolls were found to contain information relating to the locations of treasure hoards.

Cave four (4Q), located just W of Khirbet Qumran was discovered in 1952 and contained a wealth of fragments of nearly all the Biblical books (except, apparently, Esther), many familiar and unknown apocryphal writings, commentaries, liturgical texts and other literary works. Caves five to ten, in the vicinity of Qumran yielded less significant material, but cave eleven (11Q), discovered in 1956, contained several relatively complete scrolls. All the fragments recovered from the various sites are at the time of writing being cleaned, classisified and published by an international team of scholars, but it will be many years before the task is completed. In 1955 it was announced that the MSS originally in possession of the Syrian monastery had been acquired by the State of Israel, and the Dead Sea Scrolls are now housed with other ancient documents in the Heb. University of Jerusalem in an edifice known as the "Shrine of the Book."

3. Dating the scrolls. When reports were circulated concerning the antiquity of the scrolls and the early date assigned to those in the possession of Sukenik, many scholars were frankly incredulous, and almost immediately an acrimonious debate arose on the matter. Unfortunately it was conducted for the most part by those who only knew of the discoveries at second hand, and who were unaware of corroborating archeological evidence. Sukenik had assigned a date not later than A.D. 70 for the scrolls which he had studied, and if this was correct it meant that the textual evidence for the Heb. OT had been advanced by at least a millennium. They would thus be by far the oldest surviving Heb. MSS, and of priceless value for the textual critic.

Many who were skeptical were aware that literary hoaxes had been foisted previously on unsuspecting Biblical scholars, particularly in the 19th cent. When it was announced that the original cave (1Q) had been rediscovered and excavated officially, the whole matter appeared in very different perspective. The problem of dating is basically fourfold in nature, involving the date of composition of the literary works, the period when copies of the documents were made, the date to be assigned to the linen in which some scrolls were wrapped, and finally, the actual time when the jars were deposited in the caves.

It is almost impossible to answer the first question satisfactorily with respect to most of the Biblical material, with the exception of *pesharim*, or "Commentaries." Thus in the case of the Book of Isaiah, the earliest extant MS is now 1QIs[a], assigned by Burrows to about 100 B.C., and is at the most some 600 years subsequent to the draft form entrusted by Isaiah to his disciples (Isa 8:16). The Habakkuk commentary presents a twofold problem, since the *pesher* is obviously later in date than the book itself. If the commentary portion of 1QpHab is to be dated before 100 B.C., this then becomes the earliest external evidence for the text of the canonical book. The date of the *pesher* depends partly on the identification of the militant Kittim, with which the sect was concerned, and which have been identified variously with the Seleucid forces of Antiochus IV Epiphanes (175-164 B.C.), the military might of Alexander Janneus (103-76 B.C.), the occupation forces of the Rom. period in Pal., particularly during the first Jewish War (A.D. 66-70), and even the Christian Crusaders of the medieval period.

The date of composition of 1QS, 1QH and 1QM has encountered as wide a range of scholarly opinion as that of the Biblical docu-

Top: Another view of the Qumran area (note men standing in upper right). ©*V.E.*
Below: The interior of Cave 2. ©*V.E.*

ments. To what extent the contents of 1QH had been in circulation before the Christian era is hard to say, but it seems evident that the document was a copy of an earlier MS, and not the original autograph. The Qumran scrolls, whether copies or originals came from a general historical period beginning about 250 B.C. and ending with the abandonment of the Qumran site in A.D. 68. Burrows has dated 1QS and 1QIs[a] about 100 B.C., while assigning 1QM, 1QH and 1QIs[b] along with the *Genesis Apocryphon* to the first quarter of the 1st cent. B.C. He has also maintained that 1QpHab was written during the last quarter of the 1st cent. B.C., and these estimates, based primarily upon paleographic evidence, were shown to be remarkably close when correlated with subsequent archeological discoveries.

The potsherds excavated from 1Q belonged either to the Hel. period and were dated from the 1st cent. B.C., or to the Rom. period from about the 3rd cent. A.D. The pieces of cloth removed from 1Q proved to be linen of local manufacture, and were dated by means of the radiocarbon method of computation. This is based on the fact that every living organism contains a proportion of radioactive carbon-14, which is unstable and begins to degenerate when the species dies. The half life of a radioactive carbon atom is 5,500 years and computation of the age of organic material can be achieved by reducing it to carbon through burning, and then measuring the carbon-14 residue by means of a highly-sensitive radiation counter. There is naturally a small margin of error, and the present range of measurement does not exceed 30,000 years. W. F. Libby of Chicago, who had pioneered this method of dating, tested the flax from Qumran and announced that it had ceased to absorb carbon-14 in A.D. 33, with a plus or minus margin of 200 years, furnishing a complete range of from 168 B.C. to A.D. 233. The median date thus obtained confirmed the antiquity of the scrolls, and needed only to be corroborated by archeological discoveries at Khirbet Qumran.

The actual time when the jars and their contents were placed in the caves of Qumran for safety is less easy to establish. R. de Vaux maintained that the caves had formed an emergency storage place for the lit. of the sectaries, and if this is so the jars could have been deposited on several occasions during the troubled period in which the Qumran sectaries lived. On paleographic grounds it seems clear that all copies of the scrolls in 1Q had been made by A.D. 70 at the latest, and it is most probable that the MSS were hidden locally just before community life at Qumran ended in A.D. 68.

4. Contents of manuscripts. The contents of the major scrolls can now be surveyed briefly, beginning with the large Isaiah MS (1QIs[a]). In surprisingly good condition, it comprised fifty-four columns of clear Heb. script written on seventeen sheets of leather stitched end to end. It measured twenty-four ft. in length and was about a ft. wide. The text averaged twenty-nine lines to each column, and was set out in clearly marked paragraphs and sections. Despite considerable handling in antiquity there were only ten lacunae in the MS and about a dozen small holes, making restoration of the text comparatively easy. The activity of several different hands in the MS was evident, and scribal errors had been corrected in numerous ways. Certain curious marginal symbols were present in the MS, and may have served to divide up the prophecy for liturgical reading. The fairly numerous transcriptional errors in 1QIs[a] could have arisen from the MS being dictated, but aside from these the scroll lends impressive support to the Masoretic textual tradition. The orthography of 1QIs[a] exhibits certain phonetic characteristics which are less prominent in the MT, and which comprise in part a contemporary phonetic spelling designed to facilitate reading without changing the traditional pronounciation. This particular deviation is valuable in enabling scholars to know the way in which Heb. was enunciated with regard to long vowel sounds just before the Christian era, and in showing that Hebrew persisted as a living language after the 2nd cent. B.C.

The fragmentary Sukenik scroll (1QIs[b]) consisted of one large portion and several smaller sections, most of the script of which could be deciphered only by infra-red photography. When assembled into four sheets the two smaller ones, containing material from the earlier chs. of the prophecy, averaged ten inches by six inches, while the larger section, comprising the last third of the prophecy, measured eighteen inches by eight inches. The text approximated closely indeed to the Masoretic tradition, using the older form of spelling current after the Exile.

The most clearly written scroll of all was the Habakkuk commentary (1QpHab), which consisted of two parchment strips stitched together and measuring five ft. by seven inches approximately. As with the other scrolls, the letters were suspended from faintly ruled lines and the text was grouped in columns. Deterioration of the leather resulted in several lines being lost from the bottom of each column. Only the first two chs. of the canonical Habakkuk had survived in the scroll, prob. because the third, a poem, was unsuited to the exegetical aims of the sect. The commentator cited short sections of Habakkuk and then explained them eschatologically or allegorically in terms of the history of the Qumran brotherhood. Interpretative principles of the Jewish *midrashim*, or expositions, were present in the text, including cryptic and eschatological references, the mechanical rearrangement of letters in a word, the interchanging of similar letters and the shortening or division of similar words. The

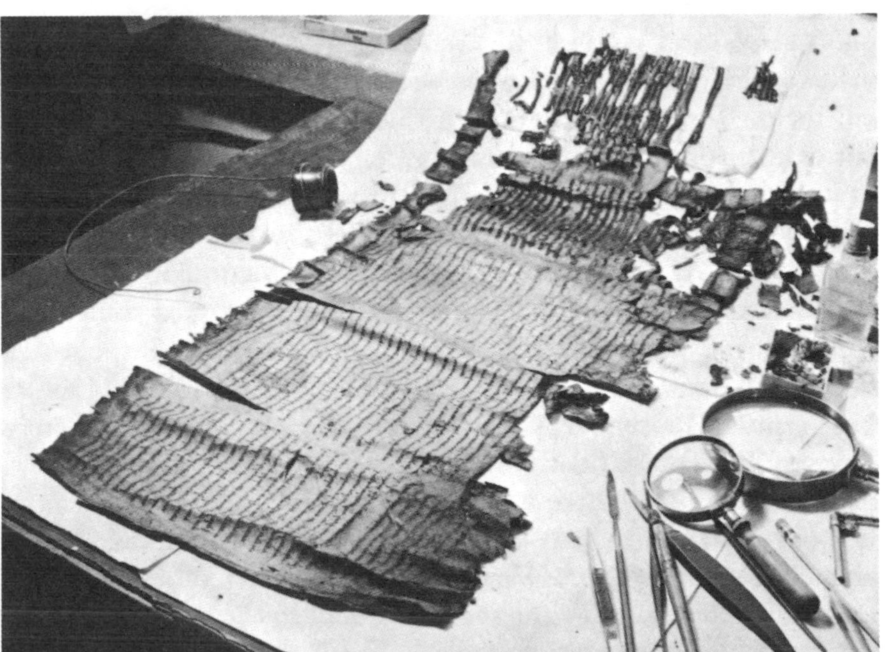

Three stages in the unrolling of a Dead Sea Scroll. The one shown is the Genesis Apocryphon, which was written in Aramaic. *Top:* The tightly-rolled scroll as found. *Middle:* The scroll partly unrolled. *Bottom:* The entire scroll unrolled. Much of the outer material was destroyed. ©*Ecol Biblique et Archaeologique, Jerusalem*

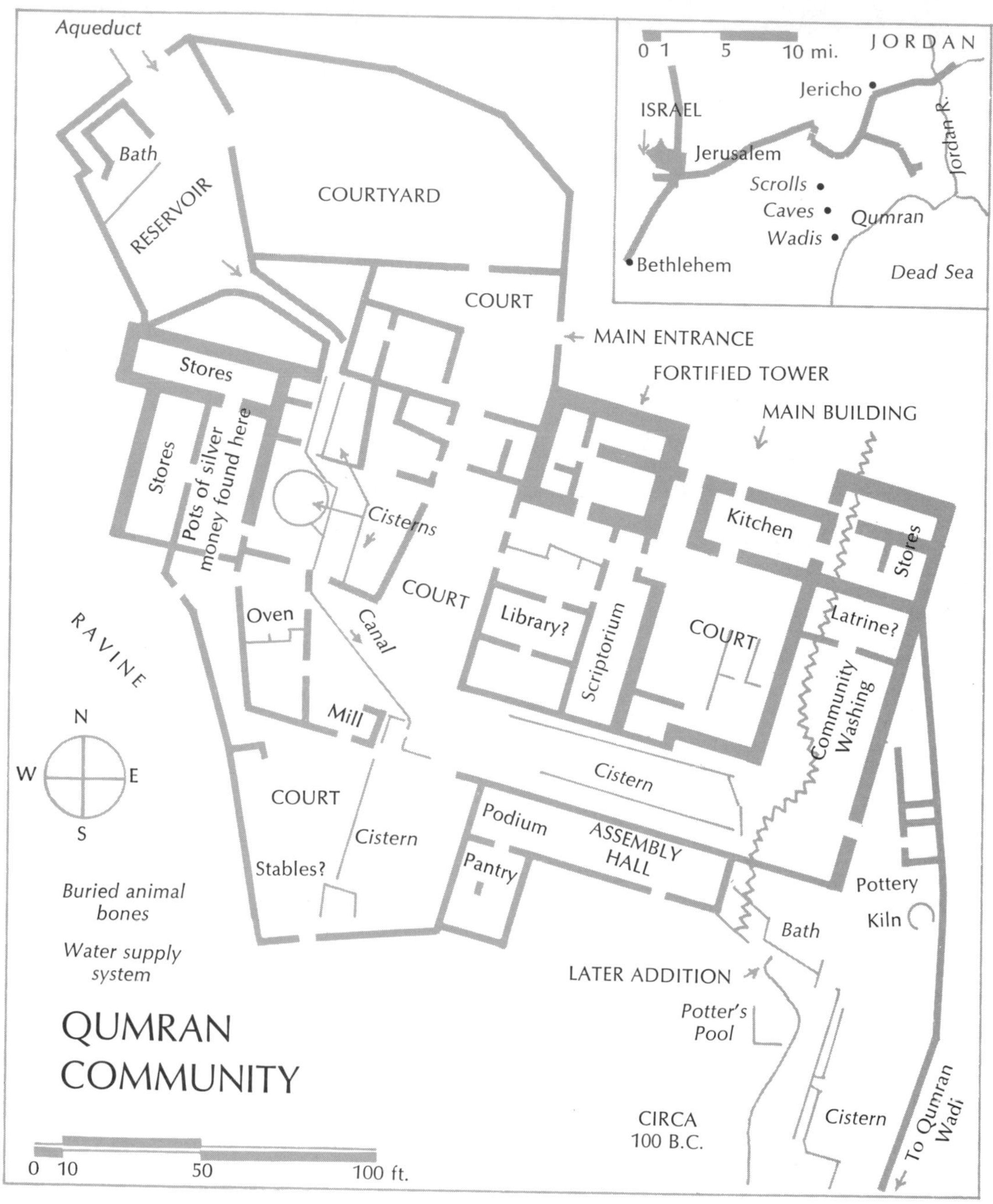

commentary did not explain the meaning of the canonical prophecy, but instead pointed out the existence of certain conditions within the sect from which the scroll originated. The opposition of a wicked priest and the ruthless Kittim were dominant concerns, for these two powers represented the spiritual and temporal opponents of the sectaries. Needless to say, their identification has provoked a good deal of contemporary discussion.

The so-called Manual of Discipline (1QS) or *Community Rule* was recovered in two separate sections, which when joined formed a document about six ft. by nine and a half inches. Originally the scroll had been at least seven ft. long, but the beginning has not survived. The script was remarkably clear, and the style of writing was similar to that of the scribe who copied out 1QIs^{a}. The text comprised eleven columns with about twenty-six lines to each column, the precise number being uncertain because of the damage sustained by the scroll. This work is by far the most important source of information concerning the religious sect at Qumran. It began with a statement of requirements from those aspiring to "enter into the Covenant," and this was followed by the liturgical form of initiation. A section of the text dealt with the Qumran doctrine of man, and this was followed by a list of community rules occupying five columns, the MS concluding with a devotional psalm.

When Sukenik acquired the Thanksgiving Hymns they were in four separate portions, one of which was very difficult to unroll. Parts of the collection were badly decayed and needed infrared photography before becoming legible. The original document had comprised fifteen columns of about twelve inches in height with up to thirty-nine lines of script per column. The overall length was prob. seven and a half ft. The calligraphy showed the activities of two scribes, and the collection of hymns numbered about twenty. They reflected two distinctive pre-Christian types of liturgical writing, namely "thanksgiving" hymns commencing with an act of praise to God and "benedictory" compositions in which a formula of blessing opened the psalm. The collection showed many points of contact with Hebrew and Ugaritic traditions, and in the matter of the personal relationship existing between God and the worshiper they were particularly close to the thought of the Psalter. These poetic writings were prob. the most original of the spiritual expressions to emerge from Qumran.

The last of the four scrolls originally acquired by the Syrian Metropolitan defied many attempts at unrolling, but its contents were finally revealed in 1954. The badly deteriorated state of the work suggested prolonged exposure to unfavorable climatic conditions, and reconstruction of the text was extremely difficult. Preliminary scrutiny had suggested that the scroll was the long lost apocryphal *Book of Lamech*, but it proved to be an Aram. VS of several chs. from Genesis, dealing in paraphrase form and midrashic insertions with the lives of the patriarchs. The original scroll had prob. measured nine ft. in length and about a ft. in width. The text had been inscribed in a clear hand, but the ink had apparently reacted on the leather to produce holes in the scroll, a situation which would suggest a hurried or careless preparation of the material.

The scroll sometimes known as the *Rule of War* (1QM) was originally issued by Sukenik under the title of "The War of the Sons of Light with the Sons of Darkness." It was preserved in good condition, and when unrolled it was nine ft. in length and almost seven inches in width. The text had been written on four sheets in eighteen columns, with the remains of another column from a fifth sheet completing the scroll. It dealt in an eschatological manner with the prosecution of a war between Levi, Benjamin and Judah as the "Sons of Light" and those enemies of Israel which included the Greeks, Philistines, Moabites and Edomites as the "Sons of Darkness." The forthcoming conflict was introduced by means of a short prologue, followed by a detailed series of directions for the conduct of the battle and several prayers to be uttered at different times by the "Sons of Light." Precisely what the sectaries had in mind when this material was written has been the subject of much debate, and it is, at the time of writing, uncertain whether they were thinking in terms of an actual military engagement or an apocalyptic Armageddon.

North wall of council chamber at Qumran. ©*Lev*

Three fragments of Daniel recovered from 1Q were found to have come from two different scrolls. Two of them were related palaeographically to the large Isaiah scroll, while the other was very similar to the script of 1QpHab. Two pieces preserved portions of the same ch. of Daniel, while the third included the point where the Aram. section of Daniel began. The text was in essence that of the Masoretes, and the chief differences had to do, like those of 1QIs[a], with the spelling of words.

Other fragments from Qumran included some 200 scraps found in the second cave (2Q), among which were portions of the Torah, the Psalter, Jeremiah and Ruth. Non-Biblical texts seemed to predominate, however, and were mainly apocalyptic or Messianic in nature. From 3Q, about a m. N of 1Q, came several hundred mixed MS scraps of Biblical and non-Biblical writings. The most significant discovery in this cave was that of two copper scrolls which had escaped destruction when the cave roof collapsed in antiquity. One scroll was in two sections, and originally the strips may have been fastened together to form a sheet of metal about eight ft. long and a ft. wide. The complete oxidization of the metal made unrolling almost impossible, and it was only in 1956 that it was decided to cut the metal into strips, a process which fortunately was executed with little textual loss. The rolls contained a list of about sixty treasure caches, and described their locations in various parts of ancient Judea, some of which cannot be identified. The lettering in the metal had been punched out hurriedly and the finished work rolled up quickly by unskilled hands, suggesting that the treasure had been disposed of and the list compiled in a time of emergency, perhaps about A.D. 68.

An estimate of the value of the items detailed in the copper scroll has placed it as high as six thousand talents, or about two hundred tons of gold and silver. Such a vast hoard of wealth seems out of character with a sect which had a renunciation of riches and communal living as two of its most important regulative factors, and a satisfactory explanation of the situation has not been forthcoming to date. Quite aside from the historical nature of this catalog, the text itself is of great importance since it was written in a colloquial dialect of the 1st cent. A.D. rather than in standard literary Heb. Prior to the discovery of the copper scrolls, the only extant representatives of this dialect were some Jewish religious treatises of which the Mishnah (2nd cent. A.D.) was the oldest.

5. Manuscript scraps. A great many fragments were recovered in 1952 from another cave (4Q) located near Khirbet Qumran. Probably over 300 books had been stored there originally, about one-third of which were canonical in nature. Fragments of every OT book with the exception of Esther were represented in the cache, along with such extra-Biblical compositions as the *Book of Enoch*, the *Damascus Document*, the *Testament of Levi*, and others. A section of Numbers (4QNum[b]) exhibited a type of Heb. text midway between the LXX and Samaritan varieties, while a portion of Samuel (4QSam[a]) contained a text which was not only close to that underlying the LXX, but also was nearer to the text of Samuel employed by the Chronicler than was the MT. Yet another fragment of Samuel (4QSam[b]) is thought to exhibit a text type which is superior alike to the LXX and the Masoretic tradition.

The fifth cave contained some almost completely decomposed fragments including portions of Kings, Lamentations and Deuteronomy, as well as an Aram. eschatological work entitled *Description of the New Jerusalem*, which was also represented in other caves. 6Q contained several hundred papyrus and leather fragments including small portions of Genesis and Leviticus written in palaeo-Heb. script, sections of Kings and five fragments of Daniel. Non-Biblical books were represented by some apocalyptic writings and a number of Aram. compositions. Five other caches were subsequently found in the Qumran area, the latest of which (11Q), discovered in 1956, yielded several scrolls in a very good state of preservation, including two MSS of Daniel and a damaged Book of Psalms. Equally notable was the recovery from the same cave of an Aram. targum of Job, which was prob. composed in the 1st cent. B.C.

The fragments found in the Murabba'at area in 1952 came almost entirely from the second cave (2Mu), and comprised 2nd cent. A.D. documents written in Gr., Heb. and Aram. Of these, prob. the most important was a papyrus palimpsest inscribed in an archaic hand which appears earlier than the 6th cent. B.C. script of the Lachish ostraca, and which was assigned by J. T. Milik to the 8th cent. B.C. It contains a short list of masculine names. Fragments of the Pentateuch and the Book of Isaiah from 2Mu exhibited minute agreement with the MT, and have been dated in the 2nd cent. A.D. Some additional light was thrown on the latter period with the recovery of a few Heb. papyri written by Simon Ben-Kokhba, the leader of the ill-starred Second Jewish Revolt against Rome (A.D. 132-135) to his forces positioned in the Wadi Murabba'at region. Other material of the same period, written in cursive Lat., showed that the fortified post at Murabba'at had been occupied by the Romans later. The fact that the letters from 2Mu had been written in Heb. is further proof of the fact that it had survived into the Christian era as a living tongue.

In 1953 Belgian archeologists found further MSS fragments at Khirbet Mird, N of Bethlehem which included Arab., Gr., Syr. and Christo-Palestinian material. All the documents recovered were of later date than those from

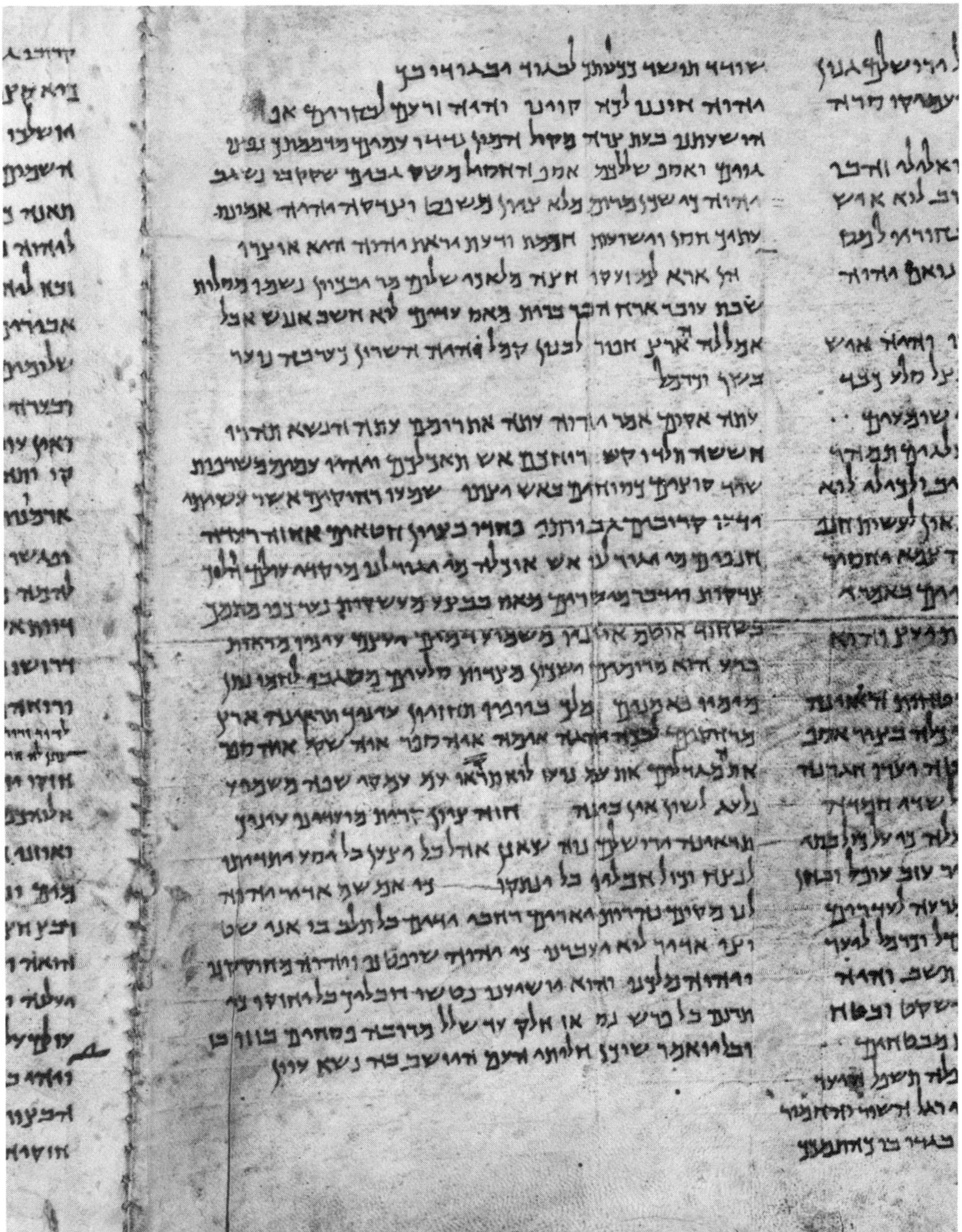

Column 27 of Isaiah manuscript from Dead Sea cave; contains Isaiah 33:1-24.

either Qumran or Murabba'at. At a place still unidentified at the time of writing there was found in 1952 a fragmentary Gr. text of the minor prophets, written on leather in a beautiful uncial hand and containing portions of Micah, Jonah, Nahum, Habakkuk, Zephaniah and Zechariah. It was dated by Barthélemy in the 1st cent. A.D., and is of great value for the textual critic in supporting the claim of the LXX to be a reliable witness to an early textual tradition. The fragments comprise a VS which is a revision of the LXX, and which was most prob. the text which influenced the VSS made from the Heb. original in the 2nd cent. A.D. by Aquila, Theodotion and Symmachus.

One of the caves. ©V.E.

6. The Qumran settlement. While the Qumran area was being excavated officially in 1949, the attention of the archeologists was drawn to some ruins on a rocky plateau about one m. S of 1Q. After preliminary soundings the excavation of the ruin or *khirbeh* was undertaken thoroughly in 1952, revealing the presence of a large complex of rooms, one of which contained broken plaster benches. There was also a large water cistern joined in antiquity by means of an aqueduct to some natural reservoirs further along the escarpment. Of particular significance was the discovery of an intact jar, identical in size and shape with the pieces recovered from 1Q, and this established beyond question an immediate link between the occupants of the ruin (known as *Khirbet Qumran*) and the MSS from 1Q. It became evident that a religious community had once lived at the site and had been responsible for the documents deposited in the nearby caves. A cemetery was found adjoining the *khirbeh* containing male and female skeletons, and this made the connection all the more sure. Subsequent campaigns at the site uncovered the entire community complex. On the NW corner of the main structure was a large fortified tower, which had apparently been buttressed following a severe earthquake in 31 B.C. when it was damaged on the E side and on the SE corner. The principal community building of an area of about 120 ft. square was located N of the refectory and kitchen. To the SW were four or five rooms which may have served as places of study and prayer. One of these, the *scriptorium*, contained the remains of plaster benches where in all probability some of the Qumran scrolls had been copied. Two inkwells of the Rom. period, one made of earthenware and the other of brass, helped to date the deposit accurately.

At the SE corner of the complex the excavators unearthed the remains of a workshop containing the tools used by the community members. A pottery kiln was also discovered nearby, indicating that the community was virtually self-supporting. Latrines, conduits and cisterns were in considerable evidence in the well-planned community settlement. From the abundance of cisterns and reservoirs it has been supposed that the religious sect placed a good deal of emphasis upon rites involving ceremonial washings. It is also true that the sheer physical needs of a community of perhaps 500 persons would require the provision of ample supplies of water. It is thought that the community derived its principal staple commodities such as grain, vegetables and meat from ‘AIN FESHKA, a date palm oasis lying

The tall, mended jars hold the scrolls found in Cave 1. The cooking pot on the shelf above is also from Qumran and dates to about the time of Christ. ©Kelso

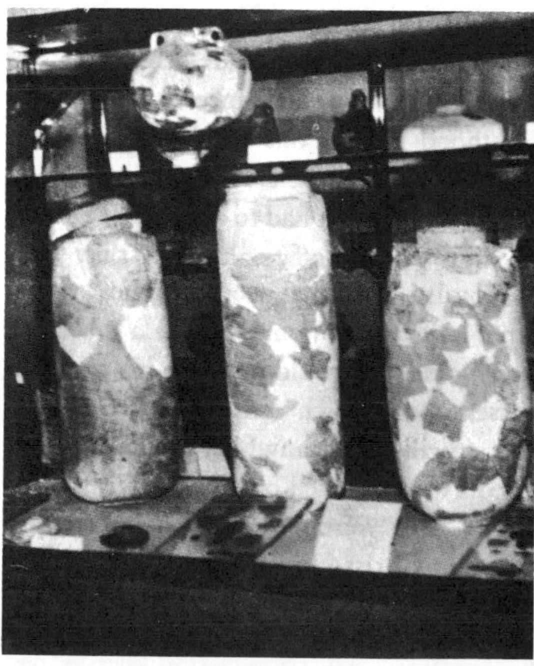

about two m. S of the *khirbeh*, on the W coast of the Dead Sea.

The potsherds and coins recovered during the excavations helped further to determine the connection between the religious sect and the Qumran scrolls. The potsherds came from three occupational levels, c. 110-31 B.C., A.D. 1-68 and A.D. 66-100 respectively. During the third season (1954) a cylindrical jar of the same shape and pattern as those from 1Q was found in a storeroom S of the principal building, reinforcing the connection between the sect and the cave deposits.

Many coins were recovered from the *khirbeh* but none from the Qumran caves, indicating that all monetary dealings took place within the settlement alone. The coin deposits have enabled an accurate dating of the various occupational levels to be made, and indicate that the first such period began during the time of John Hyrcanus (135-104 B.C.) and continued without interruption till the reign of Mattathias (40-37 B.C.), the last of the Hasmoneans. Only one coin came from the period of Herod the Great (37-4 B.C.) in contrast to the series belonging to his son Herod Archelaus (4 B.C.-A.D. 6). Other deposits represented the period of the Rom. procurators of Judaea, along with twenty-three coins of the reign of Herod Agrippa I (A.D. 37-44). Some coins came from the period following the fall of Jerusalem in A.D. 70, while about a dozen from Level III were dated in the Second Jewish Revolt.

7. The Qumran brotherhood. ***a. Origins.*** The general character of the Qumran sect has become evident through the MSS discoveries, and particularly from the contents of the *Community Rule* (1QS), although not all problems relating to the nature of the brotherhood have been solved. The sect comprised a group of priests and laymen pursuing a communal life of strict dedication to God. The mysteries of prophecy had been revealed to the founder, a priest described as the Righteous Teacher; an important feature of community life was the interpretation of Scripture in terms of the witness of the sect and the end of the age. The Righteous Teacher had been sent by God to announce the punishment which was to come upon Israel. According to the Habakkuk commentary, the Righteous Teacher knew even more of the eschatological implications of this than did the prophet himself. Though ostensibly delayed, the end would come, but a remnant would survive. This latter was the Qumran community, which had pleased God because of its fidelity to the Torah and its trust in the Righteous Teacher.

This general message was rejected flatly by the Wicked Priest and his followers, whose concerns were apparently with things other than

Museum for the Dead Sea Scrolls (The Shrine of the Book in Jerusalem, Israel)

the spirituality of the Torah. The reference to the Wicked Priest was evidently to the office of High Priest in Jerusalem, since the incumbent was spoken of as "ruling in Israel" and bearing the "true name." While a broad allusion to the High Priesthood was doubtless intended it seems clear that a specific clash between the Righteous Teacher and the Jerusalem High Priesthood had occurred at some point in the early history of the sect, for the *pesher* spoke of the Wicked Priest persecuting the Righteous Teacher and doing the latter physical harm. The issue reached a climax on the Day of Atonement, when the Wicked Priest "consumed" the Righteous Teacher and made his followers stumble, presumably a reference to the death of the leader and the dispersion of the sectaries.

However, the persecuting Wicked Priest was himself overtaken by his enemies, and in company with the "last priests of Jerusalem" he was delivered into the power of his enemies. The commentary thought in even broader terms of the destruction of the whole nation by those valiant and proud agents of divine anger in the last days, who were described as the *Kittim*. In the OT this name was used of the people of Cyprus (Gen 10:4 RSV; Isa 23:1, 12 ASV; Jer 2:10; Ezek 27:6, et al.), and in the Apoc. as a designation of the Greeks (1 Macc 1:1; 8:5 [tr. Macedonians]; mg.). In later Jewish authors the name was applied cryptically to any victorious power regardless of the particular epoch, and this tradition may be reflected in 1QM, where the Kittim of Assyria were mentioned. However, the Kittim of 1QpHab can only be either the Greeks or the Romans. While the conquering armies of Alexander were partially maritime in origin, those of his successors, the Seleucids and Ptolemies, came from Syria and Egypt, not from the "coastlands of the sea." Furthermore, the Seleucid and Ptolemaic forces do not correspond fully to certain other aspects of the Kittim as outlined in the commentary.

A more probable identification is with the Rom. armies, who accord with the description of the Kittim better than any other earlier imperial power. They came from distant maritime places, were under the command of a "guilty house," sacrificed to their standards, and venerated their weapons of war. This latter form of cult worship was apparently common in the 1st cent. B.C., when the Romans regarded the "eagles" as sacred objects and offered worship to them accordingly. Josephus recorded that this custom was still in existence in the 1st cent. A.D., for he described the way in which the Rom. legions erected their standards near the E Gate of the Temple compound and offered sacrifices to them prior to storming the Temple in A.D. 70.

If the Kittim can be identified with the Romans it may be that 1QpHab described the occupation of Judaea under Pompey in 63 B.C. In that event, the Wicked Priest may have been either Alexander Jannaeus or Aristobulus II, although assured identification is difficult. Precisely who the Righteous Teacher was is also uncertain, particularly since some of the allusions prob. referred to an office rather than an individual. Two fragmentary *pesharim* also mentioned the struggle between the Righteous Teacher and the Wicked Priest. The *pesher* of Psalm 37 described the divine mission of the Righteous Teacher and his task of occupying the Holy City and its Temple. The text of this fragment said that the Wicked Priest had been sent to kill the Righteous Teacher and to slay "the upright of the way." In portions of a Nahum *pesher* were mentioned a certain Antiochus and also a man named Demetrius, "king of Javan," presumably Demetrius III of Damascus who aided the Pharisees against their despotic ruler Alexander Jannaeus (103-76 B.C.). It is possible that the reference in the *pesher* to the Lion of Wrath "hanging up men alive" refers to the revenge of Jannaeus after a victory by Demetrius, but the cryptic use of terms in the *pesharim* makes this uncertain. Against this background the sect would seem to have been a splinter group within Judaism, originating most prob. in the days of Antiochus IV Epiphanes (175-163 B.C.), and organized as an orthodox theological group under the Righteous Teacher in the Judaean settlement at various times between 175 B.C. and A.D. 70.

b. Community life. For this the *Community Rule* is an invaluable guide to the organization of the sect, which comprised a group of priests and laymen following a communal existence in dedication to God. According to 1QS, those desirous of "entering into the Covenant" had to comply with certain preliminary procedures, after which they were initiated on a probationary basis, reaching full membership after three years. Each member was subsequently required to renew his pledge of obedience annually, when he was also reminded of those faults which could result in his expulsion from the brotherhood. The fifth column of 1QS supplied the rules for community government, from which it is evident that the sect was controlled by elders and priests for the purpose of engaging in Biblical study and participating in a sacramental type of worship.

The sect clearly regarded itself as the true Israel, awaiting the establishment of divine rule on earth. The expectation of the Messianic advent loomed large in the thought of the brotherhood, partly because the sectaries were required to follow their pattern of living according to the Torah until the coming of a prophet and two Messianic figures styled "the anointed ones of Aaron and Israel." In a document entitled the *Zadokite Work*, a religious group known as the Covenanters of Damascus, which has striking affinities with the Qumran fellowship and with which it has been identified by many scholars, there occurred the designation "the Messiah of Aaron and Israel," pointing to the expectation of a single individual. The Messianic concepts of the sect were summarized in a document from 4Q containing a series of Biblical texts. Beginning with the promise to Moses that a prophet would arise (Deut 18:18) it continued with a citation from the Balaam oracles (Num 24:15ff.) and ended with the blessing of Moses (Deut 33:8ff.), along with a quotation from a hitherto unknown pseudepigraphical work.

The *Community Rule* depicted the Messiah participating in a banquet in the New Age. Those present were assembled in order of seniority, and the presiding priest blessed the bread and wine. After this the Messiah, who was evidently occupying a subordinate position, blessed the food also. The banquet was clearly apocalyptic in nature, yet at the same time had definite sacramental qualities. The ritual could be followed at any time by variant numbers of participants from those laid down, and the sense of expectation of the events ushering in the divine kingdom was a prominent feature of the ceremony. For the sectaries, the kingdom would emerge after the Kittim of various countries had been conquered and Israel had emerged triumphant. It would be characterized by a theocratic system with a sacrificial order and a priesthood which had much in common with the thought of Ezekiel.

Ritual lustrations occupied a large place in the practices of the sect, and adequate amounts of water were provided for these purposes. The spiritual implications of such rites were stressed, making it clear that true repentance and submission to God alone determined whether or not a person was cleansed as a result of these ceremonies. The Torah was studied day and night at Qumran, and sacred festivals were strictly observed. Theologically, the covenanters are believed to have held to a dualistic view of the universe in which the spirits of light and darkness, God and evil, were placed in ethical opposition in a Zoroastrian fashion. The struggle between them would be resolved only on the Day of Judgment, a theme elaborated in 1QM in the description of the apocalyptic battle between the offspring of light and darkness and for which the sect had to prepare. Despite their tendency toward dualism, the members stressed truth, justice, humility and devotion, seeking by their disciplined life to acquire such virtues.

c. *Relation to Essenes.* The fellowship at Qumran has often been described as Essene, but despite such similarities as the monastic life, manual labor, spiritual devotion and the like, there are certain striking differences between them. Unlike most ESSENES, the Qumran sectaries practiced marriage, indulged in animal sacrifices, were non-pacifists, and avoided all contact with the outside world. Although, as Josephus has made clear, the term "Essene" was of an elastic nature in antiquity, it seems

Fragments of the Dead Sea Scrolls under glass plates. ©*P.A.M.*

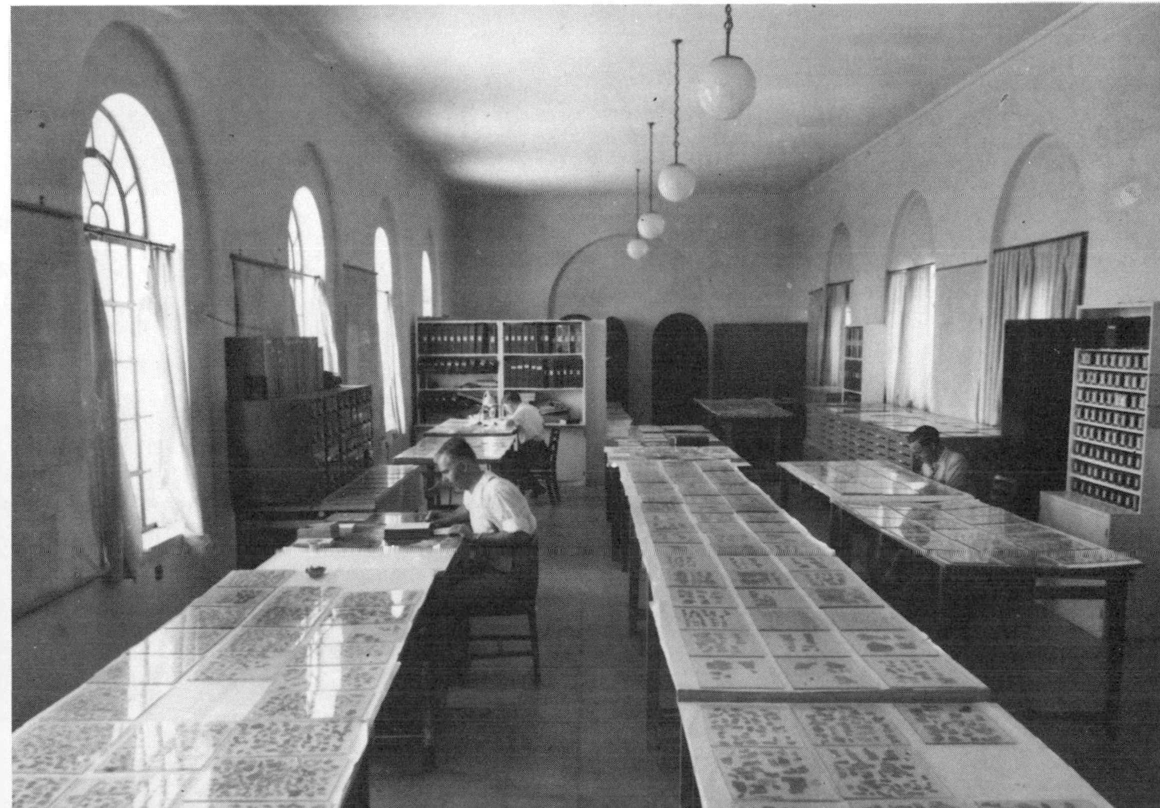

unwise at present to regard the Qumran group as typically Essene, since they may well be more closely related instead to the cave-dwelling Magharian sect of the early Christian era.

d. *Qumran and Christianity.* Some scholars have attempted to see in the Qumran brotherhood a distinct anticipation of Christianity, the most important areas being that of the Righteous Teacher as Messiah and the organizational and quasi-sacramental life of the group. The sectaries nowhere regarded their founder as the Messiah however, while their monastic life has few parallels with early Christianity. The gospel sacraments have different theological bases from those in use at Qumran, and entertain concepts of sin and atonement which were foreign to the thought of the sectaries. Suggestions that John the Baptist and even Jesus may have received some training at the settlement are entirely speculative, for in actual fact there are serious differences between the theology and practices of the Qumran group and the lives and doctrines of the Baptist and Christ, making any serious contact between them improbable. Despite the common background of divine revelation in the OT upon which both Christ and the sectaries drew, the parallels between Qumran teachings and the doctrines of Jesus are almost entirely restricted to the fifth ch. of Matthew. Echoes of Qumran diction in the NT writings include such phrases as "children of light," "life eternal," "the light of life," "the works of God" and "that they may be one." Such expressions set the NT material firmly against a 1st cent. A.D. Palestinian Jewish milieu, making unnecessary a 2nd cent. date for 2 Peter and the fourth gospel.

8. The Scrolls and the Bible. While the Qumran discoveries are extremely valuable for the intertestamentary period and for Biblical studies generally, they are particularly important for the text of the OT. A study of various MSS shows that in the immediate pre-Christian period there were at least three text types in existence, one of which was the precursor of the MT, another being a text closely allied to that used by the LXX trs., while a third was one which differed from both of these. The fragments of Samuel recovered from 4Q have shown that the text of that book which circulated before the present extant recensions was considerably longer than either the MT or the Heb. underlying the LXX VS, and that it differed in significant areas from both of them. This fact has struck a mortal blow at the idea so long cherished in critical circles of a fixed Heb. text which could be used as an assured basis for literary analysis. Perhaps most important of all is the formidable witness which the scrolls have borne in favor of the reliability of the MT and the scrupulous care with which it was transmitted. This has also reflected positively upon the LXX and Samaritan Pentateuch studies, both of which have received considerable stimulus from the Qumran discoveries.

It is now clear that no OT book can be assigned any longer to the Maccabean period, since all such books at Qumran were copies, making the originals antecedent to the sect itself, which originated in the Maccabean era. Indeed, many psalms previously deemed late have now been assigned to the Pers. period. The Maccabean dating for Daniel, long advocated by liberal scholars, now needs to be adjusted upward, whether the relationship between some scraps of Daniel from 1Q and the scrolls of Isaiah and Habakkuk is demonstrable or not. Light has been thrown by 1QIs[a] on the composition of Isaiah by the realization that the break at the end of ch. 33 in the scroll was intended to show that the book had been compiled in the ancient bifid fashion. This involved the composing of a literary work in terms of two balanced halves which complemented and paralleled each other in important areas, and often involved a good deal of skill and artistry. The concept of Isaiah as a literary bifid is compatible with a date of composition during or shortly after the death of the prophet himself. In any event, the original written prophecy antedated by several centuries the scroll found at Qumran, thereby precluding the late date assigned to some of its sections by critical scholars.

While much study of the Qumran material is still needed, it is quite clear that the MSS present no threat whatever to the Christian faith as was rumored when the discoveries first came to light. They have confirmed much that was previously known about the Scriptures, but have also shown the desirability of radical revision of certain theories cherished by some scholars. Not the least benefit is the stimulus given to the task of reconstructing as accurate a pre-Christian OT text as possible.

BIBLIOGRAPHY. M. Burrows, *The Dead Sea Scrolls* (1955); J. M. Allegro, *The Dead Sea Scrolls* (1956); F. F. Bruce, *Second Thoughts on the Dead Sea Scrolls* (1956); T. H. Gaster, *The Scriptures of the Dead Sea Sect* (1957); J. T. Milik, *Ten Years of Discovery in the Wilderness of Judaea* (1959); J. M. Allegro, *The Treasure of the Copper Scroll* (1960); R. K. Harrison, *The Dead Sea Scrolls* (1961); F. M. Cross, *The Ancient Library of Qumran* (1961); G. Vermes, *The Dead Sea Scrolls in English* (1962).

R. K. HARRISON

DEAD, STATE OF. On the subject of the condition of those who have departed this life, divine revelation is progressive. By this is meant that there is development, not from error to truth, but from a little truth to more truth, although even in the NT there is little said by comparison with what is revealed on other subjects.

I. Old Testament. The revelation given by God on this matter in the OT is extremely meager. In the early chs. of Genesis man is threatened with death if he disobeys (Gen

2:17), and when he does sin he is told that eventually he will die: "You are dust and to dust you shall return" (Gen 3:19). The fact of man's death is recorded at the beginning of the genealogy in Genesis 5, but no more is said. The genealogy itself emphasizes the universality of death with its monotonous repetition ". . . and he died"; but on the other hand, an intimation of more glorious possibilities is given in the account of Enoch (vv. 21-24) "Enoch walked with God, and he was not, for God took him." Further hints of some form of life after death have also been seen in the expression "gathered to his people" (e.g. 25:8) and in the words of the dying Jacob (47:30). In the NT (Heb 11:11-16), it is suggested that Abraham grasped the truth of a life beyond the grave, but this is never positively stated in the patriarchal narrative itself.

Genesis 37:35; 42:38; 44:29, 31 mark the first occurrences in the OT of the word *Sheol* (Heb. שְׁאוֹל), the exegesis of which normally figures largely in discussions on the OT view of life after death. This word occurs sixty-five times in the OT, and its etymology is in doubt. Most OT scholars, however, are in no doubt as to the derivation of the idea. They feel that Israel took over from her neighbors the ideas of the underworld and the afterlife which were fairly widespread in the ancient Near E.

According to this view, Sheol (cf. also Abaddon) is a deep pit far down in the earth, a place of darkness, where the "shades" of men (the Heb. word is רְפָאִים, which is not equivalent to "soul," as the Hebrews psychology thought of man as a unity, not as composed of two "parts." It is the whole man that goes down to Sheol, although the "shade" is only a thin weak replica of the man as he was on earth) have a vague shadowy existence, cut off from the land of the living, from all joys and from communion with God. Sheol is therefore something to be dreaded and avoided for as long as possible. There are no moral distinctions in Sheol, good and bad are there together.

Various Scriptures are used to substantiate this reconstruction, and these may be referred to in any of the numerous works which give this kind of account. A number of passages which express belief in some kind of moral distinctions in Sheol, or where believers look for deliverance from Sheol, or even resurrection, are either explained in other ways or are said to be among the latest parts of the OT and so to prepare the way for the development which is found in lit. of the intertestamental period.

Some evangelical scholars, however, are unhappy about this account of the OT teaching. They feel that too much from the beliefs of Israel's neighbors is read into the OT, and while they in turn may be accused by others of attempting to read too much of the NT teaching into the OT, they believe that the OT and NT revelation in the afterlife is consistent. The following points need to be considered: (1) A distinction should be made between what is felt, feared or even believed, by godly men, and what is positively revealed by God in His Word. This principle needs to be treated with caution, but it is relevant. (2) The fear of death is sometimes to be explained in terms of fear of the unknown, about which nothing has been revealed, and/or fear of exclusion from the blessings of the covenant, which in the OT were given exclusively in terms of this life. (3) The word "Sheol" may not always have the same meaning. In some passages it is used abstractly to signify the state of death (e.g., 1 Sam 2:6). In others it apparently has the meaning "the grave" (Gen 35:20). In others it has the idea of "hell," the place of punishment (Deut 32:22; Ps 9:17) which speaks of God's anger burning to the depths of Sheol. The reader is referred to the sections in L. Berkhof and J. Barton Payne for fuller statements.

In Exodus 3:6 God is recorded as saying to Moses: "I am the God of your father, the God of Abraham, the God of Isaac, and the God of Jacob." Jesus (Matt 22:31, 32; Mark 12:26, 27; Luke 20:37, 38) uses this passage to prove the resurrection of the dead, for "he is not God of the dead, but of the living; for all live to him" (Luke 20:38). With this may be linked a number of passages in which desire or hope of waking from death is expressed (Job 19:25; Pss 16:11; 17:15; 49:14, 15; 73:24), and those in which resurrection is definitely promised (Isa 26:19; Dan 12:2, and prob. Ezek 37:1-14).

II. Apocryphal and apocalyptic writings of inter-testamental period. There are certain developments of belief in these writings, and while there is no complete agreement among the various writers, there are a number of trends, some of which may have been influenced by Pers. or Gr. ideas. Belief in the resurrection of the bodies of the righteous becomes more clear-cut, possibly due to the terrible sufferings and martyrdom during the time of the Maccabees. More attention is also given to the intermediate state. Sheol (and its Gr. equivalent Hades, ᾅδης) largely refers to the place to which the ungodly go at death while awaiting judgment, while Paradise (παράδεισος, from a Pers. word for a garden or pleasure ground, sometimes thought of as the "upper compartment" of Sheol) is used to denote the state of blessedness enjoyed by the souls of the righteous between death and resurrection. At the resurrection, the wicked are consigned to Gehenna (q.v.), the righteous are raised to enjoy more fully the blessings of Paradise in terms of a new earthly Garden of Eden or a more transcendent, heavenly hope.

III. New Testament. In the NT the emphasis

in thinking on what lies after death is on the resurrection and transformation of the bodies of the righteous, which will take place at the Second Coming of the Lord Jesus Christ, and the subsequent enjoyment of the presence of God and of Christ to all eternity (1 Cor 15:20ff.; Phil 3:20, 21; 1 Thess 4:15-17, etc.). For the ungodly there will be a resurrection to judgment, resulting in wrath, perdition and eternal punishment (Matt 25:46; John 5:29; 2 Thess 1:7-10; Heb 9:27, 28). *See* articles on RESURRECTION, JUDGMENT, GEHENNA, PERDITION, LAKE OF FIRE.

On the matter of the state of the dead between death and resurrection there is more reticence. From the point of view of those remaining on earth, it is a sleep (Acts 7:60; 1 Thess 4:13, 15), and although compared with the resurrection, it is a time of "nakedness" in the disembodied state (2 Cor 5:1-5). It means, nevertheless, being "at home with the Lord" (2 Cor 5:8), being "with Christ," which is "far better" and "gain" (Phil 1:21, 23). In Revelation 6:9-11 there is a vision of the souls of the martyrs "under the altar," who ask how long it will be before their blood will be avenged. They are given a white robe, and told to rest until the full number of their brethren is complete.

Jesus told the parable of the rich man and Lazarus (Luke 16:19-31) and many have seen here further revelation on the intermediate state. However, most scholars point out that the terms and ideas are all familiar Jewish ones and the general theme is one which appears many times in the rabbis; consequently, while it may be said in this sense to be a "true life story," it is not necessarily a "true after-life story" (E. Earle Ellis, Comm. in loc.). Plummer says (in loc.) "It is no purpose of the parable to give information about the unseen world." The purpose seems to be that of showing the reversal of men's status in the Messianic age, and the impossibility of altering that status once death has intervened. However, it might still be argued that the parable does teach the general truth that at death men have a foretaste (good or ill) of the state which will be eternally theirs at the Last Judgment.

Also relevant to the discussion is a study of several passages (Luke 23:43; Acts 2:27, 28; Eph 4:8; 1 Pet 3:18-20; 4:6). These have led some to believe that between His death and resurrection, the Lord visited Paradise (the upper half of Sheol) and removed it and its inhabitants—the OT saints—into the presence of God. Some indeed have felt that the last two references justify saying that He went to hell and gave a second chance to certain lost souls by preaching the Gospel to them. However, this has not been the position of historic Christianity, and the reader is referred to a detailed discussion in the commentaries on the passages.

BIBLIOGRAPHY. S. D. F. Salmond, *The Christian Doctrine of Immortality* (1901); S. Zandstra "Sheol and the Pit in the OT," PTR V (1907), 631-641; J. D. Davis "The Future Life in Hebrew Thought During the Pre-Persian Period," PTR VI (1908), 246-268; L. Berkhof, *Systematic Theology* (1941), 679-693; H. H. Rowley, *The Faith of Israel* (1956), 150-176; L. Boettner, *Immortality* (1956); C. R. Smith, *The Bible Doctrine of the Hereafter* (1958); W. Strawson, *Jesus and the Future Life* (1959); J. B. Payne, *The Theology of the Older Testament* (1962), 443-463; D. S. Russell, *The Method and Message of Jewish Apocalyptic* (1964), 353-390; J. Jeremias TDNT I (1964), 146-149; S. H. Hooke "Life after death: Israel and the After-Life," Expt LXXVI (1965), 236-239; ibid. "Life after Death: the Extra-Canonical Literature," Expt LXXVI (1965), 273-276; C. L. Mitton, "The After-Life in the NT" Expt LXXVI (1965), 332-337; W. Eichrodt, *Theology of the OT* II (1967), 210-223.

R. E. DAVIES

DEAF (חרש ; κωφός). The Bible speaks of deafness both in a literal and in a figurative sense. People insensitive because of sin are said to be deaf to the voice of God. Isaiah, in anticipation of the spiritual awakening to be introduced by the coming of the Messiah, prophesied: "Then the eyes of the blind shall be opened, and the ears of the deaf unstopped" (Isa 35:5). He regarded deafness as a voluntary state which could be changed by choice, for he commands: "Hear, you deaf; and look, you blind, that you may see" (Isa 42:18).

Physical deafness was healed by Christ to seal His claims of messiahship, and also to illustrate that He healed spiritual deafness as well (Mark 7:32-37). *See* DISEASES OF THE BIBLE.

D. A. BLAIKLOCK

DEATH (מות ; θάνατος).

I. OLD TESTAMENT

A. Death is punishment for sin. The first reference to death in the OT (Gen 2:17), although not without its problems, nevertheless gives the basic orientation for the Biblical understanding of death. Here death is punishment for sin. This is seen further in the course of events: when Adam and Eve sinned, they were excluded from the Garden, the place of communion with God, also from access to the Tree of Life which would have prevented the onset of their dying (3:22, 23), and are consigned to a life of pain and toil which will terminate in physical dissolution (3:16-19). Theological distinctions are usually made between physical death, spiritual death, and eternal death and in general these are valid; but from the passage it appears that death in its totality is the result of sin. One must remember also that in the Biblical view, man is a psychosomatic unity. The whole man is the subject of death. In the history of the Church there have been those who have felt that physical death, the dissolution of the body, was normal and natural, and that this is only reversed by a divine provision, as shown in the Genesis narrative by access to the Tree of Life. The majority of orthodox theologians, however, have rejected this idea. The rest of the Biblical revelation, esp. that of the NT, seems to run counter to it, although it is often said that with our present physical make-up death is a biological necessity.

B. Death is a fact of human experience. It is certainly true that in much of the OT narrative, death is recorded as a universal fact of human experience (cf. the genealogical table of Genesis 5, with its monotonous repetition "and he died"), but this is not to say that the writers thought of death as "natural," or as something which was part of God's perfect will for man. It is indeed seen as inevitable for man in his present sinful and fallen state, but this is rather different. The bright exception of Enoch (Gen 5:24) gives an indication of something better and more desirable.

C. Death is something to be feared and avoided. This becomes clearer in considering the great number of places where the OT writers expressed their personal feelings, and speak of death as something to be feared and avoided at all costs (e.g. Pss 6:1-5; 88:1-14; Isa 38). It may be said that it is early death which is feared, and examples may be given (e.g., Gen 25:8) of men dying "in a good old age, an old man and full of years," with the sense of satisfaction that they have enjoyed their natural span and that they continue to live on in their posterity, accepting their death as something natural. On the other hand, Psalm 90 bears witness to the belief that even a full life-span is short and is cut off because of God's wrath.

It is true, of course, that much of the abhorrence of death expressed by the OT writers may be due to fear and avoidance of the unknown, so little having been positively revealed in the OT on the state of the dead. It is also true that in view of this, it was felt that death would cut one off from enjoyment of the covenant blessings, which in the OT were given in terms of the land, the Temple, the people and length of days. Even this fact may be used to show that death was considered as unnatural, since it might possibly separate from the living God, the God of the covenant, and therefore could not be part of God's original purpose for man. If length of days is promised for obedience (Exod 20:12) and is a sign of God's favor (Job 5:26), then the cutting off of those days, even when long, is an indication that death is something unnatural.

D. Death is not outside the control or rule of God. He can give escape from death (Ps 68:20; Isa 38:5; Jer 15:20). He can restore the dead to life (1 Kings 17:22; 2 Kings 4:34; 13:21). He kills and makes alive, brings down into Sheol and raises from there again (Deut 32:39; 1 Sam 2:6). He can take men to Himself without their dying (Gen 5:24; 2 Kings 2:11). He can bring death completely to nothing and triumph over it by raising the dead (Isa 25:8; 26:19; Ezek 37:11, 12; Dan 12:2; Hos 6:2; 13:14).

E. Death is not victorious. These last references introduce the hope expressed in the OT of victory over death. One or two of the vv. may refer to a revival of national fortunes, but others speak quite clearly of a resurrection from physical death, and to these may be added those which indicate a confidence in personal resurrection (e.g., Job 19:25-27; Pss 16:9-11; 17:15; 73:23-26). This hope, however slight, is nevertheless present in the OT, but finds its full flowering in the NT which reveals Christ "who abolished death and brought life and immortality to light through the gospel" (2 Tim 1:10).

II. New Testament

A. Death is the penalty for sin. The victory of Christ over death in His own resurrection from the dead and the consequences of this for believers, is the theme which dominates the NT in all its parts, but this is set against the backdrop of death as the penalty for sin. Paul traced back the entrance of death into the human race to the sin of the first man Adam (Rom 5:12-21; 1 Cor 15:22). No other NT writer makes this explicit connection but neither do they say anything which would militate against it; they are concerned, as is Paul in the main, rather with the empirical facts of man in sin. Indeed, the responsibility of the individual is not diminished by his involvement in Adam's fall; for the individual "the wages of sin is death" (Rom 6:23; cf. Ezek 18:4, 20). This is death in its totality, contrasted with "eternal life" in the second part of the v., and is elaborated and developed in different parts of the NT in the following ways:

1. *Physical death.* This is the result of the entrance of sin into the world through Adam. It is the lot of all men (Heb 9:27) and through fear of it and what may follow it (ibid.) they are throughout their lives in bondage (Heb 2:15; cf. Rom 8:15).

2. *Spiritual death.* All men are by nature spiritually dead, that is, alienated from God the Source of life by sin, insensible to divine things, unresponsive to His laws. This is clear from the words of Jesus (Matt 8:22; cf. Luke 15:32) as well as from the writings of Paul (Eph 2:1-3; 4:17-19; Col 2:13; cf. Jude 12).

3. *Eternal death.* Those who remain in spiritual death throughout their lives and do not believe on the Son of God, die in their sins (John 8:21, 24), remain under the wrath of God (3:36) and in the Day of Judgment will be consigned to a state of eternal separation from God, called in Scripture the second death (Rev 21:8).

B. Jesus Christ has risen from the dead and so overcame death. This is the center of the NT message, and is witnessed to in every part of the NT. All four gospels record Jesus' prophecies before the event (e.g. Mark 8:31;

9:31; John 2:19-22) and the event itself (Matt 28; Mark 16; Luke 24; John 20, 21); it was the core of the apostolic preaching in Acts (e.g. Acts 2:24-36; 3:15; 17:31); and the epistles and the Apocalypse all bear witness to its centrality (e.g. Rom 1:4; 4:25; 1 Cor 15:4-8; Heb 13:20; 1 Pet 3:21, 22; Rev 1:5). He has "the keys of Death and Hades" (Rev 1:18); He has abolished death (2 Tim 1:10); He has overcome the devil, who had the power of death (Heb 2:14); He is the Head of the new humanity, the firstborn from the dead (Col 1:18); He has caused believers to be born anew to a living hope through the resurrection of Jesus Christ from the dead (1 Pet 1:3).

This last reference introduces the blessings which come to believers as the result of Christ's resurrection and triumph over death.

In the coming of Christ, and esp. in His resurrection, the eschatological process has begun, and the life of the age to come has broken into this present age. Believers already partake of the life of the coming age (John 3:36); for them the eschatological verdict has been passed. They have already passed from death—the condition of men in this age—to life (John 5:25). Paul makes a similar point when he says that in Christ, the Second Adam and Head of the new humanity, believers have died and risen again (Rom 6:1-4; Col 3:1-3) and therefore, although they still live in this world, their attitude to sin, the law and the world is to be that of dead men (Rom 6:11; Gal 2:19, 20; 6:14).

In Christ their Head believers partake of the life of the age to come, and physical death is for them a sleep (1 Thess 4:15; cf. Acts 7:59). The sting of death has been removed (1 Cor 15:56); it cannot separate from Christ (2 Cor 5:8; Phil 1:23) and so is not to be feared, and may even be desired (Phil 1:21-23).

At the Second Coming of Christ, believers' bodies will be changed, and all traces of sin, mortality and death will be removed. Then death will be swallowed up in life (1 Cor 15:52-57).

At the judgment, death and Hades are said to be cast into the lake of fire (Rev 20:14) signifying that as God brings in the new heaven and new earth (Rev 21) the last enemy, death (1 Cor 15:26), is finally and irrevocably destroyed. *See* IMMORTALITY.

BIBLIOGRAPHY. L. A. Muirhead, *The Terms Life and Death in the Old and New Testaments* (1908); R. H. Charles, *Eschatology: Hebrew, Jewish and Christian* (1913); J. C. Lamberts, HDAC I (1915), 698-700; H. Bavinck, ISBE II (1929), 811-813; L. Morris, *The Wages of Sin* (1955); Arndt (1957), 351, 352; T. C. Vriessen, *An Outline of Old Testament Theology* (1958), 201-212; J. J. von Allmen, VC (1958), 79-83; E. F. Harrison, BDT (1960), 158, 159; L. Morris, NBD (1962), 301, 302; F. C. Grant, et al. in HDB rev. (1963), 205-207; R. Bultmann in TDNT, III (1965), 7-25; ibid. IV (1966), 896-899.

R. E. DAVIES

DEATH OF CHRIST. The New Testament writers had an absorbing interest in the death of Christ. This interest is principally interpretive; they were more concerned with the meaning of the event than with the circumstances that made up the event. Yet it is entirely misleading to suggest, as some moderns have done, that the faith of the apostolic Christians was indifferent to the historical reporting of the facts as they actually happened. The theology of the cross, first elaborated by Paul, is by no means independent of the events recorded in the narratives of the gospels. The death of Christ is both a fact and a doctrine; the two are inextricably bound together in the NT.

As the doctrinal aspects of Christ's death are discussed in another place (*see* ATONEMENT, PROPITIATION, EXPIATION), more attention shall be given in this article to the historical circumstances surrounding this event.

Paul wrote to the Corinthians that he determined to know nothing among them "except Jesus Christ and him crucified" (1 Cor 2:2). This emphasis is reflected in the manner in which the gospels report the story of Jesus' life. The spotlight focuses on the last few days of Christ's public ministry, leading up to His crucifixion. The Evangelists considered His death the great purpose of His life; Jesus lived that He might die.

When Jesus first introduced the subject of His death (Matt 16:21; Mark 8:31; Luke 9:22), it marked a turning point in His ministry. He spent less time with the multitudes and more with the Twelve; He spoke not only of the kingdom, but also of Himself, esp. the death He must die. The necessity of His death is not reported in a manner that presents Jesus as a helpless victim of overpowering opposition. Though the forces of evil that He faced were mighty, even in the last hour He could have summoned legions of angels to His rescue (Matt 26:53). Rather, His own anticipation of His death testified to Jesus' sense of vocation and destiny as the One to fulfill the role of the suffering servant of the Lord. Hence, "when the days drew near for him to be received up, he set his face to go to Jerusalem," a resolution that could not be daunted (Luke 9:51f.).

His arrival at Jerusalem began the period known as Passion Week. ("Passion" is a term used in ecclesiastical lit. to describe the sufferings of the Lord, particularly the agony of Gethsemane and the cruel treatment by the Rom. soldiers who finally crucified Him.) Though He entered the city in triumph (Matt 21:1-11 and parallels), His authority was soon challenged (21:23-27 and parallels), and as opposition stiffened, the chief priests conspired to destroy Him (26:1-5, and parallels), in which conspiracy Judas, one of the Twelve, became surreptitiously involved (26:14-16 and parallels). While Judas plotted to betray His

Part of the ancient road descending from the house of Caiaphas on Mount Zion to the Garden of Gethsemane. Jesus undoubtedly walked this very road. ©*Lev*

master for money, Jesus sent two disciples to a private residence with directions for preparing the Passover, which He observed on Thursday evening with His disciples. Jesus solemnly reminded them that He was soon to leave them, going so far as to identify the traitor, though the disciples were too incredulous and amazed to apprehend the significance of Judas' treachery.

In reporting this last meal with the disciples, the gospel writers emphasize not so much the Passover feast as such, but rather Jesus' unique handling of the bread and wine during and after the meal. We read, "Now as they were eating, Jesus took bread, and blessed, and broke it, and gave it to his disciples and said, 'Take, eat; this is my body.' And he took a cup, and when he had given thanks he gave it to them, saying, 'Drink of it, all of you; for this is my blood of the covenant, which is poured out for many for the forgiveness of sins' " (26:26-28).

Because He was soon to die, Jesus interpreted His death to His disciples. Here is illustrated how fact and meaning are united in the New Testament view of Christ's death. When they had finished eating, they sang a hymn (the paschal hymns, Psalms 113-118 and 136) and went out to the Mount of Olives. (At this point they lingered to talk, for John records a long farewell discourse concluding with the well-known intercessory prayer, John 13-17.) As Jesus spoke further of His impending death and their defection, the disciples—esp. Peter—protested their steadfast loyalty, even producing weapons ready for His defense.

The following scene, in the Garden of Gethsemane, is so steeped in pathos that it has stirred Christians through the centuries, inspiring innumerable masterpieces of art and poetry. In these familiar environs, Jesus retreated with three of His closest disciples to pray. Though their eyes were heavy with sleep, the Lord was in an agony of spirit that seems to surpass in sheer intensity anything that He suffered subsequently. As He prayed that He might be delivered—"Father, if thou art willing, remove this cup from me"—He began to sweat great drops of blood (Luke 22:42-44). Some have interpreted this statement to mean that His perspiration was large and beady, but the assimilation to blood strongly suggests the color of red, and several instances have been cited of a bleeding of the pores of those suffering from intense emotional anguish. More important than the physical aspects of the Lord's suffering is His resolute submission to His Father's will, which He achieved in and through this severe trial—a resolution without which salvation could never have been achieved. "In the days of his flesh, Jesus offered up prayers and supplications, with loud cries and tears, to him who was able to save him from death. . . . he learned obedience through what he suffered; and being made perfect he became the source of eternal salvation to all who obey him" (Heb 5:7ff.).

Interior of the Church of All Nations in the Garden of Gethsemane. Stone before altar is possible site where Jesus knelt to pray. ©*Lev*

Having surmounted this crisis, with the help of angelic comforters, the Lord rejoined His disciples as Judas appeared with a band of Temple guards to apprehend Him. The Master was identified by a kiss. (The verb bears a prefix which denotes affectionate kissing; Judas kissed Him repeatedly, a detail that underscores the perfidiousness of his act.) Without resistance, Jesus gave Himself to His captors, though remonstrating with them that they should arm themselves as if they sought a dangerous criminal. Though Peter made a quixotic defense by striking off an ear of the high priest's servant with his sword (Jesus cured him with a touch), the entire company of the disciples soon dispersed into the night, leaving Jesus to His fate (Matt 26:47-56 and parallels).

In reporting the arrest, John's gospel includes a detail not found in the synoptics, that at the first encounter Jesus' would-be captors fell backward on the ground (John 18:6). This was evidently intended to underscore the truth that Jesus was master of the situation even at the moment of His arrest, and is in keeping with the saying, "No one takes it [my life] from me, but I lay it down of my own accord" (John 10:18). (In this same vein, John also reported Jesus' answer to Pilate, when he claimed to have power to crucify Jesus. "You would have no power over me unless it had been given you from above," 19:11.)

Apprehended, Jesus was brought to the palace of the former high priest Annas, who vainly tried to extract a confession from Him, and then sent Him to Caiaphas, the high priest. Jesus was tried before the Sanhedrin, hastily assembled at daybreak (Matt 26:57-75 and parallels). After great difficulty in securing competent and consistent witnesses against Jesus, Caiaphas finally adjured Him respecting His Messianic claims, and upon the strength of His avowal, accused Him of blasphemy, the whole council concurring in the sentence of death. In this account of the trial before the Jewish authorities, the repeated denial of Peter counterpoints Jesus' indictment as a secondary theme, and underscores further the utter loneliness of the Lord in the hour of His extremity. Condemned by His compatriots, denied by His friends, the tragic element is heightened—if possible—as Judas the betrayer, in a paroxysm of remorse, confessed the innocence of Jesus, cast down the accursed silver on the pavement, and went out and hanged himself. The twisted conscience of the elders is revealed in their calloused indifference to Judas' confession and their careful use of the money so as not to offend legal scruple (27:3-10).

After many vile insults to His person, Jesus was led to Pilate's residence to obtain legal sanction of the death sentence. The Messianic issue appeared again, only now with a political twist; Jesus was accused of sedition. But Pilate showed himself reluctant to be involved, and having learned the defendant was from Galilee, engaged in the delaying tactic of sending Jesus off to Herod the king, who happened to be in Jerusalem during the Passover season. Herod received Jesus with overweening curiosity, having heard of His miracles; but when Jesus refused to break His silence, Herod sent him back to Pilate, having mocked Him with the raiment of royalty (Luke 23:8-12). The moment of truth had now come for Pilate. Compelled to adjudicate the case, yet convinced of the prisoner's innocence—his conscience being reinforced by a message from his wife—he sought to release Jesus as a common criminal according to the custom that dictated a gesture of clemency at the Passover season. Instead, the multitude clamored for the release of Barabbas, a notorious criminal; and Pilate having ceremoniously washed his hands before them, yielded to their demands, passed sentence upon Jesus, and left Him to the abuse of the Rom. soldiers (Matt 27:15-30 and parallels).

As Jesus was led out of the city of Golgotha where He was to be crucified, a passerby, Simon of Cyrene, was pressed into the service of bearing His cross. Meanwhile Jesus, in somber accents that anticipated the imminent desolation of Jerusalem, bade the disconsolate women to weep for themselves and their nation rather than for Him (Luke 23:26-31). Having reached the place of execution, He was crucified between two criminals, with a prayer on His lips for His murderers. Though reviled by spectators, soldiers, and Jewish leaders, one of the thieves sued for mercy and was assured by Jesus with the well-known words, "Today you will be with me in Paradise" (23:43). Having committed His mother to the care of John, and having given utterance in the language of Psalm 22 to His agonizing loneliness ("My God, my God, why hast thou forsaken me?") He expired with a loud cry, "Father, into thy hands I commit my spirit!". The veil of the Temple was rent by an earthquake and the sun was darkened. The centurion in charge, awed by evidence of the supernatural, exclaimed, "Truly this was the Son of God" (Luke 23:33-47).

Up to this point, the crucifixion was typically Roman—scourging, mocking, the garments becoming the spoil of the soldiers, the place of execution on an elevated spot outside the city, and the superscription over the head of the accused. At this point is introduced a concern to remove the body before sundown, a strictly Jewish matter; the Jews did not want the bodies on the cross during the Sabbath. They petitioned Pilate to hasten the death of the victims so that the bodies could be removed before sundown. The order was given, but they did not break Jesus' legs because He was already dead. A soldier, however, plunged his spear into Jesus' side—to make sure He was dead?—and water mingled with blood poured from the wound (John 19:31-37).

The report of the crucifixion in the gospels is characterized by reserve and sobriety, fitting for such an awful and solemn tragedy. It is assumed that the readers were familiar with the details. Inasmuch as crucifixion is unknown in the modern world, and because the event of Jesus' death has been idealized by the poetry and art of the centuries, some account perhaps should be given of the stark details.

Crucifixion appears to have been first used by the Persians as a form of execution, then by Alexander the Great (who crucified 2,000 Tyrians at one time), and then by the Carthaginians whence it came to the Romans. It was commonly acknowledged the most horrible form of death, worse than burning. (A fire was sometimes built under the crucified to hasten death.) In the scourging that preceded the crucifixion, soldiers often used nails or pieces of bone to heighten the pain, which was sometimes so intense that the victim died under its duress. (Pilate had Jesus flogged before passing sentence, not so much from custom, it would seem, as to excite pity and procure immunity from further punishment, Luke 23:22.) The main stake forming the cross was secured in the ground in advance, and the condemned carried the crossbar with him from the place of incarceration to the place of execution. Lying on the ground, he was tied or nailed to the crossbar, and then raised up and fastened to the main post. The body of the victim was usually only a foot or two above the ground. Midway up the main post was a peg on which the weight of the body rested, and the feet were secured by tying or nailing. Sometimes a single nail secured both feet. At this point usually some drink was given to confuse the senses and deaden the pain (Jesus refused it, Matt 27:34). A centurion with a band of soldiers was assigned to keep watch, because the lingering character of the death would allow a person to be taken down and recover, which sometimes happened. (It is reported that women among the Convulsionaires were crucified repeatedly, some remaining on a cross for three hours.)

The rapidity with which death overtook the Lord has been occasion for infidelity to suspect He only swooned, later to be revived by the coolness of the tomb. Others have sought to divine some unique fact in His medical history, such as a rupture of the heart due to the violence of the emotional stress under which He suffered. Still others have appealed to the voluntary surrender of His life implied in the expression, He "yielded up his spirit" (27:50; cf. John 10:18, "I lay it [my life] down of my own accord"). Whatever theory one may adopt of the cause of Jesus' death it is beyond all cavil that He died. Pilate expressly satisfied himself on this score by questioning the cen-

A tomb with a rolling stone for closing its entrance. Similar to the Garden tomb, this burial place was found on the back slopes of the Mount of Olives, near Bethphage. ©*Lev*

turion (Mark 15:44). It cannot be doubted that He suffered excruciating agonies before He was mercifully relieved by death.

This most brutal and degrading form of execution devised by civilized man was abolished by Constantine, prob. out of reverence for the sign under which he was said to have conquered. From this time on, the cross, the symbol of disgrace and degradation, became the chief symbol of the Christian faith.

There are two questions that have no direct bearing on the meaning of Christ's death, which are nonetheless of such perennial interest as to warrant a brief discussion. One concerns the time of the arrest, trial, and crucifixion; the other, the responsibility for these events.

As for the first question—the date of the crucifixion—was it on the 14th of Nisan (April 6) or the day following, the 15th? If the former date is chosen, not only is there a discrepancy between John and the synoptics as to the most important and conspicuous date in the life of Jesus, but also the last meal that Jesus ate with His disciples was not the Passover. This fact would cast doubts on the historicity of the synoptic accounts of the institution of the Lord's Supper and Jesus' own understanding of His impending death. The technical aspects of this question are too large for an article of this scope. Suffice it to say that when John commented that the Jewish leaders did not enter the praetorium to remain undefiled and so eat the Passover (John 18:28), or again, when the day of the trial was identified as the preparation of the Passover (19:14), the term "Passover" need not be narrowly understood of the initial evening meal, but is flexible enough to include the entire feast of unleavened bread that followed the meal that Jesus celebrated with His disciples (*see* Jos. Antiq. XVII. ix. 3 and Jos. Wars II. i. 3; also Luke 22:1). On such an interpretation, there is no discrepancy between John and the synoptics who plainly teach that Jesus partook of the paschal supper. This supper occurred on Thursday evening, as we reckon time. That same Thursday night He was betrayed, seized by the Jewish authorities and condemned by the Sanhedrin. Early Friday morning He was brought before Pilate, and before the day was over, that is before sundown, He had been condemned, crucified, and buried.

As for the question of responsibility for His death, the Church has traditionally accused the Jews of the crime of deicide, for which they were supposedly accursed to all generations. Only the hollow eyes of prejudice could fail to see that this was a pious cloak to cover a deep-seated anti-Semitism. The canonical gospels indeed indicate that Jesus' death was instigated by the Jews—which was inevitable under the circumstances—but it was made possible, approved, and carried out by the Rom. authorities. It would seem, then, that neither Jews nor Gentiles can escape the reproach of complicity in this crime. It was the sin of all humanity against heaven, an evil that God has transformed into our salvation, so making His goodness to triumph over man's wickedness.

In saying all this, the theology of Christ's death is introduced, which is the primary, almost exclusive concern of the NT apart from the gospels. The doctrine of the cross was first elaborated by Paul, who was concerned not with the historical details, but with the salvation significance of the cross. Christ "became obedient unto death, even death on a cross" (Phil 2:8f.), and by this obedience to His Father's will He accomplished man's salvation. Hence, wherever Paul went, he so preached Christ crucified as to placard Him before the eyes of all who heard (Gal 3:1). This word of the cross is God's wisdom, which is foolishness to human reason; but to those who are saved, it is the wisdom and power of God (1 Cor 1:18ff.).

Paul wrote to the Galatians that if he were to proclaim circumcision as the means of salvation, then the offense of the cross would be removed, but circumcision and the cross are mutually exclusive; therefore, he will glory in the cross that all glorying in self may be brought to nought (Gal 5; 6).

How is it that Christ's death on the cross is the decisive revelation of God in history? Because it is the means by which God is reconciled to man (Eph 2:16; Col 1:20; 2:14). The basis of the reconciling power in the death of Christ is the propitiatory power of the blood that He shed there (Rom 3:21-26). Another way of putting it is to say that He cancelled the bond that stood against man with its legal demands, nailing it to His cross (Col 2:14). Paul told the Ephesians that they were brought near by the blood of Christ, near, that is, to God, from whom, as Gentiles, they were alienated, being "strangers to the covenants of promise" (Eph 2:11f.). All of this has happened, ultimately, because God loved men even when they were sinners (Rom 5:8). Because, on the one hand, God loved man (John 3:16), and, on the other, because the wages of sin is death (Rom 6:23), therefore Christ died for mankind. This is the basic reason for the death of Christ. Historically, His death was due to the jealousy of the Jewish leaders, the treachery of Judas, the fear of the disciples, the vacillation of Pilate, the cruelty of the Romans; but on a different level, the cause of Christ's death is man's sin and God's love. Sin involved men in death, and Christ could not deal with sin effectually, except as He took the consequences upon Himself "to be made sin, who knew no sin, so that in him we might become the righteousness of God" (2 Cor 5:21).

The rest of the NT takes essentially the same view of Christ's death as is found in the epistles of Paul. Especially in Hebrews is this the case. Christ is set forth as a priest whose work is to bring sinners into fellowship with God. To do this He had to die, and to die, He had a body prepared for Him (Heb 10:5). The incarnation was for the purpose of atonement. And this atoning death was, so to speak, God's last word; He has nothing more in reserve. Christianity is final. Speaking of the cross of Christ, Watts wrote:

Here we behold God's inmost heart,
Where grace and vengeance strangely join;
Here his whole name appears complete,
His wrath, his wisdom, and his love.

Having known His "whole name" in the cross, Christians look forward to the day when, with men from every tribe and kindred and tongue and nation, they shall join in praise to the Lamb who was slain, who loved His own and loosed them from their sins by His blood (Rev 1:5; 5:9). *See* JESUS CHRIST.

BIBLIOGRAPHY. B. H. Throckmorton, ed., *Gospel Parallels,* (1949), 163-186; J. Denney, *The Death of Christ* (1951); J. Schneider, "Stauros," TWNT (1964); G. C. Berkouwer, *The Work of Christ* (1965), ch. 6.

P. K. JEWETT

DEATH, SECOND, the tr. of most Eng. VSS of the Gr. phrase ὁ δεύτερος θάνατος, found only in Revelation 2:11; 20:6, 14; 21:8. It refers to the eternal judgment of God upon sin which occurs after physical death. It is therefore synonymous with such other apocalyptic expressions as "lake of fire," "winepress of wrath," "darkness," et al. The phrase is characteristic of the repetitive and reciprocal nature of the structure of Revelation, wherein ordinal numbers e.g. first, second, third, etc., play an important part in its presentation.

W. WHITE, JR.

DEBIR de' bər (Heb. דביר and Heb. דבר). 1. A king of Eglon, a member of the confederacy of five Amorite rulers who opposed the town of Gibeon at the invitation of Adonizedek, king of Jerusalem. The Gibeonites appealed to Joshua and he and his army fought the Amorites in the Valley of Aijalon where Joshua's Long Day, q.v., occurred (Josh 10:3-39). The name Debir has been etymologized to a possible Egypt. root "back" or "shrine" but this is merely conjectural.

2. The name of one or more locations. The more frequently mentioned Debir was located in the hill country of the Shephelah to the W of Jerusalem. On the basis of W. F. Albright's excavations at Tell Beit Mirsim some seven m. S of Lachish, this site has been identified with Debir. However, insufficient topographical and archeological evidence has come to light to support this contention cf. K. Galling, "Zur Lokalisierung von Debir," *Zeitschrift des deutschen Palästina-Vereins,* 70 (1954), 135-141.

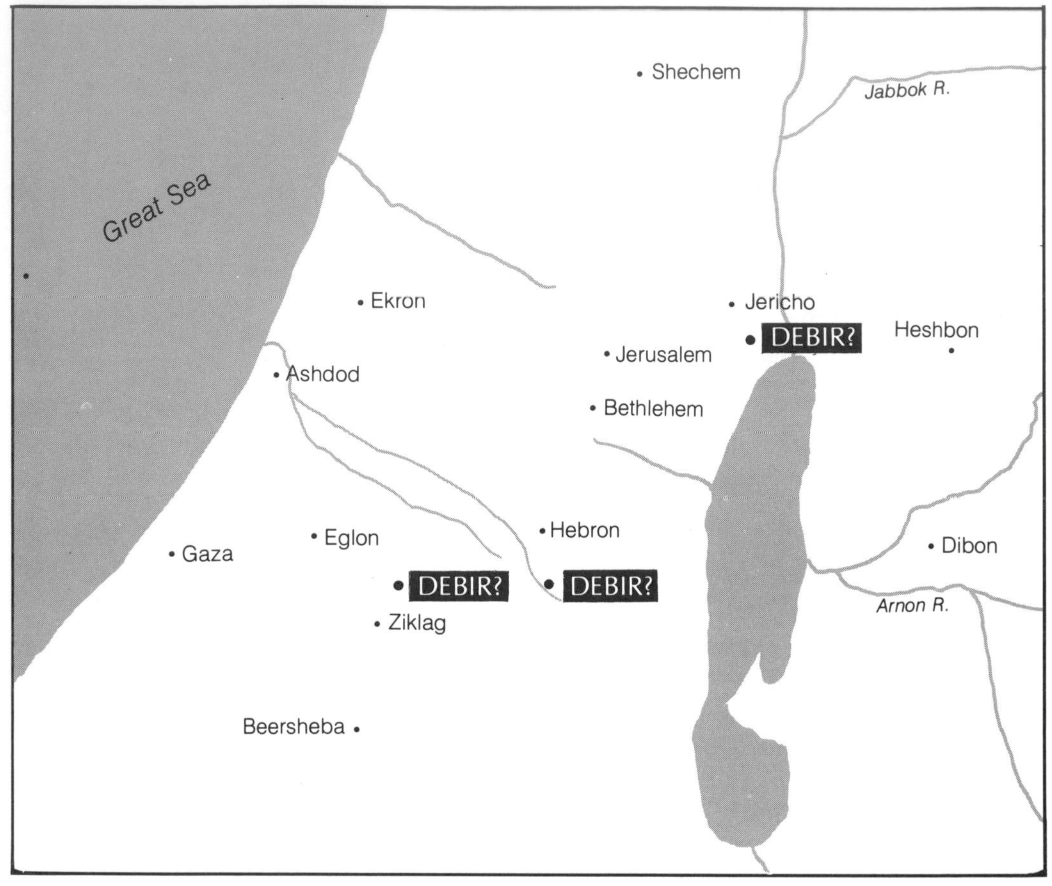

In the same article Galling proposed that the site might be modern Hirbet Rabūd esp. since this site is near a set of naturally occurring springs of various altitudes which accords well with the description in Judges 1:15, in the context of Caleb's granting of the request for land from Achsah, his daughter. Excavation of this site by Moshe Kokhavy and others in the seasons 1968, 1969 have turned up much material from the period of the Conquest. There is little doubt that this site will prove to be Biblical Debir. The origin of the name is hidden in obscurity but it prob. had some connotation of "treasure," possible "written materials," as it was later known as sacred precinct, its original name having been Heb. קרית-ספר (Josh 15:15) "city-of-writing," incorrectly recorded in Joshua 15:49 as Heb. קרית-סנה. which is meaningless, though the LXX correctly records the same name in both passages. The history of the town is woven throughout the story of the conquest and settlement of Canaan. It is first mentioned as a Canaanite royal town in the hill country of S Judea (10:38; 12:13) which was overthrown by Joshua who destroyed the Anakim, its inhabitants. The particular force involved was that under the command of Caleb (15:15-17; Judg 1:11-15). After the division of the land it became a regional center (Josh 15:49) and is mentioned along with the other towns and villages of the Shephelah which were ceded to Judah. What appears to be a different place is mentioned in Joshua 15:7 as one of Judah's N boundaries, which is located in the wadi of the Achor. This border is variously described in the OT.

3. Still another reference to the name appears in Joshua 13:26 as the name of a town in Gilead located near the Jordan. This town has the full name Heb. לֹדבר, meaning unknown. It was the refuge to which the family of Jonathan fled when Israel was defeated by the Philistines. It was the home of Jonathan's lame son, Mephibosheth, and from that place David summoned him to the palace (2 Sam 9:4-13). The last reference to the name is in the prophecy of Amos. It has been conjectured that perhaps it was lost in the Israelite wars with the Arameans and regained under Jeroboam II. In Amos the name is purposefully perverted in time-honored Sem. fashion by twisting the vowels to Heb. באדבר (Amos 6:13) "nothingness," as it was most likely a place of pagan sacrifice and heathen idolatry and a subject of great satisfaction to the corrupt monarchy. The site of this and the lesser references to the names are so far unidentified.

BIBLIOGRAPHY. W. F. Albright, "The Excavations of Tell Beit Mirsim," AASOR, vol. XII (1930-1931); vol. XIII (1931-1932); vol. XVII (1936-1937); vols. XXI-XXII (1941-1943); J. Simons, GTT (1959) par. 514 et al.; Y. Aharoni, *The Land of the Bible* (1967), 18, 136, 197, 199, 209, 230, 235, 240, 259, 270, 292, 300, 344.

W. WHITE, JR.

DEBORAH děb' ə rə. Heb. דבורה, prob. derived from the root, דבורה, meaning a *honey bee*, as in Psalm 118:12, et al. It appears as the name of three characters in the OT in its fem. form. 1. Deborah, the nurse of Rebekah, the wife of the patriarch Jacob who was buried under an oak at Bethel which was then named, "Allonbacuth," "The Oak of Weeping."

2. Deborah, the judge and prophetess (Judg 4). She is said to have been the wife of a certain Lappidoth, a name which because of its fem. form has always been the subject of much speculation. She is described as a "woman, a prophetess," the only judge thus described (4:4). Centuries later a giant palm which stood between Ramah and Bethel was called "the palm of Deborah." In the time of the oppression of the loosely knit tribes of Israel by King Jabin of Hazor, Deborah summoned Barak the son of Abinoam from Kedesh-naphtali and gave him the command of the Lord to gather 10,000 soldiers from the tribes of Naphtali and Zebulun and marshal them at Mount Tabor. When Barak requested Deborah to go with them to the battle with Jabin and his host at the river Kishon, she replied that God would deliver Jabin into the hand of a woman to be slain, thus rebuking the cowardice of the men of Israel. When Jabin's military chief, Sisera, heard of the Israelite preparations for battle he obliged by setting off for the battlefield. When Deborah gave the command, the battle was begun and Israel was victorious, and Sisera fled the battlefield to be slain by Jael, the wife of Heber the Kenite. Thus was Deborah's prophecy fulfilled, and Sisera was put to death by a woman. The next ch. (Judg 5) contains the magnificent psalm, The Song of Deborah, an original piece extant from the 13th cent. B.C. This piece of ancient poetry is one of the oldest fragments of the Heb. language in the Heb. Bible. It has beautiful lyric parallelism and contains many precise expressions drawn from Ugaritic and possibly other, older lits. It is difficult to tr. and exegete because of its antiquity and obscurity. However the joy of Israel's deliverance is stated gloriously in such lines as: "Awake, awake, Deborah; Awake, awake, Sing thou a song, Rise up Barak, and lead thy captivity captive, thou son of Abinoam," or the often cited phrase, "From heaven fought the stars, the stars in their courses fought against Sisera." The victory of Jehovah's righteousness is inspired by the prophetess, Deborah. Her psalm ends with the prayer, "So perish all thine enemies O LORD—."

3. Deborah, the mother of Tobit's father, who raised her grandson after his father's death (Tobit 1:8).

W. WHITE, JR.

DEBT, DEBTOR (משא, משאה; Cf. חוב; ὀφειλή, ὀφείλημα, δάνειον, ὀφειλέτης, *debt, loan, money borrowed, usury, interest, burden, obligation, sin*). Money, property or contract which one is bound to repay or perform for another; that which is owed or due and must be paid. The person who owes another a debt or obligation. Spiritual sense: sin, trespass (Neh 10:31; Ezek 18:7; Matt 6:12; 23:16; Luke 16:5; Rom 1:14; 8:12).

The OT, particularly in Exodus and Leviticus, records detailed stipulations and limitations regarding debts, loans, interest and contracts. Abuse of the Biblical regulations brought forth repeated admonition and condemnation from the prophets. Interesting word pictures regarding contracts and debts arose among the Israelites. The Mosaic legislation attempts to protect both lender and borrower through a system of pledges and guarantees. The ideas carry over into the NT, although the NT ethic is not so restricted and lacks detail.

It is to be expected that the OT ethic centers much on interest and usury since these were the source of both profit and abuse. In Israel lending and borrowing was not for big commercial enterprises, but to help private individuals who lacked everyday needs. Not the rich, but the poor were in debt. When greed replaced concern in loans the common people considered it unfortunate and a disgrace to be in debt because it placed the debtor at the mercy of the creditor. Jehovah, the God of mercy, would protect by manifold regulations the poor and downtrodden from the wicked oppressor. The OT legislation deals with interest and usury in such a way that both mercy and justice be done. Poverty was common in Israel, caused by over-population, high taxes, poor resources and war. The payment of interest made lending and borrowing both difficult and burdensome for both parties of a transaction in that one party had the power to charge exorbitant interest and the other could choose to default. After the Exile a whole system of guarantees and limitations was developed to protect both debtor and creditor from each other. Later the rabbis worked out ways and means by which profit might be made from capital—not interest, but usury was forbidden.

The Pentateuch indicates that a first principle of lending and assuming debts is that such a transaction was pleasing to both God and man, since it gave the lender an opportunity to help a fellow man in need as an act of love. The Heb. words used indicate the lender lifted a burden from the borrower by helping him through a crisis. Lending to the poor was considered a good deed (Ps 37:21). Since the borrower would pay back what he owed he could receive help with thanks and respect. This is why Moses forbade an Israelite to take interest from a fellow Israelite. The idea was that in a brotherhood help should be given free and not for profit. The motive should be that without Jehovah's intervention in Egypt all Israelites would be slaves: "If your brother becomes poor, and cannot maintain himself with you, you shall maintain him; as a stranger and sojourner he shall live with you. Take no interest (*neshek*) from him or increase (*tarbith*), but fear your God; that your brother may live beside you. You shall not lend him your money at interest nor give him your food for profit. I am the LORD your God, who brought you forth out of the land of Egypt to give you the land of Canaan, and to be your God" (Lev 25:35-38; Exod 22:25). This doctrine of brotherhood, however, allowed the Israelite to lend on interest to non-Israelites: "You shall not lend upon interest to your brother, interest on money, interest on victuals, interest on anything that is lent for interest. To a foreigner you may lend upon interest, but to your brother you shall not lend upon interest" (Deut 23:19, 20).

The poor who were forced to borrow were protected in other ways. It was not lawful to accept as surety objects which were a means of livelihood. A creditor could not take a widow's ox through foreclosure of a loan. One could not keep a man's garment overnight if it had been given as security for a loan (Exod 22:26, 27; Deut 24:12, 13). "No man shall take a mill or an upper millstone in pledge; for he would be taking a life in pledge" (Deut 24:6). On the other hand, Mosaic law protected the lender through a complex system of security arrangements. Pledges were of various kinds: money, movable property, garments, millstones, etc. which were surrendered to the lender at the time of the contract. Securities were not always equal to the value of money borrowed. The guarantee meant that the debtor upon his honor would pay his debts. Such contracts weighed heavily upon the borrower. When the lender took a pledge home with him it was a visible token to everyone that the debtor would repay. (See the episode of Judah and Tamar, Gen 38:12-26.) Early in Judaism a debtor could pledge a son or daughter into the hands of a creditor—the value of their labor would be charged against the interest and the debt itself (2 Kings 4:1-7). One could also give himself as a slave for surety of repayment, or he might be able to persuade a third party to be surety for him (Job 17:3; Prov 6:1). The prophets and rabbis sometimes cautioned against this procedure (Prov 22:26, 27; 27:12, 13). To alleviate the burden of the poor debts were released every seven years during the Sabbatical Year (Deut 15:1-6) and property which was seized was restored during the Jubilee Year (Lev 25:28).

In spite of all the legislation, however, Israel did not follow the Word of the Lord. The preaching of the prophets reveals that the abuse of all guarantees and pledges became a scourge of the people in later Judaism. During the days of Nehemiah, some Israelites were compelled to give up their sons to regain their vineyards (Neh 5:1-13). Rates of interest became exorbitant, a social plague, and the poor debtor became helpless. All of Israel's neighbors oppressed the poor. Lending money at interest was described vividly by the word *nashak*, to "bite like a serpent." The word for interest and usury (*neshek*) really meant "bite," indicating the attitude toward loans, debts and interest among the people. The lender would take his "bite" even before the borrower received a loaf of borrowed bread but expected a full loaf in return. The term for interest also took on the meaning of "oppress" (Hab 2:7). The Arab. parallel is the word "to gnaw." The man who borrowed on interest is pictured as being gradually gnawed away by the interest. The attitude of greed is described by a statement in the Talmud: "If Moses had known how much might be made by lending money at interest, he would never have thought of forbidding it."

The borrower gave his right hand in the transaction because it represented the power and honor to repay, as we in our culture raise our right hands when giving an oath. Ezekiel describes the sins of Israel as if they had broken all the statutes of the law regarding debts and interest (Prov 28:8; Ezek 18:8, 13, 17; 22:12). They abused the laws wholesale (2 Kings 4:1-7). Hundreds of people were reduced to actual slavery (Isa 50:1). Whereas the purpose of loans was really to help a person in need, naked commercialism killed all love and mercy, and both debtor and creditor cursed each other. Greece and Rome, too, were hard on people who defaulted on loans. Rome allowed a creditor to seize the debtor and place him in jail where he could never pay (cf. Jesus' Parable of the Debtor).

In the NT Jesus and the apostles speak of debts, debtors, creditors, money-changers, interest, and other commercial practices which carried over from OT times (Luke 7:41). This is evident from the Lord's imagery in the parable of the wicked servant (Matt 18:23-35), "Have patience with me, and I will pay you," pleads the wicked slave. But "he refused and went and put him in prison till he should pay the debt" (cf. Luke 12:57-59). Jesus speaks of a commercial system in the Sermon on the Mount; "Make friends quickly with your accuser, while you are going with him to court, lest your accuser hand you over to the judge, and the judge to the guard, and you be put in prison; truly, I say to you, you will never get out till you have paid the last penny" (Matt 5:25, 26). Although Jesus nowhere condemns interest directly, and in spite of the implications in His parable of the pounds (Luke

19:11-27) and the parable of the talents (Matt 25:14-30), His use of commercial terminology should not be construed as an approval of all business activity. His words go beyond the OT law—He has contempt for money-making (Matt 6:19-21). All such activity belongs to the kingdom of mammon. No one can serve two masters (6:24). The rich man ends in hell, but Lazarus is found in Abraham's bosom (Luke 16:19-31). In general, Jesus is hard on the improper attitude toward wealth and oppression of the poor, just as in the OT ethic. The creditor forgives just as God does (6:14). God loves all men alike regardless of social and economic status (20:1-16).

The most prominent use of the debtor-creditor terminology in the NT, however, is to picture sin and forgiveness. A debt of sin is contracted by one who has offended his neighbor and sinned against him, and thereby has sinned against God. The words of the Lord's Prayer, "Forgive us our debt (*opheiletes*), As we also have forgiven our debtors" (Matt 6:12), is easily understood against the OT commercial background. Sin implies guilt which must be paid or canceled before man is free. The Christian has such redemption through Christ. The imagery is interpreted by the words which follow: "For if you forgive men their trespasses, your heavenly Father also will forgive you" (v. 14). Other statements in the NT also take on meaning in the light of the OT. Jesus is "the surety of a better covenant" (Heb 7:22). The Holy Spirit is the guarantee of our inheritance (Eph 1:14). Paul is a debtor to preach the Gospel to both Greeks and Barbarians (Rom 1:14). Christians are "debtors, not to the flesh, to live according to the flesh" (Rom 8:12). The Gentiles are debtors to those who shared the Gospel with them (Rom 15:26, 27). The circumcised man is a debtor to keep the whole law (Gal 5:3).

BIBLIOGRAPHY. H. B. Tristan, *Eastern Customs in Bible Lands* (1894), 245-262; E. Day, *The Social Life of the Hebrews* (1901), 175-195; C. Kent, *Social Teachings of the Prophets and Jesus* (1921), 96-106; A. Rehwinkel, *New Testament World* (1950), 244-246; J. D. Derrett, *Fresh Light on St. Luke*, 16:1, NTS (Apr, 1961), 198-219; R. de Vaux, *Ancient Israel* (1961), 172, 173; S. Baron, *A Social and Religious History of the Jews* (1962), I, 161, 195, 261; H. Daniel-Rops, *Daily Life in Palestine at the Time of Christ* (1962), 246-248; L. E. Toombs, *Love and Justice in Deuteronomy* (INT, 1965), 399-411; T. B. Maston, *Biblical Ethics* (1967), 62-85.

L. M. PETERSEN

DECALOGUE. *See* TEN COMMANDMENTS.

DECAPOLIS **dĭ kăp' ə lĭs** (Δεκάπολις). The Decapolis, as its name implies (Gr. *deka*: "ten," *polis*: "city"), was, in NT times, the area of the ten towns. In such significance the term occurs in Matthew (4:25), Mark (5:20; 7:31), Pliny (*Natural History* V. 16, 17) and Jose-

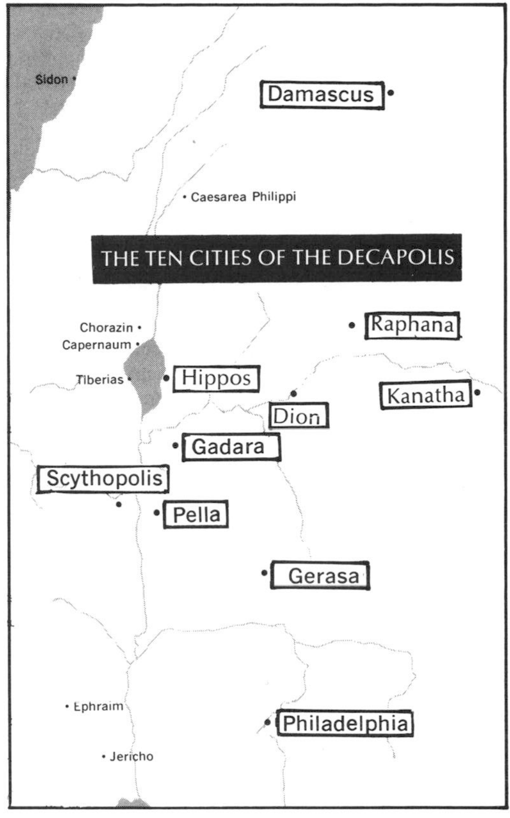

phus (War III. ix. 7). Its original meaning may have been political rather than geographical, signifying the league of ten towns that prob. took shape in the period between Herod's domination of the area and Rome's stabilization of the eastern frontier in the early days of imperial rule. The area E of the Jordan and Galilee, where nine of the ten allied communities were located, was exposed to the open and unpacified desert, and a military alliance was sound policy for a group of predominantly Gr. cities, which in characteristic Gr. fashion set some value on autonomy and political independence.

The complex of Gr. communities in eastern Pal. was a phenomenon of the Hel. diaspora, that deep penetration of the whole of the eastern Mediterranean by Gr. immigrants that followed the conquests of Alexander the Great. Two of the ten Decapolis towns, Pella and Dion, both Macedonian names, were prob. founded by Alexander's own veterans in the mid-4th cent. B.C. Almost as ancient were Philadelphia (the site of Rabbath-Amman of the OT and Amman, capital of modern Jordan) and Gadara. They were both important strongpoints by the end of the 3rd cent. B.C. Gerasa (whose extensive ruins are one of the great sights of Jordan) together with Hippos, do not seem to have attained strength and eminence until Rom. times. Most northerly of the ten towns, according to Pliny, was Damascus, one of the most ancient of the world's cities. Josephus, however, seems to exclude Damascus, calling Scythopolis the largest of the ten.

A tradition of free government was established by the Gr. immigrants, and though the cities lost such autonomy in the days of Maccabean domination, Pompey recognized the spirit of the territory when he established Rom. control in 64-63 B.C. In the words of Josephus, he "restored the cities to their citizens." Josephus, in this connection, mentions Gadara, Pella, Dion, and Hippos; but Philadelphia also dates coinage by Pompey, and must therefore have been a recipient of his beneficence. Such freedom meant that the cities of the area elected their own councils, possessed the privileges of coinage and asylum, the right of property and administration in adjacent territory, and the right of association for defense and commerce. The area was nevertheless under the overall control of the governor of the province of Syria, who was empowered to supervise political administration, law, and foreign affairs, and to levy imperial taxes. It was a system typical of Rome's multilateral concept of government and the empire's readiness to adopt and adapt indigenous forms and patterns of rule and control.

The Gr. communities of the Decapolis would undoubtedly have regarded Rome as protector and benefactor. The league, from Rome's point of view, would strengthen the desert frontier where the great caravan routes and highways of trade bent around the inner curve of the Fertile Crescent. Security was a pressing need. Information is fragmentary, but an inscr. of A.D. 40 speaks of grave menace to the town of Hauran from Bedouin incursion from the desert. Rome's long effort to stabilize her vast frontiers, and the extreme vulnerability of the desert borders in the E are facts that must be considered in the study of imperial history in Pal. Whereas it is on record that two of the Decapolis cities, Hippos and Gadara, were given by Augustus to Herod, it it possible that the League as a defensive unit, did not emerge until after Herod's death in 4 B.C., but it is as probable that it took shape sixty years earlier—as part of Pompey's reorganization of the whole of the eastern area of the Mediterranean.

Trade and commerce originally determined the pattern and progress of the Gr. communities of eastern Pal. The widest gateway to the Jordan Valley from the Mediterranean is the great fertile plain of Esdraelon. Traffic to the territories E of Jordan and the Lake of Galilee necessarily passed between the high country to the S and the lake; hence the importance of the fortress of Beth-shan (or Scythopolis, its Gr. name) and the inevitable association of the place with the ten towns that spread fanwise along the highways further E. Scythopolis is the only one of the ten to lie W of the Jordan. Israeli Beth-shean, as the ruins of the ancient town are called today, is the only Decapolis site in Israel, and not Jordanian or Syrian territory, so persistent is the shape of history in that ancient land. Scythopolis covered E-W communications between the sea and the Decapolis. On the three roads that branch eastward from this nodal point, all the remaining cities of the Decapolis were situated, except for those that lie on the N-S route from Damascus to Arabia along the edge of the desert, which forms the terminal line of all the other highways. Across the Jordan—Gadara, Hippos, and Pella marked the beginning of the three roads. From Pella, a highway ran SE to Philadelphia through Gerasa. The central road ran from Gadara, NE by E to Raphana, whose precise location is not yet established, and on to Kanatha, most easterly of the Decapolis cities, at the foot of Jebel Hauran. The third road ran N to Damascus. To these ten towns—Scythopolis, Pella, Dion, Gerasa, Philadelphia, Gadara, Raphana, Kanatha, Damascus, and Hippos—others joined themselves. Ptolemy, the geographer, listed eighteen names, omitting Raphana of the original ten. Abila and Kanata (a town apparently distinguished from Kanatha) are the most important additions.

Each of the Decapolis cities controlled surrounding territory and perhaps separated enclaves of land. This prob. accounts for the confusion between the various readings "Gadarenes," "Gerasenes," or "Gergasenes' in various texts of Matthew 8, Mark 5, and Luke 8. There is no reason why Gerasa should not have controlled a section of lakeside territory in an area geographically associated with Gadara. Generally, around Hippos was Hippene territory and villages, and around Gadara, Gadarene land (Mark 5:1 KJV). Gadara's long aqueduct reveals the extent to which the community of Gadara must have controlled territory necessary to its life, commerce, and convenience. G. A. Smith, the great Palestinian geographer, wrote, "The Decapolitan region, as Pliny calls it (V. 15), 'the borders of the Decapolis,' as it is styled in the gospels, was, therefore, no mere name, but an actual sphere of property and effective influence" (*Historical Geography of the Holy Land*, 9th ed., p. 601). The Decapolis formed a solid belt of territory along Galilee and Jordan, deeply permeated with Gr. influence, but cosmopolitan by reason of commerce, history, and geographical position. Cultural life was as vigorous as commercial activity. Gadara produced Philodemus, the Epicurean philosopher, in the middle of the 1st cent. B.C. The same town was the birthplace of Meleager, the epigrammatist; Menippus, the satirist; and Theodorus, the rhetorician tutor of Tiberius. Gerasa was also renowned for its teachers.

Top: Jerash, Forum and Street of the Columns. ©*Lev*

Below: The South Theater, built in the 1st Century; accommodated 4000 to 5000 people. Jerash was one of the chief cities of the Decapolis. ©*Lev*

Of chief interest to the student of the NT is the impact of the Decapolis on Galilee. "The Decapolis," writes Smith (op. cit. p. 607), "was flourishing at the time of Christ's ministry. Gadara, with her temples and her amphitheatres, with her art, her games and her literature, overhung the Lake of Galilee, and the voyages of its fishermen." Across the lake, five to eight m. wide, the farmers of Galilee could see a Gentile world. That world had a bridgehead in their territory at Scythopolis; and the roads, converging on that center and radiating thence must have exercised an attraction on many Jews. Perhaps the story of the Prodigal illustrates the fact with the "far country" remote only in outlook and way of life. Swine, a Gentile food, was among the farmstock of the Gadarene territory, and the wanderer of the story, trapped and ruined by an alien society, may have been no more than a hard day's journey from home. Contact between the two areas was separated only by the tenuous barrier of the river and the lake. Large crowds from the Decapolis followed Christ at an early period of His ministry (Matt 4:25). He visited the area when He returned from Tyre and Sidon, reaching the eastern shore of the lake through Hippos. The healed lunatic of Gadara, the first "apostle to the Gentiles," was sent to proclaim his blessing there (Mark 5:20). The multitudes of the later visit (8:1) were the fruit of this witness.

The Jewish church withdrew to Pella at the time of the Great Rebellion and the siege of Jerusalem, A.D. 66-70. G. A. Smith concludes: "We cannot believe that the two worlds, which this landscape embraced, did not break into each other. The many roads which crossed Galilee from the Decapolis to the coast, the many inscriptions upon them, the constant trade between the fishermen and the Greek exporters of their fish, and the very coins—thrust Greek upon the Jews of Galilee. The Aramaic dialect began now to be full of Greek words. It is impossible to believe that our Lord and His disciples did not know Greek. But at least in Gadara, that characteristic Greek city overhanging the Lake of Galilee, in the scholars it sent forth to Greece and Rome we have ample proof that the kingdom of God came forth in no obscure corner, but in the very face of the kingdoms of this world" (op. cit. p. 608).

BIBLIOGRAPHY. G. A. Smith, *The Historical Geography of the Holy Land*, 9th ed. (1902).

E. M. BLAIKLOCK

DECEIT (DECEPTION, GUILE) (מרמה, δόλος, *deceit, treachery, cunning*). Other semantically related Heb. and Gr. words are תרמית, רמיה, ערמה, שקר, משאון, ἀπάτη, πλάνη. Deceit is that which gives a false impression, the deliberate misleading or beguiling of another. Of course, it is always condemned in Scripture (cf. Jer 23:26). It cannot be justified from 2 Corinthians 12:16, for Paul was here employing irony and quoting the words of his critics. Satan is the master of deception (1 Tim 2:14; Rev 20:8, 10). No guile was found on Christ's lips (1 Pet 2:22).

K. L. BARKER

DECISION, VALLEY OF (עמק החרוץ, *valley of strict decision* or *judgment*). In Joel 3:14 this expression refers to the valley of Jehoshaphat (Joel 3:2, 12). The latter in turn seems to be a symbolical name of a valley near Jerusalem which is to be the place of God's ultimate judgment on the nations gathered to attack Jerusalem. Significantly, Jehoshaphat had witnessed one of the Lord's historical victories over the nations (2 Chron 20). The valley has been traditionally identified with the Kidron, but the location remains a problem. Perhaps the solution is contained in Zechariah 14:4, which indicates that when the Lord returns to the Mount of Olives a great valley will be opened. Since Jehoshaphat's name means "The Lord judges," possibly this newly opened valley is so named because of the Lord's judgment there.

K. L. BARKER

DECK. 1. "Deck" is used as a verb in the sense of "cover, adorn, beautify, bedeck, decorate, ornament." Heb. and Gr. verbs denoting this are עָדָה, *cover* or *adorn oneself*, יפה, *beautify, adorn*; κοσμέω, *adorn*; cf. also כהן, עשה, רבד, χρυσόω. For typical occurrences, cf. Isaiah 61:10; Revelation 17:4; 21:2.

2. "Deck" also refers to the deck of a ship, providing a floor for the space above and a roof for the space underneath. In Genesis 6:16, after "lower, second, and third," RSV supplies "decks," KJV "stories." Thus, Noah's ark had three decks. In Ezekiel 27:6 קרש, *board(s)* or *plank(s)* (of a deck), is rendered "deck" in RSV (KJV "benches"). The reference is to Tyre appropriately under the figure of a ship.

K. L. BARKER

DECREE (אסר ; גזרה ; דבר ; דת ; חק ; חקק ; טכם ; טעם ; מאמר ; קים ; δόγμα). The word occurs most frequently in Ezra, Esther, and Daniel, almost always in the sense of an official order, edict, or decision issued by a king, as by Hezekiah (2 Chron 30:5), Cyrus (Ezra 5:13), Cyrus and Darius (Ezra 6:1, 3), Ahasuerus (Esth 1:20), Nebuchadnezzar (Dan 3:10), Caesar Augustus (Luke 2:1), Caesar (Acts 17:7). Sometimes where the KJV uses "decree," the RSV uses another word more appropriate to the context as in Daniel 6:7, where the RSV has "interdict," and Daniel 2:9, where the RSV has "sentence."

The word is not found in the Bible in the theological sense of God's eternal plan for His creation although the Scriptures definitely teach God's sovereign appointments in nature and in providence. God makes decrees (Dan 4:24; Ps 2:7) and the world is subject to them.

There is a decree for the rain (Job 28:26), one for the sea and its bounds (Prov 8:29), one for the bounds of the planets (Ps 148:6). Statements like these come near to what today are referred to as the "laws of nature."

In the NT the word δόγμα is found in Luke 2:1 of the decree of Augustus, in Acts 17:7 of the decree of Caesar, in Acts 16:4 of the "decisions" (RSV) of the Church at the Jerusalem Council. It is also found in Ephesians 2:15 (RSV "ordinances") and Colossians 2:14 (RSV "legal demands") of the ordinances of the OT law.

J. C. CONNELL

DEDAN, DEDANITES de′ dən, dĕd ən īts (דדן). The name of two men in the OT and also a term applied to a people. 1. The son of Raamah, son of Cush, the son of Ham (Gen 10:7). His brother was Sheba. He is also mentioned in 1 Chronicles 1:9.

2. The grandson of Abraham by Keturah. His father was Jokshan and his brother also is called Sheba (Gen 25:3; cf. 1 Chron 1:32). The sons of Dedan are listed as Asshurim, Letushim, and Leummim.

3. As a geographical and ethnic term in several references in the prophets. (a) In the oracle concerning Arabia they are mentioned as lodging in the thickets of Arabia and are referred to as being in caravans (Isa 21:13). (b) Dedan is mentioned in a passage noting the object of God's wrath. The people of Dedan are mentioned in company with Tema and Buz and those who cut the corners of their hair (Jer 25:23). (c) In the context of a prophecy against Edom the people of Dedan are warned of God's punishment to befall them (49:8). In a similar context God's judgment against Edom includes all the territory from Teman to Dedan (Ezek 25:13). (d) Ezekiel 27:15 also mentions the Dedanites. Here RSV follows the LXX and trs. "Rhodes" instead of "Dedan." If the Heb. is correct, then the Dedanites were traders with Tyre. This would seem to be borne out by Ezekiel's statement that Dedan traded with Tyre in saddlecloths for riding, a commodity abundant among the Arabs (27:20). (e) Dedan is mentioned with Sheba in a prophecy concerning Gog (Ezek 38:13, 14).

One can conclude therefore that the Dedanites were a people of Arabia who were closely associated with Sheba. Their exact identity is not known. Extra-Biblical sources of antiquity indicate that Dedan also was an oasis on the trade routes of the peoples of Sheba, Tema and Buz. The oasis of Dedan was known as ed-daḡan as late as A.D. 1200 and remains of its buildings still survive.

El-'ulä is to be identified as the most likely site, being located fifty m. SW of Tema and one hundred and fifty m. E of the Red Sea in Central Arabia.

BIBLIOGRAPHY. J. Simons, *The Geographical and Topographical Text of the Old Testament* (1959), 21; J. Thompson, *The Bible and Archaeology* (1962), 201ff.

J. B. SCOTT

DEDICATE, DEDICATION (קדשׁ, *be holy, set apart*, חנך, *dedicate, consecrate*; ἁγιάζω, *set apart*, ἐγκαινίζω, *make new*, then *initiate, dedicate*).

Qādēš and its cognates are used of: God, denoting His apartness or holiness (Isa 6:3); places set apart for God (Jer 31:40); the Temple (2 Chron 29:5); persons set apart to God (Exod 28:3); and things set apart for sacred use (29:37). *Hānaḵ* and *ḥănukkâ* are applied to the Temple (1 Kings 8:63), the wall of Jerusalem (Neh 12:27), etc. (*Ḥănukkâ* was later applied to the Jewish Feast of Dedication [Hanukkah], q.v.; cf. *egkainia* in John 10:22.) *Hagiazō* and its cognates in the NT have connotations similar to *qādēš* (e.g., persons: John 10:36; Acts 9:13; things: Matt 23:17; places: Heb 9:1). *Egkainizō* is used of the inauguration or dedication of the first covenant (Heb 9:18) and of Christ's dedication of a new and living way (10:20).

Related to the ideas of dedication and devotion is the Heb. root *ḥrm*. The verb means "to seclude from society," usually by complete destruction, and the noun, "a thing secluded or devoted (to God)." They were generally used of Canaanite and neighboring cities, peoples, and things, which were hostile to Israel's religion and therefore to be exterminated or, in the case of certain objects, set apart for sacred use.

BIBLIOGRAPHY. Trench (1865); R. B. Girdlestone, *Synonyms of the Old Testament* (1897); BDB (1907); W. E. Vine, *An Expository Dictionary of New Testament Words* (1940); Arndt (1957); NBD (1962), under "Curse."

K. L. BARKER

DEDICATION, FEAST OF (τὰ ἐγκαίνια): A feast called the Feast of Hanukkah, celebrated annually by the Jews for eight days to commemorate the cleansing of the Temple in Jerusalem after it had been desecrated by the Syrians under Antiochus Epiphanes (1 Macc 4:52-59; 2 Macc 10:5). The restoration of the worship of God was effected by the Hasmonean, Judas Maccabaeus about 165 B.C., three years after its defilement. The Greco-Syrian Antiochus, in his excessive zeal to Hellenize his realm, persecuted the Jews, proscribed their religious observances, and erected an idolatrous altar on the altar of burnt offering in Jerusalem, where heathen sacrifices were then offered (1 Macc 1:41-64; 2 Macc 6:1-11; Jos. Antiq. xii. 5, 4). The Hasmoneans raised the cry of revolt at Modin and ultimately overthrew the forces of Antiochus. Josephus gives a vivid account (Jos. Antiq. xii. 5, 4; 7, 4). The feast falls on the twenty-fifth day of Kislev, which tallies with December (but not always). Josephus designated it "The Feast of Lights." The Apostle John called it "The Feast of Dedication" (John 10:22, only here in the NT). He correctly states the season of the year, showing his familiarity with Jewish customs. The Jews have named it "The Feast of the Maccabees," and the Talmud designated it "The Feast of Illumination." Christ, present in Jerusalem during this festival, addressed the multitude. The festival was characterized by the illumination of synagogues and homes. It was a time of joy and merriment, and no public mourning was permitted on this feast. Jewish tradition claims that Judas Maccabaeus found a cruse of oil, which was sufficient for a day, but lasted for eight. The feast is celebrated among the Jews today. The system of lighting is one light for the first day, and an additional one for each succeeding day of the festival. Second Maccabees 10:6, 7 indicated the feast was observed like the Feast of Tabernacles, with palms, branches, and the singing of psalms. On this occasion Psalm 30 (see title) was read in the ritual of the day (1 Macc 1:41-64; 2 Macc 6:10, 11).

In the celebration today, although work is allowed on these days, there is a prescribed, festive ritual. The family solemnly gathers around the father as he lights the candles with a prayer of thanksgiving to God for the liberation of His people from the persecution of the oppressor. Presents and money gifts are distributed to the children. During the evening games are played with the posing of riddles and exchange of jokes. In Europe the special table dish for the occasion was pancakes. *See* FEASTS.

BIBLIOGRAPHY. H. Schauss, *The Jewish Festivals* (1938), 208-236; B. M. Edidin, *Jewish Holidays and Festivals* (1940), 87-103; *The Jewish People, Past and Present* (1948), II, 277, 278; G. Kittel ed., *Theological Dictionary of the New Testament*, III (1965), 453, 454. C. L. FEINBERG

DEEP (THE) (צוּלָה, *deep water*; מְצוֹלָה, *depth of the sea*; תְּהוֹם, *deep sea, deep wells, deep river*; ἄβυσσος, *the deep, bottomless pit*; βάθος, βυθός, *the deep* [sea]). These words are sometimes used in an adjectival sense to mean any depth, but their chief usage refers to a lake or sea. The word *abyssos* is fig. used for the bottomless pit in Revelation. A similar usage of *teh*ôm for the underworld is debatable.

The word *ṣûlâ* is used only in Isaiah 44:27, where it seems to refer to the canals of Babylon. Its derivatives, *meṣôlâ* and *meṣûlâ* are used of the depths of the sea crossed by Israel (Exod 15:5), also of the Mediterranean Sea (Ps 107:24; Jonah 2:5).

The word *tehôm* is of more import. It is thought by some to be used mythologically of the waters of a nether world. This view sees in *tehôm* (Gen 1:2) a parallel to *Tiamat* of the Babylonian creation story. Tiamat was the demon of chaos from whose split body Marduk made the earth and sky. This Babylonian story, called *Enuma Elish*, has little if anything else in common with the Biblical account.

It should be noted that *tehôm* is not used elsewhere in the OT of mythical subterranean waters. It is used repeatedly of the Red Sea through which Israel passed (Exod 15:5, 8; Ps 77:16; Isa 51:10; Hab 3:10). It is used also many times of the Mediterranean or the deep ocean in general (Gen 7:11; Ps 107:26; Jonah 2:5). In several places the poetic parallel for the word is *yām*, "sea" or the word for "waters," etc. (Job 38:16; Pss 33:7; 135:6; Ezek 26:19; 31:4, 15). The Biblical cosmology does not picture any subterranean watery chaos. Such terms as "the waters under the earth" (Deut 4:16-18) refer only to waters below shore line as the mention of fish in them clearly shows (see the author's "Bible and Cosmology" ETSB V [1962] pp. 11-17).

It is clear that *tehôm* could not be borrowed from the Babylonian *Tiamat* because the Akkad. language lacks the laryngeal consonant "h" which a borrowed Heb. word would not acquire. It is far better to assume that the old Sem. root *thm* indicated "ocean," of which the Babylonian demon Tiamat was a personification.

The NT *abyssos* is used only nine times. In the LXX it regularly trs. the Heb. *tehôm* and thus about thirty times means merely the ocean and lakes. However, as the seas were the deepest things known to the ancients the word gained a fig. usage and is used seven times in Revelation of the bottomless pit, the abode of evil spirits. It is possible that Luke 8:31 (KJV) also shows this usage. The other reference (Rom 10:7 RSV) uses the word *abyssos* of the place from which Christ was raised. Opinions will differ whether *abyssos* refers merely to the grave, as the author believes, or to the underworld (cf. the author's "Meaning of the Word Sheol," ETSB, IV [1961], pp. 129-135).

BIBLIOGRAPHY. A. Heidel, *The Babylonian Genesis* (1951), 98-101.

R. L. HARRIS

DEER. This word apparently is not found in any modern Eng. VSS, other than in combination "fallow deer" (KJV), but this animal is clearly recognizable in hart and hind (q.v.), possibly also in doe (q.v.). Brief notes only are given under these and other related names, with more detailed discussion under this head. At least three species of deer lived in Pal. during OT times, but they were prob. not distinguished. It seems agreed that Heb. אַיָּלָה, and derivatives (see HART, HIND) applied to all three species, or at least to the larger two. Those once native to Pal. are:

1. Red deer. This formerly had a wide distribution living in all suitable wooded parts of Europe and SW Asia, and also in N Africa. Its range has been reduced and with the destruction of forest it has sometimes become

Lion pulling down red deer stag, detail from Black Obelisk. ©*B.M.*

a moorland and mountain animal. Red deer were often preserved strictly as royal game and with continuing protection they have survived even in industrialized lands. It stands between four and five ft. at the shoulder and the stag has large spreading antlers with ten or even more points, which are shed and renewed annually, as with all deer. This species disappeared from Pal. early, perhaps several centuries B.C. It became extinct in Iraq less than one cent. ago and the nearest survivors are prob. in Anatolia and Greece.

2. Fallow deer are much smaller, standing only three ft. All deer are spotted at birth but in this species the coats remain spotted at all ages, esp. in summer. Their antlers are palmate. This deer has been used as a park animal for so long and introduced so often that its distribution is confused. In early times there were two species in the Middle E, both living in hill forests. They disappeared long ago, but one, *Dama mesopotamica*, known as the giant fallow deer, survives in the Zagros Mountains of Luristan, Persia. Both red and fallow deer are herd animals for most of the year and more likely to be obtainable in quantity.

3. Roe deer are much smaller still, standing only about twenty-eight inches, with short upright antlers. In contrast to the others it is solitary and stays mostly under cover, coming out only to graze on field margins. As a result it exists almost unknown in many woodland areas and recorded facts about it are scanty, but it has long been lost to Pal. Although it was prob. the commonest kind, it was rarely depicted in ancient art whereas the others were often illustrated. All deer make excellent eating when in good condition and, being ruminants, they were clean meat to the Israelites. The first five mentions of hart and hind are all in literal contexts and they imply clearly that deer were familiar animals and regularly eaten—e.g. Deuteronomy 12:22, "Just as . . . the hart is eaten" suggests that it was a standard meat. The meat was available daily for Solomon's kitchen and it could be that he had a deer park where fallow deer were kept in readiness. All other references are fig., suggesting graceful animals, sure-footed and swift, e.g. 2 Samuel 22:34, twice repeated later, "He made my feet like hind's feet."

BIBLIOGRAPHY. H. B. Tristram, *The Natural History of the Bible*. 9th. ed. (1898) (valuable for account of conditions in mid-19th cent.); F. S. Bodenheimer, *Animal Life in Palestine* (1935); *Animal and Man in Bible Lands* (1960).

G. S. CANSDALE

DEFILE, DEFILEMENT (among a dozen or so Heb. and Gr. words used in the Bible and tr. "to defile," the most frequently used are the following: חלל ; טמא ; גאל ; *κοινόω*; *μιαίνω*; *μολύνω*). Among the OT Jews were five kinds of defilement: (1) *Physical* (S of Sol 5:3); (2) *Sexual*, either moral or ceremonial, involving either illicit intercourse (Lev 18:20) or intercourse at forbidden times (Lev 15:24; 1 Sam 21:5). (3) *Ethical* (Isa 59:3; Ezek 37:23). (4) *Ceremonial*, which meant to render oneself ceremonially unclean so as to be disqualified for religious service or worship (Lev 11:24; 15:19; 22:6). (5) *Religious* often hard to distinguish from the ceremonial, but concerned more with the heart attitude toward Jehovah (Num 35:33; Jer 3:1; Mal 1:7, 12). The gospels show that by the time of Christ the rabbis had extended the rules regarding defilement into a complex and very burdensome system (Mark 7:2; John 18:28). In the teaching of Christ and the apostles, defilement is uniformly ethical or spiritual (Matt 15:18; Mark 7:19; Heb 12:15).

S. BARABAS

DEGREE (מעלה, *step, stair, ascent*; *ταπεινός*, *of low estate* or *rank, poor*). A word of frequent occurrence in the KJV (2 Kings 20:9, 10, 11; 1 Chron 15:18; 17:17; Ps 62:9; in the titles of Pss 120-134; Isa 38:8; Luke 1:52; 1 Tim 3:13; James 1:9), but found only twice in the RSV (Luke 1:52; 2 Cor 3:18). When used of things it means "step," "stair," "ascent"; and when used of persons it means "rank," "estate." Nothing is known of the form of the sundial of Ahaz, but there is no doubt that the "degrees" upon it were "steps" (2 Kings 20:9-11; Isa 38:8). The Heb. word that it renders means "step," "stair," "ascent," and the word "degree" that the KJV trs. employed, as the OED shows, once meant "a step in an ascent or descent; one of a flight of steps," a sense now obsolete. The word also occurs in the titles of fifteen Psalms (Pss 120-134 "A Song of Ascents"). The reason for the titles is not clear, but two widely accepted views are that the Psalms were sung by the Levites as they ascended by fifteen steps from the court of the women to the court of the men—one Psalm being sung on each step; or that they were sung by the pilgrims during the ascent to Jerusalem at feast times (cf. 1 Sam 1:3; Ps 42:4; 122:4; Isa 30:29).

Applied to persons, the term "degree" means social or official rank, order, estate, grade. The KJV uses it in this sense in 1 Chronicles 15:18 (RSV "order"), 1 Chronicles 17:17 (here the Heb. text is bad and the RSV has a different reading), Psalm 62:9 (RSV "estate"). Both the KJV and the RSV use "degree" in the sense of "rank" in Luke 1:52. In James 1:9 where the KJV has "brother of low degree," the RSV has "lowly brother." In 1 Timothy 3:13, the KJV trs. *bathmòn kalón* "a good degree," whereas the RSV has "a good standing," but there is uncertainty regarding what Paul had in mind. In 2 Corinthians 3:18, where Paul says that the Christian is changed progressively into Christ's image *apò dóxēs eis dóxan*, the KJV renders the Gr. words literally, "from glory to glory," but the RSV trs. them, "from one degree of glory to another." The RSV interprets the words of Paul to mean that the Christian goes forward from one stage of glory to another, but it is possible that Paul meant that the glory seen in Christ creates a similar glory in the Christian.

S. Barabas

DEGREES, SONG(S) OF. *See* Musical Instruments.

DEHAITES, DEHAVITES (דהוא, דהיא, meaning uncertain). Identification uncertain.

In an Aram. list prepared for Artaxerxes (Ezra 4:9), the "Dehaites" are grouped with Elamites and others who were transferred to Samaria by the Assyrian king, Ashurbanipal. They were protesting the rebuilding of Jerusalem. According to some, they were the ancient inhabitants of Dehistan or Daikh, E of the Caspian Sea. However, no satisfactory identification has been made. For this reason, Hoffmann has made the plausible suggestion that the word be vocalized דהוא, "that is." This agrees with two MSS and LXX (B) *hoi eisin*. The resultant tr. would be, "the Shushanchites (or Susians), that is, the Elamites"; cf. G. Hoffmann, *Zeitschrift für Assyriologie*, II (1887), 54.

K. L. Barker

DEITY OF CHRIST. The clearest and fullest expression of the deity of Christ is found in the Nicene Creed which was originally presented at the Council of Nicaea, A.D. 325. In the Eng. *Book of Common Prayer* the tr. appears as follows: ". . . one Lord Jesus Christ, the only begotten Son of God, Light of Light, Very God of Very God, Begotten, not made." Set forth in this statement is every possible effort to make clear that Christ is "Very God of Very God." Closely allied with the word "deity" is the more general word "divinity." Deity is the stronger word, the absolute one. It can be argued that there is a "spark of divinity" in every man; not so with the word "deity."

Only one person has ever made such claims for himself—Jesus Christ. His claims embrace the idea that what He teaches God Himself teaches, that what He has done only God could do, and that in His full personality there is an absolute oneness with God. To assert Himself in any way at all, is to assert God. Anyone making the claims for himself that Jesus Christ makes for Himself must be either mad and perverted or his claims must be true. Since the former simply cannot stand in the light of other evidence available one is forced to conclude that the latter is established. Jesus Christ is what He claims to be: "Very God of Very God." The character portrayed in the gospels and reflected in the epistles will not allow man to believe that the one "altogether lovely" is a deceiver or self-deceived: "*Si Non Deus, Non Bonus.*"

In the NT He is expressly called God as seen in the order of the words in John 1:1, ". . . *καὶ θεὸς ἦν ὁ λόγος.*" The absence of the article shows *Theos* to be the predicate, and the predicate precedes the verb for emphasis: the *Logos* was not only with God, He was God. (Cf. John 1:18, "The only begotten God," Rom 9:15.) In Titus 2:13 there is a careful declaration of His deity, "awaiting our blessed hope, the appearing of the glory of our great God and Savior Jesus Christ," or, in another type of approach, the address of Thomas (John 20:28), "My Lord and my God," goes unrebuked by Christ in the presence of the disciples with their Jewish heritage (see also Phil 2:6; Col 2:9; Heb 1:8; 1 John 5:20).

OT descriptions of God are applied to Him. The descriptions, the support of oral tradition, the writers of the gospels, Paul in his Jewishness: none of these could have allowed for the treatment of Christ as He appears in Scripture apart from their acceptance of the truth of deity; indignation because of blasphemy was the normal automatic reaction of the Jews to Christ's assertions of His relationship to the Father. Take, for example, the frequency of prophetic support in Matthew's gospel: Matthew 3:3, "Prepare the way of the Lord " (note also John 12:41 with Isa 6:1; Eph 4:7, 8 with Ps 68:18). First Peter 3:15 reads, "reverence Christ as Lord," while Isaiah 8:13 reads "The Lord of hosts, him you shall regard as holy." The NT writers move much too easily between the OT God, whose name is ineffable, to Jesus' name for their point not to be self-evident.

As is attested in any systematic theology other evidences of a scriptural support for the deity of Christ are legion. For example, Christ possesses the attributes of God: omnipotence (Matt 28:18; Rev 1:8); omnipresence (Matt 28:20; Eph 1:23); omniscience (Matt 9:4; John 2:24, 25; Acts 1:24; 1 Cor 4:5); truth (John 14:6; Rev 3:7); love (John 3:16); holiness (Luke 1:35; John 6:69; Heb 7:26). "In him was life" (John 1:4; 14:6). He possesses the attributes of eternity (John 8:58; Col 1:17; Heb 1:11; Rev 21:6) or self-existence or immutability. The works of God are ascribed to Him in such things as the creation of the world, the upholding of all things by His power, the raising of the dead, and the judging of the world. His name is associated with God's name upon a footing of equality. The titles of deity are applied to Him. He is willing to receive honor and worship due only to God, and His equality with God is expressly claimed. So the arguments run. There may be reasons why the deity of Christ might be controverted, but such reasons cannot be drawn from any serious acceptance of Scripture.

Every person who knows himself to be saved and who has the assurance of communing with Christ is by the nature of the experience driven to give his Redeemer the highest place and bow before Him in worship. "Jesus Christ is the same yesterday and today and for ever" (Heb 13:8) is not only a description of Christ's eternal essence but is also a useful description of the unanimous report in every age and in every place of the presence of Christ. Christian experience, rather than speculation, compelled the formulation of the doctrine of Christ's deity. Indeed it may be said that one does not think so much of the attributes of God and then apply them to Christ as that he sees Christ and knows what God must be like.

BIBLIOGRAPHY. See Creeds, Systematic Theologies (Hodge, Strong, Berkhof); Dorner, *History of the Development of the Doctrine of the Person of Christ*, 5 vols. (1863); Schaff, *Creeds of Christendom*, 3 vols. (1877); Bruce, *The Humiliation of Christ* (1881); Sanday, *Christologies Ancient and Modern* (1910); Mackintosh, *The Doctrine of the Person of Jesus Christ* (1912).

A. H. LEITCH

DEKAR. *See* BEN-DEKER.

DELAIAH dĭ lā' yə (דליהו, meaning *the Lord drew up*) is the name of four or five, the oldest twenty-third of twenty-four priests David organized "to come into the house of the Lord" (1 Chron 24:18, 19).

When Baruch read Jeremiah's scroll Delaiah was one of all the princes who heard, referred to the king and one of three who urged him not to burn the inspired prophecy (Jer 36:12, 25).

First Chronicles 3:24 has a Delaiah among seven sons of Elioenai, a descendant of Solomon.

In the return from captivity the sons of Delaiah could not prove whether they were really Israelites (Ezra 2:60; cf. Neh 7:62). Perhaps it was a different Delaiah whose son Shemaiah helped in a final effort to stop Nehemiah by closing the doors of the Temple in Jerusalem (Neh 6:10).

W. G. BROWN

DELILAH dĭ lī' lə (Heb. דלילה), a woman of pagan extraction mentioned as the temptress of the judge Samson (Judge 16:4, et al.). No acceptable Sem. etymology for the name has been forthcoming and the comparison to Egyp. Arab. *tedellel*, "coquette" is quite fanciful. The woman was presumably a Philistine and therefore ultimately of Grecian origin speaking an ancient dialect of Gr., possibly similar to that of the earlier Mycenaeans or that of the Ionic colonies in other areas of the Eastern Mediterranean. She is pictured in the story as a courtesan who was hired by her countrymen to lure Samson into compromising his personal strength and his position as judge in Israel. In antiquity, the lot of women was closed off and separated from that of the men of her community, the singular exception was that of the bar maids and prostitutes such as Rahab (Josh 2:1). It is probable that Delilah was one of these footloose women who were severely strictured in Israel.

W. WHITE, JR.

DELIVER (DELIVERANCE). 1. "Deliver" in the sense of "give birth to." The words involved are ילד (e.g., Isa 9:6); τίκτω (Matt 1:21) and γεννάω (Matt 1:20).

2. "Deliver" in the sense of "give up or over (to)." The words are נתן (Hos 11:8), and παραδίδωμι (Rom 8:32).

3. "Deliver" in the sense of "save, rescue, redeem, set free." The primary words are (only the main verbal roots are listed, not the derivatives): נצל, "snatch away, deliver"; ישע, "save, deliver, give victory to"; גאל, "act as kinsman-redeemer, redeem, avenge, vindicate"; פדה, "ransom, deliver from bondage"; ῥύομαι, "rescue, deliver"; σῴζω, "preserve, save," synonymous with *hruomai*, though the idea of "preserve from" is predominant in *sōzō*, that of "rescue from" in *hruomai*; λυτρόω, "set free by paying a ransom, redeem"; and (ἐξ)αγοράζω, "buy (out or back)."

The words in the third category have many applications, referring either to material and temporal deliverance or to spiritual and eternal deliverance. In the NT "save" largely takes the place of "deliver" in the OT, and the emphasis is more on spiritual and eternal deliverance, although the latter is present in the OT. The following are rather typical deliverances:

a. Exodus 6:6; 15:13: from bondage. The Exodus (Israel's deliverance from Egypt's bondage) is frequently alluded to as the supreme demonstration of God's power on behalf of His OT people.

b. Psalm 33:19: from death.

c. Psalm 34:6: from troubles.

d. Psalm 107:6, 13, 19: from distresses. Concerning the Psalms, Westermann maintains that the significance of the *waw* adversative in the petition by an individual is that it indicates the change from lamentation to confession of trust or assurance of being heard, the transition from petition to praise. Thus even in Psalms of individual petition or lament there is a movement from supplication to praise for expected *deliverance* (*The Praise of God in the Psalms*, pp. 64-81).

e. Daniel 3:17, 28: from the fiery furnace.

f. Daniel 6:14, 16, 20, 27: from the den of lions. In the references cited from Daniel, the Aram. verb is the *shaphel* form שיזב, a loan word from Akkad. *ušēzib*, preterit of *šūzubu*, "rescue, save, deliver."

g. Romans 8:21: from decay (creation).

h. Isaiah 59:20 and Romans 11:26: of Israel by the Messiah (future and spiritual).

i. Matthew 6:13: prob. from Satan ("deliver us from the evil one").

j. Acts 16:31; Ephesians 2:8; etc.: from the power of sin, Satan, the second death, etc. Thus, even the basic idea of spiritual redemption or salvation is deliverance, e.g., deliverance from sin's penalty, power, and, eventually, presence.

BIBLIOGRAPHY. Trench (1865); R. B. Girdlestone, *Synonyms of the Old Testament* (1897); BDB (1907); ISBE (1939); W. E. Vine, *An Expository Dictionary of New Testament Words* (1940); Arndt (1957); C. Westermann, *The Praise of God in the Psalms* (1965).

K. L. BARKER

DELIVERER (THE) (מפלט ; מושיע ; מציל; ρυόμενος; λυτρωτής. One who rescues and removes from danger).

The word tr. "deliverer" in the KJV and also in the RSV OT are participles with a causative meaning. The root of *mᵉpallēṭ* means to "escape." This form signifies "one who makes a way of escape." The word is used in this sense to refer only to God. A typical v. is Psalm 40:17, "Thou art my help and my deliverer."

The word *môshîa'* is from the root to "save" and means "one who saves." It is used in this sense to refer to judges whom God raised up to deliver His people. It is often used of God and tr. *savior* (e.g., Isa 43:11).

The word *maṣṣîl* is from the root *nāṣal* to "deliver." It also is used with other trs. as in Psalm 7:2 to "rescue" (KJV "deliver").

All of these words are from common roots and can refer to both physical and spiritual deliverance.

The word *lytrōtēs* (Acts 7:35) is not used in secular writings. It is from the root meaning to "ransom" or "redeem" and refers to Moses' work of delivering God's people from Egypt.

The word *ryómenos* is a participle from a root meaning "save" or "deliver." It also is used for physical as well as spiritual salvation.

Of special importance is Romans 11:26 which promises that a Deliverer will come from Zion. This is taken by some to predict the salvation of national Israel. Others refer it to spiritual Israel. The quotation is from Isaiah 59:20 where the Heb. says that a Redeemer will come to Zion. The word used for Redeemer is *go'ēl* which often is used in the OT to refer to a kinsman who redeems a relative from poverty or who avenges a relative's murder. The word is used often of God as the Redeemer of the helpless. The NT quotation follows the LXX of Isaiah verbatim except for the preposition. The LXX preposition is *eneken*; the NT is *ek*; the Hebrew is *lᵉ*. It is possible that these three renderings can all be satisfied by tr., "A Deliverer shall come for the sake of Zion." Or the tr. "Redeemer" would be quite appropriate in Romans as in Isaiah.

BIBLIOGRAPHY. Commentaries in loc. and of special interest on Romans 11:26: J. Murray, *Romans*, New International (1965), II, 96-99.

R. L. HARRIS

DELOS de' lŏs (Δῆλος). A small Aegean island, regarded as the center of the Cyclades, which derive their name from their encirclement of Delos. That they do so is apparent to anyone viewing the panorama of surrounding islands and sea from the 480 ft. summit of Mount Cynthus, the central rock knoll of the island. The island itself, barren of trees and uninhabited, is covered with the remarkable ruins of a Greco-Roman town.

Delos was reputed to be the birthplace of Apollo and Artemis, and from earliest recorded history the island was honored by song and dance, and was the scene of a sacred festival which, as early as the 8th cent. B.C., attracted visitors from all parts of the Aegean world. The island was taken over by colonists of Gr. stock as early as 1000 B.C., and was already famous as a place of Hellenic life by the time the *Odyssey* was written, in the 8th cent. History, in the stricter sense of the word, begins, however, in the 6th cent., when Pisistratus of Athens (560-527 B.C.), and Polycrates, who came to power in Samos in 540 B.C., sought in turn to bring Delos within their spheres of control.

When the Pers. fleet was on its way to Greece in 490 B.C., it respected the sanctity of Delos, and when, after the clash with Persia, the Greeks set up a maritime confederacy to protect their independence (478 B.C.), Delos was chosen as the seat of the common treasury. When Athens boldly removed the treasury to Athens, Delos remained a member without tribute. Athenian control continued until the end of the disastrous war with Sparta that closed the 5th cent. B.C., when Athens lost her great naval power. A generation later (378, 377 B.C.) Ath-

ens lead a revived maritime league and again controlled Delos. With Athens' final eclipse (314 B.C.), her influence in Delos ended.

For the next cent. and a half, the island was administered by officials known as *hieropoioi*, with Ptolemaic Egypt and metropolitan Macedon, successor states of Alexander's empire, contending for power in the Aegean. Delos enjoyed the status and institutions of a city-state over this period. Monuments and inscrs. reveal the rivalries of the surrounding states —Egypt, Macedon, Pergamum and Syria— under their Hel. kings all of whom, however, seem to have respected Delian independence and the island's sanctity.

Early in the 3rd cent., Delos became the center of the Aegean grain trade. Foreign banking firms flourished and Italian names began to appear in Delian inscrs. Delos lost her neutral status when she made the mistake of supporting Perseus of Macedon in his clash with Rome. Rome, after breaking Macedon, handed Delos to Athens, which had been shrewd enough to support the victor, and Athens replaced the whole Delian population by her own colonists (166 B.C.). Delos was made a free port to damage Rhodian trade and the island rapidly became a cosmopolitan center of business commerce and the chief center of the slave trade in the central Mediterranean. It was one of the states to whom the Rom. Lucius Calpurnius Piso appealed for protection of Jewish interests in the war with Antiochus VII (1 Macc 15:15-24). When Mithridates of Pontus launched his great assault on Rome in 88 B.C., Archelaus his general massacred 20,000 Italians on Delos and the island failed to recover its commercial prosperity. The trade routes changed and the place fell into the dereliction in which it is seen today.

The French began the archeological investigation of Delos in 1873. Its mass of remains, buildings, public and private, sacred and secular and its multitude of inscrs. have notably added to the knowledge of the Gr. world and its culture.

BIBLIOGRAPHY. CAH, VIII, ch. 20 (1930) has a full bibliography; W. A. Laidlaw, *A History of Delos* (1933).

E. M. BLAIKLOCK

DELUGE OF NOAH, THE. *See* FLOOD.

DEMAS, de' mas (Δημᾶς; shortened form of Δημήτριος, or Δημάρατος). This companion of Paul is first mentioned in the greetings sent from Rome to Colossae (Col 4:14; Philem 24), but is later marked for his desertion of Paul in his last imprisonment (2 Tim 4:10). Paul speaks volumes in the few words applied to Demas: he "hath forsaken me, having loved this present world" (KJV). Demas had gone to Thessalonica; but whether this was his home, whether he continued to fall away or became a faithful preacher, one cannot say. It is highly unlikely that he can be identified with the Demetrius of 3 John 12 (cf. Don John Chapman JTS, V, 1904, pp. 364ff.). Not lack of courage but a lust for materialism seemed to be his downfall.

L. FOSTER

DEMETRIUS de me' tri us (*belonging to Demeter*). 1. The disciple whom John praised in his letter to Gaius (3 John 12).

2. The jeweler of Ephesus who raised a mob against Paul because his preaching had resulted in damage to his lucrative business of making silver images of the goddess Diana (Acts 19:23-27). The name of one Demetrius, a warden of the Ephesian temple, has been found by modern explorers; he probably was the silversmith. Three kings of Syria bore the name: Demetrius Soter or Savior (Jos Antiq. XII. x. 1-4); D. Nikator, or Conqueror (Antiq. XIII. v. 2, 3, 11); D. Eukarios, the fortunate (Antiq. XIII. xiii. 3; xiv. 1. 3).

DEMON, DEMONIAC, DEMONOLOGY. The Eng. word "demon" is derived from the Gr. δαίμων, which was used of rather anonymous influences whether of a good or bad variety. When the concept of a supernatural spirit or intelligence subsequently developed in Gr. circles, the word gradually acquired a malign connotation, and was used as a general designation of malevolent powers which were commonly assigned individuality and characteristic functions.

1. Use in Greek thought
2. Mesopotamian demons
3. Egyptian demons
4. Demonism in the OT and Apocrypha
5. Demonism in the NT

1. Use in Greek thought. The most common occurrence of *daímōn* in Homer was in connection with the idea of divinity, deity or divine power, as contrasted with θεός which denoted a god in person. A *daímōn* was thus treated as a personification of the vague powers which were associated in the Gr. mind with the activities of the major deities, and which in consequence exerted some influence upon human life. The term was also employed of an individual's genius, and thus of one's lot or fortune in life. In Hesiod the *daímōn* was sometimes regarded as one of the souls of men from the golden age who formed a connecting link between the gods and mortals. One result of this was that when δαίμονες and θεοί were mentioned in association with one another, the former were thought of as gods of inferior rank. Because the general fortunes of human life appeared to incline to a preponderance of evil, the term *daímōn* in the sense of one's lot acquired an increasingly malign connotation, esp. at the hands of the Attic poets. Despite this however, the term never completely lost its associations with the rather ill-defined powers which were believed to govern the circumstances of life, and for this reason the Greeks could think consistently of good as well as evil spirits. The latter were often thought of as ghosts, and it is interesting to note that the ghosts of heroes were commonly believed to be particularly dangerous, since for some unexplained reason they were capable only of working evil. The Greeks gave consistent credence to the idea of a guardian spirit which watched over an individual from his birth, and which could be either friendly or malign in character. Quite independently of this, evil demons were represented as attaching themselves to an individual in order to insure his untimely end. A demon which was given the title of ἀλάστωρ was credited with special powers of vengeance for the punishment of specific transgressions. Among the Gr. philosophers Thales maintained that "all things are full of gods," and the Pythagoreans made this animism more specific by teaching that all the air was filled with souls, which they described in terms of demons and heroes. These disembodied entities were responsible for sending health and disease alike to both animals and men. Beneficial relations could be established with them through rituals of purification and expiation as well as by divinatory acts and omens. Heraclitus refined the popular concept of an indwelling, controlling deity by the remark that "character is each man's demon," while to Empedocles was credited the dubious distinction of describing the rehabilitation of wicked demons by means of various phases of reincarnation. Socrates gave the impression that he was not infrequently dissuaded from following a particular course of action through receiving a divine sign or warning, and this must have suggested to his hearers the operation of that kind of fate or destiny by which individual lives were popularly supposed to be controlled. Plato held that demons, which he identified with the souls of the dead as did his contemporaries, served as interpreters between the gods and men. Reflecting the thought of Heraclitus he believed that the true guiding genius within each man was the soul, which was the gift of God. Aristotle had a rather less exalted view of the demonic situation, however, merely assenting to the popular theory that all men had demons which accompanied them consistently through life. The most convinced exponents of demonism in ancient Greece were the Stoics, whose pantheism and fatalism enabled demons to be represented as experiencing human passions and emotions, pains and pleasures. Being composed of the same substance as the human soul they enjoyed a permanent existence, and were located in an area beneath the moon. Epicurus went to the other extreme in denying the very existence of demons, and maintained that even if they did exist they could not possibly communicate with human beings in any way.

2. Mesopotamian demons. From their beginnings the Mesopotamian peoples were highly superstitious in character, due in no small measure to the influence of their natural environment and conditions of living upon their religious projections. Whereas in Egypt the quiet, regular inundations of the Nile gave a sense of order and stability to life, in Babylonia the formulation of an ordered civilization was only the result of a prolonged struggle against the unpredictable and devastating floods to which the Tigris and Euphrates were subject. The Sumerians gave definition to the religious traditions of Mesopotamia, and in formulating the concepts which were to become normative for many centuries they took a low view of the significance of human life, regarding man as constituting little more than an afterthought of divine creativity. Sumerian mythology contained numerous allusions to the underworld gods or *anunnaki* and the seven evil *asakki* or demons, which also inhabited the nether regions. The demons were popularly held to be responsible for all the misfortunes which overtook men, and were esp. credited with causing the onset of disease. In Mesopotamian thought sickness occurred when demons entered the apertures of the head and penetrated the internal organs. To forestall this activity it was necessary to resort to magical incantations, amulets, jeweled ornamentation and the like. The modern earrings and necklaces are survivals of an age when such adornments were endowed with magical power as a means of guarding the ears, nostrils and mouth against invasion by disease demons. Thus Ea, the god of the waters, was esp. invoked in incantations and spells, being venerated as the ally of humanity in its conflict with the malevolent forces of existence. Ea thus became the patron deity of those priestly orders which were trained in exorcism, the knowledge of spells, the formulating of incantations and the interpreting of dreams and omens. The spirits most dreaded by the Sumerians and their religious successors were the wraiths of those defunct persons who had not had the appropriate burial rites performed over them, or who had died under mysterious or violent circumstances. Such ghosts were popularly known as *etimmu*, and a special kind of exorcist-priest, the *ashipu*, was required to recite the proper incantations for dispelling their attacks. Such priestly activities involved a substitute for the sufferer, and the appropriate object, whether an animal, a clay image, or some other inanimate substitute, was regarded as being dead and already in the underworld. The offerings and rituals were made to the malign powers suspected of occasioning the disease, and when an incantation invoking such life-giving gods as Ea or Marduk had been pronounced, the sick person was regarded, often in an act of faith, as having risen from the dead, and by this means liberated from the malevolent power of the demon, ghost or evil deity.

The Mesopotamians gave names to the demons which they feared, some of the designations being those of actual diseases while others were the names of hostile natural powers. One demon was known as *Rabiṣu* or "the croucher," because he was thought to lie in wait secretly for his enemies (cf. Gen 4:7). Apparently the reason why demons and evil spirits were given names was that the Sumerians and the Semites of Babylonia generally laid great stress on the belief in the magical power of names. If a demon was to be expelled properly it was necessary for the exorcist-priest to know its name and use it properly in a conjuration or spell (cf. Mark 5:9; Luke

An Assyrian demon, Pazuzu, front and rear views of a bronze representation. "The ancient Semitic world was thought of as populated with these creatures, who caused every conceivable kind of trouble. Cuneiform literature abounds with omens, charms and incantations against these evil spirits. This bronze charm was made to insure the efficacy of a charm or incantation uttered against his . . . activity as evil spirit of the southwest wind" (from Unger, *Archaeology and the Old Testament*). ©O.I.U.C.

8:30). While the incidence of sickness was widely attributed to demons, almost any other kind of human activity could also be threatened by malign supernatural forces. For example, the laying of a foundation provided an occasion when demons could infiltrate the planned structure and bring about the subsequent collapse of the fabric. The Sumer. practice of making foundation deposits in all public and sacred buildings was marked by rituals which were designed to forestall the activities of the malevolent underworld powers and insure the stability of the structure against internal or external onslaught. Among the Babylonians, Assyrians and later Sem. peoples, there existed a great many non-human demons for whose creation mankind had no responsibility. The *asakki* of the Sumerians were known to the Babylonians as *utukku*, and were frequently mentioned in exorcism texts. Over the centuries the demons were accorded a realistic form, so that by the time of Ashurbanipal (669-627 B.C.) it was common for pictures or figurines of these evil powers to be made and employed for protective purposes. The *utukku* seem to have originated in the concept of ghosts, but in a developed form they were regarded as devils who lurked in the desert areas, ready to pounce upon the unwary or solitary traveler. A female demon named Lamashtu was an object of particular dread. The daughter of Anu, the Sumer. high god of heaven, she frequented mountainous regions or marshy areas looking for unprotected or straying children. Equally feared was the deity Namtar, the herald of death, who controlled sixty diseases which he was able to inflict at will upon mankind. Another deadly enemy of mankind who was associated with Namtar was Irra, the god of plagues, against whom many incantations were formulated. Another spirit of pestilence was named Ura, who was prominent in Babylonian apotropaic or protective tablets. These contained a representation of the deity in human form on one side, while on the other was inscribed an exorcist ritual or formula designed to discourage the attentions of the demon. Well known among Sem. peoples of a later age was the Babylonian female demon Lilitu, who was in effect a *succuba*, a ghostly lecher who tempted men by means of sexual dreams. The Assyrian *ardat lili*, for whom there was also a male counterpart, was supposed to roam at night until she found an unmarried man with whom to mate.

3. Egyptian demons. As with other peoples of the ancient Near E, the Egyptians believed in the presence of a multiplicity of demons against which the powers of magic had to be marshaled if everything was not to be blotted out by their malign influences. Despite a belief in demonic forces, the ancient Egyptians did not catalog their devils and evil spirits in the same way as so many other peoples did. Furthermore, such celestial phenomena as floods and storms which elsewhere were regarded as the work of demons, were attributed by the Egyptians to the gods themselves. As in Mesopotamia the incidence of disease was generally ascribed to demons, who would steal at night into the inert form of the sleeper to bring pain, fever, and perhaps even death. Powerful magical agencies in the form of charms and incantations were needed to combat such dreaded demonic influences. Demons were also thought to inhabit the air itself, hence the need for periodic fumigation of temples and palaces, esp. on the occasion of a funeral. More than any other demons the Egyptians feared the disembodied dead, who in ghostly form could devise all sorts of malicious deeds against humanity. They could only be held in check by powerful magical spells, and in the Book of the Dead they were depicted as ready even to harm souls which had newly arrived in the nether world. Insofar as demons were named in Egyp. lit. they were described functionally by such epithets as "the cutter," "the archer," "the ripper," and so on, while specifically female demons were spoken of as "the lady of the sword thrusts," "she who is violent," and the like. Because of the difficulty of distinguishing clearly in ancient Egyp. thought between a god and a demon, there is some ground for the view that the possession of a proper name served to identify a god as such. The situation is somewhat complicated by the fact that anonymous groups of demons were accorded superstitious veneration by sections of the populace from time to time, as well as by the process of development through which it was imagined that demons could become gods. Popular demonology in Egypt, however, manifested many of the characteristics found in the demonism of other nations, including the superstitious influence of days and horoscopes, the response of demons to chants, and the ability to control demons by the use of their correct names. Egyptian lit. never mentioned demons which attacked children or who were wantonly bloodthirsty, unlike the writings of the Babylonians.

4. Demonism in the OT and Apocrypha. In the earliest Heb. sources there was no specific term equivalent to "demon," and in those cases where supernatural phenomena needed to be described, the words אל or אלהים, commonly tr. "god," were employed in the narrative. Thus an inspired man was a "man of *’ᵉlōhîm*," i.e., a godly man, an expression which found its counterpart in the Hitt. phrase "man of the gods," i.e., a seer *’ᵉlōhîm* was frequently used in a descriptive sense of a formidable power, as in Genesis 30:8 ("mighty wrestlings") or Jonah 3:3 ("a 'divine' city"). In the same neutral sense the idea of a divine spirit (*rûaḥ ’ᵉlōhîm*) possessing a person was employed to account for extraordinary phenomena such as the prophetic activities of Balaam (Num 24:2) or Saul (1 Sam 10:11; 19:20-23). The adjectival use of *’ᵉlōhîm* in connection with an evil spirit occurred in 2 Samuel 16:15, 16, 23, but the Eng. VSS wrongly ascribed the provenance of the phenomenon to God. In actual fact, the use of the generic term for "god" was merely intended by the author to describe the evil spirit as "powerful" or "mighty" without any inherent demonism being conveyed. In the same way the outpouring of a positive spiritual endowment was described in Exodus 31:3; 35:31 by the expression *rûaḥ ’ᵉlōhîm* or "impressive gifts," again incorrectly rendered in the Eng. VSS by the expression "the spirit of God." Possession by a powerful extraneous spirit was described by the same phrase in relation to the ecstatic activities of Saul (1 Sam 10:6; 11:6). The exploits of Samson in the vineyards of Timnah (Judg 14:6) were attributed to the inspiration of the Lord where the proper name YHWH was substituted for *’ᵉlōhîm* as an adjective (cf. Judg 13:25). In view of the common Near Eastern attribution of sickness to demons, it is important to notice that the diseases mentioned in the OT were related in their incidence to the activity of the one God, in line with the consistent monism of Heb. thought. The plagues of Egypt came from the divine hand (Exod 9:3), and even the calamities which overtook Job, including a loathsome disease (Job 2:7), were perpetrated by the adversary (השטן) with divine permission. Similarly the expression *’ᵃḥāzanî hassābāṣ* (2 Sam 1:9) has been claimed by some scholars to denote seizure or possession by an evil power whereas in actual fact Saul was describing an attack of giddiness due to extreme emotional exhaustion. The occurrence of disease due to the activity of demonic powers has been wrongly inferred from the reference in Isaiah 53:4, where the suffering servant was "powerfully smitten" (Eng. VSS, "smitten of [by] God") as part of His affliction. A plain reading of the Heb. text makes it clear that this did not result from the activities of malign forces even though his travails included the bearing of sicknesses (*ḥᵒlî*) and pains (*mak’ôḇ*).

Yet the OT does contain some allusions to the popular demonology of pagan nations, particularly in the context of cultic worship. The term שדים (Deut 32:17) rendered in the LXX by δαιμόνια referred to foreign gods (cf. Ps 106:37), which need not have been specifically demonic in nature. In post-Biblical Heb. the word *sēḏ* became the common designation of a malign spirit, and the reference in Deuteronomy may imply only the Assyrian *shêdu* or "guardian spirit." Another allusion to pagan gods occurred in Leviticus 17:7, where the term שעירים, or "hairy ones" has been taken by some commentators as a reference to "satyrs." The literal meaning of the word is "goats," but in pagan thought the "hairy ones" were deemed to be sylvan gods or demons which inhabited waste places (cf. Isa 13:21;

34:14). Goat worship, accompanied by depraved rituals, was prevalent in Lower Egypt, and was familiar to the Israelites of pre-exodus times. This was one form of worship from which God desired to attract His people (cf. Josh 24:14; Ezek 20:7), hence the prohibition of offerings to satyrs. Whereas in Leviticus 17:7 the LXX reads *daimónia* and the Vulgate *daemones* for שׂעירים, in a similar reference (2 Chron 11:15) the LXX reads μάταια or "vain things" for שׂעירים. In attempting to understand these terms it is important not to regard late interpretations as necessarily identical in meaning with the original usage. While Arab. popular thought could envision a whole class of hirsute demons, all the OT references to "hairy ones" make it quite possible that the writers were speaking merely of wild goats or he-goats as objects of pagan veneration, not as spirits of the wilderness. While *sēd* could be given a demonic interpretation, the concrete use of the term suggests a heathen deity rather than an indeterminate afflatus. Since both Heb. terms are specific rather than generic in nature, an appropriate interpretation would seem to be required in the various passages.

A number of demons referred to either by name or title in lit. from the ancient Near E are also mentioned in certain OT passages. There is a problem of interpretation, since the fact that all such allusions occur in poetic sections raises the question as to whether they are actually anything more than mere figures of speech. (Isaiah referred to the familiar Akkad. female demon Lilitu by the Heb. name of לילית, LXX ὀνοκένταυρος; Vulg. *Lamia*; Isa 34:14.) In Mesopotamian lit. Lilitu appeared as an alluring female wraith who tempted men in sexual dreams, but by the 8th cent. B.C. she had tended to become confused in Pal. with the child-stealing hag Lamashtu. In popular thought Lilith was believed to be a night demon who prowled among ruins and lurked in desolate places, but despite this the name is not derived from the root for "night," as was once imagined. Instead it comes from the Sumer. term *lil* meaning "wind."

Another demon familiar to Near Eastern mythology was Resheph, who was mentioned in documents from such widely separated places as Mari, Ugarit, Egypt, Cyprus and Carthage between the 19th and 4th centuries B.C. Resheph was the Canaanite deity of pestilence, and in both Ugaritic and Egyptian texts was associated with violent death. The pestilence as an agent of divine power was mentioned in Habakkuk 3:5, although there was no personification, despite the poetic nature of the passage. The term occurred also in Song of Solomon 8:6 where it was used in the sense of "sparks" or "flames" (RSV "flashes") rather than pestilence. In Psalm 76:3 it was employed to describe "flashing arrows," while in Psalm 78:48 it alluded to the destruction of herds by means of thunderbolts. What appears to be the threat of a febrile condition of high mortality was mentioned in Deuteronomy 32:24, where *resep* carries overtones similar to those found in connection with Resheph in the Ugaritic texts. The idea of Resheph as a "searing flame" may have originated in Babylonia, where Girra was the god of fire as well as pestilence. Since the foregoing references occur in poetic passages it is difficult to imagine that they are anything more than thoroughly demythologized forms of literary allusion. The mention of Rahab (Job 9:13; 26:12; Ps 89:10; Isa 30:7; 51:9, 10) has been interpreted as referring to a mythological dragon slain in primordial combat by God, although this explanation is doubtful if only because the meaning of the name Rahab is uncertain. The LXX trs. were quite dubious about the allusion, omitting the word altogether in Isaiah 51:9 and refusing to recognize it as a proper name in Isaiah 30:7. In Job 9:13 and 26:12 it was tr. by κῆτος or "sea monster," and was simply transliterated in Psalm 87:4. In this latter passage, as also in Isaiah 30:9, the name was used fig. of Egypt with the implication that the proud nation would be humbled.

Some interpreters have seen further allusions to demonic influences in references to "the destruction that wastes at noonday" (Ps 91:6). The affliction in question may have been sunstroke, or possibly acute spinal meningitis, but the description is of a general nature, and although the LXX rendered קטב by *daimónion*, there is no obvious personification in the Heb. While it is true that many ancient Near Eastern peoples regarded the onset of dizziness in the heat of the day as the result of demonic activity, the nature of the Heb. expression makes it more probable that an empirical medical description, and not a demonic one, was being contemplated. Of a rather more substantial nature is the allusion in Psalm 91:5 to a phenomenon described as the "terror of the night" (פחד לילה ; LXX φόβος νυκτερινός), which may reflect the universal dread of "things that go bump in the night." It is uncertain, however, from a straightforward reading of the v., whether the terror is of an external order which produces fright or of a purely internal kind due to the mild state of shock which accompanies an unexpected disturbance of sleeping patterns. Certainly there is insufficient evidence, particularly against a poetic background, for the assumption that the author had in mind one of the many malign spirits which in ancient Near Eastern demonology were popularly supposed to perpetrate their assaults under cover of darkness.

Yet another allusion to demonic powers has been seen in the reference to the "leech" (ASV "horseleach," Prov 30:15). The Heb. term עלוקה, LXX Βδελλή, has generally been thought of as the Heb. equivalent of the late Arab. word *ilgitu* or "leech." More romantic interpretations have argued from the late Arab. word *'Aulaq* or "vampire," "ghoul," to the view that the Biblical reference was to a greedy demonic creature which fed with an insatiable appetite upon its victims. Again, it seems quite clear that poetic imagery alone is involved, and that the Heb. sage was using metaphorical language to describe the relentless pressures exerted upon humanity by certain well attested phenomena of nature and life. To regard the "leech" as an allusion to a vampire or some other demonic creature is to proceed far in advance of the available evidence. A similar criticism can be entertained regarding the supposed "seven evil spirits" (Deut 28:22), for the children of Israel were warned that disobedience of the divine commands would cause God to smite them with "consumption, and with fever, inflammation, and fiery heat, and with drought, and with blasting, and with mildew; they shall pursue you until you perish." Had this list originated from Mesopotamian sources it could be argued that such terms as "consumption" and "fever" were the official names given to the demons thought to have occasioned such diseases, as with the celebrated Babylonian "Headache" series, where a specific disease was personified and addressed as though it were a spiritual being. The fact that the Biblical utterance emerged from a specifically wilderness milieu prior to the entrance into Canaan emphatically repudiates any suggestion of either the presence or the influence of magic. Instead, Moses was promising the recalcitrant Israelites a variety of punishments which would affect their persons and their livelihood, and whose nature was already well known to them. To interpret these phenomena in demonic terms as though they were the Israelite counterparts of the agents of Irra, the Mesopotamian god of disease, is entirely fanciful and unwarranted by the evidence of the Heb. text. The poisonous "pestilence" (קטב, LXX *ὀπισθότων*, Deut 32:24) comes into the same category of afflictions which are described in empirical, non-demonic terms. The fact that in Psalm 91:6 the LXX read *συμπτώματος*, and *κέντρον* in Hosea 13:14 for *qeṭeḇ* would imply that something other than a specific demon was being contemplated, otherwise the same term would have been used with a personified force. Another passage which has been wrongly interpreted in demonic terms is Job 18:14, where the wicked man is spoken of as being brought to the "king of terrors" (מלך בלהות) . Since this occurs in a poetic section it is best seen as a euphemism for death rather than as an allusion to Nergal, lord of the Babylonian underworld, or to Osiris, the ruler of the Egyp. dead. As a general observation it should be noted that such references to pagan mythology as do occur in the OT have themselves been thoroughly stripped of their pagan associations, and appear largely as figures of popular thought or speech rather than as serious metaphysical concepts. Native to the OT Scriptures, however, was the idea of an "adversary" who was opposed to the outworking of the divine will. While OT references to his activities are few in number, they certainly depict them as being against the best interests of humanity. This character was most evident in the temptation and fall of man (Gen 3:1-19), and illustrated further in the opposition presented to David (1 Chron 21:1) and Joshua the high priest (Zech 3:1f.). The Book of Job described the adversary (השטן) as presenting himself before the Lord among the "sons of God," and showed that despite the inimical nature of his intentions he was unable to carry out his plans without the permission of God. In this sense the book describes an experiment by Satan into the nature of distinterested virtue, and while it indicates that the evil which overtook Job was to some extent the responsibility of God it also makes clear the fact that the operations of the adversary have never been free from all restraint.

During the period of the Apoc. and Pseudep., popular thought gave fuller expression to the concepts concerning good and evil spirits which had appeared in the canonical lit. This development was not uniform, for there are books such as Ecclesiasticus and Maccabees which contained almost no allusions at all to spiritual beings (cf. Ecclus 48:21; 1 Macc 7:41; 2 Macc 11:6; 15:22, 23). The Wisdom of Solomon made no reference to demons or angels except in the description of the Exodus (Wisd Sol 18:15), in which the divine word was spoken of as an active vengeful angel. Some of the Apocalypses carried the belief in good and evil spirits to great extremes, though a more moderate estimate appeared in works such as Tobit, the Testament of the Twelve Patriarchs, the Apocalypse of Baruch, 2 Esdras and the Book of Jubilees. The author of the latter composition tended to attribute a spirit to the various natural forces (cf. Jub 2:2; 10:5), while in the Testament of the Twelve Patriarchs it was the immoral tendencies of human nature which were given demonic status. Seven "spirits of deceit" were enumerated, and to these wicked elements were subsequently added sleep and the human senses. These evil forces led men into sin and then exacted retribution from them. In popular thought the demons became a distinct order of malign spirits operating under the control of Belial or Satan, the former term indicating an extremely wicked person (cf. Ps 18:4). The Apocalyptists generally thought of Satan and his allies as being overthrown by God and the powers of goodness before the new creation was ushered in (cf. Test. XII Pat; Test. Asher 1:9; 6:2; Test. Dan 1:6, 7; Test. Judah 13:3; 14:2; Test. Levi 19:1, etc.). This idea was also clearly formulated in the DSS, one section of the Manual of Discipline attributing all mortal plagues and difficulties to the "spirit of perversity" (1QS III, 22-24), whose control of evil forces was a continual embarrassment to the spirituality of the sons of light and righteousness (cf. 1QS IV, 12, 13), but who would be vanquished at the dawn of the Messianic age. This perverse spirit and his allies depicted in the Qumran writings have a great deal in common with the Iranian *druj* and the *daevas*, whose malign influences were greatly feared in Persia and elsewhere in the ancient orient.

Despite the impact of pagan thought, orthodox Jewish beliefs consistently challenged any dualistic tendencies which would cast doubt on the complete sovereignty and supremacy of God. In order to explain the ills which afflicted human beings some writers thought of Satan as the archdemon who tempted man and led him astray (cf. Wisd Sol 2:4; Slavonic Enoch 3:31). Such writers called Satan by his Gr. name *diábolos* or devil and identified him with the serpent of Eden. In the Book of Enoch another view of the origin of evil involved a presentation of a theory of demonic beginnings. Devils, it was assumed, had at one time been angels who had rebelled against God and had caused mischief on earth by mating with human wives (cf. Gen 6:1-4; Ezek 28:13-17). Because matter was thought to be evil, following Iranian dualism, these spiritual beings had thereby corrupted themselves, and could only look forward to ultimate destruction by fire. Further Pers. influence is seen in the Book of Tobit, where a specific demon named Asmodeus was regarded as a male counterpart of the Babylonian *succuba*. It is uncertain, however, whether the name is a variation of the demonic Shamedon, found in Palestinian Jewish midrashim, or whether it was actually a representation of the familiar Pers. demon Aeshma. In any event other aspects of the work exhibit clear traces of Pers. demonology. Perhaps the most rational demonology in pre-Christian times occurred in the Testament of the Twelve Patriarchs and The Ascension of Isaiah, where the evil propensities of man were personified and placed under the control of Beliar (a variant form of Belial). This avoided the fanciful practice of associating "fallen angels" with human mating procedures, and related most of the evil in the world to aberrant behavior.

During the intertestamental period most people, including the Jews of Pal., believed that the world was full of supernatural agencies working for good or ill. Just as angels were able to accomplish beneficent deeds, so demons or devils were always at hand to perpetrate calamity, sickness or misfortune. So pervasive had Near Eastern superstitions become that Jews and Gentiles alike regarded the onset of disease as the work of demonic powers. In Israel, in particular, the physician was of comparatively low repute, since God was regarded as the dispenser of sickness and health alike. When superstitious beliefs in demons arose, the best the physician could do was to treat the patient by means of charms, incantations, and the like, which was a far cry from the non-magical, empirical therapy of the Mosaic law.

5. Demonism in the NT. Whereas the subject of devils and demonism was not of particular interest to OT writers, there are many references to devils in the earliest Christian lit., and particularly in the gospels. They were generally referred to by the term *daimónion*, a diminutive form of *daimōn* but employed without any significant difference. In addition the term διάβολος was used to describe a "devil." As distinct from Classical Gr. thought, where *daimōn* was not infrequently employed in a good sense, the NT writers always thought of devils or demons as spiritual beings which were hostile to both God and men. The "prince" of these malign beings was accorded the name of Beelzebub (perhaps more accurately Beezebul), so that demons generally were regarded as his agents in human society (Mark 3:22). There were, however, a few instances (Acts 17:18; 1 Cor 10:20; Rev 9:20) where *daimónia* simply meant "pagan deities" rather than "demons." This was particularly the case when sacrificial meats offered to pagan gods were concerned, and where Paul gave special application (1 Cor 10:20) to the teachings of Christ about the impossibility of serving God and mammon (cf. Matt 6:24; Luke 16:13). Aside from this instance, there are few references to either demonism or demon-possession in the epistles. In the gospels the outbursts of demonic opposition to the work of God in Christ are most evident, and the evangelists depict Christ in continual conflict with evil forces. To expel demons was no easy matter, as the disciples discovered (Matt 17:19; Mark 9:28), and the recognition that Christ was able to accomplish this with apparent ease led His enemies to link Him perversely with demonic forces instead of recognizing His divine origin (cf. Luke 11:15; John 7:20; 10:20). This association was quickly dispelled by Christ with the comment that a house thus divided against itself would soon fall (Luke 11:17, 18). This, in turn, led to the observation that if He by the "finger of God," was able to expel demons, then indeed the kingdom of God was already present in contemporary society. Reporting the same incident Matthew attributed the power of Christ in this area to the spirit of God (Matt 12:28). Jesus shared His gifts of exorcism with His followers at the time of the mission of the Twelve (Luke 9:1), where the disciples were given power and authority over all demons, and subsequently when the Seventy were sent out (10:17) and on their return reported that even the demons were subject to them through His name. In NT times there was apparently no significant difference between demons, evil

A view of the contemporary village at Gadara, home of the "Gadarene demoniac." ©Lev

spirits (*ponēra*), and unclean spirits (*akatharta*), since in the case of the Gadarene demoniac the terms "unclean spirits" and "devils" were used interchangeably (8:27-29). In Luke 11:24 the "unclean spirit" which went out of a man returned with seven other spirits of a more wicked though still kindred nature. Demons and evil spirits were regarded in the NT as one cause of disease (Mark 1:23; 7:25), but it is interesting to note that such possession did not defile the sufferers either morally or spiritually, since they were not specifically excluded from the synagogue or the Temple precincts. The possessing spirits were uniformly regarded as evil, and had to be expelled on all possible occasions, for they were allies of Satan and thus hostile to God and man alike.

The nature of these references makes it clear that the evangelists did not treat evil as impersonal, a fact which is further substantiated by the intensely personal character of the temptations experienced by Christ (Matt 4:1-11; Mark 1:12, 13; Luke 4:1-13). Here as elsewhere the identity of the demonic force was revealed (cf. Legion, Mark 5:9; Luke 8:30), and this was done to make evident its metaphysical reality as well as to confront it by an even more powerful force which also partook of a personal character. This latter, expressed in the divine name, enabled the demons to be expelled (cf. Matt 7:22).

The concept of the "power of the name" was widespread in antiquity, and was based on the assumption that the "name" was not only a personal designation but also represented an integral part of the personality of the bearer. The superior power inherent in the name of God was reflected by the psalmist (Pss 20:7; 118:12), who entertained the defeat of pagan armies through divine intervention. In the time of Christ it was the custom in Jewish circles to commence a magical incantation against a demon with the words "I conjure you by the name." This was reflected in Acts 19:13, where certain itinerant Jewish exorcists took it upon themselves to pronounce over those who were possessed with evil spirits the name of the Lord Jesus, using with entirely unexpected results the formula, "I adjure you by the Jesus whom Paul preaches." In the NT the only names of demons mentioned are Legion and the various designations of the "prince of the devils," namely Satan, Belial and Beelzebub (Beezebul). The name "Legion" presents certain problems because while it is given as the designation of the Gadarene demoniac (Mark 5:9, 15; Luke 8:30), it is clear that it is the large number of demons who are speaking, and not the man himself. Perhaps the demons were unwilling to identify themselves and gave instead a collective name indicative of a large number, which would accord with the tradition of Matthew 12:45; Luke 8:2, that demons preferred to go about in groups. The "destroying one" (ὁ ὀλοθρευτής) (1 Cor 10:10) is not so much an evil demon as an avenging angel of God (cf. 2 Sam 24:16), while the prince of the abyss (Rev 9:11) named Apollyon or Abaddon was an angel also, not a devil in revolt against divine power.

In the gospels the term δαιμόνια was used to designate unclean spirits, although in the Lukan writings the expression πνεύματα ἀκάθαρτα was preferred (cf. Luke 8:29; Acts 5:16, etc.). They were described as entering and "troubling" ὀχλεῖν, Acts 5:16) or "overtaking" (καταλαμβάνειν, Mark 9:18) a man. Sometimes a person "possessed" them (ἔχειν, Luke 4:33), the result of which was the incidence of physical disorders (Matt 4:24; 9:32; Mark 9:18; Luke 11:14, etc.) or mental pathology (Matt 11:18; John 10:19-21, etc). Although the descriptions of disease are framed for the most part in untechnical or popular language, there does seem to have been some attempt in the NT to differentiate between demon possession and other forms of pathology. Neurasthenic conditions were allotted to the same general classification as demon possession, and these were viewed in a somewhat different light from epilepsy and lunacy. Despite this, however, the thought of the day tended to attribute the same demonic etiological factors to both varieties of mental affliction. What is significant, however, is that in certain passages (Matt 4:24; Mark 1:32; Acts 5:16; 10:38) demon possession was referred to as additional to the other kinds of diseases mentioned, which would imply that it had certain recognizable features of its own. The ancient beliefs concerning the influence of the moon over certain types of mental conditions was reflected in the case of the epileptic boy (Matt 17:14-18; Mark 9:14-27; Luke 9:37-42), whom Matthew described as "moon-struck" (σεληνιάζεται). The RSV tr. of "epileptic," apart from describing one of the symptoms, furnished no greater understanding of the pathological situation than did Matthew's popular terminology, and serves to illustrate some of the difficulties involved in understanding the recorded case histories in the gospels. In this instance, for example, it is virtually impossible to say whether the boy was suffering from a true congenital epilepsy, from infantile idiopathic epilepsy, or from some deep emotional disturbance in the subconscious mind which resulted in epileptoid attacks. For this reason it is obviously quite arbitrary to assume that demon possession was actually nothing more than a popular designation for epilepsy. In any event, modern scientific medicine has its own difficulties with epilepsy, since very little is actually known concerning the etiology of the clinical form. As a result it becomes extremely difficult on occasions for doctors to distinguish between the classical convulsive disease and glandular or emotional disturbances which may simulate it. Numerous forms of epilepsy have been described to date including hereditary types and those which may have resulted from a cerebral tumor, an apoplectic stroke, or some injury to the brain tissue. Single convulsive attacks which give the appearance of genuine epilepsy can also be precipitated by deep emotional conflicts, to which the ancients were no less liable than their modern counterparts. If such attacks are brought into focus by means of a sudden shock which produces cerebral vasoconstriction with a rapid reduction in the oxygen content of the brain, an epileptiform seizure would take place. When speaking of emotional conflicts one is attempting to designate certain processes of an ill-defined nature which operate deep within the uncharted recesses of the subconscious mind, and which are thus not readily amenable to detailed clinical delineation. It is known, however, that the vital forces of the human personality function within this area of the mind, and that there is always a significant emotional or psychic element in most diseases, and not least in idiopathic mental afflictions. If such states are to be seen in terms of the evil, destructive powers found in the subconscious mind gaining the ascendancy over the positive forces for good in the human personality, it is possible to think of all mental disorders as being to some limited extent at least the result of temporary possession of the human mind by demonic influences, a situation which could conceivably become permanent. Indeed, in so far as specific clinical conditions can be identified as emotogenic, the same considerations could apply to a significantly wider range of human afflictions. Because modern psychosomatic medical research has shown that attestable clinical disease can result from such metaphysical entities as suggestion, emotional conflicts, fear, and the like, it is no longer possible to dismiss as implausible the noxious effects which the various forms of evil, working through the personality of fallen man, can have upon individual and mental well-being. Indeed, Jesus viewed all disease in these general terms, and re-emphasized the OT concept of the individual as a *nepeš hayyāh* (Gen 2:7), i.e., a personality manifesting an essential unity of body and mind. He frequently saw the incidence of disease as the result of evil producing an imbalance within the individual personality, and His healings stressed that the will of the Father was for humanity to enjoy wholeness and salvation (John 3:16; 10:10). So important was the human mind to Jesus that many of His teachings were formulated in a way which would help His followers to achieve inward peace (Matt 11:29), as illustrated by the Sermon on the Mount.

Prominent NT cases of demon possession included the Syrophoenician's daughter (Matt 15:22; Mark 7:25), the Gerasene demoniac (Matt 8:28; Mark 5:2; Luke 8:27), the Capernaum madman (Mark 1:23; Luke 4:33), the blind and dumb demoniac (Matt 12:22; Luke 11:14) and the young woman with divinatory insights (Acts 16:16). In the case of the little Canaanite girl, her mother described her acute condition as being "seriously possessed by a demon" (Matt 15:22) or an "unclean spirit" (Mark 7:25), but aside from this there are no other clinical indications which would assist in determining precisely what constituted demon possession. The Gerasene (Gadarene) demoniac(s) behaved as though a separate personality was speaking through the man's mouth and using his physical strength to destructive ends. His psychosis was deeply entrenched, and it has been suggested that his self-imposed name of Legion furnishes a hint as to the origin of the shock which precipitated his illness, namely some atrocity committed in the area by the Rom. legion, possibly the massacre of children. Whether this is actually the case or not, the sufferer spoke as though possessed in the most literal sense, and the phenomena which accompanied his cure did nothing to dispel this notion in the minds of those who witnessed it. The Capernaum madman spoke as though he was a victim of multiple personality, and his convulsive interlude during the healing might have resulted from the discharging of long repressed emotion in the subconscious mind. The narratives concerning the blind and dumb demoniac are too vague to admit of pronouncements concerning the nature of the affliction, unlike those of the young woman with divinatory gifts, who seems in point of fact to have been little more than a fortune teller or soothsayer. While such individuals were popularly supposed to be "possessed," they certainly came into a different category from the mentally afflicted, since they were not diseased in any clinical sense. One interesting form of possession (Matt 12:43-45) showed that the spirits were sometimes concerned with moral evil. Quite obviously a man cannot effect his own moral reformation merely by expelling the "demons" within and leaving a spiritual vacuum. What is needed to sustain human efforts at reformation is the entrance of the spirit of God.

Evidences of contemporary survivals of the Biblical type of demon possession have been described from oriental countries by medical and other missionaries. Generally the phenomenon assumed the form of characteristic personality possession, and when the individuals concerned had been exorcized they subsequently led normal healthy lives. A modern psychiatrist would describe many cases of "possession" by quite different terms, which, however, prove to be no more meaningful than those of the Bible. The soundest approach to the situation is ultimately a theological one, which recognizes that because of the depravity of human nature the mind is peculiarly liable to the influence of evil. In imbalance this constitutes a form of possession, however mild, since the personality is then at the disposal of the powers of darkness to some extent.

BIBLIOGRAPHY. R. C. Thompson, *The Devils and Evil Spirits of Babylonia* (1903); *Semitic Magic* (1908); H. Kaupel, *Die Dämonen im AT* (1930); J. Trachtenberg, *Jewish Magic and Superstition* (1939); L. D. Weatherhead, *Psychology, Religion and Healing* (1951), 62-70; T. H. Gaster, IDB, I, 817-824; R. K. Harrison, IDB, I, 853, 854.

R. K. HARRISON

DEMOPHON, *Δημοφῶν*. This man was described as a district governor in Pal. during the Maccabean era (2 Macc 12:2). With him were mentioned three other governors, Timothy, Apollonius and Hieronymus, who were in favor of the Hellenizing policy of the Seleucid regime. This brought them into conflict with the more orthodox segments of Jewry, provoking local disturbances.

R. K. HARRISON

DEMYTHOLOGIZATION. *See* BIBLICAL CRITICISM.

DENARIUS. *See* COINS.

DEN OF LIONS, Aram. גב, in the phrase אריותא גב, *a pit* or trenched out "den" of lions, mentioned ten times in Daniel 6:27-24. The Babylonians and Assyrians kept lions captured in the marshlands of the Near E as beasts for hunting and as pets. They are shown in the magnificent reliefs of the Neo-Assyrian rulers Ashurnasirpal II (883-859 B.C.) at Nimrud and Ashurbanipal (668-627 B.C.) at Nineveh. The later Medo-Persian rulers continued this practice. Although no visual representation of such a punishment has survived, the condemnation to a "trial by ordeal" has many precedents in Mesopotamian-Iranian law. When Daniel was spared his accusers were condemned to the same fate (Dan 6:24). The "lion's den" is mentioned in other OT passages as a frightful and awesome place (Job 38:39-41).

W. WHITE, JR.

DENY (כחש, meaning *to deceive, lie* [Gen 18:15; Lev 6:3]; מנע, meaning *to withhold, refuse* [1 Kings 20:7; Prov 30:7] KJV; ἀρνέομαι, meaning *to say no, reject, disown* [Matt 10:33; Acts 3:13]; ἀπαρνέομαι; this compound word has same meaning as ἀρνέομαι [Luke 9:23; John 13:38]). The word "deny" is a composite of deeper meanings as can be seen from the various Heb. and Gr. words from which it is tr.

First, there is the concept of denying by lying. Sarah denied/lied that she laughed in Genesis 18:15. In Proverbs 30:9 the writer is concerned lest he come to deny God by lying about his knowledge of God. Peter denied the Lord by lying about his involvement with Jesus (Matt 26:70, 72).

Second, there is the idea of denying by withholding something from someone. The writer is requesting two things in Proverbs 30:7, and he asks that they not be denied/withheld from him before he dies. This same idea is seen in Genesis 30:2 where Jacob is expressing his anger against Rachel in that she feels that Jacob is at fault because she had not yet conceived a child. The attitude of denying oneself (Matt 16:24; Mark 8:34) would come under this second category as well. It is the withholding or the refusing of one's self-interest and personal ambition in acknowledgement of Jesus Christ.

Third, there is denial by rejecting or disowning someone or something. Many Jews of Jerusalem rejected Jesus as Messiah (Acts 3:13). Joshua established a monument as a reminder to the people that they not disown or reject the God who led them into the Promised Land (Josh 24:26). Job was concerned that he not put his confidence or trust in gold, lest he reject God (Job 31:28).

G. GIACUMAKIS, JR.

DEPOSIT (פקדון [Lev 6:2, 4]; παραθήκην [1 Tim 6:20; 2 Tim 1:12, 14]). An individual in the Biblical world left a deposit either as security or for safekeeping. Since there were no banks or security houses in the ancient world, it would not be uncommon for an individual to deposit valuables with a friend or neighbor if he were going on a trip.

Specific laws are spelled out in Exodus 22:7-13 and Leviticus 6:1-7 concerning the protection of deposits. The person to whom goods or money are entrusted, bears a heavy responsibility to watch over those goods. If it can be proven that he was negligent with that which he has been entrusted, then he is responsible to pay the owner in full.

In 2 Maccabees 3 Seleucus sends his emissary Heliodorus to confiscate the money in the Temple treasury. Onias, the high priest, attempts to discourage him by mentioning that many widows and orphans had deposits in the treasury, thus showing the practice in Jerusalem at this late period.

The deposit in the NT is primarily the Gospel which has been entrusted to the apostles and to the disciples in order that they would proclaim it and teach it faithfully. Paul attempts to impress Timothy with this fact (1 Tim 6:20).

G. GIACUMAKIS, JR.

DEPRAVITY. Scripture uniformly traces voluntary transgression to its root cause in sinful human nature. Sinful acts are the fruit of a depraved nature (cf. Prov 4:23; Mark 7:20-23).

In Biblical history man's depravity assumes particular prominence in the antediluvian period. The depravity of man is characterized by potency ("was great in the earth"), inwardness ("every imagination of the thoughts of his heart was only evil") and invariability ("evil continually"). The Flood which man's depravity called forth swept away sinners, but it could not eradicate depravity (cf. Pss 14:1-4; 51:5; 58:3). When Jeremiah contended against an external observance of religion which did not arise from inward love of God he emphasized the fact of man's depravity (Jer 17:9). In His conflict with the Pharisees our Lord drew attention to the innate perversity of man's heart (Mark 7:20-23; John 3:6). According to the teaching of Paul (Rom 5:19) all men have depraved natures, for all men have imputed to them the sin of Adam which carries with it "involvement in the perversity apart from which Adam's sin would be meaningless and its imputation an impossible abstraction" (J. Murray, NBD, p. 1191). With a chain of quotations from the Psalms Paul proves that depravity is a deep-seated and universal moral perversity (Rom 3:10-18).

Because he is depraved man turns aside from God (3:12). He is incapable of pleasing God, since even his "good" actions do not spring from the principle of love to God which finds expression in obedience to God's law (8:7, 8). Depravity is not partial, extending to part of mankind only, or to only part of man's nature. It is total. This description should not, however, be misunderstood. It does not mean that man is as thoroughly wicked as he could possibly become. Neither does it mean that the unregenerate sinner is lacking in an innate knowledge of God (1:19-21), or is without a conscience that distinguishes between good and evil (2:15, 16). Nor does it imply that the sinner does not, and cannot, approve of virtuous character, or that he is incapable of kindness toward his fellow men (Luke 11:13). Positively, it does mean that inherent corruption extends to every aspect of man's nature. He is depraved in *all* the faculties and powers of his body and soul.

The implications of the Biblical doctrine of depravity are far-reaching. First, since man is incapable of spiritual good his salvation must be entirely of grace. In particular this means that he must be renewed in all his faculties by the Holy Spirit. Second, evangelism and apologetics should proceed on the assumption that man's reason is as corrupted as his will and his affections. While the truth of the Gospel will be presented to the mind there will be the awareness that without the enlightenment of the Holy Spirit the sinner remains in darkness (1 Cor 2:14). Finally, in the realm of sanctification, true holiness will be defined not merely in terms of outward actions, but also in respect of the inward principles of positive desire for the glory of God and love of His commandments. *See* SINNER.

BIBLIOGRAPHY. J. Murray, "Sin," NBD, 1189-1193; W. Grundmann, TDNT, 267-316; J. Edwards, Works I (1834), 143-233; F. R. Tennant, *The Concept of Sin* (1912).

D. P. KINGDON

DEPTHS (מצולה, meaning *deep* [Exod 15:5; Ps 68:22]; עמק, meaning *deep area* or *valley* [Prov 9:18]; תהום, meaning *depth of sea* or *primeval ocean* [Job 28:14]; ἄβυσσος, meaning *bottomless abyss* [Luke 8:31]; βάθος [Mark 4:5; Rom 8:39]). The concept of "depths" or the "deep" in the Biblical world verged on the mysterious. The Babylonians believed that the primeval ocean is that which was the source of the universe. The ocean personified as Tiamat is ultimately defeated by Marduk, the god of Babylon, and becomes divided into the heavens above and the earth beneath. The ancient Hebrews along with other Near Eastern peoples thought of the earth as lying flat on top of a subterranean ocean. In Egyp. funerary texts part of the nether world is an underground body of water. *Tehom* in Ugaritic appears as *thm* and as the dual *thmtm* (the two deeps, U.T. #2537) and shows the division of heaven and earth.

Even though there are three Heb. words tr. as "depths" or "deep," *tehom* is by far the most common word. It is almost always in a context, either literally or figuratively, of primordial waters. Leviathan, the mythological sea monster often referred to symbolically, is said to dwell in the depths (Isa 27:1). It is evident that the concept of the after-life or the nether world is not quite as developed in the OT as it is in the NT. The spiritual world beyond the grave is somewhat obscure, even though the God of the ages has a place for believers quite separate from the dwelling place of the wicked.

Abussos is the Gr. word which is parallel to the Heb. *tehom*. It is the bottomless pit of the Book of Revelation and a place of punishment. *Bathos* is not quite as "negative" as *abussos* and is used often in a fig. way as illustrated in Paul's letter to the Romans: ". . . nor height, nor *depth*, nor any other created thing, shall be able to separate us from the love of God . . ." (Rom 8:39).

BIBLIOGRAPHY. J. Gray, *The Legacy of Canaan* (1957); C. F. Pfeiffer, "Lotan and Leviathan," EQ 32 (1960), 208f; G. L. Archer, *A Survey of the Old Testament Introduction* (1964); C. H. Gordon, *Ugaritic Textbook* (1965), 497; T. H. Gaster, *Myth, Legend and Custom in the OT* (1969).

G. GIACUMAKIS, JR.

DEPUTY. 1. נִצָּב. A ruler appointed to function in lieu of a king (1 Kings 22:47).

2. פֶּחָה, RSV "governor" (Esth 8:9; 9:3). Only in Esther does the RSV tr. it "deputy," where it refers to one type of Pers. governor.

3. Ἀνθύπατος, RSV "proconsul" (Acts 13:7, 8, 12; 19:38) and ἀνθυπατεύω, verbal form of same (18:12). The rulers appointed over the relatively stable Rom. provinces which were under the jurisdiction of the Senate as Sergius Paulus, over Cyprus, and Gallio, over Achaia.

W. L. LIEFELD

DERBE dûr' bĭ (Δέρβη). The name of this city, situated in the southeastern part of the Lycaonian region of Rom. Galatia, may derive from a dialectical word for the juniper tree. It was the most easterly locality visited by Paul and Barnabas on the journey in which they established the churches of southern Galatia. The reason for pausing at this point is plain to see

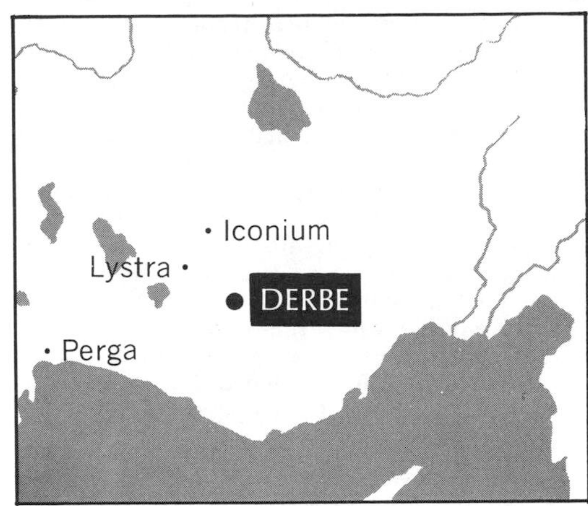

if Paul's Rom. strategy is taken into account. To proceed further E would have taken them beyond the confines of the Rom. province, and into the territory of a client kingdom (Acts 14:6, 7). Paul and Silas visited the place as they moved westward on the next journey through Asia Minor (Acts 15:40-16:1). Coming from Cilicia, Paul reached Derbe first, in passing on to Lystra.

The site of Derbe has been a matter of considerable debate. The last chapter of Ramsay's study of the cities of St. Paul (pp. 385ff.) discusses the matter at great length, but the precise locality seems to have been established in 1956 by M. Ballance, at Kerti Hüyük, some thirteen m. NNE of Karaman, or Laranda, and sixty m. from Lystra. Therefore, as F. F. Bruce remarks, the closing words of Acts 14:20 must necessarily be tr.: "and on the morrow he set out with Barnabas for Derbe." Derbe must also have been on the route of Paul's third journey, but wins no mention.

Derbe has left no great mark on history. Amyntas, ruler of Galatia from 39 to 25 B.C., held the area as part of his domain, and Derbe must have passed with the rest of his territory into Rom. hands in the year of his death (25 B.C.). From A.D. 41 to 72, it was dignified with the prefix Claudia, in recognition of its position as a frontier town of the province. This covered the period of the visits of Paul and the establishment of the Christian community in the area. Of that community, one Gaius is known. He traveled with Paul (Acts 20:4), no doubt as one of the representatives of the Galatian churches in the deputation that carried monetary contributions for the poor of the Jerusalem church.

BIBLIOGRAPHY. W. M. Ramsay, *Cities of St. Paul* (1908), 385ff.; M. Ballance, *The Site of Derbe: A New Inscription* (*Anatolian Studies*, VII) (1957), 147ff.

E. M. BLAIKLOCK

DESCENT INTO HADES (HELL) hā' dēz (Heb. שְׁאוֹל, LXX καταβαίνειν εἰς ᾅδου; κατελθόντα εἰς τὰ κατώτατα; cf. *descendit ad inferna*[*inferos*]). The descent into Hades or Hell is an article in the doctrinal tradition of the entire Christian Church. It is strange, however, that few doctrinal statements have had more research and less clarity of understanding than this single statement. Not only are the sources of tradition blurred, but Scripture passages alleged to throw light on the doctrine are denied by some authorities as source material, and those which are used as support create problems in exegesis even to every single word. Because of these obscurities, some denominations do not now include "He descended into Hades" in their liturgical use of the Apostles' Creed.

A. The tradition. This particular expression does not appear in the early Rom. Symbol but makes its first appearance in the Symbol of Aquileia by Rufinus (cf. Art., Apostles' Creed). It appeared in the Fourth Sirmian Formula in A.D. 359, in the same year in the Formula of Nice and again in Constantinople in A.D. 360. Its appearance in these creedal statements, however, reflected an earlier tradition, as it had already been mentioned by Clement of Alexandria, Tertullian, Justin Martyr, and Irenaeus. Thus there is a clear tracing to the apostolic period. The question still remains what was understood during the patristic period and in the early creedal statements. Was the descent for the deliverance of the OT saints? Was it an offer of the Gospel to those who had not heard it? Was it a victorious battle with Satan who tried to restrain Christ? None of these questions is clearly answered, and in some such form they still remain.

The Early Church had hard questions about what happened between Christ's death and resurrection, questions akin to those reflected in the Thessalonian epistles regarding what would happen to those who died before Christ's Second Advent. Two problems were particularly clear: (1) Where was Christ's spirit between death and resurrection? (2) What was the fate of those who had died before the Gospel was preached? According to the climate of opinion of the day, Christ went to Hades (the abode of the dead) precisely because He was dead and buried. What, then, was He like there, and what did He do there? As far as can be known now, the beginnings of this doctrine of the Church rest more in tradition, for which there are now no clear answers, than in Biblical interpretation which seems to have been a later development used to justify the tradition.

What can be understood of the nature of the abode of the dead in the day in which the tradition arose? There is the possibility of provisional judgment on the soul at death, awaiting the last day judgment, a provisional place of punishment (Luke 16:23), something of Gehenna (Matt 5:22, 29ff.), or the furnace of fire (13:42, 50), from which there is a possible transition to Paradise before the last day, the latter view playing into Roman Catholic hands on their position on Purgatory. What can be said then of a provisional state of salvation, as, for example, Abraham's bosom (Luke 16:22) or the kingdom of heaven (Matt 25:34; Luke 13:29; 2 Tim 4:18; 2 Pet 1:11), or Jesus' words to the thief on the cross, "Truly, I say to you, today you will be with me in Paradise" (Luke 23:43)? These questions are further aggravated in the preaching of Peter where he applies to Jesus the words of Psalm 16:10, "For thou wilt not abandon my soul to Hades, nor let thy Holy One see corruption" (Acts 2:27). Jesus had applied Isaiah 61:1 to His own ministry, "He has sent me to proclaim release to the captives . . ." (Luke 4:18), and this was suggested by some as having to do with those in the prison house of Hades.

B. Exegesis. The basic text used in support of the *Descensus* is 1 Peter 3:19, with the wider context of 1 Peter 3:17-22. Interestingly enough, the basic text does not expressly state (as does the Apostles' Creed) that Christ even descended into the realm of death, i.e., Hades. Interest is restricted to two particular facts: (1) that Christ preached and (2) that His preaching was for "spirits in prison." Of significance in interpretation is the verb for preaching. In the NT this is always the careful expression for the announcing of the "kerygma," i.e., the proclamation of the Christian Gospel that Jesus is the Christ, that the Suffering Servant is the Lord. One can assume, therefore, that this is the content of the preaching to the "spirits in prison." Whether it was a message of judgment or release on this occasion is not even mentioned, and the reader is shut up to the single idea of the proclamation of the Gospel. That He went in the spirit and not in the flesh seems perfectly clear from the context, although this raises serious questions for the Lutheran tradition with their insistence on the ubiquity of Christ's body.

Apart from the message preached, there are impossible questions about the nature of "the spirits in prison." Although there is some light shed on this by a reference to Noah (1 Pet 3:20) and a reference to baptism (3:21), the character of these "spirits" is so confusing that attempts have been made to evade the thrust of the passage entirely. Rendall Harris, for example, insists that the Scripture contains a textual error in which the name of Enoch has been dropped out, and that there is, therefore, another reference to the apocryphal Enoch (relating to Gen 6:1-4) with scriptural authority equal to that of Jude 14. Peter was trying to give support to Christians under the pressure of evil men, and reading Jude from the sixth v. through the sixteenth, one obtains the impression that there are no distinctions between angels and men, and that exceptionally evil persons often assumed superhuman proportions. The relevant passage is in 1 Enoch 67:4-69:1 and esp. 67:12, "This judgment wherewith the angels are judged is a testimony for the kings and the mighty who possess the earth." Although brilliant work has been done by Harris and supported by both Moffat and Goodspeed, there is no real evidence at all for their conjectures. Selwyn makes out of this passage that Christ's death was a proclamation to the powers of evil. "What St. Peter and St. Paul assert of these powers of evil, as the divine Master asserted before them, is that 'In Christ's death their end is sealed'." This may well be true, but there is no evidence for such an interpretation of this passage.

The simplest meaning, although still an unsatisfactory one, is that the Lord, between His death and resurrection, descended into Hades, although Peter does not say so (Hades or Sheol could be in this case a place of punishment or bliss or some such intermediate state) and preached to certain spirits in prison there. Possibly, judging from the context in 1 Peter, they could have been the fallen angels spoken of in Genesis 6:1-4 or, more likely, the spirits of that rebellious generation who perished in the flood (Gen 6:12ff.).

C. Church doctrine. 1. *The Roman Catholic position.* Christ descended into hell in the interval between His death and resurrection in the soul, and not in the body. The scene of the Descent is the forecourt of hell, the *limbus patrum*. The purpose of the Descent was to show His power and glory even in the underworld and to comfort and deliver the souls of the just held captive there, i.e., take them to heaven.

Although this is the official position, the theologians of the church are still left with many unsolved problems: (1) If Jesus promised Paradise to the thief on the cross, what is the relationship of Paradise to His time in hell, or is one to assume that Paradise is wherever Christ is? (2) Where was Jesus' abode during the forty resurrection days between His preaching in hell and His ascension? In other words, where was He when He was not manifested to His followers? (3) After the incarnation can one think of Jesus Christ apart from His humanity? If so, what was His nature when only His spirit descended into hell while His body lay in the grave? (4) Does the passage in 1 Peter refer to the Descent at all?

2. The Lutheran position. The Lutherans are faced with the difficulties of other doctrines as related to the Descent, such as the ubiquity of Christ's body and the problem of soul sleep. The Lutheran problem is intensified by the apparent discrepancies between the theological position and the popular discourses. Luther seems to give a definition in his Easter sermon of 13 April 1533 (Earl. ed [Ger] XIX, 40-54). "The Lord Christ—His entire person, God and man, with body and soul undivided—had journeyed to hell, and had, in person, demolished Hell and bound the Devil." Apparently in such a statement Luther has accepted ubiquity and dismissed its problems. In his exordium on this Easter discourse he commented, "And it pleases me well that, for the simple, it (*Descensus*) should be painted, played, sung or spoken . . . and I shall be quite content if people do not vex themselves greatly with high and subtle thoughts as to how it was carried out" (Earl. ed. [Ger] XIX, 40). Regarding the problem of the whole person, it is typical of Luther to say "Please God, the banner, doors, gate, and chains were of wood, or of iron, or did not exist at all." In short, Luther rather characteristically gives some affirmations and dismisses the explanations.

3. The Reformed position. Here there is a complete abandonment of Roman Catholic dogma. What matters is that Christ really died: *vere mortuus est.* He died and was buried and therefore went to Hades, the abode of the dead. He really died. Calvin thought that the Roman Catholic idea that the souls of the dead are confined in a prison is a *fabula.* He regarded the whole approach as "childish" (Inst. 1559, II, 16, 9.). With Augustine and Aquinas, Calvin looked upon the Petrine passage as referring to the agonies of the soul in death, what Jesus was experiencing during the hours of His death. He did not attribute the Petrine passage to the *Descensus* at all. The possibility that there is preaching to the dead and an offer of salvation after death has no basis in Scripture nor in any sound tradition of the Church in Reformed doctrine.

D. The modern emphasis. The descent into Hades is merely another way of emphasizing the depth of Christ's humiliation and His total identification with the sufferings of man in death. Furthermore, it is one more way of saying what the Creed already said; men are to reach a climax in the building up of phrases: crucified, dead, buried, descended into hell. The creedal phrase "descended into Hell" does not come out of the NT at all but develops out of the proclamation of His death and His "resurrection from the dead." James D. Smart puts it well: "Perhaps, then, 'He descended into Hell' is meant to say to us that Jesus not only shared with us our death and burial, that strange and troubling end of our familiar life, but so bound Himself into one with men that He knew the agony of man's utmost deprivation of life. . . . Hell is the existence of the man who is alone with himself with no way of access either to God or to his fellow man. The descent into hell, then, is Christ with man in hell, what no man could expect, what no man could deserve; the love of God reaching across the abyss that sin has made, bearing the pain and darkness of hell with man in order to deliver him to the brightness and joy of life with God. . . . This at last it means: that in His death He conquered death and hell, finishing the battle that He had waged throughout His life" (*The Creed in Christian Teaching*, p. 130ff.). *See* SHEOL.

Desert panorama of the wilderness of Judea, east of Bethlehem. ©*Lev*

BIBLIOGRAPHY. J. Calvin, *The Institutes*, ed. (1559), II, 16, 9; A. H. Strong, *Systematic Theology* (1907), 707, 708 (esp. good for exegesis); HERE (1922), vol. 4, 654-663; E. G. Selwyn, *The First Epistle of Peter* (1946); IB (1957), vol. 12, 132, 133; J. D. Smart, *The Creed in Christian Teaching* (1962), 130-144; B. Reicke, *Anchor Bible* (1964), vol. 37, 106-115.

A. LEITCH

DESERT (מדבר, meaning *uncultivated wilderness* [Exod 3:1; Jer 25:24]; ישימון, meaning *wilderness* [Ps 78:40]; ציה, meaning *waterless place* [Isa 41:18]; חרבה, meaning *dry area* or *wasteland* [Ps 102:6]; ἔρημος, meaning *solitary place* [Luke 1:80; Acts 8:26]).

1. Geography and culture. The "desert" or the "wilderness" is found mentioned in numerous contexts throughout the Bible. In most places it is a mild desert receiving some rain during the winter season of the year. Rain falls at intervals from November to April causing flooding at certain places because of the treeless soil, while the other six months it is extremely dry because of the *khamsin* or desert winds. The Negev in the S is the dryest area with only one to two inches of rain per year. Galilee, to the N, is at the other extreme as far as rainfall is concerned, for it receives as much as forty inches of rainfall per year. The reason for such a contrast in climate is the location of Pal. between the Mediterranean Sea and the harsh desert areas to the E. The winds from each direction are "in conflict" thus causing such extremes in climate.

The desert has had a far greater influence on the life and culture of Pal. than has the Sea. This is because of the lack of good natural harbors along the Palestinian coast, whereas to the N along the Syro-Phoenician (Lebanon) coast there are a number of excellent natural harbors. Solomon had to depend upon the Phoenicians to carry out his interests on the sea, for his own people and land were not accustomed to that way of life. There was continuous hostility between the inhabitants of the desert and those of the more fertile areas. The lure of the planted crops was more than a hungry bedouin tribe could withstand. In other periods of time when peace was negotiated, active trade took place over the desert routes bringing many goods from the S and E to Pal. The open avenue of trade or conflict with the desert kept Pal. Sem. Down through the centuries the Sem. nomads would either settle in Pal., or at least they would influence the culture to the extent that it remained Sem. in spite of the Mediterranean contacts. (Aharoni, LOB, p. 10.)

2. Biblical words. There are a number of words in the Bible which are tr. as "desert" or "wilderness." The most common and most inclusive word in the OT is *midbar*. The *midbar* not only includes the barren deserts of sand and rock, but also the steppe lands which can be classified as semidesert. These would be used for the grazing of sheep and goats at certain periods of the year. *Ṣîyyah* and *yəshimōn* tend to be a little more narrow in meaning referring to very dry and waterless areas. *Horbah* seems to carry the added meaning of wasteland—i.e. an area not only dry, but even if one could get water to it, it would prob. be useless.

The other two Heb. words which have been tr. in some VSS as "desert" or "wilderness" are better tr. as proper names. They are the words ערבה and נגב, and they identify specific desert areas. The 'Arabah is the barren plain located in the southern part of the Jordan valley, just N of the Dead Sea; S of the Dead Sea the narrow 'Arabah stretches all the way to the Gulf of Aqaba. The Negev is the great southern desert tucked between the Sinai peninsula to the W and the 'Arabah to the E.

The NT does not have quite the variety of Gr. words referring to the desert. *Erēmos* is used in relationship to the desert, not so much in reference to the desert's dryness, but more in the sense of a solitary or lonely place. In Mark 6 Jesus and His apostles went to the area around Bethsaida on the eastern shore of the Sea of Galilee. This area is called an *erēmos* or "lonely place," which even though it was classified as desert had some grassy areas (John 6:10).

3. Allegorical uses. The desert is presented both in a positive and in a negative way in its relationship to Israel. At the beginning of the nation's history, the desert was where God showed His power and concern for Israel (Jer 2 and 3). Hosea also sees God's love expressed in the desert for His people (Hos 13:5). Deborah sings praise to the God of Sinai and the desert (Judg 5:4, 5), and likewise Habakkuk as he speaks about God's deliverance of Israel (Hab 3:2-7).

The wilderness, however, also is seen as a place of sin. The golden calf scene took place in the desert (Exod 32:23). Korah's rebellion took place there (Num 16 and 17). At Shittim many of the Israelites identified with Baal of Peor (Num 25) and suffered the judgment of God.

BIBLIOGRAPHY. D. Baly, *The Geography of the Bible* (1957); Y. Aharoni, *The Land of the Bible* (1967); Y. Aharoni and M. Avi-Yonah *The Macmillan Bible Atlas* (1968); "Wilderness" *Encyclopedia Judaica* (1971), vol. 16, 511-513; E. Orni and E. Efrat, *Geography of Israel*, 3rd ed. (1971).

G. GIACUMAKIS, JR.

DESIRE (אביונה, caperberry). The word "desire" (Eccl 12:5) can be tr. "caperberry," "caper," or even "caper tree," in the Lat. Vul., the LXX and the Goodspeed VSS.

The caper is *Capparis sicula*, which grows all over Pal. and particularly around Jerusalem. The berries have an aphrodisiac effect. It is said that when the fruits fail to have a stimulating effect on men, the latter are really old! The plant grows like the ivy on walls and rocks, or spreads itself over the ground.

Capparis spinosa var. *canescens* is the wild form of the cultivated caper.

W. E. SHEWELL-COOPER

DESIRE. There are over nine different Heb. words which can be tr. into Eng. as "desire" as well as about the same number of Gr. words. Some of the words which are used are אוה ; רצון ; נפש ; משאלה ; מחמד ; חשק ; חפצ ; חמדה; תאוה ; תשוקה; *θέλειν*; *θέλημα*; *θεμησις*; *ἐπιθυμία*; *αἰτέω*; *ἐρωτάω*. Practically the whole spectrum of underlying psychological meanings are covered by the wide range of the above Heb. and Gr. words. This clearly shows how important a characteristic it is esp. as far as Scripture is concerned.

1. Craving. One aspect of this word is that of craving or covetousness. Covetousness is condemned and prohibited in the tenth commandment (Exod 20:17). Greed is seen as lying at the base of all sin and social injustice (Micah 2:1). The writers in Proverbs and Ecclesiastes indicate a number of times that envy and greed are never satisfied (Prov 27:20; Eccl 5:10). The psalmist expresses it as the "desire" of the wicked (Ps 10:3).

2. Love. Under the category of love would come friendship (Ps 133:1-3). Then there is the love/desire as expressed between a man and a woman so vividly written by the author of Song of Songs (Solomon). In Ezekiel 24:16 there is illustrated the love/desire between husband and wife. The expression of love or desire toward God is seen in Deuteronomy 19:9 and Romans 10:1.

3. Good or pleasure. This third aspect of the word desire involves delight or happiness in beauty and accomplishment. Solomon had accomplished his goal in the construction of the Temple (1 Kings 9:1). Solomon granted to the Queen of Sheba all that she desired which was good for her and her country (2 Chron 9:12). Handsomeness is called that which is desirable (Ezek 23:6). The suffering Servant of Isaiah 53 is not beautiful that He be desired (Isa 53:2).

4. Natural desires. These can be listed as hunger (Ps 145:16), protection and refuge (Ps 7:1), sexual desire separate from a love relationship (Deut 21:11).

Paul strongly stressed in the NT the conflict which takes place between the desires of the old nature without Christ and those of the new nature under the control of Jesus Christ (Rom 7). With spiritual growth the desires under the control of Christ would supersede those of the old nature.

BIBLIOGRAPHY. Ἐπιθυμία-ἡδονή, TDNT, III, 168-172 (1965); "Covetousness," *Encyclopedia Judaica* (1971).

G. GIACUMAKIS, JR.

DESIRE OF ALL NATIONS, THE. This phrase is found only in Haggai 2:7 (KJV) in a context prob. quoted in Hebrews 12:26, 27. The prophet predicts glory for Zerubbabel's temple greater in the future than in the present. The v. is often taken as a Messianic prediction like several vv. of Haggai's compatriot, Zechariah (Zech 3:8; 9:9). The RSV (Hag 2:7) trs. "the treasures of all nations shall come in" (ASV similar), taking the v. to mean that the temple will be enriched by foreign gifts or tribute. This reading changes the sing. noun "desire" to a pl. to agree with the verb. The LXX supports this reading, but the Vul., Syr., and Targ. are against it. The tr. "treasures" for this word is not witnessed elsewhere. It seems from the context that the prophet was looking to the distant future. In Haggai 2:22, 23 he apparently refers to Zerubbabel symbolically as the Messiah, just as Zechariah 6:12 does to Joshua. Haggai 2:7 possibly refers not to the arrival of the Messiah, but to the coming of the leaders of the Gentiles (Gr. *eklekta*) to join in worship in the Messianic age.

R. L. HARRIS

DESOLATION, ABOMINATION. *See* ABOMINATION OF DESOLATION.

DESSAU dĕs' ô, dĕs'ə u (Δεσσαού). ERV LESSAU. A village where the Jews joined battle with Nicanor, a general of Antiochus Epiphanes, in Maccabean times (2 Macc 14:16).

DESTINY (מְנִי) a pagan god, along with Fortune in Isaiah 65:11, ASV. One may guess that there is some similarity with the Stoic theory of fate, but the fact that the founder of Stoicism, Zeno, was a Semite is insufficient ground for asserting any historical connection.

Pagan ideas of fate or destiny vary. In Gr. mythology and in some popular forms of Mohammedanism the hour of death is determined, and perhaps the place also, but the ordinary course of life is left to chance. Stoicism, more consistently, insisted that every event was determined. Sometimes fate is supposed to be a blind, purposeless force, rather than providence, foresight, and wise planning. Again, the Stoics, particularly in later times, asserted the wisdom and foresight of God.

Though the word "destiny" does not occur in the KJV and the Gr. word does not occur in the NT, the idea, divested of pagan implications, is frequent in the Bible. God sees the end from the beginning. He has appointed a destiny for the Christian, for the unbeliever, for Israel, and for other nations. But instead of the word "destiny," the Bible speaks of providence, predestination, and last things or eschatology (q.v.).

As the Westminster Shorter Catechism says, "God's works of providence are, his most holy, wise, and powerful preserving and governing all his creatures, and all their actions."

G. H. CLARK

DESTROYER, THE (הַמַּשְׁחִית ; ὁ ὀλοθρεύων, *the destroyer*; ὀλοθρευτής, *destroyer*). A superhuman being, used as an instrument of God's wrath in the execution of His judgment. It is difficult to say whether this is a good angel used by God as an agent of destruction, or Satan or one of his minions. If a good angel, God could use it to bring both blessing and destruction.

The term is used only twice (Exod 12:23 [cf. Heb 11:28]; 1 Cor 10:10). In the Exodus passage, it is used in connection with the tenth plague of Egypt, the destruction of the Egyptian first-born. In the 1 Corinthians passage Paul warned against grumbling, as some Israelites did in the wilderness and were destroyed by the Destroyer. It is thought by some that the Destroyer referred to by Paul was the fiery serpents God sent to bring death to the complaining Israelites.

In the time of David the Lord sent an angel to smite the people by means of a plague because David had made a census of the people (2 Sam 24:16). In Hezekiah's time in a single night an angel destroyed 185,000 men in the Assyrian camp (2 Kings 19:35). The prophet Ezekiel saw in a vision a number of angels executing judgment upon Jerusalem and Judah (Ezek 9:5-7). The psalmist petitioned that the angel of the Lord would drive his enemies like dust before the wind (Ps 35:5, 6). The composer of Psalm 78:49 believed that angels could smite one's enemies upon God's command. In the OT Apoc., Jeremiah warned that the angel of God who was with the Israelites would punish them if they apostatized (Ep Jer 6:5-7), and in 2 Maccabees 3:24-26, Heliodorus was whipped by angels when he attempted to plunder the Temple at Jerusalem.

BIBLIOGRAPHY. W. Eichrodt, *Theology of the Old Testament*, I (1961), 201, 202.

S. BARABAS

DESTROYING LOCUST. *See* LOCUST.

DESTRUCTION, CITY OF. *See* HELIOPOLIS.

DEUEL dōō' əl (דְּעוּאֵל, meaning *God knows*). The fame of Deuel is in his son Eliasaph (אֶלְיָסָף "God has added"). When Moses and Aaron would take a census of the people at Sinai, Eliasaph, son of Deuel, was with them to record the male Gadites of twenty years old and up, 45,650 (Num 1:14; 2:14). When the Tabernacle was complete Eliasaph brought the large donation of a tribal leader on the seventh of twelve days (7:42, 47). He, then, was leader of Gad's host (1:24, 25).

Once in these Heb. references the name is spelled Reuel (רעואל *God is friend*), also the name of four others. In the LXX it is always with an R. The Heb. ד and ר are easily mistaken for each other.

W. G. BROWN

DEUTERO-CANONICAL BOOKS. *See* APOCRYPHA, O. T.

DEUTERONOMY (Δευτερονόμιον). **A. Introduction.** The Eng. title of Deuteronomy, meaning "repetition of the law," is derived from the LXX Δευτερονόμιον and the Vul. *Deuteronomium.* This inaccurate rendering is based on Deuteronomy 17:18 where the words "a copy of this law" (התורה הזאת משנה) are incorrectly tr. τὸ Δευτερονόμιον τοῦτο as if the Heb. had been "this copy of the law" (הזה משנה התורה). This title, however, is not inappropriate, for the book does include, along with much new matter, a repetition or reformulation of a large part of the laws. In Heb. lit. the book was known by a title taken from its opening words, "these are the words" (אלה הדברים), or simply, "words" (דברים).

B. Content. Deuteronomy claims to consist almost entirely of the farewell speeches of Moses addressed to the new generation which had grown to manhood in the wilderness. The speeches are dated in the eleventh month of the forty years of wandering (1:3) and it is stated that Moses wrote as well as spoke them (31:9, 22, 24).

The three main discourses are preceded by a brief introduction (1:1-5) and followed by an epilogue (34) which narrates the death of Moses. The first discourse is chiefly historical and hortatory, reviewing the life of Israel in the wilderness from the mountain of Horeb or Sinai to the land of Moab (1:6-4:43). This discourse contains a brief statement about setting aside three cities of refuge on the other side of the Jordan (4:41-43) and announces the following exposition of the law by Moses under the triple heading of testimonies, statutes, and ordinances. The chief part of this discourse (chs. 5-26), opens with an exposition of the Ten Commandments and develops particularly the first comandment at great length (chs. 5-11). Next follow the laws which can be considered under the categories of ceremonial (12:1-16:17), civil (16:18-18:22), and criminal (19:1-21:9). This is followed by the miscellaneous laws pertaining to family and property (21:10-25:19).

The ceremonial laws treat place of worship (12:1-28); idolatry (12:29-13:18; 16:21-17:7); clean and unclean food (14:1-21); tithes (14:22-29); remittance or release (15:1-18); setting aside of firstlings as holy (15:19-23); holy seasons (16:1-17).

The civil ordinances treat appointment of judges (16:18-20; 17:8-13); election of a king (17:14-20); regulations concerning the rights and revenues of priests and Levites (18:1-8); and rules concerning prophets (18:9-22).

The criminal laws cover the manslayer and cities of refuge (19:1-14); false testimony (19:15-21); conduct of war (20:1-20); expiation of an undetected murder (21:1-9); and crime punishable by hanging (21:22, 23).

The collection of miscellaneous laws cover such a variety of subjects as marriage with a female captive (21:10-14); right of primogeniture (21:15-17); disobedient son (21:18-21); kindness to animals (22:1-4, 6-8); prohibition of various mixtures (22:5, 9-11); twisted cords on garments (22:12); punishment of unchastity

A fragment of Deuteronomy 32 (Song of Moses) from Qumran.

(22:13-29); exclusion from the congregation (23:1-9); ritual cleanness in the camp (23:10-15); runaway slaves (23:16, 17); temple prostitutes (23:18, 19); exaction of interest (23:20, 21); vows (23:22-24); use of neighbor's fruit and corn (23:25); remarriage after divorce (24:1-4); exemption of newly-married men from war service (24:5); pledge (24:6, 10-13, 17, 18); man-stealing (24:7); leprosy (24:8, 9); wages (24:14, 15); parents and children (24:16); treatment of strangers, orphans, and widows (24:17-22); excessive punishment (25:1-3); muzzling the laboring ox (25:4); Levirate marriage (25:5-10); indecent assault (25:11, 12); weights and measures (25:13-16); and the extermination of Amalek (25:17-19).

Chapters 26 and 27 present the didactic applications of these laws and ch. 28 is a declaration of the blessings and curses which will overtake the people if they observe or neglect the prescribed statutes and ordinances.

The third discourse (chs. 29, 30) consists of a supplementary address, exhorting the people to accept the terms of the new covenant and promising them forgiveness in case of sin, if attended by wholehearted repentance. These three addresses are followed by a collection of miscellaneous materials such as Moses' farewell, his deliverance of the law to the priests, his commission to Joshua, the Song of Moses, and the Blessing of Moses (31-33).

At least three elements—historical, legislative, didactic—can be traced through the book. The references to history are usually with a didactic aim. The legislative element tends directly to secure the national well-being.

The tone of exhortation which runs through the earlier and later addresses pervades also the legislative portion. The laws are not systematically stated but are ethically expounded in order to set forth their relation to the theocratic principles laid down in chs. 5-11. The author's purpose is primarily hortatory; he is not a historian or jurist as much as he is a religious teacher.

The author wrote under a keen sense of idolatry and was deeply concerned to guard Israel against this, by insisting earnestly on the debt of gratitude and obedience it owed to its sovereign Lord. Therefore, the truths on which he dwells are the godhead of the Lord, His spirituality (Deut 4), His choice of Israel, and the love and faithfulness He has manifested toward it. From this is then deduced the need for Israel's loving devotion to Him, an absolute repudiation of all false gods, a warm and spontaneous obedience to His will, and a generous attitude toward men.

Throughout Exodus-Numbers the Lord speaks to Moses; through Deuteronomy Moses speaks to the people. Here Israel's redemptive history is tr. into living principles; Deuteronomy is more commentary than history. The purpose is to arouse Israel's loyalty to the Lord and His revealed law.

Deuteronomy clearly teaches that the relation of God to His people is more than law. The thought of the love of Israel toward her God, which is indeed laid down in the words of the Decalogue (Exod 20:6; Deut 5:10), is not required elsewhere in the Pentateuch, but in Deuteronomy is earnestly insisted upon (10:12; 12:1, 13, 22; 13:3; 19:9; 30:6, 16, 20). Appeals made to Israel to keep the commandments often are based on the recollection of God's might and of His terrible visitation, awe, fear; but the highest appeal is to the consciousness of His own free love (Deut 7:7, 8; 8:17; 9:4-6). Love indicating the people's affection and devotion to the Lord is again and again insisted upon as the true spring of all human action (5:10; 6:5; 7:8; 10:12, 15; 11:1, 13, 22; 13:8; 19:9; 30:16, 20).

The idea of Israel as "son" and the Lord as "father" is set forth in Deuteronomy. The loving God had given Israel life by redemption from Egypt; He had reared and educated Israel in the wilderness (Deut 8:2, 3, 16; 14:2). These new Israelites, born and trained in the desert, were to inherit the blessings promised to their fathers. This intimacy emphasizes the demand that Israel should cleave to the Lord (11:22; 13:4) and not follow "other gods" (6:14, 15; 7:4; 8:19, 20; 11:16, 17, 20; 30:17, 18). Because Israel was holy, she was not to join other gods (7:6). This spirit of holiness was also expressed by observing love toward neighbor, and charity toward poor, widow, orphan, Levite, stranger (10:18, 19; 24:17-21).

By means of the covenant, the Israelites became heirs of all the promises given to their fathers the patriarchs (4:31; 7:12; 8:18; 29:13). Israel was considered holy and peculiar, and esp. loved by the Lord (7:6; 14:2, 21; 26:18, 19; 28:9). They were indeed disciplined for their own good (8:2, 3, 5, 16), but also to be established as a special people, as the Lord's peculiar lot and inheritance (32:6, 9; 4:7).

The chief thought of Deuteronomy is the unique relation which the Lord, as a unique God, sustains to Israel as a unique people. The monotheism of Deuteronomy is very explicit: "Hear, O Israel: The LORD our God is one Lord." The LORD is the only God, "There is none else besides him" (4:35, 39; 6:4; 32:39), "He is God of gods, and Lord of lords" (10:17), "the living God" (5:26), "the faithful God who keeps covenant and steadfast love with those who love him and keep his commandments" (7:9), who despises graven images and every species of idolatry (7:25, 26; 12:31; 13:14; 18:12; 20:18; 27:15), to whom belong the heavens and the earth (10:14), who rules over all the nations (7:19), whose relation to Israel is near and personal (28:58). Being such a God, He is jealous of all rivals (7:4; 29:24-26; 31:16, 17), and therefore all temptations to idolatry must be removed from the land, the Canaanites must be destroyed, along with their altars and images (7:1-5, 16; 12:2, 3; 20:16-18).

The other nations feared their gods but Israel was expected not only to fear the Lord but also to love Him and cleave to Him (4:10; 5:29; 6:5; 10:12, 20; 11:1, 13, 22; 13:3, 4; 17:19; 19:9; 28:58; 30:6, 16, 20; 31:12, 13). Israel was destined to enjoy the highest privileges because the people were partakers of covenant blessings; all others were strangers and foreigners, except when admitted into Israel by special permission (23:1-8).

C. Analysis. In recent years scholars have compared the extra-Biblical covenant (suzerain—vassal) treaties of the ancient Near E with the Biblical material and some have concluded that Deuteronomy, to a great extent, follows the classic covenant pattern consisting of the following sections: preamble, historical prologue, stipulations, curses and blessings, invocation of oath deities, direction for deposit of duplicate treaty documents in sanctuaries, and periodic proclamation of the treaty of the vassal people. M. Kline (*Treaty of the Great King*) has made a detailed comparison of Deuteronomy with this classic treaty structure and made the following outline of Deuteronomy: I. Preamble: Covenant Mediator (1:1-5); II. Historical Prologue: Covenant History (1:6-4:49); III. Stipulations: Covenant Life (chs. 5-26); IV. Curses and Blessings: Covenant Ratification (chs. 27-30); V. Dynastic Disposition: Covenant Continuity (chs. 31-34).

Stylistically, this comparison of the pattern of the international suzerainty treaty is noteworthy. Deuteronomy is an exposition of the covenant concept and reveals that God's covenant with His people is a proclamation of His sovereignty and an instrument for binding His elect to Himself in a commitment of absolute allegiance. Ancient suzerainty treaties began with a preamble in which the speaker, the one who was declaring his lordship and demanding the vassals' allegiance, identified himself. The Deuteronomy preamble identifies the speaker as Moses (v. 1), but Moses, however, as the earthly, mediatorial representative of the Lord (v. 3), the heavenly Suzerain and ultimate Lord of this covenant. Following the preamble in the international suzerainty treaties there was a historical section, written in the I-thou style, which surveyed the previous relationships of lord and vassal. Benefits conferred by the lord upon the vassal were cited with a view to grounding the vassal's allegiance in a sense of gratitude and fear. All these features characterize Deuteronomy 1:6-4:49.

Following the historical section were the stipulations which constituted the long and crucial central section of the covenant. When suzerainty treaties were renewed, these stipulations were repeated but with modifications, esp. such as were necessary to meet the changing situation. So, in these Deuteronomy stipulations (5:1-26:19) Moses rehearses and reformulates the requirements promulgated in the Sinaitic Covenant. Also just as treaty stipulations customarily began with the fundamental and general demand for the vassal's absolute allegiance to the suzerain and then proceeded to various specific requirements, so Moses confronts Israel with the primary demand for consecration to the Lord (chs. 5-11) and then with the ancillary stipulations of covenant life (12:26).

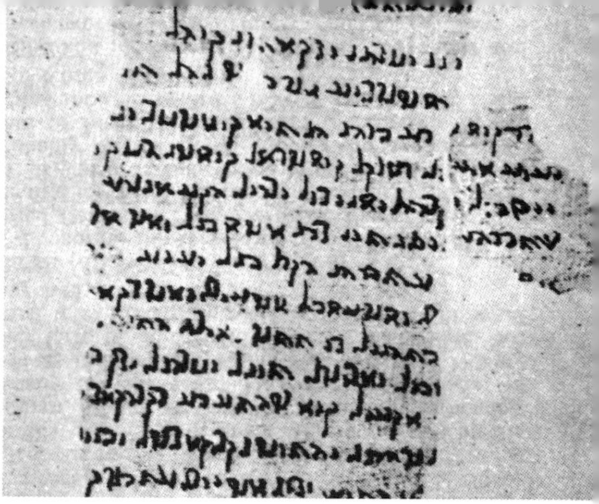

A small portion of the Nash Papyrus fragment of Deuteronomy 5. ©*B.A.*

The fourth standard division in the Near Eastern suzerainty treaties included the curses and blessings. In Deuteronomy this section is found in chs. 27-30. The final section of the covenant document has as its unifying theme the perpetuation of the covenant relationship. This succession is provided for by the appointment and commissioning of Joshua as dynastic heir to Moses in the office of mediatorial representative of the Lord (ch. 31). Included are two other standard elements in the international treaties. One is the invocation of covenant witnesses, here represented chiefly by the Song of Witness (ch. 32). The other is the direction for the disposition of the treaty document after the ceremony (31:9-13). By way of notarizing the document, an account of the death of Moses is affixed at the end (ch. 34).

The implications of this comparative evidence for the questions of the antiquity and authenticity of Deuteronomy are far-reaching. This kind of document with which Deuteronomy has been compared did not originate in some recurring ritual situations. Where, either in monarchic or pre-monarchic times, except in the very occasion to which Deuteronomy traces itself, can a historical situation be found in which such a treaty document is most appropriate?

This literary structure of Deuteronomy also has important implications for the way in which, having once been produced, this document would have been transmitted to subsequent generations. By their very nature treaties like Deuteronomy were inviolable. They were sealed legal documents; in fact, it was a practice to deposit such treaties in sanctuaries under the eye of the oath deities. There are examples in some of the extinct texts of specific curses pronounced against anyone who would in any way violate the treaty inscrs. Corresponding to these special stele curses is an injunction (Deut 4:2a): "You shall not add to the word which I command you, nor take from it."

This extra-Biblical evidence confirms and illuminates not isolated data in Deuteronomy but the Deuteronomy treaty in its very structure; this information argues against a long evolutionary process being required to produce a book like Deuteronomy.

D. Authorship. 1. *Critical views.* The traditional critical view (the Graf-Wellhausen hypothesis) claims that Deuteronomy (at least chs. 12-26) was first published in 621 B.C. when Hilkiah found "the book of the law" in the Temple during the eighteenth year of King Josiah (2 Kings 22:8). This book was written, so the critics claim, for the express purpose of promoting a religious reform, to include the abolition of the "high places," or local sanctuaries, supposed to have been perfectly legitimate up to that time, and to concentrate on the people's worship in Jerusalem. As a 7th cent. B.C. literary creation reflecting the teaching of the 8th cent. B.C. "ethical" prophets, Deuteronomy was accorded a position late in the evolutionary process which led, in Wellhausen's thought, from the primitive religion of the patriarchs through the henotheism of later times to the exalted monotheism of Deutero-Isaiah and the lit. of the exilic and postexilic period. If, however, as the critics claimed, the author was a prophet whose object was a religious reformation, and his aim was to abolish the "high places," why does he not mention them? If he wanted to centralize worship in Jerusalem, why not make it clear? Jerusalem is not even mentioned. Moreover, would a prophet of such oratorical and spiritual power as reflected in this book be afraid to proclaim his message openly, or prefer to remain unknown, write it in a book, and hide it in the Temple?

Many cogent arguments have been raised against the critical view which would date the book in the 7th cent. B.C., and connect it with Josiah's reformation. The law book discovered by Hilkiah was recognized immediately as an ancient code (2 Kings 22:13). Were they all deceived? Even Jeremiah (Jer 11:3, 4)? There were many persons who would have strong motives for exposing such a forgery. Also one wonders why such a code formulated in Josiah's time would include such archaic and anachronistic references as the command to exterminate the Canaanites (Deut 7:16, 22), and to blot out Amalek (25:17-19), the last remnants of which were completely destroyed in Hezekiah's time (1 Chron 4:41-43). It is esp. remarkable that if the document was composed shortly before the reign of Josiah, there should be no anachronisms in it betraying a post-Mosaic origin. There are no allusions to schism between Israel and Judah, no hint of Assyrian oppression through exaction of tribute, nor any threat of Israel's exile to Assyria or Babylon, but rather to Egypt (Deut 28:68). From a literary point of view it is well nigh impossible for a writer to conceal all traces of his age and circumstances, yet no Egyptologist has ever detected an anachronism in Deuteronomy.

Of course, the traditional critical view of the origin of Deuteronomy is an integral part of the documentary hypothesis; indeed, one might say that the question of Deuteronomy is the cornerstone of the documentary hypothesis. So the approach of the critics to the Book of Deuteronomy is based on their attitude toward the origin and nature of the Pentateuch itself, as well as to the whole question of the development of Israelite religion. The classical critical approach to Deuteronomy has been altered in various ways in recent years so that at the present time the origin of the Book of Deuteronomy is among the most controversial problems with the critics. Serious problems raised by late date theories have caused the critics to make various modifications which confuse and cancel each other. Almost every period has been advanced as the age in which the book was composed, while its authorship has been ascribed variously to Moses himself, Samuel or, less specifically to prophetic, priestly, and other circles. As to its origin, it has been associated with such sanctuaries as Jerusalem, Shechem and Bethel or, less precisely, to northern Israel or Judah. A convenient survey of the evolution of these differing and conflicting theories of the critics may be found in E. W. Nicholson's *Deuteronomy and Tradition* (1967).

2. *Traditional view.* The traditional view of the Mosaic authorship of Deuteronomy is based on the teaching of the Bible itself and Jewish and Christian tradition which was in full accord until the advent of higher criticism.

Deuteronomy is represented as emanating from Moses. Nearly forty times his name occurs, and in the majority of cases as the authoritative author of the subject matter. The first person is sometimes used (1:16, 18; 3:21; 29:5). It is expressly stated that Moses taught Israel these statutes and judgments in order that they should obey them in the land which they were about to enter (4:5, 14; 5:31). The book bears the message of one who is interested in Israel's political and religious *future.* A paternal mood runs throughout which marks it as Mosaic.

The Bible clearly indicates, "And Moses wrote this law, and gave it to the priests the sons of Levi. . . . When Moses had finished writing the words of this law in a book, to the very end, Moses commanded the Levites who carried the ark of the covenant of the LORD, 'Take this book of the law, and put it by the

Ruins atop Mt. Nebo. Tradition has it that Moses penned the book of Deuteronomy in this general area. © *R.B.*

side of the ark of the covenant of the LORD your God, that it may be there for a witness against you'" (Deut 31:9, 24-26). Here it is distinctly and emphatically stated that "Moses wrote this law." The simplest explanation is that Moses "wrote" the legislation itself, namely chs. 12-26. An unbroken line of tradition assigns authorship to Moses; this was accepted by the Lord Himself (Matt 19:8) and generally by the NT writers. The record of Moses' death is not as serious as some would claim. It is not out of order, even today, for an editor to furnish addenda to an autobiography, giving an account of the author's death. It will be noticed that the Book of Joshua is closed in the same way. This appendix may have been attached to the document soon after the death of Moses, or it may be, as some suppose, that what is now the end of Deuteronomy was once the beginning of Joshua. The author of the appendix could have been Joshua, the intimate friend of the great lawgiver and his successor as the leader of Israel. He was the one above all others who should have pronounced the eulogy upon his master after his death. Notice the expressions "Moses the servant of the LORD," and "Moses, the man of God." Neither of these phrases is found in the preceding part of the Pentateuch and it does not appear that Moses even assumed such titles for himself. It was a favorite method with Joshua, however, in speaking of his dead friend and leader. The words "Moses the servant of the Lord," occur more than a dozen times in the Book of Joshua, and are found in both the narrative matter and the speeches attributed to the author. The other expression also was known in his day for Caleb referred to "Moses, the man of God," in addressing him.

E. Background. 1. *Personal element.* The content of Deuteronomy contains what one would expect to find from the hand of Moses; the background reflects a Mosaic character. References to experiences which must have deeply stirred Moses' feelings crop up unexpectedly, such as "the house of bondage" (5:6), the recalling of the attack by the Amalekites (25:17), the burden of judgment (1:9-18), the murmurings of the people (9:22-24), the material of which the Ark was made (10:3), the enemies they had overcome. The references to Aaron (9:20ff.; 10:6ff.; 32:50) and Miriam (24:9) spring naturally from Moses but appear strange if merely inventions of a 7th cent. B.C. prophet.

Throughout chs. 12-26 Moses' name is absent, yet it is clearly assumed that he is the speaker. This is the more striking since his name is repeated no fewer than thirty-eight times in the narrative portions. His personality shines through by the intrusion here and there of the first person, esp. in the phrase, "I command thee," sometimes with the addition of "this day." This is particularly the case in the remarkable passage 18:15-18, with its reference to the people's memory of Horeb in v. 16. One can well imagine this intrusion with its promise coming from the mouth of Moses; but otherwise it loses much of its point. It is not easy to conceive of it as a device of a reformer, or to see how it could serve his purpose.

The personal element again appears, quite unexpectedly in 24:8, "Take heed, in an attack of leprosy, to be very careful to do according to all that the Levitical priests shall direct you; as I commanded them." The emergence of the first person in this verse is uncalled for, if not Mosaic. Then comes, "Remember what the LORD your God did to Miriam, on the way as you came forth out of Egypt." How natural for Moses to call to mind his own sister's folly and punishment; how strange if simply used by one intent on the reform of the cult!

Other incidents which must have deeply impressed Moses unexpectedly intrude into the law, such as the attack of the Amalekites (25:17), and the hiring of Balaam to curse (23:4).

The number and character of reminiscences is a striking feature. The mode of their occurrence is frequently quite incidental, such as the frequent references to Egypt and the reference to Miriam. They convey the impression that they issue from an old man who rebuked the people for disobedience as if they were children, and to display his anxiety that these younger hearers should "remember" and "not forget" his words, when he should be no longer there to guide (4:9-6:7).

There are also signs that the speaker has known the responsibility of leadership. He remembers the "ways" by which they traveled, the turnings, the treatment they received, the difficult crossings, and the places where water was attainable for the cattle.

There are names of events, all of which stirred Moses' feelings deeply, the tempting (Massah), striving (Meribah), destruction (Hormah), the burning (Taberah), the graves of lust (Kibroth-hattaavah) and the chastisement (Mosera). Is this combination of words pure accident, or is it not probable that these are the names which Moses himself attached to the events? It is significant that Moses is never praised until after his death (34:10).

It should also be noted that these reminiscences found in Deuteronomy cover the whole period of Moses' life but never transgress that limit. The author remembers the "garden of vegetables" artificially watered (11:10), the plagues which fell on Pharaoh (7:18), his household (6:22), and his land (29:2). He also recalls the Passover instituted in the month of Abib (16:1), the departure "in haste" and "at even" (16:3, 6 KJV), and the destruction of Pharaoh's army in the Red Sea "to this day" (11:4), the proving at Massah (6:16; 8:3, 16; 9:22), and the attack by Amalek (25:17-19).

Also remembered are the covenant in Horeb, the ten "words" and the "ark of acacia wood" (10:1-3), and Moses' prayer for Aaron (9:20). The words, "stamped it," and "the brook that descended from the mount" are peculiar to Deuteronomy. Also specific reference is made to the forty years in the wilderness (8:2, 19; 11:5), "great and terrible" (1:19), where were "fiery serpents and scorpions" (8:15), the manna (8:3, 16), the water from the "rock of flint" (8:15 ASV), the divine care (2:7; 8:3), and the judgment on Dathan and Abiram (11:6). Also recalled are the stay in Kadesh-barnea (1:19-46), the pillar of fire, the pitching of the tents, the mission of the twelve spies, and the long journey around Edom, Moab, and Ammon. Note also the reference "unto this place" (9:7-11:5) as the long wilderness journey terminated.

This is a formidable list when compared to the few references found in the prophetic writings. There is nothing to compare with this amount of detail in any of the speeches recorded in the historical books and much less than this would have sufficed to provide the law with a "Mosaic" setting. These reminiscences contribute nothing to the alleged program of reform attempted at a late date.

In Exodus it is related that Moses prayed for the people, but nothing is said about his prayer for Aaron. But in Deuteronomy 9:20 we read "the LORD was so angry with Aaron that he was ready to destroy him; and I prayed for Aaron also at the same time." Why should a late writer introduce this? Yet nothing could be more true if Moses were the author. Another reference (32:50) records Aaron's death, an event which must have left an indelible impression on his brother's mind, since they were both involved in the same trespass.

Could all these personal Mosaic features have been introduced by some reformer, priest, prophet, or Levite, in order to invest his collection of laws with a Mosaic dress? Is it probable that such an author would have succeeded in establishing a correspondence so natural, so close in manifold and minute particulars, and so profound? Or is it more reasonable to think that this result proceeds from a true historical connection between the book of the law and the man whose name it has always borne? On every hand if Deuteronomy is acknowledged to be a great book which exerted great influence, should it not also have a great author? Who can fill that place so worthily as the old and tried leader who brought the Israelites out of Egypt, shared their experiences and laid the foundations of their faith?

2. Historical setting. The time for these discourses in Deuteronomy is plainly stated; it was the eleventh month of the forty years of wandering which were imposed upon the people for their unbelief (1:3, 35; 2:14). If one endeavors to picture the author living in monarchic or later days he meets on every side baffling paradoxes; if, however, the author is speaking to Israel as they approach the Promised Land and are about to settle, the language is precisely what one would expect. The aim of the author is to protect the Israelite community against Canaanite influence. This is viewed as a future danger and not as in Hosea where the people are already entangled with many lovers. Deuteronomy speaks of "other gods, which you have not known" (13:2, 3), even of "new gods that had come in of late" (32:17). This is not the language of one addressing a degenerate Israel of a later age; it is language connected with entry into the land.

The historical setting, moreover, is explicit in "when you go over the Jordan" (12:10), and "when you come into the land" (18:9), and implicit throughout. The campaign against the former inhabitants had still to be fought (20:17). The remembrance of the bondage in Egypt recurs frequently, and is treated as a recent experience in the living memory of some. Close connection with the immediate past is reflected in "Remember what Amalek did to you on the way . . ." (25:17); and also the exclusion of the Ammonite and the Moabite from membership in the congregation "because they did not meet you with bread and with water on the way" (23:4).

Two of the most frequent phrases in the book are "go in and possess" (thirty-five times), and "the land which the LORD giveth thee" (thirty-four times). The occupation of the land by the Israelites had a primary place in the mind of the author. The language of promised blessings was for a people about to settle in a new land; not those settled for ages. The gods of the Canaanites are described as those of "the nations whom you shall dispossess" (12:2, 29, 30). This language is in striking contrast to Ezekiel, Haggai, or Ezra!

Where "tribes" are mentioned in Deuteronomy, they are separate entities but included in one whole; nothing to indicate a breach between N and S; Judah and Ephraim are not two kingdoms, and in fact are named only once, which is in the Blessing (33:7-17). The consistent address to "all Israel" assumes the unity of the nation; the people were addressed as a whole. For the period of the divided kingdom this was neither appropriate nor significant.

In Deuteronomy the election of Israel and the covenant at Horeb are always referred to as past events, but the inheritance of the land is always regarded as future. There is a national consciousness and a national religion, but as yet there was no central political organization. The contents are precisely suitable to the time and place (Deut 4:44-49). Anachronisms and discrepancies are not present in the text to reflect a "late" author.

It should also be noted that the primitive

nature of the laws is suitable for a time when Israel first became a nation, but insufficient if viewed in relation to the needs of the 7th cent. B.C. These laws were to be executed by judges (16:18), priests (17:9), and elders or "men of the city" (21:21) not by the king (contrast 2 Kings 15:3, 4). In this book the Lord Himself lead the people to battle as in the days of Joshua.

These laws were issued with a tone of authority which seems to proceed from a great leader. The prophets plead, but this author commands. This colors the whole legislation, and is explicit in the repeated phrase, "which I command you this day" (13:18; 19:9; 27:1).

The theology of the Deuteronomic legislation is simple and unsophisticated; it shows no advance upon that of Moses and no difference from it. The same cannot be said of the theological outlook of Isaiah or his successors. Deuteronomy reflects the optimism of the Mosaic era; the promise of the fathers, the wonders in Egypt, the people's deliverance and the covenant at Horeb. Such a combination of qualities can scarcely be due to accident, nor does it wear the appearance of design. The laws laid down in chs. 12-26 exactly correspond to the background of the Mosaic era and not to any other.

3. *Geographical features.* An analysis of the background data contained in Deuteronomy reveals geographical references too accurate for a Mosaic setting to be accidental. The account of the journeyings (chs. 1-3) is altogether realistic and quite unlike an introduction later prefixed to a collection of old laws. The views described and the features of the Moabite country reproduced reflect an eyewitness account. There is much geographical detail recorded, esp. in the opening and closing chapters, but Pal. is always viewed from the outside. The minute accuracy of the description of the land of Moab and the journey to it is esp. a striking feature (chs. 2 and 3). In contrast, Deuteronomy knows nothing of Zion or David and even these omissions are significant. If Deuteronomy comes from a late period as critics have persistently asserted, why is there no mention of Jerusalem, or even Shiloh where the Tabernacle came to rest?

Deuteronomy contains numerous notices concerning nations with whom the Israelites had then come in contact, but who, after the Mosaic period, entirely disappeared from the pages of history, such as the accounts of the residences of the kings of Bashan (1:4). The observation is made (2:10) that the Emim had formerly dwelt in the plain of Moab and that they were a great people, equal to the Anakim; this observation accords with Genesis 14:5. Deuteronomy gives a detailed account (2:12) concerning the Horites and their relations to the Edomites. An account of the Zamzummim (2:20, 21), one of the earliest races of Canaan, is given though mentioned nowhere else; the author apparently had some interest in them. All of this is most strange if viewed from a "late" period, but exactly what one would expect from Moses.

Deuteronomy uses the appellation of "hill country of the Amorites" (1:7, 19, 20, 44), but even in the Book of Joshua, soon after the conquest of the land, the name is already exchanged for "hill country of Judah" (Josh 11:16, 21).

The Book of Deuteronomy clearly reflects the personality of Moses, the historical setting of his age, and the geographical data one would expect.

F. Later influence. The influence of Deuteronomy upon the later writings and history of Israel is great. Of all the Pentateuch, Deuteronomy has been most used by the prophets, simply because it is best calculated to serve as a model for prophetic declarations.

In the Books of Joshua, Judges, 1 and 2 Samuel, and 1 and 2 Kings there are sufficient references to reveal that Deuteronomy was known and observed. When Jericho was taken, the city and its spoil were "devoted" (Josh 6:17, 18) in keeping with Deuteronomy 13:15ff. (cf. Josh 10:40; 11:12, 15 with Deut 7:2; 20:16, 17). When Achan trespassed, he and his household were stoned, and burned with fire (Josh 7:25. Cf. Deut 13:10; 17:5). When Ai was captured, "only the cattle and the spoil" did Israel take (Josh 8:27 and Deut 20:14); also note that the body of the king of Ai was taken down before nightfall from the tree on which he had been hanged (Josh 8:29), which was required (Deut 21:23; cf. Josh 10:26, 27). Joshua built an altar on Mt. Ebal (8:30, 31), "as Moses the servant of the LORD had commanded" (v. 31) and he wrote thereon a copy of the law (Josh 8:32), as Moses instructed (Deut 27:3, 8). Especially notice that the elders and officers and judges stood on either side of the Ark of the covenant between Ebal and Gerizim (Josh 8:33), as directed in Deuteronomy 11:29; 27:12, 13, and Joshua read to all the congregation of Israel all the words of the law, the blessings, and the cursings (Josh 8:34, 35), in strict accord with Moses' orders (Deut 31:11, 12). Other references make it quite clear that Deuteronomy was known in the days of Joshua.

The Book of Judges has references to Deuteronomy. The complete destruction of Zephath (Judg 1:17) may be compared to Deuteronomy 7:2; 20:16ff. Gideon's elimination of the fearful and faint-hearted from his army (Judg 7:1-7) should be compared to Deuteronomy 20:1-9. The case of Micah, who congratulated himself that the LORD would do him good seeing he had a Levite for a priest, is clear evidence that Deuteronomy was known in the days of the Judges (Judg 17:13; cf. Deut 10:8; 18:1-8; 33:8-11).

The prophets of the 8th cent. were certainly aware of the book. Hosea alludes to striving with priests (Hos 4:4; cf. Deut 17:12), removing landmarks (Hos 5:10; cf. Deut 19:14), returning to Egypt (Hos 8:13; 9:3; cf. Deut 28:68), and of the LORD's tender dealing with Ephraim (Hos 11:3; cf. Deut 1:31; 32:10). Amos also appears to have been familiar with the contents of Deuteronomy (cf. Amos 3:2 with Deut 7:6; 9:12). Amos condemns Israel's inhumanity and adultery in the name of religion, and complains of their retaining overnight pledges wrested from the poor, which was distinctly forbidden (cf. Amos 2:6-8 with Deut 24:12-15; 23:17).

The NT contains several references to, and some citations from the Book of Deuteronomy, and in these its Mosaic authorship and divine authority are generally assumed. In Hebrews 10:28 the words of Deuteronomy 17:6 are quoted as "Moses' law." Paul quoted Deuteronomy 27:26 and 21:23 with the introduction: "It is written" (Gal 3:10, 13), and similarly parts of the Decalogue (Rom 7:7; 13:9; Eph 6:2). In another passage (Rom 10:6-9) he equated the words in Deuteronomy 30:12-14 with the "word of faith" which he preached.

Jesus, in the hour of His temptation, three times quoted the words of Deuteronomy as authoritative (Matt 4:1-11; Luke 4:1-13). He called Deuteronomy 6:4, 5 the "great and first commandment" (Matt 22:38), and described the Decalogue as "the commandment(s) of God" (Mark 7:9-12; 10:17-19) or as "the word of God" (Mark 7:13). In response to the question of the Pharisees concerning divorce, He described the permission for divorce under certain conditions given by Moses (Deut 24:1) as the precept which Moses "wrote" (Mark 10:5). *See* LAW IN THE O T

BIBLIOGRAPHY. J. Reider, "The Origin of Deuteronomy," JQR, N.S. 27 (1936-1937), 349-371; G. T. Manley, "The Moabite Background of Deuteronomy," EQ. XXI (1949), 81-92; G. E. Mendenhall, "Covenant Forms in Israelite Tradition," BA, XVII (1954), 50-76; G. T. Manley, *The Book of the Law* (1957); J. Muilenburg, "The Form and Structure of the Covenantal Formulations," VT, IX (1959), 347ff.; M. G. Kline, *Treaty of the Great King* (1963); D. J. McCarthy, *Treaty and Covenant* (1963); D. R. Hillers, *Treaty-Curses and the Old Testament Prophets* (1964); O. Eissfeldt, *The Old Testament: An Introduction* (1965); E. W. Nicholson, *Deuteronomy and Tradition* (1967).

L. L. WALKER

DEVIL. This word occurs in Eng. VSS in relation to a number of terms in the OT and NT. References to devils in the OT while few in number, seem to be predominantly to foreign deities, as the term שדים (Deut 32:17), rendered in the LXX by δαιμόνια. Another similar reference occurred in Leviticus 17:7, where שעירים, LXX δαιμόνια, or "hairy ones," has been interpreted as an allusion to "satyrs." In a similar reference (2 Chron 11:15), the LXX reads μάταια or "vain things," which casts some doubt upon a specifically demonic interpretation. *Sēḏîm*, a common post-Biblical Heb. term for "evil spirits," was derived from the Assyrian *shêdu* or "guardian spirit," but the pagan gods mentioned need not have been demonic (Deut 32:17; Ps 106:37). The general topic was of little interest to OT writers, so that references to it are few. (*See* DEMON.)

By contrast devils figured prominently in the gospels. The personage of Satan (LXX διάβολος) was named in the NT as either *diábolos* or *satanâs* without any basic difference. In Job, Satan had been accused before God in a demonstration of the nature of disinterested virtue; in the NT he was depicted as one inciting to evil—the "prince of devils" (Matt 4:1; 13:39; John 13:2; etc.). Those under his control could be called devils or children of the devil (John 6:70; 8:44; 1 John 3:8, 10), and he held the power of death (Heb 2:14). Though ruler of the world, he was defeated by the death of Christ and His resurrection (cf. Matt 25:41; Rev 2:10; 12:9, etc.).

In the NT the word most commonly used for "devil" was δαιμόνιον, a diminutive form of *daimōn*, and referred to a spiritual being which was hostile to both God and man. There are numerous statements in the gospels about people being possessed by devils, a situation which manifested itself in eccentric behavior (Luke 8:27), dumbness (11:14) and epilepsy (Mark 9:17, 18). It should be noted, however, that the evangelists distinguished between sickness and possession by devils, as in Matthew 4:24, where the various categories are not identical with one another.

Christ's enemies attributed His success in expelling devils to the indwelling of Satan himself (Luke 11:15), to which Christ replied that such a situation would disrupt the entire realm of evil (11:17, 18). Jesus shared His supremacy over devils with His disciples as in the missions of the Twelve (9:1) and the Seventy (10:17). Unlike His disciples He was unconcerned when others used His name to expel devils (Mark 9:38, 39).

BIBLIOGRAPHY. E. Langton, *Essentials of Demonology* (1949).

R. K. HARRISON

DEVOTED (THINGS) (חרם [verb], חרם [noun], *devoted, accursed, to be utterly destroyed*). Devoted to the deity either for sacred use or for utter destruction.

This root is used about eighty times in the OT. The verb is usually tr. "utterly destroy" both in KJV and RSV. The tr. "devoted," though less common, is more expressive of the meaning of the root. In Arab. the word *Haram* is used for the consecrated area of the Dome of the Rock in Jerusalem. The word *harem* comes from this root and implies that the quarters of the women in a polygamous society are private and forbidden to outsiders.

The overwhelming usage of the root *ḥrm* refers to the destruction of the enemy in the total wars commanded in the conquest of Canaan, in the campaign against the Amalekites, and in similar situations. The enemy was put "under the ban," as it is sometimes expressed. An example is the city of Jericho which was thus devoted. All was to be destroyed except metals which could be purified by fire, for the Lord's treasury. Thus Achan in violating the ban actually stole from God.

There is another usage observable (Lev 27:21, 28, 29; Num 18:14; Ezek 44:29). These passages refer to offerings dedicated to holy use, which are given to the priests. Leviticus 27:21 specifies that such a field shall be the priests' in perpetuity and shall not revert to the owner in the jubilee year. Similar religious endowments are a part of Arab. law in Jordan to this day. Leviticus 27:28 declares that every devoted thing is the Lord's and is most holy. A man may not exchange a different animal for a devoted thing, as may be done in the case of certain firstlings (Lev 27:26, 27).

Devoted men are mentioned in Leviticus 27:29 as certainly condemned to death. This does not refer to those persons consecrated to the Lord by a vow and serving as slaves in the Temple. These are mentioned in Leviticus 27:1-8. Nor does it refer to the firstlings of men who were redeemed when God chose the tribe of Levi as an equivalent (Num 3:12). There is no vestige of early human sacrifice. Rather the devoted men who must be killed as directed in Leviticus 27:29 are captives from the holy wars. These captives theoretically belonged to God. Yet such foreign captives could not serve in the holy precincts. Like Agag and the Amalekites they must be put under the ban (1 Sam 15:3-33).

Before one judges Israel too harshly in this, or objects to God's commandment, he needs to remember first that he in this era has learned again the sad lesson that the most effective war is total war. Aerial bombing spares no one. The enemy in Israel's day could at least flee. It is a common observation that the culture of the conquered often conquers the victors. God did not want that, but to a degree it happened. Psalm 106:34-38 shows that misplaced mercy can result in the slaughter of the innocent. It may further be observed that when Joshua conquered Canaan, the war was more than usually justified, for he was carving out a homeland for his people from the Palestinian possessions of the Egyptian empire. In a sense, Israel had paid for Canaan many times over in blood and tears in Egypt. Remember Lincoln's second Inaugural Address, "If God wills . . . that every drop of blood drawn by the lash shall be paid by another drawn with the sword, . . . it must be said, the judgments of the Lord are true and righteous altogether." *See* ANATHEMA.

BIBLIOGRAPHY. R. de Vaux, AIs, 251-265; G. F. Oehler, *Theology of the OT* (1883), 81, 82; J. B. Payne, *Theology of the Older Testament* (1962), 329, 330.

R. L. HARRIS

DEVOTION, DEVOTIONS di vō' shən (σεβάσματα). This Gr. word means "an object of religious worship" (Acts 17:23; see 2 Thess 2:4). Devotion appears only five times in the RSV, employed once each by David and Jeremiah and three times by Paul (1 Chron 29:3; Jer 2:2; 1 Cor 7:35; 2 Cor 11:3; Col 2:23). All are trs. from different words. "Devotion" is strictly a Biblical or religious term, with worshipful overtones. It is wishful and willing commitment in acts and attitudes as in prayer and meditation.

G. B. FUNDERBURK

DEVOUT di vout' (εὐλαβής; εὐσεβής; σέβομαι). These words are variously tr. "pious," "reverent," "religious," and "to worship," and with few exceptions are peculiar to Luke from whose writings alone they are tr. "devout" in the RSV. He applied the description to Simeon (Luke 2:25), to Cornelius and his "devout soldier" (Acts 10:2, 7), and to Ananias through whom Paul recovered his sight (Acts 22:12). Others collectively were "Devout men [who] buried Stephen" (8:2); "devout converts to Judaism" (13:43); "devout women of high standing" in Antioch of Pisidia (13:50); "devout Greeks" in Thessalonica (17:4); and "devout persons," prob. proselytes, in the synagogue at Athens (17:17). Beside Luke's ten uses, Isaiah speaks of "devout men" in his oracles (Isa 57:1).

G. B. FUNDERBURK

DEW. In a dry climate, and in the hot season, dew plays an important part in water supply. Only on this basis can we understand Elijah's threat in 1 Kings 17:1, "There shall be neither dew nor rain. . . ." In areas where skies are normally clear in summer, and cooling at night, heavy dews are produced wherever (e.g., with a wind from the sea) moisture is present in the atmosphere. On the Levant Coast dew is formed on between twenty and twenty-five nights per month in summer. This dew will prob. represent the vital difference between total barrenness and a vegetation cover: it may freshen up shrubs or plants sufficiently to offer at least a meager form of pasture for flocks. It can even keep a man alive for limited periods: dew collection has been reported by several desert travelers when short of water.

Nowhere does the Bible more clearly reveal its environmental background than in the prominence given to the dew and in its treatment of dew as a symbol of blessing. It is mentioned in Isaac's blessing of both Jacob and Esau (Gen 27:28, 39) and in Moses' blessings of the tribes (Deut 33:13, 28). In Proverbs 19:12 the king's favor is likened to the dew and in Hosea 14:5 God promises that He will be like dew in blessing His people. Conversely, if the dew is withheld this is, or would be, a sign of God's displeasure (Hag 1:10).

J. H. PATERSON

DIADEM dī′ ə dem′ (צפירה, a *circle* or *something round about the head* [Isa 28:5]; צניף, primarily *to wrap, dress, roll, a headdress* in the nature of a turban; a piece of cloth wrapped around the head [Isa 62:3]; διάδημα, always indicates *the fillet, the symbol of royalty*). The Eng. word "diadem" occurs only five times in the RSV, twice in Isaiah and three times in Revelation. Diadem is strictly a royal headdress, and therefore closely akin to a crown. Several Heb. words, including the above, and *kether* may be tr. either "diadem," "crown," or "turban," depending on the context (Esth 1:11; 2:17; 6:8; Job 29:14; Prov 14:18; Ezek 21:26). In ancient times the diadem was worn by kings as a badge of royalty; hence, emblematic of power and distinction. Thus Isaiah said, "In that day the LORD of hosts will be a crown of glory, and a diadem of beauty, to the remnant of his people" (Isa 28:5). Of Zion he prophesied, "You shall be a crown of beauty in the hand of the LORD, and a royal diadem in the hand of your God" (62:3). In Revelation where John witnessed great displays of power he saw three arrays of diadems always in the pl.: The dragon wore "seven diadems upon his heads" (12:3); the beast wore "ten diadems upon its horns" (13:1); and Christ wore upon his head "many diadems" (19:12).

BIBLIOGRAPHY. Davies-Mitchell, *Student's Hebrew Lexicon* (1960), 311, 545f.; Zondervan, *Interlinear Greek-English NT* (1965), 25.

G. B. FUNDERBURK

DIAL (Heb. מעלה, a difficult root, one which is cognate to Akkad. *mēlû*, the *maqtal*, participial form of the verb *elû*, *to ascend, to go up* cognate to Heb. עלה, meaning *to go up*). The noun thus formed is used for "stairs" and often for a flight of stairs by which the shadow of the pillar or post nearby was measured. The pl., *ma'ᵃlōwṯ* appears in 2 Kings 20:11 and Isaiah 38:8 in the narrative of a sign given to Hezekiah to prove the authenticity of Isaiah's prophecy that God would heal him of his disease. In the Isaiah text the stairs are called by the name of their builder, "stairs of Ahaz," and the term is tr. by the word "degrees" as a gradation. Although "dial" (KJV and RSV), strictly speaking, is not correct, "degrees" (JPS) is even less literal. The meaning is actually that of "marks" or "gradations" and should be understood as such.

BIBLIOGRAPHY. B. Landsberger, *Der kultischer Kalendar der Babylonier und Assyrer,* (1915); R. W. Sloley, "Primitive Methods of Measuring Time, with Special Reference to Egypt," JEA XVII (1931), 166-178; S. Iwry, "The Qumran Isaiah and the End of the Dial of Ahaz," BASOR, 147, Oct. (1957), 27-33; Y. Yadin, "The Dial of Ahaz," *Eretz-Israel,* V sepher Mazar (1958), 83-90 (Heb. with Eng. summary.)

W. WHITE, JR.

DIAMOND, the most desired of all the precious stones and the hardest naturally occurring substance known (Jer 17:1). It is pure carbon and commonly occurs as octahedral crystals. Diamonds have been mined in India from the earliest times, and this must have been the source of all famous diamonds of antiquity.

DIANA. *See* ARTEMIS.

DIASPORA dī ăs′ pər rə (διάσπορα, *scattered*). The scattering of the Jews beyond the boundaries of Pal.

1. The term. *Diaspora* in Gr. was generally equivalent to the Heb. *golah* and has come into Eng. as "dispersion." There was, however, a distinction between the Gr. term which meant "scattered" and the Heb. which meant "exiled." "Diaspora" referred to a voluntary moving of the Jews to lands other than their own. It set them apart both from their kindred that remained at home and the strangers among whom the transplanted Jews lived in other lands. *Golah* referred to the Jews who were moved by force, as a result of war, exiled and sometimes imprisoned. The descendants of such exiles were a large part of the diaspora of NT times.

The Sibylline Oracles (c. 250 B.C.) noted concerning the scattering of the Jews: "Every land and every sea is full of thee." By NT times it was estimated that more Jews lived outside of Pal. (perhaps as many as three to five million) than lived in the homeland.

The primary cause of the Diaspora was deportation of the Jews into exile by their enemies. The Assyrians took Jews from Samaria to the E in 722 B.C., and the Babylonians took some from Jerusalem as early as 586 B.C. Later Pompey took Jews to Rome as slaves.

The Jews, being an industrious people, also went voluntarily to other lands where the opportunities in business and trade were better. The increasing population in Pal. kept pressure on the people there to look elsewhere, esp. to the large cities in surrounding countries, for livelihood. These circumstances helped to create the people called the Diaspora.

2. Geographic areas. Egypt had one of the largest, if not the largest, concentrations of Jewish people outside Pal. in NT times. The Jews of Egypt came close to producing a religious center to rival Jerusalem. It was from Egyp. sources that the LXX came. Whether the Egyp. or Mesopotamian settlement came first has been debated, but unquestionably the scattering of the Jews to the E was quite early. The two main Jewish centers in Mesopotamia were at Nehardea and Nisibis. Syria was said by Josephus to have had the largest percentage of Jewish inhabitants in his day. In Syria the Jews were primarily found at Antioch. There were thousands also at Damascus. Judas Maccabaeus and his brother Jonathan had brought settlements of Jews into the borders of Syria as a protection for Judea. The nearness of Syria to Pal. was enough to draw the enterprising Jews to its cities.

There is considerable evidence both inside and outside the NT for the presence of Jews in Greece and Asia Minor. Philo, the Alexandrian Jew, preserved a letter from Herod Agrippa I to the Emperor Caligula which besought him to grant religious and civic freedom to the Jews in Pamphylia, Cilicia, and a greater part of Asia Minor as far as Bithynia, also in Thessaly, Boetia, Macedonia and Corinth. The Jews seem primarily to have been in these areas because of trade opportunities. A major trade route ran through Cilicia to Syria and Pal. Other trade routes in Macedonia and Achaia collected Jews also. In addition to trade there is evidence that Antiochus III transferred to Asia 2,000 Jewish families that were loyal to him, to help insure peace.

Jews were dispersed throughout Italy. Cicero wrote of them with hate and fear (62 B.C.). Tiberius Caesar persecuted the Jewish settlement in Rome. Claudius Caesar sought to drive the Jews out of Rome and forbade their assembling in their synagogues. The Jews seem to have been in Rome even prior to the deportation of Pompey's captives from Jerusalem (63 B.C.).

Jewish settlements populated the islands of the Mediterranean as well. The letter of Agrippa I to Caligula mentioned Cyprus and Crete as possessing Jews in considerable numbers. Cyprus seems to have been the home of Barnabas, and Titus was associated with Crete.

Paul found well-established synagogues throughout Asia Minor. This was true also in Macedonia and Achaia. Habitually, he began his work among his own people in each new location.

3. Characteristics. In many lands the Jews were given places of trust and enjoyed social freedom. Often they were entrusted with military positions and, because of their loyalty, even commanded armies. They became high officials in government also.

Most Jewish settlements were autonomous in affairs that were strictly their own. In many places they had equal, or almost equal rights with the strangers among whom they lived. In religious affairs the Jews of the Diaspora were devoted to their ancestral faith. When persecution came upon the Jews away from Pal., it was nearly always because of some religious fanaticism, as it was judged by the authorities of the nations where they lived. Tiberius Caesar hated the Jews because he believed that the Jews considered their religion to be above all other religions.

In most instances the Jews of the Diaspora enjoyed freedom of religion. This seems to have been the policy of Antiochus III who moved the 2,000 Jewish families to Asia Minor. The Rom. government considered Judaism as *religio licita*, licensed religion. The Jews, therefore, did not have to appear in court on the Sabbath; and when public dole was made to the poor, no strange foods or oils were given to the Jews. If the day of public distribution fell on a Sabbath the Jews were permitted to draw their relief the next day. Although some Jews served in military forces with distinction, the Jews as a whole in Asia Minor were exempted from military service because of their peculiar food laws and Sabbath observance.

The scattered Jews maintained strong ties with Jerusalem and the Temple. Frequent pilgrimages were made to Jerusalem for the religious festivals. Gifts of money were sent regularly to the Temple. A half-shekel was expected from the Jews of the Diaspora, but no doubt many people sent much more. Nearly every country had a collection point where the gifts were gathered, awaiting the annual journey to Jerusalem. Mithridates, king of Pontus in Asia Minor confiscated 800 talents of silver on the island of Cos which the Jews had collected in Ionia for the Temple. Pomponius Flaccus, a Rom. governor of Asia Minor, confiscated on another occasion 100 gold pounds which had been gathered for the Temple from Apamea, Laodicea, Pergamum and Adramyttium. It was esp. the treasure from the Diaspora that made the Temple in Jerusalem rich and beautiful.

Some of the Jews of the Diaspora obtained Rom. citizenship. In the NT Paul would serve as an example. How Jews came by such citizenship is not known precisely. Paul apparently inherited his citizenship. Some, no doubt, were able to purchase Rom. citizenship. Other Jews were apparently rewarded with citizenship for distinguished military service to the Caesars.

Proselyting was another characteristic of the Jews outside Pal. Those Jews were propagandists of the first order and zealous missionaries. The tr. of the OT into Gr. had enabled them to communicate their religion to the people among whom they lived. The high ethical content and monotheism of Judaism combined to appeal to a considerable segment of the pagan world. God-fearers stood in large numbers on the fringe of Judaism while many other Gentiles entered fully into it.

4. Contributions. If it had not been for the Diaspora, there would have been no LXX. In addition to the LXX the Diaspora produced the Targum, trs. and paraphrases of the OT into other dialects of the E, esp. Aram. The Diaspora also gave rise to a significant body of lit. Some scholars have included the OT books of Job and Proverbs as well as some of the Psalms in that lit. The principal literary contributions were, however, the Apoc. and Pseudep. It is thought also that the synogogue had its rise in the Diaspora.

5. Influence. Jews in foreign lands were inevitably influenced by the cultural and religious environment that surrounded them. Many scholars have felt that angelology and demonology among the Jews were doctrines esp. indebted to the Diaspora. However that may be, it is unquestioned that there was a considerable

THE JEWISH DIASPORA IN NEW TESTAMENT TIMES

effort made to adjust Judaism to the thought world of the Greeks, witness Philo of Alexandria who was a foremost leader in the Hellenizing process.

It may be that the seeds of Jewish legalism were sown in the Diaspora. In the times of captivity it was not possible to carry out the Levitical requirements of sacrificial worship. The concentration of the synagogue was, therefore, directed toward the letter of the law. After the return to Pal. the preoccupation with legal observance and interpretation continued in Pharisaism.

On the other hand, the Diaspora also had an influence in the direction of personal religion. The conviction of sin was quickened; personal piety grew; spiritual elements in religion were emphasized. A universal outlook, a cosmopolitan view, came to Judaism through the mixing and mingling of Jews with people of other heritages.

6. Significance. The Diaspora was indispensable to the spread of Christianity. The Judaism of the scattered was much more open to change than was the religion of the homeland. The presence of communities of Jews across the Mediterranean world made it possible for early Christian missionaries to move quickly from one area to another, preaching a message for which the people of the synagogues had a basic preparation, not to mention the large number of Gentile God-fearers who were ready to hear the Gospel. The LXX was also invaluable to the spread of Christianity because it was the Scriptures of the early churches. The Messianic expectation of the Jews of the Diaspora had prepared to a certain extent the whole civilized world for the message of Christ.

BIBLIOGRAPHY. A. Causse, *Les Disperses D' Israel* (1929); H. W. Robinson, *The History of Israel* (1938); R. H. Pfeiffer, *History of New Testament Times* (1949); J. M. Wilkie, "Nabonidus and the Later Jewish Exiles," JTS, II (1951), 36-44; A. Schalit, "The Letter of Antiochus III to Zeuxis Regarding the Establishment of Jewish Military Colonies in Phrygia and Lydia," JQR, 50 (1951), 289-318; F. Zweig, "Israel and the Diaspora," *Judaism,* VII (1958), 147-150; N. H. Snaith, *The Jews from Cyrus to Herod* (n.d.).

H. L. DRUMWRIGHT, JR.

DIATESSARON dī' ə tĕs' ə ron. *Diatessaron* (a Gr. prepositional phrase, "by means of four") the name traditionally given to a harmony of the gospels, compiled by Tatian, a Christian apologist of Assyrian origin resident in Rome in mid-2nd cent., until returning E in A.D. 172. In one ancient source, his compilation is called *Diapente,* "by means of five." Both terms belong to Gr. music theory, meaning perfect fourth and perfect fifth respectively, these harmonies being most highly esteemed. Hence the work is defined as the "perfect harmony." The use of *Diapente* may signify Tatian's inclusion of apocryphal material from a fifth source, together with the four canonical gospels, since instances of apocryphal items are found in all sources.

It was prob. composed in Syr., but an early Lat. rendering may have been made in his lifetime. It is unlikely that its original language was Gr. The one certain Gr. fragment known is prob. a retranslation from Syr. The Diatessaron has not survived in its original form; a partially preserved Syr. commentary upon it by Ephraem (d. 378) was edited in 1963 and is the most direct source. An Armenian tr. has preserved the whole commentary. An Arab. VS of the harmony is known in several MSS. These two form the primary sources of knowledge, but may be supplemented from many others. A Pers. adaptation is known, and the harmony has left its mark in the E on the Armenian, Georgian, and Palestinian Syr. VSS; on their source, the old Syr. gospels; on quotations by Syr. Fathers; and in Manichaean lit. In the W, stemming from the early Lat. tr. mentioned, there are marked traces in the Old Lat. gospels, in Lat. harmonies adapted to the text of the Vulgate, and in vernacular harmonies in Old High Ger., Middle high Ger., Medieval Dutch, Middle Eng., and the Medieval Tuscan and Venetian dialects of Italian.

This astoundingly wide influence bespeaks Tatian's literary skill and popular devotional appeal. The harmony even in the remotest sources bears traces of the extreme asceticism (Encratism) that forbade both sexual experience and the partaking of meat and wine. Some ancient references even assert that Tatian omitted the gospel genealogies of Jesus, although many of the sources have them. Three sure signs of Diatessaric influence upon any document are the assertion that both Joseph and Mary were of Davidic descent; that a great light shone on the Jordan at Jesus' baptism; and that Jesus looked on the rich young ruler "lovingly."

BIBLIOGRAPHY. C. Peters, *Das Diatessaron Tatians* (1939); L. Leloir, *Le Témoignage d'-Ephrém sur le Diatessaron* (1962); B. M. Metzger, "Tatian's Diatessaron and a Persian Harmony of the Gospels," *Chapters in the History of New Testament Textual Criticism* (1963).

J. N. BIRDSALL

DIBLAH, DIBLATH. *See* RIBLATH.

DIBLAIM dĭb' lĭ əm or **dĭb lā' əm** (דבלים, may mean *two lumps, mouthfuls, cakes,* as of pressed figs). The father of Gomer, the unfaithful wife of the prophet Hosea (Hos 1:3).

DIBLATHAIM. *See* BETH-DIBLATHAIM.

DIBON, DIBON-GAD Dī' bŏn, Dī' bŏn găd (דיבן, דיבון ; the Moabite Stone's spelling, דיבן, and the LXX's Δαιβών, show that the י had a consonantal value; דימון ; דימונה ; LXX Δειμών, Διμωνά). 1. A Judean town toward the S, inhabited in the time of Nehemiah by members of the tribe of Judah (Neh 11:25), which seems to be the same as Dimonah, a S Judean city (Josh 15:22), possibly Tell ed Dheib.

2. A city in Moab, E of the Dead Sea, N of the Arnon River, to which reference is first made in the OT in describing Israel's victory over Sihon of the Amorites (Num 21:30), and which place together with the whole area was given to Gad and to Reuben (Num 32:3, 34; Josh 13:9), and although Dibon was built (i.e., rebuilt) by Gad (Num 32:34) and, therefore, was sometimes called Dibon-gad (Num 33:45, 46), it was part of the territory of Reuben (Josh 13:17).

Subsequently Israel did not keep continuous possession of Dibon and the surrounding country, as is evidenced by Moabite control under Eglon (Judg 3:12ff.), the conquest of the area by David (2 Sam 8:2), Moab's rebellion (2 Kings 1:1) and subjugation by Judah and Israel (2 Kings 3), although Mesha in the Moabite Inscription (c. 840 to 830 B.C.) claimed victory over Israel; and further in Isaiah's time (Isa 15) and later in that of Jeremiah (48:18, 22) this town, with others, was counted under the control of Moab, there

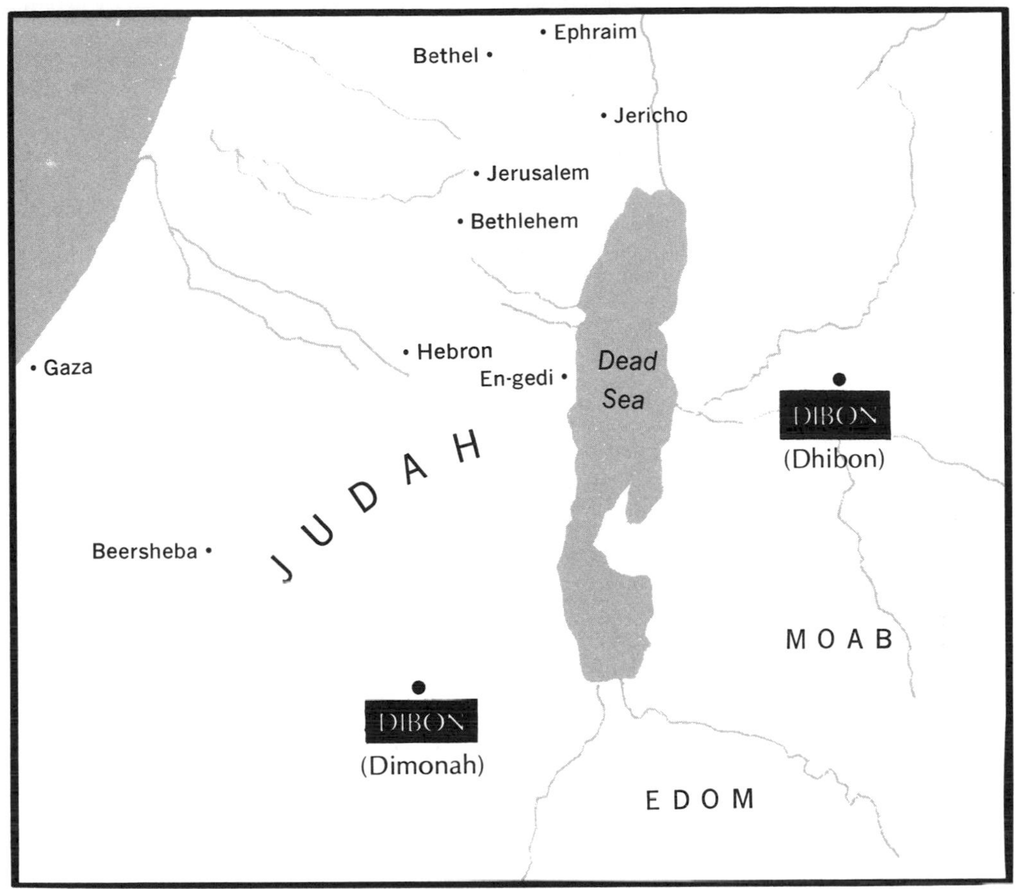

being a play on words in Isaiah 15:9, as the MT, which has Dibon in Isaiah 15:2 has Dimon in closer resemblance to the word דם, "blood."

Moab as a political state seems to have been destroyed by Nebuchadnezzar. Later Dibon was prob. under Jewish control as suggested by a coin of Hyrcanus II (63-40 B.C.) found there.

The city is not mentioned in the NT, but that the town flourished from before the time of Christ through the Arab. period is attested by the presence there of Hellenistic, Nabataean, Roman, Byzantine and Arabic sherds and coins, there being only a few literary references to the place in these periods, one being in the *Onomasticon* of Eusebius (4th cent. A.D., ed. Klostermann 16, 18ff.) which says that Dibon was a very large village (κώμη παμμεγέθης).

The modern Dhībân, located a few m. N of the Arnon Valley on the road to Kerak, adjoins the ancient tell, Dibon, where the Moabite Stone was found in 1868. The discovery indicates that this was the site of the king of Moab's capital (cf. 2 Kings 3:4, 5). Dibon was the original name; Mesha in rebuilding it gave at least a part of it the name, Qrhh (Moabite Inscription), a title which did not endure.

Archeological excavation of Dibon was undertaken by the American Schools of Oriental Research between 1950 and 1956 in the following campaigns (directors are noted): 1950-1951, Fred V. Winnett; 1952, W. L. Reed; 1952-1953, A. D. Tushingham; 1956, W. H. Morton. This excavation was of particular interest because Dibon was a Trans-Jordanian tell which had been occupied during most of Trans-Jordan's history, which would give a cross section of the country's archeological history.

The Dibon site, elevation about 2134 ft. above sea level, consists of two mounds, one occupied by the modern village, Dhībân, and the other to the NW, connected by a saddle, being the ancient tell, Dibon, in size, six acres, the SE section of the latter mound prob. being the area where Mesha built his royal addition to Qrḥh to Dibon (Moabite Inscription 1. 24, 25). There are no springs in the area.

Some conclusions derived from the seasons of excavation thus far are: the identification of Dhībân with Dibon of the Omri-Ahab-

Mesha period (c. 850 B.C.) is certain; the site was occupied in the Early Bronze period and the city was important during the medieval and early Arab, Byzantine, Roman, Nabataean and Iron II periods. Caution must be used in drawing conclusions concerning the absence of strata that could be associated with the Maccabean, Hellenistic, Persian, and Late, or Middle Bronze periods because of the restricted areas of the excavations at Dibon; 100 cisterns already found verify the statement of the Moabite Inscription on the need for such objects; and that Dibon was an agricultural center is illustrated in the discovery of grain, ovens, and storage jars for grain.

BIBLIOGRAPHY. P. Savignac, "Sur les pistes de Transjordanie méridionale," RB XLV (1936), 238f.; F. M. Abel, *Géographie de la Palestine*, II (1938), 304, 305; F. V. Winnett, "Excavations at Dibon in Moab, 1950-1951," BASOR, CXXV (1952), 7-20; A. D. Tushingham, "Excavations at Dibon in Moab, 1952-1953." BASOR, CXXXIII (1954), 6-26; W. H. Morton, BASOR, CXL (1955), 4-7; J. B. Pritchard, ed. ANET, 2nd ed. (1955), 320; F. V. Winnett and W. L. Reed, The Excavations at Dibon (Dhībân) in Moab, AASOR XXXVI, XXXVII (1964).

W. H. MARE

DIBRI dĭb' rī (דִּבְרִי, prob. *wordy*; i.e., *he talks too much*). A man of the tribe of Dan whose daughter Shelomith married an Egyp. Their son blasphemed the "name" of God and was stoned (Lev 24:10-23).

DICE-PLAYING. *See* GAMES.

DIDACHE dĭd' ə kĭ (Διδαχή, *teaching*). A writing of the Early Church. **1. The text.** The title of the document which is today commonly called the *Didaché* appears, at the beginning of the Gr. MS which is the primary text, as "The Teaching of the Lord by the Twelve Apostles to the Gentiles." It was quoted perhaps as Scripture, by Clement of Alexandria in his *Miscellanes* (I, 20). However, Eusebius classed it among the νόθοι (spurious books) in his *History* (III, 25, 4) and Athanasius said that it was not in the canon but among the books "to be read by those who newly join us" (*Festal Letter* 39). The last western indication of it before modern times seems to be a trace in Pirminius (d. 753). It is listed in the *Stichometry of Nicephorus* (c. 850) as a rejected book. It appears to have dropped out of learned discussion after that time. But in 1873 Philotheos Bryennios, metropolitan of Nicomedia, found the text of the *Didaché* in a MS dating from 1056. He published it in 1883 and quite a sensation was created as it appeared that it might be from the very early period of the Church. This MS still provides the basic Gr. text (H). There is a nearly complete variant Gr. text in the *Apostolic Constitutions* deriving from the 4th cent. and a fragment in Oxyrhynchus Papyrus No. 1782, from the late 4th cent.

Two Lat. VSS of some of the material in the first part of the *Didaché* are in existence, one dating from the 9th or 10th cent. and the other, much more extensive, from the 11th cent. E. J. Goodspeed of the University of Chicago considered this second Lat. MS, preserved at Munich and known as *de Doctrina Apostolorum*, to be the original form of the *Didaché*. This, however, does not seem to be quite the best way to solve the problem. There are also Coptic, Georgian, Ethiopic, and Arabic VSS of parts or most of the text.

2. Content. Broadly considered the *Didaché* may be divided as follows: I. The Description of the Two Ways (chs. 1-6); II. Directions for Worship, including Baptism and the Eucharist (chs. 7-10); III. Directions concerning Officers and the Conduct of Congregational Affairs (chs. 11-15); IV. Eschatology (ch. 16). These subjects are of intense interest, if the *Didaché* is an early document as it appears to be (see below under Date).

a. The Description of the Two Ways is a document by itself. It forms the first part of the *Didaché* and the last part of the so-called *Epistle of Barnabas* (q.v.). This concept, of course, is an ancient one (cf. Deut 30:15). It may also be found in the OT prophets (Jer 21:8). The Qumran *Manual of Discipline* (3:13-4:26) presents a similar concept. In the *Didaché* the contrast is life/death as it is in the OT. In *Barnabas* and the Qumran *Manual* it is light/darkness. There are other forms of the contrast. Because of the close similarity of the text it has been thought by some that Barnabas borrowed from the *Didaché* (e.g., F. X. Funk, O. Bardenhewer) or, more frequently, the *Didaché* from *Barnabas* (e.g., R. H. Connolly, F. C. Burkitt, J. A. Robinson, J. Muilenberg). It is more likely that both took the idea from a third source circulating in the Gr.-speaking Jewish diaspora. This view is finding more and more favor.

The contrast between the two ways is an ethical one. It is set forth in a form for use in teaching catechumens. It clearly reflects the moral instruction of the OT. There is a section in the *Didaché* (I, 3-6) which does not correspond to anything in the Barnabas text, however, where the background is clearly that of the Sermon on the Mount. It is not obvious that the writer was using the text of Matthew or Luke. Probably some earlier form, perhaps oral, was the source.

b. One of the areas of greatest interest dealt with by the *Didaché* is worship, since it appears that there was early information concerning baptism and the Lord's Supper. Chapter seven is devoted to baptism. Catechetical instruction is stated to be presupposed. Fasting is to precede the baptism (VII, 4). The formula of baptism is trinitarian "in the name of the Father and of the Son and of the Holy Spirit" (VII, 1). Cold running water was preferred, and prob. assumed the mode of immersion. An alternate mode was pouring (VII, 3).

The common word for the Lord's Supper in the Early Church was Eucharist (ευχαριστία). Two sections of the *Didaché* use this term: IX, 1; X, 7; XIV. It has been thought (e.g., by Gregory Dix, *The Shape of the Liturgy*, 90ff.; F. E. Vokes, *The Riddle of the Didaché*, 177-207) that the section beginning at IX, 1 describes an agape meal and ch. XIV the Eucharist proper. It is more likely that chs. IX and XIV represent an observance where the Eucharist and the agape meal are still celebrated together, while ch. XIV refers to a Sunday celebration of the Eucharist alone. Other interpretations are possible and have been defended. Assuming, as most likely, the suggestion just made, it may be noted that the thanksgiving prayers (IX, 2-4) are in the order cup-bread while the order, "eat . . . drink" (v. 5) follows and may well refer to the action. The cup-bread order, however, occurs in Luke 22:17-19 (parts of vv. 19 and 20 are omitted by the Western text) and in 1 Corinthians 10:16. The strong emphasis upon Thanksgiving and triumph in the prayers is noteworthy. The Eucharist is restricted to the baptized. Knowledge and holiness are stressed. The enjoyment of food and drink as gifts of God is noted.

The celebration of the Eucharist is appointed for each Lord's Day (XIV, 1). The use of the word θυσία (sacrifice) in this connection is not to be understood as a reference to the sacrifice of Christ. The word was a common description of prayers, alms and gifts in the usage of the time. It is the "sacrifice" of the people to which reference is being made.

c. Life and discipline. The prescriptions for conduct are, of course, influenced by the OT law and by Jewish development of that law. There is to be mutual oversight of, and assistance to, one another in the community (XV, 3). Love and prayer for others are commanded (II, 7). Division is to be avoided (IV, 3). Gifts to others are commended (I, 5; XIII, 3, 4). Hospitality is proper, both toward the leader (XI, 4) and the ordinary stranger (XII, 1, 2). Food is restricted. It may not include that offered to idols (VI, 3), and fasting is to be practical (VIII, 1). The presumption throughout appears to be that the community is a relatively poor one economically. The members are not influential in this world. They are subject to the temptations to be quarrelsome which often afflict such groups (XV).

d. The Official titles used are apostle (XI, 3-6), prophet (X, 7; XI, 3-11; XIII, 1-4; XV, 2), teacher (XI, 2; XV, 2), bishop (XV, 1), and deacon (XV, 1). The first three are applied to itinerant individuals whose stay in the community is expected to be very short. The possibility that a prophet might wish to remain is provided for, however (XIII), and is welcomed. In such a case they are to be as high priests to the community (XIII, 3). The bishops and deacons, on the other hand, are thought of as the resident equivalents of the traveling prophets and teachers, and are to be honored by the group (XV, 2).

e. The return of Christ in the future is expected (XVI, 8). The hour is unknown (XVI, 1), but there will be indications of its approach. False prophets and corrupters will increase in number and the allegiance of some people will change (XVI, 3). An individual claiming to be the Son of God will arise whose evil and deceptive actions will mislead (XVI, 4). The coming itself will be preceded by a sign extended in the sky, a trumpet peal and the resurrection of the saintly dead (XVI, 6, 7). The visible coming will follow and, according to the Georgian VS, the last judgment (XVI, 8). It behooves Christians to be watching and ready (XVI, 1).

3. Place of origin. It is impossible to be dogmatic about the locale where the *Didaché* was written. It seems likely that it did not originate in a large city where the stay of a traveling prophet or apostle might be expected to be longer than is contemplated (XI, 5; cf. XII, 2). The reference to mountains (IX, 4) may reflect the environment. Possibly it contained warm baths or springs (VII, 2). Syria is perhaps as likely a place of origin as any, in the light of these considerations.

4. Date. Speculation concerning the date has ranged over a wide period. It is clear that the references to church officers presuppose a relatively early state of affairs when traveling apostles and prophets were not too rare. There is no indication of a monarchical episcopate. The eucharistic practices seem comparatively primitive. While, therefore, speculation has ranged over the period from about A.D. 50 to the early 3rd cent., it seems most likely that a date between A.D. 70 and 110 is to be preferred.

BIBLIOGRAPHY. R. Knopf, *Die Lehre der zwölf Apostel, die zwei Clemensbriefe* (*Handbuch zum neuen Testament,* Ergänzungs-Band, *Die apostolischen Väter*, I) (1920); J. A. Robinson, *Barnabas, Hermas and the Didache* (1920); J. Muilenberg, *The Literary Relations of the Epistle of Barnabas and the Teaching of the Twelve Apostles* (1929); F. E. Vokes, *The Riddle of the Didache* (1938); E. J. Goodspeed, *The Apostolic Fathers* (1950), 1-18; J.-P. Audet, *La Didachè, Instructions des Apôtres* (1958); R. M. Grant, *The Apostolic Fathers*, I (1964); R. A. Kraft, *Barnabas and the Didaché* (ed. R. M. Grant, *The Apostolic Fathers,* III (1965). *See* also APOSTOLIC FATHERS, esp. for texts and trs.

P. WOOLLEY

DIDRACHMA. *See* COINS.

DIDYMUS **dĭd′ ə məs** (Δίδυμος, *twin*). This designation, another name for the Apostle Thomas, appears only in the gospel of John (11:16; 20:24; 21:2). The Gr. form, Θωμᾶς is a transliteration of תּוֹאָם, meaning 'twin" (Gen 25:24; 38:27; S of Sol 4:5; 7:3). Probably the Gr. equivalent, Didymus, was used among Gr.-speaking friends of Thomas. Each time the word is used in John, it is preceded by the word λεγόμενος, which does not mean, "Thomas who is commonly *called* Didymus." The theory that Jesus gave him this name because of his twofold nature, divided between doubt and faith, seems to be pure invention. More likely the designation refers to the simple fact that Thomas (q.v.) was a twin.

L. Foster

DIE. *See* Death.

DIKLAH dĭk′ lə (דִּקְלָה ; LXX Δεκλα; *date-palm*). A Sem. tribe descended from Eber through Joktan (Gen 10:27; 1 Chron 1:21). Traditionally Joktan is the ancestor of the S Arabians, but the specific place names of Genesis 10:30 are difficult to identify. See J. Simons, *The Geographical and Topographical Texts of the Old Testament*, 136.

G. G. Swaim

DILEAN dĭl′ ĭ ən (דִּלְעָן ; LXX A Δαλααν; B Δαλαλ; meaning unknown). A city in the Judean Shephelah (Josh 15:38). Though the site is not known, it is thought by some to be Tell en-Najileh.

DILL (ἄνηθον). Matthew 23:23 says: "Ye pay tithe of mint and anise." The word *anēthon* is undoubtedly "dill."

Dill

This herb is used in Great Britain as a salad, but in Scandinavia it is used as the flavoring for new boiled potatoes. It is often put into jars of pickles.

The plant is found growing wild in Israel, or in modern gardens as a cultivated plant. The seeds are aromatic, and can be used for flavoring bread and cakes.

Dill is *Anethum graveolens* and looks like parsley when growing. It is a member of the same family. Moffatt, Weymouth and Goodspeed tr. the word *anēthon* as "dill." Its Lat. name confirms this tr.

It is an oriental plant—far more so, in fact, than anise, which, though seen now in the Holy Land, was not grown there in the time of our Lord. Further, the Gr. word is *anēthon* (dill).

Dill is considered by some to be the correct tr. of fitches (q.v.) in Isaiah 28:25, but there seems to be no foundation for this.

Our Lord accused the Pharisees of rigorously tithing the dill, but ignoring the more important acts of obedience (Matt 23:23).

W. E. Shewell-Cooper

DIMNAH dĭm′ nə (דִּמְנָה ; LXX Δεμνα; *dung-pit*?). A city of Zebulun assigned to the Merari Levites (Josh 21:35), called Rimmon (19:13), Rimmono (1 Chron 6:77). Modern Rumaneh.

DIMON dī′ mən (דִּימוֹן ; LXX Ρεμμων; *dung-pit*?). A place mentioned in Isaiah's oracle against Moab (Isa 15:9). Though taken by RSV as a mistake for Dibon, it is now identified with Khirbet Dimneh near 'ain el-Megheisil. (J. Simons, *The Geographical and Topographical Texts of the Old Testament*, 1261.)

DIMONAH dī mō′ nə (דִּימוֹנָה ; LXX A Διμωνα; B Ρεγμα; *dung-pit*?). A city of the Negeb, near the Edomite border, belonging to Judah (Josh 15:22). It is generally thought to be the same place as the Dibon of Judah occupied by the Jews in the period of the return from exile under Nehemiah (Neh 11:25). The exact site is not known.

DINAH (Heb. דִּינָה). Similar names are found in use among other Sem. groups; e.g. Akkad. *Dina*, derived from words for "just," "justice" and "judge." In the context of Genesis 34:1, 3, 13, 26 Dinah is the daughter of Jacob and Leah. During an inspection of the land and a visit with the pagan women she is criminally assaulted by a certain Shechem, the son of the ruler, Hamor, stated to be a Hivite. Subsequently Jacob and the brothers of the victim return and listen to a proposal of marriage and settlement presented by the Hivites on behalf of Shechem. The sons of Jacob agreed to the plan but insisted upon the Hivite males submitting to the rite of circumcision which the Hivites unsuspectingly agreed to do. After the rite had been performed upon all the

Hivites and the strangers in their midst and the wounds were sore and debilitating, the two brothers of Dinah, Simeon and Levi, took their weapons, prob. heavy iron broad swords of the Hitt. type, and slew all the males. Apparently the ravished sister was by this time married to Shechem because they took her from his house (34:26), and despoiled all the rest of the village. For this act of wanton revenge the brothers Simeon and Levi were cursed in Jacob's final blessing (49:5-7), wherein they are said to have, "Weapons of violence their kinship" (JPS). An important aspect of the story is the fact that among the sons of Jacob acts of violence and lust were proscribed.

W. WHITE, JR.

DINAITE(S) **dī' nə' īt(s)** (דִּינָיֵא). Among those who complained to the Pers. monarch Artaxerxes against the Jews rebuilding the Temple Ezra 4:9 lists the Dinaites, the Apharsathchites (אֲפַרְסַתְכָיֵא) and Tarpelites (טַרְפְּלָיֵא) along with Persians and men from Erech, Babylon and Susa. So the KJV, ASV, etc., but RSV makes three of the proper nouns to be titles of officials, and NEB makes four. Without changing consonants the definite pl. could become the Aram. דִּינִם, "judge." The context, then, shows considerable organization in the Pers. province N of Judea.

W. G. BROWN

DINHABAH **dĭn hə' bə** (דִּנְהָבָה ; LXX Δενναβα; *give judgment*). The capital city of Bela; son of Beor; king of Edom in the period before the Israelite monarchy (Gen 36:32; 1 Chron 1:43). Outside of this reference, the site is totally unknown.

DINNER. *See* FOOD.

DIOGNETUS, ADDRESS TO **dī ŏg' nī' təs** (Διόγνητος). An apologetic address or letter of the Early Church.

This is a brilliant, lucid exposition of Christianity by an unknown author. The person addressed, Diognetus, is presumably intended to be the teacher of Marcus Aurelius who bore that name. It is written in Gr. in a rhetorical style. The foolishness of idolatry was demonstrated. Judaism was accused of unnecessary sacrifices and of ridiculous observances. In contrast, Christian character was praised. The Incarnation brought a revelation of God's truth. God "gave his own Son as ransom for us" (IX, 2).

Chapters 11 and 12 are by another hand, perhaps Hippolytus or Melito. The main body prob. dates from the late 2nd or early 3rd cent. The idea that it is the lost *Apology* of Quadratus, advanced by P. Andriessen in 1946, is not likely. The only pre-Reformation MS of the text is no longer extant, but a MS copy and printed texts are available.

BIBLIOGRAPHY. H. G. Meecham, *The Epistle to Diognetus* (1949). *See* also APOSTOLIC FATHERS.

P. WOOLLEY

DIONYSIA (Διονυσία). A series of festivals that honored Dionysus, the god of wine. The first of the feasts was the Oschophoria in the month of Pysanepsion (October to November) which celebrated the ripening of the grapes. The running of races, making of processions and singing of choruses were climaxed by a sacrifice and banquet. The smaller Dionysia was held in the month of Poseideon (December to January) and celebrated the first tasting of the new wine. A solemn procession to the altar of the god was climaxed by a sacrifice, followed by dancing and dramas. The Lenoea was the feast of the vats held at Athens in the month of Gamelion (January to February) at Lenaeon, the oldest and most sacred shrine of Dionysus. The feast was notable for its meal which was provided at the public expense, after which a procession was made to the tragedies and comedies. The Anthesteria was observed for three days in the month of Anthesterion (February to March) and celebrated the opening of the casks of new wine. The most important feature was the symbolic marriage of the wife of the high priest of Dionysus to that god. The great urban Dionysia was held for six days in the month of Elaphebolion (March to April). Processions and singing were climaxed by three days of performances of the new tragedies, comedies, and dramas.

H. L. DRUMWRIGHT, JR.

DIONYSIUS THE AREOPAGITE **dī' ə nĭ shəs** (Διονύσιος, related to Dionysus, god of vegetation). By his title prob. a member of the council of the Areopagus and a convert of Paul at Athens (Acts 17:34).

He is one of a number of prominent men who are mentioned by Luke as converts (13:12; 19:31; 26:32; 28:7). Little else is known about him except by tradition. According to Suidas he was born at Athens and studied there and in Egypt. While he was in Egypt he observed the eclipse which took place at the time of the crucifixion and theorized that God was suffering. He then returned to Athens and became a person of influence. Eusebius (HE III. iv. 10; IV. xxiii. 3), quoting Dionysius of Corinth, states that he was the first bishop of Athens. Accounts vary concerning his death. One tradition is that he was martyred at Athens under Domitian. Another indicates that he came to Rome and was then sent to Paris by Clemens I, where he was beheaded on the martyr's mount (Montmatre). He is often identified with St. Dennis, the patron of France.

Christian and Neoplatonic writings of three or four centuries later were attributed to him. *On the Celestial Hierarchy, On the Ecclesiastical Hierarchy, On the Divine Names, On the*

Mystical Theology were widely read and influential throughout the Middle Ages. Many commentaries were written on them from the 9th cent. on. The real author may have been the monophysite Peter the Iberian, 411-491.

BIBLIOGRAPHY. J. P. Migne, ed., *Patrologia graeca* III-V (1857); E. Honigmann, *Pierre l' Ibérien et les écrits du Pseudo-Denys l' Aréopagite* (1952); W. Volker, *Kontemplation und Ekstase bei Ps.-Dionysius Areopagita* (1958).

A. RUPPRECHT

DIONYSUS dī ə nī′ səs (Διονύσος). Dionysus was the god of an ecstatic and emotional cult, which appears to have reached Greece from Thrace. The cult satisfied that strange and somewhat terrifying urge in human nature that found expression in the "dancing madness," which periodically invaded Europe from the 14th to the 17th cent. and even appropriated to its mass excitement perverted forms of Christianity. The "Shakers," the Jewish Hasidim, the Moslem dervishes, and the Siberian shamans were and are other examples of such psychological maladies.

Mythology made Dionysus the son of Zeus and Semele, snatched unborn from his mother's womb when Semele was incinerated before the burning glory of Zeus that she had insisted on seeing. The babe was born in due time from his divine father's thigh in which he was sewn. Myths clustered around the young god's name, the most famous of which forms the theme of Euripides' last and strangest tragedy, the *Bacchae*, a drama which, rightly viewed, is a moving and horrifying study of the worship of Dionysus as Euripides encountered it in its northern homeland in his final years.

The Dionysiac myths are of little account. They are accretions around a form of primitive worship of vast antiquity, which came to Greece from ancient times and found new forms and adaptations as society grew more sophisticated and civilized. The drama, tragedy, and comedy, but esp. the former, had their primitive roots in the worship of Dionysus, and the Attic Dionysiac festivals produced their final splendid fruit in the magnificent theater of Aeschylus, Sophocles, and Euripides.

Beneath the mass of myth and the final shape of the ritual, it is possible to see the worship of a vegetation spirit and the fertility cult so frequently associated with such deities in primitive religion. Dionysus' cult titles confirm this. He was "the Power of the Tree," the "Blossom-bringer," the "Fruit-bringer," the "Abundance of Life." His domain was, as E. R. Dodds puts it, "Not only the liquid fire in the grape, but the sap thrusting in a young tree, the blood

Remains of the Temple of Bacchus at Baalbek. ©*M.P.S.*

pounding in the veins of a young animal, all the mysterious and uncontrollable tides which ebb and flow in the life of nature." The tidy-minded Romans turned this ancient deity into the jolly Bacchus, the wine god with his reveling nymphs and satyrs, theme of Titian and Rubens, and turned "orgia" into "orgies," not the ecstatic acts of the transforming and horrible devotion that they were in their primitive context of nature worship and religious "possessions."

BIBLIOGRAPHY. J. E. Harrison, *Prolegomena to the Study of Greek Religion* (1903); W. F. Otto, *Dionysos* (1933); E. R. Dodds, *The Bacchae* (1944); W. K. C. Guthrie, *The Greeks and their Gods* (1950); E. M. Blaiklock, *The Male Characters of Euripides* (1952), 209ff.; C. Seltman, *The Twelve Olympians and Their Guests,* ch. XIII (1952).

E. M. BLAIKLOCK

DIOSCORINTHIUS dī′ əs kə rĭn′ thĭ əs (LXX Διὸς Κορινθίος). This word is found just once, in the Apocrypha (2 Macc 11:21) in the dating of a letter which Lysias, deputy of Antiochus Epiphanes and later regent of his successor Antiochus Eupator, wrote to the Jews. The date is given as the twenty-fourth day of Dioscorinthius (in the year 165-164). The name is otherwise unknown. There are several possible explanations. (a) It may mean the month Dios (or Dius) in the Macedonian calendar, equated with the Jewish month Marḥeshwan in Jos. Antiq. I. iii. 3. The addition of -corinthios remains unexplained. (b) In Lat. MSS of the passage there are VLL, Dioscoridos a name not otherwise known as the name of a month, and Dioscurus the third month of the Cretan year. (c) Another suggestion is that it was an intercalary month such as Babylonians and Jews found it necessary to insert every two or three years, as it was realized that the lunar year fell eleven days short of the solar year (see IDB, I. 486f.).

F. FOULKES

DIOSCURI dī ŏs ku′ re (Διόσκουροι, *sons of Zeus*). The twin patrons of distressed seamen in Gr. and Rom. mythology, whose names were Castor and Pollux.

Traditionally the sons of Zeus by Leda, to whom he appeared as a swan, they were also considered to be the children of Tyndareus, king of Sparta, where they were said to have ruled and had been buried. They were esp. worshiped by the Dorian Greeks. Castor was a great charioteer and Pollux a boxer. When Pollux was offered immortality by Zeus, he chose to share death with Castor who had been killed in a fight.

As the patrons of sailors, they were identified with the two highest stars of the constellation Gemini (Twins) and appeared also to sailors during electrical storms as St. Elmo's fire.

Paul sailed from Malta to Puteoli on an Alexandrian ship which was marked by the Dioscouri (Acts 28:11). The RSV interprets this to mean "with the Twin Brothers as figurehead." It was prob. the name of the ship which carried a symbol of the gods on the masthead, or as the figurehead.

A. RUPPRECHT

DIOTREPHES dī ŏt′ rə fez (Διοτρέφης, *nourished by Zeus* or *foster-child of Zeus*). The lone Biblical reference to Diotrephes is 3 John 9 where he is reprimanded for his failure to receive the representatives sent by the author, John. Evidently he had resisted the receiving of a former letter from John (v. 9), had maligned John, refused to grant hospitality to the brethren, and urged that all others of the congregation do likewise (v. 10). John characterizes him as loving "to have the preeminence."

L. FOSTER

DIPHATH. *See* RIPHATH.

DISCERNING OF SPIRITS (διάκρισις πνευμάτων). The charismatic gift of determining the genuineness of allegedly divine messages and works.

It was recognized, not only in Christianity but also among other religious groups, that supernatural acts and utterances might come from evil as well as good sources. There was consequent need for a means of discerning the motivating spirits. The Early Church was plagued by false prophets (1 John 4:1) as Jesus and Paul had warned (Matt 7:15; Acts 20:28ff.). The outcome of predictions (Deut 18:22) or the evidence of fruit (Matt 7:15f.) could not always be waited for, and God's true message must be quickly recognized and heeded (1 Thess 5:19-21).

First John 4:1ff. applies a confessional test. The spirit in question must make a commitment to the orthodox belief in the deity and humanity of Christ (cf. v. 15). Further, there must be submission to apostolic authority (vv. 5f.), as well as evidence of Christian moral character (1 John, passim).

In 1 Corinthians 12-14 the concern is for edifying ministry. With free participation, only the divine charismatic gift of discerning of spirits could provide the needed control. Therefore the gift of discernment was given. First Corinthians 12:10 is the sole occurrence of the actual term "discerning of spirits."

W. L. LIEFELD

DISCHARGE. *See* DISEASE, DISEASES.

DISCIPLE (תלמיד ; למוד ; μαθητής; μαθητρία, *learner, pupil, disciple*).

The idea of discipleship is very old. It was common among the Greeks, rarely mentioned in the OT (1 Chron 25:8; Isa 8:16; 50:4), yet a prominent feature of later Judaism. It always involved a teacher-student relationship. Derived as it was from verbs meaning "to learn," discipleship denoted the learning process but its usage described in addition the necessity of the disciple adopting the philosophy, practices and way of life of his teacher (cf. Xen. Mem. 1. 6. 3). Physical proximity of the student to his teacher was also implied in the meaning of discipleship, although there are instances when its meaning was extended to include pupils separated from their masters by centuries (Dio Chrysostrom 38 [55]. 3-5; John 9:28, where Jews contemporary with Jesus called themselves disciples of Moses).

Discipleship is also a prominent and important concept in the NT. John the Baptist had his disciples (Matt 9:14), the Pharisees theirs (22:16), even Paul his (Acts 9:25).

Most often, however, the word "disciple" was used to denote the relationship between Jesus and His followers. In its widest sense it included all those who believed on Him (John 8:30, 31), or who came to learn from Him (Matt 5:1, 2). At one time these disciples were many (Luke 6:17) and included a cross-section of society from sinners to scribes (Matt 8:18-22; Mark 1:16-20; 2:13-15; Luke 6:14-16; John 19:38). Many of these were from Galilee, but not all (John 7:3).

The word disciple also was used more narrowly, referring to some or all of Jesus' intimate circle of friends (Matt 10:1; 11:1; Luke 9:54; John 6:8), a frequent synonym for the Twelve.

All of Jesus' disciples were learners required to "abide" in His word (John 8:31, 32). This meant not only that they were to listen to what He said, but they were also to adopt His teaching as their way of life (Luke 6:40; John 15:7, 8).

His teachings covered many topics, but the whole of it was summarized in one commandment, love (John 13:34); and although discipleship had many facets it was summed up in a single concept—obedience to this command (13:35).

Jesus' teaching was for the many to hear (Matt 5-7; 13). Because it was radical, and, esp. that about Himself, too difficult to accept (John 6:60), the majority of disciples defected (6:66). Consequently, much of what He taught about His death and resurrection (Matt 16:21), about the end of the age (Mark 13), about love, the Father and the Holy Spirit (John 14-16), etc., was given only to the inner circle (6:68).

Discipleship was initiated by Jesus (Matt 4:19, an exception being Luke 9:57), and involved a commitment to His person even more than to His teaching. (Note: to criticize Jesus' disciples was to criticize Jesus, Mark 2:18, 23, 24, and to remove the teacher was to destroy the community of disciples, Mark 14:27, 50.) This is not to say that His disciples were unconcerned with what He taught. They prob. memorized much of His teaching, as was customary for disciples to do, and no doubt were responsible for passing on this teaching as the tradition of the church (1 Cor 15:1-3).

The idea of physical adjacency inherent in the word disciple also applied specifically to Jesus' associates. It was this idea that placed such radical demands on any one desiring to be His disciple. An itinerant rabbi, Jesus was constantly on the move. To be His disciple was in a literal way to be His follower. (Note: the verb "to follow" occurs about eighty times in the gospels, and exclusively describes the relationship between the earthly Jesus and His companions. It became a synonym for disciple.) This meant, therefore, that every disciple in the strict sense had to leave his occupation (Mark 1:18, 19), his father and mother (10:29), everything (10:28), take up his cross and go forward even to death (Matt 10:38). For the disciple was not above his teacher (10:24), and what would happen to the teacher could also happen to the taught (10:25; Luke 6:40).

The expression "disciple of Jesus," was also used less strictly. It described those who were His disciples secretly (John 19:38), and by implication those who were not at all physically adjacent to Him (cf. Mark 9:38-40; 5:18, 19). This looser concept of disciple may have made it possible for the writer of Acts to use it as a general term for "Christian" (Acts 9:25 and 19:1 are the only exceptions), the original idea of being an intimate companion of the earthly Jesus now almost forgotten.

Surprisingly, the word "disciple" never appears a single time in the NT outside of the gospels and Acts. It is also instructive to discover that the verb "to follow," a synonym for disciple and used frequently in the gospels, occurs only twice outside of them to describe the relationship between the risen Lord and His adherents (Rev 14:4; 19:14). Apparently, therefore, because the writers of the epistles saw in the meaning of the words "disciple" and "follower" a disciple-teacher relationship no longer possible in the new era, they dropped them from their vocabulary lest those requirements for the disciples of the earthly Jesus —to leave one's trade, his father and mother, etc.—be universalized and made general requirements for those who would believe on Him now as the exalted heavenly Lord.

The word "disciple" was revived, however, in the writings of the early sub-apostolic Church, and given much the same meaning as that in Acts, "Christian." Ignatius, however, employed it almost exclusively to denote those who became martyrs for the sake of Christ (Trallians 5:2; Ephesians 1; 2).

BIBLIOGRAPHY. K. H. Rengstorf, μαθητής (1942), in G. Kittel's *Theological Dictionary of the NT*, tr., and ed. by G. W. Bromiley; E. Schweizer, *Lordship and Discipleship* (1960); J. J. Vincent, "Discipleship and Synoptic Studies," *Theologische Zeitschrift*, XVI (1960), 456-469; S.

Legasse, *Scribes et disciples de Jésus*, RB, LXVIII (1961), 321-345; B. Gerhardsson, *Memory and Manuscript* (1964).

G. F. HAWTHORNE

DISCIPLINE dis' ə plin (מוסר ; παιδεία). The word discipline is Old Eng. from Lat. *disciplina,* "instruction," "training," "discipline," from *discipulus,* "a learner," from *discere,* "to learn." The Heb. *musar* is tr. "correction" or "chastisement," while a kindred word *moser* means "bands" or "bonds." Greek *paideia* includes both the negative and positive meanings listed above. Paul counsels: "Fathers, do not provoke your children to anger, but bring them up in the discipline and instruction of the Lord" (Eph 6:4). He states that the commendable conduct of "the Lord's servant . . . [is] correcting his opponents with gentleness" (2 Tim 2:24f.). In his climactic admonition to Timothy, he wrote, "All scripture is inspired by God and profitable for teaching, for reproof, for correction, and for training [discipline] in righteousness" (2 Tim 3:16).

Discipline in the OT is restricted to punishment by "the discipline of the LORD" (Deut 11:2) and by parents. Consequently, the following may be observed. Punitive discipline is administered by someone in authority and in position of responsibility. It is introduced Biblically with the Mosaic law as punishment for its violation (Lev 26:23; Deut 4:36; 11:2; cf. Exod 20:20). In a liturgy on divine judgment the psalmist quotes God in saying, "You hate discipline, and you cast my words behind you" (Ps 50:17). Centuries later, when national Israel was on the brink of disaster, facing the impending judgment of the Babylonian captivity, its apostasy was recalled: "This is the nation that did not obey the voice of the LORD their God, and did not accept discipline" (Jer 7:28). Means of divine discipline included plagues, pestilence, poverty, wild beasts, crop failure, property destruction, famine, sword, captivity, fear, pining, disease, desolation, and death (Lev 26:14-39).

Besides the five already mentioned, eleven other references to discipline occur in the OT, all of them in Proverbs. The writer admonishes: "My son, do not despise the LORD's discipline" (Prov 3:11); points out that "the reproofs of discipline are the way of life" (6:23f.); that "Whoever loves discipline loves knowledge" (12:1); and that one should not hate discipline (5:12), for "He dies for lack of discipline" (5:23), and "there is severe discipline for him who forsakes the way" (15:10). With reference to parental discipline, "He who spares the rod hates his son, but he who loves him is diligent to discipline him" (13:24); "Discipline your son while there is hope" (19:18); discipline will expel folly from a child (22:15; see 23:13; 29:17).

The NT discipline is primarily of a positive nature, and is associated with love rather than law. Jesus' life and teachings, and that of His dedicated followers elevated discipline to an essential and desirable means of achieving the highest goals. Jesus' willingly self-imposed deprivations and sacrifices constitute the noblest forms of discipline (Luke 9:58; Phil 2:1-8). The same spirit is manifest in His teachings concerning self-denial and bearing crosses (Matt 10:37f.; Luke 14:25-33).

Significantly and appropriately Jesus' specially selected twelve men were called "disciples." They were learners under the great Teacher, having accepted His invitation to "Take my yoke upon you, and learn from me" (Matt 11:29). They had matriculated in His school and committed themselves to His discipline, the education required for their high calling. Following this precedent self-discipline became a chief characteristic of dedicated Christian workers. After the resurrection, and the new power given on Pentecost, Christ's followers committed themselves to learning the sacred writings and to teaching others. Paul admonished Timothy to "Train yourself in godliness" (1 Tim 4:7b); and "Do your best to present yourself to God as one approved, a workman who has no need to be ashamed, rightly handling the word of truth" (2 Tim 2:15); and "Take heed to yourself and to your teaching" (1 Tim 4:16). The writer of Hebrews mentions discipline six times, all in one ch., in the punitive manner of its OT use. He begins with the exhortation, "Do not regard lightly the discipline of the Lord" (12:5), and concludes, "For the moment all discipline seems painful" (12:11).

Ultimately discipline is in the hands of God, though it is delegated in part to institutions: government, school, church, and home. And everyone is disciplined, either by self, or society or God.

BIBLIOGRAPHY. R. de Vaux, *Ancient Israel* (1962), 147-150; E. W. K. Mould, *Bible History* (1966), 552, 581-584, 682.

G. B. FUNDERBURK

DISCOURSE OF ST. JOHN THE DIVINE. The standard Gr. form of the *Assumption of the Virgin,* edited from five MSS by Tischendorf. Translated in ANT 201ff.; cf. also NTAp. I. 429.

DISCOURSE OF THEODOSIUS. A Bohairic VS of the *Assumption of the Virgin,* and one of the main sources for the Coptic form of the legend (ANT 198ff.).

DISCUS. Throwing the discus was an athletic exercise practiced by the Greeks and an important event in the Gr. athletic festivals. It is frequently mentioned by Homer and the discus thrower was a subject of Gr. artists, Myron's *Discobolus* being world famous, though the original is lost. There is no mention of discus or discus throwing in the canonical books of the Bible and only one reference appears in the Apoc. The discus is referred to as an indication of the degree of Hellenization promoted by the high priest, Jason. Jason set up a place of exercise under the citadel (2 Macc 4:12) and the author of Maccabees describes with disapprobation the results of this innovation: "So that the priests had no more any zeal for the services of the altar: but despising the sanctuary, and neglecting the sacrifices, they hastened to enjoy that which was unlawfully provided in the palaestra, after the summons of the discus" (2 Macc 4:13, ASV [1908]).

C. E. DeVries

DISEASES OF THE BIBLE (חלי, מחלה Gr. νόσος, *disease, illness*).

A disease is a definite entity of sickness of part or all of the body, with a characteristic group of symptoms.

For a brief description of the development of medical care to cope with diseases in Biblical times, *see* Physician.

It is likely that the Hebrews were subject to the same diseases that are prevalent in the semitropical climate of the mid-East today. However, in many cases the Bible only mentions symptoms, such as fever, hemorrhage, discharge or itch, and one can only surmise what the disease entity was.

Perhaps in this discussion of the diseases of the Bible and their symptoms, it will be most helpful if they are listed in alphabetical order and then briefly described.

Alcoholism. Wine was a very common drink in Biblical days, much as coffee is now. This was good in a country like Israel. Dysentery of several kinds was endemic and drinking water easily contaminated. Wine was a safe drink because of its alcoholic content. The Bible speaks favorably of wine in several places. When Isaac gave Jacob his blessing (Gen 27:28), he said "May God give you plenty of grain and wine." Then, of course, we have the classical record of Jesus miraculously changing a huge volume of water into wine.

Some scholars seek to show that the wine was really only grape juice. This is improbable, since grape juice would quickly spoil with temperature and living conditions as they were in Biblical days. Wine was definitely wine as we know it today, and it was a good thing for the people of that day.

However, it is also true that some Hebrews used wine to excess and got themselves and others in trouble. The Bible repeatedly speaks favorably of wine, but warns frequently and emphatically against its excessive use.

There seems to be a strange chemistry in the bodies of certain people that produces a strong craving for alcohol. They start drinking it in normal manner with their food, or socially, but are unable to control themselves and go on to excess. Beer and whiskey were prob. unknown to the Jews, but excessive wine drinking can do just as much damage as other forms of alcohol intake. A true wino is a sad looking specimen of humanity, and is on his way to committing suicide through destruction of his brain, liver and other organs.

In modern times alcoholism is looked upon as a disease, and is treated as such. In Biblical days it was considered a moral problem. Chronic alcoholism is an amazingly stubborn ailment. Persons who seem to have recovered from it show relapses after months or years in seventy-five percent of such cases. Christian faith is of enormous help. Several chronic alcoholics have been instantaneously cured of alcoholism by simply accepting Jesus as their Savior and Lord. Undoubtedly there were cases like that in the old days when alcoholics returned to sincere Jehovah worship. Medication, counseling, institutional training, and Alcoholics Anonymous are valuable, but none are as effective as that mysterious experience known as "rebirth."

Atrophy. Job speaks of one of his afflictions with the words, "He has shriveled me up" (Job 16:8). The impression received of Job's physical troubles is that he was assailed with several ailments, one of which was atrophy. If we were to think of a disease most likely to make Job "shrivel up," we might think of muscular dystrophy. This is a condition in which the muscles refuse to absorb the food brought to them by the blood. Food intake may be adequate, with digestion and absorption from the gastro-intestinal tract normal, but when the food gets to the muscles it is not adequately absorbed by them. As a result the muscles grow increasingly thinner and weaker. As an example we may think of a child with muscular dystrophy being picked up by a parent. In a normal child, the muscles in its shoulders, chest, back and hips give it some solidity; but when a youngster with muscular dystrophy is picked up, he may unexpectedly slide through a parent's arms like a slippery eel, because there is so little muscular structure left. The brain is not involved, but the body in an advanced case would be much as Job described himself.

Another reference to atrophy is found in Luke 6:6. Jesus healed a right hand that was withered. This time the atrophy could have been due to injured nerves paralyzing the hand and allowing it to wither. Another likely cause is polio meningitis.

Polio is caused by a virus—an organism so small that it is not even visible with an ordinary high power microscope. The tiny virus is found primarily in the mouth and pharynx, and in the lower bowel. Food contaminated by fecal material may contain the polio virus, and this is the principal method by which it is spread. The germ is picked up by the small bowel and travels to the central nervous system. Sometimes the disease is so mild that it is not even diagnosed excepting during an epidemic. At other times paralysis of almost every degree may occur and be permanent.

Polio is more frequent in tropical climates than farther N, and it must have been a common ailment in Biblical days. The man with the withered hand may very well have had polio years earlier, with just the single hand permanently affected by it. When paralyzed muscles are not used, withering, or atrophy, inevitably occurs.

Thanks to devoted scientists—and the goodness of God—vaccines have been developed which are amazingly effective in protecting people against polio. As with smallpox, polio is now almost unheard of in our country.

Baldness. Jews usually had a luxuriant growth of hair on head and chin. It was a source of pride to them. Foreign neighbors of Israel sometimes shaved their scalps and chins as a sign of mourning (Isa 15:2), but the Israelites were strictly forbidden to follow this practice (Deut 14:1). Unavoidable baldness was considered regrettable, and sometimes disgraceful.

There were, and still are, many reasons for baldness. Perhaps the greatest is an inherited tendency. Wearing a heavy or tight hat can interfere with the flow of blood to the scalp. Advanced and debilitating diseases can be the causative factor in baldness, as also simple old age. However, the two most common causes were seborrheic dermatitis, a fungus infection with a dirty mess of greasy, yellowish crusts, and tinea capitis (ringworm of the scalp).

Blindness was common in Egypt, Israel and the Arabian countries. Poverty, unsanitary conditions, brilliant sunlight, excessive heat, blowing sand, accidents, and war injuries were some of the factors involved, but the main cause was ignorance of infectious organisms.

The blindness from birth spoken of in the Bible was prob. ophthalmia neonatorum (gonorrhea of the eyes). This has been the prime cause of infantile blindness for centuries. Women often harbor gonorrheal diplococci in their vaginas, even though they may be totally unaware of the infection. Then, when a baby is born, and it makes its passage down from the uterus, it may get some of the germs in its eyes. The conjunctiva of a baby is an ideal breeding place for gonococci, and in about three days the baby's eyes run with pus. In many cases permanent blindness results. In modern practice, antiseptic drops are placed in the infant's eyes immediately after birth, and the infective organisms that may be present are destroyed.

The other frequent cause of blindness was trachoma. The infecting organism is a virus. I have treated scores of Navajo Indians with this disease, and it was a pitiful sight to see them come in with their bleary, itching, painful eyes. Some of them had an apron of tissue, called a pannus, growing down over the cornea. Many older people had badly deformed eyelids, and some were blind. Today's sulfa drugs provide an easy and complete cure, but in former days it was a devastating illness.

A Syrian settler in Egypt whose leg shows deformation typical of infantile paralysis. From a Stele of the 13th century B.C.

Boil. It is likely that the word "boil" as used in the Bible covered many types of skin diseases, such as pustules, simple boils, carbuncles, abscesses and infected glands.

Boils, as we know them today, are usually caused by staphylococci. These germs are normally present on the surface of the skin, and do no harm unless there is some kind of injury to the skin, allowing the germs to get inside and proliferate. The body reacts with its defense of leucocytes, and in the battle that ensues germs, leucocytes and debris may form a painful pocket of pus that we call a boil. If the boil is single and comes to a head, it ruptures and recovery follows.

A carbuncle is much like a collection of boils in a limited area. The infection runs deeper than an ordinary boil and has several openings. It is commonly located in the back of the neck. It usually covers an area several inches in diameter, and sometimes is fatal.

An abscess may be minor, but frequently is deep, involving important structures of the body, such as muscles, lungs, brain, liver, spleen, kidney, bowel and appendix.

Hezekiah's boil must have been a carbuncle or deep abscess, as his life hung in the balance when he was afflicted with it. Job's boils were superficial, or they would have resulted in his death. The boils of the sixth Egyp. plague prob. were extremely painful superficial boils.

The Babylonians used boils in its broader sense. Recently archeologists dug up a Babylonian tablet which stated that if a physician cut into a boil and the patient died, the physician would have both his hands cut off. If the patient happened to be a slave, the physician's hands were spared, but he had to buy another slave for the owner of the patient. So, the doctor had to be extremely careful when he lanced an abscess or a boil.

Consumption. This word appears only twice in the Bible (Lev 26:16 and Deut 28:22). In both instances it is included in a list of disasters that would befall the people of Israel if they rejected their God. Efforts have been made to limit its meaning to tuberculosis or malaria, but it is more likely to refer to the whole group of wasting diseases, including esp. dysentery in its several forms.

Deafness may be partial or complete. There are several general areas that may be involved in deafness. The first of these is the external ear canal. With the sand, dust and drying heat of the mid-East, there must have been many cases in which the ear canal became plugged with wax and dirt, producing a serious degree of deafness. Undoubtedly many persons suffered deafness much of their lives because of dirty ears. Infections of the external ear canal were also common in tropical and semi-tropical countries.

The middle ear is another frequent source of trouble. This little chamber with its three tiny ossicles—the malleus, incus and stapes—forming a little chain from the ear drum to the window of the cochlea, and the Eustachian tube coming into it from the pharynx, serves an important function in hearing. The area may become infected by organisms coming through a ruptured ear drum, or through the Eustachian tube. Severe deafness may also be due to the ossicles becoming rigidly solidified to each other following an infection.

The inner ear is the third possible location of trouble. It is called the cochlea because it resembles a snail shell. It is really an extension of the auditory nerve. Infection of the cochlea or tumors of the auditory nerve and hearing center of the brain are uncommon, but severe when they occur.

It should be remembered that we have two ears and that it is possible to be deaf in one and not the other.

"Deaf" and "deafness" are also used fig. with reference to lack of response to the voice of God (Isa 29:18).

There is a curious reference to the deafness of an adder (Ps 58:4), "like the deaf adder that stops its ear." This prob. refers to an ancient belief that an adder, to avoid hearing the sounds of a charmer, placed one ear on the ground and stopped the other with the tip of his tail.

Demon possession. *See* DEMON. It is undeniably true that in Biblical days diseases in general were ascribed to the presence of evil spirits in the patient, although not so much in Israel as in other countries. Violent episodes, such as might occur with insane persons, or those with severe attacks of epilepsy, strengthened belief in demon possession.

Demon possession may simulate or cause diseases such as epilepsy, insanity, or aphasia, but it is distinguished from these in the Bible (see Matt 4:24; 17:15; Mark 9:17-27). Not every case of illness which Jesus cured was attributed to demonic influence, but certain instances were definitely so identified (*see* EPILEPSY).

Dropsy is an abnormal accumulation of serous fluid in the tissues of the body, or in one of the body cavities. If it is locked in the structure of the tissues, it is usually called edema. It is commonly seen due to a faulty heart or diseased kidneys. There is bloating of the face. Arms and legs may be greatly swollen and have a doughy appearance. Liver disease from alcoholism can fill the abdomen with gallons of fluid. The abdomen feels as hard as a drum, and pressure of the fluid against the diaphragm makes it difficult for the patient to breathe. If the fluid is drawn off with a hollow needle, it gives only temporary relief, and the abdomen soon fills up again.

Dwarf. Dwarfs seem normal at birth, but early in life it is noted that linear growth is abnormally slow, and after the tenth year it may stop entirely. This retardation in growth may have various reasons. One is a deficiency of the pituitary gland. This small gland near the base of the brain has various important functions, and one is to manufacture a growth hormone. When the supply of this hormone is insufficient, dwarfism results; if it is excessive, gigantism may result. Human growth hormone is almost impossible to obtain and extremely costly, but when used in cases of dwarfism due to deficiency of this hormone, it really stimulates growth. Thyroid extract seems to fortify its effectiveness.

Dwarfism may be an inherited characteristic, as in the pygmies of Africa. It may also be due, and often is, to such deficiencies as rickets, poor absorption of food from the small bowel, chronic kidney disease, and malformations of the heart.

Physical normalcy was demanded of Heb. priests, and therefore dwarfs were barred from priestly duties (Lev 21:20).

Dumbness may refer to total inability to speak (mutism), or to inability to speak clearly and coherently (aphasia) as was the case with the man mentioned in Mark 7:32, who "was deaf and had an impediment in his speech."

Dumbness in the sense of mutism may be due to stubborn uncooperativeness, to severe depression because of an external calamity (Ps 38:13), to extreme fright as seen in Saul's companions (Acts 9:17), to hysteria or to a lesion of the brain. A person born completely deaf may be mute for a long time because he is unfamiliar with sounds. However, his organs of speech may be normal, so that with proper training, he can learn to speak (think of Helen Keller).

The dumbness of sheep was not due to inability to make a sound, but is considered to be a token of submission. Idols were called dumb (1 Cor 12:2) because they had no life in them. They were unable to hear, speak or act.

Dysentery was a very common ailment among the people of the mid-East. It was due primarily to three types of organisms—amebae, bacteria and worms. In some cases the body adjusted itself to the invading organism, and there would be only sporadic attacks of diarrhea. But often it was very severe, and at times so bad it was called malignant dysentery. Plague is the most striking example of such malignancy. The stools consisted mainly of mucus, pus and blood. It was accompanied by severe abdominal pain, and frequently high fever. Passage of stools was painful with dysentery because of the irritating effect of the excretions. Hemorrhoids developed, and at times there was a prolapse of the lower part of the colon, as was the case with Jehoram (2 Chron 21:18) "His bowels came out because of the disease, and he died in great agony" (v. 19). There was also rapid loss of weight, and death might ensue within a few days. Publius (Acts 28:8) "lay sick with fever and dysentery," and we can readily appreciate his gratitude when God healed him.

Epilepsy (ἐπιληψία) is a Gr. word meaning "a seizure." This seizure may be very light, such as a twitch of the face or hands, or even a recurring sharp, but brief abdominal pain, and is then known as "petit mal." The really alarming attacks are called "grand mal." The patient suddenly falls down, loses consciousness, starts shaking all over with convulsions, chews his tongue, and foams blood from his mouth. The fit lasts from five to twenty minutes.

Epilepsy, in some form, is a very common disease with an estimated average occurrence of one in every two hundred persons. Hippocrates gave a good description of it about 400 B.C. Like many of his contemporaries, he considered it due to possession by some god or demon. Sometimes it was called the "sacred disease"; at other times "possession by demons."

In Matthew 4:24 it is listed as one of a group of diseases. In Matthew 17:15 a man called to Jesus, "Lord, have mercy on my son, for he is an epileptic and suffers terribly; for often he falls into the fire, and often into the water." Jesus said the boy was possessed by a demon. The demon was ordered out and the boy was healed.

The cause of epilepsy is obscure. It may be inherited. If just one party in a marriage has epilepsy, their offspring will prob. not have it, but if there is epilepsy in the person or family of both individuals, the danger of one or more of their children inheriting the disease is very great. Other causes are brain injury from accident, tumors on the brain, hardening of the arteries, etc.

With modern sedatives, the attacks can be almost completely eliminated, but no effective medical treatment was available in Biblical days.

Fever refers to bodily temperature distinctly higher than normal. Our bodily temperatures are beautifully controlled under normal circumstances by an inner mechanism which keeps the temperature at about 98.6 degrees Fahrenheit. The controller of this mechanism is a small gland called the hypothalamus, located near the center of the brain. It sends its commands to the liver, heart, lungs, muscles, fat, skin, sweat glands, and other organs, and has them work in unison to keep the body temperature within approximately one degree of the normal 98.6. This temperature control system is another evidence of the supreme intelligence, wisdom and power of God in creation.

Disease may overwhelm this mechanism. When an infecting organism enters the body, a tremendous battle goes on, involving millions of cells, with the body trying desperately to defeat the invading organism. This increases the metabolism of the body and fever results. Usually the body wins and the temperature returns to normal. With extremely severe sickness, the temperature may rise to as high as 108 degrees, and death may ensue.

Peter's mother-in-law had a high fever. It might have been due to flu, pneumonia, or an intestinal disease. It is assumed that malaria was common in the mid-East in Biblical times, and that this may have been the cause of her high fever. However, the Bible does not say and trying to identify the disease is pure speculation.

Fiery heat. This expression is used in Deuteronomy 28:22, "The LORD will smite you with . . . fiery heat, and with drought." What does fiery heat refer to in this text? Is it related to the high fevers associated with diseases mentioned in the same text, or to heat stroke, or perhaps to the failure of harvest due to excessive heat? Probably to all three.

The temperatures in Israel ran very high in summer, and they had no air conditioning. It is true, they were acclimatized to heat, enabling them to work in temperatures that would kill someone coming from a cooler climate, but even so, the blazing sun could injure with heat stroke.

Heat stroke is characterized by body temperatures that rise very high—106 and 107 Fahrenheit, together with cessation of sweating, and with unconsciousness. It is not difficult to envisage the distress of people in a hot country, with successive years of drought, and the dangers related to the necessity of hard, physical labor in the hot sun.

The boy who cried, "Oh, my head, my head" and then died (2 Kings 4:19) undoubtedly had an attack of heat stroke.

Headache. *See* FIERY HEAT.

Hemorrhage. In Luke 8:42-48 we have the account of a woman who had a flow ("issue" KJV) of blood for twelve years. Was this rectal or vaginal bleeding? In a primitive, semi-tropical country like Israel, there were many cases of bloody diarrhea and dysentery. The woman's trouble may have been a recurrent or chronic attack of one of these.

It is generally assumed, and prob. correctly so, that it was vaginal bleeding. If so, we would like to know approximately how old she was. If forty years, or less, she might have been concerned not only about the messiness of her condition, plus the loss of strength and weight, but also about the fact that she was unable to bear children—something that the women of that day took very seriously.

It is not likely that it was a continuous flow of blood. If it were, she would not have lived twelve years with it. More likely it was a frequently recurring experience. A common cause of this would be hormone imbalance. Her ovaries could have been secreting too much estrogen. Her menstrual periods would then have been prolonged and profuse, or they might have occurred more than once a month.

It has been suggested that fibroid tumors were the cause of her trouble. Many women have such tumors—most of the time without abnormal bleeding. Much depends on the locaion and size of the tumors. They may occur on the outer surface of the uterus. They may be smaller than marbles or larger than grapefruit.

Another frequent location is within the muscular walls of the uterus, expanding the uterus until at times it fills the pelvis like a wedge. In such cases constipation or distressing frequency in passing urine may be experienced, as well as heavy bleeding.

Other fibroids grow just beneath the mucosa on the inner walls of the uterus. Sometimes these appear as finger-like polyps that may be the forerunner of carcinoma.

Carcinoma must be expected in every case of chronic vaginal bleeding. The focus of the disease is usually in the cervix of the uterus. The cervix becomes ragged and cancer may develop in this area, spreading later to the body of the uterus and neighboring glands. It is not likely that the woman healed by Jesus had cancer, however. If that were the case, she would prob. have died before twelve years went by.

Impediment of speech. This physical difficulty is mentioned in Mark 7:32, "and they brought to him a man who was deaf and had an impediment in his speech."

"Aphasia" is such an impediment and it appears in many forms. For example, some persons are at a total loss for words when they smell something and want to give expression to their reaction. Others have the same experience when it concerns tasting food. Others have what is called "amnesic aphasia." They cannot recall certain words that ordinarily are completely familiar to them. Then there are those with motor aphasia—people who know what they want to say but cannot utter the words because the muscles of mouth and face refuse to respond. Persons with gibberish aphasia speak words and phrases that make no sense. People who stutter also have a real impediment of speech.

There are impediments of speech due to abnormalities of the face or mouth, such as a severe tongue tie, or hare lip, or a face which is badly scarred.

A rather common impediment of speech is known as auditory aphasia. Persons who were born deaf, or became deaf in early childhood—perhaps as a complication of measles—do not know what speech sounds like, and, excepting in rare cases, either do not try to talk at all, or speak with difficulty and lack of clarity. This was prob. the case of the man who was healed by Jesus, as it is recorded that he was also deaf.

Indigestion. Paul writes to Timothy "no longer drink only water, but use a little wine for the sake of your stomach and your frequent ailments" (1 Tim 5:23).

The digestive processes of the body are more evidence of the wonderful way the Lord has fashioned us. As soon as food enters the mouth, digestion starts. Our saliva contains an enzyme called "ptyalin" which starts the digestion of carbohydrates. When the food gets to the stomach, some of the carbohydrate digestion continues, but proteins get the major attention and are broken up by pepsin and hydrochloric acid. After the stomach has completed its job, the partly digested food seeps through the pylorus into the duodenum and small intestine. Here several additional digestants get to work, including secretions from the liver and pancreas. Millions of villi—like microscopic hairs—extend from the inner surface of the bowel, absorb the digested food, and pass it on to the blood and lymph vessels.

Many people feel that they have to use a whip to this system, and so add pepper, hot sauce, or chili to their food. Some of these are powerful additives. I have tried to eat chili so strong that it felt like fire on my lips, and yet was amazed to see other persons in the restaurant eating the liquid fire with gusto.

Wine is not nearly as strong as chili, but the alcohol in it is a stimulant, and its sugar content also has a tonic effect. So Paul advises Timothy to use a little of it instead of water. The word "little" is interesting. Paul did not want to give the impression of advocating any large use of wine.

Timothy was evidently not strong physically. Paul does not say why. Improper diet and nervous strain may have been factors. At all events, Timothy did not have an ulcer of the stomach or duodenum, for then wine would have been contraindicated.

Infirmity. John 5:5 (KJV) tells of a man at

the pool of Bethesda who "had an infirmity thirty and eight years." In v. 7 we read that he was an "impotent" man.

Infirmity is a word with a very broad meaning and may refer to any disease of the body, or abnormality in its structure. The implication seems to be that something happened to him thirty-eight years previously and left him with a residual incapacity so severe that he is called impotent and was unable to compete successfully with other diseased or handicapped people in getting into the healing pool of water.

This could well have been a paralysis dating back to an attack of polio in his youth. In many cases of polio both legs are left completely and permanently paralyzed. Other extremities and organs of the body may also be involved. If his infirmity had been a continuous illness, it would in all probability have run its course in far less than thirty-eight years, and ended in either recovery or death.

Inflammation. Deadly germs, esp. streptococci and staphylococci are always present on the surface of our bodies. Surgeons are well aware of this, and before they perform a major operation they must scrub their hands with a stiff brush and plenty of soap to get them as free as possible of these germs.

The first defense against these organisms is the skin itself. Skin consists of several layers of cells packed closely together and gives excellent protection against germs.

If that skin is bruised or cut, germs immediately get in and start multiplying. They promptly encounter a second line of defense. Leucocytes (white cells) go to war with the invaders.

Leucocytes are so called because, when looked at through a microscope, they appear transparent, in contrast with the iron-laden red blood cells. They are of various types, and each kind has its own job to do. I like to think of them as state police, foot soldiers, heavy artillery, and reserves.

Leucocytes are always present in the body by billions. If you can imagine a tiny cube 1 mm. in size (1/25th of an inch), think of it, when filled with blood, as containing about 5,000,000 red cells and about 6,000 leucocytes. These leucocytes are constantly on patrol throughout the body. They are present in every organ and even in the stroma between the cells of body structures. They are continuously on the watch for foreign invaders and for any debris that may be floating along.

After a bruise or cut, the leucocytes attack invading organisms. Most of the time they win their battle with relative ease and the patient does not take his injury seriously. Sometimes, when the invaders are particularly virile or numerous, they win the first battle. The call goes out immediately for additional leucocytes held in reserve in bone marrow. Within hours, the leucocyte army will not only be doubled, but new ones by the billions will go into production.

A general view of the Pool of Bethesda where Jesus healed the sick man (John 5:2-9). © *Lev*

At the site of infection, some leucocytes will absorb the invaders by a process known as phagocytosis. Microscopic examination has shown that a single leucocyte will absorb (eat) as many as 20 invaders, and some have been seen to engulf up to 100 of them. The germs are digested by the leucocytes and unwanted remnants are excreted.

As a result of this struggle, there will be inflammation with localized heat, swelling and pain. A pocket of pus may result from the debris of battle. The leucocytes can be aided by allowing the pus to escape. As healing takes place, other leucocytes (trash collectors) take the debris away. Liver and spleen are the principal organs for filtering the unwanted material from the blood. Some of it is used to manufacture new cells (re-cycling), and the balance goes primarily to the kidneys for excretion.

The inflammation may be localized, as in a single boil, or appear in multiple lesions, as predicted in Deuteronomy 28:27, and experienced by Job.

Insanity (σεληνιαζόμενος, *lunatic*, Matt 4:24 KJV; שִׁגָּעוֹן, *madness*, blindness and confusion of mind, Deut 28:28).

Insanity is an unpleasant word. Many persons think of it in the words of Proverbs 26:18—"like a madman who throws firebrands, arrows and death." It is, however, an illness of degrees, and is the result of a defect in part or all of the brain.

Insanity (lunacy, dementia) may be unrecognized in its early stages. It may start with a loss of mental alertness, loss of energy, difficulty in remembering, esp. concerning recent events, or the patient may have trouble connecting words so they make sense. He may become lost easily, show poor judgment, become depressed, gloomy, anxious, irritable, and fearful that someone is trying to hurt him (paranoia). He fails to take care of himself and may have to be given nursing care. His trouble may go on to total disorientation.

There is a form of dementia called Alzheimer's disease. It starts in middle life and is the result of gradual deterioration of the cerebral cortex. It is characterized by disorder in gait, disorientation, and hallucinations. Death usually occurs in from five to eight years. This disease is of special interest because the deterioration of the brain is similar to that seen in senility.

What brings on insanity? Perhaps the greatest factor is heredity. In some cases excessive use of drugs such as barbiturates, alcohol, marijuana, and heroin may have caused the damage to the brain. Certain illnesses, such as syphilis, pernicious anemia, epilepsy, malaria, plague and typhoid fever may be responsible. Arteriosclerosis, cerebral hemorrhage, and injury are relatively common causes. The madness predicted in Deuteronomy will result from inability of the people to cope with overwhelming disaster.

Issue of blood. *See* HEMORRHAGE.

Itch. This is another of the curses with which the Lord threatened Israelites who departed from the faith (Deut 28:27). Itch is a discomfort with which the inhabitants of the sub-tropical mid-East were thoroughly familiar.

The chief culprit in producing itch is a tiny mite known as "Sarcoptes Scabiei" and the disease it generates is known as Scabies. The female in the Scabies family is the one who does all the hard work. She digs through the upper layer of skin and makes a burrow for her home. The burrow is short—just a small fraction of an inch—but it is a definite characteristic of Scabies. A clever dermatologist, with the aid of a magnifying glass, can pull the Scabies mite out of its burrow.

While in that burrow, the Scabies mite causes intense itching, esp. at night. The victimized person scratches desperately to relieve the itching, frequently digging through the skin and starting serious infection.

The Scabies mite has a few favorite spots for burrowing. They include the inner surface of the wrist, the lower abdomen, and the glans penis.

The Scabies mite is stubborn and may exist for years (seven year itch) in unclean, untreated individuals. It is prevalent in time of war and has been known to seriously handicap soldiers.

Lice also can make life miserable with their itching. There are three well known types—the head louse, the body louse, and the crab (or pubic) louse.

Leprosy was greatly feared by the Israelites, not only because of the physical damage done by the disease, but also because of the strict isolation laws applying to leprosy, making the patients feel like feared outcasts of society.

It was in 1873 that a Norwegian by the name of G. Armauer Hansen discovered a bacillus he called "Myobacterium leprae," which he found in nearly all cases of leprosy, and abundantly so in severe cases. The more euphonious term of "Hansen's disease" is now commonly used instead of leprosy.

Leprosy appears in two principal forms. The first, and by far the more dangerous, is called "lepromatous"; and the other, more benign type, is designated as "tuberculoid."

Both start with discoloration of a patch of skin. This patch may be white or pink. It is most likely to appear on the brow, nose, ear, cheek or chin. I have seen one case of beginning leprosy with a whitish patch on the side of the abdomen. The patient said he felt no pain whatever when the skin in this patch was repeatedly pierced by a needle.

In the lepromatous type of leprosy the patch may spread widely in all directions. Portions of the eyebrows may disappear. Spongy, tumor-like swellings grow on the face and body. The disease becomes systemic and involves the internal organs as well as the skin. Marked deformity of hands and feet occur when the tissues between the bones deteriorate and disappear. Often the sensory nerve endings no longer respond to heat or injury and the unwary patient may be subject to further destruction of his limbs before he realizes his danger.

Leprosy is a long lasting disease. Untreated cases may be sick with lepromatous leprosy from ten to twenty years, death occurring from the disease itself or from an intercurrent invasion of the weakened body by tuberculosis or some other disease.

The tuberculoid type is less severe. As stated, it starts with a change of skin color in a localized area. More such patches may follow and each patch is characteristically surrounded by a low ridge. However, the tuberculoid type of leprosy tends to be limited and even untreated cases heal completely in from one to three years. What a wonderful feeling it must have been for such patients to return to their priest and be declared healed!

One interesting phenomenon in both the lepromatous and tuberculoid types is that they have recurrent periods of exacerbation and subsidence. During the period of exacerbation the lepromatous cases suffer fever, pain and prostration. This flare-up may last for hours, days or weeks, and it is during these periods that the disease is most contagious.

So far as we know, the Hebrews had no cure for leprosy other than divine intervention. In modern times, there are very effective medicines available, and leprosy patients are usually not isolated.

Lunacy. *See* article on LUNATIC.

Madness. *See* article on MADNESS.

Obesity. Judges 3:17; "Now Eglon was a very fat man"; Judges 3:22: "and the fat closed over the blade."

Surgeons who have had to cut through two to four inches of fat to get into an abdomen can easily understand what happened to Eglon. Moreover, excessive fat is located not only in a thick, greasy layer between the skin and muscles, but also in the abdomen with its thick mesentery and abundance of fat around the organs.

A panel of doctors from the American Medical Association, testifying in a U.S. Senate Committee hearing, stated that the principal causes of obesity were: 1) heredity, 2) glandular disturbance, 3) nervous worry, and 4) big appetite. Another is the desire for prestige. In countries where food was scarce and an adequate diet difficult to obtain, it was a source of pride to a person if he and the members of his family had full faces and protuberant abdomens. Once while I was in China, and in conversation with a language teacher, the teacher became enthusiastic in describing his wife, who he said was very fat and he was so proud of it. Fatness could be important in a country where the ability to obtain adequate food was uncertain, and the person might have to call

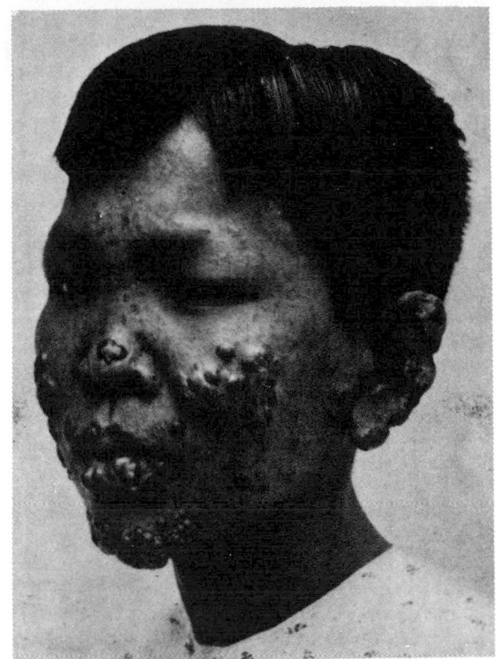

Above: Lepromatus Leprosy. *Stitt's Diagnosis*

Below: Mutilation of the hands in leprosy. *Stitt's Diagnosis*

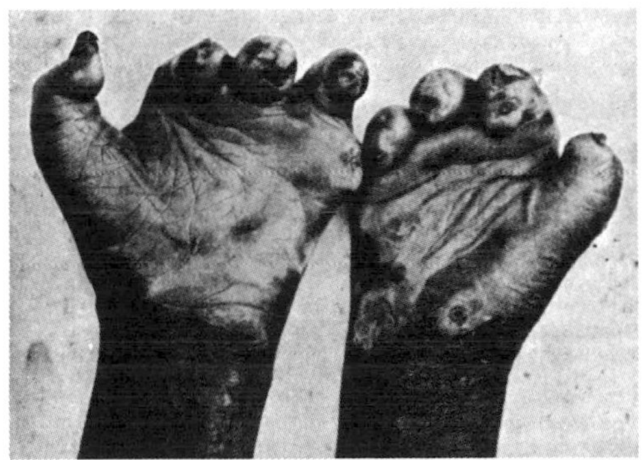

on his reserves of fat, much as a camel uses the fat in his hump.

In modern times we have been alerted to the dangers of obesity with respect to our hearts, varicose veins, arteriosclerosis, arthritis, diabetes, possible surgery, and the number of years we shall live. Diet and reasonable exercise are the ingredients of relief.

Old age. Old age is a disease if it is regarded as a gradual decrease in vitality, finally ending in death.

There is a marvelous reconstruction process going on in our bodies at all times. Old cells are constantly being replaced by new ones, and it has been estimated that a person acquires almost a complete set of new cells every seven years; but the replacement cells are not all perfect. Until we reach about twenty-two years of age, the new cells are fully as good, even better, than the ones they replace. After that age limit, replacement still goes on vigorously, but the new cells are somehow defective and become increasingly so as old age creeps up with decreasing muscular strength, vague aches and pains, loss of teeth, defective eyesight and hearing, forgetfulness and other familiar handicaps.

What is missing in the body after age twenty-two that prevents renewal cells from being just as good as the ones the body received before twenty-two? Is it a hormone? Scientists are trying to find out, and it is possible they will succeed.

Prior to Noah's time, people lived up to almost a thousand years. In later Biblical times, the average life span was much shorter than it is now. Look up the records of the lives of the kings of Judah and Israel, and note at what age most of them died! Today we may be grateful if our lives have been free from serious diseases and we may slowly, almost imperceptibly, move to the day of our transition.

Palsy. *See* the article on PALSY.

Pestilence is a word that is used frequently in the Bible. There is a striking example of David's sin that was punished with the death of 75,000 of his people by a pestilence (2 Sam 24:15) that lasted three days. Amos 4:10 speaks of "pestilence after the manner of Egypt."

Plague is the disease most likely referred to. It was endemic in Egypt and along the Mediterranean Coast of Pal. In severe outbreaks of the disease, death usually occurred within three days of the first appearance of symptoms.

Some Biblical scholars have suggested that cholera might be implicated, but according to Beeson and McDermott, "Prior to the nineteenth century, cholera was unknown outside India."

If cholera did exist in the land of Israel, it certainly would fit under the heading of pestilence. It is commonly transmitted by contaminated drinking water or by food that had been grown in fields fertilized with human excrement. It is endemic in India and oriental countries. It is characterized by a terrific diarrhea, with adult patients passing up to thirty quarts of liquid bowel movement in one day. Patients drink great quantities of water, if they can get it. In modern times, early treatment cures almost every case; but when patients are not treated, the death rate in adults is about seventy percent.

Plague. *See* PLAGUE.

Scabies. *See* ITCH *in this article.*

Scurvy. *See* SCURVY.

Skin diseases. The Hebrews had a wide variety of skin diseases and many of them are listed in the Bible. *See* CAUL, SCAB, SORE, SCURVY, TETTER and ULCER; also (in this article) **Baldness, Boil, Inflammation, Itch, Leprosy** and **Scabies.**

Starvation. Deuteronomy 28:53, "And you shall eat the offspring of your own body, the flesh of your sons and daughters."

Starvation is a matter people in the mid-East were well acquainted with in Biblical times. Periods of drought were common, and when they continued for successive years they were disastrous. We need think only of the experience of the Egyptians and Joseph. The drought was so bad that Joseph induced the Egyptians to pay for their food with their personal wealth, then with their livestock, next their land, and finally with their freedom, making them all slaves of the Pharaoh.

The craving of a hungry man for food can be extreme. Within the brain there is a small portion of brain tissue known as the hypothalamus. This organ has control of appetite and sends out agonizing sensations of hunger when the food intake is seriously inadequate. Experience of soldiers in concentration camps, such as the men captured by the Japanese at Bataan, show to what extremes men will go to get a morsel of food when they are being starved.

Civilized people have been known to resort to cannibalism. If a mother had a baby, she prepared her afterbirth as food. Parents will eat their children in extremities of hunger, and men will eat one of their comrades if he succumbs during a desperate search for food in a desert, or the sea, or when caught in a siege.

When the intake of calories is less than the body needs for its metabolism, reserve body fat is first used. When this is largely exhausted, the proteins will be called on. Meanwhile, of course, the body is gradually weakening until it dies either from starvation, or from an intercurrent disease that has gotten a foothold in the weakened body. If the water is easily obtainable, a healthy man may live from thirty to forty days without food. With no water, he will be gone in less than half that time.

Tetter. *See* the article on TETTER.

Trachoma. *See* BLINDNESS *in this article.*

Tumor. *See* the article on TUMOR and PLAGUE.

Ulcer. *See* the article on ULCER.

Worms are perhaps as nearly omnipresent and prolific as any animals on earth. Certainly the Israelites had plenty of them while living under rather primitive conditions in a semi-tropical country. The variety of them is almost unbelievable. Some of the main groups are tapeworms, flukes, roundworms, hookworms, ascariases, threadworms, and our old nemesis, the pinworm. Authorities say that there are over a half million identifiable species.

The tapeworm gets into the body when persons eat food infected with them. The worm has three or four suckers, and with these attaches itself to the upper part of the small bowel. The worms are flat, like a ribbon, and grow in segments. Sex is no problem as they are all bisexual (hermaphrodites). In the small bowel they allow themselves to be swished back and forth by the liquid food.

As long as there is plenty of food coming down from the stomach, the bowel doesn't mind the floating ribbon of tapeworm enjoying a share.

It is interesting to note that the tapeworm absorbs food through the covering of its body. It has no mouth. It would be the same as if we were able to smear peanut butter on our abdomen and have it absorbed directly through the skin.

There are beef, pork and fish tapeworms. They grow to be ten or more yards long and some live twenty-five years. Segments of the tail break off, and some of these segments are loaded with eggs. They may reach a farmer's fields when included in fertilizer and grow on the plants that the cattle eat. The embryos penetrate the muscles of the cattle. People eat the infected meat and a new life cycle begins.

It should be noted here that with tapeworms, as well as with other species of worms, the body can well tolerate a few of them, but when they overpopulate they can cause serious illness and even death.

Flukes are the small worms that our soldiers had so much trouble with in Vietnam. Somehow the eggs of flukes penetrate snails. The flukes multiply rapidly, get into water, and attach themselves with suckers to anyone sloshing through the water. They dig through the skin, enter the blood stream and reach the lungs. Ultimately they land in the veins of the liver, intestine and bladder, where they may do permanent damage.

It is estimated that one-fourth of the population of Africa is infected by these flukes. In Israel, Iraq and Iran they are endemic. Irrigation is a big help to the flukes and their snails. When the Aswan Dam was being built in Egypt and irrigation started, the pools of water came alive with flukes and started an epidemic.

Pinworms are one of our commonest worms and are well-known in the mid-East also. They have an interesting life cycle in that the female pinworm migrates to the anus, usually during the night and deposits her eggs. She then causes intense itching of the anus, and sometimes of the vagina also. The normal reaction is to scratch. Eggs get under finger nails and next day into the food, to start life all over again in the intestine. Surgeons operating for appendicitis occasionally find the appendix filled with pinworms.

The Ascaris lumbricoides is the large roundworm found in man, and it has been estimated that one in every four people of the world have it. The Ascaris has a daily output of about 200,000 eggs. It has a dangerous habit of forming bridges across the lumen of the bowel and thus occasionally causing intestinal obstruction.

The hookworm is a little fellow that sucks blood from the small bowel and causes anemia.

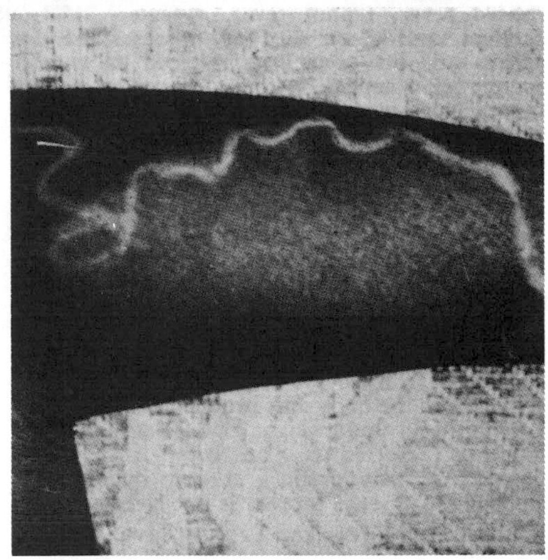

Above: Female guinea worm lying under the skin of the forearm. *Stitt's Diagnosis*

Below: Guinea worm rolled on stick for gradual extraction. *Stitt's Diagnosis*

It grows rapidly in warm, moist soil. It is able to climb stems of grass as high as three feet. Like some other worms, if they are able to reach the skin of man, they penetrate it and travel with the blood stream to the lungs. Then, in some strange way, they are able to squeeze through the walls of the alveoli of the lungs, climb up the bronchi, go down the esophagus and reach their favorite home in the bowel.

The guinea worm often is mentioned in a discussion of mid-Eastern worms. It is not as prolific as some of the others, but has an interesting life. The worm is found in shallow wells or pools used for drinking water, and thus gets into the human body. As is more often the case, the male is small and not very important except for copulation and fertilizing eggs.

The female grows until she may be a yard long. To discharge her larvae she works her way through the body till she reaches the buttocks or thighs. There she secretes a little toxin from her head and raises a vesicle. When the top is rubbed off this vesicle, she lets go of her larvae and hopes they will safely get to drinking water again. It is important to pull the long worm out of the body. This is done by grasping her head end and winding her on a stick, an inch or two a day, until she is completely dislodged. If, during this process, the yard long worm is broken and the remaining part cannot be found, a serious infection may take place.

BIBLIOGRAPHY. White and Geschichter, *Diagnosis in Daily Practice*, (1943); Reich and Nechtow, *Practical Gynecology* (1950); W. A. Dorland, *The American Illustrated Medical Dictionary* (1951); G. M. Lewis, *Practical Dermatology* (1952); G. C. Sauer, *Manual of Skin Diseases* (1959); W. A. Sodeman and W. A. Sodeman, Jr., *Pathologic Physiology* (1961); A. C. Guyton, *Textbook of Medical Physiology*, (1966); P. B. Beeson & W. McDermott, *Textbook of Medicine* (1971).

R. H. Pousma

DISH. The tr. in ERV of four Heb. and two Gr. words. 1 and 2. In Exodus 25:29; 37:16; Numbers 4:7, where the KJV, ASV have "dishes and spoons," the RSV has "plates and dishes." The Heb. word for "plates" is קערה, and refers, in these passages, to a deep and large gold dish in which oblong cakes were brought to the table, or laid upon it. The word for dishes is כף, and refers to the cups for frankincense, which were placed upon the loaves and burned on the altar of burnt-offering at the end of the week.

3. Jael brought Sisera curds in a "lordly bowl" (Judg 5:25, KJV "dish"), evidently a bowl of large size, one fit for a lord. The Heb. word is ספל.

4. "Flat dish" (צלחת) is used metaphorically in 2 Kings 21:13.

5. The "dish" (*τρύβλιον*) into which Jesus and the apostles dipped the sop at the Last Supper (Matt 26:23; Mark 14:20) was really a large bowl, made either of earthenware or bronze.

6. When Jesus said in Luke 11:39 that the Pharisees cleansed the outside of the cup and of the dish (*πίναξ*), He had in mind a shallow dish. In four other occurrences of the Gr. word in the NT the RSV trs. it "platter" (Matt 14:8, 11; Mark 6:25, 28).

S. Barabas

DISHAN dī′ shăn (דישן ; LXX Ρεισων; *a kind of antelope* or *mountain goat*). The leader of a clan of the Horites descended from Seir (Gen 36:20-30; 1 Chron 1:38-42). His people were eventually displaced by the Edomites (Deut 2:12).

DISHON dī′ shŏn (דישון, דישן, דשן, LXX *Δησων*). Its meaning may be indicated by occurrence of the common noun, דישון in a list of clean animals which may be eaten (Deut 14:5). It is tr. in LXX with *πυγαργον*, which is the Libyan antelope. The RSV trs. "ibex").

1. A chief of the Horites and fifth son of Seir whose land was appropriated by Esau and his descendants (Gen 36:21, 26, 30; 1 Chron 1:38, 41b).

2. A son of the Horite chief, Anah, and grandson of Seir. He was the brother of Oholibamah, Esau's wife (Gen 36:25; 1 Chron 1:41a, 42). A comparison of Genesis 36:21-30 with 1 Chronicles 1:38-42 suggests the Dishan in Genesis 36:28 should be read Dishon (son of Anah). The LXX has *Ρισων*.

D. H. Madvig

DISMAS. Alternate form of Dysmas.

DISPENSATION (*οἰκονομία*, *to divide, apportion, administer* or *manage the affairs of a house*, Lat. *dispensatio, to weigh out* or *to dispense*), a stewardship (Luke 16:2-4; Eph 3:2); a commission (1 Cor 9:17); a plan (Eph 1:10; 3:9); a divine office (Col 1:25) divine training (1 Tim 1:4).

A. Definition. 1. *Scriptural use.* The Gr. word tr. "dispensation" occurs in three forms in Scripture. As *οἰκονομία* it occurs in Luke 16:2 where it is tr. to "be a steward." The noun *οἰκονόμος* occurs ten times and is usually tr. "steward," an exception being Romans 16:23, where it is tr. "city treasurer." The noun *οἰκονομία* which is the direct source of the tr. "dispensation" is used nine times and is tr. in the RSV as noted above. In each of these cases the underlying thought is consistent with the lexical meaning of the word; i.e., the process of managing or supervising the affairs of another or of a house.

In four occurrences (Eph 1:10; 3:2, 9; Col 1:25) the word has the sense of a divine stewardship or administration that is being accomplished by God. In this use the word takes on the significance of "plan" as well as "administration," and is the foundation for further definition.

In *Dispensationalism Today*, Ryrie sees the passage in Luke 16 as characteristic of the use of the word *οἰκονομία*. He observes four pertinent features: (1) There are two parties involved including one who delegates duties and one whose responsibility is to fulfill those duties. (2) There are specific responsibilities involved in the arrangement. (3) A steward may be called to account for his administration of his stewardship. (4) A change may be made if there is unfaithfulness in the arrangement (p. 26).

Therefore, there seems to be two different uses of the word in the NT: the first as illustrated in the parable of Luke 16, and the second as the word comes to be used by Paul in Ephesians and Colossians when he speaks of the divine administrations of God manifest in his program on earth, with some writers making the earlier use illustrative of the latter.

2. *Theological definition.* Based on the above use of the word in Scripture, theologians have given further definition to the word in its use as describing the unfolding of God's program on earth. With variations dependent upon the system of the theologian, God's arrangement with man upon which He is working out His plan is called a dispensation.

At this point unity of perspective concerning the term seems to end. The major division is between those who are called covenant theologians and the dispensational theologians. The covenant theologian sees the Covenant of Grace as the overriding unity of Scripture and uses the concept of a dispensation to speak of the manifestations of that covenant. Charles Hodge, for example, asserts that there are four dispensations after the Fall—Adam to Abraham, Abraham to Moses, Moses to Christ, and Christ to the end. These dispensations are simply the outworking of the Covenant of Grace (*Systematic Theology* [1946], II, 373-77). Louis Berkhof more typically speaks of only two dispensations—the Old and the New.

An alternative approach for this concept in covenant theology is to speak of the Old Covenant and the New Covenant without recognizing either as a dispensation. This approach is demonstrated by Buswell in his *A Systematic Theology of the Christian Religion.*

The common characteristic of the covenant approach is that any change of administration is seen only as an aspect of the unifying Covenant of Grace. Thus its emphasis is soteriological and the change is more that of anticipation in the Old and accomplishment in the New than it is an actual change of administration.

In contrast to this methodology, dispensationalism develops its understanding of the progress of revelation as a series of dispensations, or arrangements with man that God has set forth in the course of history. The *Scofield Reference Bible* has been the primary popularizer of this approach.

Scofield defines a dispensation as "A period of time during which man is tested in respect of obedience to some specific revelation of the will of God" (p. 5). Scofield then distinguishes seven such dispensations in the Scriptures.

Other dispensational writers have not emphasized the time period aspect in their definition and have placed their emphasis on the nature of the arrangement. For example, Ryrie defines a dispensation as "A distinguishable economy in the outworking of the plan of God" (op. cit. p. 29). H. A. Ironside has stated, "There are various economies running through the Word of God. A dispensation, an economy, then, is that particular order or condition of things prevailing in one special age which does not necessarily prevail in another" (H. A. Ironside, *In the Heavenlies*, p. 67).

B. Historical uses of the word. The above distinctions made by theologians today are not necessarily characteristic of the use of the word down through church history. Since the above difference is relatively recent, it may be of value to note how the word has been used in times previous.

According to Ryrie the earliest use of the word is by Justin Martyr who distinguished the programs of God while noting the uniformity of God's righteousness. He also speaks of the present dispensation (*Dialogue with Trypho*, XCII). Berkhof identifies Irenaeus' three covenants as dispensations but Irenaeus himself does not refer to them as such. He does refer to dispensations, and speaks of the Christian dispensation.

Augustine uses the word with some frequency and states in one place: "The divine institution of sacrifice was suitable in the former dispensation but is not suitable now. . . . There is no variableness with God, though in the former period of the world's history He enjoined one kind of offerings, and in the latter period another, therein ordering the symbolical actions pertaining to the blessed doctrine of true religion in harmony with the changes of successive epochs without any change in Himself" (*To Marcellinus*, CXXXVIII, 5, 7).

Post-Reformation writers who used the term in developing their understanding of Scripture were men such as Pierre Poiret (1647-1719) who wrote *The Divine Economy*. He had seven dispensations which, although differing from the contemporary forms, include one before the Flood, one to Moses, etc., down to the millennium which is the final dispensation. Jonathan Edwards published a volume in 1699 entitled, "*A Complete History or Survey of All the Dispensations.*" He includes four dispensations since the Fall but considers the millennium to be a spiritual fulfillment in the Christian Dispensation (II, p. 720).

Isaac Watts identifies five dispensations and defines the terms as follows: "Each of these dispensations may be represented as different religion, or at least, as different forms of religions, appointed for men in several successive ages of the world" (*Watts Works*, II, 625).

There is, therefore, a variety of uses of the term down through the centuries, preceding the modern period. If there is a uniformity of description of the dispensations in this list, it would prob. have two common characteristics. (1) God has worked in varying ways with people and (2) these ways are identified with successive time periods in God's sovereign plan.

C. The current debate. The current discussion about the nature of a dispensation grows out of the development of systematic theology since the Reformation. With the return to the Word and to evangelical theological growth, theology became much more systematic. Luther's and Calvin's work became Lutheranism and Calvinism and were gradually organized into full-scale theologies.

Out of Calvinism developed covenant theology with its organization of the progress of revelation around the Covenants of Works and Grace. Within the Covenant of Grace, the change of administration was noted as the Old and New Covenants or sometimes dispensations. This concept was intended to help organize and explain the differences that are found in the Old and New Covenants with reference to the manifestations of salvation.

The Reformation also brought a return to prophetic study, and there is a rise of belief in premillennialism that is characterized by some post-Reformation groups. As was illustrated in Pierot and Watts above, this was sometimes organized into a dispensational scheme.

In the 19th cent. a member of the Plymouth Brethren, John Nelson Darby, began the process of systematizing and organizing these dispensational approaches into a systematic theology. Dispensationalism which resulted from this has come to be a significant force in American Christianity.

Ryrie defines the system growing out of this mode of thinking. "Dispensationalism views the world as a household run by God. In this household God is dispensing or administering its affairs according to His own will and in various stages of revelation in the process of time. These various stages mark off the distinguishably different economies in the outworking of His total purpose and these economies are the dispensations. The understanding of God's differing economies is essential to a proper interpretation of His revelation within those various economies" (*Dispensationalism Today*, p. 31).

Therefore, the current discussion revolves around the proper use of the term theologically. The dispensationalist does not object to the Covenant theologian's use of the word, but believes that he has not done full justice to the differences and development of the various dispensations. The Covenant theologian usually objects strongly to using the concept of the dispensations as the foundation for the unity of the Scriptures.

The primary objection to this latter use is that dispensationalism teaches two ways of salvation. A footnote to John 1:17 from Scofield is usually cited at this point. "The point of testing is no longer legal obedience as a condition of salvation, but acceptance or rejection of Christ with good works as a fruit of salvation." While the clear implication is that salvation in the OT is by works, not faith, contradicting the principle of faith, Buswell has well pointed out that this approach is not unique to dispensationalism but is also inferred in Hodge and Calvin (*Systematic Theology*, I, 316). There is a sense in which the Covenant of Works faces the same problem. It implies that man at one time could merit salvation by his works.

While there are passages of Scripture that may be interpreted to imply the possibility of salvation by works (e.g., Luke 10:28; Rom 2:6; James 2:14-26) it is clearly taught in Scripture that salvation is by faith alone. Therefore, later dispensationalists have rejected the inference of Scofield and insist that the various arrangements of the dispensations include manifestations of the faith that saves rather than being the source of salvation.

A second major objection to the dispensationalist structure is that it makes dispensations into time periods rather than stewardship arrangements. While it is admitted that the word οἰκονομία refers to the arrangement and the word αἰῶν speaks of time, there is a close connection between the arrangement and the time in which it is in effect. Most contemporary dispensationalists do not include the time factor in their definition.

A third major criticism of dispensationalists' use of the term is that it divides the Bible into time periods and fails to see the unity of Scripture. Berkhof has stated, "Since the dispensations do not intermingle, it follows that in the dispensation of the law there is no revelation of the grace of God, and in the dispensation of Grace, there is no revelation of the law as binding on the New Testament people of God" (*Systematic Theology*, pp. 291, 292). While there may be a validity to this criticism in some statements made by dispensationalists, most theologians holding this position state that in the progress of revelation there is unfolded the will of God in various economies. Rather than being terminated as a principle they grow or evolve into the next economy. The resulting process is like stair steps with each arrangement building on the preceding one, sometimes borrowing from it and usually adding to it. Thus, while there is always a manifestation of the grace of God, the dispensationalist states that the contemporary age is characterized by *grace* while the previous one is better described by the term *law*.

Another criticism that is often raised is characterized by Clarence Bass in his book, *Backgrounds to Dispensationalism*. It is his contention that dispensationalism is recent in church history and divisive within the church and by implication then, in error. While there is some validity to this argument especially in the life of Darby (see Bass, pp. 48-99), the implications of such arguments are not necessarily valid. The Reformation in the sense of church history is both recent and divisive. The key is that theology must be evaluated for its Scriptural support in a primary sense and for its impact in a secondary sense.

D. The number of dispensations. 1. *Covenant theology*. In this position the number of dispensations is widely varied. Buswell accepts none while Berkhof and most others accept two, Hodge contends that there are four in the Old Covenant and one in the New. The actual number really does not significantly affect the system.

2. *Dispensational theology*. From this perspective the number of dispensations varies somewhat, although the seven held by the Scofield Bible are the most usual. Some minimize the early ones and combine conscience and human government, while others make the tribulation a separate dispensation and then the total may be more than seven.

The crucial distinction that makes dispensationalism's approach distinct is to distinguish between God's program for Israel in the past, particularly the law, God's present program for the Church, and the future manifestation which is the millennium. Usually this scheme is accompanied by a belief that the Church will be raptured before the tribulation, further distinguishing the church age.

3. *Ultradispensationalism.* There is a distinctive branch of dispensationalism that further distinguishes the dispensations which is sometimes called Bullingerism after one of its early leaders, E. W. Bullinger. It is sometimes called the Grace Gospel Fellowship or the Worldwide Grace Testimony. While there is considerable difference among the adherents, their consistent tenet dispensationally is that they distinguish at least two dispensations in the current church age. They identify a Jewish church early in the Book of Acts and then a separate Gentile church later on. They often reject water baptism, but usually observe the Lord's Supper. Their definition of a dispensation usually includes a strong emphasis on the aspect of time as well as the emphasis on the stewardship or economy involved.

BIBLIOGRAPHY. C. I. Scofield (ed.), *The Scofield Reference Bible* (1909); L. S. Chafer, *Dispensationalism* (1936); A. H. Ehlert, "A Bibliography of Dispensationalism," *Bibliotheca Sacra* (1944-1946); O. T. Allis, *Prophecy and the Church* (1945); G. E. Ladd, *Crucial Questions About the Kingdom of God* (1952); E. Sauer, *From Eternity to Eternity* (1954); C. Stam, *Things That Differ* (1959); C. B. Bass, *Backgrounds to Dispensationalism* (1960); J. D. Pentecost, *Things to Come* (1964); C. C. Ryrie, *Dispensationalism Today* (1965).

H. P. Hook

CHART OF REPRESENTATIVE DISPENSATIONAL SCHEMES

Pierre Poiret 1646-1719	**John Edwards** 1639-1716	**Isaac Watts** 1674-1748	**J. N. Darby** 1800-1882	**James H. Brookes** 1830-1897	**James M. Gray** 1851-1935 (Pub. 1901)	**C. I. Scofield** 1843-1921 (Pub. 1909)
Creation to the Deluge (Infancy)	Innocency Adam fallen Antediluvian	Innocency Adamical (after the Fall)	Paradisaical state (to the Flood)	Eden Antediluvian	Edenic Antediluvian	Innocency Conscience
Deluge to Moses (Childhood)	Noahical Abrahamic	Noahical Abrahamical	Noah Abraham	Patriarchal	Patriarchal	Human Government Promise
Moses to Prophets (Adolescence) Prophets to Christ (Youth)	Mosaical	Mosaical	Israel—under law under priesthood under kings	Mosaic	Mosaic	Law
Manhood and Old Age	Christian	Christian	Gentiles Spirit	Messianic Holy Ghost	Church	Grace
Renovation of All Things			Millennium	Millennial	Millennial	Kingdom
					Fullness of times Eternal	

Adapted from *Dispensationalism Today* by Charles C. Ryrie,

DISPERSION, THE. *See* DIASPORA.

DISTAFF dĭs' tăf (כּישׁוֹר) KJV SPINDLE. A stick used to hold flax or wool fibers during the process of spinning (Prov 31:19). One of the virtues of a noble woman is that

"She puts her hands to the *distaff*, and
her hands hold the spindle" (Prov 31:19).

Spindle and distaff are reversed in the KJV. The RSV seems preferable for the first word, כּישׁוֹר, is from a root meaning "to be straight" corresponding to *distaff* and the other (פלך) is from a root meaning "to be round" corresponding to the *whorl* on the spindle. Moreover, the second word is tr. in the LXX by ἄτρακτον, which means "spindle."

A woman when spinning would hold the distaff under her left arm. She would take the long fibers from the distaff and attach them to the notch in the end of the spindle, which was a shaft from 9 to 12 inches long and tapered on both ends. Near the bottom of the spindle was a whorl. This was a circular weight of clay, stone, or some other heavy material with a hole in the center to allow it to be placed on the spindle. The whorl provided momentum to keep the spindle turning smoothly when it had been twirled between the thumb and forefinger. Additional fibers would be added and twisted into thread as the spindle rotated. When the thread became so long that the spindle reached the ground it would be wound around the spindle and the process repeated until the spindle was full.

BIBLIOGRAPHY. S. Driver, *Notes on the Heb. Text and Topography of the Books of Samuel* (1913), 250, 251; T. Fox, "Spinning," *Encyclopaedia Britannica* (1961), XXI, 233.

D. H. MADVIG

DISTINGUISHING SPIRITS (διακρίσεις πνευμάτων). A manifestation of the Holy Spirit in some believers, as a gift, enabling them to discriminate what is genuinely of God from what is of demonic spirits or merely the human spirit. The primary v. is 1 Corinthians 12:10. The verb for "discerning" (KJV), *diakrino*, means "to pass judgment" or "make a distinction," as when a believer having the gift of discernment tells what is really of the Spirit from words of different speakers (1 Cor 14:29). False prophets were a threat to doctrine and practice in the Early Church (2 Cor 11:12-15; 1 John 2:19; 4:1; 2 John 7, 10, 11; Rev 2:2). Many regard this gift, like apostleship, as temporary to meet this Early Church peril only (Walvoord, p. 188). It supplied, in gifted persons, what was later available through a completed NT, an authoritative standard. Not the gifted only, but all believers must exercise discernment to some degree, then as now (1 Cor 2:14, 15; 1 John 2:20, 27; 4:1-6; cf. Phil 1:10). They need caution against evil spirits using false doctrine and also counterfeits from man's own deceitful impulses and emotions.

BIBLIOGRAPHY. A. R. Hay, *The New Testament Order For Church and Missionary* (1947), 189, 203-207; J. F. Walvoord, *The Holy Spirit* (1954), 188; A. Bittlinger, *Gifts and Graces, A Commentary on I Corinthians 12-14* (1967), 45-47.

J. E. ROSSCUP

DIVES dī' vez (πλούσιος, *rich*). The name traditionally given to the rich man in the parable of the rich man and Lazarus (Luke 16:19-31). Actually, his name is nowhere given in the parable. Vulgate trs. πλούσιος, by "dives," "rich," "wealthy." The use of "Dives" by the 3rd cent. is seen in the Lat. tr. of Irenaeus (*Against Heresies*, II xxxiv. 1). *See* LAZARUS.

J. B. SCOTT

DIVINATION (קסם, *practice divination*; נחשׁ, *observe, divine, enchant*; ענן, *observe times* [KJV], *practice soothsaying.* Other relevant words include: אוֹב, *medium, necromancer, familiar spirit* [KJV]; ידעני, *wizard,* כשׁף, practice *witchcraft, sorcery*).

Divination is the practice of consulting beings (divine, human, or departed) or things (by observing objects or actions) in the attempt to gain information about the future and such other matters as are removed from normal knowledge.

1. Classification of types. The above definition suggests the need for distinguishing between what might be termed *personal* or intuitive, and *impersonal* methods. The term "divination" indicates that a divine Being provides the information. Seers, the Pythia who uttered the oracle at Delphi, and mediums who consult the dead, all are said to receive messages from a personal source or in a subjective way. Other methods, sometimes called "artificial" or "automatic," are gathered from impersonal things like the flight of birds, a sneeze, or the casting of lots.

Divination is related to magic, but is distinct from it mainly in that the latter attempts to produce certain effects while the former seeks knowledge. Nevertheless practitioners of one also might engage in the other. Note the various practices and practitioners associated in Deuteronomy 18:10 (cf., 2 Chron 33:6), which were a threat to Israel.

2. Methods of divination. a. *Chresmology.* Prognostication by seers and through oracles may be considered a form of divination to the extent that information is sought out. The OT indicates that prophets were formerly called seers, and were consulted to ascertain God's will (1 Sam 9:9). However, seers, like prophets, could be false, and Micah 3:7 links them with diviners, to whom God refuses an answer. Oracles were messages from a deity. The word also signified the place or person who transmitted them.

b. *Oneiromancy.* Dreams were thought to convey divine messages. These frequently need-

Ceremony of "opening the mouth" for giving the deceased a new body in the hereafter, an illustration of necromancy: New Kingdom. ©B.M.

ed interpretation (as was given by Joseph and Daniel). An ancient dream analyst, Artemidorus, who itinerated from city to city plying his trade, has left a vivid account of his practice. Sometimes one would sleep in a temple (incubation) hoping for a dream from the resident deity. The god of healing, Asclepius, was thought esp. communicative in this regard. Aelius Aristides, a hypochondriac orator, has related in his *Sacred Discourses* how Asclepius instructed him regarding treatment.

c. *Astrology* was an ancient means which gained in popularity, esp. in the Hel. period. On the assumption that the planets and stars were in harmony with earth and mankind, the character and fate of an individual, or even a whole nation, were determined through a horoscope based on the signs of the Zodiac (*see* ASTROLOGY).

d. *Necromancy* was consultation with the dead. This was done through a medium, who received messages through a "familiar spirit." This method received severe condemnation in the Bible (Lev 19:31; 20:6, 27; Isa 8:19f., where the KJV has the quaint rendering, "wizards that peep, and that mutter," in addition to Deut 18:10; 2 Chron 33:6). King Saul, who had banished mediums and wizards, nevertheless in desperation consulted the medium at Endor, an act for which he was judged by God (1 Sam 28:9-19; 1 Chron 10:13f.).

e. *Haruspicy*, study of the entrails of animals and esp. *hepatoscopy*, study of livers, provided a means of impersonal divination used widely from the Babylonians to the Romans. Since the liver was at one time considered the seat of life and since sacrificial animals were used, hepatoscopy was a religious practice.

f. *Augury* was the analysis of the movements of animals, and esp. of birds.

g. *Omens and portents* were of many kinds, including e. and f. above. A portent was an omen of great or supernatural character, such as earthquakes or heavenly phenomena. Typical omens were involuntary human actions, as a cough or hiccup, the actions of animals, or other impersonal occurrences. (Divination by human signs is called *cledonomancy*.) Since one who had decided on a course of action would be more affected by a contrary omen, they, and esp. portents, frequently took on a negative character.

h. *Mechanical means*. These would include *hydromancy*, divination by water (see below on Joseph and the cup), *pyromancy*, the observation of fire, and *cleromancy*. This last includes the use of plates or rods drawn at random (*sortilege*), the interpretation of the position of objects such as rods or arrows (*rhabdomancy*), and, in general, any casting of lots, or of dice, drawing straws, etc.

It will be observed that, in general, the above

methods range from the personal (seer and oracle) to the completely impersonal (lots). Yet, even omens were considered to convey the mind of God (cf. Prov 16:33; Acts 1:26).

3. History. Divination and magic are known from early times among many cultures. The OT reflects the situation in contemporary cultures: Moabite (Num 23:23), Philistine (1 Sam 6:2), and Babylonian (Isa 44:25). Egyptian magicians sought to duplicate the acts of Moses and Aaron (Exod 7:8-13, 22; 8:7, 18). Apparently Joseph learned divination performed by observing water in a cup (Gen 44:1-5, 15), although the Heb. also may be understood in a way which attributes wisdom to Joseph concerning (rather than by means of) the cup in question. The ability to interpret dreams is attributed to Joseph (Gen 37:5-11; 40:5-19), but this is understood to be a revelation from God (40:8), not a duplication of pagan techniques.

Divination in ancient Greece was originally not as much a religious function as in some other cultures. The seer was a familiar figure. Dreams and omens were of great importance throughout Gr. history. The latter were esp. sought with regard to a tentative course of action. Astrology, introduced from Babylonia, was accepted by many because of its claim to scientific accuracy. It made great gains after the unification of the world in the Hel. period and the decadence of formal religion and philosophy, which made its claim to cosmic unity and its offer of personal guidance attractive.

Oracles were offered not only at the famous shrine of Apollo at Delphi, but at that of Zeus at Dodona (the oldest shrine), and others. At Delphi the Pythia, the prophetess, sat on a tripod over a steaming fissure and communicated the oracle, which usually had to be interpreted by the "prophets" there. The ambiguity of many of these oracular interpretations is well known.

It will be noted from the above that the Greeks practiced both personal and impersonal divination. Often the personal involved "possession" by a deity, or "enthusiasm." This type did not find ready acceptance at Rome. Cleromancy, esp. sortilege, haruspicy, and various omens were popular. Augury was used to determine times for official functions that were "auspicious" (from *auspicium*, divination by the flight of birds). Such practices, though widely used, were, like astrology, spurned by some Romans. Nevertheless, they had their influence, as did the Sibylline Oracles, which had full acceptance.

4. Divination in the Bible. First it must be noted that there are several apparent occurrences of divination in both the OT and the NT. The case of Joseph has been mentioned. Daniel's interpretation of dreams is attributed to the revelatory power of the true God (Dan 2:17-23). The word used to describe Laban's claim to superior knowledge is a cognate of נחשׁ, otherwise used to describe enchantment or divination (Gen 30:27). The same word is used in the account of Balaam, who found that enchantment and divination were powerless against Israel (Num 23:23; 24:1). The Syrian Ben-hadad's servants watched for an omen (1 Kings 20:33 RSV). Numbers 5:11-31 provides for a procedure, in the case of a woman suspected of adultery, which could be considered either divination or, perhaps more precisely a means of judgment. Gideon's use of the fleece (Judg 6:36-40) is prob. to be classed with God's provisions of signs to confirm his revealed will, rather than as a means of divination. (Shortly afterward, Gideon also heard of someone's dream which indicated his forthcoming victory [7:13-15].) The incident in 1 Samuel 14:7-12 may be of the same nature. Ezekiel 21:18-23 provides a description of the devices used by the king of Babylon, arrows, teraphim (images), and liver. The use of arrows by Jonathan (1 Sam 20:20-22) and by Joash (2 Kings 13:15-19) was not for divination as some have maintained.

It is not known how the Urim and Thummim were used. It is suggested that they were two stones or other objects, possibly inscribed on opposite sides with the words Urim and Thummim. Exodus 28:30 indicates that these were kept in the breastpiece attached to the ephod worn by the high priest. Moses gave directions for its use (Num 27:21), and David employed it, asking questions which required a positive or negative answer. These answers are preceded by the words, "And the LORD said . . ." (1 Sam 23:9-12). There is no further mention of this device until postexilic times (Ezra 2:63; Neh 7:65).

In the NT, the casting of lots in Acts 1:26 is related without further comment. God indicated His will to Paul in an unspecified way through a prophet (16:6-10; 21:10ff.). Paul exorcised a "spirit of divination" who had possessed a girl (16:16ff.). Luke describes Simon the magician, whose figure reappears in early Christian lit. as the antagonist Simon Magus (Acts 8:9-13). In Acts 13:6ff. we are introduced to Elymas who is also a *magos.*

This word (*μάγος*) was used to describe the Pers. wise men and astrologers (Matt 2:1), clever people and magicians in general, or any scoundrel one might suspect or accuse of evil practices. *Magos* and *goēs* (*γοής*, "sorcerer") were words frequently employed in apostolic and postapostolic times as invectives against practitioners who were not of one's own religious persuasion. They are found in Josephus, the Church Fathers, and other lit. The Jewish Talmud contains accusations implying that Jesus had employed sorcery.

From time to time in Jewish history cabalistic practices have been followed, but, except for certain periods, divination has been rare in

Judaism and likewise in Christianity. The Church has on occasion risen to oppose allegedly magical practices, and the Salem witch hunts are esp. notorious. In the latter part of the 20th cent. occult practices again have flourished, including divination and witchcraft, requiring a fresh application of Biblical teaching.

It will be seen from the passages referred to that the Scriptures forbid divination and magic. The major passages include Leviticus 19:26, 31; 20:6; Deuteronomy 18:9-14; Isaiah 8:16-20; 44:24ff.; Jeremiah 14:13-16; 27:8-11; Ezekiel 13:6-9, 23. It will be noted that these references, given here in their full contexts, contain not only warnings against divination, but also affirmations that God speaks through His own true prophets.

BIBLIOGRAPHY. Cicero, *On Divination* (45 B.C.); A. Bouché-Leclercq, *Histoire de la divination dans l'antiquité* (1872-82); M. Summers, *The History of Witchraft and Demonology* (1926); M. Summers, *The Geography of Witchcraft* (1927); H. J. Rose, "Divination (Introductory and Primitive)," 3rd "Divination (Greek)," HERE (1928), 775-780; 796-799; H. S. Lea, *Materials Toward a History of Witchcraft* (1939); K. Seligmann, *The History of Magic* (1948); M. P. Nilsson, *Geschichte der griechischen Religion*, I, 2nd ed. (1955), II (1950); R. La Roche, *La Divination* (1957); R. H. Robbins, *The Encyclopedia of Witchcraft and Demonology* (1959); K. A. Kitchen, "Magic and Sorcery," NBD (1962); J. P. Hyatt, "Magic, Divination, and Sorcery," HDB rev. (1963); R. Alleau, *Histoire des Sciences Occultes* (1965); R. Flaceliere, *Greek Oracles*, tr. D. Garman (1965).

W. L. LIEFELD

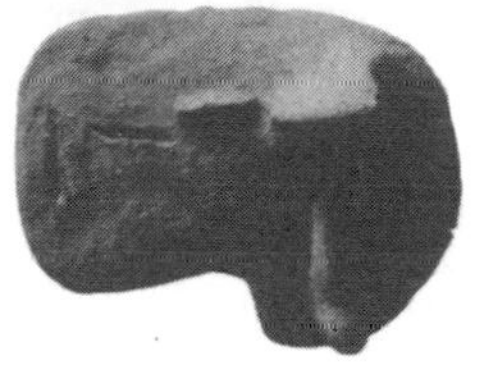

Clay models of the liver. One inscribed with omens and magical formulae for use of diviners, from about 1830-1530 B.C.: other uninscribed, from Megiddo, 1350-1150 B.C. ©*B.M. and* ©*P.A.M.*

DIVINE, DIVINER. *See* DIVINATION.

DIVINERS' OAK (אלון מעוננים, partially transliterated *plain of Meonenim* in KJV; *oak of Menonenim* in the New Scofield; tr. *fortune-tellers' oak* in BV, and *diviners' oak* in RSV and the JB.

Judges 9:37 is the only occurrence of the expression, although two other vv. may be relevant (v. 6 in the same ch. and Gen 12:6, reading "oak" instead of "plain"). The oak was in a prominent place, the "navel" (KJV "*middle*," RSV *center*) of the land, possibly on a small rise. The tr., "*diviners*," is based on the derivation of מעוננים from ענן, to "practice soothsaying." The existence of a tree in Canaan used for augury is not surprising in view of the widespread practice of divination. (*See* DIVINATION.)

W. L. LIEFELD

DIVINITY OF CHRIST. *See* DEITY OF CHRIST.

DIVORCE (כריתות ; *a cutting off*; ἀποστασιον). Divorce is a legal term for the act of removing the obligations of a marriage contract. Most societies have made some provision for the dissolution of a marriage when it does not prove satisfactory. Normally a divorce also allows the parties involved to contract a subsequent marriage.

Knowledge of the practice of divorce among the ancient Hebrews is quite sketchy. The primary references to divorce in the law (Deut 22:18-29; 24:1-4) are "case laws" referring to particular situations. No general law on divorce is present. Only Deuteronomy 24:1 alludes to the procedure to be followed. Several Biblical stories recount divorces (Gen 21:8-14; Judg 14:19, 20; 15:2, 6; 1 Sam 18:12-17). Much discussion has focused on whether Deuteronomy 24:1-4 refers to divorce because of adultery or for some lesser reason of incompatibility. However, since the law called for adultery to be punished by death (Deut 22:22), the latter is likely. Of course, many Heb. men in actual practice used divorce as a merciful response to an unfaithful wife (Matt 1:19).

Hebrew marriage was a legal contract binding a man and a woman and their families to perform certain socially prescribed roles. The contract covered the lifetime of the contracting parties; the male, however, as senior partner appears to have had the right of preparing a "bill of divorcement" and thereby terminating the arrangement.

It is important to realize that divorce is essentially a socio-political concept. Religion has been concerned primarily with challenging its abuse and with ministering to the suffering which it causes. Religiously, divorce, as Jesus later explained, lay outside God's will. Politically, it had to be allowed. A reading of OT laws concerning marriage and divorce suggests the importance of responsibility in one's family life.

The post-OT writings of the rabbis shed some light on the divorce issue. Two schools of thought emerged concerning the grounds for divorce. Rabbi Shammai restricted divorce to cases of adultery—conservative, but a liberalization of Mosaic law. Rabbi Hillel allowed divorce for almost any grievance, no matter how trivial. There is evidence that divorce was rather common in Jesus' day.

The basic ethical questions asked by Christians in discussions of divorce are: (1) Is a Christian ever justified in seeking a divorce? (2) Once divorced, may a Christian remarry?

Jesus' own teachings on the subject of divorce appear in Matthew 5:27-32; 19:3-12 and parallel passages (Mark 10:2-12; Luke 16:18). The first passage appears in the Sermon on the Mount. Here Jesus is depicted as going beyond Moses, making even more strict demands. The issue for interpretation is whether Christ was giving a "new law" for Christians or stating the extent of God's perfect will for mankind so that all might realize they are sinners in need of God's grace. Is this law or hyperbole? The second passage records Jesus' response to a rabbinical question concerning possible "justifiable" grounds for divorce. Here Jesus declares that marriage forges a unity between the couple. To dissolve this unity is contrary to God's will. Again, law or hyperbole?

In the history of Christian ethical thought two different approaches to ethics have been taken: (1) casuistry; (2) law/grace. Each takes a different approach to these teachings. The casuistic approach has been the more popular one. It sees Jesus as a new lawgiver. His teachings on divorce are the law for Christians. This law is normative and is to be applied to marital problems occurring in the life of individual Christians. The "except for fornication" clause (Matt 19:9) has been variously interpreted when applied to problems of justifying divorce under certain circumstances. Examples include subsequent discovery of premarital unchastity, extra-marital sex relations, and failure to perform marital responsibility. In Roman Catholic ethics this process becomes very elaborate. The new situation ethics is also casuistic. It glosses over Jesus' teaching on divorce and focuses on the law to love. The situationalist may justify divorce in a specific case as being "the loving thing to do." Essentially the casuistic approach seeks to determine if justifiable cause for a divorce action by a Christian can be found. This approach is often condemned on two grounds: (1) it is legalistic and devoid of the grace proclaimed in the Gospel; (2) it eases one's conscience allowing him to feel justified in his actions without suing for God's forgiveness.

The alternate approach finds Jesus' teachings to be an attack on the "cheap grace" of the Pharisees and their casuistry. Jesus' teachings on the commandments of God (Matt 5:17-48) radicalize them, removing any justification for one's doing less than the ideal. The Christian measures his actions by the ideal. Anything less is sin. Sin can be atoned only by the gracious forgiveness of God. Specifically, divorce is not the will of God; it is evil. Divorce hurts the husband and wife, the children, the families, the Church, and the community. The damage of divorce is irreparable. To divorce a woman, Jesus taught, is to brand her as unfaithful. If a man marries a divorcee, he becomes suspect. This approach finds no "justification" for divorce. Subsequently when the Pharisees challenged Jesus' authority to go beyond the commands by appealing to Moses, he responded that Moses was simply accommodating God's perfect will because of the sinfulness of the people. Moses was giving laws for the state; and the laws of the state can never be as demanding as those of the faith. This approach questions the validity of the exception clause in Matthew 5:32 and 19:9, since it does not appear in Mark and Luke. How does a radical ethic respond to those situations where divorce appears to be the "lesser evil," where divorced people wish to remarry or where a divorced person wishes to hold a place of leadership in the church? Here the emphasis shifts from law to grace. Although divorce is always wrong, God is gracious and will forgive (1 John 1:9). God forgives; Christians forgive; divorce is not the unpardonable sin. This approach to Christian ethics counsels repentance and faith.

Two passages from Paul, the "Pauline Privilege" (1 Cor 7:12-15) and the qualifications for bishops (1 Tim 3:1-7) should also be mentioned. The first is sometimes interpreted to mean a Christian can divorce an unbelieving spouse without sinning. The latter is interpreted as disqualifying divorced men from the ministry and the deaconate. Both interpretations are questionable.

In summary, the emphasis in the Bible is on contracting a successful marriage. At best, divorce is not in keeping with God's will. The family today is in a state of flux, undergoing many changes. Christians must hold fast to the "one flesh" concept and see divorce as a disruption of this relationship. Christ was right in seeing divorce being caused by the "hardness of our hearts." *See* MARRIAGE.

BIBLIOGRAPHY. C. Cavesno, "Divorce," ISBE, II (1915), 863-866; R. Patai, *Sex and Family in the Bible and the Middle East* (1959), 112-121; D. S. Bailey, *Sexual Relations in Christian Thought* (1959), 32-97, 103-110, 211-229; O. Piper, *The*

Biblical Views of Sex and Marriage (1960), 140-151; O. J. Baab, "Divorce," IDB (1962), 859.

G. E. FARLEY

DI-ZAHAB dīz′ ə hăb (די זהב, LXX καταχρύσεα, *abundance of gold*, or *sufficiency of gold*; but more prob. די זהב means *possessor of gold*). A locality listed along with Paran, Tophel, Laban, and Hazeroth to specify the place where Moses delivered the messages of the Book of Deuteronomy to Israel (Deut 1:1). The exact location of Di-zahab has not been established. The identification with Mina al Dhahab by Burkhardt as well as the identification with Me-zahab (Gen 36:39) by Sayce are no longer accepted. The context suggests a location in the E of the Arabah. The other locations which are named provide no assistance since they are also unknown. The name itself has been explained in Jewish tradition as having some connection with the golden calf which was destroyed by Moses. Another suggestion is that it was an area abounding in gold. The latter has led to the possible identification with edh-Dheibeh.

BIBLIOGRAPHY. M. Seligsohn, "Di-Zahab," *Jewish Encyclopedia* (n.d.), IV, 628.

D. H. MADVIG

DOCETISM dŏs′ ə tiz′ əm, dō′ sə—. Docetism was the term for a Gnostic sect which appeared so early in the history of Christianity that there is an answer for it in 1 John 4:2 and 2 John 7. Its error lay in its denial of the reality of Christ's human body. The Docetae or Docetists held that the body of Christ was not real flesh and blood but only a hallucination or a phantasm, deceptive and passing; that Christ's body was purely spiritual and therefore took up nothing even in the body of the Virgin of true human nature. This heresy developed easily and rapidly in one form or another because of the pagan philosophic emphasis of the time that matter is inherently evil. This being so, it was blasphemous to maintain that the spiritual Christ could have, in any sense at all, a physical body. Basilides, an early Gnostic, held to a relatively human Christ with whom the divine *nous* became united in baptism, but his followers became true Docetae. Hippolytus gave an early account of the whole system of this sect and attached to the movement the names of Saturninus, Valentinus, Marcion, and the Manichaeans. Distinction should be observed in that Docetae denied the *reality* of Christ's human body, whereas the Apollinarians denied the *integrity* of Christ's human nature. In the case of the Apollinarians there was a human nature in body and soul, lacking mind or spirit. *See* GNOSTICISM.

A. H. LEITCH

DOCTOR (διδάσκαλος, *teacher*; νομοδιδάσκαλος, *teacher of the law*). The KJV rendering of διδάσκαλος in Luke 2:46 (ASV, RSV "teacher"), and the KJV, ASV rendering of νομοδιδάσκαλος in Luke 5:17 (RSV "teachers") and Acts 5:34 (RSV "teacher"). The word διδάσκαλος is the common word for "teacher" in secular and NT Gr. The word νομοδιδάσκαλος, however, is not found in secular Gr. or in the LXX, but occurs only in Christian writings. The pl. is rendered "teachers of the law" (1 Tim 1:7). It is not of Jewish origin, although the linguistic basis of the term is found in the formula τὸν νόμον διδάσκειν, "to teach the law." The word "doctor" is simply Lat. for "teacher." In Old Eng. the word "doctor" also meant "teacher," and it is so used in the passages given above. The VSS of Wyclif, Tyndale, Geneva, and Rheims use the word "doctor"; all modern VSS use "teacher." The "teachers of the law" (1 Tim 1:7) were not Judaizers, but men who corrupted the law of Moses by allegorical interpretations and whittled away its moral precepts. Some scholars hold them to be incipient Gnostics.

S. BARABAS

DOCTRINA ADDAEI. A Syr. account of the origins of Christianity in Edessa, related to the Abgar legend recorded by Eusebius (*see* ABGARUS, EPISTLES OF CHRIST and) and to the Gr. ACTS OF THADDAEUS (6th cent.). Messengers sent by Abgar to the governor of Syria report the deeds of Jesus on their return. Abgar sends a letter, to which Jesus gives a verbal reply (in Eusebius, it is a letter): He cannot come Himself, but will send a disciple. The king's envoy also paints and takes home a portrait of Jesus (in the Acts of Thaddaeus, a towel imprinted with His likeness). After the ascension, Thomas sends Addai, one of the Seventy, who heals Abgar, makes converts, and builds a church. His deeds are said to have been recorded by the king's scribe and placed in the official records, but references to "the Old and New Testaments," to Acts and the Epistles of Paul and esp. to the Diatessaron, show that the document belongs to a later date (c. A.D. 400: Bauer, NTAp. I.438). An interesting feature is an account of the finding of the true cross by Protonice, wife of the emperor Claudius (cf. the story of Helena, mother of Constantine).

BIBLIOGRAPHY. Phillips, *The Doctrine of Addai the Apostle* (1876); see also NTAp. I. 437ff.

R. McL. WILSON

DOCTRINE (διδασκαλία, διδαχή, basically meaning *teaching*, usually emphasizing the *content* of what is taught). These two words occur forty-eight times in the NT and are tr. "doctrine" in all but two instances in the KJV. The RSV and NEB more often tr. them "teaching" or "instruction." There is no single OT word which means "doctrine," but see תורה, "law," esp. in later Judaism; למד, to "teach," or "instruct" or "learn," אמונה, "truth."

In the Gr. world, teaching (esp. *didaskalia*) implied the communication of knowledge, either of an intellectual or technical nature. For the most part it had a clear intellectual character.

Among the Jews, esp. in the OT, teaching served not for the communication of religious truth, but rather to bring the one taught into direct confrontation with the divine will. What is taught are the commandments; what is expected is obedience. Thus Moses is taught what he should do (Exod 4:15), and he in turn teaches Israel the commandments (Deut 4:1, 5, et al.), which they likewise are to teach to their children (Deut 6:1, 6, 7, et al.). Therefore, although a "doctrine" of the unity of God or of divine election is presupposed in OT teaching, such teaching is not the communication of such "doctrines" but instruction in the divine will.

For the most part the NT use of *didaskalia* and *didachē* corresponds more to the OT idea than to the Gr. That is, teaching usually implies the content of ethical instruction and seldom the content of dogmas or the intellectual apprehension of truth. For example, in the Pastoral Epistles "sound doctrine" which is "in accordance with the glorious gospel" is contrasted with all kinds of immoral living (1 Tim 1:9-11; cf. 6:1, 3; Titus 1:9; 2:1-5, 9, 10). Also the later work entitled the *Didachē*, or *The Teaching of the Twelve Apostles*, is a manual of ethical instruction and church discipline with scarcely any theological content.

In the NT this usage is strengthened by the relationship of *didachē* to *kerygma*, or preaching. It was by means of the *kerygma* that men were brought to faith in Christ (1 Cor 1:21); and the content of that *kerygma* included the essential data of the Christian message: the life, work, death and resurrection of Jesus Christ as God's decisive act for man's salvation (cf. Acts 2:14-36). Those who responded to the preaching would then be instructed in the ethical principles and obligations of the Christian life (2:42).

This relationship may be seen throughout the NT. Thus Jesus "preaches" the in-breaking of the kingdom of God (Matt 4:17; 11:28). Men are called to decision by His mighty words and deeds. But His teaching, which astonished the crowds for its authority, was replete with ethical demands (cf. the sixfold "you have heard that it was said . . . but I say to you" in Matt 5). So also Paul in his epistles often followed the kerygmatic content of his gospel with its ethical demands (Rom, Gal, Eph, Col). Such ethical demands were seen as the inevitable corollary of response to the *kerygma*.

One may note, therefore, that "doctrine" in contemporary parlance would derive more from the content of the *kerygma* than from the *didachē* in the NT.

However, since ethical instruction, or obedience to the divine will in the NT is so closely related to response to the preaching with its "doctrinal" content, it is not surprising that teaching itself eventually came to include the essential data of the faith. Thus "the elder" uses *didachē* to refer to the truth of the incarnation, belief in which, of course, should eventuate in love (2 John 9, 10).

This latter meaning of "teaching," as including the essential beliefs of the Christian faith, ultimately prevailed in the Early Church and continues in vogue today by the tr. of "doctrine" for *didachē* and *didaskalia*.

BIBLIOGRAPHY. K. H. Rengstorff, διδάσκω TDNT, II (1935), 135-165; C. H. Dodd, *The Apostolic Preaching and Its Developments* (1936); id. *Gospel and Law* (1951); D. M. Stanley, "Didache As a Constitutive Element of the Gospel-Form," CBQ, XVII (1955), 216-228; J.-L. Leuba, "Teaching," VB (Fr. orig. 1956), 414-416; J. J. Vincent, "Didactic Kerygma in the Synoptic Gospels," SJT, X (1957), 262-273; E. F. Harrison, "Some Patterns of the New Testament Didache," BS, CXIX (1961), 118-128; O. A. Piper, "Gospel (Message)," IDB (1962), II, 442-448; P. H. Menoud, "Preaching," IDB (1962), III, 868, 869.

G. D. FEE

DOCUS. KJV form of DOK.

DODAI. Alternate form of DODO.

DODANIM. *See* RODANIM.

DODAVAHU (DODAVAH) dō də vā′ hu (דודוהו; LXX Δωδια; *beloved of Yahweh*). The father of the prophet Eliezer of Mareshah, who condemned Jehoshaphat king of Judah, for his alliance with Ahaziah of Israel, and foretold the destruction of his navy (2 Chron 20:37).

DODO, DODAI dō′ dō, dō′ dī. One Dodo (דודו, *his beloved*) was the grandfather of Judge Tola of Issachar (Judg 10:1).

In the time of David a Dodo (MS B of the LXX in Chronicles has Δωδῶε, see below) was father of Eleazar, second of the three heroes of David. He distinguished himself in a battle at Pas-dammim against the Philistines, defending a plot of barley, where the Israelites left him alone, though his weary hands stuck to his sword (2 Sam 23:9, 10; 1 Chron 11:12-14). Through him God wrought great victory.

Another Dodo of Bethlehem was father of Elhanan, who belonged to David's picked thirty heroes.

A similar name Dodai (דודי, "beloved of Yah"), from Aholah, was head of the second of twelve contingents of twenty-four thousand each whom David organized (1 Chron 27:4).

W. G. BROWN

DOE dō (יעלה, [f] Prov 5:19 only; *Roe* KJV; *Doe* ASV, RSV). Although this word may be correctly used in RSV, in that *yaʿalāh* is prob. a female antelope or deer, it is in fact an inexact word meaning the female of fallow deer, hare or rabbit. It therefore needs qualification. *See* DEER.

G. S. CANSDALE

An ivory comb from Megiddo showing a dog attacking an ibex. © O.I.U.C.

DOEG **dō′ ĭg** (Heb. דאג, traditionally thought to mean *anxious*), the name of one of Saul's herdsmen (1 Sam 21:7; 22:9, et al., and in the title of Ps 52). He is said to have been an Edomite (q.v.) and the chief of Saul's shepherds. The rabbinical commentators point out that Doeg must have been a proselyte or a Jew who once came from Edom to the SE of Israel, otherwise he could not have entered the sanctuary. His name is spelled with two different vowel letters. In 1 Samuel 21:7-22:22 the name appears as, דאג, with an *aleph*; however, in the title of Ps 52 it is spelled דאוג, with the addition of the *waw* which may indicate that this was a foreign non-Sem. name and thus difficult for the Massoretes to transcribe. This conversation between Doeg and Saul about the support rendered by the priests about Ahimelech, leading finally to their slaughter, must have been a celebrated incident as it was recorded in the Psalm and Talmudic tradition. The LXX mentions Doeg as "caring for the mules" while a fair portion of the Talmudic *Neziḳin* is taken up with discussions concerning the learning of Doeg, "-The Holy One, blessed be He, said to Doeg, 'Art thou not a mighty man in Torah? Why then boastest thou thyself in mischief'?" (*Soncino Talmud, Neziḳin*, Vol III, 726). The rabbis also interpreted the variant spelling as an inclusion of an implied curse. The basis for so much supposition and legend is found in Psalm 52 which decries the misuse of gifts of wisdom, which, it is assumed, was applied to Doeg. The narrative about this rather obscure personage lends much to the outline of the history of David's reign. It is most evident that the atrocities of Saul's dominion made the people of Israel more than ready for a change in dynasty and fulfilled the words of Samuel's warning about the harsh and selfish treatment a king would bring to Israel (1 Sam 8:10, et al.).

W. White, Jr.

DOG (כלב, *κυνάριον*, *little dog*; *κύων*, *dog*, all Eng. VSS). To the Israelites all dogs were utterly unclean. In Pal. and Egypt then, as in parts of the E today, the dog was a scavenger and did in larger towns what hyenas helped do in the villages and outside the walls; though classified as a carnivore it lived on refuse of all kinds and thus was a potential carrier of many diseases, either mechanically or as a vector. The incident in 2 Kings 9, where the dogs ate Jezebel after she had been thrown off the city wall and killed, was nothing unusual, for dead bodies were sometimes thrown to the dogs. Even contact with a corpse was ritually defiling (Lev 22:4) which was also a matter of practical hygiene, for after a death from some diseases the corpse can be a dangerous source of infection. This is another example of the Mosaic laws being ahead of their time. The fact that the dog was so highly esteemed in Egypt was another point against it; it was considered a desirable goal for the human soul after death and may have been associated with the deity Anubis. The Israelites, however, were exceptional in their attitude to the dog, which was the first animal to become domesticated and which, well before they left Egypt, had been developed into many useful forms, esp. in the hunting field. There is ample evidence that Stone Age man enlisted dogs as helpers in many parts of the world. Opinions differ slightly, but it is generally agreed on anatomical and behavioral grounds that the wolf is the ancestor of all domestic dogs, which are known collectively as *Canis familiaris*. The association began when man lived by hunting, but its development must be a matter for conjecture. From clearing up the remains of a kill and taking refuse from around the encampment there could come a closer cooperation leading to defending the area of their owners against other groups; thence to the assumption of proper guard duties, herding, assisting in the hunt, etc. Dog remains have been found in the earliest Jericho stratum, while in Egypt at least three breeds can be distinguished in predynastic material and a much wider range in the Old Kingdom. A type like the greyhound was firmly established prior to 3,000 B.C. Dogs were regarded just as highly in Mesopotamia, where a big hunting mastiff was in use in the earliest Babylonian period (3rd millennium B.C.) Development of different forms went on continuously, with certain types being fixed as they became useful, esp. in herding stock and in many forms of hunting.

Because of Israel's attitude most dogs were semi-wild, like the pariahs that still haunt districts in India and other countries. Such dogs were descended from individuals that had "gone wild," when they soon lost any breed characteristics and reverted to a general type. Several possible exceptions can be found in the Biblical record. In speaking of the dogs of his flock (Job 30:1) Job can be referring only to sheep dogs, but it is not certain that Job was an Israelite. Isaiah 56:10 is a fig. passage but the expression "dumb dogs, they cannot bark" certainly suggests that it was the custom to keep guard dogs; prob. sheep dogs, since the preceding v. mentions "beasts of the field come to devour." Another is found in the incident of the Syrophoenician woman (Matt 15:26, 27), where the Gr. diminutive is used. This could refer to young dogs; more prob. to small pet dogs allowed to enter the house; but the owners were not Jewish. For the rest, the contexts, both lit. and fig., portray the dog as contemptible, whether as a filthy scavenger or "a dog that returns to its vomit" (Prov 26:11) which is one of several proverbs in which it features. To make the metaphor even stronger, David and others, always referring to themselves, spoke of a dead dog (2 Sam 9:8, etc.)

In Deuteronomy 23:18 dog seems to be a technical term, perhaps a euphemism, for a male temple prostitute, perhaps echoed by Revelation 22:15, listing those who are outside the Holy City. Just one or two mentions are neutral (e.g. Eccl 9:4), quoting the still current proverb that a live dog is better than a dead lion. Conditions have since changed radically and so allowed the dog to assume a role of assistant and companion in countries over much of the world today, even though they may still carry rabies, one of the most unpleasant diseases that can affect man.

BIBLIOGRAPHY. K. Z. Lorenz, *Man Meets Dog* (1954); F. E. Zeuner, *A History of Domesticated Animals* (1963), ch. 4.

G. S. CANSDALE

DOGMA. The noun δόγμα which is of infrequent occurrence in the NT, originally signified "an opinion" or "a judgment." It came to mean "a judgment given with authority" and so "a decree." Thus it refers to imperial decrees in Luke 2:1; Acts 17:7 (cf. Heb 11:23 where a minor variant uses it of a decree of Pharaoh). It is used also of religious decrees (Eph 2:15; Col 2:14) by which the decrees of God expressed in the Mosaic law are in view. To this realm also belongs the verb δογματίζομαι ("I submit myself to ordinances"), used once in the NT (Col 2:20). The noun is used in Acts 16:4 of the decrees of the Jerusalem Council. The verb δοκέω is from the same root and is used impersonally, with the meaning "it seemed good," in the account of the Council's proceedings (Acts 15:22, 25, 28). It may have been due to its use at such a Council that it came to be employed widely by the early Fathers with reference to official doctrinal pronouncements of the Church, the meaning the Eng. word normally bears today. It is found in this sense in Ignatius (*Epistle to the Magnesians*, 13), fairly often in Origen, and frequently from the Council of Nicaea onward.

G. W. GROGAN

DOK dŏk (Δωκ, corrupted to Δαγων, in Jos. Antiq. XVIII. viii. 1). DOCUS, dō′ cəs. A small fortress built (or rebuilt) by Ptolemy, the son of Abubus, a short distance NW of Jericho. The name of the ancient city survives in modern 'Ain Duq c. four m. NW of Jericho. The ancient site is identified with Jebel Qarantal. Simon Maccabeus and his sons Mattathias and Judas in making a circuit of the cities of the country were received at Dok by Ptolemy. After they had banqueted and had become drunk, Ptolemy's men who were lying in wait arose and killed them (1 Macc 16:15). Dok was one of several fortresses guarding the routes into the central mountain region.

BIBLIOGRAPHY. D. Baly, *Geography of the Bible* (1957), 201.

D. H. MADVIG

DOLPHIN. *See* BADGER.

DOMINION. The tr. of a number of words implying "mastery" and "sovereign authority," of which the most frequently used are the following: (1) משל, "to rule"; (2) רדה, "to tread down"; (3) שלטן, "to have power over"; (4) ממשלה, "to rule"; (5) κράτος, "strength, power"—used only in doxologies; (6) κυριεύω, "to exercise lordship"; (7) κυριότης, "lordship."

The following forms of dominion have special Biblical and theological significance: (1) God's rule over the universe (Ps 22:28); (2) man's dominion over nature given to him by God (Gen 1:26; Ps 8:6); (3) Christ's eschatological rule (1 Cor 15:24-28; 2 Thess 2:8); (4) the saints' eschatological rule with Christ (2 Tim 2:12; Rev 3:21); (5) the believer's freedom from the dominion of sin (Rom 6:9, 14; 7:1).

The word κυριότης is found in four passages: Ephesians 1:21 (KJV, RSV "dominion"), Colossians 1:16 (pl.; KJV, RSV "dominions"), Jude 8 (KJV "dominion"; RSV "authority"),

2 Peter 2:10 (KJV "government"; RSV "authority"). The context shows that in Ephesians and Colossians a rank or order of angels is meant. There is no necessary reference to evil angels, but a comparison of these passages with Ephesians 2:2; 6:12 shows that they need not be excluded. The meaning of κυριότης in Jude and 2 Peter is perplexing and has been much disputed. The answer prob. lies in one of the following suggested interpretations: (1) Angels are referred to in both passages, or only in Peter but not in Jude. (2) The reference is to the power and majesty of God, or the Lordship of Christ. (3) The reference is to legitimate authorities in the Church or to the lordship of civil rulers, who are despised and spoken against by evil men in the Church.

BIBLIOGRAPHY. H. Cremer, *Biblico-Theological Lexicon of New Testament Greek* (1892), 385; J. B. Lightfoot, *St. Paul's Epistle to the Colossians and Philemon* (1892), 152-154; G. Kittel, *Theological Dictionary of the New Testament*, III (1965), 1096, 1097.

S. BARABAS

DOMITIAN **də mĭsh' ən.** When the popular Titus died at the untimely age of forty-two, after only two years and a few months as emperor, he was succeeded by his thirty-year-old brother Domitian whom neither Titus, nor their father Vespasian, had expected to be called to the task. Domitian was no trained soldier like his two predecessors, and he came to office, a despised younger brother, embittered by his elders' contempt, a resentment all the deeper for his keen intellect. He was shrewd enough to note the parallel of his case with that of Tiberius, who succeeded the first emperor, Augustus, after being similarly passed by, humiliated, and embittered. The documents of Tiberius were his favorite reading (Suetonius, *Dom.* 20), and played some part in bringing out the worst in Domitian. It is difficult to ascertain the truth behind the distortions of writers who belonged to, or spoke for, the upper section of Rom. society, on whom the prince vented his spite, i.e., Juvenal, Tacitus, Suetonius, and Pliny.

Sensitive about his absence of military glory, a conspicuous advantage in his two predecessors, Domitian ordered an attack on the Chatti of the Main Valley, and celebrated his victory in a great triumphal celebration. The campaign salutarily removed an awkward salient in an essential frontier. It revealed, too, that Domitian, like Augustus and Claudius, had a faculty for picking able men.

Roman historiography is Rome-centered and aristocratic. It failed to record in detail that the provinces were content and well governed at the time when the pathological fears and suspicions of Domitian were reviving in Rome the hated cult of delation—that pernicious system of the common informer and the law of treason that so played into his hands. Both Tacitus (*Agricola* 45.2) and Pliny (*Pan.* 48) spoke with horror of those days when aristocracy and Senate were decimated by the jealous suspicions of the prince.

Among Domitian's victims were the Christians. He was heir to a policy and legislation established by Nero, and sporadically pursued under Vespasian and Titus both of whom had links with Pal., and entertained some fear of any movement initiated there. But Domitian, with a sharp eye for treason and enthusiastic for the Caesar-cult justly ranks with Nero as a systematic persecutor. According to Irenaeus (Iren. Her. V. xxx. 3), the Apocalypse of John was written during the reign of Domitian and reflected the emperor's anti-Christian attitude. Suppression extended to the family of the emperor, so high had Christianity penetrated. It seems even to have destroyed Domitian's arrangements for the succession. Domitian was murdered in A.D. 96, after a plot supported by his wife, who felt the insecurity of her own position. The abiding significance of his somber fifteen years as emperor is that a sharp advance was made toward complete autocracy and monarchy.

BIBLIOGRAPHY. W. M. Ramsay, *The Church in the Roman Empire*, ch. XI (1893); E. M. Blaiklock, *The Century of the New Testament* (1962), 116-126.

E. M. BLAIKLOCK

DOOR (דֶּלֶת, *door*; פֶּתַח, *doorway*; θύρα *door, doorway*). Ancient doors usually were made of wood, sometimes sheeted with metal as in the case of city gates or in large public buildings. Sometimes they were made of one slab of stone, or, rarely, a single piece of metal. Hinges on doors, as known today, were unknown; instead, doors turned on pivots set in sockets above and below. The sockets were made of stone or, sometimes, of metal. In Egypt, the hinge consisted of a socket of metal with a projecting pivot, into which two corners of the door were inserted. A wide doorway had a pair of folding doors (Isa 45:1), which could be bolted with bars of wood (Nah 3:13) or of metal (Isa 45:2; Ps 107:16). The Temple doors were two-leaved (1 Kings 6:34). Doors were provided with a bolt (2 Sam 13:17) or with lock and key (Judg 3:23). The doorway consisted of three parts: the threshold or sill, the doorposts at the side, and the lintel. Doorways often were highly ornamented (Isa 54:12) and inscribed with sentences of Scripture in literal accordance with the law of Moses, "And you shall write them upon the doorposts of your house and upon your gates" (Deut 11:20).

The word is also used metaphorically, as in John 10:7, "I am the door"; Acts 14:27, "he had opened a door of faith to the Gentiles"; and Revelation 3:20, "Behold, I stand at the door and knock." *See* ARCHITECTURE.

S. BARABAS

DOORKEEPER (*see* PORTER) (*θυρωρός*, John 18:16, 17) KJV and ASV PORTER. A person who guarded the entrance to public buildings, temples, city walls, etc. A woman is mentioned as doorkeeper of the palace of Ishbosheth (RSV following the LXX, 2 Sam 4:6). The doorkeeper of a rich man's house is mentioned by Jesus as an example of one who watches faithfully (Mark 13:34). A doorkeeper might guard the entrance of a sheepfold (John 10:3, RSV GATEKEEPER). A maid kept the door of the courtyard of the high priest the night Jesus was on trial (18:16, 17). To be a lowly doorkeeper of the Temple is preferred to a life of wickedness (הִסְתּוֹפֵף, "to act as doorkeeper," Ps 84:10). "Doorkeeper" is used sometimes in KJV and ASV to tr. שׁוֹעֵר, "gatekeeper," q.v.

D. H. MADVIG

DOPHKAH dŏf' kə (דָּפְקָה, LXX Ῥαφακα). A place where the children of Israel encamped on their journey from the Red Sea to Sinai (Num 33:12). It has been identified with Serabit el-Khadim where the Egyptians carried on mining, and where the famous "Sinaitic Inscriptions" were found (dating from about 1525 B.C. and written in a Sem. hieroglyphic alphabet). J. Simons suggests that the name be read "Maphqah," for "Mafqat" is the name of the turquoise mined there as well as the name of the district.

BIBLIOGRAPHY. J. Simons, *Geographical and Topographical Texts of the OT* (1959), 252; G. Wright, *Biblical Archaeology* (rev. 1962), 64.

D. H. MADVIG

DOR dôr (דֹּאר, דּוֹר ; LXX Δωρ, 1 Macc 15 Δωρα; this name may be related to Akkad. *duru*, "fortress"; KJV 1 Macc 15 DORA, dô' re). A fortified city on the coast of Pal. S of Mount Carmel c. eight m. N of Caesarea. It was settled in very ancient times by the Phoenicians because of the abundance of shells along the coast which were the source of a rich purple dye. Near the end of the 2nd millennium B.C. Dor was inhabited by the Tjekker, one of the sea peoples. Dor is mentioned in the Egyp. story of Wen-Amon, an emissary of Pharaoh who stopped at Dor on his way to Phoenicia.

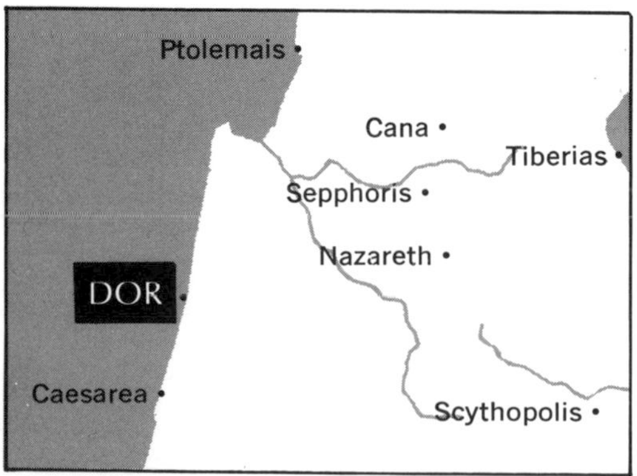

The king of Dor supported Jabin, king of Hazor, in his unsuccesful battle against Joshua at the waters of Merom (Josh 11:2ff; 12:23). Dor was one of the cities within the borders of Issachar and Asher which were assigned to Manasseh although Manasseh was unable to capture it. In later years when it was captured, its Canaanite inhabitants were subjected by Israel to forced labor (Josh 17:11ff.; Judg 1:27). Dor is listed also among cities possessed by descendants of Ephraim (1 Chron 7:29). Dor and the neighboring territory were made the 4th administrative district by Solomon.

Tiglath-pileser III (744-727 B.C.) conquered Dor and established an Assyrian governor over it. In 219 B.C. the city was besieged by Antiochus the Great. He did not capture Dor, however, for rumors of an approaching Egyp. army caused him to agree to a truce. The Phoen. cities were subject to the Ptolemies until c. 200 B.C. when they were taken by the Seleucids who made Dor and several other cities independent. In 139 B.C. Dor was besieged by Antiochus VII (1 Macc 15:10-25). Trypho, her governor, fled to Apamia where he was captured and killed. The city was rebuilt, made free, and made a part of the province of Syria by Pompey in 64 B.C.

The site of Dor is identified with modern el-Burj N of Tanturah.

BIBLIOGRAPHY. CAH (1954), VII, 190, 192; Jos. Antiq. V. i. 22; XIII. viii. 2; XIV. iv. 4; XIX. vi. 3; J. Pritchard, ANET (1955), 26; D. Baly, *Geography of the Bible* (1957), 131-133; J. Simon, *The Geographical and Topographical Texts of the OT* (1959), 272, 418, 419, 433.

D. H. MADVIG

DORCAS dôr' kəs (Δορκάς; Aram. תַּבִיתָ, meaning *gazelle*). A feminine name not uncommon to both Jews and Greeks, used in the NT to denote the Christian woman of Joppa who died and was raised from the dead by Peter (Acts 9:36-43). While Peter was healing Aeneas at Lydda, about ten m. distant from Joppa, the ailing Dorcas had died. She was held in high esteem for her outstanding service to others; and her example has inspired the founding of numerous "Dorcas societies" in congregations today. She was described as a *μαθήτρια*, the only citation in the NT where the feminine form of "disciple" is used. On the occasion of her death, two men were sent to Lydda to summon Peter. When Peter arrived the body already had been washed for burial and placed in an upper room. The widows were mourning and in deep appreciation were showing the handiwork of Dorcas as they displayed the garments she had made, perhaps for these very individuals. Like Jesus (Matt 9:25) Peter sent everyone out, and knelt and prayed. Upon the command to arise, Dorcas responded; and she was presented to the others alive. Because of this miracle many believed in the Lord.

L. FOSTER

DOSITHEUS, APOCALYPSE OF. A Gnostic document found in the Nag Hammadi library (cf. Apocryphal New Testament), and as yet unpublished. The last of five documents in Codex VII (pp. 118. 10-127. 27), it contains in its title a reference to the three Stelae (pillars or tables) of Seth, which Doresse links with an allusion in another work, the *Apocalypse of Zostrianus.* The three stelae are in fact hymns, each occupying three pages of text. In style according to Doresse it recalls some of the Hermetic documents. A Dositheus is mentioned in the Pseudo-Clementines as a rival of Simon Magus, but to link him with this apocalypse is pure speculation. For the details available see Doresse, *Secret Books of the Egyptian Gnostics* (ET London 1960), 188ff.

R. McL. Wilson

DOT (*κεραία, horn, projection,* or *extremity*) KJV TITTLE, tĭt′ əl. An accent or diacritical mark, or a stroke which distinguishes similar letters, such as ה and ד ח, and ב ר, and כ. This word occurs twice in the NT in Jesus' statements: "Not an iota, not a dot, will pass from the law until all is accomplished" (Matt 5:18), and "But it is easier for heaven and earth to pass away, than for one dot of the law to become void" (Luke 16:17).

The iota is the smallest letter in the Gr. alphabet and here it signifies *yod,* the smallest letter of the Heb. alphabet. The expression "not an iota, not a dot" signifies the tiniest details. It is used by Jesus to emphasize the enduring and unchangeable nature of the law of God (i.e., The Torah, the OT). Similar statements are found in Jewish tradition asserting that a *yod* could not be removed from the law, that the world would be destroyed if one mark which distinguishes similar letters were removed.

BIBLIOGRAPHY. A. Edersheim, *Jesus the Messiah* (1947), I, 537f.; W. Arndt and F. Gingrich, *A Greek-English Lexicon of the NT* (1957), 429.

D. H. Madvig

DOTAEA. Alternate form of Dothan.

DOTHAIM do′ thĭ əm (Δωθαιμ). The KJV, ASV tr. of *Dothaim* in Judith 4:6; 7:3, 18; 8:3 (RSV DOTHAN); a city located about fifteen m. N of Shechem. Its modern name is Tell Dotha.

DOTHAN dō′ thən (דֹּתָן, *two wells*) a place located sixty m. by road N of Jerusalem; thirteen m. N of the city of Samaria.

1. In Biblical history. The city of Dothan is a focal point in an event of the earlier days of Joseph (c. 1900-1800 B.C.). His father, Jacob, sent him to inquire about the well-being of his brothers. He found them at Dothan, pasturing their flocks (Gen 37:13-17). They put Joseph in a pit, and subsequently sold him to a passing caravan of Ishmaelites, who took him to Egypt.

A thousand years later (c. 850 B.C.), the prophet Elisha lived at Dothan. The King of Syria surrounded the city with his chariots and horsemen to apprehend the prophet, who was revealing the secret military plans of the Syrian king to the king of Israel (2 Kings 6:8-14).

2. In extra-Biblical history. In addition to the two Biblical events in which Dothan figures, the city is mentioned in the inscrs. of the Egyp. king Thutmose III (1490-1436 B.C.) as one of the Palestinian towns from which the Egyptians exacted tribute. Dothan is also referred to several times in the apocryphal book of Judith (3:9, 4:6, 7:3) in the military campaigns of Holofernes in the region of the plain of Dothan during the intertestamental period. In the early Christian period, Eusebius mentions Dothan in listing place names in Pal. (*Onomasticon,* 76, 13).

3. Identification of the site. The mound known as Tell Dotha in modern times was identified as the Biblical site of Dothan in 1851 by Van de Velde.

4. Excavation of Dothan. Archeological excavations were begun at the site of ancient Dothan in 1953 by the writer and his wife, and the Dothan expedition staff. A deep sounding the first season at the top of the slope of the mound showed that Dothan began about 5000 years ago (3000 B.C.), and, though destroyed and rebuilt many times, was a thriving town in every main period of Biblical and Near Eastern history from 3000 B.C. through NT times, with evidence of occupation in Byzantine times (c. A.D. 300-500) and the Arab. period (A.D. 600-1100) and Crusader times. A Venetian coin of about A.D. 1600 attested a possible village in this period. For the last half cent. there has been a modern village of about ten houses on the lower slopes of the mound.

The city of Dothan during the thousand years (3000-2000 B.C.) leading up to the Patriarchal period was well attested by seven levels of occupation containing Early Bronze Age sherds (3000-2000 B.C.). This evidence in the deep sounding of the first season implied the destruction and rebuilding of seven towns over this thousand year period, and parallels other such rebuilding and destruction, "when the Amorite was in the land," as found at other northern Palestinian sites, including Megiddo and Beth-shan. A heavy city wall surrounded the city in this period, still surviving to a height of sixteen ft. after it was uncovered. It prob. was twenty-five ft. high in Biblical times. It measured eleven ft. thick at the base and nine ft. thick in the upper surviving part.

In the Patriarchal period (2000-1600 B.C., Middle Bronze Age), we uncovered ten rooms of a heavily built citadel, with walls four ft. thick (ninth season, 1964). The citadel abutted against the inside of the heavy city wall, near the gateway area. This heavy construction reflected the days of minimal central power and the need for individual defense on the part of each Palestinian city. Outside the wall in this gateway area we uncovered a wide stairway (thirteen ft.) leading up to the city wall. After baring eighteen steps, we came to the edge of our property. It continued under land not ours. In Patriarchal times, water was doubtless carried up these stairs from the well a few hundred ft. down the slope in the plain of Dothan. This was the city of Dothan of Joseph's time, represented by two Middle Bronze Age levels in our archeological stratification.

The Late Bronze Age (1600-1200 B.C.) was abundantly attested by two main levels which yielded thousands of potsherds from Late Bronze pottery. The citadel of the Middle Bronze period appeared to have suffered partial destruction in the late 17th or the 16th cent. B.C., and after repairs, to have continued in use into the Late Bronze period.

One of the striking discoveries from the Late Bronze period was a tomb on the W slope of the mound, cut into the bedrock of the hill on which Dothan was built. It began as a family tomb about 1300 B.C. or shortly thereafter, and continued in use between 200 and 300 years. In it were found nearly 600 clay lamps and nearly 600 pyxis oil juglets, implying the burial of approximately that number of people. With this number of burials, there was a considerable amount of bones. Over eighty skeletons could be separately identified the first main season of the tomb project, and about the same number the second season. Years later the roof of the tomb had partially collapsed, and tons of bed rock lay on the bones and objects. In places there were several inches of "bone material," compressed together without individual bones being particularly recognizable, but representing numerous skeletons. This tomb ("Tomb 1") yielded over 3200 pottery objects —lamps, pyxis jars, craters, bowls, jugs, and almost every type of vessel used in later Late Bronze and earlier Iron I times. Also over 200 bronze objects came from the tomb; daggers, spear points, chisels, and even a bronze lamp in the shape of a typical spouted pottery lamp. All of this type of object would have been familiar to Gideon and the other judges who lived in the period either side of 1200 B.C.

The Iron I period (1200-1000 B.C.), parallel to the later part of the period of the Judges, was represented by two levels. The tomb continued in use during the earlier part of this period and when it was full, another tomb was carved out next to it ("Tomb 2"), which we discovered the eighth season (1962). It yielded 500 objects similar to many found in Tomb 1. These two tombs yielded five pottery lamps which had seven spouts on each lamp, attesting to the earlier date of the concept of the sevenfold light, a concept formerly downdated to about 600 B.C. by the Wellhausen school and subsequent followers.

The Iron II period (1000-600 B.C.) paralleled the period of the Israelite monarchy, and yielded four main levels. The lowest of these represented the Solomonic period (c. 1000-900 B.C.) and contained a large well-built structure which appeared to be the local "administrative building." In one room we found the remains of ninety-six small storage jars, all the same size, likely standard measures for collecting taxes in oil and other commodities at this local "county seat." This evidence of administrative procedure parallels the Biblical implications of Solomonic governmental organization.

The heavier walls of the "administrative building" were about four ft. thick. Two drains served the building, providing better sanitation facilities than existed in Elizabethan England nearly three millennia later.

The level representing the third city of Dothan in the days of the Biblical kings, dating to about 725 B.C., was likely the city destroyed at about the same time that the city of Samaria was taken by the Assyrian army (2 Kings 17:5, 6). The fourth city of this period, dating about 700 B.C., continued into the 7th cent. Many of the houses of this period had plaster covered courtyards. The excavation at Dothan and other sites shows that hydraulic lime plaster first came into general use in the 10th cent. B.C., prob. due to the progressive planning and inventiveness of the Solomonic regime.

We have not found a distinct level of the Pers. period (c. 500-300 B.C.), but some Pers. pottery and metal bowls have come to light. Perhaps it was a small settlement, reflecting the desolation of the Exile and postexilic period, and covered only a part of the mound which has not been excavated.

The Hel. period is well attested (c. 300-50 B.C.). The higher part of the mound yielded house walls and sherds which included a number of Rhodian jar handles having stamped inscrs. datable to this period. During the eighth and ninth seasons house walls from the Rom. period were uncovered. One sherd bore a stamp with the letters SC, standing for "*Senatus consultus.*" This is a reversal of the usual Lat. word order, "*Consultus Senatus*" (Senate consulted), implying approval of the Rom. senate, and tying in with the Rom. rule over Pal. at this time.

The higher part of the mound yielded Byzantine walls, sherds, and glass (A.D. 300-600); also Arab. period sherds (A.D. 600-1100), and on the highest part of the mound the remains of a medieval fortress-palace (12th-14th cent. A.D.). We uncovered twenty-five rooms of this structure around a courtyard. Five other adjacent depressions imply five more courtyards; if each of them has twenty-five rooms, we have a medieval feudal type structure with 150 rooms for the retainers, the servants, and the rest of a feudal type retinue. Arabic sherds

Top: A view of Tel Dothan, sixty miles north of Jerusalem. Excavated by Dr. Joseph P. Free ©*M.P.S.*

Below: Dothan valley, view northwest toward the village of Arrabe. ©*Lev*

abound on top of the mound. The Venetian coin of about A.D. 1600 has been mentioned, and the modern village of about ten houses on the lower slope.

Shepherds still come from southern Pal. to the region of Dothan to water and pasture their flocks, as they did 4000 years ago in the days of Joseph's brothers. Some doubt has been expressed (Kraeling) on the Biblical record of shepherds traveling out of "the vale of Hebron" eighty m. or more to the Dothan area. One spring week-end we counted ninety flocks on the road from Jerusalem to the Dothan area; many came from the region between Hebron and Jerusalem.

BIBLIOGRAPHY. J. P. Free, "The First Season of Excavation at Dothan," *Bulletin of the American Schools of Oriental Research*, October, 1953, 16-20; ibid., "The Second Season at Dothan," October, 1954. Succeeding seasons are described in the October issues of the BASOR for 1955 and 1956; the Dec., 1958 issue, 1-8; also 1959 and 1960 issues. For a radio-carbon date of an Iron Age level at Dothan, see BASOR, No. 147.

J. P. FREE

DOUAY VERSION. *See* BIBLE, ENGLISH VERSIONS.

DOUBLE-MINDED (*δίψυχος*). Literally the word meant "double-souled." The noun has not been found in the LXX or in secular writing. Neither is the verb found in the LXX or the NT, but it does occur in the writings of the Fathers. There it meant to be undecided or changeable, esp. referring to the indecision of accepting Christianity or belief in specific Christian doctrine or teaching. It is probable that the use of this term by the Fathers developed from the Book of James where *dipsuchos* is twice employed (James 1:8; 4:8). When James described a man as "double-minded," he used a figure of speech, as if it were possible for a man to have two minds inside himself. One mind believed, the other mind disbelieved. Such a man was a walking civil war in which faith and doubt waged a continual battle against each other. Set in context with an admonition to pray, it would be understood that the essence of prayer was the turning over of the entire mind to God. A man cannot pray and face in two directions while he is doing it. A man faced God when he prayed; thus prayer was the elimination of the "double-minded." James' second use of the term is likewise set in an admonition to draw near to God. The answer to the double mind with its wavering loyalties, indecision, divided interests and impurity was the rededication of the whole personality to Christ.

H. L. DRUMWRIGHT, JR.

DOUBLE-TONGUED (*δίλογος*). A word which occurs only once in the NT (1 Tim 3:8). It designates one of the qualifications of a deacon. He must not be double-tongued, i.e. saying one thing at one time and something else at another time. Cf. Lat. *bilinguis* which has the meaning, "hypocritical," or "false." Related forms are found in other lit. with the sense, "repeating."

BIBLIOGRAPHY. W. Hendrickson, *Exposition of the Pastoral Epistles* (1957), 131.

D. H. MADVIG

DOUGH (בצק, עריסה ; *φύραμα*). A mixture of flour with water or, sometimes, olive oil. This was kneaded in a wooden trough usually by hand, but also, when a large quantity was to be kneaded, by foot (Exod 12:34, 39; 2 Sam 13:8; Jer 7:18; Hos 7:4; fig., Rom 11:16; 1 Cor 5:6, 7). It was made chiefly from wheat and barley, but occasionally from beans, lentils, millet, and spelt (Ezek 4:9). It is not certain whether there was a class distinction between those who ate bread made from wheat and barley. A little bit of leaven (dough left to sour from the previous baking) was placed in the dough to cause it to rise—for leavened bread. For the Passover and the Feast of Unleavened Bread, no leavened bread could be used.

Some salt was sprinkled in the dough, for both leavened and unleavened bread. After the dough was sufficiently kneaded, it was put aside to allow it to rise, and then it was baked in one of a variety of ovens that were then used. *See* FOOD.

S. BARABAS

DOVE (PIGEON) (יונה, *dove, young pigeon*; גוזל, a *young pigeon*; *περιστερά*, *dove*, [*young*] *pigeon.*)

In the OT all Eng. VSS tr. "dove" approximately twenty times and "young pigeon" ten times indicating that the two names are largely interchangeable. In the OT pigeon is restricted solely to birds used for sacrifice and it is always prefaced by "young." In the NT, KJV is less consistent and when referring to sacrifices uses both pigeon and dove (once only). RSV trs. all "pigeon," but omits "young" in all cases but one. Luke 2:24 "a pair of turtledoves or two young pigeons"—brought by Mary and Joseph to obey the law concerning the birth of a first-born male.

In Eng. one refers to the pigeon family, but the wood pigeon is also called the ring dove, while the rock dove is the wild species from which domestic pigeons are descended. Palestine today has at least six members of this family; rock, ring, and stock doves of the genus *Columba*; turtle, collared and palm doves of the genus *Streptopelia.* The last of these has become common and widespread in Israel since the 1950s with the extension of farming. It seems likely that *yonah* applies in particular to the rock dove and generally to all three *Columba* species. These are generally blue-gray and distinctly larger than the other three, which are mostly rufous and vinaceous. They have their own names. (*See* TURTLE DOVE.) These birds are wholly vegetarian, taking seeds, fruits and green stuff.

The rock dove is the sole ancestor of all domestic pigeons and has a wide range in Europe, Asia, and N Africa. It nests on cliff faces and when town pigeons use ledges of high city buildings they revert to wild habits. It is likely that it was domesticated independently in several different areas. It is featured on monuments in the earliest dynasty of ancient Egypt and the first record of the pigeon being used as a table bird is in the fourth dynasty c. 2,500 B.C. It has been universally regarded as good for food and was prob. first domesticated for that purpose, later becoming important for sacrifices. It is recorded that four pigeons were dispatched in different directions to announce the coronation of Rameses III (1204 B.C.), but it is unlikely that they were taking messages. Although it is implied that pigeons were trapped (Hos 7:11, 12) it is likely that the "young pigeons" offered by the poor were domestic stock; most breeding colonies were inaccessible.

"Dove" occurs largely in fig. contexts, but some merit comment for their natural history allusions. Jeremiah 48:28: "dove that nests in the sides of the mouth of a gorge." This describes precisely their habitat in the Negev today, from where they must fly large distances to find food and water. Isaiah 38:14: "I moan like a dove." Many doves have a plaintive note and the Heb. *yonah* comes from a root with this meaning. Their courtship displays make doves an obvious symbol of love (S of Sol 1:15, etc.). Another word for dove, from Heb. ימימה Arab. YAMAMATU gives the personal name Jemimah (Job 42:14).

BIBLIOGRAPHY. Peterson et al., *Field Guide to Birds of Britain and Europe* (1954); G. R. Driver, "Birds in the OT: II, Birds in Life," PEQ (1955), 129, 130; P. Arnold, *Birds of Israel* (1962).

G. S. CANSDALE

DOVE'S DUNG (חרי יונים ; *dove's dung*, softened by Jewish scribes into the more euphemistic דב יוכים *dib yônîm*). Mentioned in 2 Kings 6:25, "a kab of dove's dung." The common name "bird's milk" or "bird's dung" is given to the bulb, *Ornithogalum umbellatum*. These bulbs have to be roasted or boiled before eating.

Today, the plant is known as "Star of Bethlehem." Linnaeus, the botanist, called the "dove's dung" *Ornithogalum*. Parkinson, the British herbalist (1800), said the roasted bulb was "sweeter than a chestnut."

The bulb, grown in Pal. at the time of the siege, was prob. roasted, and then sold for five pieces of silver.

The white flowers, borne in a large, loose group on a twelve-inch stem are star-shaped.

The LXX trs. literally.

W. E. SHEWELL-COOPER

DOWRY, three Heb. words are so tr. in the Eng. VSS. 1. מהר, "purchase price," "purchase money" (KJV) DOWRY, (RSV) MARRIAGE PRESENT. The actual meaning of the word is in effect "bride-price," a sum paid the father of the bride for her economic loss to the family. This could be paid in service (Gen 29:18). It is used specifically in the sense of money paid the father for the bride (Gen 34:12; Exod 22:16; 1 Sam 18:25). It is therefore incorrect to consider this type of payment a dowry.

2. שלוחים, "gifts given to a daughter on her leaving for marriage." Although a rather clumsy definition, it is clear enough in the two texts where it occurs (1 Kings 9:16; Mic 1:14 [KJV], "present" [RSV], "dowry").

3. זבד, "endowment," "gift" (Gen 30:20). The relative scarcity of such terms in the OT demonstrates that although common in the Near Eastern cultures around them it was not customary among the people of Israel; in fact, three of the less than ten references are in contexts concerning Gentiles. *See* MARRIAGE.

W. WHITE, JR.

DOXOLOGY dŏks ŏl' ə jĭ (δοξολογία, from *doxa*, "praise," "honor," "glory," and *logos*, a "speaking," "a· saying," "a word"; hence, "a praising," "giving glory"): is used both in song and prayer. It was sung by angels to shepherds the night Jesus came into the world (Luke 2:14). It was sung by "the whole multitude of the disciples" the day Jesus rode triumphantly into Jerusalem, Palm Sunday (Luke 19:37, 38). John reports hearing a doxology by angels around the throne in heaven (Rev 5:13), and later by "a great multitude in heaven" (Rev 19:1-3). In the OT all five books of the Psalter end with a doxology, the last comprising a whole Psalm in which "praise" appears thirteen times (Pss 41:13; 72:18f.; 89:52; 106:48; 150:1-6). In Christian liturgy the hymn known as "The Doxology" is sung every Sunday in a host of churches all over the world. It is composed of four short phrases, beginning with, "Praise God, from whom all blessings flow."

The Lord's Prayer is traditionally concluded with the doxology: "For thine is the kingdom, and the power, and the glory, for ever. Amen" (Matt 6:13n). It does not appear in some old Gr. MSS. In a different arrangement, it is in 1 Chronicles 29:11.

Paul uses the doxology rather sparingly as well as briefly. Nor does he subscribe to formula but to the spontaneous outburst of his soul at spiritual peaks (Rom 11:36; 16:27; Eph 3:21; 1 Tim 1:17). The longest and most comprehensive doxology in the NT, and one frequently used as a benediction by pastors, is in Jude 24, 25.

G. B. FUNDERBURK

DRACHMA. *See* COINS.

Seven-headed fiery dragon attacked by two gods; from Tel Asmar. ©Iraq Museum

DRAG, DRAGNET. "Drag" is KJV, ASV tr. of מכמרת, in Habakkuk 1:15, 16 (RSV SEINE). "Dragnet" is the RSV rendering of חרם, in Ezekiel 32:3 (KJV, ASV NET). The reference is to a net dragged along the bottom of a river, etc., for catching fish or used for catching game.

DRAGON. Two Heb. words תנים, תנין, are tr. "dragon" KJV in all except four passages (see below). Although almost identical these words are thought not to be cognate. (For detailed discussion on these roots see NBD, p. 322.) *Tannim* (masc. pl. of *Tan*) and, once, *tannoth* (fem. pl.) are tr. fourteen times as "dragon" (KJV) and "jackal" (ASV and RSV). In the only other occurrence (Ezek 32:2) it is tr. "whale" (KJV), "dragon" (ASV, RSV). It is tempting to regard this as a textual error for *tannin* (below), for all the other contexts have enough in common to confirm the ASV and RSV "jackal" (q.v.).

Tannin is less uniformly tr. "dragon" (7), "sea monster" (1), "serpent" (3), "whale" (2) in KJV; "dragon" (6), "sea monster" (2), "serpent" (4), and "jackal" (1) in ASV and RSV. These words are used literally in only two passages: (a) Genesis 1:21 "whale" (KJV), "sea monster" (ASV, RSV); (b) Exodus 7:9, 10, 12, serpent," all Eng. VSS. All other contexts are fig.: (a) in the Creation narrative, fifth day, and the word is clearly a general one that might be better tr. "giant marine animals"; (b) the incident of the rods that became serpents (q.v.). For the rest the tr. "dragon" is perhaps as good as any, for the use is pictorial and allegorical. There is some logic in allowing the Heb. *tannin* to have two meanings, mythological and biological, for this is true of Eng. "dragon." Defined first as a mythological monster with wings and claws, the word is also found in such animal names as komodo dragon (a giant lizard), dragon fish, dragonfly, etc.

The NT position is simpler. Δράκων, occurs only in Revelation 12:13, 16, 20, where it is used fig. for Satan. In LXX, Heb. *tannin* is usually tr. δράκων.

G. S. Cansdale

DRAGON, BEL AND THE. *See* Bel and the Dragon.

DRAM. *See* Coins.

DRAUGHT HOUSE drăft. The *Qᵉrē'* substitutes the less objectionable מוצאות, "sinks," for מחראות, "privies," in the *Kᵉtib*. LXX λυτρών, "privy," RSV LATRINE, public restroom. In purging Baal worship from Israel Jehu demolished the temple of Baal and converted it into a latrine (2 Kings 10:27). Such an action was the utmost desecration (cf. Ezra 6:11; Dan 2:5).

D. H. Madvig

DRAWER(S) OF WATER (שאבי מים, LXX ὑδροφόρος). A lowly servant class. This expression is usually coupled with "hewers of wood." Drawing water was a menial task which was often performed by women (Gen 24:13; 1 Sam 9:11). Sometimes it was assigned to young men (Ruth 2:9). It may have been customary to subject defeated enemies to this service as Israel did to the Gibeonites (Josh 9:21ff.). The well or spring was usually located outside the city walls. The water was carried into the city in water pots or goatskins by the drawer of water or on donkey back. Drawers of water are listed as the lowliest of those entering into covenant with God (Deut 29:11).

D. H. Madvig

DREAM (חלום, ὄναρ, *a dream.*) A dream is a series of thoughts, images, or emotions occurring during sleep; any seeming of reality occurring to one sleeping; a more or less coherent "imagery" sequence occurring during sleep. Fromm defines "dream" as a meaningful and significant expression of any kind of mental activity under the condition of sleep.

Psychologial description. Dreams seem to be the reappearance of thoughts which have, in some form or other, been formed in our minds. They are portions of our former conceptions and impressions revived, and randomly reassembled. Bergson conceives of a dream as being the direct link between sensation and memory; being constructed around what we have seen, said, desired, or done, and their elaboration depends on memory images collected and preserved in the unconscious since earliest childhood. The same faculties function when we dream as when we are awake, but in one instance they are tense and in the other relaxed. The fullness of our mental life is available in our dreams, but with a minimum of tension, effort, or movement.

The importance of dreams. Doubtless the primary function of the "dream" is that of the "guardian of sleep." Though a person be in a state of sleep, stimuli are still present and registering on the human nervous system. Various stimuli, simple and/or complex, single and/or mingled, may prompt certain memory images or perceptions which the mind associates with those stimuli. These stimuli the unconscious mind puts together, producing the "dream," and thus allows the person to continue in a sleeping condition, and not awake to consciousness.

Dreams attest to the infinite bounds of the human mind. They are a forceful suggestion of the manifold and extensive possibilities within the mind and soul of man, waiting to be called forth. Of this arresting quality of dreams much has been written. "The slumber of the body seems to be but the waking of the soul. . . . It is the litigation of sense, but the liberty of reason; and our waking conceptions do not match the fancies of our sleep" (Sir J. Browne). "Dreams, these whimsical pictures, inasmuch as they originate from us, may well have an analogy with our whole life and fate" (Goethe). "Dreams have a poetic integrity and truth. . . . Their extravagance from nature is yet within a higher nature. They seem to suggest to us an abundance and fluency of thought not familiar to the waking experience. . . . A skillful man reads his dreams for his self-knowledge; yet not the details, but the quality" (Emerson). "We are not only less reasonable and less decent in our dreams but we are also more intelligent, wiser, and capable of better judgment when we are asleep than when we are awake" (Fromm).

Dream analysis is the fundamental technique of psychoanalysis. The free associations which occur within the unconscious as revealed in the dream are seen as guides to the person's motivational schema and underlying dynamics. Ideas, images, and events occurring in the dream may be interpreted as symbols of repressed anxieties, fears, or wishes. Such is suggested not only by the analysts, but by playwrights such as Goethe, . . . "Inasmuch as they originate from us, may well have an analogy with our whole life and fate."

Views held by ancient Eastern culture. Ancient Eastern peoples, esp. the Jews, held dreams in high regard; they noted them, and sought out those who professed or were known to explain and/or interpret them. Dream interpreters were highly esteemed; such is witnessed in the Egyptians of Joseph's time (Gen 40; 41). Oppenheim observes that in the ancient Near E, dream experiences were noted on three clearly differentiated planes: dreams as revelations of deity which may or may not require interpretation; dreams which reflect, symptomatically, the state of mind, the spiritual and bodily "health" of the dreamer, which are only mentioned but never recorded; and thirdly, mantic dreams in which forthcoming events are prognosticated.

As used in the Old Testament. The Bible treats "dreams" as being of three origins and importances: (1) natural (Eccl 5:3), (2) divine (Gen 28:12), and (3) evil (Deut 13:1, 2; Jer 23:32).

The major use of the word "dream" in the OT is that of it being a medium of a message from God: "I the LORD . . . speak with him in a dream" (Num 12:6); "For God speaks in one way, and in two . . . in a dream . . . that he may turn man aside from his deed, and cut off pride from man; he keeps back his soul from the Pit, his life from perishing by the sword" (Job 33:14-18). In this manner, "God came to Abimelech," and spake to him (Gen 20:3), "spoke through an angel of God" to Jacob (31:10, 11), "came and spake" to Laban (31:24), and "appeared" to Solomon (1 Kings 3:5).

Another use of the word "dream" in the OT concerns the prophetic function, the foretelling of events, including: Joseph's dreams which he related to his brethren (Gen 37:5-11); the Egyp. baker's and butler's dreams and the interpretations by Joseph (40:5-22); Pharaoh's dream (41:1-32); Gideon's encouragement in the Midianite camp from hearing a Midianite relate his dream of Gideon's forthcoming victory (Judg 7:13-15); Nebuchadnezzar's dream of world empires (Dan 2:1-45); Nebuchadnezzar's "tree" dream (4:4-28); Daniel's dream of the four winds, the great sea, and the four great beasts (7:1-28). The Israelites were instructed to show discernment concerning dreams and interpreters, for they may be evil (Jer 23:28). They were not to place them above the commandments of God (Deut 13:1-5).

Dreams were indicated too, as coming from natural causes, "For a dream comes with much business" (Eccl 5:3); also as a source of empty words, "For when dreams increase, empty words grow many" (5:7).

The word "dream" is employed also as a figure of speech, an expression to denote: that which is fleeting and/or transient, "fly away like a dream" (Job 20:8), "destroyed in a moment, swept away. . . . like a dream when one awakes" (Ps 73:19, 20); the unbelievable, the overwhelming, and amazing, "like those who dream" (126:1); and as being descriptive of the vain hopes and utter ruin of the enemies of Ariel (Jerusalem), "And the multitude of all the nations that fight against Ariel . . . shall be like a dream, a vision of the night. As when a hungry man dreams he is eating . . . as when a thirsty man dreams he is drinking" (Isa 29:7, 8).

As used in the New Testament. All occurrences of the word "dream" in the gospels, being six times in Matthew, concern the person of our Lord Jesus. Through a dream: an angel spake to Joseph about Mary's conception of the Christ child by the Holy Ghost (Matt 1:20-23); the wise men were warned concerning Herod (2:12); Joseph was warned to flee with the child and Mary to Egypt (2:13); an angel told Joseph to return to Israel from Egypt (2:19, 20); Joseph was warned that Archelaus reigned over Judea in place of his father Herod so that he (Joseph) withdrew to Galilee (2:22); the wife of Pilate suffered over Jesus and warned Pilate to have nothing to do with Jesus, "that righteous man" (27:19). The only other passage in the NT using the word "dream" is a direct quotation of Joel 2:28 (Acts 2:17).

See also TRANCE, VISION.

J. M. LOWER

DRESS. Ever since the creation man has been interested in articles of clothing, and thus it is not surprising that the Bible gives considerable information as to articles worn by men and women. Sometimes the Heb. and Gr. terms are clear as to the exact nature of the items, and at other times there exists doubt as to the specific shape, size, or character of the articles.

A. Descriptions in which terms for several articles of dress occur together. Several passages in the OT and NT give descriptions of dress to be worn (including ornaments) in which a number of Heb. and Gr. terms for articles of apparel are to be found together. These and other terms are found scattered throughout the Scriptures.

Matthew 5:40 and Luke 6:29 are instructive as to the ancient practice of wearing outer and inner garments, by using the terms χιτών, "tunic," for the "inner garment" and ἱμάτιον, for the "outer." In Matthew 5:40 the χιτών, RSV "coat" or "inner garment" occurs first, because in this legal case described, the defendant, besides the more easily accessible *himation,* "cloak," was to relinquish the indispensable χιτών, the "inner" garment. However, in Luke 6:29 the *himation* is listed first, because in a robbery situation the "outer garment," ἱμάτιον would logically be stolen first, and then, the inner *chitōn*.

Fully dressed men are described in Daniel 3:21 (in an Aram. section of the book) as being attired in "mantles" (סרבל, prob. or possibly "trousers," or, even "shoes"), "tunics" (פטש, meaning uncertain, possibly "tunic" or "leggings"), "their hats" (כרבלא, prob. "helmet" or "cap"; cf. Akkad. *karballatu*), "and their other garments" (לבוש, "garment," the same word as the Heb. one); but, as can be seen, this v. is difficult of interpretation in light of the dubious meaning of the Aram. words.

Ezekiel 16:8-14 presents Jerusalem in the figure of a woman regally attired as a bride. She is pictured as clothed "with embroidered cloth" (רקמה, variegated, woven, or embroidered stuff), "fine linen" (שש, fine Egyp. linen) and "silk" (משי, a costly material for garments, according to Rabb "silk"); and she is shod "with leather" (תחש, a kind of leather or skin used for sandals) and has a "beautiful crown" (עטרה תפארת, "crown of splendor" or "beauty") on her head. She also is pictured as adorned with ornaments (עדי), such as arm bracelets (צמיד, "bracelet"), neck chain (רביד, "chain," ornament for the neck), a nose ring (נזם, used both as nose ring for women as here, and earring for men and women), and earrings (עגיל, "hoop" or "ring," prob. "earring").

Isaiah 3:18-24 presents a fairly long list of clothing and ornamental items, and materials for beautifying, among which are finery for the ankles (i.e., anklets as ornaments), headbands (שבים, "frontband"; *cf.* Arab., a "sun" or small glass neck-ornament), crescents (שהרין, "moon" or "crescent," as an ornament), pendants (נטיפה, "drop," "pendant," or "pearl"), bracelets (שרה, "bracelet"), veils (רעלה, prob. "veil"; RSV "scarf"), headdresses (פאר, "headdress," "turban"), armlets (צעדה, "armlet," a band clasping the upper arm), sashes (קשרים, "bands" or "sashes," a woman's ornament which is bound on), charms (לחש, "charms," or "amulets" worn by women), signet rings (טבעת, here "ring" as an ornament), nose rings (cf. Ezek 16:12), "festal robes" (מחלצה, "robe of state," here in Isa 3:22, dress robes of the ladies of Jerusalem), mantles (מעטפה, "overtunic" or "mantle"), cloaks (מטפחת, "cloak," that which is spread over), handbags (חריט, "bag" or "purse," made of skin or other material), garments of gauze, or transparent garments (גליון, or "tablets of polished metal," "mirrors"), linen garments (סדין, "linen cloth" or "wrapper"), turbans for women (צניף, "turban," here of women), large veils (רדיד, or "wide wrapper"), girdles (חגורה, "girdle," "loin covering," "belt") and rich robes (פתיגיל, "rich robe").

Revelation 18:16 pictures Babylon as a woman in her finery with her fine linen garments (βύσσινος, made of fine linen, "linen garment"; cf. the Heb. term in Isa 3:23) dyed with purple (πορφύρα) and scarlet (κόκκινος) and adorned with gold ornaments (χρυσίον), precious stones (λίθος τίμιος) and pearls (μαργαρίτης).

When Abraham's servant went to Nahor in Mesopotamia to obtain Rebekah as a bride for Isaac, the text of Genesis 24 speaks of items of clothing and adornment for her, such as a gold nose ring and arm bracelets (vv. 22, 47), jewelry of silver and gold and clothing (בגד, a garment, clothing or robe of any kind) (v. 53).

The kind of dress worn by Jesus and His disciples can be deduced from the instructions given by Jesus to the Twelve (Matt 10:5-15; Luke 9:1-6) and to the seventy (10:1-12) as they went out on their preaching missions. Such articles included tunics (χιτών, "tunic," "undergarment"), sandals (ὑπόδημα), belts (ζώνη, "belt," "girdle"), money bags or purses (βαλλάντιον) and staff (ῥάβδος).

The dress of Aaron, the high priest and his sons, was to some extent specialized. In Exodus 28:4 Aaron's dress was said to have included a breastpiece, an ephod, a robe (מעיל, "robe," an external garment worn over the inner tunic), a tunic (כתנת, here the high priest's embroidered tunic), a turban (צניף, here, the turban for the high priest), and a girdle (אבנט, the special girdle of the priests, and of the high priest Exod 28:4, 39; Lev 8:7; 16:4). For Aaron's sons were made the tunic (*kuttonet*) and the girdle (*'abnēṯ*, Exod 28:40; 29:9; Lev 8:13, the same girdle as worn by the high priest) and a hat or cap, different from that of the high priest, called the מגבעות (cf. Exod 29:9; 39:28; Lev 8:13).

For military dress *see* ARMOR, ARMS.

B. General terms for garments of men and women. The examples given in the preceding discussion present some of the terms for clothing given in the Scriptures. Some of these words together with others often are used to refer to clothing in general, rather than to distinguish individual garments worn.

One such widely used OT term is בגד, a word to indicate a garment or robe of any kind. It is used for the garment of the poor and needy (Job 22:6), including the widow (Deut 24:17, "you shall not . . . take a widow's garment in pledge") and the prophet (2 Kings 4:39 "lap") to the elaborate and costly robes of the wealthy (Esth 4:1; Zech 14:14) and royal robes of princes (1 Sam 19:13, the princely garments of David, Saul's son-in-law), and kings such as David (1 Kings 1:1), Ahab and Jehoshaphat (2 Chron 18:9). Likewise, *beged* refers to the filthy, torn clothes of lepers (Lev 13:45, 47), the holy garments of the priests (Hag 2:12) and the high priest (Exod 28:2). *Beged* is used prophetically for the garments of Christ which were to be divided among the soldiers (Ps 22:18; cf. John 19:24). The word is used also for the clothing of the ordinary human being (Ps 102:26; Prov 25:20; Joel 2:13).

מד, is used as a general term for clothing in the reference to the clothes under which Ehud's sword was hid (Judg 3:16) to soldier's garments (1 Sam 17:38; 18:4; 2 Sam 20:8) and to the coat of the common man (Ps 109:18).

שמלה, term also is used in the general sense of garments as in the instructions to Ruth (3:3) to "put on her best clothes" and in the reminder to Israel that in the wilderness wandering their clothing did not wear out (Deut 8:4).

High Priest in typical clothing and other articles of clothing.

Workmen's garments, resembling those of ancient times. © *M.P.S.*

The Lord is pictured as one who gives the sojourner clothing as well as food (Deut 10:18) and these garments are spoken of as such as a a man would cover himself with at night (Exod 22:26; cf. Gen 9:23). Jacob instructs his household to change their garments (Gen 35:2) and David, following the death of the child born to him of Bathsheba "changed his clothes" (2 Sam 12:20). This term can be used to refer to a captive woman's clothing (Deut 21:13), but can also indicate the garments both of men and women (22:5). Such garments could be used to hold various objects, such as military spoil (Judg 8:25), a sword (1 Sam 21:9), and kitchen equipment (Exod 12:34). This word by metathesis becomes שׂלמה, and as such is used in general for clothing i.e., in reference to the clothes of the Gibeonites (Josh 9:5) and the well preserved garments worn by the Israelites following the Exodus (Deut 29:5).

The general term כּסוּת, means "covering," "clothing," and is used for a woman's clothing (Exod 21:10), as well as for the "covering" used to keep a man warm at night (Exod 22:26, 27; Job 24:7).

The general reference to clothes in Ezekiel 27:24 is to the מכלל (a garment made perfectly or gorgeously) and to the גלום (a "wrapper" or "garment").

In the NT *ἱμάτιον*, can be used generally for clothing (as well as for the outer garment) as seen in reference to an old garment (Matt 9:16; Mark 2:21; Luke 5:36; Heb 1:11; cf. Ps 102:26), in the pl., to clothing (Matt 27:35; cf. John 19:24; Ps 22:18), and to various pieces of clothing contributed as covering for the colt upon which Jesus rode and for the road upon which He traveled (Matt 21:7, 8; Mark 11:7, 8; Luke 19:35, 36). The *ἐπενδύτης*, used in John 21:7 can mean just "clothes" or possibly "outer garments."

C. Individual articles of clothing for the body. 1. *Materials used.* Clothing could be made of sackcloth (Jonah 3:6) or of costly materials (Gen 24:53; Esth 4:4; Zech 14:14; Rev 18:16), and the material itself might be made of sack or coarse hair (שׂק, "sack," "sackcloth"; 1 Kings 21:27; 2 Kings 6:30) or of fine linen as in the case of priestly garments (Lev 6:10; 16:4); and of the fine linen garments given by Pharaoh to Joseph (Gen 41:42), of garments in the time of Ezekiel (16:10) and of the NT (Rev 18:12, 16).

Sometimes garments were made of silk (Ezek 16:10, 13). Garments of such fine materials would be known as "soft raiment" (Luke 7:25). The OT instructed that garments should not be woven out of two different materials (Lev 19:19), such as wool and linen (Deut 22:11), materials from the different animal and plant kingdoms. Some garments would contain special adornments as the collar on Aaron's robes (Ps 133:2), the embroidered or checker work on his coat (Exod 28:4, 39), and tassels, as indicated in the instructions regarding the cloak of the common Israelite (Deut 22:12). Garments ordinarily seem to have been white (Eccl 9:8; John 20:12; cf. Rev 3:5, 18; 4:4; Matt 17:2), but they were also dyed purple and scarlet (2 Sam 1:24; Prov 31:22; Rev 18:16), and were black in the case of mourning (Rev 6:12; cf. Herm. *vis* 4, 1, 10). Sometimes garments were scented with perfume as in the case of those of kings (Ps 45:8) and brides (S of Sol 4:11).

2. *Men's garments.* Men's outer garments could be expressed by the terms בגד (see Isa 36:22; 37:1 where Hezekiah and his men rend their clothes); and by שׂלמה, a new garment with which the prophet Ahijah clothed himself and which he tore into twelve pieces (1 Kings 11:29, 30).

A different Heb. term מעיל, is used in the

Arab women in typical clothing, similar to biblical dress. © *M.P.S.*

OT to indicate an "exterior garment" or "robe" worn over an inner tunic or coat. It was like the *qumbaz* of modern Pal., being a long loosely-fitting robe, prob. sleeveless, worn over all other garments. It was worn by men of rank such as kings and princes (Saul and Jonathan, 1 Sam 18:4; 24:5); foreign princes (Ezek 26:16); David (1 Chron 15:27); prophets (as Samuel, 1 Sam 15:27); and scribes such as Ezra (9:3). It was also a robe of the high priest (the robe of the ephod) made of blue (Exod 28:31; 39:22), which had skirts around which were alternatively colored pomegranates and golden bells, and an opening at the top by which it could be pulled over the head (Exod 39:22-26).

The NT term ἱμάτιον could not only refer to clothing in general but also it was used to indicate the outer garment, "the cloak," in contrast to the χιτών, the inner garment, "the coat" or "tunic." It means "cloak" in Matthew 9:20 where the woman "touched the fringe of his (Jesus) garment," and in the passage where Jesus tells His disciples to sell their "mantles" and buy a sword (Luke 22:36). The purple robe that the soldiers put on Jesus was an outer garment (John 19:2), and Christ's outer robe is to be inscribed with King of kings and Lord of lords (Rev 19:16). Those who stoned Stephen laid aside their cloaks to free their arms for their task (Acts 7:58). The tearing of the cloak was a sign of grief (14:14). The περιβόλαιον, a covering something like a "cloak" is pictured as perishable in comparison with the eternal God (Heb 1:12). The στολή, "robe," esp. a long-flowing robe, was evidently something like the outer *himation*, but of superior quality, being the best robe put on the prodigal son (Luke 15:22), the robe worn by triumphant saints (Rev 7:14) and angels (Mark 16:5). Scribes are characterized as walking around in these long robes (12:38).

The principal Heb. word to express the inner garment was the כתנת, the ordinary garment worn by man and woman next to the skin, as seen in the tunics of skin worn by Adam and Eve (Gen 3:21) and the cloth inner garment rent as a sign of extreme grief (2 Sam 15:32). It had a mouth or collar (Job 30:18), and at least in some cases reached to the ankles, and had sleeves (Gen 37:3, 23, 32). These tunic-type garments pictured in the Beni-Hasan painting of about 1890 B.C. (ANEP, 3) are sleeveless, draped over one shoulder, and about calf length. This type of garment was also worn by the high priest (Lev 16:4) and by the priests generally (Exod 29:8; 40:14).

The מכנס, "drawers," was a special priestly linen garment worn next to the skin to cover the body from the loins to the thighs (Exod 28:42) to be used by the priest when removing ashes from the altar of burnt offering (Lev 6:10) and by the high priest on the Day of Atonement (Lev 16:4).

The NT χιτών, "tunic" or "coat," was worn next to the skin (cf. Matt 5:40; Luke 6:29), and was the seamless garment of Jesus for which the soldiers cast lots (John 19:23, 24). Dorcas had made numbers of these articles (Acts 9:39).

Accessories in addition to clothing included waistcloths and girdles such as the אזור, a "waistcloth," which was a girdle of leather worn by Elijah (2 Kings 1:8), but a waistcloth of linen for Jeremiah (13:1), an article which would be loosened at night (Isa 5:27). There were also the חגור, "belt" or "girdle," used by the soldier to which was attached a sheath with its sword (2 Sam 20:8), and the חגורה, a "girdle," or "loin covering" used by Adam and Eve (Gen 3:7) and also as a belt by the warrior (1 Kings 2:5). The אבנט, was the girdle of the priests (Exod 28:40), the high priest (Exod 28:4, 39), and also of a high official

Items of women's clothing, including footwear, typical of New Testament times.

(Isa 22:21). The מזח, "girdle," was an Egyp. loan word *mḏḥ*, used in Psalm 109:19. In the NT the ζώνη is the "belt" or "girdle," made of leather (worn by John the Baptist, Matt 3:4; Mark 1:6) or of gold (Rev 1:13), used as an instrument to bind parts of the body (Acts 21:11) and to hold up the long flowing garments for ease in traveling (1 Pet 1:13). Money could also be kept in it (Matt 10:9; Mark 6:8).

A special garment was the אדרת, "mantle" or "cloak," worn by Elijah the prophet (1 Kings 19:13, 19; 2 Kings 2:8, 13, 14) evidently an insignia of his office (cf. Zech 13:4), and also by the king of Nineveh (Jonah 3:6). Such a distinctive kind of mantle, a beautiful and costly one from Shinar was that which tempted Achan (Josh 7:21, 24).

3. *Women's garments.* The term בגד could be used also for women's garments as those of the widow (Deut 24:17), as is likewise true of the שמלה (Deut 22:5; Isa 4:1), and לבוש (2 Sam 1:24; Ps 45:14). In the NT the woman wore the outer garment, also named the *himation* (Acts 9:39; 1 Tim 2:9; 1 Pet 3:3).

The inner tunic, the כתנת, was also worn by the woman, as by Eve (Gen 3:21) and the king's daughter (2 Sam 13:18, 19), and could be put off at night (S of Sol 5:3). The סדין, a "linen wrapper" or "garment," is in the list of women's lingerie in Isaiah 3:23. In the NT the women also wore a garment called the χιτών (Matt 10:10; Acts 9:39).

As to accessories, the women's girdle is mentioned in Isaiah 3:24, presumably being similar to the ordinary sash or belt worn by men.

D. Footwear. The normal covering for the foot was the sandal, expressed by the word נעל, as in reference to the sandals of the Israelites in the wilderness journey (Deut 29:5) and those worn out, patched ones of the Gibeonites (Josh 9:5; cf. 1 Kings 2:5), which evidences the general practice of wearing some sort of protective covering for the bottom of the foot. Sandals were removed in mourning (Ezek 24:17, 23) and when standing on holy ground (Exod 3:5; Josh 5:15; Acts 7:33). Evidently there were other times, however, when a person would not wear his sandals or at least when an extra pair of sandals would be carried (Matt 3:11; Mark 6:9; Luke 10:4). They were taken off when sleeping (Acts 12:8). This sandal was bound on the foot by means of a thong according to Genesis 14:23; Isaiah 5:27 (cf. Mark 1:7). Another Heb. word for footwear was the סאון (prob. a loan word from Akkad. *šênu,* "shoe," "sandal," of leather) but its one OT use in Isaiah 9:5 refers to a soldier's "boot" or "shoe."

In the NT the term for footwear is the ὑπόδημα, a "sandal" or "leather" sole fastened to the foot by straps, an article referred to in Matthew 3:11; Luke 3:16; 15:22. Another term was σανδάλιον, a leather or wood sole also strapped to the foot (Mark 6:9 and Acts 12:8).

Women, too, wore sandals as evidenced by Song of Solomon 7:1 and Ezekiel 16:10, in the latter case the footwear being of leather. Shoes were so worn as evidenced in the Beni Hasan painting (ANEP, 3) where men are shown in thonged sandals but the women in shoes with a white border around the top, completely covering the foot and coming up over the ankle.

E. Headwear. Infrequent are references to headdress. There was the פאר, a "headdress," or "turban," worn by the bridegroom (Isa 61:10; the RSV, "garland"), by priests (Exod 39:28; Ezek 44:18), and by elegant women (Isa 3:20). It could be worn as a sign of joy (Isa 61:3, "garland"), the opposite of mourning (Ezek 24:17, 23). The מצנפת was the linen turban of the high priest (Exod 28:4, 37, 39; Lev 8:9), but it could also be a sign of royalty (Ezek 21:26). The מגבעות, however, was the turban or headdress of the priest (Exod 28:40), possibly conical in shape (Exod 29:9; Lev 8:13). Compare the conical hats shown in ANEP, 46, 47, 61, 355. The כובע was the soldier's helmet (1 Sam 17:5; Jer 46:4; cf. περικεφαλαία, the helmet of Eph 6:17 and 1 Thess 5:8).

Besides the headdress of Isaiah 3:20, women wore the צניף ("turban," Isa 3:23). They also wore the face-veil (צעיף, Gen 24:65; 38:14, 19) and a wide or large veil, the רדיד, which evidently was to cover the upper part of the body (S of Sol 5:7; Isa 3:23). The more elaborate tiara or turban (μίτρα) also used by women such as Judith (16:8), does not occur in the NT.

F. Ornaments. Ornaments worn with clothing included the finger ring, טבעת, used as a symbol of authority (Gen 41:42; Esth 3:10; 8:2) and also as an instrument to seal official documents (Esth 3:12; 8:8). The חתם, the seal or signet ring was hung by a cord around the neck (Gen 38:18), and also worn on the right hand (Jer 22:24). The נזם, the "ring of gold" of Job 42:11, was the customary golden earrings of the Ishmaelites (Judg 8:24-26), and was worn by men and women (Exod 32:2, 3); but it was also used as a woman's ornamental nose-ring (Gen 24:47; Isa 3:21; Ezek 16:12). The δακτύλιος, in Luke 15:22 refers to a ring but the σφραγίς of Revelation 5:1; 7:2 is only a seal.

Royalty wore crescent-shaped ornaments (שהרון) (Judg 8:26) (as did also women, Isa 3:18) and also eardrops or pendants (אצעדה, 2 Sam 1:10), which other men and women also wore (Num 31:50; cf. Isa 3:20).

Beyond the above, women were adorned with a number of ornaments called עדי, "ornaments" (2 Sam 1:24; Jer 2:32), including jewels of silver and gold (Gen 24:53; 1 Tim 2:9). The bracelet (צמיד) worn on the wrist (Ezek 23:42) or arm (Gen 24:22, 30; Num 31:50; Ezek 16:11) and the chain for the neck

Women's hair styles at the time of Paul.

(רביד, Ezek 16:11), among others, were important items of adornments. *See* CLOTH.

BIBLIOGRAPHY. A. Edersheim, *Sketches of Jewish Social Life in the Days of Christ* (n.d.), 216-222; A. Edersheim, *Life and Times of Jesus the Messiah*, vol. 1 (1901), 620-627; vol. II, 278, 279; J. B. Pritchard, *Ancient Near East in Pictures* (1954).

W. H. MARE

DRESSER OF SYCAMORE TREES. The phrase occurs only once in the OT. Amos so designated himself (בולס שקמים, Amos 7:14) in his disavowal of descent from any prophetic line. The dresser pruned or nipped the trees to promote ripening a greater yield.

DRIED GRAPES (ענבים יבשים), included in the proscribed list of foods for Nazirites (Num 6:3). All products of the vine, even the seeds and the skins, were forbidden to the Nazirite during the time of his separation (v. 4).

DRINK, DRINKING (שתה ; שקה; πίνω). The Eng. tr. of a number of Heb. and Gr. terms used in the Scriptures in the following ways: (1) in the ordinary sense of the bodily consumption of fluids such as water, wine, grape juice, milk, vinegar, etc., but even this to be done to God's glory (1 Cor 10:31); (2) symbolic of the spiritual expression of one's faith in God (Isa 32:6; John 6:54, 55; 7:37; 1 Cor 10:4); (3) symbolic of Christ's acceptance of God's will (John 18:11) and of the disciples' participation in Christ's suffering (Matt 20:22, 23); (4) the means by which Christians participate in the sacrament of the Lord's Table (Matt 26:27; 1 Cor 10:21; 11:25); (5) "giving drink" as an indication of Christian love and compassion (Matt 25:35-46); (6) symbolic of the reception of God's judgment and wrath (Job 21:20; Ps 75:8; Rev 14:10); (7) symbolic of sinners' participation in all kinds of evil and evil practice (Job 15:16; Prov 4:17; 26:6); (8) "drink blood," symbolic of blood slaughter against one's enemies (Ezek 39:18); (9) used also to describe the process by which the earth is watered by the rain from heaven (Heb 6:7).

J. B. SCOTT

DRINK OFFERING. *See* SACRIFICE AND OFFERINGS.

DROMEDARY. *See* CAMEL.

DROPSY. *See* DISEASE, DISEASES.

DROSS (סיג Ezek 22:18; סיגים elsewhere). Literally that which is removed from metal through the smelting process; the waste matter. Generally, the dross of silver is discussed (Prov 25:4; Isa 1:22; Ezek 22:18). Dross is parallel to בדיל "alloy, tin" (Isa 1:25). In each case dross is a symbol of moral corruption (cf. Ps 119:119), sometimes describing the wickedness of Israel (Ezek 22:18).

כסף סיגים "silver of dross" (Prov 26:23, mg.) has been rightly altered by the RSV to כספסיגים, "as glaze." Ugaritic *spsg* "whiteness" or "white glaze" provided a clue to this meaning.

BIBLIOGRAPHY. W. F. Albright, BASOR 98 (1945), 24, 25.

H. M. WOLF

DROUGHT. Any community whose habitat embraced a semi-arid region on the desert's fringe would certainly be painfully aware not only of the value but also of the variability of rainfall amounts which is characteristic of such a region. The *Atlas of Israel* has an interesting series of rainfall maps for the period 1931-55; they reveal deviations from long term mean of over one hundred percent in individual years. When successive subnormal years occur (cf. 1 Kings 17:1) famine results. Numerous Bible passages see drought as evidence of God's withholding blessing from His people. *See* RAIN; PALESTINE, CLIMATE OF.

J. H. PATERSON

DRUM. *See* MUSIC, MUSICAL INSTRUMENTS.

DRUNKENNESS (שכרון, רוה ; μέθη). There are many evidences in Scripture that alcoholic intoxication was one of the major social evils of ancient times. This was true of all nations, including Israel, in the Near E and the Mediterranean world. Drunkenness was common among all classes, but esp. the rich and the members of the nobility (1 Sam 25:36; 2 Sam 13:28; 1 Kings 16:9; 20:16). The prophet Amos said that God would bring judgment upon the wealthy women of Samaria for oppressing the poor and enticing their husbands to drink with them. The fact that Eli suspected Hannah, the mother of Samuel, of being inebriated while she was engaged in prayer in the Tabernacle shows that intoxication was not unknown even in that holy place. Isaiah wrote of priests and prophets in his own time, that they reeled and staggered with strong drink and that their minds were confused with wine (Isa 28:7).

The effects of strong drink are vividly described in the OT. There are frequent references to the unsteady gait of drunkards (Job 12:25; Ps 107:27; Isa 19:14; 24:20). Drunkards stagger in their vomit (Isa 19:14); they are given to quarrelsomeness and brawling (Prov 20:1; 23:19-35); they begin to drink early in the morning and continue until late hours, till wine inflames them (Isa 5:11); their minds are confused with drink (28:7); their understanding is taken away (Hos 4:11); they neglect their duties (Prov 31:4, 5); they think they are heroes (Isa 5:22); they end their days in poverty (Prov 21:17; 23:20, 21) and in woe and sorrow (23:29-32).

Among the better known cases of drunkenness in the OT are the following: Noah (Gen 9:21), Lot (19:33, 35), Nabal (1 Sam 25:36), Uriah (who was made drunk by David, 2 Sam 11:13), Amnon (13:28), Elah, king of Israel (1 Kings 16:9), Ben-hadad, king of Syria, and thirty-two allied kings (20:16).

Priests were forbidden to drink wine and strong drink while on duty in the sanctuary (Lev 10:9). Nazirites were expected to abstain from intoxicating beverages during the period of their vows (Num 6:3, 4).

The Scriptures contain strong injunctions against strong drink (Lev 10:9; Deut 21:20; Luke 21:34; 1 Cor 5:11; Gal 5:21).

Drunkenness also is used in a metaphorical sense (Job 12:25; Isa 19:14; Jer 23:9; Ezek 23:33; 39:19; Nah 3:11).

S. BARABAS

DRUSILLA drōō sĭl' ə (Δρούσιλλα). A diminutive or pet name for Drusa, chosen no doubt by Herod Agrippa I for his youngest daughter, who happened to be born in A.D. 38 when the mad Caligula, recently made emperor, was mourning the sudden death of his twenty-two-year-old sister Drusilla. Herod Agrippa, a companion of Caligula, was in Rome at the time. Drusus, son of Tiberius had also been a protector of the young Jewish prince. It was prob. in A.D. 53 that Drusilla, in her sixteenth year, was married to Azizus of Emesa, a small principality in the N of Syria, which included Palmyra. A year later, Felix, Claudius' unprincipled freedman and that emperor's notorious appointee to the procuratorship of Pal., persuaded Drusilla to leave her husband (Jos. Antiq. XX. vii. 2). She became Felix' third wife (Suetonius, Claud. 28), and in that role appears briefly in the story of Paul's imprisonment at Caesarea (Acts 24:24-27). According to Josephus, who was at the time a member of Vespasian's household, Agrippa, Drusilla's son by Felix, died in the eruption of Vesuvius on 24 August 79. Whether his widowed mother died with him is not known. Josephus' account is ambiguous.

E. M. BLAIKLOCK

DUALISM. See THEISM.

DUKE. KJV rendering of אַלּוּף, and once (Josh 13:21) of נְשִׂיא. "prince." אַלּוּף is related to the word for thousand אֶלֶף and means "leader of an *elep*, chiliarch;" although the precise number is not to be stressed. It is commonly applied to the tribal chiefs of Edom until the time of Moses (Exod 15:15). Genesis 36 contains an enumeration of several of these chiefs. The chiefs of Judah are referred to by Zechariah (9:7; 12:5, 6). Ugaritic *ulp* means "prince, chief." The RSV renders στρατηγός as "general" in 1 Maccabees 10:65 where the KJV has "duke."

H. M. WOLF

DULCIMER. See MUSIC, MUSICAL INSTRUMENTS.

DUMAH dōō' mə (דּוּמָה ; *silence*). 1. The sixth son of Ishmael and the presumed founder of an Arab community (Gen 25:14; 1 Chron 1:30). Dumat al Gandal appears to identify with the Biblical Dumah· as the capital of a district known as Gawf. The site is an oasis half way between the head of the Persian Gulf and the Gulf of Aqabah. Royal Assyrian and Babylonian inscrs. from the 7th and 6th centuries refer to the destruction of the Adummatu which may be a reference to the descendants of Dumah.

2. A town in the hills of Judah (Josh 15:52). The *Onomasticon* refers to a town of this name. It is frequently identified with the present ed-Domeh located SW of Hebron.

3. "The oracle concerning Dumah" (דּוּמָה מַשָּׂא) appears in Isaiah 21:11. The next words mention Seir so perhaps the term is a figure from Edom. The LXX renders the word as "Idumaea."

H. JAMIESON

DUMB, DUMBNESS. See DISEASE, DISEASES.

DUNG (Dung Gate). The excrement of humans and animals. In the Bible ten different words meaning dung are used, nine of them in Heb. and one in Gr.

The term has several connotations in Scripture: (1) That which shall perish (Job 20:7); (2) That which defiles (Ezek 4:12, 15), and is used to degrade (Mal 2:3; see 2 Kings 18:27; Isa 36:12); (3) That which is unclean (Exod 29:14; Lev 4:11; 8:17; 16:27; Num 19:5), and in sacrificing consequently that which is to be disposed of and not included in the sacrifice (cf. 1 Kings 14:10); (4) That which is useless (2 Kings 9:37; Ps 83:10; Jer 8:2; 9:22; 16:4; 25:33). This meaning is seen also in 2 Kings 6:25.

In the NT Paul uses the term to refer to that which is despised and worthless. Paul counts all other things as "dung" compared with knowing Christ (Phil 3:8).

The name "Dung Gate" is found in four passages in the Book of Nehemiah and refers to one of the gates of Jerusalem in Nehemiah's day. From this gate Nehemiah surveyed the broken walls of Jerusalem in the night (2:13). It was located between the Valley Gate (3:13) and the Fountain Gate (3:15). It was repaired by Malchijah, the son of Rechab. It was near this gate that Nehemiah had the dedication of the wall when it was completed (12:31). It is most probable from the series of gates mentioned in Nehemiah, that the Dung Gate was on the Tyropoeon side of the city and led down to that valley. Perhaps dung was dumped here in the valley at one time. Today, the Dung Gate is that gate on the S side of the walled city, leading down to the spur Ophel which was the ancient city of David. (*See also* DUNG GATE.)

The Dung Gate in the Jerusalem city wall. ©M.P.S.

BIBLIOGRAPHY. National Geographic Society, *Everyday Life in Bible Times* (1967), 225, 357.

J. B. SCOTT

DUNGEON (בור, *pit*; בית הבור, *house of the pit*). The word "pit" suggests that a dungeon was a sunken room, perhaps a dry well. Joseph was placed in one in Egypt (Gen 40:15; 41:14), and Jeremiah was cast into one in Israel (Jer 38:6, 7, 9, 10, 11, 13; Lam 3:53, 55). Isaiah (42:7) uses the term in a fig. sense, saying that the Messiah would "bring out the prisoners from the dungeon." *See* PRISON.

S. BARABAS

DUNG GATE (שער האשפות, *the gate of the ash-heaps*). A postexilic gate on the S side of Jerusalem (Neh 2:13 [*dung port*, KJV]; 3:13-14, 12:31), leading to the rubbish dump in the Hinnom Valley (2 Kings 23:10). L. Vincent proposes a SW corner, the later "Gate of the Essenes" (Jos. War. V. 4. 2); but most prefer the great gate S of the City of David at the SE corner (J. Simons, *Jerusalem in OT*, in 123, 124).

J. B. PAYNE

DURA dōōr′ ə, PLAIN OF (Aram. בקעת דורא, plain of Dura). A plain somewhere in the province of ancient Babylon, in which King Nebuchadnezzar erected his golden image, referred to only in Daniel 3:1 in the OT.

The Akkad. name *dûru* (from which the Aram. comes) means "circuit," "walled place" and was common in Mesopotamian geographical names. This meaning of the Akkad. evidently prompted the LXX to tr. *dûwrā'*, "Dura," by περίβολος meaning an enclosed, or walled, area.

Of the three most likely identifications for the place, the first, near Carchemish (Polybius v. 48) was not a part of provincial Babylon, and the second, located beyond the Tigris not far from Apollonia (Polybius v. 52) is too far from the capital Babylon. Rather, the place may more likely be identified with the mounds or tells of Dura, a few m. to the S of the city of Babylon.

BIBLIOGRAPHY. J. A. Montgomery, *The Book of Daniel*, ICC (1927), 197; C. F. Keil, *Daniel* (1955), 119.

W. H. MARE

DUST (עפר, אבק, דק, *fine dust*, שחק, also *cloud*; *κονιορτός, χοῦς*). עפר is the most common, referring to loose earth, soil, powder. It was thrown upon the head as a sign of mourning (Josh 7:6), but could serve to indicate abundance collectively (Gen 13:16). Man was made of dust (Gen 2:7; 1 Cor 15:47-49) and, at death, returns to dust (Gen 3:19; Job 10:9). אבק is dust which caused boils in Egypt (Exod 9:9). It could refer to thin clouds at God's feet (Nah 1:3), similar to שחק.

H. WOLF

DWARF. The tr. of דק, "thin," "fine" (Lev 21:20) where physical handicaps which disqualify a descendant of Aaron from offering sacrifices are listed. The word is used of thin cows and ears of corn (Gen 41:3-7), of small, fine manna (Exod 16:14), of dust (Isa 29:5), and of a mere whisper (1 Kings 19:12). Although the exact meaning is not known, the idea of "withered" fits best (cf. BDB, p. 201—"thin, shrunk, withered"). The LXX and Vul. propose "eye defect," but this is unlikely.

H. WOLF

DWELLING PLACE. A frequent term tr. a number of words from the original languages. It is not always clear whether the location or the structure in which one dwells (tent or house) is in view. The common noun מושב, from ישב, "to sit," "dwell," can mean "dwelling place" (Num 24:21). It can refer to Zion as the habitation of God (Ps 132:13). "Inhabited places" fits its usage in Ezekiel 34:13, and the root meaning "seat" occurs in 1 Samuel 20:25 and Psalm 1:1. The "situation" or "location" of a city is acceptable, but lack of water and barren ground spoil it (2 Kings 2:19). מושב can even mean "those dwelling in a house" (2 Sam 9:12). The infinitive of the same root, שבת, combined with מקום, "place," means the "dwelling place" of God in heaven (1 Kings 8:30).

משכן, often denotes the particular wilderness tabernacle where God chose to abide (root שכן "to dwell, abide"). When it does not refer to this building, it is sometimes parallel to "houses" (Ps 49:11) or "tents" (Jer 30:18). The RSV renders the first, "dwelling places" and the second, "dwellings." Another synonym, מכון emphasizes "a fixed or established place, foundation" (Exod 15:17). כל מכון is tr. "the whole site" in the RSV (Isa 4:5). BDB suggests "all the extent" of Zion.

מעון, can be a "refuge" or "habitation" of jackals (Jer 9:11; 51:37) or of God in heaven (Deut 26:15). God is called "a dwelling place" or "refuge" for His own (Ps 90:1). Cf. Esther 4:14 (KJV) where "place" may refer to God.

Κατοικητήριον means the "dwelling (place)" of God in believers, the Church of Christ. Revelation 18:2 refers to destroyed Babylon as the "dwelling place" for demons.

'Αστατέω, "to be homeless, unsettled," is used by Paul in describing the deprivation of the apostles (1 Cor 4:11). The KJV reads: "have no certain dwelling place." *See* House.

BIBLIOGRAPHY. H. C. Leupold, *Exposition of the Psalms* (1959), 643, 916; J. B. Payne, *The Theology of the Older Testament* (1962), 361.

H. Wolf

DYE, DYEING. The actual dyeing process is not described in the Bible. Dyed materials are mentioned as early as the time of the Exodus. Material for the Tabernacle is described as "blue and purple and scarlet stuff" (Exod 26:1, 31). Josephus described the Temple materials as "woven of four stuffs, byssus as a symbol of the earth, whence the flax grows; purple, the sea which was dyed with the blood of fishes; hyacinth, the air; and scarlet, the fire" (Antiq. III. vii. 7).

Dyeing with its infinite possibility in color variations had its secret formulae. Not until Hel. times were many of the secrets of the formulae used in the dye industry recorded. All ancient crafts were family affairs and the best techniques and materials were trade secrets. With the rise of the new science of chemistry in the Hel. period the secret formulae were made known.

The dye used must have a natural affinity for the cloth used, or a mordant must be added to make the color fast. Wool, the most common cloth in Biblical times, was easy to dye. Natural wool came in a variety of colors running from white and yellow through tans and browns. By the use of different dyes on these various wools it was possible to make the "many-colored robes" (Ps 45:14). Linen was more difficult to dye, but linen was used in the Tabernacle (Exod 35:6) and the Temple (2 Chron 2:7). Cotton was easy to dye. Its home was India and by the time of Esther it was used in Persia (Esth 1:6). Cotton did not appear in Pal. until the intertestamental period. Some silk was dyed before it left the Far E for Antioch, while some was dyed in Mediterranean cities. Fine leather also was dyed.

The most important red used in dyeing ran from a brilliant hue to a scarlet (Isa 1:18). It was produced from cochineal insects. A cheaper commonly used dye was secured from the root of the madder plant.

The best blue dye was that extracted from the molluscs *Purpura* and *Murex* which flourished on the Phoen. coast. The expensive garments which symbolized rank and nobility were dyed purple from the secretion of the mollusc. During intertestamental times indigo came into Pal. from India. Yellows were made from safflower, turmeric and pomegranate.

The best example of dye works in Pal. came from Kirjath-sepher or modern Tell Beit Mirsim. Six dye plants were excavated by the archeologists, but it is estimated that approximately thirty installations had been constructed at the site. The size of the vats indicated that thread was dyed rather than cloth.

The dominant color of cloth described in the NT is purple (Mark 15:17; Luke 16:19; John 19:2, 5; Acts 16:14). The Gr. term πόρφυρα refers back to the purple shellfish, then to the purple dye obtained from the mollusc and finally the cloth or clothing dyed purple. When the Apostle Paul went to Philippi, Lydia from Thyatira, "a seller of purple goods" (Acts 16:14) was one of the first to respond to the Gospel.

H. Jamieson

DYSENTERY. *See* Disease, Diseases.

DYSMAS **dĭz' məs** (Δυσμᾶς; alternately *Dismas, Demas,* meaning uncertain). A name given in later apocryphal accounts to the repentant thief described in Luke 23:39-43. The Gr. *Acts of Pilate* (9. 5) name the thief on the right, Dysmas, and the unrepentant thief on the left, Gestas. Syrian sources bear the name Titus in place of Dysmas and on the left is Dumachus. The latter comes from the Gr. δύσμαχος, "hard to fight with," "unconquerable." A possible derivation for Dysmas is δυσμή, meaning "sunset" or "close of life." It was later used in the baptismal renunciation made by the candidate while facing W (Cyr. H. *Catech.* 19. 2).

BIBLIOGRAPHY. M. R. James, *The Apocryphal New Testament* (1924), 103, 104, 116, 161; E. Hennecke, *Neutestamentliche Apokryphen* (1924), 79; M. S. Enslin, "Hagiographic Mistletoe," JR, XXV (Jan. 1945), 10-24.

L. Foster

A dye plant at Tell Beit Mirsim.

Mount Ebal as viewed from Jacob's Well. ©*M.P.S.*

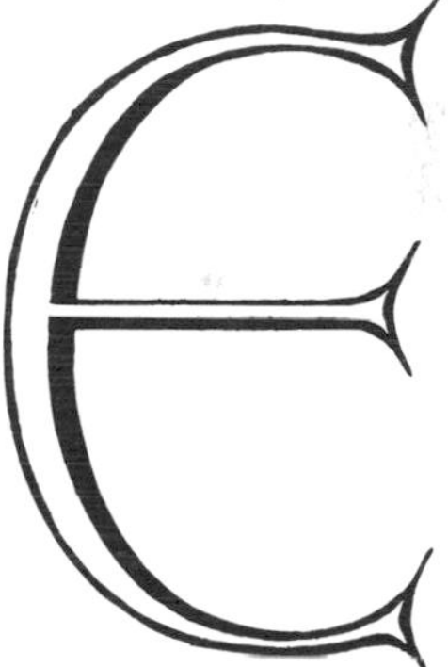

E (ELOHIST) ĕl′ ō hĭst. A document prominent in higher critical theory which allegedly was written in the 8th cent. B.C. It stemmed from the northern kingdom and reflected a more objective style than "J." "E" refers to the characteristic Heb. name for God in this source, אלהים. Critics regard it as an important source of the Pentateuch.

H. M. Wolf

EAGLE (נשר ; ἀετός; KJV EAGLE also RSV, except Prov 30:17; Lam 4:19; Hos 8:1; VULTURE RSV). Eagle occurs more than all other birds of prey and is uniformly tr. in KJV; also, with above three exceptions, in RSV. Its position at the head of the Levitical table suggests great size and this is implied in several contexts; e.g. Exodus 19:4, "I bore you on eagles' wings." Other attributes are swiftness and strength—Jeremiah 49:22, "Fly swiftly like an eagle." It flies high in the heavens (Obad 4), "Though you soar aloft like the eagle." The root represents a gleaming flash or rushing sound, a bird which streaks through the air (Driver). These facts would apply to either eagles or vultures, and Pal. is rich in these birds—golden, spotted, lesser spotted, Bonelli's, booted, imperial, tawny, Verraux's,

Eagle drawn from a silver tetradrachma from Ascalon, dated 29 B.C. ©*U.A.N.T.*

short-toed and white-tailed eagles; black bearded, Griffon, and Egyptian vultures.

In a few contexts the vulture is clearly meant—e.g. Matthew 24:28, "There the eagles will be gathered together." These scavengers hang high in the sky great distances apart, and can see when a neighboring bird drops down, so that vultures from a wide area soon collect. This is a habit of vultures generally. An ancient proverb quoted in the Talmud, says that a vulture in Babylon can see a carcase in Pal. The context in Micah 1:16, "Make yourselves as bald as the eagle" suggests the Griffon vulture, whose head is covered with short creamy down, giving the appearance, at a distance, of being bare.

Few people today, other than experienced naturalists, can distinguish between these birds, usually seen at great distances and heights, where color cannot be distinguished. Hebrew נשר can thus be taken as a name embracing them all. Several fig. passages reflect interesting beliefs (Deut 32:11), "Like an eagle that stirs up its nest," implies that a hen eagle deliberately disturbs the young, persuades them to take off, and then catches them on her wings if need be, but this has little basis in fact. Young birds spend long periods alone at the nest, esp. as they grow older. Between eight and twelve weeks, according to species, the juvenile becomes fully feathered and begins flapping and exercising its wings, finally becoming airborne. "Flying like an eagle toward heaven" (Prov 23:5), may be connected with an ancient belief that the eagle disappeared into the sun every ten years, to dive down into the sea, like the sun, and emerge refreshed. Pliny wrote of the eagle forcing her young to look straight against the sun's beam.

The biology of eagles in Pal. is too varied to treat. About three species breed in tall trees or, more often, on cliffs. The others are passing migrants or winter visitors. They feed mostly on live prey, which ranges from young deer to reptiles and insects.

BIBLIOGRAPHY. G. R. Driver, "Birds in the OT; I, Birds in Law," PEQ (1955), 5-20. *See* also Bibliography of BIRD MIGRATION.

G. S. CANSDALE

EANES (KJV) OF MAASEIAH **mā' ə se' yə** (מַעֲשֵׂיָה, מַעֲשֵׂיָהוּ) a postexilic priest who had married a foreign woman in the time of Ezra (Ezra 10:21; 1 Esdras 9:21).

EAR (אֹזֶן, *οὖς*, *ὠτίον*, *little ear*). The vital organ of hearing, while used in the physical sense often, more frequently involves the idea of understanding and obedient response. The tip of the right ear of the priests was touched with blood during their consecration (Lev 8:23f.). A servant who spurned freedom to continue in the service of his master had his ear bored with an awl to signify his continual subservience (Exod 21:6).

Several idioms involve the word "ear." "To incline the ear" means "to give attention" (Ps 88:2). גלה אזן denotes "revealing a secret to one" (1 Sam 20:2; 2 Sam 7:27). Uncircumcised ears are deaf to moral and spiritual instruction, not delighting whatever in the Word of God (Jer 6:10; Acts 7:51). Likewise, men with healthy ears sometimes do not hear (Jer 5:21), or are prevented from hearing spiritually (Isa 6:10). One with a hearing ear manifests obedience (Prov 20:12; 25:12) whereas one who "stops his ears" from listening to an evil plot declares that he wants no part of it (Isa 33:15). At the hearing of disastrous news, ears tingle (1 Sam 3:11; 2 Kings 21:12).

God is said to open men's ears with the result that they gain understanding (Job 29:11) and display obedience (Isa 50:4, 5). Christ exhorted the disciples to "let these words sink into your ears" (Luke 9:44) implying a careful and heart-searching response. Probably the "digging" of David's ears refers to this same capacity to respond to God's voice (Ps 40:6).

In contrast to idols (135:17), God's ears are not heavy (Isa 59:1, 2). Another reference to ears "heavy of hearing" appears in Matthew 13:15. Occasionally, the phrase "in the hearing of" equals "in the presence of" (1 Chron 28:8; Luke 4:21).

Cutting off ears was a feared practice of the enemy (Ezek 23:25). Peter's severing of the ear of the servant in the garden marks the only occurrence of *ὠτίον*, the diminutive of *οὖς*, signifying the outer ear (Matt 26:51; Mark 14:47).

BIBLIOGRAPHY. M. Dahood, Psalm I, in *The Anchor Bible* (1966), 246.

H. WOLF

EAR OF GRAIN, שבלת, and στάχυς, refer to the "head" or "ear" of grain (cf. Gen 41:5-7, 22-24 where Joseph interprets Pharaoh's dream—KJV "ear of corn," Isa 17:5; Matt 12:1). In Mark 4:28 the στάχυς is contrasted with the "full grain in the ear."

מלילה describes an ear of wheat which is prob. rubbed or scraped (Deut 23:25). אביב refers to fresh young ears of barley which could be roasted and which were included in the offering of first fruits (Lev 2:14). The first month (equal to April) was called אביב because of its agricultural importance. כרמל is more properly "fresh fruit, garden growth" (2 Kings 4:42).

H. M. Wolf

EARLY RAIN. *See* Rain.

EARNEST (NT ἀρραβών). The word came into Gr. from a Sem. language, perhaps from the vocabulary of Phoen. traders. Hebrew has the word ערבון associated with the verb ערב, which usually means "take" or "give in pledge." The noun is used three times in Genesis 38:17-20 (the only LXX use of ἀρραβών) for Judah's pledge given to Tamar that she would receive her hire. Right down to modern Gr., where ἀρραβών is used for an engagement ring, the word is used for a pledge in a contract.

In a derived sense an ἀρραβών in a commercial transaction came to be a down payment, as in the modern hire-purchase system (some good examples are given in MM). Both meanings, pledge and first installment, are involved in each of the three NT uses of the word. Second Corinthians 1:22 speaks of God's gift of the Holy Spirit as the pledge and foretaste of what the Christian will enjoy later (significantly the word "seal" is also used in the context). Second Corinthians 5:5 similarly says that the Holy Spirit is the earnest of that fullness of life which the Christian will enjoy after the dissolution of his earthly "tent." The Holy Spirit of promise is the earnest of the inheritance (Eph 1:14) which the Christian will finally receive. The earnest, as Behm (in TWNT) puts it, "always implies an act which engages to something bigger"; it is a pledge or deposit guaranteeing that a larger payment will be made.

F. Foulkes

EARRING. Earrings have been a popular ornament from the remotest antiquity, the earliest mention in Genesis 35:4. Earrings are frequently mentioned in the OT. The earring mentioned in Genesis 24:47 (KJV) is rendered a nose ring in the RSV. They were often regarded as amulets or talismans (Gen 35:4), as they still are in the E. Among all Oriental peoples, except the Hebrews and Egyptians, earrings were in general use by both sexes; but Exodus 32:2 shows that at least in the time of Moses they were also worn by Israelite boys. In the W they have been largely female ornaments. Judges 8:24, 25 records that the Ishmaelites wore earrings. Prior to the 4th cent. B.C., Gr. statues had the ear lobes perforated so that earrings might be hung from them. Usually they were made of gold or silver.

S. Barabas

EARTH, EARTH, CIRCLE OF THE (אדמה, *land, soil,* ארץ, *land, earth,* עפר, *dust,* γῆ, *earth,* οἰκουμένη, *inhabited earth*; חוג, *vault, horizon*). There is considerable overlapping of meaning in these words. Sometimes it is hard to define the territorial limits intended by "land" or "earth." Poetic references are even more difficult. The word for "circle," חוג, is derived either from חוג, "to draw round, make a circle" or חקק, "to trace, mark out a circle over the face of the deep." The phrase itself appears only in Isaiah 40:22, where God "sits above the circle of the earth." Job 22:14 refers to God "walk(ing) on the vault of heaven," and Proverbs 8:27 describes a "circle" placed upon the deep. This last reference, esp., suggests a boundary, and some would treat the "circle of the earth" as a protective wall, or mountains, which guard the earth from the foreboding waters around it. Such an interpretation imposes too much upon חוג, however, for it has a less precise meaning, more like "horizon." "Sphere" may likewise be reading something into חוג.

Earrings from Bible times.

EARTH, CORNERS OF THE (כנף, pl. כנפות, *wings* [of birds], *ends of garment, skirts, corners*). Once כנף occurs in the sing. (Isa 24:16). Used with "land, earth," כנפות refers metaphorically to the totality of the area involved. All five occurrences are in poetic passages. The "four corners of the land" are mentioned in Ezekiel 7:2, while Isaiah 11:12 describes the regathering of Israel from the four corners of the earth, that is, the whole world. Cf. the similar Akkad. idiom *kip̮at irbitti*. Job 38:13 emphasizes the idea of "skirts" which God grasps to shake out the wicked of the earth. (See Job 37:3.)

EARTH, PILLARS OF THE (עמודים, *pillars, columns*). A poetic expression occurring only twice. Job 9:6 speaks of the trembling of the earth's pillars during an earthquake. In Psalm 75:3, there is also an "adjustment" of the pillars at the dissolving of the earth. Heaven's pillars "tremble" at the rebuke of God (Job 26:11). Some scholars insist that these references must mean that the Hebrews conceived of a world supported by literal pillars. A more general sense of "rocky foundations" is more probable. They, also, are said to tremble (Isa 24:18).

EARTH, VAULT OF THE (אגדה, *band, thong, vault*). This infrequent word can denote the fetters of prisoners (Isa 58:6), a band of men (2 Sam 2:25) or the "vault" of heaven. "Vault" is possible only in Amos 9:6 (KJV "troop") where it is parallel to "upper chambers." The context aids little in defining its usage. (*See* EARTH, CIRCLE OF THE.)

BIBLIOGRAPHY. M. H. Pope, "Job," *The Anchor Bible* (1965), 151; E. J. Young, *The Book of Isaiah*, I (1965), 396.

H. M. WOLF

EARTHEN VESSELS, EARTHENWARE. *See* POTTERY.

EARTHQUAKE, the shaking of the ground resulting from the release of stored elastic strain energy due to the sudden deformation of a region of the earth which has been in a state of stress. The destruction with which earthquakes are commonly associated is caused by seismic waves which travel outward in all directions from a focus where fracturing or faulting occurred. The focus of most major earthquakes, and those causing most destruction, is less than 25 m. below the earth's surface. However, earthquakes as deep as 420 m. have been recorded.

About 50,000 earthquakes annually are noticed without the aid of instruments, with about 100 intense enough to cause substantial damage if their centers are near regions of habitation. The great majority of these earthquakes occur in well-defined zones, particularly in the circum-Pacific belt and in the Trans-Alpine belt, which stretches from Burma across southern Asia through Iran and Turkey, to Bulgaria, Greece and Italy. Another seismic belt corresponds with the ocean ridge system together with the apparently connected E African Rift Valley, the Levantine rift including the Jordan Rift Valley and the region of the Red Sea (Fig 1). All these major seismic regions can be related to major features of the earth's crust and in particular to the margins and relative motions of "plates" of the lithosphere in the order of 30-60 m. thick and up to several thousands of m. across.

There is considerable evidence suggesting that the present Mediterranean Sea represents only a remnant of a large ocean that once existed between Eurasia and Africa. The high seismic activity of the region is related to the general northward movement of the African and Arabian plates together with the relative motions of two rapidly moving plates which generally correspond with the regions of Greece/Aegean Sea and western Turkey. These regions and those of eastern Turkey and Iran are seismically active throughout (Fig. 1). Very destructive earthquakes have occurred in the past few years in Iran and Turkey while 60,000 and 45,000 people, respectively died in earthquakes in Cilicia, Asia Minor, in A.D. 1268 and in Corinth, Greece in A.D. 856. Hence the region of Mesopotamia, with which the beginnings of human activity in the ancient Near E is so closely associated, and the region of the Pauline journeys, have been and are both subject to considerable earthquake activity, some of it very destructive (Acts 16:26).

While the Mediterranean region is essentially one of crustal compression, the region from the Red Sea down to the E African Rift Valley is one of extension, with three crustal plates meeting at the southern end of the Red Sea (Fig. 1). The faulting and release of strain energy as these plates have moved (and are still moving) relative to one another, and parted, has resulted in considerable seismic activity. While this is largely concentrated SE of the Holy Lands, the Jordan Rift Valley represents part of a related very large fault zone which stretches northward from the entrance of the Gulf of Aqaba for over 683 m. to the foot of the Taurus ranges. The geological evidence indicates that there has been, in the region of the present Dead Sea, 67 m. of left-hand shear movement (cf. Zech 14:4) during the last c. sixty million years. This is associated with the separation of the Arabian peninsula from the African continent. The rifting took place in two main stages but this major crustal dislocation, with the associated earthquake phenomena, has been moving from c. sixty million years ago to the present, and is still active both on the major faults and also the complex set of associated faults (Fig. 2). Hence the inhabitants of the region have been familiar with

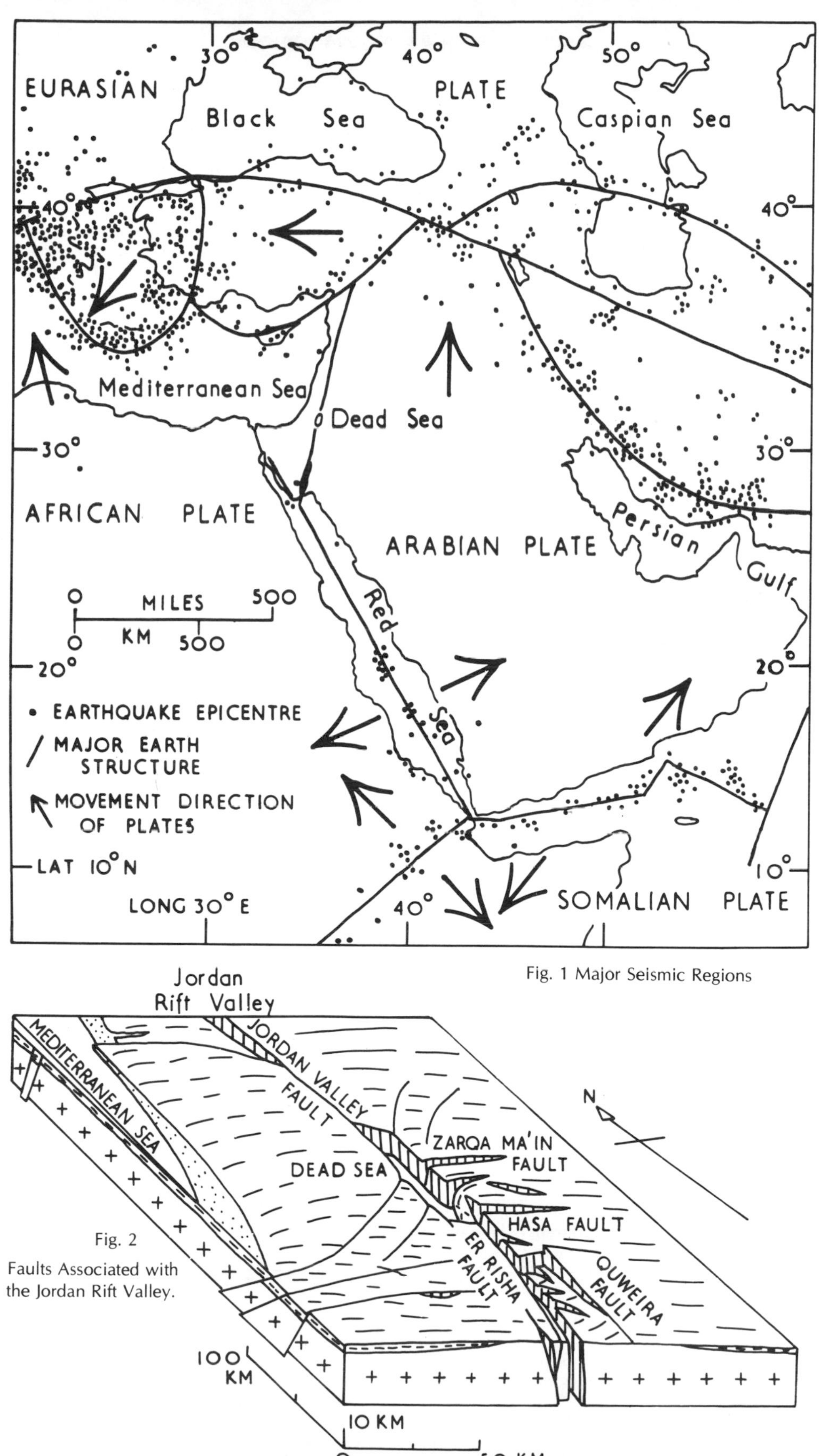

Fig. 1 Major Seismic Regions

Fig. 2
Faults Associated with the Jordan Rift Valley.

the earth shaking (cf. Ps 68:8; Isa 13:13; Hag 2:6), with even the mountains which were regarded as symbols of permanence being affected (Ps 46:3). The earthquakes during the twenty-seventh year of the reign of King Uzziah must have been severe (Amos 1:1; Zech 14:5), while the earthquakes at the time of the crucifixion and resurrection of Jesus Christ had marked effects (Matt 27:54; 28:2). Earthquakes figure prominently in indications of the nature of things to be (e.g. Matt 24:7; Mark 13:8; Luke 21:11; Acts 8:5; Rev 6:12; 11:13; 16:18). Other catastrophic events, such as landslips of unstable sediments, triggered off by earthquake activity, could explain the background to the story of Sodom and Gomorrah (Gen 19:24). Certainly one of the chief geological characteristics of Pal. has been its proneness to earthquakes.

BIBLIOGRAPHY. E. M. Blaiklock (ed.), *The Zondervan Pictorial Bible Atlas* (1965), 3-5; 438-452; H. Benioff and F. Press, "Earthquake," E Br, 7 (1970), 853-861; D. P. McKenzie, "Plate Tectonics of the Mediterranean Region," *Nature Lond.,* 226 (1970), 237-243; D. P. McKenzie, D. Davies and P. Molnar, "Plate Tectonics of the Red Sea and East Africa," *Nature Lond.,* 226 (1970), 243-248.

D. R. BOWES

EAST, CHILDREN (MEN, PEOPLE) OF THE (בני קדם). A term evidently describing nations located to the E of Pal. *Qedem* ("East") already occurs in the Egyp. *Romance of Sinuhe* (c. 1900 B.C.) as a land near Canaan where Bedouins were seen. In Genesis 29:1 Jacob journeyed to the territory of the people of the E in Paddan-aram, northern Mesopotamia. Judges 6-8 includes the בני קדם as Arabs who fought Israel with the Midianites and Amalekites. (See Jer 49:28; Ezek 25:4, 10.) Job 1:3 describes Job as the "greatest of the children of the east." Some think that northern Arabia, Edom, or Moab provides the setting of the book, a location which fits Isaiah 11:14 also. Hitti affirms that Arabia in general was the home of the children of the E.

Along with the Egyptians, the Eastern people were known for their wisdom (1 Kings 4:30). The wise men who visited the young child Jesus were also from the E (Matt 2:1-12).

BIBLIOGRAPHY. P. K. Hitti, *History of the Arabs,* 7th ed. (1960), 43.

H. M. WOLF

EAST COUNTRY (ארץ קדם, *land of the front, east*). Abraham sent the children of his concubines to this land (Gen 25:6). It lay prob. to the SE of Pal., including part of Arabia. Midian was one of the sons involved.

EAST GATE (שער המזרח, *gate of the place of sunrise*). Nehemiah 3:29 refers to this gate in Jerusalem, although it is not specifically stated that Nehemiah repaired it. The "east gate" (*haqqadmōnî*) of Yahweh's house may be the same structure. It was a temple gate (Ezek 10:19; 11:1).

EAST SEA, EASTERN SEA (הים הקדמוני). A name appearing in Ezekiel 47:18; Joel 2:20; Zechariah 14:8 for the Dead Sea. Its location on the eastern border of Israel makes the name appropriate. In the minor prophets it is opposed to the "western sea" (hinder sea), the Mediterranean.

EAST WIND. A scorching wind, the sirocco, which in Pal. and Egypt blows in from the desert most often in May and October. It withers vegetation (Gen 41:6; Ezek 17:10) and dries up fountains and springs (Hos 13:15). Sometimes it destroys houses (Job 1:19) and ships (Ps 48:7; Ezek 27:26). By an E wind God drove back the waters so that the Israelites could cross the sea on dry land (Exod 14:21). God used an E wind to bring judgment (Isa 27:8; Jer 4:11, 12; 18:17). "God appointed a sultry east wind" to afflict Jonah (Jonah 4:8). An ENE wind drove Paul's ship off course (Acts 27:14, KJV "Euroclydon"; ASV "Euraquilo"; RSV "northeaster"). The "scorching heat" (James 1:11 RSV) may be the sirocco (Gr. καύσων).

E. RUSSELL

EASTER (KJV rendering of τὸ πάσχα, in Acts 12:4; correctly tr. *the Passover* in the other Eng. VSS. KJV trs. all the other twenty-eight instances of *tò páscha* as *the Passover*). *See* PASSOVER.

The derivation of the name "Easter" is uncertain, but according to Bede (*De Ratione Temporum,* XV) it is derived from *Eastre,* a Teutonic spring goddess, to whom sacrifices were offered in April. The pagan festival prob. gave way to the Christian celebration of Christ's resurrection.

It is held by some that the annual celebration of the Lord's resurrection was observed in apostolic times. They see an intimation of Easter in 1 Corinthians 5:7, 8, which is very doubtful, however. The earliest written evidence for an Easter festival appears in the "paschal controversy" over the correct date for Easter, which began with the correspondence in A.D. 154 between Polycarp, bishop of Smyrna, and Anticetus, bishop of Rome (Euseb. Hist. V. 23-25). By this date, therefore, this festival must have been generally observed throughout the Christian Church.

J. C. CONNELL

EATING AND DRINKING. *See* FOOD.

EBAL or OBAL, Heb. עיבל, variant, עובל, a name of (1) several characters in the OT, descended from Hurrian or Edomite parentage (Gen 36:23); a son of Shobal (1 Chron 1:40); a son of Joktan (Gen 10:28; 1 Chron

1:22). (2) Name of a mountain in Ephraim, "the mount of cursing" (Deut 11:29; et al.). The term is of foreign origin.

EBAL, MOUNT ē' băl (Heb. הר עיבל, known variously as Gr. Γαιβάλ, also as Jebal and Hebal). It is a 3,080 ft. mound of rock with little vegetation N of the valley of Shechem. It is opposite Mt. Gerizim and the two mountains form a steep embankment on the sides of the valley which runs E and W. The Mt. of Ebal was the scene of the reading and reaffirmation of the law before the encampment of Israel by Joshua and the priests and elders (Josh 8:30ff.). This was a renewal of the blessing upon Mt. Gerizim and the cursing upon Mt. Ebal pronounced by Moses prior to the entrance into Canaan by the Israelites (Deut 11:29ff.). This command was reiterated in Deuteronomy 27:4ff. These mountains and the highlands S of Esdraelon were divided between the tribes of Manasseh and Ephraim. Omri, the king of the rebellious ten northern tribes, built his capital at Samaria which was later used as the name for this whole hilly region. During the period of Assyrian conquest all these cities and the areas around Ebal were depopulated and the inhabitants carried off to Mesopotamia. New Sem. peoples were deported to Samaria and the resultant fused culture with vestiges of the Jewish religious practice is called Samaritan.

Numerous small incidents have occurred in this area between the inhabitants and the invaders who periodically passed through these hills. The view from the summit of Mt. Ebal is frequently praised by 19th cent. travelers. Its height of almost 1,500 ft. above the valley proper makes it an excellent observation post; a fact not lost on the innumerable armies who crossed this land. The Muslims hold that the severed head of John the Baptist is buried here, and a small memorial building was erected over the traditional site in the Middle Ages. There are also ruins of early orthodox churches and what may have been monastic settlements which once stood on both Gerizim and Ebal. Recent excavations at the site of ancient Shechem have shown that the area was inhabited from the middle of the 4th millennium B.C., but received its greatest impetus to growth during the era of Israelite kingship at Samaria.

W. WHITE, JR.

EBED ē' bĕd (עבד, LXX Ὠβήθ, *slave, servant*; perhaps a hypocoristicon for the theophoric name, עבדיאל, "servant of God"). 1. Father of Gaal who rebelled against Abimelech (Judg 9:26-35).

2. One of the sons of Adin who accompanied Ezra on his return (Ezra 8:6).

The word is also part of the compound name, Ebed-melech (q.v.), and an element in the expression, עבד יהוה, "Servant of the Lord"

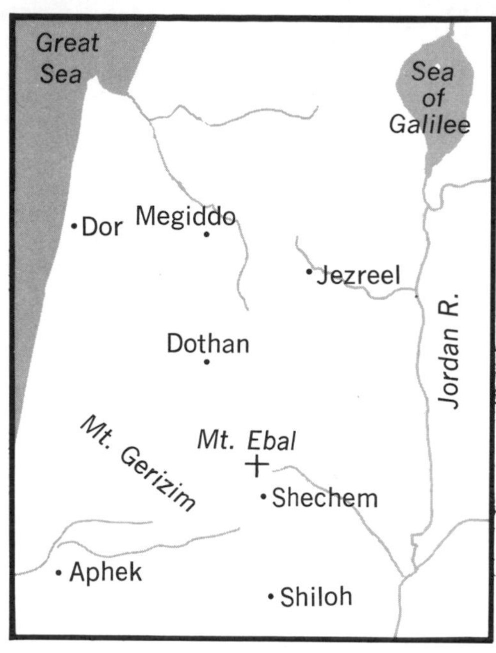

(on the concept, "slave of God" cf. E. Yamauchi, *Bulletin of the Evangelical Theological Society*, IX [1966], 31-49).

K. L. BARKER

EBED-MELECH ē' bĭd mĕl' ĭk (עבד מלך, LXX Ἀβδεμελεχ, *servant of a king, royal servant*). A common name, but in the OT specifically that of the Ethiopian eunuch in the court of Zedekiah who received permission to rescue Jeremiah from a miry dungeon (Jer 38:7-13), and as a reward his life was to be spared when Jerusalem was sacked (39:15-18).

The title of " 'ebed" or "slave" was employed in Akkad. circles to designate a class of court official hired usually for a specific purpose, in contrast to the older patriarchal institution of elders or tribal heads. David apparently initiated the title in Israel, and it occurred also in Ammon and Edom. As a proper noun, "Ebed-melech" is known from Assyrian and Nabatean sources.

R. K. HARRISON

EBEN-BOHAN. *See* BOHAN.

EBEN-EZEL. *See* EZEL.

EBENEZER, EBEN-EZER ĕb' ə nē' zər (אבן העזר; LXX Ἀβενέζερ, *stone of help*). 1. The scene of two defeats of the Israelites by the Philistines. In the first battle, the Israelites lost 4,000 men and in the second, 30,000. In the second battle, the Ark of the Covenant was taken by the Philistines; also Eli's sons, Hophni and Phinehas, were killed (1 Sam 4:1-11). The precise location of Ebenezer is uncertain. It was near Aphek, but this site has not been identified with certainty either. Some scholars believe the site of Ebenezer may be Majdel Yaba, NE of Jaffa.

2. Ebenezer also was the name given by Samuel to the stone set up by him between Mizpah and Jeshanah to commemorate an Israelite victory over the Philistines (1 Sam 7:12).

A. C. SCHULTZ

EBER **ē′ bər** (עבר, *one who crosses over*). Name of an ancestor of Abraham and of four minor individuals in the OT.

Eber is the fourth in the genealogy from Noah to Abraham (Gen 10:21-25; 11:14-17; 1 Chron 1:18-25). Practically nothing is known of him. Interest attaches to the name which has the same root as the name *'ibrî*. This latter word may be the same as a cuneiform word Ḫabiru which refers to many people of various areas and situations. It may actually not be related to *'eber*.

The meaning of the word *'ēber* is uncertain. The root means "to cross over." The form may well be intransitive and refer more to a "nomad," a "traveler." This meaning would fit the name "Hebrew," but as mentioned above, may be only coincidental.

The name *'ēber* also is applied to a Gadite (1 Chron 5:13), two Benjaminites (1 Chron 8:12, 22), and a priest (Neh 12:20). The reference in Numbers 24:24 is taken by Albright to be from the verb *'ābar* "cross over" ("The Oracles of Balaam," JBL, LXIII [1944], 226). Smick suggests "quarter," from the meaning "region beyond" or "side" (WBC in loc.).

BIBLIOGRAPHY. M. Greenberg, *The Hab/piru* (American Oriental Series, vol. 39 [1955], 90-93).

R. L. HARRIS

EBEZ **ē′ bĕz** (אביץ, LXX 'Ρεβες, which may imply an original Heb. רבץ). KJV ABEZ. A town (Josh 19:20) located in the territory of Issachar, which occupied the greater part of the fertile plain of Esdraelon. However, the actual location of Ebez is unknown.

R. K. HARRISON

EBIASAPH. Alternate form of ABIASAPH.

EBIONISM, EBIONITES (GOSPEL OF THE) **ē′ bĭ ə nĭsm, ē′ bĭ ə nīts** (אבינים, 'Εβιωναῖοι or 'Εβιωναῖται, from the term אביון, meaning *poor*, i.e., *poor men*). A term and an apocryphal gospel used to describe certain Judaeo-Christian groups in the early centuries of Christianity. Although some early sources (i.e. Tertullian) suggested that these sects took their name from an individual with the supposed name of Ebion, it is more likely that the term and title was at first one of reproach indicating their stress upon poverty and asceticism partially as a literal interpretation of Matthew 5:3.

1. Ebionite sects. The origin of these sects is shrouded in mystery; however, from the lit. of the Early Church and esp. Acts, it is clearly observable that certain Judaizing tendencies manifested themselves from the very first in the Jerusalem church. (Cf. Acts 6:1-6; 15:1f.; Gal.) After the fall of Jerusalem in A.D. 70 and again during the Bar Cochba rebellion when Hadrian destroyed Jerusalem, A.D. 132, Jewish Christianity lost its standing in Jerusalem and the church there was controlled by a Gentile bishop. It is known from the writings of Justin, Irenaeus, Tertullian, Hippolytus, Origen, Eusebius and esp. Epiphanius and Jerome that at least two Jewish Christian groups were known: one heretical in its Christology and resentful of Gentile Christianity, and the other friendly, though distinct from Gentile Christianity but orthodox in its view of Christ. Recent scholarship has distinguished three Judaeo-Christian groups sometimes loosely referred to as "Ebionites": (a) Nazarenes who accepted the supernatural birth of Jesus without developing a Chalcedonian Christology; (b) Pharisaic Ebionites who recognized Jesus as Messiah but denied His Virgin Birth and hated Paul; (c) Gnostic or Essene Ebionites who tended to gnosticize their Christology. (Cf. HERE, V, 140, 141.) As the early Christian sources indicate, generally the Ebionites were known for two doctrines: (a) adherance to the Jewish law for Jews at least if not for Gentiles and (b) a tendency to interpret the Person of Christ as merely a man on whom the Holy Spirit descended at His baptism.

The exact relationship of the Ebionites to the Dead Sea Community and/or the Essenes as well as the older sect known as the Rechabites is still a matter of conjecture, although more recent scholarship has tended to see basic similarities if not some type of direct relationship.

2. Ebionite Gospel. Only Epiphanius (d. A.D. 403) refers to a Gospel of the Ebionites. Sometimes this gospel is identified with or confused with either the Gospel to the Hebrews or the Gospel of the Nazarenes. The meager traces of this gospel in the extant quotations of Epiphanius are peculiar in their stress upon vegetarianism in the NT accounts of John the Baptist and Jesus.

BIBLIOGRAPHY. W. Beveridge, "Ebionism," HERE, V (1928), 139-145; old but still very useful; L. Wallach, "The Textual History of an Aramaic Proverb," JBL, LX (1941), 403-415; H. Hirschberg, "Simon Bariona and the Ebionites," JBL, LXI (1942), 171-191; H. J. Schoeps, *Jewish Christianity* (1969). Original sources: Justin, *Dial. c. Tryph.*, 47; Irenaeus, *Against Heresies,* I. xxvi, 2; III. xxi, 1; V. i, 3; Tertullian, *De Praescr.*, 33; Hippolytus, *Haer.*, vii. 34; ix. 13-17; Epiphanius, *Haer.*, xxx. For a good tr. of Epiphanius' quotations see M. R. James, *The Apocryphal New Testament* (1924), 8-10.

D. LAKE

EBONY (הבנים). Only mentioned once (Ezek 27:15)—"in payment ivory tusks and ebony." This could be the product of various trees, but surely it is that of the *Diospyros ebenaster* (or *ebenus*) of the family Ebenaceae—a hard and durable timber. The outside is soft and white, and the central part or heart of the trunk is hard and black. This central portion is often only two ft. in diameter.

The twenty-seventh chapter of Ezekiel mentions the luxury importations from Ceylon and India to Pal., for it is undoubtedly from these countries that the ebony came. Ebony polishes well and even today is used for carvings of elephants and the like.

The Diospyros can be date tree or date plum called D. lotus in W Asia (not the date palm).

All trs. agree on the use of the word "ebony" for *hobnim* in this single text. The LXX omits the word completely, however. It is obvious that ivory and ebony were used together by the ancient Israelites just as they are today in the E. The pure white ivory goes well as a contrast to the jet-black, polished ebony.

W. E. SHEWELL-COOPER

EBRON (עֶבְרוֹן), KJV Hebron. A town located in the territory allotted to Asher (Josh 19:28) consisting of the NW corner of Pal. bordering the Mediterranean. "Ebron" is quite possibly a misspelling of the MT for ABDON (עַבְדּוֹן) due to a scribal confusion of ד and ר. *See* ABDON.

R. K. HARRISON

EBRONAH. KJV form of ABRONAH.

ECANUS. KJV Apoc. form of ETHANUS.

ECBATANA (ACHMETHA) ěk băt′ ə nə (Aram. אַחְמְתָא, LXX Ἀμαθα, Xenophon, al. Ἐκβάτανα, meaning uncertain; *citadel, fortress, place of gathering* have been suggested). KJV ACHMETHA.

Ecbatana was the Gr. name of the capital of the empire of the Medes, and later one of the capitals of the Persian and Parthian empires,

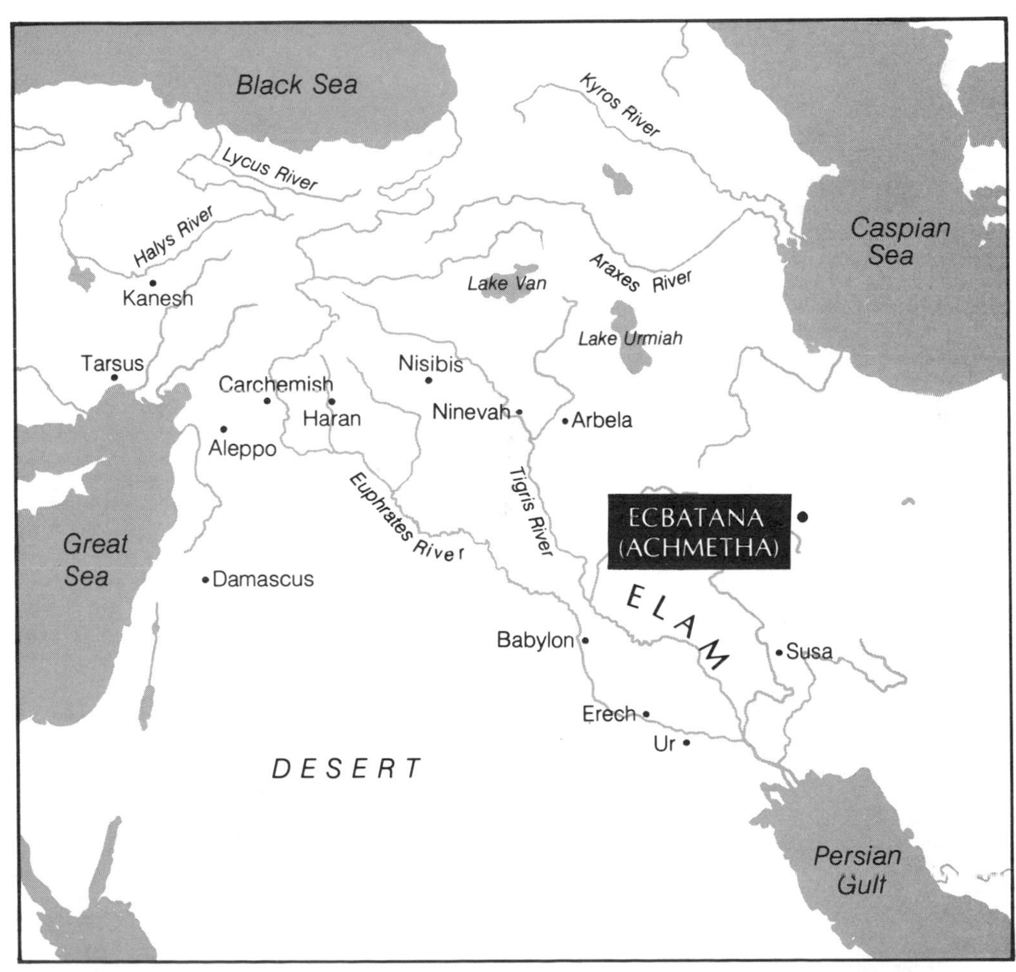

the Old Persian name of which was Hangmátana, "the place of assembly." The city is mentioned several times in the apocryphal books. In Tobit it was the home of Reguel and Sara his daughter (Tobit 3:7; 7:1; 14:13). It was fortified by the Median king Arphaxad in his war against "King Nebuchadnezzar of Assyria" (Jud 1:1, 2, 14), and to it Antiochus Epiphanes IV fled shortly before his death (2 Macc 9:1-3). The site is occupied today by Hamadan, Iran, on the plain near the northeastern foot of Mt. Alvand, c. 175 m. SW of Teheran. The city owed its importance to its strategic location on the caravan route from Mesopotamia to the Pers. plateau. The pleasant summer climate accounts for its popularity as a resort city.

According to the Greeks (Herodotus i. 96; c. 450 B.C.), Ecbatana was founded by the half-legendary Deioces the Mede c. 678 B.C., who also established the Median dynasty, but scholars question the accuracy of this tradition. The Median empire may have been established by Phraortes, the son of Deioces, who built Ecbatana to check the advance of the Assyrians. A description of the city is given by Herodotus and Polybius (x. 27). It was surrounded by seven concentric walls, the inner walls rising above the outer, since the city was on a hill. Each wall was of a different color. The citadel was also a treasure house, the city famous for its luxury and splendor. Ecbatana was captured by Cyrus the Great of Persia from Astyages in 550 B.C., and he made it his summer residence. According to Ezra 6:2, the imperial records of the time of Cyrus were kept here, and here Darius found the decree of Cyrus authorizing the rebuilding of Jerusalem. It was taken from the last Achaemenid by Alexander the Great in 330 B.C. He destroyed the walls and looted the palaces.

Ecbatana became the summer capital of the Parthian kings, maintaining its traditional reputation, but under the Sassanids it declined. After the Islamic conquest, the modern city of Hamadan took its place. The ruins of the ancient citadel of Ecbatana lie outside of the present city, and on the slope of Mt. Alvand are Achaemenid inscrs. Modern Hamadan stands on most of the ancient city which prevents extensive archeological excavations of the site. In 1923, two foundation plaques of silver and gold were found, inscribed with the name of Darius I, and also column bases of Artaxerxes II. These indicate that Darius I and Artaxerxes II built palaces in Ecbatana. The so-called tomb of Esther and Mordecai shown today in Hamadan is prob. the tomb of the wife of the Sassanid king, Yazdegird (A.D. 399-420).

BIBLIOGRAPHY. A. T. Olmstead, *History of the Persian Empire* (1948), 29, 30, 37, 38, 162; A. L. Oppenheim, *Ancient Mesopotamia* (1964), 134, 394; C. H. Gordon, *The Ancient Near East* (1965), 255, 281, 282.

A. C. SCHULTZ

ECCLESIASTES (ĭ klē' zĭ ăs'tēz) Gr. *Ekklēsiastēs*, Heb. *Qōheleth*, prob. meaning *The Assembly-speaker*, i.e. *The Preacher*.)

- I. Etymology and genre
- II. Authorship and time of composition
  - A. Linguistic affinities with Phoenician
    1. Orthography
    2. Inflections and particles
    3. Syntax
    4. Lexical affinities
- III. Other internal evidences as to authorship
- IV. Doctrinal message of Ecclesiastes
- V. Outline of the contents of the book
- VI. Final summation

I. Etymology and genre

The term *Qoheleth* is derived from the root *qāhāl*, "assembly, congregation"; hence the fem. abstract noun may have meant "the office or function of speaker in the assembly." This book belongs to the general class of Wisdom Literature, or *Ḥokhmah*, but to the special genre of the philsophical discourse—of which there are no other extant examples in ancient near Eastern lit. It purports to have been composed by "the son of David, king in Jerusalem" (Eccl 1:1), i.e. by Solomon. Since it consists of a review of his lifelong search for truly valid goals in human existence, it was doubtless a product of his old age, c. 940 B.C.

II. Authorship and time of composition

The Solomonic authorship of this book is regarded by most modern authorities as purely fictional, composed by some unknown later author upon the basis of the experiences and insights of the historic Solomon. On the basis of supposed allusions to the misfortunes of the Israelite nation down through the Babylonian Exile, as well as on allegedly late characteristics of language, *Qoheleth* has been assigned a 5th cent. date by such conservative authors as Hengstenberg, Delitzsch, Leupold and E. J. Young, and 3rd cent. or later by liberal scholars. These allegations of spuriousness (or fictional character) are not justified by the objective evidence. More recent discussions of the language of Ecclesiastes (like that of J. Muilenberg in BASOR 135, p. 135) admits that "Linguistically the book is unique. There is no question that its language has many striking peculiarities." In other words, it differs from all other books of the OT of whatever age; it equally differs from all known intertestamental Heb. works, such as Ecclesiasticus (which, however, has been greatly influenced by it) and the Qumran sectarian lit. No significant resemblances can be made out with the extant pre-Christian Heb. lit. of any period, either in respect to vocabulary, grammar or style. It is quite as dissimilar to 5th-cent. productions, such as, Zechariah, Ezra, Nehemiah, Esther and Malachi as to any of the pre-exilic period. This poses an insuperable difficulty to those who, like Delitzsch and Young, date *Qoheleth* (Qoh.) around 430, or to Beecher (in ISBE) who puts it at 400 B.C. The earliest MS fragments come from Qumran Cave 4 and date from the 2nd cent. B.C., and so there is no possibility of dating it after the sectarian period (to whose writings it is altogether dissimilar).

A. Linguistic affinities with Phoenician. The true explanation for the peculiar language and style of Ecclesiastes is to be found in its genre. As in ancient Gr. lit. the dialect or style in which each genre (such as the epic, the elegiac, the love poem, etc.) was first brought to classic perfection became a binding convention upon all who would in later ages compose in that genre, so also in ancient Sem. and Egyp. circles a peculiar style became conventional for each genre. It so happens that there are no other surviving examples of the genre to which *Qoheleth* belongs (the philosophical disquisition), and there is no literary parallel with which to compare it. There is, however, a noteworthy affinity for early Canaanite and Phoenician characteristics which makes it likely that Solomon, if he was the true author, wrote in a genre which had been cultivated in Phoenicia or in Canaanite areas of Pal. itself.

The evidence for this has been gathered in a very able article by M. J. Dahood, "Canaanite-Phoenician Influence in Qoheleth" (*Biblica* 33, 1952), in which he draws upon the linguistic data of the 14th cent. Ugaritic tablets, the *Corpus Inscriptionum Semiticarum*, and Lidzbarski's Phoenician and Punic inscrs. in *Ephemeris*. He comes to the conclusion (op. cit. p. 32) that "The Book of Ecclesiastes was originally composed by an author who wrote in Hebrew but who employed Phoenician orthography, and whose composition shows heavy Canaanite-Phoenician influence." He marshals his proofs under the following categories: (1) Phoen. orthography, (2) Phoen. inflections, pronouns and particles, (3) Phoen. syntax, and (4) Phoen. lexical borrowings or analogies.

1. Orthography. Under Phoen. spelling he lists many instances of variants as between the MT of the OT and the ancient VSS in Gr., Aram., Syr. and Lat.—variants which are most easily accounted for by an original text in which no vowel letters were written (final vowel letters were introduced into Heb. spelling at least by late 8th cent., judging by the Siloam Inscr.). Thus it was possible to supply differing final vowels affecting the number and gender of verbs (such as *na'^a^seh* "was made," in the MT of Ecclesiastes 1:13, but *na'^a^sū* "were made" in some of the VSS; or again, *hāyâ* is the MT reading in 1:16—"it came into being"—but *hāyû,* "they came into being" according to the VSS. These variants indicate that the original author spelled the first word n-'s, and the second word h-y—which remained the normal Phoen. spelling until 3rd cent. B.C. or later. Or again, 3:16 reads *haṣṣedeq* "the righteousness" in MT, but *haṣṣaddīq* "the righteous man" in the VSS.

2. Inflections and particles. As for inflections, Phoen. uses the -t ending even for fem. nouns in the absolute state; so there are nouns like *mattat* in 3:13 and 5:18 meaning "gift"—as in a 7th cent. Phoen. inscr. from Ur (op. cit. p. 46). Even more distinctive are prepositions ending in "t," like *'al dibrat* ("on account of") in 3:18 and *'ummat* ("corresponding to") in 5:14. So Phoen. uses '-l-t as well as '-l for "upon," and p-n-t as well as l-p-n for "in front of." As for the relative pronoun *shĕ*, which occurs sixty-seven times in Ecclesiastes alongside *'usher* (which is used eighty-nine times), it is very close to the Phoen. '-š ("who, what"). It occurs elsewhere in the OT largely in writings containing N Israelite elements. Closely related

Fragment of Ecclesiastes Scroll from Qumran. ©*P.B.I.*

is *mah-še* "whatever" in 1:9; 3:15, etc.—which appears as m-'-š in the 9th cent. Phoen. Kilamuwa Inscription. The same inscr. also uses the interrogative "who?" (m or m-y) five times in the sense of "whoever"; compare this with the four occurrences in Ecclesiastes (1:9; 3:15; 5:9; 9:4) where the same indefinite interrogative appears—a far higher ratio than in any other OT book. As for the definite article *ha,* "the," its sporadic and irregular use conforms perfectly with Phoen. usage, where '-y-t the sign of the accusative, often precedes a noun lacking *ha-* (contrary to the rule in Heb. grammar), just as *Qoheleth* often uses *'ēt* before an anarthrous noun. Or, he leaves out the article before an adjective modifying a definite noun—which is also good Phoen. usage. (This cannot be explained as a tr. from a late Aram. original which no longer used the emphatic state [-ā] for definite nouns only; it is now known from the 1st cent. *Genesis Apocryphon* that even by that period the emphatic was still restricted to definite nouns.) As for particles, the conditional *'illū* ("if"), used in Ecclesiastes 6:6, is found in the 11th cent. Ahiram Inscription spelled as '-l; hence it is not to be regarded as derived from Aram. *'illā'*, as some have argued. One other particle is vowel-pointed as *lāmmâ* "why?" in the MT (5:5 and 7:7); but in view of the Phoen. l-m meaning "lest," it should prob. be so construed in those two passages, where "lest" makes far better sense.

3. Syntax. As for syntax, the peculiar combination of infinitive absolute plus the independent pronoun (e.g. 4:2 reads *w^{e}šabbē^{a}, '^{a}nī* for "And I praised") occurs four or five times in Qoh., and only once elsewhere in the OT. Cf. the combination q-t-l '-n-k in the Karatepe Phoen. inscrs., and EA 113:40-42 in the Tell-Amarna correspondence, back in the 14th cent. Even the use of the independent personal pronoun as a copular verb, which occurs quite often in Ecclesiastes (e.g. 3:13 *mattat '^{e}lōhīm hî',* "it is a gift of God") is shown to be a Phoen. usage, as well as Aram. and Mishnaic Heb. For example, the 5th cent. Yehawmilk Inscription states that "He was a righteous king" (k-m-l-k ṣ-d-q h-'). (Cf. also CIS 93:1-2; Lidzbarski 36:4; and Nora Inscr. 2f.)

4. Lexical affinities. As for lexical affinities, note that Ecclesiastes uses *'ādām* for "man" in the non-generic sense (contrary to normal Heb. practice); cf. the Azitawadd 9th cent. inscr., which uses '-d-m five times and '-š (Heb. 'îš) only once. The characteristic phrase "under the sun" (*taḥat haššemeš*) occurs in no other ancient NW Sem. language except Phoen. (cf. the inscrs. of Tabnit and Eshmunazar at Sidon). Even the term *re'ût* ("a striving, a desire"), which occurs seven times in Qoh. and is usually explained as a borrowing from Aram., occurs in Punic inscrs.: once meaning "decree, decision," once meaning "pleasure, good will." An unusual pair of verbs occurs in 10:18: "By slothfulness the roof *sinks in (yimmak),* and through idleness of hands the house *leaks (yiḏlōp).*" It is most significant that these two verbs, *mākak* and *dālap,* occur nowhere else in combination except Ugaritic Text 68:17. The distinctive climax series "seven . . . eight" occurring in 11:2 (nowhere else in OT except Mic 5:5) appears at least six times in Ugaritic lit. (BASOR 76 [1939], 5-11). The distinctive phrase *šemen rōqē^{a}ḥ* occurs nowhere else besides Ecclesiastes 10:1 ("perfumer's oil") and in Ugaritic Text 120:5. But the noun r-q-ḥ "perfumer" occurs at least five times in Phoenician and Punic inscrs. It is unknown in Aram., although *ruqqû* appears in Akkad. as "compound ointment."

Dahood's article closes with an impressive assortment of mercantile terms most appropriate to a commercial culture such as characterized the Phoen. people. Thus: (a) *'āmāl* "gain, earning" (twelve times); (b) *yitrôn* "gain, advantage" (eighteen times); (c) *'inyān* "occupation, business" (six times); (d) *ḥesrôn* "lack, deficit" (six times); (e) *ḥēleq* "share, portion" (seven times); (f) *kišrôn* "success, advantage" (five times); (g) *'ōšer* "riches" (twelve times); (h) *hešbôn* "computation, reckoning" (five times); and (i) *ṣākār* "wages" (two times). These and many other terms which he lists confirm still further the theory that the genre to which Qoh. belongs was borrowed from a Phoen. prototype. Nor should it be forgotten (although Dahood does not discuss this) that Israel in the age of Solomon was more deeply involved in international trade than at any other time in its history, before or since (1 Kings 9:26-28; 10:28, 29). (Dahood attempts to retain an early postexilic date on the basis of a theory that a substantial colony of Jews took refuge in Phoenicia after the fall of Jerusalem in 587 B.C., and that the unknown author composed Ecclesiastes there; but there is not a shred of historical evidence for any such colony, and it seems unlikely that a Phoenician subject to Nebuchadnezzar's authority—apart from a revolt by Tyre resulting in the complete destruction of its mainland city—would have dared to harbor refugees from the wrath of the Chaldeans subsequent to the assassination of Gedaliah. All the refugees of whom there is any recorded knowledge fled southward to Egypt.)

In view of the prominence of the Red Sea port of Elath during Solomon's reign, there is every reason to believe that he had extensive contacts with India from whence he might have borrowed such terms as *pardēs* "park" (Sanskrit: *paridhis*) and *pitgām* "official decision" (Sanskrit: *pratigāma*), rather than from Pers. (a language rather closely related to the Sanskrit classical language of India). As for allegedly postexilic terms like *šhālaṭ* ("have dominion, authority"), the Hyksos invaders of Egypt called their ruler by the title *Salitis* back in the 18th cent. B.C., long before the time of Moses. It is beyond question that *Salitis* is derived from the root *šālaṭ*. As for *zᵉmān* "appointed time," while it is true that it appears outside of Ecclesiastes in the Heb. Scriptures, only in Esther and Nehemiah, it is also true that it was used in Akkad. as *simānu* "fixed date," and also in Arab. as *zamanun*, and in Ethiopic as *zaman*. It was a Pan-Semitic word, therefore, and no evidence for a post-Solomonic date, esp. since "a proper time," "fixed time," is elsewhere in Ecclesiastes always expressed by the classical Heb. *'ēt* (cf. 3:1-8).

III. Other internal evidences as to authorship

Apart from linguistic factors there are other internal evidences used by opponents of Solomonic authorship to indicate a later date of composition. Thus there are said to be such obvious anachronisms as to alert any Heb. reader to the fictional character of this work. The Preacher declared that he had attained more wisdom than "all they that have been before me in Jerusalem" (1:16). Since the only Heb. king before Solomon in Jerusalem was his father David, the "all that were before me" must point to a long succession of Jewish kings before Ecclesiastes was actually written. But this argument overlooks the fact that the author is not referring to kings who preceded him in Jerusalem, but rather to "wise men" or sages who were practitioners of the various genres of *ḥokhmah* lit. (cf. 1 Kings 4:31, which states that Solomon excelled even Heman, Chalcol and Darda, who were doubtless outstanding scholars who flourished in pre-Israelite Jerusalem, a city of notable influence and prestige from the days of Melchi-zedek and Adoni-zedek centuries before). A second anachronism is alleged in 1:12: "I . . . was (*hāyîtî*) king . . . in Jerusalem," which is thought to imply that Solomon was no longer king (and therefore dead) at the time this book was written. It should be pointed out, however, that *hāyîtî* can also mean, "I became king over Israel"—a perfectly natural explanation for an elderly king to give when recollecting the commencement of his reign.

Solomonic authorship is supposedly excluded by the non-royal viewpoint of the author. Instead of speaking of himself as the ruler of the land he occasionally expressed sentiments implying disapproval of, or even hostility toward, the king. See, for example, 10:17: "Happy are you, O land, when your king is the son of free men, and your princes feast at the proper time, for strength, and not for drunkenness." Or again, "Do not curse the king, not even in your bedchamber" (10:20), or 4:13: "Better is a poor and wise youth than an old and foolish king, who will no longer take advice."

In dealing with passages such as these, however, it should be understood that the author is writing as a philosopher, not as the head of a government, or even as a propagandist in his own behalf. As a keen observer of world history, both past and current, it would be inconceivable that he was unaware of the existence of gluttonous, intemperate, stubborn or misguided kings in other countries, or of the unhappy consequences to their subjects under such a rule. Just as at a later age the Rom. emperor Marcus Aurelius composed his *Meditations* not as a piece of government propaganda but (esp. after the introductory Book I) as a Stoic philosopher, so also Solomon as a scholar of wide renown, wrote this remarkable treatise on the true values of life in order to persuade men to settle for nothing less than obedience to the revealed will of God. In order to illustrate his various points, he drew upon familiar experiences and vicissitudes common to the Near E in recent and contemporary history: the downfall of the rich and proud, the sudden elevation of the ignoble and lowly to positions of prominence and honor. It is quite pointless and futile to attempt to discover in these illustrations covert allusions to the national downfall of Judah in 587, the miseries of the Babylonian exile, or the penury that prevailed in the days of Ezra and Malachi. The author is dealing with the misfortunes and hardships that befall mankind generally as individuals rather than as nations. Sentiments such as, "Better than both is he who has not yet been, and has not seen the evil deeds that are done under the sun" (4:3) point to the injustice and calamity which all too often infects society and assaults its hapless victims at all periods in human history. Even though prosperity and peace prevailed during most of Solomon's reign, his recollection of the harrowing experiences of his father during Absalom's revolt, and his knowledge of the tides of invasion and bloodshed that had always characterized the history of the Near E, all served to give him a realistic understanding of the afflictions of mankind. Indeed it was these afflictions which posed the anguished questions of meaning and value without which the adventure of life made little sense. One concludes, then, that there is nothing in the sentiments expressed or the attitudes assumed in the text of Ecclesiastes to preclude Solomonic authorship. The so-called allusions to exilic and postexilic conditions are incapable of demonstration, nor are they at all inappropriate to a 10th cent. setting. Neither in this area nor in the linguistic phenomena of the book can a convincing case be made out for non-Solomonic authorship.

IV. The doctrinal message of Ecclesiastes

The basic theme of *Qoheleth* is the ultimate futility of a life based upon earthly ambitions and desires. Any world view which does not rise above the horizon of man himself is doomed to meaninglessness and frustration. To view personal happiness or enjoyment as life's greatest good is sheer folly in view of the transcendent value of God Himself as over against His created universe. Happiness can never be achieved by pursuing after it, since such a pursuit involves the absurdity of self-deification. ". . . also, the hearts of men are full of evil, and madness is in their hearts while they live, and after that they go to the dead" (9:3). The final judgment upon all self-seeking, autonomous human effort and pursuit after meaning and permanent achievement is: "Vanity of vanities" (i.e. complete futility), "This also is vanity." Transient mortals must realize that they are mere creatures, and that they derive importance only from their relationship to the almighty Creator. "I know that whatever God does endures for ever; nothing can be added to it, nor anything taken away from it" (3:14). In other words Ecclesiastcs is really intended to be a tract for the conversion of the self-sufficient intellectual; it compels him to discard his comfortable, self-flattering illusions and face honestly the instability of all those materialistic props on which he attempts to base his security. At the end of the road for the "hard-headed" materialist lies death and physical dissolution. Only as one finds a new meaning for life in surrendering to the sovereignty of God and faithful obedience to His will in moral conduct can one find a valid principle and goal for responsible human living. There may be many aspects of God's will that man does not yet understand, nevertheless he must submit to it with unrebellious trust, and gratefully receive and enjoy the mercies of food and clothing and material comforts as He may apportion them to us. ". . . also he has put eternity ('ôlām) into man's mind, yet so that he cannot find out what God has done from the beginning to the end. I know that there is nothing better for them than to be happy and enjoy themselves as long as they live; also that it is God's gift to man that every one should eat and drink and take pleasure in all his toil" (3:11-13). It is from this perspective that the so-called "Epicurean" passages (like 2:24) are to be understood; they do not exalt mere hedonism to the status of absolute value (as some interpreters have imagined), but rather they exhort men to a wholehearted appreciation and enjoyment of God's material bounties, even while they recognize them as possessing only temporal and conditional value.

As for the alleged pessimism of *Qoheleth's* teaching, with its recurrent reminder of the inevitability and universality of death, these elements too must be interpreted in the light of the over-all purpose of the book, as defined above, and also in the light of the immediate context. Thus in the case of 4:2, "And I thought the dead who are already dead more fortunate than the living who are still alive," this is no rejection of the worthwhileness of life as such. The preceding v. makes it clear that if a person's life is to consist of nothing but oppression, calamity and sorrow, then it would have been better never to have been born at all. Or again, in 6:8 the query: "For what advantage has the wise man over the fool? And what does the poor man have who knows how to conduct himself before the living?" is to be put in focus with the main thrust of the book: apart from God and His holy will, the life of no man (whether educated or uneducated, rich or poor) has any ultimate meaning, but ends in futility. If a man's relationship to the Lord is what it should be, then it will be well with him. "Though a sinner does evil a hundred times and prolongs his life, yet I know that it will be well with those who fear God" (8:12).

It should be added that the Preacher lays great stress upon the importance of this life as the only arena of opportunity and accomplishment for man before he steps off the stage into the eternity of the life beyond. From this standpoint it is true that "he who is joined with all the living has hope; for a living dog is better than a dead lion" (9:4). Also the following v. is no affirmation of soul-sleep ("the dead know not anything") but rather a warning that the dead have no longer any expectation of a personal future with opportunities of choice for or against God, or between good and evil, such as they had prior to the grave. Nor do they have any knowledge of what goes on "under the sun," i.e. upon earth, while they wait in Sheol for the day of judgment. (In Solomon's time, of course, it was premature to reveal anything clear about the glories of heaven, since access to these glories for believers was largely delayed until the triumph of Christ's resurrection.) All of these considerations then, are intended to point men away from the specious and pretended values of this life (personal enjoyment, happiness, success, or materialistic achievements) to the one true and abiding value, fellowship with God and living in obedience to His will. Plainly this is the conclusion to which the author wishes to drive his readers, for he ends with: "The conclusion, when all has been heard is: Fear God, and keep his commandments; for this is the whole duty of man" (12:13).

It is only by dint of deleting from the received text of Ecclesiastes the vv. which speak of obedience to God and trust in Him that rationalist critics are able to construe the book as a pessimistic manifesto of skepticism which somehow found its way into the OT canon despite its heresy. No plausible motivation can be made out for the reworking of an originally Bible-rejecting book in order to make it acceptable to the believing community through the insertion of occasional pious-sounding verses. Such a theory is totally without objective foundation, and a mere product of the inventive imagination of modern higher criticism.

V. Outline of the Contents of the Book

The book is composed of four main discourses and a conclusion.

First discourse (1:1-2:26): The vanity of human wisdom
- A. Basic thesis: mere human effort and achievement are futile (1:1-3)
- B. Thesis demonstrated (1:4-2:26)
  1. Futility of the cycle of human life and history (1:4-11)
  2. Ultimate uselessness of human wisdom and philosophy (1:12-18)
  3. Enjoyments of pleasure and wealth are empty (2:1-11)
  4. Even the wise must eventually die (2:12-17)
  5. Heritage of diligent industry left to undeserving heirs (2:18-23)
  6. Duty of contentment with God's gracious providences (2:24-26)

Second discourse (3:1-5:20): Appreciate the divine laws governing life
- A. The attitude compelled by realities of life and death (3:1-22)
  1. A proper time appointed for each activity and experience (1-9)
  2. God is the only guarantor of abiding values (10-15)
  3. Punishment and death appointed for all the unrighteous (16-18)
  4. Death is, however, universal for man and beast (19, 20)
  5. Unsure of the life beyond, make the best of this present life (21, 22)
- B. The disappointments of earthly life (4:1-16)
  1. Cruelty and misery may afflict this life (1-3)
  2. Disadvantages even to success, and penalties for laziness and greed (4-8)
  3. Life's trials faced better by partners than by loners (9-12)
  4. Even success in politics is unstable (13-16)
- C. Futility of the self-seeking life (5:1-20)
  1. Folly of false sacrifices, vain words, broken promises (1-7)
  2. Sure retribution for oppressors; disappointment for the greedy (8-17)
  3. Contentment comes from thankful enjoyment of God's gifts (18-20)

Third discourse: No satisfaction in earthly goods or treasures (6:1-8:17)
- A. The inadequacy of worldly attainments (6:1-12)
  1. No lasting satisfaction in wealth or large family (1-6)
  2. No real satisfaction for either the worldly wise or the foolish (7-9)
  3. No real point to life apart from God (10-12)
- B. Prudent counsels for a sin-corrupted world (7:1-29)
  1. True values emerge in the face of sorrow and death (1-4)
  2. Pitfalls of cheap gaiety, dishonest gain, short temper (5-9)
  3. Wisdom is better than wealth in coping with problems (10-12)
  4. Both good fortune and ill come from God (13, 14)
  5. Self-righteousness and immorality both lead to disaster (15-18)
  6. Great advantages to wisdom, but sin is universal (19, 20)
  7. Be unconcerned at base malice toward yourself (21, 22)
  8. Man by mere wisdom cannot attain spiritual truth (23-25)
  9. Worst of all evils is an evil woman (26)
  10. But all men have fallen from original goodness (27-29)
- C. Coming to terms with an imperfect world (8:1-17)
  1. Wise to respect governmental authority (1-5)
  2. God's law operates despite sorrows and death (6-9)
  3. The esteemed, unpunished wrongdoer will finally meet God's judgment (10-13)
  4. Life's injustices may encourage shallow hedonism (14, 15)
  5. But God's ways are inscrutable to man (16, 17)

Fourth discourse: God will deal with injustices in this world (9:1-12:8)
- A. Death is inevitable for all (9:1-18)
  1. Death inevitable for both evil and good; moral insanity of man (1-3)
  2. At death all moral choice and knowledge of this life terminate (4-6)
  3. The godly must use opportunities of this life to the full (7-10)
  4. Success is uncertain, life-span unpredictable even for the worthy (11, 12)
  5. Yet wisdom, though unappreciated, succeeds better than force (13-18)
- B. The uncertainties of life and the baneful effects of folly (10:1-20)
  1. Even a little folly ruinous; be prudent before princes (1-4)
  2. Reversals of fortune and sad retribution for sin (5-11)
  3. Empty talk and misdirected effort mark a fool (12-15)
  4. Moral responsibility vital for nations and men (16-19)
  5. Contempt for authority brings sure retribution (20)
- C. The best way to invest a life (11:1-12:8)
  1. Kindness returns with blessing to the benefactor (11:1, 2)
  2. To alter or fathom God's laws of nature is beyond human wisdom (3-5)
  3. Wisest course is cheerful diligence and industry (6-8)
  4. There is ultimate retribution for youth spent in seeking pleasure (9, 10)
  5. Start living for God early before the infirmities of old age (12:1-8)

Conclusion: Life's meaning in the light of eternity (12:9-14)

A. Qoheleth's purpose to teach the meaning and duties of life (9, 10)
B. These admonitions more valuable than all literature of this world (11, 12)
C. God's will comes first, for His judgment is final (13, 14)

VI. Final summation

Ecclesiastes presents itself as the matured and chastened wisdom of a king who has learned from experience the futility of living for any other purpose than the glory of God. He has come to realize what a poor bargain it is for a man to gain the whole world but to lose his own soul. He had been personally favored with unlimited wealth and power to test all that the world had to offer. He enjoyed the finest of education and an unrivaled reputation for wisdom (1:16). His riches were immeasurable (2:8); he was surrounded with hosts of servants (2:7); his opportunities for carnal pleasure knew no restriction (2:3); he could afford the most extensive building projects and look with pride on their accomplishment (2:4-6). Yet in the end these false avenues to life's highest good led only to a vanished satisfaction and a sense of personal emptiness: all was "vanity," futile meaninglessness. In the end this son of David was driven back to the lessons and insights of his early upbringing, and he had to recognize that only in God can a man find real significance and lasting satisfaction. It was therefore this legacy that Solomon wished to leave behind him for his willful, headstrong people, and also for all men of subsequent generations who earnestly search for life's highest good. Paradoxically, it is not found in this life at all, but rather in God and the supernal realm of His perfect will.

BIBLIOGRAPHY. The genuineness of Ecclesiastes as a work of Solomon is defended by W. T. Bullock in *The Speaker's Commentary,* and by Dr. Charles Wordsworth (Archdeacon of Westminster), London (1868). So also the article by Gietmann in the *Catholic Encyclopedia,* V, 244-248. Taylor Lewis, the tr. of Zoeckler's *Commentary on Ecclesiastes* in the Lange series, included his personal defense of Solomonic authorship and added comments of refutation in the commentary itself.

The following works, listed according to the order of their publication, hold to a postexilic date for Ecclesiastes:

O. Zoeckler, *Commentary on Ecclesiastes* in the Lange series, repr. (n.d.); A. L. Williams, *Ecclesiastes* (1922); Fr. Delitzsch, *Commentary on Ecclesiastes,* repr. (1950); H. L. Ginsberg, *Studies in Koheleth* (1950); R. Gordis, *Koheleth: the Man and His World* (1955); H. L. Ginsberg, "The Structure and Contents of the Book of Koheleth" (in Supplement to *Vetus Testamentum,* III [1955]), 138-149; O. S. Rankin and G. G. Atkins, "Ecclesiastes" in *Interpreter's Bible,* V. (1956); E. W. Hengstenberg, *Ecclesiastes,* repr. (1960).

G. L. Archer

ECCLESIASTICUS ĭ kle' zĭ as' tə kəs (Ἐκκλησιαστικός). The longest and one of the most important books of the Apoc., known also by the title "The Wisdom of Jesus the Son of Sirach" (Σοφία Ἰησοῦ υἱοῦ Σιράχ), occasionally abbreviated to "The Wisdom of Sirach" (Σοφία Σιράχ) or simply "Sirach" (cf. the occasional Lat. form, *Siracides*).

The title "Ecclesiasticus" ("of the Church") was given to the book as early as the 3rd cent., prob. in recognition of the superior worth of the book for reading in the Church among those writings that did not hold canonical status (i.e., which were not a part of the Hebrew OT). The early Church Fathers referred to the book as the "most excellent" or (literally) "all virtuous" Wisdom (Πανάρετος Σοφία). However, the title "Ecclesiasticus" may also have been given to the book because it was early placed alongside the book Ecclesiastes, and a similar title was deemed suitable.

1. Author
2. Date
3. Place and language
4. Purpose
5. Content
6. Theological teaching and importance
7. Canonicity
8. Text

1. Author. The generalizing title "Ecclesiasticus" obscures the fact that the author of the book is known to have been Jesus the Son of Sirach (as the alternate title correctly recognizes). In this writing alone, among the Apoc., does the author include his name in the actual text. He writes, "Instruction in understanding and knowledge I have written in this book, Jesus the son of Sirach, son of Eleazar, of Jerusalem, who out of his heart poured forth wisdom" (Sirach 50:27). There is considerable textual difficulty concerning the names mentioned, and particularly noteworthy is the fact that the Heb. text apparently ascribes the book to "Simon the son of Jeshua, son of Eleazar, son of Sira." This same ascription (but in two forms, one omitting reference to Eleazar) occurs in the colophon of the MS. Probably the Heb. ascription of the book to Simon is the result of the importation of Simon's name from 50:1 and is to be regarded as erroneous. The Gr. MSS are unanimous in their ascription of the book to "Jesus the son of Sirach" both in 50:27 and in the colophon. More important than this, however, is the reference to the author of the book contained in the prologue written by the Gr. tr. of the book who was also the grandson of the author. The tr. narrates in the prologue that his grandfather Jesus, having devoted himself to the arduous study of the Scriptures, was led to produce the book which he has tr.

Who was this "Jeshua son of Sira" (to use the Aram. forms of the names)? Nothing is known of him beyond what can be deduced from the book that he authored. Due to the length of the book along with the comparatively generous number of personal references that it contains, one knows a fair amount about the author. Ben Sira, as the author may be called, seems almost certainly to have been a scribe, that is to say, a professional student of the Scriptures. This is evident not only from what the tr. indicates concerning his grandfather's serious study of the Scriptures, but also from the contents of the book. In particular, Ben Sira's glowing description of the calling of a scribe (38:24-39:11) could be seen as a veiled autobiographical sketch of his own life work of which the present book is but an embodiment.

But the calling of a scribe was not simply to study, but to practice and esp. to teach (cf. Ezra 7:10). Ben Sira was also a teacher. This would have been clear from the character of the book alone—obviously the product of a heart concerned with and experienced in teaching—were there no references to it contained in the book. The author exhorts, "Draw near to me, you who are untaught, and lodge in my school" (Sirach 51:23). From this (and the following vv.) it may be inferred that Ben Sira in his later years maintained an academy, prob. in Jerusalem. The reference is literally "house of instruction," the Heb. of which (בית המדרש) thereafter became the standard expression used for the rabbinic schools (cf. also 51:29 of the Heb. text, which refers to a group of disciples). It seems safe to affirm that in his life, as in his books, he labored "for all who seek instruction" (33:17).

Ben Sira had no narrow background. In his closing prayer he reviews his pilgrimage to wisdom and understanding. He refers to travels undertaken in his youth (51:13), which recalls an earlier mention of how an educated man gains understanding particularly by travel experience, as he himself could personally testify (34:9-12). It may even be that he traveled as an adviser on diplomatic missions, which as he suggests was at times the duty of the scribe (39:4).

Along with his thorough knowledge of the Scriptures, Ben Sira reveals in his writing a great wealth of knowledge, which may be called "worldly wisdom," i.e., that wisdom common to the sages of antiquity. One may suggest that he was not only widely traveled, but also well-read (parallels to Euripides, Theognis, and Aesop have been seen).

In terms of religious stance (*see below*), Ben Sira is most often described as a precursor of the Sadducees. Whereas his book does reveal some of the traits of the later Sadducees, it is quite appropriate also to see the book as propounding the classical ideals of Pharisaism. In the discussion of the actual teaching of the book, more information will be found concerning the religious viewpoint of Jeshua Ben Sira.

2. Date. The author of Ecclesiasticus is known (not true for the other books of the Apoc.) and also the nearly exact date of the book is known—again something rare for the writings of the Apoc. The evidence comes from the prologue supplied by the tr. This tr., whose name is unknown but who was the grandson of the author, says that he emigrated to Egypt in the thirty-eighth year of the reign of Euergetes. Two Egyp. kings bore the surname "Euergetes," Ptolemy III and Ptolemy VII, but the former reigned some twenty-five years, whereas the latter reigned no less than fifty-three years. Obviously, the Euergetes referred to by the tr. must be Ptolemy VII, whose reign began in 170 B.C., thereby putting the date of the tr's. emigration at about 132 B.C. This being the case the date of the book is most prob. to be put in the early decades of the 2nd cent. B.C. Since the book reveals no knowledge whatsoever of the catastrophic events that occurred in 168 B.C. at the instigation of Antiochus IV, such a conclusion is confirmed, and the scholarly estimates of the date of the book almost all fall between 200 and 180 B.C.

Another piece of evidence that bears directly on the date of Ecclesiasticus is the reference to "Simon the high priest, son of Onias" (50:1). The following description of his work and ministry in the sanctuary is given in the past tense, and there are suggestions that this was written after the death of Simon (cf. "in his life," "in his time" 50:1; a prayer for peace to prevail among Simon's sons is found in the Heb. of 50:23f.) Some confusion exists concerning the identity of this Simon, son of Onias (Simon I: Jos. Antiq. XII, ii, 5; XII, iv, 1; Simon II: XII, iv, 10; XII, v, 1). However, next to nothing is known of Simon I, surnamed "the Righteous," who is said to have flourished about 300 B.C. This sparseness of data combined with the fact that in the Mishna, Simon the Righteous mediates between the Great Synagogue of Ezra and Antigonus of Socho (about 180 B.C.), thus occupying a span of more than two centuries, has led some to the conclusion that Simon I is a mythical rather than a historical personage. In any event, if Simon I did flourish about 300 B.C., he was too early to have been the Simon referred to by the grandfather of our tr. who, as indicated, emigrated to Egypt in 132 B.C. Simon II, on the other hand, seems to have been high priest from about 220 to about 195 B.C. and, by virtue of the coincidence with the chronological data already reviewed, is almost certainly the Simon referred to by Ben Sira. This being the case, a date of shortly after 195 B.C. is very probable.

3. Place and language. Other matters for Ecclesiasticus are known with certainty (more than for any other book of the Apoc.). Ben Sira tells that he lived in Jerusalem (50:27), and it was doubtless there also that he maintained his academy and ultimately committed his teaching to writing. Although it is not specifically stated in the prologue, Ben Sira's grandson prob. came to Egypt from Pal. Perhaps he brought the book with him, which he later felt compelled to tr.

It is certain that Ben Sira wrote his masterpiece in Heb. The unnamed tr. asks the readers' indulgence for the imperfections of his work, adding a sentiment common to trs.: "For what was originally expressed in Hebrew does not have exactly the same sense when tr. into another language." He further remarks that the law, the prophets, and "the rest of the books" in Gr. all exhibit the same type of inevitable discrepancies with the original. The task of Ben Sira's grandson, then, is exactly parallel to the work accomplished by the trs. of the LXX in making available Heb. writings to a Greek-speaking public.

Prior to 1896, scholars knew Ecclesiasticus only through the Gr. and Syr. VSS, which served as the basis for later trs. However, in that year and succeeding years, significant portions of the Heb. text were identified among the materials excavated from the Cairo Geniza. More recently, fragments of the Heb. text have been discovered at Qumran. The net result is that today approximately two-thirds of the entire book in its original language has been acquired. Considerable debate has centered around the question of the authenticity of this Heb. text and a number of important scholars have argued that it is merely a retranslation of the Gr. VS. Whereas clearly it is a very corrupt text, this Heb. seems prob. to be representative of the original product of Ben Sira. Even the opponents of the authenticity of the recovered text, however, allow that Ben Sira must originally have written his work in Heb.

4. Purpose. Ben Sira's purpose is immediately apparent upon a perusal of Ecclesiasticus. Like the great wisdom writer who authored Proverbs, Ben Sira seeks to provide his reader with instruction in wisdom by the compilation of various epigrams and sayings designed to inculcate righteousness, or obedience to the law. Indeed Ben Sira somewhat immodestly regards himself as standing at the end of a long line of writers who upheld the teachings of the law. Thus he writes: "I was the last on watch; I was like one who gleans after the grape-gatherers; by the blessing of the Lord I excelled, and like a grape-gatherer I filled my wine press" (33:16; cf. 24:33). Ben Sira's book serves as a complete guide to right thinking and right conduct. There is perhaps a subsidiary motive in the author's mind as he emphasizes in one of the climactic sections of his book that Wisdom has made her dwelling place in Israel (24:8-12) and as he equates Wisdom with the law of Moses (24:23). In all of this, Ben Sira may be speaking to his brethren who were weakening under the constant temptations of Hellenism. He exhorts that they should not be ashamed "of the law of the Most High" (42:1ff.). Throughout the book the exhortations to the standards of conduct set by the law may be taken as countering an opposite tendency provoked by the Hellenizing influences of the day. This still remains secondary, for what argument there may be against Hellenism remains always tacit. Ben Sira's purpose is better taken as that which is so readily apparent from the content of the book. This is summed up beautifully by the tr. in his prologue when he writes that "by becoming conversant with this [book] also, those who love learning should make even greater progress in living according to the law."

5. Content. There is virtually no organization in the contents of Ecclesiasticus and no progression of thought is apparent in the book. A few proverbs and sayings will often cluster around a common subject, but beyond this rather natural occurrence, the materials are set in no particular structure. Instead, as in the case of the Book of Proverbs, the author allows himself to dart from subject to subject in a seemingly haphazard fashion. It has been suggested that the contents of the book may well consist of the notes that were used by Ben Sira in teaching at his academy.

Because of the lack of intrinsic structure in the book, it is difficult to suggest a meaningful outline of its contents. There are some natural divisions in the last ten chs. of the book formed by material that is different in character from the preceding portion of the book. The first of these (42:15-43:33) is a panegyric on the glory of God as seen in the works of creation and ends on the futility of ever adequately recounting the greatness of His works, for as the author concludes "the sum of our words is: 'He is the all'" (43:27). The following section (44:1-50:21) reviews the history of the great men of Israel, ending with a great tribute to Simon the high priest, the son of Onias. This is followed by a general doxology and prayer (50:22-24), an odd proverb (50:25, 26), and a concluding postscript identifying the author and encouraging the reader (50:27-29). The book seems naturally to end here, yet there is added an excellent thanksgiving hymn (51:1-12) and a final acrostic (in the Heb.) poem on the pursuit of wisdom (51:13-30).

In addition to the divisions found toward the end of the book, however, a number of writers have found a major division in the main portion of the book, although the latter seems at first glance to consist only of random collections of proverbs and wisdom sayings. The division has been made largely on the basis of the long poem on wisdom, which begins in 24:1. Since this is parallel to the long discourse that opens the book (1:1-20), and these two are by far the longest poems on wisdom, it has been suggested that the second opens a second volume of the same work. (It should be noted that the Book of Proverbs also begins with a long treatise on wisdom [chs. 1-9].) To some extent this conjecture may find support in the remarks that follow the second poem on wisdom. Ben Sira likens his work to the watering of a garden, but he says, "my canal became a river, and my river became a sea" (24:31), perhaps implying that his work grew to unexpected proportions. He continues, "I will again make instruction shine forth like the dawn" (24:32) and "I will again pour out teaching like prophecy" (24:33), affirmations that may well refer to a renewed activity of composition.

Perhaps a simple outline is best for a book of this nature, and the following may be suggested:

Prologue (usually not given v. enumeration)

a. Instruction in wisdom, part one (1:1-23:27)
b. Instruction in wisdom, part two (24:1-42:14)
c. The glory of God in His works (42:15-43:33)
d. The glory of God in His servants (44:1-50:21)
e. Concluding remarks (50:22-29)
f. Thanksgiving hymn (51:1-12)
g. On the pursuit of wisdom (51:13-30)

Bypassing the tr's. prologue one may devote some comments to the contents of the two main sections, which, although essentially undistinguishable, are discussed separately for the sake of convenience.

The opening poem on wisdom can be regarded as setting the tone of the whole book and not merely that of the first section alone. Ben Sira writes, "All wisdom comes from the Lord and is with him for ever" (1:1). He proceeds to argue eloquently that because this is true, wisdom can mean only one thing for man: the fear of the Lord. To fear the Lord is not only the beginning of wisdom (cf. Prov 1:7) and its root, but also its perfection and crown. To fear the Lord is to keep His commandments; therein lies wisdom (Ecclus. 1:26f.). A large proportion of the remaining teaching of the book grows out of this basic premise. In addition to the traditional Jewish piety that derives from this reverence for the law, Ben Sira includes considerable proverbial wisdom that bears no special relation to the law.

Much of the material, then, is hortatory, calling the reader to keep the commandments. Negatively, this means to keep oneself from sin. The reader is exhorted to beware of evil (4:20; 17:14), and to flee from sin "as from a snake" (21:2). Although the Lord is merciful, His mercy must not be presumed upon, for He also knows wrath (5:6; 16:11). The Lord knows all that a man does, and nothing can be hid from Him (17:15ff.). Moreover, judgment is sure to come despite all present appearances to the contrary (16:12ff.; 17:23). Consequently, only the fool presumptuously boasts "I sinned, and what happened to me?" (5:4). The punishment of the ungodly is severe (7:17) and the end of the road for the sinner is "the pit of Hades" (21:10). A man ought therefore to examine himself before judgment comes (18:20); for if he remembers the end of his life, he will never sin (7:36). It is within this basic framework that Ben Sira sets his teachings concerning the avoidance of specific sins. To give some examples, the wise man does not set his heart on wealth (5:1), does not slander (5:14), does not fall into the snare of a loose woman (9:3ff.), is not angry (10:6) or proud (10:18), avoids evil desires, gluttony, and lust (23:6), does not lie (20:24ff.), swear (23:9ff.), speak foul language (23:13), or fall victim to sexual sins (23:16ff.). On the positive side, Ben Sira exhorts his readers to find wisdom by honoring their parents (3:1ff.; 7:27f.), by humility (3:17ff.; 10:7ff.), charity to the poor and the wronged (4:1ff.; 7:32f.), sincerity in speech (5:9ff.), almsgiving to the devout (12:1ff.), and self-control (18:27ff.). These are examples drawn at random, but they help to catch the tenor of the book.

Significant religious teaching is found in the following emphases of the first section. Ben Sira speaks clearly of the sovereignty of the Lord. Everything, both good and bad, comes from the Lord (11:14). Despair and rejoicing should be minimized because the Lord can easily turn the tables (11:21ff.). Moreover, death is inevitable (14:17ff.). The right attitude is to bow before the sovereignty of God and accept what He brings (2:4). At the same time, a man cannot say that the Lord is responsible for his sinning, for as Ben Sira writes, "If you will, you can keep the commandments, and to act faithfully is a matter of your own choice" (15:15). The greatness of the Lord defies expression (18:1ff.), and His work of creation is both great and good (16:26-17:14). Man, however, is insignificant, like a grain of sand or a drop of water by comparison (18:18ff.).

Also to be found throughout these chs. is wisdom of a more common, proverbial type, which also has its place in the good life as understood by the author. Ben Sira expounds on the qualities of true and false friendship (6:5ff.; 12:8ff.), good government (10:1ff.), the right use of silence (20:1ff.), and the disagreeableness of a fool (22:7ff.). Although he cautions against an undue harshness of self-discipline ("If a man is mean to himself, to whom will he be generous?" 14:5), he urges the strict disciplining of children (7:23ff.; 22:3ff.). It is right to give heed to the wisdom of the elderly (8:8ff.), and one does well to keep virtuous companions (9:13ff.) and avoid those who are not of like mind (13:1ff.). Not only ought one to keep clear of the ungodly (12:13ff.), but one ought also to avoid giving hospitality to strangers (11:34). Among his counsels, one of the most interesting is to refrain from seeking answers to questions that transcend the limits of human understanding (3:21ff.). A host of other wise sayings are to be found throughout the chs. of this first division of the book. They are pithy and often employ a characteristic poetic parallelism. In addition to the long opening passage praising wisdom, there are other, shorter, passages devoted to the praise of wisdom (e.g. 4:11f.; 6:18ff.; 14:20ff.).

The content of the second main section of the book (24:1-42:14) is very similar to that which has just been described. Again a wide variety of subjects is discussed, and these are connected only in the loosest fashion. The opening poem on wisdom (ch. 24) is particularly noteworthy. Wisdom is personified and made to speak in the first person (cf. Prov 8). She speaks of herself in the most exalted language and invites all to come and partake of her fruit. Those who do will return for more of her delights (24:21). After this passage spoken by personified Wisdom, Ben Sira makes the striking assertion that this Wisdom is nothing other than the law: "All this is the book of the covenant of the Most High God, the law which Moses commanded us as an inheritance for the congregations of Jacob" (24:23; cf. 19:20). The material that follows contains motifs already familiar from the first section. Thus, "the fear of the Lord surpasses everything" (25:11), and the man who has gained wisdom accordingly guards against what is unpleasing to the Lord, e.g. sin in business (27:2); anger and hatred (27:30); sins of the tongue (28:13ff.); "make a door and a bolt for your mouth" (28:25); love of money (31:5ff.). A man is directed to consider the end of his life as an incentive to keep the commandments (28:6). Justice is sure to come from the Lord who will repay a man according to his deeds (35:12ff.). Offerings and sacrifices are important, but they must be offered by righteous men who keep the law (35:1ff.). Emphasis is given to the sovereignty of the Lord in all His acts. As a potter molds his clay, so does the Lord order the ways of men (33:13). Inequality (33:12) and death (41:3f.) are the results of His pleasure. At the same time, Ben Sira laments "From a woman sin had its beginning, and because of her we all die" (25:24), and elsewhere, "O evil imagination [i.e. inclination], why were you formed to cover the land with deceit?" (37:3).

There is even more teaching of the proverbial wisdom type in this second section of Ecclesiasticus than in the first. Ben Sira advises on a great variety of matters, including lending and sureties (29:1ff.), table etiquette for a guest (31:12ff.), the proper use of wine (31:25ff.), correct behavior at a party (31:31), the treatment of slaves and servants (33:24ff.), dreams and divinations (34:1ff.), and friendship (37:1ff.). Ben Sira's teachings in these and other similar areas have an attractiveness to them, being based on the two foundations of consideration for others and moderation in all things. As in the first section, again the reader is exhorted to be strict with his children ("He who loves his son will whip him often," 30:1ff.). Whereas a good wife is praiseworthy (cf. 36:24), nothing is worse than an evil wife ("I would rather dwell with a lion and a dragon than dwell with an evil wife," 25:16). In the end, however, Ben Sira's view of woman is decidedly pessimistic (cf. 42:12ff.). In one interesting passage, the reader is exhorted to make proper use of physicians and medicines in time of illness (38:1ff.). A helpful passage follows on the place of grief for the dead which is proper for a season, but is not to be prolonged since by it, "you do the dead no good, and you injure yourself" (38:21). Ben Sira knows the value of positive thinking and exhorts his reader to be glad and to rejoice, for so is his life best lived (30:21ff.). Particularly significant is the lengthy discussion of the occupation of the scribe as contrasted with that of other occupations, which though necessary, do not afford the leisure that is the *sine qua non* of the contemplative life (38:24-39:11). Also noteworthy is the prayer for national restoration (36:1-17), which is complete in itself and exactly analogous to the similar prayers of other books of the intertestamental period. Special mention is in order for the hymn of praise to God found in 39:13-35. Stylistically, attention should be called to the numerical proverbs of ch. 25, and the "better than both" comparisons of 40:18ff.

The remaining sections of the book, which are quite different in nature from the preceding, have already been described above and need not be elaborated upon.

6. Theological teaching and importance. It must first be made clear that not only is Ecclesiasticus not a theological treatise, but it also does not systematize or in any other way set in order, or even attempt to harmonize its theological teaching. Whereas it contains no small amount of such teaching, that teaching is largely incidental to the immediate purpose of the author, and often the exhortations of the book presuppose rather than delineate the underlying theological truth.

Ecclesiasticus stands solidly in the mainstream of orthodox Judaism. Ben Sira's God is the God of the Torah, the Creator who is transcendent in His glory, whose sovereignty rules the universe, and whose holiness and righteousness are absolute. God has entered into covenant relationship with Israel, esp. endowing her with wisdom in the form of the law. In this identification of wisdom with the law (ch. 24), Ben Sira makes an apparently original contribution to traditional Judaism. There is no question in Ecclesiasticus concerning the specially privileged position of Israel, and Ben Sira can make his voice heard in strongly nationalistic tones (cf. 36:1ff.). Nonetheless, the emphasis in his book is clearly upon personal piety. The individual man who possesses wisdom is the man who heeds the commandments of the law. In all of this, Ben Sira reflects his thorough acquaintance with and dependence upon not only the Torah, but also the prophets and, particularly, the Psalms.

As far as man's moral ability is concerned, Ben Sira acknowledges the existence of an evil inclination (*yeṣer ha-ra'*) within man, yet insists that it is possible for man to keep the law (15:15). The sovereignty of God and the free will of man stand in tension through the whole of the book. Man inevitably sins, and consequently every individual is deserving of punishment (8:5). Salvation, however, is possible for man because the Lord is merciful and forgives the sins of those who turn to Him (2:11; 5:7; 17:24).

A number of the theological emphases of Ecclesiasticus have been regarded as reflecting, anachronistically, a Sadducean viewpoint. In his book, Ben Sira reveals a great love for the priesthood, the Temple, and the sacred rituals performed there. When reviewing the history of God's work through the famous men of Israel, Ben Sira gives more than a proportionate amount of space to those entrusted with the priesthood. Aaron, with whom the priestly lineage begins, is given a glowing tribute that takes more space than that given to Abraham, Isaac, Jacob, and Moses combined (45:6ff.). Similarly, Phinehas the son of Eleazar is given a prominent place among the great of Israel because of his importance for the priesthood (45:23f.). Most impressive in many ways, however, is the praise showered upon the high priest Simon, son of Onias, whom Ben Sira describes in his priestly functions on the Day of Atonement with the vividness of an admiring eyewitness (50:1ff.). Similarly, the Temple is of great significance for Ben Sira (cf. 24:10; 36:13f.) as are also the religious festivals of Israel (33:7ff.).

Further, Ecclesiasticus contains no hint of the doctrine of the resurrection of the dead. Rewards and retribution are experienced in this life only. Sheol (Hades) is the abode of the dead where nothing occurs (cf. 17:27; 41:4; 14:16)—in the Gr. VS of Ecclesiasticus this view is modified somewhat (*see* 19:19, fn. where a Gr. interpolation speaks of "the fruit of the tree of immortality"). The only "immortality" acknowledged by Ben Sira is found in the memory of a name of good repute (cf. 44:8ff.). Since the attention of Ecclesiasticus is constantly focused on the present life, when the wicked prosper and the righteous suffer—a paradoxical situation for this viewpoint—Ben Sira counsels that circumstances may change quickly and thus it is not prudent to make such judgments prior to the death of the persons in question (11:21-28). The problem, however, remains, and many passages indicate that Ben Sira was not unaware of it.

This conservatism of Ben Sira in these viewpoints, reflected also in his conception of the aristocratic scribe (38:24ff.) and in his penchant for Biblical phraseology throughout the book, has been taken as indicative of a Sadducean orientation. Whereas one does not properly speak of Sadducees before the post-Maccabean age it is clear that Ben Sira does anticipate certain of their characteristic doctrines. It is, however, an oversimplification simply to categorize Ben Sira as a proto-Sadducee. In his book, he carefully counterbalances his emphasis on Temple ritual with forceful assertions of the necessity of personal righteousness. He can speak like the prophets in this regard: "The Most High is not pleased with the offerings of the ungodly; and he is not propitiated for sins by a multitude of sacrifices" (34:19; cf. 35:6ff.). Ben Sira exhibits an interest in the prophetic tradition at least equal to, if not greater than, his interest in the priestly tradition. In his "praise of great men" he seems to stress that it is prophetism that serves as the significant linking factor in the history of Israel (cf. 46:1; 47:1; 48:1, 8, 13). These facts when combined with the orthodox theology of Ecclesiasticus, make it possible to view Ben Sira as the forerunner of Pharisaic Judaism. Certainly, the juristic nature of the traditional wisdom with which Ben Sira expounds and supplements the law anticipates and parallels the oral tradition handed down in rabbinic Judaism, which was later to be codified in written form in the Mishnah.

The particular significance of Ecclesiasticus lies in its position in the literary history of Israel. The last, and in many ways the greatest of the wisdom books, it presents the culmination of the wisdom tradition. At the same time, it stands immediately prior to, and in many ways as the clear precursor of, both Sadducean and Pharisaic Judaism.

Mention must be made of one other important fact about Ecclesiasticus. Within the prologue, important information is found concerning the state of the OT canon in the 2nd cent. B.C. The tr. once speaks of his grandfather who devoted himself to the reading of "the law and the prophets and the other books of our fathers" and a little later again refers to "the law itself, the prophecies, and the rest of the books," suggesting that by 132 B.C., the OT canon had already taken its threefold division (cf. Luke 24:44). Within Ecclesiasticus are intimations of a threefold division of canonical writings (e.g. 39:1, "law," "wisdom," and "prophecies"; cf. 44:3-5), and in his praise of famous men (chs. 44-49), Ben Sira follows closely the order of their appearance in books of the Heb. Bible, although there are some strange omissions in the list (esp. Daniel and Ezra).

7. Canonicity. Ecclesiasticus was among the books that found their way into the LXX, and thus gained currency, particularly in the Early Church. It was never accepted as canonical by the Jews, although it was often quoted, and

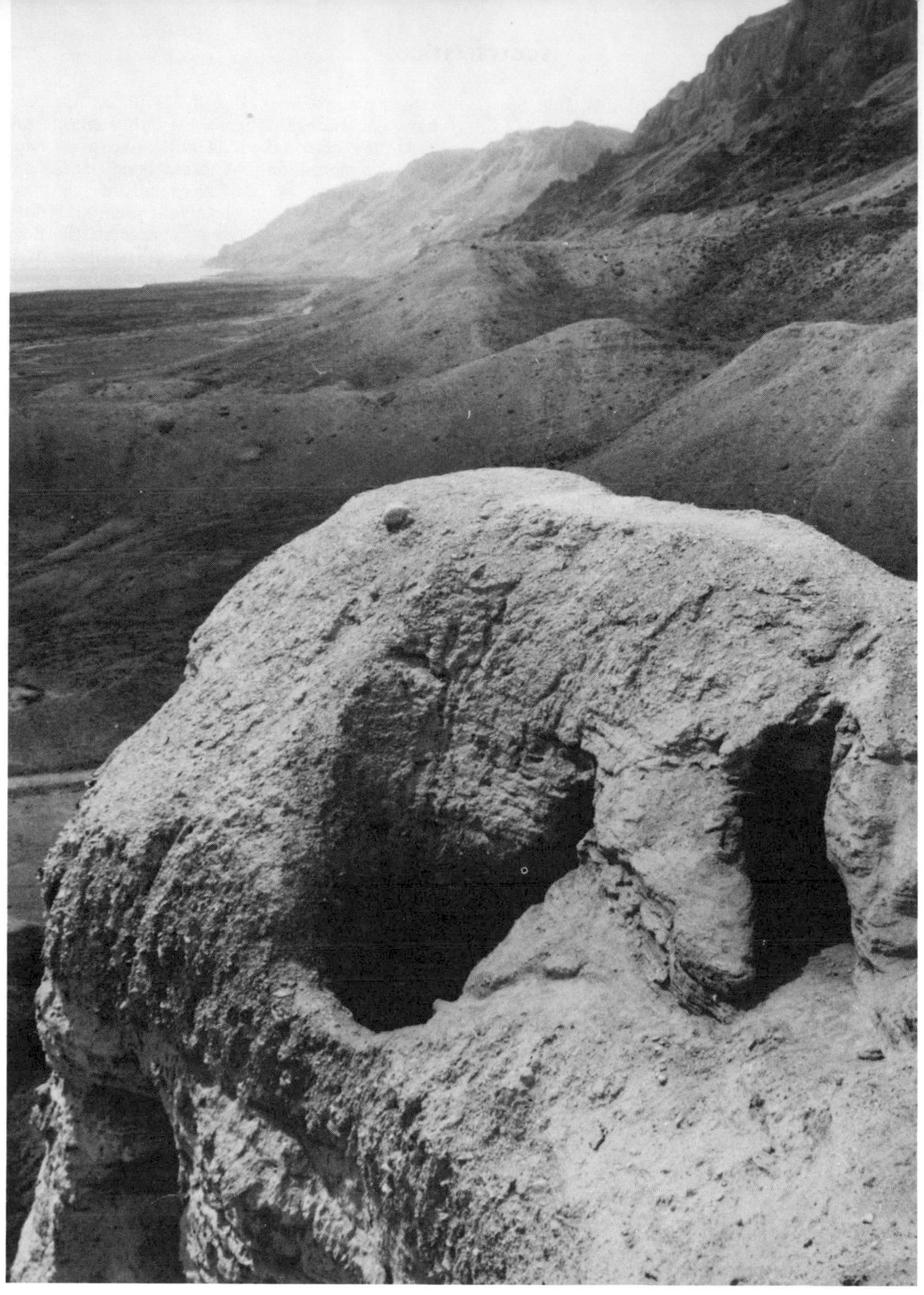

In these caves, burrowing into the escarpments along the western bank of the Dead Sea, archeologists found the Dead Sea Scrolls, which included fragments of Ecclesiasticus. © *Aramco*

it exercised considerable influence on the later rabbinic lit. A number of parallels to Ecclesiasticus in the NT, esp. in Matthew and James (*see* APOT I, p. 294f.), also testify to the early influence of the book. The patristic writers often quote from Ecclesiasticus, and on occasion refer to the book as "Scripture," but in these early centuries, although the book seems to have enjoyed a quasi-canonical status, it did not receive technical recognition of canonicity until Augustine and certain church councils of the late 4th and early 5th cent. formally accepted the book as canonical. Jerome, however, clearly set Ecclesiasticus apart from the canonical books (i.e. those of the Heb. canon). The book became an established part of the Roman Catholic canon following the decision taken at the Council of Trent in the 16th cent. Protestants, although highly esteeming Ecclesiasticus, receive it only as a book of the Apoc.

8. Text. The textual evidence for Ecclesiasticus constitutes a fascinating and difficult puzzle for scholars. There are three primary witnesses to the text: the Gr. of the LXX (tr. by Ben Sira's grandson), the Syr. of the Peshitta (made originally from the Heb. rather than the LXX), and the fragmentary Heb. MSS (about two-thirds of the book extant) from the magnificent finds of the Cairo Geniza. There are a number of secondary witnesses in the form of trs. (Old Latin, Syriac, Coptic, Ethiopic, Arabic, Armenian, Georgian, and Old Slavonic) that for the most part derive from the LXX, but which may occasionally show the influence of other primary witnesses. Not only is there question concerning the relationship of the three primary witnesses, but there is also question concerning the history of various textual representatives within each of the three recensions. Among the Gr. MSS, great divergencies in text are discovered (transpositions, interpolations, and omissions). Basically, the Gr. MSS have been separated into two categories, some going back to an earlier (original?) Heb. text, and others apparently to a later recension of the Heb. text. The Syriac Peshitta seems also to have been influenced by the hypothetical later Heb. recension. Perhaps most confusing of all, however, are the five Cairo Heb. MSS that date from about the 11th or 12th cent. These MSS reveal numerous secondary readings in common with the second group of Gr. MSS and the Syr. Do these secondary readings indicate that these Heb. MSS depend to some extent upon the hypothetical Heb. recension that seems to have influenced certain of the Gr. MSS, or are they "retroversions"—retranslations into Heb. of certain readings of the Gr. or Syr. witnesses? Whereas the latter explanation has been increasingly popular, there seems to be a new turning to the former (see Di Lella and Rüger). It is striking that the fragments of Ecclesiasticus found at Qumran seem to bear a text form similar to that of the Cairo MS(A). If a relationship to Qumran could be ascertained, the reliability of the Cairo MSS would be established. The difficulty in solving the textual problem posed by Ecclesiasticus is thus compounded by what appears to be the various signs of reciprocal influence among the three primary witnesses.

The text of the major LXX witnesses is available in the standard printed editions of the LXX. The Heb. is available in a reconstruction by M. S. Segal (*see* Bibliography). The modern Eng. VSS usually follow an eclectic text, indicating more important variants in accompanying notes.

BIBLIOGRAPHY. G. H. Box and W. O. E. Oesterley in R. H. Charles, APOT, I (1913), 268-517; W. O. E. Oesterley, *The Books of the Apocrypha* (1915), 321-348; E. J. Goodspeed, *The Story of the Apocrypha* (1939), 20-30; R. H. Pfeiffer, *History of New Testament Times with an Introduction to the Apocrypha* (1949), 352-408; M. S. Segal, *Sepher Ben-Sira Ha-shalem* (1953); H. J. Cadbury, "The Grandson of Ben Sira," HTR, XLVIII (1955), 219-225; B. M. Metzger, *An Introduction to the Apocrypha* (1957), 75-88; A. H. Forster, "The Date of Ecclesiasticus," AThR, XLI (1959), 1-9; J. T. Milik, *Ten Years of Discovery in the Wilderness of Judaea* (1959), 31f.; L. H. Brockington, *A Critical Introduction to the Apocrypha* (1961), 71-84; L. F. Hartman, "Sirach in Hebrew and in Greek," CBQ, XXIII (1961), 443-451; J. G. Snaith, "The Importance of Ecclesiasticus (The Wisdom of Ben Sira)," ExpT, LXXV (1963-1964), 66-69; O. Eissfeldt, *The Old Testament: An Introduction* (1965), 595-599; A. A. Di Lella, *The Hebrew Text of Sirach* (1966); R. K. Harrison, *Introduction to the Old Testament* (1969), 1231-1237; H. P. Rüger, *Text und Textform im hebräischen Sirach* (1970).

D. A. HAGNER

ECLIPSE. *See* ASTRONOMY.

ECUMENISM ěk′ yōō měn′ ĭsm (*οἰκουμένη*, lit. *inhabited world* but occasionally has the meaning of *cultured world* as in contrast to barbarian societies). A theological term dealing with the unity and universality of the Christian faith and the Christian Church.

The mutual concepts of unity and universality are rooted in OT concepts of the covenant and cult worship but come to fullest expression in the NT doctrine of the Church.

1. OT concepts of covenant universality and cultic unity. Ecumenism as both universality and unity are clearly observable in the context of OT Biblical theology. Israelite particularism sometimes obscures the broader concepts of the "world" and "nations" but the evidence clearly points to a profound universalism in the OT. (a) Creation and the genealogical table of nations in Genesis clearly place God's covenant people within the broader framework of universal world history (cf. Gen 1; 2; 5; 10). (b) The Abrahamic Covenant not only calls attention to Israel's elective soteriology but includes "all the families of the earth" (Gen 12:1-3; 17:1-8). (c) God's covenant with Israel at Sinai implies both a redemptive particularism as well as a universal priesthood. Yahweh calls Israel to "be a kingdom of priests and a holy nation" (Exod 19:5, 6). Indeed, the record of OT history portrays Israel's failure to serve in this servant ministry, as Yahweh's priestly *Qâhâl* (congregation) among the *Goyim* (nations). (d) During the monarchy of David there is a growing consciousness of a universal mission. (Cf. the Davidic Psalms 9:11; 18:49; 57:9.) Even more pronounced is Solomon's prayer of dedication after the erection of the Temple—that the Temple would become a place of universal worship of Yahweh (1 Kings 8:41-53). (e) The fact that the prophetic lit. consistently contains "foreign nation sections" in which judgment is pronounced upon and salvation is promised to these nations also confirms the deep-seated universalism implicit in the structure of Israel's faith. (Cf. Amos 1:3-2:3; Isa 13-28; Jer 46:51.) (f) Also one may trace in the exilic and post-exilic prophets an equal emphasis upon Israel's universal mission to the nations. What Israel had failed to be, her *diaspora* among the kingdoms of the world was to accomplish. (Cf. Jer 18:7; Ezek 3:6; 47:22; Mal 1:11.) (g) Finally, what are we to conclude about the numerous cases of Gentile participation in Israel's history as well as the examples of faith found among non-Israelites? Note the "mixed multitude" which came out of Egypt with Israel (Exod 12:38); the protection of the "stranger" (Deut 10:19); Rahab the Canaanite harlot in Joshua 2; the whole story of Ruth and her contribution to the Davidic line; Ittai (2 Sam 15:21); and Naaman (2 Kings 5).

This universalism must not hide the equally obvious fact of Israel's uniqueness and particular election. This particularism is vital and essential to the covenant relationship of Yahweh and Israel: "Now therefore, if you will obey my voice and keep my covenant, you shall be my own possession among all peoples; for all the earth is mine" (Exod 19:5; cf. Deut 7:6-16). The Deuteronomic idea of Yahweh's choosing a "place where His name will dwell" served during the monarchy to justify the establishment of a central sanctuary where not only Israel but all nations would come to worship. (Cf. Deut 12; 14:23-25; 15:20; 16:1-16; 17:8, 10; 18:6; 23:16; 31:11; esp. 33:27.) History has recorded the elaborate growth of cultic ceremony and ritualism which developed around the Temple. The centralizing of Israel's worship in Jerusalem was intended to provide the unity of Israel's covenant relationship with Yahweh. The division of the monarchy in 931 B.C. and the increase in Baalism in both the southern and northern kingdoms indicates the failure of cultic centralization as well as unity based upon a single sanctuary. With the exilic *diaspora* and the development of the synagogue, Israel had to find her unity in the recovery of that essential spirituality of God's covenantal relationship; hence, later Judaism turned to the *Shema* (cf. Deut 6:4-6) as a theological basis for her oneness before God. The debate over a centralized sanctuary never ceased in Judaism, and echoes can still be heard in Jesus' discussion with the woman at the well in Sychar (cf. John 4).

The concept of unity was vital to OT eschatology. (a) In the prophetic writings there are repeated references to Zion as the source of man's knowledge of God and salvation. "It shall come to pass in the latter days that the mountain of the house of the LORD shall be established as the highest of the mountains, . . . and all the nations shall flow to it, and many peoples shall come, and say: 'Come, let us go up to the mountain of the LORD, to the house of the God of Jacob; that he may teach us his ways and that we may walk in his paths.' For out of Zion shall go forth the law, and the word of the LORD from Jerusalem" (Isa 2:2, 3; cf. Isa 56:6-8; 66:18-21; Mic 4:1ff.). (b) The apocalyptic vision of the prophet Ezekiel in chs. 40-48 where a new Temple is seen points again to the cult as the center of Israel's faith, worship and unity. Although Ezekiel warns against "admitting foreigners uncircumcised in heart and flesh" in 44:7, his enlarged vision of the boundaries of the land obviously includes other nations: "You shall allot it as an inheritance for yourselves and for the aliens who reside among you and have begotten children among you. They shall be to you as native-born sons of Israel; with you they shall be allotted an inheritance among the tribes of Israel" (47:21-23). (c) Jeremiah's prophecy of a "new covenant" engraved on the human heart speaks of a spiritual unity transcending all institutions and legal prescriptions (Jer 31:31-34). It is the same "new covenant" which forms the basis for unity as well as universality in the NT Church as the "body of Christ." (Cf. Heb 8:8-12; note the textual variants in the institution of the Eucharist in Matt 26:17-29 and Mark 14:12-25; also observe Luke's association of the Eucharist with the kingdom and Israel in 22:28-30.) (d) And ultimately, not only the cultic unity of Israel's worship but in Israel herself—both old and new Israel—as the "people of God," there is to be seen both continuity and unity (cf. Gal 6:13-16). This can account for the prophetic interpretation of Israel's return to Pal. as a united kingdom (cf. Jer 31-34; Ezek 36; 37). Paul's discourse on Israel in Romans 9-11 also points to the continuing role of Israel in God's *Heilsgeschichte*, but it is a role in which all nations will also play a part. It is here that eschatology blends with ecumenism as both universality and unity (cf. Rev 7:1-17).

2. The "world-theology" of the NT. In the NT *oikoumenē* always is interpreted by the more frequent term *kosmos*. The latter term speaks of a divinely created world of order and humanity, of an ordered society of men, of an organic society controlled by the "evil one" and soteriologically of a world redeemed through Jesus Christ. (Cf. Matt 4:8; 5:14; 26:13; Mark 8:36; John 1:9, 10, 29; 3:16, 17, 19; 4:42; 12:31; Acts 17:24; Rom 1:18, 20; 11:15; 1 Cor 1:20, 21; 2 Cor 5:19; Gal 4:3; 1 John 2:15-17.) Although the longer ending of Mark is of questionable textual authority, there can be no doubt that the mission of the Church is coextensive with the universal redemption of Jesus Christ (cf. Mark 16:15; 2 Cor 5:14-21). *Oikoumenē* is the *kosmos* become the kingdom of Christ! (Cf. Rev 11:15.)

3. Ekklēsia as Church-church. The concept of Church-church attempts to indicate two facts about NT ecclesiology: (a) there is a distinction between the Church as a metaphysical spiritual reality transcending all historical institutional forms and the existence of the church as a local institution; and (b) the hyphen connecting Church with church points to the NT teaching that all local congregations depend for their existence upon the metaphysical, spiritual reality of the Church as the "body of Christ." At the same time, the Church always assumes and manifests itself in the reality of institutional societies who bear a distinctively Christological character. Paul's Ephesian letter presents the clearest examples of the NT idea of the Church. Speaking of Christ and the Church, Paul says "he has put all things under his feet and has made him the head over all things for the church, which is his body, *the fulness of him who fills all in all*" (Eph 1:22, 23; cf. Col 1:15-29). The "fulness of him who fills all in all" is not simply Christ but Christ and His Church! (Cf. Eph 2:19-22; 3:1-12; 5:21-33; 2 Cor 12:12, 13; Rom 12:3-8.) That the term *ekklēsia* in the NT most frequently refers to local congregations is shown by its use in the Book of Acts. (Cf. 8:1; 9:31; 11:22, 26; 12:1; Rom 16:1; 1 Cor 1:2; 1 Thess 1:1.)

Ecumenically speaking *the Church* transcends all historical, institutional and geographical expressions but is, nevertheless, manifested in all local assemblies called into being by the *kerygma* of Jesus as the Christ. (Cf. Acts 2:14-47.) The pastoral nature of the NT lit. reveals the tension of the churches always being called to be the Church.

4. Conclusions: unity, universality and institutionalism. (a) Unity: in later Christianity the term "catholic" (καθ' ὅλη), came to designate both the unity as well as the universality of the Church and is one of the clearest indications that ecumenicity soon became a concern of the post-apostolic church. (Note the third article of the Apostles' Creed.) The idea of a *kath' holē* church is found only in adjectival examples in the NT. (Cf. ἐφ' ὅλη τὴν ἐκκλησίαν, Acts 5:11; σὺν ὅλῃ τῇ ἐκκλησίᾳ, 15:22.) Ignatius (d. A.D. 107) is the first to use the term to distinguish a true church which holds to the apostolic doctrine of Christ from all other institutions founded upon heresy. The NT stress upon unity among Christians is almost too obvious to require illustration. Note, however, Christ's promise to build "His Church" and the word "church" is sing. (Matt 16:18). Christ's high-priestly prayer in John 17 to which ecumenics have always appealed is a prayer that the unity of Christians will serve apologetically the spread of the Gospel (vv. 20-26). Earlier in the fourth gospel, Christ is presented as saying "there shall be one flock, one shepherd" (10:16). Paul's repeated emphasis wherever the Church is defined as the "body of Christ" is upon her essential oneness in Christ. (Cf. 1 Cor 12:12, 13; Rom 12:3-8; Eph 4:1-16.) He answers the schism of the Corinthian church with the rebuke "is Christ divided?" (1 Cor 1:10-17).

(b) Universality: Christ's great commission is a call to a worldwide mission—"Go into all the world" (Matt 28:19, 20). The nineteen hundred years of church history is confirmation of the church's ecumenical mission and its partial fulfillment. Yet even in the 1st cent. Paul expresses his "ambition to preach the gospel, not where Christ has already been named," and he hoped that before his life was over he might travel as far as Spain—considered then to be one of the utmost western points of the world. (Cf. Rom 15: 20, 28.) In Acts 1:8, the Church's mission is coextensive with the "end of the earth."

(c) Institutionalism: the question of unity and universality have more recently raised the question of a united, universal institution which can lay claim to being "Christ's Church." No NT evidence can support any attempt to construct a monolithic institution. There is indeed clear evidence that the Church in the NT period was institutional in nature with a Christological, apostolic foundation, with ministerial offices, with a liturgical structure and with a membership concept capable of ecclesiastical discipline; but there is no evidence that a centralized organization with headquarters in Jerusalem, Antioch or Rome ever existed in the 1st cent. or was projected for future centuries. (Cf. Matt 18:15-20; Acts 2:37-47; 6:1-6; 14:23; 20:17, 28-32; 1 Cor 5:1-13; 10:14-22; 11:17-34; Eph 2:20; 4:1-16; Phil 1:1; 1 Tim 3:1-16; Titus 1:5-9.) The unity of the Early Church and the unity which the Church in all ages is called to demonstrate is her confession of Jesus as Lord and her members as servants for Jesus' sake. (Cf. 2 Cor 4:1-6.)

"Having sketched the *Heilsgeschichte* from Abraham to Christ . . . the early chapters of Genesis which tell of the Creation and the Fall, the Deluge and the Tower of Babel serve to universalize the historical experience of Israel. The strange history of Israel which culminated in Christ and the rise of the Christian Church as the new Israel has significance for the whole world of men who fell in Adam and are all included in the covenant made with Noah. . . . The Bible, then, gives us the record of God's ways with a particular community, but the story is set in a universal framework. . . . The biblical history became universal history through the emergence of the Church Catholic and it is still in the Church that history in the fullest sense is made, because it is primarily in the Church that man meets with God and makes the response which God demands. It is within the Church that the Bible is read and the Sacraments administered in the context of an act of worship through which believers are made contemporary with the great creative events of history constituting God's revelation of His will." (Norman W. Porteous, "Old Testament Theology," *The Old Testament and Modern Study*, ed. by H. H. Rowley [1951], 342, 343.)

BIBLIOGRAPHY. J. H. Maude, "Catholicism, Catholicity," HERE, III (1928), 258-261; O. J. Baab, *The Theology of the Old Testament* (1949), 183-186; E. Brunner, *The Misunderstanding of the Church* (1953); L. Newbigin, *The Household of God* (1953); J. D. Murch, *Co-operation Without Compromise* (1956); T. F. Torrance, *Conflict and Agreement in the Church*, 2 vols. (1959); J. B. Payne, *The Theology of the Older Testament* (1962); H. Sasse, "*κόσμος*" TDNT, III (1965), 868-895; K. L. Schmidt, "*ἐκκλησία*" TDNT, III (1965), 501-536; B. Vassady, *Christ's Church: Evangelical, Catholic, and Reformed* (1965); O. Michel "*ἡ οἰκουμένη*," TDNT, V (1967), 157-159.

D. M. Lake

ED (עֵד, *witness*). RSV WITNESS. An altar built by Reubenites, Gadites, and the half-tribe of Manasseh who settled E of the Jordan, as a witness of their loyalty to the God of Israel and to the tribes W of the Jordan. Not in MT or LXX; inserted in KJV, ASV (Josh 22:34).

EDAR e′ dər KJV form of EDER (עֵדֶר). This reference is to the "tower of Eder" (מִגְדַּל עֵדֶר, *tower of the flock*) located between Bethlehem and Hebron, where Jacob camped for a time following the death of Rachel (Gen 35:21). *See* Eder.

R. K. Harrison

EDDIAS. KJV Apoc. form of Izziah.

EDDINUS. Alternate form of Jeduthun.

EDEN, CHILDREN OF; HOUSE OF. *See* Beth-eden.

EDEN (GARDEN OF) (including Pishon, Phison, Pison) עֵדֶן; LXX, Ἔδεμ, the first habitation of our first parents.

1. Etymology. Two possibilities are encountered on this score: (a) either the word "Eden" is derived from the Akkad. *edinu*, or from the Sumer. *edin*, i.e. "open field"; or again (b) it is the Heb. (*'eden*) for "delight." Possibility (a) is less likely, because "open field" is not an apt designation of a "garden." Besides, the LXX frequently trs. for "garden of Eden," "park of delight."

2. Use of the word. The word *'eden* is used for garden in general; also for a territorial or geographic location; it appears as a proper name of a person; and lastly as the name of a town (Amos 1:5). *See* KB s.v.

3. Location. Three major possibilities are to be encountered under this head: (a) Armenia, (b) Babylonia, or near the head of the Persian Gulf, (c) near the N Pole. The last of these may be dismissed quickly, inasmuch as about all it can adduce by way of support is that evidence of tropical flora has been discovered as fossil remains in the frozen N. Babylonia also seems unlikely, because the river-pattern described in Genesis 2:10-14 does not agree with this claim. At least two of the streams mentioned in this Scripture (the Tigris and the Euphrates) are known to have been in days of old, as they are to this day, near to one another and springing from the Armenian highlands. This does not assign any proper place to the Pishon and the Gihon, with regard to which the conjecture has been offered, among others, that they are the Indus and the Nile. But positive identification of these two cannot be established. In fact, it seems that one must rest content with the identification of the Euphrates with the *prath* (v. 14) and of the Tigris with the *hiddekel* (cf. Sumer., *Idigna*, and the Akkad., *idiqlat*—KB). Since no such set of streams can be identified anywhere (one major stream dividing into four branches), there is great likelihood that they are correct who allow for the possibility that some major topographical change, such as might have been wrought by the great Flood, may have taken place. The only helpful fact left is that the Tigris and Euphrates still originate in the same general area, as well as do some minor streams (such as Araxes and Murat) that would come close to making up the original four mentioned in the text. For the claim seems irrefutable that the picture given in vv. 10-14 is that of a single strong stream issuing forth from the garden itself, and then subdividing into four branches which go off in the direction of the four points of the compass. No comparable situations that may be discovered correspond geographically to what is depicted here. The reverse often occurs that a number of streams in confluence combine to make one stream. The subdividing of a stream is, as far as is known, to be found only in deltas, which is not what is being described here. To try to make of the Pishon and the Gihon two of the canals that in days of old connected the Tigris and the Euphrates does not seem a happy solution of the problem. These canals originated at a much later date.

4. Description of the garden. The scriptural emphasis in reference to the garden seems to lie in the fact that it constituted a flawless background for human beings themselves flawless. It had many tokens of divine goodness and favor made accessible for the first parents. Among these tokens "trees" are mentioned first (2:9), all manner of them "pleasant to the sight and good for food." Of particular moment are two special trees, the tree of the knowledge of good and evil and the tree of life. These may well have been the center of the garden, as they certainly were as in their intrinsic importance to mankind.

Then it should be noted that as to location the garden lay "in Eden." Eden appears as a larger territory within whose confines the garden was located. Besides, the location is specified as lying "in the east," which must indicate: E from the point of location of the writer of the account, which does not help in this instance, for one does not know where the writer was.

In addition to many types of trees there were many animals, representatives perhaps of all major classes of the creatures that had been created on the sixth day (Gen 1:24f.). These creatures may have served man in many ways which became more and more apparent as time went on.

That the garden was well-watered has been indicated indirectly in the things that were said about the one river and the four rivers. In Biblical language almost always abundance of water is the major physical blessing. At the same time the care of the garden provided a suitable occupation for the first parents, but since nature had not been "made subject to vanity" the work assigned was neither too much nor too little. Lastly, everything points to the possibility that the climate was temperate, for clothing apparently was not a physical necessity.

5. The use of the term elsewhere in Scripture. It is not to be wondered that the Garden of Eden became the symbol or epitome of beauty and perfection, to which the following passages bear witness: Isaiah 51:3; Ezekiel 28:13; 31:9, 16, 18; Joel 2:3.

6. The later history of the garden. At first it must be remembered that cherubim were stationed to the E of the garden to prevent the entrance of man. It was also a matter of tradition that Cain's place of dwelling lay to the E of the garden. From there on, everything is wrapped in silence. There is always the possibility that the garden continued to exist and was the place of the manifestation of the Lord's presence to man until the time of the Flood, the cherubim involved, being in this case the ones who upheld the throne of the Almighty. The NT, basing on the term used by the LXX, uses paradise as a term descriptive of the bliss of the hereafter (Luke 23:43; 2 Cor 12:3; Rev 2:7).

BIBLIOGRAPHY. Any standard commentary on Genesis; also the current run of encyclopedias of the Bible and dictionaries of the Bible.

H. C. LEUPOLD

EDER, EDAR **e' dər** (עֵדֶר, *flock* as place name; prob. Aram. form of עֵזֶר, *helper* as personal name). 1. A watch tower (*migdal*) between Bethlehem and Hebron, where Jacob pitched his tent after Rachel's death, and where Reuben cohabited with Bilhah (Gen 35:21, 22). The JB renders it Migdal-eder. Because of its proximity to Bethlehem where David was born Micah (4:8) refers to it ("O tower of the flock," KJV, RSV, etc.) and to Ophel ("the stronghold," KJV), where David's palace stood in Jerusalem, as symbols of the royal house of David.

2. A town in the Negeb district of Judah (Josh 15:21), identified by some with el-'Adar, c. five m. S of Gaza on the right bank of the Wadi Ghazzeh. The LXX B, however, has *Ara*, suggesting that Arad (q.v.) is prob. the correct reading (Y. Aharoni, *The Land of the Bible* [1967], p. 105).

3. A Benjamite (1 Chron 8:15).

4. A Levite, descendant of Mushi, son of Merari (1 Chron 23:23; 24:30).

J. REA

EDES, EDOS. *See* IDDO.

EDICT. *See* DECREE.

EDIFICATION, EDIFY, EDIFYING (*οἰκοδομέω, to build*; *οἰκοδομή, the act of building*). The word is occasionally used in the literal sense of building (of tombs, Matt 23:29; of a house, Acts 7:47). More frequently it is used in the metaphorical sense of the building up in character, of a church (Matt 16:18) or of an individual (esp. in Paul's writings, e.g. in 2 Cor 10:8; 13:10; Eph 4:12, 16). Paul frequently used *οἰκοδομή*, but never in the literal sense. He describes the church as a building (1 Cor 3:9 and Eph 2:21), and talks of erecting it on the proper foundation (1 Cor 3:10, 12, 14). Paul says to the Corinthians that when they come together, each one having "a hymn, a lesson, a revelation, a tongue, or an interpretation," all is to be "done for edification" (14:26). He is anxious that Christians mature, that they grace Christ's cause, that they become well-founded in the faith.

The Puritans stressed edification, and influenced John Wesley (1703-91) in the matter. Wesley wrote a sermon on "The Means of Grace," in which he treated prayer, Scripture searching, and the Lord's Supper as the chief means of being built up in the faith. Elsewhere he added fasting and Christian conference (fellowship) to these three chief means of growth in grace.

The village of Dhana in Edom. This town has a plan closely approaching that of ancient towns excavated here. ©*Lev*

BIBLIOGRAPHY. J. K. Grider, *Taller My Soul: the Means of Christian Growth* (1964).

J. K. GRIDER

EDNA (from עדנה, *delight*). Wife of Raguel in Ecbatana and mother of Sarah who became the wife of Tobias (Tobit 7:2). Raguel brings the marriage scroll for the marriage of Tobias and Sarah (7:14), Edna prepares the marriage chamber and comforts Sarah (7:15, 16). She accepts Tobias as a son-in-law, her farewell to the departing couple is touching (10:12), and in turn she receives the blessing of Tobias (11:1). She is named Anna in the Vul. which also is the name of the wife of Tobit.

Masculine names (Adnah, Eden, Adna) occur from the same root (1 Chron 12:20; 2 Chron 17:14; 29:12; Ezra 10:30; Neh 12:15).

J. P. LEWIS

EDOM ē′ dəm, EDOMITES ē′ də mīts (אדום, *red*; LXX 'Εδώμ; אדומים). The designation "Edom" denoted either the name of Esau, commemorating the red vegetable soup which he received in exchange for his birthright (Gen 25:30), the land of his descendants (32:3; 36:20, 21, 30), or the Edomites collectively (Num 20:18, 20, 21; Amos 1:6, 11; Mal 1:4).

1. The territory of Edom. The land which was occupied by the Edomites was a rugged mountainous area, stretching from the Brook Zered S to the Gulf of Aqabah for nearly one hundred m., while to the E and W extending up to forty m. across the Wilderness of Edom. Although the terrain was inhospitable, there were several good cultivable areas (Num 20:17-19). Edomite territory generally has been divided into three areas, the first of which was the northern section embracing Bozrah and Punon (Feinan). It comprised a rough rectangle about fifteen m. wide and some seventy m. long, extending S from the Brook Zered (Wadi el-Ḥesa) which formed the boundary with Moab. This area ranged in elevation from about 5,000 ft. above sea level at Bozrah to nearly 5,700 feet near Teman (Tawilan), where the S limit was marked by the escarpment overlooking the Hismeh Valley. This quadrangle formed the fortified area of Edom in antiquity, being dotted with a series of strong points, particularly on the exposed E frontier. In Biblical times the King's Highway passed along the E plateau after ascending the Wadi Laban, and then passed S near to Tophel, Bozrah, and Dana until it descended into the Hismeh Valley. Sela, the capital of Edom, lay to the W of the King's Highway on the massive plateau of Umm el-Biyara, which towers 1,000 ft. above Petra (the Gr. form of Sela). The second principal area of Edom, the outlying district, comprised the region S of the Hismeh Valley as far as the Gulf of Aqabah, which was under Edomite control though not settled. Those portions of the Arabah involved were valuable for their iron and copper mines, and constituted an important source of wealth for the Edomites who worked them. In addition, trading routes connecting Mesopotamia and Egypt passed through the S extremity of this region, thus contributing further to the Edomite treasury. A third area of land, to the W of the Arabah, was occupied by nomadic tribes which were sometimes loosely associated with the Edomites (Gen 36:11, 12), but were never actually under firm Edomite control. It was through this area that the Israelites passed just prior to the conquest of Canaan.

2. Its history and population. Archeological investigations reveal that the land was occupied before the time of Esau, since from the 23rd to the 20th centuries B.C. there was a thriving civilization in the locality, after which the land remained uninhabited until the 13th cent. B.C., apart from bands of roving Bedouin. Whether the invasion of Chedorlaomer (Gen 14:1ff.) was responsible for the depopulation of the area or not is hard to say, but it is probable that Esau and his sons absorbed the original Horite settlers (14:6) when they came to Mount Seir (36:5-8). The Horites already had some tribal chiefs ruling the country (36:29, 30), and Esau took the daughter of one of these chiefs for a wife (36:2, 25). The descendants of Esau were also tribal chiefs (36:15-19, 40-43), and no doubt took over Horite functions in this respect (cf. Deut 2:12, 22).

Esau had already occupied Edom when Jacob returned from Haran (Gen 32:3; 36:6-8; Deut 2:4, 5), and the Edomites were well established in the country and living by a monarchic pattern prior to the Exodus period, having apparently abandoned the system of tribal chiefs. Unfortunately all inscrs. and written records of the Edomites have perished, and it is necessary to depend on Egyptian, Hebrew and Assyrian sources for information about them.

In this connection the mention of Edom and Seir occurs in the records of the Pharaohs Merneptah (c. 1225-1215 B.C.) and Rameses III (c. 1198-1167 B.C.) as being their tributaries, but caution has to be exercised in assessing this claim. Hebrew records (Gen 36:31-39; 1 Chron 1:43-51) indicate that the Edomites possessed kingship long in advance of the Israelites, thus further attesting to the antiquity of that particular social pattern in Edom. The Edomites were also mentioned in the 13th cent. B.C. Papyrus Anastasi VI of Egypt in connection with the passing of shepherd tribes from Edom to the lush pasturelands of the Nile delta and again in the Tell el-Armana letter No 256, dated about 1400 B.C., where Edom (*Udumu*) was described as one of the enemies of a Jordanian prince. In view of the constant OT emphasis on the closeness of racial relationship between Israel and Edom, it is probable that originally the Edomites came from Aram. However, at an early period they intermarried with the Canaanites (the "Hittites" of Gen 26:34) and prob. also with the native Horites of Seir (36:20-30), whom they absorbed (Deut 2:12), thus making Edom a composite entity.

Despite the discourtesy of being refused permission to travel through the country by the King's Highway, the Israelites were forbidden to hate their Edomite brothers (23:7, 8). In the time of Joshua the tribe of Judah was allocated territory reaching to the borders of Edom (Josh 15:1, 21) though not violating Edomite territory. During the time of the Conquest and Settlement there was no recorded contact between Israel and Edom. Two centuries later, Saul was in conflict with the Edomites (1 Sam 14:47), although some of them were in his service (1 Sam 21:7; 22:9, 18). It fell to David to subdue the country and place garrisons throughout the land (2 Sam 8:14; in v. 13 read *'ḏôm* for the incorrect *'ᵃrām*), a defeat which was made more decisive when Joab the Israelite commander, conducted a six-month campaign designed to eradicate all male Edomites (1 Kings 11:15, 16). However, some warriors escaped the slaughter, for a certain Hadad, a royal prince, fled to Egypt and was subsequently a source of annoyance to Solomon (11:14-22).

The subjugation of Edom marked an important stage in the economic growth of the kingdom under Solomon, for not merely did he secure control of the rich caravan trade by this means, but also made possible the exploitation of the copper and iron mines of the territory. Solomon also built a port at Ezion-Geber on the Gulf of Aqabah which served as the terminal point for his Red Sea trading vessels to Ophir and Arabia (9:26; 2 Chron 8:17). Archeological excavations show that, on a new site about two and a half m. W of Aqabah (Elath), there was constructed a copper and iron smeltery in the time of Solomon. Situated between the hill country of Sinai and Edom, it was ideally located for the purpose since it received the full force of the N winds howling down the Arabah rift-valley. The ore for the blast furnaces was obtained locally, and was prob. processed by slave labor.

In the time of Jehoshaphat (870/69-848 B.C.) Edom joined Ammon and Moab in an attack upon Judah (2 Chron 20:1), but the allies subsequently came to blows (20:22, 23). Jehoshaphat tried to use the port facilities at Ezion-Geber, which he apparently reconstructed after they had burned down in the preceding cent.; but his fleet was wrecked by the strong winds (1 Kings 22:48; 2 Chron 20:36, 37). At this period Edom was governed by a deputy who functioned as king (1 Kings 22:47). He was under the control of Judah, and joined the coalition between Israel and Judah in an attack on Mesha, king of Moab (2 Kings 3:4-27).

Edom rebelled in the time of Jehoram (848-841 B.C.), cutting off, sacking and occupying Ezion-Geber (8:21). Although Jehoram defeated the Edomites in battle he failed to subjugate them, and Edom became independent for some forty years. Amaziah (796-767 B.C.) invaded Edom, slew 10,000 warriors in the valley of Salt, and captured Sela their capital (14:7; 2 Chron 25:11, 12). Uzziah (767-740/39 B.C.) his successor completed the conquest and restored the port at Elath (2 Kings 14:22), but in 735 B.C. Edom regained its freedom from Judah, apparently by allying with Israel and Aram, and carried captives away from the southern kingdom (2 Chron 28:17; in 2 Kings 16:6, "Edom" should be read for "Aram"). Judah never recovered Edom, and Assyrian inscrs. show that in 732 B.C. Tiglath-pileser III compelled Kaush-malaku, king of Edom, to become his tributary, a state of affairs which lasted for a cent. with virtually no interruption.

The heavy tribute required of Edom diminished its prosperity considerably, resulting in a general decline of the kingdom and quiet acceptance of Babylonian suzerainty in 604 B.C. The Edomites allied with Nebuchadnezzar when he overthrew Jerusalem in 587 B.C., and were overjoyed at the destruction of their traditional foes (Ps 137:7; Lam 4:21, 22; Obad 10-16). Some Edomites subsequently occupied S Judah and made Hebron their capital, thus forming the Idumaea of the postexilic era. During the 5th cent. B.C. Edom proper came under Arab control, and by the 4th cent. B.C. had been overrun by the Nabataeans who entered the land from the S and E, making Petra their capital city. While some Edomites moved to Idumaea, others apparently remained and were absorbed by the Nabataean Arabs.

Known Idumaean history commenced with the Maccabean revolt, part of the military success of Judas Maccabeus comprising a victory over the Idumaeans in the Akrabattene in 164 B.C. (1 Macc 5:1-5; Jos. Antiq. XII, 8, 1). John Hyrcanus occupied all Idumaea about 120 B.C. and compelled its people to adopt Judaism (Jos. Antiq. XIII, ix, 1; XV, vii, 9). When the Romans took over Pal., the Edomites naturally fell under their jurisdiction, one result being that from Idumaea came Antipater, the father of Herod the Great, as governor of the country in 63 B.C. His son founded in 37 B.C. the final dynasty of Palestinian rulers, and after the destruction of Jerusalem in A.D. 70 the Idumaeans disappeared from history, thus ending the varied career of the Edomites. Ironically, the descendants of those who had exulted over the fall of Jerusalem in 587 B.C. were among its staunchest defenders against Rome in A.D. 66-70.

3. Edom in the OT. The traditional antagonism between Edom and Israel had its roots in the relations between Esau, identified with Edom, and Jacob, representing Israel (Gen 36:1). Perhaps there is a play on words in the description of Isaac as "smooth" (*hālāq*) and Esau as "hairy" (*sā'îr*), since Mount Halak, standing on the S border of Israel, faced the Edomite boundary of Seir (Josh 11:17; 12:7), but this may be entirely accidental. The bitter hatred of Edom for the Israelites was severely censured by almost all the prophets of Judah. Amos condemned them for their brutal practices in war, and mentioned an otherwise unrecorded border conflict (Amos 2:1) in which the Moabites burned the bones of an Edomite king to powder, thus inflicting the greatest possible personal insult upon a corpse. The whole of Obadiah was given over to a bitter denunciation of Edom and a prediction of its destruction. The principal point at issue in this prophecy was the sense of betrayal felt by the Judaeans when blood relatives, albeit hereditary enemies, turned upon them in the time of crisis which saw the fall of Jerusalem in 587 B.C., and aided the common enemy.

This tragic occurrence was perpetuated by the psalmist (Ps 137:7), who prayed for retribution for such a dastardly act. A prophetic oracle in Jeremiah (Jer 49:7-22) reflected much the same sentiments as Obadiah in predicting the desolation of Edom, a theme which also occured in Isaiah 11:14; 34:5-17 and Ezekiel 35:1-15. The Book of Malachi (Mal 1:2-4) was particularly emphatic as to the divine choice of Jacob and the uncompromising rejection of Esau as a medium of revelation. On the other hand, Zephaniah and Zechariah did not include Edom among those people who were to be punished by destruction, and in the Torah provision was made for the admission of Edomites into the community of Israel (Deut 23:7, 8). If the characters in the Book of Job, which had as its setting a locale in the Arabian desert E of Pal., were in fact Edomites, the author of this work had clearly risen far above purely national sentiments in making them the vehicles of divine revelation in the vital area of human experience involving suffering. Nevertheless, of all the neighbors of Israel, Edom, as a nation, was the only one who was not extended any promise of mercy from God.

BIBLIOGRAPHY. F. Buhl, *Geschichte der Edomiter* (1893); N. Glueck, AASOR (1935), XV, 18, 19; ibid. *The Other Side of the Jordan* (1940), 114-134; D. Baly, *The Geography of the Bible* (1958).

R. K. HARRISON

EDOS ē' dŏs (LXX B, Ἠδός, LXX A, Ἠδαΐς). KJV EDES (1 Esd 9:35). One of the sons of Nebo who had married a foreign wife. He was called JADDAI in Ezra 10:43.

EDREI ĕd' re ī (אדרעי, *strong*? [meaning uncertain]). Town name. 1. A residence city of Og, king of Bashan (Deut 1:4; 3:10; Josh 12:4; 13:12). Built on a bluff overlooking a southern fork of the Yarmuk River, along the S boundary of Bashan (q.v.) near the eastern desert. Here Og could watch for invaders from the S or from the E. Moses defeated Og in a pitched battle outside of Edrei, which was then destroyed (Num 21:33-35; Deut 3:1-6). The ruins were included in the allotment to the Machir clan of the tribe of Manasseh (Josh 13:31). Edrei is identified with modern Der'a, a town of 5,000 in southern Syria, c. sixty m. S of Damascus and thirty m. E of the Jordan. The site has ruins going back to Early Bronze times as well as a remarkable subterranean city of numerous streets, shops, rooms, and cisterns, prob. from the Hel. or Rom. period, in underlying caves in the basaltic rock (*Unger's Bible Dict.*, p. 287; HGHL, p. 576).

2. A fortified city allotted to Naphtali, near

The tombs near the entrance to the Siq at Petra, in Edom. ©*Lev*

Kedesh in Upper Galilee (Josh 19:37), possibly modern Tell Khureibeh. It is prob. the *i-t-r-‘*, #91 in the campaign list of Thutmose III at Karnak (ANET, 242; Y. Aharoni, *The Land of the Bible* [1967], 150).

J. REA

EDUCATION IN BIBLICAL TIMES. The word for education (חניך) in modern Heb. is derived from the root חנך, *to train* which is used in late Biblical Heb. "Train up a child in the way he should go . . ." (Prov 22:6). Other verbs are used to denote "training," "instructing" and "learning." Teaching and learning often took the form of repetition שנה. למד is used of the training of animals, the bullock in particular (Jer 2:24) but also of Israel (Judg 3:2; Hos 10:11). יסר is used of giving instruction (2 Chron 35:3; Prov 1:2; Isa 28:26). Derived from תורה, which is usually tr. "law" (but in fact has the wider meaning of "instruction"), is the verb ירה meaning "to instruct" (1 Sam 12:23). The object of knowledge is described as "insight" (בינה) (Prov 2:3; 9:10), as well as תורה. Derived from the roots ירה and למד, already mentioned above are two words for "teachers," מורים and מלמדים (5:13). Teachers are also described as "the wise" חכמים (Prov 13:14; 15:7) which is in Gr. σοφοι. They had "pupils" (=sons) בנים (1 Chron 25:8; Prov 2:1; et al.). Pupils were also described as "disciples" למודים (Isa 8:16; 50:4).

By NT times teachers were known as רב, or רבי or רבא "Rabbi" or מר "Master," "rabbi" is tr. as διδάσκαλος (John 1:38; 20:16) and "Master" as Κύριος. Jesus is described as "teacher" (διδάσκαλος) about fifty times in the gospels which on many occasions indicated that Jesus taught (διδάσκειν). He taught the multitudes (Mark 2:13); He taught in the synagogue (1:21). He also taught His disciples (μαθηταὶ) (Matt 5:1, 2, etc.). Mention of Jesus' disciples occurs over 200 times in the gospels. What Jesus taught is described as "doctrine" (διδαχή) (John 7:16). Having been taught by Jesus, His disciples were told to teach others also, making them disciples (Matt 28:19, 20).

I. Introduction
II. Jewish education in Old Testament times
  A. Origin and aims
  B. Development
  C. Characteristics
  D. The synagogue
    1. Origin and development
    2. Function
  E. Schools and academies
  F. Personnel
    1. God
    2. The family
    3. The place of Moses
    4. The priests
    5. The king
    6. The prophets
    7. The sages
  G. The place and use of the law
    1. Oral law
    2. Written law
  H. Education symbols, principles, and methods
  I. The Qumran sect
  J. The diaspora
  K. Conclusion and criticism
III. Hellenistic education
  A. Origin, development and aims
  B. Characteristics
  C. Influence on Jewish education
  D. Conclusion
IV. The education of Jesus
V. The education of the apostles
  A. The Twelve
  B. Paul
VI. Education in the Church in holiness and maturity

I. INTRODUCTION

The purpose of this study limits investigation to the development of education in Israel and the Early Church. But it will be necessary to say a few words about the background out of which Israel's educational ideals developed. Educational systems had evolved as early as the 3rd millennium B.C. There are a number of school texts dating from about 2,500 B.C. From these documents we learn of numerous schools for scribes in ancient Sumer. In these schools literary works were copied and studied. The study was connected with the training for the needs of the Temple, palace courts and the administration of the empire. Education of this kind was voluntary and costly, and pupils were drawn from the upper class. Subjects studied were botany, zoology, geology, geography, mathematics, languages and other cultural studies. The schools were staffed by a professor and his assistants who gave regular classroom tuition. A teacher was referred to as "father" and he referred to his pupils as "sons."

The profession of the scribes was highly regarded also in ancient Egypt. Other professions are compared unfavorably with it. Such was the prestige of this profession that a severe discipline and single-minded study could be required of those who intended to enter it. The scribal school was attached to the Temple and was called the "House of Life." Study was divided into two sections, elementary education and higher education. The elementary education consisted of the learning of writing (NB calligraphy), the study of ancient lit. and the copying of these texts. At the end of the elementary education, students transferred either to the government administration or to the priesthood. If they transferred to the government administration they received a higher education in the duties of office, composition, geography, and natural science. If to the priesthood their study was in theology and medicine.

Three points of contact or similarity may be mentioned here.

First, observe the connection of education with the Tabernacle (Temple). At an early age, Samuel was dedicated to God's service and was brought to the Tabernacle where he ministered to the Lord and was educated by Eli the priest. Samuel was not a Levite nor did he belong to the priestly class. The incident raises the question as to whether there was a school attached to the sanctuary, even in those early days. Many OT scholars now claim that around the cultic shrines in Israel there were schools of priests, who were responsible for the transmission of the law, both oral and written. If such was the case, it is a parallel situation to what took place in Egypt and the ancient Near E.

Second, notice the class of men known as scribes in Israel. They are to be compared with the scribes of Egypt and the ancient Near E, where such officials played an important part in the administration of the nation. They were friends, philosophers and guides to the kings and leaders of the nation of their time. In Israel there is little evidence for the existence of a scribal class until the exilic and post-exilic period of history. Prior to this, the stage had been dominated by such figures as Moses, the judges, the kings, the prophets and the priests. It may be that the scribal functions were carried out by some of these officials. Indeed, it has been suggested that Moses learned a great deal about the scribal activities in the course of his education in Egypt. It is not until the time of the Exile that the scribes come to the fore in Israel. Ezra is described as a scribe "skilled in the law of Moses which the LORD God of Israel had given" (Ezra 7:6). This description seems to assume that the institution of scribes had been in existence for some time. This is true in a sense because although there does not seem to have been a special class of scribes, there were those who carried out secretarial functions such as Seraiah mentioned (2 Sam 8:17; cf. 2 Chron 24:11; 26:11). (For mention of certain other scribes see also 1 Chron 24:6; 27:32; 2 Chron 34:13 and Jer 36:26.) These scribes apparently carried out secretarial functions in the king's court and in the administration of the nation. Some of the scribes also were occupied in the transmission of the law (Jer 8:8). Initially it is possible that the priests (who were Levites) combined scribal functions with their teaching duties. The later priesthood, however, developed in a different direction. The upper class became involved in politics, and other priests and Levites were involved in the intricacies of Temple worship. Biblical scholarship and exposition passed over into the hands of a special class of scribes. Ezra the scribe who was a priest marks the development of this new class (Ezra 7:6, 11; Neh 8:4, 9, 13). From the time of Ezra onward, the scribes were a special class of Biblical scholars, exegetes, official teachers and spiritual leaders.

Third, notice contact with the background of the ancient world in the reference to teachers as "father" and the pupil as "my son" (Prov 2:1; etc.). It is probable that the scribes were the "wise" of Proverbs who collated the Wisdom Lit. of the OT and became the educators of Israel.

II. Jewish education in Old Testament times

The word "Jewish" is used in an ideological or theological sense to indicate those who are Jews by religion. Consequently, the discussion at this point excludes the contribution of the early Heb. Christians, which is found in the NT.

A. Origin and aims. Educational ideas and practice begin with the birth of the nation. OT scholarship has long recognized a double origin for Israel: the first, beginning with the call of Abraham and the second, with Moses and the Exodus. The Israelites were called to understand themselves as the people of God and to come to know how they may serve the Lord who had called them. Thus the primary aim of all the educational activity was religious (Gen 18:19). The aim was to train the young to know and serve the Lord (Deut 6:7; Prov 1:7) so that throughout their life they would not depart from this way (Prov 22:6). Thus religious education centered its attention on the Torah and aimed at educating the Jews for living. It was not merely an education to make a living but was concerned with persons and character forming. Knowing was not divorced from being and doing, and good character was seen to result from a right relationship with God through the study of the Torah. The primacy of the Torah embraced the whole of life from the cradle to the grave. One was never too old or too young to learn. It embraced every aspect of life also. From the time of Ezra onward, the life of the Jews was Torah-centric. They became known as "the people of the Book." It was this that separated them from all other people.

It may be said that the Jewish aims in education were exclusively religious, neglecting cultural development. In later Judaism, the preoccupation with the Torah developed into a legalistic system of hair splitting which led to absurdities, and in many instances to the hypocritical self-righteousness of the Jews as they often appear on the pages of the NT. In spite of this narrowness, Jewish educational aims succeeded where the systems of Sparta, Athens and Rome failed. These systems failed because of faulty aims. The system of Sparta may be said to have aimed at the obliteration of the individual in the service of the state. The aim in Athens may be said to be the training of the individual in the service of culture. In Rome, the training of the individual was in the service of the state. The aim in Israel was the

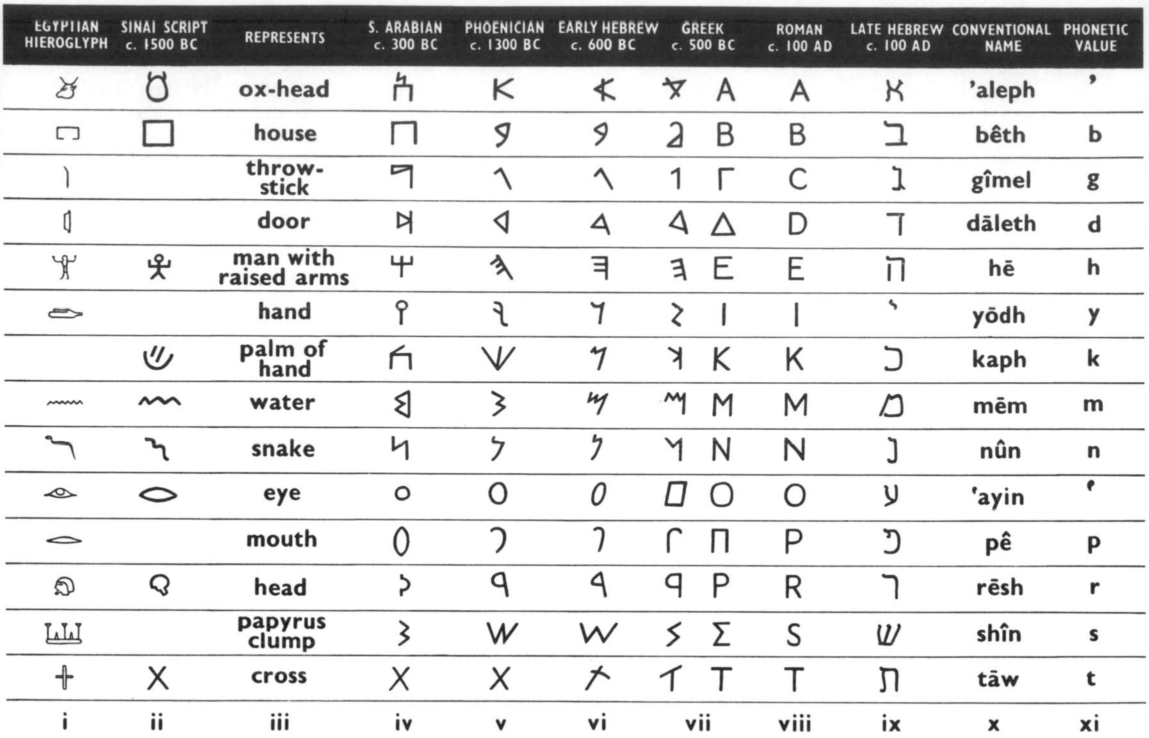

EGYPTIAN HIEROGLYPH	SINAI SCRIPT c. 1500 BC	REPRESENTS	S. ARABIAN c. 300 BC	PHOENICIAN c. 1300 BC	EARLY HEBREW c. 600 BC	GREEK c. 500 BC	ROMAN c. 100 AD	LATE HEBREW c. 100 AD	CONVENTIONAL NAME	PHONETIC VALUE
		ox-head	𐩱	𐤀	𐤀	A	A	א	'aleph	'
		house	𐩨	𐤁	𐤁	B	B	ב	bêth	b
		throw-stick	𐩴	𐤂	𐤂	Γ	C	ג	gîmel	g
		door	𐩵	𐤃	𐤃	Δ	D	ד	dāleth	d
		man with raised arms	𐩠	𐤄	𐤄	E	E	ה	hē	h
		hand	𐩺	𐤉	𐤉	I	I	י	yōdh	y
		palm of hand	𐩫	𐤊	𐤊	K	K	כ	kaph	k
		water	𐩣	𐤌	𐤌	M	M	מ	mēm	m
		snake	𐩬	𐤍	𐤍	N	N	נ	nûn	n
		eye	𐩲	𐤏	𐤏	O	O	ע	'ayin	'
		mouth	𐩰	𐤐	𐤐	Π	P	פ	pê	p
		head	𐩧	𐤓	𐤓	P	R	ר	rēsh	r
		papyrus clump	𐩪	𐤔	𐤔	Σ	S	ש	shîn	s
		cross	𐩩	𐤕	𐤕	T	T	ת	tāw	t
i	ii	iii	iv	v	vi	vii	viii	ix	x	xi

Table showing development of writing and alphabet from pictographic scripts of Egypt and Sinai. The S. Arabian script (col. 4) preserves the formal style. The earlier Phoenician (Exodus period; col. 5) and the Hebrew (col. 6) are cursive forms.

training of the individual in the service of God. The aim in Rome, Sparta and Athens failed at a moral level. Their systems did not contain the faith capable of challenging indifference and superficiality. Therefore, they lost their sense of direction and failed. It has been said "the Graeco-Roman world was decaying and dying from the dearth of true educational ideals" (W. M. Ramsey, *The Education of Christ*, p. 66). Jewish education never lost its sense of direction. Its intention was not education in academic and technical knowledge, but education in holiness (Lev 19:2). Though the people of Israel often forgot the ideals, there were always priests, prophets, scribes, sages, rabbis and teachers to remind them. God and not man was the center; righteousness, not self-interest was the aim (Exod 19:6).

B. Development. The Jewish educational system was the result of a long and gradual development from a simple origin to a complex system as it appears in NT times. Throughout the OT period there was nothing like a state educational system. Generally speaking, the boys were taught the necessary skills of agriculture by their fathers, and the girls were taught domestic skills by their mothers. But, as education in Israel meant education in living and serving God, attention must be drawn to the necessity of reading and understanding the law; hence the question of literacy in OT times. Throughout the ancient Near E, as early as the beginning of the 3rd millennium, writing was a sign of civilization. In the 2nd millennium alphabets were developed with a resulting increase of literacy. As yet, few documents from the preexilic period have been found in Pal., but many thousands have been discovered in neighboring territories. It is reasonable to assume that its proximity to other cultural centers enabled Israel to share the art of writing throughout all the periods covered by the OT. Throughout the whole of the OT period there were individuals in Israel who could read and write. Moses read the decalogue (Exod 24:12; cf. 17:14; 34:27; Num 24:4; Deut 30:10; Josh 8:31). Apparently he was helped by literate officials (Num 11:16). During the wandering in the wilderness, the priests wrote down curses (5:23). Samuel wrote down the rights and duties of kingship (1 Sam 10:25). David wrote letters to Joab

(2 Sam 11:14). Solomon wrote to Hiram, king of Tyre (2 Chron 2:1-10). Scribes recorded lists of persons (1 Chron 24:6). The prophet Isaiah wrote (Isa 8:1); Jeremiah dictated his teaching to his secretary Baruch (Jer 36:27). It is impossible to say what proportion of the population was taught to read and write. E. W. Heaton suggests that only a small proportion of the population would have been literate. Isaiah distinguishes the literate and illiterate (Isa 29:12), and he mentions a child's writing; "The remnant of the trees of his forest will be so few that a child can write them down" (10:19). Isaiah was in close touch with the aristocratic circle of the court and his casual reference cannot be used as the basis for a sweeping generalization. Far more significant of the general state of affairs is the fact that when an Israelite borrowed money he did not write an I.O.U., but gave a garment in pledge (Deut 24:13). The garment had no security value and prob. was used as a symbol of indebtedness by the illiterate.

It is quite certain that some boys were taught to read and write and it is possible that there is still some evidence of their writing exercises. The rough scribbling known as the Gezer Calendar has been plausibly interpreted as a student's effort, and in 1938 someone noticed the first five letters of the Heb. alphabet scratched in their conventional order on the vertical face of a step of the royal palace at Lachish. This inscr. has been dated in the early part of the 8th cent. B.C. It has been suggested that it was written by a boy who was just learning his alphabet. G. R. Driver has suggested that Isaiah 28:9, 10 "precept upon precept, line upon line" is a reference to a child's spelling lesson. It also has been suggested that the Israelite teacher had his boys repeat, in turn, the letters of the alphabet, a suggestion which is perhaps confirmed by the word "alphabet" itself.

It seems likely that increasing numbers of Israelites became literate as time passed. Those who could not write, but needed to transact official business simply made their mark. This was done by placing one of the letters of the alphabet at the foot of the script (Job 31:35). Another method of signing a document was to seal it. Such evidence, as we have, would suggest that prior to the monarchy and during the monarchy, education of a formal nature was only for the few. Such teaching was done in Heb., in the homes by the parents. In the exilic and postexilic periods, education expanded its scope to many more individuals and was carried out in Aram. as well as Heb. Such teaching continued to be done in the home, but also in schools and by specialized individuals such as the scribes. With the coming of the Greeks in the 4th cent. B.C., the Gr. language also was used in Israelite education. Thus, we notice a development in Israelite education from teaching in the home to a developed school system. It should be noted that from the first, nurses or guardians or teachers *in loco parentis* were employed among the higher classes (see Ruth 4:16; 2 Sam 4:4; 2 Kings 10:5; Isa 49:23).

W. F. Albright is of the opinion that there is evidence of literacy, even among the peasants by the 10th cent. B.C., i.e. during the early monarchy; thus it has been suggested that though literacy was not universal (Isa 29:11) it was widespread (see Deut 6:9; 17:18, 19; 27:2-8; Josh 18:4, 8, 9; Judg 8:14; Isa 10:19). Reference to the Siloam inscr., Lachish letters, Elephantine papyri show widespread writing of daily affairs. Further, the development of the cursive script indicates a broadening use by the masses. (1 Macc 1:56 indicates that copies of the Torah were in houses, and the Talmudic lit. and notes of students show a high degree of literacy in the days of the second commonwealth.)

With the development of literacy a change in the aims of education can be detected. The fundamental aim in Israelite education was religious, but one can distinguish two separate parts of this aim—(a) the transmission of a historical heritage. Israelites were requested to teach their history (Exod 12:26, 27; 13:7, 8, 14; Josh 4:21ff.). They were required to remember to teach the ordinances (Deut 4:9, 10; 6:20, 21; 7:17-19; 32:7). The aim was to transmit an ethical heritage (Gen 18:19—cf. Exod 20:1-17). Of course, ethical injunctions were aimed to make a good and just society (Lev 19:2ff.). Social justice is linked with the holiness of God (Amos 2:6, 7). The fear of the Lord is to lead to a good life (Prov 9:10). In fact wisdom is equated with life itself (8:35). In the Wisdom Lit. the emphasis shifts to instruction in ethical conduct of life. Here the instruction in daily existence finds many parallels in the lit. of the ancient Near E. There is instruction, for example, concerning the sex life (5:3-21). Again and again the stress is laid on the need for instruction for the good life. This is the purpose of education, to instruct in righteousness (1:2-4). The need for the continuity of this instruction continues life long (1:5).

C. Characteristics. The most important characteristic of Jewish education was the whole religious ethos and intention of the system. Consequently, the Jewish education lacked scientific character, in fact it was pre-scientific. We find nothing of physics, chemistry, biology, psychology and the other natural sciences. But the Hebrews knew many practical trades and skills, building, mining, metallurgy, wood and stone work (Exod 35:30ff.). The point of significance is this—there were no schools to teach these trades. The trades were learned in apprenticeships. As far as we know, there were no schools of music, architecture, sculpture, painting, arts or the theater, etc. The place that music plays in the worship in Israel

A class in a synagogue school. *K.C. ©F.C.*

suggests that at least this art must have been developed by systematic instruction, but there is no evidence for this. Most of the cultural arts here mentioned were associated with the heathen religions and were developed in Gr. and Rom. culture. Just as the Jewish educational system ignored the arts, so it ignored also the development of philosophy. Philosophic origins presuppose a culture alien to that of Israel. Philosophy originated in a humanistic society which believed in the power of man's intellect. Such a presupposition is alien to the Jewish dependence on divine revelation. The whole of Israel's religion, worship and educational practice was based on the firm belief that God had revealed Himself to Moses and to the prophets. It was this historical revelation that was to be communicated in the educational process.

D. Synagogue. 1. *Origin and development.* There is no account of the origin of the synagogue in the OT, the Apoc. or the NT. In spite of this lack of information, most scholars feel sure that the synagogue developed as an institution during the Exile in Babylon. In the OT, only in Psalm 74:8 is the Heb. word for "synagogue" (מוֹעֵד) used, though of course the LXX uses the Gr. word *συναγωγή* on many occasions to refer to the assembly of Israel. These references should not be understood of the synagogue as an institution in Israel. *Συναγωγή* is used fifty-six times in the NT.

Although the origin of the synagogue is uncertain, its significance could not be clearer. Scholars have suggested that the importance of the synagogue for Judaism cannot be overestimated. It was this institution that gave Judaism its character. Prior to the Exile worship in Israel had been centered on the Temple and on the sacrificial cultus. With the destruction of the Temple this focal point was removed. For the exiles even worship at Jerusalem was an impossibility. It seems that the synagogue arose as a place for instruction in the Scriptures and prayer. There are scholars who consider that the Exile does not mark the origin of the synagogue but a modification in its functions, worship becoming from then on the principal, though far from the only, purpose, with administrative functions falling into the background. Other scholars have suggested that Ezekiel 14:1, "Then came certain of the elders of Israel to me, and sat before me" (cf. 20:1) provides a probable basis for the origin of the synagogue. Levertoff ("Synagogue" in ISBE) simply asserts "It must have come into being during the Babylonian exile." After A.D. 70, Ezekiel 11:16, "Yet will I be to them as a little sanctuary" (KJV) was interpreted to mean that in the worldwide diaspora, Israel would have a synagogue in miniature to replace the lost Temple. One may conclude that from a shadowy origin the synagogue developed into the characteristic institution in Judaism by NT times.

2. *Function.* In every place in the ancient world where there was a community of Jews, there was a synagogue. In the synagogue there was no altar. The reading of the Torah and prayer took the place of sacrifice. The synagogue became the center of a new social and religious life. The Temple had centered God's presence in one place. Now there were synagogues throughout the Diaspora wherever ten adult male Jews were found, bringing God's presence to the people wherever they were.

Worship, education and the government of the community, were the purposes which the synagogue fulfilled. The purposes of worship and education often were carried forward in one activity, because in the synagogue worship took on the character of instruction. Peritz has shown that the primary function of the synagogue assemblies was the popular instruction in the law (*Encyclopaedia Biblica*, 4 Vols. 1899-1903).

According to the Mishnah (*Megillah* 4:3), the service of the synagogue consisted of five parts: (a) the Shema was read, i.e. Deuteronomy 6:4-9; 11:13-21; Number 15:37-41; (b) the synagogue prayers were recited, e.g. the eighteen benedictions, though this form of prayers may be later than the NT period. At the heart of these prayers is the theme of the restoration of Israel to the land of the fathers and return of the glory of God to the Temple, rebuilt in Jerusalem; (c) the reading of the law; (d) the reading from the prophets; (e) the benediction. Because many people could not understand Heb., a paraphrase of the lessons was given in Aram. and an exposition and exhortation drawn from it. This part of the service came after the reading in Heb. and preceded the benediction. It has been suggested that this is a later practice. Nehemiah (8:8) wrote "and they read from the book, from the law of God, clearly; and they gave the sense, so that the people understood the reading." This seems to refer to this practice. The synagogue provided a mass system of adult education in which the Torah was studied weekly. With the destruction of the Temple in the 6th cent. B.C., the synagogue came into prominence and it became the most enduring and widespread institution in Israel after the Exile. Under its influence, all Jews became students of the law and without the synagogue the Jews would have perished.

E. Schools and academies. The text of the OT suggests that the prophets were responsible for the first schools in Israel. The prophets' educational role is quite plain from the beginning. They look back to Moses as their founding figure, as the prophet par excellence (Deut 34:10). He embodied the prophetic ideal (Deut 18:15ff.), "The Lord your God will raise up for you a prophet like me (i.e., Moses) from among you, from your brethren—him you shall heed." The prophets were considered teachers of Israel as a whole. By the time of the beginning of the Israelite kingdom, there was a prophetic profession. Bands or companies of prophets (see 1 Sam 10:5, 10; 19:20) is a description of the "band of prophets." The "sons of the prophets" were the disciples who were taught by the prophets. Later on there is clear evidence of the prophets teaching their disciples (see 1 Kings 19:16; 2 Kings 2:3ff; 4:38; Isa 8:16). The prophets transmitted knowledge to their disciples (2 Kings 4:38-41). An aspect of the knowledge that was transmitted concerned medical science (cf. the practice in Egypt where theology and medicine were combined). As may be expected from a tradition that had its roots in a Mosaic prototype, the teaching of the prophets centered on the Torah, the law, taking into account the question of a relevant interpretation for the times in which they lived.

The development of schools in the more formal sense is related to the growth of the synagogue. If there is some uncertainty as to the time of the origin of the synagogue, the same is true of the origin of the school system in Israel. It does not seem likely that the school system was in operation in the time of the Exile. More likely is the suggestion that the development took place under Hel. influence, therefore in the 4th cent. B.C. or later. During the second commonwealth, literacy was widespread, books of the law being found in many houses (see 1 Macc 1:56f.). Rabbinic lit. attributes a compulsory school system to the Pharisees during the 1st cent. B.C. The Pharisees were the popular party c. 76-67 B.C. Simon ben Shetach (75 B.C.) taught people systematically. He decreed that children should attend elementary school (בת הספר) the "house of the book." The Book, of course, was the Torah, with the explanation and oral law.

The first elementary school was prob. in Jerusalem with the institution spreading to the urban centers at a later time. Joseph ben Gamala (c. A.D. 65) tried to make elementary education universal and compulsory by endeavoring to make provision for teachers in all provinces and allowing children to enter the school at the age of six or seven. Instruction was given in reading, and the Torah was studied both in its written and oral form. The curriculum in the elementary school was basically the Bible—the OT and the Apoc. The Pseudep. was not part of the formal education in school, though it had a widespread circulation. Scientific ideas were embedded incidentally in the OT—this is true also of political ideas. The OT was studied in Heb., except for a few passages in Aram., notably in Ezra and Daniel. Some apocryphal books were in Gr., but Heb. continued as the language for scholarly study. Popular readings were written down in Aram., the Targums and in Egypt, Asia Minor and Greece. Greek trs. became necessary and consequently the LXX was published to meet this need. In the elementary schools one would expect to have found study in Heb., Aram. and Gr., though the emphasis on the different languages would have differed from place to place. In the Jewish Diaspora there was more emphasis on the study of the Gr. language and hence more contact with Gr. culture. The difference between Palestinian Judaism and the Judaism of the Diaspora must not be overemphasized. Elementary education concluded about the age of fifteen, and promising students could then go on to secondary school. By NT times there was a strong attempt to make elementary education universal for all Jews wherever they were.

Academies of the rabbis were the secondary schools for promising students. The academy was called the "House of Study" (בת המדרש). It seems probable that the elementary schools studied the OT and the oral law, the Mishnah. In the secondary schools the rabbis conducted theological discussions, and these discussions now have been written down and constitute the Talmud. Each house of study was conducted by a great Pharisaic teacher (cf. Hillel and Shamai). These academies had more sanctity even than the synagogue (*Megillah* 26b-27a). Under the leadership of the rabbi, students discussed the interpretation of the Torah and its application. These discussions became the basis of normative Judaism. Paul was educated in the academy of the Pharisee Gamaliel, who was the grandson of Hillel and was prob. the leading teacher of the time. The first mention of "the House of Study" is in Ecclesiasticus 51:23. A mention of the men of the great assembly or the Great Synagogue in the Mishnah is prob. also a reference to the academies.

Under the wing of the synagogue, elementary and secondary schools grew up. The elementary school normally operated in or near the synagogue building, and the rule of the synagogue was normally the teacher's. The secondary school or the academy normally operated apart from the synagogue in the Temple precincts or in the teacher's own house. Through the influence of these three institutions, the synagogue, the elementary school and the academy, all Jews became students of the law and these institutions more than anything else made the Jews the people of the Book.

F. Personnel. 1. *God.* In the ancient world there was no such thing as a "secular culture." God or gods were presupposed in Gr. and Rom. civilization just as much as in the Heb. civilization. Nevertheless, there were important differences between the Hebraic approach to knowledge and the Graeco-Roman approach. The Hebrews believed that all truth came from God the Creator, Judge and Redeemer who revealed to man the knowledge necessary for his own welfare. Man's welfare was thought to be dependent on a satisfactory relationship to God. For the Greeks and Romans, man's mind had the potential power for the discovery of truth. Therefore, they stressed the development of reason, and this led to the study of science and philosophy. The Heb. approach to education arose from their understanding of revelation. If man was to have knowledge, he was to have it only because God had revealed Himself to man. Consequently, God was the primary educating figure in Israel. He is called "the Teacher" (Isa 30:20ff.), and as such the prophet considers that people should consult Him for knowledge rather than idols or the dead (see Isa 8:19). As the Teacher, He calls on His people to listen to Him, "Give ear, O my people, to my teaching; incline your ears to the words of my mouth!" (Ps 78:1ff.).

As *the* Teacher it is considered impertinent to ask who has taught God; "Will any teach God knowledge, seeing that he judges those that are on high?" (Job 21:22ff.). "Who has directed the Spirit of the LORD or as his counselor has instructed him? Whom did he consult for his enlightenment, and who taught him the path of justice, and taught him knowledge and showed him the way of understanding?" (Isa 40:13ff.). The presupposed answer to these questions is "no one," and this is meant to be self-evident. The content of this instruction given by the Lord is the Torah. Teaching the Torah also includes telling "to the coming generation the glorious deeds of the LORD, and his might, and the wonders which he has wrought" (Ps 78:4). The psalmist asks, "Make me understand the way of thy precepts, and I will meditate on thy wondrous works" (Ps 119:27). The teaching of the Torah and God's activity in history are inseparably linked together.

The method God used in teaching His people was a form of discipline (Deut 8:3, 5). The essence of what he taught was the Torah (Job 22:22; Ps 94:12; 119:26ff.). The future hope was that the people would be taught by God . . . "All your sons shall be taught by the LORD" (Isa 54:13). (See also Jer 31:31ff. where the hope of the new covenant was that all would know the LORD and be taught by Him.) The Torah was not taught directly by God to man. He communicated the Torah through men, through Moses, through priests, through prophets, through the Servant. The Lord remained the prototype of the teacher, but the law was communicated to Israel through Moses (Deut 4:1, 5). Through Moses, Israel is commanded to educate the coming generations (Deut 4:9ff.) "Only take heed, and keep your soul diligently, lest you forget the things which your eyes have seen, and lest they depart from your heart all the days of your life; make them known to your children and your children's children—how on the day that you stood before the LORD your God at Horeb, the LORD said to me, 'Gather the people to me that I may let them hear my words, so that they may learn to fear me all the days that they live upon the earth, and that they may teach their children so'." While God remained the source of knowledge and revelation, and the prototype of teacher in Israel, He commanded others to carry out the teaching and communicated knowledge through them. Not only did He command but He also inspired men to teach (Exod 35:31-35). When false prophets declared their message, they were upbraided because God had not revealed knowledge to them. He had not commanded them; He had not inspired them; therefore no heed was to be paid to their teaching (see Jer 14:14; Hab 2:18ff.).

2. *The family.* The OT depicts a clear, high regard for children in Israel. Children were regarded as the most precious gift of the Lord (Job 5:25; Pss 127:3; 128:3, 4). Happiness could not be understood without children (see Zech 8:5). The Lord Himself was regarded as the prototype of the loving father (Ps 103:13), and Israel was his son (Hos 11:1). It is natural that care was taken in bringing up children. Training began at an early age (Isa 28:9). Prior to the Exile, with few exceptions, children were trained in the home by the parents. Exhortations to teach were intended for families. Later they were anachronistically interpreted as an exhortation concerning formal education (Gen 18:19; Deut 11:19; Prov 22:6). The primary importance of the family was never forgotten in Israel's educational system. The family never gave up its responsibility. The parents' responsibility to teach the children provided the preliminary requirements such as literacy. But the system, whether domestic, elementary or rabbinic, was always devoted to the elaboration of duty toward God, i.e. the elaboration of the law. The aim was the perfect application of the law. It was Abraham's duty to instruct his whole household (Gen 18:19). The duty of every father was to instruct his children (Exod 10:2; 12:26, 27). The essence of what was taught

A Jewish Scribe teaching his son in the home. ©M.P.S.

was summed up in the Shema (Deut 6:4-9) which was to be taught to the children. The importance of this transmission is indicated in Psalm 78:3-6; and Proverbs 4:3, 4. It would seem that this kind of education began as soon as the child could speak, and one may perhaps describe the nature of the instruction as the culture of memory. The place of the development of memory in the educational system of Israel is of primary importance. The purpose of the instruction was that the children may grow up to know and remember, and consequently obey, the law.

In the family situation, children were trained in their everyday duties (1 Sam 16:11; 2 Kings 4:18), and artistic training was given in some cases, at least (Judg 21:21; 1 Sam 16:15-18; Ps 137; Lam 5:14). Girls learned household crafts presumably from their mothers (Exod 35:25, 26; 2 Sam 13:8). During the second commonwealth, the schools were intended only for boys. Girls learned their household skills at home (Prov 31:13-31). If there were no sons girls did the work of the sons (Gen 29:6; Exod 2:16). Some women received a relatively good education and consequently became leaders (Judges 4:4ff.; 2 Kings 22:14-20). In Proverbs mothers appear to be of equal importance as fathers as teachers (Prov 1:8; 6:20). Women were among the חכמים, "the wise," the "teachers" of the Wisdom Lit. Proverbs 31:1 indicates that Lemuel, the king of Massa, was taught by his mother. Among the higher classes, evidently nurses (guardians or teachers) were used *in loco parentis* (Ruth 4:16; 2 Sam 4:4; 2 Kings 10:5; Isa 49:23). The instance of Samuel's education by Eli should be noted, but this may be an exception for the period. The rule in ancient Israel was education by the family, by the father, to some extent by the mother, though we have noted exceptions to this rule.

3. *The place of Moses.* In Judaism, there was no more prominent teaching figure than Moses. In fact, Moses was the ideal of each class of Israelite leader or teacher. His importance arises from his relationship to the law. The Jews recognized that the law was given through Moses, but not only this, the law became known as the law of Moses (see Num 12:6, 7; Neh 9:14; Dan 9:11). After Moses, Israel's hope became bound up with the expectation of a new Moses, a prophet like Moses whom the Lord God would raise up, and to whom the people of Israel would hearken (Deut 18:15, 18). The prophecy concerning the new covenant (Jer 31:31ff.) prob. arises out of the expectation of the new Moses who would usher in a new covenant which would be effective, because "unto him," the new Moses, "the people would hearken." In the OT, Moses is characteristically described by God as "my servant" (see Num 12:7; et al.). With this in mind, it is possible that the servant of Isaiah 42:1ff., 49:1ff., 50:4ff; 52:12ff. is the fulfillment of the hope of a prophet like Moses. The servant is given as a covenant to the people (Isa 42:6). He publishes the law (42:4), and brings out the prisoners from the dungeon and captivity (42:7). His role appears to be modeled after the role of Moses. Moses offered to give his life for the people of Israel when they sinned. The Servant, in fact, gives His life for the people (see Isa 53:5).

4. *The priests.* Initially the priesthood was a delegation of Moses' office (Exod 4:10-17). Aaron was to act as Moses' mouth. He was Moses' brother and was a Levite (4:14). The function indicated was to communicate the knowledge of God revealed to Moses to the people. The primary task of the priesthood was to teach the law of Moses (Lev 10:8-11; Deut 31:9-13; 33:10; Mal 2:6, 7). In the course of teaching the Torah, they were to preserve it (Deut 17:8, 9; 31:9). As the custodians of the law, the priests kept a copy in the Temple (31:9). The custodians of the law at times failed in their duties. Not only did they fail to teach the law, they failed to keep it themselves (Ezek 22:26). The writings of the prophets are studded with critiques of the function of the priesthood in Israel. Again and again, one finds the criticism that the priests who should have taught the law had failed to do so (2 Chron 15:1-6; Ezek 7:26; Hos 4:6; Zeph 3:4; Mal 2:6-8). The priesthood, which was in essence a teaching office, failed to fulfill this function, and Israel was without a teaching priest (2 Chron 15:3). It is not surprising that when the priesthood forgot to teach the law, that the law should become forgotten and lost. Evidently this was the situation prior to the rediscovery of the book of the law in the time of King Josiah (2 Kings 22:8). The priests became involved in politics and the worship of the Temple. Their work as expounders and teachers of the law became overlooked. Consequently, the need arose for a special class of men to carry out these tasks.

It is possible that from the beginning, the teaching functions of the priesthood were restricted to trained members of this class, though Leviticus 10:11 indicates that the sons of Aaron were to teach Israel, and the prophets seem to presuppose that all priests shared in the teaching office (Mal 2:6, 7). At least some Levites were also instructed to teach (Deut 33:10; 2 Chron 35:3). Priests were not to be paid for their instruction (Mic 3:11). Instruction was carried out by the priest visiting a town (2 Chron 17:8, 9), gathering the people together and expounding the Torah (Deut 31:10-13; 2 Chron 17:8, 9). This practice continued after the return from the Exile (Ezra 8:15-20; Neh 8:7-9). The teaching was carried on by those skilled in the art of exegesis. By the return from exile, there was a body of teaching which was the property of the priesthood, and the exposition of this was one of the most important functions of the priests and Levites. Ezra was a priest (Ezra 7:1-5; Neh 8:2). But he evidently was a member of a section of the priesthood with special knowledge and ability to teach the Torah (Ezra 7:6, 10). When Ezra came from Babylon he brought with him a copy of the Torah and expounded this to the assembly of returned exiles. This assembly included teaching Levites (called מבינים Neh 8:3, 9). The purpose of this instruction was prob. to refresh the memories of the teaching Levites. The instruction was carried out from a wooden pulpit (Neh 8:4). The

The law of Moses, the textbook of the Jews, was neglected and lost by the priests. The nineteenth-century English artist W. H. Bartlatt depicts the finding of the Law in the temple during Josiah's reign. © *H.P.*

Torah was read while the reader was surrounded by his assistants, prob. Levites who assisted in the interpretation (Neh 8:7-9). During the second commonwealth, the Torah was expounded on Mondays and Thursdays, these being the market days when there would be a congregation. Later on, a three year consecutive cycle of readings was worked out for the Torah. Thus a major program of adult education was initiated.

It is possible that some priests combined scribal and teaching duties. If this is so, they were the ancestors of the scribes of the second commonwealth who were the custodians of the Torah and its interpreters. Our knowledge of Ezra, the priest, who was also a scribe, fits in with this theory (Ezra 7:6-11; Neh 8:4, 9, 13). From Ezra's time, the scribes were a special class of Biblical scholars, exegetes, official teachers and spiritual leaders in Israel. The scribes were the predecessors of the doctors of the law from Maccabean times to about A.D. 200. The scribes and the doctors of the law adapted Biblical exegesis to meet the requirements of the time, and from their teaching the Mishnah developed. The aim of these teachers was to pass on their heritage to an ever increasing number of disciples. As Moses was the originator of the priesthood, so also the scribes looked back to Moses as "the great scribe of Israel." With the coming of Ezra, the scribe, the priest began the development of the scribal schools, an institution which had more effect on Israelite education than any other.

5. The king. The teaching function of the kings is often overlooked in thinking of education in Israel. David's songs had a considerable instructional effect in Israel. The sons of David, the kings of Israel, were responsible for keeping the law as a condition for sitting on the throne of David (Ps 132:12). Jehoshaphat caused his princes to be sent throughout the land of Judah teaching the people in all the cities (2 Chron 17:7-9). The wisdom of Solomon became a proverb throughout the ancient world so that even the Queen of Sheba came to test his wisdom (1 Kings 10:1-13). The kings were not often competent for the teaching task. More often than not, they disregarded the law in their own lives and led the nation to sin against God.

6. The prophets. The role of the prophets also has its origin in the office of Moses (Deut 18:15, 18; 34:10; Hos 12:13). Moses is thought of as the prophet par excellence, with whom the Lord spoke face to face. The activity of the prophets was largely bound up with teaching the law, and bringing out its meaning in the current situation (see Isa 1:10; 8:16, 20 and esp. Zech 7:12). The activity of Elijah the prophet is depicted as a return to Moses. In his return to Horeb, the mount of God, Elijah comes to know the true meaning of his mission (1 Kings 19:8ff.).

The prophets were the critics of evil government, standing fearlessly before kings to declare to them the errors of their ways, as Elijah did before King Ahab (ch. 17, etc.). The prophets were also the friends of wise government seeking to strengthen the kings who sought to lead the people in the way of the Lord as Isaiah did with King Hezekiah (2 Kings 19). The prophets criticized injustice in the social behavior of the people (see Amos). They condemned the infidelity of Israel in forgetting Jehovah (see Hosea). They denied adamantly the false hope that because of Jerusalem and the Temple, Israel never would be enslaved by the enemy. The message of the prophets was one of judgment and doom on a nation that had strayed from the law of God. The message of judgment and doom was itself bound up with the message of the law (Deut 30). The message of the prophets was not one of ultimate doom because God in His covenant love would not permanently cast off His covenant people (see Hosea). Ultimately, He would find a way of redeeming them. In the new act of redemption, Israel would return to Him as their Lord. Consequently, an important aspect of the message of the prophets was one of returning unto the Lord, a message of repentance (Joel 2:12-14). The message of repentance was, itself, a message of hope (Isa 40, etc.). The message of the prophet involved an inspired interpretation of the law of Moses and of the historical situation in which they lived. During the first commonwealth, it was the prophets that kept the people true to their historical heritage. The prophets were to the first commonwealth what the scribes and the doctors of the law were to the second. Of course, there is a great difference in that the prophets were prepared to offer their critical judgment of the situation in terms of the word of the Lord to the people of the day, whereas the scribes and the doctors of the law offered their words as interpretations and varying interpretations of the law of Moses.

7. The sages. Moses is also the prototype of the wise man in the OT (Deut 4:5ff.). For the NT assessment of Moses as a wise man see Acts 7:22: "And Moses was instructed in all the wisdom of the Egyptians, and he was mighty in his words and deeds." The class of wise men in Israel is related in its origin to the wise men of other nations.

When the prophets ceased to proclaim the word of the Lord in their inspired and penetrating manner the need arose for those who could give guidance in the everyday matters of life. It was in this area that the sages played their part in educating Israel. They applied the Torah to the practical, everyday matters of life. This practical wisdom appears in the Wisdom Lit. of Israel. Practical or worldly wisdom does not always harmonize with the economy of God. Consequently, there are occasions in the OT when the prophets came into conflict with the professional wise men (Isa 29:13, 14; Jer 8:8ff.). On these occasions, what was put forward as practical wisdom was evidently "worldly wisdom."

Just as the prophets faced the problem of preaching a message to those who would not heed them (cf. the experience of Jeremiah), so also the wise men found that people were more ready to pursue a course of folly than to heed a course of wisdom (Prov 5:13). Although their wisdom was not always heeded, the sages were effective in building up a philosophy of education and a pedagogical system. Through them, education previously carried out with little planning or consistency was worked into a systematic whole.

G. The place and use of the law. The Jews had one textbook, i.e. the Scriptures. The Scriptures were made up of the OT canonical books. The body of writings known as the Pseudep. had no official recognition in the schools though it had a wide circulation in private homes. One should recognize that the development of these written records was gradual and over a long period.

1. *Oral law.* Scholars have debated the date of the origin of the written law. It has been suggested that in the initial stages of Israelite history, all law was in an oral form, only to be written down at a later date. Today, it would seem more likely that written and oral law developed side by side, later being crystallized into a full written tradition. The completion of the writing down of the law of the OT may not have taken place until after the Exile, and certainly the later books of the Apoc. must be dated in the Maccabean period or later. Further, the oral law developed from the time of the Maccabean period until about A.D. 220 when the Mishnah was completed in a written form. The Mishnah, of course, does not include any canonical writings of the OT but is the interpretation of those canonical writings by the rabbis. Thus, in considering the place of the law in Jewish education in Biblical times, one must take into account the development of oral law as well as written law. The Mishnah formed the earliest part of the Talmud, the more comprehensive written form of the sayings of the rabbis.

2. *Written law.* The written Torah dates from the time of Moses and gradually developed into a greater body of writings. The word Torah, or law has a number of different senses. The word can be used to describe the Ten Commandments. This is the narrowest sense. In a broader sense, the Torah or law can describe the five books of Moses, the five books of the law. In a more general sense, Torah can describe the whole of the OT. Torah may even be used to include the oral Torah of the Mishnah and the Talmud. The most basic study concerned the written law and certain passages of it received special attention. Of these passages, the great Shema is the best known. The passage begins with the Heb. word שמע, "hear"—"Hear, O Israel: The LORD our God is one LORD" (Deut 6:4).

Torah has the sense of teaching, instruction. The commandments were instruction about the way to live. Torah in the wider sense was instruction concerning the meaning and implication of these commandments. The prophets' message was Torah because they applied to their own day the meaning of the teaching of the law of Moses. By the end of the Biblical period the Jews had as their canonical writings the OT and as well as these writings they included, but gave lesser authority to, the books of the Apoc. For the most part it involved the teaching of the Pentateuch. In this, instruction in the formal matters of education, reading and writing were only a means to this end. Other subjects were incidental to the teaching of the law. Ideas of science, politics and medicine were embedded incidentally in the Torah. With this emphasis on teaching the Torah, education took the form of the culture and development of memory which is so important for the preservation of oral tradition.

The textbook for Judaism is the Scriptures, but the Scriptures came in varied languages. Although the OT was basically in Heb., there are certain Aram. passages, notably those in Ezra and Daniel. Some of the apocryphal books were written in Gr. The scholarly language for Biblical study continued to be Heb., but in postexilic times the ordinary people could no longer understand Heb. This brought about the need for Aram. trs. and paraphrases of the Scriptures i.e. the development, of the Targums (e.g., Neh 8:8).

The scattering of the Jews throughout the ancient world in the dispersion also brought about the need for the tr. of the Scriptures into Gr. This need may be viewed from two points of view. First of all, Jews who lived in the dispersion came under Hel. influence more strongly than their fellow countrymen in Pal. Many of them understood Gr. better than they did either Heb. or Aram. Second, the scattering of the Jews brought the Jewish faith to the people of the ancient world. By the early 3rd cent. B.C. there were trs. of certain books of the OT into Gr. The Letter of Aristeas (purporting to be written by a certain Aristeas to his brother Philocrates during the reign of Ptolemy Philadelphus [285-246 B.C.]) relates how Philadelphus appealed for a copy of the Heb. Scriptures for his royal library. The result was that the high priest at Jerusalem sent seventy-two elders to Alexandria with an official copy of the law. The seventy-two made independent Gr. trs. which miraculously corresponded to what we now know as the LXX. The story has accretions which are not accurate to the historical event, but it seems likely that the Pentateuch was tr. in Egypt in the reign of Ptolemy

Philadelphus. The remaining books were prob. tr. piecemeal at a later date, some time before 117 B.C. when the grandson of Sirach refers to the tr. of the whole OT. Subsequently the name LXX was extended to cover also all the books of the Apoc. (See A. Rahlfs *Septuaginta* Vol 1, pp. xxii ff.)

H. Educational symbols, principles, and methods. ***Educational symbols.*** The feasts of the Jews served to solidify national consciousness in a manner which many other races are never able to achieve except in time of war. Festivals were national holy days as well as holidays. Through them the Jew realized his dependence on God in providing food and protection. In the time before Ezra when there were no schools, the festivals were most important for education and remained so, even after the beginning of schools. The law required a father to explain great festivals to his son (Exod 13:8; Deut 4:9; 6:20, 21). Through participation in the festivals, the children would learn their meaning, and in this way the festivals became a part of life indelibly etched upon their minds. The festivals were unique opportunities for teaching the young the great truths of the Jewish faith. They provided a dramatic, vivid and intrinsically interesting way of teaching. It was a far more effective means of teaching than by abstract ideas and philosophical principles. In this way, the dealings of God with His people were effectively brought to attention by religious ceremony. All festivals were colorful and intensely interesting. The child was always at the heart of each one. This is the genius of the Jewish people. They placed the child at the center of life and by the educational media they developed, insured that the Jewish history and Jewish religion was passed on to succeeding generations.

The most important of the holy days was the Sabbath. One reason for its importance was its frequent repetition, week by week. In ceasing from their labors, the Jews indicated by their action, their faith in God to supply all their needs. The Sabbath was a day in which faith was expressed, a day of rejoicing in the Lord, a day of meeting for worship, a day of learning, a day of instruction. In a sense, the whole of the covenant faith was gathered together and symbolized in the Sabbath observance.

There were seven important festivals during OT times, a further one being added prior to NT times. Each of these festivals symbolized an aspect of Jewish faith. The first of the festivals was the Feast of Unleavened Bread (Exod 23:15), preceded by the Passover (Lev 23:5), which commemorated the deliverance from Egypt (Exod 10:2). It was one of three annual festivals and it occurred on the fourteenth day of the first month. The second of the festivals was the Feast of Weeks. It is also called the Feast of Harvest, the Day of the Firstfruits (Exod 23:16; 34:22; Num 28:26). This feast later became known as Pentecost because it was celebrated on the fiftieth day from the Sabbath beginning the Passover. This festival marked the Jewish dependence on God for the harvest. The third festival was the Feast of the Tabernacles or the Feast of Booths. It is also called the Feast of the Ingathering (Exod 23:16; 34:22; Lev 23:34, 39; Deut 16:13). The fourth was the Sabbath, which is regarded as a feast in Leviticus 23:2, 3. The fifth, the Feast of the Blowing of Trumpets (Num 29:1). The sixth, the Day of Atonement (Exod 30:10; Lev 23:26-31). The seventh was the Feast of Purim, described in Esther 9. This feast commemorated the remarkable deliverance from the intrigues of Haman. It was a day of feasting and gladness. The feast which was instituted after the completion of the OT lit. was the Feast of Dedication, commemorating and celebrating the cleansing of the Jerusalem Temple by Judas Maccabeus in 164 B.C. after its desecration by Antiochus Epiphanes. It is also called the Festival of Lights. In John 10:22 it receives its Gr. name, ἐγκαίνια.

The Tabernacle and later the Temple, embodied much educational symbolism. The structures themselves symbolized the place where God's presence was to be located. Within the structures there were several items of notable symbolic value. First of all, one notices the geography of these buildings. The Holy of Holies in its separation from the meeting places of the people symbolizes the holiness of God in His separation from all sinfulness. The furniture of the Tabernacle and later the Temple, reminded the Jews of the Exodus history, and also of the problem of sin and the means of atonement. The Temple stood for the presence of God with His people made possible by the overcoming of sin by way of atonement.

The prophets used symbolical methods to emphasize the meaning of their message to the people. Such symbolism is described as the prophetic "sign" (אות) . The method was to enact the meaning of the word declared. An instance of this is given in Isaiah 8:1ff. where the Lord tells Isaiah to take a large tablet and write upon it in common characters, and also when he is told to give his children certain names which bear out the prophetic message. Jeremiah is told to buy a linen waistcloth and cause it to be spoiled even before its first wash, to show how the Lord will spoil the pride of Judah (Jer 13:1-11). The prophet goes about with a wooden set of yoke bars on his neck to show how the people will be led into slavery by Nebuchadnezzar (28:13). When the false prophet Hananiah breaks the wooden yoke bars to show how the Lord would break the power of Nebuchadnezzar, the king of Babylon, Jeremiah then took yoke bars of iron to reinforce the point that the people really would be led into bondage. The prophet Ezekiel is told "for I have made you a sign (את) for the house of Israel" (Ezek 12:6). Ezekiel proclaimed his message of destruction and doom on Jerusalem by means of symbolic actions. He ate bread and drank water, trembling in fearfulness, symbolically portraying the destruction coming on Jerusalem and the fear that it would bring. He proclaimed the destruction of Jerusalem by drawing a picture of Jerusalem on a piece of clay, and shattering it in pieces to show how Jerusalem would be razed to the ground.

Other symbolical articles that were used at a more domestic level were the Zizith (Num 15:39-41; Deut 22:12), phylacteries (Exod 13:1-10; Deut 6:4-9; 11:13-21) and the Mezuzah (Deut 11:20).

Pedagogical principles. The basic principle of Israelite education was to begin at an early age (Ps 8:1ff.; Prov 22:6; Isa 28:9). Second, it seems to be suggested that the morning was the best time to teach, when the student is fresh (Isa 50:4). No doubt the lack of adequate lighting facilities influenced this judgment. Third, it is suggested that the subject matter should be presented to the child gradually, at a level which can be understood by the child at that stage (28:10, 13). This leads to the fourth point, that education should proceed from the known to the unknown. Fifth, the problem of forgetting is recognized and the necessity for relearning is prominently in view, e.g., "Only take heed . . . lest you forget the things . . ." (Deut 4:9). Again and again the exhortation, "remember," etc. (Exod 13:3; 20:8; 32:13; Num 15:39; Deut 5:15; 9:7; 24:9; etc.) is repeated.

Methods of instruction. Oral instruction took precedence over all other methods (Deut 5:1; Prov 1:8; Isa 1:10; 50:4). Hence the frequent exhortation to "hear," because the most important method of instruction was oral. Emphasis was placed on the need to remember, hence the frequent exhortation to "remember." Consequently there was a strong emphasis on the culture of memory in the Israelite situation. The development of memory also led to the development of means which could present the teaching in a memorable form, such as mnemonic devices for memory (Prov 31:10-31), where each new section begins with the next letter of the alphabet from א to ת. Memory is also helped by the use of משׁל, the parable, the oracle (Num 23:7), the analogy (1 Sam 10:12), the riddle (Ezek 17:2), the story with the vivid moral (2 Sam 12:1ff.).

Written instruction played an important part in Israelite education (Deut 31:19; Ps 119:18; Prov 22:20; Isa 30:8ff.). Even so, the written forms suggest the importance of the oral history of the teaching (Prov 1:8).

The importance of dramatic instruction via the various festivals and institutions already has been noted. The prophets evidently used symbolical methods also to emphasize the point of their message. They used proverb and parable (Jer 31:29; Ezek 12:22ff.; see also Mark 4 for the use of parables by Jesus, cf. Isa 28:23-29; Hos 12:10).

Instruction also was given in a catechetical form, i.e. by means of a question and answer. The use of rhetorical questions appears in Amos 3:3-8, etc. The question and answer form is found more fully in Jeremiah 15:11ff. (cf. Job), Deuteronomy 6:20; etc. Micah 6:6-8 is a catechism lesson, given in rhetorical form where the answer to the questions stated is implied. The climax comes in v. 8, "He has showed you O man, what is good; and what does the LORD require of you but to do justice, and to love kindness, and to walk humbly with your God?"

Variation of method is used in the OT. The writer of the letter to the Hebrews (1:1), said, "In many and various ways God spoke of old to our fathers by the prophets." God spoke to Moses face to face, He spoke to the prophets in visions and dreams, He spoke through omens and the casting of the lot, He spoke through nature and in the normal events of daily life. He spoke in the events of history, He spoke through the priest, the prophet and through others who were His servants. His voice was to be heard through conscience, and His will to be known through the law.

Instruction and discipline are inseparably linked together. "Know then in your heart that, as a man disciplines his son, the LORD your God disciplines you" (Deut 8:5; cf. Eph 6:4). "Apply your mind to instruction and your ear to words of knowledge. Do not withhold discipline from a child; if you beat him with a rod, he will not die. If you beat him with the rod you will save his life from Sheol" (Prov 23:12-14). Thus discipline was considered to be an integral part of instruction. Discipline was considered as a means by which the love of God fulfilled its purpose in the life of His people (Isa 54:8; Jer 31:18-20). When God disciplined Israel, it was to bring Israel back to Himself. The teacher exhorts, "My son, do not despise the LORD's discipline or be weary of his reproof, for the LORD reproves him whom he loves, as a father the son in whom he delights" (Prov 3:11, 12; cf. Heb 12:5-11). Discipline, or chastisement, is to be regarded as a mark of God's love and concern in instructing those whom He loves (Ps 94:8-13). Chastisement is at times fruitless (Jer 4:22; 5:3; Amos 4:6-12). In these instances the chastisement has a penal emphasis (Ezek 21:8ff.; Amos 4:6-12). Discipline as a means of carrying out instruction leads to an incentive of reward and punishment. Rewards and punishment are an inducement to good behavior and hard work (Isa 52:13; 53:12). As the Lord used the means of discipline as an incentive for Israel to learn so the wise teacher in Israel used discipline with his students.

I. The Qumran sect. Qumran is the name of the site on which the ruins of the community, which has now taken on the name of the site, were discovered in 1947. The community prob. took up residence in this situation in the 2nd cent B.C. Evidently the sect broke with orthodox Judaism over the question of a legitimate high priest. The interests of the sect were largely apocalyptic. They were concerned with the end time when God would destroy evil and reinstate His people. Their value judgments were puritanical and on the whole they were an inward-looking community. The purpose of the discussion of the sect at this point is to draw attention to the place of Scripture in the life of Judaism. At the heart of the buildings of the Qumran sect, there was a scriptorium, a building which was occupied for the purpose of copying and transmitting the sacred texts of Scripture. Almost all the texts are in Heb. though there are some Aram. and Gr. documents. Further, as well as canonical OT writings and Apoc. writings, there are some documents which are peculiar to the Qumran sect. There is the Manual of Discipline, the Hymn Scroll and various Biblical commentaries, as well as the already known Damascus Document. In these documents, the sect's own peculiar teaching is put forward.

J. The diaspora. The difference of the Judaism of the diaspora from that of Pal. is one of degree and not of kind. It is a mistake to think that the Judaism of Pal. wholly rejected Hel. influence. There is clear indication of Hel. influence, even in such a nationalistic group as the Qumran sect. Greek was a widely spoken language in Pal. The difference in degree is that some Jews in the dispersion lost touch altogether with their native Aram. and Heb. This also may have been true of Jews in Pal., but the difference in degree must be maintained. Many more Jews in Pal. were aware of the meaning of Aram. and Heb. than were the Jews of the dispersion. The Jews of the dispersion were more acutely aware of Hel. influence. Philo of Alexandria was aware of Hel. philosophical ideas and expressions. This is not to suggest that he was a proficient philosopher in his own time, but simply that he had contact with these areas of thought.

K. Conclusion and criticism. Jewish education primarily was religious education, based on the belief that God had revealed Himself. It was education that presupposed revelation at every point. Thus philosophy played no real part in its system. As its educational system was exclusively religious, apart from elements of science and other studies which incidentally were taught in the process of teaching religious knowledge, Jewish education lacked scientific character, in fact, was pre-scientific. It neglected culture, but in spite of this Jewish education succeeded where Gr. and Rom. educational systems failed. In a sense, the Jewish system of education failed also, because it became legalistic and hair-splitting. The aim was the perfect application of the law. Paul gives a critique of the system as one who has been inside it, a student of the law at the feet of Gamaliel. He gives two lines of attack. First, he draws attention to the status of Christ in relationship to the law, a status of superseding the law. Second, he draws attention to the fact that the law could not achieve its aims anyway. The NT writers did not disparage the law itself and the high ideal of educational responsibility it inspired in Jewish minds (Rom 2:17-20). They were convinced that the covenant was fulfilled and that the perpetuation of a system of Judaism would be a case of arrested educational development, unnecessary to those who had graduated to God's household. Further, pride in the law was an anachronism condemned because Gentile was as likely as Jew to live up to the ideals of the law, for the law sets up goals without the means of achieving them (2:14, 15; 7:13-24). The legalistic system encouraged contempt for others (2:17-24; James 1:26; 3:14-16). In the NT there are two concerns: the first is to find a means adequate for personal development, and the second is to show the success of this means by judging it with the test of "loving one another." This test was not unique, but it was not conventional to make this test central.

III. Hellenistic education

By "Hellenistic" is meant the later Gr. empire beginning with Alexander and including the Graeco-Rom. empire. It has been said that the Greeks first learned culture themselves and then they taught the ancient world. Consequently, in the Graeco-Rom. period, Hel. culture was the culture of the then known world. Of course, there were variations from place to place according to the local traditions. Hellenism is to be described as a cultural, military and political phenomenon.

A. Origin, development and aims. The educational system of Hellenism had its roots in the educational systems of Sparta and Athens. In Sparta, the aim of education may be described as the obliteration of the individual in the service of the state; in Athens, the training of the individual in the service of culture. From Sparta, the emphasis on the development of physical attributes and the training for warfare; and from Athens, the emphasis on the development of culture, carried over into Hel. education. The Greeks produced their philosophers of education and perhaps the most important of these was Plato. His book *The Republic* (one of his fifty-six books) gives a detailed account of the aims, ideals and methods of education. Plato was a student of Socrates, whom we know only through the writings of Plato. One of the most important students of Plato was Aristotle. With regard to the theory of knowledge, Aristotle rejected Plato's approach and his reaction has been likened to "a colt that kicks his mother." This saying is attributed to Plato. In spite of this, it seems that Aristotle and Plato continued on good terms. In due course, Aristotle became tutor in the court of Philip of Macedon. At this stage he began a relationship with Alexander the Great, then thirteen years old, a relationship that was to last about eight years. His influence on Alexander cannot be doubted. From Aristotle onward, the study of philosophy and the natural sciences went hand in hand.

The importance of Alexander in the spread of Hel. culture cannot be overemphasized. Alexander has been described as the apostle of Hellenism. Through his exploits, Hel. culture was spread throughout the then known world. Even when the Greeks finally bowed the knee to the strength of Rome, the Romans showed themselves to be the heirs of Greece, adopting and exploiting Hel. culture. In the Graeco-Rom. age, the spread of the Gr. language, religion, education and philosophy, continued throughout the ancient world.

In the early stages of Gr. education, education was for the aristocratic class only. The ideals which students sought to attain were those of strength, courage, skill with weapons and music. These were the Gr. virtues. Goodness was described in aesthetic rather than moral terms. The Gr. school system presupposed that every attribute of mind, body and soul, properly disciplined, is good and worthy. In Gr. thinking, in its pure form, there is no room for asceticism. The aim was the development of personality, and from this point of view it may be described in terms of humanism. The educational ideal required both intellectual and physical effort. The physical effort is not to be understood in terms of work and labor but in terms of athletic prowess. Work, in terms of labor, was for the servile class.

The Hel. educational system may be described as follows: girls received no education outside the home. For boys, the first five years of life were spent with their mothers. Elementary schools took up the years from six to fifteen. During these years, they undertook the basic learning programs. The years from sixteen to eighteen were spent in the gymnasium and activities were basically physical, music and dancing (naked) taking the main emphasis, though lit., the sciences and politics also were studied. The aim of the gymnasium was to prepare persons fit for citizenship. This kind of education was restricted to citizens who were native born. The years between nineteen and twenty were spent in military service by those who were eligible for this undertaking.

In cities which lost their citizenship (e.g. Athens), the original purpose and military nature of the organization died out in the gymnasiums. They became rather "liberal arts colleges" for the sons of aristocrats. The training became somewhat like that of a university. Athens, Tarsus and Alexandria were cities famous for their "universities." In these "universities" the ultimate in study was either philosophy or rhetoric. By the NT period, philosophy had given way to rhetoric as the ultimate study.

In such cities as had lost their citizenship in the Rom. empire, schools were open to foreigners as well as natives. The aim which Plato had outlined of preparing scholars for citizenship was now lost. Instead, these universities or schools equipped a few wealthy unoccupied young men to enjoy their own leisure time. Education at this time had lost the lofty ideals of Plato, and in fact had lost any real direction.

B. Characteristics. Hellenistic education was characterized by the belief that man's mind discovered truth. The system stressed the development of reason. This led to the study of science and philosophy. Dut to the scepticism of later philosophers and the recognition of the power of persuasive speech, philosophy gave way to rhetoric as the "queen of the sciences." Aesthetic standards, beauty, symmetry were applied rather than moral standards such as those we find in Judaism.

C. Influence on Jewish education. Scholars have recognized Hel. influence on the development of the Wisdom Lit. in Israel. This is not to say that Hel. influence is wholly responsible for the development of the Wisdom Lit. in Israel. Hellenistic influence did contribute to the later Wisdom Lit., to such an extent that it is doubtful whether there would have been a body of Wisdom Lit. had there been no Hel. influence. This influence brought about an interest in the more practical affairs of living and the development of a pedagogical system. It is doubtful whether the Jews would have developed their school system had Hellenism not suggested this system to them.

Second, there was an extensive development of writings in the Gr. language among the Jews. Notable among these is the LXX, the tr. of the OT and Apocryphal books into Gr. The need of such a tr. indicates the inroads which Hel. thought had made into Jewish ways of thinking (see C. H. Dodd, *The Bible and the Greeks*). Along the same line was the influence of Hel. thought in the writings of Philo of Alexandria (1st cent. A.D.). He shows himself to be one who is thoroughly acquainted with the popular ideas of Hellenism. It has been suggested that he was acquainted with the writings of Plato and other Gr. philosophers. Such is not necessarily true, as he may have learned what he had in common with Plato and other philosophers secondhand at a more popular level. Josephus, the Jewish historian, was acquainted with Hel. culture. Paul (Saul of Tarsus) also seems to have had contact with Hel. culture. It is possible that as a citizen of Tarsus, "no mean city," Paul received a Hel. education. However, it is more likely from the evidence of the Acts of the Apostles that Paul received a traditionally

A restoration of a Palestinian Synagogue of the 1st and 2nd century. No 1st-century edifice has remained, but the appearance was probably much like this one. The education of Jesus undoubtedly included studies at the local synagogue. ©U.A.N.T.

Jewish, Pharisaic education at the feet of Gamaliel.

D. Conclusion. For all the wealth of cultural appreciation that Hel. education brought, the fact that the Gr. standard was aesthetic rather than moral must be regarded as a fundamental weakness. By the NT period, the Greeks admired the accomplishment of rhetoric as the apex of achievement. Paul was aware of this and gives a critique of the system which gives pride of place to the art of rhetoric. His critique arises out of an involvement in the Hel. educational system. Paul also had his rival platform. He gave lectures in the "school of Tyrannus" in Ephesus (Acts 19:9). (This is the only occasion where the word σχολῇ is used in the NT.) Thus the question is raised: did Paul have a full classical training? It is more likely that he moved to Jerusalem at an early age for rabbinic training. His skill in rhetoric was prob. acquired in action. There were others who were professionals, e.g. Apollos (Acts 18:24, 28 and cf. 1 Cor 1:17; 2:1-4; 3:2; 4:19, 20; 2 Cor 11:5; Col 2:4, 8). Paul was ridiculed (2 Cor 10:10; 11:6). He was plunged into a competition for status and it is in this context that the boasting passages which are so hard to reconcile with the rest of his teaching are to be understood (passages using the Gr. words καύχησις and καυχάομαι). They make sense in the contemporary professional etiquette, while at the same time parodying that same etiquette. Among the nobility, there was a cult of glory. Winning glory was the aim of public life, and the assurance of immortality. Public figures defined their own glory for posterity. Self-magnification became a feature of Hel. higher education. To Paul's mind, such glorification of man was anathema. Even pride in the law was now excluded. Yet, in this context, he was entitled to boast (1 Cor 15:31; 2 Cor 7:4, 14). The boasting passages are in fact an attack on the Hel. system of education. They represent a total rejection of the Hel. ideal. Paul now boasts in his humiliation (2 Cor 6:4-10; 10:9-12:13). There is a new design for the glorification of man in the sufferings and glory of Christ (4:7-17; Phil 2:3-11). The death of Christ is the sole object of boasting (Gal 6:14). The man who is a Christian has rejected the world and thus shares in the passion and glory of Christ through the Resurrection. Worldly boasting is excluded for the new man in Christ Jesus. Paul specifically rejects the power of persuasive speech as the prime test of human cultivation (1 Cor 1:17ff.; 2:4ff). In the place of this system, Paul draws attention to the need for personal morality, for a system where the standard of personal goodness is the test for the claim to wisdom. Neither the service of the state nor the service of culture could make a total claim on man. Paul's critique placed the revelation of God in Christ, Christ crucified, at the heart of any system of education.

IV. The education of Jesus

There is little knowledge of how Jesus was educated, but the following may be said with a great deal of certainty. It is apparent that Jesus was born to a God fearing family. Joseph is described as a righteous man, Mary as a pious young woman. This family undoubtedly lived up to its responsibilities of teaching the young child Jesus the matters of the law and the prophets. The family, though a godly one, does not appear to belong to the Pharisaic party. Jesus' education prob. consisted of what

He was taught by His mother and father, supplemented by the teaching of the local synagogue school. What He knew of the Scriptures and the teaching therein He learned in these situations. He did not attend any of the academies of the great rabbis, as the question asked by the Jews, "How is it that this man has learning, when he has never studied?" (John 7:15) indicates. While it is true that Jesus comes according to the flesh of the seed of David, the royal line, it is true at the same time that his family seems to have been poor, of the peasant class (Luke 2:24; cf. Lev 12:6, 8). Jesus learned a trade, that of a builder, following in the footsteps of Joseph. Jesus did make trips to Jerusalem with His family, attending the Temple, and on one occasion He astounded His elders with His learning (Luke 2:47). It was His custom to go to the synagogue (4:16).

Jesus' education consisted of the teaching He received in the synagogue services, and also what he learned from those trips to Jerusalem on the great festival occasions. But all of this does not explain Jesus' teaching and authority. Of course, one may assume that He meditated long on the Scriptures of the OT. When all this has been said, however, it should be recognized that the origin of His teaching is not to be found in the home, the synagogue, or the Temple. Again and again Jesus was to claim, "My teaching is not mine, but his who sent me" (John 7:16).

V. The education of the apostles

A. The Twelve. None of the twelve apostles appear to have been learned men originally. Andrew, Peter, James and John were fishermen; Levi (Matthew) was a tax collector; some were zealots (religious nationalists), and others have unknown backgrounds. It seemed unlikely that any of these men would have had very good formal education. The best that can be expected would be that they were educated in their homes and sent to primary school, that they attended the synagogue and perhaps, on rare occasions, had trips up to Jerusalem to the Temple for the great festivals. They were, by and large, uneducated, common men. Having called these men to follow Him, Jesus taught them. They would have heard Jesus' teaching to the multitudes. Above and beyond this, Jesus taught His own disciples, secretly, apart from the multitudes (Mark 4:10ff.). Thus one must take into account the effectiveness of Jesus, the great Teacher of men. The evidence suggests that His teaching had great effect, so that after Peter and John had been instrumental in the healing of the lame man at the Gate of the Temple and had occasion as a consequence to bear witness to Jesus, Luke records the following; "Now when they saw the boldness of Peter and John, and perceived that they were uneducated, common men, they wondered; and they recognized that they had been with Jesus" (Acts 4:13). Of course it should not be forgotten that along with the effectiveness of Jesus' teaching, there was the new power of the Holy Spirit, effective in and through the lives and teachings of Peter and John.

B. Paul. Paul grew up as a Pharisee receiving a full Pharisaic education. Though Paul was a Rom. citizen, born in Tarsus (Acts 16:37; 21:39; 22:25ff.), it seems almost certain that his real home was Jerusalem, where he sat at the feet of Rabbi Gamaliel, the doctor of the law and member of the Sanhedrin (22:3). Gamaliel represents the liberal wing of the Pharisees, the school of Hillel, as opposed to the more conservative group, the school of Shammai. Gamaliel intervened on behalf of the apostles with a persuasive speech at their trial (5:33-40). It is of significance that Paul, certainly the most prolific author of the NT, was educated by one of the leading (if not *the* leading Jewish teacher) of his time. It is ironic, to say the least, that the student, unlike his teacher, pursued a course of persecuting the Church (9:1ff.), only to be converted through an encounter with the living Christ. Of all the church leaders of the NT times, it seems probable that Paul was the most adequately equipped from an intellectual point of view. Paul compares himself with his contemporaries and says, "I advanced in Judaism beyond many of my own age among my people, so extremely zealous was I for the traditions of my fathers" (Gal 1:14).

VI. Education in the Church in holiness and maturity

In NT times, the Church did not create any special educational system for teaching children. It used the existing educational system, in both the Gr. and Jewish worlds. That Christians continued to use the existing educational systems is supported by what is known of Julian "the Apostate," who in the 4th cent. attempted to drive out Christianity and restore paganism. Julian required that those who shared in Hel. education also should subscribe to its ideology. His action made it virtually impossible for Christians to be involved in Hel. education and raised the question of a separate educational system. This problem falls outside the period under consideration. In the period of the Early Church, leaders were drawn from those whose educational qualifications were taken for granted. The Church made heavy educational demands on its members. One may say that the Church was not out of touch with the need for education; it was creating a new need for it. While accepting the formal education of existing institutions, the Church in its life and order constituted a substitute schooling. An awkward dualism of religion and education began to grow up. Such a dualism led, of necessity, to a criticism from a religious standpoint of the educational systems. In the NT both the Jewish and the Hel. systems of education are criticized, the rivalry between them is condemned, and members are challenged to a new way of life which is superior to both (Eph 2:11-22; cf. Acts 20:21; Rom 1:14-16; 2:9-11; 10:12; 1 Cor 1:21-24; 12:13; Gal 3:28; Col 3:11).

The new way of life in Christ was dependent to some extent on a teaching and learning relationship. The specific training of children, however, is nowhere catered for or implied in the Church as such. The Church was concerned with adult education or "higher education" in Christ, education which presupposed the existing educational systems but discounted their end product in favor of the new man (Eph 4:11-16; Col 2:2-7). The Church had its officials whose tasks were primarily educational in function (Rom 12:6-8; 1 Cor 12:4-10, 27-31; Eph 4:11; 1 Tim 3:1-13; Titus 1:7-9; 1 Pet 4:11). The way the aims of these functions should work out in the Church is expressed in Ephesians 4:8-16 and may be set out in the following three points.

(a) The aim was the *spiritual man* (1 Cor 2:4; Gal 3:14). Christ in His ascension poured out His Spirit on all who believed (John 7:39). At the heart of the Church's educating task was the need to keep the faith of Christ crucified and risen central. Those who drifted away from their faith in Christ could not hope to grow into the new man in Christ.

(b) The believer who had received the Spirit (and the Spirit's gift of ministry) was to grow up, through the fellowship of the Church and the ministry it brought to him, into the *mature man* in Christ (Eph 4:13). This maturity was marked by a sharing in the fellowship of the Church and appreciation of its teaching. Such appreciation was not merely intellectual; which leads up to the third point.

(c) The ideal was the *loving man*. The mark of the Spirit in man and the sign of his growth and maturity is loving action. Consequently, it is evident that the Church rejects both the Gr. and the Heb. ideals. The goal is not simply private goodness in moral or aesthetic terms, but mutual service of the members of the body. The diversity of individual roles is recognized as the diversity of the gifts of the Spirit and co-operation in the power of the Spirit is emphasized. In this new body, the fellowship of the Church, there is the recognition that each believer is equipped by the Spirit and is responsible for ministering his gifts within the fellowship of the Church. Each member has an educational role in building up the body until it comes to full maturity. Each member is called to a "mutual responsibility in interdependence in the body of Christ."

BIBLIOGRAPHY. A. Edersheim, *The Life and Times of Jesus, the Messiah* (1883); E. Schürer, *The Jewish People in the Time of Jesus Christ* (E. T. 1885), 6, 90; A. Compayrē, *The History of Pedagogy* (1909); F. H. Swift, *Education in Ancient Israel to 70 A.D.* (1919); T. Meek, *Hebrew Origins* (1936); J. Orr (Ed.) ISBE Vol. 2. (1939); N. Drazin, *History of Jewish Education from 515 B.C.E. to 220 C.E.* (1940); A. C. Bouquet, *Everyday Life in New Testament Times* (1956); E. W. Heaton, *Everyday Life in Old Testament Times* (1957); W. Barclay, *Educational Ideals in the Ancient World* (1959); E. A. Judge, "The Early Christians as a Scholastic Community" (Australian) *Journal of Religious History*, Vol. 1, No. 3, 130ff. (1961); J. Pederson, *Israel, Its Life and Culture* (1961); J. D. Douglas (Ed.), *The New Bible Dictionary* (1962); G. A. Buttrick (Ed.), *Interpreter's Dictionary of the Bible* (1962); M. C. Tenney (Ed.), *The Zondervan Pictorial Bible Dictionary* (1963); T. W. Manson, *A Companion to the Bible* 2nd Ed. (1963); G. von Rad, *Theology of the Old Testament* (1962 and 1965); G. H. Blackburn, *Aims of Education in Ancient Israel* (1966); E. A. Judge (Ed.) (Australian) *Journal of Christian Education*, various articles including: E. A. Judge, "The Conflict of Educational Aims in New Testament Thought" (1966), 32-45; P. W. Peters, "The Hebrew Attitude to Education in the Hellenistic Era" (1967), 39-51; B. E. Colless, "The Divine Teacher Figure in Biblical Theology" (1967).

A. W. MORTON

EDUTH **ĕ duth'** (עֵדוּת, *warning, reminder, testimony*). Hebrew meaning not found in Eng. VSS. *See* TESTIMONY.

The *eduth* refers specifically and collectively to the Ten Commandments (*see* TEN COMMANDMENTS) on the two tablets of stone as the all important and solemn divine charge (Exod 25:16, 21; 31:18; 32:15; 34:29). These were the basic terms of the covenant made by Yahweh as Suzerain with His people. Among modern Jews a man gives his *eduth* or word that he will perform a certain obligation.

J. REA

EGG(S). In OT בֵּצִים, *eggs*; Deuteronomy 22:6, an injunction not to take a mother bird with her eggs, but the eggs only; Job 39:14 speaks of the ostrich leaving her eggs on the ground to be warmed by the sun; Isaiah 10:14 reports the boast of the king of Assyria that he will gather the wealth of the earth as one gathers eggs forsaken in a nest; 59:5 refers to reptiles' eggs.

In the NT *ᾠον*, *egg*; Luke 11:12 refers to the absurdity of thinking that a father would give a scorpion to a son who asked for an egg. Wild birds' eggs were first gathered for food (Deut 22:6), then eggs of domesticated fowl (possibly, Isa 10:14). By NT times eggs of domesticated fowl were a staple of diet (Luke 11:12). A bird's egg consists of the yolk, in which is the germ of life, surrounded by the white, an albuminous substance, and a calcareous shell which protects the contents yet can be broken by the chick when it is ready to emerge.

In Job 6:6 KJV, ASV, Moffatt tr. Heb. חַלָּמוּת, *a plant with thick, slimy juice*; *purslane*, as "white of an egg," but ASVmg, RSV correct this. LXX guessed "empty words." The word has always troubled interpreters.

E. RUSSELL

EGLAH ĕg' lə (עֶגְלָה, "calf"). A wife of David who bore him his sixth son Ithream at Hebron (2 Sam 3:5; 1 Chron 3:3).

EGLAIM ĕg' lĭ əm (אֶגְלַיִם, *two drops*). Town name. Not the same as En-eglaim.

A town on the border of Moab (Isa 15:8). Its site is uncertain. Eusebius mentions a place named Agallim, eight m S of Areopolis (Rabba), which would be along the northern border. L. Koehler identifies Eglaim with Khirbet el-Gilime, NE of er-Rabba (KB, p. 9). Y. Aharoni suggests Mazra', an oasis on the shore of the Dead Sea NE of the Lisan peninsula (*The Land of the Bible* [1967], 32).

J. Rea

EGLATH-SHELISHIYAH ĕg' lăth-shĭ lĭsh' ə yə (עֶגְלַת שְׁלִשִׁיָּה, "the third Eglath"). A town near Zoar mentioned in prophetic oracles of judgment on Moab (Isa 15:5; Jer 48:34).

EGLON ĕg' lŏn (עֶגְלוֹן, *young bull* [?], Akkad. *Ig-la-nu*). An obese Moabite king, who early in the Judges period occupied territory W of Jordan near Jericho. The military campaign of this king was assisted by the neighboring Ammonites, who attacked an area to the E of the Jabbok River (Num 21:24; Josh 12:2; 13:10, 25; Judg 11:13, 22), and also by the desert Bedouin Amalekites. The exploits of Eglon resulted in the occupation of the "city of palm trees" (Judg 3:13 KJV), but since this site (Jericho) had been destroyed in the previous cent. (if not earlier) by Joshua, the 12th cent. B.C. Moabite occupation doubtless involved the subjection of the surrounding territory, including Bethel. The Israelites were dominated by the Moabites for eighteen years, after which God raised up Ehud to deliver Israel from this humiliation (Judg 3:21). Ehud brought the annual tribute to Eglon, gained a private audience, and when the obese king stood up to receive the tribute Ehud inflicted a fatal abdominal wound upon him.

BIBLIOGRAPHY. V. Tallquist, *Assyrian Personal Names* (1914), 95.

R. K. Harrison

EGLON ĕg' lŏn (עֶגְלוֹן, most LXX MSS have substituted Adullam, q.v., but numerous variants occur e.g. 'Αγλων, 'Εγλών, et al.). An Amorite town in the western Shephelah. W. F. Albright's contention that Eglon be identified with Tell el-Ḥesī has gained general acceptance. The ancient name is preserved at nearby Khirbet 'Ajlân to where the town had been moved by Byzantine times (Eusebius, *Onomasticon*, ed. Klostermann, 48:18). The archeological excavations of W. M. F. Petrie (1890) and F. J. Bliss (1891-1893) were the genesis of modern archeology in Pal. Eight distinct levels were uncovered dating from the Early Bronze III to the Pers. Periods.

The earliest mention of Eglon is the reference to *'q3y* in the Egyp. execration texts (Posener, No. E 58). The cuneiform tablet discovered at Tell el-Ḥesī is contemporary with the Late Bronze texts from El Amarna (EA 333). The letter describes the high treason that was brewing at nearby Lachish and Jarmuth against the pharaoh.

The king of Jerusalem took action against his subjects the Gibeonites (q.v.) because they had made a pact with Joshua. The Amorite kings of Jarmuth, Hebron, Lachish and Eglon were called upon for assistance (Josh 10:3-6). The Israelites came to the rescue of the Gibeonites and defeated the Amorites. Subsequently, the five kings were captured (10:23); and during the campaign in southern Pal., the city of Eglon was conquered (10:34-37; 12:12). It was assigned to the inheritance of Judah, in the second district of the Shephelah region (15:39).

BIBLIOGRAPHY. E. Robinson, *Biblical Researches in Palestine and the Adjacent Regions* (1856), II, 388-392; C. R. Conder, *Tent work in Palestine* (1878), II, 168, 169; id., and H. H. Kitchener, *SWP, Memoirs,* III (1883), 261; W. M. F. Petrie, *Tell el Hesy (Lachish)* (1891), 18-20; F. J. Bliss, *A Mound of Many Cities, or Tell Hesy Excavated* (1898); P. Thompsen, *Loca Sancta* (1907), 14, 15, 58; W. F. Albright, "Researches of the School in Western Judaea," BASOR, No. 15 (1924), 7, 8; id., "The American Excavation of Tell Beit Mirsim," ZAW n.f. VI (1929), 3, n. 2; J. Garstang, *Joshua and Judges* (1931), 174; K. Elliger, "Joshua in Judäa," PJb XXX (1934), 66-68; M. Noth, *Das Buche Josua* (1938), 68; J. Obermann, "A Revised Reading of the Tell el-Hesi Inscription. With a Note on the Gezer Sherd," AJA (1940), 93-104; W. F. Albright, "A Case of lèse-majesté in Pre-Israelite Lachish, with some Remarks on the Israelite Conquest," BASOR, No. 87 (1942), 32-38; O. Tufnell, "Excavator's Progress, Letters of F. J. Bliss, 1889-1900," PEQ, 1965, 112-127.

A. F. Rainey

EGYPT, BROOK OF. The SW border of the Promised Land (Num 34:5), of the tribe of Judah (Josh 15:4, 47), of Solomon's kingdom (1 Kings 8:65; 2 Chron 7:8), and later Judaea (2 Kings 24:7).

The "brook" or watercourse (Heb. *naḥal*, Arab. *wady*) of Egypt is prob. the present-day Wady el-'Arish, reaching the Mediterranean at El-'Arish some ninety m. E of the Suez canal and almost fifty m. SW of Gaza. Local geography supports this identification—only scrub and desert W of El-'Arish, but cultivable terrain eastward therefrom, claimed by Judah (cf. Gardiner, JEA, VI [1920], 115; B. Rothenberg et al., *God's Wilderness* [1961], 21 end, 32 [plate 9], 57). The Biblical evidence places it westward from Gaza (cf. Josh 15:47) and Kadesh-barnea (cf. Num 34:4, 5). Identical with Heb. *naḥal-miṣrayim* is Akkad. *nahal-muṣur* mentioned by Sargon II of Assyria in 716 B.C. (ANET, 286; Tadmor, *Journal of*

Cuneiform Studies, XII [1958], 77, 78). He settled people in its "city," the Arza(ni) or Arsa which Esarhaddon's texts place on the "brook of Egypt" (ANET, 290), the classical Rhinocorura, and phonetically comparable with modern (El-)'Arish. Hence, the "brook of Egypt" should prob. not be confused with Shihor (q.v.), the old Pelusiac and easternmost arm of the Nile (never a *nahal*). Further discussion, cf. NBD, 353, 354.

K. A. KITCHEN

EGYPT, LAND OF **e' jĭpt** (Heb. מצרים; Gr. Αἴγυπτος). In the NE corner of Africa, the Nile delta and valley, with their flanking deserts, from the Mediterranean Sea to the first cataract in antiquity, to the second cataract in modern times.

I. Natural conditions
  A. The setting
  B. Topography
II. Population and languages
  A. Population
  B. Languages and scripts
    1. Languages
    2. Scripts
III. Names of Egypt
IV. Chronology
  A. Basis of Egyptian chronology
    1. Introduction
    2. Sources and limits of Egyptian dates
  B. Outline table of Egyptian dates
V. Historical survey
  A. Predynastic Egypt
  B. Archaic Egypt
  C. Old Kingdom
  D. Rise and fall of the Middle Kingdom
    1. First Intermediate Period
    2. Middle Kingdom proper
    3. Second Intermediate Period
  E. New Kingdom
    1. The 18th dynasty
    2. The 19th dynasty
      a. History
      b. New Kingdom background for the Hebrews in Egypt
    3. The 20th dynasty
  F. The Late Period
    1. The 21st dynasty
    2. The 22nd-24th dynasties
    3. The 25th dynasty
    4. The 26th dynasty
    5. Later Egypt
VI. Egyptian literature
  A. Historical outline
    1. Third millennium B.C.
      a. Old Kingdom
      b. First Intermediate Period
    2. Second millennium B.C.
      a. Middle Kingdom and Second Intermediate Period
      b. The New Kingdom
    3. First Millennium B.C.
  B. Egyptian literature and the OT
    1. Direct links
    2. An objective background for OT literature
      a. Literary criticism
      b. History and forms of literary categories
VII. Egyptian religion
  A. The gods of the Egyptians
  B. Worship and cult
  C. Funerary beliefs

I. NATURAL CONDITIONS

A. The setting. The Nile in past ages carved out a long gorge or valley northward to the Mediterranean across the African tableland; the successive phases of the process can be seen in the terraces visible in the cliffs that border the valley. Not until the valley floor had been filled with alluvial mud could there be a long, narrow strip of human settlement in the valley "flood-plain" on either river bank, and that only in the last eight thousand years or so. The Delta, formerly a bay of the sea, was formed by alluvial mud at the same time, and this region early consisted in large measure of low lying marshland, gradually and progressively reclaimed during the course of Egypt's long history. Desiccation of the Sahara steppe land forced early hunters into the Nile valley, to become its first settlers.

The course of the Nile is hindered by six outcrops or "cataracts" of granite. Eroded less easily than the Nubian sandstone or the limestone that succeeds it northward some seventy m. N of Aswan, these cataracts limited ancient Nile navigation. The first is at Aswan, and the others are counted southward to the sixth, about seventy m. N of Khartum in the Sudan. Now flooded by the new High Dam at Aswan, the valley between the first and second cataracts was Lower Nubia; southward is Upper Nubia. Nubia was the Biblical Cush (q.v.), and its history was closely bound up with that of Egypt.

Within Egypt proper, the Nile valley is rarely more than twelve m. wide. Green vegetation flourishes as far as the life-giving waters reach, but immediately beyond, all is desert, a change so sharp that one may stand with one foot on the cultivation and one on the sand. On the political map of Africa, Egypt (AR) occupies a large rectangle some 386,200 square m. in extent, but ninety-six percent of that terrain is desert, so that ninety-nine percent of Egypt's population live on and from the four percent of usable land in valley and delta. Hence Herodotus' famous dictum about Egypt being the gift of the Nile, esp. as the rainfall is of the slightest: about seven and one-half inches at Alexandria, an inch at Cairo, and nil at Aswan apart from very occasional showers or cloudbursts. Until the advent of modern regulation, the Nile has created and renewed the fertility of Egypt by its annual flood or "inundation," derived from the rains and melting snows of equatorial Africa and Ethiopia. These waters

View from top of Great Pyramid near Memphis. Sphinx is at lower left foreground. © *Har*

brought down a vast quantity of silt that was deposited as virtually a layer of new soil. The Nile begins its rise in June/July, subsiding after October. The abundance of the inundation determined that of the crops, and so prosperity or famine (cf. Joseph); modern dams are designed to retain a reserve of water and so guarantee the supply.

The long narrow valley and broad spreading delta stand in striking contrast—two Egypts, the Upper (valley) and Lower (delta). The pharaonic monarchy effectively began with the uniting of these two lands under one rule, but the ancient Egyptians never forgot the duality of their country: the pharaohs were always "King of Upper and Lower Egypt" and "Lord of the Two Lands." This conception affected the administration both in its ceremonial titles and in its practical divisions (e.g., separate viziers for S and N). The only feasible site for a capital of such a bipartite land is at the region of junction of the two areas—in the district where Cairo now stands as successor to ancient Memphis only a few m. across the river.

Some forty m. S of Cairo, but on the W bank, is the natural depression of the Fayum, connected to the Nile by a long water channel. From at least the 12th dynasty, the Fayum served as a reservoir, and by irrigation became (and is) a garden province. Further W in the Sahara desert, a string of oases owe their existence to wells of artesian water, used since pharaonic times.

Within her valley and delta, Egypt had one splendid highway, the Nile itself. Her deserts largely protected her from external invasions for much of her early history, but access routes across the Sinai isthmus and through the E desert to the Red Sea, plus contacts S up the Nile and W along the Libyan coast all gave scope for Egypt both to give and to receive cultural stimuli.

B. Topography. Within the two broad divisions of Upper and Lower Egypt, the land was divided anciently into provinces or "nomes." While various of these (esp. in Upper Egypt) may have originated as petty chiefdoms in prehistoric times, the organization of these nomes first clearly emerges during the Old Kingdom (3rd millennium B.C.), and continued to develop thereafter. As early as the 12th dynasty (1900 B.C.), Upper Egypt was already divided into the later canonical number of twenty-two such provinces (P. Lacau and H. Chevrier, *Une Chapelle de Sésostris Ier à Karnak* [1956]). The more gradual development of the Delta can be seen in the recognition of only a dozen Lower-Egyp. nomes in the 12th dynasty, the full twenty provinces being established finally only in the 2nd cent. B.C. under the Ptolemies.

The ancient Egyptians took their geographical orientation from the S, not N; hence, Aswan was in the first Upper-Egyp. nome, it

Egypt lies in the foreground of this air view of the Sinai peninsula from Gemini IX. Dead Sea is at top of photo. ©*N.A.S.A.*

was early a frontier post (first cataract) with Nubia, and a staging post when Nubia was under Egyp. control. A hundred m. to the N (some 300 m. S of Cairo), the spectacular monuments at Luxor preserve the memory of ancient Thebes (q.v.) in the fourth nome, most magnificent of Egypt's capitals during the Empire age (c. 1550-1085 B.C.), with the Karnak and Luxor temples of the god Amun, and the tombs of its pharaohs in the Valley of the Kings. Some fifty m. further N (eighth nome) stood Abydos, holy city of Osiris, the Egyp. god par excellence of the dead and of the afterlife, sacred (even before Osiris) from the earliest times. Among the cities further N in Middle Egypt, suffice it to name Hermopolis (15th nome), the seat of Thoth the god of learning, to the SE of which Akhenaten established his city for the worship of the solar disc (whence came the Amarna tablets), and also Heracleopolis (20th nome) opposite the Fayum and seat of the 9th and 10th dynasties.

The territory of Memphis (Biblical Noph), the administrative capital, counted as the first nome of Lower Egypt, and was prob. founded by the very first pharaohs; across the Nile just N of modern Cairo once stood Heliopolis (Biblical On), city of the sun god Ra. Further N was Bubastis (Biblical Pi-Beseth), famed for its cat goddess and festival, while the NE Delta contained administrative centers such as Pi-Ramessē (Raamses, q.v.) and its successor Tanis (Zoan), on or near the main route to Pal. The Delta could boast of other renowned cities: Busiris (sacred to Osiris), Mendes, and esp. Sais, an ancient city from which later came the 26th dynasty, of Neco and Hophra (q.v.). Out on the NW shore of the Delta, the Ptolemies made Alexandria their capital, developing Alexander the Great's new foundation into a vast city of Hel. culture where only a village (Rakoti) had stood before. Egyptian society was (as now) predominantly rural, and her ancient cities were not dense industrial communities, but groups of settlements with garden lands among and between them.

Detailed study of the ancient geography and topography of Egypt is very complex, esp. as the courses of the Delta branches of the Nile have varied in number and location at different historical epochs. Ancient Egyp. sources mention three main arms, classical writers distinguish seven, while today only two main streams function, from and between which a network of lesser channels, canals and drains run and intersect.

II. Population and languages

A. Population. The ultimate origins of those earliest settlers who first colonized the Nile valley remain uncertain. The predynastic (i.e., prehistoric) Egyptians who developed the beginnings of settled culture in the Nile valley show African affinities. On the eve of the formation of a literate and united kingdom in Egypt, in N Egyp. cemeteries of that epoch traces have been noted of people showing slightly different physical characteristics (e.g., in cranial capacity), the so-called "Giza race." These are thought by some to have been newcomers who infiltrated from Western Asia, fused with the existing stock, and promoted the rapid flowering of what is known as typically Egyp. culture of the pharaonic period. However, certainty on the point is not attainable. From the Old Kingdom onward, the Egyptians show from their statues, reliefs and paintings their own distinctive type, a physical type that has persisted ever since (despite all invasions), so that the Egyptians of today are the lineal descendants of their ancient predecesors, notwithstanding the transition through three civilizations in the interim.

B. Languages and scripts. 1. *Languages.* The language of the ancient Egyptians had a complex origin and very long history. It was basically an African language, perhaps of the Libyo-Berber group ("Hamitic") which was then affected in some grammatical forms, syntax, and a fair proportion of vocabulary by the impact of a Sem. language. The independent personal pronouns, for example, are closely related to those of the best known Sem. languages, and cognates in vocabulary can be readily recognized. The links between ancient Egyp. and African languages are less easy to establish clearly (partly due to lack of ancient African texts), but useful work is being done in this field. The result of the "Hamito-Semitic" fusion was what we now call ancient Egyptian, and was already established by the time of the earliest inscrs., with the first dynasties.

The main phases of the Egyp. language may be summarized as follows. *Old Egyptian* is the relatively terse form of the 1st to 8th dynasties in the 3rd millennium B.C. (Archaic period and Old Kingdom); apart from tomb inscrs., the main source for this phase is the Pyramid Texts (*see* LITERATURE and RELIGION, below), which show the most archaic forms of the tongue. *Middle Egyptian* was prob. the spoken language of the early Middle Kingdom (11th-12th dynasties, c. 2100-1800 B.C.), and is the "classical" phase of the language—it was thus used for formal writings of every kind (esp. literary) not only in the Middle Kingdom but throughout the New Kingdom (even with Late-Egyp. current), and well on into the late period, even till the Graeco-Rom. age in a modified form.

Late Egyptian was the vernacular of the New Kingdom (empire) and after, in the 16th to 8th centuries B.C., but had begun to develop before that period (traces back to 18th cent. B.C.). With Akhenaten of the late 18th dynasty, Late Egyptian came to be used regularly in written documents, esp. of current business, administration, etc.; literary and religious texts also were composed in Late Egyptian from the Ramesside age onward, alongside the Middle-Egyptian lit. "Demotic," really the name of a script, is the term applied to "later" Late

Egyptian, further developed, as attested in documents from the 8th cent. B.C. into the Rom. epoch. It was always principally the language of business and daily life, but literary and religious works in Demotic joined the existing Middle and Late Egyptian traditions.

"Coptic" was the final phase of Egyp., as it came to be used in Byzantine Egypt, developed by native Christian writers, esp. for tr. the Bible and Gr. church lit. Coptic has survived in Egypt into modern times as the liturgical language of the Coptic or indigenous church (cf. Lat. at Rome), while the everyday tongue of modern Egypt is Arabic. Coptic exhibits several dialects, Sahidic and Bohairic being the most important.

2. Scripts. The oldest is the hieroglyphs, by origin pictorial signs. Such signs may be used (i) to stand for the object depicted (ideogram or word sign), (ii) to represent the consonants of the word for the object depicted, giving the sign a phonetic value that can allow it to be used to write other words, and (iii) as a "determinative" appended to a phonetically-spelled word to indicate its general class.

However, almost as early as the hieroglyphs themselves, there appeared abbreviated or "cursive" forms of them. Writing at speed with a reed pen and carbon ink upon papyrus, or making jottings on limestone flakes or on potsherds ("ostraca"), the scribes soon developed running, even ligatured forms based on the hieroglyphs but no longer pictorial. This form of book-script we call "hieratic." It was the usual script for all documents (literary or otherwise) on papyrus while the hieroglyphs remained the monumental script on stone and wood. Both scripts were used to write Old, Middle and Late Egyptian, right on into the days of the Roman empire; i.e., for about 3,000 years.

In the 8th cent. B.C., there was developed a "shorthand" VS of hieratic, now termed demotic, and which has given its name also to the still later form of Late Egyptian expressed in this script. This, too, continued into Rom. times. With the advent of Christianity in the valley of the Nile, the need arose for ordinary people to be able to read the Scriptures. For this, the old scripts were much too cumbersome with their hundreds of signs and groups. After some experimentation ("Old Coptic"), the Egyp. Christians took over the Gr. alphabet, adding to it seven letters to represent sounds not covered by the Gr. letters. This is the only form of Egyp. that shows the vowels, and is of philological importance.

During the course of Egyp. history, various foreign loan words entered the language, esp. in the highly international age of the 14th-13th centuries B.C.; these are mainly Sem. Such attestations of W Sem. vocabulary are of great value for the study of Heb. and other Sem. languages. Occasionally, Egyp. words appear in cuneiform, e.g., in the Amarna tablets. In the Coptic of Christian Egypt, a large body of Gr. vocabulary was taken over, plus a sprinkling of Lat. and further Sem. terms.

Southward from Egypt, the Nubian kingdom and civilization of Meroe adopted Egyp. hieroglyphs, modified them to write the Meroitic tongue, and eventually developed its own cursive script. This kingdom flourished from the 6th cent. B.C. to the 4th cent. A.D. However, Meroitic is not yet fully deciphered; it would be the mother tongue of Candace's officer (Acts 8:27ff.).

III. Names of Egypt

The mod. name "Egypt" derives from Gr. *Aigyptos*, and the latter from Egyp. *Ḥa(t)-ku-Pta(ḥ)*, "Mansion of the *ka*-spirit of (the god) Pta(h)," a name for Memphis, the ancient capital. (Cf. Gardiner, *Ancient Egyptian Onomastica*, I, 124*.) This term is already attested in the Amarna letters of the 14th cent. B.C. as Hikuptah. This shows a use of the city name for the land, while conversely in Arab. the name of the land, Masr or Misr, also stands for Cairo, successor to Memphis. This Arab. term for Egypt is that attested in the older Sem. languages, including Akkad. (*Muṣri*) and Biblical Heb. (*Miṣrayim*), cf. Mizraim.

Throughout the OT, Miṣrayim stands for Egypt virtually without exception, despite sporadic attempts in the past to refer some passages to a Musri near SE Anatolia. By Musri, the Assyrian sources for their part usually mean Egypt, and sometimes a land N of Assyria; its use for N Arabia is dubious (cf. Oppenheim, ANET, 279, n. 9, for references). The only OT passages that have been seriously attributed to a northern Musri are the references to Solomon's horse and chariot trade with Misrayim and Kue (1 Kings 10:28, 29, cf. 2 Chron 1:16, 17). That Kue is Cilicia seems clear. But if so, then Misrayim could hardly be a near neighbor of Kue if Solomon's traders were to act between them. If the trade was between Egypt to the S (producing chariots) and Kue in the N (horses), then Solomon was ideally placed to be middle man between the two. On Musri (Akkad.), see P. Garelli, "Musur," in F. Vigoureux and H. Cazelles (eds.), *Supplement au Dictionnaire de la Bible*, V (1957), cols. 1468-1474, and H. Tadmor, IEJ, XI (1961), 143-150.

OT Misrayim for Egypt is paralleled not only by Akkad. Musri but also by Ugaritic *Msrm* in the 14th/13th centuries B.C. For possible origins of the term, *see* under Mizraim. The ancient Egyptians themselves had their own terms for their homeland: *Kemyt*, the "black land" (as opposed to the desert, the "red land"), *Tawy* the "Two Lands" (Upper and Lower Egypt), and *Ta-meri*, a term of uncertain meaning.

IV. Chronology

A. Basis of Egyptian chronology. 1. *Introduction.* Ancient Egypt shows a continuous history for almost 3,000 years down to the Rom. conquest (31 B.C.), a span rivalled only by Mesopotamia. Current knowledge of that history varies in accuracy and detail from period to period in relation to the available sources, and the accuracy of Egyp. chronology is similarly conditioned, as a compact survey of the basic evidence will make clear.

Before the decipherment of the hieroglyphs, the principal source of Egyp. chronology was the Epitome of dynasties and kings based on the *History of Egypt* written in Gr. by the Egyp. priest Manetho in the 3rd cent. B.C. He divided the long line of kings into thirty "dynasties" or families. This basic framework has largely stood the test of modern knowledge of firsthand Egyp. sources opened up by decipherment of the hieroglyphs, and so it is still retained today. However, it has been found convenient to group the dynasties into larger units, corresponding to the main divisions of Egyp. history, the whole now being prefaced by the Predynastic (and in practice, prehistoric) period. Thus, the three most brilliant and best understood epochs of Egyp. history are termed the Old Kingdom (3rd-6th dynasties, third millennium B.C.), the Middle Kingdom (11th-12th dynasties, early second millennium), and the New Kingdom or Empire period (18th-20th dynasties, late second millennium). Before the Old Kingdom came the formative Protodynastic or Archaic Period of the 1st and 2nd Dynasties. Between the Old and Middle, and Middle and New, Kingdoms respectively are the First and Second Intermediate Periods (7th-10th and 13th-17th dynasties), obscure periods of internal weakness. After the New Kingdom, the Late Period covers the 21st to 30th dynasties and Pers. rule prior to Alexander the Great (i.e., c. 1085-332 B.C.). The 21st to 24th dynasties are sometimes termed the "Third Intermediate Period" because of conditions reminiscent of the earlier Intermediate Periods; the 26th dynasty saw an archaizing "renaissance" until overwhelmed by the Pers. empire. After Alexander the Great, the Ptolemies ruled until supplanted by Rome. Between the limits of prehistory and Alexander, the profile of Egypt's history may be graphically set out thus:

Archaic

OLD-K	MIDDLE-K	NEW-K
1st IP	2nd IP	Late Pd.

2. Sources and limits of Egyptian dates. Besides the excerpts from Manetho preserved in defective VSS by later writers, there exist also Egyp. king lists from the New Kingdom. Despite its pitifully damaged state, the most valuable of these is the Turin Papyrus of Kings which once listed nearly all the kings of Egypt, from the mythical dynasties of gods and spirits and the first human dynasties down to the time of Ramses II, giving lengths of reigns and of groups of dynasties, etc. It thus preserves, for example, a figure of 955 years for the first eight dynasties, and gives 143 (136+7) years for the 11th dynasty, besides the reigns of many individual kings. Other lists give simply the names of kings in order, often omitting obscure periods; such are the lists of Sethos I and Ramses II in their temples at Abydos, and from the tomb of Tjenuna at Saqqara. A list of Thutmose III from Karnak (now in the Louvre) merely gives groups of selected kings. For the first five dynasties, one must add the limited but vital evidence of the Palermo Stone and other fragments from the same or a similar monument which once contained a record of all the years of the kings of the 1st to 5th dynasties, with notes of events (mainly religious).

At all periods, we possess monuments dated by the regnal years of individual pharaohs; these furnish at any rate minimum figures for reigns in default of other evidence. Genealogies of officials in which successive generations served different kings can be very helpful, esp. in the Late Period (21st-25th dynasties). Synchronisms betwen Egyp. pharaohs and the rulers of states in W. Asia in the 2nd and 1st millennia B.C. afford valuable cross-checks on dates of both areas.

Finally, there are some "external" means of control upon Egyp. dates. The Carbon-14 method is of limited utility, mainly for the prehistoric epoch. Astronomy is more serviceable for the historical period. The Egyp. calendar was 365 days long, and so ended a day too early every four years (no leap year). Thus, after some 700 years the calendar-seasons fell in the wrong natural seasons (calendrical summer in natural winter, etc.), and after some 1,453 years the calendar would coincide with nature's seasons again. The proper starting point of the Egyp. calendar happened to coincide with the "heliacal" rising of the Dog Star, Sirius or Sothis. Thus, mentions of such risings of Sothis in terms of dates of the moving calendar are of great value in helping to fix the date B.C. of such references within narrow limits. Lunar dates can be useful, if they are known to fall within a limited general time span.

This kind of evidence has made it possible to date the 12th dynasty closely to 1991-1786 B.C. (a Sothic rising, plus lunar dates), and so the 11th dynasty with 143 years before it at c. 2134-1991 B.C. A similar Sothic datum is attested for Amenophis I in the early 18th dynasty. Taken as observed at Thebes, this seems to indicate a date of c. 1551 B.C. for the start of the 18th dynasty, while lunar data for Thutmose III would place his reign in 1490-1436 B.C. This allows of good dates for the dynasty to the death of Amenophis III in about 1364 B.C. This dynasty would end by either 1315 or 1301 B.C. at the latest, depending on the date adopted for Ramses II, and affected by the vexed question of a possible co-regency of Amenophis III and Akhenaten.

In the 19th dynasty, lunar data indicates

CHRONOLOGICAL TABLE: History of Egypt

	B.C.
First and Second Dynasty	3000-2778
Old Kingdom	2778-2423
Third Dynasty (Builders of the Great Pyramids)	2778-2723
Fourth Dynasty (Builders of Pyramids)	2723-2563
Fifth Dynasty	2563-2423
Sixth Dynasty	2423-2263
Seventh and Eighth Dynasties	2263-2070
First Intermediate Period (Ninth and Tenth Dynasties)	2190-2040
Middle Kingdom (Eleventh and Twelfth Dynasties)	2160-1580
Second Intermediate Period (Thirteenth and Fourteenth Dynasties)	1785-1680
Hyksos (Fifteenth and Sixteenth Dynasties)	1730-1580
Seventeenth Dynasty	1680-1580
The New Kingdom	1580-1090
Eighteenth Dynasty	1580-1314
Ahmosis	1580-1558
Amenophis I	1557-1539
Thutmosis I	1539-1520
Thutmosis II, Hatshepsut	1520-1484
Thutmosis III	1504-1450
Amenophis II	1450-1425
Thutmosis IV	1425-1408
Amenophis III	1408-1372
Amenophis IV ("Akhenaton")	1372-1354
Smenkhare, Thut-Ankh-Amon, Ai, Haremhab	1354-1314
Nineteenth Dynasty	1314-1200
Ramses I	1314-1312
Sethi	1312-1289
Ramses II	1290-1224
Mernephtach	1224-1204
Twentieth Dynasty	1200-1085
Ramses III,	1198-1166
Late Period	1085-332
Twenty-First Dynasty	1085-950
Smendes, Herihor	1085-1054
Twenty-Second Dynasty (Libyan)	950-730
Shosenk I	950-929
Osorkon I	929-893
Osorkon II	870-847
Shoshenk II	847
Twenty-Third Dynasty (Libyan)	817-730
Twenty-Fourth Dynasty	730-715
Twenty-Fifth Dynasty (Nubian)	751-656
Shabaka	716-701
Taharka	689-663
Tanutamon	663-656
Twenty-Sixth Dynasty (Saitic)	663-525
Psammetik I	663-609
Necho	609-594
Apries (Hophra)	588-568
Amasis	568-526
Psammetik III	526-525
Twenty-Seventh Dynasty (Persian Domination: Cambyses until Darius II)	525-404
Twenty-Eighth Dynasty	404-398
Twenty-Ninth Dynasty	398-378
Thirtieth Dynasty	378-341
Second Persian Domination	341-333
Conquest by Alexander the Great	332

Many of the dates are approximate only. Some dynasties ruled at the same time in different parts of the country.

Only the rulers of importance for the history of Canaan and Israel are listed.

(based on: E. Drioton—J. Vandier)

that the redoubtable Ramses II reigned either 1304-1238 B.C. or 1290-1224 B.C. (a margin of only fourteen years), but intensive attempts to decide finally between the two dates have proved fruitless because the Egyp. and Near Eastern data contain ambiguities not yet eliminated; new material is needful. After Ramses II, the next generally agreed fixed point was not reached until the beginning of the 26th dynasty in 664 B.C. (not 663); from the Pers. conquest (525 B.C.) onward, Egyp. dates are well enough tied in with the rest of antiquity to cause little difficulty beyond details.

However, between Ramses II and 664, it is possible to suggest that Shoshenq I (Biblical Shishak) who raided Pal. in the fifth year of Rehoboam of Judah did so about 925 B.C., and so reigned c. 945-924 B.C.; some set these dates about a decade later. Shoshenq's line, the 22nd dynasty, ended with Osorkon IV who was prob. the Shilkanni mentioned by Assyrian documents of Sargon II in 716 B.C., which sets an upper limit for the rule of the 25th dynasty in Egypt. With this outline framework and a large body of scattered facts, it is then possible to produce reasonable dates for the 20th to 25th dynasties that rarely exceed a decade or so in margin of error.

Between the end of the 12th dynasty (1786) and the beginning of the 18th (c. 1551), there are some 235 years for the 13th to 17th dynasties of the difficult Second Intermediate Period. However, the 13th dynasty can be allowed 153 years for its sixty kings during 1786-1633 B.C., ruling most of Egypt until c. 1650 B.C. The 14th dynasty was a minor line local to the NW Delta, not affecting general chronology. Similarly, the "16th dynasty" consists of local Hyksos chiefs subject to the main 13th dynasty and Hyksos kings. The 15th or Hyksos dynasty itself had six rulers for 108 years (Turin Papyrus); and, being expelled in about the eleventh year of Ahmose I of the 18th dynasty, it prob. ruled most of Egypt during c. 1648-1540 B.C. until the last decade.

Going back beyond the 11th dynasty (from 2134), there is the Turin Papyrus figure of 955 years for the 1st to 8th dynasties, which may be fairly correct. The length of the 9th/10th dynasties is not really known, nor the length of their overlap with the 11th dynasty. If the 9th and 11th dynasties competed for the kingship immediately from the end of the old 8th dynasty, then 955 years before 2134 would set the start of the 1st dynasty at c. 3089 B.C.—say c. 3100 B.C. in round figures. If the 11th

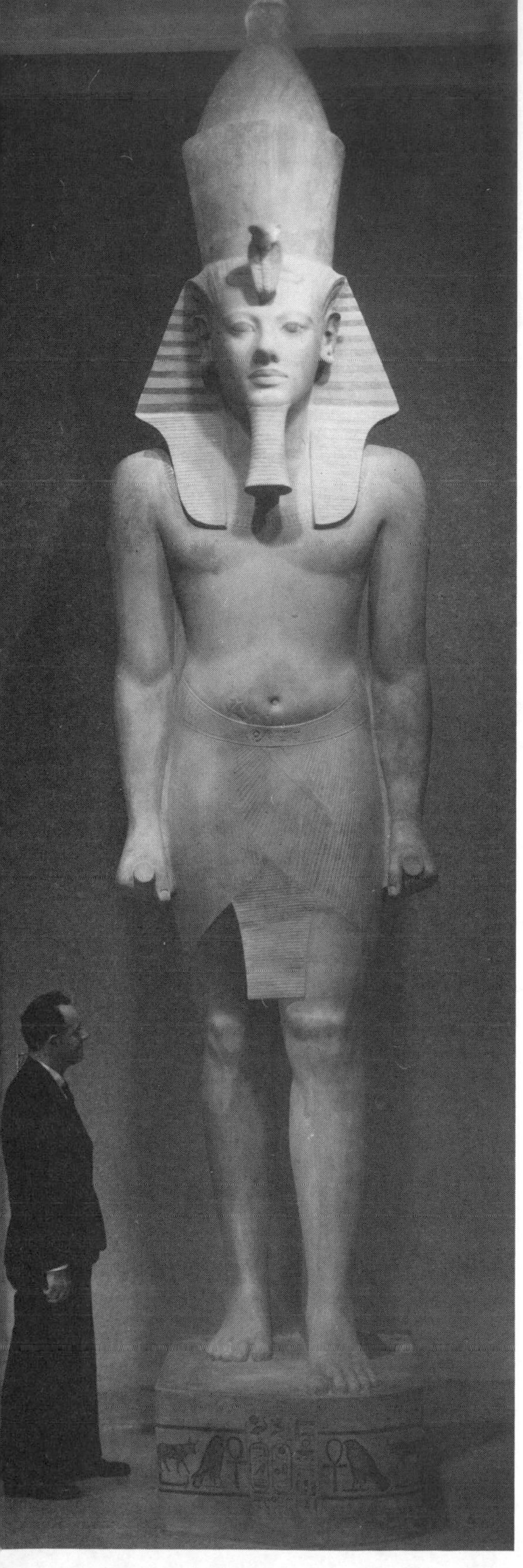

Statue of Egyptian Pharaoh. Medinet Habu. ©O.I.U.C.

dynasty was only founded some years after the 9th dynasty took over from the 8th, then the whole set of dates for the 1st to 8th dynasties would have to be raised by the amount of that interval. Conversely, if the 400 years or so usually allotted to the 1st and 2nd dynasties proved to be excessive, then the beginning of the 1st dynasty would have to be correspondingly lowered somewhat. Thus, for the 3rd to 8th dynasties, there is several decades' margin of error; for the 1st and 2nd, up to a cent. or more. Cf. following Table.

B. Outline table of Egyptian dates.

B.C.		
Before c. 3100:	Predynastic (prehistoric): Badarian, Naqada I, Naqada II Periods.	
c. 3100-2686:	Archaic Period (dyns. 1-2)	
c. 2686-2180:	Old Kingdom (dyns. 3-6)	
c. 2180-2030:	1st Intermediate Period (dyns. 7-10)	
c. 2134-1991:	11th dynasty	Middle Kingdom
c. 1991-1786:	12th dynasty	
c. 1786-1551:	2nd Intermediate Period (dyns. 13-17)	
c. 1551-1315/01:	18th dynasty	New Kingdom (Empire)
c. 1315/01-1200:	19th dynasty	
c. 1200-1070:	20th dynasty	
c. 1070-945:	21st dynasty	Late Period begins; Third Int. Period
c. 945-715:	22nd/23rd dynasties	
c. 720-715:	24th dynasty	
c. 715-664:	25th dynasty	
c. 664-525:	26th dynasty (Saite revival)	
c. 525-402:	Pers. rule ("27th dynasty")	
c. 402-341:	28th to 30th dynasties	
c. 341-332:	Renewed Pers. rule	
332-31:	Alexander and the Ptolemies	
31:	Beginning of Rom. rule.	

V. Historical survey

A. Predynastic Egypt. In Upper Egypt, the first settled societies are known as Badarian (earliest phase, Tasian). These people practiced agriculture, lived in villages (huts or tents), and made pottery (some, very fine), having flint tools and some use of copper. They had already developed some concept of an afterlife, as indicated by the furnishings of their modest burials. The following period, Naqada I (or Amratian), had some contacts abroad with S Arabia, Iran and Mesopotamia, possibly passing via Wadi Hammamat in the Eastern desert and down the Red Sea. The final period of Egyp. prehistory, Naqada II (or Gerzean), witnessed great changes by its end. By now, regular townships existed, some walled (e.g., at Naqada itself). Graves and their furnishings increased in elaboration. During this age at latest must have occurred that fusion of "Hamitic" (Libyo-Berber) and Sem. elements that went to produce the Egyp. language of the historic period. And before the end of

Naqada II, cultural influences from Mesopotamia had a tangible impact, inspiring the Egyptians to use cylinder seals, undertake monumental brick architecture, and above all to produce their own form of writing—the hieroglyphs. By the end of the period, Upper Egypt had become a unified kingdom, and another kingdom had rule over at least part of the Delta.

B. Archaic Egypt. 1st and 2nd dynasties (c. 3100-2686 B.C.). Traditionally, Egyp. history begins with the union of the Two Lands under King Menes from Upper Egypt, conquering the Delta kingdom and founding a new capital at Memphis for the 1st dynasty to rule all Egypt. It is likely that the Menes of late tradition is the King Narmer of contemporary monuments. This king dedicated a superb, shield-shaped "palette" bearing triumphal scenes that show him wearing the crowns of Upper and of Lower Egypt—perhaps direct evidence of his actually uniting the two Egypts under his rule. Seven other kings, his descendants, continued the dynasty, a period of tremendous advance in early civilization. At Abydos, each king had at this holy place a tomb surrounded by graves of the nobles of the court, well back on the desert edge, and also—rather nearer the town—an imposing "funerary palace" (possibly with provision for his continuing cult) itself surrounded in turn by the graves of palace servitors. The stele or tombstone of the fourth king, Wadji (or, "Djet"), is in beauty of execution the noblest monument of its kind. At Saqqara, on the desert edge to the NE of Memphis the new capital, magnificent brick tombs were built, combining a burial with a superstructure having a "palace-façade." These were prob. the tombs of great men of the realm who served the king at Memphis. Several scholars have suggested that some of these Saqqara tombs were the real royal tombs, the Abydos tombs being a species of cenotaph, but this is far from certain. See on the significance of these series of tombs, B. J. Kemp, JEA, LII (1966), 13-22, and in *Antiquity*, XLI (1967), 22-32. The physical furnishings of all these tombs—both at Abydos and at Saqqara—illustrates the great strides made in the applied arts: fine vases of the hardest stones, fantastically carved slate dishes, fragments of beautiful furniture employing ivory, ebony, etc., a full range of copper tools and vessels, and free use of gold (usually plundered long since). The evidence of clay sealings and of bone and ivory labels once attached to goods deposited in the tombs bear witness to a rapidly-developing and elaborate state administration already in the 31st to 29th centuries B.C. One may perceive the functioning of a treasury, state bureaus for provisions, the existence of various royal estates and institutions as economic units, and so on—all, 2,000 years before David and Solomon had to organize their state administration. Only in contemporary Sumer

Colossal head from the statue of Amenophis (Amen-hotep III), king of Egypt 1413-1377 B.C., once thought to be the pharaoh (king) at the time of the Israelite Exodus; wearing the uraeus, symbol of sovereignty. ©*B.M.*

do we have written evidence for a parallel elaboration of civilized life, but the mute evidence from Asia Minor, Syrian and Palestinian town sites, with palatial and military architecture, organized material wealth, etc., is enough to hint that, so early, much of the future Biblical Near E already had highly organized societies.

Under the 2nd dynasty, progress was for a time halted by internal dissensions, possibly epitomized in the figures of the falcon god Horus and the god Seth of Ombos (both of Upper Egypt). These troubles were prob. ended by a King Khasekhem who perhaps took the modified name Khasekhemwy, "the two powers are manifest," as symbol of a reconciliation. The Palermo Stone preserves some records of the first two dynasties, but mainly of religious ceremonies and the founding of buildings. The date-lines of the ivory and bone labels "date" their years within the king's reign by reference to such events plus the royal name. The data on these labels plus the once continuous enumeration of such years and events on the Palermo Stone are the nearest approach to historical annals for this early epoch.

The Sphinx and the Great Pyramid of Cheops. ©*M.P.S.*

C. Old Kingdom (3rd-6th dynasties, c. 2686-2180 B.C.). The rapid progress of the early dynasties, consolidated by Khasekhemwy, had laid the foundation for Egypt's first and most vigorous period of greatness, an age epitomized for many by the pyramids (q.v.) that are her most enduring monuments. The 3rd dynasty is dominated by the figures of the Pharaoh Djoser and his minister Imhotep. At Saqqara they built the Step Pyramid, the world's first great building of stone, originally nearly 200 ft. high. It stood in a vast enclosure, nearly 600 yards long by over 300 wide, which contained besides the pyramid a whole series of special buildings for the royal cult in perpetuity, all with an external finish of the finest limestone masonry. Doubtless that cult was celebrated with rituals of matching elaboration, precursors of the later attested Pyramid Texts. Imhotep was celebrated early by the Egyptians as an author, prob. of Egypt's first wisdom book (cf. later allusions, e.g. ANET, 432a, 467a), and by the Greeks as a healer and identified with Asklepios. Further step pyramids were built by Djoser's successors, but were all unfinished because of the premature deaths of most of these kings.

True pyramids came into fashion only with the 4th dynasty; its founder, Snofru, built two at Dahshur. His son Kheops built the Great Pyramid (originally 481 ft. high) at Gizeh opposite the area of modern Cairo. Khephren built the Second Pyramid and was prob. responsible for the carving of the Sphinx, a large specimen of a common royal/divine guardian figure in Egyp. sculpture. The Third Pyramid, of Mycerinus was much smaller but was expensively sheathed in granite. The step pyramids may have given tangible expression to the concept of a stairway to heaven (cf. distantly Jacob's ladder Gen 28:12, and the Mesopotamian temple towers). The true pyramid was a solar symbol, reminiscent of the *benben* stone of the sun god Ra at Heliopolis, and perhaps symbolized the rays of the sun as a ramp upon which the king might ascend to heaven.

The divine Pharaoh ruled supreme but in due course had to yield in authority to the sun god, to whom he was subordinated theologically as Son of Ra. This began in the 4th dynasty, but reached full expression in the 5th dynasty when the kings built not only pyramids but also separate solar temples in their vicinity.

Throughout the 4th to 6th dynasties, the pharaohs sent expeditions S into Nubia, establishing a foothold at the second cataract, and also in the N maintained trade relations with Byblos in Phoenicia to procure timber of the class of "cedar of Lebanon." In the 6th dynasty, movements of peoples in the Near E caused pressure on Egypt's Palestinian frontier; and so, under Pepi I, the dignitary Uni led five expeditions into Pal. to ward off this threat, the fifth of these being an amphibious operation.

In internal politics, the increasing elaboration of administration meant that the pharaoh delegated ever more authority to his ministers and officials. In the 4th dynasty the chief ministers had often been members of the royal family, from the 5th dynasty onward this ceased to be so. The steady fragmentation of power and the economic drain of tax-exempt royal endowments for temples attached to pyramids and gifts of land for the funerary cults of officials all combined to reduce the effective power of the kings, esp. in the 6th dynasty. In Upper Egypt, the provincial governors became hereditary local rulers with an increase in real local authority at royal expense. To counterbalance this trend, the pharaohs appointed special governors of the S as "overlords" for the local rulers, but this measure eventually proved inadequate. The end came with the reign of Pepi II, who acceded as a boy of six and reigned for ninety-four years; for the latter part of his overlong reign, the aged king was prob. helpless to halt the centrifugal forces in the realm.

The internal peace and security of Egypt under a strong and effective administration headed by the vizier and other ministers made possible the full development of all the civilized arts. Architecture was represented not only by the vast surfaces of the pyramids, but also by the sumptuous royal temples attached to them. Choice and costly granites and alabaster were often employed for pillars and paving, and their walls were increasingly decorated with superbly executed scenes in delicate low relief, usually painted, and mainly of ritual subjects. The tombs of the great nobility each consisted of a massive rectangular structure of stone over a burial shaft and pit; in the 5th and 6th dynasties, funerary chapels within these massifs (called *mastabas*) were brilliantly decorated with scenes in relief of daily life, etc., for the other worldly benefit of the owner, but vividly preserving the life of the epoch. Statuary in the round reach heights of excellence unrivaled at any later period in world history before the works of the Greeks.

Airview of the Pyramids of Gizeh, the three great pyramids of Egypt. ©*M.P.S.*

So much ability and brilliance in practical and visual arts did not lack counterparts in the intellectual realm, although the evidence is much more fragmentary. The gods of Egypt were already served in temples with elaborate rituals. From the time of King Unas (end of the 5th dynasty), the inner chambers of the royal pyramids were inscribed with a vast series of spells, magical rituals and religious texts now known collectively as the "Pyramid Texts," the oldest major corpus of religious lit. yet known. They served magically to insure the protection and well-being of the pharaoh in the afterlife (cf. also Literature, below, for their evidence on early literary form). Another famous document, the "Memphite Theology," prob. originated in the Old Kingdom; it shows the first known formulation of a logos type concept. Of quite another order were the "Instructions" or wisdom books composed by leading dignitaries of the monarchy from Imhotep of the 3rd dynasty to Ptahhotep of the 5th (see Literature, below). In their day, these were the quintessence of the "wisdom of the Egyptians," and inculcated the rules for a successful and "integrated" life within the society and service of the pharaoh. They aimed also at "good style" in their mode of literary expression (so, Ptahhotep). Then esp. in the 6th dynasty, we have the biographical tomb inscrs. of high officials, giving glimpses of history (e.g., Uni) associated with their personal achievements. Royal decrees in favor of temples exhibit the official style. Having arisen, flourished and passed away long before Abraham was born, this brilliant age (and its parallels abroad) is of value in several respects from the viewpoint of Biblical studies. Like the Archaic Period, it serves to underline the fact that the Biblical world was not merely the dim haunt of savages prior, say, to the Heb. monarchy or the Babylonian exile—such a conception is false, even 1,000 years before Abraham. The wealth of pictorial matter contributes to our understanding of ordinary daily life and custom in the Biblical world, and the lit. provides material toward a really factual history of literary style in the Biblical world as a setting for OT lit.

D. Rise and fall of the Middle Kingdom. 1. *First Intermediate Period* (7th-10th dynasties, c. 2180-2030 B.C.). The 7th and 8th dynasties show a rapid series of brief reigns without any notable undertakings. The pharaohs at Memphis were still recognized in Upper Egypt, if rather nominally, as shown by their temple decrees from Coptos. When their throne fell vacant, a prince from Middle Egypt (Herakleopolis)—Khety I—founded a new line (9th-10th dynasties), but the order ran into difficulties in both N and S. From Pal., Asiatics penetrated the Delta and added to unrest in the towns, while in the S the princes of Thebes established a rival line of kings—the 11th dynasty—in southern Upper Egypt from c. 2134 B.C. This period of internal stress came to an end only when the Theban King Mentuhotep II (Neb-hepet-re) reunited all Egypt by about 2030 B.C., so ushering in the Middle Kingdom proper. However, this tense age produced (or inspired) noble lit.: the earnest questings about life and death in the *Dispute of a Man With His Soul*, the demand for social justice reflected in the ornate rhetoric of the *Eloquent Peasant*, and the royal wisdom of the "Instruction" of [Khety III?] for King Merikara, that rightness of character is better than sacrifice, cf. 1 Sam 15:22 (samples in ANET, 405ff., 407ff., 414ff.).

2. *Middle Kingdom proper* (11th-12th dynasties). The 11th dynasty ended with the great Mentuhotep's second successor. Into the vacant kingship stepped the latter's former vizier as Amenemhet I to found the 12th dynasty, establishing a new administrative center (Ithet-tawy) just S of Memphis itself. In the pseudo-prophecy of Neferty, he had himself portrayed as a promised deliverer of Egypt from her ills, and announced a program of internal prosperity and external security, thus inaugurating the deliberate use of lit. for political and social propaganda. He undertook correspondingly vigorous measures for two decades, but was almost assassinated on the eve of appointing his son Sesostris I as co-regent. In the "Instruction of Amenemhat I," the old king set out the achievements of his reign, casting bitter odium on his ungrateful assailants. Thereafter, the dynasty stood on a firmer footing, and Egypt again knew an age of peace, effective government and considerable prosperity. Some kings, e.g., Amenemhat III, took particular interest in irrigation and developed the Fayum province. New wisdom books (see Literature, below) inculcated loyalty to the throne, or exalted the role of the scribes upon whom the success of the administration rested (*Satire of the Trades*).

Nubia was brought under firm control as far as the second cataract and beyond, with trade posts in the third cataract region. Trade and gold mining interests were safeguarded through massive mud brick forts of medieval proportions. Egypt also had intimate contact with Western Asia, esp. through Byblos, whose princes by the end of the 12th dynasty were writing their names in Egyp. hieroglyphs, and thereafter full length inscrs. also. The Execration Texts of the 12th/13th dynasties, for cursing the pharaoh's enemies, throw vivid light on the political geography of Syria-Pal. in the age of the Patriarchs, including references to (e.g.) Jerusalem and Shechem, and the land of Damascus under the term Upe. They show the division of Canaan into city-states and tribal areas much as is presupposed by the narratives of Genesis 12ff. Sesostris III raided Pal. as far as Shechem (cf. ANET, 230). A close guard was kept by use of forts on Egypt's Sinai frontier, and important centers were established in the E Delta, esp. near modern Qantir (*see* RAAMSES, HYKSOS). One may note as a background parallel to the men appointed to escort Abraham out of Egypt (Gen 12:20), those appointed to conduct the Egyp. fugitive Sinuhe back into Egypt (ANET, 21b). The well-known tomb scene at Beni Hasan of the magnate Khnumhotep welcoming "37 Asiatics" into Egypt under Sesostris II is the classic pictorial background for the Egyp. journeys by Abraham and Jacob (Gen 12, 46/47).

3. *Second Intermediate Period* (13th-17th dynasties). The great 12th dynasty ended with a queen. The 13th dynasty (c. 1786-1633 B.C.) saw a rapid succession of kings. At first, Egypt remained outwardly powerful, but real power now resided with the viziers, not the throne; "Asiatics" (mainly W Semites) increasingly came into Egypt, partly as slaves and in many occupations. Some Semites prob. gained a foothold as local rulers in the E Delta, and eventually one of them overthrew the reigning pharaoh, banishing the 13th dynasty to Thebes and the S. Thus was established the 15th (Hyksos) dynasty, a line of six kings that lasted 108 years, from c. 1648 to c. 1540 B.C. Historical data for this whole epoch are very meager. The settlement of Joseph and his family in Egypt may perhaps be placed c. 1700 B.C. in round figures, i.e., late 13th dynasty passing over into the Hyksos period. A Brooklyn papyrus of c. 1740 B.C. sheds light on the prison system of the day; and of about seventy servants of an official listed elsewhere on this document, over forty bear names of good Sem. origin like Joseph himself (a Menahem, a Shipra, etc.). Joseph began (Gen 39:2) as a domestic, Egyp. *ḥery-per*, "in the house," and like some of these he rose to become steward or "overseer of the house" (*imy-ra per*). The interpretation of dreams was the subject of special textbooks; in the British Museum, Papyrus Chester Beatty III is a New Kingdom copy of a work prob. much earlier than Joseph's day. Horses were known in Egypt from about the 18th cent. B.C. (skeleton from the Middle Kingdom fort, Buhen), and as horses were used for chariotry *before* being ridden as cavalry, this is prob. indirect evidence for some knowledge of the chariot in Egypt just before Joseph's time. The keeping of cattle (*see* GOSHEN) was a matter of interest to the pharaohs in the Delta (47:6), including in texts of barely a cent. or so later (ANET, 232b and n. 5). Utterly dependent on the Nile flood, Egypt always feared famine while blessed oftener with rich harvests.

E. New Kingdom (18th-20th dynasties). 1. *The 18th dynasty* (c. 1551-1315/01 B.C.). Ahmose I (c. 1551-1526 B.C.) completed the work of his elder brother King Kamose, in ejecting the Hyksos rulers from Egypt, and in the process invaded Pal. The first major step toward an empire was taken by his second successor, Thutmose I (c. 1505-1493 B.C.) who reached the river Euphrates in N Syria, and as far as the fifth cataract of the Nile in Upper Nubia. After the premature death of her husband Thutmose II (c. 1493-1490 B.C.), Queen Hatshepsut (1490-1468) ruled Egypt as real king during the minority of her stepson Thutmose III (1490-1436 B.C.). Her reign was remarkable mainly for works of peace: a great trading expedition down the Red Sea to Punt (S. E. Sudan), her superb W Theban funerary temple at Deir el Bahri, a shrine at Karnak, etc., but she did not hesitate to repress rebels in Nubia. After her death, the now mature Thutmose III conducted no less than sixteen campaigns in Western Asia, turning Syria-Pal. into an Egyp. province. The wealth, religious influences and captured peoples from Canaan entered Egypt, while Egyp. artistic canons penetrated Syria-Pal., during the ensuing period. Thutmose III was also a great

Relief of Hatshepsut. Karnak. ©*O.I.U.C.*

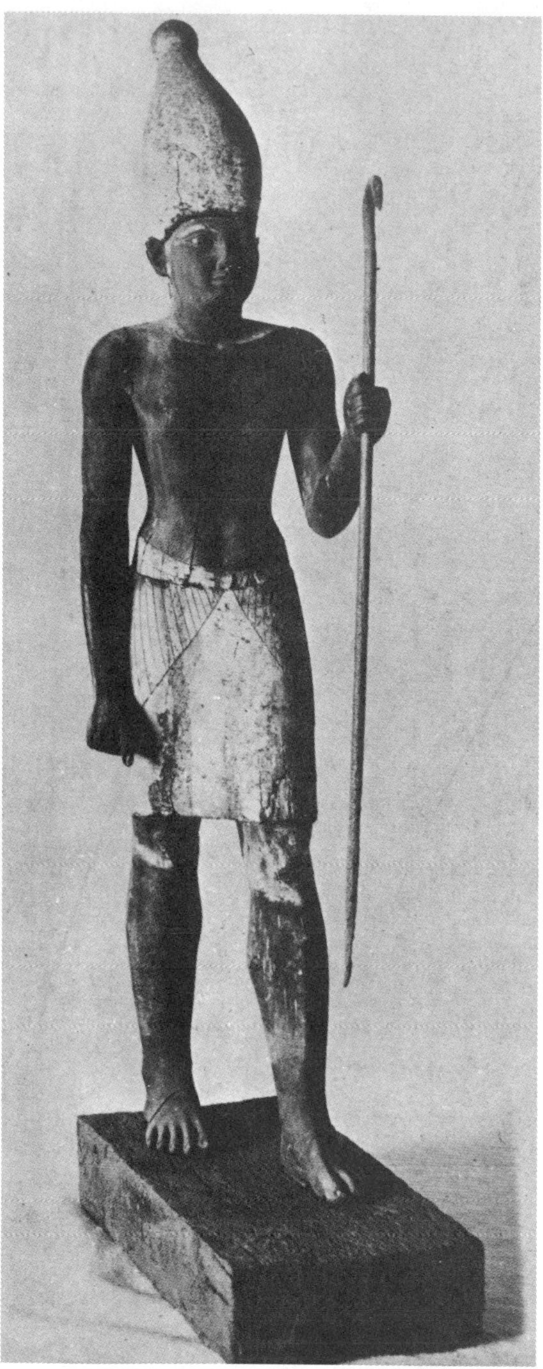

Wooden figure of Sen-Usert I wearing the white crown of Upper Egypt. ©*Cairo Museum*

builder of temples and an energetic administrator. His immediate successors maintained Egypt's power, and made marriage alliance with the strong N Mesopotamian state of Mitanni. Thus Amenophis III (c. 1402-1364 B.C.) had a reign of peace and hitherto unparalleled magnificence, still reflected by his buildings (e.g., temples of Luxor and Soleb, and the "Colossi of Memnon," sole relic of his funerary temple in W Thebes). Babylon and Mitanni courted Egypt for gold. Tensions between the monarchy and the priesthood of Amun, god of Thebes, broke out openly under his son Amenophis IV who, as Akhenàten, proclaimed the sole worship of the sun god manifest in the solar disc as Aten, abolishing the other gods (esp. Amun) and disbanding their priesthoods. Akhenaten built himself a new capital (Akhet-Aten ("Horizon of the Aten"), now El Amarna, in Middle Egypt; part of his diplomatic correspondence with Babylon, Mitanni, and the Syrian city-states was found there in 1887, becoming known as the El Amarna tablets or letters. Along with Hitt. annals and the archives from Ugarit in Phoenicia, these tablets shed a brilliant light on conditions in Canaan in the 14th cent. B.C., on the eve of the Exodus and Conquest. During Akhenaten's preoccupation with the Aten, a war betwen the Hitt. and Mitannian empires lost Egypt her N Syrian possessions, while Pal. lapsed into some disorder. With the deaths of Akhenaten and his brother Smenkhkara, the throne came to the young prince later known as Tutankhamun, famous principally for the splendors of his burial-equipment, discovered almost intact in the Valley of the Kings in Western Thebes. As he died prematurely without heir, his queen appealed to the Hitt. King Suppiluliuma I for a son of his to become pharaoh as her husband. But the over wily Hitt. delayed, so that his younger son then was murdered on his way into Egypt when the plan became known. Instead, the aged retainer Ay reigned briefly, until the general Haremhab took in hand the renewal of Egypt's now neglected internal administration.

Egypt reached the zenith of her political power and wealth in this epoch. Under the king, two viziers served for Upper and Lower Egypt and a viceroy ruled Nubia as a separate province. In Syria-Pal., the city states continued to be ruled by their own local dynasties, but on oath of allegiance to the pharaoh who regulated the succession in these states. A large and usually reasonably effective administrative organization supported these and other departments of state. A standing army was the nucleus of Pharaoh's forces. The increasingly splendid temples of the gods enjoyed rich endowments in land and settlements in Egypt and abroad, and a goodly share of the spoils of conquest. In these temples, the priesthoods performed complex rituals often of great length, both daily and for the great periodical festivals.

2. *The 19th dynasty* (c. 1315/01-c. 1200 B.C.). a. HISTORY. From Haremhab, the throne passed to a military colleague Paramessē, who reigned a brief sixteen months as Ramses I (c. 1315-14 or c. 1301-00 B.C.) but was succeeded by his able son Sethos I (c. 1314-1304 or c. 1300-1290 B.C.).

Sethos I immediately set about the reconquest of Syria-Pal., and thus collided head-on with the Hittites, not unsuccessfully. At home, he undertook the vast hypostyle Hall of Columns in the Karnak temple of the god Amun at Thebes, and built a temple in Abydos now famed for its exquisite colored reliefs. He also began building works in the Delta, and was prob. a pharaoh of the Heb. oppression. His son Ramses II (1304-1238 or 1290-1224 B.C.) doggedly fought on against the Hittites, the pyrrhic Battle of Qadesh being his most famous encounter. Eventually, both powers made peace in Ramses II's twenty-first regnal year by a treaty later sealed by dynastic marriages (*see* RAMSES, KING). Within Egypt, Ramses II erected and adorned more temples than any other pharaoh. His were the great rock temples of Abu Simbel in Nubia (two of half-a-dozen shrines), the Ramesseum (funerary temple) in Western Thebes, much at Karnak, a great court at Luxor temple, and the residence city of Raamses in the E Delta. It was perhaps in his reign that the Exodus (q.v.) occurred. His successor Merneptah (1238-1218 or 1224-1214 B.C.) beat off a massive Libyan invasion of Egypt, after a brief campaign in W Pal. on which his forces encountered some Israelites (the "Israel Stela," ANET, 376, 378). Merneptah's successors were short-lived and insignificant.

b. NEW KINGDOM BACKGROUND FOR THE HEBREWS IN EGYPT. The 19th dynasty was perhaps the most cosmopolitan age in Egyp. history, and was a fitting backdrop for the oppression, Moses and the Exodus. Official intercourse between major and minor states of the ancient world was at its height, following on from the 18th dynasty. At every level of Egyp. society, foreigners—esp. from Syria-Pal.—filled a multitude of roles in the main centers, whether the E Delta, in Memphis, or in Thebes. Ever since the expulsion of the Hyksos, a steady stream of prisoners of war had flowed into Egypt, used to help cultivate the fields and man the workshops of the state institutions and of the great temples; such slaves could also be found in small numbers in Egyp. households. In the early 18th dynasty, the veteran warrior Ahmose son of Abana lists nineteen such slaves in his tomb at El Kab (Upper Egypt), one woman bearing the good Akkad. name Ishtar-ummi (Sethe, *Urkunden der 18. Dynastie*, 11). At the other end of the scale, Amenophis II (c. 1438-1412 B.C.) lists vast numbers of captives from Syria from his (and his father's ?) campaigns there: e.g., 3,600 'Apiru, 15,200 Shasu (semi-nomads), 36,300 people of Hurri (Horites Syria-Pal.), 15,070 people of Nukhasse (in N Syria), and so on (cf. ANET, 247). These people often were installed in special settlements, e.g., at Thebes, "a settlement of Thutmose IV with Syrians (who were) spoils of His Majesty from Gezer," attached to the king's funerary temple in Western Thebes (ANET, 248a). Such people were used on building projects, like the Biblical Hebrews in the brick fields of Exodus 1:14.

Besides the famous painting of Egyptians, Semites and others making bricks, in the tomb chapel of the vizier Rekhmire under Thutmose III, an ostracon of that same official deals with building works, referring to the hauling of stone, causing to mold bricks, and to various personnel including thirty Hurru (Syrians) among others (text, Sethe, *Urkunden der 18. Dynastie*, 1174-5). Under Ramses II, the chief of militia and of royal works, Amenemonē, had charge of "the soldiers and the 'Apiru who drag stone for the great pylon" of a building of Ramses II at Memphis (Papyrus Leiden 348; tr. by Caminos, *Late-Egyptian Miscellanies* [1954], 491, 494; cf. Gaballa and Kitchen, *Chronique d'Egypte*, XLIII/85 [1968], 263-269). In the Anastasi Papyri of this general period, one official noted his work people "making their quota of bricks daily" (Caminos, op. cit., 106), while another had to complain, "there are neither men to make bricks nor straw in the neighborhood" (ibid., 188), scenes reminiscent of Exodus 5. Furthermore, a close surveillance was kept of the days worked, as is exemplified by jottings on ostraca from W Thebes concerning work on the royal tombs there. Such journals of work took special note of days worked and days "idle," in some examples even for individuals by name and giving the reasons for their absences from the job—"ill," "eye trouble," "brewing (beer)," or plain "idle." And religious holidays for festivals (cf. Exod 5:1, 3, 8) occur as "offering to the god" (so, Ostracon British Museum 5634, of the fortieth year of Ramses II). Such references occur in many other similar documents (references, Kitchen, *Ancient Orient and Old Testament* [1966,] 157, notes 17-19). When such a close check was kept on Egyp. workmen, one cannot expect foreign slaves to escape from equally close oversight.

However, the brickfields and building sites did not account for all Semites in Egypt, Hebrews or otherwise. The abilities of Bezalel and Oholiab (Exod 31:1-11) and the early career of Moses indicate otherwise. Such foreigners could be employed in all manner of callings (e.g., shepherds, weavers, brewers, wine merchants, porters, soldiers and ships' captains), including also craftsmen. One finds shipbuilders, stonemasons, coppersmiths and goldsmiths (see W. Helck, *Die Beziehungen Aegyptens zu Vorderasien* . . [1962], 372, 373, § V, for references). Some Hebrews may have

Brick made of Nile mud and chopped straw, stamped with the name and title of Rameses II, possibly the pharaoh at the time of the oppression. ©*B.M.*

Below: Tomb model of brickmakers. The central man digs mud to be placed in the basket once held by the kneeling figure. The third man *(left)* presses the mud into a frame to form a brick, three rows of which lie before him. ©*B.M.*

reached such employments. Higher up the scale, besides foreigners serving as priests (ibid., 373, 374, § VI), one finds scribes high and low, high stewards of the Kings Sethos I and Ramses II (Horites, in two cases), and cupbearers who were the trusted confidants of several pharaohs, e.g., Ben-Ozen (from Rock-of-Bashan!) under Merneptah, one Baal-mahir under Ramses III, and a Pen-Hasuri ("he of Hazor," Helck, op. cit., 369). One also notes foreign couriers coming and going over the E Delta frontier between Egypt and S. Pal. (ANET, 258b). Si-Montu, a son of Ramses II, married the daughter of a Syrian sea captain called Ben-Anath (Spiegelberg, *Recueil de Travaux*, XVI [1894], 64), while a daughter of Ramses II bore the corresponding name Bint-Anath, "daughter of (the goddess) Anath." In Ramesside Egypt, the learned scribes prided themselves on their knowledge of Canaanite, as in the Satirical Letter of this period (ANET, 477b); at a humbler level, a father reproached his son for making blood brotherhood with "Asiatics" while in the Delta (see J. Černý, JNES, XIV [1955], 161ff.). This extraordinarily rich background for the mingling of Semites and Hurrians (Horites), etc., with Egyptians in Egypt, and at all levels from court to slaves, is a fitting backcloth for the early career of a Moses—taken up by a minor princess in a Delta ḥarem of the reigning pharaoh, and brought up in an Egyp. and Sem. milieu. Like him, other Asiatics were brought up in "district harems," e.g., in the Fayum (see Sauneron and Yoyotte, *Revue d'Égyptologie*, VII [1950], 67-70; related matters, also refs. in NBD, 343b, esp. 844-845). This upbringing carries the implication that a person in Moses' position would undergo an Egyp. royal education, no mean equipment in its day. Cf. H. Brunner, *Altägyptische Erziehung* (1957), for details of Egyp. education. As a scribe, a Moses would be able easily to learn the 26 or 30 letters of the W Sem. alphabet. Apart from the Sinai texts of c. 1500 B.C., other brief epigraphs in alphabetic script are known, e.g., one mentioning *'mht*, "maidservants," on an ostracon from the Valley of the Kings at Thebes, far distant from Pal. or the Delta; and, significantly, all these are homely, everyday inscrs., not recondite. In this context, the picture of a literate Moses is no fantasy—and the Hebrews would have known the ways of Canaan in Egypt itself, long before they ever set out for the Promised Land.

3. *The 20th dynasty* (c. 1200-1070 B.C.). Siptah, last king of the 19th dynasty, was a short-lived puppet ruler, enthroned by the Syrian "king-maker," the chancellor Bay. After the deaths of Siptah and the dowager Queen Tewosret, one Setnakht briefly took the throne, founding the 20th dynasty and restoring internal order in Egypt again. His son Ramses III was the last great pharaoh of the empire. While Sea Peoples in the E Mediterranean basin and other folk moving overland brought final destruction to the Hitt. empire and to the old order of Amorite and Canaanite states in Syria, Ramses III was able in three campaigns to beat off both the Libyans and their allies in the W (years 5, 11) and the Sea Peoples on his NE (year 8) in a dramatic land and sea conflict in S Pal. and at the mouths of the Nile, so saving Egypt from invasion. His inscrs. (e.g., in his great funerary temple of Medinet Habu in W Thebes) contain the first known mention of the Philistines outside the pages of the OT. Peace and prosperity so hard won by Ramses III were transitory, ebbing away with the decay of administration, increase of graft and venality among officials, and spiraling inflation, causing great hardship to the ordinary people. His life ended with a harem conspiracy, and none of his successors—Ramses IV to XI —was able to stop the rot. In this period there first came into the open under Ramses IX a series of notorious tomb robberies in Western Thebes, from which not even the sacrosanct bodies of the pharaohs were exempted. Under these later Ramses, Thebes (and in some measure, Upper Egypt) was increasingly dominated by virtually a dynasty of high priests of Amun, until Amenhotep was displaced by the military commander Herihor in a coup d'état. Ramses XI then endeavored to stabilize the internal situation through the introduction of a "Renaissance" era whereby he as pharaoh had as his direct subordinates Herihor ruling Upper Egypt and Nubia, and one Smendes ruling Lower Egypt. Herihor also became high priest of Amun in Thebes, a dignity that remained hereditary in his family for another 130 years or more. With the death of Ramses XI, the empire formally came to an end, and the accession (c. 1070 B.C.) of his northern deputy Smendes marks for us the beginning of the Late Period.

No age is better known by documents and by visual remains than is the New Kingdom; special mention should be made of the great war reliefs and topographical lists in the Theban temples, so valuable for Syro-Palestinian geography, and of the amazing wealth of scenes of official and daily life still brilliantly preserved in many of the more than 400 tomb chapels of nobles and officials at Thebes. Both literary and non-literary papyri and ostraca throw a flood of light on lit., religion and society in the Egypt of the general period of the Exodus.

F. The Late Period. 1. *The 21st dynasty* (c. 1085-945 B.C.). In an age of decline, the only outstanding kings were Psusennes I and Siamun. This dynasty reigned in the Delta with Tanis (Heb. Zoan) as its capital, while Thebes in the S was in the hands of Herihor's descendants as military governors and high priests of Amun. They ruled almost a state within a state, acknowledging the overlordship of Tanis as long as the latter allowed their regional hegemony. Egypt's internal division and impotence ruled out any expansionist policy abroad, and helps to explain her modest international role in the age of the later judges, Saul, David and Solomon.

The first link between Egypt and the OT at this epoch is afforded by 1 Kings 11:18-22. After David's commander Joab had devastated Edom, the young prince Hadad was spirited away to Egypt by his retainers. He there grew up, married a pharaoh's sister-in-law, and had a son, "weaned in Pharaoh's house." At the death of David (c. 970 B.C.), Hadad returned to Edom; hence, one may place his period of residence in Egypt within roughly 990-970 B.C., which in the 21st dynasty would run from late in the reign of Amenemopet through the brief six years of Osochor well into the reign of Siamun. His Egyp. wife was perhaps, then, a sister-in-law of either Osochor or Siamun. The Tahpenes of 1 Kings 11:19, 20 seems simply to be the Heb. transcript of the Egyp. phrase for "queen," *ta-ḥem(t)-pa-nesu* (giving Heb. *t-ḥ*[*m*]-*p-ns*, consonantally), and not to be a proper name, cf. Grdseloff, *Revue de l'Histoire Juive en Égypte*, No. 1 (1947), 88-90 (differently, Albright, BASOR, No. 140 [1955], 32). The provision assigned to young Hadad and his retainers—a house, food allowance, and land (1 Kings 11:18)—agrees with known Egyp. custom. A thousand years before this the courtier Sinuhe on his return from Syria-Pal. was assigned the house of a former courtier plus some ground and meals were brought to him from the palace "three and four times a day" (cf. ANET, 22:295ff.). In the New Kingdom, it was normal for members of the royal family (as Hadad became, by marriage) to have a personal estate (*per*), including princes (references in Helck, *Materialen zur Wirtschaftsgeschichte des Neuen Reiches*, II [1961], 201-214), and foreigners who entered Egypt by marriage like the Mitannian queen of Amenophis III (ibid., 212:9). Some inscrs. of the 21st and 22nd dynasties show that the pharaohs and high priests sometimes built up such estates by purchase (examples, Gardiner, JEA, XLVIII [1962], 57-69; Legrain and Erman, *Zeitschrift für Aegyptische Sprache*, XXXV [1897], 12-16, 19-24). Again the reference to Hadad's son Genubath being "in Pharaoh's house . . . among the sons of Pharaoh" (1 Kings 11:20) reflects longstanding Egyp. usage, whereby the sons of officials were educated along with the royal princes at court. In the Old Kingdom, one may refer to the example of Ptah-shepses who married a king's daughter (cf. Breasted, *Ancient Records of Egypt*, I, §§ 256, 257). In the Middle Kingdom, in his "Instruction," Khety, son of Duauf, imparts his wisdom to his son while en route to the palace school (ANET, 432b and n. 1), and the official Ikhernofret was reminded of his royal training (ANET, 329b:5ff.). In the New Kingdom, references to this youthful status early in the lives of officials (as *ẖrd-n-k'p*, "pages") are very common. At that period, the sons of Syrian kinglets subject to Egypt were taken as hostages to Egypt, and were kept at court much as were Hadad or Genubath (cf. references, Helck, *Beziehungen Aegyptens zum Vorderasiens* [1962], 366, notes 73-76).

In the early years of Solomon (cf. Malamat, JNES, XXII [1963], 9-17), that monarch married the daughter of a Pharaoh who gave Gezer as a dowry (1 Kings 3:1; 9:16; etc.). The pharaoh concerned was prob. Siamun of the 21st dynasty, from whose reign a broken relief found at Tanis shows him smiting an Asiatic who holds an Aegean-looking weapon. It has therefore been suggested that Siamun had conducted a "police action" in neighboring Philistia, and perhaps also had taken Gezer then, so thereafter giving it as dowry when making the marriage alliance with his powerful Heb. neighbor.

2. The 22nd-24th dynasties (c. 945-715 B.C.). At the death of Siamun's successor Psusennes II in c. 945 B.C., the obvious candidate for the vacant throne was Shoshenq, Great Chief of the Mashwash (Libyans), whose eldest son had married the daughter of Psusennes II, and who himself seems to have had a royal mother. As founder of the 22nd dynasty, Shoshenq I obtained a firm grip on the government of all Egypt, bringing Thebes under his effective control by appointing there as high priest his second son. At the head of a reunited Egypt, Shoshenq in due course planned to deal effectively with his powerful neighbor in Pal. He harbored such political refugees as Jeroboam son of Nebat (1 Kings 11:40); and when Solomon died, allowed him to return to Pal. to precipitate the schism of the Heb. kingdom (1 Kings 12:2ff.). The divided realm of Rehoboam and Jeroboam was no match for Shishak (as the OT calls him) when he duly invaded Pal. in Rehoboam's fifth year (c. 925 B.C.); a broken stele from Karnak temple suggests that a border incident gave Shoshenq his cue to launch an attack (cf. text, Grdseloff, *Revue de l'Histoire Juive en Égypte*, No. 1 [1947], 95-97). The reality of Shoshenq's campaign is graphically illustrated by his great triumphal relief on the S wall of the Karnak temple of Amun at Thebes, naming many towns in Pal. (Epigraphic Survey, *Reliefs and Inscriptions at Karnak*, III [1954], plates 3ff.), and by a fragment of a stele of his that was actually found at Megiddo (cf. C. S. Fisher, *The Excavation of Armageddon* [1929], figure on p. 13). However, though his booty was rich (1 Kings 14:26), Shoshenq's triumph was short lived; he prob. died even before his great Karnak sculpture was completed.

Later Egyp. adventures in Pal. in this period were less successful. "Zerah the Ethiopian" (2 Chron 14:9) was prob. an Egyp. army commander of Nubian origin who under either Osorkon I or Takeloth I endeavored to emulate

Left: Nefert-iti, queen of Akh-en-Aton.

Below: Ahk-en-Aton, sun-worshiper and the first monotheistic king of Egypt, from Amarna.

Bottom: Family scene of Akh-en-Aton, Nefert-iti, and their daughters, under the sun-disc with radiating arms; from Amarna.

Shishak's success, but in vain. Later pharaohs of the 22nd dynasty had neither the ability nor the political power of Shishak. By the time of Osorkon II (c. 860 B.C.), the inner unity of the state was already prejudiced by the ambitions of the high priests in Thebes—again hereditary, but among rival branches of the reigning dynasty. Osorkon II seems to have returned to the more modest foreign policy of the 21st dynasty in similar circumstances of inner political weakness, and so to have made an alliance with Israel. A presentation vase of this pharaoh was found long since in the Omride palace at Samaria (Reisner, Fisher, Lyon, *Harvard Excavations at Samaria*, I [1924], figure on p. 247). Such an alliance would best explain how it was that, rather later on in history, Israel's last king (Hoshea) sent to "So, king of Egypt" for help against Assyria in about 725 B.C. By this date, the Egyp. monarchy had already split into two, with twin lines of pharaohs at Tanis and Bubastis (22nd dynasty) and at Leontopolis (23rd dynasty), and further sub-kings were beginning to emerge in Middle Egypt at Herakleopolis and Hermopolis. These further changes had been heralded and accompanied by bitter civil wars in Upper Egypt, sparked by rival claims on the high priesthood of Amun at Thebes (cf. R. A. Caminos, *Chronicle of Prince Osorkon* [1958], passim). No pharaoh of Egypt in 725 B.C. could possibly aid the luckless Hoshea against Assyria, and his appeal to So (2 Kings 17:4) seems to have gone unanswered. "So" may be an abbreviation for Osorkon, in this case the powerless Osorkon IV last king of the 22nd dynasty (cf. NBD, 1201, and Kitchen, *Third Intermediate Period*, forthcoming). It is unconvincing to interpret this name as "Sais," W Delta capital of the prince Tefnakht (with Goedicke, BASOR, No. 171 [1963], 64-66). A few years later, the impotence of Osorkon IV was well illustrated by his having to buy off Sargon II of Assyria from the Egyp. border by the gift of twelve large horses in 716 B.C. (cf. Tadmor, *Journal of Cuneiform Studies*, XII [1958], 77, 78).

During the period c. 730-715 B.C., two new powers arose on the Nile to contend for the mastery of Egypt. In the N Tefnakht, prince of Sais, built up a kingdom in the NW Delta, and briefly claimed kingship (c. 727-720 B.C.), and his son Bekenranef was sole king of the 24th dynasty for five or six years (720-715). From Nubia, the prince Piankhi had raided Egypt c. 728 B.C., and his successor there, Shabako, invaded Egypt in 715 and eliminated the hapless Bekenranef, thereby uniting Egypt and Cush under the 25th dynasty.

3. *The 25th dynasty* (c. 715-664 B.C.). Shabako was neutral toward Assyria, extraditing rebels when this was requested of him by the Assyrian king, in 712 B.C.; clay sealings of Shabako from Nineveh suggest further contacts. His successor Shebitku changed to a more ambitious and so more aggressive policy. It was prob. he who sent his younger brother Tirhakah (then aged about twenty or so) in 701 B.C. to oppose the Assyrian forces led by Sennacherib against Hezekiah of Judah. The title "king of Cush" accorded to Tirhakah at this juncture in the Biblical narratives (2 Kings 19:9; Isa 37:9) is his eventual title (with the kingship of Egypt) from 690 B.C., but is used by the Biblical writers writing after that date for identification purposes. This is a prolepsis of exactly the same nature as is used in Tirhakah's own inscrs. (so, Kawa Stela IV, lines 7, 8). That Tirhakah was only about nine years old in 701 B.C. (as some have suggested) is ruled out by the fact that his father Pinkhi had died within 717-713 B.C. (extreme dates), and prob. in 716 B.C. (See Kitchen, *Ancient Orient and Old Testament* [1966], 82-84 and note 29, and with fuller background *Third Intermediate Period* forthcoming.) Tirhakah's intervention failed, but Hezekiah survived. Egypt and Cush were no match for Assyria, and as king, Tirhakah experienced two disastrous Assyrian invasions of Egypt in 671 and 666/665 B.C. Finally, his successor Tanwetamani (or Tanutamon) involved Egypt in a further Assyrian invasion which resulted in the sack of Thebes in 664/663 B.C.—an event that echoed round the ancient world, and decades later furnished the prophet Nahum (3:8ff.) with an appropriate analogy when he proclaimed the fall of Assyria in her turn. The pharaohs from Cush had indeed proved to be a broken reed (2 Kings 18:21; Isa 36:6).

4. *The 26th dynasty, Saite Revival* (664-525 B.C.). Like Tefnakht half a cent. before, a prince of Sais in the Delta—Psammetichus I—arose to gain control of Egypt, and this time without a Nubian rival. Within eight years of 664, the sage Psammetichus succeeded in gaining full control of the Delta, winning over the shipmasters of Herakleopolis who ruled Middle Egypt, and finally obtaining recognition in Thebes and the S, installing his daughter as "God's Wife of Amun" (cf. Caminos, JEA, L [1964], 71-101). Like Shoshenq I, Psammetichus succeeded in reuniting Egypt internally, but with far more lasting success, resulting in a period of great prosperity. Under the new dynasty, Egypt looked increasingly for inspiration to her august past, esp. to the Pyramid Age of 2,000 years before and archaic modes were in fashion. Psammetichus established a force of Gr. mercenaries as the core of his army and encouraged Gr. traders. Abroad, Psammetichus I and Necho II supported the waning Assyria against the emerging power of Babylon, as if to keep a balance of powers in Western Asia. When Necho II marched N to support Assyria against Babylon in 609 B.C., Josiah of Judah delayed him sufficiently to seal Assyria's fate, but at the cost of his own life (2 Kings 23:29). Egypt's attempt to replace Assyria as overlord of Pal. was defeated at the Battle of Carchemish in 605 B.C., when

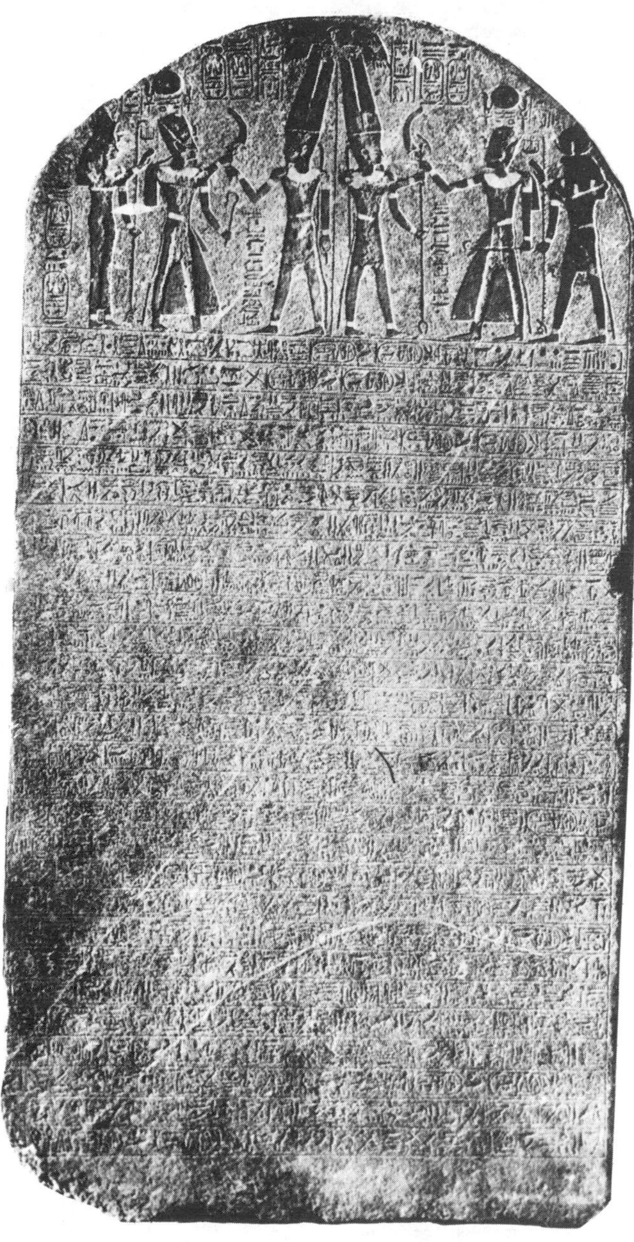

The famous "Israel Tablet" of Pharoah Mernepthah at Thebes, mentioning the departure of Israel from Egypt. © C.M.

the Babylonians ousted the Egyptians and took over the region (Jer 46:2). In 601 B.C., in a further clash, Egypt so severely mauled the Babylonian army that it had to retire for eighteen months for a refit, and thereafter Necho II remained neutral. In Judah, however, Jehoiakim then rebelled against Babylon, perhaps hoping for Egyp. aid (not forthcoming), but in 597 B.C. Nebuchadrezzar II took Jerusalem, and deported the new King Jehoiachin to Babylon. In Egypt Psammetichus II maintained the policy of neutrality in regard to Pal., but his less cautious successor Hophra (q.v.) encouraged Zedekiah in his fatal new rebellion against Babylon in 589/8 B.C., but without affording the Judaeans any real help. Later, as prophesied by Jeremiah (46:13ff.), and attested by a Babylonian text, Nebuchadrezzar II duly marched against Egypt, but perhaps came to some agreement with the new King Amasis (Ahmose II) who had displaced Hophra. Henceforth, both powers were more concerned to ward off the rising threat posed by Media. However, in 525 B.C., Cambyses of Persia took Egypt just as earlier Cyrus had taken over Media and swallowed Babylon.

5. *Later Egypt.* Under Cambyses and Darius I, Pers. rule was fair if firm, and these two kings were given pharaonic titles (27th dynasty). Hankering for their lost independence, the Egyptians revolted just before the death of Darius. They brought upon themselves the wrath of Xerxes I. Henceforth, Egypt was treated as a rebellious province, under a much less liberal regime. In turn, the Egyptians rebelled time and again, until at last during the years 400-341 B.C., they achieved a precarious independence under the kings of the 28th to 30th dynasties. Often in alliance with Greeks (either Athens or Sparta, depending on the varying shifts in Gr. politics), Egypt held off her vast foe until finally overwhelmed by the might of Artaxerxes III in 341, to be ruled again by the Persians for nine years until on his arrival in 332 B.C., Alexander the Great was hailed as a liberator.

Jewish communities in Late Period Egypt dated from the early 26th dynasty when Jeremiah was carried off by his countrymen to Tahpanhes (Daphnai) in the NE Delta (Jer 42-43). Under the Pers. regime there was a Jewish mercenary force acting as garrison on Elephantine Island opposite Aswan (first cataract). They had their own local temple, and the papyri from their settlement form the major part of the Aram. documents for the period (c. 480-400 B.C.). Egyptian independence from c. 400 may have brought this group to an end.

After the death of Alexander the Great in 323 B.C., one of his generals, Ptolemy son of Lagus, assumed the rule of Egypt. He became king as Ptolemy I in 305 B.C., founding a long dynasty. (*See* PTOLEMY.) The Ptolemies ruled as a Hel. Gr. monarchy, based on Alexandria, and ruled Egypt simply as an estate for their own wider ends. Initially, their efficient organization brought renewed prosperity, but the later decay of their administration fostered unrest among the Egyptians. With the defeat of Antony and Cleopatra, Egypt passed under Rom. rule in 31 B.C., and thereafter remained part of the Roman and Byzantine empires for seven centuries until the Islamic conquest in A.D. 641/642. From the 3rd and 4th centuries A.D., Egypt was predominantly a "Christian" land, its indigenous church—still extant—being known as the Coptic church. Monasticism found its first roots in Christian Egypt (St. Antony); the most notable native leader was Shenoute.

VI. EGYPTIAN LITERATURE

Ancient Egypt produced one of the world's first great treasuries of lit. What is extant is preserved and recovered only in part, and much remains to be fully understood, but what is available is of merit and value both in itself and as background for Biblical study.

A. Historical outline. 1. *Third millennium B.C.* a. OLD KINGDOM (2700-2200 B.C.). The oldest lit. is religious, namely the Pyramid Texts. These are a vast corpus of material inscribed in the funerary chambers of the kings of the 6th dynasty, following the example of Unis at the end of the 5th dynasty. These rituals, spells etc. were for the benefit of the dead pharaoh (see Religion below); the texts were published by K. Sethe, *Die altägyptischen Pyramidentexte*, I-IV (1908-1922), plus his *Übersetzung und Kommentar zu den altägyptischen Pyramidentexte*, I-VI (n.d.). An Eng. VS is given by R. A. Faulkner, *The Ancient Egyptian Pyramid Texts*, I-II (1969). Despite their early date, extant copies of c. 2350-2180 B.C. resting on older originals, these texts already exhibit a wide range of literary forms, appropriate to poetry for example. These forms are then attested in Egyp. lit. for 2,000 years thereafter, as well as independently in other ancient Near Eastern lit. and in the OT. The use of parallelism of thoughts in parallel lines and also of converse concepts (so, "synthetic" and "antithetic" parallelism) occurs in its simplest forms, with many detailed variations, and runs to four line groupings and even six and eight line constructions with variations. These stylistic modes of the 3rd millennium B.C. are as artistically "advanced" as anything to be found in Proverbs or the Psalter and have nothing Hel. or even postexilic about them. The literary device of "chiasmus," where elements are varied in the order A-B, B-A, is to be found, sometimes with subtle internal variations, again providing an immense time-perspective as background to the flowering of OT lit. On style in these texts, see O. Firchow, *Grundzüge der Stilistik in den altägyptischen Pyramidentexten* (1953). An almost equally famous religious effusion that originated in this period is the so-called Memphite Theology, known from a copy of the 8th cent. B.C. This is remarkable

Thut-mose IV as a sphinx treading upon his foes; throne fragment from Thebes. ©*Museum of Fine Arts, Boston*

mainly for its "advanced" concepts (early "logos" formulation) at so distant an epoch (ANET, 4-6).

Wisdom lit. in Egypt traditionally began with Imhotep in the time of Djoser and the Step Pyramid (c. 2680 B.C.), but his "Instruction" has yet to be recovered. Fragments are known for those of [Kairos?] to Kagemni, and of Hardjedef, a son of Kheops (builder of the Great Pyramid). Happily, the "Instruction" of Ptahhotep (c. 2400 B.C.) is preserved complete in two Middle Kingdom VSS.

Other literary traces occur in the autobiographies of officials in their tombs. That of Uni cites a victory hymn over his Palestinian foes; it shows a very simple poetic structure exactly like that of Psalm 136 (but with the refrain coming first in each couplet; ANET, 228 for a tr.). Sometimes the Old Kingdom tombs of the nobles preserve snatches of songs of the common folk, cf. ANET, 469b.

b. FIRST INTERMEDIATE PERIOD (2200-2030 B.C.). The noblest product from this troubled age was doubtless the *Dispute of a Man With His Soul,* esp. its moving poems on death and disillusion. For trs., cf. ANET, 405-407, and R. O. Faulkner, JEA, XLII (1956), 21-40, plus the very important comments by R. J. Williams, JEA, XLVIII (1962), 49-56, and E. Brunner-Traut, *Zeitschrift für Aegyptische Sprache*, XCIV (1967), 6-15. The *Eloquent Peasant*, a plea for social justice put into the mouth of a peasant, shows the same A-B-A structure of prose prologue, a cycle of highly poetic speeches, and prose epilogue as does Job (cf. ANET, 407-410). As the badly preserved Discourse of Sisobk appears to have had this pattern also, this A-B-A structure is evidently a proper literary form of high antiquity, and attempts to divorce the authorship of the speeches from the prologue and epilogue in Job are revealed as entirely arbitrary from a purely literary viewpoint. The "Instruction" of Merikara (cf. ANET, 414-418) is also notable.

2. *Second millennium B.C.* a. MIDDLE KINGDOM AND SECOND INTERMEDIATE PERIOD (2134-1551 B.C.). In this, the classical age of the Egyp. language, there emerges a fine group of short stories. Finest of all is the autobiography of *Sinuhe*, a courtier of Amenemhat I, who fled to Syria at his master's death (ANET, 18-22). *The Shipwrecked Sailor* is a nautical fairy tale. Middle-Egyptian stories about the Old Kingdom include the tale of King Neferkara and General Sisenet, and the *Tales of the Magicians* set at the court of Cheops. Field sports feature in the *Sporting King* and the *Pleasures of Fishing and Fowling*. Wisdom lit. is represented by propagandistic works of great skill. Apart from the pseudo *Prophecy of Neferty* (ANET, 444-446), one may notice the "Instruction" of Khety son of Duauf, a "Satire on the Trades" other than that of scribe (to encourage "civil service" recruitment), ANET, 432-434, and that of Amenemhet I to justify his regime against would-be assassins. The "Instructions" of Sehetepibra and of a Man to His Son inculcated loyalty to the throne as the path of wisdom. Religious lit. included long hymns to the Nile, Osiris and Min, as well as to King Sesostris III; less "literary" is the great corpus of Coffin Texts, spells for safety and benefit in the afterlife.

b. THE NEW KINGDOM (1551-1070 B.C.). Literature was greatly enriched under the empire. New stories included the *Foredoomed Prince*, from a world of fairy tales like that of more modern times; the *Tale of the Two Brothers* (a mythical fantasy); and the allegory, the *Blinding of Truth. The Capture of Joppa* foreshadowed *Ali Baba and the Forty Thieves*, while the *Adventures of Wanamun* in Syria (c. 1075 B.C.) is prob. a historical report, but has literary merit. Many other narrative fragments exist, including two "ghost-stories." Complete is a ribald treatment of Osirian mythology in the *Contendings of Horus and Seth*. Wisdom lit. was enriched by the "Instructions" of Aniy (ANET, 420, 421), Amennakht, a priest Amenemhet, and above all, of Amenemopet which is so often correlated with Proverbs (see below). A series of other fragments also survive, esp. praise of ancient writers (ANET, 431, 432).

New in this age is a delightful series of collections of lyric love poems, somewhat reminiscent of the Song of Solomon in style and language. Besides mythological items, religious texts include the great Hymns to Amun (e.g., ANET, 365-369), and Akhenaten's beautiful Hymn to the Aten (solar disc, ANET, 369-371). Of some merit are the stately triumph hymns of such pharaohs as Thutmose III, Amenophis III, and Merneptah (ANET, 373-375, 376, 376-378, respectively), and the touching hymns of penitence of humbler folk, a testimony to the meaning of religion to individuals in the late 2nd millennium B.C. (cf. some Pss) on a personal level (cf. Gunn, JEA, III [1916], 81-94). However, the so-called *Book of the Dead* is merely a collection of spells for the afterlife; and various "illustrated" guidebooks through the Netherworld were inscribed in the tombs of the pharaohs (Books of Gates, Caverns, of What is in the Netherworld, etc.).

3. *First Millennium B.C. The Late Period.* Most of the preserved (and original) lit. of this age is in Demotic, dating from the 6th cent. B.C. to the Rom. period. Stories include the *Cycle of Pedubastis* and *"Egyptians and Amazons,"* romances based on the rivalries of local princes in the 8th/7th centuries B.C., and the *Stories of the High Priests of Memphis*, famous magicians (esp. Khamwese, a son of Ramses II). Wisdom is well represented by the *Instruction of Onkhsheshonqy*, the *Papyrus Insinger* and variants, and works preserved in the Louvre and Brooklyn museums. Among hieroglyphic inscrs., a 22nd-dynasty priest, Nebne-

Top: Door socket from First Dynasty. *Below:* Ruins at Karnak. ©*U.M.P.*

teru, gives his ideals and counsels (Kees, *Zeitschrift für Aegyptische Sprache*, LXXIV [1938], 73-87 [esp. 78ff.], corrected by Kees, ibid., LXXXVIII [1962], 24-26), while the priest Petosiris c. 300 B.C. may in his "wisdom" even have been influenced by Heb. (texts, G. Lefebvre, *Le Tombeau de Pétosiris* [1924], three parts).

B. Egyptian literature and the Old Testament. 1. *Direct links.* Real examples of this have yet to be substantiated. Akhenaten's solar monotheism was essentially little more than the recognition of the beneficent, life-sustaining force of the sun, and offers no basis for Mosaic or ethical monotheism (cf. Religion, below). The incident in the *Tale of the Two Brothers* where a youth is wrongly accused by a woman with designs on him is similar in plot to that of Joseph and Potiphar's wife, but it occurs in a wholly different milieu in which it is the sole item of comparison. Such banal sins are only too well attested in reality (in Egypt as elsewhere) to have any bearing on direct literary connection.

A more promising link between the OT and Egyp. lit. seemed to be between the Egyp. "Instruction" of Amenemopet and parts of the Book of Proverbs; cf. such studies as that of D. C. Simpson, JEA, XII (1926), 232-239. Dependence has been argued both ways. An ostracon of Amenemopet of the 21st dynasty (c. 1070-945 B.C.) would seem to exclude Egyp. dependence on the Heb., while a proper critical study of both works in the *total* context of ancient Near Eastern wisdom lit. (instead of in isolation) shows that there is no adequate basis for making the Heb. Proverbs dependent on Amenemopet (J. Ruffle, *Amenemopet*, forthcoming). The closest points of comparison are far too often merely those which have equally good parallels in other Near Eastern wisdom writings or are banal, while some comparisons fail because they are inexact in form, content, or both.

2. *An objective background for OT literature.* In this role, alongside the literatures of Mesopotamia, the Hittites, Canaan, etc., that of Egypt is of the utmost value, and offers a vast field of study. A few examples and references must suffice to illustrate this theme; cf. already, the example of literary forms illustrated by the Pyramid Texts, above.

a. LITERARY CRITICISM. The attempts to find "hands" in the Pentateuch and Joshua-Judges must fall under the gravest suspicion in the light of Egyp. and allied literatures. With its criteria of double names of deity, humans, clans and places, synonyms in vocabulary, appeals to style, etc., and to supposedly "primitive" and "advanced" concepts, this mode of analysis was produced in the 18th cent. and fully developed in the 19th cent., when at first no objective control from directly comparable sources was available. When such material did become available (late 19th cent. onward), its help was neither sought nor properly utilized. Yet, the same kind of "phenomena" can be found in these literatures as in the OT, and are therefore quite meaningless for analysis, which should carry a sharp danger warning in OT study. Similar criticisms apply also to the methods of study used in Form Criticism (*Gattungsforschung*) and Oral Tradition (History of tradition), with equally drastic implications. Only when OT criticism can proceed from the extant structure of OT lit., in comparison with real modes of composition and attested structure clearly exhibited by the rest of the Biblical world, will a realistic, objectively based and constructive Biblical criticism become possible. (See provisionally, K. A. Kitchen, *Ancient Orient and Old Testament* [1966], 112-138, cf. 139-146, and references.)

b. HISTORY AND FORMS OF LITERARY CATEGORIES. A good example of the application of the data of Egyp. and allied literatures to OT study can be drawn from the wisdom lit., esp. in relation to the Book of Proverbs. As it stands, Proverbs 1-24, with a second collection 25-29, is labelled as Proverbs of Solomon; 1-24 includes a full title with name and rank of the author in the third person, with prologue and discourses (1-9), a subtitle (10:1) and main body of maxims (10ff.). It has been commonly suggested that 1-9 are the latest part of the whole work, of the 4th to 3rd centuries, B.C., partly because of supposedly "advanced" concepts (e.g., personification, as of wisdom), partly on the longer sentence structure, etc.; relatively little even of 10ff. need be attributed as far back as Solomon's time. However, such assumptions and analyses and datings are not supported by the comparative criteria offered by ancient Near Eastern, and esp. Egyp., wisdom lit. Thus, a title with author's name in third person plus rank occurs as normal practice in almost a score of Egyp. wisdom books, at all periods from Old Kingdom to Late Period; and such titles are to be taken seriously. The literary pattern of main title plus discourses, then subtitle and maxims, as in Proverbs 1-9; 10ff., is precisely the pattern presented by Ptahhotep back in the late 3rd millennium B.C., by Khety, son of Duauf, in the early 19th cent. B.C., and as late as Onkhsheshonqy in the 5th-3rd cent. B.C. Variety in sentence length and structure, moreover, is palpably worthless for dating purposes as late as Solomon's time, when one observes the length and elaboration of both discourses and maxims in Ptahhotep in the 3rd millennium B.C. along with the one line proverbs of Onkhsheshonqy 2,000 years *later*, "evolution" here stands on its head (or, rather, is simply inapplicable and irrelevant). Personification belongs not to Hellenism but to the ancient E from the 3rd millennium B.C. onward (cf. Kitchen, *Tyndale House Bulletin*, Nos. 5/6 [1940], 4-6). This and various other aspects may suffice to indicate that Proverbs 1-24 (and

25-29 originally separate) represents a well attested unitary literary form, with nothing later, and much earlier than Solomon.

VII. Egyptian religion

A. The gods of the Egyptians. Fundamentally, Egyp. religion was very local in its practice and horizons. The Egyptians in each district tended to worship principally their particular local deities rather than some greater figure of national or cosmic scope. As was commonly the case in ancient paganism, the gods of Egypt were in large measure the personifications of the powers of nature (e.g., fertility), and of natural phenomena (e.g., the Nile) and their supposed attributes (e.g., of falcon gods, bull gods, etc.). Some were cosmic (sun god), and some were the embodiments of certain concepts (e.g., Maat, goddess of "truth" and right order).

Insofar as various animals, plants, etc. were respected as symbols of natural powers and of mysterious forces, these in turn were considered as manifestations of the deities concerned, even as vehicles of their presence—a role that came to be shared by statues and other images, and by sacred animals (like the Apis bull of Ptah at Memphis, for example). This affected the representations of Egyp. gods in art. As early as the Old Kingdom, the gods came to be conceived in basically human form. Some, like Ptah or Osiris, were shown commonly in entirely human form. Others, by a kind of iconographic shorthand, appeared in human form, except for their heads which are shown as the characteristic heads of the animals connected with particular deities concerned. Anubis appears with the head of a jackal, Sobk with that of a crocodile, Horus and Ra commonly with that of a falcon, Thoth with that of an ibis, etc. Sometimes, they might appear in more than one form: Amun of Thebes was generally in purely human guise, but could have a ram's head.

Among local gods, Amun of Thebes represented the hidden powers of nature, and his close relative Min of Coptos embodied virility and fertility, esp. human and animal. At Memphis, Ptah was the artificer, patron of craftsmen, the Egyp. Vulcan, while the falcon headed Sokar was a local god of the dead and of new life (soon identified with Osiris). In Middle Egypt, Thoth was a god of wisdom and letters, and linked with moon worship. Further S, Hathor of Dendera was a goddess of love. The goddesses Bast of Bubastis and Sekhmet at Memphis respectively represented beneficent powers and the menace of pestilence among other things.

Among gods who had a far reaching impact, beyond merely local appeal, Ra and Osiris were by far the most important. Ra the sun-god (q.v.) had his main cult center at Heliopolis (On). He early became closely associated with the kingship, reaching theological dominance in the state in the 4th and 5th dynasties (*see*

Bes, Egyptian god of Amusement and Games. ©*U.M.P.*

PYRAMID), outrivaling Ptah of Memphis, the administrative capital. His cult also affected the forms of Egyp. temple cult generally. His impact on the monarchy is indicated by the title "Son of Ra" adopted by nearly every pharaoh from the 5th dynasty to the Rom. period, some 3,000 years in all. In the 18th dynasty, Akhenaten endeavored to make a special form of sun worship the sole religion of Egypt. Ra also affected life in the hereafter —the dead could sail over the heavens by day with him in his sacred boat, and also by night through the nether world, rising daily with him on the eastern horizon. During the Old Kingdom, the rise to prominence of Osiris provided an alternative afterlife, and in later days (by the New Kingdom), there was even a theological construction of Ra and Osiris as the risen sun by day and the night sun preceding rebirth, respectively.

The worship of Osiris perhaps came nearest to a universal religion in all Egypt, prior to the impact of Christianity. He was a funerary god who, in the Old Kingdom, became identified with Khentamentyu ("Chief of the Westerners"), the local funerary god at Abydos in Upper Egypt, a place hallowed long previously by tombs of the earliest kings. Osiris was the lord of the netherworld and of the afterlife therein, modeled partly upon earthly Egypt— his followers could sow and reap bountiful harvests, and enjoy the pleasures formerly had on earth. He held the promise of a continued existence in this afterworld, and also became identified with the Nile whose rise annually brought new life to the land. An important aspect of his cult was its "family" nature. His wife was the goddess Isis, a resourceful character as wife and mother of their son Horus who avenged his father and supplanted their foe Seth, in mythology. Here Egypt found a religion that offered something after death in terms that appealed to both men and women comprehensibly. Already accepted into the Pyramid Texts by the late Old Kingdom, the triumph of Osiris was complete from the advent of the Middle Kingdom, c. 2000 B.C., and Abydos became one of the most sacred and famed cities of Egypt. Many hundreds of memorial stelae in the world's museums (esp. Cairo) exhumed from its sands over the last cent. bear mute witness to the wish of countless Egyptians to have their names there in the presence of the "great god." In the Late Period, the influence of Osiris on other cults was most noticeable; even the great imperial god, Amun of Thebes in the 21st to 26th dynasties saw his precinct at Karnak dotted with twenty or more little shrines to various forms of Osiris. Still later, the cult of Osiris (esp. as Serapis) and Isis penetrated the Graeco-Rom. world, and the religion of Isis competed with Mithras and early Christianity, reaching far across Europe and throughout the Rom. empire. The Nile god, Hapi, was also venerated throughout Egypt, and at all periods (esp. in relation to agriculture), but he never received great temples. His worship was more often marked by seasonal riverside ceremonies, those at Memphis and Heliopolis (later, at Cairo) surviving even into modern times (the "Night of the Drop" on the traditional feast for the beginning of the annual rise of the Nile).

However, besides the local cults and gods such as Ra and Osiris with a wider appeal lasting for millennia, the history of Egyp. religion shows also the wax and wane of other gods, conditioned by political changes. Under the earliest dynasties in the Old Kingdom, Ptah of Memphis shared in the central importance of that city, but then was overshadowed by the sun god Ra. The Memphite theology from this age prob. represents Ptah's claim (against Ra) to the role of supreme god and creator of all else. By the late Old Kingdom, Osiris was gaining ground so much as even to invade the domain of Ra, i.e., royal theology; and as noted above, furnished the Egyptians with their most powerful hope in the afterlife from the Middle Kingdom onward, such that in the New Kingdom, theological accomodation even reckoned Ra and Osiris as forms of each other. Amun of Thebes well illustrates the fluctuating fortunes of a god and his city. His importance first arose when in the Middle Kingdom he became Amen-Ra (with a more universal scope) and was favored by the 12th dynasty, itself of S Egyp. origin. It was only with the all-conquering Theban pharaohs of the 18th dynasty that Amun of the hidden forces of nature became also king of the gods and virtually god of the empire, with the biggest temples ever seen. However, the disproportionate prominence of Amun and his priesthood in the state was felt as a menace by the monarchy, culminating in the deposition of Amun and the other gods in favor of the sun god by Akhenaten. However, Akhenaten's solar monotheism was shallow and (as noted above) concentrated largely on the beneficent and life sustaining force of the sun in nature; it had no moral tone or philosophical basis. The epithet "living in truth" (Maat) merely reflected Akhenaten's claim that his way, not that of the old gods, was true to the right order of the cosmos. There is here no adequate source for the emphatic moral and social monotheism of a Moses or a Sinai covenant.

In the 19th and 20th dynasties, the Ramessides curbed the power of Amun by favoring him as one of a trinity of gods: Amun of Thebes, Ra of Heliopolis, and Ptah of Memphis. One or two remarkable texts even syncretistically seek to identify the three as aspects of one great deity (cf., e.g., Gardiner, *Hieratic Papyri in the British Museum, 3rd Series*, I [1935], 28-37), a fact that shows a high level of religious thinking and speculation already in the 13th cent. B.C. In this light, the revealed monotheism of the OT need hardly

Osiris, King of Egyptian Gods. ©*U.M.P.*

Isis, sister and wife of Osiris, and their son, Horus. ©*U.M.P.*

wait until after the Babylonian exile to be expressed or formulated. In the Late Period (cf. above), Amun's fame outside of Thebes waned with the eclipse of Empire, Ptah similarly resumed the main role of local artificer—god of Memphis, and Ra continued traditionally as part of the theology of kingship—Osiris and Isis with their son Horus enjoyed the greater general popularity, while the gods and goddesses of the Delta received more prominence with that achieved by the Delta cities under Lower Egyp. kings in the later dynasties.

Finally, Pharaoh himself must be reckoned among the gods. He was their representative on earth, and among the Egyptians a man who moved in the world of the gods. The living king counted as Horus, and the dead ruler(s) as Osiris; a new king received an unchallengable right of succession at least partly by virtue of giving proper burial to his predecessor in filial fashion as did Horus for Osiris (*see* PHARAOH).

B. Worship and cult. The Egyp. temple was the house of its god in quite a literal sense. The basis of the cult was the daily ritual. This was modeled on ordinary life. In the morning, the god in his sanctuary was awakened with the morning hymn, his shrine was opened, his cult image ritually purified and dressed, and offerings presented to it (breakfast). At midday and later, lesser services of offering were celebrated. The god might give oracles, receive visitors (other gods embodied in their cult images) or himself go in procession to some other temple. His life had its necessities and duties, so to speak, as did the king or a householder. The cult so celebrated was the preserve of the priests, there was no lay congregation to witness or share in the rites.

This is illustrated and emphasized by the form of Egyp. temples, best known from New Kingdom examples. The whole sacred precinct was shut in by massive mud brick walls, pierced by one or more massive gateways. Within the area stood not only the temple of the god (and perhaps shrines of associated deities) but also the dwellings of the priests, the storehouses for offerings, quarters for livestock for offerings, temple gardens and trees, and the sacred lake—source of holy water and setting for dramatic rites. The temple itself would often be approached along an avenue lined with sphinxes on either side, leading to a great gateway between two flanking towers of inward sloping form, broader than high —the whole being termed a "pylon." Such an entrance might be preceded by obelisks and colossal royal statues; beyond it, one commonly entered an open court with colonnades. Beyond this, the privileged entered the temple proper, perhaps through a second pylon, into a great "hypostyle" hall of columns, with a central nave higher than the rest, allowing of clerestory lighting. Thereafter, one would pass through successive halls and rooms (each with its role), into ever-increasing darkness, whose mystery was heightened by rising floor levels, lower roofs, and in the dim light, the gleam of gold and glow of rich colors from painted reliefs of the king performing ritual acts. Finally came the sanctuary containing the shrine of the god, its doors bolted and sealed, guarding the cult image within. Around were sanctuaries of co-templar gods, and storerooms for the treasures and paraphernalia of the cult.

The spectacle of the outwardly powerful Egyp. gods actually dependent in some measure on the food offerings presented to them (and on images of the rites, should human agents fail) stands in striking contrast with the God of Israel (and *a fortiori*, of the NT), self-sufficient and sustaining all else, whose offering rites in Tabernacle and Temple were aimed at the benefit of His worshipers, with didactic role concerning sin and atonement and reconciliation.

Excluded from the great temples, the populace frequented lesser shrines or oratories at the gateways of the vast major precincts. Their main contact with the great gods came only on high days of festival, when the gods went forth in glittering array on stately processions. The splendor of the festivals culminated under the empire; suffice it to mention some great Theban festivals. On the Feast of Opet, Amun sailed on the river from Karnak to Luxor temple, accompanied by joyous crowds along the river bank (cf. W. Wolf, *Das schöne Fest von Opet* [1931], Luxor scenes). On the Feast of the Valley, Amun's golden barge took him to Western Thebes across river to the funerary temples of the pharaohs, while the Thebans offered to their own ancestors and made holiday at the tomb chapels, brilliantly-painted venues for the feasting (cf. S. Schott, *Das schöne Fest von Wüstentale* [1953], on rites). Both at Memphis and at Thebes, the rich festival of Sokar-Osiris attracted the multitude to see the fantastically formed golden boat of Sokar borne around the walls of town or temple, and to the necropolis (Gaballa and Kitchen, "Festival of Sokar," *Orientalia*, XXXVII [1968], 1-76). Herodotus reported on the feasts of the Delta, and the temples of Edfu and Dendera give much detail on feasts in the Ptolemaic age. Both the ordinary rituals and the festival rites of Egypt far outstrip in complexity anything to be found in the rituals of the Heb. Pentateuch. Even on an "evolutionary" basis (inherently erroneous), therefore, it would be unrealistic to make the relatively simple Heb. rituals as late as the Pers. age; by Egyp. standards, they would be more than prepatriarchal, let alone Mosaic!

C. Funerary beliefs. Belief in an afterlife was a leading feature of Egyp. religion at all periods, but as already seen was not a unity—solar and Osirian hereafters offered either the

Egyptian Temple. ©*V.E.*

Hypostele Hall (Karnak) restored. ©*U.M.P.*

Portion from "Book of the Dead"—19th dynasty. ©U.M.P.

company of Ra across the heavens or else the netherworldly realm of Osiris on a more earthly model. In either case, the body was a material abode for the soul, hence the efforts to preserve it (mummification) and the use of statutes to preserve a likeness even if the body perished. Insofar as the afterlife reflected earthly conditions, tomb pictures magically could supply the wants of the deceased, and the tomb was his eternal house, to be appropriately furnished with goods that would be magically effective—hence the wealth of Egyp. burials, a famed target of tomb robbers. While the Book of the Dead included a moral element in a form of judgment of the dead, the impact of this was weakened by resort to magic. To the materialistic nature of Egyp. eschatology, we owe a great deal of our knowledge of that civilization.

BIBLIOGRAPHY

A. Bibliographical aids. Up to 1941, see Ida A. Pratt, *Ancient Egypt, Sources of Information in the New York Public Library* (1925); and idem., *Ancient Egypt*, 1925-1941 (1942), plus the running bibliographies in JEA and *Chronique d'Égypte*. For the years 1939-1947, consult W. Federn, in *Orientalia*, XVII (1948) to XIX (1950), eight installments. Since 1947, see J. M. A. Janssen, *Annual Egyptological Bibliography* (1948ff.), continued by M. Heerma van Voss. For standing monuments and finds, absolutely invaluable is B. Porter, R. L. B. Moss, E. M. Burney, *Topographical Bibliography of Ancient Egyptian Hieroglyphic Texts, Reliefs, and Paintings*, I-VII (1929-1951), and 2nd ed., I:1 (1960), I:2 (1964), II. On recovery of ancient Egypt, see J. A. Wilson, *Signs and Wonders Upon Pharaoh* (1964); L. Greener, *The Discovery of Egypt* (1966); E. Hornung, *Einführung in die Ägyptologie* (1967).

B. Geography and topography. On earliest conditions, see Rushdi Said, *The Geology of Egypt* (1962), and W. C. Hayes, *Most Ancient Egypt* (1965), from JNES, XXIII (1964), 73ff., 145ff., 217ff., with further references. Generally, see J. Ball, *Contributions to the Geography of Egypt* (1939). On ancient topography, Sir A. H. Gardiner, *Ancient Egyptian Onomastica*, I-III (1947) is a mine of information, more careful than the vast compendium by H. Gauthier, *Dictionnaire des Noms Géographiques*, I-VII (1925-1931), and the recent survey by P. Montet, *Géographie de l'Égypte Ancienne*, I-II (1957). On classical sources, cf. J. Ball, *Egypt in the Classical Geographers* (1941). Baedeker, *Egypt and the Sudan* (1929) is valuable, and so for interrelation of land, culture and history is H. Kees, *Ancient Egypt, A Cultural Topography* (1961).

C. Language and scripts. Affinities of Egyp. and Sem., cf. Gardiner, *Egyp. Grammar*, § 3; G. Lefebvre, *Chronique d'Égypte*, XI/22 (1936), 266-292; for Old Egyptian, see E. Edel, *Altägyptische Grammatik*, I/II (1955/1964). For Middle Egyp., a full survey is Sir A. H. Gardiner, *Egyptian Grammar*[3] (1957), and a modern, compact treatment, H. W. Fairman, *Introduction to Middle-Egyptian Grammar* (in press); for Late Egyp., A. Erman, *Neuägyptische Grammatik*[2] (1933) is available but obsolescent; for lexicography, standard is A. Erman and H. Grapow, *Wörterbuch der Aegyptischen Sprache*, I-V (1926-1931), Indices= VI-VII (1950/1963), and *Belegstellen*, I-V (1937-1958) for sources used; handy is R. O. Faulkner, *A Concise Dictionary of Middle Egyptian* (1962). For Coptic, Sahidic dialect, a handy outline is J. M. Plumley, *Introductory Coptic Grammar* (1948), fuller is W. C. Till, *Koptische Grammatik* (1956). For Bohairic, cf. A. Mallon (ed. M. Malinine), *Grammaire Copte*[4] (1956), with good general bibliography. All dialects are usefully outlined in W. C. Till, *Koptische Dialektgrammatik*[2] (1961). The finest lexicon is W. E. Crum, *Coptic Dictionary* (1939), with addenda by R. Kasser, *Compléments au Dictionnaire Copte de Crum* (1964); handier is W. Spiegelberg, *Koptisches Handwörterbuch* (1921), being replaced by W. Westendorf, ibid. (1965ff.), and J. Černý, *Coptic Etymological Dictionary* (in press); none of these works include the Gr. words in Coptic, but they find a place in R. Kasser and W. Vycichl, *Dictionnaire . . . Copte* (1967ff.).

On Egyp. hieroglyphic script, see Nina M. Davies, *Picture Writing in Ancient Egypt* (1958); hieratic, G. Möller, *Hieratische Paläographie*,[2] I-III, IV (1927-1936, repr. 1965), and *Hieratische Lesestücke*, I-III (1909-1910 and reprs.).

Semitic loanwords cf. M. Burchardt, *Die altkanaanaischen Fremdworte und Eigennamen im Aegyptischen*, I/II (1909/1910), with W. F. Albright, *Vocalization of the Egyptian Syllabic Orthography* (1934) and with T. O. Lambdin, JSS, II (1957), 113-127. For Meroitic studies, see bibliography by F. Gadallah, Kush, XI (1963), 196-216 (esp. 209, 210), and outline survey by P. L. Shinnie, *Meroe, A Civilization of the Sudan* (1967).

D. Chronology. For Manetho, see W. G. Waddell, *Manetho*, Loeb Classical Library (1940); W. Helck, *Untersuchungen zu Manetho und den Ägyptischen Königslisten* (1956); Turin canon, cf. Sir A. H. Gardiner, *The Royal Canon of Turin* (1959) for its text, with data excerpted in his *Egypt of the Pharaohs* (1961), 429ff.

For Egyp. dates down to c. 945 B.C., cf. W. C. Hayes in Hayes, Rowton, Stubbings, CAH,[2] I, ch. 6: *Chronology* (1961). For Egyp. calendars and 12th dynasty dates, see R. A. Parker, *The Calendars of Ancient Egypt* (1950); Lunar dates of Thutmose III and Ramses II, Parker, JNES, XVI (1957), 39-43. On New Kingdom chronology, see E. Hornung, *Untersuchungen zur Chronologie und Geschichte des Neuen Reiches* (1964), plus K. A. Kitchen, *Chronique d'Égypte*, XL/80 (1965), 310-322, and (early 18th dynasty) Hornung, *Zeitschrift der Deutschen Morgenländischen Gesellschaft*, CXVII (1967), 11-16. For the 21st to 25th dynasties, see Kitchen, *Third Intermediate Period in Egypt* (1972-1973). For 664 B.C. as correct date for start of 26th dynasty, see Parker, *Mitteilungen des Deutschen Archäologischen Instituts, Kairo Abteilung*, XV (1957), 208-212, and Hornung, *Zeitschrift für Aegyptische Sprache*, XCII (1966), 38, 39. Ptolemies, A. E. Samuel, *Ptolemaic Chronology* (1962).

E. History. (General works at end of section).

1. Predynastic. Outline and further references, E. J. Baumgartel, CAH[2], I, ch. 9a: *Predynastic Egypt* (1965), cf. Hayes, *Most Ancient Egypt* (1965).

2. Archaic. Good surveys, W. B. Emery, *Archaic Egypt* (1961), and I. E. S. Edwards, CAH[2], I, ch. 11: *The Early Dynastic Period in Egypt* (1964).

3. Old Kingdom. W. S. Smith, CAH[2], I, ch. 14: *The Old Kingdom in Egypt* (1962); the art, W. S. Smith, *Egyptian Sculpture and Painting in the Old Kingdom*[2] (1949); Administration, cf. W. Helck, *Untersuchungen zu den Beamtentiteln des Ägyptischen Alten Reiches* (1954), and K. Baer, *Rank and Title in the Old Kingdom* (1960), esp. ch. VII. Monuments, cf. I. E. S. Edwards, *The Pyramids of Egypt*[2] (1961); A. Fakhry, *The Pyramids* (1961); Decrees, H. Goedicke, *Königliche Dokumente aus dem Alten Reich* (1967).

4. Rise and fall, Middle Kingdom. W. C. Hayes, CAH[2], I, ch. 20: *The Middle Kingdom in Egypt* (1961), and CAH[2], II, ch. 2: *Egypt from Death of Ammenemes III to Seqenenre II* (1962); G. Posener, *Littérature et Politique dans l'Égypte de la XIIe Dynastie* (1956); W. C. Hayes, *A Papyrus of the Late Middle Kingdom* (1955); W. Schenkel, *Memphis, Herakleopolis, Theben* (1965), J. von Beckerath, *Untersuchungen zur politischen Geschichte der zweiten Zwischenzeit in Ägypten* (1965); J. van Seters, *The Hyksos, A New Investigation* (1966); for Byblos, Kitchen, *Orientalia*, XXXVI (1967), 39-54.

5. New Kingdom. T. G. H. James CAH[2], II, ch. 8: *Egypt from Expulsion of the Hyksos to Amenophis I* (1965); W. C. Hayes, CAH[2], II, ch. 9; *Egypt, Internal Affairs from Thutmose I to the Death of Amenophis III*, two parts (1962); R. O. Faulkner, CAH[2], II, ch. 23: *Egypt, from Inception of Nineteenth Dynasty to Death of Ramesses III* (1966); J. Černý, CAH[2], II, ch. 35: *Egypt, from Death of Ramesses III to the End of the Twenty-first Dynasty* (1965); G. Steindorff and K. C. Seele, *When Egypt Ruled the East*[2] (1957); D. B. Redford, *History and Chronology of the Eighteenth Dynasty of Egypt* (1967), cf. Kitchen, *Chronique d'Égypte*, XLIII/86 (1968), 313-324; On Egypt and Near East see W. Helck, *Die Beziehungen Ägyptens zu Vorderasien im 3 und 2. Jahrtausend v. Chron* (1962); economics and administration, cf. W. Helck,

Zur Verwaltung des Mittleren und Neuen Reiches (1958), and Helck, *Materialen zur Wirtschaftsgeschichte des Neuen Reiches,* I-VI (1961-1965); texts of Ramses III, cf. W. F. Edgerton and J. A. Wilson, *Historical Records of Ramses III* (1936).

6. Late period. For 21st dynasty, Černý, CAH, in section above; the 21st-25th dynasties, Kitchen, *Third Intermediate Period in Egypt,* 1972-1973. Persian age, cf. G. Posener, *La Première Domination Perse en Égypte* (1936); for 26th to 30th dynasties, see F. K. Kienitz, *Die politische Geschichte Ägyptens vom 7. bis zum 4. Jahrhundert vor der Zeitwende* (1953), and Mary F. Gyles, *Pharaonic Policies and Administration,* 663 to 323 B.C. (1959). Egypt, Judah and Babylon, cf. D. J. Wiseman, *Chronicles of Chaldaean Kings* (1956); on Jewish settlements and Aramaic papyri in Egypt, cf. E. G. Kraeling, *The Brooklyn Museum Aramaic Papyri* (1953), 3-119.

7. General histories. Besides the new CAH², already cited by fascicules, see J. A. Wilson, *The Burden of Egypt* (1951), also as *The Culture of Ancient Egypt* (1956, paperback); W. C. Hayes, *The Sceptre of Egypt,* I-II (1953/1959); Sir A. H. Gardiner, *Egypt of the Pharaohs* (1961); É. Drioton and J. Vandier, *L'Égypte*⁴ (1962), well-documented; E. Hornung, *Grundzüge der Ägyptischen Geschichte* (1965). Most historical sources are in J. H. Breasted, *Ancient Records of Egypt,* I-V (1906-1907).

F. Civilization. A. Erman, *Life in Ancient Egypt* (1894); H. Kees, *Aegypten* (1933); S. R. K. Glanville (ed.), *The Legacy of Egypt* (1942), new ed. 1972; G. Posener et al., *A Dictionary of Egyptian Civilization* (1962), reliable, comprehensive, well-illustrated; L. Casson, *Ancient Egypt, Great Ages of Man* (1965). Art and Archaeology: J. Vandier, *Manuel d'Archéologie Égyptienne,* 5 vols. in 9 (1952-1969); W. S. Smith, *Art and Architecture of Ancient Egypt* (1958); J.-L. de Cenival, *Living Architecture, Egyptian* (1964). On Egypt and OT, cf. J. Vergote, *Joseph en Égypte* (1959), plus Kitchen, JEA, XLVII (1961), 158-164; P. Montet, *L'Égypte et la Bible* (1959).

G. Literature. Selections in ANET, passim. Fuller, A. Erman tr. by A. M. Blackman, *The Literature of the Ancient Egyptians* (1927), repr. with valuable new introduction by W. K. Simpson as *The Ancient Egyptians, A Sourcebook of their Writings* (1966); G. Lefebvre, *Romans et Contes Égyptiens* (1949); E. Brunner-Traut, *Altägyptische Märchen*² (1965). Valuable studies of Egyp. literature include: H. Grapow, *Bildliche Ausdrücke des Aegyptischen* (1924); G. Posener, "Récherches Littéraires," I-VII, in *Revue d'Égyptologie,* VI (1951) to XII (1960); Brunner et al., in B. Spuler (ed.), *Handbuch der Orientalistik,* I: (*Ägyptologie*), 2: *Literatur* (1952); H. Brunner, *Grundzüge einer Geschichte der Altägyptischen Literatur* (1966).

H. Religion. J. Černý, *Ancient Egyptian Religion* (1952), and H. Frankfort, *Ancient Egyptian Religion* (1951) are handy outlines. Fuller and well documented are: J. Vandier, *La Religion Égyptienne* (1949); H. Kees, *Der Götterglaube im Alten Ägypten*² (1956), and *Totenglauben und Jenseitsvorstellungen der alten Ägypter*² (1956); S. Morenz, *Ägyptische Religion* (1962), and *Gott und Mensch im alten Ägypten* (1964); H. Bonnet, *Reallexikon der ägyptischen Religionsgeschichte* (1952) is invaluable; for early periods (e.g., Pyr. Texts), cf. J. H. Breasted, *Development of Religion and Thought in Ancient Egypt* (1912, repr. 1959). On priests, cf. S. Sauneron, *The Priests of Ancient Egypt* (1960); H. Kees, *Das Priestertum im Ägyptischen Staat* (1953-1958), and *Die Hohenpriester des Amun von Karnak von Herihor bis zum Ende der Äthiopenzeit* (1964), completing G. Lefebvre, *Histoire des Grands Prêtres d'Amon de Karnak* (1929); On Egyp. temple cult, cf. H. W. Fairman, "Worship and Festivals in an Egyptian Temple" (Edfu), repr. from BJRL, XXXVII (1954), 165-203; Festivals, cf. S. Schott *Altägyptische Festdaten* (1950), and C. J. Bleeker, *Egyptian Festivals* (1967).

K. A. KITCHEN

EGYPTIAN, THE. An unnamed individual mentioned in the context of Paul's arrest and removal from the Temple precinct (Acts 21:38). In the narrative the Rom. officer (Gr. χιλίαρχος, Lat. *tribunus*) asked Paul if he was not a certain "Egyptian" who was attempting a revolt against Rome. This man was supposed to have led his four thousand dagger-bearers (Gr. σικάριος, loan word from Lat. *sikarius,* derived from *sica* "a dagger") into the wilderness. Although the Sicarii are mentioned in contemporary accounts such as Jos. Antiq. XX, 186, 204, 208 and Jos. War. II, 254-257 et al., yet the precise identification of the "Egyptian" is unknown. During the years of Rom. imperial occupation of Pal. many such revolutionaries appeared and were brought to judgment by the legions. The last revolt in A.D. 66 engaged the Sicarii and their leaders, and there is strong evidence to associate them with the defense of Masada in A.D. 73. They were the most violent and terroristic of the many national sects which appeared among the Jews under Rom. domination. Undoubtedly these groups adhered to a certain military chiliasm as is demonstrated in the lit. of the much more passive Qumran community such as the 1 Q M. One of the features of these groups was their abhorrence of Lat., hence the wonder of the tribune at Paul's use of Gr.

W. WHITE, JR.

EGYPTIAN VERSIONS. *See* VERSIONS, ANCIENT.

EGYPTIANS, GOSPEL OF THE. A *Gospel of the*

Egyptians is mentioned among other apocryphal books by Origen (in *Luc. hom.* I). Two distinct works are known under this title: (1) a document quoted by Clement of Alexandria in *Strom. III*, where he was concerned with questions of marriage and sexual morality, and *interalia* joined issue with the Encratites and other groups. In so doing he mentions their use of this gospel and gives a few extracts from a dialogue between Christ and Salome. A fragment of this dialogue is quoted in II Clement 12.1, 2, but whether the other non-canonical sayings in II Clement also derive from the *Gospel of the Egyptians* is by no means certain. A further quotation occurs in Clement's *Excerpta ex Theodoto* (67), and according to Hippolytus (*Ref.* V. 7. 8f.) the book was used by the Naassenes. Epiphanius (*Pan.* 62. 4) mentions its use by the Sabellians, but gives no information of its character.

The evidence is not sufficient to provide a basis for conclusions about the nature, content and structure of the book, but it must go back to the 2nd cent. and seems to have been of a Gnostic, or at any rate, Encratite character. Clement quoted it *against* the Encratites, but had to read his own interpretation into the text; but while he clearly places it on a lower level than the canonical gospels there is no sign that he entirely disapproved of it. It was probably the gospel of Gentile Christians in Egypt, while the *Gospel of the Hebrews* (q.v.) was that of the Jewish Christians. Parallels in the *Coptic Gospel of Thomas* (q.v.) have led to the suggestion that the *Gospel of the Egyptians* was one of its sources, but this again remains uncertain. (See further NTAp. I. 166ff.).

(2.) Completely different is a document contained in Codices III and IV of the Nag Hammadi library. Both VSS have the title "Sacred Book of the Great Invisible Spirit," but Codex III also has in the colophon the title, "*Gospel of the Egyptians.*" The description of the heavenly world from its opening pages has been tr. and discussed by A. Böhlig (*Le Muséon* 80 [1967] 5ff.). It begins with a description of the great invisible Spirit and of the emanations (Father, Mother, Son) which proceed from Him. The appearance of Barbelo and various points of agreement with the *Apocryphon of John* suggests a connection with the Barbelo-gnostic sect. (See further NTAp. I. 361ff.)

R. McL. Wilson

EHI e' ī (אחי). Listed as a son of Benjamin (Gen 46:21), but his name was given as Ahiram (Num 26:38) of which Ehi may have been a fragment. In 1 Chronicles 8:1 it is spelled Aharah.

EHUD ē' hud (אהוד, Judg 3:15, 1 Chron 7:10; אחוד, 1 Chron 8:6). A Benjamite name designating the son of Gera. ("Abihud," a personal name in 1 Chron 8:3, is prob. a mistake for "father of Ehud.") Ehud was notable for being left-handed (Heb. "hindered in the right hand"), a physical characteristic sufficiently unusual in antiquity to merit mention. This hero led the revolt against the Edomite King Eglon, who early in the Judges period had subjugated Israel for eighteen years.

Some scholars have seen in the deliverance narrative (Judg 3:15-30) two closely interwoven accounts with Judges 3:17a being a continuation of 3:15b, and vv. 18, 19 an insertion between 3:17b and 20. However, this rearrangement does nothing to clarify or enhance the narrative, which possesses its own genuine motifs typical of the exploits of heroes in the E Mediterranean Heroic Age. While Ehud was not specifically described as a "judge," the characteristic introduction and conclusion to the narrative (3:12-15a, 28-30; 4:1) indicate that the compiler of Judges clearly regarded him as such.

Before taking the annual tribute to Eglon, Ehud fashioned a thirteen inch double-edged dagger which he carried on his right thigh for convenience, being left-handed. Having publicly paid the tribute, he seized an opportunity through a ruse to speak privately to Eglon and slew the unsuspecting king. Gaining time by locking the body in the private chamber, Ehud escaped through a window and marshaled the W Jordanian Israelites to prevent 10,000 Moabite soldiers from fleeing homeward, thus insuring peace for eighty years (3:30).

BIBLIOGRAPHY. E. G. Kraeling, JBL (1935), LIV, 205-210.

R. K. Harrison

EKER ē' kər (עקר, *root*.) A man listed as a son of Ram (1 Chron 2:27), descendant of Judah. He was a member of the clan of Jerahmeel, of postexilic origin.

EKREBEL. KJV form of ACRABA **ăk' rə bə** ('Εγρεβήλ, Judith 7:18). A place described as "near CHUSI beside the brook Mochmur," prob. the modern Akrabeh, about twenty-five m. N of Jerusalem in the hill country, within a few m. of the well of Sychar.

EKRON, EKRONITE ĕk' rŏn, ĕk' rŏn īt (עקרון, LXX 'Ακκαρών; עקרוני, LXX 'Ακκαρωνίτη. Nouns derived from the root "to root out"). The northernmost of the five major Philistine cities and its inhabitants the latter of whom are mentioned in two passages (Josh 13:3; 1 Sam 5:10; LXX reads Askalonites in 1 Sam 5:10). The city is mentioned in twenty passages.

Ekron, a border town in the tribal territory allotted to Judah, was not taken before the death of Joshua (Josh 13:3; 15:11, 45, 46) but was acquired later (Judg 1:18). It is later said to belong to Dan (Josh 19:43) and Josephus (Antiq. V. 177) also mentions Ekron in his account of the press of the Danites by the Philistines.

Though Ekron is said to have been taken by Judah at the beginning of the period of the Judges (Judg 1:18) the Philistines continued to dominate it through the period of the Judges and the Kings. While the Ark was in Philistine possession, after being at Ashdod and at Gath, it was sent to Ekron (LXX reads Askalon: 1 Sam 5:10; 6:16) where its presence caused panic and from which it was returned with gifts to the Israelites at Beth-shemesh and eventually came to Kiriath-jearim (5:10ff.; 6:16; 7:1). Samuel is said to have restored Israel's territory from Ekron to Gath (7:14); again the Philistines were driven back to the gates of Ekron following the death of Goliath (17:52).

The god of Ekron was Baalzebub to whom King Ahaziah (c. 850-849 B.C.) sent to inquire of the possibilities of his recovery. The king's action brought stern denunciation from Elijah (2 Kings 1:2, 3, 6, 16).

Destruction was threatened Ekron by the prophets in their oracles against the Philistines (Jer 25:20 [LXX 32:20]; Amos 1:8; Zeph 2:4; Zech 9:5, 7). Gath had by this time disappeared from the Philistine list leaving only a group of four cities. Zechariah promised that like the Jebusites Ekron would be incorporated into Israel.

When Padi, king of Ekron, was imprisoned by Hezekiah in 701 B.C., Sennacherib both forced his release and forced Hezekiah to cede Judean territory to him. Sennacherib arrived at Ekron on his way S after taking Eltekeh and Timnah (ANET, 287, 288). Later, tribute was taken from Ekron by both Esarhaddon (ANET, 291) and Ashurbanipal (ANET, 294). After the destruction of Jerusalem in 587 B.C., Ekron is unmentioned until the Maccabean period at which time in 147 B.C. Alexander Balas gave the city as a prize for services to Jonathan Maccabeus (1 Macc 10:89). The city continued on to Crusader times.

The identification of the site of Ekron remains conjectural. Eusebius in the *Onomasticon* (ed. Klostermann, p. 22, 1. 9, 10) mentions Ekron as a large Jewish village between Azotus and Jamnia to the E. Jerome (PL. 23. 915) suggests that some identify it with *turrim Stratonis* (Caesarea) which suggestion is now completely rejected. Robinson (*Biblical Researches*, II, 226-229) identified Ekron with the village of Aqir; however, Aqir situated in a level plain four m. E of Yebnah and twelve m. NE of Ashdod and ¾ m. SW of Ramleh—in the area today of Kefar 'Ekron—has neither a tell nor potsherds from the required fifteen hundred year period of occupation; hence the identification, though still preferred by Simon and others, is rejected by Macalister and Albright.

Macalister attempted a distinction between northern Ekron (to be identified with the Danite town, (Josh 19:43) which he thought might be 'Aqir and a second Ekron (in Judah) for which he proposed Dhikerin, a location between Mareshah and Ashdod where there are caves and cisterns from antiquity.

Qaṭra, a hill three m. SW of 'Aqir, with a tell and remains from the Greco-Rom. period, was favored by Albright as fitting the description of Eusebius which places Ekron to the E of the route from Ashdod to Jamnia. The site would lend itself to the strong fortifications expected in a major Philistine city.

More recently Naveh of the Joint Archaeological Survey of the Dept. of Archaeology of the Hebrew University and the Israel Exploration Society has proposed that Khirbat al-Muqanna' (Tell Miqne), located about one third m. E of Kibbutz Revadim, S of the Sorek valley, is Ekron. Philistine sherds are to be found on the surface. The city existed from the iron age to the Pers. period, and at its height of development would have covered forty acres, which makes it the largest iron age city yet found in Pal. Sections of the wall and the city gate can be traced out. There are springs of water in the area sufficient to support a sizeable town.

BIBLIOGRAPHY. R. A. S. Macalister, *The Philistines, Their History and Civilization* (1911), 64, 65, 74-76; W. F. Albright, "The Sites of Ekron, Gath, and Libnah," AASOR, II-III (1923), 1-7; J. B. Pitchard, ANET (1950), 287, 288, 291, 294; J. Simon, GTT (1959), ## 318 (D/1), 1632; G. Naveh, "Khirbat al-Muqanna'—Ekron," IEJ, VIII (1958), 87-100, 165-170; Z. Kallai-Kleinmann, "The Town Lists of Judah, Simeon, Benjamin, and Dan," VT, VIII (1958), 145, 146 n. 4.

J. P. LEWIS

EL ēl (אֵל, *strength, power,* Assyrian *ilu,* Ugaritic *il*). Largely poetic designation of the one and only true God of Israel; often in Heb., used with the definite article, the (true) God, although no such article is needed to define the true God (Num 12:13). But the term, basically meaning "strength," can be used as an adjective and also in reference to men of might and rank (Ezek 31:11), such as Nebuchadnezzar, or it may refer to the angels (Ps 29:1).

Just as the word "god" in Eng. can be used of the true God or the gods, so this word in Heb. may mean the heathen gods, usually meaning idols (Exod 15:11; 34:14; Isa 43:10). The same root is used in the Ugaritic mythology as the name of the chief god of the Canaanite pantheon, although father-god of the pantheon *Il* played a role of lesser importance than such hero gods as Baal. Critics posit the idea that the Heb. ancestors worshiped clan deities who bore this element in their names. Old Phoen. and Ugaritic lit. use the feminine form of this word for the goddesses of the pantheon. The Heb. Bible wholly avoids this feminine usage of the word because the Heb.

A view of the Valley of Elah. ©*M.P.S.*

religion had no mythological concept of a goddess. The heathen goddesses are named in the Heb. Bible (e.g. Ashtaroth, 1 Sam 7:3). El, however, is often combined with other adjectives to create epithets of God which express His numerous attributes. Among these names are *El Shaddai*, God of the Mountain (Gen 17:1; Exod 6:3); *El 'Elyon*, God Almighty (Gen 14:18-24); *El 'Olam*, God of Eternity (Gen 21:33); *El Ro'i*, God the Seeing One (Gen 16:13); *El Rehum*, God of Compassion (Deut 4:31); *El Nose'*, the forgiving God (Ps 99:8); *El Hannun*, the gracious God (Neh 9:31); *El Kanna'*, the jealous God (Exod 20:5); etc. *See* God, Names of.

BIBLIOGRAPHY. M. H. Pope, *El in the Ugaritic Texts* (1955); J. Bright, *A History of Israel* (1959), 90, 91, 108, 109, 147 n.43.

E. B. Smick

ELA ē′ lə (אֵלָא). The father of Shimei who was the administrator in Benjamin in charge of providing for King Solomon's household (1 Kings 4:18)

ELADAH. KJV form of Eleadah.

ELAH ē′ lə (אֵלָה, LXX Ἠλα, perhaps *chief, strong, divine*, cf. "terebinth"; Noth, *Israelitische Personennamen*, pp. 38, 90). Fourth king of Israel, son of Baasha of Issachar. His reign is described briefly in 1 Kings 16:8-14. He succeeded his father in the twenty-sixth year of Asa of Judah, and was assassinated in the following year (vv. 10, 15). "Two years" (v. 8) indicates that his reign covered more than a full year; this was long enough for him to show his adherence to his father's religious policy, in defiance of the prophecy of Jehu ben Hanani, but he seems to have lacked his father's energy and leadership. It is recorded that he met his death while carousing with his chamberlain in Tirzah, though the army was at the time laying siege to the Philistine city of Gibbethon.

J. LILLEY

ELAH, VALE (VALLEY) OF (עמק האלה ; LXX, ἡ κοιλὰς Ἠλα, *of the terebinth* or *of the oak*).

A valley in the Shephelah, generally identified with Wadi es-Sant ("Valley of the Acacia"), about fourteen m. SW of Jerusalem. It is possible that the valley of Shittim, mentioned in Joel 3:18, is a reference to Wadi es-Sant (Heb. *shiṭṭah* is the equivalent of Arab. *sant*). The area is rich in acacias, terebinths, and oaks. It was the scene of the combat between David and Goliath (1 Sam 17:2ff.; 21:9). Coursing through the valley is a watercourse (or *wadi* as the Arabs call it), which runs in the period of the rains only. The bottom of the watercourse is covered with small stones, the kind David might have used for his sling.

A. C. SCHULTZ

ELAM ē ləm (עילם, LXX Αιλάμ, meaning uncertain; perhaps *high land*). 1. A son of Shem and the progenitor of the Elamites (Gen 10:22; 1 Chron 1:17). *See* ELAM, ELAMITES.

2. A priest who participated in the dedication of the walls of Jerusalem in Nehemiah's time (Neh 12:42).

3. A son of Shahach and descendant of Benjamin (1 Chron 8:24).

4. A Korahite in the time of David who was a gatekeeper (1 Chron 26:3).

5. One of the chiefs who are said to have sealed, with other leaders, the covenant of Ezra (Neh 10:14).

6. The eponym of a family of which 1,254 returned to Pal. after the Exile under Zerubbabel (Ezra 2:7; Neh 7:12; 1 Esd 5:12). It has been suggested that "the other Elam" (Ezra 2:31) with whom also 1,254 returned is the same as the Elam of Ezra 2:7. Jeshaiah, another member of this family returned with Ezra (Ezra 8:7). Still another member of this family, "Shecaniah the son of Jahaziel, of the sons of Elam," suggested to Ezra that Hebrews who had married non-Hebrew wives put away these wives and their children (Ezra 10:2-4). Six of the men of this family put away their foreign wives (Ezra 10:26).

A. C. SCHULTZ

ELAM (Country), ELAMITES ē' ləm, ē' ləm-īts (עילם, LXX Αιλάμ, meaning uncertain; perhaps *high land*).

1. Introduction. Elam is the Biblical designation of a people and a country in the southern area of the Iranian plateau in the Zagros mountains E and NE of the valley of the Tigris. It is approximately equivalent to the present Iranian province of Khuzistan. The name derives from the Elamite *Haltamti*. It is the *Elamtu* of the Assyrians and the Babylonians and the *Elymais* of the Greeks who also called it *Susiana* from the capital Susa (*Shushan*), modern Shush. Scholars are not agreed in regard to the relationship of the language of the Elamites to the other languages of the Near E. The earliest stage of the language is written in a script not yet completely deciphered, but from which there developed in c. 1600 B.C. a cuneiform writing which in its turn gave way at the end of the 6th cent. B.C. to the Elamite adaptation of the writing of the Achaemenid Pers. The language is non-Sem. The history of the Elamites is known largely from the records of other peoples which makes breaks in its continuity inevitable.

2. Early history. The Biblical record traces the Elamites back to Elam a son of Shem (Gen 10:22; 1 Chron 1:17). Scholars classify them as non-Sem. Caucasians. Archeology and anthropology shed no particular light upon Elamite origins but it is clear that Elam was influenced by the Jemdet Nasr culture during the later period of the fourth millennium B.C. The dependence culturally of Elam upon Mesopotamia that began in this early period lasted through her entire history. Elam's earliest appearance in Mesopotamian records shows it in subjection to the Sumer. Eannatum of Lagash in 2450 B.C. This further strengthened the influence of Sumer. culture upon the Elamites. Elamite dependence upon Mesopotamia continued after hegemony in the Tigris-Euphrates valley shifted from the Sumerians to the Akkadians under Sargon of Akkad (2360-2305 B.C.). It was in this period that the Elamites appropriated the Sumero-Akkad. cuneiform script with which they produced their inscrs. on clay tablets and stone. Elamites from Susa participated in the building of the temple of Gudea of Lagash (c. 2000 B.C.).

With the decline of Akkad. power Elam gained her freedom and established an independent dynasty. But the third dynasty of Ur eventually gained control of much of Elam and dominated many of the country's cities. However, the Elamites were eventually able to reassert their independence and to destroy their oppressor's capital city, carrying back to Elam the last king of the dynasty of Ur, Ibbi-Sin (c. 2030 B.C.). The destruction of Ur by the Elamites is bewailed in a Sumer. lamentation text.

At this time of Elamite history the rulers of the country were known as "governors"

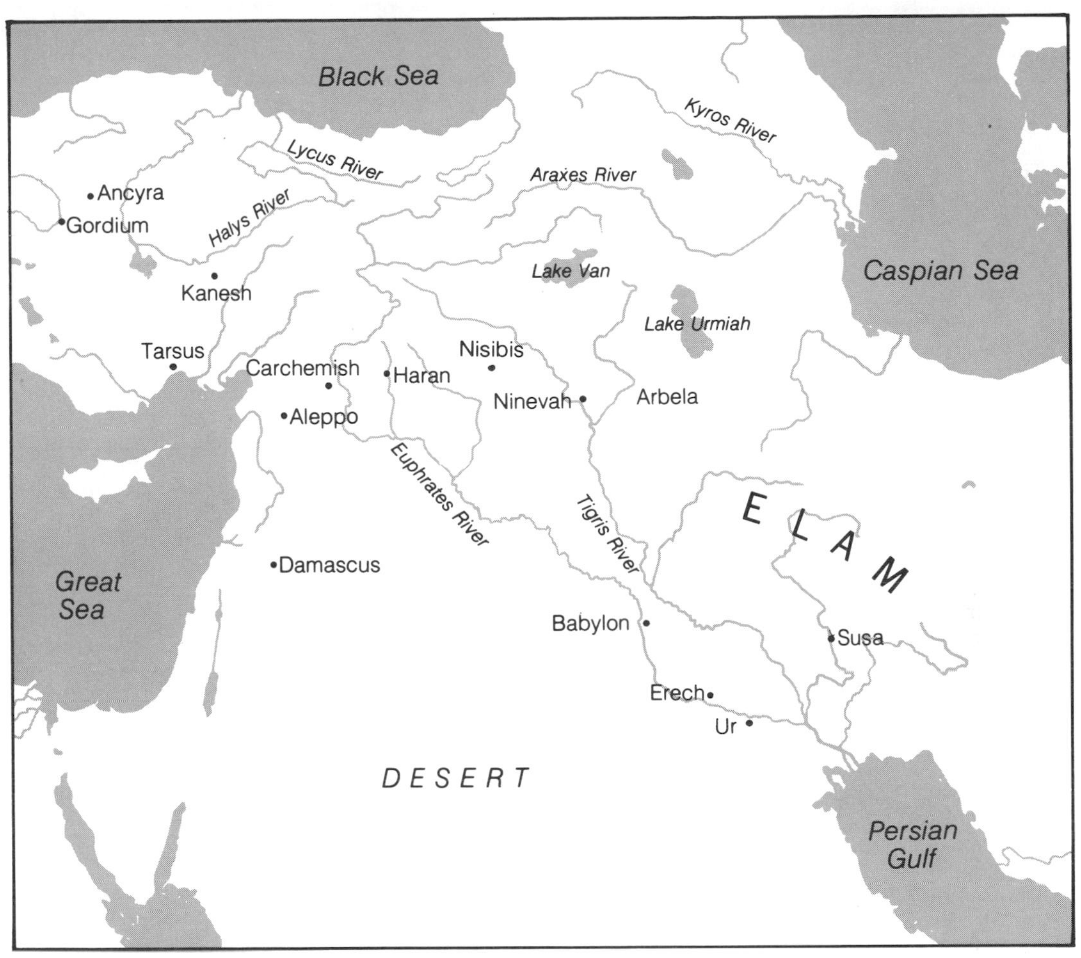

and not as kings in the Mesopotamian sense of the term. The rulers of Elam were actually feudal lords who were considered to be representatives of Inshushinak, god of Susa. A unique cultural form appeared in this period which served to determine the method of the transition of power from one ruler to another to the end of Elamite history. This was the principle of matrilinear succession in which the throne was hereditary through women so that the new ruler was the son of a sister of a member of the previous ruler's family. The quality of the succession was somewhat protected by the regulation that the successor was expected to have had some experience as viceroy, usually at Susa.

The power of Elam spread into Mesopotamia under King Kutir-Mabug who made Rim-Sin king of Larsa and through him controlled southern Babylonia as far N as Babylon. Larsa fell to the First Amorite Dynasty of Babylon under Hammurabi (c. 1728-1686 B.C.) who made Elam a province of his empire, according to his records, in the thirtieth year of his reign. The empire of Hammurabi's dynasty fell before the Kassite invasion (c. 1600 B.C.) and Elam was delivered from Babylonian domination. For the next 300 years practically nothing is known about Elam. In the last quarter of the fourteenth cent. B.C. the Kassite Kurigalzu III claims to have conquered Elam.

3. The classical period. This period begins c. 1200 B.C. when Elam again gained independence and re-emerged as an international power. A succession of capable kings expanded Elamite power and an invasion of Babylon in 1160 B.C. destroyed Kassite domination. Babylon was made a satellite of Elam. Scores of temples were built throughout the empire dedicated to Elamite deities and tribute flowed into Susa the capital. Archeological excavations at Susa have disclosed that the Elamites plundered several Babylonian cities. Among the trophies found at Susa were the stele of the Code of Hammurabi and the victory stele of Naram-Sin. Many of the captured monuments were set up in the courts of important city temples and dedicated to the gods of Elam. These Elamite successes were abruptly ended by Nebuchadnezzar I who captured and plundered Susa (c. 1130 B.C.) and once more made Elam subject to Babylon. And once again for nearly 300 years nothing is known of Elamite history.

The Babylonian Chronicle mentions Elam as an independent state in 742 B.C. and it is described in the same way in the inscrs. of the Assyrian kings Tiglath-pileser III (745-727 B.C.) and Sargon II (722-706 B.C.). The Assyrians demonstrate great diplomatic skill in playing the various claimants to the Elamite throne against each other. Elamite inscrs. begin with Shutruk-Nahhunte II (717-681 B.C.) and are an important supplement to the Assyrian inscrs. The Elamites cooperated with the Babylonian rebel Merodach-baladan against Sennacherib (705-681 B.C.) which resulted only in Elam becoming a refuge for the rebellious Babylonians humiliated by the Assyrians. Sennacherib was unable to gain a decisive victory over Elam. In at least one battle the Elamites inflicted a defeat upon the Assyrians. The struggle between the two powers continued until the later years of the reign of the Assyrian Ashurbanipal (633-619 B.C.). Ashurbanipal defeated King Teumman and in one of his reliefs shows the defeated Elamite monarch's head dangling from a tree in the palace garden where he and his queen are feasting with other nobles. Ashurbanipal placed a puppet upon the throne of Elam but he proved disloyal with the result that in 640 B.C. the Assyrian monarch invaded Elam, sacked Susa and deported many of the population to Samaria. Elam as an independent nation thus comes to an end. At the rise of the Pers. empire 550 B.C. Elam was made a satrapy paying tribute to the Achaemenid kings. Susa was maintained as an important city and was used as the king's residence for three months of the year. It was widely known for the beauty of its halls and palaces. The city was mentioned by Gr. writers such as Arrian, Ctesias, and Herodotus.

4. Elam in the Bible. Elam, the progenitor of the Elamites, with Asshur, Arpachshad, Lud, and Aram, was a son of Shem (Gen 10:22). In Genesis 14:1-17 Chedorlaomer, king of Elam, is described as the overlord of three other Mesopotamian kings. Cuneiform tablets discovered at Mari indicate that in this period Elamite mercenaries served in the armies of the kings of Mesopotamia and that Elamites traveled as emissaries as far as Aleppo and Hazor which may help to understand Genesis 14. It is impossible on the basis of present knowledge to synchronize adequately the rulers of the Mesopotamian cities and the Elamite kings.

Elam is listed among those who attacked Jerusalem and is described as a land of archers (Isa 22:6; Jer 49:35). It also is listed with the Medes among the attackers of Babylon under Cyrus (Isa 21:2, 9). Elam is listed as one of the places to which Israelites were exiled (Isa 11:11). Jeremiah lists Elam with the nations that will be forced to drink the cup of the wrath of God (Jer 25:25; cf. 49:34-39). Ezekiel numbers Elam among the nations over whose graves a lamentation shall be chanted (Ezek 32:16, 24). The Elamites are listed among the peoples settled in Samaria by the Assyrians (Ezra 4:9, 10). Cyrus (Isa 44:28; 45:1) was from the Elamite province of Anshan. The episodes recorded in the Book of Esther occurred at Susa the ancient capital of Elam in the reign of Ahasuerus the Pers. who is identified by some as Xerxes I, and by others as Artaxerxes II. In Acts 2:9 the Elamites are said to have been present, along with Parthians, Medes, and others, in Jerusalem on the day of Pentecost.

BIBLIOGRAPHY. G. C. Cameron, *History of Early Iran* (1936); G. A. Barton, *Archaeology and the Bible* (1937); E. Herzfeld, *Iran in the Ancient Near East* (1941); J. A. Thompson, *The Bible and Archaeology* (1962); J. Gray, *Archaeology and the Old Testament World* (1965).

A. C. SCHULTZ

ELASA **ĕl′ ə sə** ('Ελασά), the place where Judas Maccabaeus lay encamped when Bacchides advanced upon him in 160 B.C. (1 Macc 9:5). In the ensuing battle, Judas was killed. The site is identified with *Il'asa*, near Beth-Horon.

ELASAH **ĕl′ ə sə** (אלעשה, LXX Jer 36:3 'Ελεασα; 2 Esd 10:22 'Ηλασα; *God has made*). 1. One of Pashhur's sons who were among the priests who put away their foreign wives (Ezra 10:22).

2. A son of Shaphan, who when sent to Nebuchadnezzar by Zedekiah, carried a letter from Jeremiah to the exiles (Jer 29:3). (This is really the same name as Eleasah, q.v.)

D. H. MADVIG

ELATH, ELOTH **e′ lăth, e′ lŏth** (אילת, אילות, meaning *palm grove* or *groves*). A town on the northern end of the Gulf of Elath (or Gulf of 'Aqabah) of the Red Sea.

Deuteronomy 2:8 mentions Elath in connection with Ezion-geber and because of that some think that these two names may be in apposition. The name may have been given by the Edomite chief Elah (Gen 36:41).

Not only did the wandering children of Israel pass through Elath, but because of its strategic position it was an asset to any nation. The first mention of the place after the Exodus states that "King Solomon built a fleet of ships at Ezion-geber, which is near Eloth on the shore of the Red Sea, in the land of Edom" (1 Kings 9:26; cf. 2 Sam 8:14). Later,

Elamite Goddess En-Susinak with Genii protectors. ©V.E.

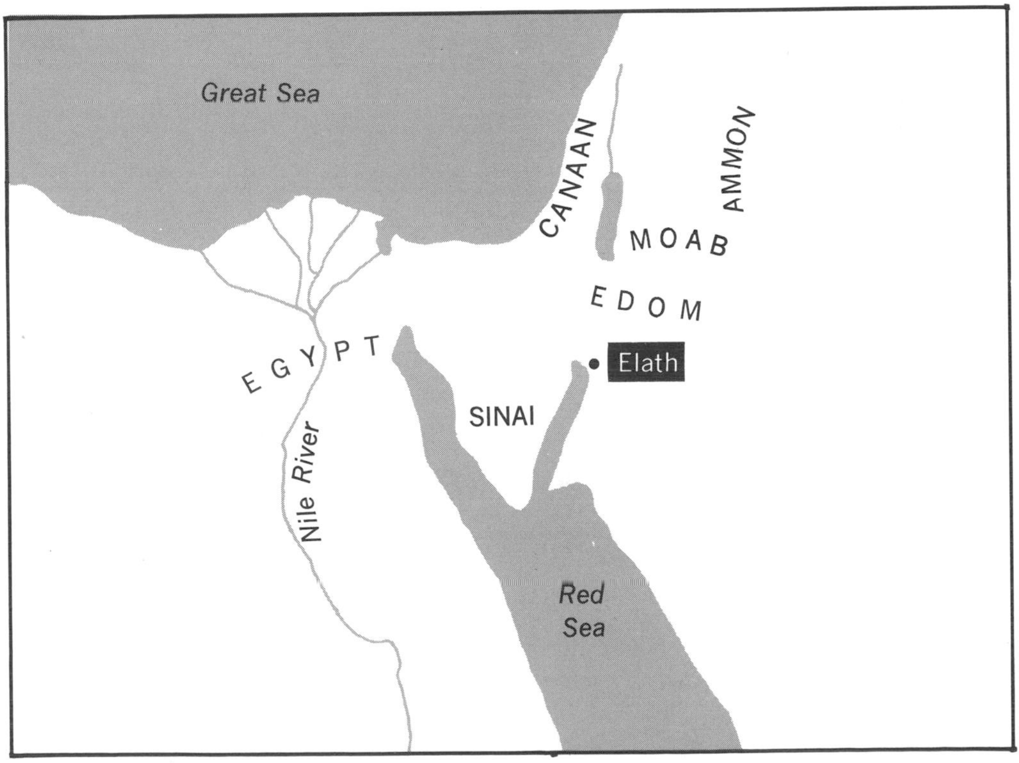

in the time of Jehoshaphat, the ships were wrecked there (1 Kings 22:48; 2 Chron 20:35ff.). There is no deep harbor and the strong northerly winds coming down the Arabah make its use as a port difficult.

Although not named, the Edomites apparently captured Elath under the reign of Jehoram (2 Kings 8:20), for Amaziah built Elah and restored it to Judah (2 Kings 14:22). His son, the next king, Uzziah (Azariah) apparently completed the rebuilding (2 Chron 26:2). But it was lost again to the Edomites under the reign of Ahaz (2 Kings 16:6). (The KJV reads "Syria" and "Syrians" for the MT *aram.*)

There is evidence that the town continued to play an important role long after OT times. Tell-el-Kheleifeh has been excavated but it is uncertain if this is Elath, Ezion-geber, or something else. The modern town of Eila, Israel, shares the same general locale but the Jordanian town of Aqabah may be covering the ancient Biblical site.

BIBLIOGRAPHY. N. Glueck, *Rivers in the Desert* (1959), 157-163; AASOR, XVIII-XIX (1939), 4-7.

R. L. Alden

ELBERITH, EL-BERITH ĕl' bĭr ĭth (אל ברית, "God of the covenant"). An alternate name for the god worshiped at Shechem, in whose temple some of the people of Shechem took refuge when Abimelech destroyed the city (Judg 9:46).

EL-BETH-EL, EL-BETHEL ĕl bĕth' əl (אל בית אל, "the god Bethel," or "the god of Bethel"), the name of the altar erected by Jacob at Bethel after his return from Paddam-aram (Gen 35:7).

ELCIA. KJV form of Elkiah.

ELDAAH ĕl dā' ə (אלדעה). One of the sons of Midian (Gen 25:4; 1 Chron 1:33). Midian was a son of Abraham through Keturah (Gen 25:1, 2; 1 Chron 1:32). The sons and grandsons of Keturah were all ancestors of Arab. tribes.

ELDAD ĕl' dăd (אלדד, *God has loved, God is a friend*). One of the seventy elders chosen to assist Moses in leading the Israelites (Num 11:16f., 24-29). When Moses found that the discontent of the people, on the journey from Sinai toward Canaan, was hard to bear, he was commanded to choose seventy elders who would share the burden of administration. When the elders gathered at the Tabernacle, the Spirit of the Lord came upon them and they prophesied. Two of those chosen, Eldad and Medad, remained in the camp, yet they received the same spirit of prophecy. Joshua was indignant because these two prophesied in the camp rather than at the Tabernacle, but Moses refused to forbid them, remarking that he wished all the Lord's people were prophets. Since their names have the same meaning, Eldad may be identical with Elidad (Num 34:21), who was the Benjamite representative among those who administered the division of Canaan. The imparting of some of the spirit that was upon Moses indicates that the endowment of the leadership abilities was due to the direct operation of the Spirit of God. The prophesying, which occurred only once, appears to have been an outward sign of this spiritual gift. There is little clue to the precise nature of the activity, but it is commonly held that it was a form of ecstatic experience (cf. 1 Sam 19:23f.).

BIBLIOGRAPHY. KD, *Numbers*; J. Lindblom, *Prophecy in Ancient Israel* (1962), 100-102; W. Eichrodt, *Theology of the Old Testament,* II (1967), 50-54.

G. Goldsworthy

ELDAD, AND MEDAD, BOOK OF ĕl' dăd, mē'-dăd. Two of the seventy elders appointed by Moses (Num 11:26ff.) who prophesied after the Spirit of God rested on them and were approved by Moses for doing so. Although almost nothing is known about these two men a rich tradition grew up around them in the later period of the Hel. and a pseudepigraphic work appeared which was purported to be the written transcript of their prophecies in the manner commonly known from the various apocalypses of the Post-Pers. era. No actual passages of this work now exist nor any citation which may be undeniably attributed to the book. The Palestinian Targumic traditions have more extensive details on the story of Numbers 11:26 and add several phrases concerning what was said by Eldad and Medad. One has the phrase, "The Lord is close by them who are in the time of trial," and the context would indicate that they prophesied about the coming of Gog and Magog at the end time of Israel, a favorite subject of speculation in the DSS and elsewhere. Only the apocryphal postapostolic epistle *The Pastor of Hermas* mentions the book and gives a quotation from it, "The Lord is near to them who return unto Him, as it is written in Eldad and Medat (d), who prophesied to the people in the wilderness" (ANF Vol. 11, 12).

W. White, Jr.

ELDER IN THE NT (*πρεσβύτερος*, lit. *older person* or *old man*; sometimes transliterated *presbyter*). This term designated three different groups in the NT: (a) older individuals comparatively speaking; (b) the religious-political leaders of Jewry and (c) the early leaders of the apostolic church.

1. Background: OT, Rabbinic Judaism and the Qumran community. According to OT terminology, the elder was a rather loosely defined term designating the religious and political leaders esp. of Israel. Biblical references show that other nations such as Egypt and Moab possessed such leaders (cf. Gen 50:7; Num 22:7). Although several Heb. terms were used to describe these leaders, three terms appear more frequently than the others: זקן being the technical term for elder but generally meaning elderly person (cf. Gen 43:7; Exod 3:16, 18; 12:21; 17:5, 6); שיבה, meaning old age or an elderly age from the verb meaning to be hoary (cf. 1 Kings 14:4); and שר, meaning chieftain, chief or ruler and often appearing in contexts where it is clearly a synonym for elder (cf. Judg 5:15; 6:6-16). In Isaiah 3:2, 3 no less than eleven different leadership positions are mentioned by the prophet; elder is one of them. Particularly important is the idea of the "seventy elders" in the OT (cf. Exod 24:1; Num 11:16).

In the first cent. A.D., the office of elder was a regular position in the Jewish synagogue. In the tractate Sanhedrin of the Mishna, the duties of this office are clearly outlined. The council of elders was responsible for the government of the Jewish community. In Jerusalem, the Sanhedrin, a council composed of seventy-one elders, acted as the supreme court for all Judaism. (Cf. Berakhoth 4:7; Nedharim 5:5; Meghillah 3:1; Edhuyoth 5:6; Ta'anith 3:8; Middoth 2:2; Ezra 10:8; Luke 6:22; John 9:22; 12:42.)

The discoveries at Qumran have revealed a covenant community in which the office of elder also functioned in much the same sense as that office in Judaism, and there is general agreement that the Qumran community did have rather significant connections with early Christianity. This is not to suggest that the Early Church adopted its ecclesiastical structure from the Qumran community. The Manual of Discipline (1QS VI) speaks of the elder (*mebaqqer*) as being second in rank behind the priests.

2. NT meaning and significance for the Church. The terms associated with this position appear over seventy times in the NT: (a) almost half of these refer to the office in Judaism (cf. Matt 15:2; 26:47; Mark 8:31; 14:43; Acts 4:5; 25:15; note: the term is not used at all in John's gospel except for the textual variant in 8:9, and this is particularly significant in the light of the negative tone of the fourth gospel toward Judaism in general); (b) five references are comparative designations of age (cf. Luke 15:25; Acts 2:17 [RSV "older men"]; Rom 9:12; 1 Tim 5:2 [RSV "old women"]; Heb 11:2 [RSV "men of old"]); (c) the remaining references are to the office in the Early Church.

In the Lukan apostolic history, the office appears without explanation as to its origin for the first time in Acts 11:30. The reference here is to the elders in the Church in Judea for whom a collection had been taken in the Church at Antioch. Later we are told that Paul "appointed" (χειροτονήσαντες, from the Gr. verb meaning "to choose or elect by raising hands or to appoint") elders in every church (Acts 14:23). The exact nature of this apostolic ordination or appointment is not described except to imply that prayer and fasting were a part of the ritual. We may assume that this unexplained appearance in contrast to the selection of the seven in Acts 6 implies a rather natural transition from the synagogue structure of Judaism to the organization of the Early Church (cf. Acts 2:46).

The question over which the Church has been divided throughout her history is the relationship of the office of elder to the total ministry of the Church. First, it should be noted that in several important ecclesiological passages the office of elder is not specifically mentioned. The offices of deacon (διάκονος) bishop or pastor (ἐπίσκοπος) as well as elder are noticeably omitted (1 Cor 12:4-11, and vv. 28-30). (Cf. κυβερνήσεις in 1 Cor 12:28 tr. as "administrators" which may be a reference to a sort of ruling elder.) In a somewhat more definitive listing of church offices in Ephesians 4:11, "pastors" (ποιμήν) and "teachers" (διδάσκαλος) are among the titles used to describe these leaders. Second, the pastoral epistles refer to only two offices: pastors or elders and deacons. In 1 Timothy 3:1-13, the text uses *episkopos* and *diakonos*; whereas, Titus 1:5-9 seems to use the terms *episkopos* and *presbuteros* almost interchangeably: "I left you in Crete . . . [to] appoint elders (*presbuteros*) in every town. . . . For a bishop (*episkopos*). . . ." In the letter to the church at Philippi, the salutation mentions only "bishops" (*episkopos*) and "deacons" (*diakonos*), and it should be noted that both terms are pl.

Two questions are raised by the NT evidence. First, what is the significance of the plurality of elders in the NT Church? Second, what is the relationship of bishop or pastor to the office of elder?

In regard to the first question, it should be observed that two possible explanations are available. On the one hand, the existing structure of the synagogue with its plurality of elders is paralleled by the NT church organization. It should be pointed out here that even in the synagogue there was a "head of the synagogue" known as the ראש הכנסת or ἀρχισυνάγωγος. The plurality in this case would not forbid the predominant leadership of one elder, perhaps referred to as a "ruling elder" (1 Tim 5:17). There is in later church history a traceable development from a plurality of elders to a presiding bishop to an episcopal hierarchical structure. The nature of the early NT Christian assemblies which often worshiped in the homes of the members may also help to explain the plurality of elders. In other words, in a given community there might be a number of elders each one responsible for the care of a particular congregation which met in his home or the home of some other Christian in the congregation. Clear examples of this are found in the NT itself (cf. Acts 16:11ff.; Rom 16:3-5).

As to the latter question, it already has been noted that by the time the pastoral epistles were written, the terms "bishop" and "elder" were used interchangeably (cf. 1 Tim 3; Titus 1). But even earlier in Paul's ministry (cf. Acts 20:17-38) when he met with the elders of the Ephesian church, he seems to relate the three terms together—elder, bishop or overseer and pastor. The idea of the elders serving as shepherds of the flock and overseeing the administration of the Church helped to distinguish the *title* of the office from its practical *functions*. In other words, the term elder originally designated those who were both naturally as well as spiritually older or more mature. Note that Paul makes specific mention of the fact that no one is to be admitted to the office of elder or bishop who is a "recent convert" or novice (cf. 1 Tim 3:6). The other terms—pastor or shepherd and bishop or overseer—refer to the functions of this office in the Church. An elder is, therefore, an older, spiritually more mature male member of the Church who is responsible for the administration of the congregation. In this latter case, it is instructive that Peter refers to himself as an elder: "So I exhort the elders among you, as a fellow elder" (1 Pet 5:1). In the later postapostolic writings of the Church, there is clear evidence that the office of pastor or bishop and elder were the same (cf. Didache 10:6).

Finally, it should be noted that the term also has a decidedly eschatological signification. In the Revelation of John, a select group is given the title "twenty-four elders" and they are called to share in the eschatological structure of redemption. NT commentators have not been agreed as to the precise reference of these "twenty-four elders" but it may be suggested that this title points again to the Jewish (OT and rabbinic) origin of the office as well as the dynamic relationship of Israel and the Church. The doubling of the number twelve may point to that spiritual unity which shall be fulfilled eschatologically and ecclesiologically in the final age! (Cf. Rev 4:4, 10; 5:5-14; 7:11-13; 11:16; 14:3; 19:4; Rom 9-11.)

BIBLIOGRAPHY. H. B. Swete, ed., *Essays on The Early History of the Church and the Ministry* (1921); K. E. Kirk, ed., *The Apostolic Ministry* (1946); E. Schweizer, *Das Leben des Herrn in her Gemeinde und ihren Diensten* (1946); W. Michaelis, *Das Ältestenamt der christlichen Gemeinde im Lichte der Heiligen Schrift* (1953); R. Reicke, "The Constitution of the Primitive Church in the Light of Jewish Documents," *The Scrolls and the New Testament* ed. by K. Stendahl (1957), 143-156; G. H. Davies, "Elder in the OT," IDB, II (1962), 72, 73; M. H. Shepherd, Jr., "Elder in the NT," IDB, II (1962), 73-75; I. Sonne, "Synagogue," IDB, III (1962), 477-491; H. W. Beyer, "ἐπίσκοπος," TDNT, II (1964), 608-622; G. Bornkamm, "πρεσβύτερος," TDNT, VI (1968), 651-681.

D. Lake

ELDER, IN THE OT (זקן, related to a word for *beard, chin*; שׂב, from שׂיב, *to be gray*, only in Ezra; LXX πρεσβύτερος). A group of adult men (perhaps all the adult men, those who wore a beard) who gathered in popular assembly, or as a kind of council in every village. They also served as local rulers. Usually they were the heads of families, but prob. were selected also on the basis of age, wisdom, ability, respect, or prowess. Pharaoh had his elders (Gen 50:7), as well as the Midianites and Moabites (Num 22:7), and the Gibeonites (Josh 9:11). The Greeks and Romans also had elders. The modern equivalent is the sheik of Arabia.

The origin of the elders in Heb. history goes back to the nomadic period in the life of Israel before the occupation of Pal., with the roots of the office prob. in the individual home within the clan. The elders were already recognized as a part of the community during the period of bondage in Egypt (Exod 3:16; 4:29). It was the elders (obviously the heads of the houses) who were instructed concerning the observance of the first passover in Egypt whereby the people might escape death (12:21). They were particularly associated with religious leadership (24:1, 9), including the offering of sacrifices (Lev 4:15). Seventy elders were selected to share with Moses the burden of the people and were given part of the Spirit that rested on Moses (Num 11:16, 17). They were often mentioned alongside the priests (1 Kings 8:3). There is one mention of elders of the priests (2 Kings 19:2).

The elders served in various capacities. A principal function was to serve as judges in disputes or to dispense justice as they sat in the gates of the city (Deut 22:15). The prophets demanded that respect for justice at the gate be shown (Amos 5:10-12; Zech 8:16) and charged that the elders had become corrupt in their administration of justice. As members of what amounted to a popular court, the elders were not to bear false witness, accept gifts, nor follow the majority in defiance of justice. Their responsibility was to condemn the guilty and acquit the innocent. Each town had its own elders (Deut 19:12) who determined if a man should be turned over to the avenger to die, thus depriving him of the protection of the cities of refuge. They determined whether a rebellious son should be stoned to death and they participated in the execution of the sentence (21:18-21). They also adjudged the validity of a husband's charge that his bride was not a virgin (22:15). They settled cases concerning Levirate marriage where a man did not want to take his deceased brother's wife (25:7-10), and served as witnesses to commercial transactions (Ruth 4:4). The elders also served as military leaders (Josh 8:10; 1 Sam 4:3). They were involved in the selection of kings of the nation. They demanded that Samuel appoint for them their first king (8:4, 5) and participated in the anointing of David as king over all Israel after the death of Saul (2 Sam 3:17; 5:3). It is most likely that it was the elders who gathered at Shechem after the death of Solomon to receive certain assurances from Rehoboam before recognizing him as king. They apparently did not acknowledge the right of automatic succession by inheritance (1 Kings 12). When Jezebel plotted the death of Naboth, she wrote the elders and nobles of Jezreel to provide false witnesses in order that Naboth might be stoned to death (1 Kings 21:8-11). Through the wise counsel of the elders Jeremiah's life was saved by remembering the prophecies of Micah (Jer 26:16-19). They were included among those carried into exile (29:1; Ezek 8:1).

The elders seemed to occupy a continuing place of importance throughout the history of Israel, from their sojourn in Egypt to the postexilic period when mention was made that they gave orders to assemble the people to deal with the question of foreign marriages (Ezra 10:8). The elders were able to survive the collapse of the royal institutions.

Nothing is said about the organization of the councils of the elders of the tribes. Their number prob. depended on the size of the local community; there were seventy-seven at Succoth (Judg 8:14). It is quite unlikely that there was a council of elders of the entire nation selected from the elders of the various tribes.

In the Mari archives of the 18th cent. B.C. down to the royal correspondence of the Sargon dynasty in the 8th, the elders appear as representatives of the people and defenders of their interests, but without administrative functions. In the Hitt. empire, the elders did control municipal affairs and settled local disputes in co-operation with the commander of the garrison. The Phoen. towns had their elders also, as non-Biblical documents attest for Byblos and Tyre.

It is difficult to determine if the officials, שרים, are equivalent to the elders. In Numbers 22:7, 14 and Judges 8:6, 16 the terms appear alternately. They also appear together in Succoth (Judg 8:14). In Job 29:9 the *śārîm* sat at the gate of the town, as did the elders of Proverbs 31:23.

BIBLIOGRAPHY. J. Pedersen, *Israel,* I-II (1926), see "elders" in Index; C. A. Simpson, *The Early Traditions of Israel* (1948), 227, 629, 630; M. Noth, *The History of Israel* (1960), 108, 226; R. de Vaux, *Ancient Israel* (1961).

F. B. HUEY, JR.

ELEAD **ĕl' ĭ əd** (אלעד, LXX Ἐλεαδ, *God has testified*). One of the descendants of Ephraim who was killed by the men of Gath while making a raid on their cattle. This tragedy moved Ephraim to call his next son Beriah, a name which in popular etymology may have been associated with the word "evil" (1 Chron 7:21).

ELEADAH **ĕl' ĭ ā' də** (אלעדה, LXX Ἐλεαδα, *God has adorned*) KJV ELADAH ĕl' ə də. A descendant of Ephraim whose father and son were both named Tabath (1 Chron 7:20).

ELEALEH **ĕl' ĭ ā' lə** (אלעלה אלעלא) . A city in Trans-Jordan on the southern boundary of the region known as Gilead. It lay over a m. NNE of Heshbon, almost due E of the northern tip of the Dead Sea. It is identified with the modern site of el'Âl. This region was disputed territory throughout the OT period. It was conquered by the Israelites as they occupied Trans-Jordan and Elealeh and surrounding towns were given to the tribe of Reuben (Num 32:3). They were rebuilt and given Israelite names (32:37, 38). The Moabites soon reoccupied the area, and the territory was in dispute between Ammon and Moab (Judg 11:13ff.). After the revolt of Mesha of Moab was successful upon the death of Ahab (c. 850 B.C.), the territory became Moabite and remained so throughout the prophetic period. Elealeh and Heshbon are mentioned as Moabite towns in both Isaiah's and Jeremiah's oracles of judgment on Moab (Isa 15:4; 16:9; Jer 48:34).

F. W. BUSH

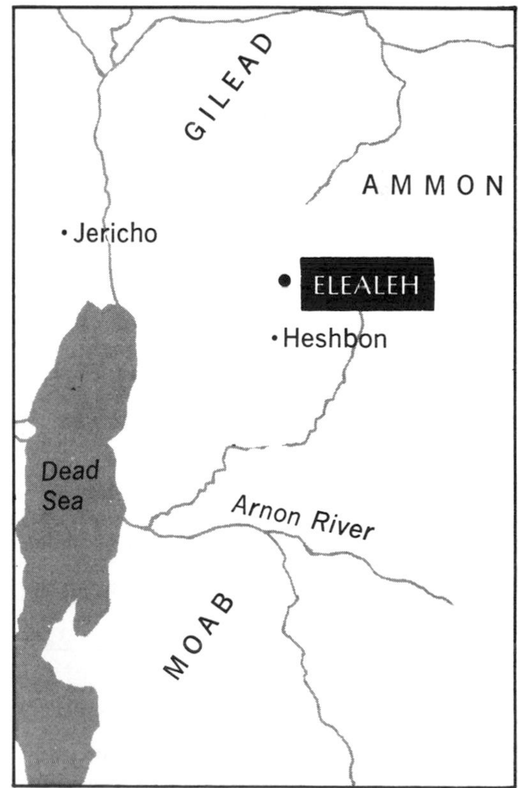

ELEASA. KJV form of ELASA.

ELEASAH ĕl' ĭ ā' sə (אלעשה, LXX 1 Chron 2:39f.; 9:43, Ἐλεασα; 1 Chron 8:37, Ἐλασα, *God has made*, in Heb. this name is the same as Elasah, q.v.). 1. A member of the tribe of Judah, the son of Helez and father of Sismai (1 Chron 2:39f.).

2. A member of the tribe of Benjamin and a descendant of Saul, the son of Raphah and father of Azel (1 Chron 8:37; 9:43). (Really the same name as Elasah, q.v.)

D. H. MADVIG

ELEAZAR ĕl' ĭ ā' zər (אלעזר, Ἐλεαζάρ, *God has helped*). Any one of six men mentioned in the OT and one in the NT. 1. The third son of Aaron. Aaron, the brother of Moses, had four sons, Nadab, Abihu, Eleazar, and Ithamar (Exod 6:23). Nadab and Abihu were killed when they offered strange fire before the Lord —possibly being drunk (Lev 10:1-11). Eleazar, the oldest remaining son married a daughter of Putiel, otherwise unknown. Eleazar's mother was Elisheba, sister of Nahshon, the chief of the tribe of Judah (Exod 6:23; Num 1:7; 1 Chron 2:3-10).

Eleazar evidently had the primogeniture rather than Ithamar. He succeeded in the high priestly office after his father's death (Num 20:25-28; Deut 10:6). Eleazar supervised the Kohathites who carried the Ark and the holy furniture upon their shoulders on the march (Num 3:30-32) and he was charged with the oversight of the Tabernacle and its furniture, also the oil, the incense, etc. (4:16). His brother Ithamar was over the Gershonites and Merarites who transported the tabernacle curtains, boards, etc. (4:28, 33).

Eleazar was prominent after the rebellion of Korah, Dathan, and Abiram (4:28, 33). He was the first appointed to prepare holy water from the ashes of the red heifer (19:4). He served as high priest to Joshua (27:19-21). His son Phinehas carried the trumpets, etc., to battle in Trans-Jordan (31:6). With Joshua, Eleazar divided the land of Pal. by lot (34:17; Josh 14:1; 17:4). In later days, his son Phinehas evidently wore the mantle (Josh 22:13; Judg 20:28). This line of priests is traced in the genealogies down to Ezra himself (1 Chron 6:1-15; Ezra 7:1-5).

It is not clear how it happened, but for a time the descendants of Ithamar superseded those of Eleazar in the Tabernacle of Shiloh. Eli was of the house of Ithamar (*see* ELI), but because of the wickedness of his house, his line was rejected. In David's day the chief men of Eleazar's line were numbered sixteen to Ithamar's eight (1 Chron 24:4).

2. The son of Abinadab who kept the Ark after it was brought back from Philistia (1 Sam 7:1).

3. One of David's first three "mighty men," son of Dodo the Ahohite (2 Sam 23:9; 1 Chron 11:12).

4. A descendant of Merari, the son of Levi (1 Chron 23:21, 22; 24:28). He had no sons.

5. A priest of the time of Ezra (Ezra 8:33) prob. identical with the Eleazar of Nehemiah 12:42.

6. One of the sons of Parosh who had married a foreigner (Ezra 10:25).

7. An ancestor in the third generation above Joseph the husband of Mary (Matt 1:15).

The name Eleazar is similar to ELIEZER, which see.

R. L. HARRIS

ELEAZURUS, ELIASIBUS. KJV and ASV forms of ELIASHIB.

ELECT, ELECTION is used as verb (בחר, *choose*; ἐκλέγομαι, *select*) to denote the action whereby an individual or group is chosen for a specific purpose; as adjective (בחיר, ἐκλεκτός) to characterize the individual or group chosen, and "election" (ἐκλογή) is the corresponding substantive. Though the verb can be used with reference to man's action (cf. Luke 10:42; 14:7; Acts 6:5), yet it is with God's action we are concerned when we use the terms "elect" and "election." It is particularly upon the differentiation involved for men that thought is focused. God makes men to differ, and Scripture is permeated with this emphasis.

I. THEOCRATIC ELECTION

Israel as a people were chosen by God for special favor and privilege and set apart from all the nations of the earth (Deut 4:37; 7:6, 7; 10:15; 14:2; 1 Kings 3:8; Pss 33:12; 76:1, 2; 105:6, 43; 135:4; Isa 41:8, 9; 43:20-22; 44:1, 2; 45:4; cf. also Gen 18:19; Exod 2:25; Jer 31:3, 4; Hos 11:1; Amos 3:2; Mal 1:2). With respect to this election the following considerations are to be noted.

A. It proceeded from God's love. The election proceeded from God's love and this love was not constrained by any eminence in might or righteousness belonging to Israel (Deut 4:37; 7:6-8; 9:4-6). Israel was the fewest of all peoples and they were also a rebellious and stiffnecked people (9:7-13). It was, therefore, of His own sovereign good pleasure that God loved them and took delight in them. Election arose from the free determinations of His loving will.

B. It was unto separation. The election was unto separation from all other nations that Israel might be holy and a people for God's own possession (14:2; Pss 33:12; 135:4), a people formed for Himself to show forth His praise (Isa 43:1, 7, 21). Repeatedly in the history of Israel it had been declared through prophet and demonstrated in the events of providence that Israel had not only been chosen to show forth God's praise but also increased, preserved, and restored for his name's sake (Exod 9:16; 32:9-14; Ps 106:8, 47; Isa 43:25; 48:9-11; 63:12-14; Ezek 36:21-24).

C. It was unto obedience. The election was unto obedience in the bond of covenant fidelity (Exod 19:4-6; 20:2-17; 24:7; Lev 18:4, 5; 19:2-4; 20:7, 8; Deut 14:1, 2; Ps 147:19, 20). Israel's privilege could never be divorced from the corresponding obligations nor from the curses incident to unfaithfulness (Deut 27:1-26; Amos 3:2).

D. It became specialized. The election became more specialized in reference to certain tribes and persons for distinct functions and prerogatives (Num 16:5; Deut 18:1-5; 1 Sam 10:24; 2 Sam 6:21; 2 Chron 6:6; Ps 78:68).

E. It did not guarantee the eternal salvation of all who were comprised in it. Of itself, therefore, it is to be distinguished from the more specific and particularized election that is unto and commensurate with salvation. This was exemplified in the OT (cf. 1 Kings 19:18; Ps 95:8-11; Isa 1:9; 10:22, 23). It is made more perspicuous in the NT. "They are not all Israel, that are of Israel" (Rom 9:6 ASV; cf. 9:7-13; 11:7-10; Heb 4:2-7). There are, however, two important observations to be made. (a) Though the ethnic election did not insure salvation, it is not to be depreciated. "What advantage then hath the Jew? or what is the profit of circumcision? Much every way: first of all, that they were intrusted with the oracles of God" (Rom 3:1, 2 ASV). To Israel pertained "the adoption, and the glory, and the covenants, and the giving of the law, and the service of God, and the promises" (Rom 9:4 ASV). The election of Israel was the channel through which God was pleased to administer His saving grace and in the fullness of time fulfill His redemptive purpose for all nations (cf. Gen 12:3; 22:18). Within this context Christ came (Rom 1:3; 9:5; Gal 4:4). (b) The ethnic election must not be dissociated from the particular election that is unto salvation. Within the context of the former there were always those who were elected to salvation, and the blessings and privileges dispensed in terms of the ethnic election provided the means through which particular election came to expression and achieved its purpose. Furthermore, at the center of the administration which constituted the ethnic election was "the election of grace" (cf. Rom 11:5) insuring the salvation of those who were the children of God and the true seed (cf. Rom 9:7, 8). This is verified in the history of the OT by the faithful in all generations.

II. Messianic election

This refers to the election of Christ (Ps 89:19; Isa 42:1; 1 Pet 2:4, 6; cf. Isa 28:16; Luke 23:35). The Father's witness to Christ on the occasion of the baptism by John (Matt 3:17; Mark 1:11; Luke 3:22) and also at the transfiguration of Jesus (Matt 17:5; Luke 9:35) bears directly on this election. The words "in whom I am well pleased" should be taken to mean "on whom my good pleasure has come to rest," and the word "chosen" in Luke 9:35 points to this conclusion. The Father's good pleasure rested on the Son for messianic appointment and investiture. The various passages cited above are in distinctly messianic contexts—chosen out of the people for kingly rule (Ps 89:19), elect as Servant (Isa 42:1; cf. Ps 2:6) and as the living chief cornerstone and sure foundation (Isa 28:16; 1 Pet 2:4, 6). This implies that the election must be conceived of within the economy of salvation and is concerned with the office to which the Son of God is appointed in order to bring to fruition God's saving purpose. We have no warrant to assume or affirm that Christ's *election* is the precondition of the election of men unto salvation even though, as will be noted, the latter was election in Christ (Eph 1:4). It is, however, of paramount significance that God the Father is the author of both and thus Christ and the elect are all of one (Heb 2:11).

III. Soteric election

Though closely related to the foregoing aspects, election to salvation is distinct. It is distinct from Israel's ethnic election in that it insures the salvation of its objects and distinct from Christ's election in that the latter is not to salvation but to office for the accomplishing of salvation. In the OT much emphasis falls on ethnic election. In the NT ethnic election recedes to the background and the terms "elect" and "election," when the action of God in reference to men is in view, are used with few exceptions (cf. Acts 13:17; Rom 11:28) of the election unto life and salvation. The revelatory data establish its characterizing features.

A. Eternal. Ephesians 1:4 is explicit to this effect. The election in Christ was "before the foundation of the world." The same is implied when Paul says that God "saved us, and called us with a holy calling, not according to our works, but according to his own purpose and grace, which was given us in Christ Jesus before times eternal" (2 Tim 1:9 ASV). Whether the concluding clause refers to the "calling" or to the "grace" (the latter alternative is distinctly to be preferred), we are, in any case, pointed to God's eternal counsel, and the analogy of Paul's teaching (Eph 1:4, 9; cf. Rom 9:11) would require that this counsel include election. We cannot think in terms of eternity because we are creatures and are temporally conditioned. But we must think of eternity and it is of faith to believe that the fountain from which salvation emanates is the eternal purpose of God. All the other features of election cannot be properly construed except as they are related to its origin in the mystery of God's eternal will.

B. Sovereign. To suppose that election is constrained by or grounded in any differentiating quality or condition in men themselves would contradict the pervasive emphasis of Scripture upon the good pleasure of God.

When Paul speaks of election in Christ before the foundation of the world (Eph 1:4), he explicates this still further in v. 5 as predestination in love unto adoption and then informs us of that in accordance with which election and predestination took place. It is "according to the good pleasure of his will." These terms are sufficient to express God's sovereign determination as the explanation, but the apostle is not content. He reiterates the thought and piles up expressions which obviate the possibility of intruding a human factor as the conditioning element. Predestination, he repeats, is "according to the purpose of him who worketh all things after the counsel of his will" (v. 11 ASV). The same accent on the pure sovereignty of God appears again in Paul. In meeting the objection that the differentiation impugns the justice of God he appeals to the word of God to Moses: "I will have mercy on whom I have mercy, and I will have compassion on whom I have compassion" (Rom 9:15 ASV; cf. Exod 33:19) and concludes: "So then it is not of him that willeth, nor of him that runneth, but of God that hath mercy" (Rom 9:16 ASV). God's sovereign will is compared to the right of the potter over the clay in order to show, not that God deals with men as clay, but that God in His dealings with men has the right to differentiate and does so as the potter makes one vessel unto honor and another to dishonor (9:19-24). It may not be pleaded that this is only Pauline doctrine. The same principle of God's sovereign good pleasure appears in the teaching of our Lord and is predicated of the Father and of Jesus Himself: "Yea, Father, for so it was well-pleasing in thy sight . . . and he to whomsoever the Son willeth to reveal him" (Matt 11:26, 27 ASV). It is thus of the essence of the NT doctrine of election to characterize it as unconditional, and this means that the source and cause reside in God's sovereign good pleasure alone.

C. Gracious. That election is all of grace is implicit in its sovereign character. In addition to the emphasis upon the good pleasure of God the Scripture expressly defines it as gracious. It is "the election of grace" (Rom 11:5) and the ultimate design is stated to be the praise of the glory of God's grace (Eph 1:7; cf. v. 12). Grace and mercy are correlative in the plan and execution of salvation and when the apostle says that the election is "of God that hath mercy" (Rom 9:16) and that He makes known "the riches of his glory upon vessels of mercy, which he afore prepared unto glory" (Rom 9:23 ASV), the reference to mercy accentuates the gracious character. In the history of revelation this feature is verified in none more than in the choice of Jacob. All the circumstances converge to point up sovereign grace as opposed to any determining factor belonging to Jacob or to his conduct (cf. Rom 9:11-13). In the theocratic election Israel was repeatedly reminded that they were not chosen because of their might or righteousness. In particular election the choice of the foolish, weak, base, despised things of the world and the things that are not is to the end that no flesh should glory before God (1 Cor 1:27-29; cf. James 2:5). The eternal fount of salvation is the grace exhibited in its actual possession (cf. Eph 2:8-10).

D. Immutable. "The purpose of God according to election" (Rom 9:11) cannot mean less than electing purpose and it is this that is said to stand. The thought is the security and inviolability of the purpose entailed in election. Various considerations show that the end contemplated in election cannot fail of realization. (a) When Jesus said that the days of tribulation would be shortened for the sake of the elect, the implication is that the elect must be saved (Matt 24:22; Mark 13:20). The gathering of the elect from the four winds, from one end of heaven to the other at Jesus' coming in glory (Matt 25:31; Mark 13:27) is the assurance given by Jesus Himself that at the end the elect will be gathered to Him by a ministry that belongs to the people of God as the heirs of salvation, the ministry of the angels (cf. Matt 18:10; Luke 16:22; Heb 1:14). (b) Since election involves determinate purpose it is impossible to conceive of this purpose as defeated and the purpose must be one correspondent with the grace of election itself. This is the tenor of various passages—elected to be holy (Eph 1:4), predestinated unto adoption (1:5), chosen unto salvation (2 Thess 2:13). The purpose according to which calling takes place (Rom 8:28) is the one that issues in glorification (8:30). (c) The security of the elect is the theme of Romans 8:33-39. The triumphant conclusion of vv. 38, 39 is continuous with and the climax to the series of questions that begins with: "who shall lay anything to the charge of God's elect?" (v. 33). (d) The "vessels of mercy" (9:23) are, by reason of the context, to be identified with the elect (cf. v. 11) and they are said to be "afore prepared unto glory" in contrast with the "vessels of wrath fitted unto destruction" (v. 22 ASV).

E. In Christ. The only place where this feature is expressly intimated is Ephesians 1:4. Much debate has arisen respecting the import. Since there are no parallel passages to shed light on the precise meaning, we shall have to be content with the unanswered questions which we are disposed to ask. Christian faith is resigned to the unsolved mysteries with which revelation confronts us. Election in Christ is, however, a datum of revelation to be received and obscurity respecting certain implications should not be allowed to eclipse the truths and relationships involved of which we do know.

God the Father is the subject of election; it is His distinguishing action and He who initiates the whole process of salvation. That the ultimate source resides in the Father is the sustained witness of Scripture and faith is greatly impaired if this is not recognized and appreciated. But this action of the Father may not be dissociated from Christ nor conceived of apart from Him. How the action of the Father relates itself to Christ we are not able to define; this belongs to His unsearchable counsel. Nevertheless it is of the essence of our faith in the Father's electing grace to know that in the fount of salvation the elect were never contemplated apart from Christ, that union with Christ was constituted in the decree of election. The people of God prize the mediation of Christ in all phases of redemption accomplished and applied. They should also prize the relation to Christ constituted in eternal election.

The election in Christ, as shown above, must be construed in messianic terms and as relevant to the economy of salvation. This economy has its source in election and election is unto the salvation of its objects. It would be proper, therefore, to infer that Christ is contemplated in His messianic identity when it is said that the elect were chosen in Him. Election must not be thought of apart from the salvation which it insures, and salvation is inconceivable apart from Christ. One must conclude that election in Christ and the election of Christ are correlative and therefore not only to be conjoined in our thought but intrinsically inseparable by reason of the terms in which Scripture enunciates them.

No phase of salvation is more basic or central than union with Christ. Redemption once wrought is efficacious because the redeemed died with Christ and rose with Him (Rom 6:2-6). At the inception of salvation in possession is the call of the Father into the fellowship of Christ (1 Cor 1:9). It is in Christ we have the forgiveness of sins and are justified (Rom 8:1; Eph 1:7). In Him we are given an inheritance and in Him sealed with the Holy Spirit as the earnest of the inheritance (Eph 1:11, 13, 14). In Christ believers die and they are dead in Christ (1 Thess 4:14, 16). In Christ they will be resurrected (1 Cor 15:22). Together with Christ they will be glorified (Rom 8:17). Election in Christ before the foundation of the world is the assurance given us that this union with Christ in all its aspects and in the richness of its grace has its source in a union constituted before times eternal. All spiritual blessing bestowed is in accordance with this election in Christ and flows from it. No spiritual blessing can be regarded as the precondition of election in Christ; every such blessing is its fruit.

The pivotal passage (Eph 1:4) has no precise parallel. It may be that Romans 8:29 expresses what is intended by election in Christ. If this is so, then "predestinated to be conformed to the image of his Son" defines the import of "in Christ" and the purpose of the latter is to inform us that election had not been conceived of or determined by God the Father except in terms of the end to which it was directed, namely, conformity to the image of the Father's only begotten. It can be said that this would provide a sufficient reason for the terms of Ephesians 1:4. In any case, Romans 8:29 informs us of what is implied in the election in Christ and, if it is not intended as definition, no other text is comparably rich in setting forth what is involved. For conformity to the image of God's Son that He might be the firstborn among many brethren is the highest conceivable destiny for creatures.

F. Obligations. All of God's revealed counsel comes to us with demand. The kind of demand is determined by the specific content of what is revealed and by the relation we particularly sustain to God. It might be supposed that only believers should be concerned with election and that to unbelievers this truth of election is sealed. It is true that unbelievers cannot know themselves as elect of God, and it would be presumption for them to entertain the faith of their election or the conviction of their non-election. But the truth of God's electing grace is revelation given to all to whom the Gospel comes. Unbelievers should be stirred by concern to use the God-appointed means for their salvation to the end that through repentance and faith they may come to know that they are elect of God. Election should be encouragement rather than discouragement to sinners seeking salvation. Election assures them that God does save and that the grace which saves is the same grace that has its fountain in election. Furthermore, the free overture of grace in Christ to all without distinction comes from God's electing grace. Hence, it is a grave error to maintain that election either as to its truth or in its proclamation has no relevance to unbelievers. No part of God's counsel may be withheld from men.

The obligations incident to election have special reference to believers.

1. *They are to make their election sure* (2 Pet 1:10). This does not mean that they are to make it sure by effecting it, by causing it to be. It is God who elects and no agency of man enters into it or contributes to it. To make it sure means to make certain that it is a fact pertaining to ourselves. How this is to be done the Scripture makes plain. It is significant that a certain order is observed: "make your calling and election sure." Though calling is likewise an act of God and of God alone, it is an act addressed to us and comes within our experience. Calling and election are always conjoined (Rom 8:28-30; 2 Tim 1:9) and from the certainty of our calling we may be assured of our election. Paul also indicates this order of thought (1 Thess 1:3, 4). It was from the "work of faith and labor of love and patience of hope" that he knew of the election of the saints, not by some esoteric or mystical insight into the hidden mysteries of God. The same process applies in the sphere of self-examination. Our thought proceeds upstream. Only from the fruit may we be assured of the ultimate root in divine election. Perplexity and confusion result from neglect of this order of human inquiry and faith.

2. The assurance of election should evoke gratitude and humility. Salvation is all of grace and that this grace takes its origin from the sovereign good pleasure of God the Father in the counsel of His will from eternal ages should fill the believer with adoring amazement that he should have been chosen in love for life everlasting. Election constrains the praise of the glory of God's grace (Eph 1:6, 12, 14) and to make it the occasion for presumption or pride is to turn the grace of God into lasciviousness. "The thought of election should drive ransomed sinners to incessant doxologies and thanksgivings, as it does Paul" (J. I. Packer, "Election," NBD [1962], p. 360). The fruit of gratitude is not license but constant care to "prove what is the good and acceptable and perfect will of God" (Rom 12:2 ASV), to be "sincere and void of offence unto the day of Christ" (Phil 1:10; cf. Col 3:12).

3. The certainty of election imparts to the believer a sense of security. Bound up with election is the immutable purpose of God. In this resides the security of God's people and nothing will separate them from the love of God in Christ Jesus (cf. Rom 8:33-39). The praise of God's grace is intensified the more believers rely upon the faithfulness and power of God. His counsel stands fast and is the guarantee that the final issue will correspond with the love that election reveals.

IV. Election to office

In the NT, as in the Old, there is election to specialized functions. It is to be distinguished from election to salvation in two respects.

The latter is specifically the action of God the Father, as has been noted repeatedly. With the exception of Acts 15:7, where Peter, by implication, is represented as chosen to bring the word of the Gospel to the Gentiles, the election to special office appears as that exercised by Christ (Luke 16:13; John 6:70; 15:16, 19; Acts 9:15).

Election to office is not *necessarily* concomitant with election to salvation. The choice of Judas Iscariot shows this. Judas' loss points up the necessity of observing the distinction because his loss is not to be construed as defeat of the election of grace or as an exception to the security it entails. The case of Judas likewise warns us that endowments for office are not of themselves the guarantee of salvation. The words of our Lord also advise us (John 17:12; 18:9) that the example of Judas is not the rule in the institution of Christ. The rule is what we find in John 15:16, 19 that those chosen to office are not of the world and bear the fruit that abides (cf. also John 17:16).

V. Elect angels

The angels that kept their first estate (cf. Jude 6) are called the elect angels (1 Tim 5:21). Election in their case differs from election as it pertains to men. These angels never sinned and so their election was not to salvation or redemption but to preservation and confirmation. Although they perform manifold functions in connection with the salvation of men, their election was not in Christ nor were they predestinated to the unsurpassable glory designed for the elect of mankind (cf. Rom 8:29; Heb 2:5, 10-16). But the services they perform for the heirs of salvation (Heb 1:14) are bound up with the confirmation they enjoy by reason of election. The elect of mankind in deriving untold blessing from the ministry of angels should know that this ministry the angels perform in gratitude to God for the election of which they are partakers.

See also FOREKNOW, FOREKNOWLEDGE.

BIBLIOGRAPHY. J. Calvin, *Institutes,* III, xxi-xxiv; J. Zanchius, *The Doctrine of Absolute Predestination* (E. T. 1930); A. Booth, *The Reign of Grace* (1949), 53-97; H. H. Rowley, *The Biblical Doctrine of Election* (1950); B. B. Warfield, "Predestination" in *Biblical and Theological Studies* (1952), 270-333; G. C. Berkouwer, *Divine Election* (1960); J. I. Packer, "Election" in NBD (1962).

J. MURRAY

ELECT LADY (*ἐκλέκτη κυρία*). This title was used in the salutation of 2 John 1:1. It has been understood to identify a Christian woman, the acquaintance of the Elder who wrote the letter. Her sister may have been his hostess at the time he wrote. "Lady" in Gr. was sometimes a proper noun, and some have thought it should have been transliterated (*Kuria* or *Cyria*) as was Gaius' name in 3 John. It is more likely that the reference was a figure of speech referring to the church to which the letter was addressed, as also the closing reference to "sister" would be understood as a designation for a Christian community. The symbolism of the church as a mother and its members as children may be hinted in 1 Pet 5:13 also. The election of God's people was a prominent idea in the OT and the figure of the Messianic community as a woman bearing children may likewise be understood in Galatians 4:25 and Revelation 12.

H. L. DRUMWRIGHT, JR.

EL-ELOHE-ISRAEL **ĕl ĕl′ ō he ĭz′ rĭ əl** (אל-אלהי-ישראל, *God is the God of Israel*). The name of an altar erected by Jacob.

When Jacob returned from Paddan-aram with his family, he purchased a portion of a field from the "sons of Hamor, Shechem's father," on which he had camped (Gen 33:18-

20). This Canaanite family ruled Shechem which made it possible for Israel to have a permanent shrine here. This later proved useful when they took the land under Joshua (Josh 24:32). On this lot Jacob erected an altar and named it "El is the God of Israel," a confessional altar or shrine which appropriated the Canaanite deity name "El" (the Mighty One) for use as one of the designations of Israel's God.

E. B. SMICK

EL-ELYON **ĕl' ĕl yōn'** (אל עליון, *Most High God*). A name of God used in a number of OT books but esp. in Genesis and the Psalms.

When Abraham paid tithes to Melchizedek (Gen 14:17-22) this is the name by which the priest worshiped God (cf. Heb 7:1ff.). This priest, "resembling the Son of God," said to Abraham,

"Blessed be Abram by God Most High,
maker of heaven and earth;
And blessed be God Most High,
who has delivered your enemies into
your hand!"

The name occurs exactly in this form again in Psalm 78:35 but there are Psalms with variations of the name. For example, Psalms 7:17 and 47:2 say the LORD (Yahweh) Most High, while Psalms 57:2 and 78:56 use God (*Elohim*) Most High. Frequently, *Elyon* (the Highest) is used by itself as a name for God (Num 24:16; Deut 32:8; 2 Sam 22:14; Pss 9:2; 18:13; 21:7; 46:4; 50:14; 73:11; 83:18; 87:5; 91:1, 9; 92:1; 107:11; Isa 14:14; Lam 3:35, 38). The sons of Elyon (Ps 82:6) are either rulers of this earth (cf. Gen 6:2) or they are the angel-princes of the heavenly sphere.

E. B. SMICK

ELEMENT (ELEMENTAL SPIRIT), ELEMENTS (*στοιχεῖον*, pl. *στοιχεῖα*). KJV tr. "elements" (Gal 4:3, 9; 2 Pet 3:10, 12); "rudiments" (Col 2:8, 20), and "first principles" (Heb 5:12). RSV tr. "elemental spirits" in Galatians and Colossians, "elements" in 2 Peter and "first principles" in Hebrews.

A variety of meanings are associated with this word in ancient religion and philosophy. It meant "one of a row," i.e., anything standing in series, such as the sounds of the alphabet. It aptly described the rudiments ("ABCs") of a system of knowledge or religion. This is prob. its meaning in Hebrews 5:12. This "principal" or "logical-pedagogical" sense also may apply to the Galatian and possibly the Colossian passages.

A natural extension of the word was to the elemental substances of the world, which is its probable meaning in 2 Peter 3:10. In later times the heavenly bodies and signs of the Zodiac also were so designated. However, the evidence for this is prob. too late to allow its consideration, in spite of the references to "new moons" in Colossians 2:16 and to calendar observances in Galatians 4:10.

The term also came to designate personified beings or "elemental spirits." These could be simply personifications of natural forces, or could be individualized as demons or, possibly, as angels. Recent scholarship has tended to interpret the language of Colossians 2:8, 20 in this way. Some interpreters have so understood Galatians 4:3, 9 as well.

Discussions on the above options usually include some of the following considerations and assumptions. The context of the Galatians passage deals with the Jewish law. The idea of bondage to the elements parallels that of bondage to the law. The description of the elements as "weak and beggarly" (KJV) may be compared to Paul's statements regarding the weakness of the law, thwarted by human nature (e.g., Rom 8:3). Therefore, the elements could here signify the rudiments of the law (Ridderbos, Bandstra). If the modifying words "of the world" ("universe," Gal 4:3 RSV) are taken to refer to the astral or spirit sphere, it is conceivable that the angels (3:19) are the elemental spirits who transmitted the law and hence have held men in bondage (so Reicke). However, nowhere does Scripture say that angels tyrannize men.

The meaning of the term in Colossians may or may not be equivalent to that in Galatians. The interest in laws, rituals, astral phenomena and seasons could have applied to either Jewish or Gentile heretics. The interpretation of the elements here as spirit beings may be supported by the reference to angels (2:18) and "principalities and powers" (2:10, 15 KJV). The reference to the "new moon" may suggest reverence of spirits behind the heavenly bodies. Similarities between the heresy of Colossians and later Gnostic speculations renders it possible that Gnostic intermediary powers are alluded to here. It also must be noted, however, that much of the language of Colossians applies to Jewish custom (2:11, 14, 16). It may be argued also that the Christian has not "died" to angels or other spirits but to the law (2:20). The interpretation is, therefore, still open to debate.

BIBLIOGRAPHY. B. Reicke, "The Law and this World According to Paul," JBL, LXX (1951), 259-276; H. N. Ridderbos, *Commentary on Galatians* (1953), 152f.; G. Delling, "*στοιχέω, συστοιχέω, στοιχεῖον*," TWNT, VII, 666-687; F. F. Bruce, *Commentary on Colossians* (1957), 231; C. F. D. Moule, *The Epistles of Paul the Apostle to Colossians and to Philemon* (1962), 90ff.; A. J. Bandstra, *The Law and the Elements of the World* (1964).

W. L. LIEFELD

ELEPH. KJV form of HA-ELEPH.

ELEPHANT. It is not mentioned by name in OT or NT, but is the producer of ivory (שן or שנהבים ; *ἐλεφάντινος*). Extinct forms of elephant roamed Pal. during the Pleistocene period, but the nearest natural occurrence of

Box from one piece of ivory with sphinxes and lions carved in high relief; from Megiddo, 1350-1150 B.C. ©*P.A.M.*

the Asiatic elephant was in the upper reaches of the Euphrates, where it was exterminated by hunters late in the 1st millennium B.C. Although other teeth, esp. of hippopotamuses, are sometimes used, true ivory comes only from elephant tusks, which are a pair of highly modified upper incisors. Ivory has been highly prized since the dawn of civilization and put to a wide range of ornamental uses, and these articles provide valuable archeological material today. (*See* IVORY, p. 590 NBD.) Most of the ivory used in Pal. and Syria came from the western race of the Asiatic elephant, now extinct, but supplies also came from India by sea to Babylon, via the Persian Gulf, or to Eilat, via the Gulf of Aqaba. The African elephant provided even heavier tusks, usually taken to Pal. overland via Dedan in Arabia, but routes were also developed across the Sahara which carried ivory, skins and even live animals of various kinds, through the Rom. era. The elephant was used against the Jews by Antiochus—"elephants two and twenty, and 300 chariots armed with hooks" (2 Macc 13:2 KJV).

BIBLIOGRAPHY. F. S. Bodenheimer, *Animals and Man in Bible Lands* (1960).

G. S. CANSDALE

ELEPHANTINE (*see* SYENE) **ELEPHANTINE PAPYRI el ə făn tī′ nī, Sé vĕ nĕ, ĕl ə făn tī′ nī pă pī′ rī** ('Ελεφαντίνη, *Elephant place* or *town*, tr. of the older Egyp. name, *Iebew*, which later Aram. papyri reproduced as Yeb; סונה, prob. סונה, for סון, *mart, trading post*, Egypt. *Sun*, Copt. *Suan*, modern Arab. *Aswan*. LXX Συήνη). Elephantine, a settlement on an island in the Nile River, opposite ancient Syene, with the modern name, Gezîret Aswan (the "Island of Aswan") in Upper Egypt, whose name has been given to certain ancient papyri of the 5th cent. B.C. which were found there.

1. Geographical location. Elephantine, known as "Yeb the fortress" (Brooklyn Aramaic Papyri, 2:2, etc.) was located at the southern frontier of ancient Upper Egypt on the narrow palm-studded island in the Nile River. It was just below the modern Aswan High Dam and opposite Syene (Aswan) which was on the E bank and from whose quarries came the sought after red granite (cf. the mineral name, *Syenite*). It served as a terminal port for deep water boat traffic because of the First Cataract just above it (cf. the phrase, "boatsman of the waters," Br. AP 12:20, for the importance of such men in this territory in the Pers. period).

2. Biblical references. Although Elephantine is not referred to in the Bible, it is prob. to be included in the reference to Syene (Ezek 29:10; 30:6), just as Herodotus in referring to stone from Elephantine (2, 175) must have included Aswan where the stones were quarried.

Sanballat and Johanan (Neh 2:10; 12:22; 13:28) are mentioned in Br. Aram. Papyrus 30:18, 29.

3. Archeological finds and excavations. It was not until 1893 and after, that, outside of the OT, quantities of Aram. papyri and ostraca appeared, chiefly from Elephantine. Most of these are now published as the Br. AP, 1-17 (5th cent. B.C.), the papyri purchased by C. E. Wilbour at Aswan in 1893; and *Aramaic Papyri of the Fifth Century* B.C. (AP 1-83, etc.), being collections of J. Euting, H. Sayce, A. Cowley and E. Sachau.

Excavations at Elephantine have been conducted by the French (1902ff.); the Germans (1906-1908); the Fathers of the Pontifico Instituto Biblico in Rome after World War I; and the Egyp. government (1932 and 1946).

Among building structures excavated were the Temple of Khnum (of the 4th to the 2nd centuries B.C.) and an earlier mud brick temple, the latter excavated by the Egyptians in 1948.

The excavations have not produced conclusive evidence regarding the exact location of

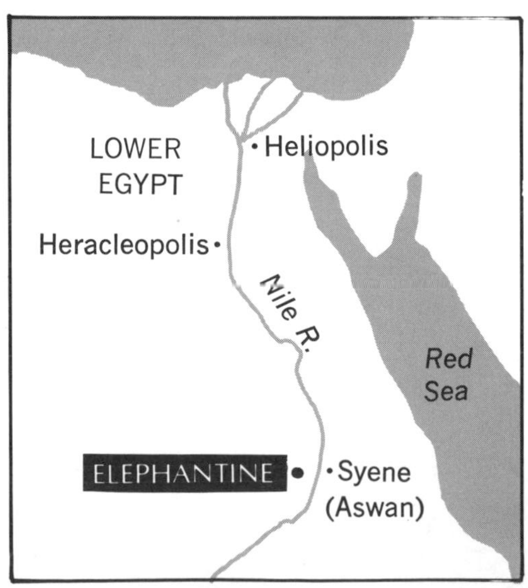

the 6th-5th cent. B.C. Jewish temple of Yahu which seems to have been located near an earlier temple of Khnum.

4. Early Egyptian history of the area. Elephantine was established as a fortress possibly as early as the 3rd dynasty, but surely so in the 6th dynasty when powerful princes of Egypt resided there. During the periods of Egyp. history from the time when Nubia was subservient to Egypt (c. 1550 B.C. to 700 B.C.) down to the period of Pers. domination (the late 6th and the 5th centuries B.C.) Elephantine undoubtedly played an important part as a frontier military post against enemies and desert tribesmen and as a fortress for keeping open the trade routes to the S.

The space was cramped at Elephantine, so there being a supplementary fort at Syene and more adequate room there for social activity, it is no wonder that inhabitants owned houses in both places, considering themselves as being both of Yeb and Syene (Br. AP 11).

5. Background and history of the Jewish colony. When the Elephantine 5th cent. B.C. Aram. papyri were written, a Jewish group was already established with houses, families and a temple dedicated to their God, Jahu, being a part of a military organization in service to the Persians, as is evidenced by letters addressed to such as "my brethren Yehoniah and his colleagues, the Judean garrison" (AP 21:1; cf. also AP 22:1; 24:33). That the Jewish colony was well established at Elephantine before 525 B.C. is proved by the Bagoas letter's (AP 30) reference to the temple's existence before Cambyses invaded Egypt. It was prob. founded early in the reign of Pharaoh Apries (Hophra of Jer 44:30; 588-566 B.C.) or later, the Egyps. evidently being friendly at that time to the erection of such a temple. Later when the Jewish garrison served under the Persians, the Egyp. attitude must have changed, as they destroyed the temple in 410 B.C. (AP 30). That the Jahu structure was subsequently rebuilt has been shown by its mention of being in existence in 402 B.C. (Br. AP 12:18, 19).

The colony and its temple evidently came to an end in the reign of Nepherites I (399-393 B.C.).

Aside from the Elephantine papyri, Aram. speaking Jews of Egypt have left only a little trace of their existence. There is a fragment of about 300 B.C. referring to Jewish persons (AP 82) and a long papyrus (AP 81) of approximately the same time which includes Jewish and Gr. names and mentions a Johanan the priest, suggesting the presence of a temple, a possible successor to the one at Elephantine. In the 1st cent. A.D. there may have been Jews in the Elephantine area (Philo, *Flaccus* 43).

6. Religious beliefs and practices of the Jewish colony. Aramaic religious syncretism seems to have been at work in the religious life at Elephantine, exampled by the listing along with Yahu the names of other gods, such as

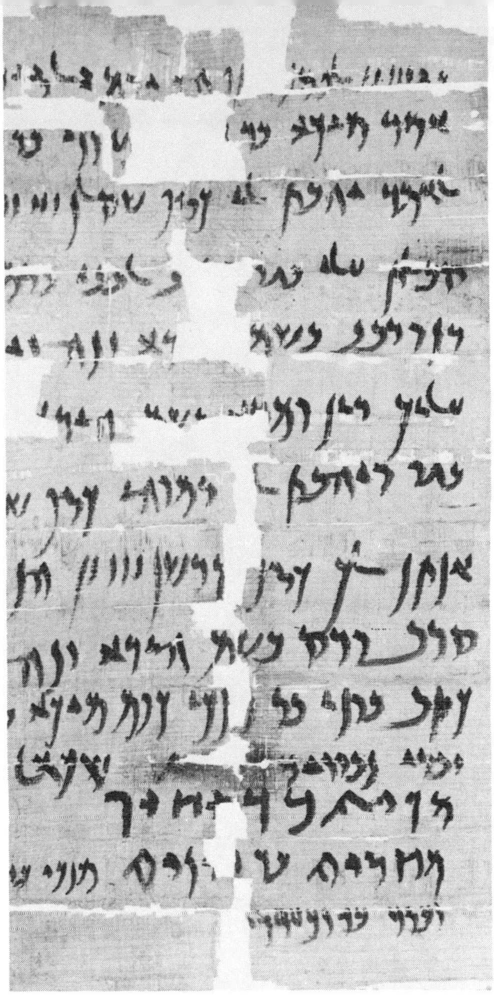

Elephantine papyrus in Aramic, dated 404 B.C., describing the gift of a house by Anani-bar-Azarih to his daughter. ©*Brooklyn Museum*

Eshembethel and 'Anathbethel (AP 22). It has been noted that the Bethel ("house of God") part of the names may be taken simply as a personification of El's house (in heaven) and as a substitute expression for El.

The Jewish colony did accommodate itself to the gods of the area which is shown in the use of the polytheistic formula, "may the gods desire your welfare" (AP 21:2, etc.).

In spite of these compromises and tendencies to syncretism, the worship of Yahu, the God of Pal., is seen in the use of the phrases, "God in heaven" (AP 38:2, 3; 40:2; cf. Dan 2:19, 44 where the same phrase is used) and "Yahweh of Hosts," *yhh sb't*, on an ostracon (cf. Ps 24:10) found by Clermont-Ganneau, which shows relationship of the colony to Jerusalem and its worship.

It is quite possible that the colony observed

Eleusis. Temple of Demeter (foreground), looking east. ©Lev

the sabbath (C-G ostracon 204, 152, 186), and it seems certain that they observed the Feast of Unleavened Bread and possibly also the Passover (AP 21).

Aramaic Papyrus 30 sheds additional light on two persons in Nehemiah, Sanballat (2:10; 13:28) indicated as the governor of Samaria; and Johanan (Neh 12:22), the son of Joiada and likely the same one whom Nehemiah chased (13:28) is mentioned as high priest, Bagoas being governor of Judea.

BIBLIOGRAPHY. A. Cowley, *Aramaic Papyri of the Fifth Century* B.C. (1923); E. G. Kraeling, "New Light on the Elephantine Colony," B.A. XV (1952, 1953), 50-67; G. R. Driver, *Aramaic Documents of the Fifth Century B.C.* (1954); W. F. Albright, *Archaeology and The Religion of Israel,* 3rd ed. (1956), 168-174; J. Bright, *A History of Israel* (1959), 327, etc.; B. Porten, "The Structure and Orientation of the Jewish Temple at Elephantine," JAOS, LXXXI (1961), 38-42.

W. H. MARE

ELEUSIS ĕl u' sĭs (Ἐλευσίς). A town fourteen m. W of Athens on the bay of Salamis and opposite the island.

A wealthy and independent town in the 8th and 7th centuries B.C. it later became a part of the city-state of Athens. It was the seat of the cult of Demeter and Persephone. Numerous archeological remains of all periods from the Mycenaean period to Rom. times survive. Most important are the temple and sacred precinct of the mystery cult.

The ceremony connected with the worship of the goddess and her daughter was elaborate, and aimed at stirring the emotions and promoting a feeling of purification and regeneration. Little is known of the rite, but it is likely that part of it involved the elevation of a sheaf of wheat, which symbolized death and rebirth. This may be the explanation of Christ's remark, "unless a grain of wheat falls into the earth and dies, it remains alone; but if it dies, it bears much fruit" (John 12:24).

A. RUPPRECHT

ELEUTHERUS ĭ lōō' thər əs (Ἐλεύθερος, *free*). A small river flowing from the Lebanon Mountains across Phoenicia to the Mediterranean Sea. It marked the northern limit of two expeditions by Jonathan the Maccabee (1 Macc 11:7; 12:30).

ELEVEN, THE (*οἱ ἕνδεκα, the eleven*). The eleven apostles (Acts 1:26) or disciples (Matt 28:16) of Jesus, remaining after the death of Judas (Mark 16:14; Luke 24:9, 33; Acts 2:14). The use of the Gr. definite article sets them apart as a group who retained their continuity with the Twelve after the defection of Judas. They became "The Twelve" again after the choice of Matthias (Acts 1:26; 6:2; Rev 21:14). Listing the resurrection appearances of Jesus, Paul wrote of the Twelve though there were at that time only eleven (1 Cor 15:5). The Eleven as such appeared only as witnesses of the resurrection appearances of Jesus, mentioned in Matthew, Mark, Luke, and Acts.

E. RUSSELL

ELHANAN ĕl hā' nən (אֶלְחָנָן, LXX Ἐλεανον *God has been gracious*=Adeodatus [2 Sam 21:19; 23:24; 1 Chron 11:26; 20:5]) The name of two men in the OT. 1. A Bethlehemite, son of Ja'are-orégim, who in David's army in the wars against the Philistines at Gob slew (KJV conjecturally adds "brother of" from 1 Chron 20:5) Goliath the Gittite, the shaft of whose spear is said to have been like a weaver's beam (2 Sam 21:19). In Chronicles the father of Elhanan is Jair and his victim is Lahmi the brother of Goliath (1 Chron 20:5).

Conjectural efforts to solve this problem are: (a) Postulate two separate giants named Goliath, one slain by David and one by Elhanan, or postulate that Goliath is a generic name for a class of giants. (b) Assume that "brother of" has fallen out of the text of Samuel. (c) Assume that Chronicles is trying to solve the problem by adding "brother." (d) Assume with Ewald and Kennedy that a story originally dealing with Elhanan has been transfered to David whose victim previously had been anonymous. (f) Assume from a tradition preserved in Jerome (*Quaest. Heb. in Libros Regnum*) and the Targum that David and Elhanan are identical. It recently has been widely assumed that David rather than being a personal name is a throne name for Elhanan. Support for this contention from the occurrence of *dawidum* in Mari texts for a leader now has been shown to be indefensible.

2. Son of Dodo of Bethlehem, one of the thirty mighty men of David who ranked next to the three (2 Sam 23:24; 1 Chron 11:26).

BIBLIOGRAPHY. A. R. S. Kennedy, *Samuel: The Century Bible* (n.d.), 300; S. R. Driver, *Notes On the Hebrew Books of Samuel* (2nd ed., 1913), 354, 355; A. M. Honeyman, JBL, 67 (1948), 23f.; V. Pákozdy, ZAW, 68 (1956), 257-259; J. J. Stamm, SVT, 7 (1959), 167ff.

J. P. LEWIS

ELI e' lī (עֵלִי, a short form of *'ēliyyâ, Jah is high*). The priest at Shiloh during Samuel's youth. He was a judge of Israel for forty years (1 Sam 4:18).

Eli is a tragic figure of whom comparatively little is known. An old man with faithless sons, he raised the child Samuel as a temple servant. Eli is remembered for his ineffective protests against the sins of his sons, Hophni and Phinehas. Because of this failure the boy Samuel was called to pronounce Eli's doom and the removal of his family from the priestly office (1 Sam 3:11-14; cf. 1 Sam 2:27-36). Finally when the army in distress called for the Ark of God to be used as a talisman of success in battle, Eli's two sons who bore it were killed and the Ark was captured. On hearing the bad news, Eli, a heavy man, fell off his

Tell Shiloh where Eli presided over the Tabernacle. ©*M.P.S.*

seat by the city gate and died of a broken neck. He was ninety-eight years old.

The wilderness tabernacle had been pitched in Shiloh for many years (Josh 18:1; Judg 18:31). Eli was a descendant of Aaron's son Ithamar as one learns from the notation concerning his successor Ahimelech (1 Sam 22:20; 1 Kings 2:27; 1 Chron 24:3). Eli's descent is not given in 1 Chronicles 6, because after the judgment on Eli's family the priestly line was reckoned through Aaron's other son Eleazar. In David's day, after the slaughter of the house of Ahimelech (1 Sam 22:18-20) it is noted that the priests descended from Eleazar outnumbered those from Ithamar, two to one (1 Chron 24:4).

The sins of the sons of Eli included both sacrilege and immorality. They paid little attention to the proper ritual of the sacrifices and less to their meaning. They used the priestly office merely for livelihood. The sordid story includes their sin with "the women who did service at the door of the tent of meeting" (RSV). The words may suggest that Hophni and Phinehas had introduced into the tabernacle worship the sacred prostitution so common at the surrounding Canaanite shrines. The comment is "the sin of the young men was very great" (1 Sam 2:17).

There was also a better side to Eli. He exhorted Hannah to godliness and blessed her for her faith. He doubtless had much to do with raising Samuel and did better with him than with his own sons. He presided over the Tabernacle in Shiloh a long time. Archeological investigation indicates that Shiloh was destroyed close to 1050 B.C. which is just the time of Eli's death. The tragedy of Shiloh was remembered until Jeremiah's day (Jer 7:12). *See* SHILOH.

R. L. HARRIS

ELI, ELI, LAMA SABACHTHANI e′ lī, e′ lī, lä′ mə sə bák′ thə nī (Aram. אלהי למה שבקתני אלהי, transliterated into Gr. [Matt 27:46] as *ἠλὶ ἠλὶ λεμὰ σαβαχθανί*). The form of the divine name with personal possessive suffix, אלי, is identical with the OT Heb. quotation in Psalm 22:1 from which the phrase is quoted. The verbal form *sabachthani*, however, is pure Aram. In the parallel quotation (Mark 15:34), the Gr. reads ἐλωΐ ἐλωΐ λαμὰ σαβαχθάνι, wherein the divine name is Aram. in form. In the many texts and VSS of this v., the two gospel readings are often interchanged, and even the Lat. varies widely, some VSS yielding "*heloi*" and "*lammasabani*." This is easily explained when it is recognized that few Gentile Christians knew any Heb., and that a mixed dialect of Heb. and Aram. was common in Pal. throughout the postexilic period. The question of which of these languages Jesus actually spoke has been discussed for centuries. It appears that He followed the custom of the time of speaking in Aram., although listening to and expounding the OT in the Heb. text. (Cf. other clues in the NT, e.g. the use of "Amen" in John [3:3, et al.] and the phrase employed in the raising of Jairus's daughter, Mark 5:41.)

The statement is of great theological significance in the comprehension of the self-revelation of Jesus. The meaning of the phrase is abundantly clear, as both evangelists immediately gloss the Aram. transliteration with the meaning, "My God, my God, why hast thou forsaken me?" (Matt 27:46; Mark 15:34). The true comprehension of the momentous meaning of the text is involved with the fact that it is quoted from a Messianic Psalm. The rabbinical commentators and the Talmud itself assumed Psalm 22 to be an expression of suffering and a plea for mercy greater than David's alone. The cry of the dying Messiah in the passion narratives refers to the mystery of Christ's two natures—the Divine co-eternal Lord-Christ was judging the human Messiah-Jesus upon the cross, and in this hour of agony when redemption was accomplished, the suffering servant cried out to the just and angry covenant God. In view of this moment, many churches have added over the centuries the phrase "he descended into Hell" to the statement regarding Christ's passion in the Apostles' Creed. At this point in the narrative of redemption, the insight is far beyond the realm of analysis and only confession is valid.

W. WHITE, JR.

ELIAB ĕ lī′ əb (אֱלִיאָב, LXX Ἐλίαβ, *My God is father*). The name of six OT men (Num 1:9; 16:1; 1 Sam 16:6; 1 Chron 6:27; 12:9; 15:18) in addition to being the name of the Simeonite ancestor of Judith (Jud 8:1) in the Apoc.

1. A Zebulonite, son of Helon, attendant of Moses in taking the census in the wilderness, leader of a host of 57,400 (Num 1:9; 2:7; 10:16) whose offering to the Lord at the Tabernacle on the third day totaled a silver plate and basin full of fine flour, a golden dish of incense, a bull, lamb, goat, two oxen, six rams, five male goats, and five male lambs for sin and peace offerings (Num 7:24-29).

2. A Reubenite, son of Pallu and father of Nemuel, Dothan and Abiram, the last two of whom were among the leaders of those who contended with Moses and Aaron in the wilderness (Num 16:1, 12; 26:8, 9; Deut 11:6).

3. A Kohath Levite, son of Nahath and ancestor of Samuel the prophet (1 Chron 6:27). Variant names are Eliel (1 Chron 6:34 [MT: 19]) and Elihu (1 Sam 1:1).

4. Eldest son of Jesse and brother of David whose physical appearance made him attractive to Samuel as a candidate for king but who at the Lord's prompting was passed in favor of David (1 Sam 16:6; 1 Chron 2:13). Eliab served Saul in the Valley of Elah when Goliath challenged the army and was angry at David for coming to the battle (1 Sam 17:13, 28). He also was the father of Abihail, wife of Rehoboam (2 Chron 11:18). It is often conjectured, following Jerome (*Quaesitones Hebraicae, ad loc.*) that Elihu of 1 Chronicles 27:18 is a variant for Eliab.

5. A Gadite warrior, third in rank of the Gadite officers, who served David at Ziklag (1 Chron 12:9 [LXX v. 11]).

6. A Levite minister, harpist, and singer at the sanctuary, as arranged by David, appointed to play *ʿalamot* (1 Chron 15:18, 20; 16:5).

J. P. LEWIS

ELIADA, ELIADAH ĭ lī′ ə də (אֶלְיָדָע, LXX Ἐλιαδάε, meaning *God knows*). In the OT three men were known by this name. 1. A son of David, born in Jerusalem (2 Sam 5:16; 1 Chron 3:8). In 1 Chronicles 14:6 he is called Beeliada, a variant spelling for Baaliada. Here Baal is substituted for El.

2. Father of Rezon, who overthrew Hadadezer and became king of Syria (1 Kings 11:23, 24).

3. A skilled soldier and a commander of 200,000 Benjaminite archers during Jehoshaphat's reign (2 Chron 17:17).

G. H. LIVINGSTON

ELIADAS. KJV Apoc. form of ELIOENAI.

ELIADUN. KJV Apoc. form of ILIADUN.

ELIAH. KJV form of ELIJAH (1 Chron 8:27; Ezra 10:26).

ELIAHBA ĭ lī′ ə bə (אֶלְיַחְבָּא, LXX 2 Sam 23:32, Ἐλιασου; 1 Chron 11:33, Ἐλιαβα, *God hides*). One of the "thirty," David's elite guard, a Shaalbonite (2 Sam 23:32). He is listed among those who are called "the mighy men of the armies" (1 Chron 11:33).

D. H. MADVIG

ELIAKIM ĭ lī′ ə kĭm (אֶלְיָקִים, LXX Ἐλιακείμ, meaning *God raises up*). There are three men in the OT and two in the NT who were called by this name. 1. The son of Hilkiah, Eliakim, with two others, was selected to negotiate with the besieging Assyrian army in 701 B.C. The trio objected to the Assyrian's use of Heb. instead of Aram. in the public conference, but to no avail. After hearing the repeated demands that Jerusalem surrender, they relayed the message to the king with great sorrow. Cf. the parallel accounts (2 Kings 18:18-37; Isa 36:3-22). Eliakim is mentioned in Isaiah 22:20-24 as destined to take his unworthy father's place in the government.

2. The second son of Josiah was enthroned by the Egyptians, after deposing Jehoahaz and changing Eliakim's name to Jehoiakim which means *Jahweh raises up*. This took place in 609 B.C. When the Babylonians took over Pal. in 605 B.C., Jehoiakim reluctantly became their puppet, but after three years rebelled and lost his life in 598 B.C. The accounts of his reign are given in 2 Kings 23:34-24:6; 2 Chronicles 36:4-8; Jeremiah 22:13-19; 25; 26; 35; 36.

3. A priest who played a trumpet at the dedication of the wall of Jerusalem under the leadership of Nehemiah (Neh 12:41).

4. Mentioned in the postexilic division of the genealogy of Jesus as the son of Abiud and the father of Azor (Matt 1:13).

5. Mentioned in the preexilic section of the genealogy of Jesus (Luke 3:30).

D. H. LIVINGSTON

ELIALIS **ĭ lī′ ə lĭs** (LXX B Ἐδιαλεις; A Ἐλιαλει) KJV ELIALI, -LĪ. One of the sons of Bani (KJV Maani) who put away their foreign wives and children (1 Esd 9:34). The name of Elialis does not appear in the parallel in Ezra 10:38.

ELIAM **ĭ lī′ əm** (אליעם, LXX Ἐλιάβ, meaning *God is kinsman*). Two men in the OT possessed this name. 1. Father of Bathsheba, the wife of Uriah (2 Sam 11:3). He is called Ammiel which means the same, only the name's components are reversed (1 Chron 3:5).

2. A son of Ahithophel of Gilo (2 Sam 23:34), and a member of the "Thirty" who were David's supreme military council and commanders of the militia. This man is also called Ahijah the Pelonite (1 Chron 11:36). Ahijah means *a brother of Jahweh.*

G. H. LIVINGSTON

ELIAONIAS. KJV Apoc. form of ELIEHOENAI (1 Esd 8:31).

ELIAS. KJV NT form of ELIJAH.

ELIASAPH **ĭ lī′ ə săf** (אליסף, LXX Ἐλισάφ, meaning *God has added*). Two men in the OT have this name: 1. A son of Deuel (Reuel) and a leader of the tribe of Gad recognized by Moses (Num 1:14; 2:14; 7:42-47; 10:20).

2. A descendant of Gershon of the tribe of Levi; this man was a leader of the Gershonites during the time of Moses (Num 3:24). He was in charge of the tabernacle coverings, the curtains of the court and the main altar.

G. H. LIVINGSTON

ELIASHIB, ELIASIB **ĭ lī′ ə shĭb** (אלישיב, LXX Ἐλιάσιβος, or Ἐλιασούβ, meaning *God restores*). Six men are listed by this name in the OT. 1. A priest chosen by David to head the eleventh of the twenty-four courses of priests who took turns serving in the sanctuary (1 Chron 24:12).

2. A high priest who gained the displeasure of Nehemiah because he made a temple storage area into special living quarters for a certain Tobiah, while Nehemiah was in the Pers. capital. Nehemiah, on his return, abolished this favoritism (Ezra 10:6; Neh 3:1, 20, 21; 13:4-9; 1 Esd 9:1).

3. A singer among the Levites during the time of Ezra (Ezra 10:24; 1 Esd 9:24). He pledged to put away his foreign wife and children when commanded to do so.

4. A son of Zattu and a layman of Ezra's time who made the same pledge to put away his foreign wife and children (Ezra 10:27; 1 Esd 9:28).

5. A son of Bani, a layman who made the same pledge (Ezra 10:36; 1 Esd 9:34).

6. A son of Elioenai whose ancestry is traced back through Zerubbabel, Jeconiah and the royal lineage to Solomon and to David (1 Chron 3:24).

G. H. LIVINGSTON

ELIASIBUS. KJV Apoc. form of ELIASHIB.

ELIASIMUS **ĭ lĭas′ məs** (Ἐλιασιμος) RSV ELIASHIB, ĕ lī ə shĭb. One of the sons of Zamoth (RSV "Zattu") who put away their foreign wives and children (1 Esd 9:28). The parallel account in Ezra 10:27 reads Eliashib, q.v.

ELIASIS **ĭ lī′ ə sĭs** (Ἐλιασις). One of the sons of Bani of the non-priestly, non-levitical families (KJV "Maani") who put away foreign wives and children (1 Esd 9:34). His name does not appear in the parallel account in Ezra 10:36, 37.

ELIATHAH **ĭ lī′ ə thə** (אליאתה, LXX Ἠλιαθα, *God comes*). One of the sons of Heman, the king's seer, who was set apart for the Temple service. Under the direction of their father they participated in Temple service with cymbals, harps, and lyres (1 Chron 25:4). The assignment of duty was done by lot. The twentieth lot fell to Eliathah, his sons and his brothers (25:27).

D. H. MADVIG

ELIDAD **ĭ lī′ dăd** (אלידד, *God has loved*). The son of Chislon from the tribe of Benjamin (Num 34:21). He was one chosen by God to divide the land of Canaan on the W side of the Jordan for the inheritance of the ten tribes. Eleazar, the priest, and Joshua, the son of Nun, were to oversee the work. He is perhaps the same as the Eldad of Numbers 11:26ff. who together with Medad prophesied in the camp of Israel. When Joshua asked Moses to forbid them to prophesy, Moses refused and said that he wished all of the Lord's people were prophets.

J. B. SCOTT

ELIEHOENAI, ELIHOENAI **ĭ lī′ ə hō′ ē nī** (אליהועיני, *unto the Lord are mine eyes*). The name of two men in the OT. 1. The seventh son of Meshelemiah of the Korahites (1 Chron 26:3). The seven sons together with their father were appointed as doorkeepers in the time of David. The KJV spells the name ELIOENAI.

2. A son of Zerahiah who was of the family of Pahath-moab (Ezra 8:4). He was at the

head of two hundred men who went up with Ezra to Jerusalem from Babylon in the reign of Artaxerxes. The name also occurs in the LXX as Ἐλιαωνίας (1 Esd 8:31).

J. B. Scott

ELIEL **ĭ lī′ əl** (אליאל, *My God is God*). The name of nine or perhaps ten different men in the OT. 1. An ancestor of Heman, a Kohathite (1 Chron 6:34). He was the great-grandfather of Samuel who was the grandfather of Heman, a singer appointed in David's day for the service of song in the house of the Lord. He is prob. the same as Eliab (1 Chron 6:27) and Elihu (1 Sam 1:1).

2. The head of the house of his father in the eastern half of the tribe of Manasseh, a famous man of valor (1 Chron 5:24).

3. One who dwelt in Jerusalem in David's day, a descendant of Benjamin (8:20).

4. Another Benjamite of the same period as number three above (8:22).

5. One of David's mighty men (11:47). A Mahavite (11:46).

6. Another of David's mighty men (11:47).

7. One of the eleven Gadites who joined David in the wilderness. These Gadites were mighty men of valor, trained for war, who were swift as a roe on the mountains. The least of these was said to be equal to 100 men (12:11). It is possible that he is the same as either number 5 or number 6 above.

8. The chief of the sons of Hebron, one of the Levites whom David gathered to carry the Ark to Jerusalem (15:9).

9. Possibly the same as number eight, but this is uncertain (15:11).

10. One of the overseers under the hand of Conaniah, the Levite, by appointment of Hezekiah (2 Chron 31:13). He had oversight of the tithes and offerings.

J. B. Scott

ELIENAI **ĕl′ ĭ ē′ nī** (אליעיני, Ἐλιωηναι, the meaning may be, *my eyes are toward Yahweh*). A son of Shimei of the tribe of Benjamin (1 Chron 8:20).

ELIEZER, ELIEZAR **ĕl ĕ ē′ zər** (אליעזר, *God is help*). The name of eleven different individuals in the OT. 1. The head servant of Abraham (Gen 15:2). According to the custom of that day, he was due to receive the inheritance of Abraham because Abraham then had no son as heir. He is designated as "from Damascus," possibly to distinguish him from other servants of the same name. He was most likely the unnamed servant of Genesis 24 who was sent by Abraham to get a wife for Isaac from among Abraham's people. If so, he was a devout man of faith.

2. The second son of Moses by Zipporah (Exod 18:4). The name was given to him by Moses because God delivered Moses from Pharaoh. He had one son, Rehabiah, who had many sons (1 Chron 23:15, 17). One of his descendants, Shelomoth, was in charge of all the treasuries of the gifts which David and the heads of the families of Israel had dedicated to God (26:25, 26).

3. One of the sons of Becher, a descendant of Benjamin (7:8).

4. A priest of Levi (15:24). He was appointed to blow the trumpet when David brought the Ark to Jerusalem from the house of Obed-edom.

5. A ruler over the Reubenites in David's day (27:16). He was the son of Zichri and the chief officer of the tribe.

6. A prophet, the son of Dodavahu, in Jehoshaphat's time (2 Chron 20:37). He was from Mareshah and prophesied against Jehoshaphat because he had made alliance with Ahaziah. God promised to destroy the king's works and consequently Jehoshaphat's ships were broken and destroyed.

7. One sent by Ezra to Iddo to get ministers for the house of God (Ezra 8:16). The name is spelled Ἐλεαζαρ in 1 Esdras 8:43.

8. One of the priests who married foreign wives and who promised to put them away and to offer guilt offerings (Ezra 10:18). It is also spelled Eliezar in 1 Esdras 9:19.

9. Another Levite who had married a foreign wife (Ezra 10:23), possibly the same as the Jonah of 1 Esdras 9:23.

10. The son of Harim, one who had married a foreign wife (Ezra 10:31). Possibly he is the same as Elionas of 1 Esdras 9:32.

11. An ancestor of Joseph, the husband of Mary, the mother of Jesus (Luke 3:29). He lived between the time of David and Zerubbabel.

BIBLIOGRAPHY. A. Edersheim, *Bible History,* I (1890), 89, 107-109; A. Edersheim, *Bible History* II (1890), 43, 57, 58; J. Finegan, *Light From the Ancient Past* (1946), 54; Wright and Fuller, *The Book of the Acts of God* (1957), 62; Margolis and Marx, *History of the Jewish People* (1958), 370; E. Young, *An Introduction to the Old Testament* (1958), 139; J. Bright, *A History of Israel* (1960), 71; C. Pfeiffer, *Patriarchal Age* (1961), 77; C. Pfeiffer, *Egypt and the Exodus* (1964), 44; National Geographic Society, *Everyday Life in Bible Times* (1967), 82.

J. B. Scott

ELIHOREPH **ĕl ə hôr ĭf** (אליחרף, *autumn God* ?). One of the high officials during Solomon's reign (1 Kings 4:3). He is further identified as a son of Shisha and one of two scribes in the reign of Solomon. His brother Ahijah was the other scribe or secretary. The suggestion that this was a title and not a personal name has no textual warrant. He undoubtedly was held in high regard by Solomon to have had such an important position and to have been regarded as a שר (prince or high officer).

J. B. Scott

ELIHU **ĭ lī′ hu** (אליהו[א], or אליאב, LXX Ἠλίου or Ἐλιάβ, meaning *He is my God* or *My God* *is Father.*) This name was carried by five men in the OT. 1. Ancestor of the prophet Samuel (1 Sam 1:1) who is called Eliab (1 Chron 6:27) and Eliel (1 Chron 6:34).

2. One of the soldiers of the tribe of Manasseh who deserted Saul to join David's army to become a commander (1 Chron 12:20).

3. A gatekeeper of the Korahites, serving at the Tabernacle during the time of David (1 Chron 26:7).

4. A brother of David, who became a leader of the tribe of Judah during David's reign (1 Chron 27:18); also called Eliab in LXX (cf. 1 Sam 16:6; 17:13, 28 [A]; 1 Chron 2:13; 2 Chron 11:18 [A]).

5. A young man, son of Barachel the Buzite of the family of Ram (Job 32:2). He became angry with Job's arguments and the failure of his three friends to answer Job. Thereupon he launched into a speech which held that suffering has a disciplinary purpose (Job 32:6-37:24).

G. H. LIVINGSTON

ELIJAH ĭ lī′ jə (Heb. אליה ; אליהו, *Yah is my God*, KJV, twice, ELIAH; Gr., LXX, Ἠλίου; Ἠλίας; KJV, NT, ELIAS) was (1) the famous 9th cent. prophet who served in the northern kingdom in the reigns of Ahab and his son, Ahaziah. One of the outstanding heroes of the Bible, Elijah was prominent in Jewish prophetic expectations; representatives of religious officialdom were sent to question John the Baptist concerning his identity and asked him if he was Elijah (John 1:21, 25). His importance in God's plan for the ages is apparent from his predicted reappearing before "the great and terrible day of the LORD" (Mal 4:5) and from his presence with Moses and the Lord upon the Mount of Transfiguration, where the three talked about the Lord's sacrificial death (Matt 17:1-13; Mark 9:2-13; Luke 9:28-36).

His identity. Nothing is known of his family and little of his geographic origin. The Bible states clearly that he was from Gilead (1 Kings 17:1), so he was certainly at some time from Trans-Jordan. He is also called "the Tishbite," which indicates his association with a place named Tishbe, whether in Napthali or E of the Jordan. The Heb. text of 1 Kings 17:1 adds that he was "of the תשבי of Gilead"; MT gives מתשבי, "of the settlers, sojourners" (cf., less accurately, KJV, "inhabitants"). LXX reads ἐκ θεσβῶν, interpreting the term as a place-name BDB (p. 986; cf. KB, p. 1042) and many commentators read מתשבה (or תשבה), followed by the RSV, "of Tishbe." Though the identity of Tishbe is not known for certain, topographers suggest the possibility of Tisib (or Listib, fr. Arab. *el Istib*), some thirteen m. NW of Gerasa. N. Glueck proposed that a textual error has obscured an original "the Jabeshite, from Jabesh-gilead" (*The River Jordan* [1946], 170; AASOR, 1945-1949, XXVI-XXVIII [1951], 218, 219, 225-227).

Personal characteristics. Elijah often is regarded as a wilderness dweller, prob. because of his Trans-Jordanian connections, his directed seclusion at the brook Cherith, his identifying apparel ("a garment of haircloth, with a girdle of leather," 2 Kings 1:8), and his NT associations with John the Baptist. His simple attire and diet did not prevent him from moving in more sophisticated circles, and he had repeated opportunities to address the king in person. Elijah was a man of great physical endurance; his feat of running before the chariot of Ahab from Mt. Carmel to the entrance of Jezreel demonstrates his excellent physical condition. His unhesitating devotion to the Lord made him a bold spokesman for what is right; he did not turn aside from vigorous denunciation of the actions of the hostile king nor did he cringe before the fanatic opposition of the priests of Baal. The human side of Elijah is evidenced in his flight from the vindictive Jezebel, when she sent him the message that she would take his life. The combination of zealous bravery and human failure gives added weight to the power of prayer exemplified in this man of God; he was "a man of like nature with ourselves," but "he prayed fervently" and God answered him (James 5:17, 18). Elijah was not only an enthusiastic religious leader; he was also an ardent patriot and his energetic service for God was coupled with a sincere concern for the nation of Israel. He also had strong interests in education; he continued the schools of the prophets founded by Samuel and he instructed Elisha in their administration. The "sons of the prophets" regarded him with respect and affection. When he and Elisha left Jericho to cross the Jordan, fifty of the sons of the prophets accompanied them and stood at some distance from them as the two crossed the river (2 Kings 2:7). When Elisha returned alone, the group at Jericho insisted that fifty men be sent to look for him (vv. 16-18), though they had known that he was to be taken away.

His career and mighty works. The Biblical account introduces Elijah with a dramatic and sudden appearance before King Ahab (1 Kings 17:1), to whom he declared that there would be neither dew nor rain except at the prophet's word. After making this prediction, he was directed by the Lord to hide himself by the brook Cherith, E of the Jordan, where he was supplied morning and evening with bread and meat carried by ravens. The identity and precise location of this stream are uncertain; Glueck and Grollenberg suggest Wadi Yâbis. When the waters of the brook dried up, he was divinely commanded to go to Zarephath in the territory of Sidon, where a widow was to feed him. Zarephath is the Sarepta of NT times (cf. Gr., Luke 4:26) and the modern Sarafand, between Tyre and Sidon.

The unfailing supplies (17:8-16). Arriving

Elijah nourished by an angel at the Brook Cherith. Engraving from a picture by Doré. ©H.P.

at Zarephath, Elijah found a widow whose supplies of meal and oil were nearly exhausted. He requested that she first bake a cake for him and later for herself and her son, and explained that this supply of flour and oil would last until the rains returned.

Raising the widow's son (17:17-24). When the widow's son became ill and died, the widow blamed Elijah for her loss, but he took the boy to his room, prayed, and stretched himself upon the child's body three times. When the boy returned to life, Elijah presented him to the mother, who then recognized the divine mission of the prophet.

The contest on Mt. Carmel and the breaking of the drought (1 Kings 18). After three rainless years the Lord instructed Elijah to present himself before Ahab. On his way the prophet met Obadiah, who was over the king's household, and told him to go to inform the king that he had come. Ahab came to meet Elijah and greeted him as "the troubler of Israel" (v. 17), but he replied that it was Ahab who troubled Israel, because he had forsaken the Lord and followed the Baals. He further challenged Ahab to bring to Mt. Carmel the 450 prophets of Baal and the 400 prophets of Asherah who were subsidized by Jezebel, the queen. Those prophets assembled as directed, along with many of the people, and God's prophet proposed a test to determine who was the true God. The prophets of Baal were to prepare a meat offering and Elijah was to do the same; the god who answered by fire and consumed the offering would be God. The efforts of the Baal worshipers proved to be ineffectual and Elijah mocked them as they tried to induce Baal to receive their offering. Finally he took charge, repaired an old altar of the Lord, prepared his offering, and instructed the people to pour four jars of water on it three times, so that the water soaked the prospective offering and everything about it. When he prayed, God answered with fire from heaven and consumed the offering, the wood, the altar, and even the dust and water about the altar. Then he commanded that the false prophets should be seized and slain, so they were put to death by the river Kishon.

Elijah next announced to Ahab that a great rain was about to fall. The prophet went to the top of Carmel and prayed. He ordered his servant to go look toward the sea and upon the servant's seventh trip of inspection a small cloud was seen. Ahab was told to make ready his chariot before the rain stopped him; the sky grew dark, and soon wind and a heavy downpour arrived, but Elijah ran all the way to the entrance of Jezreel in front of Ahab's chariot and ahead of the storm.

Elijah's flight (19:1-8). When Jezebel heard of the death of the false prophets, she swore vengeance on the prophet, who decided to flee, going to the S, to Beersheba and into the wilderness. Overcome by fatigue and strain, he despaired of life, but an angel provided food and drink for him and encouraged him to go on to Mt. Horeb in Sinai, where he found shelter in a cave.

Revelation and assignment (19:9-18). While Elijah was at Sinai the Lord spoke to him and, after sending a powerful wind, an earthquake and a fire, revealed Himself to the prophet in a "still, small voice" (v. 12). The Lord told him that he was to anoint Hazael to be king over Damascus, Jehu to be king of Israel, and Elisha, son of Shaphat of Abel-meholah, to be Elijah's successor in the prophetic office.

The call of Elisha (19:19-21). Elijah found Elisha plowing with twelve yoke of oxen. He cast his mantle upon the younger man, who immediately acknowledged the call but requested the privilege of bidding his parents farewell. The appointments of Hazael and Jehu were not carried out in the time of service of Elijah, but were left for the ministry of Elisha (see 2 Kings 8:7-15; 9:1-10).

Naboth's vineyard (1 Kings 21:1-27). When Ahab coveted the vineyard of Naboth to the point of frustration and illness, his wicked Tyrian wife arranged for his gaining the property by means of false charges which resulted in the execution of Naboth. When Ahab went to take possession of the vineyard he was confronted by the fearless Elijah, who both accused Ahab of murder and predicted the violent deaths of Ahab and Jezebel. Ahab gave indication of repentance and the Lord informed the prophet that because of Ahab's changed attitude the predicted evil would be delayed.

Elijah and Ahaziah (2 Kings 1). After the death of Ahab, his son, Ahaziah, succeeded him. The new king accidentally fell from an upper room of his palace and was seriously injured. To learn of his prospects for recovery, he sent messengers to inquire of Baal-zebub ("lord of flies"), the god of Ekron (Ugaritic, *Baal-zebul*; cf. Matt 10:25; Mark 3:22). Elijah intercepted the messengers and sent them back with the message that the ruler was soon to die. Ahaziah determined from a description of the prophet that he was dealing with Elijah and he sent a contingent of fifty men to arrest him. Elijah responded to the demand of the captain of the group by having fire from heaven destroy the would-be captors (cf. Luke 9:54, RSVmg.). A second unit suffered the same fate, but when a third captain arrived he pleaded for his life and the Lord directed Elijah to go with him in safety. The prophet personally gave to the king the prediction that he would not recover.

The translation of Elijah (2 Kings 2:1-12). When the time came for Elijah to be taken up to heaven, he and Elisha were engaged in their duties with the schools of the prophets, going from Gilgal to Bethel and to Jericho. At Gilgal and Bethel Elijah asked Elisha to stay behind, but Elisha swore that he would not leave him. The sons of the prophets and Elisha knew that Elijah was to be taken away by the Lord. Leaving Jericho the two prophets crossed the Jordan miraculously; Elijah struck the water with his mantle and the waters parted to make a way for them. He asked the younger man what he wanted as a favor from him. Elisha requested a double portion of the spirit of his master and Elijah replied that this would be granted if Elisha saw him as he left. Suddenly they were separated by a chariot and horses of fire; a whirlwind caught up Elijah as Elisha watched and cried, "My father, my father! The chariots of Israel and its horsemen!"

Elisha picked up the fallen mantle of his master, recrossed the Jordan and went to Jericho, where the sons of the prophets observed that "the spirit of Elijah rests on Elisha" (2:15). They kept urging that a search be made for Elijah; Elisha reluctantly permitted fifty men to go, but they returned without finding him.

Elijah had prophesied that the house of Ahab would be destroyed (1 Kings 21:21); when Jehu became king he used this prophecy as a basis for the annihilation of all of the relatives of Ahab (2 Kings 10:10, 17).

When Jehoram, the son of Jehoshaphat, made high places and led Judah astray, Elijah sent him a letter informing him that catastrophe would occur to the nation and to him because of his apostasy (2 Chron 21:12ff.).

Elijah and Baalism. The life of Elijah centers around the conflict between the worship of the Lord and the religion of Baalism. There were many Baals in Israel, but during the time of Ahab the prominent one was Baal-Melqart, the deity of Tyre. Ahab married Jezebel, the daughter of Ethbaal, king of Tyre and Sidon; she persecuted the prophets of the Lord (1 Kings 18:3, 13; 19:10, 14) and promoted the cult of Baal in Israel (18:19). The drought indicated the impotence of Baal, a supposed nature-god, while the survival of Elijah showed God's power to care for His own, even at Zarephath, in the home territory of Baal-Melqart. The contest on Mt. Carmel brought the nation of Israel to a place of decision and the subsequent flight of Elijah took him to the scene of earlier revelation at Mt. Horeb. The Naboth affair demonstrated the superior moral content of revealed religion, and the encounter between Ahaziah and Elijah showed that there was a God in Israel superior to Baal-zebub of Ekron. Elijah was throughout the man of God, the prophet and the spokesman of God, and his life testified to the reality and power of the one true God.

Elijah in later Scriptures. Malachi 4:5 foretold that Elijah would appear again before the day of the Lord; this prediction has both NT and future fulfillment (cf. Rev 11:6). The annunciatory angel declared to Zechariah that his son, John the Baptist, would go before the Lord "in the spirit and power of Elijah" (Luke 1:17). Though John denied that he was Elijah (John 1:21, 25), Jesus spoke of John as "Elijah who is to come" (Matt 11:14; 17:10-13). Jesus Himself was regarded by some of the Jews as Elijah (Matt 16:14; Mark 6:15; 8:28).

In His ministry Jesus used the example of Elijah's reception by the widow of Zarephath to illustrate the scarcity of faith within Israel (Luke 4:25, 26).

Elijah appeared as a participant in the scene of the Transfiguration, when he and Moses discussed with the Lord the "departure" which Jesus was to accomplish at Jerusalem. On this occasion Peter suggested that three tabernacles should be built for Jesus, Moses, and Elijah (Matt 17:4; Mark 9:5; Luke 9:33).

When Jesus was dying on the cross, He cried out to God ("Eli," "my God") and the bystanders thought he was calling Elijah (Matt 27:46-49; Mark 15:34, 35).

Paul, arguing for the principle of a remnant of Israel, referred to the 7,000 faithful worshipers in the time of Elijah (Rom 11:2). The two witnesses of Revelation 11 are not mentioned by name, but the powers ascribed to them are those of Moses and Elijah, e.g., "they have power to shut the sky, that no rain may fall during the days of their prophesying" (v. 6).

(2) An Elijah is listed among the heads of fathers' houses of the tribe of Benjamin (1 Chron 8:27).

(3) Among the priests who married foreign women in the time of Ezra was an Elijah, one of the sons of Harim (Ezra 10:21).

(4) An Elijah, a son of Elam is named among other Israelites who married foreign wives (Ezra 10:26).

BIBLIOGRAPHY. F. Krummacher, *Elijah the Tishbite* (1838); J. M. Lowrie, *Translated Prophet* (1868); A. S. Peake, *Elijah and Jezebel* (1927); R. S. Wallace, *Elijah and Elisha* (1957); B. L. Smith, "Elijah," *The New Bible Dictionary* (1962), 363, 364; S. Szikszai, "Elijah the Prophet," IDB (1962), II, 88-90.

C. E. DeVries

ELIJAH, APOCALYPSE OF. Two pseudepigraphic works have been known by this title. (1) The older is a lost book of the Pseud. known only from fragments in Coptic and an obscure reference in the works of the patristic writer Origen (A.D. 185?-254?) who stated that the difficult text, 1 Corinthians 2:9, was quoted from an Apoc., "But as it is written, 'What no eye has seen, nor ear heard, nor the heart of man conceived, what God has prepared for those who love him.' " This judgment of Origen's was supported by other ancient authorities. (2) A later post-Christian writing, part of which is dated back to A.D. 260/1 produced traditionally at the time of the Rom. emperor Valerian's capture by the Sassanian king of Persia, Sapor I (q.v.). This work tells

An oasis in the Sinai peninsula, with springs and palm trees. Elim must have been a similar place, although its exact location is uncertain. ©*M.P.S.*

of the defeat of the tyrant of Palmyra, Odenathus, the archenemy of the Jews. (3) A third though unlikely text is the Story of Rabbi Joshua ben Levi, a teacher in Lydda (Lod) who lived in the early 3rd Christian cent. In this apocryphal work the aged rabbi sees the panorama of heaven and hell with his companion Elijah.

BIBLIOGRAPHY. M. Buttenwieser, *Die hebräislhe Elias-Apocalypse* (1897); "Apocalyptic Literature," Jew Enc, Vol. I (1901), 680.

W. WHITE, JR.

ELIKA ĭ lī′ kə, ĕl′ ĭ kə (אליקא). Listed among the "thirty" mighty men of David (2 Sam 23:25). His name is omitted from a similar list in 1 Chronicles 11:27.

ELIM ē′ lĭm (אילם, *terebinths* or *oaks*). The second recorded stopping place of the Israelites on their journey from the Red Sea to Sinai (Exod 15:27; 16:1). The narrative of Exodus 15 recounts that they journeyed from the Red Sea to Marah, and from there to Elim, where there were twelve springs of water and seventy palm trees. A similar description of the place is given in Numbers 33:9f. The exact location of this oasis is not certain, for it depends upon the location of Sinai. If the traditional identification of Mount Sinai in the lower part of the peninsula is correct, Elim is likely to be one of the oases in the wadis along the main route into that area. The place now known as Wadi Gharandel is most frequently suggested. If Sinai is not in this area, the location of Elim is unknown. The suggestion that the name is a masculine pl. variation of the feminine pl. form Eloth (Elath) in 1 Kings 9:26, a location at the top of the Gulf of

Akabah by Ezion-geber, does not accord with the evidence of Numbers 33:35, which indicates that this area was reached much later on the journey.

BIBLIOGRAPHY. J. Simons, *The Geographical and Topographical Texts of the Old Testament* (1959), 252f.

G. GOLDSWORTHY

ELIMELECH ĭ lĭm′ ə lĕk (אֱלִימֶלֶךְ, *God is King*). A Bethlehemite, the husband of Naomi (Ruth 1:2), a head among the families of Judah. He went to Moab to sojourn because of a famine in his homeland. Two sons were born to him, Mahlon and Chilion, who after their father's death married daughters of Moab. Mahlon married Ruth, but died shortly thereafter. Boaz, being of the same family with Elimelech (Ruth 2:1, 3), and by right of kinship, purchased from Naomi the land formerly belonging to Elimelech. He also married Ruth, the daughter-in-law of Elimelech (Ruth 4:3, 9). From this marriage came David, a great-grandson of Ruth and Boaz. By marriage, Ruth the Gentile was brought eventually into the line of promise from Abraham to Christ.

J. B. SCOTT

ELIOENAI ĕl′ ĭ ō ē nī (אֶלְיוֹעֵינַי, *unto the Lord are my eyes*). The name of six men in the OT. 1. The son of Neariah and father of Hodaviah and six others (1 Chron 3:23, 24). He was a descendant of David and Solomon, and lived after the exile.

2. A descendant of Simeon (4:36), a chief.

3. The son of Becher, the son of Benjamin (7:8). He was a head of the family of the sons of Becher.

4. One of six sons of Pashhur, of the priestly family that had married foreign wives (Ezra 10:22). He is called Elionas in 1 Esdras 9:22. He may be the same as the trumpeter in Nehemiah 12:41.

5. One of six sons of Zattu of Israel who had a foreign wife (Ezra 10:27).

6. A postexilic priest who had a trumpet at the time of the giving of thanks at the dedication of the wall (Neh 12:41). He may be identified with number 4 above.

This name should not be confused with Eliehoenai (q.v.). KJV fails to distinguish in spelling the two distinctly different names.

J. B. SCOTT

ELIONAS ĕl′ ĭ ō′ nəs (Ἐλιωναίς, Ἐλιωνάς). A name applied to two men in the list of those who put away foreign wives at Ezra's insistence (1 Esd 9:22 KJV ELIONAS; RSV ELIOENAI; 9:32). The names in the two verses apparently correspond to Elioenai (Ezra 10:22) and Eliezer (10:31).

ELIPHAL ĭ lī′ fəl (אֱלִיפַל, *God has judged*). The son of Ur, one of the mighty men of David (1 Chron 11:35). See also Eliphalat (number 3). "Eliphelet, the son of Ahasbai, the son of the Maacathite" (2 Sam 23:34 ASV), and "Eliphelet the son of Ahasbai of Maacah" (RSV). While the Chronicles passage and the Samuel passage are parallel, and there is a similarity in the names of Eliphal and Eliphelet, the fathers' names are different. It is not unusual for men to have more than one name so that different generations would designate the same individual differently.

J. B. SCOTT

ELIPHALAT, ELIPHALET, ELIPHELET ĭ lĭf′ ə lĕt, (אֱלִיפֶלֶט, *God is deliverance*). The name of six men in the OT. The name is properly spelled "Eliphelet." 1. A son of David born in Jerusalem (2 Sam 5:16), misspelled "Eliphalet" in KJV which ignores the pause lengthening the vowel at the end of the verse. He was one of nine sons born in Jerusalem, not of a concubine (1 Chron 3:8; 14:7).

2. Another son of David born in Jerusalem, also one of the nine (3:6).

3. One of the thirty of David's mighty men (2 Sam 23:34). He was the son of Ahasbai and the grandson of the Maacathite. It is probable that he is the same as ELIPHAL of 1 Chronicles 11:35 (q.v.).

4. A descendant of Saul and Jonathan, the son of Eshek (1 Chron 8:39). He was the third of three brothers.

5. One of three sons of Adonikam in postexilic Jerusalem (Ezra 8:13). He went up with Ezra from Babylon to Jerusalem in the reign of Artaxerxes.

6. A son of Hashum in postexilic Jerusalem (Ezra 10:33). He was one of those who had foreign wives in Israel.

J. B. SCOTT

ELIPHAZ ĕl′ ə făz (אֱלִיפַז, *God is victorious*). An Edomite from Teman and friend of Job.

As one of the three of Job's friends he was wise, rich, and a ruler of men. He was their leader (42:7) and prob. the eldest. He is marked out by the courtesy with which he at first addressed Job (chs. 4, 5). Like his friends, he took for granted that Job must have committed some major sin, for only so could he explain his sufferings. But dominated, as he was, by a dream he had had of man's sinfulness before God (4:12-21), he tried to make it as easy as possible for Job to repent. In his second address (ch. 15) one senses the note of irritation caused by Job's rejection of his advice; the colors are darkened, and the applicability to Job heightened. The third address (ch. 22) is in many ways the bitterest of all addressed to Job, for Job had virtually denied the basis of his theology. He accused him without evidence of all the worst sins according to the concepts of the time. Even then his kindliness breaks through in a final offer of hope to Job of God's mercy. *See* JOB, BOOK OF.

H. L. ELLISON

ELIPHELEHU ĭ lĭf' ə le' hu (אליפלהו, *God has set him apart*, KJV ELIPHELEH). A Levite assigned to be a musician when David made preparation to bring the Ark of God up from the house of Obed-edom. He is called one of the brethren of the "second order" who followed Heman, Asaph, and Ethan who apparently sang and sounded bronze cymbals while some played lutes (*nᵉbālîm*). Eliphelehu, with others, played lyres (kinnōrôṯ) according to the Sheminith which means possibly "on the octave" (1 Chron 15:18-21).

E. B. Smick

ELISABETH. KJV form of Elizabeth.

ELISHA, ELISEUS ĭ lī' shə (Heb. אלישע. *God is salvation*; Gr., LXX, Ἐλισα, Ἐλισαιε, NT, Ἐλισαῖος; KJV, ELISEUS, Luke 4:27), was a prophet, the successor of Elijah.

His origin. Elisha was a son of a man named Shaphat, of the city of Abel-meholah, possibly modern Tell Abu Sifri, W of the Jordan and about midway between the Dead Sea and the Sea of Galilee. Elisha's name appears for the first time in 1 Kings 19:16, as the one Elijah was ordered to anoint as his successor. Elisha served primarily in the northern kingdom, from the latter part of the reign of Ahab into the rule of Joash, from roughly 850 to 800 B.C.

His call. The call of Elisha to the prophetic office was given by the prophet Elijah and was acted out in the manner characteristic of many of the OT prophets. As he passed by Elisha, Elijah cast his mantle upon him. Elisha immediately ran after Elijah and said that he would follow him as soon as he had said farewell to his parents. Like many other Biblical heroes, Elisha was a man who was close to the soil. At the time of his call he was plowing with twelve yoke of oxen (1 Kings 19:19; cf. 1 Sam 11:5). Before leaving with Elijah, he made a feast for the people by butchering two of the oxen.

His early ministry. While Elijah's ministry continued, Elisha served him (1 Kings 19:21), much as Joshua had assisted Moses. Elisha's name does not reappear in the Biblical narrative until 2 Kings 2:1, which marks the beginning of the account of Elijah's ascension to heaven and prefaces the active role of Elisha as the full successor to Elijah.

Elisha and the ascension of Elijah (2 Kings 2:1-12). Elisha accompanied the older man as he made his rounds to the prophetic schools or groups of "sons of the prophets." Just before Elijah was caught up to heaven, the two proph-

A panel from an Egyptian wall painting showing plowing and sowing. At the time of his call, Elisha was plowing with twelve yoke of oxen. © *B.M.*

ets went from Gilgal to Bethel and Jericho. At Gilgal and Jericho Elijah tested the younger man by requesting him to stay while the old prophet went on, but Elisha swore that he would not leave his master. At Bethel and Jericho the sons of the prophets asked Elisha if he knew that the Lord would take Elijah away from him that day; Elisha knew it well. The two men proceeded to the Jordan, which they crossed by a miraculous parting of the waters. Beyond the river, Elijah asked what Elisha wanted as a favor from him. Elisha requested a double portion of the spirit of the older man; Elijah answered that this would be granted on the condition that Elisha saw him as he was being taken from him. While they walked and conversed, they were separated by a chariot of fire and horses of fire; Elijah was taken up by a whirlwind as the younger man watched.

The prophetic ministry of Elisha. Elisha was now the full-fledged successor of his master and he proceeded with the same type of ministry, serving the schools of the prophets, helping the needy, performing miracles, giving advice to the king, and acting as a spokesman for God. It has been remarked that the miraculous works of Elisha are double the number performed by his predecessor, thus indicating that he had, in fact, been endowed with a double portion of the spirit of Elijah. The record of the ministry of Elisha extends to 2 Kings 13:21, which relates a miracle performed after Elisha's death; beyond this point the prophet is not mentioned again in the OT.

Deeds and miraculous works of Elisha. **1. *The parting of the Jordan*** (2 Kings 2:13, 14). Upon the disappearance of Elijah, Elisha tore his own clothes into two pieces and took up the fallen mantle of Elijah. Returning to the river Jordan he faced his first crisis. With the cry, "Where is the LORD, the God of Elijah?" he struck the waters with the mantle and the waters parted. When he came to Jericho the sons of the prophets recognized that the spirit of Elijah rested on him. They met him and did obeisance to him, but they insisted that he send a group to look for Elijah.

2. *The purifying of the spring* (2 Kings 2:19-22). The people of Jericho complained to Elisha about the quality of the water, so he threw a bowl of salt into the spring and declared that the Lord had changed the fountain. The account states that the water "has been wholesome to this day," and Elisha's Fountain is still an important source of good water for the people around Jericho.

3. *The cursing of the children* (2:23, 24). While going from Jericho to Bethel, Elisha was mocked by small boys who made fun of his bald head. He "cursed them in the name of the LORD. And two she-bears came out of the woods and tore forty-two of the boys."

4. *The defeat of Moab* (3:1-27). Jehoram, king of Israel, Jehoshaphat, king of Judah, and the king of Edom joined in a military campaign against Mesha, king of Moab. Marching through the wilderness of Edom, the armies found no water and were near despair. Jehoshaphat wished to consult a prophet of the Lord and was informed that Elisha was present. At first Elisha refused to counsel Jehoram, but after listening to a minstrel the prophet was empowered by the Lord to predict that the land would be filled with water and that the allies would defeat the Moabites (vv. 16-19). The next morning the prediction was fulfilled.

5. *The widow's oil* (4:1-7). A poor widow complained to the prophet that a creditor was about to enslave her two children. When Elisha learned that the woman owned only a jar of oil, he instructed her to borrow many empty vessels from her neighbors, and then to go into her house with her sons and fill all of those vessels from the single jar of oil, so that she could pay her debts and live on the income from the oil.

6. *The Shunammite's son* (4:8-37). A wealthy woman of Shunem proposed to her husband that they should build on their house a room for the prophet's use. In return for this kindness, Elisha foretold that in about a year the childless couple would have a son. A few years later this child suddenly became ill and died. The woman went to Mount Carmel to see "the man of God" (v. 25), who sent his servant, Gehazi, to place the prophet's staff upon the face of the child, but this had no effect (vv. 29-31). Elisha then came to the house, prayed, and stretched himself upon the body of the child, who regained life and was presented again to his mother.

7. *The poison pot* (4:38-41). During a famine, the prophet came to Gilgal and ordered his servants to prepare food for the sons of the prophets. When one of the men in ignorance placed some poisonous wild gourds into the cooking pot, Elisha threw meal into the mixture and the contents of the pot became harmless.

8. *The multiplying of the loaves and grain* (4:42-44). A man from Baal-shalishah brought twenty barley loaves and some heads of grain, which Elisha told his servant to set before a hundred men. Though the servant protested, he finally obeyed and there was food enough and some left over.

9. *The healing of Naaman* (2 Kings 5). Naaman, the commander of the Syrian army, was a leper. A captive Israelite girl who served in Naaman's household suggested to Naaman's wife that the prophet in Samaria could heal Naaman. The king of Syria sent Naaman to Israel, with a letter of introduction to the king of Israel. The Israelite king panicked, but Elisha heard of the problem and cured the commander's leprosy by having Naaman dip seven times in the Jordan River. Naaman then acknowledged the God of Israel, but Gehazi could not resist requesting a reward for the healing and was punished by becoming a leper.

10. ***The floating axe head*** (6:1-7). While constructing new buildings near the Jordan for the sons of the prophets, one of the men lost the head of a borrowed axe in the water. The prophet threw a stick into the water and the axe head floated and was recovered.

11. ***Divine espionage*** (6:8-10). On several occasions when the Syrians and Israelites were at war, Elisha saved the Israelite king by warning him of the location of the Syrians.

12. ***The Dothan episode*** (6:11-23). The Syrians attempted to capture the prophet at Dothan, but the Lord protected him with chariots of fire. When the Lord struck the soldiers blind, Elisha brought them to Samaria, where they recovered their sight. Upon Elisha's advice, the king of Israel made a great feast for them and then released them.

13. ***Famine and feast in Samaria*** (6:24-7:20). Under siege by the army of Ben-hadad of Syria, Samaria suffered such famine that cannibalism was resorted to by several women. When the king proposed executing Elisha, the prophet foretold that there would be an abundance of food the next day. During the night the Syrians fled in disarray and four lepers discovered that the Syrian camp was forsaken; they reported the good news to the city, whose inhabitants soon enjoyed abundance.

14. ***The Shunammite's property*** (8:1-6). During a seven-year famine in Israel the Shunammite woman sojourned in Philistia, and upon her return wished to recover her house and land. The woman and her son arrived to make appeal to the king while Gehazi was relating her earlier story to that ruler, who secured the restoration of her property.

15. ***Elisha and Hazael*** (8:7-15; cf. 1 Kings 19:15). Ben-hadad became ill and sent Hazael to the prophet to inquire about his recovery. Elisha's answer indicated that Hazael would become king of Syria; the Syrian smothered his ailing master and became king.

16. ***Elisha and Jehu*** (9:1-3; cf. 1 Kings 19:16). Elisha sent one of the sons of the prophets to Ramoth-gilead to anoint Jehu to be king of Israel.

17. ***Elisha and Joash*** (13:14-19). During his final illness the prophet signified in a symbolic prophecy that Joash would defeat the Syrians.

18. ***The raising of a dead man*** (13:21). A corpse hastily thrown into the grave of Elisha, when raiders approached, came to life when the body touched the bones of the prophet.

In the NT Elisha is referred to only once. Preaching at Nazareth, the Lord used Elisha's healing of Naaman as an example of the scarcity of faith within Israel; there were many lepers in Israel in the days of Elisha, but only Naaman the Syrian was healed.

BIBLIOGRAPHY. C. Geikie, *Old Testament Characters* (1888), 331-349; R. S. Wallace, *Elijah and Elisha* (1957); S. Szikszai, "Elisha," IDB (1962), II, 91, 92; B. L. Smith, "Elisha," *The New Bible Dictionary* (1962), 365, 366.

C. E. DeVries

ELISHAH **ī lī′ shə** (אלישה, *God saves*). A son of Javan and progenitor of the Japhetic nation which bears his name (Gen 10:4; 1 Chron 1:7; Ezek 27:7). Since Javan is the Heb. word for the Greeks, Elishah is to be associated with them. It is associated with islands or coastlands (Gen 10:4, 5; Ezek 27:7). Ezekiel speaks of the islands of Elishah which supplied purple dyes to the Tyrians. Its association with Greece and Kittim (Cyprus), would seem to indicate a location in the area of the N Mediterranean. Josephus identified them with the Aeolians, an ancient people of Gr. stock. Some have identified it with Carthage, a nation in N Africa, because of the similarity between Elishah and Elissa, the latter being, according to tradition, a Tyrian princess who founded Carthage. Most prob. Elishah refers to the inhabitants of the islands of the Aegean Sea. Its close association with Javan and its dye industry, which would necessitate close proximity to the sea, seem to support this identification.

T. E. McComisky

ELISHAMA **ĭ lĭsh′ ə mə** (אלישמע, *God has heard*). The name of seven different men in the OT. 1. The son of Ammihud of the tribe of Ephraim (Num 1:10). He was selected to help Moses as a representative from his tribe in the taking of the census. He is later described as the prince of the children of Ephraim (2:18). As a prince he offered for Ephraim the oblation to the Lord on the seventh day (7:48, 53). He led his host in the march through the wilderness, seventh in line (10:22). From 1 Chronicles 7:26, one learns further that he was the father of Nun and grandfather of Joshua.

2. One of the sons of David who was born in Jerusalem. His mother was a wife of David and not a concubine (2 Sam 5:16). The sons are listed as nine in number (1 Chron 3:8). In 1 Chronicles 14:7 the children are thirteen in number. Apparently the later list includes daughters as well.

3. Another son of David born in Jerusalem by the same name (1 Chron 3:6).

4. A descendant of Judah through Perez. His father was Jekamiah (2:41).

5. The grandfather of the Ishmael who killed Gedaliah (2 Kings 25:25), the governor of Israel appointed by Nebuchadnezzar, named in Jeremiah 41:1.

6. A scribe of Israel in Jeremiah's day who was one of those who heard Baruch read the words of God (Jer 36:12). Later the roll of the scroll was put in his chamber where it remained until it was taken to be read to the king (36:20, 21).

7. A priest sent by Jehoshaphat to teach God's book of the law in Judah (2 Chron 17:8). It is possible that numbers 4 and 5 above are the same. Jerome suggested this possibility.

BIBLIOGRAPHY. D. Thomas, *Documents from Old Testament Times* (1958), 221.

J. B. Scott

ELISHAPHAT ĭ lĭsh' ə făt (אלישפט, *God has judged*). One of five captains of hundreds who helped Jehoiada the priest in the overthrow of Athaliah to make Joash king (2 Chron 23:1).

ELISHEBA ĭ lĭsh' ə bə (אלישבע, *God is an oath*). Daughter of Amminadab; sister of Nahshon; the wife of Aaron; mother of Nadab, Abihu, Eleazar, and Ithamar (Exod 6:23). Since Nahshon was the leader of Judah (Num 1:7; 2:3), Elisheba was of that tribe. Her son Eleazar succeeded Aaron as chief priest (Num 20:25-28).

ELISHUA ĕl' ə shōō' ə (אלישוע, *God is salvation*). A son of David born at Jerusalem (2 Sam 5:15; 1 Chron 14:5). Apparently the same son is called "Elishama" in 1 Chronicles 3:6, but this is prob. a transcriptional error, since "Elishama" occurs again in the next line (v. 8).

ELIU ĭ lī' u (Ἠλιού). The KJV spelling of the name of an ancestor of Judith (Jud 8:1 ASV ELIHU, RSV ELIJAH).

ELIUD ĭ lī' əd (Ἐλιούδ, *my God is glory*). An ancestor of Jesus, according to Matthew's genealogy (Matt 1:14, 15). In the fifth generation before Jesus, he was the son of Achim and father of Eleazar.

ELIZABETH ĭ lĭz' ə bəth (Ἐλισάβετ, Ἐλεισάβετ, same as Heb. אלישבע, *God is my oath*; KJV, ASV, ELISABETH). The wife of the priest Zechariah (KJV, ASV *Zacharias*), and the mother of John the Baptist (Luke 1:5-66).

Like her husband, Elizabeth was of Aaronic descent; indeed, she had the same name as Aaron's wife (Exod 6:23). She and her husband are described as being righteous before God, walking before Him blamelessly by obeying all His commandments and ordinances. Her barrenness was a great trial to them, until an angel appeared to Zechariah and told him that in spite of their age, their prayer for a child would be answered, and their son would be the forerunner of the Messiah. The story recalls similar answers to prayer to Sarah and Hannah in the OT.

Elizabeth is called the "kinswoman," or relative, of Mary the mother of Jesus (Luke 1:36), but the term is too broad to indicate the precise nature of the relationship. When Mary came to visit her, the babe leaped in the womb of Elizabeth and, in the Holy Spirit, Elizabeth told Mary how greatly blessed she was and expressed her amazement that God should honor her with this visit from the mother of her Lord. There is some textual evidence in Old Latin MSS, in Irenaeus, and in Origen, that the Magnificat was originally ascribed to Elizabeth rather than to Mary.

BIBLIOGRAPHY. "Mary or Elizabeth?" ExpT, 41 (1929-1930), 266, 267; "Again the Magnificat," ExpT, 42 (1930-1931), 188-190.

S. Barabas

ELIZAPHAN ĕl' ə zā' făn (אליצפן, *God has protected*). A Heb. masculine proper name. 1. The son of Uzziel a Levite, a chief of the Kohathites who is described in Numbers 3:29, 30 as "the head of the fathers' house of the families of the Kohathites," whose responsibility was to take care of the Ark, the table, the lampstand and the vessels of the sanctuary, etc. (cf. 1 Chron 15:8; 2 Chron 29:13). An alternate form of his name is *Elzaphan* (Exod 6:22; Lev 10:4); the name remains the same, but contains a shorter form of deity element *El* for the more archaic *'Elî.*

2. The son of Parnach, a leader from the tribe of Zebulun, who assisted Moses in dividing the land into future inheritance portions for each tribe (Num 34:25).

E. B. Smick

ELIZUR ĭ lī' zər (אליצור, *God is a rock*). Son of Shedeur; a chief of the tribe of Reuben (Num 1:5; 2:10; 7:30, 35; 10:18).

ELKANAH ĕl kā' nə (אלקנה, *God has taken possession*, or *God has created*). The name of eight men in the OT. 1. One of the descendants of Korah of the family of Levi (Exod 6:24). He was the head of his father's house (6:25). He is more exactly described as the son of Assir, Korah's son. Elkanah's son was called Ebiasaph (1 Chron 6:23).

2. The father of Samuel (1 Sam 1:19). He is described as a man of Ramathaim-zophim of the hill country of Ephraim (1:1). He was the son of Jeroham an Ephraimite.

Elkanah had two wives, the favorite Hannah was barren. His other wife is called Peninnah (1:2).

Because of her grief, his wife Hannah prayed to God for a son whom she would return unto the Lord. God answered her petition and she bore Samuel who after he had been weaned was given to Eli the priest (1:28). Later Hannah bore to Elkanah other sons and daughters (2:21). In 1 Chronicles 6:27 he is listed with the descendants of Levi. Here Elkanah's father is called Jeroham. His great-grandson Heman was one of the singers in David's day.

3. An ancestor of Samuel and descendant of Levi (1 Chron 6:25, 36).

4. Another ancestor of Samuel two or three generations closer than number three (6:26, 35).

5. The ancestor of one of the Levites named Berechiah who dwelt in Jerusalem after the return of the Babylonian captivity (9:16).

6. One who joined David at Ziklag (12:6). He was one of David's mighty men.

7. One of the Levitical doorkeepers who was

appointed by David to care for the Ark (15:23).

8. One in Ahaz' reign who was next in authority to the king (2 Chron 28:7). He was slain by Zichi, a mighty man of Ephraim for having forsaken the Lord.

BIBLIOGRAPHY. F. Josephus, *Antiquities of the Jews* and *A History of the Jews,* 301; A. Edersheim, *Bible History,* IV (1890), 5; A. Pieters, *Notes on Old Testament History* (1950), 124.

J. B. Scott

ELKIAH **ĕl kī′ ə** (Ἐλκία). Mentioned in Judith 8:1 as the son of Ananias and grandson of Gideon. He was the father of Oziel; KJV ELCIA.

ELKOSH, ELKOSHITE **ĕl′ kŏsh, īt** (אלקשי). A term used to identify Nahum the prophet (Nah 1:1). It prob. refers to a place, but if so, the place is unknown.

Several possible locations have been proposed: 1. A site in Galilee called Elcesi. Jerome thought this was the site.

2. A site in Mesopotamia N of Mosul near the Tigris River. Nestorius was the first to suggest this site. A so-called "tomb of Nahum" is found at Elqush N of Mosul.

3. A site in S Judah, prob. Beit Jibrin between Jerusalem and Gaza. This supposition has the merit of Nahum's apparently having been from Judah.

4. The most apparent site, but one doubted by most scholars, is כפר נחום i.e. Capernaum, the village of Nahum. This is the village on the N shore of the Sea of Galilee where Jesus taught frequently in His earthly ministry.

It must be emphasized that there is no real evidence for any of these sites. Perhaps the site is yet to be discovered, if indeed a geographical site is intended.

J. B. Scott

ELLASAR **ĕl′ ə sär** (אלסר, meaning uncertain). Arioch, king of Ellasar, was one of the allies of Chedorlaomer, king of Elam, in his raid on the Jordan valley in the time of Abraham (Gen 14:1). Earlier scholars considered the identifications of these kings as reasonably firm with Arioch being identified with Eri-Aku, king of Larsa. Further studies have weakened this confidence. In the case of Arioch, "Eri-Aku" is now read as "Warad-Sin," and the phonetic differences between "Larsa" and Ellasar" are given more weight. Ilanzura, between Carchemish and Haran in northern Syria, has been suggested recently, but the only positive argument for this suggestion is the phonetic similarity between the two names. At present, the identification of Larsa remains uncertain.

BIBLIOGRAPHY. D. J. Wiseman, "Ellasar," NBD (1967).

A. C. Bowling

ELM (אלה, *terebinth*). Mentioned once (Hosea 4:13, KJV), "upon the hills and under . . . elms." This word "elah" is frequently tr. oak (Isa 6:13). David killed Goliath in the "elah" valley.

The tree is unlikely to be elm (*Ulmus campestris*), because this is not known in Pal. The writer feels that the *'ēlâ* must be the terebinth. In the LXX *'ēlâ* is tr. "terebinth" (*Pistacia terebinthus*), and this is undoubtedly correct.

W. E. Shewell-Cooper

ELMADAM, ELMODAM **ĕl mā′ dəm, ĕl mō′-dəm** (Ἐλμαδάμ). An ancestor of Jesus, according to Luke's genealogy (Luke 3:28). KJV ELMODAM; RSV ELMADAM.

ELNAAM **ĕl nā′ əm** (אלנעם, *God is pleasantness, delightfulness*). Mentioned only in 1 Chronicles 11:46 as the father of Jeribai and Joshaviah, two of the mighty men of David's army.

ELNATHAN **ĕl nā′ thən** (אלנתן, *God has given*). A masculine personal name; a more common form has the deity element last, *Nātān'ēl* (Nathanael). 1. Elnathan of Jerusalem, the grandfather of King Jehoiachin (2 Kings 24:8), and possibly the same Elnathan, the son of Achbor, a nobleman who did the king's bidding (Jer 26:22). Elnathan sat among the nobles while Jeremiah's message was read to King Jehoiakim (36:12). He sought to dissuade the king from burning Jeremiah's scroll, but to no avail.

2. Several other Elnathans are mentioned among the Levites who were described as "leading men" and "men of insight" in the days of Ezra (Ezra 8:15, 16). The passage tells of a search for Levites who were scarce in those days.

E. B. Smick

ELOAH **ĕ lō′ ə** (אלוה, *God*, sing. of Elohim, q.v.). It is used forty-one times in Job (replacing Elohim) and sixteen times elsewhere. These occurrences are mainly poetic and refer to the true God except in 2 Chronicles 32:15; Daniel 11:37, 38, 39; and Habakkuk 1:11 (cf. Job 12:6).

C. P. Weber

ELOHIM **ĕl′ ō hĭm** (אלהים, many suggestions for the meaning of the root but no consensus, perhaps related to "El" meaning *mighty* or *strong*). A most commonly used Heb. word for God, gods, angels, or magistrates.

It has been demonstrated to the writer's satisfaction that 14th cent. B.C. Ugaritic lit. when referring to a single deity sometimes uses the "plural of majesty" (cf. Anchor Bible, 16, pp. XXIV and 43 etc.). Since the pl. word *Elohim* when used for God in the OT is most emphatically sing. in meaning (Deut 4:35, 39; 1

Kings 8:60; 18:39; Isa 45:18, etc.), there is real probability that the Hebrews looked on it as a "plural of majesty." Often but not always when referring to the true God, the definite article is employed with the word in Heb. This usage was an overtone of the root's basic meaning, hence "the Mighty (?) One," but this is not carried over into the Eng. Bible which has simply "God" with a capital letter.

The word is frequently used to refer to heathen gods (Exod 18:11; 20:23; 1 Sam 4:8; 2 Kings 18:33, etc.). Less frequently the word refers to a heathen god in the sing., Dagon (1 Sam 5:7), Chemosh (Judg 11:24), Baal (1 Kings 18:24) etc.

There are a number of references where the word can be rendered magistrates, judges, or rulers. Noteworthy are Exodus 21:6 where the slave is brought "to God" or perhaps "to the judges" where his ear is bored, and Exodus 22:28 which may mean "You shall not revile the *magistrates* (God?), nor curse the ruler of your people" (cf. 1 Kings 21:13). Other passages should be studied in this light (i.e. 1 Sam 2:25 and Judg 5:8).

It is quite clear that the sons of Elohim are the angels in Job 1:6; 2:1; 38:7. The writer takes them to be dignitaries in Genesis 6:2, 4. The NT follows the LXX in rendering Elohim as angels in Psalm 97:7 (Heb 1:6).

See GOD, NAMES OF. E. B. SMICK

ELOHIST (ĕl′ ō hĭst). A designation for the author or editor of the so-called "E" source of the Pentateuch. Elohist is derived from ELOHIM (אלהים) the Heb. name for God characteristic of the "E" document, supposedly originating c. 750 B.C. in the northern kingdom.

ELOI, ELOI, LAMA SABACHTHANI. *See* ELI, ELI, LAMA SABACHTHANI.

ELON e′ lŏn (אילון, אלון, אלן, *terebinth*). The name of three men and a locality mentioned in the OT. 1. A Hitt. whose daughter Basemath married Esau (Gen 26:34). She caused much grief to Isaac and Rebekah. In Genesis 36:2, Elon's daughter Basemath is called Adah. (Note that in the latter passage the name Basemath is given to the daughter of Ishmael so that two of Esau's wives were actually named Basemath.) One wife is the daughter of Elon and one wife is the daughter of Ishmael. (Perhaps, since Esau had two wives of the same name, the Hitt. was given an alternate name to distinguish the two.)

2. A son of Zebulun. He was among those who came to Egypt with Jacob (Gen 46:14). From him sprang the Elonites (Num 26:26).

3. A judge in Israel from the tribe of Zebulun (Judg 12:11). He judged Israel ten years after which he died and was buried in Aijalon in the territory of Zebulun (12:12).

4. A city on the border of the inheritance of Dan betwen Ithlah and Timnah (Josh 19:43). It is identified today as Kirbet Wādi 'Alīn about one m. E of 'Ain-Shems (Beth-shemesh).

Two other appearances of the name Elon are to be noted. 1. The name Aijalon in Judges 12:12 is read "Elon" by the LXX due to the fact that in the Heb., the consonants for Aijalon and Elon are identical, and only the vowels are different.

2. A compound place-name Elon-beth-hanan is mentioned in connection with the twelve districts from which officers of Solomon were to provide food for the king and his household (1 Kings 4:9).

BIBLIOGRAPHY. F. Josephus, *Antiquities of the Jews* and *A History of the Jews*, 170; A. Edersheim, *Bible History*, III (1890), 153, 163; Oesterley and Robinson, *An Introduction to the Books of the Old Testament* (1958), 76; E. Young, *An Introduction to the Old Testament* (1958), 186; J. Simons, *The Geographical and Topographical Text of the Old Testament* (1959), 200, 349.

J. B. SCOTT

ELON-BETH-HANAN. *See* ELON.

ELOTH. Alternate form of ELATH.

ELPALET, ELPELET. KJV forms of ELIPHALET.

ELPARAN, EL-PARAN ĕl pâr′ ən (איל פארן). Mentioned in Genesis 14:6 as the southernmost point of the campaign of Chedorlaomer against the Horites in the mountains of Seir (i.e. Edom). It is said to be on the edge of the wilderness (14:6b). Now "El-paran" contains the name paran that is a wilderness area in the E central region of the Sinai peninsula whose eastern boundary was the Wadi Arabah in the N and the Gulf of Aqabah in the S. Since the mountains of Seir (the modern Jebel-esh-Shera' range) extend to the SW as far as the Gulf of Aqabah, "El of paran" on the edge of the wilderness (of paran), situated at the southern limit of the mountains of Seir, exactly describes the position of Elat (q.v.), the seaport on the northern tip of the Gulf of Aqabah. Finally, Elat (אילת) and El-paran (איל פארן) both contain the same initial element El- (איל), hence it is highly probable that they are identical, El-paran being the ancient name of Elat.

F. W. BUSH

EL ROI ĕl rō′ ī (אל ראי ; MT is defectively pointed *’ēl r*^{o}*’ī*). The name used for God in Genesis 16:13 by Hagar whose protection she experienced when fleeing from Sarai. An ambiguous phrase in Heb., "El Roi" has been rendered in two main ways: (1) "God who sees me" (cf. KJV, Gr., Vul.) and (2) "God of seeing" (RSV). Also favoring the latter interpretation is the *Jerusalem Bible*, and NEB using the title "El Roi" with "God of (a) Vision" in the footnote explanation.

M. R. WILSON

EL SHADDAI, EL SHADDAY **ĕl shăd′ ī** (אֵל שַׁדַּי, *God of the mountain(s)* or *God Almighty*). An epithet of God in the patriarchal narratives and as an archaism in many poetic passages of the OT.

The term is tr. "God Almighty" in the RSV (Gen 17:1; 28:3; 35:11; 43:14; 48:3; Exod 6:3). These are prose passages and the full term El Shaddai is used. In many other passages (Num 24:4, 16; Ruth 1:20, 21; Ps 68:15; 91:1; Joel 1:15 [cf. Isa 13:6], Ezek 1:24; Job 5:17, and thirty times more in Job) the single element Shaddai is used and tr. "the Almighty." This tr. is somewhat dubious since it is based on a Heb. root (*šādad*) which does not exactly mean "Almighty" but "to deal violently with." This meaning was first used in the LXX which frequently uses *παντοκρατωρ* ("almighty") to render El Shaddai. Some critics believe it refers to a tribal deity, a high god worshiped by the patriarchs, who were not true monotheists. They usually point to Deuteronomy 32:17 or Joshua 24:2 which recorded the fact that the Israelite ancestors served other gods "beyond the Euphrates." While this is allowed for in the Genesis account, it emphatically states that Abraham turned from this false religion to worship the true and only God. One of his many descriptive epithets was El Shaddai, a meaning of which one cannot be absolutely sure, although W. F. Albright makes a strong case for its meaning, "God of the mountain(s)" (JBL, LIV [1935], 180-193). The name Shaddai is sometimes used as a divine element in proper names (Num 7:36, *Zurishaddai*) and is attested in Egyp. documents in the name *Shaḏai-'ammi*, etc. (infra p. 243, Albright).

See GOD, NAMES OF.

BIBLIOGRAPHY. W. F. Albright, *From the Stone Age to Christianity*, 2nd ed. (1957), 15, 243, 244n., 247, 271, 300.

E. B. SMICK

ELTEKE, ELTEKEH **ĕl′ tə kə** (אֶלְתְּקֵה, אֶלְתְּקֵא). A town in the territory of Dan (Josh 19:44). It was assigned to the Kohathite Levites (21:23). The Assyrian king Sennacherib destroyed the town in 701 B.C. on his way to Timnah and Ekron. In its environs, the decisive battle between the Assyrians and Egyptians was fought (2 Kings 18:13ff.; 19:8ff.). On this occasion it is probable that the forces defeated by Sennacherib consisted of Jews along with Ekronites and Egyptians. A natural place for these allies to meet and take their stand would have been on the high road between Ekron and Jerusalem. The site is prob. Khirbet el-Muqenna', about six m. SE of Ekron and seven m. NW of Timnah.

C. L. FEINBERG

ELTEKON **ĕl′ tə kŏn** (אֶלְתְּקֹן). A town given in the city-list of the tribe of Judah (Josh 15:59). It has been tentatively identified with Khirbet ed-Deir, c. 4 m. W of Bethlehem.

ELTOLAD **ĕl tō′ lăd** (Heb. אֶלְתּוֹלַד), a place name mentioned only in Joshua 15:30; 19:4. According to a recurrent folk-etymology the name means, "the place where children may be obtained." From this it has been deduced with little evidence that it was the site of some ancient pagan temple of fertility. It was a town of Judah mentioned with Ezem (modern, Abu 'iẓam) and Hormah (modern, Tell es-sab') somewhere betwen 'Ararah and Beersheba. A variant of the name, TOLAD (q.v.) occurs in 1 Chronicles 4:29.

W. WHITE, JR.

ELUL **ē lūl′** (אֱלוּל, LXX Ελουλ, meaning uncertain; prob. derived from the Babylonian *Elulu* or *Ululu*, the month of purification). Sixth month of the year (August-September). Found only in Nehemiah 6:15 (cf. Ελουλ, 1 Macc 14:27). *See* CALENDAR.

ELUZAI **ĭ lōō′ zī** (אֶלְעוּזַי, *God is my strength* or *my refuge*). A Benjamite warrior who joined David while he was in exile from Saul at the Philistine city of Ziklag (1 Chron 12:5). He could use bow or sling with either hand.

ELYMAIS **ĕl′ ə mā′ əs** ('Ελυμαις). A province of ancient Persia, located E of the Tigris, S of Media, and N of Susiana. Susa (or Shushan) was within its territory.

The name occurs in 1 Maccabees 6:1: "King Antiochus was going through the upper provinces when he heard that Elymais in Persia was a city famed for its wealth in silver and gold." Since no such "city" is known, virtually all scholars are agreed that the text should be slightly corrected to read: "that in Elymais in Persia there was a city." Read thus, Elymais seems to be equivalent to OT Elam, q.v.

"The number and chronology of the kings of Elymais are uncertain since the only sources are their coins, but inscriptions from Tang-i Sarwak reveal that the population was Aramaic-speaking" (R. N. Frye, *The Heritage of Persia*, p. 216).

BIBLIOGRAPHY. R. Ghirshman, *Iran* (1954); IDB (1962); R. N. Frye, *The Heritage of Persia* (1963).

K. L. BARKER

ELYMAS **ĕl′ ə məs** ('Ελύμας). A Jewish magician and false prophet whom Paul found on his first missionary journey, in the retinue of Sergius Paulus, the Rom. proconsul of Cyprus (Acts 13:6-12). Sergius Paulus is described by Luke as a "man of intelligence," who when he heard that Paul and Barnabas were giving lectures on religion and ethics summoned them to appear before him so that he might hear what they had to say. In the apostolic period there were many traveling teachers and philosophers, some of whom acquired a great reputation and eventually were asked to teach at one of the great universities.

Bar-Jesus, which means "son of Jesus" or "Joshua," was a member of the proconsul's court and prob. had considerable influence over him. Ancient lit. abounds in stories of men skilled in the lore of the occult who became favorites of men in power. Juvenal (VI. 562; XIV. 248) and Horace (*Sat.* I. 2. 1), for example, mention Chaldaean astrologers and imposters who were prob. Babylonian Jews. It must not be assumed that such men were necessarily cheap frauds, like gypsy fortune tellers. Often they were the men of science of the day, better acquainted than most people of their time with the powers and processes of nature, but also learned in the strange skills of the Median priests.

Afraid that he might lose his influence over Sergius Paulus if the proconsul were persuaded of the truth of the Christian religion, Elymas spoke against Paul and Barnabas and sought to turn the proconsul from the faith. Paul, filled with the Spirit, looked intently upon him and told him that because he had opposed the truth of God he would become blind and be unable to see for a time. Immediately Elymas lost his sight; and when Sergius Paulus saw what befell the magician he believed, "for he was astonished at the teaching of the Lord" (Acts 13:12).

Josephus (Antiq. XX. vii. 2) tells of a Jew of Cyprus who was a magician and who helped the procurator Felix to win Drusilla (24:24), the wife of Aziz of Emesa, away from her husband. There is a possibility that he and Elymas are the same person.

There is a problem regarding the name of this man. Acts 13:6 says that his name was Bar-Jesus; but v. 8 refers to him as "Elymas the magician (for that is the meaning of his name)." There is clearly no connection beween the names Bar-Jesus and Elymas. The word Elymas seems to be derived from the Arab. word *'alim*, signifying "wise," and to be equivalent to Magus. The likelihood is that Bar-Jesus gave himself the name or the title Elymas because he claimed the powers of the Median priests. *See* BAR-JESUS.

S. BARABAS

ELZABAD ĕl zā' băd (אלזבד, *God has given*). 1. The ninth of eleven Gadite army officers who joined David while he was with the Philistines at Ziklag in exile from Saul (1 Chron 12:12).

2. A Korahite gatekeeper, son of Shemaiah, grandson of Obed-edom, whose offspring were well qualified for the service (1 Chron 26:7).

EMADABUN ĭ măd' ə bən (Ἠμαδαβούν, KJV MADIABUN, me dī' e bŭn). Head of line of Levites who helped rebuild the Temple under Jeshua and Zerubbabel (1 Esd 5:58; omitted in Ezra 3:9). RSV indicates Emadabun is surname to adjacent Jeshua which KJV, with some Gr. texts, omit.

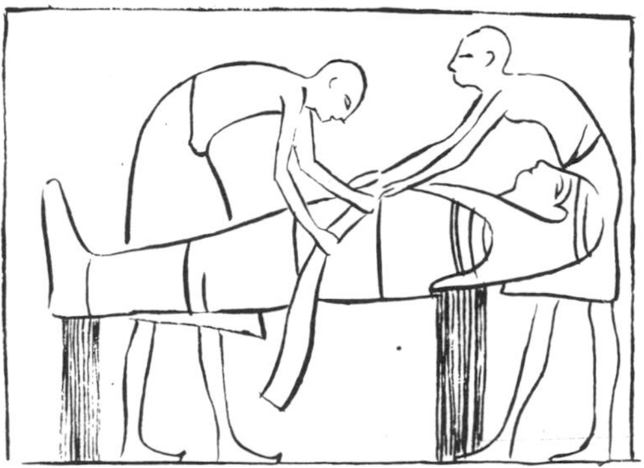

Embalming process as depicted in an Egyptian Tomb.

EMATH. Douay VS form of HAMATH.

EMATHEIS. ASV form of ATHLAI.

EMATHIS. Apoc. form of ATHLAI.

EMBALM, EMBALMING (חנט, חנטים, *to spice, make spicy, embalm*). The treatment of a corpse with various substances to preserve it from decay. The Egyptians invented embalming. They believed that the state of the soul in the after life was directly dependent upon the preservation of the body. The Hebrews, however, did not practice the art of embalming. Laws concerning the touching of dead bodies prevented the Hebrews from being innovators in medicine and human anatomy (cf. Num 5:1-4; 19:11-22). These laws, in part, reflect Heb. repugnance of Egyp. religion.

The only clear examples of embalming in the Bible are those of Jacob (Gen 50:2, 3) and Joseph (50:26). These are exceptional cases primarily due to the prestige of the persons and the necessity of preservation of the bodies until burial in their homeland of Canaan. After Jacob was embalmed he was carried by his sons to the patriarchal burial area E of Mamre, the cave of Machpelah (50:13, 14). Joseph's interment at Shechem (Josh 24:32), however, was delayed several centuries until after the Exodus (Exod 13:19). Joseph's age at death, 110 years (Gen 50:26), was viewed by Egyptians as the ideal span of life for a man.

In Song of Solomon 2:13, *ḥānaṭ* also occurs. The expression has reference to the ripening of figs, "The fig tree puts forth (lit. 'spices') its figs." Though spices are used elsewhere

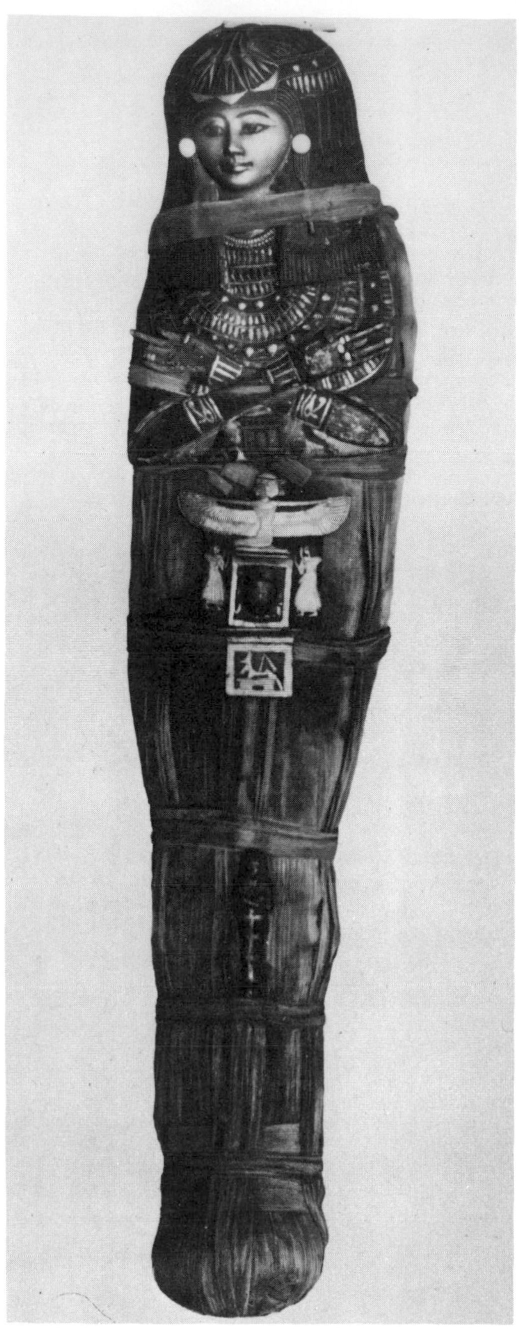

An excellent example of Egyptian embalming, the mummy of the woman Katebet, at Thebes. ©*B.M.*

in the Bible, prob. for ceremonial reasons and to counteract the stench of decaying flesh (cf. 2 Chron 16:14; Mark 14:8; 16:1; John 11:39; 19:39, 40), these instances are not to be equated with the art of embalming.

For the method of embalmment, one is particularly dependent upon two Gr. historians, Diodorus Siculus (I, 91) and Herodotus (II, 86-89). Genesis indicates forty days were required for the physicians to embalm Jacob (Gen 50:2, 3), whereas seventy days seems to have been the usual length of time.

According to Herodotus, the embalmers offered three methods which differed in elaboration and cost. In the cheapest method, the intestines were cleared out with a purgative and then the body was placed in natron for seventy days. In the second type, the body was soaked in natron after cedar oil was injected at the anus, thus dissolving the stomach and intestines. The first-class method of mummification called for the removal of the brain and all internal organs except the heart. The abdominal cavity was then washed out and filled with spices. Next, the body was soaked in natron for seventy days. It was then washed and wrapped from head to foot with bandages of linen cloth smeared with gum. Finally, relatives took the corpse, placed it in a wooden coffin of human shape, and left it upright against the wall of the burial chamber.

BIBLIOGRAPHY. R. Hutchins (ed.), *Great Books of the Western World*, VI, "The History of Herodotus" (1952), 65, 66; P. Montet, *Everyday Life in Egypt* (1958), 300-330; J. Vergote, *Joseph en Egypte* (1959); L. Cottrell, *Life Under the Pharaohs* (1960), 221-236; B. Mertz, *Temples, Tombs and Hieroglyphs* (1964), 64-113.

M. R. Wilson

EMBROIDERY. Decoration on cloth by means of ornamental needlework. Embroidered work, chiefly using geometric patterns and stylized motifs, is well attested in sculptured and painted scenes from the ancient world. Several Heb. words refer to embroidery and related skills. מעשה רקם ("work of the embroiderer," Exod 26:36) and רקמה ("embroidery," Ezek 27:16) are generally taken as referring to embroidered goods. Reasons for this conclusion are the following: Embroidery is well attested in the background cultures of the OT, and may be expected to appear in Heb. crafts also. The expressions denoting the raw materials used by the embroiderer (i.e. "blue and purple and scarlet stuff and fine twined linen," Exod 26:36) can refer to thread and yarn suitable for embroidery since they can refer to products of spinning (35:25). It should be noted, however, that some of these terms occur in contexts where they could be taken as denoting woven cloth as well as spun thread; e.g. "blue," תכלת (39:22). Exodus 35:35 distinguishes between the "embroiderer" and the weaver. Also, רקמה as a term for the varied sheen of eagle's feathers (Ezek 17:3) recalls the multi-colored brilliance of detailed decorative needlework (cf. also the "colored stones," רקמה, 1 Chron 29:2). The cumulative effect of these considerations confirms the interpretation of the two terms under discussion as denoting embroidery.

Other terms, however, lack decisive attestation. For example, the precise meanings of שבץ (Exod 28:39, RSV "weave in checker work," KJV "embroider") and תשבץ (Exod 28:4, RSV "checker work," KJV "broidered") remain unclear (*see* FILIGREE for discussion of other words derived from שבץ מעשה חשב).

Exod 26:31, RSV "skilled work," KJV "cunning work" refers to the Tabernacle hangings decorated with cherubim and to some of the priestly garments (28:6). It has been suggested that "skilled work" refers to more original designs (HDB) in contrast to the stereotyped, geometric patterns of typical "embroidery." On the other hand, some of the rabbis—perhaps with no more real evidence—thought that "skilled work" referred to decorative weaving in which the design showed on both sides (Jew Enc). It has also been suggested that the "pomegranates" (רמון, Exod 39:24) on the hem of the high priest's garment were appliqué work (NBD). It is equally possible that they were hanging ornaments of a braided or plaited sort that, like the golden bells, hung from the hem. The meanings of these terms remain unclear for lack of decisive or even reasonably clear attestation.

In the OT, embroidery symbolizes luxury and lucrative commerce (Ps 45:14; Ezek 27:16). As early as the Songs of Deborah and Barak, embroidered goods were prized as spoils of war (Judg 5:30). Most of the references to embroidered goods in the OT are to the Tabernacle, with the priestly garments. The curtain for the gate of the court and the curtain for the door of the Tabernacle were both embroidered (Exod 27:16; 26:36), whereas other hangings were of "skilled work" (26:1, 31). The high priest's girdle was embroidered (28:39), and other garments were "checker work" (28:4) or "skilled work" (28:15).

BIBLIOGRAPHY. G. M. Mackie, "Embroidery," HDB (1901); E. G. Hirsch, "Embroidery," JewEnc (1901); H. F. Lutz, *Textiles and Costumes among the Peoples of the Ancient Near East* (1923); M. S. and J. L. Miller, *Encyclopedia of Bible Life* (1944), 353-355; G. I. Emmerson, "Embroidery," NBD (1962).

A. BOWLINC

EMEK-KEZIZ **ē′ mĭk kē′ zĭz** (Heb. עמק-קציץ derived from *'emēq*, "low ground," "valley" cognate to Ugar. *'m q*, Canaanite *'amq*, Mari Akkad. *ḥamqum*, and *q'ṣīyṣ*, "cut off," cognate to Ugar. *q ṣ ṣ*, Akkad. *qaṣāṣu(m)*, appearing only in Joshua 18:21 in the list of border cities between the Dead Sea and Jericho. The site is unidentified.

EMERALD, a rich yellow-green to deep green variety of beryl (q.v.), a beryllium aluminum silicate. It is one of the most valuable of all gem stones (Rev 21:19) and owes its beauty to its color and transparency. "Fire," such as shown by diamond, is lacking. The best emeralds are deep grass-green in color (4:3) and free from flaws, although unflawed emeralds are rare and large unflawed emeralds are unknown. Many crystals contain feathery inclusions while in some, the color, due to a small proportion of chromium is variable. Emerald mines were worked 2,000 years ago near the Red Sea, in Egypt, with hundreds of shafts sunk, some to 850 ft.; however the stones were not of fine gem quality. All the fine emeralds come from mines in Colombia, which were worked by the Spaniards. They occur in calcite (calcium carbonate) veins which cut across black shales.

D. R. BOWES.

EMERODS. *See* DISEASE, DISEASES.

EMIM **ē′ mĭm** (אימים, *terrors*). Early inhabitants of the area round Kiriathaim (q.v.) E of the Dead Sea, they were defeated in the time of Abraham by the four invading kings (Gen 14:5). In the time of the conquest they were described by Moses as former inhabitants of Moab, tall like the Anakim (q.v.), and therefore called "Emim" by the Moabites (Deut 2:10, 11). Y. Aharoni, *The Land of the Bible* (1967), map 7 (p. 128).

T. C. MITCHELL

EMMANUEL. *See* IMMANUEL.

EMMAUS **ĕ mā′ əs** ('Εμμαύς, חמת, *warm springs*, in the Talmud variations of אמאוס and עימאוס, etc.; in 1 Macc 3:40, 57; 4:3; in Josephus, of 'Αμμαοῦς [Antiq XIV. xi. 2; Jewish War. II. xx. 4; III. iii. 5] and 'Εμμαοῦς [Antiq. XVII. x. 9]). Once used in the NT (Luke 24:13) as the name of a Judean village (κώμη), the direction from Jerusalem not being stated. The location is uncertain, with several sites having been suggested as fitting the geographical qualifications for the village.

Luke 24 describes two disciples journeying to Emmaus, which was sixty stadia (seven m.) from Jerusalem, and returning the same day after communing with Jesus.

The location of Emmaus must be looked for somewhere near Jerusalem, there being several possible locations ranging from four to twenty m. away, namely: el Kubeibeh; Kaloniyeh; 'Amwas; Abu Ghosh; el Khamsa; and Artas.

El Kubeibeh, seven m. NW of Jerusalem, similar to the distance in Luke 24:13, in its connection with Emmaus goes back to the times of the Crusaders who had found nearby the place Castellum Emmaus, an ancient Rom.

Approaching the village of Emmaus. ©*M.P.S.*

This Roman built road at Emmaus could be the actual place where the risen Messiah walked with the two disciples. ©*Lev*

fort, and at which place in 1878 the Franciscans found remains of a basilica of Crusader, or, possibly, Byzantine date.

Only four m. to the W of Jerusalem is the modern Kaloniyeh (cf. *colonia*), identified with an Emmaus at which Vespasian is said to have settled 800 soldiers, the location being according to Josephus, three and one half m. from Jerusalem (War VII. vi. 6). The Josephus MSS vary in reading either thirty (which has the better evidence) or sixty stadia, and if this is taken to have been the NT site, the latter reading must be accepted or the former (thirty stadia) be understood in a rather broad way.

At about twenty m. W of Jerusalem on the Jaffa road is an Emmaus where Judas Maccabaeus in 166 B.C. defeated Gorgias (1 Macc 3:40; 4:1-15), the name of which in the 3rd cent. A.D. was changed to Nicopolis, the modern designation being 'Amwas or 'Imwas. Arguments against identifying this place with NT Emmaus are twofold: 'Amwas seems to have been a city (being the seat of a toparchy, Jos. War III. iii. 5) instead of a village (Luke 24:13); and the distance of 'Amwas from Jerusalem is too great unless the variant reading, 160 stadia, of MSS Aleph in Luke 24:13 (the better reading is 60) be accepted with the resultant problem of having the two disciples traveling an arduous forty m. in one day from and to Jerusalem.

Abu Ghosh, about nine m. W of Jerusalem, also known as Kiryat el'Enab, makes claim to having been Emmaus for a Crusader church was built over a Rom. fort which contains an inscr. indicating that part of the Tenth Legion was stationed there. This place seems to be too far from Jerusalem to be identified with the Emmaus either of Luke 24 or of Josephus (War VII. vi. 6).

NT Emmaus is also conjectured to have been located at el Khamsa, over sixty stadia SW of Jerusalem, and at Artas, S of Bethlehem where Rom. baths were found.

BIBLIOGRAPHY. E. Schürer, *A History of the Jewish People*, 2nd rev. ed., II (1891), 253-255; F. M. Abel, "La distance de Jérusalem à Emmaüs," RB, XXXIV (1925), 347-367; A. Plummer, *St. Luke*, ICC (1925), 551, 552; L. H. Vincent and F. M. Abel, *Emmaüs sa basilique et son histoire* (1932); S. Caiger, *Archaeology of the New Testament* (1939), 90; R. de Vaux and A. Steve, *Fouilles à Qaryet el-'Enab Abu Ghosh* Palestine (1950); J. A. Grassi, "Emmaus Revisited," CBQ XXVI (1964), 463-467; H. L. Strack and P. Billerbeck, *Kommentar zum Neuen Testament*, II (1965), 269-271.

W. H. MARE

EMMER. KJV Apoc. form of IMMER.

EMMERUTH. Corruption of IMMER (Ezra 2:37).

EMMOR. KJV NT form of HAMOR.

EMPEROR (*see also* CAESAR). In modern usage an emperor rules an area larger than a single kingdom. In Rom. law and custom two significant ideas are found. First, however dictatorial he may have been, the emperor was thought of as exercising *imperium* (Lat.: the properly delegated authority to command in behalf of the state). By contrast, kings ruled by virtue of personal legitimacy or personal authority. Second, the emperor was the one declared ruler or *imperator* by the Rom. armies (this custom clearly contradicts the spirit of the first idea). Most historic European "emperors" traced the legal origins of their title from the Rom. emperors.

None of these distinctions are significant for Biblical usage. Cyrus, Nebuchadnezzar, and Caesar all are referred to as "king" (Ezra 1:1; Dan 3:9, and John 19:15, respectively). Moreover, in contrast to the rich theological connotations of "king" (q.v.) in Scriptures no theological concepts are attached to the office of emperor. Christ as ruler is "King of kings" (Rev 19:16) rather than "Emperor."

A. C. BOWLING

EMPEROR WORSHIP. The worship of the Rom. emperor as a divine being, the cause and occasion of the tragic rift between the empire and the Church, began spontaneously in the eastern provinces, and was recognized by Augustus and Tiberius and progressively promoted by their successors as a political measure. Such a cult had manifest usefulness as a cementing and unifying force as the principate struggled in the 1st cent., to stabilize the frontiers and establish cohesion in the Mediterranean world. "The imperial cultus," wrote Moffatt, "was instinctive rather than deliberate, developing out of certain germs within the ancient mind, such as the blend of religion and patriotism among the Persians, and the worship of the Ptolemies which shocked the pious Plutarch. Its primary aim was to foster patriotism by providing a symbol of the solidarity and unity of the Empire" (EGT, Vol 5, p. 307).

The cult, as the words quoted indicate, found origin and form in the E. From earliest times, the rulers of Egypt had been regarded as incarnations of deity and accorded divine honors and worship. When the Ptolemies, on the breakup of Alexander's vast empire, took control of Egypt, they were regarded as the successors of the Pharaohs, and similarly were honored by the Egyp. people. The Caesars were no more than the successors of the Ptolemies. Nor was it difficult for similar concepts of a divine ruler to find place in Syria and Asia Minor. The idea was indigenous. "Distance," writes Moffatt in the passage already quoted, "lent enchantment to the provincial view of the emperor. Any sordid traits or idiosyncracies retired into the background before the adoration felt for the divinity which hedged this unseen, powerful figure who was

A view of the Roman Forum in Pergamum (Pergamos). This was a center of Roman cult worship. ©*Lev*

hailed with a mixture of servility and real gratitude as 'the Saviour,' 'the Peace,' or the lord of men. Asia became a hotbed of the cult" (loc. cit., p. 308).

In Pergamum, in many ways the Asian headquarters of the cult, the worship of Rome, and Caesar as its incarnate deity, colored the city's life. The first temple of the cult was located at Pergamum as early as 29 B.C., and provided a motif for Pergamene coinage for over a cent. A second temple was built in honor of Trajan at the end of the 1st cent. and a third for Severus a cent. later. Only the first temple functioned when the apocalyptic letter was written to Pergamum, but its ritual and worship were sufficient to make the presence of the imperial power very real in the city, and were for Christians shockingly oppressive. When the imagery of the letter speaks of "One who holds the sharp two-edged sword," and of those who "dwell where Satan's seat is," it has this confrontation between Christianity and Caesarism in full view.

Ancyra served as cult-center for Galatia, as Pergamum did for Asia. Through all the provinces of the great peninsula, provincial assemblies maintained the cult, and special officials (e.g. the Asiarchs of Ephesus) saw to its proper ordering and maintenance. An extant letter of Pliny, the governor of Bithynia at the end of the first decade of the 2nd cent., showed the cult in its political operation. Pliny, a kindly but legally-minded man, had found his province in the grip of Christianity. Doubtless pressed hard by the temple wardens of the cult whose shrines were empty, and the guild of butchers whose sacrificial meat was finding no purchasers, the governor, following the lamentable anti-Christian legislation that had been on the imperial statute books since Nero or Vespasian, proceeded to suppression. Pliny writes: "Those who denied they were, or had ever been, Christians, who repeated after me an invocation to the gods, and offered adoration, with wine and frankincense, to your image, which I had ordered to be brought for that purpose, together with those of the gods, and who finally cursed Christ—none of which acts, it is said, those who are really Christians can be forced into performing—these I thought it proper to discharge. Others who were named by that informer at first confessed themselves Christians, and then denied it; true, they had been of that persuasion but they had quitted it, some three years, others many years, and a few as much as twenty-five years ago. They all worshipped your statue and the images of the gods, and cursed Christ" (Pliny, *Letters* 10. 96, 97).

Here is a vivid picture of the imperial cult in operation against a minority who were regarded as dissident and "tampering with the established processes of life: challenging, rebuking" (*The Christian in Pagan Society*, p. 15, E. M. Blaiklock). This, in fact, was the usefulness that the emperors saw in the cult, and why they gave its spontaneous appearance in the E instinctive welcome and official encouragement. Nor must the sufferings of a Christian minority under its impact obscure the fact that the empire, or the principate as it is more correctly called, avoiding the dual sense of the word empire, brought manifold blessings to the eastern provinces. Cicero's letters from Cilicia and his orations against Verres are indication enough of the exploitation and misgovernment that was common in the provinces during the last turbulent cent. of the Rom. republic. The emperors brought peace and at least some semblance of stable government. Hence, the natural adoration of him whose rule had brought such blessings. The whole system of worshiping a man must be seen in its ancient context of ruler-worship in the E, the cult of heroes in Greece, and against the background of a popular theology without the advantage of the Christian or even the Jewish idea of a transcendent God.

So far the worship of the emperor in the eastern stronghold of the cult has been the major theme. In Rome itself, the myth of a deified ruler was invented in the 4th cent. B.C. under Gr. influence, and there are instances, as Rom. power spread through the Gr. world, of Rom. officials receiving divine honors. In the city itself such notions became prominent only in the 1st cent. B.C. and were concerned mainly with the thought of the deification of the virtuous dead. Julius Caesar, who had tasted the adulation of the E, accepted divine honors in his lifetime, and was deified after his assassination. Augustus, preoccupied in avoiding his adoptive uncle's mistakes, was canny about such honors in the W, ready though he was to exploit the instinctive adoration of the E. He allowed altars, not temples, to be set up to his "genius," associated with the worship of *Dea Roma*, the deified spirit of Rome. In lit., Virgil, Horace, and others of the poets of the Golden Age, spoke commonly of the prince in a manner associated with divine things and the hero-cults. They shared, after all, the common gratitude for the gift of peace that Augustus' subtle diplomacy, clever leadership, and immense prestige had brought. The very name Augustus, bestowed by the Senate on Octavian, was indication of this drift of thought. The successors of Augustus shared his hesitation about frank acceptance in Italy of divine appellatives and formal worship. The Greeks and the provinces had no reserve, and the gradual growth of absolutism together with the spread in the W of Eastern cults finally established Caesar worship with its full ritual throughout the Mediterranean world. The cult in no way fulfilled a religious need. It was never more than a tribute of flattery, a demonstration of gratitude, a symbol of patriotism or subjection, and as such a vastly important political force.

BIBLIOGRAPHY. L. R. Taylor, *The Divinity of the Roman Emperor*; Moffatt, EGT 5308 collects a useful list of references.

E. M. BLAIKLOCK

EMPTIED. *See* KENOSIS.

ENAC. Douay VS form of ANAK.

ENAIM **ĭ nā′ əm** (Heb. עינים), a rare dual place name, "Two Eyes." The root of the word has a long and complicated history (KB p. 699). It may mean "spring" (Gen 16:7). Mentioned only in Genesis 38:14, 21, it is treated as a place name in the Rabbinical tradition, LXX, and most VSS, but KJV trs. it as "open place." Located in the high hill country SE of Jerusalem between Adullam and Timnah, a variant of the name, ENAM (q.v.) appears in Joshua 15:34.

W. WHITE, JR.

A bust of Julius Caesar. *Vatican Museum*

ENAM **ē′ nəm** (Heb. עינם) prob. a variant of ENAIM, mentioned only in Joshua 15:34 in a list of the towns of Judah and Simeon located in the Shephelah, on the road S to Timnah.

W. WHITE, JR.

ENAN **ē′ nən** (עינן, perhaps *spring*). Father of Ahira, who, as military leader of the tribe of Naphtali at the time of the wilderness wanderings, assisted in the Sinai census and brought the tribal offering (Num 1:15; 2:29; 7:78, 83; 10:27).

ENASIBUS. KJV Apoc. form of ELIASHIB.

ENCAMPMENT BY THE SEA. A descriptive term for the place where the Hebrews camped the night before God's miraculous destruction of the Egyp. chariot force in the Red Sea (i.e. Sea of Reeds). Biblical evidence indicates that it was "between Migdol and the sea" (Exod 14:2) in the vicinity of Baal-zephon (q.v.) and Pi-hahiroth (q.v.). As in the case of other sites of the early Exodus, its location is dependent upon the interpretation of the route of the Exodus (q.v.). A northern route would locate the encampment on Lake Sirbonis, a southern route would place it on the present Red Sea, and a central route would place it on one of the lakes in between. (For additional discussion of the issues involved *see* articles on EXODUS, PI-HAHIROTH, and other sites of the Exodus.)

A. BOWLING

ENCHANTER. A person who influences people or things through charms, enchantments, and spells. (For broader issues relating to magic and sorcery, *see* MAGIC, MAGICIANS.)

The work of the enchanter is universal. Although practice of the art was forbidden to the Hebrews (Deut 18:10, 11), the OT shows acquaintance with several kinds of charming. Snake charming (לחש) is referred to (Eccl 10:11; Jer 8:17; cf. also Isa 3:3). Etymological evidence suggests that the snake was originally charmed by whispering or some similar noise. The Heb. root "to bind" (חבר) occurs both as a noun meaning "charm" and as a verb meaning "to bind with a charm" (Ps 58:5; cf. Deut 18:11; Isa 47:9, 12).

In addition, Heb. נחש, is tr. "enchantment" (Num 23:23; in 24:1 the same word is properly tr. "omens," RSV; "enchantments" in KJV). "Charmers" (Isa 19:3, KJV; RSV uses "sorcerers") tr. a Heb. word of uncertain meaning (אטים).

One Aram. word, אשף, is regularly tr. as "enchanter" in the RSV (KJV tr. "astrologers"; e.g. Dan 2:10). The word occurs twice as a loan word in Heb. portions of Daniel (Dan 1:20; 2:2).

The NT texts refer to broader issues of magic, sorcery, and swindling; rather than to the more specific issue of enchantment.

(For *Bibliography, see* MAGIC, MAGICIANS.)

A. BOWLING

END OF THE WORLD (*συντέλεια τοῦ αἰῶνος, end of the world* KJV, *close of the age* RSV, e.g. Matt 13:39; also simple *τέλος, end,* e.g. Matt 24:13, 14). Terms for the miraculous and catastrophic events that will close history and open the eternal age. For a detailed, chronological reconstruction of the events associated with the end of the world, *see* ESCHATOLOGY.

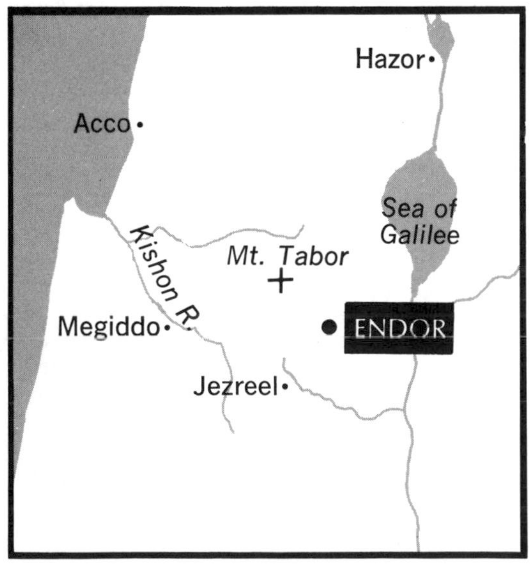

Most ideas associated with the end of the world in the OT appear as relatively subordinate details to God's future work in restoring His chosen people to the Promised Land. The gradual emergence of these details is an instructive example of progressive revelation. The miraculous and catastrophic character of some of these events shows that the restoration of God's people is not merely another event within history, but rather that it marks the apocalyptic end of history.

Some of these events are: (1) miraculous and catastrophic events in nature (Joel 2:30; Zech 14:4); (2) judgment upon the nations, particularly those who have persecuted God's people (Joel 3:9-12; Obad 15, 16; Zech 14:12-15); (3) restoration to a world of miraculous prosperity (Hos 2:22; Joel 3:18; Amos 9:11-15), political peace (Isa 2:3, 4; Mic 4:3), and peace within nature (Isa 65:23-25); (4) judgment followed by God's personal rule (Obad 21; Dan 2:44); (5) restoration to a sinless state (Zeph 3:11-13; Zech 14:20, 21); and (6) resurrection to immortality (one relatively late passage only: Dan 12:2, 3).

As an examination of the passages referred to above shows, OT apocalyptic eschatology was the end product of a gradual development that began well before the Exile. It is, therefore, erroneous to suppose that apocalyptic eschatology emerged only as the disappointed Hebrews of the Exile deserted history for an "other-worldly" hope. Rather, apocalyptic eschatology can be viewed as a normal outgrowth of the older Heb. confidence in God's working within history.

NT eschatology retains the ideas listed above and adds some new ones: (1) seen from one perspective, the end of the world had already begun with Christ's appearance as a sacrifice (Heb 9:26), though other aspects of the end are clearly future; (2) even the preaching of the Gospel can be regarded as only a preliminary for the end (Matt 24:14); (3) a distinction is made between the events introducing the earthly millennium (q.v.) and the events introducing the eternal age (one passage only: Rev 20; 21); (4) the end is associated with the personal return of Jesus Christ to earth (Matt 24:29, 30); (5) a total, catastrophic dissolution will end the present world and make room for a new, eternal earth (2 Pet 3:7-10; Rev 21:1; *see* ESCHATOLOGY).

A. BOWLING

EN-DOR ĕn′ dōr (עין דר, עין דור, עין דאר, LXX 'Αενδώρ, *āndōr, fountain of habitation*). A town in Issachar allotted to Manasseh because of the members of the tribe of Manasseh living there (Josh 17:11). Apparently, Manasseh did not drive out all the Canaanites from En-dor at the time of the conquest (17:12). It is identified with the historical *Endūr*, 4 m. S of Mt. Tabor and 6 m. SE of Nazareth, on the northern slope of Little Hermon (*Nebi Dahi*), where there are several ancient caves. In Roman days, it had a large population. In modern times, *Endūr* was occupied by Arabs who abandoned it in 1948 during the Arab-Jewish war, whereupon the Israeli established a settlement there and called it *Ein Dor*.

According to Psalm 83:9, 10, En-dor formed part of the plain of Kishon and thus a part of the battlefield of Megiddo. It was the scene of the defeat of Jabin and Sisera by Barak. En-dor was the site of the encampment of the army of King Saul before the battle with the Philistines (1 Sam 29:1). The town is perhaps most famous because Saul here sought the help of a medium in the uncertain hours before his final battle (28:7).

A. C. SCHULTZ

EN-EGLAIM ĕn ĕg' lĭ əm (עין עגלים, meaning *spring of calf* or *heifer*). This location is mentioned in reference to Israel during the golden age (Ezek 47:10). From this place S to En-gedi (about the middle of the western shore of the Dead Sea), fishermen will put forth their nets according to the prophet. This restored kingdom age wonder will be in direct contrast to the present lack of fish life in the Dead Sea.

The exact location of this site is not known, but it is prob. several m. S of Khirbet Qumran.

G. GIACUMAKIS, JR.

ENEMESSAR en' ə mes' ər (Ενεμεσσάρος, meaning uncertain). The name given to the king of Assyria (Tobit 1:2, 15, 16). It is found only in the LXX. Shalmaneser appears instead of Enemessar in the Heb., Aram., and Lat. MSS.

Several explanations have been given for this variation in name: (1) Some have tried to identify Enemessar with Senemessar. (2) Rawlinson feels that the *Shal* in Shalmaneser has been mistaken for a genitive. He transposes the *m* and *n*. Identification between Enemessar and Shalmaneser is virtually eliminated, for in Tobit 1:15 Shalmaneser is made the father of Sennacherib, whereas the father of Sennacherib was Sargon. (3) Others feel it is an unrecorded private name for Sargon. (4) In more recent times the name has been looked upon as an Assyrian compound *SARRU-KINU*, "the legitimate king," an epithet for Sargon.

C. J. BARBER

ENEMY, ENEMIES. One who feels or behaves in a hostile manner.

1. Original vocabulary. Four major Heb. words normally mean "enemy," although, on occasion, slight differences in meaning may be discerned: איב (*hostile one*), צר (*foe, hostile one*), משנא (*one who hates*), and שנא (*one who hates*). Less frequently used are שורר (*spiteful foe*, only in Pss) and צרר (*one who is hostile*). Two other words, ער (1 Sam 28:16; Ps 139:20) and שור (Ps 92:11), are not sufficiently attested to define their meaning. The former may be an Aram. loan word. One Aram. word, ער (*rival, adversary*), and a Gr. word, ἐχθρός (*enemy*), complete the list.

2. Old Testament teaching. Enmity among men, resulting in murder, is one of the first recorded results of the Fall (Gen 4:5-8). This enmity between men will someday be removed (Mic 4:3, 4). Enmity is opposed to love, a basic ethical principle even in the law (Lev 19:18). The law commanded love even for the resident foreigner (19:34).

The enmity of nature toward man is also a result of the Fall (Gen 3:17, 18). The future will include reconciliation of the parts of nature with one another, as, for example, in the case of reconciling the enmity between the animals (Isa 65:25).

Men, including God's chosen people (Lam 2:4; Isa 1:24, 25), who oppose God's purposes can become enemies of God. Scriptures hint that their hatred of God is self-destructive (Isa 26:11c: "your enemies' fire will consume them"—writer's tr.). God's vengeance on His enemies is coming (Jer 46:10), and God's enemies must be destroyed when God reigns (Ps 97:1, 3).

The OT principle of revenge (Lev 24:19-21) seems to sanction revengeful enmity against one's enemy. On the other hand, revenge may have been a necessary, though unpleasant, expedient for maintaining public order in the absence of central governmental authority. Also, the OT principle of revenge prevented the act of revenge from becoming disproportionately larger than the original crime. The revenge could not exceed in degree the crime or hurt committed. As such, the principle of revenge would not have been an unconditional warrant for personal hatred. In personal relations, the OT attitude is expressed in the warning not to rejoice in the enemy's misfortunes (Prov 24:17) and in the command to return the enemy's lost goods (Exod 23:4, 5).

Hatred toward the national enemy is expressed in strong poetical terms (e.g. Ps 137:8, 9). This hatred in behalf of the nation and God's purposes should not be confused with personal hatred. Concerning the national enemy, when the people are in God's will, their enemies are God's enemies (Gen 12:3; Exod 23:22), and God gives victory (Lev 26:3, 8; Ps 44:5). But, when they become God's enemies through sin, God fights for their enemies (Jer 21:4-6). God even raises up enemies against His sinning people (Isa 9:11). But the enemy thus raised up should not glory in his own power since he is merely God's tool (Deut 32:27; Isa 37:22-29). Israel sometimes complained that God had delivered them to their enemy without reason (Ps 89:38-45).

3. New Testament teaching. The NT specifically and unequivocally commands love both

Upper Spring of En-gedi, a place where David found refuge from Saul. ©*M.P.S.*

for the stranger (Luke 10:29-37) and the hostile enemy (Matt 5:38-44).

The message of Christ, however, may produce enmity (Matt 10:34-36). Theologically, enmity with God has been universalized and used to describe fallen mankind (Rom 5:10). "Reconciliation," then, views salvation as making enemies of God into friends of God (cf. 2 Cor 5:18-20). *See* WRATH.

BIBLIOGRAPHY. D. Philipson, "Enemy," JewEnc (1901); W. Foerster, "ἐχθρός," TDNT (1964).

A. BOWLING

ENENEUS, ENENIUS. ASV and KJV Apoc. forms of BIGVAI.

EN-GANNIM ĕn găn′ ĭm (עין־גנים, *spring of gardens*). 1. In Joshua 15:34 it is one of the towns in the second district of Judah. Beyond the fact that it was in the Shephelah (lowland) and prob. not far from Beth-shemesh there is no indication of its site. The identification with the modern Beit Jemâl is dubious.

2. In Joshua 19:21 it is a place in the tribal portion of Issachar, and in Joshua 21:29 a Levitical city given to the Gershonites. In 1 Chronicles 6:73 Anem is prob. a scribal corruption of the name. In addition it is prob. the Beth-haggan of 2 Kings 9:27 (so HGHL p. 354, Moffatt, RSV; KJV, ASV have "garden house"). There is general agreement that it is the modern Jenin. The site was never of military importance, but very fertile and lying on a secondary route out of the plain of Esdraelon.

H. L. ELLISON

EN-GEDI ĕn gĕd′ ĭ (עין־גדי, Arab. *'Ain Jidi, the spring of the kid*). KJV Apoc. ENGADDI (Ecclus 24:14). It is the name of a spring and associated streams that issue from beneath the limestone cliffs on the W side of the Dead Sea at a temperature of 80°F. It lies almost due E of Hebron. Second Chronicles 20:2 gives it the name Hazazon-tamar, but this is not likely to be the place of the same name in Genesis 14:7. It belonged to the territory of Judah (Josh 15:62). Because of the oppressive heat of the Dead Sea valley, there can never have been any large population here. In NT times, there seem to have been c. 1,000 population (Jos. War IV. vii. 2). The name Hazazon-tamar suggests the presence of palm trees, cf. Ecclus 24:14, and Song of Solomon 1:14 mentions vineyards, but both disappeared after the Muslim occupation. The modern Jewish settlement grows early vegetables. The wilderness of En-gedi (1 Sam 24:1), figuring in the story of David, is one of the bleakest parts of the Wilderness of Judah, or Jeshimon (q.v.). When Ammon, Moab, and Edom tried to invade Judah through En-gedi in the time of Jehoshaphat (2 Chron 20:1f.), it was presumably, because they hoped to achieve a tactical surprise by attacking one of the few weak spots on Judah's eastern flank. Once warning had been given, failure was inevitable. En-gedi is mentioned again (Ezek 47:10) in the prophet's vision of the transformed Dead Sea.

H. L. ELLISON

ENGINE. A battering ram (Ezek 26:9); also a device used in connection with shooting arrows or other missiles (2 Chron 26:15).

1. The word "engine" refers to a battering ram once in the OT (Ezek 26:9) where it is used against city walls. The KJV reads "engines of war," the ASV "his battering engines," and the RSV "the shock of his battering rams" (Heb. מחי קבלו, *the stroke of his forward part,* i.e., *the stroke of his battering ram*). The usual Heb. word for battering ram is כר (Ezek 4:2, et al.). The siege engine mentioned in 1 Maccabees 13:43, 44 (Gr. ἑλεόπολις) was prob. a large, portable tower including battering rams. The usual Gr. word is κριός (2 Macc 12:15).

A typical battering ram, the kind used by the Assyrians, was mounted inside of a mobile device about fifteen ft. long and half as high. It was suspended by a rope in the center so that it could be swung. The ram was used to strike at the cracks between the stones and when forced into the cracks it was then pushed back and forth to dislodge the stones. On the front of the unit was a turret adding another nine ft. to the height from which the assailants could shoot arrows or direct operations. The unit was mounted on four or six wheels for mobility.

2. According to 2 Chronicles 26:15 Uzziah "made engines . . . to be on the towers and the corners, to shoot arrows and great stones." The word "engine" (חשבון, "device," "invention," LXX μηχανή, "machine," "engine") has been understood to mean a device for the purpose of firing arrows or stones.

The same Gr. word appears in 1 Maccabees 6:51, 52 and 2 Maccabees 12:15 in similar contexts. Concerning the passage in 2 Chronicles, Yadin feels that this does not refer to a specific catapult or firing device as there seems to be no evidence of this existing anywhere at this time but that these were wooden devices with shields in the fortification of the walls to protect those who were shooting arrows and throwing stones. They protected the defenders of the city so that they could stand upright and use their weapons with comparative safety and freedom of movement. These are pictured in Assyrian reliefs.

BIBLIOGRAPHY. A History of Technology, II (1957), 698-703, 715-717; Y. Yadin, *The Art of Warfare in Biblical Lands* (1963), 16-18, 313-316, 326, 327.

C. P. WEBER

ENGLISH BIBLE VERSIONS. *See* BIBLE, ENGLISH VERSIONS.

ENGRAVER. This Eng. word covers several Heb. terms whose exact meanings are difficult to distinguish, for they are often used as synonyms.

The jeweler's engraving of the names of the tribes of Israel on onyx stones (Exod 28:11) is referred to by the two words חרש and פתח. When the engraver cuts the words "Holy to the LORD" on a gold plate the word is פתח (Exod 28:36). The term כתב refers to the engraving of the Ten Commandments on stone tablets (Deut 5:22). In Exodus 32:16 there are two terms for this same engraving כתב and חרות. Again in Jeremiah 17:1 are two terms for engraving; one is כתב and the other is חרש. In this verse, the engraving tools used are mentioned. One is an iron (steel) chisel, and the other is a diamond-tipped chisel. (The Egyptians used the diamond-tipped chisel.) Emery was also employed in this work.

The finest engraving is often referred to in Scripture as that of signet rings; the archeologist confirms this verdict. The term פתח is also used as the general word for sculpturing of any kind in either wood or stone.

Second Corinthians 3:7 has the Gr. ἐντυπόω when it refers to the engraving of the Ten Commandments on stone.

J. L. KELSO

ENGRAVING (פתוח, *engraving*; from verb פתח, *engrave*). The art of cutting letters or designs into a hard surface.

Mediums used included metal, stone and wood. An engraved plate of gold was worn by Aaron as high priest (Exod 28:36, 37). Designs were engraved as decorations on the bronze stands made for Solomon's Temple (1 Kings 7:29). Precious stones (gems) were engraved with inscrs. (Exod 28:9, onyx or carnelian; also Zech 3:9). There were engravings on the inside walls of the Temple (1 Kings 6:29), made of wood (v. 15), overlaid with gold (v. 21).

A broader term, חרש (Jer 17:1), חרת ("plow," "cut") with the noun חרש ("craftsman," "engraver"), is also used for the art of engraving (Exod 32:16, the Ten Commandments on the two tables of stone, NT ἐντυπόω, "to carve," 2 Cor 3:7; and Jer 17:1, also on stone). In addition, חצב ("hew out") is used to describe an engraving in rock (Job 19:24).

Tools used included stylus (עט), "pen," "stylus," of iron (19:24), and iron with a diamond or emery point (Jer 17:1); also חרת, "stylus" (Exod 32:4 and Isa 8:1), file, wheel, and drill. The drill was attached to a stick which was twisted by the back-and-forth motion of a bow whose string was looped around the stick. Grinding was accomplished with the aid of an abrasive.

BIBLIOGRAPHY. J. H. Middleton, *The Engraved Gems of Classical Times* (1891); ANEP (1954); C. Singer, et al. eds., *A History of Technology,* I (1954), 189, 190, 648, 649, 663-681.

C. P. WEBER

EN-HADDAH **ĕn hăd ə** (עין חדה, meaning *sharp spring*). This city mentioned only in Joshua 19:21 was included in the territory assigned to Issachar. Issachar possessed a small geographical area and its tribal location was in part of the Jezreel valley SW of the Sea of Galilee. Probable location is about three to six m. E of Mount Tabor.

G. GIACUMAKIS, JR.

EN-HAKKORE **ĕn hăk' ə rī** (עין-הקורא, *the spring of him that called*, though possibly *the spring of the partridge*).

The spring where Samson drank after slaughtering the Philistines at Lehi (Judg 15:14-19). It cannot be identified, if it still exists, for it is generally agreed that the site of Lehi remains unidentified. Attempts to locate it are made in the NBC, p. 253a, and the *Oxford Bible Atlas.* Since *lehi* also means jawbone, KJV has a most misleading tr. of Judges 15:19 suggesting that the water came from the jawbone.

H. L. ELLISON

EN-HAZOR **ĕn hā' zôr** (עין חצור, meaning *settlement spring*). There are at least five different locations with whole or part of their name being Hazor. En-Hazor was a fortified city included in the assignment to the tribe of Naphtali. This town is not the same as the royal city of Hazor which was located in the region of Naphtali NW of the Sea of Galilee. En-Hazor's exact location is unknown, but Aharoni, *Land of the Bible*, p. 150, conjectures that it might be 'Ainitha. En-Hazor is mentioned only in Joshua 19:37.

G. GIACUMAKIS, JR.

ENLIGHTEN (אור ; נגה; φωτίζω). The Heb. and Gr. words meaning "to bring light," or "to enlighten," are used in a literal sense only by the KJV in the OT (1 Sam 14:27, 29; Job 33:30; and Ps 97:4).

In all other cases of the use of the word in the Bible its sense is metaphorical. The psalmist says that God lightens his darkness (18:28 KJV "enlighten"), and that God's commandments are pure, enlightening the eyes (19:8 RSV). Pondering the omniscience of God, the prophet Isaiah asks, "Whom did he consult for his enlightenment?" (Isa 40:14).

Paul prays that God will give the Ephesians the spirit of wisdom and of revelation in the knowledge of Him, having the eyes of their hearts enlightened, for only so can they know the extent of their inheritance in Christ (Eph 1:18). The apostle also says that the God of this world, Satan, has blinded the minds of unbelievers (2 Cor 4:4). John the Baptist proclaimed that the Messiah is the true light that enlightens every man (John 1:9), and Jesus Himself more than once claimed to be the light of the world (8:12; 9:5). Paul said of the Jews of his time that they had a zeal for God, but it was not enlightened (Rom 10:2). In one of the most difficult passages in the NT the author of Hebrews says, "It is impossible to restore again to repentance those who have once been enlightened, who have tasted the heavenly gift, and have become partakers of the Holy Spirit, and have tasted the goodness of the word of God and the powers of the age to come, if they then commit apostasy, since they crucify the Son of God on their own account and hold him up to contempt" (6:4-6).

It is evident from these passages that enlightenment is the intellectual and moral effect produced upon a person by the reception of the Christian revelation. It is not a mere intellectual illumination or understanding of divine truth, for this spiritual insight manifests itself in ethical action. Christians are "sons of light," as Paul puts it (1 Thess 5:5).

J. C. CONNELL

EN-MISHPAT ĕn mish′ pȧt (עין משפט, meaning *spring of judgment*). Where this place name occurs (Gen 14:7), there is a parenthetical explanation put in by the writer of a later period which identifies En-Mishpat with Kadesh. This is an oasis located in the northeastern part of the Sinai peninsula.

ENNATAN (*See* ELNATHAN) **ĕn nā tăn** (Εννатαν). Ennatan is found only in the apocryphal book of 1 Esdras (8:44). Some trs. have emmended this to read "Elnathan" as it is in the first part of the v., for there are two occurrences of the name in the v. In the parallel lists found in the Book of Ezra (8:16), the name "Elnathan" is used three times. Ennatan is not found at all in the Book of Ezra.

G. GIACUMAKIS, JR.

ENNOM. Douay VS form of HINNOM.

ENOCH e′ nək (חנוך, LXX Ἐνώχ, meaning not certain; perhaps *dedicated one*, or *one trained up* from the root "to train up a youth" [cf. Prov 22:6]). The name of four different individuals in the Old Testament. 1. The son of Cain (Gen 4:17, 18) for whom the first city which Cain built was named.

2. The son of Jared of the godly line of Seth, who walked with God and was translated to heaven without dying (Gen 5:18-24; 1 Chron 1:3). As a hero of faith (Heb 11:5) he is known as a man who pleased God, while Jude 14 and 15 refer to the tradition that Enoch prophesied against ungodly men (cf. *The Book of Enoch*). There can be no question that the clause "and he was not, for God took him" (Gen 5:24) refers to translation; the same expression is used of Elijah's translation (2 Kings 2:11).

3. A son of Midian, the son of Abraham by Keturah; this Enoch was father of one of the tribes of Midianites (Gen 25:4; 1 Chron 1:3).

4. The first son of Reuben, the son of Jacob (Gen 46:8, 9; Exod 6:14; Num 26:5; 1 Chron 5:3).

E. B. SMICK

ENOCH, BOOKS OF ē′ nək. A number of pseudepigraphic writings ascribed to Enoch the son of Jared and father of Methuselah (Gen 5:18ff.). Enoch's evident translation to heaven gave rise to the belief that he must be knowledgeable concerning the secrets of heaven and therefore these works, all apocalyptic in character, could be appropriately attributed to his authorship.

A. Ethiopic Enoch or **1 Enoch** or simply, **The Book of Enoch.** This is a lengthy composite work of 108 chs. seemingly compiled in five sections or "books" which prob. correspond, at least in part, to the author's sources. The whole was provided with an introduction and conclusion. It may be possible to define further the structure of the book in the light of continuing study of the Qumran material.

1. *Content.* Chapters 1-5 serve as a kind of introduction to the whole work and esp. its major themes of rewards and punishment, the end of the world, and the final judgment.

Book I (chs. 6-36) is concerned largely with angels and the universe. Chapters 6-11, which come from the Book of Noah (q.v.), suggest that the fall of angels occurred because of the marriage of the sons of God with the daughters of men (cf. Gen 6:1ff.). The angels in turn taught mankind the various arts and skills of civilization and mankind became corrupted and godless. God then pronounced judgment on mankind and on Azazel who led them astray. In chs. 12-16 Enoch has a vision and, while he intercedes passionately on behalf of the fallen angels, he is finally instructed to predict their utter doom. In chs. 17-36 Enoch is escorted by the angels of light on various tours throughout the earth, to the place of punishment of the fallen angels, to Sheol, to the tree of life, to Jerusalem with its mountains, rivers and streams, and to the Garden of Righteousness.

Book II covers chs. 37-71 and is composed of three parables or similitudes. Each parable is quite lengthy compared to a parable of the gospels, for example, and each is primarily concerned with the triumph of righteousness over wickedness. The first parable (chs. 38-44) deals with the impending judgment of the wicked, the abode of the Righteous and Elect One, the four archangels and certain astronomical and meteorological secrets. The second parable (chs. 45-57) is concerned mainly with the Elect One or Son of Man sitting in judgment. He is not pictured as a human being but rather as a majestic heavenly being possessing absolute dominion over the world of men and of angels. The third parable (chs. 58-71) speaks of the blessedness of the saints, the measuring of paradise, the judgment of the kings and mighty ones and gives the names and functions of the fallen angels.

Book III is the so-called Book of the Heavenly Luminaries and covers chapters 72-82. It is an almost purely scientific treatise, showing virtually no interest in ethical questions. The author seeks to construct a uniform astronomical system from the data of the OT and argues that the measurement of time should be solar rather than lunar. Interestingly, however, the author's solar year is 364 days though he is aware of the 365¼ day year. The interest in 80:2-8 suddenly becomes ethical, however, and it is stated that in the last days the heavenly bodies as well as the earth will suffer serious disorders.

Book IV, covering chs. 83-90, consists of two lengthy dream-visions predicting the future history of Israel. Chapters 83 and 84 give the first dream-vision which, in the view assumed by the author, predicts the Flood as a judgment upon the world. The second dream-vision encompasses chs. 85-90 and, after recounting the history from the beginning to the time of Enoch, goes on to predict the history of the world to the founding of the Messianic kingdom. This history is given using a wide array of symbolism. Thus, oxen appear to symbolize the patriarchs; sheep the true house of Israel; preying beasts and birds the heathen; a sheep with a great horn possibly Judas Maccabeus, and a white bull with great horns the Messiah. The dream-vision ends with the new Jerusalem, the conversion of the Gentiles, the resurrection of the righteous and the establishment of the Messianic reign. The fact that the history as understood from the symbols goes no further than the Maccabean period is an indication of the date of this part of the work.

Book V is a work which includes exhortations for the righteous and maledictions for the wicked and occupies chs. 91-105. The structure of this section is difficult, though the theme is much the same as the rest of the work. A notable feature of this book is the Apocalypse of Weeks found in 93:1-10 and 91:12-17. The history of the world from Enoch's time and on is divided into ten weeks of unequal length, each seemingly marked by some special event. Thus, the first is marked by Enoch's birth, the third by Abraham's call, and the seventh by the publication of Enoch's writings. In the eighth week the righteous will gain the victory over their oppressors. In the ninth week the world will be made ready for destruction. In the tenth and endless week a new heaven will be ushered in.

The conclusion of the work occupies chs. 106-108. Chapters 106 and 107 derive from the earlier Book of Noah (q.v.) and relate the increase of sin after the Flood until the Messianic reign. The final chapter again returns to the theme of rewards for the righteous and punishment for the wicked.

2. *Texts and versions.* Until the discovery of the DSS, the text of 1 Enoch was best preserved in the Ethiopic MSS, twenty-nine of which are known. Most of these contain the complete work, sometimes together with certain Biblical or Apocryphal books. Within this group of MSS, two text types are distinguishable. The Ethiopic MSS are late, however, the earliest belonging prob. to the 16th cent.

Portions of the book have also been preserved in Gr. Two MSS dating from the 8th cent. or later were discovered in 1886-1887 in a Christian grave at Akhmim, Egypt, and preserve chs. 1-32:6 and 19:3-21:9. Syncellus (c. A.D. 800) preserves 6:1-10:14; 15:8-16:1 and 8:4-9:4 in duplicate form. A Vatican MS preserves 89:42-49 and Egyp. papyrii containing chs. 97-104 and 106-108 were published by Bonner in 1937. Some quotations from Enoch, esp. from 106:1-18 are preserved in Lat.

The Scrolls from Qumran now appear to provide the best representatives of the original text of the Book of Enoch, however. About ten fragmentary MSS of the work in Aram. were found in Cave IV. Five of these correspond roughly to Book I and Book IV of the work. It appears that these sections together with the last chapters of the book once formed a separate work. Book III, the astronomical section, is represented by four Aram. MSS which provide a more intelligible text than any others available to this time. The beginning of Book V is represented by one MS. It may have circulated as a separate work as well. Support for this suggestion comes from a fragmentary Gr. MS found among the Chester Beatty-Michigan papyri. The fact that there are no fragments of Book II may be due to accident or it may be that this too was a separate composition not known to the Qumran community.

It seems probable that the continued study of the evidence from Qumran will alter our estimates of the Book of Enoch somewhat.

3. *Date.* Because the book is a composite work it is necessary to speak of "dates" rather than "date." The many historical events alluded to in the course of the work serve at least as a partial means of dating. Experts in the field are not agreed concerning the question of dating. R. H. Pfeiffer (see Bibliography) gives the following dates: Introduction: 150-100 B.C.; Book I: c. 100 B.C.; Book II: 100-80 B.C.; Book V: 100-80 B.C. (except the Apocalypse of Weeks: 163 B.C.); Conclusion: 100-80 B.C. though chs. 106-107 which are from the Book of Noah may be earlier. R. H. Charles (see Bibliography) and some others, however, argue that Book I must be dated before 170 B.C. Charles also suggests a pre-Maccabean date for the Apocalypse of Weeks though recognizing the difficulty of being certain. The book itself was prob. compiled in the 1st cent. B.C., the actual dates suggested being 95 B.C., 63 B.C. and during Herod's reign (37-4 B.C.).

4. *Language.* Generally, experts in the field agree that the original language of 1 Enoch was Sem. though it is not agreed which particular Sem. language it was. It may have been Heb. or Aram. or, perhaps more prob., both Heb. and Aram. R. H. Charles assigns chs. 1-5 and 37-105 to Heb. and chs. 6-36 to Aram. Such a two-language phenomenon is also present in the Biblical book of Daniel (q.v.). The book has a distinctly poetical element and this fact has been of considerable assistance in the editing of the work.

5. *Influence.* The Book of Enoch exerted a strong and widespread influence on both Jewish and Christian lit. It appears that the writers of the Testaments of the Twelve Patriarchs, the Assumption of Moses, 2 Baruch and 4 Ezra quoted from it. There appears also to be literary dependence between the Book of Jubilees and 1 Enoch though it is not possible to be certain at all points which way the dependence runs. Charles suggested that in the earlier sections of 1 Enoch, Jubilees was used, while in the later sections the dependence was reversed. The problem is linked with the question of dating (q.v.). After the 2nd cent. A.D. Jewish lit. took little notice of the Book of Enoch, however.

Parallels with 1 Enoch from practically every section of the NT can be cited, though it is prob. going too far to say that every NT writer must have been familiar with the book. Perhaps the most familiar reference to 1 Enoch in the NT is the famous passage in Jude 14, 15. In addition to this apparent literary dependence, however, many of the concepts familiar to us from the NT appeared either first or most prominently in 1 Enoch. Thus, for example, the spiritual nature of the Messianic reign. Thus also the titles used to refer to the Messiah, such as, "Christ" or "The Anointed One," "The Righteous One," "The Elect One," and "The Son of Man." The NT concepts of Sheol, resurrection and demonology also bear striking similarities to those of Enoch.

Much of the early Patristic lit. shows acquaintance with 1 Enoch and Barnabas and Tertullian, for example, seem to rate the work almost as highly as Scripture. Gnostic and Apocryphal lit. also make use of 1 Enoch. However, by the 4th cent. A.D. the book had fallen into considerable disfavor in the W and Jerome declared it to be an Apocryphal work. Its use, however, evidently continued for a longer time in the E.

B. The Book of the Secrets of Enoch or **The Slavonic Enoch** or **2 Enoch.** This is another work ascribed to Enoch and known to us only from two Slavonic texts which were published near the end of the 19th cent. While showing some similarities with the earlier Book of Enoch, this book is by no means to be identified with it.

1. *Contents.* Second Enoch is basically an account of Enoch's travels through the seven heavens and includes certain revelations given to Enoch and Enoch's exhortations to his children. The revelations are concerned with creation and the history of mankind. In the beginning God created the world out of nothing. He also created seven heavens with all the angelic hosts and mankind as well. Just as God performed His creative work in six days and rested the seventh, even so the history of the world would span 6000 years and it would then rest for 1000 years. After this, an eternal day of blessing would begin.

The souls of men were created before the world began and also a place either in heaven or in hell for the future habitation of each soul. The soul was created good, but because of free will and because of the soul's habitation in the body, sin appeared in spite of the instruction man had received regarding the Two Ways. Men will therefore have to face judgment and only the righteous will escape the hell prepared for sinners.

The ethical teaching of the book is in many respects noble. Man should work and be just, charitable, unavenging and humble. Above all, he should fear God.

2. *Language, place of writing, author, date.* At least a part of the book was originally written in Gr. This is seen from the facts that the name Adam is derived from the initial letters of the Gr. words for the directions E, W, S and N; the chronology of the LXX is followed; the text of the LXX is used as over against the Heb. and the Gr. of Sirach and the Book of Wisdom are evidently used. Some portions of the book, however, were most prob. Heb. in origin.

The place of writing of the book is thought to be Egypt, possibly in Alexandria. This is argued from the typically Hellenistic and Philonic speculations which the book contains, the lack of Messianic teaching typical of the OT, the appearance of monstrous serpents which are typically Egyp., and the syncretistic character of the creation account. The author must have been a Hel. Jew with syncretistic tendencies.

On the question of dating, the fact that the Testaments of the Twelve Patriarchs makes use of passages from 2 Enoch implies a pre-Christian date for those portions. The use of Sirach, 1 Enoch and the Book of Wisdom by 2 Enoch implies a date after 30 B.C. The fact that the Temple is still standing in 2 Enoch implies a date before A.D. 70. Most scholars, in fact, prefer an early Christian date (e.g. A.D. 1-50) for the composition of 2 Enoch.

3. *Influence.* The book seems to have exercised considerable influence upon both Jewish and Christian lit. Its presence is felt in the Book of Adam and Eve, the Apocalypse of Moses, the Apocalypse of Paul, the Sibylline Oracles, the Ascension of Isaiah and the Testaments of the Twelve Patriarchs. Irenaeus and Origen both show traces of its influence as does the Epistle of Barnabas. Many passages of the NT can be cited for the similarity of their thought and expression with 2 Enoch.

C. The rabbinic Enoch. There is a further Enoch book which follows, to some extent the Slavonic book and is attributed to Rabbi Ishmael a prominent figure in the Barcochba rebellion. This book is referred to in the Talmud.

In this book, Rabbi Ishmael ascends through six heavens to meet Enoch (who is referred to as "Metatron") in the seventh. Here Enoch discusses some events of his own life and the life of Adam. This book reflects some of the traditions of 2 Enoch, and it is prob. these which were originally in Heb.

BIBLIOGRAPHY. R. H. Charles and W. R. Morfill, *The Book of the Secrets of Enoch* (1896); G. Beer, "Das Buch Henoch," in E. Kautzsch, *Die Apokryphen und Pseudepigraphen des Alten Testaments* (1900), II, 217-310; R. H. Charles, *The Book of Enoch* (1912; reprinted in 1921 with introduction by W. O. E. Oesterley); "Book of Enoch" in APOT, 163-281 and "The Book of the Secrets of Enoch" in APOT, 425-469; C. Bonner, *The Last Chapters of Enoch in Greek* (1937); R. H. Pfeiffer, *History of New Testament Times* (1949); S. B. Frost, *Old Testament Apocalyptic* (1952); J. T. Milik, *Ten Years of Discovery in the Wilderness of Judaea* (1959), 33, 34; H. H. Rowley, *The Relevance of Apocalyptic* (3rd. ed. 1963); D. S. Russell, *The Method and Message of Jewish Apocalyptic* (1964).

H. G. ANDERSEN

ENOCH (city) ē nək (חנוך, 'Ενώχ). Nothing is known about this city outside of that mentioned in Genesis 4:17. This city was built by Cain in honor of the name of his son Enoch. Enoch also occurs in the Bible as the name of one of Seth's descendants.

ENOS, ENOSH ē' nŏs, e' nŏsh (אנוש, 'Ενώς, *man, mankind*). Son of Seth and the grandson of Adam; an ancestor of Christ. He became the father of Kenan after he lived ninety years. He had other sons and daughters and died at 905 years (Gen 5:6-11). At his birth it is noted that "men began to call upon the name of the LORD" (4:26). The spelling Enos comes from the Gr. and is so found in Luke 3:38 (except NEB). (The KJV uses Enos throughout except for 1 Chron 1:1 where it is Enosh.)

C. P. WEBER

EN-RIMMON ĕn rĭm' ən (עין-רמון, *spring of the pomegranate*). A village resettled after the exile (Neh 11:29). Joshua 15:32 (RSV Rimmon); 19:7 (RSV En-rimmon) First Chronicles 4:32 mentions two places, Ain and Rimmon in the same area, first allotted to Judah and then transferred to Simeon. Since the site has not been excavated, it is not clear whether the name refers to two small settlements which later coalesced, or whether, as seems far more likely, one place has been divided into two by a scribal error. It is possibly also the Rimmon of Zechariah 14:10. It is generally idenified with Khirbet Umm er-Rumamin nine m. N of Beer-sheba.

H. L. ELLISON

EN-ROGEL ĕn rō' gel (עין רגל, meaning *spring of the fuller, foot,* or *spy*). A spring just S of Jerusalem in the Kidron Valley.

Today En-rogel is connected with Bir Ayyub (The Well of Job) where a gasoline-powered pump brings up the water which in olden times came up of itself. The one other source of water in E Jerusalem, 'Ain sitti Miriam (Spring of the Lady Mary) or The Virgin's Fountain, has also been a suggested identification but is a less likely candidate. They are within a few hundred ft. of each other. The latter is now thought to be the Gihon Spring of 1 Kings 1:33 et al., which necessitates its being a different place than En-rogel.

En-rogel first appears in Joshua 15:7 and 18:16 as being on the boundary between the tribes of Judah and Benjamin. It was at En-rogel that Jonathan and Ahimaaz, two of David's spies, stayed during Absalom's rebellion (2 Sam 17:17). From that point just S of the city of David they could report to David what a maidservant told them, since they themselves could not enter the city.

En-rogel was mentioned again as the coronation site during the attempted usurpation of the kingdom by Adonijah, who sacrificed animals "by the Serpent's Stone (*Zoheleth* KJV), which is beside En-rogel" (1 Kings 1:9). The identification of such a "stone" is uncertain and thus it is no help in determining absolutely which source of water was En-rogel.

BIBLIOGRAPHY. J. Simons, *Jerusalem in the OT* (1952), 48f.

R. L. ALDEN

ENROLLMENT, ENROLMENT. *See* CENSUS.

EN-SHEMESH ĕn shĕm ĭsh (עין שמש, meaning *spring of the sun*). A spring which is usually identified with modern 'Ain el-Ḥod located about three m. E of Jerusalem on the way to Jericho in the Jordan Valley. It is sometimes referred to as the "Spring of the Apostles."

The only reference to this spring in the Bible is in the Book of Joshua during the conquest and settlement period. It marked a point on the southern boundary of Benjamin and on the northern boundary of Judah (Josh 15:7 and 18:17).

G. GIACUMAKIS, JR.

ENSIGN. *See* BANNER.

EN-TAPPUAH ĕn tăp yŏŏ ə (עין תפוח, meaning *spring of the apple tree,* Josh 17:7). This spring was located at the town of Tappuah on the border between Ephraim and Manasseh in central Pal. It is usually identified with modern Tell Sheikh Abu Zarad about eight m. S of Shechem.

The town was a Canaanite stronghold which held out against the Israelites for a period of time during the conquest. The town's lands fell to the onslaught of Manasseh, but it held out until it was finally taken over by Ephraim (Josh 17:8).

G. GIACUMAKIS, JR.

The well at En-rogel, a spring just south of Jerusalem in the Kidron Valley. ©*M.P.S.*

ENUMA ELISH ə nū′ mä ĕ′ lish, the opening phrase and title of the most important Mesopotamian cosmological text. The text was written on seven tablets in the Babylonian dialect of Akkad. and used as the ceremonial epic in the New Year's ritual at the great temple of Esagila. The standard VS of the text dates from the 1st millennium B.C. but the true provenience of the epic is controversial. The text has been recovered by the excavations at Nineveh, Ashur and Kish, and several edd. and many trs. have been published. The contents of the tablets are as follows: Tablet I, the initial coming into being of the most primitive forces and gods, the rage of the sea goddess Tiamat. Tablet II, Tiamat and her monsters gird for battle against the gods who take Marduk (in some VSS Aššur) as their champion. Tablet III, the assembly of the gods decrees the outcome of the impending battle and the glory of Marduk. Tablet IV, Marduk prevails over Tiamat in a gruesome struggle and dissects the cadaver. Tablet V, Marduk constructs the cosmos and the cosmological order from the remains of Tiamat. Tablet VI, Tiamat's captive henchman, Kingu, is slain and dissected and his blood used to make mankind. Tablet VII, a list of the magical names of Marduk to which is attached a short epilogue. The text has been proposed by the followers of the pan-Babylonian school of critics as the true source of the Biblical story of creation. A brief survey of the two texts will show that they are only superficially related and that the Biblical account is of a considerably higher order of thought. The epic of Enuma Elish is of low literary quality in consideration of some of the marvelously eloquent texts such as Gilgamesh, Ludlul Bel Nemeqi and the like.

BIBLIOGRAPHY. ANET (1955); tr. by E. A. Speiser; A. Heidel, *The Babylonian Genesis* (1942); W. White, "Enūma Eliš and the OT," (thesis) Westminster Theological Seminary (1963); A. L. Oppenheim, *Ancient Mesopotamia* (1964), 177-203, 232, 264ff.

W. WHITE, JR.

ENVY (קִנְאָה ; *ardor, zeal, jealousy, envy*; φθόνος; *envy*; ζῆλος; *jealousy, envy*. The Eng. word "envy" comes from the Lat. word *invidere* "in—against"; *videre*—"to look at"), meaning "to look askance at," or "to have hatred or ill will toward another." It is a feeling of displeasure and ill will because of another's advantages, possessions, etc.; a malign feeling toward another who possesses that which one greatly desires.

1. The OT. The Heb. word *qin'āh* has a good meaning and an evil meaning. In its good sense of "zeal" and "jealousy" it is used repeatedly of God and of good men; while in its evil sense of "envy" there are comparatively few instances, and it is never used of God. Basically it means "burning," "glowing," a "getting red in the face," and thus denotes intense emotion. From this come the diverse meanings of "zeal," "jealousy," and "envy." The exact meaning is determined by the context of the passage in which the word is found. In many passages the KJV has "envy" where the RSV has "jealousy" (Gen 37:11; Num 11:29; Ps 106:16; Isa 11:13; etc.).

Both the Psalms and Proverbs warn against the temptation of becoming envious of evil men when they seem to prosper in spite of their wrongdoing (Pss 37:1; 73:2, 3; Prov 3:31; 23:17; 24:1, 19). The author of Ecclesiastes (4:4) observes that men are driven to work and to develop their skills when they envy the prosperity of their neighbors. The OT abounds in examples of the evil effects of envy —among them Jacob and Esau, Rachel and Leah (Gen 30:1), Joseph and his brothers, Haman and Mordecai.

2. The NT. There are two Gr. words rendered "envy": *phthónos*, which uniformly has an evil meaning, and *zēlos*, which, like *qin'ah*, has both a good and a bad meaning, sometimes (a) "zeal," "enthusiasm"; (b) sometimes "jealousy," "rivalry." As in the OT, in many passages the KJV has "envy" where the RSV has "jealousy" (Rom 13:13; 2 Cor 12:20; James 3:14, 16). Envy is said to have led to the crucifixion of Jesus (Matt 27:18). It is listed with the worst of sins by Jesus and by Paul (Mark 7:22; Rom 1:29; Gal 5:21). Christians are warned against it (Gal 5:26; 1 Pet 2:1). James 4:5 has "envy" in the KJV, but the passage is of uncertain meaning and has been interpreted in a variety of ways.

BIBLIOGRAPHY. R. C. Trench, *Synonyms of the New Testament* (9th ed. 1880), 86-90.

S. BARABAS

EPAENETUS ĭ pe′ nə təs (Ἐπαίνετος, *praised*). A Christian affectionately greeted (Rom 16:5) as "the first convert in Asia for Christ."

"My beloved" indicates Paul's warm affection for Epaenetus; "the first fruits of Asia" (ASV) marks his special distinction as the first convert to Christ in the province of Asia. The TR reading "of Achaia" is poorly attested; this wrong reading was prob. derived from 1 Corinthians 16:15. Such senior Christians naturally assumed positions of leadership in the Church. That Epaenetus was an accepted leader is implied in Paul's mention of him immediately after Prisca (Priscilla) and Aquila.

It is not stated that Epaenetus was the personal convert of Paul. He may have been won by Priscilla and Aquila before Paul returned to Ephesus (Acts 18:27).

This mention of Epaenetus has been used to support the claim of an Ephesian destination for Romans 16. But the mention of more than twenty others with no known Ephesian connections blunts the claim.

D. E. HIEBERT

EPAPHRAS ĕp′ ə frăs (Ἐπαφρᾶς, a contracted

Epaphras was a native of Colossae. This is the "Tell" of Colossae. ©Lev

form of 'Επαφρόδιτος, *charming*). A native of Colossae and founder of the Colossian church, who was with Paul when he wrote Colossians (Col 1:7, 8; 4:12, 13; Philem 23). He is not to be confused with Epaphroditus (Phil 2:25; 4:18), a member of the Philippian church.

Epaphras may have been Paul's convert. As Paul's representative he had evangelized Colossae (Col 1:7 RSV) and the neighboring towns of Laodicea and Hierapolis (4:12, 13) during Paul's Ephesian ministry (Acts 19:10). His visit to Paul in Rome and his report concerning conditions in the churches of the Lycus Valley caused Paul to write Colossians (Col 1:7-9).

Paul's high esteem for Epaphras is seen in the terms he applies to him, "our beloved fellow servant," "a faithful minister of Christ on our behalf" (Col 1:7), "a servant of Christ Jesus" (4:12), and "my fellow prisoner" (Philem 23). Because the last term is applied to Aristarchus (Col 4:10), the probable meaning is that Epaphras and Aristarchus alternated in voluntarily sharing Paul's imprisonment.

The unique distinction of Epaphras is Paul's praise of him for his fervent intercession for the churches in the Lycus Valley (Col 4:12, 13).

BIBLIOGRAPHY. Commentaries on Colossians in loc. H. S. Seekings, *The Men of the Pauline Circle* (1914), 147-153; H. C. Lees, *St. Paul's Friends* (1918), 146-159; D. E. Hiebert, *Working By Prayer* (1953), 67-82; H. Lockyer, *All the Men of the Bible* (1958), 110, 111.

D. E. HIEBERT

EPAPHRODITUS ĭ păf' rə dī təs ('Επαφρόδιτος, *handsome, charming*). A member of the Philippian church who brought an offering to Paul at Rome (Phil 2:25-30; 4:18).

His Gr. name, corresponding to the Lat. Venustus (belonging to Venus), indicated a non-Jewish origin. The name was common in both its Gr. and Lat. forms. It was also common in a contracted form, Epaphras. There is no evidence to identify him with the Epaphras from Colossae (Col 1:7; 4:12).

Epaphroditus was an esteemed member of the Philippian church; that he was an officer is not certain. He was commissioned to deliver the church's offering to Paul (Phil 4:18) and to stay and help him (2:25, 30). In relation to the Philippians Paul calls him "your messenger and minister to my need," sent to serve Paul on their behalf. He became dangerously ill at Rome "for the work of Christ." His sickness possibly came from exposure on the trip, but more prob. from overexertion in fulfilling his commission at Rome, "risking his life to complete your service to me."

After his slow recovery Paul felt it best to send Epaphroditus back home. He was distressed because of anxiety for him at Philippi and longed to return. Paul sent him back with the letter to the Philippians and asked them to receive Epaphroditus "in the Lord with all joy." Paul's description of Epaphroditus as "my brother and fellow worker and fellow soldier" indicates his own high esteem of him.

BIBLIOGRAPHY. Commentaries in loc. J. A. Beet, "Epaphroditus and the gift from Philippi," *The Expositor*, 3rd ser. IX (1889), 64-66; H. S. Seekings, *The Men of the Pauline Circle* (1914), 157-164; H. C. Lees, *St. Paul's Friends* (1918), 192-209; A. T. Robertson, *Types of Preachers in the NT* (1922), 230-238.

D. E. HIEBERT

EPHAH (MEASURE). *See* WEIGHTS AND MEASURES.

EPHAH **ē′ fə** (עיפה, LXX Γαφερ, Γεφαρ, Γαιφα(ρ), Γαιφα, Γαιφαηλ, *dark one*). A masculine and feminine personal name. 1. A son of Midian, related to Abraham through his concubine Keturah (Gen 25:4; 1 Chron 1:33). Isaiah speaks poetically of the young camels of Midian and Ephah (60:6). Some MSS of the LXX confuse the two sons of Midian whose names are similar (cf. Gen 25:4 and above).

2. A concubine of Caleb who bore three sons in the tribe of Judah (1 Chron 2:46).

3. A son of Jahdai in the tribe of Judah (1 Chron 2:47).

E. B. SMICK

EPHAI **ē′ fī** (עיפי, Jer 40:8). He was an inhabitant of Netophah, a city or group of villages near Bethlehem. His sons were among the officers who placed themselves under the authority of Gedaliah, the Babylonian appointed governor of Judah after the Exile. The phrase, "the sons of Ephai," is left out of the parallel passage in 2 Kings 25:23-25.

G. GIACUMAKIS, JR.

EPHER **ē′ fər** (עפר, LXX Αφερ, Γαφερ, Γοφερ, Οφερ; *a young hart, stag*). A masculine proper name. 1. A son of Midian in the line of those who descended from Abraham through his concubine Keturah. Abraham sent these descendants away eastward into the E country (Gen 25:4-6; 1 Chron 1:33). There may have been more than one clan of Midian, or the name may be used broadly of different peoples. Some who were the descendants of Abraham were helpful to Israel (Exod 3:1) while others became bitter enemies (Num 31:2ff.; Judg 6:1ff.).

2. A son of Ezrah in the tribe of Judah (1 Chron 4:17).

3. A head of a household and mighty warrior in Manasseh (1 Chron 5:24).

E. B. SMICK

EPHES-DAMMIM **ē fĭz dăm′ ĭm** (אפס דמים, *end* or *boundary of blood*). A site in the territory of Judah between Socoh and Azekah (1 Sam 17:1), where the Philistines encamped. It is elsewhere designated PAS-DAMMIM (1 Chron 11:13). Some have conjectured that the deep red color of the soil gave rise to the concept of blood. It is more probable that the site was so named because of the number of battles fought there between Israel and the Philistines. Archeologist Abel thinks the place is to be identified with *Beit Faṣed*, which is SE of Socoh. However, it has been usual to identify the place with the ruins of Damun, about 4 m. NE of Socoh. Latest atlases indicate that the site cannot be located with exactness.

C. L. FEINBERG

EPHESIANS, LETTER OF PAUL TO THE (πρὸς Ἐφεσίους). This letter has been known traditionally as the epistle written to the "saints" at Ephesus. The assignment of this destination was in accord with the evidence of the TR (1:1) and (apart from Marcion) was generally supported by the tradition of the early Fathers. However, the phrase, "who are at Ephesus and faithful" (1:1), is not in the earliest and best texts (P^{46} B, ℵ, 1739) but appears to be the result of the incorporation of an early marginal gloss. The original form of the letter was apparently without address, Tychicus (6:21) having the responsibility to introduce the letter personally to those for whom it was intended. The letter was written to the "saints" of Asia Minor (6:21, cf. Col 4:7f.). When the need arose to identify the letter more specifically with a church center, Ephesus, because of its proximity to the region involved and its importance as the chief city of Asia, was chosen. Instrumental in the assignment may have been the fact that Paul apparently had written no other letter to this important city, in spite of the fact that he had carried on an extensive and prolonged mission in its environs (cf. Acts 19:8, 10). It is possible that when the letter was read at Ephesus, the church simply appropriated it and was responsible for introducing the marginal gloss into the text. When the prestige that a church enjoyed who had been a recipient of a letter from an apostle is considered, such an eventuality cannot be excluded.

The reference to Tychichus and to the apostle's "chains" (Eph 6:20) identifies this letter with others written by Paul prob. during his Rom. imprisonment (cf. Col 4:7 and Philem 9, 13, 23). Its close relationship in subject matter to Colossians fixes rather closely the time of its composition (A.D. 60-62). The epistle focuses upon the Church, triumphant and exalted, in which Christ's reconciling activity is being demonstrated. Because of current ecumenical concerns, Ephesians has assumed a dominant place in the life and study of the Christian community.

1. Authorship and canonicity
2. Arguments against the genuineness of Ephesians
   a. Vocabulary
   b. The relationship of Ephesians to the other Pauline epistles
   c. Style
   d. Subjective questions
3. Origin and destination
4. Content and organization
5. Outline of Ephesians
6. Theology of the epistle
   a. Church
   b. Holy Spirit

1. Authorship and canonicity. The author of the letter identifies himself as Paul, the apostle to the Gentiles (1:1; 3:1). In a genuinely Pauline manner, he makes frequent personal references to himself and his activities, incorporating these statements into the body of his argument (cf. 3:3f., 7, 13f.; 4:1, 17; 5:32; 6:19f.). The vocabulary, subject matter, and general theological approach are admittedly Pauline. Moreover, the external attestation for the knowledge and use of the book as a genuine Pauline writing in the ancient Church is wholly positive. Some scholars feel they can detect its influence on 1 Peter and Acts. Strong reminiscences of it are to be found in most of the Apostolic Fathers; Polycarp, for example, includes an explicit citation of its text. It is found also in the writings of the heretical schools as well as in the Apologists. Although Irenaeus is the first to cite it as Pauline, it is clear that this was the common understanding of the Church. As such, it is included in the Muratorian Canon, in Marcion's statement of books to be accepted (though under the name of the Epistle to the Laodiceans), and in every subsequent list of Pauline writings. Its authorship was never disputed in the ancient Church nor was its place in the canon ever challenged. Nonetheless, with the rise of critical studies in the 18th cent. it soon became a "suspect" book. Its appearance in the TR under the title of "The Epistle to the Ephesians" immediately served to compromise its integrity. That Paul could have written such an impersonal letter, devoid of personal references to people with whom he had labored three years was deemed incredible. Moreover, it was judged an absurdity that Paul would write to the Ephesians in terms of "mutual hearsay" (cf. "assuming that you have heard of the stewardship of God's grace that was given to me" [3:2] or "because I have heard of your faith in the Lord Jesus" [1:15]). The whole tenor of the letter showed that it was written by someone who, although he had a great interest and concern for the people involved, had no firsthand acquaintanceship with them. For these early critics, who had no reason to be suspicious of the text (and no adequate critical text to consult in any instance), there could be only one conclusion: Paul had not written this letter.

Building on this seemingly secure conclusion, critics began to look for other evidence of the inauthentic character of this epistle. Singled out were the extraordinarily close relationship of Ephesians to Colossians, the verbose and unusually long sentences of Ephesians, the peculiar phrase, "his holy apostles and prophets" (3:5; cf. 2:20), and the presence of many "non-Pauline" words.

Just at the time when the spurious nature of the epistle seemed beyond question, however, new MS discoveries and textual studies showed that the letter had not been addressed to the church at Ephesus. This meant that the primary evidence for deciding against the authenticity of Ephesians was no longer valid. The problem became then whether the arguments dependent upon the vocabulary, style, and internal inconsistencies were sufficient or certain enough to reject an epistle that had the strongest possible external and internal attestation to Pauline authorship. On this question critical scholarship became divided. English scholars generally defended, Ger. scholars with a few notable exceptions rejected, and American scholars appeared on both sides of the issue. At the present time, the situation remains largely unchanged.

What tends to complicate the debate is the fact that (1) there is little agreement concerning the basis for rejection among the critics who reject the authenticity of the epistle; (2) many of the arguments advanced are mutually exclusive (e.g. most American scholars who reject Ephesians accept the genuineness of Colossians. Yet the arguments against Ephesians advanced by Ger. scholarship would make Colossians inauthentic as well); (3) arguments that have been shown to be invalid continue to be presented against Ephesians (e.g. arguments based on vocabulary statistics. In such instances it appears that some critics depend on the number of objections which can be raised rather than the decisive value of any given argument).

2. Arguments against the genuineness of the epistle. a. *Vocabulary*. One of the older but more persistent arguments advanced against the genuineness of the letter is the number of "non-Pauline" words it contains. F. W. Beare, in the IB states it this way. "There are, to begin with, an extraordinarily large number of *hapax legomena*—eighty-two words not found elsewhere in the NT." Johnson, in the IDB uses the same argument: "Linguistic considerations alone are not decisive; yet note that Ephesians has about a hundred non-Pauline words, of which some forty are unique in the NT."

However, every writing of Paul, including the brief note to Philemon, has a number of "non-Pauline" words. Some of these occur nowhere else in the NT (commonly called *hapax legomena*), whereas others, though they occur elsewhere in the NT, do not appear in any other Pauline writing. Out of the total vocabulary of Ephesians (529 words) 95 are "non-Pauline" (the statistics do not include the pastorals since many critics question their genuineness also). The number indeed appears imposing. Romans, however, has 292 non-Pauline words, 1 Corinthians 283, 2 Corinthians 207, and Galatians with a vocabulary of 526 words has an identical number of 95 non-Pauline words. And Philippians with 84 non-Pauline words out of a total vocabulary of 448, has a higher percentage than Ephesians. Yet these letters have been almost universally accepted as Paul's.

Every study of non-Pauline vocabulary (*see* P. N. Harrison, *The Problem of the Pastoral Epistles*; J. Schmid, *Der Epheserbrief Des Apostels Paulus*; and the very sophisticated study of K. Grayston and G. Herdan, "The Authorship of the Pastorals in the Light of Statistical Linguistics" NTS VI [1959], 1-15;

and the author's own investigation, G. W. Barker, *A Critical Evaluation of the Lexical and Linguistic Data Advanced by E. J. Goodspeed and Supported by C. L. Mitton in a Proposed Solution to the Problem of the Authorship and Date of Ephesians*) supports the Pauline authorship of Ephesians.

A modern study by Goodspeed has sent the argument based on vocabulary in a new direction. He has not based his argument on the number of non-Pauline words but on the more frequent appearance of these words in writings of the tenth decade. In a limited study he has shown that thirty-one of the thirty-two non-Pauline words studied in Ephesians reappear in Acts, Revelation, Hebrews, and 1 Peter, writings dated by him in the tenth decade. This served to confirm Goodspeed's thesis that Ephesians was written by a disciple of Paul sometime around A.D. 90. Goodspeed failed, however, to test his findings from Ephesians by similar studies of unchallenged Pauline writings. If he had done so, he would have found that Galatians, for example, has 61 words that met his criteria, 56 of which reappear in the same four writings as is true of Ephesians. Moreover, they occur with even greater frequency (433 instances to 235). The same is true of 1 Corinthians, Romans, 2 Corinthians, and Philippians. All that Goodspeed discovered was an unusual trait of a *genuine* epistle, not a proof of inauthenticity.

It has been alleged that an unusually high number of non-Pauline words in Ephesians reappear in the writings of the early Fathers, again supporting a late date for Ephesians. The facts, however, prove to be contrary. In comparable studies, Ephesians shows fewer words that appear either in the Apostolic Fathers or the Apologists percentage-wise than does Galatians or Romans. If the Apostolic Fathers alone are compared, Ephesians shows proportionally fewer such words than 1 Corinthians or Philippians. On the other hand, non-Pauline writings show a vast difference in this respect. Ephesians has the identical statistical pattern of the genuine epistles of Paul. That such a pattern could have been effected deliberately or unconsciously by an imitator seems wholly unreasonable.

The appearance of certain "key" words not before encountered is cited as an argument against Ephesians. Specifically noted are: *ἐν τοῖς ἐπουρανίοις* (5 times), *ὁ διάβολος* (2 times), *ἀσωτία, εὔσπλαγχνος ὁσιότης,* and *πολιτεία.* However, there is nothing esp noteworthy about this. Of a total Pauline vocabulary of 2,177 words, over half (1203) occur in a single epistle. Inevitably included are key terms. In Romans, Paul uses as key terms words that never appear elsewhere among the Pauline epistles: *ἀπείθεα* (5 times), *δικαίωμα* (5 times), *νικάω* (3 times), *ἀσύνετος* (3 times), *προγινώσκω* (2 times), *ἐγκεντρίζω* (6 times), *ἀπιστία* (4 times). Nonetheless these words become common terms in the later lit.

b. The relationship of Ephesians to other Pauline epistles. It has been alleged that Ephesians reads as a "mosaic," implying that it is "shot through" with expressions from earlier Christian writings (cf. Käsemann, p. 289). Goodspeed finds that out of 618 phrases in Ephesians, 550 have unmistakable parallels in the other Pauline letters either in "word or substance." Although Mitton concedes that Goodspeed has overstated the case, he still finds 250 phrases in Ephesians that have parallels in other Pauline writings—an amount far in excess of a genuine Pauline epistle. Neither Goodspeed or Mitton, however, exercised the same care to discover in their test book, Philippians, parallels to other Pauline epistles, as they did with Ephesians. They include verbatim parallels between Ephesians and the other Paulines, six consisting of a single word, twenty-eight phrases of two words, eighteen of three, and twelve of four. Of the twelve parallels consisting of more than five words, seven occur in Colossians, two are citations from the OT, and two more are formulae benedictions, and one consists of a standard Pauline introduction formula.

On the other hand, approximately one half of the parallels between Philippians and the other Pauline letters are overlooked. If one counts the number of words in Ephesians that occur in phrases that have exact verbal correspondence with other Pauline writings, the total amount will be 148. If one makes a similar count of Philippians, the corresponding total will be 129. Considering the difference in length between the two books, the results are negligible. Moreover, if one subtracts the Colossians parallels from both books, Philippians is left with 122 instances of verbatim likenesses compared to 115 in Ephesians. The evidence indicates that although there is a remarkable relation between Ephesians and Colossians, there is nothing at all unusual concerning the relation of Ephesians to the other Pauline epistles.

c. Style. It has been long observed that the style of Ephesians is remarkably unlike that of the other Pauline letters. There is a predilection for overly long conglomerate sentences, synonyms heaped one upon another, and endless genitival connections. Although the phenomena can be paralleled elsewhere in Paul (cf. Ernst Percy, *Die Probleme der Kolosser- und Epheserbriefe*) such Sem., syntactical phenomena occurs four times as often in Ephesians as in all other epistles of the Pauline corpus (cf. K. G. Kuhn, "Der Epheser im Lichte der Qumrantexte," NTS VII [1960], p. 334f.). The style has been variously described as "Hymnic-liturgical" (Goodspeed), "Meditative-doxological" (Käsemann); and "Liturgical-prayerful" (M. Barth). Yet the style phenomena in Ephesians cannot alone be used to decide the issue of its genuineness. The

A view of the theater at Ephesus. ©*V.E.*

familiar Pauline phrases are clearly in evidence and the pattern of thought is admittedly Pauline. What distinguishes Ephesians from the other epistles is not so much the presence of that which is non-Pauline, as it is the concentrated use of the Pauline language of worship.

d. *Subjective questions.* Other questions are raised by those who doubt the authenticity of this epistle. Would Paul have written two letters so much alike as Colossians and Ephesians? Would he have employed the same words (e.g. μυστήριον or οἰκονομία) but have given them new meanings? Would he have referred to the apostles as "holy," or to the Church as built upon the apostles and prophets? Could he have conceived of the Church as "universal," believed that Christ descended into Hades, or refrained from mentioning the Parousia?

The problem with these questions, however, is their subjective character. By their very nature, they defy objective analysis. Their answers depend heavily on our own prejudices of what we think would be appropriate for Paul in a given situation. There is no possibility of determining from a 20th cent. viewpoint what Paul could or could not have thought or written. It is just as difficult to enter the thought-world of "baptizing for the dead" (1 Cor 15:29), being transported "to the third heaven" (2 Cor 12:2), or "delivering someone over to Satan" (1 Cor 5:5). If any of these references had occured in Ephesians they would most certainly have constituted additional evidence for the presence of ungenuine Pauline utterances.

In summary, the internal considerations, where they can be reduced to objective, statistical data, clearly support Pauline authorship. The external data is early and weighty, and has always been recognized as tipping the scales heavily toward genuineness. What remains are those differences of style, mood, word usage, and point of view that confront us for the first time in this letter. Most critics will acknowledge that no one illustration of difficulty from this material would by itself be sufficient to cause us to question the genuineness of the writing.

It is this situation that demands confronting the question that H. J. Cadbury has so aptly framed: "which is more likely that an imitator in the first century composed a writing ninety or ninety-five percent in accordance with Paul's style or that Paul himself wrote a letter diverging five or ten percent from his usual style?" The force of Cadbury's question becomes even more formidable if one allows that the circumstances that brought forth this particular letter are undeniably different from what was true of the other Pauline letters and that they require both differences in style and subject matter.

3. Origin and destination. In the beginning of Paul's ministry, he was almost totally consumed in establishing and maintaining his churches. Little time was left to him for anything else, esp. for "writing theology" or publishing treatises on baptism or church government. If indeed he wrote at all, his letters were limited to that which was critical for the mission. His epistles from this period are consequently relatively easy to fix as to occasion, date, and purpose. They abound in personal references and make frequent reference to the local situation.

Toward the end of Paul's life, this situation changed. Paul's arrests grew more frequent and the amount of time he spent in prison became a primary factor. He was arrested at Ephesus and prob. imprisoned. He gained his freedom, but was arrested in Jerusalem. Two long years were spent in prison at Caesarea followed by two more years at Rome. Although prison itself represented no new experience for Paul (cf. 2 Cor 11:23) the curtailment of his freedom for such extended periods was new. Particularly hard to bear was the fact that his contact with his churches was limited to that maintained through intermediaries who came to visit him.

If Paul lost something by being cut off from personal contact with his churches, he was to some extent compensated by the opportunity he gained for reflecting upon the Christian mission as it had developed and as to its future. In such a review Paul could not have avoided certain conclusions: (1) The mission of the Church in the world was going to involve a longer time than was originally supposed; (2) the time could not be far distant when the apostles and their associates would no longer be available to lead the Church; (3) God's plan from the beginning must have anticipated this fact; (4) there were mysteries in God's dealing with Jews and Gentiles yet to be understood.

Paul's attention was inevitably drawn to the consideration of these questions, and the so-called "prison" correspondences logically include some refinement of the apostle's thinking on these subjects. Also the epistles of this period understandably bear less of the personal touch. Large sections of the writings seem to have been predigested. More of it seems to have originated out of the life and worship of the Christian community. If the above is assumed, it is understandable why a reconstruction of events leading to the publication of Ephesians must indeed be tenuous. Apart from the reference to Tychicus (6:21) and Paul's imprisonment (3:1), Ephesians is void of any objective clue as to occasion. What may be concluded concerning the occasion is largely dependent upon what can be inferred from a study of the subject matter, and the style and language of the text. Two elements relating to Ephesians, however, demand special attention and must be included in any such reconstruction.

1) A significant number of hymns (e.g. 1:3-12, 20-23; 2:4-10, 14-18), creedal confessions, and stereotyped liturgical formulas are included in the text (cf. Schille). It is the presence of this material in the letter that tends to transform it from prose (an epistle) to liturgical poetry (a tract). Either the subject matter has caused the author to elevate his style (which accounts for the inclusion of worship elements in it), or the author included elements of worship because he meant his tract to be used by worshiping communities in a special context (cf. Goodspeed and Mitton). Those who opt for the latter possibility are impressed with the value of the writing for the newly baptized. The opening prayer reads like a benediction given before a baptismal service (cf. N. A. Dahl), ch. 2 is practically a baptismal-homily, and chs. four to six include catechetical instructions particularly pertinent for the newly baptized. The very tone of the epistle acts to instruct the believer concerning membership in the Church. Kirby offers a more sophisticated reconstruction of the baptismal elements, seeing in the letter a Christianized form of the renewal of the covenant. Others suggest that the baptismal liturgy is not primarily meant for the instruction of catechumens but to recall to the readers their own baptism: the liturgy in which they participated, the confession they made, the hymns they sang, and the exhortation to which they gave heed. Building on this commitment, the author was anxious that his readers press on until all "attain the unity of the faith and the knowledge of the Son of God" (cf. Lane).

In any instance it seems likely that the liturgical style of the letter was not accidental (i.e. an expression of the peculiar style of the author). Either the writer chose this style deliberately because it furnished the best context for the materials he was using, or else it was dictated by the tastes of the community to which he was writing and the usage to which it would be put.

2) Ephesians has a distinct relationship to Colossians. The reference to Tychicus in both letters and the overlapping of vocabulary, style, and subject matter makes it clear that the origin of Ephesians cannot be explained apart from Colossians. The usual explanation is that Paul first wrote Colossians as a polemical epistle and then adapted portions from it for use in Ephesians. A close study of specific texts, however, makes this solution doubtful. The fact is that although there are passages where Colossians appears to offer the more original statement, there are no less than twenty-five passages where the converse is true. Equally difficult is the fact that words and phrases in Colossians are used in different combinations and with quite different meanings in Ephesians. That the same author within a limited time span should have composed *de novo* two letters to the same area with such startling alterations seems incomprehensible. A different solution is demanded.

One possibility is that the Ephesian letter was already in process of preparation when the Colossian controversy arose. Paul had been utilizing his time in prison to collect from the community appropriate hymns, prayers, and confessions, which he intended to work over into a general tract meant to instruct catechumens among the churches of Asia Minor. These plans were interrupted, however, by the crisis in the Lycus Valley triggered by a fresh invasion of Gnostic type speculation. An unwholesome asceticism was being advocated in the church along with false teaching concerning the person of Christ and His place in the cosmos. The issue was serious enough to require an immediate and specific response from Paul.

A letter was prepared and addressed to the church at Colossae. Because Paul had saturated his mind with the worship language of the area with its speculative thought in preparation of his Ephesian tract, it was inevitable that he would draw upon this ready reservoir for his epistle to the Colossians. Many of the same words and phrases that later appear in Ephesians are used, although here in a more specifically "Pauline" formulation.

Afterward, when Paul hastened to complete the Ephesian tract so that it could be sent along with Tychichus, certain overlappings of subject material occurred. Some of the things mentioned in Colossians were included in Ephesians but in a more expanded form whereas others are referred to only cursorily.

The difficult problem, then, of the differences between Colossians and Ephesians in word usage and phraseology can be accounted for in this reconstruction by

(1) the difference of purpose of the two letters;
(2) the result of adapting language drawn from worship materials to an epistolary style;
(3) the utilization by Paul of some worship materials that he collected from the churches but had not necessarily authored.

4. Content and organization. *The first main division (1:3-3:21).* The epistle begins with a simple preface (vv. 1, 2) and moves directly to a beautiful doxology or hymn of praise to God (1:3-14). In it Paul thanks God the Father for all those ways He has blessed man in Christ: that from the beginning God

(1) chose man to stand in His presence (v. 4)
(2) destined him for sonship (v. 5)
(3) redeemed him through the blood of Christ (v. 7)
(4) forgave him his trespasses (v. 7), and
(5) revealed to him the mystery of His own divine will (v. 9).

Most of all he rejoices that the time has come

when the eternal plan of God set forth in Christ for the world is to be accomplished, which is: *to bring into union everything and everybody, earthly and heavenly, through Christ Jesus.* This latter statement (v. 10) provides the climax to the hymn and at the same time introduces the theme of the epistle.

Paul proceeds by showing (1:11-14) that God's plan is already prevailing among Jews who believe as well as among Gentiles who, having received the same "guarantee" of the Holy Spirit, are now awaiting with their Jewish brethren the full manifestation of their mutual inheritance.

Paul continues with the main body of his expositions (1:15f.), which is framed as a "prayer meditation" concluding at the end of ch. 3. He prays that his readers might have wisdom to understand the significance of God's plan as it relates to them. Especially does he pray that they lay hold of the hope that God has now given them, that they be open to receiving the riches that are part of the new inheritance, and, above all, that they experience the greatness of God's power available to them. Paul stated that this power is identical to that which raised Jesus from the dead, established Him at God's right hand, and gave Him dominion over everything including the Church (1:16-23). Paul continues by showing that this power provides similar benefits to His followers (2:1-10). Though they were dead in trespasses and sins, God has made them alive, elevating them in Christ to God's right hand in the heavenlies, and giving them dominion by manifesting the Father's workmanship in their lives.

In the next section (2:11-22), the prayer formulation momentarily gives way to admonition and instruction: they are not to forget their former status as Gentiles, when they were strangers to the covenant of promise and without God. They are to compare that situation with their present circumstances as members of the household of God. They are to remember that it was only their relation to Jesus Christ that reversed their status. By joining them together to His body on the cross, Christ broke down the wall that shut them out, brought peace between them and the Jews, and reconciled both to the Father. Now together, they constitute a new worshiping community, banded together and growing into a holy temple, a dwelling place of God in the Spirit.

The prayer that Paul began in Ephesians 1:15, and amplified by a discourse on God's power (1:20f.) and what it has availed for them as Gentiles (2:11f.), is resumed in 3:1. As soon as he takes up this prayer, however, he interrupts it with an account of his own ministry. He explained how his understanding of God's mysterious intention to make Gentiles fellow-heirs and members of the same body had functioned in his own life. He also makes clear that this understanding of the mystery is the one he shares with the apostles and prophets. In spite of the primacy that is accorded apostles and prophets in this text, Paul declares that it is the Church, not the apostolate, which is to be the sign of the manifold wisdom of God to the principalities and powers in heavenly places.

Paul concludes his prayer meditation with a series of moving petitions on behalf of his readers (3:14-19) and ends with a doxology (vv. 20, 21).

The second main division (4:1-6:24). In the practical section of Ephesians, Paul offers simple words of admonition to guide the believer in each of the four spheres in which a Christian lives his life: in the church he is to maintain unity; in society, to practice purity; in the household, to manifest love and respect; and against Satan and the powers of darkness, to exercise strength.

Paul exhorts his readers to unity (4:1-16) by appealing that they maintain the kind of conduct that will give evidence of their Christian commitment. This means that the individual Christian will give himself to the practice of humility, gentleness, patience, and loving forbearance and will be actively engaged in maintaining the spirit of unity in the body of Christ. To support this commitment to unity, Paul cites the sevenfold oneness unique to the Christian faith. He then discusses individual gifts and their function, showing that diversity of service is not a contradiction to unity, but a necessary means of achieving it.

Paul began his practical exhortation by challenging his readers to walk worthily of their calling (4:1). He continues this theme in the exhortation to purity (4:17-5:20), which contrasts the Christian life to pagan values. The key term for his admonition is "walk," which occurs four times in the section: "walk not as other Gentiles" (4:17 KJV); "walk in love" (5:2); "walk as children of light" (5:8) and "walk responsibly redeeming the time" (5:15). The section includes important appeals relating to the Holy Spirit (4:30; 5:18) as well as ethical instructions on how to treat fellow Christians (4:25f.; 4:32; 5:19).

To members of households, Paul gives an exhortation to love and respect one another (5:21). He asks them to realize unity through willing subjection to one another as to the Lord and by practicing self-sacrificing love. Husbands and wives are told that marriage is a symbol of the relation that exists between Christ and His Church (5:21-33). Children are reminded of the OT commandment and slaves and masters are warned of their responsibility to manifest Christ in their dealings one with the other.

Finally Paul exhorts his readers to exercise strength against the evil forces in the world (6:10-20). Although the appeal to be armed with God's weaponry is couched in personal terms, as if in individual encounter, the section continues the concern for oneness by asking the believers to make supplication for each other and for all the saints.

Conclusion (6:21-23). The letter's conclusion is brief as its introduction, with a simple reference to Tychicus and a benediction.

5. Outline of the epistle

I. The salutation (1:1, 2)
II. The teaching (1:3-3:21)
  A. A hymn of praise and thanksgiving for the revelation of God's eternal plan in Christ (1:3-14)
    1. The plan required that God
      a. elect us in Christ before the world began (v. 4)
      b. adopt us in Him as children (v. 5)
      c. redeem us through His blood (v. 7)
    2. It provided that all things earthly and heavenly become united in Him (v. 10)
    3. It resulted in Jews as well as Gentiles receiving the Holy Spirit, a guarantee of a mutual inheritance yet to be received (11-14)
  B. Prayer meditation (1:15-3:21)
    1. That they have wisdom to understand the majesty of God's plan (1:17) and the mighty power by which God will effect it (1:19-2:10). This power worked in Christ in that it
      a. raised Him from the dead (v. 20)
      b. gave Him dominion over everything (v. 21)
      c. made Him head over the Church (v. 22).
      This power works also for the believers (2:1-10) in that it
      a. makes them alive from the death through sin (v. 1)
      b. raises them with Christ in the heavenly places (v. 6)
      c. bestows on them the riches of God's grace (v. 7)
      d. creates them anew to good works (v. 10)
    2. That they remember how God's plan has already worked for the Gentiles in that it (2:11-22)
      a. removed their alienation (11-14)
      b. made them with the Jews one new man (v. 15)
      c. gave them access to the Father through the Spirit (v. 18)
      d. made them into a holy habitation of the Father (v. 21)
    3. That they understand Paul's relation to the plan and not become discouraged at his sufferings on their behalf (3:1-13). This plan
      a. came to him by revelation (v. 3)
      b. required that Gentiles become fellow heirs with the Jews (v. 6)
      c. made him a minister to Gentiles (v. 7)
    4. That they come to spiritual fullness (3:14-19)
    5. Benediction (3:20, 21)
III. The application (4:1-6:20)
  A. Exhortation to promote unity in the church (4:1-16)
    1. The need for consecration (4:1-6)
    2. The matter of diverse gifts (4:7-16)
  B. Exhortation to a life of purity in the world (4:17-5:20)
    1. A contrast with paganism (4:17-24)
    2. The new life style (4:25-5:7)
    3. Light against darkness (5:8-14)
    4. Closing appeal (5:15-20)
  C. Exhortation for love and respect among members of Christian households (5:21-6:9)
    1. Wives and husbands (5:21-33)
    2. Children and parents (6:1-4)
    3. Servants and masters (6:5-9)
  D. Exhortation to put on God's armor against spiritual enemies (6:10-20)
  E. Final greetings and benediction (6:21-24)

6. Theology. a. *Church.* The doctrine most extensively treated in the epistle is that of the Church. Three images are used to describe it: The body of Christ (1:23; 4:3-16); the bride of Christ (5:22f.); and the temple of the Holy Spirit (2:19-22). In Ephesians the concept that best defines the Church is the body, of which Christ is head. The addition of this latter phrase represents a development in Paul's way of thinking and speaking of the Church. It appears elsewhere only in Colossians, where it has obvious connections with Paul's statement in Christology. If Christ is head over the cosmos, the fullness of Him who fills all things, the preeminent One exercising dominion over all things, then He is head also over the Church. Christ's leadership over the Church has special consequences which Paul is concerned to work out in Ephesians. For the Church is also Christ's body. Its existence as His body is dependent on the death of His body on the cross and the renewed life from the Father by which He rose from the dead. In this body He also ascended to the Father. The community of believers who have received His renewed life by the Holy Spirit constitute His body on earth. Yet, because He fills this body with His own life, He transforms its existence from one that is only earthly to one that is "heavenly" (i.e. in the heavenlies). This does not mean that the Church no longer lives an empirical life in this world. It is concern with this life in the world that caused Paul to write most of his letters to the churches. But it does mean that the ultimate origin and destiny of the Church can no longer be found in the temporal sphere, but rather in that which is hidden in the eternal purposes of God; and what God has made known is that the Church, Christ's own body, was selected from before the ages to be the fullness of Him who fills all things.

What Paul envisions as the mission of the Church extends beyond reconciliation of Jew and Gentile, beyond the healing of the fundamental divisions within humanity, beyond even the overcoming of the alienation that cuts off men from God. It is the cosmos itself for which God has designed the Church. It is His purpose to combine through the Church, all things that exist—heavenly and earthly, creature and thing, temporal and eternal. All are the object of the Church's existence, the beneficiary of the divine grace that flows from its Head. Through the Church even the angelic powers ("principalities and powers in the heavenly places") are to be brought to know the wisdom of God.

Therefore, Christ loves the Church and labors over her that she may become a vessel worthy to fulfill the purposes of God. The apostle also suffered on her behalf that she may achieve maturity. Believers also play a part in all this. They are the body of Christ, who with the head constitute the single entity with which the Father has to do. Only as the members are filled from the head can the body grow and come to its full stature as the body of Christ. To assist the body in its growth, Christ bestows upon it gifts—apostles, prophets, evangelists, pastors, teachers—who promote the training of the individual members for service so that each one may be able to fulfill his function. As each contributes his particular activity according to the gift he has received, the body increases. Because it enjoys a common life derived from its head, it grows together in love and so serves the Lord.

b. *Holy Spirit.* Although there is not much new presented in Ephesians on the Spirit there is a significant summing up of the Spirit's relation to the believer. The Spirit is given to the believer at baptism (1:13), whose presence assures him of his share in the inheritance from the Father (1:14; 5:5). He enlightens the believer's mind to make him wise toward God (1:17); furnishes access to the Father (2:18); indwells the community, enabling it to become a holy temple of the Lord (2:22); makes the believer strong with the might of God (3:16); gives revelations to the apostles and prophets (3:5); and constitutes part of the oneness and unity of the believers (4:4).

Exhortations are also advanced in Ephesians concerning the Holy Spirit. Christians are admonished not to grieve the Spirit (4:30), urged to be filled with the Spirit (5:18), and instructed to pray as those led by the Spirit (6:18).

BIBLIOGRAPHY. Commentaries and Expositions. T. K. Abbott, *A Critical and Exegetical Commentary on the Epistles to the Ephesians and to the Colossians*, ICC (1897); B. F. Westcott, *Saint Paul's Epistle to the Ephesians* (1906); J. A. Robinson, *St. Paul's Epistle to the Ephesians* (1923); J. Schmid, *Der Epheserbrief Des Apostels Paulus. Biblische Studien, XXII*, 3 and 4 (1925); E. J. Goodspeed, *The Meaning of Ephesians* (1933); E. Percy, *Die Probleme der Kolosser-und Epheserbriefe* (1946); C. L. Mitton, *The Epistle to the Ephesians* (1951); F. W. Beare, "Introduction and Exegesis of Ephesians," IB, X. ed. G. A. Buttrick (1953); G. Schille, *Liturgisches Gut in Epheser* (1953); F. L. Cross, *Studies in Ephesians* (1956); E. K. Simpson and F. F. Bruce, *Commentary on the Epistles to the Ephesians and the Colossians* (1957); M. Barth, *The Broken Wall* (1959); F. F. Bruce, *The Epistle to the Ephesians* (1961); D. Guthrie, *New Testament Introduction.* The Pauline Epistles (1961); G. W. Barker, *A Critical Evaluation of the Lexical and Linguistic Data Advanced by E. J. Goodspeed and Supported by C. L. Mitton* (1962), unpublished Harvard University thesis; F. Foulkes, *The Epistle of Paul to the Ephesians* (1963); L. Cerfaux, "The Epistles of the Captivity" in *Introduction to the New Testament* ed. A. Robert and A. Feuillet (1965); C. R. Erdman, *The Epistle of Paul to the Ephesians* (1966); J. C. Kirby, *Ephesians, Baptism and Pentecost* (1968).

Key articles. C. L. Mitton, "Important Hypotheses Reconsidered; VII, The Authorship of the Epistle to the Ephesians," ExpT, LXVII (1955-1956), 195; G. Schille, "Der Autor des Epheserbriefes," TLZ, LXXXII (1957), 334; J. Coutts, "The Relationship of Ephesians and Colossians," NTS, IV (1958), 201; H. J. Cadbury, "The Dilemma of Ephesians," NTS V (1959), 91; K. Grayston and G. Herdan, "The Authorship of the Pastorals in the Light of Statistical Linguistics," NTS, VI (1959), 1; L. Cerfaux, "En faveur de l'authenticité des épîtres de la captivité Homogénécté doctrinale entre Éphésiens et les grandes épîtres." V (1960), 60; *Récherches Bibliques*, V (1960), 60; J. T. Sanders, "Hymnic Elements in Ephesians 1-3" ZNW LVI III-IV (1965), 214; E. Käsemann, "Ephesians and Acts" *Studies in Luke-Acts.* ed. by L. Keck and J. L. Martyn (1966); R. P. Martin, "An Epistle in Search of a Life Setting," ExpT, LXXIX (1968), 297.

G. W. BARKER

EPHESUS **ĕf' ə səs** (Ἔφεσος, possible meaning, *desirable*). The city of Ephesus lay at the mouth of the Cayster, between the Koressos Range and the sea, on the western coast of Asia Minor. Like all the river valleys around the great blunt end of the Asian continent's westward protrusion, that of the Cayster was a highway into the interior, the terminal of a trade route that linked with other roads converging and branching out toward the separated civilizations of the E and the Asian steppes. This was why Ephesus was chosen by the early Ionian colonists from Athens as a site for their colony. The Greeks called a colony an "emporion," or a "way in," because their concept of such settlement was that of a gateway by which an active self-governing community could tap the trade and resources of a foreign hinterland. Ephesus filled the role precisely.

By NT times, however, the great days of Ephesus' trade were long past. Like her rival Miletus, similarly located at the end of the Maeander Valley thirty m. to the S, Ephesus had difficulty with her harbor, the essential gateway to the sea. Deforestation was mankind's ancient folly, and no part of the Medi-

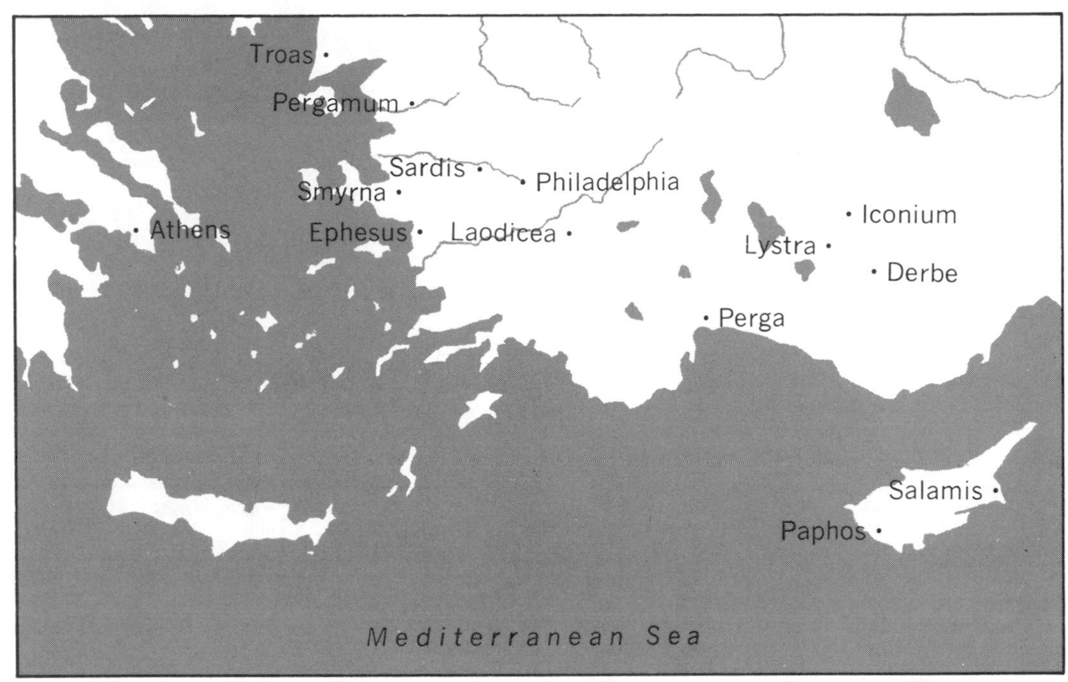

Map showing EPHESUS in relation to the rest of the New Testament world.

The Marble Street in Ephesus, view west from Agora. ©*Lev*

terranean world suffered worse than Asia Minor. The quest for timber and charcoal, the result of overgrazing, and the destructiveness of the Mediterranean goat, eternally nibbling and trampling the regenerating forest, denuded the hinterland. Topsoil slipped from the bare hillsides reft of their cover, streams became swamps, and the storm waters reached the sea laden with silt that choked the harbors. The harbor works of Ephesus may be traced today seven m. from the sea. Where once a sheltered gulf and waterway formed a safe haven for ships, there is now a reedy plain. Sir William Ramsay, most factual of archeologists, speaks in awe of the "uncanny volume of sound" which, in his day at the turn of the cent., greeted the evening visitor to the desolate levels where Ephesus once harbored her ships.

She was, none the less, over many centuries, fortunate in her engineers. The winding Maeander was silting up the harbor of Miletus as early as 500 B.C., and when that city suffered irreparable damage in the Pers. suppression of the great revolt of the Ionian Gr. cities, the choking up of her waterway passed beyond repair. It was Ephesus' opportunity, and a succession of rulers promoted the maintenance of the harbor facilities that the increased volume of trade and traffic demanded. The kings of Pergamum, most dynamic and powerful of the lesser successor states of Alexander's divided empire, did much for Ephesus, and when the Romans inherited the kingdom of Pergamum by the will of its last ruler, Attalus III, they continued the policy of promoting Ephesian trade. The Romans assumed the legacy of Pergamum in 133 B.C. and used Ephesus as the proconsul's seat. The city was proud of its name, "the Landing Place," and the title is found on a coin as late as the 3rd cent. of the Christian era. It is, perhaps, not without significance that the same coin bears the image of a small oar-propelled boat, an official's "barge," not the deep-hulled merchantmen that mark the city's pride in her sea-borne trade on the coins of earlier centuries. Paul's ship made no call there in A.D. 57. Domitian, at the end of the 1st cent., appears to have been the last ruler to attempt to repair the harbor of Ephesus, but trade had obviously declined two centuries before. By the time of Justinian, five centuries later, the battle with sand, silt, and mud was lost, and Ephesus was falling to ruins in a swampy terrain. Justinian, to be sure, built a church to Saint John on the site, in part compensation perhaps for the looting of the columns from the temple of Artemis for St. Sophia in Byzantium, where they may still be seen in the vast basilica. It is significant that the church of Saint John gave its name to the place. The Apostle John was called in Gr. "Hagios Theologos"—"The Holy Theologian." This was corrupted into Ayasoluk, the modern Turkish name for the village that stands near the site of ancient Ephesus.

Deepening economic depression and decline must have been a feature of Ephesus' life over the last cent. B.C. The city turned, as any anxious community might in such circumstances, to the equivalent of her tourist trade. Multitudes came to visit the temple of Artemis, a cult that requires explanation.

When the son of Codrus, last king of Athens, founded the city, he placed his colonists near the shrine of an ancient Anatolian goddess whom the Greeks, following the religious syncretism common in the ancient world, called after their own goddess Artemis. This was perhaps in the 10th, 11th, or 12th cent. B.C., so uncertain are dates in this borderland of legend and history. The cult thus recognized was that of a nature-goddess, associated with carnal fertility rituals, orgiastic rites, and religious prostitution. The peculiar feature in the case of Ephesus was that the cult was associated with a meteoric stone, the "image which fell down from Jupiter" of the guild-master's clever speech reported by Luke (Acts 19 ASV). Lost somewhere among the ruins, or concealed in the surrounding countryside by its last devotees, the cult-object possibly still exists. Charles Seltman, with some plausibility, suggests that it is actually a strange stone object, at present in the Liverpool City Museum (*Riot in Ephesus*, pp. 86, 87). Other elements over the course of centuries intruded into the worship, and the final form of the cult-image of Artemis of Ephesus was a strangely ornamented female figure, shrine and basket on head, a veil decorated with beasts, long necklaces, embroidered sleeves, legs sheathed with empaneled animals, and with multiple breasts, or, as some suggest, an apron covered with clusters of grapes or dates, sign and symbol of Artemis' role as the nourishing spirit of nature.

It was Croesus of neighboring Lydia (he reigned from 564 to 546 B.C.) who promoted the construction of the first temple to Artemis. Fragments of the columns that he donated, inscribed with his name, are in the British Museum. At the time, Croesus' temple was the largest of Gr. temples, and perhaps was some consolation for the loss of her independence, for it was Croesus who made Ephesus subject to Sardis. She was never, in fact, independent again. This temple, first sign of the international importance of the Artemis cult of Ephesus, stood right through the Pers. imperial dominance of the Aegean coast of Asia Minor. It was maliciously burned in 356 B.C. on the very night, the makers of omens later noted, that Alexander the Great was born of Olympias in distant Macedon.

Alexander, into whose control Ephesus passed in 334 B.C. at the beginning of his mighty "drive to the East," contributed largely to the new temple, which was destined to be a shrine of unrivaled splendor and to rank as one of the wonders of the world. It endured until the Goths sacked Ephesus in A.D. 263.

Arcadian Way at Ephesus. Large monumental column, located toward the lower end of this important street to the harbor from the center of the ancient city. ©*Lev*

The ruins have been identified in a marsh, one and a half miles NE of the city, after the discovery of Ephesus' main boulevard in 1870. It is said that the building was four times the size of Athens' magnificent Parthenon. Pheidias, Praxiteles, and Apelles all adorned it. It was widely depicted on coins. The general impression left with the archeologist and historian, who peer into the crowded past of the great city, is that the guild-master was not unjustified in his claim that "all Asia and the world" (Acts 19:27) reverenced the Ephesian Artemis. As the guild master by implication admitted, the temple was the core of Ephesus' commercial prosperity. Around the great shrine, to which worshipers and tourists poured from far and near, tradesmen and hucksters found a living, supplying visitors with food and lodging, dedicatory offerings, and the silver souvenir models of the shrine that the guild of Demetrius was most interested in making and selling. The temple was also a treasury and bank, in which private individuals, kings, and cities made deposits. Xenophon, the Athenian, described such a deposit with the "sacristan of Artemis," together with a testamentary deposition regarding the disposal of the money in the event of his not surviving the campaign ahead of him. Paul was, in fact, assaulting a stronghold of pagan religion, together with the active life and commerce associated with a vast heathen cult, in a key city of the central Mediterranean and a focal point of communication. Ephesus was also a seat of proconsular power from which the whole province of Asia could be influenced. Churches arose significantly during his stay in the three cities of the Lycus Valley—Laodicea, Colossae, and Hierapolis—in spite of the fact that Paul did not visit these centers. Radiation along the lines of communication from a point of active life accounted for such foundations. All the seven churches mentioned in the apocalyptic letters (Rev 2 and 3) were no doubt established during the same period of apostolic ministry. "A wide door for effective work has opened to me," wrote Paul, "and there are many adversaries" (1 Cor 16:9).

The preaching of Christianity in the school of Tyrannus was hitting the Artemis cult hard, so hard that the turnover in dependent trades was visibly showing the adverse effects. A riot ensued, so vividly and ironically described in Acts 19. The story is a strong, clear light on the manner in which the new faith was cutting across established forms and patterns of pagan life in the 1st cent. So it came about that Paul "fought with beasts at Ephesus" (1 Cor 15:32). He caught up a phrase of Plato from his student days in Tarsus. Plato likened the mob to wild animals. It was a dangerous situation. A fine street ran through the city from the harbor wharves at the river mouth to the great theater where the level land began to rise toward Mount Pion, a boulevard of some beauty and lined by fine buildings and columned porticoes. It was the main artery of Ephesian life, destined in later years to be even more richly adorned.

Led by the silversmiths, the mob poured down this highway. The text of Beza sometimes supplies a detail that has a ring of authenticity, and his unorthodox text adds a phrase to Acts 19:28 which may, in one flash, give a glimpse of the excited scene. Inflamed by the speech of the rabble-rouser Demetrius, delivered no doubt in the meeting house of the silversmith's guild, the audience, says Beza's version, poured "into the street." It is surely the great central boulevard that is mentioned. The noisy group swept along with them the flotsam of the town, the idlers, the visitors, the mob of any great eastern city, and flowed toward the common place of assembly—the theater on the low hillside. The greater part, says Luke in one ironical phrase, "did not know why they had come together" (19:32). It was a perilous situation, not only for Paul and his little party, but also for the Jews at large, who had every reason to fear a pogrom. The Jews had a large colony at Ephesus, and considerable privileges (Jos., Antiq. XIV. x. 12, 25). They had much to lose; hence the venture of Alexander whom the Jews "put forward," doubtless to make sure that their community as a whole was not blamed for the revolutionary views of the rabbi from Tarsus. At the sight of Alexander, who had taken some risk by his public appearance, the crowd broke into their chant, a rhythmic din that they kept up for two hours.

It is, as Ramsay says (*St. Paul the Traveller and Roman Citizen*, p. 277, 278), "the most instructive picture of society in an Asian city at this period that has come down to us. . . . In the speech of Demetrius are concentrated most of the feelings and motives that, from the beginning to the end, made the mob so hostile to the Christians in the great oriental cities." It required all the political art of the *grammateus*, no mere "town-clerk," but the city's leading official and obviously a most able man, to restore quiet and order. One phrase in his clever speech would appear to date the incident with some precision. If anything illegal had been done to rouse the just resentment of the silversmiths' guild, he said "there are proconsuls" (Acts 19:38). The historian Tacitus tells how Agrippina, the vicious mother of the Emperor Nero, had Junius Silanus, the proconsul of Asia, poisoned (Tac. Ann. XIII, 1). Silanus was a great-grandson of the Emperor Augustus, and was thus considered a menace to her son, whom Agrippina had thrust forward to the succession by all manner of intrigue and crime. The murder was committed by two men, a Rom. knight and a freedman who held the post of steward of the imperial estates in Asia. If the two villains assumed temporary proconsular power, the pl. of the official's speech is accounted for; otherwise it is without explanation. This assumption

Another view of the Arcadian Way, street leading down to the harbor. Lined with colonnades, shops and public buildings. ©*Lev*

Ruins of the Temple of Diana at Ephesus. These stones are all that remains of this Temple once classed among the seven wonders of the world. Looking west. ©*Lev*

would fix the date of the incident at A.D. 54.

Another phrase in the story is illuminating. Why did the "Asiarchs" seek to protect Paul? (*See* ASIARCH.) These officials were members of a corporation, built on the model of an earlier Gr. institution, and charged with the maintenance and protection of the Caesar cult (*see* EMPEROR WORSHIP) in Asia. It would appear probable that there was a measure of rivalry between those in charge of the newer ritual, a cult that was not yet deeply founded in Ephesus, and the custodians and champions of the vast commercialized worship of Artemis. Perhaps the Asiarchs, not yet aware of all the implications of Christianity, and as yet unhampered by any anti-Christian legislation, were not disturbed by damage to their rivals. Paul's Rom. citizenship may have weighed a little with the officers of Caesar. Whatever happened, Paul was rescued and, perhaps under some official pressure, withdrew before the irate guildsmen had the opportunity to file a formal indictment. It may also have been a consideration that weighed with Paul—that such an indictment would have had scant chance of a just hearing before such scoundrels as Publius Celer and the freedman Helios, if indeed they held brief authority in the city at the time.

It is possible from the NT to gain some idea of the progress of the Ephesian church. Although there is not the intimate insight into the doings and problems of the Ephesian Christian community, as the Corinthian epistles give, the NT provides a series of glimpses of considerable interest. First, there is the vivid story already examined. Another incident is the apostle's advice to the elders. He passed along the Asia Minor coast three or four years after the riot in Ephesus. He invited the leaders of the church to meet him at Miletus (had he given some promise to the Asiarchs not to return to Ephesus?). Paul conversed with them, and from the intimacy of almost three years' experience, warned the little community of tensions to come. That the trouble came is evident from John's letter to the Ephesian church, most prob. written when Domitian's persecution was raging.

John's letter was one of seven addressed to the Asian circuit, and prudently couched in the style of Jewish apocalyptic lit. Ephesus, as was proper, was the first church addressed, and the subject matter is light on the city, and its church, a generation after its founding. Three years of Paul's teaching in the school of Tyrannus, the nature of which may be partly glimpsed from Paul's own letter, had laid a firm basis for growth. There was much for which John could commend the Ephesian Christians; their toil, endurance, discernment, and vigor. Their lapse from first ardor and enthusiasm was due, according to Ramsay's famous thesis, to an infiltration of the Christian minority by the weariness of a civic community that had passed its prime and was living on its fading splendor.

It was natural enough in the religious capital of Asia that the sect of the Nicolaitans should be in evidence. Of this group it is fair to assume that they were Greeks who saw in their own cults a measure of true revelation, a position that might have arguments to commend it, but who carried this belief to the point of advocating unwise compromise with the debased forms of those cults in such prominence around them. Perhaps, too, they saw in the Caesar-cult only a harmless ritual of loyalty, and not an issue of man-worship on which a Christian need stake life and livelihood. Ephesus, taught by two apostles, rejected all accommodation with paganism and those who advocated the softer policy.

The question remaining is this: Was John too rigid, too extreme? Need the church, for instance, for the sake of a pinch of incense, have been exposed to the bitterness of persecution? History gives the answer. Those who accepted John's rigid rule came through that persecution refined and strengthened. They became the forefathers of all true Christianity. They laid in their suffering the foundations on which all true religion has since built. To compromise would ultimately have set Christ, where Emperor Severus ultimately placed him —in a chapel along with the images of Jupiter, Augustus, and Abraham. "The historian," writes Sir William Ramsay, "must regard the Nicolaitans with intense interest, and must deeply regret that we know so little about them. . . . At the same time he must feel that nothing could have saved the infant Church from melting away into one of those vague and ineffective schools of philosophic ethics except the stern and strict rule that is laid down here by St. John. An easygoing Christianity could never have survived; it could not have conquered and trained the world; only the most convinced, resolute, almost bigoted adherence to the most uncompromising interpretation of its principles could have given the Christians the courage and self-reliance that were needed. For them to hesitate or to doubt was to be lost" (Ramsay, *The Letters to the Seven Churches*, 300).

The last glimpse of Ephesus in the NT reveals an aging church in need of an infusion of new life, hence, the closing detail of imagery in the apocalyptic letter (Rev 2:1-7). Coins of Ephesus sometimes show a date palm, sacred to Artemis, and the symbol of the goddess' beneficent activity. "To him who conquers I will grant," wrote John, "to eat of the tree of life." The church, however, did not survive. Ignatius, writing a generation later, still accorded the church high praise. It became a seat of bishops, where a notable council was held as late as A.D. 431. Then came a long decline. The coast, with continual soil erosion of the hinterland, became malarial. The Turks came with ruin for Asia. The church died with the city. The "candlestick" was removed from its place.

A general view of the ruins at Ephesus, looking north. © *Lev*

Archeology, none the less, has shown that the prestige and magnificence of the city long outlived its declining usefulness as a seaport. Ramsay, broadly correct in his main thesis of Ephesus' decline dates its disastrous impact too early. Under Claudius in the middle of the 1st cent. and under Trajan at the beginning of the 2nd, the great theater was remodeled. Under Claudius the monumental Marble Street was built. Nero gave Ephesus a stadium. Domitian widened and beautified the great central boulevard. Adorning continued till the days of the Gothic raid in A.D. 263. (*See* ARCHEOLOGY.) It is obvious that Paul's vision had picked one of the strategic centers of the world.

BIBLIOGRAPHY. W. M. Ramsay, *The Letters to the Seven Churches* (1904); A. H. M. Jones, *Cities in the Eastern Provinces* (1937); E. M. Blaiklock, *The Christian in Pagan Society* (1951); *The Cities of the New Testament* (1965).

E. M. BLAIKLOCK

EPHLAL ĕf' lăl (אפלל, Ελφαελ, 1 Chron 2:37). A descendant of Judah through Perez and the family of Jerahmeel.

EPHOD ē' fŏd (Heb. אפוד ; LXX ἔπαμις) was a close-fitting, armless outer vest of varying length, but generally extending down to the hips. In the OT it was almost exclusively a priestly garment, or one used in the worship of God. In the Old Assyrian texts of the 19th cent. and the Ugaritic texts of the 15th the word appears as *epadu* or (fem.) *epattu* (Ug. '-p-d), and apparently denoted a close-fitting garment which some interpret as "rich vestment" (cf. de Vaux, *Ancient Israel*, p. 350), but others as a more ordinary garment (Albright in Alleman and Flack, *OT Commentary*, p. 147). The fem. *'apuddâh* also occurs (Exod 28:8; 39:5; Isa 30:22) meaning "a close-fitting garment" without cultic connotations. In the Mosaic Code it is given special prominence as part of the high priest's vestments. It was fastened around the waist with a beautifully woven girdle (*ḥēšeb*) (Exod 28:27, 28), and held together at the top by shoulder-pieces (*kitᵉpōt*) (28:12) set with onyx stones engraved with the names of the Twelve Tribes. The ceremonial breastplate (*ḥōšen*) containing twelve gem stones inscribed with the names of the twelve tribes was attached to a set of rings on the ephod. This breastplate also contained the sacred lots known as Urim and Thummim (although some authorities equate them with the twelve gems on the breastplate just mentioned).

Aaron wearing ephod and breastpiece as pictured by Aaron de Chavez, the first recorded painter to work in England. © *RTHPL.*

Less elaborate ephods were worn by the rest of the priesthood, esp. when officiating before the altar (1 Sam 2:28; 14:3); these are simply described as ephods of linen (*bad*), and prob. lacked any extensive ornamentation. Even a young acolyte like Samuel (1 Sam 2:18) wore such an ephod. A special veneration was accorded the high priestly type of ephod to such an extent that in the time of the Judges Gideon (Judg 8:27) had a replica fashioned from the gold and precious stones stripped from the Midianite warriors slain by his troops in the war. Micah the Ephraimite is said to have made an ephod for use in the worship of his silver idol, along with his *teraphim* (or images of the household gods), according to Judges 17:1-5. The high priestly ephod in the Tabernacle was apparently mounted on a model of some sort or otherwise displayed in a prominent position in the sanctuary. Probably because of the Urim and Thummim attached to it the ephod was considered of great value, esp. at crises when important decisions had to be made. When David needed to know in advance whether the people of Keilah whom he had befriended would hand him over to King Saul, he had Abiathar consult God by means of the ephod (1 Sam 23:9-12). Presumably this was done by means of the Urim and Thummim, just as in the earlier instance when Saul by that means found out that Jonathan was the one who had transgressed his ban on eating food before victory (14:18, reading "ephod" with LXX, rather than the "ark," which must have been kept at Kirjath-jearim at this time). The Urim and Thummim were drawn as "yes" or "no" answers (v. 41), eliminating the wrong choice between two alternatives.

It would appear that even in the northern kingdom ephods were made for cultic purposes in the temples of Israel (Hos 3:4). Whether these were made of woven cloth set with gold and gems, or whether they were like Gideon's of old (Judg 8:26, 27) is not clear from the evidence. No mention is made of an ephod after the fall of Jerusalem in 587 B.C. There is no evidence that a new ephod was made for the high priest after the Restoration from Babylon, although it may safely be assumed that this was done in conformity with the Mosaic Law.

BIBLIOGRAPHY. J. Morgenstern, *The Ark, the Ephod and the Tent of Meeting* (1945); M. F. Unger, *Archaeology and the OT* (1954), 212; R. de Vaux, *Ancient Israel* (1961), 349-352; H. M. Buck, *People of the Lord* (1966), 93, 94; F. Josephus, *Antiquities* iii, 7.3.

G. L. ARCHER

EPHOD (Father of Hanniel) ē′ fŏd (אֵפֹד, meaning prob. ephod, q.v.). Father of Hanniel who, as a leader in the tribe of Manasseh, was among those responsible for dividing Canaan W of the Jordan among the remaining tribes (Num 34:23).

EPHPHATHA ĕf′ ə thə (ἐφφαθά, *be opened*; Aram. passive imperative, ethpaal stem of פתח, *to open*, transliterated into Gr.). The word was spoken by Jesus to a deaf man and he was made to hear (Mark 7:34). This is one of the rare occasions that a Biblical author saw fit to quote from the Aram. the exact words which Jesus used, and the word is immediately tr. (διανοίχθητι). This may imply a connection with the words of Isaiah, "Then the eyes of the blind shall be opened and the ears of the deaf unstopped" (Isa 35:5). The word "unstopped" trs. a form of the root פתח, which is the Heb. equivalent to the root of the Aram. word that Jesus used. A repetition of Christ's actions, the Ephpheta ceremony, is included in the ritual of baptism of infants by the Roman Catholic Church (NCE, p. 462).

C. P. WEBER

EPHRAIM ē′ frĭ əm (אפרים, LXX Εφραιμ; meaning *doubly fruitful*), the younger of two sons born to Joseph in Egypt. The name of the older son was Manasseh. The mother of these sons of Joseph was Asenath, the daughter of Potiphera, the priest of On (Gen 41:50-52).

Ephraim was born during the seven years of plenty so that his boyhood years overlapped with the last seventeen years of Jacob who had migrated to Egypt during the years of plenty. In this way Ephraim had opportunity to learn of the patriarchal promises and blessings directly from Jacob.

After Jacob exacted an oath from Joseph that he would bury him in Canaan (47:27-31), Jacob adopted the two sons of Joseph as his own. Jacob's favorite wife had been Rachel whose son Joseph had been favored above all other sons until he was sold as a slave to Potiphar in Egypt. By adopting Manasseh and Ephraim as his own sons there were three tribal representatives of Rachel—Benjamin, Ephraim, and Manasseh. Joseph, who had been considered dead by Jacob, now had a double representation.

Ephraim was chosen by Jacob for the greater blessing even though he was not the first-born son of Joseph. Overruling Joseph's objections Jacob placed his right hand on Ephraim and alloted to him a greater blessing and prosperity than he did to Manasseh.

Ephraim, with Manasseh and Joseph, had imparted to him verbally the essence of the revelation God had made to the patriarchs, especially to Jacob. To Jacob there had been confirmed by divine revelation the promise that his descendants would be multiplied and that they would inherit the land of Canaan. Jacob gave the blessing in the name of the God before whom Abraham and Isaac walked, and the God who had shepherded Jacob throughout his whole lifetime. Although Jacob was about to die in Egypt, he expressed before Ephraim the firm belief that future generations would realize and experience the fulfillment of the promises to possess the land of Canaan.

Ephraim and Manasseh were allotted a particular plot of real estate in Canaan which is described as "one portion (*shekem*, shoulder) . . . which I took from the hand of the Amorites with my sword and with my bow" (48:22). This could hardly refer to the involvement of Simeon and Levi with Shechem which displeased Jacob exceedingly (ch. 34). Jacob did purchase some land from the sons of Hamor, Shechem's father (33:19). Abraham may have previously purchased some land at this place when he erected an altar at Shechem after arriving in Canaan (12:7, 8). If so this may have been referred to by Stephen (Acts 7:16). Since Jacob identifies this portion or ridge of land as being obtained by conquest, the possibility exists that this adventure by Jacob is noted only here in the Biblical account. Joseph was ultimately buried in the vicinity of Shechem (Josh 24:32). In John 4:5, 6 the tract of land which Jacob presented to Joseph's descendants is identified as being near Sychar. Four centuries later the tombs of the twelve patriarchs were known to be at Shechem according to Jerome. This likely would have included Ephraim since his tribe was so prominent in Israelite history. It may have been this Samaritan tradition that Stephen had in mind when he ascribed the burial of the "fathers" to Shechem (Acts 7:15, 16).

In subsequent history the tribe of Ephraim had a very prominent position. In Israel's encampment around the Tabernacle, Ephraim was the leader of the western camp supported by the tribes of Manasseh and Benjamin (Num 2:18-24). Among the twelve spies sent into Canaan Joshua represented the tribe of Ephraim (Num 13:8), and later was appointed as the successor of Moses (Deut 31:7). Joshua and Eleazar the high priest had the responsi-

Hill country of Ephraim. ©*M.P.S.*

bility to divide the land of Canaan among the tribes of Israel.

The Ephraimites received an allotment of land between the Jordan River and the Mediterranean Sea with the tribes of Benjamin and Dan to the S and one half of the tribe of Manasseh to the N (Josh 16:5-9). The southern boundary extended from the Jordan and Jericho westward approximately ten m. N of Jerusalem, but included Upper and Lower Beth-horons as it continued to the sea. On the N Ephraim was bounded by the brook Kanah, the cities of Shechem and Taanath-shiloh where the boundary turned southward to Ataroth and passed near Jericho on to the Jordan.

The religious center for Israel during the era of Joshua and the Judges was Shiloh in the territory of Ephraim (Josh 18:1; 22:12; Judg 18:31; 21:19; 1 Sam 1:3, 9, 24; 2:14; 3:21). The Tabernacle was erected in Shiloh by Joshua and remained there until the Ark of the Covenant was taken by the Philistines after the sons of Eli took it into the battlefield (1 Sam 4:1-11). Scholars are of the opinion that the city of Shiloh was destroyed at this time (cf. Jer 7:12). There is no indication that the Ark was returned to Shiloh.

The Ephraimites were involved in civil strife in the days of Gideon (Judg 8:1-3), and in the period of Jephthah's leadership (12:1-6).

During the Davidic and Solomonic era the tribe of Judah with its leading city Jerusalem emerged as the leading tribe, but at Solomon's death a secession was led by Jeroboam I of the tribe of Ephraim who became the first king of the northern kingdom. During the two centuries that this kingdom existed it was frequently identified as Ephraim, reflecting the fact that this was the most powerful tribe in opposition to Judah. In the books of Chronicles, Isaiah, Hosea and other prophets, the name Ephraim is commonly used for the northern kingdom.

Ephraim is to be reunited with Judah in the Messianic kingdom. The schism introduced by Jeroboam I is to be healed when the ruler of the Davidic family will rule over both Judah and Ephraim according to the prophet Ezekiel in his message concerning the final kingdom (ch. 37).

S. J. SCHULTZ

EPHRAIM, FOREST (WOODS) OF ē' frĭ əm (יער אפרים, *the forest of Ephraim* whose name is connected with *fruit-bearing.* Referred to explicitly in 2 Samuel 18:6-17 and implicitly in Joshua 17:14-18). Opinions differ as to whether the latter refers to the expansion by the house of Joseph eastward into Trans-Jordan (K. Budde, ZAW, 7 [1887], pp. 123f.; C. E. Burnes, *Israel's Settlements in Canaan* [London, 1919], pp. 20ff.) or to settlement in the forested sectors of the Ephraimite hill country itself. Two statements in Joshua 17:15 found in the MT support the first view: (1) "the land of Rephaim" ("giants" KJV) is a typical expression for Trans-Jordan (*see* REPHAIM), and (2) "the forest" is placed in juxtaposition with Mount Ephraim clearly in Cis-Jordan. Its association with Mahanaim (2 Sam 17:27), formerly Eshbaal's Trans-Jordanian capital (2 Sam 2:8, 9), firmly establishes this location. Originally this territory was granted to "the house of Joseph, to Ephraim and Manasseh" (Josh 17:17). Ephraim later lost this woodland E of Jordan to Jephthah and the Gileadites (Judg 12:1-15). LXX Lucian may have changed the text of 2 Samuel 8:6 to "the forest of Mahanaim" to modernize or clarify its location. Although the Heb. word tr. "forest" has widely divergent meaning (D. Baly, *The Geography of the Bible* [1957], pp. 83, 93), it prob. has the normal significance of the Eng. tr. because (1) Joshua commands the people "to clear ground" (Josh 17:15) and (2) Absalom's rebellion ended with his head caught in a tree.

B. K. WALTKE

EPHRAIM, GATE OF ē' frĭ əm (שער אפרים, *the gate of Ephraim,* q.v. [i.e., *double product*]). A northward (Ephraim) facing gate, 200 yds. E of pre-exilic Jerusalem's NE corner (2 Kings 14:13; 2 Chron 25:23), rebuilt by Nehemiah (Neh 12:39), and possibly equivalent to the "Old Gate" (Gate of the ישנה, Neh 12:39 [= Gate of the משנה]).

J. B. PAYNE

EPHRAIM, MOUNT ē' frĭ əm (הר אפרים, occurs thirty-two times in the OT, Josh 17:15; Judg 3:27; 1 Sam 1:1; etc.). Since it denotes the hill country in central Pal. occupied by the tribe of Ephraim, rather than a single mountain, it is better rendered "the hill country of Ephraim" (as ASV, RSV). It was more fruitful than Judaea, esp. on its western slopes and it was one of the few areas where the Israelites were able to establish themselves after the conquest under Joshua. For this reason the two main sanctuaries of the Judges' period, Bethel and Shiloh, were within its borders.

A. E. CUNDALL

EPHRAIN. KJV form of EPHRON (2 Chron 13:19).

EPHRATH, EPHRATHAH ĕf' rəth, ĕf' rə thə (אפרת ; אפרתה ; KJV EPHRATAH, ĕf' rä tä). 1. A city or area in Judaea which is connected with Bethlehem. Possibly it was originally independent but was absorbed into Bethlehem at a later date. Elimelech and his family were "Ephrathites from Bethlehem" (Ruth 1:2; cf. 1 Sam 17:12). The two places are identified in the compound form (Mic 5:2) and as the burial place of Rachel (Gen 35:19; 48:7).

2. Since the burial place of Rachel is elsewhere set in the territory of Benjamin (1 Sam 10:2; Jer 31:15) and since Genesis 35:16 suggests a considerable distance between Bethlehem and Ephrath, the parenthetical references in Genesis 35:19 and 48:7 often have been regarded as inaccurate glosses. This would indicate a third Ephrath, on the northern border of Benjamin.

3. An area in Pal. (Ps 132:6) which appears to be connected with Kiriath-jearim ("Jaar") from where the Ark was brought to Jerusalem (cf. the connection of Ephrathah, Bethlehem and Kiriath-jearim in 1 Chronicles 2:50-52).

4. The second wife of Caleb, the mother of Hur and Ashhur (1 Chron 2:19, 24, 50; 4:4).

A. E. CUNDALL

EPHRATHITE ĕf' rə thīt (אפרתי). An inhabitant of Ephrathah or Ephrath, q.v. (Ruth 1:2; 1 Sam 17:12). In addition, Ephrathite occurs in KJV (1 Sam 1:1; 1 Kings 11:26) reflecting the same Heb. original, but later VSS here tr. "Ephraimite" as KJV does in Judges 12:5.

EPHRON (the Hittite) ē' frŏn (עפרון, *fawn?*) The Hitt. from whom Abraham purchased a burial place for Sarah his wife (Gen 23:8). Ephron was the son of Zohar a Hitt. and owned a field in Machpelah, E of Mamre (Hebron) (23:17). The study of the transaction between Abraham and this Hitt. is a study in oriental shrewdness and politeness.

Apparently Ephron was willing to sell the land but for a good price (23:14). Yet he did not initially state the price, but depending on Abraham's knowledge of propriety, he offered at first to give away the land (23:11). Even when Abraham properly insisted on paying for it (23:13), Ephron did not offer to sell the land, but slyly stated the value which he put on the property (23:15). Abraham, understanding that this was the asking price, responded by purchasing it at that price (23:16).

The field formerly owned by Ephron had a cave and several trees (23:17). Sarah was buried there and later Abraham (25:9). Later on Isaac and Rebekah, and Jacob and Leah were buried at Machpelah.

Today a large Muslim stone structure covers the cave and marks the spot in Hebron where the field of Machpelah was. Visitors may see the interior of the building, but are not shown the cave.

J. B. Scott

EPICUREANS. The Epicureans are mentioned in Acts 17:18, along with the Stoics. Luke gives no information on their views, except that they rejected the idea of a bodily resurrection.

1. Moral reputation. Epicurus founded the school in Athens about 300 B.C. In a sense he effected a reform of the earlier school of Cyrenaics, whose crass slogan is partially quoted in 1 Corinthians 15:32, "Let us eat and drink [and be merry], for tomorrow we die." Contrasted with the licentiousness of the Cyrenaics, the Epicureans as judged by Gr. or generally human standards advocated a fairly pure morality.

Diogenes Laertius preserved a letter from Epicurus, which reads,

> By pleasure we mean the absence of pain in the body and of trouble in the soul. It is not an unbroken succession of drinking bouts and of revelry, not sexual love, not the enjoyment of fish and other delicacies of a luxurious table, which produce a pleasant life; it is sober reasoning, searching out the grounds of every choice and avoidance, and banishing those beliefs through which the greatest tumults take possession of the soul.

Epicureanism included even a strain of asceticism. "Sexual intercourse has never done a man any good, and he is lucky if it has not harmed him. Nor will a wise man [except in unusual circumstances] marry and rear a family" (Diogenes Laertius, *Lives of Eminent Philosophers*, X, 118, 119).

2. Hedonism. Although the Epicureans identified the aim of life as pleasure, for "No pleasure is a bad thing in itself," yet to call them hedonists, etymologically correct as it may be, is misleading. Not only "the means which produce some pleasures bring with them disturbances many times greater than the pleasures," but more profoundly, the Epicureans defined pleasure as the absence of pain. Their aim therefore was not so much the titillations of sense as it was the absence of pain, the avoidance of trouble, and freedom from annoyances.

It was this aim to avoid everything disturbing and to achieve tranquillity of mind that motivated their views both on religion and on physics. These two subjects, with the Epicureans as with other schools in the history of philosophy, were closely related.

3. Religion, source of evil. The greatest disturber of tranquillity of mind and the most prolific source of all evils is the belief that the gods punish evildoers. Lucretius (94-55 B.C.), a Rom. Epicurean, wrote, "Most often it is religion itself that inspires impious and criminal acts": e.g. the sacrifice of Iphigenia by her father. The fear of the gods disturbs man in his dreams. The thought of punishment in a life beyond the grave tortures man all his days.

Therefore the fundamental principle for a happy life is, *"Nullam rem e nilo gigni divinitus umquam,"* or, "nothing ever comes about by divine power" (Lucretlus, *De Rerum Natura*, I, 150). Confirmation of this principle is later stated: "That the world has by no means been created by divine power is clear from the fact that it contains so many flaws" (ibid. II. 180; V. 195ff.), e.g., "so much of its surface is uninhabitable, the remainder requires hard labor to produce food, the human infant is helpless, the man is harassed by wild beasts, disease, and early death."

In spite of this last reference to early death, death itself is not an evil. This must be understood, for otherwise the thought of extinction might be as disturbing as the thought of a future life.

> Accustom thyself to believe that death is nothing to us. . . . A right understanding that death is nothing to us makes the mortality of life enjoyable, not by adding to life an illimitable time, but by taking away the yearning after immortality. . . . Foolish, therefore, is the man who says he fears death, not because it will pain him when it comes, but because it pains him in the prospect. Whatsoever causes no annoyance when it is present, causes only a groundless pain in the expectation. Death, therefore, the most awful of all evils, is nothing to us, seeing that, when we are, death is not come, and, when death is come, we are not (Lucretius).

4. Atoms and freedom. All that remains, according to the Epicurean, is to frame an acceptable physics that will see mankind through the present life. If all natural phenomena can be plausibly explained in terms of atoms moving through empty space, the last reason for fearing the gods is gone. Such explanations the Epicureans give of sunlight penetrating the air, of images in mirrors, of the sun and moon, of thunder and lightning, and of many other things, but esp. of sensation and reason—all in terms of atoms moving through empty space.

These explanations need not be the absolute truth. All that is needed to show that no divine purpose rules nature is to give a materialistic account that is possible.

More important than many of these details

is the theory of free will. Two opposing theories would make life miserable. First, if God had planned the universe and determined everything, nothing would be in our power and ethics would be impossible. Second, if all the atoms were always mechanically determined, as Democritus taught, the same unacceptable conclusion would follow.

The physical theory is that the atoms generally move in straight lines, but sometimes for no cause whatever swerve just a little. Hence men, that is, human bodies composed of atoms, can sometimes for no cause whatever, move in opposition to the laws of mechanics. This is free will.

Hence, nature is to a limited extent under human control.

> The future is not wholly ours nor wholly not ours, so that neither must we count upon it as quite certain to come, nor despair of it as quite certain not to come. . . . Destiny, which some introduce as sovereign over all things, [man] laughs to scorn, affirming rather that some things happen of necessity, others by chance, others through our own agency. For he sees that necessity destroys responsibility and that chance and fortune are inconstant; whereas our own actions are free. . . . Exercise thyself in these and kindred precepts day and night . . . then never, either in waking or in dream, wilt thou be disturbed.

(Ibid., X, 124, 133, 134; *see* article on STOICISM.)

BIBLIOGRAPHY. Lucretius, *De Rerum Natura* (50 B.C.); C. Bailey, *The Greek Atomists and Epicurus* (1928). *See* also GREEK RELIGION AND PHILOSOPHY.

G. H. CLARK

EPIGRAPHY. *See* INSCRIPTION; WRITING.

EPILEPSY. *See* DISEASE, DISEASES.

EPIPHANES. *See* ANTIOCHUS IV.

EPIPHI ĕp' ĭ fī ('Επιφί). Eleventh month of the Egyp. year, June 25-July 24. According to 3 Maccabees the Jews in Egypt were registered (in order to be destroyed) under the Egyp. monarch, Ptolemy IV Philopator (221-203 B.C.) during the forty days from the twenty-fifth of Pachon (April 26-May 25) to the fourth of Epiphi. Preparations for their destruction lasted from the fifth to the seventh of Epiphi (3 Macc 6:38). The Jews were spared through a series of miraculous events.

C. P. WEBER

EPISTLE ĭ pĭs' əl (ספר, ἐπιστολή, *letter* or *dispatch . . . written communication, communication in writing* or *printing addressed to a person* or *number of persons*). While tr. "epistle" fifteen times and "letter" only nine times in the KJV NT, *epistolé* is tr. "letter" invariably in the RSV.

1. Differentiations. Preserved documents in epistolary form "might more accurately be classified as public orations, philosophical treatises, political tracts, or moral exhortations . . . [and] have all the marks of having been written for general publication" (Seitz). Robinson notes that "An epistle is a work of art; a letter is a piece of life . . . . One is like the carefully finished photograph which does you justice; the other is like a snapshot which shows you as you are." The letter is less formal, more personal and direct than is the epistle. Indeed, some of Paul's letters, esp. Romans, bear certain epistolary characteristics, as does Hebrews. Few letters, in the technical sense, are found in the OT canonical books (see 2 Sam 11:14, 15; 1 Kings 21:8, 9; 2 Kings 19:14; Jer 29; cf. Acts 9:2; Rom 16:1ff.; 1 Cor 7:1).

2. Composition and delivery. The NT letters were the earliest form of Christian lit. They, like those of the Hellenists, were written on sheets of papyrus with a reed pen and ink, then rolled or folded, tied, and often sealed for privacy and authentication (2 Kings 21:17; Esth 3:12; 8:8; Dan 12:4; Rev 5:9). Such letters were sometimes written on waxed tablets with a stylus, mainly for economy since they could be erased. As the official Rom. postal service (*cursus publicus*) was not open to private correspondence, the Christians employed members of the churches as carriers (Acts 15:22; 2 Cor 8:16-23; Phil 2:25; Col 4:7, 8). While the NT letters were written under divine guidance, as also in human wisdom, in response to specific needs of individuals or churches (1 Cor 7:1), it may be questioned whether the authors were ever aware that they were writing for all time and Christendom (2 Tim 3:16).

Sealed letter, or epistles, sheets of papyrus rolled, tied and sealed, to be delivered by messenger. ©*J.H.K.*

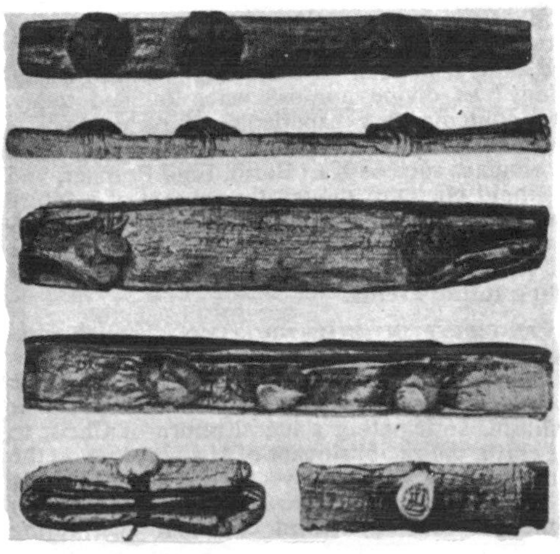

THE EPISTLES IN BRIEF
(*See* CHRONOLOGY, NT)

Title	Author	Source	Destination
1 Thess	Paul	Corinth	Church at Thessalonica
2 Thess	Paul	Corinth	Church at Thessalonica
1 Cor	Paul	Ephesus	Corinthian Christians
Galatians	Paul	Antioch, Ephesus or Corinth	Christian groups in Central Asia Minor
2 Cor	Paul	Ephesus, Macedonia	Corinthian Christians
Romans	Paul	Corinth	Roman Church
Philippians	Paul	Rome	Christians at Philippi
Philemon	Paul	Rome	Philemon
Colossians	Paul	Rome	Colossian Christians
Ephesians	Paul	Rome	Church at Ephesus
		Pastoral Epistles	
1 Timothy	Paul	Uncertain	Timothy
2 Timothy	Paul	Rome	Timothy
Titus	Paul	Uncertain	Titus
	Catholic or General Epistles Destined for Wide Reading		
James	James, half brother of Jesus	Uncertain	Christians of Dispersion
1 Peter	Peter	Uncertain	Christians of Dispersion
2 Peter	Peter	Uncertain	Christians of Dispersion
Jude	Jude, half brother of Jesus	Uncertain	Christians of Dispersion
1 John	John	? Ephesus	Early Christians, Asia Minor
Hebrews	Unknown Christian teacher	Uncertain	Jewish Christians
		Asiatic Epistles	
1 John	John		Christians of Dispersion
2 John	John	? Ephesus	"Elect lady"
3 John	John	? Ephesus	Gaius

3. Classifications. Twenty-one of the twenty-seven NT books are letters, plus two brief letters in Acts (15:23-29; 23:26-30), and seven in Revelation (2:1-3:22), which are, Seitz thinks, "simply literary introductions to a book which is itself cast in an epistolary framework." Together they constitute more than one third of the NT. Christianity is unique in that of all the other sacred books of the world, not one is composed of letters.

Four persons were usually involved in a NT letter; the writer, the secretary (amanuensis), the carrier, and the readers. It is considered, traditionally, that Paul was the author of thirteen of the NT letters; James, one; Peter, two; John, three; Jude, one; and one (Hebrews), anonymous. Paul's letters may be classified as follows: (1) eschatological (1 and 2 Thess), (2) soteriological (Gal, Rom, 1 and 2 Cor), (3) christological (Col, Eph, Phil), (4) ecclesiological (1 and 2 Tim, Titus), and personal (Philem). James is ethical; Jude is polemical; 1 and 2 Peter are pastoral; 1, 2, 3 John are pastoral; and Hebrews is largely polemical.

4. Structure and value. Structurally the NT letters closely resemble their Hellenist counterparts. Paul's general practice is typical. He begins with (1) his personal greetings, which sometimes include Christian friends or co-workers present with him, or possibly his secretary, which may account for his frequent use of the first person pl. He usually combines the Gr.-Heb. salutation-blessing, χάρις. His introductory greetings normally set the keynote for the entire letter. (2) He offers thanksgiving to God for his Christian readers. (3) Prayers for the spiritual, and sometimes temporal, welfare of his readers usually follow. (4) He treats the principal concerns of his readers, often including a doctrinal discussion of their problems that may have been raised in previous communications (see 1 Cor 7:1). (5) A practical or ethical section follows in which he applies to their needs the doctrinal principles set forth. (6) A benediction, personal messages and salutations are sometimes included (Rom 16). (7) A brief autograph, in part for authentication, usually closes the letter (Gal 6:11; 2 Thess 3:17). Marked differences between the forms of the Hellenic and NT letters occur in the secular as opposed to the Christian greetings, and in the absence of dates and places of writing in the Christian letters. The far-reaching influence of the NT letters on subsequent Christian lit. is evinced by the writings of the 2nd cent. Not all of the 1st-cent. Christian letters survived (1 Cor 5:9; Col 4:16). From the beginning these NT letters were received by the church as divinely inspired messages along with the OT Scriptures (2 Pet 3:15, 16). *See* LETTER.

BIBLIOGRAPHY. F. W. Farrar, *The Message of the Books* (n.d.), 143-157; W. M. Ramsay, *Letters to the Seven Churches* (1905), 23ff.; A. Deissmann, *Light From the Ancient East* (1911), 217-238; J. Moffatt, *An Introduction to the Literature of the New Testament* (1923), 44-58; D. M. Pratt, "Epistle," ISBE (1939), II, 966, 967; E. W. K. Mould, *Essentials of Bible History* (1951), 582-588; M. S. and J. L. Miller, "Epistles," *Harper's Bible Dictionary* (1955), 169, 170; C. K. Barrett, *The New Testament Background* (1961), 27-29; O. J. F. Seitz, "Letter," IDB (1962), K-Q, 113-115; S. Barabas, "Epistle," *The Zondervan Pictorial Bible Dictionary* (1963), 257; E. F. Harrison, *Introduction to the New Testament* (1964), 238-244; J. Stein, ed., *The Random House Dictionary of the English Language* (1966).

C. W. CARTER

EPISTLE OF THE APOSTLES. *See* APOSTLES, EPISTLE OF.

EPISTLES, APOCRYPHAL ə pŏk′ rə fəl. Interest in the apostles generally took the form of apocryphal Acts, relating their travels, miracles, and martyrdoms, rather than of letters forged in support of some doctrinal position. An exception is the Epistle of pseudo-Titus, in praise of virginity. Jesus left nothing in writing, but Eusebius preserved an apocryphal correspondence with Abgar of Edessa. The Letters of Paul and Seneca are clear propaganda, the Epistle to the Laodiceans is forged to fill a gap in the Pauline Corpus, and the Epistle of the Apostles is largely an alleged account of revelations given by the risen Jesus. Other letters are to be found in such documents as the pseudo-Clementines and the Acts of Paul. SEE APOCRYPHAL NEW TESTAMENT 3, and separate articles.

R. MCL. WILSON

ER ûr (עֵר, Ἤρ, *watcher*). 1. The first-born son of Judah by his wife Shua, a woman of Canaan (Gen. 38:3). Judah gave Tamar to Er for a wife, but the Lord slew him for his wickedness before he had any children (Gen 38:7f.; 46:12; 1 Chron 2:3).

2. A grandson of Judah through Shelah, Judah's youngest son (1 Chron 4:21). This makes this Er a nephew of the one above whom the Lord slew. Er begat Lecah.

3. A son of Joshua and an ancestor of Joseph, the husband of Mary (Luke 3:28f.). There is no OT record of this Er.

R. L. ALDEN

ERAN ĭr′ ăn (עֵרָן). The grandson of Ephraim and son of Shuthelah (Num 26:36). The Eranites descended from Eran.

Since LXX has Ἐδέν and due to the similarity between the Heb. "d" and "r" consonants, it is possible to read עֵדָן here. The parallel passage (1 Chron 7:20) does not mention "Eran" but does record an "Eleadah" as a descendant of Shuthelah.

J. B. SCOTT

ERASTUS ĭ răs′ təs (Ἔραστος, *beloved*). A common Gr. name, occurring in the NT on three distinct occasions as a companion of Paul. 1. An assistant, sent with Timothy from Ephesus into Macedonia on an errand (Acts 19:22).

2. The "city treasurer" (οἰκονόμος) of Corinth who sent greetings to the Christians in Rome (Rom 16:23). He was the steward or manager of the property or financial affairs of the city. Such officials were generally slaves or freedmen, though often wealthy. In 1929, archeologists uncovered at Corinth a Lat. inscr. reading, "Erastus, commissioner for public works [aedile], laid this pavement at his own expense." That he was the Erastus of Romans is possible, but not probable. That he is to be identified with Paul's companion of Acts 19:22 is highly improbable, although the identification has been advocated.

3. Paul's travel companion left behind at Corinth (2 Tim 4:20) mentioned without identification. He was Paul's well-known assistant. *See* 1 *above*.

It is uncertain whether any two of these men, or all three, are identical.

BIBLIOGRAPHY. For the inscr. see H. J. Cadbury, JBL, L (1931), 42-58; W. Miller, BS, 88 (1931), 342-346. For the identification, H. P. Liddon, *Explanatory Analysis of St. Paul's Epistle to the Romans* (1893), 304; G. S. Duncan, *St. Paul's Ephesian Ministry* (1929), 79ff.; R. C. H. Lenski, *Interpretation of the Acts of the Apostles* (1936), 926.

D. E. HIEBERT

ERECH ĭr′ ĕk (אֶרֶךְ, Akkad. *Uruk*, Sumer. *Unug*). The second of the cities founded by Nimrod, the others being Babel (Babylon), Accad, Nineveh, Rehoboth-Ir, Calah, and Resen (Gen 10:10, 11 RSV). Later, according to Ezra 4:9, 10, the men of Erech and others were settled in the cities of Samaria, by the Assyrian King, Osnapper (Ashurbanipal). Erech was one of the oldest, largest, and most important cities of ancient Sumer. The site is located at modern Warka c. 160 m. S of Baghdad. Originally the city was on the W bank of the Euphrates River but the river now lies some m. to the E of the site.

The original village, Kullab, was founded by the Ubaid people c. 4,000 B.C. and the founder of Erech's semi-mythical "First Dynasty" was Meskiaggasher. Uruk was the capital of the mythical hero-king Gilgamesh. From the time of Hammurabi it became part of Babylonia and shared its fortunes and misfortunes. There is perpetual reference to the city in Assyrian and Babylonian lit., and commercial documents to 200 B.C. attest its continued pros-

perity. Later in history—perhaps Assyrian times, certainly by the Parthian period—it became a sort of national necropolis.

The site of Erech was first excavated by William K. Loftus in 1850 and 1854. Later, Ger. expeditions conducted excavations in 1912-1913, 1928-1939, and 1954-1959. These revealed city walls c. six m. in circumference, encircling c. 1,100 acres; two ziggurats; and several temples from the late 4th and early 3rd millennia B.C. Also found were hundreds of pictographic tablets, seals, etc. The library found contained many documents on religious practice, some dating as late as 70 B.C. Excavations also revealed remains of canals in the immediate area of the city, while the site itself was flanked by two large streams and intersected by many canals. Poetical references imply that the city and surrounding area were regarded as once quite fertile, a contrast to the desolation of the area now.

Erech was a chief center for the cult of Anu, one of the foremost Babylonian deities. It was also a center for the worship of Ishtar.

BIBLIOGRAPHY. Loftus, *Travels and Researches in Chaldaea and Susiana* (1857); A. Falkenstein, *Archaische Texte aus Uruk* (1936); H. W. Eliot, *Excavations in Mesopotamia and Western Iran* (1950).

L. L. WALKER

ERI, ERITES ĭr′ ī, ĭr′ īts (עֵרִי, perhaps related to a verb meaning *arouse oneself*). Eri is the fifth son of Gad, the grandson of Jacob (Gen 46:16), and ancestor of the Erites (Num 26:16).

ERUPTION. *See* DISEASE, DISEASES.

ESAIAS. KJV NT form of ISAIAH.

ESAR-HADDON ē′ sər hăd′ ən (אֵסַר־חַדֹּן, [from Akkad. *Aššur-aḫ-iddin*] *Ashur has given a brother*). King of Assyria 681-669 B.C.

1. Sources. The principal events of this reign are listed in the Babylonian Chronicle, the Esar-haddon Chronicle for the years 681-667 B.C., and numerous royal inscrs. Copies of his treaties with Tyre and Medean vassals have been recovered. The OT names him as son and successor to Sennacherib (2 Kings 19:37; Isa 37:38). Some would identify him with the "great and noble Osnappar" of Ezra 4:10 (*see* ASHURBANIPAL).

2. Family. Sennacherib was murdered by one or more of his sons (*see* ADRAMMELECH and SHAREZER) in Tebet 681 B.C. (2 Kings 19:36, 37; 2 Chron 32:21; Isa 37:37, 38). This may have been in revenge for having nominated Esar-haddon, whose name implies that he was not the eldest son of the Aramean wife of Sennacherib, Naqiya-Zakutu, as crown prince. The wife of Esar-haddon (d. 673 B.C.) bore him twin sons, Ashurbanipal and Shamash-shum-ukin, whom in May 672 he had designated respectively crown prince of Assyria and of Babylonia, doubtless in the hope of avoiding internecine struggle similar to that experienced at his own accession. A daughter he gave in marriage to the Scythian chief Bartatua.

3. Rule. Esar-haddon's first task was to rally popular support, pursue the rebels into the mountains to the N, and execute the nobles who had aided them in Nineveh. This led to further operations to keep the northern trade routes open and to check the incursions of the Cimmerian tribesmen (679). In the E, the Medean chiefs were tamed by frequent raids and the imposition of vassal treaties watched over by local Assyrian garrisons. Further S, the Elamites continued to stir up the Babylonian tribes. Esar-haddon raided their territory and deported prisoners to other sites (Ezra 4:9, 10). With clever diplomacy he installed Na'id-Marduḳ of Bīt-Yakin, a son of the rebel Merodach-baladan, as local governor and secured long and loyal support. Esar-haddon was now free to devote his attention to Egypt, which was the source of intrigue within the Syrian and Palestinian city-states. He raided the Bit-Eden area (cf. Isa 37:12) and the Arabs (676 B.C.). Sidon was besieged and a treaty made with Ba'al of Tyre. Tribute was received from thirteen kings of the E Mediterranean islands and coast and twelve kings of the mainland including Tyre, Sidon, Edom, Moab, Gaza, Ashkelon, Ekron, Gebal, Ashdod, Beth-Ammon as well as Manasseh (Akkad. *Menasi*) of Judah. There is as yet no mention in the Assyrian texts of Manasseh's deportation to Babylon (2 Chron 33:11), though Esar-haddon, who had been viceroy there while crown prince, was then engaged in reconstruction of the city after its sack by his father and may have called in tributaries to help. An 8th cent. letter found at Nineveh records "10 mana of silver sent by the men of Judah" about this

King Esar-haddon holding two royal captives on leash; from Zinjirli. ©*Berlin Museum*

Historical records of Esar-haddon on an octagonal clay prism from Nineveh. ©*U.M.P.*

time. The terms imposed by Esar-haddon on his vassals, including Manasseh, are known from texts found at Nimrud. They had to assent to Ashur as their god and to teach obedience to him and Assyria to their children. Any deviation from the terms was punished by the threat of invasion and deportation. It is not surprising that the prophets and historians considered his reign as more than unusually evil (2 Kings 21:9).

In 675/4, Esar-haddon sent two expeditions against Egypt itself, having taken the city of Arzani on the border some years before and neutralized Tyre by siege works and made conciliations with the tribes of N. Arabia. Tirhakah (2 Kings 19:9) retreated to Nubia and Memphis fell. Assyrian control of the delta was by means of puppet governors. The first campaign ended by the Assyrians withdrawing with much loot "before a great storm." Soon, however, local intrigue at Nineveh must have encouraged Tirhakah to stir up open revolt in Egypt itself. It was at Haran while on the way to suppress this that Esar-haddon fell sick and died (10 Marcheswan 681) and was succeeded by Ashurbanipal.

4. Building. Esar-haddon built a new palace-fortress at Kar-Esar-haddon near Assur and in SE Calah. Temples were restored also at Nineveh, Nippur, Babylon, and other cities.

BIBLIOGRAPHY. R. Borger, *Die Inschriften Asarhaddons, Königs von Assyrien* (1956); D. J. Wiseman, "The Vassal—Treaties of Esarhaddon," *Iraq,* XX (1958), 1-99.

D. J. WISEMAN

ESAU **e' sô** (עֵשָׂו, *hairy*), son of Isaac and Rebekah, and elder twin brother of Jacob. He is also named Edom, meaning Red. As Esau grew up he became an outdoor man who enjoyed hunting. He brought venison home to his father and became his father's favorite. At the same time his brother Jacob won the favor of his mother by remaining indoors and learning to work in the house.

On one occasion Esau returned from the hunt to find his brother cooking some red pottage. Esau asked for some of the pottage, but his brother took advantage of the situation by asking Esau's birthright in exchange. Esau, reasoning that his birthright would be meaningless if he were to die of starvation, sold his birthright (Gen 25:29-34). Although Jacob took advantage of his brother's weakness, Esau is censured for the little value he placed on the birthright. He did not trust God to provide for him in his need.

Esau showed his lack of concern for the covenant promises by marrying two local girls who were not related to the people of Abraham (Gen 26:34, 35; 36:1, 2). The mixed marriages caused grief to Esau's parents, particularly his mother. When Isaac was old and feeble he decided to confer his blessing on Esau, his favorite son. Rebekah, however, determined to fool her husband into blessing Jacob instead. Esau was sent out to find the game which his father enjoyed eating. Rebekah, in the meantime, placed Esau's clothes on Jacob and induced Jacob to go to his father with the meat that she had prepared, to get the blessing intended for Esau. The deception was successful. Jacob received the blessing meant for Esau, and Esau was angered. He planned to kill Jacob, but Jacob—with his mother's aid—fled to the ancestral home in northern Mesopotamia where he married and began to raise his family. With the principal blessing given to Jacob, Esau had to be content with a lesser blessing. He would continue to be a man of the open spaces (Gen 27:39, 40), and while he would be subject to his brother, the time would come when he would regain his independence. This reflects the fact that the Edomites, descendants of Esau, were subject to Israel during times of Israelite strength. In Israelite weakness, however, Edom became an independent state. Jacob remained in northern Mesopotamia twenty years, and on his way back he sought means of appeasing Esau. Esau, however, had prospered in the region of Mt. Seir during Jacob's absence. They had an amicable reunion, after which Jacob went on to Canaan, and Esau back to the region of Edom. The Biblical account of Jacob and Esau seeks to show that the line of promise went from Abraham to Isaac to Jacob-Israel, and that the later Israelites are the descendants of Jacob. Esau, who lost his birthright and blessing, forfeited the rights of the first-born. He had, however, a satisfying life in the region of Mt. Seir. His descendants are the Edomites.

C. F. PFEIFFER

ESCHATOLOGY

I. Introduction

II. Eschatology of the OT
- A. The eschatology of the people of God
  1. The day of the Lord
  2. The messianic hope
  3. The restoration of Israel
- B. The eschatology of the individual

III. Eschatology of the Apocrypha and Pseudepigrapha
- A. Introduction
- B. The afterlife
- C. The messiah and his kingdom
- D. The resurrection
- E. The judgment

IV. Eschatology of the NT
- A. Introduction
- B. The teaching of Jesus
- C. Events leading up to the Second Coming
- D. The Second Advent
- E. The resurrection of the dead
- F. The intermediate state
- G. The Last Judgment
  1. Introduction
  2. Christ the final Judge
  3. The standard of judgment, grace, and works
- H. The divine retribution, hell
- I. The final consummation, heaven
- J. The millennium
- K. Concluding observations

I. INTRODUCTION

Eschatology (Gr. ἔσχατος *last,* and λόγος, *science* or *subject*) is a term used to designate the teaching from Scripture concerning the final consummation of all things. It is assumed throughout Scripture that history is the scene of God's redemptive activity and therefore, is moving toward a new order when sin and evil will be overcome, and God will "become all in all." It is hardly possible to overestimate the importance of eschatology to Christian faith: life without faith is empty, and faith without hope is impossible. If the "eschatology" of modern science—death for the individual, death for the species, death for the entire system of wheeling suns which we call the universe—is the only truth by which man can live, then indeed "let us eat, and drink, and be merry, for tomorrow we die." The Christian, however, does not believe that death is the last word. For him the resurrection of Christ has robbed death of its victory and brought hope and immortality to light. It is the content of this hope that the Christian doctrine of eschatology sets forth.

II. Eschatology of the OT

A. The eschatology of the people of God. In the OT one may distinguish between individual and national eschatology; the latter, in many passages, being enlarged to embrace not only Israel, but the Gentile nations as well. As the hope of Israel is the predominant eschatological note in the OT the discussion of eschatology will begin from the broader perspective of an eschatology of the people of God.

The hope of God's chosen people is the fundamental strand of OT teaching regarding the future. Eschatology is the climax of the history of Israel's salvation. God, who led the fathers out of Egypt and gave them the Promised Land, will eventually triumph over all His and their enemies; He will secure to His people complete fellowship with Himself, and eventually establish His dominion over the whole earth. Thus the promise made to Abraham, "In thee shall all families of the earth be blessed" (Gen 12:3, KJV), ultimately will be fulfilled. (If for "be blessed," one trs., "bless themselves" [RSV], i.e., wish that they might enjoy the same blessings as Abraham and his seed, it makes little difference in the ultimate meaning.) The fact that this hope is the consummation of history does not mean that it is something man will achieve by his own efforts or that man can even calculate when and how it will come about. It is rather the coming of Yahweh, who will miraculously intervene and create all things new, that makes possible the full realization of the covenant promises. For the most part, the prophets tended to depict this age of final salvation after the analogy of God's former acts of salvation history; the glorious future of Israel would be continuous with current history as they knew it. As time went on, more and more stress was laid on the qualitative difference between the present historical order and the new age of eschatological fulfillment. This is particularly true of Daniel and the later apocalyptic writers.

1. *The day of the Lord.* Perhaps the most characteristic formula in the OT to describe the eschatological drama is "the day of the Lord." The term "day" is used in Arab. for a time of battle; so in Heb., "the day of Midian" (Isa 9:4). In popular parlance, the day of the Lord is the time (not necessarily a literal day) when Yahweh will interpose on behalf of His people to save them from their enemies and alleviate the miseries that burden their lives. It is the time when the remnant, loyal to Yahweh, shall be delivered (Isa 6:13; Amos 9:9). It is the day when He shall pour out His spirit on all flesh and all who call on the name of the Lord shall be delivered (Joel 2:28-32).

This does not mean—and the prophets make the point clear—that the day of the Lord is a time of salvation alone. On the contrary, when the Lord shall visit the righteous with salvation, He shall also discomfit the wicked with judgment "Woe to you who desire the day of the Lord! Why would you have the day of the Lord? It is darkness, and not light; as if a man fled from a lion, and a bear met him; or went into the house and leaned with his hand against the wall, and a serpent bit him. Is not the day of the Lord darkness, and not light, and gloom with no brightness in it?" (Amos 5:18-20). The reason that the day of the Lord is a day of doom is that the God who saves is also a God of holiness who punishes the rebellious sinners, and Israel had thus sinned (Amos 4:12). Before the Exile, the note of judgment predominated, though the note of salvation shone through (Isa 1:25, 26; Hos 2:16f.), esp. in the latter part of Isaiah. After the Exile, the theme of salvation took the ascendancy (Ezek *passim*).

Often the day of the Lord is given wider scope, to include the Gentile nations along with Israel in the realization of the divine purpose. Sometimes nations were used as instruments of God's judgment on Israel (Assyrians, Chaldeans, Persians), although they too would be judged in turn by the Lord (cf. the prophecies against the nations in Isa, Jer, Ezek, Amos, Nah, and Hab). As in the prophecies concerning Israel, salvation was also the purpose of God toward the nations. The reign of God shall be extended "until all the earth is full of his glory" (Isa 2:2, 3; 42:4; 60; Jer 12:14-16; 16:19-21; Ezek 16:53f.; Mic 4:1-5). These events will come to pass in the "latter days" (Isa 2:2; Jer 48:47; Hos 3:5).

In Daniel's prophecy of the four kingdoms, these kingdoms were broken in pieces by a massive stone cut out of the mountains without hands (Dan 2:44, 45), which was to become a great mountain to fill the whole earth (Dan 2:34), symbolizing God's everlasting kingdom. In the same vein is the beautiful prophecy of Malachi (1:11), "For from the rising of the sun to its setting my name is great among the nations . . . says the Lord of hosts." Although the Gentiles shall be made fellow heirs of Israel's salvation, Jewish nationalism will still prevail. Israel will inherit the Gentiles (Isa 54:3). "The kingdom . . . shall be given to the people of the saints of the Most High" (Dan 7:27). The nations will do homage to Israel—"they will make supplication to you, saying: 'God is with you only, and there is no other, no god besides him' " (Isa 45:14; cf. Isa 49:23).

Though the day of the Lord is principally concerned with God's coming to mankind for salvation or judgment, it is also a time when the order of *nature itself* will be shaken with great convulsions. Scenes of gloom and dissolution are not uncommon in the prophets (Isa 2:12ff., chs. 13, 14; Hos 10:8; Joel 2, 3; Amos

5:18; Zeph 1). Along with these terrifying visions, there are those that picture a new paradisiacal order in which "the desert shall rejoice, and blossom as the rose" (Isa 35:1 KJV). "The wolf also shall dwell with the lamb, and the leopard shall lie down with the kid . . . , the lion shall eat straw like the ox. . . . They shall not hurt nor destroy in all my holy mountain [says the LORD], for the earth shall be full of the knowledge of the LORD, as the waters cover the sea" (Isa 11:6-9 KJV). The involvement of the order of nature in the eschatological drama, set forth in rapturous poetic language, expresses the essential truth that the physical world was created for man and, therefore, shares in the judgment and renewal that is his final prospect. The ancient Hebrews knew nothing of the Gr. concept of salvation by flight from the body and the world of which man is a part.

When the prophets speak of the day of the Lord, they regard it as near, esp. threatening judgment (Isa 13:6; Joel 1:15; 2:1). Of course, its exact time was known to no man; because it was a free act of God, it was not predictable as some event in the natural course of things. A presentiment of its nearness was awakened by the moral lapses and seemingly incorrigible apostasy of the people. Man's insensibility to the divine majesty seemed so frightful that the Lord must surely intervene (Isa 13; Joel 1:2; Zeph).

In this regard it should be noted that some prophecies were actually fulfilled, at least in part, by the proximate sequel of events. In the war with Syria and Ephraim (743/33), e.g., Isaiah predicted the defeat of the enemy though the hostile threat remained to Judah (Isa 7:5-7, 16; 8:4). In the siege of Jerusalem by Sennacherib (701), he prophesied its collapse (37:33-35). It was esp. the threat of Nebuchadnezzar that tended to give historic definition to the visions of eschatological doom. The eschatological dimension is actualized in the ensuing events, so that some scholars speak of the captivity and exile of Israel as an "actualizing" eschatology. Similarly, the restoration of Israel was not only a future hope but, in a limited way, a present reality in the person of Cyrus, the king of the Persians (Isa 41:2, 3, 25; 44:28; 45:1; etc.) This proximate fulfillment of the prophetic visions of judgment, in the calamities that overtook Israel from the N, and of salvation, in the restoration under Cyrus of Persia, gave meaning to the sense of imminence that informed much of the eschatological vision of the prophets.

2. The messianic hope. The messianic hope is an important element of OT doctrine, though the figure of the Messiah did not have the central place in OT eschatology that Jesus had in the eschatology of the NT. The Redeemer, in whom the pious of the OT hoped was God—"Deliverance belongs to the LORD" (Ps 3:8), and if the Messiah is a redeemer, or a savior, it is because of His divine nature.

The word "messiah" means "anointed." In the OT the word is applied to the priests, but esp. the kings, and it is this latter usage of royalty that has left the most pronounced traces in the eschatological hope of the Jewish people. By virtue of the oil of anointing, which symbolized his investiture with the Spirit of God, the king was a sacred person, consecrated as Yahweh's vicegerent in Israel. From the time of Nathan's oracle, the hope of Israel was fixed on the dynasty of David (2 Sam 7:12-16). With the humiliation of that dynasty by the Chaldeans, though the faith of Israel was severely tried, it survived in the hope of a future king who would be the true servant of the Lord, and bring justice, light, and deliverance to all nations (Isa 42:1-4, 6, 7), and to extend the covenant of God to all the earth. Visions of this coming Servant are delineated in a section of Isaiah sometimes known as "Servant Songs" (Isa 42:1-7; 49:1-6; 50:4-9; 52:13-53:12). In these passages is a certain fluid movement between the thought that Israel is the Servant and that some individual is the Servant. The corporate personality progresses toward the individual, as the prophecies progress, which justifies the classic Christian application of these Servant prophecies to the person and work of Jesus Christ. In the second chapter of his gospel (v. 32), Luke quotes Isaiah 49:6, where the mission of the Servant is expressly described: "It is too light a thing that you should be my servant to raise up the tribes of Jacob and to restore the preserved of Israel; I will give you as a light to the nations, that my salvation may reach to the end of the earth."

Another prophecy that belongs to the messianic strand of OT eschatology is Daniel 7:11ff., which refers to one coming on the clouds of heaven like unto "a son of man," having an everlasting dominion. "Son of man" appears to have been the most common self-designation of the Lord. It must be remembered that the OT does not clearly coordinate all these categories —"seed of David," "Servant of the Lord," "son of man"—as is done this side of the Incarnation. But they all have their place, even though at times they be ambiguous, in the eschatological hope of Israel.

3. The restoration of Israel. The interpretation of Israel's hope of restoration to its own land is difficult to achieve from a Christian perspective. It is, however, a prominent feature of OT prophecy. Just as the judgment of God upon His people was never separated, in the prophetic vision, from the historical event of the Exile, so the salvation of the people was never separated from the historical event of the return to the land. God said to the N: "Give up, and to the south, Do not withhold; bring my sons from afar and my daughters from the end of the earth" (Isa 43:6). Restored to the land, the people would enjoy everlasting felicity and righteousness, together with all earthly blessings (Amos 9:11-15). In the eyes of the nations they were in truth the people of God (Isa 43:2ff.).

There can be little question of the meaning of similar prophecies of restoration to the land. Though the essential element was the spiritual beatitude of the righteous through God's making His abode in their midst, nonetheless this noble vision involved an external condition of the people in the glorified land of Canaan. If the final meaning of the OT is revealed in the New, what shall be made of the fact that the NT says nothing of the restoration of Israel to the land? Paul, the only NT writer to discuss Israel's future in detail (Rom 9-11), deals only with the spiritual aspect of the promises made to the fathers. For Paul, the salvation of Israel is that they shall be grafted back into the olive tree into which the Gentiles have been grafted, through faith in Christ (Rom 11:13-36). It seems best, therefore, to take the many prophecies of restoration to the land as having their literal fulfillment in the return under Ezra and Nehemiah, when the Temple and city of Jerusalem were restored; and to construe their final fulfillment in terms of those blessings of a heavenly land, secured to all God's people in Jesus Christ. The present-day return of Israel to Pal. should indeed give one pause; yet it is difficult to see in this interesting development a clear fulfillment of prophecy, as long as the Israeli remain a nation in unbelief and their prosperity in the land is more a tribute to their technological ingenuity than to any divine, supernatural act of eschatological redemption.

B. The eschatology of the individual. As can be seen from the above, the central themes of OT eschatology—the advent of God, His judgment of the nations, and establishment of the final kingdom of righteousness—are themes that concern mankind as a whole. What of the individual? Is his life, no matter how prolonged and blessed, yet cut off by death? Does he live only in the memory of his descendants? Is the state of beatitude only for those living in "that day" when God shall create new heavens and a new earth?

It is difficult for the Christian to understand the limited place that is given in the OT to the individual, and the emphasis on the solidarity of the larger unit of the household, of the tribe, of the nation, and of the race. In the OT, the happiness of the upright man consisted in a long life in the land that the Lord had given him, and his hope in a pious and numerous seed that should live after him. Yet the Israelites did not suppose that the individual became extinct at death; from earliest times they possessed a belief in the shadowy existence in Sheol.

The etymology of the word ($sh^{e}\bar{o}l$) is difficult. It prob. derives from the same root as the words for the "hollow" of the hand, or a "hollow" place in the land. Sheol is a subterranean region, or pit, where the dead subsist in a shadowy and attenuated form; it is only a feeble reflection of life on earth. Though under God's dominion (Ps 139:8; Amos 9:2), God has withdrawn His Spirit from the denizens of that forgotten land, so that they lack energy and the vital spirit of life, being consigned to a flaccid and vacuous existence as shades. The abode of the dead is called "silence" (Ps 94:17); "the land of forgetfulness" (Ps 88:12); the dead know nothing (Eccl 9:5). Death levels all men to a common fate; it brings them to a state where the wicked cease from troubling and the weary are at rest (Job 3:17). Samuel complained at being "disquieted" by the witch of Endor (1 Sam 28:15). The most threatening aspect of death for the righteous is the fear that they will be cut off from God. "In death there is no remembrance of thee; in Sheol who can give thee praise?" (Ps 6:5). "For Sheol cannot thank thee, death cannot praise thee; those who go down to the pit cannot hope for thy faithfulness" (Isa 38:18).

Unlike the NT, the OT teaches that both the righteous and the wicked go to Sheol, and the factor of reward and retribution is not the paramount consideration. Yet it would be too much to say that the same fate awaits the righteous as the wicked, who perish under the bane of the divine displeasure. "The wicked shall depart to Sheol" (Ps 9:17), and the proud and haughty shall be brought down to Sheol, to the pit (Isa 14:15; Ezek 32:23). Scholars have frequently seen the penal character of Sheol also in Psalms 49 and 73. On the other hand, the fervent prayer, "Let me die the death of the righteous, and let my end be like his!" (Num 23:10) would seem to imply more than a desire for a prolonged and happy old age on earth.

It seems not too much to say, then, that the hope of the righteous is for a deliverance from Sheol, and that, as time went on, the deliverance was seen to imply a resurrection. The flesh of the righteous shall rest in hope, because God will not leave his soul in Sheol, but rather show him the path of life, the joy of divine presence, and the pleasures at God's right hand (Ps 16:9-11, cf. Ps 17:15; 49:15; 73:24). Job raised the question (Job 14:14), "If a man die, shall he live again?" In the light of this question, it is plausible to tr. the strong affirmation of faith in Job 19:25f. as involving the vision of God "from the flesh." Isaiah 26:19 strikes a clear note of resurrection, and in Ezekiel's vision of the valley of dry bones (37:1-14), surely the element of individual resurrection cannot be excluded. Finally, in Daniel 12:2 for the first time the resurrection of the wicked, as well as the righteous, is affirmed: "And many of those that sleep in the dust of the earth shall awake, some to everlasting life, and some to shame and everlasting contempt." The implication this prophecy contains concerning the judgment of the wicked is found as early as Isaiah 66:24, "They shall go forth and look on the dead bodies of the men that have rebelled against me; for their worm shall not die, their fire shall not be quenched, and they shall be an abhorrence to all flesh." This threat to the wicked, together with the hope of the righteous man that God will receive him to glory (Ps 73:24), summarizes the limits of personal eschatology in the OT.

III. Eschatology of the Apocrypha and Pseudepigrapha

A. Introduction. The Apoc. and Pseudep. are extra-canonical books written from the beginning of the 2nd cent. B.C. to the close of the 1st cent. A.D. Some do not touch upon the eschatological theme; others dwell upon it in great detail. Whereas many writings in the intertestamental period follow the basic perspective of the OT and conceive of the eschatological fulfillment of the divine purpose as continuous with this present age, others are strongly apocalyptic, postulating two distinct and separate ages; the present evil age under the sway of Satan, and therefore beyond redemption, and the eternal age to come, under divine dominion. Describing this eschatological hope, these books indulge in vividly imaginative representations, characterized by an increased emphasis on the individual and the afterlife. Many of these representations are developed from the OT, others reflect Babylonian, Persian, and even Greek influence. Although often conflicting with the teachings of the NT, and far from uniform within themselves, these documents constitute a nexus between the eschatology of the OT and the NT, with its heightened emphasis on the individual and its extensive use of imagery.

B. The afterlife. The realm of the dead is Sheol, a dreary, subterranean chamber in the earth. In the postexilic lit. it became a temporary rather than permanent abode, esp. for the righteous, who will leave it at the resurrection (Pss Sol 14:6, 7; 2 Macc 7:9; 14:46). In those sources that limit the resurrection to the righteous alone, Sheol is thought of as a place of punishment for the wicked who remain incarcerated there. The author of 2 Maccabees (12: 43-45) wrote that Judas Maccabeus prayed for his fellows who had fallen in battle, and who were presently in Sheol. This passage has been used as a proof text for the Roman Catholic doctrine of prayers for the dead in purgatory, though Sheol and purgatory are by no means the same.

When Sheol is thought of exclusively as a place of punisment for the wicked, the abode of the righteous is sometimes thought of as Paradise. According to the Apocalypse of Moses 33:4, when Adam died his soul was taken to Paradise. In like manner, in the Testament of Job, Job was taken by the angel of death to the throne of God's glory, to where his children had preceded him. In Baruch 21:23f.; 30:2; 4 Ezra 7:95, the souls of the righteous go to heavenly "treasuries" or chambers, awaiting the resurrection, whereas the souls of the wicked descend into Sheol.

C. The messiah and his kingdom. In the intertestamental lit. the messiah is sometimes presented as a passive ruler over a transfigured Israel (Enoch 83-90); at other times he is a warrior who slays his enemies with his own hands (Sib Oracles 3:652-660), or by the word of his mouth, ruling in justice and holiness (Pss Sol 17:27, 31, 37, 39, 41). In Enoch 37-70 he is the supernatural ruler and judge of all mankind, the most sublime view found outside the canon.

As for the messiah's kingdom, it is sometimes eternal, on a transformed earth (Enoch 1-36), inaugurated by a resurrection and a final judgment; at other times it is of temporary duration, followed by these events (Enoch 91-104; Pss Sol 17, 18; Jub, As Moses, Wisdom, etc.). In some of the lit. of this period (4 Ezra), no mention is made of a messianic kingdom. Many of the intertestamental books reiterate the OT promise that Israel will return from the dispersion to her own land.

D. The resurrection. Because it is only just that the righteous dead should share in the messianic kingdom, the idea of a resurrection became important in the lit. between the Testaments. It is generally conceived of physically, the soul coming from Sheol, or some other place, to be united with the body. Sometimes it is general—both the righteous and the wicked are raised (Apoc Moses 41:3). God will fashion men's bodies just as they were in life, so that they may be recognized (Sib. Oracles, IV, 179f., 2 Baruch 50). Sometimes the resurrection is limited to the righteous, as in certain of the Testaments of the Patriarchs; for example, the affirmation that the godly alone will be raised, esp. the martyrs (Test. of Judah 25:4), which seems to be the thought also of 2 Maccabees 7:9.

As for the nature of the resurrected body, the maimed and broken limbs of the martyrs will be restored. Enoch 62:15, 16 says the bodies of the righteous will be clad in garments of glory. In 2 Baruch 50 is expressed the quaint notion that in the general resurrection, the bodies of men will be exactly as in life; but that the bodies of the righteous will gradually change until they surpass the angels and are like the stars in glory, whereas the wicked, observing this wondrous transformation, will see their own bodies waste away and decay.

E. The judgment. The judgment is sometimes conceived realistically, i.e., as involving the destruction of the wicked by the messiah or the saints; sometimes forensically, i.e., as a court decision based on men's works. The former view is analogous to the OT prophets, the latter to the pattern of Daniel 7:9, 10, where the "ancient of days," seated on a throne, judges out of open books (cf. Enoch 47:3; 90:2-27; 4 Ezra 7:33). In some of the sources (Test Job 5:10f., Enoch 10:6; 16:1), fallen angels as well as men are judged. The judge is either

God or the messiah, and the judgment takes place either at the beginning of the messianic kingdom, or at its close, or, if no such kingdom is expected, at the end of the world. Rewards and punishments according to one's just deserts are impartially meted out. The ungodly are consigned to some place of eternal torment, generally in the lower parts of the earth where they are plagued by fire and sometimes eaten by worms. The righteous, on the other hand, enter into Paradise, which is either heaven or a renewed and transformed earth. There they will have rest from oppression and death, and enjoy the presence of God, or of the messiah, forever.

IV. Eschatology of the NT

A. Introduction. In eschatology, as in all things, the NT grows out of the Old. It also reflects the intertestamental period, insofar as this period is marked by a development of thought that is consonant with the basic thrust of the NT.

According to the NT, the Incarnation is the fulfillment of the OT promise of salvation. This fulfillment is of such a nature that it anticipates a final consummation that is still future. The historic work of Christ (His life, death and resurrection) may be called a "realized" eschatology, yet it is a partial realization that anticipates a final realization at the Second Coming of Christ, an event that is still in the future. According to the writer of Hebrews (1:2), the "last days" of which the prophets spoke, are here. As the promise of the Spirit (Joel 2:28) has been fulfilled in the outpouring of Pentecost, those who have the Spirit of Christ have already experienced the "powers of the age to come" (Heb 6:5). Therefore, the final eschatological hope of the return of Christ is not merely a hope, as though it were altogether a future event; it is a hope that has already become a historical reality. It is the consummation of what was already accomplished in the first coming, esp. in the resurrection of Jesus from the dead.

This dialectic of an eternal life that is already a historical reality, and yet remains a future hope, permeates the entire NT. It is a past reality that the apostles have seen with their eyes, looked upon, and touched with their hands (1 John 1:1); yet they confess that they still walk by faith, not by sight (2 Cor 5:7), and that only when "he appears we shall be like him, for we shall see him as he is" (1 John 3:2). In the resurrection of Christ and the quickening by His Spirit are the first fruits of the heavenly order; believers are those upon whom the "end of the ages has come" (1 Cor 10:11). At the same time, the "last day" still lies in the future; Christians are still looking for the Savior (Phil 3:20) and confess that beyond this world, there is a world to come (Eph 1:21).

B. The teaching of Jesus. What Jesus taught concerning the future is a matter of dispute. The older liberal school believed that the eschatological pronouncements attributed to Jesus in the gospels are not to be taken seriously. They viewed these pronouncements as the product of the Jewish-Christian community that adapted Jewish apocalyptic theories to Christian needs. If indeed Jesus did use such terms, it was an accommodation to His contemporaries, and men must construe them in a way that is consonant with the basic ethical principles at the core of His teaching. In such a view, a literal acceptance of the *Parousia* robs it of its true meaning. Because Christ comes as Judge, not finally in the last day, but always, in the providential moments of life, the "coming" (*parousia*) of Christ as Judge provides an impulse to moral conduct. Christ's eschatological language may be viewed as a picture of the truth of His present and continued judgment of mankind, not a description of actual future events. Even the imagery of coming in the clouds is not too much for the splendor of this thought of a present and perennial judgment.

In the school of "consistent eschatology" (Albert Schweitzer), the opposite view is taken. Jesus is interpreted as an apocalyptist for whom eschatology was anything but a peripheral matter of accommodation. Jesus regarded Himself as fulfilling the role of Daniel's "Son of man" who would come in the clouds of heaven and set up the glorious kingdom of God on earth. This interpretation of the data of the gospels has been credited with "rediscovering" eschatology in the Christian message. However, according to Schweitzer and his disciples, Jesus taught that these events were to occur in the lifetime of the generation then living. Obviously things did not turn out this way and Jesus died a disillusioned martyr, when His expectation of the imminent end of the world failed to materialize. His apostles clung to the hope He would soon return in glory, but the delay of the *Parousia* gradually compelled a major adjustment in the theology of the Church. In this process of adjustment, Jesus was metamorphosed into the Christ of dogma, having little to do with the man who lived in history.

The modern "form critical school" (Rudolph Bultmann) gives little support to this view. It is doubtful, according to Bultmann, that one can know much about Jesus beyond the fact that He heralded the coming kingdom by calling men to repentance. For Bultmann, not only did the kingdom *not* come in Jesus' lifetime, but there is no way of saying it will ever come, except the vertical act of God in each individual life, whereby the moment becomes "existential," resulting in one's living "authentically."

The view that is most faithful to the text of the gospels accords with the general position, outlined in the introduction to this article. Jesus believed that the eschatological teaching of the OT prophets received its fulfillment in His life and ministry. He began His ministry, therefore, by proclaiming that the kingdom of

God was about to be realized among men. "Repent, for the kingdom of heaven is at hand" (Matt 3:2). In fact, in the person of Jesus, the kingdom was already present. (One plausible tr. of Luke 17:21 is "the kingdom of God is in the midst of you.") At the same time, there is a sense in which the kingdom was not fully realized in Jesus' own lifetime, but remains a future hope. The day is yet coming when all men will be judged, and their final destiny determined (Matt 11:21-23; Luke 10:13-15). Men are admonished to prepare for the day that shall usher in the glorious kingdom (Mark 13:33-37; Luke 12:42-46). There is in Jesus' teaching respecting the kingdom both present reality and future expectation.

As the Messiah, Jesus looked upon Himself as the Mediator of the kingdom to God's people, both in its present form and in its glorious consummation. As for the time of the consummation, the question of its imminence is indeed central. The view that Jesus was mistaken in this matter, is by no means the only plausible reading of the evidence. The verses giving the greatest difficulty are those in which Jesus said that some shall not taste of death till they see "the kingdom of God come with power" (Mark 9:1; Luke 9:26, 27), or until they see the "Son of man coming in a cloud with power" (Luke 21:27-33; cf. Matt 16:27f.; 24:34).

The context in which these sayings are given is important to their understanding. When the disciples pointed out the magnificent Temple structure, Jesus predicted that the day would come when there would not be one stone standing upon another in that vast edifice. The startled disciples drew the conclusion that such a catastrophe could mean nothing less than the end of the world. "Tell us," they urged, "when will this be, and what will be the sign of your coming (*parousia*) and of the close of the age?" (Matt 24:3). Jesus answered this question the way it was put; that is, He wove together into a single tapestry a grand apocalyptic scene, made of two strands; on the one hand—the destruction of Jerusalem, and on the other—His own coming in the clouds "with power and great glory."

To account for this procedure, it must be remembered that He was uttering a prophecy, and that prophetic perspective involves what has been called a "timeless sequence," a telescoping of events that, in their fulfillment, may be chronologically separated from each other. (The prophets of the OT, for example, spoke of the coming of the Messiah without distinguishing between His coming in humiliation, and His coming in glory.) As an artist imposes a three-dimensional landscape on a two-dimensional canvas, so Jesus spoke of the fall of Jerusalem and the final judgment of the evil world system as *one* event—which they are theologically but not chronologically. He did this, not only because He spoke prophetically, but because the lesser event—the fall of Jerusalem—is a paradigm of the greater event, the fall of this sinful world order, when God shall judge the wicked and vindicate the righteous at the end of the age. Had nothing happened in Jesus' generation corresponding to His prophecy, then one would have every reason to believe nothing ever would, and that Jesus made a fatal mistake. But because Jerusalem and the Temple were destroyed in A.D. 70, men are confirmed in their faith that this prophecy, so strikingly fulfilled in miniature, will one day be fulfilled in the larger theater of world history. Therefore, the eschatological hope of the Second Advent, so essential to the Christian faith, is grounded in the teaching of Jesus Himself, and this teaching is by no means an illusion.

C. Events leading up to the Second Coming. The Second Advent is really a whole complex of events, some of which precede, some of which follow the appearing of Christ in glory.

The events leading up to the *parousia*, should not be used to predict the time of Christ's coming, as some have vainly done. Indeed, Jesus said that no one, except the Father, knows the day or hour of His return (Mark 13:32). Though one cannot know the times and seasons that the Father has fixed by His own authority (Acts 1:7), yet the NT has much to say about the manifestation of evil prior to the coming of the Lord, an evil that will be intensified as the time of the end draws near. Although hope is already a reality in this age, yet it is an evil age (Gal 1:4). Living in an era that is under the power of Satan, Christians are to beware of false messiahs (Matt 24:5) and antichrists (1 John 2:18, 22; 4:3; 2 John 7). Jesus compared the time of the coming of the Son of man to the days of Noah (Luke 17:26f.), and Paul warned that "evil men and imposters will go on from bad to worse" (2 Tim 3:13).

As early as the Book of Daniel, this demonic principle of evil, opposed to Christ and His kingdom, an evil that will esp. characterize the end time, begins to take on personal embodiment. Daniel's prophecy of the "little horn" (Dan 7:8, 23-26), is perhaps a veiled, apocalyptic reference to Antiochus Epiphanes, typifying some evil eschatological personage who will appear at the end of the age. Jesus warned of the "desolating sacrilege" ("abomination of desolation," Matt 24:15, KJV, cf. Dan 11:31; 12:11), and Paul spoke of "a man of lawlessness" ("man of sin," KJV) who will be revealed in his own proper time (2 Thess 2:3, 4).

This "son of perdition, who opposes and exalts himself against every so-called god or object of worship, so that he takes his seat in the temple of God, proclaiming himself to be God" (2 Thess 2:3, 4), may be the subject of the visions of evil in Revelation 13, which describes two beasts appearing, one coming up out of the sea, the other out of the land; the former representing world empire, the latter religious apostasy. Both were empowered by the dragon, who symbolizes the devil. (This

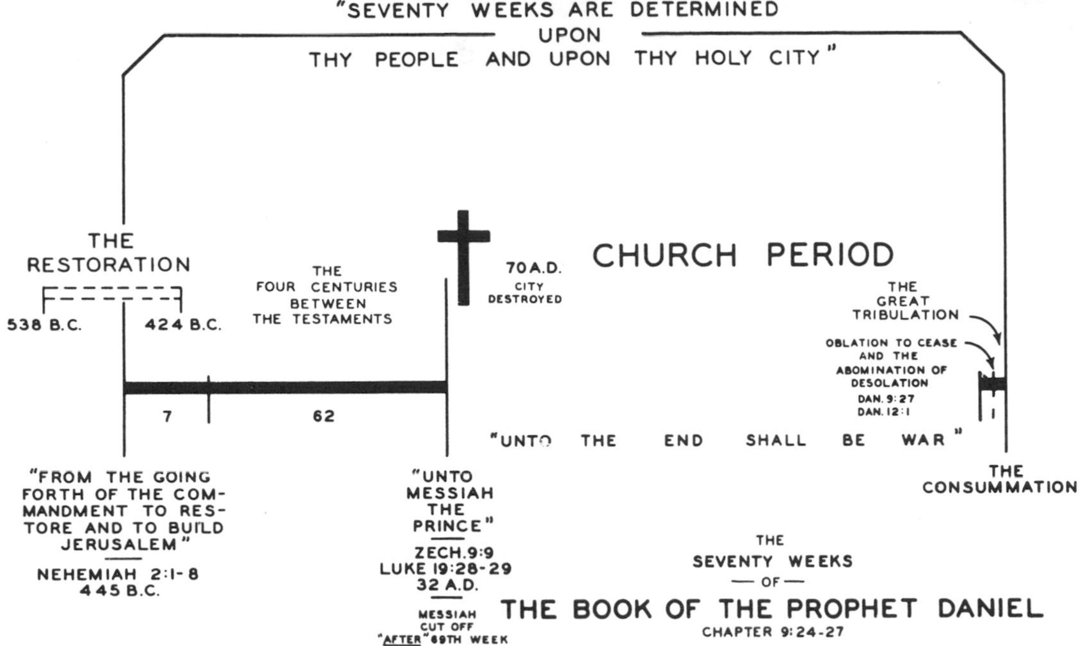

A premillennial viewpoint of *The Seventy Weeks*. Adapted from *A Survey of Bible Prophecy* by R. Ludwigson. © 1973 The Zondervan Corporation. Used by permission.

evil triumvirate—beast, false prophet, dragon—comprise a sort of demonic counterpart to the Trinity.) Many interpret both the first "beast" in Revelation and the "man of sin" in Paul as a political ruler of great power, appearing at the end of the age, who will use apostate religion to serve his blasphemous ambition to be worshiped as God (Rev 13:8, 12), following the example of the ancient Rom. emperors. Not only will he impose economic sanctions on all who will not submit to this sacrilege (Rev 13:16, 17), but he will also threaten a general and ruthless persecution against all the godly. Thus the Church of the end time, as was the Early Church, will be a martyr church sealing its witness with its own blood. This dire threat of persecution has often been seen as a fulfillment of Jesus' prophecy of a time of "great tribulation" (Matt 24:21), which will be shortened for the elect's sake (v. 22).

This time of bold defiance of heaven and persecution of the saints is also pictured in Revelation as a time of divine judgment upon the wicked, which shall culminate in the final destruction of Satan and his emissaries. Under the symbolism of trumpets and bowls, the seer of the Revelation sets forth the plagues and disasters with which God, in His wrath, shall vex and destroy the beast and those who worship him (Rev 8; 9; 14; 16). Against these terrible visitations of heaven the people of God will be protected, being sealed as His own (Rev 7:1-8) and beatified by martyrdom (Rev 7:9-17).

Other interpreters look upon these predictions of eschatological evil in personal categories, as fulfilled throughout Christian history. In such a view, there is no one anti-christ *par excellence*, nor one period that may be designated *the* tribulation, at the end of the age. All who are opposed to Christ and His Church, from Nero and his successors in ancient times to Hitler and Stalin in modern times, and any in the future, who shall emulate their example, are a manifestation of the principle of antichrist, and the Church that they persecute is the church in "tribulation."

D. The Second Advent. The event climaxing the judgments in which "this age" will end, bringing in the full salvation of the righteous in the "age to come," is the advent of Christ. Revealed from heaven with His mighty angels in flaming fire, the Lord Jesus will inflict vengeance upon those who do not know God nor obey the Gospel. At the same time, He will be glorified in His saints and will marvel at the number who have believed (2 Thess 1:7f.). The event is often described in terms that reflect the OT usage of the "day of the Lord" (Acts 2:20; 1 Thess 5:2; 2 Pet 3:10). Whether it be called "the day of God" (2 Pet 3:12) or "the last day" (John 6:39, 40, 44, 54, et al.) or just "that day" (Matt 7:22, et al.), there can be no doubt that the figure of the glorious Christ will be at the center of this final revelation of God. The NT phrases, the "day of the Lord Jesus" (1 Cor 5:5; 2 Cor 1:14); the "day of our Lord Jesus Christ" (1 Cor 1:8); the "day of Jesus Christ" (Phil 1:6); and the "day of Christ" (Phil 1:10; 2:16), all designate the

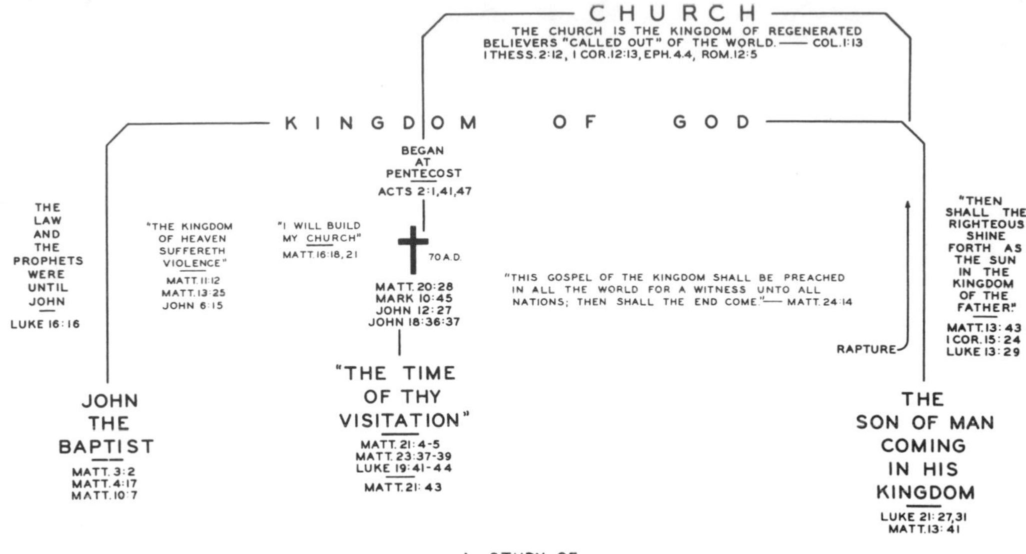

A premillennial viewpoint of *The Church and the Kingdom*. Adapted from *A Survey of Bible Prophecy* by R. Ludwigson. © 1973 The Zondervan Corporation. Used by permission.

time of the Second Advent.

Besides the general term "day" are several other technical terms used in the NT to describe the coming of Christ for the second time (Heb 9:28). The most common is *parousia* (1 Cor 16:17), which means "presence" in the sense of a "becoming present" or "arrival." It is used in Hel. Gr. of the visit of a ruler. So Jesus will "visit" this earth by way of a personal presence. Christ's appearance also is called an *apokalupsis,* that is, a "revelation" or "unveiling" (1 Cor 1:7). Then will be manifest the glory that He now has, being exalted at the Father's right hand. A third term is *epiphaneia,* from which comes the Eng. word "epiphany," meaning "appearance." In 2 Thessalonians 2:8 is a reference to the "epiphany of his parousia," which is difficult to interpret because of the closeness of the meaning of the two terms. Some have suggested that the two terms denote two distinct events, but there is nothing in the context to suggest that the *parousia* is a secret event separate in time from the *epiphaneia.* The two terms seem rather to be related as dawn to noon day, the epiphany being the full realization of the *parousia.* Scholars sometimes tr. the verse "the appearance of His coming."

Even the most cursory review of the language with which the NT describes the return of Christ shows how impossible it is to construe Christ's Second Advent as a slow, sure, spiritual conquest, in which the ideals of Jesus will yet win universal assent and His Spirit dominate the world, as in the older liberal theology (cf. Douglas MacIntosh, *Theology as an Empirical Science,* and William Adams Brown, *Christian Theology in Outline*). Rather than a tendency of history toward an ideal, the Second Coming is presented as an event, like in kind to the Resurrection and Ascension. The difference is that in His resurrection and ascension, Christ appeared "not to all the people, but to us [apostles] who were chosen by God as witnesses" (Acts 10:41). When He returns a second time, it will be a public event: "Every eye will see him" and "all tribes of the earth will wail on account of him" (Rev 1:7). It will be a *glorious* coming: "They will see the Son of man coming in clouds with great power and glory" (Mark 13:26, and parallels). It will be *personal*: the same Jesus (Acts 1:11) who walked with His disciples in Galilee and Judea, will come again to take His own to Himself (John 14:3).

E. The resurrection of the dead. Though even the wicked will be raised when Christ comes (John 5:28, 29; Acts 24:15; Rev 20:12, 13), in the NT, resurrection is principally set forth as a blessing, i.e., the redemption of the body from the power of death and the grave. The apostolic proclamation of the resurrection is based on the fact of Jesus' resurrection. It is He who, by His resurrection, "abolished death and brought life and immortality to light".

The new age manifests itself not only in Jesus' resurrection, but also in the new life that believers experience in Him (Rom 6:4; Eph 2:5, 6; Col 3:1-3), which makes the Church an eschatological community. This new order of existence, however, is preliminary and anticipatory; it is a life that will be fully realized only in the resurrection at the *parousia*. Jesus is "the firstfruits of them that sleep" (1 Cor 15:20, KJV), and "we know that when he appears we shall be like him" (1 John 3:2). There is this confident hope because many have already been delivered from death to life; "We know that we have passed out of death into life, because we love the brethren" (1 John 3:14). "If the Spirit of him who raised Jesus from the dead dwells in you, he who raised Christ Jesus from the dead will give life to your mortal bodies also through his Spirit which dwells in you" (Rom 8:11). Then shall this mortal put on immortality, this corruption shall put on incorruption, then death shall lose its sting and be swallowed up in victory (1 Cor 15:53f., free tr.).

The resurrection is not a reanimation of the "flesh" which contradicts 1 Corinthians 15:50, that "flesh and blood cannot inherit the kingdom." Rather, the new body will be "spiritual" (1 Cor 15:44), a paradoxical expression that teaches that in the life to come, the mode of existence will be neither wholly similar nor wholy dissimilar to the present mode. The body is the mark of man's creaturehood, the outward principle of his individuality. The Christian hope is not escape from the body, as a prison house of the soul, but deliverance from this mortal body of flesh and blood, to be clothed in a glorious body like that of the Lord Jesus Christ.

The concept of a bodily resurrection is a prime illustration of how the Gospel was foolishness to the Greeks. Busying themselves collecting mental bric-a-brac, the Athenians indulged Paul with condescending curiosity concerning the new gods he was setting forth; but when he propounded the idea of a resurrection of the body, they walked away mocking (Acts 17:32). This pagan incredulity has been given a new impetus by modern "scientism," the view that the realm of natural causality defines the possibilities of reality. Dead bodies just do not rise. It should not be supposed that resurrection means the reassemblage of the same atoms in the same molecular pattern that existed when the body was laid in the grave. Though such a concept is implied in some of the Jewish Ap. Lit., the NT does not speculate on the "how" of the resurrection. Paul admitted that he was telling a "mystery" (1 Cor 15:51) when he spoke of such things in answer to the questions, "How are the dead raised? With what kind of body do they come?" (1 Cor 15:35). He used the apt figure of a germinating seed to illustrate continuity with a difference. Yet, this is merely a picture drawn from nature.

Perhaps another illustration from nature may illumine the mystery of man's resurrection in a small way. In the Middle Ages, an indestructable "bone of immortality" was postulated as the nexus between the body of this life and that which would rise from the grave in the last day. By contrast, modern science teaches that the body cells, including its solid bony frame, not only turns to dust in death, but even in life perishes without a trace. In a relatively few years, the human body is renewed completely. When a man looks at a picture of a young boy, he may say, "This is I," for there is continuity at the physical level; the pattern of the hair, the pigmentation of the skin and eyes, even such individual factors as a birthmark, all underscore the sameness of the person according to his bodily nature. Yet the body of the child in the photo is not "literally" the same body; it is an entirely different body, several times removed from the one he now has. If this continuity in change can be maintained in this life, who is to say that death is such a radical destruction of the body that it cannot be overcome by the power of God?

The Christian doctrine of the resurrection rests not on any analogy of nature, but on the fact of the resurrection of Christ, which is without analogy, a setting aside of that fundamental law of entropy that has marked the entire system of nature with the sign of death. "If Christ has not been raised, then our preaching is in vain and your faith is in vain . . . you are still in your sins . . . . those also who have fallen asleep in Christ have perished" (1 Cor 15:14ff.). But, knowing that Christ has risen and become the "first fruits of those who have fallen asleep," there is hope that when He comes, all Christians shall share His resurrection, for if God raised his crucified Son, will He not raise His people by the same Spirit?

At the moment of the resurrection, those who are alive shall be changed "in the twinkling of an eye, at the last trumpet" (1 Cor 15:52) and all together shall be "raptured," i.e., "caught up . . . to meet the Lord in the air, and so we shall always be with the Lord" (1 Thess 4:17). The wicked, on the other hand, supposing they are safe, shall be surprised as by a thief in the night (Matt 24:42, 43) and overtaken by the sudden destruction that shall come upon them (1 Thess 5:2f.). Though they be working in the same field, grinding at the same mill, even sleeping in the same bed with the righteous (Matt. 24:41; Luke 17:34, 35), they shall be left behind, as were the sinners in Noah's day (Matt 24:38, 39), and the inhabitants of Sodom, when Lot departed the doomed city. Then the wheat shall be separated from the tares (Matt 13:24-30, 36-43), and the sheep from the goats forever (Matt 25:32, 33).

F. The intermediate state. What is the state of the dead who await the voice of the Son of man at the last day (John 5:25)? For the writers of the OT, the dead did not cease to exist, but entered a shadowy existence in the undifferentiated silence of the nether world. Removed from the presence of the living God, the righteous devoutly hoped that God would not abandon them to Sheol, but give them to know the joy of life in His presence (Job 19:25, 26). It was not until the inauguration of the NT age and the resurrection of Christ, that this hope was given a clearer definition. Even in the light of NT revelation, however, the question of whether the dead must await the resurrection before they enjoy the conscious fellowship of God, or whether they will "sleep" until the powerful summons awakens them from death, is hard to answer with certainty.

Originally held by certain sects of the Anabaptists and by the Socinians, the idea of "soul sleeping" has been revived in modern times by various groups of Millennial Dawnists and Adventists, and is even suggested by such a critically trained scholar as Oscar Cullmann. Paul's pithy statement, to be "absent from the body [and] to be present with the Lord" (2 Cor 5:8 KJV), a statement pregnant with hope for all Christians, is understood to reflect an immediacy of sequence in the consciousness of the individual only. When a Christian closes his eyes in death, the next moment, as far as he is concerned, he will be with the Lord, though countless millennia may have intervened. Thus the basic structure of the NT, which is death, followed by resurrection, is preserved; at the same time, the postponement of the resurrection, until the *parousia*, is maintained.

Such a view also makes possible a more consistent application of the NT emphasis on the unity of man. Traditionally, because of the interval of time between death and the resurrection, it has been taught that the soul continues in a disembodied form, intermediate between its present and its final state. This view is not without its difficulties, because it lends itself so readily to a more Gr. than Biblical mode of conception. The Greeks, suspicious of the body as evil, conceived salvation as the liberation of the soul from its fleshy prison house, that it might ascend to its proper element. They believed in immortality, but not resurrection. So concerned have some contemporary Biblical scholars been to escape this Gr. way of thinking, and to stress the Biblical concern with the redemption of the whole man, including the body, that they have affirmed that the resurrection takes place immediately upon death. The obvious teaching of the NT, that the resurrection occurs for all at the last day, is construed as a mark of man's temporal perspective. When one steps over the line in death, he shall see how, *im nunc aeternum,* "being present with the Lord" at the moment of death, and "meeting him in the air" at the *parousia,* are different ways of speaking of a simultaneous event.

Another suggestion is that in the "intermediate state" a body is given in anticipation of the resurrection body. The soul, though it has not yet been given a resurrection body, is not disembodied at death. Paul wrote to the Christians at Corinth: "Here indeed we groan, and long to put on our heavenly dwelling, so that by putting it on we may not be found naked. For while we are still in this tent, we sigh with anxiety; not that we would be unclothed, but that we would be further clothed, so that what is mortal may be swallowed up by life" (2 Cor 5:2-4). How such an "interim" body would function no one can say. If it is a glorious body, then what is the need of a final resurrection? If it is not, what is the advantage over our present mortal existence?

The Church, as a whole, has taught that while one awaits the resurrection of the body, death does not extinguish consciousness. If absent from the body, I—the essential self—am at home with the Lord (2 Cor 5:8), even though I must await the final resurrection to experience the redemption of the body. This seems to be the best, but by no means the only possible view, since it is most compatible with the fragmentary and somewhat disparate statements of the NT. In truth, the early Christians, knowing of Christ's resurrection, and assuming He would soon return to deliver them in like manner from death, were little concerned with the interval between death and the resurrection. Sometimes they spoke of the dead as "sleeping" (1 Cor 11:30 KJV; 15:20, 51; 1 Thess 4:14); sometimes as present with the Lord (2 Cor 5:8), from the analogy of the Lord's own word to the penitent thief, "Today you will be with me in Paradise" (Luke 23:43). Those who are persuaded of "soul sleeping" punctuate this passage in a different manner: "Truly I say to you today, you will be with me in Paradise." On such a reading, the fellowship in Paradise, which Jesus promised, is yet future, awaiting the voice of the archangel and the trump of God. But because "today" for the thief was his death day, and since the early Christians recalled these words of Jesus in the full knowledge of this fact, it seems they must have related "today" to the paramount concern of the man's death; otherwise "today" becomes mundane and superfluous. In like manner, it seems impossible to suppose that Stephen's final prayer (Acts 7:59), "Lord Jesus, receive my spirit," refers to some indefinite future, when his spirit would be awakened out of the sleep of death. Why should the heavens have opened upon him in the last moments of life (v. 56), only to close upon him again in death? Rather one must suppose that he joined the "spirits of just men made perfect" (Heb 12:23); that he was the first of many "souls of those who had been slain for the word of God" who cry out to the Lord from beneath the altar (Rev 6:9, cf. 20:4); that he entered into that blessed rest, a rest not from consciousness, but from labor (Rev 14:13), which is laid up for the people of God (Heb 4:9).

G. The Last Judgment. 1. *Introduction.* God

is the sovereign Lord of history, who reveals Himself not only as Redeemer, but also as Judge. He took vengeance on Pharaoh and the gods of Egypt; He rained down fire on the Sodomites; He scattered Israel among the nations for their sins. In the OT, the "day of the Lord," was a day of God's judgment of the wicked, a day of darkness and gloom.

The somber note of judgment looms large in the teaching of Jesus, who prophesied that the day would soon come when Jerusalem would be destroyed utterly (Matt 24 and parallels), the city in which the awful cry was heard, "His blood be on us and on our children!" (Matt 27:25). In a uniquely dark and sobering passage, Paul expressed the conviction (though he did not live to see the fall of Jerusalem) that a Damocles' sword was hanging over the head of his people "who killed both the Lord Jesus and the prophets, and drove us out, and displease God . . . But God's wrath has come upon them at last!" (1 Thess 2:15, 16).

The Jews, however, are no more under the judgment of God than the Gentiles. The same fate awaits the heathen who rage and imagine vain things against the Lord and His Anointed. Perhaps the most awesome vision in the Apocalypse is that of the fall of Babylon the great, symbol of the godless world order concentrated in the state and dominated by Satan (Rev 17:1-19:4). Culminating a series of bowl judgments upon the unrepentant and godless (Rev 16:2-21), the thinly veiled allusions to Rome leave little doubt as to the proximate reference of the vision. As in the prophecy of the fall of Jerusalem, so here, the implications go beyond history to a final, eschatological denouement.

2. Christ the final Judge. The one who shall administer this judgment is Jesus Christ. The day will come in which "he [God] will judge the world in righteousness by a man whom he has appointed" (Acts 17:31; 10:42). "That day when . . . God judges the secrets of men by Christ Jesus" (Rom 2:16) will be the time of the *parousia*. "When the Son of man comes in his glory, and all the angels with him, then he will sit on his glorious throne" and judge the nations, separating the sheep from the goats (Matt 25:31-36). At the end of the age, "the Son of man will send his angels, and they will gather out of his kingdom all causes of sin and all evildoers, and throw them into the furnace of fire . . . then the righteous will shine like the sun" (Matt 13:41-43).

Overpowering pictures of this last judgment are drawn by John, the seer. In one passage, the picture is in the realistic, dynamic terms of battle action. Seated on a white horse at the head of a great army, One whose name is "Faithful and True" rides forth to judge the wicked in righteousness. From His mouth proceeds a sharp sword with which He smites the nations. His robe is dipped in blood and He treads the winepress of the fury of the wrath of God (Rev 19:11-15). In another passage, the judgment is forensic in character. The judge is seated on a great white throne before which the dead stand to receive sentence, according to what is recorded in the books and according to whether or not their names are written in the "book of life" (Rev 20:11ff.).

3. The standard of judgment, grace and works. Even in this life, by virtue of God's justifying grace, Paul could declare that there is no condemnation to those who are in Christ Jesus (Rom 8:1). He who believes in Christ is justified from all things, from which he could not be justified by the law of Moses (Acts 13:39).

By contrast, he who believes not is already condemned (John 3:18). Therefore, when the day of judgment dawns, the wicked, already accused by an evil conscience, will call to the mountains to fall on them and cover them from the wrath of the Lamb (Rev 6:16). But believers need "not shrink from him in shame at his coming" (1 John 2:28), but "may have confidence for the day of judgment" (1 John 4:17).

There are some pressing questions that such a representation evokes. For one, if justification by faith has this eschatological implication; if being now justified assures one that he shall be saved from the wrath of God (Rom 5:9); if no one can bring a charge against God's elect, or condemn him for whom Christ died (Rom 8:33); is not the final judgment evacuated of all meaning? Does the believer not have a pass into the heavenly city? How then can Paul say that all must appear "before the judgment seat of Christ" to receive good or evil according to what he has done in the body (2 Cor. 5:10)? One must not make a bagatelle of such a solemn statement in the name of grace, as though it were appointed to men once to die and after this the judgment (Heb 9:27), for those who are not Christians only. Whereas the Christian, as a citizen of the heavenly country, has a "scroll" (Bunyan) and wears a "wedding garment" marking him as an invited guest to the marriage supper of the Lamb, there is surely an awesome accounting that he must render for the manner in which he has lived his life. Whereas grace and works are mutually exclusive principles in justification, grace does not exclude good works. Good works are the fruit of grace, and he whose life has been unfruitful will give answer for his lack of stewardship. The NT does not offer cheap grace.

In 1 Corinthians 3:10ff., Paul uses the figure of a building to illustrate this truth. The foundation is Jesus Christ (grace), but on this foundation each believer builds a superstructure (works). Let him take care how he does his work. If he builds with "gold, silver, [and] precious stones," his work will stand the fire of judgment; but if he uses "wood, hay [and] stubble," his works in that "Day" will be burned. "He himself will be saved, but only as through fire" (1 Cor 3:15). The importance of good deeds is also evident in the parable of Jesus that in the judgment the King will tell the righteous that in visiting those in prison, helping those who were sick, clothing the naked and feeding the hungry, they did it as to Him (Matt 25:34ff.). Without such credentials, it will do no good to call him, "Lord! Lord!" for not everyone "shall enter the kingdom of heaven, but he who does the will of my Father" (Matt 7:21).

In the judgment scene of Revelation 20, this dualism of grace and works seems to be the key to understanding the distinction between the "books" and the "book." "Books were opened" and the dead were judged by what is written in them; that is, by what they have done. But there is another book, called "the book of life," and to have one's name written in that book is salvation.

This book sometimes is called the *"Lamb's* book of life" (Rev 21:27). To say that the book belongs to the Lamb is to say that one's attitude to Christ, "the Lamb of God, who takes away the sin of the world!" (John 1:29), is decisive in the judgment. On the assumption that all men are sinners and cannot be justified by the works of the law (Rom 3:23; Gal 2:16), the NT consistently stresses that salvation is for those who confess Christ. "Every one who acknowledges me before men, I also will acknowledge before my Father who is in heaven; but whoever denies me before men, I also will deny before my Father who is in heaven" (Matt 10:32, 33; cf. 11:21-24). To the anxious inquiry of the Philippian jailor, "What must I do to be saved?" the answer is given, "Believe in the Lord Jesus" (Acts 16:31; cf. Rom 10:9).

What is to be said of those who have never heard the name of Jesus Christ? "How are they to believe in him of whom they have never heard?" (Rom 10:14). Because they could neither acknowledge nor deny the Christ, the only standard by which they can be judged is the light of nature. They stand condemned, Paul argued, because they willfully suppressed the knowledge of the truth, worshiped the creature rather than the Creator, and did what they knew to be worthy of death (Rom 1). One must not suppose that the offense of those who never heard the Gospel is the same as of those who deny Christ. It is an endemic principle of Scripture that responsibility is commensurate with knowledge. "He who did not know, and did what deserved a beating, shall receive a light beating" (Luke 12:48; cf. Acts 17:30, where reference is made to the "times of [Gentile] ignorance which God overlooked"). The degree of guilt that a man has before his Maker, only God the Judge can finally ascertain, but surely to whom less opportunity is given, of him less shall be required.

H. The divine retribution (hell). It is the common doctrine of many churches that the issue of the last judgment is not alike for all men. The righteous will be acquitted, but the wicked and impenitent will be condemned to everlasting separation from God in hell ("hell" is the common tr. of the Gr., "Gehenna," from the Heb. *ge-hinnom*, the valley of Hinnom, near Jerusalem where children were sacrificed in the fire to Molech, 2 Chron 28:3; 33:6).

Some have sought to soften this doctrine by affirming that the wicked are annihilated. The Biblical terms of "perdition," "corruption," "destruction," "death," that describe the fate of the lost, are thought to suggest the cessation of being. "Like smoke they vanish away" (Ps 37:20). Such punishment is "eternal" in that those who are annihilated never get over it. Whereas this doctrine seems to palliate the severity of the traditional view, it is by no means certain that such is the case.

> Thus repulsed, our final hope
> Is flat despair; we must exasperate
> Th' Almighty Victor to spend all his rage,
> and That must end us, that must be our cure,
> To be no more: sad cure! for who would lose,
> Though full of pain, this intellectual being,
> Those thoughts that wander through eternity,
> To perish rather, swallowed up and lost
> In the wide womb of uncreated night,
> Devoid of sense and motion?
>
> *Paradise Lost,* II, 142f.

Annihilation is not only theologically dubious, but exegetically untenable. The NT writers measure the misery of the wicked and the bliss of the righteous with the same terms. We read of "eternal" fire (Matt 18:8, 25:41), "eternal" punishment (Matt 25:46), "eternal" destruction (2 Thess 1:9), "eternal" sin (Mark 3:29). The fire is "unquenchable" (Matt 3:12); the worm "never dies" (Mark 9:48), the smoke of torment "goes up for ever and ever" (Rev 14:11). There is a lake of fire and brimstone, where the devil and his emissaries shall be tormented day and night "for ever and ever" (20:10; cf. 14:11). This same phrase, "for ever and ever," is used of the reign of the saints by the same author in the same book (22:5). The conclusion seems inescapable, therefore, that the punishment of the wicked extends interminably.

For many, such a doctrine is unthinkable. Not only do the wicked not perish eternally, but contrariwise, some suppose that finally all men will be restored to God's fellowship, because God's nature is love. The recrudescence of universalism in the contemporary lit. is marked by an appeal to the Scripture that says "God is love" (1 John 4:8), as though retributive justice were incompatible with love. But Scripture also has much to say about the holiness and justice of God, who is a "consuming fire" (Heb 12:29). In fact, love without justice is sentimental. As for the Scripture that speaks of the "restoration of all things" (*apokatastasis panton*, Acts 3:19-21 ASV), it may well be understood of the restoration of *condi-*

tions in which persons live (conditions lost by man's sin), rather than of the restoration of every individual to fellowship with his Maker.

There are, however, some striking statements on the universal scope and efficacy of the atonement in the NT. Christ took away the sins of the *world* (John 1:29); drew *all* men to Himself (12:32); propitiated the sins of the *whole* world (1 John 2:2 ASV); in Christ shall *all* be made alive (1 Cor 15:22 RSV); in Christ the *world* is reconciled to God (2 Cor 5:19). It is a fundamental rule of hermeneutics that such universal language should be interpreted in context; and always, faith in and obedience to Christ as Lord is the context for enjoying the saving benefits of His work. There is no warrant, therefore, for understanding such universal statements of Scripture as giving any hope for the salvation of those who willfully reject the claims of Christ and die in unbelief.

To be sure, the redeemed will number men from *all* nations, tribes, peoples, and tongues (Rev 7:9); the *whole world,* and not Israel only as in the OT, is embraced in God's redemptive purpose. This is not to say that every individual of mankind will be made alive in Christ and reconciled to God.

But it is commonly objected, granted that God is not only loving but holy, that it would be an intolerable miscarriage of justice that any man who has sinned threescore years and ten should suffer the consequences everlastingly. It must be remembered, however, that hell is not a place of passive suffering (as in some of Dante's visions), but rather a state of active rebellion. "Better to reign in hell than serve in heaven," said Satan. By the lives they have lived, the wicked have said, "Better to serve Satan than God," even if it be in hell. The character that one chooses in this life is irrevocably confirmed in the life to come. Sinners who chose a life without fellowship with God would prolong their lives indefinitely if they could. Can they then justly complain of hell that is just that—life without God forever? This is not to imply that the denizens of hell will be happy with their lot. They will neither be happy in hell nor aspire to heaven. Hell is frustration, the reality behind the myth of Prometheus and the rolling stone. And this restlessness is the opposite of the "eternal rest" laid up for the people of God.

I. The final consummation (heaven). As the Scripture employs terrifying figures in speaking of the fate of the wicked ("worm"—remorse, "gnashing of teeth"—frustration, "darkness"—separation from God who is light), it uses equally evocative figures in speaking of the bliss of the righteous. Theologians have called this bliss "heaven" because Scripture uses the term "heaven" to describe the abode of God (Deut 26:15); to dwell with God is man's highest beatitude. Heaven is the place where God is; and the final hope of God's people is to dwell with Him, that He may be their God and they His people, in unbroken fellowship.

Heaven is set forth in Scripture under many figures. It is the "sabbath rest" (Heb 4:9) lost in the first creation by man's sin and restored by him who said, "Come to me . . . and I will give you rest" (Matt 11:28); it is the "marriage supper of the Lamb" (Rev 19:7-9), marriage feasts being supremely joyous occasions in Biblical times; it is a lovely home, a "mansion in the sky." "In my Father's house," said Jesus, "are many mansions" (John 14:2 KJV; the Gr. means "abodes" or "dwellings," not "rooms" which convey the picture of a dormitory.) Heaven is a land, that "better country" of which the author of Hebrews wrote (Heb 11:13-16); it is a bright, white, opalescent "city," with golden streets, pearly gates, and jasper walls; a perfect cube in measurement (Rev 21:9f.); it is "Paradise Regained," a new Eden without a serpent and with the "tree of life" (Rev 22:1-5).

In this new order, God shall reign supreme. All His and man's enemies—sin, Satan, and death—shall be overcome (Rev 20:10f.; 1 Cor 15:26). His people, living and reigning with Him, will enjoy eternal life. This is the "kingdom of God," or the "kingdom of heaven," consummated (Matt 25:34, 46; Mark 10:17, 24).

The kingdom, foretold by the prophets of old, was "at hand" in the person of Jesus (Matt 4:17). God is still delivering those who believe in Christ from the dominion of darkness, transferring them "to the kingdom of his beloved Son" (Col 1:13). When Christ comes the second time, he will bring in this kingdom "with power." "Then the king will say to those at his right hand, 'Come, O blessed of my Father, inherit the kingdom prepared for you from the foundation of the world' " (Matt 25:34). At the end of the age, all evildoers having been gathered out, "the righteous will shine like the sun in the kingdom of their Father" (Matt 13:41f.).

It is difficult to know how literal or how metaphorical Scriptural representations of this glorious kingdom should be interpreted. The OT prophetic vision of the consummation involves a large degree of continuity with the present order of creation. Having beaten their swords into plowshares and their spears into pruning hooks, "they shall sit every man under his vine and under his fig tree, and none shall make them afraid" (Mic 4:1-4; cf. Isa 11:1-9). In the NT, also, is the teaching that the natural order, having been cursed for the sin of man (Gen 3:17-19), will be delivered "and obtain the glorious liberty of the children of God" (Rom 8:21). If men believe in the resurrection of the *body,* there must be some analogy of a physical and outward sort, between the present and the final state of things. If one may use the account of Jesus' appearances in His glorified humanity as a paradigm of what is to come for all believers it is plain that He did not appear to the disciples as a spirit, for He ate and drank with them (Acts 10:41), though His bodily presence belonged to another order of existence. (All of His recorded appearances, including the last one when He was "taken up" from them [1:9], contain this element of mystery, a bodily form of existence that transcends all earthly limitations.)

Along with this continuity implied in a bodily form of existence, Scripture stresses discontinuity, a radical difference between this world and the world to come, so much so that the latter may be called a *new* heaven and a *new* earth (Isa 65:17; 66:22). The Bible ends on this note of the radically new. "I saw," wrote John, "a new heaven and a new earth; for the first heaven and the first earth had passed away" (Rev 21:1). Pointing in this direction of radical change, one may interpret the reiterated vision of cosmic convulsions, characteristic esp. of Ap. Lit. In the last days, wonders shall be wrought in the heavens above and signs in the earth beneath. The sun shall be turned to darkness, and the moon to blood (Acts 2:19, 20; cf. Joel 2:28-32). The Apocalypse speaks of lightnings, thunder, and earthquakes, so great that the islands flee away and the mountains are not found (Rev 6:12ff.; 8:5; 11:19; 16:18-21). Perhaps the most graphic picture of all is in 2 Peter 3:10 that speaks of the heavens passing away with a loud noise, the elements dissolving in a fervent heat and the earth with the works thereof being burned up.

Theologians have mediated these pictures of continuity and discontinuity between a mere glorification of the present world order and a completely new creation *ex nihilo.* The Biblical words "regeneration" and "restitution" are suggestive of a mediating position. In Matthew 19:28, Jesus referred to the "regeneration" *(palingenesis* "new world," RSV) when the Son of man shall sit on His glorious throne. Peter, preaching in the portico of Solomon in the Temple, spoke of the "restitution" (*apokatastasis*) of all things at the time Christ shall return.

J. The millennium. When thinking of the relation of this world to that which is to come, some scholars and students of Scripture posit a transition period, a manifestation of the kingdom more glorious than the present, called the future millennial kingdom, but not as glorious as what shall finally be. Millennialists tend to construe prophetic visions of a future glorious age of this world as referring to this millennial kingdom, making the passages that speak of a radically new order to refer to the final state, that kingdom of glory when God shall be "all in all" (1 Cor 15:28 KJV).

Postmillennialists—who hold that Christ will return at the end of the millennium—construe the prophetic vision of a future golden age on earth, largely in spiritual terms. The Gospel of the kingdom will gradually permeate society like leaven (Matt 13:33; Luke 13:21), until men and nations shall own Christ as Lord, and justice and peace shall prevail in all the earth. As far as the *natural* order of things is concerned, the millennial age is really coterminous with the present. It is only at the close of this era of peace and righteousness that the glorious Christ shall be revealed.

Premillennialists, by contrast, have no such sanguine hope for such future accomplishments of the Church in human society. Far from accepting the Gospel, this world will remain evil until Christ Himself returns visibly to inaugurate His millennial kingdom. Giving many of the OT prophecies that speak of a coming glorious kingdom a more literal reading than postmillennialists would do, they believe that Christ will return to this world, bind Satan so that he can deceive the nations no more, and reign in a glorified Jerusalem with the resurrected saints for a thousand years (Rev 20:1-6). At the close of this period, Satan will be loosed to gather the nations to war for the last time. Both he and they shall be overwhelmed in catastrophe (Rev 20:7-10). Then they who had no part in the "first resurrection" (Rev 20:5) shall be raised to judgment and condemnation, after which the Son will turn over the kingdom to the Father (1 Cor 15:24). A threefold view of the kingdom—as manifested in this church age, followed by the millennium, culminating in the final state—is corroborated in the minds of many students of Scripture, by the structure of 1 Corinthians 15:23-28. The age began with the resurrection of Christ; it will be terminated by the resurrection of the righteous at His return; and will end when He shall deliver the completed kingdom of the Father. The premillennial view has a classic pedigree, being found in the thought of many of the ancient Church Fathers. Though it has had no place in the official theology of Roman Catholicism, nor appreciable influence in the mainstream of Protestant thought, there have been distinguished individual scholars and groups of Christians committed to some form of millennarian doctrine in all ages, including the present.

K. Concluding observations. Whether the consummation shall be attained by the triumph of the Gospel (postmillennialism), by the personal reign of Christ (premillennialism), or whether this present evil age shall be terminated and the new heaven and new earth ushered in by an immediate act of God, without analogy in history (amillennialism), it is the common confession and hope of all Christians that God shall be all in all at last. Although it is natural that the factor of man's blessedness should be emphasized, it is not this human bliss that is central in the data of Scripture nor in the doctrine of Christian hope. The *summum bonum* is to "glorify God and to enjoy him forever" (*Westminster Catechism).* The beatific vision is a vision of God. "Whom have I in heaven but thee?" asked the psalmist (Ps 73:25). One sees the caricature of Freud

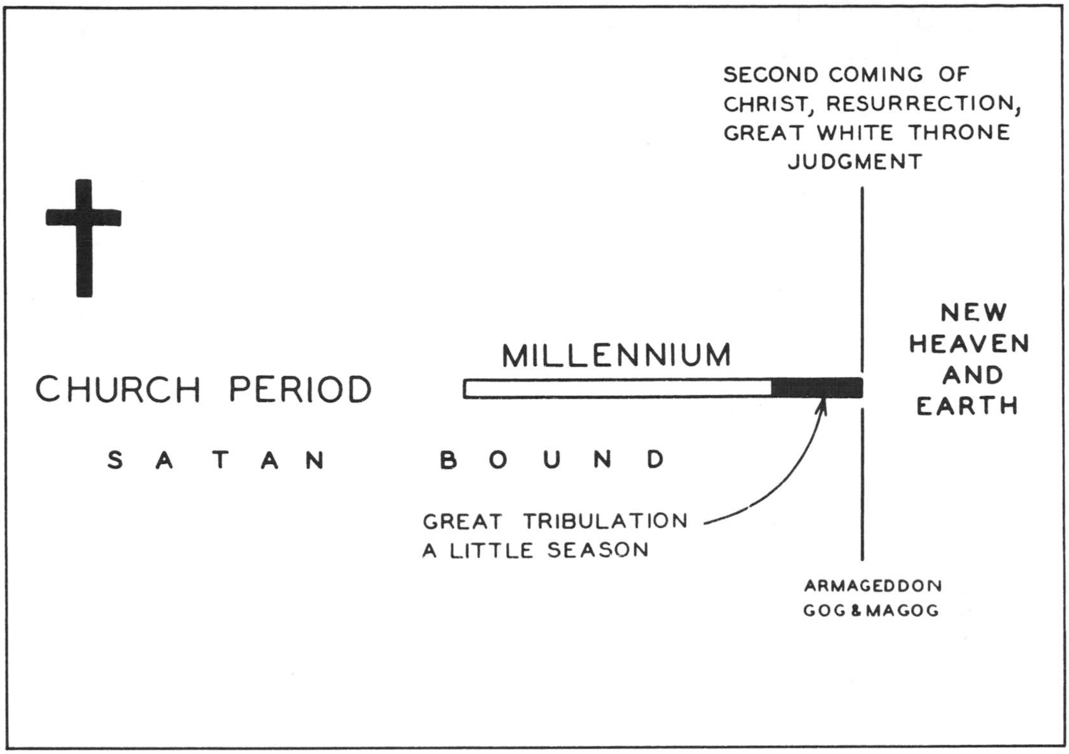

Chart of Postmillennialism.

Chart of Premillennialism.

Adapted from *A Survey of Bible Prophecy* by R. Ludwigson

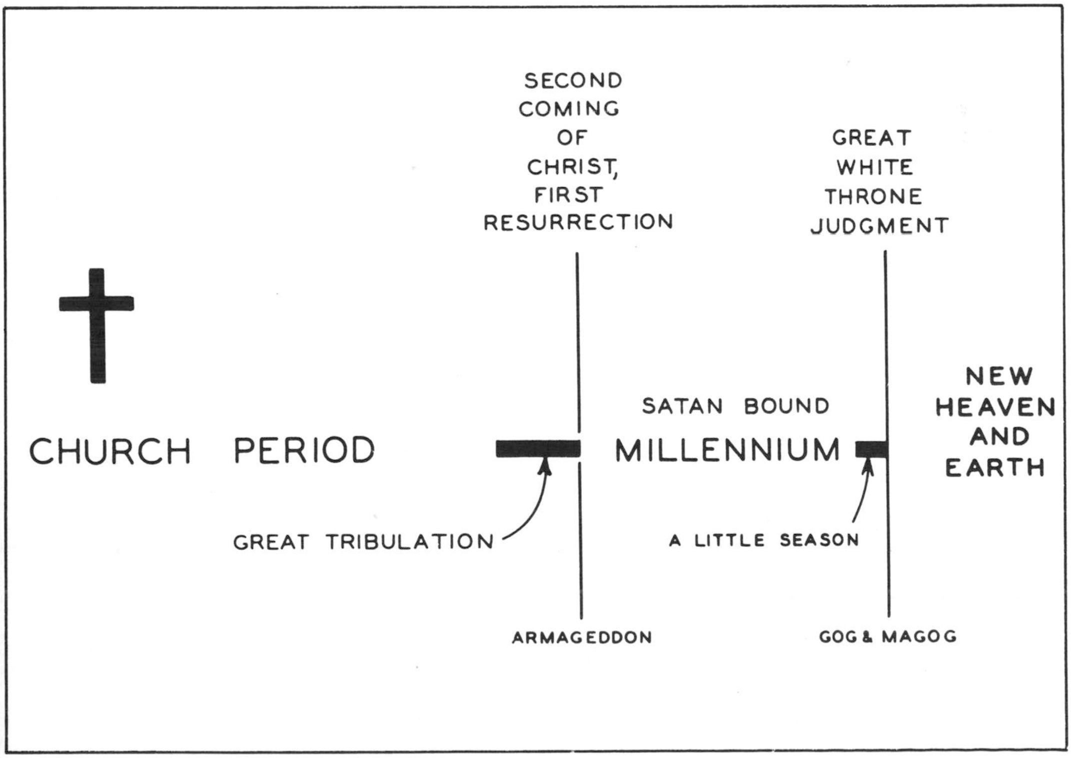

(*Future of an Illusion*) in representing Christian hope as the projection of a muted desire for happiness, which desire, being frustrated in this life, is transferred to the world to come. The goal of Christian aspiration is not "pie in the sky bye and bye," but rather *soli Deo gloria*; and when God shall be glorified in all His saints, then man will have reached the end of redemptive history, and spoken the last word of Christian doctrine.

It is, perhaps, because some unwittingly make human happiness, rather than the glory of God, an end in itself, that the question is so often asked, "How can the redeemed be happy in heaven when there is a hell?" Should they not rather ask, "How could the redeemed be happy in heaven, if those who hate God are there?" It assumes that no one can enjoy God unless he can enjoy his neighbor. Is it not true, rather, that they cannot enjoy their neighbor unless they enjoy God? Was the psalmist altogether wrong when he said, "Do I not hate them that hate thee, O LORD? . . . I count them my enemies" (Ps 139:21, 22)?

It is preoccupation, too, with the bliss of the creature rather than the glory of the Creator that has led to the oft-repeated charge that the Christian heaven is a boring place. To sit on a cushion and play a harp forever, would indeed be monotonous. Such a view overlooks the fact that the great throne scene of Revelation 4:1-5:14 presents a different picture. The center of the scene in the Book of Revelation is God, adored by His creatures who praise Him in a deafening diapason of sound. Heaven, for the Christian, is to hear the "four living creatures" sing "Holy, holy, holy, is the Lord God Almighty" (Rev 4:8), and to join their gratitude and adoration. Additional comment should be made about the "words" that the Church, following the example of inspired prophets and apostles, has used to express the Christian doctrine of hope. The current debate over theological language—"God talk"—has an obvious, if not basic, application to the eschatological statements that are made by theologians. It is alleged that the modern scientific view of time, space, and causality have rendered traditional eschatology meaningless. With a pre-scientific view of the "three-decker" universe, one can picture Christ's coming in glory on the clouds, surrounded with angelic legions, to summon the dead with trumpet sound. A look through the eyes of Einstein, a heaven of angels above, a hell of demons beneath, and a world in the middle as the stage for the awesome drama of the resurrection and judgment at the end of time, is unthinkable, it is alleged.

The problem is much older than the age of modern science; natural science may have sharpened the problem, but it did not create it. Philosophy always has been offended by a personal view of God, a God who revealed Himself in the massive form of historical events. If the doctrine of Christian hope be rejected, it is rejected because a philosophy of reality has been chosen that excludes the possibility of such hope. Such a philosophic choice does not rest upon science. Science is not a philosophy; it is a method of knowing the world of objects. Revelation, on the other hand, is concerned with the disclosure of God, who is not objective at all, but personal—the One who says, "I am." The language and thought categories of science are inadequate to describe even the mystery of *human* personality. How much less, then, should one expect an adequate description, in scientific terms, of the ultimate personal revelation of God at the last day. It is no wonder, then, that anyone who shuts himself up to the method of science will have no time for a "glorious appearing of the great God and our Saviour, Jesus Christ." Why should anyone shut himself up to a method of knowledge that makes him a mystery even to himself? The Christian theologian grants the inadequacy (not the meaninglessness) of all human language about God and the world to come, an inadequacy that will be overcome only in the consummation of all things, when faith shall become sight. In the meantime, giving up the rational autonomy of philosophy, he rests in a truth given by revelation, not discovered by reason. He believes to understand; *fides praecedit intellectum*.

BIBLIOGRAPHY. R. H. Charles, *A Critical History of the Doctrine of the Future Life* (1899); L. S. Chafer, *The Kingdom in History and Prophecy* (1915); H. H. Rowley, *The Relevance of Apocalyptic* (1941); W. C. Robinson, *Christ the Hope of Glory* (1945); G. Ladd, *Crucial Questions about the Kingdom of God* (1952); G. Vos, *Pauline Eschatology* (1952); E. Brunner, *Eternal Hope* (1954); E. Stauffer, *New Testament Theology* (1955); H. Quistrop, *Calvin's Doctrine of Last Things* (1955); J. D. Pentecost, *Things to Come* (1958); O. Cullmann, *Immortality of the Soul or Resurrection of the Dead* (1958); E. Brunner, *Dogmatics*, III, sec. IV (1962); K. Heim, *The World—Its Creation and Consummation* (1962); M. C. Tenney, *Interpreting Revelation* (1963); K. Stendahl, ed., *Immortality and Resurrection* (1965).

P. JEWETT

ESDRAELON, PLAIN (VALLEY) OF ĕz′ drĭ ē′lən ('Εσδρηλών, modification of the Heb. עמק יזרעאל, *the valley of God's sowing*, or *God will sow*, popularly "the Emek").

A lowland that transects the central ranges of Pal. separating the hills of Galilee and Samaria. Though mentioned as "Esdraelon" only in the Apoc. (Jud 1:8; 3:9; 4:6; 7:3), it forms part and parcel of the Valley of Jezreel (Josh 17:16; Judg 6:33), "the rich valley" (Isa 28:1, 4), and forms the setting for several passages of Scripture. In broadest usage, Esdraelon may include the whole plain from the sea to the Jordan, but a stricter terminology excludes both the Acre plain and (less emphatically) the valley eastward from Jezreel. It thus denotes the central triangle of lowland,

Two views of Esdraelon. *Top:* Valley looking southeast, Mount Moreh in distance. *Bottom:* Plain of Esdraelon from the Nazareth hills. ©*Lev* and ©*M.P.S.*

approximately fifteen miles along each side, with its apices at the Kishon Gorge, Jenin, and Mt. Tabor.

1. Structure. Esdraelon was formed by subsidence at the center and faulting at the periphery, and defined to the SW by the relatively continuous limestone scarp extending from Carmel to Gilboa and on the NW by the analogous if somewhat lower limestone escarpment of the Nazareth ridge. But the northeastern limits are less regular, since clear-cut fault lines are replaced here by lowland salients that isolate the limestone dome of Tabor—keystone of a vanished geological arch—and the basaltic mass of Mt. Moreh. A slight volcanic "causeway" divides the eastern from the western plain, but the basins themselves are largely infilled with alluvial loams stripped from the encircling rim of limestone and basalt, and by the dark organic soils of former swamplands.

2. Roads and passes. Enclosed within its triangle of hills, Esdraelon had its exits and its entrances, strategic keys to the Fertile Crescent. Cutting from E to W across the grain of Pal., the Emek opened a vital passage from the Mediterranean to the Jordan—the easiest lowland corridor in the length of the Syrian ranges. The western gate, guarded by ancient Harosheth, followed the ravine of the Kishon between the abrupt scarp of Carmel and the Galilean hills, whereas the eastern gate, properly the Valley of Jezreel, linked Esdraelon with Beth-shan and the fords of the Jordan.

But this E-W traverse gained added significance from its connections with N-S routeways. Since the forests and swamps of Sharon and the brusque promontory of Carmel impeded coastal movement, the "way of the Sea" turned inland for easier passage through the Samarian hill country to Esdraelon. Avoiding hard limestone uplands, the two westerly roads followed channels etched into softer chalk and reached the plain at Jokneam and Megiddo respectively, whereas the two easterly passes, following down-faulted valleys, emerged at Taanach and Ibleam. Each route had its particular advantages. The Jokneam road provided lower and more direct access from Sharon to Phoenicia; the Ibleam road, linking Samaria to Jezreel and the Jordan, was in constant use; and the Taanach route, though somewhat difficult, was an acceptable alternative to Megiddo should strategy dictate. The Megiddo route was crucial. Uniquely combining the chalk depression of the Wadi 'Ara with dry basaltic causeway, it carried the main route from Egypt across the Esdraelon marshlands and the fords of the Kishon to the Tabor gate—a further focus for traffic. For though the hills W of Tabor were not impassable and the narrow Wadi Bira led occasional traffic eastward to the Jordan, it was the easier Tabor gate that led most naturally to Galilee and Syria.

3. Settlement. Highway towns and mercantile wealth apart, Esdraelon was less significant for settlement. Its drainage retarded by narrow gorge and basalt barrier, the Kishon broadened sporadically into malarial marsh and waterlogged soils. Ancient settlements—long Canaanite rather than Israelite—clustered on the marginal lines of hills and springs, whereas the plains were grazed in patchy and seasonal fashion; the drier Valley of Jezreel was better tilled and Megiddo sent wheat to Egypt. Since 1920, however, planned colonization with eradication of malaria, drainage, well-drilling, and intensive cultivation have transformed the Emek into a rich mosaic of farmland and settlement.

4. A pattern of violence. Esdraelon, nevertheless, has been more noted for the arts of war than those of peace. Long before Thutmose III hailed the fall of Megiddo as "the capture of a thousand towns," the strategic implications were clear. The tale continued with Sisera's defeat and Gideon's victory (Judg 5:19-21; 6:33), Saul's last battle and Solomon's chariot fortress (1 Sam 31; 1 Kings 9:15), Jehu's relentless pursuit of Ahaziah and the downfall of Jezebel and Josiah (2 Kings 9:20-24, 37; 23:29). When John bore witness to the final triumph of Christ, it was Har-megiddo (Armageddon) that loomed in the Apocalyptic vision.

BIBLIOGRAPHY. C. F. Kent, *Biblical Geography and History* (1924); G. A. Smith, *Historical Geography of the Holy Land* (1931); (British) Naval Intelligence Division, Geographical Handbook Series, *Palestine and Transjordan* (1943); D. Baly, *Geography of the Bible* (1957); D. Baly, *Geographical Companion to the Bible* (1963); E. Orni and E. Efrat, *Geography of Israel* (1966).

G. R. LEWTHWAITE

ESDRAS, FIRST (1) ĕz' drəs (LXX Ἔσδρας, A, Heb. עזרא, meaning: *help*). First book of the OT Apoc. The Lat. Vul. designates it 3 Esdras, using 1 and 2 Esdras for the canonical Ezra and Nehemiah. Commonly known as the "Greek Ezra" to distinguish it from the canonical Ezra in Heb. and from the Apocalypse of Ezra in Lat. The author of the book is unknown.

1. Literary character. The similarity to the canonical books of 2 Chronicles (chs. 35, 36), Ezra (nearly all) and Nehemiah (7:73b-8:12) is obvious. There are noticeable changes in literary usage; in addition 3:1-5:6 represent a unique section, having no parallel in the OT.

Among the types of literary characteristics are the following: (1) omissions from Chronicles (see 2 Chron 35:11) and additions in 1 Esdras (see 1:23, 24); (2) word changes (e.g., 1 Esd 1:1, "held" and "offered," for "kept" and "killed" in 2 Chron 35:1); see also "temple" (1 Esd 1:2) for "house" (2 Chron 35:2); and "commandment" (1 Esd 1:6) for "word" (2 Chron 35:6); (3) elimination of many "ands" (1 Esd 1:2 with 2 Chron 35:2); (4) transposition of phrases, e.g., "in Jerusalem unto the

Lord" (1 Esd 1:1) for "unto Jehovah in Jerusalem" (2 Chron 35:1); and (5) change or addition in thought, e.g., "according to their daily courses" (1 Esd 1:2 KJV) for "in their charges" (2 Chron 35:2); "singing hymns to the Lord and praising" (1 Esd 5:60) for "to praise the LORD" (Ezra 3:10).

There is nothing in 1 Esdras which corresponds to Nehemiah 1:1-7:73a, nor is the name of Nehemiah mentioned in the narrative concerning the reading of the law (cf. 1 Esd 9:49 with Neh 8:9). Ezra is mentioned as "priest and reader" in 1 Esdras 9:39, the only place where the title occurs; Nehemiah 8:2 calls him "the priest." Possibly this data was intended to show the prominence of Ezra in his role as spiritual leader of the Restoration period.

2. Date. Due to the close relation of 1 Esdras to the canonical books of 2 Chronicles, Ezra and Nehemiah, the latter dating from the late 5th cent. B.C., and also some apparent dependence on the Book of Daniel in the LXX (see 1 Esd 4:58-60, RSV, with Dan 2:20-23), tr. in the 3rd and 2nd centuries B.C., the *terminus a quo* would be sometime in the 2nd cent. B.C. As the book is used by Josephus (Antiq. XI. V. 1-5), the *terminus ad quem* would be c. A.D. 90. Various dates have been suggested, ranging from c. 150-50 B.C.

3. Content. The historical range extends from Josiah's passover (1:1-24) to Ezra's role as leader of the people in Jerusalem (9:37-55). An annotated structural outline follows:

(1) 1 Esdras 1:1-58 (cf. 2 Chron 35; 36). Josiah's Passover; his battle with Pharaoh-Necho and resulting death; and the Babylonian invasion of Judah fulfilling Jeremiah's prophecy.

(2) 2:1-15 (cf. Ezra 1:1-11). Cyrus' decree allowing the Jewish captives to return to Jerusalem to rebuild their Temple.

(3) 2:16-30 (cf. 4:7-24). Letter from Pers. officials in Samaria to Artaxerxes asking that construction of the Jewish Temple be stopped, and the granting of the request.

(4) 3:1-5:6 (no OT parallel). Story of King Darius and three of his court guards. In answer to the question, "What thing is the strongest?" they reply, respectively, (a) wine, (b) the king, and (c) women, but truth above all. The third guard was Zerubbabel; his answer gained him permission to return and rebuild Jerusalem.

(5) 5:7-73 (cf. Ezra 2:1-4:6). The roster of returning Jews and the beginning of the restoration of the Temple in the days of Cyrus.

(6) 6:1-7:15 (cf. Ezra 5:1-6:22). Haggai and Zechariah urge the building to continue, in the second year of Darius, and after some delay, the temple was completed in the sixth year (515 B.C.).

(7) 8:1-67 (cf. Ezra 7:1-8:36). The return of Ezra and his companions to Jerusalem with a commission from the Pers. King Artaxerxes. He was to administer, rebuild and teach.

(8) 8:68-90 (cf. Ezra 9). Ezra's prayer of confession.

(9) 8:91-9:36 (cf. Ezra 10). Repentance on the part of the people, and Ezra's reforms, including judgment against mixed marriages.

(10) 9:37-55 (cf. Neh 7:73-8:12). Ezra reads the law to the people, and the Levites carry on the work of instruction.

4. Attitude toward the law. Two assertions are indicated: (1) the law was written by Moses (1 Esd, RSV, 1:11; 5:49; 7:6, 9; 9:39). The expression "the book of Moses" occurs four times and "the law of Moses" once. Further, according to 9:39, the law of Moses "had been given by the Lord God of Israel"; (2) obedience to the law was an assumed practice. Offerings were made in accordance with its directions (1:10, 11; 5:49; 7:6-9). Its words were considered a reason for rejoicing and a directive for daily life (9:37-41, 46, 47, 49-55).

After a long period of neglect and disobedience, this prevailing attitude toward the law seems to have been due in great measure to the work and influence of Ezra. According to Albright, Ezra's greatest importance "probably lay in the field of cultic reform than in that of political action." The law was established as "the normative rule of Israel's faith."

5. The story of Darius and the youths. While little background is supplied here for the story (3:1-3), Josephus (Antiq., XI, iii, 1) adds a number of details which shed a different light on the incident. Among other things, the latter reveals that "there had been an old friendship between him (Zerubbabel) and the king (Darius)."

The three wise sayings concerning what is strongest—wine, the king, and women, but, above all, truth—supply interesting insights into differing views on life, a common theme in Jewish wisdom writings.

Wine, said the first guard, is strongest, for it distorts the mental processes of those who consume it, causing them to do foolish and harmful things. Often one will reverse his normal attitudes toward his friends and his obligations.

The king is the strongest, averred the second man. He is absolute, bearing rule over even the strongest men. Obedience to the king is described by a rare word (ἐνακούουσιν), meaning "to hear to obey" (4:3). Every subject's life is at his disposal, an apt description of the oriental monarch.

Zerubbabel first named women as the strongest, yet concluded that "truth is great, and stronger than all things" (4:35). His argument for the former may be reduced to a simple syllogism: kings and wine are both great; but, women as mothers bear the men who conquer and who grow grapes; therefore, women are strongest.

Similarly, his praise of truth followed this approach: Women, along with wine and the king, are unrighteous; but, there is no unrighteousness in truth; therefore, truth is strong and prevails for ever.

The people responded to his analysis, "Great is truth, and the strongest of all!" Based on the Lat. Vul. text of 1 Esdras this statement has become proverbial: *magna est veritas et praevalet.*

At this, Darius proclaimed Zerubbabel the wisest and promised him anything he wished, and that he would be called his "kinsman" (συγγενής, 4:42).

BIBLIOGRAPHY. F. Josephus, *The Antiquities;* E. C. Bissell, *The Apocrypha* in *Lange's Commentary* (1880); R. H. Charles, ed., *Apocrypha and Pseudepigrapha,* I (1913); W. O. E. Oesterley, *An Introduction to the Books of the Apocrypha* (1946); R. H. Pfeiffer, *History of New Testament Times with an Introduction to the Apocrypha* (1949); W. F. Albright, *The Biblical Period* (1950).

W. M. DUNNETT

ESDRAS, SECOND (2) (see previous article for pronunciation and root words). The title comes from the Geneva Bible; in the Vul. it is called 4 Esdras. Sometimes called the "Ezra Apocalypse" (due to the character of chs. 3-14). Many writers regard chs. 1, 2 and 15, 16 to be Christian interpolations and give them the names 5 Ezra and 6 Ezra, respectively (e.g., Eissfeldt). See below under Date.

1. Literary character. While set in a Pers. situation (1:1-3), where the prophet Ezra received divine communication during the reign of Artaxerxes, the book is mainly apocalyptic, that is, a revelatory work on the order of Daniel 7-12. It is made up of seven visions (2 Esd 3:1-5:20; 5:21-6:34; 6:35-9:25; 9:26-10:59; 11:1-12:51; 13:1-58; 14:1-48) containing judgment against "Babylon" (Rome).

In words reminiscent of the prophet Habakkuk, the writer of 2 Esdras wrestled with the problem of evil: "How long and when will these things be? Why are our years few and evil?" (2 Esd 4:33; see also 6:59; cf. Hab. 1:2). Even when his angelic informant explained (2 Esd 4:10, 11), Ezra showed his bewilderment (4:12).

Much of the message is conveyed by symbolism. Outstanding are the fifth and sixth visions where (1) an eagle with twelve wings and three heads was encountered by a lion (11:1, 37) and (2) a man-like figure who rose from the sea and flew with the clouds of heaven was opposed by an innumerable multitude of men (13:3, 5).

2. Date. There is fairly general agreement that chs. 3-14 were composed near the end of the 1st cent. A.D., and that chs. 1, 2 and 15, 16 were added during the next cent. or two. What follows is a representative view, indicating the position of scholars as Oesterley, Metzger, Eissfeldt and others: chs. 1, 2, about A.D. 150; chs. 3-10, about A.D. 100; chs. 11, 12, about A.D. 69-96; ch. 13, about A.D. 66; ch. 14, about A.D. 100-120; and chs. 15, 16, between A.D. 240-270.

Probably the main reasons for rejecting the Pers. setting and placing the book in the Christian era are (1) the interpretation of the eagle vision (11:1-12:51) as a symbol of the Rom. empire (during the time of Vespasian, Titus and Domitian); and (2) the anti-Jewish or Christian character of much of the material in chs. 1, 2 (e.g., affinities to the gospels and the NT Apocalypse, and the anti-Jewish sentiments found in 1:24-27, 30-32, 33-35; 2:7).

3. Content. As indicated above, there are nine parts in the book, made up of an introduction and conclusion with seven visions:

(1) 1:1-2:48. The genealogy of Ezra and the record of the commands he received from the Lord to deliver the people of Israel (notice 1:4; 2:33, 42).

(2) 3:1-5:20. At Babylon, thirty years after the fall of Jerusalem, Ezra saw the contrast between the destruction of his city and the affluence of Babylon. He was perplexed over the seeming injustice, but was assured that God would solve the problem justly.

(3) 5:21-6:34. Seven days later he received a vision concerning the scattering of Israel among the nations ("O Lord, why hast thou . . . scattered thine only one among the many?"). Much of the discussion sounds similar to the Book of Job, and the solution to the problem seems to echo the Book of Revelation (on the former, see 5:35-55; on the latter, 6:17-24).

(4) 6:35-9:25. This is the longest of the visions. Eight days after the previous vision he spoke "in the presence of the Most High." Perplexity over the contrast between the many who will perish and the few who will be saved dominates this section. The judgment of mankind is vividly described. (Verses 36-105, appearing in brackets, are found in many ancient MSS but are missing from the Lat. Vul. and the KJV. It is the opinion of some that theological reasons were involved in the latter, for these vv. strongly prohibit prayer for the dead, e.g., v. 105.)

(5) 9:26-10:59. Ezra saw a woman mourning because her son had died. Then he saw a city of huge foundations. The vision was explained as follows: the woman was the heavenly Zion (10:44; cf. Rev. 21:9, 10); her son was the earthly city (10:46); and his death was the destruction which befell Jerusalem (10:48).

(6) 11:1-12:51. An eagle, having twelve wings and three heads, arose from the sea. He reigned over the earth, but was soon countered by a lion who uttered the words of the Most High against him. The interpretation identified the eagle as the fourth kingdom of Daniel's vision, and the lion as the Messiah who shall destroy the enemies of the Lord.

(7) 13:1-58. Seven days later Ezra saw "something like the figure of a man" arising from a stormy sea, and the man "flew with the clouds of heaven," language similar to Daniel 7:13. Opposed by a great multitude,

COMPARISON OF 1 AND 2 ESDRAS

	OT Ezra	OT Nehemiah	Paraphrase of 2 Chr 35-36; Ezra; Neh 8; with an original story	A Latin pseudepigraph (apocalyptic)
LXX	Ἔσδρας β		Ἔσδρας α	
Vulg.	1 Esdras	2 Esdras	3 Esdras	4 Esdras
Many later Latin MSS	1 Esdras Esdras		3 Esdras	2 Esdras (=1–) 4 Esdras (=3–14) 5 Esdras (=15–16)
English Great Bible, 1539	1 Esdras	2 Esdras	3 Esdras	4 Esdras
39 Articles VI, 1562			3 Esdras	4 Esdras
Geneva Bible, 1560	Ezra	Nehemiah	1 Esdras	2 Esdras
KJV, 1611	Ezra	Nehemiah	1 Esdras	2 Esdras

the man sent forth fire from his mouth and burned them all up. The man was the Son of the Most High (13:32) who shall destroy the wicked and gather the people of Israel from their dispersion.

(8) 14:1-48. In this final vision the prophet was commissioned to write for forty days, then would be taken to live with the Son until the times were ended. He wrote ninety-four books; twenty-four were to be made public; seventy were to be kept secret for the wise among the people. The former represented the Heb. canon (five, the Law, eight, the Prophets and eleven, the Writings); the latter prob. apocalyptic books. The Holy Spirit, sent into him as a cup full of fiery water, enabled him to write.

(9) 15:1-16:78. This final section, added in the 3rd cent. A.D., consists mainly of warnings of divine judgments against the nations. Egypt, Arabia, Parthia (Carmania), Babylon, Asia and Syria are mentioned by name. God's elect shall be delivered from the days of tribulation.

4. Theology. Second Esdras shares in common with other Jewish apocalypses a concern for the future. This concern is backed by a variety of affirmations about God and man, and by an expectation of the appearance of the Messiah (or, a Messiah) and the kingdom of God, along with a variety of beliefs about resurrection and judgment. Some of these conceptions in this book are the following:

(1) God. The favorite title is "the Most High" (at least sixty-eight times, RSV text), followed by "Lord" (at least sixty, RSV). There are various combinations, in addition, such as "Lord God" (4), "the Lord Almighty" (6) and "the Mighty One" (5). The name God occurs some twenty-one times.

One interesting variant may be noted. "Most High" does not occur in chs. 1, 2, 15 or 16, the "interpolated" sections of the book. On the other hand, the title "Lord" (and its combinations) is found many times (at least forty-three out of seventy) in these same chapters.

(2) Man. God allowed the nations to exercise free will unhindered (2 Esd 3:8). Man's ungodly nature showed itself because of his evil heart (3:20). Adam's sin resulted in a permanent moral disease, the good departing and the evil remaining (3:22). The idea of original sin showed itself in Adam (4:30). See 4:33, 38, 39; 7:22-25; 7:46-48.

Human understanding is limited (4:1, 2), and man cannot understand God's ways (4:11). When he is questioned he is unable to fathom the depths (4:1-12; 5:33-40).

(3) Resurrection and judgment. There is strong affirmation of a resurrection of the body at the end time (2:16; 7:32). The new age will soon dawn, after evil has been punished (4:26-32). The day of judgment is like a time of threshing (4:30). No one knows when this time will come (4:51, 52), but God has already determined the length of the age (4:36, 37; cf. *Sir* 36:8), and has prepared the judgment (7:70).

(4) Messiah. He is God's son who shall reign for 400 years, then die (7:28, 29). He appears as a lion who shall destroy the wicked nations (12:31, 32), and as a man arising from the sea and flying with the clouds of heaven (13:3, 25, 26). Once again he is declared to be

God's Son (13:32, 37, 52), and shall stand victoriously on Mount Zion (13:35-38).

(5) *Kingdom.* There is to be a temporary earthly kingdom (7:26-44), preceded by certain signs (6:20-24). A city shall be established (8:52; 10:27, 41-44), the heavenly Zion. After 400 years, this kingdom shall end (7:28, 29). Then comes the new age, characterized by resurrection, judgment and "the paradise of delight" (7:31, 32, 36).

While many of the lines are not clearly defined, one point is made often—the solution to the prevailing state of evil and the fate of both the good and the bad is the day of judgment, when all shall be made right by the Most High.

BIBLIOGRAPHY. R. H. Charles, *Apocrypha and Pseudepigrapha*, II (1913); ibid., *Religious Development Between the Old and New Testaments* (1914); W. O. E. Oesterley, *An Introduction to the Books of the Apocrypha* (1946); D. S. Russell, *The Method and Message of Jewish Apocalyptic* (1964).

W. M. DUNNETT

ESDRIS ĕz' drĭz (Ἔσδρις). Army officer at time of Judas Maccabeus (2 Macc 12:36). His role is not clear, and KJV (in some Gr. texts) reads GORGIAS.

ESEBON. KJV Apoc. form of HESHBON.

ESEBRIAS, ESEREBIAS. KJV and ASV Apoc. forms of SHEREBIAH.

ESEK ē' sĕk (עֵשֶׂק ; *contention*; LXX ἀδικία; *offense, wrong*). An artesian well dug by Isaac's servants in the valley near Gerar. Rather than quarrel with the native herdsmen, Isaac moved on, digging two more wells before he established an undisputed claim (Gen 26:19-22). The site is unknown.

ESHAN, ESHEAN ē' shən, ē' shĭ ən (אֶשְׁעָן, Josh 15:32). KJV is Eshean, but the more accurate Eshan is found in RSV and NASB. One of the towns taken during the conquest period which was designated for the tribe of Judah. The LXX has tr. this location as Σομα.

ESHBAAL, ESH-BAAL. *See* ISH-BOSHETH.

ESHBAN ĕsh' băn (אֶשְׁבָּן ; LXX Ασβαν; meaning unknown). One of the sons of Dishon, the Horite chieftain in the region of Mt. Seir (Gen 36:26; 1 Chron 1:41).

ESCHOL ĕsh' kŏl (אֶשְׁכֹּל ; LXX (1) Ἐσχώλ, (2) Βότρυς; Vul. *botrys*; Luther *Eskol*).

1. אֶשְׁכֹּל means *bunch, cluster*; properly the *stem* or *stalk* of a cluster viz., (a) grapes (Isa 65:8; Mic 7:1), and (b) berries or flowers hanging in clusters like grapes, e.g., dates (S of Sol 7:8), or flowers of the henna (1:14).

2. An Amorite, brother of Mamre and Aner, who apparently resided near Hebron (Gen 14:13). All three were allies of Abraham (c. 1955 B.C.) when Lot was rescued from Chedorlaomer (Gen 14:24).

3. The valley or wadi where the twelve spies found a cluster of grapes so huge that it required two men to carry it (Num 13:23, 24). Perhaps נַחַל אֶשְׁכֹּל (*valley of a cluster*) can be identified with a wadi just N of Hebron. (There is a spring called Ain-Eshkali c. two m. N of Hebron.) The vineyards in this area still produce delicious grapes.

R. C. RIDALL

ESHEK ē' shĕk (עֵשֶׁק, meaning *oppression*, 1 Chron 8:39). A family of the tribe of Benjamin descended from Saul, king of Israel.

ESHTAOL, ESHTAOLITES ĕsh' tĭ əl, ĕsh' tĭ ə-līts (אֶשְׁתָּאוֹל, אֶשְׁתָּאֻלִי), a reflexive form of the verb "to ask," possibly a place name serving to define possession (Y. Aharoni, *The Land of the Bible* [1967], p. 98); possibly modern Eshwa' (Ishwa'). Scholars have differed in their explanation of the anomaly that Eshtaol is listed as one of the cities of Judah (Josh 15:33) and also as one of cities of Dan (Josh 19:40, 41). KD harmonize the passages by assuming that the most northerly part of Judah's district was given up to the tribe of Dan on the second division of the land by Joshua (cf. Josh 18:2ff.). A. Alt, followed by most modern scholars, proposed that the Judean town list in Josh 15:21-62 is based on an administrative apportionment by the Judean monarchy (A. Alt, *Palästinajahrbuch*, 21 [1925], 100-116,=*Kleine Schriften zur Geschichte des Volkes Israel,* II [1953], 276-288; F. M. Cross and G. E. Wright, JBL, 75 [1956], pp. 202-226; K. Kalli-Kleinmann, VT, 8 [1958], 134-160; Y. Aharoni, VT, 9 [1959], 225-240). When the Danites' attempt to occupy the Shephelah ("the lowland" RSV) region around Zorah and Eshtaol encountered stiff opposition from the Amorite cities there (Judg 1:34, 35), the Danites of Zorah and Eshtaol played a principal role in relocating the tribe in Leshem (Josh 19:47; Judg 18:2, 8, 11). In the genealogy of Judah (1 Chron 2-4) the sons of its various clans are mentioned along with the names of their respective settlements in such a way that a clansman becomes the father of the place occupied; accordingly it can be determined that Judeans from Kiriath-jearim, descendants of Hur, prob. replaced the Danites in both Zorah and Eshtaol (1 Chron 2:50-53). The Spirit of God began to stir Samson, a Danite (Judg 13:24), between Zorah and Eshtaol (Judg 13:25), and he was buried there (Judg 16:31).

B. K. WALTKE

ESHTEMOA, ESHTEMOH ĕsh' tə mō' ə (אֶשְׁתְּמֹה, אֶשְׁתְּמוֹעַ), (the form *'eštemō[h]* found only in Joshua 15:50 is prob. corrupt), LXX Εσθεμω; derives from Heb. root meaning *to hear* (on the form of the name *see* ESHTAOL); modern

Valley of Eshcol just north of Hebron. ©*M.P.S.*

es-Semu'a, c. nine m. S of Hebron. The exact genealogical connection of this Judean town in the southern hill country of Judah (Josh 15:50) with the sons and grandsons of Judah mentioned in 1 Chronicles 4:1 is not known because in the received text Ezra, who begot Ishbah, the father of Eshtemoa, is unknown (1 Chron 4:17). Moreover, the exact connection between Ezra and Ishbah is unknown because the text appears corrupt. According to 1 Chronicles 4:19 Eshtemoa is a descendant of the wife of a certain Hodiah and also is a Maacathite; viz. descended from Maacah, Caleb's concubine (1 Chron 2:48). The town was later ceded to the Levites (Josh 21:14 and 1 Chron 6:57 [Heb v. 42]) (cf. A. Alt, "Festungen und Levitenorten im Land Juda," *Kleine Schriften* II [1952], 306-315). It was one of the cities where David had friends who were elders of Judah and to whom he sent part of the booty taken from the Amalekites after their raid upon Ziklag (1 Sam 30:26-28).

B. K. WALTKE

ESHTON **ĕsh' tən** (אשתון ; LXX Ἀσσαθών; *effeminate* or *uxorious*). A man enrolled in the census of Judah as the son of Mehir, the son of Chelub 1 Chron 4:11, 12).

ESLI **ĕs' lī** (Ἐσλί; meaning unknown). An ancestor of Joseph, husband of Mary, Jesus' mother (Luke 3:25).

ESORA. KJV form of AESORA.

ESPOUSAL, ESPOUSE. *See* MARRIAGE.

ESRIL, EZRIL. KJV Apoc. form of AZAREL.

ESROM. KJV NT form of HEZRON.

ESSENES **ĕs' enz** (Ἐσσηνόι, Ἐσσαîοι). A Jewish religious group which flourished in the 1st cent. B.C. and the 1st cent. A.D., and which formed the third important school of thought in the time of Christ (with the Pharisees and the Sadducees).

1. Name
2. Literary Sources
   a. Josephus
   b. Pliny the Elder
   c. Philo
   d. Hippolytus
3. Essene history
4. Essene life

1. Name. The meaning of the name has been much debated. The E Aram. term *hăssăyâ*, "pious" has been suggested as a possible origin, while other derivations have been seen in terms of the Gr. ὅσιος, "holy," ἴσος, "equal," and the Heb. חסד, "pious," עשה, "to do," *i.e.*, performers of the law, עשיר, "noble," "powerful" and אסיא, "healer," to mention a few suggestions. This confusion is understandable if the name "Essene" was never used by the sect itself as a descriptive term, which seems probable, for as early as Philo its etymology was obscure.

2. Literary sources. Josephus (Jos. War, II. viii. 2ff.; cf. Jos. Antiq. XVIII. i. 5) described the Essenes as the third of the "philosophies" or schools of religious thought in contemporary Judaism, but apart from his testimony there are further descriptions of

Essene beliefs and customs in his older Jewish contemporary, Philo of Alexandria, as well as another from the Rom. author, Pliny, the Elder. A later account furnished by Hippolytus was based on Josephus, though certain sections were apparently derived from independent sources.

a. Josephus. Though it is recognized that this author, who lived c. A.D. 37-98, tended on occasions to modify strict historical fact for apologetic and other purposes, it is nevertheless true that his description of the Essenes gives evidence of being factual and based upon first-hand knowledge. His earliest account (Jos. War. II. viii. 2ff.) of the sect was in the compilation made shortly after the fall of Jerusalem (A.D. 70), and there are several references to the Essenes in various parts of his other works, along with a shorter VS in his *Antiquities* (Jos. Antiq. XVIII. i. 5), written about A.D. 90.

In an autobiography, Josephus recorded that, as part of his study of the Jewish culture, he had joined a wilderness sect headed by a certain Bannus, with whom he stayed for three years before returning to Jerusalem and joining the Pharisees. Whether Josephus was ever actually an Essene novitiate, as he seems to imply, or not, must remain a matter of some doubt, particularly in the light of Essene admission regulations. The fullest account of the Essenes which Josephus furnished occurred in his *Wars of the Jews,* in which this third philosophical sect was depicted as espousing a stricter discipline than the Pharisees or Sadducees, and a greater sense of fellow-feeling. They rejected worldly pleasures as evil, but regarded continence and the control of the passions as virtuous acts. The Essenes rejected matrimony, preferring instead to train the young offspring of others and mold them to their own patterns of life. While not forbidding marriage for others, they felt that their own attitude was the only legitimate safeguard against the lasciviousness and infidelity of women generally.

Josephus continued to describe the communal life of the Essenes, which was based on the premise that the possession of riches was abhorrent. Those who joined the sect were required to bring their assets for the enrichment of the group as a whole, so that there would be no appearance of either poverty or riches in the community. Their common affairs were managed by stewards appointed for the purpose, whose sole aim was the well-being of the whole group. The Essenes apparently did not form a separate community, preferring instead to mingle with society at all possible levels. They were to be found in every large city, and were evidently well-received by the Jewish populace as a whole.

Essene piety had made a great impression upon Josephus, for he spoke at considerable length of their habits of worship and devotion. They began their day before dawn with an act of prayer, and following this the members of the sect pursued the various secular avocations for which they were fitted, being noted for the conscientious and diligent discharge of their duties. At noon they bathed in cold water and having reassembled in the communal dining room they partook of a simple meal after grace. They then returned to work, and in the evening repeated the procedure with regard to washing and eating.

The strict discipline of the group was indicated by the absence of strife or disturbance, and the only things which were permitted of the members' free will were acts of help to the needy and attitudes of compassion. While mercy was not allowed to usurp justice, the sect was noted for its fidelity, integrity and humanity, and such characteristics seldom made acts of strict justice necessary. Admission to this group was by way of an initial one-year novitiate, during which the beginner was expected to manifest the qualities to which the sect aspired. If he was deemed a suitable candidate he was required to undergo a further two-year period of testing, after which he was formally admitted to Essene society. At this point the candidate took oaths of fidelity and piety toward God and justice toward men, after which he was allowed to partake of the communal food as a fully accredited member of the group.

The strictness of Essene discipline was evident in the penalties prescribed for major transgressions. The offenders were banished from the sect, and being bound by oaths not to partake of common food frequently came to the point of starvation before they were taken back into the group, often out of sheer compassion. Communal life was under the control of a number of elders, who prescribed strict decorum in public meetings.

According to Josephus, the Essenes believed that, whereas the body was mortal, the soul was immortal. This gave a certain Platonic aspect to their teachings; that the body constituted the prison house of the soul, from which the latter was released at death to wing upward to the heavens. Cessation from work, and worship on the Sabbath day, were matters of punctilious observance in Essene society, and their veneration of Moses, their legislator, required them to indulge in careful study and practice of the Torah. Some Essenes were renowned for their insights into OT prophecy, and for their ability to foretell events still in the future.

Josephus noted that one order of the Essenes diverged from the general tradition on the sole issue of marriage. This group used the married state for the procreation of offspring rather than for sexual pleasure, in the belief that by refraining from marriage the other Essenes were depriving themselves of the "principal part of human life," namely, the prospect of lineal succession. They supported their position by the unshakeable argument that if everyone was to be of the same mind as the majority of the Essenes, the whole race of mankind would disappear.

In his *Antiquities,* Josephus furnished a more concise account of Essene teachings and habits of life, in which they were described as holding to a belief in the immortality of the soul, and the necessity for ascribing all things to God. They were independent of the Temple cultus to a considerable extent, and because they deemed certain of their own rites to be of purer quality than those of the Temple priests, they were excluded from the common court of the Temple. Despite this situation the Essenes were renowned for the fact that their virtue and righteousness exceeded that of the scribes and Pharisees, and at the time that Josephus was writing they showed every indication of continuing in that fashion. For him, this notable mark of spirituality was the direct product of communal living.

b. *Pliny the Elder.* Another 1st cent. A.D. author who commented on Essene life and behavior was the Elder Pliny. This man was a fellow soldier of Vespasian, and was perhaps with the Tenth Legion in A.D. 68 when it marched down the Jordan valley. In his *Natural History,* completed in A.D. 77, he included a topographical description of the W side of the Dead Sea, beginning with Jericho and ending with the mountain fortress of Masada which protected the S border of Judaea. This narrative mentioned a religious community which lived near a palm tree oasis, and it may be that this was the group at Qumran which cultivated crops at the oasis of ʿAin Feshka. Pliny described its location in general terms as being "on the W side of the Dead Sea," but N of En-gedi, and spoke of the community as "the solitary tribe of the Essenes," which was noteworthy for its renunciation of women and worldly goods. Pliny was impressed by the remarkable manner in which world-weary postulants flocked to the community seeking to follow the strict rule of life which the Essenes required of their members. Although the passage is obviously rhetorical in style, the general identification of the Qumran locality with some kind of Essene community is quite apparent.

c. *Philo.* In the writings of Philo, the Alexandrian Jew (c. 20 B.C.–A.D. 52), there is still more information about the Essenes in general, occurring in two of his works, *Hypothetica* (XI, 1-18) and *Quod Omnis Probus Sit Liber* (XII-XIII). These works, which were apparently based on a common literary source, were prob. written in Egypt before A.D. 50, and the factual descriptions which Philo has preserved can be taken as constituting valuable information about Palestinian Essenism in the early decades of the Christian era. However, his narratives need to be assessed critically, since Philo had apologetic interests in mind when writing about the Essenes. His attitude was governed by moralistic considerations, for he was utilizing his own people as an example to support the hypothesis that virtue had not vanished entirely from the contemporary Hel. scene.

He computed the number of Essenes in Palestinian Syria in excess of 4,000, as Josephus did at a later period, and thought that their name had been derived from the Gr. *hosiotēs* or "holiness." This designation he attributed not to the prosecution of cultic observances but to the resolve of the Essenes themselves to serve God devoutly and to sanctify their minds. Philo commented on the preference of the Essenes for life in villages rather than in cities, since the latter were much more likely to corrupt and deprave the person who was seeking to lead a sincere spiritual life. He also noted their diligence with respect to manual labor, and marveled at the way in which they had deliberately divested themselves of all personal wealth and property, esteeming frugality and contentment as constituting an abundance of riches. Equally significant for Philo was the pacifist attitude adopted by the Essenes, who neither manufactured nor traded in weapons of war. In harmony with this rejection of the military arts was the disavowal of any form of slavery, since they believed in the free exchange of services and held that the owners of slaves outraged the law of the equality of individuals.

The Essenes laid great emphasis on their ancestral laws, which had been mediated by divine revelation and were of supreme importance for faith and behavior. According to Philo, the Essenes observed the ethical precepts of the Torah strictly, manifesting their love for God in a variety of ways including consistent religious purity, abstinence from oaths, a love of virtue, freedom from bondage to material possessions, self-mastery, frugality, humility and contentment. Their respect for their fellows was manifested in deeds of love and charity, in their avowed sense of the equality of individuals, and in their notable spirit of fellowship. The communal life of the Essenes was particularly significant in that it was emulated nowhere else in actual practice. Their clothes and meals were held in common possession, and the wages which each person earned were put into the community treasury so that all might benefit as the need arose. The sick were cared for by those who were well, and the cost of treatment was met from the monetary reserves of the group. The elderly members of the community were accorded the respect due to their age, and in their declining years they were maintained in dignity and contentment.

Like Josephus, Philo stressed the place given in Essene circles to the study of Scripture and the manner in which they were instructed on the Sabbath day. The Essenes abandoned all work at that time and proceeded to sacred locations called "synagogues," where they were arranged in rows according to seniority, the younger ones sitting below their elders. In process of divine worship someone read a passage of Scripture, and after this another individual who was particularly competent in this area would expound after an allegorical manner anything in the section which was not clearly understood. Philo noted that the Essenes were trained in piety, holiness, justice, domestic and civil conduct, and summarized their beliefs and practices under three headings, namely, love of God, love of virtue and love of men.

In a later work, the *Hypothetics,* Philo again commented on the diligence and industry of the sect. He mentioned the common ownership of goods and money, and remarked upon their general insistence on a rule of celibacy for their members, on the ground that women and children tended to distract the community from its avowed aim of the pursuit of goodness and truth. Women who were mothers were believed to be a particularly serious menace, since they would stoop without any qualms to use their children as a means of imposing their will upon others in a fashion which would disrupt the spiritual unity of the group.

In a treatise entitled *On the Contemplative Life,* Philo devoted considerable attention to the activites of another religious group which bore some slight resemblance to the Essenes. Known as the Therapeutae, this community flourished in Egypt for some two centuries prior to the beginning of the Christian era. The Therapeutae were organized on a monastic basis, but were actually recluses who occupied their time in prayer, meditation and the study of their sacred writings, only assembling for divine worship as a community on Sabbath days and sacred occasions. According to Philo the Therapeutae prayed twice daily, at dawn and dusk, and spent the remainder of the day in meditation, reading the OT and interpreting it allegorically. In addition to this kind of study, they composed hymns and psalms in the solitude of their cells. On the weekly day of worship the Therapeutae assembled in order of seniority, and listened to a discourse given by one of the elders of the sect, subsequently returning to their cells for meditation and study. Women formed part of this monastic group, and were subjected to the same conditions of life as the men. Self-control formed the basis of their philosophy of life, which in other respects, however, was not as rigorous as that of the Palestinian Essenes, due to climatic and other factors. Although the Therapeutae may represent a late development of a pre-Christian Jewish sect which was perhaps the progenitor of the Essenes, they may be of quite independent origin. Nevertheless, the similarities between the Essenes and the Therapeutae warrant some consideration of the latter in any estimate of Palestinian Essenism.

d. Hippolytus. The evidence of a Christian writer, Hippolytus (A.D. 170-230?) can be adduced as an important supplement to the testimony of Josephus and Philo concerning the Essenes. In a treatise entitled *The Refutation of All Heresies,* he commented on the attribute of mutual love and concern which characterized Essene behavior. In describing those who renounced matrimony, Hippolytus noted that they did not admit women to their company under any considerations, even when they presented themselves as postulants and gave evidence of a desire to participate in community life on the same basis as that of the male members of the sect. They did, however, adopt young boys and train them in the ways of the Essenes, although they did not forbid them to marry should they desire to do so at a later time.

The usual regulations concerning wealth were evident in the observations of Hippolytus. While the Essenes despised riches, they were by no means averse to sharing their goods with those destitute persons who came to them for help. On joining the order the novitiates were required to sell their properties and present the proceeds to the head of the community, who was responsible for distributing them according to individual need. Hippolytus noted what must have been a rather distinctive practice in ancient Pal., namely the abstention of the sect from the use of oil, on the ground that for them it constituted defilement to be anointed.

The decorum of the sect was governed by strict rules of behavior, which apparently impressed Hippolytus as much as earlier writers. The Essenes lived and worked under the control of elders and overseers, and were required to live lives of rigorous self-discipline. Disorderly behavior was not tolerated in any form, and swearing was a particularly serious matter, since whatever anyone said in this respect was deemed to be more binding than an oath. Swearing invariably lowered the individual concerned in the esteem of the community, and diminished his reliability as a credible person.

The account of the initiation requirements furnished by Hippolytus was similar to that of other writers on the subject. There were some differences in detail, however, as for example in the observation that, during the initial one-year novitiate, those desiring admission to the sect lived in a house apart from the community meeting place, although they partook of the same food and observed the identical rules of life. Hippolytus appears to have thought in terms of a two-year probationary period rather than the three-year period indicated by Josephus. This latter author was evidently the source of much of the information which Hippolyptus furnished about the nature of the oaths which the initiate was required to swear on being admitted to the order, the various sects into which the Essenes were divided, and the theological tenets to which they adhered. However, it is quite possible that Hippolyptus was also using

Qumran, where the ruins of the Essene Community were discovered ©V.E.

Sections from the "Rules of Behavior" or "Manual of Discipline" of the Essene community. *John C. Trever*

another source of information, since there are certain significant differences between his description of the Essenes and that of Josephus. For example, Hippolytus regarded the Zealots and the Sicarii, or Assassins, as subordinate groups of Essenes, and in his description of Essene religious practices he omitted all references to the supposed worship of the sun at dawn as part of the morning devotions of the sect. Furthermore, whereas Josephus attributed to the Essenes as a whole the traditional Hellenic belief that the body formed a prison for the soul from which death was the only release, Hippolytus stated that the Essenes held to a belief in the resurrection of the body as well as in the immaterial and immortal nature of the soul, maintaining in addition that both would be reunited in the day of judgment. In view of these divergences it may be that Hippolytus was drawing upon a source of information which was closer to the real facts of the situation than the one which Josephus employed.

3. Essene history. Because of the rather spare amount of available material, any attempt at the reconstruction of Essene history must be rather tentative in nature. Furthermore, because of the difficulties attached to interpreting some of the source material, there can hardly be said to be a consensus of scholarly opinion on the matter. However, there are good reasons for assuming that the Essenes originated among the Hasideans, the "loyal ones" (1 Macc 2:42; 7:13). These people were zealous for the Jewish law at a time when Hel. ideas and patterns of life were flooding into Pal. early in the 2nd cent. B.C. This situation took a critical turn during the rule of Seleucus IV (187-175 B.C.), the son and successor of Antiochus the Great, when a dispute between the high priest Onias III and Simon, the commander of the Temple guard, nearly resulted in the plundering of the Temple treasury by Seleucus, who was anxious to pay off some of the debts which Antiochus had incurred during his struggle against the Rom. empire. The entire incident accentuated the tension in Judaea between the more orthodox Jews and those who had succumbed to the wiles of Hellenism. The latter strongly favored Seleucid ideals, and were led by Simon and his brother Menelaus, while the more orthodox segment of Jewry remained loyal to Onias III and looked to Egyp. hegemony for support. They resisted the encroachments of Hellenism vigorously, realizing that their traditional religious beliefs had nothing in common with the skepticism, irreligion, and moral degeneration of Hellenic culture.

When Joshua, the younger brother of Onias III became the leader of the Hellenizing party in Jerusalem and adoped the Gr. name Jason, he prevailed upon Antiochus IV Epiphanes, who had succeeded Seleucus IV in 175 B.C., to depose Onias and appoint himself as high priest. This was agreed to on condition that Jason achieved the Hellenizing of Jerusalem as quickly as possible, a task to which Jason lent every effort. In protest against this trend the Hasideans (or Hasidim) became involved in outbreaks of violence, some of which were directed at the Temple priesthood.

Hostilities flared up again in 168 B.C. at a time when Antiochus Epiphanes had determined to eradicate Judaism and colonize Judaea with people of Hellenic sympathies. Accordingly a royal decree was promulgated, requiring all that was characteristic of Judaism to be removed. The Temple was profaned, the sacred books of the law were burned, and the sacrificial worship of Judaism was prohibited, being replaced by pagan Gr. rites in which the people were compelled to participate on pain of death. Many of the Hasidim would have prefered to withdraw to the wilderness rather than clash openly with the Syrian regime, but the implacable hostility of the Hellenizing party gave them little choice. Many Hasideans perished in the massacres of 167 B.C., and when active resistance crystallized at Modin under the leadership of Mattathias, the surviving Hasideans threw in their lot with his guerilla forces and fought with Judas Maccabeus, the son of Mattathias. Following the success of the Maccabean revolt and the establishing of a treaty by which Lysias guaranteed the restoration of Jewish liberties (1 Macc 6:59), the nation entered a new phase of development in which the allies of the revolution began to vie with one another in a struggle for control of the new state. While a strong Hellenizing party still remained in Judaea, the majority of the people gave firm support to the Maccabeans, who became increasingly designated by their family name of Hasmoneans, and who ultimately emerged as the dominant political party, with avowed nationalistic aims.

In the course of this struggle for power there emerged the three major religious or theocratic groups known as the Sadducees, the Pharisees and the Essenes. They had in common the spiritual aspirations of the Maccabean revolt, namely a national existence for the Jews as a separate entity in the Gentile world, and a strict observance of the Mosaic law. The Sadducees were a priestly group, being well represented in the most influential ecclesiastical circles, and they enjoyed the favor of the Hasmonean rulers until the reign of Alexandra Salome (76-67 B.C.), who preferred the Pharisees, the second major party in Judaea.

These latter had won popular support under John Hyrcanus I (134-104 B.C.). but their political fortunes were uncertain until the time of Alexandra Salome, after which they maintained a dominating position in the Sanhedrin. The Pharisees and Essenes alike seem to have developed from rival groups of earlier revolutionary Hasideans, and it may be that the real division between them occurred about 141 B.C., when a formal decree was issued in Judaea which recognized Simon as hereditary high priest and governor of the Jewish people (1 Macc 14:41). The many similarities between the Pharisees and the Essenes can thus be explained in terms of their common origin. The Pharisees certainly constituted the majority party, however, and their determined pursuit of political aims in Judaea disenchanted the Essenes, who despaired of the human situation and saw the only form of salvation in terms of divine eschatological intervention. Jewish tradition depicted the Essenes as being active in Jerusalem to the time of Aristobulus I (104-103 B.C.), as mentioned by Josephus (Jos. War. 1. iii. 5; Jos. Antiq. XIII. xi. 1, 2), but by the time Alexander Jannaeus died in 76 B.C., the Essenes had made a sharp break with Hasmonean interests, and were increasingly critical of the political aims and pursuits of the other parties in Judaea. They withdrew to a large extent from public life, and this action coincided with the decline of Hasmonean fortunes when Aristobulus II came to the throne in 67 B.C.

A series of abortive attempts by the Hasmoneans to overthrow the Herodian dynasty may well have favored the pietistic aspirations of the Essenes, particularly in the time of Herod the Great (37-34 B.C.). The chief political difficulty faced by this ruler was the opposition of the populace to his claim to be the legitimate ruler of Judaea, and he offset this partly by the backing of the Rom. military power and partly by conciliating such anti-Hasmonean elements in the nations as the Essenes. In an astute political move Herod excused the Essenes, along with some of the Pharisees, from the oaths of loyalty imposed upon the Jews in the early period of his rule, thereby giving the Essenes an unprecedented degree of religious freedom. Quite possibly they returned to Jerusalem, having doubtless obtained an assurance from Herod that their peculiar legal concepts would not be flouted by the Temple priesthood. Most prob. it was at this time that the Essenes carried out their program of missionary expansion which saw the founding of Essene communities in all the villages and small towns of Judaea. The only hint of their presence in Jerusalem was the designation given to an entrance through the S wall of the city, the "Gate of the Essenes" (Jos. War. V. iv. 2).

Certainly the friendly relations which existed between Herod and the Essenes had become well known by the time of Josephus (Jos. Antiq. XV. x. 5), although there is little doubt that the Essenes generally looked with disfavor upon the doings of Herod the Great. Be this as it may, at least one Essene was employed in the royal court as late as the period immediately after the death of Herod (Jos. Antiq. XVII. xiii. 3). In A.D. 66, at the outbreak of the war with Rome, one of the Jewish generals was an Essene named John, and Josephus (Jos. War II. viii. 10) recorded that many of the Essenes were martyred by their Rom. captors. The remainder may have offered sporadic resistance to Rome until the revolt of Bar Kochba was crushed in A.D. 135, but precisely what part they played is unknown, though Bar Kochba himself may have been an Essene. Ultimately the Essenes were doubtless assimilated by the Jewish Christians or some other Jewish group which survived the Second Jewish Revolt.

A religious group which flourished in the same general period as the Essenes, and which had close affinities with them, was the ancient sect known as the Covenanters of Damascus. The existence of this group became known through the exploration of a Cairo synagogue *genizah* or storeroom in 1896. Some of the MSS recovered were subsequently published under the title, "Fragments of a Zadokite Work," a document which narrated the fortunes of a band of priests in Jerusalem who seemed to have been deposed as part of a reform movement. They named themselves the "Sons of Zadok," and under the leadership of a person known as the "Star" they moved to a location styled "Damascus," which may or may not be the historic city of that name, where they organized what came to be known as the party of the New Covenant. This sect indulged in a monastic pattern of life, and under the guidance of a notable leader described as the "Righteous Teacher" it flourished as a criticism of the secular and political aspirations of the Pharisees, and to a lesser extent, of the Sadducees also. Despite this, however, the sect maintained a close contact with the Temple at Jerusalem, as the *Zadokite Fragment* indicates, for the members maintained that Jerusalem was their holy city and the Temple their proper sanctuary. Their affinities with the Essenes appeared evident from their insistence upon fidelity to the law of Moses, the necessity for repentance as a prerequisite to entering the Covenant community, an emphasis upon upright behavior, humanitarian concerns, and other matters dear to the Essene mind.

When archeologists were excavating the Qumran caves, they unearthed some pieces of MS from the sixth cave (6Q), which were found to be equivalent to a portion of the *Zadokite Fragment.* This discovery was augmented still further by the recovery from the fourth cave (4Q) of seven fragmentary MSS which also contained sections of the *Zadokite Fragment.* Taken together, these sources would seem to point to a close relationship between the religious group known to have produced the Qumran MSS and the sect responsible for the drawing up of the *Zadokite Fragment.* Because of the close similarity of religious ideals, many scholars have regarded the two orders as identical in nature, and have suggested that the Damascus community had prob. lived at Qumran for about seventy-five years prior to the end of the first occupational period, after which they moved to Damascus.

Many of those who regard the Damascene

Covenanters as Essenes have maintained that they prob. returned to Jerusalem under some kind of concordat in the reign of Herod the Great, and that they subsequently returned to Qumran after his death, but there is no proper evidence for this supposition. There is also some doubt as to whether the sectaries of the *Zadokite Fragment* were actually Essenes, in view of their emphasis upon animal sacrifice (CDC XIII:27; XIV:1). They were doubtless related to the Hasidim movement, but evidently regarded themselves as the true sons of Zadok. Their tenets had elements in common with the Sadducees, though they differed from them in their belief in immortality (CDC V:6), the advent of the Messiah (CDC II:10) and the recognition of prophecy and the Hagiographa. Along with the Pharisees they acknowledged the existence of heavenly beings (CDC VI:9; IX:12), divine predestination (CDC II:6, 10) and free will (CDC III:1, 2; IV:2, 10). On the other hand, they forbad divorce (CDC VII:1-3), and held that the Pharisees defiled the Temple through what they considered were sexual irregularities (cf. CDC VII:8, 9).

The excavation of a ruined settlement at Qumran and its subsequent association with the MSS and fragments recovered from nearby caves (*see* DEAD SEA SCROLLS) led to a study of the nature of the religious community which had inhabited the site. One of the scrolls, the *Community Rule* or *Manual of Discipline* (1QS) furnished most of the information concerning the structure and organization of the Qumran sect. Apparently it arose as part of the Hasidean movement, and crystallized after the time of Antiochus IV Epiphanes, when the high priesthood as well as the civil and military power came under Hasmonean control. Under the leadership of a "Righteous Teacher," the Qumran sectaries withdrew to the Judaean wilderness in protest against the "epoch of wickedness" and organized themselves as a Covenant group to prepare the way for the divine coming in the New Age. Characteristic of their attitude was an avowed refusal to recognize the Jerusalem priesthood, and in the Habakkuk commentary specific mention was made of a Wicked Priest, most prob. a Hasmonean, who manifested a particularly serious degree of hostility toward the community and its leader. Apparently the sect prepetuated a framework of Zadokite priests and Levites, who would be available for the conduct of proper and legitimate sacrificial worship in Jerusalem once the unworthy priesthood had been dispossessed. The general historical background for this movement is that of the Maccabean and subsequent eras, including the period of Herod the Great. Some scholars think that the Qumran group, which they regard as Essene in nature, moved their sphere of operation to Jerusalem, only to return to Qumran after the death of Herod.

From 1QS it appears that the Qumran sectaries lived a communal life of strict dedication and obedience to God. While members of both sexes were allowed to join the group, an exacting novitiate of one year was required, and if the postulant met the stipulations of the group at the end of the second year he was enrolled as a member of the order (1QS VI: 22, 23) after an elaborate ceremony (1QS I: 18ff.). Each subsequent year the members were required to renew their pledges of loyalty to the ideals of the group (1QS II:19ff.), and delinquent members were reminded of their obligations (1QS V:20ff.). Ritual lustrations and quasi-sacramental meals were given great prominence at Qumran, and the sectaries appear to have avoided all unnecessary contact with the outside world, preferring to live and work as a self-sustaining group, unlike the Essenes who mingled freely with society. The Qumran sectaries devoted specific parts of the day and night to meditation and study of the law. In the interpretation of the latter they were considerably stricter than the most severe Pharisees, and their exposition of Scripture was in apocalyptic terms in which they themselves were to play a prominent part in realizing the coming of the New Age. Specific guidance about the latter had been given by God to the Righteous Teacher, who bestowed this esoteric knowledge upon his disciples. However, their expectations were not fulfilled in the hoped-for manner, since their settlement was destroyed in the war of A.D. 66-73, over two decades after the founding of the Christian Church.

Scholars have commonly identified the sect of the *Zadokite Fragment* and the Qumran group, and have regarded both as Essene. However there are some significant differences between Essene and Qumranic practices which merit notice. The Qumran sectaries evidently did not regard themselves as Essene in nature, since the word "Essene" appears nowhere in the DSS. Whereas the Essenes had groups in every village and town in Judaea and mingled freely with secular society, the Qumran sectaries adopted a separatist policy, and had no dealings whatever with those who stood outside their own group. Neither the Damascus nor the Qumran covenanters distrusted women, unlike most Essenes, but were in accord with the minority Essene segment which approved of marriage. The Essene novitiate appears to have lasted for about three years, whereas at Qumran it prob. did not exceed two years in length. Whereas the Essenes were strictly pacifist by nature, the Qumran sectaries were not, if their military scroll (1QM) is a true indication of their attitudes. The Qumran fellowship did not address the sun at dawn, as did the Essenes in the report of Josephus, though the author may have been referring to only one quasi-Essene group, the Sampsaeans, who followed this custom. These differences will be sufficient to show that despite the elasticity of the term

Stone pedestal at east end of General Assembly Room at Qumran ©*Lev*

"Essene" in the pre-Christian era, the Qumran group can be thus regarded only in the most general sense, and may actually be nearer in nature to certain cave sects flourishing in the 1st cent. B.C. Consequently it is difficult at the time of writing to place the Qumran covenanters firmly within the stream of Essene history.

4. Essene life. A brief summary from known sources of the Essene way of life can now be attempted. The vast majority of Essenes were scattered about the smaller settlements of Judea, avoiding the larger cities because of their contamination by Gentile elements. Strict observance of the purity laws in the Torah was a feature of Essene behavior, being matched by an equal emphasis on purity of life. They were notable for their communal ownership of property, which arose from their abhorrence of worldly wealth, and also for their hospitality to other members of their own sect. A strong sense of mutual responsibility characterized the Essene communities, in which the needy were given every care. Life was authoritarian in nature, with everything, apart from personal acts of mercy and charity, being governed by those in charge of the brotherhood. Admission to Essene groups was preceded by a period of testing for about three years, and when a candidate had proved his suitability he had to take solemn oaths of piety and obedience. Subsequent violation of these oaths could, and most frequently did, result in expulsion from the group. Daily worship was an important feature of community life, beginning with prayer at dawn, and on holy days and sacred seasons special rites were observed. The sacrifices offered at such times took place within the confines of the various Essene communities, since their emphasis upon special conditions of purity prevented them from participating actively in the worship of the cultus at the Jerusalem Temple. However, it was their practice to send to the Temple certain things which they had dedicated to God. One aspect of Essene daily worship was the study of their sacred scriptures, a task to which special expression was given on the sabbath. Scriptural study on such occasions was a communal affair, as with many other features of Essene life, with the group assembling in their meeting hall or "synagogue," according to seniority. The method of Biblical study consisted of a reading, followed by an exposition of the passage by some learned secretary. Philo recorded that the Essenes studied their sacred writings with a view to finding out their symbolic meaning, in the belief that the divine promises to the prophets of Israel were being fulfilled in their own day. In this connection some of the *pesharim* or commentaries from the Dead Sea community are illuminating, particularly if the Qumran sect was related in some way to the Essenes, since the authors of these writings commented on the text of some specific prophecy, and then proceeded to interpret what was written in terms of events which were either contemporary or expected to occur in the very near future.

The question of marriage appears to have split the Essenes into major and minor divisions, with the former section insisting on vocational celibacy as a feature of community life and the latter permitting marriage as a primary means of perpetuating the sect. Though the majority did not condemn marriage in principle, they avoided it because of its deleterious effects on community life. Because the Essenes thought of themselves as Israelite warriors fighting a

Ruins at Qumran. View southeast from the citadel. The edge of the Dead Sea is just visible at the top of the photograph. © *Lev*

holy war, as in the time of Moses and Joshua, marriage was deemed unsuitable for a long term volunteer (cf. Deut 23:9-14). Despite their strict behavior there is no doubt that they exerted a profound spiritual influence over Jewish life at the beginning of the Christian era. *See* DEAD SEA SCROLLS.

BIBLIOGRAPHY. K. Kohler, JE, V, 224-232; F. M. Cross, *The Ancient Library of Qumran* (1958), 65-106; R. K. Harrison, *The Dead Sea Scrolls* (1961), 72-101; W. R. Farmer, IDB, II, 143-149.

R. K. HARRISON

ESTHER ĕs′ tər. Esther was a Benjamite girl, whose name is immortalized in the book that bears her name. Her cousin, Mordecai, adopted her on the death of her parents (Esth 2:5-7). Her Heb. name is equated with הדסה, Hadassah, meaning "Myrtle." It is uncertain from this v. which of the two words is the original name. If Esther was the original, then Myrtle could have been a descriptive title, but since, contrary to our way of speaking of her simply as Esther, the name Hadassah is mentioned first, the probability is that this was the original name. The turning of this into Esther might have been done by her Pers. playmates, who did not understand Heb., but who, in the manner of children down the ages, approximate a strange name to one with which they are familiar. Esther could have been connected with the Pers. *stara,* with the meaning of *Star,* or even with the Babylonian goddess Ishtar. Perhaps American or British children, confronted with a playmate named Hadassah, might rename her as "Dusty."

The Book of Esther relates how she was chosen to succeed Vashti as queen. Out of a large number of virgins, she was the one to find favor with King Xerxes. At first Mordecai told her to conceal her Jewish ancestry, but later he warned (or blackmailed) her that she would not escape the massacre of the Jews that Haman was planning, and consequently she agreed to do what she could with the king. However, she insisted that the Jews in the city should fast, and presumably pray, for her.

She appeared before the king unbidden, which could have meant death for her, but the king received her kindly. She invited the king and Haman to dinner, where she had evidently planned to disclose Haman's schemes, and, if the story had been fiction, we should have heard that she now did so. For some unexplained reason she did no more than repeat her invitation for the next night. One may assume that her courage failed her at the first dinner.

On the second occasion, she exposed Haman's plot. The king was angry and went out of the room. When he returned he found Haman leaning over Esther to beg for mercy, and the king thought the worst. Haman was taken out and hanged.

Esther and Mordecai then obtained the king's permission to avert the massacre. Since the original decree could not be directly reversed, they authorized the Jews to defend themselves on the day of the massacre on the 13th day of Adar. In this way, the edge of the decree was turned, since it was unlikely that the local authorities would now support the massacre, as they would otherwise have done. In Susa, where Esther lived, she asked permission for the Jews to kill their enemies on the following day as well, and it appears that on this day the Jews took the initiative for revenge instead of merely defending themselves (9:15f.).

The Bible shows how God used Esther and Mordecai to deliver His people in an emergency. It is not known how long either of them remained in power, but certainly Esther was not the mother of any subsequent heir to the Pers. throne.

Her name does not occur in secular records. According to Herodotus and Ctesias the name of the chief wife of Xerxes, both before and after his expedition to Greece, was Amestris, who may well be identified with Vashti. Since Esther did not actually become queen for four years after the incident of chapter one (1:3; 2:16)—Xerxes was occupied with arranging and accompanying his disastrous expedition against Greece—it is likely that Xerxes retained Vashti (Amestris) as his wife during this time. He might well have continued to do so if she had not brutally mutilated a woman with whom she suspected her husband was having an affair. Rather than risk the vengeance of Xerxes, she prob. withdrew for the time, leaving him to choose his new wife, and waiting her time to come back into favor and power once more. *See* ESTHER, BOOK OF; VASHTI; MORDECAI.

J. S. WRIGHT

ESTHER, ADDITIONS TO. The apocryphal book, Additions to Esther, consists of six passages (107 vv), inserted into the Gr. text in various places. It is generally assumed that the Heb. was tr. into Gr. by an Egyp. Jew, living in Jerusalem, no later than 114 B.C. Whether all the additions were present in the text at the time of the tr. is a matter of debate. All the Gr. recensions and the Old Lat. text contain the additions in their proper place. When Jerome made his Vul. tr., he removed these passages because they did not appear in the Heb., and he placed them at the end of the book with explanatory notes indicating where they should be inserted. Subsequent editors removed the notes. Finally, when Stephen Langton (d. 1228) divided the Lat. Bible into chs., he numbered the additions, which had been placed at the end of the book, in consecutive order. This practice was followed by Luther and the Eng. VSS. In *The Jerusalem Bible* these additions are in the text, but are printed in italicized type.

1. Content. The six passages making up the Additions to Esther are identified by letters. Each passage may be briefly summarized.

Addition A (11:2-12:6) is a dream of Mordecai in which two great dragons appear ready to fight. A tiny spring grew into a great river when the righteous nation cried to God. Mordecai later overheard two eunuchs plotting against the king. He reported them and was rewarded by appointment to a high office. All this precedes Esther 1:1.

Addition B (13:1-7) is the text of the edict of Ahasuerus (Gr. has Artaxerxes) against the Jews. It is to be inserted after 3:13.

Addition C (13:8-14:19) gives the prayers of Mordecai and Esther. It follows 4:17.

Addition D (15:1-16; Lat. 15:4-19) is an elaboration of 5:1, 2 and should be inserted before 5:3. This passage describes the anger of the king at Esther's intrusion, but God changed the king's heart and attitude toward Esther.

Addition E (16:1-24) gives the text of the edict of Ahasuerus in behalf of the Jews. This passage follows 8:12.

Addition F (10:4-11:1), which follows 10:3, is the interpretation of Mordecai's dream. The two dragons are Mordecai and Haman, and the tiny spring is Esther. The "lots" of Purim are two destinies, a "lot" for the Jews and a "lot" for the Gentiles.

2. Purpose. From the content of the Additions, the following conclusions may be drawn: (1) the author wanted to strengthen the religious element in the book and so inserted the prayers; (2) the trustworthiness and historical accuracy of the text are enhanced by the exact words of the two royal edicts; (3) the author tried to improve on the story by including sections D, A, and F; (4) if 9:20-10:3 is an addition (so Brockington and others), then there is an attempt to harmonize the record with current usage.

3. Language. The Gr. text has come down in five variant forms: (1) the standard LXX (א, B, A, etc.) (2) Origen's Hexapla; (3) Hesychius; (4) Lucian; and (5) the text used by Josephus. Most scholars believe the Additions were written originally in Gr. Roman Catholic scholars argue they were all tr. from Heb. or Aram. originals. Torrey claims that the original language was Aram. (A C D F were part of the original text), and that our canonical Heb. is a late abridgment. Patton argues that there is no evidence for the existence of Sem. originals for any of the additions.

4. Date. The date of the Additions cannot be determined with accuracy. The little evidence there is points to a date near the time of the tr. into Gr., around 100 B.C.

5. Discrepancies. The many discrepancies introduced by the Additions make it difficult to accept them as original parts of the text. The attitude of Esther toward the king in 2:15-18 is not at all the same as that given in 14:15, 16. The irrevocable edict of 1:19 and 8:8 is revoked in 16:17. Haman is hanged in 7:10; crucified in 16:18. The Jews only are to keep Purim in 9:20-32, but all Persians are instructed to keep it in 16:22. Other contradictions are found when 2:16-19 is compared with 11: 3-12:1; 2:21-23 and 6:3, 4 with 12:5; 3:5 with 12:6; 5:4-8 with 14:7; and 3:1 with 16:10.

BIBLIOGRAPHY. J. A. McClymont, "Esther," HDB, I (1898), 773-776; L. B. Patton, *A Critical and Exegetical Commentary on the Book of Esther* (1908), 31-34, 41-47; J. A. F. Gregg, "The Additions to Esther," in R. H. Charles (ed.), *The Apocrypha* and *Pseudepigrapha of the Old Testament,* I (1913), 665-671; T. Davies, "Esther, The Rest of," ISBE, II (1929), 1009f.; C. C. Torrey, "The Older Book of Esther," HTR, xxxvii (1944), 1-40; *The Apocryphal Literature* (1945), 57-59; R. H. Pfeiffer, *History of New Testament Times with an Introduction to the Apocrypha* (1949), 304-312; B. M. Metzger, *An Introduction to the Apocrypha* (1957), 55-63; L. H. Brockington, *A Critical Introduction to the Apocrypha* (1961), 49-53; E. W. Saunders, "Esther" (Apocryphal), IDB, II (1962), 151f.

R. E. HAYDEN

ESTHER, BOOK OF

1. Background
2. Unity
3. Authorship and date
4. Purpose
5. Canonicity
6. Special problems
7. Contents
8. Theology and morals

1. Background. Unless the identification is rejected on other grounds, it should be assumed that Ahasuerus (1:1) is the king of Persia usually known as Xerxes I (486-465 B.C.). The Heb. form of his name, אחשורוש, corresponds to the Pers. form, *khshayarsha.* Most scholars accept this identification, and it will be assumed in this article. The LXX, however, without the benefit of access to Pers. inscrs., quite reasonably identifies the name with Artaxerxes. Josephus does the same (Antiq. XI. vi. 1), and makes him Artaxerxes I (464-424 B.C.). The Pers. equivalent of this name is *Artakhslatra,* which is not close to the Heb. name in this book. If the king was Artaxerxes I, he would have married Esther in the year when he sent Ezra to Jerusalem (Esth 2:16; Ezra 7:8), and Esther would presumably have been the queen in Nehemiah's day (Neh 2:1, 6). The only serious alternative to Xerxes is Artaxerxes II (404-359 B.C.). This identification has been urged by J. Hoschander, *The Book of Esther in the Light of History,* and A. T. Olmstead, *History of Palestine and Syria* (612-614). Apart from the fact that the Heb. elsewhere mostly has the form ארתחשסתא, for Artaxerxes, Plutarch's *Life of Artaxerxes II* allows little room for the story of Esther. He was dominated by the Queen Mother, Parysatis, who poisoned his wife, Stateira, in the fourth year of his reign (Esth 1:3). Plutarch relates that Artaxerxes afterward married two of his own daughters.

If Xerxes is the king, it is possible to bring together the Biblical and secular records. In the third year of his reign, he called together all the leading men to discuss a campaign against Greece (Herodotus VII. 8), where his father, Darius, had been defeated at Marathon in 490. This would be the assembly of Esther 1, which was in the third year (1:3). Although the search for Vashti's successor begins in this year, Xerxes does not marry Esther until the seventh year (2:16). In the intervening period he was occupied with the Gr. campaign, taking four years to collect his armies (Herodotus VII. 21). He was ultimately defeated by the Greeks at Salamis in 480. The Biblical dating indicates that he married Esther on his return. Haman's plot against the Jews took place in the twelfth year, which means that the Biblical story ends about 473. There is no record of how long Mordecai and Esther remained in power.

It has been objected that Herodotus and Ctesias speak of Amestris as queen, and she was certainly the wife of Xerxes before 482, for in this year their son, the later Artaxerxes I, was born. Amestris was queen mother (i.e. the widow of the former king) during the reign of Artaxerxes I. She also was with Xerxes during part at least of his Gr. campaign, and Herodotus relates an appalling incident at Saris (IX. 108f.). Xerxes had an affair with a married woman and her daughter, and Amestris seized the former and horribly mutilated her.

This may be linked to the Esther story, if Amestris is Vashti. Xerxes would have taken at least one wife with him, and, although he had deposed Vashti from being queen during his drunken stupor, he retained her as his wife for the time being. Her mutilation of Xerxes' mistress would have led to her falling out of favor, or even to temporary banishment, and, on his return, Xerxes was ready to take Esther as his new queen. Amestris was clever enough to wait her time and work her way back into favor, perhaps taking advantage of a reaction against Esther and Mordecai after the Jews had killed so many of their enemies. We do not know what happened to Esther eventually. *See* ESTHER; VASHTI.

2. Unity. The only section in the Heb. which some believe to break the unity is 9:20-10:3. This is largely a section that shows how the previously recorded facts of history gave rise to the specific observance of the Feast of Purim. The historical narrative has shown what actually happened on certain vital days, whereas this section tells how Mordecai selected two of these days for special observance. The recapitulation (Esth 9:24, 25) is intended as no more than a summarizing of the main

Crown Prince Xerxes. Esther may have lived under his reign. © *O.I.U.C.*

facts, and cannot fairly be said to be out of harmony with the main body of the book.

The LXX contains 107 extra vv., and these are printed successively in the Apoc. (*see* ESTHER, ADDITIONS TO). The Apoc. numbers them in chs. as though they are attached to the end of the Heb. The actual order of the whole book in the LXX, if one brings together the numberings in the Bible and in the Apoc., is as follows: 11:2 - 12:6; 1:1 - 3:13; 13:1-7; 3:14 - 4:17; 13:8 - 15:16; 5:1 - 8:12; 16:1-24; 8:13 - 10:3; 10:4 - 11:1. These additions appear to be orthodox correctives that introduce the name of God, absent from the Heb. The opening words of 11:1 state that Dositheus and Ptolemeus brought this epistle of Purim in the fourth year of Ptolemy and Cleopatra. This would be 114 B.C., and could be the year when these Gr. additions were made.

3. Authorship and date. The book is anonymous. Such references as it contains to writing are to the official court records (2:23; 6:1; 10:2) and to what Mordecai wrote when he "recorded these things" (9:20) and set down the regulations for Purim (9:20, 23, 29-32). It is possible that Mordecai himself was the author. His omission of the name of God would be accounted for if he wished to have his book inserted among the court records. There is no reason to regard Mordecai as a devout man, though he was certainly a strong nationalist. If he is to be identified with Matakas, who is mentioned by Ctesias, he had plundered the temple at Delphi on Xerxes' behalf, when others refused to do so (XIII. 58). He would have been glad at the opportunity to insult a Gentile god.

It is possible that a later author used the Pers. chronicles when he wanted to write the story of the origin of Purim, and, since the official records would naturally not speak of the Jewish god, the Jewish copyist chose to let them stand as they were.

Various periods have been suggested for the writing of the book. It must have been in circulation for some time before the LXX tr. appeared toward the end of the 2nd cent. B.C., but neither Esther nor Mordecai is listed in Ecclesiasticus 44-50 (180 B.C.). Many believe that it was written under the stress of the persecutions in the time of the Maccabees in the middle of the 2nd cent. It is, however, difficult to account for the total omission of the name of God if the book were composed by an enthusiastic Jew at such a time.

One further suggestion must be noticed, that this book derived from a cultic story that centered in a conflict of deities, namely Ishtar (Esther), Marduk (Mordecai), who were both deities of Babylon, and Humman (Haman) and Mashti (Vashti), of Elam. Since some Jewish exiles, such as Daniel and his friends, bore Babylonian names, it is quite possible that Mordecai's name is the equivalent of the common Babylonian personal name, Mardukaia, which contained the name of Marduk, and Esther's name could be linked with Ishtar also. This is not to say that the story was originally cultic. The real objection to the cultic theory is the unlikelihood of the Jews using a polytheistic Babylonian tale as a ground for a Jewish festival of deliverance; there is no evidence for Purim ever being other than a Jewish feast, which the Jews might have adopted.

The earliest post-Biblical reference to the Feast of Purim (2 Macc 15:36) records the victory of Judas Maccabeus in 161 B.C. on the thirteenth day of the twelfth month, which is said to be on "the day before Mordecai's day." The date of 2 Maccabees is prob. the first half of the 1st cent. B.C. Presumably the Book of Esther was known by that time.

4. Purpose. The primary purpose is to relate the origin of the Feast of Purim. The book gives the historical occasion, the reason for the dates, and the origin of the name. The latter is connected with the Assyrian *puru,* which is used for a small stone suitable for the casting of lots (Esth 3:7; 9:24, 26).

5. Canonicity. The book comes in the third division of the Heb. Scriptures, and is grouped with Ruth, the Song of Songs, Ecclesiastes, and Lamentations, as one of the Five Scrolls. It was one of the books to which the rabbis at Jamnia (c. A.D. 100) gave special consideration as to whether it should continue to be counted among the inspired books. The chief argument against it was that it instituted a new festival as obligatory, whereas the law of Moses was believed to have laid down all the festivals. According to the Jerusalem Talmud (*Megillah* 70d), the solution found was that the book was revealed to Moses on Sinai, but not written until the time of Mordecai.

6. Special problems. Most commentators hold that the author had access to information about the Pers. court, even though he may have written much later than the period in which he sets his story. Thus references to the plan of the palace correspond with what archeologists have discovered at Susa. Although this was built by Artaxerxes II, he was restoring a palace that had been destroyed earlier. Another palace completed by Xerxes at Persepolis was based on the same general pattern (A. T. Olmstead, *History of the Persian Empire* 272f.; 422f.). The curtains and hangings in the courtyard (1:6) would be attached to the pillars which have been found; the colors of white and blue (1:6; 8:15) were favorite Pers. colors. Reclining at the feast (1:6), the inner council of Seven (1:14), the general difficulty of access to the king (4:11), and the ban on entering the palace in mourning (4:2), the honoring of a favorite by dressing him in royal robes (6:8), the use of couriers for taking important messages (3:13), are all incidental touches that are true to facts that are known from Herodotus and other writers.

One therefore approaches problems with a bias favoring the historicity of the book. The following objections may be noted:

(a) Herodotus and Ctesias make no mention of Esther or Vashti, but Amestris appears as queen and later as queen-mother. Vashti and Amestris could be the same person (*see* Section 1).

(b) The writer is so confused over the time scale that he holds that Mordecai was one of the original captives in 597 (2:5, 6). This would make him more than 100 years old. The text could equally refer to his great-grandfather, Kish, the relative pronoun being attached to the last name in the series (2 Chron 22:9; Ezra 2:61).

(c) Esther 1:1 mentions 127 provinces, whereas Herodotus (III. 89) speaks only of 20 satrapies. Inscriptions of Darius vary between 21 and 29 provinces. There is no doubt that the larger regions, whether called satrapies or provinces, were divided into smaller units, and, if the Bible is interpreted by itself, the small unit of Judah is regularly designated by the same word as is used in Esther 1:1 (מדינה).

(d) According to Herodotus III. 84, the king had to choose his wife from one of seven families. It is not clear from Herodotus whether this was a permanent rule, or merely a temporary agreement to satisfy the six other conspirators besides Darius who had dethroned the previous usurper. Certainly Darius himself married other wives besides one from the seven, and his son Xerxes, who succeeded him, was not the son of this wife.

(e) If Purim had really been instituted by Mordecai, why is it not mentioned until it occurs as "Mordecai's day" in 2 Maccabees 15:36? Why are not Mordecai and Esther included in the praise of famous people in Ecclesiasticus 44-49? It is difficult to see where it could have been mentioned in extant lit. In Ezra's day, it would not yet have established itself on an equal footing with the Mosaic festivals, and the Book of Ezra does not mention even all of these. One cannot argue too much from the silence of Ben Sirach in Ecclesiasticus, since he also omits Ezra. As a Wisdom writer, he was not esp. concerned with individual festivals, and he may not have approved of Mordecai's methods nor of Esther's marriage to a pagan king.

The above are the chief objections that have been brought against the historicity of the book. One cannot here consider subjective objections based on opinions of whether such and such an incident is likely. There is therefore no adequate reason for rejecting the Book's presentation of itself as genuine history.

7. Contents. *Chapter 1.* The Pers. king at a seven-day feast at Susa for all his chief men deposes queen Vashti for refusing to come in and display her beauty before the men.

Chapter 2. Esther, the adopted daughter of a Jew named Mordecai, is chosen as Vashti's successor. Mordecai discovers a plot to murder the king, and passes on the information to Esther, with the result that the plot is foiled.

Chapter 3. Mordecai offends Haman, the new vizier, through refusing to bow down to him, and Haman plans his revenge by massacring all the Jews in the empire. Experts cast the lot (*pur*) to fix a lucky day for the massacre, and a date is chosen eleven months ahead. Haman sends decrees for the massacre throughout the empire.

Chapter 4. Mordecai persuades Esther to

Susa, where much of the action of the Book of Esther took place. ©O.I.U.C.

intervene, and she explains how dangerous it could be for her to approach the king unbidden. She agrees, on condition that the Jews in Susa fast, and presumably pray, for three days.

Chapter 5. Esther approaches the king and invites him and Haman to dinner. When they come, she repeats the invitation for a second dinner next day. (Did her courage fail her?) Haman's happiness is marred by Mordecai's refusal to honor him, but his wife suggests that he build a gallows and obtain the king's permission to hang Mordecai in the morning.

Chapter 6. The king, suffering from insomnia, reads the records of his reign and finds that Mordecai had not been rewarded for revealing the plot against him. He makes Haman lead Mordecai in honor through the city the next day.

Chapter 7. At the second dinner, Esther reveals the plot against the Jews, and names Haman. The king hangs him on the gallows prepared for Mordecai.

Chapter 8. The king puts Mordecai in Haman's place, and authorizes him to write further decrees allowing the Jews to resist on the day of the massacre.

Chapter 9. The Jews take advantage of this and kill any enemies who attack them. Esther obtains permission for the Jews in Susa to attack their enemies on the next day also. Mordecai then institutes the Feast of Purim on the fourteenth and fifteenth days of the month Adar, which had been days of rejoicing after the abortive massacre on the thirteenth.

Chapter 10. A summary of the greatness of the king and of Mordecai.

8. Theology and morals. The absence of the name of God does not mean the absence of the hand of God. The whole book traces how the right person was in the right place at the right time. This did not happen automatically, but 4:16 shows that fasting, which would include prayer, was part of the working out of God's plan. One is not bound to approve of the extra massacre that Mordecai ordered in Susa, with the hanging of Haman's sons (9:13-15). Mordecai was a strong nationalist, and a brave man, but his concealment of his Jewish ancestry at first (2:10) may indicate that he was more opportunistic than devout.

BIBLIOGRAPHY. L. B. Paton, ICC (1908); J. Hoschander, *The Book of Esther in the Light of History* (1923); A. T. Olmstead, *History of Palestine and Syria* (1931) and *History of the Persian Empire* (1948); B. W. Anderson, IB (1954); S. H. Horn, "Mordecai, A Historical Problem," *Biblical Research,* Chicago Society (1964); J. S. Wright, "The Historicity of the Book of Esther" in *New Perspectives on OT* (1970).

J. S. Wright

ETAM **ē′ təm** (עיטם ; LXX 'Ητάμ, Αἰτάμ; Vul. and Luther *Etam*. Meaning of Heb. uncertain; maybe *place of ravenous* [*rapacious*] *beasts*).

A town between Bethlehem and Tekoa, which Rehoboam fortified after the secession of the ten northern tribes (2 Chron 11:6). Usually the site is identified with Khirbet el-Khôkh c. six and one-half m. SSW of Jerusalem; another possibility is 'Ain 'Atān c. two m. SSW from Bethlehem.

Josephus relates that Etam was a very pleasant place c. fifty furlongs from Jerusalem, situated in fine gardens (cf. Eccl 2:5, 6) "and abounding in rivulets of water" (Jos. Antiq. VIII. vii. 3). He also states that Solomon was accustomed to take a morning drive in his chariot to Etam. According to the Talmud, the spring of Etam supplied water for the Temple at Jerusalem. This fact prob. explains the ancient aqueduct that extends seven m. from Jerusalem to three large Hel. Rom. reservoirs beyond Bethlehem. They were discovered at a late date by pilgrims and are now known as the "pools of Solomon." The lowest pool is fed by a stream called 'Ain 'Atan. The aqueduct was constructed before the Christian era and antedates the Rom. period. Pontius Pilate prob. used it as the last section of his great conduit that brought water into Jerusalem from a distance of either two or four hundred furlongs (cf. Jos. Antiq. XVIII. iii. 2 with War II. ix. 4). This action aroused the fury of the populace because Pilate had used the sacred money (qorban) for public welfare. Apparently the Jews believed that money once dedicated to Yahweh could never be employed for a secular purpose. Today Bethlehem gets water from 'Ain 'Atan by pipe line.

2. A village in the territory of Simeon (1 Chron 4:32). The site is unknown today. Some think it is the same place that Rehoboam rebuilt in the hill country of Judah (2 Chron 11:6; *see* 1 above). Others identify it with 'Aiṭūm c. eleven m. WSW of Hebron.

3. Son of Hur or maybe an entire clan in Judah (1 Chron 4:3), or perhaps the Αἰτάν (LXX—B) or Αἰτάμ (LXX—A) mentioned in Joshua 15:59a. It might even be identical with 1 above.

4. A cliff somewhere in W Judah (Judg 15:8, 11). Perhaps located near a town called עיטם but at 'Arāk Isma'īn in Wadi Isma'īn two and one-half m. ESE from Zorah. Samson took refuge in a cleft of the rock Etam after he had slaughtered the Philistines.

BIBLIOGRAPHY. F. M. Abel, *Géographie de la Palestine,* II (1938), 321; L. Koehler and W. Baumgartner, *Lexicon* in *Veteris Testamenti Libros* (1953), 699; H. J. Kraus, "Chirbet el-Choch," ZDPV, LXXII ((1956), 152-162; L. H. Grollenborg, *Atlas of The Bible,* trans. J. M. H. Reid and H. H. Rowley (1956), 149.

R. C. Ridall

ETERNAL (עולם, *long duration*; Gr. αἰώνιος, *eternal*; ἀίδιος, *eternal*). 1. Fundamentally, the Heb. noun in the sing. and pl. means *duration*, both of antiquity and futurity. Its meanings and occurrences are listed exhaustively by Gesenius (*Lexicon* pp. 761-763). Like the Eng. words "eternal" and "everlasting," commonly used in tr., the Heb. word takes color from its context. To speak of a "bondman for ever" (Deut 15:17) manifestly limits the word to the duration of a human lifetime. To refer to "the everlasting hills" (Gen. 49:26) also obviously limits the word to the geological age of a feature of the landscape. On the other hand, the word is applied to God, His abiding acts, His covenants, promises, and laws and therefore signifies the eternal and everlasting in the literal and absolute sense of the term. *Cruden's Concordance* summarizes the concept well (s. v. "eternal"): "The words eternal, everlasting, forever, are sometimes taken for a long time and are not always to be understood strictly." For example, the possession of Canaan (Gen 17:8); the hills (Gen 49:26); the throne of David (2 Sam 7:16; 1 Chron 17:14); "eternal" in the strict sense in these two contexts demands a Messianic extension of the promise; Jewish rites and privileges (Exod 12:14, 17; Num 10:8).

2. The Gr. adjective *aionios* is derived from the noun *aiōn*, and bears the basic meaning, in consequence, of "belonging to time in its duration," i.e., *constant, abiding, eternal* (*Biblio-Theological Lexicon of New Testament Greek*, Cremer, pp. 78, 79; also s.v. *aiōn*, pp. 74-79). It was found in this meaning in classical Gr.: e.g., Plato, *Rep.* 2:363D, "the fairest reward of virtue being, in their estimation, an everlasting carousal." Biblical and ecclesiastical Gr. used the word commonly, the LXX, for example, as the standard tr. of the Heb. עוֹלָם.

In the NT, its most frequent application is to ζωή, "life," and it is in these contexts that heretical sects in modern times have habitually misinterpreted the word. Ζωὴ αἰώνιος is found in Matthew 19:16, 29; 25:46; Mark 10:17, 30; Luke 10:25; 18:18, 30; John 3:15, 16, 36; 4:14, 36; 5:24, 39; 6:27, 40, 47, 54, 68; 10:28; 12:25, 50; 17:2, 3; Acts 13:46, 48; Romans 2:7; 5:21; 6:22, 23; Galatians 6:8; 1 Timothy 1:16; 6:12, 19; Titus 1:2; 3:7; 1 John 1:2; 2:25; 3:15; 5:11, 13, 20; Jude 21.

The frequency of its use in Johannine contexts is notable. The significance mingles future and present, for "eternal life" in Christian belief is not only a life of endless duration, but a quality of life in which the possessor shares by faith in God's eternal being.

In his careful essay, *More New Testament Words* (pp. 24-32), William Barclay examines the word *aionios* in classical and NT contexts, with full analysis of the meaning and its spiritual applications. Eternal life, as he points out in conclusion, were it a mere duration, could become the burden which Tithonus, in the deeply meaningful Gr. myth, found it to be. "Life is only of value when it is nothing less than the life of God—and that is the meaning of eternal life." It necessarily follows that it has no termination.

Other NT connections employ the adjective *aionios* (Matt 18:8; 25:41; Jude 7 [fire]; Matt 25:46 [punishment]; 2 Thess 1:9 [destruction]; Mark 3:29 [sin]; Heb 6:2 [judgment]; 5:9 [salvation]; 9:12 [redemption]; 9:15 [inheritance]; 13:20 [covenant]; 2 Tim 2:10; 1 Pet 5:10 [glory]; 2 Pet 1:11 [kingdom].

3. A rare word in NT contexts, but common enough at all stages of classical Gr. from Homer onwards, is *aidios*. It occurs in Romans 1:20 and Jude 6. *See* LIFE; IMMORTALITY.

E. M. BLAIKLOCK

ETERNITY

1. Biblical data
2. Theological analysis
3. Philosophy of time
4. Augustine's view
5. Some modern views
6. Practical application

1. Biblical data. Isaiah 57:15 contains the phrase, "the high and lofty One that inhabiteth eternity, whose name is Holy." This is the only verse in which the word occurs in the KJV. The same Heb. word עַד is in Isaiah 9:6, "Everlasting Father, Prince of Peace." In Daniel there occurs עָלַם in the phrases "everlasting kingdom" and "everlasting dominion." Most frequently in the OT, the word for eternity or eternal is עוֹלָם or עֹלָם, as in everlasting covenant, everlasting priesthood, underneath are the everlasting arms, the everlasting God, and some sixty other occurrences. There is also the word קֵדְמָה in Deuteronomy 33:27 "The eternal God is your dwelling place."

In the NT, αἰώνιος is used as eternal damnation, eternal life, eternal purpose, the King eternal, and so on. The Eng. word *everlasting* also trs. the same word, with perhaps a single exception, for Jude 6 has "everlasting chains" (ἀΐδιος). This latter is also the word in Romans 1:20, "his eternal power and deity."

In addition to these verbal instances of eternal or everlasting, the Bible has much to say about the nature of God. From this other material, even more than from the verbal occurrences, one must learn what eternity means.

The simplest teaching of Scripture is Psalm 90:2, "Before the mountains were brought forth, or ever thou hadst formed the earth and the world, from everlasting to everlasting thou art God." This is a denial that God ever began to exist in time. On the surface the words seem to ascribe to God never-ending duration. Involved of course is the divine creation of the world at a point of time in the finite past; practical lessons concerning the certainty of the covenant are implied, but the nature of God Himself is here characterized as one of infinite duration.

Both the OT and the NT contain anthropomorphic and other metaphorical language. God is said to have ears and eyes, and the mountains skip like rams. Metaphorical language is not unusual. Literature and ordinary conversation make frequent use of figures of speech. Therefore, when God is described as one who exists through all time, and is also described as a temporal being, the words must be determined whether they may be fig. anthropomorphic expressions.

Geerhardus Vos in his *Biblical Theology* notes that the prophets represent God as dwelling in heaven, unlimited by space, and yet they also say that He dwells in Zion and that Canaan is His land. Then Vos continues, "The same relation applied as between Jehovah and time. In popular language, such as the prophets use, eternity can only be expressed in terms of time, although in reality it lies altogether above time." One must therefore look beyond the metaphorical expressions.

2. Theological analysis. Time and temporality is usually connected with change and motion. Things in time have a beginning, they develop in stages, and come to an end. But the Bible teaches that God is immutable. Hebrews 1:10-12 says, "The heavens are the work of thy hands; they will perish, but thou remainest . . . and they will be changed. But thou art the same." The idea of immutability helps in the understanding of eternity, for if God is immutable, if He has no beginning or end, if He does not change or move, can one say He exists in time? Is not another mode of existence—eternity—necessary? Stephen Charnock wrote an excellent volume on the *Existence and Attributes of God.* In the discourse on the "Eternity of God" he says:

> "Time hath a continual succession . . . . We must conceive of eternity contrary to the notion of time; as the nature of time consists in the succession of parts, so the nature of eternity is an infinite immutable duration. Time began with the foundation of the world; but God being before time, could have no beginning in time. Before the beginning of the creation and the beginning of time, there could be nothing but eternity . . . for as between the Creator and creatures there is no medium, so between time and eternity there is no medium (Charnock: *Existence and Attributes of God* [1873], pp. 280-282).

That God is not in time seems harder for some people to understand than that He is not in space. No Christian conceives of God as bounded by space, even though space be infinite in extent. Contrariwise, space is in God, or, at least, "In him we live and move and have our being." Even when one says he has his being in God, the literal spatial meaning is not intended. We are not in God as we are in New York or Chicago.

Because it is recognized that God is not in space, and because it is usually supposed that space and time are in some way analogous, it should not be so surprising that God is not in time either, even though time be infinite. Of course, if time and space are not infinite, it is more obviously necessary to maintain that God is not in time. The reason is that if time began at the creation of the world, one must not suppose that God began to exist; therefore He must have an eternal existence outside of time.

3. Philosophy of time. The line of argument begins to clarify that in large measure the discussion of eternity is really an investigation of time. What is time? What a theologian or philosopher says of time will color his view of eternity.

Aristotle said that time is the measure of motion. Bodies move through space, and the number of motion is time. For Aristotle, the physical world always existed; motion never began and will never end; therefore time never began and will never end. In such a view, a god can be both temporal and everlasting, if he were a physical object or were in some way dependent on a body. Nontemporal eternity could be asserted of a mathematical theorem or abstract concept, for truth is not a body and does not change. Aristotle's god—the unmoved mover, a pure form, free of all matter—can also be called eternal. Although a Christian cannot accept Aristotle's concept of God, he might accept the definition of time. In this case, God would be called eternal, for obviously the Biblical God could not be subject to the numbering, or the numerable aspect, of physical motion.

Aristotle will suffice as an example of pagan antiquity. Before considering any Christian thinker, it would be wise to examine a non-Christian philosopher of modern times. Immanuel Kant defined space and time as the two a priori forms of sensory intuition.

His meaning can be explained briefly as follows: Ordinary or empirical intuitions, such as the sensations of blue, loud, rough, bitter, acrid, vary from person to person. But all men see everything as in space, and their ideas all change in time. Because the contents of experience are so varied, whereas space and time are the same, it follows that the knowledge of space and time cannot be derived from experience. The history of British empiricism, which made the attempt and failed, supports this conclusion. As a priori forms independent of experience, space, and time are not only infinite (as no object of experience can be), but they are also universal and necessary, forming the basis of the necessary truths of mathematics, none of which sort can be learned empirically.

Therefore, concludes Kant, space and time are the innate, or as he calls them, the a priori forms of intuition. The contents of experience are poured into the mind, as hot jelly is poured into a jelly glass, and they take the shape of the mind. It is similar to the ordinary phenomenon of perspective on a profounder level. One sees parallel lines converging in the distance. This convergence is due to the mind: it is the way one sees. So too, trees and rocks are in space because that is the way one sees, and sensations follow one another in time because that is the way one arranges them.

A Christian, however, cannot accept Kant's philosophy *in toto* any more than he can Aristotle's. If he accepts Kant's theory of time, consistency will require him to make God nontemporal. God has no optic nerves, no tongue, no tympanum. God has no sensations. Therefore God, though He may know things as they are in themselves, cannot impose time on them by seeing them. Nor can man impose time on God, because God is not a sensory object to be seen. His status may then be called eternal.

4. Augustine's view. Secular philosophers, such as Aristotle and Kant, paid no attention to the Christian doctrine of creation; on the other hand, Christian theologians usually pay little attention to the nature of time. Hence their ideas of eternity are confused or at least incomplete. Augustine, however, the great philosopher-theologian of the 5th cent., tried to work out a systematic theory.

Rejecting pantheism and emanationism, Augustine asked how God could create the world, time, and change out of nothing, though He Himself is immutable. God must be immutable because if He changed He would become either better or worse, and both are impossible for a perfect Being.

Genesis 1:1, "In the beginning God created the heavens and the earth," attributes a beginning to created things. Because time is somehow connected with change, it too must have been created and must have had a beginning. No time could have preceded the world, for a preceding time would require God to choose one moment rather than another for the act of creation, and this would have been irrational. But, if time began at creation, God Himself, because immutable, because unchanging, is Eternal, and with respect to Him there is no before or after.

Human misunderstandings of eternity arise through the illegitimate comparison of two heterogeneous types of duration. These two modes are based on two types of being: created, changing being, and uncreated, changeless being. Because man knows virtually nothing about the being of God, he naturally has an incomplete idea of eternity. Man's possibilities are largely confined to his own changing being and time.

Time itself, continued Augustine, is difficult enough to understand. Aristotle, brilliant though he was, misunderstood it, for time can be neither motion itself nor its numerable aspect. The same motion can occur in different lengths of time, and those motions are measured by something that is not an attribute of motion. Thus, Augustine spends several pages in his *Confessions* refuting Aristotle.

Augustine's own view begins with the admitted fact that man can and does measure time. But man cannot measure what is not present to him. Hence man could not measure past time unless, strangely, it were present. A physical past, such as a motion yesterday, cannot be present. It is past and gone; but the human mind can make the past present intellectually. Man remembers. The existence and continuity of time, therefore, are the work of man's spirit. It is the nature of mind to preserve a series of past events in the present.

Augustine's words are, "In thee, O my spirit, I measure time . . . . The impression that passing things leave in Thee remains when they are gone. It is that present impression that I measure, not the past things. It is that impression that I measure when I measure time. Therefore either that impression is itself time, or I do not measure time" (*Confessions*, XI, xxvii).

By thus making time depend on perception and memory—a view roughly similar to that of Kant—Augustine preserves the doctrine that God is eternal. An omniscient Being could not have a series of perceptions one after another, for such a series implies that the mind does not know something and later perceives and knows it. But omniscience means that the divine Mind is never ignorant of anything. He neither loses an idea He once had nor gains one He previously did not know. Therefore there can be no temporal succession in God's knowledge. He is not subject to the form of time. Finite beings, who know and do not know, are temporal; but the infinite and omniscient God is eternal.

5. Some modern views. Contemporary theologians also discuss eternity and time, but it is not clear that they have improved upon the great thinkers of the past. For example: F. R. Tennant produced a massive analysis of time, but "we still lack a theory as to the nontemporal serial order which manifests itself in time" (*Philosophical Theology*, Vol. II, p. 138), and if he does not bluntly deny that God is timeless, at least he denies creation.

Oscar Cullmann, *Christ and Time*, has a chapter entitled "Time and Eternity." It is short and disappointing. The book might better have been called *Christ and History*, for it contains no theory of time, and it is unclear whether or not he thinks that God is eternal.

Cullmann makes a sound observation when he remarks that the Scripture nowhere discusses time and eternity in any philosophical manner. As was said earlier, the nature of eternity must be gathered by implication from what the Scripture teaches about God's immutability, independence, and sovereignty. The explicit message of Scripture, instead of stating these implications, uses the idea of eternity for the practical purpose of engendering in the worshipers truth and confidence in God.

6. Practical application. Because God is eternal, His decrees must be eternal, for He could never have existed without thinking or willing them. He can accomplish His decrees because He is almighty, but He could not be almighty without being eternal. A being who is at times ignorant could not be almighty.

What confidence could man have in any of God's attributes, such as His mercy, wisdom, righteousness, goodness, and truth, unless He were immutable, eternal and almighty? How could man entertain hope of a resurrection unless God were everlasting?

How could man rely on God's covenant, if He was not eternal? The covenant is founded on the eternity of God who "desired to show more convincingly to the heirs of the promise the unchangeable character of his purpose, he interposed with an oath, so that through two unchangeable things, in which it is impossible that God should prove false, we who have fled for refuge might have strong encouragement to seize the hope set before us" (Heb 6:17, 18).

In times of distress, decline, or apostasy, the doctrine of the eternity of God provides assurance and comfort. The God who never was born cannot die; and although declension and unbelief may corrupt the visible Church, the eternal God has said, "I will build my church, and the powers of death [or the gates of Hades] shall not prevail against it" (Matt 16:18).

The concept of eternity, the philosophical theories of time, and the carefully extended implications from Scripture may seem to be too technical and far removed from a living religion, but what part of Christianity would remain if God was not eternal?

BIBLIOGRAPHY. Aristotle, *Physics IV* (350 B.C.); Augustine, *Confessions XI* (A.D. 420); S. Charnock, *Discourses upon the Existence and Attributes of God* (1860); F. R. Tennant, *Philosophical Theology,* Vol. II (1930); O. Cullmann, *Christ and Time* (1950).

G. H. CLARK

ETHAM ē' thəm (אֵתָם, meaning possibly, *fort*). The first encampment of the Israelites after leaving Succoth (Exod 13:20). Its precise location is unknown, but it was on the edge of the wilderness of Shur (15:22), a portion of which was known as the wilderness of Etham (Num 33:6-8). Probably it was N of Lake Timsah and formed part of the Egyp. fortifications guarding their eastern frontier (cf. the reference to Migdol, "watch-tower," Num 33:7). The strength of these defenses caused the Israelites to detour S, which led Pharaoh to imagine that they were trapped between the wilderness and the sea (Exod 14:1-3).

A. E. CUNDALL

ETHAN ē' thən (אֵיתָן, LXX Γαιθάν, *enduring, long-lived*). 1. A wise man to whom Solomon was compared in 1 Kings 4:31, "For he was wiser than all other men, wiser than Ethan the Ezrahite and Heman, Calcol, and Darde. . . ." The title of Psalm 89 is "A Maskil of Ethan the Ezrahite," which prob. indicates that he wrote it.

2. A son of Zerah, a descendant of Judah (1 Chron 2:6). He was the father of Azariah (2:8). Because Ethan is mentioned in connection with Heman and Calcol, both here and in 1 Kings 4:31, some understand it to be the same Ethan. They do not have the same father, however, and unless these were understood to be ancestors they must be different men.

3. A son of Zimmah, a descendant of Levi (1 Chron 6:42; cf. Joah of 6:20f.). He is a forebear of Asaph (6:39ff.).

4. A son of Kishi (or Kushaiah in 1 Chron 15:17) who was also of the tribe of Levi (6:44). This or yet another Ethan was to sound the bronze cymbals with Heman and Asaph (15:19). Notice once again a Heman connected with an Ethan as in the first two paragraphs above. Jeduthun usually appears with the names Heman and Asaph (cf. 16:41; 25:1f.; 2 Chron 5:12; 35:15).

R. L. ALDEN

ETHANIM ĕth' ə nĭm (אֵיתָנִים, pl. of *'êtān, continual, permanent, ever-flowing*). A Heb. word that usually refers to rivers that flow the year round. In 1 Kings 8:2 the word is transliterated as it names the seventh month (Tishri, Sept-Oct), the month when all but permanent rivers are dry, preceding the early rains. It dates the month Solomon brought the Ark to the new Temple in Jerusalem.

C. P. WEBER

ETHANUS ĭ' thā nəs. One of five secretaries who accompanied Ezra into forty days of seclusion to receive a complete revelation of salvation history (2 Esd 14:24).

ETHBAAL ĕth' bāl (אֶתְבַּעַל, LXX Ιεθεβααλ, *with Baal* or *man of Baal*). The king of the Sidonians whose daughter Jezebel was the wife of King Ahab of Israel.

Apart from the one statement about Ethbaal in 1 Kings 16:31, that which is known of him comes from Josephus. This ancient historian cites Menander, who mentioned a drought in the time of Ethbaal which corresponds to 1 Kings 17 (Antiq. VIII. xiii. 2). He states further that Ethbaal built the cities of Botrys in Phoenicia and Auza in Libya. Ethbaal also reigned over Tyre (Antiq., ibid.). In his work against Apion, Josephus calls this king Ithobal. Tyre had withstood a thirteen-year siege by Nebuchadnezzar of Babylon (I, xxi). Ithobal was first a priest of Astarte. He killed his predecessor on the throne and then went on to reign for thirty-two years, dying at the age of sixty-eight (Apion I, xviii).

ETHER **e′ thər** (עתר ; 'Αθέρ). One of the nine cities of the tribe of Judah (Josh 15:42) given to the tribe of Simeon (19:7). The place suggested for the city is Khirbet el 'Atr, near Beit Jibrîn. It was located in the Negev of Judah between Libnah and Ashan. The site is prob. to be sought on the border of the Negev, but thus far no positive identification of the city by competent authorities has been made. In this instance, there is a clear example of transference of two cities—Ether and Ashan, which were removed from the end of the Negev list (19:7) to one of the districts of the Shephelah country (15:42).

C. L. FEINBERG

ETHICS

- I. History of ethics
  - A. From the ancient period
    1. Plato
    2. Aristotle
  - B. From the medieval period
    1. Augustine (354-430)
    2. Thomas Aquinas (1225-1274)
  - C. From the modern period
    1. English ethics
       - a. Thomas Hobbes (1588-1679)
       - b. Ralph Cudworth (1617-1687)
       - c. Henry More (1614-1688)
       - d. Shaftesbury (1671-1713) and Hutcheson (1694-1747)
       - e. Joseph Butler (1692-1752)
    2. Utilitarianism
       - a. Jeremy Bentham (1748-1842)
       - b. Henry Sidgwick (1838-1900)
    3. Categorical imperatives—Immanuel Kant (1724-1804)
    4. Instrumentalism — John Dewey (1859-1952)
    5. Contemporary ethics
       - a. P. H. Howell-Smith
       - b. W. H. F. Barnes
       - c. A. J. Ayer
       - d. C. L. Stevenson
- II. Some Christian principles
  - A. The Decalogue and its implications
  - B. Christian presuppositions
    1. Authority
    2. Revelation
    3. Immutability
    4. Sovereignty of God

Ethics is the study of right and wrong, of the most desirable manner of life, and of the most worthy motivation. More profound than specific moral rules and guidance in particulars is that part of ethics that attempts to answer the question, Why? Why is stealing wrong? Why is honesty right? What makes one type of life higher or better than another?

This article is divided into two parts: first, a summary of the history of ethical theory, which is perforce largely secular; and, second, a discussion of Christian principles.

I. HISTORY OF ETHICS

A. From the ancient period. 1. *Plato (427-347 B.C.)*. Plato lived at the time the OT canon was completed. He was the first philosopher to discuss ethics in a somewhat systematic fashion. His ethics, far from being a mere appendage to his system or even an honorable part of it, permeated and controlled it.

In his early years he seems to have considered pleasure to be man's chief and only good, and the solution to ethical problems consisted of calculating the amount of pleasures and pains to be derived from alternative courses of action. This theory, called Hedonism, reappeared in the ancient Epicureans and the modern Utilitarians.

On a journey to Italy, after the death of Socrates in 399 B.C., Plato was converted by the Pythagoreans to a vigorous belief in the immortality of the soul. The Pythagoreans, descendants of the Orphics, were a religio-mathematical brotherhood that believed in knowledge as the way of salvation. Mathematics and certain ethical and cultic rules, if followed, would guarantee a happy immortality (*see* GREEK RELIGION).

Plato's conversion compelled him to repudiate hedonism and to adopt a form of asceticism. In the *Gorgias*, he argued that it is better to be the victim of injustice than to be its perpetrator. Contrary to the views of Callicles Plato held that a dictator, whose every command must be obeyed and who can be unjust with impunity, harms himself more than he harms others. This argument was supported by an appeal to rewards and punishments in the life after death. In the *Phaedo*, asceticism is more pronounced. Not only is pleasure not man's only good; pleasure is positively evil. This does not mean that pain is good. The point is that pleasures, pains, and all sensations rivet men's souls to their bodies. This is evil, for the body is a tomb (σῶμα σῆμα); life on earth is a punishment for previous sins; and a philosopher strives to free his soul from contamination with the body. A philosopher is one who loves truth, but truth is not obtainable by sensation. Hence, love of truth and hatred of evil are both motives for wishing to die. A philosopher must try to die. He may not, however, commit suicide, i.e. deliberately escape from his prison house, for the gods have put man on earth for a purpose, just as the Athenians imprisoned Socrates, and it is unjust to defeat the purposes of proper authority. But by philosophic study, by the avoidance of pleasures, and by a disregard for the body, a philosopher can prepare for death, gently loosen his soul from its rivets, and anticipate a pure intellectual or spiritual existence in the higher world.

In the *Republic,* Plato described man's soul as divided in three parts. The lowest of the three is the appetitive function, concupiscence, or, simply, desire; the next may be named "spunk," or the spirited principle; and the highest is reason, or the intellect. This psychology is Plato's key to his theory of virtues. Temperance is the virtue of the lowest part of the soul and consists in its obedience to the higher functions. Similarly, courage is the virtue of the second part, and wisdom is the virtue of the intellect. Then there is a fourth virtue, justice, which consists in each part minding its own business and not interfering with or disobeying the principles above it.

Plato had a parallel theory of politics. The lowest social class, the business man, must be temperate and obedient to superiors. The soldiers must be courageous and obey the rulers. The rulers are the philosophers, who alone possess wisdom. And justice is the harmony between all the classes.

In addition to such definitions of virtue, ethics must provide some implementation of morality. How is it that not all people are virtuous? Plato included the story of Leontius, who, on a walk, observed some dead bodies and the executioner standing by them. Leontius immediately had a desire to look at them, but at the same time loathing the thought, he tried to divert himself, and covered his eyes. At length he was overmastered by desire; he opened his eyes wide with his fingers and exclaimed, "There, you wretches, gaze your fill at the repulsive spectacle."

Vice then occurs when desire, either alone or with the help of the spirited element, usurps the rule of reason. A deeper question, however, is, why does not reason always rule? What enables desire to usurp the soul's throne?

Plato's answer to this question seems to have been inherited from Socrates; it is given in the early dialogue, *Lesser Hippias*, and though never later emphasized, it was never retracted.

Socrates and Plato thought that no one ever does wrong voluntarily. Evil always harms him who commits it, and no one wants to harm himself. If he does so, it must be involuntarily. That is to say, the person who does wrong does so because he thinks an evil act is good. In this he is mistaken. If he knew what was good for him, he would choose it. Choosing evil is evidence that he does not know. Ignorance therefore is the cause of vice; knowledge guarantees moral action.

In the case cited above, Leontius desired to gaze upon the corpses, and he experienced a loathing at the same time. The loathing derived from the common opinion that it is degrading to enjoy brutality, tragedy, or death. This opinion may well be true, but as long as it is merely common opinion, it is not knowledge. Therefore Leontius' desire conquered the loathing. Desire could not have conquered knowledge.

To this, the reply is often given that men and women know that cigarettes cause cancer, and yet they continue to smoke. This reply, however, is superficial because it fails to understand Plato's strict view of what knowledge is.

Christian moralists, going beyond this supperficiality, often criticize Plato's theory, not only as an inherent defect of paganism, but also as a defect in Plato's analysis of the will. It is held, and with fair reason, that the peculiar function of the will remained unrecognized until the advent of Christianity.

Another Christian objection is that Plato made the norms of morality independent of the will of God. His world of Ideas, which contains moral concepts as well as mathematical and zoological concepts, is an eternal reality superior to and independent of God. Because of the fundamental nature of this question, its discussion will be reserved for the second part of this article. Though it is easy to criticize Plato, it is more profitable at this point to consider something in Christianity that resembles what is taken to be a defect in his view of knowledge and the will. Of course, Christianity recognizes the conflict of reason and desire. This conflict is in fact sharpened by regeneration, so that Paul wrote, "For I do not do what I want, but I do the very thing I hate. . . . For I do not do the good I want, but the evil I do not want is what I do" (Rom 7:15, 19).

In addition to this psychological observation, there is something akin to Plato's view of knowledge in the doctrine of justification by faith. Romans 6 teaches that faith inevitably produces sanctification. Other passages say that faith without works is dead, and a dead faith is simply not faith at all. Therefore when a man says he has faith, but he is devoid of works, others judge that he has no faith. This situation is sometimes called dead orthodoxy. An orthodoxy that is dead is simply not orthodoxy, which is synonymous with right thinking.

So also would Plato argue. The man who does wrong may say he knows, but he does not know; for if he knew, virtuous action would be forthcoming.

2. *Aristotle.* Aristotle, unlike Plato, had very little interest in religion. Morality for him had no connection with a future life; in fact his few references to "immortality" are so vague, it is unlikely that he had any belief at all in the future existence of an individual person. For Aristotle, morality was social custom, refined of its inconsistencies by reason, and based on a view of human nature.

Aristotle formulated the problem of ethics as the search for the Good—the Good for man. In other words, there is a desire to know *that for which* man does everything else. It is the end, or purpose, of all human action.

Purposes are ordered in series. A man walks to his garage for the purpose of getting his car for the purpose of driving downtown for the purpose of getting to work on time. Whereas ethics gives proper consideration to immediate purposes, which then become the means to a more distant end, the culmination of the study is the absolutely final end, the end that is never a means to anything else, namely, Happiness.

Happiness does not mean pleasure. It is true that men choose pleasure for its own sake, as they also choose health for its own sake, but they choose health and pleasure for the sake of other things as well. Amusement and pleasure are forms of rest, and men rest, or take recreation, because they cannot go on working without relief. Pleasure, therefore, is a means to further activity. Some pleasures actually cause harm; these should be avoided. Thus it is clear that pleasure is not Happiness; the absolutely final end—Happiness—is never chosen as a means to anything else.

To ascertain the nature of Happiness, one must analyze, rather than simply accept pleasure. The way to arrive at its meaning is to see that the Good for man is related to man's ultimate purpose. Happiness is not a matter of individual choice; it is determined by human nature; it is defined by the function of man as man. The goodness of a flutist or a shoemaker resides in his function. If the flutist plays well, he is a good flutist. If flutists and shoemakers have definite functions, would it not seem strange if man as man has none and is not designed by nature to fulfill any function? If also each part of the body, the eye or the hand, has a particular function of its own, surely the human being as a whole must have a function. The good man, then, as the example of the flutist shows, is the man who performs his function well.

In a generic sense, man has many functions, including nutrition, growth, and sensation. Man, however, has these in common with plants or animals. Ethics must determine the function peculiar to man; and this is to be found, not in mere life nor even in sensation, but in rationality. Because reason, therefore, is the specific function of man, and because a thing is good if it performs its function well, it follows that the good for man is the active exercise of his soul's faculties in conformity with reason.

Such active exercise has two forms: moral and intellectual virtue. Moral virtue is not a natural property, but one acquired by habit. Since it is the nature of a stone to fall downward, and since it cannot be trained to fall upward, it is clear that natural properties cannot be altered by habit. But morality is produced, altered, and brought to maturity by habit. In the case of natural actions, the capacity precedes the activity; for example, no one acquires the faculty of sight by repeatedly seeing. It is the reverse: Man first had the senses and then used them. But with virtue, man first goes through the motions and by doing so acquires the capacity, just as one does in learning to play the piano. By acting courageously or temperately, a man becomes courageous or temperate.

Action thus produces character. If anyone practices bad fingering on the piano, he becomes a poor musician. No one begins as either a good or bad musician. Habituation determines what he becomes.

Moral virtue is a mean between two extremes, for morality has to do with feelings and actions, of which a man may have an excess or a deficiency. For example, if in a given situation a man is too fearful, he is called a coward; on the other hand, if he has no fear at all, when bullets are whistling by, he is considered foolhardy. Courage consists in feeling the right amount of fear, neither too much nor too little. This right amount is relative to the situation and to the person. More fear is proper in battle, less in a less dangerous situation. Similarly, what is courageous for an elderly person may be cowardly for a young athlete whose physical powers are so much greater.

For this same reason, practical advice on how to become virtuous would be to counteract one's inclinations. Usually this would require a greater risk of being a little too rash than a little too cowardly. If, however, anyone knew he was inclined to rashness, he should run the risk of a little cowardice, and so possibly hit the mean. The same considerations apply to temperance, liberality, and all the moral virtues.

Higher on the scale than moral virtue is intellectual virtue; for the highest level of human nature is reason, and its proper functioning is the highest purpose of man. Contemplation, therefore, is the highest activity. Its objects are the highest objects, and its exercise is more continuous than any other human function can be. It is also most self-sufficient; for whereas the moral virtues require either the presence of other people, as in the case of justice, or the possession of goods, or both, as in the case of liberality, the wise man can think and contemplate by himself, and the more he does so, the wiser he becomes.

Furthermore, contemplation is the only activity that is loved for its own sake alone. It produces no result beyond the actual act of contemplation. The moral virtues are, to be sure, loved for their own sakes; they are ends, but they are also means to other good ends, and therefore are not absolutely final as is contemplation.

Once again, contemplation is the most godlike virtue. It is man's nearest approach to immortality. Obviously the gods cannot be moral; they cannot make contracts, restore deposits, endure terrors, run risks, or temperately restrain evil desires. Contemplation can be their only activity. Hence, contemplation is man's greatest source of happiness.

In the section on Plato, the problem of the

will and its relation to knowledge was discussed. Aristotle also examined the subject. Christians may be a little disappointed because his interest was more political than theological or metaphysical, or even psychological; yet his arguments are well worth studying.

Feelings and actions, which constitute the area of morality, may be voluntary or involuntary. The former are praised or blamed, the latter pardoned and sometimes pitied. Therefore ethics must study volition and choice.

Involuntary actions are those done through (1) force or (2) ignorance. A forced action is one whose principle of initiation is entirely external to the man, who contributes nothing. Compulsion by threat or by fear, is not pure compulsion; a tyrant may threaten, or a storm at sea may "force" one to throw the cargo overboard. Such actions are partly voluntary, but are more similar to involuntary actions. They are given a measure of praise or blame according to the circumstances because the initiation of the motion is in the man.

The claim that pleasure forces a man into immorality implies that all action would be compulsory, and no one would be responsible for anything.

Ignorance is the second cause of involuntary actions, but there is a distinction. All acts done through ignorance are nonvoluntary; only when pain and repentance follow do they become involuntary. Further, acting in ignorance is not the same as acting through ignorance. The drunk acts in ignorance but through drunkenness. Every wicked man is ignorant of what he ought to do. This ignorance does not cause involuntary action; it causes wickedness. The ignorance that causes involuntary action needs further specification.

An action is involuntary if the agent is ignorant of who is doing the act. This point of ignorance occurs only in insanity. The action is involuntary also if the agent is ignorant of the thing done, as in the case of Aeschylus who did not know he was revealing the mysteries, or in the case of a man who did not know the gun was loaded; similarly, if the agent does not know the object of the action, whether a person or a thing, as, for example, a man mistakes his son for a robber in the night, or mistakes a rapier for a foil, or poison for medicine.

Therefore, "Since that which is done under compulsion or through ignorance is involuntary, the voluntary would seem to be that of which the moving principle is in the agent himself, when he is aware of the particular circumstances of the action."

In this discussion Aristotle insisted on distinguishing between an act being voluntary and its being good or evil. There is a common tendency to dodge responsibility by blaming evil actions on force or ignorance, while taking credit for good actions. Similarly, modern liberal penology tends to excuse the criminal because he was either raised in a slum or pampered in a wealthy home. But, to be consistent, this destroys responsibility for evil actions and credit for good actions alike, and dehumanizes everybody.

Next, a subspecies of the voluntary, called deliberate choice, is a better criterion of morality than feelings and actions. Children and some animals act voluntarily, but never by choice. Sudden actions also may be voluntary, but they are not deliberately chosen. What then is choice?

Choice is a subdivision within the area of the voluntary because both children and animals can act voluntarily, but not by choice. Acts done on the spur of the moment also are voluntary, but they are not chosen. Nor is choice the same as desire, anger, wish, or opinion, for animals experience desire and anger. Similarly an incontinent man acts from desire, but not from choice. Conversely, the continent man acts from choice, not from desire.

Choice is not the same as wish because one may sometimes wish for the impossible, but he never chooses it. Further, wish relates to the end of an action, whereas choice selects the means; for example, one may wish to be happy, but one must choose the method to obtain that happiness.

Nor is choice opinion. Opinion is concerned about everything, including both the impossible and the eternal. Opinion is true or false, not good or bad. Character is the result of choice, but not of opinion. Man chooses to take or avoid something, but man holds an opinion of what a thing is. Indeed, some people have fairly sound opinions, but by reason of vice choose what they should not.

Choice, then, is what is decided upon by previous deliberation. To make the concept clearer, it is necessary to describe deliberation.

Aristotle discussed the objects of deliberation and its mode of operation. The objects do not include the impossible, the eternal, nor the invariable laws of astronomy, for they cannot be altered. Nor does a man deliberate about chance events, nor about many human affairs beyond his control. Deliberation, therefore, concerns things that are in man's power, not those that occur always in the same way, but those that are variable—matters of medicine, business, and navigation, but not mathematics and spelling.

This identification of the objects of deliberation is the key to the manner or mode of deliberation. If deliberation concerns the variable, and centers on means rather than on ends, the process consists of a search for the series of means that will produce an end. In a temporal sense, the search goes backward. For example, a man decides to purchase a necklace (the object of his deliberation) as an anniversary gift for his wife. Working backward, he next selects the store where he will purchase the necklace. The store selected, he then chooses the means of transportation, to drive his car or go by bus. The goal determines the choices.

The object of deliberation and of choice is the same object, except that the object of choice has already been determined as the result of deliberation. A man stops thinking how to act when he has brought the moving principle back to himself.

Aristotle continued in much more detail which cannot be included here. To conclude this section, a comparison with the Bible may be made. The Bible does not work out a theory of voluntary action and deliberate choice. It does, however, base responsibility on knowledge, and allows for greater responsibility, greater sin, and greater punishment in proportion to the amount of knowledge. The idea is clearly expressed in Romans 1:18, 19, 32; 2:12, 13, 15. Also, Christ said, "that servant who knew his master's will, but did not make ready . . . shall receive a severe beating. But he who did not know, and did what deserved a beating, shall receive a light beating. Every one to whom much is given, of him will much be required"(Luke 12:47, 48).

(*For later theories of ethics in pagan antiquity, see* EPICUREANS, also STOICS.)

B. From the medieval period. 1. *Augustine (354-430).* In patristic and medieval Christianity, Augustine and Aquinas developed full-fledged theories by interpreting Scripture, contrasting it with and defending it against the pagan theories, but sometimes utilizing pagan theories with Biblical teachings.

Aristotle's view that the highest type of life is contemplation of truth is sometimes exaggerated, if not caricatured, as a withdrawal from the practical activities of life. Augustine's view, determined by Scripture and to a certain extent also influenced by Plato, rejects this exaggerated position. Knowledge pure and simple is not the end of life. Knowledge itself is a means to an end, and this end is blessedness. This basic Augustinian principle is embedded in the Protestant phrases, "Truth is in order to goodness," and "The chief end of man is to glorify God and to enjoy Him forever."

If knowledge were for the sake of knowledge only, it would have no purpose, no end, and therefore no direction—for example, one could spend one's time counting the blades of grass on the front lawn or measuring the lengths of random bits of string. If knowledge has a purpose, however, one will not waste time contemplating useless information.

Philosophy is not the love of knowledge, but the love of wisdom. Though wisdom is a kind of knowledge and must possess the certitude of science, there is a distinction between them, as hinted in 1 Corinthians 12:8. Not all knowledge leads to blessedness; wisdom does.

Man is both corporeal and spiritual. If the mind were divorced from the body, it would no doubt attend only to the divine Ideas; but actually one of the soul's functions is to rule the body. Therefore man must know not only the divine Ideas, but things and bodies as well. He must act, and this requires thought of inferior objects and lower ends. Of course, even Aristotle did not deny the need for moral virtues as distinct from intellectual virtues.

The concern with corporeal affairs, however, is a means to higher intellectual activity. Thought leads to action only to prepare for contemplation. Action is work, effort, pursuit. Contemplation is reward, rest, vision. The distinction is illustrated in Scripture in the persons of Mary and Martha (Luke 10:38-42). During a Christian's earthly life, there is action in view of heavenly contemplation. Morality is the preparation for the vision of God.

Attention to bodily things is legitimate, if this interest is kept in proper perspective. If a man restricts himself to the lower sphere, he is guilty of pride, avarice, and personal cupidity. Instead of subordinating himself to God, he tries to subordinate the universe to himself. Science itself is good, but man easily abuses science.

Wisdom, on the other hand, turns man from things to God. Pride is replaced by humility. Science is necessary to arrange temporal affairs, but when people subordinate themselves to God, they put their various activities in their proper places.

Why isn't everyone wise? Plato had tried to answer this question in terms of a conflict between reason and desire. Christianity, however, although it does not deny a conflict between desire and reason, has a different psychology that requires a profounder explanation of evil. This difference in psychology is revealed in an emphasis on the will. Such emphasis was lacking, or at most, rudimentary, in Plato and Aristotle; although the Stoics advanced over their predecessors in the matter of the will, there are other differences.

All things, man included, are subject to the order God has imposed on the world. Each thing, so Augustine teaches, has its proper place in the universal hierarchy. Nevertheless, for morality, man must act and act voluntarily. Even intellectual learning depends on the will. One can almost say that a man is his will. In sensation the will is required to sustain attention. A person's fingers may be in contact with an object, or his eyes may be fixed on an object, yet if he does not attend to it, he does not perceive it. Memory also requires attention, and neither understanding nor belief takes place without an act of will.

Modern terminology might define volition as a natural drive. It is a principle of action. According to Aristotle, earth, air, fire, and water have a natural tendency to seek their

A painting of St. Augustine (Aurelius Augustinus) A.D. 354-430. © *H.P.*

proper places. Earth naturally falls, and fire by nature rises. As earth has weight, Augustine felt, so man has love. Love is man's natural motor power.

Parenthetically, it should be noted that in orthodox theology, love is a volition, not an emotion. Contemporary references to God's love and man's love for God often go astray because of faulty psychology. Love toward God consists in voluntary obedience to His laws (John 14:15, 21, 23; 1 John 2:4, 5). Emotion has little to do with it.

Accordingly, Augustine argues that the moral problem is not whether to love or not to love. This would be like asking whether earth should have weight or not have weight. The problem is to love what one ought to love, for this is virtue. Because men continually fail, the problem arises whether a natural principle of motion can go astray.

The difficulty was sharper for the Christian Augustine than it was for the pagan Plato, for in addition to the psychology of the will, Augustine had to operate with the theological concept of sin. This does not refer simply to the fact that men choose evil. The pagans knew that much. The Christian concept of sin is based on original sin and the inheritance of it. Aristotle had explained evil actions as the result of bad habits, such as poor fingering on a piano. At the start, a prospective musician has neither good nor bad habits. He is neutral, and practice makes him what he becomes. But Christianity teaches that man is born in sin; he has bad habits at the outset, and this together with guilt is inherited from Adam. Therefore, sin is a much more radical defect than is acknowledged by the pagan view of evil.

Augustine gives a memorable example. When he was a boy, he and his gang stole some pears from a nearby orchard. He did not steal because he was hungry for he had pears at home; in fact, much better pears, for the stolen pears were so bad that the boys threw them to the pigs. It is wrong to steal, but if one steals because he is hungry, or even because the pears taste good, there is some superficial plausibility in the theft. Augustine's theft, however, was not so motivated. He stole simply for the fun of stealing; he enjoyed evil for its own sake; and he enjoyed it all the more because he did it with his friends who also enjoyed evil just because it was evil. Stealing pears may not be a great sin, but what depravity could be greater than a love of evil for its own sake.

The passage (*Confessions,* Book II) containing this psychological analysis of the motives of sin does not itself refer to original sin. The immediate point is merely the perversity of the human heart. This depravity cannot be accounted for on Aristotelian principles, though even at this late date some professing Christians still say that a child becomes sinful only upon committing a voluntary transgression at or after the so-called age of accountability.

Those who deny that men are dead in sin hold also that sin is not merely voluntary, but is particularly an act of free will. Volition and free will are not the same, as the article on Stoicism shows. Free will, that is, a choice that is not caused either by God, by character, by motives, or anything else, is substituted for knowledge as the basis for responsibility. Moreover, the problem is complicated by the fact that God is omnipotent. He could have made men sinless, had He so desired. This is not the case in Platonism, where God is conceived as limited in power; Plato's god does his best to restrain evil and impose order on the visible world, but the opposing forces are sometimes too much for him. Christianity teaches that God is omnipotent, so that He could even now eradicate evil. Superficial thinking attempts to say that God limited Himself. The infinite made itself finite. God undeified Himself, and hence there is sin. This reply is inadequate because limited omnipotence is a contradiction in terms, but also because it does not answer the original question: why does not God now unlimit Himself and make all men sinless? The problem is difficult, and Augustine changed his views, beginning as a new Christian with a certain form of free will and then developing a more consistently Christian and Biblical solution.

Augustine's first attack on this basic problem of ethics, *On Free Will*, was written about A.D. 390. The question is, "If sins come from the souls which God has created, and these souls are from God, how explain that sin is not borne back upon God (*referantur in Deum*)?" Or in other words, how is God not responsible for sin?

By A.D. 390, Augustine had made such little progress in grasping Christian doctrine and was still so under the influence of Plato that he denied the sovereignty of God by adopting the Platonic view that an action is wrong not because God forbids it, but God forbids it because it is wrong i.e. or some other principle independent of God. This error subtly influenced his arguments, but gradually he was able to discard Platonism.

He next contended that things superior to the human mind, i.e. God, cannot subject a man to sin or lust because being superior they are good and would not do so. Things inferior to the mind cannot do so because they are inferior and weaker. Therefore the mind or will itself causes sin, and God is not responsible.

Yet if God created the will of man good, how could man ever choose evil? Conversely, if men are born unwise and never have a good will, why are they punished? Augustine replied with another bit of Platonism that he later discarded. He wrote that perhaps souls lived in a preexistent state before birth, and that this fact (somehow, not too clearly) answers the questions (Book I, 12). In fact he soon repeated the question (I, 16): If God gave men free will, is He not responsible for their sins; for if He had not given them free will, they would not have sinned?

This is an unfortunate flaw in Augustine's argumentation. He nowhere defined free will, and without an explicit definition, one can only guess what he means. Presumably he meant an uncaused or unmotivated will. But if so, the flaw takes the form of assuming without proof that a will can operate without a cause. Therefore Augustine's immediate remark is irrelevant: God gave man a free will so that he might live righteously (which contradicts the previous statement that without a free will no one would sin), and God is not to blame if man uses free will for the wrong purpose (II, 1), just as one cannot object to wine because some use it wrongly (II, 18).

The argument becomes more theological as it progresses. If God foreknew Adam's sin, was it not inevitable? And must not man will as God foreknows? No, replied Augustine, because *must* means *no will;* therefore foreknowledge does not conflict with human ability. For example, if one man foreknows that another will sin, the former's knowledge is not the cause of the sin. As memory of the past does not exert force on the past, so knowledge of the future does not determine the future.

Apparently Augustine assumed that a man can know the future and that God discovers an independent future the way a man does. Neither of these assumptions seems sound.

For such reasons as these, Augustine concluded that it is unwise to seek a cause of volitions. When one asks what causes the will to choose, one is led into an infinite regress. The will itself is the cause, and further search is useless.

Nevertheless Augustine went further. He admitted that sinning is inevitable, for he could not escape Romans 7:18. Therefore man does not have free will; strictly speaking only Adam had free will (III, 18). Adam's descendants are punished as Adam himself was, because the descendants of a sinner are of necessity sinful. If all souls have descended from one soul, then all have sinned and deserve punishment. Furthermore, because virtue can be acquired by God's grace, the sinful state is a stimulus to progress.

Late in life, after he had gone through the Pelagian controversy (cf. PELAGIUS), Augustine wrote two more books on the same subject: *Grace and Free Will* in A.D. 426, and *Predestination of the Saints* in A.D. 429. In the former, he still used the phrase "free will," but the discussion no longer denied a divine cause of the will's action. Chapter 29 stated that God is able to convert opposing wills and to take away their hardness; otherwise, if God could exercise no causative power on the will, it would be useless to pray for the conversion of anyone. It is certain, he continued, that it is men who will when they will, but it is God who makes them will what is good. It is God who makes them act by applying *efficacious* powers to their wills. The Scripture "shows us that not only men's good wills, which God converts from bad ones . . . but also those who follow the world are so entirely at the disposal of God that he turns them whithersoever he wills and whensoever he wills. . . . For the Almighty sets in motion even in the innermost hearts of men the movement of their will so that he does through their agency whatsoever he wishes to perform through them" (chs. 41, 42).

In the latter book he wrote against semi-Pelagianism and insisted that faith is a gift of God. God causes men to believe. Augustine confessed that he had not always understood the doctrines of grace: he had thought that Romans 7 referred to the unregenerate; he had denied prevenient grace; but now he retracted his earlier errors, for he obtained mercy to be a believer—not because he had believed.

Christ Himself is the best example of predestination, for if He had had free will, He could have sinned; but Christ could not have sinned, therefore He did not have free will, but was predestinated in all that He did. In fact, in both of these books, but esp. in the last one, Augustine taught the full Protestant position, forgotten during the Middle Ages, but rediscovered by Luther and Calvin.

After Augustine, the Rom. empire in the W disintegrated under the advances of the barbarians, and learning became almost extinct. As church superstitions multiplied, theology became semi-Pelagian or worse, though what philosophy survived was mildly Augustinian.

2. Thomas Aquinas (1225-1274). In the 13th cent., however, Thomas Aquinas succeeded in overthrowing Augustinianism and in establishing Aristotelianism.

His ethics is based on the fact of a similarity and a difference between human beings and inanimate objects. The similarity, on which the difference is built, lies in the possession of a natural tendency or inclination. Earth has a natural tendency to fall. In inanimate things these tendencies are unconscious and are not subject to the being's control. Man also has a natural inclination, but it is a higher form because man is rational and volitional. He inclines to what he knows, and he controls his own conduct.

Appetite or desire is proportionate to knowledge. In animals, the knowledge is merely sense knowledge, and since this requires a bodily organ, it follows that if a dog sees or smells a bone, he automatically desires it. Man, however, has rational knowledge, which does not immediately depend on any bodily organ; therefore the will or rational appetite does not act automatically. Nevertheless the object chosen must be known.

The will naturally or automatically inclines toward the good. Just as each plant or animal naturally tends to the preservation of itself and of the species, so too man is directed to the good. In actual life, however, man is not confronted so much with the Good as with particular goods. These are not completely satisfying, and hence they do not compel the will.

In fact, not even God can compel the will. The reason is that

> what is done voluntarily is not done of necessity. Now, whatever is done under compulsion is done of necessity, and consequently what is done by the will cannot be compelled. . . . The will can suffer violence insofar as violence can prevent the exterior members from executing the will's command. But as to the will's own proper act, violence cannot be done to the will. . . . God, who is more powerful than the human will, can move the will of man . . . . But if this were by compulsion, it would no longer be by an act of will, nor would the will itself be moved, but something else against the will (*Summa Theol.* II i, 2.6, Art. 4).

On a later page (2.10, Art. 4), Thomas considered the objection,

> It would seem that the will is moved of necessity by God. For every agent that cannot be resisted moves of necessity. But God cannot be resisted, because his power is infinite; and so it is written (Rom 9:19) "who resisteth his will?"

In reply to this quotation from the canonical Bible, Thomas uses a verse from an apocryphal book:

> On the contrary, it is written (Ecclus. 15: 14) "God made man from the beginning and left him in the hand of his own counsel."

Natural inclinations, as in inanimate things, tend toward a form existing in nature; the sensitive appetite and all the more the rational appetite tend toward an apprehended form. Therefore the will chooses, not the universal good as such, but an apparent good. The agent intends the good; he never voluntarily chooses evil; when he chooses a particular apparent good that turns out to be evil, the evil is unintentional.

The intellect therefore moves the will, but not necessarily, by presenting an object to it. If the intellect offered to the will an object good universally and from every point of view, the will would choose it of necessity, if it chose at all, for it cannot choose the opposite. If, on the other hand, the will is offered an object that is not good in every respect it will not tend toward it of necessity. Hence the will can either accept or reject particular goods.

Choice is an act of both the intellect and the will. The matter of the choice comes from the intellect, but the form of the choice comes from the will. Intellect and will interact, but their acts are not to be confused. The intellect may even command the will and say, "Do this!" Even when the will obeys, it does so freely.

With all their interaction, more complicated than this brief essay indicates, Thomas steadfastly maintained the distinction between intellect and will. Augustine, as said above, virtually identified man with his will, in which case intellectual acts are simply particular volitions. After the time of Thomas, the discussion intensified. Descartes, at the beginning of the modern period, returned to a position somewhat similar to Augustine's, but these intricacies can be followed no further here.

One who has not read Thomas can have no idea of the immense amount of detail he incorporated in his writings. Basing his views on Aristotle, he argued that habit is a quality, a species of quality, which implies order to an act; it is necessary that there be habits; some habits are bodily, some exist in the soul; some habits, such as temperance and fortitude, belong to the sensitive and irrational part of the soul; science and wisdom are habits of the intellect; justice, however, is a habit of the will; and even angels have habits.

Thomas then discussed whether any habit is from nature; whether any is caused by acts; whether a habit can be caused by one act; whether any habits are infused by God; whether habits increase (which he answers in the affirmative, for faith is a habit and faith increases); and so on until he is able to show that virtue is a habit. He then continued for many long pages on virtue in general, and had something to say about a few particular virtues.

One basic factor in the ethics of Thomas, a factor that seems to deal more closely with the particular decisions of everyday morality, is the theory of natural law.

There are several types of law: eternal law, natural law, and civil law. A law is a rule that prescribes or forbids an action; it is an obligation founded on reason. There is no other regulative principle of action than reason. The unreasonable commands of a tyrant are not laws, but merely usurp that appellation.

So completely is reason the source of law that a private person is not competent to make laws. He can give advice but he cannot efficaciously lead anyone to virtue. Coercive power is vested in a public power. A father cannot give laws even to his family, for a family is part of the state. The father can indeed issue certain commands to his children, but they do not have the nature of law.

Furthermore, although there are various precepts of prudence, the first principle in practical affairs is the highest end—happiness or beatitude. Therefore law is chiefly ordained to the common, rather than to the individual, good.

The first of the three types of law is the eternal law. Since this is the plan of government laid down by God, the Chief Governor, all the plans of inferior governors must be derived from this eternal law.

Insofar as the eternal law applies to the conduct of men, it has been inscribed in man's substance and is called natural law. Because this law causes men to be what they are—it takes the form of a human inclination toward certain ends—they obey it when they yield to the legitimate tendencies of their nature.

The first and basic principle is that good should be done and evil avoided. All other precepts depend on this. Since good has the nature of an end, "all those things to which man has a natural inclination are naturally apprehended by reason as being good, and consequently as objects of pursuit" (*Summa Theol.* II, I, 2. 94, Art. 2). Thus self-preservation is the basic inclination; next comes reproduction and the care of children; in short, all virtuous acts are covered by natural law.

These laws are indelibly written in the human heart. They cannot be effaced. Men need only to observe themselves to discover them, or in Thomas' own words, "The natural law is promulgated by the very fact that God instilled it into man's mind so as to be known by him naturally" (ibid. Q. 90, Art. 4). Thomas also extended the details of what man ought to do by including the theological virtues taught by Revelation. These make his good life more Christian than that of an Aristotelian gentleman, but they are not logically deduced from his philosophic system.

Two criticisms of Thomism should be considered—one theological, one philosophical. The first is that Christian theology is inconsistent with Aristotelian ethics. The discussion of ethics depends on an assertion of free will with the assumption that man is able by practice to make himself virtuous. Man may "naturally" seek the good, but since the Fall no one is "natural." All are born in sin and are in need of grace. Therefore they cannot will to be virtuous. Although Thomas never achieved the full Christian vision of Augustine's later works, he nevertheless had some notion of predestination and reprobation. Whether the latter can be consistently combined with free will is the question. At least the consistency is not clear in the following: "When it is said that the reprobated cannot obtain grace, this must not be understood as implying absolute impossibility, but only conditional impossibility; just as it was said above that the predestined must necessarily be saved, yet by a conditional necessity that does not do away with liberty of choice" (*Summa Theol.* I, Q.23, Art. 3). Also, "Man's turning to God is by free choice; and thus man is bidden to turn himself to God. But free choice can be turned to God only when God turns it . . . man can do nothing unless moved by God. . . . It is the part of man to prepare his soul, since he does this by free choice. And yet he does not do this without the help of God moving him and drawing him to himself" (ibid. II, I, 2. 109, Art. 6).

The inconsistency involved here seems to be that Thomas made a good case for freedom from coercion, and that this freedom is compatible with predestination, for God is not a mechanical agent. Yet Thomas also held that for responsibility and morality, the freedom of an uncaused cause is required, and this is not compatible with predestination. Until a theologian clarifies himself out on these points, neither his theology nor his ethics will escape

Thomas Aquinas. ©*H.P.*

confusion.

The second objection to be considered is philosophical and ethical—the question whether Aristotle or Thomas can build an ethics on natural law. Is it actually true that men can observe what is written on their heart and discover that adultery and theft are forbidden?

It is plausible that natural law would prescribe the care and education of children. Animals instinctively care for their young, but they are not for that reason monogamous. If it be replied that a human child requires a longer period of care and that therefore a human family ought to remain together for this longer period, neither monogamy nor permanent union is thereby established. Indeed, since the state, on Thomistic principles, is to spell out most of the details left obscure in natural law, could not a rational ruler establish communal nurseries? Who is to say that Soviet laws are less rational than American?

This includes the question of theft. If property is a creation of the state, confiscatory taxation is as reasonable as Jeffersonian democracy, and laissez faire as collectivism. Thomas admits that it is always dangerous to rebel, even when a tyrant violates natural law; but how can one distinguish between a just rebellion and an unjust usurpation?

Even self-preservation is not clearly an inviolable law of nature. Military service is considered a duty, but this can lead to death. If natural law obliges, a young man would be obliged to dodge the draft. Or, on the other hand, why must suicide be considered wrong? There may be an instinct of self-preservation, but some unfortunate people have concluded that the conditions of life were so onerous that it was rational to kill themselves. This was a definite part of Stoic philosophy, and the Stoics prescribed a life of reason as strongly as Aristotle did. But if natural law cannot absolutely prescribe self-preservation, it would seem that ethics needs find a better foundation.

C. From the modern period. 1. *English ethics.* a. Thomas Hobbes (1588-1679). In the history of English ethics, the approach differs from that of medieval times and antiquity. Thomas Hobbes aimed to make ethics scientific. Thus he held that all forms of life are but complicated relationships among particles of matter in motion. This materialism serves as a basis for his psychological hedonism. Hobbes professes to have discovered by scientific observation that all men naturally desire and are motivated only by personal pleasure. Man is essentially self-seeking. "Pity is imagination or fiction of future calamity to ourselves proceeding from the sense of another man's calamity"; and "The passion of laughter proceedeth from the sudden imagination of our own odds and eminency; for what is else the recommending of ourselves to our own good opinion by the comparison of another man's inferiority or absurdity."

For Hobbes, ethics is descriptive rather than normative. He did not say what men ought to do; he described their actual conduct. Surreptitiously, perhaps he made some recommendations.

Thus he argued that the condition most unfavorable to obtaining pleasure is political anarchy. To be sure the war of each against all is man's natural state; but it is an intolerable one. No one's life is safe; and without life pleasure is impossible. Therefore everyone must surrender all his rights to the government, preferably by selecting one man and making him an absolute monarch.

This is a form of the social contract theory of government. The people enter into a covenant with each other to set up a king. Forever after it will be wrong to rebel: by the contract they retain no rights at all—therefore no right to rebel. Nor can they later claim that the king has broken the contract, for the king was never a party to the contract.

The king now, as selfish as anyone else, protects his property, i.e. his subjects, for his own good. He enforces laws that preserve life and protect property, and under such a totalitarian government man can best enjoy himself. To rebel against the king and to diminish his authority would be to revert to anarchy and misery.

Hobbes had some reason to be apprehensive of social disturbances. His age was one of confusion in England—the disaffection of the Scottish army toward the perfidious Charles I in England and the Puritans' hostility toward the Arminian and Romish tendencies in the Anglican Church. Civil war was on its way. Foreseeing this, Hobbes contended that the principle of private conscience, by which the Puritans read the Bible for themselves, conflicted with governmental authority. Similarly, the independent conscience of the Pope was destructive of peace. Therefore Puritans and Romanists were both to be repressed, and the king by his supremacy could not only legislate the rules of morality as he saw fit, but he could even decide what books make up the Bible and what they mean.

The immediate reaction to Hobbes, on the surface at least, was an attack on his egoism. More fundamental was a rejection of scientific observation as a basis for morality. If a sense of obligation is to be maintained, if the concept of duty and the authority of normative principles is to be defended, mere factual descriptions of *what is* are not enough; something more is needed to show *what ought to be*.

b. RALPH CUDWORTH (1617-1688). Therefore Ralph Cudworth returned to a Platonic or Neoplatonic theory of suprasensible Ideas. For him as for Plato, the Good—and its derivative forms—are independent of both human and divine volition: an action is not wrong because God forbids it, but God, Himself subject to the Ideas, forbids it because it is wrong.

c. HENRY MORE (1614-1687). Henry More based morality on intuitions. As one knows a rock or a mountain simply by seeing it, so in somewhat similar fashion he can have an intellectual vision of first principles. They are not deduced from anything prior or more certain: they are simply seen. Most philosophers, except the most extremely scientific, will acknowledge the legitimacy of undemonstrable axioms, but More's two dozen moral intuitions seem unnecessarily abundant.

d. SHAFTESBURY (1671-1713) and HUTCHESON (1694-1747). Shaftesbury and Hutcheson paid more attention to the conflict between egoism and altruism. If men had no sense of good distinct from personal advantage, is their argument, they would hold in equal esteem a fruitful field and a generous friend. One would hold in equal esteem a man who serves him with delight and a man who brings him the same advantage by constraint. But one does not esteem these equally. Therefore we have a sense of good other than egoistic advantage.

e. JOSEPH BUTLER (1692-1752). A much more important writer was Bishop Joseph Butler. His most influential work, used as a textbook for over a century in many seminaries, was *The Analogy of Religion to the Constitution and Course of Nature*. His system of ethics is expounded in *Fifteen Sermons*. Neither of these is founded on Platonic or intuitionist principles. Bishop Butler believed that moral obligation, and the basic theses of Christianity too, can be established by observation. Whereas not so attached to the materialistic mechanism of Thomas Hobbes, he still depended on scientific methods. This procedure served him well in his *Analogy*, for he was able to destroy English Deism on its own grounds. He could show, for example, that the immortality of the soul was a reasonable conclusion, at least as reasonable as the opposite. This, however, may be the fallacy in his thinking. Pure, unmixed observation can just as reasonably arrive at either of two incompatible positions, and arrive at them by equally reasonable, that is equally unreasonable, arguments. Similarly, in ethics one must always scrutinize an argument that professes to deduce what ought to be from what merely is.

Thomas Hobbes. ©*H.P.*

In the second of his *Fifteen Sermons*, using the text, "For when the Gentiles, which have not the law, do by nature the things contained in the law, these, having not the law, are a law unto themselves" (Rom 2:14 KJV), Joseph Butler, not noticing the intuitional or a priori thrust of the verse, argues that the purpose of man can be discovered by observation, or, more particularly, introspection, and that this purpose reveals man's nature and fixes his obligations.

Man has a conscience as truly as he has eyes; and as the purpose of the eye is to see trees and houses, so the purpose of the conscience is to see right and wrong. Furthermore, man's instincts lead him to contribute to the happiness of society in a way and with a force that no inward principle leads him to evil. Hence, man is at least more altruistic than selfish.

If it be replied that evil and selfish instincts are also natural, and that we therefore follow nature in following them, the reply is, first, that such an argument would destroy all distinctions between good and evil—everything would be indifferently natural; and, second,

Jeremy Bentham. ©*H.P.*

that observation of human nature did not result merely in the discovery that both altruistic and selfish inclinations equally exist, but rather that conscience exists as a superior, governing principle—its purpose is to sit in judgment over the others.

Butler is quite confident of the rectitude of conscientious judgments: "Let any plain, honest man, before he engages in any course of action, ask himself, Is this I am going about right, or is it wrong? Is it good, or is it evil? I do not in the least doubt, but that this question would be answered agreeably to truth and virtue, by almost any fair man in almost any circumstance."

A person, whose viewpoint is not so restricted to Eng. common opinion in the 18th cent. may wonder whether all the world in all ages has enjoyed such a universal agreement. Without pressing the Scriptural revelation of the total depravity and desperate wickedness of the human heart, but adhering solely to observation "exclusive of revelation" as Butler insists (Sermon II, paragraph 20), an observer of humanity also notes that some widows have conscientiously mounted the funeral pyres of their husbands, that some military nations have taught that suicide is honorable, that Congolese savages regard cannibalism as normal. Observation, it would seem, allows for incompatible results.

Butler next considered a most important objection. Suppose, the objection runs, that conscience prescribes for a person a line of action that would injure him. Why should he be concerned about anything other than his own personal good? If he discovers in his makeup certain restrictions of conscience, why should he not endeavor to suppress them?

Butler's answer is that personal happiness and the good of other people coincide. All the common enjoyments of life, and, even the pleasures of vice, depend on a person's regard of his fellow creatures. The satisfactions of selfishness are not to be assumed superior to the satisfaction of acting justly and benevolently. Butler wrote, "It is manifest that, in the common course of life, there is seldom any inconsistency between our duty and what is *called* interest: it is much seldomer that there is an inconsistency between duty and what is really our present interest. . . . But whatever exceptions there are to this . . . all shall be set right at the final distribution of things. It is a manifest absurdity to suppose evil prevailing finally over good, under the conduct and administration of a perfect mind" (Sermon II, paragraph 28).

Some puzzles emerge in the study of Butler's arguments. Altruism and selfishness, conscience and "reasonable self-love" may coincide, but when they do not seem to—and in the 20th cent., duty does not speak so clearly as it did in his day—should a man follow what seems to be his interest or what seems to be his duty? Is duty in fact more clearly discernible than interest? Again, "a final distribution of things" that will equalize the temporary inconsistencies is not a principle to be derived from observation. Butler's argument is circular: he must appeal to divine Providence to save his ethical theory, although he cannot prove the existence of Providence except by observing the uniform and inviolate coincidence of conscience and self-love.

2. *Utilitarianism.* a. JEREMY BENTHAM (1748-1832). In 19th cent. England Jeremy Bentham propounded the theory of utilitarianism. Based on psychological hedonism, as was the theory of Thomas Hobbes, it, too, claimed to be observational, descriptive, and scientific. From the thesis that everyone as a matter of fact seeks nothing but pleasure, Bentham somehow arrived at the position that one ought to seek, not only his own pleasure, but the greatest pleasure of the greatest number.

"Nature," writes Bentham, "has placed mankind under the governance of two sovereign masters, *pain* and *pleasure*. It is for them alone to point out what we ought to do, as well as to determine what we shall do. . . . They govern us in all we do, in all we say, in all we think."

The pleasure to be expected from prospective lines of action is to be measured by seven parameters: intensity, duration, certainty, propinquity, fecundity, purity, and extent. The latter is the number of persons to whom the pleasure extends. By calculating the amounts of pleasure to be produced from alternate lines of action, anyone should know which action he should choose.

The right action is enforced by four sanctions. Consequences, painful or pleasurable, derived through the ordinary course of nature, presumably physiological, issue from or belong to the *physical* sanction. Consequences derived through the actions of the police, the courts, and the state form the *political* sanction. Pleasures and pain received at the hands of such chance persons who spontaneously react to our conduct form the *moral* or *social* sanction. Bentham also makes religion a fourth sanction; but this *religious* sanction operates only through the other three. Bentham gives lip service to the possibility of divine rewards and punishments in a future life, but these can have no effect on man's present choices. Such consequences are not open to observation; men cannot calculate the amounts—whether those pains and pleasures are like or unlike the present kind is something beyond the realm of discovery by observation.

Bentham's utilitarianism provides a good opportunity for showing the weakness of many secular systems. In the first place, the calculation of future pleasures, on which choice and the knowledge of obligation depend, is impossible. Only in a few simple instances, and in these only roughly, can anyone estimate the amount of pleasure he as an individual will enjoy from a particular choice. To suppose that anyone can calculate the sum total of pleasures accruing to the whole human race is utterly and obviously impossible. Let anyone who wishes, try measuring along the seven parameters.

The principle of the greatest good for the greatest number is one by which dictators can justify their cruelty. When the communists starved to death millions of Ukrainians, massacred thousands of Polish officers, murdered possibly twenty million Chinese, and slaughered the Tibetans, they could justify themselves on the ground that the pleasure of future generations of communists would outweigh the temporary pain. Certainly no scientific observation can prove the contrary.

Less gruesome but even more fundamentally destructive of utilitarianism is the fact that descriptive science can discover no reason for aiming at the good of all society. Plato, Aristotle, Butler, all agree that men should seek their own good; who can urge them to seek their own harm? Why should anyone govern his actions by the good of another person? If perchance, as Butler asserted, there is never any conflict between a man's good and the good of every other human being, then self-seeking and altruism will both prescribe the same choices. But this utopian assumption contradicts observable evidence. Personal jealousies and international conflicts alike demonstrate the incompatibility of goods. Actual life is much more like Hobbes' war of each against all than like a perfect universal harmony.

b. Henry Sidgwick (1838-1900). To avoid this disastrous argument against utilitarianism, Henry Sidgwick, whose *Methods of Ethics* is the best analysis of ethical methodology so far written, relinquished the descriptive basis Bentham used, and tried to found utilitarianism on intuitions. He urged his readers to look at the matter "from the point of view, if I may say so, of the Universe." But unfortunately no one man is the universe, and therefore no one man can see things from its point of view; nor is it easy to learn why anyone ought to take any other point of view than his own. For another person's pleasure, enjoyment, or good cannot be mine.

Sidgwick was honest enough to admit that the compatibility of all individual goods can be maintained only on the basis of God's rewards and punishments. It is incapable of empirical proof. Therefore, much to his distaste, he is forced to admit the question whether a theory of ethics can be constructed on an independent basis, or whether it is forced to borrow a fundamental principle from theology (*Methods of Ethics,* pp. 506-509). His modesty, his honesty, and his almost superhuman effort to save utilitarianism seal its doom.

Hedonism in any of its forms is a teleological system. Moral acts have the purpose of producing pleasure, and they are tested by their actual consequences.

3. *Categorical imperative—Immanuel Kant (1724-1804).* A century earlier Immanuel Kant, of Germany, constructed a nonhedonistic, nonteleological system, in which the moral quality of an act was entirely independent of actual consequences.

One of Kant's chief objections to an ethics of calculation was that on such an arrangement only those who are brilliant mathematicians can be moral. On the contrary, morality ought to be within the abilities of every humble person. Furthermore, common opinion never regards a man as immoral just because he fails to obtain a great deal of pleasure. He may be imprudent or stupid, but if his intentions are sincere and good, he is considered moral. Conversely, successful calculation may prove a man clever, but is no basis for judging him to be particularly moral.

In opposition to empirical ethics, therefore, Kant put forward a theory of a priori duty. A moral precept is such because it is a categorical imperative. Some imperatives are merely hypothetical: to bisect a line, one must draw certain arcs. Such imperatives are scientific, and if anyone does not wish to bisect an arc, no obligation exists. Moral, or categorical imperatives, however, do not depend on *ifs.* It is

Immanuel Kant. ©*H.P.*

"immoral" to say that if a person wants a good reputation, he should be honest and tell the truth. One ought to be honest and tell the truth regardless of consequences, and even without being so motivated. A moral act must be motivated only by reverence for duty.

Duty then is determined, not by any pleasure accruing to the individual, but by maxims that can be universalized. If I tell a lie by making a promise I do not intend to keep, I make myself an exception to a universal maxim. The only reason I can deceive anyone by a false promise is that people expect promises to be kept. If all or even most promises were broken, there would be no promises at all because no one would believe them. Hence the intent to deceive depends on the maxim of nondeception. An individual cannot universalize the maxim of false promises because such an attempt is self-contradictory. A false promise is always and of necessity an exception and can never be a general rule. Universalization therefore, or the absence of self-contradiction, is the test of morality. The results of the action have nothing to do with it.

Kant's example of truth-telling is the best one he could have used. Others are not so convincing. For example, the maxim, "Be a miser," can be universalized; so also "Be a spendthrift." Neither of these requires the agent to be an exception to the general rule; neither is self-destructive. Similarly the maxim, "Commit suicide," contains no self-contradictions. Or, if the maxim applied to children so that the human race would become extinct, in which case suicides would no longer be possible, the maxim can be replaced, "Commit suicide on your forty-fifth birthday." Kant tried his best to show that suicide is immoral, but if he succeeded it is because of an appeal to God and not because of a categorical imperative. Kant's ethics can be saved, then, only by an admission that suicide is right and that a miser and a spendthrift are morally equal.

However, Kant's thesis faces even greater difficulties. Morality seems to presuppose freedom. Ask a man, wrote Kant, whether he can refuse to bear false witness in court when his king requires it; and the man might doubt that he would refuse, but he would not doubt that he could refuse. Duty and the categorical imperative depend on freedom.

At the same time, Kant, to escape Hume's empirical skepticism, worked out a system of epistemology, by which every atom, every motion, every physiological change, every natural desire is determined by mathematical, mechanical law. Freedom is physically, scientifically impossible. How then can freedom and morality be saved?

It must be insisted upon that free will is not the ability to indulge one's desires and natural impulses. Natural impulses are natural; they are caused by physiological conditions. A will is free only when self-caused—independent of all influences external to itself. Such freedom is impossible in the physical, visible world.

In this predicament Kant asserts that men are citizens of two worlds. Beyond the visible world there is an intelligible world, where neither matter nor mechanism can corrupt, and where causality does not break through and steal man's freedom. In that world, morality is possible.

In this world, where men's bodies are and where men's actions occur, is morality possible? Consider a particular act of theft. A man breaks the lock on a door, enters a house, and steals some cash and jewelry. All these actions are physical actions in time and space. Now Kant is adamant. There can be no freedom, he says, for bodies or actions in time; all temporal factors are mechanically determined. Some moralists have tried to preserve freedom by denying that the motions of the theft are physically necessitated, by asserting that they are produced by some sort of psychological causation. The thief is said to be free because he acts according to his own character. Kant calls this theory a wretched subterfuge. Psychological states are as much necessitated as physical motions. Logically, it follows therefore that the theft itself could have been avoided in the higher world, although the motions of the theft could not have been avoided in this world.

This conclusion is paradoxical, to say the least; and Kant refused to explain it. He wrote, "Reason would therefore completely transcend its proper limits, if it should undertake to explain how pure reason can be practical, or what is the same thing, to explain how freedom is possible . . . while therefore it is true that we cannot comprehend this practical unconditioned necessity of the moral imperative, it is also true that we can comprehend its incomprehensibility; and this is all that can fairly be demanded of a philosophy which seeks to reach the principles which determine the limits of human reason" (*Critique of Practical Reason,* T. K. Abbot's tr., pp. 189-191).

4. Instrumentalism—John Dewey (1859-1952). For American readers something needs to be said about John Dewey. He offered an empirical, scientific ethics, and therefore the criticism must center on points previously discussed; but he is not a utilitarian and his details are significantly different.

In fact, his details and their practical application may overshadow the pure theory. For example, much of the agitation against capital punishment, which is a Biblical provision for the administration of justice, stems from Dewey's teaching. Capital punishment, he argued, ignores the fact, or alleged fact, that society is as much to blame for crime as is the criminal. Criminals should not be punished—this is irrational vengeance—they should be rehabilitated and paroled. (That the solicitude of the liberals for criminals and their callousness toward the victims result in a sharply rising crime rate never occurs to such penologists.)

This loose attitude toward crime seems to contrast with an insistence on stringent government controls over all business transactions. Rejecting the ideal of liberty, Dewey, the liberal, wrote, "Find a man who believes that all men need is freedom *from* oppressive legal and political measures, and you have a man who, unless he is merely obstinately maintaining his own private privileges, carries at the back of his head some heritage of the metaphysical doctrine of free will, plus an optimistic confidence in natural harmony" (*Human Nature and Conduct,* IV. iii). That power corrupts and that politicians are as depraved as other men, and that therefore the extent of government regulation should be minimal is too theological an argument to impress Dewey. In fact, Dewey looked forward to the day when the government would control, not merely many human activities, but even men's thoughts and wishes. He saw in the future a scientific advance that would enable politicians to manipulate men as we now manipulate physical things (*Problems of Men,* pp. 178, 179).

As a pragmatist, or instrumentalist, Dewey did not believe in fixed ethical principles any more than he believed in fixed truth of any sort. "We institute standards of justice, truth, esthetic quality, etc. . . . exactly as we set up a platinum bar as a standard measurer of

John Dewey. ©*H.P.*

lengths. The superiority of one conception of justice to another is of the same order as the superiority of the metric system" (*Logic, The Theory of Inquiry,* p. 216).

Dewey used an even better analogy. Moral standards are like the rules of grammar. They are both the result of custom. Language evolved from unintelligent babblings; then came grammar. But language continues to change and grammar changes with it. So too, the rules of morality change with changing customs, from which it may be inferred, though Dewey does not explicitly use the example, that cannibalism and rape would be moral wherever they occurred frequently enough.

In consonance with this, Dewey held that nothing is intrinsically good or bad; nothing is valuable in and of itself alone; all beliefs, all actions, and all values are instrumental. They are judged by their consequences. If they solve human problems, they are good instruments.

Unless the solution sought is itself an independent or intrinsic value, it is hard to see how it can confer value on the means. For example, chess can be considered as an instrument in cementing friendships. Yet this is hardly the reason why anyone plays chess. Usually its intrinsic merit is the motivation.

Dewey, in strange company with Aristotle, might have spurned this illustration on the ground that games are too trivial. As Aristotle said, recreation is for the sake of serious work. But Aristotle said this out of a theory of human nature that Dewey could not consistently use. If nothing is intrinsically valuable, there is no ground for distinguishing recreation from serious work.

In particular, Dewey could not accept Aristotle's view that knowledge is intrinsically valuable. He castigated such a view as a retreat to an ivory tower. Knowledge and going to college are instrumental. For a young man, they are instrumental in getting a job. For a young woman, they are instrumental in getting a young man. But the job and the marriage also are merely instrumental—to raising a family and sending the children to college. Chess, however, is instrumental in restricting social contacts, therefore in avoiding marriage and its expenses, and this saving is instrumental in buying a more handsome set of chessmen. Nowhere is there any intrinsic value. The choice therefore between marriage and chess is entirely irrational.

Dewey tried to escape this criticism by asserting that there are evil ideals. Without aesthetic enjoyment, mankind might become a race of economic monsters (*Reconstruction in Philosophy,* p. 127). But could Dewey consistently maintain that monsters are intrinsically bad?

In another place he relied on common opinion and declared that no honest person can think that murder is instrumental to anything good and that everybody resents acts of wanton cruelty (Dewey and Tufts, *Ethics*, pp. 251, 265, 292). Yet it is known that the communists and other radicals use assassination as a political device (cf. Hermann Raschhofer, *Political Assassination*, Tübingen [1964]); and some Latins enjoy the wanton cruelty of bullfights.

In his opposition to wanton cruelty, Dewey has inherited a Puritan ideal. In addition to the inconsistency of relying on Protestant ethics, there is the more formidable question as to how one decides between incompatible ideals: assassination, equal justice, minority rights, wanton cruelty, and kindness. If nothing is intrinsically valuable, how could Dewey choose?

In fact, how could Dewey choose to do anything? If there are no intrinsic values, if there is no final goal, like Aristotelian *Happiness,* if man has no chief end, by which alone subordinate means become worthwhile, the ultimate ethical question arises in full force: Why continue living—why not commit suicide?

The value of life is not just one more point of detail, as if a group would discuss theft and honesty, brutality and kindness, and then discuss suicide. These particular details are subsidiary to the all-embracing question of the reason for living. Obviously a man can choose neither honesty nor theft, unless he has first chosen to continue living.

Many modern moralists, unlike Kant, refuse to face this question. F. C. S. Schiller, a pragmatist like Dewey, notes the logical possibility of a pessimism that holds life to be, not necessarily painful, but merely too dreary and boring to be worth the trouble. On the other hand, he offers no argument against this position.

This pessimistic view is not an odd affectation of a few publicity seekers. Buddhism, with its millions, is a close approximation. Granted, the Buddhists do not approve of suicide—but not because they think life is worthwhile. Suicide is rejected because they think it is not effective enough. It does not extinguish life. Hence, they try to suppress all desire, try to make no choices, and thus attain the "extinction" of Nirvana.

The failure to give a rational refutation of pessimism is the final refutation of instrumentalistic ethics. To choose an action as a means to another ad infinitum, and to find value nowhere, resembles nothing so much as the frustration of Sisyphus.

5. *Contemporary ethics.* One more contemporary view of ethics needs to be included, and it is the one that crowns the whole history of secular ethics with failure. The view (for it is not a theory but the absence of all theory) has a negative and a positive stage.

a. Negatively, P. H. Howell-Smith in his *Ethics* writes, "Moral philosophy is a practical science; its aim is to answer questions in the form 'What shall I do?' But no general answer can be given to this type of question. The most a moral philosopher can do is to paint a picture of various types of life . . . and ask which type of life you really want to lead." Ethical choices are therefore personal preferences, and no one can question another's preference for murder and rape anymore than his preference for olives and onions."

b. W. H. F. BARNES. The positive stage of this viewpoint is expressed by W. H. F. Barnes, A. J. Ayer, and C. L. Stevenson. Their point is that ethical propositions are emotional ejaculations. Barnes writes, "Many [and I do not see why he does not say 'all'] controversies arising out of value judgments are settled by saying, 'I like it and you don't, and that's the end of the matter.' "

c. A. J. AYER. Ayer is more explicit: "If I say to someone, 'You acted wrongly in stealing that money,' I am not stating anything more than if I had simply said, 'You stole that money.' In adding that this action is wrong I am not making any further statement about it. I am simply evincing my moral disapproval of it. It is as if I had said, 'You stole that money' in a peculiar tone of horror . . . the tone . . . adds nothing to the literal meaning of the sentence."

d. C. L. STEVENSON. Stevenson goes beyond Ayer in that he emphasizes, not merely one's own approval or disapproval, but chiefly one's attempt to induce the same feeling in other people. When an individual says, "Stealing is wrong," he not only means that he does not like it, but in addition he is trying to persuade someone else to dislike it also. It is similar to the ejaculation "onions taste horrible." This conveys no information about onions; it is merely an attempt to persuade another person to eat olives instead.

Suppose that the other person insists on liking and eating onions. Suppose that the other person insists on thievery and bullfights. What is to be done in such cases of moral disagreement? Here Stevenson frankly admits that there is no rational method for settling such a disagreement. The only method is eloquence and emotional persuasion.

It is true that persuasion, like bribery, sometimes works; but it does not support the conclusion that the action recommended is good or obligatory. It is not obligatory for the person persuaded, but, more to the point, it is not obligatory even for the first person. The only problem Stevenson has solved is the problem of getting other unprincipled people to do what the unprincipled persuader wants done. The real problem of ethics, however, is how to decide which action and which principles *ought* to be acknowledged. In the failure to solve this problem is where Stevenson, emotional ethics, and secularism all fail.

II. Some Christian principles

A satisfactory ethics needs principles for systematic consistency and details for practical application. Omitting the former produces chaos; omitting the latter removes all guidelines for choice and action.

A. The Decalogue and its implications. During the first cent. and a half of the Protestant Reformation, the Calvinists (Reformed, Presbyterian, and Puritan) distinguished themselves by their stress on ethics. They not only emphasized the Ten Commandments—one would naturally expect any form of Christian ethics to acknowledge the Ten Commandments as basic obligations—but they took the trouble to outline their implications. This work, initiated by Calvin in the *Institutes*, II, viii, is summarized in the *Westminster Larger Catechism*, from which several following quotations illustrate the detailed application of divine law to the moral situations of life.

"Q. 93. What is the moral law? A. The moral law is the declaration of the will of God to mankind, directing and binding every one to personal, perfect, and perpetual conformity and obedience thereunto, in the frame and disposition of the whole man, soul and body, and in performance of all those duties of holiness and righteousness which he oweth to God and man: promising life upon the fulfilling, and threatening death upon the breach of it."

"Q. 99. What rules are to be observed for the right understanding of the ten commandments? A. For the right understanding of the ten commandments, these rules are to be observed:—1. That the law is perfect, and bindeth every one to full conformity in the whole man unto righteousness thereof, and unto entire obedience for ever; so as to require the utmost perfection of every duty, and to forbid the least degree of every sin. 2. That it is spiritual, and so reacheth the understanding, will, affections, and all other powers of the soul; as well as words, works, and gestures. 3. That one and the same thing, in divers respects, is required or forbidden in several commandments. 4. That, where a duty is commanded, the contrary sin is forbidden; and, where a sin is forbidden, the contrary duty is commanded: so, where a promise is annexed, the contrary threatening is included; and, where a threatening is annexed, the contrary promise is included. 5. That what God forbids, is at no time to be done; what he commands is always our duty; and yet every particular duty is not to be done at all times. 6. That, under one sin or duty, all of the same kind are forbidden or commanded; together with all the causes, means, occasions, and appearances thereof, and provocations thereunto. 7. That what is forbidden or commanded to ourselves, we are bound, according to our places, to endeavor that it may be avoided or performed by others, according to the duty of their places. 8. That in what is commanded to others, we are bound, according to our places and callings, to be helpful to them; and to take heed of partaking with others in what is forbidden them."

"Q. 134. Which is the sixth commandment? A. The sixth commandment is, Thou shalt not kill."

"Q. 135. What are the duties required in the sixth commandment? A. The duties required in the sixth commandment are, all careful studies, and lawful endeavors, to preserve the life of ourselves and others, by resisting all thoughts and purposes, subduing all passions, and avoiding all occasions, temptations, and practices, which tend to the unjust taking away the life of any; by just defense thereof against violence; patient bearing of the hand of God, quietness of mind, cheerfulness of spirit; a sober use of meat, drink, physic, sleep, labor, and recreation; by charitable thoughts, love, compassion, meekness, gentleness, kindness; peaceable, mild, and courteous speeches and behavior: forbearing, readiness to be reconciled, patient bearing and forgiving of injuries, and requiting good for evil; comforting and succoring the distressed, and protecting and defending the innocent."

"Q. 136. What are the sins forbidden in the sixth commandment? A. The sins forbidden in the sixth commandment are, all taking away the life of ourselves, or of others, except in case of public justice, lawful war, or necessary defense; the neglecting or withdrawing the lawful or necessary means of preservation of life; sinful anger, hatred, envy, desire of revenge; all excessive passions, distracting cares; immoderate use of meat, drink, labor, and recreations; provoking words; oppression, quarreling, striking, wounding, and whatsoever else tends to the destruction of the life of any."

"Q. 140. Which is the eighth commandment? A. The eighth commandment is, Thou shalt not steal."

"Q. 141. What are the duties required in the eighth commandment? A. The duties required in the eighth commandment are, truth, faithfulness, and justice in contracts and commerce between man and man; rendering to every one his due; restitution of goods unlawfully detained from the right owners thereof; giving and lending freely, according to our abilities, and the necessities of others; moderation of our judgments, wills, and affections, concerning worldly goods; a provident care and study to get, keep, use, and dispose of those things which are necessary and convenient for the sustentation of our nature, and suitable to our condition; a lawful calling, and diligence in it; frugality, avoiding unnecessary law-suits, and suretyship, or other like engagements; and an endeavor by all just and lawful means to procure, preserve, and further the wealth and outward estate of others, as well as our own."

"Q. 142. What are the sins forbidden in the eighth commandment? A. The sins forbidden in the eighth commandment, beside the neglect of the duties required, are theft, robbery, man-stealing, and receiving any thing that is stolen; fraudulent dealing; false weights and measures; removing landmarks; injustice and unfaithfulness in contracts between man and man, or in matters of trust; oppression; extortion; usury; bribery; vexatious lawsuits; unjust enclosures and depredation; engrossing commodities to enhance the price, unlawful callings, and all other unjust or sinful ways of taking or withholding from our neighbor what belongs to him, or of enriching ourselves; covetousness; inordinate prizing and affecting worldly goods; distrustful and distracting cares and studies in getting, keeping, and using them; envying at the prosperity of others: as likewise idleness, prodigality, wasteful gaming, and all other ways whereby we do unduly prejudice our own outward estate: and defrauding ourselves of the due use and comfort of that estate which God hath given us."

In addition to official and therefore brief expositions of ethics, there are innumerable books, either on Christian ethics as a whole, or on particular problems, such as divorce, the family, alcoholism, etc., or on such Biblical sections as the ethics of the gospels and the ethics of the OT. Some of these are Biblical and orthodox; others are liberal. In general they show how much detail can be derived by implication from the Biblical material (*see* BIBLIOGRAPHY).

B. Christian presuppositions. If one of the purposes of ethics is to furnish concrete instruction applicable to everyday living, the superiority of Christianity over secular attempts is unmistakable. The Ten Commandments, however, rest on certain presuppositions that provide the more theoretical or theological basis for Biblical ethics.

1. *Authority.* The Ten Commandments derive their validity from Biblical authority. If the Bible is composed of myths, and superstitions—the product of ingenious human construction—no one would be obliged to obey its commands. Aside from the secular systems previously discussed, men could choose the Code of Hammurabi or could consider the claims of the Koran, the Vedas, and other sacred books. Christian morality, therefore, depends on Christian Revelation.

For further material on Biblical authority, *see* BIBLE, INSPIRATION, INFALLIBILITY.

Underlying the authority of the Bible is the authority of God who gave the Bible; and the God who gave the Bible is not just any kind of deity, but is One with definite characteristics.

2. *Revelation.* It is almost repetitious to insist that one of God's characteristics is the ability to speak. But the repetition is excusable because many contemporary theologians deny that God can speak. They may try to find some place for Revelation in their theology, but it is a nonverbal revelation, something other than a communication of truth. Revelation in these theologies may be the mighty acts of God in history, or some mystic experience of encounter or confrontation.

This view of revelation is worthless. Without information divinely given man could not discern which historical events were mighty acts of God—the Exodus, perhaps; but why not also Caesar's crossing the Rubicon and Stalin's capture of Berlin? What is worse, after selecting a series of events, man would be at a loss to interpret them. Would there be any difference in value between Moses' crossing the Red Sea and Caesar's crossing the Rubicon? Do these events mean that no one should eat pork, or that everyone should support civil rights, or that attendance at football games is acceptable worship? Attempts to draw practical implications from these historical events would only revert to the secular theories of developing ethics out of experience, which has been shown to be impossible.

Ethics requires definite information as to

what is right and wrong, and such information can be revealed only by a living, communicating God.

3. *Immutability.* In the present decade several books have been published on theological ethics, presumably in opposition to irreligious secularism. The type of ethics depends on the type of theology. One such book defends the concept of the "New Morality," which in these days is offered as a substitute for the Ten Commandments. Dr. James Sellers declares that men need a new morality, a new ethics, and a new theology. In support of a changing ethics he approves Paul Ramsey's statement: "At the level of theory itself, any formulation of Christian social ethics is always in need of reformulation" (*Theological Ethics,* pp. ix, 39).

The notion that the principles of ethics (not merely their applications to changing social forms, but the basic principles themselves) must always be changing requires belief in a changing God and a changing revelation. Obviously this necessitates a rejection of the Ten Commandments and derivative Biblical precepts. Though Dr. Sellers is not too clear on the nature of God, he could not be clearer in his rejection of Scripture. He defines revelation as "something [that] has happened to us in our history which conditions all our thinking" (ibid. p. 71); as for example, the death of one's mother. Concerning the Bible he says, "worse, in some places where it is not silent, it gives us advice that is manifestly bad if taken literally"; and "the Bible also illustrates its insights with outmoded or downright unacceptable examples of morality" (pp. 88, 92).

The notion of a changing morality presupposes belief in a changing God, and raises theological issues (*see* ETERNITY and IMMUTABILITY). If, on the other hand, men accept the Ten Commandments as permanent obligations, they must also accept the Biblical concept of an immutable God. Biblical morality and Biblical theology are inseparable.

The idea that the firm morality of the Bible must now be replaced with something loose is a practical danger of this present age. In opposition to Christ's specific instructions about divorce and remarriage, some denominations officially encourage their ministers to substitute their own permissive judgment; and individual ministers of various denominations approve of adultery if the two people "really love each other." All this "new morality"—actually as old as the Canaanites—stems from a rejection of the God of the Bible.

4. *Sovereignty of God.* Immutability, however, is not the only divine characteristic needed for a systematic Christian ethics. Sovereignty is even more important.

In the Platonic philosophy, the principles of ethics, though they differ in detail from those of Christianity, are sufficiently immutable. But God, the maker of heaven and earth, is not sovereign according to Plato; above God is an immutable World of Ideas to which even He must submit.

In modern times, the point at issue is exemplified in the philosophy of Leibniz. His famous phrase that this is the best of all possible worlds, a phrase Voltaire's *Candide* ridicules with brutal force, depends on the notion that various possible worlds exist in a sort of blueprint form independently of God. Because God is good, He naturally chose the best blueprint at the time of creation. Therefore the actual world is the best possible. This exactly follows Plato, who, in his *Euthyphro,* asserted that good is not good because God approves of it, but that God approves of it because it is antecedently and independently good.

The Jewish philosopher Philo, who lived at the time of Christ, though profoundly influenced by Plato, made an alteration that completely reversed Platonic and Leibnizian theology. This alteration consisted in making God supreme and in placing the World of Ideas in God's mind. Philo wrote, "God has been ranked according to the one and the unit; or rather, even the unit has been ranked according to the one God, for all number, like time, is younger than the cosmos." In this quotation, Philo subjects mathematics to the thinking activity of God. Similarly, God does not will the good because it is independently good, but on the contrary the good is good because God wills it.

To the same effect Calvin (*Institutes,* I, xiv, 1) wrote, "Augustine justly complains that it is an offense against God to inquire for any cause of things higher than his will." Later (III, xxii, 2) he says, "how exceedingly presumptuous it is only to inquire into the causes of the Divine will, which is in fact and is justly entitled to be the cause of everything that exists. For if it has any cause, then there must be something antecedent, on which it depends; which it is impious to suppose. For the will of God is the highest rule of justice; so that what he wills must be considered just, for this very reason, because he wills it."

The sovereignty of God is the key to the basic problem of ethics. Why is anything good, right, or obligatory? Neither utilitarianism, nor pragmatism, nor emotionalism can give a rational answer. Calvin has given the answer in very precise language: "the will of God is the highest rule of justice; so that what he wills must be considered just, for this very reason, because he wills it." God establishes moral norms by sovereign decree.

That this principle permeates the Bible can easily be seen. No devout Christian holds that anything external to God compelled or induced Him to create a certain number of solar satellites rather than a different number. God could have created water with a different freezing point. Similarly, there was no external cause of His choice of detail in the Mosaic ritual. Could He not have willed the Tabernacle to have been hexagonal instead of rectangular? Similarly could He not have imposed on man other commandments rather than the Ten? Was it not merely His decision to have one Sabbath each week instead of two? Or could He not have created the world in five days and have substituted a different fourth commandment to fit a six-day week? Is it not due to God's will that man differs from the animals, and could not man have been made so that, as in their case, the sixth, seventh, and eighth commandments would not apply?

The omnipotence and sovereignty of God, as the controlling concept of Christianity, solve the problems of every sphere. The power of God is the answer to scientific objections against miracles; His will is the authority for civil government and the key to political science; and similarly His precepts constitute ethics. The good or the right is not the pleasure of the greatest number, to be determined by an impossible calculation; right or justice is what God commands, to be discovered by reading the written Revelation. The sanctions are not Bentham's, nor is virtue its own reward; on the contrary, God enforces moral obligation by the joys of heaven and the pains of hell. Here is logical consistency unmatched by either the rationalist Leibniz or the emotionalist Stevenson; here is the practical detail absent in secularism; here are the sanctions Stalin and Hitler could not escape. Such is Christian ethics.

BIBLIOGRAPHY. H. Sidgwick, *A History of Ethics* (1886); N. Smyth, *Christian Ethics* (1892); W. S. Bruce, *The Ethics of the Old Testament* (1909); D. S. Adam, *A Handbook of Christian Ethics* (1925); E. W. Burch, *The Ethical Teaching of the Gospels* (1925); A. C. Knudsen, *The Principles of Christian Ethics* (1943); C. F. H. Henry, *Christian Personal Ethics* (1957); J. Murray, *Principles of Conduct* (1957); J. Sellers, *Theological Ethics* (1966); G. F. Woods, *A Defence of Theological Ethics* (1966).

G. H. CLARK

ETHICS OF JESUS. Widely lauded, and variously interpreted, the ethics of Jesus constitute not only a standing reproach of human sin and moral weakness but also a vivid picture of the kind of people His followers should and can be.

I. Interpretation
  A. Major schools of thought
    1. Absolutist
    2. Modified
    3. Reinterpreted
  B. Principal factors involved
    1. The setting
      a. In relation to the law
      b. In relation to eschatology
        (1) Consistent
        (2) Realized
        (3) Futurist
        (4) Suggested approach
      c. In relation to the Gospel
    2. The form
      a. Literary
      b. Didactic
  C. Pointers to proper interpretation
II. Contents
  A. Negative teaching
  B. Positive teaching
    1. Personal ethics
    2. Social ethics
      a. Duty to the state
      b. Marriage and divorce
III. Sanctions

I. INTERPRETATION

A. Major schools of thought. 1. *Absolutist.* A number of interpreters have understood the ethics of Jesus in ways that have emphasized the absolute nature of its demands. Though their ideas vary, they have in common that they take the teaching with the utmost seriousness. Yet, for the most part, they fail to relate it in its rigor to life here and now.

The following summary may be noted: (1) The view characteristic of Lutheran orthodoxy is that the ethical teaching is intended not so much as a guide to life but as a means of bringing us to repentance for our failure to live up to it. (2) The interim-ethic view put forward by J. Weiss and A. Schweitzer is that the rigor of Jesus' ethics was conditioned by His conviction that the eschatological coming of the kingdom was imminent. The severity of His teaching is explained by the theory that it was intended only as "emergency regulations" for the brief interim period prior to its coming. (3) The extreme dispensationalist interpretation insists that the Sermon on the Mount, at least, is the ethics of the future kingdom of God, which is to be established on earth subsequent to the Second Advent (though it is conceived as having a secondary application to the Christian here and now). (4) Superficially similar to the foregoing is the view held by Dibelius and others that the teaching is a declaration of the divine will, unconditioned by any consideration of expediency. As such, however, it is designed to shock people into action. (5) Bultmann, in his view, asserts that the stark demands of Jesus constitute an existential call for decision. (6) Finally, there is the view expounded by scholars such as Windisch and more recently by J. Knox, that the teaching was intended to be rigorous, and that its severity should be taken seriously. It must be interpreted faithfully, and applied absolutely and universally. Of those who have attempted to practice it in its full rigor, the most celebrated is Tolstoi.

2. *Modified.* Other interpretations have, in

one way or another, modified the ethical teaching of Jesus.

Early in the history of the Church, the idea of the "double standard" was applied to Jesus' ethics. According to this view, whereas the basic commands apply universally, the advice given over and above these commands is relevant only to those who voluntarily apply them to themselves. Less is therefore expected of the rank and file than of those who, for example, embrace the "religious" vocation.

Luther, although strenuously repudiating the idea of a double standard, nevertheless argued strongly for the idea of "two realms," in only one of which the rigorous teaching applies—the spiritual realm, by which he understood the sphere of personal relationships. In the temporal realm, that of the Christian-in-relation, special guidance is not needed. The law of the land and the natural law provide all the guidance that is needed.

In other ways the ethical teaching has been toned down. Some have so emphasized the fig., and esp. the hyperbolic nature of the language in which the teaching was given, as to modify it more or less drastically. Others have interpreted it in the light of the general tenor of Scripture, and have thereby reduced its severity. Some have simply toned it down to make it more practicable.

3. *Reinterpreted.* Remaining to be considered are methods of interpretation that view the teaching in a wider light than that cast by the words themselves.

Some regard Jesus' teaching as commanding or forbidding not merely the particular acts specified, but also any other action of a similar kind. This application of the teaching in terms of acts tends to focus attention on the external side of morality.

Others see the particular acts commanded or forbidden as representing the outworking of inner attitudes. These, it is held, should be embodied, not only in the acts specified but also in others. This view has a similar effect to the previous one, but focuses attention on the inner attitude rather than the outer act.

B. Principal factors involved. *1. The setting.* It is impossible to abstract the ethical teaching of Jesus from its total setting without seriously distorting it. T. W. Manson has shown that the idea of ethics as an autonomous discipline of thought is unbiblical. It is important therefore to give attention to some aspects of the religious setting of the ethics of Jesus—law, eschatology, and gospel.

a. IN RELATION TO THE LAW. Jesus came not to destroy the law but to fulfill it (Matt 5:17, 18). This means, on the one hand, that He endorsed it. This He did, first, by yielding to it an obedience that was unique. Not only in moral matters but also in its wider connotation, Jesus abode by the law (Matt 17:27; 23:23; Mark 14:12). Second, He endorsed its teaching, subsuming all under the twofold head of love to God and neighbor (Matt 22:37-40).

On the other hand, since to fulfill includes in its meaning "to bring to fullness of completion" (J. F. A. Hort, *Judaistic Christianity*, 15) Jesus reinterpreted and reapplied as well as reinforced the law. On His own authority, He rejected scribal interpretations not only of ceremonial matters, e.g. the Sabbath (Mark 2:23-28; 3:1-6; Luke 13:10-17; 14:1-6), fasting (Mark 2:18-22), and ceremonial purity (Matt 15:1-20; Mark 7:1-23; Luke 11:37-41), but also of moral issues (Matt 5:21-47). Furthermore, He reinterpreted the role of law in such a way as to elevate the moral law to a position of eminence greater even than that accorded it in the OT. He set aside the principle of ceremonial purity (Mark 7:15, 18-23); stripped away the traditions of men that served to obscure the moral demands of the law (Matt 15:3-9); and asserted the primacy of moral requirements within the law as a whole (Matt 12:1-8; cf. 23:23).

In the light of the insistence of the prophets on the worthlessness of ceremony apart from obedience to the moral law, and indeed on the primacy of the latter over the former, this is not altogether novel. But attention has been drawn by J. I. Packer in *Our Lord's Understanding of the Law of God* (9ff.) to the new "depth of exposition" and "stress in application" in the ethical teaching of Jesus. The former—seen in the obligation to love enemies and to forgive and love others as oneself—arises from the fuller revelation of the character of God in the person of Jesus Himself. The latter—seen in the stress on qualities of character such as humility, meekness, and generosity, rather than on externally correct behavior alone—reflects the positive functions of the new covenant that Jesus had come to establish, in contrast to the largely negative functions of the old covenant.

The newness of the teaching of Jesus should not be overstated. Even the antitheses of Matthew 5:21ff. are concerned with correcting the oral law and drawing out the implications of the provisions of the moral law. W. D. Davies describes them in terms of exegesis rather than antithesis.

Deeply rooted in the law and the prophets, the ethical teaching of Jesus consists of authoritative pronouncements that draw out the deepest implications of the law of God in the light of a fuller revelation of the character of God. As such, they constitute a moral demand of the highest order, even though—as will be noted later—they are not to be thought of merely in terms of legal requirements.

b. IN RELATION TO ESCHATOLOGY. (1) *Consistent.* The theory of consistent eschatology, associated with Weiss and Schweitzer, marked a vigorous reaction against the depreciation of the eschatological element in the teaching of Jesus that was prevalent at the beginning of the 20th cent. In sharp contrast to the Ritschlian view of scholars such as Harnack who maintained that the eschatological element was merely formal, the shell within which lay the kernel of the moral teaching, it was asserted that "the whole of ethics lies under the concept of repentance—penitence for the past and the determination to live henceforward liberated from everything earthly in expectation of the Messianic kingdom" (Schweitzer). A rigorist ethic, such as Jesus taught, could only be relevant for the short interim period of life to be lived under "emergency regulations" before the apocalyptic coming of the kingdom.

This theory, as Dean Inge pointed out, "makes Christ a psychological monster and His character an insoluble enigma." The Early Church did not so understand His teaching, doubtless remembering His parting words (Matt 28:18-20). Furthermore, it has been argued that the ethical teaching is not always directly colored by eschatological considerations. Indeed, as C. W. Emmet has pointed out, "where the contents of the teaching might be regarded as determined by the eschatological outlook, the eschatological motive is conspicuously absent" (*Expositor* [1912], 429). As already noted, the ethics of Jesus are deeply rooted in the ethical teaching of the OT.

(2) Realized. This reaction against consistent eschatology is based upon those statements and parables in the gospels that indicate that the kingdom of God has come in the person and work of Jesus. The ethical teaching is therefore set in the context not of the interim period prior to the coming of the kingdom, but of the kingdom itself.

This view is a necessary corrective to consistent eschatology, avoiding much of the naivety of the Ritschlian presentation of the ethics of Jesus. For it asserts that divine initiative has been put forward in the coming of Jesus that has fulfilled the scriptural prophecies. Nevertheless, it fails to do adequate justice to the evidence presented in the gospels that shows that Jesus spoke in terms of the Second Advent. Not even the modification of this view indicated by the revision of the term "realized eschatology" to "inaugurated eschatology" can deflect the cutting edge of this criticism.

(3) Futurist. The view of some dispensationalists that the ethical teaching of the Sermon on the Mount, if not the ethical teaching of Jesus as a whole, is related to the future millennial kingdom to be set up on earth after the Second Advent, would seem to indicate another presentation that fails to do justice to the scriptural data. Only strained exegesis can deny the force of Matthew 12:28, which asserts that the kingdom of God "has come." The references in the sermon to the malevolent activity of persecutors (Matt 5:11, 12, 44) and the whole context of life in a mixed society cannot be accommodated to the millennial kingdom. The proffered explanation that there is a secondary reference to the life of the Christian in contemporary society is more ingenious than convincing.

(4) Suggested approach. Though none of the above-mentioned views commends itself as adequate, each contains some element of truth. Taken together, these point the way to an understanding of the relation between the ethics of Jesus and the kingdom of God.

There is surely a sense in which the ethic is rooted in the idea of the kingdom as an eternal fact, independent of all earthly contingencies—nothing less than the sovereignty of God. This explains its absoluteness and the magnitude of its demand: "You, therefore, must be perfect, as your heavenly Father is perfect" (Matt 5:48).

At the same time, "realized eschatology" has some contribution to make to the understanding of the teaching. It is evident that it was given for action here and now. Attested by significant signs, the presence of the King was a sure indication that the kingdom of God had come. As the teacher par excellence, Jesus expounded with the full weight of His divine authority the moral principles of the kingdom to those who recognized Him for what He was.

It is equally clear that the consummation of the kingdom was—and is—still future. Present in the world and dynamically active among men, the kingdom has not yet filled the sphere of human society, and there are inadequate grounds for believing that it will do so, apart from direct divine intervention.

Therefore, Jesus' ethics can best be interpreted in terms of the dynamic concept of God's rule that has already manifested itself in His person, but will come to its consummation only as a result of new eschatological action (*see* G. E. Ladd).

c. In relation to the Gospel. There are many who see the ethical teaching of Jesus as the heart, if not the sum and substance of the Christian message. This has been particularly true of liberal Protestantism, as exemplified in A. von Harnack and the exponents of the "social gospel."

A necessary corrective to this has been provided by the distinction drawn by C. H. Dodd between κήρυγμα and διδαχή—even if the distinction has been overdrawn at times. Religion and ethics, though closely linked, are not to be confused, still less identified. Just as OT ethics had a religious basis and law was a function of covenant; so in the NT ethics and religion are not to be confused, for teaching followed preaching of the Gospel. Does the teaching of Jesus bear out the contention—which needs to be raised not only against liberal Protestantism but also against the New Morality adherents—that Christian ethics is essentially ethics for disciples? There are clear

The traditional site of the Sermon on the Mount, the Horns of Hattin seen from the hills above Capernaum. ©*Lev*

indications that it does.

Attention must be drawn, in the first place, to the fact that the ethical teaching of Jesus is essentially personalistic. He taught on the basis of His own authority ("I say to you"); called men to follow Him; and evoked a response on the basis not of compulsion nor even of compliance with legal requirements, but of loving and glad obedience to Himself (John 14:15). In His teaching, "for righteousness' sake" (Matt 5:10) and "on my account" (5:11) are interchangeable terms. Although He taught moral imperatives and His very precept of love was formulated as a command (John 13:34), and despite the fact that He took His stand on the Mosaic law, yet He was no mere lawgiver, a new Moses and no more. Whereas the law of Moses derived its sanction from the fact that it was also the law of God, the law of Christ (Gal 6:2) stands in its own right in dynamic relationship to His person.

Furthermore, in His ethical teaching, Jesus called for a radical transformation of character. "Repent and believe in the Gospel" was His first command, and response to it was, and is, the essential prerequisite. Since He taught that the heart of man is the source of moral defilement (Matt 15:19, 20), it is hardly surprising that He called for the transformation of character at its source (12:33). The tree must be made good if its fruit is to be good.

The ethical teaching of Jesus in the Sermon

on the Mount is clearly set in a context of grace. Addressed to disciples, the ethical demands are preceded by the beatitudes that, far from being rewards promised for virtuous behavior, are compelling expressions of divine grace. True, the form critics see this context as the work of the Early Church; Jeremias, for example, regards the sermon as an early Christian catechism in which scattered sayings of Jesus were gathered together in what he agrees is a context of grace. Such a setting is, however, in perfect harmony with the general setting of the ethical teaching, which—as the ethics of the kingdom—is the ethics of the new covenant, the way of life of the people of God, and the ethics of the new heart and the new spirit. Only those who have repented and committed themselves to discipleship, those who are the followers of Jesus—as T. W. Manson points out in *Ethics and the Gospel*—are the proper objects of His teaching.

2. The form. a. LITERARY. There is no evidence to suggest that the ethical teaching of Jesus was delivered systematically. Certainly in its recorded form it bears the character of scattered sayings; even the Sermon on the Mount is not an ethical treatise. Furthermore, since the sayings were often given in response to questions on particular issues, or in the context of situations in life, they express "with dazzling finality one aspect only of eternal truth, and that the aspect which on the particular occasion needed to be emphasized" (S. Cave, *The Christian Way*, p. 45). It is patently obvious that the teaching thus given was frequently expressed in fig. language. Metaphor and hyperbole, together with simile, parable and paradox, were used with great effect to give force to the teaching. One may attempt to rationalize a camel going through the eye of a needle, but the speck and the log, the gnat and the camel are not easily interpreted literally. Nor is the command to cut off the offending hand or foot, or to pluck out the eye that causes sin.

It is a cardinal principle of literary interpretation, Biblical as well as secular, that due attention should be paid to the literary form employed. This is not to say that the meaning is to be toned down, but that it should be understood in accordance with the mode in which it is expressed. It is therefore necessary to recognize metaphor, hyperbole, and the rest, and to interpret accordingly, without in any way lessening the intended force of the teaching. Not always is it easy, esp. for occidentals, to recognize oriental use of fig. language. L. Dewar's suggestion, that the teaching should be interpreted metaphorically when to understand it literally involves a *reductio ad absurdum*, remains a subjective criterion. Nevertheless, despite the difficulties, it is clear that, just as "seventy times seven" is not to be understood mathematically, so the command to pray in secret is not to be understood so as to forbid public prayer.

b. DIDACTIC. Not only the literary form of the teaching needs to be taken into account, what might be called the didactic form must also be recognized. The suggestion made by Anderson Scott that the ethical injunctions fall into different categories is worthy of serious consideration.

Not only formally expressed but also underlying the ethical teaching as a whole, Anderson Scott discerned a single commandment—love to God and neighbor. Alongside this mandate are numerous examples that serve to illustrate specific ways in which love may come to expression. The sayings about turning the other cheek, giving the cloak as well as the coat, going the second mile, and giving to all who ask, are therefore illustrations of the length to which love is prepared to go in typical situations. It would clearly run contrary to the general tenor of the teaching of Jesus to interpret such sayings merely as legal requirements to be interpreted literally and obeyed formally. Rather, they would seem to be examples of the kind of response that those obedient to the command to love will be prepared to give in provoking circumstances. The guidance provided by such examples, must, however, be balanced by other guidance given. For example, it can hardly be disputed that there are circumstances in which we are expected not to "give" (cf. Matt 7:6).

In addition to the mandate and examples, Anderson Scott finds *consilia* that he regards as sayings giving urgent advice to particular people in particular circumstances. They are, therefore, not to be taken as necessarily incumbent upon everyone. Jesus' command to the rich young ruler to sell his possessions and give all to the poor was addressed to him personally in the light of his particular spiritual condition and is not to be generalized.

This distinction should not be confused with the distinction between basic commands incumbent upon all and additional advice that is voluntary. The latter has served only to produce a double standard with its concomitant, the acquisition of merit for going beyond obedience to the commands laid upon all. The former is an aid to seeing more clearly the central thrust of Jesus' ethical teaching and the kind of practical application that may be given to it.

The emphasis upon love as the central and governing factor in Jesus' ethics is sharply distinct from the view maintained by exponents of the New Morality who advocate that "love" is the guide to moral decisions. For the love of Jesus' teaching is the love of the Father, which demands religious expression as well as ethical activism; there is no religionless ethic in the gospels.

C. Pointers to proper interpretation. The

ethical teaching of Jesus was clearly intended to be taken seriously. With all the weight of His messianic and divine authority, Jesus reasserted the fundamental moral principles of the OT law and prophets. In doing so He focused OT imperatives with a new intensity, showing that these extended to thought as well as act, to motive as well as deed. With striking clarity, He revealed the moral demands of the kingdom of God that was now active in His person, and He portrayed with bold strokes the character as well as the conduct appropriate to His followers. Couched in pictorial and vivid language of the Orient, its interpretation calls for a proper understanding of its literary and didactic form. Furthermore, the Christian who reads it in the gospels as part of the completed revelation of Scripture is duty bound to interpret it in the light of the overall teaching of Scripture.

II. Contents

A. Negative teaching. The ethics of Jesus includes His forthright denunciation of evil. The call to repent (Mark 1:15), to deny the self (Mark 8:34) and to follow Jesus involves the repudiation of one way of life in favor of another.

By comparison with the teaching of Paul, little is said in condemnation of sexual sins. This was undoubtedly because of the relatively high standard of teaching and practice among the Jews. Nevertheless, enough is said to show that Jesus regarded as fundamentally evil such things as fornication, adultery, and licentiousness (Mark 7:21-23), and, in addition, lustful desire (Matt 5:28).

Theft, murder (including the angry thought or word of Matt 5:22), and malicious acts of any kind are also condemned, as also is slander or abusive speech (Mark 7:21, 22). A number of attitudes and dispositions also find their place in Jesus' denunciation of evil. These include thoughts that are mental processes calculated to expedite malicious acts—covetousness, or the insatiable desire to have more; deceitfulness; jealousy; arrogance; and moral insensibility (7:21, 22).

Some of the sins denounced by Jesus can only be described as sins of a religious complexion. Religious observances undertaken in such a way as to foster pride received His condemnation (Matt 6:1-5; 23:5-7). Nor did He spare the hypocrisy of the Pharisees (Matt 23). Modern research that shows that the Pharisees were, by and large, as outwardly righteous as they claimed to be has caused some to question the rightness of Jesus' denunciation of them. Their hypocrisy, however, lay not so much in conscious deception as in the moral blindness and self-righteousness that blinded their sensibilities. Theirs may not have been conscious hypocrisy, but it was hypocrisy nonetheless.

B. Positive teaching. 1. *Personal ethics.* In His summary of the law, Jesus provided also a summary of His positive ethical teaching. This is found in the command to love God and neighbor (Matt 22:37-39) and the Golden Rule (7:12). Despite parallels in Judaism, such teaching was nonetheless unique. Here alone, love to God and love to neighbor are specifically linked together and related to each other. Furthermore, the command to love is given unprecedented preeminence in the teaching of Jesus. Rabbi Akiba may have quoted the OT (Lev 19:18) as the summation of the teaching of the law, but he saw it as standing alongside the rest of the law, both written and oral. Hillel may have used the Golden Rule, but only in its negative form. Moreover, Jesus radicalized love by revealing love in its fullest meaning—not only in His teaching, but also in His life. In particular, He universalized the meaning of love by specifically extending the term "neighbor" beyond the bounds of those who have a claim upon us (Luke 10:29-37; cf. Matt 5:43-47). This He demonstrated in His own life through His compassion.

Love to God is a command that is absolute and unqualified. It involves all the heart, soul, and mind. Such a love overrides all other claims, and demands the subordination of every lesser love. By comparison, therefore, love for father and mother, wife and children, brothers and sisters, is hatred (Luke 14:26; cf. Matt 10:37). Since no man can serve two masters, the love and service of God entails lack of concern for material possessions and prospects. Such things are to be regarded as expendable items in the service of the kingdom of God, and their supply is not to be a matter of excessive concern, but can safely be left in the Father's hands (Matt 6:19-34; Luke 12:13-34).

Love for neighbor is inseparably linked with love for God, though it is no substitute for it. John 15:12 indicates the extent love must go in the context of the fellowship of Christ. Love in the ethical teaching of Jesus is not merely a sentiment of affection; indeed, sentiment is not of primary importance. The parable of the Good Samaritan and the injunctions to do good without counting the cost (Matt 5:42; Luke 6:38) show that in essence is the performance of good to others.

One manifestation of love esp. emphasized by Jesus is readiness to forgive others their trespasses (Matt 6:12, 14, 15; 18:21-35; Mark 11:25; Luke 11:4; 17:3, 4). This is to be viewed not as the cause but as the result and the assurance of having received divine forgiveness. It is to be exercised without limitation of any kind, though its effect will be conditioned by the degree of willingness on the part of the offending party to receive it.

A forgiving spirit combines with the attitudes of humility, meekness, and service as characteristic of the true disciple of Jesus. The meek who inherit the earth (Matt 5:5) have a capacity to absorb evil and to overcome it with good (5:38-41; Luke 6:27-29). Anderson Scott has suggested that most of Jesus' injunctions can be grouped under two headings —"Do not press for your rights," and "Do more than your duties."

2. *Social ethics.* That there is little explicit social teaching in the gospels is not necessarily because Jesus had a foreshortened view of the future. It does indicate that Jesus was more concerned with the fundamental matter of personal ethics than with the construction of a blueprint or even the enunciation of principles designed to lead to the transformation of society. This is not surprising if He did not come to establish the kingdom in its fullness and if its consummation still awaits His second coming. It is not without significance that attempts to give full form to the kingdom of God on earth have unfailingly ended in disillusionment.

At the same time, since the kingdom is at work in the world, its presence must make itself felt, even as the presence of salt and light cannot be hid (Matt 5:13-16). This should be true at the physical and material levels of ministry as well as the spiritual, even as the presence of the kingdom in the person of Jesus touched all levels of human need. Granted that Jesus held aloof from political and military affairs, He nevertheless enunciated general principles of love and service within the community of His disciples (Mark 9:33-37; 10:35-44) and to any who are in need (Luke 10:30-37), and made pronouncements on several specific issues within the field of social ethics.

a. Duty to the state. The question raised by the Pharisees and Herodians regarding the payment of taxes was clearly designed as a trap to ensnare Jesus (Matt 22:15-22). His answer not only defeated their purpose but also clearly revealed the duty of His followers to discharge such debts as they owe to the state as well as those they owe to God. In this way Jesus distinguished the secular and the sacred without dividing them, and united the two spheres in which disciples have to live without unifying them (R. V. G. Tasker). Possible tension between the twofold duty was not resolved by this pronouncement, but the implication is clear that duties to the state must not take precedence over duties owed to God, and it can hardly be doubted that Peter and John acted in accordance with this principle (Acts 4:18-20).

b. Marriage and divorce. Another testing question prompted the teaching of Jesus on this subject (Matt 19:3-9; Mark 10:2-12; cf. Matt 5:31, 32; Luke 16:18). Again He avoided involvement in current wrangles, this time by taking His questioners back to the creation ordinance (Gen 2:24), thus showing marriage to be a lifelong union not to be dissolved by man. In answer to a rejoinder, He explained the Mosaic concession as necessitated by the "hardness of heart" of men. If Matthew's account is compared with Mark's, it may be seen that further teaching on the subject was given "in the house" in reply to questions from the disciples. The Matthaean exception was therefore given to the disciples rather than to the Pharisees. This averts the force of the argument that Jesus would hardly have allowed Himself to become embroiled in the Hillel-Shammai controversy by aligning Himself with one school—the stricter—that argued that divorce was permissible only in the case of unchastity in the wife.

Some scholars, usually anxious to preserve the absolute indissolubility of marriage, deny the dominical authority of the Matthaean exception—but without any objective evidence. Those who accept its genuineness differ in their interpretation of the meaning of *πορνεία*. Some regard it in the light of its use elsewhere in the NT (1 Cor 5:1), as referring to "marriage" contracted within the prohibited degrees, or understand it to mean prenuptial unchastity. In both these cases, the indissolubility of marriage can be maintained, since in neither case can the "divorce" envisaged be understood as other than a declaration of the nullity of the "marriage" from the beginning. On the other hand, a considerable number of scholars—evangelicals among them—take *πορνεία* to mean postmarital unchastity, and therefore envisage a situation where the marriage bond is so ruptured as to be beyond repair. In such circumstances, divorce and remarriage are not to be regarded as constituting adultery.

If this seems to be a striking conclusion, so too is the recognition of the equal rights of the sexes (Mark 10:12). Here is something without parallel in Judaism.

Jesus indicated in reply to the disciples' further question, three categories of those who are exempt from the divine plan for men and women (Matt 19:12). These may be paraphrased as those constitutionally unfitted for marriage; those involuntarily prevented from marrying; and those who refrain from entering that estate to give themselves unreservedly to the work of the kingdom of God. This is however, no elevation of celibacy over marriage, or vice versa, but a statement anticipatory of Paul's aphorism, "Each has his own special gift from God" (1 Cor 7:7).

III. Sanctions

The ethical teaching of Jesus is far more than good advice. It is authoritative to the highest degree, and its authority involves sanctions. The most striking of these is the appeal to rewards and penalties of an eschatological nature.

Rewards are offered for enduring persecution

(Matt 5:12), practicing love (Matt 6:14; Luke 14:13, 14; 18:22), humility (Luke 14:10, 11), and renunciation (Mark 10:29, 30). Rewards appear to be offered as a *quid pro quo* and are sometimes graduated according to the extent to which a duty is performed (Luke 19: 17, 19). Punishment is similarly threatened and sometimes graduated (12:47, 48).

It has often been pointed out that all this serves to underline the gravity of moral choices, and some have asserted that the rewards offered by Jesus are the inevitable issue of goodness, just as victory is the reward for success in battle. The prominence given by Jesus to the theme of reward still seems reminiscent of Judaism, with its tendency to think of virtue as meritorious.

The problem is eased when it is noted that Jesus promised rewards only to those who were prepared to follow Him from some other motive. The righteous will be astonished by their reward (Matt 25:31-46); the reward will far outweigh any claim that might conceivably be made (20:1-16); and in fact the most faithful service represents no more than our duty (Luke 17:7-10). "Reward, in fact, is not reward, but grace" (K. E. Kirk, *The Vision of God,* 144). The essence of the reward is the kingdom itself (Matt 5:3, 10) and the privilege of discipleship (Luke 14:26, 27, 33), so it is hardly likely to appeal to the self-centered. Kirk's further suggestion that the prominence of the idea of reward is a warning against undue emphasis on "duty for duty's sake" that can only lead to self-satisfaction and pride, is also worthy of notice.

The eschatological element is prominent in the sanctions of Jesus' ethics, and it will not do to regard this as purely formal, as Wilder does. Since Jesus' ethic is that of the kingdom of God that awaits its final consummation, the life of the disciple is to be lived in the light not only of His first advent but also of His second. The "futurist" eschatology of the gospels, as well as the "realized" element, is ethical through and through. The Olivet Discourse has as its primary object the exhortation to spiritual and moral watchfulness (Matt 24; cf. 25). The pure will of God lies at the heart of the matter, but this is related by Jesus not only to the past revelation of that will in the law and the prophets, and to its present manifestation in His person and mission, but also to the future consummation when "he will repay every man for what he has done" (16: 27).

BIBLIOGRAPHY. T. Walker, *The Teaching of Jesus and the Jewish Teaching of His Age* (1923); C. A. Anderson Scott, *New Testament Ethics* (1930), 1-72; K. E. Kirk, *The Vision of God* (1931), 140-146; T. W. Manson, *The Teaching of Jesus* (1931); W. Manson, *Jesus the Messiah* (1943); L. H. Marshall, *The Challenge of New Testament Ethics* (1947), 1-215; L. Dewar, *An Outline of New Testament Ethics* (1949), 1-121; S. Cave, *The Christian Way* (1949); A. N. Wilder, *Eschatology and Ethics in the Teaching of Jesus* rev. ed. (1950); C. H. Dodd, *Gospel and Law* (1951); H. Windisch, *The Meaning of the Sermon on the Mount,* Eng. tr. (1951); P. Ramsey, *Basic Christian Ethics* (1952); A. M. Hunter, *Design for Life* (1953); C. F. H. Henry, *Christian Personal Ethics* (1957); T. W. Manson, *Ethics and the Gospel* (1960); J. Jeremias, *The Sermon on the Mount* (1961); H. K. McArthur, *Understanding the Sermon on the Mount* (1961); W. Lillie, *Studies in New Testament Ethics* (1961); J. Knox, *The Ethic of Jesus in the Teaching of the Church* (1962); J. I. Packer, *Our Lord's Understanding of the Law of God* (1962); J. A. T. Robinson, *Honest to God* (1963), 110-121; W. D. Davies, *The Setting of the Sermon on the Mount* (1964); G. E. Ladd, *Jesus and the Kingdom* (1964), 274-300.

H. H. Rowdon

ETHIOPIA **ē' thĭ ō' pĭ ə.** Nubia, a country in the N Sudan, S of Egypt.

1. Terminology. In the OT, the KJV sometimes transliterates כוש as "Cush" (Gen 10:6, 7, 8; 1 Chron 1:8, 9, 10; Isa 11:11). However, the KJV usually trs. by "Ethiopia." The KJV transliterates כושי as "Cushi" (2 Sam 18:21, 22, 23, 31, 32).

The RSV transliterates the Heb. as "Cush" (Gen 2:13; 10:6-8; 1 Chron 1:8-10; Ezek 38:5) and trs. "Ethiopia" elsewhere. Also the RSV trs. כושי (2 Sam 18:21-23, 31, 32) and כושית (Num 12:1) as "Cushite," but elsewhere renders "Ethiopian."

In the NT, "Ethiopian" trs. Αἰθίοψ, whose etymological meaning is prob. "dark-faced" (Acts 8:27).

2. Location. The Biblical Ethiopia is Nubia, in southernmost Egypt and the N Sudan, not the modern Ethiopia (also called Abyssinia). Ethiopia is often associated with Egypt in the Bible (e.g. Ps 68:31; Isa 20:3-5; Ezek 30:4, 5). More specifically Ethiopia is located S of Egypt (Jud 1:10) and S of Syene (Ezek 29:10), modern Aswan, the southernmost important city of Egypt. This location of Ethiopia agrees with the Egyp. references to *K'š* (which corresponds to Heb. כוש) and with Herodotus II. 29.

3. History. The first historical reference to an Ethiopian in the Bible is the incident of the Cushite (i.e. Ethiopian) slave who carried to David the news of Absalom's death (2 Sam 18:21-23, 31, 32).

There were Ethiopian mercenaries in the army of Shishak, a Libyan king of Egypt, when he invaded Pal. about 918 B.C. (2 Chron 12: 3).

An attack on Judah by Ethiopians and Libyans (2 Chron 14:9-15), led by Zerah the Ethiopian, was repulsed by King Asa (913-873 B.C.). These attackers may have been mercenaries in the Egyp. army settled in southern Pal. by Pharaoh Shishak. Possibly these mercenaries are also the Ethiopians near the Arabs (2 Chron 21:16), though some scholars think the reference is to the close contact of the S Arabians with Africans across the Red Sea.

Second Kings 19:9 and Isaiah 37:9 mention Tirhakah's (the king of Ethiopia) attempt to check Sennacherib's invasion of Pal. in the time of King Hezekiah. The Assyrians mockingly called Tirhakah "a bruised reed" (2 Kings 18:21 KJV) and defeated him at Eltekeh. In Egypt, Tirhakah was again defeated by the Assyrian king Esar-haddon and retired to Ethiopia. These defeats of Tirhakah may be referred to by Isaiah (Isa 20:3-5). Tirhakah ruled about 689-664 B.C. as the third and last Pharaoh of the Twenty-fifth, or Ethiopian Dynasty of Egypt. The Ethiopian control of Egypt under this dynasty explains why Ethiopia was called the "strength" of Thebes, Egypt's southern capital (Nah 3:9). This brief Ethiopian empire included Egypt for about fifty years. Tirhakah's nephew and successor as king of Ethiopia, Tanut-Amon, was defeated by the Assyrian king Ashurbanipal, who destroyed Thebes in 663 B.C. (Nah 3:8).

The Letter of Aristeas 13 states that Pharaoh Psammetichus II (593-588 B.C.) used Jewish mercenaries in his campaign against Ethiopia, which is also mentioned by Herodotus II. 161. He or a Pharaoh soon after, settled a Jewish garrison on Elephantine Island to guard the border between Egypt and Ethiopia.

Ebed-melech, who secured Jeremiah's release from the cistern (Jer 38:7-13), was an Ethiopian eunuch who held a high position in the household of King Zedekiah of Judah (597-587 B.C.). He believed in God, and Jeremiah promised that he would be safe in the coming capture of Jerusalem (39:15-17).

King Ahasuerus of Persia (usually identified with Xerxes, 486-465 B.C.) included Ethiopia at one extreme of his empire (Esth 1:1; 8:9 and in the Additions of the Apocrypha, 13:1; 16:1). Darius I of Persia also mentions Ethiopia in his list of provinces.

The Ethiopians who were to follow Antiochus Epiphanes, king of the N, or Syria (175-163 B.C.), after his conquest of Egypt (Dan 11:43) may refer to mercenaries in his army. The exact meaning, however, is uncertain in this context.

Sibylline Oracles V. 194 mentions the capture of Syene by the Ethiopians. This may refer to an expedition into Egypt sent by an Ethiopian queen with the title Candace, in 24 B.C. (Strabo, XVII. i. 54).

Acts 8:27 mentions "Candace the queen of the Ethiopians." Candace was a Nubian royal title, prob. corresponding to "queen mother." The queen who ruled at Meroe (then the Ethiopian capital) with this title at that time was Amantitere (A.D. 25-41). *See* CANDACE. That her treasurer should visit Jerusalem and should be reading Isaiah is not surprising in the light of Jewish contacts with Nubia. Some have suggested that he was a proselyte or even a Jew. *See* ETHIOPIAN EUNUCH.

4. Features. The Bible several times refers to "the rivers of Ethiopia" (Isa 18:1; Zeph 3:10), presumably the Nile, the Blue and White Niles, and the Atbara. The papyrus boats used on these rivers (Isa 18:2) are pictured in Egyp. reliefs and paintings, and they are still used in modern Ethiopia. The merchandise of Ethiopia (Job 28:19; Isa 45:14) included the topaz as a precious product of that land. Egyptian records list among the imports from Ethiopia: gold, precious stones, incense, ebony, ivory, ostrich feathers and eggs, leopard skins, greyhounds, cattle, gazelles, bows, shields, and slaves. Isaiah (18:2) calls the Ethiopians "tall and smooth." Not only are some of the Sudanese tribes tall, but they also have little body hair, and very smooth skin. Jeremiah (13:23) implies that the Ethiopian's skin is black. The prophet also (46:9) lists Ethiopians with shields among the soldiers of the Egyp. army; small wooden models of shield-bearing Nubian soldiers have been found in Egyp. tombs.

5. Prophecies about Ethiopia. Some prophecies predicted that Jewish exiles in Ethiopia would return to Pal. (Isa 11:11; Ps 87:4). Isaiah (43:3) expected that Persia would take Ethiopia as reward, poetically called a ransom, for freeing the Jewish captives. Several passages speak of coming judgment on Ethiopia (Isa 20:3, 4; Ezek 30:4, 5, 9; Zeph 2:12). Ezekiel (38:5) includes Ethiopians among the forces of Gog that will attack Israel in the end times. *Sibylline Oracles* III. 320 evidently misunderstood the geography of the Ezekiel passage and misplaced Gog in Ethiopia. According to Amos 9:7, God is concerned with the Ethiopians as with Israel. Psalm 68:31, Isaiah 45:14, and Zephaniah 3:10 mention the conversion of the Ethiopians and their inclusion in the kingdom of God.

BIBLIOGRAPHY. E. A. W. Budge, *The Egyptian Sudan* (1907); J. W. Crowfoot, *The Island of Meroe* (1911); F. L. Griffith, *Meroitic Inscriptions,* I (1911) and *Meroitic Inscriptions,* II (1912); G. Reisner, "The Meroitic Kingdom of Ethiopia," JEA, IX, (1923), 34-77; E. A. W. Budge, *A History of Ethiopia, Nubia, and Abyssinia* (1928); T. Säve-Söderbergh, *Ägypten und Nubien* (1941); D. Dunham, *The Royal Tombs of Kush,* I (1950), II (1955), III (1952), IV (1957); A. J. Arkell, *A History of the Sudan* (1955); E. Ullendorff, *Ethiopia and the Bible* (1968).

J. ALEXANDER THOMPSON

ETHIOPIAN EUNUCH. A convert of the evangelist Philip, mentioned only in Acts 8:27-40. The ethnic term "Ethiopian" (Gr. Αἰθιοπία; Lat. *Aethiopia*) was applied in Rom. times to the area of E Africa, S of Egypt and beyond the mountains of the second cataract. The Acts account states that this man was the minister (Gr. δυναστής, Lat. *potens,* "ruler," "vizier") of Candace, the queen of the Ethiopians. This Candace was a name used frequently by the African queens of the island of Meroe, but the

The city of Gaza looking toward the west. This is the probable area where Philip met the Eunuch. ©*M.P.S.*

specific ruler is difficult to identify, the name appears on monuments as hieroglyphic, *k n t k y*. The practice of emasculation was widespread throughout the Near E, and such men served as chamberlains in the royal harem. It is most unlikely that this man was a Jew because eunuchs were forbidden to enter the congregation of Israel (Lev 21:20; Deut 23:1). However, there is no doubt that after the Pers. settlement of military colonies of Jews in the area of Meroe, numbers of "God-fearers" (Acts 10:2, et al.) sprang up around the local synagogue. The Ethiopian eunuch was prob. the treasurer or minister of trade and so traveled widely and could well have known either Heb. or Gr. sufficiently to read the Isaiah scroll. The purpose of the story is to present the oneness of all races and tongues in confession of Christ.

Further investigation into the early history of the missionary spread of the Gospel shows that both Judaism and Christianity were more widely distributed at an earlier period than has usually been accepted. The apparent faith of the Ethiopian in the OT prophecy is very important to the understanding of the current interpretation of Isaiah in the apostolic age. It is abundantly clear that the Ethiopian understood the passage in Isaiah 53:7, 8 as referring not to the people of Israel but to a unique personage, possibly the prophet himself. Philip interpreted the passage to refer to the life and atonement of Christ. The story in the Lucan narrative comes immediately after the events of the scattering of the church under Paul's persecution, the preaching of Philip in Samaria, and the general missionary expansion of the Gospel in concentric patterns out from Jerusalem. The fulfillment of this is seen in the eunuch's case, in the Gospel's final outreach beyond the borders of Rome to a black man of the African world. The story logically sets the stage for the conversion of the least likely candidate of all, Paul the persecutor, and through him the presentation of the message of Jesus to the Gentiles. Historical evidence indicates that it was through such sing. converts that the national churches were planted and the universal spread of the message continued.

W. White, Jr.

ETHIOPIC VERSIONS. *See* Versions, Ancient.

ETH-KAZIN ĕth kā' zīn (עתה קצין), KJV ITTAH KAZIN *ĭ'ta ka' zīn*. A town, mentioned only once (Josh 19:13), described as being on the border of Zebulun. From the mention of other towns in the same v. its location, at present uncertain, should be somewhere on the border of Zebulun and Naphtali. The site of Kefr Kenna seems most probable.

R. K. Harrison

ETHMA. KJV Apoc. form of Nebo.

ETHNAN ĕth' nən (אתנן, *hire, gift*). One of the sons of Helah from the tribe of Judah (1 Chron 4:7). Some connect the name with Ithnan (q.v.) a town in southern Judah (Josh 15:23).

ETHNARCH éth' närk (*ἐθνάρχης*, found only once—2 Cor 11:32, "At Damascus, the governor [ethnarch] under King Aretas"). Paul in recounting his narrow escape from this officer uses this peculiar title of Gr. origin. It is a composite of the words, *ἔθνος*, "a company living together," "body of people" and, *ἀρχων*, "ruler," "prince." It appears after the Hel. expansion under Alexander the Great and has various meanings ascribed by it. Usually it was the title of a governor of a town or county, who ruled for an overlord of a different race or culture than the subjects. Unfortunately none of the classical historians of the Hel. age give its origin. It is used by Strabo, the Byzantine Encyclopedists, and the LXX VS of the Apoc., e.g. 1 Maccabees 14:47 wherein it is applied to the high priest Simon as a representative of Syria. The chiefs of the seven districts of Rom. Egypt bore the title, as did the princes of the Bosporus under Caesar Augustus. The incident mentioned in 2 Corinthians 11:32f. appears to be identical to the one narrated in Acts 9:22-26. In the latter text, it is the Jews who waited night and day to kill the apostle. The two texts, however, complement each other; the ethnarch of Damascus would have been a Jew, as indicated by the use of the term for Jewish magistrates in the communities of the Diaspora (e.g. Josephus [Jos. Antiq. XIV. vii. 2 et al.] but it is replaced by the more familiar *στρατηγος*, in certain editions). The point of the text is that the Jews were incensed against Paul. Damascus was at this time under the Arabian King Aretas, the father-in-law of Herod Antipas. So unusual was it for Damascus to have an ethnarch in control that Paul mentions it and it adds immeasurably to the historicity and situation of his narrative. Such details are by the nature of their accidence beyond the reach of invention and add an incontrovertible essence of authenticity to the Scripture account.

W. White, Jr.

ETHNI ĕth' nī (אתני, LXX *Αθανι*, *gift*). An ancestor of Asaph.

The only occurrence of this man's name is in 1 Chronicles 6:41 where he appears in the genealogy of Asaph the musician. He is of the tribe of Levi through his son Gershom. In a somewhat parallel list in 1 Chronicles 6:21 Jeatherai is recorded as being the son of Zerah instead of Ethni. Both lists apparently have gaps in them, so this problem is easily explained.

R. L. Alden

EUBULUS ū bū' ləs (Εὔβουλος, *well-advised*). A friend with Paul during his second Rom. imprisonment who sent greetings to Timothy

(2 Tim 4:21). His Gr. name implies he was prob. a Gentile by birth. Apparently a member of the Rom. church, he is otherwise unknown. The name is common in papyri and inscrs.

EUCHARIST (Gr. εὐχαριστέω, *to be grateful, to give thanks*). This verb and its cognates occur frequently in the NT denoting grateful acknowledgment of benefits received esp. through the bounty and goodness of the Lord. For this reason, the term "eucharist" in ancient times came to be applied to the Lord's Supper, prob. because of the giving of thanks (εὐχαριστέω) by the Lord at the time of institution, as He gave His disciples the bread and the cup (cf. Mark 14:22; 1 Cor 11:23, 24). It first appeared as a designation of the communion meal in the letters of Ignatius (A.D. 107) to Philadelphia (c. iv) and Smyrna (c. vi). Irenaeus wrote that after the consecration "it is no longer common bread but eucharist" (*Against Heresies*, iv. ch. 18, 5). Because of this usage, early liturgies made the thanksgiving, next to the reception, the most significant part of the celebration, and this no doubt promoted the general adoption of the name. Gratitude for salvation was reflected generally in the prayers and hymns associated with the celebration of the Lord's Supper.

P. JEWETT

EUERGETES ū ûr′ jə tez (ευεργέτης, *benefactor*). A title of honor borne by two of the Ptolemaic kings, Ptolemy III (246-221 B.C.) and Ptolemy VII (145-116 B.C.). The author of Ecclesiasticus dates his work with reference to his coming "to Egypt in the thirty-eighth year of the reign of Euergetes." (*See* Prologue.) Although he is not specific about which of the two men with this title he refers to, it is apparent that he has in mind the second.

BIBLIOGRAPHY. R. H. Charles, *The Apocrypha and Pseudepigrapha of the Old Testament*, I (1963), 293.

S. BARABAS

EUGNOSTOS, LETTER OF ug nŏs′ təs. A Gnostic document contained in Codex III and Codex V of the Nag Hammadi library, but as yet unpublished. It has, however a close parallel in the *Sophia Jesu Christi*, published by W. C. Till from the Berlin Gnostic Codex. Eugnostos is a straightforward discourse, the Sophia a dialogue between Jesus and the disciples. The most recent discussion of their relationship, by M. Krause, argues that the special material in the Sophia does not fit the common material, while that of Eugnostos does. In particular the questions of the disciples are not matched by the answers of Jesus, and are therefore later insertions. This would show Christianization of a non-Christian (or *less* Christian?) text.

BIBLIOGRAPHY. Till, TU 60 (1955); Krause in *Mullus* (JAC Erganzungsband I, 1964), 215ff.; Wilson, *Gnosis and the New Testament* (1968), 111ff.

R. McL. WILSON

EUMENES ū′ mə nēz (Εὐμενής, *well disposed*). A ruler (1 Macc 8:8) to whom the Romans had allotted much Syrian territory. He was Eumenes II (197-158 B.C.), king of Pergamum, a city located between two tributaries of the ancient river Caicus in W Asia Minor. His territorial rewards resulted from the assistance given to the Romans during their war with the Seleucid Antiochus III the Great from 191 B.C.

R. K. HARRISON

EUNATAN. KJV Apoc. form of ELNATHAN.

EUNICE ū′ nīs (Εὐνίκη, *good victory*). The daughter of Lois and mother of Timothy (2 Tim 1:5; Acts 16:1). Her husband was a Gentile (Acts 16:1), but she was a Jewess, as was also her mother. Timothy had not been circumcised, undoubtedly because his father was a Gentile, but he was brought up by his mother and his grandmother in the Jewish faith. Paul wrote of Timothy that from a child his mother had taught him to know the holy Scriptures (2 Tim 3:15). She, her mother, and Timothy were prob. converted to Christianity during Paul's first missionary journey at Lystra, where Paul had been stoned and left for dead. On his second missionary journey, when he returned to Lystra, Paul was so impressed with the fervency of Timothy's spirit that he decided to take him along. Paul said that Timothy witnessed his persecutions and afflictions at Lystra (2 Tim 3:11). Without doubt the young missionary had a very remarkable mother.

S. BARABAS

EUNUCH yū′ nək (סָרִיס, 2 Kings 9:32; 20:18; Isa 39:7; 56:3, 4; Jer 29:2, et al.; Dan 1; *officer* in Gen 37:36; 39:1; 40:2, 7; 1 Sam 8:15; 1 Kings 22:9 [cf. 2 Chron 18:8]; 2 Kings 8:6; 24:12, 15; 25:19; 1 Chron 28:1; *chamberlain* in 2 Kings 23:11; Esth 1-7; LXX and NT εὐνοῦχος, *eunuch*, Gen 37:36; Isa 39:7; and LXX σπάδων, *eunuch*). A male officer of the court or household of a ruler, and often one who had been castrated. סריס, is prob. a loan word from Akkad. *ša rēši*, "he of the head," a shorter form of Assyrian *ša rēš šarri*, "he of the head of the king," indicating a courtier or confidant (cf. *Rab Saris*). The meaning "castrated one" was secondary, arising from the preference of rulers for such men in offices involving contact with the women of their households. It is therefore improbable that all those designated סריס in the OT were eunuchs, but in most cases it is not possible to decide by other than the probabilities of the context whether the meaning "official," or "eunuch official" is more appropriate. There are passages in which the sense "eunuch" seems unlikely (Gen 37-40; 1 Kings 22:9; 2 Kings 8:6; 9:32; 20:18; 23:11; 1 Chron 28:1; Jer 34:19; 52:25); whereas in others it seems probable (1 Sam 8:15; 2 Kings 24:12, 15; Isa 39:7; Jer 38:7;

Air view of the River Euphrates, showing its circuitous, treeless course. ©*M.P.S.*

41:16, and Esth). The term is applied to men of Egypt (Gen 40:2), Assyria (2 Kings 20: 18), Babylonia (Dan), Persia (Esth), and Israel.

In the NT, an Ethiopian is described as an eunuch (Acts 8:27-39), and a reference to eunuchs by Jesus is reported in Matthew 19: 12.

BIBLIOGRAPHY. Arndt, 323, 324; AIs, 121; K. A. Kitchen, *Ancient Orient and Old Testament* (1966), 165, 166.

T. C. MITCHELL

EUODIA ū ō' dī ə (Εὐοδία, *prosperous journey, success*; KJV EUODIAS, ū ō' dī es, takes it as a masc. name, but the fem. pronoun "them" [αὐταῖς] in Phil 4:2, 3 demands that both names be fem.). A Christian woman in Philippi whom Paul asked to be reconciled to Syntyche.

Clearly both were influential women in the Philippian church, where women were prominent from the beginning (Acts 16:12-15). The cause of their disagreement, whether doctrinal or personal, is unknown, but obviously it had become chronic.

Paul's impartial appeal for reconciliation implies that both were responsible for the estrangement. He realized that outside help was needed and asked his "true yokefellow" (σύζυγος) to assist them. Paul commended the two women as having "labored side by side in the gospel." *See* YOKEFELLOW.

D. E. HIEBERT

EUPATOR ū' pə tôr (Gr. Εὐπάτωρ, *of a noble father*). The surname of the Seleucid Antiochus V (163-162 B.C.), who as a boy succeeded his father Antiochus IV Epiphanes (175-163 B.C.). He made peace with the Jews in the Maccabean period, but was betrayed and killed in 162 B.C.

EUPHRATES ū frā' tēz (Heb. פְּרָת; Assyrian, *Purattu*; Old Pers., *Ufrâtu*; Gr. Εὐφράτης; modern names, *Fra Su, Shatt el Fara*) is the longest river of Western Asia. It rises in the mountains of Armenia in modern Turkey, heads W as if to reach the Mediterranean, then swings in a wide bow in Syria, and eventually joins the Tigris to become the Shatt el Arab, and empties into the Persian Gulf. The Euphrates is some 1780 m. long, considerably longer than its companion stream, the Tigris, with which it is often linked in discussion of Mesopotamia, "the land between, or in the midst of, the rivers." Among its tributaries are the Balikh and the Khabur, which are associated with the Euphrates in locating Aram Naharaim (cf. Gen 24:10), where Laban lived and the city of Haran was situated (Gen 11: 31). The ruins of many ancient cities are found along the river in Iraq; among them are Sippar, Babylon, Kish, Nippur, Uruk (modern Warka, Biblical Erech) Larsa, Ur, and Eridu. Geological and archeological investigations leave the problem of the ancient coastline unsettled.

Euphrates and the Bible. In the Bible the Euphrates is called "the river Euphrates," "the great river, the river Euphrates," or simply "the River." The Euphrates is named as one of the four streams into which the river of the Garden of Eden divided (Gen 2:14). In the covenant which God made with Abraham, the river Euphrates was designated one of the boundaries of the Promised Land (Gen 15:8; cf. Deut 1:7; 11:24). Before the conquest of Canaan the Lord again referred to the Euphrates as one of the borders of the Land of Promise (Josh 1:4). In his final address to Israel (Josh 24), Joshua stated that the fathers of Israel had lived "beyond the Euphrates" (v. 2), where they served other gods (v. 2; "beyond the River," vv. 14, 15), but God took Abraham "from beyond the River" and brought him to Canaan (v. 3). During the monarchy David defeated Hadadezer the king of Zobah, "as he went to restore his power at the river Euphrates" (2 Sam 8:3; 1 Chron 18:3). Isaiah refers to Assyria as an instrument of judgment against Israel, "a razor which is hired beyond the River" (Isa 7:20), and speaks of a threshing and ingathering of Israel from the river Euphrates to the brook of Egypt (27:12). It was to Carchemish on the river that Pharaoh Neco went to aid the Assyrians in an unsuccessful battle against the Babylonians (2 Kings 23:29; 24:7; 2 Chron 35:20). In the prophecy of Jeremiah concerning Egypt (Jer 46) the Euphrates is mentioned three times in connection with this defeat of Egypt (vv. 2, 6, and 10). The Euphrates is referred to by name four times in an acting prophecy which Jeremiah was commanded to perform against the pride of Judah and Jerusalem (Jer 13:4, 5, 6, 7). The prophet was instructed to have Seraiah throw into the Euphrates a stone-weighted document of a prophecy against Babylon, as a symbol that Babylon was to sink and never rise again (51:63). The genealogical section of 1 Chronicles states that a descendant of Reuben "dwelt to the east as far as the entrance of the desert this side of the Euphrates" (1 Chron 5:9). The river was the boundary between Mesopotamia and Syria-Pal. in the Per. period and the satrapy of the region of Syria-Pal. was called "Beyond the River" (Ezra 4:10, 11; 5:3; 6:6; Neh 2:7). In the NT the Euphrates is mentioned in Revelation 9:14 and a command was given to release "the four angels who are bound at the great river Euphrates," and the sixth angel poured out his bowl of wrath on "the great river Euphrates" (16:12).

BIBLIOGRAPHY. S. F. Langdon, "Early Babylon and its Cities," CAH (1924), I, 357-361; E. Techen, *Euphrat und Tigris* (1934); M. G. Ionides, *The Regime of the Rivers Euphrates and*

Tigris (1937); M. A. Beek, *Atlas of Mesopotamia* (1962); C. J. Gadd, "The Cities of Mesopotamia," CAH2, I, Chap. XIII (1962).

C. E. DeVries

EUPOLEMUS ū pŏl′ ə məs (Gr. Εὐπόλεμος, *skilled in war*). A Jewish ambassador who was sent to Rome by Judas Maccabeus after the victory over a general of Antiochus IV Epiphanes in 161 B.C. (1 Macc 8:17; 2 Macc 4:11). The purpose of the embassage was to enter into a peaceful alliance with the Rom. to which the latter agreed, sending written confirmation of the confederacy to Jerusalem with Eupolemus.

R. K. Harrison

EURAQUILO. ASV form of Euroclydon.

EUROCLYDON ū rŏk′ lĭ dŏn (Εὐροκλύδων). The name given in later Gr. MSS and VSS in Acts 27:14 to the wind which aroused the storm and caused Paul's shipwreck at Melita. This reading was adopted by the KJV translators—most likely because they had no earlier and better MSS. This would mean the SE wind that stirs up the waves, from Εὖρος, the E (or SE) "wind," and κλύδων, "wave." A variant of this is Εὐρυκλύδων, from εὐρύς, "broad," and κλύδων, "wave." However, better MSS have Εὐροκύλων, a sailor's term compounding Εὖρος, E wind with the Lat. *Aquilo*, N wind, making "northeaster," as ASV and RSV have it. This suits the local situation on the S coast of Crete where a southerly breeze often gives way to a NE gale.

BIBLIOGRAPHY. J. Smith, *The Voyage and Shipwreck of St. Paul* (1880), 119ff., 287ff.

J. C. Connell

EUTYCHUS ū′ tə kəs (Εὔτυχος, *fortunate, lucky*). A young man at Troas who fell from a third story window-seat during Paul's prolonged nocturnal speech (Acts 20:7-12). For a parallel occurrence, see Expr. Pap. III. 475.

Eutychus was a common slave name. He may have been a slave who had worked hard all day. He had taken a seat in the open window. Overcome by irresistible drowsiness in the hot, over-crowded room, he fell asleep and fell through the opening from the "third story." He "was taken up dead" (v. 9). As an eyewitness of the event Luke had satisfied himself of the fact. Having embraced him, Paul quieted the tumult with the assuring words, "his life is in him" (v. 10). The presence of the lad alive at dawn greatly comforted the group (v. 12).

Efforts have been made to break the natural meaning of a restoration from the dead. That Eutychus only appeared to be dead is contrary to Luke's precise statement (v. 9). Paul's act of embracing the body is not the act of one investigating a case of apparent death; it clearly recalls the action of Elijah (1 Kings 17:21) and Elisha (2 Kings 4:34). To stamp the story as an unhistorical anecdote which Luke mistook for an actual miracle in his account is contrary to Luke's known accuracy.

BIBLIOGRAPHY. W. M. Ramsay, *St. Paul the Traveller* (1896[14]), 290, 291; R. O. H. Lenski, *Interpretation of the Acts of the Apostles* (1934), 819-828; F. F. Bruce, *Commentary on the Book of the Acts* (1954), 407-409; M. Dibelius, *Studies in the Acts of the Apostles,* Eng. tr. (1956), 17-19; C. S. C. Williams, *The Acts of the Apostles* (1957), 230, 231.

D. E. Hiebert

EVANGELIST ē văn′ jə lĭst (Gr. εὐαγγελιστής, *one who announces good news*). The twin words *euaggélion,* "gospel," and *euaggelistēs,* "evangelist," came into Biblical use with the advent of Jesus. "Good news" merited "a messenger of good news." The word "evangelist" appears three times in the NT, with reference to the person, the work, and the calling.

Philip is the typical example of an evangelist. Paul and his party, after returning from his third missionary tour, "entered the house of Philip the evangelist, who was one of the seven, and stayed with him" (Acts 21:8). Earlier, Philip had conducted a successful evangelistic campaign in Samaria, and converted and baptized the Ethiopian official, sending him back home with the Gospel (Acts 8:4-40). Philip was the first of "the Seven" (deacons) elected by the Church to serve the widows, and was not an apostle or ordained minister. But he was an evangelist, for "he preached good news about the kingdom of God and the name of Jesus Christ" (8:12). So, whoever is "a bringer of good tidings" is an evangelist. Therefore God Himself is an evangelist, for "he preached beforehand to Abraham" (Gal 3:8). And so were the announcing angel (Luke 2:10), Jesus Himself (20:1), and the apostles and early converts in general (Acts 8:4).

Paul admonished Timothy to "do the work of an evangelist, fulfil your ministry" (2 Tim 4:5). Primarily, the work of the evangelist is to "proclaim good tidings" in new areas. It is the vanguard of Christianity, announcing the good news of the kingdom and of Christ where it has not been heard before. Paul, like Philip, did this kind of work, as did Timothy and other traveling Christians. They planted Christianity (1 Cor 3:6), then moved on to other virgin soil. The preacher-pastor and teacher were to shepherd and teach the flock, while the evangelist went from place to place enlisting new converts. Later, the authors of the four gospels were called "evangelists," because they were the first to proclaim the good news through writing.

The vocation of the evangelist is distinct. Paul said that Christ's "gifts were that some should be apostles, some prophets, some evangelists, some pastors and teachers, for the equipment of the saints, for the work of ministry" (Eph 4:11). Divine wisdom foresaw the growth of the Church and consequent need for workers of diversified gifts (1 Cor 12:28). Special talent is needed for pioneer proclamation of the Gospel, founding new missions, and building new churches. The evangelist is endowed with appropriate spiritual gifts to unlock pagan, heathen, and sinful doors and admit the saving Christ. *See* MINISTRY.

BIBLIOGRAPHY. W. Walker, "A History of the Christian Church" (1959), 454-472, 495, 507; D. Moody, "God Is Really Among You" in "Professor in the Pulpit" (1963), 67-75.

G. B. FUNDERBURK

EVE ēv (חוה ; LXX and NT, Εὔα). Wife of Adam.

1. Circumstances under which these names were given in the OT. The first ch. of Genesis indicates that even in this summary VS of creation it was recognized that there were two sexes ("male and female he created them" Gen 1:27). But when Eve was brought to her husband by the Creator, Adam made the pronouncement: "She shall be called woman (*'ishshah*) because she was taken out of man (*'ish*)" (Gen 2:23), which is not an instance of etymological findings but a clever play on words. It is now commonly conceded that lexicographically the first is not derived from the second. The name "Eve" originated in the experience of the Fall of man, when God had laid disabilities on the tempter, on Adam, and on his wife. Then it became apparent to Adam that the life of mankind was tied up with his wife, and he called her *ḥawwah*, a form that may bear some relation to *ḥayyah* ("to live"). This too is an instructive play on words, aiding the memory, but is not an etymological study of scientific accuracy. She was called "Eve" because she was to be "the mother of all living."

2. Her relation to Adam. Just before the creation of Eve, Adam was assigned the task of giving meaningful names to all creatures in the garden. As they came to him by pairs, it became obvious that they all had mates, but not he. Adam felt his lone station keenly. He was to appreciate the gift of a "helper fit for him." So now he had a counterpart, as did the other creatures. It is apparent that Eve served to supplement the life of Adam, for a man's life without a woman is incomplete. To this the thought is added that the purpose of having two persons united in marriage is procreation (Gen 1:28). It is also broadly indicated that the sex relationship was uniquely pure, for though naked the first parents felt no shame.

3. Her share in the Fall. The occasion for the Fall came from without, not from some native defect. By the blandishments of the tempter, Eve let herself be led to the point where she overstepped the limitation laid upon her. Alone, she took the direction of affairs into her own hands and became guilty of a gigantic fiasco. In the revulsion of feeling against the tempter, Eve shared in the antipathy that was indicated by the Lord as an enduring consequence—"enmity," lasting enmity that was to exist between her and the tempter from this time forth, being carried on through the ensuing generations by the daughters of Eve (Gen 3:15). As a continual reminder of all this, a certain burden was laid upon Eve—pain in childbearing, and being perennially attached to her husband who from this time forth was to rule over her (v. 16).

4. Historical fact or figure of speech? Is the creation of woman (Gen 2:21-25) to be accepted as an exact description of an actual event? Or must one regard the whole incident as too crude to be thought of as having transpired according to the letter? Three or four approaches have arisen as a result of such questions: (1) the woman was actually formed from the rib of man; (2) the whole experience was a vision informing man as to the actual relation of the woman to the man; (3) analogous to this, what is written is an allegory instructing man. Though substantial arguments may be adduced for each of these views, the first still deserves the preference as being most in harmony with the whole tenor of the account. What the Lord did involves an instructive symbolism to the effect that woman is to be regarded as a full equal to man in companionship. Partly for this reason, attempts to establish a root meaning for *chawwah* after the Aram. word for "serpent" (*chiwja*), prove futile and are not based on sound etymology. Also, all attempts to make the text set forth Eve as an intended correlate to Mary, introduce much into the text that is not actually there.

5. In the NT. Reference to Eve is made by Paul in two instances. "As the serpent deceived Eve" (2 Cor 11:3) is apparently a passing reference to show how easily a fall may occur, and with serious consequences. The other argument (1 Tim 2:11-14) indicates that Eve sinned in taking circumstances into her own hands. Women, argues Paul, should therefore be "silent" in the church assembly and submissive to the authority of men.

H. C. LEUPOLD

EVE, GOSPEL OF. A Gospel of Eve is mentioned only by Epiphanius (Pan XXVI. 2. 6), who also gives the only certain quotation (ibid.). On a high mountain the narrator (unidentified) sees two figures, and is thus addressed: "I am thou and thou art I, and where thou art there am I, and I am sown in all things; and whence thou wilt thou gatherest me, and when thou gatherest me, then gatherest thou thyself." The mountain setting recalls some Gnostic gospels, as does the formula, "I am thou and thou art I," often found in Gnostic, Hermetic, and magical texts. The first reference in Epiphanius suggests a link with the Ophite interpretation of the Genesis story of the Fall

(Iren. I. 28. 4, p. 234 Harvey). See further NTAp. I. 241ff.

R. McL. Wilson

EVENING SACRIFICE. The daily burnt offering of a yearling lamb. With the morning sacrifice it constituted the continual burnt offering. Each sacrifice, a lamb without blemish, was offered with a cereal ("meal," KJV "meat") offering, one-fifth peck of fine flour with a quart of oil; and a libation, a quart of wine (Exod 29:38-42; Num 28:3-8). The observance was important in the history of Israel (2 Chron 13:11, et al.). The continual burnt offering of the restored temple of Ezekiel included only the morning sacrifice (Ezek 46:13-15).

C. P. Weber

EVERLASTING. *See* Eternity.

EVI ē'vī (אוי, LXX Ευει, *desire*). A Midianite king slain by the Israelites.

Evi was one of the five kings of Midian whom the Israelites slew (Num 31:8). This was apparently an act of vengeance. Earlier, the Lord had said to Moses, "Harass the Midianites and smite them; for they have harassed you with their wiles, with which they beguiled you . . ." (Num 25:16ff.). Evi, along with the four other kings, receives mention in Joshua 13:21. There they are called "princes of Sihon."

R. L. Alden

EVIL (רע, *bad*, usually tr. *evil*; *πονηρός*, *wicked*; *κακός*, *bad*).

Often *ra'*, appearing about 800 times with its cognates in the OT, refers to what is physically undesirable, what is bad as the opposite of what is good. Rotten figs are "bad," as are poisonous herbs (2 Kings 4:41), and a ravenous beast (Gen 37:20). A child must refuse the "bad," of all sorts (Isa 7:15). It is also used of moral evil as that which is "wicked in the sight of the Lord" (Gen 38:7; Deut 4:25; Ps 51:4); and it is the same with the counterpart words of the NT (Matt 6:23; 24:48, 49; Mark 7:21-23).

Ponērós, with its noun *ponēría,* occurs 82 times in the NT; of physical evil only twice (Matt 7:17f.; Rev 16:2). *Kakos* is another generic NT term for evil, appearing 78 times with its cognates. It usually signifies moral evil—sin, disobedience to God.

Natural, or physical evil, occurs when undesirable natural occurrences tend to frustrate human life. Examples of such evils are earthquakes, tornadoes, tidal waves, disease, and imbecility. Accidents are usually thought of as instances of natural evil, although they often happen as a result of improper human decisions. A psalmist complained, "Evils have encompassed me without number" (Ps 40:12). Jeremiah asked, "Why is my pain unceasing, my wound incurable, refusing to be healed?" (Jer 15:18). Natural evil has presented a difficult dilemma for believers in God. If God is God, they ask, why do the wicked often flourish like the green bay tree while the righteous salt their bread with tears? Leslie Weatherhead confesses, "The subject of pain has haunted my thinking ever since I began to think for myself at all" (*Why Do Men Suffer* [1936], p. 9). John S. Whale has called it "this notorious problem which has vexed thought and tried faith in every age of human history" (*The Christian Answer to the Problem of Evil* [1939], p. 13).

On this problem, some have been embittered, "pan-diabolistic" pessimists (Buddha, Schopenhauer, Joseph Wood Krutch). Others have been optimists of some sort (Neo-Platonists, Spinoza, Calvin, Mary Baker Eddy), agreeing in general with Robert Browning who said, "God's in his heaven—all's right with the world" ("Pippa Passes")—and with Alexander Pope who announced, "One truth is clear, Whatever is, is right" (*Essay on Man*). Some would call themselves meliorists (esp. E. S. Brightman), and say that both good and evil are real and that men should become co-workers with God to rout evil and enhance what is beneficial to men.

It might well be that an adequate conception of the Incarnation would furnish a pointer on this problem. Perhaps Christ, who holds the solution of moral evil, is also the locus of solution for the abysmal mystery of natural evil. His enfleshment surely implies that materiality as such is not evil. His healings suggest that diseases are not necessarily the direct will of the Father. Since the Father is "to unite all things in him [Christ]" (Eph 1:10); since there is to be "a new heaven and a new earth" (Rev 21:1); and since "the whole creation has been groaning in travail together until now" (Rom 8:22), along with our groaning "inwardly as we wait for adoption as sons, the redemption of our bodies" (8:23)—it is evident that through Christ, the harbingers of redemption from all evil (natural as well as moral), which may now be experienced, are one day to be complete, "all things" being "put in subjection under him [Christ]," "that God may be everything to every one" (1 Cor 15:27, 28).

BIBLIOGRAPHY. H. W. Robinson, *Suffering: Human and Divine* (1939); C. R. Smith, *The Bible Doctrine of Sin* (1953); A. MacLeish, *J. B.* (1956); C. Marney, *Faith in Conflict* (1957).

J. K. Grider

EVIL EYE (רע עין, *evil eye*). An eye that is supposed to be capable of harming, or even killing, living beings by looking at them. The damage may or may not be intended by the owner of the eye. This belief was widespread in ancient times and has continued up to the present, although it seems never to have spread to the western hemisphere.

Methods of defense against effects of the evil eye included the wearing of charms (the camels' ornaments of Judg 8:21, according to some), repeating of oaths, and obscene gestures. A person might be held in suspicion of evil intentions if observed watching children or farm animals. The effects of the evil eye were believed to be rooted in envy so that when one expressed his admiration for animals or children he would often say, "God bless them" or its equivalent, so that his motivations would not be questioned.

In the OT the phrase seems to denote the quality of stinginess, referring to the man or his action, without reference to magical power. In Deuteronomy 15:9, "thine eye be evil against" (KJV) might just as well be tr. "you are selfish toward." Likewise, "his eye shall be evil toward" (KJV) means "he will act selfishly toward" (Deut 28:54, 56). The contexts indicate that those referred to refused to share with others who had less. Selfishness also fits the context of Proverbs 28:22, describing one who "hastens after wealth." In Proverbs 23:6 the context allows the RSV tr. "stingy." Selfishness or envy is the apparent meaning in Matthew 20:15 and may possibly be related to the situation in Matthew 6:22, 23 and Luke 11:34.

BIBLIOGRAPHY. F. T. Elworthy, *The Evil Eye* (1895); HERE, V (1912), 608-615; S. Thompson, Motif-Index of Folk-Literature, II (1956), D 2071.

C. P. WEBER

EVIL-MERODACH ē vəl mĕr′ ə dăk (אֱוִיל מְרֹדַךְ; Akkad. *Amēl-Marduk* [originally *Awīl-Marduk*], *man* [or *servant*] *of* [the god] *Marduk*; LXX Εὐειαλμαρωδέκ). Son and successor of Nebuchadnezzar (or Nebuchadrezzar) II, as king of the Neo-Babylonian empire c. 562-560 B.C.

According to 2 Kings 25:27-30 and Jeremiah 52:31-34, in the first year of his reign he released Jehoiachin, former king of Judah, from prison, even honoring him above all the other vassal kings in Babylon. It is noteworthy that administrative documents found at Babylon and containing lists of ration issues (oil), refer to a Yakukinu of Yakudu (Jehoiachin of Judah); for the text, cf. ANET (1955), p. 308. According to Berossus and the canon of Ptolemy, Evil-Merodach was assassinated by his brother-in-law, Nerglissar (prob. the Nergalsharezer who appears as a Babylonian officer, Jer 39:3, 13), who then took the throne.

K. L. BARKER

EVIL ONE, THE. *See* SATAN.

EVIL SPIRIT(S). *See* DEMON.

EVODIUS, HOMILY OF ĭ vō′ dĭ əs. A Coptic writing, the author of which claims to be Evodius, bishop of Rome (traditionally, he was bishop of Antioch) after Peter. The writer testifies that he, along with Peter, John, and others, was an eyewitness to the death of Mary and her assumption seven months later.

BIBLIOGRAPHY. F. Robinson, *Coptic Apocryphal Gospels* (1896), 44-89; M. R. James, *The Apocryphal New Testament* (1924), 194-198; W. H. C. Frend, "The Gnostic Origins of the Assumption Legend," *The Modern Churchman* (March 1953), 23-28.

C. P. WEBER

EWE. *See* SHEEP.

EXALTATION OF CHRIST. The term "exalt" is used with reference to Christ in Acts 2:33; 5:31, and Philippians 2:9, to which may be added Isaiah 52:13, where the servant of the prophecy may well be identified with Christ. (The same Gr. term is tr. "lift up" in John 3:14; 8:28; 12:32, 34, where the reference is to the sufferings of Christ.)

The terms "humiliation" (q.v.) and "exaltation" are commonly used in theology to denote the two states of Christ the mediator; the former extending from Christ's conception to His burial, and marking the period of His incarnation where the "form of the servant" was the dominant feature of His life on earth; the latter starting with the resurrection and including His ascension, His session at the right hand of the Father and His glorious second coming.

While some have attempted to interpret humiliation and exaltation as applying either to the divine or to the human nature of Christ, it appears wisest to view both in reference to Christ in the performance of His mediatorial office. It is along this line that Philippians 2:5-11 can receive the most natural interpretation.

There has been some question whether Christ's "descent into hell" belongs to the exaltation of Christ, as commonly asserted in the Roman Catholic, the Eastern Orthodox and the Lutheran traditions. The major support for this approach—and for the view that the statement of the Apostles' creed "He descended into hell" refers to a specific transaction performed by Christ between death and resurrection—is found in 1 Peter 3:19, 20. But to build such a heavy inferential superstructure of doctrine upon a passage so manifestly obscure and of which no one appears to be able to give a truly satisfactory interpretation (cf. Bo Reicke, *The Disobedient Spirits and Christian Baptism* [1946], 276 pp.) seems precarious in the extreme. Those who view the "descent" as a stage of Christ's exaltation frequently assume that He went to proclaim His victory to OT believers, so that they might share in the full benefits of His redemption (cf. Eph 4:8-10). But this picture does not fit well with the "spirits in prison, who formerly did not obey . . . in the days of Noah," about whom Peter is speaking. One may perhaps conclude that the "descent into hell" is resting on a fragile basis and that it is not of primary importance to determine whether it belongs to the humiliation or the exaltation of Christ. (Cf. F. Pieper, *Christian Dogmatics.* English tr. II [1951], 314-320. H. Bavinck, *Gereformeerde Dogmatiek,* 3d ed, III [1917], 459-469.)

The resurrection of Christ (q. v.) is the first notable stage of His exaltation (Acts 2:32; Rom 1:4). By the resurrection not only was Christ's body re-animated (as had been the case, e.g., for Lazarus), but His whole human nature was constituted incorruptible, glorious, powerful, and spiritual; that is to say, adapted to the purpose of the spirit (1 Cor 15:42-45).

In the ascension of Christ (q. v.) we see a perfecting of the glory inaugurated by the resurrection. In entering heaven Christ, the mediator, initiates a new form of relationship with His people, and prepares their ultimate reunion with Him (John 14:2, 3).

In the session at the right hand of God (Ps 110:1; Matt 22:44; and parallels in Mark 12:36 and Luke 20:42; Matt 26:64 and parallels in Mark 14:62 and Luke 22:69, if genuine; Acts 2:33-36; 5:31; 7:55, 56; Rom 8:34; Eph 1:20; Col 3:1; Heb 1:3, 13; 8:1; 10:12; 12:2; 1 Peter 3:22; Rev 3:21; 22:1) Christ exercises His kingly rule (Eph 1:20-22), sends the Holy Spirit to His own (John 14:26; 16:7), and pursues the ministry of intercession (Rom 8:34; Heb 7:25; 9:24; 1 John 2:1, etc.). (Cf. the article OFFICES OF CHRIST II. 2.)

At the Second Coming of Christ (q. v.) the ascended Lord will return to bring to completion His redemptive work, raise the dead, judge mankind and the angels, fulfill His union with His Church as the heavenly bridegroom, and inaugurate His eternal reign.

R. NICOLE

EXCELLENT, MOST EXCELLENT (NT *κράτιστος*, superlative of *κρατός*). The word "excellent" in Eng. VSS trs. a considerable number of Heb. and Gr. words. The title "most excellent" is found four times in the NT. It was used in the Gr. of those times in two ways. (a) It was the official rendering of the Lat. *vir egregius,* which meant a man of equestrian rank, that is, one of the knights who came in order after senators in Rome. Procurators were usually drawn from them. The title was applied to Felix (Acts 23:26; 24:3) and to Festus (Acts 26:25), both being procurators of Judaea. (b) It was used more generally as a courtesy title in addressing one honored for his position (Luke 1:3), e.g., Theophilus (referred to) may have justified the official use of the title. Strong reasons can be given to support the view that the author of Luke and Acts addressed an apology for Christianity to an influential Rom. governor. It is unlikely that Theophilus was a Christian, for in all probability he would then have been addressed by some such term as "brother." MM quote Zahn as saying that "there is no instance in the Christian literature of the first two centuries where a Christian uses a secular title in addressing another Christian."

F. FOULKES

EXCOMMUNICATION. The temporary or permanent exclusion of a church member from fellowship with the church.

1. Jewish practice. Under the Old Covenant excommunication was represented by the ban (חרם) placed on those who violated the Mosaic law, and as a result placed themselves outside the covenant relationship (e.g. Exod 30:33; Lev 17:4). There is reference to the threatened excommunication of those Israelites who did not come to Jerusalem in obedience to Ezra's proclamation (Ezra 10:8).

In the NT there are references to Jewish discipline in relation to the synagogue (Luke 6:22; John 9:22; 12:42; 16:2). There were different degrees of discipline, ranging from a temporary ban on contact with fellow Jews to the death penalty. The power to excommunicate seems generally to have been vested in the Sanhedrin.

2. In the teaching of Christ. The Lord clearly recognized the place of church discipline. He gave His apostles, and through them the Church, the power to bind and loose (Matt 16:19; 18:18). He indicated the procedure which should be followed in the case of offending brethren. There must first be personal admonition, but if that does not have the desired effect there must be further admonition in the presence of witnesses. Should this not succeed, then the church must be notified. If the offender refuses to listen to the church there is no alternative but excommunication (Matt 18:15-17).

3. In the apostolic era. There are several passages in the NT which refer to the exercise of discipline (1 Cor 5:2, 7, 13; 2 Cor 2:5-7; 2 Thess 3:14, 15; 1 Tim 1:20; Titus 3:10). In the church at Corinth there had been a moral breakdown which was tending to cause scandal throughout the city. To its shame, the church had taken no action, and it was therefore giving the impression that it condoned the sin which had been committed. Paul called upon the church to act. The phrase "to deliver . . . to Satan" occurs twice (1 Cor 5:5; 1 Tim 1:20) in the NT. It prob. means simply to put out of fellowship and to consign to the pagan world, which is regarded as Satan's domain. Some scholars have suggested that the infliction of some physical disease or disability might also be involved. A warning of possible physical consequences to those who partake of the Lord's Supper unworthily was given by the Apostle Paul (1 Cor 11:30).

Being deprived of Christian fellowship the offender loses any false sense of security he might otherwise enjoy by being allowed to remain in fellowship with the church. He must be brought to see the heinousness of the sin he has committed, and at the same time the world in general must be made aware that blatant sin cannot be tolerated within the Christian Church. Opinions vary as to the meaning of the Pauline phrase "the destruction of the flesh"

(1 Cor 5:5). The underlying thought may be that the offender, having been cut off from Christian fellowship, will become acutely conscious of his sin and guilt and will hate himself for what he has done.

Mention is made of action taken by a majority vote of church members, which resulted apparently in a change of heart on the part of the offender. The apostle asks that the church shall now regard the matter as closed and restore the disciplined member to full fellowship (2 Cor 2:5-11).

It seems that in the Early Church excommunication was exercised on both moral and doctrinal grounds. In the church at Corinth (1 Cor 5:1-8) the offense to which reference has already been made was one of incest. Paul intimates in his first letter to Timothy (1 Tim 1:20) that he had excommunicated Hymenaeus and Alexander because of their false teaching. A schismatic spirit was also regarded as an occasion for exclusion from the privileges of church fellowship (Titus 3:10). In the messages to the seven churches in the Book of Revelation the church of Ephesus is commended because it did not tolerate evil men, while the churches of Pergamos and Thyatira are reproved because they did not take effective action against heretical teachers or heathen abominations in their midst.

The purpose behind the exercise of church discipline is both to safeguard the purity of the church itself and to bring home to the offender his need of repentance. Those who are called upon to enforce such discipline must always be aware of their responsibility to restore the guilty party if and when he truly repents.

It is not absolutely clear from the NT what precise form excommunication took in every case. It would seem, however, that by the time the Pastoral Epistles were written, a more or less regular method of procedure had been adopted (1 Tim 5:19, 20) based on the Lord's own teaching on the subject. Formal excommunication meant not only the severance of formal links with the local fellowship, but exclusion from the church life generally. Church members were counseled not to eat or enjoy social intercourse with one who had been excommunicated (1 Cor 5:11; 2 Thess 3:14, 15). At the same time they have a continuing responsibility to admonish and exhort the erring brother to repent. It is not to be assumed that someone who has been excommunicated ceases to be in "a state of grace." It is clear that the Apostle Paul fully expected to see the disciplined offender numbered among the Lord's people "in the day of the Lord Jesus" (1 Cor 5:5).

Whereas the exercise of church discipline is open to abuse (cf. 3 John 9, 10), the necessity for it remains. The Puritan preacher, John Owen, defined discipline as "the due exercise of that authority and power which the Lord Christ, in and by His Word, has granted unto the church for its continuance, increase and preservation in purity, order and holiness, according to His appointment." Historically there has been considerable discussion whether the exercise of such discipline is vested in church officers or in the church itself as a corporate body. It is clear that when private remonstrances fail to achieve the necessary result the church must concern itself, and even though church officers may act on behalf of and in the name of the church, it is the corporate body which must assume ultimate responsibility for action taken. Church discipline must be seen not merely as a safeguard to the purity of the church, but also as a necessary means of promoting the glory of God. Those who are called upon to enforce it must themselves be sure that their motives are right and that the ultimate redemptive aim is not overlooked.

See ANATHEMA.

BIBLIOGRAPHY. J. Bannerman, *The Church of Christ* (1869), II, 186-200; D. D. Bannerman, *The Scripture Doctrine of the Church* (1887), 144-146, 176-188, 201-203; A. Edersheim, *Life and Times of Jesus the Messiah,* ii 183, 184 (1891); SHERK 236 (1909).

G. W. KIRBY

EXECUTE, EXECUTIONER. The OT makes a clear and precise distinction between murder—the illicit and violent killing of a human being (Exod 20:13), and the legal, moral act of slaying a criminal by the duly constituted authority (Gen 9:6 et al.). Unfortunately, the KJV often renders the simple Heb. verb "to do," "to accomplish" with the obsolete Tudor "execute" (Exod 12:12 et al.). In most cases the term refers to the exacting of judgment upon the nations. However, several cases of execution, legal deprivation of life, are mentioned in the OT (2 Chron 25:2-4 et al.). Criminals were to be either stoned (Deut 13:10) or hanged (Deut 21:22). But strict prohibitions against vendetta were in force (24:16). Several executions at the hands of the authorities are mentioned in the NT (Matt 14:10 et al.). Crucifixion was the Rom. method of execution. The only occurrence of the term "executioner" is in the Marcan account of the beheading of John the Baptist (6:27) where the Gr. loan-word from Lat., σπεκουλάτωρ, Lat. *speculator*, "scout," "courier," and by extension "executioner."

W. WHITE, JR.

EXILE (גולה [2 Sam 15:19], גלות [Isa 20:4], צעה [Isa 51:14], *exile, captivity*; LXX μετοικεσία, αἰχμαλωσία [2 Kings 24:16; Isa 20:4], *deportation, captivity, exile*).

1. The meaning of the term
2. The Assyrian Exile
3. The Babylonian Exile
4. The effects of the Exile

1. The meaning of the term. The terms "exile" and "captivity" are used interchangeably in the Bible. When the exile is imposed upon an individual, the choice of the place of banishment is usually left to the person exiled. However, when exile is the lot of groups of people, the place of banishment is imposed. The deportation of communities was usually practiced in the ancient world for political reasons, frequently to destroy the power of a nation considered an enemy or to colonize an area in which it was desirable, for various reasons, to create a cultural fusion. Sometimes several reasons for the imposition of exile upon a people operated at once. There are two instances of the Israelites being taken into exile referred to in the Bible. The first was the Assyrian Exile in the 8th cent. B.C.; the second the Babylonian Exile in the 6th cent. B.C.

2. The Assyrian Exile. The first deportation of Israelites recorded in the OT (2 Kings 15:29) occurred in 734 B.C. under the Assyrian monarch Tiglath-pileser III (745-727 B.C.). He marched against Pekah of Israel and Rezin of Syria because they made war against his vassal, King Ahaz of Judah, and he punished Israel by carrying some of them into exile (2 Kings 16:7-9). The captives of this deportation to Assyria were of the tribes of Naphtali, Reuben, Gad, and the half-tribe of Manasseh (1 Chron 5:26). The second deportation of the Assyrian Exile took place after the destruction of the northern kingdom and its capital Samaria in 722 B.C. after a three-year siege (2 Kings 17:1-6). It was Shalmaneser who began the siege, but his successor finally took the city. Assyrian inscrs. recording this event indicate that 27,290 people were taken captive and deported, some to the Assyrian province of Gozan in Mesopotamia and others to Media. At the same time, colonists from other Assyrian provinces were settled in Samaria and the neighboring areas to take the place of the Israelites deported. The intermarriage of these provincials and the Israelites who remained in the land resulted in the hybrid Samaritans of later Biblical history.

The exiles were transplanted mostly to depopulated areas in the provinces of Halah, Gozan, and Media, as well as in Nineveh, and apparently were permitted to live fairly normal lives. The only record of them is contained in the book of Tobit, which indicates that some of the captives were loyal to Yahweh. Others were submerged or amalgamated into the Assyrian population. The problem of the so-called Ten Lost Tribes has been greatly exaggerated. The Assyrian figure of 27,290 captives shows that only a fraction of the Israelite population was deported and that the tribes were not "lost" in the sense implied in the phrase the Ten Lost Tribes of Israel. The destruction of the northern kingdom of Israel was according to Hosea and Amos, due to the moral and spiritual degeneration of the country and not to the might of Assyrian military power, as great as that was.

3. The Babylonian Exile. The people of the southern kingdom were subjected to various deportations by the Babylonians under Nebuchadnezzar, who adopted the Assyrian policy toward conquered peoples. The first incident of this kind took place in 608 B.C. when, after the battle of Carchemish, Nebuchadnezzar advanced to Jerusalem. He spared King Jehoiakim who had rebelled against him, but carried off several of the princes of Judah, among whom were Daniel, Shadrach, Meshach, and Abednego (Dan 1:1-7).

Jeremiah mentions three deportations (Jer 52:28-30). The first of these took place in 597 B.C. after another conquest of Jerusalem by Nebuchadnezzar (2 Kings 24:1-16). The Babylonian monarch had come to Jerusalem to punish King Jehoiakim for renouncing allegiance to Babylonia, but before the siege of the city ended, the king's son Jehoiachin had succeeded to the throne of his father. Nebuchadnezzar ordered the exile of Jehoiachin and his mother along with the most distinguished men of the country, together with the treasures of the Temple and the royal palace. Among the captives was the prophet Ezekiel, who dates the chronology of his book according to the date of this captivity. Evidence of this phase of the Exile have been found by German archeologists in the form of cuneiform tablets that list among the people receiving rations of grain, "Yakin (Jehoiachin), king of Judah," and five sons of Jehoiachin, together with other Hebrews.

The second deportation recorded by Jeremiah took place eleven years after the first. In 586 B.C., Zedekiah, who was placed on the throne by Nebuchadnezzar to succeed Jehoiachin, took an oath of fealty to the Babylonian monarch (Ezek 17:13). He soon began to give evidence of disloyalty to Nebuchadnezzar who again took action against the Hebrews. The Babylonian monarch set up headquarters at Riblah on the Orontes from which he directed the campaign against Jerusalem. The siege of the city lasted from 10 January 587 B.C. to 9 July 586 B.C. when the Babylonians were able to breach the city wall built in the days of Hezekiah (2 Chron 32:5). The flight from the city by Zedekiah and his entourage was intercepted, and he was brought to Nebuchadnezzar at Riblah. He was forced to witness the execution of his sons, after which his eyes were put out, and he was taken in chains to Babylon. Approximately eighty distinguished leaders of the Jerusalem community, among them the high priest Seraiah, were taken to Riblah and executed upon the orders of Nebuchadnezzar. On 1 August 586 B.C., Nebuzaradan, the captain of Nebuchadnezzar's bodyguard, commanded that the Temple be destroyed and its treasures further confiscated. The royal palace and the city were set on fire, and the survivors (except the poorest of the land) were taken into captivity (2 Kings 24:20-25:21; Jer 39:1-10).

This Babylonian tablet relates history of Nebuchadnezzar's invasion of Judah and the siege and surrender of Jerusalem ©*B.M.*

Nebuchadnezzar appointed Gedaliah, "who is over [Zedekiah's] house," to be governor of Judea. He exercised his office in Mizpah until he was treacherously assassinated by Ishmael, who had been a fugitive in Ammon and who objected to Gedaliah's apparent cooperation with the Babylonians. This new rebellion by the Israelites led to the third deportation recorded by Jeremiah, and took place in 581 B.C. Some of the remaining Hebrews of strong anti-Babylonian feeling fled to Egypt, forcing Jeremiah, who had been given special consideration by Nebuchadnezzar, to accompany them (2 Kings 25:22-26; Jer 40-44).

The statements in regard to the number of captives taken to Babylonia are confusing. Jeremiah gives the total carried away in his three deportations at 4,600 (Jer 52:28-30). How this figure was arrived at is not clear, but it could be a reference to only men of a specific class. The number of those exiled in 597 B.C. is said in this passage to be 3,023 instead of the 8,000 as in 2 Kings 24:15, 16. In this second reference, it is stated that in 597 B.C., 8,000 men including "men of valor, seven thousand, and the craftsmen and smiths, one thousand, all of them strong and fit for war," were exiled. William F. Albright suggests that the difference in these figures, "may be partly due to the fact that the latter was only a conjectural estimate, but may also be partly due to the heavy mortality of the starving and diseased captives during the long desert trek to Babylonia." George Adam Smith concludes on the basis of his consideration of all the figures involved that the captives did not exceed a total of 70,000 men, women, and children.

The captives were settled in southern Mesopotamia. Ezekiel mentions Tel-abib, "by the river Chebar" (Ezek 3:15), which was near Nippur, SE of Babylon. Other settlements are mentioned in Ezra 2:59 and Nehemiah 7:61, as well as Baruch 1:4 (cf. Ezek 1:3; Ezra 8:15, 17). Western Sem. proper names have been found in inscrs. from Nippur, confirming that some of the exiles were settled there.

Various reasons have been given for the location of the Exile in Babylonia. One opinion is that Israel, having originated in Babylonia, was sent back home by God as a husband sends his unsatisfactory wife back home. One opinion in the Haggadah is that Babylonia being a low-lying country becomes a symbol of the nether world from which Israel was rescued according to Hosea 13:14, "Shall I ransom them from the power of the nether world?" (Tr. of the Jewish Publication Society of America.) KJV has "I will ransom them from the power of the grave," whereas the RSV has, "Shall I ransom them from the power of Sheol?' Some believe that the northern and southern kingdoms were exiled to different places so that the two groups of captives might each derive some comfort from the other's misery.

The exiles were under royal protection and generally may be described as being under liberal interment rather than in a concentration camp. Some of the captives were used to supply labor for Nebuchadnezzar's many building projects, at least in the beginning of the Exile. Some of them enjoyed special prerogatives. They could own their homes and land, and enjoy the produce of their gardens (Jer 29:4-7; Ezek 8:1; 12:1-7). This would enable them to provide for some of their physical needs. Some of the captives apparently made an adequate living in other ways (Zech 6:9-11) and even entered business in the "city of merchants," as Babylon was known (Ezek 17:4, 12). The Heb. banking house of Murashu appears in the inscrs. The lists of captives receiving rations includes along with the Heb. names, the skilled trades in which some of them worked. Jeremiah 29:5-7 indicates that the Israelites were able to accumulate wealth. Many were so successful financially that they were able to send money to Jerusalem (Baruch 1:6, 7, 10) and when the exiles were given permission by Cyrus to return home, they refused because according to Josephus, "they were not willing to leave their possessions" (Jos. Antiq. XI.i. 3). This materialism on the part of some of the exiles led to conformity to the customs of the Babylonians and cultural assimilation. The tendency to assimilate included the adoption of the Aram. language and the acceptance of idolatry and participation in pagan ceremonies, even to sacrificing their sons on pagan altars (Ezek 14:3-5; 20:31).

Socially, the Israelites were apparently permitted complete freedom. They married, established families as they pleased, and kept in touch with Jerusalem (Jer 29:6). They met in assemblies and these occasionally were religious gatherings. It was prob. on such occasions that those faithful to Yahweh found the opportunity for worship and fellowship, and the renewal of faith that served to keep alive the vision of restoration to their homeland. It was at these gatherings that Ezekiel emphasized the promises of the return and revived their confidence in the law and the Prophets (Ps 137). The high festivals of the Israelites could not be observed in captivity, but there were observances of solemn prayer, fasting, and penance (Zech 7:3-5). Observances not dependent upon the high festivals related to the Temple were practiced. These included the observance of the Sabbath, the practice of circumcision, and praying with the face turned toward Jerusalem (1 Kings 8:48-50). It is in this context that Ezekiel's emphasis upon personal responsibility and individual morality and spirituality appears (Ezek 18:20-32; 36:26, 27).

This loyal core of Israelites surrounding Ezekiel formed the nucleus of those that returned to their homeland and provided the enthusiasm and leadership for the restoration. A harbinger of freedom to come for the Israelites was the release of King Jehoiachin from imprisonment. According to 2 Kings 25:27-30, he was freed by Evil-merodach, king of Babylonia in 560 B.C. Jeremiah had prophesied that the captivity would last seventy years (Jer 25:12; 29:10; cf. 2 Chron 36:21). One way, among others, that this period may be calculated is from the time of the destruction of the Temple in 586 B.C. to the time of its reconstruction and dedication in 516 B.C.

In 538 B.C., the Persian king Cyrus destroyed the Babylonian Empire and in the same year issued a decree permitting the Jews to return to their native land (Ezra 1:1-4; 6:3-5). These accounts of the edict of Cyrus have been confirmed by archeology. The response of the exiles to the possibility of return was not widespread. Some were prosperous and comfortable in exile, whereas conditions in the homeland were unsettled, the journey long, dangerous, and expensive. The first group to return, under the leadership of Zerubbabel, governor of Judea, and son of Jehoiachin's oldest son Shealtiel, laid the foundations of the new Temple. The second group of returnees, under the leadership of Ezra, scribe and reformer, set out for Jerusalem in the seventh year of Artaxerxes, 457 B.C. He gathered the people at the Ahava River, a group of about 1,800 men, or 5,500 to 6,000 men and women besides 38 Levites and 220 servants of the Temple from Casiphia (Ezra 8). Then in 444 B.C. came Nehemiah, cupbearer to Artaxerxes and later governor of Judea, to rebuild the wall of Jerusalem (Neh 1-13). Ezra and Nehemiah, invested with royal power, were able in spite of great difficulties to establish the postexilic Jewish community. It was in this period that an "Israelite" came to be called a "Jew," a contraction of "Judah." From the list given in Nehemiah 7:5-73, it appears that the whole Jewish community numbered 42,360 men, or 125,000 people.

The skepticism with which the Biblical accounts concerning the Exile were regarded by some scholars has been dispelled by archeological reconstruction of the Near E. The position of C. C. Torrey, S. A. Cook, G. Holscher, W. A. Irwin et al. that there never occurred a Babylonian Exile and consequently no return to Judah, not only denied the validity of the Biblical historical narratives but also the prophetic Messianism that was based in large measure upon these events. Such Biblical books as Ezekiel, Jeremiah, Ezra, and Nehemiah were, according to this view, largely a fabrication of later writers. All this has changed. Archeological discoveries, such as the Lachish Ostraca and explorations in the areas concerned, have revealed evidence for the destruction of the cities of Judah by the Babylonians at the time required by Biblical chronology. The newly discovered royal archives of Nebuchadnezzar supplement the evidence from Judah in giving support to the credibility of the Biblical history.

4. The effects of the Exile. The cause of the Exile was apostasy from God and His covenant.

Map showing locale of THE EXILES (in Assyria and Babylonia) in relation to Jerusalem.

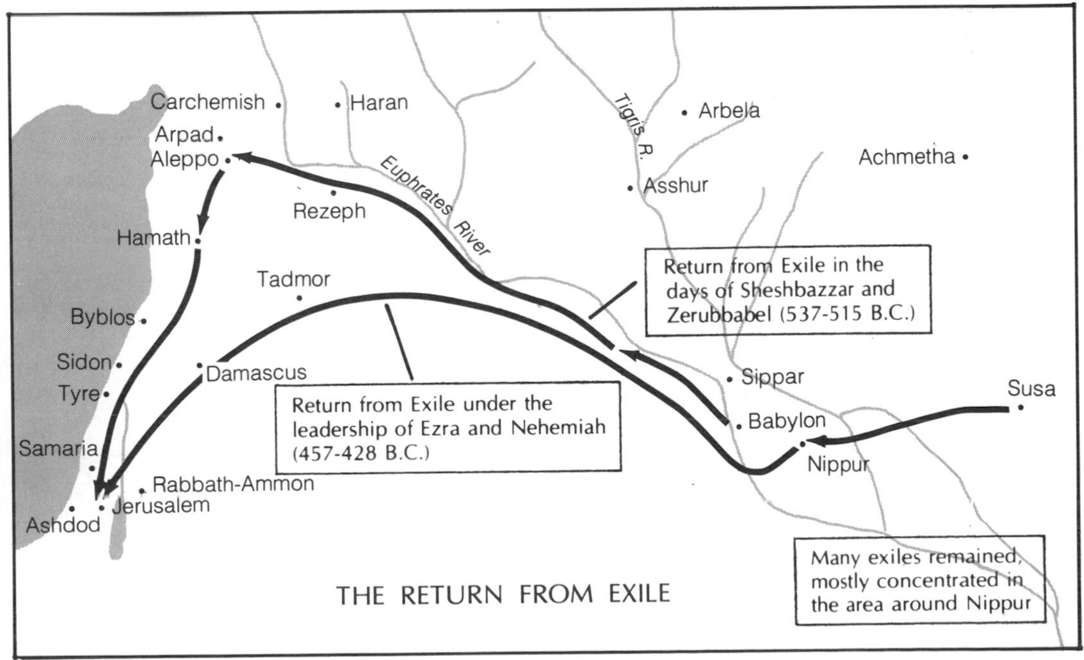

The Israelites had consistently rejected the message of the prophets and persistently continued in their sin and idolatry. The prophets constantly warned the Israelites against trusting in their own wisdom and power. The Exile was interpreted by the prophets as divine judgment that would eventuate in restoration and a revelation of God's eternal love for Israel (Isa 54:9, 10; Jer 31:3-6). It is the primary historical incident upon which Biblical Messianism is based. Among the results of the Exile for Israel was a more profound comprehension of the law of Moses and the Prophets as important for the Jews as a people. There came also a clearer grasp of the universality and sovereignty of God; that Yahweh is one and there is no god beside Him. This faith remained so unshakable that it withstood the influence and fascination of Gr. culture in spite of Hellenism's effects upon some other areas of Judaism and the rest of the Mediterranean world.

BIBLIOGRAPHY. G. A. Barton, *Archaeology and the Bible* (1937), 463-485; G. E. Wright, *Biblical Archaeology* (1960), 108-127; J. Gray, *Archaeology and the OT World* (1962), 180-198; W. F. Albright, *The Biblical Period from Abraham to Ezra* (1963), 81-89.

A. C. SCHULTZ

EXISTENTIALISM. *See* BIBLICAL CRITICISM.

EXODUS, THE ĕk' sə dəs (Gr. ἔξοδος, *a going forth*). The occasion upon which the Hebrews left Egypt under Moses.

I. ROUTE

A. The main Biblical data. The main starting point of the Israelites is given as Rameses (Exod 12:37; Num 33:5), from which was named the "land of Rameses" (Gen 47:11), identical at least in part with Goshen (q.v.; cf. Gen 47:6). Thence, they moved to Succoth (*see* PITHOM) for their first camp (Num 33:5; implied by Exod 12:37 plus 13:20; cf. phrasing of Num 33:6), and thereafter to Etham—first time—on the edge of the wilderness (Exod 13:20; Num 33:6).

Then the Hebrews were instructed to turn back from the wilderness-edge (i.e., instead of continuing eastward), so that the Pharaoh might be taught a sharp lesson in seeking to subdue them (Exod 14:1-4). Having so turned, their next camp was between Migdol and the sea (Exod 14:2, the sea later qualified in 15:22 as *yam-suph*, "sea of reeds," the Red Sea of the Eng. VSS). This was also before Pi-ha-hiroth and Baal-zephon, by the sea (14:2, 9; Num 33:7). Having proceeded from W to E without encountering a "sea" previously, they would "turn back" either northward or southward somewhat, from the wilderness edge, and so come to a "sea" and the neighborhood of the three places named. In the Pharaoh's eyes, they were "entangled in the land," shut in (to Egypt) by the wilderness.

At this juncture came the crossing through the wind-divided waters of the "sea" (Exod 14:21ff.), which brought the Israelites back eastward into the wilderness of Shur (15:22) with waterless travel for three days to Marah. Significantly, this wilderness is identified as that of Etham (Num 33:8)—so, coming here a second time, the Hebrews had made a circuit. Schematically, their route would appear as follows (A: turning N; B: turning S):—

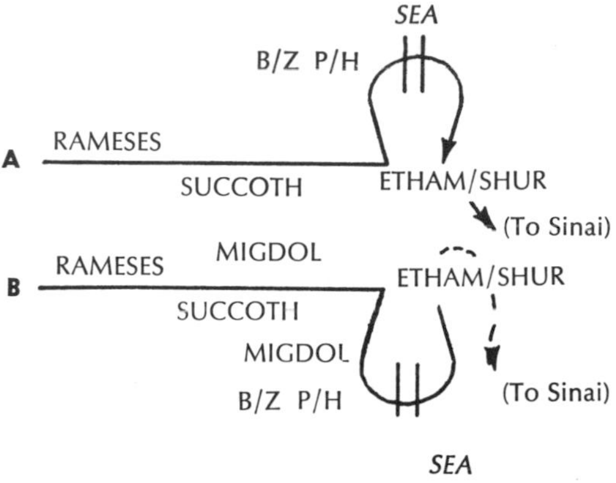

They were explicitly kept away from the way of the land of the Philistines, the direct Egypt-to-Gaza route near the Mediterranean coast, and so would have to take a more southerly route within the Sinai peninsula. On this consideration, pattern A is more meaningful than B, as A permits the Hebrews simply to continue in a southeasterly direction for Sinai, while B would land them back on the forbidden N coast route unless they further performed a sharp U-turn (not reflected by the narratives) to bring them back S again for Sinai.

B. Topographical background evidence. The starting point, Rameses, would seem beyond any reasonable doubt to have been located either at Tanis/Zoan or near Qantir 27 km. (seventeen m.) SSW. Although Tanis has hitherto been the more popular identification, Qantir would appear to be preferable on both archeological and topographical grounds. None of the quantity of Ramesside monuments at Tanis were actually found in place—all had been reused by later kings who appear to have brought them as quarry-material from elsewhere. At Qantir, evidence of palaces, the houses of high officials, temples and houses for military personnel has been found of a kind that is clearly not brought from elsewhere or (like a well of Ramses II) is definitely *in situ*. Geographically, Raamses (Egyp. Pi-Ramessē) in Egyp. documents stood on the "Waters of Ra" in a fertile district—true of Qantir, but not of Tanis. *See* RAAMSES (city). Therefore, with a high degree of probability, one may place Rameses as the starting point of the Exodus in the district of Qantir-Khatana. This fits well with the general location of the land of Goshen which was also in some measure the

The northern sector of the Wilderness of Zin, typical of the area through which the Israelites wandered. ©*Wm. White, Jr.*

"land of Rameses" (Gen 47:6, 11). This latter phrase itself corresponds in some degree to the Egyp. name of Rameses, namely Pi-Ramessē, "Estate/domain [not merely 'house'] of Ramses"—i.e., to the whole territory attached to the king's city, itself named after him. Among other tasks unspecified, the Hebrews in this area (GOSHEN, q.v.) had to labor on the building of both Raamses and Pithom (Exod 1:11) and so it seems in order to infer that Pithom should also be within reach of Goshen and Raamses. Pithom is most prob. to be sought in the Wadi Tumilatat either Tell el Maskhuta (with Succoth) or westward therefrom at Tell el Rotab (*see* PITHOM). The latter possibility in particular would place Pithom quite near the S end of Goshen, while Raamses at Qantir would be at its N end, Goshen itself extending along the territory on the E of the Waters of Ra (Bubastite-Pelusiac, the eastern arm of the Nile). A location of Raamses at Tanis rather more N would perhaps be too far N to fit these requirements, and would extend the first day's march of the Heb. multitude to up to fifty m., an unconvincingly high figure.

From a Raamses at Qantir, two routes lay before the Hebrews, a fact perhaps reflected by an inscr. of an earlier epoch (12th dynasty) from near Qantir and mentioning the settlement Ro-waty, "Mouth of the Two Roads," i.e., the place where these roads diverged: text in S. Adam, Annales du Service des Antiquités de l' Egypte, LVI (1959), 216, 223 and pl. 9; cf. Kees, Mitteilungen, Deutschen Archäol. Instituts, Kairo, XVIII (1962), 1-13, and van Seters, *The Hyksos* (1966), 141. The first road thence was the main route to Pal. going NE to Qantara and ancient Sile (Tjaru) and so by the way of the land of the Philistines to Gaza and Canaan, but this was forbidden to the Hebrews (Exod 13:17). The second way was to go SE from the Qantir district across uncultivated semi-desert terrain that extended between the main Pal. route in the N and the Wadi Tumilat on the S (cf. frontispiece map of Baedeker's *Egypt*, for the terrain). This would bring the Hebrews to Succoth (Tell el Maskhuta) near modern Ismailia, and then eastward into the wilderness proper and to Sinai. This was the "way of the wilderness" expressly taken by the Hebrews (13:18), and so too by two Egyp. slaves pursued from the Delta-residence to Succoth and beyond, in Papyrus Anastasi V, cf. ANET, 259b. Hebrew Succoth corresponds well to Egyp. Tjeku; at Tell el Maskhuta, this would make a first day's march of some twenty or so m. from just E of Qantir as Raamses.

The second day's march was perhaps briefer (fifteen to eighteen m.?), prob. ENE toward the desert now E of the Suez Canal and the El Gisr ridge, and so to the wilderness proper, named Etham or Shur. Etham is a name that lacks any convincing identification in the Egyp. texts. It can hardly be Egyp. *khetem* (*ḫtm*) "fort," because Heb. *'aleph*-breathing is a different sound, much weaker than Egyp. *ḫ*. Nor is it the *'Idm* of Papyrus Anastasi VI, 55 (ANET, 259a), as Heb. *t* appears in Egyp. as *t*, not *d*. *'Idm* is most likely Edom. However, within the Biblical data, the tacit equation of Etham with Shur (15:22 plus Num 33:8) is a useful indication. For the wilderness of Shur was also on the main routes into Egypt from Pal., i.e., on that from Gaza, El-'Arish and via Qantara into Egypt, and that which branched off S to pass into Egypt via Ismailia and Wadi Tumilat. (*See* Gen 25:18; 1 Sam 15:7; and esp. 27:8.) Thus, the wilderness of Shur/Etham (Etham, its western edges?) as extending N-S from the Mediterranean to about the latitude of Lake Timsah by Ismailia, and W-E from about the El Gisr ridge (and Suez Canal) perhaps much of the way toward El-'Arish and the "Brook of Egypt." This means that when the Israelites doubled back from the wilderness, went along by the "sea" and crossed it only to return to this same wilderness, they more prob. did so northwards from Ismailia rather than from S of it, as they thereafter went on to Sinai (scheme A, above, rather than B).

Therefore, it is possible to suggest that when the Hebrews "turned back" (Exod 14:2) from Etham, they did so by going back NNW, then N (and not SSW and S, toward Suez). If so, then Migdol, Pi-ha-hiroth and Baal-zephon would be nearer to Qantara in the N than to Suez in the S. The *yam-suph* would not be the Red Sea of today; this is no problem, as the Heb. term corresponds to Egyp. *tjuf*, "papyrus," and should here be rendered "sea of reeds" (*see* RED SEA). The Sea of Reeds would appear to be water bordered by reed-swamps in which papyrus might grow; this would fit in with the SE edges of Lake Menzaleh and the adjoining lakes that once occupied the line of the Suez Canal (Lake Ballah and southward). Thus, the Israelites prob. went N as far as the neighborhood of Lake Ballah (or its pre-Canal equivalent). If Baal-zephon is the later Tahpanhes (and Gr. *Daphnai*) as is quite likely, its location at Tell Defenneh (barely fourteen km. or eight and a half m. from Qantara) would be compatible with the situation of the Hebrews. The best-attested occupation of Tell Defenneh is later (26th dynasty, 7th-6th centuries, B.C.), but Ramesside-period remains were found there. A later Phoen. papyrus speaks of "Baal-zephon and all the gods of Tahpanhes" (N. Aimé-Giron, Annales du Service des Antiquités de l'Égypte, XL [1941], 433ff.). Migdol (q.v.) would then be an Egyp. fort on the desert land W of Lake Ballah, so far unidentified, and could not be the Migdol of the prophets, nearly thirty km. (eighteen m.) NE of Qantara, far out on the wrong side of the "sea." The name is a common Sem. word for "fort," "watchtower," taken over by the Egyptians in the New Kingdom, and there was a plurality of such places.

Pi-ha-hiroth cannot be closely identified geographically at present, but may be attested in Egyp. sources as Pa-ḥir, "the Ḥir-waters" (a canal or lake). In Papyrus Anastasi III, 2:9, Pa-ḥir is set in parallel with Shihor (old Pelusiac Nile-arm), producing natron and (3:4) flax (ANET, 471, as "Her canal"). It therefore had salt marshes and fresh water lands in common with the Sea of Reeds, and was prob. near Shihor and *yam-suph* as was true of Heb. Pi-ha-hiroth. In this latter name, Pi may be Heb. "mouth" (cf. Egyp. *ro*) for "mouth of the Hiroth (canal?)," or else it might conceivably stand for Egyp. Pi(r), "house/estate," as in Pithom, Pi-Beseth, hence "domain of the Ḥiroth." The name could appear simply as Ḥiroth (Num 33:8; no emendation needed). For the relation of Heb. Ḥiroth to Egyp. Ḥir, cf. that of Heb. Succoth to Egyp. Tjeku. Pa-hir had a royal temple vineyard under Sethos I (Spiegelberg, in *Zeitschrift für Aegyptische Sprache,* LVIII [1923], 28; VI, 31). His successor Ramses II even had a daughter named Hent-pa-ḥir ('Mistress of Pa-hir'), cf. Lefebvre, *Annales du Service des Antiquités de l'Égypte,* XIII (1914), 202:XXIII. (The Pi-Qerehet of Naville, the Pi-Hathor of Clédat, and the *Hr* and *Phrt* canals of Papyrus Anastasi III, 2:7 are all unacceptable as equivalents of Pi-ha-hiroth on philological grounds, while the Pa-ḥrn or Pa-ḥrm of Wadi Tumilat is too far S and too close to Succoth to fit the Exodus narrative.) With the relation of Pi-ha-hiroth to Baal-zephon (Exod 14:2), one may conceivably compare the occurrence of the [Waters . . *ḥ* . .] of Baal in Pap. Anastasi III, 2:8, shortly before its first mention of Pa-ḥir.

One may suggest that the famous crossing of the waters took place somewhere in the region of the present Lake Ballah; the phenomenon of the winds and waters is not unknown in modern times (cf. Ali Shafei, *Bulletin de la Société royale de Géographie d'Égypte,* XXI [1946], 278 and figs. 10, 11). Going on SE and S from such a crossing, the Hebrews under Moses would then find themselves back in the wilderness of Shur and Etham. Three days later (or, on the third day?) they reached Marah, which on such a time scale might well

The famous Israel Tablet of Pharaoh Merneptah mentioning the departure of the Israelites from Egypt.

Ramses II before Amon-Re, on a thirteenth century stela found at Beth-shan ©*U.M.P.*

Detail of the name "Israel" from Stela of Merneptah. ©*C.M.*

be as far S as the traditional 'Ayun Musa, some nine m. SE of Suez, on the Sinai side of the Gulf.

Naturally, the foregoing suggestion of a possible route of the Exodus remains in some degree tentative, but it will serve to show how well the extant Biblical data fits into the background setting as they stand; one has no need of an appeal to documentary hypotheses to solve the problem, like that offered in a well-documented study by Cazelles in RB, LXII (1955), 321-364.

II. Date

A. Introduction. During the later 19th cent. and the first half of this cent., many dates have been suggested for the Heb. Exodus from Egypt. Two in particular have enjoyed some prominence. An "early" date for the Exodus placed that event in the mid-18th dynasty under Amenophis II c. 1440 B.C., reckoning his predecessor Thutmose III as pharaoh of the oppression; the initial conquest of Canaan under Joshua then came c. 1400 B.C. (*temp.* Amenophis III). The main basis of this scheme was a linear interpretation of the 480 years between the Exodus and Solomon's Temple (1 Kings 6:1), and largely so for the data on the intervening period in Joshua-Judges, etc. A "late" date for the Exodus commonly placed it in the 19th dynasty under Merneptah, with Ramses II as pharaoh of the oppression; the conquest of Pal. would then begin c. 1200 B.C. or later. The starting point was the name of Rameses (Gen 47:11; Exod 1:11). However, neither view today seems really satisfactory; instead, one may suggest an intermediate solution, covering most of the data. No totally complete solution is yet possible, because of the lack of fully adequate data. Other famous events of ancient Near Eastern history are equally difficult to date definitively for much the same reason, so the Biblical student is in good company here.

B. The Egyptian data and background. 1. *Specific OT data.* The Exodus was from Egypt; the OT accounts do not name the Egyp. kings involved with the Hebrews, but merely refer to them as "Pharaoh." One more specific datum is the names of the "store-cities" in Exodus 1:11, Pithom and Raamses. If these can be located, archeological light on their history would help, and in the second case the very name Raamses is that used by some eleven to thirteen kings of Egypt (*see* RAMSES, King). Of these kings, Ramses III to XI (and still later, Ramses-Psusennes) can be eliminated on date: all reigned later than c. 1200 B.C. and too late for any reasonable date for the Exodus. They are also later than the Israel stela, attesting the presence of Israel in Pal. in the late 13th cent. B.C. (see below), and this also excludes Ramses-Siptah. Ramses I reigned only sixteen months, so one is left only with Ramses II. He reigned sixty-six years and did build and adorn towns and temples named after himself, and is the only likely candidate to be the king reflected in the Heb. Raamses. However, this raises the question of the status of his name at Raamses. If this town can be located, was he really its builder, or did he (as some have suggested) merely re-name an earlier foundation? (Assuming also that the "second" name came into Heb. tradition, if not at the Exodus then much later on.)

Pithom (q.v.) lay somewhere in the Wadi Tumilat, in the SE Delta. There are two possible sites: Tell el Maskhuta and Tell el Rotab. Whichever is correct, the result archeologically is the same. Both chance finds and regular excavations have produced virtually nothing before the 19th dynasty at either site; see the lists in Porter & Moss, *Topographical Bibliography of Ancient Egyptian Hieroglyphic Texts, Reliefs and Paintings,* IV (1934), 53-55. Impressive monuments of Ramses II and later times came from both sites. Hence, it would be more natural for the Hebrews to be engaged on work at Pithom (whichever be its site) under Ramses II when major monuments were installed there, than under the 18th dynasty kings who appear to have manifested almost no interest in the Wadi Tumilat region (Porter & Moss, op. cit., IV, 53, have only some usurped traces at Gebel Hassa).

The situation for Raamses is similar. The two possible sites are either Tanis or Qantir, with archeological and geographical data increasingly favoring the latter, as noted above (ROUTE). Again, the remains recovered from both locations tell a similar story. Middle Kingdom and Hyksos-age relics are followed by nothing else until the mass of monuments of the 19th and 20th Ramesside dynasties, see again Porter & Moss, op. cit., IV, 13-26 (Tanis) and 9, 10, 26, 27 (Qantir area, plus "Horbeit" monuments really from Qantir, cf. L. Habachi, Annales du Service des Antiquités de l'Égypte, LII [1954], 514-526). So many of the Ramesside works are original (usurpations being from the Middle Kingdom) that one cannot support the theory that Ramses II had merely usurped those of the 18th dynasty, for at neither Tanis nor Qantir was there anything of consequence from that epoch for him to usurp. It would appear that Sethos I began the new residence city, but that Ramses II took it over and by his vast works made it his own in fact as well as name. The appellation of "store-cities" applied to Pithom and Raamses was prob. very apposite. Each stood on a main route from Egypt to Pal., and at Raamses the "Horbeit" stelae (so miscalled) show the existence there of military contingents, requiring arsenals and stores. Raamses was at once a summer residence, a base for military campaigns, and an administrative center alongside Memphis and Thebes.

In relation to Pithom and Raamses, there is good reason to place the Exodus no earlier than the early years of Ramses II, i.e., after either 1304 or 1290 B.C., the two alternative dates for that king's accession. The term "land

The fallen statue of Rameses II now standing in the Temple at Luxor. He may have been either the pharaoh of the Oppression or of the Exodus. ©*M.P.S.*

of Rameses" (Gen 47:11) is not an anachronism, because it is not put into the mouth of either Joseph or his pharaoh but is the phrase of the later *narrator*—a point frequently overlooked. If that narrator were a Moses in the 13th cent. B.C., the phrase in question would be entirely appropriate, a definition of Goshen in terms meaningful to his contemporaries. The use of the term "pharaoh" (q.v.) for the king, without personal name appended, is current usage precisely in the Ramesside age and soon thereafter; but from the 22nd dynasty onward, the usage of Pharaoh plus personal name (cf. Pharaoh Necho) came increasingly into fashion.

2. *Other external data.* The other limiting datum comes from outside the OT, from Egypt itself; the so-called Israel stela (cf. ANET, 376-378 and refs.). This inscr. is dated to the 5th year of Merneptah, successor of Ramses II, i.e., to either 1234 or 1220 B.C. (depending on the latter's date). Its main theme is to commemorate Merneptah's great victory in smashing a massive Libyan invasion of Egypt, but at the end he also claimed that the Hittites were pacified, Canaan purged, Ascalon conquered, Gezer held, Yenoam made as if non-existent, Israel destroyed as without seed (either grain or offspring), and Pal. (Khuru) is like a widow. These names are specific and concrete, not just vague boasts, and would seem clearly to place Israel squarely in W Pal. [by Merenptah's 5th year]. These names would reflect a brief Palestinian campaign of Merneptah before his Libyan war. These apparently clear inferences and the data on which they are based have been doubted by some, but doubts of Merneptah's veracity can be discounted in the light of a less famous monument. On a stela in the temple of Amada in Nubia, Merneptah has a specially elaborate titulary, calling himself in parallel clauses "Binder of Gezer" and "seizer of the Libyans." Again, Gezer should reflect a specific event. "Seizer of Libya" is a clear allusion to Merneptah's Libyan victory, and so one may legitimately expect an equally real exploit to appear in the parallel clause—here, the capture of Gezer in Pal., and so a campaign there in the course of which the Egyp. forces happened to brush with some Israelites, these already being in W Pal.

Occasionally, scepticism has been expressed as to whether the name on the Israel stela is actually Israel and not someone (or place) else, e.g., Jezreel, with Eissfeldt, CAH², II, ch. XXVIa (*Palestine in Time of 19th Dynasty* [1965], 14). Such doubts are totally unjustified, and such a reading is highly improbable in view of the close correspondence to the Egyp. term and the Heb. for "Israel" (cf. Kitchen, *Tyndale Bulletin,* XVII [1966], 90-92, and *Ancient Orient and Old Testament* [1966], 59, note 12). Hence, one may suggest that the initial phase of the conquest under Joshua could not well have begun any later than shortly before 1234 or 1220 B.C. Thus, the Exodus, forty years of wilderness sojourn and beginning of the conquest is best located on the evidence so far within the seventy years between 1304-1234 B.C. or 1290-1220 B.C.

Some further indirect confirmation of this result may perhaps be drawn from reliefs of Ramses II as Luxor temple at Thebes, illustrating a campaign in Moab. He records the capture of "*Bwtrt* in the land of Moab" (? later Raba-Batora), and of *Daibon* (i.e., Dibon of Mesha-stela fame). See Kitchen, JEA, L (1964), 47-70, esp. 50, 53, 55, 63-67, 69, 70. It is far easier to assume that Ramses II raided Moab before the Hebrews entered that area, than to envisage the pharaoh's forces bursting into a district (e.g., Dibon northwards already populated by Israelite tribes [Reuben, Gad, Manasseh], cf. Num 21:21ff., etc.). The OT has no trace of such an event, nor does Ramses mention Israelites (as his son did, later) along with Moab and Seir. As the tradition of "all Israel" is both ancient and persistent (cf. Kitchen, *Tyndale Bulletin,* XVII [1966], 85-88), it is hard to justify the scepticism of Giveon (*Fourth World Congress of Jewish Studies, Papers,* I [1967], 194) concerning the application of the term "Israel" to the Trans-jordanian tribes, although the Egyptians certainly could have used more generalized or traditional terms like Shasu or Asiatic.

C. Exodus and conquest. 1. *Wilderness sojourn.* For the travels of Israel in the wilderness, there exists only the Biblical account. There seems no warrant for doubting the reality of the forty years, first because it is made up of lesser specific amounts (e.g., thirty-eight years in Deut 2:14, plus short spans in Num, passim, cf. NBD 215), and secondly because the purpose of this period was expressly to allow a new generation to grow up in place of the one that had rebelled (Num 14:21-23; 32:9-13; Deut 2:14). So, forty years before the lowest possible date for Joshua's initial campaigns gives 1274 or 1260 B.C. as the terminal date for the Exodus. Similarly, forty years below the highest possible date for the Exodus gives 1264 or 1250 B.C. as the highest date for Joshua's opening campaigns. With Ramses II acceding in 1304, the Exodus would fall within c. 1304-1274 and initial conquest c. 1264-1234 B.C. On the 1290 date for Ramses II, the Exodus would fall within c. 1290-1260 and the conquest begin within c. 1250-1220 B.C. The generalized round figures of c. 1280 B.C. for the Exodus and c. 1240 B.C. for the beginning of Joshua's wars would not be too far out in either case.

2. *Data in Palestine.* With these results one may correlate the Palestinian evidence. In Trans-Jordan, the early Iron-age kingdoms of Edom and Moab seem to have become real entities politically, ringed with forts, from c.

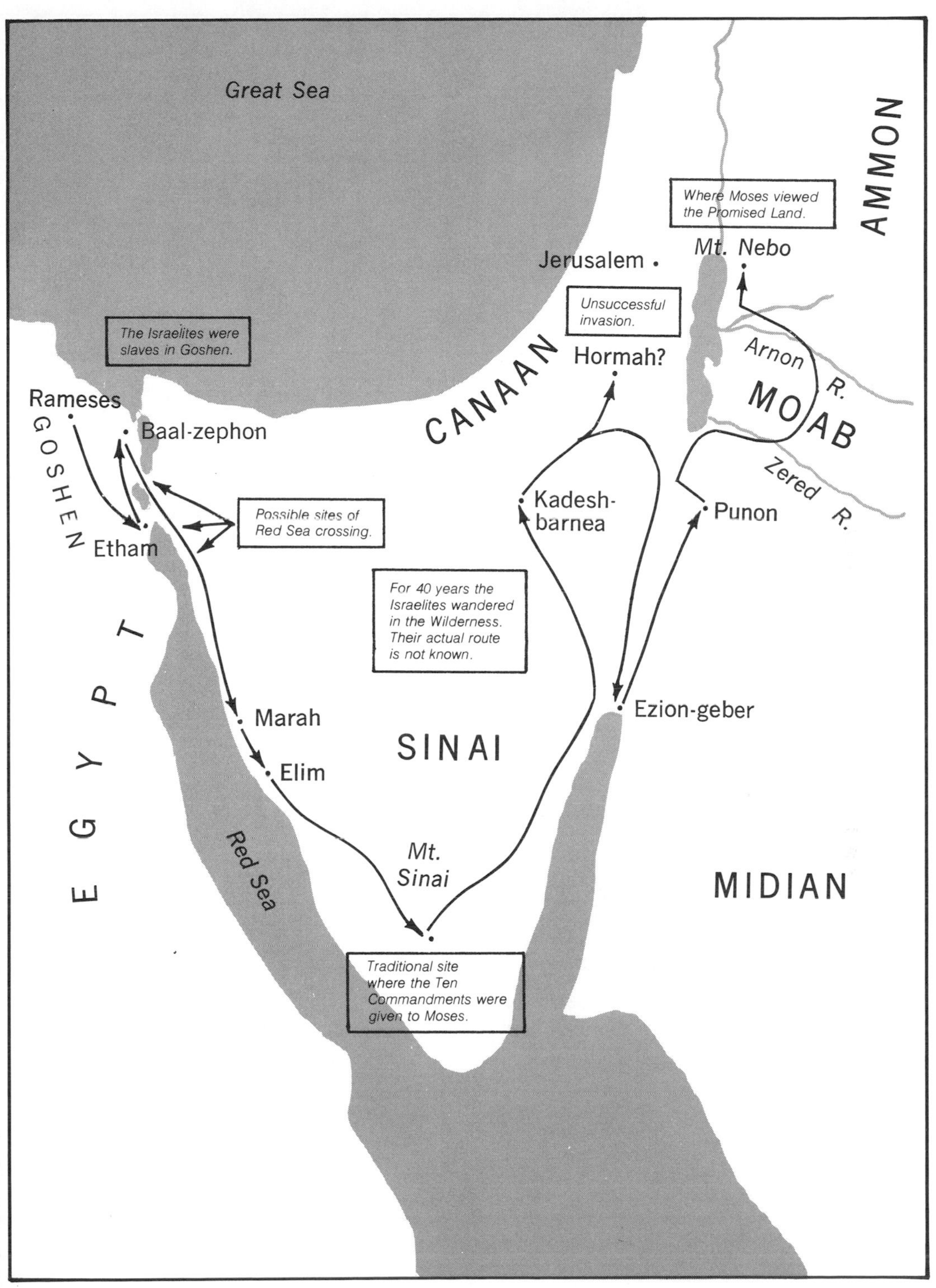
Great Sea
AMMON
Where Moses viewed the Promised Land.
Mt. Nebo
Jerusalem
Unsuccessful invasion.
Hormah?
The Israelites were slaves in Goshen.
CANAAN
Arnon R.
MOAB
Rameses
GOSHEN
Baal-zephon
Zered R.
Kadesh-barnea
Punon
Possible sites of Red Sea crossing.
Etham
For 40 years the Israelites wandered in the Wilderness. Their actual route is not known.
EGYPT
Marah
Ezion-geber
SINAI
Elim
Red Sea
Mt. Sinai
MIDIAN
Traditional site where the Ten Commandments were given to Moses.

1300 B.C. onward, in contrast to the earlier conditions with the area mainly left to nomadic tribes and occasional settlements on some routes (cf. N. Glueck, *Other Side of the Jordan* [1940], and further references, etc., in Kitchen, *Ancient Orient and Old Testament*, pp. 43, note 40 and 61 note 16). Thus, for Edom and Moab to oppose Israel (Num 20:14-21; Judg 11:17), one would prefer the Hebrew passage of Trans-Jordan to occur after c. 1300 B.C.

In W Pal., the evidence for several sites would seem to agree with this result. This is so at Tell Beit Mirsim (? Debir), Lachish (Tell ed-Duweir), Bethel (Beitin), Tell el Hesi, and esp. Hazor (Tell el Qedah). The final destructions at Canaanite Debir and Lachish could represent the exploits of Caleb after Joshua's campaigning. An important point is the change of culture visible when some of these sites were reoccupied (refs., Kitchen, op. cit., 66/68 notes 37, 45). In this picture, only Ai and Jericho appear to cause real difficulty. But there is no proof that Et Tell (destroyed c. 2400 B.C.) is Ai rather than Beth-Aven (see Grintz, *Biblica*, XLII [1961], 201-216), and the real Late Bronze Age Ai may yet await discovery. At Jericho, heavy denudation of the long-unoccupied mound has apparently destroyed nearly all of the Late Bronze levels, along with much of the Middle Bronze. Hence, the Palestinian evidence is incomplete but is not incompatible with the other data.

D. Wider aspects. The 430 years between Jacob's entering Egypt and the date of the Exodus (Exod 12:37; 12:41 eliminates the LXX 215 years); if it be reckoned back from roughly 1280 B.C., would set Joseph and Jacob at c. 1700 B.C., in the period of the late 13th dynasty leading into the Hyksos period. Such a date would be feasible on independent grounds (patriarchs with early 2nd millennium background; Egyp. conditions then). The 480 years of 1 Kings 6:1 does not so obviously correspond with the 300 or more years from about 1280 to c. 970 B.C. However, 480 is not *the* Biblical figure, but only one Biblical datum alongside others. Adding up the available figures in Exodus to 1 Kings gives not 480 but 553 years plus three unknown amounts, whereas David's genealogy in the Book of Ruth seems short for the period involved. The genealogy of Zadok the high priest (1 Chron 6:3-8) of ten generations would fit well into the roughly 300 years here invisaged. A short genealogy like David's may be selective. A larger total like the 553 years may contain partly overlapping items (e.g., judgeships), and the 480 be a portion of it. It is instructive to compare from Egypt the 500-odd years of Dynasties 13 to 17 that are known to fit into the 240 years or so between the 12th dynasty (ended 1786 B.C.) and the early years of the 18th dynasty (c. 1550 B.C.); only Judges 11:16 does not readily fit into the picture here suggested, but it requires further study.

Attempts to utilize references to the Habiru have proved rather sterile, because the term is too wide, ranging in ancient sources from c. 1800 to 1150 B.C., over the whole area of Mesopotamia, Asia Minor, Syria-Palestine and Egypt; and conditions in the Amarna tablets do not correspond with those in the Book of Joshua, and so throw no direct light on the conquest period.

BIBLIOGRAPHY. On specific points, see above in text. An outline review of older views will be found in C. de Wit, *The Date and Route of the Exodus* (1960). For a compact but fully-documented treatment of the date of the Exodus, see K. A. Kitchen, *Ancient Orient and Old Testament* (1966), 57-75.

K. A. KITCHEN

EXODUS, BOOK OF. The second book of the Bible, often called "The Second Book of Moses," as in Luther's VS and the KJV.

I. General features
  1. Name
  2. Relation to the rest of the Pentateuch
  3. Unity and authorship
  4. General structure
  5. Principal emphasis
II. Historical background
III. Contents
IV. Miracles
V. The legal sections of Exodus
  1. General remarks
  2. Relation to the law codes of other nations
  3. The originality of the laws
  4. Types of law
  5. Survey of the legal sections
  6. Laws given before Sinai
  7. The Decalogue
  8. The covenant code
  9. Regulations for the Tabernacle and for the establishment of the priesthood
  10. The laws of Exodus 34
  11. The Sabbath
VI. The higher criticism of Exodus
VII. Special problems
  1. The number in Jacob's family who went down to Egypt
  2. The new king who did not know Joseph
  3. The names of the cities Pithom and Raamses
  4. The number of Hebrew midwives
  5. The story of Moses in the bulrushes
  6. Moses' name
  7. Reuel (Jethro)
  8. "I AM WHO I AM"
  9. Borrowing from the Egyptians

I. GENERAL FEATURES

1. Name. In the Heb. Bible, this book, as the other books of the Pentateuch, takes its name from its opening words ואלה שמות, "These are the names of," or more briefly שמות

"names of," since it begins with the names of the patriarchs who went down into Egypt. The Eng. designation is taken from the LXX title, Ἔξοδος, "departure" (from Egypt), which accurately describes the first thirteen chs. of the book.

2. Relation to the rest of the Pentateuch. The narrative of Exodus is closely connected with that of Genesis, for it carries forward the history of the descendants of the patriarchs from the point where it ended in Genesis 50, even though considerable time intervened between the death of Joseph and the first events of Exodus (1:7ff.), during which the people of Israel had been brought into a position of servitude. After describing the departure from Egypt, the book tells of the giving of the law and the building of the Tabernacle. The rules for sacrifice that naturally follow make up the first part of Leviticus. Exodus is not so much an independent book, as a somewhat arbitrarily delimited portion of the section of the Pentateuch comprised in its middle three books, and the division between Exodus and Leviticus is similar to that between 1 and 2 Samuel or between 1 and 2 Kings.

3. Unity and authorship. From a very early time, Jewish tradition held that the entire book was written by Moses. Only within the last two centuries has any considerable number of writers questioned this origin, but lately it has frequently been denied, as a result of the spread of the critical theories which, beginning with Genesis, were extended to the Pentateuch, and today are widely taught (*see* section VI).

Mosaic responsibility for the contents of the book is strongly indicated. Twice the book states that God told Moses to write (17:14; 34:27), and once it says that Moses wrote (24:4). Christ declared that Moses wrote (John 5:46, 47), and He ascribed Exodus 20:12 and 21:17 to Moses in Mark 7:10. In Mark 12:26 Jesus referred to "the book of Moses." Although this latter usage does not in itself prove that Christ considered that Moses had written the entire book, it fits the common tradition, and clearly affirms the Savior's regard for the historical accuracy and inspiration of Exodus 3.

4. General structure. The book is almost equally divided between narrative and legal sections. The first nineteen chs. are almost entirely narrative, except for short legal sections in 12:14-27, 42-49; 13:1-16. The remainder of the book is largely law, except for ch. 24, which describes the adoption of the covenant, and chs. 32-34, which describe the people's rebellion, Moses' intercession, and the renewal of the covenant.

5. Principal emphases. The book has four principal emphases. The first is redemption from the oppressive power of Pharaoh. This is greatly stressed as conditioning the mind of the Israelites for all future ages, and establishing a permanent debt of gratitude to the One who delivered them from bondage. It also typically stresses the great importance of redemption from slavery to sin in the life of every one who is redeemed through Christ, typified by the Passover lamb (12:1-14). The second great emphasis is the establishment of God's covenant (19:1-24:18). This covenant is based upon the fact that God having redeemed His people, has a right to expect their allegiance and loyalty. It refers back to the redemption upon which it is based, 19:4-6; 20:2; 22:21; 23:9, 15. The people whom He has redeemed have become His covenant people. He promises them protection and continuing oversight, whereas they, in turn, are obligated to obey His righteous law. The third great emphasis is law. Declaration of the covenant begins with the great summary of the moral law in the Ten Commandments, and then goes on to present various laws important for the lives of those who are to be a holy nation and a people peculiarly devoted to God. The fourth great emphasis is worship. This is touched on in ch. 3 (vv. 5, 6), and in the rules for the Passover in ch. 12, which would place vividly before the minds of succeeding generations the nature of God's redemption and every individual's need for personal participation. It is primarily handled in chs. 25-31, which describe the arrangements for the building of the Tabernacle and the setting apart of the priests, and in the account of the actual construction of the Tabernacle in chs. 35-40.

II. Historical background

As the principal features of historical background, geographic location, and chronology are treated in the article on the Exodus, the present article will include merely a brief resumé of some of these features, with a discussion of certain archeological and historical matters.

The first twelve chs. mainly describe occurrences in Egypt during the latter half of the 2nd millennium B.C. The events of the remaining chs. take place in the Sinaitic peninsula.

Although there is much in the book that reflects the background of Egyp. life and history, there is little that specifically indicates the precise time of the events. The king of Egypt is called either "Pharaoh" or "the king of Egypt." In no instance is an Egyp. monarch mentioned by name. The statement in 1:8 that a new king arose "who did not know Joseph," strongly suggests that the expulsion of the Hyksos occurred between the death of Joseph and the birth of Moses, and makes it easy to see why the new king would have an unfriendly attitude toward those whom he connected with the Hyksos, who were also Asiatics and who had held Egypt in unwelcome subjection for a considerable time.

The problem of dating the oppression and the Exodus has been much discussed, but the data is insufficient for a final decision. Though much relevant archeological material has been found, further discoveries are needed. The names of the two store cities, Pithom and

Raamses (1:11) have been advanced as proof that the events described could not have occurred until the 19th Dynasty, because the first kings bearing the name of Raamses belonged to that dynasty. However, it would not be at all impossible that the original names should have been changed in the text to those that were known later, just as it might be said that the Dutch founded New York in 1626, even though the city did not receive this name until its conquest by the English in 1664, having been previously known as New Amsterdam. That the kings by the name of Ramses did not reign until the 19th Dynasty does not necessarily prove that a city might not have been named Raamses at a previous period, for worship of the god Re (or Ra) was prominent in most periods of ancient Egyp. history, and *mss* is a common ending in personal names. Whereas evidence of the names is therefore not conclusive proof that the events described did not occur until the 19th Dynasty, the lack of archeological evidence of previous occupation at the probable sites of both store cities constitutes important evidence in this direction (cf. EXODUS).

The Egyp. oppression is described as very severe. Some have thought that this indicates the Egyptians' mobilization of great multitudes of people to build the colossal pyramids. This is not relevant, however, as the pyramids must have been standing at least a thousand years before the time of the Exodus. Nonetheless, there is abundant evidence from the period of the 18th and 19th Dynasties of the harshness shown by Egyptians toward slaves and foreigners. The hieroglyphic sign representing a foreigner is a picture of a bound man with blood flowing from a wound in his head. This sign is used even in connection with the names of honored foreign kings with whom treaties were being made. Egyptian hatred of foreigners and severe Egyp. oppression of slaves is well evidenced and fits precisely with the events set forth in the early portion of Exodus.

Sometimes the historicity of the Exodus and of the deliverance at the Red Sea has been questioned on the ground that they are not mentioned in the known remains of ancient Egypt. This objection rests on a misconception of the nature of Egyp. archeology. Most of the day-to-day ephemeral records of ancient Egypt, and the remains of the homes of the people, are largely beneath the water table in the delta, which was the region where most of the people lived. Although the extant remains of ancient Egypt are very extensive, they consist largely of burial places and monuments erected in the desert to celebrate Egyp. achievements and victories. Defeats such as the departure of the Israelites and the failure of Pharaoh to recapture them would hardly result in the erecting of monuments.

At one time it was thought that the date of the Exodus could be ascertained by determining which Pharaoh had drowned. The passage, however, does not necessarily indicate that the king was drowned, but that he suffered a considerable defeat that included the sinking of his chariots and his host, and the drowning of his chosen captains (15:4). An argument that Pharaoh himself perished has been built on 15:19 (KJV), which says that "the horse of Pharaoh went in with his chariots and with his horsemen into the sea." The form here tr. "horse" is identical with that used in 14:9 and 23, where it clearly is used as a collective, and refers to the group of horses, rather than to an individual horse.

There is much yet unknown about the historical background of Exodus, but it can safely be said, though the dates of the events are not yet certain, that there is no reasonable ground for denying that the book could have been written by a contemporary.

III. CONTENTS

A. Preparation for deliverance from Egypt (1:1-4:28)
  1. The oppression (1:1-22)
    a. List of tribes (1:1-7)
    b. Bondage (1:8-14)
    c. Attempted killing of children (1:15-22)
  2. Preparation of God's representative (2:1-22)
    a. Moses' childhood (2:1-10)
    b. Premature attempt at deliverance (2:11-14)
    c. Flight (2:15-22)
  3. Moses' divine call (2:23-4:28)
    a. Divine compassion for Israel (2:23-25)
    b. The burning bush (3:1-6)
    c. The divine promises (3:7-22)
    d. Moses given divine credentials (4:1-9)
    e. Help for Moses' weakness (4:10-17)
    f. Return to Egypt (4:18-23)
    g. Neglect of circumcision remedied (4:24-26)
    h. Aaron provided as an associate (4:27, 28)

B. The actual deliverance (4:29-12:36)
  1. First Attempts (4:29-7:13)
    a. The people's hopes raised (4:29-31)
    b. Oppression intensified by withholding straw (5:1-18)
    c. Moses rejected by Israel but encouraged by God (5:19-6:13)
    d. Ancestry of Moses (6:14-27)
    e. Divine encouragement continued (6:28-7:5)
    f. Pharaoh rejects the evidence of miracles (7:6-13)
  2. The ten plagues (7:14-11:10)
    a. Water turned to blood (7:14-25)
    b. Frogs (8:1-15)
    c. Lice (8:16-19)
    d. Swarms of insects (8:20-32)
    e. Pestilence on the livestock (9:1-7)

f. Boils on man and beast (9:8-12)
g. Hail (9:13-35)
h. Locusts (10:1-20)
i. Darkness (10:21-29)
j. Death of firstborn predicted (11:1-10)
3. The Passover instituted (12:1-28)
4. Death of firstborn experienced (12:29, 30)
5. Pharaoh's permission for hasty departure (12:31-36)

C. The journey to Sinai (12:37-19:2)
1. Departure from Egypt (12:37-14:4)
a. The journey commenced (12:37-42)
b. Permanent regulations for Passover (12:43-51)
c. Firstborn consecrated to the Lord (13:1-16)
d. Avoidance of the Egyptian military route (13:17-20)
e. Divine leading (13:21-14:4)
2. Pharaoh's attempt to reconquer Israel (14:5-15:21)
a. Israel pursued and fearful (14:5-12)
b. Miraculous passage through the sea (14:13-22)
c. Egyptian disaster (14:23-31)
d. The song of victory (15:1-21)
3. Wilderness experiences (15:22-19:2)
a. Bitter water sweetened at Marah (15:22-26)
b. Quails and manna given (15:27-16:36)
c. God provides water (17:1-7)
d. Amalek attacks (17:8-16)
e. Jethro visits and advises (18:1-19:2)

D. The divine covenant established (19:3-24:11)
1. Preparation for the covenant (19:3-25)
2. Declaration of the moral law (20:1-17)
3. The people's fear (20:18-21)
4. Miscellaneous commands (20:22-23:19)
5. Divine promises (23:20-33)
6. Ratification of the covenant (24:1-11)

E. Commands on the mount (24:12-31:18)
1. Moses ascends the mount (24:12-18)
2. Directions for building the Tabernacle (25:1-27:21)
3. Directions for the priesthood (28:1-29:46)
4. Further instruction (30:1-31:18)

F. Interlude: The golden calf (32:1-33:23)
1. Relapse into idolatry (32:1-6)
2. The Lord's anger (32:7-10)
3. Moses' advocacy (32:11-14)
4. The people punished (32:15-29)
5. Moses' intercession (32:30-33:23)

G. The covenant reestablished (34:1-35:3)

H. Construction and erection of the Tabernacle (35:4-40:38)
1. Offerings and workers provided (35:4-36:7)
2. The parts of the Tabernacle (36:8-38:20)
3. The cost of the Tabernacle (38:21-31)
4. Garments for the high priest (39:1-31)
5. The Tabernacle completed and set up (39:32-40:33)
6. Divine manifestation of approval (40:34-48)

IV. Miracles

Exodus describes one of the few periods in Biblical history when God chose to work a substantial number of miracles. Long sections of the Bible contain no account of any such incident. The purpose of a miracle is to show that a greater than human power, namely the power of God, is involved, and to establish God's authority in the presence of doubt or apostasy.

The modern distinction between supernatural acts and providential acts is not specifically indicated in Scripture. The Eng. word "miracle" is generally used to indicate an act that involves direct use of supernatural power, but there is no such distinction in the Heb. and Gr. words that are used. In both Testaments, the words sometimes tr. "miracle" are often tr. "sign" and are frequently used in connection with actions in which no supernatural power is involved. The word אוֹת, which is tr. "miracle" in Numbers 14:22, is tr. "sign" and used as referring to the continuing observance of the Sabbath in Exodus 31:13 and 17. It would require divine omniscience to draw an exact line between what God does providentially with forces He has already established in the world, and what He does by introducing new supernatural forces. Use of the word "miracle" does not necessarily mean that a supernatural power is directly involved; it points to a sign that could rightfully be accepted by an observer as evidence that divine activity was present regardless of whether this activity was exerted through acts of providence or through direct intervention of supernatural power.

The first miracle in Exodus is the burning bush (3:2). Moses saw a flame of fire coming out of a bush and yet the bush was not consumed. There is no way of knowing whether God created something entirely new to produce this impression upon Moses or whether He made an unusual use of forces that He had already established in His universe. The account is very brief. All that is certain is that something occurred that Moses had never seen before and that he correctly considered it to be extremely remarkable.

This was soon followed by a group of miracles given to Moses to enable him to prove to the Israelites that God had really sent him (4:1-9). The first of these was the turning of his rod into a serpent. This was evidently a complete surprise to Moses, since Moses fled before it. Then God performed a new miracle by enabling Moses to seize it by the tail, whereupon it again became a rod. This double miracle was later used for the purpose of convincing both the Israelites and the Egyptians that Moses actually spoke for God (4:30; 7:10).

A view of the Red Sea, crossed over by the Israelites during their wilderness journey. ©*M.P.S.*

The second sign given to Moses for this purpose is described in 4:6, 7. Moses was permitted, after putting his hand into his bosom, to withdraw it leprous as snow, and then, replacing it in his bosom, to pull it out completely recovered.

If the Israelites should still fail to be convinced, a third sign was promised in 4:9. Moses would be enabled to take water from the river and pour it on the dry land, and it would immediately become blood.

All of these miracles, those given to Moses as signs to show the Israelites or the Egyptians, and the burning bush to attract Moses' attention, were quite beyond Moses' understanding and gave him and those before whom he later showed them clear evidence of divine intervention.

The next group of miracles consisted of the ten plagues of judgment upon Egypt. It is interesting to notice that every one of these, with the possible exception of the tenth, consists of something that might naturally occur in the land of Egypt. There are, however, four unique features that set them apart as extremely unusual events and thus give definite proof of the action of supernatural power and wisdom. These unique features are: (1) intensification, whereby the phenomenon was extremely severe; (2) acceleration, whereby all these great plagues occurred within a comparatively short space of time; (3) specification, whereby the land of Goshen was exempted from certain plagues; and (4) prediction, whereby Moses was able to foretell when the plague would occur. In the tenth plague, it was not unnatural for many children to die very suddenly from unexplained causes. The miraculous element was that the first-born of every family in Egypt would be killed. God gave an important lesson by not simply sparing the Israelites because they were Israelites, but because they obeyed God's order for a lamb to be slain for each household and the blood to be placed upon the two side posts and on the upper door posts of the houses. This indicated that every family was under sentence of death for its sin, and that only when the blood of the Lamb was shed and appropriated could punishment be escaped.

The third group of miracles was connected with the wilderness journey. Near the outset of the journey God allowed the people of Israel to become hemmed in by the sea in a place where they could easily be attacked, with no possibility of escape. Then He made it possible for them to cross over the sea on dry land, after which He brought back the waters so that when the Egyptians tried to cross they were drowned. It has been suggested that a ledge may have crossed this body of water a few ft. below the surface. When Moses stretched out his hand over the sea, "the LORD drove the sea back by a strong east wind all night, and made the sea dry land, and the waters were divided" (14:

The Colossi of Memnon on the west bank of the Nile at Luxor. ©*Har*

21). Deep water would remain on both sides, constituting a wall of protection against attack. Whereas it is possible that God introduced some new force other than the one mentioned in the Scripture, the specific statement about the E wind forcing the sea back, strongly indicates His providential use of forces He had already placed in the earth, that He caused these forces to become operative just when they were needed to perform His purpose and to display His power.

Another supernatural element in the wilderness journey was the pillar of cloud by day and fire by night by which God lead the people (14:19, 20). The movement of the cloud in the direction desired or its standing still in obedience to the Lord's will, manifest the strong supernatural element involved.

On two occasions during the portion of the wilderness journey described in Exodus, God miraculously provided water. There was sufficient water at Marah, but the people could not drink it because it was so bitter (15:23). God showed Moses a tree, which, when cast into the waters, made them sweet. At Rephidim (17:1-7) there was no water at all for the people to drink. God told Moses to smite a rock with his rod. When he did so, water flowed out. This may have been a new supernatural creation, or God may have chosen to cause a great underground stream gradually to burrow its way into the rock, perhaps over a period of years, so that when Moses struck it, an opening could be made through which an abundant supply of water would force its way. (A similar event, recorded in Numbers 20:2-13, occurred later.)

Another aspect of God's miraculous care during the wilderness journey was His provision of food. After the sweetening of the water at Marah, the people soon began to fear starvation and to long for the "flesh pots" of Egypt (Exod 16:1-3). Unlike the longer account in Numbers 11:31-35 of the provision of meat through quails and of the serious epidemic that followed, Exodus 16:11-13 includes only a brief mention of quails being provided. Here is no suggestion that a supernatural act of creating quails was involved. Quails are known to travel in large flocks only a few ft. above the ground. God caused them to migrate in great numbers just at this time, and at a height at which they could easily be struck and brought down.

Exodus 16 devotes more attention to the provision of the manna. This may have been a direct creation of God, or a supernatural intensification and miraculous increase of a natural product of the area. Somewhat similar materials have been noted in this region, which crystallize at night and fall from trees to the ground. These partial parallels fall far short of what God provided for the Israelites. It would seem that He did indeed "rain bread from heaven" (16:4; cf. Ps 78:24; 105:40).

A remarkable supernatural event is described in Exodus 20 where God spoke the Ten Commandments audibly so that the words could be understood by Moses and the listening people. This struck terror to the hearts of the people; they begged that further revelations be transmitted through Moses rather than directly from God. The wording in Exodus is not absolutely explicit that the people could understand the words beyond the mere sound of thunder, but Deuteronomy 5:24 makes it clear that the words were actually heard and understood.

It is also stated that the Ten Commandments were originally written with the finger of God on tablets of stone (31:18; 32:16). The original tablets were broken (32:19). God commanded Moses to prepare new tablets, on which the commandments would be written (34:1, 27, 28).

Exodus describes one of the great periods of miraculous divine intervention in the Scripture, yet it contains very few such occurrences as the raising of the dead by Elisha, or the walking on the water by Christ—incidents that would seem necessarily to involve the sort of creative power that God used in forming the universe in the first place. Many of its miracles may have been the use of forces that God implanted in nature and prepared long before the time of the Exodus, but became operative at precisely the time when God willed that they should occur and in response to the action of Moses, His divinely appointed leader. It is absolutely clear that whether the miracle was of direct supernatural intervention, or natural forces under a work of providence, in either case every one of them was definitely an evidence of the presence and activity of God.

V. The legal sections of Exodus

1. General remarks. Prior to the Book of Exodus, the only legal sections in the Bible are the short commands contained in the various covenants with Adam, Noah, Abraham, Isaac, and Jacob, including the law of circumcision (Gen 17:10-14). Such laws were given in connection with promises of divine blessing to God's people.

A new emphasis is found in Exodus. Every legal section in Exodus is firmly based upon a great past event—the redemption of the people from Egyp. bondage. As a sign of gratitude for what God has done, His people took upon themselves the obligation of carrying out His will. Therefore Exodus presents far more extensive and detailed legal sections than any previously given.

There is a second reason why the legal sections in Exodus are so much longer than those in Genesis. Exodus describes God's dealings not with a few individuals, but with an entire nation. If multitudes are to live together in orderly fashion, detailed regulations for the conduct of the people in many situations are necessary. The laws of Exodus have two pur-

Before the rugged slopes of Jebel Musa, the traditional Mount Sinai. © *M.P.S.*

poses: (1) to regulate the relationship of the redeemed to God; (2) to establish order and justice between man and man.

2. Relation to the law codes of other nations. A cent. ago many critics declared that the laws of the Pentateuch could not possibly have been written as early as the time of Moses, since life was then much too primitive for such advanced laws. Then the Code of Hammurabi was discovered in Mesopotamia in 1901. It was at once apparent that the laws of the Pentateuch are not too complex to have been written at so early a date, for the laws of the Code of Hammurabi, written centuries earlier, are far more complex.

Since that time, still earlier Mesopotamian law codes have been found. An extensive Hitt. law code from Asia Minor has also been discovered. Egyptian records contain references to the great scrolls of Egyp. law, but no portion of these laws has yet been recovered.

As a result of these discoveries, the critical argument was reversed, and it was suggested that much of the law of Moses had been taken over from the Code of Hammurabi or from other ancient codes. Closer examination shows this view also to be unfounded. The laws in the Pentateuch that have direct relationship to individual laws in any of these codes are comparatively few. The Code of Hammurabi is strictly a secular code and has little to say about religious matters, except for particular privileges or responsibilities of the priestly class. In contrast, fully half of the laws of the Pentateuch are concerned with specifically religious matters. Much of the Pentateuch includes regulations for sacrifice and for annual festivals or other religious services, matters that the Code of Hammurabi does not touch.

For further development in this discussion, *see* section 4 below.

3. The originality of the laws. According to the Pentateuch, the laws of Exodus were given to the people by God through Moses in the wilderness. The greater portion of these laws has no precise counterpart in anything else that has been discovered in the ancient world. The secular portion of the laws have definite contacts with laws that have been found from earlier times. This does not in any way cast question upon the authenticity of the laws as given by Moses, or upon the validity of their claim to represent God's will for His people.

It is necessary to note the nature of God's revelation. Everything that can be known with certainty about eternal things, about the origin of the universe, about its ultimate destiny, and about the future of the individual man or God's will for him, requires direct revelation from God, as He alone knows these matters. Everything of this sort that is contained in the Bible is a direct revelation, and could not otherwise be made known to man.

The case is somewhat different regarding the divine teaching about man's relation to his fellows. When the Israelites left Egypt, their minds were not blank concerning laws of human relations. The effects of many judicial enactments and customary observances become part of the outlook of every individual by the time he becomes an adult. Many matters are settled by customary procedure of the area in which a person lives, by the ideals that he hears expressed, and by the results of law cases that come to his attention. After the Israelites left Egypt, there was no reason to expect that a completely new legal system of relationship between human beings should be introduced. It was necessary at that point only to state those principles and precepts that were most urgent and vital, in order that the life of the Israelites should show forth the justice and lovingkindness of the God who had redeemed them.

4. Types of law. Although many of the laws of Exodus treat secular matters, it is impossible to sharply divide these laws into religious laws and secular laws. All were based upon the covenant obligation to the Lord, who had redeemed His people from bondage, and to whose righteous law they therefore owed obedience. Many laws were concerned exclusively with ritual or with an individual's relation to God; even most of the secular laws have a religious tinge or at least a humanitarian attitude such as is not usually found in the law of other nations of the time.

In a famous article entitled "The Origins of Hebrew Law," published at Leipzig in 1934 (Eng. tr. in A. Alt, *Essays on Old Testament History and Religion*, [1966]), Albrecht Alt suggested that light could be thrown on the origin of OT laws by dividing them into two types that he called apodictic and casuistic. He pointed out that about half of the laws in what is sometimes designated as the Book of the Covenant (Exod 20:22-23:33) are casuistic in form, in contrast to the other half. By casuistic Alt meant laws that treat specific situations, and formulate the judgment that should be given under various conditions. These laws generally begin with the particle כִּי, "if," introducing a description of the general situation. This is sometimes followed by one or more occurrences of the particle אִם (also tr. "if"), which introduces the more specific situation plus a statement of the appropriate penalty or action. Such laws give the impression of having been developed through actual cases. In the codes from Mesopotamia and in the Hitt. code, this is the most common type of law.

By apodictic type, Alt indicates laws that are categorically stated, usually without a penalty, as in the Ten Commandments, but also including those legal statements that simply end with such a phrase as "he shall be put to death" or as are preceded by the words "cursed be he who . . . ." In view of the great similarity of form between the casuistic laws in the Pentateuch and those in the codes of the highly developed nations of Mesopotamia or Asia Minor, Alt suggests that the casuistic law in the Pentateuch was taken over from the Canaanites, but that the apodictic law, in contrast, had a specifically Israelite origin.

This view of the difference of origin of the two types of law is flatly denied by G. E. Mendenhall in his article "Covenant" in the IDB, where he declares that this distinction can no longer be taken as an evidence of a different origin since he finds laws of both types not only in the covenant code of Exodus 21 to 23, but also in the Hitt. treaties and laws from Asia Minor.

In any event, derivation of these laws from the inhabitants of Pal. must be recognized as entirely conjectural, since no non-Israelite code has yet been found in that area. The Israelites were doubtless familiar with this type of law from their experience in Egypt; moreover, the patriarchs who came out of Meṣopotamia must certainly have had wide acquaintance with it. Some of these laws are very similar to laws in one of the Mesopotamian codes or in the Hitt. code from Asia Minor. Others are strikingly different.

The arduous labors of Moses in judging the people are alluded to in Exodus 18:13ff. From such labors, a body of precedents would naturally emerge. There is no evidence that the Bible claims to set forth a complete code for this sort of judgment. Doubtless many issues were decided on the basis of equity and of precedent.

In Exodus, casuistic law is not grouped by itself as distinct from apodictic law. Most of the law in Exodus, outside of chs. 21 to 24, is apodictic law. In these chs., the two types of law are about equally intermixed. The purpose of the section is not to provide a complete code for all situations, but to produce an impression of the sort of conduct that the people were expected to maintain, while giving specific guidance in a few common types of legal situations and constantly stressing the necessity of complete loyalty to the true God, utter abandonment of all fealty whatever to false gods or idols, and careful observance of the principles of benevolence and humanitarianism that God desires in His people.

5. Survey of the legal sections. The principal legal sections of Exodus, some of which shall be discussed in more detail below, are as follows:

(1) The law of the Passover (12:1-27, 43-49)
(2) The first-born set apart (13:1-16)
(3) The law of the manna (16:16, 23-33)
(4) The Decalogue (20:1-17)
(5) The "Book of the Covenant" (20:22-23:33)
(6) Regulations for the Tabernacle and the priesthood (25:1-31:17)
(7) The laws of Exodus 34 (34:10-26)
(8) Renewed emphasis on the Sabbath (35:1-3)
(9) Orders to establish the Tabernacle and the Priesthood (40:1-15)

6. Laws given before Sinai. Before the solemn and rather lengthy presentation of God's law at Sinai, three briefer legal passages occur in Exodus. The last of these, which regards the manna, was directly tied to the immediate need to regulate the collection and use of this food.

The other two legal sections that precede the experiences at Sinai did not similarly fill a definite immediate need in connection with the progress of the Israelites toward the Promised Land. On the contrary, they would seem rather to slow up and hinder this progress.

The nine great plagues had been completed, and the effect upon Egyp. determination to hold the Israelites in bondage must have been tremendous. When the last and most terrible plague occurred, the Egyptians did not merely permit the Israelites to leave; they urged them to go quickly (12:31-33). Later events proved that Pharaoh and his leaders soon regretted this decision and set out to recapture the Israelites to bring them back (14:5-9). Under these circumstances, from a human viewpoint, it must have seemed advisable at the time of the tenth plague that the Israelites should leave as quickly as possible. Yet in the midst of these circumstances the Lord gave explicit and full orders for the ceremony of the Passover (12:3-13), and, in addition, took time to lay down permanent regulations regarding the future keeping of this great annual festival and the setting apart of the first-born (12:43-49; 13:1-16). Only one conclusion is possible. More important than deliverance from bondage was the impression of great concepts upon their minds and hearts and the setting up of regulations whereby this impression would be continued and reinforced in subsequent years.

Therefore, the Passover had further lessons to stress in addition to the one great purpose of remembering the deliverance. Although the tenth plague came to force Pharaoh to let the Israelites go, it was also important to impress upon the Israelites that they also could not escape God's wrath except through a sacrifice. Nor would one sacrifice do for the nation. Each family must have its own lamb; the sacrifice was necessary. A lamb must be provided and be slain as a substitute for the sinful family. Each family was responsible before the Lord. It was necessary to interrupt the procedure of leaving Egypt to initiate this great ceremony in careful detail and beyond that, to lay down regulations for its continuous observance in future years.

7. The Decalogue. The Ten Commandments, which are contained in Exodus 20:2-17 and repeated with slight differences in Deuteronomy 5:6-21, stand apart from all other legal sections of the OT. Their importance is stressed in a very special way. Exodus 19 describes the stirring events that prepared men's minds to realize the tremendous importance of what was about to occur. It is clearly implied in Exodus 20:18, 19, and explicitly stated in Deuteronomy 5:4, that God spoke these words so that all the people could hear. All other commandments in the Bible were given through individual prophets, such as Moses. The Ten Commandments were spoken directly to the nation as a whole.

Harp with golden bull's head from Ur, reminiscent of the molten calf at Sinai. © *Hirmer Fotoarchiv, Munchen.*

In addition, the Ten Commandments were "written with the finger of God" on tables of stone (Exod 31:18; 32:16; Deut 9:10). The original tables did not last long, but were broken as a result of Moses' hot anger when he saw the people turned away in the worship of the golden calf (32:19). Thereupon God told him to hew new tables on which the words would again be written (34:1, 4, 28). When Moses repeated these laws in his farewell address, he emphasized that some of those present had personally heard them divinely proclaimed at Sinai (Deut 5:3, 4). The importance of a particular group of laws could hardly be stressed more emphatically.

The Ten Commandments summarize the ethical law. All are stated in absolute form. There is little detailed explanation. Thus stealing is forbidden, but the nature of private property, which such a law assumes, is not spelled out in detail. Murder is forbidden, but the difference between murder and justifiable homicide is left for separate explanation later (21:12-14).

The Sabbath commandment in Exodus and Deuteronomy contains hortatory statements of why it should be obeyed, and also specific detail as to its application in particular circumstances. The command regarding parents is called by Paul in the NT, "the first commandment with a promise" (Eph 6:2). Such elements are notably lacking in other portions of the Ten Commandments. No specific penalties are mentioned in any of them. Infraction of the command on coveting would be impossible for men to punish, since it is an internal, spiritual matter.

Most legal sections of Exodus include some provisions that are civil law rather than moral law; i.e., they relate to particular circumstances that might be subject to change. Nothing of this nature is found in the Ten Commandments. Nor do these Commandments include any details of ritual or ceremonial law.

Some critics have suggested that a ritual decalogue preceded the ethical decalogue of Exodus 20.

It has been questioned whether the Ten Commandments in the present form represent exactly the form in which they were originally given. The difference in wording between the Sabbath command in Exodus 20:8-11, and its counterpart in Deuteronomy 5:12-15 suggests that the command was originally either longer so as to include all that is in both forms, or shorter, being thus presented only in bare outline. To those who believe in the plenary inspiration of the Scripture, it would seem more likely that the full commandment included every word of both sections rather than that it was originally given in shorter form. Wellhausen and other critics have held that the Ten Commandments represent an advanced form of law which could hardly have come into existence until the time of the later Israelite kingdom. More recently, a number of critics have taken the view that the commandments in a much shorter and more primitive form originated in the time of Moses.

There have been various modes of enumerating the commandments. Josephus' listing (Antiq. III. c. 6, sec. 5) shows that he followed the arrangement now common in most non-Lutheran Protestant churches and in the Greek church. This arrangement was followed by Jerome and Gregory Nazianzen.

The Talmud takes the introductory statement (Exod 20:2) as the first "Word," and then combines the command on worshiping no other God with that against idolatry to form the second commandment. This is not as strange as it appears, for the Ten Commandments might also be called "the Ten Words," since the Heb. word tr. "commandment" in Exodus 34:28 and Deuteronomy 4:13 and 10:4 is more commonly tr. "word."

Augustine adopted a different mode of enumeration in which he took as the first commandment, the combination that the Talmud calls the second commandment, and then secured the number ten by considering the coveting of a man's wife as the ninth commandment and the coveting of the house or other property as the tenth commandment. This arrangement is generally followed by the Roman Catholic church and by most Lutheran divines, but strikes an obstacle in that in Exodus, coveting the house is mentioned first and coveting the wife, second.

There has been discussion as to the arrangement of the commandments on the tables. Augustine suggested that the first three were on the first table, and seven on the second table. Calvin suggested that four were on the first table and six on the second. Philo and Josephus explicitly held that five were on each table. There is no scriptural evidence on which to make a decision among these different views.

8. The covenant code. It is customary among Bible scholars to call the section from Exodus 20:22 to 23:33 "the Covenant Code" or "The Book of the Covenant." The latter title would seem to imply that this was the section read to the people by Moses, as described in Exodus 24:7, when they agreed to obey "the book of the covenant." It seems more likely, however, that the actual covenant consisted of the Ten Commandments, and that this portion was a further explanation and enlargement of the duties that would rest upon the people, rather than the actual constitution referred to in that verse, particularly in view of the reference to the Ten Commandments in 20:22.

This section consists of laws that were particularly important to present to the people at this stage of their religious life, at a time when they were looking forward to life in Canaan as the people of God (cf. Exod 3:12). Consequently its laws look forward to Canaan and imply at many points a settled life in the land that the Lord would give them, and at the same time include provisions applicable to the situation during the time when they would still be in the wilderness. It had not yet been revealed that their unfaithfulness at Kadesh-barnea would result in a forty-year period of wandering, though God knew this would happen, and He so regulated the laws that they would be applicable to both situations.

These laws divide naturally into certain sections. They begin with a reiteration of the warning against idolatry—a very important warning since they were so soon to fall into the sin of worshiping the golden calf. This is followed by specific regulations for worship in the wilderness. As the community moved through the wilderness it would be necessary to construct an altar at each place where sacrifice would be offered. General regulations for the type of altars are given (20:24-26).

A long section follows, which is mostly secular rather than specifically religious. It stresses humanitarian principles in the relation of master and servant, lays down rules for preservation of property, gives laws of compensation for personal injuries, prescribes regulations for the preservation of property rights, and then proceeds to declare specific commands against immorality, bestiality, spiritism, unkindness to the weak or the oppressed, etc.

Interspersed among these regulations, particularly toward the latter part, are comparatively simple rules for the general direction of the ritual and religious life of the people. Three annual feasts are presented and their importance is stressed. Avoidance of the Canaanite rite of boiling a kid in its mother's milk is ordered. The principle of the sabbatical year is laid down. The commands to avoid any relationship to false gods or to any false type of sacrifice are stressed, and the weekly Sabbath is emphasized.

A particularly important ordinance is the law of asylum, given in its first brief form in Exodus 21:12-14. According to the Wellhausen view this was the first stage in a development. Such an interpretation, however, is quite unnecessary. It should be noticed that it is not here said that the altar is the place of asylum. It is rather declared that a murderer is to be executed, and is not to be safe even at such a holy place as the altar. Only the man who is guilty of accidental homicide is to be protected. The words, "I will appoint for you a place to which he may flee," could have found fulfillment during the time in the wilderness through some special arrangement by Moses. After the conquest of Canaan, it was fulfilled by the establishment of the cities of refuge.

It was not the purpose of the secular portions of the Covenant Code to provide a complete set of laws for all the different types of problems that might arise, but merely to give an indication of the type of judgment to be made in certain common situations. In the main, they were a reiteration of principles already known. It contained a few specific ordinances that were vital for immediate application and presented the general attitude that God's people would be expected to maintain after entering Canaan. The purpose of this law, as far as the secular portions are concerned, was to illustrate the high moral principles and benevolent attitudes the Lord desired in the conduct of His people.

For another vital characteristic of the Covenant Code, note the discussion above in section 4, "Types of laws."

9. Regulations for the Tabernacle and for the establishment of the priesthood. During the first period of forty days and forty nights during which Moses remained on the mount, the Lord gave him instructions for the establishment of the permanent system of Israelite worship. Plans for the building of the Tabernacle were set forth in precise detail. Four times it was stressed that everything about the Tabernacle must be built exactly in accordance with the pattern that God had caused Moses to see in the mount. The language used in 25:9, 40; 26:30; and 27:8 raises the question whether the revelation was simply given in words, or whether Moses actually was shown a model of the complete Tabernacle.

The great emphasis laid on precise details of worship in these chs. and later on in the Pentateuch is in striking contrast to the very

This old Samaritan High Priest is reminiscent of Aaron and later High Priests. ©*M.P.S.*

meager detail regarding divine service for the Christian in the NT. The difference is that when the NT worship was instituted, Christ already had been crucified and raised from the dead. The great central facts of the Christian religion had occurred and had been clearly explained. The ceremonies of the Christian religion looked back to something already fully known. Since a variety of forms could remind the hearer of these vital matters, there was no longer the same need to stress precise forms of worship. In the OT, on the other hand, everything looked forward to the great events that God intended to bring about through the Incarnation and the Atonement. All this was seen by the OT believer through a glass darkly. Therefore it was necessary that the forms be strictly observed; otherwise the ceremony might fail to accomplish its purpose, or might even have the opposite effect of suggesting things that were not God's intention at all.

The details in the establishment of the Tabernacle meant much to the Israelite believer. Its place in the very center of the camp during the wilderness journey would constantly remind him of the place that God should occupy in the life of the nation and of every individual member of it. The daily sacrifices (29:38-42) would remind him that his sin constantly needed expiation and that nothing that man himself could do would provide a permanent atonement. This could be secured only by that to which the sacrifices looked forward as they pointed to the death of Christ. The place of the great brazen altar in the outer courtyard barring the entrance to the tabernacle stressed the fact that only through atonement could anyone have access to God. The laver emphasized the requirement of holiness without which no one could see the Lord. The first part of the Tabernacle, with the altar of incense and the table of showbread, demonstrated the importance of the worship of God's people and the need of constant appropriation of Christ, the Bread of Life. The veil between the holy place and the holy of holies showed how sinful man was unable to approach God until a new and living way was opened. In the holy of holies, the Ark represented the throne of God and His abiding presence with His people. This Ark would contain reminders of the time in the wilderness, such as the tables of stone, to emphasize the importance of the moral law in any relation between God and man, and the pot of manna to show God's marvelous provision in the wilderness journey and the fact of His constant presence with His people. All these matters were presented to Moses in his first period in the mount, and the necessity of carrying out the details with complete accuracy was emphasized.

10. The laws of Exodus 34. After the Covenant had been ceremonially established (Exod 24), and Moses had gone up to the mount for forty days to receive the plans for the Tabernacle, the apostasy of the golden calf occurred. Moses condemned the terrible apostasy of the people who had already fallen into idolatry, and God visited severe punishment upon those involved. Then God promised Moses that He would renew the covenant and make it possible for the tables that Moses had broken (32:15-19) to be replaced by a new set containing the basic law. Between the promise that the tables would be replaced (34:1) and the statement that such tables were actually prepared (34:27, 28) is an interesting section in which a number of the previous laws are repeated in a different order.

In this section, stress is laid on the covenant that God was renewing, and on His wonderful promises to bring His people into the Promised Land. Some of the most important of the Ten Commandments and of the religious ordinances of the Book of the Covenant are repeated, but none of its secular or casuistic laws.

When still a young man, the poet Goethe suggested that the laws of this section were the original Ten Commandments written on the two tables. Julius Wellhausen accepted this idea, though admitting that Abraham Kuenen, his important co-worker in the development of the documentary theory, resolutely denied it. C. A. Briggs in *The Higher Criticism of the Pentateuch* (1893), presented the view as definite fact, and maintained that the "ritual decalogue" of Exodus 34 was later displaced by the "ethical decalogue" of Exodus 20. However, H. Gressman (1913) and R. H. Pfeiffer (1941, 1948) strongly opposed it, insisting that Exodus 34 represents a later, rather than an earlier, form. The present tendency of many critical scholars is to feel that the Ten Commandments, although in a more simplified form, actually go back to the Mosaic period.

An apparently conclusive objection to the view that this is the primitive decalogue is that it contains not ten laws but either twelve or thirteen, depending upon how they are divided, and that hardly any two scholars agree as to which of these twelve or thirteen should be designated as later insertions to secure the number ten, which is specifically mentioned in v. 28 of this chapter. The laws of Exodus 34, however, are in no sense an earlier form of the Ten Commandments, but were simply a reiteration for the particular needs of the situation of some of the laws previously given, including some of the Ten Commandments and also some sections of the Book of the Covenant.

11. The Sabbath. Unless it be the commands against compromising with false gods or falling into idolatrous practices, no feature of the law is more repeated in Exodus than that of the maintenance of the weekly Sabbath. This was stressed in the wilderness when the manna was first given by a special supernatural arrangement concerning the times when the manna would come (16:22-30). It could not be gathered at all on the Sabbath. If more than enough for the day was gathered on any day except Friday, it would spoil during the night. On Friday, however, a double amount was given, and it would remain fresh for two days. Thus the importance of the Sabbath was stressed. Neither here nor in Exodus 20:8 was the Sabbath presented as something new, but as something that must be faithfully observed.

In the Ten Commandments, the Sabbath commandment is strongly emphasized (20:8-11), and the people were reminded that its validity rests upon the arrangement followed in the creation of heaven and earth (20:11). In the midst of the Book of the Covenant, Exodus 23:12 again urges observance of the Sabbath. In the period on the mount, when the directions for worship were being given, Exodus 31:12-17 emphasizes the importance of Sabbath observance and again mentions its relation to the creation. In the laws particularly emphasized after the punishment for the apostasy of worshiping the golden calf, Exodus 34:21 urges Sabbath observance, and Exodus 35:1-3 stresses this aspect of the life of the Israelites. Thus in the early part of this nation's experience, after its deliverance from Egyp. bondage, emphasis is given to the importance of maintenance not merely of the day of rest that man needs, but also of the ceremonial provision that pointed forward to the goal of divine rest God provides for His people (Heb 4:9, 10).

VI. The higher criticism of Exodus

The Book of Exodus occupies a prominent place in the history of the higher criticism, yet it is so closely related to the higher criticism of the Pentateuch as a whole that this aspect will be mainly discussed in the article Pentateuch. Here it should be noted that those who follow the Wellhausen theory in general have differed greatly in recent years in their interpretations of the Book of Exodus—for example, certain followers of the documentary theory attribute considerable historicity to the career of Moses, whereas others almost completely deny it.

One of the cornerstones of the documentary theory, the interpretation of Exodus 6:3, is discussed in the article Pentateuch.

VII. Special problems

1. The number in Jacob's family who went down to Egypt (1:5). Ingenuity has been expended in the attempt to prove that the number of Israelites who went down to Egypt was exactly seventy. It should be recognized, however, that this is a round number and is not intended as a precise enumeration.

2. The new king who did not know Joseph (1:8). No name is given for the new king "who did not know Joseph." There is a strong suggestion, however, that it may indicate not merely a change of monarch but a change of dynasty. This would fit well with the possibility that the kings who received the Israelites into Egypt were Hyksos, and recognized the Hebrews as being Asiatics like themselves, whereas the new king belonged to a native Egyp. dynasty after the expulsion of the Hyksos. This could be true, whether the king referred to here belonged to the 18th or to the 19th dynasty.

3. The names of the cities Pithom and Raamses (1:11). It has been alleged that the second of these names proves that the events here described could not have occurred until the 19th dynasty, because the first prominent kings by the name of Ramses belonged to that dynasty. However, this is not a necessary conclusion. It is not impossible that this place name was changed to another name by which it was known later. Also, the fact that the kings of Egypt by the name of Ramses did not reign until the 19th dynasty is not complete proof that a city could not have been named Raamses in the 18th dynasty. After all, worship of the god Ra was common in many periods of Egyp. history, and *meses* is a common ending in names at many periods.

4. The number of Hebrew midwives (1:15). The historicity of the first ch. has been questioned on the ground that so great a multitude of people as the Israelites would certainly have required more than two midwives. The allegation, however, is not vaild. The passage does not say that these were the only midwives. They are merely the only two mentioned by name. They could have been particular ones who were singled out to receive praise for their zeal in saving the lives of the Heb. male children, or they might have been the head supervisors of a large group of midwives. Professor W. F. Albright has pointed out that these are common NW Sem. women's names of the 2nd millennium B.C. (*From the Stone Age to Christianity* [1957], 13).

5. The story of Moses in the bulrushes (2:1-10). Objection has been raised to the story of putting Moses into the bulrushes and his discovery and deliverance through the daughter of Pharaoh, with the suggestion that it is an echo of the story of Sargon who was cast adrift in a boat on the water and was rescued by those who found him. Certain considerations should be noted: (1) The story of Sargon comes from distant Mesopotamia and would not likely be the basis for the invention of a story in Egypt. (2) Such instances are fairly common in all periods. To people living next to a great river it could be similar to the incident today of a child abandoned on a doorstep. The existence of stories having this theme detracts nothing from the factual nature of this narrative about Moses.

6. Moses' name (2:10). The name Moses is particularly appropriate because it would equally well fit either a Heb. or an Egyp. context. To a Heb. it would suggest the Heb. root *mashah* ("to draw out") and therefore would be a good name for the one who was providentially drawn out of the water. To an Egyp. it would suggest the common Egyp. element *mes, mesu* (or just *ms*) meaning "child" or "son," which appeared in such names as Ramses (a son of Ra, the sun god) or Tut-mose.

7. Reuel (Jethro) (2:18; 3:1). It is sometimes alleged that there is a contradiction in that the priest of Midian is called "Reuel" in 2:18 and "Jethro" in 3:1. However, if all the circumstances were known, there would prob. be no difficulty. Most people in history have more than one name, and it was common to refer to an individual by various names. There is no need of inferring any confusion or contradiction. According to the critical view, one of these names must belong to one document and the other to another document, and the use of the two names would prove that a combination of documents had occurred. If this was the case, however, the redactor who combined the two narratives would surely have felt it necessary to repeat the first name along with the second when he put the documents together. That he did not do so shows that he found no difficulty in referring to the same man by these two names. If to a redactor there appeared to be no difficulty, there is no reason why an original writer should not have used both names.

8. "I AM WHO I AM" (3:14). The cryptic statement by which God here designates Himself has been the subject of much discussion. Pointing to the use of the Heb. imperfect, some have even alleged that it shows a changing character of God. Much more probable is

Exorcists from a Bas relief in an Egyptian temple. *Top:* A magician's rod becomes a serpent; *Center:* Scarab from Tanis, depicting a snake charmer performing before three gods; *Below:* A man or a god leading four calves and carrying either a stick with a snake's head or a stick which has been transformed into a snake.

the interpretation that points to the fact that He is the only God who exists, the One who has created all things. It is interesting that in the gospel of John, the word: "I AM" is applied to Jesus many times in connection with various figures or attributes.

9. Borrowing from the Egyptians (3:22). Some interpreters have found a moral problem here caused by the KJV tr. of the Heb. שׁאל, as meaning "borrow." This is an unfortunate tr. The word is actually tr. many times in the KJV in its simple meaning of "ask," e.g., 13:14; 18:7. The Egyptians had forced the Israelites to work for many years without compensation. God declared that a certain measure of compensation would be given them as they left. They are simply to ask for things and these will be given. There is no suggestion in the v. that the things asked for would ever be returned to the Egyptians.

BIBLIOGRAPHY. J. G. Murphy, *Exodus* (1866); J. P. Lange, *Exodus* (1874); G. Rawlinson, "Exodus" in *Ellicott's Commentary* (1882); H. Gressmann, *Mose und seine Zeit* (1913); R. Smend, *Das Mosebild von Heinrich Ewald bis Martin Noth* (1959).

A. A. MacRae

EXORCISM, EXORCIST ek' sôr siz' əm, ek' sôr-sist (ἐξορκισμός, *the administration of an oath,* ἐξορκιστης, *an exorcist*). The act, and the performer of that act, of expelling an evil spirit, thereby releasing the person possessed by that spirit.

The latter word occurs once in the NT (Acts 19:13). A cognate, ἐξορκίζω, "to adjure," "to exorcise," is found in the LXX (Gen 24:3; Judg 17:2; Matt 26:63; Acts 19:13).

The concept of possession by a god or evil spirit is ancient. The Babylonians, Egyptians, and Greeks have left ample evidence. Various physical illnesses and states of frenzy were attributed to possession. Formulas of exorcism of definable types are found in ancient incantation texts. Exorcists employed such formulae, sometimes saying a specific magical word thought to have extraordinary power, and occasionally using magical objects. The demon was addressed by name if possible, as it was characteristic of ancient thought that to know the name of such a being was to control him. The exorcist might also invoke the name of a favorable deity. This was in contrast to the practice of Jesus who performed exorcisms with a touch or word of command, without invoking the name of another. It should be noted that there are many instances, particularly in Gr. lit., where possession by a demon was not considered bad. Plato attributed Socrates' impulses to a "daimon."

The OT reflects God's opposition to evildoers, but in only one case is there anything like an exorcism. This was by music rather than command, the release of Saul from an evil spirit by David (1 Sam 16:14-23). In two further instances (18:10; 19:9) this therapy did not prevent possession. Instances of recorded demonic activity in Jewish lit. increase in the Hel. period. Exorcism is described in Tobit 6:7, 16, 17; 8:3. King Solomon acquired a reputation as an exorcist in Josephus (Jos. Antiq. VIII. ii. 5) and, later, in the Talmud. Josephus testifies that he saw Solomon's methodology used effectively. Jesus' words in Matthew 12:27 imply the existence of Jewish exorcists, and some itinerant ones are mentioned in Acts 19:13.

The NT narratives assume two things, the actuality of demon possession and the victory of Christ over Satan and the demon world. Although there have undoubtedly been numerous cases of alleged demon possession throughout history which, along with reputed exorcisms, may be attributed to suggestion, insanity, etc., the cases in the NT cannot be dismissed without radical implications for NT history and theology. Second Peter 2:4; Jude 6; and Matthew 25:41 speak of the eventual doom of Satan and his angels. The actual victory was accomplished by Christ (John 12:31; Col 2:15; 1 John 3:8), who once spoke of Satan's defeat in connection with the casting out of demons (Luke 10:18). When Jesus was accused of performing exorcisms by the power of Beelzebub, he stated that these acts were accomplished against Satan, in the power of the Holy Spirit, the "finger of God," and as an expression of the kingdom, the reign of God. The various instances of Jesus' expulsion of demons cannot be understood in isolation, or merely as acts of mercy to release oppressed people, although such was also the case. All was part of the great conflict against the powers of evil, in which conflict the disciples were commissioned. Whereas the text of Mark 16:17 is uncertain, the earlier commands to the disciples are clear (Mark 3:14f.; 6:7; and parallels).

This confrontation with demons occurred at the very beginning of His ministry (Mark 1:23ff., 27, 32; Luke 4:33ff., 36). Mark distinguishes between exorcism and the healing of merely physical diseases and notes that the demons obeyed the authoritative command of Christ. In a similar passage, Matthew says the act was performed "with a word" (Matt 8:16). The woman bound by Satan was released simply by the laying on of Jesus' hands (Luke 13:10-16). The Lord's disciples, however, needed to invoke the name of Christ (Luke 10:17; so Paul in Acts 16:16ff.). The daughter of the Syrophoenician woman was healed at a distance, which rules out suggestion as an explanation of Jesus' exorcisms (Matt 15:21-28). In the case of the Gerasene demoniac (Luke 8:26-39), Jesus asked the demon's name, but it is not stated that this is related to His control of the demons. The demons on expulsion entered swine. Instances of such transference are also described in earlier, non-Biblical sources. In another case of violent behavior (Mark 9:14-29), the disciples were unable to perform the exorcism. Jesus stressed the need of strong faith and prayer on the part of the exorcist. (Some ancient MSS include the word "fasting.")

The apocryphal Acts, Justin Martyr, Tertullian, Origen, and Jerome provide evidence of the continuing involvement of early Christians in this activity. The apologists cited cases of exorcism to prove the power of Christ and the compassion of His followers. During the course of church history, matters of possession, witchcraft, etc., had great importance. Near the end of the 15th cent., James Sprenger and Heinrich Kramer compiled their code of the practices of the church against such evils, the *Malleus Maleficarum*. The next cent. saw the *Flagellum Demonum*, and in the 17th cent. there appeared the *Thesaurus Exorcismorum* and the *Rituale Romanum*. The latter, based on some of the preceding material, has been revised and published through the present time by the Roman Catholic Church. In the rites of that church, exorcism has become a preventative measure (for example, warding off demons from a baptism), as well as a curative one.

In conclusion, it should be stressed that the expulsions performed by Jesus are not called exorcisms in the NT, and that in contrast to typical exorcisms in pagan and even Jewish lit. they were devoid of magical formulae, devices, and invocations. Our Lord's authoritative commands were an expression of His victory.

BIBLIOGRAPHY. J. L. Nevius, *Demon Possession* (1894); M. Summers, *The History of Witchcraft* (1926, 1956); H. C. Lea, *Materials Toward a History of Witchcraft*, I (1939); C. William, *Witchcraft* (1941); E. Langton, *Essentials of Demonology* (1949); M. F. Unger, *Biblical Demonology* (1952); R. H. Robbins, *The Encyclopedia of Witchcraft and Demonology* (1959); J. Lhermitte, *Diabolical Possession, True and False* (1963); T. K. Oesterreich, *Possession Demoniacal and Other* (1966); K. Koch, *Occult Bondage and Deliverance* (1970).

W. L. LIEFELD

EXPIATION. This word is not used in the KJV or the ASV but the RSV has "expiation" instead of the "propitiation" of the older VSS (*see* PROPITIATION). "Expiation" is there preferred because it avoids the idea, alleged to be contained in "propitiation," that God must be appeased. It is argued that "expiation" correctly interprets the action of the Heb. verb כפר, the root meaning being "to cover" tr. in the LXX by ἱλάσκομαι, and its cognates. As explained in the article PROPITIATION, there is no real ground linguistically or theologically for altering "propitiation" to "expiation." Expiation is a necessary element in the work of propitiation, but it is not an alternative to propitiation. Expiation deals with sin and guilt in such a way that propitiation is effected toward God, and the pardoned sinner is restored to fellowship with God. The action of propitiation, therefore, is directed toward God, while the action of expiation is directed toward man in his state of sin and guilt. Wherever the action of expiation is present, the action of propitiation is always implied.

By expiation the guilty person, or rather the offense which renders him guilty in the sight of God, is covered from the eyes of the holy God who looks upon him in righteous judgment. This is, of course, no fiction, as though God were prevented from seeing what is really there. The sin is dealt with so effectively that it no longer remains as the object of God's condemnation.

The OT presents this action of covering (כפר) in several ways, usually rendered in Eng. VSS as "make atonement." Normally it was the priests who "made atonement" by the offering of sacrifice. The range of its application can be seen in the account of the Day of Atonement (Lev 16), when atonement was made for the sins of the people (vv. 30, 33) but also for the holy place, the Tabernacle and the altar (vv. 20, 33), presumably because these also were defiled through the contact of sinful men. The verb is used frequently of the effect of the blood of the sin offering (4:18, 20, 30, 31 et al.) and of the trespass or guilt offering (5:6, 16, 18) and even of the burnt offering (1:4; 14:20; 16:24). The latter has been regarded as purely a worship offering, but it is clear from these passages that all blood sacrifice had an expiatory value. Summing up this use of כפר, BDB (p. 498) says, "Underlying all these offerings there is the conception that the persons offering are covered by that which is regarded as sufficient and satisfactory by Jahweh."

The Biblical presentation of the process of expiation shows that man has been taught by divine revelation that his sin against the holy God merits death, and that this judgment can be removed only if satisfaction is made to the requirements of God's justice by the death of another in his place, usually that of an animal. Atonement is made for him, i.e., his sin is expiated by death. This fact appears even in instances where the animal sacrifices are not offered. In Exodus 32:30-32 Moses was willing to give up his own life in place of the people to make atonement for their sin (v. 30), although in fact his intercession proved sufficient. Phineas (Num 25:10-13) "made atonement for the people of Israel" by putting to death the leaders of this guilty action, thus turning aside God's wrath and stopping the plague which He had inflicted on them. (For a discussion of other non-sacrificial passages where כפר is used, see Leon Morris, *The Apostolic Preaching of the Cross,* pp. 143-150.)

While the OT stresses the substitutionary character of the offerings by which expiation for sin is made, the phrase "make atonement for" combines the ideas of making both expiation and propitiation. Both are essential for restoring the guilty to fellowship with the holy God. In the NT the atoning sacrifice of Christ also includes both factors. Therefore the RSV rendering "expiation" is inadequate to express the full import of the reconciliation effected by Christ's death and resurrection. "Propitiation" by pointing to the Godward aspect, also inevitably includes the manward expiatory value of His saving work. *See* ATONEMENT; PROPITIATION.

BIBLIOGRAPHY. C. H. Dodd, *The Bible and the Greeks* (1935), 82-95; L. Morris, *The Apostolic Preaching of the Cross* (1955); *The Cross in the NT* (1965).

J. C. CONNELL

EXTORTION (עשק, *violence, oppression, extortion, unjust gain,* esp. from the poor and needy by fraud and pillage [Deut 24:14; Ezek 22:7, 29; Jer 6:6]; ἁρπαγή, ἅρπαξ, *robbery, plunder, take forcefully, swindle* [Matt 12:29; 23:25; Luke 18:11; Heb 10:34]). The act or crime of getting another's money or property through force, under color of office, fraud, forgery, intimidation, threat, blackmail, oppression or show of right.

It has been said that as soon as a man knew another man, they began to trade and also to take advantage of each other. Numerous passages of Holy Scripture condemning fraud and extortion of various kinds indicate that even the people of God often became guilty of exploiting their fellow man. God Himself forbids all types of stealing and fraud, including extortion (Exod, chs. 21-23). "You shall not wrong a stranger or oppress him, for you were strangers in the land of Egypt" (Exod 22:21). The prophet Ezekiel warns that God will deal justly with an extortioner (Ezek 18:18) and states that extortion was a common crime of the time, "The people of the land have practiced extortion and committed robbery; they have oppressed the poor and needy" (Ezek 22:29). The psalmist preached that men who place confidence in extortion and robbery follow a vain hope (Ps 62:10).

Extortion through excessive interest, or usury, is particularly hit hard to prevent the exploitation of a fellow Israelite's misfortune (Lev 25:35, 36; Deut 23:19). The Talmud and the rabbis called usury the "abomination of abominations" and likened it to murder. The OT has no patience with the plea that the extortioner is within the law; legally or illegally, it is always wrong. One common form of extortion was to trick a man into a huge loan or pledge, then foreclose and force him to become a slave (Lev 25:39, 47). Insolvency was the common cause of people being reduced to slavery in Israel. It was not unknown that a husband would falsely accuse his new wife of not being a virgin to obtain the marriage payment (Deut 22:29). Much extortion went on along the caravan routes. Leaders of brigands would force merchants to pay tribute not to be robbed.

Jesus aimed charges of extortion, fraud, and robbery against the people of His day, particularly the Pharisees, in the sharpest terms their ears could bear: "Woe to you, scribes and Pharisees, hypocrites! for you cleanse the outside of the cup and of the plate, but inside they are full of extortion and rapacity" (Matt 23:25; cf. Luke 18:11). John the Baptist counseled repentant tax collectors and soldiers: "Collect no more than is appointed you. . . . Rob no one by violence or by false accusation, and be content with your wages" (Luke 3:13, 14). The final stroke is given by Paul: "nor thieves, nor the greedy, nor drunkards, nor revilers, nor robbers will inherit the kingdom of God" (1 Cor 6:10).

BIBLIOGRAPHY. R. de Vaux, *Ancient Israel* (1961), 172, 173; H. Daniel-Rops, *Daily Life in Palestine at the Time of Christ* (1962), 219-221; G. A. Buttrick, IDB, 201, 202.

L. M. PETERSEN

EYE (עין, cognate to Akkad. īnu, Assyrian *ēnu*, Ugaritic *'n*; ὄμμα ὀφθαλμός). The term usually appears in the dual and is the basic component of many idiomatic expressions, some of which can be traced back to Sumer. IGI, "eye." The common usage is of sight proceeding out from the eyes (Gen 13:10, et al.). The eye often is used as the symbol of understanding (3:5, et al.) and a sing. Canaanite gloss in *Amarna Letter*, 144 l. 17, "*īni-ya* [*ḫinaya*]"). A period of sorrow and a loss or diminution of the understanding as in old age is symbolized as a dimming of the eyes (Job 17:7, et al.). Often the "eyes" are used in parallel poetry as the "A" word whereas "ears" is the "B" word (Isa 6:10b, et al.). In other references, the "eyes" are the "A" word in the sense of intelligence, comprehension, whereas the "B" word is soul or body (Ps 31:9). Only in apocalyptic visions and prophetic utterances does the "eye see God." These theophanies are always in the form of the messianic incarnation (Dan 10:5, 6). In the NT, the word ὀφθαλμός, appears throughout. It is, like the Heb., the basis of many idioms: "an 'evil' eye" (one who looks with envy or jealousy, Matt 6:23 KJV); "in the twinkling of an eye" (1 Cor 15:52); "eyes of the heart or mind" (Luke 19:42). The other Gr. term is ὄμμα. A poetic term from Homer on, it appears only in two contexts, which involve the healing by Christ of blind men (Matt 20:34; Mark 8:23). In classical lit., it is usually used for the insight of intuition, "the eyes of the soul"; it may represent some specific phrase used by Christ on the occasions of the miracles and tr. into Gr. by this rarer term.

W. WHITE, JR.

A front view of Queen Nefert-iti showing use of eye paint. ©*Berlin Museum*

EYE PAINT (Heb. פוך, *black eye paint*, LXX στιμίζω, *tinge black* with antimony, ἐνχρίω στίβι', *anoint with antimony*; and Heb. כחל (verb) *to paint* eyes, LXX στιβίζομαι *to paint one's* eyelids and eyebrows *with black*). Eye paint, that substance made of mineral or other powder used by women in ancient times for beautifying the eyes.

The terms for eye paint are used only in the OT and only then found in four references: (1) 2 Kings 9:30 where Jezebel paints her eyes (Heb. *puk*; LXX *stimizo*) to allure Jehu; (2) Jeremiah 4:30 a reference in which Jerusalem presented as a harlot is pictured as enlarging her eyes (not, "face," KJV) with paint (Heb. *puk*, LXX, *enchríō stíbi*); (3) Ezekiel 23:40 where Oholibah the harlot in representation of Jerusalem, is pictured as painting her eyes (Heb. *kaḥal*; LXX, *stibizomai*); and (4) Job 42:14 in which reference Job's third daughter is called "horn of paint" or "antimony" (Heb. הפוך קרן ; LXX 'Αμαλθείας κέρας).

In the first three examples above the eye painting is connected with women of objectionable character. However, this does not mean that all such use of cosmetics is wrong, for the name of Job's daughter, as "Horn of Antimony," or "Keren-happuch" in Job 42:14 does not carry an evil connotation, since in 42:15 this daughter as well as the others is counted as best in the land.

Eye paint was used to enhance the beauty of women by "enlarging" (RSV) the eyes (Jer 4:30) and making them stand out brightly by outlining them and projecting the line to the outer edge of the eye. The gray or black mineral could also be applied to the eyebrows. Cf. the sculptor's bust of the Egyp. Queen Nefertiti, from Tell el-Amarna (ANEP, No. 404).

The material used for the eye paint mentioned in the OT was prob. the powdered minerals galena and/or stibnite; the galena being a lead ore, i.e., lead sulphide PbS, of bluish gray color and metallic luster. The stibnite was an antimony tri-sulphide, Sb_2S_3 of lead gray color and brilliant luster, a substance which the Romans called *stibium*. This mineral was listed as a part of Hezekiah's tribute to Sennacherib in the latter's annals (ANET, 288). *See* COSMETICS.

The eye paint powder before mixture with water was kept in a horn (cf. Job 42:14, "horn" of antimony), or slender reed, or in a jar.

BIBLIOGRAPHY. R. J. Forbes, *Studies in Ancient Technology,* IX (1964), 160-166.

W. H. MARE

EYES, DISEASES OF THE. *See* DISEASE, DISEASES.

EYESALVE (*κολλούριον*; variant in many MSS, *κολλύριον*). The word appears in the context of the address to the church at Laodicea (Rev 3:18). The term is a diminutive of the Gr. *kollura,* "little cake," a very common dosage form in the Hel. world. It has been suspected that this particular prescription for the spiritual blindness at Laodicea had some special reference to a product of that place, but such assumptions lack sufficient evidence to be more than speculations.

W. WHITE, JR.

EYESERVICE (*ὀφθαλμοδουλία*, a Hel. compound, *service to be seen, to please the eyes,* not therefore out of any good motivation). The term appears in nearly identical phrases (Eph 6:6; Col 3:22). The term is defined perfectly in the context in Ephesians, "Slaves, be obedient . . . not in the way of eyeservice, as menpleasers, but as servants of Christ, doing the will of God from the heart."

W. WHITE, JR.

EYEWITNESSES (*αὐτόπτης* [Luke 1:2], *eyewitness*). A specific term in classical Gr., used by the evangelist to insure the authenticity and historicity of his narrative. Another term with a similar meaning is *ἐπόπτης* (2 Pet 1:16). It is also of classical origin and was used often by both Christian and pagan writers in the Hel. and Rom. age to describe the deity as one who "oversees," the emphasis being not so much on the profundity and intensity of the gaze but in its all-inclusiveness. In 2 Peter it is used in a context nearly identical to the Lucan narrative. That Peter mentions "myths" is enlightening, as this term often was used to describe the initiated members of the Hel. mysteries. The author is thus saying, "we did not follow craftily devised myths when we made known to you the power and coming of our Lord Jesus Christ, but we were eyewitnesses of his majesty."

W. WHITE, JR.

EZAR, EZER e′ zər (Ezar only in 1 Chron 1:38, KJV editions since 1628). Name of six individuals in the OT.

1. (אצר ; LXX *'Ασαρ* et al., meaning uncertain; possibly "union" or "treasure"). A son of Seir the Horite in the land of Edom, mentioned sixth among the chiefs of the Horites (Gen 36:21, 30; 1 Chron 1:38). Three sons of Ezer are mentioned in Genesis 36:27; 1 Chronicles 1:42.

(שזר, or LXX *'Εζερ*, *'Αζερ* et al., meaning "help").

2. A descendant of Judah and father of Hushah (1 Chron 4:4).

3. A son of Ephraim who was slain by the men of Gath when he made a raid on their cattle (1 Chron 7:21).

4. The chief of the mighty men of Gad, who came to David in Ziklag when David fled from Saul (1 Chron 12:9).

5. Ruler of Mizpah and son of Jeshua, a Levite who helped to repair the walls of Jerusalem in the days of Nehemiah (Neh 3:19).

6. A priest (singer, musician) who assisted Nehemiah in the dedication of the rebuilt walls of Jerusalem (Neh 12:42).

E. L. ACKLEY

EZBAI ĕz′ bī (אזבי, LXX, *'Αζωβε*, et al., *shining, beautiful* [?]). The father of Naari, who was one of David's thirty mighty men (1 Chron 11:37). The parallel in 2 Samuel 23:35 has "Paarai the Arbite." Some MSS of the LXX of the latter passage read, however, *υἵος* (*τοῦ*) *'Ασβί*, in accordance with 1 Chronicles 11:37.

There is no consensus of opinion about harmonizing "Ezbai" with "the Arbite," though some scholars prefer the reading of 2 Samuel, citing Arab in Joshua 15:52, or reading "the Arkite" as in Genesis 10:17 and 1 Chronicles 1:15.

E. L. ACKLEY

EZBON ĕz′ bŏn (אצבון ; LXX *'Ασεβὼν*, *θασοβὰν*; meaning unknown). 1. A clan chieftain of the tribe of Benjamin, listed as the son of Bela (1 Chron 7:7).

2. The son of Gad, and as such the head of one of the clans of Gad (Gen 46:16). He is

called Ozni in the list (Num 26:15-18). Neither Ezbon of Benjamin nor Ezbon of Gad is known outside these references.

G. G. SWAIM

EZECHIAS, EZECIAS, EZEKIAS. *See* HEZEKIAH.

EZEKIEL ĭ zeʹ kyəl (יְחֶזְקֵאל ; LXX, Ἰεζεκιήλ, *God strengthens*). Ezekiel was one of the major prophets. He was the son of Buzi, a priest of the family of Zadok (Ezek 1:3); and so like Zechariah (Zech 1:1; Neh 12:12, 16) and Jeremiah (Jer 1:1), combined both the offices of prophet and priest, the Levitical influence being apparent in chs. 40-48 of his prophecy. He was reared in Jerusalem and perhaps had already entered upon the work of the priesthood when he was taken with other captives, including King Jehoiachin to Babylonia into exile by Nebuchadnezzar in 597 B.C.

The problem concerning the age of Ezekiel when he was taken into exile has been a matter of discussion, but it is most probable that he was twenty-five years old at the time. The opening statement of his prophecy, "In the thirtieth year . . . as I was among the exiles," appears to be a reference to his age at the time of his call into the prophetic ministry, which in the following verse is dated in the "fifth year of the exile of King Jehoiachin," who was also among the captives of the 597 B.C. deportation (Ezek 1:2). The summons to take up the prophetic ministry thus came to Ezekiel in 592 B.C. Both John the Baptist and Jesus began their public ministry at the age of thirty (Luke 3:23).

As a member of the Zadok family, Ezekiel was among the aristocracy taken into captivity by Nebuchadnezzar (2 Kings 24:14). The prophet therefore built the chronology of his prophecy on the years of Jehoiachin's abduction (Ezek 1:2; 33:21; 40:1). His last dated prophecy is in the year 570 B.C., the twenty-seventh year of Jehoiachin's captivity (29:17), and indicates that Ezekiel exercised his prophetic office for at least twenty-two years, his first prophecy having been announced in 592 B.C.

Ezekiel's prophetic ministry falls into two major periods. The first included the years 592-586 B.C., during which the prophet's message—directed toward Jerusalem—consisted of reiterated warnings and symbolic actions designed to bring Judah to repentance and back to her historic faith in God. The second period, which began with the year of the destruction of Jerusalem and the Temple by Nebuchadnezzar, included the years 586-570 B.C. In the course of these years, Ezekiel was a pastor to the exiles and a messenger of comfort and hope (Ezek 33-48). Thirteen years of silence separated the two periods of active prophesying, the last prophecy of the first period having been delivered in April 585 B.C. (32:17). He was not heard from again until April 572 B.C.

The conical tower over Ezekiel's Tomb in Kifl, Babylonia. ©*M.P.S.*

(40:1). It has been suggested that Ezekiel returned to Jerusalem before the city fell, but there is no real evidence for this. He was in Babylonia when the city fell (cf. 33:21, 22.)

The years of Ezekiel's captivity were the most severe years of Judah's history. The period of Assyrian domination of Judah actually began in 722 B.C. when the Assyrian Sargon took Samaria and destroyed the northern kingdom, and although Judah remained an independent kingdom, she was forced to pay tribute to the Assyrians. With the rise of Babylonian power under Nebuchadnezzar in 605 B.C. through the battle of Carchemish, the position of Judah rapidly grew worse. In that year, Daniel was in the group taken into captivity by the Babylonians led by Nebuchadnezzar. This was the first deportation, which was followed in 597 B.C. by a second when Nebuchadnezzar again invaded Judah and took the young king Jehoiachin and many of the leading citizens as captives to Babylonia (2 Kings 24:14-17). Among the captives of this deportation was Ezekiel. The third deportation of Judean captives to Babylonia by Nebuchadnezzar was in 586 B.C., the year of the destruction of the city of Jerusalem, the Temple, and the kingdom of Judah. Thus Ezekiel's life paralleled the years of the greatest crisis of Israel's history.

In Babylonia, Ezekiel was a member of a colony of captives in or near Tel-Abib on the "River Chebar," which is not to be confused with the River Chaboras. It prob. was the arm of an extensive system of canals (Ezek 3:15). Ezekiel was married (24:16-18) and lived in his own house (3:24; cf. 8:1). On the fifth day of the fourth month in the fifth year of his exile (592 B.C.), he was summoned in a vision to be a prophet of God (1:1-3:11). His description of this vision is full of mysterious imagery designed to demonstrate the omnipotence, omnipresence, and omniscience of God as they are related to the ministry of Ezekiel and the future of Judah. Ezekiel was commissioned to summon the rebellious nation to hear the word of the Lord. Another vision followed in which the prophet was given a scroll with writing on both sides. He was told to eat the words, "words of lamentation and mourning and woe" (2:10), and he found them "as sweet as honey" to the taste (3:3). He was informed that he would meet resistance (3:4-11), and he then went to the exiles and sat among them overwhelmed. He proceeded to prophesy the inevitability of Jerusalem's destruction for its persistence in sin.

It is interesting to contrast Ezekiel's inaugural vision with the experiences of Isaiah and Jeremiah. The lips of Isaiah were cleansed and then he received an audible and verbal communication from the Lord (Isa 6:6-10). Jeremiah first heard the Lord addressing him. The Lord then touched his mouth in an act symbolizing the delivering of His words to the prophet (Jer 1:4-10). For Ezekiel, however, the words for the people were written in advance and he "ate" the written words (Ezek 2:10).

Ezekiel emphasized the doctrine of personal responsibility for sin in the most vigorous terms. "The soul that sins shall die" (18:4). The message of Ezekiel in this respect constituted an important turning point in the prophetic message. With the destruction of the nation, the emphasis on national responsibility gave way to an emphasis on individual responsibility.

Like other prophets, Ezekiel enforced his spoken message from the Lord by various symbolic acts. These symbolic acts were enacted words, and they were assumed to have in themselves divine effectiveness. He drew a plan of besieged Jerusalem upon a brick (4:1-3). He lay prostrate on one side and then on the other for several days (4:4-8). He shaved himself with a sword and then divided the hair (5:1-17). Many such dramatic symbolic acts enhanced the effectiveness of the prophet's message. After the destruction of Jerusalem Ezekiel's prophecy became predominantly a message of consolation. Fully aware of the weaknesses of God's chosen people, the prophet centered Israel's Messianic hope in them, describing in glowing terms their religious, moral, political, and economic future.

Aside from Ezekiel's influence upon the NT, esp. the imagery of the Apocalypse, he exerted great influence upon the development of Judaism. He is sometimes referred to as the father of Judaism. The doctrines of personal immortality and the resurrection, and the emphasis upon the law in Judaism were all profoundly influenced by Ezekiel. His visions, frequently mysterious, affected considerably the development of Judaism's apocalyptic as well as the later mysticism of the Cabala. The prophet figured prominently in the mural paintings of the synagogue of Dura Europos completed in A.D. 255. The synagogue was removed and reconstructed as part of the national museum in Damascus, Syria. Some rabbis of the school of Shammai regarded Ezekiel as only an apocryphal book because they thought it contradicted the Mosaic law. *See* EXILE.

BIBLIOGRAPHY. G. E. Wright, *Biblical Archaeology* (1960), 88, 123, 132; H. Daniel-Rops, *Israel and the Ancient World* (1964), 203, 286-290, 313; W. Narrelson, *Interpreting the Old Testament* (1964), 285-315.

A. C. SCHULTZ

EZEKIEL, BOOK OF ē zēk' ĭĕl (יחזקאל, LXX Ἰεζεκιηλ, *God strengthens*, Vul. Ezechiel). Son of the priest Buzi, and a prophet in the Babylonian exile.

- I. The historical background of the book
  1. The fall of the northern kingdom of Israel
  2. The destruction of Assyria
  3. The fall of Jerusalem
  4. The captivity
- II. History of Ezekiel studies
  1. Early attitudes to the Book of Ezekiel
  2. Twentieth-century critical studies
  3. The locale of Ezekiel's activity
- III. The text, integrity, style and canonicity
  1. Condition of the text and its integrity
  2. The style of Ezekiel
  3. The problem of canonicity
- IV. The division and contents of the book
- V. Teachings
  1. Ezekiel's concept of God
  2. Ezekiel's concept of Israel
  3. The freedom and responsibility of the individual before God
  4. The kingdom of God in its final glory (40-48)
- VI. The NT use of Ezekiel
  1. Quotations from Ezekiel in the NT
  2. Ezekiel's influence on John
  3. Jesus and Ezekiel
- VII. Ezekiel in the history of Judaism
  1. His influence upon the mysticism of Judaism
  2. His influence upon the cult of Judaism
  3. His influence upon the literature of Judaism

I. The historical background of the book. The ministry of Ezekiel took place in one of the great critical periods of history. His book presents a clear picture of a definite historical situation because the events of his day made a profound impression upon Ezekiel. He makes allusions to contemporary events which are known to us from extra-Biblical sources. In addition to general summaries of history (e.g., 20:5-29), Ezekiel refers to specific historical events, frequently dating accurately an incident or an oracle in accordance with his chronological system which is based upon the years of the Babylonian captivity. From his situation in Babylonia as one of the captives Ezekiel describes the destruction and restoration of Israel.

1. *The fall of the northern kingdom of Israel.* The northern kingdom of Israel fell in 722 B.C. with the destruction of Samaria by the Assyrians who had grasped the hegemony of the Near E. The Assyrians invaded Judah also but were unable to take Jerusalem. In the reign of Ashurbanipal (669-633 B.C.) the Assyrian empire began to disintegrate. The Babylonians under King Nabopolassar led a coalition of the Medes, Persians, and Scythians against the Assyrians and in 612 B.C. destroyed Nineveh. In the course of the battle the last king of the great Assyrian dynasty Sin-shar-ishkun (627-612 B.C.) lost his life. The Assyrian army, however, was mustered by Ashuruballat, an army officer, for the final struggle.

At the same time there was a revival of power in Egypt and Pharaoh Neco, because of the growing Neo-Babylonian menace, decided that alliance with Assyria was the best way to accomplish his own ambitions for Egypt. It was necessary for Neco to march his army northward through Judah, to which Josiah (639-608 B.C.) king of Judah objected. Over Jeremiah's objections Josiah attempted to stop Neco at Megiddo and in the battle Josiah lost his life (2 Kings 23:29). Judah was now a vassal state of Egypt and Neco placed Josiah's son Shallum, called Jehoahaz, on the throne (Jer 22:10-12; Ezek 19:2-4). He proved to be unsatisfactory for the purposes of Neco, and after three months as king Jehoahaz was deported to Egypt. Neco now placed Jehoiakim (608-597 B.C.), an older son of Josiah, on the throne of Judah (2 Kings 23:31-36).

2. *The destruction of Assyria.* The Egyptians joined the Assyrians for the final battle against the coalition led by the Babylonians for the hegemony of the Near E. At Carchemish in 605 B.C. on the Euphrates River, the Egyptians and Assyrians were defeated by Nebuchadnezzar, who had succeeded his father as king of Babylonia (Jer 46:2). World hegemony now belonged to the Chaldeans and Jehoiakim became a vassal of Nebuchadnezzar (2 Kings 24:1). The Babylonians marched upon Jerusalem to discourage Jehoiakim's tendency to disloyalty to Nebuchadnezzar. The result was the first deportation of captives to Babylon, among whom was Daniel, Ezekiel's younger contemporary. The spiritual life of Judah suffered under Jehoiakim's leadership and he persecuted the prophets (Jer 36:1, 9, 28, 29, 30, 32). His inclinations to revolt against the Babylonians brought Nebuchadnezzar to Jerusalem again in 597 B.C. However, Jehoiakim died ignominiously just before the Babylonian's punitive expedition arrived at Jerusalem, and was buried "With the burial of an ass" (Jer 22:18, 19). He was followed on the throne by his son Jehoiachin (Coniah or Jeconiah) who three months later surrendered to Nebuchadnezzar (2 Kings 24:8-17; Jer 22:24-30; Ezek 19:5-9). The Babylonians humiliated Jerusalem and deported several thousands of the influential of the population to Babylonia. Among these exiles were Jehoiachin and Ezekiel, and the prophet dated his prophecies by the years of this captivity. As a member of the exilic community, where Jehoiachin still bore the title of king, Ezekiel avoided a chronology for his oracles based upon the years of King Zedekiah (597-586), Jehoiachin's successor (Ezek 1:1, 2).

Nebuchadnezzar made Mattaniah, Jehoiachin's uncle and third son of Josiah, king of Judah in the place of Jehoiachin and his name was changed to Zedekiah (2 Kings 24:17-25:7; Ezek 19:11-14). He proved to be spiritually and administratively incapable of meeting the demands of a difficult situation and was induced by the pro-Egyp. party in Jerusalem to break his oath of fealty to Nebuchadnezzar. He joined a coalition of anti-Babylonian nations (Jer 27:1-11; Ezek 17:13-15), news of which reached Nebuchadnezzar, who summoned Zedekiah to Babylon in the fourth year of his reign (Jer 51:59). Judah, caught between the opposing forces of the two superpowers of the Near E, was in an extremely difficult position with the pro-Egyp. and the pro-Babylonian parties each putting pressure on the king. Zedekiah vacillated for a while but finally yielded to the demands of the pro-Egyp. party and joined the rebellion against Nebuchadnezzar (2 Kings 24:20). Nebuchadnezzar's army appeared again at the gates of Jerusalem.

3. *The fall of Jerusalem.* The Babylonian siege of the city lasted a year and a half (2 Kings 25:1-3) and culminated in the razing of the city and the plundering and burning of the Temple. By the time Jerusalem fell famine had reduced the beleaguered city to desperate straits (Jer 37:21; Lam 2:4). Zedekiah, giving up all hope tried to escape by fleeing in the direction of the wilderness only to fall into the hands of the troops of Nebuchadnezzar. Ezekiel presents a symbolical portrayal of the king's flight. Zedekiah was brought before Nebuchadnezzar who was encamped at Riblah where the Babylonian passed sentence upon the Judean. He was made to witness the execution of his sons and then was blinded and brought in chains to Babylon. The prophecies of Ezekiel (12:13) and Jeremiah (Jer 34:2-5) were fulfilled. In 586 B.C. Zedekiah joined Jehoiachin in the captivity.

4. *The captivity.* Even as king of Judah appointed by Nebuchadnezzar, Zedekiah was in a rather anomalous situation. Jehoiachin had gone into captivity in 597 B.C. but there were some who believed that he would shortly return to occupy the throne of Judah (Jer 28:3, 4, 11). Jehoiachin himself may have believed in the possibility of his restoration to the throne of Judah, prompting Jeremiah's warning that this would not take place (Jer 22:24-30). It may be that the Babylonians preserved Jehoiachin in Babylon against the possibility of his return to Jerusalem. In captivity he retained the title of king and he was called "Yaukin, king of Judah" in official Babylonian records. In recently published tablets from the archives of Nebuchadnezzar dating c. 592 B.C. "Yaukin, king of Judah" and five of his sons are listed among the recipients of food rations from the royal supplies. Three jar handles stamped with the inscr. "Belonging to Eliakim, steward of Yau-qin" (Jehoiachin) found at Beth-Shemesh and Kiriath-sepher may suggest the hope of his return. Jehoiachin was released from prison by Evil-merodach, son of Nebuchadnezzar in 560 B.C., the thirty-seventh year of his captivity (2 Kings 25:27). It appears obvious that generally Jehoiachin was regarded as the legitimate king of Judah with Zedekiah acting as regent until the time of the imminent return of the exiles.

According to Jeremiah 29:4-7 many of the exiles were able to rise above the slavery and serfdom which was the lot of some of the captives. Many were able to build their own houses, plant their own vineyards, and raise their own crops. Others were successful in the business and commercial affairs of the country. Records recovered from the ruins of the city of Nippur show the names of many Jews connected with the influential banking house of Murashû and Sons. According to Ezra 2:68, 69 some of these successful Jews made substantial contributions to the return from Babylonia under Zerubbabel. The prosperity of the Jews in the Babylonian *golah* (captivity) explains why comparatively few took advantage of the opportunity to return to their homeland.

According to 2 Kings 24:14 there were 10,000 captives in the 597 B.C. deportation. There are some difficulties with the figures (cf. Jer 52:28-30) regarding the number of the exiles involved, but it has been estimated that nearly 50,000 Jews were captives in the three deportations imposed by Nebuchadnezzar. They were settled in colonies where they were permitted a reasonable degree of liberty. The principal colony appears to have been at Tel Abib, by the River Chebar, a canal mentioned in Babylonian sources as *nâru kabari*, and which passed through Nippur, a city SE of Babylon. Ezekiel lived in the colony at Tel Abib and his home became a meeting place of the elders of the exiled community (Ezek 3:24; 8:1; 14:1; 20:1). In the course of a profound theophany (1:4-28) he was commissioned to be God's messenger to the Jews of the captivity (2:3). The visions of the prophet, his allegories, symbolic actions, apocalyptic imagery, and the interpreting angel led to attempts on the part of some scholars to demonstrate that Ezekiel was psychopathic. He has been described as being a victim of paranoid schizophrenia or even catatonia. (E. C. Broome, "Ezekiel's Abnormal Personality," JBL, 65 [1946], pp. 272-292.) C. G. Howie gives an adequate answer to these conclusions and says, "Ezekiel . . . was a mystic by nature with a sensitive, artistic imagination which brought forth some of the best-known visions and symbolic figures of speech in Biblical literature" (C. G. Howie, "Psychological Aspects of Ezekiel and His Prophecy," JBL, 65 [1946], pp. 69-84). The suggested deviations of Ezekiel from his contemporaries and other prophets are accounted for by his peculiar genius.

II. The history of Ezekiel studies. 1. *Early attitudes to the Book of Ezekiel.* Shortly after the formation of the Heb. canon some Jewish scholars raised doubts about the Book of Ezekiel, classifying it among the Antilegomena. It was thought that Ezekiel at some points contradicted the Pentateuch. Benedict Spinoza in the 17th cent. suggested that parts of Ezekiel's work have been lost and that what remains has suffered from corruption. In the 18th cent. G. L. Oeder suggested that two books comprise Ezekiel, contained in chs. 1-39 and chs. 40-48. Only the first of these, according to Oeder belongs to the prophet Ezekiel. In the 19th cent. Leopold Zunz held that the entire book was spurious and was written around 400 B.C. In the early 20th cent. Hugo Winckler advocated the idea that Ezekiel was a composite work of the early Pers. period. Such opinions at the time that they were expressed were not the views of the prevailing Biblical scholarship and at the end of the 19th cent. A. B. Davidson offered what was then the representative opinion of scholarship: "The Book of Ezekiel is simpler and more perspicuous in its arrangement than any other of the great prophetical books. It was prob. committed to writing late in the prophet's life, and, unlike the prophecies of Isaiah, which were given out piecemeal, was issued in its complete form at once. The prophecies are disposed upon the whole in chronological order . . ." (*The Book of the Prophet Ezekiel*, p. iv).

2. *Twentieth-century critical studies.* In the beginning of the 20th cent. critical opinion changed radically. Liberal literally criticism

Ezekiel Prophesying. From an engraving by Dore. © *H.P.*

advocated the redactional character of the book which led to attempts to determine the amount of authentic Ezekielian material. In 1924 Gustav Hölscher published his *Esechiel: Der Dichter und das Buch*, which was a milestone in the history of Biblical criticism. It presented an entirely new view of both the prophet and his book and maintained that of the 1,273 vv. in the book only 170 could be attributed to Ezekiel. According to Hölscher 5th cent. priestly redactors were responsible for most of the book. They added all the legalistic and ritual material which completely transformed the prophet's original oracles and made of him a teacher of the law instead of a simple messenger of the people. The Ezekiel presented in the prophecy never existed, but was a fiction invented by the priestly editors of the book.

In 1932 V. Herntrich in his *Ezechielprobleme* held that Ezekiel prophesied in Pal. and that a redactor was responsible for adding the material related to the Babylonian background.

The most radical critical position was that of Charles C. Torrey who in 1930 published his *Pseudo-Ezekiel and the Original Prophecy*. Torrey's view was that the book comes from a writer who lived c. 200 B.C. and that the prophet Ezekiel never existed as a historical person. The book is a pseudepigraphon presenting a fictitious Ezekiel who is imagined to have lived in the reign of Manasseh. The Babylonian setting is the result of still later editing, according to Torrey.

In the United States William A. Irwin of the University of Chicago in 1943 published his *The Problem of Ezekiel* which was an attempt to build a critical theory upon the results of his predecessors in liberal Biblical criticism. Irwin considered the substance of the book to be Hel. Of the 1,273 vv. in the prophecy only 251 are genuine in whole or in part, the proportions of originality varying from complete genuineness down to a bare remnant of not more than a word of two. About eighty per cent of the book is spurious according to Irwin. The prophecy emerges from Irwin's methods as a patchwork of many authors, consisting of commentaries and explanations of the commentaries written over a period of several centuries. However, the prophet Ezekiel appeared as a truly prophetic personality after his genuine oracles had been disentangled from the spurious later additions.

Opposed to the opinions of critics such as the foregoing during this period were scholars who took a more conservative view. C. G. Howie in his *The Date and Composition of Ezekiel* (1950) supports the substantial correctness of the traditional view of Ezekiel and disputes the idea that the book is a composite work. Georg Fohrer also considered the major part of the book as being authentic and that whatever editing took place in the course of the history of the text did not essentially affect its content. He supports the idea of a Babylonian setting for the prophetic activity of Ezekiel (Georg Fohrer, *Die Hauptprobleme des Buches Ezechiel* [1952]). H. H. Rowley in his *The Book of Ezekiel in Modern Study* (1953) also rejected the conclusions of the popular liberal critical position and emphasized that the major content of the book belongs to the prophet.

Archeological discoveries have come to the support of the traditional view of Ezekiel. C. C. Torrey and his school attacked the historical accuracy of Ezekiel. Torrey denied that there had been a destruction of Jerusalem and Judah by Nebuchadnezzar which meant also that the Biblical account was mistaken in its history of the Captivity. This denial of the Chaldean invasion with its destruction of Judah and the resulting Captivity meant also that the Biblical account of the Restoration was false. Consequently Ezra, Nehemiah, and Jeremiah were also rejected as reliable history along with Ezekiel. The rejection of the historical accuracy of the account of what is perhaps one of the most important periods in Israel's history was also by implication of tremendous theological significance. Much of prophetic Messianology is built around the events of the destruction of Jerusalem and the Temple, the Babylonian Exile, and the Restoration.

Archeological researches have confirmed many aspects of the historical background of Ezekiel's book. The destruction of the cities of Judah by the Chaldeans has been confirmed by the evidence of inscrs. and pottery. The Lachish Ostraca recreated vividly the military campaign of the Babylonians in Judah just before they destroyed Jerusalem. Excavations in Babylon have uncovered ration lists of captives receiving grain from the supplies of Nebuchadnezzar among whom are many Jews. The fact that "Yaukin (Jehoiachin) King of Judah" and five of his sons are mentioned several times in the lists is a remarkable attestation to the Biblical records of the *golah*. Even Torrey's contention that specialists and skilled workers like gardeners were not taken captive to Babylonia as indicated in the Biblical records has been refuted by the mention of such workers in the ration lists. Archeological reconstruction of this period has come also to the support of the reliability of the record in this regard in Jeremiah, Ezra, and Nehemiah. There is also extra-Biblical evidence of the return of the captives to Jerusalem. William F. Albright says, "The substantial historicity of the Edict of Cyrus (Ezra 1:2-4; 6:3-5) in 538 has been confirmed by modern archaeological discoveries" (*The Biblical Period from Abraham to Ezra*, [1963], p. 87). All of this has contributed to a return on the part of the critical school to a more conservative position in regard to the origin of the Book of Ezekiel.

3. *The locale of Ezekiel's activity.* The problem of the locality of Ezekiel's prophetic

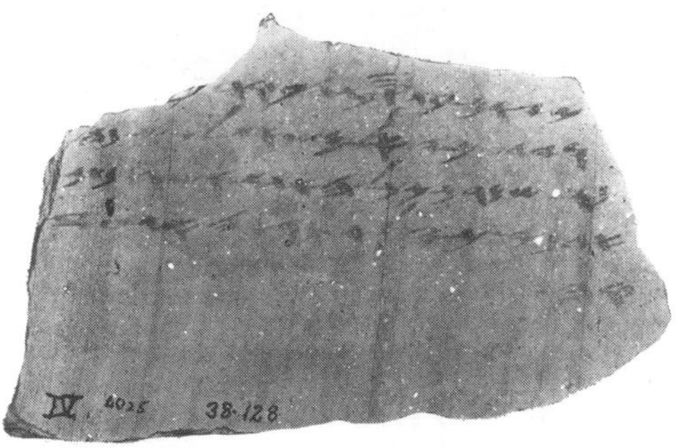

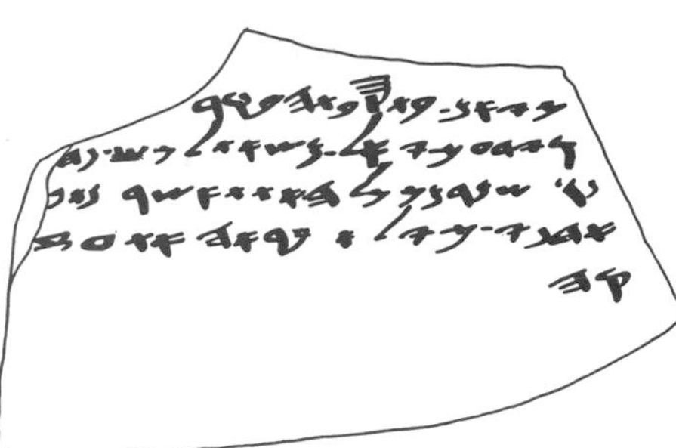

Reverse of Ostracon IV from Tell ed-Duweir with mention of Lachish; early sixth century. © *P.A.M.*

A general view of the Tell at Lachish, from which many archeological discoveries have come to support the traditional view of the authorship of Ezekiel. © *Lev*

activity is closely related to some of the aspects of the preceding discussion. The traditional position, based upon the book itself, is that the place of Ezekiel's ministry is Babylonia, in Tel Abib beside the River Chebar (Ezek 1:1). It was there that the heavens were opened and Ezekiel saw visions of God. Contrary to this view is the opinion of many of the critical school that Ezekiel prophesied in Jerusalem. This view rests upon the idea that many of the detailed descriptions of the religious, cultural, and political situation in Jerusalem are so vivid and realistic as to require that the writer was a personal eyewitness to the events and scenes described (Ezek 8; 11:1-13). The scholars who believe that Ezekiel spent his entire ministry in Judea hold that a later editor added the materials that reflect a Babylonian setting. On the other hand these same materials indicate to other scholars that the period of the prophet's ministry was divided between Babylonia and Jerusalem, first in Jerusalem and later in Babylonia. C. C. Torrey, James Smith, and Volkar Herntrich held to the Palestinian ministry of Ezekiel while Alfred Bertholet advocated the view that both areas were involved as the locale of the prophet's activity. The arguments involved in this problem are somewhat subjective in character, and it is not impossible that the entire prophetic activity of Ezekiel took place in Babylonia.

There was close contact between the exiles in Babylonia and the Jerusalem community. Consequently it was not impossible for a prophet in Babylonia to deliver prophecies and perform symbolic actions for the instruction of the people in Judah. If Ezekiel and Jeremiah were in Jerusalem together one would expect to find some indication of it not only in the Books of Jeremiah and Ezekiel, but also in the Biblical historical records of the period.

III. The text, integrity, style, and canonicity. 1. *Condition of the text and its integrity.* The MT of Ezekiel reflects the many scribal errors produced in the course of its transmission through the centuries, a phenomenon to which all ancient documents were subjected. Fortunately the LXX, as well as other trs., parallel texts, and general textual evidence have made possible reasonably reliable restoration of many passages. Hölscher and Irwin determined what they conceived to be the original and true text by means of a preconceived key to the genuine Ezekielian material. Their method was based upon what they judged to be Ezekiel's literary style and deviations from that style were expunged from the text and declared to be spurious. Emendations were made in the text to suit the requirements of the presuppositions.

A clumsy text does not necessarily indicate an irregularity or deviation from the smoothness of a pre-conceived style or a nonoriginal expression. The subjective character of the process is well described by Herbert G. May: "Literary and Historical criticism is not an exact science. The scholar can only be as honest as possible in considering and weighing all the facts. . . . There is one further warning: in a book as difficult as that of Ezekiel it is inevitable that Biblical scholars should have been much influenced by their total conception of the development and character of Hebrew religion and history" (IB, VI, 45).

2. *The style of Ezekiel.* The various literary types in the book reflect the antithetical characteristics of the prophet's personality, his seemingly contradictory moods determining the wide variations of his style, as expressed sometimes in vivid poetry and at other times in ordinary prose. Ezekiel's poetic nature is reflected in his effective use of the *Ḳinah* or dirge as in the beautiful lament over the banished princes of the royal house (19:1-14). Perhaps the greatest poetry in the book is that of the allegories of the whelps (19:2-6, 8, 9) and of the ship Tyre (27:3-9, 25-36). The description of the ship Tyre is so true to life that it is one of the most important literary sources of our knowledge of ancient navigation. The image of Jerusalem as a foundling child (16:1-63) is as beautiful as any to be found in prophecy. Ezekiel's prose style is generally without particular distinction, but is lucid and adequate to convey his message. There is some Akkad. influence in the prophet's Heb. but Aram. influence is more pronounced.

Frequently repeated typical words and phrases give support to the idea of the literary unity of the book: "walking in my statutes" (eleven times), "my sabbaths" (twelve times), "As I live, says the Lord GOD" (thirteen times), "countries" (twenty-four times), "idols" (forty times), "Then they will know that I am the LORD" (fifty times). These Ezekielian words and phrases appear in every part of the book indicating its literary homogeneity and suggesting a single author for the prophecy. The book thus bears the stamp of a single mind in its phraseology, its imagery, and in its process of thought which is developed on a plan so perspicuous and comprehensive that the evidence of literary design in its composition is unquestionably clear.

3. *The problem of canonicity.* The Book of Ezekiel became a part of the Heb. canon but in the days of the rabbis Shammai and Hillel questions arose in regard to some of the canonical books which consequently came to be thought of as the Antilegomena. Among these was Ezekiel together with Esther, Proverbs, Ecclesiastes, and Song of Solomon. The actual point at issue was not the standing of the Book of Ezekiel in the canon which was taken for granted, but the use of the book for liturgical purposes and in public readings. There is no clear evidence that there was an attempt to remove Ezekiel from the canon. The Talmud indicates (Hag 1:13a) that because of supposed contradictions to the Torah in chs. 40 to 48 of the book, it was thought its use in public was not desirable. It was anticipated that the difficulties would be solved by Elijah upon his return. It was also thought that the beautiful vision at the beginning of the prophecy would be profaned by public use or its study by any person under thirty years of age. Eventually, after burning 300 jars of oil in the course of his nightly researches Hananiah ben Hezekiah was able to find a satisfactory solution for the so-called contradictions. Others continued to be dissatisfied, and it is speculated that this situation contributed to carelessness in the transmission of the book resulting in the unusual number of corruptions in the present text. The so-called contradictions between the last part of the book and the Torah are the basis of much of the radical criticism concerning Ezekiel which presumes that Ezekiel 40-48 is a description of the revival of the Mosaic rituals. On the contrary, it is possible to see in these chs. not a revived Mosaism but a description of a future Temple with its own ceremonies which accounts for the differences.

IV. Division and contents. In its general theme the Book of Ezekiel resembles the Book of Isaiah, the first part having to do with judgment, the second with blessing. In its structure the forty-eight chs. of Ezekiel may be divided into four sections indicating the contents of the book. Within the general structure, the order of the material is, on the whole, chronological.

I. Prophecies against Israel (1-24)

A. Ezekiel's call and commission (1:1-3:15).

At the River Chebar the prophet has a vision of the glory of God and his call to prophesy to a "rebellious house" (2:5-8; 3:26, 27; 12:2-25), and to act as a guide to Israel. There is vivid description of the divine chariot which occupies a prominent place in the book (3:23; 8:4; 43:3).

B. Oracles against the people of Israel 4-24).

1. Oracles of symbolic actions describing the coming siege and destruction of Jerusalem and the Exile (4; 5).

2. Prophecies against the mountains of Israel and the land of Judah (6; 7).

3. The prophet's vision of the destruction of Jerusalem and the Temple and the departure of the glory of the Lord. It contains a description of the conditions in the city at the time (8-11).

4. Oracles of symbolic actions of the Exile (12).

5. Oracles against false prophets and prophetesses (13).

6. Oracles against idolaters (14:1-11).

7. Discourse on personal responsibility (14:12-23).

8. Allegories concerning Jerusalem; the city symbolized as a vine and as an unfaithful wife (15:1-16:52).

9. Prophecies concerning the doom and restoration of Israel (16:53-63).

10. Allegories concerning the kings of Judah, together with remarks on personal responsibility (17-19).

11. Discourse on Israel's apostasy and a prophecy of restoration (20).

12. Swords of the Lord and Nebuchadnezzar (21).

13. Description of the sins of Jerusalem and Israel (22).

14. Allegory of the two sisters Oholah and Oholibah symbolical of Samaria and Jerusalem (23).

15. Allegory of the pot; death of Ezekiel's wife (24).

II. Prophecies against foreign nations (25-32).

A. Against Ammon, Moab, Edom, Philistia (25).

B. Against Tyre represented in its wealth and beauty as the anointed cherub on the mountain of God, with a prophecy of blessing to Israel (26:1-28:19).

C. Against Sidon (28:20-26).

D. Against Egypt (29-32).

In the last two prophecies Nebuchadnezzar is named as the great agent to carry out the purposes of God.

III. Prophecies of restoration (33-39).

A. The prophet as a watchman (33:1-9; cf. 3:16-27).

B. Discourse on individual responsibility (33:10-20).

C. Ezekiel's dumbness (33:21, 22; cf. 3:22-27; 24:25-27).

D. Reaction of Ezekiel's audience (33:23-33).

E. Prophecy against the false shepherds of Israel (34).

F. Prophecies against Edom because of her support of the Chaldeans in their attack upon Judah (35).

G. Renewed prophecies concerning the restoration of the land and people of Israel (36).

H. Vision of the valley of dry bones prophesying Israel's resurrection (37:1-14).

I. Oracles of the two sticks and the restoration of Israel and Judah (37:15-28).

J. Prophecies against Gog of Magog (chs. 38; 39). These chs. describe the final assault upon the kingdom of God by the nations of the world under Gog from the land of Magog, and their destruction on the mountains of Israel in a great demonstration of the might of Jehovah to all the ends of the earth.

IV. Ezekiel's vision of the ideal theocracy of Messianic times with its restored land and Temple (40-48).

A. The Temple (40:1-44:3).

1. Ezekiel's preparation for the vision (40:1-4).

2. The Temple wall, courts, gates, chambers for the priests and the altar (40:5-47).

3. The Holy Place, the Holy of Holies, interior decoration of the Temple and its general dimensions (40:48-41:26).

4. Two three-story buildings north and south of the Temple containing the chambers for the priests (42:1-14).

5. Measurements of the whole Temple area (42:15-20).

6. The glory of Jehovah returns to the Temple after having departed from it for a time (43:1-12; cf. 10:19; 11:23).

7. The altar for the burnt offerings (43:13-27).

8.. The eastern gate (44:1-3).

B. The priesthood (44:4-45:17).

1. The statutes of the Levites (44:4-14).

2. Regulations for the Zadokite priests (44:15-31).

3. A specific area reserved sacred for the Temple, the priests, the Levites, and the prince (45:1-8).

4. The duties of the prince (45:9).

5. Correct weights and measures (45:10-12).

6. Taxes paid to the prince for the support of the Temple (45:13-17).

C. The Temple ritual (45:18-46:24).

1. Two semiannual atonement ceremonies for the Temple at the beginning of the first (March-April) and seventh (September-October) months (45:18-20).

2. The Passover Feast observed in spring (45:21-24) and the Feast of Tabernacles celebrated in autumn (45:25).

3. Sabbath and New Moon (46:1-7).

4. Regulations for entrance into the sanctuary (46:8-10).

5. The meal offering (46:11).

6. The prince's freewill offering (46:12).

7. The daily burnt offering in the morning (46:13-15).

8. Regulations for the tenure of land (46:16-18).

9. Regulations for the Temple kitchens (46:19-24).

D. The holy land (47; 48).

1. The life-giving stream (47:1-12). Flowing out of the Temple mount it transforms the desert into a paradise and the Dead Sea into a fresh-water lake abounding in fish.

2. The borders of the land of Israel, west of the Jordan River (47:21-23).

3. Aliens in Israel may acquire land in the country (47:21-23).

4. The seven tribes north of the Temple (48:1-7).

5. The area between the tribes of Judah and Benjamin is sacred for the affairs of the Temple (48:8-22).

6. The five tribes S of the Temple (48:23-29).

7. The twelve gates of the city (48:30-35). The gates are named after the twelve tribes of Israel, and the name of the city will be, "The Lord is there."

The central point of Ezekiel's prophecy is the destruction of Jerusalem. In the period before the destruction in 586 B.C., the prophet's principal purpose was to preach the importance of repentance and to demand a change in the people's way of life; to warn them that their confidence that the Egyptians could save them from defeat at the hands of the Babylonians was mistaken (17:15-17; cf. Jer 37:7); and to assure them that their city and Temple were to be inevitably and quickly destroyed. In the period after Jerusalem was destroyed, Ezekiel's main purpose was to comfort the exiled Hebrews by promises of eventual deliverance and restoration to their homeland, and to encourage them by assurances of future abundant blessings. His prophecies against foreign nations were delivered between these two periods, most of them having been spoken during the interval between the revelation to Ezekiel that Nebuchadnezzar had laid siege to Jerusalem (24:2) and the reception of the news that the Babylonians had taken it (33:21). The periods at which the prophecies on these various subjects were delivered are usually carefully noted in relation to the chronology of the captivity.

V. Teaching. A study of the teaching of Ezekiel's prophecy places him among the greatest of the Heb. prophets. He gave definite and clear expression to the great theological concepts which were at the heart of the preaching of all his predecessors in the prophetic office.

1. Ezekiel's concept of God. Fundamental to an understanding of Ezekiel's theology is his concept of God. It is the glory of God that is first drawn to our attention by the prophet. The vision by the River Chebar which formed the introduction to the call of Ezekiel to the prophetic office, was "the appearance of the likeness of the glory of the LORD" (1:28 KJV). Here Jehovah is described as the absolute ruler of all creation over which He sits enthroned. The vision is in the form of a divine throne-chariot and appears as a great cloud and fire coming from the N. The chariot is borne by four living creatures in the form of men, "each had four faces, and each of them had four wings. . . . As for the likeness of their faces each had the face of a man in front; the four had the face of a lion on the right side, the four had the face of an ox on the left side, and the four had the face of an eagle at the back," representing the whole living creation (1:6, 10, 22-28).

These figures appear again in Revelation 4:7. The vision symbolized the transcendence of God, His omnipotence, omnipresence, and omniscience. It represented the constant and diverse manifestation of God's power in the world and Ezekiel gives it a greater emphasis than any of his predecessors. This concept of

God enters profoundly into the fiber of the prophet's teaching and is woven into every aspect of his theology.

The key to the ministry of the exiled prophet was that the glory of God could be revealed in the plains of Babylonia as clearly as on the hills of Judaea. He experienced it again in the plains of Babylonia (3:23). By the power of the Spirit he beheld it in the Temple together with "the great abominations that the house of Israel are committing" in its very presence (8:3-6). He saw it leaving its accustomed place on the cherubim as the command was given to destroy the sinful city (9:3;10:4) and eventually deserting the polluted place which had become unfit for its presence (10: 18, 19; 11:22, 23). In still another vision Ezekiel saw the glory of God return to the restored city and Temple; again "the glory of the LORD entered the Temple" and he heard the voice saying, "this is the place of my throne and the place of the soles of my feet, where I will dwell in the midst of the people of Israel for ever" (43:2-7; 44:4).

This abiding sense of the glory of God has its counterpart in the title by which Ezekiel is led to speak of himself. He is the "son of man," a weak and mortal representation of fallen humanity, conscious of his limitations before the presence of the glory of God (2:1). This indicates that Ezekiel is conscious of the fact that Jehovah is a moral being with the attributes of jealousy, anger, pity, etc., but he consistently insists that the activity of Deity must be self-centered that is, the purpose of all His dealings with men, whether in judgment or in mercy, is a revelation of His own Godhead. The constantly recurring declaration (more than fifty times) is "You shall know that I am the LORD" (6:7). It is a doctrine to which the prophet attaches the utmost importance.

Ezekiel has much to say about the name of the Lord. The name of the Lord is the correlative of His glory. That name is the name of Yahweh. "I am Yahweh" (אני יהוה 6:7) is the constantly reiterated claim in the prophecy. All of Yahweh's dealings with Israel have been, are, and will be, "for my name's sake." The acts of God are designed to reveal His one immutable nature. Israel had deserved nothing but destruction in the wilderness, but He spared them for His name's sake, "that it should not be profaned in the sight of the nations" (20:9, 14, 22). Nor is it for any merit on the part of Israel that she will be returned from the Exile, but for Yahweh's name's sake. "It is not for your sake, O house of Israel, that I am about to act, but for the sake of my holy name" (36:22). Both the redemption of Israel and the judgment of the nations are examples of the sovereign expression of divine grace in accordance with the immutable character of the divine nature.

Closely related to the ideas of the glory and the name of the Lord in Ezekiel's prophecy is the concept of His holiness. The phrase "manifest my holiness" appears repeatedly as an expression of Yahweh (20:41; 28:22, 25; 36:23; 38:16, 23; 39:27). His holiness is His essential Deity. Contemporary usage of the term "holy" has lost its original and proper comprehensive sense. The Heb. root from which the word is derived (קדש) seems to denote "separation." It represents God as distinct from man and separate from the creation He has brought into being. The term comes to signify the separation of God from everything that is finite, imperfect, and sinful. It is not a merely negative concept, being used as an appropriate epithet for the Deity, not to express any specific attribute, but rather to refer to the general idea of the Godhead. It includes the whole essential nature of God in its moral reference. Yahweh swears by His "holiness" or by "Himself" without distinguishing between them (cf. Amos 4:2; 6:8). Among non-Israelite peoples when the term was used with the word "god" or "gods," it was merely an otiose epithet, "the holy gods" with no more meaning than "the gods" (cf. Dan 4:8, 9, 18; 5:11, 14; Inscription of Eshmunazar). Ezekiel uses the epithet of Yahweh, who is the Holy One of Israel, or "the Holy One in Israel" (39:7).

The term is applied also to anything which belongs to the sphere of the Holy One in Israel or has come into His presence (cf. Exod 3:5; Num 16: 37, 38), or which belongs to Him. Hence His arm, His Spirit, His Temple are "holy" as are His city, people, land, etc. The word in this sense is applied to persons, places, and things set apart for His service, and are holy by virtue of that consecration or separation to God. It expresses not a quality but a relation. Things and men that were God's shared His "holiness" but they could be "profaned," such as His sabbaths or His holy princes (7:22, 24; 20:16).

When Yahweh reveals Himself as that which He is, He "sanctifies" Himself. Consequently to "magnify" or "glorify" Himself or set His glory among the nations are acts that "sanctify." It is said of the destruction of Gog: "Thus will I magnify myself, and sanctify myself (קדש, the verbal form in the text is hithpael); and I will be known in the eyes of many nations, and they shall know that I am the LORD" (38:23, KJV; cf. 28:22, KJV; 36:23; 38:16). In the same manner men "sanctify" Yahweh when they acknowledge what He is or ascribe to Him His true nature 36:23, KJV). Yahweh is "sanctified" in the eyes of the nations by the restoration and defense of His righteous people Israel (36:23, KJV; 38:16).

2. *Ezekiel's concept of Israel.* Yahweh reveals Himself through Israel to the nations. The statement, "I acted for the sake of my name, that it should not be profaned in the sight of the nations among whom they dwelt, in whose sight I made myself known to them in bringing them out of the land of Egypt"

(20:9, 14, 22) is usually used in reference to Israel and its destinies. It is an expression of Ezekiel's philosophy of history. History, esp. that of Israel, and as Israel is seen in the context of world history, is Yahweh acting for His own name's sake, Yahweh's concern for His own name was the origin of Israel's history and accounts for its course and future promise, otherwise she would have been destroyed because of her iniquities. The thrust of the prophet's idea is indicated by the fact that in his mind He who is God over all in the highest monotheistic sense is Yahweh, God of Israel. He has become historically God of Israel to begin His revelation of Himself to the nations, and will continue in this revelation until He is known to all the earth. Consequently Yahweh cannot destroy Israel for this would invalidate or obliterate the revelation already made (20: 9, 14, 22; cf. Deut 9:28). Thus Ezekiel views Yahweh as inseparably linked with the destinies of Israel. In spite of the frequent apostasies of the people Yahweh's revelation proceeded until the nation had to be punished and forced into exile. Among the nations, according to Ezekiel, this was a setback and reflected the weakness of Yahweh. They said, "These are the people of the LORD, and yet they had to go out of his land" (36:20).

In this way the name of Yahweh was profaned, and the heathen gained a false impression of the God of Israel and knowledge of Him was obscured. The adverse effect of the Captivity included not only the nations but also many in Israel who did not understand what happened. This effect will be eliminated when the final lesson of history is revealed (39:23). Since the honor of Yahweh is historically identified with the destinies of His chosen people, the ultimate disclosure of His deity can be effected only by the restoration of this nation to its Promised Land under conditions which reflect the holiness and glory of Yahweh. The same principle involved in the temporary exile of Israel becomes the surety of Israel's final redemption. Yahweh's recovery of His people from the lands of the Diaspora restores the prestige of His name among the nations, and emphasizes the profound moral principles of His reign (39:23). At the same time it reaffirmed and clarified to Israel the historic truths that had been the subject of the preaching of the prophets in the past (20:42-44; 36:11, 37; 39:28, 29).

Ezekiel is consequently led to a doctrine of salvation which is profoundly monergistic. Everything proceeds on the basis of the sovereign irresistible grace of God. It melts the hard hearts of the people, brings them to repentance, and endows them with a new spirit motivating them to walk in His statutes and to do His will (6:9; 11:19; 20:43; 32:14).

3. *The freedom and responsibility of the individual before God.* A prominent idea in Ezekiel is the doctrine of the responsibility of the individual soul before God. He had been anticipated in his teaching by Jeremiah (Jer 31:29, 30) but propounds it with an emphasis which is peculiarly his own. The idea of the corporate responsibility of the covenant community in which people were being punished for the sins of their ancestors was a common tradition in Israel. In some respects this was an easy deduction on the part of people chosen by God to live in a particular land. It is in this connection that Ezekiel affirms the principle that "The soul that sins shall die. The son shall not suffer for the iniquity of the father, nor the father suffer for the iniquity of the son; the righteousness of the righteous shall be upon himself, and the wickedness of the wicked shall be upon himself" (18:20). On the other hand, the presence of the righteous will not avail to save a sinning nation from punishment: "even if these three men, Noah, Daniel, and Job, were in it, they would deliver but their own lives by their righteousness" (14:14).

The sense of personal responsibility was a matter of great concern for Ezekiel in his own work. The nature and limits of his responsibility were defined for him at the beginning of his prophetic ministry, and again when he began the second period of his work. It was made clear to the prophet that although he was responsible for the proclamation of the revelation vouchsafed to him, he was not responsible for its success or failure (3:16-19; 33:1-6).

The idea of personal responsibility is inseparably related to the concept of faith as personal fellowship between the believer and God, a concept that was part of the thinking of all the prophets in regard to their own relation to Yahweh. Jeremiah had anticipated Ezekiel also in the doctrine that this is the character which true faith must assume in the experience of all people. It was Ezekiel who developed the principle most logically that neither a man's sins nor hereditary guilt can prevent the work of divine grace in the life of the penitent sinner (ch. 18). Spiritual action thus takes place at the center of life. Yahweh will reign ultimately because in His people there will be a new heart and a new spirit (cf. 11:19; 18:31; 36:26). This will be the creation of Yahweh Himself.

4. *The kingdom of God in its final glory* (40-48). This final section of Ezekiel's prophecy is in many respects the most remarkable part of the book. In the form of a Messianic prophecy the prophet describes a politico-religious constitution by which his fundamental concept of holiness is expressed in the regulation of the details of the life of the redeemed community. These chs. are separated by an interval of twelve or thirteen years from the last of the other prophecies. Foregoing prophecies described the redemption and restoration of the land and the people (33-37). This section presents a description of the condition of the people in the experience of the promised redemption. The background of this picture is formed by the first thirty-nine chapters of the book. The concluding statement of the foregoing section is, "I will not hide my face any more from them, when I pour out my Spirit upon the house of Israel, says the Lord GOD" (39:29).

The controlling idea is that of Yahweh's presence in visible glory in His sanctuary in the midst of His people, together with a suggestion of the obligations this relation involves on the part of Israel. The Israelites are a righteous people knowing that Yahweh is their God and led by His Spirit. There is no indication in the passage how salvation is to be attained simply because the people have realized it and live in the consciousness of redemption. This accounts for the supernatural elements in the record with which the natural elements are commingled. It is important to realize that this commingling of these two elements is common in all of the prophets where descriptions of the ultimate destiny of Israel are concerned. It is also important to understand that the natural and supernatural features of the prophecy are to be taken literally. One should hesitate to conclude, as some do, that the supernatural features of the account such as the change in the physical condition of the area in and around Jerusalem (cf. Jer 31:38; Zech 14:10), and the effects of the river that issues from the Temple bringing fertility to the region and life to the waters of the Dead Sea (cf. Zech 14:8; Joel 3:18) are merely symbolical representations of man's future spiritual existence just because there are natural features in the description such as the people living in their natural bodies, living on the natural produce of the earth and enduring physical death. The restoration described by Ezekiel is more than the natural restoration that took place under Zerubbabel, Ezra, and Nehemiah at the close of the Babylonian captivity. Like the restoration prophesied by Isaiah (60) Ezekiel's restoration involves the final state of the people and the world. The final perfect kingdom could be realized only through Yahweh's personal presence among the redeemed when the Tabernacle of God was with men. The final words of Ezekiel's book are: "And the name of the city henceforth shall be, The LORD is there" (48:35). The name of the New Jerusalem in the midst of the restored land shall be יהוה שׁלה, "Yahweh is there," God dwelling with His people, the difference between life and death.

One also must guard against the tendency to emphasize the supernatural elements in Ezekiel's description such as the life-giving stream which issues from the Temple mount, the personal presence of Yahweh, etc., and conclude that the whole passage is merely an allegory representing the spiritual perfection characteristic of the Church in the Christian age. The literalness and reality of the prophetic program described here are quite clear. The Temple is real, as are the ceremonies and those who serve Him. Sacrifices and offerings are thought of as continuing when Israel is redeemed and the kingdom is Yahweh's by the greatest prophets (Isa 19:19, 21; 60:7; 66:20; Jer 33:18). The sacrifices and rituals are not practiced in order to secure redemption as some scholars suggest, but in order to memorialize and conserve the redemption which in the restored kingdom has already been effected. They are ceremonies of the worship of Yahweh and personal edification, for although the people are redeemed, righteous, and led by His Spirit, they are still subject to the weaknesses of their human nature. The people are not perfect but err from inadvertency. These errors of inadvertency were recognized and confessed in the acts of worship involved in the ceremonies.

The priestly character of the institutions prescribed by Ezekiel is due in some respects to the fact that the prophet himself was a priest, but more importantly to the suitability of the priestly concept of holiness to be the principle of a theocracy that was to be the reflection of the essential character of Yahweh and the relation of His people to Him.

VI. The New Testament use of Ezekiel. 1. *Quotations from Ezekiel in the NT.* There are several references and quotations from Ezekiel in the NT. The words, "he that will hear, let him hear" (3:27) may possibly have been the original of the phrase as found in Matthew 11:15; Mark 7:16; Luke 14:35; Revelation 13:9, etc. The solemn warning that judgment must begin at the house of God (1 Pet 4:17), has its original in Ezekiel 9:6. It appears to some interpreters that 2 Corinthians 6:16 contains a combination and condensation of Ezekiel 37:27 and Leviticus 26:11, 12, and 2 Corinthians 6:18 is dependent upon Ezekiel 36:28.

2. Ezekiel's influence on John. Ezekiel is more closely related to the gospel of John and the Revelation, as indicated by a definite literary kinship as well as doctrine than any other part of the NT. Gog and Magog of chapters 38:2-21 and 39:1-11 are the basis of the prophecy in Revelation 20:8, representing the forces of Satan ultimately destroyed by God.

The vision of God in 1:22-28 is reflected in various places in the Apocalypse. John says that the voice of Christ "was like the sound of many waters" (Ezek 1:24; Rev 1:15; 19:6). Other elements of this vision appear in Revelation 4:3, 6. The figure of the life-giving stream (47:1-12) flowing from the throne of God, regenerating the land with which it comes in contact is used by John in Revelation 22:1, 2. In the Revelation passage the flowing river brings healing to everything it touches and the trees along its banks yield their fruit every month as they do in the vision of Ezekiel (47:12).

John's vision of the holy city, the new Jerusalem (Rev 21:10-27) is anticipated in great measure by Ezekiel 48:15-35. In both visions the dimensions of the city are carefully described. Ezekiel 34:11-31, with its concept of a good shepherd unquestionably influenced the NT. The prophet presents the Messiah as a shepherd who seeks out His sheep, protects and feeds them. Jesus uses the same figure to describe His own work (John 10:1-39). Ezekiel's influence upon John is again seen in the account of the useless vine (Ezek 15:2-6; John 15:1-5). John uses the idea of Ezekiel's vine to emphasize his own lesson.

3. Jesus and Ezekiel. The preceding comparisons indicate that Jesus frequently referred to the Book of Ezekiel. He used the title "Son of man" in the same sense that it is used repeatedly by the prophet.

VII. Ezekiel in the history of Judaism. Ezekiel exerted important influence upon the development of Judaism. In some respects he shares with Ezra the reputation of being the father of Judaism. He prophesied in the transition period between the pre-exilic faith of an established covenant people and the postexilic faith of this same people now a legal community in a strange land. In this period of devastation and change, the prophet contributed to the safeguards which were to protect the Israel of the future against the heathenism that had brought about the destruction of the nation. There are three aspects of Ezekiel's prophecies that are of particular significance.

1. His influence upon the mysticisim of Judaism. Ezekiel's influence upon the mysticism of Judah is the result of his visions. His visions initiated that tendency in the life of Israel that resulted in the production of an extensive Ap. Lit. chiefly between the 2nd cent. B.C. and the 2nd cent. A.D. He influenced as well the development of the later mysticism of the Cabala. There is, however, an important difference between Ezekiel's apocalyptic writing and that of the later apocalyptic writing of Judaism. These later writers borrowed Ezekiel's style, but were not inspired as to the origin, content, and delivery of their message. Consequently these apocalyptic writings were not considered canonical.

2. His influence upon the cult of Judaism. Of particular interest and significance in the influence of Ezekiel is his exposition of the Temple and its ceremonies. A priest as well as a prophet, he emphasized ritualism, but not at the expense of moral values, laying the foundations for its eventual prominence in Jewish life. The direction given by the prophet in regards to the cult was followed in succeeding generations. He was the forerunner of that Judaism which developed around the Temple cult and ceremonial minutiae. The moral and spiritual influence of Ezekiel upon Judaism was equally important. The doctrines of personal immortality, bodily resurrection, and the importance of the law in Judaism were all profoundly influenced by Ezekiel. The prophet, upon the basis of the lessons of the past with its many examples of Israel's apostasy, tribulations, and exile, insists that the future restoration depends upon Israel's observance of the will of Yahweh and strict adherence to the laws expounded by its legitimate religious leaders.

3. His influence upon the literature of Judaism. Ezekiel figures prominently in much of the lit. of Judaism as well as its art. He appears in the murals of the synagogue of Dura Europos completed in A.D. 255, and in modern times in the 1956 edition of the Bible published by Teriade in Paris in the form of an etching by Chagall, "The Calling of Ezekiel."

BIBLIOGRAPHY. G. Hölscher, *Hesekiel, Der Dichter und das Buch* (1924); C. C. Torrey, *Pseudo-Ezekiel and the Original Prophecy* (1930); J. B. Harford, *Studies in the Book of Ezekiel* (1935); G. A. Cooke, *A Critical and Exegetical Commentary on the Book of Ezekiel* in ICC (1937); I. G. Matthews, *Ezekiel* (1939); T. H. Gaster, "Ezekiel and the Mysteries" JBL, LX (1941); W. A. Irwin, *The Problem of Ezekiel* (1943); C. G. Howie, *The Date and Composition of Ezekiel* (1950); H. G. May, *Ezekiel* in IB, vol. 6 (1956); H. F. Hahn, *The Old Testament in Modern Research* (1966).

A. C. SCHULTZ

EZEL ē′ zəl (אזל). According to MT of 1 Samuel 20:19, the name of a stone (so KJV). But LXX (and RSV) understand this as a mistake for "yonder cairn," a reading requiring only the transposition of two letters in Heb.

EZEM, AZEM ē′ zəm (עצם, LXX Ασομ, Ιασον, Αισεμ; *bone, mighty, fortress*). (Azem found only in KJV of Josh 15:29; 19:3.) A city in the extreme S of Canaan, assigned first to Judah (Josh 15:29), and later to Simeon (Josh 19:3; 1 Chron 4:29). The following identifications have been proposed: (1) El-Aujeh, fifteen m. SW of Rehoboth (Young); (2) Azmon of Numbers 34:4 and Joshua 15:4 (HDB, ISBE); (3) Umm el-'Azam (-'Azem, -'Izam) (GTT). The location of this last is disputed, but it is prob. about twelve m. SE of Beersheba.

E. L. ACKLEY

EZERIAS. KJV Apoc. form of AZARIAH.

EZIAS, OZIAS. KJV and ASV forms of UZZI.

EZION-GEBER ĕ′ zĭ ən ge′ bər (עציון גבר, LXX Γεσιωνγαβερ; Γασιωνγαβερ; Ασιωνγαβερ). A city located on the northern end of the Gulf of Aqabah, banked on the E by the hills of Edom and on the W by the hills of Pal. The city is two and a half m. W of Aqabah, old Elath. Cyrus Gordon believes the offshore island known as Jezirat Far 'awn ("Pharaoh's Island") is the probable site.

The Bible mentions Ezion-geber as one of

A scene at the head of the Gulf of Aqabah close to the site of ancient Ezion-Geber. ©M.P.S.

the stations along the route of the Israelites as they journeyed toward the plains of Moab (Num 33:35, 36; Deut 2:8). In the reign of Solomon the city was of great commercial significance as the port where he built his fleet of ships and manned them with Phoen. sailors. The ships sailed to Ophir and brought back gold, almug wood (ebony?), silver, ivory, apes (perhaps baboons) and peacocks (1 Kings 9:26-28; 10:11, 22; 2 Chron 8:17). No further mention is made of the city until Jehoshaphat joined with Ahaziah to build a fleet there. The ships were wrecked in port and the venture was frustrated (1 Kings 22:48, 49; 2 Chron 20:35-37).

The history of the city has been recovered through the archeological excavations of Nelson Glueck after Frank Fritz, a Ger. explorer, discovered an insignificant mound, Tell el-Kheleifeh, which he identified as Ezion-geber in 1934. The mound was about 700 ft. from the gulf (perhaps on the ancient shore-line). In 1938 and subsequent years Glueck excavated the city and confirmed Fritz's earlier identification. He identified four cities built upon one another. The first was dated in the Solomonic period. Built upon virgin soil, the city indicated a carefully laid out complex suggesting no gradual growth, but rather development at one time according to a preconceived plan. He based the claim for the

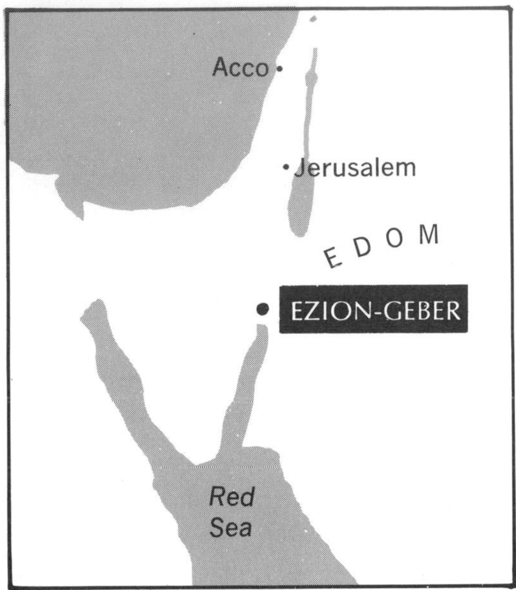

Solomonic date upon a comparison of the structure of the main gate of Ezion-geber I and that of Stratum IV at Megiddo, dated by P. L. O. Guy as belonging to the Solomonic period, and the one at Lachish, also dated in the tenth cent. B.C. Solomon was the only king in the period to possess the wealth, the power and the peaceful circumstances for such a building project. As for the earlier mention of Ezion-geber (Num 33:35, 36; Deut 2:8), these prob. had reference to a few mud huts eastward of the later city.

Referring to Ezion-geber as the "Pittsburgh of Pal.," Glueck originally believed the city to be a refinery for the copper and iron which were mined from the near-by mines of the Arabah. There were flues and air ducts in the floor and walls of the first city, and the location of the city was such, he felt, as to derive the maximum benefit of the winds which rushed through the corridor of the Arabah. In 1962 Rothenberg challenged this view on the basis of the failure of the excavations to turn up either the clay crucibles which would have been used in smelting or the slag from the refining process. Besides, the location seems to have been the best for the least number of sandstorms and at the same time have the availability of drinking water. Rothenberg points out that the finds and ground plans indicate that the city was a large storehouse for grain and supplies for caravans and a fortress guarding the southern approaches on both sides of the gulf. Glueck abandoned his earlier ideas about this being a copper refinery. The smelting was done near the mines.

The first city was sacked and burned prob. by Shishak c. 925 B.C. The Bible mentions his campaign into Pal. (1 Kings 14:25, 26; 2 Chron 12:1-9), and a topographical list preserved in the Amon temple at Karnak includes Edomite names, indicating that the strategic location at Ezion-geber would prob. have been included.

The city was rebuilt by Jehoshaphat of Judah (c. 860), who imitated Solomon by building a fleet there. A few years later the Edomites revolted during the reign of Jehoram (2 Kings 8:20-22) and burned it. The third city was rebuilt after Azariah (Uzziah) recovered it from the Edomites (2 Kings 14:22; 2 Chron 26:2), and it was renamed Elath. A seal of Jotham, his successor, was found in the third level (cf. BASOR 163 [1961], pp. 18-22). This level is the best preserved with many walls standing almost at their original height.

When Rezin and Pekah formed the Aramaen-Israelite coalition and invaded Judah, the Edomites regained Elath (Ezion-geber) and drove Ahaz's troops from the city (2 Kings 16:6). The Bible states, ". . . and the Edomites came to Elath, where they dwell to this day." The final phases of the city from the 7th to the 4th cent. B.C. saw the continued flourishing of trade, evidenced by Aram. ostraca and sherds of black-figured Attic ware. The city was destroyed in the 4th cent. and was never rebuilt. The Nabataeans later built a port city at the northern end of the gulf, but it was located at the site of the present day Aqabah.

BIBLIOGRAPHY. N. Glueck, BASOR 71 (1938), 3-17; 75 (1939), 8-22; 79 (1940), 2-18; 80 (1940), 3-10; 82 (1941), 3-11; *The Other Side of the Jordan* (1940), 89-113; B. Rothenberg, PEQ, 94 (1962), 44-56; N. Glueck, BA, 28 (1965), 70-87; C. Gordon, *Before Columbus* (1971).

W. B. COKER

EZNITE. *See* ADINO.

EZORA ĕ zôr' ə (Ἐζωρα; meaning uncertain). In the textual tradition of the story of Ezra preserved in 1 Esdras, Ezora was the father or clan leader of several men who participated in the mass divorce encouraged by Ezra (1 Esd 9:34). Cf. Machnadebai, Ezra 10:40.

EZRA ĕz' rə (עֶזְרָא, Ἔσρας, Ἐσδράς).

1. A descendant of Judah (1 Chron 4:17, but spelled עֶזְרָה).

2. Ezra, the son of Jozadak, a priest and prominent postexilic leader. His genealogy is carried back to Aaron in 1 Chronicles 6:3-15 and, with some omissions, in Ezra 7:1-5. He is called a ready scribe in the law of Moses (Ezra 7:6), and led back some 1750 men, perhaps a total of 5000 people, in a second return from Babylon. It seems clear that Ezra wrote the book bearing his name. The last two vv. of 2 Chronicles are identical with the first two of Ezra which supports the Jewish tradition that Ezra wrote Chronicles also (cf. W. F. Albright, *Yahweh and the Gods of Canaan* [1968], 182).

Ezra's return is dated in the seventh year of Artaxerxes (Ezra 7:7). The usual view has been that this was Artaxerxes I and the date therefore about 457 B.C. More recently the view has been advanced that he returned in the seventh year of Artaxerxes II or 398 B.C. The matter is adequately discussed in J. S. Wright's monograph, *The Date of Ezra's Coming to Jerusalem* (1947). The arguments for the late date are not conclusive. The first point concerns the wall (4:12ff.). There is a problem here. Verses 7-23 refer to opposition in the days of an Artaxerxes, but the rest of the context refers to the times of Cyrus (539 B.C.). It is most logical to say that this ch. includes a synopsis of the opposition met by the Jews both in building the Temple in 516 B.C. and in the efforts to build the wall under Artaxerxes I. In any case, the reference to work on a wall which was later stopped must relate to events before the completion of the walls by Nehemiah in the twentieth year of Artaxerxes I, about 444 B.C. It is quite likely that Ezra who returned with 5000 people and much treasure had secured permission to build the walls and had made a beginning. But the opposition made the work cease until Nehemiah came in 444 B.C. with a new building permit. This may explain how Nehemiah finished his work in so short a time—fifty-two days—for Ezra had already done much. Incidentally, this view suggests that Daniel's sixty-nine sevens of years (Dan 9:25) should begin with Ezra's return at about 457 B.C. The period would end about A.D. 26 with the beginning of Jesus' public ministry.

The only other argument of consequence for a late date of Ezra concerns the mention of Eliashib who was high priest in 444 B.C. (Neh 3:1). He was the father of a Jehohanan associated with Ezra (Ezra 10:6); and the Elephantine papyri mention a high priest Jehohanan in 408 B.C. The problem is not serious. Ezra's marriage reform of Ezra 10 has no date given. Jehohanan could have been made high priest at some subsequent time and lasted in office until 408 B.C. Or there may have been two Eliashibs and two Jehohanans. It was the custom to name a boy for his grandfather. Three such successive Sanballats are now known! The traditional order of Ezra and Nehemiah is still satisfactory.

Of Ezra's political office very little is known, but he clearly had influence at court. He was given a blank check by the king and authority to appoint officers (7:21-26), but is not called a governor as was Nehemiah. His faith is shown by refusing a military guard for his caravan (8:22). Nehemiah emphasizes Ezra's scribal activity. Actually, Ezra was a priest of the line of Zadok and would be expected to teach the law (cf. Neh 8). Ezra and Nehemiah led the two processions at the dedication of the walls (Neh 12:36-40).

Ezra was prominent in post-Biblical Jewish tradition. In the late book, 2 Esdras 14, he is said to have rewritten and published the twenty-four books of the Heb. canon which had been burned during the captivity. In the tradition he dictated the books rapidly under special divine enablement.

BIBLIOGRAPHY. H. H. Schaeder, *Esra der Schreiber* (1930); A. C. Welch, *Post-Exilic Judaism* (1934); J. S. Wright, *The Date of Ezra's Coming to Jerusalem* (1947); W. F. Albright, *From the Stone Age to Christianity* (1957).

R. L. HARRIS

EZRA, BOOK OF

I. Background
II. Authorship
III. Date
IV. Canonicity
V. Special problems
VI. Content

I. BACKGROUND

The books of Ezra and Nehemiah originally were regarded by the Jews as a single work, and a general introduction must treat them together. Moreover, the opening vv., when compared with the closing verses of Chronicles, show that Ezra-Nehemiah continues the Chronicler's history (*see* CHRONICLES, BOOK OF).

After recounting the history of the monarchy and the Temple until the Exile, the writer passes over the period when the Temple lay in ruins, and the key men in Judah were in Babylonia, and records the predicted return—leading to the rebuilding of the Temple through Zerubbabel (of the line of David) and Joshua (of the line of Aaron). He describes the establishment of the new Jewish community during the period 538-433 B.C.

The Jews came under the Pers. empire when Cyrus conquered Babylon in 539 B.C. The names of the Pers. kings are important for the understanding of these Books.

Cyrus (539-530). Cyrus allowed other captive peoples to return also (Ezra 1).
Cambyses (530-522).
Gaumata, or Pseudo-Smerdis (522). A usurper.
Darius I (522-486). Ezra 5, 6.
Xerxes I (486-465). Ezra 4:6. Also Esther. (Ahasuerus)
Darius and Xerxes both made ill-fated invasions of Greece.
Artaxerxes I (464-424). Ezra 4:7-23; 7:1-10:44. The whole of Nehemiah's work belongs to this reign. Some suppose that Ezra himself belongs to the reign of Artaxerxes II (*see* NEHEMIAH, BOOK OF).

II. AUTHORSHIP

Style and approach, as well as the verbal link already noted, suggest that the compiler of Chronicles and Ezra-Nehemiah is the same person. In much of the book he is a compiler, since he makes extensive use of documents and often inserts them word for word. Thus the authorship must in the first instance be applied to the individual documents.

The following form the basis of the present book:

A. Memoirs of Ezra, in the first person sing. (7:27-9:15) preceded and followed by third person narratives (7:1-26; 10) that could be based on a record made by Ezra himself, or, since they incorporate a verbatim decree and legal affairs, could come from the Temple archives.

B. Memoirs of Nehemiah. These are in the first person sing. (1:1-7:5; 11:27-43; 13:4-30).

C. Aramaic documents. Aram. was the diplomatic language of the day.

1. Letter of complaint to Artaxerxes I about the rebuilding of the city walls, and his reply (Ezra 4:8-24). Chronologically this prob. comes immediately before Nehemiah 1, which refers to a recent destruction of the walls (Ezra 4:23; Neh 1:3).

2. A letter to Darius I and his reply (Ezra 5:1-6:18). The whole incident is appropriately related in Aram.

3. The official authorization of Artaxerxes (Ezra 7:12-26).

D. Lists. Listings of names are included for various purposes.

Returned exiles, perhaps including some who came at later dates (Ezra 2 [cf. Neh 7]).

Those who returned with Ezra (Ezra 8:1-14).

Those who had married pagan wives (Ezra 10:18-43).

The builders of the wall and the sections where they worked (Neh 3).

The leaders who set their seal to the covenant (Neh. 10:1-27).

The allocation of the people in Jerusalem and neighborhood (Neh 11).

Lists of priests and Levites down to Jaddua (Neh 12:1-26). This may be the Jaddua who was high priest in the reign of Darius II (338-331).

These lists would have been filed in the Temple archives.

E. Narrative. It is not possible to say how much of the remaining narrative comes from the Chronicler himself, and how far he drew upon oral or documentary sources. The Temple staff would naturally hand on oral and documentary records of the first return and rebuilding of the Temple, and there would also be background material in the Temple to supplement the memoirs of Ezra and Nehemiah.

III. Date

The latest name mentioned in Ezra-Nehemiah is Jaddua, who was prob. the high priest in the reign of Darius III (338-331; Neh 12:11, 22). This need not mean that the Chronicler compiled his work as late as this. Copyists on the Temple staff would tend to keep a simple list of this kind up-to-date.

Since the Chronicler writes on the assumption that the Priestly Code was in force all through the monarchy, scholars who hold that P was introduced by Ezra and then later incorporated into the previously existing codes, naturally place the Chronicler sufficiently long after Ezra for this to be possible. Those who date Ezra's coming in 398 (*see* NEHEMIAH, BOOK OF) place the compilation of Chronicles and Ezra-Nehemiah in the last part of the 4th cent. B.C., although some hold that further additions were made after this.

If, however, the Pentateuch in its present form existed from the time of Moses, we are free to postulate any reasonable date for the compilation of the Books after about 430 B.C.

The identity of the compiler must remain unknown, but it could have been Ezra himself. He had the ability and aptitude as a student-scribe, and, as priest, he had access to the Temple records (Ezra 7:1-6). Talmudic tradition (*Baba Bathra* 15a) regards Ezra as the writer of Chronicles and of Ezra-Nehemiah up to his own day, though it suggests that Nehemiah completed the work.

IV. Canonicity

In the Heb. Bible, Ezra-Nehemiah is placed in the third group of Books (The *Writings*), which were the last to be recognized as inspired Scriptures (*see* CANON). Illogically it precedes Chronicles, but this may be because it covered an entirely new field, whereas Chronicles was parallel with Samuel and Kings, and so might be read as a supplement.

For its relationship with 1 Esdras of the Apocrypha, with its confusion of people and dates, *see* 1 ESDRAS, BOOK OF.

V. Special problems of the Book of Ezra

There are two periods where scholars have queried the Biblical account, and it will be convenient to consider these separately, and deal with the first here, and the other in the article NEHEMIAH, BOOK OF.

The Chronicler is said to be in confusion over the rebuilding of the Temple. Ezra 3:10 says that the foundation was laid in 536 by Zerubbabel and Joshua. The work was hindered, and lapsed until 520, when, through the preaching of Haggai and Zechariah, it was taken up again and completed by 516 (Ezra 6:15). On the other hand, according to Haggai's own words, the foundation was laid in 520 (Hag 2:18). Some suppose that only a small number returned in 537, and were content to worship on the ruined site of the Temple. A fresh party of enthusiasts came with Zerubbabel, Joshua, Haggai, and Zechariah, in 520, and laid the foundation.

The whole weight of national psychology is against this view. It is the enthusiasts who flock back in large numbers as soon as the doors are opened, without waiting for seventeen years, although even enthusiasts can be diverted by intense opposition from building the Temple to building their own houses and scraping a living for themselves (Hag 1:4, 9-11). Haggai 2:18 may not mean that the

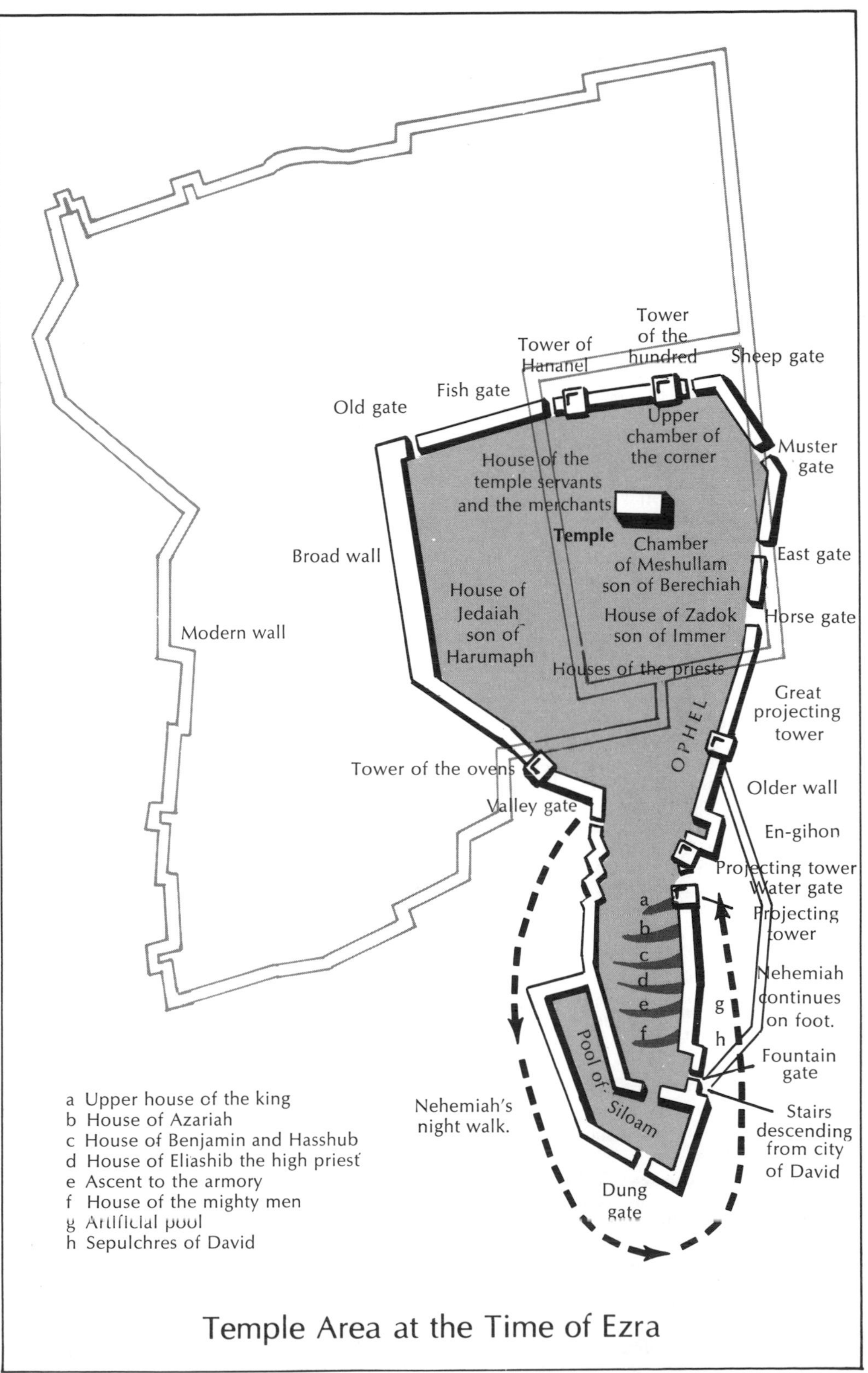
Tower of Hananel
Tower of the hundred
Sheep gate
Fish gate
Old gate
Upper chamber of the corner
Muster gate
House of the temple servants and the merchants
Temple
Chamber of Meshullam son of Berechiah
East gate
Broad wall
House of Jedaiah son of Harumaph
House of Zadok son of Immer
Horse gate
Modern wall
Houses of the priests
Great projecting tower
OPHEL
Tower of the ovens
Older wall
Valley gate
En-gihon
Projecting tower
Water gate
Projecting tower
Nehemiah continues on foot.
Pool of Siloam
Fountain gate
Stairs descending from city of David
Nehemiah's night walk.
Dung gate
a Upper house of the king
b House of Azariah
c House of Benjamin and Hasshub
d House of Eliashib the high priest
e Ascent to the armory
f House of the mighty men
g Artificial pool
h Sepulchres of David

Temple Area at the Time of Ezra

foundation had only just been laid in 520, but this interpretation is probable. If so, since so little had been done since 536, the enthusiasm of the Jews would be kindled by a fresh foundation ceremony. This would not be unusual, since Akkad. and Hitt. rituals exist for founding and repairing temples, and mention more than one foundation stone in different parts of the building (*see* J. B. Pritchard, ANET., 339f., 356).

In Ezra 3:8 Zerubbabel lays the foundation, but in 5:16 this is said to be the work of Sheshbazzar, who is spoken of there as though he were dead, whereas Zerubbabel is still alive. The Jews (5:13-17) were trying, however, to identify a missing document that they hoped would be in the Pers. archives. This document was the authorization given to Sheshbazzar, who had been appointed governor (1:8), and it would be useless to look for one with the name of Zerubbabel, although Zerubbabel had actually been the prime mover. The statement that the work had been going on ever since (5:16) is purely diplomatic, since, if they had admitted that they had stopped building, the answer would have been, "If Cyrus really gave you permission, why did you stop?"

There are variant VSS of Cyrus' decree in chs. 1 and 6. But the public decree of Ezra 1, with Cyrus's acknowledgment of Yahweh, is paralleled by extant inscrs. in which Cyrus acknowledges the Babylonian god Marduk in speaking to the Babylonians. The filed decree in 6:1-5 is naturally formal, and contains maximum dimensions of the Temple for which Cyrus was prepared to make a grant.

There is, then, no inconsistency between individual sections of the Book of Ezra, or between Ezra and Haggai or Zechariah. An interesting link may be found between the letter of complaint to Darius in Ezra 5, which might have resulted in the work being stopped, and the great mountain (Zech 4:7) that was blocking Zerubbabel's completion of the Temple.

VI. Content and outline

A. 1:1-11. Cyrus authorizes the return of the Jews under Sheshbazzar, and gives them their Temple treasures. It is known that he allowed other captive peoples to take back their idols.

B. 2:1-70. A list of those who returned, classified under various heads.

C. 3:1-13. The altar is set up for regular offerings. Later the foundations of the new Temple are laid.

D. 4:1-4. Many non-Jews, including the semi-pagan inhabitants from the N (2 Kings 17:33-41) offer to help, but are refused. They then hinder the work.

E. 4:6-23. The compiler brings together subsequent occasions of opposition, but has dated them carefully as happening in the reigns of Xerxes I and Artaxerxes I. There is no mention of the building of the Temple but only of the city and the walls. Artaxerxes orders the work to cease, and the enemies use violence to stop it.

F. 4:24-5:17. The opening words refer back to 4:5 to take up the story again. Haggai and Zechariah, who may have been infants at the original return, urge the people to take up the building again. The authorities make a formal protest, and are referred to the decree of Cyrus.

G. 6:1-22. The decree is found in the Pers. archives, and Darius orders the work to proceed. The Temple is finished in four years (516), and now returned Israelites, and others of the northern kingdom who had not gone into exile, are allowed to celebrate the Passover, once they have broken with everything pagan.

H. 7:1-28. There is a gap between 516 and 458, when Ezra is sent by Artaxerxes I to investigate and enforce the operation of the Jewish law in the province of Judah.

I. 8:1-36. Ezra's journey, with another group of exiles and gold and silver for the Temple.

J. 9:1-15. Ezra's prayer of anguish after hearing of mixed marriages with pagan peoples.

K. 10:1-44. The people unitedly investigate all the alleged cases, and almost unanimously (10:15) agree that the Jews should divorce their pagan wives. In all probability with the Jews being a minority group, the parents and families of the wives would secure proper alimony for them.

BIBLIOGRAPHY. C. C. Torrey, *Ezra Studies* (1910); L. W. Batten, ICC (1913); L. E. Browne, *Early Judaism* (1920); W. F. Albright, "The Date and Personality of the Chronicler," JBL, XL (1921); A. C. Welch, *Post-exilic Judaism* (1935); W. Rudolph, *Esra und Nehemia,* HAT (1949); K. Galling, "The Gola-list according to Ezra ii/Neh vii," JBL (1951); R. A. Bowman, IB (1954); J. S. Wright, *The Building of the Second Temple* (1958). *See also* Nehemiah, Book of.

J. S. Wright

EZRAHITE **ĕz′ rə hīt** (אזרחי ; LXX 'Εζραΐτης, 'Ισραηλίτης). Formerly understood as a patronymic for the descendants of Zerah (1 Chron 2:6, cf. the list in 1 Kings 4:31), this word is now interpreted by W. F. Albright (*Archeology and the Religion of Israel,* pp. 127, 210) to mean "aborigine, member of a pre-Israelite family." The word occurs only in the titles of Psalms 88 and 89 and 1 Kings 4:31 (MT, LXX 5:11).

G. G. Swaim

EZRI **ĕz′ rī** (עזרי ; LXX 'Εζραί; *my help*). The supervisor of the cultivators of the royal lands, listed in connection with David's controversial census (1 Chron 27:26).

EZRIL **ĕz′ rĭl** (Εζριλ; presumably = Azarel, *God has helped*). One of the sons of Ezora (q.v.) participating in Ezra's mass divorce (1 Esd 9:34). Cf. Azarel, Ezra 10:41.

The Cylinder of Cyrus is a contemporary document of the time of Ezra. ©*B.M.*

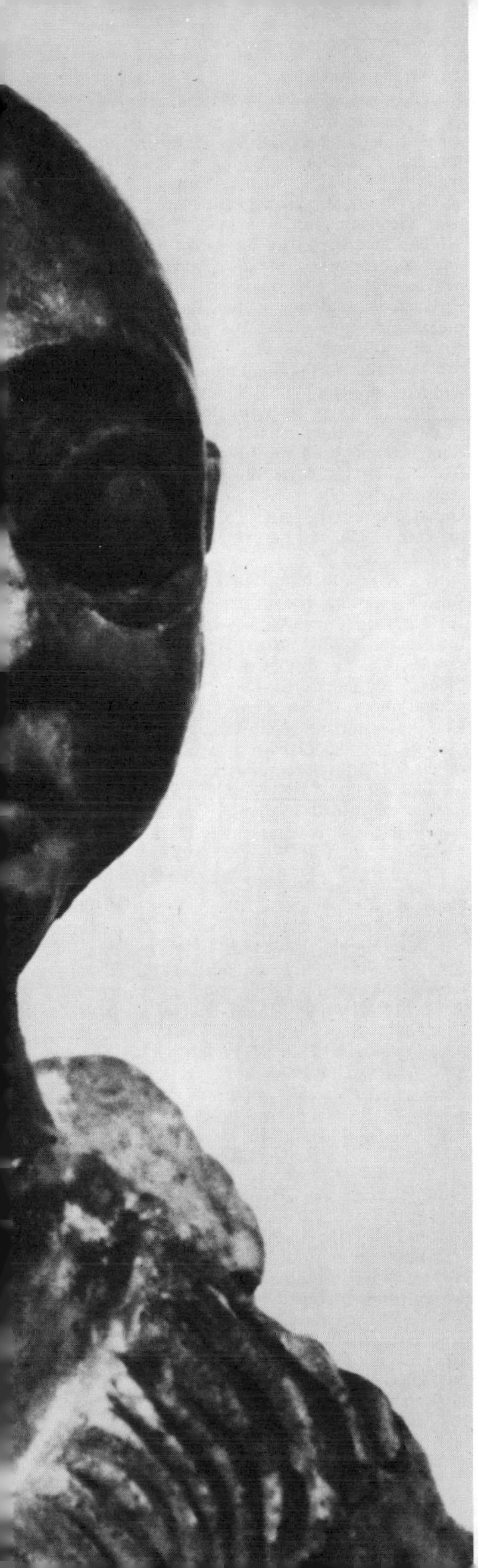

Man has been fascinated by his face since the beginning of time. This Sumerian male statuette is dated to about 2290-2255 B.C., before the time of Abraham. ©*B.M.*

FABLE, (*μῦθος, talk, tale, legend, myth*). A literary genre in the form of a short story embodying a moral and making use of animals, birds, or inanimate things like trees, as persons or actors. This form of writing was well-known in ancient lit., esp. in Sumer. and Akkad. According to Trench, a principal difference between a fable and a parable is that the former tries to inculcate maxims of prudential morality—like industry, foresight, and caution; while the latter teaches spiritual virtues.

There are two fables in the OT. In the first, found in Judges 9:8-15, Jothan, standing on Mount Gerizim and speaking to the people of Shechem in the valley below, tried to show them the folly of choosing as king a worthless fellow like his brother, who had just murdered seventy sons of Gideon. The trees of the forest asked an olive tree, a fig tree, and a vine, to rule over them, but they all refused, saying that they were too busy serving the community to waste their time waving their branches over their fellows. Finally they chose a useless bramble (representing his brother Abimelech), a dangerous choice, for conflict would result in all perishing in the forest fire.

In the other OT fable, Jehoash, king of Israel, told Amaziah, king of Judah, who had challenged him to a fight, that he would demean himself by accepting the challenge. "A thistle on Lebanon sent to a cedar on Lebanon, saying, 'Give your daughter to my son for a wife'; and a wild beast of Lebanon passed by and trampled down the thistle" (2 Kings 14:9). Jehoash was not dissuaded, and in the battle that followed was roundly defeated.

Some OT prophets employ illustrations which approach the status of fable, like Isaiah's poem about the vineyard (Isa 5:1-7), and Ezekiel's poems concerning the lioness and her whelps (Ezek 19:2-9), the vine (Ezek 19:10-14), and the great eagle (Ezek 17:3-10).

The KJV uses the word "fable" in the NT to refer to some false teachings which were coming into the Church, but in each instance the RSV more accurately trs. the Gr. word *muthos,* "myth" (1 Tim 1:4; 4:7; 2 Tim 4:4; Titus 1:14; 2 Pet 1:16). It is difficult to determine the exact nature of the heresy. It may have been a kind of Judaizing Gnosticism or an elaboration of legends out of OT narratives similar to those in Rabbinic *haggadah,* the Book of Jubilees, and Philo.

BIBLIOGRAPHY. R. C. Trench, *Notes on the Parables* (1882), 1-5; F. J. A. Hort, *Judaistic Christianity* (1894), 135ff.

S. Barabas

FACE (אנפין, אף, *face, nose*; עין, *eyes, aspect*; פנים, *face,* the commonest term; Gr. ὄψις, *face*; πρόσωπον, *face*). Not only does the word refer to the face of a man (Gen 3:19; James 1:23) but also the face of the flocks (Gen 30:40), the seraphim (Isa 6:2), the living creatures around the throne (Rev 4:7), the face of God (Num 6:25), the face of Christ (2 Cor 4:6), the face of the waters (Gen 1:2), of all the earth (1:29), the moon (Job 26:9) and the sky (Matt 16:3). The face is all the head except the brain case. Nose and eyes may stand for the whole countenance. The man himself may be meant (Deut 7:10) as in the oriental circumlocution for "I."

The face reflects feelings. "Cain was very angry and his countenance fell" (Gen 4:5) or "a glad heart makes a cheerful countenance" (Prov 15:13). The face was covered in mourning like David's after Absalom's defection and death (2 Sam 19:4), or in the doom of Haman (Esth 7:8), or by a harlot (Gen 38:15), although "covered his face with his fat" suggests prosperity and arrogance (Job 15:27). Moses hid his face in reverence (Exod 3:6) but put a veil on his face when talking with his people to dim the shine received while talking with God (Exod 34:29-35).

To seek the face is to desire an audience (Ps 105:4) but to turn away or hide the face is rejection (13:1), or to forsake the house of God (2 Chron 29:6), and to harden the face is to promise no appeal (Prov 21:29). A woman falls on her face in humility and astonishment (Ruth 2:10). Favors are granted when the face is lifted up (Num 6:25) but to spit in the face was a grave insult (Matt 26:67). Determination was evident when Christ set His face to go to Jerusalem (Luke 9:51) and calamity when the face was set against a people (Jer 44:11).

Much is said about the face of God. It means God Himself or His glory in its fullest which could not be seen by Moses before he received the Ten Commandments (Exod 33:20). When Jacob said, "I have seen God face to face," he was referring to the relationship of closest intimacy he felt because of his wrestling with the man by the ford of Jabbok and the blessing given to him. "No one has ever seen God" (John 1:18) face to face but "the knowledge of the glory of God" is seen in the face of Christ (2 Cor 4:6). "Speaking face to face" suggests that God shows His attributes even though not in their completeness, yet His servants are promised that they shall see His face (Rev 22:4) when they approach the throne of God in the new Jerusalem. The service of the priests is called appearing before the face of the Lord (Deut 10:8).

God hides His face when angry (Job 13:24), sets His face against the wicked for evil (Jer 44:11) and hides His face from sin, both to show His displeasure with it (Ps 27:9) and to show He has forgiven it (51:9).

The shewbread in the Ark was called the bread of the Presence, but a literal tr. is the bread of the face (Exod 25:30).

R. L. Mixter

FAIR. A word which, in the KJV of the Bible, renders about a dozen Heb. and Gr. words, but never in the Bible has it the meaning of *light in color; blond*: as, *fair* hair. 1. Usually it has the meaning of *beautiful* (Gen 6:2; 12:11, 14 KJV *fair,* RSV *beautiful*; Esth 1:11; Job 42:15; S of Sol 1:15, 16 KJV *fair,* RSV *beautiful*; Acts 7:20 KJV *fair,* RSV *beautiful*). 2. *Unspotted* (Zech 3:5 KJV *fair,* ASV, *clean*). 3. *Plausible, persuasive* (Prov 7:21 KJV *fair,* RSV *seductive*; Gal 6:12 KJV *fair,* RSV *good*). 4. *Good* (of weather, Matt 16:2).

S. Barabas

FAIR HAVENS (*καλοὶ λιμένες, fair harbors*). A bay near Lasea on the S coast of Crete about five m. E of Cape Matala.

Paul in the custody of a centurion sailed W from Cnidus on an Alexandrian grain ship. The weather forced them to sail on the S side of Crete. They passed Cape Salome, the eastern tip of the island and took refuge at Fair Havens. Since Fair Havens was only an open bay, the centurion, the captain and the owner of the ship decided to attempt to reach Phoenix, a harbor further to the W. They failed, and drifted in the open sea for fourteen days until the shipwreck at Malta (Acts 27:8).

A. Rupprecht

FAIRS (KJV rendering of עִזָּבוֹן, *wares*). Occurs only in Ezekiel 27:12, 14, 16, 19, 22, 27, 33. Verse 12 mentions iron, tin, and lead "exchanged for your wares" (BDB, p. 738 has "furnished as wares"). The LXX supplies both ἀγορά, "market-place," and μισθός, "hire, pay."

FAITH, FAITHFULNESS. These two concepts are central to Biblical thought. They deal with the relationship of God and men. They are in some respects correlative, for man's faith is that which responds to and is sustained by God's faithfulness. In other respects there can be a progression of thought, for faith on the part of man should lead to his faithfulness. Again, the idea of faith can move from the subjective attitude of trustfulness to "the faith"—that which God has revealed objectively through deed and word and sign in order that it should be trusted. Associated closely with the two nouns is the adjective "faithful" and the verb "have faith in," "trust," or "believe." In some parts of the Bible the verb is more prominent than the noun. As always in the Scriptures, the divine initiative is emphasized or assumed, and the fact that the living God is willing to enter into relationship with men and has shown them that He is worthy of their trust is what gives Biblical faith its distinctive character. Faith as it is demonstrated in the OT is a necessary, but incomplete preliminary to its full possibility through Christ in the NT.

- I. Faith and faithfulness in the OT
  - A. Terminology
    - 1. אמן
    - 2. בטח
    - 3. חסה
    - 4. Closely related words
  - B. Theological presentation
    - 1. Creation and providence
    - 2. Redemption
    - 3. Promises and signs
    - 4. The covenant
    - 5. Personal
- II. Faith and faithfulness in Judaism
  - A. The Apocrypha and Pseudepigrapha
  - B. Philo
  - C. Qumran
  - D. The rabbis
- III. Faith and faithfulness in Greek thought
  - A. Classical
  - B. Hellenistic
- IV. Faith and faithfulness in the NT
  - A. Terminology
    - 1. Pisteuo
    - 2. Pistis
    - 3. Pistos
    - 4. Negative words
  - B. The usage of the NT writers
    - 1. The synoptic gospels
      - a. God's faithfulness
      - b. Human faith
    - 2. John's gospel and epistles
      - a. God's faithfulness
      - b. The nature of faith
      - c. The object of faith
      - d. The basis of faith
      - e. The result of faith
      - f. The development of faith
      - g. Human faithfulness
    - 3. The Acts of the Apostles
      - a. God's faithfulness
      - b. Men's faith
    - 4. The Pauline epistles
      - a. God's faithfulness
      - b. Faith and the Gospel
      - c. Faith and justification
      - d. Faith and relationship
      - e. The life of faith
      - f. Human faithfulness
      - g. The faith
    - 5. The Epistle to the Hebrews
      - a. God's faithfulness
      - b. Man's faith
    - 6. The Epistle of James
    - 7. The Epistles of Peter and Jude
    - 8. Revelation
  - C. Faith and faithfulness in NT theology

I. Faith and faithfulness in the OT

A. Terminology. There are three main word groups in the OT, which are used to describe these ideas. There are also a number of other words and ideas which are related to them.

1. אמן. From an original meaning connected with "firmness" and "stability," there comes the idea of "trust" and "constancy" which is prominent in the OT. The word "Amen," which is used frequently in the OT and NT, shows the confident affirmation which is associated with the verb. In the reflexive (*niph'al*) the verb may be used of God (Deut 7:9) or of His servants (Num 12:7). It can be extended to witnesses (Isa 8:2; Jer 42:5) and to a city (Isa 1:21, 26). It can be used of testimony (Ps 19:8) and of promises (2 Chron 1:9). It may have no moral connotation, as when it refers to plagues (Deut 28:59). It is used slightly more frequently in the *hiph'il*, where there is the active sense of believing or trusting. This may be in an absolute form (Ps 116:10), but it is more usual for it to be followed by כִּי, "that," and object clause (Exod 4:5) or by the prepositions בְּ, or לְ. These may go with God (Gen 15:6; Isa 43:10), or with men (Exod 4:1; 19:9) or with things, usually words or messages (1 Kings 10:7; Ps 106:12). There is no reason to suppose that the prepositions are different in meaning. The Heb. words are usually rendered in the LXX by πιστεύω, "believe," or by the adjective πιστός, "faithful."

Derived from אמן are two nouns found often in the OT: אמת, and אמונה. Generally speaking, they are connected more with the passive sense of faithfulness than the active of believing, and this is reflected by the fact that the LXX renders them by ἀλήθεια, "truth," 119 times and by πίστις, "faith," only twenty-six times. They may refer to the faithfulness of God (Ps 25:10; 36:5) or to that of His servants (Josh 24:14; 1 Sam 26:23). There seems to be little difference between the two nouns, which rank alongside צדק, "righteousness," and חסד, "mercy" or "covenant love," as key words of Heb. religion. They are esp. prominent in the Psalter.

2. בטח. This word is used in the OT sixty times in a secular sense, as against fifty-seven in a religious. As an important devotional word it has a special place in the Psalter, where it is found thirty-seven times. Its sense is that of "feeling secure." This feeling may be unjustified (Judg 18:7, 27, where the word is used of an unsuspecting city) or misplaced, in human strength (Jer 17:5) or in idols (Ps 115:8). But essentially, in its positive sense, it is that attitude to God which acknowledges Him as the believer's own God (Ps 31:14). The noun בטח, has the sense of safety or security, and it can likewise be used of a true or false security. The verb normally is rendered in the LXX by πέποιθα, "trust," or ἐλπίζω, "hope."

3. חסה. The meaning of this word is "to take refuge" and in the OT it is used predominantly in a religious sense (Ps 7:1). Its chief usage is in the Psalter, where its devotional meaning is clear. The LXX renders it likewise mainly by *pépoitha* and *elpízō*.

4. There are various other words which are closely associated with the idea of faith and faithfulness in the OT, particularly those which denote hope (יחל חכה, and קוה). Of even greater importance is the word חסד because it denotes the relationship of God and man and of man and man under the covenant. It was the covenant which formed the heart of Israel's religion and which gave faithfulness and faith their fullest opportunity for expression.

B. Theological presentation. The idea of a faithful God and men who are called to faith in Him is absolutely fundamental to OT religion. It will be possible here only to outline some areas in which this is represented, even where none of the "faith words" actually appear.

1. *Creation and providence.* The faithfulness of God who has made the world and all that is in it, who orders it regularly and provides for His creatures is abundantly illustrated in a nature psalm such as Psalm 104. It is a demonstration of the fact that all is under the control of a God who can be relied upon. This produces in the believing beholder a response of exultation in His might and majesty.

2. *Redemption.* The whole sweep of God's redemption in the OT, from the call of Abraham to the establishment of the people in their own land with a place for His name to dwell in, was evidence of His faithfulness (Exod 33:1; 1 Kings 8:56). The central point of this redemption was the Exodus, which is a supreme example of the faithful God in action (Exod 15:1-17). The response of the people when God had delivered them was to believe in Yahweh and His servant Moses (14:31). The mighty acts of God had to be kept in remembrance for future generations. One way in which this was done was through the Passover service (12:24-27). Another was through the recitation of creedal forms (Deut 26:5-9; cf. Deut 6:20-24). It was intended that these should lead men of every age to faith in the redeeming God (Ps 77; Mic 6:3-5). In addition, there were psalms which were devoted entirely to the Exodus period, such as Psalm 105 which lays great emphasis on the faithfulness of God and Psalm 106 which stresses the unfaithfulness of the people. In Psalm 136 the idea of Yahweh's faithfulness in redemption is linked to His faithfulness in creation, and both are cause for praise that "his steadfast love endures for ever." When God delivers His people again from captivity, this is further evidence of His faithfulness in action calling for a response of trust from them (Isa 40-55 passim).

3. *Promises and signs.* In the OT God is not represented simply as doing things in history. He also is shown to promise them by word and by symbolic deed. The most important instance of God's promises in the OT is found in the story of Abraham. From Genesis 12:1-3 onward, the unlikely promises of God to Abraham of a land and descendants were slowly but surely, against all the odds, being fulfilled. The greatness of Abraham was found in the fact that "he believed the LORD; and he reckoned it to him as righteousness" (Gen 15:6). Faith in the God of the impossible brought Abraham into a new relationship with Him, which, of course, also needed obedience as its outworking (22:15-18). The intellectual, the moral and the spiritual aspects of faith all can be seen intertwined in his character. The faithfulness of God is written large upon his page of history.

The other particular instance where the faithful fulfillment of God's promises is noted, is in the establishment of the Davidic house (1 Kings 8:1-66). This was something clung to even in the nation's darkest hour, but inevitably with a new dimension added to it (Jer 33:14-26). The prophets had to look ahead through history to a more glorious age when the Messiah would come. There were many other cases when the prophets interpreted the times and spoke predictively in the name of Yahweh, and He performed what He said He would. In every such case they required a response of faith in their hearers.

In addition to the faithfulness of God shown in words which came true, there were signs as visible words. Notable signs were performed before the Exodus so that people might believe that God was in action redeeming His people (Exod 4:1-5). On occasion a man could receive guidance from Yahweh by a special sign (Judg 6:36-40). These were to give men confidence, provided that their attitude to Him was right (Isa 7:3-17). If men did not believe, they could not be established.

4. *The covenant.* The focus of God's faithful dealing with His people and their response to Him is in the covenant relationship which He established with them. A covenant was a binding obligation between two parties, and in the case of a covenant in which Yahweh was involved, it was always He who took the initiative and who was the dominant partner in the relationship. The basic terms of a covenant were, "I will be your God and you shall be my people"—it was a corporate relationship to Him out of which various obligations sprang. The covenant with Noah included promises of blessing to his descendants and to all flesh (Gen 6:18; 9:9-17). The covenant with Abraham was based on the promises of God, with the seal of circumcision as a reminder of God's undertaking and men's obligation (17:1-14). The covenant with the people of Israel after the Exodus was linked with that made with Abraham (Exod 2:24); it was sealed with blood and included the stipulation of obedience on the part of the people (24:7f.). Under Joshua the people renewed the covenant with promises of obedience (Josh 24:24f.). God made a covenant with David and His descendants (2 Sam 7:12-17) and the way in which this demonstrated His faithfulness is brought out most strikingly in Psalm 89.

The fact that Yahweh had entered into covenant with His people in these different ways was the basis for much exhortation to the people to be true to Him. The Book of Deuteronomy constantly dwells upon His faithfulness and the obligations of the covenant nation. The penalties of unfaithfulness also are brought home. Most of the prophets seem to have had the idea of the covenant somewhere in their thought, but in Hosea the theme of God's loyalty and man's disloyalty is absolutely basic to the whole book. The northern kingdom went into captivity because of its failure to observe the covenant (2 Kings 17:15-38), and the southern kingdom had to reform itself drastically when reaffirming the covenant under Josiah (2 Kings 23:1-4). It was Jeremiah's great achievement that he saw that outward reform could not go far enough and that unfaithfulness to an outward covenant was unavoidable. Hence the dramatic new spiritual prospects opened up through his prophecy of the new covenant (Jer 31:31-34).

The religion of the OT was dominated by the law. No Israelite could conceivably be ignorant of the fact that he was under obligation to be faithful to God. Yet at its best, Israel saw that law was not legalism and that the claims of God for their complete loyalty were based upon His prior action in loyalty to His obligations freely entered into by the divine promise (Exod 20:1-3). But when Yahweh had revealed Himself in the way that He had, the call to obedience could never be divorced from the invitation to faith.

5. *Personal.* The main thrust of the OT is concerned with God and His people as a whole, but it would be wrong to infer from that, that there was no such thing as individual, personal faith. That is abundantly illustrated at all periods of Israel's history. The personal faith of Abraham, Moses, David, or Elijah is something real and important as well as the national faith. The Psalms afford abundant examples of trust in Yahweh through thick and thin. They often are couched in tones of deep personal devotion. God's faithfulness is the one thing which can be relied upon, and it is under the shadow of His wings that the children of men take their refuge (Ps 36:5-7).

So we see faith and faithfulness in the OT. The God who acts gives signs and promises, and enters into relationship with His people. Man is utterly dependent upon Him and is called upon to acknowledge that dependence and to obey His will. The covenant is the undergirding of the nation's life and in his personal life "the righteous will live by his faith" (or faithfulness) (Hab 2:4). Any confidence in anyone or anything to the exclusion of God is condemned (Ps 146), yet there is an overflowing of the concept of faithfulness to dealings with fellow men (2 Sam 2:5). The prophets were insistent that relationship with God must lead to just dealing with neighbors, and the psalmist sees that the man who dwells with God and is truly established is the man who can be relied upon in all his dealings with others (Ps 15). Behind it all is the character of the God of the covenant whose faithfulness was proclaimed in the great congregation (Ps 40:9f.).

II. Faith and faithfulness in Judaism

A. The Apocrypha and Pseudepigrapha. While these writings drew freely upon their OT heritage, there can be seen an increasing institutionalization of the idea of faith and faithfulness. In particular, the observance of the law was closely involved with it (Ecclus 32:24). The defense of the law and institutions of Israel as an expression of faith is found movingly portrayed in the struggles of the Maccabees. In the Diaspora there grew up an emphasis upon the greatness of the God of Israel as opposed to the pointless polytheism of the nations. This is shown particularly in some sections of the Wisdom of Solomon. There also was developed the absolute use of the term "the faithful" (*οἱ πιστοί*), as the pious, contrasted with unbelievers inside and outside Judaism (Wisd Sol 3:9-15). In these processes there was some movement also toward a concept of faith which was more intellectual and less a matter of personal trust. In the apocalyptic books faith was much more connected with the future and therefore in some respects would be better described as "hope." In the coming eschatological judgment, it is the faithful remnant who will be vindicated.

B. Philo. Philo's understanding of the OT

Qumran: a view south over the ruins from the Citadel. There is considerable emphasis in the Qumran documents upon the faithfulness of God. © *Lev*

was influenced greatly by his knowledge of Gr. philosophy, in particular that of Plato. As a Jew he believed in the greatness of the one God, but rather than seeing Him as active in history he sought Him through withdrawing from the world. The phenomenal world was essentially insubstantial, and true security could be found only in a mystical relationship with the ultimate reality in God. To him we owe the description of faith as "queen of virtues."

C. Qumran. There is considerable emphasis in the Qumran documents upon the faithfulness of God. The community, inevitably as a group within a larger whole, thought of itself as a faithful remnant. As with many other groups in later Judaism, their stress was not so much upon an active personal trust in God as in a loyal obedience to His commandments. The Habakkuk commentary emphasizes both faith in the Teacher of Righteousness (esp. in the truth of His teachings) and in God's vindication of them.

D. The rabbis. What was true of the Apoc. and Pseudep. as far as the institutionalizing of faith was concerned, was even more marked in the case of much of the rabbinic lit. Faith is connected closely with obedience, and faith easily becomes faith in the tradition of the elders and obedience a legalistic keeping of the law and its many subtle interpretations. There were among the rabbis men of personal trust in the living God, but it became fatally easy for this to be obscured by an over emphasis upon the Torah.

III. Faith and faithfulness in Greek thought

A. Classical. There is a clear interrelation between the ideas of faith and faithfulness in the usage of words of the πίστις group in classical Gr. Both the adjective *pistós* and the noun *pístis* can be used in an active or a passive sense—they can refer either to trusting or to being worth trusting. The verb πιστεύω, could express trust in persons or things. There was nothing necessarily religious about these terms, although they could be used in the area of religion. But none of the words standing by themselves would immediately suggest a religious significance.

B. Hellenistic. It was in this period that *pisteúō* became one of the words which could be used regularly to denote belief that there were gods. At the same time *pistis* began to acquire a flavor of piety, for the belief in the existence of gods naturally extended to a recognition that they had some claims upon human allegiance. Likewise there followed the belief in certain theological propositions, with particular reference to the invisible world and man's relationship to it. The word group really came into its own when there was competition between various religions and each proclaimed the necessity of faith in the truth for which it claimed to stand. The concept might vary in its intellectual or moral content, but in the mystery religions it was seen as the way of illumination and salvation. While there are clear differences in the object and nature of faith between Heb. and Gr. writings, *pistis* and its cognates were ready-made for the LXX trs. when they wished to render *ĕ'mûn* and its cognates into Gr.

IV. Faith and faithfulness in the NT

A. Terminology. There is no need to emphasize the centrality of the concept of faith in the NT. The words that are used to express it are almost always those of the *pistis* group. Despite the usage of the LXX in rendering *'emeth* and *'emûnāh* by *alētheia*, that word and its cognates almost always denotes in the NT truth, reality, and genuiness. There is an association with the concept of faithfulness quite frequently because what is true is also trustworthy. By and large the field has been left entirely to *pístis* and the words related to it.

1. *Pisteúō.* This word often has a nontechnical sense even when it is dealing with religious statements. So it is possible to believe that when using a *hoti* clause (John 8:24) or the accusative and infinitive (Acts 8:37). Likewise one may give credence to a statement (Mark 13:21). When it is followed by a noun referring to a thing, the object of *pisteúō* is in the accusative (1 Cor 13:7). It is much more frequently found with the dative of the thing (John 2:22) or of the person (4:21). It is used also in the active (2:24) and in the passive (Gal 2:7) in the sense of "entrust." More important is the technical sense of Christian believing that it developed. It could be used with the dative of faith in God (Acts 16:34), in Christ (John 8:31) and in His name (1 John 3:23). There were various prepositional uses of which the most important is *eis* followed by the accusative (John 2:11), but *epi* also is found with the accusative (Rom 4:5) and with the dative (1 Tim 1:16). The verb also may be used absolutely (John 1:7) and the participle became a technical term for Christians (1 Thess 1:7).

2. *Pistis.* This is used only rarely in the NT of human fidelity (Titus 2:10) and of divine faithfulness (Rom 3:3). In the great majority of cases it means human faith in God. It is one of the great "theological virtues" (1 Cor 13:13). It can be further defined by the use of the objective genitive or by the prepositions *eís, pros, epi,* or *en.* Faith may be in God (Mark 11:22), in Christ (Rom 3:22), in His name (Acts 3:16). It also may be in things such as His blood (Rom 3:25) or the Gospel (Phil 1:27). The word *pístis* also may be used in an objective sense of the doctrine which is to be believed (Jude 3).

3. *Pistós.* The adjective *pistós* also may be used both technically and nontechnically, and in both active and passive senses. It is commonly used of the reliability of servants or stewards (1 Cor 4:2). God is supremely the One in whom confidence may be placed (1:9), but His word and His promises are also reliable (Rev 21:5). Statements of Christian truth also may be trusted (1 Tim 1:15). When *pistós* is used in the active sense to mean believing, it is only as a technical term (John 20:27). It also can be used almost as the equivalent of "a Christian" (Acts 16:1).

4. *Negative words.* There are a number of privative formations of words in the *pístis* group which may be found in the NT. *Apistéō* means to disbelieve in a general sense (Luke 24:41) or in a specific sense of being an unbeliever (1 Pet 2:7). It likewise can be used in the sense of being disloyal (Rom 3:3). *Apistós* may be used in the passive sense of "incredible" (Acts 26:8), but more often means "unbelieving" (John 20:27). The adjective can be used as a term for non-Christians (1 Cor 6:6). The noun *apistía* may refer both to unfaithfulness (Rom 3:3) and also to unbelief (4:20). The compound *oligó pistos,* "of little faith," is a word virtually found nowhere except in the synoptic gospels.

B. The usage of the NT writers. 1. *The synoptic gospels.* a. God's faithfulness. God is portrayed in the first three gospels mainly under two figures—as King and as Father. Each of these concepts is associated in some way with the idea of His faithfulness. The kingdom of God comes not out of the blue, but because the time is fulfilled (Mark 1:15). The first two chs. of Luke's gospel give a vivid picture of people who were waiting for God to fulfill His promises made under the Old Covenant (Luke 2:25, 38). Those who see the beginning of the fulfillment rejoice in His faithfulness. The Magnificat (Luke 1:46-55) is a song of praise to God who "has helped his servant Israel, in remembrance of his mercy, as he spoke to our fathers, to Abraham and to his posterity for ever" (Luke 1:54f.). The Benedictus (Luke 1:68-79) likewise is a celebration of the faithfulness of God who has acted "to perform the mercy promised to our fathers, and to remember his holy covenant, the oath which he swore to our father Abraham" (Luke 1:72f.). The opening chs. of Matthew's gospel also commemorate the faithfulness of the Lord who fulfilled what He had spoken through the prophets (Matt 1:22f.). This theme of fulfillment of Scripture is found elsewhere in the gospels, but it is a particular emphasis which is found throughout Matthew.

When God is spoken of as Father, there is conveyed the idea of His faithfulness in loving and providing for His children. This theme is particularly brought out in the Sermon on the Mount (with parallels in Luke). It is the Father who in His faithful providence "makes his sun rise on the evil and on the good, and sends rain on the just and on the unjust" (5:45). It is He who is faithful in rewarding those who do His will (6:4, 6, 18). It is He who feeds the birds of the air and clothes the grass of the field—how much more will He provide for His human children! The realization of this should lead men to trust Him in a way that will banish worry. Faith will mean taking His providence seriously and putting His claims first (6:25-34). It is absurd to suppose that human fathers with all their sinfulness would fail to give their children what they really needed. How much more is this true of the heavenly Father (Matt 7:7-11)!

b. HUMAN FAITH. The response of men to the arrival of the reign of God in their midst in the Person of Jesus Christ was to be that they should "repent and believe in the gospel" (Mark 1:15). Here faith is shown to be dependent upon the divine initiative. The kingdom comes whether men hear or whether they forbear, but the claim which it makes is faith. This faith is centered in the Gospel, or, the good news of God's redeeming action. There is therefore at least to some extent an intellectual content to faith. Its moral content is emphasized by its close association with repentance.

The miracles of Jesus were signs of the coming of the kingdom of God. In some cases faith was a necessary prerequisite for their performance by Jesus (Mark 2:5; 5:34; 10:52) and also for the forgiveness which was associated with many of the healing miracles. He was astonished at the unbelief of His own countrymen (6:5f.). During a storm on the Sea of Galilee, Jesus rebuked the disciples for their lack of faith in His ability to exercise the power of the Creator in stilling the storm (4:35-41). The same power that He had to heal was also available to those who had faith in God, for "All things are possible to him who believes" (9:23f.). The command of Jesus is therefore, "Have faith in God." Where there is such faith, the results of believing prayer will be remarkable (11:22-24). The moral and intellectual sides of faith are seen to stand together.

The unexpected faith of some which Jesus commended warmly (Luke 7:9) was in marked contrast to the unbelief of professed believers. The chief priests were aware that they had not believed John the Baptist (Mark 11:30f.). Jesus asserted that they would not believe Him if He told them that He was the Christ (Luke 22:67). They mockingly suggested that they would believe if He would come down from the cross (Mark 15:32). Even the disciples were slow to believe all that the prophets had spoken (Luke 24:25). Yet God had given them the mystery of the kingdom of God, whereas others were taught in parables to confirm them in their blindness (Mark 4:11f.). Luke emphasizes that the purpose of Satanic activity is to prevent men from believing and being saved (Luke 8:12).

An interesting and significant feature of the gospels is the portrayal of the faith which Jesus had in God. This is illustrated well by the way in which He addressed God as His Father. He could use the intimate word *Abba* and show complete dependence upon Him and His will (Mark 14:36). In a famous saying, similar in thought and style to John's gospel, He reveals the complete mutual trust between them and the possibility of others entering in some measure into the unique relationship of the Son to the Father. "No one knows the Son except the Father, and no one knows the Father except the Son and any one to whom the Son chooses to reveal him" (Matt 11:27; Luke 10:22). It is because of this relationship that He can tell His disciples to pray, "Our Father." The faith of believers in a trustworthy God is nowhere better expressed than in the Lord's Prayer (Matt 6:9-13; Luke 11:2-4). In Matthew it is set in the context of teaching about the heavenly Father who knows His children's needs, and who forgives His children's sins when they are of a forgiving disposition themselves. Here one sees clearly the personal and moral connotations of faith in God (Matt 6:7f., 14f.).

There is not revealed in the synoptic gospels the fullness of Christian faith, for that was essentially something which came after the Resurrection and Pentecost. The faithfulness of God revealed in the OT is given a new dimension with the coming of Jesus Christ and the practice of a new intimacy with Him is inaugurated through the life of His Son.

2. John's gospel and epistles. The gospel and epistles are treated together without any judgment being passed about their common authorship. It is clear that they belong to the same school of thought and the concept of faith in them is similar.

a. GOD'S FAITHFULNESS. The only use of a word from the *pístis* group ascribed to God is in 1 John 1:9 where He is said to be "faithful and just, and will forgive our sins." The word *alēthēs*, "true," is sometimes used of God in the Johannine writings and its meaning is often not far from that of faithfulness (John 3:33). There is the idea found in the synoptics of the fulfillment of Scripture (13:18; 17:12; 19:24, 28, 36f.). God is portrayed as the Author and unseen Director of the whole drama in which Jesus is the leading Actor. Yet there is relatively little that stresses directly God's faithfulness. It is rather assumed, in contrast to faith in God which is made vividly explicit throughout the gospel.

b. THE NATURE OF FAITH. There are numerous other words which are used alongside *pisteúō* in the gospel which help us to a clearer understanding of its meaning. The noun *pístis* is not found in the gospel at all and occurs only once in the Johannine epistles. The victory which overcomes the world is described as "our faith" (1 John 5:4). It may well be that the meaning here is "our creed." The reason why John did not use *gnōsis*, "knowledge," is generally understood to be that the Gnostics had made it their own. It is less easy to see why *pístis* is not used. It may be that the increasing application of it to "the faith" would have made its use somewhat misleading when John wrote. It also is possible that the use of the verb gives a more vivid representation of a dynamic relationship.

Faith is connected with knowledge. There is no question of knowledge being a stage of perfection beyond mere faith. Both are concerned with the divine origin of the mission of Jesus (*ginóskō* John 7:17; 17:8; *pisteúō*; John 11:42; 16:27-30; 17:8, 21). Both are ways of reaching the truth (8:32; 14:1), and of apprehension that Jesus is the Christ (6:69; 11:27). Faith can help men to know, but never to know in such a way that they do not need faith. Faith is also connected with obedience, for the believer is contrasted with the one who does not obey the Son (3:36).

There are some metaphorical expressions which seem to be illustrative of faith. Believing is said to be the same as "receiving" Christ (1:11f.; 5:43f.). It also can be said to be "coming to" Christ (6:35; 7:37f.). It is associated closely with loving Him also (16:27), and indeed is connected in some way or other with all the leading ideas of the gospel.

c. THE OBJECT OF FAITH. There are a number of occasions when the verb *pisteúō* is used without an object, when the sense must be something like "become a disciple" (1:7, 50; 4:42, 53; 6:47; 19:35). Far the commonest use, however, is the construction *pisteúō eis,* with Jesus as its object (2:11; 3:16, 18, etc.). This is unknown in secular Gr., and of the forty-five occurrences in the NT thirty-seven are in John or 1 John. The expression undoubtedly suggests not only intellectual credence, but also moral commitment to the person of Christ and is absolutely central to Johannine thought. There are also a number of places where *pisteúō* is followed by a *hoti* clause which describes something about the person and mission of Christ which should be believed. Men were to believe "that I am he" (8:24; 13:19), and that He was the Christ (20:31); as Martha acknowledged (11:27); that He and the Father mutually indwelt each other (14:11) and that He came from the Father (11:42; 17:8), as the disciples confessed in John 16:27, 30.

Faith in Jesus also could be described as faith in His name (1:12; 2:23; 3:18). This has reference to His character prob., but also, it is likely, to His ownership. It may emphasize the sense of allegiance and obligation which faith in Him brings. There are also references to the believing of the words of Jesus (2:22; 4:21; 14:11). The believing of Moses in the OT is linked with believing Him (5:46). Faith in Jesus was the gateway to faith in God the Father (5:24; 14:1).

d. THE BASIS OF FAITH. As such tremendous importance is attached to faith in John's gospel, the evangelist emphasizes the solid foundation which any faith in Jesus will have. The concept of evidence (*marturía*) is referred to frequently as something which leads the way to faith. John the Baptist came for the purpose of bearing "witness to the light, that all might believe through him" (John 1:7). Jesus had greater testimony than that of John to lead people to faith. There was the evidence of His deeds and the evidence of His Father Himself, but their disbelief of Jesus showed their failure to receive the Father's word (5:30-40). In the First Epistle of John it is stated that there is divine as well as human testimony to Jesus as the Son of God. It is meant to lead men to believe in Him. Those who do not are making God a liar by refusing to believe the evidence which He has given (1 John 5:6-12). Jesus likewise gives His own testimony, which men do not receive (John 3:11).

In John, faith is related to both seeing and hearing. Seeing the Son is the natural preliminary to believing as far as His contemporaries are concerned (6:40), but it was possible to see and not to believe (6:36). Seeing the Father directly was not possible, but believing was the gateway to eternal life (6:46f.). Faith would lead on to seeing the glory of God (11:40). The faith of Thomas in the risen Christ was based upon sight, but Jesus pronounced a great benediction upon those who did not see and yet believed (20:29). The idea of sight varies between the literal and the metaphorical. In the former sense it may or may not be the prelude to faith. In the latter, believing is seeing. Hearing can likewise be a purely natural process, not leading on to faith (6:60-65). Men who do not hear God's word in the words of Jesus cannot come to believe (8:43-47). On the other hand, men may hear His word and believe the Father who sent Him, and they find not judgment and death, but life (5:24).

On four occasions in John the preposition *diá*, "on account of," is used to describe the immediate cause of belief. The purpose of John's coming as a witness was, "that all might believe through him" (1:7). Many of the Samaritans from Sychar believed in Jesus because of the testimony of the woman whom He met at the well, though in the end the ground of their faith was rather His word than hers (4:39-42). Jesus prayed not only for His disciples but "for those who believe in me through their word" (17:20). It was not only the spoken word which had this effect; it was also the acted word. His disciples were urged to believe because of the works which He had done (14:11).

Some of the works were described as "signs." They were not only miracles on the physical level but also dramatic illustrations of the spiritual life which Jesus brought. They were therefore meant to bring men to believe in Jesus (2:11, 23; 4:50, 53), though often they were the cause of conflict (11:45-47; 12:9-11). No more than in the synoptic gospels is Jesus willing to provide mere wonder-working as a basis for faith (4:48).

e. THE RESULT OF FAITH. The first consequence of faith mentioned in the fourth gospel is becoming sons of God (1:12). This meant that men could to some extent enter into the relationship which Jesus had with His Father which is so integral a part of the gospel, though the words for faith and faithfulness are not used to describe it. Men may be said to receive light (12:36) and satisfaction (6:35; 7:37f.). By far the most frequent picture, however, is that of eternal life, or as it is often called, simply "life." The loving purpose of God was that the believer should have eternal life (3:15f.; 6:40). Those who believe have eternal life here and now (3:36; 6:47; 1 John 5:13). The evangelist's purpose in writing with a selection of the signs which Jesus did was to invoke faith in Jesus as Christ and Son of God and so to lead men to life in His name (John 20:31).

The blessedness of faith is contrasted with the wretchedness of unbelief. The believer is not condemned, but the unbeliever is already condemned (3:18). The believer has passed from death to life and does not come into judgment, but those who have done evil do (5:24, 29). Unless men believed, they would die in their sins (8:24), and sin was essentially unbelief in Him (16:9). There is a paradox in the gospel between the great universal "whoevers" (3:15f.; 6:40; 11:26; 12:46) and the inability of some to believe in fulfillment of prophecy (12:37-43), because they are not "of God" (8:45-47) and do not belong to Jesus' sheep (10:25f.).

f. The development of faith. It is interesting to note the ebb and flow of faith as it is dramatically revealed in John's gospel. The first person said to "believe" is Nathanael, who confessed Jesus as Son of God and King of Israel, but had greater things to see than that Jesus had seen him under the fig tree (1:45-51). After the sign at the wedding at Cana Jesus' disciples believed in Him, but as yet with imperfect faith (2:11). Many believed in His name when He had cleansed the Temple, but Jesus knew them and the nature of their faith well enough not to commit Himself to them (2:23-25). The inability of the religious leaders to believe earthly things prevented them from believing heavenly things (3:12). The Samaritans, however, believed in Him and confessed Him to be "the Saviour of the world" (4:39-42). The official whose son Jesus healed not only believed His word but "believed" with his household (4:46-53). "The Jews" could not believe because they were too concerned with prestige, and they did not even really believe Moses (5:44-47). Those who saw the feeding of the five thousand only saw and did not believe (6:36). Some even of Jesus' disciples did not believe (6:64), but Peter spoke for the Twelve when he said, "we have believed and have come to know, that you are the Holy One of God" (6:69). This faith was not shared during the ministry by His brothers (7:5). Many believed as He spoke about His origin and destination (8:30f.), but others would not believe Him when He was telling the truth (8:45-47). The blind man whom He healed said, "Lord, I believe" though not at first knowing who the Son of man was (9:35-38). "The Jews" would not and could not believe the evidence that He was the Christ (10:24-26), but at the other side of the Jordan many who remembered what John the Baptist had said about Him believed in Him (10:40-42). The death of Lazarus provided an opportunity for His disciples to believe (11:15) and before he was raised Martha confessed, "I believe that you are the Christ, the Son of God, he who is coming into the world" (11:27). After the raising many of the Jews believed in Him (11:45), so that the chief priests and Pharisees were afraid that everyone would believe in Him (11:48). The miracle continued to lead many to faith (12:11). Many others, however, did not believe in Him despite the signs (12:37), or if they did believe in Him they were afraid to admit it (12:42f.). The disciples in the last week of the ministry needed to be told to believe the mutual indwelling of Father and Son (14:10f.) though they believed that He came from God (16:30; 17:8). The fullness of faith could not come until the Resurrection (2:22) and it was the Beloved Disciple who was the first to see the empty tomb and believe (20:8). Only after the Resurrection Thomas addressed Jesus in terms of adoring wonder as "My Lord and my God!" (20:26-29). His was the first adequate confession of faith.

g. Human faithfulness. While the *pístis* words are used almost entirely in the sense of putting one's trust in Jesus or God, if the correct reading of John 20:31 is a present subjunctive, it will mean "hold the faith" (NEB), suggesting an attitude of continuing faithfulness. Only those who continued in His word were truly Jesus' disciples (8:31). They were to "abide" or remain in Him and keep His commandments (15:1-11). Their faithfulness to each other was described as "love," which was derived from His prior love for them and was the mark of true discipleship (13:34f.; 15:12).

3. *The Acts of the Apostles.* a. God's faithfulness. This theme is emphasized in two ways in the Acts. In the first place, what God has already done in Christ is proof of His faithfulness. The apostolic *kerygma* is grounded upon the fact that He has been faithful to His promises. The Incarnation showed this for, as Paul said in the synagogue at Pisidian Antioch, "of this man's [i.e. David's] posterity, God has brought to Israel a Savior, Jesus, as he promised" (Acts 13:23). His suffering and death was in fulfillment of Scripture and showed the providence of God without excusing the guilt of the human agents (2:22-24; 3:18; 13:27-29). The apostles brought "the good news that what God promised to the fathers, this he has fulfilled to us their children by raising Jesus" (13:32f.; 26:6-8). This was "the holy and sure blessings of David" (13:34). The Resurrection was one of the great pieces of evidence of God's faithfulness and is described as an "assurance" or "pledge" (*pístis*) of future judgment (17:31). The other was the presence and the power of the Holy Spirit. The outpouring of the Spirit was "the promise of the Father" (1:4; 2:33), and the receiving of the gift of the Spirit by those who repented was a promise to all those whom God called to Him (2:38f.). The return of Christ in due time would mark the establishment of "all that God spoke by the mouth of his holy prophets from of old" (3:21).

The second way in which God's faithfulness is stressed is in the way in which His present activity is seen to overrule the life of the Church and the progress of the Christian mission. It was He who "added to their number day by day those who were being saved" (2:47). His angel guided Philip to the Ethiopian eunuch (8:26-40) and released Peter from prison (12:6-11). His Spirit sent out Barnabas and Saul on their missionary journey (13:1-4), guided the Council of Jerusalem (15:28f.) and led the apostles into Europe (16:6-10). He guided Paul on his dangerous and roundabout journey to Rome (19:21f.; 23:11; 27:21-26). There are also two occasions when Paul is recorded as mentioning the faithfulness of God as Creator and Judge who "did not leave himself without witness, for he did good and gave you from heaven rains and fruitful seasons satisfying your hearts with food and gladness" (14:17; cf. 17:24-31).

b. MEN'S FAITH. This is, if anything, even more prominent a theme in Acts than God's faithfulness, to which it is the response. The verb *pisteúō* often is used without an object in the sense of believing the *kerygma* and so becoming a Christian (2:44; 4:4, 32; 5:14; 11:21; 13:12, 39; 14:1; 15:7; 17:12; 18:8, 27; 19:2, 18; 21:20). (Cf. also the adjective *pistós*, in 10:45; 16:1, 15.) The verb sometimes is followed by a noun to indicate in whom people believed—the Lord (9:42; 14:23; 18:8), the Lord Jesus Christ (11:17; 16:31; cf. 10:43; 19:4; 22:19) or God (16:34). The response seems to have been superficial only in the case of Simon (8:13). The commitment to Christ might have as a prelude believing the Scriptures (24:14; 26:27) or believing an evangelist (8:12). The initial act of faith needed to be succeeded by a constant trust in the promises of God (27:25).

The noun *pístis* does not occur frequently. It can be used absolutely (6:5; 11:24; 14:9, 27; 15:9) or with reference to Christ explicitly (3:16; 20:21; 24:24; 26:18). It also has the meaning "the faith"—the body of Christian doctrine (6:7; 13:8; 14:22; 16:5). So we see the lively exercise of faith is dependent upon an objective act of God. Faith is connected with repentance (11:21; 20:21) and has moral consequences (24:24f.). It leads to forgiveness (10:43; 26:18), cleansing (15:9) and justification (13:39). It was the result of God's calling (13:48) and was due to His grace (18:27). It was accompanied by the gift of the Spirit (10:43f.; 11:17; 19:2). It might be induced by a miracle (5:14; 13:12), by the Scriptures (17:12) or by the preaching of the Gospel (4:4; 18:8). It sometimes involved healing (3:16; 14:9). Its natural outcome was a common purpose with other believers (2:44; 4:32) and joy (16:34). Some outstanding disciples can be described as "full of faith" (Stephen in 6:5; Barnabas in 11:24).

None of the words of the *pístis* group is used to describe human faithfulness, but this idea is found in relation to God when the verb *prosménō* ("to remain") is used (11:23; 13:43). Loyalty to God and to the Christian brotherhood is implicit throughout the book and perhaps finds clearest expression in the incident involving Ananias and Sapphira (4:32-5:11).

4. *The Pauline epistles.* Neither Paul the man nor his writings can possibly be understood unless we grasp the meaning of faith to him. Ever since his encounter with the risen Christ on the road to Damascus the whole of his thinking and his life were dominated by the ideas of the faithfulness of God and the need for a responsive faith in man. If there is a systematic treatment of these themes only in Romans, their living reality bursts forth spontaneously again and again in the varied pastoral situations which he deals with in all the epistles. His entire doctrine of salvation, his entire theology, could be summed up under the heading of faith, but we shall have to concentrate on the passages where the *pístis* words or closely associated ideas are present.

a. GOD'S FAITHFULNESS. This is the solid foundation upon which all else in Pauline theology is built (Rom 3:3). The adjective *pistós* is used six times with reference to God or Christ. God is faithful in fulfilling His promises (2 Cor 1:18). He is faithful in continuing to work in and to preserve those whom He has called to Himself (1 Cor 1:9; 10:13; 1 Thess 5:24; 2 Thess 3:3). Even "if we are faithless, he remains faithful—for he cannot deny himself" (2 Tim 2:13). It is because He is faithful that there are sayings about what He has done which also are completely reliable (1 Tim 1:15; 3:1; 4:9; 2 Tim 2:11; Titus 3:8). Christian teaching as a whole can be described as "the sure word" (Titus 1:9).

We find also in Paul a fair number of references to ἔλεος, "mercy." This is the word which renders *hesed* in the LXX. In the gospels its main uses are in the twice repeated quotation of Hosea 6:6; Matthew 9:13; 12:7, and its occurrence five times in the first ch. of Luke. Paul uses it as a greeting, alongside grace and peace (1 Tim 1:1; 2 Tim 1:1) and also as a benediction (Gal 6:16). Its chief use as noun or verb (*eleéō*) is, however, in Romans 9 to 11. In these chapters Paul shows how God's faithfulness has been demonstrated despite the unfaithfulness of Israel. The word of God had not failed (Rom 9:6). There was no injustice with God, for "it depends not upon man's will or exertion, but upon God's mercy" (9:16). He has not rejected His people (11:1). The gifts and call of God are irrevocable (11:29). The purpose of God is "that he may have mercy upon all" (11:32).

Another important subject illustrating the faithfulness of God is that of His promises. This is dealt with especially in Romans 4 and Galatians 3 and 4 where the story of Abraham is in mind. Abraham was "fully convinced that God was able to do what he had promised" (Rom 4:21), and the promise was guaranteed to all his descendants (4:16). Christians, "like Isaac, are children of promise" (Gal 4:28).

b. Faith and the Gospel. Christian faith begins as a response to the *kerygma.* "It pleased God," says Paul, "through the folly of what we preach (the *kerygma*) to save those who believe" (1 Cor 1:21). He expresses the main thrust of the *kerygma* as the Cross (1:17, 18, 23, 24). The Resurrection also was something which had to be believed, for if it were not true both *kerygma* and faith would be futile (1 Cor 15:14). The relationship of faith to the Gospel is dealt with more fully in Romans 10:8-17. With relentless logic Paul shows that salvation depends upon calling upon God, which depends upon faith, which depends upon a preacher. "Faith comes from what is heard, and what is heard comes by the preaching of Christ" (10:17). Faith is defined further as confessing with the lips that Jesus is Lord and believing in the heart that God raised Him from the dead (10:9). Faith then involves an intellectual acceptance of and a moral response to the *kerygma* and it is the means by which salvation is experienced (1:16). It is connected with obedience to God's command to repent in the Gospel (1:5; 10:16; 16:26; Gal 3:2; 2 Thess 1:8). It is established by the power of God rather than the wisdom of men (1 Cor 2:5), but there was still a need of human preachers (Rom 10:14f.; 1 Cor 3:5; 15:11). Yet underlying all the human activity involved was the conviction that faith was due to grace—that it was a gift of God (Eph 2:8).

c. Faith and justification. While Paul has a number of different figures which are used parallel to one another in order to express the new relationship with God which is entered by Christian faith, the chief figure is that of justification. It means declaring a man to be in the right, giving him a right standing with God. In the case of sinful men that can be done only through faith in the Christ and His work of redemption. It is something achieved by the grace of God and is a gift to be received by faith (Rom 3:21-26). Faith which leads to justification is the correlative of grace. Grace means divine action from sheer undeserved love, and faith therefore is humble and thankful acceptance of something unearned. Because man prefers to earn things in order to have something to pride himself upon, Paul is insistent that the principle of faith understood thus is utterly opposed to the principle of works—of earning salvation by good deeds. This was a particular temptation for Jews who kept the law of Moses and had higher moral standards than their contemporaries (3:27-31; 9:30-33; 10:1-8; Gal 2:16; 3:10-14; Eph. 2:8; Phil 3:9). While Paul could in one sense regard the law as a custodian "until faith should be revealed" (Gal 3:23-26), he was anxious to show that, far from overthrowing the law by this faith, he was in fact upholding it (Rom 3:31).

In order to show the importance of faith even in the OT, he goes back behind Moses to Abraham. The faith principle can be found working in his case, for Abraham "believed God, and it was reckoned to him as righteousness" (Gen 15:6; cited in Rom 4:9; Gal 3:6). This was before circumcision was instituted (Rom 4:10) and even over four centuries before the law was given (Gal 3:17). Religion in Abraham's case was a matter of promise. God made promises to him which he believed himself, and through him they were made to his descendants. Those descendants need now to be redefined in terms of those who share the faith of Abraham (Rom 4:11f.; Gal 3:29; 4:28). For Abraham did not just believe promises, he believed also in God as one "who gives life to the dead and calls into existence the things that do not exist" (Rom 4:17). The equivalent for Christians therefore is to "be-

Abraham's Oak near Hebron where he built an altar to the Lord. © *M.P.S.*

lieve in him that raised from the dead Jesus our Lord, who was put to death for our trespasses and raised for our justification" (4: 24f.).

This then is the heart of the Gospel which had such power in the life of Paul and others (1:16), "for in it the righteousness of God is revealed through faith for faith; as it is written, 'He who through faith is righteous shall live'" (1:17; citing Hab 2:4; cf. Gal 3: 11). The emphasis of the prophet may well have been more on the continuing relationship of faithfulness than on the initial saving act of faith. The principle is the same—faith is the only way to receive righteousness and life.

d. FAITH AND RELATIONSHIP. Justification by faith means not only accepting a doctrine but also commitment to a person. It is trusting him who justifies the ungodly (Rom 4:5). While the verb *pisteúō* is generally used by Paul in an absolute sense (but it is followed by *eis* in Rom 10:14; Gal 2:16; Phil 1:29), the noun *pístis* is made more specific on a number of occasions by being related to God (1 Thess 1:8) or to Christ (Rom 3:22, 26; Gal 2:16, 20; 3:22, 26; Eph 1:15; 3:12; Phil 3:9; Col 1:4; 2:5; 1 Tim 3:13; 2 Tim 1:13; 3:15). Close to the center of Pauline thought is the idea of "faith-union" with Christ which is expressed by the phrase *en Christō*, "in Christ." It is in Him that men are sons of God through faith (Gal 3:26). The Holy Spirit also is received through faith (Eph 1:13; Gal 3:5, 14).

e. THE LIFE OF FAITH. Baptism is the sign of beginning the new life of faith (Col 2:11f.; cf. Gal 3:26f.) and wherever it is spoken of, faith is assumed to be present. But faith needs to grow (2 Cor 10:15). There may be deficiencies in it which need to be made up (1 Thess 3:10) and the aim should be fullness of faith (Rom 4:20; 1 Thess 1:5), which will however always fall short of sight (2 Cor 5:7). Having faith will lead to action (1 Thess 1:3). The faith of a community may become something which is widely known (Rom 1:8; Eph 1:15; Col 1:4; 1 Thess 1:8; Philem 5). Faith will bring confidence about death (1 Thess 4:14) and may be associated with hope (1 Cor 13:13). There are some members of the Church who may have special gifts of faith (12:9), but a loveless faith of this kind is useless (13:2). Faith also is involved in the question of religious scruples, which Paul deals with in Romans 14 and 15, where weak faith signifies over-scrupulousness. It is similar to the idea of conscience (1 Cor 8:1-13; 10:23-30).

f. HUMAN FAITHFULNESS. The adjective *pistós* is used simply for believers without distinction being made between beginning and continuing in faith. It has the specific meaning of *trustworthy* when referring to stewards of the Gospel (1 Cor 4:1f.) and ministers (Eph 6:21; Col 1:7; 4:7). Paul can believe himself to be reckoned trustworthy by the Lord (1 Cor 7:25; 1 Tim 1:12) and to have had the Gospel entrusted (*pisteúō*) to him (1 Tim 1:11; Titus 1:3). He urges Timothy to find trustworthy people to teach others (2 Tim 2:2). The idea of continuing steadfastly in faith is found also as an important theme (1 Cor 16: 13; 2 Cor 1:24; 2 Thess 1:4), though the word used is more often *hupomonē*, "patient endurance."

Faithfulness needs also to be shown to others, as it is part of the fruit of the Spirit (Gal 5:22). Faith in Christ is linked with love (Eph 1:15; 3:17; 6:23; 1 Thess 1:3; 3:6; 2 Thess 1:3). Faith and love are two of the "theological virtues" (1 Cor 13:13). Paul sums up the relationship of the two by speaking of "faith working through love" (Gal 5:6).

g. THE FAITH. There are a number of occasions where Paul refers to "the faith" as the body of Christian belief, though it is not always possible to be sure whether *pístis* is being used in this objective sense. It may be referred to as something to obey (Rom 1:5). Paul was described by Christians in Judaea as "preaching the faith he once tried to destroy" (Gal 1:23). It is possible that the objective sense is intended in 2 Corinthians 13:5 and Colossians 1:23; 2:7, though in all these cases, it may refer to the subjective exercise of faith. It is most common in the Pastoral Epistles, though there again it is not always clear which usage is involved. There is the mystery of the faith (1 Tim 3:9) and "the words of the faith" (4:6). It is possible to depart from the faith or to deny it (4:1; 5:8; 6:10) or to miss "the mark as regards the faith" (1 Tim 6:21). There are a number of other possible references (1 Tim 1:2, 19; 3:13; 6:12; 2 Tim 3:8; 4:7; Titus 1:4, 13; 2:2; 3:15).

The negative words for unbelief are also found in Paul, mainly in Romans and the Pastoral Epistles, but the adjective *apistós* is used fourteen times in the Corinthian letters.

5. *The Epistle to the Hebrews.* a. GOD'S FAITHFULNESS. This theme is first introduced when the writer shows that God can be relied upon to punish sin under the New Covenant even more than under the Old (Heb 2:1-4). He would not overlook their work and love in dealing with the readers (6:10). Emphasis is laid upon His swearing an oath when making the promise to Abraham. There were therefore "two unchangeable things, in which it is impossible that God should prove false" and this was "a sure and steadfast anchor of the soul" (6:13-20). The New Covenant is better than the Old because it is enacted on better promises, and it shows God's loving and forgiving relationship to His people (8: 6-13). The certainty of judgment for willful sin is balanced by the promises and rewards of God for the faithful (10:26-39). The promises were to be received not by men of the Old Covenant but by those of the New (10: 39f.). Even the suffering which they had to endure was evidence of the faithfulness of God (12:3-11). The kingdom which He offered was unshakable (12:25-29). It was the God of peace who had saved them through the death and Resurrection of Christ, who would equip them to do His will (13:20f.). This theme is perhaps best summarized in the phrase "He who promised is faithful" (10:23; cf. 11:11).

b. MAN'S FAITH. This is dependent upon Christ who was Himself "a merciful and faithful high priest in the service of God" (2:17). If Moses was faithful as a servant, Jesus was as a son (3:1-6). He was therefore the surety of a better covenant (7:22). He was the pioneer and perfecter of our faith (12:2). In response to Him men were to hold fast their confidence and pride in their hope (3:6). Holding their first confidence firm to the end was the only way to escape from the unbelief which was characteristic of the people of the first Exodus who failed to enter God's promised rest (3:7-4:7). This faith involved "sharing in Christ" (3:14). Men could draw near with confidence to the throne of grace to receive mercy and help (4:16). When upbraiding them for their immaturity, the writer regards repentance from dead works and faith toward God as elementary Christian teaching (6:1). He is anxious that they should be "imitators of those who through faith and patience inherit the promises" (6:12) and he urges them to seize the hope set before them by God's promises (6:13-20).

Again he urges the readers "to draw near with a true heart in full assurance of faith" and to hold fast the confession of their hope without wavering (10:19-25). They were not to throw away their confidence but to have faith and keep their souls, and he quotes Habakkuk 2:3, 4 rather more in its context than does Paul to reinforce his point (10:35-39).

Chapter 11 is one of the classical NT passages on faith. It begins with a definition: "Faith is the assurance (*hupóstasis*) of things hoped for, the conviction (*élengchos*) of things not seen" (11:1). It is the means by which there is present experience of realities which are future in time, or unseen as belonging to the spiritual sphere. It was something found in the OT and was necessary for divine approval (11:2-6). It meant trusting the God who made the world out of nothing (11:3), believing in His existence and His rewarding seekers after Him (11:6). Faith of this quality, which believed in God's power to bring the invisible to life and acted upon that belief even when it meant suffering and shame, is now abundantly illustrated from the OT. Noah (11:7), Abraham and Sarah (11:8-19), Isaac, Jacob and Joseph (11:20-22), Moses (11:23-28), and a multitude of others all displayed a faith which, "seeing Him who is invisible," endured to the end. Men of the Old Covenant could not receive the true fulfillment of the promises—that is available to us in Christ (11:39-12:2). Their faith was to show itself in faithfulness to others (13:1-6). The readers must imitate the faith of their leaders in the faithful Jesus Christ "the same yesterday and today and for ever" (13:7f.).

6. The Epistle of James. There is a fair amount of reference in this epistle to the faithfulness of God. It is He who gives wisdom to all those who ask Him (James 1:5), and the crown of life which He has promised to those who love Him (1:12). Every good endowment and every perfect gift comes from Him and with Him "there is no variation or shadow due to change" (1:17). It is He whose mercy triumphs over judgment (2:13). His coming is certain though delayed (5:7-9). He will answer the prayers of the righteous (5:15-18).

Human faith or faithfulness must be tested to produce steadfastness (1:3). When it is exercised in prayer it must be without doubting (1:6) and it can be used for the healing of the sick (5:15). "The faith of our Lord Jesus Christ, the Lord of glory" is to be held without partiality (2:1), for God has chosen the poor in the world to be rich in faith (2:5). Most significant, however, in the epistle is the discussion of the relationship between faith and works (2:14-26). James insists that faith cannot save a man unless it has action to back it up. Even Abraham, the great type of justification by faith in the OT, was justified by his action of offering Isaac. At first sight this seems to be a contradiction of Pauline teaching, but closer examination suggests that this is not likely. Faith is in this passage mere intellectual belief, such as the demons have—and shudder. Paul would never deny that such faith would need to be proved real by actions. Works are not treated as a way of earning salvation, as Paul treats them when setting them against faith. Justification also seems to be used rather differently, in the sense of outward vindication rather than of receiving a right relationship with God. It is quite probable that James was refuting perversions of Pauline teaching, but he does not seem to answer any known Pauline letter point by point. It is a healthy reminder that faith is no isolated part of religious experience, but has to determine all the actions of a man.

7. The Epistles of Peter and Jude. In the First Epistle of Peter we see emphasis laid on the faithfulness of God in the face of persecution of the Church. It is He who chose and destined Christians (1:2). It was His mercy that gave them new birth, and a safe inheritance for which they were preserved. Because of this the outcome of their faith would be the salvation of their souls (1:3-9). God's plan before the creation was revealed for their sake and this should produce faith and hope in Him (1:20f.). Their response of faith was an obedience of the truth, and they were born through the dependable message of the Gospel (1:22-25). The prophecy of Isaiah 28:16

is invoked to show that the believer will not be let down by God. The calling and mercy of God achieve this, and unbelievers are destined to fall (2:6-10). Christ left an example of trusting Himself to "him who judges justly" (2:21ff.). Whenever there is unjust suffering, they must remember that "the eyes of the Lord are upon the righteous, and his ears are open to their prayer" (3:12; citing Ps 34:15). The fiery ordeal of persecution is something to be accepted with joy because it means sharing the glory of Christ (4:12-14). Those who suffered according to God's will were to "do right and entrust their souls to a faithful Creator" (4:19). Because God cared for them and would provide them with strength and exalt them in the end, they were to trust Him with all their cares and anxieties (5:6-11). They were to resist the devil, firm in their faith (5:9). The epistle ends with a note that Peter regards Silvanus, through whom he has written, as a "faithful brother," who would presumably transmit his message reliably in writing (5:12).

In 2 Peter and Jude *pistós* and *pisteúō* are not used positively. Faith is said to be "in the righteousness of our God and Savior Jesus Christ" (2 Pet 1:1). Faith is treated as something which needs to be supplemented by virtue and various other qualities (1:5). "The faith" was something which "was once for all delivered to the saints" and had to be defended (Jude 3). It could be described as "your most holy faith" (Jude 20). Throughout the two epistles the need for steadfast faith and faithfulness is set against the background of widespread apostasy and the faithfulness of God. The judgment would come as promised (2 Pet 3:8-10) and God was "able to keep [them] from falling" (Jude 24).

8. *Revelation.* The greeting in the book invokes grace from God "and from Jesus Christ the faithful witness" (Rev 1:4f.). He is described in a similar way again as "the Amen, the faithful and true witness" (3:14) and later the man on the white horse "is called Faithful and True" (19:11). His words therefore are trustworthy and true (21:5; 22:6). His witnesses are likewise to be faithful to death, as Antipas was (2:10, 13). Those who are in the army of the Lamb are "called and chosen and faithful" (17:14). This faithfulness means not denying the faith of Christ (2:13) and keeping "the commandments of God and the faith of Jesus" (14:12). Faith therefore is very much linked with endurance (2:19; 13:10). This is what would be expected in a writing to churches undergoing persecution. Likewise there is the sense of the reliability of God whose victory and vindication of His people is sure.

C. Faith and faithfulness in NT theology. The NT sees God's faithfulness in a new way, for many of the promises made in the OT have been fulfilled, and God has so acted that there is little doubt that the others will be fulfilled also in due course. While the idea of God's faithfulness in creation and providence is given a new depth through the life and ministry of Christ, it is essentially His faithfulness in redemption which is central to NT thought. What the OT could only look forward to, the NT could look back upon. Things had come to their culmination in the life, ministry, death, and resurrection of Christ and in the gift of the Holy Spirit. The new covenant of forgiveness and the personal knowledge of God had come into its own. The faithful God had acted decisively for the redemption of the world.

The Gospel was therefore good news, to be believed and acted upon by all men. The *kerygma* recited the mighty acts of God and called men to repentance and faith on the basis of the divine initiative. So men of every nation, believing the facts of redemption on divine testimony, abandoned themselves completely to the love and mercy of God. In the face of opposition and persecution, they stood fast by the unshakable realities of the Gospel and proved in the depths of human experience that God keeps faith. *See* HOPE.

BIBLIOGRAPHY. B. B. Warfield in HDB (1906); W. H. P. Hatch, *The Pauline Idea of Faith* (1917); *The Idea of Faith in Christian Literature* (1920); G. F. Moore, *Judaism* (1927-1930); C. H. Dodd, *The Bible and the Greeks* (1935), 42-75; C. H. Dodd, *Interpretation of the Fourth Gospel* (1953), 151-186; J. Barr, *Semantics of Biblical Language* (1961), 161-205; R. Bultmann and A. Weiser, *Faith* (1961); A. Richardson, *Introduction to Theology of NT* (1961), 19-34; E. C. Blackman in IDB (1962); G. von Rad, *OT Theology* (1963-1965).

R. E. NIXON

FALCON fôl' kən. אַיָּה, *falcon* [ASV, RSV]; Lev 11:14 KJV, *kite;* Job 28:7 KJV *vulture.*

A Bedouin hunter with his trained falcons. ©*M.P.S.*

Adam and Eve banished from the Garden of Eden (by Masaccio.) © *H.P.*

See BUZZARD. Falcons are among the commonest birds of prey; Pal. has about ten species. These include Peregrine and Lanner, about eighteen inches long; also Kestrel and Lesser Kestrel, Hobby and Red-legged Falcon, eleven to fourteen inches long. These take only living prey; the biggest catch birds up to the size of a Rock Dove, but others take small rodents, lizards and insects. About half breed in Pal.; the others are migrants.

G. S. CANSDALE

FALL, THE, refers to that event recorded in Genesis 3 (cf. Rom 5:12; 1 Tim 2:14) according to which our first parents, Adam and Eve, fell from the estate of integrity in which God had created them.

1. The occasion. Adam and Eve did not themselves originate the thought that came to fruition in their disobedience to God's commandment. They were subjected to suggestion and solicitation in the form of temptation. The direct instrument of this temptation was the serpent (Gen 3:1). The narrative indicates that the serpent was of such a kind that he could be compared with the other beasts of the field and within that category. The presence and agency of a literal serpent may not be denied. Futhermore, the curse pronounced (Gen 3:14) implies a being to which its terms could apply. Behind the serpent was the activity of Satan (cf. John 8:44; Rom 16:20; 2 Cor 11:3; 1 John 3:8; Rev 12:9; 20:2). The data given in Genesis 3 is not complete and must be supplemented by subsequent revelation. The later revelation confirms the earlier and assures us that from the beginning of man's fallen history there was the sinister craft and power of the archenemy.

The focus of the temptation was direct assault upon the veracity and integrity of God (Gen 3:4, 5). It was not an impeachment of God's knowledge nor merely a denial of His power. The tempter accused God of deception and deliberate falsehood. God, it was alleged, perpetrated a lie in order to preserve His own exclusive possession of the knowledge of good and evil. Herein lies the diabolical character of the allegation. The design was the destruction of man's integrity by the breakdown of man's belief in the integrity of God. The way of integrity is unreserved and unrelenting trust in God and the giving to Him of the sovereignty and finality that are exclusively His.

2. The cause. Temptation was the occasion; it was not the *cause*. To be subjected to temptation is not sinful for the tempted. Embrace and acquiescence constitute sin. So it was with our first parents. Eve succumbed to the solicitation of the tempter and Adam to that of Eve.

The strategy of the tempter was to direct his solicitations to the woman. The silence of Scripture compels reserve concerning the reason. In the case of Eve, however, one is justified in tracing the process by which she came to the point of overt disobedience to the divine prohibition. Acquiescence in the allegation of the serpent and defection from God's Word cannot be postponed beyond the point when she "saw that the tree . . . was to be desired to make one wise" (Gen 3:6 ASV) This demonstrates that the tempter had gained her trust; she accepted as true what was a blasphemous assault upon the veracity of God and came to regard the tree as desirable in the direction that contravened the divine prohibition. She served the creature rather than the Creator.

Her failure to recoil with revulsion from the tempter's "You will not die" (Gen 3:4) is evidence that defection had already taken place and that she exemplified the invariable psychology of sin that overt action proceeds from the inward disposition of heart (cf. Prov 23:7; Mark 7:21-23; James 1:14, 15). The eating of the forbidden fruit was the expression of an inward movement of apostasy at the instance of satanic beguilement. In the case of Adam there was a difference; he was not deceived (1 Tim 2:14). What the movement of his thought was cannot be defined. But the same principle must hold that the actual volition cannot be divorced from precedent disposition of mind and heart.

The prohibition imposed upon Adam and Eve (Gen 2:17) was for the purpose of proving the ultimate criterion of faith in God, unquestioning obedience to God's commandment. In the prohibition were epitomized the sovereignty, authority, wisdom, goodness, justice, holiness, and truth of God. Transgression was no trivial offense; it was assault upon God's majesty, repudiation of His sovereignty, doubt of His goodness, dispute with His wisdom, contradiction of His veracity. All along the line of God's perfections it was what all sin is, the contradiction of God. Hence its gravity and the corresponding liabilities.

3. The consequences. ***a. Subjective.*** Man's dispositional complex was radically altered. The pivot on which this revolution turned was the changed attitude to God (3:7-10). Man was made for the presence and fellowship of God and in the presence of God would have found his supreme delight. Now he flees from God's face; shame and fear took possession of his heart. "For every one that doeth evil hateth the light, and cometh not to the light, lest his works should be reproved" (John 3:20 ASV).

b. Objective. God changed His relation to man. The reason for the rupture between God and man was man's sin, but the rupture was not onesided. After Genesis 3:9 an aspect of God's character is disclosed that previously was threatened to be in exercise (Gen 2:17) but had not been manifested and it appears in reproof, condemnation, curse, and retribution (Gen 3:14-19, 23, 24), the echoes of divine wrath. At the outset is the lesson that sin not only involves our changed attitude to God but also His changed attitude to us, not only our estrangement from God but also His alienation from us.

c. Cosmic. The Fall was an event in the spirit of man. It did not consist in physical disturbance or maladjustment, but it drastically affected the physical and non-spiritual. "Cursed is the ground because of you" (Gen 3:17). "The creation was subjected to vanity" (Rom 8:20 ASV). Man was the crown of creation and with his fall came the bondage of corruption for all over which he was to exercise dominion. Only with the consummation of redemption will the cosmos be released from the curse incident to man's sin (cf. Rom 8:19-23; 2 Pet 3:13).

d. Racial. The sequel to the fall of Adam and Eve is the catalogue of sins in the unfolding history of mankind—envy, malice, murder, polygamy, violence. The result was cumulative and "the wickedness of man was great in the earth" (Gen 6:5) and it was "filled with violence" (6:13). History shows that Adam's fall was not an isolated event but affected the whole race. Scripture reveals the reason and specifies the kind of solidarity existing between Adam and posterity explanatory of this consequence. Adam was not only the father of all mankind but he was also by divine institution the representative head. "Through one trespass the judgment came unto all men to condemnation . . . through the one man's disobedience the many were made sinners" (Rom 5:18, 19 ASV). As all died in Adam (1 Cor 15: 22), so all sinned in Adam; "for the judgment came of one unto condemnation" (Rom 5:16 ASV; cf. 5:12, 15). All mankind is reckoned as participating with Adam in his sin and therefore in the depravity which his sin entailed. This is the Biblical explanation of universal sin, condemnation, and death and no other validation of racial involvement in sin is necessary or justifiable.

e. Death. The threat pronounced upon eating of the forbidden fruit was: "thou shalt surely die" (Gen 2:17 ASV). The fulfillment of this threat is eloquently stated in Genesis 5 in the repeated formula: "and he died." Notwithstanding the longevity of patriarchal man, he cannot escape this appointment (cf. Heb 9:27). The disintegration following in the wake of the Fall, exemplified in the respects specified above, enters also into the constitution of man and separates the elements of his being (cf. Gen 3:19; Eccl 12:7). The Biblical witness is unequivocal that death took its origin from the trespass of Adam, that it is the wages of sin and not the debt of nature (Gen 2:17; 3:19; Rom 5:12; 6:23; 1 Cor 15:22).

4. The historicity. Much has been written in support of the thesis that Genesis 3 is myth or legend, not history but story, portraying what happens to all men but not an account of a unique, once-for-all series of events at the beginning of human history. Adam, it is alleged, is every man. We all sin as Adam sinned.

This might appear to be an acceptable and effective way of maintaining the Biblical doctrine that all have sinned, but the position is fraught with fallacies.

a. It is not true that all sin as Adam. There is a radical difference between Adam and posterity. We all come to be as sinners; Adam and Eve did not. The beginning of our sinfulness was not by voluntary defection and transgression as in the case of our first parents, but by divinely constituted solidarity with Adam in his sin. As a consequence we are shapen in iniquity and conceived in sin (cf. Ps. 51:5); we are "by nature the children of wrath" (Eph 2:3). We are dead in trespasses and sins not by acquisition but by imputation to us of Adam's sin and by generation. So the position in question fails to correspond with the total witness of Scripture and to assess the human situation in sin and misery.

b. *If we are all Adam, then the uniqueness of Adam as the first man is denied.* The parallel between Adam and Christ (Rom 5:12-19; 1 Cor 15:21, 22, 45-49) belongs to the way of salvation and to the integrity of the Gospel. This parallel provides the antithesis between the way in which sin, condemnation, and death came to reign and the way righteousness, justification, and life come to bear upon men. The former was by Adam, the latter is by Christ. Therefore Adam and Christ sustain unique and incomparable relations to men. The preservation of both parallel and antithesis requires that Adam should be as real and unique in his historical identity as was Christ. To aver that Genesis 3 is story but not history, that we are all Adam and sin as Adam, destroys the particularity of Adam and undermines what belongs to our history in sin and redemption.

c. *NT allusions assume the historicity of Genesis 2 and 3.* In Matthew 19:5, 6; Mark 10:7, 8 reference is made to Genesis 2:24 and the actual terms of the latter are quoted. The reference to the transgression of Adam (Rom 5:14) clearly indicates that the one man mentioned in v. 12 is none other than Adam and the one trespass of the one man (cf. vv. 15-19) is the first sin of Adam. In 1 Corinthians 15: 45, 47, 49 there is distinct allusion to Genesis 2:7. In 1 Timothy 2:13 there is reiteration of the principle stated in Genesis 2:20-23 and in v. 14 there is explicit appeal to Genesis 3:1-6, 13. These examples suffice to show that in the esteem of our Lord and of the Apostle Paul the accounts given in Genesis could be appealed to for what they purported to be. We cannot dissociate the doctrine set forth in such passages from the premises on which the inspired teachers proceeded in enunciating the doctrine. Not only is the historical character of the early chs. of Genesis involved in the question but also the authenticity and relevance of the NT allusions and appeals to them.

BIBLIOGRAPHY. J. Murray, *The Imputation of Adam's Sin* (1959); G. C. Berkouwer, *Man: The Image of God* (1962), 119-193; P. E. Hughes, "Fall" in NBD (1962); G. Kittel ed., *Theological Dictionary of the New Testament*, E-T (1963), I, 281-286; J. G. Machen, *The Christian View of Man* (1965), 161-172, 208-219.

J. MURRAY

FALLOW (GROUND) (נִיר, from the verb *to break up, freshly till*). Land that is left idle for a season after plowing and harrowing, so that weeds and insects are killed while the soil regains its fertility. נִיר occurs in Jeremiah 4:3 and Hosea 10:12 as a cognate accusative, meaning "break up your fallow ground." Exhortation to seek God and become active spiritually is implied in the figure. In Proverbs 13:23, נִיר apparently refers to fallow ground which God will bless.

Exodus 23:11 discusses the law of the sabbatical year, prescribing one year of rest every seven years for cultivated soil. Here, the verb נטשׁ, "leave, forsake," is tr. "lie fallow." Such a custom was practiced by other nations as well. Evidently Israel failed to obey this dictum during much of its history (Lev 26:34, 35).

H. M. WOLF

FALLOW DEER (יַחְמוּר, *fallow deer* [Deut 14:5; 1 Kings 4:23] KJV; ROEBUCK ASV, RSV). A traditional identification of *Bubal Hartebeest*, q.v., for reasons for considering this unlikely. Fallow deer have long been kept successfully as park animals and this is therefore a possible tr. *See* DEER for discussion of deer that once lived in Pal.

FALSE APOSTLES (ψευδαπόστολοι). Reference to false apostles occurs only in 2 Corinthians 11:13. The reasons for Paul's harsh judgment of these men are their destructive work in the Corinthian Church, and their criticisms of Paul. Paul says they led the Corinthian Christians "astray from a sincere and pure devotion to Christ" (2 Cor 11:3), and they preached "another Jesus" (v. 4). They said Paul was an inferior (v. 5) and unskilled apostle (v. 6), who received "outside" support from Macedonia (vv. 7-9). They boasted of their special religious prerogatives as Jews (v. 22). These items show they lacked the apostolic virtues and message.

They were counterfeit apostles, but not from the circle of the apostles or apostolic men. Rather, they were members of the Judaizing party whose activity in the early churches gave the occasion for Paul's classic defense of his gospel and apostleship in the Galatian epistle. In the narrative of Galatians, Peter and James figure prominently, but not as opponents of Paul. The Judaizers claimed the authority of James (Gal 2:12) but these claims were false (Acts 15:24). (See the language of 2 Cor 11 with Gal 1; 2; Acts 15; esp. "false brethren" in Gal 2:4 and 2 Cor 11:26. See Rev 2:2.)

J. C. DEYOUNG

FALSE CHRIST, ψευδόχριστος, one who makes a spurious claim to be the Messiah. The OT anticipates or allows others to promote him as such. Jesus Christ cautioned against impostors (Matt 24:24; Mark 13:22). More than twenty have been in the limelight.

The false messiah is distinct from an antichrist. The former is an impersonater or impostor usurping the title or allowing others to herald him as such. The latter, *antichristos*, mentioned only by John (1 John 2:18, 22; 4:3; 2 John 7), does not emphasize impersonation as much as opposition by one who is against Christ (J. Broadus, *Matthew,* p. 488;

Trench, SNT, p. 107). He opposes Christ by doctrines about His person and work which are contrary to truth, as in the Gnostic heresies. Antichrists active in John's day (1 John 2:18, 22) were characterized by the same spirit as the supreme antichrist whose career will be just before Jesus Christ returns (2 Thess 2; Rev 13:1-10).

Christians view Jesus of Nazareth as the genuine Messiah of Israel who, though rejected at His coming, will come again with blessing for all who receive Him, including Jews. Evidence for His authenticity sets Him apart from false christs. When He claimed to be God (John 5:17; 10:30, 37; 14:9; cf. Isa 7:14; 9:6; Mic 5:2), He displayed the character and works of God (Matt 9:6; 25:31ff.). He was recognized as God by those who spent their lives proclaiming Him as such (Matt 14:33; 16:16, 17; Col 2:9), and He never disappointed them. He fulfilled many prophecies pointing to one who would be God and man (Isa 9:6; Mic 5:2) and reaching down to the precise time when He came (Dan 9:25, 26). He died (Isa 53), then arose as verified by many evidences (Ps 16:10; Matt 28; 1 Cor 15; etc.).

False christs have differed from one another in several ways: (1) in motives, some seeking prestige, others deliverance from oppression, or clever mockery; (2) in methods, some using violence, others appealing to fasting, prayer, and a miracle that failed to occur as announced; (3) in line of messiahship, some proposing to be messiah of the house of David (2 Sam 7:4-16), others of the house of Joseph as an Ephraitic messiah; (4) in claims, certain ones heralding themselves out of self-deception or to exploit the hopes of the people, others being announced by followers and riding the crest of popular opinion, still others claiming to be a forerunner or prophet with Messiah Himself to be manifested on some date or by some miracle; (5) in influence, some swaying Jews in Pal., some in different lands, some in several countries; (6) in emphasis, certain ones being religious reformers, some political messiahs, others both; (7) in end, some vanishing to unknown places, some fading into obscurity, others being put to death by armies, royal power, or their own disappointed but wiser followers; (8) in beliefs after their deaths, some being rejected as impostors by certain of their group, others supposedly rising from the dead but without any substantial evidence, still others expected to reappear but never did so.

A few examples may be cited:

Theudas (c. A.D. 44; Acts 5:36) promised to divide Jordan for his followers to cross. They massed for a miracle, but Rom. troops massacred many and took others captive. Bar Cochba (c. 132) was named "son of a star" in expectation that he would fulfill Numbers 24:17. He led a Jewish rebellion, conquering Jerusalem for three years, where he was hailed as king and messiah. Romans retook Jerusalem and he was later slain at Bither, a stronghold, with five to six hundred thousand followers. Moses Cretensis (c. 440) assumed the name "Moses" on the island of Crete, capitalizing upon a Talmudic computation of Messiah's date. Many Jews gathered at his assurance that the sea would open for a march dryshod to Pal. Some leaped into the water and were drowned. "Moses" vanished from the scene. David Alroy (c. 1160), a Pers. Jew, led a revolt against the Moslems. His death is obscured by different traditions, and his movement came to nought. Asher Lammlein (1502), a rabbi in Italy, claimed to be a forerunner, with Messiah to appear if people would fast, pray, and give alms. A pillar of cloud and fire would lead them to Pal. Then Lammlein disappeared. Sabbethai Zebi (1626-1676) took the title "king of the kings of the earth" in Smyrna, attracting many Jewish followers. Later, he defected to the Moslem faith under charges by the Turkish government. He was beheaded. Some of his group claimed to be Messiah after him.

Other notable names have been: Menahem (A.D. 60s), Julian (529), Serene (720), David el-David (1199), Abraham ben Samuel Abulafia (1240-1292), Nissim ben Abraham (1290s), Moses Botarel (1393), David Reubeni (1525), Isaac Luria (1534-1572), Hayyim Vital Calabrese (1543-1620), Abraham Shalom (1574), Mordecai Mokiah (1680), Jacob Frank (1726), and Moses Hayyim Luzzatto (1707-1747).

BIBLIOGRAPHY. H. Graetz, *History of the Jews*, 6 vols. (1891-1898); check index for individual names; *Jew Enc*, "Pseudo-Messiahs," vol. X (1905); HERE, "Messiahs (Pseudo)," vol. 8 (1915); *Universal Jew Enc*, "Messianic Movements," vol. 7 (1942); A. Edersheim, LT, I, 171-179 (1956); A. H. Silver, *A History of Messianic Speculation in Israel* (1959 rp).

J. E. ROSSCUP

This letter written to Joshua ben Galgola, one of Bar Cochba Commanders, alerted him to the approach of Roman troops. ©Dept. of Antiq. Jerusalem

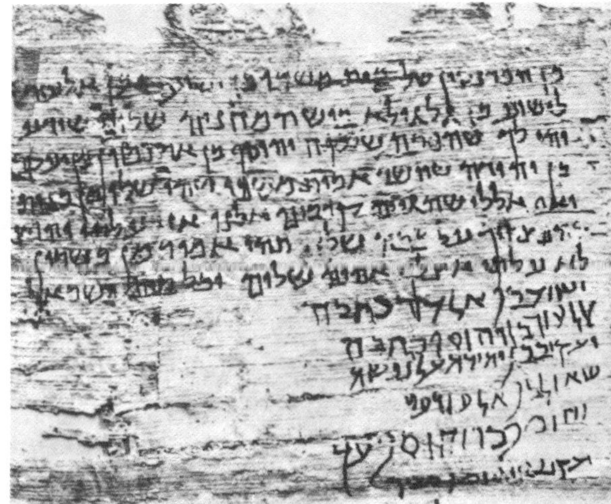

FALSE PROPHET(S), THE (נביא שקר. *prophet of falsehood, deceit*; *ψευδοπροφῆται*). Moses ordered the death of any prophet advocating the worship of another god (Deut 13:1-4). During the monarchy, false prophets were often in the majority in the court of Israel. Ahab's 800 prophets openly advocated the worship of Baal and Asherah (1 Kings 18:20). Later, 400 prophets, influenced by a lying spirit, assured Ahab of victory at Ramoth-gilead, only to be contradicted by Micaiah, the true prophet (22:6-23). Frequently, lying prophets told the leaders what they wanted to hear (Jer 5:31; Luke 6:26). Jeremiah inveighed against those who claimed to be receiving visions from God, but who counseled rebellion against Babylon (Jer 27:9). Zedekiah and Ahab were two prophets cursed because of their evil advice (29:21-23). Testing the prophets should have been a constant practice.

In the NT false prophets were plentiful (1 John 4:1) and were compared with wolves in sheep's clothing (Matt 7:15) and false teachers (2 Pet 2:1). The false prophet Bar-Jesus was smitten with blindness by Paul (Acts 13:6, 11). Christ warned of false prophets whose miracles would deceive many in the end (Matt 24:24; Mark 13:22). In Revelation 13:12-14 and 19:20, the master false prophet is described. He will support the beast through powerful signs before his destruction.

BIBLIOGRAPHY. J. B. Payne, *The Theology of the Older Testament* (1962), 56, 57.

H. M. WOLF

FALSE SWEARING, WITNESS (עד שקר, lit. *witness of deception, falsehood*; שבעת שקר, *swearing of falsehood*). Refers to damaging false testimony, esp. in court. Bearing false witness is banned in the laws (Exod 20:16; 23:1; Deut 5:20). Deuteronomy 19:16-21 subjects the false witness to the penalty he intended to inflict on the accused. Twice God is said to hate false witnesses (Prov 6:19; Zech 8:17). Jeremiah 5:2 condemns those who swear falsely, even though they say, "As the Lord lives." Note also the warning against taking the Lord's name in vain (Exod 20:7).

H. M. WOLF

FAMILIAR SPIRIT (אוב, RSV *medium*). The spirit of a dead person which a medium, in the form of magic known as necromancy, claimed to summon to consultation (Deut 18:11). In necromancy, in which the dead were consulted about the future, it was believed that either a spirit dwelt in the controlling medium (Lev 20:27), who was most commonly a woman, or that the medium had fellowship with a spirit from whom she could receive information. The word "familiar" in this term has the sense of belonging to one's family, and so to oneself; ready to serve one as a servant.

Mediums seem to have deceived their inquirers by speaking in a thin weak voice, as though it came from the ground or from a bottle (Isa 8:19; 29:4). The LXX generally represents them as ventriloquists. Nothing is known of their method of procedure.

The Mosaic law forbade the consulting of familiar spirits, and mediums were commanded to be put to death (Lev 19:31; 20:6, 27; Deut 18:11).

King Saul put away the mediums early in his reign, but, greatly worried about the outcome of his last battle, he consulted the witch of Endor and asked to speak to the prophet Samuel (1 Sam 28:3, 7, 8, 9; 1 Chron 10:13). It appears that Saul was told by the witch that she saw Samuel, and Saul himself entered into the conversation with the prophet. King Manasseh also fell into the sin of consulting mediums (2 Kings 21:6; 2 Chron 33:6); but his grandson Josiah put them out of the land (2 Kings 23:24).

Belief in the possibility of communing with the spirit of the dead was common in ancient heathendom. The Gilgamesh Epic, Tablet XII, gives evidence of it; and Acts 16:16-18 tells of a slave girl who was a medium and brought her owners much gain by her divination.

S. BARABAS

FAMILY. The center of the covenant activity of God is the family. Father, mother, children and extended relatives all play a part in the scriptural ideal.

I. FAMILY IN THE OT

The OT teaching about the family is embodied in the first chs. of the Torah. The creation of God was in a world-order and in a family-order. In the OT family relationships are concentric, that is the married couple—husband and wife—form the nucleus of the circle, the children lie in the next circle, the grandparents, cousins, and the like on a further

An artist's concept of a typical family scene in Old Testament days. © *S.P.F.*

circle. This principle is clear in the terminology. Each term is applicable beyond the mere immediate definition to the set of relations which the term represents, e.g. the term daughter (q.v.) may be applied to a number of other individuals aside from one's own female offspring, or it may be applied to any number of females who are in a specific law-relationship to the "father."

A. Terminology. The OT often uses the common Sem. term for "house" Heb. בית, as a term for the idea of "family" (Ruth 4:11). In this sense the KJV trs. "family" for *bēyt* in 1 Chronicles 13:14; 2 Chronicles 35:5, 12; Psalm 68:6, while the RSV trs. "household." The most frequently occurring term is Heb. משפחה a fem. noun which is not developed in Heb. but does appear as a noun in Ugaritic meaning "family." A secondary form שפחה, also appears in Heb. and refers to the less central relationships such as maid and menservants (Gen 30:7, 10, 12). These terms are usually tr. "family" but they actually embrace all possible range of meanings from "clan" (10:5); through "species" (8:19); to "consanguinity" (24:38). The term with all its difficult semantic range appears some 300 times in the OT, the highest frequency being in Numbers where it frequently stands for "clans" of the tribes of Israel. On one occasion the KJV mistakenly trs. the Heb. אלף, "thousand" as "family" (Judg 6:15). Usually it appears with *mispāḥāh* in the sense of a subgroup qualified numerically from the whole group (e.g. 1 Sam 10:19), "Now therefore present yourselves before the LORD by your tribes [*mispāḥāh*] and by your thousands [*'ēlēph*]." However, all such terms are simply collectives for the group and do not involve much of the elaborate social-moral connotation of the modern usage of the term "family."

B. The creation ordinances and the law. The initial statement of the relationship of man and woman in the Scripture is given in the narrative of the creation account. In the section which begins the creation of the world-order, the creation ordinances (Gen 2:4-5:1), the form of human family life is set forth. The unity of male and female in the marriage bond is set down on two levels, the fulfillment of man's need for companionship and the sexual relationship for the procreation of the race (2:18; 3:20; 4:1, 2). There is no question throughout the rest of the Bible that the monogamy of the Garden of Eden is the situation to be considered "normal" and the ordained law of marriage (Mark 10:6-9). This relationship was not to supersede the relationship to God (Deut 13:6-10; Matt 19:29; Luke 14:26) nor was it binding upon either party when separated by death (Matt 22:30; Mark 12:25 on the analogy of many OT passages). This complete reliance upon the monogamous law-order was an inherent part of the Israelite world-view and from that source has continued to be a mark of western civilization. Regardless of all evolutionary and psycho-analytic theories of explanation, the monogamous, lifelong relationship is that which is the nature of man and the creation. In view of this the creation ordinance is walled about with several other sets of strictures, the Decalogue (Exod 20:14, 17); the Levitical laws (Lev 18:6-18; 20:14-21; 21:7-15); and the customs e.g. Dowry Feast, Bride (q.v.). To the positive statement of the text and the illustration in the history of the creation there are added the various negative restrictions. It was correctly assumed by the rabbis that for every negative commendation or commandment the contrapositive statement also was true. Thus the negative statements concerning the family relationships have equally binding positive obligations.

C. Cultural developments. The OT is primarily a continuous narrative of the history of the covenant people of God. It begins with the Adamic covenant, continues through the patriarchal and tribal periods and ends with the rise and fall of the Israelite monarchy. There is a definite temporal progression, and the various changes in the cultures of the ancient Near East—the development from mesolithic to neolithic, from bronze to iron and from food-getting nomads to food-producing township settlements—all have their impact on the covenant people. In such an arrangement, the place and structure of the family underwent certain alterations. Some of these are insignificant, some positive and some absolutely contrary to the covenant and the law order itself. In the patriarchal period the story of Lot and his antagonism to the rampant sexual immorality of his surroundings (Gen 19:4-11) and of Joseph and his escape from Potiphar's wife (39:6-20) show the resistance of the covenant people to the family notions of their contemporaries. Ultimately, however, as Israel became a settled and independent political entity these cross-cultural forces worked upon the family associations of the Jews.

1. *Polygamy, Levirate marriage.* The greatest single erosion of the creation order of marriage, the polygamous marriage, appears early in the patriarchal narrative, "and Lamech took two wives" (4:19). The subsequent events of the families of Abraham, Isaac and Jacob frequently follow what is now known to have been the customs of the other Semites of the time. Analogies frequently have been drawn between patriarchal customs and the family laws of Babylon, Nuzi and Ḥatti. The concubinage of a servant girl to her mistress' husband is a specific type of polygamy widely practiced in the ancient Near East and also recorded in the patriarchal period (16:1-4; 30:1-5, 9-13). One result of this was the expansion of the family to include not only the man and his wife and their children, but also uncles, aunts, cousins, servants, concubines, slaves, travelers, employees and even prisoners of war.

All of these people came under the family covenant of Abraham (Exod 20:10, et al.). In light of this, the rite of circumcision was performed upon all males born in a Jewish house (Gen 17:23-27). One important factor of Jewish polygamy is the preservation of the dignity and rights of the concubine and her offspring. Nowhere does the OT provide for the elaborate caste systems commonplace in cuneiform descriptions of family relationships. Even a female prisoner had to be treated as a bride in binding marriage (Deut 21:10-13) and captives, whether man, woman or child, could not be sold into slavery. The offspring born to wives were to have no better inheritance than those born to concubines or slaves merely because of their inferior status. Since the polygamy of the ruling and dominating families greatly increased the degree of consanguinity and other males were either slain or forced into monogamy, the children of Israel were in a few generations a separate entity from the other nations round about them.

Since the polygamous marriage of two individuals in separate families, was in effect a covenant between the families, this also tied the few major strains of inheritance even more tightly together so that the families or clans not only grew larger, numerically, but more tightly related (Gen 34:8-22). Aside from specific rare instances the extent of polygamy or bigamy in the OT is small and in the books of Samuel, Kings and Chronicles, there is no reported polygamy on the part of commoners who lived during the age of the monarchy of Israel. Even though polygamy was accepted as a reality and legislation concerning it was ordained (Deut 21:15-17) yet the actual situations in which it occurred are hardly shown to be happy, and are forthrightly declared to be the sources of continual bickering, envy and other sins.

On the other hand the monogamous relationship is praised and lauded (Prov 5:15-19; 31:10-31). In fact, the worship of the one and only true God of Israel is presented in terms of marital devotion and fidelity (Isa 50:1; 54:6-8; 62:4, 5; Jer 2:2) while idolatry and heterodoxy are painted in images of harlotry, bigamy and incest (Hosea). A woman had no legal status in Israel and had to be under the legality or protection either of her father or husband, and if neither were living, then under a kinsman (Heb. גאל), described in great detail in the Book of Ruth. In effect, the woman was subservient to the male member of the family. The term for "husband" is Heb. באל. The word also means "master," "lord." Thus the woman was in the subordinate position in the family as declared in the law-ordinance (Gen 3:16); however, the *bā'āl* or *gō'ēl* was absolutely responsible for the rights and treatment of his female family members. In the case of the payment of the "bride price" some girls were actually sold (31:15), an unfortunate outcome of the system. The need to retain the family title to land in an agrarian society and similar customs in the nations around them seem to have induced the Jews to accept the relationship of the Levirate marriage (q.v.). Even these somewhat contrived matches appear to have been monogamous. In fact, it is doubtful if the family holdings would have been of much value if too many inheritors were forthcoming. The Levirate marriage was easily brought about, as brides were usually chosen and grooms arranged, although true love often developed between the partners. Love was not the primary motivation, which was familial not personal to begin with, the goals being clan preservation and children. As with most neolithic agricultural people, wealth was measured in the number of sons a man possessed for tilling and herding and the number of daughters for marrying and thus bearing more generations (Ps 127 which in light of Ruth 4:11, et al. refers entirely to one's children).

2. Fatherhood, motherhood, childhood. In the participant tribalism of a small agricultural village in Pal. the ages and groups of the members of the village appear to have acted in concert in most of the common tasks. The dress and activities of each group were defined strictly as were the times of their activities. As with most ancient peoples, it was assumed that any two adults of opposite sex, if alone together for any time, were engaging or had engaged in sexual activity. This principle manifests itself frequently in the events (Ruth 3:14, et al.). Fatherhood was assumed to be the prerogative of the mature male, and there is some evidence that the marriage of older men (35-55) to younger women (13-18) tended to lower the birth rate. However, prostitution also is noted in the OT and it apparently had no relation to the marriage bonds (Gen 38:14). Motherhood was construed as the natural outcome of wedlock and the plight of the barren woman is greatly lamented. The notion of male infertility is nowhere advanced. Motherhood was accompanied by an increased security that no other wife or concubine would be necessary to the husband. Although restrictions are placed upon the times of sexual relations, nothing is indicated about the frequency, and the OT generally is much more frank about the female response than have been some recent societies (3:16, et al.). Childhood is nonexistent as a class or separate period. While very young children are considered non-combatants (Deut 20:14), and while pleas are made for infants (Jonah 4:11), children who are old enough to talk are held responsible for their deeds and frequently judged (2 Kings 2:24). Progress toward manhood was marked by skill and wisdom, there being no Hebraic concept of knowledge, which was taught by the village elders. Primogeniture was strictly observed (Gen 25:24-26; 38:27-30) for both sons and daughters (25:24-34; 29:26); however, the father had the right to assign the birthright to any son he signified (49:3, 4). Because of the immediate tribalistic nature of life, most children grew up worldly wise and old before their years. While children were suckled up to three to four years of age they were considered mature at a very early age, boys at thirteen (the bar mitzvah), and girls at their first menstrual cycle. During their early years boys were kept with the women, but later on allowed to sleep in the father's quarters, while girls were kept close to their mother's activities. The harem, long a feature of the ancient Near E does not appear until the wealth and opulence of the monarchy.

Israelite girls were allowed a great deal of freedom in the small farming communities which predominated in the period of the conquest and the early kings of Israel. After the Amarna Age (fifteenth century B.C. and thereafter) when no one nation of the Eastern Mediterranean held sway over the many petty kingdoms, political marriages and courtly concubinage became commonplace.

It was during this time that Solomon and his successors built their elaborate harems and fostered many sons and daughters who were raised from infancy in the women's apartments to rule the kingdom someday. It was in this period of decadence that Israel began its final decline; almost all of the creation-ordinances and the Levitical precepts were ignored, and Israel went first through captivity and finally into the diaspora.

II. Family in the NT

The only family actually portrayed in the NT is that of Jesus, and then only scarcely and occasionally. It is clear, however, that while a vast stable of princes and princelings had been enforced by the Hel. and Rom. rulers, the common people still followed the OT family tradition. The father was still the head, the wife concerned with motherhood, and the children raised in the community obligations. The one significant change seems to have been in the growth of the synagogue and the Rabbinate which provided a modicum of participation and education for Israelite boys throughout the country.

To some extent this may have been in self-conscious opposition to the zeal for education caused by Hellenism and the paganizing schemes of the Hel. rulers. Be that as it may, it had a great effect upon the Jewish family.

As with all urbanization the growth of Rom. age towns caused more and more breakdown in the old extended family. The visit of Mary and the subsequent trip to Bethlehem show some of this shearing of the older clan ties (Luke 1:36-40; 2:4). For one thing there is a marked change in the terminology applied and the many difficult semi-social clan determinations which marked the OT pattern are no

Ritual passover supper in an orthodox Jewish home in Jerusalem. Family originally from Yemen, southern Arabia. © *M.P.S.*

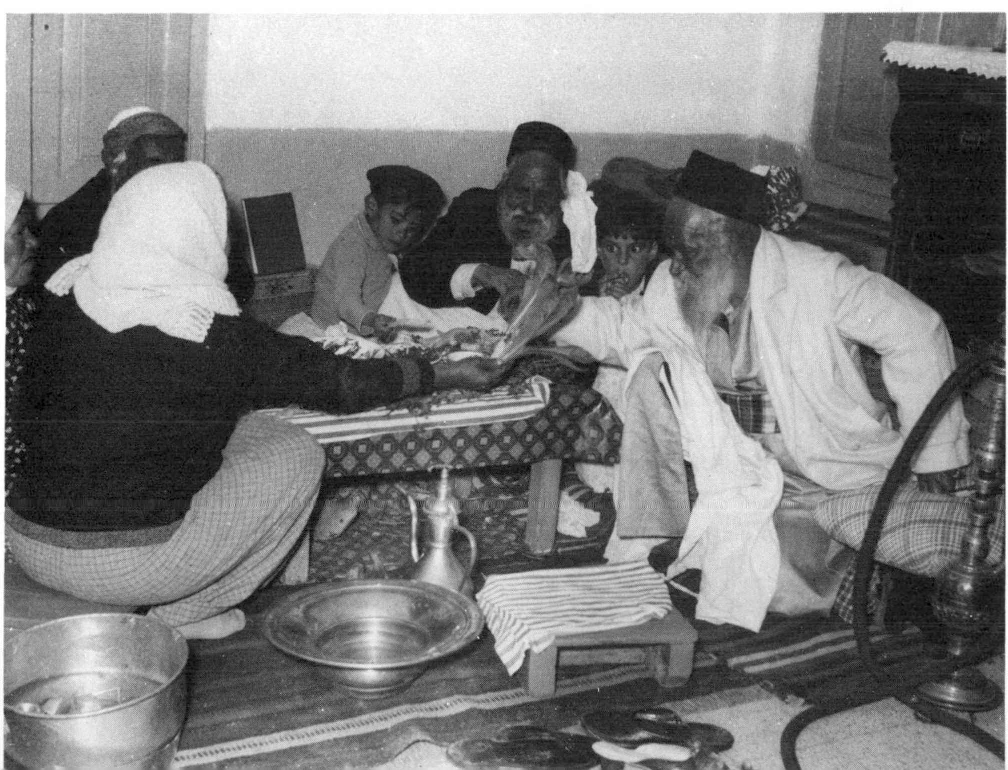

longer in use. The Gr. terminology is more precise, analytical and directly individualistic; no remnant of the ancient concentricity remains.

A. Terminology. Since the birth and early life of our Lord is accomplished under the old dispensation, the terms are simply trs. of the Heb. e.g. "house and lineage of David" (2:4). The terms are Gr. and they soon develop the more precise Hel. meanings. The most frequent is Gr. *οἰκία*, "house," but from Attic classical lit. used in the sense of "family" (Matt 13:57; Mark 6:4; John 4:53; et al.). Less frequent is Gr. *πατρία*, "family," "clan," "relationship" as in its three NT occurrences (Luke 2:4; Acts 3:25; Eph 3:15). These are both subdivisions of the tribe, Gr. *φυλή*, "nation," "people," "tribe" (LXX and Matt 19:28, et al.). More often than in the OT the relationships of individuals within the family are stressed and the terms for father, mother, husbands, wives, and children are thus foremost.

B. Jesus' teaching about the family. Much of Christ's instruction concerning the family is simply reiteration of the creation ordinances with the added responsibility of motivation (Matt 5:27-32). However, the family is used as the pattern for the forgiveness, love and longsuffering of God. In fact the use of the endearment, "Our Father," is one of the most profund insights into the nature of God revealed through Jesus' teaching. It is clear that monogramy is uppermost and the bond of love is central in such discourses (Matt 18; 19; 20).

The family as covenant and the covenant members as a family are two themes repeated in the illustrations Christ gives (19:13-15). The institution of the new covenant with its central rite of the eucharist expanded the availability of the ritual outside of the male members of the family. However, the concept of corporate or "household" salvation certainly is represented in the gospel narratives. It also is important that some of our Lord's miracles were concerned with families, their sorrows, and their relationships (Matt 8:1-13, 14, 15; 9:18-26; 15:21-28; 17:14-20; Mark 1:30, 31; 5:21-43; 7:24-30; 9:14-29; Luke 4:38, 39; 7:1-10; 8:40-56; 9:37-43; John 2:1-11; 4:46-54; 7:11-17; 11:1-46; 21:6-11.)

C. The apostolic and epistolary teaching about the family. The concept of the family was so easily extended that the apostles apparently used it in their preaching to describe, not only the Israel of the theocracy, but also the Church of Christ. Specific instructions concerning the family are given in terms of husband and wife (1 Cor 7:1-28; 11:3; Eph 5:22; Col 3:18; 1 Tim 5:8; 1 Pet 3:7). Of special emphasis is the subject of the subjection of the woman to her husband. This theme is repeated in a number of Paul's epistles and in 1 Peter 3:1-7.

In the dissolution of the family in the later Rom. republic and early empire was prob. a recurrent problem in the churches. The relation of children to parents is far less prominent than in the OT (Rom 1:30; 2 Tim 3:2; and the exhortations of Eph 6:1-4; Col 3:20, 21, and 1 Tim 4:12). In the three Johannine epistles the figure of the child is brought to its fulfillment with the repetition of the apostolic love for the Church in terms of family endearment (1 John 3:10, et al.). The legal position of children, inheritance, adoption, illegitimacy and naming all are used as figures of the application of the Atonement in the epistles (Gal 4:5; Eph 1:5; Phil 4:3; Heb 12:8; 1 Pet 1:4 et al.).

D. The family in the Early Church. The fact that the first churches were in private homes as that uncovered at *Dura Europos*, and that the initial converts were usually family groups, gave a specific character to the family image of Christianity (Acts 16:31; et al.). Symbols of Jesus as the Good Shepherd, the murder of the innocents, the scenes of Jesus' childhood are all extant in early Christian art.

In the apocryphal NT Book of Hermas, there were collected some folk stories of the childhood of Jesus. Of all Christian concepts that of its application to the family as a unit seems to have been the most appealing. Even the love of Christ for the Church is stated as the love of a husband for his wife. This image of the bridegroom and the bride is used in the final apocalyptic visions of the New Jerusalem (Rev 18:23; 21:2, 9; 22:17.) *See* DIVORCE.

BIBLIOGRAPHY. W. R. Smith, *Kinship and Marriage*, 2nd ed. (1903); T. G. Soares, *The Social Institutions and Ideals of the Bible* (1915); J. Doller, *Das Weib in Alten Testament* (1920); V. Aptowitzer, *"Spuren des Matriarchats im jüdischen Schrifttum"* HUCA IV (1927), 207-405; V (1928) 261-297; E. B. Cross, *The Hebrew Family* (1927); M. Tschernowitz, "The Inheritance of Illegitimate Children According to Jewish Law," *Jewish Studies in Memory of I. Abrahams* (1927), 402-415; M. Noth, *Die israelitischen Personennamen im Rahmen der gemeinsemitischen Namengebung* (1928); S. Feigin, "Some Cases of Adoption in Israel," JBL (1931), 186-200; E. M. Mac Donald, *The Position of Women as Reflected in Semitic Codes* (1931); C. H. Gordon, "Fratriarchy in the OT," JBL (1935), 223-231; C. H. Gordon, "The Status of Women as Reflected in the Nuzi Tablets," *Zeitschrift für Assyriologie und verwandte Gebiete*, XLIII (1936), 146-169; A. Margolius, *Mutter und Kind im altbiblischen* (1936); M. Burrows, "The Complaint of Laban's Daughters," JAOS LVII (1937), 259-276; C. H. Gordon, "The Story of Jacob and Laban in the Light of the Nuzi Tablets," BASOR 66 (1937); M. Burrows, *The Basis of Israelite Marriage* (1938); "Levirate Marriage in Israel," JBL LIX (1940) 23-33; "The Ancient Oriental Background of Hebrew Levirate Marriage," BASOR 77 (1940), 2-15; M. I. Rostovtzeff, *The Social and Economic History of the Hellenistic World*, 3 vols. (1941); D. Jacobsen, *The Social Background of the OT* (1942); E. Neufeld, *Ancient Hebrew Marriage Laws* (1944); J. Pederson, *Israel, its Life and Culture*, I-II (1946), 46-60; I. Mendelsohn, "The Family in the Ancient Near East," BA XI (1948), 25-40; A. van Selms, "The Best Man and the Bride," JNES IX (1950), 65-75;

J. Murray, *Divorce* (1952); W. H. Russell, "New Testament Adoption—Graeco-Roman or Semitic," JBL LXXI (1952), 233, 234; D. R. Mace, *Hebrew Marriage* (1953); J. Leipoldt, *Die Frau in der antiken Welt und im Urchristentum* (1954), 69-114; A. van Selms, *Marriage and Family Life in Ugaritic Literature* (1954); K. Elliger, "Das Gesetz Leviticus 18," ZAW LXVII (1955), 1-25; R. de Vaux, *Ancient Israel*, Vol. I (1957), 19-64; R. Yaron, "On Divorce in OT Times," *Révue Internationale des Droits de l'Antiquité* VI (1957); S. Kardimon, "Adoption as a Remedy for Infertility in the Period of the Patriarchs," JSS III (1958), 123-126; R. Yaron, "Aramaic Marriage Contracts from Elephantine," JSS III (1958), 1-39; I. Mendelsohn, "On the Preferential Status of the Eldest Son," ASOR 156 (1959), 38-40; A. N. S. White, *Roman Society and Roman Law in the NT* (1963).

W. WHITE, JR.

FAMINE (רעב, λιμός). *Rā'āb* and *limós* are tr. "famine"—an acute and prolonged lack of food almost always in Eng. VSS, but in a few cases they are rendered "dearth" or "hunger."

In lands dependent on seasonal rainfall, failure of the rain or its coming at an inappropriate time means the failure of crops and pasturage. In Pal. there were two rainy seasons, the "early rain" in October-November and the "latter rain" in March-April. The OT also mentions famines caused by the destruction of the food supply by hail (Exod 9:23-25, 31, 32), insects (Exod 10:15; Joel 1:4; Amos 4:9), or by the human agency of invasion (Deut 28:51) or siege (2 Kings 6:25). Famines in Egypt, as in the time of Joseph, are caused by the failure of the annual overflowing of the Nile, due ultimately to lack of rain in the interior. Famine often was accompanied by widespread disease (1 Kings 8:37; Jer 14:12; 21:9; Luke 21:11).

In the Bible famine is never regarded as a mere accident of nature, for God is the Creator and Ruler of all natural powers. Famines form part of God's ordering of the lives of His people, as with the journeys of Abraham and Isaac to Egypt (Gen 12:10) and the meeting of Naomi with Ruth (Ruth 1:1). By means of a famine God raised Joseph to a position of authority in Egypt and brought all the families of Israel into that land (Gen 41-47).

The usual stated purpose of famine, whether actual or threatened, was the judgment of God: to warn (1 Kings 17:1), correct (2 Sam 21:1), or punish His people or the heathen (Jer 14:12, 15). Jesus predicted famines as a sign of the end of the age (Matt 24:7; Mark 13:8; Luke 21:11).

Scripture tells of many famines, among them those in the time of Abraham (Gen 12:10), Isaac (26:1), Joseph (chs. 41-47), Ruth (Ruth 1:1), David (2 Sam 21:1), Elijah (1 Kings 17; 18), Elisha (2 Kings 4:38; 6:24-7:20), Zedekiah (2 Kings 25:3), Claudius (Acts 11:28)—the last prob. being the one mentioned by Josephus (Jos. Antiq. XX. ii. 5) who also gives one of the most vivid descriptions of the terrible effects of famine in a besieged city in his account of the Rom. siege of Jerusalem (Jos. War V. x. 3).

The prophet Amos used the word in a fig. sense when he says that in Israel there would be "a famine . . . of hearing the words of the LORD" (Amos 8:11).

J. C. CONNELL

FAN, FANNER (KJV rendering of מזרה, *a pitchfork with six prongs,* from זרה, *scatter, fan, winnow;* πτύον, *winnowing fork*). In Isaiah 30:24 the מזרה is used for winnowing provender. Jeremiah 15:7 mentions winnowing as the judgment of God upon Jerusalem. In the NT, the figure describes the judging activity of Christ as He separates the wheat from the chaff (Matt 3:12; Luke 3:17).

The verb also can refer to the scattering of powder (Exod 32:20) or to the dispersion of the nation Israel (Ezek 36:19). God is said to "sift" our activities (Isa 30:28).

H. M. WOLF

FARMER (אכר, *plowman, husbandman;* γεωργός, *soil-worker;* KJV *husbandman,* NEB *vine-grower,* RSV *tenant,* Matt 21:33ff.; Mark 12:1ff.; Luke 20:9ff.; NEB *gardener,* RSV *vine-dresser,* John 15:1). One who tills the soil.

In the OT, *'ikkār* (LXX *geōrgos*) is used generally for one who raises crops in fear of drought (Jer 14:4) and occupationally along with the shepherd (31:24). Other contexts, however, more specifically describe the farmer as a plowman with a team (Jer 51:23) or a worker in the vineyard (Amos 5:16; cf. 2 Chron 26:10).

The term *geōrgos* occurs generally in the NT for one who grows crops (2 Tim 2:6; James 5:7). In the parable of the wicked tenants (Matt 21:33ff.; Mark 12:1ff.; Luke 20:9ff.) and Christ's discourse on the true vine, the farmer is a vinegrower. *See* also TRADE; OCCUPATIONS and PROFESSIONS; AGRICULTURE.

M. R. WILSON

FARTHING. *See* COINS.

FAST, FASTING (צום, LXX νηστεύειν, Vul. *jejunus.* To abstain from food or the period in which the abstinence takes place.

I. OLD TESTAMENT

A. Psychology of fasting. Abstinence from food and/or drink in times of distress is practiced among many peoples. In Scripture refusal to eat when under violent emotions such as jealousy, anger, and vexation is seen when Hannah would not eat when provoked by her rival (1 Sam 1:7); when Jonathan abstained from eating in anger when his father cast the spear at him because of his relationship with David (20:34); and when Ahab refused food because he could not have Naboth's vineyard (1 Kings 21:4). This type of abstinence has nothing to do with religious fasting.

Religious abstinence in Scripture often is accompanied by the putting on of sackcloth and ashes. This self-affliction seems to have as its basic psychology to say to the Deity, "I am penitent; I am not high and mighty. You need not afflict me further." Perhaps also an appeal to the pity of the Deity is involved. The one case where a specific motive is supplied is that of David: "I fasted and wept; for I said, 'Who knows whether the LORD will be gracious to me, that the child may live?' " (2 Sam 12:22). There is the humbling of oneself before God: "Have you seen how Ahab has humbled himself before me? Because he has humbled himself before me, I will not bring the evil in his days" (1 Kings 21:29).

Patriarchal fasts are not mentioned specifically in Scripture. Fasting is mentioned first at Sinai when Moses refrained from eating forty days and nights while on the mount (Exod 34:28; Deut 9:9) and also after his breaking the tables of stone (9:18).

B. Occasions of fasting. 1. *Day of Atonement.* By the law, "afflicting one's soul" (נפש ענה; LXX *kakoun tēn psuchēn* or *tapeinoun tēn psuchēn*) from morning until evening, is strictly demanded on the Day of Atonement—the tenth of the seventh month. The penalty for infraction is to be cut off from the community (Lev 16:29ff.; 23:27-32; Num 29:7; Jer 36:6). While neither the verb nor the noun for fast and fasting occur in this section of the Pentateuch, "afflicting one's soul" equals fasting. This fast was observed by the Qumran community according to its calendar (Zad Frag 6) though the wicked priest is said "to cause them to stumble on the Day of Fasting" (1QpHab xi).

The rabbis ruled that one could not eat a quantity as large as a date on this day, and enacted other privations. According to the Mishna, *Yoma* 8:1, on the Day of Atonement it is forbidden to eat, or drink, or bathe, or anoint oneself, or wear sandals, or to indulge in conjugal intercourse. When the day fell on a Sabbath, the duty to fast took precedence over the normal manner of Sabbath observance (M. *Menahoth* 11:9).

Since this fast *par excellence* (cf. Philo, *On Special Laws* I, 186; II, 193ff.; *Life of Moses* II, 23; Jos., Antiq. 14. 16. 4; 17. 6. 4) came in the fall of the year, it might be used to indicate that the winter season was at hand, e.g., "the fast was now already past" (Acts 27:9 KJV). Romans considered that sailing was hazardous after Sept. 11 and that it ceased on Nov. 11 not to be resumed until March 10 (Vegetius, *De Re Militari* iv. 39; Caesar, *Bell. Gallico* iv. 36; v. 23); while some rabbis considered travel on the sea to be possible from Passover to the Feast of Tabernacles (SBK III, 771).

2. *Times of distress.* In addition to the Mosaic fast, Israelites fasted without specific commandment on numerous other occasions in time of distress. Some were communal affairs while others were acts of the private individual.

a. WAR OR THE THREAT OF IT. Israel fasted at Bethel in the war against the Benjamites (Judg 20:26); at Mizpah in the Philistine war (1 Sam 7:6); Saul had not eaten all day and all night before his visit to the witch of Endor (1 Sam 28:7-20). Fasting might be imposed upon warriors in a campaign (Judg 20:26; 1 Sam 7:6), though the evidence is insufficient to conclude that it always was demanded. Saul issued a curse on the man who ate before evening that he might take vengeance on his enemies the Philistines. Jonathan's breaking his father's injunction would have cost him his life had not the people intervened (1 Sam 14:24ff.).

b. SICKNESS. David fasted and wept for his son while the boy was ill, but when the boy died, contrary to the expectations of his servants, he washed, anointed himself, went to the house of the Lord and then ordered food (2 Sam 12:16ff.). The psalmist also mentions fasting for sick friends (Ps 35:13).

c. MOURNING. The men of Jabesh-gilead fasted seven days for Saul (1 Sam 31:13; 1 Chron 10:12); David and the people fasted for Saul and Jonathan (2 Sam 1:12); and the custom of fasting in mourning is considered normal behavior (12:21).

d. PENITENCE. Calamities were considered manifestations of divine anger. Acts of penitence were therefore the way to end them. Perhaps in this light is to be interpreted the fast requested by Jezebel at which the fate of Naboth was decided (1 Kings 21:9ff.). Ahab fasted—not in vain—after being threatened by Elijah for having taken Naboth's life and vineyard (21:27). The general fast at the communal reading of the law by Ezra was an act of penitence (Neh 9:1).

After the destruction of the Temple in A.D. 70 and sacrifice was no longer possible, fasting was allied in the Rabbinic view with sacrifice (T. B. *Ber* 17a). As a means of expiation it was preferred by some over almsgiving (T. B. *Ber* 32b), while others placed its value in the accompanying almsgiving (T. B. *Ber* 6a). Neither fasting nor confessing sufficed, unless they were accompanied by a practical amendment of conduct (T. B. *Ta'an* 16a).

e. IMPENDING DANGER. Jehoshaphat fasted when threatened by Edom (2 Chron 20:3). Jehoiachim proclaimed a fast in the ninth month of his fifth year (Jer 36:9). Ezra led a fast when seeking the favor of God toward his return from exile (Ezra 8:21)—a journey likely to be fraught with many dangers, but for which he did not wish to ask for mounted guards. Nehemiah fasted when he heard of the state of Jerusalem (Neh 1:4). The Jews fasted when they heard that Haman had obtained the king's decree against them (Esth 4:3); Esther and Mordecai fasted before she went before the king (4:16) and the establishment of Purim is said to deal with fasts and lamentations (9:31). The onset of a locust plague might occasion a fast in which all elements of the community—people, elders, children, and even the bride and bridegroom—participate (Joel 1:14; 2:15).

f. COMMEMORATION OF CALAMITIES. During and after the Exile special fasts were observed on the days calamities had befallen Jerusalem (M. *Ta'an* 4:6). The tenth of the fifth month was the burning of the Temple (cf. Jer 52:12, 13); the second day of the seventh month was the murder of Gedaliah (2 Kings 25:23-25; Jer 41:1ff.); on the tenth day of the tenth month was the beginning of the siege of Jerusalem (2 Kings 25:1); and on the ninth day of the fourth was its fall (25:3, 4). An inquiry by men of Bethel concerning the validity of these fasts in the fifth and seventh month brought a reply from Zechariah that obedience, justice, and kindness rather than fasting were significant in the sight of the Lord (Zech 7:1-14). The fasts were to be seasons of joy (Zech 8:19).

h. DROUGHT. By the 1st cent. a fast was the preferred method of appealing to the Lord for rain. If the fall rains did not make their appearance in due time, first individuals voluntarily fasted, but if this action was ineffective, a communal fast of three days was proclaimed. If no rain fell, three more days were proclaimed, and, if necessary, seven more days to make a total of thirteen. These were of increasing severity. At first eating and drinking after nightfall, washing oneself, anointing oneself, putting on of sandals, and marital intercourse were permitted. In the second period these were prohibited, and in the last period shops were closed except on Mondays after dark and on Thursdays. The *shofar* was blown (M. *Ta'an* 1:5ff). The individual could not dissassociate himself from the community at such times and refuse to fast (T. B. *Ta'an* 11a). These customs and other Jewish fasting practices are the subject of extended treatment in the Mishna tractate, *Ta'anit.*

3. *Preparation for revelation.* In the cases of Moses (Exod 34:28; Deut 9:9, 18) and Daniel (Dan 9:3) fasting was engaged in as a preparation for receiving revelation.

C. Length of fasts. A fast was often for one day (Judg 20:26; 1 Sam 14:24; 2 Sam 1:12; 3:35) from sunrise to sunset, and after sundown food would be taken. Or a fast might be for one night (Dan 6:18) Aram. טות. The fast of Esther continued three days, day and night, which seems to be a special case (Esth 4:16). Jesus also is said to have fasted day and night (Matt 4.2). At the burial of Saul the fast by Jabesh-gilead was seven days (1 Sam 31:13; 1 Chron 10:12). David fasted seven days when his child, born after his illicit affair with Bathsheba, was ill (2 Sam 12:16-18). Prolonged fasting brought on weakness (Ps 109: 24; cf. 1 Sam 28:20). Moses' fast for forty days (Exod 34:28; Deut 9:9), Elijah's (1 Kings 19:8), and Jesus' (Matt 4:2; Luke 4:2) are the longest recorded in Scripture.

A weakened form of fasting might involve abstinence from wine, flesh, dainty food, and from anointing oneself for an extended period such as three weeks (Dan 10:2f.).

D. Participation of beasts in fasting. The unusual custom practiced in Nineveh, including animals in a fast (Jonah 3:7), is also attested for Jews (Jud 4:10-13).

E. Display in fasting. Fasting lent itself to external show and it is this feature of the practice which the prophets attack. The most vigorous attack is that made in Isaiah 58 when people complain that they have fasted and God has not seen (Isa 58:3). In contrast to the external display of bowing one's head like a rush and spreading sackcloth under oneself (58:5), the fast pleasing to the Lord is to loose the bonds of wickedness, to let the oppressed go free, to share bread with the hungry, to bring the poor into one's house, and to cover the naked (58:6, 7). Joel called for a rending of hearts and not of garments (Joel 2:13). The Lord refused to heed the fast of Jerusalem in her degradation (Jer 14:12).

II. APOCRYPHA

The Apoc. and Pseudep. extol the merits of fasting. Judith fasted each day of the week except upon Friday, the Sabbath, and upon certain feast days (Jud 8:6). This fast extending through all the days of her widowhood is considered an extraordinary act of piety. Jeremiah and others fasted (2 Bar 5:7). Ezra fasted in preparation for receiving visions (4 Ezra 6:31; cf. 9:24). Fasting in times of danger is attested for the Maccabean period (1 Macc 3:47; 2 Macc 13:12). Reuben (Test Reub 1:10) and Judah (Test Jud 15:4) fasted in penitence. Simeon fasted two years because of his hatred for Joseph (Test. Sim 3:4). Joseph fasted during the seven years he was tempted by Potiphar's wife (Test. Jos 3:4; 4:8; cf. 10:1). Benjamin was born after his mother had fasted twelve days (Test. Ben 1:4). Fasting makes atonement for sins of ignorance (Pss Sol 3:8). Prayer, fasting, almsgiving, and righteousness are jointly praised in Tobit (Tobit 12:8). But if one fasts and sins again, his humiliation is unprofitable (Ecclus 34:26).

III. NEW TESTAMENT

John the Baptist taught his disciples to fast often (Mark 2:18; Luke 5:33). Though Jesus fasted in the wilderness (Matt 4:2; Mark 1: 13) fault was found with Jesus and His disciples for failure to fast. To this objection Jesus replied that His disciples would fast when the bridegroom was taken from them (Matt 9:14, 15; Mark 2:18, 19; Luke 5:33-35).

In what appears to be a paranomasia: "disfigure (*aphanizousin*) their faces that they may appear (*phanōsin*)," Jesus castigated insincere fasting of hypocrites whose mournful faces were to be seen of men. In the cases of almsgiving and praying, they received that which they sought, namely, the praises of men. He charged the washing of the face and the anointing of the head that the fast not be seen of men but of God who sees in secret (Matt 6:16-18).

The claim of the Pharisee in the parable to fast twice in the week is in excess of any demand made of him (Luke 18:12), but is paralleled in the church of the 2nd cent. in the exhortation to fast on Wednesday and Friday as contrasted to the fast on Monday and Thursday of the Jews (here called hypocrites; *Didache* 8:1). T. B. *Ta'an* 12 also attests the custom of fasts on Monday and Thursday and the pious might fast more often (Jud 8:6). A late source reports that Jews refrain from fasting on Sunday because of the Nazoreans (T. B. *Ta'an* 27b).

Prayer and fasting frequently are associated together. Anna served God with fasting (Luke 2:37). Certain demons could be cast out only by fasting (Matt 17:21 TR; Mark 9:29 TR); Paul fasted following his vision on the road to Damascus (Acts 9:9). Cornelius was fasting before his vision (10:30, some texts). The sending of Barnabas and Saul out on the first missionary journey was preceded by fasting (13:2, 3). Those on the ship with Paul in the storm abstained from food for fourteen days (27:33). A couple may abstain from conjugal relations by consent to give themselves to fasting (1 Cor 7:5 TR). Paul claims to be approved to the church in fasting (2 Cor 6:5) and lists as one of his sufferings "in fastings often" (11:27 KJV). These last cases may be cases of abstinence due to the unavailability of food which in the NT is also called *nesteia* (cf. Matt 15:32 RSV). Other than these cases, there is nothing in the NT epistles about fasting.

Jews of Jerusalem pledged themselves not to eat until they had killed Paul (Acts 23:12, 14). We are informed in Mishna *Nedarim* 5:6; 9:1f. that such vows were not considered binding in cases where they could not be carried out.

IV. The second century church

In the 2nd cent., in addition to fasts twice in the week (*Didache* 8:1; cf. *Disascalia* 5:14) which days are chosen specifically to differ from the Jews who fast on Monday and Thursday (cf. M. *Ta'an* 1:3-7)—a fast by the baptized, the baptizer, and other members of the community who are able, preceded the baptismal ceremony (*Didache* 7:4). The Epistle of Barnabas allegorizes fasting as it does the other demands of the law (*Ep. of Barnabas* 3:1ff). Second Clement 16:4 evaluates fasting as better than prayer. Hermas calls fasting "keeping a station," but proclaims the good life as the real fast pleasing to the Lord (Hermas, Sim. V. 1). He speaks of a fast in which only bread and water are eaten and the money which otherwise would be spent is saved to be spent on charity (*Sim.* V. 3).

BIBLIOGRAPHY. I. Abrahams, *Studies in Pharisaism and the Gospels* (1917), I, 121-128; J. F. Moore, *Judaism* (1927), II, 55ff.; 257ff.; SBK (1928), IV, 77-114; J. Pedersen, *Israel, Its Life and Culture* (1940), III, 11f.; 456f.; J. Behm, TWNT (1942), IV, 925-935.

J. P. Lewis

FAT (חֵלֶב). 1. Fat is first mentioned in the Bible in Genesis 4:4, where it is said that Abel offered the fat of the firstlings of his flock to the Lord. According to the Mosaic law, all the fat of sacrificed animals belonged to the Lord, and was burned as an offering to Him, as a sweet savor to Him (Lev 3:14-16; 7:30). The fatty portions are specified in Leviticus 3-7 as the fat of the entrails, of the kidneys, and of the liver, and also the tail of the sheep. The fat had to be sacrificed on the day the animal was sacrificed (Exod 23:18). It is sometimes asserted that the eating of any fat was forbidden to the Israelites. Deuteronomy 12:15, 16, 21-24 show that the prohibition did not apply to animals slain solely for food, but only to specified parts of sacrificed animals. The word "fat" is sometimes used in a fig. sense to signify the best part of anything, e.g., "the fat of the land" (Gen 45:18), the "fat of the wheat" (Ps 81:16 ASVmg.).

2. The KJV uses "fat" for "vat" (RSV) in Joel 2:24; 3:13, and "winefat" for "wine press" (RSV) in Isaiah 63:2 and Mark 12:1.

S. Barabas

FATHER (אָב, πατήρ). **1. The patronymic system.** Both the OT and the NT offer ample proof that the Jewish family life was patronymic or paternal in nature. As the name implies, the patronymic system traces kinship through males who play the dominant role in the family and in society (Num 1:22; 3:15). Evidence is not lacking that the patronymic system supplanted an earlier maternal kinship system. Evidence of this more primitive system is found in Genesis 36, where the "generations of Esau" are traced through his wives, and in the Book of Ruth where Leah and Rachel are recognized as the women responsible for building the house of Israel (Ruth 4:11).

Wherever the paternal system is found, both rank and property descend through the father. In general the ethnologists agree that the development of private property and the taking over by men of the chief functions of production have been the major influences in the development and extension of father power and a paternal family system.

With the development of the paternal family organization among the ancient Hebrews went a steady increase in the power of the head of the family—the patriarch—over wives, children, slaves and the "ger" or stranger within his gates.

2. Paternal privileges. In the early times the Heb. children, like their mothers, were almost completely under the authority of the father. In the rude early days of the patriarchs the controls extended even to life and death rights over them. This was made clear by Abraham's attempt to sacrifice his son Isaac as a burnt offering. However, quite early in their history the Israelites were forbidden by Mosaic law to burn their children upon the altars of Molech (Lev 18:21). The power of the patriarchal father was restricted in two other situations: he was not allowed to make his daughter a prostitute (Lev 19:29) and he was not allowed to sell her to a foreigner. The father had the authority to marry his children as he saw fit. He had also the authority to sell children as slaves but only to fellow countrymen (Exod 21:7-9).

The Heb. children owed their parents the utmost respect and reverence coupled with the most scrupulous obedience. The Mosaic law required that the child who smote or cursed his father should be put to death (Exod 21:15, 17). The stubborn or gluttonous son was condemned to be stoned by his fellows after the father and the mother had testified against him before the elders of the people of Israel (Deut 21:18-21).

The Jewish household included slaves and many times even strangers sojourning among them who placed themselves under the protection of the patriarch. For all practical purposes such foreigners were treated as members of the family as long as they remained with the family and under the control of its head.

In the Talmudic period the father was permitted to contract for the marriage of his daughter only before she reached the age of puberty. After reaching the legal age the daughter had the privilege, if she wanted, to refuse to carry out the contract. In such a case the contract became null and void. In this respect the Talmudic law was more advanced than the marriage laws of Greece and Rome. The strict rules established by the patriarchal father for his family continued to have restrictive effects upon the decisions of his children even after they reached the legal age, and therefore limited the complete application of the Mosaic law.

3. Parental responsibilities. The Jewish household was a closely knit social, religious, and economic organization. The Heb. home had also other very important functions. The family was the only educational institution for the training of the children until the time of Christ. The parents served as the chief teachers of their children, particularly the father (Deut 4:9; 6:7; 31:13; Prov 22:6; Isa 28:9). The father was expected to exercise rigid control and discipline over his children (Prov 13:24; 19:18; 22:15; 23:13).

The religious exercises taking place in the home coupled with the instruction offered to the children were prob. the most significant influences in the establishment of the strong ties and solid foundations of the Jewish family.

The Babylonian Talmud establishes the fact that the father was obligated to circumcise his son, to redeem him—if necessary, to teach him the books of Moses, to find a wife for him, and to teach him a trade as a means of livelihood. The father continued to exercise great and decisive influence over the lives of his children even after they were married.

BIBLIOGRAPHY. W. Goodsell, *A History of Marriage and the Family* (1939), 1-80; E. P. Barrows, *Sacred Geography and Antiquities* (n.d.), 469-481; G. Cornfield, *Pictorial Biblical Encyclopedia* (1964), 310-320.

P. TRUTZA

FATHERHOOD OF GOD (אָב, 'b, πατήρ). The special relationship of authority and care between God and (1) His Son, and (2) His people.

1. Father of His people. One of the most frequent comparisons in the OT is that between the father/child relationship and the God/Israel one. This is expressed in terms of a father's love for his children (Ps 103:13), his chastisement of the children he loves (Deut 8:5; Prov 3:12), and God's desire that His chastised children return to Him (Jer 3:22; 31:20). In contrast to the timeless, non-historical character of the divine fatherhood concept in the fertility cults, the OT doctrine is expressed in terms of God's dealing in history with His people, particularly in the Exodus (Hos 11), although occasionally a more general understanding can be seen, as in the Lord's being "father of the fatherless" (Ps 68:5). Although the fatherhood relation extends to the entire nation, it is concentrated in a particular way in the Davidic royal line and its perpetual rule (2 Sam 7:11-16) and in the person of the Messiah to come (Ps 2:7). Perhaps the prophetic utterance in Mal 2:10 speaks of the future extension of the fatherhood to all the world; however, the book is distinctly addressed to Israel (1:1).

2. Father of Christ. Jesus identifies Himself as being the Son of the Father. While the Jews correctly understood this as a claim to deity (John 5:18; 10:30, 33; 19:7), Jesus Himself also related His sonship to that which they enjoy "to whom the word of God came" (John 10:35). While the followers of Christ are also sons of the same Father, it is noteworthy that the expression "our" Father is never used by Christ, but rather the deliberate "my Father and your Father" (John 20:17); the "Our Father" of the Lord's Prayer (Matt 6:9) is not prayed by Christ Himself, but is instruction to the disciples as to how they are to pray; cf. Christ's continual reference to "your" father; perhaps the usage in Matthew 17:24-27 is an exception.

3. The responsibility of sons. Jesus' Messianic work is described in terms of His filial relationship to His Father. Both the task given Him (John 17:4) and the authority to perform it (John 3:35) come from the Father, as well as the people given Him as the reward for His obedience (John 17:24, cf. 10:29). The disciples' attitude to God's children should be the same as God's (the rebuke to the elder brother in Luke 15:31, 32). Their prayers should be confident ones, for their Father is more generous than a human one (Matt 7: 9-11; Luke 11:11-13).

While the NT doctrine of the new birth would seem to provide the basis for the sonship of believers, more explicit teaching is in the realm of adoption (Rom 8:14, 15; Gal 4: 6), where it is the Spirit who makes us sons, and it is also through Him that we recognize that sonship. The Christian life is a life of responsibility before our Father (1 Pet 1:17) but also a life of blessing and praise to the Father who has given us all things (2 Cor 1:3; 2 Thess 2:16; 1 Pet 1:3).

BIBLIOGRAPHY. T. J. Crawford, *The Fatherhood of God* (1868); R. S. Candlish, *The Sonship and Brotherhood of Believers* (1872); E. D. Burton, ICC *Galatians* (1921), 384-392; G. Vos, *Biblical Theology* (1948), 381-397; H. Ridderbos, *The Coming of the Kingdom* (1950), 232-284; G. Schrenk and G. Quell, "patēr" in TDNT, V (1954), 945-1022.

D. C. DAVIS

FATHERLESS, THE (יתום, ὀρφανός). The child depends upon his father to fill the many needs of his life. The relation of father and son appears to be, in the divine providence, a provision so greatly needed to secure the survival of the fatherless. Yet, there are the orphans, deprived of the care and protection of a father.

In Biblical times, as in modern times, the fatherless were considered as the most helpless and pitiable members of the human society. No clear-cut evidence is presented in the Scripture record in regard to established institutions founded for the purpose of defending their interests and caring for their needs. God has made provision for them, Mosaic law included (Deut 14:29; 24:19-21; 26:12; 27:19).

God proclaims Himself, in a special way, as "the father of the fatherless" (Ps 68:5) and their helper (10:14). The Scriptures reiterate again and again warnings given by God to those who mistreat the fatherless.

The orphan is generally coupled with the widow in the Scripture. God's protection is equally extended over both. Oppression against them is equally forbidden (Deut 16:14; 24:17, 19, 21; 26:12, 13).

In the Talmudic period to give proper care to the orphans was commended as the most praiseworthy act. *See* ORPHAN.

P. TRUTZA

FATHERS, APOSTOLIC. *See* APOSTOLIC FATHERS.

FATHER'S HOUSE, FATHERS' HOUSE (בית אב, בית אבות, οἶκος τοῦ πατρός). In the OT, while the word "house" by itself basically means a dwelling in which people live, in conjunction with "father" it indicates at least a family home (Gen 12:1; 31:14, 30; 1 Sam 18:2), that is, the head of a family and his dependents—or a household. The term also refers to the head of a family, his sons and their wives and children, and the slaves (Gen 46:31; Exod 12: 3). The term was also used of the main divisions of each tribe (Num 3:15, 20), and for the whole tribe (17:2). When used in the pl. (fathers' houses), it means the clan or a tribe (Exod 6:14; Num 3:20; 7:2).

In the NT it may mean a number of things: (1) a *home*, as in Acts 7:20, where it is said that Moses was brought up for three months in his father's house, and in Luke 16:27, where the rich man tells Abraham to send someone from the place of burning to his father's house to warn his brothers; (2) the *Temple* in Jerusalem, as when Jesus says in John 2:16, "You shall not make my Father's house a house of trade"; (3) *heaven*, as when Jesus says (John 14:2), "In my Father's house are many rooms." *See also* HEAVEN.

BIBLIOGRAPHY. R. de Vaux, *Ancient Israel* (1961), 19-23.

J. C. CONNELL

FATHOM. *See* WEIGHTS AND MEASURES.

FATLING, FATTED. (An animal, esp. a young one—a calf, lamb, or kid—fattened for slaughter). It is the tr. of four Heb. words. 1. מחים (Ps 66:15; Isa 5:17 KJV "fat ones").

2. בריא (Ezek 34:3 KJV "them that are fed," tr. "fat sheep" in v. 20 RSV, and "fat cows" in Genesis 41:2-4, 18, etc.).

3. מריא, pl. *merī'im* (2 Sam 6:13; 1 Kings 1:9, 19, 25; Isa 11:6; Ezek 39:18; "fatted beasts" in Amos 5:22).

4. משנה (1 Sam 15:9). This Heb. word does not really mean fatlings, but "of the second sort," or, "of the second birth." Some scholars have suggested that it means "of the second rank," as though the animals referred to were divided into groups according to their value; others have said that it means "of the second birth," animals considered better than the others, although Gesenius says that they were inferior. Most scholars have thought it best to amend the Heb. text into משמנים, found in Nehemiah 8:10 where it means "fatted things" and is supported by some of the ancient VSS (Targum, Syriac, and Arabic) and is followed by ERV.

In Matthew 22:4 the word σιτιστά, is tr. "fatlings" in the KJV, but "fat calves" in the RSV.

S. BARABAS

FAUCHION. *See* ARMS, ARMOR.

FAUNA. The sources of evidence are surveyed in three sections. (1) Ancient material provided by explorers, archeologists, etc. and textual evidence, including philological. (2) Study of the fauna and flora of these areas today, considered in the light of history in order to assess potential, allows any inferences to be drawn. This is treated regionally. (3) The area generally has been radically affected by man's activities which in some cases have left no sign of the original vegetation. These are discussed in some detail historically, after considering, and rejecting, the theory that the widespread deterioration of flora might be due primarily to climatic worsening since Biblical times. Many species are mentioned but their fuller description is found in individual articles.

- I. Sources of information about earlier fauna
  - A. Introduction
  - B. Ancient material
  - C. Biblical evidence
- II. Natural regions
  - A. Introduction
  - B. Desert
    - 1. Description
    - 2. Large mammals
    - 3. Small mammals
    - 4. Carnivores
    - 5. Birds
    - 6. Reptiles
    - 7. Dead Sea
    - 8. Large oases
  - C. Sand dunes
  - D. Lowlands and plains of Sharon and Esdraelon
  - E. Rift valley
  - F. Hill country
    - 1. Description
    - 2. Mammals
    - 3. Birds and insects
    - 4. Snakes
    - 5. Domestic stock
  - G. Trans-Jordan hill country
  - H. Marshlands
    - 1. Former extent
    - 2. Mammals
    - 3. Birds
- III. Results of human interference
  - A. Introduction
  - B. Climatic change or human damage?
  - C. General effect of human occupation
  - D. The Fertile Crescent
  - E. Palestine
  - F. Modern developments
  - G. Results of introducing new plants and animals
  - H. Conclusions

I. Sources of information about earlier fauna

A. Introduction. Any description of the fauna of Pal. in the Biblical period must be based clearly on reconstruction. This section considers the sources of literary and other recorded information on which this is based.

B. Ancient material. Data provided by the paleontologist largely refers to older faunas that prob. lived in climatic conditions so different that they are of only academic interest. Archeological material is becoming much more relevant now that animal remains are being examined more critically by more modern methods. In particular the work of the late F. E. Zeuner is invaluable for its treatment of bones found in human contexts, esp. because he sought to differentiate wild animals from the modified forms domesticated from them. It is fortunate that much of his work concerns Pal. and nearby lands. By its nature this material is limited largely to three groups: (1) Domestic animals. (2) Wild animals, esp. game, whose meat was eaten and whose bones, horns and antlers were used for making weapons and tools. (3) Other animals connected with superstition or religion. The great volume of dated and localized pictorial and written material resulting from excavations is an equally useful source of data. Prehistoric cave drawings are of less importance here than elsewhere.

C. Biblical evidence. The Bible itself provides not only the names of numerous animals, many from roots of known meaning, but also considerable information about them, whether stated explicitly or to be deduced from the context. It is unrealistic, however, to search the Scriptures for anything in the nature of a "check-list" of animals once found in Pal. By and large the animals are present as an integral part of the life of ordinary people. Thus the frequency with which an animal is mentioned, with its range of names, is a good indication of its importance, whether economic or ceremonial; e.g. sheep, with c. 400 occurrences, and cattle, with over 450, in OT and NT, far outnumber any other species, wild or domesticated. Biblical animals are largely confined to: (1) Domestic stock and clean wild animals used for food. (2) Animals that were a danger or nuisance to human life, stock, crops or other possessions, ranging from lions to clothes moths. (3) Familiar animals seen along roadsides, around houses, etc. including swallow, raven and sparrow. (4) A special class of unclean animals forbidden as food. As is explained in more detail where these are discussed individually, this prohibition was not just arbitrary, but was in many cases based on sound hygiene not understood or properly practiced for another 3,000 years.

There is little difficulty in identifying (1) and (2), for many are mentioned often, or occur in meaningful contexts; (3) contains a wide variety of animals, mostly rather small, not all of which can be named with certainty; (4) includes most of the doubtful names, given in what amounts to little more than two bare lists. Even here there are exceptions; Heb. פרס tr. vulture (Lev 11:13) is a good example of the help given by philology. Listed among unclean birds it is clearly a bird of prey; the name "bone-breaker" precisely describes the habits of the Black Vulture and Bearded Vulture. (*See* OSSIFRAGE.) Such ease of naming is exceptional. Some names have no known root meaning and are not known in any modern cognate form; further, they appear only in these lists. It should be noted that it is unsafe to rely on modern Heb., in which some names have been given to entirely different animals. It is believed that all animal names used in KJV, ASV and RSV have individual entries. Animals mentioned mainly in fig. contexts, in poetical, wisdom and prophetic books, are sometimes difficult but in most cases tentative identifications can be made.

II. NATURAL REGIONS

A. Introduction. Although Pal. as such no longer exists, it is a useful term for the area where much of the Biblical story was set. For a period after World War I it covered present Israel and all land W of the Rift Valley and Jordan; it is in this rough sense that it is used here. The topography is such that the regions into which this area is divided are fairly clearly demarcated; they are primarily geographical and botanical, aspects which are treated in greater detail elsewhere. These factors, in turn, determine the potential fauna, though geographical and faunal regions seldom coincide exactly, and man has had such an overwhelming impact on both flora and fauna that natural boundaries are sometimes completely masked. (*The Geography of the Bible* by Denis Baly [1957] defines these regions well.) The object of this discussion is to relate what is seen today with the original flora and fauna.

B. Desert. 1. *Description.* Much of S and E Pal. consists of desert and near desert. Surface varies from deep sand through gravel to more or less bare rock; topography from steep escarpments to almost level plains; and altitude from far below sea level to rather over 2,000 ft. above sea level. Rainfall, mostly from two to eight inches, usually occurs in a few winter storms violent enough to cause local flooding, esp. in the loess areas where the soil surface quickly forms an impervious skin, but a year often passes with no rain at all in one part of the desert or another. There is no closed cover, yet few large areas are entirely without trees or shrubs, which can draw moisture from deep in the soil, while most wadis are lined with specialized woody plants. Some soil is potentially fertile, esp. the loess, and quickly becomes temporarily covered with grass and flowering plants after rain. This is the only fresh green stuff available to the domestic stock around the desert edge, and the Bedouins' intimate local knowledge allows them to make full use of it. Even in the hills around the Dead Sea the cent. old well-trodden grazing tracks of sheep and goats are plainly visible at all seasons, though perhaps used only for a short period once a year. The desert is subject to great ranges of temperature, both diurnal and annual. In summer the ground surface temperature by day would be lethal to small animals, whose activity is therefore confined to the night; winter nights can be too cold, and animals may then be active in late evening and early morning. Within the desert there are some areas where no animals can live, and the average density of animal life is low everywhere.

2. *Large mammals.* Gazelles and Desert Oryx are the only large wild animals able to survive in such surroundings; they are big and fast enough to travel far in search of food and they stand high enough to keep above the fierce ground heat. The pale coat gives some degree of camouflage and also reduces absorption of sun heat, while with their specialized physiology they seldom need to drink water, getting most of their moisture from their food. They are few in number and are reckoned in many square m. per head. The Nubian Ibex —one of the mountain goats—is at home on some of the desert hills, including those on the W of the Dead Sea around Ein Gedi, where it is now protected. Only camels can serve as beasts of burden in desert conditions. Thorny plants provide food when they are allowed to range freely, but camels need occasional access to water, and if they are used on long, heavily loaded stages they must be well fed.

3. *Small mammals.* These are more numerous and varied. The Egyp. Jerboa, known in World War II as the Desert Rat, lives a similar life to that of the unrelated Kangaroo Rat of the California and Arizona deserts, spending the day in burrows where the lower temperature and higher relative humidity give more moderate conditions, and coming out at night in search of seeds, fruits and succulent roots. Other small rodents—several species of gerbils, jirds and sand rats—also live in dry habitats but are more typical of the desert edge, with rainfall above eight inches.

4. *Carnivores.* With their possible prey so scarce, carnivores are even more rare, and the only true cat seems to be the Caracal, or Desert Lynx; a very small pale variety of the leopard (q.v.) lives near, rather than in, the actual desert. The Fennec Fox, with huge ears, is a true desert form, smaller than the ordinary fox but with the same omnivorous habits. The slow-moving Arabian Hedgehog is well known; it feeds mostly on invertebrates and small reptiles.

5. *Birds.* The Griffon and Black Vultures, and Lammergeier, or Bearded Vulture, are in a special position. Very small numbers serve to scavenge a great area of desert, which they survey while cruising or soaring slowly from several thousand feet. Precise identification is

A typical desert vista in the Arabah. © *M.P.S.*

A gazelle near Emmaus. ©*Lev*

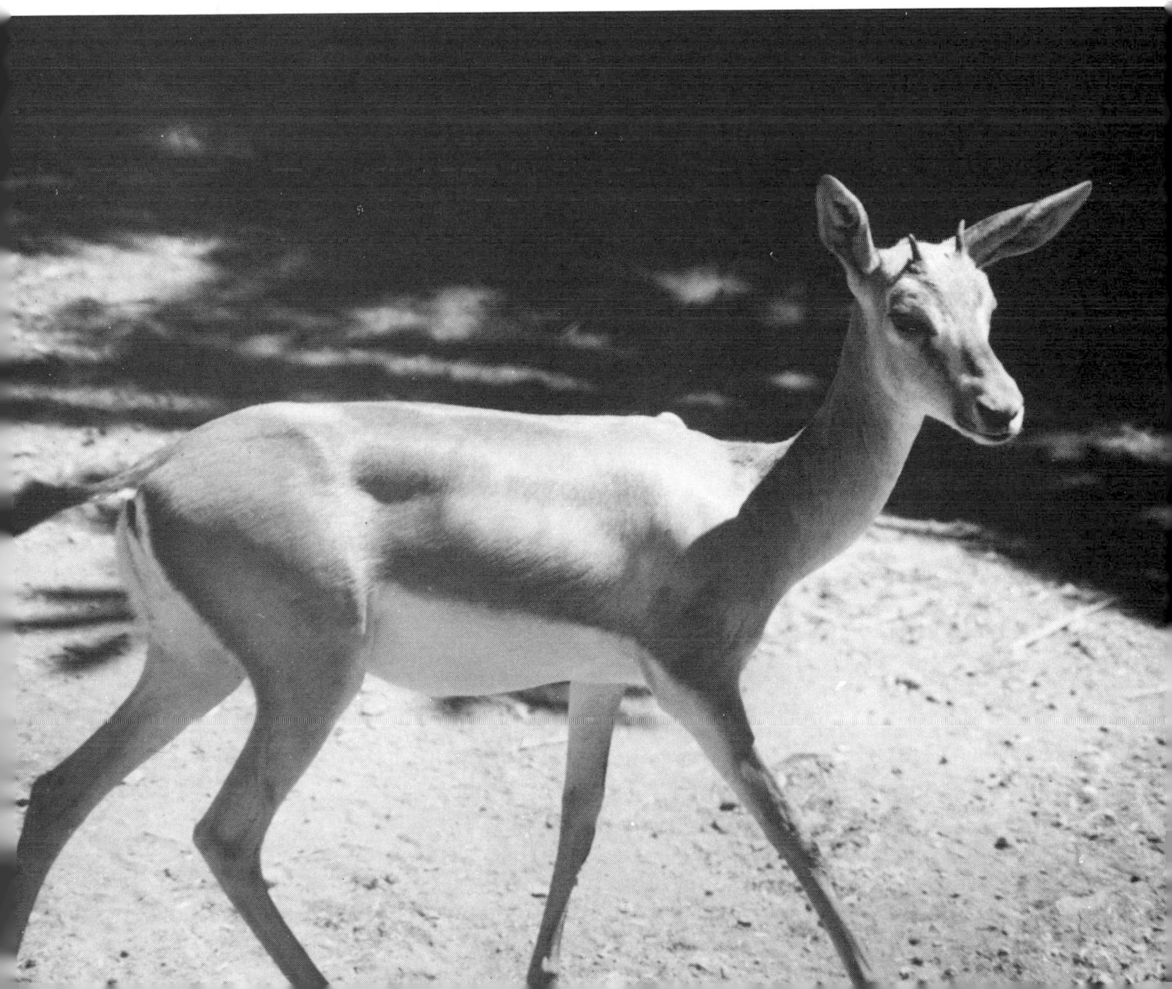

not possible, but large birds of prey high overhead would have been a familiar sight to the Israelites on their desert wanderings. In the migration seasons these included eagles, vultures and buzzards; for the rest of the year mostly vultures. Migrant birds are without doubt the most conspicuous animals of the desert, the large ones usually flying high overhead, the smaller ones traveling in shorter spells and stopping where possible for food and water. Like the Quail, which still flies N in numbers, these migrants are travelers across the desert rather than residents in it. In contrast, the Rock Dove, from which domestic pigeons are descended, nests on desert cliffs, flying far each day to find food and water.

6. Reptiles. Although the total numbers are low and their distribution patchy, the desert has a surprisingly large range of reptiles, none very big and most of them carnivorus. They include one plant-eating lizard—Uromastyx, Spiny-tailed Lizard. Having little or no internal means of regulating body temperatures, reptiles are even more restricted in their periods of activity; they must spend both the burning day and the cold parts of the night safely underground, where only a few inches from the surface the temperature range is much reduced. It is likely that some desert snakes are almost independent of water, obtaining all necessary moisture from their victims. The Sand Boa, a constrictor, lives in sandy desert and has a typical "swimming" motion to bury itself. At least four vipers are widely distributed, including two whose bites can be fatal to man (*see* SERPENT). All are highly adapted to a desert life, with a movement known as "sidewinding"; the same method of progressing over loose sand has been developed independently by the American Sidewinders, which are desert rattlesnakes. Most snakes prob. take a range of prey, but it seems that they depend to some extent on the casualties from the flocks of small migrant birds which pass N between February and May, and S again in late summer and autumn. Some desert reptiles go into a resting state, called estivation, in the hottest weather. Many species of snake can survive without food for many months.

7. Dead Sea. This is true desert, physiologically, for its high mineral content, about twenty-five per cent makes it useless for drinking, and no form of life is known to exist in it.

8. Large oases. Within the desert are large oases with ample underground water, e.g. Yotvata; or with piped spring water, e.g. Ein Gedi. The irrigated fields and orchards form an artificial habitat and attract fauna not typical of the surrounding desert.

C. Sand dunes. A feature of the Mediterranean coast, from around Gaza to beyond Haifa, is a discontinuous belt of rather mobile sand dunes, up to a few m. in width and up to 150 ft. high. These should not be confused with true desert dunes, which seldom carry vegetation. The coastal dunes enjoy reasonable rainfall but form a quasi-desert habitat, for until a layer of soil is formed water cannot be retained and only specialized plants thrive. The typical animals are those of the less extreme sandy desert—esp. the small rodents, whose tracks and entrances to burrows are seen widely, for such areas can support a denser population. Hedgehogs are also typical, the E and W species meeting somewhere in this area. As on similar coasts in other parts of the world, the dunes are to a large extent the result of human activity, by destroying woody cover and making movement of sand easier. Man is now reversing this process by fixing these dunes and thus recreating a habitat more favorable to both agriculture and animal life generally.

D. Lowlands and plains of Sharon and Esdraelon. Much of this region is potentially fertile and it has been farmed in varying degrees since the dawn of history. In recent years all suitable parts have been so intensively occupied that little or no trace of their original cover now remains. Enjoying a fair, though sometimes marginal, rainfall and once covered with forest, scrub and marshland, they are now a complex of settlements, orchards and fields, mostly irrigated. The woodlands were the home of deer, notably Fallow and Roe Deer, and possibly Red Deer also, but these were driven out long ago and the nearest survivors today are in Persia and Turkey. Lions hunted here, though not as much as in the broken hill country and lower ground beyond. Bird life is likely to be more numerous today, for farms and orchards often support a richer and larger bird fauna than virgin wodlands. Many birds are resident and they are small rather than large; migrants pass through but are less obvious, for they are traveling on a broad front and have more cover. Dense beds of milk thistles often fill road verges and odd corners left fallow, providing food for many goldfinches and cover for other small birds. It is likely that most animals familiar to the shepherds of the hill country also went down to the plains at some seasons.

E. Rift valley. From the Huleh area nearly to Jericho is a semi-tropical tract with many plants more typical of the Nile Valley, including papyrus. The lake fish most in demand is the *Tilapia*, a genus of Cichlid well represented in Central Africa, where it is one of the main food fishes of the great lakes. The deeply cut valley itself is lined in parts with almost impenetrable jungle in which wild boar, fishing cats and perhaps other large animals survive, but little is known of this area today for much of it is along a frontier where naturalists are not encouraged.

F. Hill country. 1. *Description.* Much of the Biblical narrative is set in the hills—from Galilee in the N through Samaria to beyond Bethlehem. The rainfall generally is above twenty-four inches, though it decreases rapidly

Figured bone inlays featuring a running gazelle. ©*Kelso*

on the E or leeward side. In the N large oaks can grow, but are now rare; over much of the area the naural climax is scrub, with taller trees growing in pockets of deeper soil. The olive is the commonest planted tree.

2. *Mammals.* This region once provided a wide range of animal life, for it offered both browsing and grazing, while the rock formation gave shelter for mammals as varied as the brown bear and Syrian Rock Hyrax—the coney. Deer were the most important wild ungulates, with the Pal. gazelle. The former have long been lost; the Pal. gazelle was able to survive in drier country to the S and, under protection, has made a good recovery, living in fair numbers through the Judaean hills and even on the Plain of Esdraelon, where it takes little notice of tractors working in the fields. Bears and lions are extinct here, but the striped hyena and wolf linger in small numbers. The leopard once hunted in these hills and still just survives in the Jordan Valley. Smaller carnivores are locally common—fox, jackal, mongoose and badger—and on a day's journey through these hills it is not unusual to see a run-over corpse on the road (*see* 3 F [5] below). Mole-rats push up small heaps in irregular lines wherever the soil is deep enough, but never appear above ground.

3. *Birds and insects.* The Rock partridge is heard daily at some seasons but prefers running to flying and is seldom seen. The varied cover in the hills makes it the home of many perching birds, and the smaller migrants go through without being obvious. The resident Pal. jay and Hooded crow are often seen and heard, the latter waiting on the roadside to pick up small road casualties. The larger resident birds of prey are now rare and the main scavenger is the conspicuous black and white Egyp. vulture, which still frequents garbage heaps outside towns. The Harvester Ant is busy throughout spring gathering food supplies to store underground; the trail of husks, removed before storage and thrown out, marks the entrance clearly.

4. *Snakes.* The largest venomous snake—Pal. viper—is found in the hills, as well as in most habitats other than true desert. Reaching a length of over four ft. and thickness of one inch, it must be treated with respect. It is considered responsible for more human casualities than any other snake, largely because it lives in inhabited areas.

5. *Domestic stock.* Sheep and goats have always been the main stock in the hills, the latter causing serious damage to vegetation by their browsing habits. They may even climb trees to get what they cannot reach from the ground. The rolling hills in N Galilee are more suited to cattle raising. The hills are not really camel country but camels are still kept in small numbers as beasts of burden and for farm work in a few Arab areas, notably in Samaria, around Nazareth, and in the Druse district of N Israel, where they look strangely out of place in the green countryside.

G. Trans-Jordan hill country. To the E, beyond Jordan, are further ranges of hills and broad plateau—the country of Ammon, Edom and Moab. These are distinctly drier than the western hills, which make the winds drop much of their rain, but the highest points are much higher—above 5,000 ft. above sea level—and the general conditions are more extreme, with the desert adjacent. In early times both lions and leopards were well known, though it is hard to speak with certainty of their prey. The land perhaps suited the Pers. race of Fallow Deer, which lived in poor scrub and dry woodlands. The onager was at the extremity of its range here and was still fairly common in a few places a cent. ago, though now extinct. (*See* WILD ASS.) Perhaps it came only to the edge of the hills from which the lions would hunt; in Africa zebras are their favorite prey and this could have been true of the closely related onager. Great numbers of sheep were kept in Ammon and Moab, as is suggested by the tax that Mesha King of Moab paid annually—100,000 lambs and the wool of 100,000 rams (2 Kings 3:4, 5). If the land could support such numbers, however skilfully managed, there had presumably been many wild ungulates, preyed on by suitable carnivores. Much of this area was camel country, though perhaps around rather than up in the hills, and these provided the basic transport for the traders whose routes ran straight through these lands.

H. Marshlands. 1. *Former extent.* There were once considerable areas of marshland: some, perhaps all, resulting from human activity around the former Lake Huleh, which also had much open water; on the Plains of Sharon and Esdraelon; and near the coast N of Haifa. The first was kept permanently wet by the lake through which the Jordan flowed, but the other areas perhaps dried out in part in summer. All have now been drained and reclaimed (*see* 3 F [4] below) but they once formed major barriers to invading armies and were a serious menace to health, for the most important insect living there was the *Anopheles* mosquito, carrier of malaria.

2. *Mammals.* These marshes made a suitable habitat for the fishing cat. Frogs of several kinds and water tortoises were common. When the wild boar was driven out of other parts the marshes made a safe retreat, and its main stronghold today is around the Huleh Valley and in the dense jungle lining the lower Jordan.

3. *Birds.* Above all the marshes were breeding grounds for many water-loving birds, esp. members of the heron family; they are also refuges for countless waders (shore birds) ducks, terns and herons on the N and S migrations, as well as providing winter quarters for vast numbers of coots and ducks. A group

Black-haired goats. The typical Palestinian goat is black-haired. Bedouin tents are made from the hair. These are at Petra. ©*Lev*

of brackish water fishponds on the coast midway between Haifa and Tel Aviv, reclaimed from useless marsh, is now a wild life sanctuary, and during spring migration it is alive with birds headed for their breeding grounds in all parts of Central, E and N Europe.

III. Results of human interference

A. Introduction. Large areas of Pal. and adjacent lands have become degraded through centuries of ill treatment and erosion; the flora was impoverished and the fauna diminished. In some parts, both town and country, man has used the ground so completely that no traces of original cover remain. As a direct result, the status of many animals has changed radically; a few are known, on good historical evidence, to have been exterminated from the area as a whole or from large parts of it. This change is largely quantitative, but to some extent qualitative also. Human action alone explains the position in the occupied areas; is this also true as a whole?

B. Climatic change or human damage? Only one other factor need be considered here —the climate. Has this perhaps become less favorable since the Biblical period? If this were so, it would greatly complicate the assessment of conditions, say, 4,000 years ago, for the earlier potential would have been different; it could have included some species not on the present list, i.e. those which live in more moist conditions; and excluded others, i.e. those which demand drier conditions. One school of thought claims that destruction of tree cover has an adverse effect on climate— esp. on rainfall—while the planting of trees improves it. It is true that land with good woody cover makes better use of available water; also that forest on a hill top may sometimes just cause a cloud to shed rain, but this effect is so marginal as to be negligible. It has also been claimed that there has been a longterm swing to a drier climate, by those who cannot regard Pal. with its present climate as even potentially "flowing with milk and honey"; they are also mystified that the N Negev was successfully occupied for at least two long periods, widely separated. However, all evidence is against any significant climatic change, so that the vegetation of the various regions is still potentially what it was when the patriarchs first saw Canaan. The massive reduction in area and quality of cover is due solely to man's action, direct and indirect. Regarding the Negev, botanists and agriculturalists have recently reconstructed the Nabatean earthworks at Avdat, abandoned c. A.D. 100, and used their specialized system of irrigation to establish farms and orchards, which suggests that the rainfall is no less now than it was then. Unchanged climate presupposes an unchanged climax vegetation; the fauna, dependent on this, is thus potentially the same. This somewhat simplifies the interpretation, even though man's influence through the ages has been destructive and complex. This will now be discussed in sections.

C. General effect of human occupation. With the advance of civilization and rapid increase of population, this has now become the overriding factor in nearly all parts of the world and at an increasing pace, but this process began very early, esp. in the lands around Pal. Man affects animal life mainly in two ways. First, by occupying land, turning forest and scrub into farm and raiding much larger areas for fuel, he so changed the habitat that many animals moved out; some because there was no room for them, others because they would not tolerate interference. In general, the larger species are most adversely affected; smaller kinds may be helped by human activity and become much more numerous as a result, some even becoming pests that must be controlled. Second, man took direct action against various animals, either killing them or driving them away. These fall into several classes: (1) The browsing and grazing animals, e.g. antelopes, cattle and wild horses, which were competitors with domestic stock. Many of these, and others also, were good for food or desired as trophies or totems, and were therefore hunted or trapped. (2) Beasts of prey —wolf, bear, lion etc.—which are potential enemies to man himself and his livestock. (3) Animals, other than predators, that are dangerous to life and health, e.g. venomous snakes and a wide range of noxious insects. The total result is to reduce seriously the range of many animals that were once widespread. For instance, within historic times the lion was found through much of SW Asia, but is now reduced to a small group of some 200 in the Gir Peninsula of India. The aurochs, ancestor of the main cattle stock, disappeared for good early in the 17th cent., and the wild forebears of both kinds of camels were prob. lost soon after these were domesticated.

D. The Fertile Crescent. Since the dawn of civilization man has been busy exploiting and destroying his environment, but his impact has varied from country to country and in the course of time. In Mesopotamia, for instance, long periods of comparative peace allowed the development of great cities and cultures, based on efficient agriculture. Much of the wild flora and fauna disappeared and, in time, widespread desiccation caused irreversible degradation of the habitat. This latter did not occur in Egypt, where the Nile periodically renewed the fertility of the land as well as watering it. The larger fauna survived only in regions such as mountains and deserts, which were self-protecting, and in hunting reserves which the kings established and guarded carefully for their own pleasure.

E. Palestine. As a whole this area enjoyed no such period of prolonged peace, the longest apparently being under David and Solomon; this began toward the end of David's reign and was over before Solomon's death. (Before

Large areas of Palestine have become eroded because of man's misuse. ©*Lev*

Irrigation has made previously unusable land fertile. ©*Lev*

the Heb. invasion the land had been owned by a patchwork of tribes and nations and it is doubtful if occupation was ever complete.) Century after cent. saw unrest and guerilla warfare, or massive campaigns. Except perhaps for the valley of Esdraelon, few parts were used intensively and throughout this time the wild fauna was prob. less affected than in most nearby lands. Several successive periods of deportation and scattering, with big resultant casualties, kept the population low, and Pal. continued to be a troubled area, under Gr. and then Rom. rule, until well into the Christian era. It seems likely that through most of these periods much of the natural vegetation remained untouched, and a sanctuary for wild animals, with comparatively little change in the fauna from the days of the Judges until the time of the Crusades. If this hypothesis is true the wild life which the Biblical writers from Moses onward knew was richer and much more prolific than what is there today, and it came much closer to the everyday lives of the ordinary people. A limited area would be under cultivation at any time; flocks and herds were led over wide areas to find grazing, but they were always controlled and protected, against both predators and raiders from other tribes. Under such conditions the hillside soil remained stable and safe, with little or no serious erosion. Between the rise of Islam and the end of the 19th cent. the damage was far greater than in all the preceding centuries, though it is hard to know just when this serious change began. The damage had three main causes:

(1) Livestock, esp. goats, ranged uncontrolled and destroyed vegetation of all kinds, leaving steep hillsides exposed to fierce winter rain storms, which quickly removed the thin layer of soil that had been built up slowly over many centuries. This lack of control continues in many Arab countries today; in places along the Israel/Jordan border in spring the noticeably green vegetation on the one side, where goats must always be tethered, is in marked contrast to the brown of the exposed soil on the other.

(2) Many trees, within and outside the farmed areas, were cut for firewood, charcoal and timber, with similar effect. During one period of Turkish rule a tree tax was imposed, which the Arabs avoided simply by cutting down their trees.

(3) As soil deteriorated the unit yield dropped and larger areas had to be brought into cultivation, including some of the steeper slopes. This would have been reasonably safe if conservative methods of farming had been used, with plowing only along the contours, but this principle was not generally understood, though the Phoenicians had early practiced it, and the usual result was progressive erosion. The farming of hillsides in Upper Galilee was a factor in filling much of Lake Huleh with silt and so creating swamps which were drained during the 1950s.

In such comparatively hot countries, where the variable rainfall mostly comes in heavy storms in winter and spring when the ground has least natural cover, these changes can be almost irreversible. The position can be restored only by long, painstaking effort, in contour-plowing and planting, which is highly expensive in labor, for such work can hardly be mechanized.

F. Modern developments. The 20th cent. has introduced several new factors which have complicated the position still further. The first two are direct and the others indirect in their effects.

(1) High-powered rifles brought danger to larger desert animals that had previously been approachable only with great difficulty. Fast motorized transport, and the advent of great wealth from oil, made things much worse and within a few years the Desert Oryx was high on the world list of threatened species. The Pal. and Dorcas gazelles were greatly reduced.

(2) The creation of the state of Israel attracted zoologists and naturalists from countries with a tradition of wild life conservation that was entirely new. The establishment of sanctuaries and nature reserves, with a more humane national attitude, has made Israel an area where animal life of all kinds is less harassed than it has been for a long time, and the gazelles are now safe again; but this factor cannot help the oryx, of which the nearest is well over 1,000 m. away in S Arabia. In some other states the official attitude to wild life is changing somewhat, but this cuts right across the Arab philosophy, which includes little thought for wild animals, large or small, except as something that Allah has provided for them to eat—and will go on providing. This callous disregard for wild life has added markedly to the more indirect damage that the fauna has suffered in recent centuries.

(3) The extensive tree-planting programs, both in forests and roadside shelter-belts, and in orchards, and the introduction of irrigated cultivation over large areas have created new habitats and conditions which have allowed many species, esp. birds, to improve their status radically. For instance, the Palm dove, once a largely African species, has spread so widely and become so numerous that it is locally a pest and seems to be driving out the turtle dove. The African bulbul has also come from the S and moved into gardens and orchards, being useful to man when it catches insects to feed its young, but doing damage later to ripening fruit.

(4) Land reclamation programs have been started, often with international help. The object is to restore woody cover to eroded hillsides, though often with introduced species of trees which are expected in time to produce a more useful crop than the native scrub. The end

A herdsman and his flock. ©*M.P.S.*

result can thus be different from the original climax vegetation, but always more favorable to most forms of animal life than the degraded cover which it replaces. The draining of Lake Huleh is a different type of reclamation which has resulted in a major change of land usage; the area remains useful as a resting and feeding place for migrants, but it is no longer a habitat fit for the larger wild animals and great flocks of water birds that once lived there.

(5) Intensive arable farming has resulted in serious plagues of rodents, esp. voles. These have often been attacked with permanent poisons such as thallium; the dead and dying animals have been taken by birds and beasts of prey, and these in turn have died, to be eaten with fatal results by jackals, hyenas, vultures and other scavengers. Before the danger was realized the breeding population of some of the animals concerned had been reduced to about ten per cent. Many years of protection will be needed to restore the situation fully. A similar chain of damage has been started by the use of resistant insecticides.

G. Results of introducing new plants and animals. There is still another way in which man has affected the fauna of Pal.—by the deliberate introduction of plants and animals from other lands. Among the former should be listed crops of most kinds, few of which are truly native; these are an integral part of agriculture, the general effect of which has been discussed. This is true also of domesticated animals; even if they are derived from once local species their impact on the land is quite different and this, too, is a concomitance of farming. Introduction of exotic wild animals has been on a more limited scale than in many temperate countries, where this practice has sometimes resulted in catastrophic damage, first to the vegetation and then to native animals. Such few as can be cited for Pal. are quasi-domesticated and of these only the carp is worth discussion. This cultured form has been kept in fishponds for many centuries (*see* FISHING). It is now the basis of an intensive fish-breeding industry in great complexes of artificial ponds, esp. in the Jordan Valley. Occasional escapees find their way down into the Lake of Galilee, where they are caught by net fishermen; the carp fills a manmade niche and its introduction is unlikely to affect adversely either other fish or animals of other classes, if only because it is edible and valuable, and therefore worth controlling.

H. Conclusions. The above are prob. the most important factors that have combined to produce the changed and impoverished flora and fauna that a visitor to the Holy Land sees today. The birds, esp. the small migrants, have changed least of all. The larger mammals have been reduced to a tiny remnant, seen only by the energetic enthusiast but in places responding to protection. Livestock continue to be the most conspicuous animals, but even here a major change is taking place. Intensive animal husbandry is putting cattle and sheep, and even chickens, more or less permanently into stalls or under cover, esp. in the desert settlements such as Yotvata and Ein Gedi, while the tractor is steadily replacing the ass, horse and camel in all parts for work in the fields, and the bicycle and car are taking over for personal transport.

BIBLIOGRAPHY. H. B. Tristram, *The Natural History of the Bible*, 9th ed. (1898); N. Glueck, *The River Jordan* (1946); W. F. Albright, *The Archeology of Palestine,* 2nd. ed. (1954); D. Baly, *The Geography of the Bible* (1957) (with full classified bibliography for all regions); F. S. Bodenheimer, *Animal and Man in Bible Lands* (1960) (with very detailed references to classical authors); P. Merom, *The Death of the Lake* (n.d. but c. 1961) (a pictorial record of draining Lake Huleh); F. E. Zeuner, *A History of Domesticated Animals* (1963) (with exhaustive references, esp. to scientific periodicals); D. L. Harrison, *Mammals of Arabia*, Vol. I (1964), Vol. II (1968), Vol. III (1972) (a definitive work covering the areas S of Pal.).

G. S. CANSDALE

FAWN (עפר, *young stag*; pl. עפרים, *fawns*). The word appears only in S of Sol, tr. *young stag* (2:9, 17; 8:14) and *fawns* (4:5; 7:3). The word meant originally "young animal" generally, but is now restricted to the young of certain deer, esp. Fallow and Roe Deer. It is sometimes applied to the young of antelopes, etc. The RSV trs. Genesis 49:21 as "hind . . . that bears comely fawns" on the basis of a conjectural emendation of the Heb text. The KJV renders it, "he giveth goodly words." *See* DEER and GAZELLE.

G. S. CANSDALE

FEAR (יראה, ירא ; *φόβος*, *φοβέω*). Several Heb. words are tr. "fear" in the OT, the principal ones of which are *yirah* and *yare*, noun and verb respectively. Their meaning comprises "fear," "dread," "terror," "timidity," "wonderful," "stupendous," "reverence," and "awe." The chief Gr. words for fear are *phobos* and *phobeo*, also tr. "terror," "alarm," "reverence," and "respect."

Fear in the Bible, as in common parlance, is used in many ways, all of which fall into two categories. In one it is beneficial; in the other baneful. Hence, fear is either friend or foe. In its natural sense, innate fear serves as an alarm system, or an arousal, alerting one to impending danger. Consequently, the threatened may prepare for the appropriate reaction, to fight, to flee, or to freeze. Fear of this character is nature's asset. Contrarily, if fear is not soon expelled, it sinks into the subconscious mind where it becomes "phobia," which is an unhealthy condition. In modern scientific experiments with primates and children psychologists have learned that the principal sources of innate fear are darkness, loss of support, strange things, sudden noises, and snakes. All these are potentially beneficial or harmful, and all are found in the Bible either factually or fig. Numerous other objects of man's fear may be added to this list, both from everyday life and the Bible. In the Scriptures clear distinction is made between what man should fear and should not fear.

1. Beneficial fear—the fear of God. The most prevalent use of fear in the Bible is the fear of God. Next to that is the fear of God's people. The former is the reverential or awesome side of the fear spectrum. This fear is friend.

a. As religion of God's people. The majesty and holiness of God cannot but incite fear in man. "God is clothed with terrible majesty. The Almighty—we cannot find him; he is great in power and justice, and abundant righteousness he will not violate. Therefore men fear him" (Job 37:22-24). Anything of magnitude that dwarfs man by contrast incites fear in him. As man gazes into a deep canyon, or into limitless stellar space, or across a boundless ocean, he senses a feeling of awesome fear. How much more is this effect in the presence of God who is vastly greater than all these. As the psalmist meditated on this contrast he was amazed that God would be mindful of man (Ps 8:1-4). Similarly, God's holiness transcends man's character with like effects (Isa 6:5). Naturally then, the phrases, "the fear of God" and "the fear of the Lord" occur frequently in the Bible, particularly in the OT. The Heb. deity was awesome, so naturally the Israelites were constantly called on to "fear the LORD your God" (Deut 10:20). The admonition was an instrument with two edges, rewards and restraints.

"The fear of God" is synonymous with religion, and therefore rewarding. It was considered so as early as Abraham's day. When that patriarch misrepresented his wife Sarah to Abimelech, he gave as his reason, "because I thought, There is no fear of God at all in this place" (Gen 20:11). The fear of deity was an integral part of primitive and pagan religion. Even God was called "the Fear of Isaac" (31:42). In advising Moses to appoint subordinate judges to share the judicial burden, his father-in-law, Jethro, recommended that he select "able men . . . such as fear God" (Exod 18:21). Proselytes in the NT were called "God-fearing" or those who "fear God," as Cornelius (Acts 10:2) and Paul's congregation in Antioch of Pisidia (13:16, 26).

"The fear of God" was required in the following ways: by keeping His commandments (Exod 20:20); by serving Him and keeping His statutes (Deut 6:13, 24); by hearkening to His voice (1 Sam 12:14); and by worshiping in His Temple (Ps 5:7). Moses' strict injunction to Israel was, "You shall fear your God" (Lev 19:14b). Furthermore he said, "The LORD commanded us to do all these statutes, to fear the LORD our God, for our good always, that he might preserve us alive" (Deut 6:24). From early times rewards were promised for Jehovah worship.

God's blessings on those who fear Him are numerous, mentioned frequently throughout the Bible. Satan asked the Lord, "Does Job fear God for naught," and in answering his own question declared that God had "put a hedge about him" (Job 1:9f.). And, Eliphaz asked Job, "Is not your fear of God your confidence?" (4:6). The psalmist said, "The eye of the LORD is on those who fear him . . . that he may deliver their soul from death, and keep them alive in famine" (Ps 33:18, 19). In the wisdom lit. it is stated: "The fear of the LORD prolongs life" (Prov 10:27); "The fear of the LORD is a fountain of life" (14:27); ". . . leads to life" (22:4; cf. Ps 61:5; 119:37f.). One of the most familiar Proverbs is "The fear of the LORD is the beginning of wisdom" (Prov 9:10; Ps 111:10). Similar ones are: "The fear of the LORD is the beginning of knowledge" (Prov 1:7), and "The fear of the Lord is instruction in wisdom" (15:33). David summarized religious benefits in two statements: "He fulfills the desire of all who fear him" (Ps 145:19), and "O how abundant is thy goodness, which thou hast laid up for those who fear thee" (Ps 31:19; cf. 34:9).

Isaiah's prophetic description of the Messiah was that "His delight shall be in the fear of the LORD," and "the fear of the LORD is his treasure" (Isa 11:3; 33:6c). Malachi prophesied in the words of the Lord, "But for you who fear my name the sun of righteousness shall rise, with healing in its wings" (Mal 4:2). And one psalmist sang, "Surely his salvation is at hand for those who fear him" (Ps 85:9).

Another benevolent work of the fear of God is its restraining force. Constantly the Israelites were warned of the consequences of wrong doing. Moses taught, "And now, Israel, what does the LORD require of you, but to fear the LORD your God, to walk in all his ways, to love him, to serve the LORD . . ." (Deut 10:12). One Heb. philosopher said, "By the fear of the LORD a man avoids evil" (Prov 16:6). Clearly, all these references to the fear of God mean the Jehovah religion, worship and service of God. Consequences of failure to do so are clearly stated, as in the major categories of infidelity, injustice, and insincerity.

Since spiritual infidelity, or apostasy, mothers a multitude of sins, the penalty was death, that "all Israel shall hear, and fear, and never again do any such wickedness as this among you" (Deut 13:11; cf. 17:13; 21:21). And, if the laws were not kept, "that you may fear this glorious and awful name, the LORD your God, then the LORD will bring on you and your offspring extraordinary afflictions" (Deut 28:58, 59; see v. 67). Joshua (Josh 24:14) and Samuel (1 Sam 13:14) and all the prophets uttered similar warnings.

Judicial injustices were sternly warned against

by King Jehoshaphat (2 Chron 19:5-11) and governor Nehemiah "because of the fear of God" (Neh 5:6-15). And the psalmist warned, "O kings, be wise; and be warned, O rulers of the earth. Serve the LORD with fear, with trembling kiss his feet, lest he be angry and you perish in the way" (Ps 2:10f.; cf. 90:11).

Isaiah warned against insincerity, those who "honor me with their lips, while their hearts are far from me, and their fear of me is a commandment of men learned by rote" (Isa 29:13). The extreme penalty was paid by Ananias and Sapphira for insincerity, and "great fear came upon the whole church" (Acts 5:11).

b. *As reflected on God's people.* When God made man and gave him dominion over the earth, he said, "The fear of you and dread of you shall be upon every beast of the earth, and upon every bird of the air, and upon everything that creeps on the ground and all the fish of the sea" (Gen 9:2). It is doubtless the image of God reflected in the countenance and personality of man that incites fear in lower creatures (Ps 139:14). Consequently, man "shall not fear the beasts of the earth" (Job 5:22). David (1 Sam 17:34-36) and Daniel (Dan 6:22) boldly faced savage beasts.

Moreover, God's people are feared by wicked people. As the Israelites began the conquest of Canaan, God said, "This day I will begin to put the dread and fear of you upon the peoples that are under the whole heaven . . ." (Deut 2:25; cf. 11:25). And the harlot Rahab confessed to the spies "that the fear of you has fallen upon us" (Josh 2:9). Soon the tribal kings "feared greatly" Joshua's army (Josh 10:2). Note also Absalom's rebellion (2 Sam 17:10); Jews in Persia (Esth 9:2); mariners and Jonah (Jonah 1:1-16); and Herod and the Jewish rulers (Matt 14:5; 21:46; Mark 12:12).

2. Baneful fear—the fear of evil. The other side of the ledger of fear is deficit. This fear is harmful to those who fear, and in turn makes them a source of fear. This fear is man's foe. It debilitates, disorganizes, demoralizes, and destroys.

a. *As it affects evil men.* The wicked person is destroyed by his fears. Some wise man said, "The wicked flee when no one pursues" (Prov 28:1). Numerous records confirm this. When Cain was exiled, he was seized with a fearful dread that "whoever finds me will slay me" (Gen 4:14). He had slain and was afraid someone would slay him. Likewise, Herod's guilt fears haunted him after he beheaded John the Baptist (Matt 14:1f.) In man's dreadful hallucinations he fears all kinds of evil, destitution, desolation, and destruction (*see* Job 5:21; Isa 7:25; 8:6; Rev 18:10, 15). In Elisha's day the Syrian army fled, panic-stricken, in the night, "For the LORD had made the army of the Syrians hear the sound of chariots, and of horses, the sound of a great army" (2 Kings 7:6). Later, Isaiah encouraged Hezekiah with God's promise, "Behold, I will put a spirit in him, so that he shall hear a rumor and return to his own land" (2 Kings 19:7). Fear itself is a destructive enemy. "What the wicked dreads will come upon him" (Prov 10:24). Isaiah said, God will "bring their fears upon them" (Isa 66:4). Fear disorganizes the wicked. When Belshazzar saw a man's handwriting on the wall, "the king's color changed, and his thoughts alarmed him; his limbs gave way, and his knees knocked together" (Dan 5:6). Fear also paralyzes. When the angel rolled away the stone from the sepulchre, "for fear of him the guards trembled and became like dead men" (Matt 28:4).

b. *As it affects godly men.* No matter how it works, "The fear of man lays a snare" (Prov 29:25). It takes its toll among good people. It disqualified men from fighting the holy wars. Moses left instructions that, "What man is there that is fearful and fainthearted? Let him go back to his house" (Deut 20:8). And, when Gideon screened men to fight the Midianites, he said, "Whoever is fearful and trembling, let him return home" (Judg 7:3). The good are sometimes stricken with fear as with a dreadful disease. Job said, "The thing that I fear comes upon me, and what I dread befalls me" (Job 3:25). False perception can replace faith with fear. When Jesus came to His disciples at night on the stormy sea, they "were terrified . . . And they cried out for fear" because they thought he was "a ghost" (Matt 14:26).

Christian freedom has been threatened from the beginning by fear of the wicked. "For fear of the Jews" Joseph of Arimathea was a secret disciple (John 19:38); parents of the healed blind man declined testimony (9:22); and the Twelve hid behind closed doors (20:19). Punishment and judgment are causes of fear for all (Deut 28:67; Heb 10:27, 31).

3. Banishing fear—freedom from fear. By precept and example Jesus taught His disciples to make conquest of their fears. It can be done.

a. *By the presence of God.* David said triumphantly, "I fear no evil; for thou art with me" (Ps 23:4b). Long before this, God had said to Abraham, "Fear not, Abram, I am your shield" (Gen 15:1). To Isaiah He said for Israel, "Fear not, for I have redeemed you . . . Fear not, for I am with you" (Isa 43:1, 5; cf. Zeph 3:15; John 12:15). Divine visible presence, after the first startling moments, always dispelled fears (Exod 3:6; Luke 1:30; 2:10; Matt 14:27; 17.6f.). Moreover, God's unseen presence hovers over His own and protects them. Elisha had at his command a mountain covered with "horses and chariots of fire" (2 Kings 6:17). And, Jesus had in reserve "more than twelve legions of angels" (Matt 26:53).

b. *By perfected love.* "The fear of God" in the OT yielded to "The love of God" in the NT. Though the awesome nature of God will never diminish, His Fatherly love was manifested through Jesus. His tenderness has replaced terror. Consequently, John could give the Christian antidote for fear: "There is no fear in love, but perfect love casts out fear. For fear has to do with punishment, and he who fears is not perfected in love" (1 John 4:18). The Christian should have no fear of hunger, nakedness, sickness, suffering, wicked people, death, nor judgment. All have lost their power of fear in the love of Christ. "Fear not, little flock, for it is your Father's good pleasure to give you the kingdom" (Luke 12:32). *See* WORSHIP.

BIBLIOGRAPHY. L. D. Weatherhead, *Psychology and Life* (1935), 213-237; E. S. Jones, *Abundant Living* (1942), 68-88; D. O. Hebb, *A Textbook of Psychology* (1960), 64-97; A. M. Fiske, "Death, Myth and Ritual," *Journal of American Academy of Religion* (Sept. 1969), 249-265.

G. B. FUNDERBURK

FEASTS. "Feast" is used in the Eng. Bible without distinction for both private and public celebrations while Heb. used *mishteh* for the former and *mo'ed* or *hag* for the latter.

I. OLD TESTAMENT

A. Private feasts (משתה ; LXX Γάμος, *marriage feast*; δοχή, *banquet*; or πότος, *drinking party*). The social life of ancient Israel provided many joyous occasions that were celebrated with feasts: weddings (Gen 29:22)—the celebrations of which might extend seven days (Judg 14:10, 12, 17)—the weaning of a child (Gen 21:8), the birthday of a king (40:20), and the arrival of or approaching departure of guests (19:3; 26:30). Sheepshearing was also a joyous season and the first sheared wool went to the sanctuary (Deut 18:4; cf. Gen 38:12; 1 Sam 25:4-11, 36; 2 Sam 13:23-27). Job's children held a feast at the house of each on his day (Job 1:4, 5). In the days of the monarchies there were state occasions (2 Sam 3:20; Esth 1:3ff.; Dan 5:1). Solomon dedicated the Temple with a feast (1 Kings 8:65); the queen might entertain the king (Esth 5:4, 14; 7:2, 7). Solomon celebrated his dream with a feast (1 Kings 3:15) and Ahasuerus celebrated his finding of a new queen (Esth 2:18).

Ancient Hebrews were not ascetics. Often feasts demanded no specific occasion other than gladness (Job 1:4, 5; Isa 5:12). It was a severe restriction upon participation in social life imposed by the Lord on Jeremiah when He forbade him to go to the house of feasting (Jer 16:8).

B. Communal feasts (מועד, *appointed time*; חג, *festival gathering*, esp. one observed by a pilgrimage; LXX ἑορτή, *festival*). Moses and Aaron in Egypt requested of Pharaoh permission to celebrate a feast in the desert (Exod 5:1ff.). After the Exodus the communal festivals were seasons of rejoicing (Deut 16:14). In early Israel at the yearly feast in Shiloh the girls danced in the vineyard (Judg 21:21). Elkanah annually attended the feast at Shiloh (1 Sam 1:3ff.). Later there were processions at the house of the Lord with songs and shouts (Ps 42.4). There was the ever present danger that drinking might result in drunkenness (1 Sam 1:13-15). Abuse of the festivals and false trust in their efficacy brought forth denunciations from the prophets (Isa 1:12-14). The communal festivals of Israel may be thought of in categories of: (1) weekly, (2) monthly, (3) annual, and (4) periodic events.

1. *Weekly festival—The Sabbath* (שבת, LXX σάββατον, *rest*). The seventh day, sanctified by the Lord at creation (Gen 2:1-3), but not observed until the time of the Exodus (Exod 16:23), is listed in festivals (Lev 23:1). The day commemorated both the Lord's rest at creation and the deliverance from servitude to Egypt (Deut 5:12-15). It is a sign between Jehovah and Israel (Exod 31:17; Ezek 20:12, 20).

The Sabbath was observed by strict cessation of servile work from sunset until sunset (Exod 20:12, 13; Neh 13:15-22) so that kindling a fire (Exod 35:3) and picking up sticks (Num 15:32, 33) were punishable by death (Exod 31:14; 35:2). One must remain in his place (Exod 16:29; Lev 23:3). Forming an analogy from the two thousand cubits of Numbers 35:2, the rabbis defined the Sabbath day's journey to be limited to two thousand cubits (Acts 1:12; Jos. War V. ii. 3; cf. M. *Erubin* 4:1). The topic of movements on the Sabbath is treated at length in the Mishna tractate *Erubin.*

Some Jews of the Maccabean period allowed themselves to be massacred on the Sabbath rather than to profane it by self-defense after which the Maccabees permitted self-defense on the day (1 Macc 2:38-41). Some Jews would not negotiate for peace on the Sabbath (Jos., War IV. ii. 3). The extent of permitted activities was a point of dispute between Jesus and the Pharisees. The latter permitted defiling the Sabbath when human life was in danger. Jesus contended that lesser cases of human need as well as animal need took precedence over the Sabbath (Matt 12:1ff.). The *Zadokite Fragment* (10:14ff.), denies the right to aid suffering beasts on the Sabbath but grants it for humans.

Special offerings were made on the Sabbath (Num 28:9, 19) and the twelve loaves of showbread were placed on the table in the Holy Place (Lev 24:5-8). Psalm 92 is said to be a Psalm of the Sabbath. The day was a day of holy convocation (Lev 23:3) but only after the rise of the synagogue are instruction and worship activities attested as a prominent part of Sabbath observance (Luke 4:16, 31ff.; Acts 13:14; 18:4).

Despite its restrictions, the Sabbath was a joyous occasion (2 Kings 4:23; Isa 58:13ff.) the cessation of which in the Exile was considered as a punishment from God (Lam 2:6; Hos 2:11). The prophets called for proper Sabbath observance (Isa 56:4; Jer 17:19ff.).

A Samaritan congregation praying before "Mt. Moriah" on Mount Gerizim during the Passover celebration. ©*M.P.S.*

2. *Monthly festival—the New Moon* (חדש or ראש חדש; LXX νουμήνια). At the beginning of the month special offerings were demanded by the law (Num 28:11-15; cf. Ezra 3:5). There was also a blowing of trumpets (Num 10:10; Ps 81:3). The observance was prominent in the period of the kings and an accidental uncleanness excused one from attending as did a conflict with a "daily feast." One might visit a holy man on that day (2 Kings 4:9). David's arrangements for the Levites included service on the new moon (1 Chron 23:31). A cessation of activity, not demanded in the law, seems to have been observed with laxity in Amos' day (Amos 8:5). This day with others is included in prophetic denunciations of abuses of religious observances (Isa 1:13, 14). The Exile brought a temporary cessation (Hos 2:11 [13])) but the festival continued to the end of OT time (Neh 10:33) and formed a part of Ezekiel's Temple description (Ezek 45:17) and of Isaiah's picture of the new heaven and earth (Isa 66:22, 23).

In Pauline thought new moons and sabbaths are mere shadows of good things to come (Col 2:16).

3. *Annual festivals.* a. PENTATEUCHAL FESTIVALS. These annual seasons—designated by *ḥag*, "to dance, to turn around"—requiring the appearance of all males at the sanctuary dominated the Israelite religious year: Passover, Weeks, and Ingatherings (Deut 16:16). These occasions, called "the feasts of the LORD" (Exod 12:14; Lev 23:39, 41, etc.), were times in which freewill offerings were made (Deut 16:16, 17). Some aspects of the seasons were celebrated at night (Isa 30:29). These days were of course interrupted by the Exile (Hos 9:5).

(1) *Passover* (פסח; LXX πάσχα). The Passover commemorated the final plague in Egypt in which the first-born of the Egyptians died, but the Israelites were spared by the blood on the doorpost (Exod 12:11, 21, 27, 43, 48). Thereafter the event was observed as a feast

to the Lord (12:14). The second Passover was observed in the wilderness of Sinai (Num 9:1-5).

Passover fell in the first month (Abib; Deut 16:1; the first month is called Nisan in post-exilic times: Neh 2:1; Esth 3:7) on the fourteenth day at evening (Lev 23:5). The victim was selected on the tenth day of the month (Exod 12:3) and after slaughter on the fourteenth was boiled and eaten (Deut 16:7). Neither the uncircumcised person nor the hired servant could eat (Exod 12:48). None of the lamb should be left over on the following morning (34:25). Special sacrifices were made to the Lord (Num 28:16-25). The unclean person observed the corresponding day in the second month (9:10ff.).

This night was followed by seven days—the *ḥag hammassot*—in which unleavened bread was eaten (Exod 34:18, 19; Lev 23:6; cf. Exod 12:31-34). For this reason the NT speaks of the entire season as "the days of unleavened bread" (Acts 12:3; Luke 22:1). On the first and the seventh of these days no servile work was to be done and special offerings were made upon them all.

The Passover was observed at Gilgal when Joshua brought Israel into Canaan (Josh 5:10-12). Reforms of Hezekiah and Josiah were characterized by elaborate Passover celebrations (2 Kings 23:21-23; 2 Chron 30:1ff.; 35:1-19). Passover and unleavened bread were observed by the Elephantine Jews (ANET, p. 491).

The liturgy of the Passover celebration is the subject of minute elaboration in the Mishna tractate *Passover*. Despite the assertion of Jubilees 49:16 that one cannot eat the Passover outside the sanctuary, Jesus ate with His disciples in a private house as was the custom of the times (cf. *M. Passover* 5; 8:13). In addition to the pilgrimage to Jerusalem this festival retained some features of a home celebration which reasserted themselves after the fall of Jerusalem. The Passover meal was eaten at home with bitter herbs, successive cups of wine, the blessings and reciting of the Psalms. Whether a roast was eaten or not varied from community to community (*M. Passover* 4:4). The need for each individual to feel personally that he was brought out of Egypt was stressed.

During NT times large crowds, including Greeks, attended the celebration (John 12:20; Jos., War VI. ix. 3). Jesus was a participant in the celebration (Luke 2:42; John 2:13; 6:4; 11:5) and was Himself crucified during the Passover season (John 13:1). Peter's imprisonment and deliverance was also at this season (Acts 12:3 RSV; KJV "Easter").

In Pauline thought the Passover is used fig. when Christ our Passover Lamb is said to have been sacrificed and when the disposing of the leaven is allegorized to signify the casting out of insincerity (1 Cor 5:7).

(2) *Weeks* or *Pentecost* (שבעות ; LXX *ἑορτὴ ἑβδομάδων*; NT: *πεντηκοστή*). This one day festival, thought earlier to have been the "feast of harvest" (Exod 23:16), the "feast of weeks" (34:22) or the "feast of firstfruits" (Num 28:26), is named from the fact that its date is set by counting from the sabbath of Passover to the morrow after the seventh sabbath (Lev 23:15ff.; cf. Tobit 2:1: "the feast of Pentecost which is the sacred festival of the seven weeks"). Two loaves of bread and seven lambs one year old, one bullock and two rams made up the special offering of the day. No laborious work was to be done. A free-will offering was to be made, and there was to be rejoicing with family and with the unfortunate classes of the community: the Levite, widow, orphan, and sojourner (Deut 16:9-12).

A memorial significance was given to the Feast of Weeks by the rabbis by the 2nd cent. A.D. when they designated it as the time the law was given at Sinai (T. B. *Pesahim* 68b), but the connection is not made in Scripture. The *Book of Jubilees* puts all the covenants it can find in the OT on the day of the Feast of Weeks. The Qumran Community celebrated the renewal of the covenant on the Feast of Weeks.

An ambiguity in the instructions for the day was the occasion of debate between the Pharisees and the Sadducees. The former argued that "Sabbath" (Lev 23 means the first day of Passover without regard to the day of the week (Mishna *Haggigah* 2:4). Thereby for them Pentecost could fall on any day of the week. The Sadducees (Boethusians) argued that "Sabbath" has its regular meaning in the passage and thereby Pentecost must fall on the first day of the week (cf. *M. Menahoth* 10:3; *Haggigah* 2:4).

The outpouring of the Spirit (Acts 2), took place on Pentecost and thereby the day acquired additional meaning as the beginning day of the Church. Paul hoped to extend his stay in Ephesus until Pentecost (1 Cor 16:8), but sought to be in Jerusalem at that season in a later year (Acts 20:16).

(3) *Booths* or *Tabernacles* (חג הסכות ; LXX *ἑορτὴ σκηνῶν*). The Feast of Booths or Ingatherings fell on the fifteenth of the seventh month, five days after the Day of Atonement, and occupied seven days (Exod 23:16, 17; 34:22). The first and eighth days were days of rest. Branches of palm trees, leafy trees, and willows along with fruit of goodly trees were used to make the booth in which the Israelite dwelt seven days—"That your generations may know that I made the Israelites dwell in booths when I brought them out of the land of Egypt" (Lev 23:33-43). There was rejoicing with family, servants, widows, orphans, Levite, and sojourner of the community (Deut 16:13-15). Special sacrifices for this season totaled seventy bulls. Each seventh year there was the public reading of the law (31:9-13).

The returned exiles observed this feast under

Ashurbanipal feasting with his Queen in the royal garden (660 B.C.) ©*B.M.*

Darius (Ezra 3:4) and in the time of Ezra at which time Ezra read the law and led the people in acts of penitence. The celebration is said to be different from anything done since the days of Joshua (Neh 8:13-18). Zechariah 14: 16-19 envisions all nations coming up to Jerusalem year by year to keep the Feast of Tabernacles. The punishment for those who neglect it is that upon them no rain shall fall, but in the case of Egypt the inundation of the Nile would fail.

The Feast of Tabernacles was participated in by Jesus (John 7:2, 8ff.). Josephus calls it the holiest and greatest of the Heb. feasts (Antiq. VIII. iv. 1). Both Josephus (Antiq. III. x. 4; XIII. xiii. 5) and the Mishna (*Sukkah*) enlarge upon the customs of the later observance, one chief feature of which was a libation of water drawn from the fountain of Siloam. This practice furnishes a likely background for Jesus' discourse on living water (John 7:37-39).

(4) *The Day of Atonement* (יום הכפרים ; LXX ἡμέρα ἐξιλασμοῦ) fell on the tenth day of the seventh month, Tishri (Lev 23:27-32; Num 29:7-11). Its ritual, which included the expiation for the priest and for the people and the sending away of the goat for Azazel, is described in Leviticus 16:8, 10, 26. It was a day of rest and fasting.

(5) *The New Year's Day* (ראש השפה, beginning of the year; LXX πρῶτος μῆν, first month). One of the most debated questions in current study is that of whether or not there was a New Year's Day celebration in ancient Israel. Beginning with an analogy with the Babylonian *Akitu* festival which fell in the spring of the year and celebrated the renewal of creation and kingship of Marduk, it is postulated by many scholars that in Israel *Yahweh* was crowned annually at the "New Year Feast of *Yahweh*." Mowinckel argued that the "enthronement psalms" (Pss 47, 93, 96-99) in which "*Yahweh* reigns" prominently occurs were a part of the liturgy of the day. Out of these concepts it is thought that Israel's messianic and eschatological thought developed. It is argued that Jeroboam introduced a festival in the eighth month, similar to the one held in Judah, in order that the people not be attracted to Jerusalem (1 Kings 12:32).

Opponents of the theory point out the difficulty of explaining how a spring festival got shifted to fall. Exodus 12:2 points to Nisan one as the beginning of the year. While there are special offerings on the first of the seventh month, a convocation was held in which no laborious work was done, trumpets were blown, and an offering made to the Lord (Lev 23:24-27; Num 29:1-6), the text says nothing specific about the New Year's day. The postexilic gathering on the first of the seventh month is not said to be a day of high feast (Neh 8:1), and the one occurrence of *rosh hasshanah* in Scripture (Ezek 40:1) describes a vision on the tenth of the month and not one on the first. The observance of such a feast also goes unmentioned in the Apoc., Josephus, and Philo, but is the subject of a Mishna tractate *Rosh Ha-Shanah*.

b. Postexilic festivals. Two non-pentateuchal festivals were prominent in late Judaism:

(1) Purim (פורים ; LXX φρουραὶ, *lots*) has its origin in the deliverance wrought by Esther (Esth 9:16ff.) and falls on the fourteenth of Adar (roughly March) by those in villages and unwalled towns and on the fifteenth by those in fortified cities (Esth 9:18, 19; Jos. Antiq. XI. vi. 13). The name is explained as

coming from the lot (*pur*) which Haman planned to cast to destroy the Jews. The observance of the festival is first attested by 2 Maccabees 15:36 where it is called the "Day of Mordecai." There is no mention of any religious observance connected with the day. In later observance the Book of Esther was read in the Synagogue amidst rejoicing, and food and presents were sent to friends; see Mishna *Megilla.*

(2) *Hanukkah* or *Dedication* (חנכה ; LXX *αἱ ἡμέραι τοῦ ἐγκαινισμοῦ τοῦ θυσιαστηρίου*, the days of the dedication of the altar; NT, *τὰ ἐγκαίνια*). Following the victories of Judas Maccabeus in 167 B.C. a celebration of eight days commemorating the rededication of the Temple, whose worship had been interrupted three years, was instituted (1 Macc 4:41-49; 2 Macc 10:6-8). The festival begins on the 25th of Kislev (December) and one additional candle is lighted each day until a total of eight is reached (*T. B. Sabbath* 21b). Josephus (Antiq. XII. vii. 7) calls it "lights" (*Phota*). There was no partial or total abstention from ordinary occupation nor was there a holy convocation at the beginning and end. Jesus was once in Jerusalem at this season (John 10:22).

After 160 B.C. Nicanor's day was celebrated on the thirteenth of Adar commemorating the victory over the Syrian general (1 Macc 13:51-52).

4. *Periodic Festivals.* a. SABBATICAL YEAR (שבת שבתון לארץ ; LXX *σάββατα ἀνάπαυσις ἔσται τῇ γῇ*, "a sabbath of rest will be to the land"). Each seventh year brought a cessation of agricultural activity and a release from debt. That the land might have its required rest, exile was threatened for neglect of the observance (Exod 23:10, 11; Lev 25:1-7; Deut 15:1). At the Feast of Booths there was the public reading of the law (Deut 31:10ff.).

b. JUBILEE (יובל ; LXX *ἀφέσεως σημασία*, "sign of release"). At the Day of Atonement of the forty-ninth year the sounding of a trumpet marked the onset of the Jubilee year as a period of freedom (*darom*) in the land. Property returned to its original owners. There was a price adjustment in sales in view of its approach. Sowing and reaping was forbidden (Lev 25:8-17). The *Book of Jubilees* is built around this custom, but uses a different system of calculation from that in Scripture.

II. NEW TESTAMENT

A. Jewish festivals. Allusions to the Sabbath, Passover, Unleavened Bread (Matt 26:17; Mark 14:1; Luke 22:1; John 7:2), Feast of Tabernacles, Dedication (10:22) and Pentecost (Acts 2) may be seen under the appropriate heading in the above discussion. The parents of Jesus observed Passover when He was a child (Luke 2:42) and during His public ministry Jesus may have attended as many as four Passovers (John 4:45; 5:1; 6:4; 12:1ff.). To the last of these Greeks also came (12:20). Pilate had a custom of releasing a prisoner at the feast (Matt 27:15; Mark 15:6).

THE JEWISH SACRED YEAR

MONTH		SPECIAL DAYS
Nisan	(April)	14 — Passover 15 — Unleavened Bread 21 — Close of Passover
Iyar	(May)	
Sivan	(June)	6 — Feast of Pentecost — seven weeks after the Passover (Anniversary of the giving of the law on Mt. Sinai)
Tammuz	(July)	
Ab	(August)	
Elul	(September)	
Tishri	(October)	1 & 2 — The Feast of Trumpets *Rosh Hashanah,* beginning of the civil year 10 — Day of Atonement 15-21 — Feast of Tabernacles
Marchesvan	(November)	
Kislev	(December)	25 — Feast of Lights, Dedication, *Hanukkah*
Tebeth	(January)	
Shebet	(February)	
Adar	(March)	14 — The Feast of Purim

Pan for baking unleavened bread used in Passover celebration.

The festivals were sources of allegorical interpretation for the NT writers. Christ our Passover Lamb has been sacrificed (1 Cor 5:7ff.). Sabbaths, new moons, and festival days are mere shadows of good things to come (Col 2:16, 17). The epistle to the Hebrews allegorizes the rest of the people of God to be the eternal rest (Heb 4:1ff.) and the ceremony of the Day of Atonement forms the basis for the presentation of the work of Christ as our High Priest (Heb 8:1ff.).

B. Other feasts. 1. *Social occasions.* Jesus denounced the Pharisees for seeking the uppermost seats at feasts (Matt 23:6; Mark 12:39; Luke 20:46). Levi entertained Jesus and His friends at a great feast after he was called to discipleship (Luke 5:29). Jesus suggested that the poor should be invited rather than rich friends when one gives a feast (Luke 14:13). Jesus attended the marriage feast in Cana (John 2:8ff.).

2. *Pagan feasts.* In Corinth, because of food sacrificed to idols, a problem faced the Christian as to whether or not he could attend pagan feasts. Paul grants the right to go and eat whatever is set out asking no questions for conscience sake (1 Cor 10:27).

3. *Love feast.* Certain characters with heretical tendencies are said to be blots in the "love feasts" (ASV and RSV) or "feasts of charity" (KJV—the *agapē* Jude 12).

C. The marriage feast. The marriage feast (γάμος, *marriage*) or the banquet (δεόπνον, *supper*) is the background theme of the parables of Jesus: the ten virgins (Matt 25:1ff.), the marriage of the king's son (22:2ff.), and the great supper (Luke 14:15ff.). Jesus compared His relation to the disciples to that of the bridegroom and his friends (Matt 9:15; Mark 2:19; Luke 5:34); while John the Baptist spoke of himself as only the friend of the bridegroom (John 3:29). The Book of Revelation climaxes with the invitation to the marriage supper of the Lamb (Rev 19:9). The background for this concept was laid in the prophets (Isa 25:6) and is closely related to the messianic banquet of rabbinic thought at which the righteous would dine on behemoth and leviathan. A disciple's exclamation, "Blessed is he who shall eat bread in the kingdom of God!" (Luke 14:15) called forth the parable of the great supper. The universality of the Gospel may be expressed in terms of a feast in which many from the E and the W will eat with Abraham, Isaac, and Jacob (Matt 8:11; Luke 13:29). The entire Christian life may be called a feast (1 Cor 5:8).

D. The eschatological banquet. In the prophets already the figure of speech in which God's judgment on a people as a sacrificial banquet is expounded (Isa 34:5ff.; Ezek 39:17-20). This inversion of the concept of a banquet in the Apocalypse when the birds are invited to enjoy the great supper of God is the counterpart of the messianic banquet (Rev 19:17ff.).

BIBLIOGRAPHY. G. F. Moore, *Judaism* (1927), II, 40-54; J. Pedersen, *Israel* (1940), IV, 377, 378; N. H. Snaith, *The Jewish New Year Festival* (1947); E. Auerbach, "Die Feste im alten Israel," VT, VIII (1958), 1-18; 337-343; S. J. Schultz, *The Old Testament Speaks* (1960), 68ff.; R. de Vaux, *Ancient Israel* (1961), 468-517; S. Mowinkel, *The Psalms in Israel's Worship* (1962), I, 106-189.

J. P. LEWIS

FEET, WASHING. *See* FOOT WASHING.

FELIX, ANTONIUS ăn tō′ nĭ əs fe′ lĭks (Αντωνιος Φῆλιξ). Antonius Felix was a freedman of Antonia, the mother of the emperor Claudius, and brother of the same prince's freedman and favorite, Pallas. A social reject through the formative years of his life, Claudius had fallen into the company of the freedmen of the imperial household, and it was inevitable that they should play a large part in the affairs of the principate, a situation which naturally roused the aristocratic scorn of such writers as Tacitus. It was the influence of Pallas which secured the appointment of Felix to the governorship of Judaea. Tacitus' dislike for both freedmen betrayed him into carelessness over detail in two vital chapters of the *Annals* (12:53, 54), and raised a problem of dating which at present defies final solution. Felix would naturally have been appointed to the governorship of Judaea after the recall of Ventidius Cumanus in A.D. 52. Tacitus, prob. misinformed, and finding closer research in a context so repugnant distasteful, seems to suggest some overlap between two procuratorships with Felix in au-

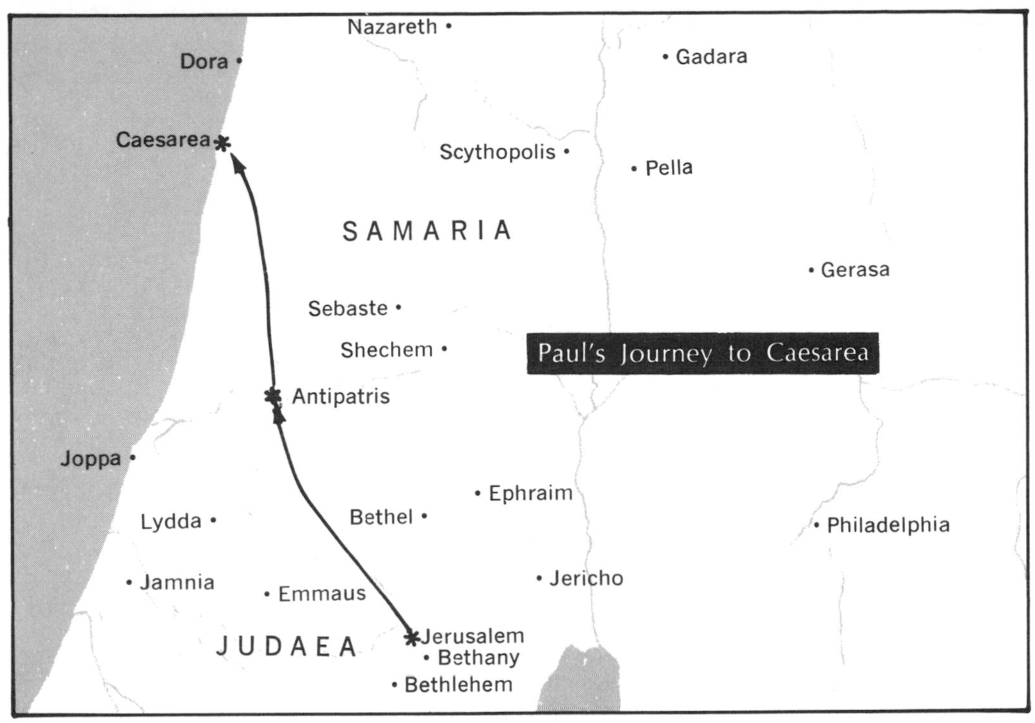

thority in Samaria and Cumanus in Galilee. There is certainly a discrepancy between the account in Tacitus and that given by Josephus (B. J. 2:12; Antiq. X:6.8), a discrepancy which ampler detail might easily remove.

Unreliable though Tacitus' account is, it is worth examining in some detail for the lurid light it throws on Felix's character and reputation. After some acid comment on honors paid by the Senate to Pallas, Tacitus proceeds in his next chapter (12:54) to show how Felix found protection from the consequences of his corruption and misrule under his powerful brother's shadow. The Jews, says the historian, were still in a state of excitement and resentment over Caligula's narrowly averted plan to defile Jehovah's Temple with his own statue. The situation was wantonly exploited by Cumanus in Judaea, and Felix in Samaria. The pair of scoundrels had connived at an almost open conflict between the rival communities, and to have claimed a share in the loot. The situation so cynically permitted got out of hand, and savage repression by both governors provoked the intervention of Quadratus, the governor of Syria, and in consequence the nearest commander with sufficient military strength at his disposal to impose a forcible solution on the distracted area. It was a further illustration of the difficulties which beset the Romans' persistent attempt to hold Palestine with the token force which was based at Caesarea, and of the fumbling and too often corrupt rule, of the minor officials who filled up the sorry list of procurators. Quadratus himself was heavily impeded by circumstances. Hesitating to deal with the influential Felix, the legate placed the full blame on Cumanus, with the result that Felix succeeded to the vacant procuratorship. Details and dating may remain uncertain, but Tacitus' laconic account is illustration vivid enough of another comment he made concerning Felix as a governor. He described him in the *Histories* (5:9) as "a master of cruelty and lust who exercised the powers of a king in the spirit of a slave." Such is the truth which emerges from the garbled story. According to Josephus, Cumanus was sole procurator in A.D. 48, and Felix in A.D. 52, which is an oversimplification. It is a fair guess that Felix, by his brother's favor, exercised some commission in Pal. under Claudius, and perhaps used his position to entangle Cumanus in administrative difficulties, and replace him. Such was the stage-setting of corruption and misrule in Pal. in the decade before the savage outbreak of the Great Rebellion. The state of the country under the rule of Felix is illustrated by the fact that the military commandant of the Jerusalem garrison found it necessary to provide an escort of 470 troopers to secure the safe convoy of one political prisoner down the guerilla-ridden mountain road from Jerusalem to Caesarea. The countryside must have been in a state of near anarchy. In Luke's account of the examination of Paul by Felix in the Rom. garrison town, the procurator appeared true to form. With him was Drusilla, the Herodian girl whom he had enticed from her royal husband, Aziz of Emesa. His disregard for Rom.

justice and his avarice are visible in the story. Such was the scoundrel before whom the apostle to the Gentiles preached of "righteousness, self-control, and the judgment to come" (Acts 24:25 ASV), and who put the consideration of such matters off until a more "convenient season." Nero recalled Felix in A.D. 57 or 58. Dates again become a difficulty. Nothing is known of his subsequent fate.

E. M. BLAIKLOCK

FELLOES fĕl' ōs (גַּב, *curve*; tr. *felloes* KJV, 1 Kings 7:33; *rim* RSV). The rims of the wheels on the ten brass lavers in Solomon's Temple. In Ezekiel 1:18 *gab* is used for the rims of the four wheels beside the four living creatures.

FELLOW fĕl' ō (חָבֵר, *companion*; רֵעַ, *friend*; עָמִית, *associate*; Gr. πλησιον, *neighbor*; μέτοχος, *partner*).

In Heb. the word sometimes tr. "fellow" include the basic *rēa*. The feminine of this word has been tr. "fellow" in Judges 11:37. In the following v. it is tr. "companion." Also the form *hábēr* alternates between the tr. "companion" and "fellow" as in Psalm 45:7; Isaiah 44:11 and Ezekiel 37:19. "Knit together as one man" is one expression comprehending the deeper significance of the word. Another Heb. form *amith* (Zech 13:7) may have a more abstract meaning as "man of my fellowship."

The Gr. forms include *plēsion* used in the feminine, but tr. "fellow"; and *métochos* (Heb 1:9), a quotation from Psalm 45:7, used in the sense of *companion*.

Another basic use of the word relates "fellow" to a person or persons, and often is used as an expression of contempt. The Heb. *ĭsh* (1 Sam 29:4) is at times tr. "fellow." The demonstrative *zĕh* (this) is also used to express contempt.

W. H. JOHNSON

FELLOWSHIP (κοινωνία, *association, communion*; μετοχή, *sharing, participation*).

The meaningful words *koinōnīa* and *metochē* are among the most powerful concepts in the Judeo-Christian Scriptures. They apply first of all to participation in a person or project and a "common" spirit. Christians share "the divine nature" (2 Pet 1:4). Fellowship in the family of God comes after the new birth (2 Cor 5:17; 1 John 3:9). Christians partake of Christ (Heb 3:14), and of the Holy Spirit (6:4).

True fellowship results in mutual love (John 13:34). A "common salvation" (Jude 3) and a "common faith" (Titus 1:4) characterize true Christians.

The significant tr. "communicate" touches the heart of the Christian spirit (Gal 6:6). He that is taught in the Word is admonished to "communicate." Fellowship exists when there is community. This was an essential strength of the early Christians. Although a minority movement, they shared the strength of belonging to each other and to God.

Where there are positive factors of "koinōnīa" there are also negative factors. These NT concepts are complementary. A Christian has no genuine "fellowship" with an unbeliever (2 Cor 6:14-16). Natures of unbelievers are different. They are children of the devil (1 John 3:10-12). Pagan ceremonies are not a part of true *koinōnīa* (1 Cor 10:20-22). Christians should have no "fellowship" with unfruitful works of darkness (Eph 5:11).

True NT *koinōnīa* is rooted in a depth of fellowship with God as Father (1 John 1:3, 6). The Fatherhood of God has significance for those who are in the family of God through the new birth.

Christians must continue to walk in the light to enjoy this fellowship. They are called to fellowship with the Son (1 Cor 1:9). The Lord's supper is a symbol of this inner fellowship (10:16).

Fellowship with the Spirit is a blessing of Christians (2 Cor 13:14).

The true *koinōnīa* is not only earthly, but continues and is consummated in heaven (Eph 2:21; Rev 21:1-4).

Some have regarded the "fellowship" (κοινωνία) of Acts 2:42 as primarily a "communism" anticipating the Marxist philosophy and economy. It would, however, seem to be a healthy balance of four elements: "teaching" or doctrine; "fellowship" in social and spiritual sharing; "breaking bread," ceremonies or rites such as the eucharist, and "prayers," devotional sharing.

W. H. JOHNSON

FELSPAR (FELDSPAR) fĕl' spar, the name of the most important group of rock-forming minerals. The feldspars are alumino-silicates of potassium, sodium, calcium or barium and are generally white, gray or pale shades of orange-red. Green feldspar (Exod 28:17; 39:10; Ezek 28:13, NEB) is generally a variety of the potassium feldspar, microcline. This is referred to as amazonstone and is sometimes cut and polished as an ornamental stone. Amazonstone occurs in the Ilmen Mts. and at other points in the Urals, in Italy and in the gem-bearing pegmatites of Madagascar.

FEMALE (נקבה ; אשה ; θῆλυς). Female designates that grouping of any species which has the capacity to produce ova and bear offspring. The female is differentiated from the male whose biological function it is to produce sperm and implant it in the ova.

The Biblical account of creation presents the idea that the biological differences between the sexes is the consequence of God's creative activity (Gen 1:1, 2, 4). The Hebrews were aware early that sex relations between males and females were necessary for reproduction (1:28; 7:1-5). The beautiful account of the creation of the female of the human kind

(2:18-24) has often been interpreted to indicate the inferiority of women. Not so! Rather, the female is pictured as helper, an integral part of man, the one with whom is experienced wholeness and completeness (2:23, 24). Anyone who has had a good marriage knows that this is the case.

Of course, the Bible partakes of the "male superiority" complex present in its culture. The account of the Fall (3:1-19) pictures the female as being the first tempted and the one who, in turn, carried the temptation to the male. To blame women for the entrance of sin into the world, as some naïvely have done, was rejected by God long ago (3:14). The prophetic utterance concerning the future relation between male and female (3:16) need not be taken as a proof text for male superiority. God may have been declaring what would happen because of sin entering the world, but not sanctioning it.

Although women appear in significant roles throughout the OT (Exod 2:1-9; 15:21; Num 12; Judg 4, 5; 1 Sam 1:1, 2, 11; Prov 31), the tenor of the accounts is that of females being subordinate. The law casts females in a secondary position also (Exod 21:7-11; Num 5:26, 27; 30:3-5; Deut 21:10-14; 22:20-22).

In the NT Paul seems to have accepted the cultural idea of the inferiority of women (1 Cor 7:11, 14; Eph 5; 1 Tim 2:12). However, it is to be noted that these references appear in the practical sections of his letters dealing with specific problems and may be instances of accommodation. His lone reference to females in the theological sections (Gal 3:28) announces the principle of the equality of the sexes. The Church has been slow in putting this principle into practice. Currently it is being challenged to do so by the Women's Liberation Movement. Among the questions which they are raising are these: Does the creation story teach the inferiority of women? Is God male? Are men and women essentially different? Or are these differences culturally determined?

BIBLIOGRAPHY. H. Luering, "Female," ISBE (1915), 1106; J. O. Hertzler, *The Social Thought of the Ancient Civilizations* (1936); D. S. Bailey, *Sexual Relations in Christian Thought* (1959), 293-303; G. Farley, "The Saint Paul Hang Up," *The Student* (April 1971), 30f.

G. E. FARLEY

FENCE (גָּדֵר, *fence*, Ps 62:3; גְּדֵרָה, KJV HEDGE, NEB WALL, Nah 3:17). It is used of an enclosing wall made of stone. The psalmist (62:3) speaks of his oppressors as a "tottering fence," i.e. ready to fall over. Dahood (*The Anchor Bible*, vol. 17, pp. 89, 92) sees this expression referring to those who are a "menace to the community" because of indulging in gossip. The leaders of Nineveh are likened to "clouds of locusts settling on the fences" (Nah 3:17).

M. R. WILSON

FENCED CITY (usually FORTIFIED CITY in RSV). Technical term for walled cities and walled villages in KJV OT. Heb. words are *"mĭb-ṣär"* (*inaccessible place*), *"bä-ṣōōr"* (*inaccessible*), and *"me-ṣōō-rä"* (*fortified place*). Other words which can designate a fortified city or village are *"mä-'ōz"* ("place of strength"; Isa 23:14; Dan 11:31) and *"me-ṣōō-dä"* ("place difficult to approach"; 2 Sam 5:7) though both more typically refer to a purely military stronghold.

A. C. BOWLING

FERRET fer' it (אֲנָקָה, *ferret* RJV; GECKO ASV, RSV Lev 11:30 only). The tr. "ferret" is not correct. *See* discussion under LIZARD.

FERRY-BOAT. *See* SHIPS AND BOATS.

FERTILE CRESCENT. This term refers to that stretch of land beginning at the Persian Gulf,

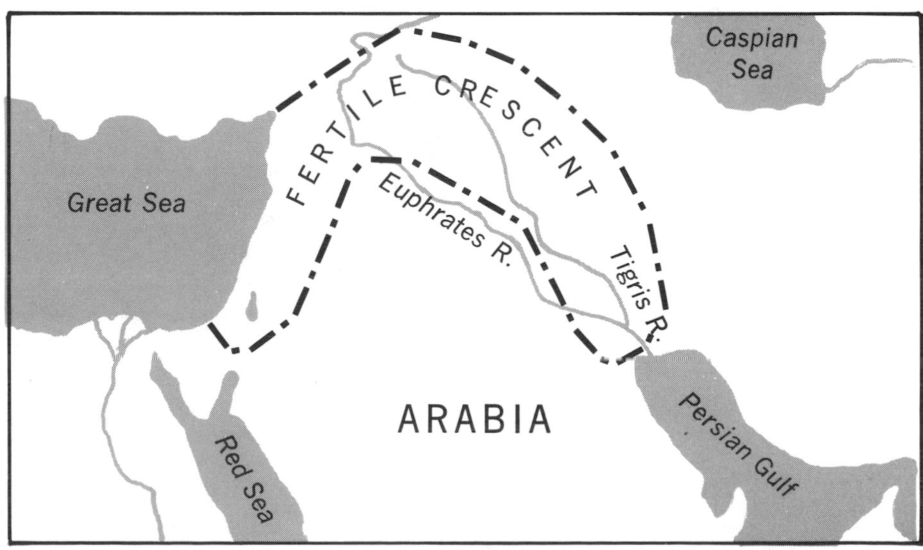

extending NW through the Tigris and Euphrates River Valley, continuing W to the NE coast of the Mediterranean Sea, turning S through Canaan, and (popularly) including the Nile River Valley. The area described is in the form of a crescent and is very fertile although the area the arc encloses is barren. The earliest records of civilization come from this area, and it was the center of civilization until the age of Greece. Egypt at the western tip, as well as Assyria and Babylonia in the E, developed in power and influence while the coastland at the E end of the Mediterranean developed commercially, but was often subjected to invading armies from either end. It is in this crossroads of humanity that God chose to place His people Israel and later to send His Son.

BIBLIOGRAPHY. L. H. Grollenberg, *Atlas of the Bible* (1956), 11ff.

C. P. WEEBER

Fertility cult objects. ©*Kelso*

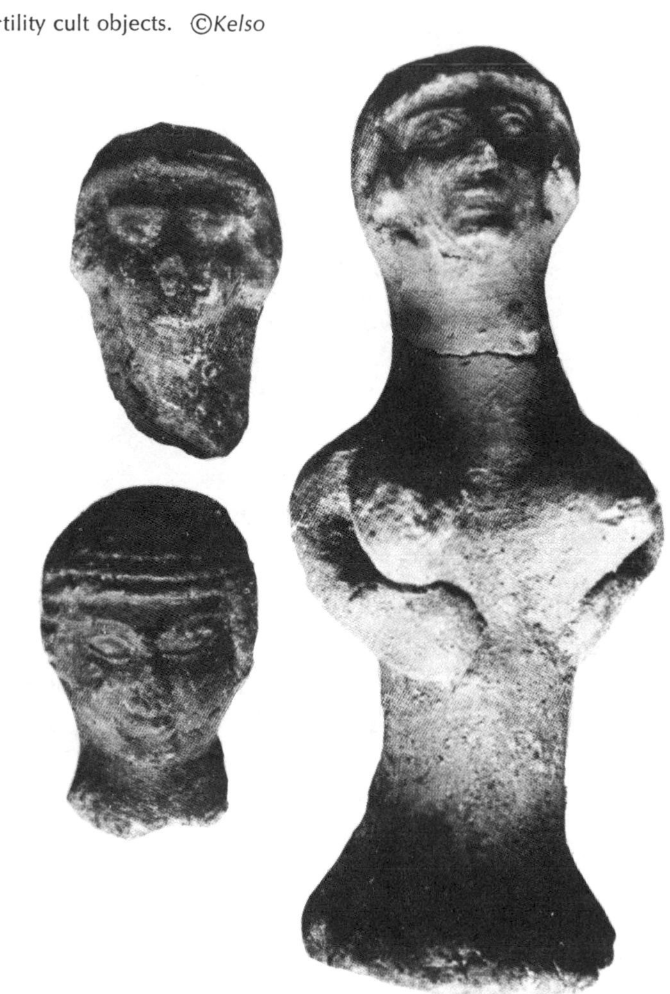

FERTILITY CULTS. Since the classic work of James G. Frazer in 1906 it has been widely held that a number of cults promoted the fertility of men, animals, and crops by celebrating the myth of a dying-and-rising god with rites of mourning and of later jubilation. The god was believed to typify the death and renewal of vegetation. A "sacred marriage" between the god, represented by the king, and the goddess, represented by a hierodule, also was believed to promote the fertility of the land. The sacred prostitution of Astarte and of Aphrodite also was directed to this end.

In Egypt Osiris was killed by his brother Seth, but was revived by his wife Isis. From the Egyp. Empire to the Ptolemaic period Osiris was associated with germinating grain. The Egyp. dead also were identified with Osiris as the prototype of "resurrection." In Mesopotamia the Sumer. Dumuzi (the Akkad. Tammuz) was originally a king of Erech, who was deified as the consort of the goddess Inanna (the Akkad. Ishtar). Although the text of the myth, "Inanna's (or Ishtar's) Descent to the Netherworld" is missing, it has been widely assumed that the goddess descended in order to resurrect her lover. Laments for Tammuz are well-known, as well as some "sacred marriage" love songs. In the Greco-Rom. period the youthful Adonis, beloved of Aphrodite, was mourned in Byblos in Lebanon. Adonis was slain by a boar in midsummer. Seeds sown in pots, known as "the gardens of Adonis," were cast into the sea or in wells. In Asia Minor, Attis, the consort of Cybele, met death by castration. The priests of Cybele, the famous Magna Mater, were castrated eunuchs.

In Greece the figure representing the dying vegetation was the goddess Persephone or Kore, whose abduction into Hades was mourned by her mother Demeter. Mysteries of Kore were celebrated at Eleusis. Some scholars have suggested that similar mysteries promising immortality were celebrated for various dying-and-rising gods, and further, that the resurrection of Christ and the preaching of Paul are in some measure dependent upon these mysteries.

The only explicit reference to any of these gods is found in Ezekiel 8:14: "Then he brought me to the entrance of the north gate of the house of the LORD; and behold, there sat women weeping for Tammuz." The Jewish month of June-July still is called Tammuz. But this prob. lost its original significance just as we no longer associate Rom. fertility rites with the month of February. "The plants of pleasantness" in Isaiah 17:10 have been interpreted as "Adonis gardens," and Hosea 7:14 has been considered to refer to ritual wailing for grain.

Other scholars have gone further in seeing the fertility-cult background as the key to the interpretation of a number of books of the OT. They argue that the Canaanite fertility cult was transmitted to Israel when the prophets exalted Yahweh as the god of the sacred marriage in place of Baal. They interpret the imagery of Jehovah and Israel as His bride as being derived from the fertility cult. Meek comments on Canticles as a Tammuz liturgy, and Gaster sees in numerous Psalms and in Joel the seasonal pattern of God's victory over His cosmic foes. Indeed, H. G. May went so far as to derive the concepts of immortality, of the suffering servant, and of the fatherhood of God from the fertility-cult background of popular Heb. religion.

In the NT Paul warned the Corinthians against the defilement of their bodies in relation with the sacred prostitutes of Aphrodite. Paul's harsh words of Galatians 5:12 concerning the Judaizers may have been an allusion to the self-mutilation of the priests of Cybele. Jerome reports that Hadrian (A.D. 135) deliberately desecrated the birthplace of Jesus at Bethlehem by consecrating it to the worship of Adonis/Tammuz.

Many scholars from Reitzenstein to Bultmann have compared the Resurrection of Christ to the resurrection of such figures as Attis, Adonis, or Osiris, and have attributed some of Paul's teachings to a dependence upon pagan mysteries.

Recent studies tend to undermine seriously the Frazerian thesis of a generically similar series of fertility cults, on the one hand, and the thesis of the dependence of Christianity upon the pagan mysteries, on the other hand.

Studies by Kramer indicate that no cuneiform text speaks explicitly of the resurrection of Dumuzi/Tammuz. A fragmentary passage does imply that Tammuz spent half the year in the underworld with his sister taking his place for the other half year. Frankfort has pointed out that Osiris is not a "dying" god but a "dead" god; he reigns as the mummy-clad king of the dead. Lambrechts has shown that the evidence for the deity and the resurrection of both Attis and Adonis do not antedate the late 2nd cent. A.D. Wagner has demonstrated that in many cases the alleged mysteries of the fertility gods are dubiously attested, and that Christianity is not dependent upon the pagan mysteries.

BIBLIOGRAPHY. A. *General*: W. Baudissin, *Adonis und Esmun* (1911); J. G. Frazer, *Adonis, Attis, Osiris,* 3rd ed. (1914); H. Frankfort, *Kingship and the Gods* (1948); P. Lambrechts, "Les Fêtes 'phrygiennes' de Cybèle et d'Attis," *Bulletin de l'Institut Historique Belge de Rome,* XXVII (1952), 141-170; *id.*, "La 'résurrection' d'Adonis," *Annuaire de l'Institut de philologie et d'histoire orientales et slaves,* XIII (1953), 207-240. B. *Fertility-Cult Interpretations of the Bible*: T. Meek, "Babylonian Parallels to the Song of Songs," JBL, XLIII (1924), 242-252; *id.*, "The Song of Songs and the Fertility Cult," in *The Song of Songs*, ed. Wilfred Schoff (1924), 48-79; H. G. May, "The Fertility Cult in Hosea," AJSL, XLVIII (1932), 73-98; T. Meek, "The Song of Songs," *The Interpreter's Bible* (1956), vol. V; T. H. Gaster, *Thes-*

pis, 2nd ed. (1961); S. N. Kramer, "The Biblical 'Song of Songs' and the Sumerian Love Songs," *Expedition,* V (1962), 25-31; *id., The Sacred Marriage Rite* (1969). C. *Criticisms of the Fertility-Cult Interpretations*: H. H. Rowley, "The Song of Songs: An Examination of Recent Theory," *Journal of the Royal Asiatic Society* (April, 1938), 251-276; E. M. Yamauchi, "Cultic Clues in Canticles?" ETSB, IV (1961), 80-88; *id.,* "Tammuz and the Bible," JBL, LXXXIV (1965), 283-290; G. Wagner, *Pauline Baptism and the Pagan Mysteries* (1967); B. Metzger, "Methodology in the Study of the Mystery Religions and Early Christianity," in *Historical and Literary Studies: Pagan, Jewish and Christian* (1968), 1-24.

E. M. YAMAUCHI

FESTAL GARMENT, FESTAL ROBE (חלפות שמלת, or חליפות בגדים, *festal garment*; KJV, CHANGE OF RAIMENT or GARMENTS; NEB, CHANGE OF CLOTHING). Though literally "change of clothes" the context often implies a (costly) gift and thus "festal garment" or clothing worn on special occasions (see Gen 45:22; Judg 14:12, 13, 19; 2 Kings 5:5, 22, 23). Another term, "festal robe" (מחלצה), is used for the robes of Jerusalem's "society women" (Isa 3:22, KJV "changeable suits of apparel"). Translated "rich apparel" (KJV, "change of raiment") for the high priest's garment in Zechariah 3:4.

M. R. WILSON

FESTIVAL(S). *See* FEASTS; FASTS.

FESTUS, PORCIUS pôr′ shəs fĕs′ təs (Φῆστος). Of Porcius Festus' life prior to his appointment to Antonius Felix' vacant procuratorship nothing is known. The date is variously given as A.D. 57, 58, 59 and 60. The discrepancy can manifestly be much narrowed. The time of the year is nowhere mentioned, nor is any gap specified between official nomination and taking office. Months of traveling time are also involved. If the date was more certain, valuable aid toward a firm chronology for Paul would be given. Nothing more than this is involved. Festus died early in his tenure of office, so the one glimpse afforded of him is the scene of his examination of Paul at Caesarea, and his consultation with Agrippa II. It is an interesting view of a minor Rom. governor at work in a most difficult situation. Festus, a welcome contrast, according to Josephus (Jos. Antiq. XX, viii, 9; XX, ix, 1), to his vicious predecessor, and to the equally corrupt Albinus who succeeded him in the procuratorship, had inherited a load of trouble from Felix' maladministration. There was a shocking breakdown of law and order in the countryside, and open armed hostility between the rival factions in the hierarchy. It was the first foreshadowing of the fearful internecine strife which was to add unprecedented venom to the ordeal of the coming rebellion, now a brief six or seven years away. Festus knew that he could not afford to alienate or offend any collaborating elements in the Jewish population, and the problem presented

Porcius Festus was procurator of Caesarea on the Mediterranean Sea. © *J.F.W.*

him by the priestly elements who were determined to be rid of Paul must be weighed and appreciated in this context. Any perceptive governor could see that tension in Pal. was fast mounting toward some sort of climax. Herein lay the difference between Festus' position and that of Pilate some thirty years before, when the same hierarchy had sought to do away with an obviously innocent man. Events had seriously deteriorated in Pal. Nor was Festus damagingly compromised by past mismanagement of the difficult Jews, as Pontius Pilate was. He was none the less under orders to do his utmost to contain an explosive situation, and, in the light of this, A. P. Gould's contention that "Paul's appeal to Caesar is the lasting condemnation of Festus," is without validity. More fortunate than Pilate in his similar conflict of duties and considerations, Festus was offered a way of escape by the prisoner's own action. He offered Paul an acquittal on the major and relevant charge of sedition, and added the proposal, not unreasonable in normal times from the point of view of the occupying power, that the ex-Pharisee should face a religious investigation before his co-religionists. It was a crisis for Paul. Perhaps with fuller information and sharper apprehension than the procurator's, Paul saw the peril of the situation in Judaea, the deepening anarchy, and the looming crisis. He cut the knot, to Festus' relief, by the exercise of his Rom. citizen's right of an appeal to Caesar. Festus was obliged by law to accept the appeal, and did so with alacrity. It solved his major problem, Paul's security. On the other hand, as a new arrival in Pal. Jewish law and Jewish religion were unfamiliar to him. He had a career to make, and the lucidity and correct terminology of a document over his signature addressed to Rome's highest court might have been a matter of deep concern to him. Hence, the eagerness with which Festus availed himself of the aid of Agrippa II, an able man, an indispensable ally of Rome in the mounting difficulties of her rule, and a person with a close acquaintance with both Judaism and Christianity. To honor where convenient the old Herodian house was also a policy as old as Augustus himself. Nowhere else in the records of 1st cent. history is so authentic a document of the empire in political action to be found.

BIBLIOGRAPHY. E. M. Blaiklock, *The Century of the New Testament,* ch. 6 (1962).

E. M. BLAIKLOCK

FETTERS. Originally used for bonds or shackles for the feet; then, by extension, for shackles and bonds in general. Relevant Biblical words are the following: Heb. כבל (*fetters*, Ps 105. 18) refers to foot-fetters as does Gr. πέδη (Mark 5:4). Two words refer to chains used as fetters or bonds: Heb. זקים (Job 36:8) and Gr. ἅλυσις (Acts 28:20). Heb. נחשתים (lit. "two bronzes"; Judg 16:21) was used for the two shackles which bound the two limbs (cf. Eng. usage of "irons" for metal shackles). This word is used for foot-fetters (2 Sam 3:34), but other examples could refer to shackles in general (e.g. 2 Chron 36:6). Greek δεσμός (Luke 8:29) refers to bonds in general. Heb. אסור (Judg 15:14) seems to have equally general application. Two typical types of shackles seen in sculptured figures are the shackles for feet, connected by a short rope which limited the victim's length of stride, and hand shackles connected to the neck by a short rope.

A. BOWLING

FEVER. *See* DISEASE, DISEASES.

FIELD (שׂדה, *open field*; שׂדי, *level place*; ארצ, *land*; בר, *open country*; חוּצ, *out-of-doors*; חלקה, *plot*; שׁדמה, *field*; יגב, *arable field*; ἀγρός, *the open country*; χώρα, *territory belonging to a particular tribe, people*; χωρίον, *a particular locality*). The Heb. word שׂדה is the most commonly used word for "field," and means an unenclosed tract of ground, whether for pasture or tillage, and varying in size from a small area to the territory of a people (Gen 14:7 "country"; 23:9; Ruth 1:6 "country"; Matt 6:28; 13:24). It is sometimes contrasted with what is enclosed, whether a vineyard (Exod 22:5), a garden, or a walled town (Deut 28:3, 16). In some passages the word implies land remote from a house (Gen 4:8) or a settled habitation (24:27).

The separate plots of ground were marked off by stones, which might easily be removed (Deut 19:14), not by fences of any kind. Flocks and herds therefore constantly had to be watched. Fields sometimes received names after remarkable events, as Helkath-Hazzurim ("the field of swords"), or from the use to which they may have been applied, as "Fuller's Field" (Isa 7:3) and "potter's field" (Matt 27:7). *See* AGRICULTURE.

S. BARABAS

FIELD OF BLOOD. *See* AKELDAMA.

FIERY SERPENT. English term (e.g. RSV and KJV) for the desert vipers which attacked the Hebrews in the wilderness as they journeyed around Moab (Num 21:4-9). Their bite was cured miraculously when the victim looked at the Bronze Serpent (q.v.) made by Moses on that occasion. The phrase trs. two Heb. terms: שׂרף (v. 8) and נחשׁ שׂרף (v. 6). These same snakes also are referred to simply as "serpents" (נחשׁ, v. 7).

The Numbers context seems to refer to a poisonous viper living in the desert regions around Biblical Moab. It has been identified tentatively with Heb. אפעה which is, in turn, identified with *Echis carinatus,* "a viper living in sandy plains" ("Serpent," IDB).

In other usages, the term *saraf* refers to legendary creatures (e.g. the flying serpents of Isa 14:29; 30:6) or supernatural angelic beings (e.g. *seraphim* of Isa 6). This raises the possi-

A fig tree with first figs. ©*M.P.S.*

bility that *saraf* is used in Numbers 21:6 not because the term normally designated a particular kind of snake, but rather to emphasize the supernatural, miraculous character of the plague. *See* BRAZEN SERPENT.

BIBLIOGRAPHY. G. E. Post, "Serpent," HDB (1905); F. S. Bodenheimer, "Serpent," IDB (1962).

A. BOWLING

FIG TREE (Heb. תאנה; Gr. σῦκη). Normally, fig or fig tree is *te'ēnâ*, as for instance in Genesis 3:7 and Jeremiah 24, but the Gr. word *sûkon* is used in Matthew 7:17; Mark 11:13-21; Luke 6:43, 44; and James 3:12. The word *paggâ* is used for green or unripe figs in Song of Solomon 2:13, and the Gr. word ὀλύνθος, in Revelation 6:13. Fig tree is *te'ēnâ* in twenty-three vv. in the OT, and *sukē* in sixteen vv. in the NT.

The fig tree is *Ficus carica*. The fruit (σῦκον) is a succulent, enlarged hollow receptacle, containing the flowers inside. The flowers are not seen unless the fruit is cut open. The land of Pal. was described (Deut 8:8) as "a land of . . . vines and fig trees"—those who searched the land (Num 13:23) "brought . . . of the figs."

Again and again the fig tree is used by God to indicate the prosperity of the Jewish nation, (1 Kings 4:25 and Mic 4:4). Figs were made into cakes called *debēlîm*, and cakes of figs were brought to David (1 Chron 12:40), while Abigail gave 200 cakes of figs to David in Hebron (1 Sam 25:18).

Hezekiah is cured of his illness by a "lump" of figs being laid on the boil, presumably as a poultice (2 Kings 20:7; Isa 38:21). The falling or the destruction of figs is used in the Bible to indicate the Lord's judgment. (*See* Isa 34:4; Jer 5:17; 8:13; Hos 2:12; Joel 1:7.)

The fig is mentioned in Genesis 3:7 when Adam and Eve pulled off the leaves in order to make a semblance of a covering—or as Moffatt puts it, a "girdle." This is far more likely than the "breeches" of the Geneva Bible.

There are today in the Holy Land both cultivated varieties of figs and wild figs. Most modern Israeli gardens contain a trained fig tree, and it is foretold in the OT that in the final days every man will sit under his own fig tree. Looked after, the fig can be a thirty ft. tall, strong tree—growing wild, it will straggle uncontrolled over the rocks and stony places.

Figs are shaped generally like pears though there are rounder varieties. At the farthest end from the stalk there is a small aperture through which a pollinating insect, called the fig wasp, may go. When the ripened fig is eaten, the little somewhat gritty seeds are "felt"—these are indeed the true fruits. The fig is the receptacle that holds them.

In the E, the fig tree produces two definite crops of fruits per season. The normal winter figs ripen in May and June and the summer figs in late August and September. Sometimes, one crop overlaps the other. The baby fruit buds are usually seen in February before the leaves appear in April each year.

It is possible to pick fruits over nine or ten months of the year in Pal. In Europe, and esp. in Great Britain, the baby figlets are killed during the winter, and so the first crop is never produced. Fig trees have lived for over 400 years. In the days of Pliny, there actually were six known varieties.

Our Lord condemned a fig tree at Passover time on Mount Olivet (Mark 11:13; Matt 21:19). This tree should have borne early ripe figs. The Lord would have known whether the tree should have been cropping. Moses had said that fruit borne on trees by the wayside could be picked by passers-by.

Young fig trees growing in the drier regions need to be mulched with dung (Luke 13:8). Even today in Pal. fig trees grow in the corners of vineyards. Fig trees must have grown well in Bethphage, which means "house of figs."

A fig tree produces masses of large green leaves and gives ample welcome shade in a hot country. This is the reason one finds a fig planted next to a well. The thick dark shade keeps the water cool. *See* AGRICULTURE.

W. E. SHEWELL-COOPER

FIGURE, the rendering of two Heb. and three Gr. terms. The Heb. סמל, "image" or "idol" is a rare term appearing only in Deuteronomy 4:16; 2 Chronicles 33:7, 15; Ezekiel 8:3, 5. The KJV reads "figure" only in Deuteronomy 4:16, it reads "image" elsewhere. The word has no clear etymology, but a similar root does appear in Phoen. The other term is תבנית, "configuration," "form," or "likeness," used widely but not frequently throughout the OT. It is variously tr. (Exod 25:9, 40) and other passages are rendered "pattern" while only Isaiah 44:13 is read "figure" (in RSV) and elsewhere. The word was applied to any type of engraved, carved or drawn image. It is probable that "image" is the best tr. The NT term most commonly employed is Gr. τύπος, a difficult term used from early Attic times in a number of contexts and varieties of meaning: "mark," "trace of," "copy," "anything formed," "figure," "pattern," "archetype," "example," and even a "symbol." Almost all of these connotations are found in the NT. It is this term which is employed frequently in the LXX to represent the Heb. terms above. The term appears in the gospels only in John 20:25; "the print of the nails" which Thomas required as the ultimate proof for his belief. In the epistles it is used in the sense of "pattern" or "example" of moral conduct (1 Tim 4:12) and as "pattern" or "method of instruction" (Rom 6:17). The most important and characteristic usage is in the sense of an event or personage who fulfills a prophetic prefigurement. Such a connotation is involved in Romans 5:14, et al. The Eng. cognate "type" often has been used to tr. this usage. Another Gr. term παραβολή, is used frequently in the gospels to indicate the form of Jesus' characteristic teaching. It appears also in Hebrews 9:9; 11:19 and is variously tr. by the VSS. The KJV renders it "figure." The notion of "pattern" is not foremost, but the word seems to indicate a fully completed exemplar, a prophetic paradigm. One other term is rendered "figure," but only in Hebrews 9:24. Elsewhere it is tr. "like figure" (1 Pet 3:21). It is a compound of *typos*, Gr. ἀντίτυπος. Such terms are exceedingly difficult and come to be almost primarily Christian in usage. From such involved formulations of the prophetic prefigurement and the fulfilling reality, the whole elaborate system of hermeneutics known as "typology" was developed.

Although the roots of such fig. views were developed in the later Platonic academy, they grew and flourished in the Medieval period. The complex exegesis of the Roman Church sought for manifold levels of meaning in the text of the Scriptures. The "types" of Christ, Mary and the various OT and NT are shown in church art and celebrated in hymns. This interpretation survived the Reformation and appealed to pietist and romanticist alike, and so they have become part of the inheritance of various groups in the modern age. In recent decades types have been less frequent in Biblical studies.

W. White, Jr.

FIGURED STONE. RSV tr. for two related Heb. expressions. From contextual usage, the expressions prob. refer to religious images carved in relief on flat surfaces. "Figured stone" was proscribed along with other pagan cult objects (Lev 26:1; אבן משכית ; KJV "image of stone"). "Figured stones" (Num 33:52 RSV; משכיות ; KJV "pictures"), together with molten images and high places were to be destroyed. In Ezekiel 8:12, the figures (Heb. משכית ; RSV "pictures," KJV "imagery") clearly are "portrayed" on walls (cf. Ezek 8:10; note: the word here tr. "portray" means "to carve" in 1 Kings 6:35). Their idolatrous significance is graphically pictured.

Such contexts recall numerous religious-magical relief figures on walls of Egyp. tombs and temples, Babylonian boundary markers with reliefs of protective deities and their symbols, and most specifically, the N Syrian practice of carving mythological scenes on upright stone slabs.

In Proverbs 25:11, משכית (RSV "setting," KJV "pictures") may refer to gold inlay in silver carved work. Psalm 73:7 (RSV "follies") and Proverbs 18:11 (RSV footnote "imagination") use the same root, but its meaning in these vv. is difficult to discern.

BIBLIOGRAPHY. W. F. Albright, *Archeology and the Religion of Israel* (1941), 160.

A. Bowling

FIGUREHEAD (παράσημος; *sign*, KJV, Acts 28:11). The symbol on the Alexandrian ship's prow upon which Paul sailed toward Rome. The figurehead was of the Twin Brothers (*Dioskouroi*), Castor and Pollux, sons of Zeus, and "good luck" deities of sailors.

FILIGREE. Ornamental work in fine wire. Archeological finds have demonstrated that filigree work was produced throughout the ancient Near E. Egyptian funerary jewelry provides some of the best examples with intricate wire reproductions of divine symbols inlaid with glazed beads and semi-precious stones.

Although the evidence is less than conclusive, Biblical scholars generally agree that some of the gold settings (משבצות ; e.g. Exod 28:13) of the high priest's garments were of gold filigree (e.g. IDB). These are the settings for the two onyx stones of the shoulder pieces of the Ephod (Exod 28:11; 39:6), the two settings on the shoulder pieces for the chains which connected the shoulder pieces with the breast piece (28:13, 14, 25; 39:16-18), and the settings for the twelve precious stones of the breast piece (28:20; 39:13); the former uses a slightly different Heb. form: משבצים .

If the above interpretation is correct, Psalm 45:13b might better be tr. "adorned with golden filigree" instead of "decked . . . with gold-woven robes" (RSV).

BIBLIOGRAPHY. F. C. Toombs, "Filigree," IDB (1962).

A. C. Bowling

FILLET (חשוק) . A band or ring binding the pillars of the Tabernacle, prob. close to the capitals (Exod 36:38). The fillets for the pillars of the court were overlaid with silver (38:10-12, 17, 19), while those for the door pillars were of gold (36:38). The root חשק is obscure, although Aram. חשק does mean "to bind, saddle (an ass)." In 1 Kings 7:33 the cognate *chišûq* means "spokes of a wheel." Some contend that the fillets were in reality rods connecting the tops of the pillars, which supplied greater stability and from which the curtains were suspended. The denominative verb חשק does not decide the issue, meaning "to furnish with fillets (or rings?)." Where Exodus 27:17 says that the pillars were "filleted with silver," the LXX has "cased with silver." There is no solid evidence that rods instead of bands are intended. Exodus 26:32, 37 says nothing about the curtains hanging from rods, whereas hooks are explicitly mentioned. If "bind" or "clasp," rather than "connect," is indeed the basic idea, the "ring" concept is more suitable. Perhaps the hooks were attached to the fillets on the pillars.

חוט, is rendered "fillet" by KJV in Jeremiah 52:21 (RSV "circumference"). It clearly means a "line, thread, cord," which could sometimes be broken easily (Jud 16:12). In this case, it refers to a line used to measure the circumference of the pillars.

BIBLIOGRAPHY. M. Noth, *Exodus* (1962), 217.

H. M. Wolf

FILTH, FILTHINESS, the rendering in the Eng. VSS of a number of terms, usually refers to ceremonial uncleanness or moral depravity and only secondarily to actual dirt. The most common OT term is Heb. תמאה, "ceremonial uncleanness" (Ezek 22:15, et al.). The word is related to a number of others all meaning "defilement" or "to defile." Less common but more graphic is Heb. צאה, צאת, "excretement," possibly cognate to similar terms in other languages for bodily discharges. The term is used of garments and furniture (Isa 4:4; 28:8; et al.) but specifically in the sense of ceremonial impurity. The term אלח appears only in Psalms 14:3; 53:3 and Job 15:16. Its meaning and etymology are obscure, but there is no doubt from the parallel terms that it means "corruption." The only known cognate is an Arab. term which refers to the souring or tainting of milk. The familiar passage in Isaiah 64:6, and possibly Ezekiel 16:6 refer to the female menses. The difficulty of these expressions is indicated by the confusion of usage among the various VSS. In the NT the conception of ceremonial cleanness is not foremost, as in the OT use of such terms. The most common Gr. word is ῥυπόω, "to make dirty," "to defile" (Rev 22:11), the noun ῥύπος, "filth," usually thought to be the oily exudate of a plant such as the hyssop (1 Pet 3:21), and the abstract concept ῥυπαρία "dirt," "filth" often used of moral or ethical depravity (James 1:21). The other more common term is αἰσχρός, "ugly," "shameful" and the like (1 Cor 11:6 et al.). The compounds of this word are exceedingly graphic of man's iniquity; e.g. αἰσχρολόγος, "foulmouthed" (Col 3:8), and αἰσχροκαρδής, "gain obtained by foul means" (1 Tim 3:8). The Scriptures continually use such terms to convey the total depravity of sin and its irremedial effects. This realization prepares man for the message of atonement and the antonyms of these terms are used to describe the state of the redeemed. *See* Clean.

W. White, Jr.

FINE(S). *See* Crimes and Punishments.

FINE FLOUR. *See* Flour.

FINE LINEN. *See* Linen.

FINER, FINING, FINING POT. *See* Refiner.

FINERY (תפארת, *beauty, glory*). The word describes the beauty of the anklets, pendants, and other items which adorned the upper-class women of Jerusalem (Isa 3:18). God promises that He will replace these luxuries with articles of shame when He judges the city.

FINGER (אצבע ; Gr. δάκτυλος). The fingers which are an extension from the palm of the hand are still a major part of the whole hand, and are mentioned when the emphasis is on dexterity and skill rather than power. Fingers often stand for the whole hand as in "your hands are defiled with blood and your fingers with iniquity" (Isa 59:3) and the Lord "trains my hands for war, and my fingers for battle" (Ps 144:1). The fingers were used in conversation by the oriental to add to the expression of the mouth, e.g. "winks with his eyes . . . points with his fingers" (Prov 6:13) and "if you take away from the midst of you the yoke, the pointing of the finger, and speaking wickedness" (Isa 58:9). Accusation was, and still is, made by pointing. Measuring by the fingers assumed .73 inch for each finger, for instance, the pillars of Solomon's Temple were thicknesses of four fingers (Jer 52:21). Much of a person's wealth could be carried in rings on his fingers.

Shaking hands signified unity of purpose (2 Kings 10:15) and spiritual guidance was bound on fingers (Prov 7:3). A finger sprinkled the sacrificial blood upon the horns of the altar of the Tabernacle and the priests received blood upon the thumbs of their right hands (Exod 29:12, 20).

A rare dominant hereditary trait is the possession of extra fingers and toes, such as of the man of great stature at Gath (1 Chron 20:6).

Rehoboam stressed the burden of his yoke upon his people by following the advice of his young men to say, "My little finger is thicker than my father's loins" (1 Kings 12:10). Jesus complained that the scribes and Pharisees laid burdens on men's shoulders, but they themselves would not move them with their fingers (Matt 23:4).

The finger of God was like the hand of God, only His creative skill is suggested in such statements as "when I look at thy heavens, the work of thy fingers" (Ps 8:3). With it He wrote the Ten Commandments on tablets of stone

A view of the central Sinai Mountains, where the Ten Commandments were given to Moses. ©*M.P.S.*

(Exod 31:18). In a miracle He made the fingers of a man's hand to appear and write on the plaster on the wall to pronounce doom on Belshazzar (Dan 5:5). Apparently the writing by Jesus on the ground in the presence of the accusers of the adulterous woman was a sentence of conviction (John 8:6, fn). Jesus said it was by the finger of God that He cast out demons, and Luke, a physician whose fingers would so often be used in healing, is the one who records this (Luke 11:20).

Not only did Jesus ask Thomas to test His reality by thrusting his finger into His side (John 20:27) but He blessed with His fingers when He healed the deaf man, and when "children were brought to him that he might lay his hands on them and pray" (Matt 19:13).

Lifting and laying on of hands for blessing was common. The position of the fingers was important in the early western church. Three upraised fingers stood for the Trinity, while the remaining two closed fingers signified the two natures of Christ.

R. L. MIXTER

FINGER OF GOD. A fig. expression used several times in the OT and once in the NT to refer to the power of God. The Egyp. magicians said, after one of the plagues of Moses which they could not duplicate, "This is the finger of God" (Exod 8:19), meaning, "This is beyond the power of man to do; it is supernatural; God must be backing Moses and Aaron." The Ten Commandments are said to have been written by the finger of God, that is, by some supernatural process, and not by any human hand (Deut 9:10). The psalmist (Ps 8:3) says that the heavens were made by the fingers of God. In something so vast and wonderful as the heavens, not *a* finger, but *all* of God's fingers were used. He made and shaped the planets and the stars. Jesus said that He cast out demons with the finger of God (Luke 11:20). In the parallel passage in Matthew (12:28) the words are "by the Spirit of God." He clearly meant that He cast out demons by the power of God.

S. BARABAS

FIR (ברוש, *cypress, pine*; fir tree, *b^erôsh*). One cannot be certain whether the fir referred to twenty-one times in the Bible is the Aleppo Pine (*Pinus halepensis*), or a Cypress (*Cupressus sempervirens*).

The Aleppo Pine grows to a height of sixty ft., bearing short, stalked cones, and will withstand considerable periods of drought. It is certainly abundant in the hilly areas of Pal., where its wood is considered almost as valuable as cedar.

Because the fir is described in the Bible as "a goodly tree," some have thought that it must be *Pinus tinaster,* which grows to a height of 120 ft., and is an important resin-producing tree.

Cypress wood is long lasting. The gates of Constantinople were made of it, and they lasted over a thousand years. Rafters were made of its wood (S of Sol 1:17). The Temple floor was covered with planks of fir (Ezek 27:5) and King David played on musical instruments made with fir (2 Sam 6:5), prob. harps and lutes.

W. E. SHEWELL-COOPER

FIRE (אשׁ ; πῦρ; see also אור, Isa 31:9; נור, Dan 3:22ff.; φῶs, Luke 22:55).

1. Instrument of service to man. Fire was used domestically for cooking, heating, and lighting. Abraham ordered Sarah to bake cakes for his angelic guests (Gen 18:6); Israelites ate roasted lamb on the night of the Exodus (Exod 12:9, 39); one cereal offering was to be "from fresh ears, parched with fire" (Lev 2:14); and when Jesus appeared to His disciples by Galilee after His resurrection, they "saw a charcoal fire there, with fish lying on it" (John 21:9). Isaiah, in rebuking unfaithful Israel, exclaimed, "No coal for warming oneself is this, no fire to sit before!" (Isa 47:14). When Jesus was before Caiaphas, "Peter was standing and warming himself" (John 18:25); and the natives of Malta "kindled a fire" for Paul and his shipwrecked fellowmen "because it had begun to rain and was cold" (Acts 28:2). A third domestic service of fire was to give light. This is reflected in Jesus' parable of the woman who would "light a lamp and sweep the house" until she found her coin (Luke 15:8); and in the comparison He made to Christians, that "men light a lamp . . . and it gives light to all in the house" (Matt 5:15). Fire was used also occupationally as in processing crude metal ore. It served the dual purpose of burning out dross and melting the ore to be molded or minted for useful purposes. Ezekiel said, "As men gather silver and bronze and iron and lead and tin into a furnace, to blow the fire upon it in order to melt it; so I will . . ." (Ezek 22:18-20; also, Exod 32:24; Num 31:22f.).

2. Instrument of destruction by man. Fire was employed as man's ultimate means of destroying property and people. In the conquest of Canaan, Joshua and the Israelite army burned the cities of Jericho, Ai, and Hazor, wholly sacrificing the first to God, and they burned the chariots of the Canaanite coalition (Josh 6:24; 8:19; 11:9, 11). They also killed and burned the whole family of Achan (Josh 7:24f.). Later the men of Judah captured Jerusalem "and set the city on fire" (Judg 1:8). King Nebuchadnezzar tried to burn the three young Hebrews, Shadrach, Meshach, and Abednego (Dan 3:19-28).

Human sacrifice by fire was an ancient practice in some primitive religions. It may have some correlation with Abraham's aborted effort to sacrifice Isaac (Gen 22:1-14). It was at times practiced by the Canaanites, for Moses warned the Israelites not to imitate them, "for they even burn their sons and their daughters in the fire to their gods" (Deut 12:31). He further commanded, "You shall not give any of your children to devote them by fire to Molech," their heathen divinity (Lev 18:21). Molech (Milcom) was made their national god by the Ammonites, resulting in the contamination of Solomon's religion (1 Kings 11:5-7). Later, Kings Ahaz and Manasseh both sacrificed their sons to Molech (2 Kings 16:3; 21:16). In the days from Ahaz to Manasseh Molech worship was centered in the Valley of Hinnom where a huge altar pyre (Topheth) stood. On it children were sacrificially burned (Isa 30:33). Josiah had it destroyed (2 Kings 23:10). This place of lowest human degradation served Jesus as a symbol of hell, which he called "Gehenna" (Matt 5:29mg.).

3. Emblem of divine presence. Though literal fire is a natural phenomenon, it has a quality of mystery, a factor invariably associated with deity. Consequently, it was an emblem of divine presence to the Hebrews. In the first Scripture reference to fire, as Abraham made sacrifice, "a smoking fire pot and a flaming torch passed between these pieces" (Gen 15:17). Fire was an emblem of divine presence to Moses in the burning bush; to Israel in the "pillar of fire"; and to Moses and Israel on Mount Sinai when the law was given (Exod 3:2; 13:21; 19:18). Elijah called down fire to consume two contingents of soldiers; and he was taken to heaven by "a chariot of fire and horses of fire" (2 Kings 1:9-12; 2:11). Elisha asked God to open his servant's eyes to see the mountain "full of horses and chariots of fire" (2 Kings 6:17). The most consistent expectancy of God's presence was at the altar at the time when burnt offerings were made. There are more than a hundred references to altar fires in the OT, including laws governing burnt offerings (Lev, Num, Deut). There are singular instances of divine fire consuming sacrifices offered by Aaron (Lev 9:24); by David (1 Chron 21:26); by Solomon (2 Chron 7:1); by Elijah (1 Kings 18:38). Also, the guest angel made a holocaust in each case with the meals offered by Gideon and Manoah (Judg 6:21; 13:20).

4. Symbol of divine punishment. The metaphorical meaning of fire as the wrath of God is used abundantly throughout the Bible. God's wrath, like fire, was both purifying and punitive. As in cooking fire destroys the harmful enzymes, making food more edible and tasty, and in smelting it burns out the dross and refines the metal for use, so God's wrath conditions man for better use. In Moses' song, God said, "a fire is kindled by my anger" (Deut 32:22). Jeremiah warned, "lest my wrath go forth like fire" (Jer 4:4; cf. 15:14). Ezekiel spoke of "the fire of my wrath" (Ezek 22:21). Zephaniah said, "In the fire of his jealous wrath, all the earth shall be consumed" (Zeph 1: 18), and Nahum said, "His wrath is

A view of the Valley of Gehenna, the Old Testament Valley of Hinnom where a huge altar pyre (Topheth) stood. ©*Lev*

poured out like fire" (Nah 1:6). Moses said, "For the LORD your God is a devouring fire, a jealous God" (Deut 4:24). The invariable use of fire in this sense is punitive, whether literal or fig. Sodom and Gomorrah were destroyed by "brimstone and fire from the LORD" (Gen 19:24). Fire from the Lord consumed 250 rebellious Levites making unauthorized offerings (Num 16:35).

The unquenchable fire (pur *asbestos*), the final reward of the wicked, was proclaimed by the prophets and emphasized by Jesus and John. Isaiah declared, "Their worm shall not die, their fire shall not be quenched" (Isa 66: 24; cf. Ezek 20:47). John said the chaff of humanity God "will burn with unquenchable fire" (Matt 3:12), and that Jesus "will baptize you with the Holy Spirit and with fire" (Matt 3:11). Jesus said, "Every tree that does not bear good fruit is cut down and thrown into the fire" (Matt 7:19). In His statement, "I came to cast fire upon the earth" (Luke 12: 49), He used fire as a symbol of judgment. The work of the Holy Spirit, by "tongues as of fire" through the proclamation of the Gospel, was to be, like Jesus, for salvation and for judgment (Acts 2:3). Jesus solemnly warned people not "to go to hell, to the unquenchable fire" (Mark 9:43).

BIBLIOGRAPHY. J. H. Thayer, *A Greek-English Lexicon of the NT* (1889), 558; Price, Sellars, Carleson, *Monuments and OT* (1958), 158, 196-200; N. K. Gottwald, *A Light to the Nations* (1959), 142f., 148-150, 207, 253f., 327f.; B. Davies, *Students Hebrew Lexicon* (1960), 66; R. de Vaux, *Ancient Israel* (1962), 406-456; H. M. Buck, *People of the Lord* (1966), 50, 263f., 431.

G. B. FUNDERBURK

FIRE, LAKE OF. *See* LAKE OF FIRE.

FIREBRAND (אוד, perhaps a curved stick used for stirring fires originally). It is used fig. in each of its three occurrences. Isaiah 7:4 describes two angry kings as "smoldering stumps of smoking firebrands" (BDB p. 15). Elsewhere, it refers to the merciful preservation of Jerusalem and Israel, plucked from the fire (Amos 4:11; Zech 3:2). In Judges 15:4 "torch," לפיד, is a preferable tr. זקים "missiles, sparks" are thrown by a madman along with arrows (Prov 26:18). זיקות prob. means "brands, sparks" in Isaiah 50:11.

H. M. WOLF

FIRE OFFERING. *See* SACRIFICE AND OFFERINGS.

FIREPAN (מחתה). A pan for carrying live or dead coals. It was used for three different functions in the sacrifice and worship of the OT.

1. It was used to carry coals to and from the altar of burnt offering (Exod 27:3; 38:3; Num 4:14), usually tr. "firepans."

2. It was used in combination with the snuffers of the golden lampstand, prob. as a tray to catch the pieces of burned wick (Exod 25:38; 37:23; Num 4:9), tr. by KJV as "snuff dishes," by other VSS as "trays," "ash-trays" or "firepans."

3. It was used as a receptacle to burn incense, live coals being placed in the pan and the incense thrown on top to burn (Lev 10:1; 16:12, 13; Num 16:6, 7, 17, 18, 37-39, 46). As such it is tr. by KJV and others as "censer," although other trs. use "firepan" or "pan."

In some passages it is difficult to determine which of these specific usages is meant (1 Kings 7:50; 2 Kings 25:15; 2 Chron 4:22; Jer 52:19), although firepans for carrying coals are prob. intended, esp. in the latter case where the same terms as occur in Exodus 27:3; 38:3; Numbers 4:14 are mentioned in the list.

F. W. BUSH

FIRKIN. *See* WEIGHTS AND MEASURES.

FIRMAMENT, the traditional rendering in the Eng. VSS for Heb. רקיע, a difficult word the root of which refers to beaten metals. A verbal form is found in Exodus 39:3, Heb. וירקעו, "and they hammered out"; the term refers to the vault of heaven. Numerous authors have assumed that the use of this term indicated a specific system of cosmology involving a hollow concavity of the celestial sphere. There is no evidence for this in the lit. of the ancient Near E or in the occurrences of this rare term. The term in Genesis 1:6 does indicate that the firmament was formed to separate the mass of waters and divide them into two layers. The name of the firmament as given in v. 8 was Heb. שמים, "heaven." The LXX reads, *στερέωμα*, "solidity," "steadfastness" (Col 2:5) which was rendered as *firmamentum* by Jerome in the Vul. and thus the Eng. "firmament." The firmament is mentioned nine times in the creation account of Genesis, twice in the Psalms (19:1; 150:1), and in Ezekiel and Daniel, but always in the context of creation.

W. WHITE, JR.

FIRST-BORN (בכור, *πρωτότοκος*, meaning *first in sequence to be born* or, fig., *first in rank, preeminent*).

Normally the word means the oldest son (Exod 6:14; 11:5). He enjoyed prerogatives over his brothers, like receiving the father's blessing (Gen 27:1-4, 35-37), preferential treatment by the father (43:33), respect as leader among the brothers (37:22), and a double portion of the inheritance, twice what any other son received (Deut 21:17). The first-born might barter away his rights, as Esau (Gen 25:29-34), or forfeit them for misconduct, as Reuben by incest (35:22; 49:3, 4; 1 Chron 5:1). The Lord claimed first-born of men and animals for Himself (Exod 13:1-16). Such animals were sacrificed and such sons redeemed, since God did not tolerate child sacrifice as in heathen customs (13:11-15). Levites as a group were designated for special service to the Lord in lieu of the first-born (Num 3:12, 13; 8:16-18). In the NT, Jesus is called the first-born son of Mary (Luke 2:7), who was a virgin before His birth, but who had other sons after Him (Mark 6:3; cf. John 7:5).

Sometimes the meaning is fig., denoting priority or supremacy. Israel was God's "first-born" (Exod 4:22; Jer 31:9). As the first-born son had special priority, Israel was privileged over other nations. Christ is the "first-born" of the Father (Heb 1:6), having preeminent position over others in relation to Him. He is "first-born among many brethren" (Rom 8:29) as one sovereign above those related to Him in the new creation. He is "first-born of all creation" (Col 1:15), a statement misunderstood by Arians of the 4th cent. and modern-day Jehovah's Witnesses who make Him a created being and not God. The proper meaning is that Christ, truly God, stands in a relationship of priority or sovereignty over all creation (Lightfoot). This meaning is correct because: (1) He is Himself creator of all (v. 16); (2) He is prior to all, having existed before it (v. 17), and also supreme over it; (3) only this view that He is God would combat the Gnostic error Paul answers, for they made Christ only a created emanation from God and such a concession by Paul would play into their hands; (4) rabbis called God Himself "first-born" as the supreme being, the "first-born of the world" (R. Bechai on Pentateuch, cited by Lightfoot, p. 47); (5) Paul claims the fullness of deity for Christ elsewhere (2:9; Titus 2:13). Paul further says (Col 1:18), and John also (Rev 1:5), that Christ is "first-born from the dead." Certain others arose before Him but later died again. He is first to rise bodily from the grave to immortality, and also the one supreme over those in this class. He is the "first fruits" of resurrection (1 Cor 15:20). *See* FAMILY.

BIBLIOGRAPHY. J. B. Lightfoot, *Saint Paul's Epistles to the Colossians and to Philemon* (1900); R. deVaux, *Ancient Israel* (1961), 41, 42.

J. E. ROSSCUP

FIRST DAY OF THE WEEK. *See* SUNDAY.

FIRST FRUITS ([1] ראשית. LXX ἀπαρχή. An adjective meaning "first" which modifies the particular product concerned. [2] בכור, LXX πρωτογένημα. From a root "to bear early, new fruit").

1. Literal. Just as the first-born of man and cattle were sacred to the Lord, so also the first production of a vineyard (Lev 19:23-25) and the first of the annual production of grain, wine, olive oil, sheared wool (Exod 23:16; 34:22; Deut 18:4), and the first of coarse meal (Num 15:20, 21), of honey and of all the produce of the land (2 Chron 31:5; cf. Prov 3:9) were the Lord's. Bread of first fruit was offered on the day of first fruit—Pentecost (Num 28:26; cf. Exod 23:16; 34:22). In a few passages *re'shit* and *bikkurim* are in a combined expression (Exod 23:19; 34:26; Ezek 44:30) without the distinction being clear, though at some periods a distinction may have been made. Except for a cereal offering (Lev 2:14-16), the priest benefitted from the first fruits (Num 18:12). The offering was brought in a basket to the sanctuary for presentation (Deut 26:1-11).

First fruits of twenty barley loaves and of fresh ears of grain supplied Elisha with resources to feed a hundred men (2 Kings 4:42). First fruits were given to priests in Hezekiah's time (2 Chron. 31:5); were pledged in Nehemiah's day (Neh 10:35) and men were appointed to oversee store chambers in which to store them (Neh 12:44; 13:31). The first fruits were included in Ezekiel's plans for worship (Ezek 44:30; 48:14).

Though the NT has no provision for the paying of first fruits, the community from which the *Didachē* arose paid first fruits of the winepress, threshing floor, oxen, sheep, bread, newly opened jars of wine and oil, of money, of clothes, and of all possessions to the prophets as being the high priests, and in the absence of prophets, gave them to the poor (*Didachē* 13:3).

2. Metaphorical. The OT custom lends itself naturally to becoming a metaphor for that which is first. First fruit is used only metaphorically in the NT. The way for some of these cases may have been prepared by Jeremiah who calls Israel the first fruit of God's harvest (Jer 2:3; cf. Hos 9:10) despite the fact that the LXX rendering of the passage obscures the metaphor (cf. 1 Clem 29:3). For Paul, believing Jews were the first fruits of the Jewish people (Rom 11:16; cf. Num 15:20f.). For James, Christians are the first fruits of God's creatures (James 1:18), and in Revelation 14:4 those who follow the Lamb are first fruits to God. Christ is the first fruit of them that slept (1 Cor 15:20, 23; cf. 1 Clem 24:1); Epaenetus is the first fruit in Asia (Rom 16:5) and the household of Stephanas, the first fruit in Achaia (1 Cor 16:15; cf. 1 Clem 42:4). The present possession of the Holy Spirit is the first fruit of the spirit (Rom 8:23), an indication of that which is to come. In the Epistle of Barnabas prophecy is said to give the first fruits of the taste of things to come (Epistle of Barnabas 1:7).

BIBLIOGRAPHY. G. F. Moore, *Judaism* (1927), II, 71; G. Delling, *"aparche"* in Kittel, TWNT (1933), I, 483, 484; J. Pedersen, *Israel* (1940), III, 300ff.

J. P. LEWIS

FISH, FISHING (דאג ; דגה; *fish*, all Eng. VSS; ἰχθύς; *fish*, all Eng. VSS; Gr. ἰχθύδιον; ὀψάριον, *fish*; small fishes; little fishes; variously in Eng. VSS. The two latter are non-specific and refer to small fishes generally. ὀψάριον is found only in John; only used for fish about to be or already cooked. This is consistent with its use in classical Gr., where it may also mean food in some contexts).

I. SPECIES AVAILABLE

The two Heb. words are always tr. "fish" but may also cover shellfish, crustaceans, etc., and sea mammals. The word "fish" is not used in the food laws of Leviticus 11:9 and Deuteronomy 14:9, 10. The latter is more concise, "Whatever has fins and scales you may eat. Whatever does not have fins and scales you shall not eat." This rule excludes all aquatic invertebrates, some of which are tasty and nutritious, but can easily cause food poisoning, also marine mammals, of which the dugong was once common in the Red Sea and the Monk Seal rare in the Mediterranean. Also the sharks, which are cartilaginous fish with rough skin but no scales; and eels, including Moray Eel, which was later a favorite Rom. food. The Catfish (*Clarias lazera*) of Galilee might also have been avoided, but this still left several excellent eating lake fishes, in particular *Tilapia* species. Known as St. Peter's fish it is now too expensive for any but the luxury trade. These fish are mouth-breeders, of a family well known to aquarists—*Cichlidae*. The Barbels (*Barbus canis* and *longiceps*) are also native to these waters. In recent years the Gray Mullet (*Mugil cephalus*) from the brackish estuary waters of the Mediterranean has been successfully introduced. The small fishes of Matthew 14:17 and 15:36 cannot be identified but can be assumed to have come from the lake. Many small fish are salted and dried, and either stored for future use or

Fishing on the Sea of Galilee. ©*M.P.S.*

used for eating as described. The most common is the Lake Sardine, or Belak (*Acanthobrama terrae sanctae*) of which large quantities are canned.

II. Fishing method

A. Nets. 1. *Cast net.* (ἀμφίβληστρον; Matt 4:18) is taken to be the net thrown by hand. This is circular, with small weights around the perimeter, and thrown so as to fall flat on the surface, enclosing a shoal. It is still used widely in Africa and parts of Asia; also occasionally on the lake for benefit of tourists! It is uneconomical where labor is expensive.

2. *Gill net.* This is perhaps the best modern equivalent of δίκτυον (Matt 4:30), and is still used for catching medium-sized *Tilapia* and other species. Long nets, supported on floats, hang near the surface, usually through the night, and are hauled up the following day. This net is used in a passive way and takes fish only of one approximate size; the smaller pass through and the larger cannot insert their heads. This is mostly used well out in the lake, and at sea, and fish are brought ashore by boat.

3. *Drag net* (σαγήνη). As described fig. in Matthew 13:47, 48 this would better fit a modern seine net several hundred yards long, which is taken by boat around a semicircle and then both ends are hauled in to the shore. All kinds and sizes of fish were taken and then sorted. Much time ashore was occupied with net maintenance including washing (Luke 5:2), spreading and drying (Ezek 47:10) and mending (Matt 4:21). Fishermen also made them in the first case. Much of this work is now greatly lightened by using artificial (drip-dry) filaments and machine-made nets.

B. Hook and line. Isaiah 19:8, "the fishermen . . . who cast hook in the Nile." Heb. חכה is also found in Job 41:1, "draw out Leviathan with a fishhook" and Habakkuk 1:15, "He brings all of them up with a hook." Another specific word (Heb. סיר דוגה) is in Amos 4:2. These are also in fig. contexts but the use of two technical words confirms that the method was general. Matthew 17:27, "cast a hook, and take the first fish that comes up" could refer to a baited hook or to another method still used by children in Galilee. A large triangle of sharp unbaited hooks, perhaps two inches across, tied on a long cord, is thrown into a shoal and snatched, sometimes hooking a fish. A watersnake may be caught by mistake and, though the reference is not obvious, this is taken locally as a commentary on Luke 11:11, "instead of a fish give him a serpent."

C. Fish spear. Job 41:7 trs. two words: "harpoons" and "fishing spears" (RSV) and "barbed irons" and "fish spears" (KJV). The target in this v. is a crocodile but this method was more often used in shallow water for taking fish. Fish-spearing from a papyrus raft is illustrated in a painting in the tomb of Simut at Thebes c. 1500 B.C. In spring the large *Tilapia* are vulnerable to such weapons when they enter the reed beds to spawn, but in such areas they are usually taken undamaged in trammel nets.

III. Fishing regions

A. Inland Palestine. Through much of its history Israel had control over the whole Lake of Galilee but this has little mention in OT, where nothing is said about its fish. In the gospels, largely because much of the Lord's ministry was based there, it is important and the word sea was synonymous with it. At least seven disciples were fishermen and lake fishing has special emphasis. Except for the carp (*Cyprinus carpio*) which may escape from fishponds and reach the lake, where they grow big, and the Gray Mullet (u.s.), the species are the same as when Peter took them. Including those already listed there are at least twenty-five species. Intensive cultivation, with manuring, in parts of the Jordan Valley makes nutrient salts available in the drainage water and fish growth should be faster. Since World War II much research has been done and modern methods introduced, including production of fry. Yield from the Lake of Galilee for 1965 was: *Tilapia* species, 304 tons; Bleak, 787 tons; Barbel, 123 tons; Gray Mullet, 55 tons; others, 9 tons; total 1278 tons. For much of its passage through Upper Galilee the Jordan is fast-flowing and unsuitable for fishing. The yield from this river and others, subject to rapid rise and fall, would have been very small. Until about 1950 the Lake of Huleh, though partly silted up, was still a useful fishing ground; this is now drained, but the fishponds that ring the reclaimed area much more than make up for the loss.

B. Marine. Varying lengths of the Mediterranean coastline were occupied by the Israelites, but they were never a seafaring people and most maritime shipping mentioned in OT and NT was foreign-owned. Any fishing which they did was prob. close inshore. "Men of Tyre also, who lived in the city, brought in fish . . . and sold them . . . in Jerusalem" (Neh 13:16). This was presumably sea fish from the Phoen. coast and because of distance it must have been preserved by salting, drying, smoking, etc. For several reasons, esp. the narrow coastal shelf with shallow water, the Mediterranean is generally poor fishing ground and even with modern methods its potential is low. The catch for 1965 was 2,910 tons, of which half was sardine. At several periods, esp. during the reigns of Solomon and Jehoshaphat, Israel had access to the Red Sea, where a range of tropical fish is found, but these could have been only of local value. The 1965 catch was only 292 tons.

C. Egypt. The Israelites looked back from the desert and longed for the fish they had enjoyed in Egypt (Num 11:5). The Nile fish were killed by the first plague and this was enough to pollute even a river of such great volume. The Nile has always been a major source of food and various methods of fishing are illustrated in ancient Egyp. art. The dense population of lower Egypt and its intensive cultivation greatly increased the area of channels available for fish, as well as making the water more fertile. Over 100 species are recorded for lower Nile, many of them edible, including carp, perch and Cichlids. This fauna has changed little since OT times.

D. Fishponds. One of only two Biblical references is in doubt. Isaiah 19:10, "[who] make sluices and ponds for fish" (KJV); "who work for hire will be grieved," (RSV). The other is Song of Solomon, 7:4, "fish pools in Heshbon" (KJV); "pools in Hesbon" (RSV). The old Moabite city of Heshbon is in Trans-Jordan, more or less level with the N point of the Dead Sea, and excavation has revealed remains of pools and conduits, so the Hebrews prob. practiced some form of fish farming. This was known early in other lands; fishponds have been found in ancient Mesopotamia and Egypt, and they are illustrated in Assyrian reliefs. Romans became experts and developed methods of raising several species of sea fish including mullet, wrasse and, above all, Moray Eels. This work needs a high degree of skill. The Romans also made fresh water ponds in occupied countries and the monks' "fish-stews" of Europe were their successors. There is no evidence about the fish kept in these ponds in Pal. Within recent years fish-farming has become an important industry in Israel, where the climate allows a fairly long growing season. Over 12,500 acres yield about 10,000 tons per annum (1965), mostly carp and much of it for the Passover market. This is an ideal pond fish, which prob. originated in E Europe, but it was not used extensively for this purpose until the Middle Ages.

A typical Tilapia of Kinneret. ©*Wm. White, Jr.*

IV. Figurative use

Of the six Heb. words for net, at least three refer to types of fish nets and all contexts are fig. esp. men trying to catch others with evil intent (Mic 7:2), or Jehovah acting in judgment on nations (Ezek 32:4) or an individual (Ps 66:11). Similar warnings are expressed in Jeremiah 16:16, "many fishers . . . shall catch them" referring to Judah; "They shall take you away with fishhooks" (Amos 4:2), speaking to Samaria. The metaphor is different in NT. "Peter and Andrew . . . were fishermen. . . . I will make you fishers of men" (Matt 4:18, 19). The kingdom of heaven is compared to a drag or seine or net (Matt 13:47). The fish became a symbol in early Christian art, almost a code word, because Gr. ιχθύς spelled out the initials of a simple creed "Jesus Christ, God's Son, Savior."

V. Fish in worship

Deuteronomy 4:18 expressly forbids making an image of fish. The fishtailed deity shown on coins found at Ashkelon is identified with Atargitis the fish goddess, whose cult originated in Syria and was spread by merchants. It does not seem to have been practiced by the Israelites at any stage. The often repeated statement that Dagon (1 Sam 5:2ff.) was a fish deity, with its name derived from Heb. דאג, has no real foundation. (*See* NBD, p. 287.)

See Trades and Occupations.

BIBLIOGRAPHY. Bulletins of Dept. of Agric. and Fisheries, Israel; W. Luther and K. Fielder, "Die unterwasser Fauna der Mittelmer Küsten."

G. S. Cansdale

FISH GATE (שער הדגים). A gate in Jerusalem. Manasseh is said to have built the outer wall of Jerusalem from W of Gihon to the Fish Gate (2 Chron 33:14). When Nehemiah rebuilt the walls; the Fish Gate was built by the "sons of Hassenaah" (Neh 3:3); and one of the choirs proceeded past it at the dedication of the walls (12:39). In Zephaniah 1:10 it is mentioned with the Mishneh or "second quarter" of the city. The majority of scholars hold that it stood in the Tyropoeon Valley in the NW wall of the city (so J. Simons, *Jerusalem in the Old Testament* [Leiden: Brill, 1952], p. 291, n. 3; yet see now M. Avi-Yonah, "The Walls of Nehemiah," IEJ 4 [1954], 242, who would identify it with the Ephraim gate). It apparently obtained its name from the fish market near by (cf. Neh 13:16). F. W. Bush

FISHHOOK. Several Heb. terms are tr. "fishhook" or "hook" by modern trs. The word חכה is used in Job 41:1, Isaiah 19:8, and in Habakkuk 1:15, to refer to the "fishhook" proper. This method of fishing was widely used in the ancient world, although it was not an important industry in Pal. Other terms used are derived from words for "thorns" or "spines" of various plants which were used for fishing or for gaffing fish. In Amos 4:2, the term דוגה סירות, "spines for fishing" uses the word סירה which refers to the thorn of the Thorny Burnet (*Poterium Spinosum*). In Job 41:2 the word חוח, "thorn, spine" is used with the meaning "hook." KB identifies it in this passage as a "thorn put into the gills of a fish to carry it home."

F. W. Bush

FISH POOL. A mistranslation in the KJV of Song of Solomon 7:5 for the ordinary Heb. word for "pool, pond" (ברכה).

FITCH, FITCHES (כסמת, קצח). In Ezekiel 4:9, the Heb. *kussemet* is used, and is believed by some to refer to the Prickly Fitch. The other three references in Isaiah 28 are *qeṣah,* prob. the black cummin.

Fitches are members of the Ranunculus family, and produce an abundance of black seeds. It is these that are used as pungent flavoring.

The tr. "fitch" is unfortunate, as the *qeṣath* is not a vetch. The plant undoubtedly is the *Nigella sativa,* sometimes called "The Nutmeg Flower," though it certainly is not a true nutmeg. This Biblical Nigella is related to the annual grown in the garden, called "Love in the Mist." Its flowers are like the buttercup, and the fruit pods contain large quantities of tiny black seeds.

In the Holy Land, the Arabs call it "kasah," which is similar to the *qeṣath* of the Hebrews. The use of these seeds in bread is said to make it more wholesome.

The plant is still grown in Pal. and the seeds are beaten out of the capsules with a flail.

In Isaiah 28:25 the idea seems to be that the seeds of the Nigella are broadcast liberally, while the seeds of the true cummin had to be sprinkled lightly.

W. E. Shewell-Cooper

FLAG. A word that appears in the KJV of the Bible three times, but not in the RSV. In Exodus 2:3, 5 it is said that the mother of Moses laid the ark of bulrushes "in the flags by the river's bank," and that Pharaoh's daughter saw "the ark among the flags" (RSV "reeds"); in Isaiah 19:6 (KJV) the prophet predicts that in the divine judgment that will come upon Egypt the Nile will dry up and "the reeds and flags (RSV 'rushes') shall wither." In both passages the Heb. word is סוף, a general term

Reeds

denoting sedgy plants such as grow along the Nile and its canals today. The Red Sea (Exod 10:19) is literally the "Sea of Reeds" (ים סוף). The third appearance of the word is in Job 8:11 (KJV), where Bildad asks a rhetorical question, "Can the flag (RSV 'reeds') grow without water?" The Heb. word here is אחו, a generic word for marsh grasses or reeds. The KJV trs. the same Heb. word "meadow" in Genesis 41:2, 18, where it is said that the seven well-favored kine (RSV "cows") of Pharaoh's dream came out of the river and "fed in the meadow" (RSV "reed grass").

S. Barabas

FLAGON. This word is used in the KJV to tr. Heb. אשישה (2 Sam 6:19; 1 Chron 16:3; S of Sol 2:5; Hos 3:1.) The RSV, ASV and all modern trs. have understood it correctly as a pressed cake of raisins. The Eng. word "flagon" is also used by modern Eng. trs. along with other words such as "jar, pitcher, pot," etc., to represent several Heb. words of similar meaning without any agreement or uniformity.

F. W. Bush

FLAGSTAFF. This is the tr. used by the RSV and other modern VSS for Heb. תרן (Isa 30:17; KJV "beacon"). The word clearly means "mast (of a ship)" in Isaiah 33:23 and Ezekiel 27:5. In the latter Tyre is pictured as a ship for which a cedar of Lebanon is used for a mast. In Isaiah 30:17 the word is used to picture the solitariness and conspicuousness of the survivors of the people of Israel after the judgment of God has come upon them: they will be like a תרן, "mast, pole" on a mountain top.

F. W. Bush

FLASK. The Eng. word "flask" was not used by the KJV trs., but several of the modern trs. have used it to render a number of Heb. words without much agreement or uniformity. It is used by the RSV and other modern trs. to render the Heb. word פך (2 Kings 9:1, 3; in 1 Sam 10:1 the same word is tr. "vial" by the RSV and other modern VSS). Jeremiah 19:1, 10 (RSV) uses it for בקבק, although other modern trs. use "jar" or "jug" in this passage and the same word in 1 Kings 14:3 is rendered by the RSV as "jar." At least one modern VS has used "flask" for אסוך (2 Kings 4:2) and for צפחת (1 Kings 17:12, 14, 16). The difficulty in tr. such terms is a dual one: (1) the words used are so rare or their meanings so difficult to determine, that one does not know the exact connotation of the word; and (2) even when one knows the connotation more exactly, there is no Eng. word with the same range of meaning.

F. W. Bush

FLAT NOSE. The KJV tr. of חרם, used only in Leviticus 21:18 to describe one of the conditions that rendered a man unfit for priestly service. Although the root is not known elsewhere in Heb. (except perhaps for החרים in Isa 11:15, see Driver JTS 32 [1931]: 251), cognates in other Sem. languages, esp. Arab., suggest some such meaning as "having a slit or split nose or lip." So it was taken in the Talmud, see M. Jastrow, *A Dictionary of the Talmudim* (New York: Pardes, 1950), Vol. I, p. 503. It possibly referred to the condition that often accompanies a cleft palate.

F. W. Bush

FLAX (פשתה, λίνον). The word *pishtâh* occurs in Exodus 9:31; Isaiah 42:3; and 43:17. This could be tr. "wick." *Pēshet* occurs seven times (Josh 2:6; Judg 15:14; Prov 31:13; Isa 19:9; Ezek 40:3; Hos 2:5, 9), but the word can be tr. "linen." In Matthew 12:20, the *linon* is a quotation from Isaiah 42:3.

Flax was grown in Pal. before the arrival of the Israelites, for Rahab (Josh 2:1, 6), hid the two spies under the stems of flax she had drying on the flat roof of her house. The cloth made from local-grown flax would have been welcomed by the Jews, whose clothes, after their long trek, might have been wearing out.

Solomon congratulates a good wife who separates the fibers of the flax and makes fine linen (Prov 31:13). Fine flax is mentioned in Isaiah 19:9, when it is obvious that white cloth and thin white linen were made.

It is obvious that the Egyptians knew about growing flax. Making linen for Pharaoh gave Joseph fine linen clothes, and after the Israelites had escaped from Egypt, and had "spoiled the Egyptians," they were able to make fine

Flax

linen priestly garments for Aaron and his sons.

Solomon knew the value of linen, and seems to have made it a state monopoly. Linen was used also as sails for yachts (Ezek 27:7). In the NT linen towels and napkins are mentioned (John 11:44; 13:4). Linen also was used for the wrappings of dead bodies (Mark 15:46).

It is generally believed that the flax was *Linum usitatissimum* which grows two to four ft. high and bears beautiful blue flowers (there are occasionally white varieties). The plants were grown until they were ripe, when they were pulled up whole and laid out to dry. To lose a crop of flax was serious, and could be one of God's punishments (Hos 2:9).

The capsules of flax are called "bols," and the bolled flax is the mature flax, ready for harvesting and drying. Bundles of flax are soaked in water for three or four weeks. This causes what is called "retting"; i.e., the fibers separate, and it is only then that the threads can be combed.

Of course, the best linen was used for wrapping the body of our Lord, while "the church"—the bride of the risen Lord—is "arrayed in fine linen" (Rev 19:8 KJV) and the angels themselves are robed in pure white linen also (15:6 RSV).

Linen is the oldest of textile fibers, and was evidently graded into three types—(a) coarse (Ezek 9:2); (b) better texture (Exod 26:1); (c) really fine and expensive (Esth 8:15).

Incidentally, the Talmud gives full instructions as to how orthodox Jews should harvest, bleach and prepare linen used by the rabbis.

W. E. SHEWELL-COOPER

FLAYING. *See* CRIMES AND PUNISHMENTS.

FLEA (פרעש), *flea* all Eng. VSS. The flea is mentioned twice (1 Sam 24:14 [all Eng. VSS]; 26:20 [not RSV]). These are metaphorical passages which confirm the tr., for killing fleas as they hopped actively around was a familiar occupation. Fleas (*Pulex* and *Ctenocephalides* species) belong to a small and highly specialized insect family. The adults are bloodsuckers and each species normally concentrates on one host. The larvae are not parasitic but live on rubbish, so that human species thrive where there is dirt. In the dry conditions of Pal. fleas often swarm and may be regarded with indifference by the local folk. Besides causing much discomfort, fleas can transmit several diseases, in particular bubonic plague (*see* MOUSE).

G. S. CANSDALE

FLEECE (גז, גזה [the latter being simply the feminine form of the former], lit. "something cut"; more specifically גז צאן [Deut 18:4] "a cutting from the flock, i.e. fleece", גז כבש [Job 31:20] "a cutting from a lamb, i.e. fleece," or גזת צמר [Judg 6:37] "a cutting of wool, i.e. fleece"). The root means literally "to cut down, off," hence, used of sheep, "to shear," used of hair, "to cut, shave (off)," used of crops, "to mow." The verb is used only of sheep or hair in the OT, but the word גז "something cut" not only means "fleece" but also "mown grass" (Ps 72:6; Amos 7:1). The verb means "to mow, prune, trim" frequently in Mishnaic Heb. It is the coat of wool freshly sheared from a sheep. Gideon requested that a fleece be covered with morning dew, while the ground remained dry and then the opposite (Judg 6:36-40) as a sign that God intended to deliver Israel through him. It is specified as one of the first fruits that is the Levitical priest's due from the people (Deut 18:4), while Job could testify that the poor man could bless him from his heart because he had been warmed by the fleece from his lambs (Job 31:20). *See* SHEEP.

F. W. BUSH

FLESH (in the OT). Three words in the OT are used to tr. "flesh," as follows: בשר, which occurs 269 times; שאר found sixteen times, and טבחה, occurring three times and tr. "flesh" on one occasion only (1 Sam 25:11 KJV). Whereas the last of these words referred solely to slaughtered meat (1 Sam 25:11; Ps 44:22; Jer 12:3) the other two were used in relation to the principal physical constituent of the human body as well as in connection with food and animal sacrifices.

1. Literal usage. The word *bāsār*, Ugaritic *bshr,* seems to be most closely related to the Akkad. *bishru,* whose meaning embraced such concepts as flesh and blood or a family relationship by blood. Its earliest connotation may have been that of the flesh immediately beneath the skin, but this is uncertain at present. In common usage *bāsār* signified the soft muscular tissues of the body, both of men (Gen 2:21; 2 Kings 5:14, etc.) and animals (Gen 41:2; Deut 14:8; etc.). Such organic bodies were still regarded as flesh even when dead (1 Sam 17:44), and only lost their characteristics when they returned to the earth in the form of dust (Eccl 12:7). All OT writers based their concept of flesh in a literal sense on the words of Genesis 2:7 and 7:22, which describe flesh as the clay (the "dust" of the Eng. VSS) from the ground which had been made to live as the result of divine creativity. Animal flesh alone could be used for food (Gen 9:4; 40:19, etc.), although the hygienic prescriptions of the Mosaic law (Lev 11:2-47) made a careful distinction between animals and birds which were fit for food and those which, because of their particular eating habits, were unsuitable for human consumption. Although the term *s*e*'er* was far less frequently used in the OT, it was nevertheless of considerable antiquity, related etymologically to the Akkad. word *shîru,* "flesh," and may have been distinguished from the Akkad. *bishru* in that the former was prob. thought of as the inner organic tissues of the body which were richly supplied with blood vessels and which therefore bled profusely when seriously damaged. As with *bāsār*, *s*e*'ēr* denoted the body or flesh in general (Prov 11:17 KJV; Mic 3:2 KJV, RSV etc.), or the whole constituent human being (Ps 73:26; Prov 5:11). With reference to the animal creation it also denoted flesh to be used as food (Exod 21:10 KJV; Ps 78:20, 27 KJV).

2. Metaphorical use. Aside from its purely literal incidence, the Hebrews generally employed the term "flesh" in a figure of rhetoric known as *synecdoche* as a means of referring to the human body either partially or as a whole. Synecdoche is a rhetorical form which is based on contiguity and, as the Gr. name implies, involves the understanding of one element or concept simultaneously with another. Thus the individual can be substituted for the class, the more general for the less general, the concrete for the abstract, and so on. In this sense the word "flesh" could denote humanity in a comprehensive sense, and by extension the expression "all flesh" could include the animal creation (Gen 6:13 RSV; Lev 17:14 KJV, etc.). Similarly the concept of "flesh" served as an acceptable substitute for the human personality, since the body constituted its spatio-temporal extension (Job 19:26 RSV; Ps 16:9 KJV). This was thoroughly consistent with the tradition of creativity (Gen 2:7) where God breathed the living breath into the clay which He had fashioned into human shape and man became a *nepes hayyāh*. This expression was rendered in the KJV and ASV by "living soul" and in the RSV by "living being," but the true emphasis of the Heb. is not so much upon "soul" or "existence" as upon the fact that, by virtue of special creativity, man is an integrated living personality. For this reason the ancient Hebrews found no difficulty whatever in attributing emotional or psychosomatic functions to bodily organs other than the brain, whose workings were unknown to them, because the fact that the individual constituted an integrated personality meant that psychic and somatic functions necessarily interpenetrated one another at the various levels of existence. This realization, which was expressed widely and in differing ways in the OT writings, has formed the basis of modern psychosomatic medical research. It need occasion no surprise, therefore, to discover that under this figure of rhetoric the "flesh" could be used to designate the personality in its total reaction to life (Ps 63:1 [Heb 63:2]), where the psalmist paralleled the idea of the soul thirsting with the flesh fainting. By extending the psychosomatic concept in a particular direction and fixing it upon one of the internal organs which gave vitality to the "flesh" or personality, it was possible in poetic thought to conceive of the "heart and flesh" singing for joy (Ps 84:2, [Heb 84:3]). By contrast, the heart of the psalmist had been stricken within him, so that his knees became weak with fasting and his body gaunt with hunger (Ps 109:23, 24). Because of his physical appearance his enemies knew that he was enduring emotional and spiritual affliction. The author of Lamentations (3:4) complained that the outpouring of divine anger had made his flesh and his skin waste away and had broken his bones, implying that affliction had brought his entire personality to a low level of expression. The term "flesh" was used also in this same fig. sense as a euphemism for parts of the human body which were associated with sexual activity. The reference to the normal menstruation of the female is directed to the functioning of the womb (Lev 15:19). In another reference to a bodily discharge (15:2, 3, 7), the term *bāsār* alludes to the male genitalia and to a venereal secretion, as contrasted with the benign emissions (15:16-18). Such euphemisms are seen also in the substitution of "hands" and "feet" for the male or female genitalia (e.g., Deut 28:57; Ruth 3:4; 1 Kings 15:23; Isa 6:2, etc.), while a similar usage has been preserved by the KJV rendering of "flesh" (Ezek 16:26; 23:20). The circumcising of the "flesh" is a more familiar way of avoiding a direct reference to the *membrum virile* (Gen 17:14, etc.).

A second fig. use of the term "flesh" involved a rhetorical device known as *metonymy,* which is somewhat different from synecdoche. Instead of naming the thing itself, metonymy describes it in terms of some significant accompaniment or adjunct; whereas in synecdoche the name substituted is generally cognate in meaning, in metonymy the meaning is often less closely related to the substituted term. In the latter figure the instrument can do duty for the agent, the container for the thing contained, the maker for the thing made, the name of a passion for the object of desire, and so on. By using *bāsār* or *sᵉʼēr* in this way the Hebrews could think of "flesh" in terms of natural or family relationships. Thus Adam spoke of his helpmeet as specifically "bone of my bones and flesh of my flesh" (2:23), and the brothers of Joseph expressed the same sentiment (37:27). Two terms were employed (Lev 18:6; 25:49) to express the concept of a somatic relative, while *sᵉʼēr* was used to designate both sides of family descent (Lev 18:12, 13). Under the patriarchal system the unit of natural relationship could reach beyond the family to include the township (Judg 9:2) or the people as a whole (2 Sam 5:1).

3. Theological implications. Although the term "flesh" frequently denoted the vitality of individual personality, there are several instances where human flesh was associated with weakness and frailty. The mortal nature of man was implied (Gen 6:3; cf. Job 34:15), while God was mentioned as excusing human sin on the ground that men were only flesh after all (Ps 78:39). Flesh as weakness was compared unfavorably with spirit as strength (Isa 31:3), and a similar figure occurred in 2 Chronicles 32:8, revealing the weakness of the king of Assyria, described as "an arm of flesh," as contrasted with the mighty power of God. On occasions the use of the expression "all flesh" has direct implications of weakness (Isa 40:6), where humanity was compared to grass which is frail, short-lived, and easily consumed (cf. Pss 37:2; 90:5; 103:15). The dependence of "all flesh" upon God for day to day sustenance was emphasized in Psalm 136:25.

From the comprehensive concept of "flesh" as representative of the people (2 Sam 5:1) it is possible to argue toward the use of *bāsār* along the lines of corporate personality. This is by no means out of harmony with other aspects of OT thought, since the covenant relationship between God and Israel was based upon this general concept. Consequently, the forgiveness of national sins of inadvertence could be entertained in the Heb. sacrificial system just as readily as atonement could for individuals, both procedures not uncommonly involving animal *bāsār*. Taking the religious implications of corporate personality one stage further, it was because of the uncovenanted mercies of God to Abraham and his descendants that all the nations of the earth would be able to bless themselves (Gen 12:3; 18:18, etc.).

The OT theology of human personality, noted above, is of a dynamic order which emphasizes the psycho-physical unity of human nature. Although this "flesh" was regarded in the OT as generally weak, there is no single element in Heb. thought which corresponds to the NT view of the "flesh" as the central principle of fallen humanity. While the flesh for the Hebrews was frail, it was not regarded as sinful, and the nearest approach to the idea of moral weakness seems to be in Psalm 78:39. Salvation for Ezekiel constituted that regeneration which would replace a stony heart with one of flesh (Ezek 36:26), which contains the idea that the flesh is perverted.

BIBLIOGRAPHY. J. A. T. Robinson, *The Body* (1952), 11-16; N. W. Porteous, IDB, II, 276; J. A. Motyer, *Baker's Dictionary of Theology* (1960), 222f.

R. K. HARRISON

FLESH IN THE NEW TESTAMENT. There are three basic ways in which the word σάρξ is used in the New Testament. At the one extreme are those places where no negative moral judgment is implied and the word flesh bears no connotation of evil at all. At the other extreme are those places where a negative moral judgment is made and σάρξ becomes descriptive of man's baser nature or is defined as being simply sinful. Bridging the two extremes is a set of uses where σάρξ is not sinful *per se*, but tends in that direction.

I. Flesh As Non-Sinful. There are three subdivisions here and in none is sinfulness implied.

First, σάρξ is seen as the physical substance from which men are made. The basic and most obvious use is when the meaty or fleshy parts of the body are in view (Rom. 2:28; Col. 2:13; James 5:3; Rev. 19:21) and here flesh may even be distinguished from bones (Luke 24:39). Men share this with animals, which also are fleshy, but Paul is careful to say that it is not the same kind of flesh (1 Cor 15:39). An extension of this idea is where σάρξ describes the body as a whole, physically considered (1 Cor 15:39; 2 Cor 7:5; Gal 6:12,13; Col 2:1). The flesh is man's contact with the world at large and other human beings. The term σάρξ may also be used to describe the physical substance which one inherited from his parents or what united him with others of like descent (Rom 4:1; 9:3,8: Heb 12:9). Jesus is said by Paul to be united with his ancestors in this way as well (Rom 1:3; 9:5).

Second, taking the idea of physical substance one step farther, the term σάρξ is used to define humanity as such; that is, corporeality (flesh) and humanity are made to coincide. This idea is not wholly different from the above, but it looks at flesh from the side of humanity rather than as the vehicle in which humanity resides. Flesh becomes in fact an aspect of humanity as such. Here σάρξ becomes a commonplace designation for a man or mankind in general (Mark 13:20; Luke 3:6; Acts 2:17; Rom 3:20; Gal 2:16). Σάρξ is synonymous with person or human being (John 17:2) and "flesh and blood" means a human being (1 Cor 15:50; Gal 1:16). Here, too, Jesus is said to take part in our common humanity (John 1:14; 1 Tim 3:16; Heb 10:20; 1 John 4:2).

Because our essential being is corporeal, the term σάρξ may be used to set humanity apart from beings who are not physical, but spiritual, whether it be God (Matt 16:17), or a spirit in the abstract (Luke 24:39), or spirits, concretely, whether they be demonic or otherwise (Eph 6:12). Also, while we are alive we are described as being in the flesh, but after we are gone we no longer have fleshly existence and are presumably as the angels, i.e. spiritually existent, until the resurrection of the body (1 Cor 7:28; Phil 1:24; Heb 5:7).

Third, there is the symbolic use of the word σάρξ made by Jesus in John 6:51-56 where eating His flesh means participating in the benefits of His death. In this passage Jesus says that He is the living bread and the one who eats of it shall live forever. He defines that bread as His flesh which is to be given for the life of the world. He then affirms that His flesh, like the living bread, must be eaten in order for a man to live. All of this points symbolically to a genuine participation in the benefits of Christ's self-offering.

II. Flesh As Weak. Although the above category implies no necessary or inherent weakness or sinfulness, it tends in that direction. The flesh is called weak (Matt 26:41) although the Spirit might be willing; i.e., the flesh is not always a fit medium through which the higher element of man may act. The law which tells us of God's requirements is weak not in itself, but because of the flesh (Rom 8:3); the flesh simply does not cooperate. The flesh is subject to physical infirmity (Gal 4:13) or may more comprehensively designate the whole person as weak (Rom 6:19). The flesh is mortal (2 Cor 4:11), and what is born of flesh (John 3:6), that is, what is human only is irreversibly so. It can never be more than it is. The flesh gives rise to pride when one glories in the externals related to it (Phil 3:4). The flesh is unavailing and ineffectual when it comes to spiritual warfare (2 Cor 10:3) and cannot add to what God has done by His Spirit (Gal 3:3).

In none of this is there necessarily sin, but the weakness of the flesh is that it cannot, in its present state, fight off temptations and lusts and therefore is the place where sin may make its malevolent entrance into human lives.

III. Flesh As Sinful. In this category a negative moral judgment is made. Here the term is used to define the lost condition of man before the life-giving Spirit of God makes His entrance. When we were "in the flesh" we were lost (Rom 7:5; 8:5,6,8). Akin to this, in Paul's allegory concerning Hagar and Sarah to be "born after the flesh" is to be lost (Gal 4:29). Because Paul has used the word *σάρξ* to mean being lost, he is careful to point out that the Christian is not in the flesh, but in the Spirit (Rom 8:9). A lost man is in the flesh and dominated by sin, thus the ideas of sin and flesh may blend together. The flesh becomes the baser side of man defining either the impulse to sin itself or at least the seat of it (Rom 7:18, 25; 8:5b, 12,13; Gal 5:17,19; 6:8; 1 Pet 3:21; 2 Pet 2:10,18; 1 John 2:16). The flesh (man's base nature), as it were, lurks about seeking a chance to break loose and wreck havoc on man (Gal 5:13). An extension of this correlation of sin and flesh is seen where *σάρξ is* sin (Jude 23), or where by extension the word *fleshly* becomes an adjective meaning sinful, and qualifies other ideas. Hence one may have a fleshly body (Col 2:11) or a fleshly mind (Rom 8:7; Col 2:18). The word *σαρκικός* is used in this way as well, meaning base or sinful (e.g. Rom 7:14; 15:27; 1 Cor 3:1; 1 Pet 2:11). Indeed, the flesh may be defined as simply "sinful" (Rom 8:3). Here too Paul is careful to say that the Christian is not dominated by the flesh. Just as the believer is not in the flesh (Rom 8:9) so he has crucified the flesh, with its affections and desires (Gal 5:24). In this connection it is significant that Paul nowhere says the flesh will be resurrected; for him it is the body that will be raised to newness of life (see e.g. 1 Cor 15:44). This is because *σάρξ* connoted sin to Paul and the word body was a more neutral term. The flesh, man's fallen nature, will not be raised again.

What is the connection between the conception of flesh as an earthly substance and flesh as debased? The link seems to be sin. Flesh is not sinful *per se*, as made by God, but now, as fallen, the flesh is sinful because all men are *de facto* sinners. It is through the flesh that sin makes its most dramatic entrance (lust), and hence flesh and sin may become almost synonymous terms; but it must be remembered that the mind may generate desires that are sinful too (Eph 2:3), and that there is uncleanness of the spirit, as well as of the flesh (1 Cor 7:1). However, the Christian is freed from his bondage to the flesh, for although the flesh is contrary to the Spirit attempting to prevent the believer from doing what he would (Gal 5:17) it is fighting a losing battle. To walk in the Spirit is not to do the desire of the crucified flesh (Gal 5:16), because we are no longer debtors to the flesh (Rom 8:12) but alive through the Spirit and heirs of God destined to be glorified together with Christ (Rom 8:16,17).

W. A. ELWELL

FLESHHOOK. KJV tr. of מַזְלֵג (1 Sam 2:13, 14) or מִזְלָג (Exod 27:3; 38:3; Num 4:14; 1 Chron 28:17; 2 Chron 4:16), tr. by modern versions as "fork." It was one of the implements used in the Tabernacle (Exod 27:3; 38:3; Num 4: 14) and the Temple (1 Chron 28:17; 2 Chron 4:16). A three-pronged instrument was used by the priest to remove the portion of meat due him from the boiling pot (1 Sam 2:13, 14). It is not clear whether this is the same instrument as above since the vocalization of the word is different.

F. W. BUSH

FLESHPOT, FLESH-POT (סִיר הַבָּשָׂר, meaning *pot of flesh* or *meat*). These pots were large metal kettles which were used for the cooking of meat. Other purposes for which the pots were used are the boiling of water and for washing.

The specific reference to fleshpots is found in Exodus 16:3 where the Israelites spoke about how well they fared in the land of Egypt. Their complaint includes the statement that in Egypt they "sat by the fleshpots and ate bread to the full." Some scholars have felt this statement to be somewhat strange, since meat was not a part of the poor man's diet. However, Numbers 11:4, 5 appear to indicate that fish also was considered as flesh.

G. GIACUMAKIS, JR.

FLINT, an opaque black, gray, brownish-black or smoky brown variety of very fine grained silica (silicon dioxide) possibly with some hydrated silica. Flint, which is allied to chalcedony (q.v.) is not as hard as many gem stones (Ezek 3:9), but is harder than steel and is used as an abrasive. It commonly occurs as hard, tough, structureless nodules (cf. Isa 50: 7), particularly in chalk deposits which, to a large extent, consist of calcareous remains of

Flint object

minute organisms together with varying proportions of detrital sandy (siliceous) and clayey material. The concretionary nodules of flint represent the redeposition, from percolating ground water, of silica derived from the solution of small scattered sponge spicules, originally scattered through the chalkstone (q.v.). The nodules tend to be found mainly along bedding planes in the chalk where there was some detrital silica. This is the case for the flint nodules occurring in the chalks and chalky limestones of northern Samaria, parts of western Galilee and over large areas of Jordan E of the Jordan Rift Valley. In Jordan, particularly, the relatively soft chalkstone has been eroded away, mainly by the wind, and has left the hard impervious nodules as residual flint gravels.

Flint fractures into shell-like shapes as the result of either a blow or under thermal action (heat or frost). The flakes, which at their edges may be pale gray or yellowish-brown, afford sharp cutting edges. Because of this, and the hardness of the material, flint was extensively used by prehistoric man for weapons and tools.

BIBLIOGRAPHY. E. S. Dana, *A Textbook of Mineralogy,* 4th ed. (revised by W. E. Ford) (1932), 472, 473; E. M. Blaiklock (ed.), *The Zondervan Pictorial Bible Atlas* (1969), 438-452.

D. R. BOWES

FLOAT, FLOTE. *See* SHIPS AND BOATS.

FLOCK. A word used to tr. three Heb. and two Gr. words: עֵדֶר ; used to refer to a group of sheep or goats, or both together (Gen 29:2; S of Sol 4:1; Joel 1:18); also used fig. of Judah as the flock of God, the object of His special care (Isa 40:11; Zech 10:3). צֹאן ; also used to refer to sheep or goats (Gen 4:4; 38:17), the context sometimes making clear that it does not include both (1 Sam 25:2), and to Judah (Ps 77:20; Jer 23:2); מִקְנֶה, "cattle" (Num 32:26). ποίμνη, ποίμνιον. These Gr. words are used exclusively in a fig. sense of the Church (Matt 26:31; Luke 12:32; Acts 20:28, 29; 1 Peter 5:2, 3).

S. BARABAS

FLOGGING. *See* CRIMES AND PUNISHMENTS.

FLOOD (General) is the tr. of a number of different expressions (פרץ מים, *a burst of water*; מַיִם נחלות, *rushing water*; שבלת, *a flowing stream*; שטף, *flood, overflow*; מבול, *deluge*, used mainly of GENESIS FLOOD; Gr. κατακλυσμος, *deluge*; πλεμμυρα, *spring freshet*; πόταμος, *river.* Floods have been part of the many vast cycles of nature throughout all of the years of earth's geological history. These cycles may be seasonal annual rainfall or melting of winter snows, or sporadic and unpredictable, caused by great hurricanes and monsoon storms. There are also massive seacoast floods caused by high winds and tides. As man began to build his centers of living near the great river systems and ocean ports, and as the population increased, the incidence of landslides, tsunami waves, and cycles of flooding became disasters.

Flash floods are sudden violent bursts of water surging down narrow mountain valleys or desert gullies previously dry. They occur in mountainous areas where high slopes are relatively bare of vegetation, but do not generally last long. The illustration of Jesus concerning the men who built their houses on rock and sand, and who passed through a flood is prob. an allusion to this phenomenon (Matt 7:25, 28; Luke 6:48).

Tsunamis are low seismic sea waves, generated by earthquakes. The energy wave can travel across oceans, fastest in deepest water, up to 600 mph. One of the earliest such waves recorded wiped out cities of Crete, Greece, and other Aegean seaports after the eruption of Santorini volcano about 1500 or 1400 B.C.

The terms *mabbul* and *kataklysmos* are applied almost completely in the OT and NT respectively to the GENESIS FLOOD. The other terms are used to describe either the natural floods that occur from time to time, or else are used fig.

BIBLIOGRAPHY. J. Strong, *The Exhaustive Concordance of the Bible* (1890); W. G. Hoyt, and W. B. Langhein, *Floods* (1955); L. B. Leopold, M. G. Wolman and J. P. Miller, *Fulvial Processes in Geomorphology* (1964); A. N. Strahler, *The Earth Sciences,* 2nd Ed. (1971).

W. U. AULT

FLOOD (Genesis)

I. The Biblical account
  A. Reason
  B. Date
  C. Place
  D. Ark
  E. Animals
  F. Cause
II. Sumerian, Babylonian and other traditions
III. Interpretations—universal and non-universal
IV. Theories to explain the cause of the Flood
  A. Canopy theory
    1. Ice ages
    2. Climatic change
    3. Mammoth extinctions
  B. Rapid melting of glacier ice
  C. Fountains of the deep (Isostasy)
V. Evidence cited for the Flood
  A. Universal (?) language
  B. Flood tradition
  C. Diluvea
VI. Catastrophism vs. uniformitarianism—flood geology
  A. Unconformities
  B. Aeolian deposits
  C. Redbeds
  D. Rain
  E. Evaporite deposits
  F. Fossil sequence

G. Mass extinctions
H. Coal
I. Cyclothems
J. Age of fossil fuels
K. Sediments
L. Serious flaw
M. Geologic time table
VII. Conclusions

I. THE BIBLICAL ACCOUNT

The Biblical account of the Deluge at the time of Noah is found in Genesis 6-9. The relative amount of space in Scripture and details given for this event in human history seem to underline its importance. In the NT it is cited as an important event. Two recent writers, Ramm (1956) and Heidel (1946), present rather extensive objective, and scholarly treatments of the Flood, and the reader is referred to these works. We accept the Genesis account of the Flood as factual and true, a historical event; but we cannot interpret, explain or add to the words given in Genesis without introducing uncertainty. Many theories have been advanced to explain specific aspects of the flood and thus make the account fit a particular interpretation. Some of these theories can be briefly evaluated on the basis of established archeological and geological data.

A. Reason. The reason for the Flood was "the wickedness of man . . . the earth was corrupt in God's sight, and the earth was filled with violence" (Gen 6:5-11). But "Noah was a righteous man, blameless in his generation . . . [who] walked with God" (Gen 6:9). God commissioned Noah as a preacher of righteousness to warn the people, and to prepare a large ark to preserve human and animal life during the Flood.

B. Date. The date when the Flood occurred is not known. Conservative Christian writers, e.g. Unger (UIGOT, p. 194) and Ramm (RCVSS, p. 233) believe that the Deluge took place "long before 4000 B.C.," based on archeological remains. The genealogical methods used for computing dates are at best only estimates, having uncertainties of perhaps thousands of years. (*See* ANTEDILUVIANS for discussion of genealogies.) It appears that most writers on the subject would place Noah between 5,000 and 15,000 years ago, but without satisfactory basis. Fifteen thousand years would cover the recessional stages of melting and flooding of the last continental ice sheets, but not the migration of man into North and South America.

Layers of fine sediment from a flood of very limited extent have been found at several ancient cities of Mesopotamia. In archeological lit. we find the use of terms "pure river silt" and "clean uniform clay" to apply to the eight foot layer of river sediment at Ur dating from the mid-Obeid Period, and later "evidences of a large flood" at Shuruppak during the Jemdet Nasr Period, and still later a "layer of sediment" (or "similar stratum" compared to that at Ur) one and one-half ft. thick at Kish and "some distance above the Jemdet Nasr Period." Hence these terms applied to flood sediment must be taken in the general sense to indicate their fine-grained size and not in the technical sense to distinguish between silt and clay or to indicate composition. Finnegan suggests that the flood at Shuruppak or Kish may be the one referred to in the Sum. king List. Barton indicates that "there is no real proof" that either of the sediment layers (Ur or Kish) were deposited at the time of the Biblical Flood. In fact, the evidence from pottery examined by Frankfort has shown that the two "inundations were not even in the same century." He concludes that there is "no evidence that these deposits . . . mean more than that for a time the Euphrates and Tigris changed their beds and flowed for a time over parts of Ur and Kish that had previously been inhabited" (FLAP, p. 24, BAB, p. 41.)

Some so-called "Pre-Flood Seals" and "Pre-Flood Tablets" found at Fara and Ur, and at Kish respectively beneath "layers of silt" (HBH) are most likely older than the silt, but whether they pre-date Noah is open to question. Ramm indicates that there are four such "flood deposits" separated in time by about 600 years, therefore they cannot be cited as evidences of Noah's flood" (RCVSS, p. 233). They cannot be used to date the Flood.

So far, we know of no bonafide materials, either archeological or geological, which are known with certainty to derive from the Flood of Noah. This must not be construed to mean that we do not believe the Biblical Flood to be a historical event, but rather that we have not found or recognized any flood remains evidencing it. Any material evidence, if it can be produced, could and would be studied by varied physical and chemical analytical techniques. For example, any particular sediment or sedimentary rock frequently has characteristics revealing information concerning the source rock and its proximity, and the processes of weathering, erosion, transportation, and deposition of the sediment. These factors are varied and diverse as represented by the present day accumulation of sediment.

Archeologists have discovered several ancient historical records of the Flood from Sumerian and Babylonian sources in Mesopotamia. These show remarkable similarities to the Genesis account and are discussed later.

Frequent stories about finding Noah's ark have all proven fictitious, and even recent expeditions to Mt. Ararat (Ağri Daği), variously given as 16,254 to 16,946 ft., have produced no convincing evidence. Berossus reported that "the vessel being thus stranded in Armenia, some part of it yet remains in the Corcyraean Mountains." Genesis 8:4 indicates that the ark "came to rest upon the mountains of Ararat." Wright indicates that this is some indefinite place in the highlands of Armenia and not Mount Ararat. (ISBE, 11, pp. 821, 823.)

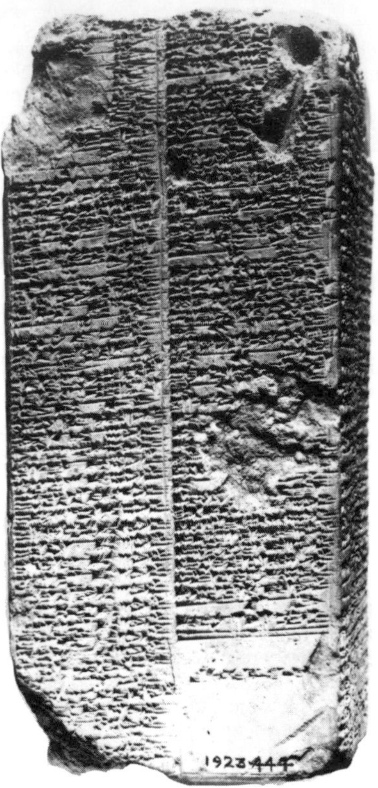

A Sumerian Prism (called the Weld Prism), found at Kish and dated about 2000 B.C. It gives an outline of world history, naming ten kings who ruled before the flood. ©*ARAMCO*

A few recent writers, not geologists, appeal to terrace gravels and unconsolidated sediments as evidence of flood deposits but this is untenable. None of the terrace gravels are known to correlate world wide, and the more recent ones date throughout 1.6 million years of the Pleistocene Epoch. The divisions of the Pleistocene Epoch are discussed more fully later. Any organic materials such as plant debris, humic soil layers, or wood from the ark could be reliably dated by radiocarbon.

C. Place. Essentially all writers concur that Noah lived in Mesopotamia and built the ark there. The Sumer. King List indicating ruling cities before and after the Flood in Mesopotamia, lends strong support (BAB, p. 317).

If the date for Noah is placed too far back the Persian Gulf would have been non-existent as a gulf. It would simply have been an extensive lowland traversed by the confluenced Tigris and Euphrates Rivers and subsequent tributaries. During the prolonged Wisconsin Ice Age of perhaps 40,000 years or more, when vast ice sheets covered some six million square m. of North America and Eurasia, sea level was about 330 ft. lower than today. In its last stages the North American ice sheet had several advances with periods of retreat (melting back) in between. The last glacial maxim, the Tazewell, occurred at 17,000 BP (before present) and the last readvance, the Cochrane, at 8,000 BP.

Consequently, before 17,000 BP and possibly until 8,000 BP, mankind likely inhabited extensive areas of the continental shelf, now below sea level. Areas like the Persian Gulf should be fruitful areas to explore for buried remains of early man. However, even the oldest Sumer. flood stories refer to cities in post-glacial Mesopotamia and not to an extended lowland area as discussed above. A possible exception may be found in BAB, p. 318, tr. the Babylonian cunieform text. Column III, lines 23-25, reads "Dumuzi the hunter (?), whose city is *among the fishes*, ruled 100 years." This it might be noted, does not prove, but fits well with, a date for Noah and the Flood within the last 8000 years.

D. Ark. Noah was commanded (Gen 6) to make an ark of gopher wood, with three decks and rooms, covered inside and out with pitch, with a roof, and finished "to a cubit above," and with dimensions: 300 cubits long, 50 cubits wide, and 30 cubits high. The gopher wood (Heb. *'atsē*) is thought to be cypress, which Ramm points out the Phoenicians used for their ships, as did Alexander to build his fleet at Babylon (RCVSS, p. 229). The ark was essentially a rectangular box with one door. Apparently the roof was to be finished to within a cubit of the walls leaving an opening all around for ventilation (HGEOTP, p. 234). The length of the cubit is uncertain since there were long and short cubits, royal cubits, Egyptian cubits and Talmudic cubits with lengths ranging from eighteen to twenty-five inches. The legal cubit of the Talmudists was twenty-two inches. Regardless of which cubit was used, the ark was built with dimensions perfect for floating, the approximate ratios of which have been copied by modern ships (RCVSS, p. 230). Covering the ark within and without with pitch (*see Bitumen*) would make it waterproof with a flexible covering.

E. Animals. The animals, birds, and creeping things coming into the ark to Noah, all in pairs and some by sevens, was nothing less than a miracle. Taxonomists report that there are presently about 4500 species of living mammals and 8650 species of living birds. There are some, but comparatively few, species of each which are known to have become extinct in the last few thousand years (SPEAK, p. 7, PCDZ, p. 302; ABW, p. 11).

F. Cause. The flood waters are attributed to rain and to factors not understood. The windows (sluice gates) of heaven were opened, and all the fountains of the great deep burst forth (Gen 7:11). If the waters covered the highest mountains as they stand today it would require some eight times as much water as presently existing on earth. There were certainly high mountain ranges at the time of the

Flood because the highest mountain ranges of today were uplifted many millions of years ago—the Alps and Himalayas around 35 million years ago, the Rockies and Sierra Nevada about 80 million years ago, and the Andes about 10 million years ago. Hence, it is highly improbable that, due to any normal natural process, the elevations of ocean floor and the highest mountain peaks at the time of the Flood a few thousand years ago were different from present elevations by more than a few feet. Conjectures on the meaning of "windows of heaven" and "fountains of the deep" are no more than theories and must be recognized as such until such time that substantiating evidence is discovered. We can say with confidence that there is no adequate source of subterranean waters. Water has a specific gravity of one which is about one-third that of average crustal rock. The oceans and continents have been traversed by gravity surveys sufficient to make this generalized statement. No such subterranean reservoirs have been found.

II. Sumerian, Babylonian and other traditions

Remarkable supporting evidence for the Biblical Flood comes from ancient clay tablets found in Mesopotamia. Below is a comparison showing some of the similarities and differences between the several sources. Barton (BAB, pp. 317-336) gives a tr. and comparison of the Babylonian accounts. Wright (ISBE, II, p. 823, 824) compares the Genesis and Babylonian accounts which are ably summarized by Ramm (RCVSS, pp. 247, 248). Similarities: (1) The Deluge is a divine punishment for man's wickedness. (2) The ark floats inland in Mesopotamia. (3) Both accounts agree in general regarding the collecting of animals for preservation, but the Babylonian account doesn't mention the number seven for clean animals. (4) Birds are sent out in both accounts, but the order in Genesis is a raven and a dove (twice), while in the cuneiform the dove and raven are reversed and a swallow is added. (5) Both accounts have an altar after the Flood, but the Babylonian account is polytheistic. (6) The accounts both agree in indicating that the human race will not again be destroyed by a flood.

The differences are: (1) The cuneiform inscr. is polytheistic: Genesis is monotheistic. (2) The different names used are not reconcilable at present. (3) The dimensions of the ark in Genesis are reasonable, being similar to the dimensions of modern shipping. Those given by the cuneiform and Berosuss are not reasonable. The cuneiform gives 140 x 140 x 140 cubits, and Berossus gives the length as 5 stadia (3000 ft.) and width as 2 stadia (1200 ft.). (4) In the cuneiform the deluge results from a quarreling among the gods, and the survivors escape through a mistake which angers the god Bel. In Genesis the holiness, justice and mercy of God is evident even in His punishment of the wicked. (5) Both accounts indicate rain as a source of water, but the Biblical account gives "fountains of the deep" and the Babylonian tablet indicates a raging sea and wind. (6) The Babylonian tablet relates the slaughter of animals for food, a mast and pilot for the ship, and the lading of the ship with silver and gold. (7) The duration of the Flood in the Bible is a year and seventeen

The eleventh Tablet of the Assyrian version of Epic Gilgamesh. It records the Babylonian version of the Flood. © *B.M.*

Figurines made by pre-Flood people.

days, while in the Babylonian tablet it is fourteen days.

III. Interpretations

Interpretations of the Genesis account of the Flood have been categorized as either 1) universal or 2) not universal (limited, local, regional), depending on whether it is held that all the high mountains of the world were covered by liquid water at the same time.

Wright (ISBE II, p. 824) asks the question "Was the flood universal?" Ramm (RCVSS, pp. 236, 238) notes that the Church generally has held to a belief in a universal flood and many Christians still do, but most "recent conservative scholarship of the church defends a local flood." Arguments generally presented in defense of a universal flood are:

1. The language of Genesis 6-9 is universal —the waters prevailed so mightily upon the earth that all the *high* mountains under the *whole* heaven were covered; the waters prevailed above the mountains, covering them fifteen cubits deep. And all flesh died . . . everything on the dry land in whose nostrils was the breath of life died . . . only Noah was left and those with him in the ark.

2. Universality of flood legends among all people, attributed to the descent of all races from Noah.

3. World-wide distribution of diluvia deposits.

4. Sudden death of many woolly mammoths frozen in Alaskan and Siberian ice; an inferred milder climate to support the necessary flora for food in contrast to frozen conditions which prevail presently; and the reported observation that these animals died by choking or drowning and not by freezing.

5. The so-called depletion of the species

claimed by "flood geologists." They argue that there are relatively fewer species living today compared to the number evidenced in rock strata and attributed to the Flood.

Those who hold that the Flood was less than universal do so because of the seemingly insurmountable physical problems involved, viz.:

1. The amount of water needed to cover Mt. Everest would be about eight times as much as that presently on the earth, and there is no known source for such an amount of water, and no way of getting rid of the water afterward.

2. The unique distribution of animals, for example, the kangaroo in Australia, Tasmania, and New Guinea (Wallabies) and the problem of getting them to Mesopotamia and back again without populating other parts of the world.

3. The practical logistics of housing so many species of mammals (4500), and birds (8650), and other terrestrial life in a three story ark about one acre in floor plan (3 A total), and caring for them for one year.

Since Scripture records the Flood as a natural-supernatural occurrence and not as a pure and gigantic multiple miracle, they argue, it is only logical to assume that the practical problems presented by a universal flood indicates that such an interpretation is incorrect and not intended by the inspired account. Indeed from other Scripture references such universal language expressions obviously do not mean universal in the absolute sense (see discussion later.)

Several non-universal flood interpretations have been suggested:

1. That all the highest mountains were not covered by liquid water but perhaps were covered by snow and ice, or were simply not meant to be included.

2. That the Flood was universal only with respect to mankind—a) that flooding covered lowlands world-wide and that the habitation of mankind was limited to these lowlands, or b) that flooding was limited to the Mesopotamian area as was the distribution of mankind.

3. That the entire record must be interpreted phenomenally; that is, if the Flood was local, though spoken of in universal terms, so also was the destruction of man local though spoken of in universal terms.

These interpretations involve many assumptions and must each be viewed only as theories of interpretation. Factors involved in the above

A pre-flood tablet, with pictographic inscription, found under the flood deposit at Kish, in Babylonia. ©*F.M.*

Annipadda's Foundation Tablet, a marble slab found by Dr. Woolley in a cornerstone of a Temple near Ur. This is one of the oldest historical documents ever found, dating back to soon after the Flood. ©*B.M.*

interpretations will be discussed in the next section.

IV. Theories to explain the cause of the Flood

Since the account of the Flood in Genesis is simple and brief there are many unanswered questions. Many of these questions may remain unanswered indefinitely but they have generated numerous theories. It is important to remember that essentially all discussion to explain the *cause* of the Flood are theories and are not to be considered on a par with the data from the inspired Scriptures. By inspiration we mean that under God's guidance the original autographs of the Scriptures were factual and accurate within the intended meaning of the writer. The Genesis account describes historic persons, places, and physical phenomena. The favored viewpoint (interpretation) should be one that appears to have the best agreement with Scripture and with information derived from our present knowledge of the physical universe. Theories propounded in such a way that show disregard for basic knowledge or that consist of conjecture having little or no basis in fact should be labeled, perhaps, as science fiction. A number of theories which cluster around the miraculous are of this type because they assume physical phenomena which have no basis in fact.

There is a sense in which the whole phenomenon of the Flood was supernatural; i.e., God said to Noah, "I will bring a flood of waters upon the earth" (Gen 6:17). However, the deluge is not called a miracle in Scripture. It is stated in terms of physical phenomena seemingly emanating from the earth alone. Writers who hold to a universal flood are driven to postulate miraculous phenomena for the source of the water and its subsequent removal from the earth; or they postulate a miraculous change in the height of the mountains and depth of the ocean basins. Ramm ably reminds us that much of the weight of evidence for a local flood view stems from showing the imponderable difficulties of a universal flood (RCVSS p. 240).

We must emphasize that it is not a question of what God can or cannot do. Rather, the question is "What did God do?" Those who hold to a local flood view believe in the omnipotence of God as much as those who hold to a universal flood. The problem is not one of inspiration of the Scripture but one of interpretation. The problems arising from the universal flood and the questions of interpretation have prompted writers to postulate various supposed physical phenomena to effect the universal flooding of the earth, or to associate the worldwide flooding of all lowlands (or lands to a certain arbitrary elevation) with the rapid melting of continental glaciers at the end of the Wisconsin Ice Age.

A. Canopy theory. The canopy theory and ice lens theory are similar in that they suggest a source of flood water which is beyond the atmosphere, and these both suffer from the same problems.

The canopy of water theory postulates that the earth was initially enveloped by a layer of water or water vapor beyond our atmosphere, supposedly formed during the early (prob. high temperature) history of the earth. This canopy of water was the source for the water which flooded the earth.

The ice lens version is similar, suggesting that the water required to flood the earth initially existed as an ice lens or perhaps a satellite (moon) of the earth. This ice mass was broken up and precipitated on earth causing the great ice age (vast continental glaciers) and the Flood.

We are reminded that to envelop the earth with water to a depth to cover Mt. Everest, 29,028 ft. elevation, would require some eight times as much water as presently on earth. Even if there were naturally existing extraterrestrial sources of water precipitated on the earth by some physical phenomena, the subsequent removal of the water would be a stupendous miracle, for there is no known existing mass of water above the atmosphere today. Water in the atmosphere comprises only 0.001 per cent of the total water on earth.

Both the canopy and ice lens theories propose the precipitation on earth of presumably fresh water. This would greatly dilute the world's oceans and could be verified in several ways. If this were the case then geochemical studies of marine water and marine organisms predating the Flood would be expected to differ from those of today. Precipitation is substantially different isotopically from sea water. Oxygen in precipitation is isotopically lighter in mass by about 0.7 per cent in the mid-latitudes and by 3 per cent in the Arctic. Hydrogen in precipitation is lighter by about 7 per cent in mid-latitudes and by 30 per cent in the Arctic. Although no isotopic study has been directed solely at the problem of possible recent dilution of the oceans, there is ample oxygen isotopic data available on marine samples from the present back millions of years. The study of paleo-temperature (ancient temperature) measurements is possible because of the verification that certain marine organisms build their shells of carbonate in which the oxygen composition is isotopically in equilibrium with that of the ocean water and is temperature dependent. Also, the hydrogen and oxygen isotopic data on ancient brines (trapped residues of ancient sea water) is typically that of present day oceans. The geochemical data has shown no evidence of a large dilution—say a dilution of times eight or even a dilution of times three or times two—a few thousand years ago.

Keil and Delitzsch consider (v. III, p. 146) the problem of the great amount of water needed and that possibly the loftiest mountain peaks were not covered, and that Genesis 7:19, like Deuteronomy 2:25 and 4:19, has been regarded as a rhetorical expression which is not of universal application. However, they maintain that even if mountain peaks higher than Ararat (there are more than forty) were not covered, we must regard the flood as universal because the few peaks uncovered would be insignificant in comparison with the surface covered, and no human beings could exist upon these mountains covered with perpetual snow and ice. Their suggestion does not help the problem much since over three times as much water as is present on earth would still be required.

Some writers suggest that there were no high mountains on earth at the time of Noah. Such a suggestion cannot be taken seriously because the Himalayas and Alps were uplifted gradually from the Tethyan geosyncline in post Eocene time over many millions of years beginning about thirty-five to forty million years ago. Most other major mountain ranges are much older.

The ice lens or ice planet suggestions apparently were conceived first because of the requirement of much water to effect the Flood, and secondly as a result of assuming that the ice age was a catastrophic event of "extreme suddenness" (PBFIE, p. 101ff.). It is rather ill conceived, making numerous assumptions without established evidence, and the theory does not account for the disposition of the excess water after the Flood. The theory is esp. inadequate in that it ignores most of the evidence for the glacial periods.

1. *Ice ages.* There was not just one glacial period—precipitated suddenly a few thousand years ago and lasting for one year—when continental glaciers covered much of the northern part of continents in the northern hemisphere, but there is adequate evidence that there have been four periods of extensive continental glaciation throughout much of the Pleistocene Epoch (the last 1.6 million years). The continental ice sheets slowly spread outward and generally southward from the several areas of snow accumulation on each of the northern continents. In North America the place of major snow accumulation was the vast area around Hudson Bay. These phenomena of snow accumulation, changing to glacial ice under pressure, and spreading outward from areas of accumulation are well known, being presently observed in the interiors of Greenland and Antarctica and in numerous valley glaciers under study in the high mountain ranges.

The continental glaciers each took thousands of years to advance, lasted for tens of thousands of years, and took several thousand years to retreat (melt back). The last major ice sheet in North America is called the Wisconsin. Along most of its southern front it did not advance as far S as the much earlier and successively older Illinoian, Nebraskan, and Kansan ice sheets did. During the Wisconsin period there were subperiods covering thousands of years when the glacier was receding followed by minor readvances. Fairbridge gives data on some of these subperiods of readvance—Tazewell (about 17,000 BP, before present), Carey (about 15,000 BP), Valders (10,500 BP), and Cochrane (8,000 BP). Just prior to the Valders subperiod the glacier had retreated from the area around Two Creeks, Wisconsin on the shore of Lake Michigan so that a black spruce forest had grown there. This spruce forest was pushed over, buried and preserved by the fine glacial sediment about 11,300 BP (radiocarbon dates on wood, Broecker and Farrand, 1963).

2. *Climatic change.* Another assumption made for the canopy theories is that the earth's climate abruptly changed at the time of the Flood (PBFIE, p. 110) from widespread subtropical to temperate over most of the earth to that of the ice ages. This assumption ignores the dates and great length of time shown for the repeated build up and advance of continental glaciers, as already discussed, and also the various ages of the flora remains cited as evidence for change in climate. Repeatedly in the past there were long periods of widespread subtropical conditions but one cannot at random claim one of these as evidence and ignore the time aspect of when such conditions prevailed.

The last interglacial (Sangamon or Riss-Würm) with mean temperatures of about 75°F (24°C) prevailed for thousands of years prior to approximately forty or fifty thousand years ago. Present day mean temperature is about 30°F. These interglacial periods did not come on abruptly, but the change happened over thousands of years, as evidenced by ocean bottom sediments and the dating by the thin varve layers of glacial lake sediments formed during recession of the glaciers. Many of the widespread climatic changes of the past took place over millions of years. For example, the gradual change which occured during the Miocene and Pliocene Epochs of the Tertiary Period, covered some twenty-five million years.

3. *Mammoth extinctions.* The extinction of woolly mammoths which are found frozen in the glacial ice and permafrost areas of Alaska and Siberia have been cited by non-scientific writers as evidence of a sudden catastrophe which deepfroze the whole population with fresh grass still in the mouths and undigested food in the stomachs. It is alleged that this is evidence of an abrupt change in climate.

Again, important data have conveniently been omitted. The woolly mammoth, mastodon, woolly rhinoceros, and other associated animals are cold weather animals native to the colder latitudes. Drumm indicates that the woolly mammoth "had heavy fur and a layer of fat beneath the skin, both adaptations of extreme cold." Contrary to popular opinion, the mammoth carcasses were "not as fresh as

TABULATED CHRONOLOGY OF THE FLOOD

1. The making of the ark (Gen. 6:14)	
2. Collection of the animals (Gen. 7:9)	7 days before the rain started
3. Fountains of the great deep were broken up and the windows of heaven were opened	Second month, 17th day in Noah's 600th year
4. Rain (Gen. 7:12)	40 days and 40 nights
5. All the high hills covered (Gen. 7:19)	
6. Water prevailed upon the earth (Gen. 7:24)	150 days
7. Water returned from off the earth (Gen. 8:3)	150 days
8. Ark rested upon the mountains of Ararat (Gen. 8:4)	Seventh month, 17th day
9. Waters decreased (Gen. 8:4)	
10. Tops of mountains seen (Gen. 8:5)	Tenth month, 1st day
11. Noah waited (Gen. 8:6)	40 days
12. Noah sent forth raven and a dove; dove returned (Gen. 8:7-9)	
13. Noah waited (Gen. 8:10)	7 days
14. Noah sent forth dove again (Gen. 8:10); dove returned with olive branch (Gen. 8:11)	7 days
15. Noah waited (Gen. 8:12)	7 days
16. Noah sent forth dove which did not return (Gen. 8:12)	7 days
17. Noah removed covering; face of the ground was dry (Gen. 8:13)	1st month, 1st day, Noah's 601st year
18. Earth dried; Noah left ark (Gen. 8:14)	2nd month, 27th day

quick-frozen meat." Its remains have been found associated with typical tundra plants and animals. The Beresouka mammoth, discovered in northern Siberia near the Beresouka river in 1899, had undigested food in its stomach—"remains of grasses, sedges, the alpine poppy and buttercup" (DMM, pp. 7, 12). Scientific opinion places the extinct mammoth within their usual arctic habitat and attributes each death and burial to normal accidents such as falling over a cliff or into a crevass, caught in a blizzard or a mud flow, etc., in situations where they were quickly frozen and preserved.

Drumm also estimates the mammoth population in late Pleistocene prior to extinction as about 50,000 (ibid). The woolly mammoth has been extinct so long that no mention of it is known from the legends of living people, but paleolithic man left drawings of it on the walls of a cavern at Combarelles, France. Beside the nearly complete Beresouka carcass about fifty others less complete have been found frozen in Alaska and Siberia (DWHG, p. 35). Radiocarbon dates of the carcasses show that they lived and died 11,450 to 39,000 BP. Significantly they did not all die at the same time but over a period of time, 37,000 years or longer, and the most recent one over 10,000 years ago. The existence of frozen mammoth carcasses which are 39,000 years old is strong evidence that the north tundra regions of the earth have remained frozen and therefore have not been covered by a flood during this time. Such evidence would appear to be fatal to Patten's theory, for he postulates that the ice age came suddenly, froze the mammoths, and caused a world-wide flood. However, he does not explain how the mammoths remained frozen during a year long flood which was violent with huge tidal waves so that it transported all types of sediment but left all the mammoths and associated animal remains undisturbed in their cold habitat.

Kowalski (MWPE, pp. 356, 357), discussing possible causes of the extinction of mammoths, calls attention that the mammoth's adaptation to cold climate preclude life in the present southern steppes of Eurasia with their warm dry summers. The present-day tundra north of the Arctic Circle, with its long polar nights and abundant winter snowfall, is very different from the steppe-tundra of the late Pleistocene with no polar night and possibly light snowfall.

In summary, the extra-terrestrial ice theory as the cause of the Flood as presented by Patten is invalidated by 1) the existence of more than one period of glaciation in the Pleistocene Epoch; 2) the duration of the Wisconsin period of glaciation for 40,000 years or more; 3) the duration of the combined periods of glaciation during the Pleistocene Epoch (perhaps as much as 1.6 million years); 4) the evidence of extensive glaciation during the latter part of the Paleozoic era, viz., the Permian period (200 to 300 million years ago) and also during Huronian time of the Precambrian era (some 600 to 700 million years ago); 5) the existence of widespread subtropical and temperate climate numerous times in the past, the last being about 60,000 years ago (there is the existence of widespread subtropical and changes); and 6) the supposed catastrophic mass extinctions by freezing at a recent date do not accord with the facts.

B. Rapid melting of glacier ice. There is much evidence that during maximum glaciation (greatest extent of continental glaciers) the world mean sea level was over 300 ft. lower than today. If the Greenland and Antarctic ice caps were to completely melt, sea level would rise another 300 to 400 ft. During maximum glaciation much of the presently submerged continental shelf areas were dry-land coastal regions inhabited by man. It has been suggested by Fairbridge that a period of relatively rapid melting of the glaciers and flooding of the extensive coastal regions accompanied by torrential rains could have generated the numerous flood stories among many peoples. Data is also cited to indicate that the mean sea level rose during some oscillations of the glaciers at approximately thirty ft. per cent. The greatest and fastest rise was about 6000 BP and the highest mean sea level was about ten to twelve ft. higher than at present.

In the absence of any other confirming evidence, the above should be taken only as a suggestion. We do not know the date of Noah's Flood, or that the human population inhabited only the coastal regions at that time. Fossil man, Australopithecines to Homo sapiens, seems to have ranged far inland. Furthermore, an appeal to world-wide flooding to generate the numerous flood stories implies that all of mankind today did not derive from Noah.

C. Fountains of the Deep (Isostasy). Another theory that has been suggested to explain the mechanism of flooding of the earth indicated in Genesis 7:11, 17—"the fountains of the great deep were burst forth . . . and the waters increased greatly upon the earth"—is that the ocean floor was uplifted and the continental masses, esp. the mountain ranges sank.

Isostasy or isostatic equilibrium is the geologic phenomenon which describes the various segments of the earth's crust, for example, the deep ocean floors or parts of continental masses as floating more or less independently in the plastic (or hot and viscous) mantle of the earth. The principle can be illustrated by barges in a river. When loaded, they float lower than when unloaded. Also, even though two identical barges were loaded with the same weight, if one were loaded with solid rock having a density of 3.3 and another with somewhat more bulky rock having a density of 2.8, then the bottom of the barges would each float at the same level in the water but the load of the second barge would stand at a higher elevation. Illustrating still further, if the second barge had a much heavier load than the first in addition to being more bulky (lower density), then its lower surface would float lower and its upper surface higher than that of the first barge. This is precisely the comparison that geophysical data indicates between the crust of the earth in the ocean basin and the continents. The few miles of water (low density) added to the dense basaltic rock composing the ocean floor, averages a higher density than the very thick crustal plates consisting mostly of low density granitic and sedimentary rock. As mountain ranges are slowly unloaded by erosion they continue to rise.

Improbability (miracle?). The isostatic adjustment of the earth's crust to loading is a slow response because of the viscosity of the mantle substratum. Parts of the continent, where unloaded of their burden of glacial ice 8 to 10,000 years ago, are still rising measurably (adjusting isostatically). Thus it can be seen that to suggest that the ocean floors raised and the mountains sank without any known physical cause and within a few months time would invoke nothing less than a gigantic miracle. It is evident that the highest mountain ranges, e.g. the Himalayas, Alps, Andes, and Rockies could not have been depressed several miles independent of the continents and raised again without leaving telltale fault trenches and gouge (ground up rock) zones. To suggest that the convection cells in the earth's mantle, proposed by geophysics on much evidence, localized selectively and greatly speeded up by a factor of a billion or more, is again suggesting nothing less than a world-wide miracle.

Again we remind the reader that there is no known scientific evidence which would allow us to expand on the meaning of "fountains of the deep." There certainly are no vast atmosphere reservoirs, or subterranean reservoirs of water beneath the floor of the oceans. Seemingly the simplest miracle would be to create and then remove the additional water required for the year long Flood. But the Scriptures nowhere call the Flood a miracle, or indicate that God created much water for this occasion, or that the continents and mountains sank beneath the waters. Rather, we are told that the waters rose and prevailed exceedingly until the high hills and mountains were covered.

V. Evidence cited for the Flood

A. Universal (?) language. John Pye Smith, Ramm, Filby and others feel that the weight of the argument is in favor of a local flood. The universality of language is not sufficient proof for a universal flood in face of the inherent problems and absence of any confirmatory evidence. Similar expressions are found in 1 Kings 18:10; Job 37:3; Psalm 22:17; Matthew 3:5; John 4:39; and Acts 2:5 but they are not pressed for universality. Did literally all countries of the world come to Egypt to buy grain (Gen. 41:57)? Did the American Indians live in fear because of Joshua's conquest of Canaan (Deut. 2:25)? Likewise the NT reference to the universality of sin passing on all men has a notable exception in Jesus Christ (Rom. 1:8) (RCVSS, p. 241). Our attitude must be one of desiring to know all the facts in the case by weighing all the evidence before drawing our own conclusions, rather than being committed immovably to a position. If we are seeking truth we will be willing to change when the facts warrant it.

B. Flood tradition. Traditions of a flood (or floods) are widespread among many peoples. This is generally taken as evidence that all people of the earth descended from Noah. The Deluge was so impressive that they carried the story with them as they spread out over the earth, changing and corrupting the story down through the millenniums. Ramm points out that flood stories are not found everywhere; e.g. Japan or Egypt and few in Africa (RCVSS, p. 242). But Wright (ISBE, II, p. 822) and Filby (FFR, p. 52) discuss many flood legends, among them China, Siberia, Kamchatka, the Americas, and Africa. Filby indicates that they are "much less common in Africa which is represented by Egypt, Sudan, Nigeria, Congo, and South Africa."

Filby concludes that "there is no other story of an ancient event in all the world so widely accepted," and the cumulative weight of evidence is "that the present human race has spread from one center and even from one family . . ." (ibid). Even if the Flood accounts are taken as evidence for the universal destruction of mankind in the Flood, they cannot be interpreted to indicate the extent of inundation of the high mountains without making assumptions about the distribution of antediluvian man. It must also be admitted that there is no proof that the traditions all refer to the same flood.

C. Diluvea. Over a hundred years ago worldwide diluvea was cited as proof of Noah's Flood. Such views were held by the then prominent geologist, Wm. Buckland in his *Reliquiae Diluvinae* (1823), and non-geologist Cuvier and others. Buckland, however, recanted his views in 1836 because of closer study of these unconsolidated geologic materials which had been quite unspecifically designated. Unconsolidated stream and glacial alluvial deposits of widely differing ages had been erroneously grouped together. Many streams will leave valley terrace gravels as do glacial lakes during the retreating stages of the glacier and high sea level stands of former interglacial warm periods.

VI. Catastrophism vs. Uniformitarianism

Moore (1970) helpfully reviews the debate between catastrophic and uniformitarian viewpoints of geology during the 19th century. He wisely counsels writers that to understand the history of the warfare of the past "is valuable both as a warning to avoid repeat performances and as an aid to better understanding of the present debate."

Catastrophists variously attributed certain types of rock strata to Noah's Flood. With the development of many analytical techniques and ensuing detailed studies of geological strata, numerous sedimentary phenomena are recognized, none of which indicate a universal flood. The times of formation of the various strata in question also are known to represent not one point in time but many geologic epochs and periods over thousands and millions of years. Today no qualified geologists hold to the catastrophic viewpoint, essentially because there is no evidence for it.

Some recent writers on the Flood take an anti-uniformitarian position, but it is significant that none are geologists. They do not seem to realize that an anti-uniformitarian position, to be valid, requires them to demonstrate, in the cause and effect relationship of the physical and chemical laws of the universe, the variability which they propose. In nearly every case such a writer, after disclaiming uniformity, will then proceed to present a scheme which, to make it plausible to the reader, employs the uniformity of cause and effect in the natural phenomena which he proposes. To every Christian the nature of the Judaeo-Christian God of Scripture, in whom is no variableness, neither shadow of turning, should not only fit well with the uniformitarian concepts but would seem to demand them. In fact, if it were not for uniformity of cause and effect in nature, it would be impossible to recognize a miracle (an act of the Supernatural). We conclude that the non-uniformitarian view is incorrect and that such writers are inconsistent. The Christian should intuitively accept uniformitarian principles as the usual course of nature because a belief in miracles and the Supernatural requires it.

Flood geology, otherwise known as catastrophic geology, is an attempt by some (Price, Morris and Whitcomb) to explain all the geologic formations as due to the Flood of Noah. Basically it is an attempt to claim all the great thicknesses (many miles) of sedimentary strata as physical evidence for the Flood. The writings of these non-geologists exhibit a basic lack of understanding of even the fundamental principles of geology. Kulp (1950) and Ramm (RCVSS, pp. 179-188) have reviewed a number of basic points that completely invalidate the flood geology approach. Many types of geologic features could not have formed under water, others could not have formed in a short period of time, and countless other features show varied, sequential, and definite space and time relationships that require varied environments and much time. A few of these are:

A. Unconformities. Essentially all erosional unconformities, whether formed on horizontal strata of marine origin or on formerly horizontal strata which have been tilted at an angle or folded and faulted, are formed by subaerial erosion. This is subsequently covered by a different sequence of horizontal strata frequently deposited after the region in question has again become covered by marine waters. An example of this is the early Paleozoic strata, the Tapeats sandstone of Cambrian age, which overlies the Grand Canyon Series of late Precambrian age. The early Paleozoic strata in the Colorado Plateau show a gradual ingress of the sea from W to E on a time scale of millions of years.

B. Aeolian deposits. Thick deposits of wind-blown sand showing beautiful cross bedding, e.g., the Navajo sandstone of Zion National Park, the Windgate and Entrado sandstones, give evidence of extensive deserts prevailing during the Triassic and Jurassic periods when these thick wind-blown sands were deposited. The Silurian and Permian were also periods when widespread deserts prevailed in North America.

C. Redbeds. Subaerial exposure of sediments during deposition in the near shore environment, produced on fluviatile floodplains, or by migrating shorelines due to fluctuations in sea level or continental elevations, results characteristically in redbeds. Good examples of this are the extensive Devonian redbeds of the Catskills, the Triassic redbeds of the ancient fault troughs of eastern U.S., and the Old Red Sandstone of Great Britain.

D. Rain. The Flood of Noah is sometimes coupled with the assumption, on the basis of Genesis 2:5, that there was no rain before the Flood. That there were hundreds of millions of years of rain throughout the history of the earth is evident from the existence of rivers, flood-plains, glaciers, fresh water lakes, water erosion and transportation of sediments, and many others, among them fossil raindrop imprints in formerly soft mud now preserved in sedimentary rock.

E. Evaporite deposits. The sequence of sedimentary strata from Silurian and Permian periods contain extensive beds of salt. Noteworthy are the Silurian salt deposits of western New York (aggregate thickness, 250 ft.), the Silurian and Devonian of eastern Michigan (aggregate thickness of Silurian alone is 1600 ft.), the Delaware and Midland Basins of the Permian period in New Mexico and Texas which precipitated nearly 2000 ft. of anhydrite and salt in the Castile formation and 2400 ft. in the overlying Salado formation, and enormous Permian salt deposits in Kansas and Jurassic anhydrite deposits in the Williston Basin on the northern Great Plains. Similar salt deposits are found in other parts of the world. There is no way that these precipitate beds of salt could be intercalated with other basin strata in a submarine environment of a great flood. Rather, salts are precipitated from saline water which is saturated because of intense aridity and evaporation, and the thick layers are evidence of continual but limited inflow of sea water from the ocean. Interlayering of halite, sylvite, cancrinite and other salt and potash evaporite minerals is controlled by slight variations in geochemical conditions (temperature, pH, etc.). It is calculated (DWHG, p. 301) that to produce the Permian salt of Kansas, Texas, and New Mexico alone (3 x 10^{13} tons) would require the evaporation of 22,000 cubic miles of sea water of normal salinity.

F. Fossil sequence. The sequence of fossils in the strata of the world or in the stratigraphic column in any one region simply cannot be explained on the basis of a one year flood. The fossil species are not hopelessly mixed. Rather, many index fossils, distinctive of a given geologic period have been recognized and used successfully by geologists around the world. Different brachiopod species, for example, which are index fossils for different periods, may have distinctive morphological features but be quite similar in shape and size. There is no way that these fossils could be selectively winnowed out of world-wide flood waters and deposited in their respective strata except that they lived at different times and were buried where they lived. Likewise, Cenozoic mammals and birds are not found in the Mesozoic strata, and Mesozoic reptiles (dinosaurs) are not found in the Cenozoic strata. On the other hand, fossil flora and faunal assemblages in a given stratum often allow one to deduce a picture of paleoclimatic conditions distinctive to and consistent with the marine, littoral, or terrestrial environment.

G. Mass extinctions. It is repeatedly and erroneously claimed by some writers that the mass extinctions of animals all occurred simultaneously a few thousand years ago during the Flood. Fossil evidence does not show a mass extinction several thousand years ago. Rather, there have been extinctions throughout geologic times since the Cambrian, but some periods are characterized by extensive extinctions of many species. Noteworthy are the Permian about 225 million years ago and the Cretaceous about 65 million years ago. It is erroneously claimed by some that the woolly mammoth, mastodon, woolly rhinoceros, saber tooth tiger, and others were wiped out simultaneously in a common world cataclysm which left many carcasses frozen in tundra and glacial ice. However, the paleontologic data shows that of about fifty such carcasses found, they were entombed from 11,450 to 39,000 years ago. In fact, the radiocarbon dates available at this writing show that most of the woolly mammoths died before 30,000 years ago. The time element completely vitiates the catastrophic ice or flood theory with respect to the mammoths.

H. Coal. Kulp (1950) cites characteristics of coal formation which would preclude it from being formed in a world-wide flood. There is much evidence that the vegetative matter grew right where it accumulated.

I. Cyclothems. The coal beds of the Pennsylvania period throughout Pennsylvania, Ohio, Indiana and Illinois show cycles of deposition. The organic matter collected where it grew in great swamps much like it does today forming peat, which under suitable conditions of arrested decay and burial can form coal. In eastern Ohio tree roots and stumps in some coal beds are still in place in the underclay in which they grew. Typically, after a long period of accumulation (about 100 ft. of vegetative matter will form 1 ft. of coal and some coal beds are many ft. thick) the swamp would be inundated and the layer of peat would be covered by sediments which formed shale, limestone, or sandstone in sequence. About 100 such cycles of deposition, cyclothems, are recognized in eastern Ohio. This alternation, from terrestrial swamps to near shore sandstone or shale deposition to marine limestone environment and back again repeatedly, rules out flood geology as a reasonable possibility. Cannel coal, formed almost entirely from pollen accumulation in open water patches of the swamp gives evidence of lengthy selective accumulation.

J. Age of fossil fuels. If any deposits of coal, petroleum, asphalt, oil shale, or black organic shales were formed within the last 40,000 years from plants or animals still living at the time of formation, then the deposit could be dated reliably by radiocarbon. Anyone who proposes a recent origin for any of these deposits should diligently try to verify the assumed age by dating them.

K. Sediments. Flood geology cannot explain how the proposed gigantic tidal waves could fill the Rocky Mountain seaway (Cordilleran geosyncline of the Cretaceous which subsequently uplifted to form the Rocky Mountains) with billions of km^3 of sediments from the W, and the Appalachian geosyncline (Paleozoic trough which uplifted to become the folded Appalachians) with terrestrial sediments from the E, and at the same time not scatter the terrestrial sediments into the ocean basins. The fact that continents were not denuded of even their loose sediment demonstrates the non-existence of such hypothetical gigantic tidal waves. The Genesis account does not give the faintest suggestion of tidal waves; rather, Noah and the ark appear to quietly ride out the Flood.

Furthermore, Genesis seems to indicate the existence of the Tigris and Euphrates Rivers in Mesopotamia before and after the Flood. Thus even transient geomorphological features like river systems and regolith (loose rock material) survived the Flood with no demonstrable change.

Another serious question to be faced by advocates of the various flood theories, is what would happen to all the neritic (shallow) marine life, for example, immobile coral and bottom dwellers if suddenly the depth of water were increased by several miles, and that by the addition of non-marine or fresh water. Both the increased pressure and decreased salinity would have a devastating effect on marine life. There is no evidence of such a recent massive extinction or decimation of the population.

L. Serious flaw. Perhaps the most serious flaw exhibited in flood geology treatment is the incompatibility with the scientific method. To hold to the flood geology theory of catastrophism in the face of all the evidence to the contrary, much data and analytical techniques must be rejected, even though they can be demonstrated repeatedly by observation and measurements. Clearly this is not an objective approach. An objective approach allows and demands that one change his interpretations when established data warrants it.

M. Geologic time table. A geologic time table of many consistent data-points over 3000 million years (or 4500 million years including meteorites and lunar rock samples) has been obtained on geological materials by several independent, established radioactive methods. This is confirmed by many research scientists in numerous countries around the world. No one has been able to alter the rates of radioactive decay by physical, chemical, or radiation techniques. It appears that God, the Creator, has provided man with a built in geochronometer with which to unravel the time problems of the universe. These indicate that the solar system is about 4500 million years old which is compatible with Genesis in that it gives no age—"In the beginning"—and with our eternal God who existed even before He created time.

VII. Conclusions

In conclusion, the predominance of qualified Christian scholarship appears to favor a local flood interpretation because of the lack of evidence for and the problems attendant on a universal flood. There is, and has been no lack of writers who propose a catastrophic universal flood. However, they present little that is new, and no data that is convincing. The serious Bible student will not seek to support the physical aspects of Bible history with pseudo-science. In the final analysis the true interpretation of the Biblical flood account will fully accord with true science. At this time we may favor one viewpoint over another but must seek continually to integrate all the pertinent data which seem well established.

BIBLIOGRAPHY. J. P. Smith, *On the Relation Between the Holy Scriptures and some parts of Geological Science* (1840); G. A. Barton, *Archaeology and the Bible* (BAB) (1937); G. F. Wright, "Deluge, of Noah, The", in Orr, J. and others (ISBE), v. 1 (1939), 821ff.; J. Finegan, *Light from the Ancient Past* (FLAP) (1946); A. Heidel, *The Gilgamesh Epic and Old Testament Parallels* (1946); C. F. Keil and F. Delitzsch, *Biblical Commentary on the Old Testament* (1949); J. L. Kulp, "Deluge Geology," J. Amer. Sci. Affiliation, v. 2, No. 1 (1950), 1-15; M. F. Unger, *Introductory Guide to the Old Testament* (1951); B. Ramm, *The Christian View of Science and Scripture* (1954); H. H. Halley, *Bible Handbook*, 22nd Ed. (1959); R. W. Fairbridge, "The Changing Level of the Sea," *Sci. Amer.* (May 1960), 70-79; J. L. Austin, *Birds of the World* (1961); V. J. Stanek, *The Pictorial Encyclopedia of the Animal Kingdom* (1962); W. S. Broecker and W. R. Farrand, "The Radio-carbon age of the Two Creeks Forest Bed, Wisconsin," Geol. Soc. Amer. Bull., v. 74 (1963), 795-802; J. Drumm, *Mammoths and Mastodons: Ice Age Elephants of New York* (1963); R. F. Pennak, *Collegiate Dictionary of Zoology* (1964); H. M. Morris and J. C. Whitcomb Jr., *The Genesis Flood* (1966); D. W. Patten, *The Biblical Flood and the Ice Epoch* (1966); P. S. Martin and H. E. Wright, Jr., (eds.) *Pleistocene Extinction* (1967); C. O. Dunbar and K. M. Waage, *Historical Geology*, 3rd ed. (1969); F. A. Filby, *The Flood Reconsidered* (1970); J. R. Moore, "Charles Lyell and the Noachian Deluge," J. Amer. Sci. Affiliation, v. 22, No. 3 (1970), 107-115.

W. U. Ault

FLOOR (גרן, meaning *threshing floor*, Deut 15:14; Judg 6:37; 1 Kings 22:10, etc.; Aram. אדרי קיט־, meaning *summer threshing floor* Dan 2:35; קרקע, meaning *bottom* or *floor*, 1 Kings 6:15, 16 etc.; ἅλων, meaning *threshing floor*, Matt 3:12; Luke 3:17.)

The most common use of the word *floor* in the Bible is in relation to the threshing floor. These floors near the town or village were a flat platform of stone or clay often in the open to insure the blowing wind for winnowing. Either walking animals or dragging sleds were used to separate the grain from the stock. Then it was winnowed by tossing it into the air.

Another use of the word is as the floor of a building. This is esp. seen in 1 Kings 6 in reference to the Temple. In Amos 9:3 the same word refers to the "floor" (NASB) or "bottom" (RSV) of the sea. *See* House.

G. Giacumakis, Jr.

FLORA. The Linnean Society, prob. the oldest Botanical society in the world, of Burlington House, London, says that there are in the plant world 111 natural orders. The Royal Horticultural Society, in its *Dictionary of Gardening,* published in 1951, gives the following explantion for the term "Natural Order": "E.g., family: a group of one or more genera, having close natural affinity, the term is now more usually applied to a group of families nearly related to one another."

The R.H.S. also says that genus (genera) is a group of species with common structural characters, which may be supposed to have derived in the remote past from some common ancestor. The main characters on which reliance is placed in defining "genera" are found in the flower, fruit and seed.

The number of species in a genus may be extremely large, or may be only one, so much structurally isolated from its nearest relative as to stand by itself. The name of the genus in designating a plant is placed first and invariably has a capital initial letter.

In this Biblical encyclopedia, the rules of the Royal Horticultural Society's dictionary have been adhered to. The correct Lat. names have been given in each case, as far as the writer can ascertain them; the generic name has been given, together with the species, and in some cases, the common Eng. name as well.

Of the 111 natural orders recognized by the Linnean Society, some fifty-four are found in the Bible, either in the OT or NT, while a few appear in the Apoc. It must be remembered that the Bible is largely an Eastern book, and the natural orders that are included are those normally found in the Middle E.

In order to cover the whole Flora of the Bible methodically and intelligently, the natural orders are dealt with in alphabetical order.

Classification of Biblical plants

1. Cereals
   a. Barley (Gramineae)
   b. Beans (Leguminosae)
   c. Lentils (Leguminosae)
   d. Millet (Gramineae)
   e. Wheat (Gramineae)
2. Fruit trees
   a. Almond (Rosaceae)
   b. Apple (Rosaceae, Solanaceae)
   c. Fig (Moraceae)
   d. Mulberry tree (Moraceae)
   e. Nuts (Anacardiaceae, Juglandaceae)
   f. Olive tree (Elaeagnaceae; Oleaceae)
   g. Palm tree (Palmaceae)
   h. Pomegranate (Punicaceae)
   i. Sycamore (Moraceae)
   j. Vine (Vitaceae)
3. Vegetables and gourds
   a. Cucumber (Cucurbitaceae)
   b. Endive (Compositae)
   c. Garlic (Liliaceae)
   d. Leek (Leguminosae, Liliaceae)
   e. Onion (Liliaceae)
4. Flax (Linaceae)
5. Flavors and condiments
   a. Anise (Umbelliferae)
   b. Fitches (Ranunculaceae)
   c. Mint (Labiatae)
   d. Mustard (Cruciferae)
   e. Saffron (Iridaceae)
   f. Salt (Chenopodiaceae)
6. Balms, drugs and incense
   a. Aloes (Liliaceae)
   b. Balm (Zygophyllaceae)
   c. Cane, calamus, sweet cane, sweet calamus (Gramineae)
   d. Cassia (Compositae)
   e. Cinnamon (Lauraceae)
   f. Galbanum (Lauraceae)
   g. Henna (Lythraceae)
   h. Myrrh (Burseraceae, Cistaceae)
   i. Spikenard, nard (Valerianaceae)
   j. Spices (Leguminosae)
7. Costly timbers
   a. Algum, almug timber (Leguminosae)
   b. Ebony (Ebenaceae)
   c. Gopher wood (Pinaceae)
8. Forest trees and shrubs
   a. Acacia tree, acacia wood (Loranthaceae)
   b. Bay tree (Lauraceae)
   c. Box tree (Buxaceae)
   d. Bush, thornbush (Compositae)
   e. Cedar (Pinaceae)
   f. Fir, fir tree (Pinaceae)
   g. Juniper (Leguminosae)
   h. Laurel (Lauraceae)
   i. Hyssop (Labiatae)
   j. Mallow (Chenopodiaceae)
   k. Myrtle (Myrtaceae)
   l. Oil tree, wild olive (Elaeagnaceae)
   m. Oak (Fagaceae)
   n. Pine (Pinaceae)
   o. Storax tree (Styracaceae)
   p. Terebinth, turpentine tree (Anacardiaceae)
   q. Willow (Salicaceae)
9. Lilies and roses (Amaryllidaceae, Apocynaceae, Iridiceae, Liliaceae, Nymphaeaceae, Ranunculaceae, Rosaceae)
10. Reeds and rushes
    a. Cattail (Typhaceae)
    b. Flag, meadow, reeds (Butomaceae)
    c. Reeds (Gramineae)
    d. Rush, papyrus, bulrushes (Cyperaceae)
11. Thorns and thistles
    a. Brier (Rosaceae)
    b. Thistle (Compositae)
    c. Thorn (Compositae)
12. Weeds and nettles
    a. Cockle (Caryophyllaceae)
    b. Nettle (Acanthaceae, Cruciferae, Urticaceae)
    c. Tares (Gramineae)
    d. Wheel, rolling thing, whirling dust (Compositae, Cruciferae)
13. Wormwoods and poisons
    a. Bitter herbs (Rutaceae)
    b. Gall, hemlock (Cucurbitaceae)
    c. Wormwood (Compositae)
14. Hedges and fences
    a. Brambles, thorns (Rosaceae)
15. Other plants
    a. Caper (Capparidaceae)
    b. Mandrake (Solanaceae)

Acanthaceae: The only plant mentioned in this natural order is the *Acanthus syriacus,* tr. "nettles" (Job 30:7; Zeph 2:9). This is a common weed in Pal., growing strongly and having spiny leaves.

Amaryllidaceae: Only one plant mentioned is in this natural order—the *Narcissus tazetta.* This is what is called today a Polyanthus Narcissus, and is tr. as "rose" (Isa 35:1 KJV). It is very sweet smelling, and is plentiful in the Sharon Plain. It grows on the hills around Jerusalem and Jericho.

Anacardiaceae: There are three trees that are grouped in this natural order—*Pistacia lentiscus*, tr. "a little balm" (Gen 43:11)—a shrubby, evergreen dwarfish tree, which produces a scented gum from its branches when pierced; *P. terebinthus*, which seems to be mentioned seven times, often as *elah* . . . (1 Sam 17:2), also as "elms" (Hos 4:13), and as "turpentine tree" (Ecclus 24:16). This species of *Pistacia* which has a variety known as *palaestina*, is an oak-like, deciduous tree, growing twenty to twenty-four ft. high, which produces almost invisible flowers, followed by pretty, red fruits. When the branches are pierced, a Cyprus turpentine oozes out. *Pistacia vera* is tr. "nuts" (Gen 43:11 KJV), and this spreading tree can grow to a height of thirty ft. It bears light-colored nuts, containing greenish-yellow kernels, which are sweet to the taste.

Apocynaceae: Mentioned in the Apoc. only, and tr. as "rose" or "rose plant" (Ecclus 24:14; 39:13). This is prob. the *Nerium oleander*, or, to give it its common name, oleander. It is a beautiful flowering shrub, which grows up to twelve ft. tall, bearing masses of white or pink flowers. These are often double, and it is claimed for this reason that they have a rose-like look. The leaves are evergreen, but they are poisonous.

Araliaceae: Only one plant is included under this natural order—the ivy, *Hedera helix* (2 Macc 6:7). No one doubts that this is the common Eng. or British ivy, which was plaited into wreaths, and often worn on the head like crowns by those who were to go in procession in the temple. As a plant, the ivy was dedicated to the wine god, Bacchus, by the Greeks in Biblical days. Today, the plant has lost its heathen connotation.

Burseraceae: A natural order of thirteen genera and 320 species, all of which are shrubs and trees which grow in the tropics only. The flowers are generally small and unisexual, the fruits are capsules or drupes, and most of the species produce resins or balsam.

Commiphora abyssinica (synonym *C. africana*) is a small, thorny tree from which the myrrh is obtained; both the wood and the bark produce a strong scent. This is the Heb. word *mōr*. . . . It was said originally that the myrrh undoubtedly came from *Commiphora myrrha*, but *C. myrrha* was called *Balsamodendron myrrha* many years ago, and recently the botanists have renamed the plant *Canarium*—from *canari*, the Malayan name.

The myrrh found in Exodus 30:23; Psalm 45:8; Matthew 2:11—to mention only three of the twelve references—undoubtedly came from the plant normally called *Commiphora*, but the writer is not certain to which special species this refers.

Butomaceae: The plant found in this natural order is *Butomus umbellatus*, the flag mentioned in Job 8:11 (KJV), and prob. the word "meadow," so tr. in Genesis 41:2. The word used here is Egyp. and not truly Heb. and would appear to be a reed grass or flowering rush, as the Royal Horticultural Society's dictionary calls it. This would be eaten by the cattle, and would grow in the marshy sides of a river.

Buxaceae: In this natural order is found *Buxus longifolia* only. This is the box tree of Isaiah 41:19 and 60:13. It is also mentioned as "boxtrees" in 2 Esdras 14:24 (KJV). The box is a slender, hardy evergreen, which may grow twenty ft. high. The wood is hard and polishes well, and so is much used for carving, wood engraving, furniture and the like. Because this tree is not found in Pal. today it has been argued that it could not have been there in Biblical days. It is far more sensible to believe that the trees were so popular and coveted that they became extinct in that country.

Capparidaceae: If the word "desire" (Eccl 12:5) should be tr. "caper berry," then the plant is *Capparis sicula*, and within this natural order. The common caper is found growing profusely in many parts of Pal., and esp. on the hilly slopes round about Jerusalem. It can cover ruins like ivy, or it can spread over the ground. Not only are the berries picked, pickled and used in the kitchen, but the little unopened flower buds are also popular when pickled in vinegar. It is claimed that the caper buds or berries have a stimulating effect, particularly on men!

Caryophyllaceae: Only one plant is mentioned from this natural order—*Agrostemma githago*. This is surely the "corn cockle" (Job 31:40). The Heb. word לאשה could mean *noisome weeds*. The corn cockle, however, is a common weed in fields of wheat in Pal. It is a strong grower and can be a great nuisance. It can grow two and three ft. tall. The blooms are much like those of the Campion, and can be white, red or purple.

Myrrh

Chenopodiaceae: There is only one plant in the natural order *Atriplex halimus*, commonly called the Sea Purslane. Here the reference is to the "mallows" (Job 30:4 RSV). The Heb. word מַלּוּחַ has a salt connotation to it. Therefore, it seems that it is a saltwort, often called "orach." The halimus species is the Sea Purslane. It is naturally found round about the Dead Sea. There are incidentally over twenty species of *Atriplex* in Pal.

Cistaceae: There are three possible entries under this natural order—*Cistus salvifolius, C. creticus* and *C. villosus*. It all depends how one trs. the word לוט "myrrh" (Gen 37:25; 43:11). The scented product could indeed have come from one of the flowering rock-roses whose Lat. names are found above. The name "ladanum" . . . is spelled "ladan" in Arab.—"labdanum" in some old writings. This is a gummy, dark-brown, blackish substance, which will ooze out of the foliage and little stems of the Cistus plants. This gum is very fragrant. It is collected by drawing a piece of material over a bush, and the substance sticks to the cloth and can afterward be removed. It is wondered whether *Cistus creticus* really ought to go into this list, as it is not predominently Palestinian.

Compositae: There are nine plants that can be included in this natural order. The first is the *Anthemis palaestina*—the chamomile, with its aromatic leaves and daisy-like little flowers. This is very common in Pal., where the plants are in flower from February to May and June. The plants are dried like hay, and can be burned, as Scripture suggests (Luke 12:27, 28).

The second in this group, *Artemesia herba-alba,* the wormwood, mentioned many times (Deut 29:18 KJV, Prov 5:4 RSV, Jeremiah 9:15, and goes on through Lamentations, Hosea, Amos, and on to Revelation 8:11). All wormwood has an acrid smell, and the leaves taste bitter. The ancient Jews thought the plants to be poisonous. *Herba-alba* is the most common species in Pal.—there is a camphor fragrance to it.

There is also *Artemesia judaica,* which is found only in a few parts of Pal. now. It is included because one cannot be absolutely sure to which species Scripture refers.

It is thought that the thistle mentioned in Genesis 3:18; Hosea 10:8 and even 2 Kings 14:9 and 2 Chronicles 25:18, is the Star Thistle, *Centaurea calcitrapa.* The problem here is that one cannot obviously be sure of the species, let alone the genus. There are other thistles found in Pal. today like *Centaurea iberica* or *Centaurea verutum.* As the writer states under "Thistle" there is a possibility that "bramble" would be a better tr. or even "thorn bush."

If the bitter herbs found in Exodus 12:8 and Numbers 9:11 are chicory, then the plant is prob. *Cichorium intybus.* It could as easily be the *C. endivia,* the "endive," which is much used as a salad today. In Great Britain, roots of chicory are forced in heat and in the dark, in order to produce the golden chicons used as a salad. In Pal., the leaves of both these plants would be eaten as growing, and this is why they were described as tasting bitter. The bitterness is removed today by blanching, which is the etiolation of the leaves by keeping out the light.

The next plant to be found in this natural order is *Saussurea lappa,* which is found as the word "cassia" (Ps 45:8). This, as will be found under "Cassia" is known as the Orris root. The plant is a perennial with strong roots, and looks like a thistle when growing, often six feet high.

The *Gundelia tournefortii* is best described as a prickly, milky herb with headlets of six to seven flowerets. The leaves are leathery, thick and rigid, having prominent veins; the plants usually are easy to find around Nazareth and Jerusalem, and near the sea of Tiberias. This is one of the plants thought to be the "rolling thing" (Isa 17:13), now known as the *Gundelia.* It is a thistle-like plant, which can curl up into a ball and so rolls in the wind. It collects sometimes in the hollows or dips. The Heb. experts in Pal. at the present time feel that the Heb. word *galgal* should be tr. Gundelia, and there is, of course, some similarity in the name.

Notobasis syriaca is a very common Palestinian plant found growing on the roadsides and in the fields. The stems are erect and branching, and the leaves are glabrous above and hairy below, and they are edged with spines. The flowerets are tubular. This is one of the thistle-like plants which may find a place in Scripture, being, say, the Syrian this-

The globe thistle, one of the common "thistles" and "thorns" of Palestine. ©*M.P.S.*

A mustard tree. ©*M.P.S.*

tle mentioned in Isaiah 34:13 or Job 31:40. It would certainly have been a commonly-known thistle to Job.

Xanthium spinosum is the Burrweed or Clot Burr found at the roadsides, bearing tripartite, green leaves, wedge-shaped at base, with strong yellow spines. This may be the plant referred to in Isaiah 34:13 and Hosea 9:6. The Clot Burr, as it is called, is very prickly. The plants are usually three ft. tall and produce tiny green flowers at the top of the stems.

Cruciferae: It seems that three plants can be included in this natural order in the Bible. First of all the "wheel" (Ps 83:13 KJV), the rolling thing (Isa 17:13 KJV, and even the rose plant (Ecclus 24:14). This is presumed to be the *Anastatica hierochuntica.* This tumbleweed of Pal. is known in Great Britain as the Resurrection Plant. It grows flat on the ground and after flowering and seeding, the plant curls up to form a hollow ball. Later, the stem breaks in two and the ball rolls away in the wind. As it travels it sows the seeds it contains. This spreads the weed everywhere. Thousands may be seen in Pal., rolling about and traveling at a fast rate in gales.

The second plant is the mustard, the *Brassica nigra,* and is found in Matthew 13:31 "a grain of mustard seed," and 17:20; Mark 4:31; Luke 13:19; and lastly, Luke 17:6. The Gr. word is σίναπι. In Pal. the plant was grown for the oil it produced and not for the yellow condiment so much used today. This annual plant normally grows four ft. high, but the writer has seen in Pal. plants growing to a height of fifteen ft.

The third plant in this natural order is *Sinapsis arvensis,* the nettles found in Proverbs 24:31—"nettles had covered the face thereof." These nettles are prob. charlock—a very common weed in fields of wheat. It looks like mustard, having yellow flowers and grows about three ft. high.

Cucurbitaceae: If the gall mentioned in Deuteronomy 29:18; Psalm 69:21; Jeremiah 8:14, and Lamentations 3:5, is the *Citrullus colocynthis,* then this must be included in the Cucurbits. This may be described as a clambering plant like a squash or marrow, bearing round, orange-like fruits, with a very hard skin. It is a very common plant in Pal.; the fruits look tempting, but when eaten are found to be extremely bitter, and indeed, poisonous.

The second plant found in this natural order is the cucumber, *Cucumis sativus* (Num 11:5 and Isaiah 1:8). It is said that these were much eaten because they were easy to grow and were cheap, by the children of Israel when in bondage in Egypt. Whether the cucumbers they ate were the normal ones grown today, or the *Cucumis chate,* the writer cannot tell. This species has been described as being somewhat variable in shape; the fruit being fusiform, or cylindrical, and a foot long or more. It develops a woody rind and is picked before it reaches the ripe state, and is then cooked and eaten. This information (concerning the *C. chate*) was supplied by Sir George Taylor, Director of the Royal Botanic Gardens, Kew, England.

Cynomoriaceae, sometimes called **Balanophoraceae.** *Cynomorium cocineum* is a parasitic plant found in the salt marshes and in the sand dunes, as well as in the Plain of Jericho toward the Dead Sea. It bears a crimson petal-like leaf called a spathe, which makes it very conspicuous. Some people have thought that the roots Job ate (Job 30:4) were the roots of *Cynomorium.*

Cyperaceae: The only plant that is found under this natural order is *Cyperus papyrus.* This plant was almost a menace along the sides of the Nile in Biblical days, and was the bulrush from which the papyrus paper was made (Exod 2:3; Job 8:11; Isa 19:6; 58:5). These rushes are said to have grown as high as sixteen ft. and could be three inches thick. It is no wonder when they were growing in a mass that they could hide little Moses floating in his basket made with the same flags.

Ebenaceae: There is little doubt that the ebony found in Ezekiel 27:15 is *Diospyros ebenum.* This is the best of many kinds of ebony. Large trees can be produced whose heart wood is usually jet black, though occasionally streaked brown or yellow. It is extremely heavy and strong. The *Diospyros lotus*

Olive branches loaded with fruit. ©*M.P.S.*

also is found in this natural order, being the date plum, sometimes called *Diospyros ebenaster*. This, however, in the writer's opinion, is not the tree that is referred to in Scripture.

Elaeagnaceae: Though in this natural order there are three genera and about forty-five species, the only one that seems to appear in the Bible is the oleaster, *Elaeagnus angustifolia. Elaia* means "olive," and this perhaps gives the connection between the olive tree mentioned in 1 Kings 6:23 and 1 Chronicles 27:28. The oleaster is a deciduous tree growing some twenty ft. high, with spiny branches and narrow, oblong leaves. The flowers are yellow within and silver without, and the fruits are yellowish, oval, with silvery scales. They are mealy and sweet. Some writers have called this tree the Wild Olive, but this does not mean that it is truly related to *Olea europaea.*

Fagaceae: Oaks are mentioned again and again in Scripture, starting in Genesis 35:4, and ending in Zechariah 11:2, though it is true that the scarlet of Revelation 18:12 is prob. the dye from the Kermes Oak tree. It is difficult to know for certain which oaks were grown in Pal. at the time, but there is little doubt that the list included the Valonia oak, *Quercus aegilops*, which produces the largest acorn cups and acorns of any species. The tree is widely spread in the Eastern Mediterranean region. It undoubtedly includes also the Kermes Oak, or Grain Tree, so called because it is the host plant of the Kermes insect (*Chermes ilicis*) which produces a remarkable scarlet dye. The leaves are thick, hard and prickly; the acorns solitary on a short stalk, more than half enclosed in the cup. This is the most pleasing of the dwarf evergreen oaks. There is a variety of *Coccifera* called *Pseudo coccifera,* which is also found in Pal., and it is said that Abraham's oak tree at Mamre was this variety.

The *Holm Oak, Quercus ilex,* could also be included because it is a native of the Eastern Mediterranean, being an evergreen tree of good size, often from eighty to ninety ft. high. The acorns are usually ¾″ long, produced two or three together on a short stalk. There has been a suggestion that *Quercus lusitanica* should be included, but this is a native of Spain or Portugal. There is a variety *infectoria,* which is found in Asia Minor, but the only tree the writer has seen is small and elegant, with grayish foliage. It does not therefore seem to fit in with the Biblical descriptions.

Gramineae: This natural order concerns the family of grasses in which there are 400 genera and 5,000 species at least. They are all monocotyledons. The starch seeds sometimes also rich in protein, make a number of species of this natural order valuable food for man and beast. The leaves of some other species are used today for their fiber and for paper making.

The first plant of nine or ten found in the Bible in this natural order is *Andropogon aromaticus* (synonym *Calamus aromaticus*), found as the "sweet calamus" (KJV, Exodus 30:23; S of Sol 4:14; Ezek 27:19). This is the ginger grass of the E which all kinds of cattle love to eat. The foliage, when cut, smells of ginger, and when eaten tastes of ginger, while from the grass may be obtained a ginger-oil.

A second plant is prob. the *Arundo donax*, the reed found in 2 Kings 18:21; Job 40:21; Isaiah 42:3; Ezekiel 40:3 and Matthew 11:7. It is the Giant Reed or Persian Reed, which can grow to a height of eighteen ft. and was used for fishing rods, walking sticks, and even musical instruments.

There is little doubt about the next in this list—the "barley" of Exodus 9:31; Leviticus 27:16; Deuteronomy 8:8; Ruth 1:22; 2 Samuel 14:30; Job 31:40, and so on. The barleys are *Hordeum*; the spring-sown barley, *Hordeum vulgare*; the winter-sown barley, *Hordeum hexastichon*; and the common barley, *Hordeum distichon.* Bread made from barley was considered food for the poor, hence the poor boy who had five small barley loaves and two fishes. Gideon being poor also is referred to as a cake of barley (Judg 7:13). Today, barley is made into beer, but it was not so in Biblical days. Barley is an easy crop to grow in the E because it puts up with drought better than wheat, and it is ready for harvest four weeks earlier than wheat as a rule.

Panicum miliaceum is the old Lat. name for the true European "millet." This is the millet found in Ezekiel 4:9, and prob. in Ezekiel 27:17, where the word *pannag* . . . is used. This bears a very small grain. The grass itself does not grow more than two ft. high. In Biblical days it was used for food, but today it is almost entirely bird seed. Large fields of millet

"The tares and the wheat . . . some seed fell among thorns." ©*M.P.S.*

are still grown in Pal. in some parts.

If the "sweet cane" mentioned in Isaiah 43:24 is *Saccharum officinarum,* then this must be included in the Gramineae. It is a strong growing perennial grass, looking something like sweet corn, maize or mealies. It certainly was not made into sugar until perhaps the 7th cent., but it may have been sucked and chewed by the Israelites as a kind of "sweet" or "candy." The sweetening of drinks in Biblical times was undoubtedly by the addition of honey.

Once again one cannot be absolutely sure about *Sorghum vulgare,* which is possibly the reed mentioned in Matthew 27:48 and Mark 15:36. This is the name given to a millet widely grown in warmer countries under such names as *durra* . . . or the Egyp. Rice Corn, the Tunis Grass, used for forage, and the Kaffir Corn.

The Triticums are the wheats found again and again in Scripture as corn (Gen 40:2), as bread and wheat and flour (Exod 29:2), as wheat (Judges 6:11), as parched corn (1 Sam 17:17), and even as ground corn (2 Sam 17:19). As in the case of barley, there is winter sown wheat and spring sown wheat, both *Triticum aestivum*; the bearded wheat, *Triticum compositum*; the one grained wheat, *Triticum monoccum*; and the Egyp. wheat, *Triticum tungidum*. Today in Pal., *triticum durum* and *Triticum vulgare* are grown almost entirely. Wheat has always been one of the most important crops of Pal., and has been called "the staff of life." The word "corn" in the KJV is the old Eng. word for grain and has nothing to do with maize or American corn.

Lolium temulentum is an annual, called the Bearded Darnel, sometimes referred to as tares, which is found in the fields of grain around Jaffa and Jericho.

Iridaceae: Two plants, the writer feels, are included in this natural order: (1) The *Crocus sativus*, and (2) the *Iris pseudacorus*.

This is a family of some fifty-seven genera and over 800 species. Most are tuberous or rhizomatous plants of great importance to the gardener.

The *Iris pseudacorus* is the yellow flag iris which grows three ft. high, and is found in Europe as well as in the Middle E. The flowers are bright yellow and almost scentless. This is presumed to be the lily (Hosea 14:5; Ecclus 39:14; 50:8).

There were numerous irises grown in Pal., but this species is the one that grows by the water side, and so fits the full description in Ecclesiasticus 50:8, "as lilies by the rivers of waters." The other species grow largely on the hillsides.

The *shûshan*, tr. "lily," seems similar to the Arab. word *sûsan,* given to Iris species in Pal.

The saffron (S of Sol 4:14) is prob. the *Crocus sativus* or saffron crocus. This was grown in very large quantities in Saffron Waldon, Essex, for the saffron powder used to flavor cakes and puddings. Four hundred crocus stigmas are needed to produce one ounce of saffron powder.

This crocus is fairly common in Pal. today, and was certainly known to Joshua.

Juglandaceae: The name of this natural order is derived from *Jovis glans,* i.e. Jupiter's Acorn. There are sixteen species, all of them deciduous trees bearing walnuts—the common walnut being *Juglans regia*—a tree which will grow to a height of 100 ft. Not only are the nuts much prized but the wood is classed as one of the best timbers. It is much used for furniture.

This is the tree referred to in Song of Solomon 6:11. *Juglans regia* is not indigenous to Pal., but must have been introduced long before Solomon's time. The beautiful shade as well as the fragrant leaves and delicious nuts the trees give would have been much beloved by Solomon's relatives and friends.

Labiatae: This natural order contains 160 genera and 3000 species, only two of which are found in the Bible. Curiously enough though, the family is widely distributed—particularly so in the Mediterranean region. It is a natural order that contains most of the culinary herbs like marjoram, thyme, savory, rosemary, sage, basil, horehound, and so on.

There are two plants found in this natural order, the first being *Mentha longifolia,* seen as "mint" (Matt 23:23 and Luke 11:42). This is the common house or hairy mint, which grows three ft. high and has pale purple flowers. Why some have suggested this could be *Mentha sativa,* the writer cannot understand, because this is really a cross *Mentha arvensis* x *Mentha spicata,* and it is doubted whether it was in existence in the NT days.

The second plant is "hyssop," *Origanum maru,* called *'ezôb* in the Heb. It is a shrubby plant, growing about forty inches high with erect, stiff, hairy branches, and long, hairy, thick leaves. The flowers are purplish, being borne in oblong spikes. It is quite common in Pal. and Syria (Exod 12:22; Lev 14:4; 1 Kings 4:33; Ps 51:7).

Lauraceae: A family of forty-five genera and 1000 species, mostly tropical and sub-tropical trees and shrubs, usually evergreen—all parts being aromatic. Only two species are found in the Bible—the *Cinnamomum cassia* and *Laurus nobilis.*

Cinnamomum is a genus of about forty species of evergreen trees, all of which would seem to be natives of SE Asia. The *Cinnamomum cassia* yields "cassia bark," which is sometimes used as an adulterant in the true "cinnamon," which is *Cinnamomum zeylanicum.* The cassia is mentioned in Exodus 30:24 and Ezekiel 27:19, and it obviously was imported—prob. from Ceylon.

Laurus nobilis is the Bay Laurel, an evergreen aromatic tree, growing often sixty ft. high. The flowers are small and greenish-yellow, often inconspicuous. The leaves are dark, shining green. This is prob. the green bay tree (Ps 37:35 KJV). It has been called bay laurel, sweet bay and bay tree. It certainly must have been a strong growing evergreen tree or shrub.

This bay is a native of Pal., and if we accept the word "towering" instead of "spreading" (Ps 37:35) then we get the rendering "spreading himself like a green bay tree," and this is exactly what *Laurus nobilis* does. The writer has two in his own garden. It certainly is an easy tree to grow, and a very leafy one.

Leguminosae: A family of trees, shrubs, perennial and annual plants, diverse in habit. There are about 430 genera and some 7000 species. This is the family which has nodular outgrowths on its roots. These nodules are formed by bacteria which have the power of using the free nitrogen in the air. The plants therefore benefit and further, the nodules may be left behind for the benefit of crops that are to follow. Thus the "legume" plant may be said to enrich the soil at no cost to itself.

There appear to be eight plants in this natural order mentioned in the Bible. The first one is *Acacia nilotica,* which is one of the plants which some critics suggest may be the answer to the miracle of the burning bush (Exod 3:2). It is on the species, *Acacia nilotica,* that the parasitic plant mentioned under *Lauraceae,* grows.

The *Astragalus tragacantha* is prob. the plant referred to under "spices" (נכאת, Gen 37:25; 43:11; Isa 39:2). It is difficult to be sure, but because the words are like the word used by the Arabs, *necaat'* for gum "tragacanth," one jumps to the conclusion that the species referred to are from the plant *Astragalus tragacantha,* an evergreen shrub, much branched and very thorny—only growing three ft. high as a rule.

Cercis siliquastrum is the Judas tree, which can grow to forty ft., but is usually smaller. The flowers are produced directly on the trunk and branches, giving the idea of the tree "bleeding." The flowers are purply-red or rose. This is the tree that Judas is supposed to have hung himself in, and every year in the spring the trees "bleed," i.e. produce small blood-like flowers in abundance (Matt 27:5) on the stems.

Genista raetam is the white Broom or juniper bush—very graceful indeed. The white sweet-pea-scented flowers are followed by pods about ⅜" long. Its synonym is *Retama raetam.* This is prob. the juniper tree mentioned in 1 Kings 19:4, 5 under which Elijah sat, and may well be the plant of Psalm 120:4. The bush may grow to ten ft. high in Pal., so it could have given Elijah plenty of shade.

Lens esculenta is the lentil mentioned in Genesis 25:34, when Jacob gave Esau a soup, or when Barzillai brought food to David (2 Sam 17:28). This is a vetch-like annual plant —twelve to eighteen inches high, which produces pale blue colored sweet-pea-like striped flowers, followed by pods containing one pea-like seed which splits up into the lentils known and used today.

Pterocarpus santalinus—the name comes from *pteron,* "wing," and *karpos,* "fruit," because the pods are surrounded by broad wings. *Pterocarpus draco* is the Dragon Gum Tree and *Pterocarpus indicus* is the Burmese rosewood. The *P. santalinus* is presumed to be the Almug Tree (1 Kings 10; 11, 12; 2 Chron 9:10).

Since no one quite knows where Ophir is, it is difficult to pinpoint the species of tree referred to, but it may well be the Red Sandalwood. If this is correct, one may certainly add another Legume, *Trigonella foenum-graecum* from *treis* meaning "three," and *gonu,* "angle," because the flowers have a triangular appearance. This is the annual fenugreek, which was eaten as a salad by the Egyptians and Israelites. The plant grows up to two ft. high, quite erect, and produces tiny white flowers. Years ago this plant was used in medicine and as a vegetable. It *may* be the plant referred to in Numbers 11:5 as "leek."

The fenugreek bears seeds which are eaten, and the writer was told when in Cairo that the plants are cut when on the young side, and are popular even today as salad.

Faba vulgaris is undoubtedly the bean mentioned in 1 Samuel 17:28 and Ezekiel 4:9. Its synonym is *Vicia faba,* the broad bean. It bears white flowers with large blue-black spots on them. The pods are large and thick, often seven or eight inches long. It has been widely cultivated for years.

Liliaceae: This is a large natural order, containing over 200 genera and 2000 species distributed all over the world. Most of the species are perennials, but a few are annuals. Most of the members of the family are bulbous, but these are those with corms and rhizomes.

There are ten species mentioned in the Bible, starting with the onion, *Allium cepa.* It is said that it came originally from Persia. This vegetable was known and eaten in Egypt in the days of Moses. Numbers 11:5 talks of the great desire of the children of Israel for onions when they were on the march to the Promised Land. The Egyptians' onions even today are among the best, since they ripen so well in that country.

Allium porrum is the leek—it should now be called *Allium ampeloprasum porrum.* This is a plant whose main stem is blanched when it can be two ft. or more long and one inch across. This is also the pot leek which is stouter and shorter, say, one foot of ivory white stem, two inches or more thick. The nomadic Israelis longed for vegetables in the wilderness (Num 11:5). Leeks make good soup, and are said to be good for the throat.

Allium sativum is the garlic (Num 11:5). This produces oblong ovate offsets around the planted bulb or clove. This is a world-wide extremely popular plant. It is claimed that this is the only plant containing freely assimilable sulphur. It is used medicinally for this reason, and if planted around peach trees prevents an attack of the Leaf Curl disease. The Jewish Talmud believes in garlic, and recommends the bulbs for seasoning dishes.

Aloe comes from the Arabian word *alloeh.* The cultivation of the plants goes back to the earliest of days. There are over 200 species, 110 of them being found in Africa. The aloe mentioned in Holy Writ is *Aloe succotrina.* It was first introduced into Great Britain in 1697. It was lost in the intervening years, and was rediscovered in 1905 in Cape Province, South Africa, by Dr. Marloth. The stem can be four ft. long, and the flowers on the top are pale red. The leaves are thick and tapered—they are pale or glaucous, sometimes blotched toward the base.

The *Hyacinthus orientalis* mentioned, is believed by some (S of Sol, chs. 2, 6) to be lilies. This hyacinth is certainly indigenous to Pal., and is found largely in the rocky parts. This is the Common Hyacinth, much grown today in its various forms. The Goodspeed tr. affirms the use of the hyacinth for lily in a passage as Song of Solomon 2:1—"I am a rose of Sharon, a lily of the valley." The wild Palestinian plant is very graceful, and it is wondered whether it is now in cultivation.

Two lilies should be included in this natural order—*Lilium candidum* and *Lilium chalcedonicum.* The former is the Madonna Lily or White Lily. The flowers are pure white, rarely tinged with purple without. The length of the stem varies from two ft. to five ft. It is known to have grown in the E in Biblical days. The *Lilium chalcedonicum* produces bright scarlet flowers, olive brown at the base. The stems are stiff, and three to four ft. long. *Lilium candidum* is a poor claimant for inclusion, as a matter of fact, but for the fact that in 1925 the first of the wild candidum lilies was discovered by students—and subsequently others were found growing. It is now therefore worth saying that *Lilium chalcedonicum* could be the plant in Song of Solomon 5:13—"his lips are lilies, distilling liquid myrrh." The writer prefers Moffat's tr.: "lips are red lilies, breathing liquid myrr." This, as Song of Solomon suggests, is a plant of great beauty. This lovely scarlet lily may have been rare in the Holy Land, but there is little doubt that it was known then. In fact, it is catalogued at The Royal Botanic Gardens at Kew, England, as a Palestinian plant.

Ornithogalum umbellatum, commonly called the Star of Bethlehem, because of its starry white satiny flowers, has bulbs 1½ inches thick, and the stems are often one ft. high. The writer has seen it growing in Pal. and in the Maltese Islands. It is a very close relation to the popular South African Chincherinchee, *Ornithogalum thyrsoides.* Its name comes from the Ornis (a bird) and Gala (milk). The flowers are supposed to resemble the white excreta of birds when seen growing in stony places. It has been given therefore the name of Doves' Dung (2 Kings 6:25). Some think that the baked bulbs of this plant were sold in the famine.

Tulipa is named after the Turkish word for Turban, which the flower is said to resemble. It is a genus of over one hundred species of bulbs. A special classification was made by Sir Daniel Hall in his book: *The Genus Tulipa* (1940).

Tulipa montana, which it is claimed is mentioned in the Bible, has solitary flowers opening nearly flat. They are crimson-scarlet with a small, black blotch. The stems are about five inches long, the bulb about ¾-inch thick. This is a synonym of *Tulipa ursoniana,* a native, it is claimed, of Persia. *Tulipa sharonensis,* which also has a claim to OT reference, has a solitary wide bell as a flower, dark scarlet in color, with a dark olive blotch, narrowly margined yellow. The stem is six inches long, and the bulb one inch thick. This is undoubtedly a native of Pal., and prob. the only tulip that is.

The text referred to in Song of Solomon 2:1 "Rose of Sharon" may be read as *Tulipa montana,* but more likely as *Tulipa sharonensis*—note the similarity of the species name.

Linaceae: A family of nine genera and over 150 species, found all over the temperate and warm regions of the world. These are mostly trees and shrubs—several of which are very ornamental.

The only Biblical species is *Linum usitatissimum,* known as the Common Flax. This is an annual about eighteen inches high, with an erect stem. The flowers are of a beautiful blue color. Varieties have been chosen by man for their value as fiber in the making of linen, and incidentally for the oil content of the seeds, known as linseed oil.

It is agreed that from flax has come the oldest of fibers that makes very good linen. It presumably is the main vegetable material used for cloth in Bib. days. It was common enough for the flax to be blanched on the flat roofs of houses in Pal., as Rahab was doing when she was visited by the spies in Joshua's days (Josh 2), about 1400 B.C. Evidently, three types of linen were made from Flax—a coarse linen (Ezek 9:2), a superior type of linen (Exod 39:27), and a very fine beautiful linen (1 Chron 15:27). The priests, of course, wore pure white linen garments. Mummies were wound in linen cloths by the Egyptians. In the NT times table napkins or serviettes (John 11:44), and the sails of ships on the Nile and in the Mediterranean were produced from linen.

Altogether, linen or flax appears in some fifty-three vv. in the Bible, and sometimes two or three times in one verse. It starts in Genesis 41:42 when Pharaoh clothed Joseph in fine linen. Linen was part of the priestly clothing (Exod 28; Lev 6:10). Samuel was clothed with a linen ephod when he performed his duty in the Temple (1 Sam 2:18), and so was David (1 Chron 15:27).

The good woman (Prov 31:13) worked with flax to make linen. Jeremiah in the parable was told to get a linen girdle (Jer 13:1), while the Lord Himself told of a man who was rich and wore fine linen. It ends with the armies in heaven that were clothed in fine linen (Rev 19:14).

Loranthaceae: A family of evergreen shrubs and herbs usually with berry-like fruits. There are twenty-one genera and over 700 species in the NT, but only one may be said to be in Holy Writ. Some suggest that the burning bush (Exod 3:4) was the crimson flowered plant—the strap flowered Acacia, *Loranthus acaciae*—Lorus meaning "strap" and *anthos* "flower." This is a parasitic plant which is found growing on Acacias in Pal., and is crimson flowered. The claim is that the flame-like blossoms looked like fire to Moses when growing on a bush—a rather unlikely explanation, since Moses would prob. have been familiar with this plant.

Lythraceae: A family of twenty-one genera and fifty species, found everywhere except in the colder regions. They may be herbaceous perennials, shrubs or trees.

The only plant found in this genus in the OT is *Lawsonia inermis,* the henna plant—a shrub growing to a height of ten ft. bearing rose-colored flowers in panicles. There is a white variety and a species called *miniata,* which bears cinnabar-red flowers. The latter was not seen in Pal.

This plant is always cultivated in the E for the production of a dye. Even today, the leaves are imported into Europe for the making of cosmetics.

Actually, in the OT the word "henna" does not appear, but it seems obvious that the word "camphire" (S of Sol 1:14, and 4:13) is really henna.

Moraceae: A family of fifty-five genera and over 1000 species, most of them trees and shrubs, but including some plants whose stems contain milky juice, found in the tropics.

The only three plants in this natural order are *Ficus carica*, the common fig; *Ficus sycomorus,* known as the Sycamore fig, and *Morus niger*, the common or black mulberry. This can grow to a height of thirty ft. with fruit clusters one inch long, dark red, sub-acid and sweet. It is grown in some countries for the fruit, but in Great Britain for the beauty of the leaf and trunk. It is a tree indigenous to W Asia.

The Sycamore fig is said to be the sycamore of the Bible. The synonym is *Sycomorus antiquorum.* It is sometimes called the mulberry fig—it certainly is not what we today call the sycamore or buttonwood which is *Platanus occidentalis.* This sycamore fig is found in different texts (1 Kings 10:27; 1 Chron 27:28; Ps 78:47; Amos 7:14).

The *Ficus carica* is the ordinary fig mentioned again and again in the OT and NT. The Jewish nation is pictured as an olive tree. The fruit was considered part of the staple diet of the Israelites (Micah 4:4; Zech 3:10). Figs are mentioned some fifty-seven times altogether. Even at the beginning of time, Adam and Eve tried to make garments or girdles with fig leaves.

Myrtaceae: A natural order of some seventy genera and 2800 species, usually growing in sub-tropical and tropical areas. The shrubs or trees are invariably aromatic and evergreen. The flowers are usually showy.

Myrtis communis is the Common Myrtle—a densely-leaved shrub with downy shoots. It can grow fifteen ft. tall. The solitary flowers are small and white and scented when bruised. These are followed by a purple-black berry, half an inch long.

In Nehemiah 8:15, myrtle branches are re-

Right: First and second figs. © *M.P.S.*
Left: A young fig tree. © *Lev*

ferred to, as they are in Isaiah 41:19; 55:13, and Zechariah 1:8. This is quite a common tree in Pal. The leaves, flower petals, and the fruits are all used in perfumes. Myrtle is a symbol of peace and justice to the Jews.

Nymphaeaceae: This is the family of water plants. There are eight genera and over sixty species found almost everywhere in the world except the Arctic regions. The flowers of this family are as a rule striking and beautiful.

Nymphaea lotus is the only species mentioned in the Bible (Job 40:21, 22). It is the Egyp. lotus. The flowers, which open on four nights only, are large and scentless—the leaves are large and flat.

It is prob. this lily mentioned in 1 Kings 7:22, "upon the top of the pillars was lily-work," or in 2 Chronicles 4:5 "its brim was made like the brim of a cup, like the flower of a lily."

It is obvious that the children of Israel knew of water lilies which they would have seen in Egypt. It is known as "the bride of the Nile."

Oleaceae: This natural order contains twenty-one genera and nearly 400 species, generally speaking in sub-tropical areas, or certainly in warm temperatures. Some genera include plants of economic value like the Fraxinus. Most others are ornamental. There is only one plant to be included, *Olea europaea*. This is the well-known olive, a round-headed, much branched tree often forty ft. high. The flowers are small and white, the berries are oval green or black, containing one long seed each.

The olive is mentioned again and again in Scripture, from Genesis 8:11, when the dove brought an olive leaf to the ark; to Paul's parable in Romans 11:17-24.

Again the olive tree is used like the fig as a picture of the Jewish nation. It is the symbol of prosperity— the symbol of blessing, strength and beauty.

Kings were anointed with olive oil, even as they are today in Great Britain (1 Sam 10:1). Psalm 52:8, gives the picture of a happy man —"I am like a green olive tree in the house of God." Hosea 14:6 gives the idea of beauty —"his beauty shall be as the olive tree."

Even the sick can be healed by faith, prayer and anointing with oil (James 5:14).

Palmaceae: A big natural order of 150 genera and over 1100 species, found in the subtropics and tropics. The palms are of great importance economically, and it is said that all the wants of man are produced by members of this natural order, i.e. food, building materials, ropes, baskets, wax, oil, alcoholic drinks, betel nuts for dyeing, and so on.

The *Phoenix dactylifera* is the palm tree—the date palm, a well-known tree in Pal. in

A date palm with ripe fruit. ©*M.P.S.*

the olden days. Almost every part of the date palm is valuable, the fruit, the stones, the leaves, the trunk, the crown, the branches.

Tāmār, the Heb. name of the palm tree is often given to girls. Absalom's sister, the beautiful girl, was called Tamar, because this stood for elegance and grace in the estimation of the Jews of her day.

The tree, which can grow some eighty ft. high, stands out often in the plain, esp. as at the apex of this straight up-and-down tree, there is a beautiful large cluster of deeply serrated and feathery leaves.

The custom in the E is to cut off the male inflorescence and hang it in the top of a female tree, to insure complete fertilization.

Pinaceae: A natural order of twenty-four genera and over 300 species, all of which are found in the temperate regions of the world. The family contains many trees of great economic importance, all of them conifers.

Pinus pinea is the Stone Pine or Umbrella Pine, a tree which will grow eighty ft. high, with a long, clean trunk. The cones are produced singly or two or three together, egg-shaped, and four to six inches long. These take three years to mature. The seeds found in the cones are large, and contain an edible kernel. In South Africa these are called Donna Ball "pits." The root system is not very extensive, and many trees are blown over.

Often called *Apinus pinea*, this tree is much grown in Pal. It is the "green fir tree" referred to in Hosea 14:8 (KJV). It was certainly found in Pal. at that time, so the experts agree.

There are *Pinus brutia* and *Pinus halepensis* to be reckoned with, or so some experts have suggested. *Pinus halepensis* is the Aleppo Pine or Jerusalem Pine, and *Brutia* is not a separate species, but is a variety of *halepensis*. It is true that in the past it was thought a separate species, and so the Royal Horticultural Society's dictionary has as the synonym for *Pinus halepensis brutia—Pinus brutia* or *Pinus pyrenaica*. The variety *brutia* has a branch system less dense than *halepensis,* and the cones on the branches point forward. This pine will withstand long periods of drought, and is an excellent tree for places which are too dry for most conifers. The true *Pinus halepensis* may grow to a height of sixty ft. and the young shoots are gray with a glaucous bloom to them. The cones are short-stalked and point backward on the branches.

Once again the writer searches for the true meaning of such passages as Isaiah 41:19 and Isaiah 60:13, where the pine tree is mentioned, 1 Kings 5:8 and 2 Chronicles 2:8, where fir trees are featured. Both could well be *Pinus halepensis* and/or its variety *brutia.*

Cedrus libani is the Cedar of Lebanon, growing up to 100 ft. high. The cones are barrel-shaped, four inches by 2½ inches wide. They are beautiful trees and the timber is first-class. The synonym is *Cedrus patula*.

In the OT, cedars are mentioned in forty-four different texts, and sometimes two or three times in a text. "Cedar trees beside the waters"

This great, venerable Cedar of Lebanon is known as "God's Cedar." ©*M.P.S.*

appear in Balaam's prophecy (Num 24:6); at the building of the House of the Forest of Lebanon by Solomon cedars were used (1 Kings 7:2). Also at the building of the Second Temple cedars were used (Ezra 3:7). The Psalms are full of cedars (Ps 104:16). Isaiah is fond of mentioning cedars (Isa 44:14), and so is Ezekiel (Ezek 17:22; 31:3ff.). Zechariah ends the mentioning in 11:1 and 2—"the cedar is fallen."

Tetraclinis articulata comes from the Lat. *tetra*, "form," and *cline*, "bed." It is a tender, evergreen tree, which seldom grows taller than thirty ft., with erect, feathered branches divided into a fine spray. It bears solitary cones at the ends of the shoots. Its synonyms are *Callitris quadrivalvis* and *Thuja articulata*. The wood is yellow or red, quite fragrant, and is often marked prettily. It is used in making furniture for this reason. From its trunk exudes a hard resin called sandarac, which is made into varnish.

This is the thyine wood mentioned in Revelation 18:12, i.e. the Sandarac Tree, sometimes known as the citrum tree or even citrus tree, though it has nothing to do with oranges and lemons.

Cupressus sempervirens comes from the Lat. *kus*, "to produce" and *parisos*, "equal." This indicates that the species grows symmetrically. It is an evergreen tree now used for ornamental purposes when young. The tree grows like a pyramid but when old it spreads. It is interesting to note that the juvenile leaves and the older ones are quite dissimilar.

C. sempervirens is the Mediterranean Cypress. There are two main forms, one very erect, 150 ft. high, and the other spreading. The cones are 1¼ inches long and one inch wide, as a rule. The wood is useful for furniture—it is quite fragrant. An oil may be distilled from the leaves and shoots.

This is the tree in all probability from which planks were cut to make the ark; gopher wood is mentioned in Genesis 6:14. Isaiah 60:13 talks about the cypress tree. Noah's example, incidentally, was followed by Alexander the Great, who also built his ship from the cypress wood. Moffatt seems to think that the Almug tree is the Cypress (2 Chron. 2:8).

Juniperus is a genus containing almost fifty species of hardy or half-hardy shrubs and trees, nearly all of them growing in the northern hemisphere. The one species which is found in the southern hemisphere is the Sharp Cedar, *Juniperus oxycedrus*. This is a tree which grows up to thirty ft. high, with prominently-angled branches, and bearing globose half-inch wide cones, reddish-brown when ripe. An essential oil, which is said to have medicinal properties, is distilled from the fragrant wood of this tree. It is known as Oil of Cade. If this tree is to be included, then it is because of the word ערער, tr. *heath* (Jer 17:6). *'Ar'ar* is, the writer understands, the name given by the Arabs to this particular Juniper. It is therefore likely that the words of Jeremiah 17:6 could be "He shall be like the Sharp Cedar in the desert." There is a similar reference (48:6), though the Heb. word here appears to be *'ărô'ēr*.

Juniperus sabina is known as the Savin. It is a shrub which may grow to fifteen ft. in height, and the branches are divided into fine sprays. A strong odor is released when a shoot is bruised; this comes from what is known as an oil gland. This oil, which can be distilled, is said to have diuretic properties. The cones look waxy-white. *J. sabina* is said to grow well in Pal.

Platanaceae: This natural order contains only one genus, *Platanus orientalis*. There are six or so species which bear unisexual flowers—the sexes apart. The fruits are one-seeded nutlets, packed into round balls. This *Platanus orientalis* is known as the Oriental Plane, and grows to a height of 100 ft. The fruit balls it bears may be anything from two to six on a pendulous stalk. The tree is extremely long-lived.

This plane tree is well-known in Pal., growing chiefly in the valleys and plains. The Heb. word *'armôn* tr. "chestnut tree" (Gen 30:37), and "chestnut trees" (Ezek 31:8), is prob. this plane tree, because the literal tr. of the Heb. word is "naked." Even in London, where these trees are grown abundantly, large pieces of bark are constantly peeling off, leaving the trunk underneath looking white, i.e. naked.

Punicaceae: There is only one genus which contains two species, all of which are deciduous small trees or shrubs. The most popular species is *Punica granatum*, the pomegranate, which is

A pomegranate tree. ©*M.P.S.*

Anemones ("lilies of the field") growing in the Jerusalem area. ©*M.P.S.*

a very popular fruit in Pal., where it ripens well. The writer has seen it growing to a height of thirty ft., bearing beautiful scarlet flowers 1¼ inches across, followed by yellow and crimson fruits, which may be as wide as 3½ inches. The tr. pomegranate is undoubtedly correct. It is mentioned again and again in the OT. The beautiful little colored pomegranates decorated the hem of the robe of the high priest (Exod 39:26). The Israelites took a poor view of the fact that there were no pomegranates growing in the Wilderness (Num 20:5). Saul lived under a pomegranate tree (1 Sam 14:2). Pomegranates were carved to beautify the Temple (1 Kings 7:18). The beauty of the pomegranate is shown in Song of Solomon 4:13 and the death of the pomegranate in Joel 1:12. Pomegranates were certainly promised by God to His people (Deut 8:8), and were regarded as a definite blessing. They are certainly very sweet and delicious to eat on a hot day in Pal., esp. when picked straight from the tree.

Ranunculaceae: This is a very large family containing forty-eight genera with something like 1300 species. They can be shrubs or herbs, and nearly all of them have acrid sap, some of which can cause blisters when handled.

The *Anemone coronaria* is found in this natural order. It grows today very popular cut flowers—red, blue, violet or yellow. It undoubtedly grew wild in Pal. in our Lord's time, and esp. on the Mount of Olives, and was therefore most prob. the lilies to which he referred as being more beautiful than "Solomon in all his glory" (Luke 12:27).

The second plant in this large order is *Nigella sativa,* about which the Royal Horticultural Society says: "said to be the Fitches mentioned in Isaiah 28:25, 27. The seeds are often sprinkled on cakes in Palestine."

This Nigella is commonly called the Nutmeg flower and must not be confused with the annual plants called Devil-in-the-Bush, or Love-in-the-Mist. It was cultivated for its aromatic seeds, which even today are used in the E for flavoring curries.

Rhamnaceae: Here we have a natural order of forty genera and 500 species. The great majority of them are found in the tropics. This natural order is closely related to the Vitaceae family.

Paliurus spina-christi in this natural order is a shrub growing to a height of ten ft. as a rule. It bears greenish-yellow flowers and interesting fruits which are one inch wide and look like a wide-brimmed hat. *Paliurus bergatus* is a synonym of *P. spina-christi.* This shrub will grow in any ordinary soil and loves full sunshine. The Royal Horticultural Society dictionary says that it is one of the legendary trees from which the crown of thorns was made (Matt 27:29; John 19:2).

Zizyphus is a genus of approximately forty species of evergreen or deciduous shrubs and trees, living in the warm, temperate or tropical regions. The flowers are invariably small and greenish or yellow. The two species which may be mentioned in the OT are *Z. lotus,* a deciduous small tree with tiny flowers and ovoid-roundish yellow fruits. *Z. spina christi* is an evergreen with ovate, oval leaves and minute woolly flowers in short clusters. The fruit in this case is black, half an inch wide, and when ripe is edible. *Z. lotus* is prob. the shady tree mentioned (Job 40:21, 22, although Moffatt in his tr. uses the words "lotus trees"). These are certainly found in Pal. and Syria. In the case of *Z. spina christi,* there is reason to suppose that this shrub with its thorny branches could be the thorns indicated in Judges 8:7; Isaiah 9:18; and perhaps also Matthew 7:16. This thorny shrub undoubtedly grows happily throughout Pal., and could therefore be the plant referred to in the passages mentioned.

The thorns mentioned in Genesis 3:18; Psalm 58:9; Proverbs 15:19; Isaiah 10:17 and Hosea 2:6, to give but a few examples, may well be those of the buckthorn, and there is a Palestinian species, *Rhamnus palaestina,* often called *Rhamnus punctata,* var. *palaestina,* which grows to a height of five or six ft. and has evergreen leaves and extremely thorny branches.

Rosaceae: A family of some ninety genera and 2000 species, which are found all over the world. The *Prunus amygdalus communis,* often quoted as being mentioned in the OT is really *Prunus communis,* the almond, a tree which will grow in the E to a height of twenty ft., and produces two-inch long velvety fruits, containing smooth stones in which are the almonds. Almond trees are mentioned in Ecclesiastes 12:5 and Jeremiah 1:11, and the Heb. word *shāqēd* is also tr. "almond" in Genesis 43:11 and Numbers 17:8.

Some claim that *Prunus armeniaca* must be included under this natural order. This is the apricot, a tree that will grow thirty ft. high, and produces white or pinkish flowers, followed by delicious yellow fruits, tinged with red. It has a synonym, *Armeniaca vulgaris.* The only reason that this has any right to be included is that there are those who claim that the tree in Genesis 3:6 was an apricot. (*See* APPLE.)

Rosa phoenicia is a strong climbing rose with hooked prickles and white flowers, two inches across. It came to Great Britain from Syria in 1885, and the Royal Horticultural Society's dictionary thinks that it may have been one of the parents of the Damask Rose. This species of rose should be included, because of two possible references in the Apoc. (2 Esd 2:19; Wisd of Sol 2:8).

Rubus is a genus of some 400 species, and contains all the members of the bramble family— raspberries, blackberries, boysenberries, and so on. The *Rubus sanctus* is usually called the Palestinian Bramble, and is closely related to *Rubus ulmifolius,* a semi-evergreen, spreading shrub, with downy, purply stems, covered with broad spines. The flowers are rosy-red, but the fruits are of no value for food. These, it is thought, may be the thorns and briars found in Judges 8:7; Isaiah 7:25; 9:18.

Writers of the 1800s have used the term *Rubus fruticosus,* which was a comprehensive Linnaean term for brambles. Today, however, this so-called species has been split up into many other species and even varieties.

Ruscaceae: Sanders Encyclopaedia (1955) states that *Ruscus aculeatus* is in the natural order *Ruscaceae* or *Liliaceae. Ruscus* itself is a genus of four evergreen sub-shrubs with creeping root stocks. The species thrive in shady places. *R. aculeatus* is the Butcher's Broom, which is found all round the Mediterranean region, and is really lovely when covered with red berries. Unfortunately, there seem to be more male forms than female, and so the brilliant, berried types are seldom seen. It is the Heb. word *sillôn* tr. "brier" or "pricking briar," which gives an indication, for some claim this Heb. name to be similar to *sullaon,* the name the Arabs give to the extremely prickly stiff Butcher's Broom, this being of course *Ruscus aculeatus,* which is well-known in Palestine, and can be seen around Mount Carmel. The problem is that the Heb. word in Ezekiel 2:6 is *sārābîm,* and there is reason to believe, therefore, that it may have been *Ruscus hyrcanus,* which is closely related to *R. aculeatus.*

Rutaceae: This is a family of 100 genera and 900 species, most of which are found in South Africa and Australia. They are usually shrubs or trees, and several of them are useful because they yield oil.

An almond tree in blossom in Palestine. ©*M.P.S.*

Ruta chalepensis, synonym *R. angustifolia,* is a sub-shrub, growing to 2½ ft., bearing yellow half-inch wide flowers. It is well-known in the Mediterranean regions.

Ruta graveolens is called the Herb of Grace, commonly known as Rue, and is an acrid evergreen shrub, semi-woody, growing to a height of three ft. with erect shoots. The flowers are ¾ inch wide, and of a rather dull yellow color. The leaves have a very strong odor, and in Great Britain are often used in claret cup.

Ruta chalepensis is included, because it is said to be a common plant in Pal., but *Ruta graveolens* seems to the writer to have precedence, because it is the herbal rue used even today, and it is herbs to which our Lord refers (Luke 11:42). *R. chalepensis* is included to give this species the benefit of the doubt.

Salicaceae: This is a family of two genera only, but with 330 species, all of which are shrubs and trees. The flowers are catkinlike, and generally appear before the leaves. The poplars produce catkins that hang, and the willows catkins that hold themselves upright.

Salix alba is the white willow with pendulous branches of beautiful shape. The young shoots are silky and the catkins often two inches long.

The weeping willow is, of course, *Salix babylonica,* which may grow fifty ft. high, with its branches hanging down, and looking extremely beautiful in the winter as well as in the summer (*see* Ps 137).

The willows of Leviticus 23:40 some have claimed as the Balsam poplar, *Populus taca-*

mahaca, but this seems to be a North American tree and not one known in Pal.

In the case of the willows mentioned in Job 40:22; Isaiah 15:7 and 44:4, there is every chance that the tree is *Salix safsaf*, which is a common Palestinian willow, and, in fact, the name used today by the peasants for this tree is *safsaf*. It is a tree with reddish-brown branches, which loves to grow by water and is happy growing in the upper parts of the Jordan for this reason.

Salix acmophylla is another species which likes to grow near water, and is found in Pal. It was once thought to be a variety of *safsaf*. The branches are reddish, and the catkins erect, oblong and cylindrical.

If, however, the willows mentioned in Leviticus 23:40; Psalm 137:2, are *Populus euphratica*, as Moffatt and Goodspeed suggest, then it is a tree which also grows on the banks of the Jordan, and which some feel is the mulberry (2 Sam 5:23 KJV).

Populus alba is considered by some to be the green poplar that Jacob took (Gen 30:37), because the leaves are green above and snowy-white beneath, and the shoots would therefore suit this schemer well. This poplar is also mentioned in Hosea 4:13. It is a species that likes to grow in wet places.

Solanaceae: A natural order of seventy genera and 1800 species, rarely trees. Large numbers of the family are of importance economically—for instance, the potato, the tomato, the capsicum, the aubergine, and even tobacco. Two Biblical plants are to be included in this natural order.

Lycium europaeum is the Boxthorn, and within the genus there are a hundred species of shrubs, usually thorny. Most of them bear bright red fruits profusely. It is thought that *L. europaeum* occurs in Scripture, whose synonym is *L. mediterraneum*. This is a rambling, spiny shrub, bearing globose fruits, and is found in the Mediterranean region. Is this the bramble mentioned in Judges 9:14, even though allegorical?

The *Mandragora officinarum* is the Mandrake or Devil's Apples. There are three species of perennials within this genus, no one of them very beautiful. All of them, however, seem to have legends attached to them. The Royal Horticultural Society's dictionary states that *Mandragora officinarum* is the Mandrake of Genesis 30. It may also well be the Mandrake of Song of Solomon 7:13. It is claimed to be the original loveapple.

Amid the arguments about the true tr. of the word *shāmîr* (Isa 10:17; 55:13; Mic 7:4; Heb. 6:8), most agree that the plant is prob. *Solanum incanum*, the Palestinian nightshade, sometimes called the Jericho Potato. This is found on roadsides and in waste places in the Lower Jordan Valley and around Jericho, and is extremely prickly. The fertile flowers produce yellow berries.

Styracaceae: This natural order contains six genera and about eighty species of trees and shrubs. Most of these are found in Mexico, Texas, Java or Japan, but *Styrax officinalis* is definitely popular in the Mediterranean region. This is a small tree or shrub which can grow to a height of twenty ft. bearing pendulous clusters of fragrant white flowers. The stems yield a fragrant resin when punctured, known as Storax.

It has been claimed that the sweet spice called Onycha (Exod 30:34) is the *Styrax benzoin* which grows wild in Sumatra, and produces a resin called benzoin with which Friar's Balsam is made. The writer doubts that there would have been an export from Sumatra to Pal. in Biblical days. There is no difficulty, however, about *Styrax officinalis*, because this is known to have grown in Asia Minor, and could therefore easily be the Sweet Storax found in Ecclesiasticus 24:15. Here is a tree which even today is easy to find in Pal. in the lower hills.

Tamaricaceae: This natural order comprises four genera and 100 species of small trees or shrubs, usually heath-like, often found by the seaside or in desert places.

Tamarix aphylla is one of the species that may be mentioned in the OT, its synonym being *T. articulata*. It is a small tree or bush, some twenty ft. high, bearing pink flowers one-eighth of an inch across. It was called at one time *Tamarix orientalis*.

Tamarix tetrandra is a glaborous shrub, growing twelve to fifteen ft. high, with tiny pink flowers packed into cylindrical spikes, usually two inches long. Possibly the shrub underneath which Hagar cast the child (Gen 21:15) could be the *Tamarix aphylla*, because bushes of this species now grow in the desert where it is thought Hagar wandered with her child. The Tamarisks certainly grow in sandy soil. The shrub is unlikely to have been the species *tetrandra*, though this may be found in Western Asia.

Typhaceae: A natural order of one genus and possibly fifteen species, all of them being marsh plants. The flowers are closely crowded with the male blooms above and the female blooms below.

The Biblical plant is the Small Reed Mace, *Typha angustata*, which grows four ft. high, producing dark green leaves half an inch or so wide, convex beneath and channeled above toward their base. The flower spikes are brown.

The reed mace is sometimes called Cattail from the "Olde English"—"Cattes Tayles."

If the plant were the true Cattail, it would be *Typha latifolia*, growing eight ft. high. This, it is claimed, is the reed with which our Lord was smitten (Mark 15:19) and the reed put into our Lord's hand as an imitation scepter in Matthew 27:29. Whether, however, *Typha latifolia* grew in the Holy Land at that time, the writer has been unable to discover.

Umbelliferae: This natural order has approximately 180 genera and 1400 species. Most of these grow in the northern temperate regions, but some are distributed in the Middle E. The flowers are invariably produced in compound umbels, hence the name of the natural order.

In this natural order the first is *Peucedanum graveolens,* an annual with yellow flowers in a large umbel. It was originally called *Anethum graveolens,* and is found under this name in some books. This is undoubtedly the anise mentioned in Matthew 23:23, but its proper name is dill. This plant is grown for its seeds which are used in a similar way to caraway seeds. Dill water given to babies comes from the distillation of this seed. The Douay Bible uses the word anise, but Goodspeed, Moffatt and Weymouth tr. the Gr. word *anēthon* as dill. Crudens Concordance includes the word dill in the reference to this plant.

Coriandrum sativum is an annual which grows about eighteen inches high. The name comes from the word "coris"—a bug. This alludes to the unpleasant odor of the leaves. The flowers are pale mauve or white and the fruits globose. The seeds are used in flavoring sweets or candy, in bread, mixed spices, some curry powders, and alcoholic drinks like gin. The seeds smell unpleasant when unripe, but the odor disappears when they are dried. The seed is mentioned in Exodus 16:31 and Numbers 11:7, merely because manna was likened to it. The plant, however, was and is grown in Pal.

Cuminum cyminum is a half hardy annual herb with aromatic fruits that are used in flavoring. It produces a pink or white flower, grows six inches high, and is known to have been popular in the Mediterranean region. To the uninitiated, it is a member of the "carrot family," and the seeds are larger than those of the caraway. They were and are still used in Pal. as a spice or flavoring. Sowing the seeds is mentioned in Isaiah 28:25, and the tithing of the seeds in Matthew 23:23.

Though *Ferula* is a genus of about eighty species of herbaceous perennials, only one appears to be mentioned in Scripture, *Ferula galbaniflua.* This bears yellow flowers on short, thick stalks, and the little fruits that follow are oblong and elliptic. The special gum, galbanum, exudes from the lower part of the stem, as well as from the bases of the leaf stalks. The name "galbanum" is found in Exodus 30:34, and in Ecclesiasticus 24:15.

Commercially, an incision is made in the young stem three inches above ground level, and as a result, a milky juice appears which in a short time hardens and becomes the galbanum used commercially as an anti-spasmodic in medicine, as well as for certain varnishes. It is not known for certain whether this plant grew in Pal., or whether the galbanum was imported from Persia.

Urticaceae: This is a natural order of over forty genera, containing 500 species, the great majority of them tropical shrubs, trees and herbs. The word "urtica" comes from the Lat. "uro," "to burn" because the plants are largely stinging nettles. The perennial nettle is *Urtica dioica,* and the dwarf annual nettle is *Urtica urens. Urtica coudata* is found in waste places in Pal., having erect branching stems. It bears small, greenish flowers. As these three nettles are found in Pal., it is wondered whether they are those referred to in Isaiah 34:13 and Hosea 9:6, and certainly Goodspeed and Moffatt think of them as species of nettles. The writer agrees. The species *Urtica pilulifera* is also found on waste ground round about Jericho and Jerusalem, where it is commonly known as the Roman Nettle. This would therefore be included also.

Valerianaceae: In this natural order, there are eight genera and 350 species. The flowers are usually numerous but small, and they are often showy. The only Biblical plant that seems to fall into this natural order is the *Nardostachys* which gets its name from *nardos* (a fragrant shrub), and *stachys* (a spike). This is a genus of two species and the spikenard mentioned in Song of Solomon 1:12; 4:13; Mark 14:3 and John 12:3, and is the ancient spikenard known to man for generations.

This *Nardostachys jatamansi* bears rose purple flowers in a small terminal panacle. The plant was not grown in Pal., but was imported in sealed alabaster boxes as a delicious perfume. It is found growing in the cold, dry upper areas of the Himalayan mountains, and was given the name Jataman*see*—spelled in this way by the Hindus in their country. It is the roots and woolly, young stems that are carefully dried and made into an ointment or perfume.

Vitaceae: A natural order of eleven genera and 450 species of shrubs, most of which are climbers. These are widely distributed in the sub-tropical and tropical regions. The flowers are small and regular, but sometimes uni-sexual. The fruit is a berry.

If the unprofitable vines mentioned in the Bible are the ornamental types, then *Ampelopsis orientalis* is prob. the one referred to, since this grows in Pal. and Syria, bearing tiny, red fruits resembling red currants. Its synonym is *Vitis orientalis,* because it was thought at one time to be a member of the Vine genus.

The true grapevine is *Vitis vinifera,* said to have been originally a native of the Caucasus region, and it was certainly known to Noah. The fruits are oval or globose, amber-colored, or black with a blue bloom. For "wild grapes," see Isaiah 5:4; "strange vine" (prob. wild grapes), see Jeremiah 2:21; and for the true vine, see references throughout the Bible (Gen 9:20; Num 13:20; Ps 80:8; S of Sol 7:8; Jer 2:21; Ezek 19:10; Zech 3:10; Matt 26:29; John 15:1 and Rev 14:18).

Zygophyllaceae: A family of twenty-six genera and 250 species, all of which grow in the warmer regions. Rarely are they annuals, occasionally are they herbs, but usually they are sub-shrubs or shrubs. Generally speaking, the flowers are solitary, though occasionally there are two together. The fruit is generally a capsule, hardly ever a drupe or berry.

Balanites aegyptiaca has hermaphroditic, green flowers. The leaves are woolly, and the plants as a whole are found in desert places, esp. between Jerusalem and Jericho. It has been thought that the balm in Genesis 37:25; Jeremiah 8:22 and 51:8, refers to the resin or gum, *Balanites aegyptiaca.* This is commonly known as the Jericho Balsam, because it grows abundantly in the desert areas around Jericho, often twelve to fifteen ft. tall. The fruits of this shrub are boiled for the sake of the oil content, which is said to possess healing properties, hence the text: "Is there no balm in Gilead?" (Jer 8:22). The Douay Bible makes the tr.: "Is there no rosin in Gilead?" and for this reason, soon after it was published, the edition was known as the Rosin Bible.

W. E. Shewell-Cooper

FLOWERS (מגדל [a towering plant]; נצה [a blossom]; נצן [blossom]; פרח [flourishing flower]; ציץ [open flowers]; ἄνθος [a flower]).

There are several different Heb. words used for flowers in the OT, some, it will be seen, having a particular emphasis on the type of flower, i.e., open or fading.

Today, botanists and horticulturalists are careful to give all flowering plants Lat. names which describe properly the genus, the species, and sometimes the strain or variety as well. In Biblical times, flowers were given local names, which could mean one plant in one district and quite another plant in another district. The London Plane tree means quite a different tree in Scotland, for instance—even today.

It is curious, some people say, that flowers are mentioned so little in Holy Writ, but in Pal. there were no gardens as they are now known, merely farm fields to grow crops in, and groves of trees around the houses to provide shade. Even today in agricultural Spain there are no gardens around farm workers' houses. Further, flowers were not used in vases in the home in Pal. in those days—there were no occasional tables for bowls of blossoms—and no large windows through which the sun could shine.

There were undoubtedly plenty of wild flowers, but these would have been taken for granted, and hardly even noticed. It is claimed that in the plains and on the mountains could be found 500 different species of wild flowers that are now actually grown in Great Britain, and another 500 species in addition that are indigenous to Pal. also.

Our Lord, as He preached, must have stood on mountain sides, which were carpeted with thousands of wild flowers of all kinds. In fact, this is what He may have had in mind when He said: "Consider the lilies . . ." (Matt 6:28 or Luke 12:27), using this word to cover all the beautiful wild flowers at His feet at the same time.

Flowers that are specifically mentioned are lilies—Lily of the Valley; rose (though not the true rose); saffron or *Crocus sativus*; Star of Bethlehem or *Ornithogalum umbellatum;* poppy (if we believe the milk-like juice was used in the vinegary drink given to our Lord at the crucifixion); and the Rock Rose from which the "onycha" of Exodus 30:34 may have come. These flowers are dealt with under their own headings, where the "pros and cons" of the meanings are discussed.

W. E. Shewell-Cooper

FLUTE. *See* Music, Musical Instruments.

FLUX, BLOODY. *See* Disease, Diseases.

FLY (זבוב, *fly* all Eng. VSS; ערב, *swarms of flies,* Exod 8:21ff. all Eng. VSS; *divers sorts of flies,* Ps 78:45 and Ps 105:31 KJV; and *swarms of flies* ASV, RSV).

The latter Heb. word refers to one incident only—the fourth plague. In popular language the word *fly* is about as widely used as *worm.* Technically it is applied to members of the order *Diptera* (two-winged) which are true flies, but it is given to many other insects also—Dragonfly, Firefly, Sawfly, etc. Flies of many kinds abound in Egypt; some of them are biting and blood-sucking, and become a pest because of their numbers. There is nothing in the context to identify the kind, or perhaps kinds, of flies concerned, but the fact that the flies were *on* the people suggests that they may have been biting flies such as *Stochomys calcitrans.* Commentators like Hort and K. A. Kitchen (NBD, p. 1002) see a connection between the fourth and sixth plagues, with the fly serving as the vector for a skin disease, perhaps a modified form of the anthrax that struck the cattle in the fifth plague.

Apart from being used in association with Baal (q.v.) Heb. *zebub* is found only twice. In Ecclesiastes 10:1 the context is proverbial: most ointments were scented with spices and other perfumes, and unless covered they attracted flies, which quickly drowned in the greasy base, causing it to spoil (*see* Bee).

G. S. Cansdale

FOAL (עיר meaning *donkey, stallion,* or *colt*; but more often בן meaning *son of—*). The word "foal" refers to the young of a horse, donkey, or zebra. In the Bible it is used in relationship to the young of a donkey. It is often interchanged in some tr. with the word "colt" (Gen 32:15; 49:11).

The most common way in the OT and NT to designate a "foal" or a "colt" is to use the phrase "the son of a donkey" (Zech 9:9 and Matt 21:5).

G. Giacumakis, Jr.

FODDER (בְּלִיל, meaning *mixed fodder* or *mash* for domestic animals Job 6:5; 24:6; Isa 30:24 . Verb form found in Judg 19:21). This word is used in the OT for the food of donkeys or oxen. It was usually mixed from that which remained after a crop had been harvested and threshed. Isaiah 30:24 indicates the practice of salting the mixture in order to fulfill the animals' salt needs. In some VSS this Heb. word is tr. as "provender" (RSV Isa 30:24).

G. GIACUMAKIS, JR.

FOLD. A pen in which to keep sheep or goats; in the NT, the Church. גדרה, *a place walled in, a hedged* or *fenced place* (Num 32:16; Zeph 2:6). דבר, *pasture land, fold* (Mic 2:12). מכלה, *restrained place* (Ps 50:9; 78:70; Hab 3:17). נוה, *home* (KJV, ASV, Isa 65:10; Jer 23:3; Ezek 34:14). Αὐλή, *a court-yard* (Rev 11:2). Ποίμνη, *flock* (KJV, John 10:16). Folds were used chiefly as a protection from wild beasts at night. They consisted of a walled enclosure preferably near a place providing water. Often there was a tower within them. Sometimes flocks of more than one shepherd were kept overnight in the same fold, with one shepherd taking care of the animals. In the morning the sheep would be carefully counted when the shepherds came to reclaim their flocks.

S. BARABAS

FOLLY (אולת, *badness*; כסילות, *stupidity*; נבלה, *emptiness*; סכלות, *thickheadedness*; תהלה, *insipidity*; ἄνοια, *senselessness*; ἀφροσύνη, *heedlessness*.) The above, with their variants, are the words in the Bible commonly tr. "folly." Other related terms are פתי, *simplicity*; ἄσοφος, *unwise*; μωρία, *foolishness*.

1. Old Testament. Folly is the opposite of wisdom. It is not imbecility, insanity, or error. It is wrongheadedness. It has to do with practical insights into the nature of things that lead to success or failure in life. Wisdom and folly in the Bible rest on the principle of adjustment to a higher law for a practical purpose. Folly involves rejection or disregard of the revealed moral and spiritual values on which life is based. The fool sins against his own best interests and rejects God (Ps 14:1). This idea of folly is expressed in various ways.

a. 'Iwwelet is a common word, esp. in Proverbs, conveying the general idea of moral badness. The fool is hasty (Prov 14:29), self-sufficient (12:15), impervious to instruction (15:5), given to unrestrained anger (17:12), and stupid in his persistence in evil (26:11).

b. Kesīluth and its cognates are the most frequent words for folly. They are most common in Proverbs and Ecclesiastes. The root indicates thickness, sluggishness, or plumpness. This slow, self-confident person is ignorant (Eccl 2:14), thoughtless (Prov 10:23; 17:24), contentious (18:6), indolent (Eccl 4:5), and brutish (Ps 49:10). Disregarding moral ideals, he is a victim of stupidity.

c. Nebālāh, most common outside the Wisdom Literature, denotes a wicked person as an evil character, shamelessly immoral. The word is often associated with base and unnatural lewdness (Gen 34:7; Deut 22:21; Josh 7:15). Isaiah 32:6 describes in detail the destructive attitudes and conduct of this wicked man. Abigail described her husband, Nabal, as "this man of Belial" or "ill-natured fellow," "for as his name is, so is he" (1 Sam 25:25).

d. Siklut comes from a root meaning "to be stopped up." It is generally taken to denote thickheadedness. However, it denotes more than mere foolishness. It is associated with madness (Eccl. 2:12).

e. Toholāh (Job 4:18) is thought to be related to the Ethiopic *tahala,* "to err."

f. Tiplāh is from a root that means tasteless, unseasoned, insipid, unseemly. It is used of fish that are not salted. Folly, then, is conceived in terms of that which is absurd and unworthy of human beings (Job 24:12; Jer 23:13).

g. Petī is used of the simple, the impressionable ones, who are easily led into folly because of their lack of wisdom (Prov 1:22).

2. New Testament. Though fewer words are used, the NT has analogies for most of the OT meanings.

a. Anoia basically means "without understanding." It is sometimes a madness expressing itself in rage (Luke 6:11).

b. Aphrosune also means "ignorant" and "without understanding," but with a moral as well as an intellectual reference (Mark 7:22).

c. Mōria reflects the moral reprobation of the OT *nebālāh* (Matt 5:22). It is more than intellectual deficiency.

d. Asophos describes one as lacking in wisdom (Eph 5:15).

As folly in the OT accounts was so deeply rooted in the mind and heart of man that only the revealed law could extirpate it, so in the NT man is a victim of folly until the Gospel dawns on him (Rom 2:20; Titus 3:3-5). The highest wisdom is revealed in the Gospel. Sinful man is so radically wrong in his relation to the moral world that he decries the Gospel as foolishness (1 Cor 1:21-25). Yet it is his only hope of becoming wise. *See* WISDOM.

W. T. DAYTON

FOOD. That which sustains the body or soul, called "meat," "victuals," "bread" in KJV, and "bread," "food," and "provisions" in RSV, represents a variety of words in MT: אכל, מאכל, אכלה—all meaning that which is eaten; לחם, "bread"; and מזון, "sustenance." These words are most frequently βρῶμα or τροφή in the LXX and NT.

I. Literal
  A. Food supplies
  B. Food of animals
  C. Food for humans
    1. Plant foods
      a. Cereal grains
      b. Nuts
      c. Vegetables
      d. Fruits
    2. Animal products
      a. Flesh
      b. Dairy products
    3. Condiments
  D. Food availability
  E. Food of special periods
  F. Food preparation
  G. Food prices
  H. Eating habits
    1. Posture
    2. Time of eating
  I. Prohibited foods
  J. Clean and unclean birds
  K. Food offered to idols
  L. Sharing food
  M. Life and food
II. Metaphorical use

I. Literal

A. Food supplies. Despite recurrent droughts (Gen 31:40 KJV; 2 Kings 4:38; Jer 14:1, 4-6; Hag 1:11), hail (Hag 2:17 RSV), other calamities (Amos 4:6-10) and resulting famines (Gen 12:10; 26:1; 41:1ff.; 1 Kings 18:2; 2 Kings 4:38), and periodic want brought on by the ravages of war (2 Kings 6:25), Pal. was to Biblical writers a land "flowing with milk and honey" (Exod 3:8, 17; Num 13:27; etc.; cf. Deut 8:8), in which food could be eaten without want (8:7-9; Josh 24:13; Judg 18:10). The description left by the fugitive from Egypt, Sinuhe, c. 1920 B.C., is in agreement: "Figs were in it, and grapes. It had more wine than water. Plentiful was its honey, abundant its olives. Every (kind of) fruit was on its trees. Barley was there, and emmer. There was no limit to any (kind of) cattle. . . . Bread was made for me as daily fare, wine as daily provision, cooked meat and roasted fowl, besides the wild beasts of the desert, for they hunted for me and laid before me, besides the catch of my (own) hounds. Many . . . were made for me, and milk in every (kind of cooking) (## 80-90; ANET, pp. 19, 20).

Scarcity was a warning or a punishment from God sent upon His unfaithful people (Lam 4:9, 11; Amos 4:6). According to Sirach the necessities of life include salt, wheat flour, milk, honey, the blood of the grape and oil (Ecclus 39:26). The land produced a variety of food stuffs.

B. Food of animals. The Lord supplies His creatures their proper food in due season (Ps 104:27, 28)—a grace attributed in the Egyp. hymn of Ikhnaton to his god Aton. For the carnivorous such as the lion, there is flesh (Dan 6:24; 7:5; Nah 2:12); for the wolf, there is prey (Ezek 22:27); for the scavenger, there is carrion (Jer 16:4; 19:7; 34:20; Ezek 32:4); and the dog returns to his vomit (2 Pet 2:22). For the plant eaters there is herbage (Jer 14:6); for the ox there is grass (Dan 4:15, 25; 5:21) and straw (Job 6:5; Isa 11:7; 65:25). Swine feed on the carob pod (Luke 15:16); horses on barley and straw (1 Kings 4:28); the birds eat seed (Matt 13:4); and the locust devours plants (Joel 1:4ff.).

C. Food for humans. 1. *Plant foods.* a. CEREAL GRAINS. The fields of Pal. produced wheat (חטה, LXX σῖτος; Gen 30:14; Ezek 4:9; etc.); barley (שעורה, LXX κριθή; Ruth 1:22; 2:23); millet (דחן, LXX κέγχρος; Ezek 4:9), and spelt (כסמת, LXX ὄλυρα; Exod 9:32; Isa 28:25; Ezek 4:9).

Corn (Indian maize) was unknown to the Biblical world. This term of the KJV should be understood as the cereal grains. In times of famine, grain was obtained in Egypt (Gen 41:49) where flax, barley, wheat, and spelt were produced (Exod 9:31, 32). Grain (דגן, or שבר, LXX σῖτος [renders nine words]) might be shelled out as one went through the fields (Deut 23:25; Matt 12:1ff.). One of Elisha's friends brought fresh grain to the prophet (2 Kings 4:42-44). When harvested, grain was ground into flour (קמח, or סלת, LXX σεμίδαλις) and made into bread (לחם, LXX and NT ἄρτος) which was the staff of life (Isa 3:1). There are more than two hundred references to bread in Scripture. Bread is often a synonym for food in general. Bread was at times baked on coals (1 Kings 19:6), first on one side, and then properly turned over to bake the other (Hos 7:8).

A subsistence diet consisted of bread and water (Gen 21:14; 1 Kings 18:13; 22:27). In times of famine children cry for bread and wine (Lam 2:12). Both wheat bread and barley bread were used. In numerous cases barley bread (Judg 7:13; 2 Kings 4:42) or barley cakes (Ezek 4:12) are encountered. It was from five barley loaves that Jesus fed the five thousand (John 6:9, 13). Millet and spelt (KJV "fitches") also could be used for bread (Ezek 4:9). Cakes baked for the queen of heaven formed a part of a Canaanite cult (Jer 7:18).

Grain might be parched and eaten (קלי, LXX πεφρυγμένα χίδρα, et al. Lev 23:14; Josh 5:11; Ruth 2:14; 1 Sam 17:17; 25:18; 2 Sam 17:28). The diet of the laborer at noon might consist of parched grain and wine (Ruth 2:14). Grain might be crushed and spread out to dry as was done over the well where Ahimaaz and Jonathan were hidden (ריפה, LXX παλάθας, cakes of preserved fruit; 2 Sam 17:19; Prov 27:22).

b. NUTS. Jacob sent to Pharaoh a present of produce of the land which included pistachio nuts (בטנים, LXX τερέμινθος) and almonds (שקד, LXX κάρυον) along with balm, honey, gum and myrrh (Gen 43:11).

c. VEGETABLES. The wilderness generation complained over lack of cucumbers (קשאים, LXX σικύοι); melons (אבטיח, LXX πέπονας) leeks (חציר, LXX πράσα); onions (בצלים. LXX κρόμμυα); and garlic (שום, LXX σκόρδα) which they had enjoyed in Egypt (Num 11:5). Later generations in Pal. doubtless enjoyed many of these. There were beans (פול, LXX κύαμος) and lentils (עדשים, LXX φακός, 2 Sam 17:28); and cucumbers (Isa 1:8; Jer 10:5). There were the bitter herbs of Passover (מררים, LXX πικρίδιον Exod 12:8; Num 9:11); and the garden plants: mint, dill, and cummin (Matt 23:23). A dinner of herbs might suffice for the poor man (Prov 15:17; Rom 14:2). In times of want the carob pod (κεράτια) ordinarily used for cattle (*M. Sabbath* 24:2) might be eaten. There was also sweet cane (קנה הטוב, LXX κινάμωμον) from a distant land (Jer 6:20).

d. FRUITS. The grape (ענב, LXX ἄμπελος) produced wine and vinegar (חמץ, LXX ὄξος, Ruth 2:14) and raisins (Num 6:3; 1 Sam 25:18; 1 Chron 12:40; Hos 3:1). Fresh grapes might be eaten while passing through a vineyard (Deut 23:24). The spies brought a large cluster of grapes borne on a pole between two of them (Num 13:23). Sour grapes set the teeth on edge (Jer 31:30; Ezek 18:2). Wine (יין, LXX οἶνος) which cheers God and men (Judg 9:13) and makes glad the heart of man (Ps 104:15) might lead to intoxication as it did in the case of Noah (Gen 9:21), Lot (Gen 19:33, 35), and Nabal (1 Sam 25:37). It is therefore a mocker (Prov 20:1). The OT has a variety of words for intoxicants. The butler squeezed the grapes into Pharaoh's cup (Gen 40:9ff.). The Nazirite refused all products of the grape (Num 6:1ff.; Judg 13:4, 14; Jer 35:1ff.). Cakes of raisins (צמוק, LXX σταφίς) were eaten frequently (1 Sam 25:18; 30:12; 2 Sam 16:1) as well as being used in the worship in Canaanite cult (Hos 3:1). In the NT that which comes from the grape is the "fruit of the vine" (γένημα τῆς ἀμπέλου; Matt 26:29).

The olive (זית, LXX ἐλαία) was perhaps eaten both green and ripe as today, though this is not specifically stated. Olives were beaten into oil (Exod 27:20).

The fig (תאנה. LXX and NT συκῆ) was eaten fresh (Jer 24:1ff.) and dried (1 Sam 25:18; 30:12; 1 Chron 12:40). The first fig of the season (בכורה, LXX πρόδρομος σύκου) was a special delicacy (Isa 28:4; Jer 24:2; Hos 9:10; Mic 7:1; Nah 3:12). Every man under his vine and every man under his fig tree with none to make them afraid is considered the ideal state (Mic 4:4). Dried figs (דבלה, LXX παλάθη ἐκ σύκων) were used for boils (2 Kings 20:7; Isa 38:21) and also eaten on journeys (1 Chron 12:40).

The pomegranate (רמון, LXX ῥόα; Exod 28:33; Num 13:23; 1 Kings 7:20; S of Sol 6:11; 8:2; Joel 1:12) and the apple (תפוח, LXX μῆλον; Prov 25:11; S of Sol 2:5; 7:8; 8:5; Joel 1:12) were available. The date palm (תמר, LXX φοῖνιξ; Judg 4:5; Ps 92:12; Joel 1:12; John 12:13) and the sycamore (שקמה, LXX συκάμινος Amos 7:14) are in Scripture but no reference is made to their fruit as food. Summer fruits of unspecified variety are often mentioned (Jer 40:10, 12; Amos 8:1ff.).

2. *Animal products.* a. FLESH. (בשר, LXX κρέας; Judg 6:20 etc.). In the KJV "meats" is a term for food in general and is not limited merely to flesh. For the Israelite the domesticated animals: oxen, sheep, and goats supplied meat. The mother and offspring were not to be slaughtered on the same day (Lev 22:28). The kid of the sheep (כבש, LXX ἀμνός; 2 Sam 12:3) or goat (גדי עז, LXX χίμαρος ἐξ αἰγῶν) was a preferred dish (Gen 31:38; 37:31; Lev 4:23, 28; Luke 15:29). The stalled ox (שור, LXX μόσχος; Prov 15:17; cf. Amos 6:4; Hab 3:17) or the fatted calf was reserved for slaughtering on special occasions (1 Sam 28:24; Matt 22:4). For such waste over the return of his brother the elder brother objected (Luke 15:30). After the Exile there was a Sheep Gate in Jerusalem doubtless so named because the sheep market was near (Neh 3:1).

Nimrod is said to be a mighty hunter (Gen 10:9). A variety of game existed to be hunted. Deuteronomy 14:5 lists seven varieties (cf. Lev 17:13). There was venison (ציד, LXX θήρα, game; Gen 27:3), the wild goat (אקו, LXX τραγέλαφος), the ibex (דישן, LXX πύγαργος), the mountain sheep (זמר, LXX καμηλοπάρδαλις; Deut 14:5), the roebuck (יחמור, LXX βούβαλος), the gazelle (צבי, LXX δορκάς), the hart (איל, LXX ἔλαφος; Deut 12:15), and the antelope (תאו, LXX ὄρυξ; Isa 51:20, RSV, KJV "wild ox"; Deut 14:5).

In the wilderness the people missed the fish (דג, LXX ἰχθύς) they had enjoyed in Egypt (Num 11:5). Fish were in Galilee and in the sea (Jer 16:16; Eccl 9:12; Ezek 47:10; Neh 13:16; Matt 4:18; Luke 11:12) and in later times were sold in the Fish Gate (Neh 3:3). No specific species are mentioned except good and bad (Matt 13:48) and they are big and small (Jonah 1:17; Mark 8:7; John 21:11). Dried fish were available (Neh 13:16). Peter, Andrew, James, and John were fishermen prior to their being called to discipleship (Matt 4:18, 21). The five thousand were fed fish (Matt 15:34; Mark 6:38). The fish net formed the basis of one of Jesus' parables (Matt 13:47-50).

From the insect family four types of locusts were eaten: (1) ארבה, LXX βροῦχος; (2) סלעם, LXX ἀττάκης; (3) חרגל, LXX ὀφιομάχος; (4) חגב, LXX ἀκρίς (Lev 11:22f.; cf. Matt 3:4).

Various fowl were eaten (1 Kings 4:23); the partridge (קרא, LXX νυκτικόραξ, 1 Sam 26:20; Jer 17:11); the quail (שלו, ὀρτυγομήτρα, Exod 16:13; Num 11:32); the pigeon (יונה, LXX περιστερά, Lev 12:6, etc); the turtledove (תור, LXX τρυγών, Gen 15:9), and the sparrow (στρουθία, Matt 10:29; Luke 12:6). After the Pers. period chickens, the female of which is the ὄρνις (Matt 23:37) and the male is ἀλεκτόρα (26:34), were available.

b. Dairy products. Dairy products included milk (חלב, LXX γάλα) of the cow, the goat, and the sheep (Deut 32:14; Prov 27:27) and was kept in skins (Judg 4:19). Use of camel milk also may be inferred from Genesis 32:15. Curds (butter, KJV) (חמאה, LXX βούτυρον, Gen 18:8; Deut 32:14; Judg 5:25; Isa 7:15, 22) and cheese (גבינה, LXX τυρός; Job 10:10 or חלב חריצי, LXX τρυφαλὶς τοῦ γάλακτος, 2 Sam 17:29) were eaten.

Honey (דבש, LXX μέλι, Deut 32:13; 1 Sam 14:25; Ps 19:10; Prov 16:24) both wild and domestic were known (Judg 14:8, 9; Matt 3:4). Honey was forbidden in offerings to God (Lev 2:11).

Eggs (בצה, LXX ᾠόν, Deut 22:6; Isa 10:14) were used.

3. Condiments. Food was seasoned with salt (מלח, LXX ἅλας, Ezra 6:9; 7:22; Job 6:6). The covenant of salt signified fellowship and friendship (Num 18:19; 2 Chron 13:5; Ezra 4:14). Salt was obtained by evaporation, and for this the Dead Sea furnished an inexhaustible supply (Ezek 47:11). Not always pure, there was the possibility of its becoming mixed with foreign matter until it lost its power (Matt 5:13). Lot's wife became a pillar of salt (Gen 19:26). All cereal offerings required salt (Lev 2:13) and Ezekiel prescribed it for all other offerings (Ezek 43:24; cf. Mark 9:49 TR). Elisha cast it into the spring to make the water suitable for use (2 Kings 2:20, 21).

Use of pepper is not mentioned in Scripture, but the condiments mint, anise, and cummin (Matt 23:23), coriander seeds (Exod 16:31; Num 11:7) and mustard (Matt 13:31; 17:20; Luke 13:19; 17:6) made food more palatable.

D. Food availability. One is not to suppose that all this abundance was available at all times and places. Patriarchal fare was doubtless scant. For guests there was bread freshly baked, curds, milk, and the slaughtered young calf (Gen 18:6, 8). Jacob, on the other hand, dined on bread and pottage of lentils, and for this Esau sold his birthright (25:34); and at other times there might be other pottage to make a meal (2 Kings 4:38). Roasted grain and wine (Ruth 2:14) or bread and wine (Gen 14:18) might make up the meal of the ordinary man. Victory in battle occasioned feasting from the supplies of the vanquished.

Settled life in Pal. brought a greater variety of foods. Abigail brought to David and his men two hundred loaves, two skins of wine, five sheep ready dressed, five measures of parched grain, a hundred clusters of raisins, and two hundred cakes of figs when David was fleeing from Saul (1 Sam 25:18). Ziba brought two hundred loaves of bread, one hundred clusters of raisins, one hundred summer fruits and a skin of wine to David as David fled from Absalom (2 Sam 16:1). At David's return Barzillai brought to him wheat, barley, meal, parched grain, beans and lentils, honey, curds, sheep, and cheese from the herd (2 Sam 17:28, 29). Solomon's daily supplies included: fine flour, meal, oxen, pasture-fed cattle, sheep, harts, gazelles, roebucks, and fatted fowl (1 Kings 4:22, 23). Tables of the rich were more luxurious than those of nomads and included "lambs from the flock, and calves from the midst of the stall" (Amos 6:4). An army on the march might have bread, a cake of figs, and clusters of raisins (1 Sam 30:12). Jesse sent to his sons parched grain and bread and sent to the commanders cheeses (1 Sam 17:17). Foreign trade added to the variety of foods. Tyre trafficked in wheat, olives, early figs, honey, oil, and balm (Ezek 27:17).

E. Food of special periods. Adam in Eden was granted permission to eat of every green plant and of the fruit of all trees except of the tree of the knowledge of good and evil (Gen 1:29; 2:16, 17). At the time of the Flood Noah took into the ark food of all that is eaten for himself and for the animals (6:21). At the end of the Flood he was informed that flesh was permitted (9:3). Many scholars conclude from the silence of Scripture and from this data that early man until the time of the Flood was vegetarian.

When Israel hungered in the wilderness, the Lord supplied manna which was gathered to the extent of an homer per person (Exod 16:16, 22). Manna was white and tasted like wafers made of honey (16:31). It could be ground, baked, and boiled to make cakes that tasted as cakes of oil (29:23; Num 11:7, 8). Manna continued through the forty years until Israel crossed Jordan and came to Gilgal (Josh 5:12). Paul describes manna as spiritual food (1 Cor 10:3). When the people desired meat, the Lord supplied quail (Exod 16:13; Num 11:31; Ps 105:40).

Elijah was fed bread and meat by the ravens when he was at the brook Cherith (1 Kings 17:6). Under the law the priests ate of the sacrifices (Exod 29:3ff.; Lev 2:3, 10; 6:16-18; Deut 18:1; etc.) and of the shewbread (Lev 24:9; 1 Sam 21:6; Matt 12:4). Some portions of certain offerings were consumed by the offerer (Lev 7:15, 19, 20; 2 Chron 25:14); the tithe was consumed before the Lord (Deut 12:17; 14:23) as were the firstlings (15:20).

Daniel and his companions in Babylon refused the king's dainties and wine and ate vegetables (זרעים, LXX ὄσπριον, pulse; Theod. σπέρμα, seed) and drank water instead (Dan 1:8ff.). During the time of exile, when laws of clean and unclean could not be observed, unclean food was eaten (Ezek 4:13; Hos 9:3). Judith carried with her wine, oil, parched grain, a cake of dried fruit and fine bread, when she went to Holofernes' camp (Jud 10:5). Judas Maccabeus and his companions lived on what grew wild, in order to escape defilement (2 Macc 5:27). Also to avoid ceremonial uncleanness Josephus and his companions lived on figs and nuts (Jos. *Life* 3).

The food of John the Baptist was locust (*akris*) and wild honey. *Akris* are insects and the effort to identify them with the carob pod has nothing to commend itself (Matt 3:4). Jesus and His disciples bought food from time to time as they journeyed (John 4:8; 13:29).

F. Food preparation. Though royal houses may have had male bakers (Gen 40:16) and both male and female cooks (1 Sam 8:13), and though some lesser figures like Samuel had cooks (9:23), the division of labor with the Israelites, as with us, made food preparation the woman's work (Gen 18:6; 1 Sam 8:13; Prov 31:15). Either a wife or a slave might be engaged (Gen 18:6, 7). Tamar took dough, kneaded cakes, baked them, and served them to Ammon (2 Sam 13:8). Flour must be ground daily and the cessation of the sound of the grinding of the mill is the end of a civilization (Eccl 12:4; Jer 25:10; Matt 24:41; Rev 18:22). Since it was necessary for the continuance of life, the upper millstone could not be taken as a pledge for debt (Deut 24:6). Dough consisting of flour and water kneaded in kneading troughs and baked in an oven to make bread formed the staff of life (Isa 3:1). When baked in haste, it was unleavened bread (Gen 19:3; Deut 16:3) but when baked with leaven which was formed from a bit of sour dough left from a previous baking, it was the more usual bread. Bread may be baked on coals (1 Kings 19:6). In Jerusalem the bakers had a special street in Jeremiah's day (Jer 37:21).

Meat was boiled in pots (1 Sam 2:13; Ezek 24:3-5) or roasted (1 Sam 2:15). The latter was used for small animals (Prov 12:27, KJV) and for the lamb at Passover which was eaten with unleavened bread and bitter herbs (Exod 12:8, 9). There are six different names for the types of pots or caldrons used in boiling. Water was first boiled and the meat added (Ezek 24:3 RSV) with salt. The broth left over also was eaten (Judg 6:19; Isa 65:4). Fish were broiled on coals (Luke 24:42; John 21:9).

G. Food prices. One knows little of the exact prices of food in ancient times. One *se'ah* of fine flour and two of barley sold for a shekel (2 Kings 7:1, 16). In times of want an ass's head brought eighty shekels of silver (6:25).

Clay figure bending over a trough kneading dough: from a cemetery of 900-600 B.C. at Ez-Zib. ©P.A.M.

Josephus (Antiq. IX. iv. 4) assumes that it was used for a condiment (cf. 2 Kings 18:27). Two sparrows sold for a penny ("assarion," Matt 10:29). In the Apocalypse a quart of wheat is worth a denarius and three quarts of barley are worth a denarius (Rev 6:6). Later prices may be seen in *M. Menahoth* 13:8.

H. Eating habits. 1. *Posture.* Early Israelites prob. sat on the ground while they ate while the host might stand by to serve (Gen 18:8). Isaac sat when he ate (27:19) as did Jacob's sons (37:25), the Levite and his concubine (Judg 19:6), Saul (1 Sam 20:5, 24) and Samuel (1 Sam 9:22). Those fed by the miracle of the Lord sat on the ground (John 6:10). Tables were used quite early. Adonibezek had seventy captive kings at his table (Judg 1:7). "Thou preparest a table before me . . ." sings the psalmist (Ps 23:5). In NT times crumbs fell to the dog under the table (Matt 15:27; Mark 7:28). Jesus sat at a table when Mary anointed him (John 12:2).

The guests at Esther's banquet reclined on couches (Esth 7:8). Reclining on the left elbow was a normal posture in NT times (John 13:23). It is likely that the guests dipped food from the common dish. The Pharisees were strict in demanding the prior washing of hands (Mark 7:3). A blessing said over food was also an established custom in the 1st cent.

2. *Time of eating.* The OT has no reference to a meal earlier than noon; however, too much should not be made of the silence. The disciples of Jesus ate an early morning meal on the seashore after a night of toil (John 21:12). The main meals were at noon and in the evening. Peter could argue that the apostles were not drunken at nine o'clock. The custom of two meals prob. goes back to Scripture: "At even ye shall eat flesh and in the morning ye shall be filled with bread" (Exod 16:12). The ravens brought Elijah food in the morning and evening (1 Kings 17:6).

In Egypt there was a mid-day meal (Gen 43:16) as there was among laborers in Pal. (Ruth 2:14). It was at the sixth hour (noon) that Jesus rested at the well in Samaria while His disciples went to buy bread (John 4:6). Peter's intended noonday meal was being prepared when messengers from Cornelius arrived (Acts 10:9ff.). This meal is the ἄριστον ([RSV and KJV: "dinner" *see* DINNER], Matt 22:4; Luke 11:38; 14:12). Supper came after the work was done (Ruth 3:7; Judg 19:16ff.). In some cases it might be prepared by a servant who had previously done field work all day (Luke 17:7ff.). This meal has no special name in the OT, but is the δεῖπνον of the NT (John 12:2; 13:2; 21:20; 1 Cor 11:20; RSV and KJV "supper").

I. Prohibited foods. In Eden every herb and tree yielding seed was for food (Gen 1:29) and only the fruit of the tree of knowledge of good and evil was forbidden (2:16, 17; 3:1ff.). Prohibitions of eating of the sinew of the hip (not otherwise attested in the OT) is traced to Jacob's wrestling with the angel (Gen 32:32). Josephus thought this to be the broad sinew [sciatic nerve] (Jos. Antiq., I. xx. 2). In Rabbinic legislation a punishment of forty stripes is meted out to the transgressor (*M. Hullin* 7:1, 3).

Under the law, food regulations dealt with meat and not with vegetable products. There is no basis either in Scripture or in Rabbinic lit. for Justin Martyr's accusation in *Dialogue* 20 that certain vegetables are prohibited. Recabites and Nazirites abstained from the produce of the vine (Num 6:2; Judg 13:14; Jer 35:1ff.), and Josephus, *Life* 2, speaks of a certain Bannus who was a vegetarian, but these are exceptional cases. The argument that early man was vegetarian is based on the prior silence of Scripture connected with the specific permission to eat meat given to Noah (Gen 9:3).

The eating of blood, prohibited in the days of Noah (Gen 9:4) and prohibited by the law (Lev 19:26; Deut 12:16, 23, 24, 25; 15:23; 1 Sam 14:34) was further prohibited in the apostolic letter (Acts 15:20, 29). Flesh of an animal found dead (Lev 7:24; Deut 14:21), flesh of an animal torn by beasts (Exod 22:31; Lev 7:24; 22:8), and a limb torn from a living animal are forbidden foods. The eating of fat (חלב, LXX στέαρ; Lev 3:16, 17; 7:23) and the fat tail (אליה, LXX ὀσφῦς; Exod 29:22; Lev 3:9) is prohibited and carried the death penalty when this food was a part of a sacrifice (7:25). These parts belonged to the Lord (Gen 4:4; 1 Sam 2:16; 2 Chron 7:7). After the Exile the eating of "fat things" (משמן, LXX λίπασμα, KJV "fat") is commended (Neh 8:10; cf. Isa 25:6).

Deuteronomy prohibits the taking of the mother bird and eggs and young ones at the same time. The mother bird is to have her freedom (Deut 22:6, 7).

J. Clean and unclean foods. Laws of clean and unclean animals, already in part alluded to in the days of the patriarchs (Gen 7:2, 3) are the most significant regulations of the law in matters of food. These laws deal with quadrupeds, fish, birds, and insects (Lev 11:1-27; Deut 14:3-21). For quadrupeds, those which have parted hoofs and chew the cud alone are edible. The camel, the rock badger, the hare, and the swine are specifically rejected by name (Lev 11:4-8; Deut 14:8). It is specifically stated that swine's flesh is an abomination (Isa 65:4; 66:3, 17).

Of fish, those which have fins and scales are edible (Lev 11:9-12). Of birds, a list of twenty are specified which are to be rejected (11:13-19). Of insects, the ones which have legs and leap may be eaten. The locust and grasshopper are specifically mentioned as being edible; while other flying, swarming, and crawling things are rejected (11:20-23). Distinctions in food broke down in times of want (Ezek 4:13).

Peter in his vision rejected the command to eat animals not conforming to these categories

(Acts 10:12-15). Jesus is said to have done away with distinctions concerning foods (Mark 7:19). These were regulations of the first testament that have lost their significance (Heb 9:10) and cannot confirm the faith (13: 9). The effort to try to connect these regulations of the law with modern laws of hygiene is arbitrary and breaks down when applied in details. It has no more to commend it than the earlier allegorical exegesis of the same laws.

The rabbinic prohibition of eating milk and meat at the same time is based on an exegesis of Exodus 23:19; 34:26; Deuteronomy 14:21 ASV: "Thou shalt not boil a kid in its mother's milk" (cf. *M. Hullin* 8:4). Ugaritic discoveries have, from a reconstructed text (Gordon, 52:14), called attention to a similar practice on the part of the Canaanites to that forbidden in Scripture.

K. Food offered to idols. A special problem with food faced the early Christian when he asked whether or not he could eat food previously offered to idols. The apostolic letter enjoined abstinence "from what has been sacrificed to idols" (Act 15:29 RSV). When questioned about that offered to idols, Paul answered that food does not commend one to God. The kingdom of God is not meat and drink. One may eat what he is disposed to—whatever is sold in the market (1 Cor 10:25)—without asking questions for conscience's sake; but if the eating causes a brother to stumble then the Christian abstains for the sake of his brother's conscience (Rom 14:13ff.; 1 Cor 8:1-13).

L. Sharing food. Sharing one's food with the hungry was demanded by John the Baptist as a sign of repentance (Luke 3:11). In the OT Job claims this trait among his virtues (Job 31:17). Those who are hungry are to be fed (Matt 25:35, 36). The duty extends to the hungry enemy (Prov 25:21; Rom 12:20). Faith that refuses to feed the brother or sister that is hungry is dead faith (Jas 2:15-17).

M. Life and food. As important as it is, food is not the chief ingredient of life. "Man does not live by bread alone, but . . . by everything that proceeds out of the mouth of the LORD" (Deut 8:3; cf. Matt 4:4; Luke 4:4). Failure of food should not destroy faith in God (Hab 3: 17, 18). Life is more than food (Matt 6:25, 32; Luke 12:22, 30).

II. METAPHORICAL USE

The basis for a metaphorical use of food is laid in the prophets when Isaiah rebukes those who spend their substance for that which does not satisfy (Isa 55:1ff.). Food is a frequent metaphor in the NT. Jesus' comparison of Himself to the bread of life (John 6) is the chief fig. use of food in Scripture. As Israel ate manna in the wilderness, so Christ gives of Himself to the believer that he may eat of His flesh and drink His blood and have life in himself. The one eating this food shall never want.

In answer to the question of whether anyone had given Him anything to eat, Jesus answered "My food is to do the will of him who sent me, and to accomplish his work" (John 4:34). This, of course, did not imply that He could dispense with earthly food. Continuing the metaphor, the new believer is to desire the pure milk of the Word (1 Pet 2:2). Elementary teaching is milk for babes while advanced matters are solid food for the mature (1 Cor 3:2; Heb 5:14).

The preservative power of salt illustrates the powers of the disciple in the world (Matt 5: 13; Mark 9:50). Its seasoning power is a figure of the proper choice of speech (Col 4:6).

The one who overcomes will "eat of the tree of life" (Rev 2:7). *See* COOKING.

BIBLIOGRAPHY. J. Behm, *Brōma,* TWNT (1933), I, 640-643; J. B. Pritchard, ANET (1950), 19, 20; H. N. and A. L. Moldenke, *Plants of the Bible* (1952); A. C. Bouquet, *Everyday Life in NT Times* (1954), 69-79; M. S. and J. L. Miller, *Encyclopedia of Bible Life* (1955), 199ff.

J. P. LEWIS

FOOL. *See* FOLLY.

FOOT (Heb. רגל, *foot*; פעם, *foot, footfall*; כן, *foot, base, stand*; Gr. πούς, *foot*). In man, the lowest extremity of the leg, but in an animal, any of the four terminal parts of the legs. The feet of God (Exod 24:10) with thick darkness under his feet (Ps 18:9), a glorious place (Isa 60:13), are fig.; for a spirit has no flesh or bones. The reference to the presence of hands and feet of the resurrected Christ revealed that Christ still possessed a body (Luke 24:39). Great care was needed for the feet in the E, since people wore sandals or went barefoot, hence the washing of feet showed needed and refreshing hospitality (Gen 18:4). This was the lowest task of servants, performed by the youngest or least skilled upon the part of the body most likely to be defiled. Christ's example in washing His disciples feet showed both humility and complete devotion (John 13:5). A widow in the Early Church washed the feet of saints (1 Tim 5:10). Undoing the latchet of a sandal was an equivalent task. By contrast, the disciples shook the dust off their feet to predict judgment on unhearing and unhospitable towns and villages (Matt 10:14).

The feet of the Israelites were miraculously preserved during the long journey in the wilderness (Deut 8:4). Feet suggest movement, "the feet of him who brings good tidings" (Isa 52:7). Angels guard the feet of one "who dwells in the shelter of the Most High . . . lest you dash your foot against a stone" (Ps 91: 1, 12).

Interesting ideas are conveyed by the feet. Taking off the shoes was not only proper before entering a house, but also in the presence of God (Exod 3:5). Solomon commanded, "Guard your steps when you go to the house of God" (Eccl 5:1).

To bare the foot in public expressed mourning (Ezek 24:17) or shameing (Deut 25:9), but to take off a sandal and give to another confirmed a transaction of redemption and exchange (Ruth 4:7). The phrase tr. by the KJV in 1 Samuel 24:3 is "to cover his feet," but this becomes "to relieve himself" in the RSV. A wicked man could communicate by scraping or tapping with his feet (Prov 6:13). Unlike present day usage, the foot was not used to measure, except possibly the foot's length not granted to Abraham (Acts 7:5).

A learner sat at the feet of his teacher (Luke 10:39) as Mary did, yet no churchman should ask the poor to sit at his feet (James 2:3) to show discrimination. Jairus fell at the feet of Jesus in humility, respect and supplication (Mark 5:22). Feet were embraced or kissed in adoration (Luke 7:38). Egyptian monuments picture conquerors treading on the vanquished as a method of insult. The Lord promised to trample the Assyrian under foot (Isa 14:25).

"My foot has held fast to his steps" is a poetical claim to a consistent walk (Job 23:11) which has not "let the foot of arrogance come upon me" (Ps 36:11) nor let his foot offend him (Mark 9:45). In the body of Christ, a foot should not envy the hand (1 Cor 12:14, 15).

R. L. MIXTER

FOOTMAN (רגלי, or איש רגלי meaning *men on foot*—Exod 12:37; Num 11:21; also means *footsoldiers* or *infantry*—Judg 20:2; 1 Sam 4:10; 15:4; 2 Sam 10:6; 1 Kings 20:29; etc.) The main use of this word outside of the Pentateuch is for military purposes. It is used to distinguish between the soldier who marches and fights on foot and the soldier who rides on horseback or in a chariot.

Its use in the Pentateuch seems to be broader than just military because of the tribal context. There it is used to contrast between adult men and children.

KJV also uses the word "footman" in a context that calls for the word "guard" (1 Sam 22:17) as well as in a context which calls for "courier" (Jer 12:5).

G. GIACUMAKIS, JR.

FOOTSTOOL (כבש, *footstool*; הדם, *stool*; ὑποπόδιον, *footstool*). A low stool for supporting the feet of a person seated upon a pretentious seat, as a throne. In the RSV the word is used in a literal sense only once (2 Chron 9:18) where it is said that Solomon's throne had six steps and a footstool of gold; in the KJV a literal use is found in James 2:3 (RSV "feet"). The thirteen other times the word is used are fig., and in all of them it is God who makes use of the footstool. All of the NT references, except for James 2:3 (KJV), are quotations from the OT. The fig. uses of the word fall into the following groups: (1) Of the earth; heaven is the throne of God and the earth His footstool (Isa 66:1; Matt 5:35; Acts 7:49). (2) Of the Ark of the covenant in the Tabernacle (1 Chron 28:2). (3) Of the Temple (Pss 99:5; 132:7; Lam 2:1). (4) Of the enemies of the Messianic King who have been subdued by Him (Ps 110:1; Matt 22:44; Mark 12:36; Luke 20:43; Acts 2:35; Heb 1:13; and 10:13).

S. BARABAS

FOOT WASHING (better feet washing). Though never a major rite in the Mosaic ritual, the washing of hands and feet of the priests did have a place (Exod 30:17-21). It may indeed be that all ablutions of the Bible are ritual rather than sanitary, though they rise out of assumed sanitary practices (de Vaux, *Ancient Israel, Its Life and Customs,* p. 460). Guests ordinarily were offered water and vessels for washing the feet (Gen 18:4; 19:2; 24:32; 43:24; Judg 19:21). As a special act of affection or humility the host(ess) might even wash his/her guests' feet (1 Sam 25:41). A "sinful woman" spontaneously and gratefully so served the Lord (Luke 7:36-44).

At the Last Supper the Lord, taking a towel and basin during the meal (John 13:4-10), proceeded to wash the disciples' feet and to wipe them with the towel. It was not to observe a custom, for the disciples were mystified by it. There is no doubt that Jesus gave it the spiritual significance of symbolic cleansing of the believer from the defilement of present sin as baptism symbolizes cleansing from all guilt—the one partial and temporary (νίπτω), the latter complete and permanent (λούω imperfect tense): "He who has bathed does not need to wash, except for his feet" (John 13:10). This is the main lesson rather than humility (viz. note in *Scofield Bible,* loc cit). Whether or not it is an ordinance (viz. John 13:14, 15) must be decided on the basis of whether or not it meets the three qualifications of a church ordinance: (1) instituted by Christ, (2) of universal, and (3) permanent application. A number of smaller denominations developing out of the "Left Wing of the Reformation" (Bainton) believe it to be an ordinance, citing in addition to John 13, 1 Timothy 5:10. The National Fellowship of Brethren Churches has developed quite a cogent theology and defense of it as an ordinance (viz. H. A. Hoyt, *This Do,* Brethren Missionary Herald Co., Winona Lake, Ind., also C. F. Yoder, *God's Means of Grace* o.p.).

R. D. CULVER

FORBEAR fôr bâr′ (חדל, *to cease, leave off, desist, abstain or refrain from, forbear*; ἀνέχομαι, *to bear up under provocation, to hold oneself back, to put up with, to forbear*).

FORBEARANCE fôr bâr′ əns (חדל, *a ceasing, a leaving off, forbearance*; ἀνοχή in secular Gr. *armistice, truce, temporary suspension of hostilities*; in NT, *a holding back, a deferring of punishment, forbearance*; μακροθυμία, *patience, longsuffering*).

There are many words in the OT and NT which are used to express the idea of forbearance. In the OT there is דמם, *to be silent, cease, stand still* (Ezek 24:17); חשך, *to restrain, spare, withhold* (Prov 24:11); משך, *to extend, protract* (Neh 9:30 et al.). But the preferred word is חדל, listed above (Exod 23:5; Zech 11:12). In the NT there is ἀνίημι, *to send back, let away, refrain from* (Eph 6:9); φείδομαι, *to spare* (2 Cor 12:6); στέγω, *to bear* (1 Thess 3:1, 5). But the preferred words are ἀνοχή and μακροθυμία, listed above (Rom 2:4; 3:25; Eph 4:2).

In its religious meaning forbearance is characteristic of the God of Biblical revelation. Jehovah, the God of Israel, was extremely patient with the perverse and recalcitrant people He had elected. In their wickedness He bore with them (Neh 9:30) and proved Himself merciful and gracious, slow to anger, and abounding in steadfast love (Ps 103:8). Thereby He revealed and exercised His forbearance, i.e. His disposition to hold back or restrain His wrath and to delay the divine punishment which must eventually fall upon the sin which is not covered by repentance and atonement.

God's forbearance is not an easy and indifferent "tolerance" of sin. For sin God has only negations. Neither will God absolve the unrepentant sinner. The final judgment will call all men into account and seal their destiny for good or ill. But in this age, in the day of grace, He is long suffering. He is both slow to punish and unwilling, even in the face of opposition and alienation, to withdraw His overtures toward peace or cancel His invitation to be reconciled.

God's forbearance is celebrated in the NT no less than in the OT. Jesus hinted both at it and at His kinship with the Father when He asked, "O faithless generation . . . How long am I to bear with you" (Mark 9:19). The Apostle Paul proclaims it in Romans 2:4; 3:25; 9:22, where he teaches that God has shown forbearance for a number of reasons: to show His wrath (upon sin), to make known His power, to disclose the riches of His glory for the vessels of mercy, and principally, to lead men to repentance. The same is declared by the Apostle Peter who, faced with the scoffers' question "Where is the promise of his (Christ's second) coming?" (2 Pet 3:4), answered "The Lord is not slow about his promise as some count slowness, but is forbearing toward you, not wishing that any should perish, but that all should reach repentance" (2 Pet 3:9).

Christians who wish to lead a life worthy of the calling to which they have been called, are obliged, in imitation of their Lord, to forbear one another in love, with all lowliness, meekness, and patience (Eph 4:2). That is, they are to exercise calm patience under provocation, avoid resentment and retaliation, be slow to judge and punish, and be ever ready to forgive (Phil 4:5; Col 3:13; 2 Tim 2:24).

H. Stob

FORD (מעבר ; מעברה). A shallow place in a stream where it may be crossed on foot. Fords were of great importance in OT times because of the absence of bridges, which were first built in large numbers by the Romans. Scripture often mentions the fords of the Jordan, which could be crossed in many places (Josh 2:7; Judg 3:28; 12:5, 6). There seem to have been two principal fords across the Jordan—at Jericho (Josh 2:7; Judg 3:28; 2 Sam 19:15), and at Bethabara, where John baptized (John 1:28 KJV). In time of flood, when the melting snows of the Lebanon mountains caused the Jordan to overflow its banks, it was impossible to cross the Jordan (Josh 3:15). Near the Dead Sea the Jordan is about 100 ft. wide, and from five to twelve ft. deep.

The crossing of the Jordan is mentioned in connection with Jacob (Gen 32:10), Gideon (Judg 8:4), David (2 Sam 10:17; 17:22), Absalom (2 Sam 17:24), and others. Under the leadership of Joshua the Israelites crossed the Jordan on dry land, not by fording it since it was then in flood, but by a tremendous miraculous act of God. Jesus crossed the Jordan on numerous occasions when He journeyed between Galilee and Jerusalem by way of Perea instead of passing through Samaria.

Mention is also made in Scripture of the ford of the river Jabbok (Gen 32:22) and the fords of the river Arnon (Num 21:13; Deut 2:24; Isa 16:2).

S. Barabas

FORECAST (חשב, meaning *to think, plan*). This word is used in KJV (Dan 11:24, 25) in the context of planning evil against a person. ". . . he shall forecast his devices against the . . ." and ". . . they shall forecast devices against . . ." RSV and NASB use the tr. instead "to devise against."

FOREHEAD (מצח, μέτωπον, literally meaning *between the eyes*). The use of the word "forehead" in the OT conveys several meanings. It

A shallow place in the Jabbok. ©*Lev*

is used in a literal sense (Exod 28:38) when Aaron was instructed to wear the plate of pure gold on his forehead. Likewise in 1 Samuel 17:49 and 2 Chronicles 26:19, 20 it is used in a literal sense to refer to specific wounds or leprous marks on the forehead. A fig. use (Ezek 3:8, 9) illustrates that the direction of the forehead shows determination or defiance.

In the NT all the references are in the Book of Revelation. They refer to the fig. or literal marks, seals, or names found on the foreheads of those who are servants of God as well as those who reject God. These marks often show the contrast between these two types of individuals (Rev 7:3; 9:4; 13:16; 14:1; 20:4).

The forehead was also the place where the harlot might advertise her intentions (Jer 3:3; Rev 17:5).

G. Giacumakis, Jr.

FOREIGNER (נכרי, תושב, גר ; ἀλλότριος, ἀλλογενής. A "non-citizen," roughly equivalent to an "alien," dwelling in a country either as a temporary guest, perhaps for purposes of trade, or as a permanent resident alien). The three Heb. words which refer to foreigners are tr. in a variety of ways—foreigner, alien, stranger, sojourner—and are practically indistinguishable in meaning. *Nokrī*, rendered "foreigner" in the RSV, is in the KJV so tr. only twice (Deut 15:3; Obad 11); usually the KJV trs. it "alien" (Deut 14:21; Job 19:15; Ps 69:8; Lam 5:2) or "stranger" (Gen 15:13; Exod 2:22). *Gēr* and *tōshāb* are sometimes used together in the same passage with no apparent difference in meaning (Lev 25:35; 1 Chron 29:15; Ps 39:12). A whole clan or tribe might be sojourners in Israel, as e.g. the Gibeonites (Josh 9) and the Beerothites (2 Sam 4:2). Solomon's census shows that the number of aliens in the land of Israel was quite considerable (2 Chron 2:17).

The word "foreigner" and its equivalents was applied not only to non-Israelites residing in Pal. more or less permanently, but also to Israelites making their home for a time in other lands (Gen 23:4; 26:3; 47:4; Exod 2:22; Ruth 1:1).

Foreigners in Israel enjoyed certain limited religious and civic privileges and were subject to certain laws. They could offer sacrifices (Lev 17:8; 22:18, 19), but were not permitted to enter the sanctuary unless they were circumcised (Ezek 44:9). They could take part in the three great annual religious festivals attended by all Israelite males (Deut 16:11, 14). They were not permitted to eat of the Passover unless they were circumcised (Exod 12:43, 48), and the Passover prohibition of the use of leaven applied also to them (Exod 12:19). Like the Israelites, they were forbidden to work on the Sabbath and on the Day of Atonement (Exod 20:10; 23:12; Lev 16:19; Deut 5:14); and like them also they were stoned to death for reviling or blaspheming God's name (Lev 24:16; Num 15:30). They heard the law read to all the people in the Sabbatical year (Deut 31:10-13).

There was one law for the foreigner and the native (Exod 12:49; Lev 24:22), and in legal actions they were entitled to the same justice as the Israelites (Deut 1:16) and were liable to the same penalties (Lev 20:2; 24:16, 22). Israelites were warned not to oppress foreigners, since they themselves were once strangers in the land of Egypt (Exod 22:21; 23:9; Lev 19:33, 34). Foreigners were to be loved and treated like native Israelites (Lev 19:34; Deut 10:19), for God loves them (Deut 10:18) and watches over them (Ps 146:9; Mal 3:5). Needy foreigners were to be given assistance (Num 35:15; Deut 10:19). They were to share in the special triennial tithe (Deut 14:29) and in the produce of the Sabbatical year (Lev 25:6), as well as in the gleanings of the olives, grapes, and grain at the time of harvest (Lev 19:10; 23:22; Deut 24:19-21). They were entitled to asylum in the cities of refuge (Num 35:15; Josh 20:9). It was forbidden to oppress them when they labored as hired servants (Deut 24:14).

Like Israelites, they were forbidden to eat blood (Lev 17:10, 12), but, unlike them, they might eat animals that had died a natural death (Deut 14:21). Israelite laws of sexual morality applied to them as well (Lev 18:26). Although there were certain prohibitions of marriage between them and Israelites, the OT contains many instances of marriage between them (Gen 34:14; Exod 34:12, 16; Deut 7:3; Josh 23:12).

Foreigners naturally suffered some disabilities. They could not take part in the deliberations of the clan, tribe, or nation. The law prohibited a foreigner from becoming a king of Israel (Deut 17:15). They had to pay interest for money they borrowed (Deut 15:3; 23:20); and when, during the Year of Jubilee the debts of Israelites were cancelled, theirs were not (Deut 15:3), and when Heb. slaves were freed, they remained in bondage (Lev 25:45, 46).

Ezekiel, however, foresaw the time in the Messianic age when they would share in all the blessings of the land with God's own people (Ezek 47:22).

S. Barabas

FOREKNOW, FOREKNOWLEDGE is to know beforehand and is used of the knowledge which men may possess on the basis of information given or revelation received (Acts 26:5; 2 Pet 3:17). Apart from these two instances, however, the term both as verb and substantive (προγινώσκω, πρόγνωσις) is used of God's knowledge (Acts 2:23; Rom 8:29; 11:2; 1 Pet 1:2, 20) and hence in theological usage it is upon God as subject that thought is focused.

In the sense of cognition God's foreknowledge belongs to His omniscience and embraces all persons and things. Scripture throughout teaches God's all-comprehending prescience and knowledge. Nothing is hid from Him (cf., e.g., Job 28:23, 24; 37:16; Pss 44:21; 139:1-4; Isa 46:9, 10; 48:2, 3, 5; Jer 1:5; 1 Cor 2:10, 11; 1 John 3:20). There is no ground for dispute respecting God's foreknowledge in this sense. An implication, however, is liable to be overlooked. If God foresees all that comes to pass, then with God there is no uncertainty of occurrence. Hence, certainty respecting all that comes to pass is involved in foreknowledge no less than in foreordination, and foreknowledge provides no escape from the certainty which foreordination asserts and determines. It is of Biblical faith to believe that for God there are no contingent eventualities and believers should be assured that all the circumstances of their life are well known to Him who is their God and Savior.

The crucial questions respecting foreknowledge arise in connection with those passages cited above which expressly deal with salvation (esp. Rom 8:29; 11:2; 1 Pet 1:2). There can be no question but "whom he foreknew" (Rom 8:29) and "the foreknowledge of God the Father" (1 Pet 1:2 ASV) are predicable of the elect and of those only. Romans 8:29, 30 introduces a chain of events that issues in glorification and those embraced in this chain are designated as "God's elect" in v. 33. In 1 Peter 1:1 those concerned are called "elect." The question is: What is the import of "foreknew" and "foreknowledge" and, more particularly, what relation does the former sustain to predestination (Rom 8:29) and the latter to election (1 Pet 1:1, 2)? It is widely maintained that the foreknowledge in these texts is the prescience of God, His foresight of faith or, more accurately, His foresight of certain persons as believing. Whom God foresees as believing He predestinates and elects to salvation.

If this were the intent of Paul and Peter, it would not be unworthy of them and not contrary to the general tenor of Biblical teaching. God's foresight of all persons and actions is, as noted, Biblical doctrine, and He foresees His people as believing. There is, however, an important consideration, derived from Scripture teaching, to be kept in mind. It is that faith itself is not an act or activity of man's autonomy; it is not something of which men are capable. It is a gift of God. This was the teaching of the Lord expressly (John 6:37, 44, 45, 65) and by implication (3:3-8). It is Paul's teaching (Rom 8:5-9; Eph 2:8-10; Phil 1:29) and Peter's (2 Pet 1:1). Hence the faith which God foresees is the faith which He has determined to give. To use the Lord's language, the faith God the Father foresees is the coming to Christ which is the result of His own effectual drawing (John 6:44), of the learning which He imparts (6:45), and of His own giving (6:65). Foresight of faith, therefore, does not eliminate the sovereign differentiation which God causes to be in His saving operations; it throws one back on God's sovereign will to work effectually to the exercise of faith. No escape from the sovereignty of God's will in salvation is provided by this view of foreknowledge.

The most significant passage (Rom 8:29) requires further examination and the relevant considerations indicate that a different interpretation from that discussed above should be adopted.

1. It is to be noted that Paul says "whom he foreknew." The persons in view are the object of the verb "foreknew" and they are the object without any qualification or further characterization. The view that supposes foresight of faith or foresight of persons as believing is required to supply a characterization which the apostle does not add. Unless there is a compelling reason for this addition one has no right to append it. We must ask the question: Is there a meaning of the word "foreknew" that can properly belong to it and which avoids the necessity of importing something that has no warrant in the text itself? If such a meaning can be found, a meaning supported by Scripture usage, then an interpretation based upon the need for a qualifying importation is ruled out. This alternative is valid. There is ample evidence for an interpretation in which "whom he foreknew" is intelligible and appropriate without further explanation.

2. "Foreknow" is a compound in which the word "know" is the main ingredient. The first part in Eng., as in Gr., indicates simply that the knowing is beforehand. So it is necessary to focus attention on the term "know" and determine its precise force. It is used frequently in Scripture in the sense of simple cognition. It is used also often with a richer meaning in which the thought of distinguishing affection and will enters. When "know" is used in this sense there is differentiation in the word itself. The instances are numerous in both Testaments (cf., e.g., Gen 18:19; Exod 2:25; Ps 1:6; Jer 1:5; Hos 13:5; Amos 3:2; Matt 7:23; 1 Cor 8:3; Gal 4:9; 2 Tim 2:19; 1 John 3:1). The distinguishing connotation lies on the face of this usage. "Know" means to know with distinguishing regard, affection, and purpose and comes to be synonymous with love. This is all the more apparent in the OT when the distinction inherent in the word "know" in the examples given is frequently expressed by the word love (cf. Deut 4:37; 7:8, 13; 10:15; 23:5; 1 Kings 10:9; 2 Chron 9:8; Jer 31:3; Hos 11:1; 14:4; Mal 1:2). The inference is inescapable that to "know" is the same as to "love" and that with the distinguishing affection and purpose which this term frequently conveys in Scripture. Hence, to "know beforehand" is to know with peculiar regard and love from before the foundation of the world (cf. Eph 1:4) and "foreknew" (Rom 8:29)

can have the persons as direct object with no further qualification.

3. Corroboration is found in Ephesians 1:5. That there is an identity of theme in the two passages needs no demonstration. When Paul says, "In love having predestinated us unto adoption," he intimates that predestination is conditioned by love and springs from it. When foreknowledge is interpreted, as the analogy of Scripture and the terms of the passage dictate, Romans 8:29 expresses the same relationship with the additional emphasis upon the coextensiveness of this love and predestination to be conformed to the image of God's Son. There is no duplication of thought in either passage. The love focuses attention upon the electing grace, the predestination upon the high destiny to which those embraced in electing love are appointed. The order of thought is similar to Ephesians 1:4, where election in Christ is said to be to the end of being holy and without blame. Electing love is not fruitless affection. It always moves to a goal commensurate in magnitude with the love that impels.

4. The idea of mere foresight of faith does not comport with the governing thought of Romans 8:28-30. The accent in this passage falls upon God's determinate action, upon His monergism. It is God who predestinates, calls, justifies, and glorifies, and this emphasis appears in confirmation of the assurance of v. 28 and in elucidation of the purpose in accordance with which those concerned are called. Foresight, however true of God it is in itself, suggests a passivity out of agreement with the total thrust of the context. Only the efficient action involved in electing love measures up to this requirement. It is not the foresight of what will be but the foreknowledge that causes to be.

These considerations show that in this all-important passage "foreknowledge" as applied to God is not to be construed in terms merely of prescience, and so one may not proceed on the assumption that in other instances this diluted sense obtains.

In Romans 11:2 the reference to the people whom God foreknew is most appropriately taken of the people of Israel as a whole after the pattern of Romans 11:28. Every consideration would point to the conclusion that the choice of Israel in love, is in view. The notion of mere prescience is obviously inadequate. Although the full force of the distinguishing love of Romans 8:29 cannot be applied to 11:2, yet the same basic meaning obtains, namely, the love on God's part by which Israel had been chosen and set apart (cf. Deut 4:37 et al. as cited earlier). What is in view is the theocratic election of Israel, and Paul is assuring us that the love animating this election has abiding relevance and is the guarantee that Israel has not been finally rejected. This instance is additional evidence for the pregnant force of foreknow.

In 1 Peter 1:20—"foreknown indeed before the foundation of the world" (ASV)—foreknown is contrasted with manifested and, in reference to Christ, the distinction is between design from eternity and realization in the fullness of the time. It is apparent that the notion of "foreseen" before the foundation of the world falls short of Peter's intent. The thought is that Christ was chosen and provided before the world began, but was manifested in the end of the times. If the idea expressed by "foreknown" does not rise to that of "foreordained," the difference is scarcely perceptible. In any case this instance shows that "foreknow" can properly express the thought of the ordination and appointment of God's design and counsel.

Before proceeding to the discussion of the substantive (πρόγνωσις) it is necessary to take account of two other terms: προοράω (Gal 3:8) and προβλέπω (Heb 11:40). In the former it may not be insisted that anything more than foreseeing is expressed (cf. Acts 2:25, 31). However, if "the Scripture" is personified and in reality means God, more could be intended than that of foreseeing and might well mean "determining beforehand" after the pattern of 1 Peter 1:20. The term which means more literally to "foresee" is used in the sense of "provide," and the rendering "foresee" would be inappropriate (Heb 11:40). The interest of this passage is to show that a term closely corresponding to foreknow and, like foreknow, may express simply the thought of foreseeing can be and is used with a much more active connotation and furnishes evidence parallel to the distinctly determining force of foreknow as demonstrated above.

The usage respecting the verb "foreknow" in each instance where God is the subject demonstrates that in the NT the term possesses an active and ordaining force that the Eng. equivalent would not of itself readily suggest. This must be borne in mind in dealing with the two instances of the substantive "foreknowledge." The meaning of the verb creates strong presumption that the same force is present in the noun. It should be noted that Acts 2:23 is distinctly similar to 1 Peter 1:20 for the predetermining counsel of God respecting Christ is the thought in both passages. First Peter 1:2 is similar to Romans 8:29 because foreknowledge conditions election in the former as it conditions predestination in the latter. This parallelism is a factor not to be discounted.

In Acts 2:23 there are several considerations bearing upon the interpretation of "foreknowledge."

1. The term indicates that the counsel of God involved in the crucifixion of Christ was prior to the event; it was *beforehand*. The analogy of other passages (Eph 1:4; 1 Pet 1:20) would require that this priority was eternal, before the foundation of the world.

2. The words with which foreknowledge is conjoined, "determinate counsel" (ὡρισμένῃ

βουλῇ), denote the immutable purpose and decree of God. Stronger terms to express predetermination could not be found. It may not be argued that appeal to God's foresight of the crucifixion and of all the circumstances associated with it would be inappropriate in conjunction with the emphasis upon determinate counsel. Foreknowledge could relevantly draw attention to God's eternal omniscience in order thereby to assert that the efficient decree was made in the light of comprehensive knowledge of events and implications. But this notion of foreknowledge does not take proper account of the construction. It was, Peter says, "by the determinate counsel and foreknowledge" that Jesus was delivered and the agency or instrumentality that is exercised *by* the determinate counsel is applied also to the foreknowledge. This implies for the foreknowledge an efficiency comparable to that of the fixed counsel. The mere notion of prescience does not possess this quality. The thought requires an active, determining element of which prescience falls short (cf. Rom 8:29). It is not simply conjunction of counsel and foreknowledge that the text mentions but a conjunction of determining decrees, and foreknowledge for this reason requires the strength of foreordination. It may not be objected that there is virtual duplication of ideas. It is characteristic of Scripture to emphasize something by adding a virtual synonym. Here, however, this is not necessarily the case. Foreknowledge points to the *pre*-ordination, determinate counsel to the immutable decree.

3. It is significant that the writer of 1 Peter 1:20 is the speaker in Acts 2:23. The determinate force of "foreknow" in 1 Peter 1:20 is an index to the meaning of the noun in Acts 2:23. Since the two passages deal with God's counsel respecting Christ, conclusive evidence would have to be available if differentiation on the question at issue were to obtain. This evidence does not exist. As maintained above, the considerations point to an identity in respect of active, determining will.

4. It would not be legitimate to press unduly the analogy of Acts 4:28. It is conceivable that the terms of 4:28 were intended to express foreordination in a way that 2:23 does not. Yet, since other considerations evince that foreknowledge in 2:23 carries the force of foreordination, it is not possible to discount the unequivocal terms of 4:28 in interpreting 2:23. They both reflect on the same subject. Peter is the speaker in the one case; he is closely associated, if not the actual spokesman, in the other. There is proximity in the literary composition. It would be natural to regard them both as enunciating the same doctrine. If so, the foreknowledge of 2:23 would have to perform the service of "foreordained to come to pass" in 4:28.

It must be concluded, therefore, that the exegetical considerations claim for "foreknowledge" the same determinant force as is apparent in the use of the verb "foreknow." What is to be said for 1 Peter 1:2?

1. If one proceeds on the assumption that "according to the foreknowledge of God the Father" is taken with the words "elect sojourners" (vs. 1 ASV), then the foreknowledge of God is to be regarded as conditioning election and causally prior to it. As indicated earlier, the similarity to Romans 8:29 is apparent. The considerations adduced in connection with Romans 8:29 against the notion of mere prescience would be equally valid: foreknowledge here is not qualified any more than "foreknew" in Roman 8:29 and the pregnant meaning applies as much to "knowledge" as it does to the word "know."

2. In 1 Peter 1:2 there is another factor pointing to the active force of foreknowledge. The foreknowledge of God the Father is coordinated with "sanctification of the Spirit" and "sprinkling of the blood of Jesus Christ." Foreknowledge is the source or, at least, the pattern of election, sanctification the sphere within which it comes to effect or the means by which it is operative, and sprinkling of the blood of Christ, the end to which it is directed. One cannot think, therefore, of foreknowledge in less efficient terms than sanctification of the Spirit and sprinkling of Christ's blood. There is in this case what has been apparent in other contexts, namely, the active force that foresight does not possess. It is this quality that imparts to the foreknowledge of God the Father the efficiency in reference to election which the construction would lead one to expect. Foreknowledge is itself causally operative and determining.

3. Since the predetermining character of foreknow and foreknowledge is necessary in the other instances, one should expect the same meaning in 1 Peter 1:2, and, unless compelling reasons for exception should exist, the analogy of usage would throw its weight in favor of the same interpretation.

The upshot then is that "foreknow" and "foreknowledge," when applied to God in Scripture, designate much more than what belongs to the attribute of omniscience. In each instance these terms refer to God's determining will and, though each passage views this will from the aspect appropriate to its own context, yet the terms take on the strength of "foreordain" and "foreordination" and in some cases express the same thought. It is also significant that they are used only in reference to what falls within the sphere of salvation. In terms of Scripture usage and, strictly speaking, foreknow and foreknowledge do not designate God's all-inclusive determining will, but His will as it concerns the provisions and objects of saving purpose.

BIBLIOGRAPHY. See Elect, Election.

J. Murray

FOREORDAIN, FOREORDINATION (Gr. *προορίζω, decide beforehand*) is applied in Scripture to both persons and events. As applied to persons it means to appoint to a fixed destiny; as applied to events, to make certain their occurrence. The corresponding term in the NT is *προορίζω* and in every instance God is the subject. In four cases (Rom 8:29, 30; Eph 1:4, 11) the predestination of the elect to the glory of adoption and of conformity to the image of God's Son is in view, in the two other cases (Acts 4:28; 1 Cor 2:7) the predetermination of what has come to pass. To foreordain and to predestinate are synonymous, but the former is more appropriate for events, the latter for persons.

Although *προορίζω* occurs infrequently, that to which it refers is pervasive in both Testaments. In the OT the thought is expressed in terms of God's undefeatable purpose (cf., e.g., Job 23:13, 14; Ps 33:11; Prov 16:33; Isa 14:24-27; 37:26). In the NT other terms such as *βουλή* (Acts 2:23; 4:28; Eph 1:11), *θέλημα* (Acts 21:14; Rom 1:10; 15:32; Gal 1:4; Eph 1:5), *εὐδοκία* (Matt 11:26; Eph 1:5, 9), *εὐδοκέω* (Gal 1:15), *πρόθεσις* (Rom 8:28; 9:11; Eph 1:11; 2 Tim 1:9) indicate the extent to which it is permeated with the conception of God's foreordaining, sovereign, and all-controlling will. Acts 2:23 and 4:28 are particularly instructive. They show conclusively that the sinful acts of men are embraced in the determinate counsel of God and occur in accord with what his counsel foreordained to come to pass. Yet this effective foreordination in no way curtails or interferes with the responsibility and guilt of the perpetrators of iniquity. It is in the indictment of the men of Israel with the crime of the crucifixion that the reference to God's counsel and foreknowledge occurs. Both agencies are present but the differentiation in respect of purpose must be maintained.

J. MURRAY

FORERUNNER (Gr. *πρόδρομος*), a *hapax legomenon* in Hebrews 6:20, the term is classical in origin and has a range of meanings. Although used primarily of military forces who "rush ahead" or of special guides of the army who "attack suddenly" the term is used also in a metaphorical sense for any precursor. The author of Hebrews uses it of the person of Christ into the Holy of Holies (Heb. קדשים-הקדשה; Exod 26:33-35; 40:20, 21). This meant that the ancient order of priests which started with Melchizedek (Gen 14:17-20) now came to its fulfillment and completion in the last priest, the Messianic priest-sacrifice. Christ is therefore the precursor of all believers who may now enter into the presence of Jehovah Himself (Rom 8:15; Gal 4:6).

W. WHITE, JR.

FORESAIL. *See* SHIPS AND BOATS.

FORESHIP. *See* SHIPS AND BOATS.

FORESKIN (ערלה, Gen 17:11, 14, 23-25; Exod 4:25; Lev 12:3. Verb form means *to have a foreskin* or *be uncircumcised,* Hab 2:16; Gen 17:14). The rite of circumcision was to take place on the eighth day after birth. The cutting of the foreskin from the penis was considered an important religious ceremony because of its spiritual significance. The act of circumcision symbolized the covenant which God made with Abraham and his descendants. Once one identified with the covenant, it was to be followed by obedience to God's commandments. A fig. use is also seen (Deut 10:16): "Circumcise therefore the foreskin of your heart. . . ." Obedience was necessary to follow God. This is esp. clear in the NT references to circumcision.

G. GIACUMAKIS, JR.

FOREST (חרש, *a thicket,* or *wooded height*; יער, *thicket, wood*; פרדס, *park, the garden ground,* or *paradise*).

The word "forest" occurs thirty-eight times in the Bible, thirty-five times as *yaar*—an outspread place; once as *ḥoreš* or thicket (2 Chron 27:4); once as *ya'ârâh* (Ps 29:9); and once as *pardēs,* i.e. *park* (Neh 2:8). Four special forests are mentioned—the Forest of Carmel, found in Zebulun on the S border of Asher; the forest of Hareth, S of Judah on the borders of the Philistine Plain; the Forest of Lebanon (1 Kings 7:2; 2 Chron 9:16), which refers to an armory or treasure house which King Solomon built in or near Jerusalem, and the Forest of Arabia. The real Forest of Lebanon was near Tyre. This ran almost parallel to the seacoast, NE through Syria. The situation of the Forest of Arabia (Isa 21:13) is not known.

The Lebanon Forest undoubtedly was by far the biggest one in the Pal. region. Remember that 100,000 lumberjacks worked solidly for fifty-five years in these forests to provide sufficient cedar for Solomon's Temple, palaces and treasure house. Millions of feet of lumber floated down from Tyre to Joppa, the port of Jerusalem, over that period. This forest not only grew cedars, but firs and almug trees as well.

There is evidence that in ancient times great forests covered Syria and Pal., but by the time the children of Israel occupied the land, much of the forest land had been ruined by the greed of man. It is, for instance, believed that there was a date palm forest in the Jordan valley from Lake Gennesaret to the Dead Sea. Even in the days of Josephus, A.D. 37 to 95, there was a forest of date palms near Jericho, seven m. long.

There must have been Kermes oak forests, even if small, in the mountainous regions of Pal. It is on this oak (*Quercus coccifera*) that the scale insect lives which produces the scarlet dye used by the Israelites.

There are references like Psalm 50:10 "every beast of the forest is mine," or in Isaiah 9:18 "in the thickets of the forest," or in Hosea 2:12

Kibbutz Qiryat Anavim, in area of complete reforestation, northwest of Jerusalem. ©*Lev*

—"I will make them a forest," which seem to refer to forests as a whole, and not to any particular one. In Deuteronomy 20:19, we read "The tree of the field is man's life" (KJV). The cutting down of forests invariably leads to soil erosion and often to a desert. Such unprotected soil dries out, and is blown or washed away. Deuteronomy 20:19 warns against destroying trees.

W. E. SHEWELL-COOPER

FORETELL, FORETOLD (*see* PROPHECY; προεῖπον, Mark 13:23; προκαταγγέλλω Acts 3:24; προλέγω, 2 Cor 13:2). The actual use of the word "foretell" is found tr. only three times in the KJV, all of which are in the NT. In the RSV and NASB the word or phrase which is used instead is "saying beforehand" or "announcing beforehand."

The concept of foretelling is very old and goes back to the role of the prophet. The prophets dealt primarily with their contemporary situation, but in light of future events.

G. GIACUMAKIS, JR.

FORFEIT (חרם; ζημιόν). The word appears only once (Ezra 10:8) in the KJV, but eight times in the RSV (Deut 22:9; 2 Kings 10:24; Ezra 10:8; Prov 20:2; Hab 2:10; Matt 16:26; Mark 8:36; Luke 9:25). The Heb. word *ḥāram* has the basic meaning of consecrating something to God for sacred use, but it later acquired the idea of paying a penalty for a crime, fault, etc. and of losing the right to something. Where the law said that Israelites must not sow their vineyards with two kinds of seed, lest the whole yield be forfeited to the sanctuary (Deut 22:9), it meant that the crop would become God's (Temple property). The penalty for refusing to comply with Ezra's order that all Israelites appear in Jerusalem within three days was the forfeiture (relinquishing) of their property to the Temple treasury (Ezra 10:8). The Gr. word ζημιόν found in Jesus' saying, "For what will it profit a man if he gains the whole world and forfeits his life" (Matt 16:26; Mark 8:36; Luke 9:25), occurs also in 1 Corinthians 3:15; 2 Corinthians 7:9; and Philippians 3:8, where the RSV renders it "suffer loss." The primary meaning of the verb is "to suffer loss," "receive damage" (MM).

S. BARABAS

FORGE, FORGER. The two trs. of this Heb. word in the KJV (Job 13:4 and Ps 119:69) are in a context calling for a fig. use of this word. Lexicographers have come to define this word, טפל as "to smear" or "plaster over" and the contemporary VSS have tr. the word accordingly.

The forger of metals and his furnace, however, is to be found several times in the pages of Scripture and in Ap. Lit. Jeremiah (6:27-30) compares the Judeans to "bronze and iron" having impurities and needing the refining process of God. Both Ezekiel (22:18, 20) and Isaiah (48:10) speak of God's fury melting Israel in the crucible. Likewise in the apocryphal book of Ecclesiasticus a number of references are noticed concerning the forging of metals (31:26; 38:28).

G. GIACUMAKIS, JR.

FORGIVENESS (סליחה, *pardon, forgiveness*; also forms of נשא, *to lift up, bear, pardon*; סלח, *to pardon, forgive*; כפר, prop. *to cover*, hence *to pardon*, and of several other terms meaning *to let pass, take away, hide, wash, purify, trample under foot*, etc.; ἄφεσις, *release, forgiveness, pardon*, of sins [prop. *the letting them go*, as if they had not been committed], *remission of their penalty*; also forms of ἀφίημι, *to send away, leave, omit, let go* [a debt], i.e., *remit, forgive*, and χαρίζομαι, *to show one's self gracious, grant forgiveness, bestow*).

1. Human and divine forgiveness. In the Bible there are instances of both human and divine forgiveness. This does not mean, however, that there is a basic difference between them. God is self-existent and eternal, while man is dependent and temporal, but both are personal beings and as such are similar in their attitudes and actions. Therefore Jesus could teach His disciples to pray, "And forgive us our debts, as we also have forgiven our debtors" (Matt 6:12), and could conclude the parable of the unmerciful servant with the statement, "So also my heavenly Father will do" (Matt 18:35).

2. God's greater readiness to forgive. Though according to the Bible human and divine forgiveness do not differ essentially, God is acknowledged as far more forgiving than man. The clearest OT statement to this effect is that of Isaiah 55:8, 9: "For my thoughts are not your thoughts, neither are your ways my ways, says the LORD. For as the heavens are higher than the earth, so are my ways higher than your ways and my thoughts than your thoughts." These words are often taken to point to God's otherness, to His remoteness and inscrutability; but read in their proper context, they point to something far more comforting and thrilling. Immediately preceding them is one of the most striking assurances of God's pardon in all the Bible, and as an explanation of its truth the passage states that His thoughts and ways are higher than man's. They evidently are that because they are truer, nobler, better, wiser, and morally and spiritually more exalted. When injured or wronged, men tend to bear a grudge and seek revenge; they are apt to insist on their rights and demand restitution. Not so God: He will show mercy and abundantly pardon.

This greater readiness of God to forgive is strikingly exemplified by Jesus. When Peter asked him, "Lord, how often shall my brother sin against me, and I forgive him? As many as seven times?" Jesus said to him, "I do not say to you seven times, but seventy times seven" (Matt 18:21f.). It is also clearly evidenced by the wonderful truth declared in John 3:16 and confirmed by the cross. In the light of this truth, all human readiness to forgive fades into relative insignificance.

3. Distinctiveness of the Biblical teaching of God's forgiveness. It is noteworthy that divine forgiveness is distinctively a Biblical concept. Zoroaster of Persia had a high ethical concept of God but knew little of His redeeming love and mercy. According to Him there was no hope for the wicked, who in crossing "The Bridge of the Separator" fell off it into hell (see J. H. Moulton, *Early Religious Poetry of Persia,* p. 71). Hinduism believes in the inexorable law of Karma, according to which a man's deeds, both good and bad, work themselves out in one life after another. The only escape from the wheel of reincarnations is found in becoming wholly apathetic or in attaining insight into some allegedly releasing truth. Buddhism, too, has its law of Karma and knows of no such divine forgiveness as that set forth in the Bible. The idea is present in Islam, but not as prominent as in Judaism and Christianity. It is in the Bible that it comes to its own; and subsequently it has remained an important feature of the Hebrew-Christian tradition, one that for its adherents lifts this tradition above all other religions and marks it as definitely superior.

4. Instances of forgiveness in the Bible. a. *Human.* In the OT Esau forgives Jacob (Gen 33:1-17); Joseph, his brothers (Gen 45:1-15; 50:15-21); Moses, the people of Israel (Exod 32:11-14, 30-33) and his sister (Num 12:11-13); David, Absalom (2 Sam 14:21, 33) and Shimei (2 Sam 19:18-23); Solomon, Adonijah (1 Kings 1:52f.). In the NT Jesus and Peter speak of forgiving others (Matt 6:12, 14f.; 18:21-35; Mark 11:25; Luke 17:3f.); and Paul forgives, and enjoins the church at Corinth to forgive a member who has caused pain to the others (2 Cor 2:5-11). In Colossians, among the attributes of the new nature believers are to put on, Paul lists forgiving each other, if one has a complaint against another. "As the Lord has forgiven you," he says, "so you also must forgive" (Col 3:13; cf. Eph. 4:32).

In some of these instances no term signifying forgiveness is used; but the attitude and deed are there, though not in every case to an equal degree nor always for the same reason. Esau's forgiveness of Jacob seems quite genuine and wholehearted, prompted by Jacob's evident recognition of guilt and his humility and goodwill. Joseph's forgiveness is likewise genuine. But Solomon's forgiveness of Adonijah is definitely conditional—likely for political reasons—and when in Solomon's opinion he oversteps the bounds laid down he is executed (1 Kings 2:22-25). Jesus characteristically expects a man's forgiveness to be from the heart and counsels Peter never to stop forgiving his brother.

b. *Divine.* As in the case of human forgiveness, divine forgiveness in the Bible is often implied rather than explicitly stated. In the story of the Fall of man, judgment is pronounced upon Adam and Eve and they are expelled from the Garden of Eden; but Abel presently appears as one accepted by God.

Enoch some generations later walks with God. Noah is singled out as a righteous man; and after the Flood Abraham becomes the friend of God and a covenant is established with him.

In instances where forgiveness is explicitly mentioned, divine like human forgiveness is variously motivated and conditioned. There are a number of factors that are said, or assumed, to affect God's attitude. One is a man's weakness (Pss 78:38f.; 103:12-14; Amos 7:2f.); another, his ignorance (Luke 23:34; Acts 17:30); a third, circumstances beyond his control (Num 30:5, 8, 12); a fourth, the presence of men who do justice and seek truth in sinful communities (Jer 5:1, 7); a fifth, sufficient chastening (Isa 40:2); and a sixth, God's reputation. In Numbers 14:20 God's pardon is granted after Moses' manifest zeal for the glory of His name and God's apparent interest in it. It is true that in this case the pardon is hardly complete. Those receiving it will not see the Promised Land (Num 14:21-25). But the purpose achieved by it points to an important feature of divine forgiveness. A similar purpose is found in Psalm 25:11: "For thy name's sake, O LORD, pardon my guilt, for it is great," and in Daniel 9:19: "O LORD, hear; O LORD, forgive; O LORD, give heed and act; delay not, for thy own sake, O my God, because thy city and thy people are called by thy name." The persons uttering these prayers clearly expect God to find the highest reason for His forgiveness within Himself. They assume that it is both His nature and His glory to forgive.

This is in accord with a further characterization of God's motive in forgiving. "For we do not present our supplications before thee on the ground of our righteousness, but on the ground of thy great mercy," says Daniel just before the prayer quoted above. Here the prophet indicates an important reason for God's forgiveness. He is merciful, compassionate (Ps 78:38), and abounding in steadfast love (86:5). Justice would warrant His rejecting, disowning, and punishing the sinner; love prompts Him to forgive (Exod 34:7; Num 14:18; Neh 9:16f.; Pss 86:5; 103:11f.; Mic 7:18-20; John 3:16).

5. Who is forgiven and what. From the preceding it is obvious that it is man in every instance who is forgiven, whether by God or other men. In no case does man forgive God. The presupposition throughout is that God is holy and righteous and never in need of forgiveness, while all men are sinful and in need of it. Were God in need of forgiveness He would be subject to a principle higher and more perfect than Himself, which is inconceivable, for then He would not be truly God. But men, not animals or unconscious objects, are in need here. Forgiveness in any meaningful sense of the word presupposes guilt, and guilt understanding, moral consciousness, and responsibility. As agents endowed with these qualities, men are repeatedly guilty of injury and wrong done to others and of offense given to God. Consequently bad attitudes, evil intentions, and perverse deeds on their part call for forgiveness. Admittedly, these attitudes, intentions, and deeds may largely be what they are because of what a man is due to his intelligence, disposition, experience, and training, as the latter in turn may be influenced by his heredity and environment. Yet insofar as they are not forced upon a man, but willingly accepted by him, insofar as he approves them and knowingly identifies himself with them, he is responsible for them. To this extent, he is not a helpless victim of them, but a guilty agent. It is on this supposition that the Bible judges men according to their endowments, opportunities, and knowledge (Matt 11:20-24; 25:14-30).

The analysis of the human situation and of man's need of forgiveness is not yet complete. Underlying and informing man's various evil attitudes, intentions, and deeds is apt to be a deeper factor that requires attention. It is nothing less, in fact, than a wrong commitment of life. Deuteronomy 6:5 says, "You shall love the LORD your God with all your heart, and with all your soul, and with all your might," and Leviticus 19:18, "You shall love your neighbor as yourself." "On these two commandments," said Jesus, "depend all the law and the prophets" (Matt 22:40). The very essence of sin in all its forms and the real determinant of the wrong one does to a neighbor would seem to be, primarily, the violation of the former and, secondarily, the violation of the latter of these commandments. In pride, man cherishes himself, and his ability and worth, supremely rather than God; in greed, material wealth; in sensuality, bodily desires. In all of them he subordinates his fellow man. As a result, his rights and opportunities are trampled on and curtailed. Jeremiah 2:13 states: "For my people have committed two evils: they have forsaken me, the fountain of living waters, and hewed out cisterns for themselves, broken cisterns, that can hold no water." This was true not only of ancient Israel, but also is true of men today. This is what must be forgiven. Basically sin and human wrong are a matter of living by a wrong scale of values. This scale must be changed to achieve a harmonious, meaningful life; living by it one must be forgiven, if he is to be reconciled with God and his fellow men (see Vincent Taylor, *Forgiveness and Reconciliation*, 3).

It has been said that nature does not forgive. Physical, mental, and social consequences of human deeds work themselves out according to dependable processes. It is to be observed, however, that even the consequences of evil deeds may in God's providence serve higher ends for one who knows he is forgiven. God ordained and ordered nature, and by anticipation, He has correlated its events with the exigencies of various human situations. Not only this: the influence of God's Spirit in men's lives can also counteract the effects of sin in them. Furthermore, a changed and forgiven man can in dependence on the same processes mentioned above initiate a new and better series of consequences. Nature in a sense may not forgive, but it will respond to new endeavor.

In Matthew 12:31f., Mark 3:28-30, and Luke 12:10, Jesus speaks of blasphemy against the Spirit as a sin that will not be forgiven. Calvin holds that they alone are guilty of this sin "who, with evil intention, resist God's truth, although by its brightness they are so touched that they cannot claim ignorance" (*Institutes of the Christian Religion*, III, 617). One might ask, Resist God's truth to what extent? With what degree of evil intention and knowledge? The nature of this sin cannot perhaps be precisely stated in one short sentence. Certainly Calvin's characterization of it is not perfect, let alone complete. It would seem that the unpardonable sin presupposes such spiritual perversity and blindness that neither the truth of God appeals nor does its true light appear. It may also presuppose such indifference as cares not for forgiveness or such hostility as flippantly derides what is holy. At all events, this sin apparently implies a situation in which true repentance never eventuates. He who truly desires forgiveness and would sincerely repent, need not fear that he has committed it.

6. Conditions of forgiveness. a. *Human.* The foregoing notes that there were different reasons why men in the Bible forgave others. A question is, Are there any conditions according to the Bible that offending persons must meet to expect forgiveness? Some passages do not speak of any. "Lord, how often shall my brother sin against me, and I forgive him?" (Matt 18:21), asks Peter, and Jesus tells him how often. There is no reference made to any condition the offender must meet. The parable that follows Jesus' answer to Peter clearly implies that forgiveness is being sought; and in a comparable passage (Luke 17:3f.) repentance is specified as a condition. Moreover, though repentance on the part of the offender is not always mentioned, in some of the instances cited above it was evidently present. It may be concluded that a man must forgive his fellow man, if he repents; he should himself repent when he is the offender, and should in any case be ready to forgive. Should he ever forgive the impenitent man who knowingly has done wrong? Doubtless as far as personal offense or injury are concerned, though not as far as violation of moral principle goes. It was obviously an absence of personal offense and his compassion for his spiritually blind persecutors that made Stephen pray the notable prayer he did (Acts 7:60).

b. *Divine.* As in the case of human forgiveness, so in the case of God's forgiveness, some passages of Scripture fail to specify repentance as a ground or condition (Pss 65:3; 85:2; 86:5; 103:3, 10; Isa 46:12f.; Jer 31:31-34; 33:1-18; Ezek 36:16-38; Mic 7:18-20; Acts 13:38f.; Eph 1:7; Col 1:14; 2:13; 1 John 2:2). In other passages repentance is clearly called for (Lev 26:14-45; 1 Kings 8:46-50; 2 Chron 7:14; 30:18f.; Pss 32:3-5; 51; Isa 1:27f.; 55:6f.; 59-61, esp. 59:20; Jer 18:7-11; 26:3; Lam 3:42; Ezek 18:31f.; Zech 1:3; Mal 3:7; Matt 4:17; Luke 13:3, 5; Acts 5:31; 8:22; 1 John 1:9). Omission of its mention in the first instances may be explained by the fact that in these it was either understood, or God was not so much forgiving sin as achieving other ends (Ezek 36:20-23, 32, 35f., 38). He also may have been moving His people to repentance by His action (36:31).

On this question of the condition, or conditions, required for forgiveness, recent and contemporary theologians differ. Karl Barth represented an extreme position. He held that all of life apart from God's own action in it falls under the judgment that it is sin. Christians live solely by God's forgiveness. Even repentance has been made for them (*Dogmatics in Outline*, 150ff.).

Paul Tillich spoke of the unconditional character of the divine act in which God declares him who is unjust just. Transcending justice destroys in man what must be destroyed, if reuniting love is to reach its aim. This which must be destroyed is the *hubris* of trying to conquer the evil in one's being as such, and to reach reunion with God by one's own good will. Such *hubris,* said Tillich, avoids the pain of surrendering one's own goodness to God's sole activity in a reunion with Him, a surrender that occurs in him who accepts the divine acceptance of himself, the unacceptable. The courage of this surrender is the central element in the courage of faith (*Systematic Theology*, III, 226).

Emil Brunner emphasizes the need of repentance as a condition of forgiveness (*The Divine-Human Encounter*, 98ff., 149ff.), a view shared by Rudolf Bultmann, Frederick C. Grant, H. R. Mackintosh, Ernest F. Scott, Vincent Taylor, and Benjamin B. Warfield, as well as the Westminster Confession of Faith (ch. XV). Nor does Brunner stop here. Instead he goes on to take exception to a one-sided advocacy of the doctrine of forensic justification. He says, "God not only *declares,* He *creates* a new man . . . . We not only believe in the new man, but in faith we put him on" (101). Repentance for him entails condemning the old man within and putting him off; it means accepting the death of Jesus Christ as a divine judgment upon oneself (101, 151).

The late Herman Bavinck of the Netherlands, like Brunner, underscored the requirement laid down in the Bible for God's forgiveness. Specifically, he held that regeneration, faith, and conversion are conditions for the forgiveness of sins and other benefits of the covenant of grace (*Gereformeerde Dogmatiek*, IV, 160). One's entry into the kingdom of heaven depends on them (202). But, unlike Brunner, he adhered to a rather strict theory of forensic justification. The forgiveness of sins is not brought about by faith nor gained by man's endeavors. It is found completely in Christ, precedes faith, and is accepted only by faith (201f.). All works are excluded from the faith that is reckoned as righteousness (168). G. C. Berkouwer of the Free University of Amsterdam seems in substantial agreement with him, except that he significantly distinguishes between works of the law and works of faith in the writings of Paul (*Faith and Justification*, 104ff.). For him, however, these works of faith give form to faith; they show its nature, rather than themselves constituting part of the basis of God's acceptance of man.

From the foregoing, the diversity of thought on this question is evident. Yet it is clear that repentance as a condition of forgiveness of sin has been, and is, widely recognized, and that it is well supported Scripturally. It is also clear in the Bible that with the advent of Jesus Christ repentance as a condition is definitely associated with His suffering and death. To His disciples on the day of His resurrection Jesus said, "Thus it is written, that the Christ should suffer and on the third day rise from the dead, and that repentance and forgiveness of sins should be preached in his name to all nations" (Luke 24:46, 47). "The blood of Jesus . . . cleanses us from all sin" (1 John 1:7). "He himself [Christ] bore our sins in his body on the tree" (1 Peter 2:24; cf. Acts 2:38; 13:38f.; 26:18; Rom 5:8-11; 1 Pet 1:18f.; 3:18; 1 John 2:1, 12; 3:5).

How are such passages to be understood? In the light of them, Brunner is doubtless right when he sees the death of Jesus Christ as a divine judgment upon oneself; and one may add a judgment which the truly penitent man, when confronted with it, will accept as his due and thus be assured of God's forgiveness. The sinner can by faith take the cross of Christ into his life, he can identify himself with Christ on the cross, and so be crucified with Him (Gal 2:20). He can die to sin that he may live to righteousness (1 Pet 2:24), the righteousness that Christ has shown but he admittedly has failed to achieve, and will never achieve fully. In this way he rejects his sinful self and returns to the Shepherd and Guardian of his soul (1 Pet 2:25); he is healed by Christ's wounds and brought to God (1 Pet 2:24; 3:18).

A further condition of God's forgiveness is found in another teaching of Jesus which He stated explicitly on at least three occasions. The first statement occurs in the Sermon on the Mount. After formulating the Lord's Prayer Jesus says, "For if you forgive men their trespasses, your heavenly Father also will forgive you; but if you do not forgive men their trespasses, neither will your Father forgive your trespasses" (Matt 6:14f.). Equally clear and unqualified is His comment at the close of the parable of the unmerciful servant, referred to earlier in this article. This servant refused to forgive his fellow servant a debt, though his master had forgiven him a much greater one. His master thereupon revoked his cancellation of the debt and delivered him to the jailers until he should pay in full. "So also," said Jesus, "my heavenly Father will do to every one of you, if you do not forgive your brother from your heart" (Matt 18:35). The third statement is found in Mark 11:25: "And whenever you stand praying, forgive, if you have anything against any one; so that your Father also who is in heaven may forgive you your trespasses." The import of this teaching of Jesus is plain: a man must forgive others to be forgiven by God. This requirement evidently rests on the genuineness of one's repentance. A person who seeks forgiveness but does not forgive others hardly knows what he is asking for and is not worthy of it.

Ethically, too, repentance is required for receiving the forgiveness of God. God is holy and righteous. He is "of purer eyes than to behold evil" (Hab 1:13). Because He is self-existent and the great Creator and Upholder of all including the highest principles of reality and life, personal offense given Him by man can hardly be distinguished from moral violation. In view of this, for Him to forgive without requiring repentance would be like condoning sin or being indifferent to it. It would also mean that He did not deal with man as the responsible moral agent He has made him. Hence, God is for man, but not as a sinner; only as a potential saint. He accepts the unacceptable, but only as the unacceptable becomes acceptable by repenting, that is, by acknowledging God's righteous judgment of him in Christ and by committing his life wholly to God. *See* RECONCILIATION; REPENTANCE.

BIBLIOGRAPHY. A. Ritschl, *The Christian Doctrine of Justification and Reconciliation* (1900), 38-79; C. T. Ovenden, "The Forgiveness of Sin," HJ, V (1906-1907), 587-599; D. White, *Forgiveness and Suffering* (1913); B. B. Warfield, *The Plan of Salvation* (1915); H. R. Mackintosh, *The Christian Experience of Forgiveness* (1927); H. Bavinck, *Gereformeerde Dogmatiek,* IV (1930), 159-214; F. H. Wales, *The Forgiveness of Sins* (1940); P. Lehmann, *Forgiveness, Decisive Issue in Protestant Thought* (1940); E. Brunner, *The Divine-Human Encounter* (1943), 98-103, 149-151; P. Tillich, *Systematic Theology,* I (1951), 286-289; R. Bultmann, *Theology of the New Testament,* I (1951), 22-26, 33-40, 72-74, 85, 114-121, 135-144, 270-285; R. V. Taylor, *Forgiveness and Reconciliation* (1952); G. C. Berkouwer, *Faith and Justification* (1954), 103-122; K. Barth, *Dogmatics in Outline* (1959), 149-152; P. Tillich, *Systematic Theology,* III (1963), 217-245; Editorial, "Beyond Forgiveness," ChT, IX (1964), 31, 32; J. G. Emerson, Jr., *The Dynamics of Forgiveness* (1964); H. McKeating, "Divine Forgiveness in the Psalms," JTS, XVIII (1965), 69-83.

P. H. MONSMA

FORK. The rendering of three Heb. words and one Gr. word. 1. מַזְלֵג. A three-pronged implement used at the altar in the Tabernacle and Temple to remove from the pot in which the sacrifice was boiled that portion of the meat which was intended for the priests (1 Sam 2:13, 14; KJV, ASV "fleshhook"; Exod 27:3; 38:3; Num 4:14; 1 Chron 28:17; 2 Chron 4:16, KJV "fleshhooks").

2. מִזְרֶה. A pitchfork prob. with six prongs, used in winnowing grain (Isa 30:24, KJV "fan"). Used fig. in Jeremiah 15:7, KJV "fan." Bezalel, the chief architect of the Tabernacle, was also a skillful metal artificer, and among the implements he made for it were bronze forks (Exod 38:3; cf. 27:3). David provided gold to make implements, including forks, for the Temple (1 Chron 28:17), and Huram-abi made some of bronze (2 Chron 4:16).

3. Πτύον. John the Baptist said that when the Messiah came He would take a winnowing fork in His hand and purge the floor of chaff and burn it with unquenchable fire (Matt 3:12, KJV "fan").

S. BARABAS

FORM CRITICISM is the analytical study of the "forms" assumed by various categories of tradition, esp. in its oral, preliterary phase. The Ger. word *Formgeschichte*, "form history," suggests, as the Eng. term does not, a study of the history of the tradition as revealed by the development of its "forms." While the word *Formgeschichte* in the field of Biblical criticism does not appear to have been current before the publication of the first edition of M. Dibelius's *Die Formgeschichte des Evangeliums* in 1919, the discipline itself was not new. The similar term *Formengeschichte* occurs in the subtitle of E. Norden's *Agnostos Theos* (Leipzig, 1912)—"Inquiries into the *history of the forms* of religious language." As far as the gospels are concerned, A. Menzies anticipated some of the most characteristic features of the form-critical approach in *The Earliest Gospel* (London, 1901). The pioneer of form criticism in Biblical study was H. Gunkel, who applied it to Biblical lit. as early as 1895, in his *Schöpfung und Chaos* (a comparison of Gen 1 and Rev 12). Gunkel's most fruitful application of this method (already applied by others to the lit. of the heroic ages of Greece and Northern Europe) was to the Psalter, which he classified according to its *Gattungen* ("literary types"), assigning to each *Gattung* its life-setting—a life-setting almost invariably to be found in Israel's worship (cf. his *Die Psalmen*[4] [Bonn, 1926] and *Einleitung in die Psalmen* [Göttingen, 1933], completed by J. Begrich). It is perhaps no accident that M. Dibelius had his interest in comparative religious study first aroused by Gunkel.

1. Classification. The main classification of gospel material naturally recognizes the distinction between narratives and sayings. The terminology of classification differs from one form critic to another, but outstanding categories of narrative in the gospels are (a) pronouncement stories (paradigms, apophthegms), (b) miracle stories (in which healing narratives are prominent), (c) stories about Jesus (e.g. the baptism, temptation and transfiguration narratives), while outstanding categories of sayings are (a) wisdom sayings, (b) prophetic and apocalyptic sayings, (c) community rules, (d) "I" sayings, (e) parables. There are other ways of classifying the gospel material, and whichever way is adopted, a fair amount of overlapping is inevitable.

One important result of classification and cross-classification of the material is that a Messianic picture of Jesus is consistently yielded: "We can find no alternative tradition, excavate as we will in the successive strata of the Gospels" (C. H. Dodd, *History and the Gospel* [London, 1938] p. 103). Especially on the European continent, form critics warn scholars not to conclude that this picture goes back into the conditions of the actual ministry of Jesus; many of them hold that this study can take one back only to the Christ of the primitive Early Church preaching.

Classification in itself is not of prime importance; more important are two things closely connected with it in the history of form criticism, i.e. the theory of the composition of the synoptic tradition propounded by K. L. Schmidt and adopted by many colleagues and successors, and the quest for the life-setting.

2. Composition. Schmidt's thesis in *Der Rahmen der Geschichte Jesu* (Berlin, 1919) was that the synoptic, i.e. the Markan tradition consisted originally of isolated units, brought together by Mark in such a way as to form a consecutive narrative with the aid of "editorial cement" lacking any historical value of its own. The passion narrative, admittedly, did exist as a connected record from earliest days, partly because of its being repeatedly recalled in the cult (cf. 1 Cor 11:26), but otherwise material simply did not exist to make a coherent life of Christ, or even a continuous account of His ministry, possible. C. H. Dodd ("The Framework of the Gospel Narrative," ExpT XLIII [1931-1932], pp. 396 ff.) argued that the "editorial cement" in Mark, when considered in isolation from the units of tradition which it joined together, presented an independent outline of the gospel story, comparable to outlines which can be discerned in some of the epistles and the speeches of Acts (e.g. Acts 10:37-42). Dodd's argument has not found much acceptance outside Britain, but it cannot be easily refuted.

3. Life-setting. In form-critical terms, the life-setting usually means the setting in the life of the primitive Christian community which determined the preservation of certain elements in the tradition about Jesus and the form in which they were preserved. An interest in this life-setting should not preclude an interest in the earlier life-setting in the ministry of Jesus. Although the possibility of establishing this earlier life-setting except in a handful of instances is widely denied, it should not be given up too quickly. W. Manson, for example, gave cogent reasons for believing that the setting given in Mark 11:20-24 to Jesus' saying about mountain-removing faith corresponds to the original historical and geographical setting (*Jesus the Messiah* [London, 1943] pp. 29f.).

But in its more extreme formulations the doctrine of the life-setting rules that if a saying or action ascribed to Jesus in the gospels reflects the post-Easter faith of the Church, it should be regarded as a creation within the Church, and that no saying or action ascribed to Him can confidently be taken as authentic if a parallel saying or action is elsewhere ascribed to a Jewish rabbi. It is unlikely that the Church never took over some of Jesus' historical teaching and it is equally unlikely that Jesus never said or did anything comparable to the word or action of some rabbi; nor need one take too seriously the insistent view that in such cases the burden of proof lies on those who maintain the authenticity of the gospel tradition.

Yet the life-setting approach helps one to appreciate the circumstances of the Church's worship and witness within which the gospel tradition (Johannine as well as synoptic) was molded and transmitted, and in so far as form criticism makes it possible to move back from the setting in the Early Church to the setting in the ministry of Jesus (e.g. by removing, as it sometimes does, a later Hel. layer which has overlain an earlier Palestinian layer), it makes its own special contribution to the understanding of the gospels and appraisal of the works and words of Jesus.

BIBLIOGRAPHY. K. L. Schmidt, *Der Rahmen der Geschichte Jesu* (1919); E. Fascher, *Die formgeschichtliche Methode* (1924); V. Taylor, *The Formation of the Gospel Tradition* (1933); F. C. Grant (ed. and trans.), *Form Criticism: Two Essays by R. Bultmann and K. Kundsin* (1934); R. H. Lightfoot, *History and Interpretation in the Gospels* (1935); E. B. Redlich, *Form Criticism* (1939); M. Dibelius, *Die Formgeschichte des Evangeliums*[3] (Tübingen, 1959), Eng. tr., *From Tradition to Gospel* (1934); R. Bultmann, *The History of the Synoptic Tradition*, Eng. tr. (1963); C. K. Barrett, *Jesus and the Gospel Tradition* (1967); K. Koch, *The Growth of the Biblical Tradition: The Form-Critical Method* (1967); N. Perrin, *Rediscovering the Teaching of Jesus* (1967).

F. F. BRUCE

FORMER RAIN. *See* RAIN.

FORNICATION (πορνεία, meaning *unchastity* or *immorality*). Some form of πορνεία appears forty-seven times in the NT.

Four different NT meanings are obvious. 1. In 1 Corinthians 7:2 and 1 Thessalonians 4:3, Paul is warning unmarried people about the temptation to fornication. In both cases he advocates marriage to prevent a single life of sexual immorality. In both cases fornication refers to voluntary sexual intercourse of an unmarried person with anyone of the opposite sex. The meaning is specific and restricted. In four other passages fornication is used in a list of sins which includes "adultery" (Matt 15:19; Mark 7:21; 1 Cor 6:9; Gal 5:19). Since adultery involves a married person, the meaning of fornication in these passages is specific and restricted, involving voluntary unchastity of unmarried people.

2. In two passages (Matt 5:32; 19:9) fornication is used in a broader sense as a synonym of adultery.

3. In some passages fornication is used in a general sense referring to all forms of unchastity (John 8:41; Acts 15:20, 29; 21:25; Rom 1:29; 1 Cor 5:1; 6:13, 18; 2 Cor 6:17; 12:21; Eph 5:3).

4. In other passages fornication refers to harlotry and prostitution (e.g. Rev 2:14, 20, 21). Since fornication has many shades of meaning, the meaning must be determined by the context of each passage.

Out of seven lists of evils in the writings of Paul, the word fornication is included in five of them (1 Cor 5:11; 6:9; Gal 5:19; Eph 5:3; Col 3:5) and is first on the list each time.

Jesus related fornication to adultery when he said "Everyone (πᾶς ὁ) who looks at a woman lustfully [with a thought of sexual intercourse] has already committed adultery with her in his heart" (Matt 5:28). R. C. H. Lenski interprets the "everyone" to include both men and women and both married and unmarried. Thus Jesus was saying that sexual intercourse of unmarried people (fornication) is as evil as extra-marital sexual intercourse (adultery).

Note that possible unmarried people are included in the meaning of fornication in all of those passages where it refers to adultery, immorality, harlotry, et al. Those who state that the NT makes no reference to premarital sex relations and gives no advice on the personal and social problems involved are overlooking the NT use and meaning of the word fornication, esp. in such passages as 1 Corinthians 7:2 and 1 Thessalonians 4:3. *See* ADULTERY.

BIBLIOGRAPHY. D. S. Bailey, *The Mystery of Love and Marriage* (1952), 50-53; D. R. Mace, *Hebrew Marriage* (1953), 221-267; L. Kirkendall, "Premarital Sex Relations: The Problem and Its Implications," PP (Pastoral Psychology) (April, 1956), 43-46; W. G. Cole, *Sex and Love in the Bible* (1959), 230-267; O. E. Feucht (Editor), *Sex and the Church* (1961), 48f., 70f., 216f.; J. T.

Landis and M. G. Landis, *Building a Successful Marriage* (1968), 165-184; H. J. Miles, *Sexual Understanding Before Marriage* (1971), 204-206.

H. J. MILES

FORT, FORTIFICATION, FORTIFIED (FENCED) **CITIES.** The main Heb. and Gr. words meaning *fort, fortification, stronghold, refuge, fortified (fenced city)* are the following: מבצר ; משגב ; מעון ; מצורה ; מצודה ; מצד ; *οχύρωμα*. Every town and city in the Near E in ancient times was normally encircled by ramparts and defended by towers and fortified gates. Reports describing the large fortified cities of the Canaanites struck fear into the Israelites; and after their conquest of these towns, they rebuilt the broken defenses and improved them where they could. The walls of a city were usually of large dimensions, anywhere from fifteen to twenty-five ft. thick; and often there were two or even three of them. Some of them were well over twenty-five ft. in height. They were made of rough or cut stone, with the upper courses made of brick, or even wood. Walls were rendered less assailable by having a trench, or fosse, dug around them. Towers, or bastions, were built at the corners and other places on the wall where attack was to be apprehended (Zeph 1:16, KJV; 2 Chron 14:7). These towers protruded from the walls for some ft. so that the defenders of a besieged city could assail the attackers with available weapons. Since gates were an obvious point of weakness, most towns had no more than one or two. The gates were ordinarily of two leaves, and for greater security against fire were often overlaid with bronze (Ps 107:16; Isa 45:2). Since no city could hold out for long without a supply of water, it was of prime importance that a town be built where an abundance of water was available. Sometimes long tunnels were made to a source of water outside the walls. The Bible in a number of places tells of fortifications which the kings of Israel and Judah erected to protect their chief cities. Solomon, e.g., fortified Jerusalem, Megiddo, Hazor, and Gezer (1 Kings 9:15); Rehoboam fortified fifteen cities in Judah (2 Chron 11:5-12); and Asa fortified Geba and Mizpah (1 Kings 15:22).

BIBLIOGRAPHY. R. de Vaux, *Ancient Israel* (1961), 229-240; G. E. Wright, *Biblical Archaeology* (1962).

S. BARABAS

FORTUNATUS **for′ chə nā′ təs** (Φορτουνᾶτος, Gr. form of Lat. *Fortunatus, blessed* or *fortunate.* Both Lat. and Gr. forms occur in papyri and inscrs.). A prominent member of the Corinthian church, mentioned only in 1 Corinthians 16:17, but some MSS also insert it in v. 15. He is named second in a three-man delegation which brought a letter from the church (1 Cor 7:1) to Paul at Ephesus. Their presence "refreshed" Paul, giving him the desired contact with that church. They apparently returned with our 1 Corinthians, which the subscription in the TR affirms.

Some forty years later Clement (*Ep. ad Cor.* LIX) mentions a Fortunatus whom he distinguishes from his messengers to Corinth. The commonness of the name and the time lapse make identification uncertain.

BIBLIOGRAPHY. R. C. H. Lenski, *Interpretation of I Corinthians* (1935), 797-800.

D. E. HIEBERT

FORTY. One of the favorite numbers of the Israelites, often having symbolical significance. It was frequently used as the approximate time span of a generation and to designate an extended period of testing, repentance, vigil, or punishment. It is associated with important new developments in the unfolding drama of redemption (e.g. the Flood, the Exodus, Elijah and the prophetic era, the life of Christ, and the birth of the church).

The following are a few of the many examples of the use of the number forty in Scripture: At the time of the Flood it rained for forty days, and the waters subsided for an equal period (Gen 7:4, 12, 17; 8:6); Moses was forty years old when he visited his brethren (Acts 7:23), was forty years in Midian (Acts 7:29, 30), was on the Mount forty days (Exod 24:18), and prayed for Israel for forty days (Deut 9:25). The Israelites wandered forty years in the wilderness (Num 14:33; 32:13). David and Solomon each reigned forty years (2 Sam 5:4; 1 Kings 11:42). Jonah called on Nineveh to repent within forty days (Jonah 3:4); Jesus fasted in the desert forty days (Matt 4:2) and remained on earth forty days after His resurrection (Acts 1:3).

S. BARABAS

FORUM OF APPIUS **ăp′ ĭ əs** (*τὸ Ἀππίου φόρον, market of Appius*). A traveler's stop on the Appian Way forty-three m. S of Rome, where Paul was met by brethren from Rome on his way to the capital under guard (Acts 28:15).

It was also the northern terminus of a canal which ran through the Pontine marshes to Feronia, providing public transportation in boats towed by mules (*Strabo* 5.233). Horace (Sat. 1.5) vividly described the Forum as an unsavory place crammed with boatmen, innkeepers, and wayfarers, who cheat, carouse, and quarrel, the disturbance compounded by the gnats and frogs of the marshes.

A. RUPPRECHT

FOUNDATION (יסד, *to found*; *καταβολή founding*, and *θεμέλιος, foundation stone*).

The word is used in both a literal and a metaphorical sense. The ancients realized the necessity of sinking the foundations of a house down to the bedrock (Luke 6:48f.). The foundation of Solomon's Temple consisted of large (12 x 15 ft.), costly, and carefully dressed blocks of stone (1 Kings 5:17). The Babylon-

Excavating the ruins of a house at Kiriath-sepher dating back to the days of Isaiah and Jeremiah. Its foundation is easily discernible © *JK*

ian records show that the laying of a foundation was sometimes accompanied by human sacrifice; such sacrifice is prob. suggested in 1 Kings 16:34, where it is said that Hiel built Jericho "at the cost of Abiram his first-born, and set up its gates at the cost of his youngest son Segub." The word is used metaphorically for the ultimate basis on which a thing rests (Job 4:19; Ezek 13:14; Matt 7:25; Luke 6:48) and for anything immovably established, like the inhabited world (Ps 18:15), the mountains (Deut 32:22), and the vault of heaven (Amos 9:6). The church is built upon the foundation of the apostles and prophets, with Christ as the cornerstone (Eph 2:20). *See* HOUSE.

S. BARABAS

FOUNDATION, GATE OF THE (שער היסוד). A gate of Jerusalem mentioned in 2 Chronicles 23:5 in the account of Athaliah's execution (2 Chron 23:1-15); also called "the gate Sur" (2 Kings 11:6; LXX, "gate of the ways"). It is possibly the same as the horse gate (Heb. סוס) of 2 Chronicles 23:15; 2 Kings 11:16, leading to the king's palace. This gate was prob. a connection between the palace and Temple.

W. H. Mare

FOUNTAIN (בור, *pit, well, cistern,* referring to the hole or excavation in which water may be found; ביר, a variant of the former term; מבוע, from נבע, *flow, spring, bubble up*; מעין, *spring,* also עין, possibly related to עין, *eye*; מקור, a *hole,* a *well*; Gr. πηγή, *spring*), a source of fresh running water.

In a country like Pal., which depends largely on rainfall for water, there are usually three sources from which it may be obtained: springs, wells, and cisterns. All three were used from the earliest recorded times, and the words listed above were used to describe them. Each has been tr. *fountain* as meaning a source of water.

1. בור describes a cistern or well, a hole in which water may be found; but it may be used of any excavation in the earth. *Bir* (Jer 6:7) is prob. only a vocal variant of *bor,* and refers definitely to a well.

2. מבוע, derived from נבע, *to bubble* or *to spring,* denotes a bubbling spring, prob. on the surface of the ground (Eccl 12:6; Isa 35:7; 49:10).

3. עין, which is the most common Heb. word for *spring,* occurs frequently in the OT, esp. in the prefix which denotes some particular spring; e.g. En [Ain] -gedi (1 Sam 24:1), or En [Ain] -rogel, near Jerusalem (2 Sam 17:17; 1 Kings 1:9). A cognate form is used both literally (Gen 7:11) and figuratively of a source of wisdom or learning (Prov 18:4).

4. מקור, derived from קור, *to dig,* originally denoted a well, but is used of a spring, frequently in a fig. sense (Prov 25:26).

5. There are only 12 uses of πηγή in the NT, variously tr. by *well* and *fountain.*

Springs or fountains were essential to life, and the early settlements in Pal. usually clustered around a spring. Fortified cities grew up beside them, and often enclosed the spring in order to insure an ample supply of water in case of siege. In the war with the Philistines the Israelite army camped by the fountain in Jezreel, where there was abundant water for their forces (1 Sam 29:1), and the Samaritan woman encountered Jesus at the well of Jacob near Sychar (John 4:6) when she went to replenish the supply for her household. *Fountain* is used fig. of a source of wisdom (Prov 18:4) or of salvation (Jer 17:13) or of cleansing (Zech 13:1).

M. C. Tenney

FOUNTAIN GATE, the RSV rendering of the Heb. place name, שער העין (KJV), "gate of the fountain" (Neh 2:14; 3:15 and 12:37). It was one of the gates of the city of Jerusalem in the SE section of the wall restored after the return. It is thought to have been down below the Pool of Siloam along the vale of Kidron.

FOURSQUARE, a term appearing frequently in OT descriptions of buildings such as the wilderness Tabernacle (Heb. רבע, "square" [RSV]; "foursquare" [KJV]). The term also is tr. simply "square" (1 Kings 7:5; et al.). It is derived from the term for "four" (Heb. ארבע) as in the ancient phrase *"kibrātim arbaim,"* "four shores" (L. W. King, *Letters and Inscriptions of Ḥammuṛabi* [1898] 57.5, 94.23, 95.5). The term appears in Exodus predominantly, and in the LXX is tr. by the Gr. τετράγωνος, "foursquare" which appears in the NT as a *hapax legomenon* in Revelation 21:16, in the context of the description of the holy city, the Jerusalem of the Apocalypse.

W. White, Jr.

FOWL (צפור, *fowl, bird, sparrow. See* SPARROW for discussion. עוף, *fowl* [61], *bird* [9] KJV. *Fowl* [1], *bird* [68], *insect* [1] [Lev 11:20] RSV. עיט, *bird* [1], *ravenous bird* [1], *fowl* [4] KJV, *bird* [6] RSV; πετεινόν, *bird* [5], *fowl* [9] KJV; ὄρνεον, *bird* [1], *fowl* [2] KJV. In NT RSV tr. *bird* throughout). The usage of Eng. "fowl" has changed radically since the 16th cent. Then it was a common word for birds generally; "bird" (also Old Eng.) was first used for young birds, but a more general meaning was already being attached to it. "Fowl," as a general word, is now listed as obsolete, and "bird" has replaced it in all but a few specialized uses; e.g. popular for domestic chicken; hunted birds are wildfowl. A fowler (Ps 91:3) is still one who traps or shoots wild birds. RSV retains "fowl" for birds that are eaten (*see* Chicken), but otherwise trs. birds. Greek πετεινόν and πτηνόν mean "winged" and have general meaning, though most often tr. "bird." One or two fig. passages, e.g. James 3:7 may have wider meaning. *See* Sparrow.

G. S. Cansdale

FOWLER (יקוש) ; One who traps and hunts wild birds. In ancient times birds were caught or killed in many different ways—with decoys, traps, nets, snares, lures, bait, slings, bows and arrows, bird lime smeared upon branches, birdcalls, and setting dogs. Birds were a favorite food esp. of Egyptians; and many Egypt. paintings exhibit scenes of fowling. The Egyptians were expert at killing, preserving, and preparing for the table all kinds of birds. Even today countless birds migrate N and S across Pal. in the spring and fall, preferring to fly over land rather than across the Mediterranean. Birds were used for food, as caged pets, and for sacrifice. In the Mosaic legislation it was forbidden to take the mother bird with the eggs

Fowling in the marshes, from ancient Egyptian paintings, Davies and Gardner.

or young, lest the species should become exterminated (Deut 22:6, 7). The word is used often in a metaphorical sense to represent evil men who set snares to catch the unwary and bring them to moral and spiritual ruin (Ps 91:3; 124:7; Prov 6:5; Jer 5:26; Hos 9:8).

J. L. Kelso

FOX (שׁוּעָל, *fox* Eng. VSS except Ps 63:10 and Lam 5:18, *jackal* RSV; ἀλώπηξ, *fox*).

There is general agreement about this tr., but foxes and jackals are alike in size and form, and can easily be confused. Three species of fox live in Pal. and Egypt—the Red Fox, which is found in a number of forms over much of the old world, and two desert species, with large ears, the better known of these being the small Fennec Fox. Foxes are largely nocturnal, esp. in hot dry country, and spend the day safely and comfortably in their holes, or earths, as the Lord pointed out (Matt 8:20). Their fondness for fruit, esp. grapes, is mentioned (S of Sol 2:15). The passage in Judges 15:5ff. has caused considerable comment. The action was certainly far from humane, as were many things done by Samson and his enemies, but the effect of releasing 150 pairs of foxes (more prob. jackals, which would be more easily caught in numbers) in ripe corn would be devastating. A similar cruel custom is recorded in Rom. times when foxes with torches tied to their tails were hunted in the circus at the feast of Ceres. Brer Fox has appeared in stories and fables since Gr. and Rom. times, but in Pal. and Iraq the jackal usually takes its place. In these stories the fox is cunning and crafty, and the Lord used this metaphor in one of His rare critical comments when He referred to Herod as "that fox" (Luke 13:32). *See* JACKAL.

G. S. CANSDALE

FRACTURE. RSV rendering of the Heb. שׁבר, "break." It is a common verb in the OT but is tr. "fracture" in Leviticus 24:20 only, KJV "breach." KJV renders the same verb "breach" in Psalm 60:2; Proverbs 15:4; Isaiah 30:26; Jeremiah 14:17; Lamentations 2:13. Modern rendering of "break" is to be preferred.

FRAME. The Old Testament. 1. Five Heb. words tr. "frame" in the RSV refer to parts of the Tabernacle and Temple or to things inside them. a. מוט (KJV "bar"), a bar or frame from which the lampstand and the vessels of service of the Tabernacle were suspended when they were carried (Num 4:10, 12). b. מסגרת (KJV "border"); a brace around the table of the presence to hold the legs firm in their places (Exod 25:25, 27; 37:12, 14); panels for the stands of the molten lavers in the Temple (1 Kings 7:28-36; 2 Kings 16:17). c. קרשׁ (KJV "board"), the wooden frame of the Tabernacle over which the curtains and skin coverings were spread (Exod 26:15-29; 35:11; 36:30-34; 37:12, 14; 39:33; 40:18; Num 3:36; 4:31). d. שׁלבים (KJV "ledge"), another word for the brace referred to in b. above (1 Kings 7:28, 29). e. שׁקוף (1 Kings 6:4 KJV "lights"; 1 Kings 7:4, 5 KJV "windows"; Ezek 41:16 KJV "windows").

2. מבנה ; in Ezekiel 40:2 where the KJV has "the frame of a city," the RSV has "a structure like a city."

3. Three Heb. words refer to the human form. a. יצר (Ps 103:14). b. עצם (Ps 139:15, KJV "substance"). c. ערך (Job 41:12, KJV "proportion").

4. A number of Heb. verbs are rendered "frame" in either the KJV or the RSV or in both. a. In the famous Shibboleth passage (Judg 12:6) the KJV has "he could not frame to pronounce it right." The Heb. text, however, has no word for "frame," and is therefore best tr. by omitting it, as the RSV does, "he could not pronounce it right." b. צמד "combine," "join" (Ps 50:19—KJV "frameth"; RSV "frames"). c. יצר, "form," "fashion" (Ps 94:20—KJV "frameth"; RSV "frame"; Jer 18:11—KJV "frame," RSV "shape"). d. נתן, "to give." In Hosea 5:4, where the KJV has "They will not frame their doings to turn unto their God," the RSV and most modern trs. regard "their doings" as the subject of the verb; the RSV reads, "Their deeds do not permit them to return to their God."

The New Testament. 1. συναρμολογέω, "to fit" or "join closely together" (KJV Eph 2:21—"fitly framed together"; RSV "joined together"). 2. καταρτίζω, "to fit out" (Heb 11:3—KJV "framed"; RSV "created").

S. BARABAS

Frankincense

FRANKINCENSE (לבונה ; λίβανος). Frankincense occurs fourteen times in the OT and twice in the NT. Most of the references in the OT are instructions as to how and how not to use this scent (Lev 2:1; 5:11). In Song of Solomon 3:6 the references are to frankincense as perfume. The references in the NT are Matthew 2:11, where frankincense is one of the gifts the wise men brought, and Revelation 18:13, which deals with the fall of Babylon.

Frankincense is derived from the resin of the tree *Boswellia.* There are three species from which gum may be obtained, i.e. *B. carterii, B. papyrifera,* and *B. thurifera.* The gum is collected during the summer; it is customary to peel the bark back first, and then to make a deep cut with a sharp knife.

The Heb. name *l^ebônâ* and the Gr. word *libanos* both mean "white." This is presumably because when the gum first exudes from the bark it is of an amber color; later when removed from the tree, the resin produces a white dust on its surface. The gum, when warmed and burned, produces a sweet, pleasant odor.

The children of Israel imported frankincense from Arabia—this was produced near Saba or Sheba.

In the Apoc. there is a reference (Ecclus 50:8) to a locally-grown tree, whose outline and growth would be known to the Hebrews. In this particular case, there is reason to believe that the tree may have been *Commiphora opobalsamum,* whose resin can produce perfume.

Boswellia trees are related to Turpentine trees; the star-shaped flowers are pure white or green, tipped with rose. The tree has leaves similar to the Mountain Ash.

If Moffatt's tr. of Song of Solomon 4:6 and

4:14 is correct, the following results: "I will hie me to your scented slopes, your fragrant charms . . . with . . . all sorts of frankincense." This use of the word "sorts" could mean that the gum had come from the three species of Boswellia trees. On the other hand, the Douay VS renders the phrase "All the trees of Libanus," and some have thought that this meant that the gum came from the forests of Lebanon, thus giving rise to the Heb. word "lebonah." One could get fragrant wood from pines and junipers which grew in Lebanon. The dried, powdered wood may, of course, have been used to adulterate the pure powdered frankincense and thus make it less expensive.

BIBLIOGRAPHY. G. Van Beek, "Frankincense and Myrrh in Ancient Arabia," JAOS, Vol. 78 (Sept. 1958) 141-151.

W. E. SHEWELL-COOPER

FRANKISH VERSIONS. *See* VERSIONS (ANCIENT).

FREE, FREEDOM, FREELY. *See* LIBERTY.

FREEDMAN, FREEMAN (ἀπελεύθερος; ἐλεύθερος). NT terms to indicate an emancipated slave in the first word and a condition of freedom in the second.

Apeleutheros is used only in 1 Corinthians 7:22 in the NT, and there in a fig. sense of "being made free by the Lord."

Eleutheros is employed to indicate political and social freedom, as is brought out in 1 Corinthians 7:21, several times being included in lists setting forth different religious, social, and economic groupings of society, as Jew, Greek, barbarian, slave, free, king, etc. (1 Cor 12:13; Gal 3:28; Eph 6:8; Col 3:11; Rev 6:15; 13:16; 19:18). The word can also indicate independency of action (1 Cor 9:1; Matt 17:26; Rom 6:20; 7:3; 1 Cor 7:39; 9:19) as well as spiritual freedom in Christ (John 8:36; 1 Pet 2:16; cf. Gal 4:26).

W. H. MARE

FREEDMEN, SYNAGOGUE OF THE (συναγωγὴ τῶν Λιβερτίνων). The term occurs in the NT in Acts 6:9. It refers to those who together with Cyrenians and Alexandrians and others opposed Stephen. They apparently opposed him on theological grounds, but were not able to withstand the wisdom by which he spoke.

To oppose Stephen they hired false witnesses who accused Stephen of speaking blasphemous words against Moses and God.

As a result, a mob gathered and he was arrested and accused before the council. Their only accusation was that he said Jesus would destroy the Temple and change the customs of Moses.

It has never been fully established just who these men of the Libertines were and just where their synagogue was. It has been identified with Raymond Weill's discovery of an inscr. of a synagogue in Jerusalem. This discovery in 1920 mentions the building of a synagogue by Theodatus, son of Vettenus, priest and chief of the synagogue. The name Vettenus obviously refers to the Rom. family of which he or his father was a slave. When the Jews were freed from their Rom. masters and returned to Jerusalem they became known as "freedmen."

The above mentioned synagogue is the oldest archeological evidence of a synagogue in Pal. In Tacitus' *Annals* II. 85, he recalls that Jews were expelled from Rome about A.D. 19.

Some believe the term should read not "Libertines" but "Libyans" and that they were Africans, but this is highly speculative and unnecessary.

BIBLIOGRAPHY. W. F. Albright, *The Archaeology of Palestine* (1949), 172.

J. B. SCOTT

FREEWILL OFFERING. *See* OFFERING.

FRET, FRETTING. In all, seven separate Heb. terms are so tr. by the Eng. VSS. 1. חרה, the common verb "to be angry," which appears frequently (Gen 44:18, et al.) often is tr. "fret yourself/himself," when it occurs in the *hithpa'el* form, lit. "cause oneself to be angry" (Ps 37:1, 7, 8, et al.)

2. מאר, "painful" appears only in Leviticus 13:51, 52; 14:44 and in Ezekiel 28:24 (KJV) "pricking," (RSV) "to prick"; the same root metathesized appears in Ruth 1:20, "Do not call me Naomi, call me Mara (bitterness, pain)." The VSS therefore are incorrect and the word should be understood as "cause yourself pain."

3. רעם, "to thunder," "to cause trembling," (KJV) "make her fret" (RSV) "to irritate her" should be understood in its secondary meaning "be humbled" as in Ezekiel 27:35 (KJV) "troubled," (RSV) "convulsed" should be understood as "humbled."

4. פחתת, a peculiar form occurring as a *hapax legomenon* in Leviticus 13:55, derived from the rare root, פחת, "hollow out" (2 Sam 17:9, et al.) which in turn is a metathesized form of the common Sem. פתח, "bore," "open" (Mal 3:10), *patāhu(m)*, "open." The use of this verb in Isaiah 48:8 is identical to its use in Akkad. lit., *patāh uzun*," "his ears were open." The Leviticus passage should thus be tr., "if the lesion has not changed its color and the lesion is not spread, it is unclean; you shall burn it in the fire; it is a fistula, whether the infection is internal or external." (N.B. the word also can be used in the medical sense of "sinus.")

5. רגז, "be agitated," "to tremble" (Deut 2:25, et al. frequently). KJV mistakenly trs. this term as "fret" only in Ezekiel 16:43; RSV "enraged" should be tr., "Because you have not remembered the days of your youth, but have provoked me . . ." as in Job 12:6 (KJV).

The tassels (or fringes, KJV) at the four corners of the upper garment of male Jews.

6. זעף, "be angry," "be embittered" (Isa 30:30) mistakenly tr. "fret" by KJV only in Proverbs 19:3, properly tr. by KJV in 2 Chronicles 26:19.

7. קצף, "be wrathful," "wrath," an Old Canaanite term, occurs as a gloss in *Amarna Letter*, 93:5; 82:51. Akkad. *ašāšu*(*m*), "to be afflicted," "troubled," is mistakenly tr. "shall fret themselves" by KJV and JPS in Isaiah 8:21. It should be tr. "they will be enraged" (RSV). Undoubtedly much of the difficulty with these words is due to the wide semantic range given "to fret" in Tudor Eng. so that it became a catchall for the more difficult and oblique Heb. verbs.

W. WHITE, JR.

FRIEND, FRIENDSHIP (אהב, רע, *companion, friend,* among other terms; φίλος, *friend,* φιλία, *friendship*; also ἑταῖρος, *comrade, mate*).

Besides friendship in the form of hospitality (*see* HOSPITALITY), there are many explicit references to friends or friendship in the Bible. The range of the connotations of these terms is wide. Apart from being merely a term of familiar, kindly address (Matt 20:13; 22:12), "friend" may mean a well-disposed acquaintance, dependable companion, or helpful neighbor (Gen 38:20; Jer 6:21; Luke 11:5-8; 14:10; 15:6, 9), a political adherent (1 Sam 30:26; 2 Sam 3:8; 15:37; 1 Kings 4:5; John 19:12), or a person dear as one's own soul (Deut 13:6). There are false friends as well as true ones (Prov 18:24); friends who fail one (Job 6:14, 27; Lam 1:2; Zech 13:6) as well as friends who prove faithful (Ps 35:14; Prov 17:17; John 15:13). There are those who are selfish (Prov 19:4, 6f.) and those who seek the welfare of others (27:6, 10).

Friendship with Jesus depended on a common commitment of life with Him (Matt 12:46-50; John 15:14).

Perhaps the most notable instance of human friendship in the Bible is that of David and Jonathan (1 Sam 18:1-4; 19:1-7; 20:1-42; 2 Sam 1:25f.).

The highest friendship the Bible speaks of is friendship with God (2 Chron 20:7; Isa 41:8; James 2:23), whose direct opposite, enmity with God, is friendship with the world (James 4:4).

BIBLIOGRAPHY. H. Black, *Friendship* (1903); S. Dodds, *Friendship's Meaning and the Heart of God in Nature* (1919), 7-43; G. Kittel, ed., TWNT, V (1954), 16-23.

P. H. MONSMA

FRINGE, FRINGES (ציצית ; κράσπεδον). In the time of Christ every Jew was constantly reminded of his duties toward God by three mementos: (1) The *tephillin*, or phylacteries, which every male Jew was required to wear at morning prayer, and which consisted of little parchment cases with enclosed Scripture portion; (2) the *mezuzah,* a small oblong box containing Scripture verses which was fixed to house and room doors; (3) the tassels (KJV "fringes") at the four corners of the upper garment of male Jews.

The Israelites were commanded (Num 15:37, 38) "to make tassels (KJV 'fringes') on the corners of their garments throughout their generations, and to put upon the tassel of each corner a cord of blue." A similar ordinance is found in Deuteronomy 22:12, "You shall make yourself tassels (KJV 'fringes') on the four corners of your cloak with which you cover yourself." The purpose of the tassels was to remind the Israelites of the commandments of the Lord, and not to depart from His will.

There has been much speculation about the precise meaning of the injunction about the cord of blue upon each tassel, but it is usually taken to mean that in some way the tassel was to be attached to the garment by this cord of blue.

There are a number of references to these tassels in the NT. The woman who had an issue of blood had faith that she would be healed by merely touching the fringe of Jesus' garment (Matt 9:20), and many brought their sick that they might do likewise (Matt 14:36). Matthew (23:5) records Jesus' condemnation of the scribes and Pharisees who made their tassels long in order that they might be highly regarded by men.

Monuments from Egypt and the Near E show that many types of tassels were worn by non-Jews in ancient times, though not for the same purpose.

Jews gradually ceased to wear these tassels outwardly, as prescribed in the law, chiefly to avoid exposure to heathen and Christian persecution. They therefore devised a kind of undergarment (or vest) covering the chest and back, with four corners where tassels were attached. Modern orthodox Jews still wear it, or a prayer shawl which likewise has tassels attached to the corners. However the "blue thread" is no longer regarded as necessary.

BIBLIOGRAPHY. TNDT, IV, 904.

S. Barabas

FROG (צפרדע ; Βάτραχος. *Frog* in all Eng. VSS).
The only OT mention of this common amphibian is concerning the cause of the second plague. Many species are found in the marshes and rivers of the Middle E and the Nile Valley, the most common being *Rana esculenta*, the Edible or Green Frog. It is sometimes known as the River Frog because it stays in water most of the year and not only in the breeding season. It reaches a length of about three inches. Many people dislike the cool moist feel of a frog's skin, but the reaction of the Egyptians was far more severe, because to them the frog was also unclean. This finds an echo in the only NT occurrence (Rev 16:13). This plague followed closely on the first, by which the Nile became gravely polluted. This may be seen as the immediate cause of the frogs leaving the rivers and invading the houses. The magicians could produce frogs by sleight of hand, but could not drive away the plague that God had sent. In the hot dry air frogs quickly became dehydrated and died, the result being physically unpleasant as well as abhorrent. It is ironic that frogs are useful in keeping down insects, such as caused the following plagues.

G. S. Cansdale

FRONTLETS (טוטפת). A word occurring in only three OT passages (Exod 13:16; Deut 6:8; 11:18). The expression, "as frontlets between your eyes," is coupled each time with a similar expression connected with the hand, "as a sign upon your hand." In the Exodus passage God said that the Feast of Unleavened Bread was to remind the Israelites of their deliverance by Him from Egypt, and was to have the same value as marks upon the hand and the forehead. In Deuteronomy Moses told the Israelites that the law was to have a very important place in their lives. They were to bind it upon the hand and have it as frontlets between the eyes. It appears that the injunction was intended to be taken metaphorically, and not literally, as the later Jews understood it, when they wrote four passages of the law (Exod 13:1-10, 11-16; Deut 6:4-9; 11:13-21) on small bits of parchment, which they enclosed in little boxes, which were worn, bound on the arm and brow, at morning prayer. These "tephillin" were reverenced as highly as the Scriptures. It is usually thought that the phylacteries worn by the Pharisees (Matt 23:5) were the same as the frontlets.

S. Barabas

FROST, two Heb. words are so tr. 1. קרח, which means both "snow" (possibly "ice") as in Psalm 147:17; and "frost" as in Genesis 31:40, KJV, et al. It is used as a sign of God's power and sovereignty over nature.

2. חנמל, a *hapax legomenon* in Psalm 78:47; some other VSS read "great hail stones." The parallelism is difficult and no known etymology exists except for a variety of folk etymologies selected from the Arab. lexica. The climate of Pal. is widely divergent from the hills around the Sea of Galilee to the desert of the southern Sinai. Although snow is rare and scattered it does fall in the higher elevations. Frost will develop rapidly from the drop of temperature caused by the convection currents over the desert. Violent falls of hail stones, swirling snow showers and frozen dew all are features of the variable climate.

W. White, Jr.

FRUIT (PRODUCTS) אב (fruit budding); יבול (fruit increase); לחם (fruit as food); מאכל (fruit as food); מלאה (fruitfulness); נוב (fruit); ניב (fruit); פרי (fruit); תבואה (fruit, produce); תנובה (fruit, increase of); זמרה (fruit, best); פרה (fruit, to bring); יב (fruit, to bring forth); מלאה (fruit, first ripe).

In the NT, γένημα, "fruit produce"; καρπφορέω, "to bear fruit"; ἄκαρπος, "without fruit."

The word "fruit" appears 215 times in the Bible, 106 times as the Heb. word *p^e^rî* and 63 times as the Gr. word *karpos*.

The word "fruit" often is used fig. as well as factually. For instance—fig. in Leviticus 25:19 RSV—"the land will yield its fruit," or Deuteronomy 28:4—"Blessed shall be the fruit of your body." Psalm 104:13—"satisfied with the fruit of thy work." Proverbs 11:30—"the fruit of the righteous." Song of Solomon 2:3—"His fruit was sweet to my taste." Isaiah 3:10—"They shall eat the fruit of their deeds."

Factually, as in Genesis 3:2—"we may eat of the fruit of the trees." 2 Kings 19:29—"plant vineyards, and eat their fruits." Jeremiah 11:16—"a green olive tree . . . and of goodly fruit"; whereas our Lord in Matthew 26:29 and Luke 22:18 refers to "the fruit of the vine," and in Matthew 21:19 forbids the fig tree to bear fruit.

The various fruits mentioned in the Bible are found under their own headings.

In an Eastern country, the fruits grown are those indigenous to the area. The most important fruit tree is prob. the vine, which occurs again and again from Genesis 9:20 to Revelation 14:19. The olive is almost as important, and occurs first in Genesis 8:11, when a dove brings an olive leaf, and continues to Revelation 11:4, when two olive trees are described. The fig is the third claimant—it is first mentioned in Genesis 3:7 when Adam and Eve used fig leaves to cover themselves, and last in Revelation 6:13, where useless figs are shed.

A date palm; an olive tree; pomegranates.
©*Lev*

These three fruit trees are all used in parabolic form to describe the Jewish people. In Jeremiah 11:16 we read "The LORD called thy name a fair green olive tree." In Psalm 80:8, the text says: "Thou didst bring a vine out of Egypt," obviously referring to the children of Israel, while the Lord used the fig tree in Luke 13 to describe the barrenness of the Jewish nation.

As to the kinds of fruits mentioned, there is the apple, which, as is said, is prob. an apricot; there is the blackberry, as in Luke 6:44; the fig; the melon—prob. a water melon (Num 11:5); the mulberry, mentioned three times (2 Sam 5:23, 1 Chron 14:14, 15, KJV); the olive; the date palm; the pomegranate (1 Sam 14:2); the vine, the sodom vine; and goodly fruit, prob. an orange or lemon; the locust bean—a fruit borne by trees, mentioned by inference in Luke 15:16. This makes twelve fruits in all.

The almond could be included, though it is really the seed of a fruit. The balm mentioned in Genesis 37:25 and Jeremiah 8:22 prob. comes from the fruit of the Balanites Tree. There are two species of myrrh, which bear oval, plum-like fruits. The cucumber is a fruit, though we classify it as a vegetable (Num 11:5). The walnuts grown in Solomon's garden (S of Sol 6:11) also may be regarded as fruits. The mandrake in Genesis 30:14 bears a yellow fruit like a large plum, called by the Arabs "devil's apples."

It may be that other fruits were grown by Solomon, because in Song of Solomon 4:16 one reads "choicest fruits." It is believed that Solomon collected fruit trees from many different parts of the world.

The term "does not bear good fruit" (Matt 3:10; Luke 3:9; Rom 1:13) may refer to seedling trees which bear quite useless fruit. The "hasty fruits"—*bikkûr* (Isa 28:4, KJV) are really fruits which ripen early in the summer and must be eaten immediately, while the "summer fruit" in Amos 8:1, 2, refers to the last of the ripened fruits, i.e. the end of the season.

W. E. SHEWELL-COOPER

FRYING PAN (Heb. מרחשת, from the root, רחש), a rare phenomenon of an Aram. loanword which appears in the sense of "to creep" (B. Landsberger, *Die Fauna Des Alten Mesopotamien nach der 14 Tafel der Serie HAR-RA=Hubullu* [1934], p. 127), but what exactly the connection between the two words is semantically is as yet undetermined (Lev. 2:7; 7:9).

FUEL (Heb. אכלה, in the phrase, מאכלת אש, *food for fire* [Isa 9:5, 19; Ezek 15:4, 6; 21:32]) used of fuel on the analogy that fire consumes material. The fuels of antiquity all were derived from vegetable hydrocarbons. Woods and barks were burned along with rushes, straw, twigs, sticks, thorn bushes, chaff and roots. The only animal material was dung, which burned slowly and gave off a detestable odor. The process of making charcoal certainly was discovered by the beginning of the 2nd millennium B.C., as it was used to gain the necessary temperature for the smelting of copper and the alloys needed to make bronze. Since many of the richer homes and temples utilized charcoal and the braziers upon which it was burned were imported, the OT has a number of foreign cultural-words which are used to describe them, e.g. Heb. כיר (Lev 11:35); Heb. אח (Jer 36:22, 23).

W. WHITE, JR.

FULFILL, FULFILLMENT. To deal fully with all that is involved in the idea of fulfillment would require a study of several broad theological themes, because it is a key concept of Christian thought. It will be possible here only (1) to indicate the various Heb. and Gr. words which represent the idea and to bring out their significance; (2) to show the relationship between promise and fulfillment and to bring into focus the relevance of the OT; (3) to analyze the various types of fulfillment illustrated in the Bible; and (4) to note the special NT ideas of fulfillment.

1. Discussion of the terms used. The main Heb. words used are מלא, and כלה ; the first focuses on fullness, the second on completeness. In the LXX πληρόω frequently trs. the Heb. מלא and carries with it the same idea of fullness. Its primary sense is filling up, but its main Biblical importance rests in its secondary sense of bringing to fulfillment. In the NT two compounds, *anaplēróō* and *ekplēróō* are used in addition to the frequent use of the root verb with much the same meaning. The first of these compounds is found in the papyri in the sense of completing contracts and is used in 1 Thessalonians 2:16 of the Jews for filling up the measure of their sins, but in Matthew 13:14 the same term is used for the fulfillment of prophecy. The second word is used in the NT only in Acts 13:33 of God fulfilling His promises.

The Gr. forms τελειόω, τελέω and συντελέω are also associated with the idea of fulfillment, but with the special emphasis on the idea of completeness. Thus *teleióō* is used of the fulfillment of Scripture in John 19:28 (cf. Luke 2:43, where it is used in a temporal sense of the finishing of the period of days). *Teléō* is used of the fulfillment of prophecy in Acts 13:29 in the sense of "completing," while *sunteléō* occurs in Mark 13:4, where it describes the accomplishment of what Jesus had predicted.

2. The relation of promise to fulfillment. Fulfillment presupposes previous prediction, and it is essential to understand the nature of the prediction to appreciate the significance of the fulfillment. The OT concentrates the promises in the covenant relationship and in the Messianic hopes. The OT was in fact forward-pointing and takes on its true meaning only in the light of the consummation found in the NT. The OT is to the NT as promise is to fulfillment. The Apostle Paul makes much of the promises made to Abraham in his Roman epistle (ch. 4). These promises he clearly sees to have been fulfilled in Christ. It was the glory of Abraham's faith that it staggered not at the difficulties inherent in the fulfillment, because he was convinced of the inviolability of the promise. This is typical of the OT revelation. It was never represented as being complete in itself. There was always something more glorious to follow.

The early Christian appeal to OT citations is a striking reminder of the importance of the idea of fulfillment for primitive Christian theology. The Acts speeches are full of such citations and so are the gospels. Moreover, in the epistles there are frequent appeals to the OT fulfillments, and various formulae of citation are employed to bring out the nature of fulfillment.

The essential link between the Testaments is never more clearly seen than under this concept. It is fundamental to the Scriptural presentation of God that He must keep His promises. The Scripture cannot be broken (cf. John 10:35), and for this reason fulfillment is certain. It was no more than might be expected. However, fulfillment did confirm the faith of those who either at the time or else later recognized that some former prediction of God had come to pass. It was this sense of thrilling fulfillment that gave to primitive Christianity a remarkable air of joyfulness. The age to come had arrived. Promise had merged into fulfillment. More will be said later about this under the fourth sub-section.

3. Various types of fulfillment. The idea of fulfillment will clearly vary according to the nature of the prediction. For the sake of clarity some classification of these types is necessary. (a) The first class consists of cases of *immediate fulfillment*. An example from the OT is seen in the prediction of the prophet Ahijah that Jeroboam's wife would suffer the loss of her child as soon as she arrived home (1 Kings 14:12). A NT example is the withering of the fig tree at the command of Jesus (Mark 11:12-14, cf. Matt 21:18, 19), or the prediction of Peter's denial a few hours before it happened (Matt 26:34, 75). (b) The second class consists of cases of *delayed fulfillment.* Under this classification there are two main groups: those instances where fulfillment has already taken place and those instances where as yet the promises remain unfulfilled. The former group gives assurance that the latter will yet be fulfilled. Under the former group must be classed all those Messianic predictions which found their fulfillment in Jesus Christ, for instance, the seed that would bruise the serpent's head (Gen 3) and the Servant passages in Isaiah. In these cases the delay in fulfillment spanned many centuries, and yet there was no hesitation in the minds of Christians that Jesus was the perfect fulfillment of all the ancient predictions. Examples of prophecies yet to be fulfilled are numerous. In the OT there are various prophecies relating to Israel which are as yet unfulfilled and others which in quite recent years have seen remarkable fulfillment in the reconstitution of the nation of Israel. In the NT there are many eschatological predictions which await fulfillment at the end of the age. (c) The third class consists of cases of both *immediate and delayed fulfillment.* It is important to recognize this class since it has occasioned most difficulty in the interpretation of prophetic utterances. A notable illustration is the eschatological discourse in Mark 13 where the predictions of Jesus received a partial fulfillment in the fall of Jerusalem, but will be consummated only at the Parousia. The line of demarcation between the immediate and the future was not clearly defined for the original hearers, but subsequent events have shown the words to possess a double aspect. Sometimes an event which had originally a specific local significance is symbolic of a deeper fulfillment later, as for instance Isaiah 7:14. (d) A fourth class comprises cases of what might be called *extended fulfillment.* Where a prediction has a fulfillment after a brief interval of time which adequately satisfies the prediction, it may yet receive a further application in a sense different from its original significance. Thus in the NT some OT predictions are applied to the times of Christ, which were not normally considered to be Messianic. The prophecy of the slaughter of the innocents (Matt 2:17, 18) had a different meaning in its original context (Jer 31:15). This process will explain many of the OT citations used in the NT. They had a meaning which was hidden from the people originally addressed, but which was nevertheless a true fulfillment. In these cases the recognition by Christians of the fulfillment of an ancient prediction was regarded as an important feature of God's dealing with them.

4. Fulfillment in the NT. The early Christians were deeply impressed with the fact that the salvation events centered in Jesus Christ were fulfillments of Scripture. "According to the Scriptures" was a fixed part of the primitive preaching and tradition (cf. 1 Cor 15:3ff.). The gospels contain many instances of events which are said to have happened in fulfillment of OT *Testimonia.* This is particularly true in Matthew's gospel, where a group of twelve such testimonies are introduced with some such formula as "that it might be fulfilled which was spoken . . ." These formulae may at first give the impression that the people concerned with the action were acquainted with the fact that prophecy was being fulfilled, but the citations are for the most part the evangelist's own commentary on the events. It was in retrospect that the details in the life of Jesus were fulfillments (cf. Matt 12:17ff.). But one of the key factors in the interpretation of fulfilled prophecy was the conviction that all things were planned, working toward a climax. This conviction undoubtedly came from Jesus Himself. When He appeared to the disciples after the resurrection, He said, "These are my words which I spoke to you, while I was still with you, that everything written about me in the law of Moses and the prophets and the psalms must be fulfilled" (Luke 24:44). This was the cue for their understanding of the OT.

There is ample evidence that Jesus was conscious of the processes of fulfillment both in His life and His death. When John the Baptist asked whether Jesus was the Coming One, Jesus in reply echoed the words of Isaiah 35: 5, 6, and when Judas shared the same dish with him at the supper table Jesus stated that the Son of man goes as it is written of Him (Mark 14:21). At the commencement of the ministry in Luke's story, Jesus read a passage of Scripture in the synagogue and then declared that Scripture had been fulfilled in their hearing. This consciousness stayed with Him throughout His public ministry. In John's gospel this idea is most clearly expressed. Jesus was sent to fulfill a divine mission. He was moving toward a specific "hour" which would climax His work. All the evangelists are convinced that the death and resurrection of Jesus occurred in fulfillment of Scripture and this is equally apparent in the speeches in Acts. It is through the Scriptures that Jesus is revealed to be the long promised Messiah.

It is in the Acts and esp. in the epistles that the theological importance of fulfillment is fully brought out. It formed an integral part of the primitive *kerygma.* Was it developed in the epistles? It is clear from the repeated refrain in 1 Corinthians 15:3, 4, that the Apostle Paul took it from earlier tradition. The frequency with which he cited Scripture shows that it became an integral part of his theological outlook. This may best be illustrated from the most theological of his writings, the Epistle to the Romans. He begins by noting that God had promised the Gospel beforehand in the Scriptures. The Gospel was itself fulfillment. The theme of the whole epistle is founded on an OT quotation, Habakkuk 2:4. The argument of the epistle is frequently buttressed from Scripture (Rom 3). The promise is prominent in

Romans 4 and the Adam motive in Romans 5. The discussion in Romans 9-11 is impregnated with the problems of fulfillment and is frequently supported by the appeal to Scripture. Also in the ethical section (Rom 12-15), Scripture is repeatedly quoted under the formula, "It is written" (cf. 14:11; 15:9ff., 21). The closing doxology (Rom 16:25-27) refers to the prophetic writings. What is true of this epistle is true of Paul's approach generally. The same is true for the other NT epistles. Hebrews may be described as an epistle of fulfillment, as the superiority of the new order over the old is developed. In 1 Peter some of the major ideas of the Book of Exodus have their fulfillment in Christ.

The NT makes clear that the present age will reach its consummation in the fulfillment of the promise of the *eschaton* (the last time). The return of Christ is predicted (Matt 25:31; Mark 8:38), and the details given show that the event is still future. The *eschaton* will be a time of judgment (John 12:48), but in the mercy of God judgment is delayed. Although the present period is a time of partial unfulfillment, the end is certain. It will be a time of great glory for the Son of man and for His people. His kingdom will be established and all the promises concerning it will be fulfilled.

BIBLIOGRAPHY. W. J. Beecher, *The Prophets and the Promise* (1905); R. V. G. Tasker, *The OT in the NT* (1947); O. Cullmann, *Christ and Time* (1950); W. G. Küemmel, *Promise and Fulfillment* (1961); G. von Rad, *OT Theology,* II (1965), 319-387.

D. GUTHRIE

FULLER (כבס, *to trample* or *tread*; γναφεύς). One who cleans, shrinks, and thickens newly shorn wool or cloth. Also in ancient times the fuller often dyed cloth. The root of the Heb. word כבס, meaning "to tread," suggests what was chiefly involved in the fuller's art. Before material could be used for a garment, it was necessary first to free it from the oily and gummy substances that adhered to the raw fiber. This was done by first washing the material with some cleansing substance like white clay, putrid urine, or nitre which was made from the ashes of certain plants that grew in Egypt. Soap was unknown in ancient times. The material was then washed free from the alkali by many changes of clean water or by boys treading on it in a running stream. After that it was placed in the sun to dry and bleach. Because of the odors given forth in the process of fulling, the fuller's shop was usually outside the city (2 Kings 18:17; Isa 7:3; 36:2).

In Malachi 3:2 God is compared to a refiner's fire and to fullers' soap. In the NT the word is used only once (Mark 9:3), where the garments of Jesus at the time of His transfiguration are described as being whiter than any fuller on earth could whiten them.

BIBLIOGRAPHY. R. J. Forbes, *Studies in Ancient Technology* (1956), IV, 81-89.

J. L. KELSO

FULLER'S FOUNTAIN. *See* EN-ROGEL.

FULLER'S SOAP. Heb. phrase, וכברית מכבסים, consisting of a term ברית, "alkaline salt," "natural lye" extracted from the Asiatic soap plants such as *Mesembrianthemum cristallinum*; *Salicornia solacea*; *Salsala kali* and the like (cf. I. Löw, *Die Flora der Juden* [1924-1934]) which are reduced by burning to produce a pasty mass used as a bleach, esp. in the presence of olive oil. The other term is the common Sem. term כבס, "to tread," "knead" and thus to wash in the Near Eastern fashion.

W. WHITE, JR.

FULNESS OF TIME. This expression (Gal 4:4) indicates the "right" or "proper" time for Christ's advent. The expression does not mean the "full term" of pre-natal human life ("born of woman") but rather the right time chosen by the Father ("God sent forth"). This "right time" was determined by God's plan of redemption prepared for by historical developments: the completion of the OT era, Messianic expectation, cultural, political, and religious factors in the Rom. world. This provided fertile soil for the ministry of the Messiah, the founding of the Church, and the rapid spread of the Gospel.

J. C. DEYOUNG

FUNDAMENTALISM. *See* BIBLICAL CRITICISM.

FURLONG. *See* WEIGHTS AND MEASURES.

FURNACE. The tr. of a number of Heb. and Gr. words. 1. אתון, *furnace*; prob. a loan-word from Akkad. *utūnu,* "oven," as used for baking bricks or smelting metals. The word is found in Daniel 3:6, 11, 15, 17, 19, 20-22, 26, and refers to the furnace into which Shadrach, Meshach, and Abednego were cast. Both history and archeology reveal the cruelty of some punishments under ancient oriental despots.

2. כבשן, *kiln*, for lime or pottery. A kiln was made of limestone, was dome-shaped, and had openings at the top and bottom for the escape of smoke and the supplying of fuel. When fuel was being burned, a thick, dark column of smoke issued forth. In the account of the destruction of Sodom and Gomorrah it is said that "the smoke of the land went up like the smoke of a furnace" (Gen 19:28). The ashes of a kiln would be fine as dust (Exod 9:8, 10). When God met the Israelites at Mt. Sinai, "the smoke of it went up like the smoke of a kiln" (Exod 19:18).

3. כור, *smelting-pot* or *furnace* for smelting metals. In the Bible the word is used only in the metaphorical sense of suffering permitted

by God in punishment or discipline. The deliverance of Israel from Egypt was like being taken from the midst of an iron furnace (Deut 4:20; 1 Kings 8:51; Jer 11:4). God told Israel that He had refined them in the furnace of affliction (Isa 48:10). Gold is refined in a furnace (Prov 17:3; 27:21).

4. עֲלִיל. The word is used only in Psalm 12:6 where it is said that the promises of God are absolutely trustworthy, like silver purified seven times in a furnace—real sterling.

5. מוֹקֵד, *burning mass.* Found in Psalm 102:3, "For my days pass away like smoke, and my bones burn like a furnace" (KJV "hearth"; ASV "firebrand"). The various trs. of the Eng. VSS seem to be rather arbitrary.

6. תַּנּוּר, *a portable stove* or *fire-pot.* Translated "furnace" four times in the KJV (Gen 15:17; Neh 3:11; 12:38; Isa 31:9), "fire pot" in the RSV (Gen 15:17); "oven" in the RSV Neh 3:11; 12:38; Mal 4:1); "oven(s)" KJV and RSV (Exod 8:3; Lev 2:4; 7:9; 11:35; 26:26; Ps 21:9; Lam 5:10; Hos 7:4, 6, 7; Mal 4:1); and "furnace" in the RSV (Gen 19:28; Isa 31:9).

7. Κάμινος, *furnace, oven.* The LXX uses *kāminos* to tr. *'attūn, kibshān,* and *kūr.* In Matthew 13:42, 50 and Revelation 9:2 it is used as a synonym of "hell," the destiny of those who are finally impenitent. In Revelation 1:15 it is said of the one who is "like a son of man" (Rev 1:13) that "his feet were like burnished bronze, refined as in a furnace" (1:15). Refined bronze is a hard metal, symbolizing the crushing power of Christ when He deals with His enemies.

It will be seen that almost always the word "furnace" occurs in the Bible in a metaphorical sense of God's punishment or of His tempering the character of man.

Furnaces were used for smelting iron from the ore; melting and refining gold, silver, brass, tin, and lead; firing pottery and other ceramic products; firing bricks; and making lime.

The metal industry flourished as early as 2000 B.C. Many mining and smelting camps along the edge of the Arabah have been found. The largest was at Mene'iyyeh, c. twenty-one m. N of the Gulf of Aqabah. There was another at Khirbet en-Nahas, fifty-two m. farther N.

The largest copper mine in the whole of the ancient Near E was found at Tell-el-Kheleifeh (Ezion-Geber), at the S end of the Wadi Arabah. It was built in the 10th cent. B.C., most likely by Solomon, who also built a fleet of merchant ships there for carrying on trade. The shelter was oriented so that the strong prevailing wind from the N would blow into the flues, making the use of bellows unnecessary. Charcoal was used for fuel. This smelter was in use up to the 5th cent. B.C.

A number of smelting furnaces have been discovered in Pal. itself, some used to smelt copper, others iron. Four were found at Tell Jemmeh, two at Ain Shems, and others at Ai and at Tell Qasile near Tell Aviv.

BIBLIOGRAPHY. N. Glueck, *The Other Side of the Jordan* (1940), chs. 3, 4; N. Glueck, *The River Jordan* (1946), 145-147; R. J. Forbes, *Studies in Ancient Technology* (1958), VI, 66ff.; C. Singer, etc. (Eds.), *A History of Technology* (1954), 391-397, 577; G. E. Wright, *Biblical Archaeology* (1962), 135-137.

S. BARABAS

FURNACES, TOWER OF THE. *See* OVENS, TOWER OF THE.

FURNITURE (כְּלִי, *article, utensil, vessel*). Since the word *keli* basically means "anything made," "finished," or "produced," the Eng. VSS tr. the word in a variety of ways: furniture, furnishings, instrument, thing, stuff, utensils, vessel. It is often used of the various articles of furniture, implements, and vessels of the Tabernacle which God asked Moses to make according to the pattern shown to him in the Mount—the brazen altar and laver, the table of showbread, the golden lampstand, the altar of incense, the ark and mercy-seat (Exod 25:9 KJV "instruments," RSV "furniture," KJV "furniture," RSV "utensils"; 31:9 KJV "furniture," RSV "utensils"; 35:14 KJV "furniture," RSV "utensils"; 39:33 KJV "furniture," RSV "utensils"; 40:9 KJV "vessels," RSV "furniture"; 1 Chron 9:29 KJV "vessels," RSV "furniture").

When Nehemiah discovered that Tobiah had been given a furnished chamber in the Temple, in anger he threw all the household furniture out of the room (Neh 13:8 KJV "stuff").

In Genesis 31:34 the Heb. word כַּר, is tr. "furniture" in the KJV, but "saddle" in the RSV. The reference is to a "basket-saddle." It was in this that Rachel successfully hid the household gods from her father.

Household furniture in Biblical Pal. was very simple. Handwoven curtains separated the men's and the women's quarters. Beds were found only in the homes of the wealthy; the average person used sleeping mats, which were rolled up when not in use. Since houses were primarily a place for sleeping, and people spent most of their time out of doors, there was little furniture in the house. Mats spread on the bare floor served in place of tables and chairs. Sometimes stone or wooden benches, covered with carpet, were placed along the walls. With the wealthy it was different, as evident in the denunciation of the grandees of Samaria by the prophet Amos, who, he said, luxuriated in beds of ivory and lazily stretched themselves upon couches (Amos 3:12; 6:4).

BIBLIOGRAPHY. M. S. and J. L. Miller, *Encyclopedia of Bible Life* (1944), 246-252.

S. BARABAS

FURROW (גדוד, Ps 65:10; מענה or מענית, Ps 129:3; 1 Sam 14:14; תלם, Job 31:38; 39:10; Hos 10:4; 12:11. All these words carry the meaning of *plow path* or *plow trench*). In the KJV two other Heb. words are tr. as "furrow." The word found in Hosea 10:10 is better tr. as "guilt." The word found in Ezekiel 17:7, 10 is better tr. as "bed" (of plants).

The furrow or plow trench was usually made with a single-handled wooden plow pulled by an animal. Iron was available after David's period, but wood continued to be used in many instances. *See* AGRICULTURE.

G. GIACUMAKIS, JR.

FUTURE LIFE. *See* ESCHATOLOGY; IMMORTALITY.

Gabbatha, or the "pavement," in Jerusalem, possibly the place where Pilate judged Jesus. ©*Lev*.

GAAL gā' əl (געל, LXX Γααλ, *scarab*, or *loathing*). The son of Ebed who with a select group of men from among his relatives gained the confidence of the inhabitants of Shechem and stirred them up to revolt against Abimelech (Judg 9:26-41). While they were having a great banquet, Gaal and the men of Shechem became drunk and scoffed at Abimelech. In the midst of their revelry, Gaal boasted that with adequate support he could overthrow Abimelech. When Zebul, the ruler of Shechem heard this, he sent word to Abimelech urging him to quell the rebellion at once. He advised Abimelech to set an ambush around the city during the night. The next morning as Gaal and Zebul stood in the city gate watching, they saw the troops of Abimelech arise from hiding and approach the city. Zebul challenged Gaal to make good his boast to overthrow Abimelech. Gaal and his men were defeated and driven from the field, and they were repulsed from the city by Zebul. The next day Abimelech captured Shechem, destroyed it, and sowed it with salt. This was seen by the Scripture writer as the just judgment of God on the Shechemites who supported Abimelech in the assassination of his seventy brothers.

D. H. Madvig

GAASH gā' ăsh (געש, *shake*, *quake*). A name used to identify a mountain and a wadi of the same vicinity. The mountain locates the burial site of Joshua, in the hill country of Ephraim (Josh 24:30; Judg 2:9). The wadi is referred to as the area from which Hiddai (Hurai), one of David's mighty men, came (2 Sam 23:30; 1 Chron 11:32). Probable location is about twenty m. SW of Shechem.

J. B. SCOTT

GABA. KJV alternate form of GEBA.

GABAEL găb' ĭ əl (Γαβαήλ). 1. A member of the tribe of Naphtali and an ancestor of Tobit (Tobit 1:1).

2. A brother or son of Gabrias who lived at Rages in Media with whom Tobit left ten talents of silver for safekeeping (1:14; 4:20). Having been prevented by political conditions from recovering the money himself, Tobit sent his son Tobias to get it.

D. H. MADVIG

GABATHA găb' ə thə (Γαβαθά). A eunuch who plotted against King Ahasuerus. The plot was discovered by Mordecai (Add Esth 12:1, 2). He is the same as "Bigthan" (Esth 2:21) and "Bigthana" (Esth 6:2).

GABBAI găb' ā ī, gă b' ī (גבי, *tax collector*). One of the chiefs from Benjamin who willingly lived in Jerusalem after the return from the Exile (Neh 11:8). The text is doubtful.

GABBATHA găb' bə thə (Γαββαθâ; Aram., גבחתא, *open space*, or גבתא, meaning uncertain: *ridge* [?] *height* [?]). A location in Jerusalem, where Pilate judged Jesus.

John 19:13 identifies Gabbatha as the "Hebrew" (Aram.) name for Gr. Λιθόστρωτον, q.v., *Pavement* ("of stone"), which is otherwise unknown. Attempts to equate Gabbatha with Γαβάθ (Gibeah) = λόφος, "ridge" or "crest" in Jos. War, V. 2. 1 (Arndt, p. 148), or with Lat. *gabata*, "platter," hence a dish-shaped area (C. C. Torrey, ZAW, 65 [1953], 232, 233), remain speculative. The fact that Gabbatha lay outside the praetorium, or governor's residence (John 19:9, 13), would indicate either the palace of Herod in the W part of Jerusalem or the fortress of Antonia in the E. The latter, at the NW corner of the Temple area, is favored by L. Vincent's identification at this spot of 2500 square yards of pavement, beneath the present church of the Dames de Sion, as belonging to the NT fortress. The stone slabs are over one yard square and one ft. thick, some still bearing marks suggestive of Rom. soldiers' games (cf. John 19:2, 3, 24).

At Gabbatha, Pilate sat on the βῆμα, "judicial bench," and ultimately acceded to the pressure of the Jewish leaders, delivering Jesus to them for crucifixion (19:16).

BIBLIOGRAPHY. HDB, II, 74, 75; M. Burrows, BA, 1 (1938), 17-19; Arndt, 704 (πραιτώριον); L. Vincent, *Jerusalem de L'AT* (1959), 216-221.

J. B. PAYNE

GABBE, GABDES. ASV and KJV forms of GEBA.

GABRIAS gā' brĭ əs (Γαβρίας). The brother or father of Gabael who lived at Rages in Media with whom Tobit deposited ten talents of silver (Tobit 1:14; 4:20).

GABRIEL gā' brĭ əl (Heb. גבריאל, Gr. Γαβριήλ), the name of a supernatural messenger seen by Daniel in his vision in Daniel 8:16 and 9:21 only in the OT. The name has been etymologized as a compound meaning, "God is great," and other names similar to it have been proposed in the apocalyptic and legendary writings of the Jews. In the apocryphal and mystical kabbalistic writings this angel is joined with the archangel Michael (Dan 10:13, 21; 12:1) and Uriel and Raphael around the throne of God. However, the narrative of Daniel's vision states clearly that the sound heard by Daniel was (Heb. קול-אדם) "voice of a man" so that there is no reason to suppose that this messenger of the Almighty had an appearance or powers apart from man. In the apocryphal books of 1 and 2 Enoch, the character and position of Gabriel are defined in terms of the Jewish folklore. In the Aram. Targ. he is written back into several accounts of the OT and is the angel to whom the finding of Joseph's brothers, the burial of Moses and the slaughter of the Assyrian armies of Sennacherib are all ascribed. It is not clear what the exact sources of these embellishments may have been, but it is highly possible that they were, in fact, aspects of the Pers. demi-gods derived from the elaborate hierarchy of the Iranian pantheon. The simplicity of the account in Daniel is a far removed step from the involved tales of the rabbis.

The angel plays a role in the Lucan account of the Incarnation, as Gabriel is the messenger who announces the birth of John the Baptist to his father the priest, Zechariah, in the Temple (Luke 1:19) and the birth of the Messiah to the Virgin Mary (1:26). His action in both places and the acceptance of his message is similar to the appearance recorded in Daniel. He indicates his authority as one who stands in the presence of the Almighty and thus follows His bidding and bears divine authority for His message. The mythical encrustation of the ages has not dimmed the simple narrative of the angelic announcement, and the Scripture envisions no such creature as the artists of the Renaissance often depicted, a half-man and half-bird derived from late Gr. sculpture. A most interesting aspect is the rarity with which such heavenly visitations are mentioned in the Bible, and in each of the four cases are directly connected to the fulfillment of the Messianic promise. Speculations on the mechan-

ism and details of these angelic announcements have troubled the Church throughout the ages.
W. WHITE, JR.

GAD găd (גָּד ; LXX Γάδ, *fortunate, good fortune*, perhaps after the god of fortune, Gad, גָּד). A son of Jacob and his descendants, the tribe of Gad.

A. The seventh son of Jacob (Israel). The first-born of Zilpah (Gen 30:10, 11), Leah's maid. His younger full brother was Asher. He was born to Jacob during his sojourn with Laban in Paddan-aram during the seven years he was working to pay for his second wife, Rachel. When Gad was born Leah exclaimed, "With good fortune!" (KJV "a troop cometh" following *qere*) whence the name "Gad" (good fortune).

Nothing is known of the life of Gad other than that which is known of the family as a whole (*see* JACOB). At the time when he went with Jacob and his family down to Egypt to sojourn, Gad had seven sons: Ziphion (Zephon), Haggi, Shuni, Ezbon (Ozni), Eri, Arodi (Arod), and Areli (Gen 46:16, variants from Num 26:15, 16). On his deathbed, Jacob blessed Gad, "Raiders (mg. 'a raiding troop'; the Heb. גְּדוּד, 'troop,' 'raiders,' is to be considered a play on words, being similar to the word 'Gad') shall raid Gad, but he shall raid at their heels" (Gen 49:19). The tribe would be subject to attacks by raiding parties (prob. the Ammonites) but Gad would return them.

B. The tribe of Gad, descendants of the son of Jacob. 1. *In the wilderness.* At the first census (Num 1:24, 25), males twenty years old and upward fit for military service numbered 45,650. This is out of a total for Israel of 603,550 (vv. 44-46), which number did not include the tribe of Levi. At the end of their wanderings in the wilderness, the Gadites numbered 40,500, a substantial decrease (26:15-18). The number of non-Gadite Israelites during the same period increased slightly, the total (including Gad) was 601,730 (Num 26:51; *see also* 1 Chron 5:18).

The leader of Gad at the beginning of the wilderness wanderings was Eliasaph (Num 2:14; 10:20) the son of Deuel (2:14, Reuel). He was appointed to assist Moses in the first census (1:14). He brought the representative offering from the Gadites for the dedication of the altar (7:42-47).

In the encampment, Gad was a member company of the camp of Reuben, which camped to the S of the tent of meeting. Reuben camped next to the tent of meeting followed by Simeon with Gad on the outside (2:10-14). In the marching formation, the camp of Judah led, followed by the Gershonites and Merarites who carried the Tabernacle. Then came Reuben, Simeon, and Gad, followed by the Kohathites carrying the holy things, and then the rest of Israel (10:11-21).

When Moses sent men to spy out the land of Canaan the representative from Gad was "Geuel the son of Machi" (13:15).

2. *The time of the conquest.* After the defeat of Sihon, king of the Amorites, and Og, king of Bashan, the Gadites, along with the Reubenites, who were very rich in cattle and needed grazing land, saw that this land (Gilead, Transjordan) was good for cattle, and they requested from Moses that it be given to them as their inheritance (Num 32:1-6). This was given to them upon the promise that their fighting men accompany the children of Israel over the Jordan River, and help to drive out the inhabitants of Canaan until the task was done (32:28-32). Of this Moses later said, "He [Gad] chose the best of the land for himself, for there a commander's portion was reserved" (Deut 33:21). The relationship of Reuben and Gad prob. stemmed from their position at the S of the Tabernacle where Gad was part of the camp of Reuben. The other member, Simeon, received his inheritance to the W of the Jordan as the southernmost of the tribes (Josh 19:1-9).

At the entrance to Canaan, just before crossing the Jordan, Joshua (after the death of Moses) reminded the two and one-half tribes that the men of war were to accompany the rest of Israel W of the Jordan (1:12-18). When the children of Israel passed over the Jordan before the conquest of Jericho, the armed forces of Reuben, Gad, and the half-tribe of Manasseh who went with them, leaving their children behind, amounted to about 40,000 (4:12, 13).

After the defeat of Ai, the Israelites stood by Mount Gerizim and Mount Ebal for the blessing and the curse (8:33-35), according to the words of Moses (Deut 27:11-14). Gad and Reuben were among those designated for Mount Ebal.

Chart showing THE LOCATION OF GAD IN THE ISRAELITE CAMP.

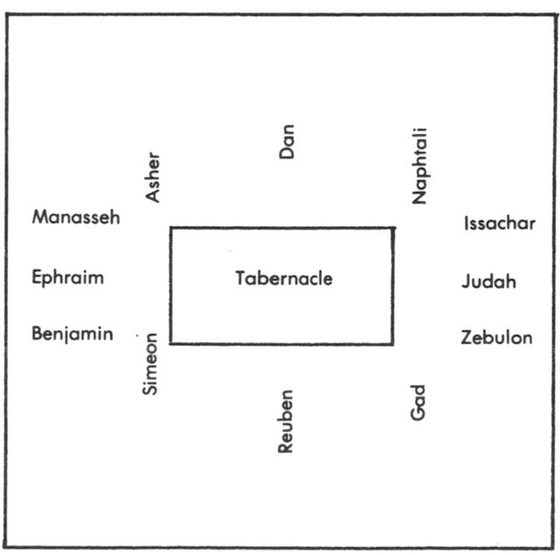

After the conquest, Joshua officially released the Gadites to return home (Josh 22:1-6). When they crossed back over the Jordan with the Reubenites and the half-tribe of Manasseh, they built an altar of great size by the Jordan. When the rest of the Israelites heard of it they gathered together to make war with the two and one-half tribes. The explanation was that this was not an altar for worship of false gods but was a witness that these tribes belonged with the commonwealth of Israel and were always to be included in the worship of the Lord. The explanation pleased the rest of the Israelites and a civil war was prevented (Josh 22).

3. *Tribal inheritance.* In the wilderness, Gad had been a part of the standard of the camp of Reuben on the S side of the tent of meeting (Num 2:10, 14). This association continued when they asked Moses for an inheritance to the E of the Jordan (32:1-5). Moses granted to them (and to the half-tribe of Manasseh) the former kingdoms of Sihon, king of the Amorites, and Og, king of Bashan (32:33). At this time, the land was not divided into tribes, but the Manassites settled in the N (32:39-42), and the Reubenites and Gadites settled in the S (32:34-38). The locations of the towns belonging to Gad and Reuben mentioned here show that at that time their allotments intermixed. For example, Gad "built" Dibon and Aroer (v. 34), which were near the southern border of Reuben (the Arnon River, Deut 3:12, 16) opposite from the territory later given to Gad and actually listed as cities given to Reuben (Josh 13:16, 17). Mesha (king of Moab at the time of Ahab) referred to the inhabitants of Ataroth (Num 32:34) as Gadites "from of old" (Mesha inscr., I. 10), indicating that the Gadites continued to occupy Ataroth (deep in Reubenite territory) after tribal boundaries were fixed. Moses listed the territory of Manasseh separately but that of Gad and Reuben together (Deut 3:12-18). The latter included the area E of the Jordan from Chinnereth (Galilee) to the Salt Sea.

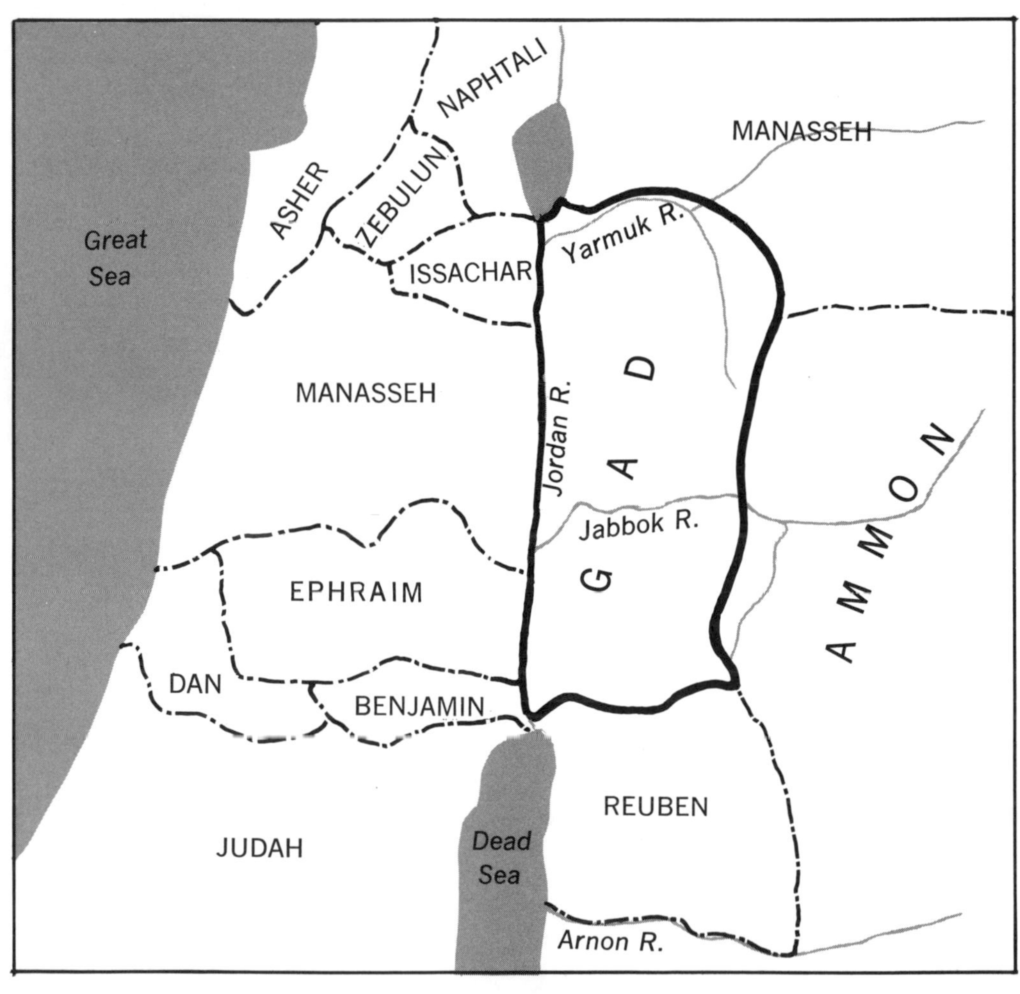

The whole area of the two and one-half tribes is delineated a second time (Josh 12:1-6; 13:8-13). The border on the W was the Jordan; on the S, the Arnon; to the N, the border of Geshur and Maacath; and to the E, apparently the border of the Ammonites (to the Jabbok River). Joshua described the inheritance of Gad individually (13:24-28). The border in the N was from the southern tip of the Sea of Chinnereth eastward with Manasseh as a border, including Ramoth-gilead (a city of refuge, Josh 20:2). On the W was the Jordan. The border on the S was Reuben, just to the N of Heshbon (13:26), which belonged to Reuben (v. 17) but is listed as a Levite city from the tribe of Gad (Josh 21:39; 1 Chron 6:81). To the E were the Ammonites, the border being E of Aroer (Josh 13:25; near Rabbah, modern Amman; not Aroer on the Arnon, v. 16).

Israel's possession E of the Jordan, esp. that of Gad and Manasseh, was called Gilead (q.v.), a geographical term not clearly defined. At times Gilead was used in place of the tribal name (Judg 5:17).

The cities for the Levites from the tribe of Gad were Ramoth, Mahanaim, Heshbon, and Jazer (Josh 21:8, 38, 39; 1 Chron 6:63, 80, 81). Of these, Ramoth in Gilead was a city of refuge (Deut 4:43; Josh 20:8).

4. *The time of Saul and David.* During the reign of Saul, when the Philistines oppressed Israel, some of the Israelites crossed the Jordan and migrated to the land of Gad (1 Sam 13:6, 7). The two and one-half tribes are tied together again in 1 Chron 5. They produced an army of 44,760 and defeated the Hagrites "because they trusted in" God (vv. 18-21). If this is the same event as v. 10, it happened during the reign of Saul, who, because of lack of trust, was losing his battles.

When David was in exile at Ziklag building up a following of trained fighting men, there came Gadites to join him, "mighty and experienced warriors, expert with shield and spear, whose faces were like the faces of lions, and who were swift as gazelles upon the mountains" (1 Chron 12:8). Earlier, Moses had said of Gad, "Gad couches like a lion, he tears the arm, and the crown of the head" (Deut 33:20). Bani the Gadite was one of David's thirty mighty men (2 Sam 23:36). The Reubenites, Gadites, and the half-tribe of Manasseh are listed together as sending a contingent of 120,000 armed men to David's coronation. (Other tribes were listed individually.) Moses had said, ". . . he [Gad] came to the heads of the people" (Deut 33:21). Gad is included in the numbering of the children of Israel by Joab at David's command (2 Sam 24:5). David appointed Jerijah, chief of the Hebronites, along with his brethren, 2,700 men of ability, to the oversight of Trans-Jordan, including the Gadites, for matters "pertaining to God and for the affairs of the king" (1 Chron 26:29-32). A number of these men had been found in Jazer in Gilead (perhaps formerly from Hebron).

5. *Later history.* During the time of Israel's monarchy, the Gadites are not usually referred to separately but share in the history of Gilead. When Hazael, king of Syria, defeated the Israelites, he took much of Trans-Jordan, including the territory of Gad (2 Kings 10:32, 33); Ramoth-gilead had fallen earlier (2 Chron 22). The region was prob. restored under Jeroboam II (2 Kings 14:23-28), but the two and one-half tribes were taken captive by Tiglath-pilneser III (744-727) and were transplanted into parts of his kingdom (1 Chron 5:26). Later, the Ammonites moved into the Gadite territory (Jer 49:1).

Gad is included in the division of the land mentioned in the restoration (Ezek 48:27) and also as the name of one of the gates of the city (48:34). Among the 144,000 Israelites sealed are 12,000 Gadites (Rev 7:5).

BIBLIOGRAPHY. N. Glueck, "Explorations in Eastern Palestine, III," AASOR, XVIII-XIX (1939), 151-251; Id. IV, XXV-XXVIII (1951); D. Baly, *The Geography of the Bible* (1957), 217-231.

C. P. WEBER

GAD (DAVID'S SEER), găd (גָּד, LXX Γάδ, *good fortune*). A prophet, or seer, who served King David. He was with David when David sought refuge for his father and mother in Moab during the time he was hunted by Saul. Upon Gad's advice, David left the stronghold in Moab and entered the forest of Hereth in Judah (1 Sam 22:3-5).

After he had ill-advisedly conducted a census of the people, David became conscience-stricken and confessed his sin to the Lord. The next day Gad brought David a message from the Lord. He was to choose one of three punishments—three years of famine, three months of defeat at the hand of his enemies, or three days of pestilence. David chose to suffer by pestilence, and 70,000 men perished. God relented just as the angel of the Lord was standing on the threshing floor of Araunah (Ornan the Jebusite, 1 Chron 21:15). Gad directed David to build an altar to the Lord on that very spot. After David had offered sacrifices, the plague was stopped (2 Sam 24:10-25; 1 Chron 21).

Gad wrote a document recording the life and activities of David (1 Chron 29:29) and assisted David in establishing arrangements for the Temple musicians (2 Chron 29:25).

D. H. MADVIG

GAD (DEITY, A GOD) găd (גַּד, LXX Gen 30:11 τύχη, *fortune, troop* KJV; Isa 65:11 δαίμων, *fortune* RSV, *that troop* KJV). A god of fortune, or good luck, worshiped by certain Sem. peoples. He is usually mentioned with Meni, "Destiny." Isaiah proclaimed that the worshipers of Gad and Meni would suffer judg-

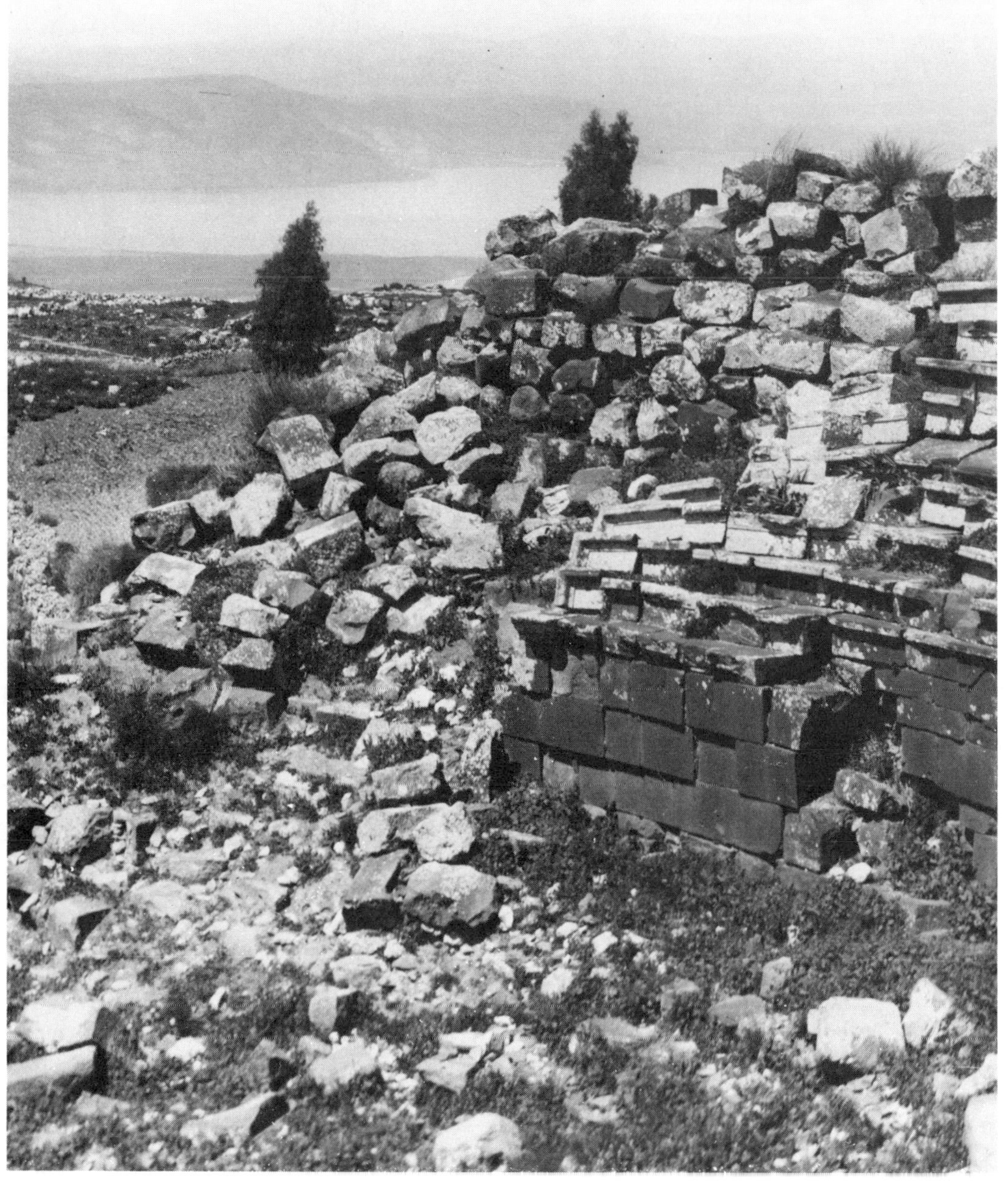

The possible site of Gadara (probable capital of Perea in time of Christ) overlooking the Sea of Galilee. Remains of Roman theater in foreground. Sea of Galilee in background. ©*M.P.S.*

ment (Isa 65:11). Some scholars find a reference to this deity in Leah's naming of her son Gad (Gen 30:11). The popularity of the worship of this god among the Canaanites is manifested by the place names, Baal-gad (Josh 11:17; cf. 12:7; 13:5) and Migdal-gad (Josh 15:37), and the personal names, Gaddi and Gaddiel (Num 13:10, 11). Gad has frequently been equated with the Babylonian god Marduk and with Jupiter.

D. H. MADVIG

GAD, VALLEY OF (TOWARD) (נחל הגד). The phrase "toward Gad," occurs in the RSV (2 Sam 24:5). The KJV has "the river of Gad," whereas the ASV has "the Valley of Gad." It identifies the point where David's census began. The "Aroer" of the context is prob. the city on the N bank of the Arnon, and therefore the "river" or "valley" would be the Arnon.

J. B. SCOTT

GADARA, gă d' ə rə GADARENES, -renz (Γαδαρά; Γαδαρήνες). A city of Transjordania, about six m. SE of the southern end of the Sea of Galilee, one of the cities of the Decapolis; the inhabitants of the city and surrounding countryside, which were predominantly non-Jewish.

1. The gospels. The only NT reference to Gadara (Matt 8:28), is the account of the healing of two demoniacs and the drowning of the swine in the Sea of Galilee. The parallel passages (Mark 5:1; Luke 8:26; cf. v. 37), though mentioning the one demoniac, refer to the same episode.

In each gospel reference there is a textual variant concerning the spelling of the name. The RSV reading of "Gadarenes" (Matt) and "Gerasenes" (Mark and Luke) is correct according to the textual evidence, and suggests some difficulty in identifying the place. This problem of harmonization is resolved if one remembers that each reference is to the country (ἡ χώρα) of the Gadarenes-Gerasenes. The geography and history sources show that the area designations prob. overlapped; Gadara was the chief city of the immediate area, whereas Gerasa may have referred to a wider area including the lesser city of Gadara. Matthew gives a specific reference to the Gadarenes, Mark and Luke a more general reference to Gerasenes. The third reading "Gergesenes," although it has poor MS evidence and obviously is a late, confused effort to harmonize the synoptic texts, yet gives the best location for the incident near the village of Gergesa. Although topographical maps show hills all along the SE shore of the Sea of Galilee, geographers who visited the area say the only place to locate the drowning swine incident is a strip of steep coastline near Gergesa, the present-day Kersa (cf. GERASA, GERGESA).

2. History. Several references to Gadara appear in Josephus. In the Maccabean wars, Alexander Jannaeus took the city after a ten-month siege (Jos. Antiq., XII, iii. 3; Jos. War, I. iv. 2) and demolished it. After the Rom. conquest it was rebuilt by Pompey in 63 B.C. (War. I. vii. 7) and made a "free" city. Gabinius made it the capital of one of the five districts of occupied Pal. Herod the Great received it as a gift from Augustus in 30 B.C. (Jos. Antiq. XV. vii. 3; Jos. War. I, xx. 3). Herod ruled it harshly and was sustained in his policy by the emperor (Jos Antiq. XV. x. 3). At Herod's death it was annexed to Syria (Jos. Antiq. XVII. xi. 4; Jos. War, II. xviii. 1). During the rebellion of A.D. 68-70 it fell quickly to Vespasian, who burned it and plundered the countryside (Jos. War, III. vii. 1). Rebuilt again, it flourished, as coins from the city show, until A.D. 240. It had a Christian church from the 2nd cent. and was the seat of a bishop from A.D. 325 until the Moslem conquest.

3. Archeology. Gadara is identified today as Muqeis, or Umm Qeis, overlooking the S valley of the Yarmuk river. The ruins are extensive, including remnants of two amphitheaters, a basilica, a temple, colonnades, large residences, and an aqueduct, all showing the size, beauty, and importance of the city.

Another Gadara is mentioned by Josephus as "the capital of Perea" (Jos. War, IV. vii. 3), but he may have confused it with Gerasa.

BIBLIOGRAPHY. W. A. Thomson, *The Land and the Book* (1882) 333-338, 353-359; A. Plummer, *Gospel According to St. Matthew* (1909), 132, 133; M. F. Unger, *Archaeology and the New Testament* (1962), 139-141.

J. C. DEYOUNG

GADDI gă d' ī (גדי, LXX Γαδδί, may mean *fortune*) KJV Apoc. CADDIS, *kăd'ĭs* (1 Macc 2:2).

1. The son of Susi of the tribe of Manasseh, one of the twelve spies whom Moses sent from the wilderness of Paran to spy out the land of Canaan (Num 13:11).

2. A name of John (KJV Johanan) the son of Mattathias and brother of Judas Maccabeus, all of whom were leading figures in the Jewish struggle for independence (1 Macc 2:2).

D. H. MADVIG

GADDIS Gă d' əs (Γαδδί, 1 Macc 2:2). This was the surname of John (KJV Johanan), the son of Mattathias and eldest brother of Judas Maccabeus. With the latter he joined in the struggle for Jewish independence in the 2nd cent. B.C.

GADFLY (קרץ, meaning uncertain, perhaps "nipping" [KJV: "destruction"]). A stinging insect.

Gadflies include both botflies (*Oestridae*) and horseflies (*Tabanidae*). They approach their victims, such as livestock, with a loud hum and inflict painful bites. The term is applied metaphorically to Nebuchadrezzar (Jer 46:20), described as a gadfly coming from the N upon Egypt. This he did in 568-567 B.C. It has been suggested that the plague of flies visited upon the Egyptians (Exod 8:20, 31 [MT 8:16-27]) was a plague of gadflies. Here the Heb. word is עָרֹב, which prob. means simply, "swarm."

K. L. BARKER

GADI Găd' ī (גָּדִי, *my fortune*). This man was the father of King Menahem of Israel who usurped the throne from SHALLUM (2 Kings 15:14-20). Gadi may be short for GADDIEL (גַּדִּיאֵל, "God is my fortune").

GADITES. Members of the tribe of GAD.

GAHAM gā' hăm (גַּחַם, *flame, burning brightly*). This man was listed as the second son of Nahor, the brother of Abram, by his concubine Reumah (Gen 22:24).

GAHAR gā' här (גַּחַר, LXX Γααρ). The sons of Gahar were among the Temple servants (KJV Nethinim) who returned with Zerubbabel from exile in Babylon (Ezra 2:47; Neh 7:49).

GAI gā' ī (גַּיא, LXX Γεθ, Γαι, *valley*, RSV *Gath*, KJV *the valley*). A locality mentioned in 1 Samuel 17:52 together with Ekron as the limit to which the Israelites chased the Philistines after the victory of David over Goliath. The absence of the article in MT argues against tr. "the valley" as in KJV. The last half of the verse, as well as the reading of the LXX and the Syriac, strongly suggests the reading "Gath" as in RSV.

D. H. MADVIG

GAIN. In the OT this word is the rendering of three Heb. nouns: בֶּצַע, "gain made by violence," "unjust gain" or "profit" (Judg 5:19 KJV "gain," RSV "spoils"; Job 22:3; Prov 1:19; 15:27; Isa 33:15; 56:11; Mic 4:13); מְחִיר, "price," "hire"; in Daniel 11:39 it means "reward," "gain" (RSV "price"); תְּבוּאָה, "increase," "fruit" (Prov 3:14). Two Heb. verbs also are thus rendered: בָּצַע, "to gain by violence" or "dishonestly" (Job 27:8 KJV); זָבַן, "to gain," "buy" (Dan 2:8).

In the NT there are three Gr. nouns that are tr. work: ἐργασία, "work," "business" (Acts 16:16, 19; 19:24 KJV "gains," RSV "business"; κέρδος, "gain" (Phil 1:21—Paul says that for him to live is Christ and to die is gain, 3:7); πορισμός, "a means of gain" (1 Tim 6:5, 6—Paul says that godliness with contentment is great gain). Three Gr. verbs mean "to gain": κερδαίνω, "to make gain" or "profit" (Matt 16:26; 18:15; 25:17, 20, 22, KJV "gain," RSV "made"; Mark 8:36; Luke 9:25; Acts 27:21—KJV "gain," RSV "incurred"; 1 Cor 9:19, 20, 21, 22, KJV "gain," RSV "win"); προσεργάζομαι, "to gain besides," by working or trading (Luke 19:16 KJV; RSV "made"); ποιέω "to make" (Luke 19:18 KJV; RSV "made").

J. C. CONNELL

GAIUS gā' yəs (Γάϊος, Gr. form of Lat. Gaius, *rejoiced, I am glad*). A common name. 1. A Macedonian Christian; as Paul's companions in travel, he and Aristarchus were seized by the mob during the Ephesian riot (Acts 19:29).

2. A Christian of Derbe, one of the group waiting for Paul at Troas (Acts 20:4). They apparently were the delegates from the churches who went with Paul to Jerusalem with the collection. The variant reading Δουβέριος in Codex D makes him a Macedonian from Doberius. With this reading he could readily be identified with 1. above.

3. A Christian in Corinth; one of two men whom Paul names as having been baptized by him, contrary to his usual practice (1 Cor 1:14, 17). He doubtless was the same as the Gaius who was Paul's host when he wrote Romans from Corinth on the third journey (Rom 16:23). That he was host also "to the whole church" implies that the Corinthian church met in his spacious home. Tradition has made him the bishop of Thessalonica. Some would identify him with the Titius Justus of Acts 18:7.

4. The addressee of 3 John. John had a deep affection for him, commended him for his hospitality, and desired his continued support for missionaries being sent out by John. There is no evidence to identify him with any of the above.

BIBLIOGRAPHY. E. J. Goodspeed, "Gaius Titius Justus," JBL, 69 (1950), 382, 383.

D. E. HIEBERT

GALAAD. KJV and Douay VS forms of GILEAD.

GALAL gā' lăl (גָּלָל, LXX Γαλαλ, perhaps *A rolling away*). 1. One of the Levites who returned to the tribe's possessions from exile in Babylonia (1 Chron 9:15).

2. The son of Jeduthun and grandfather of Obadiah (or Abda, Neh 11:17), one of the Levites who returned to the tribe's possessions from Babylonian exile (1 Chron 9:16).

D. H. MADVIG

GALATIA (Γαλατία). The word bears two senses in ancient history and geography. In its first and ethnic meaning, it signifies the kingdom of Galatia in the northern part of the inner plateau of Asia Minor, made up of parts of a territory formerly known as Cappadocia and Phrygia. The name derives from the fact that this area was occupied by "Gauls," a Celtic people who, in one of the final movements of the two thousand-year-old folk-wanderings of the Indo-European tribes, crossed the Hellespont at the unwise invitation of Nicomedes I, king of Bithynia, who sought allies in a civil war, and penetrated the Asia Minor peninsula in 278 B.C. After a typical period of raiding and plundering, the nomad invaders were finally pinned and contained in a tract of high territory extending from the Sangarius to a line E of the Halys. This was the achievement of Attalus I of Pergamum in 230 B.C. From this tribal area the Celts continued their petty harassment of their neighbors, and after the battle of Magnesia in 190 B.C., which marked the beginning of Rom. interest and dominance in Asia Minor, the Republic inherited the Gallic problem.

Rome sent Manlius Vulso to subdue the tribesmen, and he did so with effectiveness in a campaign of 188 B.C. With typical Rom. diplomatic skill, the Republic was able to use the Galatians as a check on the dynamic kingdom of Pergamum, and also to retain their allegiance when Mithridates of Pontus launched his strong attacks on Rome in Asia Minor. Galatia, as a tribal region, was organized on a Celtic pattern, the three ethnic groups Tolistobogii, Tectusages, and Trocmi, occupying separate areas, with distinct capitals—Pessinus, Ancyra, and Tavium respectively. Each tribe was divided into four septs or wards, each under a tetrarch. The combined council of the three tribes had provision for periodic meetings and retained collective jurisdicition in cases of murder. So coherent was their community, that its Celtic character survived into the empire, and Jerome is evidence for their retention of their Gallic speech into the 5th century. Part of Pompey's organization of Asia in 63 B.C. appears to have been the establishment of a paramount ruler in Galatia. Deiotarus, tetrarch of the Tolistobogii of W Galatia, was of considerable help to Pompey in the third Mithridatic War. He was rewarded by Pompey in 64 B.C. with part of neighboring Pontus, and twelve or thirteen years later received from the Senate of Rome the district of Lesser Armenia and the kingship over the area of his control, together with the resultant royal title.

The Galatian king naturally followed Pompey in the civil war between Pompey and Julius Caesar, and was deprived of his territorial acquisitions by Caesar on his victory. In 45 B.C. he was accused before Caesar of various acts of insubordination, and was defended by the great orator Cicero, whose speech for the accused survives. Deiotarus had prudently befriended Cicero's son, during the orator's governorship of Cilicia. After Caesar's assassination in the following year, Deiotarus regained control of his lost territory, and bought recognition from Antony. He supported Brutus and Cassius in the renewed civil war, again a wrong choice, but one hardly to be avoided when the "tyrannicides" lay across his communications with Rome. By a timely desertion to Antony at Philippi, Deiotarus retained his kingdom, and in 42 B.C., after murdering a rival tetrarch, he acquired all of Galatia and associated regions. These details of petty history are important because they mark the course of the evolution of the ethnic region of Galatia into the multi-racial Rom. province, and the freedom with which Rome habitually varied frontier lines to suit administrative expediency.

Deiotarus died in 40 B.C., and was succeeded by his secretary, Amyntas, who had commanded the Galatian auxiliaries of Brutus and Cassius at Philippi, and had shared in, or prompted, the desertion of the Galatian contingent to Antony. Antony rewarded Amyntas in 39 B.C. with a Galatian kingdom which ultimately included parts of Lycia, Pamphylia, and Pisidia. Amyntas accompanied Antony to Actium, when Antony and Octavian clashed in the final phase of the civil strife which saw the end of the Roman Republic, and history repeated itself. A Galatian prince was, by force of geographical and political circumstances, on the wrong side. Again, a timely desertion, this time before the actual armed clash of Actium's decisive naval battle, won the favor of the victor. Octavian, soon to emerge from the long strife as the Emperor Augustus, confirmed Amyntas in all his royal possessions.

Amyntas died in a campaign against unruly highlanders on the mountainous southern marches of his realm. It was in 25 B.C. that Augustus, engaged in the long task of establishing the Rom. peace, and organizing its frontiers, seized the opportunity to convert Amyntas' realm, augmented by parts of Phrygia, Lycaonia, Pisidia, and possibly Pamphylia, into a province called Galatia. The precedent of including slices of contiguous territory under Galatian control had been set by Pompey. Augustus' principate merely adapted, adopted and applied precedents which had been established at least since the days of the great Pompey. Portions of Paphlagonia and Pontus were afterward incorporated into the province, which was normally governed by a praetorian legate until A.D. 72. In this year Cappadocia and Lesser Armenia were included in the Galatian provincial boundaries, and the augmented province was placed under consular legate. Another reorganization under Trajan saw Galatia again reduced in A.D. 137. Under Diocletian the province had shrunk almost to the old ethnic area of the original Galatian tribal lands. The chief cities in the 1st century were Ancyra and the Pisidian Antioch. Within the province of Galatia were also the other towns visited by Paul in his fruitful first journey into Asia Minor—Iconium, Lystra, and Derbe, all of which included large populations of Romans and other Italian expatriates, Greeks, and Jews.

The precise meaning of the term Galatia is of some importance in NT studies and involves a modern controversy which cannot be said to be completely resolved. It is beyond question from the full account given in Acts 13 and 14, that Paul visited urban centers in the southern part of the province, and established Christian communities there. On the very slender evidence of Acts 16:6, some have contended that he also visited northern Galatia, the habitat of the Celtic stratum of the population, and also established churches there. It was to these churches, marked by their volatile, excitable, Celtic congregations, that Paul addressed the strictures of his letter "to the Galatians." The opening clause of Acts 16:6, of which so much is demanded, runs in KJV: "Now when they had gone throughout Phrygia and the region of Galatia . . . ." W. M. Ramsay cogently demonstrated that the clause described a single area and is to be rendered "the Phrygian Galatic region." Roman provinces were administratively cut into "regions." Rome's tampering with ancient boundary lines has been noted above, and was a feature of her government and organization in Asia Minor. Part of the onetime kingdom of Galatia was incorporated in the province of Galatia, as it was constituted after the death of Amyntas. Another part belonged to the province of Asia. It is reasonable then to interpret the opening clause of the verse under discussion as a reference to the section of Phrygian territory which was included in the new province of Galatia. This is an interpretation clearly supported by the rest of the verse concerning the constraint felt by the apostle not at that time to extend his activities into the neighboring province of Asia by moving westward from Pisidia.

This is not the proper place to discuss Acts 18:23 where the same geographical expression is encountered in reverse. R. J. Knowling has a lucid and sufficient comment upon it in EGT II. 341, where he quotes periodical lit. relevant to the controversy. A. Souter has also a brief clear statement (HDB p. 277). At any time epigraphy, in a rich archeological field, may provide evidence which will remove all perplexity. In the meantime, while the brevity of Luke's account of Paul's activity over considerable tracts of his ministry, and even his occasional complete silence, may be granted, it seems clear that the Galatian churches known to the NT were those founded in the more sophisticated and multi-racial parts of the province. Such foundations were certainly consonant with Paul's obvious Gentile strategy. Christian communities may have been established in the northern Celtic reaches of the province at a comparatively early date, but if so their foundation must have been due to unrecorded diffusion from the more civilized S, and not to the personal penetration of the ethnic area by the apostle.

The strong consensus of modern scholarship would therefore agree that the Galatians addressed in Paul's famous letter were the southern communities of his own planting, and it would follow that the "churches of Galatia," of which Paul makes mention to the Corinthians (1 Cor 16:1) were the same group. Did Paul ever use the term Galatia in other than its Rom. sense? He was a self-conscious Rom. citizen, and used language from that point of view, not in a parochial sense. He may even be observed rejecting an available alternative term and turning a Lat. word into Gr. ("Illyricum," Rom 15:19 is an example). The Galatians to his mind could not be the inhabitants of an ethnic area. They were the inhabitants of a province, and in his context the whole body of Christians from that area, regardless of race. It is on historical grounds rather than linguistic, and on the fact that there is no clear evidence either of a visit to N Galatia, or a facet of Pauline policy which would make such a visit likely, that it may be assumed with some confidence that the Galatians addressed were the Christian communities of Pisidian Antioch, Iconium, Lystra, and Derbe. A balanced brief review of the arguments arrayed for both N and S "Galatian Theories," with due weight given to arguments advanced for the former, is to be found in R. A. Cole's small commentary on the Galatian letter (pp. 16-20, Tyndale NT Commentaries).

It remains to mention the listing of Galatians among those to whom the first general epistle of Peter is addressed. The bearer of the letter obviously moved in a southward bending curve from E to W through the northern half of Asia Minor, the long deep tract of territory N of the Taurus Range. Facilities for travel were abundant, and the fact that church communities in Pontus, Galatia, Cappadocia, Asia, and Bithynia were addressed reveals the active Christian life apparent in the peninsula. Nothing, however, can be deduced about the pattern of Galatian Christianity, for however deeply the faith may have penetrated northern ethnic Galatia, an epistle couched in terms so general, a circular, in fact, cannot be supposed to have omitted the strong Christian communities in the multi-racial S.

BIBLIOGRAPHY. W. M. Ramsay, *Saint Paul the Traveller and Roman Citizen* (1898); *An Historical Commentary on the Epistle to the Galatians* (1900); F. Stahelin, *Geschichte der Kleinasiatischen Galater* (2 Auflage, 1907); W. M. Ramsay, *The Church in the Roman Empire* (1911); A. H. M. Jones, *Cities of the Eastern Provinces* (1937); R. A. Cole, *The Epistle of Paul to the Galatians* (1965); E. M. Blaiklock, *Cities of the New Testament* (1966).

E. M. Blaiklock

GALATIANS, EPISTLE TO

1. Introduction
2. The author
3. The historical background
4. The Judaizers
5. Destination and readers
6. Date and place of writing
7. Theme and purpose
8. Contents and outline
9. Characteristics and special features

1. Introduction. The Epistle to the Galatians

is one of Paul's greatest and most important letters. It contains in substance what the apostle taught and which he had received by divine revelation (Gal 1:12). Many have characterized the letter as a "short Romans." Indeed, Romans may well be an expansion of Galatians. A comparison of the two epistles reveals that they are similar in theme and contents—both teach boldly the Pauline doctrine of justification by faith and the ethical imperatives which are the fruits of the Gospel of love.

Great men in the Church have esteemed Galatians highly. It has been the source of strength and guidance for many. For the reformers of the Reformation Era it was Galatians, more than any other single book, which became the manifesto of freedom and revival of Biblical truth. The epistle was a favorite of Luther. In it he found strength for his own faith and life and an arsenal of weapons for his reforming work. He said of the letter: "The Epistle to the Galatians is *my own little epistle.* I have betrothed myself to it; it is my Katie von Bora" (name of Luther's wife). Luther lectured on Galatians extensively and his *Commentary on Galatians,* one of his early books of the Reformation, did much to expound the dominant theme of the reform movement, the doctrine of justification by *faith alone,* to the common people. Dr. William Ramsay, the famous Eng. scholar, described Galatians in this manner: "It is a unique and marvelous letter, which embraces in its six short chapters such a variety of vehement and intense emotion as could probably not be paralleled in any other work." Farrar had this estimate of the letter: "The words scrawled on those few sheets of paper were destined to wake echoes which have lived, and shall live forever and ever—they were the Magna Charta of spiritual emancipation." Another scholar has said the Galatian letter is "the pebble from the brook with which the Reformers smote the papal giant of the Middle Ages" and that it was the cornerstone and battle cry of the Protestant Reformation. Dr. Merrill Tenney writes, "Few books have had a more profound influence on the history of mankind than has this small tract, for such it should be called. Christianity might have been just one more Jewish sect, and the thought of the Western world might have been entirely pagan had it never been written. Galatians embodies the germinal teaching on Christian freedom which separated Christianity from Judaism, and which launched it upon a career of missionary conquest. It was the cornerstone of the Protestant Reformation, because its teaching of salvation by grace alone became the dominant theme of the preaching of the Reformers" (*Galatians: The Charter of Christian Liberty,* p. 15).

It is true that the letter, because of its extremely high doctrinal content, its apologetic nature, and its lack of poetic beauty, has not always been well known or highly favored in some eras of the Church's history, but since the Reformation it has come into its own and has been recognized particularly for what it meant to the Early Church. Its bold succinct definition of the beloved Gospel *in terms of people* in the third chapter was like an ancient "shot heard around the world" and its note of freedom has struck the inner cords of millions of oppressed hearts. No words on human worth and equality and the universality of Christianity have ever matched these: "Now that faith has come, we are no longer under a custodian; for in Christ Jesus you are all sons of God, through faith. For as many of you as were baptized into Christ have put on Christ. There is neither Jew nor Greek, there is neither slave nor free, there is neither male nor female; for you are all one in Christ Jesus" (3:25-28). The church of the Protestant Reformation has always prized its doctrinal contents, esp. its mighty statement and defense of justification by faith alone and its glorious defense of spiritual liberty against any form of legalism. It has always been an impregnable citadel against any attack on the heart of the Gospel, salvation by grace through faith: "For all who rely on works of the law are under a curse; for it is written, 'Cursed be every one who does not abide by all things written in the book of the law, and do them.' Now it is evident that no man is justified before God by the law; for 'He who through faith is righteous shall live'; but the law does not rest on faith, for 'He who does them shall live by them.' Christ redeemed us from the curse of the law, having become a curse for us" (3:10-13). In short, in Galatians we meet for the first time the great Pauline teaching of justification by faith which has helped people to understand the love of God and the person and work of Jesus Christ.

2. The author. The Church has always believed that the Apostle Paul wrote the Epistle to the Galatians. Except for one or two extremely radical scholars, no one has ever attacked the genuineness of Galatians, that is, that the letter came from the Apostle Paul. Biblical scholars both ancient and modern attest to the Pauline authorship. Most radical critics have agreed not only to Pauline characteristics but also Pauline authorship. Noted scholars today in their writings on Galatians no longer discuss the matter. The obvious reason for this situation is that from every possible consideration—ancient attestation, the literary style, the doctrinal content, the historical background, literary analysis—the letter leaves no room for doubt. Everyone admits that, if there ever lived a man like Paul who is known from other books he wrote, then Galatians must have come from him.

Dr. Findlay once said: "No breath of suspicion as to the authorship, integrity, or apostolic authorship of the Epistle to the Galatians has reached us from ancient times." The great scholar Lightfoot wrote: "Its every sentence so completely reflects the life and character of the Apostle of the Gentiles that its genuineness has not been seriously questioned." In recent decades the letter has stood as a solid wall against any criticism that would deny any of the letters of Paul. The external testimony of the ancient church leaders to the Pauline authorship of Galatians is unambiguous. One of the earliest Church Fathers, Clement of Rome, refers to the letter in his writings. Polycarp and Barnabas knew of Galatians, as did Hermas and Ignatius. Even Marcion, who excluded entire blocks of the NT writings from his early canon, placed the letter on his choice list and refers to it by title. Justin Martyr uses the third chapter of the letter to interpret the OT in the light of Paul's doctrine. Both the faithful man and the heretic assume it was written by Paul. Early Gnostic interpreters used the epistle. Irenaeus, Tertullian and Clement of Alexandria quote the letter and refer to Paul as the author.

The internal evidence is just as strong and certain as the witness from without. Most important, the author of the letter courageously calls himself "Paul an apostle—not from men nor through man, but through Jesus Christ and God the Father" (1:1). And in the body of the letter an almost unprecedented statement of Pauline authorship is found "Now *I, Paul,* say to you that if you receive circumcision, Christ will be of no advantage to you" (5:2). All of the personal and historical references in the first two chapters fit perfectly into the mission activity and life of Paul recorded in Acts. The letter exhibits the mind and fervor, logic and style of Paul in every detail. His doctrine of freedom in Christ is like that emphasized in other of his writings (5:1). His contention against the law as a way to salvation and his love of faith and justification are unmistakably Pauline. Parallels in his letters, such as the use of Abraham and the OT, are easily found: "Abraham 'believed God, and it was reckoned to him as righteousness' " (3:6; Rom 4:3-5); or the Jew-Gentile dilemma as exposed in his opposition to Peter: "If you, though a Jew, live like a Gentile and not like a Jew, how can you compel the Gentiles to live like Jews?" (2:14; Eph 2:4-19); or the discussion of circumcision (2:12; 5:2-6; 6:12-16; Rom 4:9-12); his teaching of the Holy Spirit (5:16-25; Rom 5:5) or his ethical teaching based upon the gospel of faith and freedom (5:13-23; Col 3:1-11) all of which match the teaching, and often the phraseology, of Paul exactly. A forger could not have imitated the mind and style of the Pauline teaching and paranesis, or placed himself into the Galatian situation with the feeling and understanding of the apostle. The burning issues of the middle of the 1st cent. of the Church's history when Paul traversed the old Rom. world are those prominent in the epistle. How could another writer have placed antithesis between two great leaders of the time—Peter and Paul? Those few critics who have placed the writing of Galatians after the death of Paul, did the same with such great letters as 1 and 2 Corinthians and even Romans—a view of the NT situation which cannot be considered worthy of solid NT scholarship.

3. The historical background. Paul's personal experience in his conversion is directly related to the question of the epistle: faith or works? Obviously this is why he writes with such fervor and conviction in absolute categories. Assuming that he was converted about A.D. 32 and wrote Galatians in A.D. 48 or 49, he had more than fifteen years of spiritual preparation for his missionary treks and epistolary efforts. He speaks of his conversion in Heb. before the crowd at the Temple in Jerusalem (Acts 22:1-21. cf. Acts 9:1-19) and before King Agrippa in Caesarea (Acts 26:1-32) and defends his doctrine of salvation by faith. In both addresses, before both friend and foe, his purpose is to offer his conversion as the greatest proof of his discipleship and the truth of his doctrine that a man is saved by faith and not by works. In his first letter to Timothy he described his conversion in glowing terms of grace as the epitome of the validity of the Gospel which he expounded and defended so magnificently in Galatians: "Though I formerly blasphemed and persecuted and insulted him; but I received mercy because I had acted ignorantly in unbelief, and the grace of our Lord overflowed *for me* with the faith and love that are in Christ Jesus. The saying is sure and worthy of full acceptance, that Christ Jesus came into the world to save sinners. And I am the foremost of sinners" (1 Tim 1:13-16).

His most effective use of his conversion experience in behalf of the Gospel of grace is in Galatians itself: "For I would have you know, brethren, that the gospel which was preached by me is not man's gospel. For I did not receive it from man, nor was I taught it, but it came through a revelation of Jesus Christ. For you have heard of my former life in Judaism, how I persecuted the church of God violently and tried to destroy it; and I advanced in Judaism beyond many of my own age among my people, so extremely zealous was I for the tradition of my fathers. But when he who had set me apart before I was born, and had called me through his grace, was pleased to reveal his Son to me, in order that I might preach him among the Gentiles, I did not confer with flesh and blood, nor did I go up to Jerusalem to those who were apostles before me, but I went away into Arabia" (Gal 1:11-17).

For Paul it all began on the Damascus Road and there was no road back. He penned Galatians to plead with all Christians to take only the Damascus Road—any other road leads to "another gospel." These events preceding the

The House of Ananias near Straight Street in Damascus, where Paul began to learn the lessons he shared with the Galatians. © *M.P.S.*

writing of Galatians help explain the letter itself and make it clear that only such a man could have written it. He is alone with his Lord in Arabia, perhaps for several years, meditating, thinking, dialoging, preparing (Gal 1:13-17). The urge to tell others moved him to return to Damascus, prob. around A.D. 34, 35. It is enemy territory now—former friends make the fiercest enemies. A plot to take his life in Damascus caused him to seek shelter in Jerusalem (Acts 9:26-28; Gal 1:18). It was a short visit of two weeks and his enemies tried to kill him once more, but his brethren whisked him away to Caesarea where he boarded a ship and made his way to his home town of Tarsus (Acts 9:29-31; Gal 1:21-24). All of this strife for the new convert against his former "friends" makes up the marrow of the Galatian letter and gives it the light and heat of newfound freedom in Christ. The years spent in Tarsus and Cilicia, on the fringe of the Galatian area into which he pushed on his first missionary journey, comprised more spiritual and mystical preparation for the road ahead.

Always the brethren know of Paul's whereabouts and of his fervor for Christ. It is prob. true that he preached and defended this Gospel in Cilicia between the years A.D. 36-43 because later the Apostolic Council sent communications to the Gentile brethren in Antioch and Cilicia (Acts 15:24). And in Acts 15:41 Luke writes that Paul was going to strengthen the churches of Syria and Cilicia. His first journey took him much farther W, so he must have witnessed in this area during his so-called "silent years." All the while the pressure between the (gospel of) "freedom men" and the "legal men" was building up until it reached the heated pitch of the Galatian polemic.

According to an accepted order of events, however, the first missionary journey intervened (Acts 13:1-14:28). The church in Antioch was growing tremendously. The Jerusalem brethren asked Barnabas to journey to Antioch and to assist and lead the work. More workers were needed and Barnabas went to Tarsus to get Paul and brought him to Antioch. Paul worked in Antioch with Barnabas (Acts 11:26) and other leaders in Antioch (Acts 13:1). There was scarcity of food and famine in Jerusalem, and Paul and Barnabas were asked to take a collection of food and grain to the brethren in that city. After a few weeks in the Holy City they made their way back to Antioch to resume the work there. The gospel of freedom should not be contained—it is for all men. John Mark went with them (Gal 2:1-21; Acts 12:24, 25). Then we are told that the Holy Spirit Himself instructed the young church: "Set apart for me Barnabas and Saul for the work to which I have called them." With fasting and prayer the church "laid their hands on them and sent them off" (Acts 13:2, 3).

The first mission odyssey began—a portent

Site of ancient Derbe where Paul fled after the strong Jewish opposition in Iconium. © *V.E.*

of many more to come. John Mark joined the mission group. They left from Seleucia and sailed to Cyprus. Astounding events in Salamis and Paphos! The power of the gospel of freedom was felt by Rom. officials and magicians. Luke describes one of the great gospel events of ancient times: "Then the proconsul believed, when he saw what had occurred, for he was astonished at the teaching of the Lord" (Acts 13:1-13). They left the island and headed for the mainland of Asia Minor. Perga in Pamphylia, Antioch of Pisidia—the strategy was to visit the cities and towns of the area, the heavily populated areas. Christ has freed all men and all men must hear the good news (Acts 13:38, 39). They preached the Kerygma: Jesus is the Messiah, fulfiller of the Old Testament. Many believed in the risen Lord. John Mark left the expedition at Pamphylia and returned home —perhaps the work was too difficult and free for the young Jerusalemite. Preaching in the synagogues of Antioch gave rise to opposition because of Jewish law. The extent of the inner division was beginning to be felt outwardly. "When the Jews saw the multitudes, they were filled with jealousy, and contradicted what was spoken by Paul, and reviled him. . . . the Jews incited the devout women of high standing and the leading men of the city, and stirred up persecution against Paul and Barnabas, and drove them out of their district" (13:45-52). We are reminded that in Galatians Paul did not neglect to chastise severely to correct the error.

Iconium up in the hill country was next—again the Jews stirred up opposition. Paul would long remember the work of these "Judaizers," or "lovers of law," as we call them today. Then came Lystra. Here the apostle was stoned; Derbe was next, the quiet receptive city—but everywhere it was much the same as it was in Iconium: "But the people of the city were divided; some sided with the Jews, and some with the apostles" (Acts 14:2-4). Sometimes both Gentiles and Jews were ready to stone them. Always "the unbelieving Jews stirred up the Gentiles and poisoned their minds against the brethren" (Acts 14:2-20). Already one can hear the clarion call of Galatians: "O foolish Galatians! Who has bewitched you, before whose eyes Jesus Christ was publicly portrayed as crucified? Let me ask you only this: Did you receive the Spirit by works of the law, or by hearing with faith?" (3:1-4). But the legalistic enemies with their problems of circumcision were still working openly in the Galatian congregations (Gal 5:6-12). They must be counteracted; it takes only a little leaven to spoil the whole group (Gal 5:9). "You were called to freedom, brethren. . . . in Christ Jesus neither circumcision nor uncircumcision is of any avail, but faith working through love" (Gal 5:13, 6). This was the real issue and carried over into the Apostolic Council (Acts 15). Against this foil the Epistle of Galatians was written and finds its meaning.

4. The Judaizers. Almost without exception, Biblical interpreters who have written a commentary on Galatians believe that the letter was written primarily to counteract the activities of the Judaizers in Galatia. The mischievous work of these "legal men" is described in general in the previous section on the historical background; a more specific, though brief, treatment of these "Old Testament Christians" might be useful in aiding the reader to understand more fully the contents and the theological issue of Galatians. Who was a Judaizer and why was he called thus? The term is derived from a coined Lat. word *Iudaizo* meaning "to be or live like a Jew." It is a religious designation rather than a national description. Bible students have called these opponents of the early Christian missionaries Judaizers because of their fundamental belief that Gentiles should live like Jews; that is, follow the Mosaic Law and Jewish customs and traditions, when and after they became Christians. It is not that Judaizers were wicked people or that they did not have good intentions; *for them* the issue was a matter of principle and from God Himself. But the implications of their insistence upon Jewish ceremonial law for the young Christian Church, both theologically and socially, were volatile and divisive indeed.

The situation was brought about by the teaching of Jesus Himself on the law, the doctrine of grace and of God's love for all men, on the one hand; and, on the other, by the mixture of Jews and Gentiles in the early Christian churches. It was one thing to preach grace to Jews only (and it may be assumed that Jewish Christians may have misunderstood the requirements of the kingdom even as they worshiped Christ); it was quite another task to preach the Gospel of Christ and freedom to Jews, Greeks, Syrians and Mr. Everyman in the same congregation, esp. if it were still in the Jewish synagogue. After all, the Jewish person had been circumcised, he knew the glory of Israel, he knew the pride of Judaism with its one God and high morality; but the poor Gentile, what did he have? The Jew could easily summarize it for him: false gods, fornication, immorality, drunkenness, etc. Surely, it was not enough just to give up these practices and simply believe—that was really cheap grace—but if one really wanted to be a Christian, like Jesus Himself, he should really be a Jew first and then both a Jew and a Christian. No doubt many early Gentile Christians attempted to imitate their Jewish fellow believers, or at least tried not to offend them, but when it came to circumcision, for adults particularly, with its accompanying irritation, annoyance and inconvenience, esp. when the apostles said there was "neither circumcision nor uncircumcision in the kingdom," the reluctance for a Gentile to accede became strong indeed. Thus the issue finally boiled down to circumcision and few other things (Acts 15) and not even the Apostolic Council settled the matter. This is why it is rather fruitless to debate on these grounds whether or not Galatians was written before or after the Council—the issue was so emotional and tense that several councils and apostolic epistles could hardly bring peace entirely.

The tension was tightened by the fact that the first churches in Pal. were Jewish (Christ came for the Jews, too; the kingdom was for *all* men). Paul himself said "Jew first and also . . . the Greek" (Rom 1:16); and by the method of Paul and his co-workers of going to the Jewish synagogues outside of Pal. as their first contact for preaching the Gospel in an area or city. In these synagogues were also men who were "devout converts to Judaism" (Acts 13:43) and people described as "men who fear God," Gentiles who were "proselytes of the gate" and not fully converted to Judaism or involved in the synagogue, but who liked its high moral character and monotheism. These "fringe people" were made to order for the new church. Yet Paul tried to be "all things to all men" and in preaching to the Jews (even though there were Gentiles in the audience) showed again and again that the prophets and John the Baptist and Jesus Himself taught that all the OT was preparatory to the Messiah and the new kingdom (Acts 13:26-41). At the same time Paul made it plain that the Gospel was no addendum to Judaism, no mere supplement to the law, but the end and fulfillment of the law and the antithesis to it. The new kingdom would go beyond the boundaries of Israel, not just nationally but also theologically and socially—even though Jesus the Messiah came from David's line, now "every one that believes is *freed from everything* from which you could not be freed by the law of Moses" (Acts 13:39).

The doors of the new church were thrown open to everyone—to Jews, Jewish proselytes, Gentiles, publicans, sinners—*and everyone had direct access to God through Christ by faith.* Paul was saying out loud what for so long had been in the scrolls and parchments of the OT, in Pentecost, in Jesus' ministry, in the calling of publicans as apostles, and he was practicing it in a new social situation. As a result large numbers of people of all kinds, Gentiles and slaves, came into the church *without circumcision*, not through the synagogue, not by doing all the laws and customs of the OT, but directly. These people came in "Just as I am, without one plea"; they took the apostles at their word. But this was too much for Jews who had grown up in Judaism and their true thoughts and attitudes began to come to the surface. No one wanted to deny a Gentile the privileges of membership, but surely there was more to it than just believing. Perhaps it was not so much that they as Jews had to bear the burden of the law all those years "till Christ came" (although Luke writes that "when the Jews saw the multitudes [in Antioch of Pisidia], they were filled with jealousy," Acts 13:45), but the great glory and validity of the OT. Was not the OT from

Moses by God's will? Were all God's covenants, rites, symbols, His relationship to the Commonwealth of Israel, and everything else to be discarded just because Christ came? Were the ancient people of God, the children of Abraham, simply to disappear from history?

It is not surprising, then, that strong-minded Jewish people became vigorous Judaizers. They came from within the new church. One gets the feeling from following their activities in Acts that they were not from the congregations or synagogues in the mission churches, but men from other churches who followed Paul about undoing his work. While they were primarily of Jewish origin, it is not impossible that there may have been some misguided Gentile proselytes among them who had gone through the demands of Judaism and were circumcised when they joined the Christian Church and wanted all other Gentiles to do the same. Luke calls them simply "unbelieving Jews" (Acts 14:2). It was easy for them to operate in the church which was in the stage of transition from a Jewish nationalistic group to a Gentile–Jewish membership, whether the Jews or the Gentiles were in a majority in a given congregation. The Judaizers reasoned as follows: They did not come to destroy Paul's work or the Gospel, but to fulfill and complete it (Gal 3:3). The Messiah's coming only culminated and sanctified the OT. Israel was still the most important and would always be Israel. Only Gentiles could join Israel, Israelites could never join Gentiles. The Sabbath and circumcision and all the other ordinances were by no means obliterated. They were covenants between God and His people forever. Christ never freed men from the law; He confirmed it. Faith alone, without circumcision, without the law, would leave Christianity incomplete. In fact, Paul and his co-workers were false apostles; they were not telling the full truth. The other apostles had never said this; it was only Paul who was the libertine. Would not his teaching result in moral tragedy, in every dangerous and immoral act? Would faith not lead to license instead of liberty? Their attack upon Paul, therefore, may be considered threefold: (1) On the apostolic authority of Paul, (2) Paul's gospel is an incomplete gospel, (3) Paul's gospel with its attitudes toward law, will lead to immorality (cf. Rom. 3:1-5; 6:1).

In Galatians Paul answers this threefold attack. He knew that they were striking at the very heart of the Gospel. They were describing what might be called an "Old Testament Christian," a true Israelite who believed in the coming Messiah and kept all the law besides. It is possible that a Judaizer might do all the things demanded by the law, including circumcision, and, as long as he did not think he was thereby esp. pleasing God by these acts (the error of the church of the Middle Ages) it would do no harm; but what about demanding all this of a Gentile before he can be considered a good Christian? This was the burning issue. It was fought by Judaizers supposedly on theological or Scriptural grounds. Faith was not enough to make certain of God's grace and salvation. Besides accepting Jesus Christ as the Messiah, a new convert also should join the Jewish nation and observe its laws and customs which came from Moses, generally epitomized in the refusal to eat with Gentiles (Gal 2:11-14; 4:10). The Christian must be saved by faith *and* works, faith *and* Judaism, grace *and* law on an equal basis. In the Jerusalem church the Judaizing tendency had not become an issue because the Christians there were all of Jewish origin and had been circumcised before coming to faith. Perhaps they even continued in their old ways. In Antioch and in Asia Minor the situation was different. In the mission fields the Gentiles often outnumbered the Jews. In their teaching and preaching Barnabas and Paul had not insisted upon circumcision since faith made a person a member of the kingdom (Gal 3:26). To do anything else would have destroyed God's universal grace and supplanted faith with works. It would have meant that Jewish people who became Christians had somewhat of a head start over all Gentiles and the Gentiles had a built-in handicap before God. The entire letter to the Galatians is actually built around this argument. Paul says the Christian does not have the choice of a "both-and," but it is an "either-or"—the choice lies only between grace or law, faith or works, either Moses or Christ (5:2-6). For Paul the mixing of a tiny requirement of man's obedience to any law shakes the foundation of salvation by grace alone. Grace excludes all works, not just highly publicized public deeds, but the most insignificant private deed if motivated for salvation by works. Any and all works in the doctrine of salvation were of the devil and destroyed man's only hope and comfort for certainty in salvation. The heart of Christianity for Paul is God's free grace in Christ Jesus and anything else is a sword thrust into the heart of Christianity. This is why Paul's thermometer rose so high against these false teachers, not only because their doctrine was a perversion of the Gospel, but because it sounded so reasonable and natural to Jewish Christians who in turn wished to impose these impossible demands upon Gentile Christians. The Judaizing trap is an ancient snare—many Christians in the past have fallen into it and no doubt many more will. It is difficult to find the proper place and distinction between law and Gospel. Faith alone does not mean "no works"—these are of the Spirit (Gal 5)—but it does mean that the Gospel saves and not laws, customs or ceremonies. Paul ends Galatians with a comment on this key point. *Both* Jew and Gentile have joined Christ and the one new church, on an equal basis. "Neither circumcision counts for anything," he says, "nor uncircumcision . . . but *a new creation*. Peace and mercy be upon all who walk by this rule, upon the Israel of

God" (6:15, 16). The term Israel had to be re-defined for both parties. Messiah had come.

5. Destination and readers. The epistle opens with the words: "Paul an apostle . . . and all the brethren who are with me, To the churches of Galatia" (1:1, 2). This letter is the only Pauline epistle which is specifically directed toward a group of churches, unless it be Ephesians as a circular letter. Who were the "Galatians"? Where were these churches located? Answers to these questions have caused a great deal of discussion in the past half cent. and have influenced scholars much in determining the date and the readers of the letter.

The nomenclature "Galatia" was used for centuries to designate the territory in the N and central part of Asia Minor to which a large number of Gauls migrated (or invaded) from Europe about 275 B.C. (compare the Lat. *Gallia*, Gaul). By 230 B.C. the territory assumed rather fixed boundaries and these Gauls, or Galatians, lived in this small kingdom, had their own government, and developed their own customs. In 25 B.C. the territory was taken over by the Roman Empire and made a Rom. province. King Amyntas (36-25 B.C.) was the last ruler of this old Galatian territory, but before his death he added some parts of Phrygia, Pisidia, Lycaonia and even Isauria to his small kingdom. The Romans added several other adjacent territories to Old Galatia, combined the entire area with the territory to the S, and named the entire country "Galatia." It is possible, then, that in Paul's day during Rom. times there were two "Galatias," the first being the Old Galatia in the northern part of Asia Minor and the second being the reorganized territory of the N and the S and both together called Galatia. Bible students have called the territory of Old Galatia the "Territory Hypothesis," Geographical Galatia, Galatia Proper, Ethnographical Galatia and Northern Galatia. The combined larger territory which Rome organized has been termed Political Galatia, Provincial Galatia, "Province Hypothesis," and Southern Galatia. Although Bible students speak of N Galatia and S Galatia, one should not be mislead by the terms as if there was a Galatia in the N and another Galatia in the S. It should be remembered that the province of Galatia included both the old Galatia and the new territory to the S. The situation might be illustrated by drawing a horizontal line through the middle of the State of Illinois and then for a moment hypothetically assuming that the northern part of the state was settled as a territory in early pioneer days and was called Illinois; later the lower part of the present State of Illinois was included in the state and the entire state was called Illinois. Similarly the entire combined province of Galatia was simply called Galatia by the Romans.

The important question for the letter to the Galatians is: In what way did Paul and Luke use the term? Was Paul referring to the old territory of Galatia proper or was he using the term in the Rom. provincial sense? Or to put the question in a more specific manner, was the apostle referring to unnamed churches in the old territory of Galatia in the N, or was he referring to the churches of such towns as Derbe, Lystra, and Iconium which he founded on his first missionary journey? The answer to this question is significant as it relates to the people to whom the letter was addressed, the date, and the historical setting. If the epistle was not written until Paul visited the northern Galatian territory on his second or third journey and long after the Apostolic Council, the epistle would have a much later date and be written to unknown readers. If, on the other hand, the term "Galatia" refers to the cities he visited on the first missionary journey, it is possible to date the epistle early, even considering it one of the first letters the apostle wrote.

The first view has been called the "Northern Galatian Theory" by Biblical scholars. It was early defended by an able scholar by the name of J. B. Lightfoot in a commentary on Galatians (1890), and assumed that Paul's visit to Galatia took place during the second and third journeys when he traveled through the region of Phrygia and Galatia (Acts 16:6). This view holds that Paul traveled through such towns as Pessinus, and Ancyra, and Tavium and finally reached Troas after a long journey. Acts 18:23 indicates that he made a similar tour on his third missionary journey.

Today, however, most scholars believe that Paul wrote his letter to the churches in the southern part of the province of Galatia. This proposal has been named the "Southern Galatian Theory" or the "Province Hypothesis." A famous Eng. scholar, Sir William Ramsay, championed the view, believing that "the churches of Galatia" were those founded on the first missionary journey and that they were later re-visited on other journeys (Acts 16:1-6; 18:23). If this view is correct, it answers in a natural manner certain questions regarding the destination of the letter. Several considerations undergird the hypothesis: (1) It has been shown that Paul in his writings generally uses provincial names of Rom. districts or provinces, never the territorial identification (Achaia, Macedonia, Illyricum, Dalmatia, Judea). In the Rom. sense Judea meant all of Pal. (2) It would also seem strange that Paul would make no appeal to the significant decision of the Apostolic Council, authority which he could easily have used in his defense of the Gospel against the Judaizers, if he wrote the letter after the council. The fact that the council is not mentioned prob. means it had not taken place. (3) It has been suggested that the Northern Galatian Theory does not explain why the Judaizers did not invade the important churches in S Galatia. (4) The internal evidence from the letter itself seems to indicate that Paul is speaking to the churches in the southern part of the

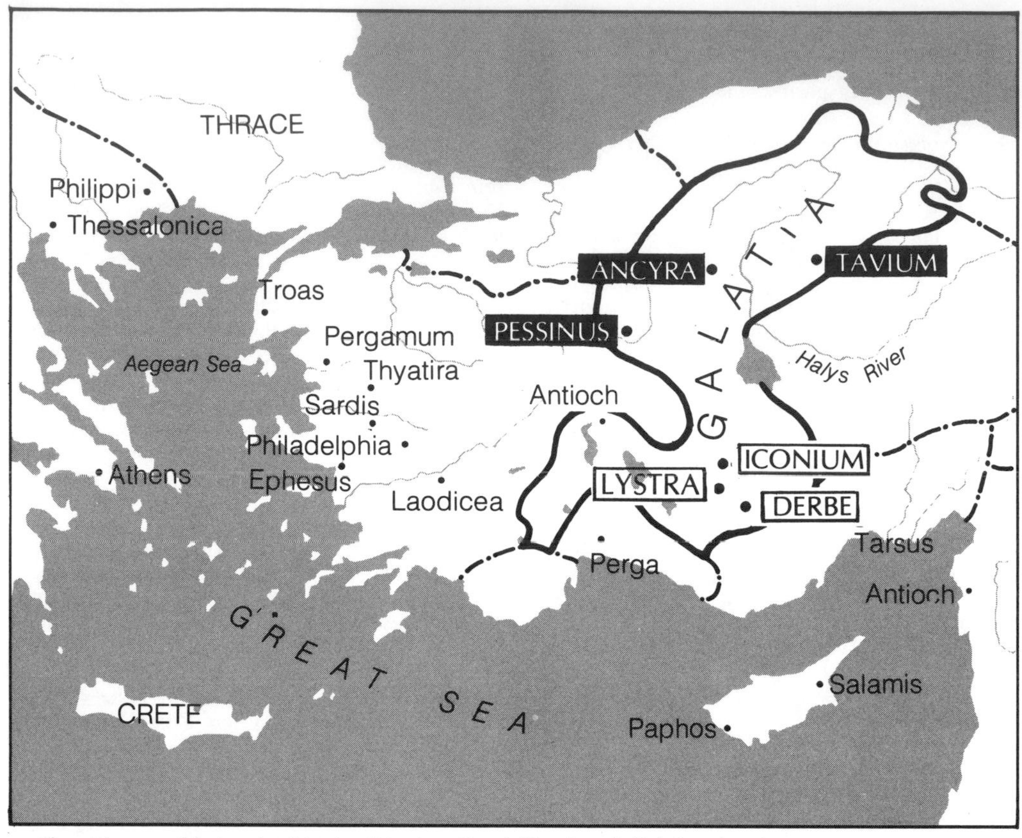

The cities possibly involved in the "Northern" and "Southern" Galatian theories.

Rom. province of Galatia. Paul's activities up to the time of writing, as we have seen, can be more easily explained if the letter was written early. One can also explain Paul's altercation with Peter (Gal 2:11) with greater ease if this took place before the first church council. (5) Barnabas is mentioned in the letter as a person well-known to the readers but he was with Paul only on the first missionary journey as far as is known. (6) In 1 Corinthians 16:1, where Paul speaks of Galatia, he evidently has in mind the southern section because Derbe is included (Acts 20:1-4). (7) Paul's sickness (Gal 4:13) can be explained easier if he were speaking of southern Galatia since he would hardly, as a sick man, have gone into the northern part of the province, a bleak desolate country. (8) The issue of faith versus works with the Judaizers was prominent in southern Galatia, as we see from Acts 16:1. There is no evidence that the Judaizers went to northern Galatia.

For these reasons most scholars follow the more natural Southern Galatian Theory to answer the questions: To whom did Paul write this letter? Where were the churches of Galatia located? The Judaizers had been following Paul throughout his first missionary journey and after he returned to Antioch he was informed of the trouble they were causing. He immediately sat down and wrote these churches the firm and passionate letter which we know as Galatians. The Northern Galatian Theory must base its evidence upon two rather obscure passages (in Acts 16:6 and 18:23). It also has further difficulties in the understanding of the terms Phrygia and Galatia. Again, there is no real evidence that Paul founded churches in northern Galatia—he was interested in hurrying on to Europe rather than preaching in this area.

Some scholars hold that Paul was opposing two sets of opponents in the letter; not only a Jewish or Judaizing tendency but also a Gnostic element. They say certain anti-gnostic statements quite clearly show this, as in 4:8-11; "How can you turn back again to the weak and beggarly elemental spirits, whose slaves you want to be once more? You observe days, and months, and seasons, and years! I am afraid I have labored over you in vain." His words in 4:19-21 seem to bear this out because he lashes out with all his might against every desire and act of fleshly libertinism. The Spirit of God, says Paul, not the "beggardly elemental spirits" are in control of man and his destiny through the power of love and faith (cf. Marxsen, pp. 50-54). It may well be true that both elements may have been represented in the churches of Galatia, perhaps at times even a combination of the two. Scholars have conclusively shown that a Jewish-Gnostic tendency existed early in the Church.

6. Date and place of writing. The date and place of writing follow closely upon the identification of the recipients of Galatians. Those who advocate the Northern Galatian Hypothesis have assigned the letter to Ephesus during the third missionary journey about the time Romans was written. Others who uphold this theory believe that it may have been written during the second missionary journey about A.D. 52. Scholars who support the Southern Galatian Theory generally place the writing of the letter just before the Apostolic Council. Those who believe the letter was written prior to the Council place it in Antioch of Syria, while those who believe it was written during the second or third missionary journeys choose Corinth or Ephesus as the place of writing. All things considered, it seems best to place the writing of Galatians at about A.D. 48 just prior to the Apostolic Council. According to this view Paul wrote the letter on the eve of the council in order to take care of the emergency in Galatia. It is possible that Paul did not know such a council would be held, nor would he know its outcome. Peter's speech in Acts 15:7-11 may also take into consideration the views stated in Galatians. It is granted that not all of the evidence demands the writing of the letter before the Apostolic Council and some of the problems in chronology are difficult. One must agree that the argument that Galatians speaks of the Apostolic Council is not overwhelming. If Paul were detailing his visits to Jerusalem, he certainly would not exclude specific mention of the Apostolic Council.

7. Theme and purpose. The theme of Galatians is *Christian freedom* in terms of salvation by grace and freedom from the law as the way to salvation. In this it partakes of the objective of the great letter to the Romans. Another way of asking the major question of the letter is: What is the place of the law in Christian theology? Is Christian salvation a question of faith *and* works, or faith *without* works? No one denied that the law was given by God and that it was divine. But did the new Pauline emphasis on grace and faith wipe out the law completely? Paul's answer is negative and his statement of the relationship between law and Gospel in the letter becomes a dominant leitmotif. The law has its place in God's plan but it is not the old Pharisaical or legalistic approach. The law tells a man what sin is. If there is no law one cannot transgress law; and if there is no transgression against law there is no sin.

Furthermore, for Paul the law drives a man to despair and causes him to throw himself upon the grace of God in one great act of faith. The honest legalist knows from experience that he can never completely obey the law for God and that the law only condemns. Only grace and faith give true life and liberty to the total man. In this letter then, the apostle's great theme is Christian liberty which praises the grace of God.

The Judaizers attempted to answer this question of the law and the Gospel by opting for a legalistic system. Their argument was subtle and rational. If a Jew became a Christian, naturally he must bring Judaism with him into the Christian faith. Was not the Jew there first? Was not the law from God? It was so simple. A Jew must always remain a Jew. On the other hand, if a Gentile wished to become a disciple of Christ, he had to become a Jew to qualify. Were not all of God's promises, even of the Messiah, promised to Jews alone? Christianity, like Judaism, was for Jews only. This was a new kind of slavery, worse than the old. It also faced man with demands he could not meet and drove all love for God and man from his heart. What hopes the poor Gentiles had were dashed to pieces. Everything in the letter is gathered about the theme of freedom in the grace of God, whether it be Paul's own biography, his altercation with Peter, the works of a Christian (Gal 2:19-21), the case of Abraham, the desires of the flesh and the compulsion of the Spirit, the doctrine of love, or forgiveness (6:15). Vehemently the apostle writes against the folly of salvation by works: "All who rely on works of the law are under a curse . . . Christ redeemed us from the curse of the law, having become a curse for us" (3:10-13). In some way, each issue of the epistle has something to do with this theme.

The purpose of the letter is knotted to the theme. Paul wished to combat legalism and the Judaizers. Legalism always has, and always will, take the heart out of Christianity and transplant a heart made of stone. Only the Spirit gives life. The heart of Christianity is God's free grace in Jesus Christ. Let the law do the honorable work of showing a man his sin, but do not let it save man from sin. Paul's purpose was to keep the new kingdom from being another Jewish sect—he preached a universal Gospel of grace intended for all men (Gal 3:26). The Judaizers were not only teaching coercion to the Mosaic law, but also a work righteousness (Gal 5). Paul wished to keep the new Christian converts true to the Gospel of freedom which Christ had taught and confirmed on the cross. His letter to the Galatians, as it did in Galatia, has blocked the path of many a man who since then would change Christianity into a new paganism or another type of Judaism. It stands as a challenge to all men who would take away the grace of God, the truth of the Gospel, and joy and freedom that goes with it!

8. Contents and outline. The contents of the letter to the Galatians must compel the Christian's *personal* attention. This is not just a theological or polemical essay which, like a Gr. debater, may take either side without impunity. The subject matter of this treatise of the Gospel involves *every man* and his eternal salvation or judgment. The news of Judaizers' success caused great turmoil and even tempestuous anger in the apostle's heart. He divided his wrath between the Judaizers for preaching such heresy and the Galatians for believing it. It is not only that the Galatians would lose their liberty; they would lose their God and His eternal salvation in Jesus Christ. Justification by faith rather than by works must stand at all costs.

The letter begins with the normal greetings to the readers. There is no indication of the thrust of the Word to come. The first two chapters form a defense of Paul's apostolic authority. The best way to illustrate his point is to relate his own activities and show that the Gospel came by revelation from God and not from Paul or even the other apostles, for if one apostle can be attacked, all may be attacked. So certain is he of the Gospel's freedom that he even opposed the respected and renowned Apostle Peter about his vacillation between Jews and Gentiles. Chapters 3, 4 and 5 are freighted with Paul's defense of the Gospel—teaching the positive truth to oppose error. He sets forth his doctrine of justification by faith to refute the Judaizers and as a vehicle of the Spirit to bring the Galatians back from their apostasy. The Galatians themselves knew they did not receive salvation by keeping the law—few of them had ever followed any law. The same is true, Paul says, of the great heroes of the OT, particularly Abraham, the father of the Jews. The purpose of the law was never to save, but to convince man that his salvation is from God. In chapter 5 the apostle defends the other end of the valley—he fights off the antinomian who would say, "Yes, Paul, let us teach faith and not law and works—what do you have then? Have you not opened the very floodgates of sin and human desire? If there is no law and every man is free, will not immorality, hate, murder and every other human passion run wild so that the last situation is worse than the first?" Paul carefully illustrates that on the contrary, the Gospel, like a beautiful tree, brings forth fruits of the Spirit of every kind. Good works do not make a good man, but a good man does good works. This is true liberty—doing the will of the Spirit of God from the compulsion of the Gospel. There are, Paul says, many fruits of the flesh, but the Christian is under grace and empowered by the Spirit of God Himself, to do good, a much greater power than any human attitude or desire. At the end of the letter the apostle takes the pen from the scribe and attests the truth of the document by inscribing his own name in his own hand.

A Defense of Christian Liberty
Outline

Theme: Freedom of the Christian man—the doctrine of *justification by faith alone vs. salvation by faith AND works.* (Not F vs. W, but: F vs. F & W.)

I. *Introduction* (1:1-5)
   1. The writer and the addressees (1:1, 2)
   2. The apostolic greeting (1:3-5)

II. *The Apostle Paul defends Christian liberty by defending his apostolic authority* (1:6-2:21)
   1. Paul's defense forms the purpose and occasion of the letter (1:6, 7)
   2. Paul was never a mere man-pleaser (1:8-10)
   3. He received his Gospel directly by revelation from Christ Himself and not from men (1:11-20)
   4. The time he spent in Syria and Cilicia shows that the Christians of Judea did not know Him personally. This means he is an apostle and that the Gospel is true (1:21-24)
   5. Paul's dealings with the other apostles and with the Judaizers shows his Gospel is true (2:1-10)
   6. His rebuke of the Apostle Peter should convince all of his sincerity (2:11-16)
   7. Paul's personal testimony of his apostleship and doctrine (2:17-21)

III. *The Apostle Paul defends and explains the doctrine of justification by faith alone* (Chaps. 3; 4)
   1. First of all, Paul admonishes the Galatians again (3:1-5)
   2. Paul cites the example of Abraham's faith to recall the foolish Galatians (3:6-9)
   3. Paul explains justification by faith by speaking of Christ being made a curse (3:11-14)
   4. Paul speaks of justification under the picture of the covenant or testament (3:15-18)
   5. The apostle inserts a statement in his argumentation about the purpose and use of the law (3:19-22)
   6. Paul offers a summary argument which unites all believers into one, not under law, but in the Gospel of Christ (3:26-29)
   7. Paul speaks of justification by faith under the picture of an heir (4:1-7)
   8. Paul inserts another rebuke to the Galatians for leaving the doctrine of justification (4:8-11)
   9. A personal appeal (4:12-20)
   10. The allegory of the two sons (4:21-31)

IV. *The Apostle Paul relates the doctrine of justification by faith to the Christian life* (chaps. 5; 6) (Paul's definition of good works and defense of the Gospel against immorality)
   1. Paul re-states his reasons the Galatians should hold fast to the doctrine of justification (5:1-12)

2. The apostle states his definition of law and good works for the justified person (5:13-26)
3. Individual responsibility for ethical growth (6:1-10)

V. *Concluding remarks of the letter to the Galatians* (Recapitulation) (6:11-18)
1. Paul says he wrote the letter personally (6:11)
2. He speaks once more about the problem in Galatia, comparing the false teachers and himself (6:12-15)

9. Characteristics and special features. The entire letter is "special" and a "feature event" in Christianity. For a clear understanding of Christianity there is no better introduction than Galatians. It is highly doctrinal but yet extremely personal. The gullibility of the Galatians for such patent error is a personal affront to the apostle who had been God's instrument in bringing the Gospel to them. Almost a third of the Gospel is a statement of personal biography. Paul himself was an object lesson of the Gospel and often uses this method (cf. 1 Tim 1:1-12). Not even the casual reader can overlook the fervor of personal faith: "*I* have been crucified with Christ . . . *I* live by faith in the Son of God, who loved *me* and gave himself for *me*" (Gal 2:19, 20).

The epistle is a sharp defense of the Christian faith. "The tone of the book is warlike. It fairly crackles with indignation though it is not the anger of personal pique but of spiritual principle. 'Though we, or an angel from heaven, should preach unto you any gospel other than that which we preached unto you, let him be anathema' (Gal 1:8), cried Paul as he reproved the Galatians for their acceptance of the legalistic error" (Tenney). Paul was answering those who challenged him on two counts: The truth of the Gospel, and Paul's right to preach it.

The letter is also highly emotional. Words run like a torrential mountain stream. He begins sentences which he does not have time to finish; he quotes his words to another apostle but then flies aloft in a soliloquy as he dwells on what Christ had done for his own person. He talks to his readers as if he were on a great stage and his readers personally before him. One time he can be angry and heated, at other times pleading and conciliating. He speaks of the glory of Christ and His doctrine, but also of the beauty of the fruits of the Spirit. He asks question after question which he proceeds to answer himself. The letter shows the sensitivity of one who has experienced the depths of God's grace. He speaks of love fulfilling the whole law and walking in the Spirit as in a peaceful verdant valley. Yet he can trumpet forth with such dicta as this: "Do not be deceived; God is not mocked, for whatever a man sows, that he will also reap. For he who sows to his own flesh will from the flesh reap corruption, but he who sows to the Spirit will from the Spirit reap eternal life" (Gal 6:7, 8). The letter to the Galatians shows beautiful eloquence and deep pathos. It manifests wrath against false teachers, tenderness with respect to the erring, and urgent pleading to the faithful. The heart of the Gospel is found in its substance and in the life of freedom it advocates. The letter is most valuable for the full understanding of the Word of God. Scarcely another epistle emphasizes the "alone" of "by grace alone," "through faith alone," as does this letter. No presentation of the Gospel can equal this letter in the force with which it presents the powerful claim of the pure grace of God.

Another special feature of this great letter is that it deals directly with basic concerns of man in his relationship to God and his life on earth. It reveals the basic nature of man in that he tends to turn from truth to untruth because deception seems more delectable than truth (1:6-9); it points up the basic premise upon which man is received by God, namely the grace of God in Christ (2:11-21); it shows the all-sufficiency of Christ's atonement for the sins of all men and the gift of salvation through His saving work (2:15, 16); it reveals that God chooses to give His Gospel through other men whom He has called to be His ambassadors (2:6-10); it teaches the relationship between legal requirements and the gospel of freedom and human responsibility (2:17-21); it exhibits a brief but profound statement and understanding of the doctrine of justification by grace through faith (2:15, 16); it shows a proper use and understanding of the OT (3:15-18; 4:21-31); it speaks in no uncertain terms about the equality of all men under God in Christ (3:23-29); the unity of the Church is emphasized repeatedly (5:6); it teaches the work of the Spirit and His power in the lives of men (5:6-25); its admonition to forgiveness is held up as a basic fruit of the Gospel (6:1-5); in short, the letter teaches the basic elements of Christianity in brief and unforgettable form.

BIBLIOGRAPHY. M. Luther, *A Commentary on St. Paul's Epistle to the Galatians* (1535); G. S. Duncan, *The Epistle of Paul To The Galatians, The Moffatt New Testament Commentary* (1934); S. A. Cartledge, *A Conservative Introduction to the New Testament* (1941); H. Thiessen, *Introduction to the New Testament* (1951); M. C. Tenney, *The New Testament: A Survey* (1953); R. Stammand; O. Blackwelder, "The Epistle to the Galatians," IB, Vol 10 (1953); M. C. Tenney, *Galatians: The Charter of Christian Liberty* (1954); J. A. Allan, *The Epistle of Paul the Apostle to the Galatians* (1954); W. Barclay, *The Letter to the Galatians and Ephesians* (1958); M. Franzmann, *The Word of the Lord Grows* (1961); Feine-Belma-Kuemmel, *Introduction to the New Testament* (1965); W. Marxsen, *Introduction to the New Testament* (1970).

L. M. PETERSEN

GALBANUM (חלבנה ; χαλβάνη). This is the Syrian gum of Exodus 30:34. It is a fourth of the sacred perfumes of the OT, called "pure and holy." Galbanum is the brownish gum or resin of the plant, *Ferula galbaniflua*, a Mediterranean herbaceous perennial. It has thick stalks, yellow flowers, and fern-like green foliage. The gum exudes from the lower part of the stem.

Galbanum, when collected, is in both irregular and symmetrical drops. It may be yellowy-green or lightish brown, and has a musky, pungent smell. The particular value of Galbanum is the fact that it "holds" the scent of a mixed perfume, and allows of its "distribution" over a long period. It is also mentioned in the Apoc. (Ecclus 24:15).

W. E. SHEWELL-COOPER

GALEED gălʹ ĭ əd (גלעד, LXX βουνὸς μάρτυς, *heap of witness*). The Heb. name that Jacob gave to the heap of stones erected as a memorial, or witness, to the covenant of reconciliation and nonaggression between himself and Laban, his father-in-law (Gen 31:44-54). Laban called the heap of stones *Jegar-sahadutha,* which means "heap of witness" in Aram. Jacob and Laban sealed their covenant with a communal meal. The erection of a stele or stone-heap as a memorial of some important event or treaty was common in the history of Israel (cf. Gen 28:18; Josh 4:3, 9; 22:26-28). This story may well provide the reason why this territory in Trans-Jordan has been named Gilead.

D. H. MADVIG

GALGAL, GALGALA. Douay VS and KJV forms of GILGAL.

GALILEAN(S), the name applied by both Jews and Gentiles to the inhabitants of the portion of Syria-Pal. N of the Plain of Esdraelon and the Valley of Jezreel, and spreading E to the shores of the Lake of Galilee and W to the Mediterranean Sea. This area was little settled by the Jews after the return from the Exile. John Hyrcanus and his successors, such as Alexander Jannaeus, conquered this area and incorporated its mixed population of Aramaeans and Hel. peoples into the Jewish state. The VS of the OT known as the Aram. Targums was popular among these people. Although they were thereafter Jews their mother tongue was Aram. Under the Hasmonaean state many Jews from the S migrated and settled in Galilee and thus became Galileans. Pharisaism and the anti-Hel. and Rom. movements, such as the Zealots, flourished among the hill people of Galilee so that the revolutionary leader and founder of the Zealots was himself called Judas of Galilee. Josephus in a famous excursus distinguishes between Northern and Southern Galilee (Jos. War, Exc. II). All the inhabitants were known by the term, Gr. Γαλιλαῖος, derived from Heb. גליל הגוים, "Galilee of the Gentiles" or more properly, "The District of the Gentiles." The inhabitants of this area even though subsequently Jews and loyal to Israel always were considered somewhat inferior by the more southerly countrymen. Josephus, however, who was of Galilean descent himself wrote, ". . . the Galilaeans are fighters from the cradle and at all times numerous, and never has cowardice afflicted the men or a declining population the country" (Jos. War, Exc. II, G.A. Williamson tr.). At one point Josephus was, in fact, the governor of Galilee. The region and its peoples are mentioned outside the Gospel narratives (Acts 9:31; 10:37; 13:31). It was to these people that John the Baptist and Jesus Christ had preached and from this group that the first circle of our Lord's disciples were drawn and His closest apostles chosen. Apparently Joseph was from a family that had migrated from Bethlehem in Judea to Galilee, as shown by his return there with Mary upon the command of Caesar Augustus (Luke 2:4) Since farming, herding and fishing were the common callings of the country folk of Galilee, their experiences are apparent in Jesus' parables. In all four of the gospels, and in Acts, it is clear that Galileans were easily distinguishable to their fellow Jews by their speech. The classic passage is, of course, the accusation by the bystanders against Simon Peter and his denial (Mark 14:70; Luke 22:59). The characteristic of this speech was no doubt its Aram. vocabulary, accent and syntax. The direct speeches of Jesus Christ recorded in the gospels (Mark 5:41 and 15:34), as well as the strong Aramaisms which were tr. into Gr. (e.g. John 3:3ff.), leave little doubt that our Lord's mother tongue was this same Galilean Aram. Their use of this Aram. marked the Galileans not only linguistically but also religiously, as they seem to have utilized the Aram. VS of the OT. This concept of the Galilean origin of the apostolic language and band possibly was known to some of the Rom. authors of the time, but is not commented upon by any of the pre-Nicene Fathers of the Church. After the Rom. overthrow of the Jewish state in A.D. 70, many Jews and Jewish Christians fled from Jerusalem to Galilee, thus making the Galileans a center of the Jewish culture. Interest in Galilee and the Galileans was renewed after the introduction of the now discredited "Galilean Hypothesis" by the romantic author, E. Renan, *La vie de Jesus* (1863). *See* GALILEE.

BIBLIOGRAPHY. E. Stapfer, *Palestine in the Time of Christ* (1885); D. Baly, *Geographical Companion to the Bible* (1963); C. F. Pfeiffer and H. F. Vos, *The Wycliffe Historical Geography of Bible Lands* (1967).

W. WHITE, JR.

GALILEE gălʹ əʹ le (גליל, הגלילה, ἡ Γαλιλαία, literally *the circuit* or *district; Galilee*). The geographical area in Pal. bounded on the N by the Litani (Leontes) River, the W by the Mediterranean Sea to Mt. Carmel, the S by the northern edge of the Plain of Esdraelon (though at times the plain itself is included), and on the E by the Jordan valley and the Sea of Galilee.

I. Ancient boundaries. Little information is available to determine the boundaries of Galilee during OT times. The term is first employed during Israel's conquest of Canaan. In the hill country of Naphtali the town of Kedesh is said to be in Galilee (Josh 20:7; 21:32; 1 Chron 6:76). During the kingdom period, Galilee appears to encompass the territory of Naphtali (2 Kings 15:29), the tribal area of Asher (provided Cabul is the same city in 1 Kings 9:11-13 and Josh 19:27), and possibly the tribal district of Zebulun (Isa 9:1). It may be concluded that the OT Galilee is substantially the same as the above definition.

In the intertestamental period, Maccabean lit. includes the Plain of Esdraelon in Galilee (cf. 1 Macc 5:35; 10:30; 12:47, 49). Josephus describes Galilee as being bordered by Phoenicia and Syria, bounded on the N and W by Tyrians, to which Mt. Carmel belonged, on the S by Samaria and Scythopolis as far as the Jordan River, and on the E by the Trans-Jordan (Jos. War III. iii. 1). The region of Galilee in the NT appears to encompass this same area (Matt 4:13-15, 25; 28:16; Mark 1:28; 3:37; Luke 8:26; 17:11).

II. General description. The region of Galilee is approximately sixty m. long from N to S and thirty m. wide from W to E. Of all the regions of Pal. Galilee contains the coolest, most picturesque and lush mountainous district. The terrain is diversified, containing volcanic and limestone hills with alluvial fertile plains. It has been compared with portions of the Carolina and Virginia piedmont. The entire region is watered by springs, heavy mountain dew, and an annual precipitation of about twenty-five inches.

A. *Lower Galilee.* Lower Galilee's natural and historic boundaries include the fault of Esh-Shaghur (present Acre-Safed highway) to the N, the Mediterranean Sea from Acco to Mt. Carmel on the W, the Esdraelon valley or the Carmel and Gilboa ranges (depending upon the historical period) to the S, and the Sea of Galilee and Jordan valley to the E. The region is the most level of all the hill country of Pal. but is divided into sections by a series of four basins which bisect its low mountain ranges latitudinally E to W through cross folding and faulting. None of the names of these four valleys is known from the Bible. The basins begin just to the N of the Nazareth ridge with the Tur'an basin. To its N lies the steep slope of Jebel Tur'an (1,780 ft.). The larger basin of Sahl el-Battuf (Beth Netufa) constitutes the second basin, bordered on its N with hills to the height of 1,710 ft. North of these hills lies the Halazun (Sakhnin) basin with Jebel Kammana (1,950 ft.) rising to its N. The last valley is the long narrow Esh-Shaghur basin (Plain of er-Ramah or Beth Hakerem) which abuts the steep slope which rises almost vertically 1,500-2,000 ft. to the mountain plateau of Upper Galilee. The most distinct landmarks in lower Galilee are the Horns of Hattin, Mt. Tabor, and the Hill of Moreh.

The plain of Esdraelon, often considered the southern portion of Lower Galilee, is the largest valley bisecting the central mountain range of Pal. and the only one which joins the coastal plain with the Jordan valley. This valley is known as the valley of Armageddon (named after the site of Megiddo, Rev 16:16), where the great battle of the last times will be fought. Its length from Mt. Carmel to Beth-shan (Scythopolis) is about thirty m. and its greatest width about fifteen m. The fertility of this valley is compared with the delta areas of the Tigris-Euphrates, Nile, and Mississippi. This is due to the decomposition of volcanic deposits, basaltic subsoil, and the many springs. Two ancient valleys combined to make this larger one. The valley of Jezreel, named for the capital of the Omride dynasty, which set on a spur of Mt. Gilboa, formed approximately an equilateral triangle of twenty m. long sides, the vertices being Jokneam to the W, Tabor to the E, and Ibleam to the S. The eastern end of the Plain of Esdraelon was called the valley of Bethshan.

The plain of Acco (Acre; plain of Asher) on the Mediterranean coast from Carmel to the Ladder of Tyre crosses the western end of Lower and Upper Galilee. It was Asher's allotment, but they never possessed it entirely. The ten m. wide section in Lower Galilee lay between Mt. Carmel and Acco (Acre), composed mostly of marshes and sand dunes. The stream Kishon flowed through it, coming from and connecting it to the Plain of Esdraelon.

B. *Upper Galilee.* Upper Galilee differs from Lower Galilee in many ways. While the mountain elevation of Lower Galilee remains below 2,000 ft. the highest peaks of Upper Galilee surpass 3,000 ft., Jebel Jermuk the highest at 3,900 ft. From these high mountains N of the Esh-Shaghur basin the mountain plateau of Upper Galilee slopes to about 1,500-1,800 ft. above sea level in the N before dropping into the gorge of the Litani (Leontes; Kassimiyah) River which separates Upper Galilee from the Lebanese mountains. This mountain plateau is not uniform as in Lower Galilee and is not divided by a series of valleys. It is composed of bare ridges of hard Cenomanian limestone and flat-topped mountains of softer Senonian chalk. Rugged contours, broken by many peaks, divide the area into natural pockets. Most people feel that this area was more wooded in the past than it is today. Rainfall is heavy and consistent, helping to create small rivers: major ones are the Ga'aton, Keziv, Amud, and Litani.

Most of Christ's ministry was around the Sea of Galilee. This is a view looking across the Sea of Galilee to the hills of Gadara. © *Lev*.

The upper Jordan valley forms the eastern sector of Upper Galilee. The valley begins at the Biblical site of Ijon (c. 1,800 ft. elevation), initially bounded on the W by the Litani River and on the E by Mt. Hermon (c. 9,100 ft. elevation). This valley, fertile and well-watered, is prob. the land or valley of Mizpah (Josh 11:3, 8) which formed the OT border between Israel, Phoenicia, and Aram. It extends approximately nine m. to the area of Abel-beth-maacah and Dan where it rapidly descends to about 300 ft. elevation. Here at Dan and Baniyas two of the spring sources of the Jordan River are located. All the sources of the Jordan join together about five m. S of Tell el-Kady. During Biblical times they flowed through a marshy valley about ten m. to a small Lake Huleh, blocked in by masses of basalt. Today this marsh and lake have been drained and form the fertile Huleh valley. Just S of this lake the river Jordan reaches sea level and continues to flow for another ten m. through a rocky basalt gorge (hills stand more than 1,200 ft. above the stream) to the Sea of Galilee situated about 685 ft. below sea level. This sea, approximately thirteen m. long and seven and one-half m. wide, is nestled between the hills of Lower Galilee on the W and the plains of Bashan on the E.

As in Lower Galilee, the plain of Acco forms the western region of Upper Galilee. It runs along the coast from Acre to the Ladder of Tyre (Rosh Haniqrah) for about twenty m., its average width being two m. The shore is rocky and without sand dunes, offering no natural harbors of any significance.

III. Ancient history. Though the records are scanty concerning the occupation of Galilee prior to Israel's conquest of Canaan, there are traces of settlement and occupation as early as the Chalcolithic and Early Bronze ages (c. 4,000 to 2,000 B.C.) at such sites as Megiddo and Beth-shan. The Egypt. Execration texts of the 20th and 19th centuries B.C. curse certain towns in the Galilean area of Pal. (e.g. Acco, Achshaph, Beth-shan; possibly Kedesh and Beth-shemesh). Later Egypt. control over this region is demonstrated by the campaign lists of Thutmose III, Rameses II, et al. Subsequent loss of control by Egypt and the confusion among the Palestinian city states is evidenced in the El-Amarna letters (c. 14th cent. B.C.) of Egypt.

A. Tribal divisions. Israel gained initial supremacy in Galilee through Joshua's victory over the Canaanite league at the Waters of Merom (Josh 11:1-11). Jabin, the king of Hazor, was the leader of this alliance. Galilee was apportioned among four tribes (19:10-39): Asher received western Galilee with the coastal plain of Acco; Issachar settled in the eastern part of the Jezreel valley and the hills to its N; Zebulun inherited the central part of Galilee between the Plain of Esdraelon and the Sahl el-Battuf valley; Naphtali occupied a large area in eastern and central Galilee. Archeological surveys demonstrate that the Israelite settlement occurred in the largely unsettled interior regions of Lower and Upper Galilee, though Upper Galilee is not a region which enters much into Biblical history. None of these four tribes (except perhaps Issachar) succeeded in driving the Canaanites out of their district (Judg 1:30-33). During the apostate and anarchial period of the Judges, Deborah and Barak, with men from the tribes of Zebulun and Naphtali, defeated the Canaanite oppression by swooping down from Mt. Tabor and claiming victory at the river Kishon in the Plain of Esdraelon (Judg 4). Gideon removed the Midianites' and Amalekites' tyranny by his surprise attack against them near the Hill of Moreh (ch. 6). Neither victory was permanent.

B. Kingdom period. Saul, the first king of Israel, unified the tribes and thereby brought Galilee and the Via Maris (the major trade route) under his control. The balance of power soon shifted to the Philistines who proceeded to shut up the Israelites in the hill country. David freed Israel from the Philistine threat and made Israel the leading nation of the Near E. Galilee came under David's control. In payment for helping to construct the Temple, Solomon offered Hiram of Tyre twenty cities in Galilee. When Hiram examined those towns, he was not pleased with them and appears to have returned them to Solomon (1 Kings 9:10-14; 2 Chron 8:1, 2).

Following the division of the nation into the kingdoms of Israel and Judah, Asa, king of Judah, summoned Ben-hadad I, the Syrian, to aid him in his fight against Israel by invading Galilee. Ben-hadad promptly wasted the land of Naphtali and the whole circle of Kinneret (1 Kings 15:20). Galilee continued as an area of conflict between Israel and Aram (Syria). Omri and Ahab recovered the territory lost by Israel, but parts were lost again by Jehu to Hazael (2 Kings 10:32). Hazael continued his battles with Jehoahaz of Israel (13:22). Finally Jeroboam, the son of Joash, king of Israel, delivered the region of Galilee for a short time (14:25ff.). With the invasion of the Assyrian king Tiglath-pileser III in 734 B.C., the chief cities of Galilee passed into his hands (15:29; 16:7). Though some Israelites still remained in Galilee after this attack (2 Chron 30:10f.), the Israelite period of dominion over Galilee ended quickly with Samaria's fall to Assyria in 722 B.C. The kingdom of Israel, including the region of Galilee, was assimilated by Assyria. "Galilee of the nations" (Isa 9:1) prob. referred to the mixture of Jews and Gentiles then living in that area.

C. New Testament times. Following the Babylonian captivity, information about the history of Galilee is sparse, though the area was continually inhabited. It was ruled by Babylon, Persia, Greece, and the Seleucid empire until the Maccabees conquered parts of it and began the process of Jewish resettlement. Jews were already in Galilee in 165 B.C. when Simon the Maccabee brought numbers of them to live in Judea (1 Macc 5:14ff.). Josephus recounts Aristobulus I's conquest of Ituraea (Jos. Antiq XIII. xi. 3), and most feel that Galilee was treated similarly to Ituraea in that both were Judaized.

Under Rome Herod the Great was made military commander of Galilee in 47 B.C. He subdued the various bands of thieves which plagued the country (Jos. Antiq. XIV, ix, 2). When Herod came to his throne in 37 B.C., a period of peace and prosperity came to Galilee which continued until the banishment of his son Antipas in A.D. 40. At Herod's death in 4 B.C., Galilee fell to Antipas who made his capital at Tiberias on the western shore of the Sea of Galilee, naming it after the emperor.

Herod Antipas reigned over Galilee throughout Jesus Christ's entire life with the exception of his infancy. Jesus was born in Bethlehem of Judea, was raised in Nazareth of Galilee and made Capernaum at the N end of the Sea of Galilee the headquarters of His ministry. There was a considerable Jewish population in Galilee at this time which would explain, in part, Christ's following there. Most of His ministry was around the Sea of Galilee. The Sermon on the Mount, His Transfiguration (though no mountain has been identified with certainty for this event), nineteen of his thirty-two parables, and twenty-five of his thirty-three recorded miracles occurred in Galilee. The Messiah received His warmest welcome in Galilee, but the Jews from the S regarded the northern Jews with some contempt, feeling that nothing good could come out of Nazareth (John 1:46; 7:52) and that a claim of a Messiah from Nazareth could hardly be taken seriously (Matt 21:11). Late in Jesus' Galilean ministry, when opposition had increased, He spent considerable time in Upper Galilee.

Galilee was added to the territory of Herod Agrippa I in A.D. 40. Zealots were arising in Galilee, some found among the disciples of both John the Baptist and Christ. In A.D. 40 Caligula ordered Petronius, the governor of Syria, to erect the emperor's statue in the Temple at Jerusalem. Thousands of Jews gathered for forty days at Tiberias and Ptolemais in protest of this proposed sacrilege. Such reactionary pressure caused Petronius to give up the idea. Agrippa I died in A.D. 44 and parts of Galilee came under the dominion of Herod Agrippa II until A.D. 100. As Rome continued to administer the remainder of Galilee, the Galileans struggled for independence. With Vespasian's invasion around A.D. 70, the whole area came under Rom. rule. After Herod Agrippa II's death in A.D. 100, Galilee was joined to the Rom. province of Syria.

When Jerusalem fell in A.D. 70, Galilee became the seat of Jewish learning. The Mishnah was compiled and written in Tiberias followed later by the composition of the Talmud. Later Tiberias became the center of the Massoretes' work of preserving the OT text. The Sanhedrin likewise moved to Sepphoris after A.D. 70 and then to Tiberias.

IV. Transportation. The major trade route from Damascus to Egypt is called the Via Maris (the Way of the Sea). From Egypt this route enters Galilee from the SW through the pass of the Wadi 'Ara at Megiddo (alternative passes were at Taanach and Jokneam). At Megiddo the road branches: one way runs NW to the plain of Acco along the Phoen. coast to Anatolia; the second artery moves E to Damascus between the Hill of Moreh and Mt. Tabor to Kinneret on the NW corner of the Sea of Galilee, then N to Hazor where one branch of it continues due N to Ijon and the other branch crosses the main ford of the Jordan River about two m. S of Hazor and continues to Damascus; the third route leaves Megiddo heading E to Beth-shan, past Ashtoreth, the capital of Bashan, and joins the King's highway to Damascus. Canaanite fortresses guarded this route: Hazor in the N; Bethshan at the junction of the Esdraelon and Jordan valleys; Ibleam in the Esdraelon valley; and Megiddo, Taanach, and Jokneam at the passes leading S. Most minor routes throughout Galilee run E-W following the E-W basins crossing Lower Galilee. N-S traffic is most difficult due to the many ranges and faults which run in every direction in Upper Galilee. Roads in Galilee usually follow the spurs rather than the valleys when climbing on to the mountain plateau, because a wadi leaving a plateau usually becomes a steep valley, often impassable. The main road from Acco (Ptolemais) to Tiberias went just N of Sepphoris across Lower Galilee joining the Nazareth-Tiberias road. Another significant artery ran through Upper Galilee from Tyre to Abel-beth-maacah at the base of Mt. Hermon. This highway system put the region of Galilee in contact with the entire Near E.

V. Flora and fauna. The Galilean hills are considered to have been heavily forested in early times with an abundance of trees: olive, fig, oak, walnut, cedar, cypress, balsam, fir, pine, sycamore, bay, mulberry, and almond. The valleys were fertile and well-watered. Wheat was abundant in the upper Jordan valley; pomegranates thrived near Mt. Carmel; and the grapes of Naphtali were famous. Grains were plentiful.

The major fauna of Galilee is fish. At least twenty-two species have been classified from the streams and the Sea of Galilee.

VI. Settlement patterns. Galilee was open and easily accessible to the outsider. Yet Upper Galilee and portions of Lower Galilee with their rugged terrain made sections of the area easily fortified and naturally defensible. Almost any group could defend themselves. As a result many varied groups did survive. The population became heterogeneous with Jews, Aramaeans, Itureans, Greeks, and Phoenicians living together. Upper Galilee gave the northern portion of Pal. an area of escape during troubled times.

Josephus estimates at his day that the population of Galilee was about 3,000,000. Many villages had a population of at least 15,000, he says (Jos. War III. iii. 2). This could help explain the crowds that followed Jesus. In the valleys the villages often kept to the edges of the basin or up the slopes due to flooding in winter. In Lower Galilee two sub regions proved less attractive to habitation than any other: the SW area between the present Nazareth-Sheparam road and the Jezreel valley; the SE region from Tiberias to the N edge of the Beth-shan valley which includes four steep scarps. Neither area is easy to cultivate nor has ever been thickly populated. The more notable cities of Galilee have been Kedesh, Hazor, Korazim, Bethsaida, Capernaum, Beth-shan (Scythopolis), Nazareth, Megiddo, Jokneam, Ibleam, Acco (Ptolemais), Sepphoris, Jotapata, Cana Nain, Achziv, and Tiberias. Sepphoris and Tiberias were Rom. administrative centers in Galilee, Sepphoris being located about four m. NW of Nazareth. The NT does not record Jesus' presence in either of these two cities.

The men of Galilee were known to be courageous (Jos. War III. iii. 2). The OT notables were Barak, Gideon, Jonah, and Elijah. Eleven of Jesus' twelve apostles were Galileans.

BIBLIOGRAPHY. G. A. Smith, *The Historical Geography of the Holy Land* (1896), 379-481; W. Ewing, "Galilee," ISBE (1929), 1163-65; D. Baly, *Geography of the Bible* (1957), 184-192; S. Abramsky, *Ancient Towns in Israel* (1963), 174-250; D. Baly, *Geographical Companion to the Bible* (1963); Y. Aharoni, *The Land of the Bible* (1967), 19-33, 41-49, 121-353.

R. H. ALEXANDER

GALILEE, SEA OF (ἡ θαλασσα τῆς Γαλιλαιας, meaning *the sea of Galilee*). Also called "sea of Tiberiah" (John 6:1; 21:1), the "lake of Gennesaret" (Luke 5:1), and "the sea" (Matt 8:24, 32; Mark 2:13; John 6:16, 17; et al.). The OT refers to it as "sea of Chinnereth" (Num 34:11; Josh 13:27) and "sea of Chinneroth" (Josh 12:3). First Maccabees 11:67 refers to the sea as "the water of Gennesaret." Today it is known as "the sea of Galilee," "lake of Kinneret," or "Lake Tiberias." This is the harp-shaped lake in the Jordan valley due E of Lower Galilee and Acre bay just N of the intersection of the Yarmuk and Jordan Rivers, and W of the plains of Bashan.

1. Setting. To many the focal point of the whole region of Galilee is the Sea of Galilee. It lies E of Lower Galilee in the great Jordan rift valley, about sixty m. N of Jerusalem. The mountains of Upper Galilee rise NW of it to the height of about 4,000 ft. above sea level, while the hills immediately E and W of the lake ascend abruptly to heights of about 2,000 ft. above sea level. This creates a sharp drop of approximately 2,650 ft. from the mountain tops down to the lake's surface where the foot of the hills often abuts the lake. The main formation of the surrounding terrain is limestone overlaid with volcanic lava, broken at times with an out-cropping of basalt. The high tablelands of Bashan, Hauran, and Gaulanitis to the E of the sea are composed of black basalt and some diorite. Since the Sea of Galilee is located in the Jordan rift, it has been subject to destructive earthquakes.

Three major valleys adjoin this lake: the two plains formed by the northern entrance and the southern exit of the Jordan River and the plain of Gennesaret to the NW. The upper Jordan valley begins at the Biblical site of Ijon (c. 1,800 ft. above sea level) near the foot of Mt. Hermon which towers about 9,100 ft. above sea level and can be observed easily from the southern shore of the Sea of Galilee. This fertile and well-watered valley (prob. the land or valley of Mizpah in Josh 11:3, 8) spreads approximately nine m. S to the region of Abel-beth-maacah and Dan where it rapidly drops about 300 ft. in elevation. The major spring sources of the Jordan River are located in this area. Two smaller streams which feed the Jordan, the Bareighit and the Hasbani, form a small waterfall near Metullah as they leave this plain and drop to the Huleh valley. The two major streams of the Jordan, the Banyasi and the Liddani, spring up close to one another at Banias and Tell el-Kady respectively, considered the locations of the later towns of Caesarea Philippi and Dan. These four streams join together about five m. S of Tell el-Kady and flow through the marshes of the valley approximately ten m. to the small Lake Huleh. A few m. S of this lake the Jordan River reaches sea level and drops at a rate of about sixty ft. a m. for another ten m. through a rocky basalt gorge to the small plain which enters the Sea of Galilee situated about 685 ft. below sea level. The Jordan River is the major source of water in this lake. At the southern tip of the lake the Jordan exits through a broad fertile valley which has been heavily populated from ancient times to the present. The Yarmuk River flows into the Jordan from the E about seven m. S of the lake. The plain of Gennesaret with its average width of one m. enters the lake from the NW.

2. Description. Looking down upon the Sea of Galilee from the heights of Safed, the lake looks harp-shaped (the meaning of the Heb. term from which the word "chinnereth" is derived) with the bulge to the NW, and is deep blue. It is truly a beautiful sight. The ancient rabbis used to say that "Jehovah has created seven seas, but the Sea of Galilee is His delight." It reminds one of a Scottish loch surrounded by barren hills. The surface of the lake is set anywhere from 680 to 695 ft. below sea level. The fluctuation is due to seasonal and annual climatic variation, but most Israelis fix its norm at 685 ft. below sea level. From the entrance of the Jordan at the N to the southern tip of the lake is normally taken to be about thirteen m., though again opinions vary from twelve to fifteen m. The width in the N of the lake at its greatest distance between el-Mejdel on the W to the mouth of the wadi Semak on the E is usually understood to be seven and one-half m., though variations in this width range from five to eight m. Opinions concerning the sea's depth fluctuate from eighty ft. in the more shallow areas to the maximum of 160 ft. The lake's circumference is a little over thirty-two m., while the average quantity of clear sweet water in it is estimated at 4,562 cubic meters. Around most of the lake the beach is pebbly with a scattering of small shells. Several hot mineral springs are found on the shore, two of the more notable ones located at et-Tabgha in the NW corner and 'Ain el Fulīyeh about two m. S of modern Tiberias. The climate is tropical due to the low elevation, having temperatures which range higher than the uplands. As a result of this climate and the fertility of the soil in the plains surrounding the lake, the region is most productive. The harvesting of wheat and barley crops takes place about one month earlier than in the hill country. Wild flowers and oleanders fringe the shoreline.

The territory around the lake is varied and interesting. Moving E from the entrance of the Jordan past the site of Bethsaida, the mountain slope of the high plateau of Bashan drops almost vertically into the sea. This is broken only by the wadi Semak entering the lake due E of Magdal. The ancient site of Gergesa was perhaps located near the mouth of the wadi. Approximately three m. S of Wadi Semak, located high above the present town of Ein Gev, lie the ancient ruins called Sussita, prob. the site of the Decapolis city named Hippos. The ribbon of plain between the coast and the mountains broadens into the Jordan valley to the S as one reaches the southern end of the lake. Six m. SE of the lake, on the other side of the Yarmuk River, lies the ancient site of Gadara. Somewhere in this SW portion of the Sea of Galilee the event of the swine rushing headlong into the lake occurred (Mark 5:1-20), though the exact location is much debated. The Jordan valley S of the lake is considered the most fertile plain among those touching the sea. The Jordan exits from the lake on the W side of this valley, just S of the ruins of the ancient city of Khirbet Kerak. The ribbon type plain on the E is found once again on the western shore running eight and one-half m. N. The Rom. capital of Tiberias, built on the slope of the western hills, is located near the northern end of this narrow plain shortly before it intersects the m. wide fertile and well-watered plain of Gennesaret. This plain is watered from the W by the wadi el-Ḥamam which contains the ancient site of Arbela high on its S rim overlooking the

A view of the north shoreline of the Sea of Galilee, where the Jordan River enters. ©*Lev*

A majestic view toward the Sea of Galilee from the Horns of Hattin. ©*M.P.S.*

plain. Magdal lies on the southern side of this plain near the lake. Moving N toward the Jordan's entrance there is a shallow vale through which a road to the N passes shortly before arriving at et-Tabgha with its hot springs. Two m. further Tell Hum displays the well-preserved ruins of the 3rd cent. A.D. synagogue of Capernaum. Within the next two m., the entrance of the Jordan River is reached.

3. Products. The small valleys around the Sea of Galilee have fertile alluvial soil, hot climates, and are well-watered. These conditions produce abundant crops of wheat, barley, figs, grapes, and vegetables. Concerning the region's fertility, Josephus declares: "One may call this place the ambition of Nature, where it forces those plants that are naturally enemies to one another to agree together: it is a happy contention of the seasons, as if each of them laid claim to this country, for it not only nourishes different sorts of autumnal fruits beyond men's expectation, but preserves them a great while. It supplies men with the principal fruits—grapes and figs continually during the ten months of the year, and the rest of the fruits, as they ripen together through the whole year" (Jos. War III. x. 8). Arbela was noted for its linen.

Fish was the major commodity from the lake, being found in great abundance and in over twenty-two different species. The best fishing was at the N end of the lake where the Jordan enters. Among the apostles, Peter, Andrew, John and James were fishermen.

4. Commerce. Commercially the major industries of the region surrounding the Sea of Galilee were agriculture, dyeing, tanning, boat-building, fishing, and the curing of fish. From the latter the lake gained fame throughout the Rom. world. Major routes of trade passed by or over this lake. The eastern branch of the *Via Maris* touched the NW corner of the sea at the plain of Gennesaret. This was the major route from Egypt to Damascus and Mesopotamia. The produce from the mountain plateau to the E of the lake often was shipped across the lake on its way to the Mediterranean. The hot mineral springs along the lake's shore brought multitudes to be healed. Mineral baths are still offered today.

5. Population. The area immediately surrounding the Sea of Galilee is considered to have been the most heavily populated region of Galilee throughout history. Some maintain that in NT times there were nine cities around the lake, each said not to have a population less than 15,000. Such cities included Tiberias, Magdala, Korazim, Bethsaida, Hippos, Capernaum, Gadara and Kinneret (G. A. Smith, *The Historical Geography of the Holy Land*, 447). The fertile well-watered valleys and warm climate were prob. the major cause for this dense population. Ruins of palaces, hippodromes, theaters, and baths built by the Greeks and Romans found on the lake's shores also indicate a large population during the time of Christ. The eastern side of the sea was largely Gentile and constituted part of the region known as the Decapolis.

6. Storms. The position of the lake in the Jordan rift below sea level with the high mountains to the E and W creates a natural condition for storms. The cool air masses from the mountain heights rush down the steep slopes with great force causing violent eruptions of the lake. Such tempests are not infrequent and are extremely dangerous to small craft.

7. Biblical history. It is noticeably strange that this fertile and beautiful lake is only mentioned in the OT with respect to the land's borders. The sea of Chinnereth forms part of the eastern boundary of the land which the Lord was giving to Israel (Num 34:11). Joshua 12:3 recounts the lake again as part of the land's eastern border after the conquest under Joshua. Joshua 13:27 refers to the Sea of Chinnereth as the NW boundary of the land alloted to the tribe of Gad. Apart from these references the OT is silent concerning this lake.

In contrast, the Sea of Galilee is one of the most important centers of NT events. The headquarters of Jesus' Galilean ministry was on the N shore at Capernaum. Peter, Andrew, and Philip were residents of Bethsaida, a town which Jesus often visited, and one of the towns along with Korazim and Capernaum that He cursed for rejecting His ministry. John and James, the sons of Zebedee, were fishermen upon the Sea of Galilee. In light of the fact that the medicinal mineral springs made the lake an invalid resort, it is interesting that Christ performed ten out of His thirty-three recorded miracles beside this sea, many of them miracles of healing (Mark 1:32-34; 3:10; 6:53-56). Most of his time was spent in the NW part of the lake between Tiberias and Capernaum. It is never recorded, however, that Jesus entered the capital at Tiberias which Herod Antipas had constructed and patterned after the Greek "polis." Jesus and His disciples often walked through the grain fields of Gennesaret. Christ drew many illustrations for His Gospel message from these fields and the activity of the lake (cf. wheat and tares; parable of the sower; being fishers of men; casting the net into the sea; et al.). On a hill near this lake He preached the Sermon on the Mount (Matt 5-7). On its shores he multipled the loaves and fishes to feed 5,000 (Matt 14:13-21) and healed demoniacs (Mark 5), lepers (Luke 5:12-16) and Peter's mother-in-law (Luke 4:38). On its waters He walked (Mark 6:45-52). He calmed the storms on this lake (Mark 4:35-41). Certainly the Sea of Galilee was geographically central to Christ's ministry.

Herod the Great ruled over this region from 37 B.C. until his death when his son, Herod Antipas, began to govern the area. Antipas moved his capital to Tiberias, and from there

Top: Fishermen with their nets on the Sea of Galilee. ©*M.P.S.*
Bottom: A view by telephoto lens looking northeast across the Sea of Galilee. Capernaum is seen across the lake, and snow-capped Mount Hermon in the distance. ©*M.P.S.*

he ruled over this territory throughout the entire life of Christ with the exception of His infancy. Galilee was added to the realm of Herod Agrippa I in A.D. 40, and when he died in A.D. 44, parts of the Sea of Galilee came under the jurisdiction of Herod Agrippa II until A.D. 100.

With the fall of Jerusalem in A.D. 70, Jewish scholarship moved to Galilee. Tiberias became the center of the composition of the Mishnah and the Talmud. Later it was the home of the Masoretes who did the masterful work of preserving the OT Heb. text. Even the Sanhedrin ultimately moved to this city.

BIBLIOGRAPHY. G. A. Smith, *The Historical Geography of the Holy Land* (1896), 439-463; W. Ewing, "Sea of Galilee," ISBE (1929), 1165, 1166; D. Baly, *The Geography of the Bible* (1957), 197, 198; S. Abramsky, *Ancient Towns in Israel* (1963), 209-209, 231-238; Y. Aharoni, *The Land of the Bible* (1967), 30, 31.

R. H. ALEXANDER

GALL (ראש χολή). The poisonous herb mentioned eight times in the OT (e.g., Deut 29:18; Ps 69:21; Lam 3:19), has been described as "venom from a snake," so bitter and poisonous was it thought to be. It is likely therefore, not to be the same herb that was mixed with the vinegar given to the Lord (Matt 27:34). In fact, trs. have used the word *rō'sh* to mean hemlock—a poisonous plant (Hos 10:4).

Unfortunately, wormwood also is rendered as "hemlock," and hemlock rendered as "gall," so there is obviously some ambiguity.

The poisonous bitterness may come from the *Colocynth* (*see* VINE OF SODOM). It is the inner pulp which is poisonous and strongly bitter. On the other hand, the gall in Matthew 27:34 may be an herb to give a slightly bitter taste. The drink offered the Lord could have been a normal Rom. alcoholic beverage.

The belief that the gall comes from the poppy, whose juice is certainly bitter, is feasible. A solution of poppy heads in water could describe that mentioned by the text in Jeremiah 9:15—"water of gall to drink." Since one cannot really pinpoint the full meaning of the word "rō'sh" might easily be any poisonous or semipoisonous bitter herb grown in Pal. at that time.

W. E. SHEWELL-COOPER

GALL (OF LIVER) (מררה, מרורה ; χολή). The gall mentioned in Job 16:13 obviously refers to the bile from the gall bladder. The gall of bitterness in Acts 8:23 may be the bitter herb, or the liquid from the bladder—for the Gr. word *cholē* means "anything bitter" or bile.

The bitter internal secretion produced inside the gall bladder can cause extreme bitterness and disgust, when by mistake left inside a cooked hare or rabbit. The Biblical usage of the word indicates despair, just as the ghastly taste of the gall bile has a "despairing" effect on men.

W. E. SHEWELL-COOPER

GALLERY (אתיק, etymology and meaning uncertain; suggested are *gallery, porch, balcony portico, colonnade*). A long, narrow balcony(?).

The Heb. word occurs in Ezekiel 41:15f.; 42:3, 5 as a part of the description of the Temple that Ezekiel saw in a vision. These "galleries," with other features, distinguished the Temple of Ezekiel's vision from that of Solomon. Some have compared the structure of this building, apparently with terraces or recessed upper stories, with the design of the Babylonian ziggurat or stage-tower temple.

KJV also has "galleries" (S of Sol 7:5), but this should prob. be corrected to read, "tresses, locks of hair" (cf. RSV). A different Heb. word is involved (רהט, the meaning of which is also uncertain).

K. L. BARKER

GALLEY (אני, *fleet*). A long, low seagoing vessel, propelled by sails and oars, or by oars alone.

Hebrew is used collectively of "ships, fleet," but אניה, denotes "a unit of a fleet," i.e. "a single ship." It is the former that is employed in Isaiah 33:21 ("fleet with oars"). Obviously, the reference is to galleys propelled by oars and used primarily as warships. The passage teaches that the Lord is Jerusalem's defense. She will be like a great city protected by river-canals, into which no hostile ships ("galleys") may venture. Thus, the galley of antiquity could be either a small or large vessel and was usually manned by oarsmen ("rowers," Ezek 27:8). It is of interest to observe that the Heb. root under discussion is attested as a Canaanite gloss in the Amarna Letters: *anaya* (245:28).

K. L. BARKER

GALLIM **găl' ĭm** (גלים, *heaps*, LXX Γαλλεί[μ], B: Ῥομμα). Identification uncertain.

The village was located in Benjamin, N of Jerusalem, near Gibeah of Saul and Anathoth. The Heb. OT refers to it (1 Sam 25:44; Isa 10:30). However, LXX also mentions it as a town situated in Judah. Here, the reference is Joshua 15, *between* vv. 59 and 60, where there appears a list of cities that apparently was inadvertently omitted from the Heb. Bible in the process of text transmission. In this list, Gallim is grouped with towns lying SW of Jerusalem.

K. L. BARKER

GALLIO **găl' ĭ ō** (Lucius Junius). Proconsul (KJV "deputy") of Achaea in A.D. 51-52 or 52-53 in residence at Corinth (Acts 18:12-17).

The son of the rhetorician M. Annaeus Seneca and brother of the philospoher Seneca, he was born Marcus Annaeus Novatus at Cordova in Spain. Adopted by the rhetorician, Lucius Jiunius Gallio, he was trained by him for administration and government (Tac. Ann. 16. 17). He was a notably affable man. Seneca dedicated his treatises *de Vita Beata* to him and in the preface of the *Naturales Quaetiones* describes him as a man universally beloved.

An inscr. from Delphi shows that he was proconsul of Achaea after the 26th acclamation of Claudius as emperor. Therefore, his term of office was in 51-52 or 52-53. According to Pliny, the climate of Achaea, by Gallio's own statement, made him ill. He went to Egypt after his term of office to recover from a lung hemorrhage. He then returned to Rome and became *consul suffectus* early in Nero's reign. He was involved with his brother in a conspiracy to overthrow Nero, and, though temporarily pardoned, he was soon thereafter either forced to commit suicide or was put to death by order of Nero (Dio Cassius, *History* 62.25. Seutonius, *Rhetoric*).

While Gallio was residing at Corinth as proconsul of Achaea, a Jewish mob dragged the Apostle Paul before the rostrum and charged him with persuading men to worship God contrary to law. Gallio, concerned primarily with Rom. law, dismissed the case as a matter among Jews without letting Paul defend himself. Even when the mob seized Sosthenes, the ruler of the synagogue, and beat him in front of the rostrum, Gallio did not exercise his prerogatives (Acts 18:12-17).

BIBLIOGRAPHY. O. Rossbach in *Pauly Wissowa*, RE s.v. "Annaeus 12."

A. Rupprecht

GALLON. *See* Weights and Measures.

GALLOWS. *See* Crimes and Punishments.

GAMAD (MEN OF) gā′ măd (גמדים, possibly *valorous men*, LXX *φύλακες*, *guards, sentinels*). KJV GAMMADIMS găm′e dĭmz. Men of Gamad are said to be in Tyre's towers (Ezek 27:11). LXX and ASV tr. the term; KJV and RSV take it as a proper name. Cf. *Kumidi* in Amarna letters.

GAMAEL. Apoc. alternate form of Daniel.

GAMALIEL gə mā′ lĭ əl, a proper name, Heb. גמליאל, of two persons named in the Bible.

1. A chief of the tribe of Manasseh who was chosen to aid in the wilderness census (Num 1:10; 2:20; 7:54, 59; 10:23).

2. Also a famous Jewish sage mentioned twice in the Acts (5:34; 22:3). He was the head of a large family of prominence תנאים, or teachers whose words are quoted in the Mishnah. The one mentioned in Acts is known as Gamaliel *ha-zaqen*, "Gamaliel the Elder," and lived during the first Christian cent. Tradition states that his grandfather was none other than Hillel the Elder. However, as with many other legends about him, this statement is unsupported by reliable documents. He often is confused with his grandson also named Gamaliel, and like the first a patriarch of the Sanhedrin. The elder Gamaliel is quoted in the Mishnah, the rabbinic commentary on the Torah, in a number of passages. His legal actions are of an intensely practical nature dealing with such matters as the invalidation of a bill of divorcement through a duplicity of names, the problem of leavening dough by mixed lots of leaven and the extension of the Sabbath prohibition on journeys of mercy. However, some rather legendary and superstitous material also is attributed to his teaching and his followers. He was accorded the highest of all Jewish titles for teachers, that of Rabba/on (cf. John 20:16). His memory has been one of the greatest favor and gentility in rabbinic tradition. His precise opinion in regard to the early Christian Church has been the subject of much debate in ecclesiastical circles. A tradition of the pseudep. *Clementine Recognitions,* a much disputed early Medieval document, that Gamaliel embraced Christianity toward his death in A.D. 70 is totally without foundation. In the first mention in Acts he is pictured as advocating a course of moderate pragmatism in regard to the captive apostles. In the second instance, he is mentioned by Paul in his defense before the crowd in Jerusalem where Paul claims Gamaliel as his teacher. Considering the meager mention of Gamaliel in the Mishnah as inconclusive, it does appear that each of his enactments was liberalizing and humanitarian in its underlying motive, and this accords well with the speech quoted in Acts and with Paul's favorable mention of him as a man held in the highest esteem by the Jews. It may well be that Paul mentioned his name as a veiled suggestion that in his own case the policy of Gamaliel be adopted by the crowd. It is noteworthy that Paul casts no aspersions on the ability or insight of Gamaliel in regard to the law of Judaism. Yet he assumes that such a teacher's pupil would feel no compunction about persecuting the new and thriving "way." Paul does not again mention Gamaliel as his new-found faith had irrevocably broken off his association with the Jewish sage.

W. White, Jr.

GAME (ציד, צידה, KJV, VENISON). The Heb. term refers to game of any kind, although properly venison is the flesh of the deer. Game hunting was not a popular Heb. pastime, but was carried out mostly for reasons of hunger or the depredations of wild animals. However, men such as Ishmael (Gen 21:20) and Esau (Gen 25:27), were renowned for their hunting skills. Game consisted chiefly of partridge, gazelle, and hart meat (Deut 12:15), along with roebucks in the time of Solomon.

R. K. Harrison

GAMES. Though many amusements, entertainments, diversions, and games were known in the Near E in Bible times, there are, however, few references to them in the Bible. In interpreting the activities of the ancients, it is often difficult to distinguish sacred and secular, ritual and amusement. Furthermore, entertainment ranged from the enjoyment of fine arts to the sadistic pleasure of the physical torture of captives or slaves, from the refined performances in the Gr. theater to the cruel gladiatorial contests of Rome. Since material is considerable from antiquity concerning amusements—but little relating directly to the Bible—it is best to sketch ancient amusements generally and to note relevant Bible passages.

1. Children's games. Children love to play. The prophet Zechariah described prosperity and peace as a time when "the streets of the city shall be full of boys and girls playing in its streets" (Zech 8:5). Children's active games are depicted on Egyp. tomb walls from the period of the Old Kingdom, e.g. in the mastabas of Ptahhotep and Mereruka. Though often the scenes are difficult to interpret and the hieroglyphic legends are enigmatic in a number of instances, the activities can be described with some certainty—wrestling bouts, gymnastic games, and other exercises involving agility. Archeological excavations have unearthed dolls and simple mechanical toys of several kinds from Egyp. burials. A number of balls have been found, and it is probable that most of these were for children's play. Children also engaged in games of make-believe. Jesus described the unresponsive and stubborn generation to which He ministered as being "like children sitting in the market places and calling to their playmates, 'We piped to you, and you did not dance; we wailed, and you did not mourn' " (Matt 11:16, 17).

2. Adult amusement: active sports. It appears that in Pal., hunting and fishing were means of livelihood rather than recreation. As a shepherd, David defended his flock against incursions of predatory animals, killing marauding bears and lions by hand (1 Sam 17: 34-36); but this was performed from duty, not for amusement. On the other hand, kings and nobles of Egypt and Assyria hunted dangerous animals for diversion; reliefs, paintings, and inscrs. tell of their hunting exploits. Wealthy officials in Egypt participated in fishing or waterfowling for fun. Their sport, pursued in the marshy areas of the river, was termed *shmh-ib,* "distraction of heart," equivalent to "recreation," or "enjoyment." The most sporting type of waterfowling was done with a throwstick, or even with bow and arrow; but birds were also captured with a clapnet. Fishing was usually represented as a form of harpooning or spearing, but sometimes the tomb-owner is shown using hook and line; bowfishing also is represented in ancient Egypt.

Swimming was practiced, apparently as a practical skill and not as a recreation. In the Bible, swimming is mentioned (Isa 25:11; Ezek 47:5), but not as an amusement.

Competitive athletics existed from very early times, but found its greatest development in the Gr. games (*see* ATHLETE, ATHLETICS). Wrestling, in particular, was well-known; evidence for it comes from both Mesopotamia and Egypt. In Egypt hundreds of wrestling groups are shown in the tomb art (*see* WRESTLE). Running, boxing, rowing, archery, and singlestick, or wandfighting, were also known. Participation often appears to be associated with the military or religion, and little of competitive sport could be called amusement for the participants. There is evidence from Medinet Habu and elsewhere that such competitions were performed to entertain the king and officials, or as part of the celebration of religious-political festivals.

In the OT, runners are mentioned as bearers of messages for the army or the king (cf. 2 Sam 18:19ff.). Job lamented, "My days are swifter than a runner" (9:25). The psalmist indicates that "a strong man runs its course with joy" (19:5). Swiftness of foot was a desirable manly quality, and the passage from the Psalms indicates that pleasure was derived from the exercise of strength in running.

Dancing and various acrobatic or rhythmic movements were associated with religious ritual, festivals, and even funerals. Miriam and the Israelite women played timbrels and danced after the Israelites crossed the sea (Exod 15:20). Dancing was associated with the occasion of the worship of the golden calf at Mount Sinai (1 Cor 10:7). When the Ark of the covenant was brought to Jerusalem, "David danced before the LORD with all his might" (2 Sam 6:14). Social dancing was unknown, and dances involving persons of both sexes are not depicted.

Various forms of ball playing were practiced in Egypt; women are shown taking part in such games at Beni Hasan. Possibly there was even a form of ritual in which a ball was struck with a stick or club. Playing ball is not mentioned in the Bible, though a reference to a ball appears (Isa 22:18).

3. Sedentary, or inactive games. Sedentary games are widely evidenced throughout the Near E, esp. board games of various kinds. Beautiful gaming boards and boxes have been found, as well as informal playing squares crudely scratched on flat rock surfaces. Playing draughts appears in the Book of Gates and is represented in the funerary art. Scenes at the High Gate of Medinet Habu show Ramses III and female members of his family indulging in such play. The representation of the playing board is found even in hieroglyphic writing as the biliteral sign *mn*.

Dice were used for determining moves in certain board games. The casting of lots is often referred to in the Bible, but always as a means of making decisions, whether of identity, procedure, or possession. Roman soldiers who crucified Jesus cast lots for His seamless tunic (Matt 27:35; Mark 15:24; Luke 23:34; John 19:23, 24; Ps 22:18).

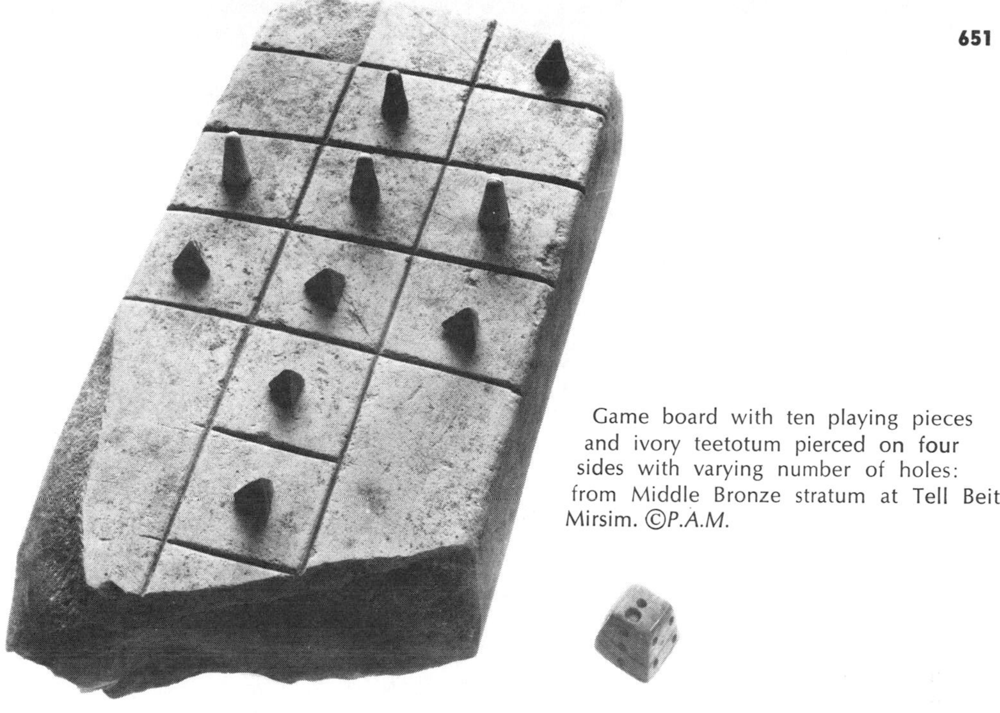

Game board with ten playing pieces and ivory teetotum pierced on four sides with varying number of holes: from Middle Bronze stratum at Tell Beit Mirsim. ©*P.A.M.*

A game board of ivory and ebony veneer, ivory pins, and knuckle-bones, for playing "Hounds and Jackals"; from a Theban tomb. ©*Met. Museum of Art.*

4. Spectator, or passive amusements. The ancients were apparently more inclined to participate than to watch, but one may suppose that there were many spectators who observed religious ceremonies and royal festivities, with their attendant entertainment. The Philistines who congregated at the temple of Dagon in Gaza called for Samson to be brought to provide entertainment for them (Judg 16:25, 27).

People enjoyed hearing stories told, and eloquent speeches were appreciated, as in the Egyp. story of the Eloquent Peasant (cf. Ezek 33:32). The NT Athenians took an avid interest in telling or hearing something new (Acts 17:21).

Magicians amused people in ancient Egypt, as the Papyrus Westcar shows, but the Egypt. magicians mentioned in the Bible were involved in serious matters (cf. Gen 41:8; Exod 7:11, 22; 8:18, 19). Magicians in Babylon were also mentioned at the time of Daniel (Dan 1:20; 2:2, 27).

Throughout the ancient Near E, banquets were held for entertainment. Many banquet scenes are shown in the Egyp. tombs, and many references to feasts appear in the Bible. Participants enjoyed abundant food and drink—sometimes to excess—and were entertained by dancers and musicians. Such entertainment was common at Egyp. banquets, and it is evident that Salome's dancing at the celebration of Herod's birthday pleased the viewers (Matt 14:6; Mark 6:22).

Music was an important diversion of antiquity. The ancients, like their modern descendants, were well aware of melody and rhythm. The beat of the drum or the clapping of hands, the playing of flute, trumpet, or stringed instruments, and the use of the human voice are clearly represented in the tomb art and well documented in the Biblical lit. (cf. Ezek 33:32). Music was, of course, important in religious ceremonies and at affairs of state, but it was common at private parties and even in the solitude of the shepherd's care for his sheep. David provided music for Saul as an amusement, a therapy, and even as a spiritual exercise (cf. 1 Sam 16:18, 23).

The Hellenization of the Near E introduced many Gr. amusements. Hippodromes, stadiums, and theaters sprang up as Gr. culture pervaded the earlier lands of the Bible. The NT missionary efforts enlarged the immediate geography of the Biblical narrative and widened its cultural horizons as well. Paul alluded to the Gr. athletic games (*see* ATHLETE, ATHLETICS). He also declared that the apostles had been made a *θέατρον* ("a theater, a spectacle") "to the world, to angels, and to men" (1 Cor 4:9). In the same epistle he also mentioned the Rom. amusement of watching fights with wild animals (*θηριομαχέω*, 1 Cor 15:32). The pagan world of the NT period was as absorbed with amusements as is the present age. The Christians were acquainted with the culture of their time, but they did not occupy themselves with it unduly, nor did they become engrossed in its less desirable features.

BIBLIOGRAPHY. E. Falkener, *Games Ancient and Oriental* (1892); I. Lexova, *Ancient Egyptian Dances* (1935); H. Hickmann, *45 siècles de musique dans l'Égypte ancienne* (1956); C. DeVries, *Attitudes of the Ancient Egyptians toward Physical-Recreative Activities* (unpublished Ph. D. dissertation, 1960). Hickmann, *Musikgeschichte in Bildern.* Ägypten (1961).

C. E. DE VRIES

GAMMADIM(S). KJV form of GAMAD (MEN OF).

GAMUL gā′ məl (גָּמוּל, *weaned* [?]). Gamul was listed as a chief of the Levites, being appointed by lot as the head of the twenty-second course of priests (1 Chron 24:17).

GANGRENE. *See* DISEASE, DISEASES.

GAR. KJV Apoc. form of GAS.

GARDEN (גַּן ; גַּנָּה ; גִּנָּה, *a royal garden*; κῆπος, *an orchard* or *plantation*). The three most important events in the Bible took place in a garden: (1) Sin entered in (Gen 3); (2) The Lord Jesus accepted the fact that He must go to the cross (Matt 26:36-46); (3) He was put into a sepulcher and rose again (John 19:41).

God planted the first garden (Gen 2:8). Complete irrigation was provided (2:10), and God Himself loved walking in the garden in the cool of the day (3:8).

Kings liked gardens. Ahab, for instance, wanted to make a scented garden of herbs near his palace, and his wife had Naboth murdered so that he could do it. It was so important to him. Ahaziah fled down the garden path and through the orangery or head gardener's house and so escaped (2 Kings 9:27), but Jehu followed him and killed him. Years later, at the siege of Nebuchadnezzar, many of the Heb. soldiers fled the same way. Manasseh had a garden in Jerusalem and was buried there (2 Kings 21:18).

Solomon waxed lyrical about gardens in the Song of Solomon (4:15)—"a garden fountain"; (6:2) "to pasture . . . in the gardens and to gather lilies"; (4:16) "Let my beloved come to his garden." In Ecclesiastes 2:5, it says: "I made myself gardens."

A garden is used to express joy, peace and satisfaction (Jer 31:12)—"their life shall be like a watered garden," while a fruitless life is described as "a garden without water" (Isa 1:30).

Foreign potentates delighted in watered gardens. Esther saw the beautiful courtyard gardens of King Ahasuerus (Esth 1:5). The king found that a walk in his gardens calmed him when he was angry (Esth 7:7).

The garden of nuts (S of Sol 6:11) was prob. a grove of walnut trees. Moffatt therefore

A view of the Garden of Gethsemane. ©*Lev*

calls it a walnut bower—and it is a Pers. bower at that, as this was the species grown in Pal. *See* EDEN, GARDEN OF.

W. E. SHEWELL-COOPER

GARDENER (*κηπουρός*). Mentioned only in John 20:15: "Supposing him to be the gardener." Of course, spiritually He is the Gardener, for He waters and cares for His plants who must stay where He puts them, and bear "fruit" a hundredfold.

By inference, however, gardeners are mentioned elsewhere in the Bible. Adam and Eve were gardeners tending the Garden of Eden. Cain became a gardener growing vegetables and fruits when Abel was a farmer.

In Luke 13:8 it is surely a gardener who asks whether he may not organically manure a tree which had become unproductive.

Gardeners tended the groves or gardens of a nature-loving heathen God, Baal (2 Kings 10: 19-23). Paul was a tentmaker, but he may have been a keen amateur gardener also, for he knows about the "stocks" of fruit trees and grafting. Isaiah used a gardener's metaphor of taking cuttings (Isa 17:10). Solomon's writings suggest that he was an interested amateur gardener, also.

W. E. SHEWELL-COOPER

GAREB gâr' ĕb (גרב ; *itch, scab*). 1. An Ithrite warrior singled out for recognition among David's "thirty" heroes (2 Sam 23:38; 1 Chron 11:40). According to 1 Chronicles 2:53, the Ithrites were a family of Kiriath-jearim (q.v.), but some scholars prefer to understand Gareb to be a native of the village of Jattir (q.v.), a reading that requires only a change of pointing (*see* S. R. Driver: *Notes on the Hebrew Text of the Books of Samuel,* 2nd ed. [1913], 372).

2. A hill not far from Jerusalem, mentioned by Jeremiah as a landmark for the future limits of the city (Jer 31:39). Scholars have not agreed on the site, not even on the direction from the city.

G. G. SWAIM

GARIZIM. KJV Apoc. form of GERIZIM.

GARLAND (לויה, Prov 1:9, 4:9; פאר, Exod 39:28; Isa 3:20; 61:3, 10; Ezek 24:17; στέμμα Acts 14:13). These two Heb. words and one Gr. word can carry the meaning of "wreath," "headdress," or "chaplet." While the word "garland" occurs only once in KJV (Acts 14:13), it occurs at least six times in RSV and a number of times in other modern trs. A "garland" or a "wreath" was one of the prizes given to the victor in a particular sports event. The references in Proverbs and Isaiah refer to the head dress of a maiden or woman. It was also at times worn by priests either on the head or as a part of the total dress.

In the Book of Acts "garlands" were among the offerings and sacrifices brought by the priest of Zeus to honor Paul and Barnabas.

G. GIACUMAKIS, JR.

GARLIC, GARLICK (שומים) . Garlic is mentioned only once in the Bible (Num 11:5)—"the leeks, the onions and the garlic." Though the mention of garlic refers to the bulbs grown in Egypt, there is no doubt at all that this crop subsequently was grown in the Holy Land, and was used in cooking.

This flavorsome vegetable is mentioned because the Israelites were tired of the simple manna and longed for the pleasant varieties eaten in Egypt.

The bulbous perennial garlic is *Allium sativum*. When planted, it produces a number of smaller surrounding bulbs, which are called cloves.

Garlic has been used medicinally as a digestive stimulant, and its juice as an antiseptic.

W. E. SHEWELL-COOPER

GARMENT(S). *See* DRESS.

GARMITE (גרמי, meaning obscure, but perhaps it comes from גרם, which means "bone" 1 Chron 4:19). This gentilic name is attached to the name of Keilah found in a genealogy of the descendants of Caleb. It is difficult to ascertain the reason for this description. Perhaps it had to do with his appearance as bony or with his strength.

G. GIACUMAKIS, JR.

GARNER (אוצר, Joel 1:17; מזו, Ps 144:13; ἀποθήκη, Matt 3:12; Luke 3:17; all three mean *treasury, repository* for grain, or *barn*). The noun use of "garner," which is now obsolete, has been the tr. of the two Heb. words above. אוצר occurs frequently throughout the OT and carries the idea of treasure, treasury or storehouse (Josh 6:19; 1 Kings 7:51; Prov 15:16; etc). מזו with the same meaning is found only once in the Book of Psalms. The more current trs. tend to be either "granary" or "treasury." In the NT the noun form has been tr. as "barn" in most modern VSS.

The verbal use of this word with the idea of gathering is more common in Eng. and still used. Both RSV and NASB use it in this way in Isaiah 62:9.

G. GIACUMAKIS, JR.

GARNET gârn' et, a common and widely distributed accessory rock-forming mineral, particularly in micaceous schists and in some igneous rocks. The color of this silicate mineral varies greatly, being dependent upon the varying proportions of calcium, magnesium, manganese, aluminum, chronium and titanium present. It is used as a gemstone, particularly the deep red magnesium-aluminum variety pyrope and the brownish red to deep red iron-aluminum variety almandine in which the color sometimes inclines to purple. Two other varieties also show purple color (Exod 28:18; 39:11; Ezek 27:16; 28:13 NEB): (i) the manganese-aluminum variety spessartite, which is generally dark hyacinth red to brownish red, but sometimes with a tinge of violet, and (ii) the magnesium-iron-aluminum variety rhodolite which shows delicate shades of pale rose-red and purple.

D. R. BOWES

GARRISON (מצב, 2 Sam 23:14; מצבה, 1 Sam 14:12; נציב, 1 Sam 10:5; 13:3, 4). A garrison is a group of troops usually assigned to a fortress or to a strategic frontier area primarily for defensive purposes. Larger military units would be needed for an offensive drive. Garrisons were placed by the Philistines in the Judean region of Israel (1 Sam 14). Once David brought these garrisons under his control, he then placed his own garrisons in Edom and Syria.

G. GIACUMAKIS, JR.

GAS (Γας, 1 Esd 5:34). This personal name is found listed in a subdivision of Temple servants. It is specifically listed under the sons of the servants of Solomon. "Gas" is only in the apocryphal book, for it has been omitted in the parallel passage in Ezra 2:57.

G. GIACUMAKIS, JR.

GATAM (געתם, perhaps meaning *burnt valley*, Gen 36:11, 16; 1 Chron 1:36). In the genealogy of Abraham's descendants through Sarah, he was the fourth son of Eliphaz, the son of Esau, and an Edomite clan chief.

GASHMU. KJV and ASV form of GESHEM.

GATE (שער, *to divide*; דלת, *gateway*; פתח, תרע, *πύλη, πυλών, θύρα*). The entrance into a palace, camp, temple, etc., but esp. a city. Although the principal purpose of city gates was to make entrance and exit through its walls possible and to make the city secure, they were also used for many public purposes in the economy of the state.

They were the civic centers of the city. Since the city dwellers worked on farms outside the city walls, everyone passed through

The Golden Gate into the old city of Jerusalem. ©*Lev*

the gates every day. It was there, in an open square by the gate, that people met their friends or discussed news (Gen 19:1; 23:10; 34:20; 2 Sam 15:2; Neh 8:1; Ps 69:12).

It was at the gate that the elders of the city sat for the administration of justice. The Mosaic law directed that rebellious sons be brought before the elders of the city at the gate (Deut 21:19). The manslayer had an opportunity to present his cause before the elders of the city of refuge at the entering in of the gate (Josh 20:4). Boaz consulted the elders of Bethlehem at the gate concerning Ruth's property (Ruth 4:1).

It was at the gate that kings sat to meet with their subjects and made legal decisions. When David heard of the death of Absalom, he sat at the gate and the people came before him to express their sympathy (2 Sam 19:8). The king of Israel joined by the king of Judah sat at the entrance of the gate of Samaria and had the prophets prophesy before them (1 Kings 22:10). Zedekiah sat at the Benjamin gate when he was told that Jeremiah had been dropped into a cistern by his enemies (Jer 38:7). When Jerusalem fell to the Babylonians, all the princes of Babylon came and sat in the middle gate (39:3). Hezekiah brought his military commanders together in the square at the gate of the city and told them not to despair over the threatened siege of Jerusalem (2 Chron 32:6).

The priests and prophets sometimes delivered their discourses, admonitions, and prophecies at the gate (2 Kings 7:1; Neh 8:1, 3; Jer 17:19, 20; 36:10).

The first legal transaction on record in the Bible, that of Abraham's purchase of the cave of Machpelah as a burial place for Sarah, was completed at the gate of the city of Hebron (Gen 23:10, 18). The gate was the market place of the town (2 Kings 7:1).

Criminals condemned to death were punished outside the gates of the city (1 Kings 22:10; Acts 7:58). Assyrian sculptures give numerous examples of execution by impalement outside the city walls and of burying outside the city gates. The dead were buried beyond the gates (Luke 7:12; Heb 13:12).

The town good-for-nothings resorted to the gate (Ps 69:12).

Gates consisted of two halves (Isa 45:1), and were made of wood, perhaps studded with nails, or of wood covered with sheets of copper or iron, or of metal (1 Kings 4:13; Ps 107:16; Isa 45:2; Acts 12:10). Occasionally gates were made of a single slab of stone, like the doors leading into the tombs of the kings near Jerusalem, which consisted of a single stone seven inches thick.

Gates were secured by strong locks of brass, iron, or wood (Deut 3:5; 1 Sam 23:7; 1 Kings 4:13; 2 Chron 8:5; Ps 147:13). The keys for gates were large, sometimes more than two feet in length (Isa 22:22).

Since the gates of a city were the weakest point of its defenses, they were strengthened by towers (2 Chron 14:7; 26:9; 32:5; Ps 48:12). Usually there was an outer and an inner gate, with rooms for the keepers at the sides, and often a room above the gate (2 Sam 18:24, 33). The width of the principal gate was about thirteen or fourteen feet. The other gates were low and narrow, permitting the entrance only of pedestrians or a single ass. Gates were of course closed and guarded at night (Josh 2:5, 7; Neh 7:3).

In the Bronze Age, the city walls had only one or two gates, seldom more. In the Iron Age the gates were more numerous. A number of Bronze Age and Iron Age gates have been preserved, notably at Gezer and Megiddo. The city of Babylon, which was forty m. in circuit, had one hundred bronze doors. Jerusalem had fifteen, each with a different name. The great wall surrounding the Temple at Jerusalem had nine gateways, with a massive two-storied gate-house over each one. One of the gates, called "Beautiful," was built entirely of Corinthian brass (Acts 3:2, 10).

The word "gate" often is used in a fig. sense. It frequently signifies the city itself, as when God promised Abraham that his posterity should possess the gate of his enemies (Gen 22:17), meaning that they should have power or dominion over the cities of their enemies. To "possess the gate" was to possess the city (24:60). To sit "among the elders of the gates" was a high honor (Prov 31:23), whereas "oppression in the gates" was synonymous for judicial corruption (Job 31:21; Prov 22:22). The gate is also a symbol of strength, power, and dominion (Ps 24:7; 87:2; Isa 60:18). Gates are pictured as howling and languishing, lamenting and mourning in time of a city's calamity (Isa 3:26; 14:31; Jer 14:2). Mention is made of the gate of heaven (Gen 28:17); the gate of the Lord (Ps 118:20); the gates of death (Ps 9:13); the gates of Sheol (Isa 38:10); the gates of Hades (Matt 16:18 ASV, KJV). When Jesus contrasted the wide gate and the narrow gate (Matt 7:13), he had in mind the broad main gate at the entrance into a city and the small ones that allowed only pedestrians and single animals to pass through.

BIBLIOGRAPHY. M. Avi-Yonah, *Views of the Biblical World* (1960), II 94, 107, 221, 262; III 137, 151; R. de Vaux, *Ancient Israel* (1961), 152 153, 155, 166, 167, 233, 234; G. E. Wright, *Biblical Archaeology* (1962), 74, 129, 132, 133, 135, 156, 163.

S. BARABAS

GATE BETWEEN THE TWO WALLS. This gate is mentioned only three times in the OT (2 Kings 25:4; Jer 39:4; 52:7). All three references are in the same context. Jerusalem was under siege by Nebuchadnezzar's army in 587 B.C. Zedekiah and his army fled eastward by night through the "gate between the two walls" to the Jordan Valley. One of the identifying fac-

Detail of Ishtar Gate of Nebuchadnezzar II at Babylon, from reconstruction in *Staatliche Museen zu Berlin.*

tors about this gate is its location near the "king's garden" which in Nehemiah 3:15 is said to be near the Pool of Siloam (Shelah). This pool at the southernmost part of Jerusalem lay between the main city wall and an outer wall. Several scholars have identified this gate as being the same as Nehemiah's Fountain Gate.

G. GIACUMAKIS, JR.

GATE, THE BEAUTIFUL (ἡ Ὡράια πύλη or θύρα, *the beautiful gate*, or *door*). A gate in Herod's Temple, q.v.

Whereas the "Beautiful Gate" of the NT Temple is known only from Acts 3, the phrase prob. refers to that entrance way, famous for its imported Corinthian bronze doors, which was the only E gate from the surrounding Court of the Gentiles into the Court of the Women (Jos. War. V. 5. 3). It was once identified with the single E gate that led from the Kidron Valley, through the outer wall and "Solomon's Porch," into the Court of the Gentiles—a fact that may account for the name of the later entrance way, now itself sealed up, that was built over it and called "Porta Aurea" (Ὡράια), the "Golden Gate."

After Pentecost, a man lame from his mother's womb, was laid daily at the Beautiful Gate to ask for alms, and was miraculously healed by Peter and John in the name of Jesus Christ (Acts 3:2, 10).

BIBLIOGRAPHY. J. Simons, *Jerusalem in the OT* (1952), 371; A. Parrot, *The Temple of Jerusalem* (1957), 85-88.

J. B. PAYNE

GATE, EAST. The most magnificent gate of Jerusalem, called the "Beautiful Gate" in Acts 3:2, 10. It was called the King's Gate after the return from the Exile (1 Chron 9:18) and had a special keeper as early as Hezekiah's day (1 Chron 31:14; cf. Neh 3:29). The Water Gate is also known as the east gate in this period (Neh 12:37 RSV).

The east gate plays an important role in Ezekiel's visions in the following ways: (1) the cherubim of the vision recorded in the tenth ch. are said to have stood at the door of the east gate of the house of the Lord with the glory of God over them (Ezek 10:19); (2) at the door of the gateway, Ezekiel also was shown by the Spirit twenty-five men guilty of iniquity and wicked counsel in Jerusalem (11:1, 2); (3) it was the first gate to be measured in Ezekiel's vision during the twenty-fifth year of exile (40:1-16); (4) it was the gate where Ezekiel saw the glory of God enter the Temple after which the glory of the Lord filled the Temple (43:1-4); (5) and it was the gate that was opened for the prince when he offered a burnt offering or a peace offering to the Lord, and was to be shut after he departed (46:12).

J. B. SCOTT

GATE, VALLEY (שער הגיא, 2 Chron 26:9; Neh 2:13, 15; 3:13). The Valley Gate is mentioned in two OT contexts. The first mentions that Azariah or Uzziah built "towers in Jerusalem at the Corner Gate and at the Valley Gate . . ." (2 Chron 26:9). This gate is mentioned again in the days of the return (c. 440 B.C.) as the place where Nehemiah began his inspection night walk. He went out of the gate heading S around the Pool of Siloam and then N past the Fountain Gate until there was no more space for his mount to walk. After the inspection tour, he returned again to the Valley Gate. This gate was on the western side of the city facing the Tyropoeon Valley.

G. GIACUMAKIS, JR.

GATH gǎth (גַּת, *winepress*). One of the five cities of the Philistines (Gaza, Ashdod, Ashkelon, Ekron, Gath), all located on or near the coast of Southern Pal., and each ruled by its own king (Josh 13:3; 1 Sam 6:17). Gath was an old Canaanite city, and among its inhabitants, who were called Gittites (2 Sam 6:10, 11; 15:18, 19, 22), were the Anakim, a people of extraordinary height who lived in the hill country of Pal. generally. The Anakim were cut off by the Israelites in the general campaign under Joshua (Josh 10:36-39; 11: 21, 22), but a remnant was left in Gaza, Ashdod, and Gath (11:22). Like all towns of any importance in ancient times, Gath was a walled city (2 Chron 26:6).

Early in the history of Israel the men of Gath slew some Israelites for raiding their cattle (1 Chron 7:21; 8:13). When the Philistines captured the Ark of the Lord, they kept it successively in Ashdod, Gath, and Ekron, and then sent it back to Israel after many of the Philistines had died (1 Sam 5:6-10; 6: 17). In the days of Samuel the Philistines took cities from the Israelites, but after they were routed at Ebenezer the cities were restored (7:14). However, the Philistines continued to be a source of trouble for the Israelites in the lifetime of Samuel (1 Sam 9:16; 10:5; 13: 3, 5, 19; 14:21; 17:1; 23:27). The giant Goliath who was slain by David was one of the Anakim from Gath (17:4, 23; 2 Sam 21:20, 22; 1 Chron 20:5-8). Among some Anakim from Gath slain by David and his servants was a man with six fingers on each hand and six toes on each foot (2 Sam 21:18-22; 1 Chron 20:6-8). When the Philistines saw that their champion Goliath was dead, they fled from the pursuing Israelites to their own cities as far as Gath and Ekron (1 Sam 17:52). During the years of David's flight from King Saul, he twice took refuge in Gath. On the first occasion, to save his life he feigned madness (1 Sam 21:10-15; Ps 56:1); on the second, he was accompanied by his wives and 600 followers, and was kindly received by Achish the king who gave him the city of Ziklag in which to live (1 Sam 27:1-28:2; 29). The likelihood is that for this favor David rendered Achish personal service in war (1 Sam 28:1). David's lament over the death of Saul and Jonathan

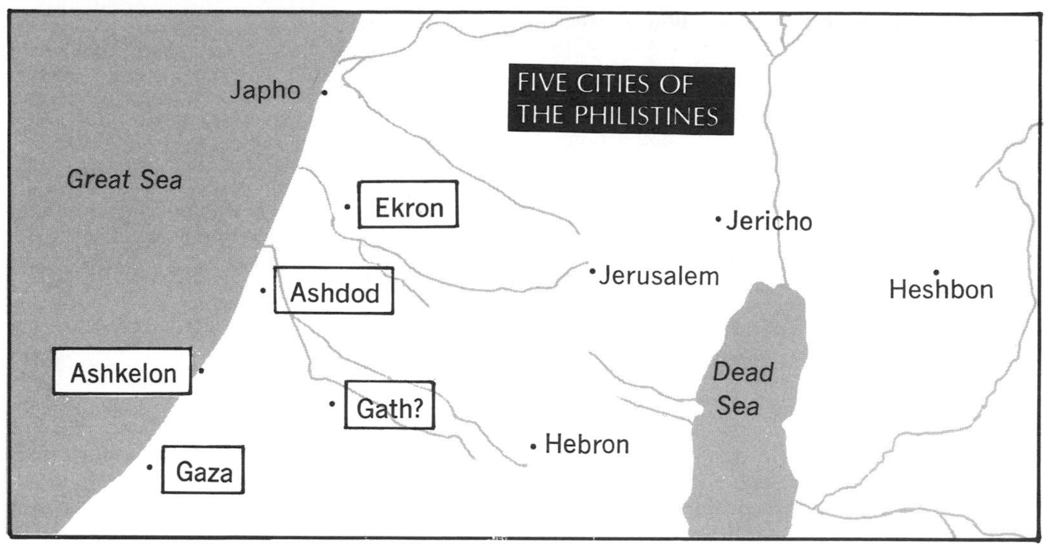

mentions the Philistine cities Gath and Ashkelon (2 Sam 1:20). The Obed-edom to whom David entrusted the safekeeping of the Ark is referred to as a Gittite, but it is not known whether he was a follower of David from Gath or whether he was a native of the Levitical city of Gath-rimmon, and therefore a Kohathite Levite (Josh 21:24, 25). Sometime during the reign of David—it is not certain exactly when—he defeated the Philistines and took from them the city of Gath and its villages (1 Chron 18:1). When David fled from Jerusalem after he had heard of Absalom's conspiracy to seize the throne, 600 Philistine followers from Gath accompanied him, and also Ittai the Gittite, who shared the command of the army with Joab and Abishai and who refused to accept David's kind invitation to dissociate himself from him (2 Sam 15:18-22; 18:2, 5). It is said in 1 Kings 2:39-42 that two of the servants of Shimei, who had insulted David with gross language when David fled from Absalom, ran away to Gath and that Shimei pursued them there and brought them back, although he had been ordered by Solomon not to leave Jerusalem under any circumstances. Solomon's son Rehoboam restored the fortifications of Gath (2 Chron 11:8-10), which had either been destroyed by David or had been allowed to fall into disrepair. Hazael, king of Syria, captured Gath during the reign of Jehoash (2 Kings 12:17), but Jehoash later recaptured the city from Hazael's son Ben-hadad. Uzziah, king of Judah, made war on the Philistines and broke down the walls of Gath (2 Chron 26:6), indicating that the Philistines must have retaken it from the Israelites.

In 715 B.C. Sargon II, king of Assyria, brought a heavy defeat upon Ashdod and Gath which, instigated by Egypt, sought to include Palestine, Judah, Edom, and Moab in an anti-Assryian league. It is not known whether Gath was then destroyed; but for some reason the later prophets omit it in the lists of Philistine cities (Amos 1:6-8; Zeph 2:4-6; Jer 25:20; Zech 9:5). The city drops out of history, and its very location is a matter of dispute. Scripture indicates a site in the Shephelah, not far from the border of Heb. territory and from Ekron in N Philistia. Various places have been proposed as its location, the most widely accepted being Tell es-Safi, c. twelve m. N of Ashdod, and Tell Sheikh Ahmed el-'Areini, near 'Araq el-Menshiyeh, c. fifteen m. E of Ashkelon and c. seven m. S of Tell es-Safi.

There were several other places with the name of Gath in Pal., since the culture of the vine was a major occupation in ancient Israel. Some of the Gaths, like Gath-hepher (2 Kings 14:25) and Gath-rimmon (Josh 19:45; 21:24, 25; 1 Chron 6:69), have an additional element added to the name to distinguish it from other Gaths, but often the name stands alone, and it is difficult to decide exactly which Gath is meant. Four or five Gaths are known from sources outside the Bible, for example in the Amarna Tablets.

BIBLIOGRAPHY. W. F. Albright, "The Sites of Ekron, Gath, and Libnah," AASOR, II-III (1923), 7-12; B. Mazar (Maisler), "Tell Gath," IEJ, VI (1956), 258, 259; D. W. Thomas, *Documents from Old Testament Times* (1962), 59; C. F. Pfeiffer, *The Biblical World* (1966), 249, 250.

S. BARABAS

GATH-HEPHER **găth heʹ fər** (גַּת־הַחֵפֶר, *winepress of digging*) KJV GITTAH-HEPHER, gĭtʹ e hē fer. A town on the border of Zebulun and Naphtali in the tribe of Zebulun (Josh

19:13) and the home of the prophet Jonah. The town is prob. to be identified with Khirbet ez-Zurra, about three m. NE of Nazareth. Nearby, to the N, is the village of Meshhed, which is the traditional site of Jonah's tomb. Archeological evidence for the occupation of this site during the time of Jonah has been found. Jerome reported visiting this tomb in his lifetime.

J. B. SCOTT

GATH-RIMMON gă̄th rĭm' ən (גת רמון, *wine-press of Rimmon*). 1. A city of the tribe of Dan (Josh 19:45). It was one of four cities of the tribe of Dan allotted to the Kohathites of the family of the Levites (21:24), and designated a city of refuge (1 Chron 6:69). Its probable location is at Tell ej-Jerisheh, four and one-half m. NE of Joppa.

2. A city of the one-half tribe of Manasseh, W of the Jordan, possibly to be identified with Rummaneh, NW of Taanach (Josh 21:25). Many scholars believe that the name came in as the result of a scribal error in recording Joshua 21:25. Verse 24 contains the name of the Danite Gath-Rimmon. If this is true, then the second Gath-Rimmon should in reality be the "Bileam" of 1 Chronicles 6:70. This conclusion is strengthened by the fact that the LXX B in Joshua 21:25 has Ἴβαθα (*Bileam*), but omits Gath-Rimmon. Bileam is located about fifteen m. SE of Megiddo.

J. B. SCOTT

GAULANITIS gôl' ə nī' tĭs (Γαυλανῖτις). A district E of the Sea of Galilee, from Hippos in the S to Seleucia in the N. The name derives from the ancient town of Golan (Γαυλών; גולן), located by archeologists about seventeen m. E of the Sea of Galilee near the modern Arab town Sheikh Sa'd.

Moses designated Golan as one of three cities of refuge "beyond the Jordan . . . . Golan in Bashan for the Manassites" (Deut 4:41, 43). Under Joshua this status continued, and the Gershonites were assigned to the city (Josh 20:8; 21:27; 1 Chron 6:71). Undoubtedly Golan was the chief city of the district S of Mt. Hermon settled by the tribe of Manasseh.

The city is not mentioned in the NT, although there is an interesting parallel between Acts and Josephus. Josephus identifies a certain revolutionary leader Judas as from Gaulanitis (Jos. Antiq. XVIII. i. 1) whereas Luke identified him as a Galilean (Acts 5:37). Josephus also called him a Galilean (Jos. Antiq. XX. v. 2; War II. viii. 1) proving Luke's identification correct and suggesting that he was prob. born in Gaulon and active in Galilee. Neither source confuses Galilee with Gaulanitis.

During the Herodian dynasty, Gaulanitis was inherited by Philip after Herod's death, and continued as a part of his tetrarchy from 4 B.C. until A.D. 34. Philip's capital was Bethsaida, rebuilt and renamed Bethsaida Julias for the daughter of Augustus Ceasar. Jesus traveled freely in this area (Mark 6:45; 8:22, 27).

It passed to the rule of Agrippa I in A.D. 37 until his death in A.D. 44. In A.D. 53, Agrippa II received it and continued to hold it until the Jewish revolt began in A.D. 66. The area was subject to the early campaign of the Romans against the Jewish revolutionaries (Jos., War IV. i. 1).

The land is part of the E Jordan plateau country and the soil is fertile. During the time of Christ the area was heavily populated.

BIBLIOGRAPHY. E. G. Kraeling, *Rand McNally Bible Atlas.*

J. C. DEYOUNG

GAULS gôlz (Gr. Γαλάτις). An ancient name for the inhabitants of the land area from the Atlantic Ocean to the Rhine River and extending from the English Channel to the Pyrenees and extended W of the Alps. It was applied by the classical peoples to the Germanic tribes of the region. They were subdivided by Julius Caesar and other authors into Belgae, Celtae and Aquitani as early as 100 B.C. Their presence, however, was known far earlier although was not specified. As wave after wave of Indo-European peoples migrated across the steppes of Eurasia during the 3rd and 2nd millennia into northern Greece, the Danube Valley, the forests and coastal plains of modern Germany and France, they often brushed the borders of the great river valley civilizations of the ancient Near E. They may have been included in the peoples mentioned by such names as Togarmah (Gen 10:3). The scarce remnants of their languages are Germanic and show similarity to the Gothic dialects of the Danube Valley. Their art as known from excavations of old Rom. sites in Northern Europe shows grotesque zoomorphic figures and finely wrought designs related to the Persian and Sarmatian art of the Indo-Iranian plateau.

W. WHITE, JR.

GAUZE, GARMENTS OF (גליון, RSV Isa 3:23, meaning *papyrus garments*; also means *tablet*, Isa 8:1). The Heb. word occurs only twice. Its meaning in Isaiah 8:1 is some type of tablet prob. made of papyrus. The difficulty lies in the Isaiah 3:23 passage. The immediate context is a criticism of the "daughters of Zion" and including a statement that the Lord will take away a number of their dress items of beauty. KJV mentions "glasses" and ASV "handmirrors," whereas RSV has "garments of gauze." Holladay* defines this Heb. word as "papyrus garments" in his attempt to capture the meaning of a very fine material.

(*William L. Holladay, ed.: *A Concise Hebrew and Aramaic Lexicon of the Old Testament*. An Eng. tr. based on the 2nd and 3rd eds. of Koehler-Baumgartner [1971]).

G. GIACUMAKIS, JR.

A scene on the Golan (Gaulanitis) Heights, east of the Sea of Galilee. © *Lev*

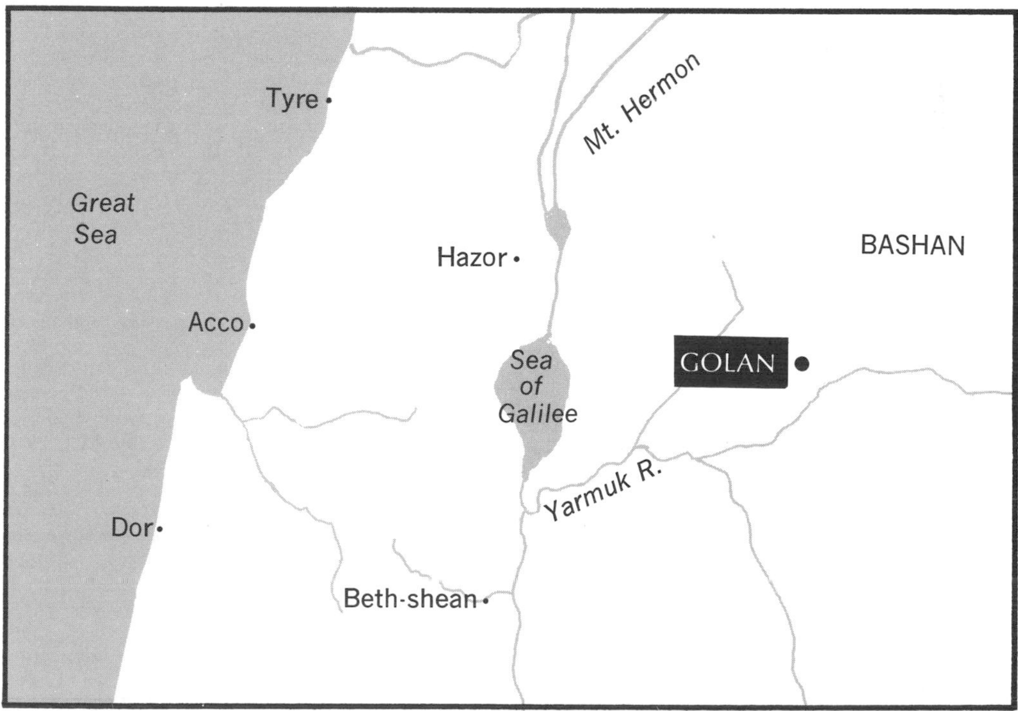

GAZA gā' zə, the more usual Eng. pronunciation of the past; gä' ze, the pronunciation more currently in use because of the prominence of this area, populated basically by Arabs, in the modern Middle East situation (עזה, *strong*; עזז, עזתי, *be strong*, Akkad. *Hazzatu*, *Hazzati*, *Azzat*; Egypt. *Gadātu*, *Gedjet*; LXX and NT Γάζα, Mod. Arab. Ghazzeh). KJV AZZAH, ā' ze, in Deuteronomy 2:23; 1 Kings 4:24; Jeremiah 25:20; **GAZITES gā' zīts, GAZATHITES gā' zə thīts.** The southernmost of the five chief Philistine cities in SW Pal., located a short distance inland from the Mediterranean Sea, on a route to Egypt.

1. Location. Ancient OT Gaza was located about fifty m. SW of Jerusalem and about three m. inland from the Mediterranean Sea. The town was about twelve m. S of Ashkelon, another important Philistine city, and on the important caravan and military route that extended to the SW and then W through the sands close to the Mediterranean Sea to Pelusium and the Egyp. Delta. Through Gaza, military expeditions were made from Egypt to Palestine, Syria, and the countries of Mesopotamia. It was vital, in any military campaign, for opposing enemies to hold this city as a rest area to or from the desert.

2. Geographical characteristics. The OT Gaza lay on and about a hill c. 100 ft. above a fertile plain. It was a natural location for a city because of fifteen fresh water wells that provided for adequate agricultural produce and the physical needs of a large population. It was inevitable that this town should develop as a trade center for caravans and a place where armies could restock their water supplies.

3. The earliest history of Gaza. The earliest OT reference (Gen 10:19) goes back to the pre-Abrahamic period in which the territory of the Canaanites is described as extending from Sidon in the N to Gerar and Gaza in SW Pal. Other early inhabitants of Gaza and the southern end of Pal., evidently prior to the time of Moses, were called Avvim (Deut 2:23; cf. vv. 19-23). Later, in Joshua's day, the Avvim together with the Canaanites were still associated with S Pal., but the Philistines were then in control of Gaza and the surrounding area (Josh 13:3, 4).

4. Early extra-Biblical references to Gaza. The Annals of Thutmose III present Gaza as an important town, which Thutmose and his Egyp. army seized and at which he stayed on his first campaign into Pal. involving the battle of Megiddo (1468 B.C. ANET, 235). Compare also the Taanach Letter No. 6, which among others was written to a prince Rewašša by an Egyp. official, Amenophis, who mentions his being in the town of Gaza, *Hazati*, (W. F. Albright, "A Prince of Taanach in the Fifteenth Century B.C.," BASOR 94 [1944], 24-27; Albright conjectures that this Egyp. governor, Amenophis, who resided at Gaza may have been the later Egyp. Pharaoh, Amenophis II). A little later in the 15th-14th cent. B.C., during this period of Egyp. domination of Pal. including the Gaza-Ashkelon area, the Tell el-Amarna No. 320, although not mentioning Gaza, refers to nearby Ashkelon in such terms as to reflect on the greater importance of the nearby official Egyp. residence at Gaza (ANET, 490). Another Amarna letter, No. 289, mentions Gaza as well as the whole land as loyal to Egypt, although there was trouble from the advancing 'Apiru (ANET, 489). Very possibly, the word *'Apiru* could mean the *Hebrews*. After the conquest of Pal. under Joshua, Judges 2:20-3:1 indicates there was much land to be subdued. The Egyptians c. 1200 B.C. could speak of still having influence over Gaza and other places S of Canaan (Papyrus Anasti I, of the late Nineteenth Egyp. Dynasty, ANET, 478).

5. Gaza and Israel. Joshua 10:41 is the first Biblical reference which mentions Israel's contact with this Philistine town, describing the fact that Joshua in his conquest defeated all of S Pal. including the area from Kadesh-barnea to Gaza. Joshua 11:22 adds that the ancient Anakim people in Israel were destroyed except in certain Philistine cities including Gaza, which cities were really in the control of the Philistines (Josh 13:3). This town was allotted to Judah (Josh 15:47), who then had the responsibility of trying to conquer it (Judg 1:18, 19). Judah did not succeed, at least for long, because the Midianites, Amalekites, and others made attacks at will on Israel as far as Gaza (Judg 6:4), and in the time of Samson, the Philistines were well in control of this town (Judg 16). Samson had made inroads on Philistine power (Judg 14; 15), including his eluding and humiliating his Gazite enemies by ripping off the doors of the gate of their city and carrying them off to Hebron (16:1-3), but evidence of complete Philistine control of Gaza was their humiliation of Samson in the prison at this city (16:21).

Later mastery of the city and area by the Philistines is evident when the king of Gath and the other Philistine rulers sent the captured ark back to Israel with a trespass offering of gold (1 Sam 6:17).

In the time of the united monarchy, Solomon most likely had the mastery over even a border area such as Gaza—in the light of 1 Kings 4:24, which states that this king "had dominion over all the region west of the Euphrates, from Tipsah to Gaza, over all the kings west of the Euphrates."

Amos (mid-8th cent. B.C.) pronounced the Lord's condemnation on Gaza because they had conquered a people and delivered them as slaves to Edom (Amos 1:6, 7).

In the time of Assyrian ascendancy, Tiglath-pilezer III (744-727 B.C.), in connection with his campaigns against Syria and Pal. (733-732), told how he received tribute of gold, silver, antimony, linen garments, etc.,

Village of Gaza looking west toward the sea. ©*M.P.S.*

from a number of cities, including Gaza and its king Hanno (ANET, 282). Hanno eventually fled to Egypt and returned with the Egyptians to fight against Sargon II (721-705 B.C.) in a battle S of Gaza (c. 721-720). Following defeat he was deported to the city of Ashur (ANET, 283-285). Gaza became Assyrian, but the Philistines were still in the region, for a little later Hezekiah, king of Judah, in rebellion against Assyria, "smote the Philistines as far as Gaza and its territory" (2 Kings 18:8). A few years later another Assyrian king, Sennacherib (704-681) made a campaign against the cities of Judah and conquered them (701 B.C., 2 Kings 18:13), and when he threatened Hezekiah and Jerusalem, the Lord overthrew his army (2 Kings 18:17-19:35). In arrogant boasting in his annals, Sennacherib told of shutting up Hezekiah in Jerusalem "like a bird in a cage," and how he took away sections of Judah and gave them to Sillibel, king of Gaza, and to other Philistine rulers (ANET, 288). Sil-Bel, king of Gaza (possibly the same ruler or a successor) with other rulers from the seacoast were forced to furnish building materials for the palace of Esar-haddon (680-669) at Nineveh (ANET, 291), and to Ashurbanipal (668-633); the same king is said to have brought heavy tribute and in submission kissed the Assyrian king's feet (ANET, 294). With this background in mind, Zephaniah (638-608) prophesied the overthrow of Gaza and the area (Zeph 2:4-7), which came about in stages in the succeeding centuries, as under Alexander Jannaeus (96 B.C.).

Jeremiah (47:1) speaks of Pharaoh conquering Gaza as does also Herodotus (2, 159) as he mentions Pharaoh's conquest of "the great Syrian city of κάδυτις" (i.e., Gaza); which occurred in connection with Pharaoh Neco's military expedition in 609 B.C. across Syria to fight the Babylonian king Nebuchadnezzar, conqueror of Assyria (Jer 46:2; cf. 2 Kings 23:29; 2 Chron 35:20; Jos Antiq. X. v. 1). Jeremiah also prophesied (Jer 25:20) that Nebuchadnezzar would conquer Gaza and all the land of the Philistines, which was fulfilled as witnessed to in the Inscriptions of Nebuchadnezzar (605-562 B.C.); the king of Gaza and others were ordered to carry on official duties in the Babylonian court (ANET, 307, 308).

6. Gaza in postexilic and intertestamental times. Despite the conquests already mentioned, Gaza and the Philistines maintained some power and influence, as is indicated by Zechariah's prophecy against them (9:5, 6). In the time of the Pers. invasion, Polybius (Hist 16, 22a) tells how brave the people of Gaza were. Later, under the Persians, the city with the help of Arab-hired soldiers (Arrian, Anab. 2, 26, 27), resisted a two-months' siege by Alexander the Great (332 B.C.) before finally falling to him (Diodorus 17, 48; Jos. Ant. XI. viii. 3; Polyb. 16, 22a), after which it became more and more a Gr. city (Josephus calls it πόλις Ἑλληνίς, Antiq. XVII. xi. 4.; War II. vi. 3). In subsequent years Gaza became the possession at times of Syria and then of Egypt. A few years prior to the Maccabean revolt, Gaza came more permanently under the control of Syria, following the victory of Antiochus the Great, at Panias (198 B.C.; cf. Polyb. Hist. 16, 22a).

In Maccabean times Gaza surrendered to Jonathan Maccabeus (1 Macc 11:61, 62). Later after the city had requested help from Ptolemy of Egypt against Alexander Jannaeus and that help failed, Alexander made a one-year seige against Gaza, conquered it, and slaughtered its people (96 B.C.; Jos. Antiq. XIII. 1. 3). In a real sense Alexander made Gaza ἔρημος, or deserted, a fact so indicated by ancient writers as Jos. Antiq. XIV. v. 3; Strabo 16, 2, 30.

Under Pompey, who conquered Syria c. 63 B.C., Gaza, such as it was, received its freedom (Jos. Antiq. XIV. iv. 4) and a little later, about 57 B.C., was rebuilt under the order of the Rom. general, Gabinius (Jos. Antiq. XIV. v. 3). In 30 B.C. Gaza came under the control of Herod the Great (Jos Antiq. XV. vii. 3; War I. XX. 3), but after his death it reverted to the province of Syria (Jos. Antiq. XVII. xi. 4; War II. vi. 3) as the imperial coins of Gaza, which begin to show up after Herod's death, demonstrate.

7. Gaza in NT times and later. The only NT mention of this city is Acts 8:26 in reference to " 'the road that goes down from Jerusalem to Gaza.' This is a desert road." A problem arises as to how the word ἔρημος, "desert," is to be handled: whether to refer it to the feminine word "road," as the RSV, "This is a *desert road*," or, as the TEV, Am. Bible Society, "This *road* is *no longer used*"; or to refer to the feminine noun *Gaza* with the meaning, "deserted" (i.e., "old") *Gaza*, as some have done. Strabo (16. 2, 30) had an understanding that Gaza had remained deserted (ἔρημος) after its destruction by Alexander the Great whom he seems to have confused with Alexander Jannaeus.

Diodorus (19, 80) spoke of an old Gaza. Some think there was a new Gaza built a bit S of the old city as maintained by some ancient geographers (*see* Schürer, II, 1, 71), and that Josephus' reference to Gaza as among coast towns (Antiq. XIV. iv. 4) also refers to this new city. The old Gaza no doubt became inhabited again after Alexander Jannaeus' destruction since it lay on the main caravan road (cf. also Diodor. 19, 80 Loeb. ed., and Arrian, Arab 2, 26, 27), and it and the new Gaza may well have continued together even into the NT period. However, that the old Gaza would then be called ἔρημος, "desert" in Acts 8:26, in reflection on its condition over a hundred years before does not sound likely. Rather, since the "road" is emphasized in Acts 8:26, it seems better to refer the concept "desert" to it, pointing out that it is the road that leads over to the desert way to Egypt.

In A.D. 66, Gaza was attacked and destroyed

A small family party of Palestine gazelles shelters under a thorn tree in the almost waterless Negev, near Eilat.

by the rebellious Jews (Jos War II. xviii. 1), but evidently only partially, for Gaza coins show up from the years A.D. 68-74 (Schürer, 2, 1, 72). In the 2nd and 3rd centuries A.D., the city prospered as a center of Gr. culture, and the Church only after hard struggles firmly established itself there at about A.D. 400. From A.D. 635 on, except for a brief time during the Crusades, Gaza was in Arab hands, until the late 1960s.

The modern city of Gaza rests on the old site, thus no significant archeological work has been possible. *See* PHILISTINES.

BIBLIOGRAPHY. E. Schürer, *A History of the Jewish People,* sec. div., vol 1 (1891), 68-72; G. A. Smith, *The Historical Geography of the Holy Land* (1896), 181-189; J. B. Pritchard, *Ancient Near Eastern Texts* (1955), 529; E. G. Kraeling, *Rand-McNally Bible Atlas* (1956), 417, 418.

W. H. MARE

GAZARA. ASV Apoc. form of GEZER.

GAZATHITES. *See* GAZA.

GAZELLE (צְבִי, *roe, roebuck* KJV; *gazelle* RSV; *gazelle* [all fig. uses, e.g. Deut 12:15]; *roe* [all fig. uses, e.g., Prov 6:5]; ASV עפר צביה, *young roes that are twins*; KJV *fawns, twins of a gazelle*; RSV Δορκάς, *gazelle.* Acts 9:36, "Tabitha, which means Dorcas or gazelle" confirms the Heb. tr. and there is nothing to support the tr. "roe," so its ASV retention in all fig. and poetic contexts is incorrect). The Roe Deer was once found in parts of Pal. (*see* DEER). Gazelles are medium-sized antelopes inhabiting dry grasslands and desert and extend, comprising about twelve species, from central Africa through Pal. and India to the Gobi Desert of Mongolia. The Gr. name is still found in the scientific name of *Gazella dorcas*, one of the two species found in W Pal. today. The other, much more common, is the Pal. gazelle; this is one of the smallest, standing just over two ft. at the shoulders. Gazelles are usually of pale brown or sandy color, often with a dark line along the side demarcating the almost white underparts. This provides good camouflage, but their main defense is speed, and all four fig. passages outside Song of Solomon refer to this. In Song of Solomon the word is used as a symbol of grace and beauty, and the name today still suggests these attributes.

At one time gazelles were widely distributed in Pal. and common enough to provide a useful amount of meat. This is clearly implied in Deuteronomy 12:15 and 22 where it is mentioned almost as a standard commodity. When Isaac asked Esau to go and kill some game ("venison" KJV), this could have meant any wild game, but by living in the Beersheba area—the gateway to the Negev—a gazelle would be the most likely target for Esau's arrow. Gazelle meat is sometimes rather dry but good enough for eating.

The spread of cultivation reduced the numbers of gazelles progressively, though the creatures are not unduly worried by the presence of men, and will feed around or even in farms and close to tractors if allowed to do so. Wealth allowed desert hunting for sport in cars, quickly reducing numbers to the danger point. In most Arab countries there is still little or no control, but with protection by game laws and reserves in Israel, stocks have recovered and their survival is much more hopeful. *See* DEER.

G. S. CANSDALE

GAZER. KJV alternate form of GEZER.

GAZERA. 1. 1 Maccabees 4:15; 7:45; 13:43, etc. sometimes spelled GAZARA. This is another way of writing the name of the OT city of Gezer.

2. 1 Esdras 5:31=GAZZAM found in Ezra 2:48 and Nehemiah 7:51.

GAZEZ gā′ zĭz (Heb. גָּזֵז, prob. derived from the word for shearing sheep, גזז). The word occurs as the name of a Calebite family only in 1 Chronicles 2:46 twice. It means something like "born at shearing time." They were a son and a brother of Haran; the older commentators thought them to be a son and grandson of Caleb.

W. WHITE, JR.

GAZITES. People of GAZA.

GAZZAM găz′ əm (Heb. גַּזָּם, traditionally derived from a noun for *caterpillar*, Amos 4:9). The name of the progenitor of some of the families of the Nethinim who returned to Jerusalem with Zerubbabel (536 B.C.), mentioned only in Ezra 2:48; Nehemiah 7:51. Mentioned as Gazera in 1 Esdras 5:31 (Gr. Γαζηρα).

W. WHITE, JR.

GEAR, RSV rendering of the Gr. σκεῦος, KJV "sail" in the context of Acts 27:17. The word is common enough in the NT, but the meaning is often uncertain. The range of meanings includes: (1) "thing," "inanimate object" (Mark 11:16, et al.); (2) "vessel," "dish," "container" (Luke 8:16); (3) "a designated vessel," "chosen object" such as a person's body (1 Pet 3:7, et al.); (4) "used of a woman, as the vessel of her husband" (1 Thess 4:4). With modifying adjectives it may refer to the equipment of various trades, such as shipping. It usually is assumed that the meaning in Acts is something like a kedge, possibly "light anchor" for warping a ship.

W. WHITE, JR.

GEBA gē′ bə (גֶּבַע, *hill, height*). KJV GABA, gā be (Josh 18:24; Ezra 2:26; Neh 7:30). A city of Benjamin, NE of Gibeah and E of Gibeon. (Josh 18:24); and assigned to the Levites (Josh 21:17; 1 Chron 6:60). Saul and Jonathan encamped there when the Philistines were at Michmash (1 Sam 13:16; KJV *Gibeah*). It was there that David began to smite the Philistines 2 Sam 5:25; but cf. 1 Chron 14:16). Asa built a fortress there with stones from Ramah (1 Kings 15:22; 2 Chron 16:6). As the N limit of Judah, Josiah defiled the high places where the priests had burned incense from it to the S limit, Beersheba (2 Kings 23:8). It is coupled with Ramah in the lists of those returning from Babylon (Ezra 2:26; Neh 7:30; KJV GABA), and it is one of the cities where Benjaminites lived after the Exile (Neh 11:31) and from which singers came and sang at the dedication of the Temple (Neh 12:29). It was one of the stopping points of the Assyrian army on its approach to Jerusalem (Isa 10:29). In Judges 20:33 and 1 Samuel 13:3 it may be confused with Gibeah. It is to be identified with modern Jeba, seven m. NE of Jerusalem, and two m. E of Ramah.

J. B. SCOTT

GEBAL gē′ bəl (גְּבַל, *boundary*; Ugar. *Gbl*; Egyp. *Kubni*; Gr. Βύβλος; Akkad. *Gubla*); GEBALITES, gē′ bel īts; GIBLITES, KJV gĭb′ līts.

1. A Phoen. city on the Mediterranean N of Beirut, called Byblos by the Greeks; modern Jebeil. The inhabitants were called Gebalites (Giblites, KJV, Josh 13:5).

Once a flourishing port and trading center known to the Greco-Roman world as Byblos and to the Assyrians and Babylonians in earlier times as Gubla. Its most valuable export was pine and cedarwood from Lebanon. The city was also noted for shipbuilding and stonecutting.

Excavation began in 1921 at Gebal by Pierre Montet, later joined by Maurice Dunand. The work has revealed successive layers of occupation. Traces of ancient magnificence in the ruins of its wall, castle, and temple were uncovered. Occupation of the site has been traced to Neolithic times. By the latter half of the fifth millennium, villages were in existence all over W Asia, including Gebal. Remains have been found of a people in late Chalcolithic Gezer and Gebal of small, slender, bony structure, long-headed, and delicate of feature. They lived in rectangular or circular huts, used silver for personal ornaments, and buried their

The village of Geba. ©*M.P.S.*

A general view of the ruins at Gebal (Byblos). ©*M.P.S.*

dead in large earthen pots.

Late in the fourth millennium, as the protoliterate culture flourished in Mesopotamia, there was widespread cultural exchange. Even at that early period, Egypt was in contact with Gebal. Seal impressions found there suggest that a major route of exchange lay through Pal. and Syria.

In c. 2800 B.C., fire swept through the city causing a setback in its progress, but it was reconstructed on an even grander scale. It was at this time that Egypt was experiencing her great classic flowering—the Old Kingdom period. She had not yet organized an Asiatic empire, but was already protecting her commercial interests there with military force. Gebal was virtually a colony during this period, supplying the cedars of Lebanon, which were of vital importance to Egypt. The temple of Baaltis in Gebal received votive offerings in great quantities from Egypt all through the Bronze Age.

Before the end of the third millennium, Canaanites in Gebal had developed a syllabic script modeled on the Egyp. hieroglyphics. A number of these inscrs. on copper have been found. The names of the kings at the end of the third millennium indicate that the rulers were Semites, prob. Amorites.

At the beginning of the second millennium, the most prosperous period of Egyp. history was about to begin—the Middle Kingdom period. Egypt enjoyed prosperity during the twelfth dynasty that was rarely matched in all her history. Most of Pal. and southern Phoenicia were under Egyp. control at this time. Gebal was an Egyp. colony. Objects found in tombs there bear the cartouches of rulers of the twelfth dynasty. The native princes wrote their names in Egyp. characters and vowed their loyalty to the Pharaoh.

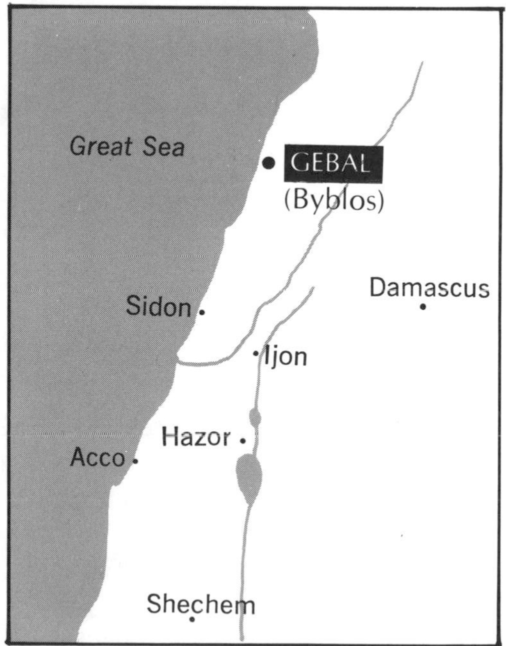

As the Middle Kingdom was coming to an end (c. 1797 B.C.), the twelfth was followed by the weak thirteenth dynasty. There was a brief revival under Neferhotep I (c. 1740-1729), when nominal authority was exercised over Gebal.

During this period Mari reached its zenith (1730-1700) under Zimri-lim and had widespread trade with many cities, including Gebal.

Gebal is mentioned in the Amarna letters. King Rib-addi of Gebal sent more than fifty letters to the king of Egypt proclaiming his allegiance and complaining of imminent invasion by the Habiru. At the beginning of the reign of Rameses II (c. 1290-1224), Gebal was a border fortress for the Egyp. province of Canaan and in 1194 was destroyed by the Sea Peoples in their march on Egypt. A period of extreme Egyp. weakness followed, c. 1080, so that Gebal, which was almost as Egypt. as Egypt herself, received the royal representative, Wen-Amon with mockery and insolence, demanding cash for the trees he had been sent to acquire for constructing a sacred barge.

The sarcophagus of Ahirim of Gebal (c. 1000) was discovered with inscrs. of a Phoen. type script. These inscrs. use the twenty-two consonants of the Heb. alphabet and are written from right to left. The Gebalites were considered master builders and able seamen (1 Kings 5:18; Ezek 27:9). Joshua 13:5 mentions their land as not conquered.

Gebal paid tribute to a number of the Assyrian kings during their era of domination. Tribute was paid to Ashurnasirpal II (883-859), Tiglath-pileser III (745-727), Sennacherib (705-681), Esarhaddon (681-669), and Ashurbanipal (669-627). The Gebalites also were dominated in turn by the Babylonians, Persians, Greeks, and Romans. The remains of a castle built by the Crusaders in the 11th cent. A.D. are there.

2. A geographical area S of the Dead Sea, near Petra of Edom (Ps 83:7).

BIBLIOGRAPHY. E. Robertson, "Jebeil," EBr, XII (1957), 985; J. Bright, *A History of Israel* (1959); L. Cottrell, ed., *The Concise Encyclopedia of Archaeology* (1960), 123; M. Noth, *The Old Testament World* (1966), 213, 214; Y. Aharoni, *The Land of the Bible* (1967).

F. B. HUEY, JR.

GEBER ge' bər (גֶּבֶר, *man, strong one*). The name of two men listed among the twelve officers appointed to provide food for Solomon's household. 1. Ben-geber (1 Kings 4:13) in charge of the district around Ramoth-gilead, E of the Jordan.

2. Geber (1 Kings 4:19) the son of Uri, in charge of the district of Gilead, also E of the Jordan, but prob. S of Ramoth-gilead.

J. B. SCOTT

GEBIM ge′ bĭm (Heb. גבים). A village of Benjamin mentioned only in the poetic listing of the conquests of Assyria (Isa 10:31). The term means lit. "pit," "pits" and is located by the prophet between Madmenah and Nob; in fact Gebim is the "B" word with Madmenah as the "A" word. Neither location has ever been confidently identified. They prob. were locations outside of Jerusalem itself. Eusebius mentions a town Gr. Γηβα, which he states is Biblical Gebim, the modern name of the place is Wādi el-ğīb by ğifnā (GTT p. 175, n. 158) and there is no evidence that Eusebius is in fact correct (Eusebius, *Onomasticon*, P. de Lagarde ed. [1870], p. 74, 1, 2).

W. White, Jr.

GECKO. *See* Lizard.

GEDALIAH gĕd′ ə lī′ ə (גדליהו, גדליה, *Yah* [i.e. *Yahweh*] *is great*). Name of several men.

1. Gedaliah, a Jeduthunite, a Temple musician under David (1 Chron 25:3, 9).

2. Grandfather of Zephaniah, the prophet (Zeph 1:1).

3. Gedaliah, son of Pashhur, one of Jeremiah's opponents (Jer 38:1-3).

4. A priest in Ezra's time who had married a foreign wife (Ezra 10:18).

5. Gedaliah, son of Ahikam, son of Shaphan, governor of Judah after the fall of Jerusalem to the Babylonians (2 Kings 25:22-26; Jer 40:6-41:18). His family's political moderation, shown by his father's protection of Jeremiah, prob. made him acceptable to the Babylonians (Jer 26:24). Mizpah, his headquarters during his two month rule, served as a rallying point for various groups of Heb. soldiers and nobility. He avoided political intrigue in rejecting the scheme of Johanan, son of Kareah, to murder Ishmael, son of Nethaniah. He, many Jewish leaders, and the Babylonian garrison, were assassinated by Ishmael. Gedaliah's partisans, fearing Babylonian reprisals, then fled to Egypt forcing Jeremiah the prophet to go with them. The events associated with his death made it impossible for a Jewish community to survive in Pal. under Babylonian control. The Jewish community, in effect, disappeared until the return of new leadership from Babylon. Jewish tradition recognizes the importance of his death in remembering its anniversary as a fast day. A contemporary seal inscribed "of Gedaliah who is over the house," has been found at Lachish.

BIBLIOGRAPHY. J. H. Greenstone, "Gedaliah," Jew Enc (1901).

A. Bowling

GEDDUR. KJV Apoc. form of Gahar.

GEDEON. (Heb 11:32) KJV and Douay VS form of Gideon.

Impression made by a scaraboid (seal) inscribed "lgdlyh ashr 'lhbyt," "belonging to Gedalia who is over the house." This may well be the GEDALIA who was made Governor of Judah by the Babylonians in 583 B.C. (2 Kings 25:23.) Found at Lachish, 6th-century B.C. Twice actual size. ©*B.M.*

GEDER ge′ dər (Heb. גדר), a place name, a village of the Canaanites mentioned only in Joshua 12:13 in proximity to Debir (q.v.). The name prob. means "wall" or "bulwark," and similar names are frequent in the OT, e.g., Gedor (Josh 15:58); Gederah (15:36); Gederoth (15:41, et al.) A citizen of the place, Gederathite, Heb. גדרת, a certain Jozabad, is mentioned in 1 Chronicles 12:4 as one of the men who rallied to David at Ziklag. Since they were all Benjamites Geder must have been located on the Western slope of the Judean hill country in the Shephelah.

W. White, Jr.

GEDERAH gĭ dĭr′ ə (גדרה, *stone-walled sheep pen*) 1. One of fourteen sites in the Shephelah (lowland hills) listed in Joshua 15:33-36. Together with Nataim, Gederah is listed as inhabited by clans of skilled craftsmen who served as potters for the king (1 Chron 4:23; KJV has "hedges" for "Gederah"). Several modern names have been suggested as preserving the ancient name and thus identifying the site. Jedirah (note: "J" is equivalent to "G"), about halfway between Gezer and Zorah, is most frequently suggested but without universal acceptance.

2. Jozabed of Gederah (Heb. Gederathite; 1 Chron 12:4), a Benjamite, would seem to be from a Gederah in Benjamin. Modern Jedireh and Khirbet Gudeira in the territory of ancient Benjamin are possible sites.

3. New Testament Gadara (q.v.) is prob. derived from the same or a related Sem. name.

A. Bowling

GEDEROTH gĭ dĭr′ ŏth (גדרות, *stone-walled sheep pens*). Associated with Beth-dagon and Makkedah in a list of towns SW of Jerusalem in the Shephelah (lowland hills; Josh 15:37-41). If the lists of Joshua are accurately transmitted, Gederoth is distinct from Gederah (q.v.; Josh 15:36). In the time of Ahaz, Gederoth was one of several towns occupied by the Philistines (2 Chron 28:18). Its general location can be deduced from its associations in the list of Joshua. A "Kedron" known from the Maccabean Wars (1 Macc 15:39; 16:9; cf. also "Gedor" of 1 Macc 15:39, 40), which is itself identified with modern Qatra, is a suggested identification. Available evidence does not permit a firm identification.

A. BOWLING

GEDEROTHAIM gĭ dĭr' ə thā' ĭm (גדרתים, *two sheep pens*). Last of fourteen names in Joshua 15:33-36 (*see* GEDERAH). However, the LXX treats "Gederothaim" as a noun and translates it as "[Gederah] and her sheep pens" (Gr. *καὶ αἱ ἐπαύλεις αὐτῆς*). This requires emending the last "m" of Gederothaim to "h." The MT contains fourteen names without Gederothaim, but the differences between the MT and the LXX list could raise questions about other names also. The identification of the site, and even if it is a genuine place name, remains uncertain.

A. BOWLING

GEDOR ge' dôr (גדור, *wall*). 1. An ancient city in the hill country of Judah (Josh 15:58) near Hebron. Penuel may have been the founder of the city (cf. 1 Chron 4:4). It is possibly to be identified with Khirbet Gedur near Bethlehem.

2. Another place in Judah, mentioned in 1 Chronicles 4:18. Possibly the same as (1) or (3).

3. A town of Benjamin and the home of Joelah and Zebadiah (1 Chron 12:7) who with others joined David at Ziklag. It is possible to identify this site with (1) above making Jered its founder (cf. 1 Chron 4:4, 18). It may be identified with Khirbet Gadeirah, N of El Jib.

4. A site mentioned twice in Judah's genealogy (1 Chron 4:4, 18) near Soco and Zonoah. The location is unknown.

5. A city S of the hills of Judah (1 Chron 4:39). It is described as a land very broad, quiet, and peaceful, formerly belonging to Ham. The settlers here were Simeonites.

6. The son of Jeiel of Gibeon, a Benjaminite and an ancestor of Saul (1 Chron 8:31; 9:37).

J. B. SCOTT

GE-HARASHIM gĭ hăr' ə shĭm (גיא חרשים, *valley of craftsmen*). 1. A Kenizzite craft clan of the tribe of Judah whose ancestor was Joab, son of Seraiah, son of Kenaz (1 Chron 4:14; KJV VALLEY OF CHARASHIM). Apparently their settlement was known as "Valley of Craftsmen" because craftsmen had settled there. Then the clan itself came to be designated by the place name (1 Chron 4:14).

2. A geographic location near Lod and Ono (Neh 11:35; "valley of craftsmen" in KJV and RSV) which was resettled by Benjamites after the Exile. It is prob. the same as the site settled by the Kenizzite craft clan mentioned above. Its association with Lod and Ono points toward identification with one of the valleys bordering the Plain of Sharon. Wadi esh-Shellal and Sarafand el-Kharab have been suggested (IDB). Alternatively, it is suggested that Hirsha, E of Lod (modern Lydda) marks the site. These identifications imply that a Judahite clan lived outside the boundaries of Judah. This is readily explained in terms of the easy geographic mobility of skilled craftsmen.

A. BOWLING

GEHAZI gĭ hā' zī (גחזי גיחזי, prob. *valley of vision*). The young servant of the prophet Elisha. The strengths and weaknesses of his character are readily apparent in the three passages where he is mentioned by name.

In the story of the wealthy Shunammite woman (2 Kings 4:8-37) is the first time Gehazi is mentioned. His master, Elisha, had been provided a chamber by this woman and was desirous of repaying the favor in some way. Gehazi perceptively alerted Elisha to the fact "she has no son, and her husband is old" (v. 14). Elisha predicted the birth of a son which came to pass the following spring. When the child had grown up he died one day of a head ailment (vv. 18-20). Immediately, the Shunammite woman, in bitter distress, rushed up to Elisha at Mt. Carmel. Gehazi was rebuked by Elisha for trying to thrust her away after she caught hold of the prophet's feet. Gehazi was then sent on ahead to Shunem with Elisha's staff to place on the woman's son. The child, however, did not come to life until the prophet came, prayed and lay upon him (vv. 32-35).

Unlike the incident above, 2 Kings 5:20-27 pictures Gehazi as a man of covetousness and distrust. After Elisha had cleansed Naaman the Syrian of leprosy, and refused the gifts offered him in appreciation, Gehazi deceitfully sought the reward. He overtook Naaman's chariot. By fabricating a story in Elisha's name he deceitfully got for himself "two talents of silver in two bags, with two festal garments" (v. 23). The sagacious prophet, however, knowing of the incident, harshly rebuked the deception of his servant by issuing a curse: "Therefore the leprosy of Naaman shall cleave to you" (v. 27).

In a final account (2 Kings 8:1-6), while Gehazi related to the king the great things Elisha had done, the Shunammite woman appeared with her son. She had returned from Philistia after a seven year famine. When Gehazi attested the identity of both, she requested of the king restoration of her house and land. This, the king granted, along with all the produce her fields had yielded since she had been gone.

Though unnamed, the "servant" in 2 Kings 4:43 and 6:15, may be Gehazi.

M. R. WILSON

GEHENNA gĭ hĕn' ə (*γέεννα*, lit., *valley of Hinnom*, Eng. VSS *hell*). In the NT the final place of punishment of the ungodly. The word de-

The Valley of Gehenna-Hinnom (Jerusalem) looking south from The Church of St. Peter's of Gallicantu, across Valley of Gehenna to the Potter's field. The monastary to the lower left is still adjacent to the place (cliffs) where Judas traditionally hanged himself. ©*Lev*

rives from the Heb. גיהנם, the Valley of Hinnom, or more fully, the Valley of the son(s) of Hinnom, situated to the S or SW of Jerusalem, usually identified with the Wadi-er-Rababi. It is first referred to in Joshua 15:8 and 18:16 as marking the boundary between the inheritance of the tribes of Judah and Benjamin. (In recent times, until the Arab-Israeli war in June 1967, it was divided in two by the border between Israel and Jordan.) During the reigns of Ahaz and Manasseh, at Topheth (prob. lit. "fire-place") in the Valley of Hinnom, human sacrifices were offered to the heathen god Molech (Moloch; 2 Chron 28:3; 33:6). Josiah in his reforms "defiled" Topheth and thus prevented any further use of the valley for that purpose (2 Kings 23:10). Jeremiah (7:30-33) announces that the name of the valley will be changed to the "Valley of Slaughter" because when the Lord judged Judah for her sins, the number of dead would be so great that they would be thrown into the valley to lie there without burial. In later times the valley seems to have been used for burning refuse, and also the bodies of criminals. From about the 2nd cent. B.C., the Valley of Hinnom came to be thought of as the place of final punishment for the enemies of God. This arose either from the earlier associations or from Jeremiah's prophecy or from the later practice just referred to. The Book of Enoch is the earliest witness to this (but cf. even in the OT itself, Isaiah 30:33; 66:24). In later thought, Gehenna was thought of as the eschatological fire of hell, still prob. considered as a *place* (esp. in Rabbinic thought), but now no longer locally outside Jerusalem. The term is used in the NT in this sense. J. Jeremias stresses the sharp distinction in the NT (as in pre-NT Judaism) between Hades and Gehenna—Hades receiving the ungodly only for the intervening period between death and resurrection, Gehenna being their place of punishment after the last judgment. Apart from James 3:6, where the tongue, compared to a fire that sets on fire the whole cycle of nature, is said to be itself set on fire by Gehenna, the remaining eleven occurrences are all in the synoptic gospels.

In the Sermon on the Mount, Jesus warned that even mental or verbal infringements of the commandments render one liable to Gehenna (Matt 5:20), and He said: "If your right eye causes you to sin, pluck it out and throw it away; it is better that you lose one of your members than that your whole body be thrown into hell" (Matt 5:29f.). He also held out the threat of Gehenna to any who "causes one of these little ones who believe in me to sin," and repeated the warning already quoted above (Mark 9:42-47; Matt 18:9). In Matthew 10:28, cf. Luke 12:5, He told His disciples to fear none but God, who alone is able to cast both body and soul into Gehenna.

The last two occurrences are in Matthew 23, in our Lord's vigorous denunciation of the Pharisees. In v. 15, He accused them of so indoctrinating any proselyte that they cause him to become twice as much a child of Gehenna as themselves. The Hebraism "child (or 'son') of Gehenna" means one fit for and doomed for Gehenna. In v. 33, He concluded: "You serpents, you brood of vipers, how are you to escape being sentenced to hell?"

The other NT writings, although not using the word "Gehenna," use equivalent expressions—of judgment, wrath, fire, destruction, perdition, Tartarus, the lake of fire (q.v.)

There is evidence among the rabbis, both those of the strict school of Shammai and the more liberal school of Hillel, of beliefs that consignment to Gehenna will either result in annihilation or will be purgatorial, and therefore will be ultimately followed by blessedness. These beliefs are not explicit in the NT.

BIBLIOGRAPHY. A. Edersheim, LT, II (1886), 791-796; BDB (1906), 161; SBK, IV (1928), 1029-1118; R. A. Stewart, *Rabbinic Theology* (1961), 157-160; NBD (1962), 390, 518, 519, 527; J. Jeremias in TDNT, I (1964), 657, 658.

R. E. DAVIES

GELBOE. Douay VS form of GILBOA.

GELILOTH gĭ lī' lŏth (Heb. גְּלִילוֹת), a difficult feminine pl. form of the familiar place name, Gilgal (q.v.). It appears only in Joshua 18:17, ". . . and thence goes to Geliloth, which is opposite the ascent of Adummim." An almost identical reference occurs in Joshua 15:7 ". . . looking toward Gilgal, that is opposite the ascent of Adummim" (JPS, modified). Obviously with such a close similarity a number of evident emendations have been suggested. It is necessary to note that the description in 15:7 deals with the boundaries of Judah after the conquest was begun while the description in 18:17 deals with the borders of the tribes of Benjamin. Therefore it is highly possible that for purposes of such identification, two different terms are meant. The word Gilgal simply means a "circle," most likely "a circle of stones," and so there are a number of separate Gilgals mentioned in the text. It is probable that the Geliloth was an area, not simply the one location specifically mentioned in 15:7.

W. WHITE, JR.

GEM. *See* JEWELS AND PRECIOUS STONES.

GEMALLI gĭ măl' ī (Heb. גְּמַלִּי), a son of Ammiel, a Danite, one of the ten spies sent by Moses into the Promised Land who returned with a dismal report and was judged by God and left to die in the wilderness, mentioned only in Numbers 13:12. The name Gemalli has been interpreted in various ways like "camel driver" or the like, but evidence is lacking.

W. WHITE, JR.

GEMARA gə mä' rə (Aram. גְּמָרָא). In Jewish lit., the term that indicates the commentary of the Mishna in the Talmud, which was developed in the early centuries A.D.

The term Gemara possibly comes from the Aram. verb גמר, meaning "to complete" and indicates the commentary of the text of the Mishna, which was based on academic discussions of Jewish scholars in Palestine and Babylon. The Mishna consisted of the code of Jewish laws, drawn up about A.D. 200, which brought illumination to the text of the Mosaic laws and made further application of those laws to human experiences. The Gemara commentary together with the Mishna was called the Talmud.

This Gemara material was developed mainly by two schools: (1) The Palestinian, the material of which came basically from Tiberias in the 3rd and 4th centuries A.D.; and (2) the Babylonian, which was produced in such academies as those at Sura, Nehardea, Sipporis, and Pumbeditha, from the 3rd to the end of the 5th centuries A.D.

The Gemara teachers, called Amoraim (i.e., interpreters), in their commentary on the Mishna treated this document as they did the OT, inspired and holy.

BIBLIOGRAPHY. M. L. Rodkinson, *The Babylonian Talmud,* 2nd ed., rev. (1916), xv-xix; *Hebraic Literature,* tr. from the Talmud, etc. (1944), introd. by M. H. Harris.

W. H. MARE

GEMARIAH gĕm' ə rī' ə (Heb. and Aram. גְּמַרְיָה), a proper name used from the time of the monarchy known to apply to at least four individuals. The name is apparently understood as, "Jehovah has brought to pass." 1. A son of a certain Hilkiah, and an emissary to Nebuchadnezzar from King Zedekiah who carried Jeremiah's message to the captive Jews (Jer 29:3).

2. A son of Shaphan the scribe. It was in his chamber in the Temple that Baruch read the scroll of Jeremiah to the people. When his son, Micaiah, brought in the news of the reading and the princes and officials sent for the scroll to be read, Gemariah with several others remonstrated with King Jehoiakim when he hacked off pieces of the scroll and burned them (Jer 36:10-12, 25).

3. A son of a certain Hissilyahu mentioned in Lachish Ostracon I, a potsherd written during the era of Jeremiah.

4. An official of the Jewish military colony at Egypt. Elephantine, he is mentioned in two of the Aram. papyri (Cowley 22, 33) as the son of a certain Yedoniah.

W. WHITE, JR.

GENEALOGY **je ne ŏl′ ə je** (יחש ; γενεαλογία, *γένεσις, genealogy, to reckon by genealogy, generation*). The ancestry or descent of individuals in the Biblical record.

1. Introduction. Genealogies are often given in the Bible and have various uses in the unfolding story of redemption. Inasmuch as history necessarily clusters around great men, the connected history of God's dealing with men involves listing men in their connections with others of various ages. Genealogies and chronologies form the connecting link from early days to the end of the Biblical period. Usually other ancient histories are partial and piecemeal. By means of genealogical records, God has given a connected history from Adam to Christ.

Genealogies also have lesser uses in the sacred record. God's blessings were often passed on in the family line and these genealogies express the covenant connections of ancient Israel. Military duty was by families. Certain offices such as the priesthood, the Levitical work, and the kingship, were hereditary, and genealogies trace the perpetuation of these offices. Also, land tenure in Israel was carried on chiefly through male descent. Genealogies therefore certified the title to ancestral holdings. Finally, in a tribal or semitribal community, a man's genealogy was his identification and means of location. It is roughly equal to the addresses of modern houses. People are located by country, state, city, and street. In a similar way, Achan, for example, was identified as of the tribe of Judah, the family of Zerah, the household of Zabdi, the son of Carmi (Josh 7:17, 18). Such a brief genealogy gave only the first two or three and the last two or three links of the man's ancestry.

2. Principal genealogies of Scripture. The ancient history of the race is compressed into the first chs. of Genesis. Except for a few incidents, this history consists of the listing of famous men and nations. There are two genealogies before the Flood (Gen 4; 5) and two after (Gen 10: 11). These genealogies have been the subject of much study because of their importance and their position at the head of Bible history.

Genesis 5 and 11 are obviously similar, giving the line from Adam to Noah and from Noah to Abraham. Each ch. gives the age of a man at the birth of his son and the years that remained to him thereafter. Each genealogy consists of ten links (remembering that LXX and Luke record a son, Cainan, after Shem) followed by a family of three sons who were not triplets, though the record refers to them as born at the same time. It is natural to believe that these genealogies are schematic, naming only the chief men in easily memorizable form. That they are true genealogies, giving the descent of ancient men, there is no reason to doubt. It will be considered later whether or not they are complete. These genealogies are compared by some to the lists recorded on Sumer. tablets of the kings who reigned before and after the Flood. There is no similarity in names. The reigns of the Sumer. kings are extremely long; those after the Flood progressively shorter until the last few reigns are nearer the normal. The last links name a king or two who are historically known. Some have held that the Biblical lists derive from the Sumer. and thus are legendary. It seems just as possible to believe that both lists derive from the ancient tradition of the race and represent early tradition. The Biblical tradition is much more believable and by God's providence and inspiration has preserved the true outlines of the past.

The genealogies in Genesis 4 and 10 are different from those in chs. 5 and 11. Genesis 10 is frequently called the "Table of Nations," tracing the expanding migrations of the various sons of Noah and their successors. It can be shown that these successors are not given in straight genealogical lines. These are colonizations of peoples rather than merely lists of descendants. For instance the "sons" of Ham (Gen 10:6) include the Ethiopians, Egyptians, Libyans (prob.), and the Canaanites, a wide variety of peoples. The Canaanites themselves included Sidon, a city; Heth, progenitor of the Indo-European Hittites; the Amorites, a Semitic people; and others. That Canaan begot Sidon his first-born is not intended to be a reference to sonship, but an indication that the city Sidon was peopled early in the history of the land of Canaan. The chapter is aptly called "the earliest ethnological table in the literature of the ancient world" (*New Scofield Reference Bible* [1967], p. 15).

Actually this difference between chs. 10 and 11 of Genesis is borne out by the Heb. wording. In Genesis 10, the word "begot" represents a different form of this Heb. verb without the causative element. It usually refers to a mother bearing a child. It also refers to Moses as fig. begetting Israel (Num 11:12) or God bearing Israel (Deut 32:18), or God begetting the Messiah (Ps 2:7). The word when used of men apparently is used of general relationships, as expressed in Genesis 10, the Table of Nations and not literal fatherhood.

The same remarks apply to Genesis 4:17-22. The so-called genealogy of Cain includes doubtless some names of individuals who are progenitors of races and craftsmen, and who founded cities bearing their own names. The comparison with Genesis 10 and the fact that the same Heb. verb form is used in both cases makes it apparent that the list of names in Genesis 4 also includes peoples and movements.

In the rest of the Pentateuch there are many shorter genealogies. These genealogies usually first present a brief reference to the worldly descendants, followed by a more detailed history of the godly line.

Abraham's family outside of Isaac is given very briefly in Genesis 25. This is followed by the family of Isaac (Gen 25:19). The chief men in the family of Esau are listed in ch. 36, followed by the family of Jacob in Genesis 46. Part of this genealogy of Jacob is repeated (Exod 6:14-25), but the family of Levi is expanded there to give the genealogy of Moses, the son of Amram, son of Kohath, son of Levi. It is clear that Kohath was actually one of Levi's three sons and head of a clan. Amram was possibly Moses' own father and head of a household. There were intervening links between Kohath and Amram because by Moses' day the Levites numbered 22,000 males (Num 3:39). Many generations must have intervened. But the ancestry of Moses given in Exodus 6 places him within the tribe of Levi.

The history of the time of the judges is given in a chronological rather than genealogical format. The judgeship was not hereditary but charismatic, i.e., God individually called the judges to their tasks. The period of the judges is spanned by one brief genealogy—that at the end of the Book of Ruth. Actually Ruth is a book belonging in the time of the judges and in old Heb. listings was counted as a part of Judges. In Ruth 4:18-22, the line of Ruth's husband, Boaz, is traced back to Perez, the son of Judah, and onward to David the great king. This genealogy, repeated in Chronicles and the NT, is our only record of the detailed ancestry of Israel's chief monarch. This genealogy is incomplete, however. It speaks of Nahshon, the chief prince of Judah in Moses' day (Num 2:3). His son, Boaz' father, is given as Salmon, whereas Ruth 2:1 says Boaz was of the family of Elimelech. Clearly there were other intervening links between Nahshon and Boaz and prob. more than two links between Boaz and David.

For the history of the monarchy, the only genealogy of any extent is that of King David, whose line is traced in the books of Kings through eighteen generations to the captivity. The genealogy of the high priests is not given in the histories, though it was known and is given in the collected genealogies of Chronicles. The genealogies of the prophets are not given, for like that of the judges, their office was charismatic and not hereditary.

The remaining genealogies of any consequence in the OT are those of Ezra (Ezra 7:1-5), Joshua, the high priest (Neh 12:10, 11), and those remarkable lists of names in 1 Chronicles 1-9 where many previous genealogies are brought together and others are added.

First Chronicles 1 comes straight out of Genesis, usually quoted directly from the early genealogies. Following this are genealogies of the twelve tribes as far as they are preserved, in this order: Judah, Simeon, Reuben, Gad, Levi, Issachar, Benjamin, Naphtali, Ephraim, Asher, and Benjamin. Dan and Zebulun, tribes of the extreme N, are missing, though some have surmised that the second mention of Benjamin is a copyist's mistake for Zebulun; this is, however, questionable.

These tribal genealogies are, naturally enough, strong on the ancestries of famous people. David's line is traced down to six or seven generations beyond the capitivity (1 Chron 3:9-24). Samuel's line is given twice (6:22-30 and 6:33-38; cf. 1 Sam 1:1; 8:2). Aaron's line is traced down through Eleazar to David's time (1 Chron 6:50-53) and also to the captivity (6:3-15) whence it is taken on to Ezra in Ezra 7:1-5. The line of Saul is also given briefly (1 Chron 8:33-40). Curiously nothing is known about Moses' descendants. His sons Gershom and Eliezer are mentioned only once (Exod 18:3, 4).

Many of the names and the incidental references to habitation and family events are found only in Chronicles. The author (now admitted by many critical scholars to have written c. 400 B.C.) obviously had access to ancient books of genealogies. Such books are referred to in Nehemiah 7:5, 64 and Ezra 2:62. It is quite possible that the author of Chronicles (Ezra or Nehemiah?) copied out of the book that Nehemiah had found. As is to be expected, some of the names are slightly different from those in the older lists. In some cases there may have been alternate names for a man. In other cases the names have suffered slightly in copying. This precise copying of names and numbers was notoriously difficult.

In American culture, genealogies are seldom kept, but in other cultures genealogies are more extensively preserved. The writer has had students from Korea and from India who possessed family records back forty generations and felt this to be not unusual. He has talked with an Arab in Jerusalem who named his child Edessa because his ancestors suffered in the persecutions of Edessa (3rd cent.). Such genealogies were kept even more in ancient times. A man living in China claims to be the seventy-seventh in direct descent from Confucius. In tribal cultures and in the settled life of ancient nations, such genealogies were apparently common.

The genealogies of Christ are recorded in Matthew 1 and Luke 3. Joseph and Mary were prob. well aware of their ancestry. The two lists differ after the mention of David, and some have found here a contradiction. Others have suggested that the genealogy in Matthew is that of Joseph; the one in Luke is of Mary (cf. the excellent treatment of Luke's genealogy in John Lightfoot's commentary, *Hours with the Hebrew and Talmud, Horae Hebraicae et Talmudicae* [1859], *in loc.*). It appears that

Mary is enigmatically referred to as the daughter of Heli in the Talmud (quoted by Lightfoot also in H. L. Strack and P. Billerbeck, *Kommentar zum Neuen Testament* II [1929], p. 155). Joseph apparently was the son-in-law of Heli. But the genealogy of Joseph in Matthew loses its point, for Joseph was not the biological father of Jesus. Comparison with 1 Chronicles 3:19, however, will indicate that Matthew's list is not a true genealogy. Matthew 1:12 says Salathiel begat Zerubbabel. First Chronicles 3:19 shows that Salathiel died without children and Zerubbabel was actually his nephew. This was uncommon in a usual genealogy, but it was frequent in lists including men who claimed the title to a throne. If the kingly line ran out, the nearest male relative assumed the title. Thus the "genealogy" in Matthew is a list of the heirs to the throne of Judah. Joseph had that title and passed that title on to his foster son, Jesus. It has further been pointed out that Joseph had the title to the throne of Judah, but being descended from Jehoiachin he could not reign, as he lay under Jeremiah's curse (Jer 22:30). Jesus as the foster son received Joseph's title to the crown, but being born of the virgin Mary He escaped Joseph's curse. (For other views, cf. J. G. Machen, *The Virgin Birth of Christ* [1930], 204-209.)

3. Genealogies incomplete. As mentioned above, it is clear that many OT genealogies are incomplete. There are four links from Levi to Moses (Exod 6:16-20), but the descendants of Levi in Moses' day were 22,000 males (Num 3:39). The genealogy from Ephraim, Levi's nephew, to Joshua seems to show eighteen links (1 Chron 7:20-27). In the NT Matthew 1:1 names just three links from Christ to Abraham. The full genealogy, or list of kings (Matt 1:2-17), omits the names of Ahaziah, Joash and Amaziah and also Jehoiakim, in contrast to the lists of kings in the OT. The genealogy of Ezra (Ezra 7:1-5) has only five links from 456 B.C. back to Zadok, David's high priest in about 960 B.C. Obviously, only the more famous men are mentioned.

These facts are necessary to know before examining the genealogies in Genesis 5 and 11. Attention already has been called to their schematic form. The assumption that the post diluvian genealogy is complete leads to some strange results. For example, the years given from the birth of a father to the birth of his son total 292 years from the Flood to the birth of Abraham, 467 years to his death. Shem lived 502 years after the Flood. Noah lived 350 years after the Flood, and he would have been a contemporary of Abraham. Arphaxad, Shem's son, also lived until Abraham was 148 years old. Yet the record of Abraham says nothing about any contact with these ancient worthies. The record implies that Noah and his sons were long gone before Abraham was told to leave his kindred and start fresh in Canaan. Also the numerous peoples pictured as recolonizing the world (Gen 10) could hardly have repopulated and spread so widely in ten generations. It is far easier to realize that Genesis 11 is incomplete. It is also held that some of these names are actually family or clan names.

Furthermore, any view that holds the Flood to have destroyed all men all over the earth, must place the Flood earlier than 292 years before Abraham who lived about 2000 B.C. There is a record, practically continuous, of Egyp. dynasties going back to almost 3000 B.C.—1000 years before Abraham. The city of Jericho in the Jordan valley shows many layers of mud brick going back long before 3000 B.C., which any destructive flood would surely have washed away. The genealogy of Genesis 11 is clearly incomplete. The one found in Genesis 5 is likely incomplete also. The date of 4004 B.C. assigned to Creation by Ussher in the 17th cent. is wrong. He assumed these genealogies were complete.

Actually the genealogies in Genesis 5 and 11 may be considered as links in the ancient tradition of mankind. Some consider a generation about thirty years long. From another viewpoint a generation is the period from birth to death—nearer seventy years or longer (*see* GENERATION). From the latter viewpoint the time from Abraham back to the Flood would be at least the sum of the lives of these patriarchs, about 2,263 years. Probably the Flood was still earlier. There seems to have been an abrupt change of climate about 9000 B.C. which would fit the genealogies well enough if the Flood was connected with that event.

4. Other references. A word may be said about NT usages of the word genealogy. The foolish questions and genealogies mentioned in Titus 3:9 prob. refer to matters such as Paul referred to tracing his own ancestry from the tribe of Benjamin (Phil 3:5). Such trust in pedigree for merit before God was vain and far removed from the practical uses of genealogies in the OT.

BIBLIOGRAPHY. Commentaries in loc. (esp. ICC, Curtis and Madsen on Chronicles); W. H. Green, "Primeval Chronology," BS (1890), 285-304 (quoted extensively in Buswell, *see below*); P. W. Crannel, ISBE II (1929), 1183-1196; J. G. Machen, *The Virgin Birth of Christ* (1930), 204-209; J. O. Buswell Jr., *A Systematic Theology of the Christian Religion,* I (1962), 325-343.

R. L. HARRIS

GENEALOGY OF (JESUS) CHRIST. 1. Of the house and lineage of David. The Davidic ancestry of Jesus Christ is an accepted fact in the NT (Matt 21:9; Mark 10:47f.; Rom 1:3). Apart from the two genealogies in Matthew and Luke, little attempt is made elsewhere to emphasize this fact. It is presented rather as historical truth. Joseph, the legal father of Jesus, was "of the house and lineage of David" (Luke 2:4). Along with other Jews of his time, Joseph treasured his family records.

Genealogical registers were kept with great care, because they figured in legal matters concerning property, marriage, and religion. Centuries ago, as in the days of Ezra and Nehemiah, such lists were kept and supervised (Ezra 2:62; 8:1; Neh 7:5). In Joseph's case, his membership in the line of David had Messianic overtones (Jer 23:5f.; Ezek 34:23). The charge of falsification ought not to be laid against the NT writers, because the expectation of a Davidic Messiah was not uniform in Judaism of that time. Some looked for a Messiah from the seed of Aaron, others from Levi. In fairness to the gospel writers, the two genealogies should be taken with seriousness. Both present Jesus as a descendant of David, and make it clear that Joseph was the legal, not the actual, father of Jesus. Matthew traced the line from Abraham and David in forty-one links to Joseph, whereas Luke reversed the official method and worked back from Joseph to David, Abraham, and all the way to Adam, employing 77 names (Matt 1:1-17; Luke 3:23-38). The slightest comparison of the two genealogies reveals striking differences, the most difficult of these is the fact that both lists trace their line through Joseph, despite the fact that almost none of the names from David to Joseph coincide. The apparent discrepancy between the lists has always constituted a severe problem to interpreters.

2. The genealogy in Matthew. Certain distinctive features stand out in Matthew's genealogy. Two high points in OT revelation figure prominently in the list—David and Abraham, both men being partners to God's covenants with Israel. Matthew intended that the pedigree of Jesus stand out sharply at the very beginning of his gospel, and it holds the first place of honor. His genealogy is structured in three sets of fourteen generations each. He arrived at this scheme through selection and omission in accord with OT practice. The device served to aid the memory, and indicated the main line of descent without sacrificing accuracy. Matthew may have chosen the number fourteen because it matches the numerical value of David's name in Heb. letters, but this is no more than a theory. Another peculiar feature of Matthew's list is the inclusion, almost incidentally of four women—Tamar, Rahab, Ruth, and Bathsheba. Rahab was a Canaanite from Jericho, Ruth was a Moabitess, and Tamar and Bathsheba were famous chiefly for their participation in public scandal. Quite apart from the character and nationality of these women, the very occurrence of their names in an official Jewish genealogy is a distinct feature. Undoubtedly, Jesus was known by His enemies as the son of an illegitimate union. He was known as the son of Mary, not Joseph (Mark 6:3), which in a male society was a dishonorable title. Later Jewish tradition developed the malicious rumor. Therefore, Matthew, desiring to offset the gossip, inserted with some relish the names of some OT characters whose reputations were not beyond reproach, but who were instrumental in the Messianic line. In Jesus' case, however, the rumors arose to counteract the miraculous character of His birth by a virgin. Jesus is presented in Matthew's genealogy as a legal male descendant of David through adoption by Joseph, and heir to the Davidic throne.

3. The genealogy in Luke. The Lukan genealogy is less official and legal in form. It is not placed at the beginning of the gospel, but is tucked away in the third ch., after the baptism of Jesus. The order is inverted, proceeding backward in time from Joseph to Adam, and includes almost twice as many entries. The most startling feature of the list is its total dissimilarity to Matthew's in the period between Joseph and David, with only two names common to both (other than Joseph and David), namely, Shealtiel and Zerubbabel. Luke traced his line through Nathan, son of David, and named Heli as grandfather of Jesus, whereas Matthew traced his line through Solomon, the royal son of David, and named Jacob as grandfather.

4. Two solutions to the discrepancy. Attempts have been made from earliest times to resolve the apparent contradiction. Assuming no colossal mistake in either gospel, two valid explanations are possible. Either both lists are properly those of Joseph but reckoned in a different way, or one is the family tree of Mary, not Joseph. Annius of Viterbo (c. 1490) proposed a theory that whereas Matthew gives the legal descent through Joseph, Luke presents the physical descent through Mary; a method that can be traced back to the 5th cent. A.D. Certainly, Mary is the chief figure in the birth narrative of the third gospel, and belongs herself very prob. to the house of David (1:27; 2:4). The article that is universally used in the list for each entry is noticeably absent from the name of Joseph (3:23), which leads to the interpretation that the list proper begins with Heli, not Joseph. Joseph's name is introduced into the list only to fill in the gap between Jesus and His grandfather Heli. The text would read then: "Jesus, being the son (as it was supposed, of Joseph) of Heli, etc." Luke's list would be the register of Mary's family, beginning with Heli her father. This theory is attractive, but suffers from the suppression of Mary's name in the list. It is, however, clearly possible, and would provide a simple solution to the problem of the double genealogy. The fact that Mary was related to Elizabeth, a daughter of Aaron, is not an insuperable difficulty if we suppose this relationship came through the mother rather than the father. The main weakness is in the failure of Luke to make this point explicit if that was his intention. The theory could be strengthened by supposing that Mary had no brothers, and

THE TWO GENEALOGIES					
Matthew	**Both**	**Luke**	**Matthew**	**Both**	**Luke**
—	—	1 Adam	(21) Ozias	—	40 Joseph
—	—	2 Seth	(22) Joatham	—	41 Juda
—	—	3 Enos	(23) Achaz	—	42 Simeon
—	—	4 Cainan	(24) Ezekias	—	43 Levi
—	—	5 Maleleel	(25) Manasses	—	44 Matthat
—	—	6 Jared	(26) Amon	—	45 Jorim
—	—	7 Enoch	(27) Josias	—	46 Eliezer
—	—	8 Mathusala	Jehoahaz	—	—
—	—	9 Lamech	Jehoiakin	—	—
—	—	10 Noe	*omitted*	—	—
—	—	11 Sem	(28) Jechonias	—	47 Jose
—	—	12 Arphaxad	(Jehoiachin)		
—	—	*Cainan*	Zedekiah	—	—
—	—	13 Sala	*omitted*	—	—
—	—	14 Heber	—	—	48 Er
—	—	15 Phaleg	—	—	49 Elmodam
—	—	16 Ragau	—	—	50 Cosam
—	—	17 Saruch	—	—	51 Addi
—	—	18 Nachor	—	—	52 Melchi
—	—	19 Thara	—	—	53 Neri
—	(1) Abraham ... 20	—	—	(29) Salathiel ... 54	—
—	(2) Isaac ... 21	—	—	(30) Zorobabel ... 55	—
—	(3) Jacob ... 22	—	(31) Abiud	—	*Rhesa*
—	(4) Juda(s) ... 23	—	(32) Eliakim	—	56 Joanna
—	(5) Phares ... 24	—	(33) Azor	—	57 Juda
—	(6) Esrom ... 25	—	(34) Sadoc	—	58 Joseph
—	(7) Aram ... 26	—	(35) Achim	—	59 Semei
—	(8) Aminadab ... 27	—	(36) Eliud	—	60 Mattathias
—	(9) Naasson ... 28	—	(37) Eleazar	—	61 Maath
—	(10) Salmon ... 29	—	—	—	62 Nagge
—	(11) Booz ... 30	—	—	—	63 Esli
—	(12) Obed ... 31	—		—	64 Naum
—	(13) Jesse ... 32	—	—	—	65 Amos
—	(14) David ... 33	—	—	—	66 Mattathias
(15) Solomon	—	34 Nathan	—	—	67 Joseph
(16) Roboam	—	35 Mattatha	—	—	68 Janna
(17) Abia	—	36 Menan	—	—	69 Melchi
(18) Asa	—	37 Melea	—	—	70 Levi
(19) Josaphat	—	38 Eliakim	(38) Matthan	(38) Mattha(n)(t) ... 71	71 Matthat
(20) Joram	—	39 Jonan		Matthan and Matthat	
Ahaziah	—	—		may be the same	72 Heli
Joash	—	—	(39) Jacob		
Amaziah	—	—		(40) Joseph ... 73	—
omitted	—	—		(41) Jesus ... 74	

Adapted from *A Guide to the Gospels* (London 1948) by W. Graham Scroggie

that Joseph became the son and heir of Heli by virtue of his marriage to Mary.

The second possible explanation considers the Lukan genealogy to be the family tree of Joseph, as Matthew's is. Both gospels stress that Joseph was of the house of David (Matt 1:16; Luke 1:27; 2:4). It is natural to suppose that both writers intended to provide Joseph's ancestry. Matthew's purpose was to trace the line of official succession to the Davidic throne, whereas Luke's informal aim was to enumerate the actual physical ancestors of Joseph back to David. This solution was originally proposed by Julius Africanus (c. A.D. 220) in a letter to Aristides, as reported by Eusebius (Euseb. Hist. 1:7). Julius believed that the law of levirite marriage could be invoked to remove the tension between the two lists—that Joseph was really the son of Heli, with Heli and Jacob as uterine brothers, born of the same mother but of different fathers. If either one had married the widow of the other, Joseph could be reckoned in that sense a son of either. A neat twist can be put on the theory by identifying the two grandfathers of Joseph (Matthan in Matthew, and Matthat in Luke). In that case, Heli might have married the widow of a childless Jacob, and begotten Joseph, in which case Joseph would be the actual son of Heli, but the legal heir to Jacob. In both lists then, the ancestry of Jesus is traced through Joseph, his legal father. Because Matthew wished to present the successive heirs to David's throne, he began with David's ancestry and worked forward to Jesus. Because Luke wished to record the actual line of physical descent, he began with Joseph and worked backward through his actual ancestors. The chief weakness of the second explanation is the series of happy coincidences required to make it function.

A final solution to so intricate a question may never be found. Enough is known, however, to show that the apparent discrepancy between the two genealogies is not insoluble.

BIBLIOGRAPHY. A. T. Robertson, *A Harmony of the Gospels* (1922), 259-262; J. G. Machen, *The Virgin Birth of Christ* (1930), 203-209; E. Stauffer, *Jesus and His Story* (1960), 22-25.

C. H. Pinnock

GENERAL, the chief military authority of an army (OT Heb. שַׂר), a difficult term in the Sem. languages as it may bear a wide range of meanings from "king" in Akkad. to "chieftain" in Heb. Translated as "general" by KJV in 1 Chronicles 27:34 only; elsewhere as "prince" (Gen 12:15 et al.), RSV COMMANDER and elsewhere "prince." These terms are relative to the situations in which they appear, and often are impossible to equate with any modern military terminology. The RSV uses it also in Revelation 6:15 (KJV "chief captains") for Gr. χιλίαρχος, "leader of a thousand troops," "military tribunes" (Acts 25:23 RSV).

W. White, Jr.

GENERATION (דור, תולדות [pl.]; γενέα; γένεσις; γέννημα; γένος, *generation, period, race*). A group of lineal descendants; a step in lineal descent. The Biblical words correspond closely to the Eng. word "generation." A further meaning of "race," or "nation" is possible in some cases.

The Heb. word דור is of broader meaning and includes the thought of an era of time, a period and thence a generation. The word has no reference to begetting. The phrase ודור דור "an age and an age" means "eternity," "forever." The same phrase is used in Ugaritic texts. The word is used (usually in the sing.) of many generations to come, as well as of a specific living generation, such as the one which died in the wilderness (Deut 2:14). The average length of a generation is often assumed to be forty years, for in the wilderness all the men over twenty died within that time. This would give a measure not of the period from a man's birth to his children's birth (more like thirty years), but would give the measure of a lifetime sixty years or more. This is apparently the meaning of Genesis 15:13, 16. Four generations equal 400 years if a generation be counted as a long lifespan. There is no statement in the Bible that the forty-year span of the rule of Solomon, of David, and of four of the judges was a round number for one generation. The forty-year figure in the Moabite Stone has also now been shown to be an accurate figure (F. M. Cross and D. N. Freedman, *Early Hebrew Orthography*, American Oriental Series, vol. 36 [1952], 39, 40).

The word תולדות comes from the root meaning "to bear a child" and is used in many OT genealogies. It may well refer also to family history in general (Gen 2:4; 6:9; 25:19; 37:2).

In the NT, the word γενέα is usually tr. "generation" (in the KJV, thirty-six times), but is also tr. "age," "nation," and "time." It is used in the genealogy of Matthew 1. Many times Jesus speaks of the faithless and perverse generation (Matt 17:17, etc.) where the reference could equally be to the Jewish nation (cf. Phil 2:15). In the RSV, such passages are tr. by "generation."

A problem v. is Matthew 24:34 and parallels. Some argue for the strict meaning and claim that Christ mistakenly expected the end in His own time. Others note that standard lexicons and other studies allow the meaning "race" or "clan" or "nation," and hold that the v. predicts the continuation of the Jewish people until Christ's return. Zahn's Commentary (in loc.) argues that "this generation" of Matthew 24:34 refers to the "this generation" of 23:36, and is in contrast to "that day and hour" of Matthew 24:36. The former expression refers to troubles applicable to the disciples' own day; the latter refers to eschatological events.

BIBLIOGRAPHY. G. F. Moore, *Judges* (on the number *forty*), ICC, xxxviii (1903); H. L. Ellison, "Kings" (on the number *forty*), NBC 307; C. H. Dodd, *The Authority of the Bible* (Torchbook, 1958), 233; H. A. Kent, Jr., "Matthew," WBC, 973 (on Matt 24:34).

R. L. HARRIS

GENESIS jĕn′ ə sis (בראשית, using the first word of the book *in beginning*, LXX γένεσις, *beginning*).

This article assumes that authorship of Genesis may rightly be attributed to Moses. No statement in the book makes that claim, nor does any other OT book. The NT makes assertions, as we shall see, that point to Mosaic authorship of the book. With this assumption and the case standing as it does, it is almost impossible to treat the material of this article under the captions usually resorted to, except in a general way. The captions to be by-passed are "background" and "date." In like manner headings such as "place of origin," "destination" and "occasion" can receive only brief treatment. For if Moses wrote the book, he would have completed the task at least before 1240 B.C., the latest possible date for Israel's crossing the Jordan after his death. "The place of origin would have been the Sinaitic peninsula or the Plains of Moab." No definite "occasion" for writing the book could be fixed. The "purpose" of writing is nowhere stated in the OT. It could be surmised with some validity that the book was written to lay the groundwork for the remaining books of the Pentateuch. The material therefore falls into the following outline:

1. The importance of the book
2. Outline
3. Author
4. Unique problems
5. Theology
6. Content

1. The importance of the book. Men have waxed eloquent in singing the praises of this, the first book of the Bible, and justly so. It contains first of all great theology, and has been rightly labeled as "the starting point of all Theology" (Fritsch, *The Layman's Bible Commentary*). It gives a basically adequate answer to the question how the world originated, how man originated, how sin came into the world, how man fell from grace, how God gave the hope of redemption to fallen man, how sin spread, how a great judgment was visited upon the sinful world in the Flood, how a remnant of the human race was providentially saved, how the human race again spread abroad still proudly asserting itself. All this is presented from a theological point of view. The rest of the book deals with the unique preparations that were made to let redemption grow out of one branch of the human family under the guidance of the Father of all mankind.

Aside from its theological importance there is its importance as great lit. Genesis compares favorably with other works of lit. that give their own national version of Creation and the Flood. The skill of the author in portraying God's activity in the guidance of creation and of history is inimitable. The charm with which the important characters of sacred history are set forth has entranced young and old through the ages. The manner in which the tale keeps moving from one climax to another is most effective. From the standpoint of good lit., the book has never lost its appeal through the ages.

Of the many things that could yet be said in praise of the importance of Genesis, is the rare combination of depth and simplicity. Subjects most vital to man, involving his deepest needs and aspirations, are dealt with in an almost childlike simplicity, which allows the young mind to catch the essence of the divine revelation with comparative ease. Like all inspired Scripture the first book in the series is still the stream through which the lamb can wade and through which the elephant must swim.

One fact stressing the extreme importance of this book is yet to be noted, and that is the frequent references to it made both by the rest of the OT as well as by the NT. True, many of the references made by the OT writers are not made by page and verse; but they are there and they stand out. To mention one summarizing example from the NT, Luke 24:27 represents the risen Lord as tracing back Messianic prophecy to Moses and all the prophets. Genesis can hardly be set aside in a reference so broad.

2. Outline. No one outline can do full justice to the contents of Genesis. It is almost immediately apparent to him who takes the book in hand that chs. 1-11 comprise a separate unit, even as do chs. 12-50. Various terms have been used to cover this difference, such as "Primeval History" and "Patriarchal History" (Fritsch, *The Layman's Bible Commentary*). Or, for that matter an outline may be used which is actually presented by the book itself, an outline which comprises ten headings, built on the Heb. word *tôl^{e}dôt*, which is most aptly tr. "history." So ten histories (2:4; 5:1; 6:9; 10:1; 11:10, 27; 25:12, 19; 36:1; 37:1) are offered by the book, some dealing with important characters (Terah, Isaac, Jacob, Joseph), some dealing with important categories, like heaven and earth or the sons of Adam and of Noah; others with minor characters, like Ishmael, Esau, etc. This outline is the most effective, although it does not penetrate into the depth of issues involved; but it does emphasize that God guided the history of mankind through His dealings with individual characters that He felt free to use for the good of the rest of mankind.

Interesting is another approach made of a recent date (Frey, *Botschaft des Alten Testaments*) which finds four major subjects treated, labeling them as: The Book of Beginnings (1-11); The Book of Faith (12-25); The Book of Struggle (26-35); and The Book of Guidance (*Füehrung*) (36-50).

Still other outlines may have their validity, for it is extremely difficult to press the rich contents of so striking a book as Genesis into the mold of an outline that may be helpful. Usually an outline catches some important feature of the contents and fails to do justice to other features.

3. Author. The approach most popular still in our day is practically that of source analysis—many writers producing many sources, which have all been skillfully woven together into one grand whole by an unknown editor (commonly called the Redactor, and referred to as R).

This article will not attempt a portrayal that covers the whole of this approach but without undertaking any direct refutation it will attempt at least to sketch the newer developments that have taken place in this field. Around the turn of the cent. the major sources were designated as J, E, D, and P—J operating mostly with the divine name Yahweh (also spelled Jahweh); E, using the divine name Elohim by preference; D marked by material that is both hortatory and legal in character, as such material appears in Deuteronomy; and P setting forth the kind of material that priests would cultivate and cherish, such as the provisions of Leviticus (Lev 1-16).

Presently it began to appear to scholars that even past the Mosaic Age it would be far more likely for a nation like Israel to preserve the record of its experiences not in books, such as might be kept in a literary age, but in living tradition that was passed on by word of mouth from generation to generation. Attention was directed to tradition as the major source of Israel's history. This should have set aside the entanglement with the problems of the written sources. Still the so-called achievements in this latter field were kept and operated with as having achieved relative validity. It was not realized that men cannot operate with both approaches simultaneously. But it must be admitted that with this shift of emphasis the richness of the traditions of Israel began to be studied and appreciated as never before.

In the meantime the search after sources had produced findings that gave even the adherents of these hypotheses of sources some serious misgivings. For example the P source had been broken down into component parts labeled consecutively as P, P^g, P^1, P^2, P^3. Similar additional subsources were discovered for J and the rest—an obviously impossible array of sources that even the most astute ingenuity of scholarship could hardly accept seriously. The minor sources were dismissed and new reconstruction of at least JEDPR were and are being attempted.

The inadequacy of this approach again became evident in that entirely new sources were demanded on every side. The original J had been broken up into J^1 and J^2. J^1 really had nothing in common with J^2 except possibly the use of the divine proper name Yahweh. So, chiefly championed by Eissfeldt, L (Lay Source) was suggested as a helpful substitute for J^1. It was also found necessary to bring another new source into the picture labeled N (nomadic stratum). In addition Noth felt that there was quite a bit of evidence for the similarity that is rather obvious when J and E are viewed side by side; and so he advocated a G source (*gemeinsame Grundlage*—common foundation) for both. A bit earlier men like Robert H. Pfeiffer had postulated an S source (S or Seir). Some appeared on the scene advocating that a K (Kenite) source is also clearly in evidence. Besides sources such as G^2, L^2, and J^2 were currently approved in many cases.

It must be admitted that some writers roundly reject the validity of the newest sources, and claim that such proliferation defeats its own purpose and causes only confusion. One writer from this camp ventures the assertion that recourse to other than the basic standards like JE and P "has proved to be so much tilting at windmills" (Fritsch, *The Anchor Bible*).

One trend of source criticism as it still prevails in our day should, in passing, be noted. Much attention is given in such studies to the way in which a book may have originated. Surprisingly little is made of the contents and message of the book. So a thorough and much used textbook of introduction to the OT devotes about 150 pages to critical problems and only casually touches upon a few matters of true interpretation, indicating the meaning and value of the contents of the books treated. In the second place it is rather significant that even so notable a work as the IB, in an introductory article by the general editor makes the admission: "For fifty years no full-scale commentary has been produced in the English language on the whole Bible." During these "fifty years" source criticism had its day and dominated all Pentateuchal studies. Meager were the fruits it produced in constructive interpretation during its heyday.

This leads to the other side of the question: If the critical approach has yielded so little fruitage and has so many obvious weaknesses with its theory of multiple authorship, also of Genesis, what has the conservative approach to offer by way of substitute? Answer: The possibility of Mosaic authorship advocated in a number of forms. We admit freely, to begin with, that nowhere in the Bible is there a direct and unmistakable claim maintaining the Mosaic authorship of Genesis in particular. But a number of factors point in this direction. That Moses wrote at least certain portions of the books that were traditionally ascribed to him may be noted (see Exod 17:14; 24:4, 7; 34:27; Num 33:2). In Leviticus at least thirty-five times expressions are used like, "And the LORD spoke unto Moses (and Aaron)." If the exact words are referred to, the words that the Lord spoke, the measure of probability is high that they were committed to writing as soon as received. Deuteronomy 1:1 also is significant. Unusually important are the passages: Deuteronomy 17:18; 27:1-8; 31:9, 24, all of which bear reference to written material dating from Moses.

It could be argued feasibly that if Moses resorted to writing in the cases just referred to, he may well have written the rest of the framework that surrounds these portions written by him. It also appears as feasible that the material from Exodus to Deuteronomy demands some such substructure as Genesis, a fact that Moses could well have sensed and taken steps to provide such a broader base, using such materials as were accessible at the time, in the form of ancient traditions that had been well preserved. Such an approach to the problem has as much to commend it as the hypothetical results of modern criticism, a fact which is tacitly admitted even by the trs. of the RSV, which captions the first book, as did the KJV trs.: "The First Book of Moses."

When passages like John 5:46f. (in which Jesus refers to the "writings" of Moses) are introduced to indicate that Jesus Himself may have asserted in them that Moses was the author of the writings commonly attributed to him, they cannot be dismissed casually with the statement: "Jesus was not at the time discussing the authorship of the Pentateuch." It all depends on how far one cares to extend the authority of the words of Jesus. That He incidentally combined with His statement a claim that Moses wrote these books could indeed have been done in the interest of reassuring His followers on this additional important question for years to come. It is true that "Moses" in this context could mean the writings commonly attributed to Moses. It is equally true that it might be a pronouncement on the authorship of these writings.

It is quite proper, therefore, for the *Wycliffe Bible Commentary* to come forth with the assertion (p. 1): "It is safe to claim Moses as the responsible author of the book" (Moody Press, Chicago [1962]). Or one may say, with *The New Bible Commentary* (ed. Francis Davidson, Eerdmans Publishing Co., Grand Rapids [1958]): "No reason has yet been produced which categorically requires that the belief in the Mosaic authorship should be abandoned" (p. 75). We hold the theory of Mosaic authorship of Genesis to be fully as feasible as the theory of source analysis.

It cannot be denied that it is eminently reasonable to believe that Moses used available documents or solid traditions currently in circulation, in the compiling of Genesis.

Nor is it unreasonable to hold with the

Bible Commission of the Roman Catholic Church, of 1906, that though Moses was the author of the Pentateuch, he may have employed qualified persons as secretaries to work under his direction for the compiling of certain source materials; cf. *Echter Bibel,* etc. Allowance may even be made for post-Mosaic editorial additions or alterations of a later date. By this we mean that the names of towns as they are listed here and there in Genesis, may have been changed to agree with the names that these towns held at a later date, a perfectly legitimate modernizing.

There is also another view on the authorship of Genesis advocated by Aalders which allows for the possibility that an author may have compiled the work "at a comparatively later date" (prob. during the early days of the monarchy) but will have "made use of the extensive Mosaic literature together with some pre-Mosaic material" (*The New Bible Commentary*, p. 34, Eerdmans Publishing Company [1958]).

4. Unique problems. Quite a number of unique problems are encountered when one enters upon a study of Genesis. Almost the first to stare the student in the face is the problem of the apparent conflict between the modern world-view and that of this book. The difference of approach could even be magnified to the point where the two viewpoints are regarded as utterly irreconcilable. However one need not be unduly alarmed at the prospect. It is now commonly conceded that obviously the writer of the Genesis creation-account cannot have had the intention of providing a scientific theory of creation, cast in terms of modern science. He was so guided by the Spirit of inspiration that he set forth basic truths of revelation in terms that were precise enough as to the truth conveyed, but yet were elastic enough to allow for the possibility of present-day scientific approaches that have been well established. The emphasis in the account of Genesis lies upon the omnipotence and mercy of the Creator. A God who can be loved and worshiped is represented in action in a manner calculated to bring a man to his knees as he beholds what God did to bring this world and man into being. The time factor involved is certainly a subject of secondary importance. In fact, in the manner in which the account is written, it is quite clear that certain processes that may have required the lapse of a large measure of time are allowed for. Without a question the well-ordered nature of God's creation as well as the wisdom with which all things were made, all stand forth rather prominently. Many scientists can gratefully accept Genesis and many theologians gladly accept the numerous validated findings of science.

Of an entirely different nature are the instances in the Scripture that seem to fail to fit smoothly into the picture of interpretation. There is the question of the historical character of the old patriarchs: Did Abraham, Isaac, and Jacob actually live and do the things recorded here? Did these events actually take place in their lives? That they were uniquely led by divine providence is rather apparent. But does an unusual measure of providential leading make an account unhistorical? More of God's overruling power may have been manifested in one man's life than in another. Besides, archeology has done valiant service in demonstrating in the record of the lives of the patriarchs that the background of these lives corresponds precisely with the state of affairs that prevailed in these lands as archeology retraces these records. Unger remarks, "The great service archaeological research is performing in this early period of Biblical history is to demonstrate that the picture of the patriarchs as presented in Genesis fits the frame of contemporary life. . . . Today archaeology compels a more general respect for the historical quality of the patriarchal stories." He adds that it "has had a momentous role in dealing a fatal blow to radical theories and in compelling a greater respect for the historical worth of the patriarchal narratives" (Merrill F. Unger, *Archaeology and the OT,* Grand Rapids: Zondervan Publishing House [1954], p. 120. See also G. E. Wright, *Biblical Archaeology*, Philadelphia: Westminster [1957], Ch. III, pp. 40ff.)

A matter that could cause the careful reader of Genesis some measure of difficulty is the fact that after one has read the largely narrative account of Genesis, the style of the record becomes so radically different in vocabulary and subject matter as one gets into material such as Exodus 21-23. Could one and the same man be found to have such diversity of style as is here in evidence? A still different style appears as one explores the material of Deuteronomy. But is not this difficulty alleviated by the simple observation that at these points a total change of subject-matter is to be found? The writer is no longer telling how God dealt with the patriarchs, but is recounting laws that he set forth for the guidance of the nation. Style and vocabulary had to change under such circumstances. So, too, they had to change again when Moses, before his end, addressed touching admonitions to the nation he had guided for so many years, as is the case in much of the material that goes to make up Deuteronomy.

Is not the argument convincing that J largely and almost exclusively used the name Yahweh for the divine being, whereas E used Elohim? Cannot this speak strongly in favor of a clear separation of these two sources? No easy solution to the problem involved has yet been offered by either side in the argument. Criticism can hardly offer a valid parallel where a writer of the Mosaic period can be shown to have known only one name for the Deity. Besides, the obvious fact that names are to be used according to their meaning is totally ignored in this case. Observe, by way of a good

"Adam and Eve Seal" found near Nineveh in 1932 by Dr. E. A. Speiser who dated it about 3500 B.C. ©*U.M.P.*

A fragment of a Creation Tablet, from Nineveh, with Assyrian account of creation. ©*B.M.*

parallel, the fine distinction that the NT makes in the use of the two names "Jesus' and "Christ." Add to this the many exceptions where J uses Elohim and E uses Yahweh.

Is there not a large measure of agreement among critics as to the major issues of source analysis? Answer: First of all, issues of this sort are not settled by majority vote. The majority often has been wrong. Besides, a large number of passages can be cited from the pen of critics admitting many unsolved problems. Critics are today more than ever before divided over the results of their investigations. Bentzen admits that "the present situation concerning the question of the Pentateuch . . . is rather in suspense. Especially among the scholars of the younger generation there exists a definite scepticism toward the Documentary Hypothesis" (A. Bentzen, *Introduction to the OT*, Copenhagen: G. E. C. Gad [1958], Vol. II, p. 23). Nielsen, writing as a representative of an Oral Tradition theory objects to the older literary criticism: "One can and must doubt whether the method by which literary criticism *finds* difficulties in the text and afterwards *solves* them is the right one. In other words one may doubt the correctness of the fundamental view and the methods of literary criticism." (E. Nielsen, *Oral Tradition* London: SCM Press [1954], p. 94.) Observe also how many findings are couched in cautious terminology, using frequently words such as "could" and "might."

Somewhat striking besides is the fact that after many sources have been detected by the methods of criticism there are still certain materials left over that cannot be traced to any of the sources or redactors with which men operate, like the famous ch. 14 of Genesis. (Cf. also: Exod 15:1-19; 19:3b-8; and Deut 32.)

Attention also should be drawn to the fact that when the theology of Genesis is set forth the custom prevails to present not the theology of the book as a whole but to fragmentize it into the separate theologies of J, E, P, etc. The total impact of the book is lost, and the hypothetical theologies of unidentified writers are emphasized. The form in which the book has providentially come down to us is ignored, though the editor, or redactor—whoever he may have been—may have been highly praised by the present-day writer for his skill in organizing. It is not the theology of Genesis that is offered, but the hazy theologies of J, E, and P.

There is another unwholesome trend which may be observed in dealing with the book as a whole, the trend which thinks in terms of the incredibility of the history of the early patriarchs. It is taken for granted that one cannot accept as facts the things set forth as having been experienced by the fathers of old. Their encounter with the divine being in assumed human or angelic form, their providential deliverance from danger, the overwhelming instances of divine providence particularly in the life of Joseph—all these are thought to tax belief beyond what confidently may be accepted. Subjective feelings are not the final measure of miracles.

5. Theology of Genesis. This is not a theology of the various so-called sources, but a theology of the book as a whole.

On the doctrine concerning God some distinct points of view emerge and some features obviously are missing. A full-rounded concept of God could hardly be conveyed by one brief book, esp. since the doctrine of God also was subject to more abundant revelation as time went on.

The God who does appear in this book is sole and supreme monarch of the universe and of His people. A latent monotheism is to be discovered in the book. It is a long while until statements like Deuteronomy 6:4 can appear, but Genesis prepares for them. It is equally obvious that this God of the patriarchs is omnipotent: He can create whatever He is pleased to bring into being, and He does all his work by the use of His potent word. He knows all things, though this fact is hinted at rather than fully revealed. He knows of the hiding of our first parents in the garden, and of Sarah's secret laughter in the tent. He is present also far from the ancestral home, as Jacob to his amazement discovers (Gen 28:16); he is virtually omnipresent.

In His workings God is supremely wise, for all things that He creates bear the stamp of being most excellently adapted to their designed use and purpose. An integrated universe comes into being from His hands. At the same time concern for the well-being of His creatures leads Him to give abundant evidence of His deep mercy and love, esp. toward those creatures who are the crown of His creation, the children of men.

This God reveals Himself to His children. Some measure of mystery surrounds the manner in which He does it. The sacred writers were not given a revelation concerning how revelation in days of old came from God to men, at least not as far as the mechanics of the method were concerned. God did at times appear (one may not be able to say precisely in what guise) and in these theophanies He spoke understandably to the chosen recipients of His revelation. Sometimes His message was conveyed to men in the stillness of the night in a dream (31:11); sometimes the mysterious agent "the angel of the Lord" functioned on such occasions (again 31:11). These experiences on the part of the patriarchs were real and do not savor of an overly lively display of religious credulity.

A rather clear picture of who and what man is also begins to appear in the context of this book. Man is a creature, made according to a preconceived design, with a material as well as a non-material side to His being. He is from the outset a creature that has a free will, for He can assent to, or He can say, "No," to temptation. God's image is stamped upon man. True, what the image of God precisely embraces is nowhere defined but it is asserted with emphasis that this belongs to His native endowment (1:27). Equally mysterious is the somewhat representative character of the first man ("in Adam all die," 1 Cor 15:22). He is the first of human beings in more than in the mere sense of numerical priority. Again this representative character is not set forth in so many words.

This man is represented from the outset as a superior being as he comes forth as God's handiwork, free from the taint of sin. Being led by the tempter, he allows himself to aspire to be like God, and rises in proud disobedience against the express will of his Creator, taking of the fruit "whose mortal taste brought death into the world and all its woe." The immediate consequences of this willful act are seen to be an unwholesome fear of God, a desire to shun His presence, and a sense of shame, together with many other distortions of what had been a "good" character. Sin's capacity for rapid growth is indicated by the record that tells how the first son of our first parents slew his own brother in cold blood. In fact, as the record points out, sin rages up and down through the world, filling it with violence, even to the point where the Creator Himself had to use drastic means—the Flood—to curb this monstrous evil. When a new development sets in and the children of men increase in numbers, soon they are defying the basic ordinance of the Almighty and are building a rallying point in the form of a huge tower. That man stands in need of help from on high is, by this account, represented negatively rather than positively. It soon becomes obvious that sin again is reaching horrible dimensions, when the abnormal development of Canaanite sexual depravity comes to light, or when the incident of Sodom and Gomorrah throws its lurid light on the pages of Sacred Writ.

That there is a grace mighty to save also soon becomes apparent. For hardly had Adam fallen, even before his well-deserved punishment is appointed, when strong evidence appears that God will not deal with men after their sins in ruthless justice, nor reward strictly according to their iniquities. He gives a rich promise, as Genesis 3:15, rightly interpreted, clearly shows. It is promised that one capable of breaking the power of the evil one will in due time appear, born of a woman. An incidental trace of the unmerited grace that God will make operative is to be found also in this that the Creator provides garments for these children of His whom He had to oust from the blessed garden of Eden (3:23). In a similar manner God's attitude toward fallen man is indicated by the rainbow in the sky after the great Flood, which was a token of grace indicating a stable world-order not again to be visited by a Flood. In fact, God's undeserved goodness found solid expression finally in the covenant that He made freely with Abraham, not because of Abraham's superior merit but because of the Lord's abounding favor (Gen 15).

So there are to be found the basic elements of redemption even at this early date: grace on the part of God; faith on the part of man. For Genesis 15:6 plainly states that when Abraham believed the Lord's promises, "He reckoned it to him as righteousness," a passage that figures prominently in the upbuilding of Paul's theology (Rom 4:3, 9, 22, 23). Genesis comes close to saying that a man is justified by faith apart from the works of the law.

It may also be noted that some clear thoughts on the subject of judgment are set forth in this early record. Abraham knows God as the God who is the fair and unimpeachable judge of all the earth (Gen 18:25). There are no soft notions of an indulgent father of mankind, but a sense of the necessity of divine justice visiting sin's consequences upon the guilty—thoughts like this are strongly underscored by incidents like the destruction of Sodom (19:1-28).

Even more strongly the concept of divine providence is maintained and exemplified. In that food is expressly provided in creation for man's needs, divine providence shows its face. The unique manner in which the patriarchs are guided and guarded in their ways conveys the same thought. In fact, perhaps nowhere in Scripture is the evidence of providential guidance exemplified more prominently than in the narrative that centers about Joseph.

6. Content. The record of Creation, it is contended in our day, was handed down from generation to generation in a long tradition. It was perpetuated in a record that went from mouth to mouth. Those who were qualified to give it shape and form did so with masterful skill and great theological insight, being no doubt skillfully guided by the Spirit of God. Was it in final form as it came to Moses, or did Moses perhaps give it some final form? God only knows.

The account as given in the first two chs. has something majestic about it. Being sanctified prose, it still reads almost like a great epic poem. It moves in solemn cadences to a great climax in the record of God's Sabbath, having just before recorded the sublime story of the creation of man. At the same time, in words coming from the lips of the divine Creator, it maps out with surprising effectiveness God's mandate to man, to "have dominion" over all created things. This includes man's control progressively advancing from step to step subduing all creatures under his dominion (1:28). Man had rare duties and rare prerogatives and a nobel destiny outlined for him by God. Man was not left to his own devices to determine what his Creator expected of him. Still the mandate was given with such latitude of movement for man that God could hardly have stressed man's moral accountability more heavily.

In ch. 2 God's work of creation, how it proceeded and what it involved, is more fully unfolded. These details could have been inserted at their proper place in the time sequence of ch. 1, but that would have interrupted the marvelous progression that is so much in evidence in ch. 1. There was something of lowliness in the story of man—he was fashioned "of dust from the ground" (2:7). This fact so effectively disclosed at this point counterbalances the story of the high dignity that marked the previous chapter's account. All this in spite of the fact that man had the distinct imprint of the image of God in his being.

Woman's position over against man is also more fully outlined in the account of 2:21ff. What had in ch. 1 been stated all too briefly ("male and female he created them") is now expanded in a report also most instructive and helpful. There is no clash between these two accounts. They obviously are intended to supplement one another.

For man's moral growth and development God had in deep wisdom provided two trees (2:9) with important directives for man's instruction in regard to the tree of knowledge. One must regard their nature as being almost sacramental. The full possibilities of the tree of life have not been perpetuated in the traditions relative to this second tree. One still gains the impression that nothing needful for man's future development had been omitted.

Basic for the understanding of man, as far as man can understand the deep things of human nature, is some instruction about the origin of evil. This is provided in ch. 3. Many questions are left unanswered, perhaps because the mystery of iniquity is too great for mankind to fully comprehend it. The record of the Fall reveals some basic guidelines that dare never be overlooked. Man, as he came from the hand of God, was without moral deficiency. Sin did not originate from within man. A personal tempter brought it into the world. Man let himself be beguiled by the mysterious serpent. At a much later time it is made obvious that in the last analysis this tempter was none other than Satan (Rev 12:9). It is impossible to determine why the tempter is not more clearly identified. Man was not cursed as a consequence of the Fall, although grievous burdens were laid upon him lest he forget the deep tragedy of the whole experience—that the ground is cursed and brings forth thorns and thistles; toilsome labor and death are to be his lot. But, the case is not hopeless. In some strange way Adam was enlightened to see that, from the woman, life would come for man-

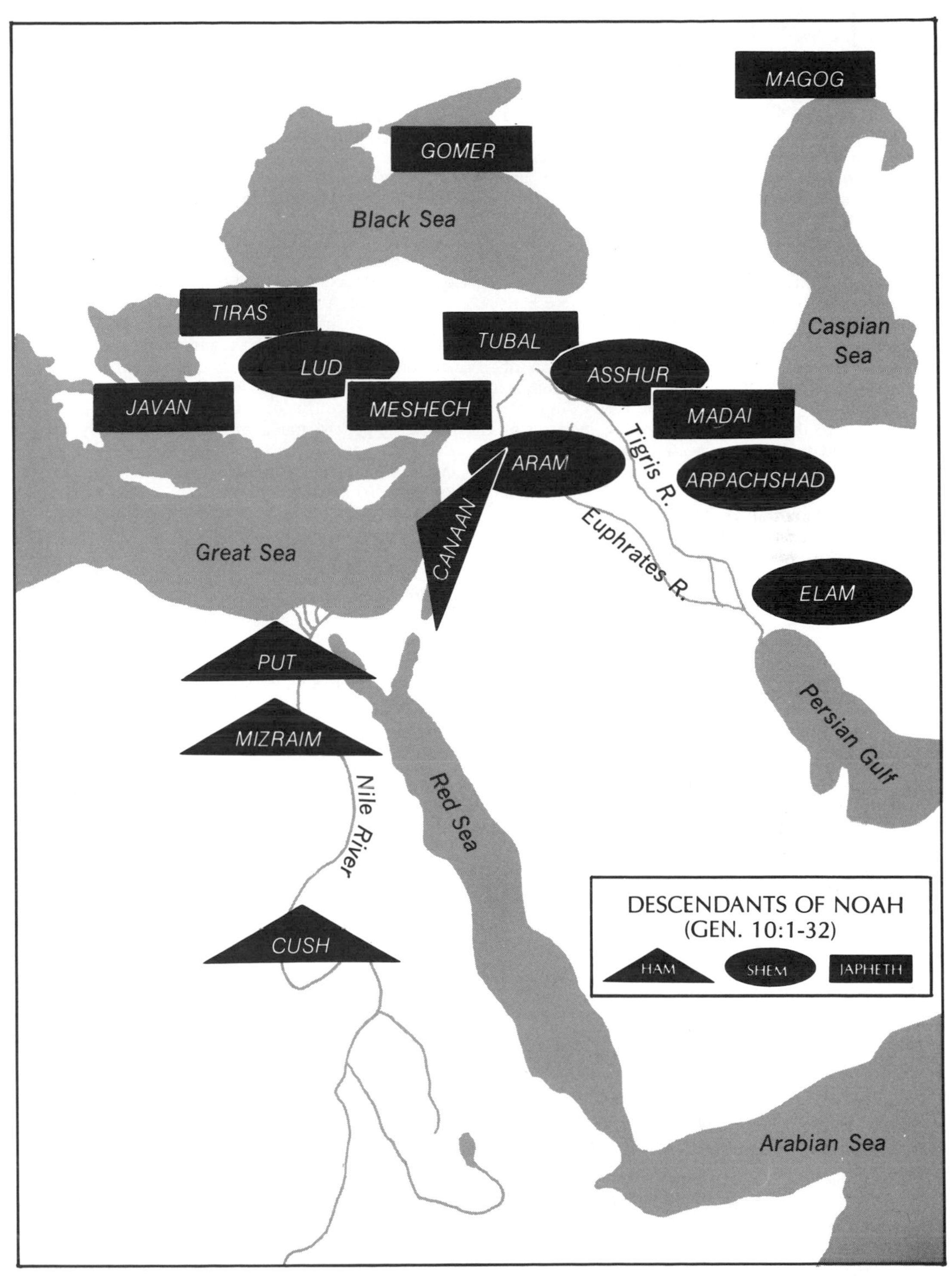

The nations of the Ancient World with particular emphasis on Canaan.

kind; for he designates his wife by the name "of Eve," which word means "life." Further indications of hope for fallen man appear also in this that one born of woman is to administer a crushing defeat ("crush the head") to the tempter in the course of time, a promise reiterated in Romans 16:20. Additional evidence of God's merciful attitude toward fallen man appears in this that he made personal provision for clothing those who had now become aware of a certain shameful nakedness (Gen 3:21).

Something of a deeply mysterious nature also surrounds the tree of life. It was for man's own good that he was barred from access to this tree. For to have partaken of it would have meant irremediable involvement in the state of sin and so the loss of the hope of redemption (v. 22). The ch. has the memorable close that shows cherubim guarding the entrance to the Garden of Eden lest man eat of the second forbidden tree and be caught in the toils of hopeless death.

In ch. 4 the slaying of Abel shows what horrible potentialities lie in sin. At the same time, this fratricide was the first step in the direction of separating the human race into two groups—the beginning of the sharp antithesis —church and world. Those who were the lineal descendants of Cain (properly called "Cainites") from this point on are seen to live a life immersed in this world and its delights and pursuits. In the seventh generation from Adam this group reached a more intense development of worldly values (nomadism, music, mastery of metals, 4:20-24). On the other hand Seth (4:25f.) was the ancestor among whose descendants the worship of the Lord flourished —public worship even at this early date. The people of this group may be designated as "Sethites." The table of ancestry of the Cainites is given in 4:17-25. The line of descent of the Sethites is presented in ch. 5. Both groups must be noted if one is to understand how the history of the nations unfolds.

Of the successive stories that cover the material of Genesis, the first "story"—that of heaven and earth—runs from 2:4 to 4:26. It is rightly designated as being the story of heaven and earth because the interests of both areas are deeply involved in these two. The second story—that of Adam—runs from 5:1 to 6:8, and indicates in its closing remarks how esp. the Sethites forfeited their identity by letting their children intermarry with the godless Cainites. From that point on, corruption grew so fast it was not long before only one righteous man was left on the face of the earth—Noah.

This then leads to the story of Noah (6:8-9:29), a period of history which was dominated by the lone figure of this venerable patriarch. Within this story is contained the record of the universal Flood, telling particularly how God mercifully spared Noah and his family in the days when He wiped out all living creatures that were left outside the ark. The rainbow as token of God's covenant mercy overarches this story and brings it to a gracious conclusion.

That we may not forget that all human families, as far as we are able to detect, stem from the stock of Noah, the next story—10:1-10:32—gives the genealogies of the sons of Noah and so traces the whole human family back to a second common ancestor—Noah.

In spite of their ancestral unity, it was not long before a new rift in the races of mankind developed as a result of man's manifest disobedience to the command of the Lord in that they refused to keep spreading abroad on the face of the earth and sought to concentrate their strength and accomplishments about the great tower as rallying point. The mysterious confusion of tongues resulted, which helped to make obvious how deeply divided sinners had become from one another in spite of their common ancestry. This confusion could well have been allowed by the Almighty in order to prevent the consolidation of future opposition to the divine will.

The story found in 11:10-32 (the descendants of Shem) makes it obvious that the writer is aiming to concentrate on some part of the family of Shem, and that he knew well how the families of the earth were integrated.

With ch. 12, beginning actually with 11:27, there is the special history of the chosen race, although this story is captioned as being that of Terah. In some way, perhaps as a prominent figure among his contemporaries, Terah could at first have outranked Abraham, but there can be no doubt that the Abraham story runs from 11:27 to 25:11. Terah seems to have died comparatively early and to have vanished from the scene at Haran.

The story of the call of Abraham (12:1ff.) is of the utmost importance. It is, of course, basic for the understanding of the sacred history that follows. It towers above the accompanying narratives though it is not even said in what manner God appeared to Abraham. It is stated that in a surprising act of faith, Abraham obeyed the call. (Note: In 12:3 the KJV tr. "in thee shall all families of the earth be blessed" has much to support it, esp. in view of the Messianic implications indicated in Gal 3:15-18.)

Genesis 12:10ff. gives an unbiased and entirely truthful account of Abraham's sojourn in Egypt with Sarah. It becomes apparent that though Abraham may have manifested surprising courage of faith in accepting the challenge of his call, yet he was far from being a perfect saint. Recent discoveries, however, relieve Abraham of some of his alleged weakness. It appears that in the Hurrian society of Mesopotamia there remained traces of a fratriarchal organization. The other marriage and inheritance laws and customs of the patriarchs also have been brilliantly illustrated by the Hurrian

Bilingual cuneiform tablet giving the Sumarian and Akkadian accounts of the creation of the world by Murdak and Aruru, 6th century B.C. Babylonian from Sippor. © *B.M.*

The Gilgamesh Seal of Utnapishtim, the Babylonian "Noah." The Gilgamesh epic tells the Babylonian account of the Flood. ©*U.M.P.*

culture evidenced by the documents from Nuzi. There are marriage documents from Nuzi in which a wife, unrelated by blood to her husband, is adopted into the status of sistership. This legal status of sistership for a wife brought with it certain rights and protections. This special status was characteristic of the upper classes of society. The Hittites, it appears, did not recognize this peculiar custom. Apparently the wife-sister relationship was expected to give a woman a status that would make her free from improper approaches and thus make her husband safe in an unfriendly land. Abraham claimed this protection for both her and himself. It did not work in Egypt where Hurrian law was not followed. God in His providence preserved Sarah and Abraham anyway. Abraham tried it again in Gerar with the same result. Possibly he also tried it elsewhere with good results. Isaac later tried it again, prob. before a different Philistine king, with no better success. The whole strange situation is seen to be in accord with Nuzi law and good ethics in the early patriarchal times. The data are given extensively by Speiser (E. A. Speiser, *Oriental and Biblical Studies,* Philadelphia, Univ. of Penna. Press [1967], pp. 68-72).

Abraham's nephew, Lot, had associated himself with Abraham in the departure from Ur of the Chaldeans. Nevertheless, as later developments show, his family did not constitute good material for incorporation with the chosen race. A separation had to take place. It ultimately appears that Lot gravitated toward Sodom, apparently finding a certain attraction for the type of life that prevailed in those wicked cities. Remarks like 13:13 indicate that an unusual measure of depravity was beginning to prevail in Canaan. The passage 15:16 points in the same direction.

There were more facets to Abraham's character than we might first suppose. He even filled the role of a deliverer from the perils of war, and as a warrior of no mean ability himself. He displayed fine family loyalty for his nephew, going to battle for him (ch. 14).

Chapter 15 records how God made a covenant with Abraham, promising him many descendants and also revealing to him that before better days came, a troubled and painful future awaited his descendants down in the land of Egypt. The shift of location down into Egypt did not come upon Abraham's descendants as a total surprise. Both the stay in that land plus the affliction there incurred, together with the disclosure that God would ultimately deliver the nation—all these coming events were communicated already to Abraham.

In this connection the sacrifice that was made according to 15:7-11, 17 is merely the record of the sacrifice by which the covenant was sealed in a formal fashion. The "smoking fire pot" (15:17), and "a flaming torch" (15:17), constitute one single picture and symbolize light, for light is the symbol of God's presence. God Himself indicated by this sign language that He personally had entered into a compact with Abraham. All this involved sign language, which in those days was readily understood.

Chapter 16 introduces a time of waiting. The fulfillment of God's promises did not come quickly. The period of waiting was a time of testing of the faith. Only under due tensions will faith grow and mature. This period of waiting extended over a number of decades. Under such circumstances people are inclined to resort to devices that are calculated to help God along. In the last analysis such devices are questionable and give evidence of a lack of faith. In this case they gave rise to family tensions, jealousy, friction, estrangement. Hagar bore a son, but he was not to be a child of promise. Abraham still had to wait quite a number of years before the true son appeared. Though the procedure followed was sanctioned by prevailing customs of that day, it still did not meet with divine approval, nor conform to the original promise God had given.

In the next chapter (17) further promises were given to Abraham, but nothing more. Faith subsists on promises. It is even indicated to this man approaching the age of one hundred years that a number of nations would trace back the beginning of their existence to this venerable patriarch. For the present, Abraham had to content himself with a unique sign of the covenant—circumcision. At least two constructive thoughts must be associated with this rite, one, the removal of impurity, and second, the sanctifying of life at its source, which rightly may be classed as a thought involving Messianic implications. In the obedience of faith, Abraham sees to it that he and his whole household take the obligations of this half-sacramental rite upon themselves. At the same time, Abraham learns that Ishmael will not rank as the son of promise. He will achieve some distinction as a son of Abraham. The promised one must be waited for, until the time is ripe in the Lord's sight.

A high point in the relationship of the two contracting partners in the covenant is reached in ch. 18. The Lord condescends to meet with Abraham as an intimate friend, sharing food with him and sharing some of His divine secrets of judgment, as a man would with a confidential associate. A major catastrophe is about to occur near Abraham's home. God would have him know what it is and what it involves, and He comes in a special visit to apprise the man of what is about to take place. Abraham appears to good advantage. Being a man of faith, he is not self-centered. Impending calamity rouses deep sympathy on Abraham's part and shows him to be bold in prayer and much concerned about the well-being of others. Abraham's prayer for Sodom and Gomorrah is not petty haggling, but intercession at its best.

Chapter 19 deals with ugly things. Sin has made tremendous inroads into the lives particularly of the Canaanites. Sin in its more repulsive forms is in evidence. It is not to be wondered at that the Almighty Himself, through His angels, takes the desperate situation in hand, and thereby sets up a severe warning for all the inhabitants of the land. Homosexuality in its grimmer aspects, venting its spite on helpless strangers, is the particular sin in which the iniquity of these people found its expression. For the sake of the intercessory prayer of a righteous man, the Lord spares at least those few persons in the city who may be less infected by this basic immorality. Even in that family group one member perishes, Lot's wife, one who takes divine commandments somewhat lightly and is disobedient to a clear divine warning. The conclusion of the ch. indicates how one family that was saved had been infected by the unholy example of the surroundings in which the family had lived for a few years.

The episode that transpires in ch. 20 is not a doublet of the one recorded in 12:10ff. The location, the characters involved, and the details of the two are quite different from one another.

In its opening account, ch. 21 gives indication how great the happiness was that reigned in the household of Abraham at the birth of the son long promised. Isaac's name in itself already means laughter; and the laughter referred to in this connection is not the laughter of amusement, but laughter of joy unspeakable over the fact that God had so faithfully kept His promise. When the two sons of Abraham grew up and failed to get along well together, this led to the dismissal of the son of the slave woman. Though her expulsion was divinely sanctioned, God compensated to her what she had to forfeit and gave to Ishmael also the hope of a challenging future, all for the sake of His servant Abraham.

Chapter 22 contains one of the best known of the stories of the OT. It should be noted in particular that the idea of offering a son to the Lord in a physical sacrifice on an altar did not originate with Abraham. God, however, does not follow mere whimsies in dealing with the children of men. It may well be that Abraham needed to be put to the test in this way, that he might become aware of the fact that he was threatened by the danger of loving this child of his old age more than even the Lord Himself. He had to face the issue squarely: Whom did he love the most, the Lord or Isaac? Hard though the test was, the Lord did not suffer Abraham to be tested above that which he was able. That God "provides" (v. 14) in the most difficult emergencies was the point that particularly impressed Abraham. Abraham had virtually made the spiritual sacrifice of his son to the Lord. At the same time, this episode may be regarded as a standing protest against child sacrifice: such sacrifice is not willed by God. It also must be obvious that this sacrifice has Messianic overtones. God was willing to offer His own Son for the saving of mankind (Rom 8:32). There is much about this ch. that still perplexes the children of God. It has unplumbed depths.

Chapter 23. An overly detailed account of the transactions connected with the purchase of a burial ground when Sarah died seems to be what this ch. presents. Possession of the land of Canaan was an item that loomed up large in the thinking of all Israelites from the time when first God promised this land to Abraham. Why should He not want at least token possession in the case of his wife's place of burial? Viewed thus, the incident takes on increased importance as the act of a man of faith. With quiet dignity Abraham goes through all the necessary legal transactions to acquire at least this much of the soil of the land.

Chapter 24. This tale could be viewed as a somewhat romantic one charmingly told. It is far more than that. Perhaps there was hardly a woman to be found in the land who was not in some manner infected with loose and ungodly Canaanite thinking and immoral idolatry. To have secured a wife for Isaac from this type of stock would have imperiled the faith and the morals of the descendants of Abraham. With fine discretion Abraham commissions the servant of his house (Abraham was by this time, no doubt, too old to undergo the rigors of journey to Mesopotamia) and instructs him on the subject of the issues involved in this transaction. The servant was a man worthy of so fine a master and carried out his commission in the spirit in which it was given. Rebekah's prompt acceptance could well have been regarded as token that the servant's prayer at the well had been answered.

Chapter 25. Abraham's second marriage with Keturah is a matter of historical record. Everything relating to the great father of the people of Israel is important. Most likely this marriage was entered upon after the death of Sarah. The children of this marriage are the fathers of the nations that had been foretold as coming from Abraham's line (17:5). At this point the Ishmael story is woven into the narrative. As a descendant of Abraham, Ishmael is important; aside from that he merits brief attention (vv. 12-18). Then comes the beginning of the Isaac story (25:19-35:29), covering a major section of the Book of Genesis. In the Isaac story, Isaac stays pretty much in the background, being overshadowed in the first part of it by Abraham, as long as his father still lived, and then yielding place to his more famous son, Jacob. All this is partly due to the fact that Isaac was an ordinary person, pushed into the background by characters more important and more aggressive than he. He had the misfortune of being the son of a great father. Besides, it was the nature of the man Isaac to be unaggressive and somewhat phlegmatic by disposition. He stayed put quietly, inaugurated no new policies, hardly did an original thing. He perhaps never asserted himself. Two sons are born of this father, one of them uniquely a child of promise (v. 23). These twins also present quite a contrast, being radically different in disposition from one another (vv. 19-34). In the brief sketch given they are effectively set off one against the other. In Jacob's acquiring of the birthright of the first-born, Jacob should not be unduly blamed. Preeminence had been promised him before his birth (v. 23). Furthermore Esau displayed little of a sense of appreciation of higher values in that he so readily disposed of his prerogative, selling his birthright. Such a sale of a birthright was not unique. An instance is recorded in the Nuzi texts, where a birthright was sold for three sheep! (C. F. Pfeiffer: *The Biblical World,* Grand Rapids: Baker [1966], p. 423.) It becomes quite obvious on reading the chapter that Jacob was the man who was better suited for outstanding leadership in the family.

Chapter 26 contributes some scenes from Isaac's life. None are particularly striking; some are similar to those found in Abraham's life. He repeated his father's procedure when he dwelt near Gerar (later in the land of the Philistines) by claiming his wife as his sister. The grace of God watched also over Isaac. He had a dispute about wells with some of the shepherds of the general area, just as did his father, but he remained in the pattern of life established by his father. Verses 23-25 give the account of the one instance in his life when the Lord appeared to him and renewed the promises that had in the previous generation been granted to Abraham. Isaac, for all that, enjoyed the great respect of his neighbors, and even of kings, and must have been more of a prominent figure than is sometimes supposed (26:26ff.). That he too was a man of faith goes without saying.

Chapter 27. This ch. tells how Isaac blessed his sons. Though in no sense can one condone the deception that Jacob and Rebekah planned to perpetrate, it should be noted from the outset that every participant in the action was more or less at fault. Jacob's fault already has been conceded. Rebekah was the originator of the deception practiced. Isaac, no doubt, knew of the word spoken by the Lord (25:23), but chose to try to invalidate it because of his favorite Esau. Esau on his part acted as though he had never sold his birthright. Out of all this moral confusion and deception came a result that was in harmony with the Lord's will in regard to the matter. Overruling providence controlled the final issue. The man of God's choice was given the better blessing, and was thereby marked to all intents and purposes as the man that carried the line of promise in this chosen family.

Chapter 28. In the light of the entire outcome in this instance, Isaac clearly confirmed the blessing that he had unintentionally at first bestowed upon Jacob (28:4). Nothing less than the ultimate murder of his brother was in Esau's mind, yet he refrained from committing it while his parents were still alive. No other course was left open for Jacob than to leave the land, not in headlong flight, but in an adventure to which his parents consented. There is good ground for believing that Jacob by this time was truly repentant of his misdeed in the matter of securing his father's blessing. For this reason God appeared to him with gracious promises for reassurance and guidance, in the well-known Bethel incident, marked by the ascending and descending of angels on a ladder. They served as symbols of God's providence and protection and served to comfort a lonely, homesick and penitent sinner. Jacob had not realized that God's providence would manifest itself away from the familiar setting of the ancestral home. He had never fully comprehended the meaning of God's omnipresence. The words of the vow (v. 20ff.) are not an expression of mercenary bargaining of a shrewd man cautiously looking out for his own advantage. Jacob is merely reiterating the promises that the Lord had just made to him (v. 15). Jesus refers to this incident in a manner that shows that the passage also foreshadowed His own intimate communion with His heavenly Father (John 1:51). It still must be noted that Jacob vowed to establish a shrine to mark the spot of his memorable experience.

Chapter 29. One of the lovely Biblical romances is presented at the beginning of this chapter. It was love at first sight, at the well. To have seven years pass like seven days marks a man deeply in love. At this point it becomes obvious that Laban is a crafty fellow, who will stop short at nothing where his own material advantage is at stake. Crafty Jacob has a craftier prospective father-in-law. They are matching wits continually. He who has so subtly deceived his brother must learn what it means to be deceived. So divine retribution goes to work to correct Jacob's wayward propensities. In spite of all the craftiness of men, the Almighty keeps the situation totally under His control. Divine providence overrules human craft and cunning.

There is another unpleasant side to the matter. Jacob became a bigamist. True, it was by accident rather than by design. Nowhere in the narrative is a word of censure spoken on Jacob's bigamy, but in its own way the sacred record shows how sinful and unwholesome such a situation could become. It resulted in family intrigues and petty bickerings; in lack of family discipline and petty jealousies; in fact, in an entirely unwholesome atmosphere. That spiritual values had to be pushed into the background under such circumstances is obvious. Besides, on a broader scale tensions were building up between Jacob's family and Laban's. Mistrust and manifold connivings were the order of the day, until the situation became unbearable. Jacob had to leave Mesopotamia and return to the land of promise. He received divine sanction for the return. Providence was able to retrieve some good from the unwholesome ways of men. It should yet be noted that the significant names that were given by the mothers to the twelve sons of Jacob indicated that a spark of faith still was glowing beneath the surface of things.

Chapter 30. As the family grew so did the flocks grow in size so as to become very large. Jacob resorted to a number of devices to get the advantage over his father-in-law in the matter of acquiring the new-born stock. It is not said that the devices employed produced results, but it is indicated that it pleased the Lord to let Jacob rather than Laban acquire wealth of herds. All this tended to increase the feelings of rivalry and jealousy that prevailed between the two camps.

Chapter 31. Finally, the situation became unbearable for Jacob. God intervened on Jacob's behalf and approved of his return to the land of his fathers. His wives were entirely on his side, for their father had treated their husband shamefully. Again, quite cleverly Jacob took advantage of a situation that allowed him to make the most of the distance between the two herds. As soon as word was brought to Laban, he set out on an expedition calculated to exact revenge. Again the Lord intervened and forbade Laban from resorting to any punitive measure. He smoothly played the part of the father-in-law who had been deprived the opportunity to take affectionate leave of his daughters and grandchildren. One thing Laban could charge against those who had fled: some one of their number had taken Laban's household gods (teraphim). No one except Rachel knew that it was she who did it. For according to the witness of the Nuzi documents, possession of the household deities guaranteed the right to the ancestral inheritance. By a clever ruse (not entirely honest), Rachel prevented her father from discovering the offender and the gods; and all this gave rise to a burst of indignation on Jacob's part that relieved feelings long pent up. This explosion seemed to clear the atmosphere and led at least to some kind of half-amicable settlement between the two parties. When a heap of stones was raised to commemorate the agreement, Laban still implied, in a memorable word, full of suspicion and mistrust, that Jacob was a man who could under no circumstances be trusted (v. 49) and had to be restrained by solemn oaths and pledges. For the sake of peace, Jacob entered upon the prescribed agreement and the matter was regarded as settled.

Chapter 32. The tension of the narrative builds up. A report came to Jacob that Esau was approaching with 400 men, gathered, beyond a doubt, for the purpose of executing the revenge that Esau had vowed to take after he lost the paternal blessing. Jacob could not begin to muster an equal force, though he had a goodly number of shepherds. Humanly, Jacob was almost at his wit's end. Then it was that Jacob was granted a vision of a host of angels at Mahanaim near the confluence of the Jordan and the Jabbok. This host never apparently went into action, but they were revealed as indicating the protective resources that the Lord could have put into action for Jacob. Repeatedly Jacob resorted to prayer. He also resorted to careful precautionary measures to appease his brother, setting up sizable numbers of sheep, oxen, camels and asses as a gift for Esau. He who in such situations submitted gifts to another, acknowledged the superior position of the one for whom the gifts were intended, a wise move of appeasement. By sending these gifts, one after the other, the calculated impact of the act was reinforced. Should Esau prove hostile, some of the groups involved might have effected an escape. As night approached, Jacob brought the remainder of his herds and personnel across the ford of the river. Then he had recourse to desperate prayer, wrestling with a mysterious man (perhaps the angel of the Lord) through a good part of the night. No one will ever completely understand the mysterious encounter involved. Somehow Jacob knew that his opponent was God and insistently sought His blessing. Men rightly believed in those days that he who encountered God face to face must die (Exod 33:20). When Jacob named the place Peniel (Gen 32:30, "face of God") he commemorated the fact that he had survived the experience of direct encounter with God.

Chapter 33. The event took an entirely unexpected turn. Beneath a hard surface there dwelt in Esau's character a soft emotional nature. At the sight of his brother all thoughts of revenge were dispelled. The brothers embraced, kissed, and wept. The hour of extreme danger was past. God had also intervened and had somehow moved Esau's heart and directed it toward kindliness. Esau would have established closer bonds of fellowship, but the more sober Jacob recognized the somewhat unstable emotional character of his brother and contented himself with the reconciliation that had been effected. This episode of sojourn in Mesopotamia is brought to an effective close by the erection of an altar at the point of entrance into the land of promise, an altar commemorating God's grace and protective care. From this point on, a number of highly revealing incidents are reported that indicate the course that events are taking. The first of these is the Dinah incident.

Chapter 34. This incident indicates how carefree Jacob's children moved about among the Canaanites, seemingly unaware of the moral contamination that Canaan represented. Dinah carelessly associated with the young people of the land and paid the price. Her seducer, a young Canaanite prince, was ready to enter upon matrimony. An agreement was reached with the family of Hamor, but treachery lurked behind it all. The brothers of Dinah were determined to take thoroughgoing vengeance on all the people of the town. Suddenly, the sons of Jacob appear in a very unfavorable light—they are murderers, truce-breakers, men given to waging bloody feuds. They are not at all men worthy of the caliber of their ancestor Abraham. They are beginning to represent a high state of deterioration. It is becoming apparent that Israel as a tribal group cannot continue to stay in Canaan without paying the price of total moral corruption. Something like the bondage in Egypt is imperative. Jacob's sons executed a horrid blood-bath, recklessly endangering their own family safety, and giving themselves a bad name. Minority groups that they were, they could easily have been exterminated if the native Canaanites had banded together for purposes of reprisal. Jacob freely admits that possibility as he rebukes his sons for their rash and wanton murder. Divine providence, undeserved though it was, watched over the group, for God had high purposes in mind for this race.

Chapter 35. Jacob had made a significant vow (28:22) at the time when he was about to leave the borders of the land of promise. God helped him remember this and fulfill his vow, establishing a sanctuary at Bethel. At the same time, God explicitly laid His promises, formerly made to Abraham and Isaac, upon Jacob, the bearer of the line of promise. The change of name to "Israel" was confirmed at this time. Before the permanent settlement in Canaan took place, Benjamin was born and Rachel died at his birth, to Jacob's great grief. In one brief v. inserted at this point, it is indicated that even the first-born of the sons of Jacob had become infected with typical Canaanite immorality, committing incest with a secondary wife of his father. Jacob, however, upon his return to the ancestral home, found his father still alive. Rebekah had died. In a way she paid the price for her participation in Jacob's treachery to gain the father's blessing, for she never lived to see him again after he left the land. Not long after this Isaac also died.

Chapter 36. The whole ch. is concerned with the story of Esau. So much attention is given to the line of Esau because he was Jacob's brother. In later years the descendants of Esau—the Edomites—displayed a very unbrotherly attitude toward Israel. Israel kept alive the sense of kinship by chs. like this.

Chapter 37. The intriguing Jacob story runs from this point to the end of the book. Jacob, however, is overshadowed somewhat by his illustrious son Joseph. Still, Jacob is always behind the scene and the controlling factor in most of that which is done. Just because Joseph informed on his brothers in his earlier youth, he can not be quickly written off as a cheap tattletale or a spoiled young man. In his attitude toward his brothers he did betray a measure of immaturity and indiscretion. On the other hand, Jacob's preference for Joseph can easily be understood. Most, if not almost all of the brothers, had displayed a lack of spiritual character. The evidence about Joseph indicates that he had godly qualities from his youth. God chose to reveal the future to the young boy. His father recognized his spiritual kinship with this son. He apparently had privately resolved to appoint Joseph as the head of the household to succeed himself. The "long robe with sleeves" (37:3), was to mark Joseph as his potential successor. Jacob erred in the manner in which he went about this disclosure. Without a doubt Joseph was a brilliant young man of admirable character. His brothers being what they were, one could hardly have expected them to take any different attitude toward him than they did.

The brothers of Joseph had rashly penetrated into the very area of danger not too far removed from the city of Shechem. Fearing for their safety Jacob dispatched Joseph to check on them, little dreaming that Joseph would thereby be exposed to danger. In fact, it amazes the reader that the great-grandchildren of father Abraham should be capable of thinking in terms of murder of their brother, just because they were jealous of him. So, on beholding him approaching, they planned to dispose of him. Reuben, the first-born, had enough of a sense of right and wrong left, to advocate at least a cooling-off period. He hoped to liberate his brother later. Judah proposed to sell him to traders so that he could be brought to the slave-market in Egypt, hardly a kindly alternative. With a certain callousness the brothers send the "long robe with sleeves" dipped in blood to their father, utterly deceiving him and causing him untold grief. He who had excelled in deceit in his younger years is now deceived by his own sons and the experience is painful.

Chapter 38. While Joseph faced a precarious future in Egypt, strange and unholy things were marking the careers of his brothers back in Canaan. This ch. furnishes a typical example of the growing moral degeneracy of the family, esp. in the case of Judah, who became involved, though in a sense unintentionally, with his own daughter-in-law. The ugly mess is described in all its repulsiveness. While Joseph languished in prison his brothers were corrupting themselves. To have been exposed to this type of Canaanite corruption could have ruined the family. Going down to Egypt, or something similar, had become a necessity.

Chapter 39. Joseph's career began at the lowest rung of the ladder. He was at first only a common slave, but he seems to have had such unusual gifts of administration and such perseverence in the faithful use of them that his

Tomb painting of Semitic people coming down into Egypt.

master, Potiphar, soon discovered what a rare treasure he had in Joseph. Besides, the obvious blessing of the Lord was also in evidence. Joseph became master, or steward, of Potiphar's household. A sudden danger confronted the goodlooking young man—his master's wife became enamored of him. That Joseph's adherence to the ancestral religion was more than something learned by rote became apparent. In the hour of temptation, Joseph disclosed the deep well-spring of his whole life in the word: "How then can I do this great wickedness, and sin against God?" (39:9). Love spurned turns to hate. Joseph, entirely in the right, is libelled, thrown into prison (slaves had no legal rights) and allowed to languish there for years. God seemed to have forgotten him, but Joseph had not forgotten God. He served Him just as faithfully in prison as he did when he was a free man. The prison warden recognized faithful service, and put him in charge of all prison administration. The whole experience served indirectly to prepare Joseph for the sudden rise to high position that was presently to occur.

Chapter 40. Busied with the affairs of the prison, quite unexpectedly a new avenue of activity opened up to Joseph—the gift of dream interpretation. The royal butler and the royal baker, both officials of the royal household, but languishing in prison for reasons unknown to us, had dreams in the same night. Without his design or plan, Joseph unexpectedly began to function as interpreter (cf. 37:5ff.), and the sequel proved that his interpretation was entirely correct. A glimmer of hope seemed to appear on the scene for a moment, for Joseph pleaded with the butler to remember him when liberated. The butler readily promised—and promptly forgot his promise.

Chapter 41. Pharaoh had two dreams which God used to convey knowledge to one farther removed from Him. When the news of the dreams spread, the butler was suddenly reminded of his promise and hastened to the king to inform him of Joseph's ability. Joseph is speedily summoned for appearance in court. He interpreted the dreams with such obvious authority that the correctness of his interpretation was immediately apparent to all. Important is Joseph's confession in this connection: "God will give Pharaoh a favorable answer." Joseph's loyalty to the Lord had not wavered. He offered suggestions for the king to proceed in the existing situation. With amazement the king admits the brilliant helpfulness of the suggestions given, and, after brief consideration, appointed Joseph as national food administrator. At once he launched into his new career with becoming zeal and energy. He inaugurated a policy of grain reserves to be accumulated during the impending seven years of plenty. In all the busy whirl of activity, home and the ancestral family are not forgotten (vv. 50-52). The seven years of plenty passed swiftly, only a few vv. in the record being given to the subject. Against this broad backdrop of history play the events of the history of that little group up in Pal. that constitute the family of Joseph.

Chapter 42. The thread of the narrative of the family of the chosen people is resumed. The famine was not limited to Egypt, but affected Canaan too. The news of Egyp. grain supplies reached Jacob's ears. Necessity compelled him to send his sons down to the old granary of the nations—Egypt. Almost at once upon entering the land they encountered Joseph, never even remotely aware of his identity. Joseph followed a course of procedure with the object of discovering whether they were the same cruel, impenitent rascals that he had found them to be back in their homeland. When the collective prison sentence was pronounced, Reuben, speaking for all, reminds them how they merited just what they are now receiving, when they treated Joseph as they did near Dothan. Joseph was deeply moved to discover that a change for the better seems to have taken place. One night in prison sufficed for present purposes; only Simeon was remitted to prison as hostage for them all. When the money given for the grain was found in the bag of one of their number on the way home, they all saw the hand of God in what was happening to them. The corrective measures were beginning to bear their fruit. That Simeon did not return added to Jacob's grief, which was still further enhanced by the prospect of not being able to go down to Egypt unless their youngest brother was brought along.

Chapter 43. The grain brought from Egypt was consumed, and a second journey to Egypt became imperative. The whole plan of Joseph was designed for the rehabilitation of the brothers, not as subtle revenge, which was farthest of all from Joseph's thoughts. When Jacob at first remonstrated, being unwilling to risk sending Benjamin along, it was Judah who pledged his life for Benjamin's and finally persuaded his father to take the hard step involved.

Chapter 44. Upon arriving in Egypt, the brothers found a situation created by Joseph which put them to the test as to whether they would sacrifice one of their number selfishly for their own safety. Once they had sacrificed Joseph to their unscrupulous ambitions. Would they now do the same with regard to Benjamin? The missing cup incident brought them all back to Egypt, to the food administrator. Benjamin appeared to be guilty. Would they give him up and save their own lives? Judah stepped into the breach. In a deeply moving speech, he volunteered to stay behind in prison, if only Benjamin were allowed to go home. Twenty years before this such an attitude would have been impossible.

Chapter 45. The carefully designed plan had fully achieved its purpose. Joseph had to reveal himself to his brothers. Immediately they were filled with grave apprehensions. Joseph, however, pointed out the providential side of all that had transpired. The existence of a future nation, to which God had assigned a most important role, was being safeguarded. Steps were promptly taken to move Jacob and his household into the protective care of Joseph.

Chapter 46. God had answered the prayer of His servant, renewing His promise to Jacob and guaranteeing his return to Canaan in due time. Ample provision was made for the family of Jacob by assigning to it the good pasture land of Goshen. Everything was made official by presenting Jacob at Pharaoh's court.

Chapters 47 and 48. The physical needs of the family were amply guaranteed for the duration of the famine. Some account of how the famine was met in Joseph's administration follows quite properly at this point. Briefly the successive steps taken were disclosed: Money was exhausted; cattle were sold for grain; and finally the Egyptians, on their own suggestion, were compelled to sell themselves and their lands. These measures were not tyrannical but a matter of desperate necessity. Jacob finally died as he had lived his last years, by the light of God's promises.

Chapter 49. This ch. records the blessing with which Jacob blessed his sons before his end. He turned prophet before his end and spoke by divine enlightenment. Outstanding among the blessings was the word applicable to Judah (vv. 8-12). Verse 10 brings a reference to a somewhat vague figure ("until he comes to whom it belongs"). This implies that the qualities of leadership, inherent in the tribe of Judah, shall blossom forth in one individual to perfection. The marginal tr. "until Shiloh comes" indicates this approach more clearly. For "Shiloh" is "a man of rest." In this man Judah's strivings come to rest; this man brings peace. Reuben (vv. 3, 4) was passed by. So were Simeon and Levi (vv. 5-7). Preeminence was appointed for Judah (vv. 8-12).

Chapter 50. After Jacob's death a memorable meeting of the twelve sons took place. The eleven were still apprehensive that Joseph had merely postponed the revenge that he might take upon his brothers until the father had passed from the scene. But nothing was farther from Joseph's thoughts than revenge. The full scope of God's dealings is beautifully described in the momentous word (v. 20): "You meant evil against me; but God meant it for good." Joseph passed from the scene reassuring his people that God would remember them. In token of faith that it would be so, Joseph exacted a promise of his brothers that when they should leave for the true homeland they would take his bones along for burial. On the note of faith and hope rests this first Biblical book, a solid foundation stone of all of God's later revelation to men.

BIBLIOGRAPHY. A massive Bibliography might be added. For the good of the average reader, only such of the many works consulted as may be accessible to him are included and, for the most part, such as are specifically referred to in the above article. B. Pritchard, *Ancient Near Eastern Texts* (1950), 1-10, 60-100; C. A. Simpson, *The Interpreter's Bible* (1952); M. F. Unger, *Archaeology and the Old Testament* (1954); G. E. Wright, *Biblical Archaeology*, Ch. III (1957), 40ff.; H. Yunker, *Echter Bibel*, Das Alte Testament (1958); *The New Bible Commentary*, ed. F. Davidson (1958); C. T. Fritsch, *The Layman's Bible Commentary* (1958); G. von Rad, *Genesis*, tr. by John Marks (1962); C. Westermann, *A Thousand Years and a Day*, tr. by Stanley Rudman (1962); K. M. Yates, *The Wycliffe Bible Commentary* (1962); H. Frey, *Botschaft des AT, Genesis* (1964).

H. C. LEUPOLD

GENEVA BIBLE. *See* BIBLE, ENGLISH VERSIONS.

GENIZAH gə ne' zə, gə net' sə (גניזה, hiding, *storehouse*). A place in a synagogue set aside for the storage of unwanted written and printed material of a religious nature. These items are called *Shemot* ("Names") because they contain the name of God and cannot be abused. They consist of worn out, heretical and otherwise unfit books, MSS and even scraps of paper. Generally, the accumulated material is periodically removed and buried in a cemetery (also called genizah), sometimes with a pious person. During the 19th cent., many old MSS were discovered and removed from the Ezra Synagogue near Cairo. The Cairo Genizah yielded many thousands of fragments, including some of the original Heb. of Ecclesiasticus.

BIBLIOGRAPHY. P. E. Kahle, *The Cairo Genizah*, 2nd ed. (1959).

C. P. WEBER

GENNAEUS gə ne' əs (Γενναῖος, *noble*, KJV GENNEUS). Father of Apollonius, Syrian governor who troubled Jews at time of Antiochus V (2 Macc 12:2).

GENNESARET gĕ nĕs' ə rət (Γεννησαρέτ). A small plain located on the W side of the Sea of Galilee.

1. Name. The name Gennesaret should be associated primarily with the area mentioned in two NT references (Matt 14:22; Mark 6:45). After feeding the 5,000, Jesus' disciples crossed over the Sea of Galilee to Bethsaida (6:45), then crossed back again (6:53) and came to land at Gennesaret. Sometimes, however, the name is not restricted to the district, for Luke speaks of the lake of Gennesaret (Luke 5:1), referring to the Sea of Galilee (cf. 1 Macc 11:67, Jos., Antiq. XVIII. ii. 1; War III. x. 7). In this usage, the name of the lake derives from the name of the plain. A small town in the area also bore the name Gennesaret. Some sources read "Gennesar." E. G. Kraeling, on the basis of the Aram. and Josephus, thinks the short form "Gennesar" would have been current in NT times. The Arabs call the little plain *el Ghuwer*.

2. Description. It is a small plain bordering on the W shore of the Sea of Galilee between

The Plain of Gennesaret and the Sea of Galilee, viewed from Bethsaida. ©*M.P.S.*

Capernaum and Magdala. The plain is about four m. long, running N and S along the sea coast, and up to about two m. wide.

The land is level, rising gently from the level of the Sea of Galilee, which is 650 ft. below the Mediterranean. Hills rise sharply on three sides. The main road from Capernaum to Tiberias runs through close to the sea shore.

During the time of Christ, this plain was the garden spot of Pal. Josephus eloquently described the beauty and fertility of the land (Jos. War III. x. 8). The soil was rich like that of the Nile delta. The climate ranges from hot to temperate. Plenty of water for irrigation was available from streams flowing out of the surrounding hills, and from several flowing springs. The land produced an abundance of wild trees and flowers, as well as important crops such as grapes, figs, olives, walnuts (Josephus), rice, wheat, vegetables, melons. The rabbis spoke of this plain as "the Garden of God" and a "paradise." *See* GALILEE, SEA OF.

BIBLIOGRAPHY. Thomson, *The Land and the Book*, II, 293f.; Hastings, HDCG, I, 640, 641; E. G. Kraeling, *Rand McNally Bible Atlas* (1956).

J. C. DEYOUNG

GENNESARET, LAKE OF. *See* GALILEE, SEA OF.

GENTILES gĕn′ tīlz (גוים, LXX ἔθνη; Vulg., *Gentiles, Gentes*). The Heb. is derived from an Akkad. loan word meaning a "gang" or "group," such as workmen. The term was originally a general expression that stressed political and social affiliations rather than bonds of kinship, and thus was used of "nations" in the widest sense. The list of the descendants of Noah (Gen 10:2 et al.) showed the affinity of all Near Eastern nations in antiquity, but with the description of the offspring of Abraham the OT narratives found it desirable to make a distinction between them and other contemporary peoples. This, however, was not undertaken in any narrow or exclusive sense (cf. Gen 12:2; 18:18; 22:18; 26:4). When the Israelites entered into a special relationship with God in the Covenant at Sinai (Exod 19:6), they became conscious of nationhood, and thereafter the sense of uniqueness and separation as the people of God was brought to bear upon all their relations with neighboring peoples (cf. Exod 34:10; Lev 18:24, 25; Deut 15:6).

The way in which the blessings of the Covenant between God and Israel would permeate the lives of other nations was outlined in Deuteronomy 28:1-14. This passage continued the spiritual traditions of the promise of God to Abraham (Gen 12:1-3), where those nations that had been living under a curse would receive blessing through the influence of the newly chosen people. The reflexive form of the verb "bless" (Gen 12:3; KJV, ASV, "be blessed," RSV, "bless themselves") makes it clear that the nations will not blend their separate identities in a common form of humanity, but that each will receive the blessing suited to its character and destiny. This motif was well understood in the ancient Near E, and is exemplified in such OT narratives as the blessings bestowed upon the sons of Jacob (Gen 49:1-27), or the benediction of Moses upon the Israelites (Deut 33:2-29). The benefits mentioned in Deuteronomy 28:1-14 were conditional upon the adherence of the Hebrews to the ideals of the Sinai covenant; but given this situation, Israel could expect to be promoted to a place of prominence among the nations. Once the latter saw that the Israelites exemplified divine holiness, they would become subservient, and in the period of the universal peace that would follow, all the benefits of prosperity would be poured out upon mankind. No political or social imbalance of the kind that would allow one nation to prosper at the expense of another would be permitted (cf. Mic 4:1-4), and in this general sense the nations would be pursuing their own way of life under the auspices of a covenant relationship.

The Mosaic tradition of a nation chosen out of all the peoples and fitted for the role of ministering priests for the whole of mankind found responsive echoes in the monarchy (cf. 1 Kings 8:41-43), the preexilic period (Isa 19:24, 25; Jer 4:2) and the postexilic era (Zech 8:13; 9:9, 10). This high ideal was virtually nullified by the trends of Hebrew history from the time of Joshua onward, which show that covenant holiness was seldom at the forefront of Heb. thinking. So pervasive were Gentile customs that the Hebrews ultimately succumbed to their allurements, and with the disavowal of the covenant relationship came threats of punishment for Israel. Between 722 and 525 B.C., the Heb. people shared the curse of the nations by being scattered in captivity among them. From then on, the only hope of realizing the ancient ideal of the Torah lay in the survival of a faithful minority of Israelites who would return to their homeland and try to revive the historic spiritual mission of Israel to the world.

The threat of contamination by paganism in the Gr. period led the Jews to adopt a rigorous, exclusive attitude toward non-Jewish peoples, so that by the time of Christ the term "Gentile" had become one of scorn. Yet the Gentiles had a place in prophecies relating to the kingdom, whether as the conquered who would enhance Israelite glory (Isa 60:5, 6), or as themselves seeking the Lord (11:10) and worshiping Him (Mal 1:11), when the Messiah came to illumine them (Isa 42:6) and bring salvation to the world (49:6). In this tradition the gospels hailed the work of Jesus as fulfilling the promise to Abraham (cf. Luke 2:32), and the Savior Himself began His ministry in "Galilee of the nations" (lit. tr.; RSV, "Gentiles"; Matt 4:15). Among the many contacts that Christ had with the Gentiles, it is noteworthy that the mission of the Seventy (Luke 10:1 seq.) was to the "nations," whereas His entry into Jerusalem revealed Him as the Messianic king who would bring peace to the nations (Matt 21:5; cf. Zech 9:9, 10). The evangelistic and baptismal commission of the primitive church was for the whole world (Matt 28:19, 20; Mark 16:15; Luke 24:47; Acts 1:8), whereas Paul saw in Christ's atonement the outpouring of the blessings of Abraham on the Gentiles (Gal 3:

A section of the inscription from Herod's Temple forbidding Gentiles to enter the Inner Court of the Temple. ©V.E.

14). Through Israel's neglect of her spiritual mission to the world, however, the riches of God would be mediated through the Gentiles.

BIBLIOGRAPHY. H. H. Rowley, *The Missionary Message of the Old Testament* (1944); J. Jeremias, *Jesus' Promise to the Nations* (1958).

R. K. Harrison

GENTILES, COURT OF (THE). The large outer portion of Herod's temple complex. The area, paved with marble, was used for business such as selling sacrificial animals and money exchange and was prob. the place from which Christ drove those so engaged (Matt 21:12; John 2:14-17). This part of the Temple was not considered sacred and was open to Gentiles. The walls gave shade from the hot sun and it was a common gathering place (similar to a park) and a thoroughfare (*see* Temple).

C. P. Weber

GENUBATH gĭ nōō′ băth (גנבת). The son of Hadad, the Edomite, who fled to Egypt from Edom when Edom was invaded by David's army under the leadership of Joab, and all the males of Edom were killed. Genubath was born to Hadad and the sister of Tahpanes, Pharaoh's wife. He was weaned by Tahpanes and was raised among the sons of Pharaoh (1 Kings 11:20).

C. P. Weber

GEON. KJV Apoc. form of GIHON.

GEORGIAN VERSION. *See* VERSIONS, ANCIENT.

GEPHYRUN gĕ fī′ run (Γεφυρούν). According to the ASV, the name of a city (2 Macc 12:13), location unknown, which in the latter part of the v. is identified as Caspin, q.v. The KJV takes Gephyrun as an infinitive from γεφυρόω, tr. by the phrase "to make a bridge." The RSV assumes Gr. γεφύραις (from γέφυρα, *bridge, dam, mound*), and trs. "with earthworks." If this account is to be connected with the following campaign, the city may be in Trans-Jordan, possibly Gilead. The city was defeated by Judas Maccabeus. Earlier identification with Ephron depended on Gephyrun being a proper name.

C. P. WEBER

GER gûr (גֵּר, *sojourner, alien*). The transliteration "ger" does not occur in standard Eng. VSS, as it is tr., generally by "stranger." In Israel, the גֵּר was generally subject to the same laws as nationals (Num 15:15, 16) and was to be well-treated (Deut 10:17-19), as Israel had been a sojourner in Egypt. Israelites were considered sojourners ("gerim") with God (Lev 25:23). Note concept in NT (Eph 2:19; 1 Pet 2:11). *See* SOJOURNER.

C. P. WEBER

GERA gĭr′ ə (גֵּרָא ; LXX Γηρὰ; *sojourner* [?]). A favorite personal name among the people of the tribe of Benjamin from patriarchal times (Gen 46:21) until the time of the Exile (1 Chron 8:3-7). Although the name was used by the Phoenicians, it does not occur in the scriptural account of Israel outside the tribe of Benjamin. When the expression "the son of Gera" is applied to Ehud the Judge (Judg 3:15) and to Shimei, who cursed David during the rebellion of Absalom (2 Sam 16:5; 19:16-18; 1 Kings 2:8), it is not clear whether this is meant to give the personal name of their respective fathers, or to identify them as members of the clan of Gera. The latter seems more likely, and is the view of the majority of scholars. Certainly most of the names in lists such as that in Genesis 46:21 refer to heads of clans, but strangely Gera is missing from the similar list in Numbers 26:38-41.

G. G. SWAIM

GERAH. *See* WEIGHTS AND MEASURES.

GERAR gĭr är (גְּרָר, LXX Γεραρά). A town and district S of Gaza and SW of the southern border of Canaan near the Mediterranean Sea.

All the Biblical references are to be found in Genesis (10:19; 20:1, 2; 26:1, 6, 17, 20, 26) except for 2 Chronicles 14:13, 14.

In its first occurrence (Gen 10:19) Gerar is used as a reference point for identification of the southern end of the territory of the Canaanites, and is identified as in the same general area as Gaza.

In 1 Chronicles 4:39, 40, the LXX prob. correctly has Gerar in place of the Heb. Gedor, Gerar being the place where the sons of Ham had lived (Gen 10:19, 20).

Abraham with Sarah, his wife, is said to have dwelt in Gerar (in the district between Kadesh and Shur), where they came in contact with its king, Abimelech (20:1, 2). This same ruler, or another in the royal line who had the same title, Abimelech (cf. the use of *Caesar* in this way), is also called king of the Philistines in a similar encounter that Isaac and his wife Rebekah had with him (Gen 26:1, 6ff; cf. also 26:26). Following these experiences, Isaac encamped in the valley of Gerar (26:17), which was prob. the present Wadi esh-Shari'ah where Isaac dug wells and experienced difficult relations with the herdsmen of the area (26:20).

In 2 Chronicles 14:13, 14, Asa, king of Judah, with the help of God, routed Ethiopian invaders and pursued them to Gerar and plundered that whole region.

Although the Philistines did not occupy this area until several hundred years after Abraham (who lived about 1900-1800 B.C.), for clarification the Genesis account speaks of Abimelech both as king of Gerar (Gen 20:1, 2), the common name of the place, and as king of the Philistines (26:1), meaning that he was king over a part of the area later called Philistia, or that he was ruler over ancestors of the people who were later called Philistines.

Gerar was known in the intertestamental and early Christian centuries; it appears on the late 6th cent. Madeba map.

The town Gerar, if correctly identified with Tell Abu Hureirah, was situated about nine m. SE of Gaza, and about fifteen m. NW of Beer-sheba. This site has been excavated and shows a long period of occupation, including that part of the Middle Bronze period (1800-1600 B.C.) when the patriarchs lived. Tell Jemmeh, nearer the coast, has also been identified as Gerar.

BIBLIOGRAPHY. J. Finegan, *Light From the Ancient Past* (1959), 146; Y. Aharoni, *The Land of the Bible*, tr. A. F. Rainey (1967), 149, 174, 210, 259.

W. H. MARE

GERASA, GERASENES (Γέρασα, Γερασηνες). A city in Transjordania, situated about thirty-five m. SE of the S end of the Sea of Galilee, one of the cities of the Decapolis; the inhabitants of the city.

1. The gospels. The NT references (Mark 5:1; Luke 8:26; cf. v. 37) describe Jesus' healing of the demoniac "Legion" and the drowning of the swine in the Sea of Galilee (cf. Matt 8:28). The textual evidence shows that the MSS preserve three variant spellings of the name in each gospel. The best text in Matthew reads "Gadarenes," in Mark and Luke it reads

Remains of the ancient ramparts of Tell Jemmeh, which has also been identified as Gerar. © *M.P.S.*

"Gerasenes," whereas some MSS preserve "Gergesenes" and "Gergustenes" (cf. Gadara).

Because some confusion exists in the gospel MS evidence and perhaps in other source material, absolute certainty cannot be attained; but the following identification seems correct.

2. Gergesa (Γέργεσα). This town is not to be confused with either Gerasa or Gadara. Gergesa is located, with relative certainty, midway along the E bank of the Sea of Galilee; Gadara is six m. SE from the S end of the Sea of Galilee; and Gerasa is some thirty-five m. SE.

The fact that Matthew places the healing of "Legion" in the "country of the Gadarenes" whereas Mark and Luke place it in the "country of the Gerasenes" may be harmonized on the historical grounds that geographical boundaries overlapped, and on the exegetical consideration that "country" embraced a wide area around the cities. Further, the conclusion seems warranted that there was confusion in some MSS of Gerasa with the more likely site for the miracle near Gergesa. In any event, the apparent differences in the texts prob. led to the substitute reading "Gergesenes," a reading that was suggested by a study of the ge-

Gerasa (modern Jerash). Stairs leading to the "Cathedral" which is the Propylea or entrance to an older pagan temple. © *Lev*

ography of the area. This solution is as old as Origen (*Commentary on John,* VI, 24) who, faced with the textual problem, suggested that the precise site of the healing of "Legion" was Gergesa, the small town in the territory of Gadara, but hardly in the more remote territory of Gerasa. Origen says this is a good example of how Biblical writers simply were not concerned to precisely identify certain sites. Most scholars today would agree with Origen that near Gergesa was the precise site for the healing of "Legion." It was a small village about midway along the E shore of the Sea of Galilee. This agrees with the general description of the site (Mark 5:1; Luke 8:26). In this immediate area, steep hills come down to the shoreline and fit the story of the swine rushing headlong into the sea. No other place on the E side of the sea fits this requirement of the story. The mountainside has caves and hewn tombs where, according to Mark and Luke, the demoniac had taken shelter. The site is identified today with the town of Kersa, or Gersa, just below Wadi es-Samak.

3. Gerasa. Gerasa is identified from various sources as a city in Arabia, Decapolis, Gilead, or Perea. Since all of these areas overlap, one may take the references as meaning the same place. Gerasa was a city situated near the Jabbok River about eighteen m. E of the Jordan, about twenty m. SE of Pella, and twenty m. N of Philadelphia. Archeologists identify it with the modern Jarash. At this distance from the Sea of Galilee, Gerasa could not have been the site of the healing of "Legion." It is doubtful that Jesus ever visited it. This location agrees with the description given by the ancient writers. Ptolemy says Gerasa was a city in Coele-Syria, thirty-five travel m. from Pella. Pliny described it as a city of the Decapolis founded after the Rom. conquest of Syria in 65 B.C. Josephus mentions it with Pella and Golan as being taken by storm during Alexander Jannaeus' campaign E of the Jordan in about 83 B.C. (Jos. War I. iv. 8). In his description of the boundaries of Perea, Josephus mentions Gerasa as one of the cities on the eastern boundary between Perea and Arabia, the other border cities being Philadelphia and Sebonitus (Jos. War III. iii. 3). Gerasa is mentioned next by Josephus in connection with the Jewish rebellion against the Romans in A.D. 70.

Apparently Gerasa was rebuilt by the Romans before the revolt began, prob. about A.D. 65. Before the war it was a Gentile settlement. In retaliation for the massacre of the Jews at Caesarea, the Jews sent several raiding parties into the Gentile cities of the Decapolis. These forces plundered Gerasa, Philadelphia, Pella, and others (Jos. War II. xviii. 1), and apparently occupied these cities with Jewish patriots.

The next allusion to Gerasa concerns its capture during Vespasian's campaign. He dispatched Lucius Annius with a force of cavalry and an army of foot soldiers, who took the city on the first attack, slaughtering a thousand young men, taking their families captive, plundering and burning the city and the surrounding towns (Jos. War IV. ix. 1).

In the 2nd cent. Gerasa was rebuilt in splendor and remained prosperous for several centuries. It was a leading city of Syria in commerce, culture, and religion. The pagan religions continued among the Gentile population as is evidenced by the ruins of the temple of Artemis. But Christianity early became important in the city; several churches were built during these centuries, so that by the 5th cent., Gerasa could send a bishop to the Council of Chalcedon.

4. Archeology. Excavations at the modern Jarash (by the British and American Schools of Oriental Research and Yale University) clearly show that Gerasa was a large and important city already in Jesus' time. The excavations uncovered what is to date the best preserved Rom. city in Pal. These ruins date from the 2nd to the 7th centuries and show that the city flourished during this period as a center for religion, culture, and commerce. The forum, with a semicircle of columns still standing, was paved with large cut stones. A main street with columns on both sides leads out of the forum. The modern village Jarash is situated on the hillside above the ruins, built with stones from the ruins. Ruins of the temple of Artemis, some columns still standing, are on another hillside above the ruins. The city was large and well planned. Its architecture was of the Corinthian order, quite lavish and imposing, with columns from three to four ft. in diameter and about thirty ft. high. The ruins also show evidence of a dozen churches, dating in the Byzantine period (4th-7th centuries) indicating that this once was a large Christian community. An inscr. noted the official establishment of Christianity and discontinuance of pagan worship in the 5th cent. (Cf. HDB, II, p. 158, 159 for a detailed description.)

BIBLIOGRAPHY. W. A. Thomson, *The Land and the Book* (1882), 333-338, 353, 359; C. H. Kraeling, *Gerasa, City of the Decapolis* (1938); *The Westminster Historical Atlas to the Bible* (1946), 64, 117; M. F. Unger, *Archaeology and the NT* (1962), 139-141; E. Lohmeyer, *Das Evangelium des Markus* (1963), 93f; C. F. Pfeiffer, *The Biblical World* (1966), 252-254.

J. C. DeYoung

GERIZIM gĕr′ ə zĭm. A mountain in central Samaria, near Shechem and about ten m. SE of the city of Samaria, esp. important as the center of worship for the Samaritans. From Mount Gerizim and Mount Ebal (about three m. NE) the sacred sites of Shechem and Jacob's well are visible.

The most important reference to Mt. Gerizim is in John 4:20-23. The woman referred to "this mountain" as the worship center for the Samaritans. She said, "Our fathers worshiped

Mount Gerizim, towering above the ruins of the ancient ramparts of Shechem. ©M.P.S.

on this mountain." Jesus answered "neither on this mountain nor in Jerusalem . . . but . . . in spirit and in truth" shall men worship the Father.

The area is sacred to Jews as well as Samaritans. Here, Abraham and Jacob entered the Promised Land (Gen 12:6; 33:18). Jacob built an altar, dug a well, and purchased a burial ground at Shechem. The Israelites used it for a burial ground for the bones of Joseph (Josh 24:32). Both Mt. Gerizim and Mt. Ebal were the sites used when Joshua gathered all the people of Israel to Mt. Gerizim and Mt. Ebal for the ceremony of taking possession of the Promised Land. According to the command of Moses (Deut 11:29; 27:11-14) Gerizim was to be the mount to pronounce the blessing on godliness, while Ebal would be the mount from which would be declared the curse of God upon wickedness. There Joshua read the law of Moses in full to the whole assembly (Josh 8:30-35) gathered before Gerizim and Ebal, but he built an altar only on Mt. Ebal (Josh 8:30).

Joshua called Israel back to Shechem, under the shadow of Gerizim and Ebal, to renew the covenant, which he did in this manner: "he took a great stone, and set it up there under the oak in the sanctuary of the LORD" (Josh 24:26). This site was sacred to the Israelites in the early days of their occupation of the Promised Land. In the movement toward centralization of worship at Jerusalem under David and Solomon, other worship centers were not looked upon with favor. When the division of the kingdom took place, Jeroboam made Shechem the capital of the northern kingdom (1 Kings 12:25), discouraged worship at the Temple in Jerusalem, and substituted calf worship at Bethel and Dan. He thereby instigated a new and separate religion, centering at Shechem and Mt. Gerizim.

After the king of Assyria resettled northern and central Pal. with pagan peoples he sent a priest of Israel back to Samaria to teach them the religion of the Jewish remnant (2 Kings 17:24-34). In this way, the worship of God was preserved, but also perverted.

The story of the origin of the Samaritan cult and temple prob. has apocryphal elements. On the basis of Nehemiah 4 and 13:28 and traditions, Josephus (Jos. Antiq. XI. viii. 2, 4) wrote that the event leading to it was the marriage of Manasseh, a son of a high priest at Jerusalem, to the daughter of Sanballat, a Gentile official at Samaria. Manasseh was ordered to divorce his pagan wife or leave the priesthood but Sanballat promised to build a rival temple for him. Some date this in the time of Alexander the Great, 330 B.C., others a cent. earlier. The temple was prob. destroyed by the Maccabees around 110 B.C. (Jos. Antiq. XIII. ix. 1; War I. 11. 6).

BIBLIOGRAPHY. Hastings, HDCG, I, 644, 645; E. G. Kraeling, *Rand McNally Bible Atlas* (1956), 158, 159.

J. C. DeYoung

GERON **gĭr′ ŏn** (Γέρων, *old man, senator*). Geron, proper name in the ASV, is tr. "old man" in the KJV and "senator," which fits both Gr. and context, in the RSV. Geron had the responsibility under Antiochus Epiphanes of compelling the Jews "to forsake the laws of their fathers" (2 Macc 6:1).

GERRENIANS, GERRHENIANS **gûr rĕn′ e ənz** (Γερρηνων, A Γεννηρων). Lysias, in fighting against Judas Maccabeus in 162 B.C., was forced to return to Syria because of a deterioration of affairs in Antioch. Before going N he made peace with the Jews and left Hegemonides in command from Ptolemais to the (land/city) of the Gerrenians (2 Macc 13:24 KJV). Both the text and the exact geographical reference are problematic. Because the context seems to call for a location in the S near the Egyp. frontier, it is commonly taken to be Gerar (qv., APOT I, p. 151). The Syr. understands this place to be Gezer (q.v.). Gerrha, which might be the obvious choice on the basis of the Gr. spelling, lay inside Egyp. territory, and so is impossible.

G. G. Swaim

GERSHOM **gûr′ shəm** (גרשום, prob. a foreign name of unknown meaning; perhaps unusual form from *gä′räš*, *to drive out,* meaning *fugitive*, Exod 2:22; 18:3 are better taken as deliberate puns than as popular etymologies). 1. Variant of Gershon (e.g 1 Chron 6:16ff.).

2. The leader of the clan of Phinehas (i.e. "sons of Phinehas") in Ezra's return from Babylon (Ezra 8:2).

3. Moses' oldest son and a clan name for some of Moses' descendants. Of Moses' son the Bible offers only genealogical data and, prob., the account of his circumcision (Exod 4:24-26).

Turning to Gershom's descendants Judges (18:30) tells of the family of Jonathan, the son (i.e. descendant) of Gershom, the son of Moses (variant text from KJV "Manasseh") which served illegally—as priests for Dan until the Captivity.

In David's bureaucracy the Gershomites appear along with the sons of Eliezer, Moses' other son (1 Chron 23:15-17). Of these, Shebuel was "the chief" (i.e. leading family?) of the Gershomites and Rehabiah was the chief of the Eliezerites.

Jehdeiah is listed as an officer of the "sons of Shubael" (variant of Shebuel; ?), and Isshiah for the "sons of Rehabiah" (1 Chron 20; 21). Comparison with ch. 23 indicates that these are variant designations for the Gershomites and the Eliezerites respectively. That is, in 1 Chronicles 24 the two clans are designated by their "chief" or leading families rather than by their ancestral names.

Shebuel, an individual contemporary with David, of the Gershomites was David's chief treasurer. The designation of the Eliezerites as "his brethren, from Eliezer" may indicate that the Gershomites were the dominant of the two clans (1 Chron 26:24, 25).

A. Bowling

GERSHON **gûr′ shən** (גרשון ; either a foreign name of unknown meaning or an unusual derivative from גרש ; *see* Gershom). 1. The oldest son of Levi since Gershon usually heads the list of sons (e.g. Gen 46:11). Apart from genealogical data, the Bible records only that he was born before Jacob went to Egypt.

2. Name of the Levitical line descended from Gershon, son of Levi. Discussion of the Gershonites will be organized according to the following chronological periods: a. The Exodus and the wanderings, b. The conquest, c. The monarchy, and d. The return from exile.

a. The Exodus and the wanderings. In Numbers, the Gershonites are divided into two "families" (i.e. "clans"): Libni (designated as "Ladan," 1 Chron 23:7; *see* Gershom for examples of clans with two designations) and Shemei (Num 3:18, 21). Gershonites, "from a month old and upward" were numbered at

7,500 (3:22). They camped immediately to the W of the Tabernacle (3:23) and were responsible for carrying the Tabernacle (i.e. the ten linen curtains), the "tent" (i.e. the eleven goats' hair curtains), the tent's "covering" (i.e. the two skin coverings), the door curtains for the Tabernacle, the curtains for the court, the door curtains for the court, the tying cords for all the curtains, and other unspecified equipment (3:25, 26; 4:25, 26). Two wagons and four oxen were allotted to them for their burdens (7:7).

b. The conquest. The Gershonites were assigned lands within the holdings of Issachar, Asher, and Naphtali in Pal. proper, and in the holdings of the half tribe of Manasseh in Trans-Jordan (Josh 21:6, 27-33; 1 Chron 6:62, 71-76; 1 Chron 6:1-43 uses "Gershom" for "Gershon"). This assignment of land placed the Gershonites in the northernmost extremes on both sides of the Jordan.

c. The monarchy. Although their northern homelands were far from Jerusalem, Biblical evidences show that the Gershonites shared in the central religious life of the nation. Apparently, there were recognized arrangements whereby outlying religious personnel shared in the worship of the central shrine. One hundred and thirty Gershonites helped bring the Ark to Jerusalem (1 Chron 15:7; again "Gershom" for "Gershon"). A Gershonite, Asaph, the son of Berechiah, was the chief of the Temple musicians under David (16:4, 5). The later prominence of the Asaphite clan of Temple musicians prob. originates from this office. Heman, the son of Joel, is another important Gershonite official (15:17); "son of Joel" may refer to a Gershonite clan thus designated (see below). Other offices held by Gershonites are exemplified by the three clans (or three individuals; the records are not clear), Jehieli, Zetham, and Joel who were "in charge of the treasuries of the house of the LORD" (26:21, 22; cf. 23:8). "Jehiel" later appears as the name of an individual office holder (29:8). Despite the unanswered questions which these passages leave, they indicate that the Gershonites played a significant role in the centralized administration of the nation.

Though the passage should be used cautiously in view of the possibility of textual corruption, 1 Chronicles 23:7-10 seems to list ten prominent Gershonite clans who shared in regular Temple worship in David's religious bureaucracy: The sons of Ladan (i.e. Libni) include the clans of Jehiel, Zetham, and Joel; the sons of Shemei (v. 9; perhaps the same as the Shemei descended from Libni through Jahath; cf. 1 Chron 6:39-43) include Shelemoth, Haziel, and Haran; and another group called "sons of Shemei" (v. 10) includes Jahath, Zina (Zizah of v. 11), Jeush, and Beriah.

Gershonites maintained their importance in the later monarchy. Several Gershonites participated in Hezekiah's cleansing of the Temple (2 Chron 29:12-15). Joah, son of Zimmah, and Eden, son of Joah ("son of Zimmah" and "son of Joah" may be clan designations), are mentioned along with two Asaphites, Zechariah and Mattaniah.

Futher participation by Gershonites in public religious life is seen in the preaching of Jahaziah, an Asaphite, in the reign of Jehoshaphat (20:14ff.) and in Josiah's Passover celebration (35:15).

d. The return from exile. The only Gershonite clan mentioned in the restored Jewish community is Asaph (q.v.).

For a treatment of the Gershonites based upon documentary criticism, the reader should consult IDB.

BIBLIOGRAPHY. W. C. Allen, "Gershon," HDB (1900); relevant names in E. L. Curtis, "Genealogy," HDB (1900); T. M. Mauch, "Gershon," IDB (1962).

A. BOWLING

GERSON. KJV and ASV Apoc. form of GERSHOM.

GERUTH-CHIMHAM gĭr′ ōōth kĭm′ hăm (כמהם גרות, *the inn of Chimham*, KJV HABITATION OF CHIMHAM). Unidentified place near Bethlehem (perhaps named after son of Barzillai, 2 Sam 19:37-40), where Johanan and company stayed while planning descent to Egypt after the murder of Gedaliah whom Nebuchadnezzar had appointed governor over what was left of Judah after 586 B.C. (Jer 41:17).

C. P. WEBER

GERZITES. *See* GIRZITES.

GESEM. KJV Apoc. form of GOSHEN.

GESHAN gĕsh′ ən (גישן, KJV GESHAM, gē′ shem). Son of Jahdai, presumably a descendant of Judah through Caleb (1 Chron 2:47). Gesham occurs only in later editions of KJV.

GESHEM gĕsh′ əm (גשם ; perhaps Heb. *rains, bulk, substance;* but prob. local dialectal Arab. name of unknown meaning; *gäsmu'* in Neh 6:6 KJV; RSVmg.) One of Nehemiah's opponents in the rebuilding of the walls of Jerusalem (2:19; 6:1ff.). He was important enough to serve as witness to the Jews' alleged treason (6:6). His title, "the Arab," may identify him as the governor of Edom (IDB), but scholars have more generally identified him with a N Arabian king referred to as "Gashm, son of Shahr" in an inscr. from Dedan in Arabia and as "Gashm, king of Kedar" in an Aram. inscr. from Egypt. Probably, both Tobiah and Geshem had friendly contacts with the nomads and seminomads who were then infiltrating into Pal. from the S. Furthermore, N Arabian kings profited economically from the trade routes extending from Arabia through Pal. to the Mediterranean coast. A resurgent Jerusalem threatened both of these interests.

BIBLIOGRAPHY. A. T. Olmstead, *History of*

the Persian Empire (1948), 295; K. A. Kitchen, "Geshem," NBD (1962); M. Newman, "Geshem," IDB (1962).

A. C. Bowling

GESHUR, GESHURITE(S) gĕsh′ er, gĕsh′ ə rīts (גְּשׁוּר, גְּשׁוּרִי, meaning uncertain, possibly *bridge*). A country E of the Jordan and a people near Sinai.

1. A country E of the upper Jordan in Syria. The area of these people, along with the Maacathites, was one of the borders of the territory given to Jair, the Manassite (Deut 3:14). The same boundary is mentioned in Joshua 12:5 as the limit of that which the Israelites took. The people are listed in Joshua 3:11, 13 as among those which the Israelites did not drive out but at the time of writing were existing within Israel. Geshur, along with Aram (Syria), took Havvoth-jair (formerly possessed by Jair, the Manassite) and other places from the Israelites (1 Chron 2:23).

Absalom was the son of David by Maacah, daughter of Talmai, king of Geshur (2 Sam 3:3; 1 Chron 3:2). When Absalom killed his half-brother Amnon, he fled to Geshur for the protection by his grandfather, Talmai, for three years until he could return safely (2 Sam 13:37, 38). At this time Joab brought him back to Jerusalem (2 Sam 14:23, 32; 15:8).

2. A people S of the Philistines near Sinai, whose land was not taken originally by the Israelite forces at the time of the conquest (Josh 13:2). When David was in exile with Achish, king of Gath, he and his men made raids upon the Geshurites (and other peoples) and led Achish to believe that he was attacking his own people (1 Sam 27:8).

BIBLIOGRAPHY. L. H. Grollenberg, *Atlas of the Bible* (1956), 150.

C. P. Weber

GESSEN. Douay VS form of Goshen.

GESTURE(S). Any movement of head, hand, or other part of the body to convey meaning to an observer, as to secure his attention or to guide his action; to emphasize what is being said or is about to be said; or to express strong feeling. A variety of words and phrases convey the different actions of persons in the Bible. People of the ancient orient were much more given to what westerners of today would regard as extreme expressions of such emotions as grief, despair, joy and friendship.

Gestures were used to communicate either with or without speech. Thus, when Zachariah was visited by an angel to inform him that he would have a son, he was struck dumb and had to make signs to express himself (Luke 1:22). When John the Baptist was born his kinfolk made signs to the father to inquire what he should be called (Luke 1:62). Peter beckoned to his partners with his hands to help him with the huge load of fish (Luke 5:7); and again with his hand he cautioned the gathered church people after he was released from prison by a heavenly messenger (Acts 12:17). Peter motioned to the beloved disciple to seek from Jesus whom He meant would betray Him (John 13:24). Paul gestured as he began to speak to the Jews in the synagogue at Antioch of Pisida (Acts 13:16), as he did elsewhere (Acts 21:40; 26:1). In Caesarea Felix motioned to Paul to speak in his defense against the Jewish leaders (Acts 24:10). It may be noted here that when the Jews interrupted Paul's speech from the tower of Antonia following his arrest, they showed their indignation by waving their garments and throwing dust into the air (Acts 22:23, 24). Stretching out the arm was occasionally used as a signal to attack or go forward, in the assurance that God would work on behalf of His people. Moses did this at the Red Sea in connection with the parting of the waters, and again at their return upon the Egyptians (Exod 14:16, 21, 26, 27). Joshua does the same with a javelin his hand at the attack on Ai (Josh 8:18, 19, 26). The stretching out of the arm often is used fig. of God to express His mighty acts in Israel's interest (e.g., Isa 23:11; cf. Acts 4:30). Jesus stretched forth His hand toward His disciples to indicate that they were His true mother and brothers and sisters (Matt 12:49). Ahasuerus the king gave the traditional gesture of acceptance when he held out the scepter to Queen Esther as she approached the throne unbidden at a critical time (Esth 4:11; 5:2).

Bowing was a common gesture of greeting and reverence. Abraham so greeted his visitors as he was encamped at Mamre (Gen 18:2); and so did Lot when they visited him at Sodom (Gen 19:1). Jacob bowed himself seven times as he approached Esau with whom he hoped for reconciliation (Gen 33:2). David fell on his face and bowed three times as he met with Jonathan to say farewell when he would have to flee to escape from Saul (1 Sam 20:41). The two men also kissed each other and wept, another common practice in Bible times, esp. when feelings were strong. Esau and Jacob embraced and wept when they met after their long estrangement (Gen 33:4). Joseph kissed his brothers and they wept when his identity was made plain in Egypt (Gen 45:15). Such wholesome gestures of love and friendship could be used hypocritically for base purposes, and Joab did this when he kissed Amasa while concealing the sword with which he murdered him (2 Sam 20:9). Judas also planted the false kiss of betrayal upon Jesus to deliver Him up to His enemies (Matt 26:49).

Considerable freedom is shown in the variety of postures or gestures in prayer and worship. Solomon, Ezra, Daniel, and Stephen all knelt to pray (1 Kings 8:54; Ezra 9:5; Dan 6:10; Acts 7:60). Bowing was frequent. Eliezer so worshiped (Gen 24:26); Elijah bowed with his face between his knees (1 Kings 18:42); the Baal worshipers bowed (1 Kings 19:18); people generally did so (Neh 8:6). People would stand as they prayed, as Hannah and Solomon did, and, of course, the hypocrites in public (1 Sam 1:26; 1 Kings 8:22; Matt 6:5; Mark 11:25). Men would lift up or spread their hands when they prayed (2 Chron 6:13; Ezra 9:5; Pss 88:9; 143:6; 1 Tim 2:8). And we recall the strong gesture of penitence by the tax collector when he struck his breast, not lifting his eyes to heaven (Luke 18:13).

Hands were joined to pledge fidelity or friendship (2 Kings 10:15) or were extended in blessing (Lev 9:22), laid on animals for sacrifice (Lev 1:4), or clapped to express joy (Ps 47:1). Weeping expressed either sorrow (Jer 9:10) or joy (Gen 46:29). The head might be lifted in pride (Ps 83:2); or covered in grief, perhaps with putting ashes, earth, or dust on it (Josh 7:6; 1 Sam 4:12; 2 Sam 13:19). Shaking or wagging the head could express contempt (Ps 64:8). Tearing garments would express grief, consternation or outrage (Gen 37:34; Matt 26:65). Shaking the dust off the feet against a town condemned it for its rejection of God's witness (Matt 10:14; Acts 13:51). Inclining the ear would indicate a readiness to listen (Isa 55:3); a "stiff necked" people would not do so (Jer 17:23).

The Gospel writers take note of various gestures of Jesus during His ministry. He looked with love upon the good but unyielding rich young man (Mark 10:21). In dealing with a deaf man with impaired speech, Jesus put fingers in the ears, spat and touched the tongue, looked to heaven, sighed, and then gave the healing word (Mark 7:33-35). He sighed over men's hardness of heart (Mark 8:12). He looked around with indignation in the synagogue when the leaders opposed His sabbath healing of an afflicted man (Mark 3:5). He picked up little children and laid hands on them to bless them (Mark 10:16). In the final hours in Gethsemane, Jesus knelt and fell on His face and prayed out of the deep agony of His heart (Matt 26:39; Luke 12:41).

BIBLIOGRAPHY. G. M. Mackie, "Gestures," HDB, II (1900), 162f., W. I. Walker, "Gesture," ISBE, II (1925), 1220f., "Gesture," HED (1952), 222f.

N. B. BAKER

GETHER **ge' thər** (גתר). One of the sons of Aram in the Table of Nations (Gen 10:23). The Heb of 1 Chronicles 1:17 lists him simply as among the "sons of Shem" without distinguishing sons from grandsons.

GETHSEMANE **gĕth sĕm' ə nĭ** (Γεθσημανεί). A "place" RSV, or "plot of ground," χωρίον (Matt 26:36; Mark 14:32), which was E of Jerusalem across the Kidron Valley (John 18:1), on the Mount of Olives (Luke 22:39). This place was a garden or enclosure (κῆπος, John 18:1) in the olive grove, and likely contained an olive press. Hence the meaning of the name Gethsemane is "oil press" from גית שמני and should be taken as referring to a certain place on the hillside. Further, both Matthew and Mark give the impression that Gethsemane was a place arrived at only after traversing part of the orchard hillside (Matt 26:30, 36; Mark 14:26, 32).

According to Luke (21:37) and John (18:2), Jesus frequently retreated to this hillside and "garden" for rest, prayer, and fellowship with His disciples. He did so on the night of His betrayal. After the Last Supper and the singing of the Passover hymn, He left the upper room, (possibly located in S Jerusalem near the Zion Gate), crossed the Kidron Valley, and ascended the Mt. of Olives, across the valley from the Temple. Upon entering the area, Jesus spoke to the disciples about their being scattered as sheep, His resurrection and reunion with them in Galilee, and the temptation of Peter and of their going to deny Him (Mark 14:26-31). Then He took Peter, James, and John on into the "garden" of Gethsemane, and charged them to watch. Going a stone's throw further, He prayed three times for deliverance (Mark 14:32-42). His prayer-agony complete, He went out to meet His betrayer.

The precise site of Gethsemane is a matter of contention in Christian tradition; different sites are identified by Western, Russian, Armenian, and Greek Orthodox Church authorities (cf. Kraeling's map, p. 396). It is generally agreed that Gethsemane was situated on the hillside above the road from Jerusalem to Bethany, but the precise site can be ascertained only by tradition. The oldest tradition, dating from Empress Helena's visit to Jerusalem in A.D. 326, fixed the site of Gethsemane at the Church of the Tomb of the Virgin, and the place of Jesus' prayer a stone's throw up the hill (Luke 22:41). This would place the site about equal distance from St. Stephen's Gate and the Golden Gate. It would have been directly across from the Temple.

The tradition that eight very ancient olive trees mark the site is prob. not well founded, since Josephus records that Titus (A.D. 70) cut down all the trees E of the city (Jos., War VI. i. 1).

BIBLIOGRAPHY. Hastings, HDCG, I, 646, 647; E. G. Kraeling, *Rand McNally Bible Atlas* (1956), 394-404; *The Westminster Historical Atlas to the Bible* (1956), 107-109.

J. C. DEYOUNG

GEUEL **gū' əl** (גאואל). One of the twelve spies sent out by Moses to reconnoiter the Promised Land (Num 13:1-33). He was the son of Machi and represented the tribe of Gad (13:15).

GEZER **ge' zər** (גזר, LXX Γαζερα, Γαζηρ, Γαζηρα, once Γαδερ [Josh 12:13 A]). A major city of the northern Shephelah.

1. Discovery. The true site of Gezer was

The Church of All Nations at the Garden of Gethsemane in Jerusalem. ©*Lev*

first identified by C. Clermont-Ganneau during 1870-1873. His investigations led him from Khulda to Tell el-Jezer beside the village of Abu Shusheh. In 1874, he found some bilingual inscrs. (Heb.-Gr.) on the rocks surrounding the tell that read ΑΛΚΙΟΥ תחם גזר, "the confines of Gezer, (of) Alkios."

2. Location. Ancient Gezer was situated on the northwestern edge of the Shephelah. It commands a good view of "the plain of Ono" (Neh 6:2), across which passed the main N-S route of the Levant. The lateral trunk road leading into the hill country via Beth-horon led directly to Gezer before meeting the coastal route.

3. Excavation. Two major excavations were carried out by R. A. S. Macalister at Gezer in 1902-1905 and 1907-1909. A Rowe made a small sounding in 1934, but his finds have not been published. The Hebrew Union College—Biblical and Archeological School in Jerusalem—has recently begun a new series of excavations under the guidance of G. E. Wright, with W. G. Dever as director. The Chalcolithic, Early Bronze I, II, and III, and Middle Bronze II as well as the Late Bronze, Iron, Persian, Hellenistic, and Roman periods are all found at Gezer. From Macalister's report it seems that the Solomonic age is not represented, but Y. Yadin has now shown that a true Solomonic gate had been mistaken by Macalister for part of a Hell. public building.

4. History. *a. Canaanite period.* Gezer is first mentioned in Thutmose III's list of towns conquered (in his first campaign) in Canaan. The name is written q-dj-r (No. 104). Thutmose IV erected a stele in his funerary temple mentioning Khurri (Horite) prisoners from Gez[er] who were brought to Egypt (ANET, p. 248). A fragmentary cuneiform tablet found at Gezer has an enigmatic allusion to nearby Gittim (Gath or Gittaim) and has been linked by Albright, et al., with a campaign by Thutmose IV. Gezer and its princes played important roles in the intrigues among Canaanite cities during the Amarna age, e.g. the ruler of Gezer seems to have been a leader in the attempt by the *'apiru* to seize the territories of other princes loyal to Pharaoh. He and his successors sought to occupy key towns guarding the approach routes to Jerusalem. Pharaoh Merneptah called himself "the reducer of Gezer"—a boast evidently based on his conquest of the city during a campaign depicted on his victory stele (ANET, p. 378).

b. Israelite period. During the conquest under Joshua, Israel defeated Horam, king of Gezer, when he came forth to support Lachish (Josh 10:33). Gezer's relation to the ascent of Beth-horon is reflected in its being mentioned after the latter town as being on the border of allotment given to the sons of Joseph (Josh 16:3 [LXX vs. 5]). Gezer was given to Ephraim (1 Chron 7:28) who failed to expel the Canaanites (Josh 16:10; Judg 1:29); later the indigenous population was put to forced labor. The Levitical Kohathites were allotted Gezer as one of their cities in the Ephraimite tribal inheritance (Josh 21:21; 1 Chron 6:67 [MT 6:52]). After David established his capital at Jerusalem (Jebus), the Philistines tried to assert their authority over the hill country by means of the approach routes to Jerusalem, but David chased them as far as Gezer (2 Sam 5:25; 1 Chron 14:16). When Solomon came to power, Gezer was taken by the Egyptian Pharaoh and burned with fire (1 Kings 9:15-17); it was then given to Solomon as dowry for Pharaoh's daughter. Solomon refortified it along with other major chariot cities and strategic towns, e.g. Hazor, Megiddo, Beth-horon, etc. The gates at Gezer were almost identical to those at Hazor and Megiddo; Hazor had a casemate wall in this period like that at Gezer, but Megiddo had a salients-and-recesses wall along with its stone houses in the Solomonic period (*contra* Yadin). When Pharaoh Shishak invaded the land in the fifth year of Rehoboam, he launched his drive into the hill country by attacking Gezer (no. 12 on his list); from there he was able to penetrate the uplands and threaten Jerusalem (1 Kings 14:25-28; 2 Chron 12:1-12).

Gezer does not appear in the history of the divided monarchy until its conquest by the Assyrian monarch Tiglath-pileser, either in his campaign against Philistia (734 B.C.) or his subsequent attack on Israel (733 B.C.). The Assyrian monarch left a relief depicting his siege of the city (ANEP, No. 369), and two tablets in Assyrian cuneiform found on the tell itself show that the conqueror established a colony at Gezer. But stamped jar handles and a shekel weight all marked "for the king" reveal that Gezer had returned to Judean control, at least under Josiah and possibly in the reign of Hezekiah.

c. Persian period. Other jar handles stamped "Yehud" and "Yerushalem" indicate that Gezer was part of, or had relations with the post-exilic province. First Esdras 5:31 says that "sons of Gezer" (*υἱοὶ Γαζηρα*) returned from captivity in Babylon—but the Heb. parallel texts (Ezra 2:48; Neh 7:51) have "sons of Gazzam," which is prob. correct. A stone slab and a scaraboid with the name of Pharaoh Nepherites (398-393 B.C.) suggest that Gezer was witness to the conflict between the 29th Egypt. dynasty and the Pers. empire.

d. Intertestamental period. Prior to the establishment of the Hasmonean kingdom, Gezer was a Gentile city to which the defeated Seleucid forces could retreat (1 Macc 4:15; 7:45). Bacchides included it in his chain of strongholds (1 Macc 9:52; Jos. Antiq. XIII. i. 3).

The High Place at Gezer, with row of monolithic pillars. ©*Lev*

Later Simon besieged and took it (1 Macc 13:43-48 has Gaza but Jos. War, I. ii. 2; Antiq., XIII. vi. 7 correctly read Gezer [Gazara]). There he established his son John with a garrison (1 Macc 13:53; 14:34). Antiochus Sidetes tried to force Simon to surrender Gezer (1 Macc 15:28-35; 16:1-10), but only under the reign of John Hyrcanus did he succeed (Jos. War. I. ii. 5; Antiq. XIII. viii. 3); after Antiochus' death, the Rom. senate supported Hyrcanus' efforts to retrieve Gezer (Jos. Antiq. XIII. ix. 2). During the subsequent Rom. rule in Judea, Gezer was reduced to a small village. By the Byzantine era it had been completely overshadowed by another town 4½ m. S-SE, viz. the Emmaus-Nicopolis of Eusebius (Onom 66:19-68:2, ed. Klostermann) and the Medeba map.

Further archeological investigation of Tell Gezer will certainly illuminate many aspects of her history and material culture. The famous "high place" discovered by Macalister has now been relocated by the Hebrew Union College expedition; its date is still not certain but appears to belong to the Middle Bronze Age. The Solomonic gate and casemate walls have also been uncovered again. It is hoped that the eastern part of the gate, untouched by Macalister, may provide more accurate stratified evidence of its construction phases.

BIBLIOGRAPHY. C. Clermont-Ganneau, *Archaeological Researches in Palestine,* II (1899), 224-275; id., "Nouvelle inscription hébraique et grecque," RB, VIII (1899), 109-115; T. Pinches, "The Fragment of an Assyrian Tablet Found at Gezer," PEQ. QSt (1904), 229-236; A. H. Sayce, "Note on the Assyrian Tablet," PEQ. QSt (1904), 236, 237; C. H. W. Johns, "Note on the Gezer Contract Tablet," PEQ. QSt (1904), 237-244; W. M. F. Petrie, "Notes on Objects from Gezer," PEQ. QSt (1904), 244, 245; R. A. S. Macalister, *Biblical Sidelights from the Mound of Gezer* (1907); id., *The Excavations at Gezer* (1912); W. F. Albright, "Egypt and the Early History of the Negeb," JPOS, IV (1924), 131-161; W. R. Taylor, "Some New Palestinian Inscriptions," BASOR, No. 41 (1931), 27-29; W. F. Albright, "Two Little Understood Amarna Tablets from the Middle Jordan Valley," BASOR, No. 89 (1943), 7-17; id., "The Gezer Calendar," BASOR, No. 92 (1943), 16-26; id., "A Tablet of the Amarna Age from Gezer," BASOR, No. 92 (1943), 28-30; R. B. K. Amiran, "The 'Cream Ware' of Gezer and the Beersheba Late Chalcolithic," IEJ, V (1955), 240-245; Y. Yadin, "Solomon's City Wall and Gate at Gezer," IEJ, VIII (1958), 80-86; A. Malamat, "Campaigns of Amenhotep II and Thutmose IV to Canaan," *Studies in the Bible (Scripta Hierosolymitana,* VIII, 1961), 228-231; G. E. Wright, "Gezer," IEJ, XV (1965), 252, 253; J. F. Ross, "Gezer in the Tell el-Amarna Letters," *Bulletin—Museum Haaretz,* VIII (1966), 45-54; H. Darrell Lance, "Gezer in the Land and in History," BA, XXX (1967), 34-47; W. G. Dever, "Excavations at Gezer," BA, XXX (1967), 47-62; J. F. Ross, "Gezer in the Tell el-Amarna Letters," BA, XXX (1967), 62-72; W. G. Dever, H. D. Lance, and G. E. Wright. *Gezer I, Annual of* HUCBAS, vol. 1 (1970).

A. F. RAINEY

GEZRITES. KJV form of GIRZITES.

GHOR (ghaur or **ghōr).** The Arab. term for the low-lying plain of the Jordan valley from the southern end of the Sea of Galilee in the N to the northern end of the Dead Sea in the S. Its eastern border is formed by the relatively straight cliffs formed when the eastern mountains of Trans-Jordan fall off to the valley below along the fault line of the Jordan rift. Its western border is much more irregular, being formed by the western mountains of the Cisjordan range, which protrude into and recede from the valley of Ghor quite brokenly, cut in several places by steep valleys. The largest of these valleys is that of the Jālūd River which comes into the Jordan valley about seven m. below the Sea of Galilee, emptying the plain of Jezreel to the NW. The Ghor is broad and expansive, as it is at its widest region (about twelve m., E to W) just N of the Dead Sea. Within this valley the Jordan River winds and twists its way from the Sea of Galilee to the Dead Sea (see Grollenberg, *Atlas of the Bible*, pl. 26, p. 17).

F. W. BUSH

GHOST (נפש ; πνευμα, *soul, spirit,* cf. German *Geist, spirit; see also* FAMILIAR SPIRIT).

1. In KJV usage, the Old Eng. word "ghost" is equivalent to the modern word "spirit." The Gr. word πνευμα is tr. "ghost" twice (Matt 27:50; John 19:30) and "spirit" 268 times apart from the title "Holy Spirit." This name occurs four times and the form "Holy Ghost" occurs about eighty-five times. Doubtless the tr. "Holy Spirit" should be uniformly adopted in conformity with modern Eng. usage.

The Heb. word נפש is tr. "ghost" twice (Job 11:20; Jer 15:9), "spirit" 230 times and "wind" 90 times. In the four times that "ghost" is tr. נפש or πνευμα, it is used in the phrase "giving up the ghost," an old Eng. expression for dying. This expression is also used fifteen other times to tr. various words for "expire." The word "ghost" in KJV never refers to the modern idea of a ghost.

2. Also in KJV usage, the Old Eng. word "spirit" is sometimes equivalent to the modern word "ghost" (Matt 14:26; Mark 6:49), where it trs. the Gr. word *phantasma* ("apparition"). In the OT, the expression "familiar spirit" trs. the Heb. אוב and refers to an alleged disembodied spirit, a ghost in the modern sense. This word is used in the record of Samuel's reappearance to Saul (1 Sam 28:7-19).

3. Apparently, the attitude of the disciples when they saw Jesus walking on the water mirrors the beliefs of the Jews in the time of Christ—that ghosts, or spirits, not only surround them in the invisible world, but could on occasion reveal themselves to human eyes (Matt 14:26; Mark 6:49; Luke 24:37).

F. E. Hamilton; R. L. Harris

GHOST, HOLY. *See* Holy Spirit.

GIAH gī' ə (גִּיחַ). An unidentified site on the route of Abner's flight from Joab and Abishai after he killed Asabel following the defeat of Eshbaal's forces by those of David (2 Sam 2:24). It is given as a place better known to the contemporaries of the author than the hill of Ammah. An accepted understanding of the v. has not been achieved and the text may be corrupt.

F. W. Bush

GIANTS. This word was used by the KJV to tr. four different Heb. words (1) גִּבּוֹר (Job 16:14 KJV); (2) נְפִילִים (Gen 6:4; Num 13:33); (3) רְפָאִים (Deut 2:11, 20; 3:11, 13; Josh 12:4; 13:12; 15:8; 17:15; 18:16) and (4) רָפָא or רָפָה (2 Sam 21:16; 21:22; 1 Chron 20:8). In (1) the word simply means "mighty man, hero, warrior" as it is tr. by all the modern VSS; in (2), (3), and (4), the meanings of the terms are unknown, and, although none of them mean "giants," they may refer to giants (see below). Hence, the great majority of modern VSS simply transliterate the terms in almost all the places that they occur.

The word "giant" in Eng. may have two meanings. It may refer to a race of beings of superhuman size and strength who appear in the mythology and folklore of most ancient peoples, often at war with the gods; or it may be used to refer to human beings of abnormal and unusual size, usually due to a disease of the pituitary gland, properly referred to as "gigantism." In modern times medical accounts record a woman 8 ft. 4½ in. tall, while claims have been made in modern times of giants as tall as 9 ft. 3 in. That "giants" occur in the OT in the latter sense admits of no doubt. Goliath of Gath, whom David slew, was "six cubits and a span" in height (1 Sam 17:4). If the ordinary cubit (q.v.) is meant, this represents a height of c. 9½ ft. Compare also Og, king of Bashan, whose "bed of iron" was 13 cubits long and 4 cubits wide (13 ft. x 5 ft.) (Deut 3:11), and the Egyp. whom Benaiah slew, who was 5 cubits tall (c. 7 ft. if the ordinary cubit is meant, 1 Chron 11:23). Second Samuel 21:15-22 records the exploits of David and several of his men against Philistine giants (although only one is said to be "a man of huge stature," 2 Sam 21:20; 1 Chron 20:6).

The Rephaim and the Anakim (q.v.), who were among the original inhabitants of Pal. (cf. Gen 15:18-21; Num 13:28, 33) prob. concern "giants" in the second sense mentioned above. Although neither one of these terms means "giants" and are unquestionably ethnic terms (both are named with lists of ethnic terms Gen 15:19-21, Num 13:28, 29) it is quite certain that they were regarded as races of people of inordinate size (see esp. Num 13:32, 33; Deut 9:2). However, that the Hebrews regarded them as giants in the first sense mentioned above (as is often held) seems highly improbable. The only passage that could suggest such is Numbers 13:33, and it is best understood as an emotional reaction of intimidated men to the power and size of the Canaanite people and fortified cities.

The only passage that may refer to giants in the first sense is Genesis 6:1-4, where the Nephilim (q.v.) are mentioned. Many hold that this passage refers to the stories of giants on earth who are descended from union between gods and humans and that it is used by the author (chs. 1-11) as a measure of the effects of human sin (see, e.g., Von Rad, *Genesis*, Philadelphia: Westminster [1961], pp. 109-112).

F. W. Bush

GIANTS, VALLEY OF. *See* Rephaim, Valley of.

GIBBAR gĭb' är (גִּבָּר). The ancestor of one of the families who returned with Zerubbabel from exile (Ezra 2:20 RSV). The parallel passage in Nehemiah 7:25 has "sons of Gibeon." Since the returning exiles begin to be listed by their city rather than their ancestor in the immediately following entry in Ezra 2:21, it is not certain which is the original reading.

F. W. Bush

GIBBETHON gĭb' bə thŏn (גִּבְּתוֹן *mound, height, ridge*). A Philistine city assigned to Dan (Josh 19:44) and to the Levites (21:23). It was while Nadab, son of Jeroboam, was besieging Gibbethon that Baasha murdered him and assumed the crown of Israel for himself (1 Kings 15:27). Later, the Israelite army was again trying to wrest Gibbethon from the Philistines when word reached them that Zimri had murdered Baasha's son, Elah, and proclaimed himself king. On hearing this, the army proclaimed Omri king, and Zimri committed suicide (1 Kings 16:15-20). The city (modern Tell Melat) was an important fortress on the eastern branch of the Way of the Sea, the route used by Thutmose III in his Syrian campaigns, and by Esarhaddon in his attack on Egypt.

G. G. Swaim

GIBEA gĭb' ĭ ə (גִּבְעָא). One of the descendants of Caleb (1 Chron 2:49). His father was

Sheva who was born to Caleb through his concubine Maacah (1 Chron 2:48).

GIBEAH, GIBEATH gĭb' ĭ ə, gĭb' ĭ əth (גִּבְעָה, גִּבְעַת ; *hill*; LXX Γαβαα, Γαβεε, sometimes βουνός, *hill*). To form an adequate understanding of the problems of identification connected with this name, the reader should carefully compare the Heb. spellings of the following forms, all of which come from the same root and have approximately the same meaning; גֶּבַע, גִּבְעָה, גִּבְעַת, גִּבְעוֹן, respectively represented in Eng. as "Geba," "Gibeah," "Gibeath," and "Gibeon." Because much of Pal. is hilly country, it is not surprising that a name meaning "hill" was widely used. Unfortunately, the MT exhibits considerable confusion in the use of these names, a confusion not clarified by the LXX, which neither follows the MT consistently, nor has any other regularly observed practice in its treatment of this name.

Gibeon, properly the chief city of the Hivites who tricked Israel into an alliance to avoid being massacred (Josh 11:19), is confused with Gibeah of Saul (2 Sam 21:6) and with Geba (1 Chron 14:16 is identical with 2 Sam 5:25, except that the former has Gibeon where the latter has Geba). "Gibeath" is simply a different grammatical form (the construct state) of the word "Gibeah"; i.e., in Heb., these two forms are the same name occurring in different forms because of the grammatical context. No attempt should be made to distinguish cities here on the basis of this variation in the form of the name, in spite of the fact that "Gibeath" (Heb.) occurs in Joshua 18:28 where the construct form is not expected. "Geba" and "Gibeah" properly refer to different places, but they are nevertheless frequently confused. In Judges 20:31, the highway can hardly go from Gibeah to Gibeah; surely Geba should be the reading here. Two vv. later, the MT has Geba where Gibeah seems more likely. In Judges 20:10, there can be no doubt that the Geba of the MT refers to Gibeah (so RSV). J. Simons finds the usage in 1 Samuel so fluid as to create the impression that the masculine (Geba) and feminine (Gibeah) forms were used interchangeably (669, 670; *see* BIBLIOGRAPHY). If this assumption is made, the reader will ask himself each time he sees one of these names, which place the context calls for, rather than relying on the form in the MT to distinguish the localities with any degree of finality. It has been argued that 1 Samuel 13:16 refers to the same place as 1 Samuel 14:16, presumably Geba (Jeba'), which is much closer to Michmash than Gibeah (Tell el Fûl), and therefore more suitable as the location for the Israelite army in opposition to the Philistine forces in Michmash. It is certain that Saul would keep some of his forces in his capital city (Gibeah, cf. 1 Sam 13:2), and it is possible to make sense out of the text as it stands. Scholars have not been able to agree on any reconstruction of the exact course of events in this war. Perhaps the best approach for the nonspecialist in these matters is to avoid basing any arguments on the use of one name instead of another until he is certain of his ground, bearing in mind that leading geographical and archeological authorities disagree on several readings.

After the readings have been ascertained, and Geba (q.v.) and Gibeon (q.v.) set aside—there are several places called Gibeah.

1. First, a Gibeah is listed with the cities in the hill country of Judah (Josh 15:57). It is identified with el Jab'ah, c. ten m. NW of Beit Immar. It is not mentioned elsewhere in Scripture—unless it is identical with the home of Micaiah, the mother of Abijah, king of Judah (2 Chron 13:2).

2. Another Gibeah, located in the hills of Ephraim, belonged to Phinehas, grandson of Aaron, and provided the burial place of Eleazar the priest (Josh 24:33). The site is of no importance in the Bible, but it was known to Josephus (Jos. Antiq. V. i. 29). Its location is unknown.

3. The Gibeah of 1 Samuel 10:10 is distinguished as "Gibeah of God" (RSV Gibeath-elohim in 1 Sam 10:5). Though some have identified it with Ram Allah, and others with Gibeah of Saul, it is prob. Geba. Ram Allah is too far N to fit Saul's itinerary as described here, and he apparently reached Gibeah-elohim before arriving at home (cf. Simons, 669, 670).

4. Finally, there is the Gibeah of Benjamin (1 Sam 13:15), or Gibeah of Saul (11:4), which was first identified with Tell el Fûl by a German, Cross, in 1843. This identification was confirmed by W. F. Albright by excavation in 1922-1923. By far the most important city by this name in the Biblical account, it first comes into prominence in the Book of Judges.

A Levite from the hill country of Ephraim, returning N from Bethlehem, hesitated to spend the night in Jebus (Jerusalem) because it was still controlled by the Jebusites. He preferred to press on to Gibeah of Benjamin. When he arrived in Gibeah, no one invited him into his house in spite of the fact that he had his own provisions with him. Finally, a man from Ephraim who lived in Gibeah came along and offered hospitality, but soon the men of the city surrounded his house and demanded that the traveler be surrendered to them for homosexual abuse. To avert this, the Levite thrust his concubine out to the mob. After raping her all night, the revelers released her at dawn. The Levite took her home, dismembered her body, and sent pieces of her throughout the land of Israel, calling for vengeance on the barbarous inhabitants of Gibeah. When the whole tribe of Benjamin defended the culprits, a bloody intertribal war broke out; over 40,000 Israelites and 25,000 Benjaminites died. Apparently, the Israelites felt more than vindicated by this "victory," for they then proceeded to murder all the inhabitants of Jabesh-gilead except for 400 young virgins, to obtain wives

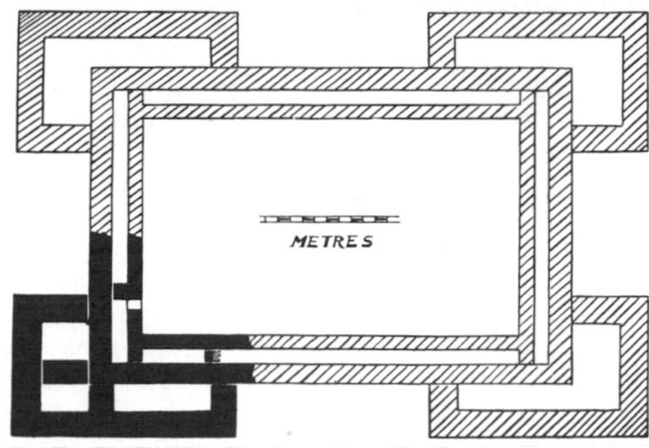

An eleventh-century fortress at Gibeah of Saul, preserved at only one corner.

for the 600 Benjaminite survivors of Gibeah (Judg 19-21). As this did not provide enough girls for 600 men, they conspired with the Benjaminites to abduct women from the annual religious feast at Shiloh.

The obvious parallels with the story of Lot's heavenly messengers in Sodom add to the impression that this city was the very paradigm of evil. (Hosea picked up this connotation in Hos 9:9 and again in 10:9.) If it could be shown that the author of this account actually knew the story of Sodom, he should be credited with an unusual subtlety of style because he nowhere makes the parallel explicit. Nor should it go unnoticed that a later inhabitant of Gibeah, Saul, son of Kish, hacked up a yoke of oxen and sent the pieces throughout Israel as a call to war to free Jabesh-gilead from a siege conducted by Nahash the Ammonite (1 Sam 11:7). Imagine the psychological impact on the Israelite warrior upon the receipt of a piece of gory meat from Gibeah of Benjamin!

At first reading, the story in Judges appears almost as a propaganda piece written to discredit Saul's claims to the throne, but the fact that Saul killed his own oxen in his bid to rescue the inhabitants of Jabesh-gilead, the same city that was massacred to provide wives for the earlier people of Gibeah, goes far to offset any propaganda value that the story might have. In fact, Saul could now be seen as the man from Gibeah who undid an earlier wrong. Later, when Saul became king, Gibeah remained his chief residence (1 Sam 10:26; 15:34; 23:19). The fortress of the city was destroyed for the second time (the first time having been in the battle to avenge the Levite) either during Saul's lifetime or at the time of his death, possibly during the same battle that cost him his life. The fact that the carbonized remains of the wood used in the construction of Saul's fortress are of cypress and pine indicates that the territory of Benjamin still supported coniferous forests at this period. The fortress was rebuilt almost immediately on the same plan but fell into disuse shortly after David succeeded in reuniting the country.

When Albright first excavated the site, he thought that the next fortification, a watchtower, was built by Asa (1 Kings 15:22, reading Gibeah instead of Geba), but when he returned to the site ten years later, the absence of Iron II pottery convinced him that this fortress must date from the late 9th or early 8th cent. The use of almond indicates the loss of the earlier conifers. This tower was destroyed later in the 8th cent. possibly in the Syro-Ephraimite War, or by Tiglath-pileser III or Sennacherib (cf. Isa 10:29). It was rebuilt in the 7th cent. and destroyed once more, this time presumably by Nebuchadnezzar in 597 or 586 B.C.

After several centuries, the tower was built again, and this time a village grew up on the eastern slope of the hill which lasted about a cent. and a half until its destruction in or about the time of the war between Ptolemy V and Antiochus III. Still, the site retained its attractiveness, and Josephus wrote of a village there in Rom. times—a village that finally came to an end with the destruction of Jerusalem and the dispersion of the Jews in A.D. 70 (Jos. War V. ii. 1). This village is of particular interest because a stone manger dating from approximately the time of the birth of Christ was found there, and it is possible that the Savior's first bed was a similar structure.

BIBLIOGRAPHY. W. F. Albright: *Excavations and Results at Tell el-Fûl (Gibeah of Saul)*, AASOR, iv (1922-1923); W. F. Albright, "A New Campaign of Excavation at Gibeah of Saul," BASOR, 52 (1933), 6-12; L. A. Sinclair, *An Archaeological Study of Gibeah (Tell el-Fûl)*, AASOR, xxxiv-xxxv (1954-1956), 5-52, plates 1-35; J. Simons: *The Geographical and Topographical Texts of the Old Testament* (1959), §§ 669, 670 passim.

G. G. SWAIM

GIBEAH OF SAUL gĭb′ ĭ ə (גִּבְעָה, *hill*). A city located within the boundaries of Benjamin, Gibeah is designated as "Gibeah, which belongs to Benjamin" (Judg 19:14; 20:4), "Gibeah of Benjamin" (Judg 20:10; 1 Sam 13:2, 15; 14:16), "Gibeah of the Benjamites" (2 Sam 23:29; 1 Chron 11:31) and "Gibeah of Saul" (1 Sam 11:4; 15:34; Isa 10:29).

The city appears first in the Biblical account as the site of an atrocity against a concubine of a journeying Ephraimite. War was waged against Benjamin because of the tribal refusal to bring the guilty to justice. The conflict destroyed the city and almost eliminated the tribe (Judg 19; 20). The first king of Israel, Saul, came from Gibeah (1 Sam 10:10, 26). As Saul's capital the city was important in the conflicts with the Philistines (1 Sam 13:2; 14:2, 16).

The prophets of the 8th cent. saw Gibeah as a significant symbol (Isa 10:29; Hos 9:9; 10:9).

Albright's excavation at Tell el-Fûl three m. N of Jerusalem in 1922-1923 and 1933 established an impressive correlation between the archeological evidence and the Biblical history of Gibeah of Saul. Further confirmation came as the result of P. Lapp's excavation in 1964.

There is no running water on the tell but numerous cisterns, silos and pits excavated out of the solid rock were cleared by the archeologists. Such construction made possible the existence of a sizable community at the beginning of the Iron Age in the time of King Saul. Ceramic evidence indicates the site was occupied in the time of Jeremiah. Life at the site continued uninterrupted by the destruction of Jerusalem in 587 B.C. until around 500 B.C.

After a lapse of several hundred years Tell el-Fûl was occupied in Maccabean times with the heaviest population being about 100 B.C. It was finally destroyed by Titus in his campaign against Jerusalem and never again occupied.

Of special interest in all the archeological campaigns was the tower fortress at the top of the tell. This building dates to the time of King Saul. Later rebuilding preserved on the early foundation drew the attention of visitors in the middle of the 19th cent. The only modification of Albright's interpretation of the fortress was occasioned by the finding of the wall of the structure on the N of the exposed walls. This demonstrated the fact that the fortress had a N-S rather than an E-W alignment.

H. M. JAMIESON

GIBEATH-ELOHIM. *See* GIBEAH.

GIBEAH-HA-ARALOTH. *See* GIBEAH.

GIBEON **gĭb' ĭ ən** (גִּבְעוֹן, LXX Γαβαών, meaning *hill*). A city about six m. NW of Jerusalem.

1. Biblical record. Gibeon is first mentioned in connection with Joshua's assault on the hill country. After taking Jericho and Ai, his march would have taken him N of Jerusalem. A delegation from Gibeon came to him, however, under the guise of having taken a long journey (Josh 9:3ff.). Joshua made a peace treaty with them before learning that they had come from nearby Gibeon. The treaty also included the towns Chephirah, Be-eroth, and Kiriath-jearim (9:17).

This treaty caused several problems. Upon discovering the ruse, Joshua did not destroy them but put them in servitude to the Israelites as "hewers of wood and drawers of water" (9:23). Their action precipitated what is now called the Battle of Beth-horon. Joshua 10 records that Adonizedek, king of Jerusalem, and the other Amorite kings planned to attack Gibeon; but Joshua, now committed to defend Gibeon by treaty, fought against them. Joshua and his army, after a night march, slaughtered many at Gibeon and chased the remainder over the Beth-horon pass. God sent hailstones and later had the sun stand still at the command of Joshua (10:6-14).

The occupants of Gibeon were Hivites (perhaps Horites or Hurrians) according to Joshua 11:19. After the division into tribes, Gibeon became a part of Benjamin (18:25; 21:17).

Another problem was Saul's apparent intolerance of non-Israelite peoples in Israel. Second Samuel 21:1ff. alludes to Saul slaughtering many Gibeonites. Later, in David's day, the Gibeonites demanded revenge on the house of Saul. Since they would not accept money in payment for the blood, David finally yielded up seven of Saul's sons whom the Gibeonites promptly hung. Only Mephibosheth was spared.

The famous contest between the twelve soldiers of Abner and the twelve of Joab at the pool of Gibeon had nothing to do with the people of Gibeon themselves (2 Sam 2:12ff.). Because all twenty-four of the young men died, the name Helkath-hazzurim (the field of the sword edges) was given to that site in Gibeon. Since the war by representation was indecisive, Joab chased Abner across the Jordan but failed to apprehend him.

The last major happening at Gibeon was Solomon's going to the high place to sacrifice (1 Kings 3:4; 2 Chron 1:3ff.). While there he had the dream in which God asked him what gift he desired, and the famous king chose wisdom. That high place is mentioned twice again (1 Chron 16:39; 21:29).

Five hundred years later, Melatiah the Gibeonite and other men of Gibeon helped Nehemiah rebuild walls (Neh 3:7; cf. Neh 7:25).

The false prophet Hananiah, whose death Jeremiah foretold, was from Gibeon (Jer 28:1ff.). There was also a personal name, Gibeon, in the genealogies (1 Chron 8:29; 9:35).

2. Archeological results. During the summers of 1956, '57, '59 and '60, James B. Pritchard directed the expeditions of the University of Pennsylvania Museum to el-Jib, the modern Arab. name of Gibeon. These expeditions not only thoroughly excavated the most famous feature of both ancient and modern Gibeon, viz., the great pool (2 Sam 2:13; Jer 41:12), but they also revealed other interesting aspects of the city. Although el-Jib, because of the similarity of the sound, had been suggested as the site of Gibeon as early as 1838 by Edward Robinson, no certain proof came until the archeologists unearthed many jar handles, twenty-four of which bore the name "Gibeon." Other handles bore the typical names of Amariah, Azariah, and Hananiah. The jars may have been used in connection with the wine industry of Gibeon. Cut into the solid rock of the hill were some sixty-six cavities, or cellars, in which the wine could be stored at a constant temperature. In the immediate vicinity were the other accouterments of wine making: presses, troughs, etc.

The dead during the Rom. period were buried most exquisitely in the necropolis of Gibeon. Several tombs plus a columbarium were excavated. These produced some of the finest pottery specimens.

"Tel el Ful-Gibeah of Saul" two miles north of Jerusalem, looking northeast. ©*Lev*

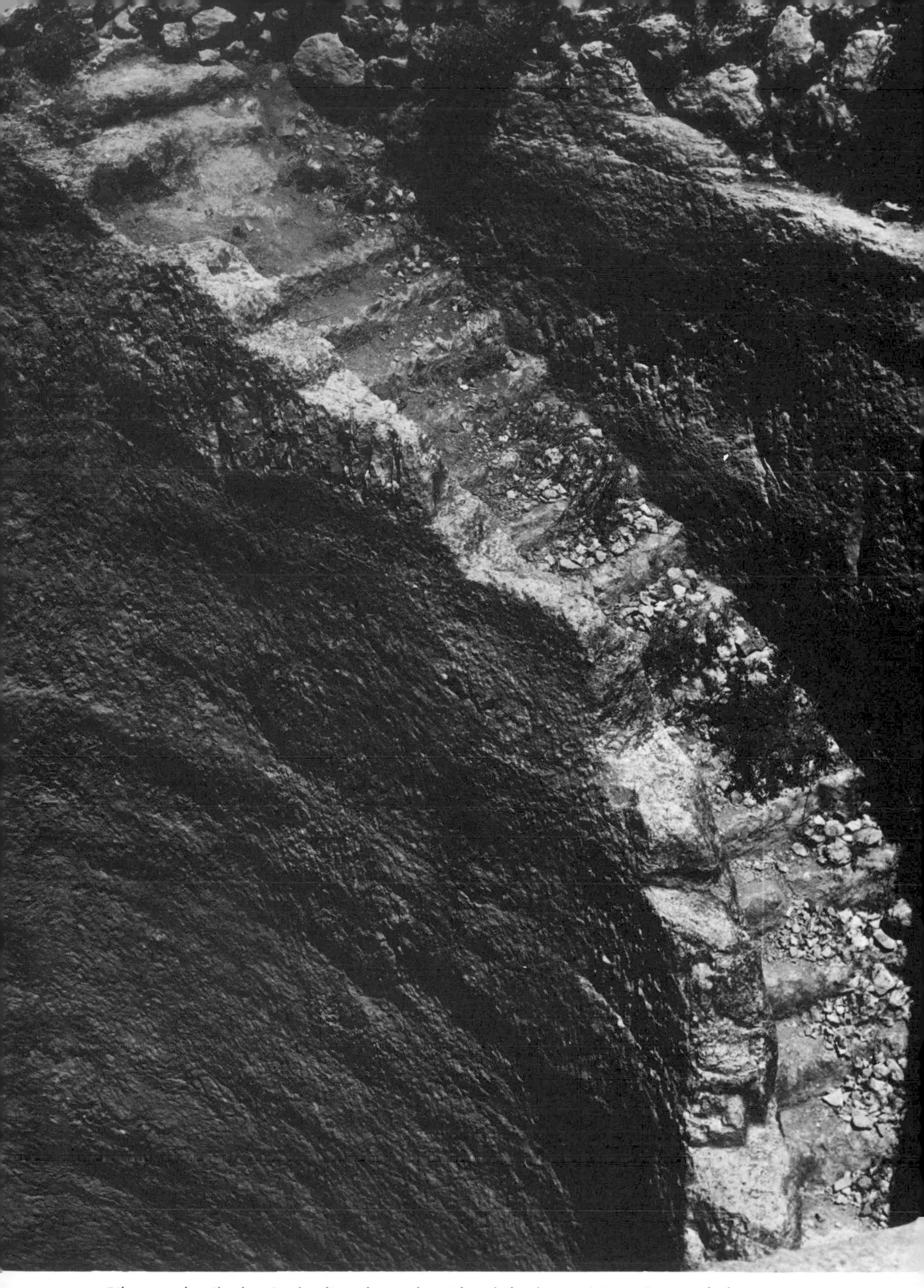

Gibeon—detail of stairs leading down the side of the large cistern. Some scholars believe this may have been a granary. ©*Lev*

By far the most spectacular feature was the great pool, thirty-seven ft. in diameter and eighty-two ft. deep with a circular staircase of seventy-nine steps cut out of the rock. This pool is one of the best-known archeological attractions. Actually the pool was never used to hold water but was part of a rather complete waterworks that assured the citizens of water even during times of siege. To reach the water required the descent of seventy-nine steps of the circular "pool" and then a tunnel 167 ft. long that descended ninety-three more steps. At the bottom was the cistern room filled with water from the main spring outside the city wall. This tunnel also was cut from the solid rock, although the crookedness of it indicates that the engineers followed the natural fissures of the rock. *See* WATER.

BIBLIOGRAPHY. J. B. Pritchard, *Gibeon, Where the Sun Stood Still* (1962).

R. L. ALDEN

GIBEONITES gĭb' ĭ ən īts (גִּבְעֹנִי). The inhabitants of the city of Gibeon.

The gentilic form Gibeon is used many times less than the name of the city itself. In fact, six of its eight occurrences are in 2 Samuel 21 (vv. 1-4, 9). Saul slew the Gibeonites, apparently because he did not want people other than Israelites serving in their midst (Josh 9:21). David sought to appease them with silver and gold, but the Gibeonites would be satisfied with nothing less than blood. So David yielded to them seven sons of Saul, and they were hung in the first days of the barley harvest (2 Sam 21:9).

Two other men in the OT were called Gibeonites: Ishmaiah, "a mighty man among the thirty and a leader over the thirty" (1 Chron 12:4), and Melatiah, who helped Nehemiah repair the wall (Neh 3:7).

The Gibeonites were some of the most ancient occupants of Canaan in view of the fact that they made peace with Joshua after he began conquering other Canaanite cities (Josh 9). Joshua 11:19 indicates that the inhabitants of Gibeon were Hivites.

R. L. ALDEN

GIBLITES. KJV form of GEBALITES. Inhabitants of GEBAL.

GIDDALTI gĭ dăl' tī (גִּדַּלְתִּי, "I have magnified [God]"). One of the sons of Heman who functioned as a singer in the Temple under his father's direction (1 Chron 25:4, 6, 7). The twenty-second of the twenty-four divisions of service fell to him (25:29). Several of the last nine names of v. four are quite unexampled in Heb. nomenclature. This has led to a number of attempts to interpret them either as a v. of a psalm or a list of psalm incipits, see J. M. Myers, *I Chronicles* (*Anchor Bible* [1965]), p. 172f. H. L. Ellison has suggested that "some early scribe saw the possibility of reading this petition in the names of Heman's sons and altered them slightly for his purpose"

Tunnel cut in the rock at Gibeon, leading down 93 steps from inside the city wall to the spring at the base of the hill. ©*Lev.*

(NBC, p. 351). However that may be, there is no question but that the author of Chronicles understood them as names.

F. W. BUSH

GIDDEL **gĭd′ əl** (גדל). 1. The name of a family of Nethinim or Temple servants who returned with Zerubbabel from the Exile (Ezra 2:47; Neh 7:49). The name Cathua appears instead in 1 Esdras 5:30.

2. The name of one of the families of the "sons of Solomon's servants" (1 Esd 5:33), who returned with Zerubbabel from the Exile (Ezra 2:56; Neh 7:58). The "sons of Solomon's servants" were descendants of foreigners or prisoners captured in war who were subjected to forced labor (cf. Josh 9:23; 1 Kings 9:21).

F. W. BUSH

GIDEON **gĭd′ ĭ ən** (גדעון, LXX Γεδεών, *a cutting down* or *a hewer*). The son of Joash, the Abiezrite, from the tribe of Manasseh, and the fifth recorded judge of Israel (Judg 6-8). Also called JERUBBAAL (*let Baal strive, contend*; Judg 6:32; 7:1, et al.) and JERUBBESHETH (*let shame strive, contend*; 2 Sam 11:21).

1. Background. During the period of the Judges there was no predetermined or planned leadership such as under a monarchy where the son of the king would rule after the death of the king. God raised up individuals to meet special circumstances, who acted as rulers, judging Israel. The Israelites were unorganized and the tribes disunited. This left them open to oppression by neighboring tribes. "In those days there was no king in Israel; every man did what was right in his own eyes" (Judg 21:25). The Israelites repeatedly fell into sin and idolatry; after which God gave them over to their enemies. At the time of Gideon, the oppressors were the Midianites and the Amalekites who periodically plundered the land, destroying what they could not carry away. With their crops destroyed at each planting, the starving Israelites cried to the Lord. God sent a prophet to rebuke them for their disobedience. After seven years of suffering God delivered the Israelites by the hand of Gideon.

2. Call of Gideon. The angel of the Lord (Judg 6:11ff., simply the Lord) appeared to Gideon at his home in Ophra (not positively identified) while Gideon was threshing wheat covertly to hide it from the Midianites. When the stranger informed Gideon that he was to deliver Israel, he asked for proof to validate the message. At the angel's request, Gideon prepared food and presented it to the angel who caused the food to go up in flames, and the angel promptly vanished. It should be noted that the dynamic leadership of Gideon that followed was not the result of public demand, personal desires for leadership, or a high opinion of his own abilities, but only as a result of the knowledge that God had called him and was leading him. For this reason Gideon asked for and received proof of God's call both at this time and later. That night, following the Lord's instructions, Gideon and his servants pulled down the altar of Baal, erected an altar to the Lord, and offered a bull, using the wood of the Asherah that was by the altar of Baal. When the townspeople learned of this the following morning they wanted to put Gideon to death. But Gideon's father, Joash, refused to deliver Gideon to them, saying that if Baal was a god he could contend for himself and did not need their help. Thus, Gideon was given the name Jerubbaal, "let Baal contend."

3. The battle against Midian. The Midianites and the Amalekites came in from the E, crossed over the Jordan, and set up camp in the Valley of Jezreel by the hill of Moreh. The Spirit of the Lord came upon Gideon; he gathered the Abiezrites and sent messengers to the rest of the Manassites and also to the tribes of Asher, Zebulun, and Naphtali, asking them to join him in fighting the Midianites. Although Gideon had already acted on faith he again asked for a sign—an additional miracle to help him in the difficult job ahead and to give faith to others who might have witnessed the event. On one night he left a fleece of wool on the threshing floor, asking for dew on the fleece, but not on the ground. On the following morning he wrung a bowl of water from the fleece although the ground was dry. The next night he asked for the reverse, so he found the fleece dry and the ground wet with dew. Then Gideon and his army of 32,000 men set up camp beside the spring of Harod on Mount Gilboa.

The Lord made it clear that the coming victory was His and not of superior Israelite might. He thus requested Gideon to send the "fearful and trembling" back home. This conformed with the laws for military exemption (Deut 20:1-8). The majority, 22,000, returned home, leaving 10,000. Still too many, the Lord set up another test based on the method of drinking water. The text as it stands does not seem clear. According to some commentators, the majority got down on their knees, put their faces down to the water, and drank it directly; whereas 300, upright, used their hands to put the water to their mouths. The phrase "laps the water with his tongue, as a dog laps" (Judg 7:5) is made somehow equal with "lapped, putting their hands to their mouths" (7:6), both of these being opposed to those who kneel down. The comparison made between the dog and the "300" is the standing position. This may have indicated that the 300 were more alert and cautious, as their physical position left them ready for action.

An alternate view (*see* YADIN) is that the 300 fell prostrate and put their mouth to the water, lapping as a dog laps whereas the rest knelt "putting their hands to their mouths." The last phrase would have to be put at the end of the v. as a textual emendation. The virtue of the 300 in this instance would be

At the well of Ain Harod, known as Gideon's Fountain, at the foot of the mountains of Gilboa. ©*M.P.S.*

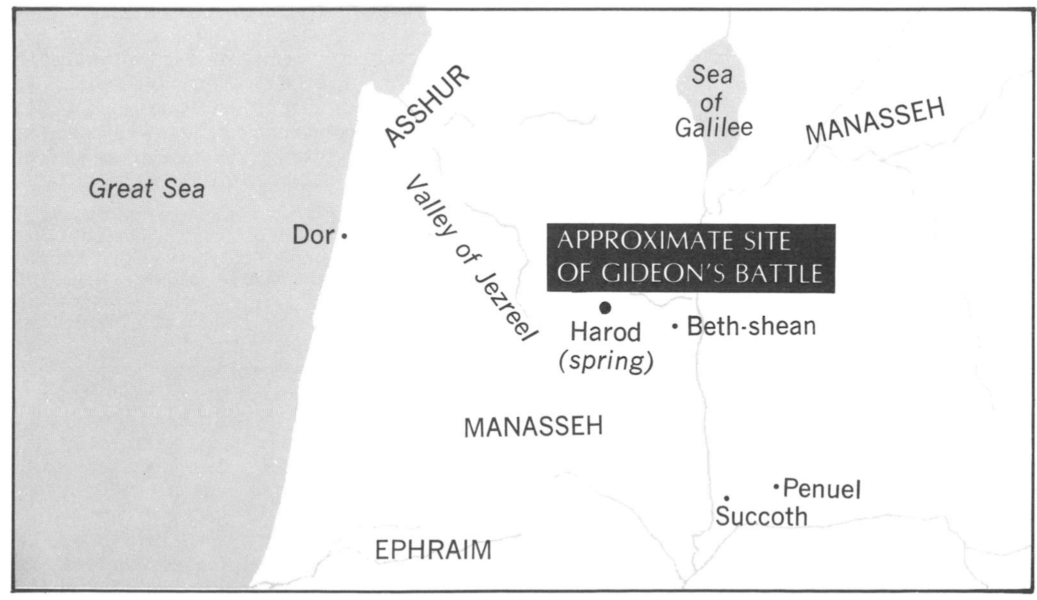

their willingness to suffer the discomfort of lying in the dirt, if it was the most efficient way of accomplishing a goal. The important part, however, is that only 300 remained. Gideon kept the 300 and sent the rest home.

Having left Gideon with a fighting force of only 300 men, the Lord saw fit to encourage him again. Leading him to the camp of Midian, the Lord caused Gideon to overhear a man relating his dream to a friend. His friend understood the dream to foretell the defeat of Midian at the hand of Gideon. This may have been an indication of insecurity among the Midianite forces. In any case, it gave Gideon the confidence to proceed with his plans.

That same night Gideon divided his men into three companies and gave them instructions for the attack. They surrounded the camp of Midian with torches hidden inside overturned jars in one hand, and trumpets in the other hand. At the beginning of the middle watch (about midnight) following the lead of Gideon, they blew the trumpets, smashed the jars, and shouted. The sudden light and noise frightened the Midianites and the Lord caused them to fight among themselves and to flee while Gideon and his men stood in their places around the camp. The places to which the Midianites fled (Judg 7:22) are not positively identified but seem to indicate that they went E, crossing the Jordan (and possibly S into the tribe of Ephraim). For an evaluation of the battle from a military standpoint, cf. *Bibliography*, the last three entries.

4. Clearing out of Midianite troops. God used just 300 men to defeat the Midianites, but the work of destroying the defeated enemy, now spread across the countryside, remained to be done. For this Gideon sent again to Manasseh, Asher, and Naphtali, and also to Ephraim for assistance to seal off the fords of the Jordan blocking their escape. The Ephraimites caught and killed the two princes of Midian —Oreb and Zeeb—and brought their heads to Gideon.

The men from Ephraim complained that they had not been asked to help with the initial battle. Gideon answered with tact and wisdom that Ephraim had slain the princes of Midian and that Gideon himself had done nothing as great as this. The soft answer turned away their wrath. This is in contrast to a similar situation faced by Jephthah, a later judge. The men of Ephraim asked Jephthah why he had fought the Ammonites without asking Ephraim for assistance (Judg 12:1-6). Jephthah answered them correctly and logically, but although the answer was a good one it did not prevent the conflict between the Ephraimites and Jephthah, whereas Gideon's diplomatic answer made peace with Ephraim and averted a civil war.

Gideon pursued Zebah and Zalmunna, the kings of Midian, eastward across the Jordan. On the way he asked for provisions for his 300 men from the towns of Succoth and Penuel. Both towns refused him, so after threatening them, he proceeded. Gideon caught Zebah and Zalmunna with their army off guard. (Only 15,000 men were left as 120,000 had already fallen.) The surprise attack again routed the Midianites. Zebah and Zalmunna tried to flee but were caught.

Returning to Succoth, Gideon took thorns and briers from the wilderness and used them to whip the men of Succoth. He also broke down the tower of Penuel and killed men there. When he learned that Zebah and Zalmunna had killed his brothers, Gideon killed them also.

5. Aftermath. From the golden earrings taken in the spoil, Gideon made an ephod (q.v.), which he put in his city, Ophra. Although Gideon was so devoted to the Lord that he refused to rule Israel, saying that the Lord should rule over them, the ephod became a "snare to Gideon and to his family," and all Israel as it became an object of worship. The land, however, had rest for forty years as a result of his leadership. Gideon had many wives, who bore him seventy sons. He died "in a good old age," and it was not until after his death that the Israelites again departed from God.

Gideon also had a son by a concubine, Abimelech (q.v.). After Gideon died, Abimelech slew his seventy brothers (except Jotham, the youngest) and set himself up as ruler (Judg 9).

6. Character and influence of Gideon. The writer of Hebrews includes Gideon as one of the heroes of the faith. He certainly learned to trust God for the impossible. He gave evidence of wisdom in the art of warfare and, also, wisdom along with patience and humility in dealing with the Ephraimites. In contrast, he took revenge against Succoth and Penuel. His error in making and worshiping the ephod may be attributed, at least in part, to the ignorance and low moral standards of that time.

Israel later remembered her deliverance by Gideon as one of national importance (Ps 83:11; Isa 9:4; 10:26). The name of Gideon has become popular in Christian circles and has been used to name groups such as Gideons International, a Bible distributing organization.

BIBLIOGRAPHY. J. M. Lang, *Gideon and the Judges* (1890); S. Tolkowsky, "Gideon's 300", JPOS, V (1925), 69-74; A. Malamat, "The War of Gideon and Midian: A Military Approach," PEQ (1953), 61-65; Y. Yadin, *The Art of Warfare in Biblical Lands* (1963), 256-260.

C. P. WEBER

GIDEONI gĭd' ĭ ō' nī (גדעוני) the father of Abidan, the leader of the tribe of Benjamin in the wilderness wanderings (Num 1:11; 2:22; 7:60, 65; 10:24). He is mentioned only as the patronym in his son's name.

GIDOM gī' dəm (גדעם, *their cutting off* [?]). A place mentioned in connection with the flight of the Benjaminites from the rest of

Israel after Gibeah's (q.v.) rape of the Levite's mistress (Judg 20:45). It is known only from this one reference.

GIER EAGLE jïr e′ gəl. Also spelled GEIR and GEIER. (רחם, *gier eagle* KJV; vulture, carrion vulture ASV, RSV; פרס, *gier eagle* ASV; *ossifrage* KJV, RSV). First used in 1615 for *vulture*, stemming from a Teutonic root still found in Ger. *Geier* (vulture). Now obsolete and found only in combination—Gyr Falcon, and Lammergeier, for Bearded Vulture. Found only in lists of unclean birds in some VSS (Lev 11:18). *See* OSSIFRAGE and VULTURE.

G. S. CANSDALE

GIEZI. Douay VS form of GEHAZI.

GIFT, the rendering of a number of Heb. and Gr. words in Scripture, was a feature of most personal encounters in the archaic-religious state. Although many of the nuances of the original meanings are lost, many of the terms can be differentiated by context. The KJV renders "gift" for twelve different Heb. words, many of which have less than four occurrences. The four most frequent are: 1. מנחה, "offering," "present," "offering gift" (Judg 6:18, KJV "present"); 2. מתן, and a similar term מתנה, "gift" (Num 18:7, et al.); the root of both of these terms is נתן, the common Heb. verb "to give"; 3. שחד, "present," "bribe" (KJV) "gift" (RSV) "bribe" (Exod 23:8, et al.); 4. תרומה, "contribution," usually applied to religious or votive gifts, "offering" (RSV) "offering" (KJV) "gift" (Prov 29:4), all other passages "offering." Gifts are presented not only to one's immediate family to mark a betrothal, marriage, birth or death, but also to superiors in political and religious hierarchy and to the palace and Temple. The ultimate gifts are those given to God as tokens of faith and dependence. However the OT insists upon the sincerity of the heart.

In the pastoral, Neolithic and Bronze Age societies of the OT gifts were almost always in kind (Gen 24:22, et al.), while in the period of the Second Commonwealth and the NT coinage is the basis of both exchange and giving. In the NT the KJV renders eight Gr. words by "gift." Of these occurrences only three basic roots are represented. The most frequently used is Gr. *δίδωμι*, an ancient Indo-European term with cognates in Hittite, Sanskrit and the Pre-Italic dialects of Italy. It means simply to "give" and two NT nouns are derived from it: 1. *δόμα* (Matt 7:11, et al.), and 2. *δόσις* (James 1:17). Their usage is nearly interchangeable and they are modified by the identical adjectives. The other verbal root is: *δωρέω*, which appears in the NT only in the Middle Voice, *δωρέομαι*, "present," "give" (Mark 15:45; 2 Pet 1:3 only.) Two nouns are derived from this root also, 1. *δῶρον*, "gift," "present" often used of offerings (Matt 2:11, et al.), 2. *δώρημα*, "gift" (James 1:17; Rom 5:16). Another term used in the NT is restricted entirely to the spiritual realm of God's blessings, *χάρισμα*. It is used of both physical and non-material favors. It is a term common in Hel. usage but defined in a new and specific way by the NT itself.

W. WHITE, JR.

GIFT OF HEALING. *See* SPIRITUAL GIFTS.

GIFT OF TONGUES. *See* SPIRITUAL GIFTS; TONGUES, GIFT OF.

GIHON (SPRING) gī′ hŏn (גיחון; LXX Γηων, *a bursting forth*). The more important of the two springs that supplied water to Jerusalem in OT times. It was Gihon that determined the original site of the city on the hill called Ophel, just W of the spring. Because it lay outside the wall of the fortified city, the pre-Israelite inhabitants cut a tunnel down through the rock of Ophel to provide protection for those drawing water when the city was under siege. It is generally thought that David's men gained access to the city through this tunnel (2 Sam 5:6-9). The fact that Gihon was chosen as the proper place to anoint Solomon as David's successor (1 Kings 1:33, 38, 45) may have been symbolic; just as David became master of the city at Gihon, so did Solomon. In any event, the selection of this site underscores its ceremonial as well as its strategic importance. It is hardly surprising that an aqueduct was later constructed to make the water more

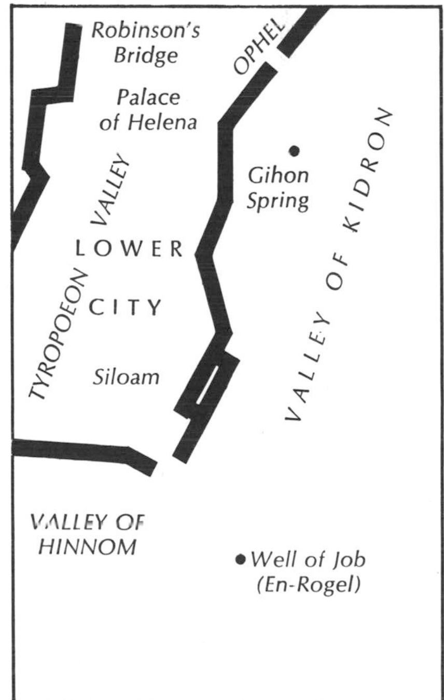

accessible (Isa 7:3). Some two and a half centuries after Solomon's accession, when Sennacherib attacked Judah (2 Chron 32), Hezekiah built a new water system, constructing the famous Siloam tunnel to provide a safer means of getting Gihon's water into the fortified area (2 Chron 32:30) and re-fortifying the wall in its vicinity (2 Chron 33:14). In postexilic times, the demand for water outgrew this supply, and the city constructed aqueducts to bring in water from farther away. Pontius Pilate either built or repaired one of these aqueducts, using Temple funds.

BIBLIOGRAPHY. G. E. Wright and F. V. Filson, *The Westminster Historical Atlas to the Bible*, 2nd ed. (1956), 105; K. M. Kenyon, *Jerusalem: Excavating 3000 Years of History* (1967), 15, 16, 31, 69-77.

G. G. SWAIM

GIHON (RIVER) **gī' hŏn** (גִּיחוֹן ; LXX Γαών, *a bursting forth*). One of the four "heads" into which the river of Eden divided after leaving the Garden (Gen 2:10-14). Suggested identifications of the Gihon include the rivers Araxes, the Nile, the Shatt el-Hai, the Karun, and even a Babylonian canal. All such identifications seem to overlook the fact that the Tigris and Euphrates, two of the other "heads," do not flow out of a common source; hence the account does not literally fit today's geography. (Cf. Ecclus 24:27.)

G. G. SWAIM

GILALAI **gĭ lā' lī** (גִּלֲלַי ; meaning uncertain). A priestly musician who participated in the dedication of the rebuilt wall of Jerusalem under Ezra (Neh 12:36). His name is omitted from the LXX account.

GILBOA, MOUNT **gĭl bō' ə** (גִּלְבֹּעַ; LXX Γελβουε; etymology unknown). A mountain or range of mountains, about eight m. long and from three to five m. wide, lying to the E of the Plain of Esdraelon, on the border between Samaria and Galilee. The highest peak, Sheikh Burqān, is only 1,696 ft, above sea level, but it falls off rather abruptly on the E to the Jordan, 2,000 ft. below. The western slope inclines more gradually to the Esdraelon, 300 ft. above sea level. On these western slopes occurred the last battle and the death of Saul and his three sons, Jonathan, Abinadab, and Malchishua (1 Sam 31; 2 Sam 1; 21:12). The Philistines prepared for war when Israel pressed into the plain and threatened to cut off Philistine access to the Way of the Sea (the major trade route from Egypt to Damascus). When they attacked, the Israelite warriors fled, and Saul was seriously wounded. Rather than fall into the hands of his lifelong enemies in this condition, Saul took his own life, one of the few suicides mentioned in the Bible.

The name Gilboa (which always has the definite article in Heb. except in 1 Chron 10) occurs in Scripture only in connection with the death of Saul; from before the time of the

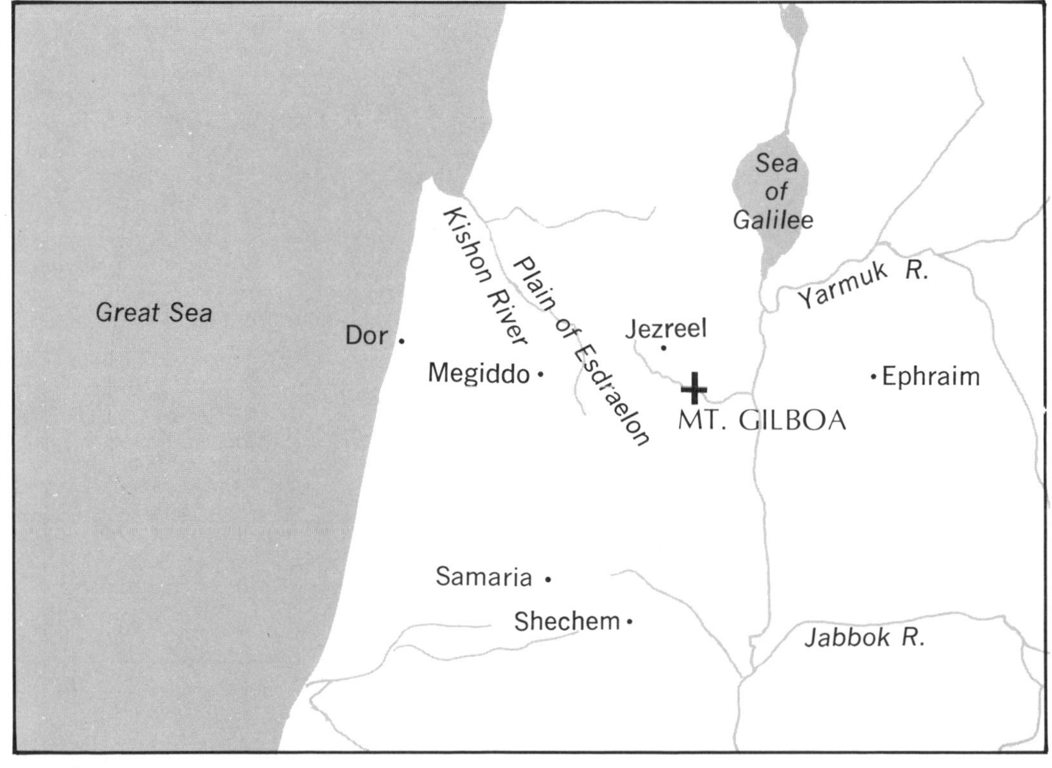

Israelite conquest, notorious battles were fought in this vicinity. It was at nearby Megiddo that Thutmose III fought the Canaanites, nearly 850 years before Neco's forces killed Josiah on their way to do battle against the Assyrians (2 Kings 23:29). Deborah's battle against Sisera was greatly aided by the Brook Kishon, which takes its rise on Gilboa (Judg 5:21). It was not far from here that Gideon routed the Midianites (6:33).

Jezreel (q.v.), summer capital of the house of Omri (1 Kings 18:45; 2 Kings 9:15), was situated on a western spur of Gilboa, about 200 ft. above the plain, commanding both the Way of the Sea (the major trade route from Egypt to Damascus) and the highway from the Mediterranean to the Jordan. Here Jehu, subverted by Elisha, murdered both Joram of Israel and his mother Jezebel, and from here he pursued and murdered Ahaziah of Judah (2 Kings 9; cf. Hos 1:4).

BIBLIOGRAPHY. G. A. Smith, *The Historical Geography of the Holy Land,* 25th ed. (1931); Y. Aharoni, *The Land of the Bible: A Historical Geography* (1962; Eng. tr. by A. F. Rainey, 1967).

G. G. SWAIM

GILEAD gĭl' ĭ əd (גִּלְעָד, meaning uncertain; Apoc., GALAAD).

1. A mountainous region E of the Jordan. Often mentioned in the OT, in its broadest sense it can be applied to all of Israelite Trans-Jordan (cf. Josh 22:9ff. where it is contrasted to the Land of Canaan, i.e., Cisjordan). The term was applied to the entire central section of Israelite Trans-Jordan (2 Kings 10:33). The name is also applied to a tribe known as Gileadites, parallel to Reuben and Dan and equivalent to Gad (Judg 5:17). There was also a town called Gilead (10:17), which is prob. modern Khirbet Jel'ad.

a. *Location.* Gilead was located in the foothills N of the Plain of Mishor. It was bounded on the W by the Jordan River, extended near the Yarmuk on the N, to the S-N branches of the Jabbok and the Arabian desert to the E, and to the Arnon on the S. Its cities included Jabesh-gilead, Mahanaim, Mizpah, Ramoth-gilead, and Succoth. In NT times, as a part of the kingdom of Herod the Great and his son Herod Antipas, it was known as Perea. The name is still preserved today in Jebel Jel'ad, Khirbet Jel'ad, and 'Ain Jel'ad S of the Nahr ez-Zerqā (Jabbok). The Wādi Yābis preserves the name of Jabesh in Gilead. The name Ramoth of Gilead is preserved in Tell Ramith, SW of Der'a.

Rising from the Jordan Valley on the W, 700 ft. below sea level, Gilead rises to heights of more than 3,300 ft. It is a well-watered hill country, thickly wooded (as Absalom found at the cost of his life), and is still well forested with Mediterranean pine and evergreen oak. It is also known for its grapes, olives, fruit trees, and pasture lands. It was also proverbial for the "balm of Gilead" (Jer 8:22; 46:11), an ointment with medicinal value.

b. *History.* The N part of Gilead was settled as early as the 23rd cent. B.C. It was occupied by the Amorites and Moabites at the time of the Israelite entrance under Moses. Sihon, the king, would not allow the Israelites to pass through his land, which resulted in warfare that ended with the land in the possession of the Israelites (Num 21). The tribes of Reuben, Gad, and the half-tribe of Manasseh did not want to cross over the Jordan with the other tribes, as the Trans-Jordan territory appealed to them. Moses agreed to give them the land after exacting a promise that they would first help the other tribes subdue the land W of the Jordan, a promise they fulfilled (Josh 22). The sons of Machir of the tribe of Manasseh were given Gilead and settled there (Num 32:39). Moses was allowed to see the land of Gilead as far as Dan from the top of Mount Nebo just before his death (Deut 34:1). Gilead seems to have been a mixture of Gadite and Josephite elements (Num 32:39f.; Josh 13:24-31). Ramoth-gilead was early designated as one of the cities of refuge (Josh 20:8).

During the period of the early settlement, the tribes E of the Jordan enjoyed a measure of security and did not even come to help their kinsmen W of the Jordan in their struggle with Sisera (Judg 5:17). During the time of the Judges, the Ammonites oppressed the people of Israel in Gilead as part of their attempt to expand their land. The people chose Jephthah, an outcast Gileadite and mighty warrior, as their leader to deliver them. He drove out the Ammonites and secured the land for the Israelites (Judg 11). However, a feud arose between the Ephraimites and the Gileadites because they were not called to participate in the struggle against the Ammonites. The Ephraimites were routed, and when they tried to flee back across the river, they found that the Gileadites had taken possession of all the fords. Anyone who attempted to cross was tested to see if he was an Ephraimite by asking him to say Shibboleth. If he said Sibboleth, they seized him and slew him (Judg 12).

The Ammonites continued to be a threat to the Gileadites in subsequent history. Saul's first great military victory after becoming king was his rescue of the city of Jabesh-gilead, which was being threatened by Nahash, king of the Ammonites (1 Sam 11). After Saul's defeat and death at the hands of the Philistines, Abner established Saul's son Ish-bosheth as king over Gilead (2 Sam 2:8, 9). It was to Mahanaim in Gilead that David fled when Absalom rebelled against him (17:24), and it was in Gilead where the decisive battle was fought that resulted in the death of Absalom and the return of the kingdom to David (ch. 18). Gilead was included in the census made by David (2 Sam 24:6).

Forestlands in Central Gilead. ©*Lev*.

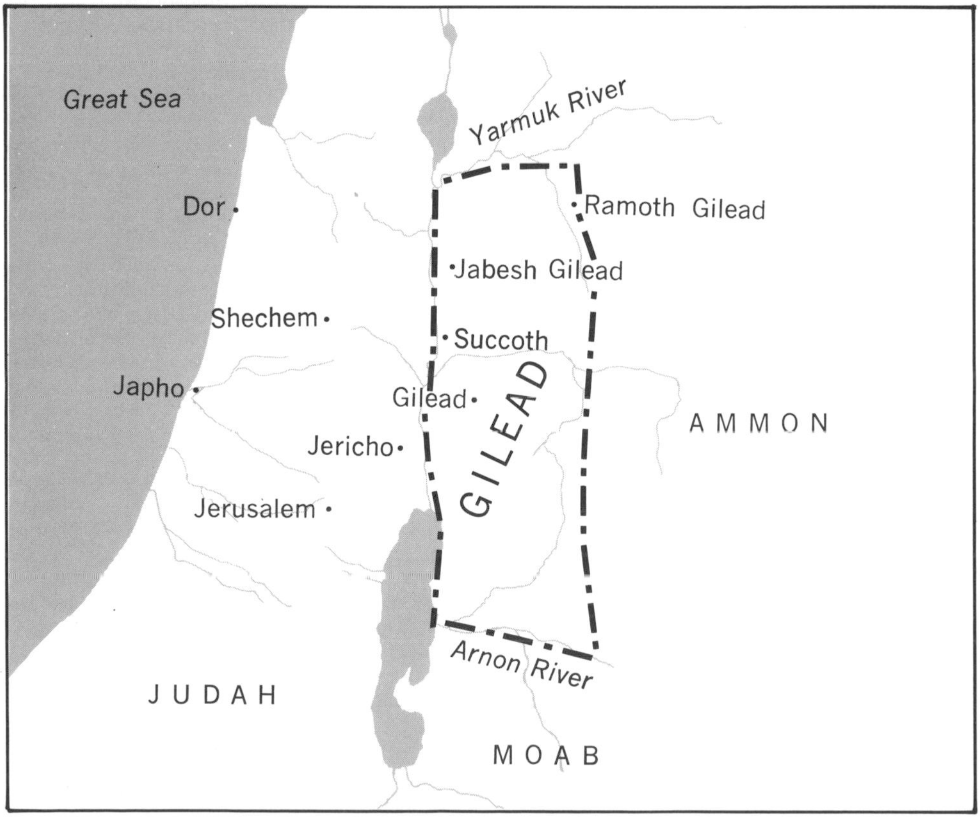

Great Sea
Yarmuk River
Dor
Ramoth Gilead
Jabesh Gilead
Shechem
Succoth
Japho
Gilead
GILEAD
AMMON
Jericho
Jerusalem
Arnon River
JUDAH
MOAB

Elijah was from Gilead (1 Kings 17:1). During the ninth and eighth centuries, Damascus (Syria) was a constant threat to the Israelites. Amos condemned Syria for her extreme cruelty, particularly toward Gilead (Amos 1:3-5). He condemned the cruelty of the Ammonites toward innocent women of Gilead in time of war (Amos 1:13). Hosea said Gilead was a city of evildoers (Hos 6:8). Israel and Judah entered into an alliance to wrest Ramoth-gilead from the king of Syria (1 Kings 22:1-4), resulting in the death of Ahab on the battlefield. Jehu made some kind of protective alliance with Shalmaneser III (c. 837 B.C.), but it did not keep Hazael from seizing part of Israel, including Gilead (2 Kings 10:33). As a result of a conspiracy by Rezin of Syria and Pekah of Israel, Tiglath-pileser III invaded the two countries in his campaign of 734-732, utterly destroying the coalition. He occupied parts of Israel, dividing the annexed territory into three provinces, named in the Assyrian lists according to their respective capitals: Megiddo (Magiddu), Dor (Du'ru), and Gilead (Gal'aza). He carried part of the population captive to Assyria (2 Kings 15:29).

In an attempt to restore the empire of David, Josiah seized the territory of the former kingdom of Israel that had been Gilead. When Babylon overran the land, no changes were made in the provincial organization established by the Assyrians. Ezekiel 47 and 48 mention the provinces of Hamath, Damascus, Hauran, and Gilead, already known from the Assyrian period. Jeremiah looked to the time of restoration of Gilead to Israel (Jer 50:19), and Obadiah foresaw its restoration to Benjamin (Obad 19). In the postexilic period Tobiah was the Persian appointed governor of the territory of Ammon which had been joined to the province of Gilead. In 163 B.C., Judas Maccabeus with his younger brother Jonathan campaigned in Gilead (Galaad) with some success, but his power was not sufficient to hold the area permanently, so he took the Israelite population to Judea that wanted to remain members of the Jerusalem religious community (1 Macc 5:9-54). Gilead in NT times was part of Perea.

2. The son of Machir and grandson of Manasseh. Eponym of the tribe or territory known as Gilead (Num 26:29, 30; 27:1; 32:40; 36:1; Josh 17:1; Judg 5:17; 1 Chron 2:21; 7:14).

3. Father of Jephthah (Judg 11:1).

4. A Gadite tribe (1 Chron 5:14).

BIBLIOGRAPHY. M. Noth, *The History of Israel* (1960), 158, 274, 371; J. Gray, *Archaeology and the Old Testament World* (1962), 16; M. Noth, *The Old Testament World* (1966), 62; Y. Aharoni, *The Land of the Bible* (1967), 331, 354, 360.

F. B. HUEY, JR.

GILEAD, BALM OF gĭl' ĭ əd (צרי גלעד). An aromatic gum of supposed medicinal value (Jer 8:22; 46:11; 51:8). Though it is not clear whether it was produced in Gilead (q.v.), it was traded both S into Egypt (Gen 37:25; 43:11) and N into Tyre (Ezek 27:17), and the texts imply that the market was controlled by the people of Pal. For a botanical discussion see HDB I, pp. 235f. *See* BALM.

G. G. SWAIM

GILGAL gĭl' găl (הגלגל, [only Joshua 5:9 and 12:23 omit the article], LXX Γάλγαλα, meaning *the circle*). The name of several towns of uncertain location, the most important was Joshua's encampment near the Jordan which later became a religious center.

1. The Gilgals of the Bible. To fit all the references to Gilgal in the Bible into one locale is impossible; from two to six separate cities bearing the same name have been suggested. The fact that Gilgal is a common and easily explained name makes a multiplicity of the same name more likely. The word prob. has reference to a circle of stones, although no etymology is given. There is a play on the word whose root is the same as the verb "roll" (Josh 5:9). Usually the name is preceded by a definite article, as were many names that were evidently made from common nouns.

a. The Gilgal near Jericho. This is the Gilgal most frequently mentioned. After the Israelites under Joshua crossed the Jordan, they camped at Gilgal (Josh 4:19). There they built a monument of twelve stones, but the Scripture does not indicate whether or not they were arranged in a circle. Also, at Gilgal, the rite of circumcision was performed (5:8) and the Passover celebrated (5:10). From this site, the Israelites set out to march around Jericho for seven days. Apparently, Gilgal was their base camp as they made attacks on the hill country, for Joshua was found at Gilgal by the Gibeonites after Ai was destroyed and after he had built an altar on Mt. Ebal (8:30; 9:6). From Gilgal, the Israelites left to defend Gibeon and returned to Gilgal victorious (10:15, 43). This is prob. the same Gilgal referred to in Judges 2:1 and 3:19. After Joshua had completed most of the conquest (Josh 18:1), the central sanctuary, including the Ark of the covenant, was transferred to Shiloh. Gilgal must have continued as a prominent city, however, because it was one of three cities on Samuel's circuit (1 Sam 7:16). Also, there Saul was made king (11:14, 15). Saul used Gilgal as a base of operations against the Amalekites, and at Gilgal he sought to placate Samuel after he had disobeyed by salvaging some cattle for booty and permitting the enemy king to live. Samuel uttered the famous maxim, "To obey is better than sacrifice . . ." (15:22) and subsequently "hewed Agag in pieces before the LORD" (v. 33).

The Gilgal near Jericho is generally accepted as the place against which the prophets

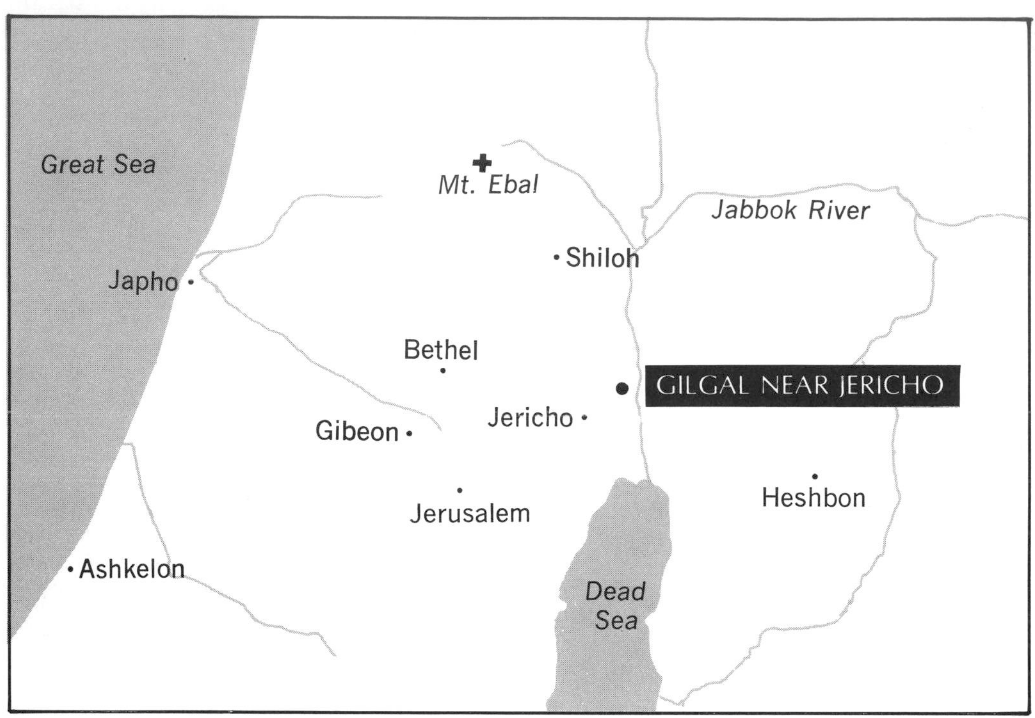

Hosea and Amos preached. Hosea 9:15 states, "Every evil of theirs is in Gilgal; there I began to hate them." Later Hosea indicated that it was a place of sacrifice (Hos 12:11). Both Hosea and Amos connect Gilgal closely with Bethel, assuming that "Beth-aven" (4:15) is a sarcastic alteration of the real name (Amos 4:4; 5:5). On the other hand, because of Gilgal's close connection with Bethel, many scholars think that the Gilgal mentioned in Hosea and Amos is different from the Gilgal near Jericho. Perhaps it should be connected with the one of 2 Kings 2:1 (*see below* under par. "b."), which most consider a separate town bearing the same name.

b. *The Gilgal of Elijah and Elisha.* This town seems more distinct from the one near the Jordan. The narrative of 2 Kings 2:1-4 indicates the route of the two prophets as "from Gilgal" (v. 1) "down to Bethel" (v. 2), and "to Jericho" (v. 4). Although the matter of "down to Bethel" can be explained as being the chronicler's perspective, such a route would indicate that Bethel was between Gilgal and Jericho, which would exclude the Gilgal near the Jordan. Since this reference connects Gilgal so closely with Bethel, perhaps the modern town of Jiljiliah, seven m. N of Bethel, is the site. At this Gilgal, Elisha threw herbs in the pot of death and made the stew harmless. There are no immediate contextual hints concerning the location of this town.

c. *The Gilgal in Galilee.* "The king of Goiim in Galilee" is on a list of conquered monarchs (Josh 12:23). This reflects the LXX (Γεὶ τῆς Γαλιλαίας). The KJV trs. the MT more accurately, "the king of the nations of Gilgal." No certain identification of this Gilgal is known, but because the other places before and after it in the list are in the N, most historians suggest that it is located between the Mediterranean and Galilee, N of Samaria.

d. *On the boundary of Judah.* Among the features of the boundaries of Judah (Josh 15) is a Gilgal "which is opposite the ascent of Adummim, which is on the south side of the valley" (v. 7). Because of the context, this cannot be either the Gilgal near Jericho or any of the others suggested above. In the determination of Benjamin's territory, which bordered on the N of Judah, is a Geliloth "which is opposite the ascent of Adummim" (Josh 18:17). The two major Gr. MSS support alternatives of this form (Josh 18:17). The names mean essentially the same thing, but Geliloth is a fem. pl. form.

e. *Near Mt. Ebal.* Another Gilgal is referred to in Deuteronomy 11:30. Reading the v. by itself presents no problem in associating it with the Gilgal by Jericho, but the preceding v. indicates that it is near Mts. Ebal and Gerizim.

2. Archeology and Gilgal. James Muilenburg has done extensive research on the location of Gilgal. His answer to the Gilgal by Jericho is the modern Khirbet el-Mefjir, located a little over one m. NE of Tell es-

Sultan, or OT Jericho. This site is not without problems or competitors. A major problem is that, until recently, there was no evidence that it was a very old site. Furthermore, the remains of the sumptuous Ummayyad palace of the caliph Hisham (A.D. 724-732) are there. The strongest alternative site for Gilgal is Khirbet en-Nitleh, three m. SE of Jericho. Many Byzantine ruins cover Khirbet en-Nitleh, and this has led many to assume it is Gilgal. Apart from the Bible references to Gilgal noted above, Josephus is the best and oldest witness. He locates Gilgal fifty stadia from the ford of the Jordan (accepted by nearly all as being at al-Maghtas) and ten stadia from Jericho (Jos. Antiq. V. vi. 4). If both Muilenburg and Josephus have the same Jericho and the same ford in mind, then Gilgal can only be Khirbet el-Mefjir, because en-Nitleh is too close to the river. Muilenburg found pottery of the Iron Age in a sounding of Khirbet el-Mefjir, which sets its occupation back at least to 1000 B.C. and dispels the major source of criticism.

The discussion so far deals just with Gilgal near Jericho. The one or more Gilgals of the Bible may be connected with the modern towns of Jiljiliah, seven m. N of Bethel (2 Kings 4:38); Jidjulah, four m. N of Antipatris (Josh 12:23); and Juleijil, two and one-half m. SE of Nablus (Deut 11:30).

BIBLIOGRAPHY. F. M. Abel, *Géographie de la Palestine*, II, (1938), 337ff.; J. Muilenburg, "The Site of Ancient Gilgal," BASOR, 145 (Dec. 1955) 11-27.

R. L. ALDEN

GILGAMESH **gĭl gă' mĕsh;** the name of a legendary king of the Sumer. city of Erech, who was undoubtedly a historical figure who later became in epic and legend the hero par excellence. He must have lived in southern Mesopotamia about the end of the 4th or beginning of the 3rd millennium B.C. It was as the great hero and personification of the human condition in the cuneiform lit. of later ages that he became famous. In the Sumer. lit. he figures as the central character in a great many poetic myths: *Gilgamesh and Agga of Kish, Gilgamesh and the Bull of Heaven, Gilgamesh and the Land of the Living, Gilgamesh, Enkidu, and the Nether World* and others. The portrayal of the character of Gilgamesh ascribes to him not only positive heroic virtues, strength, loyalty, etc. but also negative, debased aspects, e.g. trickery, tyranny and the like. This literary tradition passed to the Sem. Akkadians and their Babylonian successors and he is mentioned frequently in Akkad. lit. The greatest cycle of stories woven around him is the *Epic of Gilgamesh* in twelve tablets. The contents of the twelve tablets are as follows: Tablet I: Gilgamesh has ruled his city of Uruk tyrannically and so the gods prepare a counter protagonist, a wild man, Enkidu. Gilgamesh is warned that Enkidu can be foiled by a prostitute. Tablet II: Enkidu is seduced and becomes like other men; he wrestles with Gilgamesh and the two become fast friends. Tablet III: Enkidu and Gilgamesh go to battle the monster *Huwawa,* make preparations for the combat and set forth. Tablet IV, Tablet V: the combat. Tablet VI: Ishtar attempts to entice Gilgamesh into an affair and has the Bull of Heaven fashioned to punish him when he spurns her. Gilgamesh and Enkidu kill the Bull. Tablet VII: As a punishment for impiety the gods kill Enkidu by means of a pestilence. Tablet VIII: Gilgamesh's lament for Enkidu. Tablet IX: Gilgamesh beside himself with grief wanders over the earth seeking immortality. Tablet X: Gilgamesh continues his wanderings and carries on dialogues with various mythological characters about the nature of mortality. He finally comes to the magical land of Utnapishtim, the Sumer. who was destined by the gods to survive the deluge. Tablet XI: The account of the Flood as told in high style epic v. by Utnapishtim. Tablet XII: It has been found to be a direct tr. from an Old Sumer. text and laments for the mortality of Gilgamesh. Although the whole of the poem is of great interest to Biblical students, the Tablet XI with its detailed description of the Flood has been studied for many years. It is a brilliant and gripping tale and is strangely, but not precisely, similar to the account in Genesis. In the 19th cent. some Ger. scholars of the pan-Babylonian school saw this cycle and the character of Gilgamesh as a possible type of Christ and the messianic

A portion of the Gilgamesh Epic. ©*B.M.*

office. This has been totally rejected by all but a few authorities. A magnificent relief in the Louvre Museum from the palace of Sargon II at Khorsabad is thought to show a gigantic figure of Gilgamesh strangling a lion.

BIBLIOGRAPHY. R. C. Thompson, *The Epic of Gilgamesh* (1930); A. Schott, *Das Gilgamesch-Epos* (1934); A. Heidel, *The Gilgamesh Epic and Old Testament Parallels* (1946); *Gilgameš et sa légende*, études recueillies par P. Garelli (1960); S. N. Kramer, *The Sumerians* (1963), 45-49, 130, 131, 134ff., 185-205, 255ff.

W. WHITE, JR.

GILOH gī' lō (גִּלֹה ; *rejoicing*). A city in the mountains of southern Judah (Josh 15:51). It was the home of David's counselor, Ahithophel (2 Sam 15:12; 23:34 RSV GILO). It is generally identified with modern Khirbet Jala, a few m. NNW of Hebron. On the derivation of the name, *see* S. R. Driver, *Notes on the Hebrew Text of the Books of Samuel,* 2nd ed. (1913), 312.

G. G. SWAIM

GILONITE. *See* GILOH.

GIMEL gĭm' əl. The third letter of the Heb. alphabet (ג), pronounced *g* as in *go*. It corresponds to gamma in Gr. It heads the third section of the acrostic Psalm 119, since all the vv. of this section begin with this letter.

GIMZO gĭm' zō (גִּמְזוֹ, *sycamore*). One of several cities wrested from Ahaz by the Philistines (2 Chron 28:18). These losses, combined with an Edomite invasion, caused Ahaz to appeal to Tiglath-pileser of Assyria for help (28:16). Not mentioned elsewhere in Scripture, it is modern Jimzu, a few m. N of Gezer.

GIN jĭn (פַּח, *trap, snare*; מוֹקֵשׁ, *trap, lure, snare*). An old tr. of either of two Heb. words, "gin" in the meaning of trap or snare is not used in the RSV or NEB. Properly, פַּח refers to the trap, מוֹקֵשׁ to the lure that draws the victim to the trap (*see* S. R. Driver on Amos 3:5; *Cambridge Bible for Schools and Colleges*, vol. 25, 2nd ed. [1915], 161). The meaning of מוֹקֵשׁ also becomes extended from the bait to the snare (Ps 140:5). "Gin" occurs in KJV, Job 18:9; Psalm 140:5; 141:9; Isaiah 8:14; Amos 3:5.

G. G. SWAIM

GINATH gī' năth (גִּינַת, meaning uncertain). The father of Tibni who contended with Omri for the throne of Israel when Zimri committed suicide after murdering Elah, son of Baasha (1 Kings 16:21f.).

GINNETHO, GINNETHOI, GINNETHON gĭn' ə thō, gĭn' ə thoi, gĭn' ə thŏn (גִּנְּתוֹי, גִּנְּתוֹן, meaning uncertain, perhaps *gardener*; LXX Γαναθων). The two forms are identical in Heb. except for the length of the last letter; Ginnethon is attested in Ugaritic. The Biblical Ginnethon was a priest and founder of an important family in the days of Zerubbabel and of the chief priests Jeshua (Neh 12:4, 7) and Joiakim (12:16). He was one of the signers of the solemn covenant detailed in Nehemiah 9 and 10 (10:6).

G. G. SWAIM

GIRDLE (אֵזוֹר, *waistcloth*; אַבְנֵט, *girdle, sash*; חֲגוֹר, *belt*; חֲגוֹרָה, *belt, loin-covering*; חֵשֶׁב, *sash, band*—part of the Ephod; ζωνή, *belt, loincloth*). The girdle was that article of clothing that bound up the undergarment or tunic. It was made of leather (2 Kings 1:8; Matt 3:4) or cloth (Lev 16:4; Jer 13:1) or even (fig.) gold (Dan 10:5; Rev 1:13). The sash of the high priest was highly decorated with embroidery (Exod 28:39; 39:29). The primary function of the girdle was to hold the tunic out of the way so that it would not impede movement (Luke 12:35, 37; 17:8). This use is referred to metaphorically (Isa 11:5; Eph 6:14; and 1 Pet 1:13). As a belt, it held both the sword (Judg 3:16; 1 Sam 25:13; 2 Sam 20:8) and the purse (Matt 10:9). *See* BELT.

G. G. SWAIM

GIRGASHITE gûr' gə shīt (גִּרְגָּשִׁי ; LXX Γεργεσαῖον). A Canaanite tribe appearing often in lists of peoples dispossessed by the Israelites (Gen 10:16; 15:21; Deut 7:1; Josh 3:10; 24:11; 1 Chron 1:14; Neh 9:8). No indication is given of the tribe's locality. The city name Karkisha, known from cuneiform Hitt. texts, has been suggested as the same name. One scholar has proposed that גִּרְגָּשִׁי be understood as "client (Heb. גֵּר) of (the god) Gesh," a Sumer. god of light introduced to Pal. c. 2000 B.C. More likely related is the personal (and tribal?, cf. *bn grgš*) name *grgš*, which appears in Ugaritic texts from the 13th cent. B.C.

BIBLIOGRAPHY. B. Maisler, ZAW, I (1932), 86, 87; W. F. Albright, JPOS, xv (1935), 189; C. H. Gordon, *Ugaritic Textbook* (1965), 381, no. 619.

H. A. HOFFNER, JR.

GIRL (יַלְדָּה, tr. "girl" [Joel 3:3]; both boys and girls [Zech 8:5]). In NT, Gr. diminutives κοράσιον, from κόρη, "girl," and παιδίσκη from παῖς, as fem., "girl," are sometimes tr. "girl" in RSV, NEB; "slave girl" in Acts 16:16.

GIRZITES gûr zīts, a Canaanite tribe of the period of the conquest under Joshua, mentioned only in 1 Samuel 27:8. The text has as *Kethibh*: Heb. גִּרְזִי, "Ge/irzites" while the Qere yields: Heb. גִּזְרִי, "Gezrites," "inhabitants of Gezer." The LXX reads, Γεζραῖος which supports the Qere reading and which, in turn, would be the natural gentilic formed from the common Sem. root, Gezer, as in the Amarna Letters, *Gazri*. There is little doubt this name refers to ancient Gezer, although the common critical objection that Gezer was too far N for it to be involved in this account is not without some merit. The additional critical proposal that the term Girzite is a mere scribal dittograph from Geshurite (q.v.) is untenable since the corrected form Gezrite or Gezerite is quite proper. There is also the possibility that the Kethibh reading of "Ge/irzites may refer not to Biblical Gezer but to Mt. Gerizim, which would fit better the historical and geographical situation in 1 Samuel 27:8."

W. WHITE, JR.

GISHPA, GISPA. *See* HASUPHA.

GITTAH-HEPHER. KJV form of GATH-HEPHER in Joshua 19:13.

GITTAIM gĭt′ ĭ əm (Heb. גִּתַּיִם), a refuge near Beeroth in Benjamin mentioned in both 2 Samuel 4:3, as the city to which two captains under Saul's son fled, and in Nehemiah 11:33 as the location of one of the resettled groups of Israelites after the return. The name appears to be a dual, prob. derived from Heb. גַּת, "a winepress." Apparently the second place was NW of Jerusalem and not distant from Hazor, the modern Khurbet-Hazzur with which it is mentioned. Since such a name would be common enough in the hill country of northern Pal., there may be two separate locations involved.

W. WHITE, JR.

GITTITES. *See* GATH.

GITTITH gĭt′ ĭth (Heb. גִּתִּית), a feminine noun used exclusively in the titles of three Pss, 8, 81 and 84. Three meanings are possible. It describes a musical instrument made or used in the Philistine city of Gath (Josh 11:22); the Targ. suggests that it was a type of melody from Gath; or it may also refer to the Heb. word, גַּת, a "wine press" (Neh 13:15), and thus mean a song sung at the grape harvest.

W. WHITE, JR.

GIZONITE gī′ zə nīt (Heb. גִּזוֹנִי), appears only in a list of David's mighty warriors (1 Chron 11:34), a masculine gentilic derived from an ancient place-name. Traditionally understood as a patronymic, but more likely of Old Canaanite origin. Location presently unknown; however, the man described by the term Gizonite is stated in 2 Samuel 23:32 to have been, in fact, the son of Jashen which makes the geographical ascription of Gizon more certain.

W. WHITE, JR.

GIZRITES. Alternate form of GIRZITES.

GLASS (Gr. ὑαλίνη) a generally transparent or translucent, lustrous, hard and brittle substance which has passed from a fluid condition, at high temperature, to a solid condition with sufficient rapidity to prevent the formation of visible crystals. Glass is formed in nature in three main ways. Rarely a silica glass is formed in small amounts when lightning strikes sand. The concentrated heat fuses the sand. The melt immediately solidifies forming a fragile tube of silica glass sometimes several ft. long. Such tubes are called fulgarites and are generally found in desert environments. Rarely, also, natural glass is formed as the result of localized melting of rock in a large fault zone, the glass generally being black and referred to as pseudotachylite. The most common natural occurrence of glass is as obsidian, a glassy volcanic rock of acidic composition used by early man for making small implements. Early sources of obsidian for countries of the Middle E were the Aegean region and Ethiopia. Later obsidian was obtained from Armenia and possibly from Lipari and Pentellera.

Manufactured glass consists primarily of a combination of silicic acid and alkali (sodium or potassium). Probably it originated somewhere in the eastern Mediterranean lands, possibly in Egypt, with the Egyptians making small glass-covered objects from about 4000 B.C. The first glass vessels appear to have been made c. 1500 B.C. In Egypt and in other coastlands, like Syria, soda glass was produced. This contains sodium and calcium silicates and is made by fusing white pure sand (silicon dioxide) free from iron compounds, soda-ash (sodium carbonate) and limestone (calcium carbonate) or lime (calcium oxide) in fireclay pots or tanks at 1375°C or above. The soda-ash was obtained from seaweed ash. Bohemian or potash glass contains potassium instead of sodium and was developed in well-wooded countries, particularly Germany, the potassium being derived from charcoal, particularly beech charcoal.

An oven used to manufacture glass at Tyre. ©*Har.*

The ingredients of glass are rarely in a pure state, the sand generally containing some iron impurities. The green color they cause, due to ferrous silicate, may be neutralized by adding pyrolusite (manganese dioxide) (Gr. *pyr* "fire," and *luo* "I wash"). The resultant glass may be clear and transparent (Rev 21:18) and look like still water (Rev 15:2). However, if there are numerous minute air bubbles left in the glass, it is translucent (Rev 21:21 NEB) and has the appearance of ice (Rev 4:6 NEB).

In modern times a mirror (cf. 2 Cor 3:18; James 1:23 NEB) is a sheet of polished glass silvered at the back. However, in ancient times it was a polished sheet of metal, called a *speculum* (cf. 1 Cor 13:12).

BIBLIOGRAPHY. J. R. Partington. *A Textbook of Inorganic Chemistry*, 6th ed. (1950), 760, 761; J. McNab, "Glassware," *Collier's Encyclopedia*, 11 (1964), 143-152.

D. R. BOWES

GLASS (MIRROR). *See* MIRROR.

GLASS, SEA OF (θάλασσα ὑαλίνη). In a description of heaven (Rev 4:6), before the throne of God is what seemed like a sea of glass, clear as crystal. Around it were gathered the beings who participated in worship before the Lamb opened the sealed book (ch. 5). Later, the sea appeared to be mingled with fire (Rev 15:2); appropriate to the judgments that were about to be poured out on the earth. Around the sea, the victorious saints sang the song of Moses and the Lamb, connecting this episode with the celebration of Israel's victory over Egypt beside the Red Sea (Exod 15). The crystal sea fitly symbolizes the purity of God; the mingled fire speaks of His holiness inflamed by just wrath.

E. RUSSELL

GLAZING, the RSV rendering of the Heb. כסף סיגים (KJV) "silver dross." It is thought that the term *s p / b s q* which occurs in the Ugaritic *Tale of Aght* II, vi: 36, means "white glaze" and this meaning has been applied in Proverbs 26:23, the only occurrence in the Bible. The Heb. phrase prob. refers not to Silver (Ag) but to a shiny metalic oxide of Lead (Pb), PbO which has been used for millennia as a pigment, litharge and as a glaze on pottery.

W. WHITE, JR.

GLEANING, GLEAN glĕn' ĭng, glĕn. 1. Heb. לקט, *pick* or *gather up, glean,* is used of the gathering of grain by the poor, following the reapers, as provided for in the Mosaic law (Lev 19:9; 23:22) and beautifully exemplified in Ruth 2, where the word occurs repeatedly. Boaz' generosity was rewarded with romance.

2. Heb. עלל, *do a thing a second time, glean,* used of a similar practice with grapes or olives, for which the law is stated (Lev 19:10; Deut 24:21). Concerning grapes (Judg 8:2; Jer 6:9; 49:9; Mic 7:1); concerning olives (Isa 17:6); concerning both grapes and olives (Isa 24:13). In Judges 20:45 KJV, ASV, used of killing men fleeing from a battle; RSV "cut down."

E. RUSSELL

GLEDE glēd. The Heb. ראה, in Deuteronomy 14:13 is prob. a textual error for דאה, a "bird of prey," possibly the kite (Lev 11:14), from a root meaning "fly swiftly," "dart through the air." Probably some kind of hawk, an unclean bird whose use for food was forbidden. The Heb. letters ר and ד were easily confused in copying MSS.

E. RUSSELL

GLORY

1. Terminology
   a. Old Testament
   b. New Testament
2. The glory of God
3. The glory of God in creation and in man
4. The glory of Christ
5. Eschatological glory

1. Terminology. a. *Old Testament.* Several words such as the Heb. אדרת, הדר, הוד, טהר, תפארה; and the Aram. יקרא, have been tr. "glory." In fact, twenty-five different Heb. words are tr. δόξα in the LXX. However, the most frequently used word is כבוד. It means "difficult," "weight," "heaviness," "worthiness," "reputation," or "honor." It can be used of men to indicate that a person is a man of weight or substance; he has wealth, which is his כבוד. Hence, when Joseph refers to his wealth and position in Egypt, he says, "You must tell my father of all my splendor (כבוד) in Egypt" (Gen 45:13; cf. 31:1). Joseph was a man of wealth and position and was held in high esteem in Egypt, with servants and clothes reflecting that position. Thus he could speak in this way. Haman also recounted all the splendor (כבוד) of his riches (Esth 5:11; cf. Ps 49:16f.; Isa 16:14; 17:4; 61:6; 66:11). The Temple was a splendid building and was described as a place of "fame and glory" (1 Chron 22:5; cf. Isa 60:7). The magnificent garments of Aaron were "for glory and for beauty" (Exod 28:2), and the gorgeously apparelled king's daughter is "all glorious" (Ps 45:13 ASV; cf. RSVmg.). A crown (used metaphorically) is a glory (Job 19:9). Michal, Saul's daughter, used the equivalent verb in the sense of reputation, when she sarcastically said to David, "How the king of Israel honored himself today!" (2 Sam 6:20). She felt he had behaved in an undignified manner (cf. Job 29:20; Ps 4:2; Prov 21:21; Eccl 10:1).

When used of a kingdom, כבוד can refer to armies or peoples. Isaiah 8:7, "The king of Assyria and all his glory," illustrates this usage, as does Proverbs 14:28: "In a multitude of people is the glory of a king" (cf. Ps 78:61; Isa 17:3; 21:16). The amazement of the Queen of Sheba at the splendor and dignity of Solomon's court (1 Kings 10:5) illustrates what is involved with reference to nations. It is used with reference to nature in the phrase "the glory of Lebanon" (Isa 60:13; cf. Isa 35:2).

In many instances the word signifies brightness. This is esp. the case in Ezekiel. The vision of the glory of God that Ezekiel saw was characterized by brightness (Ezek 1:4, 14, 28; 11:22f.). Consider also Exodus 24:17, where the appearance of the God of Israel was like a devouring fire. He was gloriously majestic. All these meanings, "splendor," "reputation," "worth," etc., can be combined in applying the word to God to describe His intrinsic worth and majestic splendor.

b. *New Testament.* Κλέος, "renown," is tr. "glory" once (1 Pet 2:20 KJV and ASV; RSV "credit"). Otherwise *δόξα* is used. This word is derived from *δοκέω*, "I think." In classical lit. it means "opinion" or "reputation." The derived Eng. word, "dogma," retains the idea of opinion. Δόξα is used only once with the meaning of "opinion" in sacred lit. and that in a pseudepigraphic writing (4 Macc 5:18). Otherwise the meaning of *δόξα* coincides with the LXX usage where it translates כבוד. Plato used *δόξα* with the idea of outward splendor as opposed to reality; but this usage is not found in the NT. It is used in the sense of reputation or fame in John 12:43: "They loved the praise of men more than the praise of God" (cf. John 5:41ff.; 7:18). The use of the word in the sense of "fame" ties up with the classical "opinion." Individual opinions coalesce into one big opinion—fame.

Many illustrations can be given in which the word coincides with the OT use of כבוד. Brightness can be seen in Luke 2:9, "the glory of the Lord shone around them" (cf. 2 Cor 3:9); man's outward splendor in Matthew 6:29; "Solomon in all his glory" (cf. 1 Cor 11:15, where a woman's hair is her pride [*δόξα*]); national splendor in Matthew 4:8, "the kingdoms of the world and the glory of them" (cf. Rev 21:24); the glory of an evangelist in his converts (1 Thess 2:20).

Chiefly, however, the word refers to the revelation of God in Christ. "He reflects the glory of God" (Heb 1:3). John expresses the idea when he writes, "we have beheld his glory" (John 1:14). It was seen in the miracles (2:11) and in the transfiguration (2 Pet 1:16f., etc.). He is the Lord of glory (James 2:1). In His incarnate life, the glory of God is seen. The word, as in the LXX, indicates the outshining of the divine glory, but with particular reference to the outshining in Christ. The subjectiveness involved in "opinion" is gone, and in its place is an objective fact—the glory of God in Christ.

2. The glory of God. The major use of the word is to describe God's glory. Stephen summed up OT ideas when he referred to "The God of glory" (Acts 7:2). For Israel, the glory of God surpassed all other aspects of glory. Although the word could refer to armies or wealth, Israel must trust in neither of these, but in the Lord (Isa 31:1, 3; cf. Ps 20:7; 62:7). When Israel departed from God, Jeremiah rebuked them saying, "Has a nation changed its gods, even though they are no gods? But my people have changed their glory for that which does not profit" (Jer 2:11). Yahweh is Israel's glory. When He would forget Israel, He would change their glory into shame (Hos 4:6f.). Israel insulted God's glory when it created images of Him (Isa 42:8; 48:11). Glory belongs to God and He is the glory of Israel.

This glory belongs to God intrinsically. The Lord's Prayer sums this up, "thine is . . . the glory" (Matt 6:13 RSVmg.; cf. 1 Chron 29:11). It is not some accidental feature of God's character, but an essential quality in it. His name is majestic (Ps 8:1; cf. 102:15). The inherent glory of God is obviously in mind in such references as Psalm 29:2, "the glory of his name," or as in Psalm 63:2 where, when God is looked upon, His "power and glory" are seen. Other references are as follows: "The Lord is high above all nations, and his glory above the heavens!" (Ps 113:4). "Great is the glory of the LORD" (Ps 138:5). "They shall fear the name of the LORD from the west, and his glory from the rising of the sun" (Isa 59:19; cf. Ps 79:9; 96:8). When Isaiah saw the majestic holiness of God, the seraphim also said, "The whole earth is full of his glory" (Isa 6:3). So majestic is God's glory that to see His face is to die (Exod 33:20) and it is considered remarkable that any should see His face and live (Gen 16:13; 32:30; Deut 4:33; 5:24; Judg 6:22f.). Paul writes of "the glory of the immortal God" (Rom 1:23). The glory of God is such that if it be taken away, He is no longer God. Man's glory —wealth, reputation, etc.—may be taken from him, but he is still man; but God cannot be God without His glory. For this reason He is jealous about it; man must not infringe upon it. The intention of God is that man and all creation should give glory to Him. Man must not glory in his wisdom, might, or riches, but rather in understanding the Lord (Jer 9:23f.). He who boasts must "boast of the Lord" (1 Cor 1:31). Man is expected to show forth God's excellencies (1 Pet 2:9 ASV). This is well summed up in the Westminster Shorter Catechism; "Man's chief end is to glorify God." Man must not take to himself glory that belongs to God.

Much less must man attribute God's glory to idols. "My glory I give to no other, nor my praise to graven images" (Isa 42:8; cf. 48:11; cf. Rom 1:23). Calvin shows that in the decalogue, God, having demanded exclusive worship in the first commandment, prohibits image worship in the second. The prohibition arises from an apprehension of God's glory—glory of such a nature that no earthly form can be given to it (Deut 4:15); it cannot be represented by an idol. Calvin says, "As often as any form is assigned to God, his glory is corrupted by an impious lie." Isaiah is forthright on this point (ch. 40ff.). He asks, "To whom then will you liken God, or what likeness compare with him?" (Isa 40:18). He then shows the folly of representing such a glorious person by an idol (cf. Isa 41:7; 44:9ff.; 46:5ff.). Paul speaks likewise to the Athenians (Acts 17:29): "We ought not to think that the Deity is like gold, or silver, or stone, a representation by the art and imagination of man." God's glory is God Himself, and as such He cannot be represented by any human image; nor does He need any such image to glorify Him—in fact, in so representing Him we dishonor Him.

Whereas the glory of God is His essentially and inherently, the major emphasis of Scripture is on the glory in its manifestation. It describes the self-revelation of God's being and character. Isaiah summarizes this point, "Arise, shine; for your light has come, and the glory of the LORD has risen upon you" (Isa 60:1f.). When Moses requested to see God's glory, he was told, "I will make all my goodness pass before you, and will proclaim before you my name" (Exod 33:18ff.). Isaiah uses the impressive phrase, "The glory of his majesty" (Isa 2:10, 19, 21). He had in mind a frightening revelation of God Himself. In Numbers 14:22, the revelation of His glory is associated with the signs in Egypt. A few quotations will show how much weight the glory of revelation receives among theologians. "The glory of God is thus in effect the term used to express what we can comprehend, originally by sight, of the presence of God on the earth" (A. Richardson). "The glory of God is when we know what He is" (Calvin). More tersely, and yet clearly, Bengel writes, "The Glory is the Divinity manifest."

Specific examples of the appearance of the glory of God may now be considered. When Moses received the law at Sinai, "the appearance of the glory of the LORD was like a devouring fire on the top of the mountain in the sight of the people of Israel" (Exod 24:16-18; cf. Deut 5:24). The glory was also manifest in the cloud that accompanied Israel, and particularly when this cloud was associated with the Tabernacle and Temple. The tent was to be sanctified by God's glory (Exod 29:43). When the Tabernacle was erected, "the cloud covered the tent of meeting, and the glory of the LORD filled the tabernacle" (Exod 40:34ff.; cf. Lev 9:6, 23). So impressive was the cloud of glory that Moses could not enter the Tabernacle. The same phenomena appeared in the Temple (1 Kings 8:10f. where the cloud and the glory are again equated, cf. 2 Chron 5:13f.; Ezek 44:4). In 2 Chronicles 7:1f., fire and the glory of the Lord are associated (cf. Exod 40:38; Lev 9:23f.; Num 9:16; Ezek 43:2, 4, 5; Zech 2:5).

The cloud of glory also appeared to vindicate and protect God's servants, particularly Moses and Aaron. When the Israelites grumbled at scanty provision, God's glory appeared in a cloud (Exod 16:7, 10). The same occurred when they were in danger because of the spies' report (Num 14:10). At Kadesh, the people grumbled because of lack of water, and God's glory appeared (20:6). It also appeared to settle matters in the dispute with Korah, Dathan, and Abiram (16:19ff.). In the NT, a bright light arrested Saul of Tarsus on his way to Damascus to persecute the followers of Christ (Acts 9:3; 22:6). The death of Aaron's sons (Lev 10:2f.) may be considered as God vindicating His glory in the sanctuary (cf. Isa 2:10, 19, 21). God manifests Himself in judgment and brings the pomp, pride, and rebellion of men to nought. In so doing, He protects His servants. Being jealous of His own glory and honor, He is also jealous about the welfare of His people. In this pleasing way, the glory of God appears in the history of His people.

Attention is often drawn to the somewhat physical way in which God's glory is mentioned in the OT. Examples of this are the cloud and fire, already mentioned, and the vision of God granted to Moses (Exod 33:18ff.; 34:5ff.) in the form of a tangible theophany. The Israelites saw His glory (Deut 5:24f.). Ezekiel is particularly noticeable in this connection; his vision of the glory of God had many physical characteristics. He gives a vivid description of "the appearance of the likeness of the glory of the LORD" (Ezek 1:28), which makes this clear. He describes it in many ways, such as a bright shining phenomenon resembling the rainbow (Ezek 1:28; cf. 3:12ff.; 3:23; 8:4; 9:3; 10:4; 10:18f.; 11:22f.; 43:2). A physical manifestation is also involved in the vision to Isaiah (Isa 6:1ff.; cf. Jer 17:12).

Too much stress can be laid on this evidence, as so to say that the God of the Hebrews was a physical being. As Ezekiel described the glory of God, he was describing something he saw in a vision, apart from that in Ezekiel 39:21. The vision would have tangible form—it cannot be otherwise—because it is not an abstract idea but a concrete revelation. This does not mean that something physical was present. To the Hebrews, in any case, God was not an absolute abstraction, but one with whom they could have contact, and anthropomorphic terms were inevitable. The Hebrews did not, however, view Him as human, or earthly in shape and motion. Taking the Scripture as a whole, such physical conceptions are balanced out by the ethical ideas that attach to God's glory. In Isaiah 6 is a concrete vision, but the reaction of the prophet is not merely one of awe at God's majestic holiness but of humility before His moral attributes. Ezekiel also connects glory with judgment (39:21). It is associated with righteousness in Psalm 97:6, "The heavens proclaim his righteousness; and all the peoples behold his glory" (cf. Isa 40:4.; 60:1ff.). Paul sums up sin as a falling short of God's glory (Rom 3:23; cf. Rom 1:23; 3:7; 5:2; 2 Cor 3:18). Ephesians 1:17 describes the actions of God, the Father of glory, in the realm of wisdom and understanding. It would be a mistake to associate this word primarily with the physical. It endeavors to describe the indescribable God, and human terms are inevitable, but it is not a balanced Scriptural view to say that in Ezekiel, or anywhere else, glory is viewed as exclusively physical.

Because the glory of God is so much involved in His self-disclosure, man cannot ignore the revelation in Scripture itself, which is a light shining in a dark place (2 Pet 1:19f.). Whereas the most glorious revelation is Christ, the extant knowledge of this revelation is in Scripture. The word "glory" thus embraces the whole Biblical knowledge of God.

3. The glory of God in creation and in man. The glory of God appears in creation as well as in theophanies. Revelation itself presupposes the existence of the world to which revelation is made. To receive this revelation the world must be something of worth. An aspect of the glory of God belongs to creation. Psalms 8; 148; and 150 view the whole of nature as praising God (cf. Ps 29:1f.; 104:31). It all glorifies God. Psalm 19:1ff. expresses the idea very well, "The heavens are telling the glory of God," as does also Psalm 29:9, "The voice of the LORD makes the oaks to whirl, and strips the forest bare; and in his temple all cry, 'Glory!'" Paul has the same conception in mind in Romans 1:19ff. Though even "his eternal power and deity" are obvious in nature, the evils and idolatry of men dishonored His glory. Heavenly and earthly bodies each have their own distinctive glory (1 Cor 15:40). In nature and in the world's history, God's glory is evident.

At present, many aspects of nature seem against the glory of God. Men concentrate on nature and forget God, or meet one of the maladjustments of nature and curse Him. The blight on nature is a consequence of man's sin (Gen 3:17). Ultimately this shall be removed and "the earth will be filled with the knowledge of the glory of the LORD, as the waters cover the sea" (Hab 2:14; cf. Num 14:21; Ps 72:19; Isa 6:3). Nature, animate and inanimate, man included, one day will give due glory to God. Then "the glory of the LORD shall be revealed, and all flesh shall see it together" (Isa 40:5; cf. Luke 3:6).

In reference more particularly to man, the word כבוד is used in some OT passages to describe man's self, or soul. Jacob thus uses it, "O my soul, come not into their council; O my spirit (כבדי), be not joined to their company" (Gen 49:6). The LXX trs. the word as "liver" here, giving the vowel pointing of *kebedi*, "liver," instead of *kabodi*, "glory." Some suggest that this tr. should be followed, in view of the Heb. tendency to use organs of the body to describe psychological experiences. However, whereas the LXX supports this tr. here, in other instances it does not, but uses the term δόξα (*see* Job 29:20; Ps 4:2 KJV; 7:5 LXX; 16:9 ASV; 30:12; 57:8; 108:1). These passages are poetic, and such usage is to be expected. At the same time, this is not poetic license; a great truth is enshrined. Man is made in God's image, possessing a glory that distinguises him from the animals. He is "the image and glory of God" (1 Cor 11:7). The poetic usage points to man's glory.

At creation, man glorified God. Even including man, God could say creation was very good (Gen 1:31). Man was intended to glorify God and at first he did this. He truly uplifted God in creation, giving Him the glory due to His name (Ps 96:8; cf. 66:2). This still remains to be the duty of man, however poorly he fulfills it. The case of the healed Samaritan leper (Luke 17:18) illustrates this. The advice (though hypocritically given) in John 9:24, "Give God the praise," is still correct practice. The following considerations make clear that glorifying God covers all of life. Christians are to receive each other "for the glory of God" (Rom 15:7). The speaking and ministry of the Christian are to be "in order that in everything God may be glorified through Jesus Christ" (1 Pet 4:11). All of life must be for His glory (1 Cor 10:31). Our bodies must be kept pure for His glory (6:20; cf. Phil 1:20). The duty of man is fulfilled in the believer who is being changed "from one degree of glory to another" (2 Cor 3:18). On earth they reflect favorably on the honor of God (Eph 1:6; 1 Pet 2:9).

Although the whole duty of man is to glorify God, it is possible for man to become the mighty rebel and take to himself what really belongs to God. Calvin, having quoted Jeremiah 9:23f. and 1 Corinthians 1:29, says, "We never truly glory in Him until we have utterly discarded our own glory . . . whoso glories in himself glories against God." This perfectly sums up what the Lord says about the sin of receiving glory one from another (John 5:41ff.). In glorifying God, self-boasting must be excluded (Rom 3:27; Eph 2:8f.). The whole trouble with man since the Fall is his attempt to become as God (Gen 3:5), and as a result he does not fulfill his true destiny. He ruins his glory when he is a rebel. Man is truly glorious only when he looks on God as God and man as man.

4. The glory of Christ. Whereas man failed to glorify God, Christ glorified His Father completely, so that at the end of His earthly life He could say, "I glorified thee on earth, having accomplished the work which thou gavest me to do" (John 17:4). He did what no man ever did; He glorified God in all He was, said and did (cf. Heb 2:6ff.).

OT Israel expected the Messiah to be glorious. In the wilderness wanderings they possessed a forward look. The Tabernacle was to be sanctified by God's glory when erected (Exod 29:43). This forward look was present in the whole history of Israel; none of the religious achievements was final; more was to follow. This is exemplified in the following Scriptures: "Over all the glory there will be a canopy and a pavilion" (Isa 4:5); the dwellings of the root of Jesse "shall be glorious" (11:10); "the LORD of hosts . . . will manifest his glory" (24:23); "the glory of the LORD shall be revealed, and all flesh shall see it together" (40:5). Such longings and hopes find fulfillment either in the Incarnation or the parousia of the Messiah.

The glory of Christ existed before the Incarnation, since He was preexistent. Christ (John 17:5) refers to the glory He had before the world was made (cf. v. 24). Second Corinthians 8:9 refers to His riches, and Philippians 2:6, to Him being "in the form of God." This glory must have been personal glory, entirely divorced from any activity in revelation.

John 1:14, "the Word became flesh . . . we have beheld his glory," associates glory with the incarnate life, which was completely glorifying to God, and which also was full of His own personal glory. He glorified God in making Him known (John 1:18; 17:4, 6). Westcott, commenting on John 2:11, remarks regarding the fourth gospel, "It represents the whole human life of Christ, under its actual condition of external want and suffering and of external conflict and sorrow, as a continuous and conscious manifestation of Divine glory."

Also important to consider is the Shekinah glory, which is often associated with ἐσκηνῶσεν, "dwelt," or "tabernacled" (John 1:14; cf. Rev. 21:3). Shekinah is derived from the Heb. שכן, "to dwell," and is used of God's presence among men. The word is not a direct tr. of כבוד except once in the Targums (Zech 2:9), but in the LXX, δόξα is tr. from both שכן and כבוד. The Targums used this word to avoid any localization of God. Rabbis spoke of Moses' face being bright because he shared the Shekinah. The idea in the NT can also be associated with the cloud that overshadowed (ἐπισκιάζειν) Christ at the Transfiguration, when a voice came from the majestic glory (2 Pet 1:17; cf. Luke 2:9; Acts 7:2; Rom 9:4). "The cherubim of glory overshadowing the mercy seat" (Heb 9:5) also carries this idea.

The glory of Christ, although always present, was also largely veiled in the Incarnation. It flashed out in miracles (John 2:11; 11:40) and words of wisdom, but largely there was "no beauty that we should desire him" (Isa 53:2). He was just a carpenter to many. Paul maintains that because none of the rulers of this world recognized Christ for what He was, they put Him to death (1 Cor 2:8). He was crucified in weakness (2 Cor 13:4). The glory was there, but the god of this world so blinded men that they saw His humanity only and not "the light of the knowledge of the glory of God in the face of Christ" (2 Cor 4:4, 6; cf. Heb 1:3). The same is still true.

The only instance where His glory became fully apparent was at the Transfiguration (Matt 17:1ff.; Mark 9:2ff.; Luke 9:28ff.; cf. 2 Pet 1:16ff.). The cloud, the symbol of the divine presence, came over the disciples and Jesus, and His exceeding great glory was seen in His countenance and even in His garments. The Transfiguration is not recorded in John, for John looks beyond the outward appearance and sees the whole life and death of Christ as a continuous demonstration of the glory of God. The glory of Christ was also seen after His ascension, in the revelation to Stephen (Acts 7:55f.; cf. 6:15), and in the vision that converted Saul of Tarsus (Acts 9; cf. Acts 22; 26). All men are to honor the Son even as they honor the Father (John 5:23). To do this they must see His real glory. The redeemed of the Lord do see it and in heaven they glorify Him as they should (Rev 5:12f.).

It is easier to see the glory of Christ in miracles and the transfiguration than in the humility of His death; yet this event was His crowning earthly glory. He did not go to it as a helpless victim but as "a victorious being to His crowning." His sufferings were an entrance into His glory (Luke 24:26). Several other vv. refer to the glory of the cross. For instance, "The hour has come for the Son of man to be glorified" (John 12:23f.), and, "the hour has come; glorify thy Son" (John 17:1; cf. Luke 9:31; John 7:39; 12:16; 13:31f.; 17:4). In Hebrews 2:9 He is spoken of as being "crowned with glory and honor because of the sufferings of death," and in Revelation the slain Lamb is viewed as worthy of glory (Rev 5:12). The Gospel, which centers in the cross, shows the riches of His glory (Col 1:27; cf. Eph 1:18). Paul gloried in the cross (Gal 6:14). The cross did not enhance His personal glory; it was rather a glorious accomplishment by an already perfectly glorious person.

After His death came the glory of His resurrection and ascension. They are involved in the glory that followed His death (Luke 24:26). God glorified Him by His resurrection and ascension. He was raised from the dead by the glory of God the Father (Rom 6:4). After being raised, God gave Him glory (1 Pet 1:21). He has been taken up in glory (1 Tim 3:16) and is now in glory at God's right hand (Acts 7:55f.; cf. Mark 16:19; Acts 2:33; 3:13; 3:21; 1 Cor 15:27; Eph 1:20; Phil 2:9ff.; Heb 1:3f.). Whereas His whole life was glorious, the resurrection and ascension vindicated all His claims and overshadowed with glory the victory of the cross. This glory was not new, but a resumption of the glory He had before the Incarnation (John 17:5, 24).

5. Eschatological glory. Earlier conceptions and hopes are gathered up in the word glory when it is used eschatologically. The NT era is the last hour (1 John 2:18) and is in many ways the fulfillment of OT eschatological longings. The glory of the Lord was truly revealed (Isa 40:5; cf. Ps 97:6; 102:16; Isa 24:23; 58:8; 59:19). The NT accepts this and applies it to Christ, but it also contains its own eschatological longings. Romans 8: 18ff. describes longings for the deliverance and glorification of nature. First Corinthians 15 and 1 Thessalonians 4:13ff., have the hope of glory prominently in view (cf. Col 1:27).

The future glory of Christ receives the major emphasis eschatologically. He shall come in "the glory of his Father" (Matt 16:27; Mark 8:38; Luke 9:26). He shall come on the clouds with "power and great glory" (Matt 24:30; Mark 13:26; Luke 21:27). He shall sit on His glorious throne (Matt 19:28; 25:31; cf. Dan 7:13f.). Even when His teaching regarding the cross upset the disciples, the sons of Zebedee saw His future glory (Mark 10:37). The glory that always was His, will no longer be hidden; it will be revealed (1 Pet 4:13; cf. Titus 2:13).

Popularly, heaven is spoken of as glory. The idea is not absent in Scripture, "the voice was borne to him by the Majestic Glory" (2 Pet 1:17). Psalm 73:24 refers to being received to glory. In heaven we shall see Christ's glory (John 17:24).

The future of the Christian may be considered as the restoration of the δόξα lost at the Fall. Man must have been radiant with God's glory when the divine image was unimpaired (Gen 1:31). This idea is also reflected in Psalm 8:5ff., where man is viewed as crowned with glory and honor. The ideal is, under present conditions, realized only in Christ (Heb 2:5ff.). For man, in Christ, there is in the words, "we do not yet see everything in subjection to him" (v. 8), the idea that this also shall be seen in due course. Scripture elsewhere puts the matter more clearly, showing that man shall have the glory restored to him. Christ is the true image of God (2 Cor 4:4; Col 1:15) and we are even now "being changed into his likeness from one degree of glory to another" (2 Cor 3:18). Christ is in us as the hope of glory (Col 1: 27). Ultimately, redeemed man shall be conformed to this image (Rom 8:29). They shall be like Him (1 John 3:2) and be satisfied with beholding His form (Ps 17:15). Our bodies shall be like His glorious body (Phil 3:21). We shall have a new eschatological body (1 Cor 15:42f.). The Christian, having had the glory restored to him, will become what he was originally intended to be. The wise shall shine (Dan 12:3). He shall share a glorious inheritance (Eph 1:18). The riches of God's glory will be shown in us (Rom 9: 23). Christ will be glorified in His saints (2 Thess 1:10). Crowns shall be given at that day (2 Tim 4:8; cf. 1 Pet 5:4). We shall "appear with him in glory" (Col 3:4). The word that sums up the final state of the believer is "glorification."

BIBLIOGRAPHY. J. Calvin, *Institutes of the Christian Religion* (1559, 1949 ed.), I, 90-92, II, 68-70, 273; W. Sanday and A. C. Headlam, *Epistle to the Romans*, ICC (1907 ed.), 84, 85; B. F. Westcott, *The Gospel according to St. John* (1908), 100, 101; I. Abrahams, *The Glory of God* (1925); L. H. Brockington, "The Presence of God, a Study of the Use of the Term 'Glory of Yahveh,'" ET, LVII (Oct. 1945), 21-25; E. G. Selwyn, *The First Epistle of Peter* (1949), 250-258; A. M. Ramsey, *The Glory of God and the Transfiguration of Christ* (1949); W. H. Rigg, *The Fourth Gospel and its Message for Today* (1952), 46-80; W. Hendriksen, *The Gospel of John* (1959 ed.), 85-89; E. Brunner, *The Christian Doctrine of God* (1962 ed.), 285-287; A. Richardson, *An Introduction to the Theology of the NT* (1962 ed.), 64-67; B. Ramm, *Them He Glorified* TDNT, II (1964), 233-255; L. H. Brockington, "Presence," RTWB (1965 ed.), 172-176; R. H. Preston, "Transfigure, Transfiguration," RTWB (1965 ed.), 267-269.

M. R. Gordon

GLOSSOLALIA. *See* Tongues, Gift of.

GLUTTON, GLUTTONOUS, GLUTTONY (זלל, *light, worthless*). The law whereby a father and mother charged their son with conduct worthy of death (Deut 21:21); the vice rebuked (Prov 23:21). The words were repeated for emphasis (Prov 23:20; 28:7 ASV, RSV). Greek φάγος, "one who eats," i.e. "too much" (Matt 11:19; Luke 7:34). The Matthew and Luke references were accusations made against Jesus. Titus 1:12 KJV reads "slow bellies," ASV has "idle gluttons," RSV, NEB "lazy gluttons."

E. Russell

GNASH, GNASHING OF TEETH (חרק ; βρύχω, τρίζω, βρυγμός, *strike* or *grind the teeth together*). The Heb. (poetic) expresses the hate and scorn of enemies (Job 16:9; Ps 35:16; 37:12; 112:10; Lam 2:16). The Gr. βρύχω refers to the rage of Stephen's enemies (Acts 7:54), RSV "ground their teeth." The Gr. τρίζω describes the epileptic's grating sound by gnashing (Mark 9:18). The Gr. noun βρυγμός occurs repeatedly in the sayings of Jesus (Matt 8:12; 13:42, 50; 22:13; 24:51; 25:30; Luke 13:28) concerning the remorseful gnashing of teeth by those excluded from heaven.

E. Russell

GNAT (כנם, כן, κώνωψ, *lice* KJV, ASV, *gnats* RSV, Exod 8:16ff; *gnat*, Matt 23:24, all Eng. VSS). Found in proverbial form in NT: "straining out a gnat and swallowing a camel." This corrects a confusing tr. in KJV "strain *at* a gnat." It refers to the orthodox habit of straining wine or drinking it through a piece of cloth to avoid ritual contamination by taking forbidden meat. Probably a general word for a small fly. The Gr. word is found today in *Conopidae*, a family of two-winged flies.

See LICE for full discussion of cause of third plague in Egypt.

G. S. CANSDALE

GNOSTICISM, a term derived from Gr. γνῶσις, knowledge, and variously applied to movements within, or in relation to, early Christianity.

1. Connotations. Until fairly recently the term was generally applied collectively to the majority of those 2nd cent. movements which called themselves Christian or borrowed heavily from Christian sources, but which were rejected by the main stream of Christian tradition (represented in such fathers as Irenaeus, Hippolytus and Epiphanius). Neither the fathers nor the groups themselves, however, apply the title in this sense, the former using it only of certain groups and designating the whole simply "the heresies," the latter using the distinctive name of the particular group. There are, however, certain common features, among them a dominating concern with knowledge. Since these common features (indicated below) appear in some other forms of contemporary Hel. religion, and since a concern for knowledge is evident in the NT, there is now a tendency to use the term more widely. Some employ it of any form of dualistic teaching with sharply opposed principles of good and evil which offers knowledge as a key to the struggle, and others apply it to the myth of a supramundane Redeemer found in some forms of Hel. religion apparently derived from Eastern, prob. Iranian, sources. From different points of view, therefore, the term has been applied to the Qumran sect, Paul, the fourth gospel and the Alexandrian fathers. It seems best for the moment to use the term of the 2nd cent. Christian and post-Christian movements, without prejudice to the question of their significance for Christian origins.

2. The common features of Gnosticism. Anyone who reads through the books of Irenaeus or Hippolytus against heresies will be struck by the wide variety of these movements. There are Gnostic systems which make testing intellectual demands, others which depend on mumbo-jumbo and sleight of hand. There are Gnostic leaders who are (it comes through most reluctantly) high-minded ascetics, and others who are licentious charlatans. Nevertheless, they all offer knowledge—and in a form or degree not to be found outside their own teaching. This concern for knowledge links the higher and the lower forms of Gnosticism. At its lowest, the knowledge offered related simply to power and secrets of the future—the same sort of things as those for which people consulted astrologers and fortune tellers, but put into a religious setting. In its higher forms, it is related to abstract speculation, grappling with problems which had long been obstacles for educated pagans: how came good and evil into the world, and how do they relate to God? Sometimes, too, it is special knowledge about Jesus which is proffered, on the basis of secret, closely guarded sources. The essential content of the knowledge offered in many of the systems we know of is summarized in a passage preserved in Clement of Alexandria: "who we were, and what we have become, what we were, where we were placed, whither we hasten, from what we are redeemed, what birth is, what rebirth" (*Excerpta ex Theodoto* 78.2). Implied in this is the thought of the individual soul entering the world from the outside, and passing from it: and the Gnostic sought the key both to the origins of an evil world, and to his salvation from it.

Knowledge and salvation were keynotes of much 2nd-cent. religion: this is what people wanted from the mystery religions and explains their contemporary popularity. The Gnostic teachers sought to provide for these longings in a way which was both Christian and compatible with the basic assumptions about God and the world held by most people of the day. These assumptions might be formed by contemporary philosophy, by mythology, or by astrology; and in different Gnostic systems, these factors appear in differing degrees. What they have in common is a desire to be contemporary.

There was nothing peculiarly Gnostic about the common assumptions: these can be found in, e.g., the anti-Christian writer Celsus, whom no one would call a Gnostic. Celsus believed that God is so utterly transcendent that He can have no direct contact with the world; that matter is inherently evil and can have no contact with God; and that men, or at least some men, have within them a spark of the divine which is now incarcerated in the material prison of the body. Man is thus a creature of mixed origin, a mixture of incompatibles (Origen, *Contra Celsum*, passim). It is for such reasons as these that Celsus regards Christianity as self-condemned: the claim that God became man is impossible, since God and matter could not mix. (The old myths talked of the gods appearing in human shape: no one suggested that they *were* human while in it.) The Gnostics, however, are trying to square Celsus' assumptions with the Christian proclamation. Not surprisingly, both have to give something: the proportions, and thus the degree of closeness to traditional Christianity, vary in the different systems. In some, such as the system of Valentinus (who was at one time a serious candidate for the bishopric of Rome), a fairly orthodox Christian confession could be made, though there was little room for it in the system itself; in others, such as (apparently) the Ophite sect, all pretense at continuity with mainstream Christianity was given up, though this did not prevent large scale borrowings from the Bible and Christian tradition. And, of course, the movements evolved and changed; Basilides, for instance, seems to have held a reasonably orthodox view of Christ (Hippolytus *Refutation* 7. 26); but within fifty years, Irenaeus tells us that followers of Basilides believed that Jesus was never crucified (*Against Heresies* 1. 19. 11f.).

Of the movement as a whole, however, we can say: (a) It is rationalistic. It is seeking to answer questions outside the scope of the OT and the apostolic witness, and to do so on wholly non-Biblical assumptions. (b) It is mystical, in the sense of seeking identification with and absorption in the divine (see, e.g., the spectacular Ophite liturgy quoted by Origen, *Contra Celsum* 6.31). (c) It is mythological, employing a system of mythology to express truth, as an essential supplement to (or in some cases substitute for) the Biblical tradition.

3. The Gnostic crux. The collision of Christian and Gr. assumptions directed attention to the origin of evil in the world. For those reared on Gr. assumptions this might be formulated as, How does the divinely originated soul become imprisoned in matter, and how can it escape? For teachers believing in the love and goodness of God these posed particular problems. The general answer is to give a mythological scheme, in which redemption becomes a drama played out among cosmic forces—the "principalities and powers" of the NT—the astral forces in a good deal of contemporary religion.

4. The revision of Christian theology. The central Christian tradition represented in the apostles maintained the peculiar features of the Jewish faith in which it had been born: monotheistic, historical, eschatological, ethical, and exclusive. The Redeemer continued to be styled "Christ," a direct tr. of the Heb. "Messiah." The Jewish concern with God's interventions in human history was retained and enlarged—preaching concentrated, indeed, on the historical events of the life and death and resurrection of Jesus. Though the law was abandoned, the idea of a moral commitment directly watched over by God remained. The peculiarly Jewish belief in the resurrection and last judgment was retained, and the Jewish Scriptures continued to be read. And though the idea of a people of God defined by physical descent disappeared, the solidarity of a single "Israel of God," in continuity with the OT Israel, meant the continuing consciousness of a single worshiping community, a "third race" alongside Jew and Gentile. Gnostic reformulation was bound to collide with all these elements.

The doctrine of God. God is conceived as remote from all the material creation. The gap between is filled by a hierarchy of intermediary beings, in a descending order of magnitude. These are aeons, usually linked in pairs or syzygies (usually male and female), and are collectively given the name "the *pleroma*" (fullness). The earliest may be the result of God's creative act; the others emanate from them. There are different myths as to the origin of our world; but all agree that it was a mistake, an accident, the work of an ignorant being or the mischief of an antigod. One picture of the material universe is that of an abortion self-generated by the inordinate desire of a female aeon (*Sophia*, "wisdom"); and some systems attempt to reconcile this view with such passages as John 1:3 by describing the Logos in creation as giving form to the misshapen abortion, which thus combines the principles of good and evil. In other systems, of which the most influential was that of Marcion, creation is the work of a Demiurge, an inferior divinity.

The Old Testament. Clearly such a scheme does not reflect the Creator/Vindicator God of the OT. Accordingly, teachers like Cerdo and Marcion frankly abandon the OT, and regard themselves as liberating the Church from the fetters of the Judaizers. Since one can only be really radical with the OT by being really radical with the NT, many of those who wished to keep contact with the apostolic writings were forced to try to accommodate the OT. A long, thoughtful letter from the Valentinian theologian Ptolemy (in Epiphanius, *Panarion* 33) offers a tripartite division of the OT: part is from God, part from Moses acting as law giver, part from the elders; part is eternal, if incomplete; part was temporary and is now abrogated; part is symbolical, and is now transformed.

Nature of authority. The Ptolemy already mentioned tells his correspondent, "You will learn the order and the begetting of all these [aeons] if you are deemed worthy of knowing the apostolic tradition which we have received from a succession, together with the confirmation of all our words by the teaching of the Saviour." That is, he is claiming access to a superior source of secret knowledge. Valentinian and other "right wing" Gnostics paid lip service to the same authority as the mainstream Church: the Lord and His apostles. They had to show that they possessed reliable knowledge conveyed by the apostles (and thus ultimately from the Lord) which other Christians did not. The Valentinians claimed a tradition from a disciple of Paul called Theudas; the Basilidians from Peter via one Glaukias, and from Matthias. More exotic groups often chose James the Lord's brother as their source, or Thomas (*Didymus,* "the Twin," being taken to be the Lord's twin) as being very close to the person of the Savior. The now famous Gospel of Thomas (Logion 12) insinuates that Thomas is a source of tradition superior to Matthew and Peter, the apostles associated with the first two gospels.

Incarnation and atonement. If God's transcendence implies the impossibility of His contact with matter, how could God take a human body, still less suffer in one? There are several Gnostic answers, depending on the degree of closeness to the central Christian tradition. Some reject the idea of incarnation altogether: Christ was only an "appearance" of God in human form, He only *seemed* to suffer. Others spoke of the divine Logos resting on the righteous but human Jesus—but being withdrawn at the Passion (the cry of dereliction, Mark 15:34, was held to be evidence of this). Others again used the traditional language, but emphasized not the historical events of the incarnation, but the relations between the disordered elements of the Pleroma, which the incarnation righted. For Basilides the important fact seems to be that Jesus had within Himself all the elements of creation; His passion is related to the ordering of its confusion (Hippolytus *Refutation* 7.27). He is basically interested in the question, Whence comes evil? rather than the question, How is sin forgiven? Likewise Valentinus in the *Gospel of Truth* (discovered at Nag Hammadi) uses traditional language about the cross without finding a clear place for this very mundane event in his complex drama of redemption among the aeons.

Sin and salvation. Evil is associated with matter, ignorance, formlessness, distortion. Consequently salvation is to slough off defilement rather than to receive forgiveness for offenses. Salvation comes as illumination dispelling ignorance, triumphing over the material. The Gospel is principally a means of men *knowing* the truth; the cosmic bodies receive the same instruction.

Judgment and resurrection were a constant source of difficulty for those who sought immortality in *escape* from the body. Resurrection, and the whole eschatological dimension associated with it, is noticably missing from Gnostic schemes.

The Church and Christian life. Some schools divided mankind into three according to the predominant element in their constitutions—the material (who were unsalvable), the "psychic" who could receive some purification, and the spiritual, the elite capable of receiving the deep mysteries. Naturally the third class were the Gnostics, the mass of Christians forming the second class. The church becomes the club of the illuminated not the society of the redeemed. The view that the material is the seat of evil, leads to asceticism, celibacy and vegetarianism in some systems, and paradoxically to license in others, where "liberation" from matter meant its effects were inconsequential.

5. The origins of Gnosticism. Continental scholars have often argued that Gnosticism is of pre-Christian origin, the figure of a cosmic redeemer being taken over from Eastern, specifically Iranian, sources, which are also the prime source of its dualism. Some would even see the essence of Gentile (indeed, Pauline) Christianity as the superimposition of the Gnostic Redeemer on the historical Jesus. No one has yet shown, however, that the Gnostic Redeemer existed before Christian times, and the Qumran documents have shown that Pauline and Johannine language about knowledge was firmly rooted in Jewish tradition. R. M. Grant has even suggested that Gnosticism itself is of Jewish origin: the fruit of unorthodox speculation working upon an apocalyptic framework which the fall of Jerusalem in A.D. 70 had caused to be re-evaluated. Certainly the Nag Hammadi documents suggest the effect of Jewish speculation. The "Colossian heresy" combined Jewish and ascetic features, philosophical activity, and veneration of astral powers (Col 2:16-23), and when Paul speaks of the whole *pleroma* dwelling in Christ (Col 1:19), it is tempting to see him taking the word which the Gnostics used of their scheme of intermediary beings, disinfecting it and replacing it, as it were, by Christ. But neither the Colossians nor the Corinthians, nor the groups attacked in the Pastoral epistles or 1 John, display a Gnostic system of the type reflected in the 2nd-cent. movements. The Corinthians delighted unduly in knowledge (1 Cor 8:1; 13:8) and wisdom (1 Cor 1:17ff.), were unhappy about the thought of resurrection (1 Cor 15), included both those who questioned whether a Christian could marry (1 Cor 7) and those whose "liberation" left them indifferent to their bodies' actions (1 Cor 6:12-18). Others possessed "*gnosis* falsely so-called" (1 Tim 6:20), had mythologies and genealogies (1 Tim 1:4), spiritualized the resurrection (2 Tim 2:18), played with "Jewish fables" (Titus 1:14), and knew both severe ascetism (1 Tim 4:3) and sexual laxity (2 Tim 3:6). The elder feared the teachers of a docetic, "phantom" Christ (1 John 4:1-3). All these show what fertile soil the Early Church provided for Gnostic teaching; but show no sign of the systematized Gnosticism of the 2nd cent.

The Hermetic lit., some of which is pre-Christian, with its mystical quest for illumination and rebirth, also often reminds one of some Gnostic documents; and the mystery religions (with the notorious problems of dating material which they present) afford other parallels. All this simply reflects what was indicated earlier, that Gnosticism was a natural fruit of the 2nd cent. of religious quests of the Hel. world, with its Gr. assumptions, Eastern religion, and astrological fatalism. These tendencies did not together constitute a system: but, coming into contact with a system or articulated preaching they could form one. Coming into contact with Christianity, they took the Christian Redeemer and gnosticized Him, took the Christian preaching and tore it from its OT roots, took the Biblical tradition and sought to make it answer the problems of Gr. philosophy, took the Christian convictions about the end and purged away such offensively Jewish features as resurrection and judgment. Gnosticism was parasitic, and took its shape from the system to which it attached itself. Looked at from another point of view, it was cultural, an outcome of the attempt to digest and "indigenize" Christianity. It need not surprise us, therefore, that some of the same tendencies appear in other 2nd-cent. Christians, even among those who brought about the eventual defeat of Christian Gnosticism. It may be hard for us who have been formed in another thought world, who do not have the same inbred assumptions, to understand either the attractions of the Gnostic systems, or the agonies and difficulties of many mainstream Christian theologians. It is the measure of their greatness that, sharing so much with the Gnostics intellectually as they did, by faithfulness to the historic Christ and the Biblical tradition they produced an "indigenous" Greek-Gentile Christian thought which retained the primitive preaching and the whole of the Scriptures.

Being a phenomenon arising essentially from a particular historical and cultural situation, Gnosticism was not likely to outlast that situation long. The crisis for Gnosticism prob. came with the emergence of the genuinely Iranian, radically dualistic religion of Mani (d. A.D. 277), which was spreading in the Rom. empire from the 3rd cent. onward. Manicheism must have faced many Christian Gnostics with a crucial choice: it could not long be possible to occupy a middle ground between mainstream Christianity and the books of Mani.

6. The sources of Gnosticism. Until recent years the Gnostic writers were known almost entirely through the writings of their antagonists. Of these Irenaeus, *Against Heresies,* Hippolytus, *Refutation of all Heresies,* and Epiphanius, *Panarion*, provide extracts, often sizable, from Gnostic works. The last twenty years have seen the gradual publication of items from a Gnostic library discovered at Nag Hammadi in Egypt and containing Coptic tr. of works of very diverse character. These include as well many works further from the Christian tradition, and some Manichean ones, the *Gospel of Truth* of (prob.) Valentinus and a *Gospel of Thomas* consisting of sayings attributed to the risen Lord and including a number of Gnosticized variants on synoptic sayings. While there is much still to be done in the study of these documents, the conclusion which emerges so far is that the early fathers, for all their trenchancy of language, hardly give a misleading impression.

BIBLIOGRAPHY. H. E. W. Turner, *The Pattern of Christian Truth* (1954); R. Bultmann, *Primitive Christianity in its Original Setting* (Eng. tr. 1956); R. McL. Wilson, *The Gnostic Problem* (1958); R. M. Grant, *Reader in Gnosticism* (1961); H. Jonas, *The Gnostic Religion,* 2nd ed. (1963); R. M. Grant, *Gnosticism and Early Christianity,* 2nd ed. (1966); R. McL. Wilson, *Gnosis and the New Testament* (1968); W. Schmithals, *The Office of Apostle in the Early Church* (Eng. trs. 1971) 114-230.

A. F. WALLS

GOAD (מלמד, from למד, "to learn," Piel, "to teach," דרבנה ; κέντρον). A sharp stick used for prodding cattle, particularly during plowing. It could have an iron tip (cf. 1 Sam 13:21—a problematic v.) and also could be utilized for cleaning plows, prob. with a blade on the other end. Shamgar used an oxgoad as a spear while killing 600 Philistines (Judg 3:31). The lack of real weapons because of the Philistine iron monopoly occasioned this usage.

In a metaphorical sense, the words of the wise (Eccl 12:11) are compared to goads as they encourage and rebuke. The only NT reference to goads concerns Christ's rebuke to Paul on the Damascus road for kicking against the goads, the divine leading (Acts 26:14). *See* PRICK.

H. M. WOLF

GOAH gō' ə (געה, KJV has GOATH). A section in or near Jerusalem appearing only in Jeremiah 31:39. It is one of the boundaries prophesied for the rebuilt city. The hill Gareb is mentioned just before it in the verse.

GOAT. Six Heb. words for *goat* are tr. fairly uniformly in all Eng. VSS. The figures in brackets are all KJV (עז [fem.], *goat* [55] *she-goat* [5]); this is the basic word for *goat* generally used in nonsacrificial contexts; also used for sacrificial animals, esp. sin offering, where it cannot be differentiated from שעיר ; hence בני עזים, *kids of the flock* [1]; עתוד, *he-goat* [18], *goat* [18], *ram* [2]; hence by derivation, "chief one" KJV, "leader" RSV, Isaiah 14:9; used most often for the peace offerings made by the various families after the completion of the Tabernacle; most other passages are also sacrificial, with few lit. and fig. שעיר, *goat* [23] *he-goat* [1] *kid* [30] also *devil* [2] and *satyr* [2]; with the single exception of the first occurrence [Gen 37:31, a goat killed to provide blood for putting on Joseph's robe] this is used only for the sin offering and scapegoat; גדי, [male], *gedîyyāh* [fem.], *kid* [10], hence גדי עזים [7]; except for Isaiah 11:6, "leopard shall lie down with the kid," all are literal and only one is sacrificial—a special burnt offering [Judg 13:19]; prob. used only for kids of up to a few months, otherwise too young for standard sacrifices; תיש, *he-goat* [4], three in lit. contexts, and likely to be a nickname; צפיר, *goat* [2], *he-goat* [1], hence צפיר עזים, *he-goat* [4], a late word, prob. Aram., three times for sin offering and four times symbolic [Dan 8]; ἐρίφιον, *young kid, goat* [1]; ἔριφος, *kid, goat* [1], *kid* [1]; τράγος (masc.), *goat* [4]; these occur too rarely to show usage but *trágos* is found only in Hebrews 9 and 10, referring to *sāîr*, the sin offering; two general terms are also used for *small cattle*, i.e. sheep and goats, mixed or separate, צאן, a collective term for the group; שה, a member of such a group, almost always sing. (*See* SHEEP for more detailed discussion.) עדר, tr. *flock, drove* or *herd*, used mostly of sheep, but occasionally of goats, e.g. Song of Solomon 4:1, "like a flock of goats." The sexes are properly called he-goat and she-goat, but billy [-goat] and nanny [-goat] are much used. The young are known only as kid.

1. Origin and domestication. Many authorities consider the goat was the first domesticated ruminant. The main wild ancestor is still alive —the Bezoar, or Cretan Wild Goat (*Capra*

Goats on a Palestinian hillside. ©*M.P.S.*

aegagrus), which is reddish-brown in summer and gray-brown in winter. Its overall range is from India to Crete, but its numbers have been much reduced; it has disappeared from many areas, and elsewhere is very rare. A few remain in the mountain parts of Crete and an island of the Cyclades. Other wild goats from farther E have contributed to the stock, but the position is complicated. (*See* Zeuner, ch. 6.) All are hill animals and very sure-footed; they are browsers as much as grazers. Two factors add to the problem of dating: first, for some time the tame form did not differ markedly from the wild. Second, in many cases even experts cannot distinguish some bones of sheep and goats.

The earliest accepted evidence for domestication is from the Neolithic pre-pottery levels of Jericho, with carbon dating of 6,000-7,000 B.C. The remains of some horns show damage suggestive of close confinement. Material from N Iran is of similar age, prob. indicating an earlier origin from which both areas were supplied. Among the early goats, two types are recognized—with corkscrew and with scimitar horns. Gradually the variety increased in size, proportions, color and hair type; but the wide range of breeds now seen, esp. in Europe, is of modern origin. These show a wide range of colors, including black, white and parti-colored. The only Biblical mention of color is the spotted and speckled goats of Genesis 30. Ancient Egyp. art illustrates all these.

2. Uses. The goat was first kept for its milk. The meat was eaten, normally, of young only, e.g., Judges 6:19, "Gideon . . . prepared a kid," the standard meal for a stranger arriving unexpectedly. Later, the kid was less highly rated. Luke 15:29ff. compares it unfavorably with the fatted calf. Goatskins became the standard material for water bottles in countries of limited rainfall, and the hair was spun and woven into cloth. It seems that the sheep was tamed fairly soon after the goat (*see* SHEEP). Sheep began to replace goats in the areas where it could thrive, i.e. the less hilly places with better grazing, largely because it yielded much better meat, with ample fat, and wool instead of rather coarse hair. The goat was still valued as a milk-producer, but when the domestic cow became available, the goat was more and more confined to the rougher and drier areas. By the time of the patriarchs, sheep and cattle prob. greatly outnumbered goats. Milk is mentioned forty-two times in the OT; only four are specifically goats' milk, three of which refer to the prohibition against seething (boiling) a kid in its mother's milk (Exod 23:19, etc).

3. Damage to vegetation. Second to man, and with man's help, goats have been the most important land-destroyers in history (*see* FAUNA). In Mediterranean lands, they climb trees and destroy them by eating twigs and leaves. This is illustrated in ancient art. The goat is hardy, and if allowed to escape it can quickly establish itself and develop a feral race. The damage to vegetation continues, sometimes until the habitat is destroyed and, if it is an island, goats die of starvation.

4. Place in Biblical narrative. Numerous references in OT and NT show that the goat was important to the Hebrews, though the range of names and total numbers are far below the sheep and cattle. Goats are spoken of only once in thousands. "The Arabs also brought . . . seven thousand seven hundred he-goats" (2 Chron 17:11). In most W countries, the problem of dividing sheep from goats (Matt 25:32f.) would never arise, for flocks are unlikely to mix and the two species are not easily confused. This is not so, however, in many lands around Pal., where they often run together and native breeds may be alike in size, color, and shape. The usually up-turned goat tail may be the only obvious difference. Apart from one symbolic passage (Dan 8), the goat seems to have no fig. significance, but some seventy percent of the occurrences refer to animals for sacrifice. This would seem to have been its main importance to the Hebrews (*see* above). In addition, goats' hair was the material woven by Heb. women to cover the Tabernacle (Exod 26:7), and it is still used in tentmaking by the Bedouin. The context of scarlet, fine linen, etc. may imply superior quality cloth, perhaps comparable to cashmere from the Kashmir goat today. It is likely that long-haired races from farther E had become established by this time. In general, little can be inferred from the context about the natural history or habits of the goat.

BIBLIOGRAPHY. G. S. Cansdale, *Animals and Man* (1952); F. E. Zeuner, *A History of Domesticated Animals* (1963).

G. S. CANSDALE

GOATH. KJV form of GOAH.

GOATSKINS (תחש, *αἴγειον δέρμα, skin of a goat*). תחש usually occurs with עור or עורות, "skin(s)," to describe a covering for the Tabernacle (Exod 26:14), the Ark of the covenant, and several other articles in the Tabernacle (Num 4:6-14). Rendered "badgers' skin" in the KJV, תחש remains of dubious origin, although apparently a kind of leather. Women's shoes were made of תחש (Ezek 16:10 KJV).

Some connection with Arab. *tuḫas*, "dolphin," has been suggested. This term could refer to the dugong, "sea cow" found in the waters of Egypt and Sinai. The time of the Exodus suits the locale well.

A single NT reference (Heb 11:37 RSV), lauds the great men of faith who, among other deprivations wore the skins of sheep and goats.

BIBLIOGRAPHY. J. P. Free, *Archaeology and Bible History* (1956), 106.

H. M. WOLF

GOB **gŏb** (גּוֹב, גֹּב, *locusts*). A town mentioned only in 2 Samuel 21:18 and 19 where David's men twice battled the Philistines and the family of Goliath. It was presumably close to Philistine territory since Gath occurs in vv. 20 and 22. The parallel in 1 Chronicles 20:4 locates the battles in Gezer rather than Gob. The LXX and Syriac have "Gath" in place of "Gob" in Samuel. Although the MT of Samuel may be corrupt here, it should be noted that the name "locusts" fits the practice of sometimes naming towns after animals or insects.

H. M. WOLF

GOBLET (כֵּלִים, *vessels, utensils*). Esther 1:7 mentions "different kinds" of golden goblets (KJV "vessels") for the royal wine at Ahasuerus' feast. The sing. "goblet" occurs in Song of Solomon 7:2 (KJV) for אַגַּן, properly "bowl, basin."

GOD

I. Biblical view grounded in God's self-revelation
II. Scholastic view based on rationalistic proofs
III. Modern transition from speculative theism to naturalism
    A. Neo-Protestant reactions and concessions
        1. Liberal theology
        2. Dialectical theology
        3. Existential theology
        4. Ecumenical chaos
    B. Secular views and death-of-God speculation
IV. Evangelical evaluation of influential current views
    A. Avoidance of empirical orientation
    B. Correlation of religion with all human concerns
    C. Emphasis on human decision and initiative
    D. Dilution of the supernatural character of revelation
    E. Distortion of sacred Biblical motifs.
    F. Attempted reformulation of transcendence
    G. Tenuous role of reason in religion

I. Biblical view grounded in God's self-revelation

Evangelical Christianity traces to divine self-revelation all authentic information about God's reality, perfections, and purposes. This supernatural disclosure is universally given in nature, history, and conscience, and in the special redemptive events of Judeo-Christian history climaxed by the incarnation of the Logos. In the inspired Scriptures God has addressed to man, as fallen and sinful, an objective, propositional declaration of His nature and work centering in redemptive rescue.

The Bible reveals God as the eternal Spirit, the infinite Creator and preserver, judge of all the universe, and redeemer of all who put their faith in Him. Its characterization of the living God is everywhere related to divine disclosure. The summary by the Westminster divines remains highly serviceable: "God is a Spirit, infinite, eternal, and unchanging in His being, wisdom, power, holiness, justice, goodness and truth." Whereas modern theory expounds love as the core of divine being, and deprives other attributes of equal ultimacy in the divine nature, this statement defines love (as a manifestation of goodness) in a way that does not subordinate the righteousness and justice of God.

II. Scholastic view based on rationalistic proofs

The medieval scholastics tended to shift discussion of the case for theism from revelation to speculation, and as a result the exposition of God's nature acquired rationalistic metaphysical overtones. Thomas Aquinas, in the 13th cent. shaped the traditionally official theology of the Roman Catholic Church. His *Summa* contended that, apart from any appeal to divine revelation, the existence of God, and the existence and immortality of the human soul, are logically demonstrable, as a necessary inference from the universe. Thomas also asserted that man thus acquires a knowledge only of the divine existence but not of the divine essence. He further distinguished between univocal and analogical knowledge, denying that man's knowledge of God coincides at any point with God's knowledge of Himself. The scholastics thus compromised the importance and primacy of divine revelation and rested the case for theism first and foremost on natural theology.

III. Modern transition from speculative theism to naturalism

With the rise of modern philosophy, speculative theism further displaced Biblical theism. From Descartes onward, the case for the supernatural is typically referred to nature and to man; no longer is it grounded in an appeal to special divine disclosure, the incarnate Logos, and the inspired Scriptures. Medieval theorizing had prepared the way for this speculative trend, and Protestant reformers vigorously protested it, as seen in the writings of Calvin and Luther. Descartes, a distinguished Jesuit mathematician, remained a professing Catholic despite his assertion of skepticism as a philosophical method. He predicated all truth, including proof of God's existence, upon prior establishment of the reality of the self. From innate ideas he derived the existence of God as perfect being, omniscent, omnipotent, and infinite. Descartes' scheme embraced a curious circularity: in the clearness and distinctiveness of man's ideas he grounded man's certainty of knowledge regarding his own existence and God's, yet he invoked God's veracity as the guarantee of this knowledge.

By its speculative rather than scriptural orientation of the question of God, modern philosophy was led to successive and extensive revisions of Christian doctrine. Unitarian theism insisted on the unipersonality of God as against trinitarianism, so that the divine triunity was an early casualty. God's role as creator remained, although pantheists viewed the universe and man in terms of emanation rather than of creation *ex nihilo*. Divine redemptive activity was less and less understood in Biblical categories.

Yet, in its beginnings, modern philosophy (Descartes, Leibnitz, Spinoza, Locke, Berkeley, Kant, Hegel) was theistic or idealistic rather than naturalistic in intention and mood. But once the case for theism abandoned revelation as its ground, and a Biblical basis was ignored, the exposition of the supernatural was increasingly vexed by instability. The ground of belief was shifted away from divine disclosure to human reason, experience, intuition, or other facets of man's awareness. Although supernaturalistic in its beginnings, modern philosophy moved swiftly and suddenly toward naturalism.

A. Neo-Protestant reactions and concessions. Kant, although a professed theist, had surrendered all cognitive knowledge of metaphysical realities; he considered God a regulative ideal demanded by man's moral nature but insisted that knowledge of suprasensible reality is unattainable. In the *Prolegomena to Any Future Metaphysics* Kant mentions the possibility of an analogical noncognitive notion of God: "a concept of the Supreme Being sufficiently determined *for us,* though we have left out everything that could determine it absolutely or in itself"—thus discarding "objective anthropomorphism" (sec. 58). Here one readily finds anticipations of more recent theological emphases.

Hegel stressed Reason, but transmuted the Christian emphasis that God is revealed as truth and spirit into a spiritual monism; his pantheistic theory of the Absolute forsook the scriptural doctrine of God as a reality transcendent to nature and man. Although he retained a trinitarian approach, Hegel recast history as the differentiation of the Infinite into finite manisfestations by a dialectical process. He deliberately chose the term *Geist* as a governing principle. He thrust aside Kant's restrictions on man's competency to know metaphysical truth, but his abortive doctrine of the Holy Spirit led to unbiblical notions of man's reason as the candle of the Lord. In *The Spirit of Christianity* he miscarried the Biblical view of man in the image of God to a perverse emphasis that man as spirit can grasp and comprehend the divine Spirit in his present condition apart from mediated revelation, and sought to reinforce this notion by an exegesis of selected passages from John's gospel. In deference to his speculations of evolutionary pantheistic immanence, he erased the adverse noetic consequences of the fall of man, concealed the need of once-for-all divine revelation and redemption, and through his false metaphysics misstated even the doctrine of general revelation. This denial of God's transcendence, and of divine wrath against man as sinner, and of the need of miraculous redemption—predicated on immanentistic evolutionary assumptions—became decisive elements of classic rationalistic modernism.

1. *Liberal theology.* During the late 19th cent. and into the second decade of the 20th, the religious philosophies of Kant and Hegel were theologically most influential. Kant had differentiated God from man and the universe but he had condemned man to cognitive ignorance of the supernatural; his concealment of the reality and intelligibility of divine revelation inspired a vast variety of anti-metaphysical theologies. Hegel promoted human competence in the realm of metaphysics by unabashedly making man a part of God; thus he obscured the real presence of God in his transcendent confrontation of man as a finite creation and moral rebel. In either event the religious spirit of the age set itself over against revelation in the Biblical understanding, and consequently lent itself to arbitrary notions of deity.

Despite the fabulous supernaturalisms advanced by the metaphysical idealists of the 19th cent., or perhaps encouraged by it, the modern movement in philosophy continued away from theism toward humanism or naturalism; idealistic theory was constantly beset by waning faith in God. Karl Marx, in revolt against Hegel, described the real world not as an evolutionary manifestation of Absolute Spirit, but as a process of dialectical materialism—with economic determinism as its critical center. John Dewey retained the term God while he rejected the supernatural; empirical scientific method had become for him the sole arbiter of what modern man can know and believe. The humanists welcomed liberal Protestant concessions that disowned the miracles of the Bible, but pressed the modernists additionally to reject the absoluteness of Jesus of Nazareth on the ground of its equal incompatibility with empirical methodology as the definitive criterion of knowledge. The perverse misunderstanding of divine revelation led on, therefore, not only to a rejection of idealistic speculative theology, with its confusion of God's acting and speaking with man's history and religious life, but automatically and uncritically also to rejection of the God of Biblical revelation so long obscured and nullified by the heaven-absorbing idealists.

Freed from dependence on and answerability to Biblical revelation, modern religious philosophers swiftly and successively assailed one or another facet of the inherited Judeo-Christian view of God. Naturalists waged a comprehensive frontal attack on the basic emphasis that God is Spirit—an immaterial and invisible mind and will. The naturalistic philosophy could tolerate no reality superior to and independent of the space-time continuum; whatever gods it accommodated were simply capitalized aspects of the space-time process. But lesser assaults on the Christian definition of God were also common. As had John Stuart Mill in the 19th cent., so Edgar S. Brightman in the 20th rejected the infinity of God for a finite deity. Henry Nelson Wieman, contrary to the traditional emphasis on God as eternal and unchanging, dignified the moving front of the evolutionary process as divine. Not a single divine attribute affirmed by historic Christian theology was undisputed in the recent modern period; in fact, many neo-Protestant theologians not only denied a distinction between divine goodness or benevolence and justice, but some even promoted a "new morality" that in God's name approved conduct contravening the divine commands in Scripture.

An overview of early 20th cent. theological speculation will disclose its oscillation between innate, historical, and experiential approaches to the doctrine of God. Belief in God was grounded in finite man's feeling of anxiety or cosmic loneliness; or as an awareness of divinity involved in man's sense of absolute dependence; or viewed as a subjective necessity of human nature; or as a precognitive intuition; or as a psychic response to the mystery of the universe. Or this belief was derived from empirical reflection upon nature, or affirmed as a requirement of man's moral nature, or regarded as an inference either from the decline of civilization or from supposed evolutionary progress.

2. *Dialectical theology.* The Hegelian orientation of 19th cent. religious thought underlay the anthropocentric character of much of its theology. All questions about God were raised in the context of human experience on the assumption of an essential kinship and partial identity of the human and divine Spirit. This secularizing religious trend was called into judgment by the theology of crisis through its vigorous reassertion of special divine revelation—the Word of God confronting man from without, and making an absolute demand upon him. Yet the single most influential factor shaping neo-Protestant theology had perhaps been Kant's anti-metaphysical dogma that the limits of human reason exclude cognitive knowledge of supernatural reality. Even Barth, who strove energetically to rise above Ritschl's disparagement of knowledge in favor of trust as the essence of Christian experience, held in his earliest writings that the quest for conceptual knowledge of God characterizes speculative philosophy and not prophetic-apostolic declaration. Even when Barth later insisted that the believer has religiously adequate knowledge of God, he hedged this concession: the believer acquires this knowledge only as a bonus of personal divine confrontation. Thus Barth still left in doubt the universal validity of the believer's conceptions of God even on the basis of special revelation. Neo-Protestant theology has characteristically shunned metaphysics as an illicit concern, or at least as outside the orbit of divine revelation. It depicted the Biblical interest in divine transcendence as simply kerygmatic—that is, as expressive of faith-constructs rather than of cognitive trust about supernatural reality; hence, the religious exposition of divine transcendence was distinguished from philosophical affirmations about metaphysical transcendence in a way that stripped cognitive rights from the theologians and conferred them—if any—wholly upon the philosophers.

Nonetheless the rise of neo-orthodoxy after World War I marked a new theological era increasingly predicated on divine transcendence, special revelational disclosure, and wrath against sin. By the 1930s, crisis theology, or dialectical theology as it was widely designated, achieved the open collapse of classic modernism as a formative theological influence in Europe. Both Barth and Emil Brunner espoused the view that God meets human beings paradoxically in the Word, and personally makes that Word his own. Against Ritschlian theology, Barth insisted that divine wrath has NT as well as OT reality: Jesus' crucifixion supremely exhibits the fact that God meets man in wrath and grace in the NT as he met Israel in the OT. Yet Barth carried forward the modernist subordination of divine righteousness and wrath to love, and inadequately related the latter to the core of God's being. In expounding God's perfections, Barth considers righteousness and mercy, wrath and love, simply as variants of the same scriptural theme.

For all the neo-orthodox reaffirmation of divine transcendence, its delineation of divinity was vulnerable through its compromise of the historical evangelical acknowledgment of scripturally revealed truths about God. The dialectical theology had the merit of restoring some elements of Judeo-Christian revelation, but it obscured others, and in fact explicitly rejected propositional scriptural revelation. Barth's warning that modernism's loss of the self-revealing God made unavoidable the loss of God Himself, was too indefinite. The lesson taught by neo-orthodoxy is that the loss of an inscripturated revelation leads to the loss of the Judeo-Christian God who acts and speaks for Himself.

3. *Existential theology.* Rudolf Bultmann's existential theology, projected as a counterthrust to the Barthian view, soon won its way. Bultmann insisted that Barth's essential emphasis that God transcendently reveals Himself in personal confrontation requires neither the Biblical miracles, nor a correlation of revelation with the Biblical history. Bultmann therefore dismissed interest in the historical Jesus, and shifted the center of Christian faith to the kerygmatic, or apostolically-proclaimed Christ. Barth's theological effort to sustain quasi-objectivity for God, against an approach that seemed wholly to subjectivize God, proved unavailing; Bultmann's alternative emphasized the reality of God while wholly dispensing with larger remnants of an evangelical theology on which Barth had insisted.

Many contemporary theologians assail the modernist theology of the recent past for suppressing the once-for-all uniqueness of the Christ-event in its exposition of divine revelation. Yet this criticism proceeds not from evangelical but rather from existential motivations. It is charged that the entire past theological tradition—both evangelical and modernist—misunderstood the "true" nature of the revelation event, now redefined as recurring personal confrontation. This reconstruction of the doctrine of revelation rests on a radical exaggeration of God's transcendence by current dialectical and/or existential theologians. Consequently they deny that revelation is mediated objectively in historical events or in human concepts and language, and dismiss the revelatory status of Scripture in order to insist on contemporaneous disclosure. Sören Kierkegaard's emphasis on the leap of faith that alone bridges the gulf between eternity and time, his notion of the moment filled with eternity, inspired this correlation of faith and Christ-event in contrast to the Biblical and evangelical understanding of revelation. Here the Christ-event no longer bears the meaning of an occurrence open to historical investigation, nor is "once-for-allness" associated with a content of revelation mediated by divinely chosen prophets and apostles.

In the Bible the events of holy history—supremely the crucifixion and resurrection of Jesus Christ—carry a revelation-meaning that the inspired writings define in the context of prophecy and fulfillment. But Bultmann's philosophical bias forces his dismissal of all history as ambiguous; instead he assimilates revelation wholly to contemporary personal experience. Bultmann disavows as revelation the sacred truths delivered once-for-all by the Bible prophets and apostles; revelation he redefines rather as an eschatological event that happens again and again in the existential response of persons throughout the life of the Church.

Barthian dialectical theology was unable to stem a declension to the existentialism of Bultmann, with its "demythologizing" of the miraculous elements of the NT. The Bultmannian approach in turn was unable to arrest a further decline. For the so-called Mainz radicals, Herbert Braun and Manfred Mezger, reduced God to the anthropological dimension of love in intrapersonal relationships. From the left, existentialist theologians have been pressed to indicate on what ground they insist that it is only in the Word (Christ) that God confronts men (Schubert Ogden), or why, quite apart from insistence on the supernatural, *agape* in interpersonal relationships may not as authentically define divine confrontation and response?

Recent modern theology emphasizes the hiddenness of God, mainly on the basis of dialectical or existential projections of divine revelation as extra-rational. A passage from a recent book by J. Rodman Williams serves to illuminate this ready transition of existential theories to the secular point of view:

> "Existentialism, philosophical and theological, atheistic and non-atheistic, non-Christian and Christian, is quite closely related to the obscurity of God. It matters not whether this be the 'silence of God' (Sartre), the 'absence of God' (Heidegger), the 'concealment of God' (Jaspers), the 'non-being of God' (Tillich), or the 'hiddenness of God' (Bultmann). . . . The obscurity of God might indeed be called 'the Eclipse of God' (*Contemporary Existentialism and Christian Faith* [1965], pp. 63f.).

Evangelical theologians have resisted attempts to equate such treatments with Luther's stress on the hidden God. G. C. Berkouwer rightly indicts a "completely unbiblical concept of God" that separates the God of revelation from the lives of believers and compromises "the absolute trustworthiness and sufficiency" of His revelation (*Divine Election* [1955], 125). Berkouwer repudiates the conception of a God who discloses just enough of Himself to keep man in despair of ever knowing the real God. God is hidden to the worldly-wise and proud; He is revealed to the humble who seek grace. The problem of revelation is not divine paradox but human pride. The paradox theologians, Berkouwer notes, postulate an inverted natural theology, by locating the offense of Christianity in an abstract dialectic (based on the supposed infinite qualitative difference between God and man) rather than in its demand for repentance and rescue (*The Work of Christ* [1965], 34).

4. *Ecumenical chaos in theology.* By the last third of the 20th cent. the neo-Protestant ecumenical scene was in complete disarray respecting the nature and reality of God, and in Protestant circles only evangelical scholars championed the case for Biblical theism on the ground of revelation and reason.

B. Secular views and death-of-God speculation. Some philosophical theologians attempted a revival of interest in ontology. Among these was Paul Tillich, who defined ontology, however, not to designate a spiritual reality "beyond the world," but to refer to a structure of orders of being supposedly encountered in man's meeting with reality; the immanent ground of being replaces the supernatural transcendent God. His notion that the modern scientific world-view annuls any possibility of faith in the supernatural God of the Bible is patently arbitrary. The supernatural has been a problem for every secular world-view, prescientific or scientific. The transcendent Creator-Redeemer God of the Bible was no less alien to the thinking of Plotinus and Seneca, Descartes and Hegel, than to Bishop John A. T. Robinson. The bias against the Biblical view springs from a readiness to taper the methods of knowing reality to empirically-based rationalism.

Reinhold Niebuhr countered Tillich's view by insisting that God is a mysterious source of order above and beyond the orders and evils of the world. But Niebuhr, too, rejected objectifiable knowledge of God, and grounded affirmations of divine transcendence in the supposed dialectical experience of man in relation to the divine. Hence, the assertion of transcendence implied an epistemological predicament rather than metaphysical affirmation defining God's perfections.

The recent secular tendency to rest the case for theism wholly upon empirical scientific investigation of reality rules out in advance the existence of a supernatural God, by delimiting the field of reality to areas of inquiry that fall within this methodology. But it has also provoked the rise of linguistic theology, which defends the validity of language about trans-empirical supernatural reality as functionally meaningful, but not as conceptually true. But if religious language merely reflects a psychological or experimental necessity in man, and the cognitive validity of religious ideas is ruled out, then no reason can be adduced for preferring one religion to another, or any to none.

One outcome of modern theological declension toward a wholly secular view of life was the emergence of "death of God" speculation, which revived a theme already found in Nietzsche. Some writers, like Gabriel Vahanian, by their reference to the "death of God" simply refer factually to the modern cultural development wherein the reality of God has increasingly become an irrelevance. A Jewish rabbi has said, "God is dead as seen from Auschwitz."

Others, like Thomas J. J. Altizer, contend that in the crucifixion of Christ, God literally died, and that since the events of the gospels the human Jesus alone has formative significance for Christianity.

It is noteworthy that neo-Protestant theological formulations have had a shorter survival span as the decades have passed. Of all the short-term options in neo-Protestant theology, the death-of-God view has most swiftly run its course. The vast majority of theologians today readily identify themselves with the comment of John B. Cobb Jr., that the reality of the referent of "God" as part of one's intellectual conviction is "a matter of life or death" for one's spiritual existence as a Christian. Already the contemporary scene shows signs of a new quest for God. Theological concentration on this theme is still more evident in theological journals and in paperback publications than in larger tomes, but the call for new devotion to systematic theology is also heard. This mood does not characterize all branches of the Church; in Europe young seminarians disillusioned by the constantly changing frontiers in theology are taking a "wait and see" attitude that defers specific commitments, while in America, where more of the old liberalism survives on seminary campuses than elsewhere, many students doubt that a theology is possible, and more are unable to identify their commitment in terms of specifics.

IV. Evangelical evaluation of influential current views

The 20th cent. has been an age of extensive travel in theology no less than in tourism. The doctrine of God has emerged in recent modern thought as a main departure point for highly novel excursions. Although the many speculations about deity so conflict and compete that no identifiable "contemporary view" of God exists, a number of distinguishing features characterize some of the more influential modern theories. A survey of the slant and emphasis of these more recent views will aid us in comparing and contrasting them with the historic Christian doctrine of God, and in assessing the current trend in the light of the Biblical revelation of God.

A. Avoidance of empirical orientation. Recent modern theology exhibits a marked disinclination to base the case for theism on empirical arguments from man and the world, and a tendency rather to view the traditional proofs of God as an endeavor to confirm or justify a belief antecedently held or received on other grounds.

The contemporary outlook, in other words, avoids the view of Aquinas, who held that by experience alone, apart from revelation, one can logically demonstrate God's existence by the so-called "fivefold proof." Except by a rather small circle of scholars seeking to revive an emphasis on "natural theology," empirical evidences, where now adduced, are cast at most in a supportive role. There is a divided response to the critical theory of Kant, who limited the content of man's knowledge to sense experience and rejected rational metaphysics, but postulated God as a "regulative" ideal. Those who exalt scientific empiricism as the only method of verification tend to shun faith in the supernatural entirely, and are prone to promote a wholly secular theology, although some linguistic theologians perpetuate the notion that the role of religious theory in man's life is psychological rather than cognitive. But much recent modern theology connects the case for theism with divine revelation, by stressing God's self-demonstration in His words and ways as the basis of faith, or moves behind empirical considerations to man's primal ontological awareness of a religious reality.

For the wrong reasons some influential Christian spokesmen in the recent past have totally dismissed all empirical considerations.

Kierkegaard espoused the view that, as absolutely different, God the "wholly Other" poses a limit to human reason. He asserted the certainty of God's existence, but held that the philosopher must leap to a conclusion beyond proof and evidence, because faith by nature supposedly involves an act of will that cannot be rationally justified. Whereas Kant made non-cognition of God a basis for faith, Kierkegaard tied faith in God to a direct paradoxic divine-human confrontation. So radically did Kierkegaard disjoin eternity and time that man's epistemological predicament assertedly requires a divine Teacher who gives truth in the form of Absolute Paradox—the infinite in the form of a servant.

The bankruptcy of natural theology became a leading motif of neo-orthodox theology (*see* esp. Barth's *Church Dogmatics* I/1 and I/2), and then of existential theology. These movements emphasize personal revelational disclosure and individual response; they repudiate objective metaphysical knowledge on any basis, and disparage universally valid truths about God. Barth considered the theological anthropology of Hegelian idealism a special target, since it viewed man and nature as extensions or manifestations of God. To Barth, all association of divine revelation with man and the universe seemed objectionably to imply that these are God's necessary environment. Hence Barth's insistence that there is no way "up" to God by proofs or arguments from human consciousness or nature led him at the same time to repudiate a general divine revelation in man and the world.

Emil Brunner, however, championed general revelation. He refused to brush aside the speculative arguments for God as insignificant, and stressed that philosophical theism is the closest approximation of God possible to reason independent of special revelation. But, like Barth, he insisted that the living God is known only in paradoxic personal confrontation.

Dooyeweerd likewise eliminates metaphysics as a rational science. Yet he insists on a revelation of God in nature, a general Word-revelation, which man as sinner holds down and perverts. God's common grace conserves the fallen cosmos, but provides no basis for the autonomy of reason in the natural sphere, and no ground for natural theology; common grace can itself be understood only in terms of God's special grace in Christ.

Contemporary expositions of Thomistic philosophy have acquired a defensive character, partly because neo-Protestant theology reasserted the priority of special revelation, and partly because of evangelical and other criticisms of the medieval "fivefold proof." Whereas Aquinas appealed in his pursuit of natural theology to reason without faith, in order to arrive at reason with faith, and whereas neo-Protestant theologians like Barth promote a theology of faith beyond reason, evangelical thinkers like J. Gresham Machen, Edward John Carnell, Gordon H. Clark, and Cornelius Van Til emphasized faith and reason, or revelation and reason, to combine the priority of divine revelation with the intelligible revelational significance of man and the universe. Clark shows that the Thomistic arguments and their modern reconstruction are invalid (*Religion, Reason and Revelation* [1961], 36ff.).

George F. Thomas grants that the empirical fivefold proof does not yield logically certain knowledge of God, but holds that they "approximate" the truth, and espouses a modified form of Aquinas' arguments. More significantly, he relates the empirical arguments to a belief in God otherwise arrived at, and hence as making faith more reasonable (*Religious Philosophies of the West* [1965], 320). This reconstruction leaves in doubt the serviceability of the arguments as empirical proofs.

Among evangelical scholars, J. Oliver Buswell Jr. and Stewart Hackett have revived emphasis on the empirical arguments for God. Buswell grants that the theistic arguments cannot logically prove God's existence, but assigns them the force of probability (*A Systematic Theology of the Christian Religion* [1962], 72); he adds to the Thomistic arguments an inductive form of the ontological argument, and holds that the arguments establish "a presumption in favor of faith in the God of the Bible," and that unbelief is morally culpable (ibid., p. 100). He stresses that personal faith is a divine gift, but that the Holy Spirit uses the inductive arguments in persuading and converting sinners. It may be replied, however, that the arguments supply an occasion rather than the rationale for faith, and that the Spirit actually reinforces unsuppressed facets of the *imago Dei* in the context of God's revelation.

A. N. Whitehead made no effort formally to demonstrate God's existence, but rather appeals to man's religious intuition and seeks to confirm God's existence in conjunction with metaphysical considerations. Somewhat akin to the cosmological argument is his appeal from the "forms of definiteness" (rather than from their existence) to a primordial mind as their causal support, if not their absolute creator. Similarities to the teleological argument underlie the movement from the subjective aim of actual entities seeking satisfaction through value experience, to God as the final cause presenting "lures for feeling." Whereas the cosmological-teleological appeal survives in the emphasis that the world's order and value are best explained by God's purpose to realize maximal good, religious intuition plays an essential role, and from it Whitehead derives assurance that God will conserve whatever good is attained in the world. More recent statements of process philosophy have been provided by Charles Hartshorne, D. D. Williams and Schubert Ogden.

The importance of man's primal ontological awareness has been reasserted in a variety of ways. Frederick Herzog stresses a precognitive feeling of reality that raises the religious question in every man's experience. Tillich considered the sense of human finitude as at the same time an awareness of God, or the Ground of Being. Even John B. Cobb, Jr., who carries Whitehead's philosophy more fully in the direction of natural theology, concedes an elemental human intuition that the order of the world requires a transcendent explanation. William Horder thinks the worldwide sense of awe and reverence over the mystery of the universe evokes theological language, but that God the Mystery reveals Himself only to the response of personal faith. But it is apparent that the Barthian denial of any human point-of-contact for divine revelation is under increasing pressure. The significance of man's primal ontological awareness of a religious reality is again being probed, and while most contemporary discussions shy away from cognitive implications, a climate is emerging in which the traditional evangelical understanding of man's intuitive experience of God can find new visibility.

Clark insists that it is impossible to construct a valid logical argument for the existence of an infinite God from finite empirical data—whether man or the world, and rests the case for theism wholly upon rational a priori considerations rooted in divine revelation.

Cornelius Van Til contends that the unbeliever cannot reach a theistic conclusion based on empirical proofs because nonbelievers and believers assertedly view reality on wholly divergent premises. While the believer derives the knowledge of God from revelation rather than from nature and man, the theistic evidences serve to confirm the believer's faith in the reality and nature of the living God.

The doctrine of God in contemporary thought is now widely connected to divine self-revelation, or to intuitive considerations, or to both; an empirical grounding of the case for theism is now largely avoided, and appeals to man and the universe most frequently appear as attempts to justify or confirm belief in God already held and acquired in another way.

B. Correlation of religion with all human concerns. The schematic correlation of the claims of religion, philosophy, history, and science into a comprehensive world-life view holds intellectual fascination even for the contemporary mind. Despite the anti-metaphysical mood of our age, the most formative and influential writers integrate theological perspectives with the main concerns of modern life and learning in a synthetic overview. Even theologians whose knowledge-theory leads them to disown universally valid religious truth, propound systematic treatises relating their theological principles to all life and experience. Barth has written the largest and profoundest *Church Dogmatics* since the Thomistic age. Although he detaches Christian revelation from commitment to any particular world-view (*Church Dogmatics,* III/2, p. 447), he nonetheless discusses philosophy, science, and history on the margin of dialectical revelation. Much of the power of Tillich's speculative ontology is surely due to the fact that his *Systematic Theology* propounds a philosophical apologetics addressed not simply to believers but to man as man; theological perspectives assertedly grounded in revelation are correlated with philosophical considerations derived from an analysis of the human predicament. Whitehead's philosophical vision derives its appeal in large measure from his attempt to synthesize metaphysical interests (the cosmical attributes of God asserted by the classic philosophers) with the personal perfections of the living God of Biblical revelation in their bearing on major scientific developments and universal human concerns; he blends Judeo-Christian and Greek motifs in a bold religious ontology that seeks to vindicate ultimate meaning, purpose, and value while emphasizing the limitation of science in an age when the scientific outlook is widely correlated with naturalism. Teilhard presents scientific and confessional approaches side by side in his rational synthesis of experimental, historical, philosophical, and religious concerns.

Dooyeweerd gives Judeo-Christian revelation a significance for every frontier of human theory and action in a radical critique of theoretical thought, and insists that Christian philosophy not only best explains the meaning of reality and life but it also unmasks the basically alien religious motives of the secular alternatives.

Clark insists that Christian presuppositions alone can suggest a satisfactory world-view, that for their solution the problems of science and history and ethics and politics require theistic premises, and that all mediating positions between Biblical Christianity and atheistic naturalism are reducible to incoherence.

It is evident that the dialectical-existential revolt against rational persuasion, and the recent anti-mind mood, have not destroyed the modern interest in intellectual synthesis. Those thinkers influential in serious circles today seek convincingly to correlate their explanation of reality and life with the whole range of human concerns.

C. Emphasis on human decision and initiative. The diminishing modern emphasis on divine election, divine creation, divine revelation, and divine redemption, as scripturally understood, has dwarfed interest in the Biblical view of God and stunted its power in modern life. The modern stress on human competence in respect to man's present fortunes and final destiny suppresses a recognition of God's decisive role in man's life and affairs. It is significant that a vigorous reassertion of even isolated aspects of the Biblical view—as in the neo-orthodox emphasis on divine initiative—tends to revive interest in the historic Christian conception of God. But a lasting impact is thwarted because the scriptural view is fragmented and combined with current speculations.

The Bible doctrine of divine election is a stark reminder that nobody would escape divine wrath were it not for God's gracious intervention in a fallen world. The declaration that God in sovereign mercy elects a fallen remnant to salvation in Christ notifies all sinners that the slightest hope of their redemptive rescue depends wholly upon divine initiative. This emphasis pervades Clark's exposition of election, which combines the traditional Reformed view that God mercifully elects some and justly reprobates others, with the "supralapsarian" position that God willed to save some and to reprobate others before He willed to create any. This ties the bare possibility of salvation to the gracious will of God alone; whatever difficulties this exposition of election may pose, it wholly inverts the popular modern notion that man is the sovereign master of his destiny.

The modern theologians who retain and reformulate the doctrine of election usually destroy the urgency of personal decision for Christ. Despite many divergences in their theology, Barth and Brunner dismiss Calvin"s view that God's decree of election predetermines the redemption of some and reprobation of others. Yet they cannot dilute the scriptural view into mere foreknowledge—since the Biblical references to foreknowledge also imply foreordination—and the resultant effort to preserve a crucial role for divine election leads to highly fanciful theories. Barth regards Christ as the electing God and elected man; since all mankind is comprehended in the election of the man Jesus, and none are excluded, universal election seems the logical and inevitable outcome. Brunner too insists that election is only in Christ, but avoids universal salvation by asserting an area outside Christ, in line with traditional theology; yet his postulation of a possibility of decision-for-Christ after death and hence of salvation for everyone in the life to come robs the doctrine of election of force.

Berkouwer criticizes these arbitrary compromises. He rejects as wholly speculative Barth's notion that the historical Jesus is the electing One who embraces all mankind. He emphasizes that Scripture views this lifetime as decisive for spiritual destiny, whereas universalism and an open-ended doctrine of salvation destroy the urgency of present commitment. Berkouwer agrees with Barth and Brunner in rejecting reprobation as a logical corollary of election; moreover, he shares Barth's contention that election is not a discrimination by sovereign divine decree prior to grace, a happening predetermined in eternity, but rather is a present event. He does not, however, clarify why what is now happening cannot also have been a matter of past divine foreordination.

Most recent expositions dilute the doctrine of election still further. George Thomas limits both divine foreordination and foreknowledge; God is not the ultimate cause of all events, and divine knowledge does not extend to future contingent events. Here divine initiative is compromised beyond the tolerance of both Reformed and Thomistic theology.

Reinhold Niebuhr existentializes the doctrine of election—along with the concepts of "creation-fall-redemption." It remained for Bultmann, however, to dismiss an eternal divine decree as sheer myth, although insisting that God so determines man's life in addressing him that by faith he is compelled to speak of Him. The atheistic existentialists retain the dramatic emphasis that human decision defines man's ultimate destiny, but dispose entirely of Bultmann's "ghost-God." The confrontation of the transcendent becomes for them simply the claim of man's higher destiny upon his consciousness; in man's own response lies the power to decree the future course of history and the universe.

For Tillich, the immanent "Ground of Being" structures all selves and things and preserves them. If any doctrine of election survives, it signals little more than the universal "givenness" of things in its bearing on the finitude of life, rather than a divine decree to rescue doomed persons from sin's penalty and power.

Whitehead's denial of divine omnipotence weakens God's concrete causal power in the universe, and removes any assured final outcome of history. Whitehead sees God as the source of the order of nature wherein new values arise, and as the final cause that guides creatures in conceiving these, but God has only a persuasive relationship to the world of temporal entities as the source of its subjective aims.

Teilhard wholly sacrifices the election motif to a progressive spiritual evolution in space-time, though organic humanity, to a Center in the universal activity of the cosmic Christ that maximizes the personalization of all humanity. Redemption is not grounded on the historical death of Jesus; Christ's incarnation, rather, enables Him to subdue, control, and purify the evolutionary ascent of consciousness.

Although he protests recent assertions of God's metaphysical dependence upon the world, George Thomas compromises both God's sovereignty and foreknowledge by suspending God's steadfast purpose upon changing human situations and acts. On the basis of the "divine repentance" passages in the Bible he rejects God's absolute unchangeableness, incorporates temporal succession into God's eternity, and admits change into divine immutability.

As a main characteristic, therefore, modern religious thought inflates human initiative and contracts divine freedom. This suppression of the Biblical view of the Creator and Redeemer who by His sovereign decision fashions a special calling for mankind, and as Lord of the Covenant provides salvation for some of His fallen creatures, has fatal consequences for the doctrine of God in modern life. For such a diminution of the role of sovereign divinity in relation to human destiny presumes to make man the master of his fate at every critical turn, and by the same token, dispenses with God in the strategic decisions of life, relating him only to secondary human concerns. But the God of the Bible refuses to let history take its own course, and to abandon the course of events to man's arbitrary will; He works out His sovereign goal in the lives of men, and makes even those who resist Him fulfill His purpose.

Just as a weakened doctrine of God's predetermination deprives divine decision of forceful significance for human destiny, so recent expositions of divine creation likewise obscure

God's effective causal power in the universe, and particularly in relation to man's existence. Radical secular theologians, who contend that science has discredited miracle and has debased the supernatural, necessarily deprive the Biblical view of creation of intellectual value.

Bultmann thinks nature is controlled only by immanent forces and that modern science precludes the miraculous; therefore he dismisses as an illusion the view of God as a creative source. Tillich, too, dispenses with the supernatural; God survives not as Creator, but as a quasi-pantheistic ground of all being. Niebuhr expounds the creation doctrine in terms of existential experience rather than of causal explanation, and Brunner similarly substitutes the newer notion of divine address in interpersonal confrontation for the traditional understanding of divine creation in terms of cosmic causality. Even Barth's view, that Genesis is "saga" rather than myth or fairy tale, seems to equivocate about the causal-historical implications of creation.

Whitehead finds evolutionary theory and the newer views of matter incompatible with materialism, but he allows no finality to any formulation of truth, whether philosophical, scientific, or religious. Whitehead readily combines Gr. and medieval emphases; the personal energy and sovereignty of God are adjusted to a rational teleological order partly immanent in God. As a result, God's love and purpose for the world are viewed as necessary expressions of His nature, and divine will and initiative are restricted. Whitehead writes: "It is as true to say that God creates the world as that the world creates God" (*Adventures of Ideas,* 528). The assimilation of God to immanent process is seen in Whitehead's emphasis that the plurality of individual units of becoming (actual entities) that compose the world, and exemplify creative novelty, arise through *concrescence* as an interplay of newly arising and perishing aspects. Panpsychism is evident in Whitehead's relating of all entities to a larger world of objects through the experience of feeling (prehension); eternal objects are potentially present components of actual entities—much as the eternal ideas or forms in classic Gr. speculation—and through them actual entities assertedly gain a mental pole along with the physical, and are guided toward a "satisfaction" that requires the interdependence of God and the world. Measured by the scriptural doctrine of creation, his theory grossly distorts the Judeo-Christian revelation of a sovereign Creator independent of the universe and vastly diminishes the creative causal energy of God.

Teilhard's philosophy combines faith in God's creative origin of the world with the scientific possibility that the world arose by accident; his retention of the creation-concept seems, therefore, to serve little rational purpose. His exposition of the omnipresence of potentially divine substance relies more heavily on motifs derived from Leibnitz and Kant than from Moses. Teilhard asserts that the simple primordial elements of reality, harboring an inner spiritual energy, have evolved progressively into different orders of advancing complexity of psychic concentration. In creating the final universe devout human beings collaborate with Christ to promote world spiritualization through the ascendency of spiritual forms while the incarnate Word simultaneously penetrates the world of reality. Such a view is far removed from the more Biblical emphasis of Oscar Cullmann that the crucified and risen Christ inaugurated a new age and a new creation on the basis of supernatural conquest of sin and death. Teilhard looks for the completion of an ongoing creation through cosmic evolution guided by a partially immanent Logos as its spiritual center, whereas Cullmann foresees the supernatural rescue of a fallen race and cosmos through the redemptive historical incarnation of the transcendent Creator.

So heavily has the theology of the recent past indebted itself to the dogma of evolutionary progress that divine or superhuman forces survive mainly in the guise of an immanent directive principle. Statements on the beginning of things lack Clark's firm emphasis that the cosmos owes its origin and purpose to an omnipotent creative Logos, and Dooyeweerd's insistence that God as sovereign supernatural Creator is the source of cosmic existence, order, and enduring meaning.

To affirm God as Creator, as Biblical Christianity does, is to depict everything else as creature and creation—contingent in reality, dependent for its existence and survival, and vulnerable to doom and disappearance. That alongside God nothing need have been or need be, except for a divine decision and deed; that all the days of man's years—many or few—are a time for existence and survival and destiny that the sovereign Creator has given; and that God's will and power alone keep us from slipping over the brink of non-humanity, or non-creatureliness, or of non-existence—all this is implied in a recognition of the Creator God. But where religious philosophy entertains all premises but divine creation by a supernatural will and act; where the appearance of men and things is discussable only in a context of pre-existent materials and perpetual process; and where miracle is disallowed—while all marvels of the universe are readily referrable to chance—there the Creator God already counts for so little that the term creation is retained only by falsifying its proper universe of discourse. The modern secular world-view does not discuss man in dependence upon God, and in distinction from Him, but in the context of the cosmos, and in differentiation from organic-chemico-biological processes and from the lower animals.

Hence, this lordly capstone of evolutionary emergence does not consider himself threatened and terrified by nothingness as a real alternative facing finite creatures. What does the almighty Maker of heaven and earth any longer mean to homo sapiens who speaks universally of gods but is deeply sceptical about the living God who speaks as Lord of the universe? What recognition then remains for a sovereign Creator who might withdraw His support of the cosmos or repent that He had made man?

Modern gods mark in actuality a reversion to the antique Epicurean philosophy or world-view in which atoms gain more importance than spirit. Epicurean speculation generously lodged its gods in the interstellar spaces, in the vacuums between the worlds; modern evolutionary speculation has reserved room for the supernatural only in some neutral zone between philosophy and mythology, or at the frontier between learning and liberation.

It is not God as Creator only who is exiled by this secular mentality but also God as Redeemer. For when differentiation of the cosmos from primeval chaos and its reality and continuance are no longer referred to the divine Creator, what force then remains for a doctrine of incarnation whereby God refuses to let fallen mankind slip over the abyss of nonexistence, by Himself mercifully assuming creation's cause after the Fall, and by declaring that man remains the object of God's purpose for the cosmos in transporting human nature into the world to come? It is a matter of self-congratulation for modern secular man either that he banishes God as a contemporary irrelevance in a culture satiated by the spirit of naturalism, or that, despite his own achievements, he tolerantly retains God as a partner for the promotion of his own purposes.

D. Dilution of the supernatural character of revelation. Wherever an evolutionary view of man and the world eclipses God's causal energy in creation and redemption, the doctrine of divine revelation either undergoes a parallel distortion, or mediating theologians hopefully shift to revelational encounter the whole weight of the case for God's reality.

If the creation concept is severed from miracle and attached to immanent process, and the redemption motif is reduced to a divine-human mutual assistance pact, the doctrine of revelation is in turn readily subverted into the notion of human discovery, and retains little to commend it as divine. Whitehead, for one, shuns the term revelation entirely, replacing transcendent disclosure by man's rational quest. He insists, moreover, that religious experience carries no direct intuition of a personal God, and renounces all title to final truth, refusing to credit the special claim of Judeo-Christian religion. His doubts about ultimate personality lead on inevitably to a rejection of transcendent revelation; loss of God as personal implies the necessary forefeiture of the Biblical disclosure.

Whitehead's dismissal of divine disclosure more consistently reflects philosophical implications than does Tillich's retention of the idea of revelation alongside his disavowal of personality in God. Tillich dismisses a supernatural divinity as merely the product of myth and cult, and reinterprets the traditional doctrine within the context of his own special metaphysics. Revelation he identifies not with an objective universal disclosure of the supernatural God through the Logos, but with a mystical a priori; the divine is assertedly disclosed in the depths of everyman's experience as an intuition of the Unconditioned. The content of this supposed revelation is conditioned by man's temporal-historical existence and is not cognitive but symbolic. Tillich rejects a literal historical incarnation of the Logos; the orthodox doctrine is viewed simply as the way Christian faith expresses the triumph of New Being, even as the cross is for Tillich but a symbol of the self-negation of the finite. Tillich's "theological answers" to philosophical problems thus speculatively subvert the self-revealing God of the Bible, for he deliberately erases the divine perfections of supernatural transcendence and personality, and substitutes a conjectural doctrine of divine disclosure.

If Tillich's depersonalization of God destroys revelation in Biblical dimensions, Teilhard's *inter*-personalization of all reality through "christification" is hardly a preferable option. For by postulating Christ as the spiritual center of the universal cosmic process, Teilhard obscures the uniqueness of *agape* historically revealed in Jesus of Nazareth and erodes the possibilities of once-for-all revelation. Teilhard sees the life, death, and resurrection of Jesus as a highly polished mirror of the mystery of the universe, reflecting the prospect of ultimate metamorphosis for ourselves and our environment through personal renunciation and fulfillment. When one recalls Teilhard's emphasis that in the realms of knowledge and of faith quite divergent explanations are possible, he soon senses that this theory of evolutionary cosmic transformation speculatively replaces revelation by gnosis and obscures man's radical corruption and redemptive need.

Whereas Cullmann, too, holds that Jesus inaugurates the new creation as a prospect known to faith rather than to empirical proof or logic, it is faith in the Biblical witness on which he insists. The incarnate Logos is both the critical center of general history and the decisive center of salvation history in God's redemption of man and the cosmos. Cullmann thus defines divine revelation in terms of historical saving events and their scripturally-given meaning, in welcome contrast to recent existential and dialectical theories.

Nor does Niebuhr convincingly preserve the factuality of divine revelation in his emphasis on a dialectical tension between Christ as infinite norm and man's trans-rational spirit. Niebuhr's radical contrast of the eternal and the temporal deprives divine revelation of direct historical exposure, even in the life and teaching of Jesus of Nazareth. Only man's existential freedom to transcend nature and history anchors Niebuhr's idea of revelation, which he disjoins from rational or conceptual information. The result is an anti-rational, anti-historical view of divine-human relationships, propounded in terms of dialectical paradox. This underlies Niebuhr's hostility to acceptance of the literal truth of the Bible and to the evangelical view of revelation that rules out the self's supposedly ideal freedom from rational categories. Niebuhr's alternative has more costly consequences than its loss of rational and historical revelation, its surrender of objective divine communication identifiable with scriptural information about God and His works, its shattering of the identification of Christ the divine norm with Jesus of Nazareth. For Niebuhr's speculative revolt against objectively given divine disclosure, and his attenuation of salvation history into existential self-analysis, also jeopardizes the very reality of God. Bultmann's view had deprived revelation of historicity and objectivity, let alone verbal intelligibility; existentially expounded, revelation became merely a source of spiritual knowledge about ourselves rather than information about God and His redemptive intervention in history. Here anthropology displaces theology and revelation tells us nothing about God as a distinct being. By their further reduction of the notion of revelation, the Mainz radicals Braun and Mezger equated God's identifiable reality with interpersonal relationships.

To his credit, Barth, even if belatedly, sought to remedy certain weaknesses of "kerygmatic" theology by connecting revelation somewhat more firmly with conceptual thought and historical events. At the outset crisis-theology disparaged conceptualization, verbalization, and historical mediation of the Word of God in its emphasis on personal revelation. Since divine revelation assertedly occurred outside the normativity of thought and on the rim of history, sacred events and sacred Scripture were regarded at best as pointers to revelation, which was located exclusively in direct interpersonal confrontation. A hallmark of "kerygmatic" theology—both dialectical and existential—was its insistence that revelation is a special faith-knowledge for believers only, not truth valid for all men whether or not they accept it. But as existential theologians inspired by Bultmann increasingly disparaged the importance of Biblical history and of intelligible knowledge of God, Barth more fully asserted the quasi-historical and quasi-intellectual character of revelation. Thus Barth modified dialectical revelation to include a conceptual knowledge of God and held the historical environment to be an indispensable suburb of revelation. This was, of course, still a long way from a rational revelation consisting of universally valid propositions about God, and from historical revelation in the traditional evangelical understanding; as Barth saw it, the adequacy of theological concepts is assured only by a subjective miracle of grace, and revelational history remains outside the range of scientific historical inquiry. The very ambiguity of a theology of revelation that denied objectivity and universal validity, and yet insisted on quasi-historical and quasi-propositional divine disclosure, was too great a liability to forestall further dilution of Barth's view by existentialist theologians. The Barthian era began with a bold call to faith in the self-revealing God, while it rejected the Bible as God's objectively-given Word; evangelical theologians saw in both dialectical and existential dogmatics a threat to faith in God and to revelation alike. The theological drift of the recent past indicates that loss of the Bible as the Word of God issues sooner or later in the loss of the self-revealing God as well. Attempts to revive faith in the revelation of the Judeo-Christian God that "derevelationize" the Bible—that is, refuse to identify the Bible with revelation, and in fact contrast Scripture with revelation—dilute the concept of revelation and dissipate its theological power. The recent modern notions of revelation cannot bear the weight of the case for Biblical theism, and readily suppress the supernatural features of the Christian view in deference to humanistic emphases.

E. Distortion of sacred Biblical motifs. Another noteworthy feature of contemporary theology lies in the conspicuous reliance on sacred motifs of Biblical theology even by mediating and speculative scholars. Whereas the scriptural motifs are often distorted through an alien and arbitrary content, their ready retention attests that no framework has been found to interpret human experience superior to the controlling themes of the Bible.

For all Niebuhr's existential transmutation of Biblical concepts into a subjective tension in human experience between the ideal and the actual, he appropriates the whole range of sacred scriptural motifs from creation, and fall through resurrection and second coming, and structures his theology by them.

Tillich, too, despite his explicit repudiation of the supernaturalism of the Bible, symbolically retains not only the "fall" (a cosmic alienation or ontological predicament rather than a historical event), "salvation" (ontological reunion), "the cross" (self-negation), "parousia" (fulfillment of creaturely existence in the eternal), and "hell" (a degree of spiritual nonfulfillment), but also "Father, Son, and Spirit" as a metaphorical depiction of a threefold dialectic of separation and reunion.

Teilhard combines an evolutionary "christification" of reality, through Christ as the universal principle of vitality and cohesion, with the entire gamut of traditional terms—from creation, incarnation, kingdom of God, death, and resurrection, parousia, and Omega as the end—reinterpreted almost to the point of semantic illegitimacy.

Whitehead, too, poetically adopts many familiar Judeo-Christian concepts while annulling important essentials of scriptural theism; thus he speaks of God's love, wisdom, guidance, purpose, and salvation, whereas he leaves divine personality in doubt.

We are not saying merely that the Judeo-Christian revelation of reality is so comprehensively authentic that no serious interpreter can expound main features of the human scene, however speculatively, without unwittingly borrowing some of the elements inherent in the Biblical view. That is also true. But here we are noting that so effectively do the controlling motifs of the Judeo-Christian revelation of God and the world explain the human predicament that brilliant modern writers are reluctant to abandon these scripturally-derived categories, even if they proceed to re-interpret them in highly speculative ways.

F. Attempted reformulation of transcendence. The definition of divine transcendence remains a critically controversial feature of contemporary theology, for it governs one's view of God's relationship to man and to the whole range of being and life. The understanding of transcendence is confused today because even modern writers who deny the supernatural retain the term as a central feature of their religious philosophy. It is now widely used merely to depict an existential relationship, not to describe an ontological perfection. But Judeo-Christian theology has no authentic Biblical character unless one moves beyond the existential confusion of the self with God, to a supernatural transcendent reality.

Bultmann refers to the transcendent unknown, but he insistently dismisses the miraculous and supernatural as synonymous with the mythological. He insists that as a metaphysical reality God is inaccessible to all objective description, in other words, that we have no ontological knowledge of God. God has reality only for faith; only if we describe existential relationships do we avoid mythological language about God. The result is that all affirmations of transcendence concern facets of man's own existence, not some independent entity. Although Bultmann insists on God's reality, his existential orientation of transcendence is vulnerable to further dilution, as when the Mainz radicals Braun and Mezger discuss interpersonal relationships as God's only identifiable reality.

Tillich denies the supernatural and transcendent as an objective reality above and beyond the world. In the context of total divine immanence he speaks, however, of the transcendence of the infinite Ground of all being, or the infinite *Abgrund* that swallows all finite being. The Biblical ontology of an infinite-supernatural realm alongside finite created beings is here displaced by a speculative nonsupernatural ontology consisting of nonsupernatural Being itself, finite being, and "nonbeing," their differing interrelations describable in terms of transcendence.

So far has contemporary theological thought drifted from Biblical moorings that its speculative expositions of transcendence deviate radically from the Judeo-Christian revelation of God's relationship to the created world. Once again, an excessive view of divine immanence is gaining ground to condition God's relation to the world process, and divine transcendence is compromised to restrict God's power to what He is actually doing in the world. At worst, transcendence is expounded simply as a human relationship or experience and not at all as a divine perfection. The distinction is clearly emphasized by the French Communist theoretician Roger Garaudy, who insists that transcendence is not a supernatural perfection but the human ability to progress through continuing evolution.

Niebuhr's existential orientation of theology issues in an ambiguous supranaturalism. He rejects ontology, or a static rational description of metaphysical reality. He depicts man's capacity for self-transcendence (the extension of self-consciousness in infinite regression) as a dimension of the eternal; the transcendence of God is expounded by way of analogy from human self-transcendence. Yet he does not relate the human self, as Tillich does, to the ground and aim of every self, but rather to another self, the personal God. He does not reject, as Tillich, a two worlds supernaturalism as the background of a transcendental view of man and history, but insists that God is a mysterious source of order above and beyond the orders and evils of the world. Yet he explicitly repudiates Biblical supernaturalism as prescientific and crude, and precludes all rational objectification of God, so that his views constitute more an assault on the metaphysically transcendent God of miracle and objective revelation than an exposition of a coherent alternative. His provisional dualism of the transcendent and the historical rests not on the supernatural as a separate order of existence, but rather on a dialectical tension that structures man's self-consciousness that intuits God as free and outside the normativity of reason. But Neibuhr's exposition weakens rather than preserves, let alone strengthens, the Biblical revelation of divine transcendence. For while he seeks to preserve the distinction between man and God by an epistemological construct, Niebuhr nonetheless obscures God's ontological distinctiveness, since he ascribes to man —despite a doctrine of creation—such aspects of noncreated reality as infinity and freedom as integral elements of human self-transcendence. Elements of divine and human attributes thus are no longer fully distinguishable, but somehow blend together into a mutual identity that subverts the Biblical doctrine of transcendence.

Teilhard considers the supernatural not a finished realm of being but a transforming ferment, and God is viewed, moreover, as partly immersed in cosmic reality. Platonic and Gnostic more than Biblical in orientation, this exposition is correlated with modern evolutionary theory. God's omnipresence is viewed as a creating, preserving action of spiritual transformation that controls the evolution of the cosmos; however, the last emerging term of the evolutionary series, Omega, also stands above or outside this process as a transcendent center of psychic concentration. But Teilhard's importation of change into the supernatural, and the involvement of God in evolutionary process as a necessary feature of His being and work, seriously compromises the Biblical view.

In expounding divine immanence, Whitehead, too, subordinates essential aspects of ultimate reality to change. God is an eternal principle of order transcending the processes of nature, yet He is not wholly beyond process and growth. God is a unique, concrete actual entity with both conceptual and physical prehensions. In His "primordial" (conceptual) nature, God is infinite, eternal, unchanging, aboriginal, and independent, transcending temporal actual entities. But He lacks fullness of actuality and consciousness, and requires temporal actual entities; hence, Whitehead postulates God's "consequent" nature as meshed to the creative advance of the world, conscious but always incomplete, and involved in time and change. Care for the world is a necessary expression of His nature. This interdependence of God and the world, on which Whitehead insists, seriously distorts the Biblical view that the transcendent Creator is not dependent on the creation, while it is completely dependent on Him. In Whitehead's view, God's "primordial" nature initiates the realization of values in temporal actual entities, through provision of subjective aims as final causes. But it is as true on Whitehead's theory to say that through the conservation of values the world "completes God" as that God completes the world, since supposed deficiencies in the divine nature are overcome through God's prehensions of the temporal world.

George Thomas criticizes Whitehead's formulation of divine transcendence as obscuring the personality of God, and seeks to avoid his "excessive" statements of God's potentiality and involvement in change. The result is a somewhat higher compromise between the Biblical revelation and modern theory, even if it aims to adjust God's relation to the world agreeably to historic Christian perspectives. While Thomas affirms that God as supernatural mind and will has transcendent personality and power, He conditions divine power in respect to absolute possibility and limits divine foreknowledge. He resists the exclusion from the divine nature of all divine potentiality; God's eternity does not exclude succession in time and experience. He discards the traditional Christian exposition of God's absolute independence, eternity, immutability and perfection, and admits incompletion into the divine nature, and asserts that His immutability does not exclude change. He thinks that "the problem of the relation between permanence and change, actuality and potentiality in God's nature has yet to be worked out in a satisfactory way" (op. cit., p. 133). Thomas rejects the traditional theistic insistence on God's unchangeableness, supposedly in view of Biblical reference to God's "repentance" (cf. Jer. 18:8); God's steadfast purpose is made to respond to changing human situations and acts.

Charles Hartshorne also builds upon and goes beyond Whitehead's view to affirm pantheism. Whereas for a pantheist like Spinoza God is identical with the world, for a pantheist like Hartshorne God as a concrete reality includes the world in Himself; although His abstract essence transcends particular actual entities. The deviation from Whitehead is seen in the fact that in the latter's metaphysics God transcends the world both in His essence and experience; He is conditioned by the world, but does not include it, nor does it determine Him, although it is immanent in God who transcends it. Hartshorne too develops a view of God's supposed "incompleteness" and "relativity" to the world alongside insistence on the "absoluteness" and perfection of the divine essence. But this Whiteheadian theory nonetheless compromises the transcendence of the God of the Bible by its notions that only in His "primordial nature" is God eternal, unchanging, and infinite, and that in God's "consequent" nature these metaphysical attributes are subordinated to a divine dependence on the world. Through this subordination of permanence to change, and of reality to process, a danger arises, as George Thomas remarks, of a further decline "to the immanentism of Hegelian idealism, which affirmed that the Absolute Spirit realizes itself and comes to consciousness only through its manifestation in the world, or even to theistic Naturalism, which seems to regard God as nothing more than the value-producing aspect of the creative process itself" (ibid., p. 386).

Edgar S. Brightman, most influential of American personalists, stressed that personality but not substance is the ultimate principle that explains all else, and emphasized God's unique personal reality in distinction from finite, created selves. Contrary to most personalists, however, he, too, depicted God as finite. Against the existential and anti-rational rejection of the objectivity of God, personalism distinguishes God from other selves as the Supreme Mind who so mediates between finite minds and objects that knowledge is possible. Most personalists consider God as nontemporal and supertemporal, and hold that He can initiate change without enmeshing Himself in it. Whereas panpsychists, like Hartshorne, consider everything in the universe to be mind or soul of which material substances are simply a phenomenal form, personalists like A. C. Knudson, R. T. Flewelling and Brightman hold rather that nature is the rational externalization of divine causality under space-time forms.

God is immanent in the world not substantially or existentially, but volitionally and functionally. Nature has phenomenal reality, not ontological reality. It is said to be a part of God, the energized and externalized divine thought of the Personal Infinite under the forms of space and time, and in conformity with law and evolutionary process. This theory imperils God's free immanence in nature. Although personalists speak of a created universe, it is difficult to see how a divinely imagined universe would differ from a real universe consisting solely of God's thoughts; hence, either divine ideas are necessarily creative, or creation is an illusion. Moreover, miracle is precluded. Contrasted with nature, finite created selves are held to be other than God. Hence, God's transcendence consists not in otherness to nature and man, but rather in that He is more than nature, and other than man. In view of the problem of evil, Brightman contended that God's nature includes an uncontrollable irrational surd, so that God is finite. But even where personalists assert divine infinity they obscure God's transcendence not only by their confusion of nature with God, but by their insistence on the continuity of human values and the divine, and their rejection of a doctrine of special divine initiative and disclosure contrary to revealed religion. Divine revelation is held to be functional rather than cognitive. Although personalists emphasize logical coherence, their rejection of rational revelation and their suspension of the interpretation of reality and life on empirical considerations leaves vulnerable all affirmations about the living God. It is noteworthy that, although personalism has lost momentum, the most influential movement in contemporary theology has combined the exposition of God as person with the unique divine self-revelation affirmed in the Judeo-Christian salvation history and Scriptures.

Only in the dialectical theology shaped by Barth does contemporary neo-Protestant thought assert God's sovereign independence and transcendence of the universe in direct opposition to the recent modern exaggeration of divine immanence. Barth unreservedly affirms God as the sovereign supernatural Creator—ontologically, morally, and epistemologically transcendent, and standing to His creation in a relation of free immanence.

Transcendence is not here developed primarily as a dimension of human experience, as in the case of existential theory, but defines the supernatural and miraculous freedom of God in respect to the created universe. Existentialist philosophy is surely right in going beyond scientific naturalism to recognize a significant freedom in man, even beyond the freedom of mind over matter or of will over natural process admitted in some forms of idealistic metaphysics. It recognizes in human experience a transcendence of the cosmos involving the self's own history, bounded only by the outer limits of man's existence. But simply because it expounds a transcendence immanent in human existence and in the cosmic process, it cannot assuredly affirm man's inescapable relation to a transcendent God who defines His origin and destiny. If what we know in spiritual confrontation is ever and always an aspect of human experience, so that we cannot surely discriminate this "beyond" from our alter ego, God may be a term for the pious content of human consciousness. When religious experience is uncertain whether it is shaped by the concrete confrontation of God or by the elevation of a phase of man's own consciousness to divinity, because the divine is presumed to be identical with man's deepest, or highest, or inmost self, the question of obedience or disobedience to God easily becomes one of spiritual schizophrenia. Existential theory obscures the intelligible revelation of One who transcends man from without, and as Creator qualifies man to transcend the limits of other creatures, implicating him in knowledge of and decision for or against his Maker, establishing his ineradicable responsibility to the Eternal, and offering the gracious prospect of redemptive renewal and unending communion with the living God.

While Barth does indeed shatter the existential limitations of transcendence, his dialectical theology seriously distorts important aspects of the Biblical view. From the outset the emphasis on ontological transcendence—as against immanentistic world views—rejected all necessary involvement of deity in nature, spoke of God "begrounding as the Ungrounded" (rather than Tillich's "Ground of all being"), and emphasized that "whoever says God says miracle" (*Commentary on Romans,* 4:3-5). The assertion of epistemological transcendence traced all knowledge of God to divine self-disclosure, with the Logos as the revealer of the uniquely transcendent God; while that of moral transcendence emphasized that God is the sovereign source of the distinction between right and wrong and the holy judge of sinful creatures. But Barth's doctrine of transcendence was almost deistic in overtone, particularly in its epistemological emphasis; the reduction of all knowledge of God to paradoxic statements cancelled the conceptual value of all affirmations about God's perfections. Barth's earlier writings limit the mind's knowing faculty, in respect to the divine, to the practical (as opposed to the cognitive reason), and eroded the knowledge of God directly mediated by the words and teaching of the Bible. This exaggerated notion that divine transcendence rules out universally valid truths about God even on the basis of revelation underlies Barth's strictures against a general divine disclosure in nature as well as against any religious a priori or intuitive knowledge of God in man as divinely created; direct personal revelation, paradoxic rather than propositional, was the sole remaining option.

Sören Kierkegaard's influence had left its clear mark upon the statements of transcendence fashioned both by dialectical theologians and existential theologians. Kierkegaard stressed the radical disjunction of eternity and time and the unqualified otherness of God, and this in turn required a distorted view of revelation and redemption. The extreme segregation of eternity and time, more Platonic than Biblical in focus, so divorced God's revelation from human history and human concepts and human language that the knowledge of God was deprived of all claim to objectivity and universal validity, and the historicity of the redemptive acts was imperiled.

While in theology the negative result of these emphases did not become fully evident until after Bultmann's forfeiture of the importance of the mediation of Jesus of Nazareth, the existentialist orientation of philosophy had long taken an atheistic course under the inspiration of Heidegger. Before that, of course, Nietzsche had espoused the thesis that God had become man's rival or enemy, and more recent existentialists like Sartre and Camus stressed the silent or absent God. In *The Myth of Sisyphus* (1943) Camus contends that whereas men ought to accept the nonrationality of life, and pretend to be happy, they kill themselves intellectually by propounding theologies of hope and consolation. The God-affirming existentialists, like Dostoevski and Kafka, insist that man can be truly himself only before God. Bultmann's version of existentialism was consciously projected as a restatement of the NT aimed to interest modern secular man in the God who meets men in faith—but Heidegger lampooned Bultmann's reinterpretation as an attempt "to make theism out of my atheism."

Cullmann's noteworthy effort to overcome the radical existential disjunction of eternity and time has the merit not only of anchoring divine revelation in the stream of history, but allows for scripturally revealed knowledge of God's acts and their meaning. Not every historical occurrence stands in direct historical connection with the historical mission of Jesus Christ, but He is the controlling center of Biblical salvation history and from this midpoint all history is to be understood and judged. Yet quite in line with the paradox theologians, who formulate divine transcendence so as to erase man's cognitive knowledge of the eternal world, Cullmann shuns interest in metaphysical truth or ontological affirmations about God's being as scripturally off-limits. Moreover, he violates this reticence over ontology by insisting that time is in God, thus exchanging one vulnerable position (that time cannot become the bearer of divine disclosure) for another (that time is an aspect of divine self-experience).

The correlation of extreme divine transcendence with metaphysical agnosticism was inherent in the dialectical and existential exaggeration of the eternity-time relationship. Although Barth in later years struggled to moderate the tensions to give human thought about God a more significant role on the basis of revelation, Brunner in later stages of his theology stressed transcendence so radically that he spoke as readily of divine mystery as of God's revealing activity. It is noteworthy that insofar as death-of-God writers like Altizer and Van Buren have had an exposure to the Christian understanding of God, their views have been mainly derived from the dialectical theology of the recent past in which an almost deistic doctrine of transcendence has thinned to unintelligibility and erased from history the content of God's self-revelation.

But paradox theologians have not been the only contemporary thinkers to shun ontological concerns while emphasizing divine transcendence. Dooyeweerd does not share the recent modern infatuation with dialectic and *Existenz,* but is nonetheless critical of metaphysics as a misguided finite aspiration to exceed human limits and to inherit the eternal mysteries. Critics have not been slow to point out that Dooyeweerd's own exposition of the nature of the real world, particularly of the cosmonomic ideas, is itself thoroughly metaphysical. But more important than the inconsistencies in Dooyeweerd's own views is the basis on which he presumes to reject metaphysical knowledge. For the Dutch philosopher holds that reality is meaning, and that God is the origin of all meaning, but He does not restrict meaning to logical meaning; the ultimate cosmological principle has the character, so Dooyeweerd contends, of law rather than of logic. Law, he asserts, is the boundary between God and the cosmos, and reason is subordinated to law as an explanatory principle. The central motif of Scripture is consequently expounded as nontheoretical; although divine Word-revelation is presented to faith, this is not given as concrete Word-revelation.

A twofold tendency therefore characterizes the renewed emphasis on divine transcendence—on the one hand, even scholars who repudiate pantheism are disposed to involve the being of God in cosmic process, and to define God's nature and ways through a theory of religious knowledge that annuls the reality of transcendent revelation; on the other hand, even where scholars preserve divine transcendence a disposition remains to obscure the rational quality of revelation, and the role of divine Mind in relation to human thought and meaning, so that the reassertion of transcendence implies no recovery of ontological knowledge.

G. Tenuous role of reason in religious experience. The weakest link in the case for theism in recent modern theology is the tenuous role assigned to reason in relation to supernatural realities. The significance of reason in the religious realm is now constantly demeaned both in defining God's own perfections, and man's special status as a creature destined for spiritual knowledge. The great theological emphasis of the past, that God is the infinite Mind, the ultimate source of truth and its universal ground, who seeks man's worship "in spirit and in truth," has fallen victim to our antimetaphysical, antirational age. Theologians hurry over, and sometimes entirely ignore, the rational perfections of God, as if Biblical Christianity discloses God only as sovereign Will. Emphasis on impenetrable divine mystery is made a badge of piety in dogmatics, and claims to a logically consistent knowledge of God's nature and ways are deplored as irreverent pretension. The exaggeration of eternity-time tensions in the dialectical theology fostered by Kierkegaard has moved reason to the margin of religious experience and substituted a blind leap of faith for intelligible human response to the divine claim upon man's total being. Widening concessions to evolutionary naturalism tend to relate man's reflective self-consciousness solely to developmental processes, and all thought, theology included, is viewed as conditioned by contemporary history and culture. Even those aspects of knowledge-theory are now ignored, which over long centuries constrained great thinkers of all ages to insist that only a Supreme Mind mediates the interaction between finite minds and their cosmic environment that makes valid knowledge possible. Theologians who go so far as to assert that God created reason, as does Brunner, will then under the spell of a dialectical theory of religious confrontation, insist that man's reason cannot grasp God, and that spiritual response is ideally extracognitive. Only in later writings does Barth preserve a measure of significance for the conceptual aspects of revelation; even then, however, his assertion that on the basis of personal miracle the believer's concepts of God gain individual adequacy (but not universal validity) simply grants too little too late. Berkouwer allows more room for the rational significance of revelation, but tends also to shun rational consistency and coherence while emphasizing that the truth of God is known to faith—a tenet that does not of itself settle the question of the relation of faith and reason.

Dooyeweerd does indeed stress the human mind's uniqueness: the self can abstract modal aspects from experience, transcend time, and synthesize logical and nonlogical aspects of experience because of its unique relation to God, the divine source of meaning. Much of this had been said by personalists, unfortunately in a context of philosophical idealism that ruled out a Biblical view of revelation and reason. Dooyeweerd's frame of reference is evangelical theism, on the commendable premise that Judeo-Christian thinkers should organize the data of human experience through criteria derived from revelation. The satisfactory identification of those categories is prob. not Dooyeweerd's contribution; also his formulation of the connection of revelation and thought is not adequate. But his sure stress on God as the origin of all meaning deserves reinforcement today.

No less important is a revival of the historical Christian emphasis that God is logically explanatory of all else, particularly in a wayward age when weary minds despair of the adequacy of frail human hypotheses to explain the drift of our times, let alone the drama of human destiny. That God is a personal, living, immutable Mind; that reason is an eternal Divine perfection; and that truths are the eternal thoughts of God, are emphases not absent among evangelical theologians in our day, though perhaps none better than Clark has sensed their great importance for this turning time in the history of dogma. In his writings one often finds a reminder of the further implications that the laws of reason are descriptive of the activity of God's will, that the logical structure of the cosmos is grounded in the Logos, that God is the ultimate ground of intelligibility, and the laws of logic are an essential element of the *imago Dei* in man, that divine revelation is intelligible or rational and that God is to be known through conceptual categories, that language as well as thought must be related to a theistic basis, and that the medium of human concepts and words therefore poses no barrier to the precise communication of the Word of God.

In summary, these are some noteworthy features of recent modern theology: the shift from an empirical-grounding of the case for theism to divine revelation or to primal intuition; the special influence of writers whose explanation of religion is correlated with the whole range of human concerns; the emphasis on human decision and initiative in deciding man's destiny and the ultimate future; the dilution of the supernatural character of revelation, or the attempt, where this orientation is retained, to support the reality of God by revelational encounter alone; the profanation or distortion of sacred motifs by religious interpreters who find in them a superior framework for the comprehension of the human situation; the faltering attempt to preserve the category of transcendence by theologians who reject or modify the Biblical view of God; the tenuous role assigned to reason in the recent modern expositions of the supernatural.

By the same token it may be said that modern religious thought now often speaks of God without discriminating the living God from false gods by the criteria of revealed religion, and that it postulates new characteristics of divinity, and hence new gods and newly authoritative writings.

In the Bible the true God is known by these

marks: that in eternity past He decreed both to create a remnant of creatures who would share His fellowship forever, and to redeem them through the incarnation of His Son in human nature, that He created the universe out of nothing in an orderly way, and man in His image for obedient fellowship; that He made known His holy will and, when the first parents violated it, banished them from paradise but offered redemptive rescue; that He showed His displeasure over sin by the Noahic flood, while renewing the promise of salvation for the godly remnant; that He chose Israel as a special people to worship and serve Him in a sacred land—sending Moses as lawgiver, and declaring the standards by which all nations were to be judged, and by which the Jews were to honor Him; sending prophets to keep hope alive in the coming Redeemer, and to warn them of the evil of their ways in view of the divine purposes in time and eternity; raising up a priesthood to enforce the need of sacrifice, and anticipating the day when the Great High Priest would Himself be the sacrificial offering for the sins of men; that He came in the fullness of time as the incarnate Logos, and in Jesus Christ lived a sinless life among men, displaying His power over Satan, sin, and death, and inviting men by the Gospel of His crucifixion and resurrection for sinners to receive new life and the forgiveness of sins, and the sure prospect of eternal bliss; that He ordains the Church as a witness to the spiritual blessings available through Jesus Christ, its living Lord, and as a mirror to the world of the reality of the kingdom of heaven; and that He will climax history by the vindication of righteousness centering in the return of the Messiah in power and glory for the judgment of the nations, the resurrection of the dead, the conformity of believers to the image of their risen Redeemer, and the final doom of the wicked.

The God of the Bible is the God who reveals Himself, who speaks for Himself through chosen prophets and apostles, who addresses His words and truth to men in the written Scriptures; and who comes in the flesh to withstand the fiercest temptations of Satan by the confident appeal: "It stands written!" What stands written in the Bible remains for His followers the authentic delineation of the nature and will of God. Modern religious thought has no superior access to the God of the ages; it can at best clarify the revelation of God in Christ and the Bible, but if it ignores the Bible and Christ in its exposition of divinity, it must inevitably substitute a modern deity for the God of Abraham, Isaac, and Jacob and God manifest in Jesus Christ, and the best that can be said for such a deity is that it is subject to change without notice and subject to burial without mourners. But with the Father of lights "there is no variation or shadow due to change" (James 1:17), and the loss of this deity, of the true and living God, must inevitably mean the loss of human dignity, direction, and destiny in a universe whose Logos—whose word and meaning, and true life and light—is eclipsed.

BIBLIOGRAPHY. E. Brunner, *The Christian Doctrine of God* (1949); H. Bavinck, *The Doctrine of God* (1951); K. Barth, *Church Dogmatics*, Vol. II/1, II/2, *The Doctrine of God* (1957); P. E. Hughes, *Creative Minds in Continental Theology* (1960); H. Gollwitzer, *The Existence of God as Confessed by Faith* (1965); N. F. S. Ferre, *The Living God of Nowhere and Nothing* (1966).

C. F. H. HENRY

GOD, CHILDREN (SONS, DAUGHTERS) OF

(בְּנֵי and בנת אלהים, *sons* and *daughters of God*; τέκνα θεοῦ, and υἱοί θεοῦ, *sons of God*).

The Fatherhood of God and the sonship of man are valid definitive concepts in Biblical terminology. With reference to father and children, the earthly family bears a true resemblance to the heavenly family. In retrospect, the likeness is evident throughout the Bible, coming into sharp focus in Jesus. The Bible story begins with the natural sons of Adam; continues with the chosen sons of Abraham; and concludes with the spiritual children of redemption. All are God's children in one way or another.

1. Created children
   a. Angelic beings
   b. The whole human race
2. Chosen children
   a. Israel
   b. Jesus and Israel
3. Converted children
   a. The unique sonship of Christ
   b. Children of God by faith
   c. Characteristics of God's converted children

1. Created children. In a general sense, all created personal beings are children of God. They are products of His workmanship, and bear His image.

a. Angelic beings. Angelic beings are depicted as children of God. On witnessing the glorious creation of the earth, "all the sons of God shouted for joy" (Job 38:7). Could it be that God addressed Himself to them when He said, "Let us make man in our image, after our likeness" (Gen 1:26a)? Of course the beloved Son "was in the beginning with God; all things were made through him" (John 1:2f.; cf. Heb 1:2). But angels did not enjoy an equal sonship relation with Jesus, "For to what angel did God ever say, 'Thou art my Son, today I have begotten thee'" (Heb 1:5; cf. Ps 2:7)? However, Jesus compared the final state of man with angels. Then they would not marry, and "they cannot die any more, because they are equal to angels and are sons of God, being sons of the resurrection" (Luke 20:36).

The debatable passage in Genesis 6:1-4 relates that "the sons of God" married "the daughters of men," from which union came giants, "the mighty men that were of old, the men of renown." These, contrary to some opinions, were not angels, but natural men who were sons of God by creation. They bore in human form the image of God on one hand, and on the other hand were able to reproduce themselves. In this early age, "When men began to multiply on the face of the ground," the fact that men of divine image could not only reproduce male offspring but also daughters who were fair and beautiful was a startling revelation. Moreover, that there was sex attraction, resulting in marriage, whereby the chain of reproduction was established, was exciting enough to report in semi-mythological terms. Another pertinent factor in this brief report was God's announcement to reduce man's span of life on earth from the former longevity to 120 years. This brief passage may serve well as an appropriate epitaph of the forefathers, "the men of renown" (v. 4) of a bygone age.

In another ancient record, angelic beings are called children of God. "Now there was a day when the sons of God came to present themselves before the LORD, and Satan also came among them" (Job 1:6; 2:1). Similar ideas are expressed in the Psalms: "Ascribe to the LORD, O heavenly beings (sons of gods), ascribe to the LORD glory and strength" (Ps 29:1); and, "Who among the heavenly beings is like the Lord?" (89:6).

b. *The whole human race.* All people on earth are children of God by creation. In the process of creation, "God said, 'Let us make man in our image, after our likeness; and let them have dominion over . . .' all other creatures on earth. "And God said to them, 'Be fruitful and multiply, and fill the earth and subdue it' " (Gen 1:26-28). Thus God endowed man with two qualities resembling His— to reproduce His likeness and to rule. Just as natural children resemble their parents, men and women resemble God, for He made them in His likeness. Like God, man is rational, emotional, volitional, and spiritual, endowed with freedom of choice. Like a lost child, man is restless for his heavenly Father. Everyone's genealogy may be traced back to God, just as Luke traced Jesus' human lineage through long generations via "Seth, the son of Adam, the son of God" (Luke 3:38). Another writer says, "He reflects the glory of God and bears the very stamp of his nature" (Heb 1:3). Jesus was God in human form; therefore, man resembles God, his Father. Nebuchadnezzar identified the person in the fiery furnace with the three Hebrews as a supernatural being. "The appearance of the fourth is like a son of the gods" (Dan 3:25b), but in human form. Conversely then, man resembles God, his Maker and Father, in an amazing way. Even the pagan poet, Aratus of Greece, wrote, "For we are indeed his offspring" (Acts 17:28). Likewise, every person on earth can validly claim that he is a child of God by virtue of creation. People of every race, age, and sex are by nature children of God.

2. Chosen children. Since man is a free moral agent, he may be an obedient child of God or a rebellious one (Ezek 20:21). In the days of Noah, disobedience was so prevalent that God punished man with the Flood (cf. Eph 2:2). Man continued to sin and lose his way, so God chose some of His children to help reclaim the others.

a. *Israel.* God called Abraham to be the progenitor of the Jewish race, chosen to bring salvation to the world (John 4:22). So, the select race was called variously, "children of promise" (Gal 4:28); "Sons of the living God" (Hos 1:10); "children of Israel" (Exod 10:20). Even of these, God said, "The children rebelled against me" (Ezek 20:21a); and, He called to them, "Return, O faithless children. . . . they know me not; they are stupid children" (Jer 3:14; 4:22). But, the Father's love reformed a remnant, who again sang, "Be glad, O sons of Zion, and rejoice in the LORD, your God" (Joel 2:23).

b. *Jesus and Israel.* Jesus fulfilled God's purpose in His chosen children, while confirming God's plan in the race. He said to the Syrophoenician woman, "Let the children first be fed, for it is not right to take the children's bread and throw it to the dogs" (Mark 7:27). In this strong metaphor, in which Jews were God's children and Gentiles were dogs, Jesus was emphasizing the fact that in personal human service He "was sent only to the lost sheep of the house of Israel" (Matt 15:24). Concerning Zacchaeus, He said, "Today salvation has come to this house, since he also is a son of Abraham. For the Son of man came to seek and to save the lost" (Luke 19:9f.). The lost eventually included the Gentiles, for the Father's love included all, "not wishing that any should perish" (2 Pet 3:9). His inclusive love was also portrayed in Jesus' parable of the lost sheep (Luke 15:3-7). And, the chosen race (Deut 14:2) came to full fruition in the chosen Son (Luke 9:35).

3. Converted children. As the Christian era dawned, a new concept of the children of God was preached. John the Baptist thundered out the explosive truth to the Jews: "Do not presume to say to yourselves, 'We have Abraham as our father'; for I tell you, God is able from these stones to raise up children to Abraham" (Matt 3:9). Henceforth, divine sonship would be reckoned on a new basis.

a. *The unique sonship of Christ.* Jesus was the Son of God in a unique way. He was God's "Son, whom he appointed the heir of all things, through whom also he created the world" (Heb 1:2; cf. John 1:3). He appeared at baptism with "glory as of the only Son from the Father" (John 1:14). He called Himself God's "only Son" (John 3:16), and "the Son of God" (John 10:36); and, God out of a cloud called Him "my beloved Son" (Matt 17:5). On numerous occasions, Jesus called God "my Father," "my heavenly Father," and similar terms (18:35; 26:39). Moreover, He subordinated His lineage of David to divine lineage (Mark 12:35f.).

b. *Children of God by faith.* Through Jesus Christ all the children of Adam as well as those of Abraham are eligible to be eternal children of God. "For in Christ Jesus you are all sons of God . . . . and if you are Christ's, then you are Abraham's offspring, heirs according to promise" (Gal 3:26, 29). "It is not the children of the flesh who are the children of God, but the children of the promise" (Rom 9:8). The criterion for becoming spiritual children of God is faith not flesh. "That which is born of the flesh is flesh, and that which is born of the Spirit is spirit" (John 3: 6), and, "all who are led by the Spirit of God are sons of God" (Rom 8:14). Jesus told some Jews they were not Abraham's children, neither was God their Father, warning them, "You are of your father the devil" (John 8:44). Through Christ sonship is offered to all who believe. "But to all who received him, who believed in his name, he gave power to become children of God" (John 1:12).

c. *Characteristics of God's converted children.* Spiritual children resemble God in lives of obedience to Him. If you love your enemies, do good, be merciful, and lend to the selfish, "your reward will be great, and you will be sons of the Most High" (Luke 6:35f.). "See what love the Father has given us, that we should be called children of God" (1 John 3: 1). Christians are to "walk as children of light" (Eph 5:8), for they are "all sons of light" (1 Thess 5:5). Jesus cherished and taught the Fatherhood of God and the sonship of man. He said, "Call no man your father on earth, for you have one Father, who is in heaven" (Matt 23:9). He taught His disciples to address God in prayer with "Our Father who art in heaven" (6:9). And, "Blessed are the peacemakers, for they shall be called sons of God" (5:9).

BIBLIOGRAPHY. E. Russell, *Chapel Talks* (1935), 119-121, 125-129; *Oxford Annotated Bible* (1962), 1296-1298; 1306; 1342; 1367; 1453; 1482-1486. F. F. Bruce, *Second Thoughts on the Dead Sea Scrolls* (1956), 22.

G. B. FUNDERBURK

GOD, NAMES OF. Distinctive of the Hebrew-Christian system is the use of the names for deity as instruments for divine disclosure. The several names, simple and compound, employed in both the OT and the NT are not mere human designations or constructs. Rather they are revelatory instruments, appearing at nodal points in the career of the Israelitish people, and reflecting God's self-revelation.

Israels' feeling for names reflected the general attitude toward nomenclature which was common to ancient peoples. With them a person's name was not a mere designation of familial relationship—not a mere possession—but something distinctly personal. While there is no evidence that in Israelitish usage of names these were held (as in some cultures) to possess magical power, yet names were held in serious regard. This was true concerning personal names; and the same seriousness is apparent in the employment of designations for deity among OT peoples.

In Sem. culture, names were frequently used to designate a characteristic of the person named. The feeling seems to have been that *nomina sunt realia.* An example of this type of usage is found in the case of the name of Jacob, meaning "supplanter," whose subject was in actual fact a crafty and self-seeking person.

1. God's name: general considerations. In some parts of Scripture, God's name is regarded in a strictly sing. sense, and the principles surrounding its usage are collectively applied to the several designations of Him. Thus we have in the Decalogue, "Thou shalt not take the *name* of the LORD thy God in vain" (Exod 20:7, KJV). The usage here is generic and is intended to exclude any fraudulent or flippant use of any of the terms by which God was designated.

The third commandment is thus intended as a safeguard placed upon the structure of divine names as a revelatory instrument. The entire pattern of names was to be held in respect as a vital part of the self-disclosure of Deity, so that no aspect of His revealed nature should be regarded frivolously.

It should be noted that it is the use of the name, rather than its derivation, that is most significant in OT usage. While etymology is a highly relevant study in this connection, its conclusions cannot by themselves be accepted as definitive for the understanding of divine names. Nor can the fact that the Hebrews used names for God which were current in the ancient world be held to militate against a special use of names as revelatory in OT times.

It is to be noted that within the divine nomenclature of the OT, there are varying combinations of designations with respect to the "transcendence-immanence" question. These suggest that to the Hebrews, God was understood as being both hidden and present. Again, there is evidence that He was understood in both transcendent and anthropomorphic modes so far as His personal qualities were concerned.

The NT understanding of both the divine names and the divine nature continues and simplifies the OT usage. The names employed to designate the Deity are fewer, and less emphasis is laid upon names themselves as indicative of the nature of God. Whereas in the OT usage nuances and compound verbal structures are employed to convey the qualities of the Deity, in the NT there are characterizations, direct and indirect, which serve to elaborate men's understanding of God's nature.

2. Basic names for God in the OT. Much of OT criticism, particularly of the liberal variety, has pivoted about the use of two divine names, אל, and יהוה. These, taken together with the name אדונ (usually transliterated as *Adonai*) form what may be considered the basic OT designations for the Deity. These are, as well, simple names, as contrasted with a group of compound names, to which attention will be given later.

The name *El* is one of the oldest designations for deity in the ancient world. It forms the basic component for the general term for God in Babylonia and Arabia, as well as with the Israelitish people. That the conceptions which were sometimes attached to the term *El* in the world of antiquity were unworthy of the God of the Bible is clear, but this does not diminish the significance of the occurrence of the term in the racial stocks of the Middle E. It is a very old term, and many feel that it is reasonable to infer that the term has been retained from a primeval revelation, an Uroffenbarung.

The term *El* seems to suggest power and authority. In this connection, John P. Lange says:

> Power, greatness, vastness, height, according as they are represented by the *conceptions* of the day, carried to the fullest extent allowed by the knowledge of the day; this is the ideal of *El* and *Elohim*, as seen in the etymological congruity of the epithets joined to those in Genesis. (*Commentary on the Holy Scriptures*, I, 109n.)

Thus the original meaning of *El* may have been: (a) to be strong; (b) to have extended sphere of control; or (c) to possess binding force. Walther Eichrodt suggests that:

> It is worth noting that whichever of these meanings we adopt stresses the distance between God and man. In this they are in basic conformity with the basic characteristic of the Semitic concept of God, namely, that what is of primary importance is not the feeling of kinship with the deity, but fear and trembling in the face of his overwhelming majesty. Another point which it is necessary to remark is that they do not identify the Godhead with any natural object, but describe it as the power which stands behind Nature, or the overruling will manifested in it (*Theology of the OT*, p. 179).

The name *El* as applied to God is general and inclusive, and includes the primary significance of power or ability (Gen 17:1; 28:3; 35:11; Josh 3:10; 2 Sam 22:31, 32; Neh 1:5; 9:32; Isa 9:6; Ezek 10:5). Many feel justified in concluding that its employment and wide currency witnesses to a primeval monotheism, from which polytheism represented a lapse. Attention will be given to the frequent use of the pl. form *Elohim* in the OT in a later section. For the present, it needs to be said that the name *El* bears not only the connotation of might, but also the idea of the transcendence of the Deity.

If the name *El* was a general term for the divinity in the thought of the peoples of the Bible Lands and Middle E of antiquity, the name *Yahweh* (transliterated *Jehovah*) was a specifically Israelitish name for God. The basic meaning of the term seems to be: "He which Is" or "He who is truly present."

It is difficult to ascertain how widely this name was used during the Patriarchal era, though it was current in Abraham's day. It was given new emphasis and significance to Moses (Exod 3:15, 16; 6:3, 6. Cf. Gen 12:8) beyond what was understood by Abraham as he built his altar between Bethel and Ai (Gen 12:8). *Yahweh* was revealed as an intensely personal name. Ortho-graphically, it was indicated by the tetragram YHWH, and current transliterations supply vowels variously.

If it be correctly understood that the name was known as early as the birth of Enosh (Gen 4:26) and that Abraham had a knowledge of it, then it follows that the revelation to Moses in Exodus represented a deepening and more personalized usage of the name. It is possible that earlier disclosures of the name had been obscured or even largely lost.

The Mosaic use of the term (including the new significance attached to it) set the pattern for subsequent Heb. thought. With Moses, the name seems to have gained general currency and specific acceptance; but more important, it became intimately associated with the life of Israel as a people. That is it became the token

A list of the various names of God from the Scriptures.

God *(el, elah, elohim, eloah)*
Jehovah (JHWH)
God *(tsur* — 'rock') (Isa. 44:8)
God *(theos)* N.T.)
(N.T.)
Lord *(kurios) (adonai)* (O.T.)
Godhead *(theotes)* (Col. 2:9) *(theios)* (Acts 17:29)
Godhead *(theiotes)* (Rom. 1:20)
Highest (Most High) *(elyon)* (Ps. 18:13, etc.)
Highest (Most High) *(hupsistos)* (Matt. 21:9, etc.)
Holy One (of Israel) *(qadosh)* (Ps. 71:22, etc.)
Mighty One *(el)* (Ps. 50:1) *(gibbor)* (Deut. 10:17, etc.)
God of Gods (Deut. 10:17)
Lord of lords (Deut. 10:17)
Light giver (Maor) (Gen. 1:16)
Father *(ab)* (O.T.: Ps. 89:26, etc.)
Father: *(pater)* (John 5:17, etc.)
Judge *(shaphat)* (Gen. 18:25, etc.)
Redeemer *(gaal)* (Job 19:25)
Saviour *(yasha)* (Isa. 43:3) (O.T.)
Saviour *(soter)* (Luke 1:47) (N.T.)
Deliverer *(palat)* (Ps. 18:2, etc.)
Shield *(magen)* (Ps. 3:3, etc.) (also: Buckler) (Ps. 18:30)
Strength *(eyaluth)* (Ps. 22:19)
Almighty *(shaddai)* (Gen. 17:1, etc.)
God of seeing *(el roi)* (Gen. 16:13)
Righteous One *(tsaddiq)* (Ps. 7:9, etc.)
Lord of Hosts *(elohim tsebhaoth)* (Jer. 11:20)

of a special and crucial self-revelation of God to a special people—a disclosure which tied together the mighty acts involved in the Exodus and Israel's self-consciousness as a nation. These acts in turn prepared the way for the intimate involvement of Israel with Yahweh at Sinai.

Thus the name *Yahweh* was tied in inseparably with Israel's national awareness and was inescapably involved in Israel's unique covenant relation with Deity. Vital to this was the fact that *Yahweh* had taken the initiative, and had stepped visibly and unmistakably into Israel's national affairs.

It is significant that the use of this name for God was unique with the Israelites. The other Sem. peoples do not seem to have known it or at least did not use it in reference to the Deity except as contacts with the Heb. people brought it to their attention. It was the special property of the covenant people.

It is significant also, that the name came to have such significance that the scribes avoided pronunciation of it. Scribal usage involved circumlocutions and as well the use of alternate names. This bears witness not only to the significance of the name as a basis for the feeling for nationhood, but also to the respect which the people felt for the supernatural source of their history.

This is another way of saying that the name *Yahweh* was, in the Israelitish consciousness, set over all that which was merely naturalistic. This does not imply necessarily that the Hebrews saw in the name a metaphysical meaning (as for example Aristotle's formula of "essence equals existence") in the "I AM WHO I AM" of Exodus 3:13, but rather, that they understood *Yahweh* as being existent and active in the here and now.

In this connection, Eichrodt suggests that the name *Yahweh*

> goes much further than the divine names hitherto in use in its emphasis on the concrete nearness and irruptive reality of God, and contrasts vividly for this reason with their generalized statements (earlier names) on the rule and guidance, the exaltedness and eternity of the divine. (Op. cit., p. 191.)

It seems clear that the revelation and the grasp of the name *Yahweh* by the Israelitish people marked a landmark in spiritual awareness and in national religious experience. With the Exodus the Deity assumed in the mentality of Israel a specifically redemptive role. His "mighty acts" were specifically saving acts, and were so understood. In the deliverance at the Red (or Reed) Sea, *Yahweh* had shaped the forces of nature to serve the ends of grace, and had brought His power to bear upon the nation in a time of historic emergency and crisis.

It is understandable in the light of this, that the events of the Exodus formed the core of the Heb. *kerygma*: "I am Yahweh your God, who brought you out of the land of Egypt, out of the house of bondage" (Exod 20:2). Here is emphasized the specialized quality of God's self-disclosure to the Heb. people. It goes without saying that objections have been raised to the specificity which is implied here. Such thinkers as Douglas Clyde Macintosh have held that for God to have revealed Himself esp. and exclusively to the Heb. people would have been an act unworthy of Him, and one ultimately immoral. It is at this point that a sharp antithesis between merely human thought and the Biblical insight appears.

The OT insight is that God has taken the initiative in restoring the knowledge-bond which existed between God and fallen man, a bond which was fractured at the fall. And it was through His revelation to Israel of Himself under the name of *Yahweh* or *Jehovah* that the unfolding of saving history became visible. The unveiling of God's nature by the giving of this name to Israel was of supreme significance to the entire Biblical system.

Another of the basic names for deity which occurs frequently in early Israelitish history is *Adhon* or *Âdhônāy*, usually transliterated as *Adonai.* Its root form, *Adon*, does not seem to have been in common use among Sem. peoples generally, but was used mainly by the Hebrews. In the OT it was used in reference to human beings possessing authority.

In Joshua 3:11 God is called "Lord of all the earth"; most frequently the pl. form, *Adonai* (literally "my Lords") is employed. In its earliest usage it was evidently a more transcendent term, indicating God's role as one high and above all things. In later usage, it came to indicate a more personal and intimate relation between the Deity and His people. It thus involves not only gradations of relationships but also obligations and duties. The name was frequently used, not only for, but with the name *Yahweh.* In the latter usage, the significance would seem to be that while Yahweh does indeed enter into relationship with His people, He is not to be localized or regarded as the God of any specific place.

3. Combined or secondary names: OT. In addition to the three names which are frequently regarded to be basic in Heb. usage, there are several compound or otherwise grammatically qualified forms of divine name in the OT. Belonging to this group for lack of other special classification would be the extended form of אל, אלוה, (pl. אלוהים). The form *Eloah* (or *Eloha*) is used chiefly in the Book of Job, being found some forty times there.

The pl. form, *Elohim* (often called "the plural of intensity") is used over 2000 times in the OT to refer to Israel's God. It is frequently used with the article *ha-'elohim*, bearing the significance of the one true God. The major significance of the usage seems to be that the

Hebrews went beyond the usual Sem. name *El* as a fitting designation for their Deity, whom they regarded as being above and beyond all other gods.

Among the compound names for God in the OT, the name אל שדי represents a clear progression in the self-disclosure of God to the Hebrews of the patriarchal period. As *Ei Shaddāy* or "the almighty God" the Deity is seen to be not only creator and sustainer of the universe, but also the initiator and keeper of covenants. As such He is seen to move clearly in the human sphere, shaping natural forces to spiritual ends.

The name seems to have had Babylonian connections; the Heb. word *sadu* being related to the older Sem. word meaning "mountain." While some have understood the name *El Shaddāy* as "sustainer," this seems to rest upon a confusion upon the part of the translators of the LXX, who incorrectly associated the word *sadu* with a term meaning "breast."

The correct understanding of the name, as being derived from the name "mountain," seems to suggest strength, stability, and permanence. It has been suggested that the name is basically poetic, thus indicating majestic stability, the reliable refuge, the unmoved pillar. The disclosure of the name is associated closely with the giving of the Covenant as recorded in Genesis 17. The events associated with this point in Israel's history were intimate and personal ones, centering in the birth of Isaac, the institution of circumcision, and the provisions made for Hagar and Ishmael.

It is significant that this name for the Deity became current in the patriarchal period, in which God's providences toward the Heb. people were manifested most intimately and also uniquely to the race of Abraham. In this period, the name *El Shaddāy* was an important verbal aid in the pedagogy of the Hebrews. It may be said that in a sense this name formed a bridge in the Heb. mind between the epoch in which *Elohim* was the chief designation for the Deity, and the period of the re-emphasis on the intensely personal and redemptive name, *Yahweh* or *Jehovah*.

The names אל עלם, and אל אלין, which are both compounds of the original Sem. form *El*, represent variant emphases. The former of these bears the meaning of "God of ancient days" or "God of eternity." The chief usage of this name, in Genesis 21:33, suggests the permanence of the Deity, His exaltation above the changes and contingencies of time. He is conceived to be above the flux of natural phenomena. The ideas contained in this designation were esp. common in the era of the prophets, continuing into the time of the Exile. *El Ôlām* (or *El'ôloām*) as a name calls attention to God's eternal duration, His agelessness and His perpetuity amid the changing tides of natural and human events.

The name *El 'Elyôn* (Gen 14:18; Num 24:16) denotes the Deity as "the Most High," the highest and therefore supreme Being. In the use of this name for God, the Israelites gave expression, not in the first instance to the exclusiveness of their God (which was amply expressed elsewhere), but to His supremacy.

This name, which occurs in very early Heb. history, seems to have receded in use until about 1000 B.C., at which time it came again into use, esp. in the poetic lit. of the OT. Here the omnipotence of God is the point of stress. It occurs also in postexilic times, notably in Daniel 7:25, 27.

The name אלהים צבאת, often transliterated as *Elohim Sebā'ôt* and tr. "God of Sabaoth," means literally "God of Hosts." It is employed to indicate God's role as the One who controls all created agencies and beings. The name is associated with the Ark of the Covenant (e.g. 1 Sam 4:4; 2 Sam 6:2) and is employed frequently by the prophets. That it was not merely an appellation equivalent to "Warrior God" is evident from its large use (nearly 250 times) by the prophets.

That the term does not suggest a merely national or racial deity is witnessed by the prophetic usage which links *Yahweh Sebā'ôt* with judgment upon both Israel and the environing nations. Thus the "Lord of Hosts" was conceived as being sovereign over *all hosts*, both "things in heaven and things on earth." The name suggests exaltedness, transcendence, and omnipotence.

The use of this name implies also a universalistic tendency in Israel's religion during the period of the monarchy. As Eichrodt points out, it suggests that the early concept of a high God in Israel was sustained (*op cit.* 193). It follows that during the period of the monarchy, the Hebrews continued and sustained an earlier exalted concept of the Deity, and that their cultic usage was shaped and conditioned, not by purely national or tribal sentiment, but by a Yahwist faith which possessed universalistic conceptions.

The name צור ("Rock") occurs five times in the song of Moses (Deut 32:4, 15, 18, 30, 31) and a number of times in Psalms, Isaiah and elsewhere. The connotation is fig.; the name suggests Gods' role as a fortress or shield. It occurs in Deuteronomy in a context which suggests both God's greatness and His righteousness. The same combination occurs in Psalm 92:15: "He is my rock, and there is no unrighteousness in him."

In Deuteronomy 32:15, Moses chides ישורון (meaning "Upright One," no doubt an ironical reference to Israel) for forgetting *Tsûr* who as Maker is the source of Israels' security. In verse 31 of the same chapter, Israel's *Tsûr* is contrasted with the enemies' "rock." Here the reference is to God's strength, as well as to His special relationship to the Israelitish nation, in which He confuses their enemies, and causes them to triumph in the face of vastly overwhelming numerical odds.

The name קדש ("Holy One") appears in the Psalms, and esp. in Isaiah, where it is employed over thirty times. The term implies separation from all that is unworthy and unrighteous, and carries the connotation also of power, distance from man and the world, and in a certain sense aloofness and inaccessibility. At the same time, God is declared to be "the Holy One of Israel"; thus the motif of transcendence which might have been the major thrust of the term is modified by the suggestion of *specialness* with reference to Israel.

Two names are employed which indicate the greatness of God, אביר ("Mighty One") and גבור ("Mighty"). The first is employed in connection with the names of Israel or of Jacob; taken with a proper name, it is a poetic title of power. The second has the same significance, and is found in connection with the names both *El* and *Yahweh* (Isa 9:6; 42:13; Jer 32:18).

The name Abhīr (Gen 49:24) indicates a Mighty One who strengthens the hands of chosen men, and whose presence is symbolized by the Ark of the Lord (Ps 132:2, 5). The name is intimately connected with Israel's salvation (Isa 49:26).

The name צדק ("Righteous One") is applied to the Deity in His role as covenant-keeper, and as utterly true to Himself. There is a clear implication of divine justice in the name; Pharaoh is shown to recognize this (Exod 9:27) as is also the psalmist (Pss 129:4; 145:17).

Two names for God which are *hapax legomena* are אל רעי and אל ברית. The former occurs in Genesis 6:13 and its use is attributed to Hagar as she fled into the Negev from the ire of Sarah. The name *'El Rô'î* is capable of being tr. "God of Vision" or "God of Seeing." It seems from the context that the latter is intended in Genesis 6:13.

The name *'El Berit* occurs only in Judges 9:46. The basic meaning is "God of the Covenant"; the reference in Judges is to the name of a sanctuary at Shechem, from whose treasury the citizens of Shechem gave seventy silver shekels to Abimelech to aid him in his struggle for kingship of the city. The actual relation of the sanctuary in the city to the motif of "covenant" is unclear, but some covenant agreements between the sons of Jacob and the Shechemites were prob. implied in Jacob's acquisition of land there (Gen 33:19).

From the foregoing, it seems clear that in OT usage, the names describe functions or activities of God, although intrinsic and even metaphysical implications are not wholly absent. More significant still, they represent stages in a progressive self-disclosure of the Deity, a revelation which utilized situations (esp. crucial ones) as vehicles. The entire revelatory process was safeguarded by the third commandment, which prescribed not only a certain economy in the use of divine names, but a scrupulous adherence to norms of truth in connection with their employment.

4. Names for God in the NT. The employment of names for the Deity in the NT tends to simplify the nomenclature of the OT. The most common name is, of course, Θεός, which occurs more than one thousand times. It connotes, in one name-form, the names *El* and *Elohim* and their compounds and is expressive of essential deity. The term emphasizes self-sufficiency, self-determination and absolute righteousness. ("God, Names of" in ISBE, II, 1268, art. by Edward Mack.)

In general, NT usage of the name *Theos* takes for granted some familiarity with OT conceptions of the divine Being, whose existence is usually assumed. As *Theos* He is present in depth in all things, yet is independent of the created universe. While being no stranger to the world, He is in His essential being transcendent, unmixed with created realities.

The name Κύριος ("Lord") occurs with great frequency in the NT. It seems to gather together within itself the combined meaning of the Heb. name *Adonai*, of which it is the verbal equivalent, and *Yahweh* or *Jehovah*. The name is applied to both Father and Son, and at times is the chief signification for Jesus Christ. In the gospels it appears as the direct equivalent of *Adonai* (Mark 1:3), and as a close correlate to the name *Theos* (John 20:28). In the post-resurrection narratives, esp., it appears as a direct name for Jesus Christ (Luke 24:34; John 20:18; 21:20).

Thus, in the unfolding of the message of the NT, the richness and variety of OT nomenclature for the Deity was presupposed. This is expressed, not only in the wide range of usages of the names *Theos* and *Kurios*, but also in the carrying over in tr. of attributive names from the OT, such as *Highest*, *Most High*, and *Almighty* which correspond respectively to *'Elyôn*, *Abhīr* and *Shaddāy*. (See, e.g. Luke 1:35, 76; Rev 4:8; 11:17; 21:22.)

The most distinctive development in the use of divine names in the NT is the introduction of the name *Father*. While the idea of "God as Father" was foreshadowed in the OT, particularly in the relationship existing between Yahweh and Israel, and in the more intimate strains of the devotional lit. (Pss 68:5; 103:13) it remained for our Lord to make the usage concrete and intimate. The term was completely natural to Him, and as the divine Son He employed it frequently (Matt 7:21; 10:32; Luke 2:49; 11:13; John 12:49). It is noteworthy that His first recorded words (Luke 2:49) indicate His awareness of being about His Father's affairs, and that His last discourse on earth centered upon "the promise of my Father" (Luke 24:49).

While our Lord claimed that God was Father to Him in a unique sense (see John 5:18) yet that fatherhood was something to be shared (Matt 7:11; Luke 11:13). As the

Redeemer and Son, He ever called attention to the Father who had sent Him into the world. The ease with which He employed the name made it natural for the early Christian community to speak of God as "the Father of our Lord Jesus Christ." It follows that our Lord's language was not philosophical but filial. The name *Father* gave dimensions to the understanding of the Deity which neither the name *Theos* nor the title *Kurios* could afford.

The thrust of the language of the NT epistles is that God is the Father of all men in the sense of being the creator and sustainer of all, while at the same time there is an essentially Christian sense in which God is the Father of the regenerate. It is within the context of Christian redemption that the name *Father* comes to its fullest significance.

5. God's nature as revealed by names. It has been noted that God's existence is not argued in detail in Holy Scripture. The names by which He revealed Himself in the OT period were, as has been noted, descriptive largely of the divine activities and functions. It was mentioned further that there was an elaboration of functions (and by implication, of nature also) in the plurality of names.

This does not, of course, rule out the possibility that the employment of the varied designations afforded to the Hebrews—and to men and women of the Christian era—a propositional understanding of God's essential nature. The twin qualities of spirituality and personality shine through the OT nomenclature rather clearly. Back of this was the more basic understanding of God's sovereign freedom. He is portrayed as being above any determination outside Himself. He existed before the world and is in no way dependent upon the cosmos for His existence.

As the Almighty, He is unique in the quality of His freedom. This uniqueness has for its corollary the unitary quality of His being. He thus answers to the Shema (Deut 6:4): "Hear, O Israel: the LORD our God is one LORD." This view, which by the period of the return from the Exile had been indelibly impressed upon the mentality of the Hebrews, sums up the Jewish view of God.

As sovereignly unique and exclusively unitary, God appears also as sovereign Father. This latter concept developed alongside the regal understanding of Jehovah, and in NT times became a dominant motif. It goes without saying that each of these conceptions is morally and ethically based, this being a corollary of God's holiness.

As almighty, God is shown to act, not merely from the fact of irresistible power, but in accordance with that holiness (Lev 11:44; 1 Sam 2:2). This quality demands that all that is associated with him shall also be holy: the priests, the Ark, the Tabernacle, and the people. The purity thus enjoined is not merely a ritual characteristic, although the so-called Holiness Code (Lev 17-26) has profound ritualistic overtones. But at the same time, the Code has strong practical and ethical overtones. In the section dealing with blessings for obedience, God the Lord demands separation from evil as a condition to His making His dwelling with Israel.

The NT usage of designations for God sheds light upon the question of God's love. While in the OT there were racial and national limits to the exercise of divine love, in the NT God's love and benevolence is clearly shown to extend to the whole of mankind. This is the clear implication of the words "God *is* love" (1 John 4:8). The supreme evidence for this is, of course, shown to be found in the Incarnation of the Word, and in the sufferings, death and resurrection of the Incarnate One (1 John 4:9, 10).

Something needs to be said, finally, with respect to the relation of God's nature (and esp. as this is revealed through the employment of divine names) to the created world. This question assumes its sharpest form in the issue of transcendence *versus* immanence. The name *El*, with its strong overtones of power, clearly suggests God's transcendence. The element of distance applies both to the relation of God to man, and of God to the world. The accent falls upon *His* majesty (Neh 9:32; Ps 68:34, 35; Ezek 10:5) in OT usage and in His role as the Lord of history, Creator of all things and Ruler of the ages in the NT (1 Tim 1:17).

In the name *Yahweh* are combined the two motifs of transcendence and immanence. On the one hand, He was a God of power and ability (Exod 3:14; 20:2) but at the same time, One who was vitally operative in human events. His nearness was, in general, seen in terms of proximity and availability to persons (e.g., Moses and the Israelitish people). The term Covenant seems to bring the two motifs into close relationship, for the Mighty Deliverer was also Lawgiver and Provider.

It is significant that the understanding of Deity, particularly as it is revealed progressively through divine names in both Testaments, is singularly free from the twin extremes of Deism and Pantheism. On the one hand, God is declared and shown to be concerned with the affairs of the created universe and particularly the needs of mankind; on the other, He is intensely personal and thus distinct from all of the empirical universe.

It is noteworthy that the thrust of the Scriptural view of Deity avoids the peril of envisioning transcendence in exclusively spatial terms, and as well, that of seeing His immanence in terms of a mixture (or identification) of Him with created realities. Rather, God *as spirit* (John 4:24) is essentially and intrinsically independent, and at the same time irreducible to corporeal or material existence.

While many feel that the employment of the pl. form *Elohim* leaves the way open to the NT view of a plurality of *Personae* in the One divine Essence, the doctrine of the Trinity rests primarily upon other grounds than that of the use of names for the Deity. But these names do play an indispensable role in the total movement of history-and-thought by which the eternal God has made Himself known to the sons of men. To say the least, these names inform us, not only *that God is*, but also "that he rewards those who seek him" (Heb 11:6).

BIBLIOGRAPHY. J. P. Lange, *Commentary on the Holy Scriptures* (n.d.), I, 109n; A. E. Suffrin, "God (Jewish)," HERE, Vi (1914), 295-299; E. Mack, "God, Names of" ISBE, II (1915), 1264-1268; W. T. Davison, "God, Biblical and Christian," HERE, VI (1922), 252-269; W. R. Matthews, *God in Christian Thought and Experience* (1930),89-110; C. F. H. Henry, *Notes on the Doctrine of God* (1948), 75-91; T. Rees, "God," ISBE, II (1955), 1250-1264; W. Eichrodt, *Theology of the Old Testament*, I (1961), 178-203; R. T. A. Murphy, "Nature of God in Biblical Theology," *New Catholic Encyclopedia*, VI (1962), 560-562; H. B. Kuhn, "God: His Names and Nature," *Fundamentals of the Faith* (1969), 35-55; L. F. Hartman, "God, Names of," *Encyclopaedia Judaica*, VII (1971), 674-679.

H. B. KUHN

GOD, SON OF. *See* SON OF GOD.

GODHEAD. The term "Godhead" is a doublet of "Godhood" and is used to designate the state, dignity, condition or quality of a deity, or in Christian theology, of the self-revealed God. The terms occur as early as A.D. 1225, sometimes bearing the more explicit sense of the one divine essence in distinction from personal or hypostatic distinctions within God's nature. Although encyclopedias a generation ago carried rather extensive essays under these headings (Bradley, *A New English Dictionary on a Historical Basis*), the terms have fallen into increasing disuse, though Godhead occurs more frequently than Godhood. B. B. Warfield noted that the disfavor of substantives ending in -head "has been followed by a fading consciousness . . . of the qualitative sense inherent in the suffix. The words accordingly show a tendency to become simple denotives" ("Godhead," ISBE, II, 1268b). Most contemporary expositions simply use the term as a strong synonym for "God." *The Random House Dictionary of the English Language* (1966) uses the capitalized "Godhead" for "the essential being of God; the supreme Being." But Webster's *Unabridged* now lists first the lower case "godhead" in the sense of deity or divine nature, and in secondary meanings curiously employs the capitalized form for "one of the Trinity" as well as for "the triune God" and "the Deity." It is true that the term "Godhead" was used from the 16th cent. to designate the divine nature of Jesus Christ, as well as the essential nature of the triune God.

The word "Godhead" was used by KJV trs. to tr. three related Gr. words in three different passages; τὸ θεῖον (Acts 17:29); θειότης (Rom 1:20); θεότητος (Col 2:9). The first word was in general Gr. use for "the divine," which pagan religions saw in almost everything, and Paul employed it in addressing a heathen audience, but in a context that urges personal faith in the living God. The second word was used by non-Christians both of Artemis at Ephesus and also later of the imperial cult, and emphasized that quality that gives the divine, as deity, the right to man's worship; Paul uses the term in association with the Creator's power upon which all creatures are dependent. The third word, which emphasized deity at the highest possible level, is applied by Paul to the incarnate Logos: all the fullness of the Godhead dwells in Christ bodily.

The term "godhead" or "godhood" cannot be applied to the divine essence in distinction from the attributes, since the glory of God is precisely the totality of His attributes, and the attributes constitute His essence. God's being is a living unity, in the sense that each attribute is identical with His essence; the attributes are human distinctions, but they have their basis in the divine nature, and are affirmed in view of God's self-revelation. God is the infinite and eternal Spirit, the source, support, and end of all things. He is revealed in Scripture as Lord, Light and Love—the sovereign creator, preserver, and judge of the universe; the righteous source of moral and religious truth; and the Father of spirits, whose provision of redemption for sinners through the gift of His only Son is the supreme manifestation of *agape*.

The Biblical emphasis on divine immutability (Ps 33:11; Heb 1:12; James 1:17) has been under special attack in recent modern theology. It is now often argued by neo-Protestant writers that this insistence on the immutability of God is a by-product of speculative Gr. notions of God as a static being, whereas the God of the Bible allegedly is a God of "becoming" as well as of "being." Adduced in support of this idea are the passages about God's "repentance" or supposed change of mind, coupled with a process philosophy of creation (as by Samuel Alexander and A. N. Whitehead) as including growth in God's experience through His relation to the world; sometimes the doctrine of the Trinity is similarly invoked, in view of the incarnation of the Logos and of the two natures of Christ.

The word "repent" is indeed used of Yahweh in numerous OT verses (1 Sam 15:35; Ps 106:45) but the sense is anthropomorphic, and hardly inconsistent with the overall emphasis on God's changelessness (Num 23:19; 1 Sam 15:29; Ps 110:4) (A. Richardson, *A Theological Word Book of the Bible* [1950], 191). The tendency of modern evolutionary theory, moreover, has been to exaggerate the immanence of God and to modify His transcendence and independence of the universe (*see* GOD). The God of the Bible—of predestination, creation, calling, justification, reconciliation, and glorification—is assuredly not an isolated static being, but He is not on that account changeable and mutable. Expositions of the incarnation and atonement of the Logos promotive of the notion that the Godhead suffers, and correlating this denial of divine impassibility with doubts about divine immutability, are usually predicated on the prior abandonment of the Chalcedonian doctrine of two natures.

C. F. H. HENRY

GODLESS. This term does not occur in the Eng. Bible. The idea occurs in Ephesians 2:12 where ἄθεος is rendered "without God." *See* GODLY; GODLINESS.

GODLINESS (*εὐσέβεια*). In non-Biblical Gr. lit. this term connotes an attitude of due respect either toward gods or toward men. In the Bible it nearly always concerns an attitude toward God.

1. Right attitude toward men. In 1 Timothy 5:4, *eusebeia* is rendered "religious duty" (RSV), "piety" (KJV) and refers to proper concern and provision for one's own family.

2. Toward God. In most NT occurrences eusebeia is tr. "godliness," though once in KJV as "holiness" (RSV "piety"; Acts 3:12). The word occurs several times in Paul's Pastoral Epistles. The corresponding adjective εὐσεβής is used in Acts 10:2 to describe the character of the centurion Cornelius (tr. "devout"), which illustrates the meaning in the NT. The related Gr. term which includes the word for God is θεοσέβεια, which occurs but once in the NT (1 Tim 2:10) and is tr. "who profess religion" (RSV); "professing godliness" (KJV).

3. Hypocritical godliness. A merely formal profession of godliness is contrasted with true godliness (2 Tim 3:5): "the form of religion" (RSV); "a form of godliness" (KJV).

4. Basic idea. Godliness means more than morality and more than mere religious profession. The power and reality of a vital union with God are implied. *See* GODLY; GODLESS.

BIBLIOGRAPHY. HBD (1923), II, 221, 222; ISBE (1929), II, 1270.

J. G. VOS

GODLY. Several Heb. and Gr. expressions are tr. by this term in Eng. VSS. חסיד (Ps 4:3; 12:1; 32:6) means basically kindness; the godly man is the man who has experienced and reflects the gracious kindness of God. In Malachi 2:15, "a godly seed," אלהים "of God" is used; a "godly seed" means offspring spiritually and ethically in a right relationship to God. In the NT "godly" (adjective) is tr. from εὐσεβής in 2 Peter 2:9, the idea being pious, reverential. The same Gr. word is rendered "devout" in Acts 10:2 (of Cornelius). As adverb, "godly" is tr. from the related Gr. term εὐσεβῶς in 2 Timothy 3:12 RSV; Titus 2:12.

In another class of NT passages "godly" is tr. from Gr. phrases containing the name God θεός, gen. θεοῦ as in 2 Corinthians 1:12, ("godly sincerity"); 11:2 ("godly jealousy"); 1 Tim 1:4 ("godly edifying"). In 3 John 6 KJV, "after a godly sort" (RSV, "as befits God's service") is literally "worthily of God," ἀξίως τοῦ Θεοῦ. In 2 Corinthians 7:9, 10, 11 "godly is κατὰ Θεόν, "according to God."

Summary. The term "godly" describes persons or actions which are more than merely moral and/or religious. It includes the ideas of personal relationship and sincere practical devotion to the true God. *See* GODLINESS.

BIBLIOGRAPHY. HBD (1923), II, 222. ISBE (1929), II, 1270.

J. G. VOS

GODS (אלהים ; θεός (sing.), θεοί (pl.).

1. False divinities. The Biblical terms are used generically to mean gods, divinities, objects of worship, sometimes meaning the true God, and sometimes meaning the false divinities of paganism. Academic treatments of cultural anthropology usually betray strong influence of the theory of human evolution, maintaining that the difference between "true" and "false" religion is one of degree rather than of kind, and that there is a basic continuity between the idolatry of primitive paganism and the ethical monotheism of the great OT prophets, the NT apostles and Christ. Over against this idea, Scripture teaches that the original religion of mankind was monotheism, and that belief in and worship of gods as distinguished from the worship of the true God is to be regarded as a corruption of the primitive monotheism which appears at the beginning of the OT. Actually, the factual data discovered by field researches in anthropology tend to confirm the Biblical view. Various "primitive" tribes recognize the reality and power of a supreme God who created the universe, but they do not worship Him. It has also been shown that the oldest known religion of China was monotheism, the worship of Shang Ti, the supreme ruler, which is much older than any of the historical religions of China. The Apostle Paul outlined the downward process by which belief in the one true God, known but not worshiped, thanked or served, deteriorated to the most debased forms of polytheism and idolatry (Rom 1:18-25).

2. Treatment in OT. The first mention of idolatry or polytheism in the Bible occurs in connection with the history of Jacob, whom Laban accused of having stolen his "gods" (Gen 31:30), actually the images of household divinities (31:19). The Philistine champion Goliath "cursed David by his gods" (1 Sam 17:43). Through the course of OT history and until the end of the Babylonian Captivity in the 6th cent. B.C., there was a constant struggle to maintain consistently the purity of monotheism against the constant tendency to lapse into polytheistic belief and worship. There is a typical example of this long con-

Symbol of god Ashur (fertilizing a date palm) from the cast of a relief from the palace of Ashurnasirpal. Original in British Museum. 885-860 B.C. © *O.I.U.C.*

tinued polemic against false gods in Psalm 115:1-8. By the time of the return from the Babylonian captivity this tendency of the people of Israel to recognize and honor other gods was effectively and permanently corrected; from then on, to be a Jew was to be a strict monotheist and a hater of idols.

3. The plural form אלהים. used of the true God. This usage, which occurs throughout the OT, is not to be understood as implying any recognition of or concession to polytheism, or plurality of being or essence. The form is pl., but when used for the true God the meaning is sing. The pl. form accompanies the strictest monotheism of teaching. The pl. form may be explained as a pl. of majesty, as earthly rulers call themselves "we," or it may be regarded as a veiled hint of the doctrine of the divine Trinity, later to be revealed explicitly in the NT.

4. The term "gods" applied to men. The usage of Psalm 82:6, "I say, 'You are gods, sons of the Most High, all of you; nevertheless, you shall die like men, and fall like any prince,' " and its quotation by the Lord in John 10:35, 36, presents a difficulty. Men are called "gods" and the term actually is used in contrast to "men." "You are gods . . . nevertheless, you shall die like men." It must be remembered that the context both in Psalm 82 and John 10 is one of strictest monotheism. Jesus' statement that those who were called "gods" were those "to whom the word of God came" indicates that members of the covenant nation of Israel were meant. The generally accepted interpretation is that in these two passages "gods" refers to the judges or other rulers of OT times, who are called "gods" not because they were divine, but because they were dignitaries clothed with an authoritative commission from God.

5. Treatment in the NT. The later Judaism in the context of which the NT revelation was given by God was the strictest possible monotheism. Among and around the Jews, however, were Gentiles who were polytheists and often idolaters. Hence, the NT emphatically contradicts all claims for divinity of any others than the one true God. In the face of the manifold idolatry of Athens, Paul proclaimed the God "who made the world and everything in it" (Acts 17:24 RSV). At Ephesus Demetrius the silversmith objected violently to the preaching of Paul because the latter had said that "gods made with hands are not gods" (Acts 19:26). Paul stated his monotheism over against the prevalent polytheism emphatically in 1 Corinthians 8:4-6, ". . . 'there is no God but one.' For although there may be so-called gods in heaven or on earth—as indeed there are many 'gods' and many 'lords'—yet for us there is one God, the Father, from whom are all things and for whom we exist, and one Lord, Jesus Christ, through whom are all things and through whom we exist."

6. Demonic character of pagan gods. In using the term "god" for the objects of pagan worship, Scripture does not mean to imply their objective reality, but only their subjective existence in the minds of their worshipers. Amaziah king of Judah, after decisively defeating the Edomites, brought back to Jerusalem a collection of Edomite idols, which he then set up and worshiped (2 Chron 25:14, 15), and was rebuked by a prophet of Jehovah for worshiping gods which were manifestly unreal and helpless, since they had not been able to save their own people, the Edomites, from conquest by Judah. Evidently Amaziah, though a worshiper of Jehovah, found it difficult to hold a pure enough monotheism to regard the Edomite gods as mere lifeless images. What is important to note is not merely Amaziah's inconsistency, but the Lord's rebuke to him through the prophet.

In 1 Corinthians 10:19-21 Paul sets forth the demonic character of pagan divinities: ". . . what pagans sacrifice they offer to demons and not to God." While the pagan divinities are non-existent and mere figments of human imagination (Rom 1:21-25), still the worship offered to them was claimed and appropriated by demons, who of course are objectively real and concerned to oppose the truth of God.

BIBLIOGRAPHY. A. H. Strong, *Systematic Theology* (1912), 56, 531-532; ISBE (1929), II, 1270-1272; G. Vos, *Biblical Theology* (1948), 73, 74, 255-257; O. T. Allis, *The Five Books of Moses* (1949), 152-155, 246, 324; M. F. Unger, *Archeology and the OT* (1954), 202, 278, 279, 167-178; TCERK (1955), I, 464, 465; Von Allmen, *A Companion to the Bible* (1958), 145, 146; M. F. Unger, *Biblical Demonology* (1958); *Archaeology and the NT* (1962), 259, 260; J. B. Noss, *Man's Religions* (1963), 50-117; B. W. Anderson, *Understanding the OT* (1966), 412.

J. G. Vos

GOEL gō′ ĕl (גֹּאֵל, *redeemer*). The present active participle of the word which means "to redeem," "to act as a kinsman," or "to do the part of the next of kin."

The term is found frequently in the OT as describing the person who is next of kin and his respective duties.

One of his duties is to buy back what his poor brother has sold and cannot himself regain (Lev 25:25, 26) He is also the recipient of the restitution which may be due to a next of kin (Num 5:8).

He is to avenge any wrong done to a next of kin, particularly murder (Num 35:12, 19, 21, 24, 25, 27). As avenger, he had power to kill the murderer. Cities of refuge were established throughout Israel for those who accidentally killed another, and in those cities the slayer could not be harmed (Deut 19:6, 12; Josh 20:3, 5, 9).

Ruth illustrates the responsibility of the redeemer to purchase land belonging to one deceased who was next of kin; to marry his widow and to raise up children for the deceased (Ruth 2:20; 4:14).

It is quite appropriate then that the term became applied to God in His relationship to men. As Redeemer He would buy back what the poor sinner sold (his life) and could not regain. God also would avenge the wrong done to believing sinners by His judgment against the devil and sin. Furthermore, like a husband, God would marry the church, His bride. All of these concepts of God are seen in Scripture. They begin in the OT but are fully developed in the New.

Jacob first spoke of God as his Goel from all evil (Gen 48:16).

Job also expressed intimate knowledge of his Goel, presumably God (Job 19:25).

The psalmist calls God his Goel and strength (Ps 19:14). Note also Psalms 78:35; 103:4.

The Book of Proverbs calls God the Goel of the poor orphan (Prov 23:11).

It is Isaiah who most elaborately develops the concept of God as Goel. He uses the term in reference to God thirteen times. As Israel's Goel God will: rescue helpless Israel (Isa 41:14); destroy Babylon (43:14); be king of Israel (44:6; 47:4); teach them to profit and lead them in the way (48:17); be their Savior (49:26; 60:16); be their husband (54:5); show everlasting love for them and compassion (54:8); and be their Father (63:16). All of this is conditioned on their turning from transgression (59:20).

The LXX uses several different words to tr. the Heb. גאל. Three of them are λυτρούμενος, ῥυσάμενός, and ἐξαιρουμενός. All are participles in form.

These words appear in the NT quite appropriately in reference to God and esp. Jesus Christ.

Christ is said to give His life a ransom (λύτρον) for many (Matt 20:28). He gave Himself up to redeem (λυτρόω) us from iniquity (Titus 2:14).

Peter tells us that we were redeemed (λυτρόω) not by gold and silver but by the blood of Christ (1 Pet 1:18 19).

Note also the use of ῥύομαι and ἐξαιρέω (Rom 7:24; Gal 1:4; Col 1:13; 1 Thess 1:10).

From the use of this term it is clear that quite early God's people understood the concept of God as Goel. Christ quite appropriately, in the flesh, did become the Goel who purchased with His blood our lives and who wrought vengeance on our enemy, Satan. He further became our bridegroom and the Church, His bride.

BIBLIOGRAPHY. H. Rowley, *The Old Testament and Modern Study* (1951), 221; Oesterley and Robinson, *An Introduction to the Books of the Old Testament* (1958), 83; W. Eichrodt, *Theology of the Old Testament* (1961), 309; C. Pfeiffer, *Ras Shamra and the Bible* (1962), 43.

J. B. Scott

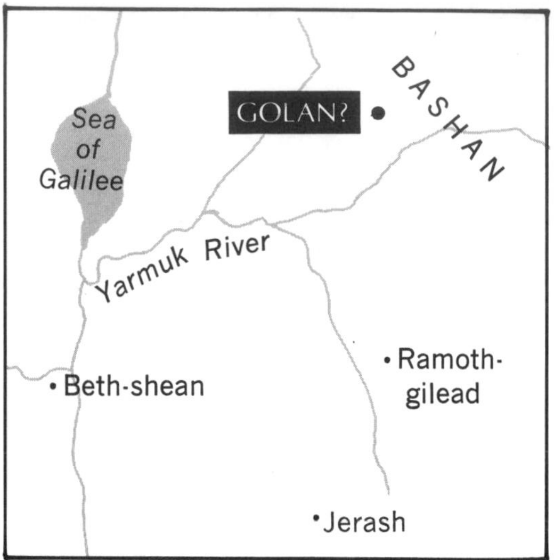

GOG **gŏg** (גּוֹג, meaning unknown). A son of Joel, from the tribe of Reuben (1 Chron 5:4). In Ezekiel (38:2; 39:1-16) another "Gog" from the land of Magog is called the prince of Meshech and Tubal. He may be the same as Gyges, king of Lydia (c. 660 B.C.), the Assyrian *Gugu*.

GOG AND MAGOG **gŏg, mā′ gŏg** (גּוֹג, מָגוֹג). Gog is the ruler of Magog and the prince of Meshech and Tubal, the demonic and sinister leader of ungodly peoples far distant from Israel, whom he leads in a final assault against the people of God, but is ignominiously defeated by the intervention of Yahweh upon the mountains of Canaan. The conflict is described in Ezekiel 38; 39 and in summary form in Revelation 20:7-9.

The origin of the name "Gog" is unknown. He has been identified with Gyges of Lydia, who is said to have expelled the invading Cimmerians with Syrian help; with Gaga, mentioned in the Amarna letters; with another Gaga, a Babylonian deity; and with Gagi, a ruler of the city of Sabi.

Magog was prob. located between Cappadocia and Media; Josephus says it refers to the Scythians (Jos. Antiq. I. vi. 1). In Revelation 20:8, Gog and Magog symbolically represent the godless nations of the world. With Gog are associated many peoples: Meshech and Tubal, of whom he is prince; Persia, Cush, Put, Gomer, Sheba, Dedan, and Tarshish—all of whom come from widely separated parts of the earth—a mighty host, like a cloud, to do battle against Israel under the mighty Gog. But God's judgment comes upon the enemies of Israel. Every kind of terror is summoned by Yahweh against Gog whose defeat is so great that his vast armaments serve as fuel for Israel for seven years and whose dead are so numerous that it takes all Israel seven months to bury them.

Gog appears again in Revelation 20:7-9, where Satan is depicted after the millennium as gathering the nations of the whole earth, that is, Gog and Magog, against the saints and the beloved city, but they are destroyed and cast into the lake of fire.

There are three major divergent interpretations of the story of Gog. Some hold it to present a literal description of a future attack on Israel by certain identifiable nations led by Russia. Others regard it as a symbolic description of some future event—either the final conflict of the nation Israel with unidentified foes, or the final catastrophic struggle between the Church and the forces of the world. Still others look upon it as a prophetic parable illustrating, not a specific historical event, but a great truth—that whenever in history evil forces array themselves to destroy God's people, He comes to the aid of His own.

BIBLIOGRAPHY. P. Fairbairn, *The Interpretation of Prophecy* (1856), 484-493.

S. BARABAS

GOIIM **goi′ ĭm** (גּוֹיִם). KJV "nations, heathen gentiles"; RSV "nations"; prob. a loanword from Akkad. *gayūm,* "tribe". Geographical name associated with NE Syria.

Goiim is the name of the territory ruled by Tidal (Gen 14:1) and by an unnamed king in the Galilee region (so LXX) defeated by Joshua (Josh 12:23). The latter is prob. the same as the Galilee of the Goiim (Isa 9:1; RSV "nations"). Harosheth-hagoiim (Judg 4:2, 13) may be a specific locality within the same area of Galilee. The location of Goiim has depended usually on the proposed identification of Tidal. The common link with Gutium (Kurdistan) implies an error in the Heb. consonants and is unlikely. If Tidal is a Hitt. or Syrian name (*Tudhalia*) then the identification of Goiim with a region in Syria would fit the Biblical references. It would further support the view that the kings were drawn into a coalition from each of the quarters of the Babylonian empire (Hatti/Goiim representing the W, Ellasar-Assyria the N, Elam the E and Shinar/Babylonia the S). Goiim cannot be understood as a collective reference to non-Israelite peoples (cf. Gen 25:23; Isa 26:2; Zeph 2:9).

D. J. WISEMAN

GOLAN **gō′ lən** (גּוֹלָן, perhaps meaning *round*). A city assigned to Manasseh in Bashan. It was a Levitical city given to the Gershonites (Josh 21:27; 1 Chron 6.71) and had been chosen by Moses as one of three places of refuge E of the Jordan (Deut 4:43; Josh 20:8). It was located in the N, although the exact site is still undetermined. Josephus describes the district of Gaulanitis in Bashan as a fertile area containing a large population. Golan was the scene of both defeat and later, victory for Alexander (Jos. Antiq. XIII, xiii. 5). It belonged to the tetrarchy of Philip.

Eusebius notes that Gaulan or Golan was a large village whose name became attached to the adjoining country. Most prob. it corresponds to modern Jaulan, an area bounded by Mt. Hermon on the NE, the Jordan and the Sea of Galilee on the W, and the Jarmuk on the S. The excellent site of Sahem el-Jolan, four miles E of the river el-'Allan may well mark the ancient city of Golan.

H. M. Wolf

GOLD (Heb. זהב ; בצר ; חרוץ ; כתם ; סגור ; פּן ; Gr. *χρυσος*). One of the precious metals which has a bright-yellow color, high density (19.3) and high melting point (1063°C). It is the most ductile and malleable of metals and can be beaten into leaves of less than 0.0001 mm. in thickness. Gold usually occurs in the native state but sometimes as gold tellurides. Native gold is generally alloyed with 10-15% silver (q.v.), sometimes with copper (q.v.), and also with iron, platinum, palladium and rhodium. The more silver present, the whiter the color, while the presence of copper makes the color orange-red. The natural alloy containing 15-45% silver was used for many early coins and is called *electrum*. This word in Gr. also means amber, while in ancient Egypt the term *asem* was used, Like silver and copper, the crystal structure of gold is a face-centered cubic lattice in which each atom has twelve neighboring atoms touching it.

Gold is widely distributed in the earth's crust, but generally only in small amounts, with the average proportion in the crust being one part per thousand million. It is found in various igneous rocks, particularly those containing quartz, and their metamorphic derivatives, including the Precambrian Aqaba Granite Complex which occurs on either side of the Red Sea and from which much of the sedimentary rocks of the Holy Lands were derived. Gold also occurs in many such sedimentary rocks, particularly those resulting from deposition in river channels and along old shore lines. The gold used in ancient times largely or entirely came from alluvial deposits. These occur on the slopes of hills not too far distant from the source of gold-bearing veins or as sands and gravels deposited by rivers in regions with auriferous bed rock; e.g. rich gold deposits were known in the valley of the River Pactolus in Lydia, Asia Minor. In such deposits, the gold is separated from the sand and gravel using a current of water which carries off the particles of lower density leaving the high-density gold flakes, which sink. The gold is then separated from any remaining material by amalgamation with mercury. The gold-mercury amalgam is then heated to vaporize the mercury leaving a crude bullion (*see* Metals and Metallurgy).

Even in pre-dynastic times the Egyptians made use of gold to embellish stone vessels and to make the handles of flint knives. The washing of gold ores is depicted on Egypt. monuments of the 1st dynasty (2900 B.C.) with gold

Gold mask of King Tut-ankh-amon, son-in-law of Akh-en-Aton found in his tomb at Thebes. ©C.M.

occurring in Egypt between the Nile and the Red Sea (Mine, Mining, q.v.). Gold also occurs in Arabia (Gen 2:11; cf. 1 Kings 10:2) and was imported by Solomon from Ophir (1 Kings 10:11). While this locality is often considered to be in Arabia, in the time of Solomon it was thought of as an overseas Eldorado (cf. Ps 45:9; Isa 13:12) to which joint Heb.-Phoen. expeditions sailed in the "ships of Tarshish." Punt in Somaliland, Zimbabwe in Rhodesia and Surparaka in India have been suggested as possible locations. Rich gold deposits were also known in ancient times in Lydia, in the lands of the Aegean and in Persia. Later, deposits were worked in Italy, Sardinia and Spain while in the time of the Rom. empire the chief source of supply appears to have been Transylvania.

Gold ornaments and utensils have been used since the Bronze Age, with the Sumerians c. 3000 B.C. using gold for domestic and ritual vessels and objects and for personal ornament. Corresponding use of gold is recorded for

Biblical times (e.g. 2 Chron 9:20; Exod 25:11; Gen 41:42, respectively). However the main use of gold has been, and still is, in relation to money and wealth (e.g. Gen 13:2; Judg 8:26; 1 Kings 10:14). It is taken as the representation of the most valuable of man's material possessions (cf. Ps 19:10; 1 Pet 1:7) while visions of things referring to the new Jerusalem speak of pure gold (Rev 21:18).

BIBLIOGRAPHY. E. S. Dana, *A Textbook of Mineralogy,* 4th ed. (revised by W. E. Ford) (1932), 401-403; J. R. Partington, *A Text-book of Inorganic Chemistry,* 6th ed. (1950), 745-747; E. M. Blaiklock (ed.), *The Zondervan Pictorial Bible Atlas* (1969), 438-443; R. D. Barnett, "Ophir," E Br 16 (1970), 991, 992.

D. R. Bowes

GOLDSMITH. The goldsmith, like the silversmith, was called a refiner or purifier, צוֹרֵף, in Heb. (Mal 3:2, 3). His major work was to hammer gold into shape, or cast it in a mold to form the object desired. The goldsmith fashioned both gold and goldplated idols (Jer 10:9; 51:17). Gold plating was placed over an idol carved from wood, using nails to hold the gold plate in place (Isa 41:7). Probably the goldsmiths, mentioned in the Heb. Nehemiah 3:8, 31, 32, were jewelers. See also Gold and Artificer.

BIBLIOGRAPHY. R. J. Forbes, "Studies in Ancient Technology," vol. VIII, ch. 5 (1964).

J. L. Kelso

GOLGOTHA gŏl' gə thə (Γολγοθα, *skull*). The Aram. name of the place near Jerusalem where Christ was crucified.

1. The Biblical record. The name Golgotha actually appears but three times in the Bible, in parallel passages of the gospels (Matt 27:33; Mark 15:22; John 19:17). The word is Aram. גֻּלְגַּלְתָּא, "the skull" essentially the same as the Heb. גֻּלְגֹּלֶת, "head" or "skull" (cf. Num 1:2; Judg 9:53; 2 Kings 9:35; 1 Chron 10:10; et al.). The root letters are the same as in the word for "roll" (גלל), and the connection is easily made to the roundness of the head. Luke, as usual, does not use the Sem. word but renders the name into Gr. as *κρανίον*, which comes over into Eng. as "cranium." This is tr. "Calvary" (from the Lat. *calvaria*) but as "skull" in the RSV.

That Golgotha was near Jerusalem is without question, though hints in the Biblical record are few. Hebrews 13:12 indicates that Jesus suffered "outside the gate." Therefore, Golgotha was not within the city wall in NT times, although not far outside (cf. John 19:20). Matthew 27:39 indicates that Golgotha was by a well-traveled road (cf. Mark 15:21). Furthermore, it was visible from some distance according to Mark 15:40 and Luke 23:49. This has led many to think of it as a hill, but nowhere in the Bible is that so stated.

2. The location of Golgotha. Although many places around the holy city have been suggested as the site of Calvary, only two are serious contenders for the spot of both the crucifixion and the burial.

One primary claim to the site is the Church of the Holy Sepulchre, whose history goes back to the 4th cent. It is within the walls of the old city today, but its supporters maintain that the NT city wall would place it outside the city. Because modern buildings heavily cover all real estate in the area, no excavation is yet possible to determine just where that northern NT wall was.

The location of this site can be traced to the Christian Rom. emperor Constantine. Eusebius, a contemporary historian, commissioned Bishop Marcarius to find Golgotha and the tomb. This was nearly 300 years after the crucifixion. The Church of Constantine was then built on the site of Hadrian's Aphrodite temple and named in honor of St. Helena, the emperor's mother. Legend has it that upon excavating for the tomb, a fragment of the true cross was found that effected miracles of healing, and thus certified the site. The tradition that this is the site is very old but it is mostly tradition. Earlier, the pagan emperor Hadrian had deliberately obscured many Christian holy sites with his temples.

The other major contender for the site of Calvary is known today as the Garden Tomb and/or Gordon's Calvary. Suggested by Otto Thenius in 1842, General Charles Gordon declared in 1885 that this was the site of the crucifixion and burial, found some 250 yards NE of the Damascus Gate. There are some arguments to support the location, as well as some serious criticisms.

Gordon's Calvary is a hill, or knoll and is certainly outside the city walls (both modern and NT). The most serious problem with the Holy Sepulchre's location does not affect this choice. A garden and a tomb (in fact, several tombs) are in the immediate vicinity. Those who contest this identification maintain that the hill was part of a ridge that is still visible on the N wall of Jerusalem adjacent to Herod's Gate. Thus is was not a separate hill in NT times. The tombs are at least of Byzantine vintage, but no one can say whether they are older than that. The topographical feature of the hill that makes it look like a skull would not have been present in NT times. In fact, this hill, which is called by the Jews, "the Grotto of Jeremiah," is thought to be a mine site developed only in the past two or three centuries. A better explanation of "the place of a skull" would be that either the hill was bare rock, or it served as a cemetery.

Protestants prefer the latter site because the organization that owns the land has landscaped it to make it resemble their concept of Joseph of Arimathea's garden. The Church of the Holy Sepulchre is, of course, a building

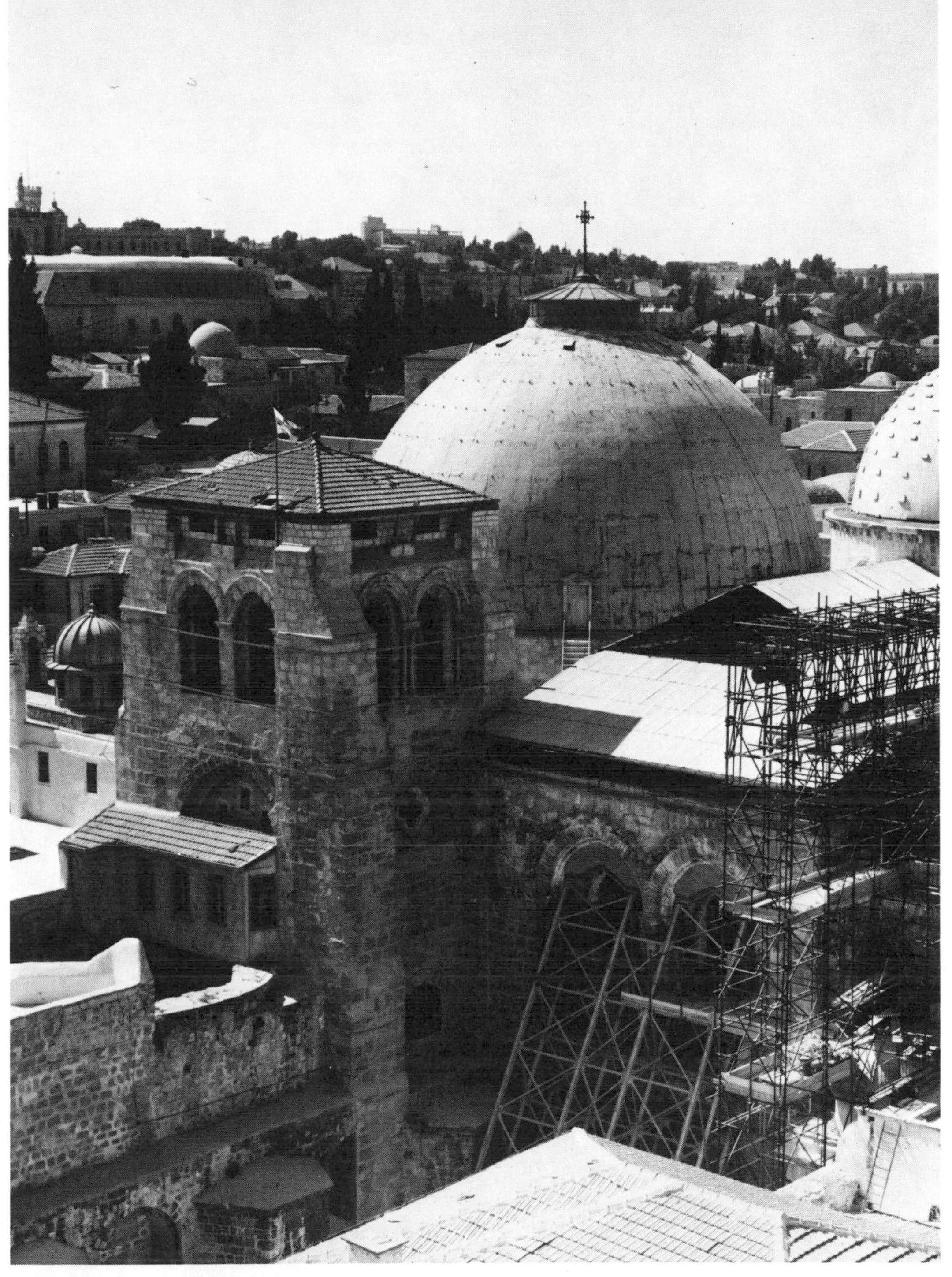

Church of the Holy Sepulchre built over the traditional site of Calvary. ©*Lev*

The other contender for the site of Calvary is known as Gordon's Calvary, pictured above. © Har

on top of a site. It is highly decorated and the scene of much activity. It requires a good imagination to see a garden tomb there.

BIBLIOGRAPHY. J. Jeremias, *Golgotha* (1926); G. Dalman, *Sacred Sites and Ways* (1935), 341-381; C. Marston, *The Garden Tomb, Jerusalem*, London, The Garden Tomb Association (1941); *Jerusalem: The Garden Tomb of Golgotha* [no author], London, The Garden Tomb Association (1945); L. T. Pearson, *Where Is Calvary?* (1946); J. Simons, *Jerusalem and the O T* (1952), 282-343; A. Parrot, *Golgotha and the Church of the Holy Sepulchre* (1957); C. C. Dobson, *The Garden Tomb and the Resurrection* (n.d.); L. E. Cox Evans, "The Holy Sepulchre," PEQ (July-Dec., 1968) 112-136.

R. L. ALDEN

GOLIATH gə lī' əth (גלית). A Gittite warrior during reign of Saul (late 11th cent.). Representing the Philistines at Ephes-dammim, he challenged the Israelites in the valley of Elah (about fifteen m. W of Bethlehem) to send an opponent. His challenge went unaccepted until David visited the battleground to bring food to his brothers. David felled the giant with a stone shot from a sling and cut off his head with Goliath's own sword (1 Sam 17).

The height of Goliath was six cubits and a span, over nine feet (17:4). His coat of mail was 5,000 shekels, about 125 pounds; his spearhead, 600 shekels, about 15 pounds (17:5, 7). His sword was kept at Nob under priestly jurisdiction and later given to David by Ahimelech, the priest, when David fled from Saul (1 Sam 21:9; 22:10).

In 2 Samuel 21:19 the slaying of Goliath is attributed to Elhanan, but in 1 Chronicles 20:5 Elhanan slew Lahmi, brother of Goliath. The passages appear to come from one source and the critical difference may have been the miscopying of a few consonants. If 2 Samuel is correct as stands, this Goliath could have been a son of David's opponent.

This event illustrates warfare of the time; that most of the army was ill-trained and no match for the well-trained elite who often engaged in individual combat. (*Note* Egyp. Sinuhe and Homerian battles.) Thus, Jonathan could fight the Philistine garrison single-handed (1 Sam 14:6-15), and Moses withstood a number of shepherds (Exod 2:16-19). These men depended on God, but their attempts were not foolhardy; rather they were acting rationally and therefore could expect God's help.

BIBLIOGRAPHY. E. J. Young, *Introduction to the Old Testament* (1963), 197, 198; Y. Yadin, *The Art of Warfare in Biblical Lands* (1963).

C. P. WEBER

GOMER gō' mər (גמר, meaning perhaps *completion, perfection*). Son of Japheth; wife of Hosea. 1. Son of Japheth and grandson of Noah (Gen 10:2, 3). Father of Ashkenaz, Riphath, and Togarmah. His offspring are prob. the Cimmerians (Akkad. *gimmirrai*, Gr. Κιμμέριοι). Gomer (the Cimmerians) is mentioned in Ezekiel 38:6 as supporting an attack on Israel that will fail because the Lord is defending His people. (Some feel that "men of Gamad," Ezek 27:11, is copyist's error for Gomer.) The Cimmerians were forced out of S Russia by the Scythians and crossed over the Caucasus into Asia Minor at the end of the 8th cent. B.C. In the following cent., they fought the Assyrians, conquered Urartu, then subdued Phrygia and Lydia, and fought Gr. cities on the W coast.

2. Wife of Hosea, an 8th-cent. prophet in Israel during the reign of Jeroboam II. Daughter of Diblaim (Hos 1:3). The Lord asked Hosea to marry a harlot. He married Gomer and by her had children to whom were given illustrative, or symbolic, names. The marriage to a harlot pictured the Lord's marriage to His people who had gone astray into idolatry. Some moralists have questioned the propriety of Hosea marrying a harlot and have proposed the possibility that she was pure at the time of her marriage, but that both the Lord and Hosea knew that she would fall into sin. Hosea is later told to marry again, "an adulteress" (3:1); some feel that this is the same woman after she had left Hosea, being bought again and asked to abstain from harlotry. Whether or not this is Gomer, it illustrates that though God's people sin the Lord loves His people and wants them to return to Him, but to refrain from sin. Some feel that these are not actual marriages but simply illustrations.

BIBLIOGRAPHY. N. Snaith, *Mercy and Sacrifice* (1953), 27-38; *The Cambridge Ancient History*, III (1960); G. A. F. Knight, *Hosea* (1960), 27-29, 40-65; J. M. Ward, *Hosea* (1966), 3-71.

C. P. WEBER

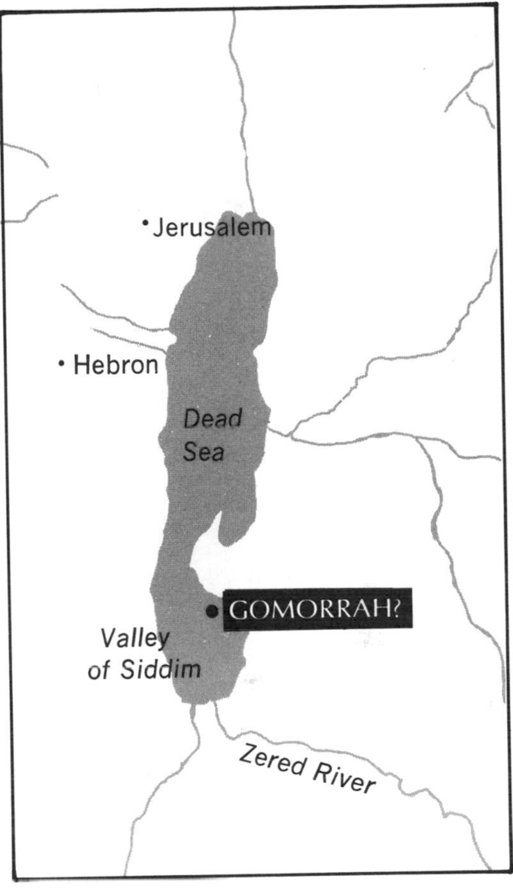

GOMORRAH gə môr′ ə (עמרה, LXX, Γόμορρα; meaning unknown). A city located in the Valley of Siddim, prob. at the S of the Dead Sea.

Together with Sodom, the cities became infamous because of the way in which they were destroyed. Sodom and Gomorrah became bywords for the judgment of God. Isaiah referred to its sin and its consequent destruction twice in his first ch. (v. 9f.), and once later (13:19). Jeremiah resurrected the horror of its destruction (Jer 23:14; 49:18; 50:40). Both Amos (4:11) and Zephaniah (2:9) pronounced divine threats in terms of the two famous cities of the plain. In the NT, Jesus, Paul, Peter, and Jude alluded to these ancient examples of God's retributive wrath (Matt 10:15; Rom 9:29; 2 Pet 2:6; and Jude 7).

Gomorrah is first mentioned as the S or E extent of the Canaanite territory (Gen 10:19) Later, Lot, Abram's nephew, chose to live in Sodom. It was then that four eastern kings under the leadership of Chedorlaomer attacked the five cities of the plain (Gen 14). Genesis 18 and 19 record the meeting of Abram with the angels and their warning to Lot of the imminent destruction of Sodom and Gomorrah. Lot escaped and "the LORD rained on Sodom and Gomorrah brimstone and fire" (19:24).

The location of Gomorrah is unknown. There are theories that it was at either the N or S end of the Dead Sea. Both arguments have strengths; both have weaknesses, but the most accepted view is that Gomorrah and the other cities are sunken beneath the shallow waters of the Dead Sea S of the Lisan peninsula.

BIBLIOGRAPHY. W. F. Albright, BASOR, 14 (1924), 5-7; AASOR VI (1924-1925), 58-62; F. G. Clapp, "The Site of Sodom and Gomorrah," AJA (1936), 323-344; J. P. Harland, "Sodom and Gomorrah, The Location and Destruction of the Cities of the Plain," BA, V (1941), 17-32; VI (1943), 41-54.

R. L. ALDEN

GONG. *See* MUSIC, MUSICAL INSTRUMENTS.

GOOD, GOODS (טוב ; יטב; ἀγαθός; ἀγαθόν; καλός; καλόν). The words "good" and "goods" appear in the Scriptures hundreds of times with a wide variety of related meanings that often shade off into one another.

As an adjective, "good" is used to express the following ideas:

1. *Kind, gracious*: "Yet the men were very good to us" (1 Sam 25:15); "For thou, O Lord, art good and forgiving" (Ps 86:5); "The Lord is good, a stronghold in the day of trouble" (Nah 1:7).

2. *Profitable, advantageous*: "It is no longer good for anything except to be thrown out and trodden under foot by men" (Matt 5:13).

3. *Befitting, appropriate*: "This time the counsel which Ahithophel has given is not good" (2 Sam 17:7); "Your boasting is not good" (1 Cor 5:6).

4. *Good, full measure; considerable*: "Then she went, and sat down over against him a good way off" (Gen 21:16); "Joseph . . . fell on his neck, and wept on his neck a good while" (46:29); "it will be given to you; good measure" (Luke 6:38).

5. *Highly esteemed*: "A good name is better than precious ointment" (Eccl 7:1).

6. *Agreeable, pleasant*: "So when the woman saw that the tree was good for food" (Gen 3:6); "a word in season, how good it is!" (Prov 15:23).

7. *Upright, righteous*: "I will instruct you in the good and the right way" (1 Sam 12:23); "He has showed you, O man, what is good" (Micah 6:8); "He makes his sun rise on the evil and on the good" (Matt 5:45).

As a substantive, "good" has the following uses:

1. *Material possessions, goods*: "Give no thought to your goods" (Gen 45:20); "But if any one has the world's goods and sees his brother in need" (1 John 3:17).

2. *Moral goodness*: "There is none that does good" (Ps 14:1, 3); "he knows how to refuse the evil and choose the good" (Isa 7:15); "And why not do evil that good may come?" (Rom 3:8).

The words rendered "goods" in the KJV are often differently tr. in the RSV, of which the following are some examples. "The LORD shall make thee plenteous in goods"; "The LORD will make you abound in prosperity" (Deut 28:11). "And he carried away all his cattle, and all his goods which he had gotten"; "and he drove away all his cattle, all his livestock which he had gained" (Gen 31:18). "And they took strong cities, and a fat land, and possessed houses full of all goods"; "And they captured fortified cities and a rich land, and took possession of houses full of all good things" (Neh 9:25). "He shall make him ruler over all his goods"; "He will set him over all his possessions" (Matt 24:47). "Father, give me the portion of goods that falleth to me"; "Father, give me the share of property that falls to me" (Luke 15:12). "I am rich, and increased with goods"; "I am rich, I have prospered" (Rev 3:17).

In the Bible, the supreme good is never a matter of speculation, as it was in ancient Gr. philosophy. In the Bible, "good" is considered as happiness, pleasure, knowledge, etc. God Himself is The Good; there is no good apart from Him. He is the source of all goodness. No man can know The Good unless he knows God in a right relationship and does His expressed will. "No one is good but God alone" (Mark 10:18).

Since God is good, all that He does is necessarily good. He declared His own creation good (Gen 1). The disorder, disruption, evil, and sin that now prevail throughout His world are the result of the rebellion of moral beings originally created good.

God's revelation of Himself in history was an increasing revelation of His goodness. He made man in His image for fellowship with Himself. Even when man flouted Him in the Fall, God's loving interest in him continued; He showed His goodness by immediately taking steps to undo the disastrous effects of the Fall. His election of Israel as His people, the Exodus, the giving of the law, His many deliverances of Israel, the promise and preparation for the coming of the Messiah—all these were evidences of God's goodness; as were the Incarnation, the atoning death of His Son, the resurrection, Pentecost.

The Scriptures make clear that history is not haphazard, but that God is working out a plan in history—the consummation of all things in His Son Jesus Christ. In this plan, God's children have an important part (Eph 1). Some day His goodness will be acknowledged by all of His creation; and He will be all in all.

Because of the Fall, man is by nature corrupt and is capable of doing nothing that is really good (Rom 7), but because of God's provision in Christ and the Holy Spirit, he can live a life of obedience to and fellowship with his creator.

S. BARABAS

GOODMAN (איש, *man, husband*, οἰκοδεσπότης, *master of the house*). KJV rendering in Proverbs 7:19 (RSV "husband") and in Matthew 24:43; Mark 14:14 and elsewhere. In Matthew 13:27 and 20:1 the more modern "householder" appears, which is the consistent RSV rendering. *See* HOUSEHOLDER.

GOPHER WOOD (עצי גפר . Lit. *wood of gopher.*) Noah was commanded to construct his ark out of this wood. גפר occurs only in Genesis 6:14 and has defied attempts to identify it with any finality. Scholars have frequently emended גפר to כפר, "pitch," which occurs at the end of the verse: ". . . and cover it inside and out with pitch." כפר is another *hapax legomenon*, but note Akkad. *kupru, kupur*, "pitch." "Wood of pitch" could be a resinous wood, such as the conifers. Cypresses are another possibility, since they often were selected for shipbuilding purposes.

If גפר does equal כפר it could indicate an

initial foreign phoneme, medial between ג and כ. This occurs with the velar plosives כ and ק in כרבע and קרבע, a word for helmet with a probable Hitt. origin (1 Sam 17:5, 38). The meaning still remains dubious, however.

H. M. WOLF

GORE (נגח, Qal and Piel, *push, thrust at*). Exodus 21:28-32 discusses laws relating to an ox that gores people. Generally, it has a military connotation of pushing away the enemy (Deut 33:17; Ps 44:5; Dan 8:4). Zedekiah fashioned horns of iron for Ahab, symbolic of irresistible weapons (1 Kings 22:11). The hithpael means to "engage in thrusting with, wage war with," describing the unsuccessful efforts of the king of the S (Dan 11:40). Ezekiel 34:21 condemns the "fat sheep" of Israel who "thrust at" the diseased with their horns.

H. M. WOLF

GORGIAS gôr' jəs (Γοργίας). A general selected by Lysias (regent over Syria under Antiochus Epiphanes) along with Ptolemy and Nicanor to destroy Judah (1 Macc 3:38). He was a "man of experience in military service" (2 Macc 8:9), a friend of the king (1 Macc 3:38), and later a governor (2 Macc 10:14) of Idumea (2 Macc 12:32).

Guided by Jews opposing Judas Maccabeus (q.v.), Gorgias once took "five thousand infantry and a thousand picked cavalry" and left camp by night to attack Judas by surprise (1 Macc 4:1ff.). But Judas learned of it and attacked the weakened gentile camp. Finding Judas gone, Gorgias' men returned to their own camp, and seeing it in flames, they fled.

Gorgias defeated Joseph and Azariah because "they did not listen to Judas and his brothers" nor "belong to the family of those men through whom deliverance was given to Israel" (1 Macc 5:59-62).

Later, when governor of Idumea, Gorgias almost lost his life as one Dositheus, on horseback, seized him and started to drag him away. He was rescued by a Thracian horseman and escaped (2 Macc 12:32-35). Following this, Gorgias' men were routed (v. 37). (The KJV with some Gr. MSS reads Gorgias in v. 36, in place of Esdris.)

C. P. WEBER

GORTYNA gôr tī' nə (Γόρτυνα, Γορτύν). A city of south-central Crete in the plain of Messara, on the River Lethaeus, about ten m. from the sea.

Next to Knossos it was the most powerful city on the island. According to Plato it was founded by a colony from Gortyn in Arcadia (*Laws* 4). In classical times it and Knossos in league controlled the island, but in later times they were in almost continual warfare (Strabo X). Gortyna allied with Rome in 197 B.C. against Philip V and soon became the most important city of the island. Under the Empire it was the capital of the province of Crete and Cyrenaica.

Much of the ancient city has been excavated by Italian archeologists, who in 1884 discovered the Gortyn Law Code. It is dated in the middle of the 5th cent. B.C. and deals mainly with laws concerning family rights.

Gortyna is listed among the autonomous cities to whom the Romans sent a letter in c. 139 B.C. guaranteeing the rights of the Jews (1 Macc 15:23). That there were Jews on Crete is clear from statements by Josephus (Jos. Antiq. XVII. xii. 1; War II. vii) and Philo (*Leg. ad Caium* 36).

A. RUPPRECHT

GOSHEN gō' shən (גשן ; LXX Γεσεμ, (Gen), Γοσομ, (Josh); meaning uncertain).

1. Goshen in Egypt. Geographically, Goshen is closely linked with the land and city of Raamses. In Genesis 47:6, 11, the pharaoh assigned Goshen to Joseph's family, the later narrator describing it as "the land of Rameses." Goshen and the land of Rameses are thus largely identical. At the time of the Exodus, the Hebrews were still in Goshen (Exod 8:22; 9:26), but began their exodus from Rameses (Exod 12:37; Num 33:3), which city they had helped to build (Exod 1:11). As the Hebrews also had to work at Pithom (Exod 1:11), Goshen should preferably be within reasonable reach of Pithom. Furthermore, Goshen lay on a route from Pal. into Egypt, and was *en route* for the residence of Joseph's pharaoh (cf. data in Gen 45:10; 46:28, 29; 47:1-6). As Joseph (on any reasonable date for the patriarchs) belongs in the Middle Kingdom or Hyksos periods, his ruler's residence must be one of that general epoch not too far removed from the later Raamses of the 19th dynasty. Finally, Goshen was a good place for keeping cattle (Gen 46:34; 47:6) and had room for settlers.

Raamses has been located at either Tanis (Zoan) or near modern Qantir (more likely; *see* RAAMSES). As Pithom is indubitably to be

Plowing in the Land of Goshen. © *M.P.S.*

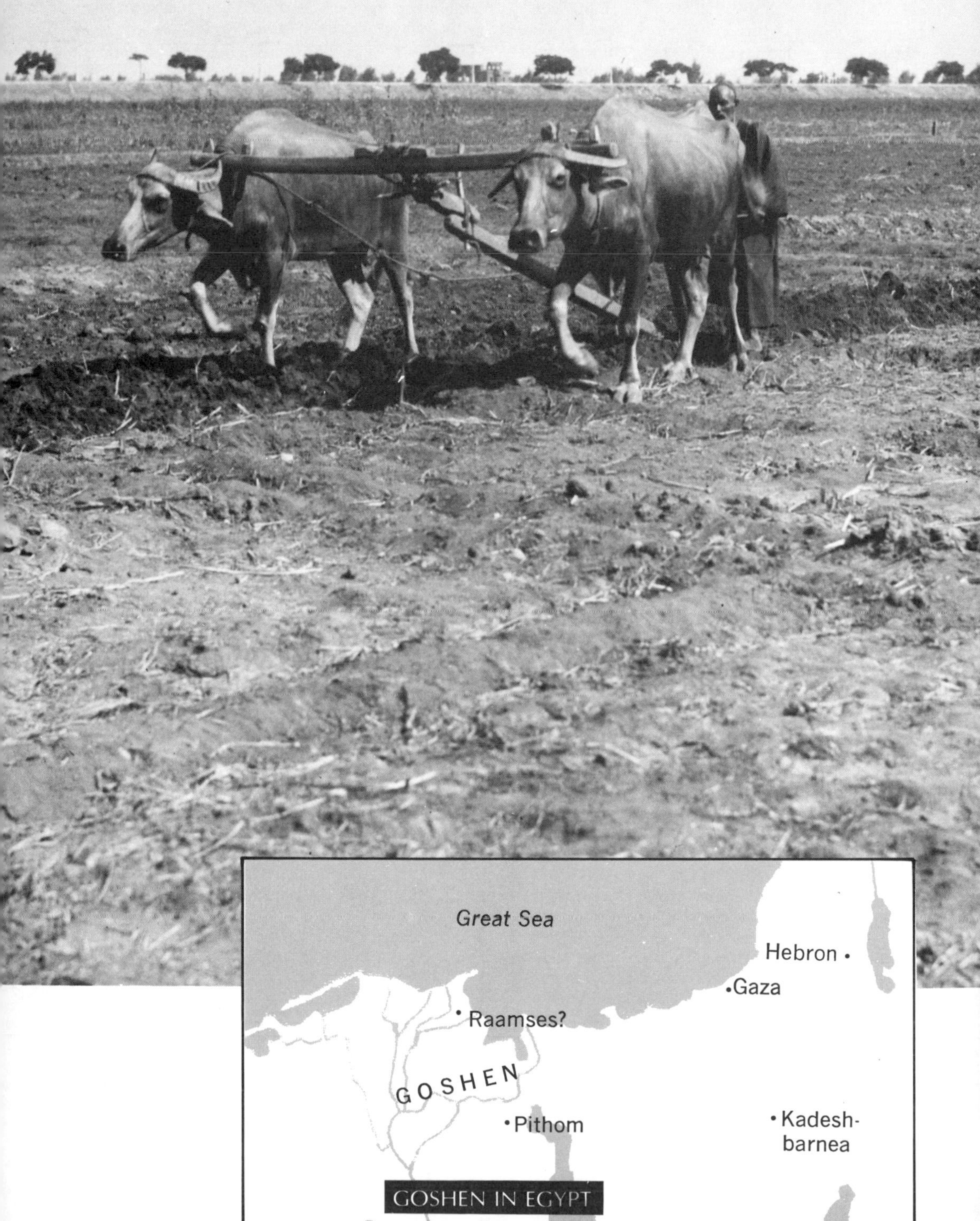

located in Wadi Tumilat in the SE Delta (*see* PITHOM), Goshen can readily be placed in the territory between Saft el Henneh in the S (at W end of Wadi Tumilat) and Qantir and El Salhieh in the N and NE. It could hardly be still further extended up to Tanis.

This suggested extent would allow Joseph to meet his family in the northern part of Goshen, if they came in by the El-'Arish route via Qantara toward Qantir; they would perhaps meet Joseph near El Salhieh. A series of discoveries by Egyp. scholars in the E Delta makes it highly probable that a royal residence existed in the 10th and 12th-13th and Hyksos dynasties (including the "Hyksos" town of Avaris) in the same region favored centuries later by Ramses II for his Delta residence of Raamses. Attested by temples and a palace, this residence was the administrative center for the E Delta and Palestinian affairs.

The LXX tradition calls Goshen "Gesem of Arabia," this "Arabia" being an epithet of the 20th Lower Egyp. nome (province), prob. extending from Faqus to Saft el Henneh. It is not quite certain whether the Egypt. inscrs. actually offer an equivalent for Heb. Goshen. One toponym in Egyp. is so written that it could be read either *Šsmt* or *Gsmt*. Brugsch and Naville accepted the reading *Gsmt* and equated this with Goshen/Gesem. Gardiner preferred to maintain the sole reading *Šsmt*, keeping it identical with a known place name. Both Montet and van Seters have revived the reading *Gsmt* and its identification with Goshen. A final verdict is not yet possible, but either way, the topography is not affected.

The role of Goshen as a cattle-raising area fits well into the conditions of the Egyp. Delta, with its bull cults (Otto, *Beiträge zur Geschichte der Stierkulte in Aegypten* [1938], 6-9, 32, 33) and prominent animal-husbandry (Kees, *Ägypten* [1933], 10). In the late Hyksos period, the Theban princes even sent their cattle to pasture in the Hyksos-controlled Delta (JEA, III [1916], 103). Under Ramses III, Papyrus Harris I has cattle of the god Amun pastured by the Waters of Ra in the very region of Biblical Goshen, alongside other districts (Gardiner, *Ancient Egyptian Onamastica,* II [1947], 167*).

2. In Palestine. Joshua 10:40, 41 records Joshua's campaigns over the hill country, southland (Negeb), lowlands (Shephelah) and slopes (Ashedoth) of W Pal., specifying the area from Kadesh-Barnea to Gaza and "all the country of Goshen, as far as Gibeon"; Joshua 11:16 also mentions Goshen as an area. This "land of Goshen" is perhaps named after the town of Goshen in the hill country assigned to Judah (Josh 15:51), either at Tell el Dhahiriyeh (so, Abel) 12 m. SW of Hebron, or somewhat further E (so GTT, sections 285-287, 497).

BIBLIOGRAPHY. On Egyp. Goshen, cf. E. Naville, *Goshen and the Shrine of Saft el Henneh* (1885); A. H. Gardiner, JEA, V (1918), 218-223; Naville and Gardiner, JEA, X (1924), 28-32 and 94, 95; J. van Seters, *The Hyksos* (1966), 146, 148 and references.

K. A. KITCHEN

GOSPEL (MESSAGE)

I. VOCABULARY AND BACKGROUND

In the NT εὐαγγελίζεσθαι means "to announce good news," and εὐαγγέλιον signifies "good news," "gospel," while εὐαγγελιστής is a "preacher of the gospel," "evangelist." The substantive εὐαγγέλιον appears most frequently in the writings of Paul (some sixty times).

A. Jewish background. In the OT the equivalent verb is בשר, which has the general meaning of "proclaiming good news" and is frequently used to signify "bringing news of victory." It is sometimes associated with the words "righteousness" ("deliverance"), "salvation" and "peace" (e.g. Ps 40:9; Isa 52:7). The participle מבשר is employed in later chs. of Isaiah to denote the messenger who announces the victory of God, the good news of God's kingly rule (e.g. Isa 52:7; cf. 61:1), and the expectation of such a מבשר persisted as a hope in rabbinic Judaism. The substantive בשרה, εὐαγγέλιον, is not found in the OT with a religious meaning.

B. Greek background. Among the Greeks εὐαγγελίζεσθαι was used often in the context of announcing a victory and εὐαγγέλιον means both "good news" and "reward for good news." Εὐαγγέλιον, in sing. and pl. also was used in the Rom. imperial cult to signify the "glad messages" of the birth of a future emperor, of his coming of age and of his accession to the throne. This aspect of the imperial worship is traced generally to Eastern influence, and it is not held that the NT message has been derived from the Rom. cult, but we can see that men would already associate a religious content with εὐαγγέλιον before the advent of Christian preachers.

II. THE MESSAGE OF JESUS

A. The kingdom of God. Like John the Baptist, Jesus proclaimed the advent of the kingdom of God (Matt 3:1; 4:17). In summarizing His ministry, NT writers declare that He traveled the country preaching the good news of the kingdom and healing (e.g. Matt 4:23; 9:35; Luke 8:1; 16:16). "Kingdom" signifies "kingly rule," the almighty, sovereign purpose of God and His royal authority, with its consequences for individual and community alike. In Mark 1:14f. Jesus comes preaching the Gospel of God, and the substance of His message is that men must make the response of repentance and faith in view of the drawing near of God's kingdom. But this Gospel of the kingdom involves more: it bears a close relation to the person of Jesus Himself. Jesus was conscious of His Messiahship (Luke 4:16-21) and of His Sonship (Matt 11:27) and of the fact that the kingdom was His Father's kingdom (26:29). With His sense of Messianic kingship He claims that God's sovereign purposes, revealed in the Scriptures, find historical and visible realization in Himself and His ministry (Matt 13:16f.; Luke 10:23f.; John 5:39). One may say, in fact, that Jesus, as the revelation of the Father (John 14:9f.), is Himself the complete expression of the sovereign rule of God. He is *αὐτοβασιλεία*, the kingdom personified (cf. Matt 19:29; Mark 10:29; Luke 18:29; and see K. L. Schmidt, TDNT, I, 589). G. Friedrich has pointed out the importance of Jesus' Messianic consciousness in this connection, for if He knew that He was the Son of God, who was to die and rise again, then He also realized that He Himself was the content of the Gospel message (TDNT, II, 728). This brings us to the fact that the kingdom which Jesus proclaimed was totally unlike that of contemporary expectation. One theme dominates Mark 8:27-10:45, which represents Jesus teaching His disciples, in emphatic, stereotyped language, that the One whom they have acknowledged as Messiah must suffer and die (Mark 8:31; 9:31; 10:33f.). The climax of that section is Mark 10:45, where Jesus describes His mission in terms reminiscent of the Suffering Servant of Isaiah 52:13-53:12. His purpose was to serve and to die as a ransom for many, thus advancing God's kingdom, in obedience to the sovereign will of the Father (John 10:11, 17, 18).

B. The invitation to the needy. Because of His identity and His mission, Jesus invites men to Himself. Following the statement of Jesus' Messianic consciousness, we have the offer of rest to those burdened by the yoke of the law (Matt 11:28). The good news is proclaimed to the poor and oppressed (Matt 11:5; Luke 4:18; cf. Isa 61:1) and the "I am" sayings of John's gospel are invitations to experience the divine provision for the needy. To respond to the invitation, through repentance and faith (cf. Mark 1:14), is to experience salvation (Luke 19:9), to enter the kingdom (18:18, 22, 24), to gain a new and eternal relationship in the family of God (John 3:3-8, 16; cf. Matt 6:9; John 20:17). This is more than a casual invitation: the parables of Luke 15 reveal the divine initiative in seeking and saving, and Jesus shows that initiative in action, for His purpose in coming was to make the good news known to all Israel (Luke 4:43) and to seek and save the lost (19:10), a purpose of which the urgency and yearning are well revealed by the lament over Jerusalem (Matt 23:37).

C. The responsibility of the hearers. Jesus is to be exalted in glory (Mark 14:62) and is to be the final judge of men (Matt 7:22, 23; 25:31-46). He therefore demands that men should determine their response to Him, for to reject His offer means death (Mark 8:34-38; cf. Matt 7:13f.), and to ignore is to reject, for neutrality is impossible (Luke 11:23). Once the step of discipleship has been taken, new responsibilities emerge, for ethical requirements are inherent in the message of Jesus. The offer of rest provides also a new yoke of obedience (Matt 11:29), for here again Jesus is God's royal authority personified and it is ***His*** instruction which is to be obeyed (Matt 5:22, 28, 32, 34, 39, 44; 7:24-27), since that instruction reveals the will of the Father (Matt 7:21, 24; John 7:16f.; 14:10). Disciples of Jesus have the responsibility to live, individually and communally, in a manner worthy of their relationship to God, in humility, holiness, compassion and trust (Matt 5-7; 18), for their relationship with the Father is one in which He reigns over their life (cf. Matt 5:3, 9, 10, 19, 20; 6:33), and their character must consequently reflect that of God Himself (5:48). Because of the world in which they live, disciples must bear witness to their Master (5:13-16; Mark 8:38), and they must fulfill lives of faithful service in view of the final judgment (Matt 25).

D. The privilege of believers. R. H. Strachan has pointed out that since the kingdom was the Father's kingdom, Jesus taught an identity of purpose and activity between the kingship and the fatherhood of God (IB, VII, 13). Those who submit to the kingdom are brought to the Father (John 14:6), and they know the experience of divine forgiveness (Matt 18:23-35; Mark 2:5-11; Luke 7:40-48) and peace (John 14:27). Believers have the sovereign protection and provision of the heavenly Father (Matt 6:25-34; 7:7-12; Luke 12:4-7, 22-32), a loving care which not only removes anxiety throughout life, but which is eternal in its scope (John 10:29). The depth of relationship with the Father into which the message of Jesus brought His followers is reflected in their use of the intimate term "Abba" (Mark 14:36; Rom 8:15; Gal 4:6). Jesus speaks not only of His disciples' privileged position as children of the Father, but also of the instruction and guidance which they may expect from the Holy Spirit (Luke 11:13; 12:11f.; John 14-16), who provides the power which is necessary for living the life of the kingdom (Acts 1:8). Finally Jesus tells of the future blessedness which awaits His followers, when they will share the glorious consummation of His own kingly authority (Luke 12:32; 22:29f.) and the eternal security of His Father's home (John 14:1-6).

III. The Message of the Apostles

It will be convenient to consider the apostolic Gospel message under the two well-known classifications, missionary preaching (*kērygma*) and Christian teaching (*didachē*), although it must not be supposed that these two aspects of the message were always rigidly separated.

A. Missionary preaching. The apostles, too, announce the kingdom of God (Acts 1:3; 8:12; 19:8; 20:25; 28:23, 31). For them also Jesus is the kingdom personified, for the person and work of Christ are frequently the objects of the verb εὐαγγελίζεσθαι (e.g. Acts 5:42; 8:35; 11:20; 17:18; Gal 1:16; Eph 3:8; 1 Pet 1:11f.). In contrast to the "glad messages" of the imperial cult, there is now proclaimed the one Christian εὐαγγέλιον of the kingdom of God, a message of which some might be ashamed (cf. Matt 11:6; Rom 1:16; 1 Cor 1:17, 23), since it is essentially connected with the person and history of Jesus. It is not naturally accepted (2 Cor 4:3), but needs to be accompanied by the revelatory power of the Holy Spirit (1 Cor 1:17; cf. 2:4; 1 Pet 1:12).

In his Gospel preaching to pagans (Acts 14:15-17; 17:22-31) Paul seeks to present the Christian message in the way most appropriate to his hearers' circumstances and cultural background. The same is true of the missionary sermons made to Jews and God-fearers in Acts, but it often has been noted that in these addresses one finds the frequent occurrence of certain definite themes. The question of a stereotyped kerygmatic pattern has been much discussed, but space forbids a detailed treatment here. Reference may be made to the works listed in the Bibliography. Among scholars who support some form of stereotyped *kerygma* are: Grosheide, Dibelius, Dodd, Hatch, Hunter, Leijs, Glasson, Craig, Gärtner, Bartels, Ward, Russell. These writers often differ widely from one another in their analyses, but the work of C. H. Dodd has had great influence upon English-speaking scholars. T. F. Glasson has modified Dodd's analysis to list the essential kerygmatic elements as: (1) the resurrection, (2) the fulfillment of OT prophecy, (3) the death of Christ, (4) the offer of forgiveness, (5) the apostles as witnesses. Among scholars who would reject, wholly or partially, a rigid kerygmatic pattern are: Evans, Filson, Baird, Wood, Mounce, Sweet. F. V. Filson analyzes the *kerygma*, but maintains, as do H. G. Wood and R. H. Mounce, that *kerygma* and *didaché* frequently were intermingled in Christian preaching, while C. F. Evans, followed by J. P. M. Sweet, prefers to think of many differing *kerygmata* rather than of the *kerygma*. In the present article it is assumed that by his presentation of frequently repeated themes in the Acts sermons Luke wished his readers to understand that these were the characteristic emphases of apostolic missionary preaching. It also is assumed that the essential *kerygma* consists of the elements which are most commonly preached, for it appears to be a sound method to follow Glasson's principle of including only the items that are most frequently mentioned, rather than to form a synthesis by utilizing each different particular which may be discovered.

We notice first, however, that a kerygmatic structure has been claimed also for other parts of the NT, particularly for certain "traditional" passages in Paul's epistles. One passage of special importance for Paul's understanding of the *kerygma* is 1 Corinthians 15:1-11, which will be examined in more detail. In v. 2 Paul says that he will remind his readers "in what terms" he had preached to them, and in v. 3 he uses the technical vocabulary employed in Judaism for transmitting and receiving tradition, which might suggest the existence of an authoritative pattern for Christian preaching. Jeremias, among others, maintains that Paul is claiming to have communicated the facts and doctrines which had been given form by his predecessors in the faith (*The Eucharistic Words of Jesus* [1955], 128ff.). Consequently Paul claims the same preaching as the other apostles (v. 11; cf. Gal 1:8; 2:1-9). What then is that preaching? It contains a statement of the death of Christ (1 Cor 15:3f.), an allusive reference to the forgiveness and salvation offered by God ("for our sins," v. 3), an emphasis upon Scriptural evidence (vv. 3f.), a stress upon the Resurrection, corresponding to what is perhaps the most characteristic emphasis of the Acts sermons (vv. 4-8), an insistence upon apostolic witness (vv. 5-8, cf. v. 15). It is apparent that there is an inherent logic in this combination of facts and doctrines. The death of Christ, the first article in Paul's summary, was from the beginning a fact of the utmost importance, if not as a soteriological event, certainly as an apparent mystery requiring some explanation and apology. The Resurrection, therefore, provided an emphatic vindication of Jesus, an overwhelming proof that He was not a rejected sinner, but the appointed Christ of God. This argument is then complemented by the fact of apostolic witness, which furnishes yet stronger evidence for the validity of the *kerygma*. The further proof, from the Scriptures, would be an essential element of apologetics in a Jewish milieu: with the Jews' strong awareness of God's action in past history, Christian preachers would need to demonstrate that their message was the culmination of the previous revelatory activity of God. It seems, therefore, both natural and logical that apostolic missionary preaching should consist of a reference to the death of Jesus, three proofs of the validity of the *kerygma*, and a concluding statement of the significance of the events preached: that forgiveness now is offered to those who believe. These five themes correspond to the items in T. F. Glasson's analysis of the *kerygma*. There may be yet another argument contained within 1 Corinthians 15:1-11. Before his conclusion Paul tells his readers (vv. 8-10) that he, like the other apostles, has experienced not only the vision of the resurrected Christ, but also the supernatural help of God in his life. Such a statement, set in general terms—that men can experience supernatural power, and that this power has a connection with Christ—would be another strong argument for the validity of the Christ-centered *kerygma*. It is not surprising to find that such a proof is sometimes used in close conjunction with the elements mentioned above. One may summarize six themes under the following titles: (1) death theme, (2) resurrection theme, (3) witness theme, (4) Scripture theme, (5) power theme, (6) forgiveness theme.

The above emphases form the essence of the missionary message in Acts. They occur as follows: (1) death theme: 2:23, 36; 3:13-15; 4:10f.; 5:30; 10:39; 13:28f.; cf. 26:23; (2) resurrection theme: 2:24-36; 3:15; 4:10f.; 5:30f.; 10:40; 13:30, 33-38; cf. 26:23; (3) witness theme: 2:32; 3:15; 5:32; 10:39-42; 13:31; cf. 26:16, 17, 22; (4) Scripture theme: 2:17-21, 25-28, 34f.; 3:18, 21-25; 4:11; 5:30f.; 10:43; 13:16-23, 27, 29, 33-36, 40f.; cf. 26:22; (5) power theme: 2:15-20, 22, 33, 38; 3:12f., 16, 19-21; 4:9f.; 5:32; 10:38; 13:17-23, 40f.; cf. 26:22; (6) forgiveness theme: 2:21, 38-40; 3:19, 26; 4:12; 5:31; 10:43; 13:38f.; cf. 26:23. An examination of the passages will show that the themes are presented in ways appropriate to the audience. For example, in Acts 2 and 3 the statements about the death of Jesus effectively contrast the crime of the hearers with the attitude of God; in Acts 10 and 13 more detailed information is given than was necessary in Jerusalem; and in Acts 13 the allusions to OT facts and to God's sovereign power are worked into a typical form of synagogue address.

What, then, is the origin of these particular emphases? The obvious source to whom to look would be Christ Himself. Bo Reicke notes that Jesus sent the disciples on preaching missions in the gospels, and it would be natural to assume that their preaching then was modelled on His, esp. as they were His representatives and considered as an extension or multiplication of His person. Some scholars have argued for an even closer connection between the teaching of Jesus and that of the apostles. B. Gerhardsson, for example, maintains that Jesus taught in rabbinic fashion, with extensive use of memorization, and that the apostles and Early Church transmitted fixed forms of tradition derived from Christ, in the way that Judaism transmitted the oral Torah. Gerhardsson's thesis has been criticized widely (e.g. by Morton Smith) and it seems improbable in its detailed outworking, but the practice of memorization was so much an accepted feature of ancient education that it does seem possible that the disciples would have learned at least some parts of Jesus' teaching by heart, and it does appear that many items of the apostolic message may be traced back to Jesus. Note the following: Servant of God, and Messiah (Mark 10:45; 14:61f.), the argument from supernatural power (Mark 2:9ff.; Luke 11:20), the importance of personal testimony (Matt 10:27; Mark 4:19; 10:38), stereotyped references to Jesus' death and resurrection (Mark 8:31; 9:31; 10:33f.), proof texts from the OT (Mark 12:10f., 35ff.). The most common kerygmatic elements occur also in Luke 24:19f., 25-27, 44-49. C. F. Evans holds that Luke has simply read back the *kerygma* into the Gospel and has presented it in a dramatic form in preparation for the Acts sermons, but it does not seem unreasonable to believe that Luke 24 is an accurate record of events, that the risen Christ answered His disciples' questionings, and that the emphases of His explanation later found expression in their preaching.

Man's concentration upon particular emphases of the missionary Gospel must not blind one to the fact which we have noticed at the beginning of this section, that the one central theme, dominating and unifying all the secondary themes, is Christ Himself. The Gospel is the Gospel of the glory of Christ (2 Cor 4:4).

B. Christian teaching. 1. *The privilege of believers.* Paul possessed an overwhelming sense of the privileged position granted to him by the grace of God (Eph 3:8), and not to him only, but to all believers, for the good news of Christ is that the priceless blessing of salvation is a free gift (Rom 3:24; 6:23), given by the grace of God (Eph 2:8; cf. Acts 20:24) to all who will accept it by faith (Rom 3:22, 25). This Gospel is God's secret which He has made known to His people (Eph 6:19; Col 1:26). It brings salvation (Eph 1:13; cf. 1 Cor 15:2), for it is God's own power for saving (Rom 1:16): it reveals the righteousness of God, that gracious, delivering activity by which God rescues the sinner and justifies the ungodly (1:17; 3:26; 4:5). A stress upon justification, God's gracious, free acquittal of guilty sinners who trust in Christ, is esp. characteristic of Paul's presentation of the Gospel message (e.g. 4:5ff.; 8:34). The Gospel tells of forgiveness and of reconciliation with God achieved through the cross of Christ (Rom 5:10f.; 2 Cor 5:19), for Christ made reconciliation and came proclaiming the good news of peace (Eph 2:16, 17; cf. 6:15). Just as the appearance of Christ on earth was "the beginning of the gospel" (Mark 1:1; cf. Acts 1:1), so in the context of Ephesians 2:15-18 the total work of Christ is summarized in the words "He preached peace" (cf. Isa 52:7; 57:19). That peace is available for the whole of humanity, for the good news unites Jews and Gentiles and mediates salvation to both alike (Eph 3:6). All believers have experienced spiritual rebirth from God (1 Pet 1:3; 1 John 3:9; cf. John 3:3), know the privilege of adoption as God's own sons (Rom 8:15ff.; Gal 4:5f.; Eph 1:5), and are set in a new order of existence (2 Cor 5:17), for there is "a new creation": the believer is "in Christ"; he is united with Christ (Rom 6:1-11); he is in "the kingdom of God's beloved Son" (Col

1:13). In this new life in God's family the Gospel brings the news of the strength which comes from God (Rom 16:25), for the gift of the Holy Spirit enables believers to live in a way that pleases God (8:1-17, 26f.). The writer to the Hebrews reminds one that Christians also have constantly the help and care of Christ as the perfect High Priest, who fully understands and sympathizes with the character and circumstances of His people (Heb 2:14-18; 4:14-16), and 1 Peter 2:21-25 is an assertion of the understanding which Christ has for His afflicted followers (cf. 1 Pet 5:10). The Christian already is triumphantly secure in the loving care of God, from which nothing can separate him (Rom 8:28-39), and he is equally secure after death (2 Cor 5:1-8). Christ is exalted in glory over the whole universe (Eph 1:20ff.; Phil 2:9; Col 1:15-17); believers share already in His exaltation (Eph 1:3; 2:6), and are yet to share in His future majesty in the restored universe (Rom 8:17-19; 1 Cor 15:20; Col 1:5, 27; 2 Tim 2:12; Heb 2:10).

2. The responsibility of believers. In apostolic teaching, as in that of Jesus, ethical requirements are inherent in the Gospel message. The new and privileged position which the believer has received by God's grace is intended to lead directly to righteous living (Eph 2:10). Note the clear ethical implications of the words found in 2 Corinthians 5:21; Colossians 1:22f.; 2:6f.; Titus 2:11-14. The Gospel is "the glorious gospel of the blessed God" (1 Tim 1:11); it is God's address to man, and when God thus speaks, man must listen and yield obedience (2 Cor 9:13; cf. Rom 1:5; 16:26). The believer must lead a life which is equally "worthy of God" (1 Thess 2:12) and "worthy of the gospel of Christ" (Phil 1:27). In his ethical teaching Paul often argues explicitly from the well-known facts of the Gospel proclamation by which the churches were established. For example, based on such essential facts about Christ are the exhortations to mutual concern (Rom 15:1-3), to humility and brotherly love (Phil 2:1-11), to forgiveness (Eph 4:32), to conjugal love (5:25ff.), to holiness and purity (Rom 6:4; 1 Cor 6:15-20), and to confidence and hope (1 Cor 15:20; 1 Thess 4:13f.). Christians are "called to be saints" (Rom 1:7); they are united with Christ (6:1-11); they must therefore lead a sanctified life. Their union with Christ involves other responsibilities too. Christ has suffered, and His followers must share that experience (8:17; 1 Pet 2:21). Christ has brought the Gospel, and now Christian believers, who have responded to that good news, must themselves bear it to others (Rom 10:15; cf. Isa 52:7; Eph 6:15; 2 Tim 4:5). An identity of purpose has been apparent in the apostolic teaching and that of Jesus. Sometimes actual words of Jesus are employed in ethical instruction (e.g. Acts 20:35) and sometimes one finds striking similarities to the Sermon on the Mount (e.g. James 1:2, 4, 5, 20, 22; 2:10, 13; 3:18; 4:4, 10ff.; 5:2ff., 10, 12). Finally, as in the teaching of Jesus, there is an insistence upon future judgment: the message of judgment is intrinsic to the Gospel (Rom 2:16), and believers are to live constantly in the light of the judgment seat of Christ (Rom 14:10; 1 Cor 3:10-15; 2 Cor 5:9f.; 1 Pet 5:4; cf. 2 Pet 3:11f.).

IV. Summary

The message of Jesus is ultimately an invitation to men to commit themselves wholeheartedly to Him, and to experience fully the relationship with the Father which is insured by that discipleship. The message of the apostles is the same, but has now been filled out, from a deepening Christian experience, with the proclamation of all the saving activity of God revealed in the total ministry of Christ, who is the climax of all God's purposes (cf. 2 Cor 1:20).

BIBLIOGRAPHY. F. W. Grosheide, "The Synoptic Problem. A Neglected Factor in Its Solution," EQ, III (1931), 62-66; C. H. Dodd, "The Framework of the Gospel Narrative," ExpT, XLIII no. 9 (1932), 396 ff.; M. Dibelius, *From Tradition to Gospel,* Eng. tr. (1934), 15-30; C. H. Dodd, *The Apostolic Preaching and Its Developments* (1936); W. H. P. Hatch, "The Primitive Christian Message," JBL, LVIII (1939), 1-13; A. M. Hunter, *The Unity of the New Testament* (1943), 23-25; F. F. Bruce, *The Speeches in the Acts* (1945); R. Leijs, "Prédication des Apôtres," *Nouvelle Revue théologique,* LXIX (1947), 606ff.; A. Rétif, "Qu'est-ce que le kérygme?," *Nouvelle Revue théologique,* LXXI (1949), 910-922; A. Rétif, "Témoignage et prédication missionnaire dans les Actes des Apôtres," *Nouvelle Revue théologique,* LXXIII (1951), 152-165; R. H. Strachan, "The Gospel in the New Testament," IB, VII (1951), 3-31; C. T. Craig, "The Apostolic Kerygma in the Christian Message," JBR, XX (1952), 182-186; T. F. Glasson, "The Kerygma: Is Our Version Correct?," HJ, LI (1952-1953), 129-132; B. Reicke, "A Synopsis of Early Christian Preaching," *The Root of the Vine. Essays in Biblical Theology,* ed. A. Fridrichsen (1953), 128-160; B. Gärtner, *The Areopagus Speech and Natural Revelation* (1955), 30-32; M. Dibelius, *Studies in the Acts of the Apostles,* Eng. tr. (1956), 165ff., 178; C. F. Evans, "The Kerygma," JTS, n. s. VII (1956), 25-41; F. V. Filson, *Jesus Christ the Risen Lord* (1956), 41-54; W. Baird, "What is the Kerygma?," JBL, LXXVI (1957), 181-191; R. Russell, "Modern Exegesis and the Fact of the Resurrection," *Downside Review,* LXXVI (1958), 329-343; W. Barclay, "Great Themes of the New Testament," ExpT, LXX no. 7 (1959), 196-199; W. E. Ward, "Preaching and the Word of God in the New Testament," *Baptist Review and Expositor,* LVI (1959), 20-30; H. G. Wood, "Didaché, Kerygma and Evangelion," *New Testament Essays. Studies in Memory of T. W. Manson,* ed. A. J. B. Higgins (1959), 306-314; R. H. Mounce, *The Essential Nature of New Testament Preaching* (1960); R. A. Bartels, *Kerygma or Gospel Tradition—Which came first?* (1961), 97-112; B. Gerhardsson, *Memory and Manuscript* (1961), 234, 274-280; H. N. Ridderbos, *The Speeches of Peter in the Acts of the*

Apostles (1962); M. Smith, "A Comparison of Early Christian and Early Rabbinic Tradition," JBL, LXXXII (1963), 169-176; B. Gerhardsson, *Tradition and Transmission* (1964), 42f.; K. L. Schmidt, βασιλεύς κτλ, TDNT, I (1964), 576-590; G. Friedrich, εὐαγγελίζομαι, εὐαγγέλιον, TDNT, II, (1964), 707-736; J. P. M. Sweet, "The Kerygma," ExpT, LXXVI no. 5 (1965), 143-147.

D. R. JACKSON

GOSPEL ACCORDING TO THE HEBREWS. *See* HEBREWS, GOSPEL ACCORDING TO THE.

GOSPEL OF THE NAZARENES. *See* NAZARENES, THE GOSPEL OF.

GOSPELS. Christianity is a historical faith. It is rooted in the Incarnation and committed to Jesus of Nazareth. Understandably, there is a tremendous interest in the life and teachings of Jesus and in those primary documents that present Him.

I. USE OF THE TERM

Originally, the term "gospel" had reference to the message of salvation through Christ, and only later was the term used to designate written documents. Gospel (εὐαγγέλιον), which means "good news," was not used in a religious sense in the cult of the Rom. emperor. His accession to the throne and his decrees were "good tidings" to the people. More important, however, is the Heb. antecedent, בשר, used in the OT (Isa 40:9; 52:7; 61:1). The "servant of the LORD," who was to come, would declare good news to men. Jesus came preaching the Gospel (Matt 11:5; Luke 4:18); in fulfillment of prophecy. "The time is fulfilled, and the kingdom of God is at hand" (Mark 1:15). Jesus Christ, the bearer of the Good News, was Himself the content and substance of the Gospel. In Paul's epistles, the Gospel is the testimony to Jesus (Rom 1:3). The word is always sing. An evangelist is one who bears the good tidings (2 Tim 4:5). At the beginning of the 2nd cent., the term began to be used for the written account of salvation (Did. 15:3f. 2 Clem. 8:5). There was, however, only one Gospel. The person who declares another gospel is anathema (Gal 1:8f.). The four works called "the gospels" are really four records of one Gospel. Justin Martyr was the first to use the word in the pl. when he wrote of the "memoirs composed by the apostles called Gospels" (Apol. 66:3). By that time, the danger of confusion had passed, though still it was the "Gospel according to Matthew," not Matthew's gospel. God's grace had broken into history, and the news of it was the Good News. An evangelist was not the writer of a gospel, but a bearer of the message itself. The four gospels were intended to do that too, and remained anonymous. These works constitute a new literary phenomenon. They are not biographies as such, for they omit much material normally found in a biography, such as character development, background facts, and chronology. They are more like biographies than anything else. They are historical in form; their primary aim is to present the data in such a way that the Good News will be very apparent. This accounts for the heavy emphasis in each gospel upon the closing days of Jesus' earthly life and His resurrection. The gospels are not literary productions; their writers were not literary men. They followed no conventional pattern or form. Each sought to give a portrait of Christ as he saw Him from his perspective. In the days of oral tradition, when eyewitnesses were available to pass on information vital to Jesus' life and ministry, the need for written gospels was not great. The spoken word was regarded more highly than the written accounts. With the gradual disappearance of eyewitnesses, by death, the need became acute for written records. Fortunately for the Church, such accounts had already been in process of compilation and composition long before the first generation died (*see* articles on various gospels for dates). The spread of the Church throughout the world did as much as anything else to create the demand for written gospels. Luke composed his two-volume work to meet such a need (Luke 1:1-4). Written documents were needed for instructing new converts and for teaching the people, as well as for use in public worship. By the end of the 2nd cent. the four gospels were almost universally accepted, not only as authentic, but as canonical—on a par with the OT Scriptures. Valuable testimony from Clement of Alexandria, Tertullian, Papias, and Irenaeus, indicates that the gospels all originated from the apostolic age. Few ancient documents have such attestation so close to the date of their composition. Their writers had no ambition for literary glory; they desired only to record the message of salvation.

II. ORAL TRADITION

Criticism of the gospels has been concentrated recently on the shadowy area of transmission from event to its recording. Most of the material in the gospels existed for a time in an oral stage, when it was handed down by word of mouth, before being incorporated into a written gospel. Jesus was a preacher of the Good News. He gave His disciples close instruction privately (Mark 4:34), and they remembered His words and deeds long after

His death. Form criticism is a method of analysis that seeks to trace this process of transmission. It arose out of some dissatisfaction with the fruits of source criticism, which could not penetrate behind the written materials themselves. Form criticism is, however, inevitably somewhat imaginary because it delves into the few decades after the Resurrection during which the gospel materials were handed down about which there is little historical information. Unfortunately, form criticism became allied to an attitude of historical pessimism. Although the investigation of the oral stage is itself quite worthy, form criticism has become synonymous with the attempt to discredit the historical integrity of the NT documents.

Form criticism treats the gospels as primary witnesses—not to the life of Jesus—but to the beliefs and practices of the primitive church. Although the attempt to find the life-situation of the materials in the gospels is legitimate, it is quite another matter to assume without proof that the accounts were invented to meet the needs of the church community. Therefore, the reconstruction of units of tradition is highly speculative. One scholar will find a totally different life-situation for a story or saying than another. If form critics would allow for more life-settings with a pre-Easter situation, their whole endeavor would look less suspicious. That the community should first frame its own traditions, and then convince itself of their historical integrity is hardly plausible. It is dangerous to start with a hypothetical theory of how the materials were handled, while ignoring the plain testimony in the text to the contrary. The presence of eyewitnesses in the Church certainly had a restraining effect on the free creation of historical traditions. The gospel accounts did not grow out of the Church's need for them; rather the Church grew out of the facts they recorded. Primitive Christianity was stamped by the impact of the person and work of Jesus. The theory that the community wrote the first life of Jesus in isolation from all reliable recollections about Him, is a speculation without foundation and without probability. The Church was "colored" by Jesus, not Jesus by the community. Early Christians were interested in stories of Jesus during His historical ministry. The apostles who played a decisive role in the formation of the Church were in a position to supply such information. The idea of the free creation and flow of tradition unhindered by historical fact is fanciful and romantic. The presence of the apostles prevented the very situation the form critics assume. There is no positive evidence that the needs and problems of the Early Church were read back into the gospels. Certain of these problems are well known, such as the admission of the Gentiles, tongues, dietary laws, and church government; none of these problems received any significant treatment in the gospels. On the other hand, there are features in the gospels that do not reappear in Acts or the epistles, such as parables, the "son of man" title, and the "kingdom of God." All the data suggests that a clear boundary existed between the history before and after Easter. There is just not enough time available for the developments assumed by the form critics. The "biology of the saga" requires a time lag of centuries for the development of a coherent cycle of myths. There was no time in the 1st cent. for the creation, collection, and collation of community sagas. The Gospel story broke into the light of history in a very short time. Form criticism as a method has been vastly overrated. Jesus gathered disciples around Him. These disciples treasured the deposit of His teaching and passed it down in the community that they led after His resurrection. A convincing parallel to what went on in the oral stage of the gospel material would be the rabbinic method of transmission, which was marked by a high degree of accuracy and continuity. The presence of eyewitnesses in the Church during the whole period of oral tradition puts a severe limiting factor upon all radical form criticism.

As long as the care employed in transmission is respected, form criticism can aid the understanding of the history of the gospels in their preliterary stage. The advance in knowledge from this source has not been great. Clearly, the early preachers gave prominence to the passion of Jesus, and presented the account in connection with the general shape of Jesus' life. As converts were instructed, further stories and sayings of Jesus were added from the memory of the apostles to meet the needs at hand. The catechesis was no doubt largely oral in form, but possibly also accompanied with written accounts. Tradition connects an early tract with the apostle Matthew, and it may have been one of many (cf. Luke 1:1) primitive written gospels that assisted the teachers in their work.

III. Written gospels

A. The four gospels. 1. *Matthew.* The first gospel breathes the atmosphere of the OT, and makes the transition from the Old to the New a smooth one. At the outset, the writer provides a genealogy linking Jesus to David and Abraham through his legal father Joseph. His interest in connecting Jesus with messianic prophecies of the OT is apparent throughout. All the significant events in Jesus' life—His birth, birthplace, home, ministry, and death—were in direct fulfillment of OT predictions. Most of the NT manifests the same concern with prophecy, but Matthew demonstrates it to a remarkable degree. Although he does not state his purpose, as Luke and John do, Matthew endeavors to prove that Jesus is the Messiah. To achieve this, the writer gave his gospel a strongly Judaic flavor. Numerous details about contemporary Jewish life and religion are included. Interest in the kingdom of heaven and the messianic king is sustained throughout. Matthew gives great prominence to the teaching ministry of Jesus. He preserved five long blocks, and inserted them into the Markan narrative. This feature made Matthew a handy teaching manual in the primitive Church. Since Mark is notably short of teaching, the inclusion in Matthew of extensive sermons is a distinct advantage. Narrative and discourse alternate. The pattern of act and word, of *kerygma* and *didachē* is striking. One of the curious features of Matthew is the tension between universalism and particularism. On the one hand, Jesus came exclusively to "the house of Israel" (Matt 15:24), and refused to go into the way of the Gentiles (10:5). Not a "jot" or a "tittle" would pass from the law (5:18f.), and the disciples were expected to observe Pharisaic instructions (18:2f.). Alongside this narrow particularism is a universalism. The coming of the Magi, the flight into Egypt, the Great Commission, all point to the universal implications of this gospel. The tension is resolved by observing the progress of saving history. Prior to His death, Jesus exhausted Himself in taking the Good News to the nation Israel who refused it. Near the end of His life, Jesus predicted, "The kingdom of God will be taken away from you and given to a nation producing the fruits of it" (21:43). Out of His death and resurrection sprang a "new Israel," a spiritual heir to the promises of God, drawn from every nation under heaven.

Matthew is a long edition of Mark. The writer incorporated almost the whole of Mark, abbreviated some of the stories, and added a large amount of non-Markan material. Whereas Mark gave Matthew his framework, Mark did not determine Matthew's purpose. Matthew's emphasis differs from Mark's. The first gospel is an apologetic tract, and the note of fulfillment is prominent. An insistent tradition in the ancient Church ascribed to Papias held that the first gospel was originally written in Aramaic or Hebrew. Opinions differ widely over what this may mean. It would seem reasonable, however, to locate the underlying genius of Matthew's gospel and its origins in the earliest Jewish Christian Church.

2. *Mark*. The second gospel is direct and to the point. It is a gospel, not a biography. Mark's readers already knew the story. It is a passion narrative with a preface; the entire movement of the action is toward the cross. The absence of teaching material accents this fact. The gospel is a brief, simple record of our Lord's life and ministry, which fills in some details in the apostolic preaching. In accord with apostolic preaching, it begins with John the Baptist and ends with the Resurrection (cf. Acts 10:36-43; 13:24-37). The skeleton, or framework, of Jesus' life was given in sermons, but further detailed information was required for use in instructing the people. Obviously, the passion narrative was preserved in definite historical sequence, and it is likely that this was true also of the other material. Mark made no attempt to provide a tight chronology, but it is going too far to suggest he ignored it altogether. In the Early Church, the gospel of Mark was overshadowed by Matthew. Mark contained so little not found in Matthew, whereas Matthew had so much more than Mark. Few wrote commentaries upon it, and eventually the idea circulated that it was a mere abstract of Matthew. Not until recent times was its identity known as the kernel to the first gospel.

Mark begins and ends abruptly. The approach is blunt and direct. Mark is a gospel of action; movement is more important than discourse. The impression from Mark is a factual, eyewitness account of the life of Jesus. Fascinating details are included in the narration, without any hesitation to get directly to the action. Mark excludes the birth narratives. Jesus' deeds are reported rather than His words. He repeatedly uses the adverb "immediately." Frequently he notes that Jesus taught here and there, but does not pause to tell what He taught. The explanation of this vividness given by the primitive Church was to find Peter's testimony behind Mark. "Mark became Peter's interpreter and wrote accurately all that he remembered, not, indeed, in order, of things said or done by the Lord." Mark derived his material from the public testimony of Peter the apostle. This would indeed explain the living character of Mark's work. Many have pointed out the Aram. influences on the second gospel. Mark may well have drawn upon Peter's sermons and lectures, and used them along with other material to construct his gospel. His work has a freshness and confidence of detail that is hard to explain in any other way.

From all indications, Mark was written from Rome for Gentile readers. A comparison of Mark 15:21 and Romans 16:13 makes a Rom. origin probable, as does the presence of an unusual number of Latinisms in the Gr. text. There is also an absence of the Judaic atmosphere so noticeable in Matthew. A comparison reveals that almost every instance of Jewish coloring in Matthew is lacking in the Markan parallel. Mark had Gentile readers in mind in writing his gospel. Where he had to include Palestinian customs, he took pains to explain them (e.g., Mark 7:3f.), although this would be extraneous for a Jewish audience. Similarly, the Aram. expressions that Mark did retain are given a Gr. tr. (e.g. 14:36). Mark is "the gospel of Jesus Christ, the Son of God" (1:1) His central aim was to present the person of the Messiah. Jesus is the Son of God, the glorious Son of man, and the Redeemer. Mark presents a high Christology throughout.

3. *Luke*. The third gospel is the longest and the most comprehensive in range and scope. Luke and Acts constitute the largest contribution to the NT of any single writer. Renan called the gospel of Luke the most beautiful book in the world. It is an attractive account that leaves a deep impression on the reader of the personality of Jesus. To have the intention of the writer expressly stated in a prologue (Luke 1:1-4) is fortunate. Without doubt, the aim of the author was primarily historical accuracy and integrity. His own statement of purpose takes precedence over any speculative theory. He was dominated primarily by a historical concern. The prologue indicates that the writer was well educated, as his excellent prose reveals, and possessed critical historical judgment. He was of the deep conviction that the believer needed to have a solid historical foundation for his faith in Christ, and this he sought to provide. Although in the last cent. scholars doubted the trustworthiness of Luke's work, recent research has vindicated his integrity in a spectacular way. At numerous points, Luke ties his account in the gospel and Acts, to secular history, and his accuracy has repeatedly been proven. He did not, however, write a secular history as such. His aim, in common with all the evangelists, was to trace the ministry of a unique Person. Like the others, Luke presents history that contains important theological significance. The author presents the beginnings of a movement that in the short space of three decades established itself in the capital of the Rom. empire. It began quietly in Judea, and extended itself to the center of the world's stage. History itself gave Luke his theme.

As would be expected, Luke's scope is indeed comprehensive; his gospel covers more of Jesus' life than any other. He writes about the birth of John the Baptist (1:5-25, 57-80), the annunciation to Mary (1:26-38), the adoration of the shepherds (2:1-20), the visit to the Temple (2:41-52). He includes an account of Jesus preaching in Nazareth (4:16-30), the miraculous draught of fishes (5:1-11), the woes (6:24-26), the raising of the son of the widow of Nain (7:11-17), the woman saved by Jesus (7:36-50), the women who served Jesus (8:1-3), the Samaritan villages that refused His message (9:51-56), the parable of the Good Samaritan (10:30-37), Mary and Martha (10:38-42), the friend at midnight (11: 5-8), the blessedness of those who obey the Word of God (11:27f.), the parable of the rich fool (12:13-21), many or few stripes (12: 47f.), the call to repentance (13:1-9), the healing of another woman (13:10-17), the departure from Galilee (13:31-33), the healing of a man with dropsy (14:1-6), teaching on humility (14:7-14), the parable of the prodigal son (15:11-32), of the unjust steward (16: 1-13), the hypocrisy of the Pharisees (16:14f.), the parable of the rich man and Lazarus (16: 19-31), the servant's duty (17:7-10), the healing of ten lepers (17:11-19), on the kingdom of God (17:20f.), the parable of the unjust judge (18:1-8), of the Pharisee and the publican (18:9-14), Zacchaeus (19:1-10), the two swords (22:35-38), Jesus before Herod (23: 6-16), the weeping women (23:27-31), the penitent thief (23:39-43), the burial of Jesus (23:55f.), the road to Emmaus (24:13-35), the appearance of the risen Christ at Jerusalem (24:36-49), and the Ascension (24:50-53).

Luke's universalism is evident in numerous places. The good news the angels brought was for all men (2:14). Simeon foresaw that Christ would be a light for the Gentiles (2:32). John the Baptist was the voice of one crying in the wilderness in fulfillment of Isaiah 40:3-5, which includes a line Luke cites, "and all flesh shall see the salvation of God" (Luke 3:6). Non-Israelites are on a par with the Jews (4:25-27; 9:54; 10:33; 17:16). Luke shows that he is interested in all manner of people. Numerous individuals emerge in his narrative unknown elsewhere—Zechariah, Elizabeth, Zacchaeus, Cleopas. Luke presents several case studies of social outcasts being transformed by the Gospel. He mentions thirteen women not found elsewhere in the gospels. Children, also, often appear in his record. This is a gospel of the manhood of Jesus. Everywhere His teaching attracted wide popular interest, and His compassion for the poor and the destitute shone through. The entire ministry of Jesus was an outworking of the saving purpose of God in history.

4. *John.* John, as does Luke, gives a clear statement of his purpose (20:30f.). John is presenting to the believer and unbeliever alike, the historical data upon which saving faith rests. The gospel was intended to be both an evangelistic and a pastoral instrument. John selected a set of signs that he believed would convince his readers of the divinity of Jesus Christ and led them to place their trust in Him. He was concerned that the messianic faith of the Church should be filled with the proper content. There are indications in the gospel that its writer was in a good position to provide this content; the narration gives constant hints of being recorded by an eyewitness. On several occasions, John reveals a detailed knowledge of Jewish life and custom in the period before the fall of Jerusalem. He was aware of the political situation in Pal. He had an intimate knowledge of the geography of the land. His account abounds with personal allusions and details absent from the synoptic narratives. Undoubtedly, the author intended his readers to take his gospel as real history, not as mere symbol or allegory. The fourth gospel is fully as trustworthy historically as the other three, and at certain points more precise and detailed than they. It is reasonable to assume the historicity of the whole account since historical errors cannot be demonstrated in the fourth gospel. The present state of Johannine criticism represents a complete reversal to that of earlier times. John's style is as simple as his thought is profound. He regularly uses only common words and paratactic constructions. Although John purposely limited the range of vocabulary, the effect is dignified and compelling. It abounds with theological theme words that recur again and again (i.e., water, light, bread, love, truth).

The first half of the gospel (1:1-12:50) presents the revelation of Jesus to the world, and is structured around seven signs. The words of Jesus are for the most part occasioned by the miracles in the narrative. The discourses are rather long, often argumentative, and frequently set in the southern ministry of Jesus, in Judea. Jesus' activity around Jerusalem was more directly polemical because the hostility to him was greater there than in Galilee.

Like Matthew, John presents Jesus as the Messiah of OT hope. Jesus approached Israel with a rightful claim to her loyalty. He was disturbed that His own people did not receive Him (1:11; 5:39, 45f.). The imagery of bread, shepherd, and the Spirit, all root back to OT prophetic passages. John does not quote texts in the way Matthew does, but OT texts continually underline his thought. All the Scriptures point to Jesus. He is the fulfillment of the OT longing.

B. Relationships. 1. *The synoptic problem.* The first three gospels are called the "synoptic" gospels because they can be viewed together, their similarities noted and their differences examined. A considerable amount of material is common to all three, or to two out of three. Some 606 vv. out of Mark's total of 661 appear, although somewhat abridged, in Matthew, and 380 reappear in Luke. Only 31 vv. in Mark have no parallel in either Matthew or Luke. In addition, there are some 250 vv. common to Matthew and Luke that have no parallel in Mark. Obviously, this synoptic relationship can be viewed in different ways. Many solutions have been proposed, but none has won unanimous agreement.

One of the stable findings of synoptic criticism has been the priority of Mark. It is a striking fact, that whereas the order of Mark and Matthew may agree against Luke and the order of Mark and Luke may agree against Matthew, the order of Matthew and Luke never agrees against Mark. In other words, Mark is the stable factor. Most prob., Mark was the source common to the other two, which they generally followed, but sometimes altered. This common material is almost entirely narrative. The non-Markan material common to Matthew and Luke, on the other hand, almost entirely comprise the sayings of Jesus. This observation has lead to a further hypothesis—the existence of a sayings source, represented by Q. Once the theory of Markan priority is accepted, the existence of Q follows. The 250 vv. of common material between Matthew and Luke possess a considerable measure of verbal agreement, and occur in much the same order in each gospel. Scholars differ as to the extent of this proposed second source. It might conceivably have contained narrative itself originally. From the data now available, it seems to have been a sayings source only. The need for Q could be bypassed if it is assumed that Luke used Matthew directly; but his alteration of Matthew's careful ordering of the sayings is difficult to explain, unless he had access to information that informed him of their rightful historical sequence. The purpose of Q can easily be imagined in the Early Church. As a collection of Jesus' teachings, it would have been a useful manual of church order and teaching.

Some scholars have gone on to detect some homogeneity in the material peculiar to Matthew and Luke. Matthew's special material has a Judaistic tone, however; its existence as a source is highly speculative. Luke includes even more special material, which he doubtless collected during his historical research.

2. The synoptics and John. The independence of John from the other three gospels is significant. There are few incidents in the life of Jesus common to the synoptics and John. Major events and extensive speeches are peculiar to John alone. The presentation of the style of Jesus' ministry is different. There are certain chronological tensions.

What is the explanation of these differences? John may either be supplementary to, independent of, interpretive of, or a substitute for, the synoptic gospels. If John's readers knew Mark, for example, John could afford to pass over Mark's account, and include stories and sayings not found there. If he wrote independently of Mark, on the other hand, it seems improbable that John could have failed to mention certain historical events, even if he wrote at a very early date before the synoptic gospels circulated. Nevertheless, the theory is gaining popularity. It is argued that John knew the oral tradition behind the synoptics, but wrote independently of them. The fact that John wrote about Jesus' activities in different locations than those mentioned in the synoptic gospels, would explain the lack of parallels. Besides, it is quite possible to harmonize the chronology of John with that of the other three, as Stauffer has recently shown.

The gospel of John preserves an excellent historical tradition of the life of Jesus, which is increasingly being appreciated.

IV. The fourfold gospel

From the first, the four gospels were considered to be various accounts of one gospel. Soon after the composition of John, the four accounts began to circulate as a fourfold corpus of Scripture. The reply to Marcion (Marcion repudiated Matthew, Mark, and John), called the anti-Marcionite prologues, prove that the four gospels were accepted as one collection. About A.D. 170, Justin's disciple Tatian composed a harmony of the gospels called the Diatessaron, which became a favorite in the

Assyrian church for some years. To Irenaeus, the fourfold gospel was as fundamental as the four corners of the world or the four winds of heaven. Clement of Alexandria, Tertullian, and Origen all agree that these four accounts are the only authentic accounts of the life of Jesus from apostolic times.

V. HISTORICAL VALUE

The Christian faith rests upon historical foundations; the four gospels are primary evidences for its authenticity and validity. An attack on their historical integrity is an attack against the credibility of Christianity itself. Many NT critics still regard the gospel tradition as community fiction handed down by anonymous and miscellaneous individuals. In the light of the evidence, such attempts to discredit the gospel records must be discounted. Historical pessimism is utterly unwarranted. The textual witness for the NT documents is incredibly good, surpassing any comparable instance in Greek or Latin lit. The internal data indicates that all of the gospels were written inside the 1st cent., and contain eyewitness accounts of the highest veracity. The concerted attempt of form critics to undermine their integrity is based upon huge speculation. The Christian faith could scarcely rest upon a more secure basis than what the four gospels provide. *See each gospel account*.

BIBLIOGRAPHY. B. H. Streeter, *The Four Gospels* (1924); V. Taylor, *The Formation of the Gospel Tradition* (1933); T. W. Manson, *The Sayings of Jesus* (1949); F. C. Grant, *The Gospels* (1957); K. Aland et al, *Studia Evangelica* (1959); R. Bultmann, *History of the Synoptic Tradition* (1963); C. H. Dodd, *Historical Tradition in the Fourth Gospel* (1963); N. B. Stonehouse, *Origins of the Synoptic Gospels* (1963); B. F. Harrison, *Introduction to the New Testament* (1964); W. G. Kümmel, *Introduction to the New Testament* (1965); D. Guthrie, *New Testament Introduction, Gospels and Acts* (1966).

C. H. PINNOCK

GOSPELS, APOCRYPHAL. The canonical gospels are not biographies, and record only a small part of the life and work of Jesus. Later a growing biographical interest led to the composition of works intended to fill the gaps, most of them based on imagination or drawing on myth and legend. The *Infancy Gospels* recount tales of His childhood, or carry the story back to the birth and childhood of Mary. The passion and resurrection, the descent into hell, and the terrors of the underworld are described with additional detail (*Gospel of Peter, Acts of Pilate,* Bartholomew lit.). The Gnostics in particular composed "gospels" containing revelations given in the period between the Resurrection and the Ascension. Rarely can one look for the survival of authentic early tradition, and only in the earliest of these documents. (See APOCRYPHAL NEW TESTAMENT 2 and separate articles.)

R. MCL. WILSON

GOSPELS OF THE CHILDHOOD OF JESUS. *See* APOCRYPHAL N.T.

GOSSIP. A gossip is one who repeats idle talk or rumors about others. Gossip need not be, but often is, malicious. The word is not found in the KJV, but is found in the RSV in both Testaments. In the OT it is the tr. of two Heb. words. (1) רָכִיל, Proverbs 20:19 (KJV "talebearer") warns against associating with gossips, who reveal secrets and speak foolishly. The same word is found in Leviticus 19:16, where the RSV trs. it "slanderer," and in Proverbs 11:13, where the RSV renders it "talebearer."

(2) דִּבָּה, found in Ezekiel 36:3 (KJV "infamy"), where the enemies of Israel are told that they will be punished for their sins against Israel, including "evil gossip." The same Heb. word is found in other places in the OT, and is rendered "whisperer," "evil report," "ill report," or "slanderer" (Gen 37:2; Num 13:32; 14:36, 37; Ps 31:13; Prov 10:18; Jer 20:10; Ezek 36:3).

In the NT the word appears three times, and in each case it is the rendering of a different Gr. word. (1) ψιθυριστής (Rom 1:29 KJV "whisperers"); listed among the sins of which the heathen are guilty. (2) ψιθυρισμός (2 Cor 12:20 KJV "whisperings"; among the sins which Paul feared existed in the Corinthian church. (3) φλύαρος (1 Tim 5:13 KJV "tattlers"); a sin to which idle persons are susceptible.

S. BARABAS

GOTHIC VERSION. *See* VERSIONS, ANCIENT.

GOTHOLIAS. KJV and ASV Apoc. form of GOTHOLIAH.

GOTHONIEL gō thŏn' ĭ əl (Γοθονιήλ, the Heb. עָתְנִיאֵל). An ancient Heb. name going back at least to the time of Moses. The GOTHONIEL mentioned in Judith 6:15 was the father of Chabris, a city elder of Bethulia.

GOURD (קִיקָיוֹן, the *Palma christi*; פַּקֻּעֹת, *wild cucumbers*). The word "gourd" is mentioned five times in Jonah 4, while "wild gourds" appear in 2 Kings 4:39. It is the marginal notes in the KJV and ASV that suggest the alternative tr. "Palm-Christ." This is the castor bean plant, *Ricimum communis*. This plant has huge leaves, which provide excellent shade. It could be used growing over a bower, and grows rapidly. In England, the castor oil plant grows to a height of four ft., but in the E it makes a large shade-giving tree. It is certainly a native of Asia. In Moffatt's tr., Jonah's booth is called a hut, and the castor oil tree could easily have grown behind it to provide thick shade and coolness.

Augustine, however, believed that the plant that gave Jonah shade was a true gourd, and it could easily have been. Gourds climb; they

Wild gourd.

have very broad leaves; and they grow quickly in the E, lengthening themselves by as much as twelve to eighteen inches a day. They wither and die quickly when attacked at their base by insects like wireworms.

Gourds are, of course, relatives of the cucumber and of the squash—much eaten in the U.S.A. and Canada. In fact, the gourd could have been one of the winter squashes like the Hubbard, *Cucurbita maxima.* They climb up pergolas and fences even today in Pal.

The gourd in 2 Kings 4:39 is prob. the poisonous *Citrullus colocynthus,* known in Great Britain as Bitter Apple. It has a leaf like a squash, and the fruit could easily, therefore, have been mistaken for an edible squash.

The cry, "death in the pot" (2 Kings 4:40), was never fully substantiated, for nobody died. The stew, therefore, may not have been poisonous, but strongly purgative and bitter. Those who partook would therefore have had an acute pain. The adding of the meal could have been God's miraculous answer, or the fact that the wise prophet knew that meal would neutralize the bitterness.

In the ASV of 1 Kings 6:18, there is a reference to gourds in the margin, i.e. instead of "carved with knops and open flowers," the words read "carved with gourds." This information is repeated in 1 Kings 7:24, where "knops" were cast in two rows. The carving of little gourds alternated with open flowers would have been very attractive.

Renaissance painters used plants in their pictures to give a symbolic meaning. Gourds were used as symbolic of salvation, and this may be the reason why they were used in the Temple (1 Kings 7:24).

W. E. SHEWELL-COOPER

GOVERNMENT. The Bible begins with God, and all thinking on human government must also begin there. Exclusive stress on human autonomy and self-sufficiency in government leads either to ruthless tyranny or to anarchy. The ideal is an ordered society subject to law with the consequent possibility of a normal life in the community—this becomes possible in so far as the Biblical conception of the state is, in some measure at least, actually realized.

1. Its source
2. The nature of the state
3. Government in Israel
4. Government in general
    a. Its divine authority
    b. The duty of obedience
    c. The limits of obedience
    d. The limits of disobedience
    e. Prayer for the government
    f. Participation in government

1. Its source. Human sovereignty as it is exercised in the state has its source in divine sovereignty. The starting point is the doctrine of creation. God the Creator made all things. All that is owes its beginning to His creative act and to His sustaining power. This inevitably implies God's sovereignty over His creation. Since all is dependent upon Him, so everything is subject to Him, whether the solar system, the world of nature, or human society.

This creative activity is the work of the Trinity. God created (and creates) through the agency of His word and the Spirit of God was (and is) present in life-giving power (Gen 1; cf. Prov 8:22-31; John 1:1-4; Col 1:15-17; Heb 1:1-3). The Son is not only the One through whom the Father created all things, but "in him all things hold together" (Col 1:17). Hence, the sovereignty of God in creation is exercised through Christ. He is not only the Savior of His people but also the Lord of all creation.

This sovereign authority of God over men is expressed in law. Prior to the Fall God dealt with Adam in terms of law. The prohibition of the forbidden fruit was the expression in legal terms of the absolute rights of the sovereign God. Adam's disobedience was thus lawbreaking, and as such, because the law was the expression of God's will, it was a personal affront to God Himself.

Sin, however, is not only culpable so that all the world is guilty before God, but it has adverse consequences in the sphere of man's relationship with his fellows. God's purpose in creation was that men should subject the created order to their control and live in harmony with each other. Sin entered, however, as a divisive influence so that men ceased to contribute to each other's welfare. Instead, they preyed on each other. Hence, it is in the natural course of events that in place of a harmonious society, murder and lust, theft and war appear as symptoms of a humanity that has lost its bearings spiritually.

The law of God declared to man in his fallen condition is His gracious corrective. This applies both to the law written on the conscience of every man and to the revealed law of the OT. Whereas law has a redemptive function in that it shows men their sin and so turns them to the Savior, it has also a secondary but none the less important function of restraining men from reaping the consequences of their own sinfulness.

God remains the God of Grace, even in face of Adam's sin and men's persistence in willful defiance of their Creator. This grace is seen not only in His redeeming work by which He saves His elect, but also in His gracious dealings with men in general, "for he makes his sun rise on the evil and on the good, and sends rain on the just and on the unjust" (Matt 5:45). If men were left to their own devices they would destroy each other. Certainly, social life would be impossible. So God has graciously imposed restraints that ordered social living is possible.

These restraining influences may be seen in the various sanctions to which men submit themselves—the pressure of conscience, the influence of the family, the customs and standards of the community. The concern in this article is, however, with one particular sphere in which God's gracious restraint is seen; namely, the state, which in Scripture is always viewed as divinely instituted.

2. The nature of the state. The term "state" in this article is employed in its widest sense. There is a wide gulf between the primitive jungle tribe and the highly sophisticated community of a technological society; there is a deep gulf between the totalitarian regime of a fascist or communist dictatorship and the freedom of a democracy. None the less, all of these have certain fundamental characteristics. Each group is a community and not merely a collection of warring individuals. They are not bound together necessarily by national ties, for many different ethnic groups may be knit together under one state, while on the other hand, a single ethnic group may be divided into two states. What constitutes a state, at the rudimentary tribal level and at the most advanced level, is the common submission of a community to law. Whether it be a tribal chief, a dictator, or a democratically elected parliament, there is an organ of government and that government exercises authority over those who are subject to its jurisdiction. This authority is expressed by laws which are promulgated (whether the unwritten code of the tribe or the precisely drafted legislation of the modern state). Law is not mere exhortation to the people to conform; it is enforced. The government must have the means of compelling its subjects to obey the law and must have the power to impose penalties on those who disobey.

There is no explicit description of the state in Scripture. There is no attempt to define precisely what constitutes the prerogatives of government. All that has been said above is implicit in Biblical teaching, whether it is expressed in the narratives of God's dealings either in mercy or judgment with nations; in the record of God's word to kings and those in authority, or in the attitude to the state, either adopted by God's people or prescribed for them by prophets and apostles and by Christ Himself.

There are two spheres in which human authority is exercised in Scripture—among the people of God, and among men in general. In the OT Israel appears as a nation under God in a special sense, but the other nations are also subject to Him and although they may not acknowledge the fact, yet the authority exercised even by pagan kings was entrusted to them by the God of Israel. Similarly in the NT there is the company of the redeemed where the kingly rule of Christ is gladly accepted. There is also the Rom. empire in which the believers find themselves under civil control. However, this is not a realm where God's sovereign power is not present; for the NT writers echo the prophets of the OT that "the governing authorities . . . . have been instituted by God" (Rom 13:1).

The authority of God exercised among His people is an anticipation of the final consummation of the purposes of God when every knee shall bow. That same authority mediated through the agency of human rulers is a standing witness to God's common grace, even to men in a state of rebellion against Him. Although some features of government as exercised in Israel are common to any properly ordered state, because of the peculiar position of the chosen people, it is best to consider them separately before looking at the wider aspects of the Biblical view of the state.

3. Government in Israel. The ancient nation of Israel was unique in that it was organized as a theocracy. Although the precise form of government varied during the nation's history, the underlying conviction was always there in the OT that the Lord is the true ruler of His people. Whoever exercised rule over the nation, the ultimate authority belonged to God.

The Lordship of God over His people is seen in the way that leaders and kings owed their appointment to Him. Moses was commissioned directly by God to lead the people out of Egypt. It was under his leadership that they ceased to be a collection of tribes and were constituted a nation, the people of the Covenant. Joshua, his successor, owed his position to the same divine commission, and in the stormy days after his death the judges who ruled were raised up by God—"Then the LORD raised up judges who saved them out of the power of those who plundered them" (Judg 2:16). In the rise of the monarchy there was the same firm insistence on divine appointment, as Saul was first selected and then rejected, and as David was summoned to the throne by Samuel, God's prophet. The king in Israel was "the LORD's anointed." He was not merely the head of the civil administration or the commander of the army. He was essentially the representative of the kingly rule of God. His government of Israel embodied and illustrated the sovereign authority of the Lord.

This meant that in Israel the ideal of creation began to be realized. Because of the sinfulness of the men called to govern the nation this realization was all too often sadly impaired. Nonetheless, a nation was established distinct from the other nations which surrounded it, in which God's purposes for man whom He had created were to some degree manifested. God's original purpose for man was that he should live in submission to his Creator, in harmony with his fellows, and in enjoyment of the bounty of nature. Sin by contrast brought rebellion against God, division among men, and discord into the whole created order. Whereas the original purpose envisaged the communion of men with God, the sad consequence of man's sin was the judgment of God, leading to exclusion from God's presence and to misery.

All this was reflected in ancient Israel. Insofar as they submitted to God's law the original pattern of creation began to be seen. When a godly ruler on the throne led the people in submission to the law, the result was unity in the land between the different tribes. There was peace and security against the disruptive forces from without. "Every man under his vine and under his fig tree" (1 Kings 4:25) enjoyed the fruit of the land but when they rebelled against God the warnings of Deuteronomy were realized. The nation was divided; they faced plague, pestilence, and famine; they became subject to their enemies, and finally they were banished from the land.

There was also the eschatological element. The glimpses of the glory enjoyed in the land were flickering tokens of the surpassing glory to come at the end of the age, when the Israel of God would be brought into perfect submission to His rule. On the other side, the sin and the consequent judgments were tokens of the solemn outcome of the final "day of the LORD," when the nations that knew not God were consumed by the fire of His wrath.

There is, of course, the important Messianic element in the history of government in Israel. Just as the anointed prophet and priest foreshadowed the Word made flesh, the great High Priest at Calvary, so the king of Israel was a foreshadowing of the Messianic king. Thus Jesus began His ministry preaching the gospel of the kingdom. The rule exercised by the kings of Israel failed to declare adequately the sovereignty of the Lord because of the sinfulness of even the best of the kings. In the Messiah there is no such imperfection, in Him God's rule is perfectly manifested.

Within the Church, Christ's kingship is the dominant truth. The government that is exercised by the spiritual leaders within the redeemed community is really the mediation of the royal government of Christ. To a greater degree than in Israel, the ideal of creation is realized. However, because the Church is comprised of men who although justified, are still sinful, the final realization is yet future, and the Christian still prays, "Thy kingdom come."

This consideration of government in Israel and in the Church of Christ has not been a mere parenthesis in the discussion of the Biblical view of the state. Apart from its positive value in stressing the ultimate authority of all human government, it needs to be related in a Biblical fashion to the wider issues, for it is at this point that historically there has been much confusion. There has been a failure to see the unique character of the theocracy in Israel with the subsequent misguided attempt to organize nations on a theocratic basis. In a similar way some Christians have viewed the government of God exercised within the Church as the blueprint for society, so that the laws of the Church become the pattern for the laws of the land.

In the 16th cent. many of the Reformers were clearly dominated by the theocratic ideal. The godly prince of the OT found his fulfillment in the Lutheran, Reformed, or Anglican ruler so that the magistrate had a responsibility to protect the Church and to enforce the moral standards that the Church declared. In its more ugly manifestation the magistrate also assumed the further responsibility of defending the "truth" and resisting "error" to the extent of punishing offenders.

This concept of the Christian state fails to do justice to the Biblical understanding of the new Covenant. It is true that there is in Scripture one Covenant of Grace. However, within that one Covenant there is the period of preparation and of fulfillment. When Jeremiah rejoiced in the prospect of the glories of the new Covenant and when the writer of Hebrews discoursed at length on the implications of this new Covenant they were not using empty words. The OT was a period when God was graciously at work, but it was still a preparatory period. It looked forward to the age of the Messiah, the Gospel age, the age of fulfillment.

The restrictive national character of the old covenant was shattered by the divinely commanded inclusion of the Gentiles. There is no longer a theocratic nation, as men and women of every tribe and nation are gathered into the Church. The godly prince of the OT finds his fulfillment in the Messiah. To look for a modern counterpart to David or Hezekiah is to miss the concept of the unique kingship of Christ. It may be that the ruler is a true believer, but that does not give him the status that the theocratic concept requires, for in the kingdom of God there is only one king, Christ Himself.

For this reason the Anabaptist wing of the Reformation movement (in its more sober and Biblical manifestations) insisted on the separate spheres of church and state. The Church is the realm of God's special grace where God governs His people by means of those whom He ordains and whom the Spirit endows with gifts for their task. The state is the realm of God's common grace extended to all men. The government, although it is of divine authority, will reflect Christian standards only insofar as the members of that government themselves exercise Christian values.

In other words, a Christian man who reaches a position of authority in the state will be motivated by his faith in the same way as a business man is influenced in his decisions by the standards of integrity and righteousness that are his because he is a Christian. This does not mean that the Christian politician can submit a nation including both believers and unbelievers to a pattern of conduct which belongs properly to believers only. The separation of church and state is not a mere slogan, but is rooted in the Biblical doctrine that there are two realms; secular government and the spiritual household of God. God is at work in both, but each enjoys a relative autonomy—relative, that is, in view of the overriding fact of God's final authority.

4. Government in general. a. *Its divine authority.* The more general aspects of human government overlap with some of the elements already discussed concerning Israel and the Church. All authority is ultimately from God and, although men may either ignore or reject God, He still remains King. Men scheme and plot and kill to seize power. Nations go to war and national boundaries change. Dictatorship gives way to democracy or vice versa. But above and beyond all political changes and the ebb and flow of national powers, the Lord God omnipotent reigns.

Daniel, the prophet, insisted on this derived character of all government when he reminded Nebuchadnezzar that "the Most High rules the kingdom of men, and gives it to whom he will, and sets over it the lowliest of men" (Dan 4:17, 25). This same Nebuchadnezzar was humbled by God, and at another time he was used to carry out God's purposes. "Now I have given all these lands into the hands of Nebuchadnezzar, the king of Babylon, my servant" (Jer 27:6). The word of the Lord to Belshazzar declared that the fall of his kingdom and the rise of the Medo-Persian empire was by the decree of God (Dan 5:28). When Cyrus acted to liberate the Jews, it was because the Lord stirred up his spirit (2 Chron 36:22; cf. Isa 44:28).

The judgment of God upon nations stresses the same truth that all government is derived from God, and therefore when rulers misuse the responsibility entrusted to them they are liable to God's judgment. So Pharaoh was overthrown, a great OT illustration of God's supremacy. The prophets declared the same theme, as in the prophetic warnings to the nations by Isaiah, Jeremiah, and Ezekiel. Not only Judah and Israel, but pagan nations as well were subject to the moral law, and all alike came under the lash of Amos' passionate invective.

The NT contains the same position. The state for most believers was the Rom. empire, paganistic and powerful. But it was established by divine decree. So Christ accepted the authority of Caesar as the legal authority in civil affairs (Matt 22:15ff.) even though Caesar controlled Pal. by force of arms. Peter counseled the same attitude. Christians were to "honor the emperor" (1 Pet 2:17). Paul in the emphatic statement already quoted (Rom 13) insisted that all human authority is derived from God.

Most significant is the fact that divine authority over government is independent of the moral character of the leaders who control the government. Nero was a blackguard, yet the same word applies—he was to be honored. An institution like the family or the state is devised and established by God, and yet many of those involved may fall far short of the ideal. To destroy the institution, however, is to produce an intolerable chaos. A father may behave like a brute and forfeit any right to respect, but this does not give cause to despise or repudiate the vital necessity of family life and parental authority. No more does the failure of one ruler to administer justly give the right to anarchic overthrow of authority. God in His own way deals with such men. In spite of individual failure, the authority of the office still stands.

b. *The duty of obedience.* The obvious corollary to the divinely given authority of the state is the obligation to submit to the laws of the land. Obedience to duly constituted civil authority is written into the canons of Christian conduct. To honor the emperor did not mean for Peter simply to pay lip service to the dignity of his office. It meant a readiness to obey the laws that the emperor promulgated, and to submit if need be to the penalties imposed on disobedience. The issue of disobedience for conscience sake will be discussed later.

Obedience to the government was practiced by Jesus Himself. He lived in the midst of nationalistic resentment of the alien rule of Rome (one of his disciples, Simon the Zealot, was drawn from this background). It would have been easy for Him to fan the embers of bitterness into a flame of opposition to the Rom. occupation, but this He refused to do. The currency bearing Caesar's head was a reminder of the benefits of stable government. The use of that currency was an implicit acknowledgment of the authority of the government that had issued it. Therefore they must obey Caesar in practical ways by paying the tax with the same coinage used to enjoy the privileges of Rom. rule. Rome was an alien occupying power, but her government was a fact of the providential ordering of God Almighty. Therefore they must obey, for to refuse to pay the tax would be to rebel against God (see Matt 22:15-21).

When standing before Pilate, the Lord affirmed the same attitude. The man who tried Him was unworthy of his office, and the trial was a travesty of justice. Nonetheless, Pilate was the governor and as such was the representative of the imperial government, and therefore to him Jesus submitted. When Pilate began to bluster there was a firm word of rebuke—"You would have no power over me unless it had been given you from above" (John 19:11)—but in His general attitude He maintained the same approach as He had earlier in the garden when He rebuked Peter for using his sword and submitted quietly to arrest.

The Apostle Paul followed his master in this as in all other things. His frequent assertion of the essential legality of his actions in the eyes of Rom. law is an implicit acknowledgment of the authority of that law. It is a standard to which he saw himself called to conform. When in the final stages of his prolonged imprisonment at Caesarea he made his appeal to Caesar, he was acknowledging the supreme authority of the emperor whose laws he had obeyed and to whose justice he now appealed.

When he spoke in explicit terms about the authority of the state and the responsibility involved in citizenship he expressed a reflection of his own personal attitude. As already noted (Rom 13), he emphasized the divine institution of the state.

God's purpose in thus ordaining the power of government is a gracious one. It is to restrain evil and punish wrongdoers. Thus the demands of the law for honesty and preservation of life reflect the demands of God. The justice of the law carried out upon evil reflects in some measure the righteous judgments of the Judge of all the earth.

This realization lifts the Christian's obedience to a new level. He does not obey merely because it is the best policy and because disobedience to the law if detected will lead to punishment. He obeys "for the sake of conscience." Seeing the hand of God in the demands of the state, hearing the voice of God in the just requirements of the powers that be, and believing himself to be a man not simply subject to the laws of the state but to the authority of God, he yields a willing obedience.

The same applies (Rom 13) to the payment of taxes, an echo of Jesus' teaching about Caesar's rights. Since the state is divinely ordained and since obviously it requires money to carry out its divinely appointed function the citizen must pay taxes to furnish the necessary resources. The Christian, says Paul, will pay taxes for conscience' sake. There will be no manipulation of his tax returns, no defrauding of the tax authorities. The tax demand note is a requirement with heaven's seal upon it, and there must be a scrupulous honesty in complying with it.

Crete was noted for its turbulence, but Christians even in such an atmosphere were to show a different spirit. Paul wrote to Titus (3:1) to remind the Cretans of their responsibility, "to be submissive to rulers and authorities." This injunction was linked with the requirement that they should be "ready for any honest work." Obedience to the demands of the government means not only an avoidance of what is illegal but also a positive participation in any task that is obviously the responsibility of a loyal citizen.

There is a unanimity in the apostolic teaching. Peter who once used his sword in Gethsemane had learned his lesson. Whether it is the emperor as the supreme authority, or the various governors who are his representatives, all must be seen by the Christian to be sent by God Himself. Government is viewed not simply in its restraining and punitive capacity but in its positive role of promoting the public good. The state praises those who do right (1 Pet 2:14). This public recognition of worth is an implicit acknowledgment of the responsibility of the state to promote moral standards in the community. If the state acts to provide education or welfare for its citizens the Christian citizen should recognize the positive side of the state's function and should readily pay his taxes to provide the means for accomplishing these programs. This submission is rendered "for the Lord's sake." This involves not only an honest compliance with the state's requirements but an ungrudging and ready obedience, since it is not merely a government that makes the demand, but the Lord Himself.

c. The limits of obedience. There are, however, limits to the obedience that the state may demand. No one is entitled to qualify his response on the ground of personal inconvenience or of personal dislike of any particular legislation. Once such considerations are substituted for submission a condition of subjectivism exists, which if unchecked leads to anarchy. A question of conscience, however, is in a different category. It is one thing when the state imposes repressive measures that may be very hard to accept, or even when the state acts unjustly. In such cases submission is due. It is a very different matter when the demands of the state conflict with the law of God. What is the Christian to do if the government commands him to act in a way that is plainly contrary to Scripture?

Where there is a conflict of loyalties the higher one must take precedence, "We must obey God rather than men" (Acts 5:29). Although the Lord was quite insistent that one must render to Caesar the things that are Caesar's, He added an important and qualifying requirement, "and to God the things that are God's" (Luke 20:25). Caesar had a divinely given authority to which submission was due, but his authority was always subject to a higher authority, God Himself. If Caesar then went beyond his prerogatives and required from men something that God forbade, then Caesar must be disobeyed.

It must be stressed, however, that disobedience must be limited only to matters of conscience. In every other point the Christian must remain a loyal citizen. It is only at the point where his loyalty to God is in danger of being violated that he must take his stand. This point emerged in Peter's first epistle. He wrote about the likely persecution and suffering that Christians would face. They must be prepared to endure trial for Christ's sake. At the same time he reminded them that it is only in the cause of righteousness that such resistance to the state is permissible. If a Christian suffered the consequences of other unlawful actions he need expect no word of commendation from God (1 Pet 4:12, 13).

d. *The limits of disobedience.* A further question arises: what form should this legitimate disobedience take? If for conscience sake one cannot obey the dictates of the state, how should he show his resistance? Should the disobedience be active or passive? This is no academic issue for it constantly recurs as an existential problem. Is it right, for example, when a dictatorship is repressing the country in general and the Church in particular, for a Christian to take part in a conspiracy to overthrow the government? Is it right for Christians to participate in civil disobedience or should a Christian's resistance be that of suffering only?

Any active participation in subversion is apparently ruled out by the basic Biblical insistence on the divine authority of government. To take steps to overthrow an existing government is to deny this fact. It means that men have rejected what is a fact of God's providence and this the Christian cannot do. He must suffer for conscience sake and await God's hour of deliverance. It may be that God will use an armed revolt to overthrow a tyranny, for God uses men's schemes and plans even when those who formulate them are not His people and their action may be contrary to His revealed will. However, the Christian cannot himself share in the planning or initiation of such a rebellion. Until the existing regime has manifestly been overthrown, his calling is to submit.

In the matter of civil disobedience guidance must come from Biblical principles rather than from explicitly stated Biblical mandates or prohibitions. Neither the OT nor the NT envisaged the type of state as the Western democracies of today, but rather the Bible knew only the authoritarian regime where the subjects' only duty was to obey. Clearly the situation is different in a democracy where opposition to the government's policies is both allowable and desirable. Indeed, organized political opposition to the government (the political party in power) is the life blood of democracy. No Biblical injunction is violated here. The "powers that be" in a democracy are the people themselves acting through their elected representatives. If then by educating public opinion, pressure is brought to bear on the government, or if by the use of the vote the political party in power is defeated it is still consistent with submission to the duly constituted authorities.

Civil disobedience, however, is in a different category. It is one thing to agitate for a particular position, or even to organize demonstrations. These are within the law. But once an activity goes beyond the law, at that point it becomes illegitimate for the Christian. There are times when it is difficult to come to a clear decision. There are areas of action that are neither black nor white, but an indefinite gray. At such times the Christian whose attitude to the law is governed by such phrases as "for conscience sake" or "for the Lord's sake" will give the law the benefit of the doubt.

A situation may also arise when there is a revolt leading to civil war with two competing authorities claiming to be the rightful government. Should the Christian take sides? What is his attitude to be? Again, he must admit that in the confusion that prevails at such a time, it is hard to come to a firm conclusion because of the lack of information, and also because of the misleading propaganda that usually issues from both sides. The Christian will stand on his basic position. Since he has accepted the existing government as the one appointed by God he will continue to treat it as such until it is quite clear that a *de facto* situation has made the *de jure* situation unreal and empty. Recognizing that God has often used rebellion to sweep away a corrupt government he will not cling blindly to the status quo but will be ready to submit with an equal obedience to the new government. One extreme is the readiness to side with any movement that looks likely to topple an unjust government. The other extreme is the conservatism that makes the Christian reluctant to accept the inevitability of a change that is already a fact, and yearn after a day that is gone. The middle course between these extremes is not easy to chart, but unless the Christian constantly relates himself to the basic Biblical principles, the way will not be merely difficult to chart, but well nigh impossible.

e. *Prayer for the government.* Paul urged that prayer should be offered "for kings and all who are in high positions" (1 Tim 2:1-4).

Clearly he was not concerned with the formal prayer that make a brief and perfunctory mention of the government in the public worship of the Church. On the contrary, he embraced the whole range of prayer as he called for "supplications, prayers, intercessions and thanksgivings." The Christian is to be as fervent in his prayers for the government as he is in what he might be tempted to consider as more spiritual concerns.

It is also important to note that Paul did not add any moral or spiritual qualifications in designating those for whom we are to pray. He knew only too well that a blackguard like Nero might be on the throne as emperor. His own experience verified the corruption that could exist at lower levels of government. His prolonged captivity at Caesarea had been due largely to the hope of a bribe on the part of the corrupt and immoral Felix, the governor. But Paul did not qualify his exhortation in any way. If a man is in a position of authority, whatever may be his personal character, he must be prayed for. Even if he is an avowed enemy of the Gospel and a bitter persecutor of the Church, he is still to be the object of intercessory prayers.

Paul knew from experience the resistance to the Gospel on the part of the Rom. authorities, who always viewed with suspicion any group which might prove to be a source of disaffection or subversion. The Christians might claim to be unconcerned with political issues, but the fact that they did not conform to the general social pattern marked them out as politically suspect. The likelihood of continuing and intensified persecution was present. To pray for the government was really to pray for the well-being of the Church. Paul gave as the aim of this praying, "that we may live a quiet and peaceable life, godly and respectful in every way" (2:2). He was declaring his concern not merely that Christians might enjoy peace, but also that they might be enabled to live as good citizens, respecting the government.

Christians at peace are never Christians at ease. Peaceful conditions in Church and state mean opportunities for preaching the Gospel. Paul followed this in his own experience. Roman roads were open to travelers because of the protecting might of the Rom. legions stationed at strategic points throughout the empire. Those roads provided opportunity for the missionary of Christ who wanted to spread the Gospel. Obviously it was a vital matter that these lines of communication be kept open. In modern times civil war and consequent anarchy are closing doors of opportunity. This call to pray for governments in all parts of the world is a continuing aspect of missionary intercession.

Paul also knew from experience the value of citizenship as a barrier against injustice. He would not use any external powers to forward the Gospel for "the weapons of our warfare are not worldly" (2 Cor 10:4). At the same time, when he was subjected to injustice or to the possibility of mob violence or assassination, he was ready to appeal to the authorities. In Philippi he was insistent that the authorities in the town must themselves be subject to Rom. justice, which they claimed to administer. In the final resort, as Paul faced the plots of the Jews against his life, he was ready to invoke his right as a citizen to appeal to Caesar. The stable government of Rome was therefore not only a condition of peaceful existence but, also was a valuable instrument for restraining unjust attacks on Paul's life. To pray for Paul's evangelistic work, to pray for his protection in carrying out that work, and to pray for the government, were not different areas of intercession, but aspects of the same basic concern.

Paul did not have in view simply the stability of the social order when he urged people to pray for rulers. He was also concerned for them as individuals, who are as much in need of the Gospel as any other sinner without God and without hope. He doubtless recognized the possibility of unbelief bordering on incredulity with which many Christians might receive the request that they pray for the emperor's conversion. They might well have doubted whether there was any likelihood of such a remote possibility being realized. Paul reminded them of the width of God's purposes of grace. "God our Savior . . . desires all men to be saved and to come to the knowledge of the truth" (1 Tim 2:3, 4). Taken in its immediate context the words "all men" would seem to refer to all sorts and conditions of men. God's purpose embraces not only the weak things of the world, who comprise the bulk of the Church, but also rulers. When Paul emphasized God's choice of the humble to confound the mighty (1 Cor 1), he did not exclude altogether those from a more exalted social or intellectual position—his phrase was "not many" rather than "not any." Therefore He declared that the gracious purpose of God reaches out to kings, so that prayer for them should petition their conversion.

There may come a time when the government of the day has gone far beyond its rights, and blatant unrighteousness and injustice control a nation. However, the Christian cannot, even then, have recourse to violent means to overthrow such a regime, but he can pray. In the Revelation is described such a conflict between the Church and the persecuting state. Therein is a symbolic glimpse of the souls of those who had been slain "for the word of God and for the witness they have borne." They were crying to God for vindication, "O Sovereign Lord, holy and true, how long before thou wilt judge and avenge our blood on those who dwell upon the earth?" (Rev 6:10). This prayer in heaven may well be echoed on earth. The Christian may be prepared to suffer for his testimony, but he is not inactive. God is his vindicator and to God he commits his cause, for in this matter his cause is no more a personal matter since it is the cause of the Gospel itself. The psalms provide inspiration for prayer at such a time (Pss 35:1; 43:1; 119:154) and also provide the ground of hope. The rulers may defy the Lord and His Christ, yet God still reigns. "He who sits in the heavens laughs; the LORD has them in derision" (Ps 2:4). The solution may be in the ruler's conversion or in his overthrow, but in either case it will be the power of God that will effect it, and believing prayer is faith's laying hold upon this divine power.

f. Participation in government. Is it right for Christians to use their vote? Can the Christian conscientiously enter political life and stand as a candidate for election either at the local or national level? These are questions that are obviously relevant only in a democracy where such possibilities exist. A similar question confronts Christians who live under some form of dictatorship. Is it right for a believer to accept employment that involves carrying out government policy? Does the believer's attitude to the world commit him to a policy of withdrawal from political affairs?

As noted above in the matter of obedience to the state the political context of the Biblical writers was different from a democratic situation of today, though very similar to that of many contemporary dictatorships. The Bible does not give definite precept or prohibition, but does provide guiding principles.

An appeal to the situation in Israel seemingly is ruled out because of the unique character of the theocracy. The ruler or king in Israel was involved not only in civil but in spiritual functions. However there is abundant OT illustration of the attitude of godly men toward Gentile and pagan governments. Joseph accepted a position of authority in Egypt, Daniel in Babylon, and Mordecai in Persia. Their positions are attributed to God's providence. Naaman continued to serve the king of Syria, and Obadiah remained in the service of Ahab, whose apostate northern kingdom approximated the surrounding heathen nations. In the NT there is no hint of the Ethiopian eunuch being called upon to renounce the office he held in the court life of his country. The same applies to Cornelius, the Rom. centurion in Caesarea, Sergius Paulus the pro-consul in Cyprus, and the Philippian jailer. When Paul sent greetings to the Philippian church he associated with him "those of Caesar's household." Although it might be argued that these were prob. only slaves in the palace, it is not probable that Paul would single out palace slaves for special mention. More likely they had an official status that would be of particular interest to a church in Philippi, which was a Rom. colony.

Some might accept the legitimacy of employment by government who would question the Christian's entry into political life. In the latter case it is a choice freely taken, and it involves a man not merely in carrying out the policy of the government but in helping to formulate it. Can a Christian thus be involved? Does the call to come out and be separate not apply here?

One preliminary point needs to be made. There would seem to be no fundamental difference between using one's vote and entering actively into political life. In both cases one is taking an active part. One vote may seem a very insignificant cog in a great machine, but a few hundred such votes can change the whole future of a country. Whether or not to allow a Christian to enter politics is basically the same issue as the question—to vote or not to vote.

The continuing principle of submission to the powers that be must again be the starting point. Assuming a democratic situation, that authority is vested in the people themselves, the men who actually rule the country are there as representatives of the people. The means by which they reach their position of authority are part of the constitution of the social order in which they live. According to the NT the ruler has divine authority, and in a democracy that power is vested in the people. Thus the procedure for electing representatives shares in that divinely given authority. To exercise the vote is thus simply to comply with the standing requirement of Scripture.

As far as active participation in politics is concerned, a Christian should only enter if he is strongly motivated by Christian principles of service. A Christian entering a political career encounters special problems. The lust for power, the unfair denigration of opponents, the dubious methods used to finance the party, the underhand and sometimes dishonest methods employed, deceit for the sake of party advantage—these are some of the features of political life that make it a particularly thorny area for a Christian. Yet, it is in the darkness that the light is needed to shine all the more brightly. Salt is not to be stored but to be used where corruption is likely. The Christian politician thus becomes a moral preservative in an area where corruption is too often an ugly reality. Also, a Christian politician can exert his influence in forming and passing the best possible legislation.

Another live issue is the attitude of the church to the political struggle. Many contend that the church has a political role and should be ready to exercise its powers in a lobby aimed at influencing government policy. The NT reply to this would surely be to stress the respective roles of the church and state. The task of the Church, as church, is to preach the Gospel, edify the believers, and lead men to worship the living God. Individual Christians may enter the political field but they will do so primarily as citizens, not as representatives of a church lobby. However, their convictions will be influenced by the presuppositions of the Christian faith and they will aim to realize in social life patterns of truth and equity. In this they will be strengthened by their membership in the Church and by the fellowship they experience there.

The Church as a body aims not primarily at improving the social order but her main objective is the salvation of men. The social improvement that may result when many men are saved is desirable, but when the Church forsakes her primary task of preaching the Gospel to engage in political enterprises her true mission is lost.

A further consideration is Paul's attitude to the standards in the Church and those in the world. Dealing with the problem of discipline at Corinth he is quite insistent that high standards be maintained in the Church. As for the world outside, he cannot judge them, for they are not subject to the Scripture that provides the criterion of judgment in the life of the Church (1 Cor 5:9-13). The Church therefore cannot insist that the state must conform to standards that are only applicable to Christians. The Christian in political life will know the standards, and in his own life he will strive to realize them. Knowing that unregenerate men can be restrained but not regenerated by legislation, and realizing that politics in a democracy is the art of the possible, he must be prepared to work for something less than the ideal lest he makes the best to become the enemy of the good.

Such an active role obviously brings its own problems of conscience. There can come a point when compromise is impossible and when a policy to which one is so committed is a clear violation of the law of God. In such an eventuality the Christian in a dictatorship must do what Daniel did in a similar situation, and face the consequences of disobedience, whereas the Christian in a democratic country has no option but to resign.

BIBLIOGRAPHY. J. Calvin, *Institutes of the Christian Religion*, Book 4 (Beveridge tr. 1943); J. Wesley Bready, *The Evangelical Revival and Social Reform* (1938); H. F. R. Catherwood, *The Christian in Industrial Society* (1964); C. F. H. Henry, *Aspects of Christian Social Ethics* (1964); C. F. H. Henry, *Christian Personal Ethics* (1965); D. Möberg, *Inasmuch* (1965); L. Verduin, *The Reformers and their Stepchildren* (1966); A. G. Dickens, *Reformation and Society in 16th Century Europe* (1966).

H. M. CARSON

GOVERNOR(אלוּף, אלף, חוקק, משל, נגיד, נשיא, סגן, פחה, פקיד, שד, שליט, תרשתא; *ἡγέομαι, ἡγεμών, ἡγεμονεύω, ἐθνάρχης, εὐθυνω, ἀρχιτρίκλινος, οἰκόνομος*). A person appointed to govern a country, province, or town. In the OT, the various Heb. words for governor are sometimes used in a vague way to refer to any person of higher rank who exercised some kind of authority; consistency is not observed in their use. Although the above Heb. words are rendered "governor" in the KJV, in the RSV they are tr. in a variety of ways: clan, commander, governor, leader, officer, chief officer, prefect, prince, ruler. The Heb. word most commonly rendered "governor" is פחה (1 Kings 10:15; 2 Chron 9:14; Ezra 5:3, 14; 6:6, 7, 13; 8:36; Neh 2:7; 5:14, 15; Esth 3:12; 8:9; Jer 51:23, 28; Ezek 23:6, 23; Hag 1:1; Mal 1:8). It refers to the ruler of a district under a king, e.g. Chaldean and Persian governors (Ezek 23:6, 23; Esth 3:12; 8:9), the Persian Tatnai, whose satrapy included Palestine, Phoenicia, and Egypt (Ezra 5:3; 6:6); and Nehemiah and Zerubbabel as governors of Judah (Neh 5:14; Ezra 6:7).

Coins of Herod and Caesar.

The Gr. words tr. "governor" are sometimes used with technical accuracy, sometimes somewhat loosely. *Ἡγέομαι*, and its derivatives are the words most frequently used, usually for Rom. subordinate rulers.

In the NT period, the various territories under Rom. rule were constituted in various ways, and their governors were of different ranks. The rulers of senatorial provinces, which were kept under control without difficulty, were appointed by the senate and called "proconsuls," their term usually running for one year. Governors of imperial provinces, which were apt to cause trouble for Rome, were appointed by the emperor personally for an indefinite term of office and were called "legates." The governor of a subdivision of an imperial province was also appointed by the emperor, and was called a "procurator." The NT mentions the following governors who were proconsuls: Sergius Paulus, governor of Cyprus (Acts 13:6f.); Gallio, governor of Achaia (18:12); and the unnamed governors of the province of Asia, who lived at Ephesus (19:38). Quirinius, governor of Syria, was a legate (Luke 2:2). The governors of Judea, which was a part of the imperial province of Syria, were Pilate (Matt 27:2; 28:14), Felix (Acts 23:26), and Festus (Acts 26:32), all of whom were procurators.

The KJV sometimes uses the word "governor" in an obsolete sense. In the account of the marriage at Cana, "the governor of the feast" and "the ruler of the feast" (John 2:8, 9 KJV) are the same person. He was the ἀρχιτρίκλινος, the steward, whose duty it was to take care of all the banquet arrangements—the tables, seating, food, etc. In Galatians 4:1, 2 "tutors and governors" is better tr. in the RSV as "guardians and trustees." The word "governor" in James 3:4 refers to the pilot or steersman of a ship; the RSV has "pilot."

BIBLIOGRAPHY. J. Finegan, *Light from the Ancient Past* (1959).

J. L. KELSO

GOZAN gō' zăn (גּוֹזָן, Akkad. *guzanu*, Ptolemy Γαυζανῖτις). City and region of the upper valley of the Khabur River (Biblical Habor, a tributary of the Euphrates). The capital, modern Tell Halaf, is by the Khabur River where it crosses the border between Syria and Turkey, some 200 m. E of the NE tip of the Mediterranean Sea. The region was conquered by Assyria (2 Kings 19:12; Isa 37:12), and Tiglath-pileser III, king of Assyria, transported Israelites from Trans-Jordan to Gozan (1 Chron 5:26). It is also one of the areas to which Israelites were deported after Samaria fell to Assyria in 722 B.C. (2 Kings 17:6; 18:11). Gozan was excavated, beginning in 1911, by Baron Max von Oppenheim, who discovered a new culture with excellent pottery.

C. P. WEBER

GRABA. KJV Apoc. form of HAGABAH.

GRACE (Gr. χάρις). In summary form the Christian message is "the gospel of the grace of God" (Acts 20:24). While the single pregnant term "grace" expresses its central and distinctive message, Christianity practically created the word "love," ἀγάπη, although the verb ἀγαπάω was right there. It was otherwise with the term "grace," χάρις, for here was a word in general exchange. It had yet to be virtually born again and baptized into Christ's spirit to express all that the NT sought to convey by it. Taken up into the message of Christ the word *charis* was to become filled out with a new and enriched content.

Charis is, then, a frequent term both in classical Gr. and in the OT. Its connotation in the former context is "attractiveness" or "charm," and in this sense it joins with the verb χαίρω, "to rejoice," "to be glad." The word appears about 170 times in the OT Gr. with the meaning of "favor" where it renders the Heb. *chen* (cf. e.g. Gen 6:8; 19:19; etc.). While the OT has many expressions to convey the reality of God's saving acts on behalf of men, *charis* never is used in this connection. "Not even the higher conception of the Divine *hesed* or mercy is able in Judaism to achieve the place occupied by *charis* in Christianity. While the gracious love of God to men had been the real foundation of the prophetic religion of the OT . . . it has to be noticed that even there the salvation of God was based not upon *charis* but upon the sovereign power and glory of God, upon His 'righteousness,' or 'judgment,' or 'torah'" ("Grace in the New Testament," W. Manson in the *Doctrine of Grace,* ed. W. T. Whitley, p. 37). As far, then, as the OT is concerned, "Of the two common English renderings of *chen* itself, favor and grace, the former is nearly always preferable" (C. Ryder Smith, *The Biblical Doctrine of Grace,* p. 8). The process by which the word *charis* came to approximate the NT idea runs somewhat as follows: (1) the primary reference of *charis* appears to have been to the state of being charmed or delighted. Plutarch, for example, speaks of the "charm" of Homer's poetry and of the talkative person whose unreasonable chatter destroys the *charis* of his deeds (*De Garrulitate* iv, v). (2) The word then took on a subjective sense with the thought of "kindly," or "courteous," i.e. "a generous disposition." It is a virtual equivalent for the idea of the willing of good to someone. (3) From this there developed the concrete connotation suggesting a "favor" or "boon." A favor is the expression of good will. As exhibiting an attitude of the will and feelings it is to be taken as a token of kindness. (4) As grace implies not only a giver but also a receiver so it came to denote the gratitude felt by the recipient for the favor bestowed and the thanks by which the gratitude is expressed.

While the NT reflects all these significations, it uses *charis* in the main with the enriched meaning which comes to it through the work of Christ. Grace is almost a synonym for salvation.

Always, however, *charis* had the underlying idea of a bestowal of help by an act of one's free generosity. Aristotle could therefore define *charis* as "helpfulness towards someone in need, not in return for anything" (μὴ ἀντί τινός) nor that the helper may get anything, but for the sake of the person who is helped (*Rhetor*. ii:7). Before Bethlehem the concept of a God of grace who gives Himself appears nowhere. Philo speaks much of God's "grace," but always in the sense of giving gifts to men. He does confess that "Often when I get rid of a foul suggestion in my mind by a rush of good thoughts, it is God flooding my soul with his grace" (τῇ ἑαυτοῦ χάριτι) (*Leg. Allegor*. ii:9). Even here, although the idea of an undeserved favor is recognized, Philo never rises to the faith that God's presence can enter a human heart. God giving Himself in Christ His Son who finds a dwelling-place in the life of the believer is "the gospel of the grace of God."

I. The synoptic gospels and grace
II. The Pauline doctrine of grace
  A. Grace and the Trinity

1. The grace of Christ
2. The grace of God
3. Grace and the Holy Spirit

B. Grace and justification

C. Grace and law, works and nature

III. Grace in the other NT writings

I. THE SYNOPTIC GOSPELS AND GRACE

The word "grace" was never used by our Lord except on four occasions in the ordinary sense of "thanks" (Luke 6:32, 33, 34; 17:9). It is entirely absent from both Matthew and Mark. Luke alone of the three synoptists mentions it on four other occasions, three of which have the sense of favor (1:28, 30; 2:52). The fact that Jesus never used the term *charis* in any other way than that of "thanks" is significant for two reasons: (1) it tells against the reiterated view that the Early Church constantly read back into the teaching of Jesus' own faith and sought to justify that faith by crediting its utterance to Him, and (2), it makes evident that Jesus could not have used a word to convey what, for example, Paul afterward sought to express by the word *charis,* for the reason that His own death and resurrection were the facts which were to give to the concept its real meaning.

Luke's use of the word in 4:22 may, however, be taken as a link with the peculiar post-Calvary significance of it. The KJV has here "they wondered at the gracious words . . . mouth," the ASV "at the words of grace," the ERV has "at the words of grace," the NEB "words of such grace." In the light of these variant trs. the phrase τοῖς λόγοις τῆς χάριτος must mean more than that they marveled at Christ's charm as a speaker, or at His winsomeness as an orator. Luke uses the term in its aesthetic meaning to underscore the attractive quality of what Jesus said, but He evidently had more in His mind. Luke uses the phrase "the word of his grace" (Acts 14:3), as equivalent to the Gospel (cf. 20:24). Something of this objective sense is to be read in the use of *charis* in Luke 4:22. This is strengthened by an examination of the context. The context is a quotation from Isaiah 61:2, and our Lord asserts its fulfillment in His coming. The allusion is made more gracious still by His omission of any reference to the divine vengeance which the original passage contained (cf. Isa 61:2; Luke 4:22). Luke intends to convey that the people did not simply marvel at the charming way Jesus spoke, or at its fascinating effects. Jesus was indicating that His presence in the world was to have a result wider and deeper than any nationalistic aid to the people of Israel. This was more than a hint of the Gospel as "grace for all." While Luke of all the synoptic writers was impressed by the gracious manner of Christ's teaching he wishes his readers also to be aware of the gracious matter of His teaching. The words of our Lord caused marvel because they came as "words of grace about grace" (A. B. Bruce).

Throughout the gospels in several ways the category of grace was demonstrated in Christ's acts and teaching. He came to fulfill a divine commission. The recurrent phrase "I am come" (cf. Matt 9:13; 10:34; Luke 12:51, etc.), accentuates this acceptance. He had come as the Father's beloved Son to seek and to save that which was lost. That is grace! By His attitude Jesus demonstrated what is meant by grace. He sought out the sinful. This is the new note of the Gospel. Judaism taught that God was ready to be gracious, but was inclined to leave the first step with the sinner. The distinctive thing with Jesus was His taking of the deliberate initiative on God's behalf. That is grace! The whole tendency of His teaching was in the same direction. There are passages in His recorded proclamations, the logical drift of which is that salvation is a matter of God's free generosity. In, for example, the sequel to the story of the Rich Young Ruler (Mark 10:17-31), the astonished disciples ask, "Then who can be saved?" They are answered that the ultimate right to enter the kingdom of God and be saved lies with God. Christ enunciates the Gospel of grace in contrast with the gospel of law and works. Several critical writers introduce the term "grace" at this point to bring out the essential meaning of Christ's reply. A place in His kingdom is not gotten by anything given up for God. It is given by the Father, and the Father's giving is the Father's grace. "What are we to get?" ask the disciples with the parable of the laborers in the vineyard in mind (Matt 20:1-8). They are reminded of the folly of bargaining with God. The final principle of God's dealing with men is a matter of grace. The parable of the Pharisee and the Publican shows clearly that "grace is grace" because, though wholly concerned with moral goodness, it does not at all depend upon how moral we are (John Oman, *Grace and Personality,* p. 189). The symbolism of the Last Supper makes clear that Jesus wished to indicate that the divine purpose of grace was focused in His cross. The blood of the cross inaugurated a new covenant and was essential to God as a means and medium of His saving work. It was no *post factum* explanation of what had happened. From the beginning, the life and work of Christ were read in the category of grace. The story of the cross was not given as an account of how the life of Jesus ended, but as revealing the basis upon which God's grace is assured and secured.

Two broad facts are clear from the record of the gospels. On the one hand, it is evident that the saving initiative is with God; and, on the other hand, any plea to human merit is ruled out. While Jesus is not the source of the term *charis* which describes these two facts, His own person is the source of the "grace" of which the whole NT speaks. It was the Apostle Paul who took these twin ideas and included them under the one pregnant term χάρις. In this sense grace is specifically a Pauline concept.

II. The Pauline doctrine of grace

While all the shades of meaning noted earlier are to be found in the NT, not all of them together convey the richness which the term acquired in the theology of Paul. For him "grace" was nothing less than the unsought and unbought saving activity of God which made him a debtor forever. The Damascus road encounter with the risen Jesus brought to focus the two basic ideas which unite in the word *charis*—that the saving initiative is with God and human merit is of no avail. By "grace," then, is meant that salvation is from first to last a gift of God. God's saving relation to man has its beginning and ending in His own eternal purpose as the counterfoil of history. He loves because He would love; saves because He would save. God acts in grace; acts without waiting for a sign or a nod from us: this is grace.

The idea of the absoluteness of grace in man's salvation is specially indicated by the fact that Paul never begins or ends his letters without a reference to grace. In neither case is he adhering to the merely conventional (cf. James 1:1, only NT writing with conventional use; see letter from Jerusalem Council, Acts 15:23—note conventional "farewell" v. 29). By beginning as he does, Paul is suggesting the supremacy of grace as the source from which flow all the blessings of the new order into which God's unmerited favor has brought the redeemed soul. Everything rests on God's free grace in Christ. Coming at the close the use of *charis* was a new thing in epistolary lit. In so using it the apostle was virtually authenticating his position as an apostle to whom the grace of God had come in such abundance. At the beginning Paul always associates "grace" and "peace," while in his salutations the close connection of the two concepts is not always immediately seen. The apostle seldom concludes without some reference to "peace." The two words seem always to be associated in his mind and the term "peace" comes somewhere in the context (cf. 2 Cor 13:11-13; Eph 6:23, 24; 1 Thess 5:23-28; 2 Thess 3:16-18, etc.) As the first word of greeting and the last word of salutation "grace" sums up for the apostle the totality of the blessings which come from God through Christ. "Grace" is the source, "peace," the stream. "Grace (χάρις), denotes the love of God manifested in the form of pardon towards sinful men; and peace (εἰρήνη), the feeling of profound calm or inward quiet which is communicated to the heart by the possession of reconciliation" (Godet, *Commentary on Romans*, vol. 1, p. 140).

At the end of 2 Thessalonians, Paul adds to that which he had already dictated, the "grace" conclusion with his own hand (3:17, 18). Such, he declares is his sign (σημεῖον) in every epistle. There is no reason to suppose with Bengel that he was in the habit of appending the "grace" in a specifically picturesque style of his own, although it may be agreed that if he could have done so he well might, for the word was engraven in multicolors upon his own heart. Paul had a purpose other than personal in adding his "grace" benediction. His letters were, as Dryden has said, "absent-sermons," and the last word for any church as well as the first is "grace." This must remain the dominant note of the celestial symphony as a Pauline epistle dies away.

A. Grace and the Trinity. 1. *The grace of Christ.* In the salutations the connection of grace with Christ is not as explicit as in the benedictions. The general formula in the latter case is "The grace of our Lord Jesus Christ be with you" (cf. Rom 16:20; 1 Cor 16:23; 2 Cor 13:14; Gal 6:18; etc.). Paul bases his trinitarian benediction on the order of experience (2 Cor 13:14). It is the grace of Christ which makes real the love of God—"first the experience of grace of Jesus, and then, through that and only through that, the certainty of the loving Fatherhood of God (cf. James Moffatt, *Grace in the New Testament,* p. 151; James Stewart, *A Man in Christ*, pp. 140f.). In 2 Corinthians 8:9 Paul sees the grace of Christ displayed in "the poverty" which for our sakes He accepted that we might become "rich." It is by "the grace of Christ" we are called, and to preach any other gospel is anathema (Gal 1:8). Thus in 2 Thessalonians 1:12 the grace of God and of the Lord Jesus Christ are associated. Paul then sees grace as founded on the absoluteness of Christ. Only an absolute Christ can meet man's absolute need. Paul never sets before man a relative Christ: a relative Christ might reduce Him to our condition, but only by removing Him from our need. To be absolute Christ must have originated on God's side; must have that origin and nothing less. Paul preached absolute grace because He proclaimed an absolute Christ. To Paul the self-sacrifice of Christ was one and the same with the grace of God.

2. The grace of God. Paul steadfastly declared that grace is given by God (cf. Rom 15:15; 1 Cor 1:3; 3:10; 15:10, etc.), and in no meager fashion either (Rom 3:24; 5:20; 2 Cor 4:15; 9:8, 14; 12:9; Eph 1:7; 2:7; 1 Tim 1:14). The grace of God is for Paul God's "radiant adequacy." The phrase "the grace of God," "signifies the generous love or gift of God by which in Christ salvation is bestowed on man and a new world of blessings opened" (Manson, op. cit. p. 43).

3. Grace and the Holy Spirit. In the Epistle to the Hebrews the Holy Spirit is referred to as "the Spirit of grace" (10:29; cf. Zech 11:10). It is by the Holy Spirit that the love of God manifest in the grace of Christ is made real to believing hearts. Both the individual and the church are the dwelling place of God through the Spirit (cf. 1 Cor 3:16; 12:11, 13;

Eph 1:12; 2:22; etc.). In this connection note must be taken of the association between "grace" and "power." God's special "favor" and God's diversified "favors" are alike the result of divine grace (cf. Rom 1:5; 12:3; 15:15; 2 Cor 8:9; Eph 4:7; etc.), it is therefore natural to conceive of the relation between them in terms of "power" (1 Cor 15:10). This association between "grace" and "power" is given special emphasis in 2 Corinthians 12:9: "My grace is sufficient for you, for my power is made perfect in weakness" (cf. 2 Tim 2:11; 1 Pet 4:10). By referring to *charis* as the active power of God, "grace" may be thought of as the presence of the Holy Spirit. For the presence of the Holy Spirit is "power" (cf. Luke 4:14; 24:49; Acts 1:8; 8:10; 10:38; etc.). Between "grace" as divine "power" and "power" as the presence of the Holy Spirit there is, then, a vital kinship. The experience of being "full of the Holy Spirit" and being "full of grace and power" is hardly to be distinguished (cf. Acts 6:5-8; 1 Cor 12:4-11; Eph 4:7-13).

In spite of this association, however, the Holy Spirit is not to be confused with the grace of God, as is done, for example, by N. P. Williams. He argues for "a frank equation of 'grace' with the Person of the Holy Spirit" (*Grace of God*, p. 110). This is to confuse association with identification; and in the end is to throw doubt upon the Trinitarian conception of the Godhead which is authentically Biblical. It is therefore rightly said that "the grace of God is the grace of the Father, Son, and Holy Ghost." It is called "the grace of the Lord Jesus Christ," because . . . the Incarnation of the Son of God is its crowning expression; and it is esp. associated with the Holy Ghost in the Christian, because we live under the new dispensation consequent upon the accomplishment of Christ's redemptive work and His appointment of "another Comforter." "Grace is, nevertheless, the grace of the indivisible Trinity and is not to be equated with any one Person of the Trinity" (O. Hardman, *The Christian Doctrine of Grace*).

B. Grace and justification. Paul begins his exposition of justification by referring to God's "grace as a gift" (Rom 3:24 RSV). To be declared righteous before God by virtue of our acceptance in Christ is altogether of God's spontaneous compassion. The grounds of our justification are variously stated (cf. Rom 5:9, 18, 19; 1 Cor 6:11). While justification is based upon the objective mediatorial work of Christ for mankind, the channel by which this saving act is made effective in human experience is "faith." Faith is the instrumental, not the formal cause: and has the meaning of a living personal trust in a perfect redemption and a present Savior (*see* FAITH). The summary scheme of salvation is, then, "by grace . . . through faith" (Eph 2:8). Grace points back to the ultimate source of God's act of justifying the sinner by His sheer goodwill and mercy. Faith, as man's response to God's act in Christ, is a divine work in us—itself a gracious and gratuitous gift of God. From first to last the justification of the sinner is a matter of grace: "But if it is by grace, it is no longer on the basis of works; otherwise grace would be no longer grace" (Rom 11:6).

Paul sees "the abundance of grace and the free gift of righteousness" (5:17), as greater and more powerful than the original taint of nature even when the added stains of actual sinful acts are taken into reckoning, for "where sin increased, grace abounded all the more." And grace reigns through righteousness to eternal life through Christ our Lord (5:21; cf. Titus 3:5). This does not allow any idea of "cheap grace" (Bonhoeffer). Paul will not admit to the perversion of God's free generosity in an antinomian direction. (Cf. Rom 6:1f.; Jude v. 4.) He insists rather that the grace of God which hath appeared for the salvation of all men trains them to renounce sinful passions and to await "our blessed hope, the appearing of the glory of our great God and Savior Jesus Christ" (Titus 2:11-14). Instead of sinning "that grace may abound," the believer is called upon to "grow in grace."

Paul's experience had taught him that God gives and God forgives. He was sure that "all is of grace"—here is the sovereignty of grace. This was the logic of his own sense of being overwhelmed by the mercy of God. The Gospel which he received and preached taught him that faith was something not confined to his own people after the flesh; and faith was, he knew, man's response by the action of grace to God's initiative. If faith was not limited to Israel neither could grace be. He was assured then that "grace is for all"—here is the sweep of grace.

In no place does Paul state that grace is given to all men. In Romans (3:22-24; 5:17f.) and Titus (2:11), the word "all" certainly is found. In each case it is clearly restricted by reference to the immediate context. In the first the "all" (Rom 3:23), does mean "all men" in a parenthesis about sinners. The declaration that "they are justified by grace as a gift" (RSV), points back to "all them that believe" in v. 22. In ch. 5, the "acquittal and life for all men" (v. 18) must be read in connection with the assurance that "those who receive the abundance of grace and the free gift of righteousness reign in life through one man Jesus Christ" (v. 17). The RSV trs. Titus 2:11, "For the grace of God has appeared for the salvation of all men"; this could too easily lead to a universalist conclusion if isolated from the whole drift of the NT. The preferable tr. is: "For the grace of God hath appeared to all men, bringing salvation." In the three passages, then, the most that could be concluded is that salvation is offered to all men: in none of them is it declared that all men are saved (cf. John 1:16; 3:16; etc.).

C. Grace and law, works and nature. Paul

declares that man is justified by faith (Rom 3:28), apart from the deeds of the law (cf. JUSTIFICATION). Throughout he clearly puts the law and grace into antithesis. To follow the law as a way of obtaining salvation is but to increase one's debt (Gal 5:3), and to fail of the grace of God. But "Christ is the end of the law unto righteousness to every one that believeth" (Rom 10:4 ASV). The law "met its end in Christ," yet it was not just "ended" by Him. He is Himself its "end" as a means of attaining to a righteousness acceptable to God (*see* LAW). The Gospel reveals the righteousness of God by faith. At the same time the law is not abolished, but has found its fulfillment in Him; here is the "grace of law" (*see* RIGHTEOUSNESS; SALVATION).

Grace, too, cancels out works as a means of attaining salvation (Rom 11:6). A reward is not reckoned of grace (4:4); thus to receive "grace" is to renounce "works" as a means of justification. The association of faith and works in salvation is impossible for then would "grace be no more grace."

It has been contended that nowhere does the NT in general and Paul in particular oppose "grace" and "nature." This is argued to justify the medieval maxim, "*Naturam non tollit gratia sed perficit*"—"Grace does not destroy but perfects nature." The contention is false. For that is not rightly regarded as grace which is but a superadded gift, a *donum superadditum*, to man's native powers. That is not grace which is a mere extra to man's initial efforts. Christ did not come to supplement man at his best, but to redeem man at his worst. Throughout the NT and esp. underscored in Pauline theology is the assertion that what is reckoned to be of the individual's own origination is assigned to "nature," whereas "grace" is what is given gratis to man. It is the plain teaching of the Gospel that man has no natural endowments and no moral deeds which merit favor with God; for if he had grace would not be grace, and man would have something wherein to glory.

III. GRACE IN THE OTHER NT WRITINGS

Although the term *charis* is less used outside the Pauline writings, its occurrences show that the Pauline sense was everywhere the Christian understanding of God's method of dealing with men. There is a close kinship of ideas between Paul and the Epistle to the Hebrews on the subject of grace. The supreme evidence of "the grace of God" is in Christ's tasting death for every man (2:9). Having a great High Priest we can come for timely help to "the throne of grace" (4:16). Man must beware lest he "outrage the Spirit of grace" (10:29 RSV), or fail to obtain grace (12:15). Rather we are to "have grace" (KJV) or "be grateful" (RSV), whichever tr. of 12:28 be preferred. It matters little since that only is grace which is received gratis; and what comes gratis demands gratitude (cf. "Grace and Gratitude" in *The Sense of the Presence of God*, John Baillie). In 13:9 the writer contrasts the strengthening of the heart by "grace" with that which comes from "foods." It is by this strengthening of grace that the believer is equipped with everything good to do the will of God (13:21). Throughout this epistle, however differently expressed, there is the same idea of grace as throughout the rest of the NT.

The Petrine epistles are no less undergirded by the same sense of indebtedness to God. God is the "God of all grace" (I, 5:10). It is to the humble He gives grace (I, 5:5; cf. James 4:6; Prov 3:34). Standing in the "true grace of God" (I, 5:12), men and women become "heirs together of the grace of life" (I, 3:7). This grace is now ours (I, 1:10), and yet there is grace coming to us at the revelation of Jesus Christ (I, 1:13). The sum of the believer's aim must be to "grow in the grace and knowledge of our Lord and Savior Jesus Christ" (II, 3:18).

James, too, assures grace for the humble (4:6). Humility is at the same time a fruit of grace and a reason for "greater grace" (4:6). Christ is the perfect law of liberty so that the liberty into which we are brought is not lawlessness but that which is of God (1:15, 27). To be "rich in faith" (2:5) is to do what God requires. No empty inactive faith saves (2:14f.). The wisdom which is "from above" produces the "fruit of righteousness" (3:17, 18). Indeed, in all things man can be but a humble receiver of "every good gift and every perfect boon." From Him comes every "act of giving" (δόσις). Of His own will are we brought into salvation by means of the "implanted word" which is able to save our souls (1:18, 21). Basic to all a man is and does is then for James God's generous acceptance of those who "draw nigh" to Him (4:8).

Six times in the Johannine writings does the term "grace" occur. This scantiness, however, is not esp. significant, for John tends to give "love" the idea "grace" has for Paul. A difficult use is that of "grace for grace" (in the gospel; 1:16). But the intention seems to be to stress the newness and adequacy of God's favor: here is grace on top of grace, and grace following grace—more grace on the foundation of grace and more waves flooding the shore of life from the ocean of grace. An almost exact equivalent phrase is found in Philo (*De Post. Cain*, 43), with the meaning of "benefit upon benefit." The term coming in the salutation of 2 John (v. 3) and Revelation (1:4, 5) has a Pauline sense, while nothing could be more apt than that the NT itself should conclude with the renewed benediction, "The grace of the Lord Jesus be with all the saints" (22:21). Here the distinctive word of the Christian message finds its climax. In Paul the special emphasis is that grace reaches down to our need: in the Apocalypse with its special stress on the sovereignty of Christ there is the assurance that grace reigns from the throne.

The free generosity of God through the self-giving of Christ is throughout what is meant by grace. Christ's self-sacrifice is the supreme demonstration of grace (2 Cor 8:9; cf. Phil 2:5ff.). And for man, He is the incarnate grace of God made available to faith. By grace we are called (Gal 1:15), and justified (Rom 3: 24), and sanctified (Rom 6:14). By grace we have an eternal consolation and a good hope (2 Thess 2:16), and the strength to endure (2 Tim 2:1). Even liberality is a blessing when conducted in the "grace" of Christ (2 Cor 8:1, 6, 9, 19; 9:8, 15).

BIBLIOGRAPHY. J. Oman, *Grace and Personality* (1917); L. S. Chafer, *Grace* (1922); E. Jauncey, *The Doctrine of Grace* (ch. 3) (1925); N. P. Williams, *The Grace of God* (1930); J. Moffatt, *Grace in the New Testament* (1931); W. T. Whitley (ed.), *The Doctrine of Grace* (1932); O. Hardman, *The Christian Doctrine of Grace* (1937); A. R. Vidler, *Christ's Strange Work* (1944); J. Murray, *The Covenant of Grace* (1954); J. N. D. Anderson, *Law and Grace* (1954); H. Kuiper, *By Grace Alone* (1955); E. F. Kevan, *The Evangelical Doctrine of Law* (1955); C. Ryder Smith, *The Biblical Doctrine of Grace* (1956); P. S. Watson, *The Concept of Grace* (1959); G. A. F. Knight, *Law and Grace* (1962); E. F. Kevan, *Salvation* (ch. 2) (1963); E. F. Kevan, *The Grace of Law* (1964); H. D. McDonald, *I and He* (chs. 5, 6) (1966).

H. D. McDonald

GRAFF, GRAFT (ἐγκεντρίζω, *graft in*[*to*]). The usual procedure of inserting a slip of a cultivated tree into a common or wild one. In Romans 11:17-24, however, the metaphor is used "contrary to nature" (v. 24), of grafting a wild olive branch, the Gentiles, into the good olive tree, the place of blessing under the Abrahamic covenant. Such a process is unnatural, which is precisely the point. Normally, such a graft would be unfruitful. The branches refer fig. to being in the place of spiritual blessing and fruitfulness. "That unbelieving Jews (branches of the good tree) were broken off that Gentiles might be grafted in, afforded no occasion for glorying on the part of the latter. Jew and Gentile alike must enjoy the divine blessings by faith alone. So Jews who abide not in unbelief shall, as 'the natural branches, be grafted into their own olive tree' " (W. E. Vine, *An Expository Dictionary of New Testament Words,* II, 171).

K. L. Barker

GRAIN (בר, *wheat*; דגן, *wheat, grain* (of cereals); שבר, *wheat, grain* (as food stuff); צרור, *pebble*; κόκκος, *kernel, grain*; σῖτος, *corn*). The word "grain" appears in the KJV eight times and in the RSV 117 times. On the other hand, "corn" appears in the KJV 101 times and in the RSV not at all. The reason is that in America, corn means maize or Indian corn, which was unknown to the ancient world, whereas in Britain "corn" is the general term for grain, including all the cereal plants, but esp. wheat. The most important agricultural products in ancient Israel were grain, wine, and oil—usually mentioned in that order (Deut 7:13; 11:14; etc.). There are many Heb. words connected with the raising and processing of grain, such as גרש, "crushed grain" (Lev 2:14, 16; שבלת, "ear of grain" (Gen 41:5, 6); KJV "ears of corn"; קמה, "standing grain" (Exod 22:6; Deut 16:9); ערמה, "heap(s) of grain" (Ruth 3:7; Neh 13:15; Jer 50:26); קלי, "parched grain" (Lev 23:14; Ruth 2:13; 1 Sam 17:17; 25:18); ריפות, "crushed grain" (Prov 27:22).

In Pal. all grain was grown during the winter. It was planted soon after the beginning of the rainy season in October. After the rainy season in March and April, the barley began to ripen and the wheat followed from a week to a month or more later, depending upon the altitude. About the first week in June the reaping began and the whole family, including the children, participated. Reaping was done with a hand sickle. The grain was then threshed on a bare, flat circular stretch of ground by having an ox or some other animal drag a threshing sledge round and round the floor. The threshed grain was then winnowed by tossing it into the air with a shovel to let the wind blow away the chaff. After that the grain was cleaned with a sieve and stored in jars, to be ground into flower with a handmill whenever there was need for bread.

Normally, the bran was not removed from the meal; when it was, it was called "fine flour." Newly ripened grain was eaten either fresh (Deut 23:25; Matt 12:1) or roasted and eaten as grits (Lev 2:14, 16). Rye and oats are not mentioned in the Bible, although oats were raised in Pal. The following kinds of grain are mentioned in Scripture:

1. Wheat. (חטה) . This was the most esteemed grain and was grown wherever the climate made it possible. The best wheat was grown in the fertile valleys of Jezreel, Samaria, and Galilee, and in the Hauron in Trans-Jordan, which in Rom. times was one of the great granaries of the empire.

2. Barley. (שערה) . This was the next most common grain of Israel. It was less expensive to grow than wheat because it could be raised on poorer soil, and it also had a shorter growing season. The ordinary food of the poor was barley bread (Judg 7:13; Ezek 4:9; John 6:9). Barley was also used to feed horses and cattle (1 Kings 4:28).

3. Spelt. (כסמת) . This was a hard-grained variety of wheat of poor quality. It was grown in Egypt (Exod 9:32) and in Pal. (Isa 28:25). Sometimes it was mixed with regular wheat to make bread (Ezek 4:9).

4. Millet. (דחן) . This grain was fed to poultry, but was also eaten by man. Ezekiel

A grain-vat (Roman). ©*Lev*

was commanded to use it as an ingredient of the bread he was ordered to prepare (Ezek 4:9). It is possible that the דחן includes other allied species of cereals, esp. Sorghum vulgare, a taller grass much cultivated in India and SW Asia.

In the NT various aspects of grain farming were used as illustrations by Jesus—the parables of the sower (Matt 13:3-23; Mark 4:3-20), the wheat and the weeds (Matt 13:24-30), the seed growing secretly (Mark 4:26-29), the rich man and his barns (Luke 12:16-21), and the metaphor of the grain of wheat buried in the ground to produce fruit (John 12:24); and by Paul, who also used the image of the buried grain of wheat, as a symbol of the resurrection of the body (1 Cor 15:37).

Grain stored in jars has been found in a large number of cities excavated by archeologists. Garstang, for example, found jars filled with wheat, barley, millet, and oats in the burned debris of Jericho; and it has been suggested that the full jars are evidence that the city was destroyed after the harvest had been gathered.

BIBLIOGRAPHY. M. S. and J. L. Miller, *Encyclopedia of Bible Life* (1944), 1-24; D. Baly, *The Geography of the Bible* (1957); R. Bridges and L. A. Weigle, *The Bible Word Book* (1960), 87; G. E. Wright, *Biblical Archaeology* (1962), 79.

S. Barabas

GRANARY. *See* Store-house; Store Cities.

GRAPE(S). *See* Vine, Vineyard.

GRASS (דשא, *tender*; חציר, *hay*; ירק, *green*; עשב, *herb*; χόρτος, *fodder*). Grass in its various forms is mentioned fifty-eight times in the Bible, sometimes as grass for grazing (Job 6:5), and in Jeremiah 50:11—"wanton as a heifer at grass"; sometimes as hay (Ps 37:2), and sometimes pictorially as in Isaiah 40:7—"the grass withers; the flower fades."

The prophets and psalmists describe man's days as grass, i.e. Psalm 103:15, "as for man, his days are as grass," and Isaiah 40:6, "all flesh is grass." In the NT also, the apostles take up the same theme. First Peter 1:24 states: "All flesh is like grass and all its glory like the flower of grass. The grass withers, and the flower falls," and James 1:11 states: "For the sun . . . withers the grass."

Grass also is used Biblically to describe plants as a whole. Our Lord says: "If God so clothes the grass of the field, which today is alive and tomorrow is thrown into the oven, will he not much more clothe you" (Matt 6:30). He was speaking primarily of flowering plants (*see* Lily), but there is a general reference to green plants.

It is wondered whether the Sorghum grass, *Sorghum vulgare,* was used by the hundreds of thousands of Israelites on the first morning of the Passover. It would have been difficult to obtain so much Hyssop (q.v.), but Sorghum grass was abundant, and was used in those days to make brushes.

The millet (Ezek 4:9) is an annual grass, bearing hundreds of small seeds.

W. E. Shewell-Cooper

GRASSHOPPER. *See* Locust.

GRATE, GRATING (מִכְבָּר, *anything twisted* or *woven, lattice-work*). An element of the altar of sacrifice.

The word occurs in Exodus 27:4; 35:16; 38:4, 5, 30; 39:39. This "grating" is described as a network of bronze (Exod 27:4) that surrounded the lower half of the altar (27:5). Therefore, the מִכְבָּר was apparently a "grating," or network, of bronze underneath a projecting ledge around the "brazen" altar of burnt-offering. Four rings were attached to it. Poles were then passed through the rings, and the altar was carried by them (27:4, 7). Various functions have been attributed to the grating itself; e.g., to support the fire, to protect the altar, to support the ledge above it, etc.

K. L. Barker

GRATITUDE (εὐχαριστία [1] *thankfulness, gratitude*; [2] *the rendering of thanks, thanksgiving*; [3] *Lord's Supper, Eucharist*, 1 Cor 10:16). The condition or quality of being grateful; an emotion or sentiment of thankfulness. A warm sense of appreciation for a kindness received; accompanied by a feeling of good will toward the benefactor, and a desire to repay the favor.

The term "gratitude" is absent from the KJV and occurs only once in the RSV (Acts 24:3) where it is a tr. of *eucharistía*. This Gr. word appears fifteen times in the NT and four times in the LXX (Esth 8:13; Wisd Sol 16:28; Ecclus 37:11; 2 Macc 2:27)—thus only one time in the canonical OT, and this in a disputed passage. (*See* the copy of Artaxerxes' letter in the text of the LXX.) In the KJV NT *eucharistía* is tr. "thanksgiving" nine times (2 Cor 4:15; 9:11, 12; Phil 4:6; Col 2:7; 4:2; 1 Tim 4:3, 4; Rev 7:12), "giving of thanks" three times (1 Cor 14:17; Eph 5:4; 1 Tim 2:1), "thanks" two times (1 Thess 3:9; Rev 4:9), and "thankfulness" one time (Acts 24:3).

Eucharistía has been employed since the time of Hippocrates (5th-4th cent. B.C.) and Menander (4th cent. B.C.). It is found in both Philo and Josephus. It is common in the inscrs., but there is perhaps only one known example in the papyri, viz., in a letter to a Gymnastic Club by the Emperor Claudius: he expresses gratification for games which were performed in his honor. In profane Gr. *eucharistía* never occurs in the sense of "thanks" or "giving of thanks"; in Biblical Gr. this usage is confined always to a religious sense. Origen equates εὐχαριστία with εὐχαριτία, "the mark of fine training."

No motif more adequately recalls the nature of Biblical faith than "gratitude" (or thanksgiving). With three insignificant exceptions (Luke 17:9; Acts 24:3; Rom 16:4) thanks invariably is rendered unto God. It appears only within the context of the covenant relationship. Moreover, it is always prompted by a concrete act of the covenant God in human affairs.

In the OT the verb "give thanks" is ידה, the basic meaning of which is "throw" or "cast"; the fem. noun is תודה ("thanksgiving"). Thanksgiving comprises the special note of the Psalter; yet Israel's gratitude to Jehovah rings throughout her history. King David appointed certain Levites "to invoke, to thank, and to praise the Lord" (1 Chron 16:4). This practice was continued by Solomon (2 Chron 5:13; 7:6), Hezekiah (31:2), and by the exiles who returned from Babylon (Neh 11:17).

Thanksgiving was prominent in Israel's cultic worship. Festival processions en route to Zion filled the air "with glad shouts and songs of thanksgiving" (Ps 42:4). Their entrance into the Temple was with thanksgiving (95:2; 100:4); the service itself contained melodies of gratitude (147:7). All the tribes ascended to Jerusalem "to give thanks to the name of the Lord" (122:4).

Israel thanked Jehovah because He ever remained faithful to His covenant with His people (100:4). God's faithfulness was manifested in many ways as He protected the Jewish nation from external foes (7:17).

In the NT thanksgiving to God both for His work (Luke 17:16) and for His person (Luke 2:38) is a major theme. The concept of thanksgiving abounds in Paul's epistles (Rom 1:8; 7:25; 2 Cor 9:15; Col 1:12; 1 Tim 1:12). The NT writers urged their fellow Christians to be grateful (Eph 5:4; Col 3:15; Heb 13:15; James 1:2, 9; 1 Pet 4:12-14). Among the Gentiles a lack of gratitude was coupled with an absence of the true faith (Rom 1:21).

Gratitude is pleasing to God (Ps 92:1) because (1) it is commanded (Ps 50:14; Phil 4:6), (2) Christ set the example (Matt 11:25; 26:27; John 6:11; 11:41), and (3) the heavenly host is engaged in it (Rev 4:9; 7:11, 12; 11:16, 17). It appears in psalms (1 Chron 16:7) and ministers were appointed to express it publicly (1 Chron 16:4, 7; 23:30; 2 Chron 31:2).

Gratitude should be offered (1) to God (Ps 50:14), (2) to Christ (1 Tim 1:12), (3) through Christ (Rom 1:8; Col 3:17; Heb 13:15), (4) in the name of Christ (Eph 5:20), (5) in both private (Dan 6:10) and public worship (Ps 35:18), (6) at the remembrance of God's holiness (Ps 30:4; 97:12), (7) before eating (John 6:11; Acts 27:35), (8) upon the completion of great tasks (Neh 12:31, 40), (9) in everything (1 Thess 5:18), and (10) at all times (Eph 1:16; 5:20; 1 Thess 1:2).

Gratitude can be expressed for (1) the goodness and mercy of God (Ps 106:1; 107:1; 136:1-3), (2) the gift of Christ (2 Cor 9:15), (3) Christ's power and reign (Rev 11:17), (4) deliverance from indwelling sin (Rom 7:23-25), (5) the nearness of God's presence (Ps 75:1), (6) our desire to give for God's work (1 Chron 29:6-14), (7) the supply of our physical needs (Rom 14:6, 7; 1 Tim 4:3, 4), (8) victory over death and the grave (1 Cor 15:57), (9) wisdom and might (Dan 2:23), (10) triumph of the Gospel (2 Cor 2:14), (11) the reception of God's Word (1 Thess 2:13), (12) conversion of souls (Rom 6:17), (13) faith (Rom 1:8; 2 Thess 1:3), love (2 Thess 1:3), and zeal (2 Cor 8:16) manifested in others, (14) grace bestowed upon others (1 Cor 1:4; Phil 1:3-5; Col 1:3-6), (15) ministers appointed by God (1 Tim 1:12), (16) all men (1 Tim 2:1), and (17) everything God permits (2 Cor 9:11; Eph 5:20).

Gratitude ought to be accompanied by (1) intercession for others (1 Tim 2:1; 2 Tim 1:3; Philem 4), (2) prayer (Neh 11:17; Phil 4:6; Col 4:2), and (3) praise (Ps 92:1; Heb 13:15).

Believers are exhorted to be grateful (Ps 105:1; Col 3:15). They should (1) resolve to offer (Ps 18:49; 30:12), (2) abound in faith with (Col 2:7), (3) magnify the Lord by (Ps 69:30), (4) enter God's house with (100:4), (5) come before God with (95:2), (6) offer habitually (Dan 6:10), and (7) present sacrifices of (Ps 116:17).

The wicked are averse to thanksgiving (Rom 1:21); hypocrites mar it with boasting (Luke 18:11). Biblical examples of true gratitude are (1) the Levites (2 Chron 5:12), (2) David (1 Chron 29:13), (3) Jonah (Jonah 2:9), (4) Daniel (Dan 2:33), (5) Simeon (Luke 2:28), (6) Anna (Luke 2:38), and (7) Paul (Acts 28:15). Gratitude lay at the very heart of Biblical faith because it formed the only proper response to what God had done for His people.

The Dead Sea scroll of Thanksgiving Psalms or *Hodayoth* (1QH) contains c. thirty-five fragmentary or complete hymns in which the author renders thanks for acts of God's kindness. Most of these psalms begin with the expression, "I thank thee, O Lord." Their style is reminiscent of the Heb. Psalter.

BIBLIOGRAPHY. J. Smith and R. Lee, *Handfuls On Purpose,* VI (1947), 70; J. Calvin, *The Institutes of the Christian Religion* (1949), II. viii. 16; III. xx. 28; W. G. Scroggie, *The Psalms,* IV (1951), 251; M. Luther, *Lectures On Galatians,* Vol. XXVI in *Works* (c1963), 43, 138, 283, 376f.; H. H. Rowly, *A Companion to the Bible* (1963), 132; W. Eichrodt, *Theology of the Old Testament,* II (1964), 271, 299, 372; G. Von Rad, *Old Testament Theology,* I (1967), 224-226.

R. E. PERRY

GRAVE בעי (found in the KJV of Job 30:24, an obscure verse, but not in the RSV); קבורה (tr. as *grave* in the KJV and RSV); קבר (tr. as *grave* by KJV, but sometimes as *tomb* in the RSV); שׁאול, *she'ōl* (always *grave* in the

Tomb, with sculpture memorial provided by an American, in the Catacombs near Rome. © Lev

Jewish catacombs at Beth-Shear'im near Haifa. One of the main entrances. ©*Lev*

KJV, but *Sheol* in the RSV); שחת (Job 33:22—KJV *grave*; RSV *pit*); ᾅδης (1 Cor 15:55—KJV *grave*; RSV *death*); μνῆμα (Rev 11:9—KJV *grave*; RSV *tomb*); μνημεῖον KJV *grave*; RSV always *tomb*).

In contrast with the Greeks and Romans whose custom it was to cremate the dead, with the Jews it was a matter of piety, as Tacitus says (Hist. V. 5), "to bury rather than to burn dead bodies." Embalming was not done in Israel, although corpses were often anointed with spices; also coffins were not used. Among ancient Jews graves were simply dug in the earth, as they are in modern times. However, usually the dead were placed in a family tomb, either a natural cave or in a cave hewn out of rock on a hillside. In the cave there were shelves on which the bodies were laid. The entrance was closed with a large circular stone set up on its edge. Once a year the entrance to the tomb was whitewashed. Ordinary graves were marked by a heap of crude stones, but often pillars were set up as memorials to the dead. The graves of the prophets and holy persons were carefully maintained. In NT times, the place of burial was uniformly outside the city or village; only kings and prophets were allowed to be buried within the city. The lack of proper burial was regarded in ancient times as a great indignity or judgment of God—one of the worst calamities that could befall a person. *See* BURIAL.

BIBLIOGRAPHY. R. de Vaux, *Ancient Israel* (1961), 56-61.

S. BARABAS

GRAVEL (חצץ, *gravel*, and מעה, *grain* [of sand]). Small pebbles.

חצץ is used fig. in Proverbs 20:17 of a liar, showing the consequences of deceitfulness, and in Lamentations 3:16 of the Lord's dealings with a sufferer ("He has made my teeth grind on gravel"). The plural of מעה occurs in Isaiah 48:19, where RSV correctly trs. it as "gravel" (this once legitimate connotation of Eng. "gravel" is now obsolete).

K. L. BARKER

GRAVEN IMAGE (פסל, from the root meaning "to carve"). An image carved from wood, stone, or metal. The difference between a graven and a molten image was that the former was carved, and the latter was cast from molten metal.

The Israelites were expressly forbidden to make any idolatrous representations of deity, whether graven (Exod 20:4, 5; Deut 5:8) or molten (Exod 32:4; 34:17). The second commandment in the Decalogue prohibits the making of such images in the form of anything seen in the heavens, on the earth, or in the sea. All ancient peoples except the Israelites made graven images to represent the various gods. The Israelites were commanded by Moses to

Bronze god (graven image) overlaid with gold and silver; from Minet el-Beida, 1500-1300 B.C. © *Louvre*

destroy all Canaanite forms of idolatry, including graven images (Deut 7:5; 12:3). In spite of this, throughout their history (Judg 17:3, 4; 2 Kings 21:7; Isa 42:17), until the return from the Babylonian captivity, they often succumbed to the idolatrous ways of their neighbors.

There has been considerable discussion concerning whether or not all imitative art is forbidden by the second commandment. In deciding this question, it must be kept in mind that certain figures were in fact made by God's own command. Both the Tabernacle and the Temple contained many objects that required the arts of carving and engraving, e.g. the two cherubim in the holy of holies (Exod 25:18, 20); the floral ornamentation of the golden lampstand (25:34); the embroidered hangings of the sanctuary (ch. 26); and the bronze serpent (Num 21:8, 9). In the Temple, moreover, there were various figures on the walls, and the molten sea rested on twelve bronze oxen.

BIBLIOGRAPHY. J. Pedersen, *Israel: Its Life and Culture,* III, IV (1947); W. Eichrodt, *Theology of the Old Testament,* I (1961), 115-119.

S. Barabas

GRAY (שׂיבה, *hoary head, old age*). A color produced by a mixture of black and white.

The Heb. verb (שׂיב) and the noun (שׂיבה) denoting "gray" are used of "gray hair" as an indication of "old age," and they may often be rendered thus. "Gray" does not occur in NT. There is an interesting related passage in the Ugaritic Tale of Aqhat (VI: 36, 37): "Glaze will be poured on my head, lime upon my pate" (both as a sign of hoariness and old age; for the word, "glaze," and its attestation in Prov 26:23, cf. K. A. Kitchen, *Ancient Orient and Old Testament,* p. 163).

K. L. Barker

GREAT, GREATNESS, a number of words are so tr. Two Heb. terms are tr. often: 1. גדול, "great," "of large proportion," applicable to man, animals, mountains, weight, age, dimensions, etc. (Gen 1:21, et al.) 2. רב, "many," much, numerous, an ancient Sem. root. The Akkad. appears in the OT in the compounds Rab-Mag, "Chief of Magi" (Jer 39:3); Rab-Saris, "Chief Eunuch" (Jer 39:3; 2 Kings 18:17); Rab-Shakeh, "Chief Officer" (2 Kings 18:17, et al.; Isa 36:2, et al.). The term refers to the quantity of things and the severity of action (Gen 6:5, et al.). The Heb. lang. has a peculiarity which allows the intensity of verbs to be indicated by an internal or suffixal modification. In many passages these morphological distinctions are indicated by adding the adjective "great" or the adverb "greatly" in the tr. (Ezek 30:16; Hos 1:2, et al.). In respect to human beings the concept "great" or "greatness" implies some characteristic about the person. It is connected with the reputation, "name," of the individual. All such titles in the Sem. lang(s). are functional.

In the NT two Gr. words are so tr.: 1. μέγας, "large," "great" can be applied in a qualitative as well as quantitative sense. It appears in many aspects, "large, spacious" (Mark 14:15); "older" (Rom 9:12); "rich" (Heb 10:35); "loud" (Rev 1:10); "important" (Eph 5:32) and many similar meanings. The other common Gr. term is πολύς, "much," "many," "numerous" used mostly and far more frequently than *megas* in a quantitative sense (Matt 7:22, et al.).

W. White, Jr.

GREAT BIBLE, THE. *See* Versions (English).

GREAT LIZARD. No reptile is known by this name now. *See* Lizard.

GREAT OWL. *See* Owl.

GREAT SEA (הים הגדול) . A Biblical name for the sea that lies between the European and African continents; better known as the Mediterranean Sea.

It was sometimes called simply "the sea" by the Hebrews (Num 13:29; Josh 16:8; Jonah 1:4). It was referred to most often as "the Great Sea" (Num 34:7; Josh 9:1; Ezek 47:15) because of its size. It was also called the "western sea" (Deut 11:24; 34:2; Joel 2:20; Zech 14:8; "hinder," "utmost," or "uttermost," KJV), because of its location in relation to the land of the Hebrews. Once it is called "sea, to Joppa," RSV; "sea of Joppa," KJV (Ezra 3:7), and once "sea of the Philistines" (Exod 23:31). In the NT the general term "seaside" (θάλασσα) is found (Acts 10:6, 32).

The Mediterranean is 2,196 m. in length from Gibraltar to the Lebanon coast and varies in width from c. 600 m. to 100 m. with a maximum depth of c. 2.7 m. It is the main existing fragment of a great ocean called by geologists Tethys that existed at least from the late Carboniferous period to early Tertiary times. Because it is largely an enclosed sea, its saline content is abnormally high. Its divisions include the Aegean, Ionian, Adriatic, Tyrrhenian, and Ligurian seas. Only a narrow strip along the Palestinian coast receives any appreciable amount of rainfall, and the rapid transition to arid desert country is quite pronounced in the E and on the S.

Many great Mediterranean civilizations of ancient times were maritime powers (Egyptians, Phoenicians, Greeks, Romans) but seafaring and sea-trading played almost no part at all in Israel's history and economy. In spite of the long coastline, the sea exerted only a marginal influence on Israel. This fact may best be explained by the absence of good harbors along the Palestinian coastline. There have been a few harbors of relative importance along the coast, e.g., Ashkelon, Dor, Joppa,

One of the most important cities on the Great Sea is Joppa. This is an airview showing Joppa and the Tel-Aviv shoreline, with the Plain of Sharon in the background. © *M.P.S.*

and Acco, but a large part of the shoreline, particularly in the S, is backed by a strip of shifting sand, sometimes several m. in width, that blocks the approach to the shore. By contrast, the coastline of Syria played an important part in the development of that area, for there are many excellent natural harbors along the Syro-Phoenician coast. Therefore, maritime trade was highly developed there even in the most ancient periods. Byblos was a noted maritime power in the third and second millennia and Canaanite Tyre and Sidon during the early centuries of the first millennium B.C.

Solomon built a fleet of ships at Ezion-geber on the Red Sea and operated it with the assistance of the Phoenicians (1 Kings 9:26, 27). Jehoshaphat's fleet was wrecked at Ezion-geber (22:48). However, the Hebrews never did undertake a similar venture on the Mediterranean.

The cosmic sources of water that were conceived in mythological imagery to be dragons are absent in the Genesis account of Creation, so little was the influence of the sea on the Hebrews. Though *tehom* (deep) (Gen 1:2) may be related etymologically with *tiamat* (dragon), there is no direct derivation or association implied. Several scriptures make it clear that the Hebrews believed that God had absolute power over the seas (Ps 89:9; Isa 23:11; Jonah 1:4, 9).

In the early Christian era, the Mediterranean world was ruled by Rome. Her supremacy in the W was established by the defeat of Hannibal of Carthage in the battle of Zama in 202 B.C. In the E, conquest by Pompey in 63 B.C. made the Mediterranean (as the Romans liked to call it) "Our Sea." Under the rule of Augustus (d. A.D. 14) and his successors, the Mediterranean world experienced for two centuries the *Pax Romana,* a period of peace which it had never had before or has enjoyed since.

BIBLIOGRAPHY. W. F. Albright, *Archaeology and the Religion of Israel* (1942), 148, 149;

J Finegan, *Light from the Ancient Past* (1946), 209, 210; H. G. Wells, *The Outline of History* (1949), *see* Index; T. Herdman, "Mediterranean Sea," EBr, XV (1957), 209; M. Noth, *The History of Israel* (1960), 13; Y. Aharoni, *The Land of the Bible* (1967), 9, 16.

F. B. HUEY, JR.

GREAT SYNAGOGUE. *See* SYNAGOGUE.

GREAVES. *See* ARMS, ARMOR.

GREECE, GRECIA

1. The name
2. Geography
3. Prehistory
4. The Mycenaean civilization
5. The city-states
6. Colonization
7. The Persian wars
8. The Confederacy of Delos
9. The Golden Age
10. The collapse
11. The fourth century
12. The empire of Alexander
13. Hellenism

1. The name. Greece, Lat. *Graecia*, whence *Graeci* or Greeks, was a geographical term properly applicable to an Indo-European group in the NW corner of the southeastern Mediterranean peninsula of Europe, opposite the "heel" of the Italian peninsula. It is a not infrequent phenomenon of geographical nomenclature that an area and its inhabitants acquire a name abroad from that area or contact first familiar to those who bestow and perpetuate the name. Hence "Palestine" from the name of the Philistine tribe settled on the southwestern corner of the land, the "Gaza Strip" of today. The French provided the term "Franks" for all Europeans among the people of the Middle E, whose first significant contact with the W was with the armies of the French Crusaders. The Greeks themselves called their country Hellas, and the people Hellenes, though there seems to be some evidence that this name too was originally applicable to a small tribe in southern Thessaly (Homer, Il. 2.683, 4). The name seems to have spread S in the wake of the Dorian invasions, the last wave of tribal migration to infiltrate the peninsula. Although Homer, the earliest Gr. writer used the term Hellenes and Pan-hellenes, the Greeks generally were named by him in tribal appelations—Achaeans, Argives, Danai; so in the OT, Javan and Dodanim may refer to Ionians (the Greeks of Asia Minor) and Danai. The name Greece (KJV Grecia) occurs specifically three times in Daniel (8:21; 10:20; 11:2) and once in Zechariah (9:13). "Grecians" in the NT is ambiguous, referring sometimes to Greeks proper (Acts 11:20—in which contexts KJV usually employs "Greeks" quite correctly: John 12:20; Acts 14:1; 16:1), and sometimes to Jews domiciled in the Hel. cities (Acts 6:1; 9:29).

2. Geography. Europe fronts the Mediterranean with three peninsulas, two of them formed by the seaward intrusion of the continent's mountain system. Geographically considered, Greece is the shattered southeastern end of the mountain core of southern and central Europe. J. B. Bury remarked that Illyricum in the E would have closely resembled Spain in the W if its structure had been cut off N of Thessaly. It would have been a solid mass of land almost touching Asia in the E, as Spain almost touches Africa in the W. But Greece, the southern and seaward extension of this land and mountain mass, has features of its own to mark it off geographically from Spain's firm square and Italy's spined ridge of land. Greece is a mountainous headland of tumbled terrain, narrow valley plains, ranges, peaks, broken from W to E across its midst by a deep rift, indented by the intruding sea, and scattered around by several groups of islands, notably those of the Ionian Sea (incongruously on the Adriatic shore though Ionia was in western Asia Minor), and of the Aegean (the Sporades, and the Cyclades). The Dodecanese islands and Crete, though not part of Greece proper, were geographically, ethnologically, and historically associated with the mainland. The geography of the whole area was determined by the submergence in the Mediterranean of a mountain complex that begins with the Alps, sweeps E, N and S and finds ultimate emphasis in the Taurus Range of Anatolia and in the strong E-W formations of Crete. In peninsula, upland, and island, as Bury said (*History of Greece*, p. 1), one can trace the ribs of a framework "which a convulsion of nature bent and shivered, for the service, as it turned out, of the human race."

It is a notable fact that Gr. history cannot be extricated from its landscape. The rugged peninsula, where the tribes of the Hellenes found precarious lodging place, was no land made for unity. It drove its inhabitants into the arms of the sea. Island, narrow coastal plain, and river valley provided foothold and dwelling. The convulsions of nature that had tumbled the land, and almost divided it in two, had decreed of old that the Greeks should invent the city-state, and thereby democracy and dialectic philosophy, and that history in the dynamic little land should be fragmented, varied, and full of strife.

The very niggardliness of nature, sparing of topsoil and tilth land even before the human folly of deforestation, set ancient limitation on the size and growth of communities, and turned men's eyes seaward to open highways of trade and colonization. Like the Phoenicians, hemmed between the mountains and the sea, with the incomparable cedar growing on Lebanon behind, and navigable water before, the Greeks became inevitably seafarers, colonists, internationalists. It was the fiat of geography born of geology.

The temple of Apollo in Corinth (Greece). Corinth commanded all of the land routes from central Greece into the Peloponnesus. © *Lev*

3. Prehistory. Perhaps the beginnings of Gr. history proper can be set about the year 800 B.C., the date of the epic poems, when the Aegean world was emerging from a Dark Age of some four centuries. "Prehistory" covers the preceding twenty centuries, and those civilizations that have left their rich remains for archeology to recover and to leave traces of their history, their rise and fall, and their dominant personalities in myth, legend, and tradition.

Stone age cultures have left traces from the Thessalian plain in the N to Crete in the S. The Bronze Age came to the Aegean perhaps by way of Asia Minor in the third millennium B.C., and mass migration, prob. of the Indo-European peoples who colonized most of Europe, began at this period with wandering groups following the sun, and infiltrating the mainland and the archipelago.

The first civilization of consequence reached its full flower in the island of Crete, which from its geographical position was in contact with the eastern end of the Mediterranean and Egypt, as well as exposed to the human pressure of the N and the Aegean. This, the "Minoan" civilization, a name derived from the legendary king, Minos, was based on sea power and sea-borne trade. It was cultural, artistic, and influential. Spacious, unwalled palaces speak of the wealth, ability, and security of the islanders. In the excellence of the work of architect, painter, and goldsmith the Minoan culture rivaled Egypt. Two forms of script have survived. "Linear B" has been deciphered, and proves to be a primitive Gr., but it is impossible to say whether this fact does more than indicate the race of a dominant minority, or even a language of trade. If the Cretans were an early wave of Indo-European invasion, perhaps overlaying a neolithic or "Mediterranean" aboriginal stock, that would at least suggest a pattern that history is in the habit of repeating—for example, the successive waves of infiltration into Britain—the Belgae, Romans, Germanic tribes, Scandinavians, each divided into numerous ripples. The W coast of America, and the S Pacific islands can demonstrate the same periodicity of occupation. The Cretan civilization collapsed about 1400 B.C., somewhat mysteriously, and due perhaps to a complex of natural disaster, social upheaval, and invasion from the N.

4. The Mycenaean civilization. The infiltrating tribes of the third millennium before Christ took longer to organize on the mainland. In Crete, whether it was first settled, or only taken over and ruled by members of this Indo-European folk-wandering, the island itself imposed a certain unity, and a framework for development, which was rapid as far as such distant evidence can be read, and certainly distinguished.

The first mainland settlements were around Corinth, the Argolis, and on Aegina. From these focal points they spread N into the fertile Boeotian plain, where Thebes was later to be dominant, S to Messenia, and W to the Ionian islands, chiefly to Ithaca. This so-called Helladic civilization was not a high or affluent one, except that their pottery was of a fine quality. It is not certain whether these villagers and pastoralists spoke an Indo-European speech. They were not literate.

The first recognizable Greeks came with fire and sword, if the archeological record of conflagration and ruin is read aright, c. 2000 B.C. They may be called the Achaeans, and it is not certain whether they came through Asia Minor or down the Balkan peninsula. It was the contact of this Middle Helladic civilization with Crete that, from 1600 B.C. onward, produced the Mycenaean civilization. It was a fruitful union in which some have sought to see "Minoan imagination yoked to Helladic restraint and order." The phrase might mean more, if there were more certain knowledge of the ethnic relationships of the tribes and peoples concerned.

The Mycenaean civilization takes its name from the great fortress of Mycenae in the eastern Peloponnesus, and the period of its greatness is notable for the building of great palaces and mighty fortifications, the development of a strong militaristic feudalism, and vast wealth. The fact that Linear B script is found on the mainland and in Crete may mean that by the 15th cent. Mycenae had actually conquered Crete. Certainly the destruction of the Cretan civilization about 1400 B.C., which prob. followed the ruin of Crete from natural causes, such as earthquake, and internal strife, can hardly have been other than the work of Mycenaean invasion.

About 1200 B.C. occurred an event difficult to assess, the Trojan war, which, as Rom. Horace wrote, found a poet who has lived in the imagination of the world. Troy lay on an escarpment with a narrow intervening coastal plain on the Asiatic shore of the Dardanelles. It was an old post of power, as the stratified remains of nine Troys heaped on the site indicate. The story of Helen and the great expedition to recover her, need not concern the reader. The Trojan conflict certainly concerns a clash of nations, or a vast internecine upheaval, the interpretation depending upon who they were who held the Trojan stronghold. The orthodox view is that the subsequent decline of the Mycenaean civilization was due to the blood-letting, the destruction, and the social strain of this great military adventure. The divided, broken, and weakened culture was ripe for the so-called Dorian invasion.

This was another wave of the same folk-migration that had marked the last millennium. The orthodox view is that the more primitive Dorians like the Saxons, assaulting a weakened Roman-Britain, came in as a destructive force, and gave Greece and the Aegean a Dark Age of four centuries, across which the Homeric poems look, preserving for another age the folk memories of epic strife in which Myceneae went down before the Dorians.

Professor Rhys Carpenter, late of Bryn Mawr, has suggested another view. His climatological studies, linked with the archeology of the period, seems to indicate that the Mycenaean civilization died of drought when the rain belts of southern Europe, determined by the meteorological and climatological conditions in the Sahara area, moved N. In consequence the great centers of Mycenae were slowly depopulated, as a weakened people sought the rainier coasts and westward-facing slopes watered by the Zephyr winds. The Dorians inherited an empty land, if this thesis can be maintained, and a good land, as the more favorable and moist weather pattern gradually reestablished itself in Greece and the Aegean. The final answer to this question of history awaits further knowledge.

5. The city-states. From 800 B.C. onward, Greece was reorganizing itself. Civilization, recovering from the trauma of invasion, was building new patterns of life. The city-states emerged as scattered villages syncretized for protection. The villages of Attica, for example, merged their strength under the masters of the Acropolis, and the power of Athens began its momentous growth; so, too, Thebes and Sparta. In the process, monarchy passed to oligarchy. In the process, too, individual "tyrants" arose. In the Greek sense of this word, which appears to be merely a Lydian term for "ruler," a tyrant was not necessarily a cruel despot. But since "power corrupts," as Lord Acton put it, "and absolute power corrupts absolutely," there came the coloring that the word inevitably took on.

In this period, the history of Greece is necessarily varied and fragmented. Athens successfully resisted "tyranny" in 630 B.C., and Solon, a rich member of an emerging industrial class, in 594 B.C. was given power to institute constitutional reforms on broadly democratic lines. After another crisis of tyranny from 561 to 528 B.C., finally in 507 B.C., one Cleisthenes introduced a genuinely democratic constitution in which the assembly of citizens had sovereign power. Sparta, meanwhile, in which a Dorian group sought over a

The Acropolis of Athens with the Parthenon which dominates the scene. Paul visited Athens on his second Missionary journey and addressed the Council of the Areopagus there (Acts 17:18). ©*M.P.S.*

long period to maintain a kind of "apartheid" over a subject population, organized herself on the basis of the savage code of the half-legendary Lycurgus—a rigid, uncultured, military society, whose most lamentable achievement was the destruction of Athens in the great war of 431 to 400 B.C., a conflict from which Athens never quite recovered.

All the city-states functioned independently in all the processes and relationships of peace and war. They present a picture of universal history in microcosm. Whereas it is true that there is properly no history of Greece, but rather the history of the Gr. states, it is also true that, despite this ultimately fatal political disunity and dismemberment (with the local jealousy and debilitating petty nationalism that made it impossible for Greece to face Persia, then Macedon, and finally Rome, as a unit of power), there was a consciousness of spiritual oneness. The great sanctuaries of Olympia with its pan-Hellenic games, and Delphi with its oracle, called the "common hearth of Greece," stand for a sense of common origin, common heritage, and common destiny, which, had it found wider political expression, might have changed European history. The world today faces the same vast problem, and Greek history assumes challenging significance.

6. Colonization. Greek migration to islands and more remote spots along the Mediterranean coastline began with the pressure of the Dorian inroads, or the climatological changes that are alleged to have played their simultaneous part. In discussing the geography of Greece, it was pointed out that the limits imposed by nature on the arable land available enforced emigration. The process continued over several countries. It was, after all, only the maritime extension and projection of the migratory movements that had populated the Mediterranean basin.

From 770 to 550 B.C., with trade vigorous in the inland seas, the process of colonization assumed immense significance for human culture and future European history. Colonies were planted, in the familiar form of city-states, on the coasts of Spain, of Southern France, the whole of southern Italy and Sicily, the Black Sea, and the African coast to the Gulf of Syrtis from almost the Nile Delta. Greek colonies generally did not penetrate or seek to subdue the hinterland. They remained independent, and some of them, Massilia, Tarentum, Syracuse, for example, became powerful

Another view of the Parthenon. ©*Walvoord*

states. Rome, in its early growth, and southern Italy generally, were strongly influenced by the transplanted Greek civilization of what came to be called Magna Graecia, the complex of Greek city-states right around the western and southern coasts of Italy from Cumae to Tarentum.

7. The Persian wars. Ionia was the name given to the Greek settlements on the western end of Asia Minor. In the 7th cent., these city-states, in which Greek art, science, and philosophy had struck their first roots, fell under the control and domination of Lydia, the inland empire based on Sardis. In 546 B.C. Lydia fell under the expanding power of Persia, which was reaching for the Aegean, as it was also pressing into India and Egypt in one of history's great movements of imperialism. In 499 B.C. the Ionian cities rose in revolt against Persia, and Athens, helping the rebels in their hopeless fight, incurred the wrath of Darius, the Pers. king. He attacked Attica from the sea in 490 but was repulsed at his point of landing, at Marathon, by the Athenians.

Ten years later, Xerxes, Darius' successor, dispatched by land and sea a mighty army determined to overwhelm Greece. Halted for a brief time at Thermopylae, by the famous Spartan Three Hundred, the great armada rolled into Attica and burned Athens, whose population had withdrawn to the island of Salamis. In the strait of Salamis, in one of the decisive battles of the world's history, the Greek fleets, about half Athenian, shattered the Pers. naval arm, upon which the vast expedition depended for communications and supply. Xerxes could do nothing else but withdraw. He left a strong army in Boeotia, and the Greeks, attaining an unusual measure of unity, mustered 110,000 men and broke the remaining remnant of the Pers. invasion at Plataea. Salamis and Plataea were decisive. Asia was not to dominate Europe. The Turks were the only comparable foe, twenty centuries later. A remnant of the Pers. fleet was broken up at Mycale, also in 479 B.C., and Greece was free to continue her system of government, which found its most significant expression in Athens.

8. The Confederacy of Delos. After their victory at Mycale, the confederate Greeks decided to pursue the war against Persia and liberate the Asiatic Greeks. A fleet was fitted out and placed under the command of the

Spartan Pausanias. The Spartans had from the first shown a strong disinclination to incur responsibilities on behalf of the Asiatic Greeks, or to embark on maritime enterprises. In 476 the allies, disgusted with the arrogance of Pausanias, transferred the command to the Athenians, and Pausanias was recalled to answer to charges of treasonable correspondence with Persia. His successor's orders were disregarded, and Aristeides, the Athenian, was acknowledged as admiral, an arrangement in which the Spartans were forced to acquiesce. The Peloponnesian squadron returned home, and Athens, now left to take the lead, entered into a compact with the allies. This was the origin of the Confederacy of Delos. Its object was the expulsion of the Persians from Europe and the security of the Greeks of Asia Minor and the adjoining islands. A definite obligation, either in ships, men, or money, was imposed upon every member, and general conditions were regulated in a common synod, appointed to meet annually in the temple of Apollo at Delos, where the treasure was placed. Special officers collected the money, ships being sent around the Aegean every spring for this purpose. The first assessment of tribute amounted to 460 talents, payable partly in ships, partly in money.

Such was the Confederacy, at first, without doubt, a just league for resisting the Persians and protecting the Aegean Sea against piracy —a league due to the fear of the Ionians, not to the ambition of Athens. How the transition from leadership to empire took place is not difficult to conjecture, for in any confederacy where there is one member unusually prominent, such a result must follow.

Within ten years the Persians had been driven from Europe and restricted to the inland of western Asia Minor. Then, as the danger from Persia became more remote, the necessity for personal service seemed to many of the allies no longer imperative, and their distaste for its duties led them to commute it for a money payment. The result of this was to put Athens in possession of a steady revenue for a constantly increasing navy, and to inspire her citizens with the idea that they were military overlords with a body of tribute-paying subjects. This change in the relations between Athens and the allies became further intensified when the treasure was removed from Delos to Athens about 455 B.C., and the management of the affairs of the Confederacy fell almost exclusively into Athenian hands. Even before this, however, there had been revolts and attempts to secede, all of which had been sternly suppressed by Athens; these became increasingly frequent, as the rule of Athens grew more despotic and her misappropriation of the tribute to her own needs became more open. Under the administration of Pericles, discontent reached a dangerous height. The tribute now amounted to 600 talents, not an excessive sum considering the number of members. The only outgoings, for many years, had been the support of sixty Athenian triremes in the Aegean; there was a surplus of nearly 10,000 talents in the Athenian acropolis, and vast sums had been expended by Pericles on the beautifying of Athens and other purely Attic interests. It was useless for Pericles to urge in answer that, as long as Athens secured the safety of the allies, she was justified in dealing with the surplus revenue as she chose. Clearly, the original object of the Confederacy had been lost, and Athens had become—partly from force of circumstances, and later from design—the mistress of the 249 cities whose names stood upon her tribute lists in the time of Pericles; of these Chios, Samos, and Lesbos alone still possessed navies.

Thus was the scene set for the clash with Sparta that came inevitably in 431 B.C. and ended the period of Athenian greatness, and half a cent. of astounding creativity, to which a paragraph must be devoted.

9. The Golden Age. It is the fate of empires to be viewed differently by their immediate beneficiaries, and by those who pay, or imagine that they pay the bill. So it was with Rome and Britain, and with Athens. Athens, first gratefully accepted as a leader, became the burdensome imperialist. At the same time, in the eyes of the Athenians, and all who from then till now have been entranced by the spectacle of her achievement in the realms of art, thought, lit., and the mind's creativity, a Golden Age was enjoyed.

The Greeks had emerged from a day of grimmest peril in the wars with Persia. The Athenian response to this challenge was an

Temple of Athena Nike on the Acropolis, Athens (c. 426 B.C.).

Temple of Zeus at Pergamum. ©V.E.

outburst of spiritual energy scarcely paralleled in history. In a mood of exaltation that believed all things possible to the conquerors of Persia, the people of Attica set to work. They equipped their farmlands with buildings which, three generations later, their Theban enemies found it worthwhile to dismantle and transfer bodily to Boeotia. They rebuilt their shattered city and filled it with monuments, some of which have survived the battering of twenty-three centuries, and stand today a monument to the worth of human effort when willing hands work as one under the inspiration of a grand idea. "In this work," says a modern historian, "Periclean Athens displayed a vitality far superior to that of postwar France. When the French recovered the battered shell of Rheims Cathedral, they performed a pious restoration of each shattered stone and splintered statue. When the Athenians found the Hekatompedon burned down to the foundations, they let the foundations lie, and proceeded, on a new site, to create the Parthenon" (A. J. Toynbee, *The Study of History,* II, p. 110).

Socially, the characteristics of that age were two. There was first a notable union between culture and democracy (we are not concerned at the moment with the differences between Athenian democracy and ours, nor to assess the part slave labor played in Athenian culture and self-expression). In 5th cent. Athens, democracy, in a real and significant form, was certainly known. That reality found a voice in lit. The partnership between culture and the Athenian way of life was no artificial product of such patronage as that by which Maecenas rallied the pens of Rome to the service of a new regime. The praise was spontaneous, an undercurrent rather than a stream.

When Aeschylus, for example, wrote his *Prometheus Bound,* he had primarily no political end in view. His theme was the vast problem of suffering and pain. He was hazarding the bold solution of a doctrine of perfectibility applied to God Himself. It was the ancient question of the prophet Habakkuk that the poet had in mind in his tremendous drama of the tormented demigod. And yet the notions of freedom that filled the air and the writer's mind color the whole picture and find involuntary expression in the passing remark, the aside, the ejaculation. For instance:

For tyranny, it seems, is never free
From this distemper—faithlessness to friends.
Wilt thou thus kick against the pricks, aware
That our harsh monarch owes account to none?

* * *

is it plain to you?—
The tyrant of the gods is violent
In all his ways

* * *

But who shall strip his tyrant sceptre from him?
Himself by his own empty-headed counsels.

* * *

Nay, let him reign supreme and work his will
For his brief day—he shall not rule for long.

The same passion for freedom and hatred of all tyranny color the characterization. It marks Hermes as the cunning menial of a royal court; Io as the maiden victim of the unbridled selfishness of kings; Oceanus, so confident and comfortable, as the compromising lover of soft ease, on whose acquiescence all dictatorship is built; and Oceanus' daughters as the unexpected opposition, whose innocence and ignorance, when fired with knowledge, are ready to face death for a name and an ideal.

The first two books of Thucydides present the same phenomenon. In the reported words of friend and foe, this historian depicts Athens. The climax is the funeral oration, whose words are carved on a thousand war memorials. It was the first winter of the Peloponnesian War, that conflict a generation long that closed the ch. of Athens' greatness. The bones of those who had died in battle were carried to the Cerameicus beyond the Dipylon Gate. There, as the custom was, an orator spoke in praise of the dead. On this occasion Pericles mounted the platform. Whether Thucydides reported his speech, paraphrased it, or transformed it, matters little. Under Pericles' name, its moving sentences stand in the historian's pages as a tribute of love and patriotism difficult to match in lit. "Athens alone of cities when put to the test excels her reputation. She alone gives her foes no reason to grudge her victory, and her subjects no cause to complain of an unworthy mistress . . . . we shall need no Homer to sing our praise nor poets, whose verse may delight for the moment but whose fancies will be destroyed by fact . . . For such a city these men have nobly fought . . . This land in which for generations the same people has ever dwelt, through the merits of our ancestors was handed down to us as a land of liberty . . . . We live under a political system which does not seek to emulate the institutions of our neighbors . . . . We are indeed an example to some, but an imitation to none . . . . We have a deep respect for those in authority and for the laws, especially those which have been ordained for the benefit of the oppressed, and for those unwritten laws which disgrace the breaker of them in the eyes of his fellow men . . . . We put our trust in the readiness of our stout hearts for the deeds demanded of us . . . . To sum up, I declare our city to be the education of Hellas" (Thuc. 2.)

Illustration might proceed. The early plays of Euripides show the same burning patriotism. Athens in these dramas is ever the refuge for the broken and oppressed. Even a Medea may find asylum there, much more the persecuted children of Heracles and the broken Heracles himself. Athens' very people tread more nobly:

The sons of Erechtheus, the olden,
Whom high gods planted of yore,
In an old land of heaven upholden,
A proud land untrodden of war.
They are hungered and, lo, their desire
With wisdom is fed as with meat;
In their skies is a shining of fire,
And joy in the fall of their feet.
(Euripides, *Medea* 824-833 [Murray])

Such ideals sanctified the Athenian struggle with Sparta in its opening years. They could not fail to find a response in the heart of Euripides. The strong awareness of the faults of democracy, and of his own democracy in particular, which was later to inspire satiric portraits of soldiers, and the horror at Athens' own crimes that was to find expression in the *Trojan Women* and ultimately in Euripides' own secession, had not yet gained control. The mood of the *Medea* was unchanged. In that play, the kindly man of Athens, his heart swifter than his head when moral right became a challenge, gave unthinking sanctuary to a criminal. The *Heracleidae,* written in the fourth year of the war is set in the temple of Zeus at famous Marathon. In these precincts, so redolent of Athenian memories, the children of Heracles sat as suppliant refugees. An Argive herald demanded their surrender. It was as simple as that. On such an issue Athens went to war. The play is vibrant with patriotism. Athena moves behind the scenes wrought in the gold and ivory of every democratic excellence. Athens appears as the home of liberty.

Says Iolaus, guardian of the refugees:
God's altar shall prevail,
And the free land whereunto we have come . . .

And the chorus to the arrogant ambassador:
Thou shouldst have shown respect to this free land . . .

And Iolaus again:
If this shall be, if she but ratify
Thine hests, free Athens then no more I know.
Nay, her sons' nature know I, know their mood:
They will die sooner, for in brave men's eyes
The honour that feels shame is more than life . . .

Demophon concluding all argument:

This city which I hold
Is not to Argives subject, she is free . . .

There, too, a man could speak his mind:
King, this advantage have I in your land,
I am free to speak and in my turn to hear.
None, as from other lands, will first expel me.

* * *

Ever she chooseth, this our land,
To help the helpless ones in justice' cause.
So hath she borne for friends unnumbered toils.

(*Heracleidae,* passim.)

Such an attitude is based, sings the chorus in a song that has the simplicity of a Heb. psalm, on truest piety:

O land
thy path is in justice
O never abandon
thy fear of the Lord.
Who denieth it in thee
close rideth to madness,
when these signs are showing.
For behold God revealeth
clear tokens. He taketh
away evermore the high mind
of the wicked.

(*Heracleidae*, 901-909)

These illustrations must suffice to indicate the reality of the partnership between culture and democracy. The quiet grandeur of Sophocles with its suggestion of a spirit at rest in its environment, and the still perfection of 5th-cent. art displaying life and not reaching painfully for the hidden and the unknown, might illustrate the same theme.

The second characteristic, noted by Pericles in the passage already quoted, was the ability of the age to produce noble leadership and the willingness of the mass to follow. It is not for nothing that the age bore the name of Pericles. With the death of Pericles, says Thucydides, there vanished the outstanding moral example of the time. He had never been led by personal ambition to a pursuit of selfish ends. He was incorruptible. He knew how to restrain the multitude without infringing liberty. He led because he would not flatter, daring, when occasion called, even to provoke. "Thus Athens became a democracy in name, but in fact a monarchy of the foremost citizen," the historian declares.

Bust of Plato. ©*H.P.*

The achievements of the age were tremendous. Here is the record in brief. Of the world's four supreme tragic artists, three of them appeared in 5th-cent. Athens—Aeschylus, Sophocles, and Euripides. "When the spirit of enquiry meets the spirit of poetry," says Macneile Dixon, "tragedy is born." They met in the vigor of those days. And yet it is difficult to realize that those who watched the half-Shavian drama of Euripides were the sons and daughters of those who saw the first performance of the *Agamemnon* of Aeschylus. In Euripides is realism, the study of such characters as the streets of Athens knew—the self-satisfied husband, the embittered foreign bride, the children of a broken home in time of war, the shellshocked boy, the epileptic, the ambitious soldier, the cold athlete. The ruler, faced with problems beyond his understanding, the phenomena of religious revival, the moral wreck of war, and the woes of the conquered, live intensely on his stage. In Aeschylus, Shakespeare and Ezekiel are combined. Imagine the fruitful mingling of the tragic power of the dramatist with the spiritual insight and religious fervor of the prophet. Imagine a gift of language that combined the daring and richness of the Englishman's speech with the color of the Hebrew. Such variety made Aeschylus, and such variety of genius marked Athens' tragic stage.

The age produced the finest of the world's historians. In granting this palm to Thucydides, cold, detached, scientific, yet brilliantly imaginative, one should not forget Herodotus, the mighty traveler and collector of facts. There is a sense in which the two were spiritual kin. They both ransacked the world for facts. They both sought a law behind phenomena. The validity of Herodotus' generalizations on the Envy of the Gods is beside the point. The quest for the principle puts him into the ancestry of Spengler and Toynbee. Herodotus was the first Gr. to seek behind events for the forces that determine them. He shared the honor with the prophets of Israel.

The age produced the noblest European mind. Plato was at once the greatest thinker and the greatest writer of Athens and the ancient world. Plato, like Paul, was as "one born out of due time." He survived the cent. that gave him birth. Most of his work is 4th cent., not 5th; and the 4th cent. was ushered in by a judicial crime, rare in the annals of Athens —the murder of Socrates. The tragedy of 399 B.C. was proof that the glory was departing, and if the mind of Plato, like the mind of Thucydides, lived on and found bitter food for thought in a twilight era, that is Plato's misfortune and the world's. One sees through Plato's personal crisis into the crisis of ancient society. That is why his work is a document of decadence, an utterance of opposition. If Plato lacked the serenity of a happier past, those who seek for truth in our own anxious day will have the deepest sympathy for his preoccupations, for truth was Plato's quest. It is that passion that made him one with the Athens of calmer years. As he drew to the end of his *Republic,* described by Sir Richard Livingstone in 1947 as "the greatest secular prose work of all time," he wrote significant words: "Is there not another quality which philosophers should possess?" "What quality?" "Truthfulness: they will never intentionally admit falsehood to their minds . . . and is there anything more akin to wisdom than truth?" "How can there be?" "Can the same nature be a lover of wisdom and a lover of falsehood?" "Never!"

The 5th cent. produced some of mankind's noblest art. Much of the revolt against classical Gr. art is the reaction of a dissatisfied and unhappy age against the serenity of a more stable society that believed it knew where perfection lay and expressed itself with confidence.

In language, itself an art, Athens produced what is perhaps the most perfect instrument of human expression in the history of speech. Words are the symbols of creative thought. Language reflects the quality of the minds that give it shape and form. If the spirit of Athens at her best was permeated with the passion for truth, one should expect to find that mood tr. into the forms of speech—the amazingly subtle verb, the rich facilities of the article, the brilliant invention of the particle that Attic Gr. carried to final perfection—that enabled the written sentence without stage directions to express irony, deprecate, cock an eyebrow, curl the lip, shrug the shoulders, and represent, in short, to the reading eye the animation of the living voice. These are only three of the many qualities that made Attic speech perhaps the world's most powerful and exact linguistic medium. For vivid conversation and the expression of abstract thought this is most certainly true.

10. The collapse. This glory withered in a generation. Its monuments remained in stone and written speech. Personalities survived like people "left on earth after a judgment day." Looking back one can see, nevertheless, that the disastrous Twenty-seven Years' War with Sparta was a conflict in which "one unhappy generation of Hellenes dealt their own Hellas a mortal blow, and knew that her blood was on them and their children" (Toynbee, op. cit. 3.292). Those who watched thought of Aeschylus and Herodotus, and murmured three Gr. words that were part of the century's contribution to historical thought—*κόρος, ὕβρις, ἄτη*. With considerable loss of moral content the words may be tr. "surfeit," "arrogant behavior," and "disaster." The first suggests the demoralization that comes with prosperity or too complete success, the relaxing of the moral fiber in the favored of fortune; the second implies the consequent loss of mental and moral balance reflected in over-confidence and outrageous action. The third word, also oddly Hebraic in force, contains the notion of the mad blind impulse, by which the spirit, morally ripe for disaster and in the grip of sin unpardonable, is driven into the catastrophic folly of attempting the impossible. However differently the thought of another age may view the relations of cause and effect, the formula covers Athens.

The war with Sparta revealed the ravages of decay. It becomes obvious, as the record proceeds, that "Ichabod" was written, and that Athens was in full career for the sorry days half a cent. later that felt the lash of Demosthenes' tongue. The marks of decadence are worth studying.

There first appeared the divorce of culture and democracy. The phenomenon may be illustrated by the thought of three penetrating minds. First take Plato, last though he was in time of the three. Plato's last work, the *Laws,* was inspired by a profound hostility to Athenian democracy. It was democracy, in Plato's view, that brought devastation by its crazy militarism upon the very world in which Athenian culture found its air and nourishment.

To turn from the philosopher to the historian and the dramatist is to find in both similar phenomena of opposition. During the summer and winter of 416 B.C., occurred an event of small military importance to which Thucydides sees fit to devote no fewer than twenty-six paragraphs of his fifth book. The Athenians had besieged and captured the little island of Melos, massacred its men, and enslaved its women and children. The island was in no sense a vital strategic base. It was without natural wealth. Why then this bulky place in the historian's narrative? Because Thucydides saw that society was a moral phenomenon, that what men think determines what men do and are, that systems and institutions form, maintain themselves, and fall with the growth, subsistence, and decay of an "êthos." In the Melos crime, Thucydides saw Athens passing from *ὕβρις* to *ἄτη*. As his manner was, Thucydides proceeded to reveal the moral background of the episode by means of speeches. The debate he reported between the Athenian envoys and the Melian Council had no doubt a solid basis in fact, but its truth is rather psychological than factual. In cold deliberate words, the Athenians explained to the little Senate that it suited their convenience that Melos should join the Athenian bloc. They did not suggest that the Melians had in any way wronged them, nor indeed did they lay claim to any shadow of right in such a demand. It was simply Athens' policy that the islands should submit to her. Melos therefore had to make her choice. She was free to submit or be destroyed.

Is it safe, the Melians answered in bitter irony, for Athens thus to flout all morality? Empires after all are mortal and there is world opinion. "We shall risk that," the Athenians answered. The Melians pleaded their neutrality, threatened Spartan intervention, expressed their determination to die rather than be slaves. "A lamentable error of judgment," said the Athenians. The cynical exposition of immoral power politics fills page after page.

"They put to death," Thucydides quietly concluded, "all the Melians whom they found of man's estate, and made slaves of the women and the children. . . ." So ends one book. The peace of desolation descended on Melos. The next book begins: "And the same winter the Athenians sought to sail with a greater fleet than ever before and conquer Sicily. . . ." Sail they did, in a burst of mad ambition, to ghastly and complete disaster.

In the same city, another brilliant mind was brooding over the same dark action. The next spring, when the shipyards of the Piraeus were roaring with preparation for the great Sicilian adventure, Euripides produced his most bitter and tragic play, the *Trojan Women*, which, to quote Murray, "set a flame of discord for ever between himself and his people." This somber drama is a masterpiece of black tragedy, a passionate protest against the evils of war difficult to match in all lit. It is a picture of war from the point of view of babes and women set amid the very blood and mud and smoke of shattered Troy. It is the morning after the night of swords. It is conquest seen when the heat of battle is over, and nothing remains but to wait and think. The reader who turns the last page of this terrible drama is not surprised that a few years later Euripides abandoned the city whose glories he had once so movingly extolled, and went away to conclude his life's work, an exile in distant Macedonia.

These three illustrations suffice to mark the reality of the contention that a significant feature of Athens' decline was a revolt of noble minds and a dissolution of the partnership that once existed between culture and the Athenian way of life. Aristophanes might provide similar illustrations. The savage satire of his comedies, and the nostalgic praise of a vanished age that strews them, both reveal an indignant and discontented spirit at war with growing decadence.

The second mark of the age of decline was a collapse of morale. In his third book, Thucydides paused and drew up a balance sheet of war. It is difficult to realize that some of the words are twenty-three centuries old. His austere prophecy that such evils as he saw "will, according to human nature, happen again in much the same way," has proved too unhappily true. He described the sanguinary end of the Corcyraean revolution, and continued: "Later the whole Hellenic world was convulsed, struggles being made everywhere by the popular chiefs to bring in the Athenians, and by the ruling class to introduce the Spartans. In peace there would have been neither the pretext nor the wish to make such an invitation; but in war with an alliance always at the command of either faction for the hurt of their adversaries and their own advantage, opportunities for bringing in the foreigner were never wanting to the revolutionary parties. The sufferings that revolution entailed were many and terrible, such as have occurred and always will occur so long as human nature remain the same. In peace, states and individuals have better sentiments because they do not find themselves confronted suddenly by imperious necessities; but war takes away the easy supply of daily wants, and proves a rough schoolmaster, that brings most men's characters to the level of their fortunes. . . . Reckless audacity came to be considered the courage of a loyal ally; prudent hesitation, specious cowardice; moderation was held to be the cloak for unmanliness, ability to see all sides of a question, inaptness to act on any. . . . Oaths of reconciliation being proffered on either side to meet an immediate difficulty only held good so long as no other weapon was at hand. . . . The cause of all these evils was lust for power arising from greed and ambition, and from these passions proceeded the violence of parties once engaged in contention. . . . Meanwhile the moderate part of the citizens perished between the two" (Thuc. 3:82, 83).

The third mark of decadence was the deterioration of leadership. The entry of the "Man in the Street" upon the stage of Athenian history before the close of the 5th century B.C. is one of the unmistakable symptoms of social decline. Few will advocate an aristocracy of wealth but an aristocracy of character all healthy people must possess or perish.

The rise of the Athenian "Common Man" was no egalitarian process fostered in politics and education. The war, which ruined the landed aristocracy and exalted, as war does, the industrialist, doubtless played a leveling part; but the chief reason was the decay of social discipline and morality already noted. This was aided by a vast refugee problem and the pauperization that follows invasion. Character deteriorated over wide areas of the populace. Leadership became a quest for power and no longer a patriotic privilege. Party politics and class conflict naturally took shape. The "sailor crowd" of Plato's and Euripides' contempt emerged. This led, meanwhile, to a loss of all view of the common good and supported this leader or that in equal pursuit of selfish advantage. The proletariat so clearly pictured later in Demosthenes' orations—selfish, emotionally unbalanced, venal, narrow-minded, self-assertive, irresponsible, and slothful—appears in clear outline in the documents. It bore the marks of mortal disease.

Athens lost her men of worth and leadership. She lost them in the spirit, she lost them in the flesh. The literal loss of blood in great wars and plagues has played a significant if unmeasured part in the decline of nations. The dilution of the old Rom. stock and the vast loss of life from Hannibal to Caesar contributed much toward the modification of the Rom. character and its ultimate deterioration. The gaps made at Passchendaele and on the Somme sixty and more years ago are still visible in public life, and today suffers from the human loss of yesterday. Athens' heavy casualties in the generation's war with Sparta and in the Great Plague may in the end have determined her failure to rise and triumphantly rebuild her battered greatness. Her talent was literally poured away. A brief return to comparative prosperity brought no resurgence of the spirit and no return to the old level of achievement.

In international politics, Athens' failure to create a commonwealth was another and final decisive factor. The forces that shaped the globe did good and ill when they tumbled the geography of Greece in confusion. The atomization of the Gr. people produced the city-state, the medium in which individualism took shape, and this in turn produced philosophy and democracy. The sharp differences of outlook, which environment also determined, proved a barrier to unity. Enlightened Greeks talked of Hellenic unity, but in spite of abortive and halfhearted efforts, unity was never achieved until the sword achieved it—in the hands of the dictator of Macedon, and later of Rome. In the Delian League that Athens built by her naval power after the Pers. war, Athens had her opportunity. She failed to grasp it and secure even that measure of loyalty from subject allies that proved Rome's narrow margin of salvation in the war with Hannibal. The modern world on which history has served notice to unite or perish should mark the fact. Athens missed her moment and it never came again.

11. The fourth century. The story of the great war between Athens and Sparta and their respective allies, whose two long episodes fill the last generation of the remarkable 5th cent., has not been told in detail. Athens struggled back to a measure of life, but the dash and vitality of her great days were gone, and the cent. was scarcely forty years old when Macedonia, considered heretofore the barbarous N. began to rise like a menacing cloud on the horizon.

Philip II of Macedonia was a dynamic dictator of the sort the first half of the present cent. has known. His northern kingdom was new, young, and potentially rich. It needed only ruthless leadership, and that Philip could give. It was not exhausted, like the rest of Greece,

Philip II of Macedonia (382-336) B.C. © *H.P.*

by war and tension. In natural resources, gold and timber, it was wealthy. Its men were raw, strong, and numerous.

Philip began to press into Thessaly, and menace the S. Athens had many spheres of influence and vital areas of control in his path, and her interests were menaced more than those of any other state. How Philip subverted Athenian strength, deceived, tricked, instigated revolt, softened morale by corrupted politicians and fifth columnists, and finally destroyed opposition in open war, is a story not unfamiliar to the 20th cent. Its gloom is relieved only by the heroism of the famous orator Demosthenes, who tried in his fine Philippic orations to rouse his weary and decadent people to rise and unite and beat back the menace to their liberty. Demosthenes' light was soon put out. Athens and Thebes were defeated at Chaeronea in 338 B.C., and Macedonia was virtual master of Greece.

To unite Greece, now cowed by Macedonian imperialism, Philip took up the challenge of a great crusade against Persia. In the midst of preparation he was assassinated, but his son, Alexander, a cultured youth educated on the Athenian tradition by Aristotle, took up the legacy of his father.

12. The empire of Alexander. The project was not as mad as it might seem at first sight, and a curious event had some significance. At the beginning of the 4th cent. B.C., an army of 10,000 Gr. mercenaries had been stranded in Persia; the rebel governor for whom they had fought was dead, and his native army dispersed. Their officers were treacherously murdered. The rank and file took up the challenge, and cut their way out to the Black Sea, through the Armenian mountains and the snows. An Athenian named Xenophon wrote the stirring story in a book. There is little doubt that the tale had much to do with a decision of the dashing young Alexander, who succeeded his father as king of Macedon in 336 B.C. An empire out of whose heart and depths a little Gr. army could boldly march was ripe for conquest.

Bust of Alexander. ©*B.M.*

Alexander was right. He needed a cause to unify Greece, and the old sin of Persia—the invasion of a cent. and a half before—was as good an excuse as any for aggression. With his well-drilled military machine, which he led magnificently, Alexander marched through the loose-knit Pers. empire, and when he died at the age of thirty-two, he was master of a realm that stretched from the Ionian Sea to the Punjab, and from the Caucasus to the Libyan Desert and the borders of Ethiopia. Nor was there anyone to challenge it. Rome, still a city-state, was at grips with the petty problems of security in Italy.

13. Hellenism. Thus was Hellenism born. Alexander, with his strangely international outlook, might have done much with his vast empire. He died, and the great, amorphous mass of conquered territory was divided into four areas of control—metropolitan Greece and three kingdoms. Egypt, which had always been safely defined by the deserts that hemmed the valley of the Nile, fell into the hands of Ptolemy, one of Alexander's marshals, and the dynasty he founded endured for three centuries, until the suicide, in fact, of Cleopatra last and most amazing of the line in 30 B.C.

The second successor-kingdom, which had much to do with Pal., was that of Seleucus, another general of Alexander, who eventually asserted his independence from metropolitan Macedon, and found himself in control of all the wide northern sweep of lands through which Alexander had marched. Seleucus' boundaries were ill-defined, and wavered with the ebb and flow of strength at Antioch. At one period, a Gr. kingdom was carved out in the eastern marches, which covered modern Afghanistan and NW India. It disappeared in the flux of history, lying as it did beyond the ultimate reach of Rome; but coinage reveals a considerable realm that had its years of power. In the W, the kingdom of Pergamum, which its ruler bequeathed to advancing Rome in 133 B.C., was cut from the Seleucid realms. Other kingdoms, too, limited Antioch's westward power from time to time. It was, indeed, a progressive disintegration of its ill-coherent mass that brought an end to Syrian imperialism, and, gradually restricting the borders of the old successor-empire of Seleucus, left Asia Minor and the Middle E finally a vacuum of power that invited and found Rome's effective intervention. The successful revolt of the Jews under the Maccabees in the 2nd cent. is a recorded illustration of the gradual process by which the Seleucid empire declined.

Thus history brought Roman, Greek, and Jew together, made Paul of Tarsus with his triple culture possible, and set the scene for modern Europe. Each contribution was essential history. The Rom. peace provided the framework for the first activity of the Church. It was on a Jewish stage that the events of the gospels took place. It was Paul, a Jew, who first wrought out the synthesis of the Testaments, but a Jew steeped in Hellenic thought, and writing habitually in the language of the Greeks. Alexander thus brought Gr. and Jew together by opening the way for the second great movement of Gr. colonization. The culture of the Greeks penetrated as far E as Gr. arms had moved, and Hellenism—that subtle blend of language, way of life, and mode of thought—was a stimulus and a catalyst felt far beyond the limits of Gr. nationhood.

BIBLIOGRAPHY. (General only; *see* other headings, e.g., Alexander, Athens, Hellenism for special bibliographies); J. B. Bury, *History of Greece* (1913); CAH, vols. II to IX; H. D. F. Kitto, *The Greeks* (1951); G. Dix, *Jew and Greek* (1953).

E. M. BLAIKLOCK

GREED (בטן ; LXX ὑπάρχωσιν; נפש ; LXX ψυχή; NT πλεονεξία, πλεονέκτης). (1) Eager, unrestrained, insatiate longing, esp. for wealth or gain; avarice, cupidity, covetousness; (2) immoderate or ravenous hunger, esp. for food or drink; (3) in a good sense: keen, avid desire for knowledge, holiness, etc. The term "greed" is not found in the KJV but it appears seven times in the RSV as follows:

1. Job 20:20: *beṭen*, "belly," "body," "womb"; as seat of passion, "avarice"; LXX *hypárchosin*, "possessions"; Vul. *venter*, "entrails"; Luther *Wanst*, "belly"; KJV "belly"; ASV "within."

2. Ezekiel 16:27: *nepes*, "seat of emotions and passions," e.g. "desire"; LXX *psychás*, "wills"; Vul. *animas*, "minds"; Luther *Willen*, "wishes"; KJV, ASV, Moffat "will"; Berkeley "preferences." *Nepesh* occurs 756 times in the OT.

3. Habakkuk 2:5: *nepes*; LXX *psychē*, "desire"; Vul. *anima*, "soul"; Luther *Seele*, "heart"; KJV, ASV "desire."

4. First Corinthians 5:11: *pleonéktēs*, "one who is greedy for gain," "a covetous person"; Vul. *avarus*, "eagerly desirous of something, esp. possessions," "avaricious," "covetous," "greedy"; Luther *Geiziger*, "miser"; KJV, RSV, ASV "covetous"; Moffat "lustful"; NEB "grasping"; Berkeley "greedy." *Pleonéktēs* has been used since Herodotus. It occurs four times in the NT; once on a vellum fragment of Oxyr. Pap. from perhaps the 3rd cent. A.D.

5. First Thessalonians 2:5: *pleonexía*, "greediness," "avarice," "insatiableness," "covetousness," lit. "a desire to have more"; Vul. *avaritiae*, "a greedy desire for possessions"; Luther *Habsucht*, "avarice"; KJV, RSV, ASV "covetousness"; Moffat "self-seeking"; Berkeley "money." *Pleonexia* occurs in Herodotus, Thucydides, LXX, *Epistle of Aristeas*, Philo, Jos., *Testaments of the Twelve Patriarchs*; ten times in the NT. The RSV "cloak for greed" (subjective gen.) means "pretext for avarice."

6. Second Peter 2:3: *pleonexía, u.s.*; Vul. *avaritia*; Luther *Habsucht*; KJV, ASV "covetousness"; Moffat "lust." *Pleonexía* is a genuine vernacular term (cf. MM).

7. Second Peter 2:14: *pleonexía, u.s.*; Vul. *avaritia*; Luther *Habsucht*; KJV, "covetous"; RSV, ASV "covetousness"; Moffat "lust." (For *pleonexía* in a good sense cf. Epictetus ii. 10.9.)

In Scripture "greed" is depicted in a bad sense only. It is defined as (1) idolatry (Eph 5:5; Col 3:5), (2) vanity (Ps 39:6; Eccl 4:8), and (3) the root of all evils (1 Tim 6:10). God (1) abhors (Ps 10:3), (2) forbids (Exod 20:17), and even punishes (Job 20:15; Isa 57:17; Jer 22:17-19; Mic 2:2, 3) greed.

Greed is (1) characteristic of the wicked (Rom 1:29) and slothful (Prov 21:26); (2) inconsistent in believers (Eph 5:3; Heb 13:5)—esp. ministers (1 Tim 3:3); (3) originates in the heart (Mark 7:22, 23), (4) engrosses the heart (Ezek 33:31; 2 Pet 2:14), and (5) is never satisfied (Eccl 5:10; Hab 2:5).

It leads to (1) foolish and harmful lusts (1 Tim 6:9), (2) departure from the faith (6:10), (3) falsehood (2 Kings 5:22-25), (4) theft (Josh 7:21), (5) poverty (Prov 28:22), (6) misery (1 Tim 6:10), (7) injustice and oppression (Prov 28:20; Mic 2:2), (8) domestic affliction (Prov 15:27), and (9) murder (1:18, 19; Ezek 22:12).

It is commended only by the wicked (Ps 10:3); believers hate (Exod 18:21; Acts 20:33). Both Isaiah (5:8) and Habakkuk (2:9) denounced it; Jesus warned His disciples to beware of it (Luke 12:15).

This sin can cause one to miss heaven (1 Cor 6:10; Eph 5:5). It shall abound in the last days (2 Tim 3:2; 2 Pet 2:1-3) but those who hate it will be rewarded (Prov 28:16). Believers ought to (1) pray against (Ps 119:36), (2) mortify (Col 3:5), and (3) avoid those guilty of (1 Cor 5:11).

Biblical examples are (1) Laban (Gen 31:41), (2) Balaam (2 Peter 2:15; cf. Jude 11), (3) Achan (Josh 7:21), (4) Eli's sons (1 Sam 2:12-14), (5) Samuel's sons (8:3), (6) King Saul (15:9, 19), (7) Ahab (1 Kings 21:2-16), (8) Gehazi (2 Kings 5:20-27), (9) Jewish nobles (Neh 5:7; Isa 1:23), (10) Jewish people (Isa 56:11; Jer 6:13), (11) Babylon (Jer 51:1-12), (12) a young man (Matt 19:22), (13) the Pharisees (Luke 16:14), (14) Judas (Matt 26:14, 15), (15) Ananias (Acts 5:1-10), and (16) Felix (24:26).

BIBLIOGRAPHY. J. Calvin, *Institutes of the Christian Religion* (1949), III. vii. 9; M. Luther,

Selected Psalms II, Vol. XIII, *Works* (c1956), 392f.; T. Laetsch, *The Minor Prophets* (1956), 151, 161f.; D. M. Lloyd-Jones, *Studies in the Sermon on the Mount*, II (1962), 86-96.

R. E. Perry

GREEK LANGUAGE, the Indo-European, Hel. language of the inhabitants of the Gr. islands.

I. Origin and classification
II. Mycenaean Greek
III. The Greek dialects
  A. Homeric
  B. Ionic
  C. Attic
IV. Hellenistic Greek
V. Koine Greek
  A. The Septuagint
  B. The non-literary papyri
  C. The later classical authors
VI. The character of New Testament Greek
  A. Phonological system
  B. Morphological system
  C. Parts of speech
    1. The noun and adjective
    2. The pronoun
    3. The prepositions, conjunctions, adverbs and particles
    4. The verb
  D. Lexical system
  E. Hebraic influences on New Testament Greek
VII. The study of New Testament Greek

I. Origin and classification

Although Gr. has been a primary subject of western scholarship since its rediscovery in the Renaissance, its grammatical and lexical qualities were interpreted in the light of Lat. until very recently. To date no systematic structural or generative grammar has yet been produced. Therefore, it is necessary to combine the classical analysis of Gr. with what recent linguistic insights have so far appeared. The origin of the Gr. language is lost in antiquity as are the initiation of most of the other languages which were spoken around the shores of the Mediterranean in the early 2nd millennium B.C. There is no doubt, however, that Gr. is related to the Indic-Anatolian language groups, esp. Hitt. (q.v.) and the better known Sanskrit. Recent evidence has demonstrated that as much influence may have come from one of the W Semite groups, such as the inhabitants of Ugarit (q.v.) or the maritime peoples of the most ancient Aegean. A careful survey reveals that a number of quite distinct dialects fall under the heading Gr., and that in some cases these are divergent enough to be considered as separate tongues entirely. It is highly unlikely that an Egypt. speaker of Gr. of Paul's time could have understood much of a poem of Pindar or a modern Gr. novel without great effort and intense previous study. There is no question that the common colloquial dialect which came into being as a result of the Alexandrian conquest (322 B.C.) was as widely comprehended and popular as any language before the age of printing. Greek as a linguistic system may be classed with Estonian, Rumanian, the Indic dialects and the Slavic languages into the still comprehensible category of Indo-European. As with similarly highly inflected languages, Gr. proceeded through definite historical stages to lose many of the complex forms and difficult syntheses found in Sanskrit and Russian. As this came to pass a simple addition or subtraction of words came to bear the meaning of the sentence. The result was to increase vastly the vocabulary while simplifying the syntax and adjusting the morphology. Certain of the relative and conditional aspects of the ancient elaborate forms were maintained and are commonly found in the Gr. Bible.

II. Mycenaean Greek

It is now widely accepted that the earliest known Gr. dialect was that utilized by the merchant-traders of the Aegean and eastern Mediterranean, known from the remains on Cyprus and other locations. Their language was decisively identified as Gr. in 1956. It is known from a number of inscrs. in the Linear "B" Syllabary (*see* Writing, VII.) The language shows affinities with both later Gr. dialects and W Sem. inscrs., of the same or later eras. Many place names, commodities and titles which appear in later texts, including the Gr. Bible, first occur in the Mycenaean economic records. To date no ritual or literary tablets have been forthcoming. The syllabic spelling presents some difficulties in recovering the proper pronunciation; however, some of the resultant forms demonstrate clearly the transition from Hitto-Sanskrit to the later classical Gr. usage. There is a strong possibility that the organization of the Linear "B" system and some of its phonetic equivalents were derived from the hieroglyphic Hitt. system. Any search for the origins of Gr. language and its semantic relationships must begin with the Mycenaean materials which must have been innovated if not yet widespread by 2100 B.C. This early stage of Gr. speech was soon superseded by later dialects which were dispersed with the increase of trade.

III. The Greek dialects

The Greeks of antiquity had only indistinct ideas of their own origins and divided their various sub-groups and dialects into several different systems. Much of this grouping was done on the basis of a combination of legend and folk etymology. The major divisions are still held to be valid; Doric, Ionic and Aeolic. It is now widely accepted that Aeolic, of which there is but scant literary evidence extant, should be replaced in classification by Achaean. Since most of the Doric influence was in the western areas of Gr. domination it may be simply denoted as W Gr. Among the remaining dialects denoted E Gr., are Arcado-Cypriot and the most important of all, Attic-

Ionic. Since these were the dialects of the Grecian cities which colonized other areas of the ancient Near E and Mediterranean world, the Attic-Ionic became the dialectal grouping which most influenced the Gr. Bible.

A. Homeric. The Homeric dialect is an offshoot of the Attic-Ionic, but at a stage before any real Attic lit. existed. Because of the popularity and preservation of the epics of Homer and other pieces in the same speech, the Homeric became a literary norm for centuries. Of special interest is the fact that the origin of the Homeric epics and the stage of the language they represent is contemporaneous with the classical Heb. of the 10th to the 8th centuries B.C., so that good and valid comparisons can be made between the philological and linguistic situation of the Psalms and the Homeric works. The problem of whether or not the Homeric text was reorganized and perhaps updated in later ages is a valid concern, although some—in fact longer portions of the text—seem to have been little affected.

B. Ionic. The Ionic dialect contains some of the great works of classical lit., Herodotus, Hippocrates, et al. It is marked by a complexity of forms and innumerable foreign loanwords and phrases. The dialect predominated from the area of Smyrna to Miletus on the W. coast of Asia Minor. This was the background tongue of many of the churches which sprang up in the region of the Lycus Valley. After the Rom. conquest of this area the terms and modes of the ancient Ionic speech still lingered on in occasional references. Certain peculiarities of the NT Gr. syntax are attributed to Ionic influence. The most important Ionicism being the "infinitive of purpose with verbs of motion," Matthew and Mark use such constructions frequently (e.g. Matt 5:17), Gr. "*οὐκ ἦλθον καταλῦσαι ἀλλὰ πληρῶσαι*," "I am come not to abolish, but to fulfill." Other Ionicisms also are found throughout the vocabulary of the NT. They, as much as any other single factor, separate the NT style from its Attic origins.

C. Attic. The complex, sophisticated dialect of Athens, the vehicle of the philosophy of Plato and Aristotle is denoted as Attic. It became important in the 6th cent. B.C. and remained in evidence well into the Hel. age. The characteristics of Attic over against the NT idiom may best be seen in the simplifications introduced by the Koiné. The Attic maintains all the classic moods: indicative, subjunctive, optative, imperative and infinitive. The dual number and various specialized constructions, such as the sequence of moods and a bewildering maze of particles are rigidly adhered to in Attic texts. The intensity of the NT style is enforced by its avoidance of many of the sophistical artificialities of Attic style. The NT dialect however, was considered crude and rough by many admirers of the polish and subtlety of Attic prose. The reduction of forms to an analytical system was accomplished by the transference of Gr. to large populations of non-Gr. speakers. The result of this frictional process is denoted Hellenic.

IV. Hellenistic Greek

After the conquests of Alexander the unity of the previously independent and autonomous Grecian states was assured. The further incorporation of the older archaic-religious-states of the E brought about the establishment of a universal, vernacular Gr. supported by a generalized and uniform Hel. culture. Although the tongue of the Macedonian court was Attic, the *lingua franca* which evolved was simplified considerably and influenced by the other dialects. Attic intermingled with its natural dialectal sibling, Ionic. In the phonology this meant the softening of the double "t" and the replacement of difficult consonant clusters, "rs" by simpler "ss" and "rr." Undoubtedly many of the tonal and stressive aspects of Attic pronunciation also were dropped. The elaborate particles and hair-splitting distinctions between manifold prepositions were too difficult for foreign speakers to master and fell away from the emerging vernacular. The abundance of literary models, schools of rhetoric and the traditionalism of the times created an opposition to the vulgarizing influences in what has been called "Atticism." This was a conscious usage of archaizing speech, obsolete terms and forms, in an attempt to regain the purity and finesse of the 4th cent. B.C. Athenian style. Needless to add the achievement of this imitation depended directly on how carefully one was schooled in the Attic conventions. Among the NT writers, Luke-Acts, Hebrews, Jude and some passages in the Pauline writings show similarities with the Attic style as it was understood during the first Christian cent. On the other hand, John's gospel, epistles and Revelation and First Peter show the least effect of the classical dialect. One important advance of the new popularity of Gr. as a trade and business tongue was its written form in a phonographized alphabetic system. In almost all cases it soon supplanted the older sylabaries of the Semites and Ural-Altai. This meant that many more common people could learn to read and, although never great by modern standards, literacy certainly increased manifold with the development of the Hel. dialect, so much so that it was easier for Jews to quote the Gr. tr. of the OT, the LXX, than to transliterate or retranslate the Heb. original.

V. Koine Greek

The term koine, Gr. *κοινή*, means "common," "everyday," in an adjectival sense and has been applied to the non-literary type of Hel. dialect. The *koiné* is singularly the language of the NT, certain ephemeral types of papyri and possibly the writings of the Stoic philosopher, Epictetus (A.D. 60-140). In essence, the NT speech is the conversation of the street and market place. It is with rare exception uninfluenced by the Attic tendency within the Hel. speech of the time. The pattern for tr. Sem. thought into Indo-European garb was set in the LXX.

A. The Septuagint. The actual speech of the LXX varies widely from book to book, however, the underlying literary vehicle is *koiné*. The history and development of the LXX is an involved process much of which is irrecoverable like the other phases of the vernacular it seeks to communicate. The effort for simplification often glosses over difficult parallelistic constructions in the Heb. and often resorts to paraphrase.

The LXX is the largest body of text in the *koiné* dialect. At points the tr. drew upon purely Gr. concepts for its rendering of Hebraic expressions while in other passages the Heb. was followed so closely to be unintelligible in Gr. The LXX, since it was the tr. of the OT, the oracles of God to Israel, held a place of supreme authority among the early Christian writers both canonical and patristic. The relative date of the LXX at the beginning of the Hel. age makes its text a primary source for the early stages of *koiné*. The fact that a number of diverse traditions were involved confuses the issue of differentiating the *koiné* elements from those of the late Attic style. The overwhelming majority of NT allusions and quotations from the OT are derived from one or another VS of the LXX. This propensity often blocks from view the current usage of some constructions at the time of the production of the NT canon as the LXX was already a slightly older VS with an earlier diction.

B. The non-literary papyri. Since the last cent. approximately sixty thousand fragments of ephemeral, daily correspondence written on papyrus material have been published. These documents provide the largest single class of extra-Biblical materials available for comparison with the NT. They have provided parallel citations for a large number of NT hapax legomena and demonstrated the continuing trend in *koiné* Gr. away from synthetic and toward analytic forms of expression. The spellings, morphology and syntax of the non-literary texts is widely variant and discloses a similar linguistic situation to that of the NT authors, specifically the use of *koiné* by writers for whom it was a learned literary means of expression. With all Hel. style, the polish and precision of Attic Gr. is sacrificed for immediacy, stress and exclamation. The outcome is a dialect which is capable of outright drama and portrayal of life as it is lived rather than as it may be analyzed. The papyri yield all manner of subjects, lists, bills, suits, briefs, orders, memoranda, notes, receipts, official communications, business contracts and love letters. These represent many strata of Hel. society and give many mundane titles of the various functionaries of the Greco-Rom. world. The vast percentage of papyri has been recovered from Egypt but some have been forthcoming from other areas of the Near E. The wide divergence of social background and degrees of literacy represented in the papyri affords a linguistic lower limit considerably below the level of the NT which accords well with the other sources of *koiné* daily speech. The true position of the NT idiom in its situation in life can be studied. Also in the same style are inscribed materials on potsherds, and ostraca, which often represent the very extreme of the ephemeral written records. Such contents as "chits" or tallies for tax purposes, business and construction memoranda have been preserved on ostraca. Also in this regard are epigraphic inscrs. on stone which vary from official monumental stele to the universal graffiti scrawled by the semi-literate of all periods of history on the privy walls of all nations. The sum total of the non-literary written materials has increased vastly the knowledge of the Gr. language and the world in which it flourished. It represents the largest single advance in the study of the NT since the days of their composition.

C. The later classical authors. The primary source from ancient non-Biblical writings for educated *koiné* Gr. is the collected discourses of the Stoic Epictetus. The statements were set down by his disciple Arrian (A.D. 95-175) in two works, an *Encheiridion*, "Manual," and a group of *Diatribai*, "Lectures," of which four books are extant. The language is Hel., but restrained and educated as well as precise. Many syntactical, lexical and conceptual parallels may be located in the epistles of Paul. Another class of writers who used the newly developed *koiné* idiom to a large degree were the scientific writers. Clear similarities to their works are found in the NT text. Chief among these are: Archimedes, mathematician of Syracuse (287-212 B.C.); Aristarchus, astronomer of Samos (c. 320 B.C.); Eratosthenes, mathematician and geographer of Alexandria (295-235 B.C.); Euclid, geometer of Alexandria (306-240 B.C.); Hipparchus, mathematician of Alexandria (190-125 B.C.) and Posidonius, mathematician of Rhodes (135-51 B.C.). Undoubtedly the nature of their writings allowed for little that is similar; however, it is remarkable that there are any parallel usages at all, in fact, quite a large number exist. In the same fashion that the non-literary texts give a lower extremity of *koiné* speech so the literary references show that *koiné* was applicable to abstruse and specialized thought. In this regard it was in no wise inferior to Attic.

VI. The character of NT Greek

Although NT Gr. varies from both the classical dialect and the main branch of Hel., it is a consistent self-contained vehicle of communication, the aspects of which have been studied with great profit for the full

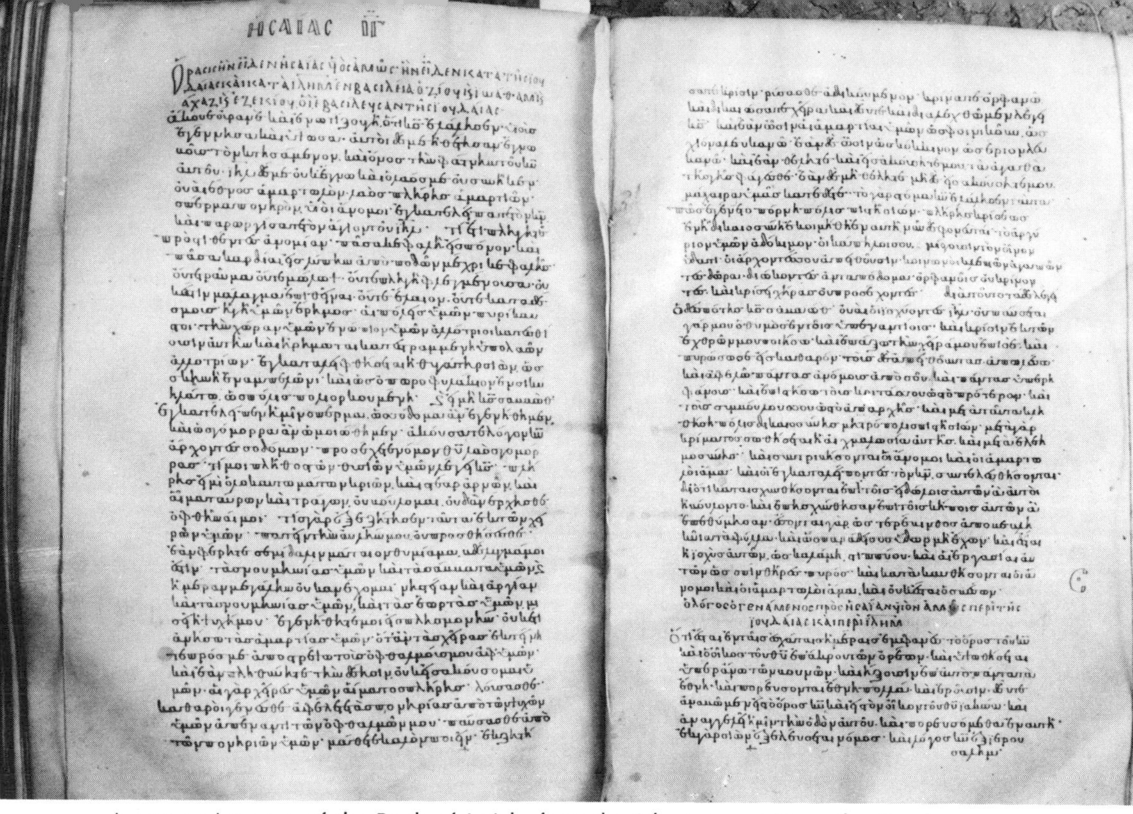

A manuscript page of the Book of Isaiah, from the 9th century A.D. in the Greek of the Septuagint (LXX). This volume is in the Greek library at Jerusalem. ©M.P.S.

understanding of the NT text. A brief outline of its phonology and morphology follows. For syntactical arrangements consult the Bibliography below (8).

A. Phonological system. The phonological or sound system of NT Gr. was widely divergent from classical speech. The pronunciation of the Attic dialect was too complex and artificial for the ears and needs of the Hel. kingdoms of the E. Specifically, the following phonography was in evidence. The vowels were: α, as in "father"; ε, as in "wet"; η as in "they"; ι, as in "sit," never as in "fight"; ο, as in "sought"; υ, a sound not common to Eng. but common to Ger., a purse-lipped *eu* sound; and ω, elongated and held as in "slow." The diphthongs or double vowels were: αι, as in "aisle"; αυ, as in "sow"; ει, in "they " (often confused in the MSS with η, above); ευ, a sound not common in Eng. remotely similar to the American colloquial explicative, "whew," interjected by someone suffering through an unusually hot day; ηυ, an elongation of ευ, but nearer to "wayward"; οι, as in "oil"; ου (not a true diphthong) but similar to "group"; υι, as in "queen"; and the unique, ωυ, which appears only in the transliterated form Μωυσῆς, the LXX and NT equivalent of OT "Moses." Pronunciation is uncertain at best. The consonants were little altered from classical Gr., however, the elisions and nasalizations which gave to Attic its musical quality were largely lost. Generally the following were equivalent to modern Eng. β, b; δ, d; κ, k; λ, l; μ, m; ν, n; π, p; τ, t; φ, f; ψ, ps; however a number were distinct, γ, consistently pronounced as in "get," never Gallicanized as in "garage"; ζ, z as in "haze"; θ, th as in "thistle"; ξ, x or ks as in "text"; ρ, r a most difficult sound to deduce precisely because of its many possible shadings and stresses, but prob. slightly trilled or burred closer to American "roared"; σ, s (softly) as in "stress"; and χ, ch the initial glottal in "cough." The classical accentuation marks and other complicated diacriticals were disregarded except for the "rough" breathing mark ʿ, placed over an initial vowel or diphthong and indicating the sound "h" as, Gr. ἁμαρτάνω, *hamartanō,* "to sin"; and the ʾ , "soft" or "smooth" breathing indicating the vowel itself is to be pronounced. Punctuation did exist in both classical and later periods but the system used by the various authors of the NT is not extant, except possible material in the fragments from Qumran, Cave 7.

B. Morphological system. Greek like all other Indo-European languages, alters the meaning and forms of individual words by the addition and alteration of prefixes and suffixes, a process known as "inflection." Although the morphology of the NT words was much simplified from the former Attic system, it was considerably more extensive than in any of the major European languages with the exception of Slavic. Generally speaking, the degree to which Gr. words must be altered to fit other morphological units in the sentence or construction, a process called "concord," is more extensive than Eng. However, Gr. words were inflected by clear and consistent principles so that the ambiguity of Eng. spelling and formation never occurs. Because of the flectional principle which governs the morphological units or "words," the word order of Gr. is more flexible than Eng. or Ger. An example of the inflection is given as: Gr. "ὁ θεὸς ἀγάπη ἐστίν" (1 John 4: 16), "God is love," which may be analyzed as: *Ho* (masc. sing. subjective form of the definite article) + *the* (root of proper noun for God, masc. sing.) + *os* (masc. sing. subjective ending) *agap* (root of common noun for love, fem. sing.) +*ē* (fem. sing. subjective ending [note: the word for love does not have the article preceding it so it is not definitized, therefore the sentence cannot be reversed into "Love is God"] *es* (root of indicative stem of irregular verb) + *ti* (masc. sing. active voice) + *n* (movable, suffixal ending to make pronunciation of construction more precise). Of special importance, as in the above illustration, is the flection of the Gr. verb. This is at its peak in the elaborate tense system which allows more consistent sequences to be indicated in individual verb forms than in Eng.

C. Parts of speech. 1. *The noun and adjective.* The common forms and meanings of the various inflections of the Gr. noun and adjective are basically similar and are indicated in the following tables:

Stem Formative	*Case—# Suffix*	*Meaning*	*Name*
λογ, (*log-*)	ος, (*-os*)	"a word"	nominative
λογ, (*log-*)	ου, (*-ou*)	"of a word"	genitive
λογ, (*log-*)	ῳ (*-ō*)	"to/for a word"	dative
λογ, (*log-*)	ον, (*-on*)	"a word"	accusative (obj)
λογ, (*log-*)	οι, (*oi*)	"words"	nominative
λογ, (*log-*)	ων, (*ōn*)	"of words"	genitive
λογ, (*log-*)	οις, (*ois*)	"to/for words"	dative
λογ, (*log-*)	ους, (*ous*)	"words"	accusative (obj)
χωρ, (*chōr-*)	α, (*-a*)	"a land"	nominative
χωρ, (*chōr-*)	ας, (*-as*)	"of a land"	genitive
χωρ, (*chōr-*)	ᾳ, (*-a*)	"to/for a land"	dative
χωρ, (*chōr-*)	αν, (*-an*)	"a land"	accusative (obj)
χωρ, (*chōr-*)	αι, (*-ai*)	"lands"	nominative
χωρ, (*chōr-*)	ων, (*-ōn*)	"of lands"	genitive
χωρ, (*chōr-*)	αις, (*-ais*)	"to/for lands"	dative
χωρ, (*chōr-*)	ας, (*-as*)	"lands"	accusative (obj)

There is also a neuter class of nouns and a neuter system for adjectives, but it differs little from the masc. except for nominative sing., which has a final "s" and the nominative and accusative pl. which is formed with a simple "ā" suffix similar to the fem. sing. nominative form. Two major classes of nouns are those which have complicated vocalic endings which undergo elision and those having stem formatives ending in a consonant which is elided in the declension of the system of nouns.

2. *The pronoun.* The pronouns are treated as adjectives for the most part. Since the Gr. verb has personal suffixes the subject pronoun is rarely if ever expressed in classical Gr., but in NT *koiné* this principle was breaking down, and so constructions such as, "You know," where the pronoun is written although it is inferred in the verbal suffix, do occur (John 21:15). The usage seems to imitate the Heb. in most cases (see below). The distinction of anarthrous (without the article) nouns and articular (with the article) nouns is important when pronouns are involved or substituted. The resultant forms are more precise yet more complicated than Eng.; e.g. "He has blinded their eyes and hardened their hearts" (Isa 6:10 as rendered in *koiné* Gr. in John 12:40) appears as, "He has blinded (of them) the eyes and hardened (of them) the hearts" in a painfully literal tr. The distinction usually made in Eng. between pronouns "I, you, he, she, it" and the like as opposed to adjectives "this, that" is ineffective in *koine*.

3. *The prepositions, conjunctions, adverbs and particles.* The Gr. prepositions are first and foremost functional in that they indicate the relationship of the nouns and pronouns to the rest of the construction. Much of the exactness of meaning in the NT is imparted by the prepositions. No single Eng. meaning can be assigned to a Gr. preposition, as subtle differences develop from the formulation and flection with which each preposition is used. The Gr. conjunctions are less complicated than Eng., and offer few difficulties in tr. The adverb is less frequent than in Eng., even though it may be easily formed from the masc. pl. genitive by altering the final "n" to "s." Adverbs often stand in grammatical senses where they would be improper in Eng. as replacements for prepositions. The most difficult of all the Gr. parts of speech are by far and away

A facsimile page from the Septuagint, a fragment of the Sinaitic manuscript, photographed from one of the scraps found by Dr. Tischendorf at Mount Sinai. ©*M.P.S.*

the particles. The NT has possibly eighty per cent fewer than the best Attic prose, but even so, many are of such indirect and stylistic importance that they are left untranslated in the Eng. VSS. They serve a special function in introducing the more unusual modal constructions of the Gr. verb. However, they are not as crucial in the NT as in Attic lit.

4. *The verb.* The Gr. verb bears considerably more of the total meaning of any construction than its Eng. counterpart. It may be implemented with a series of pronominal suffixes denoting not only the person initiating the action, 1, 2, or 3, but also the number whether sing. or pl. as follows:

Present Indicative Active Voice		
λύω	, *lyō*	"I loose, I am loosing"
λύεις	, *lyeis*	"you (thou) loose, you (thou) are loosing"
λύει	, *lyei*	"he, she, it looses, he, she, it is loosing"
λύομεν	, *lyomen*	"we loose, we are loosing"
λύετε	, *lyete*	"you (pl.) loose, you (pl.) are loosing"
λύουσιν	, *lyoysin*	"they loose, they are loosing"

The single Gr. form not only contains both subject and verb but also may signify either indefinite or progressive action depending upon the context. With certain phonological modifications the suffix system shown above is utilized for all tenses and moods of the verb. In Gr. as in Eng., the form of the verb must indicate concord in person and number with its subject in the construction. The possibility of redundancy based on the verbal suffixes often is exploited for many more degrees of emphasis than is possible in Eng. A full synopsis of the potential forms with a suggestion of their more common meanings using only the first person sing. suffix appears below.

PRESENT SYSTEM				
Active Voice				
Indicative	Present tense	λύω	, *lyō*	"I loose, I am loosing"
	Imperfect tense	ἔλῡον	, *elyon*	"I was loosing"
Subjunctive	(always present)	λύω	, *lyō*	"I would/should loose"
Optative	(always present)	λύοιμι	, *lyoimi*	"May I loose" (very rare in NT)
Imperative	(always present)	λῦε	, *lye*	"You (Thou) loose!" no first person
Infinitive	(all inclusive)	λύειν	, *lyein*	"To loose"
Participle	(verbal noun or adjective)	λύων	, *lyōn*	"loosing"
Middle Voice	(Subjunctive, Optative, Imperative, Infinitive and Participle are the same for the Passive Voice)			
Indicative	Present tense	λύομαι	, *lyomai*	"I loose for myself," (intent)
	Imperfect tense	ἐλῡόμην	, *elyomēn*	"I was loosing for myself"
Subjunctive	(always present)	λύωμαι	, *lyōmai*	"I would/should loose for myself"
Optative	(always present)	λῡοίμην	, *lyoimēn*	"May I loose for myself"
Imperative	(always present)	λύου	, *lyoy*	"You (Thou) loose for thyself"
Infinitive	(all inclusive)	λύεσθαι	, *luesthai*	"To loose for one's self"
Participle	(verbal noun or adjective)	λῡόμενος	, *lyomenos*	"loosing for one's self"
Passive Voice				
Indicative	Present tense	λύομαι	, *lyomai*	"I am being loosed"
	Imperfect tense	ἐλῡόμην	, *elyomēn*	"I was being loosed"

Further forms identical to those of the Middle Voice as noted. Many verbs are not used in the Active Voice at all and are developed only in the Middle and Passive. In such cases the Middle Voice is tr. as though it were the Active. The oblique moods, the Subjunctive and Optative do not appear in the Future.

FUTURE SYSTEM				
Active Voice				
Indicative	Future tense	λύσω	, *lysō*	"I shall loose"
Infinitive	(all inclusive)	λύσειν	, *lysein*	"To be about/prepared to loose"
Participle	(verbal noun or adjective)	λύσων	, *lysōn*	"about to loose"
Middle Voice				
Indicative	Future tense	λύσομαι	, *lysomai*	"I shall loose for myself"
Infinitive	(all inclusive)	λύσεσθαι	, *lysesthai*	"To be about/prepared to loose for one's self"
Participle	(verbal noun or adjective)	λῡσόμενος	, *lysomenos*	"about to loose for one's self"
Passive Voice				
Indicative	Future tense	λυθήσομαι	, *lythēsomai*	"I shall be loosed"
Infinitive	(all inclusive)	λυθήσεσθαι	, *lythēsesthai*	"To be about/prepared to be loosed"
Participle	(verbal noun or adjective)	λυθησόμενος	, *lythēsomenos*	"about to be loosed"

The past tense system in Gr. has an added aspect called the "Aorist." This fully developed system denotes action completed in respect to the time of the statement. In effect, it is an idea of indefinite past experience with respect to the continuation of the past. It is of fundamental importance in the NT where many statements regarding the work of God in history are related in the Aorist system. Unfortunately no simple equivalence with Eng. or even within Gr. itself is forthcoming, and its true force must be gained from the context in which it appears. So frequent is the Aorist that two types of Aoristic formations developed in Gr. the First and Second Aorist, both of which are found in the NT.

AORIST SYSTEM				
Active Voice				
Indicative	Aorist	ἔλῡσα	, *elysa*	"I loosed"
Subjunctive	Aorist	λύσω	, *lysō*	"I should/was motivated to loose" (with the understanding that I did)
Imperative	Aorist	λῦσον	, *lyson*	"Loose!" (in past sense)
Infinitive	Aorist	λῦσαι	, *lysai*	"To have loosed"
Participle	Aorist	λύσᾱς	, *lysas*	"Having loosed" (a very important form)
Middle Voice				
Indicative	Aorist	ἐλῡσάμην	, *elysamēn*	"I loosed" (for myself)
Subjunctive	Aorist	λύσωμαι	, *lysōmai*	"I (ought) have loosed" (special applications)
Imperative	Aorist	λῦσαι	, *lysai*	"Loose! for thyself" (in past sense)
Infinitive	Aorist	λύσασθαι	, *lysasthai*	"To have loosed for one's self"
Participle	Aorist	λῡσάμενος	, *lysamenos*	"Having loosed for one's self"
Passive Voice				
Indicative	Aorist	ἐλύθην	, *elythēn*	"I (in past time) was loosed"
Subjunctive	Aorist	λυθήναι	, *lythō*	"I should/was motivated to have been loosed" (with the understanding that I was)
Imperative	Aorist	λύθητι	, *lythēti*	"Be (thou) loosed" (in past time)
Infinitive	Aorist	λυθῆναι	, *lythēnai*	"To have been loosed"
Participle	Aorist	λυθείς	, *lytheis*	"Having been loosed" (important form)

The Perfective System is fully developed in Eng. only with the use. of the modal auxiliary verb "has" or "had," as in "He had had a drink of water." In most contexts it can be tr. by Eng. past tense but frequently in Gr. its exact meaning can be ascertained only from the context. Some common and exceedingly important verbs take only perfective forms but have present or imperfect meanings. The notion of "perfect" is used in this grammatical sense in regard to completed actions in past time. It places stress on the continuing results of the action fulfilled in the past but effecting the present time of the statement. A pluperfect also appears which emphasizes past actions in past time with an existing result in past time.

PERFECTIVE SYSTEM				
Active Voice				
Indicative	Perfect tense	λέλυκα	, *lelyka*	"I have loosed"
	Pluperfect tense	ἐλελύκη	, *elelykē*	"I had loosed"
Infinitive	Perfect tense	λελυκέναι	, *lelykenai*	"To have loosed"
Participle	(verbal noun or adjective)	λελυκῶς	, *lelykōs*	"Having loosed"
Middle Voice				
Indicative	Perfect tense	λέλυμαι	, *lelymai*	"I have loosed for myself"
	Pluperfect tense	ἐλελύμην	, *elelymēn*	"I had loosed for myself"
Infinitive	(Perfect tense)	λελύσθαι	, *lelysthai*	"To have loosed for one's self"
Participle	(verbal noun or adjective)	λελυμένος	, *lelymenos*	"Having loosed for one's self"
Passive Voice				
Indicative	Perfect tense	λέλυμαι	, *lelymai*	"I have been loosed"
	Pluperfect tense	ἐλελύμην	, *elelymēn*	"I had been loosed"
(all other forms identical to Perfective Middle Voice above). One other major subset of the Perfective System appears in Gr. as the Future Perfect Passive.				
Indicative	Perfect (Future) tense	λελύσομαι	, *lelysomai*	"I shall have been loosed"
Infinitive	Perfect (Future)	λελύσεσθαι	, *lelysesthai*	"To have been loosed"
Participle	(verbal noun or adjective)	λελυσόμενος	, *lelysomenos*	"Having had been loosed"

It frequently has been said that the precision and depth of meaning available to the Gr. language rendered it the perfect vehicle for the thought of Plato and Aristotle. In the same manner the directness and precision of *koiné* made it the ideal vehicle for the "Word of God."

D. Lexical system. The lexica of NT Gr. was drawn from many sources, classical usage, Hel. simplifications, foreign expressions and Heb. and Lat. words. All these combine to make a unified speech, but the etymology of many terms is irrecoverable. There are very few terms which have simple 1:1 equivalents in Eng. Therefore, it often is necessary to treat the tr. of one Gr. term in totally different fashion in a number of different contexts. Since Gr. is highly inflected the meanings of many words must be taken as related to the phrases in which they occur, so that no mere root meanings will everywhere suffice. The vocabulary of the NT is not large; less than twenty-five words occur over 150 times. There are however, only a restricted number of hapax legomena. So many sources are now known for *koiné* Gr. from non-literary texts that the meanings of all words with only a few exceptions can be located in the extra-Biblical sources. Many compounds appear in *koiné*, and older confined prepositions give way to broader ones. The monosyllables common to classical speech are replaced by fuller polysyllabic terms. Words with difficult forms tend to be reduced; however, certain irregular verbs dominate the NT vocabulary. The meanings of many terms shifted and in most cases either softened or faded; few really violent concepts survived the centuries. The intent to give emphasis to speech is seen in the frequent use of adjectives and their derivatives. A wide variation between the various authors of the NT in their use and number of words is apparent, and due to the differences in their education and background. However, an even greater cause of this difference is the variation in subjects which they treat. The historical book, describing as it does places and activities, tends to a larger vocabulary than the epistle.

E. Hebraic influences on New Testament Greek. Before the discovery of the non-literary texts, all variations in speech from the Attic which were found in the NT were attributed to Hebraic influence. This number is now reduced drastically, but there are Heb. allusions in the text. Many of these appear to be attempts to reproduce Heb. syntax in Gr. prose. Many phrases in the gospels are reminiscent of Heb. constructions. The writings of John show an especial affinity for the vernacular forms of speech and for constructions found in the LXX and the DSS. It is therefore perfectly proper to refer to both Hebraisms, possibly Aramaisms, and Septuagintisms within the NT lexica. Undoubtedly the transliteration of many names into the LXX set a pattern followed by the NT writers. The striking of all such Sem. idioms is the frequent use of καί, "and," often with some additional adverb to imitate the Heb. *waw*, "and" so common in the Pentateuchal narratives. There is no doubt that this gives the text an immediacy and urgency absent from Attic and Hel. Gr. Another such case is the frequent use of instrumental ἐν, "by," "by means of" as in 1 Corinthians 6:11 "—you were justified in (by means of) the name of the Lord Jesus Christ" for the Heb. בְּ, "by means of." In many passages these subtle variations from the Hel. idiom indicate the pattern of speech actually used by the Lord and His disciples during His ministry.

VII. The study of NT Greek

The text of the NT slowly appeared and was assembled at several centers during the apostolic age. With the barbarian invasions which overtook the W Rom. empire after the 4th cent. A.D., the knowledge of Gr. was lost to all but the clergy of the Byzantine church with its center at Constantinople. In time the Western Church under the rising Vatican forbade any Scriptures but the Vul. VS of St. Jerome (A.D. 340-420). It was only through the Jews of Spain and the displaced scholars who fled before the advance of Islam that any knowledge of the NT tongue was preserved. Of all the accomplishments of the Renaissance and the Biblical humanists this shines the brightest, that they infused life into the study of the *koiné*. Distinct periods in the study of the language and the text of the NT are distinguishable in the late Medieval, Renaissance, Reformation and Early Modern phases of Western civilization. The careful scientific study of the language began in the 17th cent., but it was not until the efforts of lower critical scholars such as Constantin von Tischendorf, and the papyrologist Adolf Deissmann recovered both the text and the comparative non-Biblical material in the 19th cent. that NT scholarship came into its own. Modern *koiné* scholarship has utilized all of the statistical and linguistic tools of the 20th cent. to discuss and expand the meaning of the NT in its idiom. The work of James Hope Moulton, an Englishman, and Archibald Thomas Robertson, an American, with a number of scholars in Germany raised the study of the *koiné* and its unique style to a fully recognized science in its own right. In the meantime, the work of the lexicographers was growing even more rapidly, and year by year the list of words appearing only in the NT has shrunk until it is hardly worthy of mention. The early work of word collecting reached a plateau with the lexicon of Walter Bauer and has matured even further with the appearance in Ger. and Eng. of the *Theological Wordbook* edited by Gerhard Kittel. Yet many more problems remain to be solved and the fascination of the speech of the apostles lingers on undiminished by the ages.

BIBLIOGRAPHY. Classical Greek studies: W. Wackernagel, *Altindische Grammatik* (1880); Pauly-Wissowa, *Real-Encyclopädie* (1894-); W. W. Goodwin, *A Greek Grammar* (1895); K. Brugmann, *Grundriss der vergleichenden Grammatik der indogermanischen Sprachen* (1896-1916); F. Bechtel, *Die griechischen Dialekte,* 3 vols. (1921-1924); C. D. Buck, *Comparative Grammar of Greek and Latin* (1933); O. Hoffmann and A. Debrunner, *Geschichte der griechischen Sprache,* 2 vols. (1953, 1954); E. Schwyzer, *Griechische Grammatik,* 2 vols. 2nd. ed. (1953); C. D. Buck, *The Greek Dialects,* rev. ed. (1955); L. R. Palmer, *Achaeans and Indo-Europeans* (1955); J. Chadwick, "The Greek Dialects and Greek Prehistory," *Greece and Rome* 2nd. series III (1956) 38ff.; M. Ventris and J. Chadwick, *Documents in Mycenaean Greek* (1956); A. Thumb and A. Scherer, *Handbuch der griechischen Dialekte,* pt. 2 (1959); E. Vilborg, *A Tentative Grammar of Mycenaean Greek* (1960); J. Chadwick, "The Prehistory of the Greek Language," CAH rev. ed. (1963); ed. H. Birnbaum and J. Puhvel, *Ancient Indo-European Dialects* (1966).

Old Testament and New Testament Greek studies: E. de W. Burton, *Syntax of the Moods and Tenses in New Testament Greek* (1893); J. W. Burgon, *The Traditional Text of the Holy Gospels* (1896); J. H. Moulton, W. F. Howard and N. Turner, *A Grammar of New Testament Greek,* 3 vols. (1906-1963); L. Radermacher, *Neutestamentliche Grammatik* (1925), A. Deissmann, *Light From the Ancient East* (1927); G. Kittel, et al., *Theologisches Wörterbuch zum Neuen Testament* (1933 -) Eng. tr. TDNT (1964 -); E. Mayser, *Grammatik der griechischen Papyri aus der Ptolemäerzeit* (1934); A. Rahlfs, *Septuaginta,* 2 vols. (1935); A. T. Robertson, "Language of the New Testament," IDB vol. III, 1826-1832 (1939); J. H. Moulton and G. Milligan, *The Vocabulary of the Greek Testament Illustrated from Papyri and Other Non-Literary Sources* (1942); L. Radermacher, *Koine* (1947); B. M. Metzger, *Lexical Aids for Students of New Testament Greek* (1955); F. Rienecker, *Sprachlicher Schlüssel zum Griechischen Neuen Testament* (1956); W. Bauer, *A Greek-English Lexicon of the New Testament and Other Early Christian Literature* (1957); ed. G. D. Kilpatrik, 'Η *Καινὴ Διαθήκη* (1958); ed. K. Aland, F. L. Cross, J. Danielou, H. Riesenfeld and W. C. van Unnik, *Studia Evangelica* (1959); eds. A. Huck, H. Lietzmann and F. L. Cross, *Synopsis of the First Three Gospels* (1959); C. F. D. Moule, *An Idiom Book of the New Testament Greek,* 2nd. ed. (1959); B. de Solages, *A Greek Synopsis of the Gospels* (1959); J. Barr, *The Semantics of Biblical Language* (1961); F. Blass and A. Debrunner, *A Greek Grammar of the New Testament and Other Early Christian Literature* (1961); K. Beyer, *Semitische Syntax im Neuen Testament* (1962); M. E. Thrall, *Greek Particles in the New Testament* (1962); E. Nestle, *Novum Testamentum Graece cum apparatu critico curavit* (1963); M. Zerwick, *Biblical Greek* (1963) ed. K. Aland, *Synopsis Quattuor Evangeliorum* (1964); E. van N. Goetchius, *The Language of the New Testament* (1965); E. Risch, "Griechisch," *Lexikon der Alten Welt* (1965) cols. 1165-1171; N. Turner, *Grammatical Insights into the New Testament* (1965); ed. S. Benko, *The Catacombs and the Colosseum* (1971).

The study of New Testament Greek: C. Tischendorf, *Novum Testamentum Graece* 8th ed. maj. (1869-1872); M. R. Vincent, *A History of the Textual Criticism of the New Testament* (1899); F. G. Kenyon, *Recent Developments in the Textual Criticism of the Greek Bible* (1932); *The Text of the Greek Bible* (1937); B. M. Metzger, *Chapters in the History of New Testament Textual Criticism* (1963); L. Deuel, *Testaments of Time* (1965) 257-347; F. P. Dinneen, *An Introduction to General Linguistics* (1967) 70-113.

W. White, Jr.

GREEK RELIGION AND PHILOSOPHY

A. Greek religion

1. Homeric religion
2. Primitive religions
3. Mystery religions
4. Forms of worship

B. Greek philosophy
1. The Pre-Socratics
2. The age of Plato and Aristotle
3. The Hellenistic age

A. Greek religion. This account of Gr. religion is divided into three parts: the classical Homeric religion of the Olympic deities; an earlier religion of fear, some practices of which continued into the classical period; and the mystery religions that later displaced belief in Zeus.

1. Homeric religion. Classical Homeric religion acknowledged Zeus as its chief god. Zeus was not in any sense the creator of heaven and earth. Neither was he the prime mover, the *ens perfectissimum,* nor the eternal self-existing being; he was the son of a previous god.

Originally there was Chaos, then came Gaea (Earth) who married Uranus (Heaven), and in addition to several monsters this pair produced the Titan gods Kronos, his sister Rhea —whom he married—Tethys, and Oceanus, and others.

When Uranus imprisoned his monster offspring, Gaea persuaded Kronos to castrate Uranus, and from his blood the Giants and the fearsome Furies, pursuers of evildoers, came into being.

Kronos and Rhea gave birth to Zeus. Fearing that one of his sons might unseat him, Kronos wished to devour Zeus as he had devoured some of his other children; but Rhea hid Zeus and saved his life. When of age Zeus overthrew Kronos and the race of Titans. Zeus thus became the chief deity, the god of the sky; his brother Poseidon became god of the sea, and another brother, Hades, became lord of the underworld.

Zeus, by his sister-wife Hera, was the father of Ares, god of war; but Athena, goddess of wisdom, sprang full grown from her father's forehead. Zeus seduced Leto, his niece, who gave birth to Apollo and Artemis. He also seduced Dione, the daughter of Tethys and Oceanus, to beget Aphrodite, the goddess of love. Zeus's main occupation, pausing only occasionally to hurl a thunderbolt, seems to have been seducing both goddesses and mortal women. Zeus also set the example, so frequently followed by his worshipers, of unnatural vice with boys.

Other gods are: the crippled smithy Hephaestus who married Aphrodite (who also became the mother of Aeneas by Anchises of Troy); orgiastic Dionysus, the god of drunken revelry; Demeter, goddess of agriculture, sister of Zeus, by whom she had a daughter Persephone, who was abducted by Hades, but was finally compelled to live in the underworld for only three months a year—an arrangement that

Statue of Aphrodite. ©H.P.

produced winter. In addition to these main gods and goddesses were innumerable local spirits of caves, springs, trees, mountains; there were the evil demons, gorgons, and sirens; the lovely nymphs, and the half-man, half-horse centaurs.

The mythology, the stories, the dealings between the gods and men are told chiefly by Homer in his *Iliad* and *Odyssey*. Hesiod and the other sources sometimes give variations on the Homeric accounts. For the present purpose, these will be omitted and attention centered on the Gr. concept of the future life.

Little did the concept of the future life encourage morality, as in the conduct of Zeus. All men, good and bad alike, met the same fate in Hades. The only exceptions were a few heroes who were changed into demigods, and a few exceptionally wicked men who had perpetrated special crimes against the gods. For example, Tantalus killed his son Pelops, roasted the body, and served it to Zeus for dinner. For this crime Tantalus had to stand forever in water, which, when he was thirsty and stooped to drink, would recede and disappear; and when he reached up to pick fruit from branches near his head, a wind tantalizingly blew the branches out of reach. Another example is Sisyphus. Zeus had abducted Aegina, daughter of Asopus. Sisyphus told Asopus what had happened and where Zeus had taken his daughter. For this "crime" against Zeus, Sisyphus was condemned to roll a heavy stone up a hill; every time he got it near the top, it rolled down again. All other men descend at death to Hades.

Hades, however, is not a place of punishment. It is simply the abode of the dead, where, as Homer describes, "flit the shades of worn-out men." Memory remains, but reason is extinct. No information about those still living trickles down. The dead do not even know whether their friends and family have died. Dismal darkness replaces the sunlight and joy of the upper world. Achilles, himself a king, remarked, after he arrived in Hades, that a menial position on earth was superior to that of a king in the underworld.

The Homeric religion is often pictured as one of happy enthusiasm in the vigorous game of life. The Greeks admired athletes and warriors; they lusted and reveled in drunken feasts; they admired beauty and produced triumphs of sculpture and architecture; and they celebrated their interests in song and story. They could be happy, however, only through deliberate thoughtlessness, for their religion gave them no hope. Death ended it all, and utter dreariness was their uniform fate.

2. *Primitive religions.* Earlier religions were not any better. In the Homeric religion there was no fear of the gods. It is true that one had to make proper sacrifices to have a prosperous voyage or to receive some gift; one had to treat them with due respect and attend the public rites—but with ordinary precaution no one was going to get hurt. Contrariwise, the gods of the earlier religion, which lasted perhaps into the 6th cent., were malevolent spirits to be appeased. The practices of this religion continued on through antiquity even though their significance, with certain gruesome details altered, had been forgotten.

The Anthesteria, a three day spring festival in honor of Dionysus, during which everyone got drunk, preserves elements of a placation of ghosts. One of the sacrifices of this festival is not offered to Dionysus at all; nor, unlike the usual Gr. sacrifices, is it eaten by the people. Eating symbolizes either communion or identification with the god. The refusal to eat seems to indicate that the god, ghost, or spirit is being sent away. On the second day of this festival they chewed buckthorn, presumably to get rid of spirits; and a vase painting of the feast shows ghosts emerging from a *πίθος*, which was ostensibly a wine jar, but it could have been a casket for the dead.

In the autumn the Eleusinian rites were celebrated. In connection with Hades' rape of Persephone, her mother Demeter in remote antiquity established her temple and worship in Eleusis (a town about fifteen m. W of Athens). These rites became immensely popular, waning only upon the advent of Christianity, but briefly revived by Julian the Apostate.

It was a mystery religion, a secret society, forerunner of many similar secret religions of later times; and so well were the secrets guarded, by severe punishment and by devotion to Demeter, that very little is known of the secret details. A large part of the rites had to do with the purification of women. They washed suckling pigs in the ocean and threw them into a chasm. Sometime later the women dug up the decayed flesh, put it on the altar, and served it as a fertility charm. It is thought that in earlier days, the women used their own babies instead of baby pigs.

Another evidence of an earlier savage religion is in the worship of Isis, which the Greeks took up at the beginning of the Christian era. Although a late importation into Greece, this Egyp. religion seems to have incorporated a much earlier, purely Gr. ritual, in which the initiates stood under a slain bull on a scaffold, and were baptized in its blood. After this baptism they ate the bull's flesh. Vase paintings seem to hint its origin in human sacrifice.

3. *Mystery religions.* Later history brought other forms of religion. With the defeat of the Persians at Salamis, a great victory for the Olympian deities, Homeric religion became more and more a purely civic and patriotic exercise. The gain in patriotism was a loss in religion. Classic worship did not stimulate morality, it had never held out the hope of eternal life, and personal interest and devotion were still further minimized.

Delphi in Central Greece. Ancient cultural place near Mount Parnassus and the Gulf of Corinth. Theater and Temple of Apollo in the foreground.

At the same time, philosophy and science undermined belief in the myths: it was the clouds and not Zeus that produced rain; the sun was not a god, but a hot stone; and so on. Sophism, though refuted by Plato and Aristotle in the 4th cent., made that century an age of secular individualism. In the 3rd cent., credulity seemed to triumph.

Pure secularism could not satisfy the majority of the people. They were economically prosperous, but this prosperity came through Alexander's destruction of the Gr. city-states. Rome later absorbed the whole territory. This development eradicated Zeus and patriotism, and left the individual in the hands of capricious Luck, Tyche, now deified. The situation stimulated the need for a more personal religion, and in such a climate mystery religions developed. Some of them may have been continuous with the early rites of fear, but they were so altered as to become religions of hope. Such mysteries existed as early as 400 B.C.; Orphism and the Eleusinian mysteries existed in some form even earlier; but they proliferated in the cent. before and the cent. after Christ.

In general, the mysteries were secret societies whose secrets or mysteries would guarantee a happy future life to their initiates. None of the mysteries included any concept of a resurrection of the body, but in opposition to the idea of Hades they asserted the possibility of a blessed immortality.

Some were more moral than the usual Gr. religion. Orphism, with its theory of the transmigration of souls, taught that wrongdoing is punished in this life, but if not, then in the future life. The Pythagoreans were a philosophic school and a religious brotherhood. One of their more moral principles was that of friendship, out of which came the story of Damon and Pythias. They also enforced a set of rules or taboos: members were not to eat beans, for earth spirits came up from below through the hollow stalks and reside in the beans; linen clothing, not woolen, was required; and they would not sit with the left leg crossed over the right. Chiefly, they held that salvation comes by knowledge; this principle motivated their serious and principal work in mathematics.

4. *Forms of worship.* After the Apostle Paul looked around Athens, he remarked that the city was "very religious"; it even had an altar to an unknown god. Strabo agreed with the apostle, for his description of one locality is, "All the region is full of shrines of Artemis, Aphrodite, and the nymphs . . . There are also many shrines of Hermes on the roads, and of Poseidon on the sea shore."

There were more than 200 shrines in Athens. Besides the great temples—triumphs of architecture, many shrines were of modest construction, some without any roofed building, just stone altars in the open, or a post with the head of Hermes on it.

Parenthetically, in Acts 14:12, the people did not call Barnabas Jupiter and Paul Mercury, as in the KJV, but they called Barnabas Zeus and Paul Hermes. In Acts 19:28 the goddess is Artemis, not Diana.

There was no central religious authority, and the ritual at any one shrine had no definite connection with the others. One god had many local shrines, and he was worshiped under such different aspects of his nature and with such different traditions that he was hardly the same god.

The large temples were staffed with priests to care for them, to manage their wealth, and to regulate the dense traffic of state occasions. There were priests for lesser places; but there was no organized priesthood. No particular moral or educational qualifications were required of the priests; rather the qualification was a handsome physique. The office, at least in the larger temples, brought them honor and respect such that they could serve as ambassadors and emissaries in time of war.

The term of office was usually one year; sometimes it was held for life; sometimes, hereditary; sometimes the priest was selected by lot; sometimes the office was sold to the highest bidder. For many of the lesser shrines there was no priest at all; anyone, esp. the father of a family, could offer his sacrifice by himself. Sacrifices were even offered at home: parts of the animal were burned on the hearth and the family ate the rest.

Even in the slaughter houses and butcher shops, such sacrifices were burned before the gods. For this reason, immature Christians refused to eat meat at banquets, suspecting it had been offered to idols. In 1 Corinthians 8, the apostle tells the church that such scruples are foolish, for "food will not commend us to God." At the same time, the mature Christian must avoid wounding the weak conscience of these ignorant Christians. Later, they may learn that all food is clean.

Before the sacrifices were burned, the worshipers examined the pieces, liver, and entrails; if they were firm and of good color, it was a propitious omen. Divination was one of the most frequent features of Gr. worship. In addition to the parts of the sacrificed animals, signs of the future were seen in the flight of birds, lightning from Zeus, eclipses, meteors, etc. That Troy would be captured in the tenth year was indicated by a serpent devouring a sparrow and her eight young (*Iliad* II, 308).

The use of natural events as signs declined from 400 B.C. on, and reliance was put on oracles, sacrifice, and astrology.

B. Greek philosophy. Greek philosophy in general had little interest in Gr. religion. The philosophic development, a minority movement in any age, is divided into three stages: the Pre-Socratics, whose chief interest was science; Plato and Aristotle, who attacked the

The altar before the steps to the Temple of Apollo at Pompeii. ©*Lev*

problem of epistemology; and the Hel. age with its largely ethical emphasis.

1. *The pre-Socratics.* Pre-Socratic philosophy began with Thales, a resident of Miletus in Ionia, who predicted the solar eclipse of 28 May 585 B.C., and so imposed scientific law on hitherto unorganized observations.

He and his fellow Milesians Anaximander and Anaximenes, though they differed on minor details agreed on the following five universal principles: (1) all things have emerged from a single underlying substance (because unity needs no explanation whereas it would be necessary to give a reason why there were ninety-three instead of merely fifty-four elements and no such reason can be found); (2) this substance is eternal: it never came into being and will never cease to be; (3) the substance is inexhaustible, prob. infinitely extended in space; (4) our immediate world or cosmos is limited in space and in duration, but other worlds preceded it and will follow upon its dissolution (it is doubtful that the Milesians asserted the existence of many worlds at one time); (5) motion, the processes of nature, the constant change in all things, is spontaneous—the substance is not dead, but alive, and the impetus to change is immanent in it rather than the effect of an extraneous cause.

The assertion of one substance leads to a problem that plagued antiquity and has not been satisfactorily answered to this day. If all things originate from one substance, each thing must or at least can turn into anything else. Observation shows that the bread we eat becomes both hair and fingernails, or, more generally, wheat can become man, dog, and donkey. Water can become fire—the wood of a tree has come from water, and wood burns —and earth can become air. For example, lead comes from uranium, whose properties are far different. How can the existence of qualitative differences be explained, esp. if basically everything is the same stuff?

Thales seems to have appealed merely to observation: water becomes steam or air as it changes into fire, and the fire in the lightning turns to rain. This really leaves little basis for Thales' view that water is the cosmic substance and that fire, air, and earth are derivatives. Anaximander made all four derivatives from an unobservable "boundless" substance. It was a stuff in which the qualities of earth, air, fire and water were so mingled that it had no quality of its own. The process by which the ordinary "elements" with their qualities came from the boundless was a whirling motion, somewhat similar to that of a cream separator.

Anaximenes, the last of the Milesians, identified air as the original substance (because water and earth fall, but air supports itself), and explained the emergence of qualities by condensation and rarefaction. Thus the concept of a natural, mechanical law is the contribution these first philosophers made to civilization.

Heraclitus (c. 525-475 B.C.) lived near Miletus in Ephesus. His attention was not focused on the generation of qualities, as in later philosophies, but on the fundamental problem of motion itself. If the cosmic substance changes spontaneously, then change is universal: "all things flow" and "no man can step into the same river twice." On the second stepping the river would not be the same because the water would not be the same, and even the bed and banks would have eroded somewhat. Since the river is its bed, banks, and water, therefore nothing remains the same.

This applies to persons too. A man cannot step twice because it is not the same man: "In the same rivers we step and we do not step; we are and we are not." Thus persons and things do not exist; for when we say that something exists, we mean that it does not change, it stands still, it remains what it is and does not become something else. If it is blue and two inches wide, it stays blue and two inches wide. But if everything is in motion, then blue must change, and every quality and dimension is becoming different. Therefore nothing exists.

However, although everything changes, there is one thing that does not change—only it is not a "thing." There is a *law* of change that does not change. Heraclitus called it the Logos. The Gr. words bear two meanings, so that Heraclitus' sentence can be translated either as "This theory, always true, men do not understand," or as "This Logos, always existing, men do not understand."

If a law be considered a reality, what becomes of the view that the only reality is a single, physical, cosmic stuff? Can *corporeal monism* admit the reality of an incorporeal law? This question Heraclitus in his own day could not understand. He identified the basic substance as fire and at the same time gave it the characteristics of a directing intelligence: "Wisdom is one thing: to understand the mind that governs all things through all"; and "the thunderbolt directs the course of all things"; and "this cosmos, the same for all, none of the gods or men has made, but it always was and is and ever shall be an everliving fire, kindled in measures and extinguished in measures." Unable to distinguish, Heraclitus confused physical fire with a mechanical law of measurement, and both with a directing mind, which men today would say is neither a law nor a body. Thus problems multiplied and philosophy developed.

The Pythagoreans (alluded to in the section on Gr. religion) formed a school in southern Italy about this time and continued all through antiquity. They were mathematicians. Pythagoras himself, a contemporary of Heraclitus, is said to have discovered the Pythagorean theorem: the square of the hypotenuse of a right-angled triangle equals the sum of the squares of the other two sides. Without their geometry, astronomy would not have been able to make much headway. Their headway was considerable, for Eratosthenes about 300 B.C. measured the circumference of the earth with an accuracy about just one per cent off modern estimates. Still, people think antiquity believed the earth to be flat.

The next philosopher, Parmenides (c. 475 B.C.), the chief member of the Eleatic school in Elea, southern Italy, addressed himself directly to the difficulties in Heraclitus and corporeal monism. Parmenides had been preceded by the poet Xenophanes (c. 590-500 B.C.?), who attacked the stupidity and impiety of Gr. polytheism. He insisted that there was but one God. Parmenides, not so religious, asserted merely that there is One.

He was troubled by a contradiction and therefore an absurdity in previous philosophy. How can a true monist assert a pluralism? How can one thing be another? How can a rational theory be irrational?

Thales had said fire is water, and Heraclitus said water is actually fire, but "pure" logic shows clearly that fire means and can only be fire, nothing else. To say that fire is water is like saying a square is a circle.

Not only so, but worse, Parmenides denied that water is water. Undoubtedly the two instances of water have the same meaning, but the word *is* denotes existence. Therefore the sentence means water is an existence. If fire cannot be water because the two words do not have the same meaning, water cannot *exist* because the two words mean different things. It is false that water is water, because it is false that water is. Water does not exist.

What, then, exists? Only that which can be asserted without contradiction or absurdity. Therefore only the existent is existent, or, Being is.

Being cannot have originated or come into being. It cannot have come from nonbeing, for nonbeing never has existed for anything to come from it. Nor can Being have come from Being, for Being is Being without any coming. Therefore origination is impossible and Being is eternal, immutable, and changeless.

If Being is changeless, there can be no motion. The earlier philosophies contradicted themselves by asserting both unity and motion, both one body and many differences, both identity and change.

Parmenides could not divest himself of the common notion that reality is corporeal. His one Being therefore was a solid, spherical, homogeneous body. Admittedly men see fire, water, and their differences; men see motion and change—but when men *see* rabbits jumping out of a hat or a man climbing a rope hanging from nothing, they *know* it is not so. Sensation must submit to reason. Absurdities cannot be true.

The Pluralists, however, could not repudiate sensation. There is a world of many different things; and if corporeal monism is absurd, let us retain motion, reject monism, and assert corporeal pluralism. This can be done in three ways.

Empedocles (c. 490-430 B.C.) asserted that there were four elements: earth, air, fire and water. Their basic qualitative differences are eternal, and the problem of their origination—either from a boundless or from one of them considered as original—is side-stepped. Other differences were somehow to be explained by chemical combinations; for example, bone is $W_2F_4E_2$. The theory of a finite number of qualitatively different elements was much later adopted by 19th cent. chemistry.

Empedocles could not, however, totally ignore the threat of Parmenides. Each element and each atom must be eternal and unchangeable like the Parmenidean Being. If so, motion is no longer spontaneous; matter, no longer alive, is inherently inert, and extraneous moving forces are necessary—two forces, Love and Hate, one to cause mixture and combination, the other to cause dissolution.

Anaxagoras immediately saw that one moving force was sufficient, for every mixing is a separation from previous combinations. Then too, whereas Empedocles was clumsy in clarifying the distinction between inert, corporeal elements and the newly assumed principles of motion, Anaxagoras described his single principle as a mind, totally separate from matter, the wise director of the cosmos. After all, if men's minds direct their bodies, why should not a universal mind direct the Universe? As Socrates complained later on, however, Anaxagoras had difficulty in carrying through this part of his theory and never really transcended the mechanistic position.

Empedocles also had made a second mistake that Anaxagoras corrected. It may be good to assume four original qualitative differences, but four are not enough. Since Parmenides had shown that origination is irrational, a philosopher to be a pluralist must assume that every quality is original and eternal. Hence, instead of earth, air, fire, and water, the elements are hair, blood, fingernails, wood, bone, and so on to infinity.

If an infinite number of original qualities seems awkward, and if four are not enough, there is only one other possibility for atomistic pluralism: an infinite number of atoms, of all shapes and sizes, but without any qualities at all.

Democritus (c. 460-370 B.C.), a native of Abdera in Thrace, with Leucippus, produced the classic theory of atomism. Each atom is impenetrable and indivisible, the characteristics are purely mechanical or geometrical. Qualities, such as hot and cold, wet and dry, do not exist in reality: they are subjective effects of mechanical action in the organs of sensation. For example, if in a compound body the smooth surfaces of the atoms are on the exterior, we receive a sensation of coolness when we touch it; but if the points and sharp edges of the atoms are on the surface, our sensation is one of heat. The atoms themselves are neither cold nor hot, blue nor red, bitter nor sweet, and so on.

Democritus found it unnecessary to posit a moving principle. Each atom moves when and because another atom hits it. There is no point asking what started the first atom on its first motion. There is no first atom and there never was a first motion.

However, whereas neither mind nor spontaneity is needed, Democritus, to explain motion, had to invent the concept of empty space. If all space were completely filled with solid atoms, none of them could budge. The Ionians did not need empty space, for their cosmic stuff was alive and nonatomic. Parmenides, too, had virtually equated empty space with nothing, for only body is real. Empedocles and Anaxagoras had not yet seen the implications of pluralism. So the credit for this concept belongs to Democritus, although the later philosophers did not regard it as much of a credit.

The pre-Socratic period, with its scientific interests, may be said to end with the destructive arguments of Zeno, the Eleatic, a disciple of Parmenides.

First, the clever story of Achilles and the tortoise proves that motion is impossible. Reduced to its bare, essential mathematics, it argues that for an atom to move to a far point, it must first traverse half the distance; before it can get half way, it must go a quarter way; and before it arrives at the quarter mark, it must arrive at the eighth mark. To start at all, it must exhaust this inexhaustible infinite series; therefore it cannot start. And therefore motion is impossible.

Similarly, at any moment of an arrow's alleged flight, it is at rest because its extremities coincide with two points in empty space. But since the flight takes place wholly within a series of moments, the arrow is always at rest and never moves.

Also, sensation is impossible. When an ocean wave "thunders" against the rocks, no atom produces an audible sensation; but the wave is nothing but atoms, therefore it produces no sound.

Finally, if there must be space for an atom to exist in, there must be a superspace for space to exist in, and a super-superspace. It would be better never to start such a useless series. Pluralism is refuted.

2. *The age of Plato and Aristotle* was introduced by the Sophists. The reaction of these men to the failure of atomism explains why science receded in importance and epistemology became the pressing problem.

The early pre-Socratic attempt to give a rational account of the universe failed because Parmenides had shown that corporeal monism is absurd. Zeno had shown that corporeal pluralism is absurd, but if one body cannot furnish an explanation, and if many bodies cannot, and since there must be either one body or many, it follows that the universe cannot be explained at all. Knowledge is impossible.

This skeptical conclusion is supported by the Pythagorean theorem. Further study of this early triumph in geometry revealed the existence of irrational numbers, such as the square root of two. If irrationality is embedded in pure mathematics, surely any further knowledge is impossible.

Ordinary Greeks had always acknowledged certain moral truths as well. The murder of parents was wrong—everyone knew that; and so was the neglect of funeral rites, and so on. But the Pers. wars had acquainted the Greeks with a foreign code of conduct, the old Gr. morality began to break down, and soon no one could know any ethical truth. All knowledge is impossible.

If knowledge is impossible, there is no use wasting time on mathematics, astronomy, or ethical principles. A wise man must renounce the life of the intellect and exercise his volition. The problem is to set a goal and achieve it.

The more ordinary Sophists therefore gave lectures in vocational education. They taught navigation or wrestling. The name Sophist, with its evil connotation of making the worse appear the better argument, got its reputation because most ambitious young men wanted to be instructed in politics. Therefore the Sophists taught the devices of oratory, the knack of swaying audiences and gaining votes. Neither the personal aim nor the political policy is subject to intellectual ethical principles. Simply willing it, or, better, achieving it, makes it right.

Two outstanding Sophists, who, though they may have taught oratory to young politicians, also reflected on the more profound philosophical aspects of their practice. Gorgias, with an Eleatic background, taught that (1) nothing exists; (2) if anything existed, no one could know it; and (3), if anyone could know it, he could not teach it to someone else.

Protagoras, with a Heraclitean background, accepted the proposition (1) all things constantly change; (2) knowledge, since men do not wish to discard the word, is perception; and (3) "Man is the measure of all things, of the existence of the things that are and the non-existence of the things that are not."

The Man-measure theory meant that everything is as it appears, no matter to whom. A wind is chilling to a man with a fever; the "same" wind feels exhilarating to a man in good health. It is not the same wind because a wind is an appearance due to the combination of certain external motions and one's sensory organs. The wind is the perception. Since two people cannot have the same sensation, for my toothache is not yours, two people never sense the same thing. Each person lives in a separate world of his own perceptions. Therefore whatever a man thinks is true, that is true for him, and no one else can judge. This is the theory of relativism, the denial of fixed, eternal truth.

This theory was resurrected by William James and John Dewey and pushed to incredible extremes by French existentialism in this day, and it has become widely accepted in American education. If Plato can make a pertinent reply, his usefulness cannot be said to have ended in antiquity.

Plato, interested in mathematics, science, and very particularly in ethics and politics, was obliged therefore to defend, first of all, the possibility of knowledge.

His preliminary answer to Sophism was that it is self-contradictory. Since Protagoras holds that all beliefs are true, and since many people believe that Protagoras' theory is false, their belief must be true and Protagoras must admit the falsity of his own position.

Or, again, if everything is constantly changing and nothing remains fixed, then, as blue does not remain blue and chilling does not remain chilling, neither can seeing remain seeing nor perception perception; from which it follows that if perception is knowledge, it immediately changes into "not-knowledge."

The key to the situation and the great absurdity is that in this view everything is relative *except* relativism. There is no fixed truth *except* the fixed truth that nothing is fixed. Relativism is always asserted absolutely.

Finally, Protagoras had located sensation in the sense organ, so that one eye could sense and know, when the other was closed and could not know. But, replies Plato, this reduces man to a wooden horse of Troy: one soldier sees out of one eye, another does not see out of the opposite ear. Man, however, is not such an aggregate of separate senses. It is the man who senses, not the eye or the ear. The senses unite in one power, the soul or the mind, and it is this power that uses the organs.

The eye cannot see a sound and the ear cannot hear a color; but the man perceives both the color and the sound, compares them, and judges that they are different. This is what the horse of Troy could never do.

At this stage of the argument, Plato makes his great, constructive contribution. When corporeal monism met its fate at the hands of Parmenides, the pluralists thought that the fault lay in the monism. When Zeno exploded pluralism, the Sophists gave up hope of rationality. Plato's genius saw another possibility. If neither corporeal monism nor corporeal pluralism can explain the universe, the fault must lie in corporealism. Reality cannot be material. Or, conversely, if knowledge is to be possible, there must be a noncorporeal reality.

In the refutation of Protagoras, Plato had asserted the existence of a soul or mind, necessary to judge disparate sensations. This soul is, of course, incorporeal. Knowledge also requires incorporeal objects for the soul to know. Plato calls these objects Ideas, and his early dialogues explain at length why such objects must exist.

The easiest argument to understand is the one based on the occurrence of common qualities. There is a very small steel cube; here are two ivory dice; here are some blocks that children play with. We call them all cubes. What then is *cube*? If it were one of the physical objects, the others would not be cubes because the others are not that one. If *cube* were the aggregate of all of them, none of them would be a cube because none is the aggregate. Furthermore, all these cubes could be destroyed, but Cube would remain. Hence Cube cannot be a physical thing; it is an eternal, unchangeable, supersensible object of thought. It is a single, unique Idea, whereas the physical objects are a plurality.

So it is with all common qualities. When two or more objects are similar, the similarity is real. It is something that exists: there *is* such a similarity, but these realities are not bodies.

A second argument is that thought and science require such an object. A geometer does not study this one triangle drawn on the blackboard. A physician does not study this one case of measles. The object of geometry is Triangle, and the object of medicine is Health. There are many drawn triangles, of all sizes, equilateral, isoceles, and scalene; but there is only one, definite Idea of triangularity. If a particular triangle drawn on a blackboard were the Idea of triangle and the object of knowledge, then knowledge would disappear when it was erased, for knowledge cannot be knowledge of the nonexistent. To know means to know something. To know nothing means not to know. Hence Ideas exist.

Since Ideas are not sensory objects that can be seen with the eyes, Plato must answer the inescapable question how they can be known. His example is the Idea of equality. When a man sees two peas in a pod or two pebbles on a beach, he carelessly says they are equal. Stopping to think, he knows well enough that they are not exactly equal. It would be better to say they approximate equality. This example shows, first, that the concept of equality cannot be abstracted from experience because equality is never found in experience; and, second, that men actually know equality before they have ever seen two pebbles. They must have known equality before their first experience because at that time they are ready to use the concept in judging that the two pebbles are not equal but approximate equality. Men have to have the concept before they can use it as a norm in judging.

True enough, as youngsters, men may never have consciously thought of equality until the moment they saw the pebbles. At that moment the pebbles remind them of an equality they know without ever having sensed it. Since sensation begins at birth, it follows that before birth men's souls must have existed in the Ideal world where they were in contact with all the Ideas. What is ordinarily called learning is therefore reminiscence. As the lyre of Simmias reminded men of Simmias, although it does not look like him, so the two pebbles, though not strictly equal, remind men of the absolute equality they previously knew but had as youngsters forgotten.

The soul therefore is immortal. It existed before birth and continues to live after death. Because of the soul's immortality and because the Ideas—Ideas of Justice, Temperance, Piety—are immutable, one can reject the relativistic ethics of the Sophists. Knowledge is possible; ethical knowledge can be taught as well as geometry; and both are valid at all times and in all places.

Since intellect and truth have displaced Sophism's unbridled will, the good life is not a life of pleasure, but of knowledge. Pleasures rivet the soul to the body and the body is a tomb (*σῶμα σῆμά*, an old Orphic adage of ascetic tendency). The philosopher detaches himself from sensation as much as possible and prepares for pure communion with the Ideas after death. In the *Phaedo*, a relatively early or middle dialogue, Plato is moderately ascetic. In the late dialogue *Philebus*, he recognizes that some pleasures are harmless and even necessary to life. Their admission into the good life, however, is strictly controlled by intellect, knowledge, and truth.

Having thus solved the problem of knowledge and ethics, Plato returned to cosmology. His mathematical physics, his astronomy in the *Timaeus*, and his invention of the eight-note scale, cannot be reproduced here, nor his adoption of a heliocentric theory later perfected by Aristarchus; but the relation he envisaged between God and the world needs mention.

The supreme Being, to which nothing is superior or equal, is the world of Ideas. These Ideas—of Equality, Courage, Man, and so on—are not merely an ordered series of concepts. They are indeed an ordered system, with the Idea of Good in the highest position, on which all other Ideas depend for existence and in whose light alone men can know them. Beyond the status of ordered concepts, the world of Ideas is a living mind. The relatively late dialogue *Sophist* gives the arguments, and the conclusions are further worked out by the Neoplatonists.

Modern students, who have been taught to believe that the world is basically an aggregate of inanimate atoms, must be reminded that in ancient times and even in modern times this has been the minority view. Most philosophers —Hegel and Leibniz, the Stoics and Plato— have held that the universe is a living being. It is all the more natural to conceive of the world of Ideas as a mind.

Independently and eternally existing, yet lower in rank than the Ideas, is "God," or the Demiurge, the personal Maker of heaven and earth.

The Demiurge is confronted with another independent and eternal being, or, rather, nonbeing; viz. chaotic space. Since the Demiurge is good and devoid of envy, he wishes to make space good too. To this end he fashions a world-soul and through it produces the visible world here below by using the world of Ideas as a model, or blueprint, and imposing its order on space or matter.

The visible world therefore, like the world of Ideas, is a living being. Note also that it is not created, as the Hebrew-Christian view has it, but is made out of preexisting stuff. Whereas a particular fashioning may occur at a definite time, the process, as explained below, is without beginning or end.

Unfortunately space is inherently recalcitrant. It cannot be made perfect; that is, neither Equality nor Justice, not even Horse and Man, can be perfectly exemplified here below. What is still worse, in a sort of rebellion, the world collapses at intervals and needs to be remade.

Thus cosmological history is cyclical as all natural processes are. World follows world, reincarnation follows reincarnation, as day follows night, forever. For the relation of Platonic philosophy to Christian theology, *see the articles on* Philo Judaeus, Augustine and the latter part of Ethics.

Aristotle (384-322 B.C.) was Plato's student but not Plato's disciple. The great difference was carried over into Christian theology, for as Augustine's tendencies, dominant until A.D. 1250 were Platonic, so Thomas Aquinas eventually succeeded in making Aristotelianism the official philosophy of Roman Catholicism.

The intricate detail of Aristotle's work is enormous and in many ways admirable. His theory of the syllogism, with perhaps only one alteration in the Middle Ages, was not carried further until A.D. 1850. He wrote several volumes of zoological observations. The eight books on *Physics* define motion and its several species, discuss time, place, and infinity, and propose a theory of a finite universe. The work concludes with the ponderous cosmological proof of the existence of the Prime Mover, or God, who sits on the circumference of the heavens, blissfully ignorant of the world below.

Aristotle was as greatly opposed to skepticism and sophism as Plato was; but he thought that a world of Ideas beyond the visible world was redundant, that reminiscence of a previous life contradicted the testimony of man's consciousness, and that sensation was a satisfactory basis for higher forms of knowledge.

Therefore he asserted that the primary realities are physical individuals, such as Socrates and Mt. Olympus. These primary realities are objects of perception, and all learning comes through sensation.

Strictly speaking, men neither see, hear, nor touch other men. Men see colors, hear sounds, and touch the hard or the soft. These are the special senses and the special sensibles. Some sensations come through two senses: men see and touch magnitude, shape, number, rest, and motion. Beyond the special senses is a *common sense,* common at least to sight and touch, and five common sensibles. By this common sense, men also compare disparate sensations, for comparison requires the two objects to be presented to a single judge; and as these objects are perceived by sense, the judge must be a sense—not any special sense, but the common sense.

There is also perception *per accidens*: A man does not perceive another man because he is a man but because he is a white object. Thus the perception of the primary realities is "accidental."

Higher forms of knowledge, however, transcend sensation and primary realities. There are secondary realities, viz., species or concepts. Socrates is only one of several men seen, and there are other mountains besides Mt. Olympus.

The common quality in all men or all mountains is the species or concept. It is as unchangeable as a Platonic Idea, but it is not learned in the Platonic manner.

Briefly, the learning process begins in sensation, upon which follow memory images. From these images, the intellect by a process of abstraction detaches the concept, the secondary reality, the definition of the species. This concept or form can be abstracted because it is embedded in the sensory matter, rather than existing independently in an Ideal world.

The intellect that does the abstracting is really two intellects. First, there is the passive intellect. As the sense organ requires the stimulation of a sense object before there is any sensation, so there must first be an object of thought before there can be any thinking. Unlike the sense organ, however, which has various corporeal qualities of its own, the mind before it thinks is actually nothing. If it had qualities, these, like colored glasses, would distort the objects of thought, in which case man could never have accurate knowledge. When the mind thinks it receives the qualities, or, better it receives the object it thinks and thus becomes the object it thinks.

Corresponding to this passive intellect which becomes all things, is the active intellect that makes all things. One might suppose that the intellectual objects themselves would stimulate the mind and raise it from possibility to actuality—but no: as color must be actualized by light before it can be sensed, so the active intellect must disengage the concepts or forms from their corporeal matrix and thus actualize them for reception into the passive intellect.

Aristotle further says:

> it is this [active] intellect which is separable and impassive and unmixed, being in its essential nature an activity. . . . This intellect has no intermittance in its thought. It is, however, only when separated that it is its true self; and this, its essential nature, is alone immortal and eternal. But we do not remember [the activity of this intellect before our birth] because this [active intellect] is impassive, while the intellect which can be affected is perishable and without this does not think at all (*De Anima,* III 5, 430 a 17-25).

Aristotle. From a sculpture after a Greek original. ©*H.P.*

When Aristotle in another place asserts that the active intellect enters a human being "from without," commentators wonder whether or not the eternal, active intellect is God. In the Middle Ages the Mohammedan philosopher Averroes identified the active intellect as God and therefore denied individual immortality. Thomas Aquinas had an individual intellect for each person and so tried to support belief in a future life. In any case, Aristotle's theory hardly fits into Christian doctrine, for even on Thomas's interpretation his active intellect is eternal, not merely immortal, and has therefore existed as long as God Himself.

Something more must be said about abstraction. So far only the concepts of man and mountain have been actualized. People who lived their life on great plains might never get the concept of mountain; but there are other concepts so basic that without them a person could not think at all. These concepts are called the categories.

The word "category," in Gr. as well as in ordinary Eng., means simply a classification. In philosophy, however, it means the fundamental, inescapable classifications. Whereas Parmenides identified the verb "is" with the meaning of "exist," Aristotle insisted that there are ten different meanings of the verb "to be."

These nine categories are: substance, quantity, quality, relation, and five others that are not discussed at much length.

Substance or reality, primary and secondary, has already been mentioned. Quantity, quality, and relation are supposed to be quite distinct, though Aristotle's arguments do not seem conclusive, and if not, the system is seriously defective. At any rate these concepts are the result of further abstraction, and therefore, unlike the Kantian categories, are empirically based.

Beyond this Aristotle must establish the fundamental principles of the various sciences. First of all, the law of contradiction is the law of all being. It is an ontological law and not merely a law of thought; it is a law of thought because it is first a law of being.

In addition to the law of contradiction, which covers all subjects, each science has its own fundamental laws, without which it could not be kept separate from other sciences. No one of these laws can be so restricted as to cover only a part of a science, nor so general and remote as to combine uncombinable subjects. Geometrical truths, for example, cannot be demonstrated on arithmetical principles. Thus the ideal of a single all-inclusive science is excluded. Today one wonders how Aristotle would explain analytic geometry, not to mention cybernetics, or the contemporary reduction of chemistry to physics. He is honest enough, however, to say "It is hard to be sure whether one knows or not, for it is hard to be sure whether one's knowledge is based on the principles of each genus or not; and it is precisely this that constitutes knowledge" (*Posterior Analytic,* I 9, 76 a 26).

After manifold sensations, memory, and wide experience, the intellect abstracts the fundamental laws. This is the process of induction and intuition; and although the processes of opinion and calculation are sometimes mistaken, intuition is foolproof and unfailingly accurate. It is consoling to know that at least part of the time men cannot possibly be mistaken, even if they cannot be sure what part of the time it is.

The most direct contact of Aristotle's philosophy with Christian theology is in his cosmological proof of the existence of God. The argument is extremely intricate; only its general character can be indicated in a brief statement of its five stages.

First, motion is eternal: it never began and will never end. Second, since motion presupposes a mover, there must be a single, eternal mover. Third, this eternal cause of motion cannot itself be in motion. Fourth, the unmoved Mover has no magnitude. And fifth, "The mover must of necessity be situated at the center or on the circumference, for these are the principles of a sphere. Now, the things that move most rapidly are those nearest the mover. Since, then, the rotation of the outer sphere is the quickest motion, there is where the mover must be" (Physics VIII 10, 267 b 6).

3. The Hellenistic age. After Plato and Aristotle, after Alexander had extinguished the independence of the Gr. city-states, and with the rise of Rom. influence came the Hel. age. As the pre-Socratics had been interested in science, and Plato and Aristotle in epistemology, the Hel. age thought it time to emphasize ethics. The Epicurean and the Stoic schools arose about 300 B.C.

Although ethics presupposes that the epistemological problem has been solved, these schools emphatically rejected the Platonic solution, and agreed with Aristotle only on the point that knowledge is based on sensation. They even defended the possibility of knowledge in their own way. Both Epicureanism and Stoicism continued in existence for over five centuries, but they had less and less success in persuading philosophers that they possessed the secret of knowledge. The Epicureans were widely despised, and Stoicism faced difficult criticism. Neither did the school of Aristotle conquer the world; rather it went into eclipse. Plato's Academy turned skeptical. If any philosophy can be said to have surpassed the other at this time, it was skepticism.

A skeptical school was founded by Pyrrho about 300 B.C., continued by Arcesilaus (315-240), who was actually a Platonist, the brilliant Carneades (219-129), the relatively insignificant Agrippa, about A.D. 100, who made an excellent summary of the arguments, and Sextus Empiricus a cent. later.

The Stoics had asserted the occurrence of a sensory impression so clear and distinct that its veracity could not be doubted. Carneades replied that there is no specific difference discernible among impressions. Dreams and illusions, while they last, are as vivid and convincing as sensations. Furthermore that man cannot distinguish between twins and mistake Castor for Pollux shows that two different objects can produce the same impression. If knowledge is based on sensation, as the Stoics say, there is no sure knowledge.

Aenesidemus, about the beginning of the Christian era, added that the sense organs of animals differ from those of men: dogs receive different odors; birds, different sounds; and flies receive visual impressions different from man's. Why should man assume that his sensations are more accurate pictures of reality than those of the animals. Indeed, animal lovers emphasize the greater acuity of their humble friends.

Agrippa reduced the skeptical arguments to five basic points, which emphasize the logical difficulties of nonskeptical philosophies. First, opinions differ on all subjects. Second, to prove the truth of one opinion, philosophers have recourse to a second, and so on ad infinitum. Third, to escape this regress, they go around in a circle. Fourth, they make an assumption, which only begs the question. Finally, all objects are relative to the subject, as Aenesidemus so clearly showed, and hence nothing can be known as it really is by itself.

If knowledge is unattainable, what becomes of ethics and the daily decisions of life? One rule of action adopted by skepticism was, "It makes no difference." One day a skeptic, about to cross a road, jumped back to avoid a four-horse chariot. A friend chided him on his inconsistency: he should not have jumped out of the path of the chariot because it made no difference. "But," replied the skeptic, "that is why I jumped back—it made no difference."

Sextus Empiricus tried to accommodate skepticism to the needs of living. Anticipating pragmatism and John Dewey, he held that the senses were made, not for knowledge, but for use; and when men are hungry they should eat. If someone objects that a statement such as this, relative to the purpose of sensation, purports to be knowledge, Sextus replies that adherence to such principles must be motivated, not by reflection, but by a conscious lack of reflection. Medical theories founded on cosmology are worthless, but empirical medicine can cure disease. Without claiming to know anything, men can formulate practical rules and become proficient—not in science, but in art. Medicine is an art; man did not learn it, he practiced it. Man is a doer, not a knower.

The reaction against skepticism and against Stoicism became prominent and effective with the work of the Neoplatonist Plotinus (A.D. 205-270).

Neoplatonism, previously thought to have originated with Plotinus' teacher, Ammonius Aaccus, can be found in the generation that followed Plato. Not only are characteristic Neoplatonic themes found in Speusippus and Xenocrates, the first and second presidents of the Academy after Plato, but Aristotle him-

Bust of Socrates. ©*H.P.*

self gives, even if mistakenly, a Neoplatonic interpretation of Plato. Nevertheless, it was not until Plotinus wrote six books of nine tractates each, the Enneads, that Neoplatonism displaced all the other schools of antiquity.

The weak point in Stoicism, by reason of which the skeptics could so greatly embarrass them, was their empiricism and materialism. Even apart from the skeptics, the Stoics themselves were troubled to give a corporeal explanation to the incorporeal phenomena of meaning or significance, space, and time. Because these difficulties had become acute, the time was propitious for Plotinus to insist that knowledge presupposes spiritual realities.

In one of the first tractates he wrote (Ennead IV 7, *On the Immortality of the Soul*), Plotinus rejects the Epicurean atomic soul, the Stoic wax soul, the behavioristic theory of harmony, the Aristotelian form of the organic body, and puts in their place a pure spiritual being.

Briefly, the arguments are that life cannot be explained as an arrangement of inanimate particles, for an arrangement requires a prior arranging mind. Further, if a soul were a material quantity and could be split into inanimate parts, the phenomenon of multiple births could not be explained; each pup of a litter of puppies is a complete dog, he does not have half a soul, part of a soul, but an entire and integral soul. The characteristic of a soul is to remain essentially the same through infinite division, to be entire at every point, to have the derivative part equal to the whole, and this is the characteristic not of body but of incorporeal spirit.

Plotinus analyzes sensation to support the same point. Perception requires the presence of the whole object in the entire unitary soul. If the soul were not unitary but extended, it would be impossible to judge that the perceived color white is different from the perceived taste sweet.

Thought even more clearly than perception requires an incorporeal soul. Even the materialistic Stoics admit that men can think of empty space and conceptual meaning. No material soul could grasp these immaterial realities.

Seemingly the discussion envisages an individual soul, like that of Socrates. If, however, the essential characteristic of soul is to remain the same and be entire at every point; and if all souls are one in species, as the Platonic argument on common qualities requires; and if, finally, a philosopher is bound to assert the unity of the universe, all souls must unite in a single world-Soul.

Although Plotinus investigates psychology in great detail, he does not use this material to build up an empirical argument to prove the existence of a world-Soul. For this purpose, general Platonic principles are sufficient. He does show how the presupposition of a world-Soul accounts for psychological details, and he thus escapes opposing objections.

One of these objections is that if your soul and my soul are one soul, then I would feel your toothache. Plotinus replies that a single soul in two bodies gives two different combinations, so that unitary Humanity moves when I move but is simultaneously at rest in you. Hence two people will have different impressions, though their soul is one. An analogy is found in a single person when the left hand does not feel the pain the right hand feels. In this case, the soul is entire and complete in each hand, but the impressions are different. So, also, with different persons.

A question arises why the world-Soul, so superior to man's, descends and contaminates itself by entering man's bodies and becoming their souls. The answer is that the existence of the world presupposes some principle of duality; the Soul is inherently productive; therefore it descends of necessity and produces men's souls and the world that lies even below us. This descent is not all loss, for the Soul's contact with the sensible world heightens its appreciation of the intelligible realm.

Above the Soul is the Divine Mind, or World of Ideas. Were there no such mind, an explanation of human intelligence would be impossible. On occasion men withdraw themselves from the insistent sense impressions and impetuous desires of everyday life and give themselves over to the calm subject of geometry or some deeper philosophical reflection. Men may even go beyond reflection and enjoy the beauty of union with the divine. Here men are in the realm of Ideas, far above the level of perception.

Stressing the viewpoint of Plato's *Sophist,* Plotinus makes it clear that the Ideas are not just a collection of hypostatized concepts, but are in truth a living mind. At this point, a modern student who has heard of Berkeleyan idealism, or a Christian who makes God's decree dependent on God's activity of thinking must take care not to misunderstand Plotinus. "Not by its thinking movement does movement arise. Hence it is an error to call the Ideas intellections in the sense that upon an intellectual act in this principle one such Idea or another is made to exist" (V ix 7). Mind and its objects are not different, the latter inferior to the former: Mind *is* what it thinks.

Philosophy, however, since its purpose is to discover unity, cannot stop with the Mind or World of Ideas because here duality still remains. There is a multiplicity of Ideas. In knowledge there are subjects and predicates. Unity requires a further ascent above and beyond duality, therefore beyond knowledge, to the ineffable One. Rational argument shows the need of postulating this One; but to be unified with it, man must leave reason behind and experience the One in a mystic vision.

Four times during the six years of Porphyry's study under him, Plotinus enjoyed this communion. This is a state in which ordinary consciousness is suspended. The soul no longer knows whether it has a body, and cannot tell whether it is a man, a living being, or anything real at all. Knowledge is somewhat like seeing sense objects on a cloudy day. In the vision a man sees the Source of the light that made knowledge possible, and he sees it directly in all its brilliance. This experience is not abnormal; it is the exercise of a faculty which all have but few use; he who has seen, says Plotinus, knows what I mean.

After Plotinus, Neoplatonism continued to the end of antiquity. Only one name, however, needs to be recorded—Proclus (A.D. 410-485). The future was to be in the hands of Christianity. Plotinus himself seems to have known nothing of orthodox Christianity, though he wrote one tractate against the Gnostics.

Augustine was rescued from Manichaeism and skepticism by neoplatonic arguments. Because of this, he gave a Platonic slant to Christian theology, though as he matured in his Christian understanding, he dropped many Neoplatonic details as inconsistent with the Scripture.

In the E., an unknown Christian writer appropriated a section of Proclus's writings. Working up two volumes of strong Neoplatonic and mystical cast, he issued them under the name of Dionysius the Areopagite. This insured their acceptance during the superstitious Middle Ages, seducing even the brilliant Thomas Aquinas, and contributed to the development of pantheism (in John Scotus Eriugena) and to a widespread vogue of mysticism.

In A.D. 529 the emperor Justinian closed the moribund school, and thus Gr. philosophy came to its end.

BIBLIOGRAPHY. A. *Religion*. Homer, *Iliad*, and *Odyssey* (c. 1000 B.C.); G. Hermann, *Orphica* (1805); C. A. Lobeck, *Aglaophamus* (1829); J. Harrison, *Prolegomena to the Study of Greek Religion* (1903); E. Caird, *The Evolution of Theology in the Greek Philosophers* (1904); A. Fairbanks, *A Handbook of Greek Religion* (1910); W. Jaeger, *Paideia*, tr. by G. Highet (1939); M. P. Nilsson, *Greek Popular Religion* (1940); M. P. Nilsson, *Greek Piety* (1948); G. E. Mylonas, *Eleusis* (1961); W. H. Hale, *Ancient Greece* (1965);

B. *Philosophy*. V. Brochard, *Les sceptiques Grecs*, (1887); L. Robin, *La Théorie Platonicienne des Idées et des Nombres* (1908); R. D. Hicks, *Stoics and Epicurean* (1910); A. E. Taylor *Plato, the Man and his work* (1927); M. C. Nahm, *Selections from Early Greek Philosophy* (1934); G. H. Clark, *Selections from Hellenistic Philosophy* (1940); P. Merlan, *From Platonism to Neoplatonism* (1953); G. H. Clark, *Thales to Dewey* (1957).

G. H. CLARK

GREEK VERSIONS. *See* VERSIONS, ANCIENT.

GREEN (ירק, *green, greenness, herbs, greens*; χλωρός, *yellowish* or *pale green*). A color produced by a mixture of blue and yellow; the color of the foliage of growing plants.

The Heb. root *yrq* usually refers to vegetation. There is an adjective, רענן (from רען), that is employed principally to describe the luxuriance of trees, but also anything that is luxuriant, fresh, flourishing, and healthy. דשא, means simply "grass" (Psa 23:2). Although other words (חי, לח, אב, and רטב) are sometimes rendered as "green," their basic connotation is that which is living, moist, fresh, growing or flourishing, and new. In the NT, χλωρός is used of grass (Mark 6:39; Rev 8:7); in Revelation 6:8 it is tr. "pale." Greek ὑγρός, "moist, green," is attested in Luke 23:31.

K. L. BARKER

GREET, GREETING, a salutation on meeting or an opening address in a letter or message. Heb. שלום, has been a traditional greeting in the Near E. The term is cognate to meaning "completeness," "welfare" and secondarily "peace." Although this is the common traditional tr. the word has come to mean in its modern semantic range something like "hello." Although popular colloquial speech rarely is recorded in the OT, the passage in 1 Samuel 25:5 seems to contain a commonplace phrase of greeting, Heb. לחי ואתה שלום, however the actual meaning is obscured. It should be tr. as, "Long life to you and peace," but this is admittedly conjectural—(KJV) "greet," (RSV) "salute." In a similar greeting instance in 1 Samuel 1:17 *šālōm* also appears, but in a possible greeting situation in Ruth 4:1 it is not used. However the NT utilizes the Gr. equivalent of the Heb. expression εἰρήνη (Mark 5:34; Luke 10:5, 6). The terms in both OT and NT mean much more than a simple social convention. Like the OT *šālōm*, as in 2 Samuel 8:10; 11:7 where it is used to inquire after someone's health and welfare, the NT uses *eirēnē*, following the LXX (Acts 16:36; James 2:15, 16).

Another aspect of greeting in the ancient Near E and the Hel. age was the effusion of natural emotions. In the W since the 18th cent. this practice has been frowned upon but no such false stoicism existed in Bible times. So men are often mentioned in both the OT and NT hugging, kissing and embracing upon meeting (Gen 27:26; Exod 4:27; 1 Sam 10:1, et al.; Luke 7:38; Rom 16:16, et al.). In the OT the word *šālōm* is associated by the earliest Messianic prophecies with the coming of the "servant of the Lord." The first overt use is in Genesis 49:10, "the peace bringer comes" (KJV), "Shiloh" (RSV), "to whom it belongs." In the famous passage, Isaiah 9:6, "Prince of Peace" is one of the divine titles of the Messiah, Heb. שר-שלום. Obedience before the coming of the Messiah is a sign of peaceful participation in His kingdom (Isa 60, et al.). The salutation to the Messiah is of profound religious importance. "Serve the LORD with fear, with trembling, kiss his feet, lest he be angry" (Ps 2:12, RSV)—"kiss his feet," reprehensible and inexcusable. This religious meaning makes the mockery of Judas even more horrible (Matt 26:49; Mark 14:45; Luke 22:47). The authors of the epistles thus commend the "peace" of God through the Messiah Christ to their readers (Rom 1:7, et al.).

W. WHITE, JR.

GREYHOUND (ערזיר מתנים, Prov 30:31, *greyhound* KJV, ASV; *strutting cock* RSV). The Heb. is generally reckoned obscure and speculation is pointless.

G. S. CANSDALE

GRIEF, GRIEVE (חלה, *to be pained, concerned*; חלי, *anxiety*; עצב, *to be afflicted inwardly*; λυπέω, *grief*). The KJV and the RSV also tr. eight more words as grief. Beyond this agreement, the KJV trs. twenty-seven additional Heb. words and seven other Gr. words as grief that the RSV often treats differently. In all, the KJV has 122 "grief verses" whereas the RSV has but 66. The suggested difficulty in determining what grief means and whether or not a situation entails grief is further indicated in the fact that the two VSS overlap in only twenty-two places.

In modern usage grief is mental distress associated with death or other keenly felt loss, whereas the older Eng. usage included a wide range of meanings such as physical or psychological pain, disease, injury, anxiety, and any displeasure or hardship. The difference is vivid in the following passages where the KJV uniformly uses the words grief or grieve, but the RSV substitutes as follows: "made life bitter" (Gen 26:35); "indignant" (34:7); "in dread" (Exod 1:12); "exceedingly bitter" (Ruth 1:13); "vexation" (1 Sam 1:16); "bitter in soul" (30:6); "displeased" (Neh 2:10); "very angry" (13:8); "offended" (Job 4:2); "embittered" (Ps 73:21); "loathed" (95:10); "disgust" (119:158); "vexation" (Eccl 1:18). From this frequent use of words that indicate subjective feeling, it is evident that the RSV prefers to think of grief (except when equated with mourning) as inner feeling. On the other hand, the KJV, in a less rigorous fashion, allows grief to refer to both internal dispositions and external conditions indiscriminately.

Changes in the Eng. language, a wider selection of attitudinal categories resulting from rationalistic and dualistic thought, and improved knowledge of the ancient languages account for the sharp variations in the two VSS. But this leaves unsettled a prior question concerning the meaning of grief for the Heb. mind or the NT writer. Undoubtedly, the Biblical writers had experiences similar to those indicated in the RSV and accordingly used a wide variety of words. The prevailing Heb. frame of reference however, would not have led them to use language primarily as a vehicle for categorizing and labeling mental dispositions. Unoriented to 18th and 19th cent. perspectives, as the RSV, the outlook of the KJV tends to reflect more accurately the Heb. notion of grief.

An article in TDNT enhances the discussion. It suggests that the Biblical writers considered the emotions and attitudes only indirectly, and naturally focused attention on the external circumstances in human experience. The *cause* of the grief was the true grief. Envisaging a world fallen in all detail and under the judgment of God (Gen 3:16f), their perspective went beyond analysis of personal feeling. Grief was related to the groaning in travail of the whole creation as Paul expressed it (Rom 8:22), which reflects a prevailing OT sentiment. Grief, however, was not simply punishment or a final state for man; by including the idea of suffering, it was related to the Messiah (Isa 53:4) who was to be the hope of redemption from the guilt indicated by the universal fact of grief (cf. Isa 35:10; 1 Pet 1:3-7).

Contrary to the prevailing Gr. practice of contrasting grief with pleasure, the NT made grief and grace complementary (John 16:20f.; Heb 12:11). Paul contrasted a "godly grief" that leads through repentance to salvation with a "worldly grief" that produces death (2 Cor 7:10). A spiritual notion of grief that includes various kinds of suffering (2 Cor 4:8-10; 11:23ff.; 12:10) also explains how the Christian is not necessarily hampered by the present course of suffering in life, but may by God's help transcend and transvaluate grief. In verses such as John 16:20; Romans 6:6; 2 Corinthians 4:8; Galatians 6:14; Philippians 1:29; 3:10; James 1:2; and 1 Peter 2:19, this pattern of grief in complementary relationship with grace can be discerned. *See* SUFFERING.

BIBLIOGRAPHY. Trench (1880), 237-239; W. L. Walker, "Grief," ISBE (1929), 1305, 1306; R. Bultmann, "λυπή, λυπέω," TDNT, IV (1942), 313-324; R. Bridges, L. A. Weigle, *The Bible Word Book* (1960), 157, 158.

T. M. GREGORY

GRIND, GRINDING. A procedure by which grain was reduced to flour through being pulverized between two large stones. Small hand mills sometimes had holes in the center of the top stone through which the grain was poured. Larger community mills were often powered by animals (Matt 24:41; Mark 9:42).

R. K. HARRISON

Two types of grindstones. *Left:* Hellenistic from the coast of Palestine. *Right:* A grindstone from the Roman era. ©*White*

GRISLED. The KJV archaic term used to tr. the pl. adjective ברדים, "spotted," "speckled." A better rendering would be "dappled." In Zechariah 6:3, 6 it referred to the color of certain horses and prob. meant "mottled," "spotted" or "dappled gray" (Zech 6:3, 6; cf. Gen 31:10, 11.

GROVE (*see also* ASHERAH; אשרה, *Asherah* or her *cult object*; אשל, *tamarisk tree*).

"Grove" is an incorrect tr. (KJV) of both Heb. words above. This mistranslation of אשרה is based on LXX rendering, "groves" (ἄλσος, ἄλση). Asherah was a Canaanite fertility or mother goddess and consort of El (cf. Ugaritic *'atrt, Athirat*); and also the wooden cult object or "sacred pole" by which she was represented. Apparently, the plurals Asherim and Asheroth refer only to her images or cult objects. The contexts show that Asherah was a goddess (or an object representing her) who was worshiped along with Baal (Judg 3:7; 2 Kings 23:6). In the time of Elijah, 400 prophets of Asherah ate at Jezebel's table (1 Kings 18:19). Naturally, Jezebel (a Phoenician/Tyrian) would have promoted the worship of Asherah and Baal. Such worship was denounced by the spiritual leaders of Israel. The Amorite name Abdi-Ashirta ("servant of Asherah") appears in the Amarna Letters. In Ugaritic, reference is made to "Athirat of the Tyrians." The word itself is prob. derived from the word meaning "walk, tread" (cf. Ugaritic *Athirat Ym*, "Athirat of the sea," which perhaps meant originally, "she who treads the sea"; cf. further W. F. Albright, *From the Stone Age to Christianity*, pp. 231, 310, and W. L. Reed, *The Asherah in the Old Testament*).

K. L. BARKER

GUARD(טבח, משמעת, משמר, רוץ ; σπεκουλατώρ, κουστωδία, στρατοπεδάρχης). One or more men assigned to protect a person or thing. In ancient times oriental monarchs had attached to their persons a body of picked men to protect them and carry out their wishes on important confidential matters. In Egypt and Babylon the members of the guard were known as "slaughterers," "butchers" (טבח), but precisely why is not known. Potiphar, to whom the Midianites sold Joseph, was the captain of Pharaoh's guard (Gen 37:36; 41:10, 12), and Nebuzaradan held the same position in Nebuchadnezzar's bodyguard (2 Kings 25:8; Jer 52:12). The men who formed the royal bodyguard were usually foreigners. David had a corps of 600 foreign mercenaries, made up of Cherethites and Pelethites, of whom Benaiah was the captain (2 Sam 20:23). They accompanied David on his flight from Absalom (2 Sam 15:18), and formed Solomon's escort on the day he was crowned (1 Kings 1:38, 44). Members of the Israelite royal guard were known as רצים (runners), that is, outrunners. They appear in the reign of Saul (1 Sam 22:17). Later, when Absalom and Adonijah attempted to seize the throne, they provided themselves with fifty runners as a part of the royal ceremonial (2 Sam 15:1; 1 Kings 1:5). In the time of Rehoboam, the guardroom stood at the entrance to the palace, and it housed the bronze shields that the guards carried when they accompanied the king to the Temple (1 Kings 14:27, 28; 2 Chron 12:10, 11). Jehu's guard went with him to Samaria to assist in the destruction of the worship of Baal (2 Kings 10:25).

Herod Antipas ordered a member of his guard (σπεκουλατώρ) to bring to him the head of John the Baptist on a platter (Mark 6:27). Pilate told the Jews to make the tomb of Jesus secure with a guard of soldiers (κουστωδία) —undoubtedly, Temple police. In Acts 28:16 the clause, "the centurion delivered the prisoners to the captain of the guard" (στρατοπεδάρχης), found in the KJV, is not a part of the RSV text because of poor textual attestation.

BIBLIOGRAPHY. R. de Vaux, *Ancient Israel* (1961).

J. L. KELSO

GUARD, COURT OF THE (חצר המטרה, *court of the guard*).

The word מטרה (from נטר [cf. נצר]) occurs in Nehemiah 3:25; Jeremiah 32:2, 8, 12, and in several vv. of Jeremiah chs. 33, 37-39. It evidently refers either to the open court in the palace complex or to the guardrooms of the palace guards, which served as a place for detaining prisoners in Jerusalem, at least during the siege of that city. Thus, it was a temporary prison. Jeremiah was confined there, but he was permitted to continue his prophetic ministry and to conduct certain business transactions with the assistance of Baruch, his secretary.

K. L. BARKER

GUARD, GATE OF THE (שער המטרה ; LXX πύλη τῆς φυλακῆς). KJV PRISON GATE. A gate of the city of Jerusalem. It is likely the same as the Muster Gate (Neh 3:31) at the NE corner of the city near the Temple compound. At the dedication of the wall, the second group sent by Nehemiah to march in procession on the wall stopped at the Gate of the Guard (12:39).

D. H. MADVIG

GUARDIAN (ἐπίτροπος, *guardian*, which means basically *a person to whom some task or property has been entrusted*). Matthew 20:8 mentions one entrusted with paying laborers. The ἐπίτροπος, "steward," of Herod was named Chuza (Luke 8:3, RSV). The cognate word ἐπιτροπή is used in Acts 26:12 of Paul's authorization by the high priests to persecute Christians. A governor with authority from the emperor was also called ἐπίτροπος. Lysias's important office was as ἐπίτροπος of Antiochus

(2 Macc 11:1; 13:2; 14:2). Paul illustrated the position of Jews under the law by means of a minor in a household (Gal 4:2). Under Greek, Roman, or Jewish law, a boy was under authority until a certain age. Under Rom. law the ἐπίτροπος was the legal guardian of a child, potentially if his father was alive, actually if he had died. Trustees (οἰκονόμοι) were responsible for his financial affairs until he was twenty-five. When he came of age, he was free, and entered into his inheritance. *See* STEWARD.

F. FOULKES

GUDGODAH. *See* HOR-HAGGIDGAD.

GUEST. 1. OT (קראים ; LXX *κλητοί, called ones*; KJV *called*; ASV *invited*, 2 Sam 15:11). A word used to denote persons invited to certain events or occasions—guests of Absalom and Adonijah at their abortive attempts to usurp the throne (2 Sam 15:11; 1 Kings 1:41, 49); guests of a loose-living woman (Prov 9:18); and those who are called by God (Zeph 1:7). The RSV uses "guest" as a free rendering of העם קראתו, *the people (whom) I called* (1 Sam 9:24) and of גרי ביתי, *the sojourners of my house* (Job 19:15).

2. NT (*ἀνακείμενος, one reclining*; *συνανακείμενος, one reclining* or *with one reclining*; KJV *them that* [*which*] *sat with him*, Matt 14:9; Mark 6:22, 26). A word used to denote persons invited to a banquet or feast—guests at King Herod's birthday party (Matt 14:9; Mark 6:22, 26); guests in the parable of the wedding feast (Matt 22:10, 11). "Guest" is used in the RSV to tr. *οἱ υἱοὶ τοῦ νυμφῶνος, the bridegroom's attendants* (Matt 9:15; Mark 2:19; Luke 5:34), and *ἐξένισεν, he received as guests* (Acts 10:23).

D. H. MADVIG

GUEST ROOM (*κατάλυμα*). KJV and ASV GUEST CHAMBER. The room in which Jesus and His disciples ate the Passover on the eve of the crucifixion (Mark 14:14; Luke 22:11). The same Gr. word is tr. "inn" in Luke 2:7. It was a room that provided facilities for temporary lodging or for banqueting. This Gr. word is used in the LXX for the place where Samuel and Saul feasted together (1 Sam 9:22, Heb. לשכה, *room*, or *hall*; ASV *guest chamber*; RSV *hall*; KJV *parlor*).

D. H. MADVIG

GUIDEPOSTS (תמרורים). KJV HIGH HEAPS. A word that occurs only in Jeremiah 31:21, where the structure of the v. suggests that it is a synonym of waymark. It is the word that is used in modern Heb. for "roadsign."

GUILE (מרמה, *deceit*; רמיה, *deceit, slackness*; *δόλος, deceit, cunning, guile, bait*). Guile is a restricted type of deceit. In some Biblical contexts, features of its use are the following: (1) No harm is intended toward the one addressed, even though he is deceived. (2) The personal interest of the deceiver is the motivating factor calling forth the deception. (3) The method of deception employed is cunningly and subtly persuasive.

Jacob's deception of Isaac by placing the skin of an animal on his arms is a clear example of the three features above, which both the ASV and RSV tr. rightfully as "guile" (Gen 27:35), but which the KJV describes more indiscriminately as coming "with subtilty." Other OT appearances of the word "guile" are not clear instances of "guile" as described above because they are hortatory or promissory in nature (Pss 32:2; 34:13; 55:11 in both KJV and ASV, but not in RSV). Strangely, the RSV has the word "deceit" in Psalm 34:13, but when this v. is quoted directly in 1 Peter 3:10, the tr. uses "guile." The sons of Jacob promise friendship with the defilers of their sister if they will practice circumcision (Gen 34:13). The ASV calls this promise "guile," but the KJV and RSV are more accurate in speaking of this as "deceit," because clearly from the start vengeful evil was intended.

In the NT, the major Eng. trs. agree in six places where "guile" is preferable to the more common "deceit" as a tr. of δόλος. Illustrative of the above criterion is Paul's evaluation of the charge against him of being insincere and crafty in his presentation of Christianity to the Corinthians (2 Cor 12:16). Paul contended that even if he did use guile (which he denied), it was because he loved them and wanted them to love him. Admitting he wanted to persuade men of the truth of Christianity, Paul claimed his appeal was always honest and without guile (1 Thess 2:3). But the tr. "deceit" would have sufficed (1 Pet 2:1; 3:10) for this list of sins and exhortations because they are presented without precise differentiations.

"Guile" as a word is best known in the Bible where Jesus says of Nathanael, "Behold, an Israelite indeed, in whom is no guile" (John 1:47). This is a common laudatory phrase without the connotation of sinlessness; only of Christ could it be said "He committed no sin; no guile was found on his lips" (1 Pet 2:22).

T. M. GREGORY

GUILT, the legal and moral condition that results from a violation of God's law as expressed through the covenant, i.e., from sin. In OT and NT thought there is little or no clear distinction made between sin, guilt and punishment (cf. Gen 4:13 where all three occur together). Older Eng. trs. therefore tend uniformly to employ the word "sin" where modern trs. reflect the greater precision of modern Eng. usage. For example, "guilt" occurs only twice in the KJV, but it occurs 109 times in the RSV; "guilty" occurs 25 times in the KJV, 46 times in the RSV. Among the more important of the Biblical words tr. or implying guilt are the Heb. אשם ; רשע ; and עון ; and the Gr. ἁμαρτία ("sin" *see* SIN); ἔνοχος ("liable, answerable, guilty"; *see* Mark 14:64; 1 Cor 11:27; James 2:10; etc.); ὑπόδικος ("liable to judgment or punishment, accountable"; *see* Rom 3:19); ὀφείλημα ("debt"; see Matt 6:12); ἀδικία ("wrongdoing, wickedness"; *see* Rom 1:18); ἀνομία ("lawlessness"; *see* Rom 6:19); and αἰτίον ("guilt, complaint"; *see* Luke 23:4, 14, 22). For a wider view of the subject area of which guilt is a part, *see* SIN.

1. Old Testament concept. In general in the OT sin, guilt and punishment are all implied in the various words used by the Biblical authors to denote the violation of God's commandments and its results. Guilt may be incurred, increased, purged, pardoned, remembered, removed, borne or taken away. (a) The word אשׁם usually refers to both moral and ritual transgression. Joseph's brothers say to each other, "In truth we are guilty (אשׁם) concerning our brother" (Gen 42:27; *see* also Gen 26:10; Lev 4:3, 13, 22, 27; 5:2, 3, 4, 5, 17, 19; 22:16; Num 5:6; Judg 21:22; 1 Chron 21:3; 2 Chron 19:10; 24:18; 28:13; 33:23; Ezra 9:6, 7, 13, 15; 10:10; Pss 5:10; 68:21; Prov 30:10; Isa 24:6; Jer 2:3; 50:7; 51:5; Hosea 4:15; 5:15; 10:2; 13:1); (b) Psalm 32:5 speaks of "the guilt (עון) of my sin" (the word occurs seventy times in the OT, but not all imply the notion of guilt; *see* Exod 28:43; Num 14:18; 1 Sam 20:8; 2 Sam 14:32; 19:19; Hosea 12:8); (c) Numbers 35:31 speaks of the "murderer who is guilty (רשׁע) of death" (*see* also Deut 25:1; 1 Kings 8:32; Job 10:7; Ps 18:23; Isa 5:23; 50:9).

To be guilty of sin is to incur God's wrath both collectively (Exod 20:5, 6; Isa 65:7; Jer 14:20) and individually (Deut 24:16; Ezek 18:2-4, 14-20). At first guilt could exist without the individual's awareness of sin, but along with individualization of guilt came the necessity of subjective knowledge (*see* Hempel, 155f.). For the psalmist and the prophets, to be guilty of breaking God's laws involves universal shame and repentance (Ps 38:1-12; 53:2, 3; Isa 1:4, 5). A sincere desire to have God remove one's sins or even a willingness to forgive a neighbor's wrongdoing leads to forgiveness and a restoration of purity (Pss 32:5; 51:1-12; 79:9; Dan 9:4-19 (esp. 9, 16, 19; Ecclus 28:2). The idea of sin as a legal *indebtedness* to God, important for an understanding of NT usage, occurs in later Judaism; the Aram. חוב ("debt"), is in fact, the term commonly used by the rabbis for sin (see Targ. Onkelos on Num 14:19; Exod 34:7; Isa 53:4, 12).

2. New Testament concept. The idea of guilt is much less frequent in the NT. Although the word ἁμαρτία usually means "sin," it also occasionally implies guilt, esp. the guilt of all men for Jesus' death. In the synoptic gospels, esp. Matthew, guilt often occurs in the context of forgiveness of sin understood as a debt owed to God (Matt 6:12; 18:21-35; etc.). Guilt as the result of lawlessness (ἀνομία, equivalent to the Heb. עון) is also implied in the synoptics (Matt 7:23; 13:41) in the context of the judgment of God.

Paul deepens the understanding of guilt by universalizing and internalizing the debt to God which results from sin. He thinks of the actual removal of sin by Christ's death as well as payment of the debt through the justification which God through faith grants the repentant sinner (Rom 3:24f.; Eph 1:7; Col 1:14; etc.). To be ἐν Χριστῷ means to be free from condemnation and guilt (Rom 8:1ff.); it means that the verdict of "guilty" is reversed.

Guilt is also seen in a Hebraic way as the consequence of sin by other NT writers; *see* John 9:41 (ἔνοχος); James 2:10 (ἔνοχος); and 1 John 3:4 for important examples.

BIBLIOGRAPHY. J. G. Simpson, "Guilt," HDCG, 1 (1906), 696-698; J. R. Willis, "Guilt," HDB, 1 vol. ed. (1909), 320-322; F. R. Tennant *The Concept of Sin* (1912); H. F. Hall, "Guilt," ISBE, 2 (1915), 1309, 1310; H. R. Mackintosh, "Sin (Christian)," HERE, 11 (1921), 538-544; C. A. Beckwith, "Guilt," SHERK, 5 (1950), 95, 96; L. Morris, "'Asham," EQ, 30 (1958), 196-210; J. Hempel, "Ethics in the OT," IDB, 2 (1962), 153-161; S. J. De Vries, "Sin, sinners," IDB, 4 (1962), 361-376; J. Barr, "Guilt," HDB rev. (1963), 354, 355; J. Heuschen and B. Vawter, "Guilt," *Encyclopedic Dictionary of the Bible* (1963), 912-918; G. Quell, G. Bertram, G. Stählim and W. Grundmann, "ἁμαρτάνω, ἁμάρτημα, ἁμαρτία," TDNT, 1 (1964), 276-316, esp. sections on Guilt; J. Lachowski, "Sin (in the Bible)," *New Catholic Encyclopedia,* 6 (1967), 850-852; P. Schoonenberg, "Sin," *Sacramentum Mundi,* 6 (1970), 87-92.

L. R. KEYLOCK

GUILT OFFERINGS. *See* SACRIFICE AND OFFERINGS.

GULL (שׁחף, Lev 11:16, Deut 14:15 "the sea gull, the hawk, after their kind," RSV; "cuckoo" KJV; "sea mew" ASV). To find the tr. "sea gull," RSV has gone back to some of the early VSS (LXX and Vulg.). Driver rejects this, for it conflicts with his hypothesis that the list consists mainly of birds of prey, and he suggests "Long-eared Owl"; but perhaps "gull" should not be rejected so quickly. It is doubtful whether a bird as rare and local as this owl, which is strictly nocturnal and found in woods, would be separately named and banned. In contrast, the gulls are numerous, diurnal, and conspicuous. Ten true gulls and eight other members of the family are recorded in Pal.; five are only rare stragglers, but the others migrate. Those that come from the S often fly up the Gulf of Aqaba to make a landfall at Eilat, before traveling overland. The winter visitors are the commonest, including lesser Black-backed and Black-headed Gulls; their flocks may run into hundreds and they may be seen on the Mediterranean and Red Sea coasts, on the Lake of Galilee and around the great complexes of fishponds. Only the Herring Gull nests in Pal., and the Black, Common and Little Terns. Most gulls are scavengers and would certainly rank as unclean. It seems much more reasonable to specify them than such uncommon skulkers and the cuckoo and Long-eared Owl.

BIBLIOGRAPHY. G. R. Driver "Birds in the OT," I, Birds in Law PEQ (1955), 5-20.

G. S. CANSDALE

GUM (נכאת ; LXX θυμίαμα, *incense*) KJV SPICERY (Gen 37:25); KJV, SPICES (Gen 43:11). A gummy or resinous substance used as incense. It is the product of the *Astragalus tragacantha,* a fair sized shrub with small pale yellow blossoms. It grows over a wide area in Pal. and the Near E. The gum is gathered by rubbing the plant with a ball of cotton. This gum was one of the goods carried to Egypt by the Ishmaelite traders who bought Joseph (Gen 37:25). It was also among the "choice fruits" of S Pal. sent by Jacob to Joseph in Egypt (Gen 43:11).

BIBLIOGRAPHY. W. Walker, *All the Plants of the Bible* (n.d.), 194.

D. H. MADVIG

GUNI gu' nī, GUNITES -nīts (גוני, הגוני ; LXX Γωυνι, and various other spellings). 1. The second son of Naphtali and grandson of Jacob (Gen 46:24; 1 Chron 7:13). His descendants are called Gunites (Num 26:48). 2. A member of the tribe of Gad who settled in Gilead. He was grandfather of a certain Ahi who seems to have been a leader in the tribe (1 Chron 5:15).

D. H. MADVIG

GUR gûr, THE ASCENT OF (גור ; LXX Γαι). An incline near Ibleam where Ahaziah was mortally wounded by Jehu's men as he fled from the threat of assassination after the death of Joram (2 Kings 9:27). The LXX reading suggests that it should be tr. "valley" and not as a place name. W. F. Albright, however, has affirmed its identification with a Canaanite city, Gurar, which is mentioned in a 15th cent. tablet discovered at Taanach.

BIBLIOGRAPHY. W. F. Albright, "A Prince of Taanach in the Fifteenth Cent. B.C."; BASOR, XCIV (1944), 21.

D. H. MADVIG

GURBAAL gûr' bāl (גור בעל, *sojourn of Baal*; LXX ἐπὶ τῆς πέτρας, *upon the rock*). A city in the Negeb inhabited by Arabs, whom Uzziah conquered with the help of God (2 Chron 26:7). Its site has not been discovered. The reading of the LXX has suggested to some that the NT requires emendation.

BIBLIOGRAPHY. J. Simons, *The Geographical and Topographical Texts of the OT* (1959), 371.

D. H. MADVIG

GUTTER. 1. (צנור. *pipe* or *water shaft*; LXX παραξιφίς, *dagger*) RSV WATER SHAFT. The tunnel that David recommended to his soldiers as a way of entering Jerusalem to conquer it (2 Sam 5:8). It has been identified with "Warren's Shaft" in the SE hill that leads from the spring Gihon to within the city wall and dates back to pre-Israelite times.

2. (רהטים ; LXX ληνοῖς, *watering trough*) RSV RUNNEL. The trough from which the flocks of Laban drank and where Jacob placed peeled rods in his effort to control the markings on the newborn lambs (Gen 30:38, 41).

BIBLIOGRAPHY. J. Simons, *Jerusalem in the OT* (1952), 168-175.

D. H. MADVIG

GYMNASIUM (γυμνάσιον, *a place for exercise*; γυμνός, *naked*). In Greece the gymnasium was originally a place of training for the Olympic games and other athletic contests. By the 4th cent. B.C. it had become as well an educational and cultural center for Gr. youths, and was regarded as an essential feature of a city. It derived its name from the fact that the competitors exercised naked. The gymnasium consisted of a number of large buildings, which contained not merely places for each kind of exercise—running, boxing, wrestling, discus throwing, etc.—but also baths, a covered portico for practice in bad weather and in wintertime, and outside porticos where philosophers and writers gave public lectures and held disputations. Most of the education of boys and young men was obtained in gymnasiums. In Athens there were three great gymnasiums, each consecrated to a particular deity, and each made famous by association with a celebrated philosopher: the Academy, where Plato taught; the Lyceum where Aristotle held forth; and the Cynosarges, which was the resort of Antisthenes and his followers, the cynics.

The Gr. institution of the gymnasium never became popular with the Romans, and was held in horror by orthodox Jews. Nevertheless, a gymnasium was erected in Jerusalem by Hellenizing Jews, under the leadership of the high priest Jason, in the time of Antiochus Epiphanes, who tried to compel the Jews to give up Judaism (1 Macc 1:10, 14; 2 Macc 4:7-9). Strict Jews opposed it because it introduced heathen customs and led Jewish youths to exercise naked in public and to be ashamed of the mark of their religion, circumcision. It existed until the destruction of Jerusalem by Titus. Paul alluded to the exercises of the gymnasium several times: boxing (1 Cor 9:26), wrestling (Eph 6:12), and racing (1 Cor 9:24; Gal 5:7; Phil 3:12-14). *See* ATHLETE.

S. BARABAS